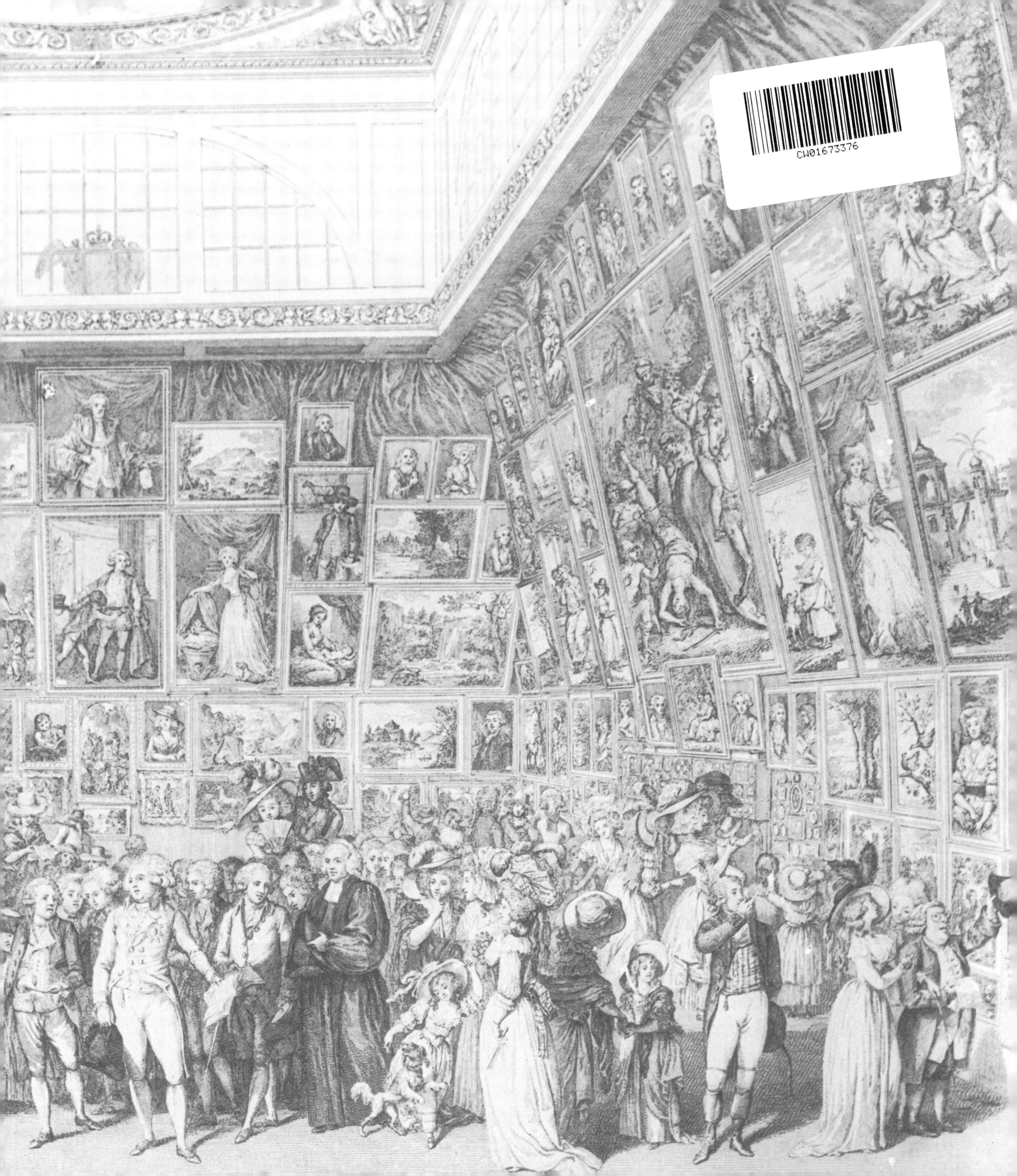

NATIONAL PORTRAIT GALLERY

MID-GEORGIAN PORTRAITS 1760-1790

Dedicated to

RICHARD J. B. WALKER
Picture Adviser to the Ministry of Works 1949–76
picture cataloguer

NATIONAL PORTRAIT GALLERY

MID-GEORGIAN PORTRAITS 1760–1790

JOHN INGAMELLS

National Portrait Gallery
2004

Published in Great Britain by National Portrait Gallery Publications, National Portrait Gallery, St Martin's Place, London WC2H 0HE

For a complete catalogue of current publications please write to the address above, or visit our website at www.npg.org.uk/publications

ISBN 1 85514 519 7

A catalogue record for this book is available from the British Library.

Design: Guilland Sutherland

Production: Ruth Müller-Wirth and Geoff Barlow

Printed in Hong Kong by Paramount Printing Co.

The publisher would like to thank the copyright holders for granting permission to reproduce works illustrated in this book. Every effort has been made to contact the holders of copyright material, and any omissions will be corrected in future editions if the publisher is notified in writing.

The National Portrait Gallery is grateful to the Paul Mellon Centre for Studies in British Art for its very generous support in the production of this book.

CONTENTS

PHOTOGRAPHIC ACKNOWLEDGMENTS

The compilers are grateful to all museums, institutions and private owners who have allowed their pictures to be reproduced in this book. They wish to extend particular thanks to the Paul Mellon Centre for Studies in British Art (London), Christie's and Sotheby's. They have endeavoured to credit all copyright and reproduction rights holders. Credits are found in the captions and as cited below (brief title, artist, page).

The Royal Collection © 2003, Her Majesty Queen Elizabeth II: Zoffany *Tribuna* xvii; Arne by Bartolozzi 19; Queen Charlotte by Ramsay 104, by Zoffany 105, by Gainsborough 105, by Beechey 106; Garrick by Hogarth 187; George III by Zoffany 198, by Gainsborough 199; Harcourt by Sievier 236; Keppel by Reynolds 307; Markham by Hoppner 333; Reynolds by himself 395; Rodney by Reynolds 406; Zoffany *The Royal Academicians* 508, *The Tribuna* 14.

National Trust properties with House collections
Ickworth, The Bristol Collection: 3rd Earl of Bristol by Gainsborough 71; 4th Earl of Bristol by Vigée Le Brun 73; Petworth House, The Egremont Collection: Egremont attributed to Hoare 156; Macartney by Reynolds 320; Saltram, the Morley Collection: Bartolozzi by Reynolds 40; Reynolds by Kauffmann 396; Uppark, the Featherstonhaugh Collection: Charlotte by Dance 104; George III by Dance 197; Upton House, The Bearsted Collection: Beckford by Romney 46; Waddesdon Manor, The James A. de Rothschild Collection: Emma Hamilton after Reynolds 229.

ARRANGED ALPHABETICALLY BY PRIVATE OWNER OR PLACE:

Mead Art Museum, Amherst College: Amherst by Reynolds 12 (Joshua Reynolds, Sir Jeffery Amherst 1717-97, oil on canvas, 1765, 50 x 40 in. museum purchase, AC1967.85).

Courtesy of the 13th Duke of Argyll: Conway by Gainsborough 113.

Auckland Art Gallery, Toi o Tamaki: Siddons by Beach 433.

by courtesy of the Wedgwood Museum Trust Ltd, Barlaston, Staffordshire:
Barbauld by Wedgwood 30; Bentley by Rigaud 54, by Wedgwood 54; Sir William Hamilton by Wedgwood 234; Stuart by Wedgwood 449; Wedgwood by Stubbs 480, by Reynolds 480.

Reproduced by permission of the Marquess of Bath, Longleat House, Warminster, Wiltshire, Great Britain: Thurlow by Reynolds 458

© Bildarchiv Preussischer Kulturbesitz, Berlin, 2003. Staatliche Museen: Wilkinson by Gainsborough 487.

Museum of Fine Arts, Boston; Photograph © 2003 Museum of Fine Arts, Boston: John Smart, Self portrait: Watercolour on ivory, Museum of Fine Arts Boston, Otis Norcross Fund 54.935: Smart Self portrait 438.

Museum of Fine Arts, Boston: Washington by Stuart 474 (Photograph © 2003 Museum of Fine Arts, Boston) Washington at Dorchester Heights, 1806, oil on panel 274.95 x 180.34 (108¼ x 71), Museum of Fine Arts, Deposited by the City of Boston L-R 30.76a).

The Trustees of the Bowood Collection: Lansdowne by Mosnier 310.

The Mistress and Fellows, Girton College, Cambridge: More by Opie 348.

by kind permission of the Provost and Scholars of King's College, Cambridge: Anstey attributed to Beach 15.

© by the President and Fellows of Queens' College, Cambridge: Venn by Chamberlin 466.

Master and Fellows of Trinity College, Cambridge: Hinchliffe by Peters 259; Watson by Romney 475.

Dean and Chapter of Canterbury: North by Romney 363.

His Grace the Archbishop of Canterbury: Archbishop Moore by Romney 345.

Amgueddfa ac Orielau Cenedlaethol Cymru/National Museums & Galleries of Wales: Mrs Piozzi by Roche 383; Wilson by Mengs 491.

The Devonshire Collection, Chatsworth; reproduced by permission of the Duke of Devonshire and the Trustees of the Chatsworth Settlement: Duchess of Devonshire by Reynolds 145, 146; Duke of Devonshire by Batoni 148; Garrick by Liotard 186; Mrs Garrick by Liotard 190.

Courtesy: Crawford Municipal Art Gallery, Cork: Burke by Barry 79.

Detroit Institute of Arts: Heathfield by Brown 251 (Sir George Augustus Elliott, K.B., First Lord Heathfield of Gibraltar, 1788/91, Mather Brown, City of Detroit Purchase, Insurance Recovery Funds. photograph © 1986 The Detroit Institute of Arts).

© Courtesy of the National Gallery of Ireland (Dublin): 4th Earl of Bristol by Hamilton 73; Cavallo by Hurter; Edgeworth by Hamilton 153; Hone, self portraits 262; Lifford by Dickinson 316.

By permission of the Governors of Dulwich Picture Gallery: De Loutherbourg by Gainsborough 141; Sheridan by Gainsborough 429.

In the collection of the Heriot-Watt University and Archive [Edinburgh]: Watt by Chantrey 479.

Courtesy of the Lewis Walpole Library, Yale University [Farmington]: Orford by Ramsay 371.

Trustees of the Firle Settlement: Gage by Martin 175.

Galleria degli Uffizi, Florence, su concessione del Ministerio dei Beni e le Attività Cultarali: Kauffmann Self portrait 299; Zoffany Self portrait 499.

Glasgow Museums: Art Gallery and Museum, Kelvingrove: Dale by an unknown artist 133.

© Hunterian Art Gallery, University of Glasgow: Black by Raeburn 57; Hunter by Ramsay 276, by Grignon 277.

by courtesy of the Trustees of the Goodwood Collection: Richmond by Reynolds 400, by Romney 400.

Wadsworth Atheneum, Hartford: Hinchliffe by Copley 259 (1947.365, Purchased of Charles D. Childs from J.J. Goodwin Fund).

Reproduced by courtesy of Abbot Hall Art Gallery, Kendal, Cumbria: Greene by Romney 217.

By kind permission of the Earl of Leicester and the Trustees of the Holkham Estate: Fox by Reynolds 167, by Opie 168.

In the collection of Lennoxlove House, Haddington: Argyll by Hamilton 16.

Lincolnshire County Council – Usher Gallery: Banks by West 28.

Board of Trustees of the National Museums and Galleries on Merseyside (Lady Lever Art Gallery, Port Sunlight): Argyll by Reynolds 17; Emma Hamilton by Vigée Le Brun 230.

National Museums, Liverpool, Walker Art Gallery: Stubbs by Humphry 451.

Bridgeman Art Library, London: Cholmondeley by Batoni and by Reynolds 109; Archbishop Moore by Lawrence 345

© Copyright The British Museum: *RA 1787* by Martini after Ramberg xv; Ashburton by Downman 21; Burney by Nollekens 82; Camden by Dance 89; Cavendish by Alexander 96; Cheesman by Edridge 108; Foote by Godfrey after Colson 162; Mrs Garrick by Cruikshank 190; Gordon by Wilson after Polak 211; Hoole by Turner after Humphry 264; Howard by Holloway 266; Hull by Downman 271; Jennings after Beugo 287; Lewis by Dance 315; Lyttelton by Townley after Cosway 319; Thicknesse by Hoare 455; Wilson by Hastings after Beaumont 491; Wolcot by Dance 495; Zoffany Self portrait 499; *Nine Living Muses* after Samuel 515; Cervetto by Chalon 517; *Sketches at Print Sales* after Sandby 534.

By permission of the British Library: Cornwallis by Devis 122.

Photographic Survey, Courtauld Institute of Art: Ashburton by Reynolds 21; Baring by Lawrence 32, by West 33; Bartolozzi by Reynolds 40; Charlotte by Dance 104; Le Despencer by Knapton 142; Duchess of Devonshire by Reynolds 145, 146; Devonshire by Reynolds 148, by Batoni 148; Egremont ascribed to Hoare 156; Fox by Reynolds 167, by Opie 168; Garrick by Liotard 186, by Reynolds 188; Mrs Garrick by Liotard 190; George III by Dance 197; Gilpin by Garrard 207; Grafton by Dance 213, by Hoppner 213; Emma Hamilton after Reynolds 229; Harcourt by Gardner 235; Howe by Gainsborough 268; Hunter by Home 275, by Flaxman 275; Kauffmann by Dance 300; Macartney by Reynolds 320; Montagu by Romney 343; Mornington by Owen 349; Norfolk by Lawrence 362, by Lonsdale 362; Orford by Carriera 371; Reynolds Self portrait 394, by Kauffmann 396; Sandwich by Reynolds 419; Smeaton by Gainsborough 441; Thurlow by Reynolds 458; Willis by Russell 489; Reynolds *The Society of Dilettanti* 530, 531.

Art Archive, Garrick Club: Baddeley by Spicer 24; Colman after Zoffany 112; Dibdin by Arnold 149; Foote after Reynolds 163; Henerson after Gainsborough 252, by Beach 253; Holland by H.B. 259; Hull by Graham 271; Palmer by Russell 377; Quick by Samuel de Wilde 389, by Gainsborough Dupont 389.

Courtesy of the Guildhall Art Gallery, Corporation of London: Camden by Reynolds 90; Cornwallis by Copley 122; Copley *Defeat of the Floating Batteries* 250; Wilkes by Roubiliac 485.

Reproduced by kind permission of ING Bank NV, London Branch: Baring by West 33.

Reproduced by kind permission of the Dr Johnson's House Trust: Carter by Read 94.

By courtesy of the Director, National Army Museum, London: Coote by Nollekens 117; Carter *The Siege of Gibraltar* 510.

© National Maritime Museum, London: Affleck by Penny ; Barrington by Reynolds 36; Bentham by an unknown artist 53; Cook by Hodges 115, by Dance 115; Gardner by K.A. Hickel 179; Emma Hamilton by Schmidt 231; Howe by Copley 268; Kempenfelt by Kettle 302; Keppel by Reynolds 307; Sandwich by Gainsborough 419; Schanck by an unknown artist 421.

© Royal Academy of Arts, London: Bacon by Dance 24; Barry by Dance 38; Bonomi by Rigaud 61; Chambers by Reynolds 99 (Prudence Cuming Associates), by Dance 99; Charlotte by Reynolds 105; Cipriani by Dance 109; Copley by Dance 119; Cosway by Dance 125; Gainsborough Self portrait 177 (Prudence Cuming Associates); George III by Reynolds 199; Gilpin by Dance 207; Hone Self portrait 262; Hunter by Chamberlin 277 (Prudence Cuming Associates); Reynolds Self portrait 395 (J. Hammond); Paul Sandby by Dance 415; Thomas Sandby by Dance 417; Serres by Dance 422; Stubbs by Dance 451; Wheatley by Dance 481; Wilton by Roubiliac 493, by Dance 493; Zoffany by Dance 500; Singleton *President and Members of the Royal Academy* 536.

Reproduced by kind permission of the President and Council of the Royal College of Surgeons of England; photograph The Conway Library, Courtauld Institute of Art: Hunter by Flaxman 275.

Reproduced by kind permission of the President and Council of the Royal College of Surgeons of England; Hunter by Home 275.

© The Royal Society: Banks by Chantrey 30; Maskelyne by van der Puyl 334; Smeaton by 'Rhodes' 440, after Brown 440.

© Tate, London 2003: Bartolozzi by Abbott 40; Blackstone by Gainsborough 58; Gainsborough by Zoffany 177; Keppel by Reynolds 307; Reynolds Self portrait 395; Sandby by Cotes 415; Siddons by Lawrence 435; Copley *Death of Chatham* xii, 533.

Victoria and Albert Museum. V&A Picture Library: Bacon by Russell 23; Delany attributed to Hoppner 139; Henderson by Stuart 253; Sheffield by Borckhardt 428; Smart Self portrait 438; Walker by Barry 468; Whitehead by Doughty 483; Wilton by Hayman 492.

© The Warburg Institute: Howard by Bacon senior 267; Johnson by Bacon senior 295; Reynolds by Flaxman 397; Robinson by della Valle 402

Trustees of Dr Williams's Library: Priestley by Artaud 387.

Louisiana State Museum: Jones by Moreau 297 (Gift of Miss Jessie V. Wise).

Maidstone Museum and Bentlif Art Gallery, Clement Taylor Smythe Collection: Jefferys after W. Jefferys 285.

© Manchester Art Gallery: Tooke by Brompton 461.

In the collection of the Earl of Mansfield: Mansfield by Martin 330, by Reynolds 332.

National Gallery of Victoria, Melbourne, Australia: Zoffany Self portrait 499 (Johann Zoffany 1733–1810 German/English, Self-portrait as David with the head of Goliath 1756, oil on canvas 92.2 x 74.7 purchased with the assistance of the Isabella and Mary Curnick Bequest and the Art Foundation of Victoria 1994); Temple by Ramsay 454 (Allan Ramsay 1713–84, British, Richard Grenville, 2nd Earl Temple 1762, oil on canvas 234.3 x 152.4, Everard Studley Miller Bequest, 1965).

Middlesex Hospital; UCL Hospitals, NHS Trust: Northumberland by Pine 365.

Reproduced by permission of the Trustees of the Middlesex Guildhall Collection: Northumberland by Gainsborough 365.

Montclair Art Museum, Montclair, New Jersey: Whitefoord by Stuart 482 (Gilbert Stuart, Caleb Whitefoord 1782, oil on canvas 30¼ x 25⅛, Montclair Art Museum, Montclair, New Jersey Museum purchase, Clayton E. Freeman Fund, 1945.110).

Monticello, Thomas Jefferson Foundation, Charlottesville, Virginia, photograph Edward Owen, Monticello: Paine by Trumbull 373.

The Montreal Museum of Fine Arts: Mulgrave by Reynolds 333 (1963.1399, Miss Olive Hosmer Bequest. Photograph Montreal Museum of Fine Arts, Christine Guest).

Bayerische Staatsgemäldesammlungen, Neue Pinakothek, München: Kauffmann self portrait 299.

New Britain Museum of American Art: Arkwright by Brown 18 (Charles F. Smith Fund 1957.8. Photo credit: E. Irving Blomstrann).

Legislative Assembly of New Brunswick, Fredericton: Sheffield by Shee 428.

By permission of the Literary and Philosophical Society of Newcastle upon Tyne: Hutton by Gahagan 279, by Morton 279.

Yale Center for British Art, Paul Mellon Collection: Charlemont by Batoni 101; Dollond by Hoppner 151; Gage by Copley 175; Mortimer Self portrait 351; Strahan by Chamberlin 446; Mortimer *Caricature Group* 529.

All rights reserved, The Metropolitan Museum of Art, New York: C.R. Burney by Gainsborough 82; Cosway Self portrait 124; Franklin by Houdon 173; Romney Self portrait 410.

By kind permission of His Grace the Duke of Norfolk, Arundel Castle: Norfolk by Lawrence 362, by Lonsdale 362.

The Marquis of Normanby, Mulgrave Castle: Mulgrave by Gainsborough 353.

Collection of the Duke of Northumberland, Syon Park: Northumberland by Barry 366.

The Department of Manuscripts and Special Collections, The University of Nottingham: Newcastle by Carriera 360.

The Warden and Fellows of All Souls College, Oxford: Blackstone by Bacon 58; North by Howard 363.

from the collection at Parham House & Gardens, West Sussex, England: Beckford attributed to Pine 44.

Courtesy of the Pennsylvania Academy of Fine Arts, Philadelphia; Washington by Peale 472 (Gift of Maria McKean Allen and Phebe Warren Downes through the bequest of their mother Elizabeth Wharton McKean 1943.16.2); Franklin by Martin 172 (Gift of Maria McKean Allen and Phebe Warren Downes Downes through the bequest of their mother Elizabeth Wharton McKean 1942; photograph presented to the NPG 1936).

Philadelphia Museum of Art: Charlemont and Leeson by Ghezzi 101 (1978-70-290, bequest of Anthony Morris Clark).

By permission of the Earl of Rosebery: Gibbon by Reynolds 205; Rodney by Gainsborough 406.

Courtesy of the Huntington Library, Art Collections, and Botanical Gardens, San Marino, California: Abel by Gainsborough 4; *Concerto Spirituale* by Rowlandson 23; Cumberland by Romney 132; Granger by Baillie 214; Siddons by Reynolds 434; Watt by Raeburn 478.

Trustees of the Stansted Park Foundation: Bessborough by Liotard 56.

The Manor House, Stanton Harcourt: Harcourt by Gardner 235.

The Royal Academy of Fine Arts, Stockholm. Photograph Nationalmuseum, Stockholm: Reynolds by von Breda 396.

By kind permission of the Marquess of Tavistock and the Trustees of the Bedford Estates: Bedford by Reynolds 48; Fitzpatrick by Nollekens 161.

Collection of the Robert Hull Fleming Museum, University of Vermont, Gift of Mr and Mrs Douglas Burden 1953.9: Seward by Romney 423.

Waddesdon, The Rothschild Collection, Rothschild Family Trust: Garrick by Reynolds 187.

Warrington Borough Council: Libraries and Information Services: Macaulay by Moore 325.

National Portrait Gallery, Smithsonian Institution, Washington DC: Copley Self portrait 119 (77.22, Gift of the Morris and Gwendolyn Cafritz Foundation and matching funds from the Smithsonian Institution); Paine by Watson after C.W. Peale 372 (69.74, National Portrait Gallery, Smithsonian Institution, Washington DC); Washington by Houdon 472 (78.1, Gift of Joe L.and Barbara B. Albritton, Robert H. and Clarice Smith, and Gallery purchase); Washington by Stuart 473 (2001.13, acquired as a gift to the Nation through the generosity of the Donald W.Reynolds Foundation).

National Gallery of Art, Washington DC: Image © 2003 Board of Trustees, National Gallery of Art, Washington: Duchess of Devonshire by Gainsborough 146 (1937.1.93, Andrew W. Mellon Collection); Hamilton by Romney 234 (1970.17.133, Ailsa Mellon Bruce Collection); Huntingdon by West 278 (B-30,828, John Davis Hatch Collection 1978); Paine by Jarvis 373 (1950.15.1, Gift of Marian B. Maurice); Reynolds by Stuart 396 (1942.8.21, Andrew W. Mellon Collection); Sheridan by Gainsborough 429 (1937.1.92, Andrew W. Mellon Collection).

Smithsonian American Art Museum, Washington DC: Lifford by Reynolds 316 (1956.11.46, Mabel Johnson Langhorne Bequest)

Courtesy of the Bishop of Bath and Wells: Beadon by Abbott 42.

Courtesy, Winterthur Museum: Washington by Trumbull 473.

York Museums Trust, York Art Gallery: Carr by Nollekens 93.

FOREWORD

It has long been an ambition of the National Portrait Gallery to complete the sequence of collection catalogues from 1500 to 1860 and this has now been magnificently achieved with the publication of the catalogue by John Ingamells on Mid-Georgian Portraits. Without the especially generous support of the Paul Mellon Centre for Studies in British Art and the initiative of its director, Dr Brian Allen, this volume would not have been possible.

Detailed catalogues of the collection are essential to the life of the National Portrait Gallery, informing as they do many aspects of our work: texts on the walls in the galleries, educational projects, the Portrait Explorer and distant access via the website. Additionally, the iconographies included here for each sitter provide a record of portraits in public and private collections across the United Kingdom and abroad.

John Ingamells spells out the history of publishing collection catalogues in his Preface below. Here I should like to put on record the importance of his own work which completes the run of catalogues covering the collection from 1500 to 1860. I should also like to thank Jacob Simon, Chief Curator, and all those other staff at the National Portrait Gallery who have helped to make this volume possible.

SANDY NAIRNE
Director, National Portrait Gallery, London

PREFACE AND ACKNOWLEDGMENTS

Detailed historical catalogues for the National Portrait Gallery were first proposed some fifty years ago by the then Director, Sir Henry Hake. The first volume, *Seventeenth-century Portraits*, appeared in 1963 compiled by the Keeper, David Piper. It was followed by catalogues by other Keepers: Roy Strong's *Tudor and Jacobean Portraits* in 1969; Richard Ormond's *Early Victorian Portraits* in 1973, and John Kerslake's *Early Georgian Portraits* in 1977. Ormond explained the ambitious long-term plan in his Introduction:

> Tudor and Jacobean portraits, and those of the seventeenth century, each have a catalogue to themselves; there will be two for the eighteenth century, one for the Regency, two for the Victorians, one for the Edwardians, and at least two for the modern period

In 1977 Richard Walker, then recently retired from the Government Art Collection, was commissioned to compile *Regency Portraits* which appeared in 1985. Such an external appointment was symptomatic of change as Keepers within the Gallery became increasingly involved with special exhibitions, outstations and administration. *Mid-Georgian Portraits*, sponsored by the Paul Mellon Centre for Studies in British Art, resumes Hake's grand design and completes, after forty years, the run of catalogues from 1600–1850.

It describes portraits of sitters who flourished within the period 1760–90 or, put another way, those not included in John Kerslake's *Early Georgian* catalogue which covered the period 1714–60, or Richard Walker's *Regency Portraits*, which covered the period 1790–1830. Such catalogue divisions inevitably produce anomalies: Jeremy Bentham and Hannah More appear as mid-georgians, but would be happier within the regency; Mrs Sheridan appears without her husband, and Fox is here without Pitt. Both Benjamin Franklin and George Washington appear as British subjects (at the declaration of independence in 1776 they were respectively aged 70 and 44).

The catalogue describes in all 467 works of art, of which 245 are paintings, 121 drawings, 44 miniatures and 25 sculptures; the remaining 32 are medallions (14), medals (11), waxes (5) and prints (2). The earliest image is of 1737, the last of 1843. There are 322 identified sitters (of whom 18 appear in groups only) and 21 unidentified.

The catalogue has been compiled principally from the vast resources of the Heinz Archive at the National Portrait Gallery, and I have drawn heavily upon the researches of others, as the list of Abbreviations and the footnotes reveal. Many have generously responded to written enquiries and I would particularly like to acknowledge help received from Hugh Belsey, Margie Christian, Andrew Cormack, Judy Egerton, John Kenworthy-Browne, Alex Kidson, Alastair Laing, Stephen Lloyd, David Mannings, Sir Oliver Millar, David Moore-Gwyn, Lady Jane Roberts, Francis Russell and Lavinia Wellicome.

As a guest in the National Portrait Gallery I have been treated with courtesy and patience, and by none more than Jacob Simon, who also made important emendations to my text. I am particularly grateful for additional help received from Lucy Peltz, Sophie Plender, Helen White and Erika Ingham. The staff of the Heinz Archive, the art handlers and the protean publications department have all assisted willingly, and I remain grateful to them.

The text has been edited and set at the Paul Mellon Centre by Guilland Sutherland, whose patience and great skill have been much exercised.

Above all I wish to thank Brian Allen, Director of the Paul Mellon Centre for Studies in British Art, for making this whole enterprise possible.

JOHN INGAMELLS
May 2003

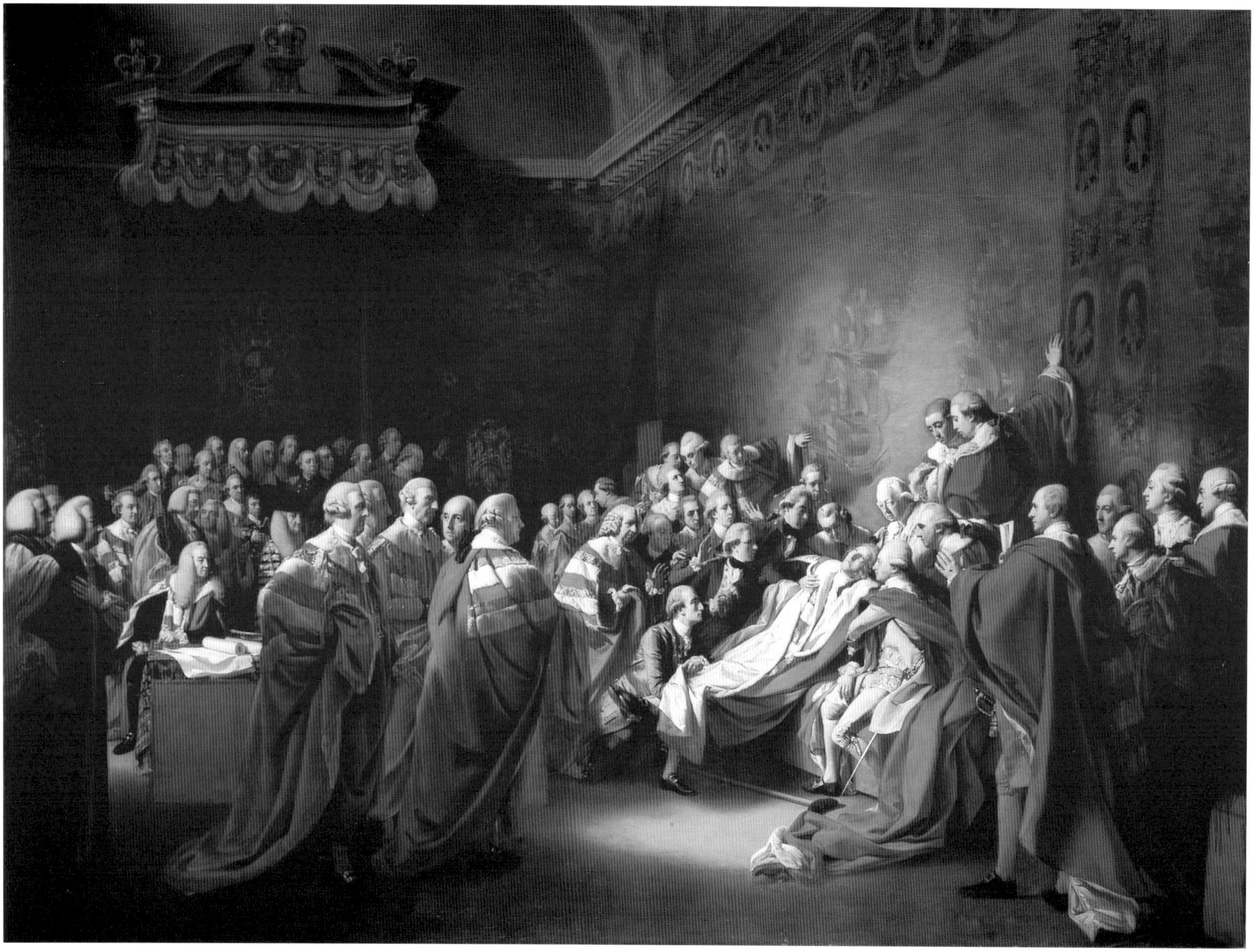

The Death of Chatham by J.S. Copley 1779-81 (Tate Gallery); and see Comparative Groups, p.532.

INTRODUCTION

(unfootnoted quotations are from the catalogue which follows)

The Period 1760-90

Copley's great picture *The Death of Chatham* shows the House of Lords debating the American colonies in April 1778. After the Duke of Richmond had proposed the withdrawal of all British troops Chatham, the architect of Empire, rose to oppose him but collapsed; within weeks he was dead. It was Chatham who had led the country through the triumphant final phase of the Seven Years War with France (1757-63), establishing a vast sea-borne Empire. After the war he had been a maverick figure, his instability aggravated by ill health, but no-one subsequently could match his inspiring qualities as a political leader. There had been short-lived governments formed by Bute, Grenville, Rockingham and Grafton, before the passive Lord North contrived some form of stability.

North's chubby features are marginalized in Copley's picture, while Rockingham cranes forward from a distance; Grafton, who was against the war, is absent (perhaps at Newmarket), Grenville was already dead, and Bute had withdrawn from public life to botanise. Shelburne (later Marquess of Lansdowne), briefly to be a future prime minister, peers down behind Chatham; the phlegmatic Duke of Devonshire appears distraught; Lord Mansfield, the lord chief justice, alone remains seated; Thurlow, later Lord Chancellor, stands next to Lord North in the background; Hinchliffe and Markham are among the Bishops. These were distinguished names, but Chatham had been a hero. Edmund Burke and Charles Fox, the other familiar names in the political history of these times, were not members of the House of Lords, the one distinguished as an orator and political theorist, the other the genial and wayward Whig, whom George III, a monarch obsessed with propriety, could not abide. When American independence was ratified in 1783 it was Chatham's young son, William Pitt, who restored the country to some stability before the French Revolution of 1789 led to a second great war against France.

It might seem in retrospect that the period 1760-90, marked by the loss of the American colonies, was otherwise an interval between two great French wars, but there was never a completely settled peace and frequent domestic disputes gave rise to spirited public argument. There were distant military conflicts in the West Indies, Gibraltar and India, all primarily against the French. Warren Hastings contrived the growth and affluence of the East India Company through a mixture of military aggression, bribery and despotism, but his consequent trial in London on charges of corruption, with Burke as his accuser, was inconclusive. Of naval and military commanders, Keppel, Howe and Rodney, Heathfield, Coote and Cornwallis, displayed spirit, often in adversity, but here was no Nelson or Wellington. It was the sheer carelessness of the Navy Board that caused the loss of the *Royal George*—and Cowper's moving elogium for Admiral Kempenfelt. The greatest seaman of the time was unquestionably James Cook, a navigator of peaceful intent.

The authority of the Crown and the role of Parliament were constantly debated. Blackstone's *Commentaries* codified English law and defined the King's sovereignty within his dominions, while Denning moved in the House in 1780 that 'the influence of the Crown has increased, was increasing and ought to be diminished' (which did not prevent him being created Lord Ashburton two years alter). There was then the radical wing pursuing an elusive concept of liberty, embodied in such figures as Alderman Beckford, the provocative John Wilkes, and Tom Paine with his *Rights of Man*—but by the time of a French republican war such protest had become indistinguishable from treason. Paine and the scientist and radical dissenter Joseph Priestley were among those forced into exile. But the greatest domestic violence came from the Gordon Riots of 1780, when the Protestant Association, led by the volatile Lord George Gordon, rioted against Catholic concessions and when Lord Mansfield's house in Bloomsbury Square was sacked and burned. It is not without irony that Gordon died in Newgate converted to Judaism.

The year before Chatham's death the economist Adam Smith commented that England 'seems to breed neither Statesmen nor Generals', but 'men of great professional abilities in different ways, great Lawyers, great watch makers and Clockmakers, etc. etc.'[1] Away from the metropolis the mechanical genius of Watt and Brindley, the experiments of Priestley and Cavendish, and the factories of Arkwright, Boulton and Wedgwood, ushered in an industrial revolution. 'Soon shall thy arm, Unconquer'd Steam! Afar/ Drag the slow barge, or drive the rapid car', enthused Erasmus Darwin.[2] Mass employment was at hand and by 1790 Manchester presented a shocking prospect for a traveller like John Byng: 'who but a merchant cou'd live in such a hole; where ... the hearty husbandman [is] suck'd into the gulph of sickly traffic'.[3] But the prosperity of Empire was founded on such industry and trade.

Despite the onset of such fundamental change culture remained essentially retrospective. It was, of course, the preserve of the educated. Hume could casually suggest that 'at twenty Ovid may be the favourite author, Horace at forty, and perhaps Tacitus at fifty'.[4] Samuel Johnson (now known best for his conversation as Boswell chose to preserve it) could read a book of Virgil's *Aeneid* each night, or debate the comparative merits of Homer and Virgil with Burke who, it was said, always had a ragged copy of the Roman poet's works by his elbow. Chatham's eloquence was compared to that of Cicero; as he died his son was reading to him the account of the death of Hector from the *Iliad*. His Empire begged comparison with that of Augustus, a

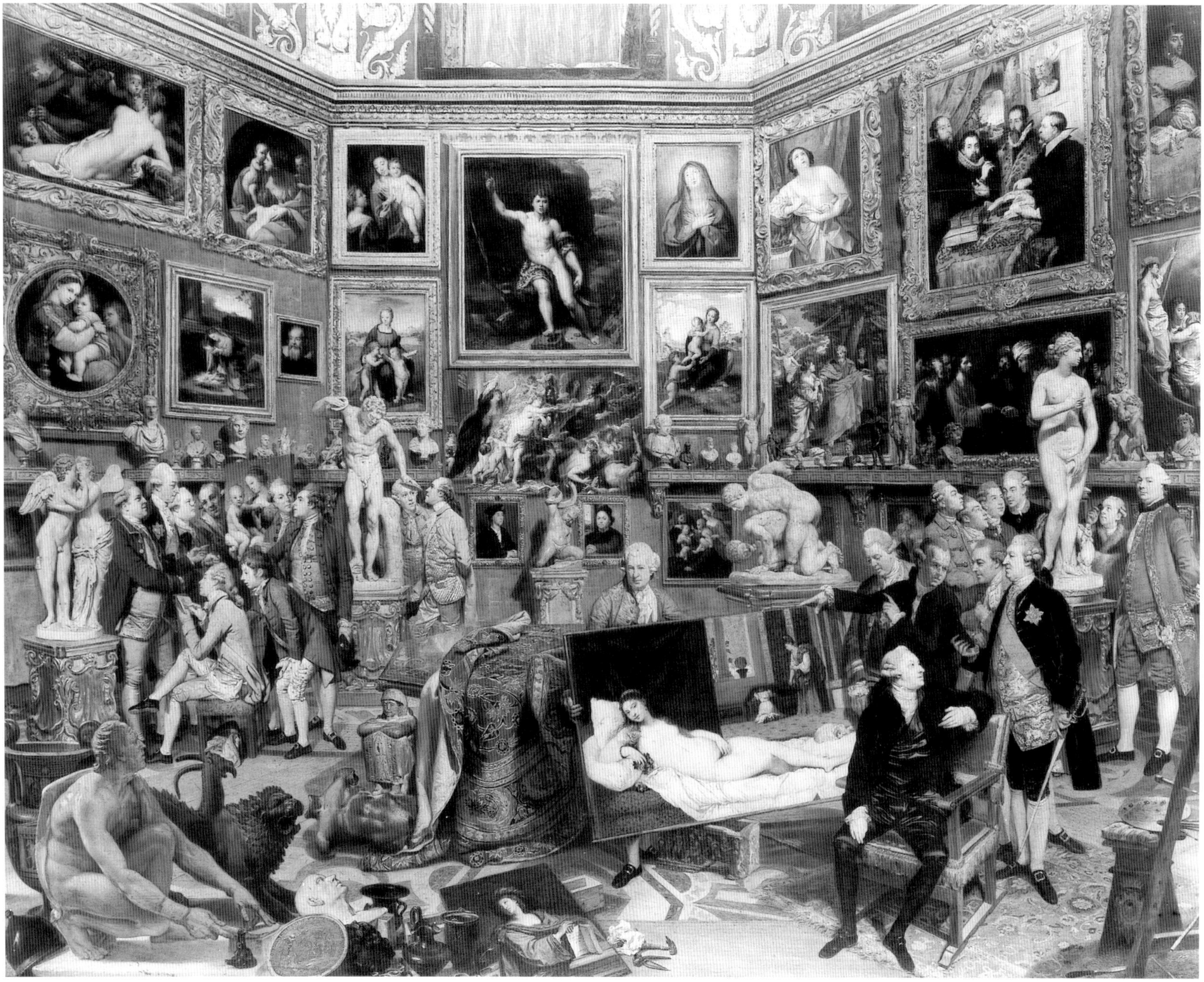

The Tribuna, Florence by Johann Zoffany 1772-78 (The Royal Collection)

stature which encouraged those histories of Britain by Goldsmith, Hume, Catharine Macaulay, Macpherson, Robertson and Smollett. None was a Tacitus and the most substantial historian of the period, Edward Gibbon, began the publication of his admonitory *Decline and Fall of the Roman Empire* to coincide with the American declaration of Independence.

'Shall we for ever make new books, as apothecaries make new mixtures, by pouring only out of one vessel into another,' Sterne had asked, and he was not alone in his questioning.[5] Goldsmith, for one, treated contemporary manners, and Cowper, who was to translate both the *Iliad* and *Odyssey*, suggested in *The Task* the virtue of a new and gentle introspection. But when in 1794 it was decided to place statues within the crossing of St.Paul's of recently deceased benefactors of the English people it was the idiom of Augustan Rome that prevailed. Sir Joshua Reynolds, John Howard (the prison reformer), Sir William Jones (the oriental scholar) and Samuel Johnson, all appear with Roman hair and, apart from Reynolds (whose statue appeared some years after the others), loose classical drapery, which now seems particularly unfortunate for Johnson's cumbrous figure. Reynolds had painted him four times, describing his huge shabby figure thinking, reading or frowning—intimate portraits born of friendship and respect.

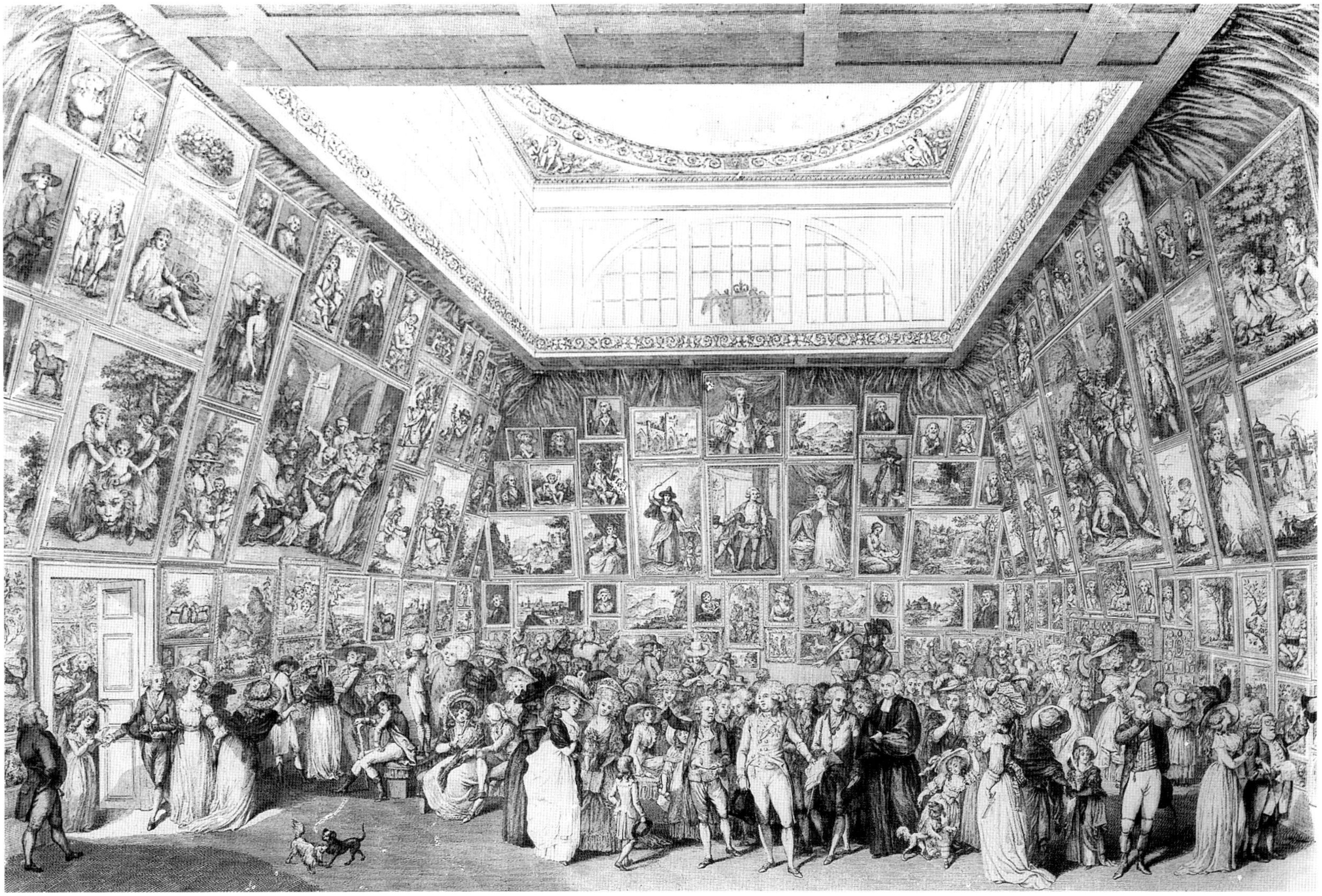

The Exhibition of the Royal Academy 1787 P.A. Martini after J.H. Ramberg (NPG archive)

Portraiture 1760–90

The years 1760–1790 are sometimes described as the Golden Age of British portraiture. The period covers the mature work of Reynolds and Gainsborough; the founding in 1768 of the Royal Academy which introduced both formal instruction and the competitive exhibition picture; the growth of reproductive engraving which could rapidly enhance the reputations of both artist and sitter, and a marked increase of relatively knowledgeable patrons (many of whose fortunes derived from the expanding overseas trade). We see them in Zoffany's *Tribuna* of 1772–78, British travellers on their grand tour stopping in the great room in Florence to consider classical and renaissance works of art such as furnished an ideal for the artists whom they would later patronise. It is a little ironic that in devising his composition Zoffany removed some fourteen portraits from the walls, to replace them with history pieces of baroque splendour.

Two self portraits by Reynolds provide another measure of the period. In 1748 he painted himself peering intently at the spectator (himself), his palette and brushes to hand (NPG 41); his costume is drab and the surround dark. Thirty years later, the self portrait he presented to the Royal Academy describes a very different figure. He stands nonchalantly, hand on hip in a pose acknowledging Van Dyck, a bust of Michelangelo beside him; he wears the dress of an honorary Doctor of Civil Law at the University of Oxford, a scroll in his hand, the tools of his trade nowhere to be seen. It is a sophisticated assertion of the dignity of his profession. In 1768 he had been knighted as the first President of the new Royal Academy.

Annual exhibitions of works by living artists were first held in London in 1760 by the Society of Artists and lasted until 1791. From 1761 they competed with the annual exhibitions of the Free Society of Artists that lasted until 1783. But neither Society was ultimately able to withstand the annual exhibitions held by the Academy from 1769 under Royal patronage (in France the Salon, also under Royal patronage, had begun in 1737). The first Academy exhibitions were held in unimposing premises in Pall Mall, but in 1780 the institution moved into much grander rooms in Somerset House, designed by its Treasurer, Sir William Chambers.

Each year portraiture comprised the largest single element of the exhibition, despite the President's repeated assertion, given in his *Discourses* to the Academy students, that history painting was the noblest form of art. It was a question of market forces. The call for portraiture, a traditional vanity, was (and is) unending, while the auction houses had long dealt with subject pictures of every description. It remains a little ironic that of the two great portrait painters of the time, Reynolds would rather have painted histories and Gainsborough landscapes but, as the latter once wrote, 'A Man may do great things, and starve in a Garret, if he does not conquer his Passions and confirm to the common Eye in chusing that branch which they will encourage & pay for'.[6]

Academy exhibitions encouraged grand portraiture. Established figures from Court, Church and State, jostled principally by actors (Garrick's iconography is here exceeded only by that of George III), vied for public attention. We can see the new rhetoric in the Reynolds of 1773 of Lord Bute (NPG 3938) parading his Garter regalia, while much of his nobility derives from the *Apollo Belvedere*, or his Sir William Hamilton of 1777 (NPG 640), an elegant, extensive description of connoisseurship and diplomatic rank; or the Gainsborough of 1783 of Lord Sandwich (an inadequate first lord of the Admiralty) standing whole length in a Van Dyck manner by the Greenwich Hospital as an object of casual splendour. Such flattering and public declarations could only benefit artist and sitter. Small wonder that in 1783 Lord Mansfield, who had just sat to Copley for a somewhat stiff whole length (NPG 83), was being urged to become 'the Patron of Painters worth patronizing, Romney, Gainsborough and Reynolds'.

Inevitably only a small percentage of British portraits was first shown at the Academy, and the overall majority of sitters was not from Court, Church, State or Stage. Less successful and less learned painters abounded – there were 196 in London alone in 1777.[7] Nothing is known of the A. Reddock of Falkirk who painted Andrew Meikle (NPG 5001), inventor of the threshing machine; Romney tried, with only limited success, to improve an indifferent portrait by Rhodes, otherwise unknown, of the engineer John Smeaton (NPG 80); James Watt sat in Birmingham to Von Breda for a gawky picture (NPG 186A). Yet perhaps such modest, well-intentioned likenesses may now tell us as much about a sitter as the sophisticated pictures of Reynolds, which many contemporaries considered not very resembling,[8] however informative they might be concerning character, status and the artist. It was observed that Rigaud's group portrait of Chambers, Wilton and Reynolds (NPG 987) contained 'strong and expressive Resemblances; but the Integrity which led the artist to copy so exactly the Vulgarity of the President's Countenance will not recommend him to his favour'.

With the increase in portraiture came a commensurate growth of the print trade, and particularly of the mezzotint. Reynolds proclaimed that he would be immortalised by the mezzotints of James McArdell. In 1784 Warren Hastings was being urged to sit to Gainsborough and to have 'some mezzotints scraped from it [which] will be 1000 times more valuable to your Friends, and creditable to you than the many bad pictures which are now extant of you'. Having commissioned Abbott's portrait of William Cowper (NPG 2783), John Johnson alleged that friends were 'crazy to have prints of it'; Boswell wanted Jones's engraving of his portrait by Reynolds to be 'in every print seller's window like a portrait of Fanny Kemble'. At the other end of the print market the *Gentleman's Magazine* and other monthlies regularly included (often woeful) engraved portraits, broadcasting portraiture on an unprecedented scale. James Granger systematically gathered portrait engravings for his *Biographical History of England* (1769). It may be noticed that this same biographical curiosity coincided with the first coherent history of English artists and engravers compiled by Horace Walpole 1762–71 from the manuscripts of George Vertue, and to Boswell's *Johnson* in 1791, a prototype of English biography.

The increasing enthusiasm for portraiture ('iconomania') could also result in fraudulence. Nothing within our period quite matches the manufacture of General Wolfe,[9] but for quite different reasons John Howard had to be packaged. He viewed 'with abhorrence' any attempt at having his portrait taken. A profile was drawn from memory and from it grew, not only a handsome bust length by Mather Brown (NPG 97), but also the statue in St Paul's. Yet we do not really know what he looked like. And there is the case of John Paul Jones, privateer and American naval hero. When he first threatened British waters, engraved portraits quickly appeared showing a dark, swarthy privateer. It was only later that he was discovered to be 'a sensible little fellow ... with a Scot's sandy hair and hazel eyes'.

The Collection 1760–90

The National Portrait Gallery was founded in 1856, to house 'Portraits of the most eminent Persons in British History', the Trustees being instructed to look 'to the celebrity of the person represented rather than to the merit of the artist'. 'Eminent' and 'celebrated' are ultimately subjective categories and, when one adds availability as a necessary third criterion, it is easy to understand why the collection was sometimes regarded as eccentric. By 1858 questions were being asked in the House:

> On looking over the list of portraits already acquired, there are some whose claims to be there I cannot understand. For instance there is the portrait of Mr Murphy [NPG 10]. I should like to know who he is and what he has done to have a place in the National Portrait Gallery? Again there is a portrait of 'La Belle Hamilton' [NPG 20], a very pretty woman no doubt in her time, but I am not aware that it is of any national interest to preserve her portrait.[10]

Long before, in 1786, a correspondent in the *Gentleman's Magazine* had chosen to stress the 'melancholy' truth that

> for these last twenty years, the epiphets of famous, celebrated, &c., have scarcely ever been applied except to persons answering to some of the following descriptions, viz. 1st, rebels; 2dly, strumpets; 3dly, rogues, highwaymen, &c. 4thly, atheistical or deistical writers.[11]

Wilkes and John Paul Jones were rebels, Emma Hamilton a strumpet, James Price, John Herbert and William Dodd were rogues, and Paine and Priestley atheistical or deistical writers; but history, *The Dictionary of National Biography* and the National Portrait Gallery have judged them worthy.

There have been inevitably some eccentricities, such as Charles Morris (NPG 739), punch maker and bard to the Sublime Society of Beef Steaks. In 1900 the *Westminster Gazette* had to explain that it was a ghost story that made the 2nd Baron Lyttelton (NPG 128) 'worth preserving in the National Portrait Gallery'. The drawing of Sir Watkin Lewes (NPG 2439), was discovered by George Scharf 'in one of the drawers of the table desk when I took office' and was eventually registered in 1929. Four interlopers arrived through mistaken identities: Johann Bodmer (acquired as Fuseli), the 8th Earl of Lauderdale (as Gainsborough), Thomas Greene (as Romney) and John Simpson (as the actor John Palmer). Burke's portrait by Barry (NPG 854) was received as William Combe by Cosway.

Approximately one third of the sitters are artists,[12] actors, writers and musicians, and a third are Peers, politicians, and army and navy officers. There are eighteen women (a ratio of one to twenty). Some sitters may now appear over-exposed: there are nine images of Garrick, eight of Johnson, seven of Hastings and six each of George III and Fox. Meanwhile the collection lacks good portraits of, for example, Hume and Rodney, and there is no portrait of Sir William Jones, whose statue, as we have seen, is in St Paul's. How satisfactory it would be to rediscover that head of Tom Paine by Romney, described by the artist's son as such that 'if Paine had not been notorious by his mischievous writings, this portrait alone would have rescued his name from oblivion'.

There are many outstanding portraits – the early Reynolds self portrait (NPG 41), Sam Foote by Colson (NPG 4904), the Reynolds of Warren Hastings (NPG 4445), Romney's Self portrait (NPG 959) or, for sentimental reasons, his last unfinished portrait of *Adam Walker with his Family* (NPG 1106)- but perhaps two might be singled out. The first by Reynolds shows the thirty-year-old Joseph Banks (NPG 5456); 'no painter', wrote Tom Taylor, 'could have so expressed the hungry heart of a man smitten with the passion of exploring and inquiring, unless he had felt a deep and intelligent sympathy with his sitter'. The second portrait was drawn by Romney of the poet William Cowper (NPG 1423) and is among the most haunting images in the collection. Cowper, diffident and shy, didn't care for his own portraiture; Romney was almost a kindred spirit, with a nervous and melancholy cast of mind. Cowper looks wide-eyed, intense and unforgettable.

1 Adam Smith, 6 June 1776; quoted by I.S. Ross, *The Life of Adam Smith*, 1995, p.292.
2 *The Economy of Vegetation*, 1792.
3 C. Bruyn Andrews & F. Andrews, eds., *The Torrington Diaries*, 1954, p.259 [1790].
4 *Of the Standard of Taste* [1757].
5 *Tristram Shandy* [1760-67], V, ch.i. George Crabbe enquired in *The Village* [1783] 'From truth and nature shall we widely stray, where Virgil, not where fancy, leads the way?' Northcote was to tell Hazlitt (in 'Conversation the Fourth' [1830]) that neo-classicism was like 'pouring liquors from one vessel into another, that become staler and staler every time.'
6 J. Hayes ed., *Letters of Gainsborough*, 2001, p.74.
7 Kearsley's *Gentleman's and Tradesman's Pocket Ledger* (Leslie & Taylor 1865, I, p.169n).
8 E K Waterhouse, *Three Decades of British Art*, 1965, p.65.
9 For whom, see Kerslake, *Early Georgian*, I, pp.314-20.

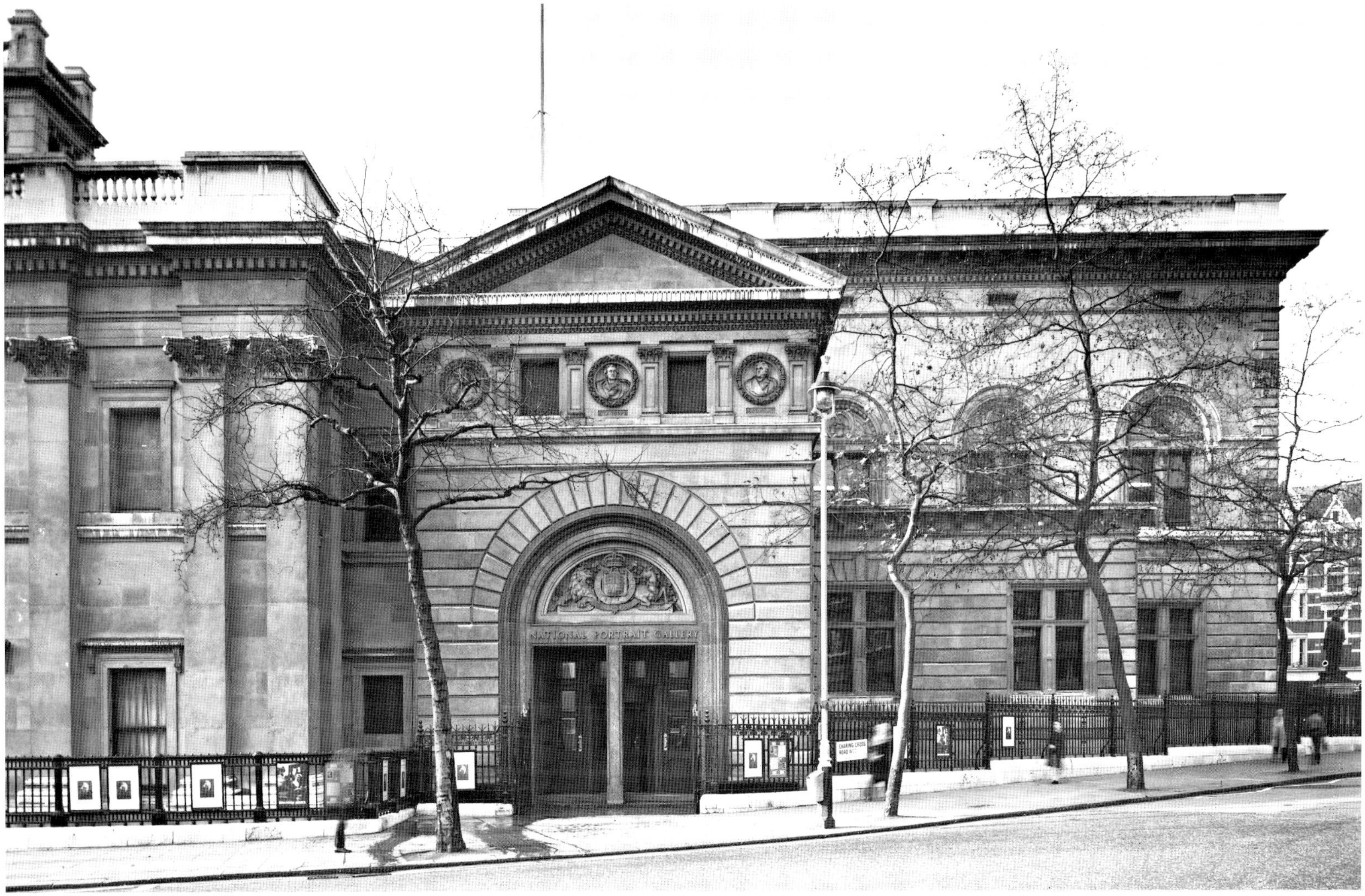

The National Portrait Gallery

ABBREVIATIONS

AG
Art Gallery

Allen 1987
B. Allen, *Francis Hayman*, 1987

Angelo 1904
H. Angelo, *Reminiscences*, 2 vols., 1904

Apples to Atoms 1986-87
Apples to Atoms, Portraits of Scientists from Newton to Rutherford, NPG travelling exhibition, Science Museum, Norwich, Grasmere, Coalbrookdale, 1986-87

AQ
Art Quarterly, published by the Detroit Institute of Arts, –1973

Archer 1979
M. Archer, *India and British Portraiture 1770-1825*, 1979

Archer 1986
M. Archer, *The India Office Collection of Paintings and Sculpture*, 1986

Arnason 1975
H.H. Arnason, *Houdon*, 1975

Artists at Work 1981-82
NPG travelling exhibition, Plymouth, Wolverhampton, Hull, Preston, 1981-82

Ashton 1992
G. Ashton, *Catalogue of Paintings at the Theatre Museum, London*, 1992

Ashton 1997
G. Ashton, *Pictures in the Garrick Club*, ed. K.A. Burnim & A. Wilton, 1997

Barry 1983
W. Pressly, *James Barry, The Artist as Hero*, exhibition catalogue, Tate Gallery, 1983

Bayne-Powell 1985
R. Bayne-Powell, *Catalogue of Portrait miniatures in the Fitzwilliam Museum*, Cambridge, 1985

Bayne-Powell 1995
R. Bayne-Powell, *Catalogue of Miniatures in the Holburne Museum and Crafts Study Centre*, Bath, 1995

Beach 1934
E.S. Beach, *Thomas Beach*, 1934

Beckford 2001
D.E. Ostergard ed., *William Beckford 1760-1844: An Eye for the Magnificent*, New York, Dulwich, 2001-02

Bell 1938
C.F. Bell, *Annals of Thomas Banks*, 1938

Bemrose 1885
J. Bemrose, *The Life and Works of Joseph Wright, commonly called 'Wright of Derby'*, 1885

Beningbrough
Beningbrough Hall, Yorks., National Trust property and NPG outstation

BFAC
Burlington Fine Arts Club

BI
British Institution

Binyon
L. Binyon, *Catalogue of Drawings by British Artists in the British Museum*, 4 vols., 1898-1907

Bone 1999
R. Walker, 'Henry Bone's Pencil Drawings in the National Portrait Gallery', *Wal. Soc.*, LXI, 1999, pp.305-67

Boswell
Boswell's Life of Johnson, ed. G.B. Hill & E.F. Powell, 6 vols., 1934-64

BPG
British Portrait Gallery within the Manchester *Art Treasures* exhibition, 1857

Brown 1980, 1987
L. Brown, *A Catalogue of British Historical Medals 1760-1960: The Accession of George III to the Death of William IV*, 1980; *The Reign of Queen Victoria*, 1987

Brown 1982
D.B. Brown, *Ashmolean Museum, Oxford, Catalogue of the Collection of Drawings*, iv, *The Earlier British Drawings*, 1982

Burke Corr.
T.W. Copeland *et al.* eds., *The Correspondence of Edmund Burke*, 10 vols. 1958-78

Burke LG
Burke's *Landed Gentry*

Burl. Mag.
The Burlington Magazine

Burney 1991
A. Ribeiro ed., *The Letters of Dr Charles Burney, I, 1751-1784*, 1991

Burnim 1998
K.A. Burnim & P.H. Highfill, *John Bell, patron of British Theatrical Portraiture*, 1998

Busco 1994
M. Busco, *Sir Richard Westmacott*, 1994

Byron 1981
A. Byron, *London Statues: A Guide to London's outdoor statues and sculpture*, 1981

Caffrey 2000
P. Caffrey, *Treasures to Hold, Irish and English Miniatures 1650-1850 from the National Gallery of Ireland Collection*, 2000

CAG
City Art Gallery

cat.
catalogue

Cavanagh 1997
T. Cavanagh, *Public Sculpture of Liverpool*, 1997

Caw 1903
J.L. Caw, *Scottish Portraits*, 2 vols., 1903

Chamberlain 1910
A.B. Chamberlain, *George Romney*, 1910

Chantrey 1847
Etched Reminiscences of the Models by Sir Francis Chantrey in the University Galleries Oxford, 1847

Chantrey 1994
A. Yarrington, I.D. Lieberman, A.Potts, M. Baker, 'An Edition of the Ledger of Sir Francis Chantrey, RA, at the Royal Academy, 1809-1841', *Wal. Soc.*, LVI, 1994

Churchill
W.A. Churchill, *Watermarks in Paper, in Holland, England, France, etc., in the XVII and XVIII centuries and their interconnection*, 1935

CL
Country Life

Clark 1985
A.M. Clark, ed. E.P. Bowron, *Pompeo Batoni*, 1985

Clifford 1952
J.L. Clifford, *Hester Lynch Piozzi (Mrs Thrale)*, 2nd ed. 1952

CMAG
City Museum & Art Gallery

Coffin & Hofstetter 2000
S. Coffin & B. Hofstetter, *The Gilbert Collection, Portrait Miniatures in Enamel*, 2000

Comerford 1999
P. Caffrey, *John Comerford and the Portrait Miniature in Ireland c.1620-1850*, exhibition catalogue, Kilkenny Archaeological Soc., 1999

Commons 1754-1790
L. Namier & J. Brooke, *History of Parliament, The Commons 1754-90*, 5 vols., 1964

Commons 1790-1820
R.G. Thorne, *History of Parliament, The Commons 1790-1820*, 7 vols., 1986

Cooksey 1991
J.C.B. Cooksey, *Alexander Nasmyth*, 1991

Copley 1995a
C. Rebora, P. Staiti *et al.*, *John Singleton Copley in America*, exhibition catalogue, Boston, New York, Houston, Milwaukee, 1995–96

Copley 1995b
E.B. Neff, *John Singleton Copley in England*, exhibition catalogue, Washington, Houston, 1995–96

Cormack 1970
M. Cormack, 'The Ledgers of Sir Joshua Reynolds', *Wal.Soc.*, XLII, 1970, pp.105–69

Cosway 1995
S. Lloyd, *Richard & Maria Cosway*, exhibition catalogue, Edinburgh, NPG, 1995–96

Cotton 1857
W. Cotton, *A Catalogue of the Portraits painted by Sir Joshua Reynolds*, 1857

CP
G.E.C[ockayne] *The Complete Peerage*, 13 vols., 1910–59 [reprint, 6 vols., 1982]

Croft-Murray
E. Croft-Murray, *Decorative Painting in England 1537–1837*, 2 vols., 1962, 1970

Crookshank & Webb 1990
A. Crookshank & D. Webb, *Paintings and Sculptures in Trinity College Dublin*, 1990

Cross 2000
D.A. Cross, *A Striking Likeness, The Life of George Romney*, 2000

CS
J.C. Smith, *British Mezzotint Portraits*, 4 vols., 1878–84, with supplementary vol. by C. Russell 1926; reference is given to the numbered lists of individual engraver's works

Dance 1977
D. Goodreau, *Nathaniel Dance*, exhibition catalogue, Kenwood, 1977

Dance Plates
[supplement to *Dance Portraits*], 1854, see Appendix II

Dance Portraits
A Collection of Portraits sketched from the Life since the Year 1793 by George Dance Esqr. R.A. and engraved in imitation of the Original Drawings by William Daniell, A.R.A., 2 vols., 1814, see Appendix II

Davies 1946
M. Davies, *National Gallery Catalogues, The British School*, 1946

Dawson 2000
A. Dawson, *Portrait Sculpture, A catalogue of the British Museum collection*, 2000

Delany 1861–62
Lady Llanover ed., *The Autobiography and Correspondence of Mary Granville, Mrs Delany*, 3 vols., 1861, a second series of 3 vols., 1862 [these vols. are referred to as I–VI]

Devis 1980
E.G. D'Oench, *The Conversation Piece: Arthur Devis & His Contemporaries*, exhibition catalogue, New Haven, 1980

Devis 1983
S.V. Sartin, *Polite Society by Arthur Devis*, exhibition catalogue, Preston, NPG, 1983–84

DNB
Dictionary of National Biography

Duleep Singh 1928
Prince Duleep Singh, *Portraits in Norfolk Houses*, 2 vols., 1928

Earland 1911
A. Earland, *Opie and his Circle*, 1911

Eidlitz 1928
R.J. Eidlitz, *Medallic Portraits of Matthew Boulton and James Watt*, 1928 (privately printed New York; NAL 73.A.130)

Egerton 1998
J. Egerton, *National Gallery Catalogues, The British School*, 1998

Eimer 1998
C. Eimer, *The Pingo Family & Medal Making in 18th-century Britain*, 1998

Erffa & Staley 1986
H. von Erffa & A. Staley, *The Paintings of Benjamin West*, 1986

Evans 1982
D. Evans, *Mather Brown: an early American artist in England*, 1982, with numbered catalogue

Evans 1999
D. Evans, *The Genius of Gilbert Stuart*, 1999

exh.
exhibition

Farington
Joseph Farington, *Diary*, 16 vols., 1978–98 (reference is made to the date of an entry)

Farrer 1908
E. Farrer, *Portraits in Suffolk Houses (West)*, 1908

Farrer 1921
E. Farrer, *Portraits in Suffolk Houses (East)*, 1921, 3 vols., typescript NPG archive

Forrer
L. Forrer, *Biographical Dictionary of Medallists*, 8 vols., 1904–30

Foskett 1964
D. Foskett, *John Smart*, 1964

Foskett 1972
D. Foskett, *A Dictionary of British Miniature Painters*, 2 vols., 1972

Foskett 1979
D. Foskett, *Collecting Miniatures*, 1979

FRS
Fellow of the Royal Society

FS
Free Society of Artists, London

FSA
Fellow of the Society of Antiquaries

Fulcher 1856
G.W. Fulcher, *Life of Thomas Gainsborough*, 1856

GAC
Government Art Collection

Gainsborough 1953
E.K. Waterhouse, 'Preliminary Check List of Portraits by Thomas Gainsborough', *Wal.Soc.*, XXXIII, 1953

Gainsborough & Reynolds 1994
Gainsborough & Reynolds, Contrasts in Royal Patronage, exhibition catalogue, The Queen's Gallery, 1994

Garlick 1989
K. Garlick, *Sir Thomas Lawrence: a complete catalogue of the oil paintings*, 1989

Garrick Letters 1963
D.M. Little & G.M. Kahrl, *The Letters of David Garrick*, 3 vols., 1963

George
M.D. George, *British Museum, Catalogue of Political and Personal Satires*, vols.V–VII, 1935–1942 (V nos.4839–636, VI nos.6361–8283, VII nos.8284–9692)

Georgian Playhouse 1975
I. Mackintosh & G. Ashton, *The Georgian Playhouse, Actors, Artists, Audiences and Architecture 1730–1830*, exhibition catalogue, Arts Council, 1975

Gibson 1977
R. Gibson, *Catalogue of Portraits in the Collection of the Earl of Clarendon*, 1977

GM
Gentleman's Magazine

Grasmere
Dove Cottage, the Wordsworth Museum, Grasmere

Graves RA
A. Graves, *The Royal Academy of Arts, a Complete Dictionary of Contributors and their work from its foundation in 1769 to 1904*, 8 vols., 1904 (reprint 1970)

Graves & Cronin
A. Graves & W.V. Cronin, *A History of the Works of Sir Joshua Reynolds*, 4 vols., 1899–1901

Gray 1894
J.M. Gray, *James and William Tassie, a biographical and critical sketch with a catalogue of their portrait medallions of modern personages*, 1894

Greene 1986
F. Owen, *Thomas Greene, Romney's Friend and Patron*, Kendal, 1986 (n.p., including Greene's diary of his tour in France with George Romney in 1764)

Grimaldi 1873
Rev. A. Grimaldi, *A Catalogue of Paintings, Drawings & Engravings by and after William Grimaldi*, 1873

Groseclose 1995
B. Groseclose, *British Sculpture and the Company Raj, Church Monuments and Public Statuary in Madras, Calcutta, and Bombay to 1858*, 1995

Grove
G.G. Grove ed., *A Dictionary of Music and Musicians*, 1st ed., 1879–89

Guelph 1891
Royal House of Guelph, exhibition catalogue, New Gallery, London, 1891

Gunnis 1968
R. Gunnis, *Dictionary of British Sculptors*, 1968 ed.

Hailstone 1869
E. Hailstone, *Portraits of Yorkshire worthies, selected from the National Exhibition of works of art at Leeds*, 1868, 2 vols., 1869

Hamilton 1972
P. Jaffé, *Lady Hamilton*, exhibition catalogue, Kenwood, 1972

Hamilton 1984
F. Cullen, 'The Oil Paintings of Hugh Douglas Hamilton', *Wal. Soc.*, LI, 1984, pp.165–208

Harcourt Papers
E.W. Harcourt ed. *The Harcourt Papers*, 14 vols., [1880–1905]

Harding
G.P. Harding, *List of Portraits in Various Mansions of the United Kingdom*, 3 MS vols., NPG library, 1804–20

Harvard Catalogue
L.A. Hall, *Catalogue of the Dramatic Portraits in the Theatre Collection of the Harvard College Library*, 4 vols., 1930–34

Hawkesbury 1903
Lord Hawkesbury, 'Catalogue of the Pictures at Hardwick Hall', *Derbyshire Archaeological and Natural History Society*, XXV, 1903, pp.103–158

Hawkesbury 1904
Lord Hawkesbury, 'Catalogue of the Portraits, Miniatures, &c, at Castle Howard, Yorkshire, and Naworth Castle, Cumberland', *Transactions of the East Riding Antiquarian Society*, XI, 1904, pp.35–122

Hawkesbury 1904a
Lord Hawkesbury, 'Catalogue of Portraits at Compton Place (Devonshire) and Buxted Park (Hon H.B. Portman), Miniatures at Devonshire House (Devonshire)', *Sussex Archaeological Society, Collections*, XLVII, 1904, pp.82–108

Hawkesbury 1906
Lord Hawkesbury, 'Catalogue of Portraits, Miniatures, &c., at Kirkham Abbey and 2 Carlton House Terrace, in the Possession of Lord Hawkesbury', *Transactions of the East Riding Antiquarian Society*, XIII, I, 1906, pp.1-139

Hayes 1970
J. Hayes, *The Drawings of Thomas Gainsborough*, 2 vols., 1970

Hayes 1975
J. Hayes, *Gainsborough*, 1975

Hayes 1992
J. Hayes, *Catalogue of British Paintings, The Collections of the National Gallery of Art, Washington*, 1992

Hayes 2001
J. Hayes ed., *Gainsborough Letters*, 2001

Hayley 1809
W. Hayley, *A Life of George Romney*, 1809

Henning 1977
J. Malden, *John Henning*, exhibition catalogue, Paisley, 1977

Hermitage 1997
B. Allen & L. Dukelskaya eds., *British Art Treasures from Russian Imperial Collections in the Hermitage*, 1997

Hewetson 1958
T.W.I. Hodgkinson, 'Christopher Hewetson, an Irish Sculptor in Rome', *Wal. Soc.*, XXXIV, 1958, pp.42-54

Hewetson 1986
B. de Breffny, 'Christopher Hewetson', *Irish Arts Review*, III, 3, 1986, pp.52-75

Hickey, *Memoirs*
Memoirs of William Hickey, ed. A. Spencer, 4 vols., 1913-25

Highfill
P.H. Highfill, K.A. Burnim & E.A. Langhans, *A Biographical Dictionary of Stage Personnel in London, 1660-1800*, 16 vols., 1973-93

Hilles 1952
F.W. Hilles, *Portraits by Sir Joshua Reynolds*, 1952

Historical Portraits
Historical Portraits 1700-1850, The Lives by C.R.L. Fletcher ..., 2 parts, 1919

Hoare 1990
E. Newby, *William Hoare of Bath*, exhibition catalogue, Victoria Art Gallery, Bath, 1990

Hull Grundy 1984
H. Tait ed., *The Art of the Jeweller, a Catalogue of the Hull Grundy Gift to the British Museum*, 2 vols., 1984

Huntington 2001
R. Asleson & S. Bennett, *Catalogue of British Paintings at the Huntington*, 2001

Hyde 1977
M. Hyde, *The Thrales of Streatham*, 1977

ILN
Illustrated London News

India Office
Oriental & India Office Collection, British Library

Ingamells 1981
J. Ingamells, *The English Episcopal Portrait 1559-1835*, 1981

Ingamells 1997
J. Ingamells, *Dictionary of British and Irish Tavellers in Italy 1701-1800, compiled from the Brinsley Ford Archive*, 1997

Ingamells 2000
J. Ingamells & J. Edgcumbe eds., *The Letters of Sir Joshua Reynolds*, 2000

Johnson 1976
E.M. Johnson, *Francis Cotes*, 1976

Joppien & Smith
R. Joppien & B. Smith, *The Art of Captain Cook's Voyages*, 3 vols., vol.3 in two parts (text & catalogue), 1985-88

JSAHR
Journal of the Society for Army Historical Research

Kauffmann 1968
A.M. Clark *et al.*, *Angelika Kauffmann und ihr Zeitgenossen*, exhibition catalogue, Bregenz, Vienna, 1968-69

Kauffmann 1998
B. Baumgärtel *et al.*, *Angelika Kauffmann Retrospektive*, exhibition catalogue, Dusseldorf, Munich, Chur, 1998-99

Kay Portraits 1842
A Series of Original Portraits and caricature etchings, by the late John Kay, with biographical sketches and anecdotes, 2 vols., 1842

Kerslake *Early Georgian*
J. Kerslake, *National Portrait Gallery, Early Georgian Portraits*, 2 vols., 1977

Kettle 1927
J.D. Milner, 'Tilly Kettle', *Wal. Soc.*, XV, 1927, pp.47-104

Kidson 1999
A. Kidson, *Earlier British Paintings in the Lady Lever Art Gallery*, 1999

Kirby Talley 1978
M. Kirby Talley, 'Thomas Bardwell', *Wal. Soc.*, XLVI, 1978, pp.91-163, with numbered catalogue

Kloss 1992
W. Kloss *et al.*, *Art in the White House*, 1992

Knox 1930
K.McC. Knox, *The Sharples*, 1930

L.
F. Lugt, *Répertoire des catalogues de ventes publiques 1600-1925*, 4 vols., 1938-87 (sales numbered consecutively throughout)

Lawrence 1964
K. Garlick, 'A Catalogue of the paintings, drawings and pastels of Sir Thomas Lawrence', *Wal. Soc.*, XXXIX, 1964

LeFanu 1960
W. LeFanu, *A Catalogue of the Portraits and other paintings drawings and sculpture in the Royal College of Surgeons of England*, 1960

Lennox-Boyd 1989
C. Lennox-Boyd, R. Dixon & T. Clayton, *George Stubbs, The Complete Engraved Works*, 1989

Leslie & Taylor 1865
C.R. Leslie & T. Taylor, *Life and Times of Sir Joshua Reynolds*, 2 vols., 1865

MA
Magazine of Art

McKay & Roberts 1909
W. McKay & W. Roberts, *John Hoppner RA*, 1909

McKechnie 1978
S. McKechnie, *British Silhouette Artists and their Work 1760-1860*, 1978

MAG
Museum and Art Gallery

Mag.
Magazine

Malone 1797
E. Malone ed., *The Works of Sir Joshua Reynolds*, 2 vols., 1797

Mander & Mitchenson 1955
R. Mander & J. Mitchenson, *The Artist and the Theatre, the story of the paintings collected and presented to the National Theatre by W. Somerset Maugham*, 1955

Mander & Mitchenson 1957
R. Mander & J. Mitchenson, *A Picture History of the British Theatre*, 1957

Mander & Mitchenson 1980
R. Mander & J. Mitchenson, *et al.*, *Guide to the Maugham Collection of Theatrical Paintings*, 1980

Mannings 2000
D. Mannings, *Sir Joshua Reynolds*, 2 vols., 2000; reference is made to the numbered catalogue in vol.1

Marchant 1987
G. Seidmann, 'Nathaniel Marchant, Gem-Engraver 1739-1816', *Wal. Soc.*, LIII, 1987, pp.5-105

Mason 1973
C.B.L. Barr & J. Ingamells, *A Candidate for Praise, William Mason 1725-97, Precentor of York*, exhibition catalogue, York, 1973

Master Drawings 1993-95
Master Drawings from the National Portrait Gallery, NPG exhibition catalogue, Tulsa, Miami, Washington, Ottawa, NPG, Manchester, Carlisle, Canterbury, 1993-95

Miles 1977
E.G. Miles, *Thomas Hudson: Portraitist to the British Establishment*, University Microfilms, 2 vols., 1977; reference is made to the numbered catalogue in vol. 2

Miles 1995
E.G. Miles, *American Paintings of the Eighteenth Century, The Collections of the National Gallery of Art, Washington*, 1995

Millar 1963
Sir Oliver Millar, *The Tudor, Stuart and Early Georgian Pictures in the Collection of Her Majesty The Queen*, 2 vols., 1963, reference is made to the numbered catalogue in vol.1

Millar 1969
Sir Oliver Millar, *The Later Georgian Pictures in the Collection of Her Majesty The Queen*, 2 vols., 1969, reference is made to the numbered catalogue in vol.1

Mortimer 1986
J. Sunderland, 'John Hamilton Mortimer, his Life and Works', *Wal. Soc.*, LII, 1986

Musgrave MSS
Sir William Musgrave, MS lists of portraits in private collections, BM Add. MSS 6391 and 6392 [see *Wal. Soc.*, LIV, 1988, pp.454-502]

NAL
National Art Library, Victoria and Albert Museum, London

NG
National Gallery

NHMF
National Heritage Memorial Fund

Nichols *Anecdotes*
J. Nichols, *Literary Anecdotes of the Eighteenth Century*, 9 vols., 1812-1815

Nichols *Illustrations*
J. Nichols, *Illustrations of the Literary History of the Eighteenth century ... intended as a sequel to The Literary Anecdotes*, 6 vols., 1817-31; supp. vols.7 & 8 by J.B. Nichols, 1848, 1858

Nicolson 1968
B. Nicolson, *Joseph Wright of Derby*, 2 vols., 1968; reference is made to the numbered catalogue in vol.1

Northcote 1819
J. Northcote, *The Life of Sir Joshua Reynolds*, 2 vols., 2nd ed. 1819

Northcote 1996
J. Simon, 'The Account Book of James Northcote', *Wal. Soc.*, LVIII, 1996, pp.21-126

NPE 1867
Second special exhibition of National Portraits (William and Mary to MDCCC), South Kensington, 1867

NPE 1868
Third and concluding exhibition of National Portraits (fortieth year of the reign of George the third to MDCCCLXVII), South Kensington, 1868

NPG
National Portrait Gallery

NPG *Burney Diaries*
Diary and Letters of Frances D'Arblay 1778-1840, ed. C. Bennett, 6 vols., 1904-05, with extra illustrations collected by F. Leverton Harris, 20 vols. folio

NQ
Notes and Queries

NT
National Trust

O'Donoghue
F. O'Donoghue, *Catalogue of Engraved British Portraits in the British Museum*, 6 vols., 1908-25 [vols.1-4 by O'Donoghue, vol.5 by O'Donoghue & H.M. Hake, vol.6 by Hake]

OP 1906
Illustrated Catalogue of a loan exhibition of Portraits of English historical personages who died between 1714 and 1837, exhibited in the Examination Schools, Oxford, 1906

Oppé 1947
A.P. Oppé, *The Drawings of Paul and Thomas Sandby in the Collection of His Majesty the King at Windsor Castle*, 1947

Oppé 1950
A.P. Oppé, *English Drawings, Stuart and Georgian periods, in the Collection of His Majesty the King at Windsor Castle*, 1950

Park 1926
L. Park, *Gilbert Stuart*, 4 vols., 1926 (numbered catalogue, I nos.1-528, II nos.529-948 and Washington nos.1-111; III & IV plates)

Patch 1940
F.J.B. Watson, 'Thomas Patch . . . with a catalogue of his known works', *Wal. Soc.*, XXVIII, 1940, pp.15-50

Peale 1992
L.B. Miller, *In Pursuit of fame: Rembrandt Peale*, exhibition catalogue, NPG Washington, 1992-93

Penny 1992
N. Penny, *Catalogue of European Sculpture in the Ashmolean Museum*, Oxford, 3 vols., 1992

Phillips Sitter Book
MS copy by J.D. Milner 1899 of Thomas Phillips's sitter book 1796-1843; NPG library

Phillips 1854
Samuel Phillips, *The Portrait Gallery of the Crystal Palace*, 1854

Pine 1979
R.G. Stewart, *Robert Edge Pine, A British Portrait Painter in America 1784-88*, exhibition catalogue, Washington, 1979

Piozzi Letters
E.A. & L.D. Bloom ed., *The Piozzi Letters*, vols.1-5, 1989-99

Poole
Mrs R.L. Poole, *Catalogue of Portraits in the possession of the University, Colleges and City and County of Oxford*, 3 vols., 1912, 1925

Portland Cat 1936
R.W. Goulding & C.K. Adams, *Catalogue of the Pictures belonging to His Grace the Duke of Portland at Welbeck Abbey, 17 Hill Street, London, and Langwell House*, 1936

Pressly 1981
W.L. Pressly, *The Life and Art of James Barry*, 1981; the catalogue has separate numbering for paintings, drawings and prints

Pressly 1993
W.L. Pressly, *A Catalogue of Paintings in the Folger Shakespeare Library*, 1993

Prown 1966
J.D. Prown, *John Singleton Copley*, 2 vols., 1966

Pyke 1973
E.J. Pyke, *A Biographical Dictionary of Wax Modellers*, 1973

Pyke 1981
E.J. Pyke, *Wax Modellers (Supplement)*, 1981

RA
Royal Academy

Rackham 1924
B. Rackham, *Catalogue of the Schreiber Collection, Victoria and Albert Museum*, III, *Enamels and Glass*, 1924

Rackham 1930
B. Rackham, *Catalogue of the Schreiber Collection, Victoria and Albert Museum*, II, *Earthenware*, 1930

Raspe 1791
A Descriptive Catalogue of a general collection of ancient and modern engraved gems ... by James Tassie, modeller; arranged and described by R.E. Raspe, 2 vols., 1791

Read 1982
B. Read, *Victorian Sculpture*, 1982

Redford
B. Redford, ed., *The Letters of Samuel Johnson*, 5 vols., 1992-94

Reilly 1973
R. Reilly & G. Savage, *Wedgwood the Portrait Medallions*, 1973

Reilly 1989
R. Reilly, *Wedgwood*, 2 vols., 1989

Reilly 1994
R. Reilly, *Wedgwood Jasper*, 1994

Reynolds 1986
N. Penny & D. Mannings, *Joshua Reynolds*, exhibition catalogue, Royal Academy, 1986

Reynolds 1992
D. Mannings, *Sir Joshua Reynolds: The Self Portraits*, exhibition catalogue, Sudbury, Plymouth, 1992

Reynolds 1996
G. Reynolds, *European Miniatures in The Metropolitan Museum of Art*, 1996

RHA
Royal Hibernian Academy

RIBA
Royal Institute of British Architects

Ribeiro 2000
A. Ribeiro, *The Gallery of Fashion*, 2000

Riccio 2000
B. Riccio ed., *Mary Berry un'inglese in Italia, diari e corrispondenza dal 1783 al 1823*, 2000

Rigaud Memoir
W.L. Pressly ed., 'Facts and Recollections of the XVIIIth Century in a Memoir of John Francis Rigaud Esq., R.A.', by Stephen Francis Dutilh Rigaud, *Wal. Soc.*, L, 1984, pp.1-164

Roberts 1907
W. Roberts, *Sir William Beechey RA*, 1907

Rogers 1878
J.J. Rogers, *John Opie and his Works*, 1878

Romney 1830
Rev. John Romney, *Memoirs of the Life and Works of George Romney ... also some particulars of the life of Peter Romney, his Brother*, 1830

Romney 2002
A. Kidson, *George Romney*, exhibition catalogue, Liverpool, NPG, San Marino 2002

Roworth 1992
W.W. Roworth ed., *Angelica Kauffman, a Continental Artist in Georgian England*, 1992

Royal Society 1980
N.H. Robinson, *Royal Society Catalogue of Portraits*, 1980

RSBA
Royal Society of British Artists

Russell Album
album of 244 photographs of pictures by John Russell, compiled c.1900; NPG archive

SA
Society of Artists, London

SBA
Society of British Artists, Suffolk Street, London

Scarisbrick 1994
D. Scarisbrick, *Jewellery in Britain 1066-1837*, 1994

Schidlof 1964
L.R. Schidlof, *The Miniature in Europe*, 4 vols., 1964

Schiff 1973
G. Schiff, *Johann Heinrich Füssli, oeuvre kataloge*, 2 vols., 1973

Schimmelpenninck 1858
Life of Mary Anne Schimmelpenninck, ed. C.C. Hankin, 2 vols., 1858

Simon 1997
J. Simon, *The Art of the Picture Frame*, NPG, 1997

SK
South Kensington

SKM 1865
Special Exhibition of Portrait Miniatures, South Kensington, 1865

Smart 1999
A. Smart, ed. J. Ingamells, *Allan Ramsay, a complete catalogue of his Paintings*, 1999

Smith 1905
J.T. Smith, *A Book for a Rainy Day*, ed. W. Whitten, 1905 [first pub. posthumously 1845]

Smith 1920
J.T. Smith, *Nollekens and his Times*, ed. W. Whitten, 2 vols., 1920 [first published 1828]

SNPG
Scottish National Portrait Gallery

SSB
Sir George Scharf's Sketch Books (NPG archive)

Steegman
J. Steegman, *Portraits in Welsh Houses*, 2 vols., 1957, 1962

Stephens
F.G. Stephens, *British Museum, Catalogue of Political and Personal Satires*, vols.I-IV, 1870-1883 (I nos.1-1235, II nos.1236-2015, III/i nos.2016-3116, III/ii nos.3117-3804, IV nos.3805-4838)

Strickland 1913
W. Strickland, *Dictionary of Irish Artists*, 2 vols., 1913

Thackray 1995
J.C. Thackray, *A Catalogue of the Portraits, Paintings and Sculpture at the Natural History Museum, London*, 1995

Thraliana 1942
K. Balderstone ed., *Thraliana*, 2 vols., 1942

Treasures 1995-96
Treasures from the National Portrait Gallery, NPG exhibition, Fukushima, Nagoya, Kitakyushu Hiroshima, Tokyo, 1995-96

Trumbull 1982
H.A. Cooper, *John Trumbull*, exhibition catalogue, Yale University AG, 1982

TSB
Sir George Scharf's Trustees' Sketch Books (NPG archive)

Vases and Volcanoes 1996
I. Jenkins & K. Sloan, *Vases and Volcanoes: Sir William Hamilton and his Collection*, exhibition catalogue, British Museum, 1996

Vertue III
G. Vertue, Note Books, III, *Wal. Soc.*, XXII, 1934

Waagen
G.F. Waagen, *Treasures of Art in Great Britain*, 3 vols., 1854; supplementary vol. 4, *Galleries and Cabinets of Art in Great Britain*, 1857

Wal. Corr.
Horace Walpole's Correspondence, ed. W.S. Lewis, 43 vols. + 5 index, 1937-83

Wal. Soc.
Walpole Society

Walker 1862
W. Walker jr., *Memoirs of the Distinguished Men of Science of Great Britain living in the years 1807-8*, 1862

Walker 1976
R.J.B. Walker, *A Check List of Portraits in the Department of the Environment Picture Collection*, 1976

Walker 1988
R.J.B. Walker, *A Catalogue of paintings, drawings, engravings and sculpture in The Palace of Westminster compiled during 1959-77*, 4 vols., 1988 [typescript in NPG archive]

Walker 1992
R.J.B. Walker, *The eighteenth and early nineteenth century Miniatures in the Collection of Her Majesty The Queen*, 1992

Walker 1997
R.J.B. Walker, *Miniatures, a selection of miniatures in the Ashmolean Museum*, 1997

Walker 1998
R.J.B. Walker, *Miniatures in the National Portrait Gallery*, 1998

Walker *Regency*
R.J.B. Walker, *National Portrait Gallery, Regency Portraits*, 2 vols., 1985

Walpole Anecdotes V
F.W. Hilles & P.B. Daghlian eds., *Horace Walpole Anecdotes of Painting*, V, 1937

Walton 1999
E. Bell, 'Life and Work of Henry Walton', *Gainsborough's House Review*, 1998/99, pp.40-104

Ward 1981
A. Ward *et al.*, *The Ring from Antiquity to the Twentieth Century*, 1981

Ward & Roberts 1904
H. Ward & W. Roberts, *Romney, A Biographical and Critical Essay with a Catalogue Raisonné of his Works*, 2 vols., 1904

Waterhouse 1941
E.K. Waterhouse, *Reynolds*, 1941

Waterhouse 1958
E.K. Waterhouse, *Gainsborough*, 1958

Waterhouse 1981
E.K. Waterhouse, *Dictionary of British Eighteenth-century Painters*, 1981

Webster 1970
M. Webster, *Francis Wheatley*, 1970

Whinney 1964
M. Whinney, *Sculpture in Britain 1530-1830*, 1964

Whitbread 1984
S. Deuchar, *Samuel Whitbread and British Art*, exhibition catalogue, Museum of London, 1984

Whitley 1915
W.T. Whitley, *Thomas Gainsborough*, 1915

Whitley 1928
W.T. Whitley, *Artists and their Friends in England 1700-1799*, 2 vols., 1928

Whitley 1930
W.T. Whitley, *Art in England 1821-1837*, 1930

Whitley 1932
W.T. Whitley, *Gilbert Stuart*, 1932

Williamson 1894
G.C. Williamson, *John Russell*, 1894

Williamson 1897
G.C. Williamson, *Portrait Miniatures*, 1897

Williamson 1902
G.C. Williamson & H.L.D. Engleheart, *George Engleheart*, 1902

Williamson 1904
G.C. Williamson, *The History of Portrait Miniatures*, 2 vols., 1904

Williamson 1905
G.C. Williamson, *Richard Cosway*, 1905

Williamson 1906
G.C. Williamson, *Catalogue of the Collection of Miniatures, the property of J. Pierpont Morgan*, 4 vols., 1906-08

Williamson 1907
G.C. Williamson, *John Downman*, 1907

Williamson 1914
G.C. Williamson, *Catalogue of a Collection of Miniatures, The Property of HRH Prince Ernest Augustus ... Duke of Brunswick-Lüneburg*, 1914 (privately distributed)

Williamson 1918
G.C. Williamson, *Ozias Humphry*, 1918

Williamson 1920
G.C. Williamson & Lady Victoria Manners, *John Zoffany, R.A., his life and works*, 1920

Williamson 1921
G.C. Williamson, *Daniel Gardner*, 1921

Williamson 1924
G.C. Williamson & Lady Victoria Manners, *Angelica Kauffmann, R.A., her life and works*, 1924

Wraxall
The Historical and Posthumous Memoirs of Sir Nathaniel Wraxall 1772-1784, 5 vols., 1884

Wright 1985
M.H. Fabian, *Joseph Wright, American Artist*, exhibition catalogue, NPG Washington, 1985

Wright 1990
J. Egerton *et al.*, *Wright of Derby*, exhibition catalogue, London, Paris, New York, 1990

Wunder 1991
R.P. Wunder, *Hiram Powers*, 2 vols., 1991

Zoffany 1977
M. Webster, *Johan Zoffany*, exhibition catalogue, NPG, 1977

EXPLANATION

Sitters are discussed in alphabetical order as follows

A brief biography, often with contemporary quotations (identified by author and date) concerning the sitter's appearance and behaviour.

Abbreviations pertaining to the individual sitter.

Description and discussion of individual works in the collection; where there is more than one image they are arranged in order of date.

The heading cites, in order, accession number, artist or attribution, and date. A date in square brackets [1773] indicates the date of the original image from which a portrait derives.

Measurements, height before width - metric (imperial).

Notes on condition - confined to the more obvious peculiarities; conservation reports on the majority of objects are in the NPG archive.

Description to supplement the illustration (compiled before colour illustration was agreed).

Exhibitions: including longer-term loans to out-stations (e.g. Beningbrough); records of long-term loans pre-1939 are incomplete.

Reference: a discriminating list; where there is a recent oeuvre-catalogue, mention of previous catalogues is generally omitted, as are all references confined to illustrations. Further references are provided by exhibition catalogues (as listed under Exhibitions) and footnotes.

Iconography: a chronology of other known portraits of the sitter, principally derived from the NPG Heinz Archive. Dates are taken where necessary from previous publications, or from exhibitions or engravings (as cited). Reference is made wherever possible to an illustration or to an illustrated catalogue, but no attempt is made at a comprehensive bibliography. Works illustrated within the text are marked with an asterisk.* Theatrical portraits and/or historical scenes are listed selectively in summary form at the end. Posthumous works are listed with discretion.

Doubtful Portraits are summarily listed and not indexed.

The alphabetical sequence of named sitters is followed by Group Portraits, Unidentified Portraits and Comparative Groups, see Contents.

LIST OF SITTERS

Abel, Karl Friedrich (1723-87)
Acton, Sir John Francis Edward, 6th Bt (1736-1811)
Adam, John (1721-92)
Adam, Robert (1728-92)
Affleck, Philip (1726-99)
Allan, George (1736-1800)
Allan, Mrs Ann (1741-87)
Amherst, Jeffery Amherst, 1st Baron (1717-97)
Angelo, Henry (1756-1835)
Anstey, Christopher (1724-1805)
Argyll, Elizabeth, Duchess of (1734-90)
Arkwright, Sir Richard, Kt (1732-92)
Arne, Thomas (1710-78)
Ashburton, John Dunning, 1st Baron (1731-83)
Bach, Johann Christian (1735-82)
Bacon, John, senior (1740-99)
Baddeley, Robert (1733-94)
Bakewell, Robert (1725-95)
Banks, Sir Joseph, Bt (1743-1820)
Barbauld, Mrs Anna Letitia (1743-1825)
Baretti, Giuseppe (1719-89)
Baring, Sir Francis, 1st Bt (1740-1810)
Barré, Isaac (1726-1802)
Barrington, Hon. Samuel (1729-1800)
Barry, James (1741-1806)
Bartolozzi, Francesco (1727-1815)
Beach, Thomas (1738-1806)
Beadon, Richard (1737-1824)
Beaufort, Daniel Augustus (1739-1821)
Beckford, William (1709-70)
Beckford, William (1760-1844)
Bedford, John Russell, 4th Duke of (1710-71)
Bentham, Jeremy (1748-1832)
Bentham, Sir Samuel Johnson, Kt (1757-1831)
Bentley, Richard (1708-82)
Bentley, Thomas (1730-80)
Berry, Mary (1763-1852)
Bessborough, Frederick Ponsonby, 3rd Earl of (1758-1844)
Black, Joseph (1728-99)
Blackstone, Sir William, Kt (1723-80)
Bligh, William (1754-1817)
Bodmer, Johann Jakob (1698-1783)
Bonomi, Joseph (1739-1808)
Boswell, James (1740-95)
Boulton, Matthew (1728-1809)
Boyce, William (1711-79)
Boydell, John (1719-1804)
Bridgewater, Francis Egerton, 3rd Duke of (1736-1803)
Brindley, James (1716-72)
Bristol, Augustus John Hervey, 3rd Earl of (1724-79)
Bristol, Frederick Augustus Hervey, 4th Earl of (1730-1803)
Brown, Lancelot (1716-83)
Bruce, James (1730-94)
Buller, Sir Francis, 1st Bt (1746-1800)
Burke, Edmund (1730-97)
Burney, Charles (1726-1814)
Burney, Charles Rousseau (1747-1819)
Burns, Robert (1759-96)
Burrow, Sir James, Kt (1701-82)
Bute, John Stuart, 3rd Earl of (1713-92)
Camden, Charles Pratt, 1st Earl (1714-94)
Carleton, Hugh Carleton, Viscount (1739-1826)
Carlini, Agostino (c.1718-90)
Carnac, John (1716-1800)
Carr, John (1723-1807)
Carter, Elizabeth (1717-1806)
Cavallo, Tiberius (1749-1809)
Cavendish, Henry (1731-1810)
Chamberlin, Mason (1722-87)
Chambers, Sir William, Kt (1723-96)
Charlemont, James Caulfeild, 1st Earl of (1728-99)
Charlotte, Queen (1744-1818)
Cheesman, Thomas (1760-1835)
Children, George (1742-1818)
Cholmondeley, George James Cholmondeley, 1st Marquess of (1749-1827)
Cipriani, Giovanni Battista (1727-85)
Cobb, James (1756-1818)
Coke, Thomas (1747-1814)
Cole, Thomas (c.1730-96)
Colman, George (1732-94)
Conway, Hon. Henry Seymour (1719-95)
Cook, James (1728-79)
Coote, Sir Eyre, KB (1726-83)
Copley, John Singleton (1737-1815)
Cornewall, Folliott Herbert Walker (1754-1831)
Cornwallis, Charles Cornwallis, 1st Marquess (1738-1805)
Cosway, Richard (1740-1821)
Cowper, William (1731-1800)
Cramer, Wilhelm (1746-99)
Crewe, John Crewe, 1st Baron (1742-1829)
Cumberland, Richard (1732-1811)

Dale, David (1739-1806)
Dance, Nathaniel (1735-1811)
Dancer, Daniel (1716-94)
Darwin, Erasmus (1731-1802)
Day, Thomas (1748-89)
Delany, Mrs Mary (1700-88)
De Loutherbourg, Philippe Jacques (1740-1812)
le Despencer, Francis Dashwood, 15th Baron (1708-81)
Devis, Arthur (1712-87)
Devonshire, Georgiana, Duchess of (1757-1806)
Devonshire, William Cavendish, 5th Duke of (1748-1811)
Dibdin, Charles (1745-1814)
Dodd, William (1729-77)
Dollond, Peter (1730-1820)
Doughty, William (1757-80/82)
Edgeworth, Richard Lovell (1744-1817)
Egmont, John Perceval, 2nd Earl of (1711-70)
Egremont, Charles Wyndham, 2nd Earl of (1710-63)
Farmer, George (1732-79)
Fawcett, Sir William, KB (1728-1804)
Fielding, Sir John, Kt (1721-80)
Finch, Lady Charlotte (1725-1813)
Fitzpatrick, Hon. Richard (1747-1813)
Foote, Samuel (1720-77)
Fourdrinier, Henry (1730-99)
Fox, Charles James (1749-1806)
Francis, Sir Philip, KB (1740-1818)
Franklin, Benjamin (1706-90)
Gage, Hon. Thomas (1721-87)
Gainsborough, Thomas (1727-88)
Gardner, Alan Gardner, 1st Baron (1742-1808)
Garrick, David (1717-79)
Garrick, Mrs Eva Maria (1724-1822)
George III (1738-1820)
Gibbon, Edward (1737-94)
Gilbert, Thomas (c.1719-98)
Gilpin, Sawrey (1733-1807)
Gilpin, William (1724-1804)
Glynn, John (1722-79)
Goldsmith, Oliver (1728-74)
Gordon, Lord George (1751-93)
Grafton, Augustus Henry Fitzroy, 3rd Duke of (1735-1811)
Granger, James (1723-76)
Graves, Richard (1715-1804)
Green, Valentine (1739-1813)
Greene, Thomas (1737-1810)
Gresse, John Alexander (1741-94)
Griffith, Mrs Elizabeth (1727-93)
Guilford, Frederick North, 2nd Earl of (1732-92)
Gwyn, Mrs Mary (c.1752-1840)
Gwynn, John (1713-86)
Haldimand, Sir Frederick, KB (1718-91)
Hall, John (1740-97)
Hamilton, Emma, Lady (1765-1815)
Hamilton, Sir William, KB (1730-1803)
Hamilton, William (1751-1801)
Harcourt, William Harcourt, 3rd Earl (1743-1830)
Harris, James (1709-80)
Harrison, John (1693-1776)
Harrison, Robert (1715-1802)
Hastings, Warren (1732-1818)
Haward, Francis (1759-97)
Hawkins, Sir John, Kt (1719-89)
Hearne, Thomas (1744-1817)
Heathfield, George Augustus Eliott, 1st Baron (1717-90)
Henderson, John (1747-85)
Herbert, John (1723-99)
Hill, Sir Richard, 2nd Bt (1732-1808)
Hill, Rowland (1744-1833)
Hinchliffe, John (1731-94)
Holland, Charles (1733-69)
Home, John (1722-1808)
Hone, Nathaniel (1718-84)
Hoole, John (1727-1803)
Horsley, Samuel (1733-1806)
Howard, John (1726?-90)
Howe, Richard Howe, 1st Earl (1726-99)
Hull, Thomas (1728-1808)
Hume, David (1711-76)
Hunter, John (1728-93)
Hunter, William (1718-83)
Huntingdon, Selina, Countess of (1707-91)
Hutton, Charles (1737-1823)
Impey, Sir Elijah, Kt (1732-1809)
Ireland, Samuel (1744-1800)
Irwin, Sir John, KB (1722-88)
Jefferys, John (1751-84)
Jenkins, Thomas (1722-98)
Jennings, Henry Constantine (1731-1819)
Johnson, Samuel (1709-84)
Jones, John Paul (1747-92)
Kauffmann, Angelica (1741-1807)
Kelway, Joseph (c.1702-82)
Kempenfelt, Richard (1718-82)
Kenyon, Lloyd Kenyon, 1st Baron (1732-1802)
Keppel, Augustus Keppel, Viscount (1725-86)
Kerrich, Thomas (1748-1828)
Lansdowne, William Petty, 1st Marquess of (1737-1805)
Lauderdale, James Maitland, 8th Earl of (1759-1839)
Leeds, Francis Osborne, 5th Duke of (1751-99)
Lennox, Mrs Charlotte (1720-1804)
Lewes, Sir Watkin, Kt (1740?-1821)
Lewis, William Thomas (c.1746-1811)
Lifford, James Hewitt, 1st Viscount (1712-89)
Liverpool, Charles Jenkinson, 1st Earl of (1727-1808)
Lynch, Sir William, KB (c.1730-85)
Lyttelton, Thomas Lyttelton, 2nd Baron (1744-99)
Macartney, George Macartney, Earl (1737-1806)
Macaulay, Mrs Catharine (1731-91)
Macpherson, James (1736-96)
Malone, Edmond (1741-1812)
Mansfield, William Murray, 1st Earl of (1705-93)
Markham, William (1719-1807)
Maskelyne, Nevil (1732-1811)
Mason, William (1725-97)
Meikle, Andrew (1719-1811)
Mendip, Welbore Ellis, 1st Baron (1713-1802)
Metcalfe, Philip (1733-1818)
Miller, Patrick (1731-1815)
Milne, Colin (1743-1815)
Molini, Pietro (1729/30-1806)
Montagu, Edward Wortley (1713-76)
Montagu, Mrs Elizabeth (1720-1800)
Moore, Dr John (1729-1802)
Moore, Archbishop John (1730-1805)
More, Hannah (1745-1833)

Mornington, Anne, Countess of (1742-1831)
Morris, Charles (1745-1838)
Mortimer, John Hamilton (1740-79)
Mulgrave, Constantine John Phipps, 2nd Baron (1744-92)
Munro, Sir Hector, KB (1726-1805)
Murphy, Arthur (1727-1805)
Murray, Hon. James (1719-94)
Mylne, Robert (1733-1811)
Needham, John Turberville (1713-81)
Newcastle, Henry Clinton, 2nd Duke of (1720-94)
Norfolk, Charles Howard, 11th Duke of (1746-1815)
North, Hon. Brownlow (1741-1820)
North, Dudley Long (1748-1829)
Northington, Robert Henley, 1st Earl of (c.1708-1772)
Northumberland, Hugh (Smithson) Percy, 1st Duke of (1715-86)
Onslow, George Onslow, 1st Earl of (1731-1814)
Oram, Edward (fl.1766-99)
Orford, Horace Walpole, 4th Earl of (1717-97)
Paine, Thomas (1737-1809)
Paley, William (1743-1805)
Palmer, John (1742-98)
Patch, Thomas (1725-82)
Phelps, Richard (1718?-85)
Phillip, Arthur (1738-1814)
Pigot, George Pigot, Baron (1719-77)
Piozzi, Gabriel (1740-1809)
Piozzi, Mrs Hester (1741-1821)
Prescott, Robert (1725-1816)
Price, James (1752-83)
Priestley, Joseph (1733-1804)
Quick, John (1748-1831)
Raikes, Robert (1735-1811)
Ramsay, James (1733-89)
Rennell, James (1742-1830)
Reynolds, Sir Joshua, Kt (1723-92)
Reynolds, Richard (1735-1816)
Richmond and Lennox, Charles Lennox, 3rd Duke of (1735-1806)
Robertson, William (1721-93)
Robinson, Sir Thomas, 1st Bt (1702?-77)
Rochford, William Henry Nassau de Zuylestein, 4th Earl of (1717-81)
Rockingham, Charles Watson-Wentworth, 2nd Marquess of (1730-82)
Rodney, George Brydges, 1st Baron (1719-92)
Romaine, William (1714-95)
Romney, George (1734-1802)
Rossi, John Charles Felix (1762-1839)
Roxburghe, John Ker, 3rd Duke of (1740-1804)
Russell, John (1745-1806)
St John, St Andrew St John, 14th Baron (1759-1817)
Sandby, Paul (1731-1809)
Sandby, Thomas (1721-98)
Sandwich, John Montagu, 4th Earl of (1718-92)
Schanck, John (1740-1823)
Serres, Dominic (1719-93)
Seward, Anna (1742-1809)
Seward William (1747-99)
Sharp, Granville (1735-1813)
Sheffield, Anne, Countess of (1764-1832)
Sheffield, John Baker Holroyd, 1st Earl of (1735-1821)
Sheridan, Mrs Elizabeth (1754-92)
Sibthorp, Humphry (1713-97)
Siddons, Mrs Sarah (1755-1831)
Simpson, John (c.1738-before 1789)
Smart, John (1742/3-1811)
Smeaton, John (1724-92)
Smith, Adam (1723-90)
Snelling, Thomas (1712-73)
Spencer, Lord Robert (1747-1831)
Spode, Josiah I (1733-97)
Spode, Josiah II (1754-1827)
Staunton, Sir George Leonard, 1st Bt (1737-1801)
Steevens, George (1736-1800)
Stillingfleet, Benjamin (1702-71)
Strahan, William (1715-85)
Strange, James Smith Stanley, Lord (1717-71)
Stuart, Mrs Elizabeth (1762-99)
Stuart, James (1713-88)
Stubbs, George (1724-1806)
Suckling, Maurice (1725-78)
Taylor Sir Robert, Kt (1714-88)
Temple, Ann, Countess (1709-77)
Temple, Richard Grenville-Temple, 2nd Earl (1711-79)
Thicknesse, Philip (1719-92)
Thurlow, Edward Thurlow, 1st Baron (1731-1806)
Tooke, John Horne (1736-1812)
Toplady, Augustus Montague (1740-78)
Townshend, Lord John (1757-1833)
Tyrwhitt, Thomas (1730-86)
Upper Ossory, John Fitzpatrick, 2nd Earl of (1745-1818)
Vancouver, George (1757-98)
Venn, Henry (1725-97)
Vesey, Mrs Elizabeth (1715?-91)
Vincent, William (1739-1815)
Walker, Adam (1731-1821)
Walker, John (1732-1807)
Washington, George (1732-99)
Watson, Richard (1737-1816)
Watt, James (1736-1819)
Wedgwood, Josiah (1730-95)
Wheatley, Francis (1747-1801)
Whitefoord, Caleb (1734-1810)
Whitehead, William (1715-85)
Wilkes, John (1725-97)
Wilkinson, John (1728-1808)
Willis, Francis (1718-1807)
Wilson, Richard (1714-82)
Wilton, Joseph (1722-1803)
Wolcot, John (1738-1819)
Woodfall, William (1746-1803)
Wright, Joseph, of Derby (1734-97)
Zoffany, Johann (1733-1810)

THE CATALOGUE

INDIVIDUAL SITTERS

IN ALPHABETICAL ORDER

ABEL, Karl Friedrich 1723-87

Musician, b. Cöthen, Sachsen-Anhalt; played in the court band at Dresden 1748-58 before coming in 1759 to London, where he shared a house with J.C. Bach 1762-73; chamber musician to Queen Charlotte; d. London.

'A tall, big, portly person, with a waistcoat, under which might easily have been buttoned twin brothers' (Henry Angelo, 1828).

5947 THOMAS GAINSBOROUGH c.1765

Canvas 125 x 100 (49¼ x 39½) lined (late 19th century);[1] cleaned 1988. Described by Fulcher in 1856 as 'distinguished by its careful execution, beauty of colouring, and deep expression',[2] and by Scharf in 1864 as 'much worn & ill treated'.[3] The surface is generally abraded and there are tears in the face (from left eye to end of nose), bottom right, and in the upper-right background; *pentimenti* indicate slight alterations to the shoulder and collar; on the left, behind a blue-green area, infra-red photography reveals a drawing of the *Three Graces*.*

Pale-brown eyes, powdered wig; wearing a gold, green and maroon flowered waistcoat and a deep red coat; a six-string viola da gamba between his knees.

Collections: [possibly J.V. Durrant sale, Christie's 28 April 1838, lot 263 'Abel playing the Viol da Gamba', bt. Bond; Robert Bond sale, Christie's, 16 February 1839, lot 73, bt. Knapp] Dr Hoskins FRS, 1856;[4] H.F. Long 1864;[5] [H.M. Bray 1866];[6] Puttick & Simpson, 7 June 1866, lot 157, but not sold;[7] [B. Barnett, London, 1876];[8] Dr W.H. Cummings;[9] his sale, Christie's, 17 December 1915, lot 145, bt. Sulley; with Tooth 1919; Carl P. Dannett, New York, by 1923, by descent; Leger, from whom purchased 1987 with the aid of the National Heritage Memorial Fund.

Exhibitions: *Gainsborough*, Grosvenor Gallery, 1885(46) lent Cummings; *Gainsborough's Circle at Bath*, Bath, 1988(18); *Gainsborough*, Ferrara, 1998(9).

Reference: W. Roberts, *Gainsborough's Portrait of Abel*, 1916;[10] *Gainsborough* 1953, p.1; Waterhouse 1958, no.3; Hayes 1970, under no.27; L. Stainton, *Gainsborough and his Musical Friends*, Kenwood, 1978, under no.17.

Abel and Gainsborough were close friends, sharing a love of life and a passion for the viola da gamba. Gainsborough became a skillful performer on the instrument and his careful portrayal of the overhand grip of the bow in both NPG 5947 and NPG 5081 reflect his under-

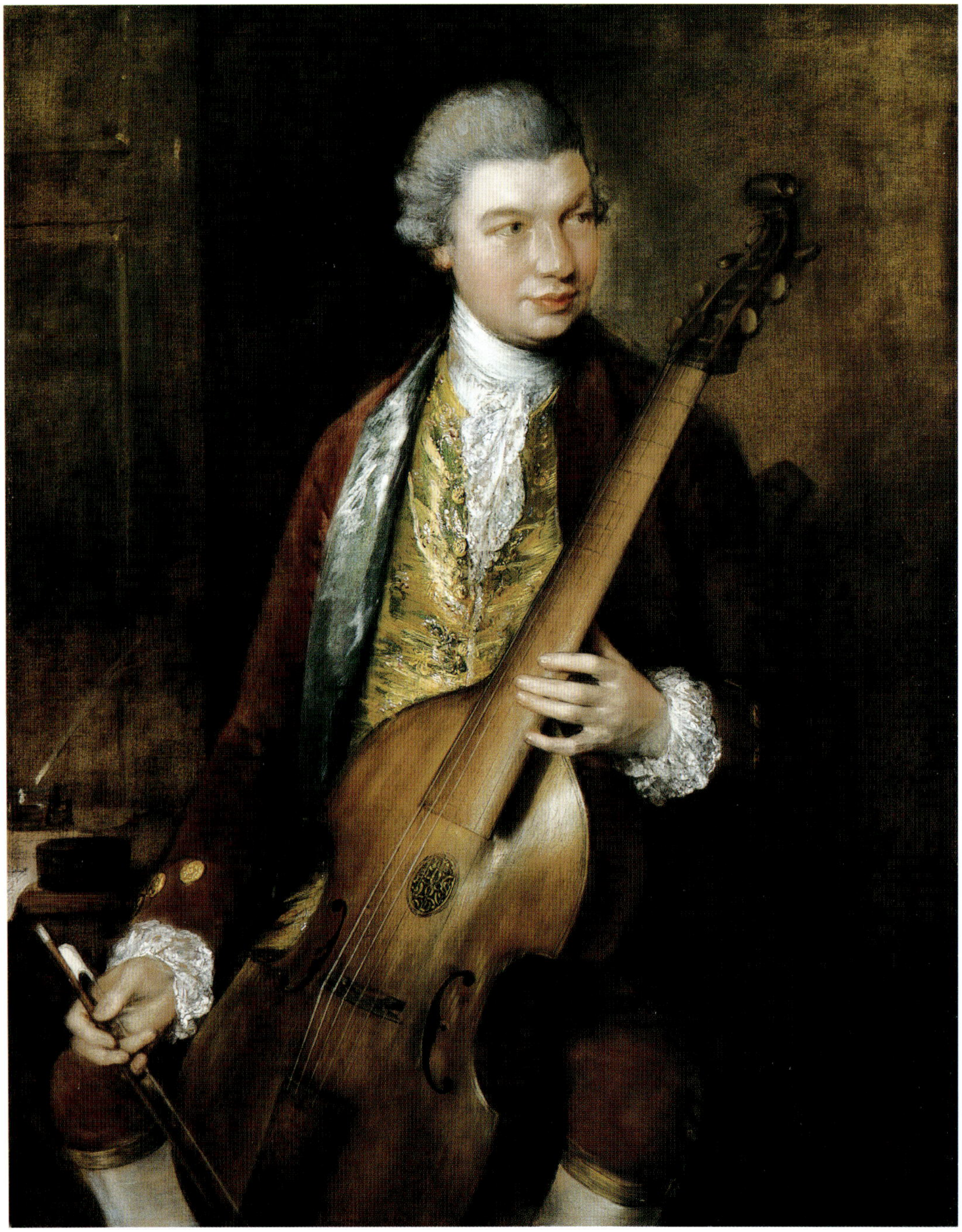

ABEL NPG *5947*

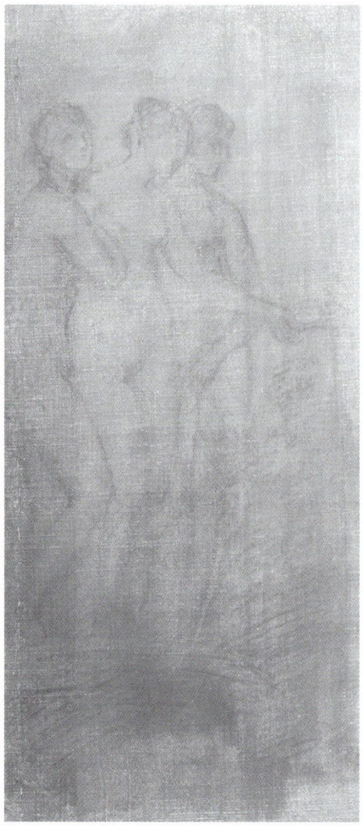

ABEL NPG *5947 (infra-red detail)*

standing. In return for his tuition Abel received from Gainsborough some paintings and many drawings, Henry Angelo recalling that the walls of his apartment 'were covered with them, slightly pinned to the paper-hangings'.[11] Gainsborough was painting a self portrait for him (see Gainsborough NPG 1107) when Abel died. Gainsborough then wrote that he would 'never cease looking up to heaven - the little while I have to stay behind - in hopes of getting one more glance of the man I loved from the moment I heard him touch the string'.[12] On the background wall of NPG 5947 Gainsborough had first included a drawing of the *Three Graces*, an appropriate (but for him uncharacteristic) emblem of *amicitia*.[13]

Between 1885 and 1988 the appearance of NPG 5947 was known, if at all, only through a photograph, while Gainsborough's whole length of Abel, which he exhibited in 1777, was acquired by the Huntington in 1925 and became relatively familiar. In 1958 Waterhouse observed, from a photograph, that the features in NPG 5947 did not altogether agree with the Huntington portrait, and in 1970 Hayes commented that it was not certainly a portrait of Abel. Then in 1975 the related drawing by Gainsborough, NPG 5081, was rediscovered and in 1988, when NPG 5947 also reappeared, it became apparent that it predated the Huntington whole length by some twelve years and that the likeness was not inconsistent. A date of c.1765, proposed by Hayes in 1998,[14] is indicated by costume and the sitter's apparent age (and perhaps by the appearance of the *Three Graces*, a motif used by Reynolds in 1765, see note 13 below).

1 Stretcher stamped: *G. Morrill, Liner.*
2 Fulcher 1856, p.108. The 1st ed. of Grove, 1879, identified a 'three-quarter length' painting by Gainsborough of Abel playing the viol-da-gamba as that 'bequeathed by Miss Gainsborough to Mr Briggs and ... sold in London in 1866', but see NPG 5081 below.
3 TSB 8/45.
4 Fulcher 1856, p.216.
5 Letter from Long to Scharf, 12 February 1864 (NPG archive), who sketched the portrait at Farrer's, 12 February 1864 (TSB 8/45).
6 He offered a 'kit cat sized' portrait of Abel by Romney to the NPG (letter of 2 March 1866; NPG archive).
7 According to W. Roberts, *Gainsborough's Portrait of Abel*, 1916, p.6; the sale is not identified in Lugt.
8 In June 1876 Barnett offered to the NPG a 'half-length' portrait by Gainsborough of Abel playing the double bass (letters of 26 & 28 June 1876; NPG archive).
9 Label verso: *W.H. Cummings Esq,/ Brackley Villa,/ Thurlow Park Road,/ Dulwich.* Waterhouse 1958, no.3, stated Cummings bought the picture c.1870; Cummings (1831-1915) was principal of the Guildhall School of Music.
10 Privately printed, 7pp., presumably when the portrait was on the market after the Cummings sale.
11 Angelo 1904, I, p.146. See also Whitley 1915, p.362, and Hayes 1970, I, p.94: Abel once gave Gainsborough a viola da gamba 'in return for two valuable landscapes, and several beautiful drawings' (*Morning Herald*, 25 August 1788) and there were 32 Gainsborough drawings in Abel's sale, Christie's, 13 December 1787 (when Gainsborough bought another viola da gamba).
12 To Henry Bate, 20 June 1787 (Hayes 2001, p.164).
13 Precisely the design used by Reynolds in 1765 for *Lady Bunbury sacrificing* (Mannings 2000, no.279).
14 *Gainsborough*, Ferrara, 1998(9).

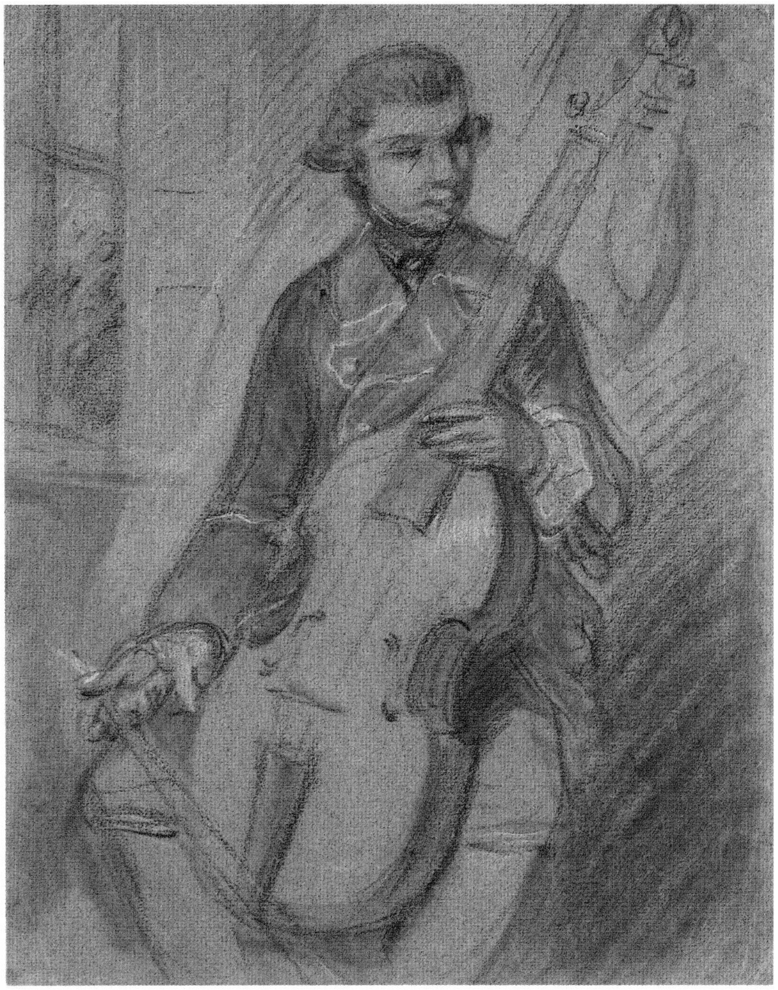

ABEL NPG *5081*

ABEL NPG *5081 verso*

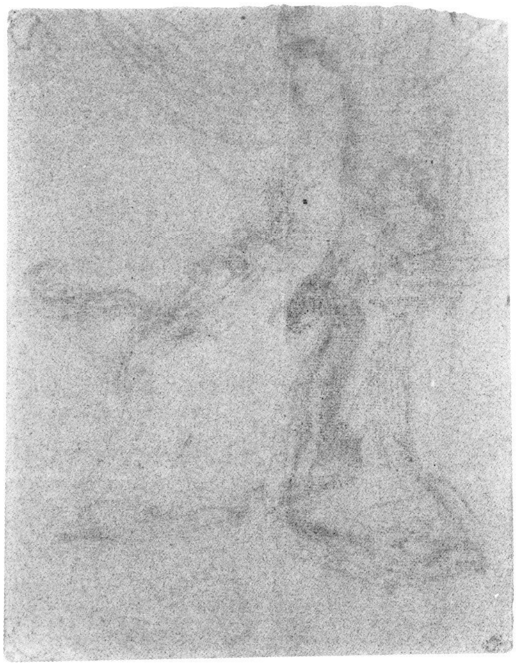

5081 THOMAS GAINSBOROUGH C.1765

Black and white chalk with stump on blue paper[1] 31.5 x 25 (12½ x 10) maximum, the top left corner irregular; verso the counterproof of a drawing* of a whole-length seated woman.[2]

Collections: The artist's daughter, Margaret Gainsborough (1752-1820), by whom bequeathed to Henry Briggs; his sale, Christie's, 25 February 1831, lot 106, bt. Crompton;[3] bt. c.1935 by Hubert Gregory, Harrogate;[4] Sotheby's, 1 April 1976, lot 66, bt. Agnew, from whom purchased 1976.

Engraving: R. Lane 1825 (*Studies of Figures by Gainsborough*).

Exhibitions: *Gainsborough and his Musical Friends*, Kenwood, 1977(17); *Gainsborough*, Paris, 1981(89); *Gainsborough Drawings*, Washington, Fort Worth, New Haven, 1983-84 (32); *Gainsborough's Circle at Bath*, Bath, 1988(24); *Music hath Charms*, Orleans House, Twickenham, 1988(103); *Master Drawings 1993-95*(22); *Gainsborough*, Ferrara, 1998(56).

Reference: Hayes 1970, no.27 (as ownership unknown); M.I. Wilson, *Apollo*, CV, 1977, p.109.

A compositional study for NPG 5947, differing principally in showing the coat buttoned up, the neck of the viola da gamba higher above his shoulder, and a window on the left. The instrument is less accurately drawn; it has four instead of six strings and is pierced by two F-shaped, instead of C-shaped, holes (cf NPG 5947).[5]

1 When examined in the British Museum in December 1976, a secondary watermark was found (*VI* or *IV*).
2 Directly related to a Gainsborough drawing in the Kupferstichkabinett, Berlin (4432, Hayes 1970, no.56, pl.200).
3 Assuming that NPG 5081 was the drawing described by Fulcher 1856, p.216: 'one of Gainsborough's favourite drawings was a portrait of Abel. It was bequeathed by Miss Gainsborough to Mr Briggs, at the sale of whose pictures it was purchased by Mr Crompton'. See Hayes 1970, I, pp.96–97, and NPG 5947 above.
4 'I bought it over 40 years ago as part of a job lot at a sale in Yorkshire' (*Yorkshire Post*, 2 April 1976).
5 See Huntington 2001, pp.94–95.

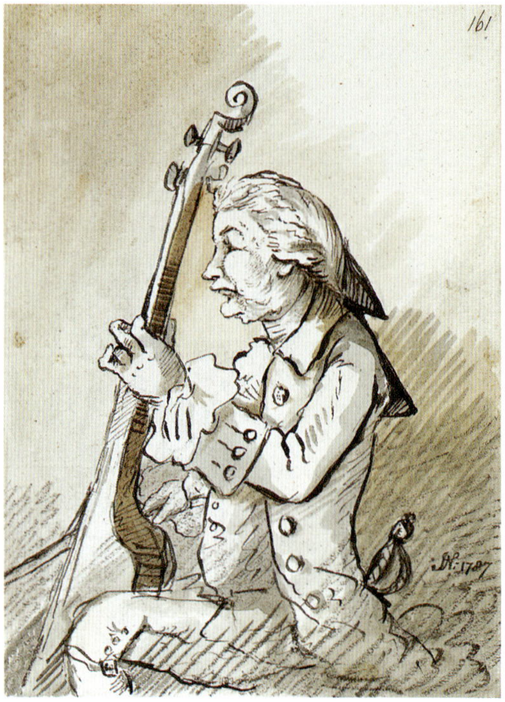

ABEL NPG *5178*

5178 JOHN NIXON 1787

Pen and wash on paper 17.7 x 11.4 (7 x 4½), the image 15.5 (6⅛) high; some staining; signed in monogram and dated lower right: *JN:1787*; inscribed below: *A Solo on the Viola di Gamba/ Mr Abel.*, and numbered, top right, in ink *161*.

Playing the viola da gamba, wearing an old-fashioned coat, a bag wig and sword.

Collections: French Hospital of La Providence, Rochester; Christie's, 22 November 1977, lot 41, bt. Baskett, from whom purchased 1978.

Engraving: W.N. Gardiner, *A Solo on the Viola di Gamba Mr Abel* (July 1787).[1]

Gardiner's etching was printed immediately after Abel's death in June 1787; it shows minor differences, the viola being a little taller, with both pegs clear of Abel's head.

1 George 8264.

ICONOGRAPHY

c.1765 Painting and drawing by Thomas Gainsborough, see NPG 5947 and NPG 5081.

1766 Drawing by Francesco Bartolozzi, exhibited SA 1766(7).

1777 Painting by Thomas Gainsborough,* whole-length at table, his viola da gamba across his knee. Huntington Art Collections, San Marino, Calif. (25.19; *Huntington* 2001, no.15); previously acquired by Queen Charlotte after Abel's death and her sale, 25 May 1819, lot 93. Exhibited RA 1777(135). A small half length version attributed to Gainsborough, exhibited *English Conversation Pieces*, 25 Park Lane, 1930(119, as Sebastian Bach) and *Gainsborough*, 45 Park Lane, 1936(25, as J.C. Bach 1735–82) lent Lady Hillingdon. A head of Abel by Gainsborough in an American private collection (possibly Dupont sale, Christie's, 10 April 1797, lot 16, and sold Parke-Bernet, New York, 5 April 1944, lot 17) relates directly to the Huntington portrait.

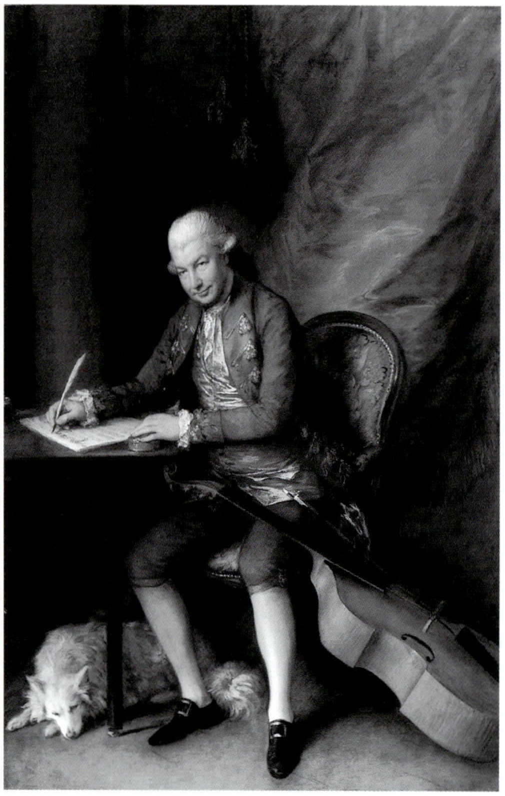

ABEL by Thomas Gainsborough 1777 (Huntington Art Collections, San Marino, California)

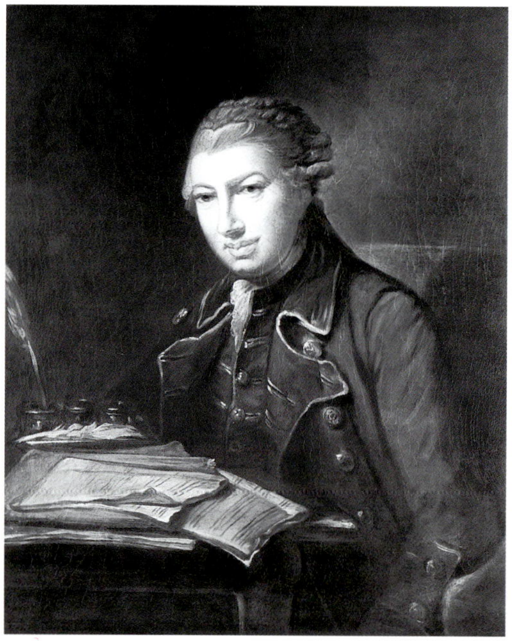

ABEL unknown artist c.1780? (Faculty of Music, Oxford)

1780 Painting by C-J. Robineau, half-length at keyboard. Royal Collection (Millar 1969, no.1048). A version ascribed to Fuseli was wrongly identified as Haydn (R. Hughes, *Haydn*, 1962, p.87).

c.1780? Unattributed painting,* half-length seated with papers and a quill. Faculty of Music, Oxford, given by Dr Philip Hayes before 1795 (Poole, I, p.162: 'Gutch says this is the work of an artist named Teeds'). The head resembles that of the 1777 Gainsborough.

1787 Drawing by John Nixon, see NPG 5178.

c.1790 Caricature by Thomas Rowlandson,* see J.C. Bach.

Undated Unattributed drawing exhibited *Music Loan Exhibition*, London, 1904 (cat., p.234, lent Lionel Benson).

ACTON, Sir John Francis Edward, 6th Bt 1736-1811

Sicilian minister, a Catholic of English extraction, b. Besançon; served with the French and Tuscan navies; knight of the Order of St Stephen 1767[1] (but see below); in 1779 reorganised the navy in the Kingdom of Naples, where he became chief minister 1789, grand chancellor 1795 and prime minister 1799-1806; knight of the Order of St Januarius 1783 (or 1785, with the Order of St Stephen),[2] of St Ferdinand 1801 and of the Golden Fleece (Spain) 1802; suc. as 6th Bt of Aldenham Park, Shropshire, 1791; m. 1800 his niece, Mary Anne Acton (c.1782-1873); d. Palermo.

1 *Dizionario biografico degli Italiani*, II, 1960, pp.207-9.
2 W. Betham, *Baronetage*, II, 1802, pp.18-19.

'a thin genteel looking man; not handsome, but neat and quiet and gentlemanlike' (Lady Palmerston, 1794).

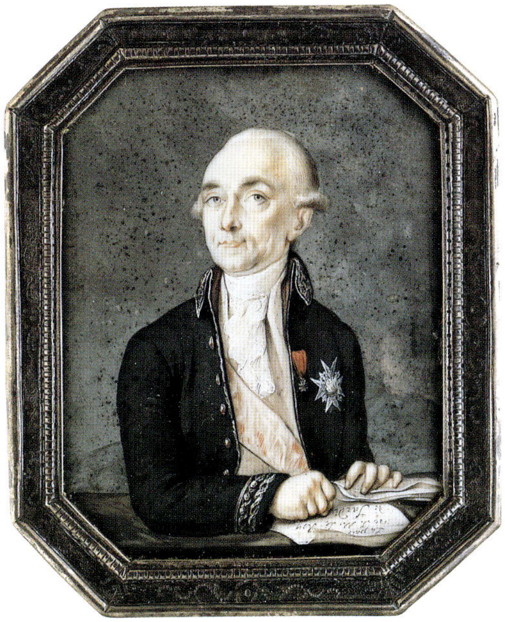

ACTON NPG *4082*

4082 PETER EDWARD STROEHLING c.1793

Watercolour and bodycolour on ivory 10 x 7.8 (4 x 3); some areas of ivory have been left untouched in the head; considerable spotting in the background and darker areas; signed bottom left: *Stroely*; the backing paper inscribed: *Il Ministre/ Jean Edouard Acton*; engraved silver frame.

Clear grey eyes, white hair; dark blue-grey coat with silver lace and a rust-coloured lining; white shirt and neckcloth; wearing the pink ribbon and star of St Januarius and the badge of St Stephen; before him a paper inscribed: *La paix/ de S.M. Le Roy/ de Sardin...*; in the background an eruption of Vesuvius.

Collections: G.A. Kenyon, Dublin, from whom purchased 1958.

La paix de S.M. Le Roy de Sardin probably concerns the defeat of the French assault on Sardinia in 1792-93; Stroehling is said to have been in Naples c.1792, before going to Vienna and St Petersburg in 1796.[1] Acton was chief minister 1789-95, as described on the contemporary backing of NPG 4082.

1 Schidlof 1964, II, p.790.

ICONOGRAPHY

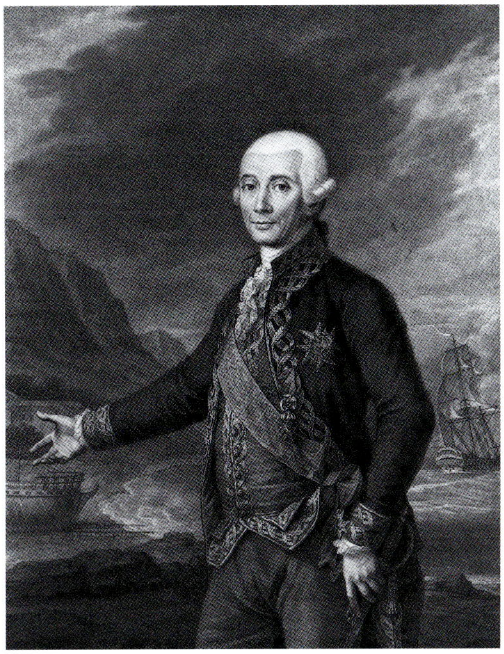

ACTON F. Bartolozzi after Carlo Marsigli c.1790 (NPG D7112)

c.1790 Drawing by Carlo Marsigli, three-quarter length standing wearing the ribbon and star of St Januarius and the badge of St Stephen. Engraved F. Bartolozzi* c.1790 (*Lieutenant Général de la Marine, Conseiller et Secretaire d'Etat de Sa Majesté Sicilienne ayant le Département des Affaires Etrangeres, de la Guerrre de la Marine, et du Commerce, &c*).

c.1790 Painting by G.M. Griffoni, half length wearing the ribbon and star of St Januarius and the badge of St Stephen. Coughton Court.

c.1793 Miniature by P.E. Stroehling, see NPG 4082.

1795 Marble bust by Antonio d'Este,* wearing the ribbon and star of St Januarius and the badge of the Gold Cross of Malta(?), inscribed and dated. Christie's, 8 December 1981, lot 130, from the collection of the Hon. Robert Acton.

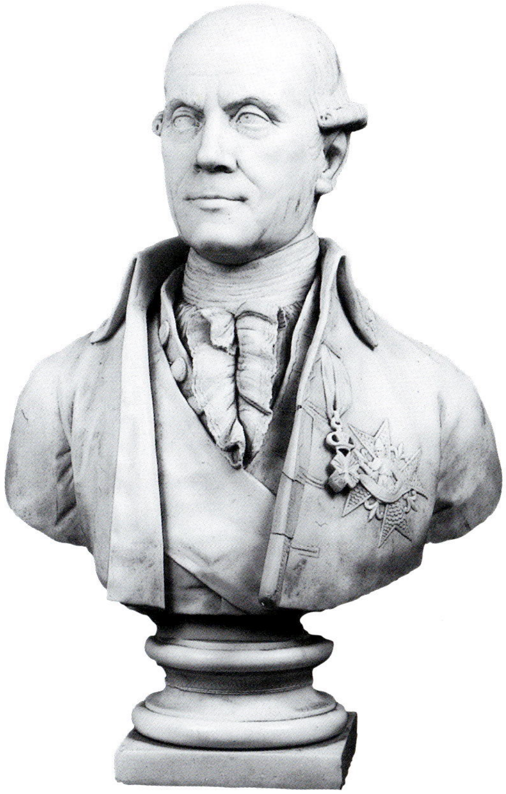

ACTON by Antonio d'Este 1795 (Christie's)

c.1800 Miniature by N-F. Dun, half length, blue coat with the ribbon and star of St Januarius and the badge of St Stephen. Sotheby's, Geneva, 13-15 November 1995, lot 286.

1802 Unattributed painting, dated and illegibly signed, three-quarter length standing, wearing the ribbon and star of St Ferdinand, the star of St Januarius, the blue ribbon and star of an unidentified Order, and the badge of St Stephen; a distant view of Naples. Private collection (illus. P. Gunn, *The Actons*, 1978, f.p.102).

Undated Unattributed miniature, bust length. Coughton Court. Possibly that exhibited SKM 1865(2917) lent H.E. Acton.

ADAM, John 1721-92

Architect; 1st s. of William Adam, architect of Edinburgh, bro. of the architects Robert and James Adam; he retired from practice c.1770, to act as steward of the family fortunes.

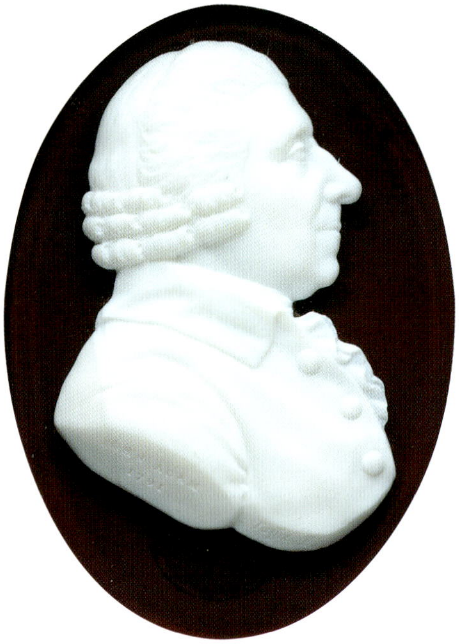

John ADAM NPG *4612*

4612 JAMES TASSIE 1791

Glass paste 7 (2¾) high; incised on the truncation: *IOHN ADAM/1791* and: *Tassie F*; set on ruby glass.

Collections: K.E. Houston sale, Sotheby's, 15 January 1968, lot 68, bt. Hugh Leggatt, by whom presented through the National Art Collections Fund 1968.

Reference: Gray 1894, no.2.

Dating from the last year of his life, this appears to be the only authentic likeness of John Adam; there is a companion Tassie medallion of Mrs John Adam (Scottish NPG, PG 1964).

ICONOGRAPHY

c.1765 Painting traditionally attributed to Francis Cotes,* three-quarter length seated, left hand on his cheek (the coat apparently unfinished). Private Scottish collection. The identity is traditional, but the attribution to Cotes is doubtful; there is a pendant portrait of Mrs John Adam at Blair Adam.

1791 Medallion by James Tassie, see NPG 4612.

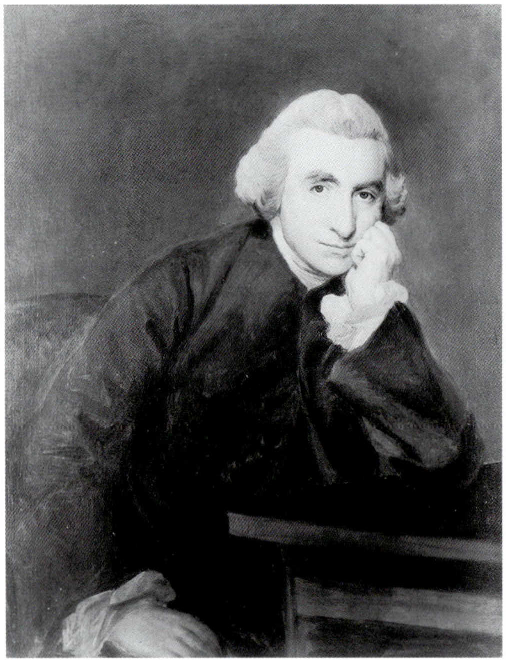

John ADAM attributed to Francis Cotes c.1765 (Private Scottish Collection)

ADAM, Robert 1728-92

Architect, 2nd s. of William Adam, architect of Edinburgh, bro. of the architects John and James Adam; in Italy 1755-57; FRS 1761; Architect of the King's Works 1761-68; MP 1768-74.

'I see ... why nobody could hit the likeness. The features were hard and irregular, and at the same time expressed the utmost sweetness, spirit and genius' (John Clerk, 1792).

Abbreviation

Brown 1978: I.G. Brown, 'Commemorative Portraits of Robert Adam', *Burl. Mag.*, CXX, 1978, pp.444-51

2953 attributed to GEORGE WILLISON c.1770-74

Canvas 127 x 101.5 (50 x 40) lined; slight *pentimenti* on fore-edge of book and on his right hand; retouchings round the nose, stockings and chair seat.

Grey eyes, white powdered wig, deep brown coat with brown buttons; silver waistcoat with turquoise gold-edged lapel and gold buttons; white breeches; green damask chair; holding an unlettered elephant folio.

Collections: By descent at Penicuik House from the sitter to his sister Margaret, his niece Susannah Clerk, and his nephew William Clerk (d.1847), by whom bequeathed to Adm. Sir Charles Adam (d.1853) of Blair Adam;[1] by descent to Lt.-Com. C.K. Adam; Sotheby's, 19 May 1926, lot 35 as English School, bt. Batsford,[2] from whom purchased 1938.

Exhibitions: Scottish NPG, July 1939; *English Taste in the 18th century*, RA, 1955-56(409 as unknown artist); *Lord Mansfield*, Kenwood, 1971(60 as attributed to Willison); *Age of Neo-Classicism*, Victoria and Albert Museum, 1972(276 as attributed to Willison); *Bicentenary Exhibition*, Register House, Edinburgh, 1974; *Art in Scotland 1650-1760*, Scottish NPG, 1989(99 as Martin); *Robert Adam & the Emperor's Palace*, National Library of Scotland, Kenwood, 1992-93, as Martin.

Although Adam was for a time the most fashionable architect in London, and by no means averse to self-advertisement, his portraiture presents a meagre study. Contemporary references are confined to portraits painted in Rome in 1756 by Allan Ramsay and Laurent Pêcheux, of which the first is untraced. When, after his death, James Tassie was commissioned to produce a medallion, he could find as a guide only the death mask taken by Nollekens (untraced) but, while the Adam family considered the result to show 'something of the general air of the face', the features were considered 'not like'.[3] In 1821 two unattributed portraits were offered for sale by the family, one showing him 'earlier in life', conceivably the Pêcheux,[4] the other conceivably NPG 2953 (see note 1).

NPG 2953 is generally considered to be the only life-size portrait of Robert Adam in existence but, owing to a lack of documentation and comparative material, the identification cannot be proved absolutely, as Kerslake first emphasised.[5] It depends largely on the provenance but, as Tait has argued, Robert Adam's niece Susannah Clerk and Admiral Sir Charles Adam, the grandson of his brother John, must have known 'either what he looked like or what his appearance was supposed to be'.[6] Lt.-Com. Adam, writing in 1932, said the portrait had always been known at Blair Adam as Robert Adam[7] and the features sufficiently agree with those shown by Pêcheux and Tassie (but do not include the wart on the right cheek). There is at least a strong family likeness in the two portraits of James Adam, by Allan Ramsay c.1754 and the so-called Batoni dated 1763 (once thought to show Robert Adam).[8]

NPG 2953 lacks the quality of both these James Adam portraits; the drawing is hard, the elegance rather forced – and the safety of the folio volume is disregarded. Costume suggests a date of c.1770, but an attribution has proved contentious. Sold in 1926 as English School, it was subsequently attributed to Zoffany in 1936, to an unknown artist in 1948, to Willison in 1971 and to David Martin in 1989. Of these names Zoffany may be discounted and Martin's work provides no completely persuasive comparison,[9] although his studio chair has been provisionally identified in NPG 2953.[10] The attribution to Willison, first suggested (verbally) by Robin Hutchison, is supported by comparison with Willison's Archibald Douglas of 1769;[11] since Willison was in India 1774–78, a date before 1774 would be implied.

The anonymous folio volume may refer to Robert Adam's *Ruins of the Palace of Diocletian at Spalatro*, published in 1764[12] or, less likely, to the first volume of Robert and James Adam's *Works in Architecture*, published in 1773.[13] But if either of these celebrated volumes was intended, it is odd that they were not identified.

A 20th-century copy is at Blair Adam.

1 Provenance as cited by A.A. Tait, *Burl. Mag.*, CXXI, 1979, p.38. It is remotely possible that NPG 2953 was one of the two portraits of Adam in the Adam sale, Christie's, 3rd day, 11 July 1821 – lot 85 in the Christie's copy of the sale cat. is marked *1.10.– A*, probably indicating it was bought in. See also note 4 below.

2 Listed in a 1938 Batsford cat. *Old and Rare Books*, no.103 (as by Zoffany and holding the first volume of Robert and James Adam's *Works in Architecture*). Acording to a letter from Lt.-Com. Adam (26 November 1932; NPG archive) the portrait was sold without his authority when he was serving abroad.

3 Margaret Adam to John Clerk, 13 February 1793; see Brown 1978, p.451.

4 Lot 86, showing Adam 'earlier in life', fetched 7s., compared with prices between one and two guineas for the other Adam portraits in this sale. The sale cat. had previously been misread so that both Robert's portraits, which were unattributed, were described as by Fragonard (A.T. Bolton, *Architecture of Robert and James Adam*, II, 1922, p.337, and Whitley 1930, p.15). Fragonard and Adam were together in Rome in 1756–57.

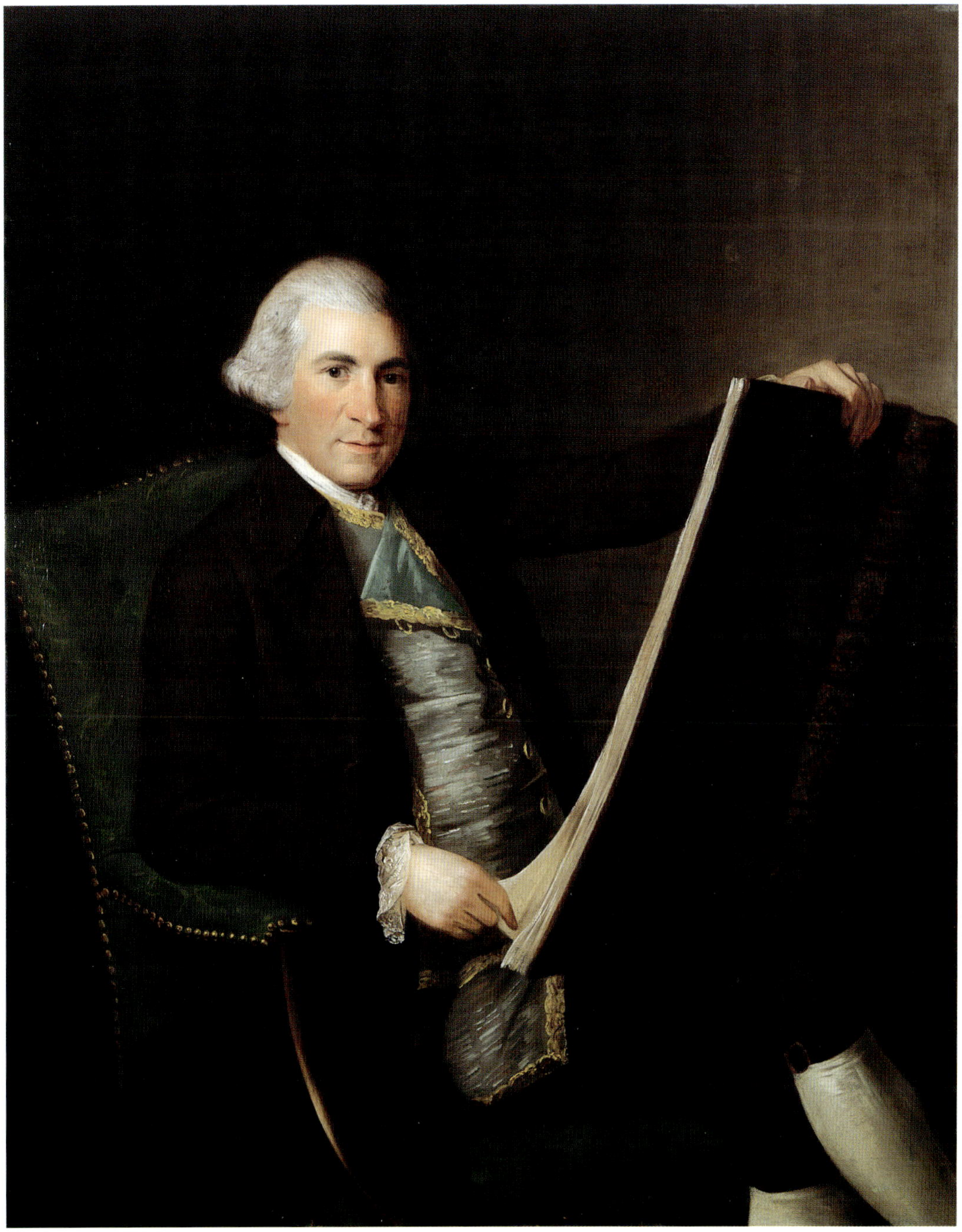

Robert ADAM NPG 2953

5 J. Kerslake, *Burl. Mag.*, CXX, 1978, p.762.
6 A.A. Tait, *Burl. Mag.*, CXXI, 1979, p.38.
7 Letter of 26 September 1932 (NPG archive).
8 Respectively, Smart 1999, no.3, and J. Fleming, *Robert Adam and His Circle*, 1962, pl.88 (see Doubtful Portraits below). These may have been lots 83 and 84 in the Adam sale, Christie's, 11 July 1821 ('Fragonard, Portrait of James Adam, Esq when young', and [unattributed] 'Portrait of ditto, executed later in life').
9 An opinion shared, for example, by Lucy Dixon (organiser of the Martin exhibition at St Andrews, 1997).
10 J. Holloway, *Patrons and Painters*, 1989, p.130.
11 Private collection; exhibited *Boswell*, NPG, 1967, no.31 illus.; Willison's portrait of Gen. Robert Clerk (private collection) uses comparable flecked lights on the uniform facings, while his Boswell (Scottish NPG) has a related cross-legged pose.
12 Suggested, for example, by D. King, *Complete Works of Robert and James Adam*, 1991, p.vii, and S. Parissien, *The Adam Style*, 1992, p.9.
13 Suggested in the 1938 Batsford cat. (see note 2) and G. Beard, *Work of Robert Adam*, 1978, p.35.

ICONOGRAPHY

Aspects of Adam's iconography have been surveyed by J. Steegman & C.K. Adams, *Architectural Review*, XCI, 1942, p.77, and by I.G. Brown in 1978 (see Abbreviation above).

1755–56 Painting by Allan Ramsay. Painted in Rome, where Adam called it 'near finishd' on 24 May 1755, but it was still incomplete, or undelivered, on 8 November; listed with the Adam family in London 1781 (Smart 1999, no.601).

1756 Etching by G.F. Piranesi, an imaginary classical medal with the profile heads of Piranesi and Adam, within the dedicatory plate of Piranesi's *Campus Martius*, etched in 1756 and published in 1762 (illus. G. Beard, *Work of Robert Adam*, 1978, pl.10). The Adam profile was separately engraved, pub. W. Richardson 1808 (illus. *Connoisseur*, IX, 1904, p.31). A curiosity, of limited use as a likeness.

1756 Miniature by Laurent Pêcheux,* bust length, showing a wart on his right cheek. Private Scottish collection. Exhibited *Lord Mansfield*, Kenwood, 1971(58), reasonably identified with the Pêcheux portrait painted in Rome described by Adam on 8 November 1756 as a head and shoulders to be finished within two weeks (A. Smart, *Allan Ramsay*, 1992, p.293n24). Probably the miniature of Robert Adam offered for sale from Blair Adam at Sotheby's, 11 June 1926, lot 86.

c.1770–74 Painting attributed to George Willison, see NPG 2953.

before 1791 'Bust of Mr R. Adam in plaister by Hokings', Adam sale, Christie's, 22 May 1818, lot 10; the sculptor identified as James Hoskins (Gunnis 1968, p.211).

before 1792 Silhouette with Adam's sister, Mrs Mary Drysdale, in 1792, from which John Clerk of Penicuik modelled a clay bust (Brown 1978, p.448).

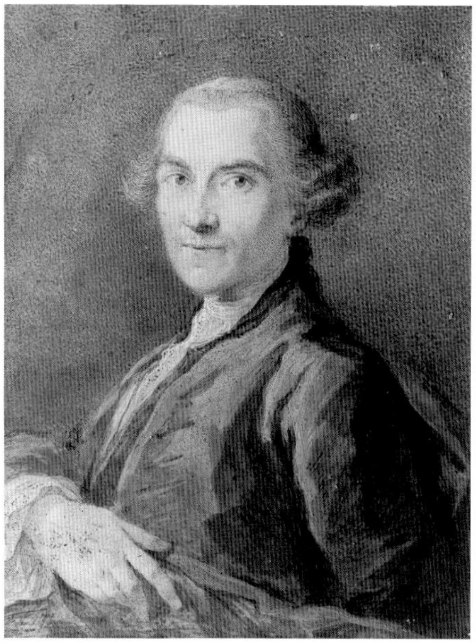

Robert ADAM by Laurent Pêcheux 1756 (Private Scottish Collection)

1792 Death mask and bust by Joseph Nollekens (Brown 1978, pp.445–46). Nollekens designed a monument for Adam incorporating a bust; preparatory drawing in the Victoria and Albert Museum (E.4369.1920; illus. J. Physick, *Designs for English Sculpture*, 1969, p.11).

1792 Medallion by James Tassie, undraped classical bust, smooth faced (Scottish NPG, PG 201; Gray 1894, no.5). A comparable ivory relief is at Blair Adam (illus. J. Lees-Milne, *Age of Adam*, 1947, pl.44). Although this profile looks younger than the other Tassie medallions, it probably dates from after April 1792 (see below).

1792 Medallions by James Tassie, using the same profile, showing two warts (on his cheek and below his ear, cf. Pêcheux 1756 above): a draped classical bust (Scottish NPG, PG 434; Gray 1894, no.6), and with wig, coat and neckcloth, dated 1792* (Scottish NPG, PG 262; Victoria and Albert Museum, 414.1323.1885; Gray 1894, no.4). On 1 April 1792 Tassie wrote 'Nolleckens did mould the face after decease from that we will be enabled to make a model' (Brown 1978, p.446).

DOUBTFUL PORTRAITS

Attributed to Batoni, sold Christie's, 26 June 1964, lot 106 (Clark 1985, p.373, as not by Batoni); by Raeburn, Aberdeen AG (illus. J. Greig, *Raeburn*, 1911, pl.4), and unattributed, RIBA, London (illus. J. Swarbrick, *Robert Adam & His Brothers*, 1915, p.26, and see *Burl.Mag.*, XCVI, 1954, p.102).

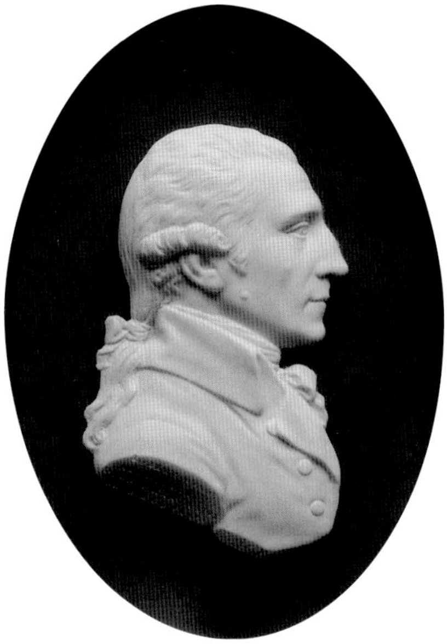

Robert ADAM by James Tassie 1792 (Scottish National Portrait Gallery)

On 11 May 1772 'Mr Adams of the Adelphi' is entered in Reynolds's sitter-book, but there is no known portrait. On 11 and 16 November 1780 a 'Mr Adams' sat to Romney (Ward & Roberts 1904, I, p.93). Adam has been identified in plaster medallions by Zucchi in the ceiling of 20 Portman Square and above a fireplace at Mersham-le-Hatch (the former showing him some ten years older than the latter; J. Lees-Milne, *Caves of Ice*, 1983, pp.36–37).

AFFLECK, Philip 1726-99

Naval officer; served with distinction in the West Indies 1780–81 and 1790–93; captain 1759; rear-admiral 1787; vice-admiral 1793; admiral June 1795;[1] 'a zealous and brave officer ... and a faithfully affectionate friend' (*GM*, 1799).

1 His brother, Sir Edmund Affleck (1725–88), was also a naval officer: captain 1757; Bt. 1782; MP 1782–88; rear-admiral of the blue 1784.

1579 LEMUEL FRANCIS ABBOTT C.1793

Canvas 76 x 64 (30 x 25¼) lined and restored 1978; original canvas inscribed: *Admiral Philip Affleck/vice-Admiral of the white/(Brother of Sir Edmund)/Admiral Philip died unmarried/ Decr 22nd 1799.*

Blue eyes, white wig, wearing an admiral's full-dress uniform of 1787–95: white neckcloth and cream waistcoat with gold buttons, blue coat with gold facings and buttons.

Collections: By descent to Philip Affleck of Dalham Hall, Suffolk; his sale, Robinson & Fisher, 24 May 1906, lot 158 (as by F.L. Abbott), bt. Leggatt, from whom bt. by H.J. Pfungst and presented 1910.

Exhibition: *War at Sea*, Yorktown, Va., 1978.

Affleck's return from the West Indies in 1793 indicates the probable date of NPG 1579. The head, which closely resembles that drawn by Russell in 1787, seems to have been quoted by Young in his mezzotint based on a much earlier portrait by Edward Penny (see below).

The attribution to Abbott is traditional and convincing.[1] The Affleck sale of 1906 contained a second portrait of the Admiral by Abbott, lot 160, probably that showing his right hand in his waistcoat, of which there are examples in the National Maritime Museum (BHC 2506) and with the Wernher Foundation (on loan to the Ranger's House).

1 Cf. A.C. Sewter, *Connoisseur*, CXXXV, 1955, pp.179, 183. NPG 1579 was attributed to Penny in NPG, *Complete Illus. Cat.*, 1981, p.5.

ICONOGRAPHY

c.1770 Painting by Edward Penny,* small whole length, seated in captain's uniform of 1767–74. National Maritime Museum (BHC 2505). Engraved J. Young 1792, the head made older (resembling that of NPG 1579), the uniform changed to admiral's full dress (as NPG 1579) – an earlier state retained the captain's coat but with admiral's cuffs; H.R. Cook 1809, following the Young mezzotint, as bust-length oval, lettered *Admiral of the White Squadron*, but in captain's full-dress uniform of 1774–95 (the lapels differing from those originally painted by Penny). A later painted version with admiral's uniform was with Chichester Antiques in 1949.

1783 Silhouette by William Wellings, *Captain Affleck*, sold Christie's, 19 May 1980, lot 38.

1787 Pastel by John Russell, half-length oval, in captain's uniform of 1774–95. Mrs E. Lovell, London, 1894 (illus. *Russell Album*, p.25). Exhibited RA 1787(378) as Captain Affleck.

c.1793 Painting by L.F. Abbott, see NPG 1579.

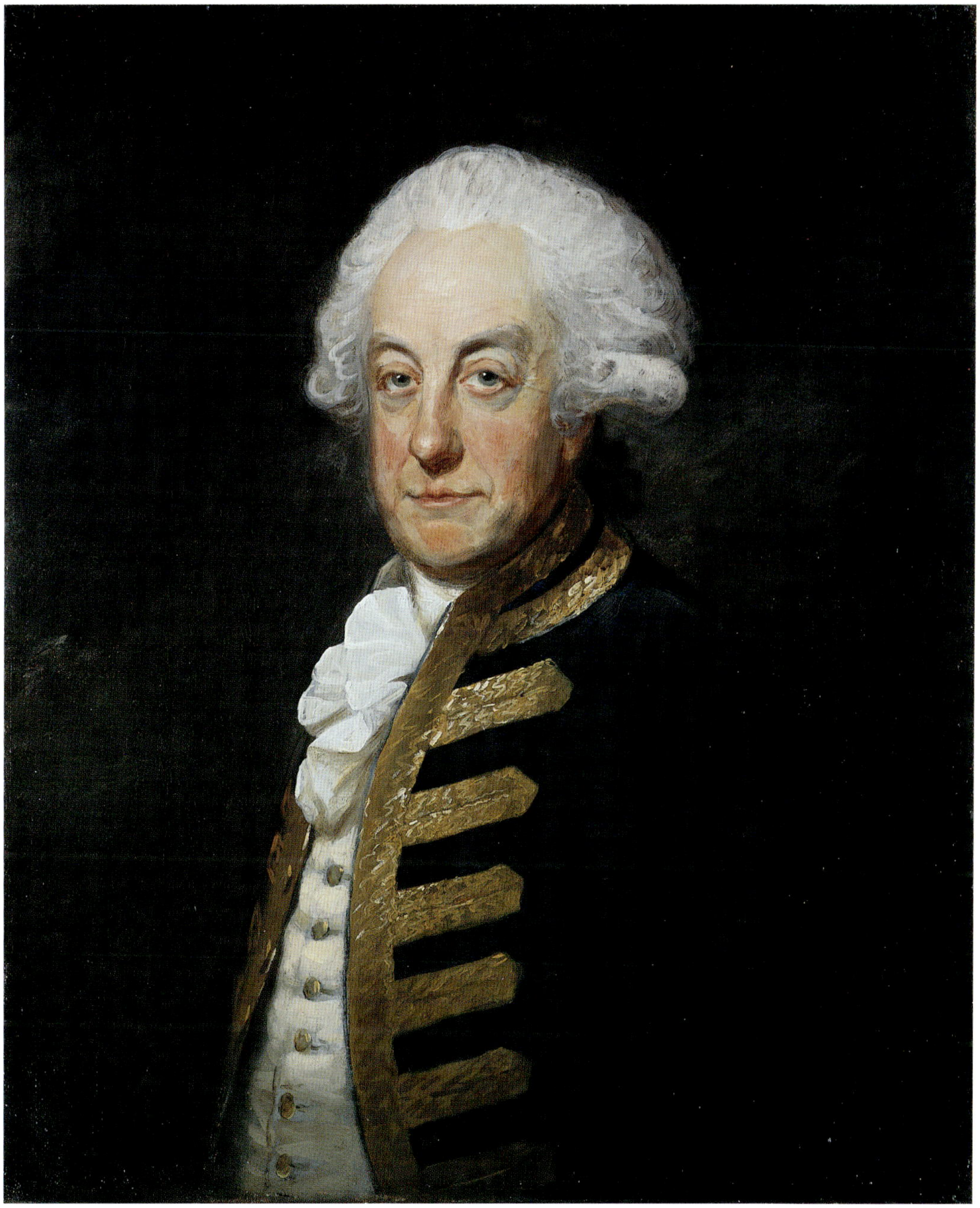

AFFLECK NPG 1579

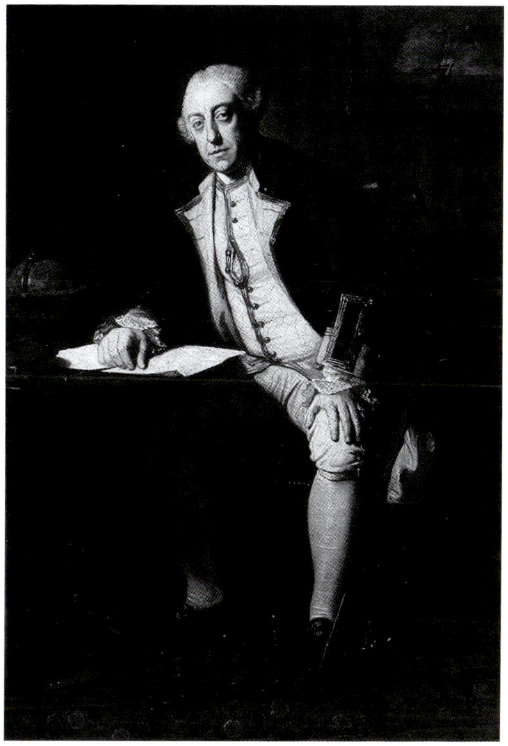

AFFLECK by Edward Penny c.1770 (National Maritime Museum)

AIKIN, Anna, see **BARBAULD**

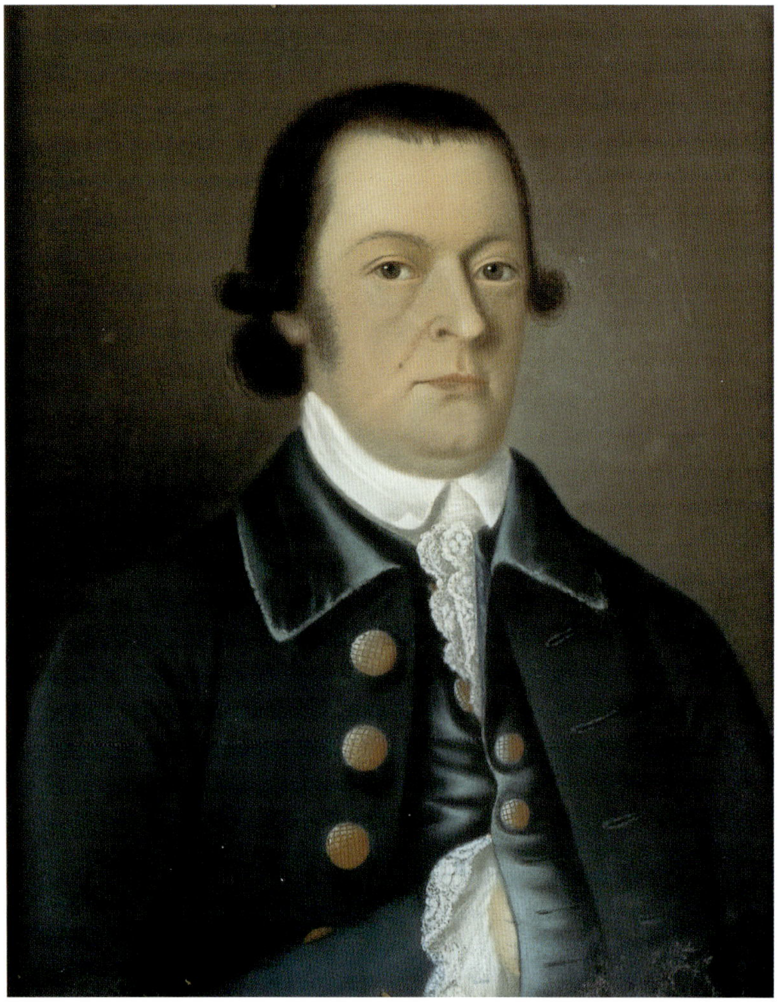

ALLAN NPG *4307*

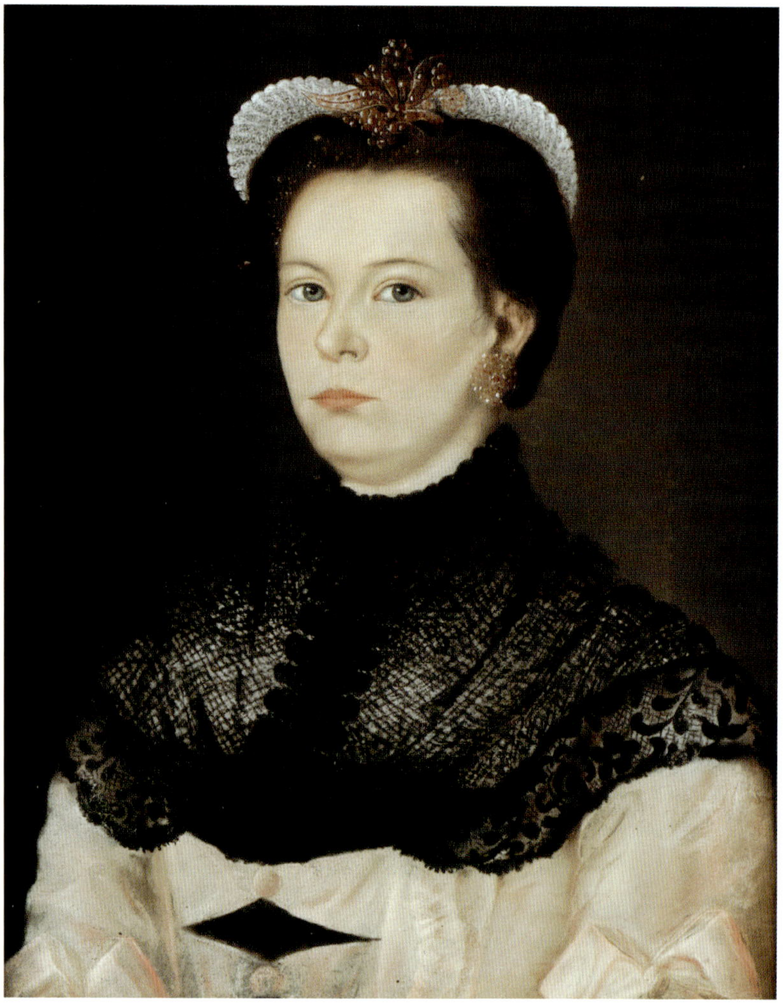

Mrs ALLAN NPG *4308*

ALLAN, George 1736-1800

Antiquary, of Blackwell Grange, Darlington; attorney and collector of manuscripts; from c.1768 he maintained a private press producing antiquarian books and pamphlets; m. 1) 1766 Ann Nicholson (see NPG 4308); FSA 1774.

'he wrote almost a quire for every day he lived. His habits were very regular and temperate ... he rose at half past seven, very seldom took any exercise, and scarce ate any animal food at all. About three glasses of wine was his allowance at dinner. He drank tea but seldom ate supper' (Nichols *Anecdotes*).

4307 UNKNOWN ARTIST C.1770-75

Pastel on pale blue paper laid on canvas 57 x 46 (22½ x 18) sight;[1] damp marks below right.[2]

Blue eyes, black hair, wearing a royal blue suit with silver buttons.

Collections: Motcomb Galleries, 3 April 1963, lot 245 (with the pendant of his wife), bt. Mr & Mrs C.J. Duveen, by whom presented 1963.

Pendant to the pastel of the first Mrs Allan, see NPG 4308, whom he married in 1766; the proposed date is based on the sitters' estimated ages. The modesty of the portraits agrees with their character, their residence, The Grange, being 'distinguished as the seat of benevolence and the virtues', but 'ostentatious ornaments [were] not displayed there.'[3] Portraits of Allan and his first wife were recorded at Blackwell Hall (another residence of the Allan family) in 1850, but no portraits were identified at the Blackwell Grange sale, 17-19 March 1954.[4]

1 Stretcher 59 x 47 (23¼ x 18½). The canvas is marked in chalk *313/1* and *43*.
2 Early-19th-century label attached to the frame: *Portrait of Geo. Allan Esq/the celebrated Antiquary/ Grange Hall*.
3 Nichols *Anecdotes*, VI, p.127n.
4 Information supplied by C.K.C. Andrew, County Archivist, Northallerton, in a letter to C.K. Adams of 22 April 1963 (NPG archive); he had consulted W.H. Longstaffe, *Memorials of the Families of Allan, Hylton, and Clervaux*, 1850.

ICONOGRAPHY

c.1770-75 Pastel by an unknown artist, see NPG 4307.

c.1785 Drawing by J. Hay, with the antiquary and historian of Durham, William Hutchinson (1732-1814), seated at table with manuscripts. Engraved J. Collyer 1814* (for Nichols *Anecdotes*, VIII), the plate originally intended for the first volume of Hutchinson's *History of Durham*, published in 1785 (Nichols *Anecdotes*, VI, p.351).

1792 Pastel by Henry Spicer, half length, holding a book, two volumes of Camden's *Britannia* on a shelf behind him. Christie's, 9 October 1989, lot

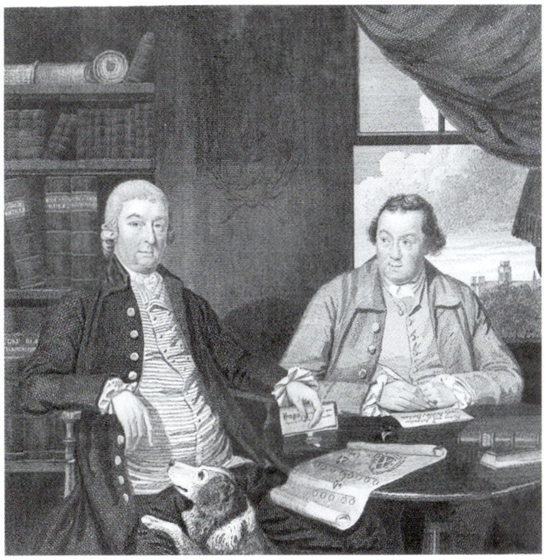

ALLAN (left) with William Hutchinson, J. Collyer after J. Hay c.1785 (NPG D 8392)

41. Spicer also painted in 1792 the sitter's sons, George (1767-1828) and James (1772-95), sold Motcomb Galleries, London, 3 April 1963, lot 244; Bonham's, 28 February 1980, lot 47, and (George alone) Phillips, 13 October 1989, lot 225.

ALLAN, Mrs Ann, *née* Nicholson 1741-87

Dau. and heiress of James Colling Nicholson of Scruton, Yorks.; m. 1766 the antiquary George Allan (see NPG 4307).

4308 UNKNOWN ARTIST c.1770-75

Pastel on pale blue paper laid on canvas 57 x 46 (22½ x 18) sight.[1]

Blue-grey eyes, dark brown hair with a Pulteney cap, a black shawl worn over a white dress with pink bows and buttons; she wears a red and white jewel in her cap and girandole earrings.

Collections: See NPG 4307 above.

See NPG 4307 above.

1 Stretcher 59 x 47 (23¼ x 18½). The canvas is marked in chalk 245/2 from the 1963 sale. Early-19th-century label attached to the frame: *Portrait of the Wife of? Geo. Allan Esqre/ the Antiquary.*

AMHERST, Jeffery Amherst, 1st Baron 1717-97

Army officer; commander of British forces in North America 1758-64 and governor of Virginia 1759-68; KB 1761; cr. Baron Amherst of Holmesdale 1776 and of Montreal 1788; field-marshal 1796.

'In his person he was tall and thin, of an adust habit, with an aquiline nose and an intelligent countenance. His manners were grave, formal and cold. ... I have scarcely ever known a man who possessed more stoical apathy or command over himself (Sir Nathaniel Wraxall, 1815).

150 THOMAS GAINSBOROUGH c.1785

Canvas 73.5 x 60.5 (29 x 23¾); lined; a drip of red paint bottom centre left across the spandrel; cleaned 1989.

Pale grey eyes, powdered wig, wearing the ribbon and star of the Bath and the uniform of a full general of c.1784:[1] red coat with two epaulettes, black facings and gold lace and buttons; cream waistcoat, his black hat beneath his arm. Within a painted oval.

Collections: Bequeathed by the sitter to Mair, his private secretary;[2] by descent to Maj. Arthur Mair, Edinburgh, from whom purchased 1862.

Engraving: J. Scott 1874.

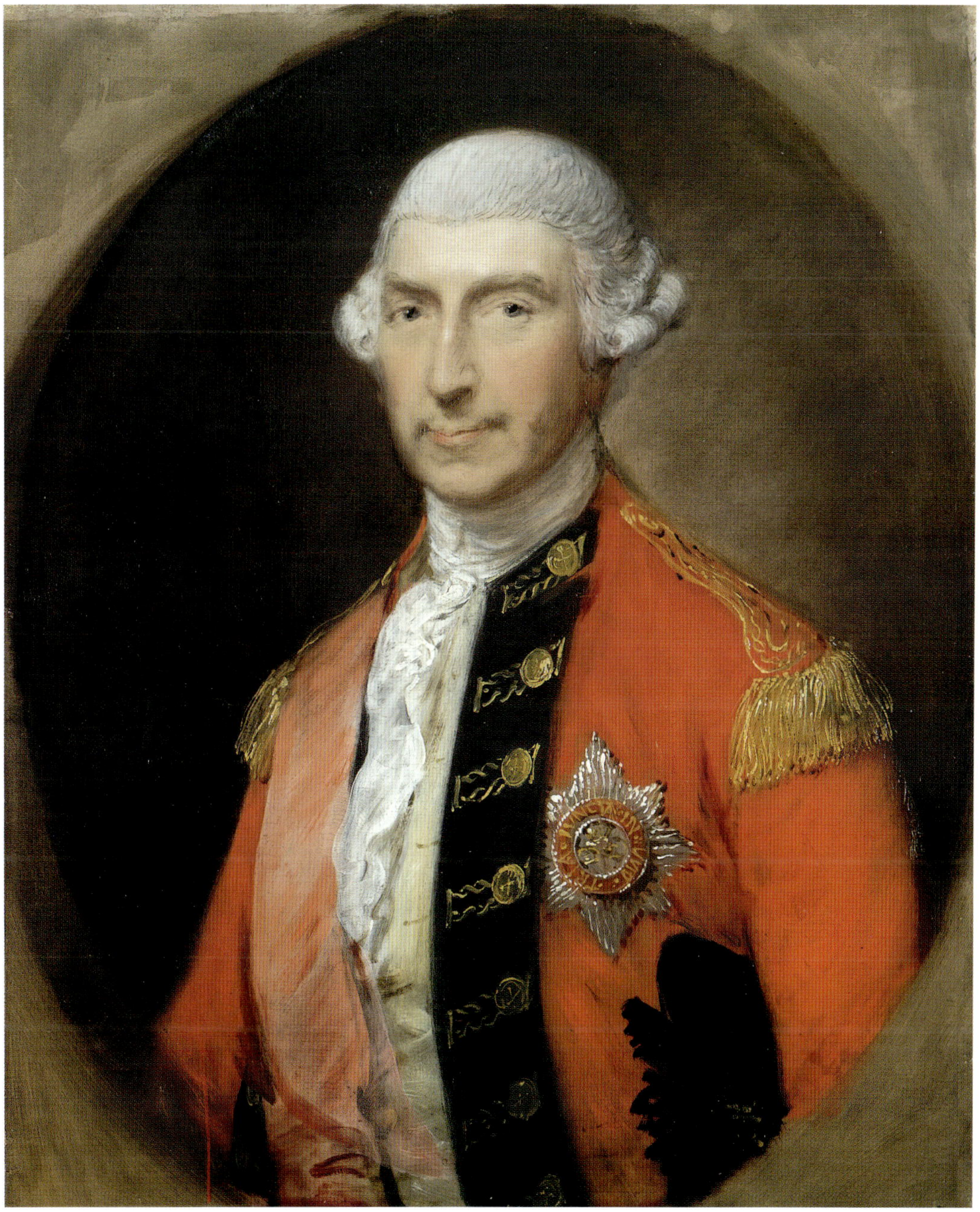

1st Baron AMHERST NPG 150

Exhibition: *Art Treasures*, Manchester, 1857 (BPG 297) lent Maj. Mair; National Gallery -1920.

Reference: *Gainsborough* 1953, p.3; Waterhouse 1958, no.15.

NPG 150 is a replica of the portrait in the Mead Art Museum, Amherst College, Amherst, Mass., which descended from the Amherst family.[3] The uniform is very sketchily painted.

1 Note from Maj. N.P. Dawnay, 1951:'uniform of a full general of c.1784 buttons evenly spaced and two epaulettes; only full generals had two epaulettes before 1791'; and see Dawnay, *JSAHR*, xxi, 126, 1953, p.73.
2 Letter from J. Gibson-Craig, 8 July 1862 (NPG archive).
3 Christie's, 12 February 1932, lot 96; Mead Art Museum (P1940.5); exhibited *The Grand Tradition, British Art from Amherst College*, Miami Beach, etc, 1988-89(7).

ICONOGRAPHY

1756 Painting by Joshua Reynolds, half length, bareheaded in armour. Hardwick Hall (Mannings 2000, no.53).

1757 Engraving by F-G. Aliamet, bust-length oval in uniform (for Smollett's *History of England*). Copied for the *Universal Mag*. Of slight iconographic worth.

1758 Painting by Joseph Blackburn, half length in uniform. Mead Art Museum, Amherst, Mass. (illus. *British Art*, Mead Art Museum monographs vi-vii, 1985-86, p.4, fig.6). Copied by H.R. Burdick 1918 (L. Park, *Proc. of the American Antiquaries Soc.*, 32, ii, 1922, pp.278-79).

1765 Painting by Joshua Reynolds,★ three-quarter length in armour wearing the ribbon and star of the Bath, his helmet resting on a map of Montreal, with troops sailing down the St Lawrence in the background. Mead Art Museum, Amherst, Mass. (AC 1967.85; Mannings 2000, no.54). Exhibited SA 1766(138). Engraved J. Watson 1766, R. Purcell, H.T. Ryall 1832. Versions in the McCord Museum of Canadian History, McGill University, Montreal, and in the National Museum of Cuba.

1765-68 Painting by Joshua Reynolds, half length in the uniform of a general officer, red coat with the star of the Bath, blue or green facings on lapels and cuffs, holding a paper inscribed ... *Louisberg 1758*. NG Ottawa (Mannings 2000, no.55). Exhibited *Pageant of Canada*, Ottawa, 1967(105 attributed to Thomas Lawrenson c.1785). A replica in a Canadian private collection 1987 descended from the Amherst family (previously sold Sotheby's, 29 January 1964, lot 6 as Beechey). A bust-length miniature copy by Ozias Humphry 1768, with a different coat collar but

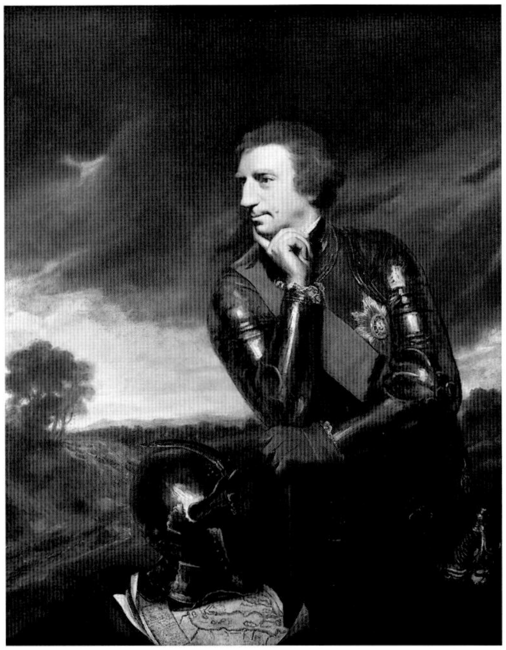

1st Baron AMHERST by Joshua Reynolds 1765 (Mead Art Museum, Amherst College)

showing the ribbon and star of the Bath, sold Christie's, 10 July 1984, lot 101; engraved J. Hall 1792.

1768 Wax medallion by Isaac Gosset, exhibited SA 1768(150). Two waxes by Gosset of 'Lord Amhurst' were listed at Clumber House (cat., 1923, nos.377, 387). An unattributed wax sold Christie's, 23 November 1983, lot 133 as 'Lord Amhurst'.

1779-81 Painting by J.S. Copley,★ *The Death of Chatham*, see Comparative Groups.

c.1779 Painting attributed to R.E. Pine, three-quarter length in general's uniform with red coat and black lapels and cuffs, standing by a cannon. Sotheby's, 14 March 1990, lot 57, from the Elveden Hall sale, Christie's, 21 May 1984, lot 67. Pine painted Amherst's brother, William, in 1779 (Mead Art Museum, Amherst, Mass.).

1782 Etching by J. Sayers, whole-length standing, in general's uniform (George 6053).

c.1785 Painting by Thomas Gainsborough, see NPG 150.

before 1787 Medallions by James Tassie, in armour with ribbon and star of the Bath, of two similar patterns (Gray 1894, no.16): a larger (Scottish NPG, PG 456, plaster replica), and a smaller, modelled by [Sarah] Brown (*Connoisseur*, CXXIX, 1952, p.137). The larger type reproduced by Wedgwood (illus. Reilly 1973, p.49).

Amherst appears indistinctly in a number of history pictures, including those by West, *George III*, 1779 (Royal Collection; Erffa & Staley 1986, no.549); by Hayman, *The Humanity of General Amherst*, c.1760-61 (Beaverbrook AG, Fredericton; a study for the lost Vauxhall picture of 1761; a rejected design by Hayman, sold Sotheby's, 18 December 1963, lot 139); by Pine, *Lord Amherst on the Heights of Abraham* (Christie's, 20 July 1990, lot 319), and by Reynolds, *Sir Jeffery Amherst*, c.1768? (Yale Center for British Art, B1981.25.512; Mannings 2000, no.56).

Amherst's hanging monument with a trophy of arms, in the church of St Nicholas, Sevenoaks, is by William Tyler, a sculptor Amherst had previously encouraged (Farington, 3 December 1799).

ANGELO, Henry 1756-1835

Fencing master; christened Henry Charles William, s. of Domenico Angelo Malevolti,[1] an Italian fencing master who came to England c.1755; succeeded to his father's fencing academy in London 1785-1817; his *Reminiscences* were published in 1828 and 1830.

1 For the confused surnames of the family, see C. Swynnerton, *The Ancestor*, VIII, 1904, pp.1-72; Henry's grandfather was Jacopo Tremamondi, under which surname Henry appears, for example, in *DNB*; his grandmother was Caterina Angela Malevolti.

5310 MATHER BROWN C.1790

Canvas 76 x 63 (30 x 24¾); lined; cleaned 1976; signed in red above his arm on the right: *M Brown*.

Brown eyes, grey hair, wearing a red scarf, a white coat with a black collar, and a yellow glove on his right hand.

Collections: L.I. Davidson; Sotheby's, 14 July 1976, lot 106, bt. Leger, from whom purchased 1980.

Exhibition: Leger, *18th-century English Paintngs*, 1978(5).

Reference: Evans 1982, no.185.

Sold in 1976 (with Hone's portrait of 1769, see below) as an unknown fencer, but the sitter closely resembles the engraving by Scott after J.R. Smith and the figure of Angelo in Rowlandson's *Mr Henry Angelo's Fencing Academy* (see 1787 below). Angelo was acquainted with Brown, as the first owner of Brown's portrait of the celebrated West Indian fencer, Joseph Saint-Georges.[1]

1 See Evans 1982, p.225; Angelo 1904, II, p.78.

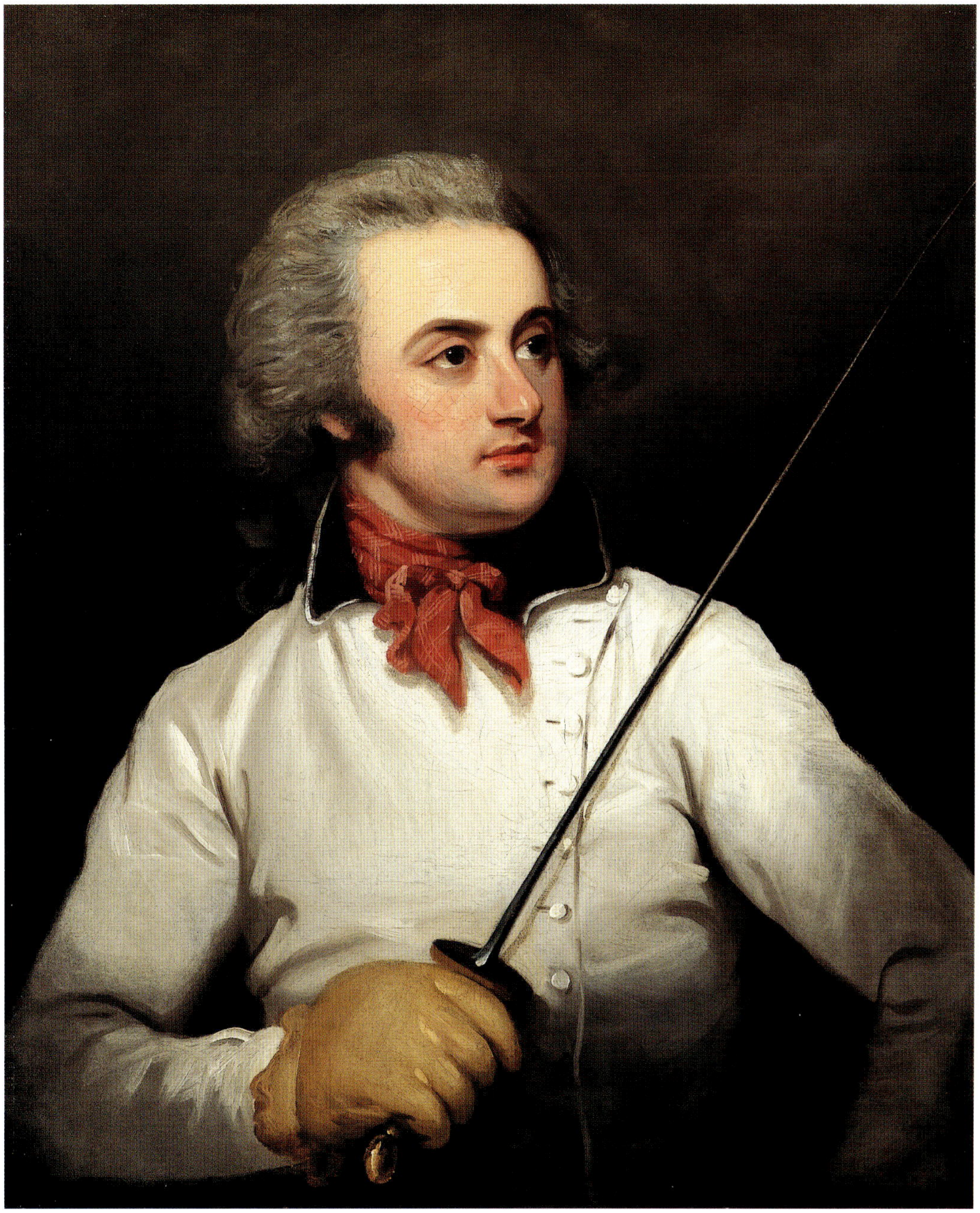

ANGELO NPG 5310

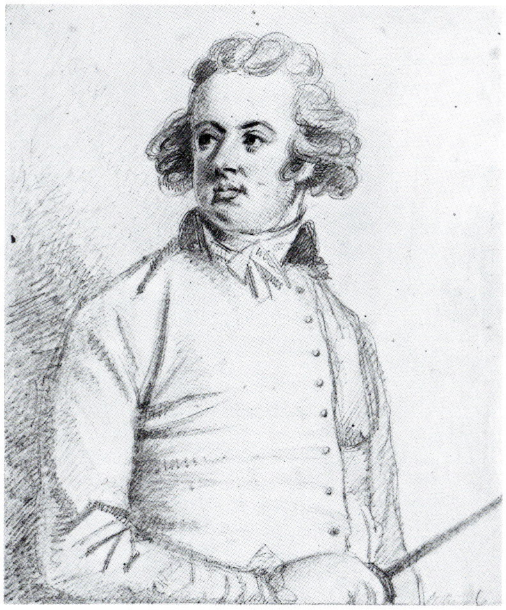

ANGELO copy of a print by B.F. Scott 1791 after J.R. Smith (NPG D 4092)

ICONOGRAPHY

1769 Painting by Nathaniel Hone, as a child, half-length seated, drawing. Sotheby's, 14 July 1976, lot 105 (sold with NPG 5310). Exhibited RA 1769(54).

1787 Watercolour by Thomas Rowlandson, *Mr Henry Angelo's Fencing Academy*, with Angelo standing on the right beneath Mather Brown's portrait of St George. Cecil Higgins AG, Bedford (illus. *Art Treasures in England*, RA, 1998, no.216). Etched by Rowlandson. A drawing by Rowlandson, *Henry Angelo and Madam Cain Fencing*, Yale Center for British Art (B1981.25.2671; J. Egerton & D. Snelgrove, *British Sporting and Animal Drawings*, 1978, no.14), is of no use as portraiture.

c.1790 Painting by Mather Brown, see NPG 5310.

before 1791 Drawing by J.R. Smith, engraved B.F. Scott 1791 as *A Fencer*. Apparently wearing the same dress as in NPG 5310. An early-19th century pencil copy of the mezzotint,* approximately the same size, inscribed *Williams*[?] and identified as *St George the celebrated Swordsman Picadilly 1799* (cf. under 1787 above) is in the NPG reference collection (D 4092).

1792 Painting by Samuel De Wilde, full length as Mrs Cole in Foote's *The Minor*. Garrick Club (Ashton 1997, no.12). Angelo played this part *en travesti* once on 29 March 1792. Engraved W.S. Leney 1792 (illus. Burnim 1998, p.89); C. Cook 1809.

1797 Miniature by George Place, exhibited RA 1797(1025, a frame with six portraits).

1801 Miniature by William Lane, exhibited RA 1801(922).

Two caricature drawings by John Nixon, *Angelo as Sir Andrew Aguecheek in 12th night*, 1796, and *Angelo in his garrett with Nixon and Samuel Maynard*, were sold Christie's, 5 November 1974, lots 87 and 69.

ANSTEY, Christopher 1724–1805

Miscellaneous writer; translated Gray's *Elegy* into Latin 1762, wrote the *New Bath Guide* 1766, and a series of letters in verse, after which, Walpole considered, came 'nothing but doggerel and stupidity'.

'habituated to the charms of literary ease and retirement, passionately fond of sports of the field, ... in the enjoyment of a competent and independent fortune, [he] found leisure for the study of the Greek and Roman authors, and the poetry and polite literature of his own country' (John Anstey, 1808).

3084 WILLIAM HOARE, *with his daughter* c.1776–78

Canvas 126.5 x 101 (49¾ x 39¾) cleaned 1979 when a previous lining was undone and the canvas marouflaged to sundeala board; there is an overall craquelure and old tears have been repaired, the most prominent to the left of his head and above his right wrist.

Brown eyes, grey powdered hair, wearing a white neckcloth, blue suit, writing (deliberately illegible) verse; the girl has brown eyes and wears a white dress with a pink sash, and a cap of ruched silk gauze; in her hand a doll with a fantastic head-dress and pink dress.

Collections: *This Portrait of my honoured father by Hoar of Bath is given by the wish of my eldest Brother, the late Revd. Christopher Anstey* [1755–1827] *to myself for Life, after my death to my Brother Thomas Anstey* [c.1770–1843] *for life and after his death to our nephew Christopher John Anstey absolutely./ A.A. Calvert*;[1] the Rev John Filmer Anstey [b. c.1825, s. of Thomas]; his dau., Caroline Mary Anstey, Mrs Samborne-Palmer, by whom bequeathed 1940.

Engraving: without the child, by W. Bond 1807, as *Aetat 52* after Lawrence (see below).

Exhibitions: [RA 1779(130, *A gentleman and his daughter half lengths*), see below] *Childhood*, Camden Arts Centre, 1967(32); *Hoare*, Bath, 1990(39); *Innocence and Experience*, Manchester, Hull, Nottingham, Glasgow, 1992–93(7); *The New Child*, Berkeley, Memphis, Tenn, Omaha, 1995–96 (cat. pl.30); *Gainsborough*, Tate Gallery, 2002–03(74); Beningbrough 1979–.

The little girl tries to distract Anstey from his verse composition with a fashionably dressed doll, whose excessive hair style recalls his own *New Bath Guide* of 1766 (letter xii):

> Those tresses, which Venus might take as a favour,
> Fall a victim at once to an outlandish shaver;
> When lo! on a sudden, a monster appears,
> A horrible monster, to cover her ears;-.[2]

A version of the composition, with the child omitted, was engraved in 1807 for Anstey's *Poetical Works*[3] as from a drawing by Lawrence, the plate giving Anstey's age as fifty two, i.e. c.1776. The composition, and even the girl's head-dress, resembles Wright of Derby's *Rev Thomas Wilson and Miss Macaulay* painted in Bath c.1776.[4] Hoare made a bust-length etching of Anstey in 1778–79 (see below). Such evidence suggests NPG 3084 dates from soon after 1776; it may well have been the portrait of *A gentleman and his daughter half lengths* exhibited by Hoare in 1779 (see above). Such dating implies that the little girl is one of Anstey's younger daughters.[5]

In 1913, when NPG 3084 had acquired attributions to both Gainsborough[6] and Lawrence,[7] Horace Buttery suggested it was by Hoare,[8] an attribution subsequently supported by the discovery of an early nineteenth-century label (quoted above) on the frame. The head from NPG 3084 appears to have been copied in the portrait attributed to Simmons in the Victoria Art Gallery, Bath (see below c.1780).

1 Label, presumably c.1830 formerly on the frame, probably written by Arthur, the sitter's youngest son (cf. c.1765 below), found beneath a second label: *Portrait of the late Christopher Anstey Esqr. Author of the Poetical New Bath Guide by Hoare/ J T Anstey* [d. 1843].
2 See A. Ribeiro, *The Art of Dress*, 1995, pp.49–50; Ribeiro 2000, pp.130–32, and Anstey's 'Epistola poetica familiaris', *Works*, 1808, pp.403–04.
3 Edited by his son John Anstey (1757–1819) and published in 1808.

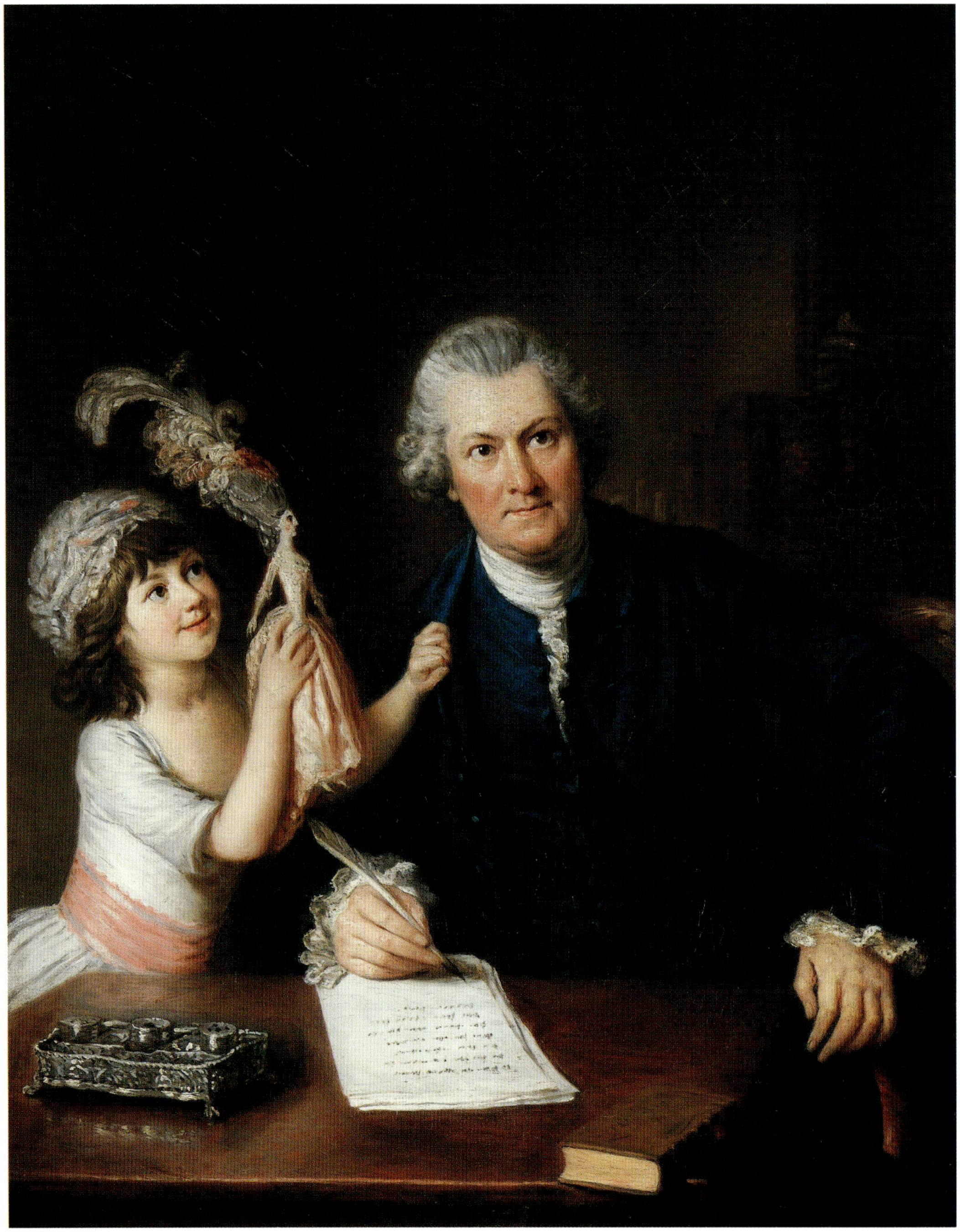

ANSTEY NPG *3084*

4 Illus. *Bath History*, VI, 1996, p.138.
5 Anstey had four daughters: Mary Ann (1763-1829; see *GM*, XCIX, 1829, i, p.381) and Elizabeth (both unm.); Caroline (Mrs Henry Bosanquet) and Sarah (Mrs Thomas Sotheby); note by J. Simon from the Wills of Anstey and his wife (PRO B 11/1432 and 1530).
6 So described on a photograph of 1913 (NPG archive).
7 W. Armstrong, *Lawrence*, 1913, p.110 (see also Engraving).
8 He also associated it with the RA 1779 exhibit (letter to Mrs Samborne-Palmer, 24 June 1913; NPG archive).

ICONOGRAPHY

c.1750-55 Painting attributed to Thomas Hudson, three-quarter length. Victoria AG, Bath (1984.23; illus. *Connoisseur*, XX, 1908, p.29, as possibly by Hoare). Previously attributed to Gainsborough (exhibited as such *International Exhibition, Royal Pavilion*, Paris, 1900, p.46). The identity is traditional and negotiable.

c.1755 Enamel by Christian Zincke, half length, engraved C. Bestland as *aetat xxxi*, with arms of Anstey and Calvert.

c.1765? Unattributed painting, half-length seated, copied by J. Thurston and engraved F. Engleheart 1822, *from an original picture in the possession of Arthur Anstey Calvert.*

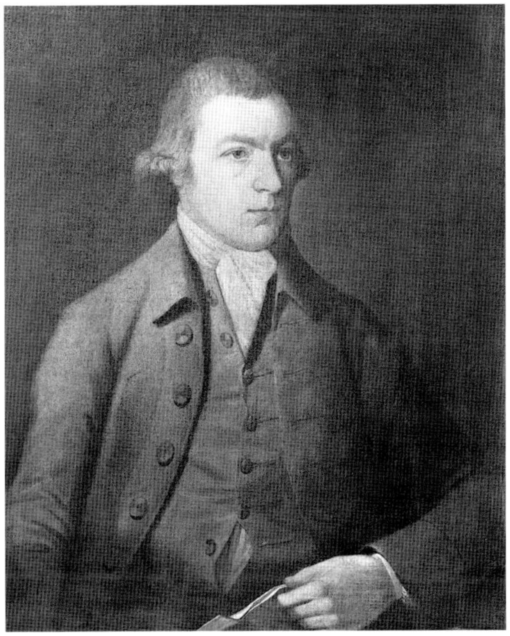

ANSTEY attributed to Thomas Beach c.1770? (King's College, Cambridge)

c.1770? Painting attributed to Thomas Beach,* half length. King's College, Cambridge.

c.1776-78 Painting by William Hoare, see NPG 3084.

1778 Etching by William Hoare, bust length. Example in the NPG reference collection (D 9493)* signed[?] *Wm Hoare ft 1779*. Pencil copy by G.P. Harding, NPG reference collection (D 5635) inscribed: *Mr Anstey/.. tey author of the Bath Guide/From an etching by W Hoare of Bath// W. Hoare fct/1778.* ~~*Wm Ty.*~~

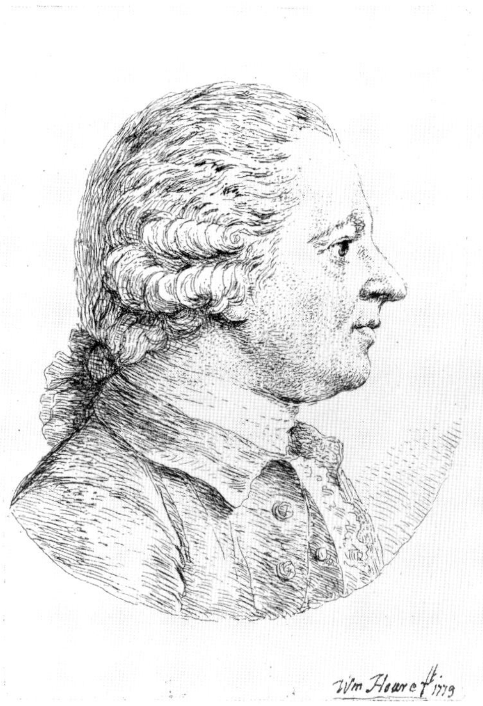

ANSTEY etching by William Hoare 1778 (NPG D 9493)

c.1780 Painting attributed to John Simmons (d.1780) and formerly to Thomas Beach, half length, painted oval. Victoria AG, Bath (1955.2). The head relates closely to NPG 3084.

c.1790 Painting by J.R. Smith, small oval three-quarter length, wearing spectacles. Sotheby's, 12 February 1998, lot 222, from the Anstey family.

1793 Miniature enamel on glass, by Jacob Spornberg, bust length, with his wife. Holburne Museum, Bath (M 207; McKechnie 1978, no.1573). Two more enamels of 1793 by Spornberg, showing ladies from the Anstey family, were sold Christie's, 8 March 1995, lot 101, and Bonhams's, 30 June 1998, lot 81, both from the collection of Lady Sackville.

A miniature, whole-length seated in library, seen in 1858 by Scharf in Bath (SSB 52/30) when attributed to Zoffany.

DOUBTFUL PORTRAITS

See Unidentified Portraits NPG 1339. A painting attributed to Gainsborough, seated by a window, 'aged 40', with H. Hughes-Stanton 1902 and possibly Christie's, 28 January 1905, lot 19.

ARGYLL, Elizabeth, Duchess of, *née* Gunning 1734-90

Celebrated beauty; 2nd dau. of Col. John Gunning of Castle Coote, Co. Roscommon; m. 1) 1752 James Hamilton, 6th Duke of Hamilton (1724-58), 2) 1759 John Campbell, 5th Duke of Argyll (1723-1806); the mother of four Dukes (the 7th and 8th of Hamilton and the 6th and 7th of Argyll); lady of the bedchamber to the Queen 1761-84; cr. Baroness Hamilton 1776.

[*with her sister Mary*] 'two Irish girls of no fortune, who are declared the handsomest women alive. I think their being two, so handsome and both such perfect figures, is their chief excellence, for singly I have seen much handsomer women than either: however, they can't walk in the park, or go to Vauxhall, but such mobs follow them that they are generally driven away' (Horace Walpole, 1751).

4890 FRANCIS COTES 1751

Pastel on blue paper 59 x 44 (23¼ x 17¼) laid down on canvas; signed in black, lower right: *FC*(monogram)*otes pxt./1751.*

Blue-grey eyes, dark hair, wearing an ermine-trimmed blue cape over a blue and pink dress with gold trimming.

Collections: Sir George Russell, 4th Bt, in 1889,[1] by descent to Lady Marjorie Russell; her sale, Christie's, 6 June 1972, lot 104, bt. Leggatt for the NPG.

Engravings: R. Brookshaw 1751; J. McArdell 1752; A. Miller.

Exhibitions: *British Art*, Grosvenor Gallery, 1889(230) lent Sir George Russell; *British Art*, RA, 1934(808) lent Arthur Russell (later 6th Bt); *Masque of Beauty*, NPG, 1972(55); *Master Drawings* 1993-95(21).

Reference: Johnson 1976, no.16; Simon 1997, pp.66, 161.

NPG 4890 not only marked the arrival in London of the beautiful Elizabeth Gunning, but also significantly helped to establish the young Francis Cotes, who went on to make several portraits of the Gunning family.[2] McArdell's mezzotint was prominently advertised in April 1752 as obtainable only from Cotes's residence in Cork Street;[3] by then Elizabeth Gunning was Duchess of Hamilton.

A pastel replica belongs to the Croome Estate[4] and a copy in oils remains at Inverary Castle. Cotes used the same head for another half length (with a corsage), almost certainly a pastel,[5] known only through an engraving by Houston.[6] This in turn was engraved anonymously with minor differences in the dress,[7] the plate becoming the source of an oval Battersea enamel.[8]

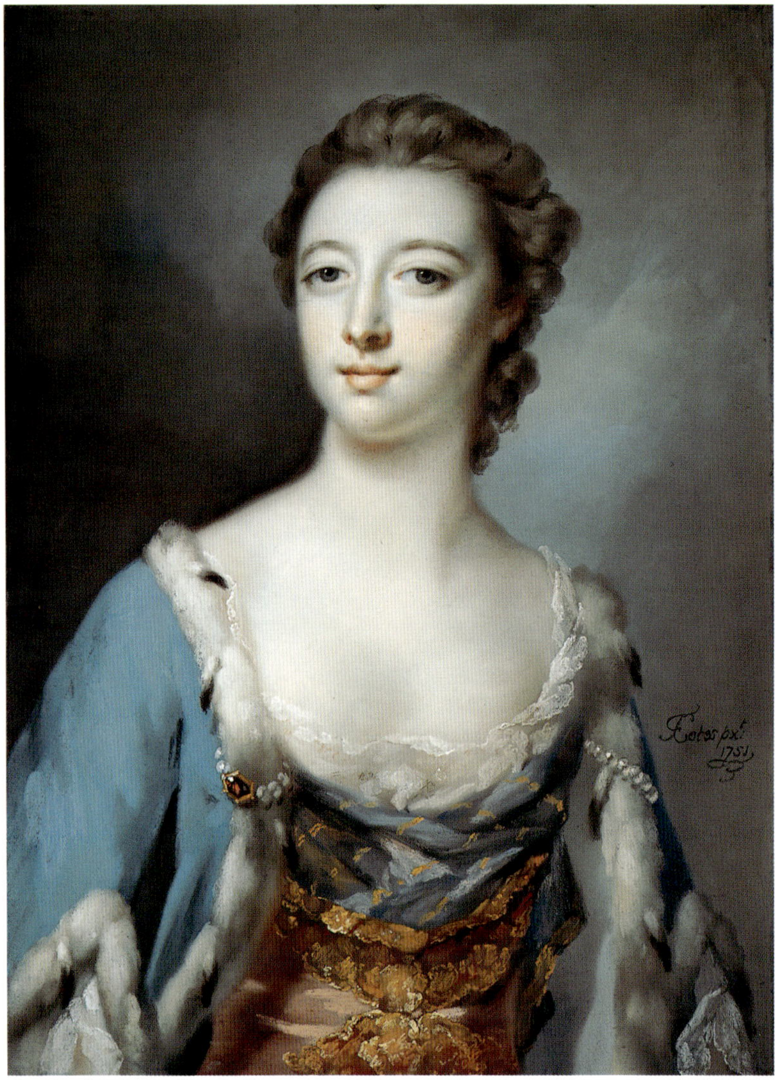

Elizabeth, Duchess of ARGYLL NPG *4890*

1 (1828-98), m. Constance, dau. of Lord Arthur Lennox (7th s. of the 4th Duke of Richmond). Johnson 1976, no.16, stated NPG 4890 descended directly from the sitter. It may just be seen in a photograph of the drawing room at Swallowfield, illus. Lady Russell, *Swallowfield*, 1901, f.p.304.

2 See Johnson 1976, p.9; a Cotes portrait of one of the Miss Gunnings was celebrated in verse in September 1750 (*GM*, XX, 1750, p.423).

3 *London Advertiser*, 6 April 1752, see Johnson 1976, p.9.

4 Illus. C. Gordon, *The Coventrys of Croome*, 2000, pl.xiii. The sitter's sister Maria (d.1760) m. the 6th Earl of Coventry.

5 Johnson 1976, no.31.

6 Illus. *Connoisseur*, XII, 1905, p.162.

7 A reduced version of the same print called *Madame Vestris as Mrs Page*.

8 Examples in the Victoria and Albert Museum (414.1411.1885; illus. *Connoisseur*, LXXXIX, 1932, p.169) and Sotheby's, 28 February 1972, lot 156.

ICONOGRAPHY

As Elizabeth Gunning

1751 Pastel by Francis Cotes, see NPG 4890.

As Duchess of Hamilton

1752 Miniature by Nathaniel Hone, half length. Sotheby's, 15 March 1984, lot 50.

c.1752 Painting by Gavin Hamilton,* whole length as Diana, wearing grey and crimson, the Hamilton colours. Lennoxlove. Engraved J. Faber 1753. A version belongs to the Croome Estate (illus. C. Gordon, *The Coventrys of Croome*, 2000, p.172, just visible) and a half length is in the Scottish NPG (PG 814).

Half-length variants, with a dark lace shawl round her arms, in the Scottish NPG (PG 1444) and at Inverary Castle; this type was closely imitated in a pastel by Anne Forbes, of which there are versions in two Scottish private collections.

c.1752-54 Painting by Gavin Hamilton, half length, her head veiled. Private collection (illus. *Scottish Art Souvenir*, RA, 1939, p.21 as with Sir Alexander Gordon-

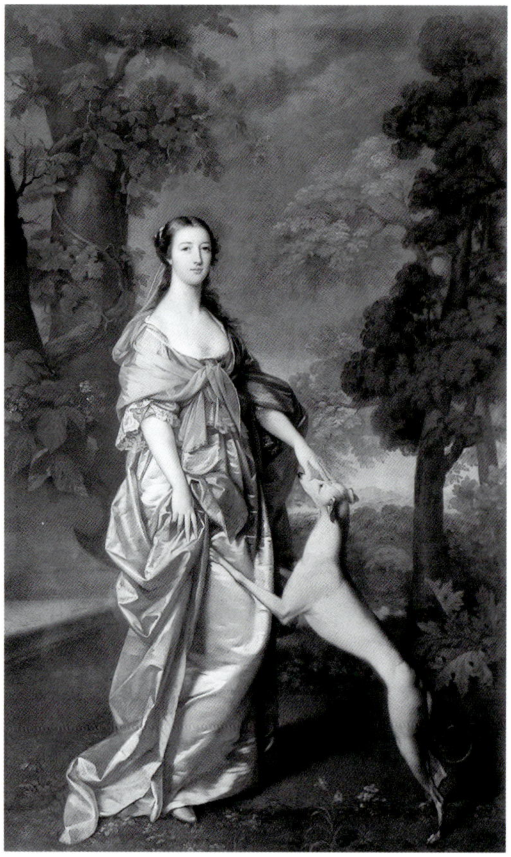

Elizabeth, Duchess of ARGYLL by Gavin Hamilton c.1752 (Lennoxlove)

Cumming). Exhibited NPE 1868(849) lent Sir W.G. Gordon-Cumming. Left unfinished at the wish of the Duke of Hamilton (cf. *Scottish Art*, RA, 1939, no.30).

1758-59 Painting by Joshua Reynolds,* whole length, with a Peeress's mantle. Lady Lever AG, Port Sunlight (LL 3126; Mannings 2000, no.810). Exhibited FS 1760(47). A studio replica of c.1764 is in the Yale Center for British Art (B1977.14.68: Mannings 2000, no.811) and a copy in the California Palace of the Legion of Honor, San Francisco (1941.31).

As Duchess of Argyll

1760 Painting by Allan Ramsay, half length. Sotheby's, 18 November 1992, lot 42 (Smart 1999, no.567, as unidentified, probably Elizabeth Gunning), from the collection of the Duke of St Alban's. The resemblance to her portraits by Cotes, Hamilton and Forbes makes the identity most likely.

before 1762 Painting by Joseph Highmore, the *Duchess of Hamilton* 'by Memory'; Highmore sale, Langford's, 5 March 1762, lot 40.

c.1763 Painting by F-H. Drouais, half length, her hands in a fur muff. Inverary Castle (illus. *French Art in the 18th century*, RA 1967-68, no.209). Painted in Paris together with a portrait of the Duke.

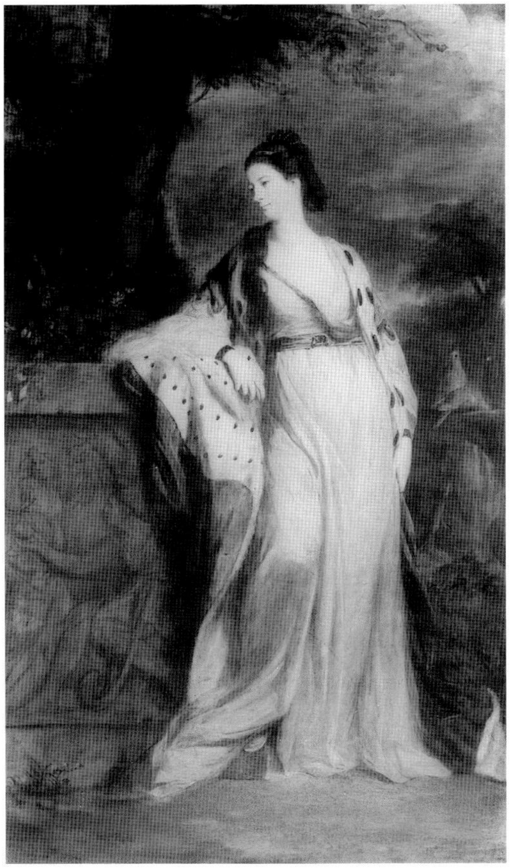

Elizabeth, Duchess of ARGYLL by Joshua Reynolds 1758-59 (Lady Lever Art Gallery, Port Sunlight)

1767 Painting by Francis Cotes, whole-length standing, by an urn. Inverary Castle (Johnson 1976, no.219, fig.83). Exhibited SA 1767(35). A three-quarter length version, formerly with Lady Marjorie Russell, sold Christie's, Scotland, 14 November 1985, lot 515.

c.1770 Pastel by Katherine Read, half-length oval, with lace head-dress. Inverary Castle. Engraved J. Finlayson 1770 (illus. *Connoisseur*, XII, 1905, p.229 and LXXXVIII, 1931, p.377), R. Lowry 1771, J. Cook 1843. Presumably the pastel of the Duchess of Hamilton which Read exhibited SA 1770(299). Versions exhibited *Art Treasures*, Manchester, 1857 (BPG 316) lent Mark Philips (SSB 49/20), and sold Christie's, 22 November 1968, lot 27 as N. Hone; a miniature copy on card by William Derby exhibited SKM 1865(1846) lent by the Earl of Derby (illus. J.J. Foster, *British Miniatures*, 1898, f.p.118).

1775 Terracotta bust by J-B. Lemoyne, exhibited *Virtue and Vision, Sculpture and Scotland*, Edinburgh, 1991(room no. 3, n.n.) lent by the Trustees of the Earl of Argyll.

Undated Unattributed miniature, inscribed *verso* with the sitter's name and the initials *PC*, exhibited *Guelph* 1891(572) lent by the Duke of Hamilton.

Undated Silhouette, life-size bust-length. Inverary Castle.

DOUBTFUL PORTRAITS

Pastel by Cotes at Brodick Castle (Johnson 1976, no.45); miniature formerly at Welbeck Abbey (*Welbeck Abbey Miniatures*, 1916, p.158, no.231); unattributed oval painting at Baddesley Clinton (NT Guide, 1998, p.18).

Untraced miniatures, called Elizabeth, Duchess of Argyll, include four exhibited *Guelph* 1891: 536 by B. Denner lent Sir C.W. Dilke; 1019 unattributed enamel lent J. Whitehead (presumably that exhibited BFAC 1889, xvi 30, and Whitehead sale, 2nd day, 5 August 1915, lot 305); 1083 by N. Plimer lent J.L. Propert (presumably that exhibited BFAC 1889, xxxvi, 28 as A. Plimer); 1199 by Cosway lent J. Whitehead..

ARKWRIGHT, Sir Richard, Kt 1732-92

Cotton manufacturer at Cromford, Derbyshire; b. Preston, he began as a barber in Bolton; his use of the water frame and the carding machine revolutionised the cotton industry; a creator of the factory system; Kt 1786.

'a plain, almost gross, bag-wigged, pot-bellied Lancashire man, with an air of painful reflection, yet also of copious free digestion' (Thomas Carlyle, 1839).

136 studio of JOSEPH WRIGHT of Derby [1789-90]

Canvas 75 x 63 (29½ x 24¾) lined; old damage upper right, the surface somewhat rubbed.

Pale blue eyes, powdered wig, red-brown coat, yellow, green-striped waistcoat with yellow buttons bearing green crosses, white neckcloth.

Collections: Said to have been given by the sitter to Erasmus Darwin;[1] his daughter-in-law Lady Darwin, from whom purchased 1861.

Exhibition: *Regency Portraits*, Kenwood, 1986.

Reference: Nicolson 1968, under no.2; *Wright* 1990, p.198.

NPG 136 derives from Wright's remarkable whole-length portrait* painted in 1789-90 (in the collection of the sitter's descendants),[2] in which Arkwright's huge figure is seated by a table bearing a set of rollers for the spinning of cotton, the source of his prosperity and perhaps of his own invention, his stern expression and clenched left hand suggesting the 'Tyrant ... more absolute than a Bashaw' described by Boulton.[3]

Wright's undated accounts record 'a full length of Sir R Arkwright £52.12.0' and 'a 3qrs [i.e. 30 x 25 in.] copy of Sir R Arkwright £12.12.0',[4] the latter very probably the half length painted for Jedediah Strutt, now in the Science Museum, London, which Nicolson described as 'the only [half length] that has strong claims to be an original'.[5] NPG 136 is one of three other half lengths which appear to be at least from Wright's studio, the other two being with the sitter's descendants and in the Helmshore Textile Museum.[6] The abraded surface of NPG 136 complicates assessment, although Nicolson considered it to be 'also excellent' and Egerton considered it a replica. It was listed as a studio production in 1981[7] and the provenance suggests a studio replica commissioned for a friend.

Half-length copies are in Manchester City Art Gallery (1968.239) and the Castle Museum and Art Gallery, Nottingham (1887-5);[8] an oval copy was sold Sotheby's, 12 February 1998, lot 220, and a small pastel copy of the whole length, attributed to J.R. Smith, was with Sabin in 1964.[9]

1 Lady Darwin [Jane Harriot, widow of Sir Francis Secheverel Darwin, Kt] to Scharf, 15 November 1861 (NPG archive): 'This portrait of Sir Richard Arkwright (by Wright of Derby) was presented by him to Dr Darwin in addition to a fee of £1000 in compensation for his time and trouble for appearing in London to give evidence at the trial in which Sir Richd Arkwright was proved to be the sole inventor of the spinning jenny'. Arkwright was a close friend and the sum seems surprising; Darwin and Watt had supported Arkwright's claim to the patent for his 'water-frame' in the Court of the Common Pleas in February and June 1785 (on the first occasion Arkwright's patent was upheld, but on the second it was dismissed, due to an inadequate specification); NPG 136 must date from 1790 or after, see note 2; Darwin subsequently attended Arkwright in his final illness and wrote a warm obituary notice of him in the *Derby Mercury*, 9 August 1792 (D. King-Hele, *Erasmus Darwin*, 1999, pp.204-06, 274).

2 Nicolson 1968, no.1; *Wright* 1990, no.126. Engraved J.R. Smith 1801 (the painting dated 1790), and as a three-quarter length by H. Meyer 1829, J. Jenkins 1833, and J. Posselwhite 1835.

3 Quoted by A. Burton, *Josiah Wedgwood*, 1976, p.198. For Arkwright, see also Nicolson, I, pp.164-69.

4 Nicolson 1968, I, p.175; Bemrose 1885, p.120, misquoted another entry, 'Mrs Arkwright half length £26.5' as 'Mr Arkwright ½ length 26.0.0', cf. Nicolson, I, p.176.

5 See Nicolson 1968, no.2; subsequently sold Christie's, 21 November 1986, lot 84; Sotheby's, 9 March 1988, lot 44, and acquired by the Science Museum in 1989.

6 Purchased 2002; from the Haigh Hall, Lancs., sale, Rogers, Chapman & Thomas, 5 November 1946, lot 1708, and Sotheby's, 4 July 2001, lot 58.

7 NPG, *Complete Illus. Cat.*, 1981, p.16.

8 Illus. *Connoisseur*, XCIV, 1934, p.324.

9 Illus. *Connoisseur*, CXLV, 1960, p.267; ex Christie's, 11 December 1959, lot 135.

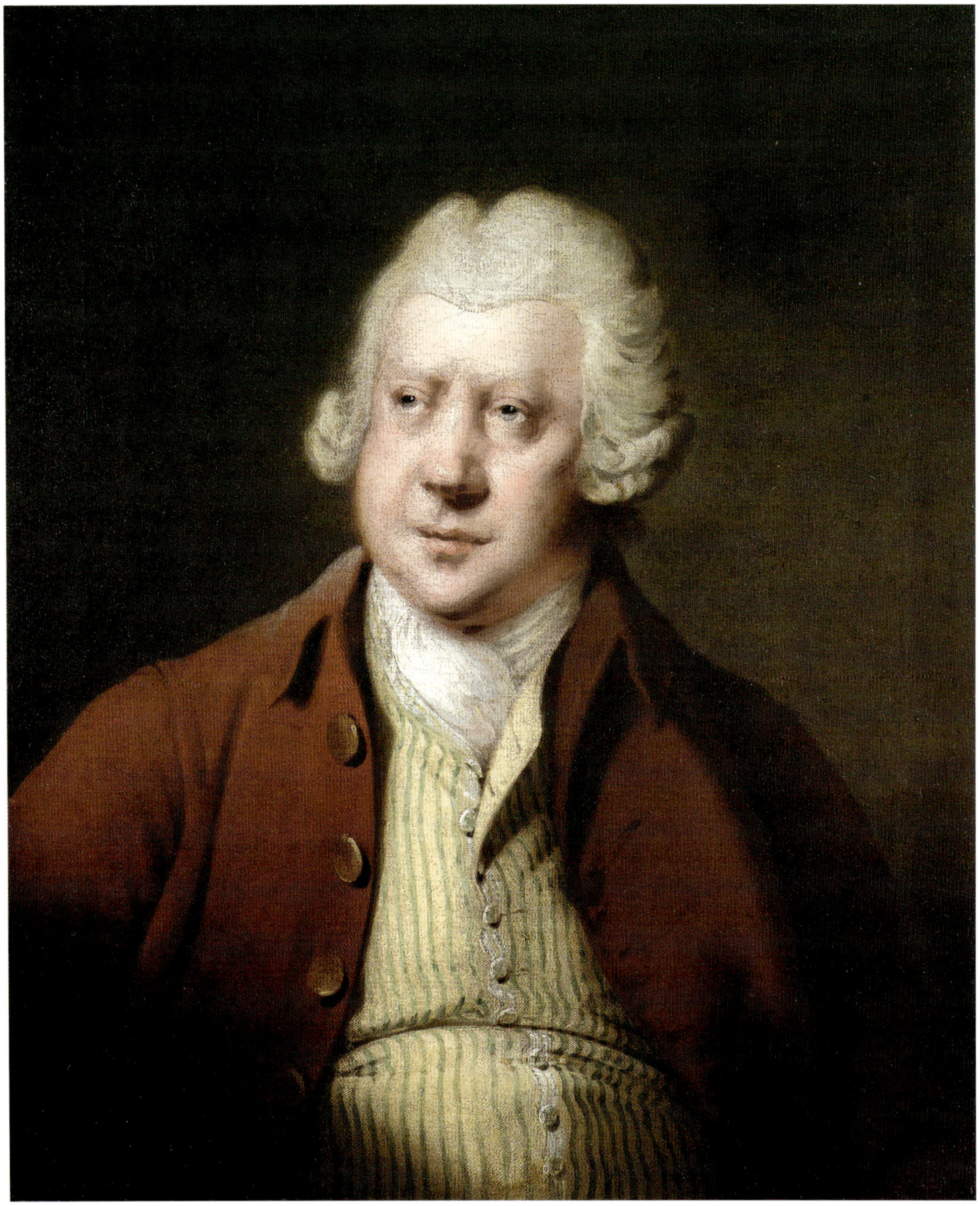

ARKWRIGHT NPG *136*

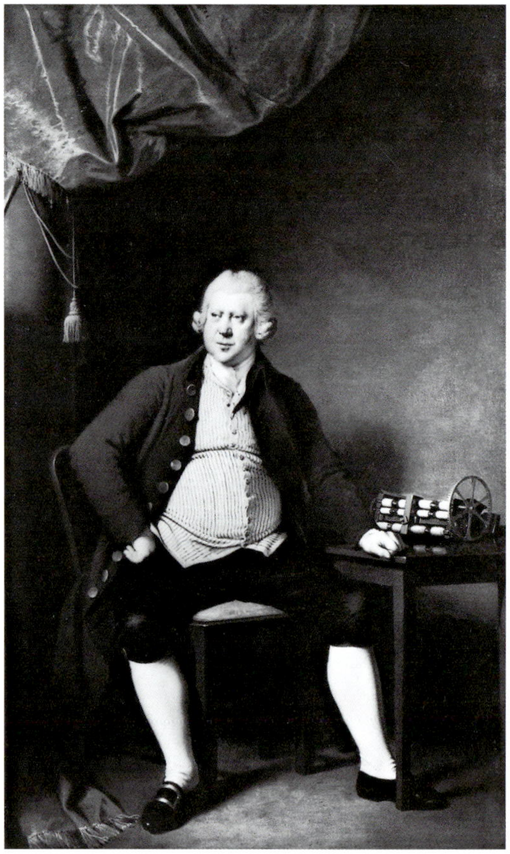

ARKWRIGHT by Joseph Wright of Derby 1789-90 (Private Collection)

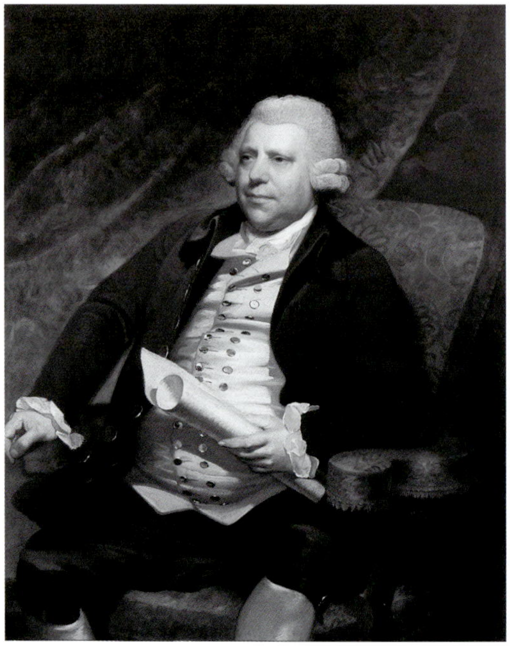

ARKWRIGHT by Mather Brown 1790
(New Britain Museum of American Art)

ICONOGRAPHY

c.1785-90 Unattributed painting, three-quarter length seated wearing a red coat, his right arm over chair back. Untraced. Exhibited NPE 1867(800) lent Philip A. Hurt.

1789-90 Painting by Joseph Wright, see NPG 136.

1790 Painting by Mather Brown,* three-quarter length seated. New Britain Museum of American Art, Conn. (Evans 1982, no.7). Painted for Arkwright's London house in the Adelphi; in 1790 Arkwright also bought from Brown the *Death of Cato* and a whole length of George III (R.S. Fitton, *The Arkwrights*, 1989, pp.200-01).

Posthumous

1810 Bust by W.J. Coffee (Gunnis 1968, p.109).

1839 Medallion by William Barton, exhibited Mechanics' Institute, Derby, 1839.

mid-19th century plaster statue by Thomas Duckett, whole-length seated. Destroyed (Gunnis 1968, p.133).

ARNE, Thomas 1710-78

Composer of operas, masques, oratorios and incidental music for plays, including Shakespeare's; the song *Rule Britannia* was part of his masque *Alfred* of 1740.

[Garrick] 'ignorant of what [Arne's] musical merit may have been had such an utter contempt for his vanity, and general Character, that he hardly ever qualified him wth any other title in Private, than the *Rabscalion*' (Charles Burney, 1749-51).

1130 after FRANCESCO BARTOLOZZI [c.1770]

Hand-coloured etching, the image 28.8 x 23 (11⅜ x 9).

Black coat and hair ribbon, red topped stool, blue curtain; the music headed *Rule Brittania*. Titled: *HARMONY AND SENTIMENT/ 'By Music minds an equal temper know;/ Nor swell too high nor sink too low;/ Warriors she fires with animated sounds;/ Pours balm into the bleeding lovers wounds'* [*Rule Britannia*].

Collections: Presented by Sir Lionel Cust 1898.

Exhibition: *Thomas Arne*, British Library, 1978.

Reference: C.J. Holmes, *Burl. Mag.*, XXVII, 1915, pp.182, 187.

NPG 1130 ultimately derives from the caricature drawing by Bartolozzi* at Windsor[1] which, in turn, as Oppé suggested, may have been inspired by a caricature by P.L. Ghezzi[2] of the Italian musician Filippo San Felice. The Bartolozzi may date from c.1770 according to costume and the sitter's age; it was engraved anonymously in 1782,[3] the plate differing in detail in the coat buttons, the cuff buttonholes, the elaborated organ case, and the omission of the candlestick. A second, more finished, Bartolozzi drawing, sold Christie's, 8 May 1975, lot 153, compares more closely with this engraving.[4]

NPG 1130 popularises the Bartolozzi design: the figure is extended to three-quarter length, and a stool, upright organ case and curtain are added, together with the music of *Rule Britannia* and the execrable verses from the text.

1 Oppé 1950, no.47, pl.39.
2 Engraved in 1758; illus. Oppé 1950, p.25, fig.5.
3 Published by William Humphrey; inscribed: *Done from an Original Sketch by F. Bartolozzi* (George 8240); it has been attributed to Gillray (Christie's, 8 May 1975, lot 153). Other engraved versions by W.N. Gardiner after J. Nixon (George 8240a) and H. Adlard; a later engraved version by J. Greatbach 1838 (for G. Hogarth's *Memoirs of the Musical Drama*, II, 1838). A crude, reversed, copy in oil, attributed to J. Cruise c.1830, with Ralph Griffin 1915.
4 A weak copy sold Sotheby's, 22 March 1944, lot 43.

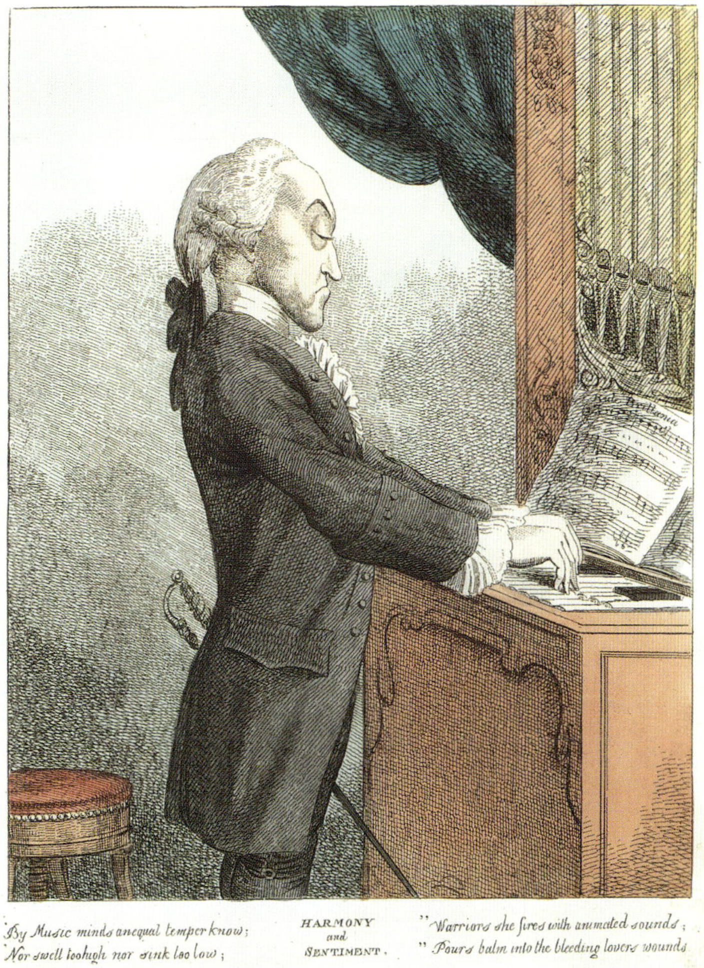

ARNE NPG *1130*

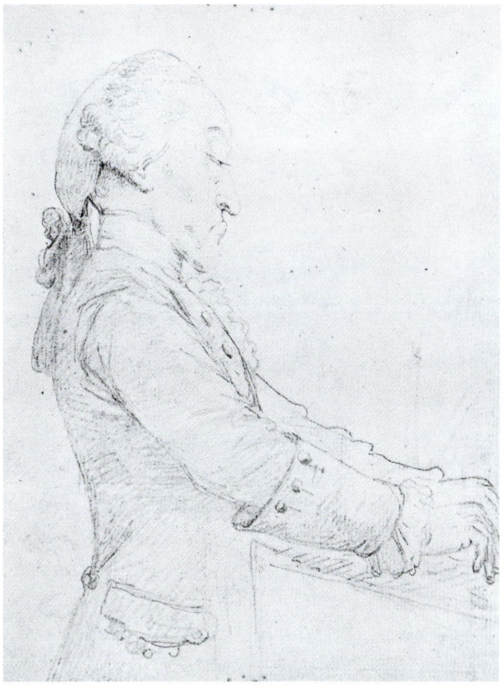

ARNE by Francesco Bartolozzi 1770 (The Royal Collection)

ICONOGRAPHY

1764 Drawing by Thomas Worlidge, profile head. Cottonian collection, Plymouth CMAG. The identity of this physically unattractive profile rests principally on an early inscription on the verso.

c.1770 Drawing by Francesco Bartolozzi, see NPG 1130.

c.1770? Painting by Robert Dunkarton, half-length oval, a sheet of music in his left hand. Untraced. Engraved W. Humphrey* 1778; anon. for the *Universal Mag.* 1784; Rhodes 1794; Drayton (as after R. Smirke) 1801 (for Bowyer's *Historic Gallery*). Copied by E.F. Burney as a half-length oval medallion portrait within an architectural design as frontispiece for Arne's *Concertos* (Christie's, 8 May 1975, lot 150), engraved J. Heath 1793.

An anon. etched caricature, whole length playing the violin, is in the Harvard College Theatre collection (*Harvard Catalogue*, I, p.35, no.8).

Posthumous

1865–67 Sculpture by H.H. Armstead, full-length figure. Albert Memorial, London (south frieze).

DOUBTFUL PORTRAITS

Arne has been very tentatively identified in J.H. Mortimer's *Caricature Group*, see Comparative Groups.

Unattributed drawing, Christie's, 8 May 1975, lot 151 (illus. *Musical Times*, 1901, p.714); paintings by Willem Verelst, 1748 (Royal College of Music); by Johann Zoffany (private collection; probably the composer's son, Michael Arne); and called Gainsborough (Eton College, illus. P. Scholes, *Companion to Music*, 1938, pl.2).

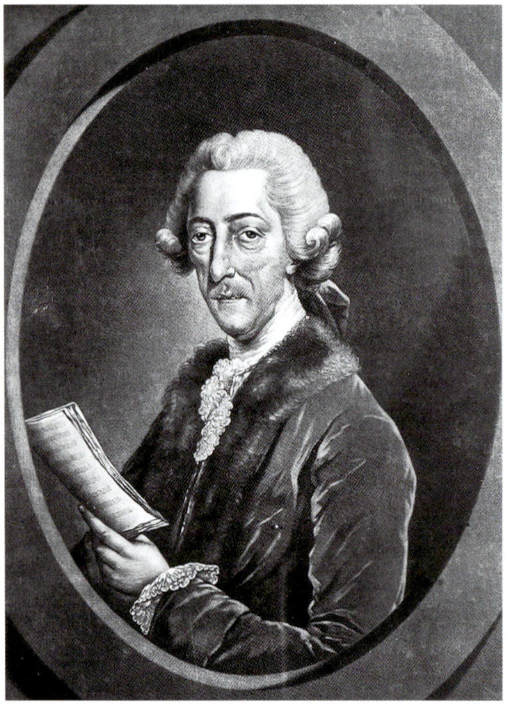

ARNE W. Humphrey 1778 after R. Dunkarton (NPG D 7360)

ASHBURTON, John Dunning, 1st Baron 1731–83

Advocate; condemned general warrants in 1765; MP 1768–82 and solicitor-general 1768–70; defended Admiral Keppel 1779 and in 1780 carried in the House the resolution that 'the influence of the Crown has increased, was increasing and ought to be diminished'; cr. Baron Ashburton 1782; 'there is not a man, of any profession ... [of] a more manly mind, a more firm and determined integrity' (Burke).

'Never perhaps did Nature enclose a more illuminated mind, in a body of meaner and more abject appearance. It is difficult to do justice to the peculiar species of ugliness which characterised his person and figure, although he did not labour under any absolute deformity of shape or limb.' (Sir Nathaniel Wraxall, 1815).

'Sober Sense and great acuteness are mark'd very strong in his Face, but if this was all, I should only admire Him as a great Lawyer; but there is a Genius ... shines in all [He] says' (Thomas Gainsborough).

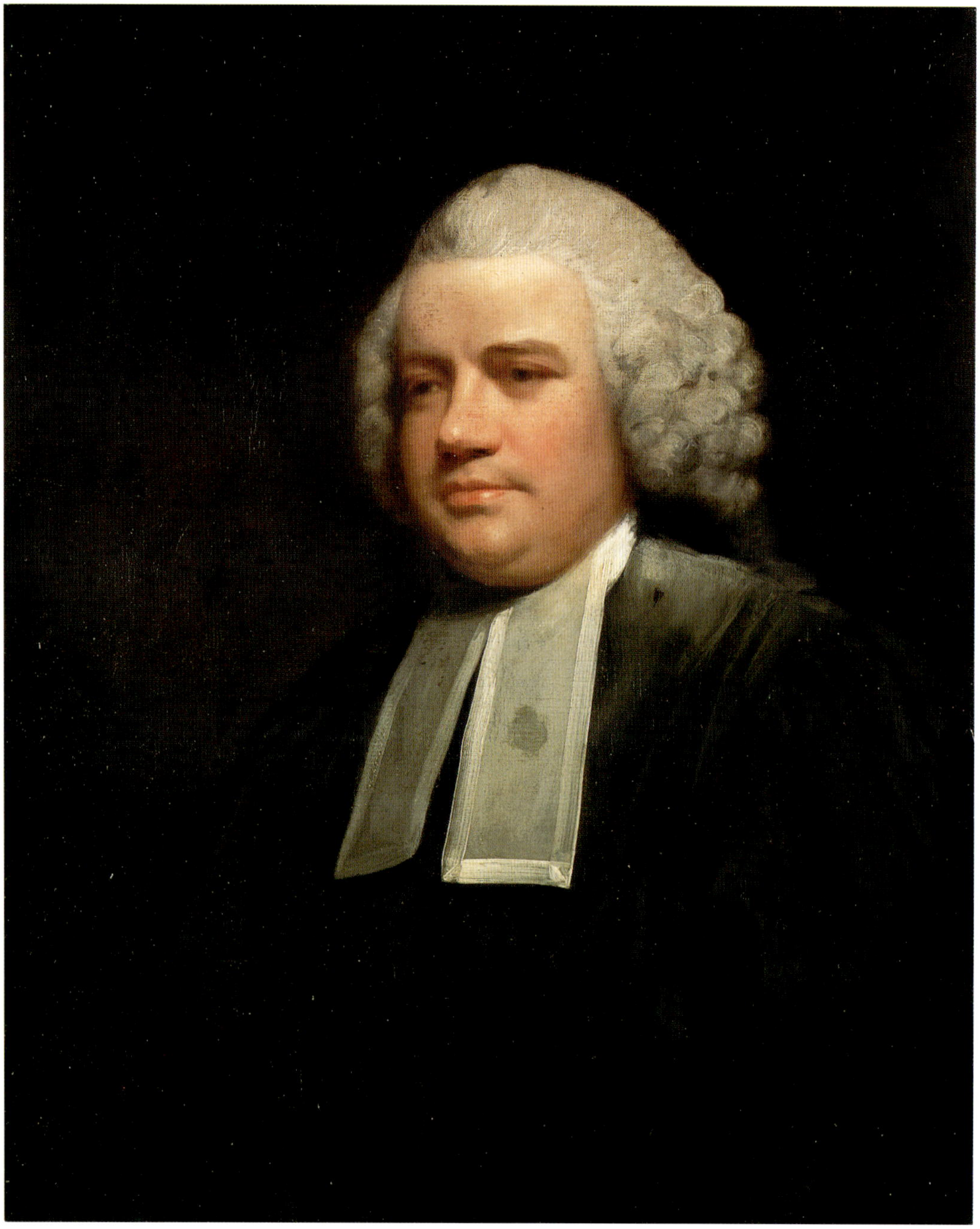

1st Baron ASHBURTON NPG 102

102 studio of JOSHUA REYNOLDS [c.1772]

76 x 62 (30 x 24½) lined; there are discoloured retouchings in the face, bands and shoulder.

Blue eyes, powdered wig, wearing councellor's robes, with white bands.

Collections: Sir Elijah Impey; Miss E.B. Impey's sale, Christie's, 8 March 1845, lot 105, bt. Graves; Thomas Baring,[1] by whom presented 1860.

Exhibitions: NPE 1867(894); *Portraits of departed Worthies*, Exeter, 1873(67); *Bishop Richard Challoner*, Westminster Cathedral, 1981(180).

Reference: Graves & Cronin, I, pp.269-70; Waterhouse 1941, p.64; Mannings 2000, no.539.

'The portly, positive, black-browed Dunning; whose peculiar ugliness ... can only be understood from Reynolds' picture of him',[2] had sat to Reynolds probably in 1772 when there were appointments in February, March, June and November. NPG 102, a studio replica of the now untraced original,[3] appeared in Reynolds's account book, sometime before August 1775, as '[Mr Dunning] given to Sir Elishay Impey' 35 [gn.]. Impey was in India 1774-83 and there was a family tradition that he had asked Reynolds to paint the portrait 'in durable colours to stand the climate of India'.[4] Sir Francis Baring, Dunning's brother-in-law, described the portrait as an 'extraordinary likeness', adding that artist and sitter were 'countrymen and much acquainted'.[5]

Copies were sold Christie's, 30 May 1930, lot 108, and from Bowood in 1952.[6] An oval minature copy by Henry Spicer 1794, inscribed as after Ozias Humphry, was sold Bonham's, 8 September 1999, lot 112.

1 The great-nephew of the 1st Baron Ashburton and brother of the 1st Baron Northbrook. Dymond 1876, p.110, alleged the portrait was formerly in the collection of Lady Ashburton.
2 Leslie & Taylor 1865, I, p.439.
3 It is now known through the oval engraving by F. Bartolozzi of 1787, see Mannings 2000, no.538.
4 E.B. Impey to A. Graves, 17 March 1845 (NPG archive).
5 Farington, 25 June 1806.
6 See Mannings 2000, nos.538a and 538b.

ICONOGRAPHY

c.1772 Painting by Joshua Reynolds, see NPG 102.

1775 Anon. engraving, bust length in gown and bands, right hand raised.

1778 Drawn and engraved by Robert Stewart, bust-length oval profile.

1778 Silhouette sent by Shelburne (Lord Lansdowne) to the Abbé Morellet, with others of himself, Col. Barré and Townsend (*Lettres de Morellet*, ed. D. Medlin & J-C. David, I, 1992, pp.387, 425).

1780 Anon. engraving, profile bust in wig and bands.

1781 Drawing by John Downman, half-length profile to left. Sotheby's, 16 March 1984, lot 69. A crayon drawing of Ashburton, 'an excellent likeness ... by an unknown artist [bearing] the initials J.D. and the date 1780', belonged to 'a lady of Ashburton' in 1876 (Dymond 1876, p.111).

1782 Drawing by John Downman,* similar to his 1781 drawing but in reverse. British Museum (1967.10. 14.185. With an inscription by the artist, saying that it was borrowed by Reynolds after Ashburton's death in order to complete his portrait (Williamson 1907, pp.xvi-xvii).

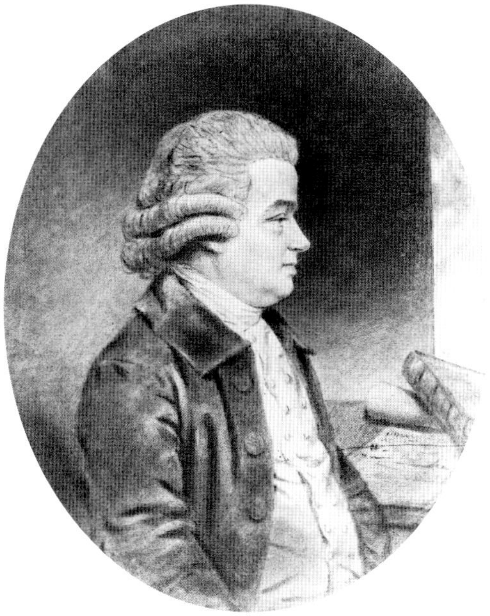

1st Baron ASHBURTON by John Downman 1782 (British Museum)

1782 Etching by J. Bretherton, bust-length, in gown and bands.

1782 Painting by Joshua Reynolds, three-quarter length in chancellor's robes. 5th Baron Ashburton, 1899 (Mannings 2000, no.540). Engraved F. Bartolozzi 1790; W. Bond 1809. A copy with Bearne's, Torquay, 1994. Probably similar to the portrait painted for the Corporation of Bristol, requested in December 1782, delivered in 1784, and destroyed by fire 1831 (Mannings 2000, no.541).

Posthumous

1786-87 Painting by Joshua Reynolds, three-quarter length seated in chancellor's robes, with his wife, Elizabeth Vowler. Tate Gallery (N 6244; Mannings 2000, no.542). His portrait derived from the 1782 sittings, his wife's portrait added after his death. See also 1782 Downman.

1787-88 Painting by Joshua Reynolds,* three-quarter length seated in chancellor's robes, with Col. Barré and Lord Lansdowne. Private collection (Mannings 2000, no.543). Engraved J. Ward; G.F. Storm 1847. His portrait derived from the 1782 sittings.

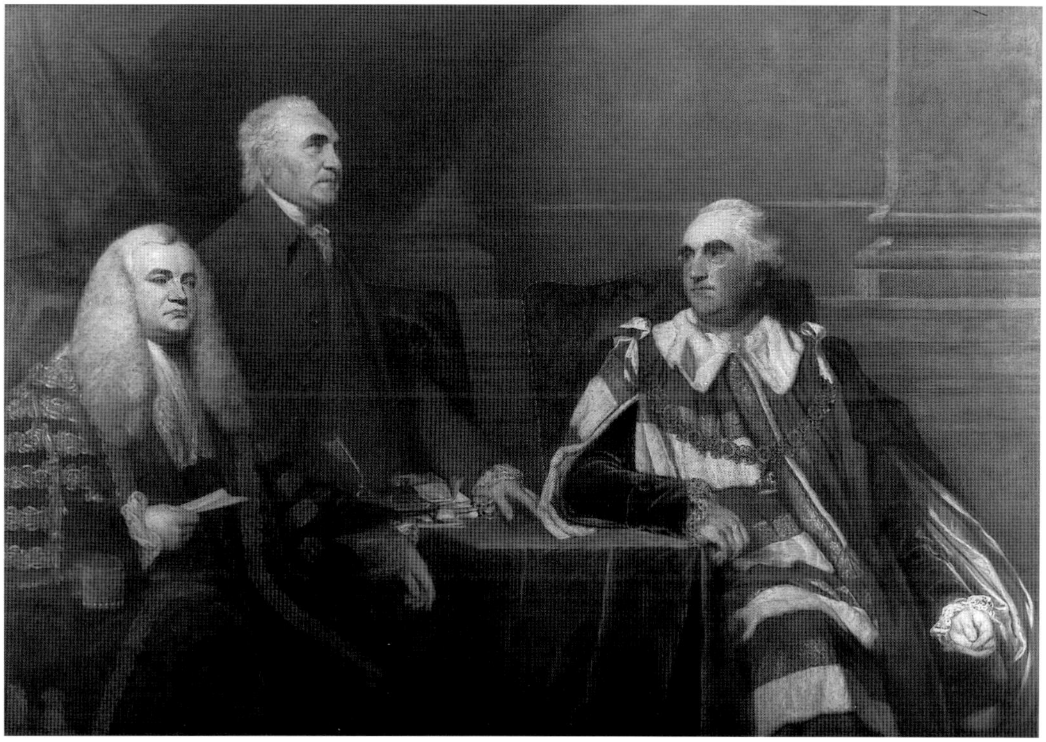

1st Baron ASHBURTON (left) with Isaac BARRÉ and the 1st Marquess of LANSDOWNE (right), by Joshua Reynolds 1787-88 (Private Collection)

1795 Miniature by George Chinnery, exhibited RA 1795(508, the late Lord Ashburton).

DOUBTFUL PORTRAIT

Painting attributed to Reynolds, sold Sotheby's, 23 November 1966, lot 49.

BACH, Johann Christian 1735-82

Composer, 'the English Bach'; b. Leipzig, 11th s. of J.S. Bach; studied in Bologna from 1756; organist at Milan Cathedral 1760-62; came to London 1762 and made music master to the Queen; prior to his marriage in 1773, he shared house with K.F. Abel; d. London.

Abbreviation

Terry 1967: C.S. Terry, *J.C. Bach*, rev. ed., 1967

5557 THOMAS GAINSBOROUGH [1776]

Canvas 75.5 x 62 (29¾ x 24½) lined.

Brown eyes, powdered hair, lace neckcloth, wearing a pink coat with silver trim and a rich blue waistcoat with silver trim; a diamond ring on his little finger.

Collections: Painted for the sitter;[1] Anna Robson (d.1857), widow of Thomas Mudge; her daughter Charlotte Walcott;[2] Walcott sale, Christie's, 4 July 1874, lot 91, bt. in; Christie's, 3 July 1875, lot 70, bt. in; bt. privately by Sir Charles Mills, later 1st Baron Hillingdon; by descent to the 5th and last Baron; purchased from the Trustees of the Hillingdon Estate 1983.

Exhibitions: *Gainsborough*, 45 Park Lane, London, 1936(17) as 'Sebastian Bach'; *Gainsborough and his Musical Friends*, Kenwood, 1977(9); *Century of Keyboard Instruments*, Cambridge, 1983.

Reference: *Gainsborough* 1953, p.5; Waterhouse 1958, no.32; Terry 1967, pp.151, 160; M.I. Wilson, *Apollo*, CV, 1977, pp.109-10.

Gainsborough remained a close friend of Bach, even though the composer once described his bassoon playing 'as the veritable praying of a jack-ass',[3] and he helped decorate the concert rooms in Hanover Square jointly owned by Gallini, Abel and Bach.[4] Gainsborough's portrait has been described as conveying excellently Bach's 'assured, confident, kindly' character.[5]

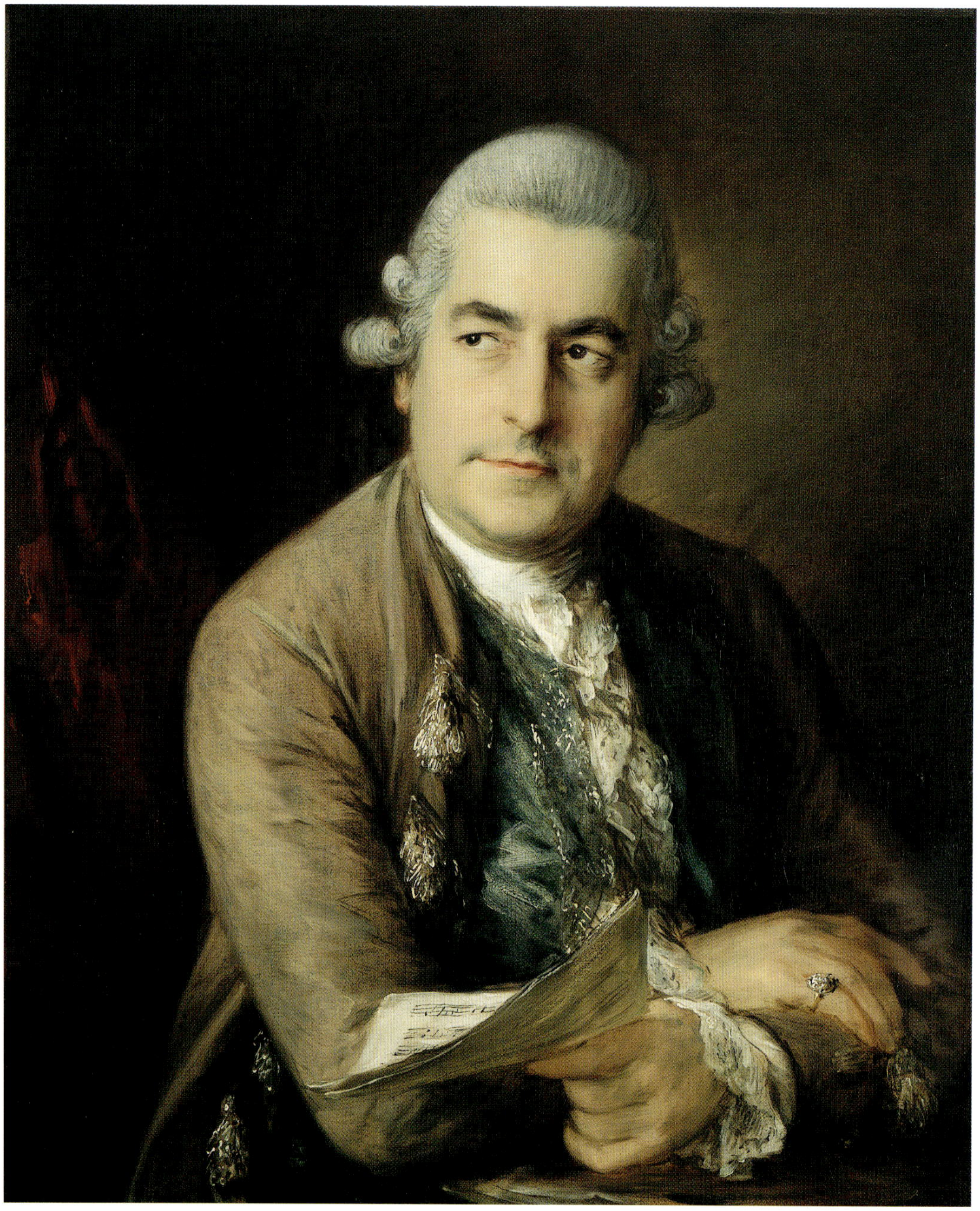

BACH NPG 5557

NPG 5557 is an almost indistinguishable replica of the portrait now in the Civico Museo, Bibliografico Musicale, Bologna,[6] commissioned by Bach's teacher, the composer and historian G.B. Martini. On 22 May 1776 Bach told Martini his portrait was already finished, but he did not send the 'excellent portrait of myself by one of our best painters' until 1778.[7] The delay may have been due in part to the painting of the replica,[8] as had happened with the portrait of Garrick, NPG 5054, a portrait equally notable for intimate characterisation within a half-length format.

1 As stated by Terry 1967, p.151n2; Hayes 1975, p.218.
2 The stretcher bears the seal of the Robson family and is inscribed: *The property of Mrs Mudge / widow of Mudge / & of her daughter Charlotte.*
3 Angelo 1904, I, pp.142-43, and see Terry 1967, pp.92-93.
4 See Whitley 1915, p.114; Terry 1967, p.141.
5 L. Stainton, *Gainsborough and his Musical Friends*, 1977, under no.9.
6 Exhibited *Romantic Art in Britain*, Detroit, Philadelphia, 1968(19); *Gainsborough*, London, 1980(118), and Paris, 1981(47); *Gainsborough*, Ferrara, 1998(19).
7 Terry 1967, pp.151, 160.
8 M.I. Wilson, *Apollo*, CV, 1977, p.109; Stainton (at note 5).

ICONOGRAPHY

c.1754 Painting by Georg Mathieu, half length. Kunstbibliothek, Berlin (illus. Terry 1967, pl.3). The identification is traditional.

1776 Painting by Thomas Gainsborough, see NPG 5557.

Posthumous

1782 Design for a monument by Agostino Carlini, incorporating a medallion portrait, engraved F. Bartolozzi 1782 (illus. Terry, 1967, pl.32) and J.F. Schröter 1789.

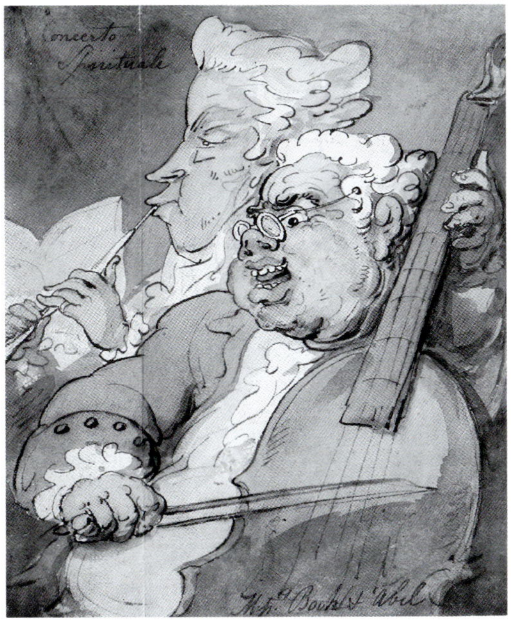

Concerto Spirituale with BACH (right) and ABEL by Thomas Rowlandson c.1790 (Huntington Art Collections, San Marino, California)

c.1790 Caricature by Thomas Rowlandson,* inscribed *Concerto Spirituale* and *Messrs Boch* [sic] *&* *Abel* (Huntington Art Collections, San Marino, Calif., 59.55.1099), appears to show Abel playing the oboe with J.C. Bach on the viola da gamba.

Undated Plaster bust, said to have been made in London, and a miniature by E.H. Abet [E.A. Abel?] belonged to members of the Bach family in, respectively, Bückeburg and Hamburg in 1792 (E. Gerber, *Historisch Biographisches Lexicon*, 1792, II, pp.61, 68).

DOUBTFUL PORTRAITS

Unattributed half-length, Trinity College of Music, London, and version sold Sotheby's, 22 July 1993, lot 571 (illus. Terry 1967, pl.6 as J.C. Bach); by Gainsborough, Cincinnati Art Museum (*Musical Quarterly*, 74, 2, 1990, pp.295-302, but cf. Waterhouse 1958, no.485).

BACON, John, senior **1740-99**

Sculptor; ARA 1770, RA 1778; began work for the Coade stone manufactory in 1769 and was later favoured by George III; a prominent dissident.

'Mr B. was about five feet eight inches in stature, of a fair complexion, and interesting countenance, expressive of his natural vivacity, tenderness, and address' (Richard Cecil, 1801).

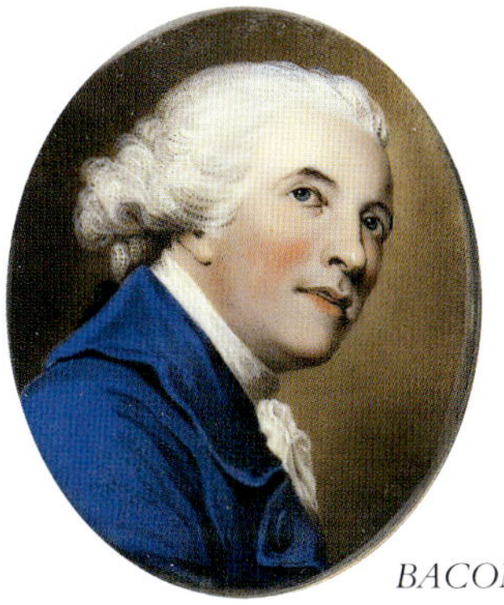

BACON NPG *6289*

6289 WILLIAM BATE after MASON CHAMBERLIN [1785]

Enamel on copper 5.8 x 4.6 (2¼ x 1¾); signed lower right *WB* in yellow. Verso, a lock of fair hair within a frame of plaited (darker) hair.

Pale blue eyes, white powdered hair, wearing a bright blue coat.

Collections: Alan Evans, by whom bequeathed to the National Gallery 1974; lent to the NPG until permanently transferred in 1994.

Reference: Walker 1998, no.50.

Copied from the three-quarter length portrait by Mason Chamberlin of 1785, see below.

ICONOGRAPHY

1785 Painting by Mason Chamberlin, three-quarter length seated, holding a design for the Chatham monument in Westminster Abbey [1779-83]. Private collection. Exhibited RA 1785(50). Engraved anon. 1790 (half-length oval; *European Mag.*). See NPG 6289.

1792 Pastel by John Russell (signed and dated 1792/1800), half length, carving a royal bust. Private collection (illus. Williamson 1894, f.p.54). Russell exhibited portraits of Bacon at the RA in 1792(133) and 1801(153). A version, bearing monogram and date 1792, was with A.J. Fink, Baltimore, in 1951 (illus. *Exhibition of the Pennsylvania Soc. of Miniature Painters*, Philadelphia, 1951, no.225).

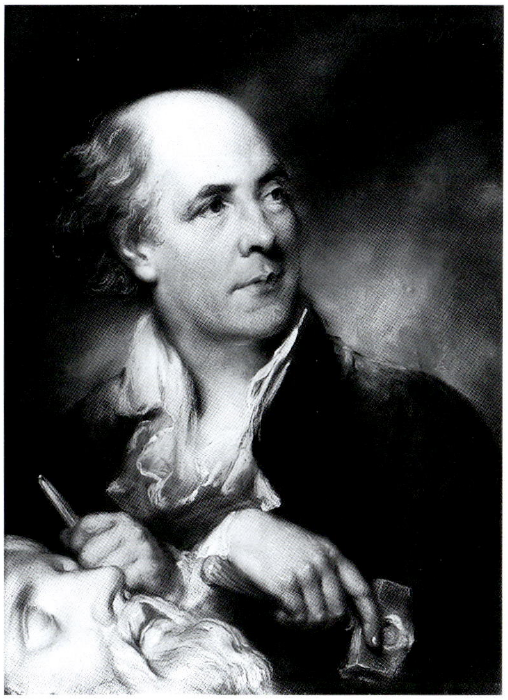

BACON by John Russell 1792 (Victoria and Albert Museum)

1792 Pastel by John Russell,* similarly posed to the preceding, but without wig and with an open shirt. Victoria and Albert Museum (P.5.1957). Engraved J. Collyer 1801; W.C. Edwards 1830 (head only, as *J. Russell R.A. 1792*); A. Roffe 1830. Version sold Sotheby's, 15 July 1999, lot 116. Copied by John Jackson, drawing in the British Museum (1852.2.14.382).

Two pastels of Bacon were lent by his descendants to the Russell exhibition, Graves Galleries, London, 1909(8, 21).

1793 Drawing by George Dance,* profile bust, dated 13 April 1793. Royal Academy. Engraved W. Daniell 1809(*Dance Portraits*). A second drawing exhibited *Sublime and the Beautiful*, Sabin, 1973(1), illus. cat.pl.1.

1795 Painting by Henry Singleton,* *President and Members of the Royal Academy*, see Comparative Groups.

1798 Bust by John Bacon jr., exhibited RA 1798(1053). Drawn by W. Brockedon (British Museum, 1867.11.19.1/4008).

Posthumous

1864 Art Union medal by J.S. Wyon, the verso reproducing Bacon's monument to Samuel Johnson in St Paul's (Brown 1980, no.2797). Exhibited RA 1864(970). Example in NPG reference collection D 2907.

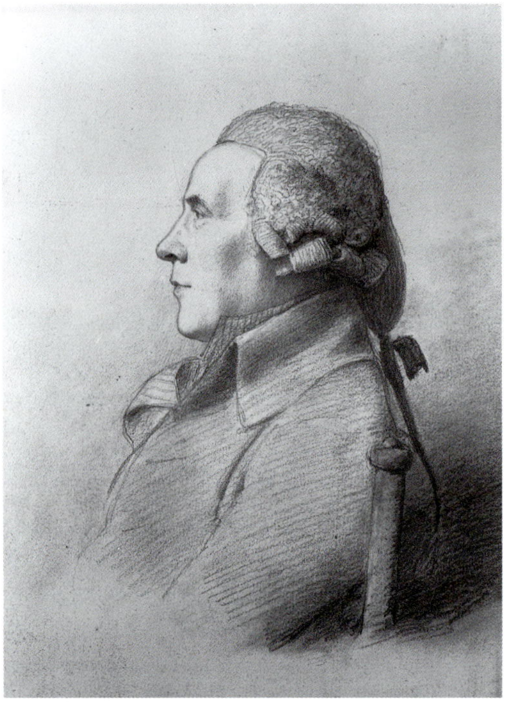

BACON by George Dance 1793 (Royal Academy of Arts, London)

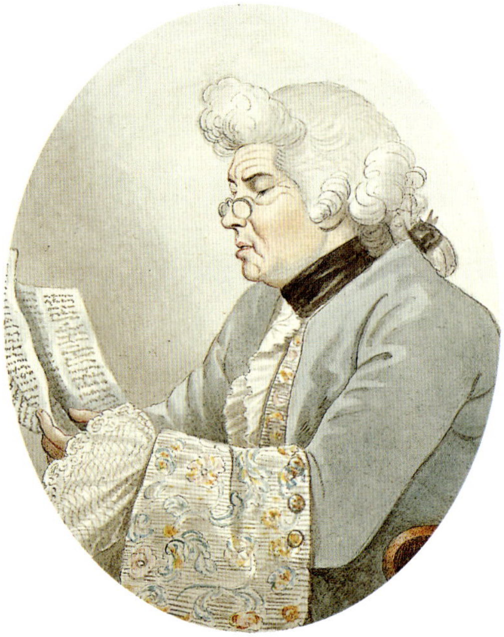

BADDELEY NPG *2541*

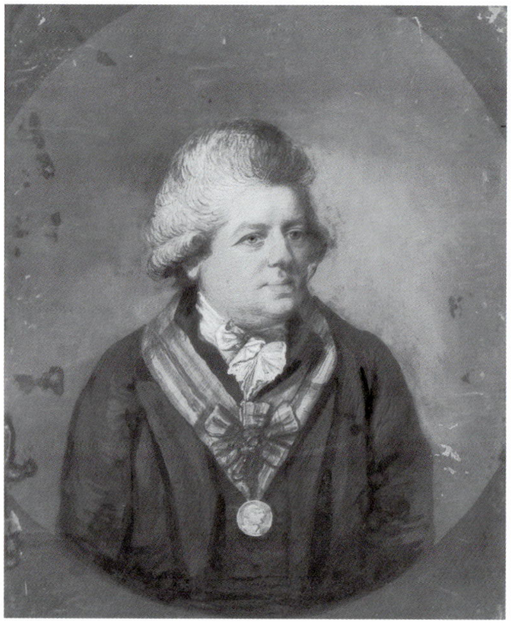

BADDELEY by Henry Spicer c.1790? (Garrick Club)

DOUBTFUL PORTRAIT

The figure of Joseph Wilton in the group by J.F. Rigaud, NPG 987, was once thought to be Bacon.

BADDELEY, Robert 1733-94

Actor; originally a pastry cook, by 1763 he was established at Drury Lane, excelling as a low comedian.

'With crab-apple phiz, and a brow that's disdainful,/ See Baddeley smile with fatigue that is painful;/ From his dissonant voice, and the form of each feature,/ You'd swear him the favorite child of Ill-nature' (Anthony Pasquin, 1786).

2541 SYLVESTER HARDING, *as Canton in The Clandestine Marriage* 1794

Watercolour and ink on paper 15.5 x 12.5 (6⅛ x 4⅞) oval, laid down between two sheets of paper.

Blue-grey velvet coat with black collar and silver floral patterned trim.

Collections: Purchased from A.W. Holliday 1932.

Engraving: S. Harding 1794 (*Mr Baddeley in the Character of Canton in the Clandestine Marriage*).

Baddeley is shown in character as Canton in Colman and Garrick's *Clandestine Marriage*, a role he played first at Drury Lane in 1766 and last on 30 September 1794 (he died on 19 November).

NPG 2541 relates closely to the superior pen drawing in the Garrick Club which bears the same inscription as Harding's print cited above. Ashton attributed the Garrick drawing to Richard Cosway[1] and suggested that, with NPG 2541, it may derive from a lost original, perhaps by Cosway.

1 Ashton 1997, no.19.

ICONOGRAPHY

See also the *Harvard Catalogue*, I, p.45, and Highfill, I, pp.201-02.

1780-85 Miniature by John Smart, bust-length oval. Royal Collection (illus. Walker 1992, no.310).

1781 Painting by Johann Zoffany, full length as Moses in Sheridan's *School for Scandal*. Lady Lever AG, Port Sunlight (LL 3535; illus. *Cat. of Earlier British Paintings*, 1999, p.183). Exhibited RA 1781(246).

c.1782 Painting by George Carter,* *The Immortality of Garrick*, see Comparative Groups.

c.1790? Drawing by Henry Spicer,* bust-length oval, as a member of the School of Garrick, wearing the Shakespeare Ribband and Favour. Garrick Club (Ashton 1997, no.22). Members of the School of Garrick, a club which lasted until the early 19th century, wore small medallions bearing the image of Shakespeare, and a multi-coloured ribbon 'in imitation of the Rainbow' as an emblem of the great variety of Shakespeare's genius (Ashton 1997, p.6).

1792 Painting attributed to Thomas Hardy, half-length wearing the Shakespeare Ribband, see c.1790? above. Garrick Club (Ashton 1997, no.21). Engraved W. Ridley 1793. This portrait is identified by Ashton as that exhibited RA 1792(164).

1794 Drawing attributed to Richard Cosway and etching by Sylvester Harding, see NPG 2541.

Other depictions of Baddeley in character include paintings by Zoffany as Jollop in Foote's *Mayor of Garratt*, 1764 (private collection) and as Canton in *The Clandestine Marriage*, 1772 (Garrick Club; Ashton 1997, no.23), and by De Wilde as Grubbin in Steele's *Tender Husband* (Garrick Club; Ashton 1997, no.20); drawings by Thomas Parkinson as Trinculo in *The Tempest* (British Museum; Burney i, no.105) and by Mather Brown as Peter in *Henry VI part ii* (British Museum; Burney i, no.102; illus. Evans 1982, no.315).

BAKEWELL, Robert 1725-95

Stock-breeder; succeeded in 1760 to his father's farm at Dishley Grange, Leicestershire, where he produced new breeds of sheep, oxen and black horses, and experimented with the feeding and housing of stock.

'In person, Mr B. was tall, broad set, and, in his later years, rather inclined to corpulency. His countenance bespoke intelligence, activity, and a high degree of benevolence' (*GM*, 1795).

5949 JOHN BOULTBEE c.1788-91

Canvas[1] 71 x 91 (27¾ x 35¾) cleaned and lined 1988; *pentimenti* along back of horse and in the cows in the mid-distance.

Blue eyes, wearing a black hat, buff coat and black boots, mounted on a bay hunter, his prize cattle beyond.

Collections: Robert Fowler (d.1791);[2] by descent to his great-great-nephew, George Price, from whom bt. by James Bliss 1891; by descent to Miss P.E.J. Williams; Sotheby's, 15 July 1987, lot 139, bt. Leggatt for the NPG.

One of four similar portraits of Bakewell, the other three lacking the foreground dog. In the signed portrait in the Leicester Museum and Art Gallery (bought in 1967) Bakewell wears a green coat; it is probably the prime version.[3] The other two, at the Brooksby Agricultural College, Melton Mowbray,[4] and with the Royal Agricultural Society, appear to be copies; neither head, for example, has the quality of the Leicester or NPG versions, one of which must have provided the original from which F. Engleheart engraved the half-length portrait of Bakewell in 1842.[5]

The attribution to Boultbee is traditional. A Leicestershire painter, he was living at Loughborough at least in 1787-88; in 1788 he exhibited 'a favourite horse of Mr Bakewell' at the RA, and in 1791 another Bakewell horse by Boultbee was engraved by F. Jukes.[6]

1 Bearing tax stamp *1377 165 11*.
2 The sitter's friend and a fellow stock-breeder. The provenance cited is that given by Sotheby's in 1987.
3 Illus. E. Moncrieff, *Farm Animal Portraits*, 1996, p.14; *CL*, CLVII, 1975, p.1710.
4 Illus. *Jnl. of the Royal Agricultural Soc. of England*, 136, 1975, f.p.57.
5 Illus. A.S. Turberville, *English Men and Manners of the 18th century*, 1929, p.145 (and *CL*, CLVII, 1975, p.1709, in reverse).
6 See W.S. Sparrow, *Connoisseur*, XCI, 1933, p.156.

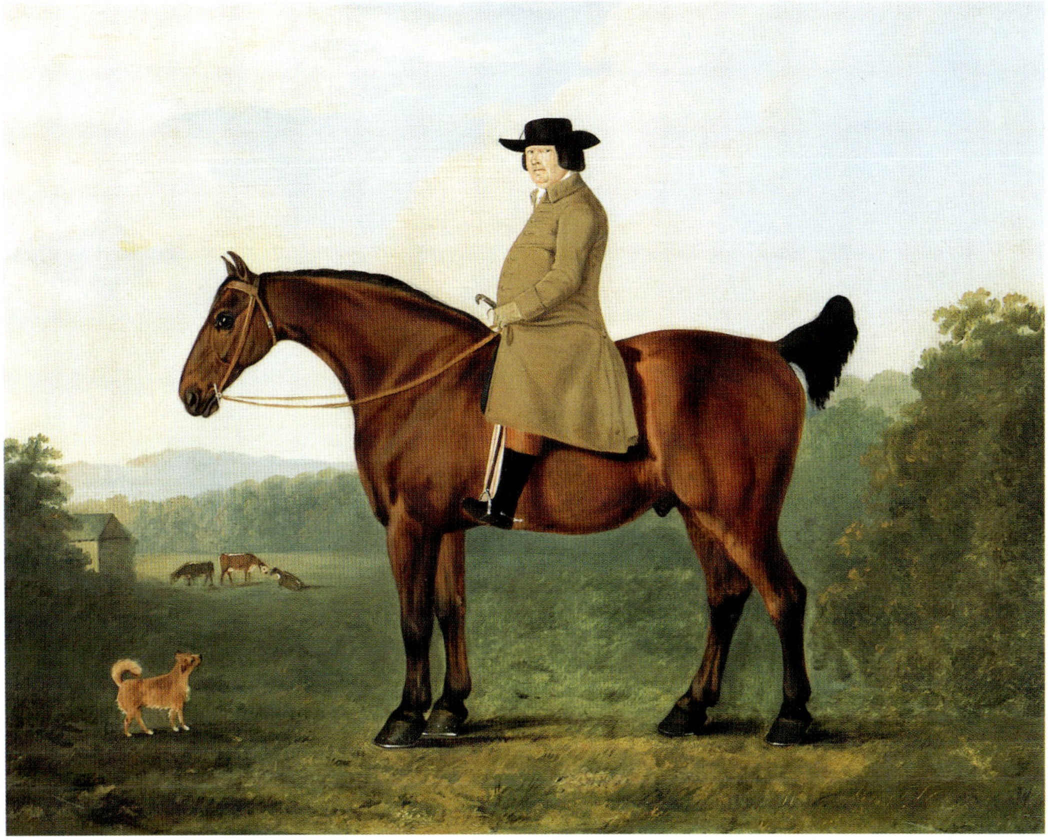

BAKEWELL NPG *5949*

BANKS, Sir Joseph, 1st Bt 1743-1820

Botanist and traveller, of Revesby Abbey, Lincs.; FRS 1766; DCL 1771; President of the Royal Society 1778-1820; Bt 1781; KB 1795; GCB 1815.

'He is awkward in his person, but extremely well bred, in the best mode of English breeding, where good breeding may be fairly pronounced the highest of all countries. In short he is one of the many instances to prove that personal graces are far from essential to politeness' (Lord Glenbervie, 1816).

'He is tall, largely made, with a manly countenance, expressive of dignity and intelligence' (*European Mag.*, 1802).

Abbreviation
Letters 2000: *Letters of Sir Joseph Banks, a selection*, ed. N. Chambers, , 2 vols., 2000

5868 JOSHUA REYNOLDS 1771-73

Canvas 127 x 101.5 (50 x 40); lined; the surface is slightly abraded and there are numerous retouchings.

Grey-blue eyes, dark hair, wearing a fur-lined deep red coat, white neckcloth and shirt, gold waistcoat and grey breeches, sitting in a green upholstered chair; on the table covered by a green cloth, the foremost paper inscribed: *Cras Ingens Iterabimus aequor* ['tomorrow we will sail the high seas again'; Horace, *Odes*, I, vii, 32].

Collections: By descent from Dorothea, Lady Banks, through her nephew, Sir Edward Knatchbull, 8th Bt, to Sir Wyndham Knatchbull, 12th Bt (d.1917); his heir, the 4th Baron Brabourne, from whom bt. 1918 by the 1st Viscount Cowdray; his son, Clive Pearson, Parham Park;[1] by descent to Clive Gibson, from whom purchased by private treaty sale through Agnew 1986, with the aid of the National Heritage Memorial Fund, the National Art Collections Fund and The Pilgrim Trust.

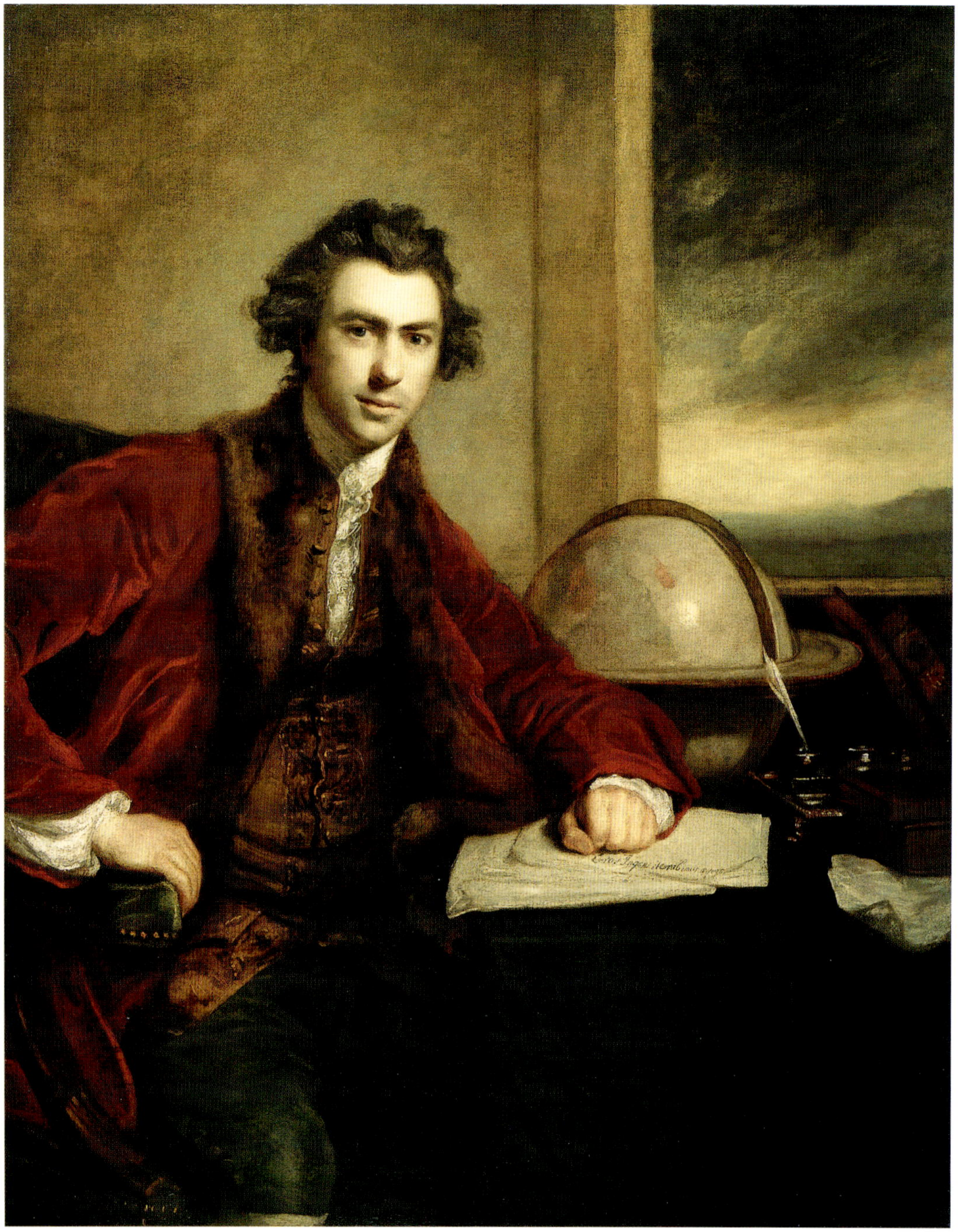

BANKS NPG *5868*

When this portrait was painted Banks was enjoying considerable acclaim for his part in Cook's Pacific voyage in the *Endeavour* in 1768–71. Boswell had met 'the famous Mr Banks' in March 1772, 'a genteel young man, very black, and of an agreeable countenance, easy and communicative, without any affectation',[2] and Reynolds was already familiar with his remarkable botanical and ethnographical collections. In 1772 Banks was invited to accompany Cook's second Pacific voyage (perhaps the first reason for the inclusion of the Horace quotation, *cras ingens iterabimus aequor*),[3] but in May he withdrew, following his impractical demands for space on board.[4]

Banks's name appears in Reynolds's sitter book in November and December 1771, and in January, February and March 1772; between July and December 1772 he was travelling in the Hebrides, Iceland and the Orkneys, but he met Reynolds immediately on his return and the last sitting took place in March 1773. A payment of 70gns. was made to Reynolds by a Mr Hodgkinson[5] on 15 January 1774. The portrait has long been admired, for its intellectualism, power and energy,[6] but above all for its characterisation: 'no painter could have so expressed the hungry heart of a man smitten with the passion of exploring and inquiring, unless he had felt a deep and intelligent sympathy with his sitter'.[7]

A small bust-length oval version, in which the fur-collared coat is blue, was painted by Daniel Chodowiecki c.1780 (with a pendant of Dr Solander; both in the Gemäldegalerie, Berlin; 491A & B).

1 NPG 5868 was no.136 in the Parham Park picture list of c.1957; it hung in the green room (*Parham Park Guide*, 1974, p.21).
2 *Boswell for the Defence*, 1960, p.56.
3 In a letter to his sister Sarah Sophia, Banks mistakenly wrote that 'the motto of the print is taken from a part of Virgil's Eneid, where Eneas encouraging his people says ...' (*Letters* 2000, no.9, where dated February 1773 – but he must have been referring to Dickinson's plate, which was published on 30 January 1774).
4 His explanatory letter to Lord Sandwich, first lord of the Admiralty, dated 30 May 1772, is printed in *Letters* 2000, no.7.
5 Cormack 1970, p.145; Possibly his uncle, Robert Banks-Hodgkinson (1722–92).
6 O. Millar, *Burl. Mag.*, XCI, 1949, p.83. See also D. Shawe-Taylor, *The Georgians*, 1990, p.94.
7 Leslie & Taylor 1865, I, p.429.

Engravings: W. Dickinson 1774; S.W. Reynolds 1820.

Exhibitions: RA 1773(239); BI 1813(125) lent Banks; *Reynolds*, Arts Council, 1949(11); *Bicentenary Exhibition*, RA, 1968–69(110); *British Painting*, Sydney, Melbourne, 1977–78(38); *The Arrogant Connoisseur*, Manchester, 1982(193a); *First Impressions*, British Museum, 1988; *Treasures for the Nation*, British Museum, 1988; *Terra Australis*, Sydney, 1988(96); *Portrait in British Art*, NPG, 1991(37).

Reference: Graves & Cronin, I, p.47; Waterhouse 1941, p.63; Simon 1997, pp. 65, 161; Mannings 2000, no.106.

853 THOMAS LAWRENCE c.1795

Pencil on paper 24.7 x 20 (9¾ x 7⅞) laid down on paper.

Wearing the ribbon of the Bath.

Collections: Probably Lysons sale, Bruton, Knowles & Co, Gloucester, 21 April 1887, lot 321 ('pencil sketch'), bt. Colnaghi,[1] from whom purchased 1891.

Exhibitions: *Cook's Voyage*, Plymouth, 1968; *Captain Cook*, Sydney, 1970; *Matthew Flinders*, Museum of Lincolnshire Life, 1974; *The Garden*, Victoria and Albert Museum, 1979; *Haydn*, Eisensstadt, 1982(624); *Lawrence*, New Haven, Fort Worth, Richmond, 1993(42).

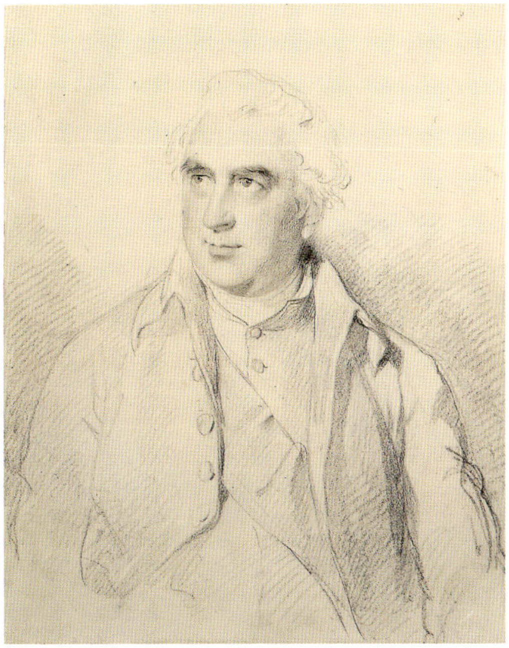

BANKS NPG 853

Reference: *Lawrence* 1964, p.213 (as probably c.1806); Garlick 1989, p.143.

Previously dated c.1806, to agree with the portrait Lawrence painted for the Royal Society, see below, but NPG 853 shows a younger man and probably shows Banks soon after he was made KB in 1795.

1 Martin Colnaghi told Scharf: 'I purchased the Drawing of Sir Joseph Banks at a Sale in Cheltenham & with it a very beautiful Drawing by Lawrence of Mrs Siddons' (11 December 1890; NPG archive).

885 THOMAS PHILLIPS 1810

Canvas 141 x 112 (55½ x 44) lined; discoloured varnish; repaired tear across left shoulder; numerous small retouchings, a broad craquelure in lower area.

Grey eyes, white hair, grey suit and stockings, with ribbon and star of the Bath, white neckcloth; green upholstered chair; deep red drape to right; to the left a paper inscribed: *On … Diseases / of Whea … / by / Sr Josh Bank*..[see below].

Collections: Commissioned by Thomas Murdoch (1758-1846); his son, Sir Thomas Murdoch KCMG;[1] his son, Charles Stewart Murdoch, from whom purchased 1892.

Exhibitions: *Science and Music in 18th century Bath*, Bath, 1977(192); *Chantrey*, NPG, Sheffield, 1981; *Apples to Atoms* 1986-87.

Reference: *Phillips Sitter Book*, July 1810, no.304 (*Jos. Banks, 3rd Time, for Mr Murdoch. l.h.l.* [i.e. long half length]

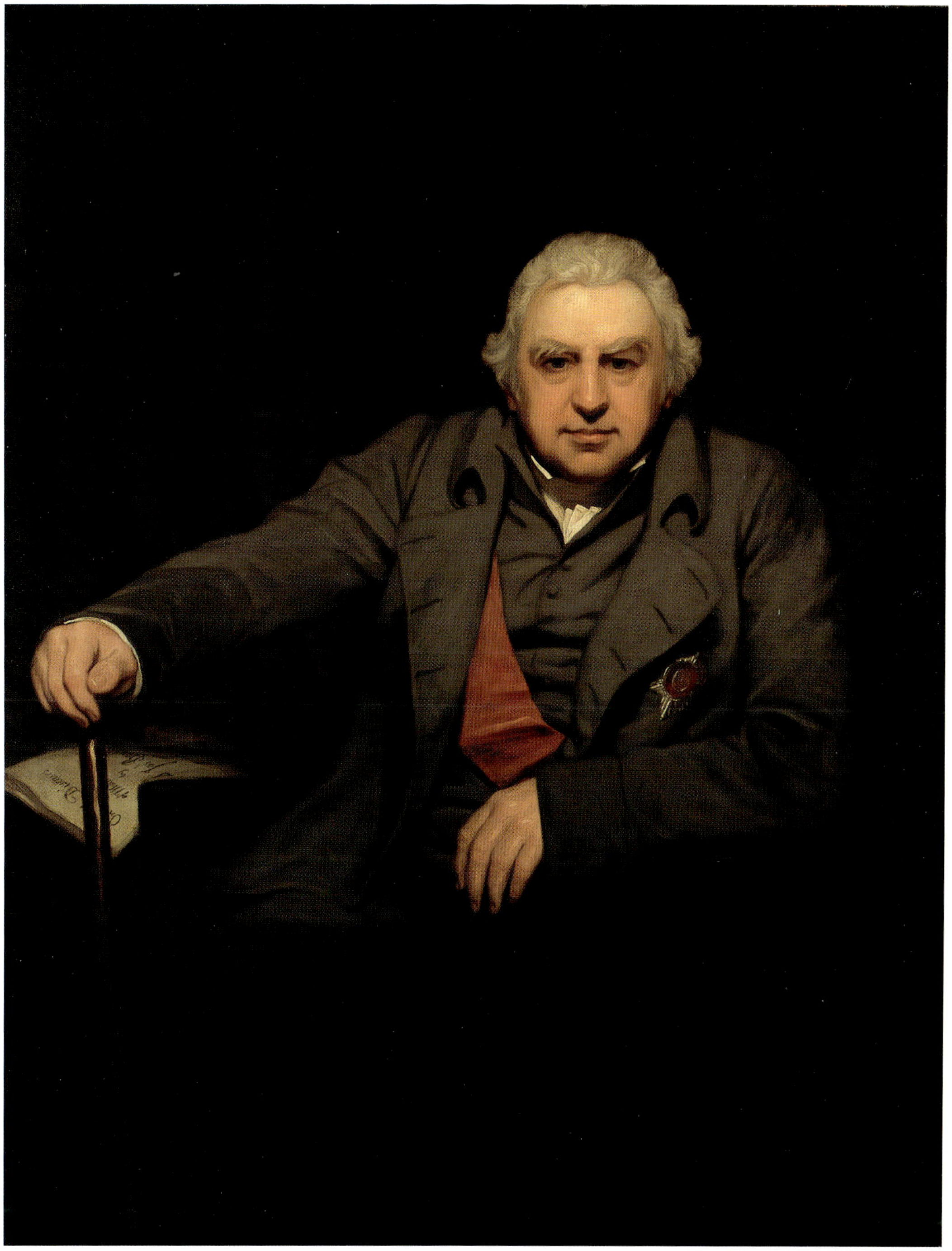

BANKS NPG 885

The manuscript Banks holds must refer to his *Short Account of the Disease in Corn, called by the Farmers the Blight, the Mildew, and the Rust*, completed in January 1805.[2]

Between 1808 and 1814 Phillips painted three types of portraits of Banks (see below), of which NPG 885 is an example of the second. Head and pose derived from the first type of 1808, showing Banks as President of the Royal Society. Another version of this second type, painted in March 1810 for Sir Everard Home, is with the Linnean Society.[3] Phillips subsequently painted Thomas Murdoch who commissioned NPG 885.[4]

1 Who had previously offered it to the NPG in December 1867 (sketched by Scharf, May 1868, TSB 13/65).

2 A later edition of March 1806 additionally treated rust on barberry and its ability to carry infection to wheat, see H.B. Carter, *Sir*

Joseph Banks, 1988, pp.404-05.
3 *Phillips Sitter Book*, 20 March 1810, no.290; another entry for 30 May 1810 reads: *Sir Jo. Banks 2nd time for Mr E.H. no.301*, partially erased.
4 Exhibited RA 1817(73); sold Christie's, 24 November 1972, lot 136.

1075 see Groups, *Men of Science living in 1807-08* by JOHN GILBERT, FREDERICK SKILL and WILLIAM & ELIZABETH WALKER 1858-62

ICONOGRAPHY

An inclusive survey, including a Portraiture-Bibliography, appears in H.B. Carter, *Sir Joseph Banks, A guide to biographical and bibliographical sources*, 1987, pp.297-316; see also R. Joppien, 'Banks and the world of art in Great Britain', in R.E.R. Banks *et al.* eds., *Sir Joseph Banks: a global perspective*, 1994, pp.87-103.

1771-73 Painting by Joshua Reynolds, see NPG 5868.

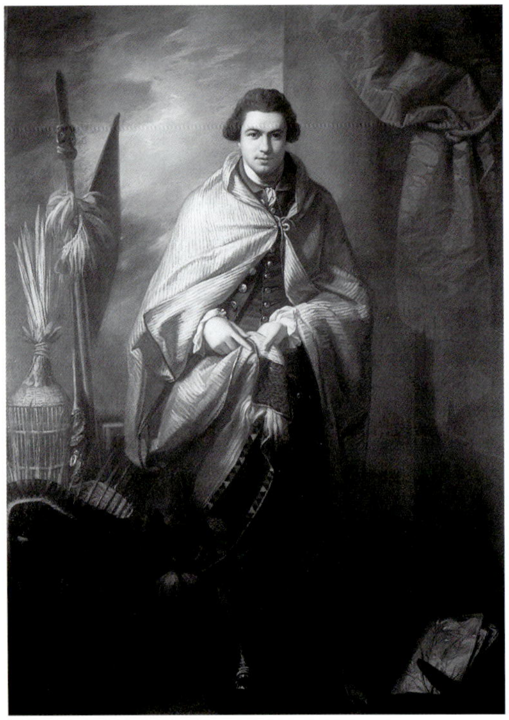

BANKS by Benjamin West c.1771-73 (Usher Gallery, Lincoln)

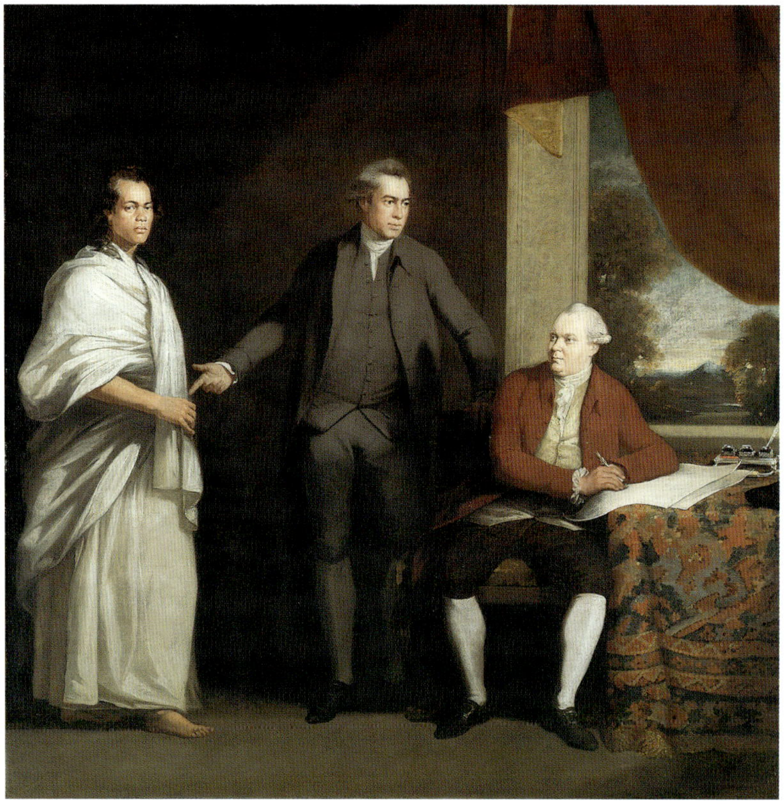

BANKS (centre) with Omai and Dr Solander by William Parry 1776 (acquired jointly by the National Portrait Gallery, the National Museums and Galleries of Wales and the Captain Cook Memorial Museum, Whitby, in August 2003)

c.1771-73 Painting by Benjamin West,* whole length, wearing a cloak of New Zealand flax (a drawing of flax by Parkinson at his feet) with a Tahitian head-dress. Usher Gallery, Lincoln (UG 89/9; Erffa & Staley 1986, no.586). Exhibited RA 1773(310, 'a whole length of a Gentleman with a New Zealand mantle around him'. Engraved J.R. Smith 1773 and 1788.

1775 Wedgwood medallion, modelled by John Flaxman (illus. Reilly 1973, p.55).

c.1775 Drawing by Thomas Hearne, bust-length oval. British Museum (1867.4.13.536). Traditionally, but not securely, identified as Banks. Hearne was in the Leeward Islands 1771-75.

1776 Painting by William Parry,* Banks standing between Omai and Dr Daniel Solander. Private collection. Banks's head was etched in 1800 by J. Owen (*Public Characters of 1800-01*). Omai, brought in 1775 from Tahiti whither he returned in 1776; Solander (1756-82), botanist, Banks's professional companion, 'the mildest, gentlest, most obliging of men'. A sepia copy by Frederick Peake sold Christie's, 2 April 1965, lot 35.

1777-78 Painting by Joshua Reynolds,* *The Society of Dilettanti*, see Comparative Groups.

1779 Wedgwood medallion, modelled by John Flaxman (illus. Reilly 1973, p.56). Apparently the medallion of Banks described by Josiah Wedgwood as 'A good head, & a very strong likeness, but the original does not seem to have sat in an over pleasant mood' (2 September 1779; Reilly 1973, p.56). A medallion by James Tassie listed by Gray 1894, no.27; he had never seen an example and supposed it may have been the same as the Wedgwood example (see also c.1788 below).

1786 Drawing by Paul Sandby, profile head with hat, one of the series of heads drawn at print sales. Royal Collection (Oppé 1947, no.417/22, fig.23). Engraved anon.,* *Sketches taken at Print Sales*, see Comparative Groups.

1788 Pastel by John Russell,* half length holding drawing inscribed *Carte de la Lune par J. Russell.* Lord Brabourne. Exhibited RA 1788(420). Engraved J. Collyer 1789; W. Ridley 1802 (reduced, *European Mag.*); W. Wright. Russell also drew Lady Banks in 1788 (private coll.), engraved J. Collyer 1790.

c.1788 Wedgwood medallion, the model attributed to John Flaxman (illus. Reilly 1973, p.56).

c.1793 Drawing attributed to Nathaniel Dance. AG of New South Wales, Sydney (acquired 1926 from Mrs John Lane as by Henry Edridge). A copy at 2 Carlton House Terrace in 1905 was listed as 'After H. Edridge, 1793' (Hawkesbury 1906, no.211).

c.1795 Drawing by Thomas Lawrence, see NPG 853.

before 1796? Pastel by James Sharples, and a miniature drawing from it by Ellen Sharples (illus. Knox 1930, p.105). Bristol CMAG (*Cat. of the Sharples Coll.*, Bristol, 1910, nos.19 and 68). The original probably dates from before 1796 when Sharples first went to

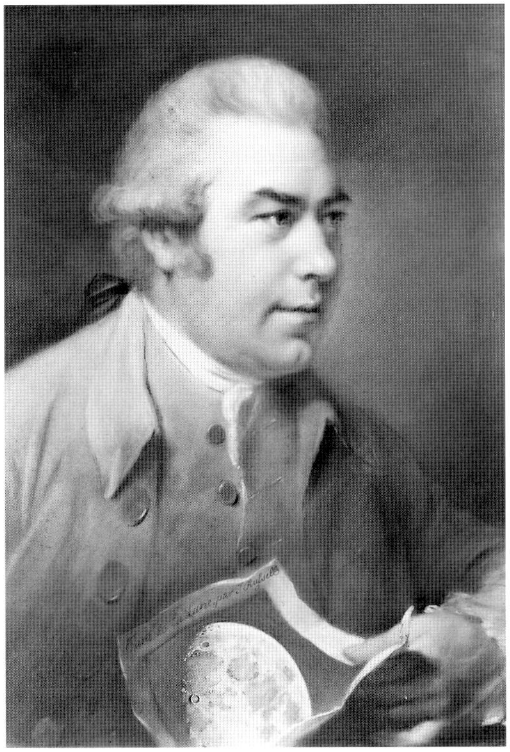

BANKS *by John Russell 1788 (Lord Brabourne)*

America, but he was again in England 1802–09. Mrs Sharples was finishing miniature copies of Banks in November/December 1803, which she 'improved' in March/April 1805 (Knox 1930, pp.117–18); she exhibited a miniature of Banks RA 1807(843).

1803 Drawing by George Dance,* profile bust, dated 27 June 1803. National Library of Australia, Canberra (NK 2093). Engraved W. Daniell 1811 (*Dance Portraits*); a tracing by Daniell in the Yale Center for British Art (B1975.4.1129); a pencil copy of the engraving, initialled *R.W.P.*, in the Natural History Museum, London (illus. Thackray 1995, no.7).

1803 Painting by Rembrandt Peale, bust length in grey coat wearing the star of the Bath. Academy of Natural Sciences of Philadelphia (*Peale* 1992, pl.5).

1804 Bust by George Garrard, wearing a fur cape over classical tunic with ribbon of the Bath. Burghley House. Exhibited RA 1804(952).

1806 Painting by Thomas Lawrence, three-quarter length as President of the Royal Society, wearing the ribbon and star of the Bath. British Museum, bequeathed by the Rev Daniel Lysons 1834 (Garlick 1989, no.59). Exhibited RA 1806(72). Engraved A. Cardon 1811; T. Woolnoth 1823; H. Robinson 1831, and T. Phillibrown.

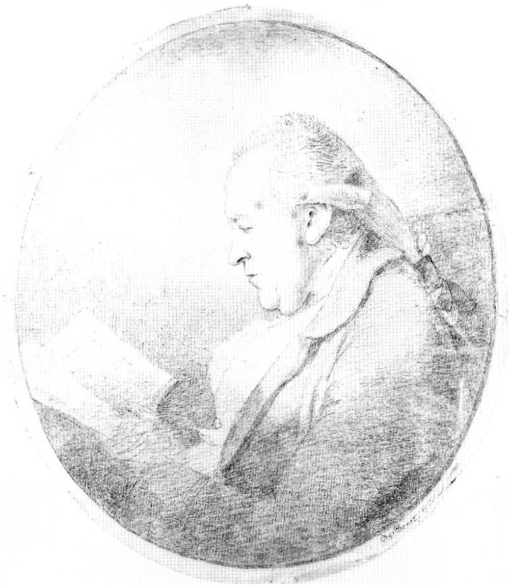

BANKS *by George Dance 1803 (National Library of Australia, Canberra, NK 2093)*

1806 Bronze bust by Anne Seymour Damer, wearing the star of the Bath. British Museum (MLA1814.3.12.1; Dawson 2000, no.2), presented by the artist 1814; exhibited RA 1813(912). Probably from the terracotta exhibited RA 1806(838). Plaster casts in the Natural History Museum and the British Library.

1807 Painting by Solomon Williams, exh. RA 1807(544).

1808 Painting by Thomas Phillips, half length as President of the Royal Society, holding a copy of Sir Humphrey Davy's Bakerian lecture of 1808 in his left hand. State Library, Sydney, New South Wales (Dixson Collection), commissioned by the Spanish astronomer Jose Mendoza y Rios. Exhibited RA 1809(134, as 'in the Chair as President of the Royal Society'). Engraved N. Schiavonetti 1812 and, reduced, W. Holl 1829 and C.E. Wagstaff 1833.

In 1808 Phillips asked Banks whether he would subscribe to a print; Banks replied that there were already three prints of him in the Print Shops, 'one from a Picture of Sir Joshua, an admirable mezzotinto; another from the Pencil of the President, & a third, a most decided Likeness, from a Crayon picture of Russell'; he added 'much as I admire the Burin of Schiavanetti [sic], *I should, was I to direct, Employ Sharp'* (*Letters* 2000, pp.287–88).

A version dated 1815, with a paper lying in the foreground inscribed: *On an improved reflecting circle* (a paper by Joseph de Mendoza read at the Royal Society in 1801), was commissioned by the Royal Society (illus. *Letters* 2000, p.289), cf. Groups NPG 1075. A replica sold Sotheby's, 6 April 1993, lot 51, is in the National Library of Australia, Canberra; a late copy, from the Brabourne collection, is in the County Hall, Maidstone; an enamel copy by Henry Bone dated 1815, exhibited RA 1816(708), sold Christie's, 3 March 1971, lot 16; his preparatory drawing NPG albums (*Bone* 1999, no.28).

1810 Painting by Thomas Phillips, see NPG 885.

1812 Impression from a gem by William Brown, exhibited RA 1812(620).

1814 Painting by Thomas Phillips, three-quarter length, short hair, wearing Windsor uniform (dark blue coat with red facings and gold lace), with the star and ribbon of the Bath, holding a drainage map for the south Lincolnshire fens. Guildhall, Boston, Lincs., commissioned by the Corporation of Boston in 1813. Exhibited RA 1814(52). Reduced version sold Sotheby's, 24 November 1999, lot 69.

1814 Marble bust by Peter Turnerelli, undraped. Royal College of Surgeons, London (illus. LeFanu 1960, pl.4). Turnerelli carved two marble busts in 1814; as the Curators of the College of Surgeons were dissatisfied with that intended for them, Turnerelli agreed to work further on both and allow them to choose (LeFanu 1960, p.6); the second bust is presumably that now in the National Maritime Museum.

1814 Medal by Thomas Wyon sr., exhibited RA 1814(392).

1816 Drawing by Thomas Phillips, profile with tie-wig. From a sketchbook in a private collection. Etched by Mrs Dawson Turner.

1816 Impression from a medal die by William Wyon, exhibited RA 1816(886). Medal by Thomas Wyon jr. and William Wyon 1816 (Brown 911).

1816 Cameo by Benedetto Pistrucci (see H.B. Carter, *Sir Joseph Banks*, 1988, p.516). Presumably the bust to left with the date 1819 engraved after Pistrucci by Mrs Dawson Turner.

1818 Marble bust by Francis Chantrey, undraped. NG of Victoria, Melbourne (*Chantrey* 1994, no.40b). Probably that commissioned by G. Watson Taylor in 1818 (and sold as by Thomas Banks, Watson Taylor sale, 15th day, 25 July 1832, lot 165). Marble exhibited RA 1818(1105). Replicas with the Royal Society,* with slight drapery, presented by the artist in 1819; the Linnean Society, presented by

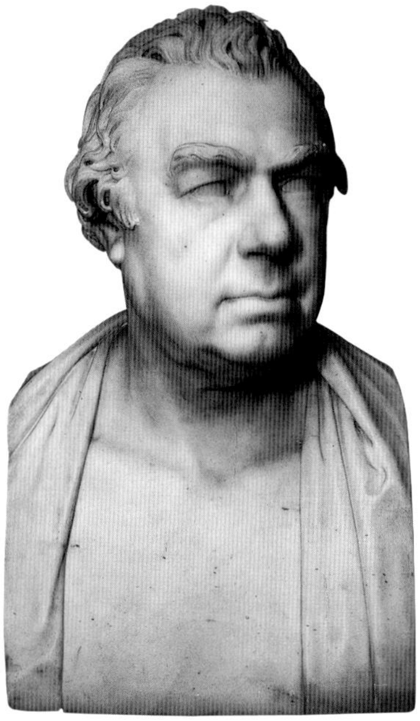

BANKS by Francis Chantrey 1818 (The Royal Society)

subscribers 1822, and at Petworth, completed 1839 (see also *Chantrey* 1994, nos.40b, 131b, 137b, 284b).

Plaster exhibited RA 1816(953); plaster model in the Ashmolean Museum, Oxford (Penny 1992, III, no.680) and a plaster dated 1818 is in a private collection.

See also Unidentified Portraits NPG 316A/172.

c.1819 Drawing by W.M. Craig, half-length seated. Engraved H. Robinson, a crude portrayal.

1820 Medal by William Wyon, 'the Banksian Medal' for the Royal Horticultural Society (Brown 1980, no.1041).

Posthumous

c.1820 Engraving by L. Rados after A.L.F. Sergent-Marceau (using the Thomas Phillips frontal head).

1821 Painting by Thomas Phillips, three-quarter length seated, with botanical drawings spread on a table. Royal Horticultural Society, by whom commissioned 1820. Engraved S.W. Reynolds and S. Cousins 1822. Phillips copied 'with some variations in drapery etc from [his portrait] belonging to the Royal Society [see 1808 above], instead of that in the possession of Sir Everard Home [see NPG 885]' (Royal Horticultural Society minutes, 16 August 1820, as quoted by C. Miller, *Thomas Phillips*, MA report, 1977, p.xiv).

1822 Impression from a medal die by William Wyon, from the bust by Chantrey, exhibited RA 1822(921).

1821-27 Marble statue by Francis Chantrey, seated, a paper held in his lap. Natural History Museum (*Chantrey* 1994, no.141a; figs.95-97; Dawson 2000, no.1), commissioned by the Linnean Society 1821 and first placed in the British Museum. Exhibited RA 1827(1123). Engraved S. Cousins before 1833. The pose of the upper torso resembles the drawing of c.1793 attributed to Dance. Plaster model, reduced to head and shoulders, in the Ashmolean Museum, Oxford (Penny 1992, III, no.623).

DOUBTFUL PORTRAITS

Drawing by Francis Chantrey, see Unidentified Portraits NPG 316A (172). Paintings by Francis Cotes (Johnson 1976, no.129); attributed to Reynolds (Christie's, 3 May 1884, lot 202); by Gainsborough (Waterhouse 1958, no.39); by West (Erffa & Staley 1986, no.647); unattributed paintings: whole-length youth (Parham Park, ex Revesby Abbey; illus. *CL*, CIX, 1951, p.1887; J. Gascoigne, *Banks and the Enlightenment*, 1994, p.84); half-length youth (Sotheby's, 21 March 2001, lot 44); half-length middle-aged man (Newby Hall); miniatures by Andrew Dunn (illus. D. Foskett, *British Portrait Miniatures*, 1963, p.149) and Nathaniel Hone 1768, exhibited *British Portrait Miniatures* 1965(178) lent Lord Beauchamp.

Engravings wrongly called Banks include those by S.W. Reynolds 1834 after Reynolds (cf. Mannings 2000, no.230), and by Mackenzie 1801, from a portrait belonging to Maxwell Garthshore.

BARBAULD, Mrs Anna Letitia, *née* Aikin 1743-1825

Miscellaneous writer; her first poems published in 1773; m. 1774 the Rev Rochemont Barbauld (who d. insane 1808) and settled in Palgrave, Suffolk, where they maintained a school until 1785 when they moved to London; her later work was centred on literary criticism.

'I remember Mrs Chapone's saying to me ... '[Mrs Barbauld] is a very good young woman, as well as replete with talents; but why must one always smile so? It makes my poor jaws ache to look at her' (Fanny Burney, 1798).

'She had a brilliant complexion, light hair, blue eyes, a small, elegant figure, & her manners were very agreeable' (Henry Crabb Robinson, 1805).

4905 see Groups, *Portraits in the characters of the Muses* by RICHARD SAMUEL 1778

ICONOGRAPHY

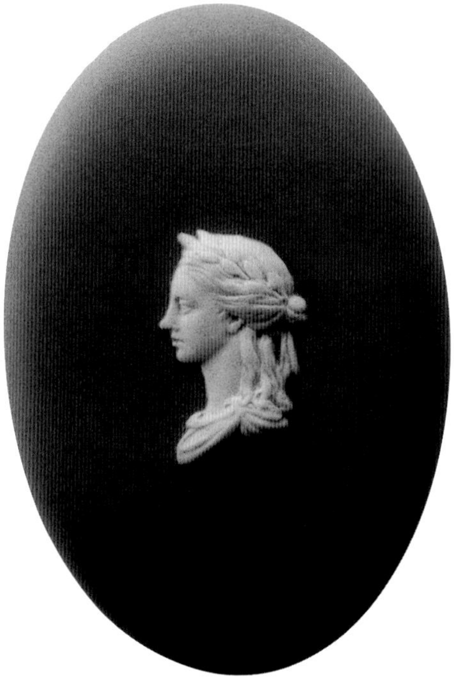

BARBAULD Wedgwood 1775 (Wedgwood Museum, Barlaston)

1774 Wax by Joachim Smith, bust-length profile with leaves in her hair, sent to Wedgwood in January 1775, two blue-ground medallions* being completed by July (Reilly 1973, p.57). Engraved T. Holloway 1776 (facing an oval of Mrs Montagu with an elaborate surround), and 1785 (*European*

Mag.). On 3 July 1775 Wedgwood wrote that the medallions of Mrs Montagu and Mrs Barbauld were not modelled as a pair 'neither in size nor character' (see Montagu).

1778 Painting by Richard Samuel, *Portraits in the characters of the Muses*, see Groups NPG 4905.

1786 Version of the Smith wax of 1774, bust-length profile wearing bonnet, engraved G. Noble (*New Lady's Mag.*).

1798 Engraving by J. Chapman, half-length oval wearing a bonnet (illus. *Romantic Women Writers*, Grasmere, 1994-95, no.7).

1825 Anon. silhouette, bust length (illus. B. Rodgers, *Georgian Chronicle*, 1958, front.).

Undated Unattributed drawing, engraved H. Meyer, bust-length, elderly, wearing a bonnet.

DOUBTFUL PORTRAIT

Unattributed half-length oval, Danton sale, Skutch, Baltimore, 18 February 1930, lot 18.

BARETTI, Giuseppe 1719-89

Writer and linguist; b. Turin, he came to London 1751; friend of Johnson and Reynolds, whose *Discourses* he translated into Italian; published a *Dictionary of the English and Italian Languages* in 1760; secretary for Foreign Correspondence at the RA from 1769.

'The person of Baretti was athletic, his countenance by no means attractive, his manners apparently rough, but not unsocial, his eye when he was inclined to please or be pleased, when he was conversing with young people, and especially young women, chearful and engaging ...' (*European Mag.*, 1789).

6248 after JOSHUA REYNOLDS [1773]

Canvas 75 x 63 (29½ x 24¾) lined;[1] the surface is much rubbed.

Wearing a grey coat, lightly powdered dark hair, sitting in a red-upholstered chair; a red-stone ring on the little finger of his left hand; a maroon curtain behind him.

Collections: Possibly bt. from Thomas Weaver by the 2nd Baron Kenyon c.1841;[2] by descent to the 5th Baron Kenyon,[3] by whom bequeathed 1993.

Exhibition: *Art Treasures*, Wrexham, 1876(307).

Reference: Mannings 2000, no.107g.

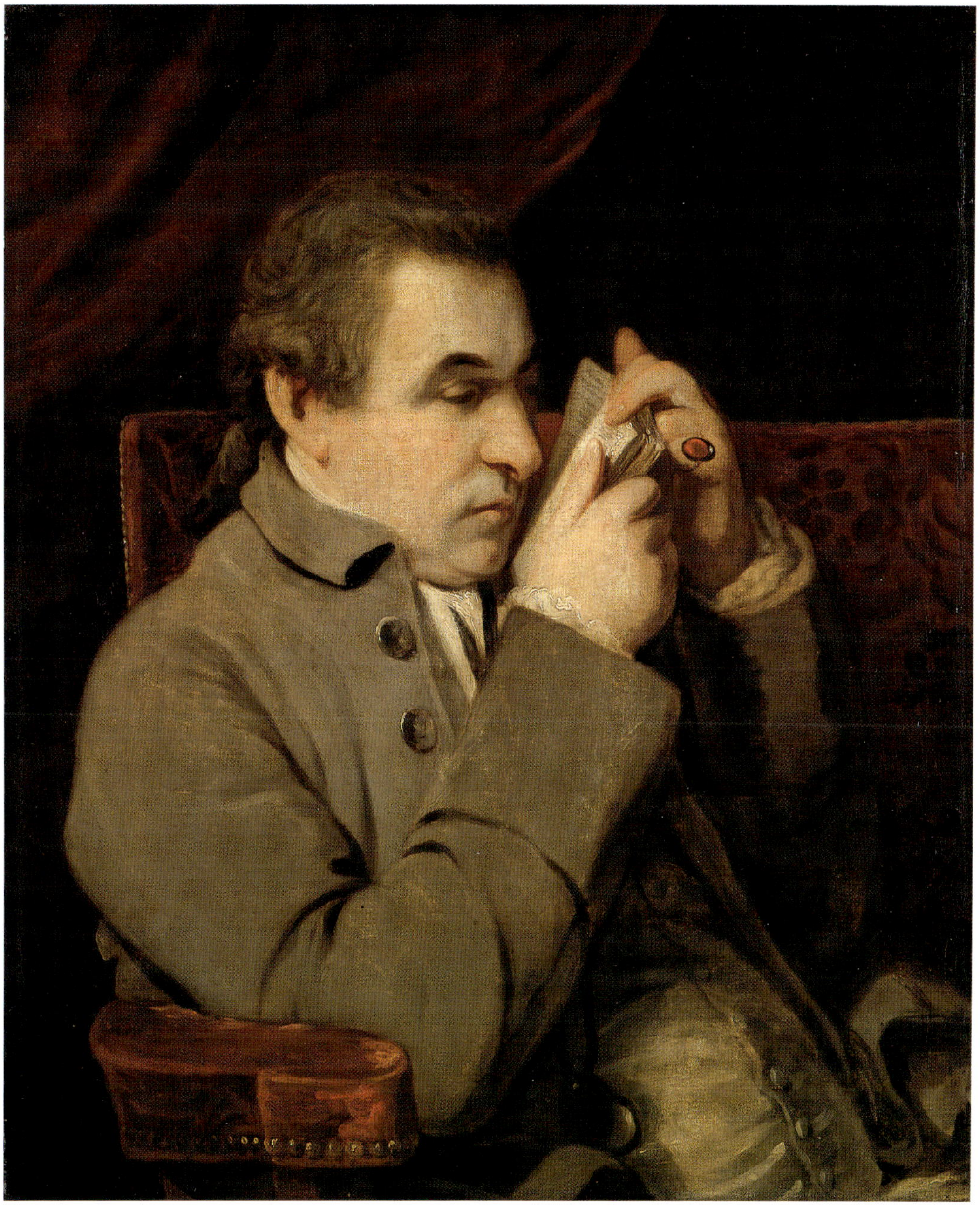

BARETTI NPG *6248*

The original portrait by Reynolds, painted in 1773, was commissioned by Henry Thrale, who had employed Baretti that year as a tutor in Spanish and Italian for his children; it first hung in the library at Streatham and is now in a private collection.[4] For Reynolds, Baretti was a gentleman of 'a peaceable, quiet disposition', exceedingly near sighted.[5] To some extent his portrait was a response both to the portrait by Barry exhibited in 1773 (see below) and to popular criticism of Baretti who, acquitted on a murder charge in 1769, had been termed a 'notorious Italian bloody minded sycophant'.[6]

NPG 6248 is apparently an early copy; Steegman recorded a traditional attribution to Reynolds's pupil William Doughty, but there is no proof. Copies include one inscribed as by James Northcote (Christie's, 22 November 1985, lot 124), another descended through the family of Sir Robert Chambers, and a grisaille in the John Herron Art Institute, Indianapolis.[7] Copies in miniature are recorded by John Bogle (Christie's, 12 October 1982, lot 60), George Engleheart 1793,[8] and Peter Paillou (Sotheby's, 9 April 1992, lot 170).

1 The stretcher was optimistically inscribed, apparently in the early 19th century: *Baretti / undoubtedly Painted by Sir Joshua Reynolds*.
2 A letter from Weaver to Lord Kenyon, dated 15 January 1841 (faded photostat in NPG archive), alleged he had acquired a portrait of Baretti, possibly NPG 6248, at the sale of the artist Boultbee (not recorded in Lugt).
3 Listed at Gredington by Steegman, I, p.159, no.71.
4 Formerly at Holland House; Mannings 2000, no.107; exhibited RA 1774(224); BI 1843(52); NPE 1867(576) lent Lady Holland; *Boswell*, NPG, 1967(59); *Reynolds* 1986(85); engraved J. Watts 1780; J. Hardy 1794; W. Bromley 1789 and S.W. Reynolds.
5 See D. Robinson in G. Sutherland ed., *British Art 1740–1820*, 1992, pp.81–94.
6 *Morning Chronicle*, 30 April 1773 (Pressly 1981, p.69).
7 See Mannings 2000, nos.107a–107k.
8 Williamson 1902, pp.48, 53, illus. f.p.52.

ICONOGRAPHY

1773 Painting by James Barry,* half-length seated reading with an eyeglass. John Murray (Pressly 1981, no.44). Exhibited RA 1773(361).

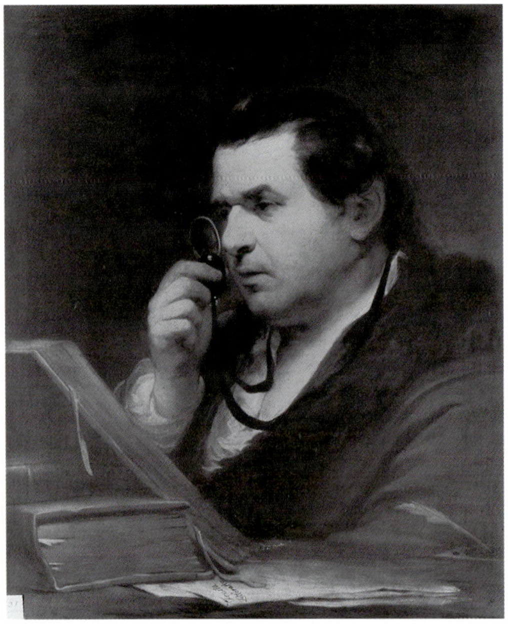

BARETTI by James Barry 1773 (collection of John Murray)

1773 Painting by Joshua Reynolds, see NPG 6248.

1789 Relief medallion by Thomas Banks. Marylebone Chapel (illus. Bell 1938, pl.xiii). Derived from the Reynolds portrait of 1773.

DOUBTFUL PORTRAITS

See Unidentified Portraits NPG 3024. Painting by Pierre Subleyras, Louvre (RF 1981–38), now identified as Jacques-Antoine de Lironcourt (exhibited *Subleyras*, Paris/Rome, 1987, no.100).

BARING, Sir Francis, 1st Bt 1740–1810

Merchant banker, his grandfather a Lutheran pastor at Bremen; founded the commercial house of Baring Brothers; MP 1784–90 and 1794–1806; Bt 1793.

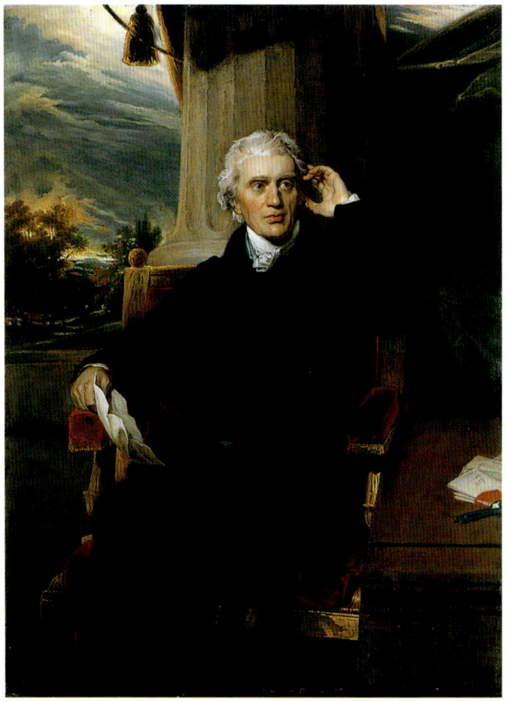

'a Chearful man & perfectly unassuming' (Joseph Farington, 1806).

'in person he is of the middle size, and very thin' (*Public Characters of 1805*).

1256 CHARLES MUSS 1823 after THOMAS LAWRENCE [1806–07]

Enamel on bombé copper panel 31.2 x 23.6 (12¼ x 9¼); some small matt areas in the darks; inscribed in yellow, bottom centre: *Portrait of Sir Francis Baring Bart. From a Painting by Sir Thos. Lawrence / Painted in Enamel by Chas Muss 1823.*

Blue eyes, own white hair, wearing black; he sits in a red-upholstered chair, a green curtain to the right; in his right hand a paper inscribed *Hope & Co*; on the table a paper inscribed *Hope 1807*.[1]

Collections: By descent to the sitter's great-grandson, the 1st Earl of Northbrook, by whom presented 1900.

Copied from the left-hand figure in Lawrence's celebrated portrait of the senior partners of Baring Brothers,* in which Sir Francis sits with his brother, John Baring, and son-in-law, Charles Wall.[2] His attitude was variously explained: Beechey thought he was turning away from Wall who was announcing a deficit, and Sir George Beaumont that he was being distracted by the sound of thunder.[3] But it was perhaps the attitude of a

BARING NPG 1256

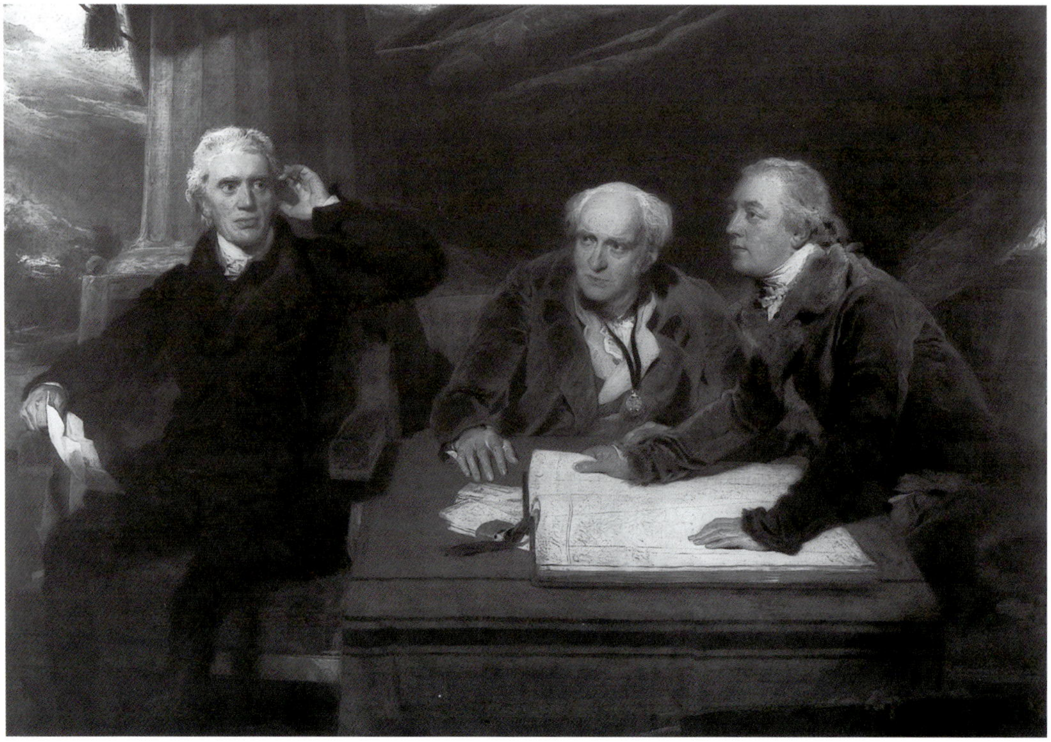

BARING (left) with John Baring and Charles Wall (right) by Thomas Lawrence 1806–07 (Private Collection)

partially deaf man, for his obituarist stated that the 'one obstruction [he] had to contend with from his earliest days [was] an incurable deafness'.[4]

There is a half-length version of the single figure in a private collection,[5] together with a related drawing attributed to Lawrence, showing his right hand resting in his lap. Muss also made enamel copies of several paintings from Baring's collection.[6]

1 Hope, the powerful Dutch merchant firm based in Amsterdam, with whom Baring worked closely.
2 Private collection; Garlick 1989, no.62; exhibited RA 1807(210); engraved J. Ward 1807–09 for private circulation (the sons not wishing their father to be seen with a ledger before him). A pendant to Reynolds's 1787–88 group portrait of Baring's political friends, *Lord Lansdowne, Lord Ashburton and Colonel Barré*.
3 Farington, 8 May 1807.
4 *GM*, LXXX, 1810, ii, p.293.
5 Exhibited *Hampshire Houses*, Winchester, 1938(1).
6 Exhibited RA 1817 and 1819.

ICONOGRAPHY

1804 Painting by Benjamin West,* three-quarter length seated. ING Bank NV, London (Erffa & Staley 1986, no.587). Cut from a group portrait of Baring's family containing six figures; exhibited NPE 1868(47) lent Lord Northbrook. Enamel copies by Henry Bone dated 1804 and 1806 (private collection, and Christie's, 6 July 1965, lot 32; preparatory drawing in the NPG Bone albums (*Bone* 1999, no.29).

1806–07 Painting by Thomas Lawrence, see NPG 1256.

1807 Drawing by Thomas Lawrence, profile bust, dated Nov 6 1807, lithographed by W. Evans.

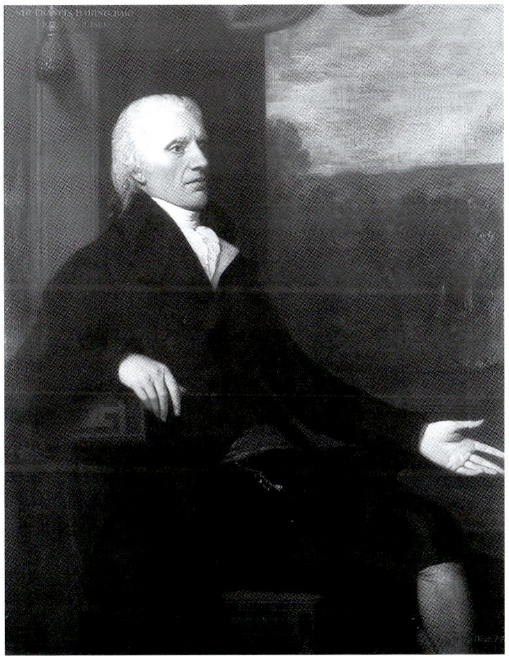

BARING by Benjamin West 1804 (ING Bank NV, London Branch)

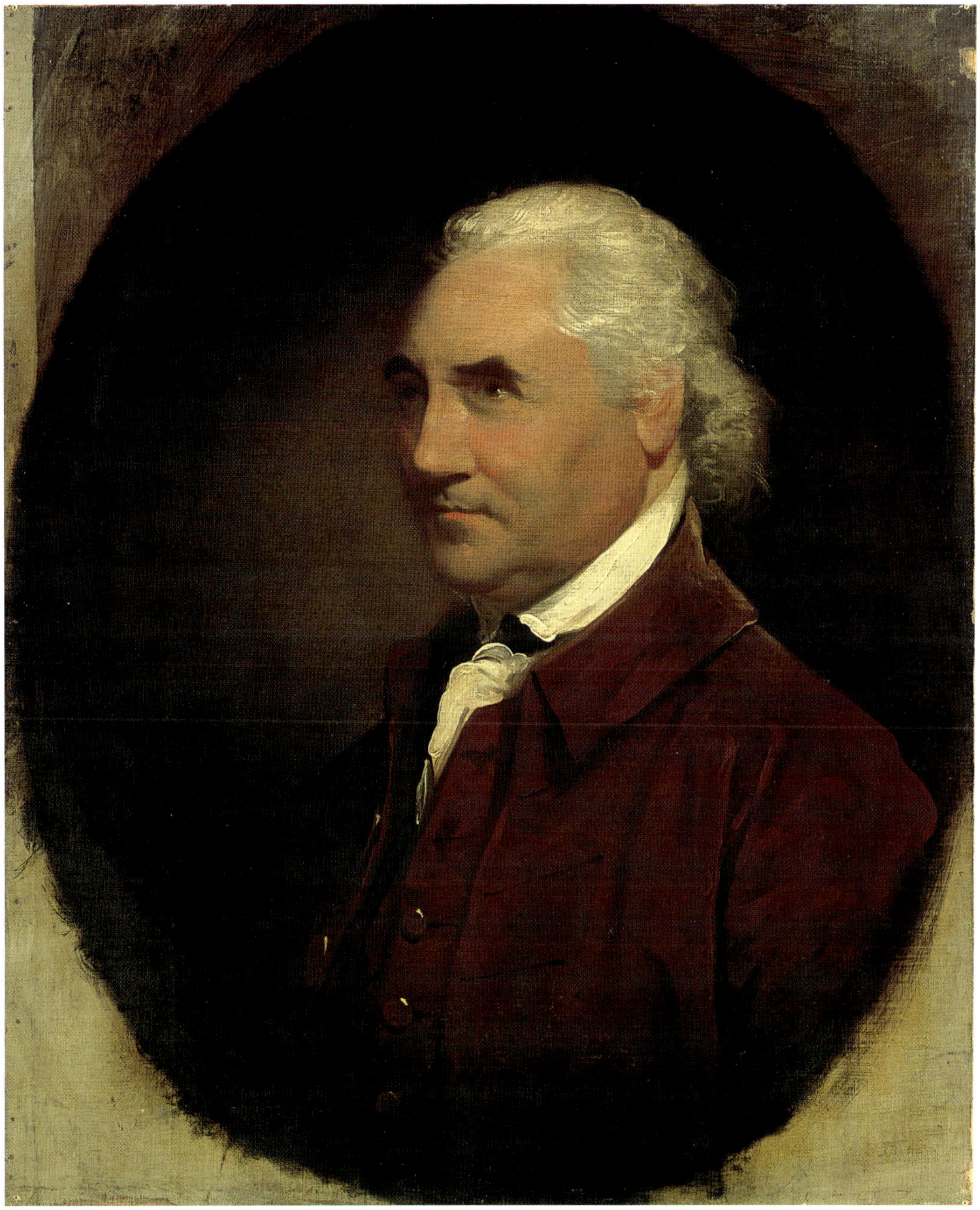

BARRE NPG 1191

BARRE, Isaac 1726–1802

Soldier and politician, of Irish Huguenot descent; served under Wolfe at Quebec; MP 1761–90, the defender of American citizens as the sons of Liberty; he lost his sight in 1790.

'A black, robust man, of a military figure, rather hard-favoured than not[,] young, with a peculiar distortion on one side [the left] of his face, which it seems was owing to a bullet lodged loosely in his cheek, and which gave a savage glare to one eye' (Horace Walpole, *Memoirs of George III*).

'[in 1781 he was] of athletic frame and mould, and endowed with extraordinary powers of voice . . . deprived already of one eye, and menaced with a privation of both, advanced in years, grey-headed, and of a savage aspect, he reminded the beholders when he rose of Belisarius rather than of Tully' (Sir Nathaniel Wraxall, 1815).

1191 GILBERT STUART [1785]

Canvas 75 x 62 (29½ x 24½) lined; some abrasion and discoloured varnish; *pentimenti* by cheek and chin.

Brown eyes, own white hair, deep red-brown coat and waistcoat with gold buttons, white collar and neckcloth; within a painted oval, the spandrels a light grey-green below and darker above.

Collections: Given 'by the sitter to his first cousin Colonel Phipps',[1] grandfather of Maj. H. Barré Phipps, from whom purchased 1899.

Reference: Park 1926, no.54; Whitley 1932, p.54.

A half-length replica of the kit-cat portrait dated 1785[2] in the Brooklyn Museum of Art, differing in detail in the waistcoat and coat buttons and omitting the left hand holding the printed proposal for Barré's 1780 Bill to appoint *Commissioners to examine Public Accounts of the Kingdom*.[3] Stuart later recalled that Barré, with Lord St Vincent and the Duke of Northumberland, had unexpectedly called on him and offered financial help, which he refused:

> They then said they would sit for their portraits. Of course I was ready to serve them. They then advised me I should make it a rule that half price must be paid at the first sitting. They insisted on setting the example, and I followed the practice ever after this delicate mode of their showing their friendship.[4]

When Stuart withdrew from the RA exhibition of 1786 it was said that his portrait of Barré 'would have counted largely to the Exhibition in the sum total both of money and skill'.[5]

Another half-length replica, showing the head more strongly lit and a light silk waistcoat, is in the Yale Center for British Art.[6] A small half-length copy was at Bowood in 1954.[7]

1 Letter of 1 September 1898 from Maj. H. Barré Phipps, who believed the portrait to be by Reynolds (NPG archive). A Barré Phipps (c.1774–1863) of St John's College, Cambridge, was probably b. in Minorca, s. of a Capt. Isaac Phipps (J. A. Venn, *Alumni Cantabrigienses* II, v, 1953, p.117).
2 According to the engraving by Hall; for the Brooklyn portrait, see Park 1926, I, no.53, illus., III, p.35 (once sold as Admiral Barrington by Hoppner).
3 Engraved J. Hall 1787; W.T. Fry, from a drawing by W. Evans, 1817. A copy by Duke made in 1873 for the American consul-general in Paris (letter of 1 June 1873 from General J. Meredith Read; NPG archive).
4 *Public Advertiser*, quoted by Whitley 1932, p.54.
5 W. Dunlap, *History of the Arts of Design in the United States*, [1834], 1965 ed., I, p.223 (Stuart's undated account was given to Charles Fraser).
6 B1981.25.615; formerly at Saltram (Lord Boringdon), later with Lord Amherst; illus. *In the Minds and Hearts of the People*, NPG Washingon, 1974, p.138.
7 Photograph, Witt Library.

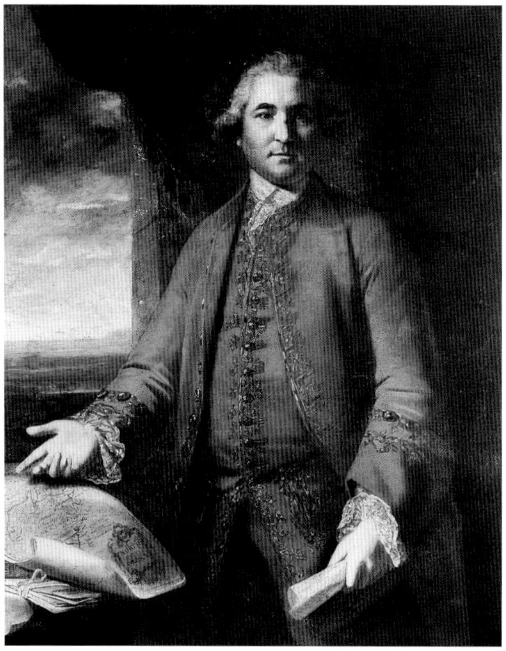

BARRE by Joshua Reynolds 1766 (Private Collection)

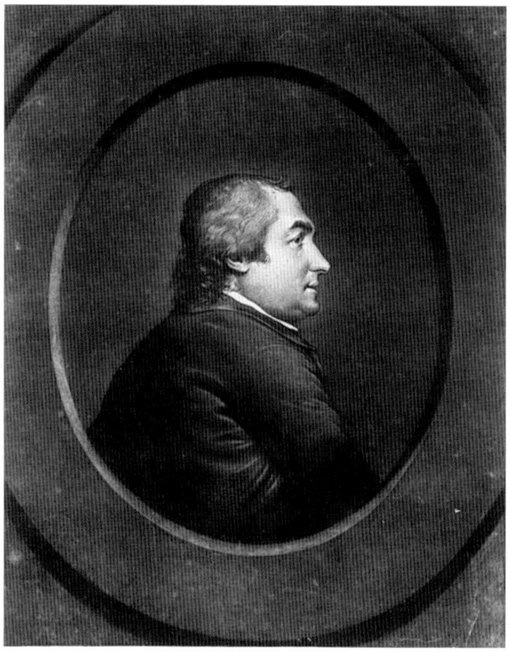

BARRE R. Houston after H.D. Hamilton 1771 (NPG archive)

ICONOGRAPHY

1765 Painting commissioned in 1765 by the town of Boston, Mass., for Faneuil Hall, with another of Henry Conway.

1766 Painting by Joshua Reynolds,★ three-quarter length standing in red military coat. Private collection (Mannings 2000, no.114). Exhibited NPE 1867(680) lent Lord Camden. Reynolds appears to have painted a second portrait for Lord Shelburne (Mannings 2000, no.115).

1770 Painting by Benjamin West, *The Death of Wolfe*, in which Barré appears immediately behind the dying Wolfe. NG Ottawa, replica in the Royal Collection (Erffa & Staley 1986, no.93). Engraved W. Woollett 1776.

1771 Pastel by H.D. Hamilton, half-length profile, exhibited SA 1771(259). Engraved R. Houston 1771.★

1774 Anon. engraving, bust-length profile, *The Martial Orator*. A weak likeness compared with the Houston plate of 1771.

1778 Silhouette sent by Shelburne (Lord Lansdowne) to the Abbé Morellet, with others of himself, Dunning (Lord Ashburton) and Townsend (*Lettres de Morellet*, ed. D. Medlin & J-C. David, I, 1992, pp.387, 425).

1780 Anon. engraving, bust-length oval (*London Mag.* 1780).

1782 Etched caricature by J. Sayers, whole-length standing (George 6066).

1782 Anon. engraving, bust-length oval, right eye closed (*Universal Mag.* 1782).

1785 Painting by Gilbert Stuart, see NPG 1191.

1787–88 Painting by Joshua Reynolds,★ half-length standing, with Lord Ashburton and Lord Lansdowne. See Ashburton.

Undated Miniature by 'I.H. Hunter', presumably J.H. Hurter, exhibited SKM 1865(86) lent Lord Cremorne.

Undated Watercolour by L-C. de Carmontelle. Musée Condé, Chantilly (from the Cheney sale, Sotheby's, 30 April 1885, lot 294).

DOUBTFUL PORTRAIT

Painting attributed to H.D. Hamilton, sold Christie's, 18 April 1986, lot 121.

BARRINGTON, Hon. Samuel 1729-1800

Naval officer, 5th s. of the 1st Viscount Barrington; captain 1747; captured St Lucia 1778; rear-admiral 1778; fought at the siege of Gibraltar 1782; lieutenant-general of Marines and admiral 1787.

740 UNKNOWN ARTIST c.1785

Canvas 76 x 59.5 (30 x 23½) lined; *pentimenti* on his right shoulder and some retouchings, mainly in the coat.

Light brown eyes, powdered hair, wearing the undress uniform of a rear-admiral: black collar, dark blue coat with gold trim and white waistcoat with gold buttons. Inscribed upper left, beneath the Barrington arms:[1] *The Honourable Samuel Barrington, / Admiral of the Blue Flag, / 4th Son*[2] *of John Viscount Barrington.*

Collections: Presented by the 7th Viscount Barrington 1885.

Exhibition: *War at Sea*, Yorktown, Va., 1978.

NPG 740 relates closely to the portrait by Gilbert Stuart painted in 1785 and the angle of the head is the same as in the Reynolds portrait of 1779 (see below). The hard handling and the inaccurate inscription and arms suggest it is not the prime version. A more softly-handled version (Christie's, 24 November 1972, lot 130), is dated 1791 and signed by George Arnald, then a young landscape painter; it might be assumed he was dating a copy (Barrington last saw active service in 1790); a third version, probably the original, remains with the sitter's descendants.

1 *Quarterly, 1st and 4th three chevronels gu., a label of as many points az. for Barrington, 2nd and 3rd part per chevron, sa. and or, in chief two griffins wings elevated or* [the Barrington supporters – plus each gorged with a label of three points or.]
2 But he was the fifth son.

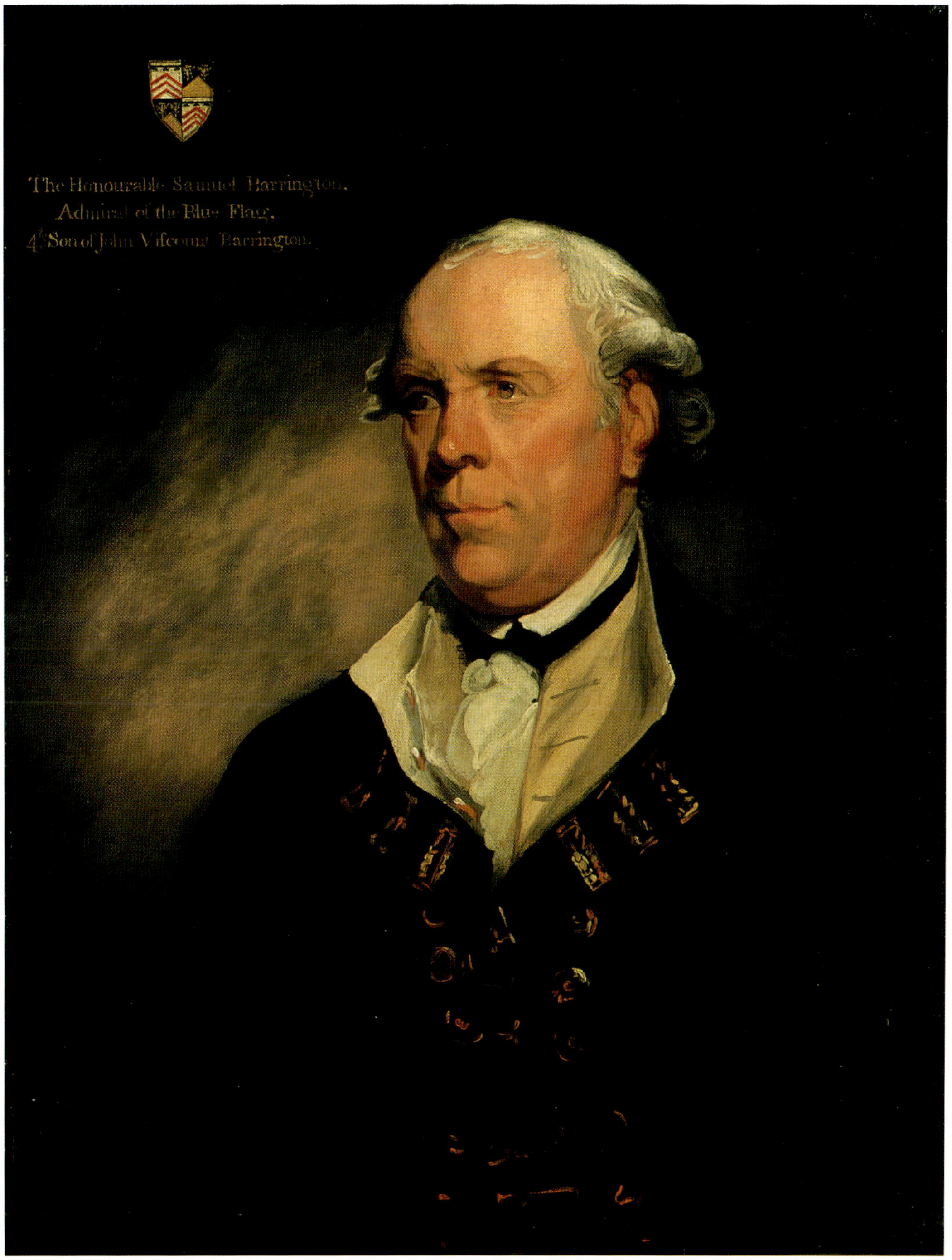

BARRINGTON NPG *740*

5519 JOHN SINGLETON COPLEY c.1790

Canvas 19 x 19 (7½ x 7½) lined; a painted roundel, the spandrels left grey-green.

Blue eyes, his own thin white hair; wearing an admiral's undress uniform.

Collections; The artist's son, Lord Lyndhurst; his sale, Christie's, 5 March 1864, lot 54 ('Portrait of Admiral Barrington, small circle, engraved'), bt. Anthony; Dr J.P. Edison, New York; Mrs Leo L. Pollok; Knoedler's, New York; Christie's, 16 July 1982, lot 66, purchased.

Reference: Prown 1966, II, pp.343, 412.

NPG 5519 appears to be a sketch for the untraced medallion portrait which, with another of Lord Howe, flanked the *Relief of Gibraltar* by Dominic Serres, exhibited in 1791 beneath Copley's huge *Defeat of the Floating Batteries** (Guildhall Art Gallery, 43; see Heathfield). It is not clear what subsequently happened to the *Relief* and the medallions; the Corporation was enquiring after them in 1794,[1] and an engraving of them all together by W. Sharp (the medallion portraits) and R. Pollard (the battle scene) was published in 1810.[2] Copley also painted a rectangular half-length version for the Barrington family, which remains with the sitter's descendants.[3]

An anonymous circular miniature copy, with a differing background, was sold Bonham's, 14 May 1991, lot 199.

1 See Prown 1966, II, pp.331-35.
2 Illus. Prown 1966, II, fig.585; Copley 1995b, p.162.
3 Illus. Prown 1966, II, fig.597; exhibited NPE 1867(739) lent Lord Barrington; engraved J.T. Wedgwood; W. Ridley 1800.

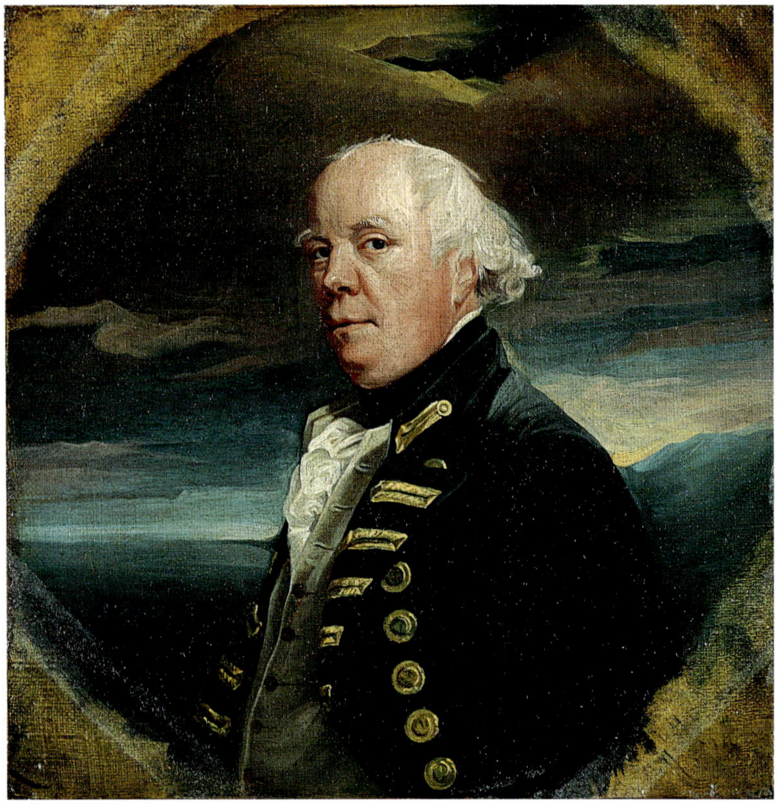

BARRINGTON NPG 5519

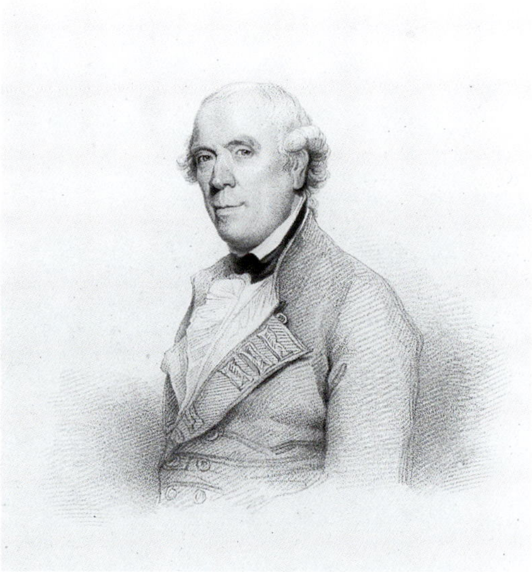

BARRINGTON F. Bartolozzi after Gilbert Stuart 1785 (NPG D 13735)

ICONOGRAPHY

c.1765 Painting by Benjamin Wilson, half length in captain's uniform. Engraved R. Earlom 1779 lettered *Admiral of the Blue*; anon. 1779 (bust-length oval). Wilson knew the sitter's brother Daines Barrington.

c.1770 Painting by Nathaniel Dance, half length in captain's uniform (National Maritime Museum, BHC 2533).

1779 Painting by Joshua Reynolds,* half length in flag officer's full-dress uniform. National Maritime Museum (BHC 2534; Mannings 2000, no.120). Engraved R. Earlom 1780; S.W. Reynolds; J. Chapman 1801; H.T. Ryall. Replicas were painted for officers serving under him and Mannings (nos.120a–120g) recorded seven versions, including those at Somerley; in the Burrell Collection, Glasgow; the Brooks Museum of Art, Memphis, Tenn.; Reading Museum, Reading, Pa., and sold Sotheby's, 17 January 1985, lot 5 (from the St Louis City Art Museum). An unattributed oval miniature copy, dated 1796, sold Christie's, 26 June 1980, lot 53, and a miniature enamel copy by J.H. Hurter exhibited SKM 1865(91) lent Lord Cremorne.

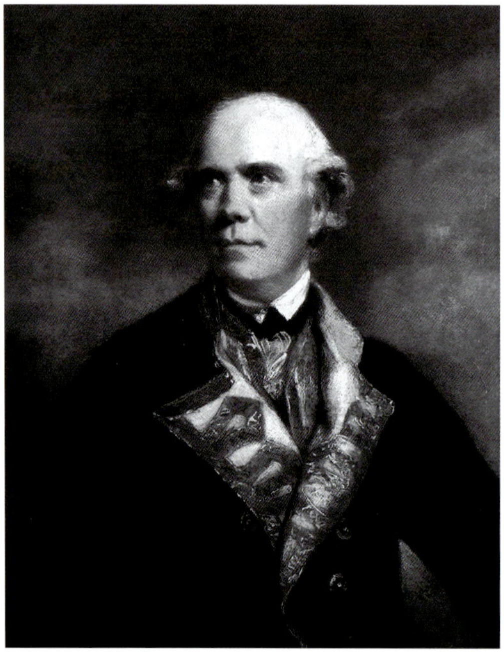

BARRINGTON by Joshua Reynolds 1779 (National Maritime Museum, London)

1785 Painting by Gilbert Stuart, half-length oval in admiral's undress uniform. Exhibited RA 1785(127). Engraved F. Bartolozzi 1812.* Autograph versions at Saltram and with J.H. Morgan, Farmington, Conn. in 1937 (illus. Park 1926, III, p.37). A miniature version by Philip Jean, showing slight differences in the uniform, was engraved J. Collyer 1790.

c.1785 Unattributed painting, see NPG 740.

before 1787 Chalk drawing by Thomas Lawrence. Bath period (listed by W. Armstrong, *Lawrence*, 1913, p.178).

1788 Painting by Mather Brown, exhibited RA 1788(220).

c.1790 Painting by J.S. Copley, see NPG 5519.

DOUBTFUL PORTRAIT

Gilbert Stuart's three-quarter length portrait of Isaac Barré was sold as Admiral Barrington by Hoppner, Christie's, 19 July 1912, lot 109 (Park 1926, I, no.53).

BARRY, James 1741–1806

Portrait and history painter; b. Cork, studied in Italy 1766–71; exhibited RA 1771–76; ARA 1772, RA 1773 and professor of painting 1782; between 1777 and 1782 he decorated the Society of Arts rooms in the Adelphi; in 1799 his criticism of the RA led to his expulsion; d. in poverty.

'[on his face] one could see lines prematurely engraven by the workings of [an] impassioned mind, so that he appeared older than he really was' (Edward Fryer, 1809).

'His face was striking ... it had vulgar features, but no vulgar expression. It was rugged, austere, and passion-beaten; but the passions traced there were those of aspiring thought, and unconquerable energy ...' (W.H. Curran, 1855).

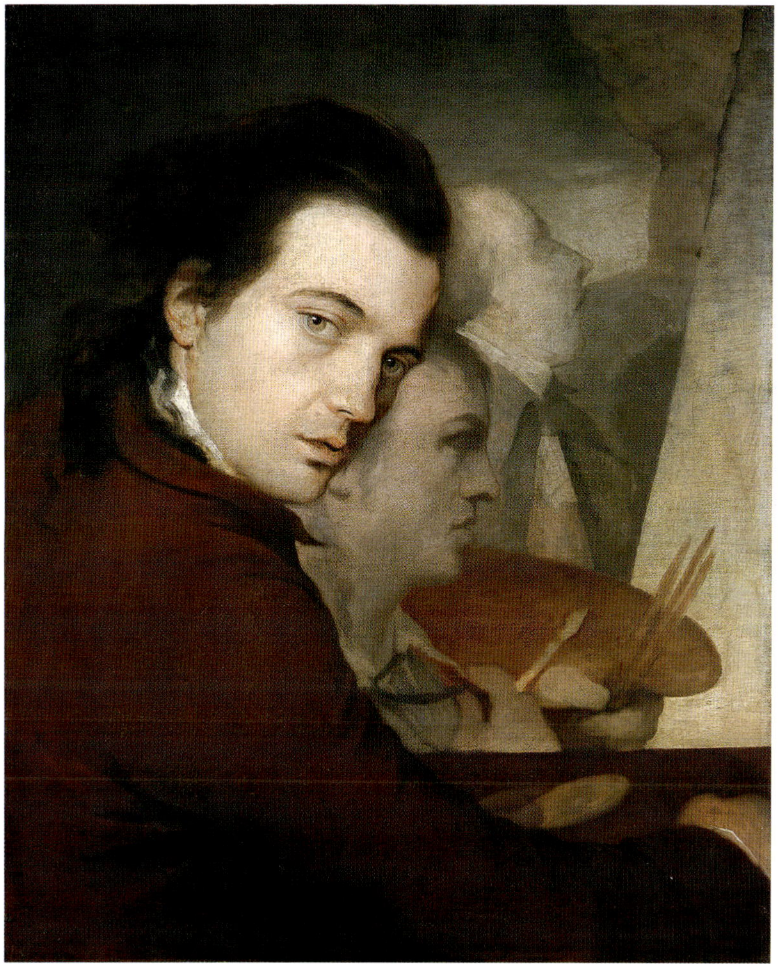

BARRY NPG 213

213 SELF PORTRAIT 1767

Canvas 60.5 x 50 (23¾ x 19¾); lined, cleaned 1976.

Light brown eyes, dark brown hair, wearing a red-brown coat.

Collections: Barry sale, Christie's, 1807, lot 73 ('Three Portraits in one Picture, Barry, Jas. Paine, and Lefevre of the French academy, then students at Rome, in 1767'), bt. S.W. Singer; W. Anthony, from whom purchased 1866.

Exhibitions: Tate Gallery 1956–74; *British Self Portraits*, Arts Council, 1962(42); *British Artists in Rome*, Kenwood, 1974(86); *Zwei Jahrhunderte Englische Malerei*, Munich 1979–80(140); *Barry*, Tate, 1983(15); *Genial Company*, Scottish NPG, 1987(28); *Grand Tour*, Tate Gallery, Rome, 1996–97(28).

Reference: Pressly 1981, p.236, no.37.

This challenging portrait was painted at a time when the artist was describing himself as a 'pock-pitted, hard-featured little fellow'.[1] It is the earliest of the self portraits, and was described in 1807 (see above) as painted in Rome in 1767, showing Barry with two fellow artists, James Paine jr. (1745–1829) and Dominique Lefèvre (c.1737–69). They appear in the background as colourless figures studying the Belvedere torso (seen upper right) which, for Barry, was the greatest surviving work of antiquity.[2]

Which of the background figures is Paine and which Lefèvre is not altogether clear. When NPG 213 was painted Paine was twenty-two and Lefèvre thirty. Lefèvre was certainly a painter, but no portrait of him is known.[3] In 1981 Pressly suggested it was Paine who held the palette,[4] but a comparison with the aquiline profile shown in his portrait by Reynolds of 1764[5] might suggest he is the further figure. Although Paine's artistic interests were widespread, in 1767 he described himself as a sculptor[6] and Barry wrote from Rome in February 1767 that a model Paine had made of *Venus and Adonis* had earned him 'no small degree of credit'.[7] Paine remained a loyal friend of Barry[8] and it would be more appropriate if he were the more prominent figure.

1 Barry, *Works*, 1809, I, p.172 (letter to the Burkes, Rome, 8 July 1769).
2 *Ibid.*, p.447.
3 The pupil in Paris of the painter J-M. Vien, he had won the prix de Rome in 1761 and was in Rome by 1764.
4 Pressly 1981, p.236; apparently the first attempt to identify Paine and Lefèvre. Pressly's identifications have since always been accepted and may, of course, be correct.
5 Ashmolean Museum, Oxford (Mannings 2000, no.1376).
6 As a subscriber to his father's *Plans* (H. Colvin, *Biographical Dictionary of British Architects*, 1995, p.726).
7 Barry, *Works*, 1809, I, p.82.
8 On hearing of Barry's final illness Paine recalled their long acquaintance, 'notwithstanding every peculiarity of disposition' and 'his very rare, and high abilities' (letter to 'Cooper', 15 February 1806, bound into the NPG copy of Barry's *Works*, 1809, I).

441 WILLIAM EVANS c.1805

Black crayon and wash on paper, sight size 15 x 11 (5⅞ x 4⅜), on a sheet of paper 36 x 30 (14 x 11¾) folded back down each edge; inscribed in pencil *James Barry R.A.* (the inscription on a folded area); the image is stained and faded.

Collections: Col. Francis Cunningham, from whom purchased 1877.

Engravings: C. Picart 1809; a larger plate 1822 (*Gallery of Contemporary Portraits*); Brocas jr., 1810 (*Hibernia Mag.*).

Reference: Pressly 1981, p.302.

Picart's engraving, used as the frontispiece for Barry's *Works*, described NPG 441 as drawn 'from an original Cast, taken a short time before his Death' (a contemporary annotation in the NPG copy of Barry's *Works* alters 'short' to 'some'). The mask referred to was conceivably made, as Pressly first supposed,[1] by W.J. Coffee in preparation for a Coade stone bust (but see

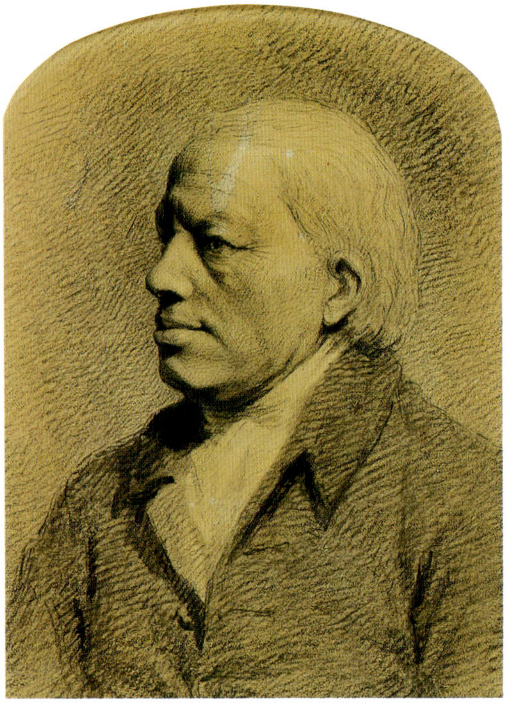

BARRY NPG 441

below). Through Picart's engraving, it became the most familiar image of Barry, and drawings by John Jackson,[2] William Blake[3] and J.M. Brighty[4] were based upon it.

Despite his appearance in NPG 441, Barry's final years were spent in isolation and fearful squalor. Robert Southey remembered him c.1803 wearing a faded old coat of green baize 'covered with incrustations of paint and dirt', living alone 'in a house which was never cleaned' and afraid to venture out by day lest 'the Academicians would waylay him and murder him'.[5]

1 Pressly 1981, pp.225n34, 301.
2 Private collection; Pressly 1981, p.302.
3 In a copy of Barry's *Account of a series of Pictures in the Great Room of the Society of Arts*, 1783; formerly in the collection of Sir Geoffrey Keynes (Pressly 1981, p.301) and considered 'a characteristic pencil recollection ... of the strange Irishman's ill-favoured face: that of an idealized bulldog, with villainously low forehead, turn-up nose, and squalid *tout ensemble*' (A. Gilchrist, *Life of Blake*, 1945 ed., pp.41, 370n).
4 Engraved J. Romney, a crude whole length, seated at his easel in a dressing gown. A later derivative engraving by L. Chapon 1867 from a drawing by A. Paquier is listed by Pressly 1981, p.302.
5 Southey to A. Cunningham, 23 July 1829; *Life & Corr. of the Late Robert Southey*, 1850, vi, p.54 (quoted by Pressly 1981, p.188).

ICONOGRAPHY

See also Pressly 1981, pp.237, 240–41, 254, 301–2.

Self Portraits

Pressly has observed how Barry's self portraits proclaim the artist, yet such pride was evidently accompanied by 'feelings of insecurity about his ability to perform adequately' (Barry 1983, p.150).

1767 Painting, see NPG 213.

1776 Painting,* *Ulysses and a Companion fleeing from the Cave of Polyphemus*, with the artist as the companion and Edmund Burke as Ulysses. See Burke 1776.

1777–84 Painting, *Crowning the Victors at Olympia*, part of the *Progress of Human Culture*, in which Barry appears as the Greek painter Timanthes sitting by a statue of Hercules ('who is crushing Envy'). Royal Society of Arts, London (Pressly 1981, no.24). Engraved J. Barry 1791.

c.1780 Painting, bust length. Victoria and Albert Museum (564.70; Pressly 1981, no.63).

c.1780 Drawing, bust-length cameo profile. Royal Society of Arts, London (Pressly 1981, no.61).

c.1780–1803 Painting,* half length, as the Greek

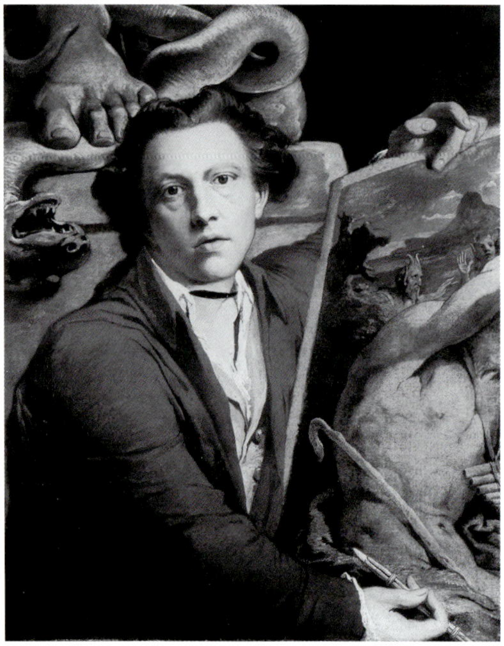

BARRY *Self portrait c.1780–1803 (National Gallery of Ireland)*

painter Timanthes, holding a picture of satyrs with a sleeping cyclops. NG of Ireland (971; Pressly 1981, no.67). The head painted c.1780, the remainder completed in 1803. Engraved J. Heath 1804; W.C. Edwards (for Cunningham's *Lives*); Ridley & Holl 1806 as a bust-length oval (*European Mag.*).

c.1800–05 Drawing, half length, right hand at chin. Ashmolean Museum, Oxford (330; Brown 1982, p.177, pl.xvii; Pressly 1981, no.63).

c.1800–05 Drawing, bust-length profile. Pierpont Morgan Library, New York (Pressly 1981, no.62).

c.1800–05? Ink drawing, bust length, spectacles on forehead. Tate Gallery, Oppé Collection (T 10438; Pressly 1981, no.68 as possibly a self portrait).

c.1800–05? Drawing, bust length, spectacles on forehead, quill in right hand. With W. Barry McCarthy in 1908 (illus. *Art Journal*, 1908, p.317).

c.1802 Drawing, half length, head on right hand. Royal Society of Arts, London (Pressly 1981, no.64). Engraved J. Barry, with some variations (illus. Pressly 1981, p.193). C.T. Warren, who bought this drawing at Barry's sale in 1807, described it as a 'favourite candle light study of [Barry's], but never intended to be made public as it was his intention that no portrait of him should be seen past the meridian of his life' (quoted by Brown 1982, p.178).

By other Artists

1766–71 Caricature drawing attributed to Nathaniel Dance, whole length, at Rome. British Museum (1868. 6.12.2136; Pressly 1981, p.301–02, and 1983, illus. p.13).

c.1775 Drawing by James Northcote, half length, seated, his right hand over his eyes. NG of Ireland (2584; illus. *Barry* 1983, p.14).

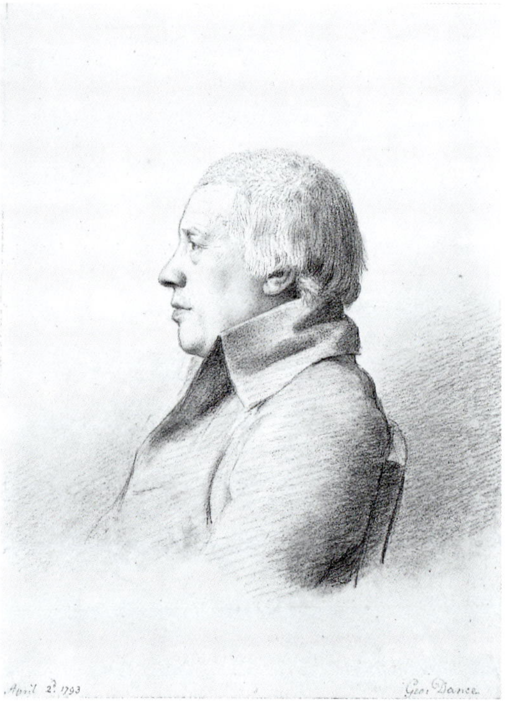

BARRY *by George Dance 1793 (Royal Academy of Arts, London)*

1793 Drawing by George Dance,* profile bust, dated 2 April 1793. Royal Academy. Engraved W. Daniell 1809 (*Dance Portraits*); tracing by Daniell in the Yale Center for British Art (B1977.14.4192). Fuseli commented on this drawing 'This fellow looks like the door of his own house' (Smith 1905, p.204).

1795 Painting by Henry Singleton,* *President and Members of the Royal Academy*, see Comparative Groups.

1800 Engraving by J. Owen, bust profile (*Public Characters of 1800-01*).

c.1805 Drawing by William Evans, see NPG 441 above.

1808 Bust by W.J. Coffee, offered to the Society of Arts, see NPG 441 above.

1819 Coade stone bust, probably modelled by Joseph Panzetta. Commissioned by Dr Clarke and Dr Edward Fryer of Greenwich, and four Coade stone copies were produced; one for St Paul's Cathedral (illus. *Barry* 1983, p.20), one for the [Royal] Society of Arts in London and two for Dr Fryer. Today one is in a private collection and the St Paul's bust remains in situ (see A. Kelley, *Mrs Coade's Stone*, 1990, pp.138-39).

1834 Engraving by E. Scriven 1834, 'from an original medallion' (Arnold's *Mag. of the Fine Arts*).

DOUBTFUL PORTRAITS

Paintings by L-G. Blanchet (Royal Society of Arts, London; illus. Pressly 1981, p.14); by Opie (NG of Ireland, 614), and unattributed (Sotheby's, 25 June 1979, lot 425; illus. *Connoisseur*, LXXV, 1926, p.130 as a self portrait).

BARTOLOZZI, Francesco 1727-1815

Engraver; b. Florence, he was brought to London by Richard Dalton, the King's Librarian, in 1764; engraver to the King, and RA 1768; he left England in 1802 to became director of the Academy of art in Lisbon.

Abbreviation

Tuer 1882: A.W. Tuer, *Bartolozzi and his Works*, 2 vols., 1882

222 JOHN OPIE c.1785-90

Canvas 90 x 70.5 (35½ x 27¾); lined, areas of retouching in the hand, cheeks, chin, the chest (above his hand) and upper right background.

Brown eyes, white powdered wig; wearing a red scarf, white neckcloth, black coat and dark grey waistcoat, holding a porte-crayon in his right hand; a red curtain behind him.

Collections:[1] 'Bromley the engraver';[2] bt. from Adamson of Bedford Street, London, by G.P. Everett Green and presented by him 1866.

Exhibition; *Opie*, Arts Council, 1962-63(34).

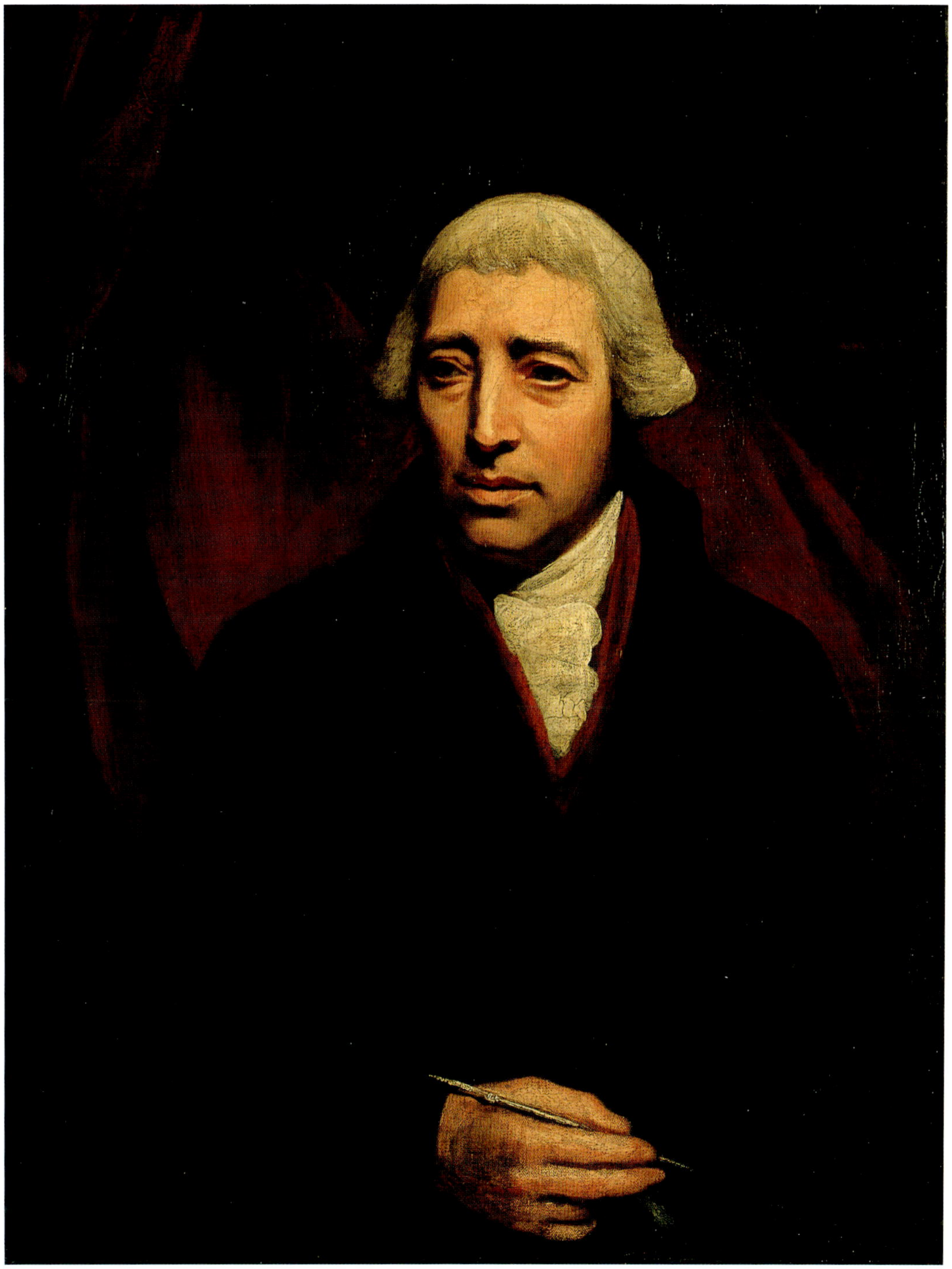

BARTOLOZZI *NPG 222*

NPG 222, a vigorous, broadly-brushed portrait, was acquired in 1866 as by Opie and the attribution has remained unquestioned. Both Earland and Rogers mistakenly stated that 'a large mezzotint' had been made from it.[3] The head resembles that painted by Pellegrini in 1795, see below.

1 Stretcher marked *June 24.50* and *2=111* (not Christie's, 24 June 1850, lot 111).

2 Note made by Scharf in 1866: 'from the collection of Bromley the engraver bought by Mr Green through Adamson, a print-seller of Bedford Street' (NPG archive). 'Bromley the engraver' could have been James Bromley (d.1838), J.C. Bromley (d.1839) or William Bromley (d.1842).

3 Rogers 1878, pp.70-71; Earland 1911, p.262. Repeated in the Arts Council exhibition cat., 1962.

3186 see Groups, *Carlini, Bartolozzi and Cipriani* by JOHN FRANCIS RIGAUD 1777

ICONOGRAPHY

A summary is given in Tuer 1882, I, p.5.

c.1762 Drawing by Angelica Kauffmann, half length. Victoria and Albert Museum (Vallardi sketchbook, E.443.1927). Tuer 1882, I, p.5, listed 'a fine portrait' of Bartolozzi painted by Angelica Kauffmann, then with C.C. Fuller of London, later sold Robinson & Fisher, 15 October 1932, lot 32.

c.1770 Drawing by G.B. Cipriani, full length asleep in a chair. Royal Collection (Oppé 1950, no.125, pl.40).

1772 Painting by Johann Zoffany, *The Academicians of the Royal Academy*, see Groups NPG 1437.

c.1773 Painting by Joshua Reynolds,* half length wearing a fur-collared red coat. Saltram (Mannings 2000, no.126). Engraved R.S. Marcuard 1784 (oval); T. Watson 1785; J.G. Haid.

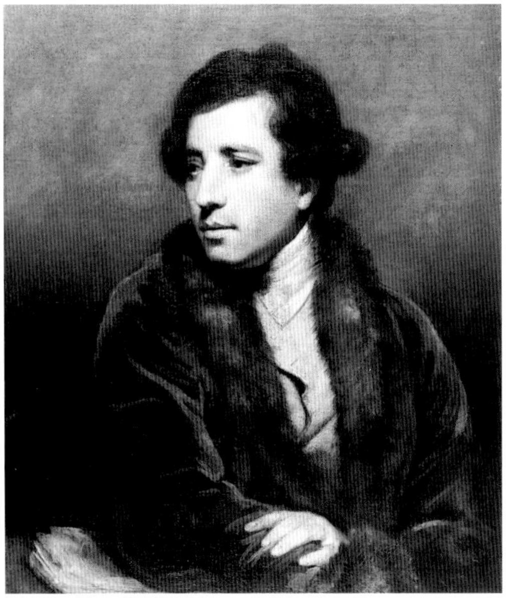

BARTOLOZZI by Joshua Reynolds c.1773 (Saltram, The National Trust)

1777 Painting by J.F. Rigaud, with Agostino Carlini and G.B. Cipriani, see Groups NPG 3186.

1778 Drawing called Bartolozzi, medallion bust. Christie's, 12 November 1968, lot 12, where identified as from the Molteno sale, 6 June 1817, lot 44, and said to have been described by Mrs Esdaile as an 'original portrait of Bartolozzi by himself', but this may be questioned. Engraved R. Ménageot. A similar profile drawing called George Dance, sold Sotheby's, 11 July 1990, lot 33.

c.1785–90 Painting by John Opie, see NPG 222.

1789 Pastel by John Russell, half length. Private collection in 1894 (illus. Williamson 1894, f.p.32). Engraved S. Smith. Drawn at the request of Russell's pupil P.W. Tomkins.

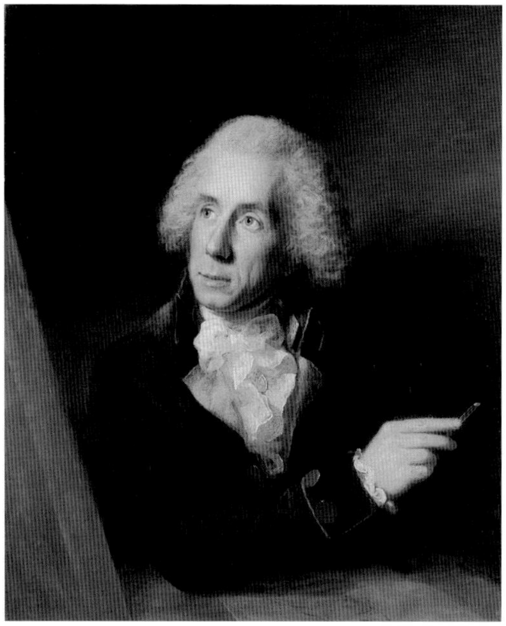

BARTOLOZZI by L.F. Abbott c.1790-95 (Tate Gallery)

c.1790–95 Painting by L.F. Abbott,* half-length seated, a burin in his right hand, an engraved plate on the table before him. Tate Gallery (T 1067).

1793 Drawing by George Dance, profile bust, dated 31 March 1793. Royal Academy (illus. *Art Journal*, 1890, p.109). Engraved W. Daniell* 1809 (*Dance Portraits*); tracing by Daniell in the Yale Center for British Art (B1977.14.4188) with, verso, a reversed image in pencil.

1795 Painting by Domenico Pellegrini, three-quarter length seated at table copying a painting from an easel. Venice, Accademia (illus. *Le portrait en Italie*, Petit Palais, Paris, 1982, no.39). Exhibited RA 1795(196). A bust-length version was in a Milanese private collection in 1935. A related, crude, whole-length engraving by J. Romney 1817, is lettered *G.M. Brighty del.*, and *Drawn by Himself*.

1795 Painting by Henry Singleton,* *President and Members of the Royal Academy*, see Comparative Groups.

1795 Miniature by Pierre Violet, exhibited RA 1795(385). An undated pastel miniature by Violet in a Grangerised copy of Tuer 1882, sold Christie's, 16 April 1980, lot 161.

c.1795 Miniature by L-A. Arlaud, bust-length oval. With J.W. von Rehling Avistgaard 1912 (illus. *Exposition de la Miniature à Bruxelles*, 1912, pl.xviii, no.82).

1797 Painting by James Green, exhibited RA 1797(976).

1797 Watercolour by Pierre Violet, half-length profile. Albertina, Vienna (illus. cat., *Die Englische Schule*, 1992, p.90). Engraved J. Bouilliard 1797.

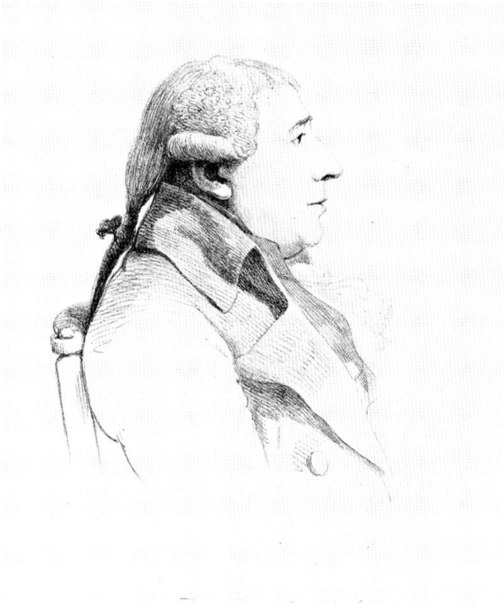

BARTOLOZZI W. Daniell after George Dance 1793 (NPG D 12186)

c.1800 Drawing by Henry Edridge, three-quarter length seated, a snuff box in his hands. British Museum (1867.4.13.535). A second drawing by Edridge in the British Museum, bust-length to right, appears to show him older (1845.8.18.5).

1802 Portrait by William Artaud, three-quarter length seated, a porte-crayon in his right hand, exhibited RA 1803(497). Engraved Pastorini & P.W. Tomkins.

c.1802 Drawing by Giovanni Vendramini, bust-length oval, engraved E. Scriven 1832, the head comparing with that painted by Artaud in 1802. Vendramini was a pupil of Bartolozzi.

c.1810 Drawing, self portrait, whole length seated to left. Museu Nacional, Lisbon (illus. *Album Cifka*, Lisbon, 1948, no.36).

c.1813 Painting by Roberto Focosi, half-length seated, a glass in his left hand, a burin in his right, engraved by L. Rados 1813. The plate, published soon after Bartolozzi's death, shows him with a dark wig looking much younger than his years.

DOUBTFUL PORTRAITS

Bartolozzi has been tentatively identified in J.H. Mortimer's *Caricature Group*, see Comparative Groups. Drawing attributed to J.K. Sherwin in the Royal Collection (Oppé, 1950, no.588); caricature by Rowlandson (Yale Center for British Art, B1975.3.132; illus. P. Noon, *English Portrait Drawings & Miniatures*, 1979, p.71); a watercolour by

Charles Ansell perhaps includes Bartolozzi (British Museum, 1890.05.12.5); miniature by Violet exhibited RA 1804(692) showed Bartolozzi's son, Gaetano; unattributed wash drawing of c.1795-1800 (NPG reference collection D 608).

BEACH, Thomas 1738-1806

Portrait painter; b. and d. in Dorset; pupil of Reynolds 1760-62; exhibited SA 1772-83, RA 1785-90 and 1797; worked much of his life in Bath.

'no man ever possessed a more friendly and benevolent disposition. He was a good scholar, and exemplary in the exercises of religion and charity.' (*GM*, 1806).

3143 SELF PORTRAIT 1802

Canvas 75.5 x 62 (29¾ x 24½) lined; pentimenti down each side of his coat; signed bottom left: *T Beach / 1802/ Painted by Himself.*

Grey eyes, own white hair, wearing a light grey-brown coat with black velvet collar; within a painted oval.

Collections: By 1934 with Knoedler, from whom purchased 1943.[1]

Reference: Beach 1934, p.54, no.9.

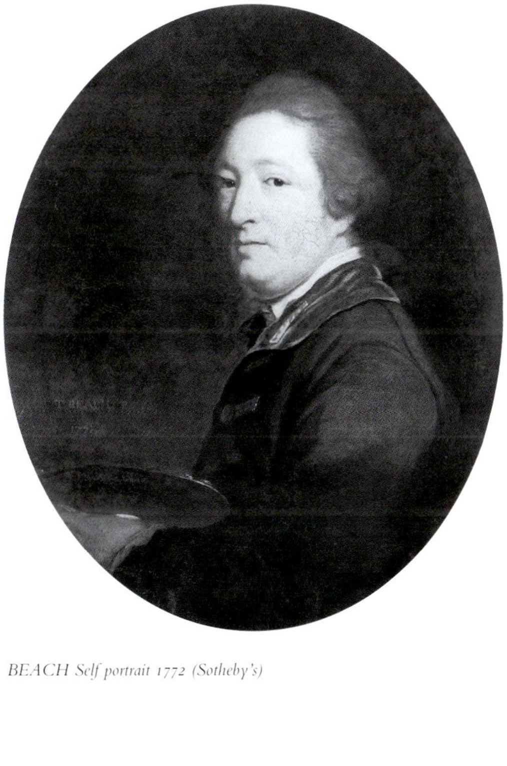

BEACH Self portrait 1772 (Sotheby's)

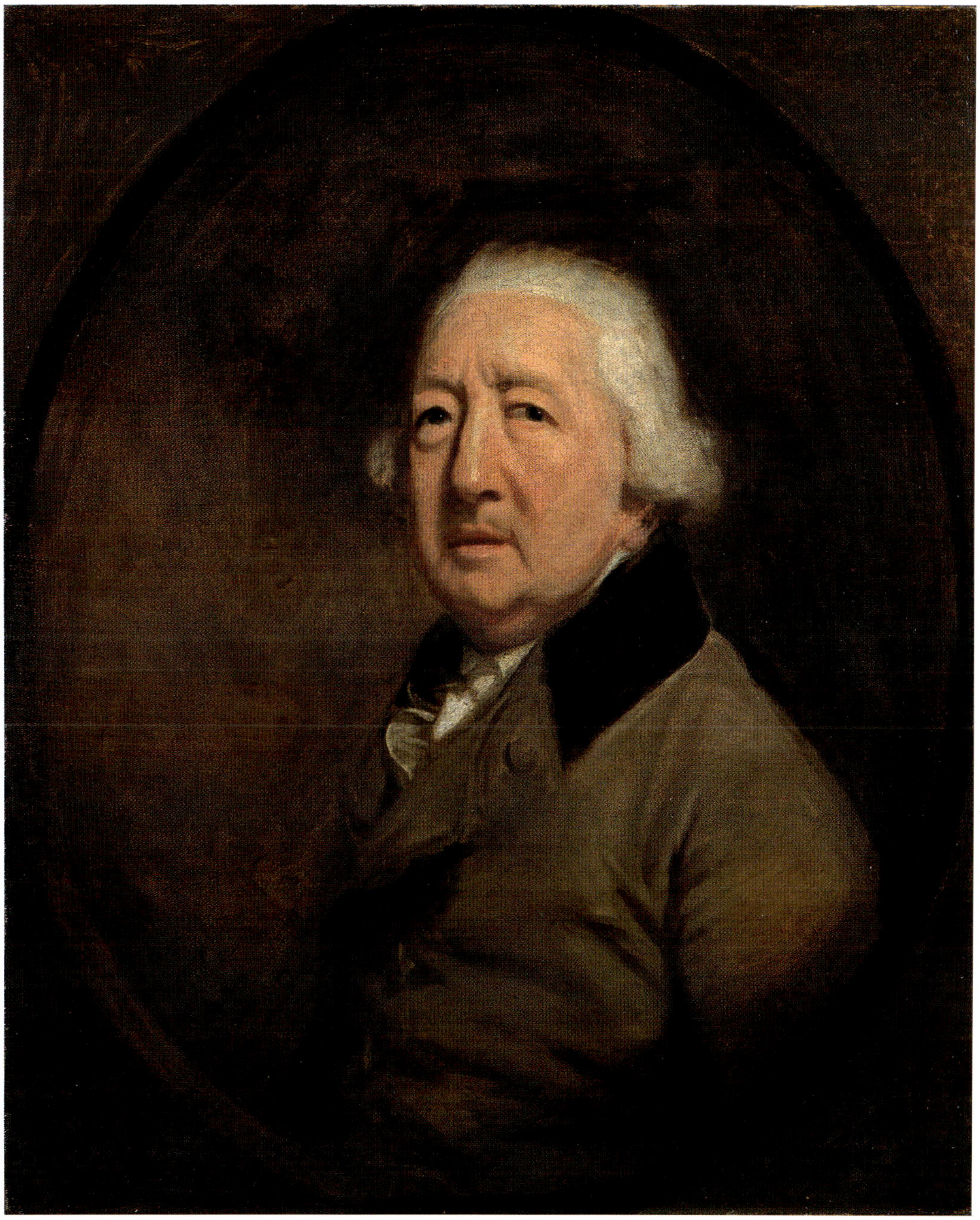

BEACH NPG *3143*

The last of Beach's self portraits, painted in Bath, where he lived 1799-1804 before returning finally to Dorchester. Closely resembling the self-portrait of 1801 (see below), with minor changes to the neckcloth.

1 Letter from Knoedler's, 17 March 1943, stated they 'had reason to believe that it was purchased in North Dorset or thereabouts in 1928'. Listed with Knoedler in Beach 1934.

ICONOGRAPHY

Self portraits (paintings)

1772 Half-length oval,* holding palette. Sotheby's, 30 January 1985, lot 50. The date has also been read as 1771.

1780 *An Academic Conversation*, sold Christie's, 8 March 1957, lot 71 as *Mr Talbot and Members of the Phelips Family of Montacute House* (in poor condition). Exhibited SA 1780(15), when it was noted that Beach in a green coat appeared in the left foreground (Whitley 1928, II, p.367).

1783 Exhibited SA 1783(30, 'An Artist, oval').

c.1785? Small half-length oval holding brush and palette, with his sister Frances (b.1741). Maj. W.G.H. Beach 1947 (Beach 1934, no.11, illus. f.p.32, as dated 1770, but the sitters' apparent ages suggest it is later).

1801 Half length, painted oval. Beach family in 1934 (illus. Beach 1934, front.). Exhibited *British Art*, RA, 1934(248). Copied by Cecil Round 1895. Closely resembling NPG 3143.

1802 See NPG 3143.

DOUBTFUL PORTRAITS

Two so-called self portraits: sold Christie's, 14 November 1997, lot 31, and sold Sotheby's, 23 March 1977, lot 74.

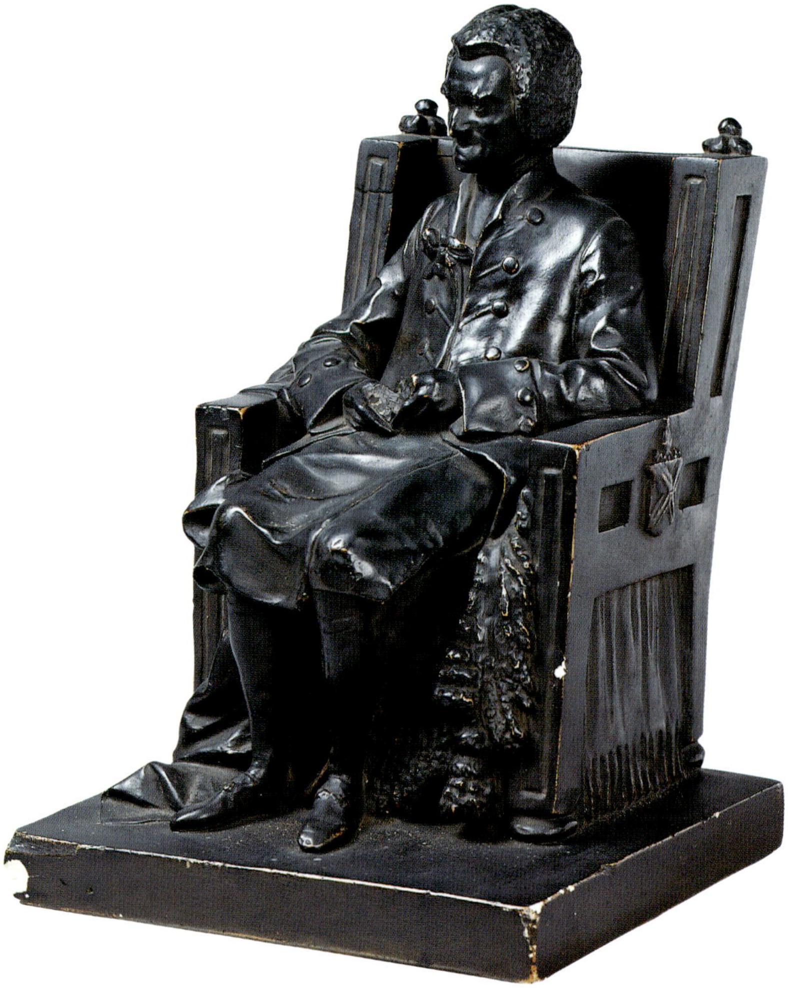

BEADON NPG *4901*

BEADON, Richard 1737-1824

Prelate; master of Jesus College, Cambridge 1781-89; vice-chancellor, Cambridge University, 1781-82; Bishop of Gloucester 1789-1802 and of Bath and Wells 1802-24.

4901 LUCIUS GAHAGAN 1823

Plaster statuette painted black 23.5 (9¼) high, inscribed on the reverse: *Richard Beadon / the Right Revd / the Lord Bishop / of Bath & Wells // Lu Gahagan / fecit Bath - / June 25 / 1823.*

In civilian dress, hands in his lap.

Collections: Bought in Bath by Cyril Humphris and presented by him 1972.

Reference: Ingamells 1981, p.120.

Executed when Beadon was already semi-retired; 'for the last few years of his life he was rendered incapable of discharging his episcopal duties by the infirmities of old age' (*DNB*).

ICONOGRAPHY

1789-95 Painting by L.F. Abbott, half length, wearing rochet and chimere, holding a small blue book. Jesus College, Cambridge. Engraved G.S. Facius. A replica is in the Bishop's Palace, Wells.*

1823 Statuette by Lucius Gahagan, see NPG 4901.

DOUBTFUL PORTRAIT

Painting recorded with the Church Council of St Margaret's, Stanford Rivers, Essex, in 1969.

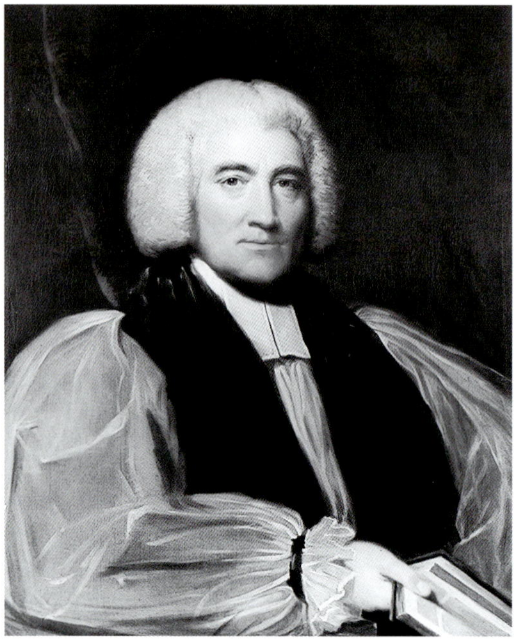

BEADON by L.F. Abbott 1789-95 (Bishop's Palace, Wells)

BEAUFORT, Daniel Augustus 1739-1821

Geographer, s. of a Huguenot pastor whom he succeeded as rector of Navan, Co. Meath, 1765-1818; published an ecclesiastical map of Ireland, with a *Memoir*, 1792.

5255 UNKNOWN ARTIST c.1800-05

Pencil on paper 11 x 9 (4⅜ x 3½), the image squared off at 9.8 x 8.6 (3⅞ x 3⅜), titled in margin below: *DANIEL AUGUSTUS BEAUFORT, L.L.D.*

Collections: Bought in Chester by Robert Bayne-Powell and presented by him 1979.

Exhibition: *The Quiet Conquest*, Museum of London, 1985(200).

Dated on comparison with the painting by Danloux of 1796 (see below); Beaufort here appears to be somewhat older.

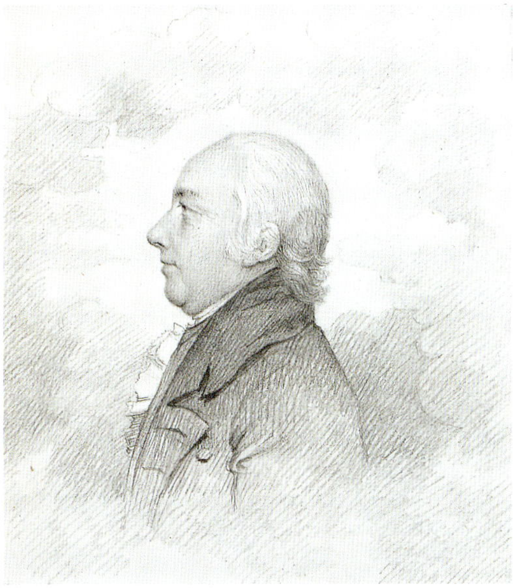

BEAUFORT NPG 5255

ICONOGRAPHY

1796 Painting by H-P. Danloux,* half-length oval. Sotheby's, 22 November 1967, lot 16, with a pendant portrait of his wife. These portraits were commissioned in 1796 at 6 gn. each (letter from C.C. Ellison, 8 September 1985; NPG archive).

c.1800-05 Unattributed drawing, see NPG 5255.

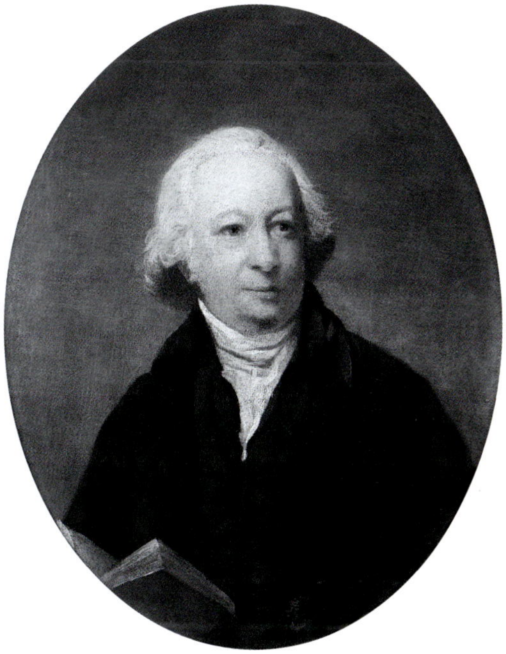

BEAUFORT by H-P. Danloux 1796 (Sotheby's)

BECKFORD, William 1709-1770

West India merchant; MP 1747-70; alderman 1752, sheriff 1755-56 and lord mayor 1762-63 and 1769-70 of the City of London; a supporter of Wilkes, on 14 March and 23 May 1770 he took to the King 'humble Addresses' of protest concerning the Middlesex elections, on the second occasion answering the King with an unprecedented address.

'He had boldness, promptness, spirit, a heap of confused knowledge, ... Vainglory seemed to be the real motive of all his actions ... the turbulence of Beckford, his imposing noise, and his great wealth, concurring to his authority' (Horace Walpole, *Memoirs of George III*).

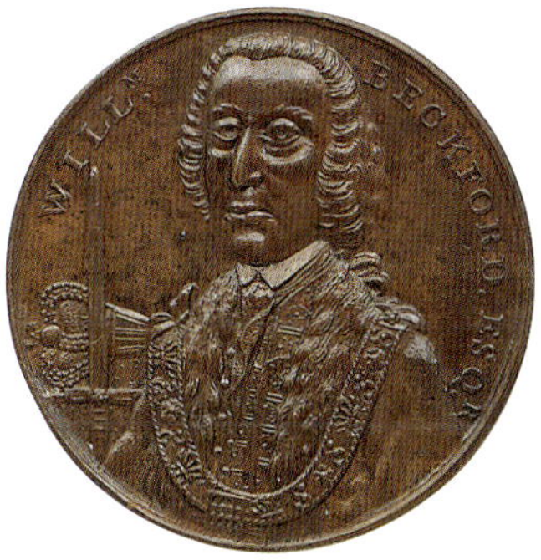

William BECKFORD senior NPG 5758

5758 JOHN KIRK 1770

Bronze medal 4.2 (1⅝) diameter

Obverse: bust portrait to left as lord mayor, inscribed: *WILLM. BECKFORD. ESQR.*

Reverse: *THE. ZEALOUS. / ADVOCATE. &INVA / RIABLE. PROTECTOR / OF. THE. RIGHTS. PRIV / ILEGES & LIBERTIES / OF THE PEOPLE.* and in the exergue: *OBIIT.21.JUN. 1770 / ANNO.AETATIS. / 65*

Collections: Purchased from Noel Warr 1984.

Reference: Brown 1980, no.141.

Commemorating Beckford's death in 1770; a crude image apparently derived from the anonymous mezzotint of 1769. Kirk produced a second medal in 1773, see below.

ICONOGRAPHY

1766 Bust by J.F. Moore, exhibited FS 1766(209). Possibly the unidentified plaster bust of Beckford at Stourhead (exhibited *William Beckford*, Bath, 1966, no.9) and presumably related to Moore's statue of 1767, see below.

1767 Statue by J.F. Moore in mayoral robes, his right hand held up before him, his left resting on a scroll (*whenever the Public is in Danger* ...); the figure of Britannia on the cippus. Ironmongers' Hall, London, presented by William Beckford jr. 1833 (illus. Gunnis 1968, f.p.240). Engraved anon. (as lately exhibited in Pall Mall). Exhibited FS 1767(89) when identified by Walpole as Beckford (*Wal. Soc.*, XXVII, 1939, p.72).

1769 Engraving by R. Houston (pub. 29 September 1769), half-length seated holding a scroll: *London Petition / Instead of punishing, confering Honours on a Paymaster the Public Defaulter of unaccounted Millions...*, with his two sheriffs, James Townsend and John Sawbridge (who rests his elbow on *Locke on Govt.*).

c.1769 Anon. engraving,* whole-length standing in mayoral robes with gold collar, left foot in front of right leg, his right hand gesturing to an open paper inscribed *The Humble Address ...*, titled: *This being the second Time of his Mayoralty & the third Time of Representing that City in Parliament*. A weak image; the head seems to provide the basis for the bust-length oval engraving by A. Benoist as well as Kirk's medal of 1770, see NPG 5758.

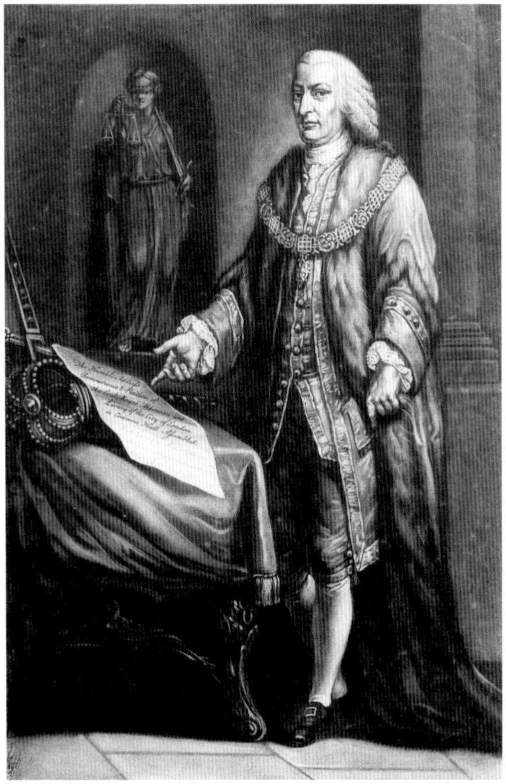

William BECKFORD senior, anon. engraving c.1769 (NPG D 675)

c.1769 Drawn and engraved by John Dixon, whole-length standing, his left hand on the *Magna Charta*, his right holding *Bill of Rights*, caption includes *This being the second Time ...* Altered from Dixon's plate of Benjamin Heath after R.E. Pine (G.S. Layard, ... *Engraved British Portraits from altered Plates*, 1927, p.59).

c.1769 Painting attributed to R.E. Pine,* whole length in mayoral robes, looking left, his left hand on a table on which lies the sceptre; with a distant view of St Paul's. Parham Park, from the 13th Duke of Hamilton sale, Christie's, 6 November 1919, lot 56 as Romney.

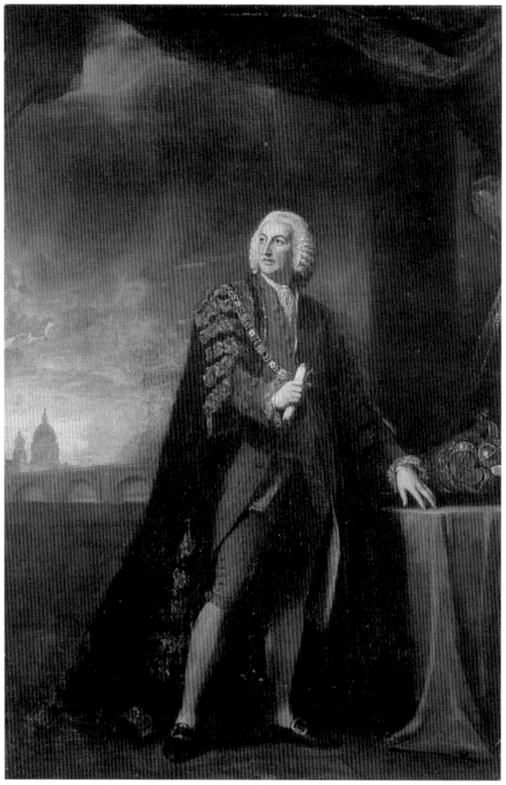

William BECKFORD senior, attributed to R.E. Pine c.1769 (Parham House)

1770 Anon. medal in mayoral robes (Brown 1980, no.142).

1770 Medal by John Kirk, see NPG 5758.

Following Beckford's death the City Aldermen commissioned a statue for the Guildhall; several designs were submitted before the commission was given to J.F. Moore.

1770 Terracotta statuette by Nathaniel Smith, whole length in mayoral robes, his left hand resting on a paper inscribed *The hum/Addres* .... Victoria and Albert Museum (A.48.1928) with an ink drawing of the figure (4910.12; both illus. J. Physick, *Designs for English Sculpture*, 1969, figs.104-5).

c.1770 Model for a statue by Agostino Carlini, engraved F. Bartolozzi 1772 from a drawing by Biagio Rebecca, as *rejected by by the Court of Aldermen in January 1771*; H. Meyer 1829 (three-quarter length); J. Chapman 1798 (bust length).

1771 Sculpture by John Rickets jr., exhibited FS 1771(203).

1772 Statue by J.F. Moore in mayoral robes, the head closely resembling that of the 1767 statue, his right hand held up before him, his left gesturing towards a table; flanked by the seated figures of London and Trade and Commerce. Guildhall, London (illus. Whinney 1964, pl.133A). Engraved C. Grignion sr. 1771 and anon.

1773 Medal by John Kirk (Brown 1980, no.170 and see under no.166).

Anon., and crude, engravings include two whole lengths as lord mayor; one, perhaps another design for a monument, with his right hand resting on the shoulder of a seated Britannia, his foot on the prostrate figure of Tyranny.

DOUBTFUL PORTRAITS

Statuette by the youthful John Flaxman, listed by Mrs Esdaile in the collection at University College, London (MS list 1925, NPG archive), presumed destroyed during the 1939-45 war. Painting attributed to Tilly Kettle (Palace of Westminster, from Sotheby's, 25 June 1952, lot 130; illus. *Beckford* 2001, p.299); miniature attributed to Jeremiah Meyer, sold Christie's, 30 March 1976, lot 40.

BECKFORD, William 1760-1844

Dilettante, the only legitimate child of William Beckford (1709-70); MP 1784-94 and 1806-20; shunned by English society for his homosexuality, he spent much time abroad; author of *Vathek, an Arabian tale*, 1786; builder of Fonthill Abbey 1796-1818; his 2nd dau. m. the 10th Duke of Hamilton.

'[Beckford] seems to possess very extraordinary talents. He is a perfect master of music, but has a voice, either natural or feigned, of an eunuch. ... His person and figure are agreeable' (George Selwyn, 1782).

'He is shrewd, whimsical and fickle, petulant and rude; proud and vain, ... at such perpetual variance with himself, that, like an egg put into boiling water, he proves hard and soft in a couple of minutes' (Beckford of himself, 1791).

Abbreviations

Alexander 1967: Boyd Alexander, 'Portraits of William Beckford', *Register of the Museum of Art, University of Kansas*, III, 8-9, 1967, pp.6-13

Chapman 1930: G. Chapman and J. Hodgkin, *Bibliography of W. Beckford*, 1930, pp.115-19

5340 JOSHUA REYNOLDS 1782

Canvas 70.5 x 58 (27¾ x 22¾) lined; cleaned 1981, when overpaint, as indicated by the 1835 engraving, was removed from the background areas to reveal the sky and curtain; a shrinkage craquelure in the flesh and white neckcloth; pentimenti show alterations to his left shoulder.

Grey eyes, light brown hair, wearing a black coat with white lace cravat; a bright red curtain top left, the background passing from a bright blue at the top, through warm umber to a hot orange.

Collections: Bequeathed by the sitter to his daughter, Susannah, Duchess of Hamilton;[1] by descent to the 13th Duke of Hamilton; Hamilton Palace sale, Christie's, 6 November 1919, lot 52, bt. Knoedler, from whom bt., 1920, by Mrs George Elkins, later Mrs S.P. Rotan (d.1977), Philadelphia; Alexander Gallery, London, from whom purchased 1980.

Engravings: T.A. Dean 1835 (front. for Beckford's *Alcobaça and Batalha*); F. Bromley 1862.

Exhibitions: RA 1782(10); BI 1861(174); Scottish NPG, 1883(110); *Reynolds*, Grosvenor Gallery, 1883-84(186); *Guelph* 1891(115); *Georgian Art*, 25 Park Lane, London, 1931(31); *Travels in Italy*, Manchester, 1988(96); *Vom zauber des Rheins ergriffen*, Bonn, 1992.

Reference: Graves & Cronin, I, pp.74-75; Chapman 1930, p.117, no.5; Waterhouse 1941, p.73; Mannings 2000, no.149.

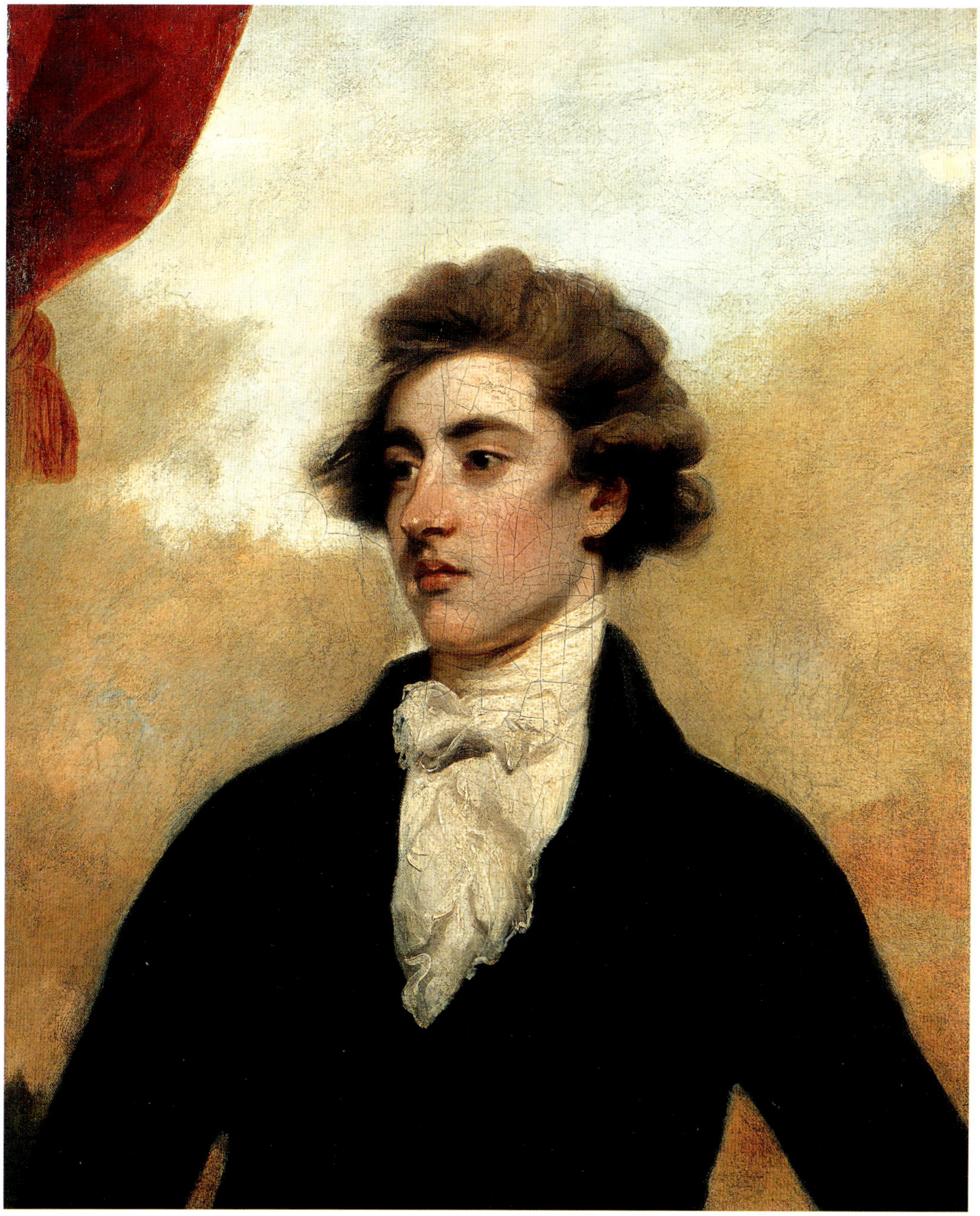

William BECKFORD junior NPG *5340*

Beckford was sitting to Reynolds in February and March 1782. He had attained his majority and succeeded to his vast wealth the previous September and he was to go to Italy for a second time in May, while the portrait was being exhibited at the Royal Academy. A contemporary review then found 'nothing remarkable' about it.[2] Beckford did not pay Reynolds the 50 gn. for his picture until 10 February 1785,[3] by which time scandal was changing his life dramatically; fifty years later he could describe the picture as 'a distinguished work of Sir Joshua's, painted in one of his happiest moments - moments I should never forget were I to live a thousand years'.[4] It was also in 1835 that Dean's engraving of NPG 5340 was published showing a uniformly dark background, oddly appropriate for the outcast in Lansdowne House, but probably indicating that the sky was already overlaid with the 'luminous ... golden brown' otherwise first described in 1883,[5] which was not removed until 1981.

The background of NPG 5340 now seems to resemble a hot evening sky, curiously at odds with Beckford's dark coat; Mannings observes that such a background 'is most unusual' in Reynolds's work.

1 On Beckford's death the portrait was listed among his possessions as showing him 'when about eighteen years of age' (Alexander 1967, pp.9, 13n30).
2 *St James's Chronicle*, quoted by Graves & Cronin.
3 50gn. then being Reynolds's price for either a 'Head' (24½ x 18½ in.) or a 'Three-quarters' (30 x 25 in.), see Cormack 1970, p.105. The sum Beckford paid in 1785 has previously been transcribed as £5 (Cormack 1970, p.145) or £557 (Graves & Cronin), but see Mannings.
4 To an unnamed correspondent, 19 July 1835, Beckford MSS; quoted by Alexander 1967, p.9.
5 J.M. Gray, *Notes on the Edinburgh Loan Exhibition of 1883*, p.32.

ICONOGRAPHY

c.1766 Painting by Andrea Casali, as a boy, oval whole-length seated. Lennoxlove (illus. *Beckford* 2001, p.298). According to Beckford's sister, 'the strongest resemblance ... a sweet pretty picture' (Chapman 1930, p.115, no.1). Casali undertook much decorative painting at Fonthill before leaving England c.1766 (see Croft-Murray, II, p.182).

c.1770 Painting attributed to William Hoare, as a boy, with two hounds. Mrs Lovette West, New York, in 1967, from the Hamilton sale, Christie's, 6 November 1919, lot 11 (as N. Dance, *Portrait of a Boy;* illus. W. Beckford, *The Vision and Liber Veritatis*, 1930, ed. G. Chapman, front.). The identification is traditional.

1777-78 Painting by A.R. Mengs. 'The portrait I would like to recover is the one Mengs did when I was at Geneva coming out of the sea, and in the best of all costumes- that of paradise' (Beckford to Franchi, 20 October 1824; Alexander 1967, p.10).

1777-78 Portraits by J-D. Huber, made in Geneva. Beckford recalled that Huber 'did various portraits of me', one with a 'pink bath robe-de-chambre' (Alexander 1967, p.10). An unfinished pencil sketch shows Beckford standing behind the artist's son François who plays the clavichord (Beckford MSS; Alexander 1967, p.10).

1781-82 Painting by George Romney,* whole length. Upton House. Alastair Laing, *In Trust for the Nation*, NG, 1995, no.9, commented 'although the portrait conveys all the arrogance of a rich, handsome and precociously published youth, its conventionality suggests that it may in fact have been painted at the wish of his Methodistical but dangerously possessive mother'.

1782 Painting by Joshua Reynolds, see NPG 5340.

1787-88 Two portraits painted in Madrid by 'Kauffmann', an unidentified relative of Angelica Kauffmann, doubtless one of her three cousins who served in the bodyguard of Carlos III of Spain (Chapman 1930, p.118, no.6).

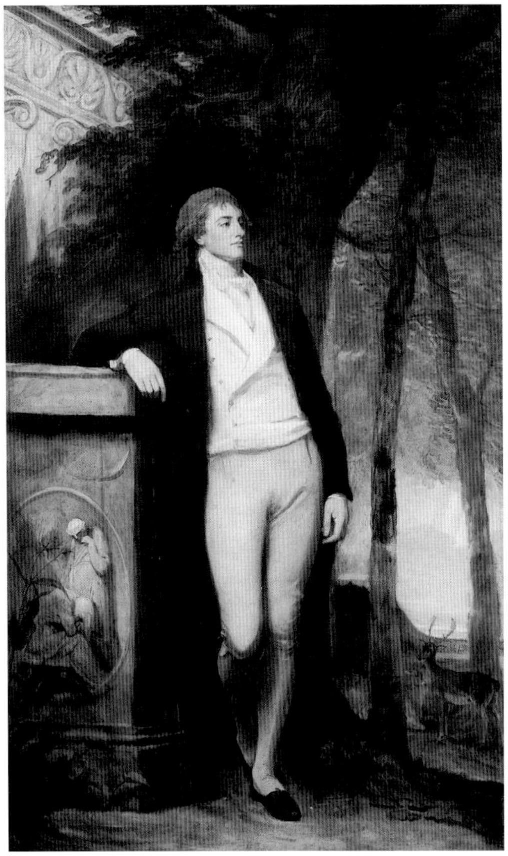

William BECKFORD junior by George Romney 1781-82 (Upton House, The National Trust)

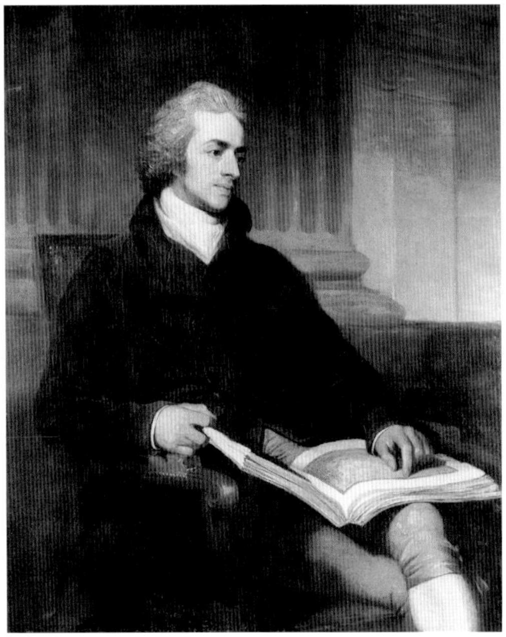

William BECKFORD junior by John Hoppner c.1800 (Salford Museum and Art Gallery)

1797 Painting by J.P. Sauvage, undraped medallion, engraved J. Singleton 1797 (*European Mag.*); A. de St Aubin 1801 (illus. *Beckford* 2001, p.99); S. Freeman 1844. A related engraving (with coat) published G. Smeeton 1823 (illus. L. Melville, *Life and Letters of William Beckford*, 1910, p.228).

c.1800 Painting by John Hoppner,* three-quarter length seated. Salford MAG. Probably painted after 1799 when Beckford finally returned to England having been abroad 1787-88, 1793-96 and 1798-99 (see Boyd Alexander, *Life at Fonthill*, 1957, pp.343-44).

1817 Anon. engraving after William Behnes, *A Dialogue in the Shades*, half length with spectacles, with his bookseller Clark and William Caxton (illus. Alexander 1967, p.7; a variant, showing Clark without his wig, illus. Boyd Alexander, *Life at Fonthill*, 1957, f.p.70, and see pp.344-45). Beckford's likeness compares with an anon. caricature in the Beckford MSS on a letter of 1 April 1803 (illus. Boyd Alexander, *England's Wealthiest Son*, 1962, p.39).

c.1825-30? Drawing by Lucius Gahagan, on horseback (illus. H. Bridgeman & E. Drury, *The British Eccentric*, 1975, p.117, without source).

1842 Lithograph by John Doyle, on horseback (illus. Beckford 2001, p.262). In old age Beckford, 'dressed in the manner of a country squire and in the fashion of the regency,' would ride out on a grey Arab, attended by a small retinue (B. Fothergill, *Beckford of Fonthill*, 1979, p.330).

1844 Painting by Willes Maddox, on his deathbed. Brodick Castle (illus. *Beckford* 2001, p.404). A reduced version in a private collection (illus. *ibid.*, p.405).

DOUBTFUL PORTRAITS

An unattributed miniature said to represent Beckford, wearing blue coat, powdered wig and black cravat, formerly with Lord Harrowby, was stolen in 1937 (Alexander 1967, p.10). Unattributed painting (Scottish NPG, PG 342); miniature by A. Plimer (H. Drake in 1903; illus. G.C. Williamson, *Andrew & Nathaniel Plimer*, 1903, f.p.48); painting by Richard Cosway (Sotheby's, 19 November 1969, lot 38); unattributed painting (T. Mowle, *Beckford*, 1998, pl.28; Bridgeman & Drury, *The British Eccentric*, 1975, p.115).

BEDFORD, John Russell, 4th Duke of
1710–71

Statesman, 2nd s. of the 2nd Duke of Bedford; suc. as 4th Duke 1732; FRS 1741; KG 1749; first lord of the Admiralty 1744–48, lord-lieutenant of Ireland 1756–61 and lord privy seal 1760; minister plenipotentiary for the Treaty of Fontainebleau 1762–63 and lord president of the council 1763–67.

'about the middle size, very good complexion, rather round, or what is called jolly' (John O'Keeffe, 1826).

755 THOMAS GAINSBOROUGH c.1770

Canvas 76 x 63 (30 x 24¾); inscribed lower left: *John / Duke of Bedford* and *T Gainsborough.*

[not available for examination]

Pale blue-grey eyes, grey powdered hair, wearing a scarlet coat and waistcoat with the ribbon and star of the Garter, his black hat under his left arm.

Collections: Painted for the sitter's daughter, Caroline, who m. the 3rd Duke of Marlborough; thence by descent; Blenheim sale, Christie's, 3rd day, 31 July 1886, lot 239, purchased.

Exhibitions: NPE 1867(455); RA 1882(16); *Gainsborough*, Grosvenor Gallery, 1885(38); Beningbrough 1979–80; *Gainsborough*, Paris, 1981(36); British Embassy, Paris, 1981–.

Reference: *Gainsborough* 1953, p.8; Waterhouse 1958, no.56; M. Beal & J. Cornforth, *The British Embassy, Paris*, 1992, p.53.

The Duke had been a particular patron of Gainsborough from 1755 when he commissioned two landscapes for Woburn. NPG 755 was painted near the end of the Duke's life, when his eyesight was troublesome and his health poor (he suffered a paralytic stroke in the spring of 1770)[1] and his drawn features are in marked contrast to those in the Gainsborough heads of 1764 and 1768.[2]

The execution was much praised by Passavant and Waagen,[3] and Scharf made a particular study of it in 1875[4] before acquiring it in 1886. A version, probably by Gainsborough Dupont, is in the J.P. Speed Museum, Louisville, Ky.[5] An unidentified portrait of the Duke of Bedford which had remained in Gainsborough's studio was in the Dupont sale in 1797, and later at Cassiobury.[6]

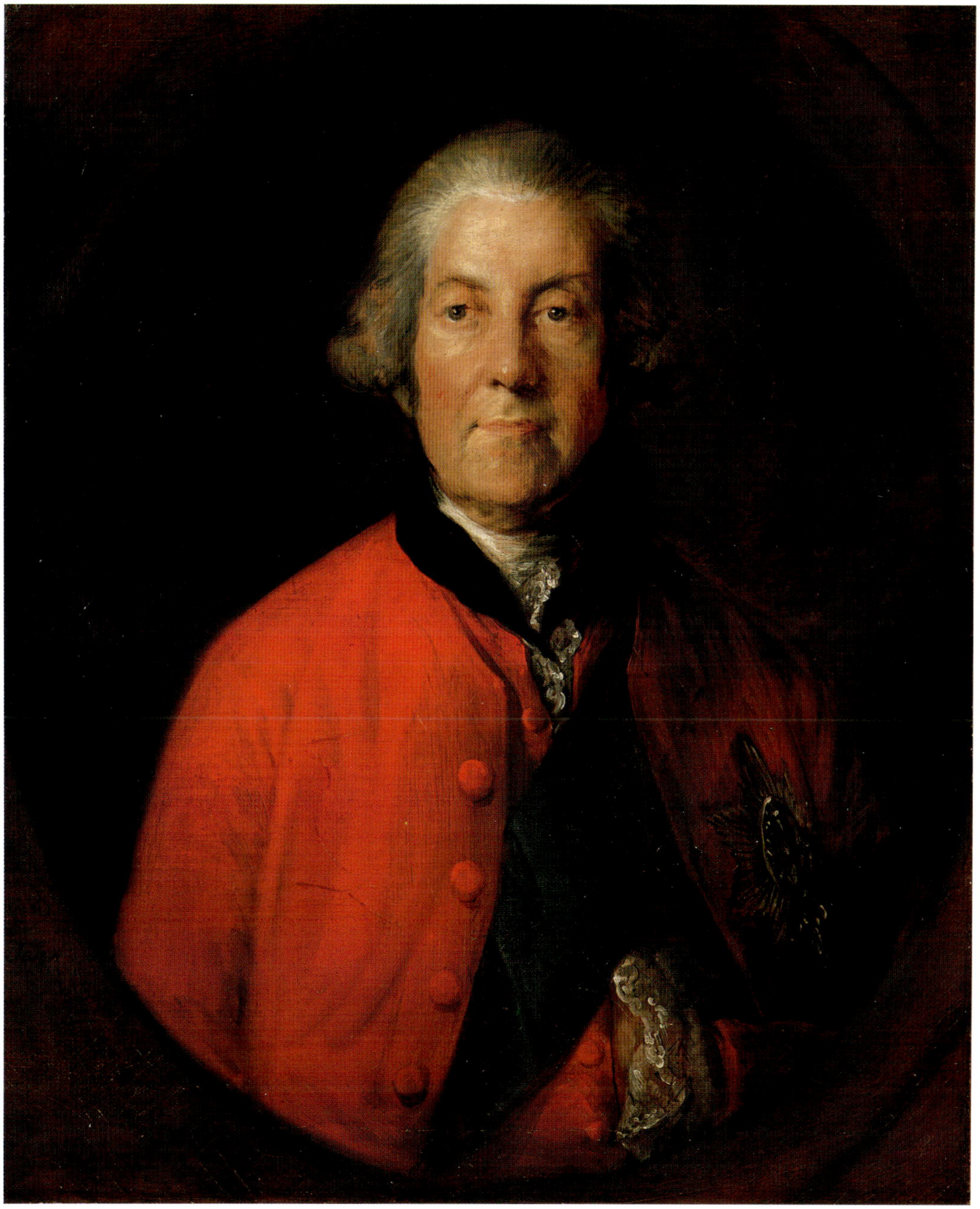

4th Duke of BEDFORD NPG 755

1 See *Wal. Corr.*, XXXVI, p.58, and XXIII, p.262.
2 See J. Hayes, *Connoisseur*, CLXVII, 1968, p.223.
3 J.D. Passavant, *Kunstreise durch England und Belgien*, 1833, p.178; Waagen, III, p.130 ('superior to many of the portraits by this master in faithful and careful execution').
4 SSB 92/68.
5 Descended from Edward Bray (d.1816); Whitwell Hall sale, Hollis & Webb, 17 April 1950, lot 194.
6 Christie's, 10 April 1797, lot 31, bt. Lord Malden (5th Earl of Essex); listed by Harding II, p.215, at Cassiobury.

ICONOGRAPHY

1747 Painting by George Knapton, halflength, with hat, the star of the Garter on his red coat. Society of Dilettanti.

c.1755 Unattributed painting, three-quarter length seated, wearing the Garter ribbon, with a drawing for the west front of Woburn Abbey (by Henry Flitcroft, commissioned in 1747, completed 1761). Woburn (cat. 1890, p.89 as in Tavistock town hall; illus. *Apollo*, LXXXII, 1965, p.437). Formerly attributed to Gainsborough.

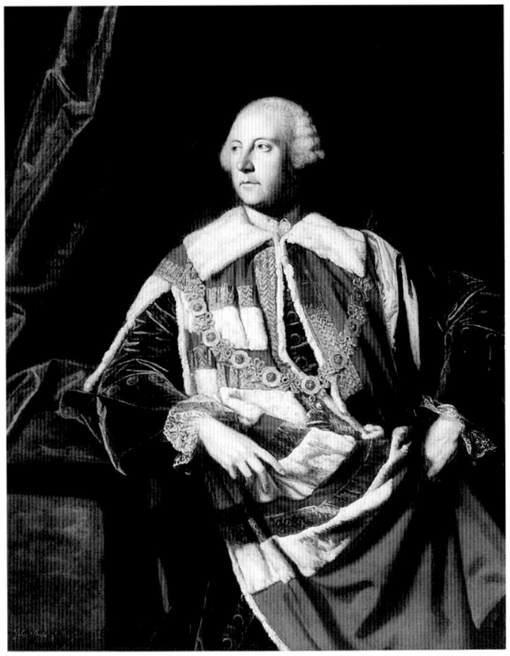

4th Duke of BEDFORD by Joshua Reynolds 1759-62 (Woburn Abbey)

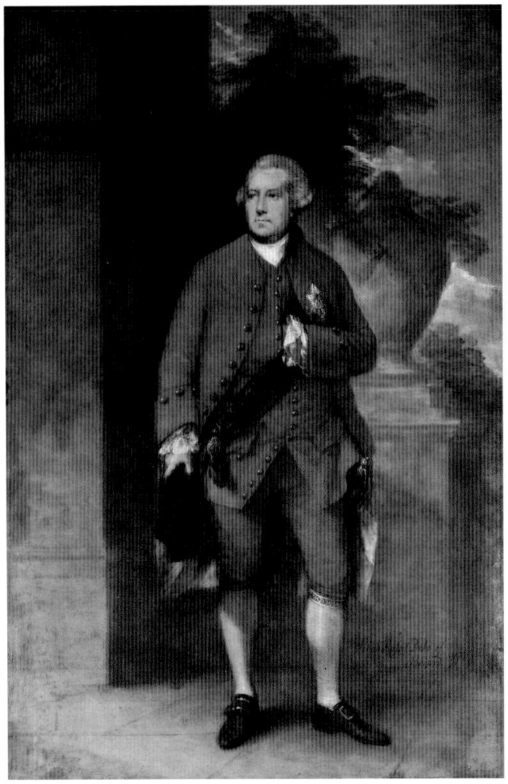

4th Duke of BEDFORD by Thomas Gainsborough 1768 (Trinity College, Dublin)

1759-62 Painting by Joshua Reynolds,* three-quarter length in Garter robes. Woburn Abbey (Mannings 2000, no.1560). Engraved H. Robinson 1832. A bust-length enamel copy by Henry Bone also at Woburn, the preliminary drawing dated 1823 in the NPG Bone albums (*Bone* 1999, no.48). A copy at Woburn (cat., 1890, no.236) once attributed to Francis Cotes, and two miniature copies by William Grimaldi of 1808 and 1810 are also recorded (Grimaldi 1873, pp.22, 24, nos.135, 163).

1764 Painting by Thomas Gainsborough, half length, wearing the ribbon and star of the Garter. Woburn Abbey (illus. *Connoisseur*, CLXVII, 1968, p.219). Engraved W. Greatbatch from a drawing by G.P. Harding 1842 (for Bedford's *Correspondence*); J. Thomson 1822, within an elaborate cartouche, lettered *Bentley pinxt.* (Orford, *Memoirs of George II*). Gainsborough painted two replicas, now untraced (see Waterhouse 1958, under no.54) and an old copy is also at Woburn (*Gainsborough* 1953, p.8).

1768 Painting by Thomas Gainsborough,* whole-length standing, wearing the ribbon and star of the Garter. Trinity College, Dublin, presented by the sitter 1768 on his appointment as chancellor. Miniature copy by Thomas Hickey, Dublin Mansion House. A three-quarter length version of 1769, his left hand in his waistcoat, at Woburn (illus. G.S. Thomson, *Russells in Bloomsbury*, 1940, p.240).

c.1770 Painting by Thomas Gainsborough, see NPG 755.

c.1770 Marble bust by Joseph Nollekens, wearing the ribbon and star of the Garter. Trinity College, Dublin, presented 1774 (illus. Crookshank & Webb 1990, p.116).

DOUBTFUL PORTRAIT

Miniature attributed to Veronica Stern, sold Christie's, 2 January 1970, lot 52, possibly shows the Duke's son, Lord Tavistock (in Italy 1761-62).

BENTHAM, Jeremy 1748-1832

Jurist and philosopher; visited his yr. bro. Samuel in Russia 1785; published *Introduction to the Principles of Morals and Legislation* 1789; settled at Forde Abbey, Somerset, 1814; his later writings included the *Rationale of Punishments and Rewards* (1825) and the *Constitutional Code* (1827, 1830).

'He is a small man. He stoops very much (he is eighty-four) and shuffles in his gait... His eye is restless, and there is a fidgety activity about him...' (Henry Crabb Robinson, 1831).

'Bentham's dress was peculiar out of doors. He ordinarily wore a narrow-rimmed straw-hat; from under which his long white hair fell on his shoulders, or was blown about by the winds. He had a plain brown coat, cut in quaker style - light brown cassimere breeches, over whose knees outside he usually exhibited a pair of white worsted stockings - list shoes he almost invariably used; and his hands were generally covered with merino-lined leather gloves. His neck was bare: he never went out without his stick 'dapple', for a companion' (Sir John Bowring, 1863).

Abbreviation

Fuller 1998: C. Fuller ed., *The Old Radical: Representations of Jeremy Bentham*, 1998 (University College, London)

196 THOMAS FRYE and studio 1760-62

Canvas 180.5 x 120.5 (71 x 47½) lined; the varnish is much discoloured and the surface heavily ironed; there are several repaired tears, e.g. below his left wrist, by his right thigh and across the left lower leg; many darkened retouchings; an inscription on the lining canvas, presumably copied from the original: *Jeremy Bentham/ Octob, 1760 Etatis Suae 13°.*

Grey(?) eyes, fair hair, wearing a pink suit and black academic gown; dark green curtain to the left and a green cloth on the table on which is an open bound manuscript illegibly inscribed; beneath it a book, *CICERO OPERA*; on the folded paper lying on the table is written Bentham's Latin ode on the death of George II and the accession of George III.[1]

Collections: Presented by the sitter's father to the 1st Marquess of Lansdowne 1784; bt. from a pawnbroker before 1832 by Sir John Bowring, by whom presented 1865.[2]

Exhibition: *Childhood*, Camden Arts Centre, 1967(29).

Reference: M. Wynne, *Burl. Mag.*, CXIV, 1972, pp.80, 84; Fuller 1998, p.25.

Thirty years after it was painted, this intriguing but indifferent celebration of Bentham's precocity was given by his father to the 1st Marquess of Lansdowne (formerly the 2nd Earl of Shelburne), the philosopher's close friend and patron. Bentham senior wrote to him explaining the circumstances of the portrait:[3]

> The Portrait, at least the capital Part of it, I mean the Head, was done by Frye, a Painter of no small eminence in his Time, and was then look'd upon as a very striking Resemblance, how little Likeness so ever there may appear to be now; but, by the Death of Frye before it was finished, the Under-Part was the work of a different, and I am sorry to say, an indifferent Hand. The two Stanzas inscribed on it were part of a Copy of Verses of my son's own composition in the Collections of the University Verses upon the occasion of the Death of the late King, and the accession of His present Majesty, and were introduced into the Picture for the purpose of denoting the Time when it was drawn, He then being a Member of Queen's College Oxford, to which he was admitted when he was but thirteen years of age, and where he took his Degree of A.B. at the age of sixteen, and his subsequent Degree of A.M. by the Time he was twenty; by which, as I was informed, he became the youngest Graduate that had ever been, in the regular Course of Education, at either of our Universities.
>
> With respect to the Violin which makes a Part of the Picture, it gives me occasion to mention that before he was five years old he wanted much to know the meaning of Musical Notes, and being told that they could not be explained but by some means of some Instrument a Friend made him a Present of a kind of Violin called a Kit, and as he had an Ear, he was soon capable of playing several Tunes.

Bentham senior's account is borne out by the softness of the head compared, for example, with the dreadful hands. The inscription copied on the verso, if accurate, might only refer to the painting of the head by Frye (who died on 3 April 1762); Bentham was in his thirteenth year 13 February 1760–12 February 1761; he had matriculated at Queen's College, Oxford, on 26 June, and his ode was completed on 28 November 1760.

1 Full text as given in *Bentham Works*, X, 1843, p.41, with, in square brackets, the parts legible in NPG 196:
In Obitum Serenissimi Regis Georgii 2di et Georgii 3ii Inaugorationem// [Eheu Geor]gi! Jamne Britannica/ [Gestare taedet sceptra piâ manu/Linguisque p]erculsum [Senatum/Et populum Patre] destitutum?/Te triste Fatum sustulit invidens/Tantum Britannis et decus et bonum;/Sed tu beatos inter, alte/ Sceptra tenens potiore regno./Quamvis ad instar fulminis, horrido/Gallum phalanges diruit impetu,/Semperque nobis a cruento/Praesidium fuit hoste tutum./Illumque Regem rudis Americus/Agnovit armis, indomitus prius;/Et Georgii longe remotus/Arma videns trepidavit Afer./[Ne spem Britanni ponite; protinus/En surgit alter Georgius; ille

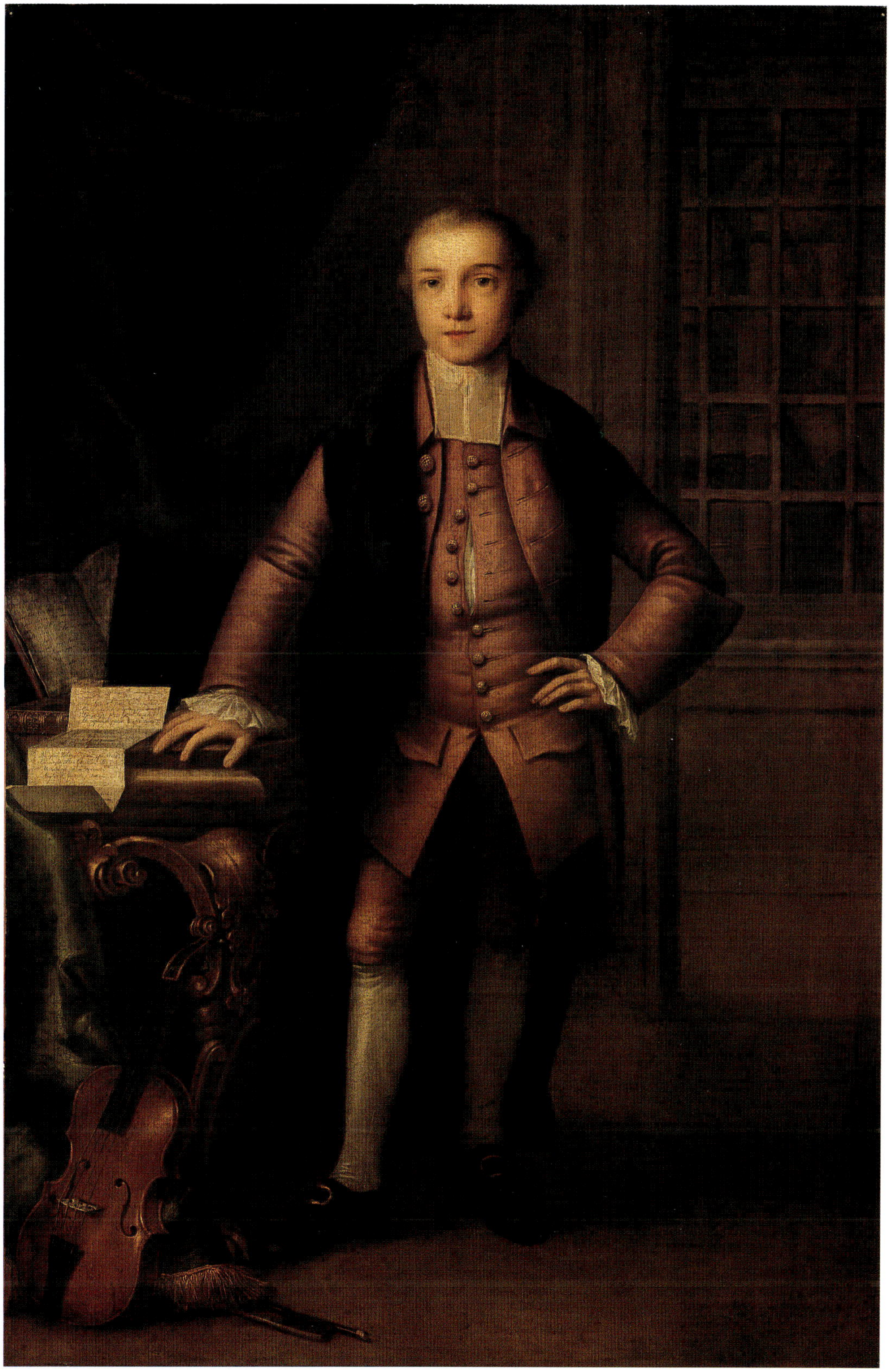

Jeremy BENTHAM NPG 196

avi/Virutibus, fama, et corona/Angliaca, potietur] haeres./Et si favebit prospera moribus/Fortuna prorsus labe carentibus,/Et rara Virtus Sanctitasque/Par pretium meritis habebunt,/Nil Georgii non perficient manus;/Redditque fessis Marte diutino/Pacem Britannis; atque clemens/Jure reget populum volentem//Jer. Bentham e Coll:Reg.Oxon:/28 Novembre, 1760.
[On the death of George II and the accession of George III: Alas poor George, the sceptre lies no longer in your blessed hand, government no longer hears your voice, your people have lost their father. Envious Fortune has taken you away, the glory of the British people. You take your sceptre to a greater, higher and blessed Kingdom. When we were struck, like lightning, by the fierce attacks of Gallic hordes, he protected us against a cruel enemy. Even the wilds of unconquered America acknowledged his arms, while distant Africa trembled before him. But despair not, Britannia, another George arises, a worthy heir to his father. Should Fortune preserve him from adversity, and Virtue and Goodness give just reward, he will prevail, bringing peace to a tired country and wise rule to his grateful people. Jeremy Bentham, Queen's College, Oxford, 28 November 1760].

2 Bowring was Bentham's literary executor, and the (most unprofessional) editor of the first edition of Bentham's *Works* 1838-43. He told Scharf (letter of 23 May 1865; NPG archive) 'I bought the picture at a pawnbrokers - it having at his [Bentham's] father's death ... [been] 'ignominiously expelled' [in Bentham's] phrase - but he recognised it - claimed it as an old acquaintance ...'. Scharf had first been approached by another Bentham pupil, Joseph Parkes (letter from Ramsgate, 22 May 1865; NPG archive), saying that he had 'written to Sir John Bowring to write the proper letter of offer...'.

3 Dated 24 November 1789; from the archive at Bowood, sold Christie's, 12 October 1994, lot 8. Lansdowne acknowledged the gift in a brief letter of 25 November (*Bentham Works*, X, 1843, p.225).

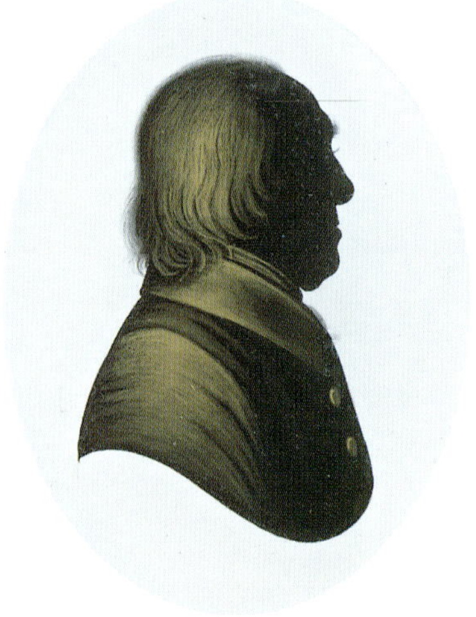

Jeremy BENTHAM NPG *3068*

3068 JOHN FIELD 1822

Plaster 5.7 (2¼) high, the profile in flat brown paint with highlights in gold powder; the label, formerly verso, of *Miers & Field / 111 The Strand, London,*[1] has been inscribed: *Jeremy Bentham a good likeness*[2] and, in an earlier hand: *From the Original./to his dear Niece,/ Sarah Jane Bentham/ 2.5.p.5 Aug 1823.*

Collections: Given by the sitter in 1823 to his niece Sarah Bentham (see above); her brother George Bentham (d.1884), whose collections passed to Sir Joseph and Lady Hooker who sold it, with other Bentham material, to the British Museum in 1897; transferred to the NPG in 1939.[3]

Exhibition: *Silhouette*, NPG, 1972(16).

Reference: Fuller 1998, p.55.

Another example in University College, London, is inscribed *J. Bentham Aged 75. 1822 / As good a likeness as can be conceived – done in this way.*[4] In 1823 Bentham's nephew George took three such silhouettes for his sisters in Paris, one of them evidently NPG 3068.[5]

In November 1822 Bentham had sent to Field and Miers hair for silhouette memorial rings (incorporating smaller images of the head alone); in his Will he left twenty-seven rings to his friends and employees, of which one, given to the Scottish publisher William Tait, is with University College.[6]

1 John Miers d.1821; Field then worked with his son as Miers and Field until 1830.
2 This hand recurs on the label NPG 3069, see Samuel Bentham.
3 For this provenance, see note under Samuel Bentham, NPG 3069 note 3.
4 Fuller 1998, p.55.
5 *Ibid.* A version with plaited hair beneath the truncation illus. McKechnie 1978, no.756, as c.1833, coll. M.A.H. Christie.
6 Illus. Fuller 1998, p.55, pl.vii.

413 HENRY WILLIAM PICKERSGILL 1829

Canvas 207 x 141 (81½ x 55½) lined 1895; a widespread drying craquelure has been partly retouched; the varnish is discoloured; the impress of an arch-topped slip apparent in the surface.

Blue eyes, white hair, wearing a claret-coloured coat with dark collar and cuffs, black breeches and stockings; a brown cloth on the table on which the books are lettered, from the left: *BENTH[AM] ON MORAL AND LEGISLA[TION]*, *DIARIO[S] DAS COR[TES E] CONSTIT[UINTES] DA NACA[O] PORTUG[EZA] TOMO I*, and *LOCKE*.

Collections: Purchased from the artist's sale, Christie's, 16 July 1875, lot 351.

Engraving: C. Fox 1838 (bust only).[1]

Exhibitions: RA 1829(127); NPE 1868(266); *Romantic Icons*, Grasmere, 1999(13).

Reference: Fuller 1998, pp.30-31.

Of the books displayed, Locke had long been Bentham's mentor ('without Locke, I could have known nothing'); the Portuguese journals had been sent to him on receipt of a Portuguese edition of his works and as a mark of respect while he was drafting material for a new constitutional code for Portugal; his *Moral Legislation* (the second edition of which appeared in 1823) had assumed considerable importance for him within his writings.

NPG 413 was described by Bowring as 'of all the pictures painted [of Bentham], ... incomparably the best. It is distinguished, indeed, by every kind of excellence'.[2] A reduced version, formerly owned by Sir John Bowring, was acquired by University College, London, in 1965.[3]

1 The steel engraved plate is in the NPG archive, presented by Sir William Thiselton-Dyer, J.D. Hooker's son-in-law, in 1892.
2 *Bentham Works*, X, 1843, p.536.
3 Illus. Fuller 1998, no.5, pl.iii and cover.

ICONOGRAPHY

For an inclusive account, see Fuller 1998.

1760-62 Painting by Thomas Frye, see NPG 196.

1789-90 Painting probably by Gainsborough Dupont, half length. University College, London, presented by Sir John Bowring 1866 (illus. Fuller 1998, pl.iii). Bentham mentioned sitting in London to an unnamed artist in December 1789 (*Corr. of Jeremy Bentham*, IV, 1981, p.115) and in 1843 the portrait belonged to Bowring (*Bentham Works*, X, 1843, p.223) who in 1866 attached a discursive label to the verso describing, *inter alia*, the history of the Frye portrait, NPG 196.

1805 Bust of 'Bentham Esq' by Peter Turnerelli, exhibited RA 1805(740).

1822 Silhouette by John Field, see NPG 3068.

On 17 February 1823 Bentham wrote that a second edition of his Moral Legislation *(see* NPG *413 above) was about to be published, 'in which is a portrait which they made me sit for. It seems well engraved: I have seen it; and people say it is like ... The first of March, or the first of April, comes out a number of the European Magazine, with another portrait of me by another hand. Considerable expectations are entertained of this likeness. When you see a copy of a print of 'the House of Lords at the time of the Queen's Trial', in hand by Bowyer, ... you will, if Bowyer does not deceive me, see the phiz of your old friend ... No fewer than five times, within little more than a year, have I been plagued with people, to waste in this way '* (Bentham, *Works*, X, 1843, pp.535-36).

1823 Drawing by James Stephanoff, engraved J.G. Murray 1823, *The House of Lords, during the Important Investigation of 1820* (the trial of Queen Caroline), including Bentham (standing far right) as one of 140 attendants (illus. Walker *Regency*, II, pl.1590). A fictitious grouping.

1823 Painting by William Derby, half-length seated, engraved J. Thomson 1823 (*European Mag.*; illus. *John Joseph Merlin*, Kenwood, 1985, A11). According to Bowring the portrait was 'not a succesful one' (Bentham, *Works*, X, 1843, p.536).

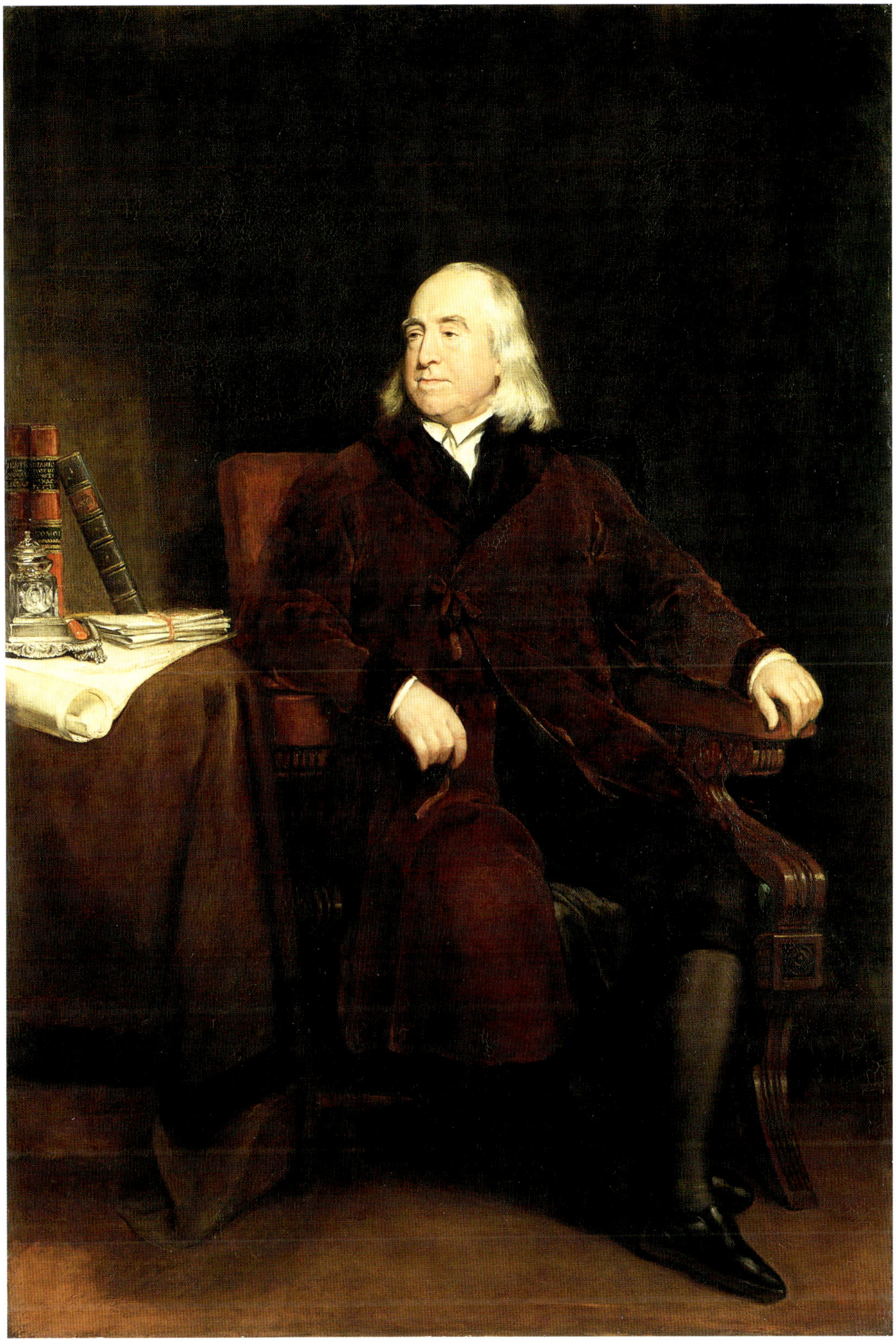

Jeremy BENTHAM NPG 413

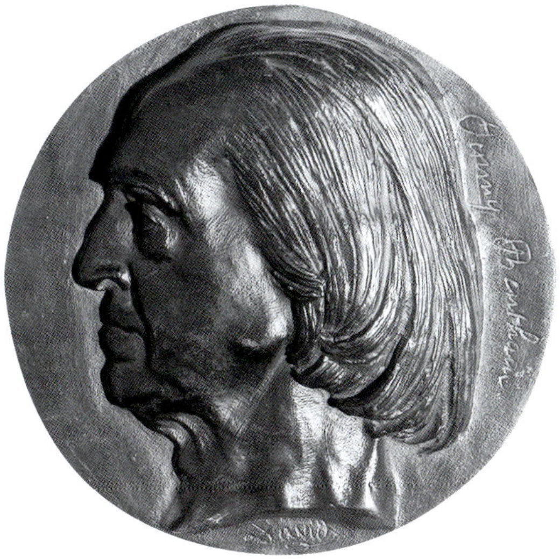

Jeremy BENTHAM *by David d'Angers 1828 (Christie's)*

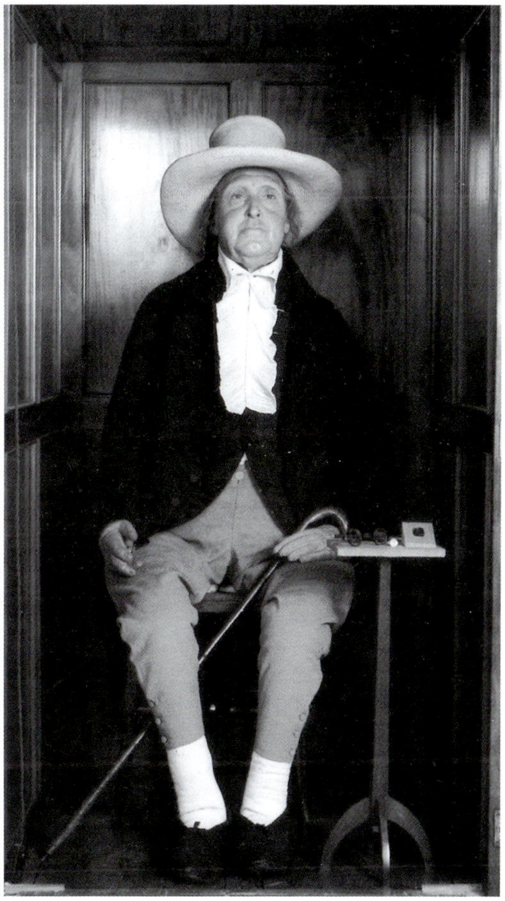

Jeremy BENTHAM, *the auto-icon 1832 (University College, London)*

1823 Painting by W.H. Worthington, half length, engraved by the artist 1823 (illus. Dawson 2000, p.40); S. Freeman 1832 and S. Leith 1843.

1825 Painting by Aimée Pagès, half length. Private collection (from Christie's, 26 June 1914, lot 41). Anon. lithograph 1825 (*Jérémie Bentham*). Bentham, who had been made an honorary French citizen in 1792, was in Paris September-October 1825 and on 1 November he wrote that the portrait 'is to be exhibited one year in Paris, the next in London and then lapse to me' (Fuller 1998, p.38).

1825 Marble bust by P-J. David d'Angers, undraped, inscribed: *A JEREMIE BENTHAM / PLVRIORVM MAXIMA FELICITAS*. Senate House, University of London. Exhibited RA 1829(1180). A bronze belongs to University College, London (illus. Fuller 1998, pp.11, 39) and a plaster is in the musée des Beaux-Arts, Angers. Copied as a medallion by John Wilson (the partner of William Tassie), exhibited RA 1833(1047), see Gray 1894, no.35. Gray also recorded a version in Wedgwood paste.

c.1825 Unattributed bronze bust, with his own long hair. British Museum (MLA 1897.4.15.1; Dawson 2000, no.6) bought in 1897 with other Bentham material from Sir Joseph Hooker (see NPG 3068). Resembling the engraving by Worthington (see 1823 above).

1827 Drawing by R.M. Sully, half length. Harvard Law School. Engraved anon. (illus. Fuller 1998, p.42). Other versions include a traced copy, also in the Harvard Law School, and an engraving by C.W. Appleby showing bookshelves behind. A second drawing by Sully made in 1827, a slight sketch of Bentham seated writing, is in the British Museum (1909.6.1.1; illus. Fuller 1998, p.42).

1828 Bronze medallion by P-J. David d'Angers* (J.G. Reinis, *Portrait Medallions of David d'Angers*, 1999, no.69).

1829 Painting by H.W. Pickersgill, see NPG 413.

Posthumous

1832 Death mask. A cast in the Department of Anatomy, University of Edinburgh, from the Edinburgh Phrenological Society (*Death Masks and Life Masks*, Edinburgh University, [1988], p.8).

1832 Bentham's mummified head is in University College, London (illus. N. Harte & J. North, *The World of University College*, 1979, p.9).

1832 Drawing by H.H. Pickersgill, of Bentham's corpse, engraved W. Taylor (illus. Fuller 1998, p.51), see below. H.H. Pickersgill was the son of H.W. Pickersgill, see NPG 413.

1832 Auto-icon,* Bentham's clothed skeleton with a wax head, seated, with a stick, wearing a high-crowned hat. University College, London, since 1850. Bentham's Will directed that his body should first be the subject of a lecture, then dissected and finally preserved, according to his essay 'Auto-Icon; or, Farther uses of the Dead to the Living'; the process was completed by 1833, the body set in the attitude 'in which I am sitting when engaged in thought' (see Fuller 1998, pp.9-14, 51-52).

1832 Commemorative medal by T. Halliday (Brown 1980, no.1568).

1837 Drawing by Margaret Gillies, half length, engraved for the *Monthly Repository* 1837 (illus. C. Yeldham, *Gillies*, 1997, pp.24, 156). Probably made from the auto-icon which was kept in her studio for sometime before 1850.

1837 Drawing by G.F. Watts made from the auto-icon (see 1832), seated beneath a tree. Queen's College, Oxford (Poole, II, p.134; illus. Fuller 1998, p.53). Exhibited NPE 1868(250). Engraved J. Posselwhite c.1835 (half length; illus. Fuller 1998, p.54). Watts later described this as having been painted when he was 'a mere lad' (MS notes by Mrs Watts; NPG archive).

From his drawing Watts made a sketch in oil (University College, London; illus. Fuller 1998, p.20, pl.vi) and there are two finished paintings: one sold Christie's, 8 June 1956, lot 126 (exactly agreeing with the drawing), the other, with a slightly different waistcoat and showing binding at the bottom of the trousers, last sold Christie's, 14 July 1994, lot 88.

1869 Statue by Joseph Durham. Burlington House, London (rear façade; illus. Fuller 1998, p.46).

1922 Mural by Henry Tonks, *The Founders of University College*, showing Bentham receiving the plans for University College from the architect William Wilkins (a fictitious episode). Flaxman Gallery, University College, London. An elaborate tempera sketch and several preparatory drawings also belong to the College (illus. Fuller 1998, pp.48-49, pl.v).

DOUBTFUL PORTRAITS

Painting by Andrew Geddes in Queen's College, Oxford (Poole, III, p.134), and a version in a private collection, possibly show William Tooke (1777-1863).

BENTHAM, Sir Samuel Johnson, Kt 1757-1831

Naval engineer, yr. bro. of Jeremy Bentham; worked in Russia 1780-91 as a naval engineer; Potemkin made him colonel in 1784, and brigadier-general and Kt of St George 1789;[1] returned to England 1791 as an inspector for the navy office; revisited Russia 1805-07 and on his return became commissioner of the navy.

1 In his obituary *GM*, CI, 1831, ii, p.91, he was described as 'Sir Samuel Bentham K.S.G. ... He was allowed to wear the insignia of the order of St George of Russia, 16 July 1789'. The ribbon of this Order was orange with three black stripes.

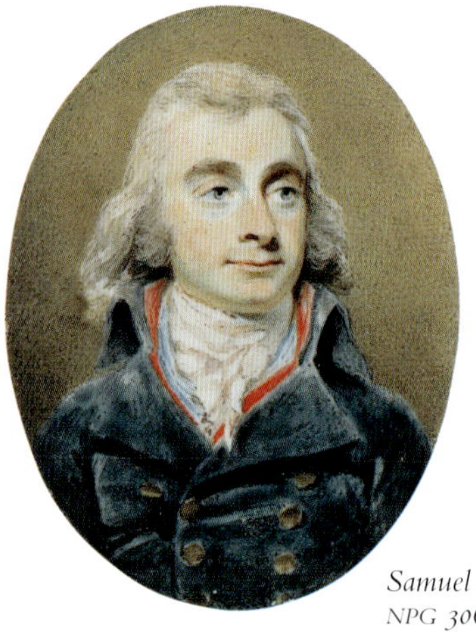

Samuel BENTHAM
NPG 3069

3069 HENRY EDRIDGE c.1795-1800

Watercolour and bodycolour on ivory 6.2 x 4.7 (2½ x 1⅞); white in the cravat has darkened. An early-nineteenth-century ink label removed from the verso inscribed: *Samuel Bentham* with above and below added in ink,[1] apparently reinforcing older pencil inscriptions: *Sir* [before Samuel Bentham] [*Lady?*] *Hookers/ Brother of Jeremy Bentham/ Father of G. Bentham FRS/ Pres. Linn. Soc./ by Eldridge* [sic].

Blue eyes, grey powdered hair, wearing a white neck-cloth, and blue coat over a scarlet waistcoat with a pale blue lining; warm ochre background.

Collections: According to the inscription (see above): the sitter's son, George Bentham,[2] whose collections passed to Sir Joseph and Lady Hooker who sold it, with other Bentham material to the British Museum in 1897;[3] transferred to the NPG in 1939.

Reference: Binyon, II, p.122, no.52.

A slightly larger, and possibly slightly later, miniature by Edridge is in the Victoria and Albert Museum, see below.

1 This hand recurs on the label of Jeremy Bentham NPG 3068.
2 George Bentham (1800-84), botanist, president of the Linnaean Society 1861-74; in 1854 he presented his family collections and books to Kew, where he worked with both Sir Walter and Sir Joseph Hooker.
3 With much Bentham correspondence (*Corr. of Jeremy Bentham*, III, 1971, pp. xvii-xviii) and see also the painting of 1784 listed in the iconography below and, for Jeremy Bentham, NPG 3068 and the bronze of c.1825.

1075 see Groups, *Men of Science living in 1807-08* by JOHN GILBERT, FREDERICK SKILL and WILLIAM & ELIZABETH WALKER 1858-62

ICONOGRAPHY

1784 Painting by a Russian artist,* half length wearing the dark green coat with scarlet facings of a Russian lieutenant colonel. National Maritime Museum (GH 232); sent by the sitter from Russia in 1784 to his father in England, and presented to Greenwich Hospital 1895 by Sir Joseph Hooker (by whom previously offered to the NPG in 1894; TSB 38/54).

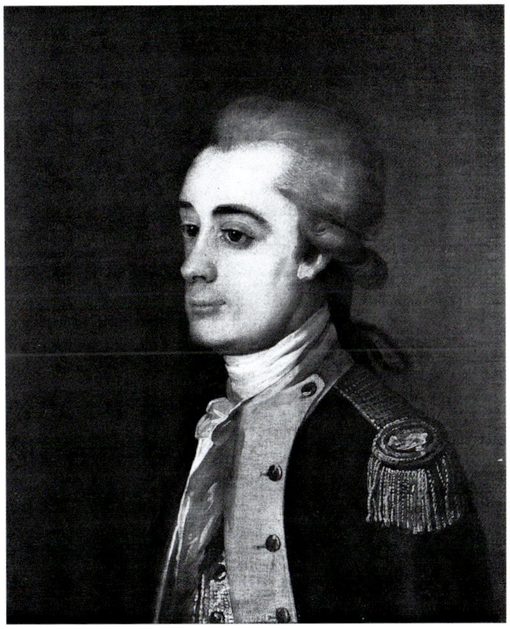

Samuel BENTHAM by an unknown Russian artist 1784 (National Maritime Museum, London; Greenwich Hospital Collection)

c.1795-1800 Miniature by Henry Edridge, see NPG 3069.

c.1795-1800 Miniature by Henry Edridge, bust-length oval, dark coat, his own white hair (a little shorter than in NPG 3069). Victoria and Albert Museum (47.1886; illus. Rackham 1930, fig.131). Originally presented by the sitter's widow, Mary, Lady Bentham (d.1858), to the Museum of the Commissioners of Patents, South Kensington (*Patents Cat.*, 1858, no.57) before transfer to the Victoria and Albert Museum; see Groups NPG 1075.

Richard BENTLEY
NPG 5885

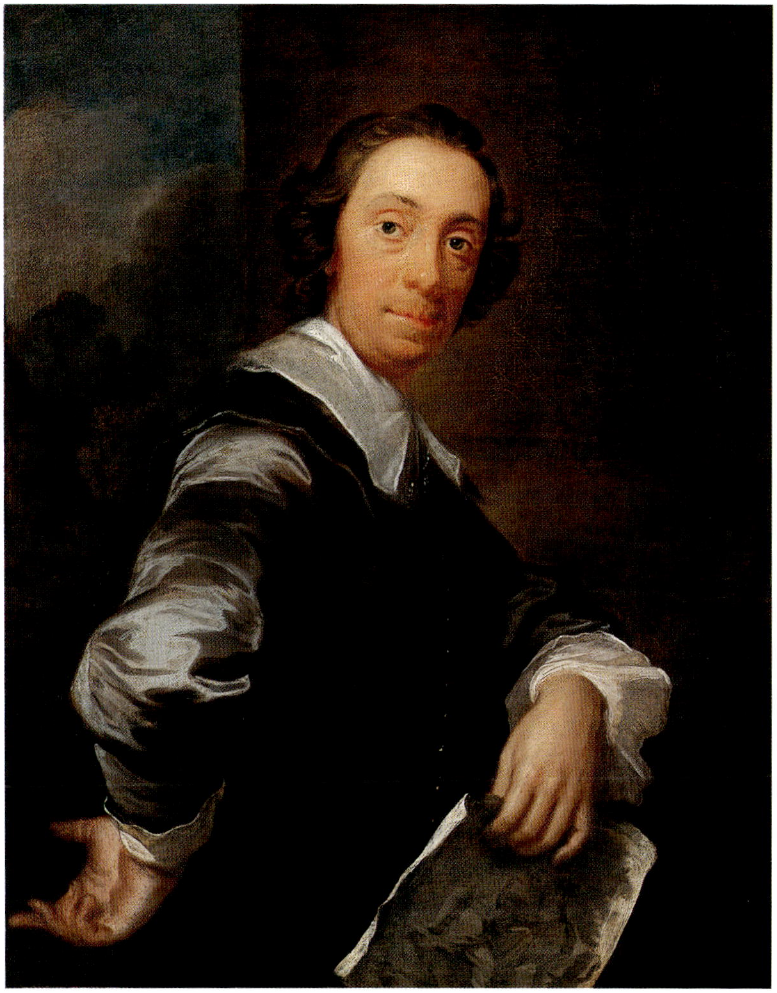

BENTLEY, Richard 1708-82

Designer, illustrator, occasional author, s. of the classical scholar Dr Richard Bentley; one of Horace Walpole's Committee of Taste at Strawberry Hill 1750-61.

5885 JOHN GILES ECCARDT 1753

Canvas 41 x 33.5 (16¼ x 13¼) lined, cleaned 1986; dated *1753* bottom right, below shield of arms; the surface is rather rubbed; prominent craquelure behind right shoulder and by his chest; pentimenti show the cloak originally fell down behind his right arm and that the collar and the fingers of left hand have been slightly modified.

Blue eyes, fair hair; wearing Van Dyck dress, a silver blue tunic beneath a buttoned grey cloak; the drawing in his left hand is a design for Melancholy drawn for the illustrated edition of Gray's *Odes* (see below); bottom right is the Bentley shield of arms (*or, three bends sable*).

Collections: Horace Walpole, 4th Earl of Orford; Strawberry Hill sale, 19th day, 22 May 1842, lot 31, bt. Money; 9th Earl of Waldegrave sale, Christie's, 10 February 1900, lot 35, bt. Renton; 'the Joel family until c.1950';[1] sold Sotheby's, 9 July 1986, lot 42, bt. Leggatt for the NPG.

Engravings: J. Heath 1798 (oval); W. Greatbach 1857 (both reversed and omitting his right hand and the shield of arms).[2]

One of six Eccardt portraits commissioned by Horace Walpole for Strawberry Hill (see Orford, NPG 988). They hung together in the blue bed-chamber, in which the chimney-piece was designed by Bentley.[3] Walpole described NPG 5885 as 'Mr Richard Bentley; from Vandyck. He holds in one hand his own design of the figure of Melancholy drawn by him for the edition of Mr Gray's Odes'.[4] Eccardt took his composition from Van Dyck's portrait of Adam de Coster as engraved by Pieter de Jode the younger[5] and the alterations to the cloak described above modified Van Dyck's design. Bentley's illustrations for Gray's *Odes* were prepared in 1751-52 and published in March 1753; his drawing of Melancholy, the tail piece for the *Hymn to Adversity* and much admired by Gray,[6] is now in the Lewis Walpole Library, Farmington, Conn.

A small watercolour copy by G.P. Harding (omitting the shield of arms), was sold Bonham's, 30 June 1999, lot 126.[7]

1 As cited in the 1986 sale cat.
2 Both illus.: *Wal.Corr.*, XXXV, f.p.643 (Heath); *Walpole and Strawberry Hill*, Orleans House, Twickenham, 1980, p.55 (Greatbach). See also note 7.
3 Engraved T. Morris for Walpole's *Description of Strawberry Hill*, 1784, f.p.28.
4 *Ibid.*, p.29.
5 New Hollstein *Van Dyck*, II, 2002, no.56.
6 *Wal.Corr.*, IX, p.143.
7 From the collection of Mrs Richard Bentley (widow of the publisher Richard Bentley, 1794-1871); almost certainly used by Greatbach for his 1857 engraving, see above.

BENTLEY, Thomas 1730-80

Merchant, scholar, and potter; travelled in France and Italy 1753; settled as a merchant in Liverpool 1754, where he helped found the Warrington Academy 1759; a friend of Joseph Priestley, who admired his 'excellent taste' and 'improved understanding', even though he was 'but an unbeliever'; from 1769 the business partner of Josiah Wedgwood, running the London showroom.

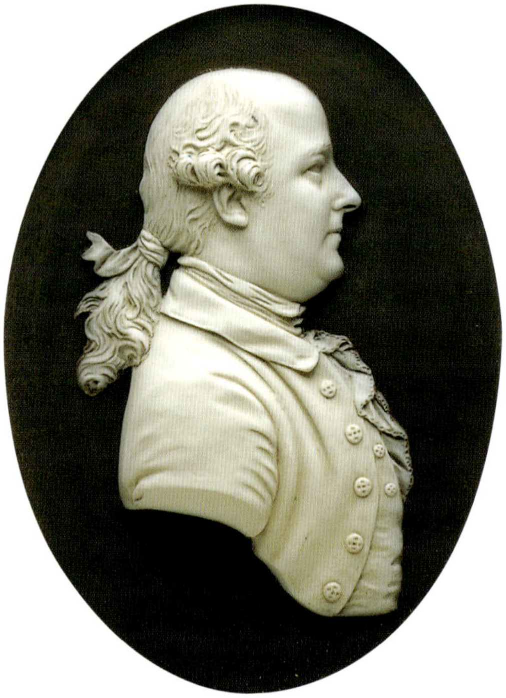

Thomas BENTLEY NPG *1949*

1949 after JOACHIM SMITH [1773-74]

Modern cast from original Wedgwood mould, white jasper on black dip 9 (3½) high. Stamped verso: *WEDGWOOD BENTLEY* and *BB637*.

Collections: Presented by Josiah Wedgwood & Sons 1922.

Exhibition: *Regency Portraits*, Kenwood, 1986.

Modelled by Joachim Smith as a companion piece to a medallion of Josiah Wedgwood. Most of the surviving examples (for example in the Wedgwood Museum, Barlaston, and in Manchester City Art Gallery) are with black dip.[1]

1 Reilly 1973, p.60, and 1994, p.14.

ICONOGRAPHY

1773 Painting by J.F. Rigaud,* three-quarter length, reading Socrates; on a table lie plaques of Socrates and the Three Graces with books including Xenophon's *Memorabilia* ('contemplating the analogy between moral and natural beauty'). Wedgwood Museum, Barlaston. Exhibited RA 1773(249). Formerly attributed to Joseph Wright. Version in the Walker AG, Liverpool (2548; *Wal. Soc.*, L, 1984, p.54, fig.11).

1773-74 Wedgwood medallion by Joachim Smith, see NPG 1949.

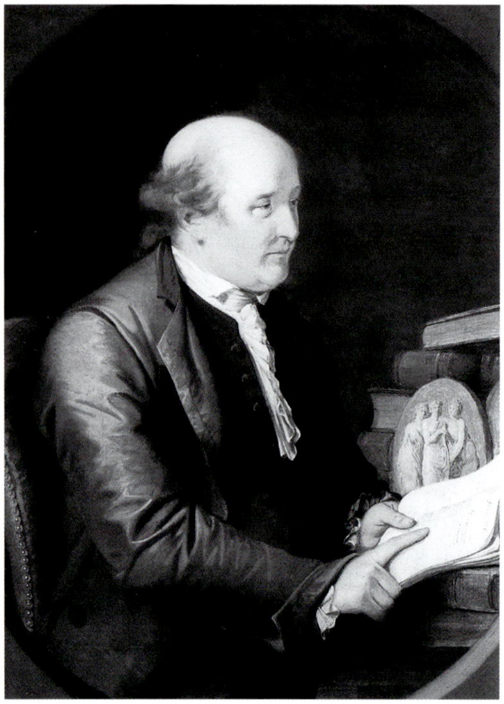

Thomas BENTLEY by J.F. Rigaud 1773 (Wedgwood Museum, Barlaston)

1778 Wedgwood medallion, attributed to William Hackwood; a second version differs only in the fall of the hair round the neck (both illus. Reilly 1973, pp.60-61).

1780 Medallion portrait on a monument by Thomas Scheemakers. St Nicholas, Chiswick (illus. A. Burton, *Josiah Wedgwood*, 1976, f.p.177). Commissioned by Josiah Wedgwood and probably derived from the Wedgwood medallion of c.1780.

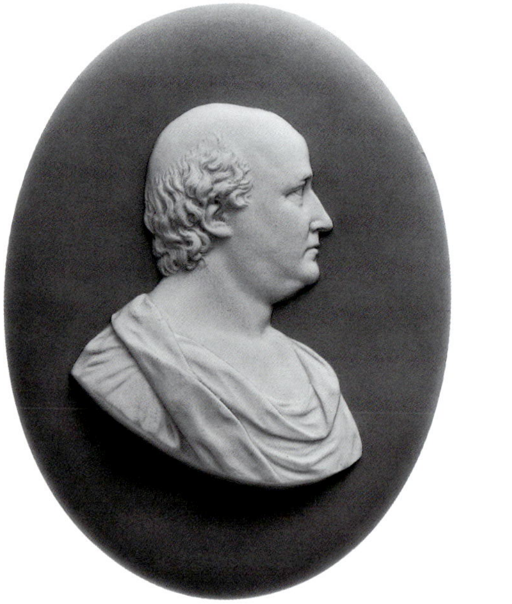

Thomas BENTLEY Wedgwood c.1780 (Wedgwood Museum, Barlaston)

c.1780 Wedgwood medallion,* attributed to William Hackwood; the head balder than in the 1778 medallion; possibly a memorial (Reilly 1973, p.61).

Another Wedgwood medallion, considerably larger than the preceding, recorded in the Wedgwood oven book in October 1782 (Reilly 1973, p.61, and 1994, p.357).

A painting by William Caddick was listed in the collection of James Boardman of Liverpool in 1851 (*DNB*).

BERRY, Mary 1763-1852

Occasional writer and traveller; Horace Walpole's literary executrix; her *Works* (1844) included plays and historical studies; from 1791 she lived with her sister Agnes (1764-1852) at Little Strawberry Hill, a house given them by Walpole.

'[she] understands Latin, and is a perfect Frenchwoman in her language ... sweet, with fine dark eyes, that are very lively when she speaks, with a symmetry of face that is the more interesting from being pale ... [her face] is formed for a sentimental novel but is ten times fitter for a fifty times better thing, genteel comedy' (Horace Walpole, 1788).

'[She] has an interesting and engaging manner. She appears to be 2 or 3 and thirty. Indifferent health is expressed in her countenance' (Joseph Farington, 1793).

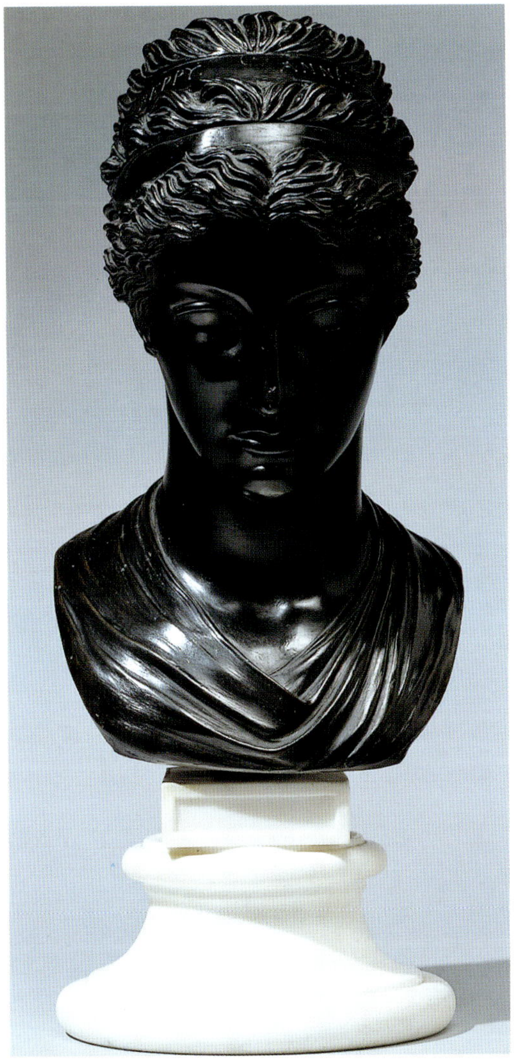

BERRY NPG *6395*

6395 ANNE SEYMOUR DAMER [1793]

Bronze bust with black patinated surface 34.5 (13½) high, on a marble plinth 11.5 (4½) high, in two sections; inscribed on socle: *ANNA.SEYMOUR.DAMER/ FECIT.*; the upper hair band inscribed in Greek letters: *MARIA BERRY ANNA SEYMOUR DAMER EP.* [*epoiese*].

Collections: A 'Lady of title'; Christie's, 10 December 1991, lot 91, bt. Eric Clapton; Christie's, 1 July 1997, lot 85, bt. Hazlitt, Gooden & Fox for the NPG.

Artist and sitter were close friends within Horace Walpole's circle; a drawing, attributed to Cosway, shows them both reading in the library at Strawberry Hill.[1] Damer's self portrait of 1778 in the Uffizi, Florence, displays an earnest classicism,[2] and NPG 6395, with its classical Greek references in style and inscription, similarly emphasises Mary Berry's *gravitas* (it was suggested that she might have lacked a certain 'playfulness of thought').[3]

NPG 6395 clearly derives from the terracotta bust on a square base, dated 1793, now in a private collection.[4] Horace Walpole had a terracotta at Strawberry Hill which he first mentioned in 1795[5] and at different times listed as 'a bust in terra cotta of Miss Mary Berry by Mrs Damer 1794',[6] and a 'Bust of Miss Mary Berry, in terra-cotta, most [?]beautiful, 1795'.[7] Was it the 'bronzed bust of Mary Berry, by Mrs Damer', in the Strawberry Hill sale, 22nd day, 19 May 1842, lot 22?[8] Meanwhile in 1840 Greatbach had engraved a similar looking bust (with the square socle) from the collection of Sir Alexander Johnston.[9]

1 Sotheby's, 14 March 1956, lot 626.
2 Illus. Walker, *Regency*, II, pl.338.
3 Lady Theresa Lewis, *Journal and Corr. of Miss Berry*, 1865, III, p.515.
4 Illus. *The Grace of Friendship*, ed. V. Surtees, 1995, f.p.148.
5 22 August 1795; he told Mary Berry that he had breakfasted 'in the closet where your bust is' (*Wal. Corr.*, XII, p.144).
6 See *Wal. Corr.*, XLIII, p.155 (the comment made in Walpole's extra-illustrated *Description of Strawberry Hill* 1784 now in the Lewis Walpole Library, Farmington).
7 In his 'Book of Visitors at Strawberry Hill 1784-1796' (*Wal. Corr.*, XII, p.274).
8 *DNB* (Berry) stated Walpole had 'a white marble bust' of Mary Berry by Damer.
9 Illus. *Wal. Corr.*, XII, f.p.144. Sir Alexander Johnston (1775-1849), distinguished colonial lawyer, owned other Horace Walpole items engraved by Greatbach, see Orford iconography 1755-59. W. Greatbach made his plate from a drawing by G.P. Harding (reissued 1857 with Damer's name replacing Harding's).

ICONOGRAPHY

c.1771-72 Painting by Johann Zoffany, Mary and Agnes standing in a park with a large dog (illus. Williamson 1920, f.p.158). Private collection. Engraved H. Adlard 1865, *from a painting in the possession of Colonel Ferguson of Raith*. Painted when the artist was a neighbour of the Berrys at Chiswick (see *Zoffany* 1977, no.70).

before 1784 Watercolour by Agnes Berry, Mary and Agnes in the grounds at Strawberry Hill (listed in H. Walpole, *Description of Strawberry Hill*, 1784, p.95).

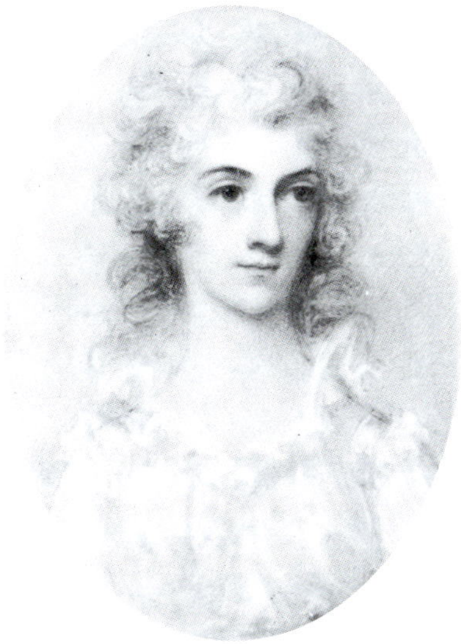

BERRY by Anne Foldsone 1790 (Private Collection)

1790 Miniature by Anne Foldsone (Mrs Anne Mee),★ bust-length oval in white dress. Private collection, from the Strawberry Hill sale, 22nd day, lot 60 'A pair of miniature Portraits of the Misses Agnes and Mary Berry, 1790, signed H.W. by Miss Foltson' bt. in (illus. *The Grace of Friendship*, ed. V. Surtees, 1995, f.p.148; Riccio 2000, p.132, on both occasions

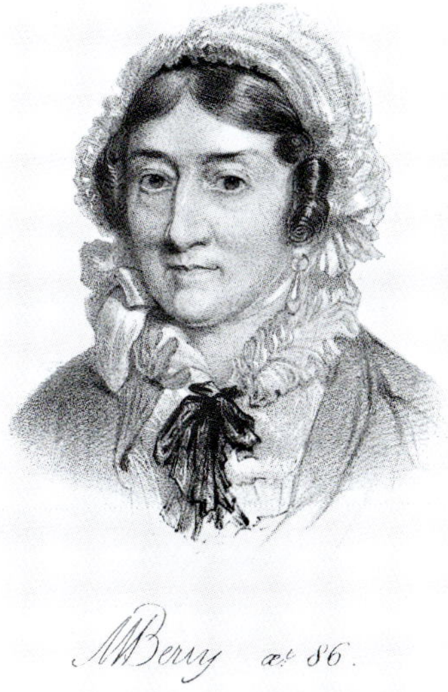

BERRY H. Robinson 1850 after J.R. Swinton (NPG D 18480)

described as in the British Museum). Engraved H. Adlard 1865. The companion piece of Agnes Berry in the same collection. Commissioned by Walpole just before the sisters departed for Italy in October 1790, but he did not receive them until October 1791 (by which time the artist had become for him 'a prodigy of dishonest impertinence'; *Wal. Corr.*, XI, p.193).

1793 Bust by Anne Seymour Damer, see NPG 6395.

1797 Watercolour by Anna Tonelli, oval. Private collection; Strawberry Hill sale, 11th day, 6 May 1842, lot 69 'Portrait of Two Young Ladies, by Mrs Tonelli', bt. in. Presumably the portrait exhibited by Tonelli RA 1797(435, *Portraits of Two young Ladies*). The artist had visited Strawberry Hill in July 1794 (*Wal. Corr.*, XII, p.246).

1800 Miniature by Mrs Francis Wheatley, exhibited RA 1800(835).

c.1800 Wax by Samuel Percy, half length with bonnet. Victoria and Albert Museum (A.14.1970; illus. *Pickpocketing the Rich*, Bath, 2002, p.24).

1816 Drawn and engraved by F. Gerard, three-quarter length seated with a straw hat (pub. Drouart, Paris).

1850 Drawing by J.R. Swinton, half length, wearing a bonnet, engraved H. Robinson 1850;* anon. 1851. An anon. seated three-quarter length portrait appears to use the same head (illus. L. Melville, *Berry Papers*, 1914, f.p.196).

DOUBTFUL PORTRAITS

Miniature by George Engleheart of c.1795-1800, Richmond Borough Council (illus. Williamson 1897, f.p.12; a pendant to an Agnes Berry in the same collection); version with A.J. Fink, Baltimore, in 1950; drawing by Paul Sandby at Windsor (illus. *Wal. Corr.*, XI, f.p.12; Oppé 1947, no.288); engraving by H. Adlard 1865, 'from a Miniature in the possession of Viscountess Palmerston'.

BESSBOROUGH, Frederick Ponsonby, 3rd Earl of 1758-1844

Whig politician; sty. Viscount Duncannon before suc. as 3rd Earl of Bessborough 1793; m. 1780 Henrietta, dau. of the 1st Earl Spencer; MP 1780-93; an admirer of Fox, under whom he served briefly as a lord of the Admiralty in 1782 and 1783; an avid print collector and a member of Brooks's; 'a man of the most amiable and mild manners' (*CP*).

2076 see Groups, *Mr Fox and his Friends* by WILLIAM LANE c.1813

999 see Groups, *The Trial of Queen Caroline* 1820 by GEORGE HAYTER 1820-23

ICONOGRAPHY

1773 Pastel by J-E. Liotard,* half-length seated. Stansted Park. Exhibited RA 1773(176).

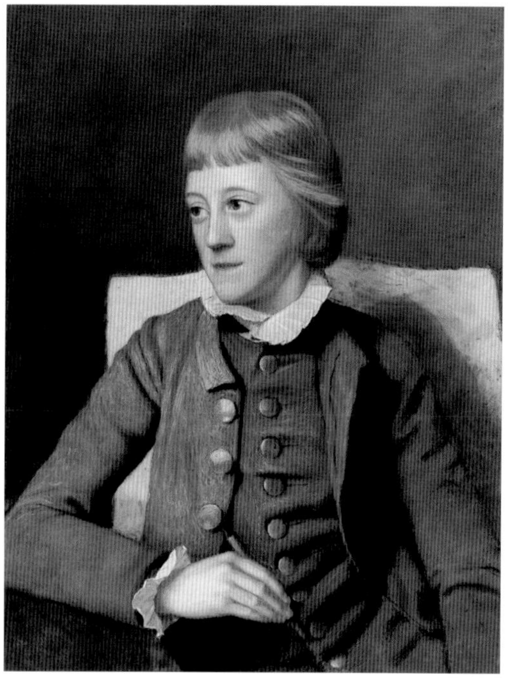

3rd Earl of BESSBOROUGH by J-E. Liotard 1773 (Stansted Park Foundation)

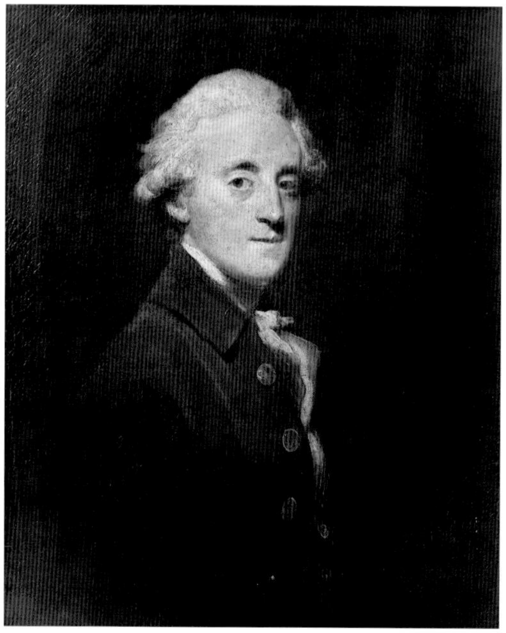

3rd Earl of BESSBOROUGH by Joshua Reynolds 1785 (Althorp)

1785 Painting by Joshua Reynolds,* half length. Althorp (Mannings 2000, no.1459). Miniature versions by W.R. Birch, in a blue coat (Sotheby's, Stansted Park, 5 October 1999, lot 465), and Richard Cosway, in a green coat (Victoria and Albert Museum, P.44.1910; illus. *Cosway* 1995, pl.23).

c.1785-90 Unattributed painting, mounted on a black horse. Private collection (illus. J. Ponsonby, *The Ponsonby Family*, 1929, p.102).

1811 Portrait by William Lane, exhibited RA 1811(360). Probably the source for the head in Lane's *Mr Fox and his Friends* of c.1813, see Groups NPG 2076.

1820-23 Painting by George Hayter, *The Trial of Queen Caroline*, see Groups NPG 999.

DOUBTFUL PORTRAIT

Engraving, *Frederick Viscount Duncannon, drawn from the life by W.H. Brown Engraved C. Warren* 1791 (*The Senator*) appears to be a copy of the 1789 Reynolds portrait of George James Cholmondeley (Mannings 2000, no.363).

BLACK, Joseph 1728-99

A pioneer in the chemistry of gases, and the originator of the theory of specific and latent heat; b. Bordeaux; professor of medicine at Glasgow University 1755 and from 1766 professor of medicine and chemistry at Edinburgh, where he also practised as a private physician.

'The aspect of Dr Black was comely and interesting. His countenance exhibited that pleasing expression of inward satisfaction, which, by giving ease to the beholder, never fails to please. His manner was unaffected and graceful; he was affable, and readily entered into conversation, whether pious or trivial' (Alexander Chalmers, 1812).

3238 JAMES TASSIE 1788

Glass paste medallion 6.7 (2⅝) high, incised on truncation: *JOSEPH BLACK MD/ 1788* and: *Tassie f.*

Collections: Sotheby's, 18 April 1945, lot 110, bt. Leggatt for the NPG.

Reference: Gray 1894, no.37.

Related wax models are in the Victoria and Albert Museum (A.84.1965) and the Wedgwood Museum, Barlaston, the latter used for the Wedgwood medallion first produced in 1788.[1] Gray also records a much smaller version (¾ in. high).[2] The Tassie profile was twice engraved: by Mackenzie 1801 and by J. Beugo (after J.

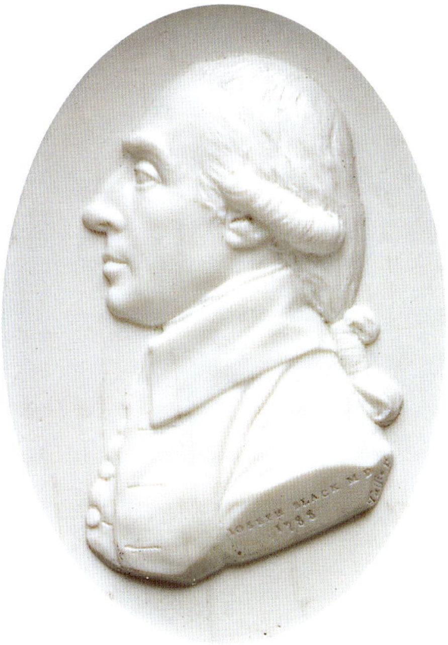

BLACK NPG 3238

Brown). A wax portrait of Black dated 1788, attributed to Tassie, was sold Sotheby's, 12 December 1985, lot 287.

1 Illus. Reilly 1973, p.64 (as from a model by William Tassie, sic).
2 Gray 1894, no.38; Vernon sale, Christie's, 20 April 1882, lot 45.

ICONOGRAPHY

c.1770 Painting by David Martin, half length. Edinburgh University (illus. D. Talbot Rice & P. McIntyre, *Edinburgh University Portraits*, 1957, pl.10).

c.1785-90 Unattributed chalk drawing, bust-length oval. Scottish NPG (PG 283).

1787 Painting by David Martin,* three-quarter length holding up a glass U-tube. Royal Medical Society, Edinburgh, on loan to the Scottish NPG. Black's lectures at Edinburgh, which involved a certain degree of showmanship, attracted large audiences.

1787 Three etchings by J. Kay (*Kay Portraits* 1842, I, nos.xxii, xxiii, xxv): half length in gown lecturing (illus. H. & M. Evans, *John Kay*, 1973, pl.14); whole length walking (illus. D. Daiches et al., *Scottish Enlightenment*, 1996, p.111) and *Philosophers* - a half length with Dr James Hutton (illus. W. Ramsay, *Joseph Black*, 1918, f.p.118). A drawing by the anatomist Thomas Pole copying one of these etchings, belongs to the Royal College of Surgeons, London (LeFanu 1960, no.20).

1788 Medallions by James Tassie and Wedgwood, see NPG 3238.

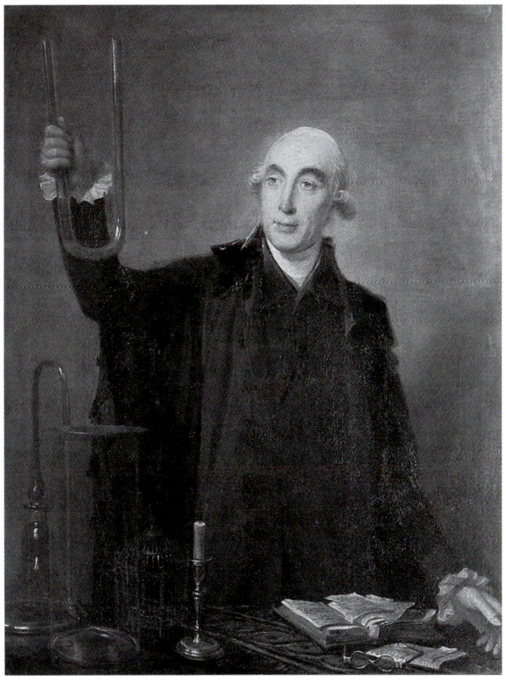

BLACK by David Martin 1787 (Royal Medical Society, Edinburgh)

c.1790 Painting by Henry Raeburn,* half-length seated. Glasgow University. Engraved J. Rogers 1855; J. Heath 1800; T.A. Dean 1830; J. Posselwhite c.1835; C. Cook. A version sold Christie's, Amsterdam, 19-20 February 1997, lot 54.

1799 Medal by N. Macphail (Brown 1980, no.466).

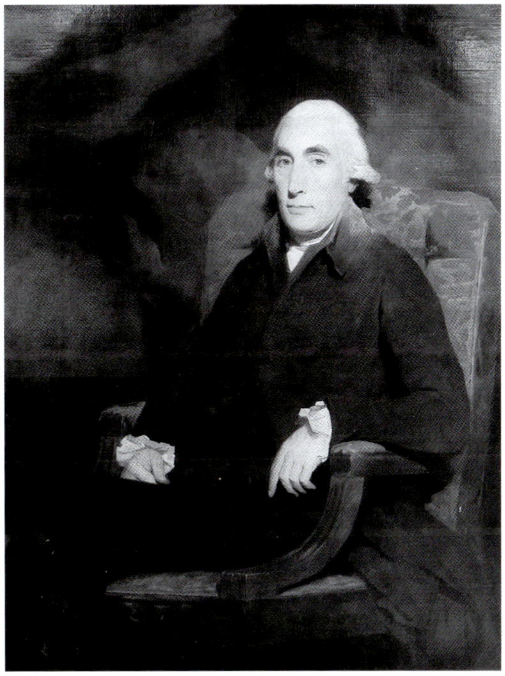

BLACK by Henry Raeburn c.1790 (Hunterian Art Gallery, Glasgow)

Undated Caricature drawing, half-length standing, a flask in his left hand. Andersonian Library, University of Strathclyde (illus. D. Daiches et al., *Scottish Enlightenment*, 1996, p.104).

Undated Engraving by Robertson after Thornton, half-length oval, wearing a cloak.

BLACKSTONE, Sir William, Kt 1723-80

First professor of Law at Oxford 1758-62; BCL 1745; DCL 1750; his *Commentaries on the Laws of England* 1765-69, defining the legal authority of the Crown-in-Parliament, brought him a fortune; principal of New Inn Hall, Oxford, 1761-66; MP 1761-74; solicitor-general to the Queen 1763 and justice of the Court of Common Pleas 1770; Kt 1770.

'physically as well as mentally he was lethargic; he grew stout, and came more and more to dislike all forms of exercise, and he seems really to have died from the want of it' (*DNB*).

388 UNKNOWN ARTIST c.1755

Canvas 125.5 x 101.5 (49½ x 40) lined; discoloured varnish; retouchings in the head and in the right background; pentiment above his left shoulder.

Brown eyes, white powdered wig; wearing white bands, a black suit beneath a scarlet and rose DCL gown; he holds a sealed document and sits in a carved, maroon-upholstered chair.

Collections: Philip Goode (b.1782), solicitor of Howland Street, London, by 1858;[1] he bequeathed his 'original portrait of Sir William Blackstone by Sir Joshua Reynolds' to his wife and thence to his younger son; sold by order of Chancery [Joseph v. Goode etc], Furber, Price & Furber, 22 October 1873 ('valuable portrait of Judge Blackstone painted by Sir Joshua Reynolds'); Price & Furber, sold Christie's, 31 January 1874, lot 300; purchased from Graves, March 1874.

Engravings: Scriven 1826 (*from the original ... by Reynolds*); R.B. Parkes 1874.

Reference: Graves & Cronin, I, pp.87-88.

Although NPG 388 long bore an attribution to Reynolds, this is untenable; the figure sits uncomfortably and the composition overall is inelegant.

1 The sitter's grandson, William Blackstone (1810-81), had sold the Gainsborough portrait (see below 1774) in 1835, see Davies 1946, p.62; NPG 388 was possibly sold by the family at the same time.

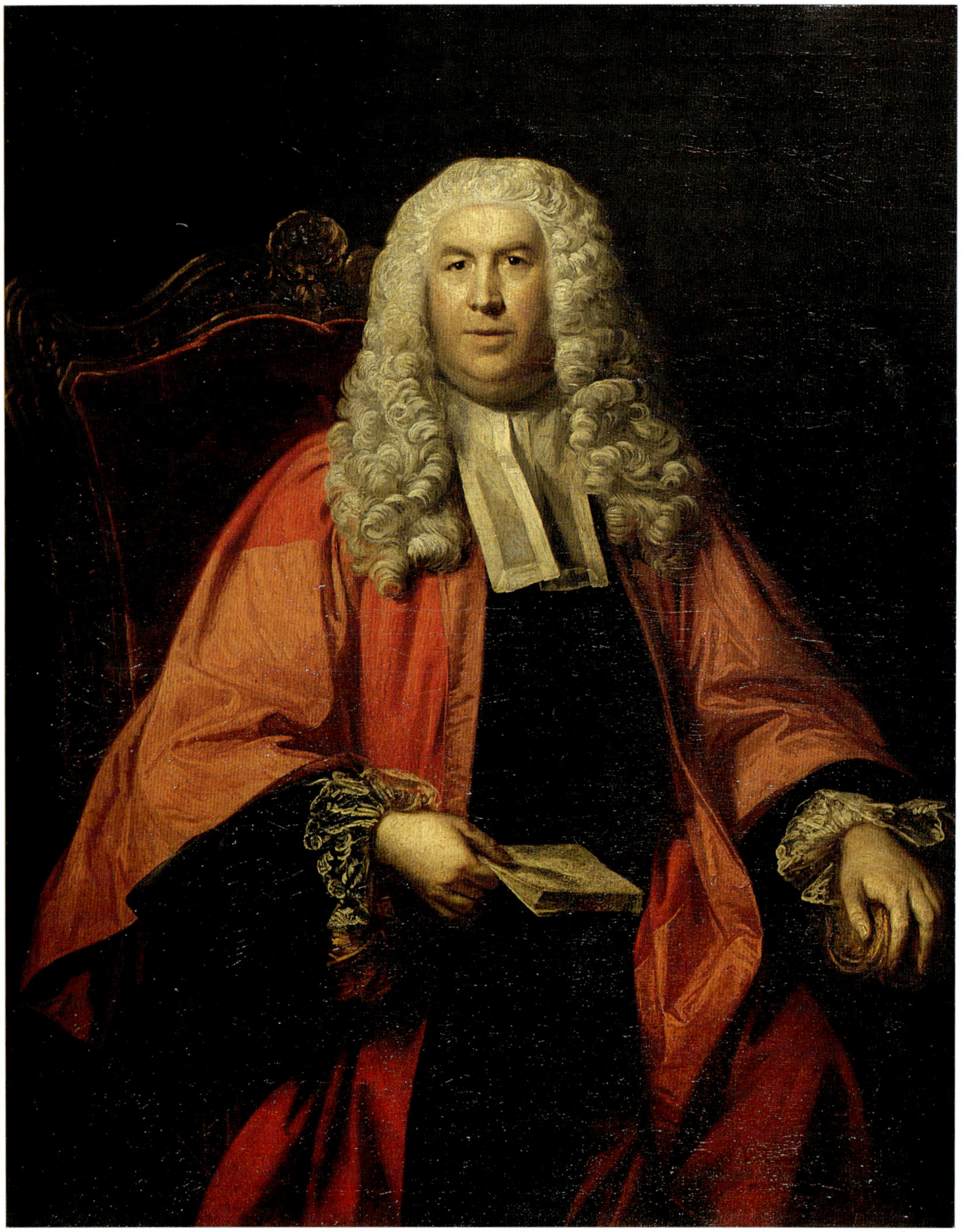

BLACKSTONE NPG *388*

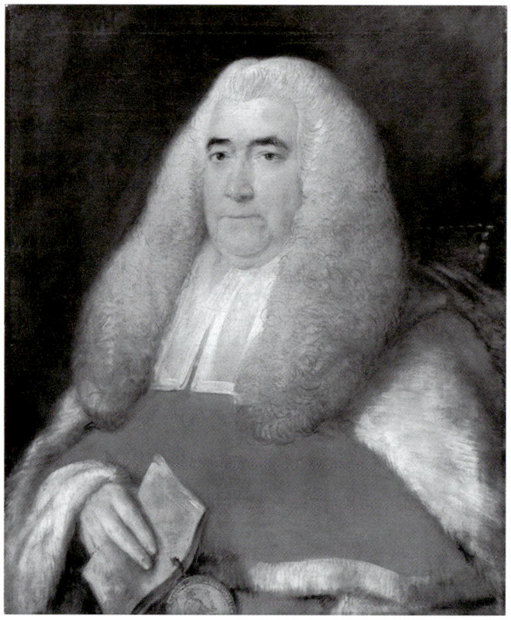

BLACKSTONE by Thomas Gainsborough 1774 (Tate Gallery)

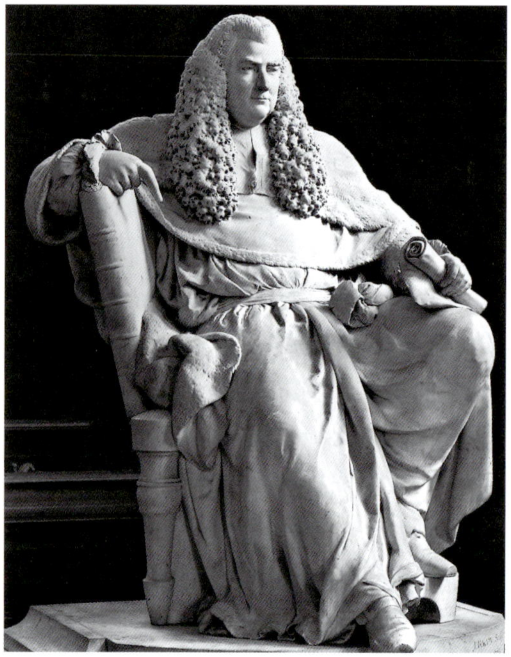

BLACKSTONE by John Bacon 1784 (All Souls, Oxford)

ICONOGRAPHY

c.1755 Unattributed painting, see NPG 388.

1763–68 Painting by Tilly Kettle, standing three-quarter length, in DCL robes. Bodleian Library, Oxford (*Kettle* 1927, pl.xvia).

1774 Painting by Thomas Gainsborough,* half length in judge's robes. Tate Gallery (N 2637; Waterhouse 1958, no.67). Engraved J. Hall 1778 & 1793, and many times as an oval, e.g. by W. Ridley 1798, J. Chapman 1800 and J. Hopwood 1805. Versions at Wallingford Town Hall (in 1966) and with F.T. Sabin in 1933; copies at All Souls, Oxford (Poole, II, p.194); Bodleian Library, Oxford, by John Rising 1808 and anon. (Poole, I, pp.107–08); Middle Temple, London, by John Bridges.

Posthumous

1782 Painting by Walker, exhibited FS 1782(256).

1784 Marble statue by John Bacon sr.,* whole length, with his *Commentaries*. All Souls, Oxford (Poole, II, p.194).

Undated Carved wooden medallion. Lincoln's Inn, London.

1925 Marble statue by Paul W. Bartlett. Law Courts, London, presented by the American Bar 1924.

DOUBTFUL PORTRAIT

Miniature by Charles Dixon at the Harvard Law School.

BLIGH, William 1754-1817

Naval officer; accompanied Cook's third and last voyage 1772-75; returning from Tahiti in 1789 as captain of the *Bounty*, his crew mutinied, setting him adrift with eighteen companions; he sailed over three thousand miles to the Dutch East Indies and arrived home in March 1790; FRS 1801; governor of New South Wales 1805-10; rear-admiral 1811, vice-admiral 1814.

'According to family tradition he was a man below the average height, robust, and active. Dr Arnold describes him in his later days as 'corpulent' ... [a fellow officer described him as] 'a very choleric gentleman, but at the same time, a very just man' (George Mackaness, 1931).

Abbreviation

Callender 1936: G. Callender, 'The Portraiture of Bligh', *The Mariner's Mirror*, XXII, 1936, pp.172-78

1138 GEORGE DANCE 1794

Pencil, with traces of pink on the cheek and lips, on paper 25.7 x 19.5 (10 x 7⅝) faded; signed and dated in pencil lower left: *Geo: Dance/ May 31st.1794;* laid down on a contemporary washed mount lettered: CAPN BLIGH.

Collections: The artist's grandson, the Rev George Dance; his sale, Christie's, 1 July 1898, lot 21, bt. Colnaghi for the NPG.

Exhibitions: *Captain Cook*, Oregon, 1974-75(132); *Mutiny on the Bounty*, National Maritime Museum, 1989(157).

Reference: Callender 1936, p.175.

Shown in civilian dress while he was at home on half pay following his return from the second successful breadfruit voyage (1791-93). No engraving of this drawing is recorded.

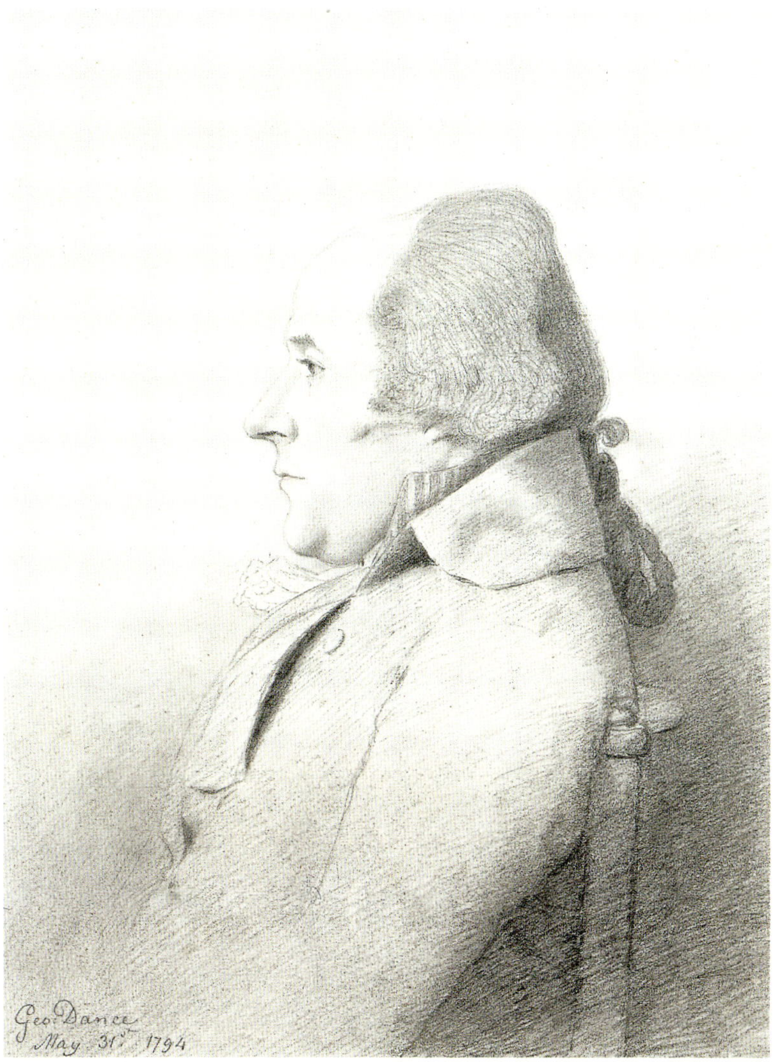

BLIGH NPG *1138*

4317 JOHN SMART c.1801

Pencil and watercolour 15 x 9.5 (5⅞ x 3¾); the watercolour confined to the head; an area of pale wash upper left and some soiling; inscribed *Capn Bligh* and verso: *Captain Bligh of / the Director*; stamped NPG and, verso, with the Ingram collector's mark.

Clear brown eyes, own white hair, in the undress uniform of a senior captain.

Collections: Mrs Busteed, the artist's great-granddaughter; her sale, Christie's, 17 December 1936, lot 34; Sir Bruce Ingram, from whose executors purchased 1963.

Engraving: J. Parker & G. Noble 1803, as part of the *Commemoration of the XIth October MDCCXCVII.*[1]

Exhibitions: *Masters of Maritime Art*, Colnaghi, 1937; *Mutiny on the Bounty*, National Maritime Museum, 1989(193).

Reference: Walker 1998, no.70.

One of Smart's eighteen portrait studies for the commemorative engraving, published in 1803, of the *Battle of Camperdown* (1797) in which Bligh commanded the *Director*. Eleven were formerly in the Ingram collection, the others being of Admirals Duncan and Onslow; Captains Burgess, Drury, Essington, O'Brien, Trollope, Walker and Wells, and Lieutenant Phillips. The remaining studies were of Captains Byard, Fairfax, Gregory, Hotham, Inglis, Knight and Mitchell.[2]

1 See Callender 1936, pp.175-76.
2 See Foskett 1964, pp.33-34.

BLIGH NPG *4317*

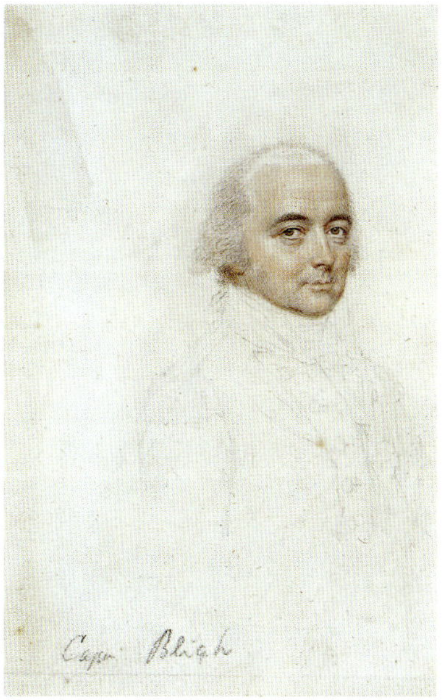

ICONOGRAPHY

c.1776 Painting attributed to John Webber, half length as midshipman. Sotheby's, 8 April 1992, lot 35; by descent from the sitter's family (illus. *John Webber*, Bern, Manchester, 1996, p.139.

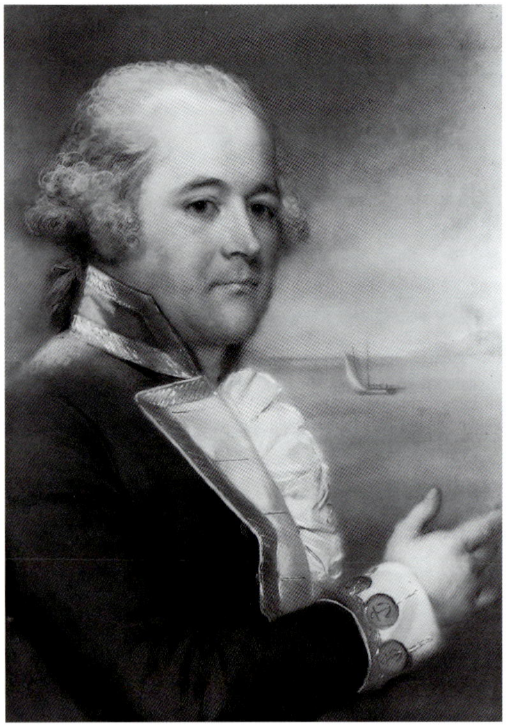

BLIGH by John Russell 1791 (Captain Cook Memorial Museum, Whitby)

1791 Pastel by John Russell,* half length as a post captain. Cook Memorial Museum, Whitby. Exhibited RA 1791(188). Engraved J. Condé 1792 (illus. Callender 1936, f.p.175); H. Adlard 1860 (illus. G. Kennedy, *Bligh, the man and his mutinies*, 1989, f.p.146).

1794 Drawing by George Dance, see NPG 1138.

1801 Wax model by G. Leader, exhibited RA 1801(1026).

c.1801 Miniature by John Smart, see NPG 4317.

1805 Drawing by H.A. Barker (the sitter's son-in-law), bust-length oval in civilian dress. State Library of New South Wales, Sydney (illus. *ILN*, 2 May 1936; O. Rutter, *Turbulent Journey*, 1936, f.p.216; Callender 1936, f.p.174).

1814 Miniature by Alexander Huey, half length as rear-admiral. Quaritch 1994 (illus. G. Kennedy, *Bligh, the man and his mutinies*, 1989, f.p.147). Exhibited RA 1814(462).

c.1814 Unattributed miniature, bust-length oval as vice-admiral. State Library of New South Wales, Sydney (illus. O. Rutter, *Turbulent Journey*, 1936, f.p.260). What appears to be a version (illus. G. Mackaness, *Life of Bligh*, 1931, I, front.) was rejected as a likeness by Callender (1936, p.176). A whole-length portrait of 1906 by J.R. Ashton (artist's collection, Sydney, 1937), used the head from this miniature.

DOUBTFUL PORTRAITS

Miniature (Mrs Oakes of Epping, New South Wales, 1931; illus. G. Mackaness, *Life of Bligh*, 1931, ii, front.); miniature by Shee, 'Admiral Bligh at age of 21', exhibited *Royal Naval Exhibition*, Chelsea, 1891(1875), lent Mrs C.F. Glennie; silhouette sold Sotheby's, 29 October 1979, lot 88; engraving by J. Chapman, as a rear-admiral wearing the Camperdown medal (illus. *CL*, CLXXXIII, 1989, p.123; cf. Callender 1936, p.177).

BODMER, Johann Jakob 1698-1783

Philosopher, translator, teacher at the Zurich Collegium.

3027 HENRY FUSELI 1778-79

Pencil on paper 39.8 x 31 (15⅝ x 12¼), within an oval mount 32.5 x 24.8 (12¾ x 9¾); laid down on paper; an oval frame sketched in lower right; the paper is stained and has a pale wash in the lower right area in the spandrel; the principal lines in the head have been scored through.

Collections: Miss James sale, Christie's, 1st day, 22 June 1891, lot 73 as Fuseli by G.S. Newton; William Ward, 1893; presented by M.H. Spielmann 1939.

Exhibitions: *Die Nibelungen*, Munich, 1987-88(139); *Füssli*, Stuttgart, 1997-98(2).

Reference: Schiff 1973, no.581.

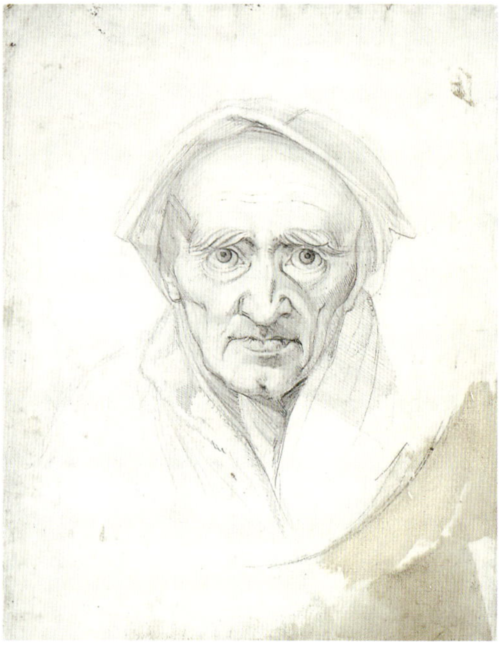

BODMER NPG *3027*

Bodmer is an uninvited guest. NPG 3027 was acquired as a self portrait by Henry Fuseli[1] and was listed as such in 1949 and 1970,[2] before being correctly identified by Schiff in 1973 as a preparatory study for Fuseli's *Self portrait in conversation with Bodmer* of 1778-81 (Zurich).[3] A second study of Bodmer by Fuseli, in the Huntington Art Collections, San Marino, Calif. (64.7),[4] agrees more closely with the finished painting.

1 For whose portraiture in the NPG, see Walker *Regency*, I, pp.195-97; II, pls. 451-55.
2 NPG *Cat.* 1949 and *Concise Cat.* 1970.
3 Exhibited RA 1781(141); Schiff 1973, no.366.
4 Schiff 1973, no.582; *British Portrait Drawings*, San Marino, Calif., 1982, no.14.

BONOMI, Joseph 1739-1808

Architect; b. Rome, he came to England in 1767, working with the Adam brothers until 1781; revisited Italy 1783-84; ARA 1789.

3089(1) WILLIAM DANIELL after GEORGE DANCE [1793]

Pencil with the outlines drawn over in red crayon, on paper 25.5 x 20 (10 x 7⅞) laid down on paper; irregular perforations round the edges, slight staining; inscribed bottom centre in pencil: *Guiseppi Bonomi*; NPG stamp lower right.

Engraving: W. Daniell (*Dance Plates*).

Collections, Reference: see Appendix II.

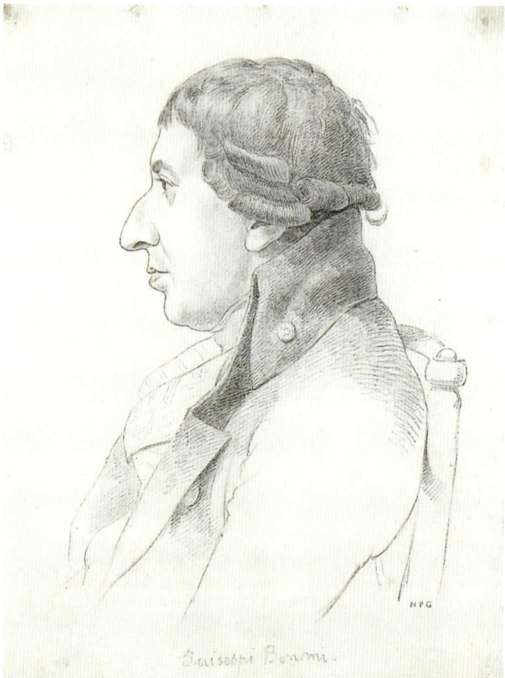

BONOMI NPG *3089(1)*

NPG 3089(1) differs from the original drawing by Dance at the Royal Academy (which is dated 4 August 1793) in having much less hatching.

ICONOGRAPHY

1793 Drawing by George Dance, see NPG 3089(1).

1794 Painting by J.F. Rigaud,* half length at table, a porte-crayon in his raised right hand, dividers in his left. Royal Academy. Exhibited RA 1794(229). Rigaud's son recorded that Bonomi, 'a man of great judgement and classical Taste in art', was a great friend of his father (*Rigaud Memoir*, p.91).

1808 Painting by J.F. Rigaud, untraced; mentioned by the artist's son: 'about this time [1808] he painted the portraits of ... Joseph Bonomi, the Architect' (*Rigaud Memoir*, p.135).

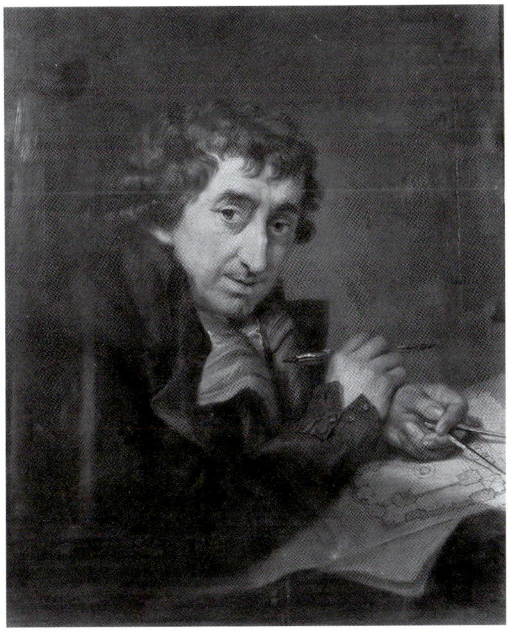

BONOMI by J.F. Rigaud 1794 (Royal Academy of Arts, London)

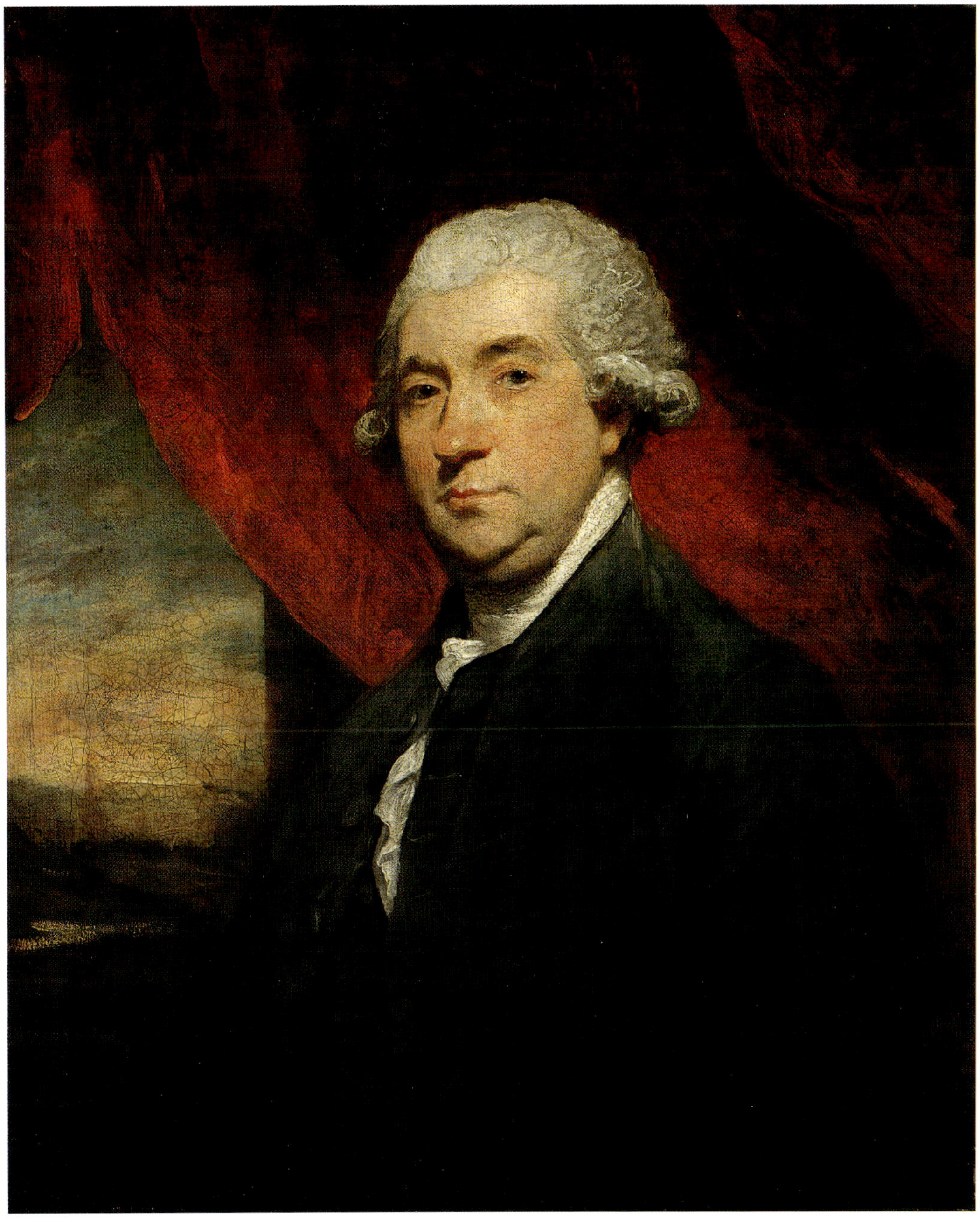

BOSWELL NPG *4452*

BOSWELL, James 1740–95

Scottish advocate, diarist, biographer of Dr Johnson; published the *Journal of a Tour to the Hebrides* 1785 and the *Life of Johnson* 1791.

'He has a good manly countenance, and he owns himself to be amorous. He has infinite vivacity, yet is observed at times to have a melancholy cast. He is rather fat than lean, rather short than tall' (James Boswell, 1763).

'His clothes were always too large for him; his hair, or wig, was constantly in a state of negligence; and he never for a moment sat still or upright upon a chair' (Charles Burney, c.1786).

4452 JOSHUA REYNOLDS 1785

Canvas 76 x 63 (29½ x 24½) lined; cleaned 1966; drying cracks in the face, the landscape and the edges of the curtain.

Blue-grey eyes; powdered wig; slate-grey coat and waistcoat; a deep red drapery above.

Collections: By descent from the sitter to Sir James Boswell, 2nd Bt of Auchinleck, whose dau. Emily Harriet (d.1898) m. Richard, 5th Baron Talbot of Malahide; given by the 7th Baron Talbot to Sir Gilbert Eliott, 10th Bt, in 1949; sold by his son, Sir Arthur Boswell Eliott, Sotheby's, 7 July 1965, lot 125, bt. Leger for the NPG, the purchase made with the aid of two private donors, the Johnson Club, the National Art Collections Fund and a Government grant.

Engravings: J. Jones 1786; reduced plates: anon. 1787 (*European Mag.*), B. Granger 1802, W.H. Worthington 1826, E. Finden 1835, S. Freeman 1855, G.W. Hutin; R. Graves.

Exhibitions: RA 1787(113); *Boswell*, NPG, 1967(90); *Georgian Playhouse* 1975(96); *Reynolds*, RA, 1986(136).

Reference: Graves & Cronin, I, pp.99-100; Mannings 2000, no.214.

Boswell wrote to Reynolds on 7 June 1785 explaining that, although he could not afford 'any expensive article of elegant luxury', he 'would regret very much that there should not be at Auchinleck [the Boswell family seat in Ayrshire] my portrait by Sir Joshua Reynolds, with whom I have the felicity of living in social intimacy'. He accordingly proposed paying for such a portrait from his legal earnings over the next five years. Reynolds began the portrait on 5 July 1785 and there were sittings on 8 July and 15 August; on 10 September Boswell recorded in his diary, 'Breakfasted with Sir Joshua and had my picture finished'.[1] On that day Reynolds endorsed Boswell's letter of 7 June, but the account was never settled and Reynolds eventually forgave the debt in 1791, the year Boswell's *Life of Johnson* was first published with a fulsome dedication to him. Malone described the portrait as 'a perfect and very characteristic likeness'.[2] The engraving by John Jones was published on 17 January 1786 and the *Morning Herald* alleged that Boswell tried to have it shown in every printseller's window, like a portrait of Fanny Kemble.[3]

NPG 1675 (see below) is a studio version and NPG 4344 (see below) a late nineteenth-century bust-length watercolour copy by J. Brownlee Hunter.[4] An early copy (in a private collection in Philadelphia in 1970) was lithographed with a plain background in the mid-nineteenth century. Versions were exhibited at Manchester 1857 (BPG 305) lent by James Crossley (described as 'formerly the property of Boswell's son, James'); at Edinburgh 1885(46) lent by Mrs George Mounsey, and at the New Gallery 1891(313) as after Reynolds lent by Philip Norman (sold Christie's, 24 June 1932, lot 72).[5] In the younger Boswell's sale, Sotheby's, 3 June 1825, lot 3287 was a 'Portrait of Jas. Boswell esq. copied by S. Harding in 1795 from a picture by Sir Josh. Reynolds, painted in 1789', and lot 3289 'a three-quarter-length portrait of James Boswell, esq., in oil'.[6] A miniature version by Thomas Day was sold Christie's, 11 July 1985, lot 387.

1 For this account, see I.S. Lustig & F.A. Pottle eds., *Boswell: The Applause of the Jury 1782-1785*, 1982, pp.308-09, 317, 321, 337, 340; Leslie & Taylor 1865, II, pp.476-77.

2 Quoted in James Boswell jr. sale cat., see *GM*, XCV, 1825, i, p.607.

3 I.S. Lustig & F.A. Pottle eds., *Boswell: the English Experiment 1785-1789*, 1986, p.97n7.

4 Presented by J.B.L. Munro 1963 in memory of the Rev J.

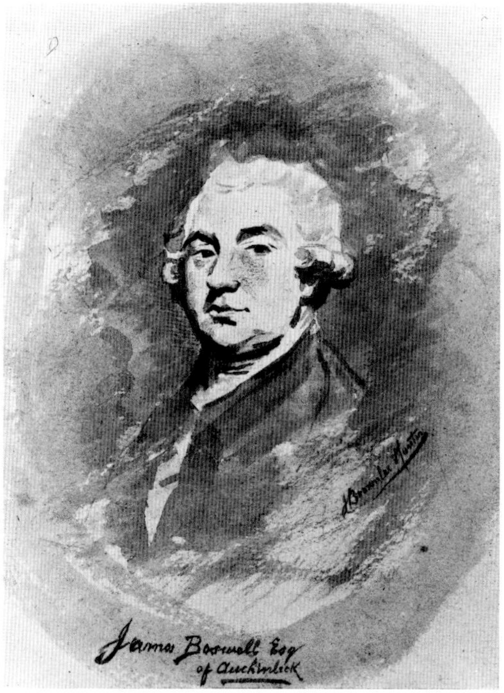

BOSWELL NPG *4344*

Lorimer Munro. 17.2 x 13.2 (6¾ x 5¼); signed *J Brownlee Hunter*, and inscribed *James Boswell Esq /of Auchinleck*.

5 Another copy by 'Thompson' from the collection of 'Spanish Phillips' (the painter John Phillips, 1817-67), was sold Christie's, 9 May 1846, lot 2; a version belonged to the Long Island Historical Society c.1910.

6 *GM*, XCV, 1825, i, p.607.

1675 studio of JOSHUA REYNOLDS [1785]

Canvas 75 x 62 (29½ x 24½) lined; much disfigured by extensive drying cracks.

Collections: Sir Robert Peel after 1845[1] and before 1865; bought by the National Gallery 1871 (no.888); lent to the NPG 1912; ownership transferred to the Tate Gallery 1954 and to the NPG 1957.

Exhibition: Parliament House, Edinburgh, 1973.

Reference: Graves & Cronin, I, pp.99-100; Waterhouse 1941, p.79; Davies 1946, p.121, no.888 (all describing NPG 1675 as the original portrait); Mannings 2000, no.214b as copy.

Until the discovery of NPG 4452, this was considered to be Reynolds's original portrait of Boswell and was associated with references properly applicable only to NPG 4452.

1 Not in the Peel cat. in the *Cabinet de l'Amateur*, IV, 1845/6 (see Davies 1946, p.121).

4344 J. BROWNLEE HUNTER after JOSHUA REYNOLDS, see NPG 4452

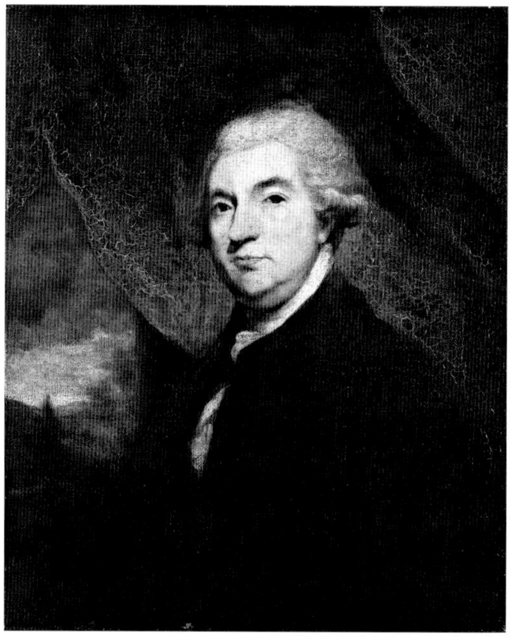

BOSWELL NPG *1675*

2755 after THOMAS LAWRENCE c.1790-95

Pencil and wax crayon on paper[1] 17.3 x 14.5 (6¾ x 5¾) laid down on paper; there is a small tear in the middle of the right-hand edge, some staining and the corners are torn; inscribed below: *Your faithful and / affectionate humble servant / James Boswell* in facsimile of the sitter's autograph from his letter to Reynolds of 7 June 1785 (see NPG 4452 above).

Collections: Presented by Harold Hartley 1935.

Exhibitions: Bodleian Library, Oxford, 1934;[2] *Samuel Johnson, Londoner*, Royal Exchange, London, 1964.

Reference: *Lawrence* 1964, p.217 as copied from the engraving, see below.

Copied from the anonymous lithograph published in 1831 in J.W. Croker's edition of *Boswell's Life of Johnson*. Croker had been 'favoured by Mrs Denham with a pencil sketch of Mr Boswell in later life, by Sir Thomas Lawrence, which, although bordering on caricature, is so evidently characteristic, and (as the editor is assured) so identically *like* that he has had it copied [i.e. lithographed], and thinks it will be acceptable as a lively illustration of both the mind and manners of Mr Boswell—busy self-importance and dogmatical good-nature were never more strongly expressed'.[3] The Denham drawing is now in the Yale University Library.[4]

A related but less finished drawing, inscribed (apparently by Joseph Farington) *James Boswell Esqr from memory by T. Lawrence*,[5] is in the Tate Gallery (T 8151; Oppé collection); a somewhat caricatured copy in blue chalk, from the collection of L.G. Duke, was

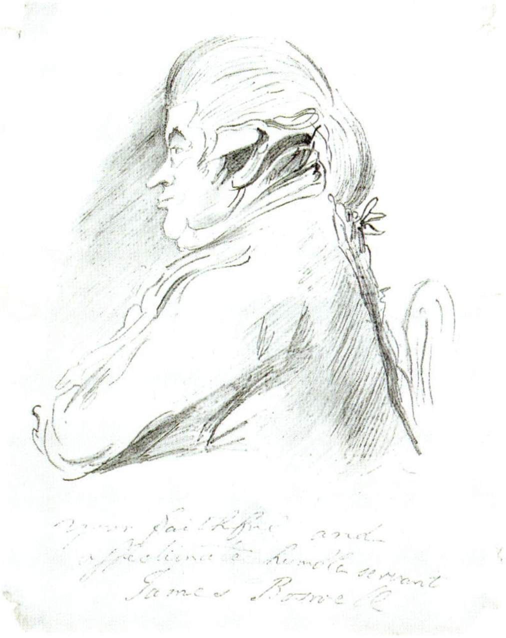

BOSWELL NPG 2755

sold Sotheby's, 11 March 1971, lot 51; an etching in the British Museum (1925.5.11.238) of a closely related head is inscribed *S Lysons* (presumably Samuel Lysons, the owner of Lawrence's drawing of Horace Walpole, see NPG 3631).

1 Water-marked *C Penny/London*, indicating a probable date of 1820–40, as suggested by Peter Bower, letters of 12 & 13 February 1990 (NPG archive).
2 Letter from the Bodleian, 17 December 1934 'the sketch has been on exhibition in this Library since November 7' (NPG archive).
3 J.W. Croker ed., *Boswell's Life of Johnson*, 1831, I, p.xxx; the lithograph appeared as the frontispiece for vol.VI.
4 Illus. *Boswell*, NPG, 1967(100). See *Lawrence* 1964, p.217.
5 As noted on the NPG archive photograph.

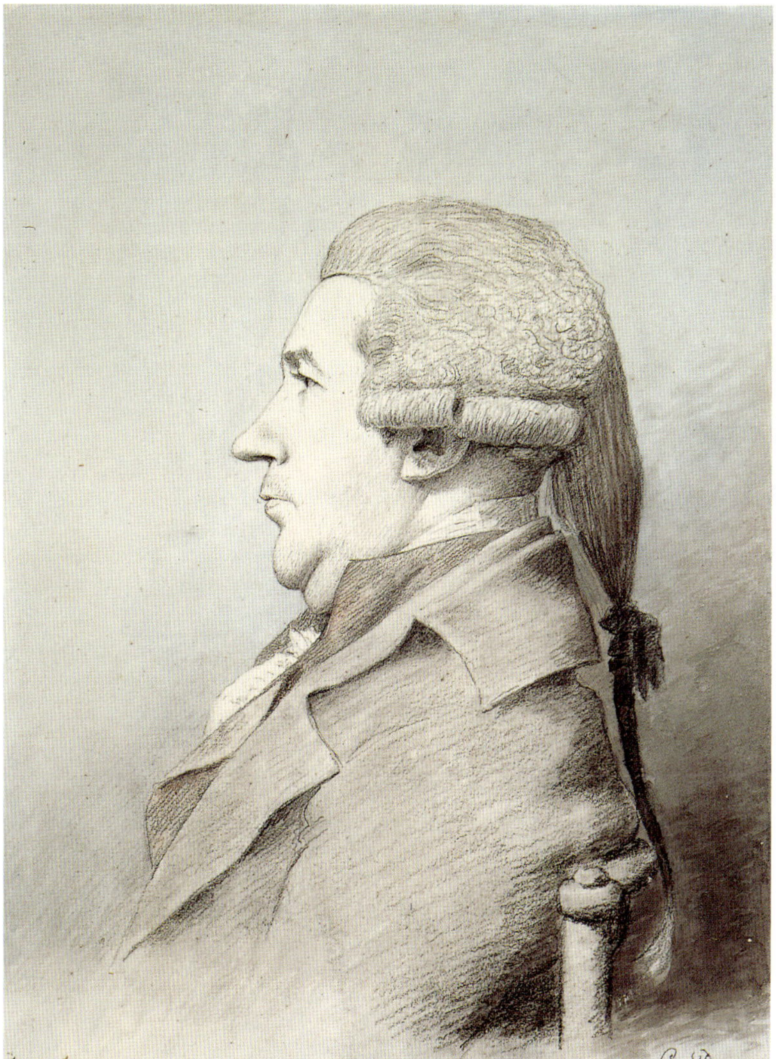

BOSWELL NPG 1139

1139 GEORGE DANCE 1793

Pencil, with traces of pink on the lips and waistcoat, grey wash on the coat and a blue and grey wash in the background, on paper 25.2 x 18.8 (9⅞ x 7⅜) faded, with minor damages behind head and upper right; signed in ink, bottom right: *Geo: Dance.*; a reinforced ink inscription, bottom left: *April 28th.1793*; laid down on a contemporary washed mount.

Collections: The artist's grandson, the Rev George Dance; his sale, Christie's, 1 July 1898, lot 22, bt. Colnaghi for the NPG.

Engravings: W. Daniell 1802 (*Dance Portraits*); W. Hawksworth 1848; etching by B. H.

Exhibitions: RA 1795(586); *Johnson and the Lichfield Circle*, Lichfield, 1959(2); *Belle de Zuylen et son époque*, Paris, Amsterdam, 1961(79); *Rousseau et le pays de Neuchâtel*, Neuchâtel, 1962(12); *Rousseau*, Bibliothèque nationale, Paris, 1962(358); *Garrick and his Contemporaries*, Stratford-upon-Avon, 1969(52); *George Dance*, Geffrye Museum, 1972(79); *George Dance*, Bath Preservation Trust, 1982; *Johnson and the Midlands*, Lichfield, 1984(38).

A copy with a plain background, probably by William Daniell, was on the London art market in 1991; another in reverse by J.T. Smith, presumably after Daniell's print, last sold Sotheby's, 19 July 1979, lot 100.[1]

1 Illus. *Connoisseur*, CLXXVII, 1971, p.69.

ICONOGRAPHY

1765 Drawing by Angelica Kauffmann, half length, hands in a muff. Victoria and Albert Museum (Vallardi sketchbook, E.387.1927; illus. *Hommage an Angelika Kauffmann*, Vaduz/Milan, 1992–93, p.25), provisionally, but plausibly, identified as Boswell, who visited Kauffmann in Rome with Dance on 18 February 1765 (see P. Walch, *Burl. Mag.*, CXIX, 1977, p.108, no.43).

1765 Painting by George Willison,* three-quarter length. Scottish NPG (PG 804). Executed in Rome. Possibly the portrait of Boswell by Batoni listed at Auchinleck in 1767 (Clark 1985, p.369).

A miniature made in Rome at the same time, 'painted by [James] Alves from a large portrait done by Willison', now untraced, was being sent to Scotland in July 1765 (J. Dennistoun, *Memoirs of Sir Robert Strange*, 1855, II, p.33).

1765 Painting by Thomas Patch. 'Patch has by this time encanvass'd you, and I dare say made us so ridiculous as his Genius will admit' (Godfrey Bagnall to Boswell, Milan, 17 August 1765; Ingamells 1997, p.108).

1769 Drawing by Samuel Wale, engraved by J. Miller, full length in the dress of an armed Corsican Chief, as he appeared at the Stratford Shakespeare Jubilee (illus. *Boswell*, NPG, 1967, no.26).

1785 Painting by Joshua Reynolds, see NPG 4452, NPG 1675 and NPG 4344.

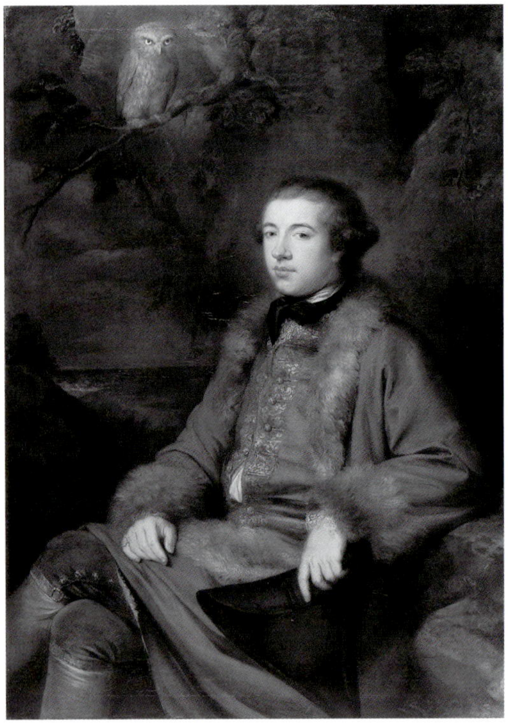

BOSWELL by George Willison 1765 (Scottish National Portrait Gallery)

c.1790-95 Pen and wash drawing by George Langton, whole-length standing. Gunby Hall (illus. *CL*, XCIV, 1943, p.863). Engraved E. Finden 1839.

c.1790-95 Drawing by Thomas Lawrence, see NPG 2755.

1792 Miniature by W. Hanneman, exhibited RA 1792(248).

1793 Drawing by George Dance, see NPG 1139.

Posthumous

1908 Bronze statue by Percy Fitzgerald. Lichfield Market Place. Fitzgerald also included a medallion of Boswell on his statue of Samuel Johnson, St Clements Danes, London, dated 1910. A crudely modelled and unattributed bust is at Auchinleck (illus. I. Finlayson, *Moth and the Candle*, 1984, p.262).

DOUBTFUL PORTRAITS

Painting attributed to Henry Singleton, called *Boswell and his Family* (Scottish NPG, PG 1250); a closely related drawing, attributed to J.T. Smith, called *Boswell and his Family* (Yale Center for British Art, B1977.14.5145; from the L.G. Duke collection, Sotheby's, 11 March 1971, lot 51 as Lawrence, *a study for a family group*). Pen and ink caricature by Lawrence (private collection; illus. *Boswell*, NPG, 1967, no.101) cannot show Boswell; see Edward Gibbon c.1790?.

BOULTON, Matthew 1728-1809

Manufacturer; b. Birmingham, inheriting his father's buckle-making business in 1759; built the Soho Manufactory 1765 and within two years was considered 'the most complete manufacturer in England in metal'; joined by James Watt 1774, with whom he developed the Boulton & Watt steam engine; FRS 1785; with Erasmus Darwin founded the Lunar Society in 1766 to discuss the widest range of scientific issues.

'He was in person tall, and of a noble appearance; his temperament was sanguine, with that slight mixture of the phlegmatic which imparts calmness and dignity; his manners were eminently open and cordial' (Mary Schimmelpenninck, 1858)

'Few men have had his abilities & still fewer have exerted them as he has done and if to them we add his urbanity, his generosity and his affection for his friends, we shall make up a character rarely to be equalled' (James Watt, 1809).

Abbreviation

Boulton 1970: J.G. Pollard, 'Matthew Boulton and Conrad Heinrich Küchler', *Numismatic Chronicle*, 7, X, 1970, pp.260-318.

1532 UNKNOWN ARTIST c.1770

Canvas 57.5 x 50 (22½ x 19¾) lined; cleaned 1977; there are losses in his right cheek and upper lip and in the background areas; painted over a full length portrait of a seated man (probably of 1730-40).

Brown eyes, grey powdered hair, brown coat, yellowish waistcoat, white neckcloth.

Collections: According to Robert Price, from whom it was purchased in 1909, NPG 1532 hung at Soho, the sitter's Birmingham home, until the death of Matthew Robinson Boulton in 1836, when it was presented by his wife's sister, Miss Wilkinson, to Mr John Thomas, the Head Clerk at Soho Foundry, on whose death 'it was presented by his widow to my Father who succeeded him in office and who was 40 years in the Firms service and it passed to me on his death in 1895'.[1]

Exhibition: *Regency Portraits*, Kenwood, 1986.

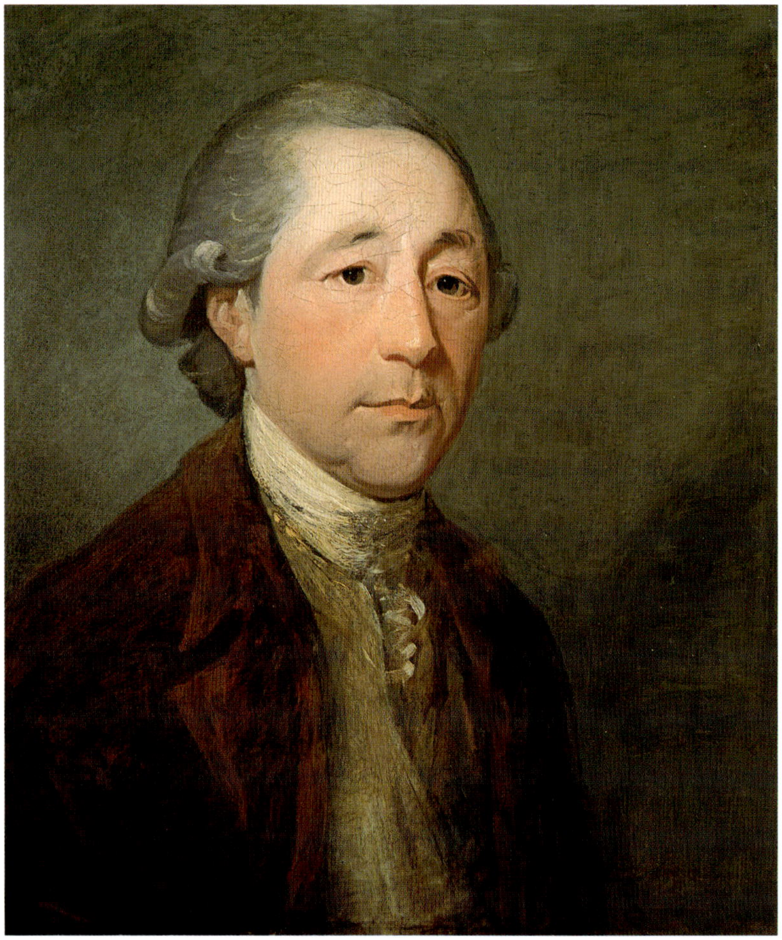

BOULTON NPG 1532

Lionel Muirhead, the historian of Boulton and Watt, described the Miss Wilkinson referred to in the provenance as one who 'drew not at all badly' and 'keen on employing others who were struggling artists, & she probably either made this copy herself, or employed someone to do it for her, & this is probably the explanation of her giving it away'; he considered it likely that NPG 1532 was a copy,[2] and his judgment seems supported by the fact that it is painted on a recycled canvas.

The features closely resemble those of the half-length portrait by J.S.C. Schaak dated 1770 in the Birmingham Museum and Art Gallery (see below) and of an unattributed half-length pastel showing Boulton examining a small urn (with Sotheby's, 1976; photograph NPG archive).

1 Letters of 6 and 28 January 1909 from Robert Price (NPG archive).
2 Letter of 10 February 1909; NPG archive.

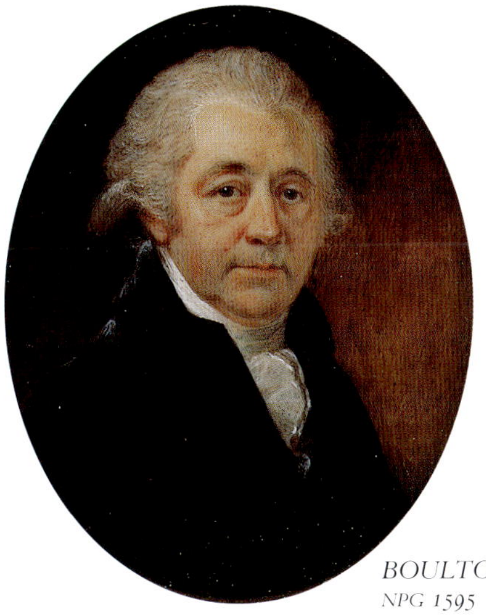

BOULTON
NPG 1595

1595 attributed to ANNE BEECHEY, after WILLIAM BEECHEY c.1799

Watercolour and bodycolour on ivory 7.9 x 6.4 (3⅛ x 2½)

Brown eyes, dark blue-grey coat, powdered wig.

Collections: Purchased from Frank T. Sabin 1911.

Reference: Walker 1998, no.98.

Copied from her husband's three-quarter length portrait exhibited at the RA in 1799,* see below. Lady Beechey exhibited a miniature of Boulton with his wife and daughter RA 1799(783).

1451 SARAH BROWN 1807

Pink wax profile portrait 7.6 x 5.7 (3 x 2¼); incised on the truncation: *S Brown 1807*; unevenly worn, with extensive powdering.

Collections: Purchased from Francis Draper 1906.

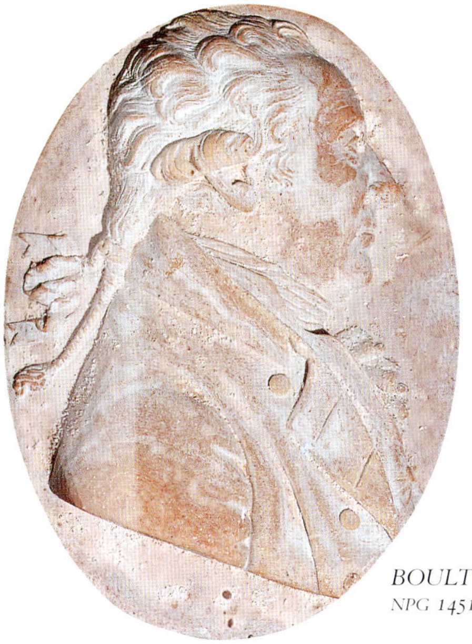

BOULTON
NPG 1451

NPG 1451 appears to be an original portrait, most closely resembling the medallion by C.H. Küchler, see below. Sarah Brown, whose husband, W.D. Brown (c.1753-1820), was Boulton's confidential clerk, practised as a wax modeller in Handsworth, Birmingham.[1] Pyke records a pink wax portrait by her, also dated 1807, of a Mr Woodward (possibly the John Woodward remembered in Boulton's will).[2]

1 See Pyke 1973, p.20.
2 Private collection (illus. Pyke 1973, pl.38).

1075 see Groups, *Men of Science living in 1807-8* by JOHN GILBERT, FREDERICK SKILL and WILLIAM & ELIZABETH WALKER 1858-62

ICONOGRAPHY

1767 Wax by Isaac Gosset (see *Boulton* 1970, p.298n3).

1770 Painting by J.S.C. Schaak,* half length, wearing a dark suit with gold frogging. Birmingham MAG (Tew Park sale, 3rd day, Christie's, 28 May 1987, lot 403).

c.1770 Painting by an unknown artist, see NPG 1532.

1786 Bust by I.J. Waeyenberghe, drawn by John Philipp (*Collectanea delineatorum varium*, 1792-1811, pl.21).

1792 Painting by C.F. von Breda,* three-quarter length seated, a magnifying glass in his right hand, a cameo in his left; on the table mineral specimens including bluejohn fluorspar; a distant view of the Soho factory. Institution of Civil Engineers, painted for John Rennie. Engraved S.W. Reynolds 1796; reduced plates by R. Page 1823 and Mackenzie. A signed and dated replica in Birmingham MAG was purchased in 1987.

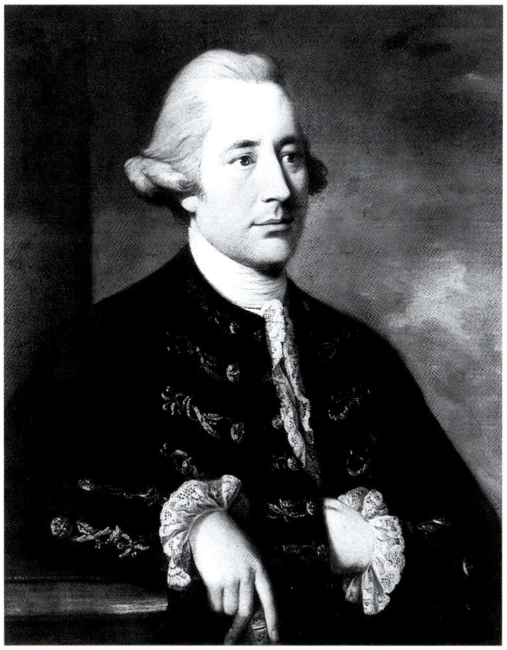

BOULTON by J.S.C. Schaak 1770 (Birmingham Museums and Art Gallery)

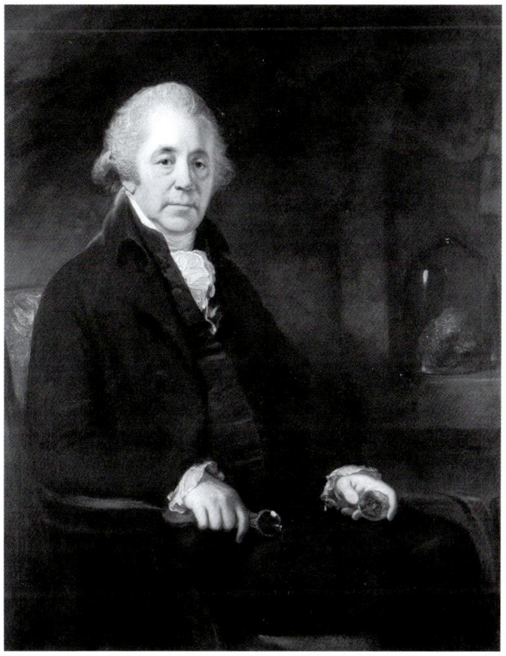

BOULTON by William Beechey c.1799 (Sotheby's)

1797-1801 Painting by L.F. Abbott,* half length, hands crossed over a book inscribed *MINT*. Birmingham MAG (20'08). Exhibited NPE 1867(799) lent by Rev W.K.R. Bedford. 'Mint' doubtless refers to Boulton's Soho Mint set up in 1788 and to his production of the new copper coinage for Great Britain in 1797.

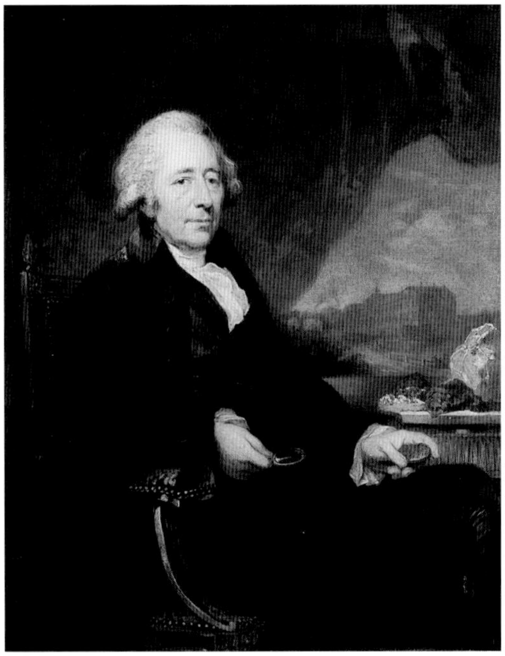

BOULTON BY C.F. von Breda 1792 (Birmingham Museums and Art Gallery)

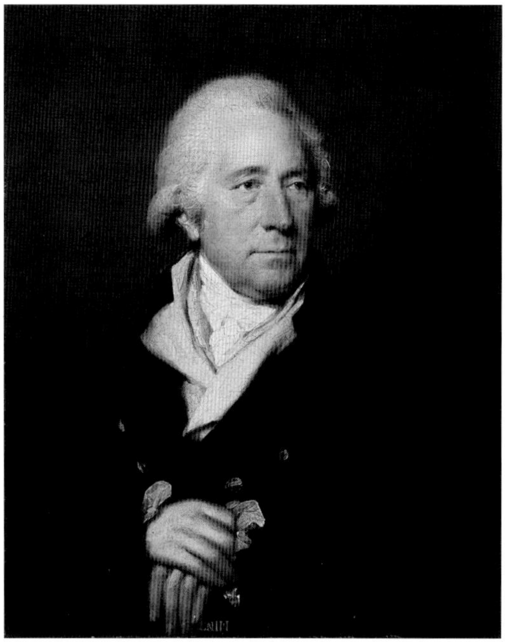

BOULTON by L.F. Abbott 1797–1801 (Birmingham Museums and Art Gallery)

1799 Painting by William Beechey,★ three-quarter length seated, closely comparable with the portrait by Breda of 1793. Private collection (by descent from the sitter). Exhibited RA 1799(209). Engraved W. Sharp 1801, A. Cardon 1822, W. Ridley 1809, W. Holl 1865. See NPG 1075. A replica at Doldowlod (sold Sotheby's, 10 March 2003, lot 34) made for James Watt was paid for in January 1810 (Steegman, II, p.209, no.9), see Groups NPG 1075. See also NPG 1595.

1799 Miniature by Anne Beechey, with his wife and daughter, exhibited RA 1799(783).

1800 Enamel by William Grimaldi, exhibited RA 1800(808). A duplicate and a pencil drawing by him listed in Grimaldi 1873, pp.19, 49.

1803 Wax by Peter Rouw. Fitzwilliam Museum, Cambridge (CM.146-1985). Exhibited RA 1803(816). An example dated 1806 in the Birmingham Assay Office.

Rouw exhibited another wax(?) RA 1812(683). A large wax by him, dated 1814, differing from the 1803 wax in the cut of the coat collar and the wig tie, is in the Victoria and Albert Museum (1058.1871; illus. D.R. Reilly, *Portrait Waxes*, 1953, fig.37).

c.1803 Medal by C.H. Küchler with Boulton's Medallic Scale (French text) on the obverse (Brown 1980, no.462; *Boulton* 1970, p.295).

1807 Medallion by Sarah Brown, see NPG 1451.

c.1807? Plaster cast after an unidentified artist, profile bust. Sotheby's, 30 November 1964, lot 83 (Bruce Ingram collection). Possibly by Nathaniel Marchant who promised to supply his portrait of Boulton in August 1807 (*Boulton* 1970, p.298n3), although no portrait by him of Boulton is listed by Seidmann (*Marchant* 1987).

Posthumous

1809 Memorial medals: by C.H. Küchler, and two derived from the 1803 wax medallion by Peter Rouw, one unattributed, another by Peter Wyon (Eidlitz 1928, nos.3, 5–7; Brown 1980, nos.659–61).

Undated Medallion in white enamel by Catherine Andras (Gray 1894, p.71; Eidlitz 1928, no.9) and another by B. Pistrucci (Gunnis 1968, p.306).

1809–18 Marble bust by John Flaxman for Boulton's monument. St Mary's, Handsworth, Birmingham (illus. Whinney 1964, pl.154A). Replica dated 1818, descended through the family, formerly at Tew Park. Plaster in the Science Museum (1929-1044) exhibited *Watt Bicentenary*, Science Museum, 1936, no.18, as Chantrey.

1814 Medal by G.F. Pidgeon, based on the Rouw wax of 1803. Exhibited RA 1814(387). Medal struck at Soho 1819 'from the Medal by Pidgeon', engraved J. Bate (Brown 1980, no.976; *Boulton* 1970, pp.316–18).

1819 Medallion by P. Taylor, exhibited RA 1819(1116).

1839 Medal by André Gallé (Eidlitz 1928, no.12; *Boulton* 1970, p.317n1).

1871 Medal by Joseph Moore, with James Watt (Brown 1987, no.2922).

1956 Bronze group of Boulton, James Watt and William Murdoch by William Bloye. Birmingham, Broad Street (illus. J. Bennett, *Discovering Statues, Central and Northern England*, 1968, p.29).

DOUBTFUL PORTRAITS

Marble bust by Benjamin Cheverton, 'reduction after Chantrey'. Birmingham MAG (illus. E. Silber, *Birmingham Sculpture*, 1990, p.18); miniature attributed to the circle of P. Paillou c.1790, sold Sotheby's, 6 March 1997, lot 10.

A portrait of 'Mr Bolton' by the Birmingham artist James Millar was exhibited RA 1784(160).

BOWMONT, Marquess of, see ROXBURGHE

BOYCE, William 1711–79

Organist and composer; composer to the King 1736; organist at the Chapel Royal 1758; wrote the air for *Heart of Oak*; published *Lyra Britannica* from 1745, and edited *Cathedral Music* 1760–78; his later life affected by deafness.

'mild and gentle in deportment, above all resentment against such as envied his reputation, communicative of his knowledge, sedulous and punctual in the discharge of his duties' (Sir John Hawkins, 1788).

4212 JOHN RUSSELL 1776

Pastel on Whatman paper 60.5 x 48 (23¾ x 19) indistinctly signed in red chalk above his right sleeve *Russell / 1776*; inscribed verso: *Dr Boyce / Painted by J Russell* (in red, probably an early nineteenth-century hand); some spotting in the head and coat and the surface is rubbed across his chin and in the upper part of the coat.

Brown eyes, pale grey coat with gold buttons.

Collections: [Commissioned by George III for Samuel Wesley, his Court Musician, together with pastels of Handel, Corelli and Kelway, see NPG 4213; thence to the Simms family 'in payment of a debt'[1]] Miss Leat, Yelverton, 1915; Mrs Mary Simms, Yelverton, from whom purchased 1961.

Exhibition: RA 1777(310, 'Portrait of Dr Boyce', oval, in crayons).

1 This provenance was given by Mary Simms in letters of 19 January and 6 February 1961. NPG 4212 was listed as 'missing' by Williamson 1894, pp.48, 127.

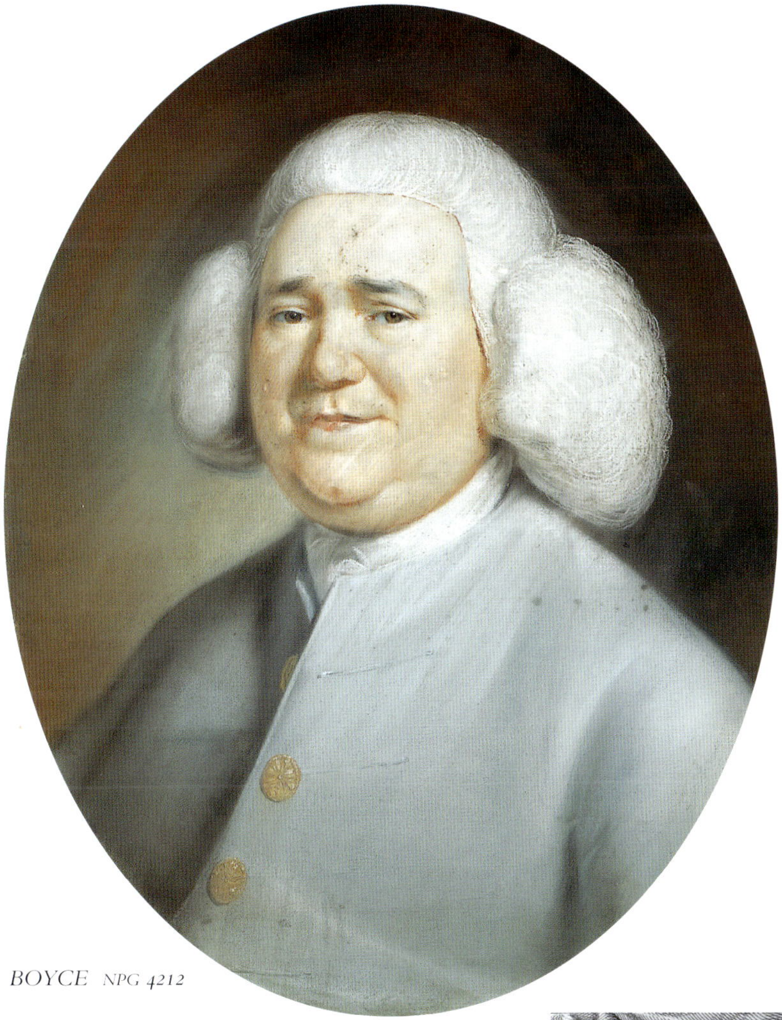

BOYCE NPG 4212

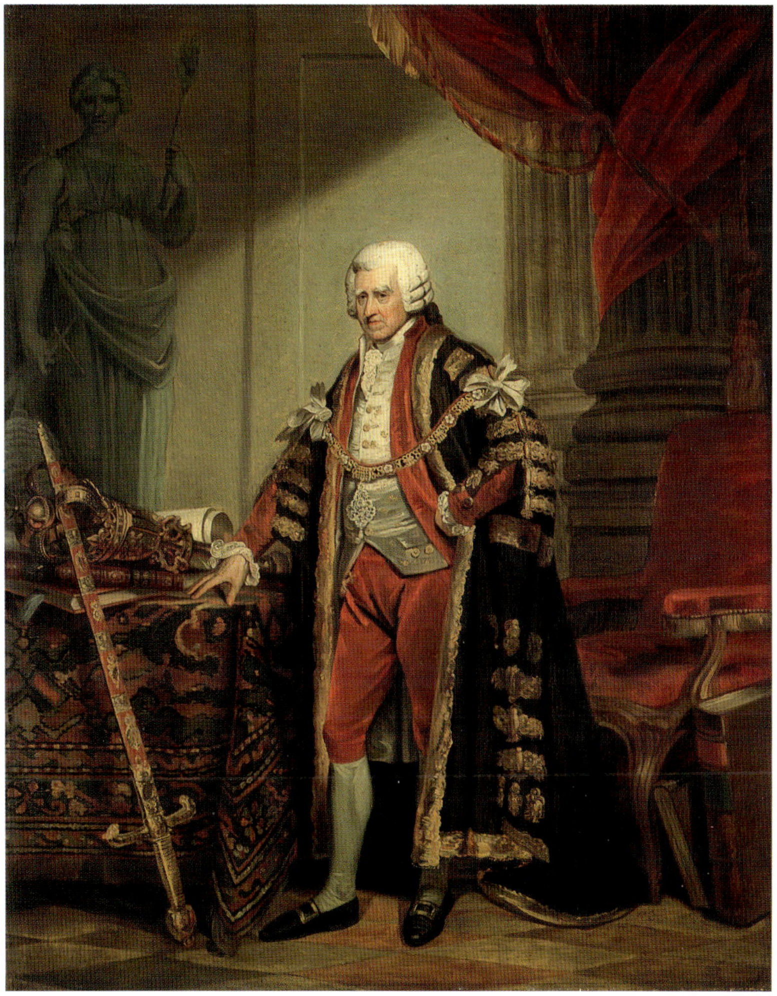

BOYDELL NPG 934

ICONOGRAPHY

c.1745-50 Painting by Thomas Hudson, whole length, the *Solomon Serenata* of 1743 in his right hand. Examination Schools, Oxford (Poole, I, p.162). Exhibited NPE 1867(427).

1764 Portrait by 'a Gentleman at Westminster', exhibited SA 1764(73).

1775 Drawn *from the Life* and engraved by J.K. Sherwin,* three-quarter length seated composing, 1775 and 1788. Also engraved G. Vincent. A painting apparently copied from Sherwin's engraving was with W.W. Zambra in 1927.

1776 Pastel by John Russell, see NPG 4212.

Vignette drawing by R. Smirke, engraved Drayton 1801 (Bowyer's *Historic Gallery*).

DOUBTFUL PORTRAITS

Painting, called Joshua Reynolds, small three-quarter length seated, exhibited *Portraits of Musicians*, Albert Hall, London, 1885(5) lent John Rendall; unattributed painting at the Royal College of Music.

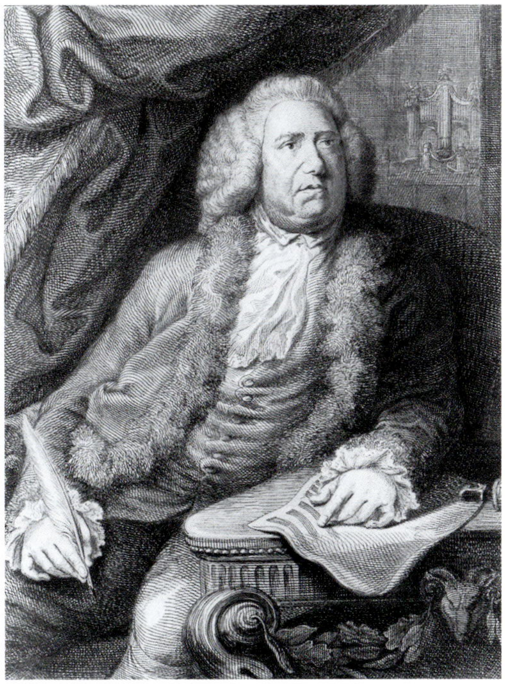

BOYCE drawn and engraved by J.K. Sherwin 1775 (NPG D 14149)

BOYDELL, John 1719-1804

Engraver and print seller; alderman 1782, sheriff 1785, and lord mayor 1790 of the City of London; his *Collection of Prints* began publication in 1769 and eventually ran to nine volumes; commissioned a series of large history paintings for engraving for his Shakespeare Gallery from 1786, but the collapse of the French market led to the Gallery being auctioned in 1805.

934 after WILLIAM BEECHEY [1801]

Oak panel 53.5 x 42.5 x 1 (21 x 16¾ x ⅜); discoloured varnish.

Grey eyes, white powdered wig, wearing a red velvet suit with gold buttons and silver waistcoat, beneath his mayoral robes: dark gown with gold trim, ornate gold collar, black shoes with brass buckles; a red-upholstered chair and red drape to the right; on the table covered by a Turkey rug, the mace and ceremonial sword, two books one lettered SHAK/SPEAR; in the left background a statue of Justice.

Collections: Henry Graves[1] by May 1863;[2] bequeathed by him 1892.

Reference: Roberts 1907, p.105 (as by Beechey).

A reduced, accurate copy of the whole-length portrait by Beechey commissioned by the Corporation of London in 1800 to commemorate Boydell's mayoralty and now in the Guildhall Art Gallery (82). In 1863 Graves, the owner, suggested NPG 934 may have been painted by the elder [Thomas Frank] Heaphy or by Miller.[3] The size suggests the copy may have been made preparatory for an engraved plate, but none is known.

1 He had acquired Boydell's business at 90 Cheapside from Hurst & Robinson in 1825; NPG 934 may have been part of the furnishings.
2 When the portrait was first offered to the NPG; it was then sketched by Scharf (TSB 8/8) who noted that it was 'blotchily but clearly painted'.
3 Letter to Scharf, 26 May 1863 (NPG archive). Graves owned another portrait of Boydell by Miller, see below.

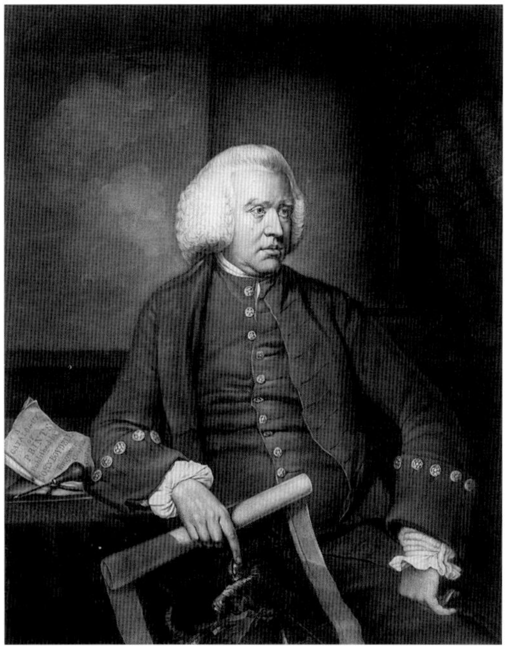

BOYDELL *V. Green after Josiah Boydell 1772 (NPG D 13738)*

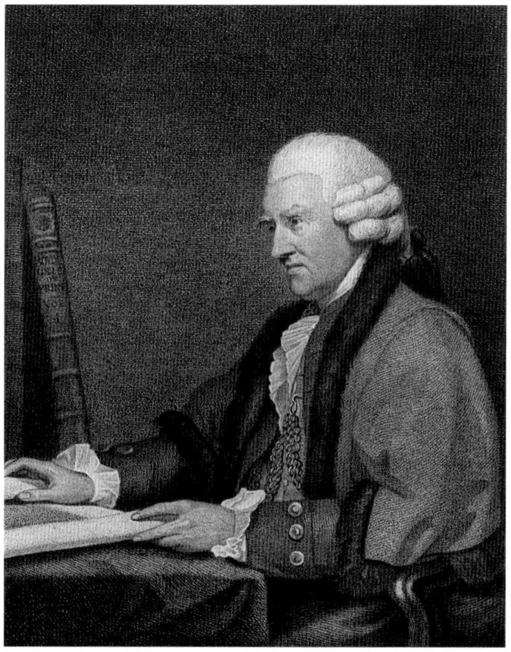

BOYDELL *G. Facius after Gilbert Stuart 1785-86 (NPG D 13737)*

ICONOGRAPHY

1763 Pastel by William Pether, exhibited FS 1763(156), see *Wal. Soc.*, XXVII, 1939, p.74.

1772 Painting by his brother Josiah Boydell, three-quarter length seated, a half-rolled engraving of Salvator Rosa's *Jason and the Dragon* in his right hand, and on the table *A Catalogue of Prints Published by John Boydell Engraver Cheapside London*; in the background three volumes of Boydell's *Collection of Prints*. Untraced. Engraved V. Green* 1772. Boydell's engraving of Salvator's *Jason* was published in 1765 (it was then in the collection of Lord Bessborough and is now in the Montreal Museum of Fine Arts).

c.1780 Unattributed painting, with his wife, half-length oval, beneath his elbow papers lettered *The Houghton Collection / Vol 1 Pub. / Boydell 1779*. Sir Thomas Adams Grammar School, Wem. Boydell's two folio volumes of engravings from the Houghton Collection were published in 1788, but he had previously issued prints in batches of ten; four numbers had been published by 1780 (*Wal. Corr.*, I, p.385n6).

c.1780-85 Drawing by Paul Sandby, profile head, one of the series of heads drawn at print sales. Royal Collection (Oppé 1947, no.417/24a), Engraved anon.,* *Sketches taken at Print Sales*, see Comparative Groups.

1785-86 Painting by Gilbert Stuart, half-length seated in alderman's robes, by a table with open books and standing volumes lettered *Boydells Coll of Prints VII and orks of VI*. H.W. Sage, New York, 1926 (Park 1926, I, no.104, illus. III, p.69). Engraved G. Facius* (the prints volume marked *I*) 1802; H. Meyer 1814 as alderman of London (and for *British Gallery* 1822); J. Hopwood (half length to right) and J. Owen (head only 1799). See also Copley NPG 2143.

1787 Painting by C. Borckhardt, half-length profile, engraved B. Smith 1810 (illus. Smith 1920, II, p.184). Presumably the miniature by Borckhardt exhibited RA 1787(315).

1789 Caricature by James Gillray, *Shakespeare Sacrificed* 1789, with a full-length figure of Boydell (George 7584; illus. T. Clayton, *The English Print*, 1997, p.208).

1790 Watercolour by Francis Wheatley, *Interior of the Shakespeare Gallery*, 1790, includes the tiny figure of Boydell (Victoria and Albert Museum, 1719.1871).

c.1790 Painting by William Miller, three-quarter length standing in mayoral robes. Exhibited NPE 1867(542) lent Graves.

1791 Pastel by Alexander Pope, half-length in mayoral robes. Christie's, 16 November 1965, lot 181. Presumably the pastel exhibited RA 1791(163). Engraved J. Condé 1792 as *Lord Mayor of London 1791* (*European Mag.*).

1791 Marble bust by Thomas Banks, with mayoral chain, inscribed *Banks del. F. Smith sc.* St Margaret's, Lothbury (illus. Bell 1938, pl.xx, and see p.85). Exhibited RA 1791(662). A plaster is in the Victoria and Albert Museum (A.19.1931).

Banks also carved for Boydell's Shakespeare Gallery a group of Shakespeare between the Dramatic Muse and the Genius of Painting (now New Place, Stratford-on-Avon), which was first engraved (G. Vitalba 1792) showing a medallion portrait of Boydell set in the base.

1792 Painting by John Graham, three-quarter length. Stationers' Hall, London. Exhibited RA 1792(352) as the late Lord Mayor for Stationers Hall (illus. *Scottish Art Review*, XIV, 4, 1975, p.19). A weak half-length engraving by F. Sansom from a drawing by R. Stachwell (for the *Wonderful Museum*, c.1800) apparently derived from this portrait.

1793 Enamel by Henry Bone, exhibited RA 1793(461).

1795 Miniature by G.F. Joseph, bust-length oval. Sotheby's, 14 September 2000, lot 366. Exhibited RA 1795(516).

1801 Painting by William Beechey, see NPG 934.

1802 Miniature by James Green, exhibited RA 1802(674).

1804 Drawing by Joseph Parry, engraved B.A. van Assen, whole length in aldermanic gown (illus. Lennox-Boyd 1989, p.5).

BRIDGEWATER, Francis Egerton, 3rd Duke of 1736-1803

Founder of British inland navigation; suc. as 3rd and last Duke of Bridgewater 1748; settled at Old Hall, Worsley, Lancs., 1759, devoting his life to the industrial development of his estates; with James Brindley constructed the Worsley-Manchester canal ('the Bridgewater Canal'), opened in 1761, and the Longford Bridge-Runcorn canal, opened in 1767.

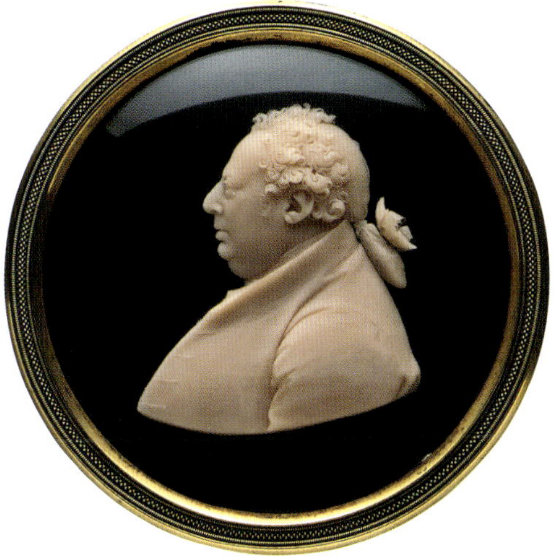

3rd Duke of BRIDGEWATER NPG *4276*

4276 PETER ROUW 1803

Pink wax 7 (2¾) high, incised on the truncation: *P.ROUW/SCULPR LONDON 1803*; the original backing paper inscribed in ink, probably by the artist: *A Portrait of the / late Duke of Bridgewater // Peter Rouw/ Sculptor / Portland Road/ London / 1803 // Published as the Act Directs.*[1]

Collections: Sotheby's, 17 June 1962, lot 137, bt. Eccleston Galleries, from whom purchased 1962.

Exhibition: presumably RA 1804(941, 'the late Duke of Bridgewater').

The profile relates closely to the drawing by Craig of 1788 (see below) but exhibits finer detail.[2] Another wax medallion is at Tatton Park.

1 The writing agrees with that on the vestigial backing of Rouw's wax of Hastings of 1806, see NPG 5065.
2 NPG 4276 was illus. as after Craig, *Connoisseur Year Book 1964*, p.98.

ICONOGRAPHY

1766 Anon. engraving,★ whole length, gesturing towards the Barton aqueduct on the Worsley-Manchester canal (from Whitworth's *Advantages of Inland Navigation* 1766); copied by T.D. Scott 1862.

c.1780? Miniature by Richard Crosse, bust length. Tatton Park (illus. *Apollo*, CXIX, 1984, p.364).

1788 Drawing by W.M. Craig, half-length profile, engraved E. Scriven 1835 (lettered with signature and date *29th Septr 1788*); J. Heath. A variant engraving by C. Picart (after *J.M. Craig*) 1812 - as a seated half length, his head slightly drooped, the details of the coat altered (this plate copied by T.D. Scott 1862).

1803 Wax by Peter Rouw, see NPG 4276.

DOUBTFUL PORTRAIT

Marble bust by Joseph Nollekens dated 1800, sold Sotheby's, 21 July 1978, lot 223, as Fox, might show Bridgewater.

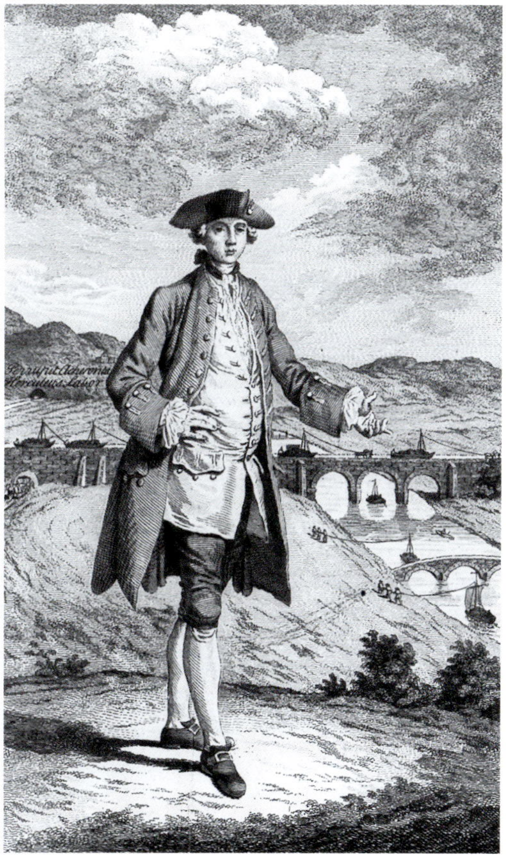

3rd Duke of BRIDGEWATER anon. engraving 1766 (NPG D 1374)

BRINDLEY, James 1716-72

Civil engineer, his reputation made through canal construction; he built one for the Duke of Bridgewater and seven through subscription, which collectively became the core of the British canal network.

'... who handles Rocks as easily as you would Plumb-Pyes and makes the four elements subservient to his will. He is as plain a looking man as one of his own Carters; but when he speaks, all Ears listen.' (*Aris's Birmingham Gazette*, 1767).

6170 FRANCIS PARSONS 1770

Canvas 129 x 99 (50¾ x 39); lined; repaired tears centre left above his right hand and left eye; cleaned 1986.

Blue eyes, grey powdered hair; wearing a white neckcloth, brown suit with brass buttons; with his theodolite[1] and a view of the Barton aqueduct beyond.

Collections: See below; the sitter's descendant Charles Brindley Beddoe by 1886;[2] by descent to his grandson Patrick Matthews, from whom purchased 1992.

Engravings: R. Dunkarton 1770, reissued 1773; H. Cook 1832; J.T. Wedgwood (*after Dunkarton 1773*).

Exhibitions: SA 1771(128); lent to the NPG 1985-92.

NPG 6170, according to the provenance and Dunkarton's reversed engraving,[3] appears to be the original portrait by Parsons. It alludes to the Barton aqueduct on the Bridgewater canal, an undertaking which led to Brindley being described as 'one of those great geniuses which nature sometimes rears by her own force, and brings to maturity without the necessity of cultivation'.[4] In 1769, just before Parsons painted him, Brindley had made his survey for the Chesterfield canal.

There was some dispute over the payment to Parsons, as Josiah Wedgwood told Thomas Bentley:

> Mr Parsons ... took Mr Brindley's Portrait which he was to have had, but they had a little fracas about the terms, Mr Parsons demanded 60 guineas for the piece & frame, Mr Brindley meant to make Mr Parsons a handsome present for the picture, but did not like the mode of demanding so much from him, & in short told him he wod not have it. Mrs Brindley always wish'd to have the picture, & she begs you wod be so good to see Mr Parsons & tell him so, & that now she is at liberty, she readily complys with his terms, & hopes he will not refuse her the picture, if it is not already disposed of. She has set her heart much upon having it.[5]

Bentley obliged and the widow got the portrait 'after Parsons had made one or more copies'.[6]

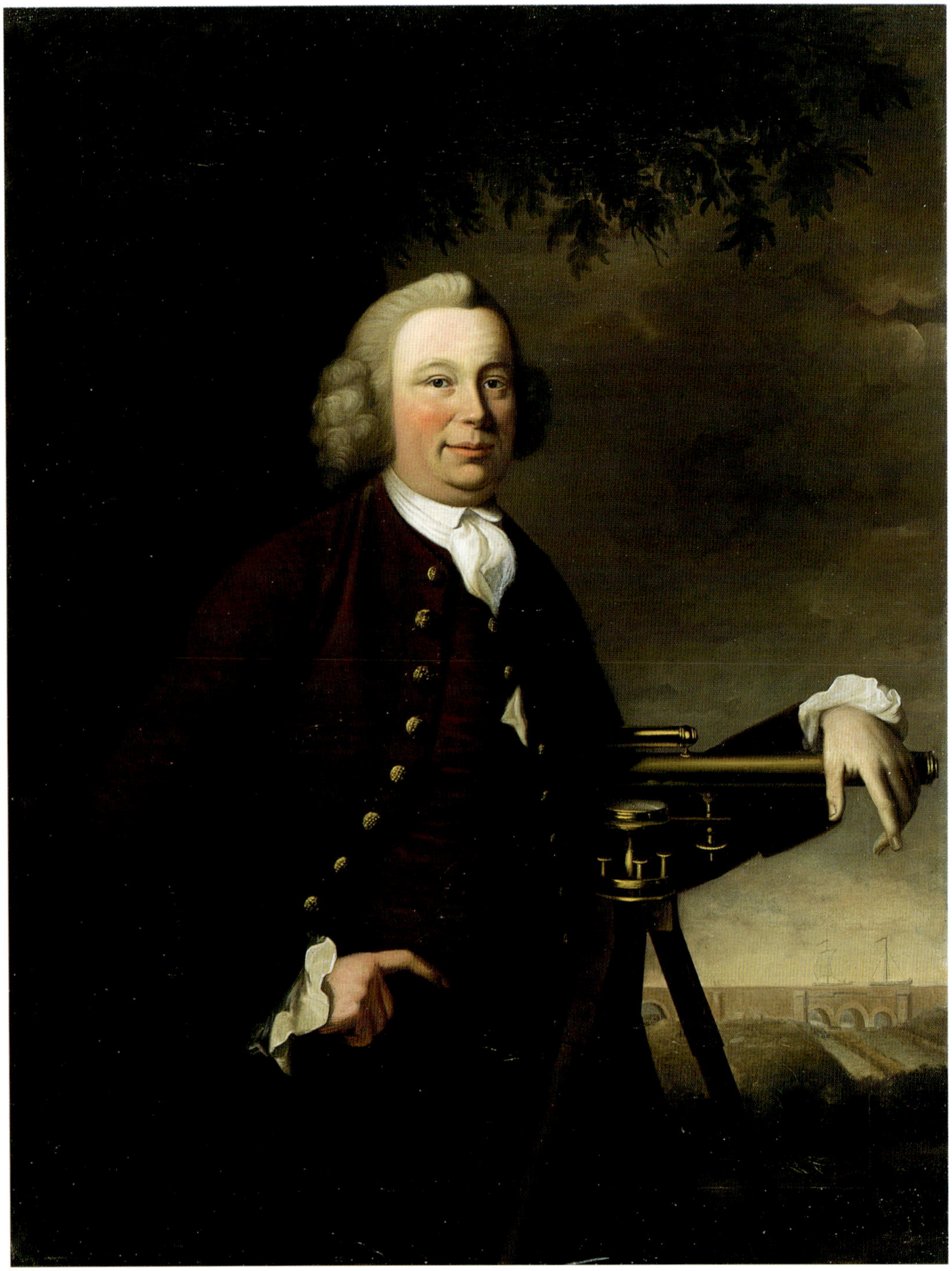

BRINDLEY NPG *6170*

Reversed copies, probably derived from Dunkarton's engraving, are in the Stoke-on-Trent Museum,[7] and with the Institution of Civil Engineers, London (half length, without hands). A version, probably autograph, showing variations in the left hand and background details, is in Salford Art Gallery and was several times engraved.[8] A Wedgwood medallion, for which there remains only documentary evidence, presumably also derived from the Parsons portrait.[9]

1 One of Brindley's theodolites belonged to Mrs A.H. Ackroyd, Southampton, in 1976 (see H. Bode, *James Brindley*, 1976, p.41).
2 He wrote to Scharf, 25 May 1886 offering his portrait of Brindley painted 'by Sir Joshua Reynolds at the request of the Duke of Bridgewater'. An old label verso bears the name *Marrian Beddoe*, a great-aunt of Matthews.
3 But Dunkarton reversed the buttons on the coat and waistcoat, so that they appear on the correct side.
4 *GM*, XXXVI, 1766, p.33.
5 Letter of 18 September 1772, nine days before Brindley's death (E. Meteyard, II, 1866, pp.240-41). I am most grateful to Christine Richardson for this reference - and other Brindley information.
6 Meteyard, II, 1866, p.244.
7 Illus. A. Burton, *Josiah Wedgwood*, 1976, f.p.80 (with the apt observation that 'the right arm appears to have been borrowed from a friend').
8 Illus. *Presents from the Past*, Bolton, Oldham, Stockport, 1978, p.35; engraved as a half length by Thomson 1822, W. Holl 1861 and for the *Universal Mag.*; and as a bust-length oval by P. Condé 1793 and 1810 (*European Mag.*; illus. *Historical Portraits*, I, f.p.252), and anon.
9 See Reilly 1973, p.72.

ICONOGRAPHY

An unattributed miniature and a silhouette were listed with Brindley's descendants in 1959 (J.H.D.M. Campbell, 'Notes on James Brindley', *Derbyshire Miscellany*, Feb. 1959).

Posthumous

Statues in Stoke-on-Trent by Colin Melbourne 1990, and in Coventry by James Butler 1998.

BRISTOL, Augustus John Hervey, 3rd Earl of 1724-79

Naval officer; 2nd s. of John, Lord Hervey; m. secretly in 1744 Elizabeth Chudleigh (who subsequently and bigamously m. the 2nd Duke of Kingston); captain 1747, retiring from active service 1762; lord of the Admiralty 1771-75; rear-admiral 1775, vice-admiral 1778; MP 1757-75; suc. his bro. as 3rd Earl of Bristol 1775.

'but let it be remembered that his failings were those of a warm temper and unguarded disposition; his virtues were those of a heart formed for everything amiable in private, everything great in public life' (Constantine, 1st Baron Mulgrave, 1780).

1835 WILLIAM SILAS SPANTON c.1900 after JOSHUA REYNOLDS [1762-63]

Canvas 126 x 100.5 (49½ x 39½) lined; the flesh areas appear rubbed and craquelure in the darker areas has been retouched.

Blue-grey eyes, powdered hair with black ribbon; wearing the uniform of a captain with above three years service; over the canon a battle plan inscribed *Marlborough Dragon Cambridge* - referring to the attack on 1 July 1762 on Moro Castle, Havana,[1] the action described in the distance.

Collections: Purchased from Leggatt[2] 1919.

Reference: Mannings 2000, no.894a.

A copy of the Reynolds portrait of 1762-63, now in the Manor House Museum, Bury St Edmunds,[3] which was engraved by Edward Fisher as *The Honble Augustus Hervey Captn in His Majestys Navy / Colonel*

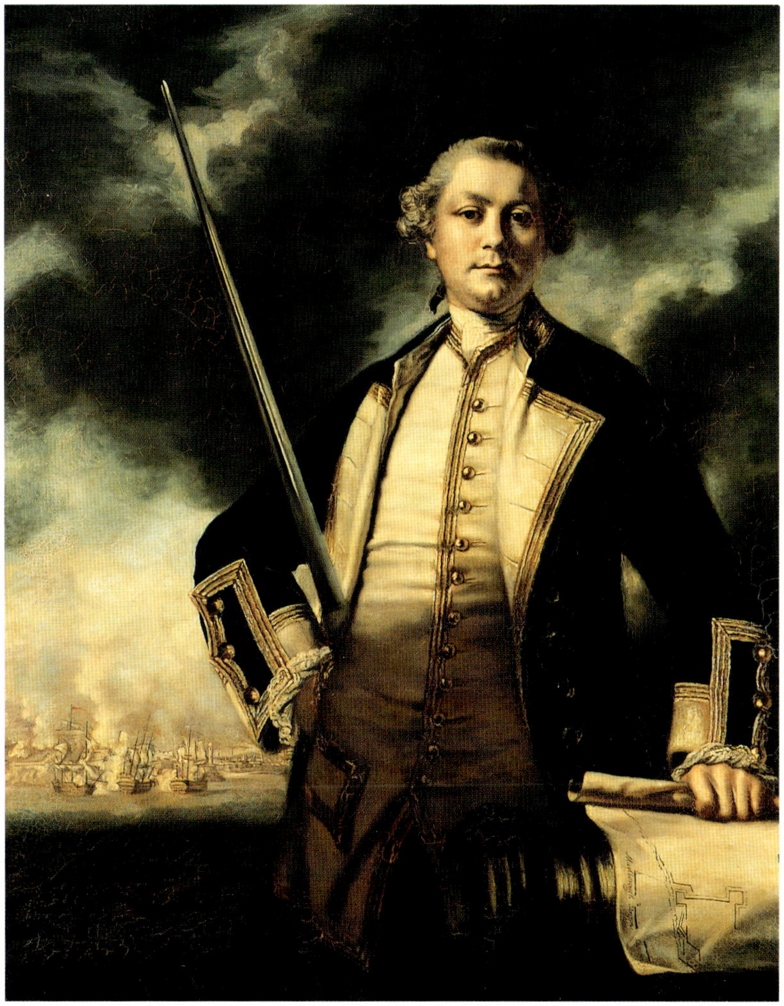

3rd Earl of BRISTOL
NPG 1835

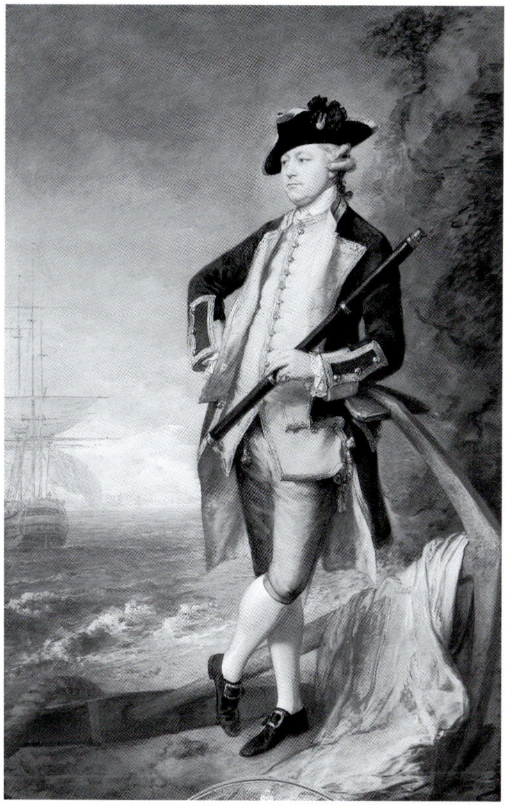

3rd Earl of BRISTOL by Thomas Gainsborough 1768 (Ickworth, The National Trust)

of Marines and Commander in Chief of / His Majesty's Ships in the Mediterranean 1763.

Despite the lined canvas and the craquelure, NPG 1835 was painted c.1900 by the professional copyist Spanton who, in March 1922, wrote how pleased he was that the NPG had 'one of my copies ... namely that of [the 3rd Earl of Bristol] from the picture in the Guildhall, Bury St Edmunds'.[4] Spanton had made two copies of the Reynolds in 1896-99,[5] one for the Marquess of Bristol (which remains at Ickworth),[6] the other for George Hervey.

A bust-length oval version, painted by Reynolds in 1763-64, is at Wilton.[7]

1 *GM*, XXXII, 1762, p.410; [1 July 1762] 'the *Cambridge* of 80 guns, the *Dragon* of 74 guns, and the *Marlborough* of 66, went in and lay against the fort.. . They continued firing for above three hours, which the fort received and returned with great steadiness. At length the ships were ordered off. The *Cambridge* and *Dragon* suffered much ...'. Hervey's ship was the *Dragon*.

2 Leggatt first wrote to to J.D. Milner in November 1918 (NPG archive): 'Mon Cher Ami, I have lately bought a finely painted copy of Sir Joshua's portrait of Augustus John Hervey 3d Earl of Bristol (Admiral) the original of which hangs in the Guildhall Ipswich [sic]. Is he suitable for your gallery? The portrait cost me 37£ size 50 x 40 v fine frame'.

3 Mannings 2000, no.894; also engraved S.W. Reynolds and other weak, bust-length, plates by Harding, A. Walker, and anon. for the *London Mag.* 1775.

4 To J.D. Milner, 31 March 1922 (NPG archive).

5 C.S. Willis, letters of 23 February and 10 March 1937 (NPG archive).

6 Also a lined canvas.

7 Mannings 2000, no.895.

ICONOGRAPHY

1747 Miniature by Maria Clementi taken in Turin for Admiral John Byng (*Augustus Hervey's Journal*, 1954, p.59). A bust-length oval miniature attributed to Nathaniel Hone of a youthful Captain remains at Ickworth.

1750 Small portraits painted by J-E. Liotard in Paris. In January 1750 Hervey sat to Liotard 'tho' the likeness he took looked well, yet I think him no painter ... I gave 16 louis for a small picture of me'; in April 'at the painter Liotard we [Hervey and Madame Caze] met for three hours almost every morning and had our pictures done over and over again for each other'; he gave Madame Caze a case with his picture and in September gave his sister Mary his picture 'in a bracelet set with diamonds' (*Augustus Hervey's Journal*, 1954, pp.97, 101, 107).

1750-51 Painting by Francis Hayman, whole-length standing in captain's uniform taking leave of his family. Ickworth (see B. Allen in *The British Portrait*, 1991, pp.139-41, illus). H. Gravelot, J-E. Liotard and D. Serres painted other parts of this picture.

1762-63 Painting by Joshua Reynolds, see NPG 1835.

1768 Painting by Thomas Gainsborough,* whole length, wearing a captain's uniform and holding a telescope. Ickworth (Waterhouse 1958, no.82). Exhibited SA 1768(60); *In Trust for the Nation*, NG, 1995 (8). Engraved J. Watson 1773; C. Tomkins. Half-length versions by Ozias Humphry at Ickworth and sold Christie's, 19 June 1970, lot 45; a bust-length miniature version by Richard Cosway at Ickworth (illus. *Connoisseur*, XV, 1905, p.5). See also Kempenfelt NPG 1641.

DOUBTFUL PORTRAIT

Painting, bust-length panel, sold Christie's, 25 June 1859, lot 72 (TSB 55/110).

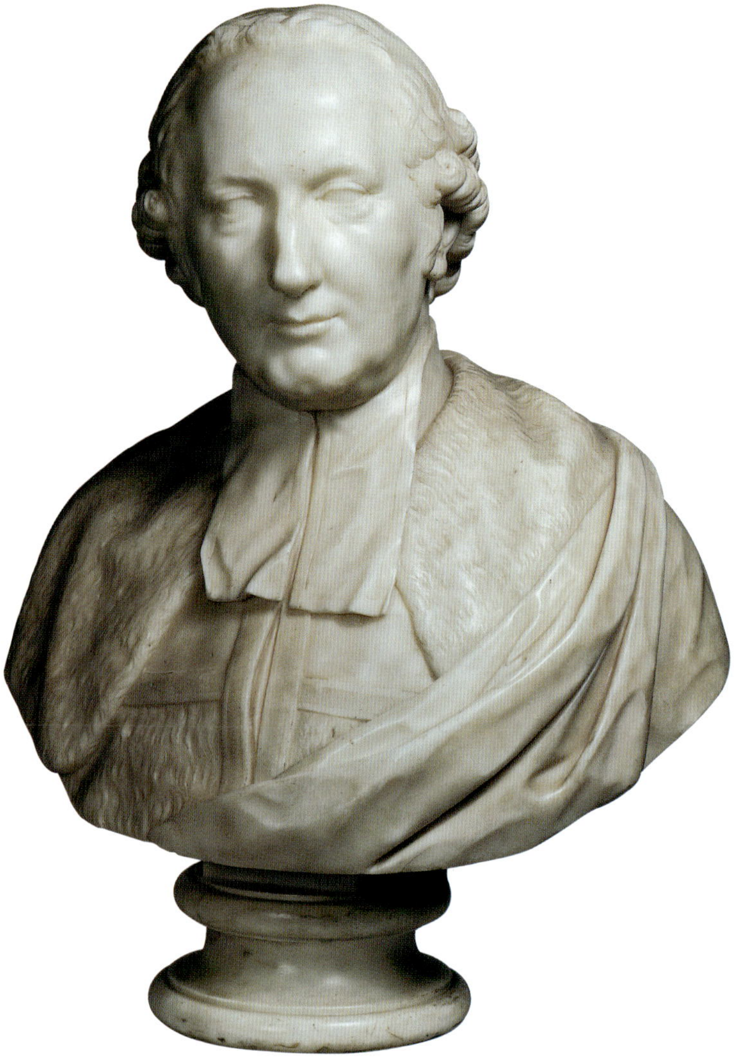

4th Earl of BRISTOL NPG *3895*

BRISTOL, Frederick Augustus Hervey, 4th Earl of 1730–1803

Prelate and traveller; 3rd s. of John, Lord Hervey, suc. his bro. Augustus 1779 as 4th Earl of Bristol; Bishop of Cloyne 1767–68 and of Derry 1768–1803; FRS 1782; travelled in Europe, principally in Italy, 1765–66, 1770–72, 1777–79, 1785–87, 1788–90 and 1792–1803; d. Rome.

'Middle or rather low of stature, of slight frame and countenance, lively in carriage and manners, quick in his speech, blunt, sometimes even rude; ... his manners seem careless, but agreeable, courtly and affable' (Goethe, 1797).

'one of the greatest curiosities alive ... his figure is little, and his face very sharp and wicked ... the last time I saw him he was sitting in his carriage between two Italian women, dress'd in white Bed-gown and Night Cap like a witch, and giving himself the airs of an Adonis' (Catherine Wilmot, 1803).

Abbreviation

Childe-Pemberton 1925: W.S. Childe-Pemberton, *The Earl Bishop*, 2 vols., 1925

3895 CHRISTOPHER HEWETSON c.1778

Marble bust 65 (25½) high, inscribed behind the shoulders: *CHRISTOPHORVS.HEWETSON.FECIT*

Wearing a bishop's fur-lined robes.

Collections: Mortlock, Meldreth Hall, Cambs.; Gerald Kerin, London, from whom purchased 1953.

Exhibitions: *Italy and the Grand Tour*, Norwich, 1958(31); *Il Settecento a Roma*, Rome, 1959(301); *Italian Art and Britain*, RA, 1960(458); *Irish Portraits 1660–1860*, NPG, 1969(163).

Reference: *Hewetson* 1958, p.50; *Hewetson* 1986, p.57, no.13.

Identified by Hodgkinson in 1953[1] and possibly contemporary with the Batoni portrait of 1778 (see below), to judge by the sitter's apparent age and wig;[2] an alternative dating of c.1770 is unsubstantiated.[3] A version at Ickworth, conceivably after Hewetson, differs only in the bands and cape; it had been attributed to Joseph Wilton.

In 1795 Hewetson accepted ('for the love of Bread and Cheese') a commission from Lord Bristol for a colossal marble portrait of Pitt, apparently never completed,[4] and there was probably a further commission for a bust of Lady Caroline Crichton, Lord Bristol's grand-daughter (private collection, Belfast).[5]

1 Note on file.
2 As suggested by R.B. Ford, *Apollo*, XCIX, 1974, p.428.
3 Ingamells 1997, p.494.
4 *Hewetson* 1958, p.50; *Hewetson* 1986, p.58, no.21.
5 See *Hewetson* 1986, p.55, no.5.

ICONOGRAPHY

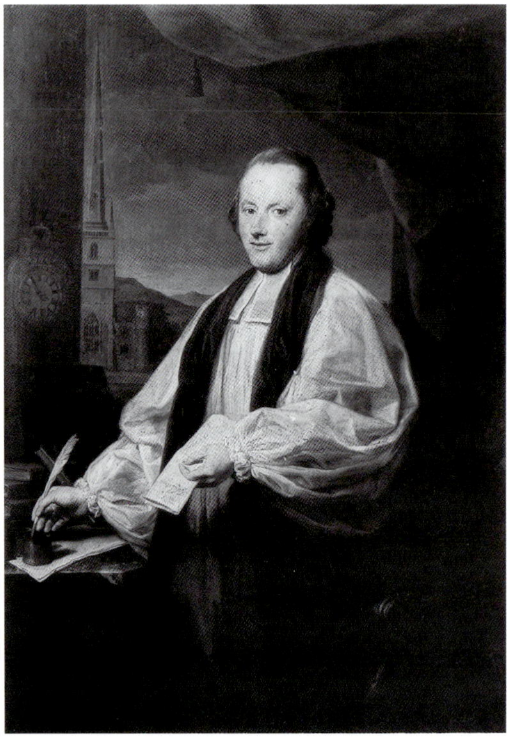

4th Earl of BRISTOL by Pompeo Batoni 1778 (Sotheby's)

c.1760 Painting attributed to Johann Zoffany, half-length oval in clerical dress, an open book showing an engraved *Expulsion from Paradise*. Ickworth (illus. Childe-Pemberton 1925, I, f.p.48). Painted before he became Bishop.

c.1760? Miniature by Gervase Spencer, formerly set in a marble paperweight. Ickworth.

1771 Painting by William Hoare, half-length seated, presenting his son to Lord Chatham. Christie's, 16 June 1950, lot 149 (illus. Childe-Pemberton 1925, I, f.p.98).

Apart from the miniature by Shelley of c.1780-85, subsequent portraits were painted in Italy

1778 Painting by Pompeo Batoni,* three-quarter length standing in rochet and chimere holding a paper inscribed *Act of Toleration*, with the spire of Derry cathedral (completed in 1778) behind him. Sotheby's, 8 April 1987, lot 21 (Clark 1985, no.402). The topographical detail was evidently added.

c.1778 Marble bust by Christopher Hewetson, see NPG 3895.

c.1780 Painting formerly attributed to Angelica Kauffmann, whole-length seated, the paintings on the back wall including a view of Derry cathedral. Ickworth (illus. *Connoisseur*, LIX, 1921, p.4). Engraved J. Bromley.

c.1780-85 Miniature by Samuel Shelley, bust-length oval in clerical dress with brooch. Ickworth.

Another version, without brooch, at Ickworth (from Phillips, 2 May 1984, lot 553).

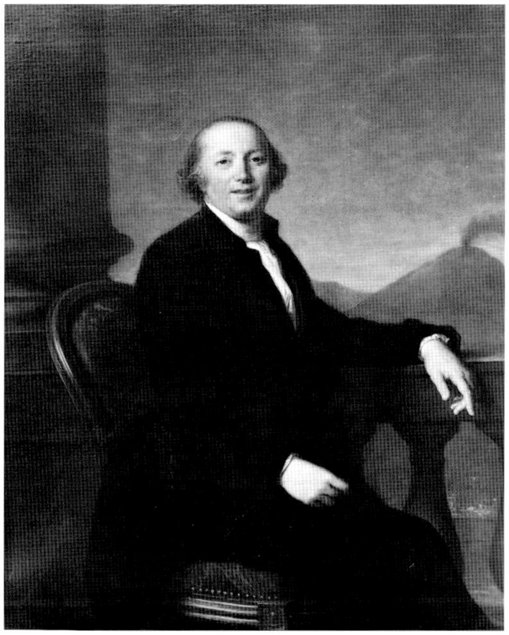

4th Earl of BRISTOL by E. Vigée Le Brun 1790 (Ickworth, The National Trust)

1790 Painting by Elisabeth Vigée Le Brun,* three-quarter length seated in clerical dress, with a distant view of Mount Vesuvius. Ickworth.

1790 Painting by Angelica Kauffmann, three-quarter length seated in clerical dress, by a bust of Maecenas. Christie's, 16 June 1950, lot 150 (illus. *Apollo*, XCIX, 1974, p.430).

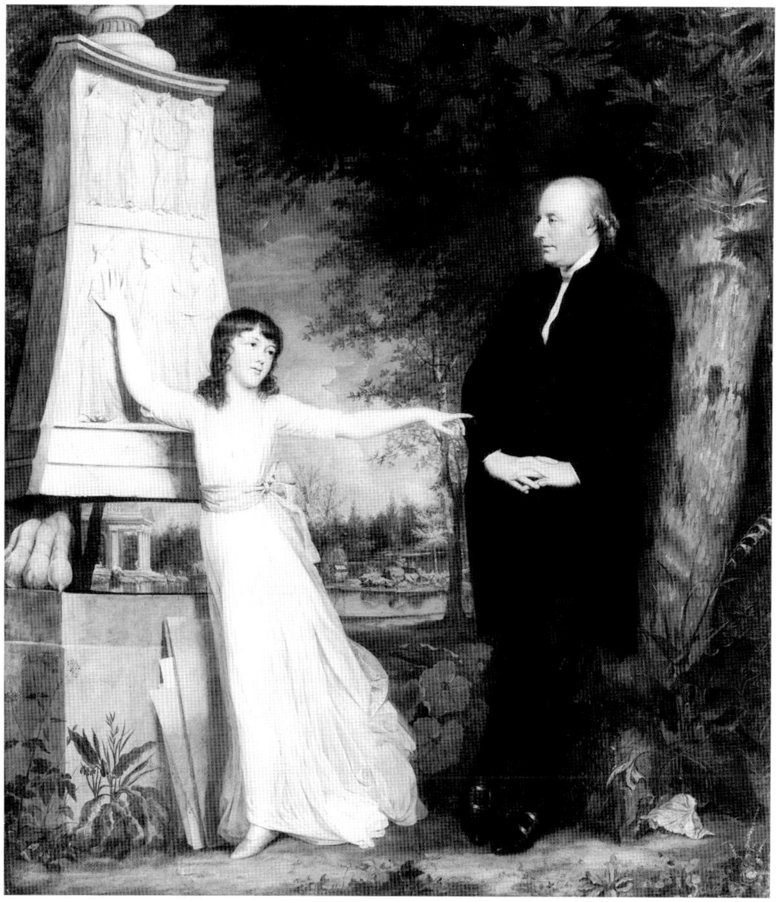

4th Earl of BRISTOL with his grand-daughter by H.D. Hamilton c.1790-93 (National Gallery of Ireland)

1790 Pastel by H.D. Hamilton, seated on the Janiculum Hill in clerical dress. Ickworth (illus. *Apollo*, XCIX, 1974, p.433).

c.1790? Unattributed miniature, bust-length oval in clerical dress, showing white shirt front. Ickworth.

c.1790-93 Painting by H.D. Hamilton,* whole-length standing in clerical dress, in the Borghese Gardens, Rome, with his grand-daughter Caroline. NG of Ireland (4350). An unattributed miniature sold Sotheby's, 22-24 September 1992, lot 559, wearing a jewelled brooch, used a comparable face mask.

c.1790-95 Miniature, formerly attributed to John Comerford, bust-length oval in clerical dress, wearing a miniature set in diamonds (said to be of the Countess of Lichtenau, who was with Lord Bristol in Italy 1795-97). Christie's, 6 July 1971, lot 75 as Continental School (illus. Childe-Pemberton 1925, II, f.p.494; listed in *Comerford* 1999, p.66). Since Comerford's earliest activity in Ireland dates from 1793 he can hardly have received a sitting from Lord Bristol, then permanently abroad.

c.1795 Miniature by an unknown Italian artist, half-length oval, wearing a light coat over his clerical dress; holding an elevation of his Irish house, Ballyscullion (started in 1787), with a distant view of Vesuvius. Ickworth (illus. *CL*, CLIII, 1973, p.1362).

Other miniatures recorded by George Engleheart (formerly with R. Bayne-Powell) and William Grimaldi (Grimaldi 1873, p.29, no.249).

Undated wax by Isaac Gosset listed at Ickworth by Gunnis 1968, p.176.

In his final year at Rome he was described as 'the patron of all modern artists, whose wives he not only associates with as his only female company, but has their pictures drawn as Venuses all over the House' (Catherine Wilmot, Rome 1803).

The many satires of the 4th Earl include *The Right Rev Volunteer*, 1784 (George 6653), *The Irish Patriot*, 1784 (George 6662), *The Patriotic Prelate*, 1785 (George 6819), and *A Whisper over the Channel* by James Sayers, 1785 (George 6805).

DOUBTFUL PORTRAIT

Miniature sold Christie's, 15 May 1979, lot 76 (illus. Childe-Pemberton 1925, I, f.p.28, as by Murphy).

BROME, Lord, see **CORNWALL**

BROWN, Lancelot 1716-83

Landscape gardener and architect; master gardener at Hampton Court 1764; d. Fenstanton, Hunts.

'His truth, his integrity, and his good humour, were very effectual, and will hold a place in the memory of his friends' (Horace Walpole, 1783).

6049 NATHANIEL DANCE c.1773

Canvas 75.5 x 63.5 (29¾ x 25) lined; inscribed, lower right: *LAUNCELOT BROWN Eq:/ of Fenstanton Hunts./ "Capability Brown"/ B.1716 D.1783.*

Blue eyes, powdered hair, wearing a blue coat and waistcoat; his chair has dull red damask upholstery.

Collections: By family descent from the sitter's third son, the Rev Thomas Brown (d.1829), whose grand-daughter m.1848 Frederick Morrice; by descent at Brampton Hall;[1] lent to the NPG from 1971 by Mrs Margaret Morrice (d.1985); her nephew Michael Morrice, from whom purchased 1989.

Engraving: J.K. Sherwin c.1783 (after death, with Mason's epitaph; the plate does not exactly match Dance's painting, e.g. in the alignment of cuff to buttons).

Exhibitions: RA 1907-08(176); *English Landscape Gardening*, Arts Council, 1951(21); *Dance* 1977(27); *Capability Brown and the Northern Landscape*, Newcastle, Leeds, Middlesborough, Barnard Castle, 1983(1); Beningbrough 1979–.

This is the only authentic likeness of Brown. Brown paid Dance twenty guineas on 2 March 1774,[2] which might indicate that NPG 6041 was painted the previous year. It has otherwise generally been dated c.1769.[3] There is a good but bland version at Burghley (where Brown was active for twenty-five years on behalf of the 9th Earl of Exeter); an oval copy was formerly with Derek Sherborn[4] and see NPG 1490 below.

1 Where listed in Farrer 1921, p.152, no.3.
2 Information from Dance's bank account at Drummonds, supplied by Deborah Turnbull (letter of 2 November 1987, NPG archive). Romney and Wright of Derby, for example, were then charging 15 gn. for a 30 x 25 canvas and 30gns for a 50 x 40 (P. Wills, 'Capability Brown's account with Drummonds Bank', *Architectural History*, 27, 1984, pp.382-91, confined himself to clients' payments to Brown).
3 Cf. *Dance* 1977, no.27.
4 Acquired in or before June 1954 from Robinson & Fisher, possibly, lot 60, 24 June 1954 ('A Gentleman, oval, English school').

1490 after NATHANIEL DANCE [c.1773]

Canvas oval 75 x 63 (29½ x 24¾) lined; general retouching particularly evident in the dark background areas, face and coat.[1]

Blue eyes, powdered hair, dark blue-grey coat, grey-blue waistcoat.

Collections: [See below]; Warren Trevor of Chester; Christie's, 4 March 1907, lot 45, bt. in; purchased from Trevor 1908.

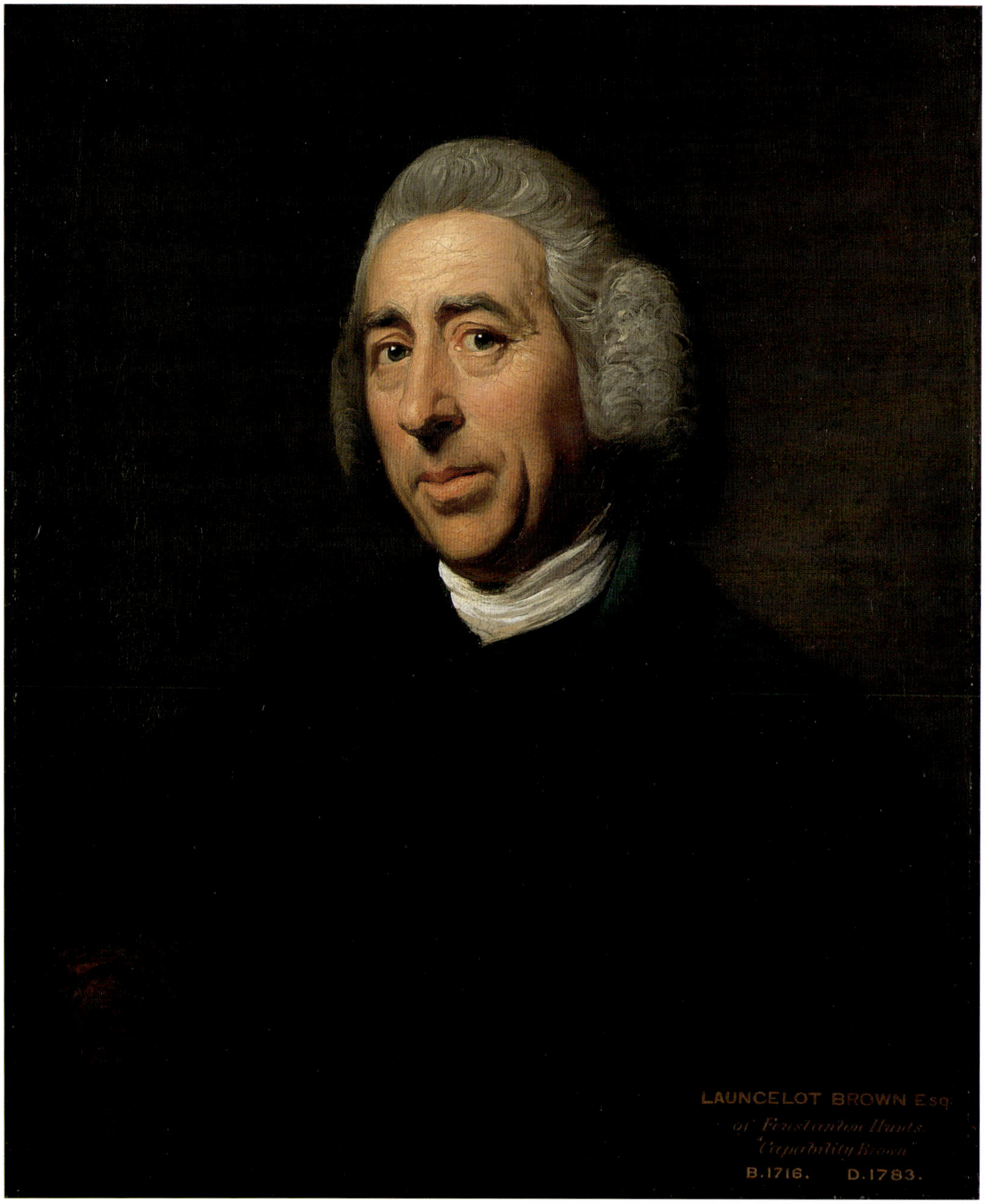

BROWN NPG *6049*

Exhibitions: *The Gothick*, Brighton, 1975(D6); *The Arrogant Connoisseur*, Manchester, 1982(175).

A copy from Dance's half-length, see NPG 6049 above; the oval format eliminates the chair back, and the angle of his right arm differs slightly.

A similar, or the same, oval portrait belonged in 1887 to H.H. Humm of Topsham, Devon, who then alleged that it was 'taken from the life and handed by Miss Brown to Mr English JP from whom I received it'; it was declined by the Gallery in June 1887.[2]

1 MS excerpt on Lancelot Brown from Bryan's *Dictionary* is pasted in the lining canvas.
2 TSB 32/74 and 183/3; letters in NPG archive.

ICONOGRAPHY

c.1773 Painting by Nathaniel Dance, see NPG 6049 and NPG 1490.

c.1780? Painting attributed to Richard Cosway, half length, the head based closely on the Dance pattern but with his own hair. Private collection, descended from the sitter's son-in-law Henry Holland (illus. D. Stroud, *Capability Brown*, 1975, front.). Exhibited *Cosway* 1995, no.3, where dated c.1770). An oval enamel version, inscribed *W.H. Craft fecit: 1789*, with Asprey 1992 (illus. Foskett 1979, p.290, pl.74a).

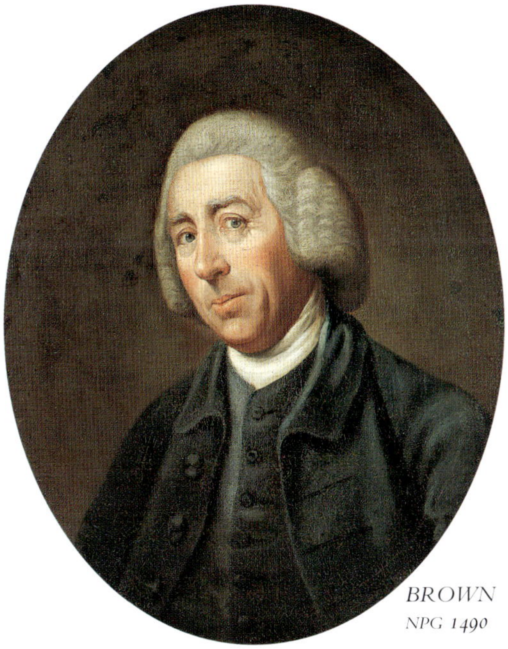

BROWN
NPG *1490*

1782 On 28 February 1782 Brown paid thirty guineas to Thomas Gainsborough, the artist's standard charge for a half-length portrait (information from Dance's bank account at Drummonds, supplied by Deborah Turnbull, letter of 2 November 1987, NPG archive).

DOUBTFUL PORTRAITS

Painting by M.F. Quadal (York CAG; illus. *Preview*, 91, 1970, p.831); drawings attributed to William Hoare (Corsham Court; illus. *CL*, LXXXVII, 1940, p.14) and by Richard Cosway, in a group of four (Capt. H. Lovegrove 1975; illus. D. Stroud, *Capability Brown*, 1975, pl.53, f.p.208).

BRUCE, James 1730-94

African explorer, b. Kinnaird, Tayside; in Italy 1762-63; British consul, Algiers, 1763-65; travelled through north Africa, Crete, Syria and Egypt, and stayed in Abyssinia 1768-72, receiving from the King the investiture of the district of Geesh; in Italy October 1773 to January 1774; FRS 1776; his accounts of his travels, initially disbelieved, were published in 1790.

'His Figure is almost Gigantic! He is the tallest man I ever saw, & exceeding well made, neither too fat or lean in proportion to his amazing height. I cannot say I was charmed with him, for he seemed rather arrogant, ... he is a very manly character, & looks as dauntless & intrepid, that I believe he could never in his life know what fear meant' (Fanny Burney, 1774).

'a man of uncommonly large stature, six feet four inches, and latterly very corpulent' (*Kay Portraits* 1842).

5008 JOHN SMART 1776

Watercolour and bodycolour on ivory 3.7 x 3 (1½ x 1¼) signed above the sitter's right shoulder *J S/1776* in black. The back of the gold frame is copiously, and rather incoherently, inscribed with a description of Bruce's travels in Latin.[1]

Brown eyes, powdered club wig, lilac waistcoat and jacket with a lace neckcloth.

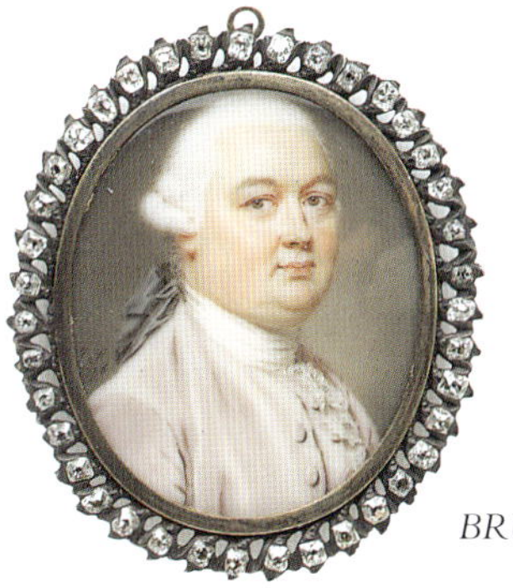

BRUCE NPG *5008*

Collections: Alfred Hill; Sotheby's, 13 May 1942, lot 84, bt. Berry;[2] E. Grosvenor Paine, Mississippi, who sold it to J.D. Goetze, Kansas City, c.1952-53; Sotheby's, 25 November 1974, lot 165, unsold; purchased from Sotheby's, with the aid of a donation from A.J.B. Kiddell, 1974.

Engravings: R. Stanier 1790 lettered *James Bruce of Kinnaird Lord of Geesh, vitam impendere vero* (*European Mag.*); anon. late 18th century.

Reference: Walker 1998, no.65.

1 *Europa Asia Africa peragratis extrema rerum usque fontes Nili pervenit. Inde per Nubiae deserta reversus est Altiora Aggressurus si quid superfuisset. Semel naufragium passus in terram Natavit semel ex Acie Vulneratus Excessit. Ter caeso excercitu Incolumi evasit. Hic Amor et Virtus Comitas & Fides tantis Laboribus finem Posuere & Premium* [he travelled through Europe, Asia and Africa to the source of the Nile. Thence he explored the Nubian desert. He swam ashore from shipwreck and was wounded in battle. Three times he survived hostile attacks. After such extraordinary experiences he is now rewarded with virtue, friendship and trust.]

2 The NPG were the underbidders.

ICONOGRAPHY

1759 Miniature by Gervase Spencer, wearing a blue coat. Jeffery Whitehead sale, Christie's, 2nd day, 5 August 1915, lot 319; presumably that exhibited without attribution *Guelph* 1891(955).

1762 Painting by Pompeo Batoni,* half-length in an elaborately trimmed red coat. Broomhall (Clark 1985, no.257). A replica Scottish NPG (PG 141; Clark 1985, no.258). A miniature copy, now untraced, was made by Victoria Stern in 1762, and a later copy sold Sotheby's, 11 April 1979, lot 101.

1774 Painting by Johann Zoffany,* *The Tribuna, Florence* (see Introduction) in which Bruce appears on the extreme right, standing next to the *Venus de Medici*. Royal Collection (Millar 1969, no.1211). Bruce was

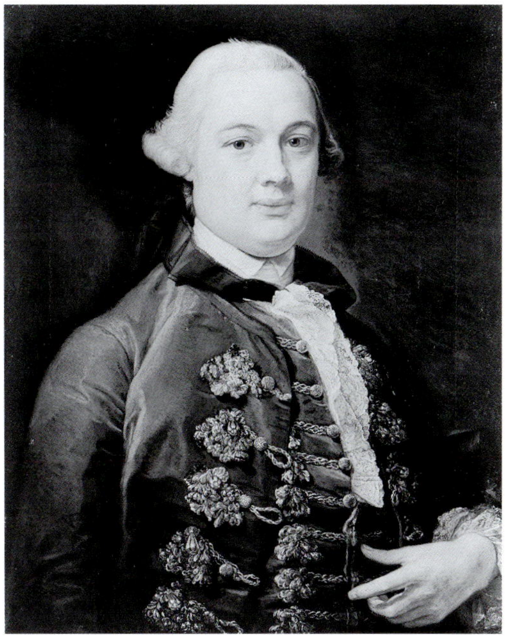

BRUCE by Pompeo Batoni 1762 (Scottish National Portrait Gallery)

in Florence in January 1774; Zoffany worked on the picture in Florence between 1772 and 1777.

1775 Painting by David Martin, half-length painted oval. Broomhall. Exhibited SA 1775(157). Engraved J. Heath 1790 (for Bruce's *Travels*, the picture then in the possession of Sir John Henderson of Fordel); W.C. Edwards 1830; S. Freeman 1855; W.H. Lizars; A half-length wash drawing after Martin is in the Scottish NPG (PG 1667), and a version was in a private collection 1998.

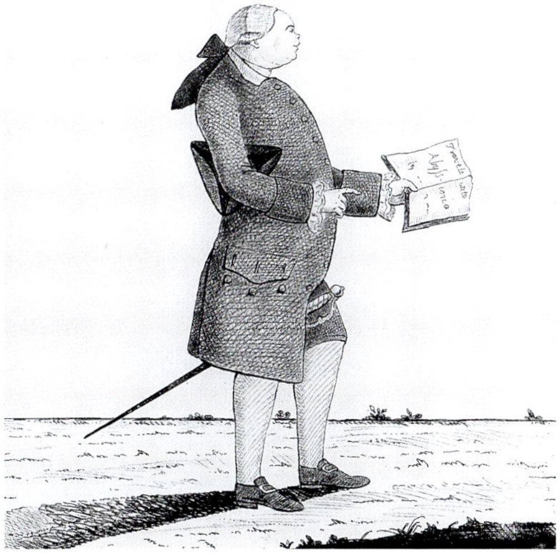

BRUCE etching by E. Topham 1775 (NPG D 13789)

1775 Etching by E. Topham,* *Abyssinian Traveller*, whole-length caricature (George 5317).

1776 Miniature by John Smart, see NPG 5008.

1790 Engraving by J. Heath, medallion (Bruce's *Travels*, vol. v).

1791 Etching by J. Kay, *Travells Eldest Son in Conversation with a Cherokee Chief*, whole-length standing with the Edinburgh traveller Peter Williamson (*Kay Portraits* 1842, I, no.lix; George 7978).

DOUBTFUL PORTRAITS

See Unidentified Portraits NPG 100. Miniature attributed to J. Bogle, Scottish NPG (PG 1460); watercolour on ivory, Holly House, Montrose; paintings by G. Weichert (Royal Geographical Society; TSB 1/5 and 4/32) and unattributed, sold Christie's, 26 September 1997, lot 48.

BRYDGES, George, see RODNEY

BULLER, Sir Francis, 1st Bt 1746-1800

Judge; KC 1777; appointed puisne judge of the King's Bench 1778 on the recommendation of Lord Mansfield (whose portrait he owned, see NPG 172); Bt 1790.

'short of stature, but of handsome features, with a piercing eye and a commanding forehead' (*DNB*).

'Gay, facetious, liberal in his conversation and opinions, he despises the petty prejudices of the day' (*Public Characters of 1798-99*).

458 MATHER BROWN 1792

Canvas 125 x 99.5 (49¼ x 39¼) lined; widespread craquelure prominent on his right knee, above his right cuff and in the dark upper areas; strip-lined and revarnished 2001.

Blue eyes, white wig, wearing judicial robes: red cape and gown trimmed with white fur with a black sash; he sits on a 'Gothic' throne, a green drape with gold tassels above him; a view of Westminster Abbey to the right.

Collections: Presented by the Society of Judges and Serjeants-at-Law 1877.[1]

Engravings: F. Bartolozzi 1794 (see below); J. Owen, 1799 (bust length; *Public Characters of 1798-99*); Orme jr. 1800 (*European Mag.*; half-length oval).

Exhibitions: RA 1792(391);[2] long loan to the Royal Courts of Justice; *Lord Mansfield*, Kenwood, 1971(26); *Art on the Line*, Courtauld Gallery, 2001(36).

Reference: Evans 1982, no.31.

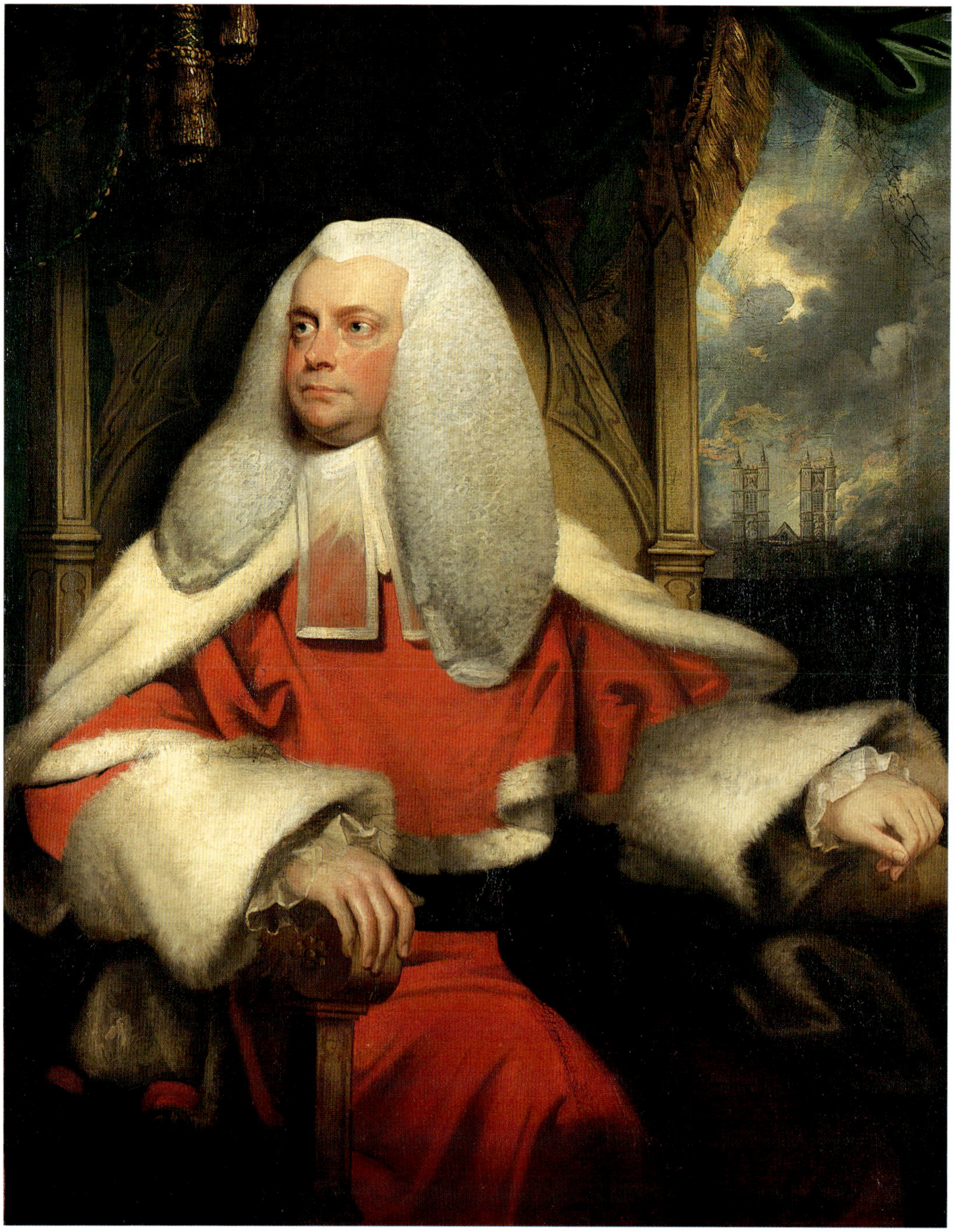

BULLER NPG *458*

A preliminary chalk study for the head is in the Scottish National Portrait Gallery (PG 451).[3] The reversed stipple engraving by F. Bartolozzi* first published in 1794[4] differs from NPG 458 in detail: Buller sits in a plain chair, his left hand[5] rests on papers lying on a table beside an ink well, and the folds of the robes and curtain are differently disposed. A version, descended from the Buller family, shows a book in his right hand and Lincoln's Inn instead of Westminster Abbey in the distance.[6]

1 Evans 1982, p.201, records that NPG 458 was said erroneously to have been sold by Lord Haldon (by F.P. Seguier, *Dictionary of Monograms*, I, f.151v; BL), but this was the Buller family's version sold Christie's, 28 February 1891, lot 52, – the same day as the Haldon pictures were sold.

2 Evans assumes that NPG 458 was the version exhibited.

3 Illus. Evans 1982, fig.93.

4 Reissued in 1823 as *M. Browne Pinxt-F. Bartolozzi Direxit*.

5 That is, the right hand in NPG 458.

6 Sold Sotheby's, 9 July 1980, lot 117a, and Christie's, 13 February 1981, lot 24; Evans 1982, no.32.

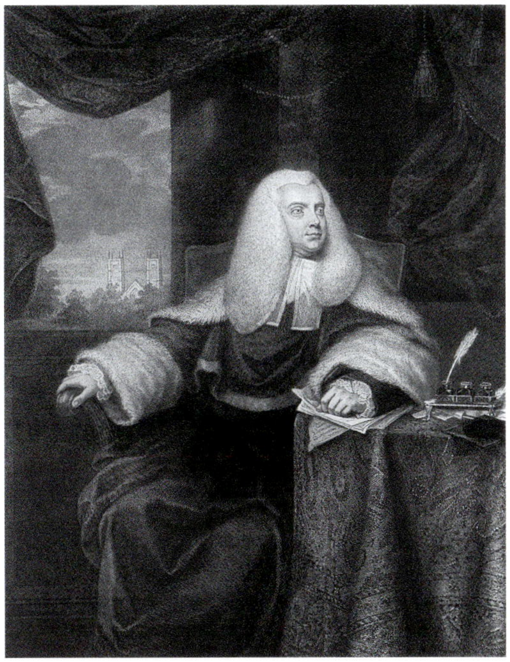

BULLER F. Bartolozzi after Mather Brown 1792 (NPG D 13739)

BURKE, Edmund 1730-97

Politician and writer; edited the *Annual Register* 1758-64; MP 1765-94; secretary to Lord Rockingham 1765-66; published *Thoughts on the Present Discontents* 1770, and *Reflections on the Revolution in France* 1792; led the impeachment of Warren Hastings from 1787.

'his Irish accent ... was as strong as if he had never quitted the banks of the Shannon' (Sir Nathaniel Wraxall, 1815).

'He was five feet ten inches high, erect, well-formed, never very robust ... near sighted ... he almost constantly, from about the year 1780, wore spectacles ... His countenance was such as a painter would find it difficult precisely to draw (and indeed I always understood they complained of the difficulty); its expression frequently varying, but always full of benevolence' (Sir James Prior, 1826).

Abbreviation

Prior 1826: J. Prior, *Memoir of the Life and Character of the Right Hon Edmund Burke*, 2nd ed., 2 vols., 1826

655 studio of JOSHUA REYNOLDS [1767-69]

Canvas 75 x 62 (29½ x 24½); canvas stamped *J Middleton;*[1] cleaned and relined 1987.

Grey eyes, dark brown hair, dull grey-green coat, a black eyeglass ribbon.

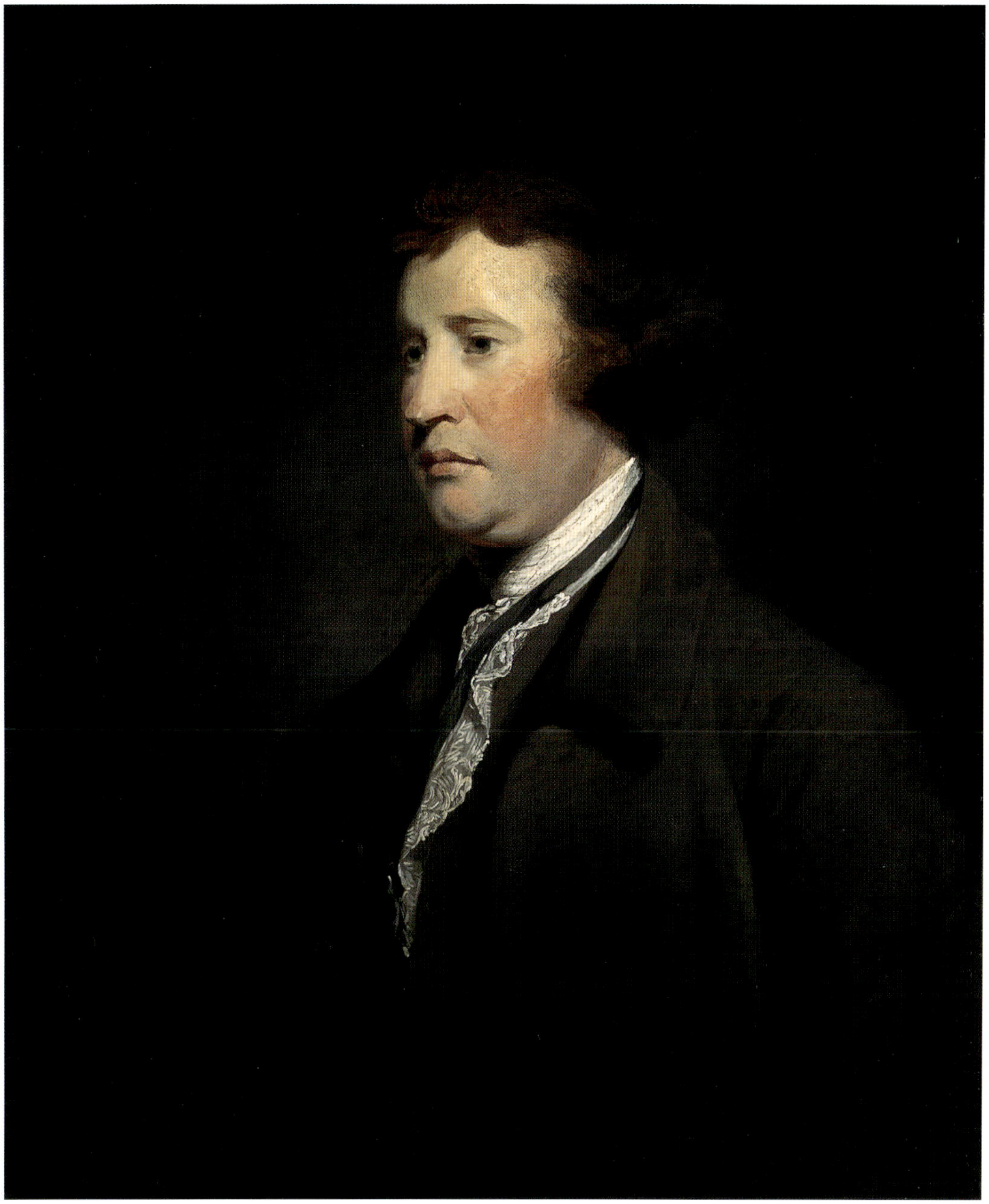

BURKE NPG 655

Collections: Thomas Haviland Burke (d.1852), the sitter's great nephew;[2] his son, E. Haviland Burke; sold by order of the Court of Chancery,[3] Christie's, 4 July 1874, lot 81, bt. in; Christie's, 24 June 1876, lot 100, bt. George Attenborough, from whom purchased 1882.

Engraving: C.E. Wagstaff 1834.

Exhibitions: RA 1871(161) lent E. Haviland Burke; *The Past We Share*, Dallas, 1967(16); *Johnson*, Arts Council, 1984(67); *The Raj*, NPG, 1990-91(148); *Romantic Icons*, Grasmere, 1999(7).

Reference: Graves & Cronin, I, pp.130-1; Waterhouse 1941, p.59; Mannings 2000, no.284a.

A near-contemporary copy of the original Reynolds portrait that was given by the sitter's widow to the Earl Fitzwilliam (private collection); it was first engraved by James Watson in 1770 and was once described as the best portrait of Burke.[4] When NPG 655 was acquired a second, weaker copy was already in the collection (purchased in 1874; NPG 389);[5] it was lent to the National Gallery of Ireland 1884-1916 and was sold by the Trustees in 1916 to Mrs Walter Hayes Burns, mother-in-law of Earl Harcourt; it was last sold Christie's, 27 October 1961, lot 32.

Other copies include those in the Victoria Memorial Hall, Calcutta (by Edward Dyer); the Bristol Council House, the Palace of Westminster and the Royal Albert Museum, Exeter (both these last once attributed to Northcote). An enamel copy by Henry Spicer, inaccurately inscribed 'from a crayon Pictor painted by Ozias Humphry', sold Christie's, 7 November 1988, lot 84,[6] was possibly that exhibited RA 1795(487). The head from the Reynolds portrait was used in an anonymous engraving showing Burke as *The British Cicero*, the *Magna Charta* in his left hand.

1 A supplier, known to Reynolds, whose business lasted until c.1840. Comparable canvas stamps appears on the canvas used by Opie for his 1792 portrait of Burke (SSB 92a/21), see below.
2 After Burke's death, his widow (d.1812) lived at Butler's Court, Beaconsfield, with her niece, Mrs Haviland (d.1816), and her son, Thomas Haviland [Burke] (Prior 1826, II, pp.405-06, and *Burke LG*, 1868, pp.182a-182b, pages of uneasy pretence, not retained in later editions).
3 The property was disputed in Chancery in 1874 between the children of Thomas Haviland Burke, E. Haviland Burke v Mrs Mary J. Evezard.
4 Mannings 2000, no.284; Prior 1826, II, p.411.
5 From Col. Penleaze, brother-in-law of Capt. William Phillips (d.1873), whose father Charles Phillips (1787-1859) was the first recorded owner.
6 A portrait by Humphry of Edmund Burke's brother, Robert, was copied in enamel by Spicer, see Williamson 1918, pp.239, 277, 295, illus. f.p.188 (previously exhibited SKM 1865, no.2229, lent T. Moreton Wood).

854 after JAMES BARRY [1774-75]

Watercolour and bodycolour on ivory 6 x 5.2 (2⅜ x 2⅛)

Brown eyes, fair hair, red-brown coat, white neckcloth.

Collections: Purchased from G. Redford 1891 (as William Combe by Richard Cosway).

Exhibitions: *Samuel Johnson, Londoner*, Royal Exchange, London, 1964; *Gillray*, Tate, 2001(100f).

Reference: Walker 1998, no.63.

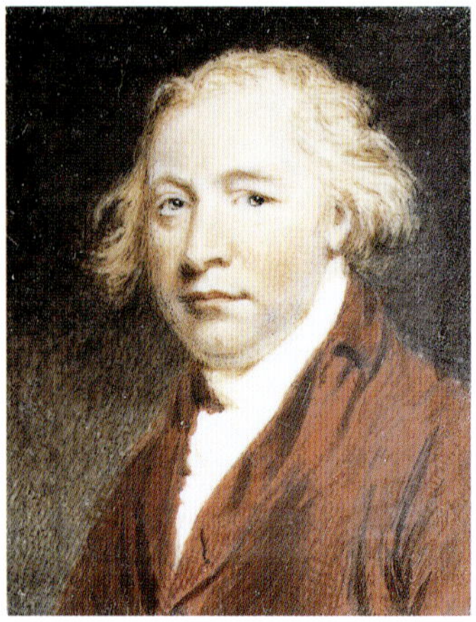

BURKE NPG *854*

Acquired in 1891 as a portrait of William Combe, NPG 854 had been correctly identified by 1906.[1] It is copied from the three-quarter length portrait, 'truly that of an orator', commissioned by Dr Richard Brocklesby from James Barry in 1772 and now untraced.[2] Complicated by Barry's neuroses and in particular by his jealousy of Reynolds, to whom Burke was sitting at the same time, the commission was only completed after an anguished exchange of letters between Barry and Burke in July 1774.[3] Two full-size copies are recorded: in the National Gallery of Ireland (128)[4] and sold Sotheby's, 20 July 1987, lot 35.

1 When a new label was drafted (NPG archive).
2 Pressly 1981, no.46a.
3 *Burke Corr.*, III, pp.4-9.
4 Pressly 1981, no.46b.

1607 THOMAS R. POOLE 1791

Pink wax 8.6 (3⅜) high, inscribed on truncation: *1791/Poole*; the wax partly discoloured and some black paint cracking on the supporting glass. Label formerly verso reads: *The Rt Honble Edmund Burke / Modelled from the Life / by T.R. Poole, / Medallion Modeller, / to his Royal Highness the / Prince of Wales.*[1]

Collections: Presented by G.B. Croft-Lyons FSA through the National Art Collections Fund 1911.

Reference: Pyke 1973, p.113.

A likeness approved by Burke's biographer James Prior,[2] who preferred it to Hoppner's portrait of 1795-1801 (see below). Other examples show slight differences in the hair ribbon and neckcloth, e.g. two in English private collections,[3] that engraved by T.W. Fry in 1823 (with the date 1795)[4] and that dated 1797 of which is there is a cast in the Scottish National Portrait Gallery (PG 1878 as James Tassie).[5]

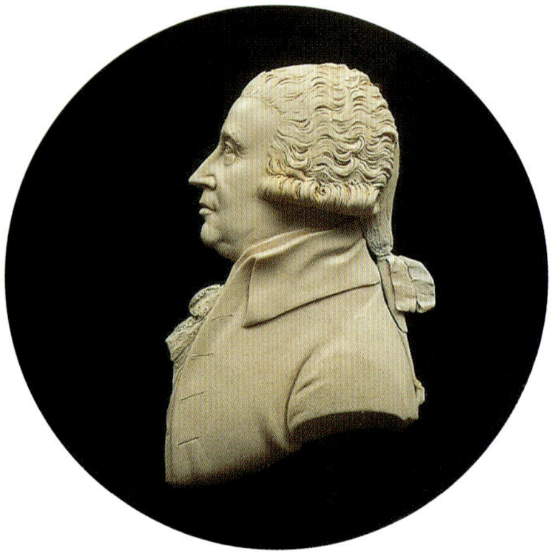

BURKE NPG *1607*

1 An ink inscription, formerly verso, reads: *The Model to be hung in a side Light*, and there was also a printed list of Poole's prices, headed: 'Mr Poole's Models are durable in any Climate', and ranging from 2 guineas for a copy of a Gentleman's medallion, to 10 guineas 'in Clerical Habit or Regimentals'; 'Mr Poole continues to model free of expence, the Head of a Gentleman, on receiving a guarantee for twenty Copies'.
2 Prior 1826, II, p.411.
3 Listed by Pyke 1973, p.113; photographs NPG archive.
4 Other undated examples in the Victoria and Albert Museum (A.31.1970); sold Sotheby's, 2 June 1975, lot 134, and 24 July 1978, lot 57 (see Pyke 1981, p.33).
5 Gray 1894, no.55; another example exhibited *Benjamin Franklin and his Circle*, New York, 1936(208 as Tassie).

745 see Groups, *The House of Commons 1793-94* by KARL ANTON HICKEL 1793-95

ICONOGRAPHY

For caricatures, to which Burke was subject throughout his political career, see N.K. Robinson, *Edmund Burke, A Life in Caricature*, 1996.

In 1774 Burke told his protégé James Barry 'I never thought my portrait a business of consequence … I have been painted in my life five times; twice in little and three times in large. The late Mr Spencer and the late Mr Sisson painted the miniatures. Mr Worlidge and Sir Joshua painted the rest' (13 July 1774, *Burke Corr.*, III, 8).

c.1755? Painting by Thomas Worlidge. Burke mentioned his portrait by Worlidge in a letter of 13 July 1774 (see above). It has been tentatively associated with the portrait sold Sotheby's, 14 July 1999, lot 45 (illus. *Burke Corr.*, I, f.p.xv), exhibited Belfast, *Great Irishmen*, 1965 (25, as attributed to Thomas Worridge [*sic*]).

before 1763 Miniature by Gervase Spencer. Mentioned by Burke in a letter of 13 July 1774 (see above); Spencer is not known to have worked after 1763.

1766 Miniature by S. Cocks (a name otherwise unrecorded; possibly a misreading of S. Cotes) previously listed at Hatfield (cat., 1891, p.119).

before 1767 Miniature by Richard Sisson, mentioned by Burke in a letter of 13 July 1774 (see above).

1766-67 Unfinished painting by Joshua Reynolds,* with the 2nd Marquess of Rockingham, see Rockingham.

1767-69 Painting by Joshua Reynolds, see NPG 655.

c.1771 Painting by James Barry, half length. Trinity College, Dublin (Pressly 1981, no.38). Possibly from the artist's sale, Christie's, 10-11 April 1807, lot 71, as 'Edmund Burke, demonstrating his position on the Sublime and Beautiful, painted about the year 1771'.

1774 Painting by Joshua Reynolds,* half length. Scottish NPG (PG 2362; Mannings 2000, no.285). Painted for Henry Thrale's library at Streatham House; conditionally bequeathed to the NG of Ire-

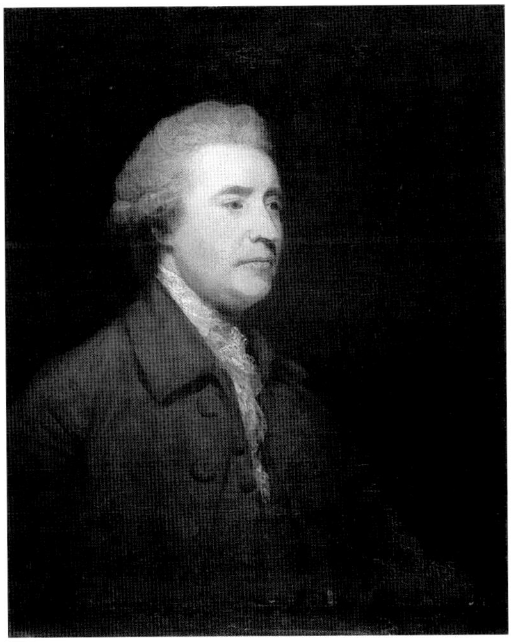

BURKE by Joshua Reynolds 1774 (Scottish National Portrait Gallery)

land in 1930; transferred to Edinburgh 1969. Probably exhibited RA 1774(224). A copy by E.F. Burney (Burney 1991, I, p.290n15) remains untraced.

1774-75 Painting by James Barry, see NPG 854.

1776 Painting by James Barry,* *Ulysses and a Companion fleeing from the Cave of Polyphemus*, with Burke as Ulysses, Barry as his companion. Crawford AG, Cork (Pressly 1981, no.48). Exhibited RA 1776(18).

1776 Painting by George Romney, half length. Commissioned by the Duke of Richmond (Ward & Roberts 1904, II, p.22; and see Richmond and Lennox, NPG 4877). Engraved J. Jones 1787* and 1790. A good version at Churchill College, Cambridge; a copy was painted for Ernst Brandes of Hanover in 1786; a miniature copy sold Sotheby's, 18 December 1995, lot 143, and a closely related drawing sold Christie's, 16 November 1965, lot 182, as by Lawrence, but possibly copied from the engraving.

1777-84 Painting by James Barry, *Distribution of Premiums in the Society of Arts*, part of the *Progress of Human Culture*, in which Burke appears as an isolated figure on the right. Royal Society of Arts, London (Pressly 1981, no.26). Engraved J. Barry 1791.

1782 Etching by J. Sayers, whole length, with spectacles (George 6055; illus. N.K. Robinson, *Edmund Burke, A Life in Caricature*, 1996, p.32).

c.1784? Painting by Thomas Hickey, small whole length with Charles James Fox. NG of Ireland (258). Given in 1789 by William Burke in Bengal to William Hickey who described it as Burke

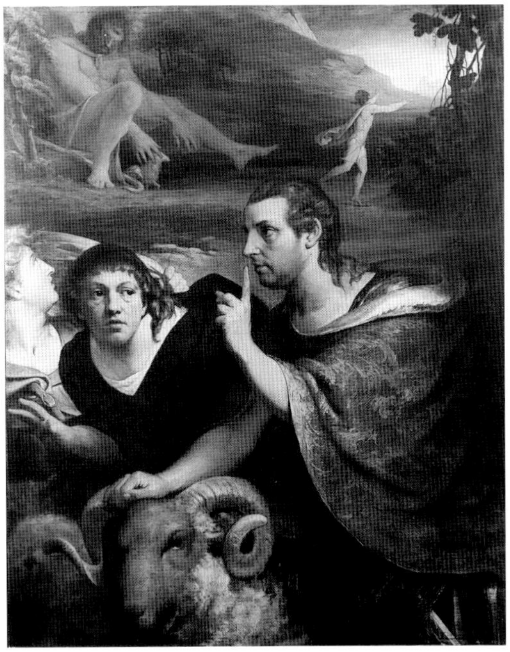

BURKE as Ulysses guiding a Companion (James BARRY) by James Barry 1776 (Crawford Municipal Art Gallery, Cork)

'reading the famous India Bill [of 1783] prepared and brought into prominence by [Fox]. It was but an indifferent performance' (Hickey, *Memoirs*, III, p.349). Hickey went abroad in 1780 and the picture was almost certainly made up.

1785 Marble bust by John Hickey. Formerly at Wentworth Woodhouse. Engraved J. Ward. Replicas: British Museum (destroyed 1941; MLA1825.11.12.1; Dawson 2000, no.10), and Trinity College, Dublin (illus. Crookshank & Webb 1990, p.30). William Burke gave a copy to William Hickey in Bengal in 1789; it appears in Thomas Hickey's portrait of William Hickey (illus. Archer 1979, p.214; Hickey, *Memoirs*, III, p.349).

before 1791 Wax by E.G. Mountstephen (J. Hassell, *Memoirs of George Morland*, 1906, p.22). An example formerly at Holland House (cat., 1904, no.254). Mountstephen left England in 1791.

1791 Design for a medal by Charles Taconet, exhibited RA 1791(278).

1791 Wax by T.R. Poole, see NPG 1607.

c.1791 Miniature by W.H. Brown, wearing spectacles, engraved W. Ridley 1798; a version engraved R. Scott.

1792 Painting by John Opie, small half length, a book in his right hand. Private collection (illus. *Burke Corr.*, VI, front). The original canvas is inscribed and dated; the Duke of Dorset's payment to Opie on 5 July 1792 is preserved (C.J. Phillips, *History of the Sackville Family*, II, pp.411, 441; SSB 92a/21).

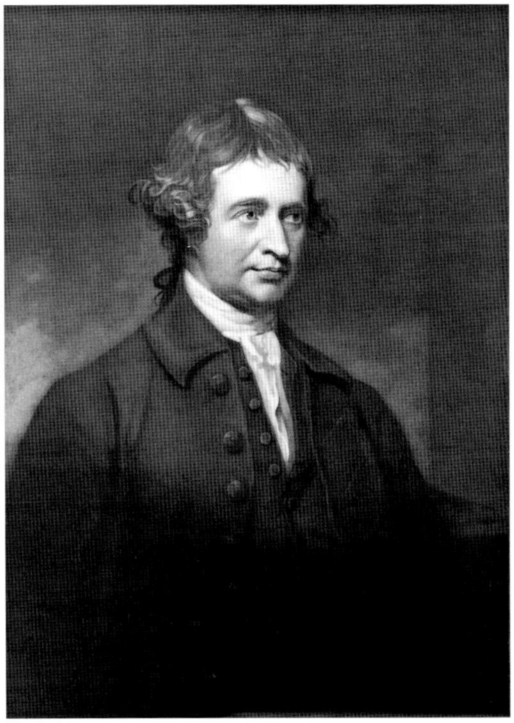

BURKE J. Jones after George Romney 1776 (NPG D 11081)

1793-95 Painting by K.A. Hickel, *The House of Commons 1793-94*, see Groups NPG 745.

1795-1801 Painting by John Hoppner, whole length in LL.D robes. Trinity College, Dublin (McKay & Roberts 1909, p.35; illus. Crookshank & Webb 1990, p.29). Commissioned by the College in 1795; 'the figure, features, and complexion are like his, but the countenance as a whole by no means does him justice' (Prior 1826, II, p.410).

1797 Bust by R.K. Porter, engraved J. Chapman 1797, T. Nugent 1798 'After a bust from the life by R.K. Porter'. An engraving by W.B. Daniel 1808, profile bust *all'antica*, probably from the same source, and an anon. marble bust sold Christie's, Adare Manor, Ireland, 9-10 June 1982 lot 205, also resembles this type.

A marble bust listed at Knole in 1924 (C.J. Phillips, *History of the Sackville Family*, II, p.255), remains untraced.

1797 Death mask, ordered by Queen Charlotte. A cast in the Department of Anatomy, Edinburgh University, from the Edinburgh Phrenological Society (*Death Masks and Life Masks*, Edinburgh University, [1988], p.4).

1797 Medallion by William Tassie, *all'antica* (Gray 1894, no.54). Cast in Scottish NPG (PG 406).

Posthumous

1850 Bust by Christopher Moore. Plaster[?] exhibited Crystal Palace (Phillips 1854, no.450).

1858 Statue by William Theed jr. Palace of Westminster (Walker 1988, III, p.13). Modello exhibited RA 1858(1179).

1868 Statue by J.H. Foley. Trinity College, Dublin (illus. Crookshank & Webb 1990, p.30). A reduced plaster version is also in the College; a reduced bronze dated 1865 is in the Royal Collection, and another, undated, sold Phillips 19 July 1995, lot 120.

1900 Bronze statue by J.H. Thomas. Colston Avenue, Bristol.

DOUBTFUL PORTRAITS

Miniature of c.1765 by Nathaniel Hone (NG of Ireland, 7315; illus. Caffrey 2000, p.175). So-called Wedgwood medallion modelled by Lochée (illus. Reilly 1973, p.76), not related to the Tassie medallion Gray 1894, no.55.

BURNEY, Charles 1726–1814

Musicologist, composer; Mus.D Oxford 1769; FRS 1773; author of *A General History of Music* (1776, 1782 and 1789); fa. of Fanny Burney.

Abbreviation

Scholes 1948: P. Scholes, *The Great Dr Burney*, 2 vols., 1948

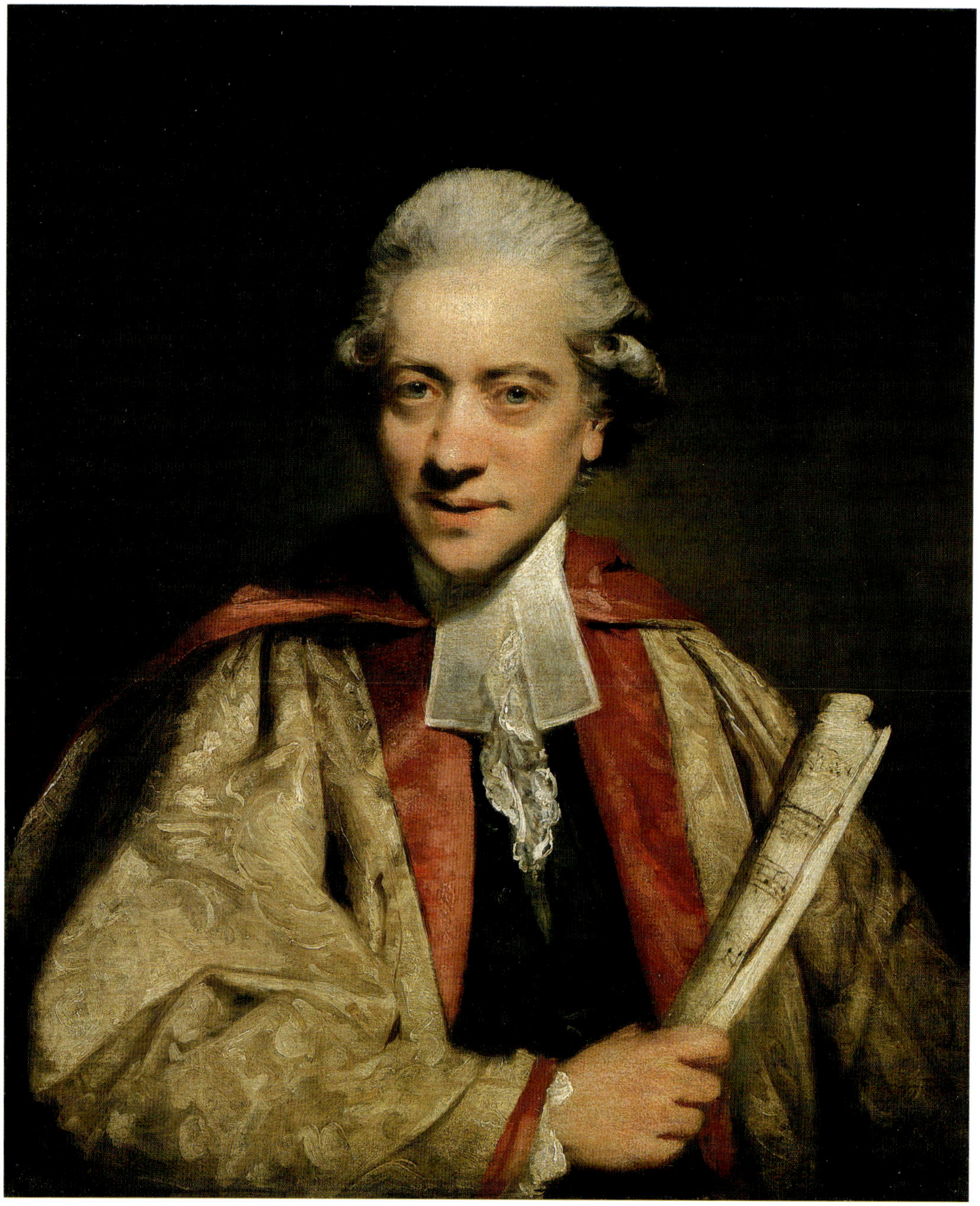

BURNEY NPG *3884*

3884 JOSHUA REYNOLDS 1781

Canvas 75 x 62 (29½ x 24½); lined.

Blue eyes, powdered hair, wearing the Oxford Doctor of Music gown of cream damask with red hood and facings, over a black suit.

Collections: Commissioned by Henry Thrale for his library at Streatham; Mrs Piozzi sale, Squibb, 10 May 1816, lot 66, bt. Charles Burney, the sitter's son; by descent to J.C. Burney-Cumming, from whom purchased 1953.

Engravings: F. Bartolozzi 1784; J. Owen 1798 (head only; *Public Characters of 1798-99*); S.W. Reynolds; H. Adlard; J. Scott 1878.

Exhibitions: RA 1781(16); BI 1813(118); BI 1848(116); NPE 1867(690); RA 1877(116); *Boswell*, NPG, 1967(66); *The Eye of Thomas Jefferson*, NG Washington, 1976(70); *Johnson*, Arts Council, 1984(56); *John Joseph Merlin*, Kenwood, 1985(A2); *Norfolk and the Grand Tour*, Norwich, 1985(107); *Reynolds*, RA, 1986(125).

Reference: Graves & Cronin, I, pp.134-35, & IV, p.1476; Waterhouse 1941, p.72; D. Piper, *Connoisseur*, CXXXIII, 1954, p.179; Mannings 2000, no.290.

NPG 3884 was the last of the series of portraits commissioned from Reynolds by Henry Thrale for his library at Streatham; it filled 'the last chasm in the chain of Streatham worthies' and hung between portraits of Baretti and Burke.[1] Within two months of its completion Thrale had died.

On 4 January 1781 Mrs Thrale wrote that her husband had ordered Burney 'to sit tomorrow' and, she added, 'I shall have the dear Doctor every morning at breakfast. I took ridiculous pains to tutor him to-day, and to insist ... on his forbearing to write or read late this evening, that my picture might not have blood-shot eyes'.[2] On 11 February she wrote that Burney 'sits for his picture in the Doctor of music's gown; and Bartolozzi makes an engraving from it to place at the head of the book [the second volume of Burney's *History of Music*]. Sir Joshua delights in the portrait, and says 'twill be the best among [the Library set]'.[3] On 25 February Burney confirmed to his son 'I have lately sate for my Picture to Sr Jos. Reynolds, for my Friend Mr Thrale (for wch he has 50 Gs)'.[4] It was well received at the Royal Academy and appears to have been criticised only by John Joseph Merlin (from motives of jealousy concerning his own portrait by Gainsborough)[5] and by Samuel Johnson (who grumbled 'we want to see *Burney* & he never comes to us in that dress').[6] Bartolozzi's plate was subsequently admired, although Burney's friend Thomas Twining found 'some unlikeness mixed with it; & it is, I think, principally about the nose'.[7]

Burney also told his son (25 February) that 'Coz. Ned' [E.F. Burney] was then 'making two Copies of my picture, (wch every body says is very like ..), one for Padre Martini at Bologna, who has many years been desiring to have my Picture, & another for the Music School at Oxford, at the request of Dr Hayes'.[8] Martini's copy remains in the Civico Museo, Bibliografico Musicale, Bologna,[9] and the Oxford portrait is now in the Ashmolean Museum, Oxford; a third copy by E.F. Burney is in the Yale University Library (Osborn collection),[10] and an unattributed miniature copy on copper remains with family descendants.[11]

A drawing in black and red crayon, the same size as Bartolozzi's 1784 engraving after NPG 3884, plausibly inscribed in a later hand *Drawn by Bartolozzi after Sir J Reynolds*, is in the NPG reference collection.[12] Bartolozzi's plate was used as the frontispiece for some copies of the first volume of Burney's *General History of Music* originally published in 1776.[13]

1 *Thraliana* 1942, I, p.475. For the Streatham library portraits see, for example, N. Tscherny, *Burl. Mag.*, CXXVIII, 1986, pp.4-11. A bibliography is provided in *Burney* 1991, p.321n21.
2 Mrs Thrale to Fanny Burney, Streatham, 4 January 1781; *Diary and Letters of Madame d'Arblay*, II, 1842, pp.5-6; see also Leslie and Taylor 1865, II, p.313; *Burney* 1991, p.321n19.
3 C. Barrett ed., *Diary & Letters of Madame D'Arblay*, 1904, I, p.459.
4 *Burney* 1991, pp.321-22. The Reynolds ledgers show that Mrs Thrale paid 35 gn. for the portrait (Cormack 1970, p.164).
5 See C. Carrett ed., *Diary & Letters of Madame D'Arblay*, 1904, I, p.505; *John Joseph Merlin*, Kenwood, 1985, pp.33-35.
6 *Burney* 1991, p.321n27.
7 To Charles Burney, 12 November 1784 (*Burney* 1991, p.411n3).
8 *Burney* 1991, pp.321-22.
9 Illus. Scholes 1948, I, front.
10 Burney sale, Christie's, 20 June 1930, lot 123 as E.F. Burney after Reynolds, the attribution accepted by Waterhouse 1941, p.72. Offered to the NPG in 1933. Illus. K. Chisholm, *Fanny Burney*, 1999, f.p.108.
11 For these copies, see Mannings 2000, nos.290a-d, and *Burney* 1991, pp.321-22nn19, 26, 28, 29.
12 *NPG Burney Diaries*, I, iii, front.
13 See R. Lonsdale, *Dr Charles Burney*, 1965, p.493.

BURNEY NPG *1140*

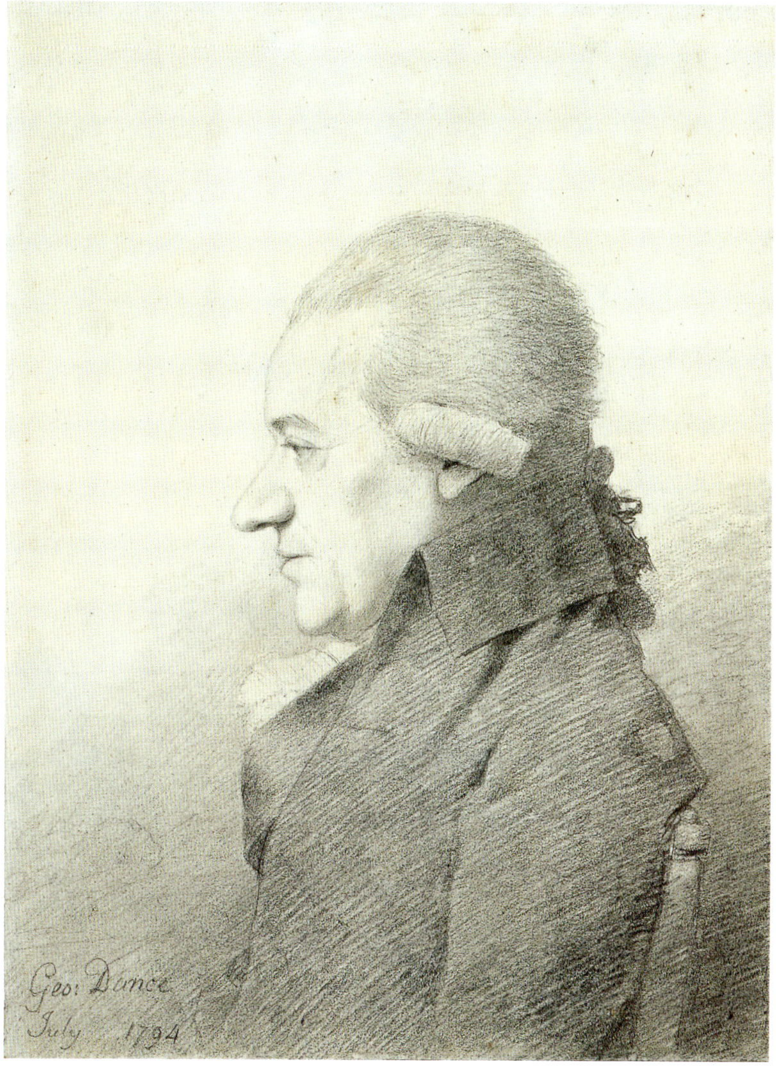

1140 GEORGE DANCE 1794

Pencil on paper 25.4 x 18.9 (10 x 7½) signed, bottom left: *Geo: Dance / July 1794*; laid down on a contemporary washed mount (which is damaged centre left and lower right).

Collections: The artist's grandson, the Rev George Dance; his sale, Christie's, 1 July 1898, lot 26, bt. Colnaghi for the NPG.

Exhibitions: RA 1795(618); *George Dance*, Geffrye Museum, 1972(80); *Bi-centenary of Burney's General History of Music*, Guildhall, Kings Lynn, 1976; *Approaching Tintern Abbey*, Grasmere, 1998.

No engraving is recorded.

ICONOGRAPHY

1770 Drawing by Joseph Nollekens, profile bust inscribed *Dr Burney at Calis in the year 1770*. Yale University Library, Osborn Collection (illus. *Burney* 1991, p.71).

1778 and 1782 Paintings by Frances Reynolds. Untraced. Burney sat to her in October 1778 and July 1782 (*Burney* 1991, pp.258, 346). The portrait has previously, but unconvincingly, been associated with the engraved portrait of 1785 (see below; Scholes 1948, II, f.p.155).

1781 Painting by Joshua Reynolds, see NPG 3884.

1781-84 Painting by James Barry, *Commerce*, part of the *Progress of Human Culture*, in which Burney appears submerged in the Thames surrounded by water nymphs. Royal Society of Arts, London (Pressly 1981, no.25). Engraved J. Barry 1791. Barry began his large canvas in 1777, but Burney's head is taken from the Reynolds portrait of 1781.

1785 Anon. engraving, bust length (*European Mag.*; illus. Scholes 1948, II, f.p.155).

1794 Drawing by George Dance, see NPG 1140.

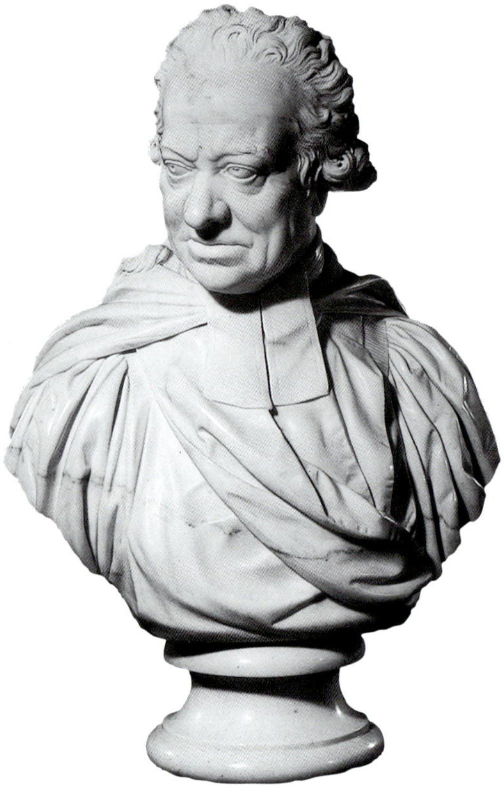

Charles BURNEY by Joseph Nollekens 1802 (British Museum)

1802 Marble bust by Joseph Nollekens,* wearing academic dress. British Museum (MLA 1944.7.4.1; Dawson 2000, no.11). Exhibited RA 1802(1059). Nollekens's receipt for 40 gn. from Burney's son for a bust of Dr Burney, dated 25 September 1801, is in the Pierpont Morgan Library (information from J. Kenworthy-Browne). A plaster in the Bodleian Library, Oxford, presented by Burney before 1806 (Poole, I, p.112; illus. *CL*, CLVII, 1975, p.1510), and another with family descendants. A bust, presumably of the Nollekens type, was presented to the Prince of Wales (*DNB*; untraced). A pen drawing, evidently made from the bust, sold Phillips 4 June 1979, lot 84 (not identified).

c.1810? Pen drawing caricature by John Nixon, bust length. Christie's, 14 March 1978, lot 52 (illus. *CL*, CLXIII, 1978, p.1794).

Silhouette c.1790 called *The Burney Family* (illus. *Connoisseur*, XXV, 1909, p.219; E.N. Nevill Jackson, *Silhouette, Notes and Dictionary*, 1938, pl.43).

DOUBTFUL PORTRAITS

Painting attributed to Nathaniel Dance (Manchester CAG, 1934.489); drawing by J.H. Mortimer (British Museum, 1997.3.22.1); pastel by Daniel Gardner (private collection; illus. Williamson 1921, f.p.128).

BURNEY, Charles Rousseau 1747–1819

Harpsichordist, violinist and composer; m. 1770 his cos. Esther Burney, dau. of his uncle Dr Charles Burney.

1860 EDWARD FRANCESCO BURNEY c.1775–80

Watercolour and pencil on paper 19.6 x 17.2 (7¾ x 6¾) laid down on paper; contemporary inscription in ink, above: *Mr. C R Burney*. Some staining and fading, and a small loss below the bridge of the violin.

Executed in shades of grey with a touch of pink on the lips.

Collections: Presented by Dr Guy Bellingham-Smith 1920.

Exhibitions: *John Joseph Merlin*, Kenwood, 1985(A5); *Master Drawings* 1993–95(32).

The attribution to E.F. Burney, the sitter's younger brother, is traditional; the distinctive use of clear tonal washes is characteristic of his work. NPG 1860 is dated according to the sitter's apparent age.

ICONOGRAPHY

c.1765 Painting by an unknown artist, said to show C.R. Burney standing playing the violin, with his father Richard Burney (b.1723–92) and wife Esther Burney (b. c.1748). Private collection, by descent within the Burney family (illus. Scholes 1948, II, f.p.40, as by Thomas Hudson).

1775–80 Painting by Thomas Gainsborough,* half length holding a libretto. Metropolitan Museum of Art, New York (50.145.16; Waterhouse 1958, no.96).

c.1775–80 Drawing attributed to E.F. Burney, see NPG 1860.

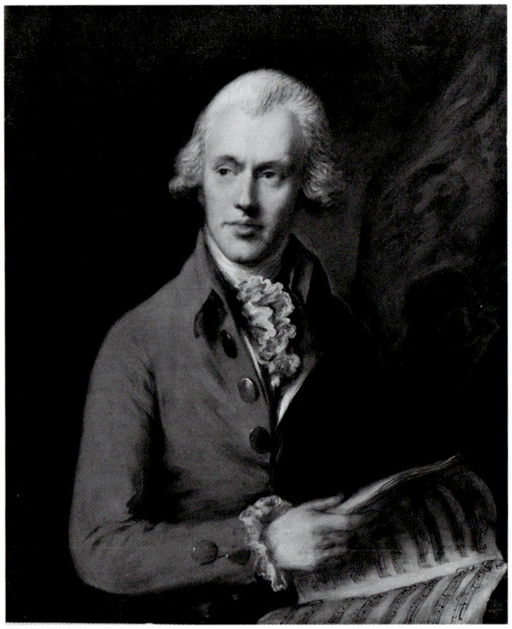

C.R. BURNEY by Thomas Gainsborough 1775–80 (Metropolitan Museum of Art, New York)

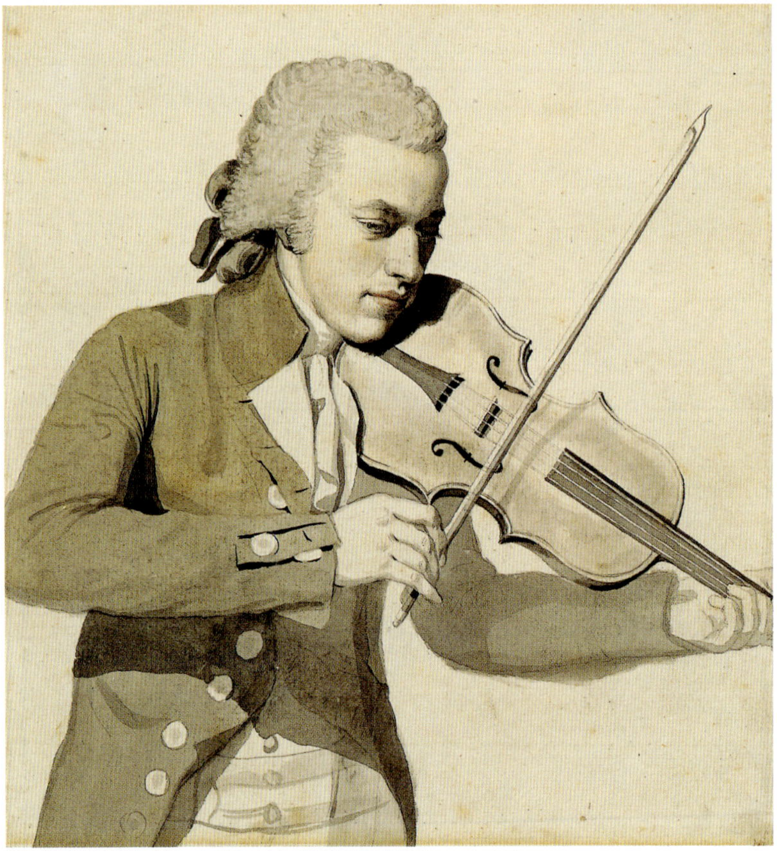

C.R. BURNEY NPG 1860

BURNS, Robert 1759-96

Poet; b. Alloway, Ayr; *Poems Chiefly in the Scottish Dialect* published in Kilmarnock 1786; d. Dumfries.

'He had a pair of good dark eyes ... [his hair] was very lank and unbecoming whenever I beheld it - he had a sensible brown, coarse face, and a very clumsy figure, particularly as to shoulders' (Charles Kirkpatrick Sharpe; *NQ*, 1869).

Abbreviations

Burns Corr. 1987: J.A. Mackay, ed., *Robert Burns The Complete Letters*, 1987

Hadden 1898: J.C. Hadden, *George Thomson, friend of Burns; Life and Correspondence*, 1898

Skinner 1963: B. Skinner, *Burns: Authentic Likenesses*, 1963

46 ALEXANDER NASMYTH [1787]

Canvas 40.7 x 29 (16 x 11½) lined; pentimenti show the sitter's right arm and shoulder were moved slightly to the right; the surrounding oval was extended slightly downwards, destroying the symmetry of the border and causing wide drying cracks along the lowest part of the figure; a general craquelure has been retouched throughout; inscribed (probably signed) in oil paint verso: *A N Pinxit*, subsequently modified in ink to read: *Sir Hy Raeburn / A Nasmyth Pinxit*.

Dark brown hair, brown eyes, wearing a dark green coat, grey waistcoat and white neckcloth.

Collections: George Thomson (1757-1851); his son William Thomson[1] who sold it c.1851, through John Scott of Colnaghi, to John Dillon, by whom presented 1858.

Exhibitions: *Burns*, Glasgow, 1896(15); *Thomas Carlyle*, NPG, 1982(59); Kenwood, *Regency Portraits*, 1986; *Romantic Icons*, Grasmere, 1999(22).

Reference: Skinner 1963, pp.7, 13; Cooksey 1991, pp.62-63(N7).

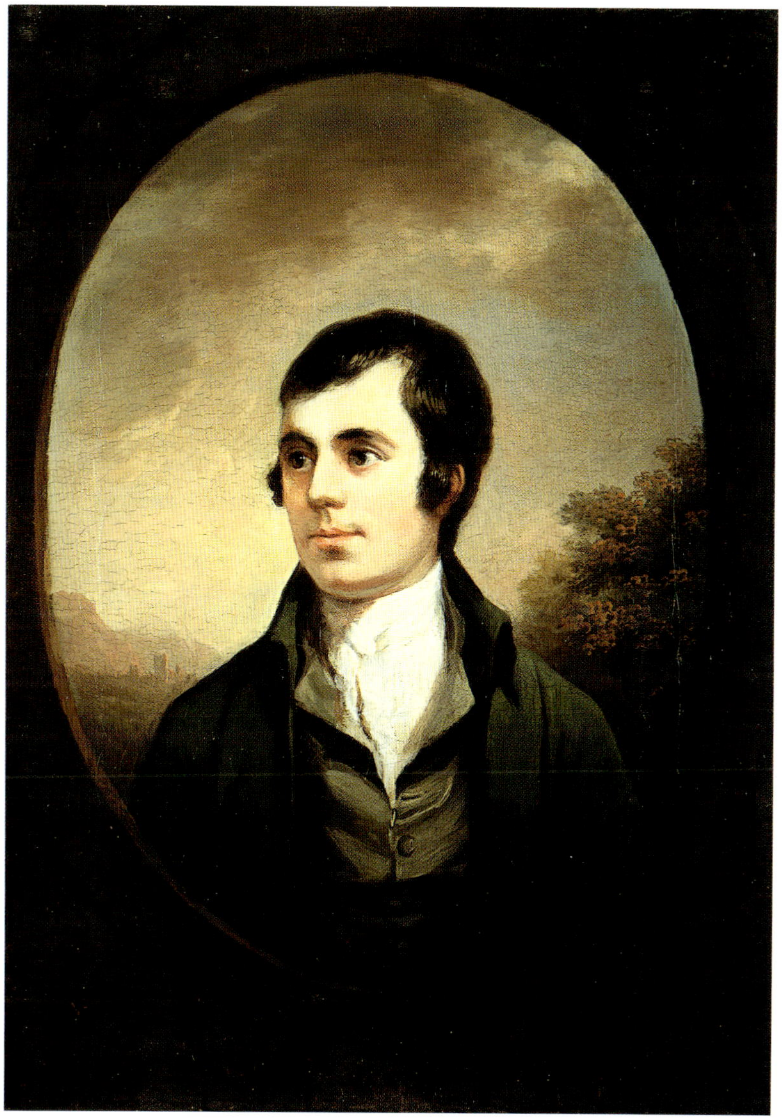

BURNS NPG *46*

A copy by Nasmyth of a portrait he painted early in 1787, now in the Scottish National Portrait Gallery (PG 1063) and inscribed *Painted from Mr Robert Burns by his friend Alexr. Nasmyth, Edinr. 1787*. It had been commissioned by the Edinburgh publisher William Creech, to be engraved by John Beugo* (for the edition of *Poems Chiefly in the Scottish Dialect* published in Edinburgh on 21 April 1787) and Burns recalled sitting 'half a dozen times'[2] for the portrait. Nasmyth, a landscape painter who shared Burns's radical disposition, had undertaken the commission reluctantly and it was said that the portrait 'was never entirely finished' since he was 'afraid to proceed any further, lest he should spoil it'.[3] Beugo received further sittings for the engraving, which was under way in February 1787.[4] His plate was particularly admired by the poet's brother, Gilbert, who once considered it 'showed more character and expression than the picture itself', although he allowed that the Nasmyth was 'certainly a pretty good likeness'.[5]

Two Nasmyth copies, NPG 46 and the picture now in the Glasgow Art Gallery (generally known as the Auchendrane portrait, from the residence of its first owner), were apparently made some thirty years later. Both show minor differences ('fortuitous vagaries', Skinner termed them), apart from slight variations in horizons, clouds and trees. The overall handling of NPG 46 is somewhat coarser (e.g. in the hair, the flesh tones and the shadows around the eyes) and shows a dark green, instead of a dark grey, coat and a plain grey, instead of a striped silk, waistcoat. The Glasgow version has a more vividly striped waistcoat and different buildings on the left; it is inscribed, apparently by the artist:

> ... *by Alexander Nasmyth being one of three pictures painted by him. The original picture painted by him in Edinburgh in 1787 is now in the possession of Mrs Burns, Dumfries* [Scottish National Portrait Gallery], *the second is in the possession of George Thomson, Edinburgh, 1824* [NPG 46] *and this picture is in the possession of E. Cathcart Esquire-Edinburgh* [Glasgow Art Gallery] *A.N.1824*.

NPG 46 was painted for George Thomson, from September 1792 the correspondent of Burns concerning songs for Thomson's *Select Collection of Original Scottish Airs* (5 volumes, 1793-1818), and after the poet's death a less than scrupulous editor of his contributions and correspondence. The circumstances of the commission were recalled by James Nasmyth, the artist's son:

> In the year 1820 it was determined by many of the Chief Citizens of Edinburgh to have a Public Dinner in Commemoration of Burns - and as it was well known that *the only authentic* Portrait of the Poet was that which my Father had painted of him, and given by him to Mrs Burns, my Father was requested to ask her for the loan of the Portrait. ... Thomson was most anxious to possess a Portrait of the Poet and got Mrs Burns permission to allow my Father to make a copy of his own picture while it was under his charge. My father made the copy accordingly and the Portrait of Burns now in the National Portrait Gallery *is that copy*.[6]

But it seems that Thomson had not received his copy in October 1821, since he was then trying to borrow the original Nasmyth from Mrs Burns as a model for Flaxman and Stothard to copy.[7] Thirty years later, at the age of ninety-three, Thomson asserted that his portrait of Burns was 'the best extant', and for an intriguing reason:

> It is a duplicate painted by Alexander Nasmyth from the one he painted from the life for the poet's family; but my duplicate had the peculiar advantage of passing through the hands of my kind and highly-talented friend Sir Henry Raeburn,[8] who, on my solicitation, did me the great favour of revising and retouching the face in my own presence, and gave much of that lustre to the eyes which I well remember in the living man, and upon which I could not help gazing during the only day I ever had the pleasure of dining in his delightful company at Mr James Simpson's, the bookseller.[9]

Thomson's son, William, alleged that it was 'at my Father's suggestion' that Nasmyth had 'consented to its being touched upon and finished by Sir Henry Raeburn'.[10] These accounts of course agree with the modified inscription on the verso of NPG 46 and the portrait was duly catalogued between 1859 and 1866 as by Nasmyth and Raeburn.[11] But the participation of Raeburn seems unlikely or irrelevant, as Scharf in 1889, Gray in 1894 and Skinner in 1963 made clear.[12] It would do him no credit, but it cannot be disproved (and since he died in July 1823, his intervention would also bear on the date).

Raeburn had previously copied the original Nasmyth portrait. In 1803 he had been commissioned by the publisher Thomas Cadell to make a copy 'of Burns the poet, from the original portrait painted by Mr Nasmyth', and his copy was delivered early in 1804.[13] An engraving of Burns 'from an original Picture by Raeburn' was advertised by Cadell in 1823 as having been 'lately published' in the 1820 edition of James Currie's *Works of Burns*, but that engraving is lettered W.T. Fry after Nasmyth; it shows Burns in his striped waistcoat and looking a little more wistful and with his hair rather more compact than in the 1787 portrait.[14]

Nasmyth's portrait became the standard image of Burns and copies abound. Nasmyth himself produced a whole-length variant in 1827-28, see below. An apparently contemporary version, allegedly descended from the poet's mother (known as the Swinton portrait), now belongs to the University of Edinburgh.[15] David Allan's drawing of *The Cottar's Saturday Night* of 1795 (National Gallery of Scotland, D 961) included an adaptation of the Nasmyth head which was much admired as an incidental likeness.[16] Skirving, who never met Burns, made an attractive red-chalk copy of the head (Scottish National Portrait Gallery, PG 745) which was elaborated in an engraving by Paton Thomson in 1798.[17] After Burns's death the portrait was constantly engraved for successive editions of his works, the more important plates being by Edward Mitchell, Paton Thomson 1805, and William Walker and Samuel Cousins 1830 (this last particularly admired by Nasmyth, who thought it a 'more true & lively remembrance' than his own painting).[18] Such prints facilitated duplication by painters who included the artist's daughter Margaret Nasmyth, John Cowan, Henry Harwood, John Gilfillan and Stewart Wilson.

1 On 17 June 1851 he wrote to the Edinburgh bookseller W.F. Watson concerning the sale of his 'Portrait of Burns, painted jointly by Nasmyth and Sir Henry Raeburn' (National Library of Scotland, MS 587, ff.16-17).

2 To George Thomson, May 1795 (*Burns Corr.* 1987, pp.673-74). Much later the artist's son, James Nasmyth (1808-90), an erratic source, alleged that the portrait 'was rapidly painted. It was done in the course of a few hours' (S. Smiles ed., *James Nasmyth's Autobiography*, 1883, p.33).

3 William Hall, letter in the *Kelso Chronicle*, 29 January 1892.

4 Skinner 1963, p.14. Burns to John Ballantyne, 24 February 1787, and to the Rev Hugh Blair, 3 May 1787 (*Burns Corr.* 1987, 114, 288).

5 Gilbert Burns to George Thomson, 2 July 1821 (Hadden 1898, pp.379-80). Beugo's plate was reversed by the Irish engraver Patrick Halpen for the pirated Dublin edition of Burns *Poems* 1787 (illus. Mackay, *Burnsiana*, 1988, p.21).

6 James Nasmyth to George Scharf, 18 May 1872 (NPG archive).

7 Thomson to Stothard, 7 October 1821 (National Library of Scotland, MS 685 f.20, kindly communicated by Helen Smailes); Thomson specifically told Stothard the loan would 'afford you an opportunity of copying the likeness' for the Parnassus ceiling in the Advocates Library in Edinburgh. Was this the loan which James Nasmyth, often unreliable in his reminiscences, associated with a Burns Dinner? A drawing by Flaxman from the Nasmyth head was sold Christie's, Edinburgh, 1 November 2001, lot 8.

8 Who painted an undated (but late), half-length of Thomson, now in a private collection.

9 To Robert Chambers, August 1850 (Hadden 1898, p.135).

10 William Thomson to John Scott of Colnaghi, 23 July 1851 (NPG archive).

11 From 1859-1866, in the 2nd-4th editions of the NPG cat., it was called Nasmyth and Raeburn; the 5th edition of 1881 omitted Raeburn's name. In 1889 Scharf explained that 'about 1872, a communication was received from Mr James Nasmyth, expressing his full conviction that Sir Henry Raeburn had no part in the portrait' and Raeburn's name was accordingly withdrawn (*NQ*, 7/viii, 1889, p.422; Nasmyth's assertion, which would be of limited academic worth, has not survived). In 1869 NPG 46 had been described as "a sort of a kind of a replica 'painted for George Thomson, and retouched by Sir Henry Raeburn', as the catalogue has it, but I should guess it to have been executed by Nasmyth after the poet's death, and without the original portrait before him" ('Chitteldrog', *NQ*, 4/iv, 1869, p.318).

12 G. Scharf, *NQ*, 7/viii, 1889, pp.422, 482. J.M. Gray, *MA*, XVII, 1893-94, p.240; Skinner 1963, p.12, considered that 'the evidence of the painting itself contradicts completely the implications of the pen-and-ink inscription'.

13 See J. Grieg, *Raeburn*, 1911, p.xxvi, citing letters from Raeburn to Cadell & Davies, dated between 14 November 1803 and 22 February 1804.

14 J.M. Gray to G. Scharf, 1 December 1892 (NPG archive). See also J. Mackay, *Burnsiana*, 1988, p.18.

15 J.H. Burnett *et al.*, *University Portraits*, second series, Edinburgh 1986, pp.31-32; see also G.G. Neill Wright, *Burns Chronicle*, 3rd ser., v, 1956, f.p.17.

16 Illus. *MA*, XVII, 1893-94, p.243, with detail of the boy's head; see also *Burns Corr.* 1987, p.673; one of a series of pictures commissioned by George Thomson to illustrate his *Scotish Airs*.

17 Once in the collection of the engineer George Rennie, who considered it the 'the most beautiful thing I ever saw' (J.P. Muirhead, *Mechanical Inventions of James Watt*, 1854, II, p.366); Walter Scott called it 'the only good portrait of Burns'. See *Raeburn's Rival, Archibald Skirving*, Scottish NPG, 1999, no.103, pl.19.

18 S. Smiles ed., *James Nasmyth's Autobiography*, 1883, p.33.

ICONOGRAPHY

Basil Skinner observed that none of the 'authentic' portraits (as discussed above and listed below 1786-96), 'with the possible exception of the Beugo engraving and the Miers silhouette, can claim our whole and unqualified acceptance in all respects' (Skinner 1963, p.5).

1786 Painting by Peter [Patrick] Taylor, half length in broad-brimmed black hat. Scottish NPG (PG 1356). Painted from the life in Edinburgh. A three-quarter length version, also in the Scottish NPG (PG 446), engraved J. Horsburgh 1830 (J.M. Gray, *MA*, XVII, 1895, p.238-39; Skinner 1963, pp.6-7, 14). A statue by John Greenshields 1830, based on the Taylor portrait is in Camperdown, Victoria.

1787 Painting by Alexander Nasmyth and engraving by J. Beugo,* see NPG 46 above.

1787 Silhouette by John Miers,* bust length. Scottish NPG (PG 113). Other silhouettes are recorded by John Field, Samuel Houghton and George Bruce (Skinner 1963, pp.9, 15).

1795-96 Miniature by Alexander Reid, bust length. Scottish NPG (PG 341). Presumed to be the miniature described by Burns in Dumfries early in 1795: 'I am just sitting to Reid in this town for a miniature; & I think he has hit by far the best likeness of me ever was taken'; later he thought the artist had spoiled it (*Burns Corr.* 1987, p.609; Skinner 1963, pp.9-10, 15).

Posthumous

1796-98 Red chalk drawing by Alexander Skirving, a head, after Nasmyth. Scottish NPG (PG 745). See NPG 46.

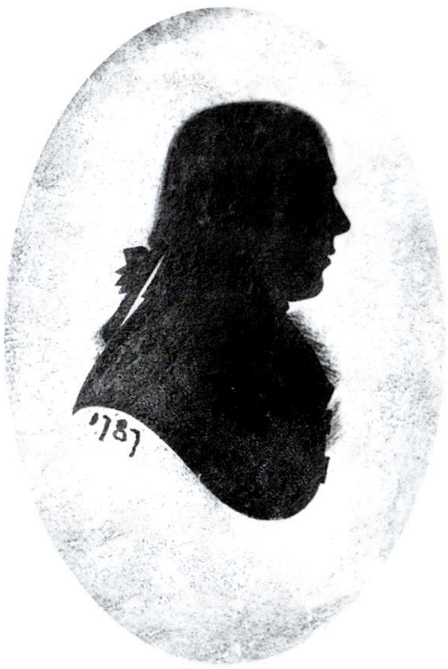

BURNS by John Miers 1787
(Scottish National Portrait Gallery)

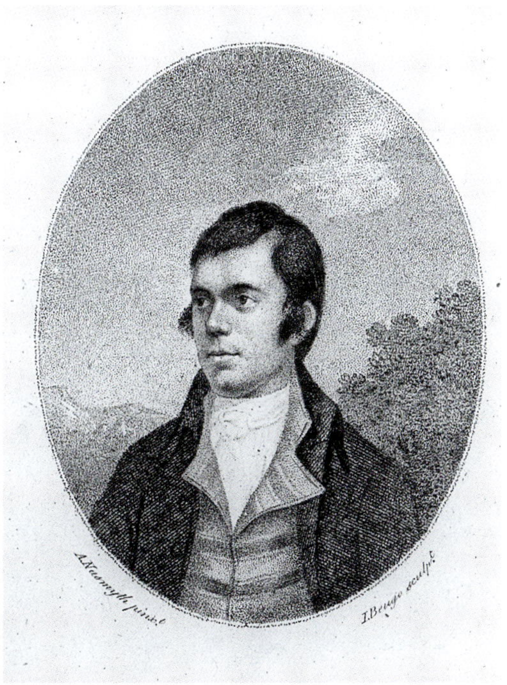

BURNS J. Beugo after Alexander Nasmyth 1787 (NPG D 13790)

c.1797 Wax by John Dell. Victoria and Albert Museum (A.39.1970; illus. Pyke 1973, pl.72).

1801 Medallion by William Tassie, ultimately based on the Reid miniature of 1795. Plaster copy in the Scottish NPG (PG 425).

1807 Medallion by John Henning. Paisley Burns Club. Plaster copy in the Scottish NPG (PG 1275).

1819 Marble monument by Peter Turnerelli, Burns ploughing with the figure of Inspiration above. Dumfries National Monument. The figure replaced by a copy by Hermon Cawthra 1936.

1822-26 Marble statue by John Flaxman, completed by Thomas Denman. Scottish NPG (PGL 139; illus. Whinney 1964, pl.149A), lent by the City of Edinburgh; originally placed in the Burns monument on Calton Hill, Edinburgh. A fund for the monument had been raised by George Thomson, who gave a plaster model to Col. W.N. Burns in 1847 (now Edinburgh City Art Centre); a clay model is in the Soane Museum. There are many bronze reductions.

1827-28 Painting by Alexander Nasmyth, whole length in broad-brimmed black hat, his arms folded, standing in a landscape with Alloa bridge. Scottish NPG (PG 1062). Engraved W. Miller 1828. Commissioned by Robert Chambers for Lockhart's *Life of Burns*, 1828, and worked up from a pencil sketch made at Alloa in 1786 (Scottish NPG, PG 1380; illus. Skinner 1963, f.p.8), the head based on the 1787 portrait. A version by William Tannock was sold Sotheby's, 30 April 1980, lot 228.

1844 Statue by David Dunbar, exhibited Westminster Hall. A cast of Burns skull taken by Dunbar c.1834 is in the Scottish NPG (PG 183). A bust by Dunbar, probably a plaster, exhibited Crystal Palace (Phillips 1854, no.410).

1845 Bust by Patric Park. Burns monument, Ayr.

In the second half of the nineteenth century the production of Burns statues and busts began in earnest. His bust by John Steell was placed in Westminster Abbey in 1885, but his memory was celebrated principally by Scots at home or abroad. The Andrew Carnegie libraries in America each contained an obligatory bust of Burns (nearly three and a half thousand) and many remain scattered throughout America, Canada and Australia (see J. Mackay, Robert Burns, *1992, pp.723-24). The Burns industry, from paintings to soap tablets, has been reviewed by J. Mackay,* Burnsiana, *1988, and for the Burns memorials, see E. Goodwillie,* World Memorials of Robert Burns, *1911.*

BURROW, Sir James, Kt 1701-82

Legal reporter; master of the crown office 1724; FRS 1737 and president 1768 and 1772, FSA 1741; Kt 1773; his miscellaneous essays include five on earthquakes and one on Oliver Cromwell.

3090(8) after ARTHUR DEVIS [1780]

Black crayon on paper 22 x 13 ($8\frac{5}{8}$ x $5\frac{1}{8}$); within a drawn border 21 x 12 ($8\frac{1}{4}$ x $4\frac{3}{4}$), the oval image 15.3 x 11 (6 x $4\frac{1}{4}$); laid down on paper; the surface is rubbed and there is some staining in the bottom right corner; lettered below: *Sir James Burrow Knt* with inscriptions along the bottom edge: *Pinxit* and *Basire.*

Collections: Purchased from Appelby 1940.

A pedantic drawing, the head and bands matching both in size and substance, those in Basire's 1780 print after Arthur Devis.[1] The absence of Basire's ornate detail from the gown and coat may suggest it was taken from the plate. An ink drawing of Burrow by Basire was listed in 1824.[2]

Devis's original painting, showing Burrow in his legal robes standing whole length in a medieval courtyard, remains untraced; it has been described as his last known work.[3]

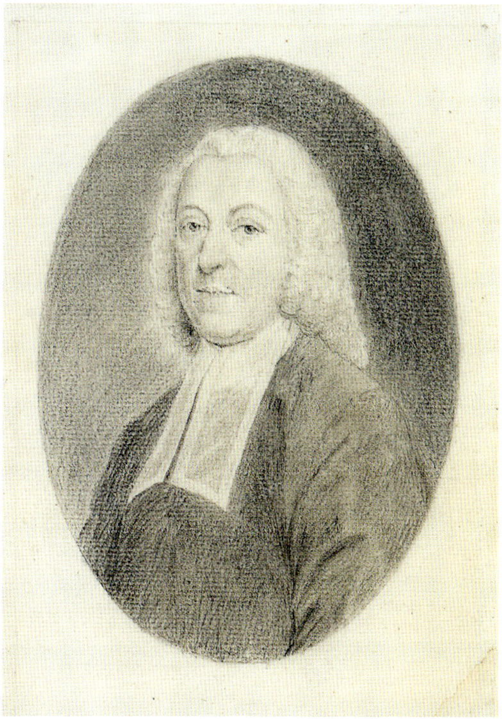

BURROW NPG *3090(8)*

1 *Painted by Arthur Devis - Drawn & Engrav'd by James Basire 1780*; the caption describing Burrow as FRS, FSA and an honorary member of the *Societé des Antiquités at Cassell.*
2 Rodd's priced sale cat., 1824, p.6, no.15.
3 *Devis* 1980, no.24.

ICONOGRAPHY

c.1742 Painting by J-B. Van Loo, three-quarter length seated. Royal Society, presented by the sitter 1777 (illus. *Royal Society* 1980, f.p.48).

c.1747-49 Three paintings by Arthur Devis, whole-lengths seated in a landscape.

a) attributed to Devis, 1747; holding his hat, accompanied by two dogs. Montreal Museum of Fine Arts.

b) with a leaning tree behind him. Private collection, from Uppark, said to have been one of twelve portraits by Devis commissioned by Sir Matthew Featherstonhaugh (*Devis* 1980, no.22).

c) 1749 with an upright tree behind him. Uppark (*Devis* 1983, no.25).

1780 Painting by Arthur Devis, see NPG 3090(8).

DOUBTFUL PORTRAITS

Paintings by Joseph Highmore, half length dated 1740 (formerly in the collection of Sir Thomas Butler), and attributed to Jonathan Richardson, three-quarter length (Royal Courts of Justice, London).

BUTE, John Stuart, 3rd Earl of 1713-92

Tutor to George III when Prince of Wales; prime minister 1762-63; suc. as 3rd Earl 1723; KT 1738, KG 1762; trustee of the British Museum from 1765 and president of the Society of Arts from 1780; his *Botanical Tables* c.1785 dedicated to Queen Charlotte, 'solely for the amusement of the Fair Sex'.

'a Scotchman, who, having no estate, had passed his youth in studying mathematics and mechanics in his own little island, then simples in the hedges about Twickenham, and at five and thirty had fallen in love with his own figure, which he produced at masquerades in becoming dresses, and in plays which he acted in private companies' (Horace Walpole, *Memoirs of George II*).

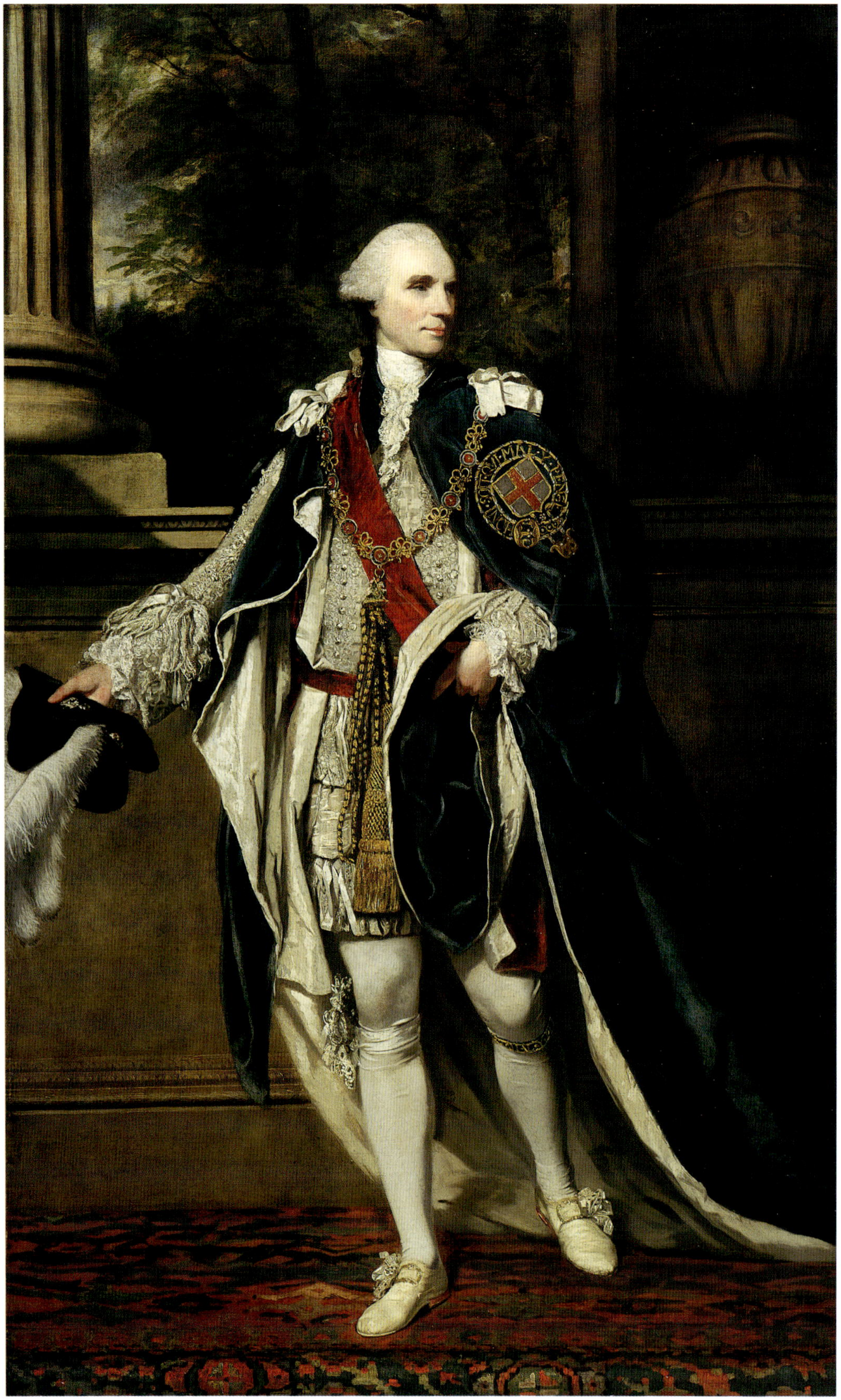

3rd Earl of BUTE NPG *3938*

3938 JOSHUA REYNOLDS 1773

Canvas 239 x 146 (94 x 57½) lined.

Grey eyes, powdered wig, wearing the robes of the Garter, the plumed hat in his right hand.

Collections: By family descent to the 3rd Earl of Wharncliffe (d.1953); purchased from his estate with the aid of the National Art Collections Fund 1958.

Exhibitions: *Art Treasures*, Manchester 1857 (BPG 290); NPE 1867(448); *Guelph* 1891(108); lent to the NPG from 1953.

Reference: Graves & Cronin, I, p.137; Mannings 2000, no.1720.

The pose, derived from the *Apollo Belvedere*, displays Bute's legs to advantage. NPG 3938 is virtually identical to the Reynolds whole length which remains in the Bute collection,[1] differing only in that the plumed hat is in his right hand instead of on a table, sky and trees replace an indoor setting, and the floor is carpeted rather than tiled. The execution of the Garter badge is disinterested.

Bute's name appears in Reynolds's sitter book nine times between 12 October and 25 December 1773. On 27 October 1773 Northcote, then working in the Reynolds studio, wrote that he was copying Lord Bute's face 'as there is to be two whole-lengths made of him'; he goes on:

> his picture by no means gives me an idea of his character, if it be as the world says. He is a tall genteel figure with a mean Scotch face; his skin very yellow and small blue eyes, with a smile on his face which gives a look of vast good humour and humility. Sir Joshua has made an extraordinary fine head of him. He [Bute] must find it very different from the time when he was forced to have bruisers behind his coach to protect him, for now he comes in a chair without any servants and often walks home.[2]

Payments for two whole lengths were made by Lord Bute on 25 October 1780.[3] A half-length version attributed to Northcote, with the inscribed date 1780, is also in the Bute collection.[4]

1 Mannings 2000, no.1719.
2 15 December 1773, quoted in Whitley 1928, II, pp.294–95.
3 Cormack 1970, p.146.
4 Exhibited *Lord Mansfield*, Kenwood, 1971(39).

ICONOGRAPHY

1716 By Mrs Howard, whole length, when three years old. Mountstuart in 1798 (Musgrave MSS 6329, f.84).

c.1725–30 Painting by William Aikman, whole length in tartan. Bute Collection (J. Holloway, *Patrons & Painters*, 1989, pp.59, 61, illus.).

1758 Painting by Allan Ramsay,* whole length in Court dress with the collar of the Thistle. Bute House (Smart 1999, no.69). First engraved W.W. Ryland 1763, R. Purcell 1763, and many times thereafter. Preliminary drawing in the NG of Scotland (D 233; illus. Smart 1999, fig.673). Versions in a Scottish private collection and sold Christie's, 24 June 1960, lot 101; a copy by William Mosman in Marischal College, Aberdeen, and a bust-length enamel attributed to Francis Sykes in the Gilbert collection (illus. Coffin & Hofstetter 2000, no.57).

1763 Painting by Joshua Reynolds,* whole length with his secretary Charles Jenkinson. Private Col-

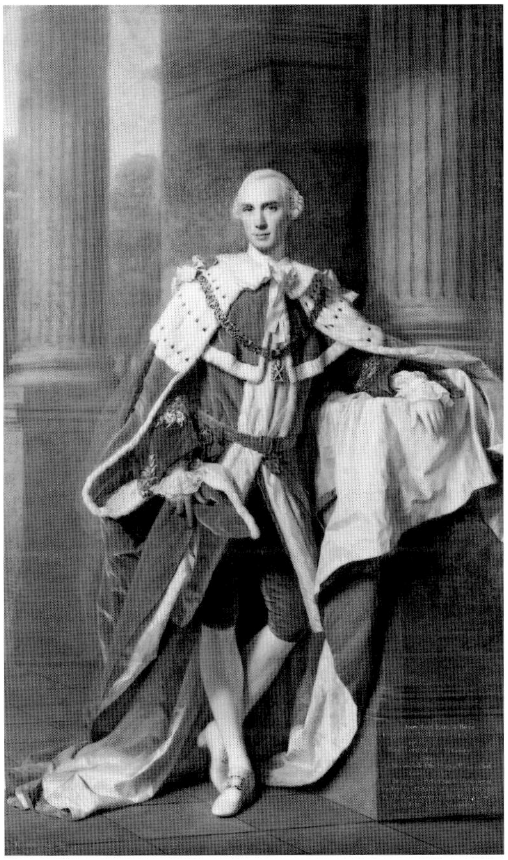

3rd Earl of BUTE by Allan Ramsay 1758 (Bute House, Edinburgh, National Trust for Scotland)

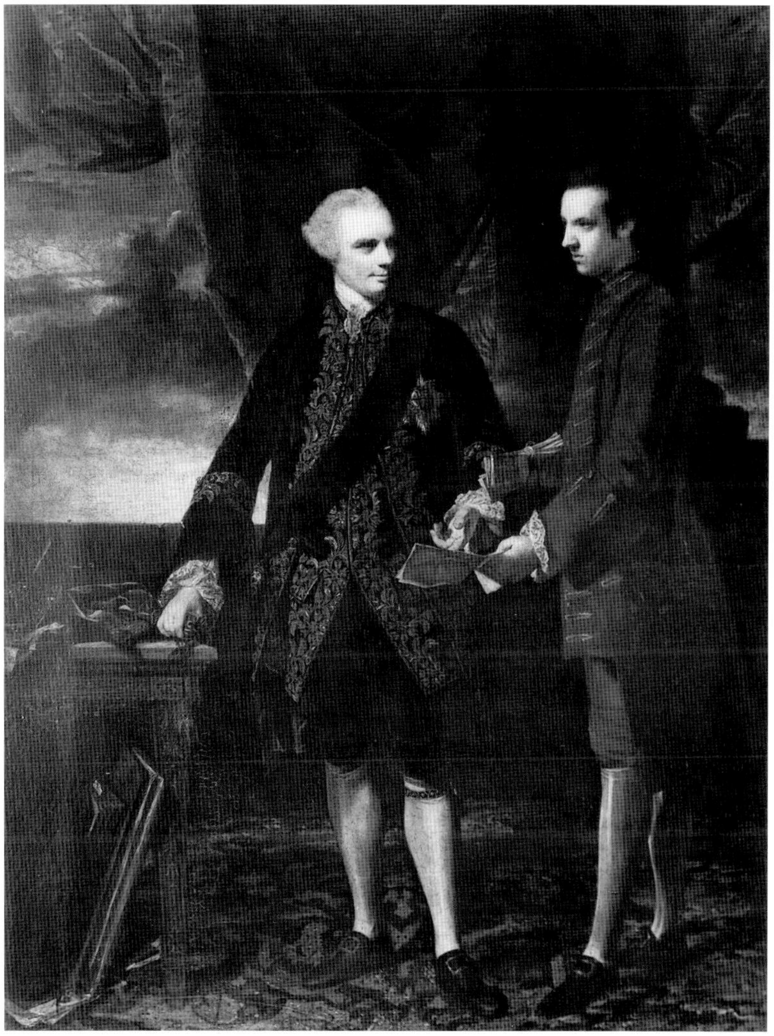

3rd Earl of BUTE (left) with Charles Jenkinson (later Lord LIVERPOOL) by Joshua Reynolds 1763 (Private Collection)

lection, given to Lord Mount Stuart by George III (Mannings 2000, no.1722). An oil sketch by Reynolds is in a private collection (Mannings 2000, no.1721); a watercolour copy by G.P. Harding 1817 (formerly at Buxted; Hawkesbury 1904a, p.20, no.8) was itself copied in pastel by May Lancaster Lucas (formerly in Lord Liverpool's collection; Hawkesbury 1906, p.50, no.71).

1767 Miniature by Luke Sullivan, bust-length oval. Victoria and Albert Museum (699.1904; illus. Rackham 1930, fig.80).

1773 Painting by Joshua Reynolds, see NPG 3938.

1789 Painting by J.C. Ibbetson showing Bute, a small whole-length figure, within a group at Cardiff Castle. Bute collection (illus. R. Clay, *Ibbetson*, 1948, pl.24).

An oval miniature by Richard Crosse listed at Earlywood in 1986.

DOUBTFUL PORTRAIT

Painting formerly attributed to Allan Ramsay (Scottish NPG, PG 308).

CAMDEN, Charles Pratt, 1st Earl 1714–94

Attorney-general 1757–62; chief justice of common pleas 1762–66; lord chancellor 1766–70; lord president of council 1782–83 and 1784–94; FRS 1742; Kt 1761, cr. Baron Camden 1765 and Earl Camden 1786.

'His eminently judicial qualifications shone forth conspicuously when he rose into the proper sphere. His unwearied patience, his unbroken suavity of manner, his unruffled calmness of temper … went far to constitute a perfect judge' (Lord Brougham, 1843).

'By nature and habit Camden was an indolent dilettante and a temperate epicure ... [his] person, though small, was handsome, and a genial smile animated his regular features and fine grey eyes' (*DNB*).

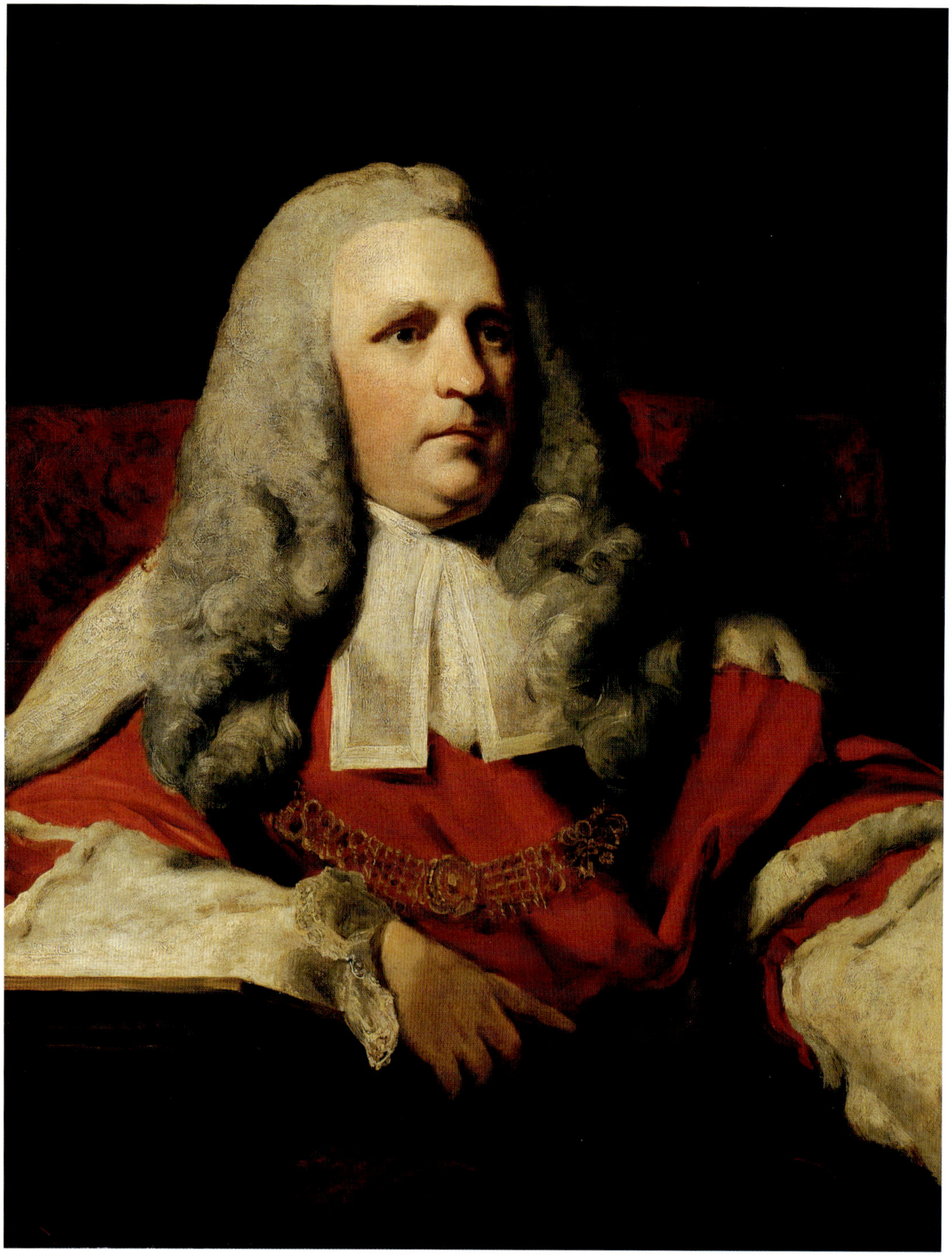

1st Earl CAMDEN NPG 459

459 after JOSHUA REYNOLDS [1765–66]

Canvas 90 x 70 (35½ x 27½) lined and heavily ironed, with discoloured retouching in the right background.

Grey eyes, wearing the red robes of the chief justice trimmed with white fur and the SS collar; seated in a red chair.

Collections: Presented by the Society of Judges and Serjeants-at-Law 1877.

Exhibition: Ministry of Works 1900–39; Law Courts 1958–

Reference: Graves & Cronin, II, p.770; Mannings 2000, no.1476a.

A copy from the whole-length Reynolds, probably of 1765–66, now in a private collection;[1] as with NPG 459, the condition of the original leaves much to be desired.

1 Mannings 2000, no.1476; engraved J.G. Haid 1766 (as from a portrait *painted by Mr Reynolds in the year 1764*), J. Romney 1817, T. Cooke and H. Meyer 1811 (half length, from a drawing by J. Jackson).

336 NATHANIEL DANCE 1767-69

Canvas 125.5 x 100.5 (49½ x 39½) lined 1970; discoloured varnish; marked shrinkage craquelure bottom centre.

Grey eyes, wearing the lord chancellor's black silk robes faced with gold braid, his gold waistcoat just visible; he holds an unlettered grey book and his chancellor's purse stands on a red cloth by his side; a deep red damask curtain above.

Collections: Purchased from the 6th Baron Rokeby 1872.

Exhibition: Crown Estates Office 1986-.

Lord Camden assumed the office of lord chancellor in 1766 and the identical version of NPG 336 in King's College, Cambridge, has been dated 1767-69 by Goodreau.[1]

A variant, differing only in that he wears a black broad-brimmed hat, for which there is a pencil study★ for the head in the British Museum (1905.10.19.14),[2] is represented by versions formerly in the collections of Lord Kenyon[3] and the Marquess of Camden,[4] and a third is in the Palace of Westminster.[5] A copy is in the Law Courts (GAC 0.132),[6] and unattributed miniature copies are in the Victoria and Albert Museum (P.30.1929) and formerly in the collection of Mrs Hore-Ruthven.[7] The type was several times engraved.[8]

1 See *Dance* 1977(22), illus.; also exhibited *Cambridge Portraits from Lely to Hockney*, Cambridge, 1978(15), illus.
2 Illus. *Connoisseur*, LXV, 1923, p.25.
3 Steegman, I, p.159, no.72.
4 Exhibited *Dance* 1977(22) and *Treasures from Kent Houses*, Canterbury, 1984(23), illus. Known as Reynolds c.1931 (note by Steegman, 17 November 1931, NPG archive).

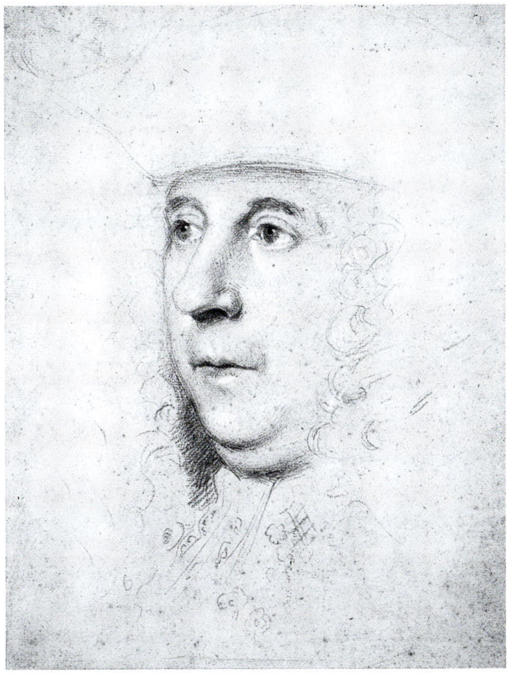

1st Earl CAMDEN by Nathaniel Dance 1767-69 (British Museum)

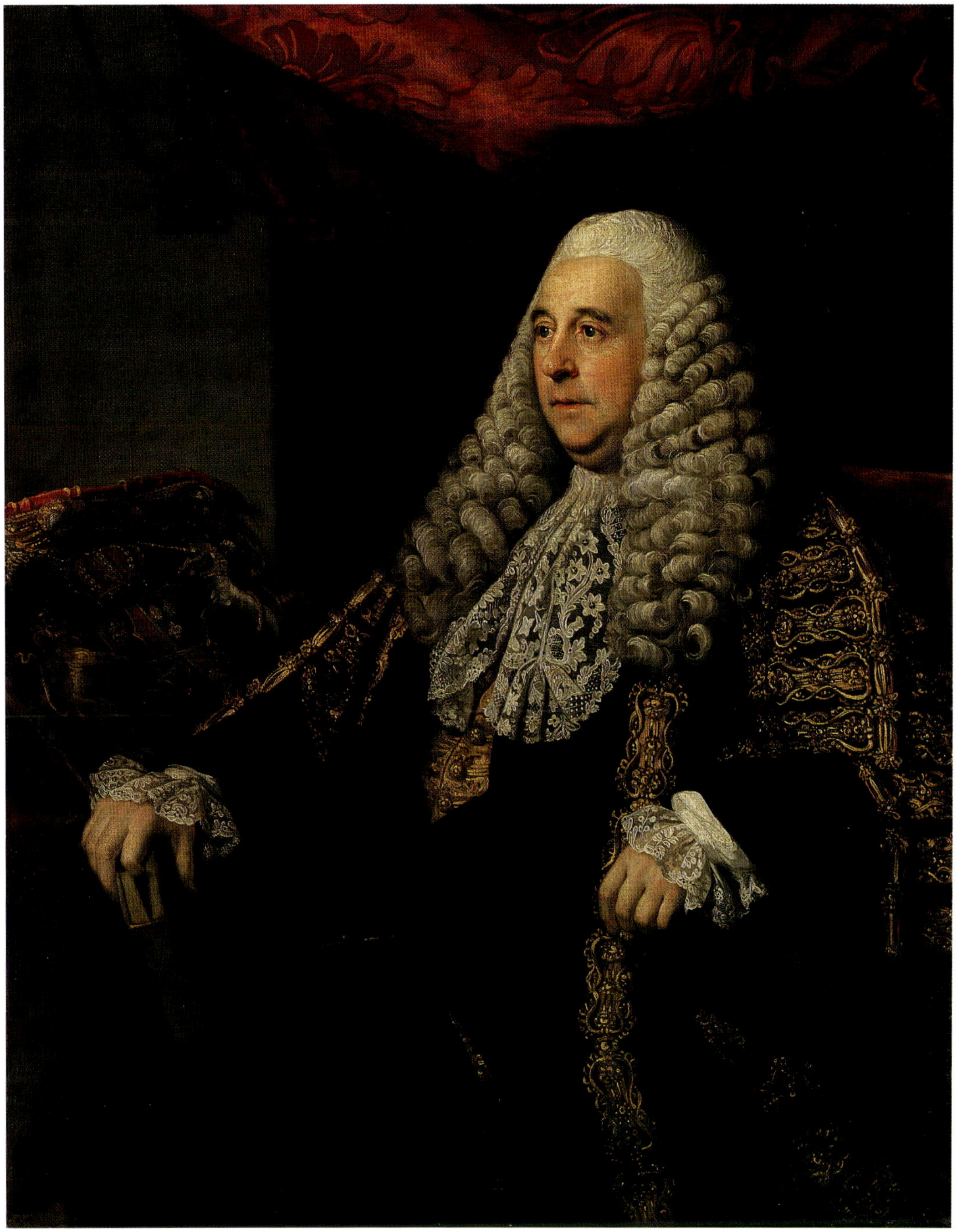

1st Earl CAMDEN NPG 336

5 Walker 1988, I, p.47; exhibited *Lord Mansfield*, Kenwood 1971(21).
6 Walker 1976, p.12.
7 Steegman, II, p.11, no.28.
8 H. Robinson 1833 (from a drawing by W. Derby), T. Phillibrown and G. Gabrielli 1875.

1759 Painting by Benjamin Wilson, standing three-quarter length in black gown and bands. Harvard Law School. Exhibited FS 1760(70). Sketched by Scharf in 1859 and 1872 (TSB 3/40 and 18/33 & 34).

In a series of judgments in 1763-65 Camden maintained that the general warrants issued by the government for the arrest of the radical John Wilkes were illegal; his judgments brought him popular acclaim and he received the freedoms of the cities of Dublin, Bath, Exeter and Norwich, while the City of London placed his full-length portrait by Reynolds within the Guildhall (see 1764-65).

1764 Painting by Thomas Hudson, whole length in judicial robes. Exeter Guildhall (where sketched by Scharf in 1884; SSB 109/72). Anon. related mezzotint 1765, a rolled *Magna Charta* in his left hand, standing by a statue of Britannia bearing a plaque lettered *amor populi*; lettered ... *in honorem tanti viri/ anglicae libertatis lege assertoris fidi*...

1764-65 Painting by Joshua Reynolds. * three-quarter length, reduced in 1968 from a whole length, standing in judicial robes. Guildhall AG, London (40; Mannings 2000, no.1475). Engraved J. Basire 1766 (exhibited FS 1767, no.18); S-F. Ravenet 1766 (*The Great Assertor of English Liberty*; exhibited SA 1767, no.264), his preparatory drawing in the British Museum (1890.5.12.66); J.G. Haid; T. Cooke; H. Wallis 1843. A half-length copy sold Sotheby's, 8 April 1992, lot 48, and a small whole-length version in an American private collection 1925 (see Mannings 2000, nos.1475a & b).

1765 Painting by William Hoare, whole-length standing, in judicial robes, the *Magna Charta* by his right hand. Assembly Rooms, Bath. Engraved J. Spilsbury 1766 (reduced).

1765-66 Painting by Joshua Reynolds, see NPG 459.

1766 Medal by Thomas Pingo, designed by James Stuart (Brown 1980, no.97; Eimer 1998, no.35). Exhibited FS 1767(225). A Wedgwood medallion of 1776 (illus. Reilly 1973, p.81) derived from this medal and there are related engravings by T. Holloway 1786, W. Ridley 1798 (for *Junius* 1799) and J. Hopwood 1805.

1766 Wax by Isaac Gosset, exhibited SA 1766(205). A medal of 1777 by John Kirk is described by Brown 1980, no.210, as after Gosset.

Medals by John Kirk were otherwise struck in 1766, 1773 and exhibited SA 1776(220), see Brown 1980, nos.96, 176.

1767 Marble bust by Joseph Wilton, exhibited SA 1767(215). A derivative bust by William Behnes 1830 is at Bayham Abbey.

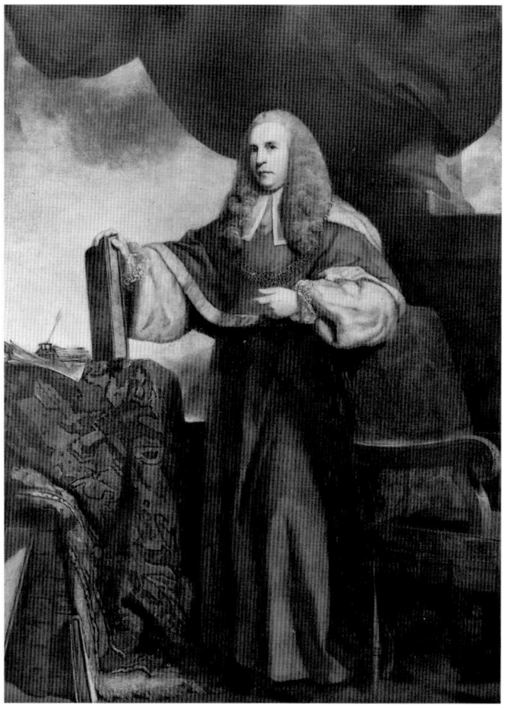

1st Earl CAMDEN by Joshua Reynolds 1764-65 (Guildhall Art Gallery, London)

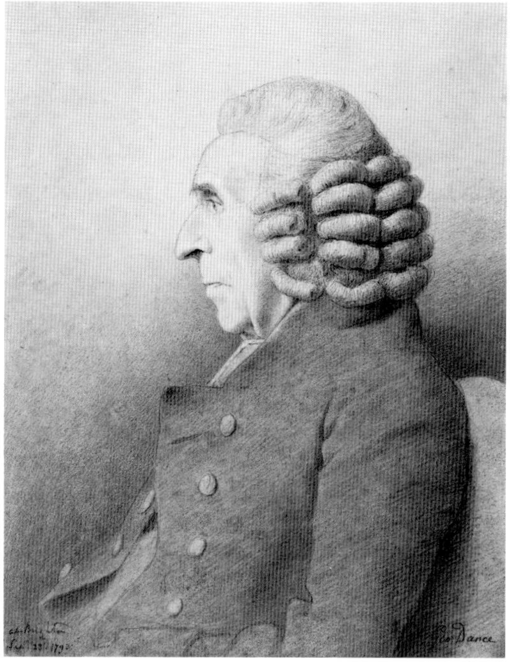

1st Earl CAMDEN by George Dance 1793 (British Museum)

1767 Painting by Joshua Reynolds, three-quarter length seated. Christie's, 31 July 1947, lot 94 (Mannings 2000, no.1477). A copy from Bayham Abbey on the London art market 1976.

1767-69 Painting by Nathaniel Dance, see NPG 336.

c.1767 Anon. engraving, whole-length as lord chancellor.

c.1770 Anon. engraving, half length in private dress (NPG reference collection, D1196).

c.1778 Painting by Joshua Reynolds, three-quarter length in private dress. Private collection (Mannings 2000, no.1478).

1779-81 Painting by J.S. Copley,* *The Death of Chatham*, see Comparative Groups. A drawing from the head of Camden attributed to Bartolozzi is in the Metropolitan Museum of Art, New York (55.106.7; illus. *Metropolitan Museum of Art Bulletin*, XIV, 1956, p.123).

1780 Painting by Richard Cosway, whole length seated in judicial robes, turning towards a bust of Lord Chatham. Private collection (illus. *In the Minds and Hearts of the People*, New York Graphic Soc., 1974, p.192). In March 1780 Camden told his daughter he was sitting to Cosway (see *Pictures from Ulster Houses* 1961, no.72).

1781 Anon. engraving, bust-length with ermine over dark coat (*London Mag.*).

1782 Painting by Thomas Gainsborough, three-quarter length seated in private dress. Private collection (Waterhouse 1958, no.110). Exhibited RA 1782(126). Engraved F. Bartolozzi 1795.

c.1782? Wedgwood medallion, tentatively dated 'as late as 1782' (illus. Reilly 1973, p.81; Reilly 1994, p.330).

1793 Drawing by George Dance,* profile bust, dated 23 September 1793. British Museum (1967.10.14.66). Exhibited RA 1795(577). Engraved J. Ogborne 1794 (see Farington, 13 November 1794); W. Daniell (*Dance Plates*). A smaller version was made for Camden's daughter (D. Stroud, *George Dance*, 1971, p.174), possibly that exhibited Sabin, *Sublime and Beautiful*, 1973(20). Camden wrote to Dance 'expressing the pleasure which He had in the general admiration of Dances profile drawings' (Farington, 11 October 1793).

1805 Anon. etching, whole-length seated in judicial robes; pub. W. Miller.

A second state of J. Faber's mezzotint of Allan Ramsay's Thomas Burnet was altered to represent Camden (CS 52).

A medallion bust of Camden appears in George Willison's *Allegory of the Douglas Cause*, 1769 (exhibited Moubray House, Edinburgh, 1951, no.79a).

CARLETON, Hugh Carleton, Viscount 1739-1826

Chief justice of common pleas in Ireland 1787-1800; cr. Baron Carleton of Amer [I] 1789 and Viscount Carleton of Clare [I] 1797.

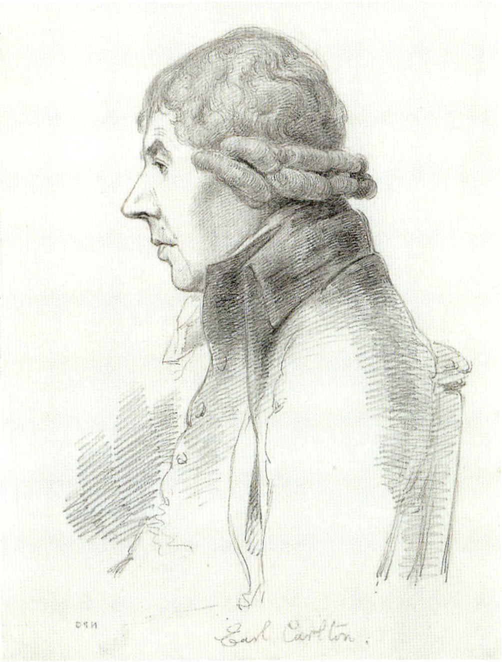

1st Viscount CARLETON NPG 3089(3)

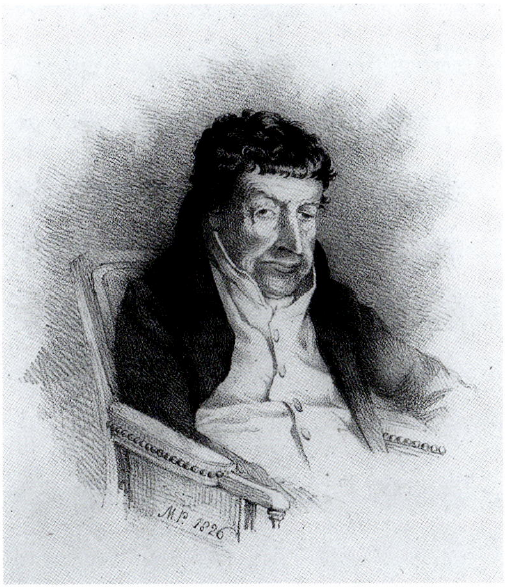

1st Viscount CARLETON engraved by M.P. 1826 (NPG D 13791)

3089(3) WILLIAM DANIELL after GEORGE DANCE [1799]

Pencil with the outlines drawn over in red crayon, on paper 25.5 x 19.5 (10 x 7¾) laid down on paper, on card; irregular perforations round the edges, slight staining; inscribed below in pencil: *Earl Carlton*; reversed NPG stamp lower left (showing through from the verso).

Engraving: W. Daniell (*Dance Plates*).

Collections and Reference: see Appendix II.

Dance's original drawing, dated 1799, was in the Dance sale, Christie's, 1 July 1898, lot 29, bought by J.L. Rutley.

ICONOGRAPHY

1787-93 Painting by Gilbert Stuart, half length. Formerly at Somerley (Strickland 1913, II, p.414; Park 1926, I, no.141). Painted in Dublin.

1799 Drawing by George Dance, see NPG 3089(3).

1826 Engraving by M.P.,* half-length seated, looking miserable.

CARLINI, Agostino c.1718-90

Sculptor; b. Genoa, he was in London by 1760, when he exhibited at the SA; a foundation member of the RA 1768, where he exhibited between 1769 and 1787 and became Keeper 1783.

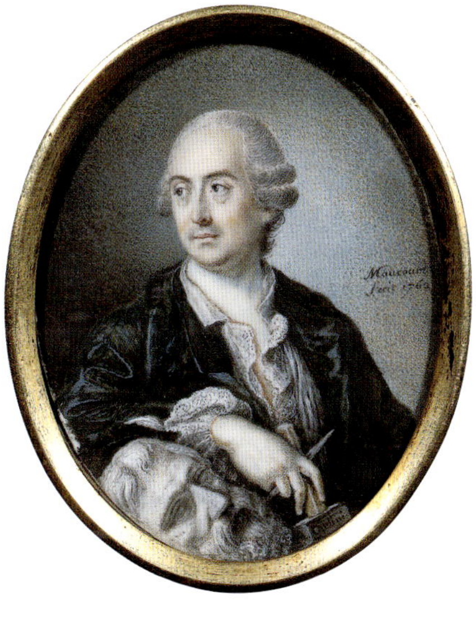

CARLINI NPG *5388*

'When Carlini was Keeper of the Royal Academy, he used to walk from his house to Somerset place, with a broken tobacco-pipe in his mouth, and dressed in a deplorable great coat; but when he has been going to the Academy-dinner, I have seen him getting into a chair, and full-dressed in a purple silk coat, scarlet gold-laced waistcoat, point-lace ruffles, and a sword and bag' (J.T. Smith, 1828).

5388 CHARLES MAUCOURT 1762

Watercolour and bodycolour on ivory 7.6 x 6 (3 x 2⅜); signed and dated, centre right: *Maucourt/fecit 1762*.

Grey eyes, powdered wig, wearing a loose blue gown with black collar and a white shirt; holding a chisel and mallett, inscribed *A. Carlini*, in his right hand which rests on a carved bearded head.

Collections: Sotheby's, 28 April 1981, lot 38, bt. Leggatt for the NPG.

3186 see Groups, *Carlini, Bartolozzi and Cipriani* by JOHN FRANCIS RIGAUD 1777

ICONOGRAPHY

1762 Miniature by Charles Maucourt, see NPG 5388.

1772 Painting by Johann Zoffany,* *The Academicians of the Royal Academy*, see Groups NPG 1437.

1777 Painting by J.F. Rigaud, see Groups NPG 3186.

1788 Wax by Peter Rouw, exhibited RA 1788(639).

CARMARTHEN, Francis, Marquess of, see LEEDS

CARNAC, John 1716-1800

Army officer of Huguenot descent; went to India 1754 where he became an associate of Robert Clive; colonel in the East India service 1765; returned to England with Clive 1767; FRS 1772; MP 1768-74; returned to India 1776 as a member of the Bombay council until his dismissal following the surrender to the Marathas at Wargoon in 1779; stayed in Bombay for the rest of his life, selling his English estates in 1783.

6284 OZIAS HUMPHRY 1786

Watercolour and bodycolour on ivory 5.2 x 4 (2 x 1½); signed and inscribed on card backing: *O:H: pt:/ 1786/ Calcutta*, visible through an aperture in a deep blue enamelled backing; dark hatching is now prominent in the hair, collar and chin; a border of braided hair is set within the gold frame.

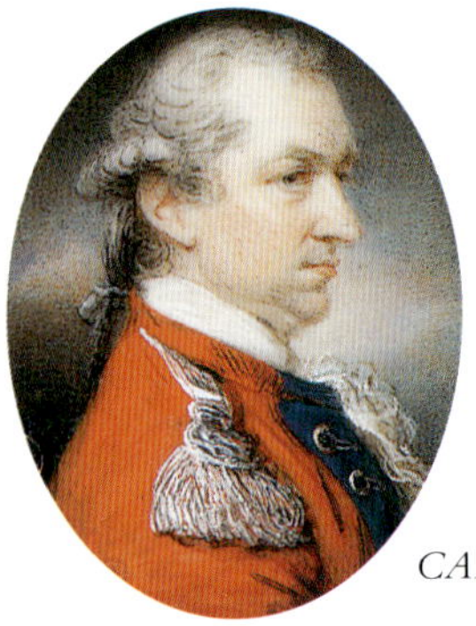

CARNAC NPG *6284*

Clear grey eyes, grey powdered hair tied with a black ribbon, red coat with silver epaulette, blue facings and silver-edged blue buttons.

Collections: Francis Wellesley sale, Sotheby's, 3rd day, 30 June 1920, lot 459;[1] Hon Frederic H.A. Wallop (d.1953), by whom lent to the Victoria and Albert Museum 1927-49; his nephew Alan Evans; by whom bequeathed to the National Gallery 1974; lent to the NPG until permanently transferred 1994.

Reference: Archer 1979, p.200; Walker 1998, no.66.

The identification is probably correct, although the earliest reference to it ('Colonel Carnac') appears to have been the 1920 Wellesley sale catalogue (cited above). Carnac had arrived in Calcutta on 16 December 1786 and Humphry had returned there in mid-November.[2] There are no significant comparable portraits, Carnac being otherwise identified as a minor figure in history paintings by West and Zoffany (see below).

1 Described as 'one of the finest miniatures by Humphry that has ever been sold'.
2 Archer 1979, pp.173, 191, 198.

ICONOGRAPHY

c.1774- Painting by Benjamin West, *Lord Clive receiving from the Mogul the Grant of the Duanney*, in which Carnac stands by Lord Clive. Lord Plymouth; commissioned by Robert Clive to illustrate an event of 1765 (Erffa & Staley 1986, no.101). Exhibited RA 1795(28). A key published by J. Baker identified the figures. A replica of c.1818 is in the India Office (British Library; Erffa & Staley 1986, no.103).

1786 Miniature by Ozias Humphry, see NPG 6284.

c.1795 Painting by Johann Zoffany, *Death of the Royal Tyger*, in which Carnac is seated in a howdah on the left-hand elephant. Untraced. Engraved R. Earlom 1802, as representing *the attack and death of the royal tiger near Chandernagur, in the Province of Bengal, in the year 1788 ...* (illus. Archer 1979, p.169). The date of the hunt does not agree with the dates of residence of all the participants and the picture was probably a reminiscence painted in England (see *Zoffany* 1977, no.113).

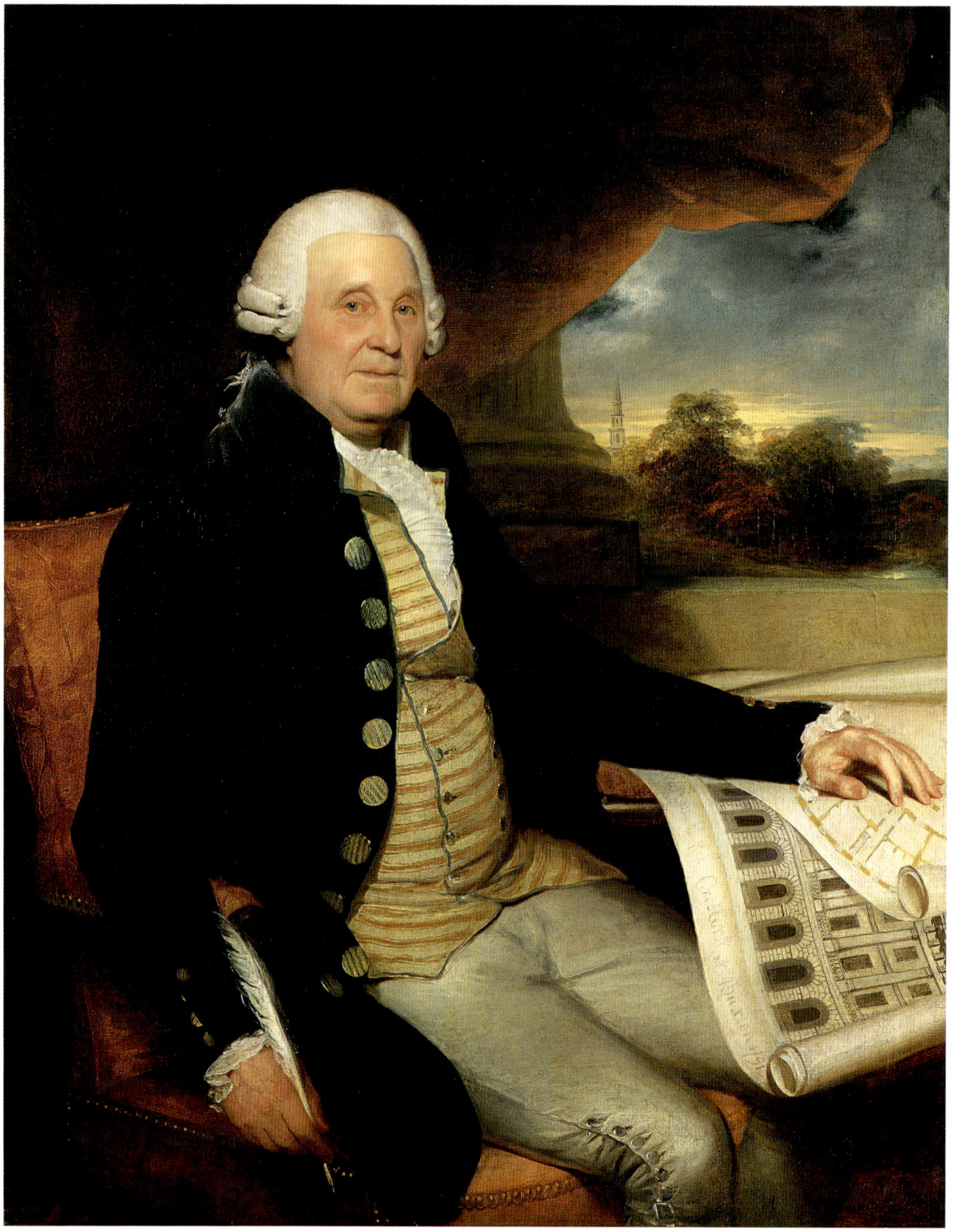

CARR NPG *4062*

CARR, John 1723-1807

Architect, 'invariably competent and scholarly'; from 1750 lived in York where he was lord mayor 1770 and 1785; retired to Horbury, his native village, 1789; d. Askham Richard, York.

Abbreviations

Carr 1971: J. Ingamells, 'Portraits of John Carr', York CAG, *Preview*, XXIV, 1971, pp.842-47

Wragg 2001: B. Wragg, ed. G. Worsley, *John Carr of York*, 2001

4062 WILLIAM BEECHEY 1791

Canvas 127 x 100.5 (50 x 39½) lined;[1] marked craquelure in curtain; retouching on base of column and in his right sleeve; inscribed verso: *John Carr / of Askham Richard / co York Esquire / 3 times Lord Mayor / of York/by/ Sir Wm Beechey*

Pale blue-grey eyes, powdered bag wig, wearing a deep blue-grey coat with gold buttons, a yellow waistcoat with orange and green stripes and silver buttons, white neckcloth; and light nankeen breeches; a red leather chair and curtain. On the table an elevation of the crescent at Buxton and a plan inscribed *...vation of the Crescent at Buxton 1791;* in the distance the church at Horbury and autumnal trees.

Collections: By descent to Col. R.G. Parker of Browsholme Hall, Yorks.;[2] his sale, Christie's, 9 May 1958, lot 20, bt. Leggatt for the NPG.

Engraving; C.H. Hodges 1793.

Exhibitions: *Jubilee Exhibition*, Bradford, 1930; Kendal, 1962-78; Beningbrough 1979-.

Reference: Roberts 1907, pp.199-200; *Carr* 1971, pp.843-44; Wragg 2001, p.82.

The date 1791 painted on the plan of the Buxton Crescent is probably the date of the portrait (the Crescent having been built in 1779-84). The distant church spire is that of St Peter's, Horbury, Yorks., which Carr had built in his native village at his own expense between 1790 and 1794 and where he was buried; it does not appear in the engraving by Hodges and was probably therefore an early addition.[3] Ribeiro has observed that although Carr's dress is fashionable, he is wearing a very old-fashioned wig.[4]

A half-length version in York Mansion House, wearing the mayoral chains of office, was presented to the Corporation by the sitter in 1803;[5] a reduced version is in the Cooper Gallery, Barnsley, and a recent copy by Andrew Festing is in Fairfax House (York Civic Trust).

1 The stretcher bears the label of Robert Rose picture cleaner.
2 In 1845 Mary Anne Carr, the heiress of the Carr property, m. Thomas G. Parker of Browsholme Hall (H. Colvin, *A Biographical Dictionary of British Architects*, 1995, p.218n).
3 See Wragg 2001, pp.158-60; although not complete until 1794, the elevation was engraved by T. Malton in 1791 (illus. Wragg 2001, p.83).
4 Ribeiro 2000, pp.141-42.
5 Illus. *Carr* 1971, pp.843-44; Wragg 2001, p.27.

ICONOGRAPHY

1791 Painting by William Beechey, see NPG 4062.

c.1795-1800 Pastel attributed to John Russell, half length wearing a light brown coat. York CAG (illus. *Cat. of Paintings*, II, 1963, pl.32), from Carr's descendant, C.H. Wybergh.

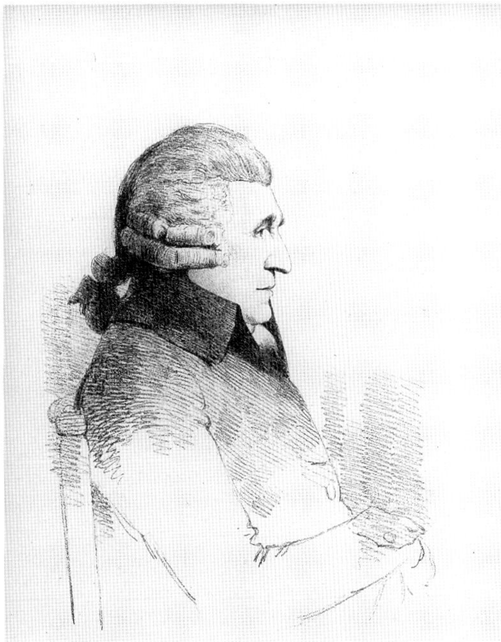

CARR W. Daniell after George Dance 1796 (NPG D 12178)

1796 Drawing by George Dance,* profile bust, dated 5 June 1796. Dance sale, Christie's, 1 July 1898, lot 30. Engraved W. Daniell 1814 (*Dance Portraits*). The sitting recorded by Farington (5 June 1796).

1800 Marble bust by Joseph Nollekens,* bald with a classical drape. York CAG.

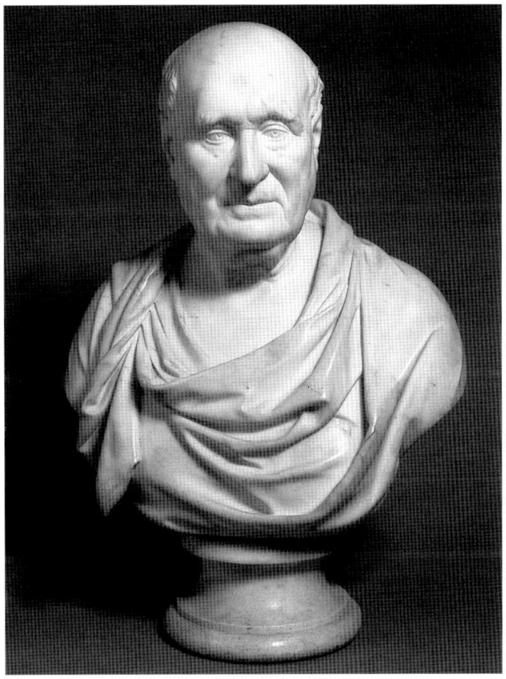

CARR by Joseph Nollekens 1800 (York City Art Gallery)

CARTER, Elizabeth 1717-1806

Writer and linguist, translated Epictetus 1758; 'my old friend Mrs Carter could make a pudding as well as translate Epictetus from the Greek, and work a handkerchief as well as compose a poem' (Johnson).

'I never saw age so graceful in the female sex yet; her whole face seems to beam with goodness, piety, and philanthropy' (Fanny Burney, 1780).

Abbreviation

Pennington 1807: Rev Montagu Pennington, *Memoirs of the Life of Mrs Elizabeth Carter*, 1807 (with a brief survey of her portraiture, p.339); the author was her nephew and executor

28 THOMAS LAWRENCE 1788-89

Pastel on vellum, irregular oval image 34.3 x 28.5 (13½ x 11¼) maximum size 35 x 29.5 (13¾ x 11⅝), the spandrels filled with test marks of the pastels.

Brown eyes, white lace cap tied with a pink ribbon, dark brown silk dress, white neck frill with pink bow, a black silk shawl round her shoulders; an eye-glass hangs from a black ribbon round her neck.

The original backing (now separately preserved) inscribed: *The Portrait of Elizabeth Carter / in Crayons by Sir Thos Lawren- / Taken in 1788 or 1789/ Bequeathed by Mrs Frances Bowdl*[er] *to Mrs Smith, Niece to/ Mrs Carter, & Wife of /* [erasure] *Geo: Smith Esqre / Somerset House / London*

Collections: Drawn for Mrs Bowdler of Bath, by whom bequeathed to Mrs Hannah Carter Smith (the sitter's niece, latterly of Malines), from whom purchased, through William Twopeny, 1858.[1]

Engraving: C. Watson 1808 (as *Thomas Lawrence delt. 1788*).[2]

Exhibitions: RA 1790(145);[3] *Lawrence*, NPG, 1979(56); Beningbrough 1979-.

Reference: *Lawrence* 1964, p.259;[4] Garlick 1989, p.166.

An ivory medallion copy by C.H. Geerts of Louvain is in Deal Town Hall, presented by Mrs Hannah Carter Smith (who latterly lived in Malines) in 1854 (it is set as a cover for a volume of six letters from Mrs Carter to Miss Highmore, with a covering letter describing Geerts's work).

1 Mrs Smith to Lord Stanhope, Malines, 7 January 1858, supplies this provenance (NPG archive), and see the inscription originally on the verso, quoted above. Mrs Smith (b. c.1788) was the younger daughter of John Carter, the sitter's brother.
2 Illus. *Romantic Women Writers*, Grasmere, 1994-95, no.1.
3 'A Portrait of a Lady', identified by Graves as Elizabeth Carter.
4 But said to have been in the Lawrence sale, Christie's, 18 June 1831, lot 43 [see below c.1800]; engraved C. Watson 1806, and purchased by the NPG in 1958.

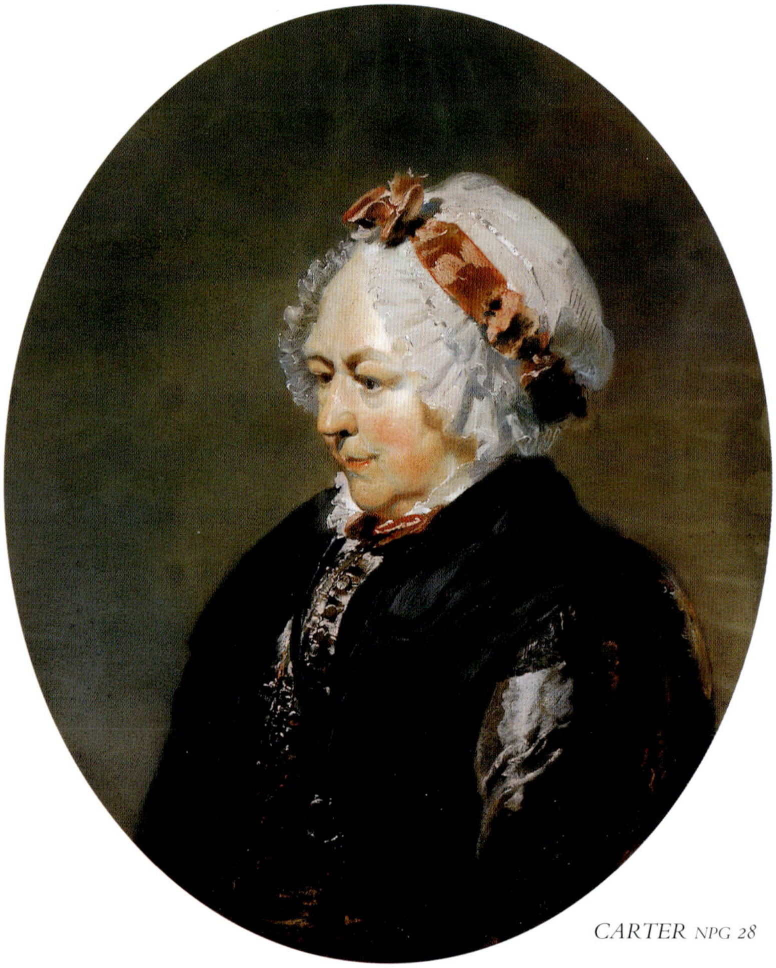

CARTER *NPG 28*

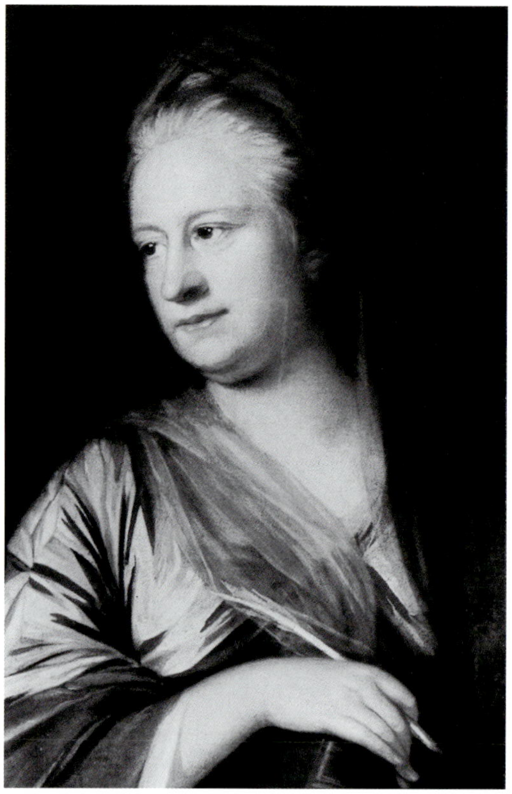

CARTER by Katherine Read c.1765 (Dr Johnson's House, London)

4905 see Groups, *Portraits in the characters of the Muses* by RICHARD SAMUEL 1778

ICONOGRAPHY

1741 Painting by William Fayram, half length as Minerva, her hand resting on a volume of Plato. Two versions, both in private collections, one formerly with Lord Treowen. The attribution is based on the association of the portrait with the poem by Alcaeus, 'To Miss Carter's being drawn in the Habit of Minerva, with Plato in her Hand' which begins with the line: 'Say, Fayram, say, whose is th'enliv'ning face,' (*GM*, XI, 1741, p.271).

c.1745? Painting by Joseph Highmore, three-quarter length standing, a book in her left hand; two allegorical figures behind may represent fame and learning. Deal Town Hall, presented by the sitter's nephew, the Rev Montagu Pennington, 1815. Exhibited *Johnson*, Arts Council, 1984, no.15. Mrs Barrett, a direct descendant of the sitter, said the date of portrait was 1738 when Elizabeth was 21 years of age (letter 24 August 1976; NPG archive), but costume suggests it may be later. Elizabeth Carter was a close friend of Highmore's daughter Susannah.

1756 Portrait by Hester Mulso. Catherine Talbot wrote to Elizabeth Carter, 12 August 1756: 'I had great pleasure in seeing in Mr Richardson's [the novelist Samuel Richardson] hands an exceeding like picture of you, drawn by Miss Mulso this last summer' (*Letters between Mrs Elizabeth Carter and Miss Catherine Talbot*, 1819, II, p.104).

c.1765 Painting by Katherine Read,* half length, a scarf round her head. Dr Johnson's House, London, bequeathed by Mrs Pennington-Bickford 1948. 'Painted for Mrs Montagu by Miss Read upwards of forty years since, was given by Mr Montagu to the author, and is reckoned a very good likeness' (Pennington 1807). A version with Mrs Erle-Drax in 1978.

1778 Painting by Richard Samuel, *Portraits in the characters of the Muses*, see Groups NPG 4905.

c.1780–85 Miniature, unattributed, bust-length oval, wearing bonnet and shawl. with John Lane 1920 (illus. Smith 1920, I, p.172).

c.1780–85 Wax cameo by Joachim Smith, bust-length oval, with bonnet. Engraved Mackenzie* 1806 and 1807, *from an original Cameo in the possession of Lady Charlotte Finch*; Pennington 1807 described the 1807 engraving as from a cameo in her Ladyship's possession, done by Joachim Smith, about twenty-five years ago in wax, 'a very good and striking likeness.'

1781 Miniature by J.H. Hurter, bust-length oval, with white bonnet. Sotheby's, 21 June 1956, lot 71. Exhibited SKM 1865(49) lent by Lord Cremorne.

1788–89 Pastel by Thomas Lawrence, see NPG 28.

c.1800 Unfinished painting by Thomas Lawrence, half length with bonnet. Lawrence sale, Christie's, 18 June 1831, in lot 43; W.H. Carpenter sale, Christie's, 16 February 1867, lot 55 (Scharf sketch in sale cat.; NPG archive). Pennington 1807 described a portrait begun by Lawrence 'a few years ago, which promised to be a great likeness, but was not finished'. In May 1809 there was some correspondence between Lawrence, Farington and Cadell & Davies concerning this unfinished portrait (Farington, 10 May 1809).

J.T. Smith mentioned 'Mrs Carter, of whom Mrs Nollekens was in possession of a portrait, most exquis-

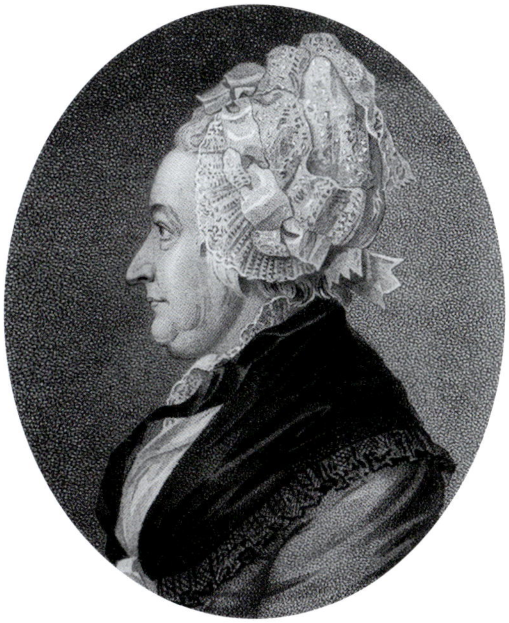

CARTER Mackenzie after Joachim Smith c.1780-85 (NPG D 13793)

itely engraven by Hayward [otherwise unrecorded], from a picture by Lawrence' (Smith 1920, I, p.62).

Undated 'portrait of Mrs Eliz. Carter in Indian ink, by Corbould' [the miniaturist Richard Corbould?], Lawrence sale, Christie's, 27 June 1830, lot 8, possibly, as Kerslake noted (NPG archive), the ink profile inserted into the front end-paper of Pennington 3rd ed. 1816 (NAL, Dyce 46K 24, 7314).

Undated Unidentified portrait painted for 'Mrs Rooke, came afterwards into the possession of Mrs Blosset, since deceased, who has left it, by her will, to the author' (Pennington 1807).

A profile engraving by Joseph Brown 1861 (*Delany* 1861-62, I, f.p.79) appears to be taken from a miniature; if of Mrs Carter it must date from c.1750-60.

DOUBTFUL PORTRAITS

Paintings by J. Kitchingman, bust-length oval, engraved J.R. Smith 1781; attributed to Michael Dahl, Christie's, Wateringbury Place, 1 June 1978, lot 345; 'school of Kneller', sold Carter Hall, Millwood, Va., Sotheby Parke-Bernet, 18 September 1976, lot 278; attributed to Reynolds, sold Christie's, 13 April 1877 lot 547. A miniature in Dr Johnson's House, London.

CAULFIELD, James, see CHARLEMONT

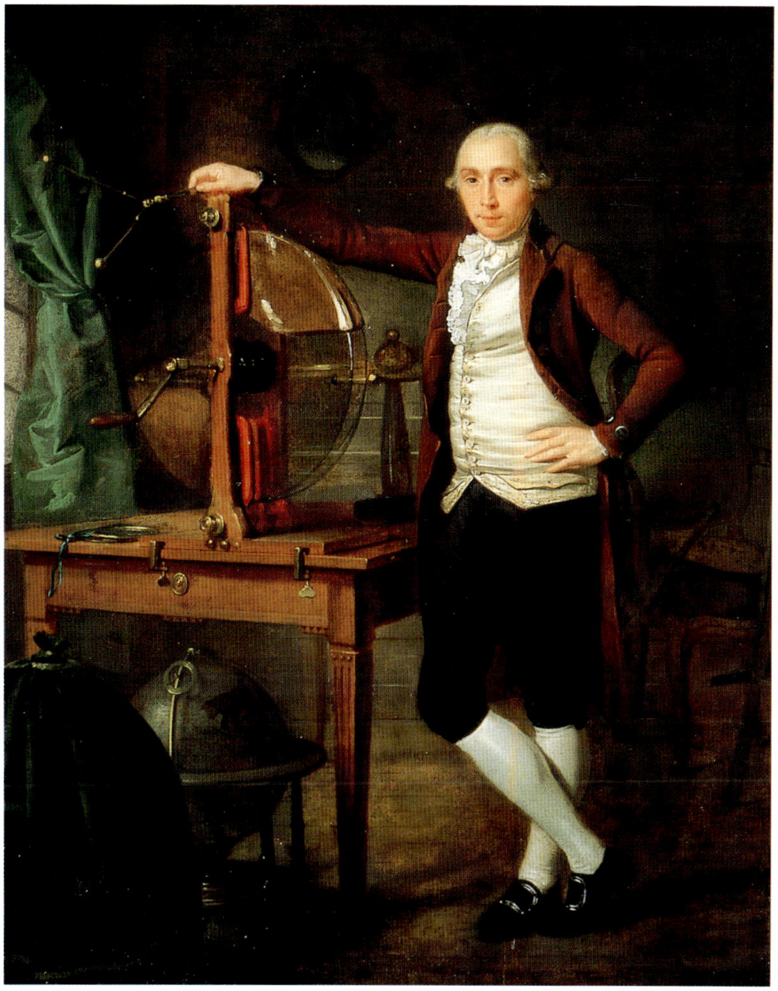

CAVALLO NPG *1412*

CAVALLO, Tiberius 1749-1809

Natural philosopher; b. Naples, he came to England 1771; published *A Complete Treatise of Electricity* 1775, the first of many scientific publications; FRS 1779; in collaboration with Dr James Lind (1736-1812), he also practised as a silhouette artist (see under Impey).

1412 UNKNOWN ARTIST c.1785

Oak panel 59.5 x 51.5 x 1.3 (23½ x 20¼ x ½) of three vertical members (13.6, 27.4 and 10.5 wide); the surface somewhat rubbed; old worm holes and a vertical split 33.5 from the left-hand edge; cleaned 1974 when the left-hand window was revealed.

Brown eyes, white hair, white neckcloth and ruff, brown coat with silver buttons, cream waistcoat, dark blue breeches, white stockings and black shoes with silver buckles; an easel and a palette lying on a chair; prominent on the table stands a twin-plate electrical machine of the later 1770s.[1]

Collections: Purchased from George H. Gabb[2] 1905.

Exhibitions: *Faces as Art*, NPG, 1976; *The Room in View*, NPG, 1996-98.

There remains an element of doubt concerning the identity. NPG 1412 was first offered in March 1905 as a portrait of Humphry Davy (for whom see Walker *Regency*) but two months later the owner was calling him Cavallo.[3] Costume suggests a date in the 1780s and the combination of scientific and artistic attributes[4] make the identification plausible. The likeness agrees with the Trotter engraving of 1787, but the Dance drawing and the Lind silhouette suggest heavier features (see below).

1 It may be compared with Cuthbertson's uninsulated twin-plate machine illus. W.D. Hackmann, *John & Jonathan Cuthbertson*, 1973, p.61, and first illus. in Cuthbertson, *Algemeene-Eigenschappen van de electriciteit*, 1782, II.

2 In March 1935 Gabb said he had bought it at Christie's in 1904 as Sir Humphrey Davy (note in NPG archive) – but such a purchase is not identifiable.

3 'I have gone into the question very carefully as to the portrait being that of Sir Humphrey Davy. As a scientific chemist, myself, I may say ...' (28 March 1905), but by 27 May Mr Gabb was writing to say how important a figure Cavallo was in the evolution of electro-therapeutics (NPG archive).

4 For Cavallo as silhouettist, see McKechnie 1978, pp.194-95, 382, and *Apollo*, XXII, 1935, pp.287-89.

ICONOGRAPHY

1783 Miniature by J.H. Hurter,* bust-length oval. NG of Ireland (3611).

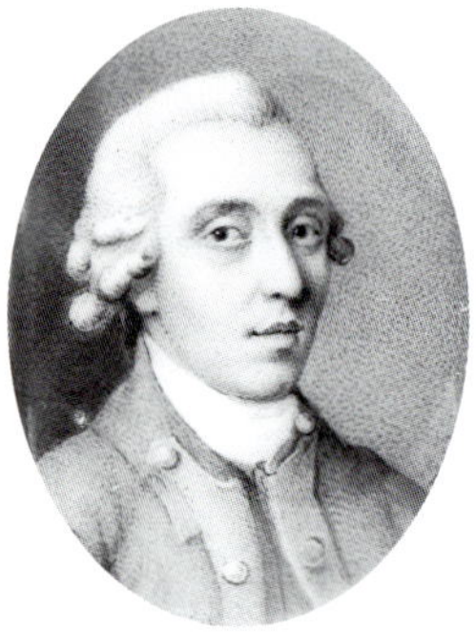

CAVALLO by J.H. Hurter 1783 (National Gallery of Ireland)

c.1785 Unattributed painting, see NPG 1412.

1787 Engraving by T. Trotter, bust-length oval (*European Mag.*); anon. reversed oval.

1792 Silhouette, bust length to right, inscribed *Mr Cavallo 1780*[?] / *Dr Lind*. British Museum (1980.U.1093). A reversed example, inscribed *Mr Cavallo / Jany.1792*, is also in the British Museum (1980.U.1094 illus., *Apollo*, XXII, 1935, p.288; McKechnie 1978, p.292). The heavy features resemble those seen in Dance's drawing of 1799.

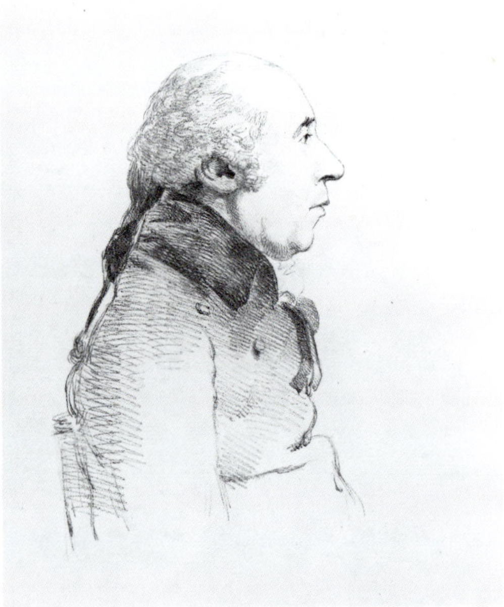

CAVALLO W. Daniell after George Dance 1799 (NPG D 12121)

1799 Drawing by George Dance, profile bust, dated 28 May 1799. Christie's, 20 November 1973, lot 163. Engraved W. Daniell* 1809 (*Dance Portraits*).

CAVENDISH, Henry 1731-1810

Scientist, 1st s. of Lord Charles Cavendish (3rd s. of the 2nd Duke of Devonshire); led a reclusive life of great simplicity devoted to experimental science; produced a paper on 'Factitious Airs' 1766; in 1777-78 he concluded that water was a combination of oxygen and hydrogen; after his paper on 'Experiments on Air' 1784, the originality of his work was needlessly disputed; he subsequently measured the density of the Earth.

'I ... recollect the shrill cry he uttered as he shuffled quickly from room to room, seeming to be annoyed if looked at, but sometimes approaching to hear what was passing among others. His face was intelligent and mild, though, from the nervous irritation which he seemed to feel, the expression could hardly be called calm. It is not likely that he ever should have been induced to sit for his picture ... His dress was of the oldest fashion, a greyish green coat and waistcoat, with flaps, a small cocked hat, and the hair dressed like a wig (which possibly it was) with a thick clubbed tail. His walk was quick and uneasy ...' (Lord Brougham, 1845).

1075 see Groups, *Men of Science living in 1807-08* by JOHN GILBERT, FREDERICK SKILL and WILLIAM & ELIZABETH WALKER 1858-62

ICONOGRAPHY

c.1800? Drawing by William Alexander,* whole length walking to left. British Museum (1.8.137), see Groups NPG 1075. Engraved C. Rosenberg. An enlarged half-length version is in the Science Museum.

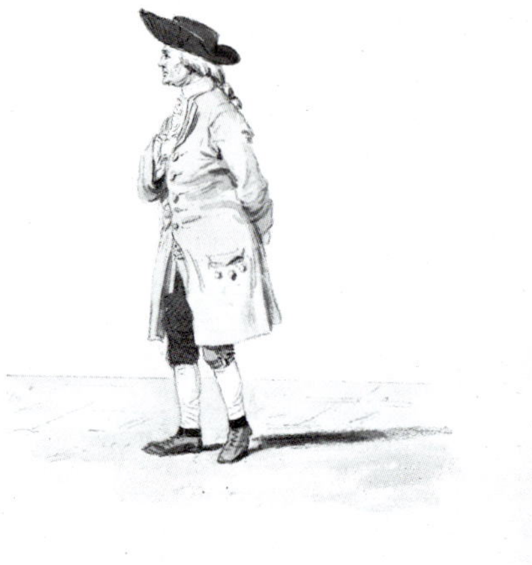

CAVENDISH by William Alexander c.1800? (British Museum)

CAVENDISH, William, see DEVONSHIRE

CHAMBERLIN, Mason 1722-87

Portrait and landscape painter; pupil of Francis Hayman; foundation member of the RA 1768, where he exhibited 1769-86.

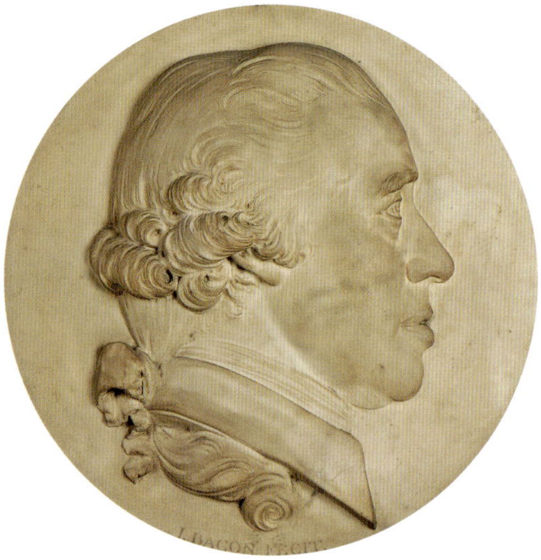

CHAMBERLIN NPG *2653*

2653 JOHN BACON senior 1785

Marble relief 40.5 (16) diameter; small chip off the temple, the surface slightly soiled; incised, below centre: *I BACON FECIT* and verso: *MASON CHAMBERLIN 1785*.

Collections: Purchased from Alice M. Huckle 1934.

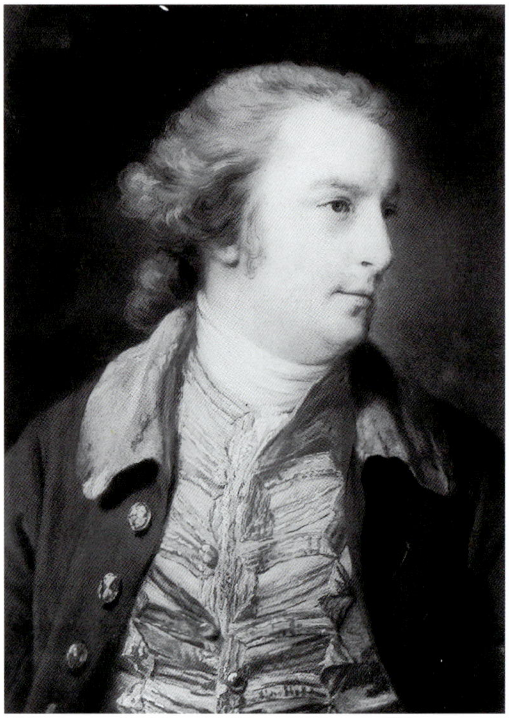

CHAMBERLIN by Francis Cotes 1766 (Christie's)

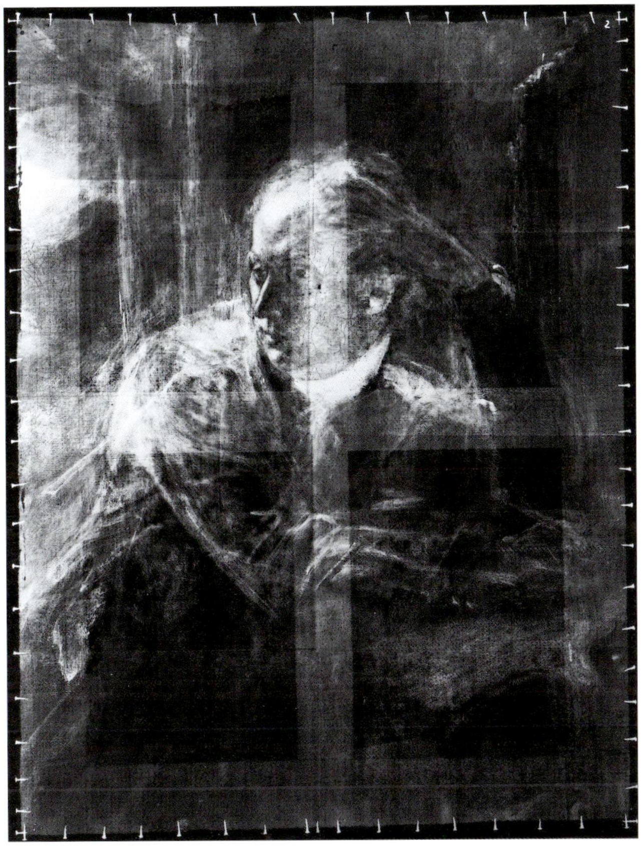

CHAMBERS NPG *27 x-ray mosaic*

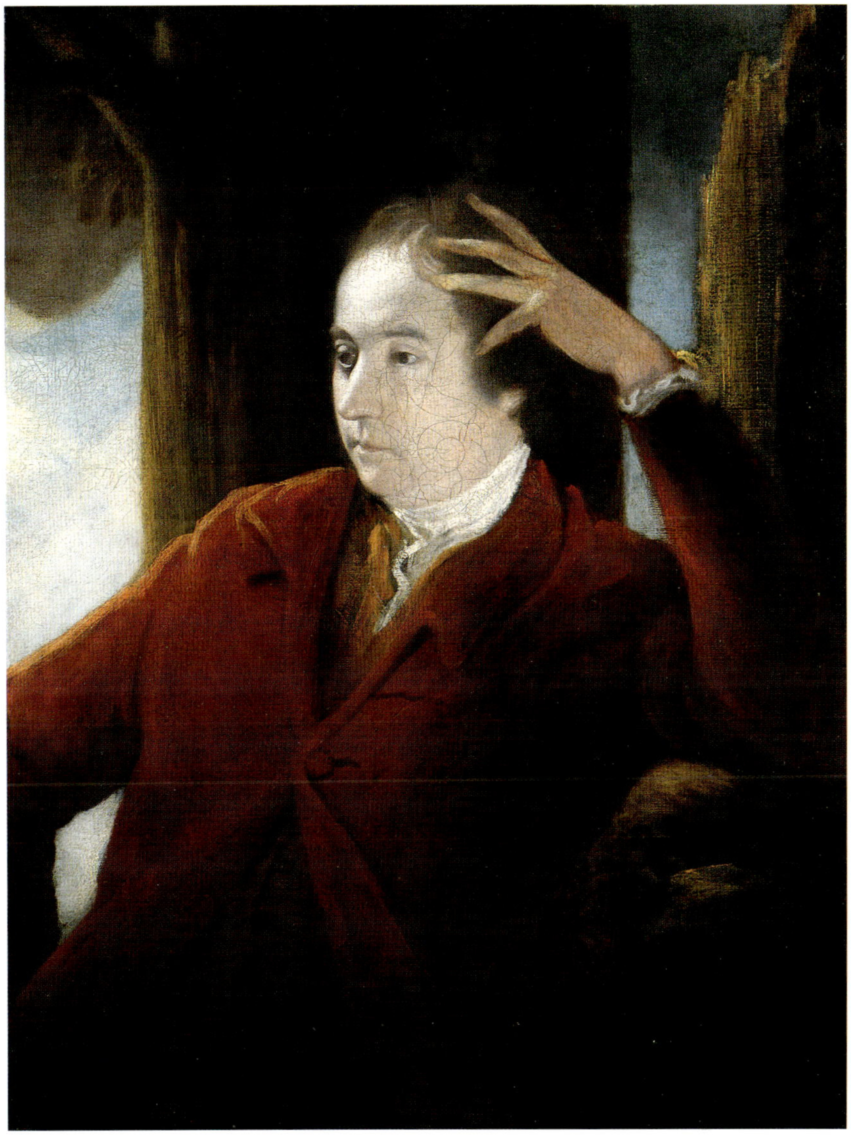

CHAMBERS
NPG *27*

Sculptor and painter apparently exchanged portraits: Chamberlin exhibited a portrait of Bacon at the RA 1785(50), showing him holding a design for the Chatham monument in Westminster Abbey (see Bacon).

ICONOGRAPHY

1766 Pastel by Francis Cotes,* half length. Christie's, 9 June 1964, lot 213.

1772 Painting by Johann Zoffany,* *The Academicians of the Royal Academy*, see Groups NPG 1437.

1784 Self portrait, exhibited RA 1784(164).

1785 Marble relief by John Bacon sr., see NPG 2653.

CHAMBERS, Ann, see TEMPLE

CHAMBERS, Sir William, Kt 1723-96

Architect; b. Gothenburg, s. of a Scottish merchant; sailed with the Swedish East India Company 1740-49; studied in Paris and Italy 1750-55; Architect to the King 1761; comptroller of the office of works 1769 and surveyor 1782; treasurer RA 1768; Kt of the Polar Star (Sweden) 1770 and allowed to assume the rank of an English knight 1772; FRS 1776.

'His Sense is middling, but his appearance is gentell & his person good which are most material circumstances' (Robert Adam, 1755).

Abbreviations

Harris 1970: J. Harris, *Sir William Chambers*, 1970

Harris 1996: J. Harris & M. Snodin, eds., *Sir William Chambers*, 1996.

27 JOSHUA REYNOLDS c.1756-60

Canvas 90 x 70.5 (35½ x 27¾) lined; the flesh tones are faded and marked by shrinkage craquelure, the surface generally abraded; the hand, coat and background trees suggest an unfinished picture, and x-radiography* confirms fundamental changes in the composition; originally the body was turned to the left, the arms crossed, left hand on right arm, resting on a table on which lay papers.

Brown eyes, greyish hair, wearing a deep red coat and brown waistcoat; in the background two straight tree trunks, one broken.

Collections: Given by the sitter's son, George Chambers, to Mr West; Christie's, 24 May 1845, lot 31, bt. B.S. Smith;[1] purchased from West's widow, Mrs M. West, January 1858.[2]

Exhibitions: Royal Dublin Society, 1861(Portrait Gallery 488); *Chambers*, London, Stockholm, 1996-97(3); Beningbrough 1979–.

Reference: Graves & Cronin, I, p.163; Harris 1970, pp.15, 173; Mannings 2000, no.344.

A composition resolved with difficulty. Chambers was first portrayed as a professional architect with (we may assume) plans before him, and then cast in the nobler role of thinker. Such elevation anticipates Reynolds's later comment that 'though he was President [of the Royal Academy], Sir Wm. was Viceroy over him'[3] (see also Groups NPG 987) but, more immediately, the changes may relate to Chambers's rapid social advancement. He had returned from Italy in 1755 already acclaimed as 'a prodigy for Genius, for Sense & good taste',[4] and within two years was appointed architectural tutor to the Prince of Wales, later George III, and was devising the exotic decoration of Kew for the Dowager Princess of Wales. In 1761 he was appointed, with Robert Adam, joint-architect to King George III.

NPG 27 is undocumented and is dated by the sitter's apparent age; it evidently took some time to complete.[5] Payments made in 1763 by Mrs Catherine Chambers for her portrait by Reynolds of c.1756 (Kenwood),[6] had previously been associated with NPG 27 (e.g. by Graves & Cronin).

1 Sent in by 'West' and presumably bt. in; I am grateful to Margie Christian for her help in identifying this lot.
2 Mrs M. West of 8 Upper Berkeley Street, Hyde Park Square, London, wrote on 26 January 1858: '[the portrait] formerly belonged to Capt Chambers son of Sir William and was given by him to his friend Mr West my late Husband' (NPG archive). George Chambers, who m. Jane, dau. of Lord Rodney, became something of a vagabond according to Farington (23 July 1817).
3 Farington, 10 December 1804 (and see 11 December).
4 By Robert Adam (cf. Ingamells 1997, pp.194-95).
5 Harris 1996, p.1, suggested that NPG 27 may have coincided with Chambers's appointment as Architect to the King.
6 Cormack 1970, pp.113, 116; see Mannings 2000, no.342 as c.1756.

4044 JEREMIAH MEYER c.1775

Watercolour and bodycolour on ivory 4 x 3.3 (1⅝ x 1¼); craquelure below hairline across forehead.

White powdered wig, brown eyes, plum coloured coat, wearing the badge of the Polar Star.

Collections: Bequeathed by Miss Eugenie F.E. Pebardy,[1] god-daughter of Frederick Harman, great grandson of the sitter, 1958.

Exhibitions: *Master Drawings* 1993-95(25); *Chambers*, London, Stockholm, 1996-97(9).

Reference: Harris 1970, p.173 (as Victoria and Albert Museum); Walker 1998, no.53.

NPG 4044 dates after 1770 when Chambers was awarded the Polar Star, and he appears slightly younger

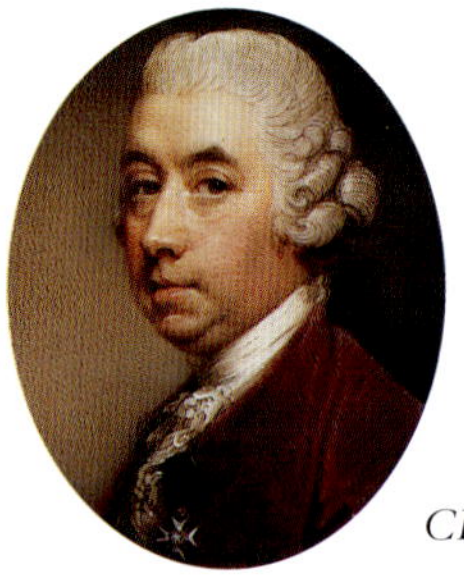

CHAMBERS NPG *4044*

than in the Reynolds portrait of 1778. The attribution to Meyer was first made by Graham Reynolds in 1958.[2]

1 She also owned a pendant containing a lock of Chambers's hair, miniatures of Chambers's daughter Selina and of her husband, William Innes, two pastel portraits of his daughters by Francis Cotes, and a miniature of his granddaughter, Mrs Samuel Harman, by A.E. Chalon – all now in the Victoria and Albert Museum.
2 As stated in a letter from C.K. Adams to the Pebardy solicitors, 21 February 1958 (NPG archive).

3159 HOUGHTON after JOSHUA REYNOLDS [1778-80]

Ink and grey wash with touches of red crayon on paper 24.8 x 21 (9¾ x 8¼); the image area discoloured through exposure.

Holding a plan with two rows of three columns each.

Collections: Mrs M.F. Warner; Sotheby's, 2 June 1943, lot 10 (with three others), bt. Arthur Spencer (Siddons Gallery, London), from whom purchased 1943.[1]

Exhibition: *Royal Family at Kew*, Richmond, 1994.

A pedantic copy of the Reynolds portrait of 1778-80 in the Royal Academy (see below). The old mount was inscribed in pencil: *Dr Wm Chambers / by Houghton / after Reynolds*, possibly the silhouettist Samuel Houghton (d.1796).

1 One of eight drawings; see also Unidentified Portraits NPG 3160.

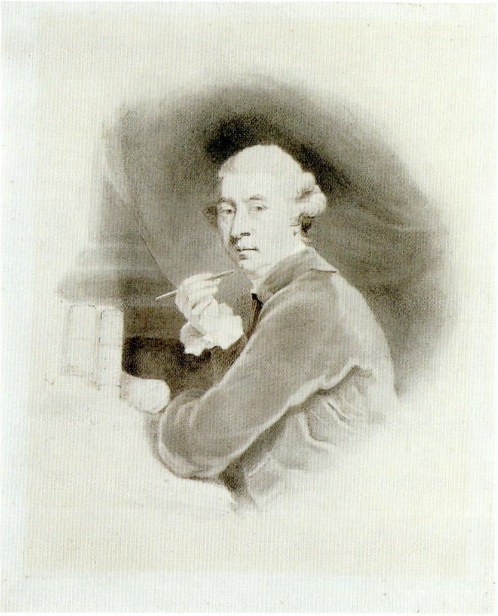

CHAMBERS NPG *3159*

987 see Groups, *Chambers, Wilton and Reynolds* by JOHN FRANCIS RIGAUD 1782

ICONOGRAPHY

A brief survey appears in Harris 1970, p.173.

1752-53 Painting by L-G. Blanchet, with volumes of Vitruvius and Palladio. Untraced (see Bowron & Rishel, *Art in Rome in the 18th century*, 2000, p.327).

c.1756-60 Painting by Joshua Reynolds, see NPG 27.

c.1760-65 Painting by Joshua Reynolds, unfinished half length. Musée des Beaux-Arts, Brussels (Mannings 2000, no.345). Engraved S.W. Reynolds 1794. Versions sold Sotheby's, 9 November 1960, lot 94, and in a private Scottish collection.

1764 Pastel by Francis Cotes,* half length. Scottish NPG (PG 629; Johnson 1976, no.137). Engraved R. Houston 1771-72; W. Bromley 1792 and 1796. A contemporary pastel copy in the RIBA; a good version in oil at Somerset House (GAC 0.252; illus. *Connoisseur*, XCIV, 1934, p.142).

1768 Drawing by P-E. Falconet, medallion (British Museum, 1881.6.11.152). Engraved D.P. Pariset 1769, and *Parriset* (rectangular, titled *Architect to the King*).

1772 Painting by Johann Zoffany,* *The Academicians of the Royal Academy*, see Groups NPG 1437.

The figure of Chambers alone was engraved as a whole length by J. Romney 1817.

1775 Chalk drawing by Robert Dunkarton. Paul Tyler in 1970 (Harris 1970, p.173).

c.1775 Miniature by Jeremiah Meyer, see NPG 4044.

1776 Miniature by George Engleheart, bust-length oval. Wellesley sale, Sotheby's, 13 February 1958, lot 6 (with other miniatures of the family), by descent from the sitter. Engleheart's fee-book records five miniatures of Chambers in 1776 and another in 1782 (Williamson 1902, pp.23, 25, 80).

1778-80 Painting by Joshua Reynolds,* three-quarter length seated, with a distant view of Somerset House. Royal Academy, commissioned by the Academy (Mannings 2000, no.346). Engraved V. Green 1780; J. Collyer 1785; G. Murray 1794; W.C. Edwards (bust length) 1830. Copies include those in the musée des Beaux-Arts, Brussels, by Thomas Robson (Warrington MAG) and by H.P. Briggs (see Mannings 2000, nos.346a-d) and a bust-length oval miniature copy on porcelain in an English private collection. See also NPG 3159.

1782 Miniature by George Engleheart, see 1776.

1782 Painting by J.F. Rigaud, Chambers with Sir Joshua Reynolds and Joseph Wilton, see Groups NPG 987.

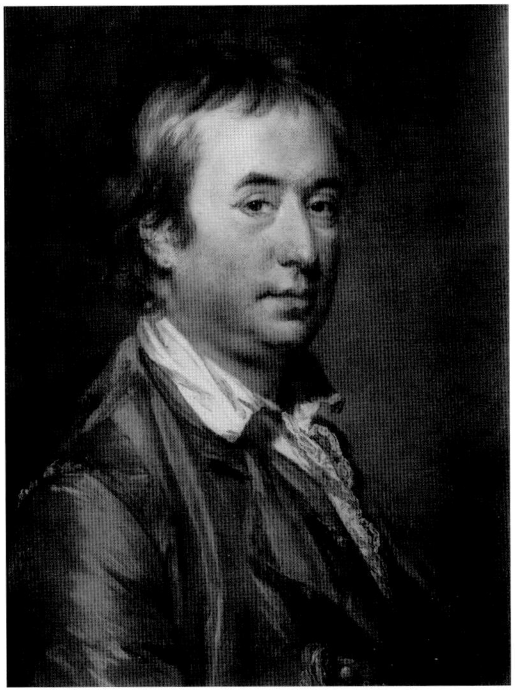

CHAMBERS by Francis Cotes 1764 (Scottish National Portrait Gallery)

before 1785 Portrait in the collection of Lord Bessborough in 1785 at Roehampton, a house designed by Chambers in the 1760s (Musgrave MSS 6391, f.199v).

1787 Wax portrait medallion by Charles Peart; used for the Wedgwood medallion of 1788 (illus. Reilly 1973, p.87).

1788 Painting by C.F. von Breda, half length. RIBA, on loan to the Victoria and Albert Museum (RIBA 3-2001; illus. *History of the King's Works*, VI, 1973, pl.1). Commissioned by Chambers. Exhibited RA 1788(197).

1790 Bust by François Le Masson, exhibited RA 1790(534).

1793 Drawing by George Dance,* half-length profile, dated 17 March 1793. Royal Academy. Engraved W. Daniell 1809 (*Dance Portraits*). Fuseli commented: 'What a *grate*, heavy, *humpty-dumpty*, this leaden fellow is' (Smith 1905, p.204). A second drawing exhibited *Sublime and the Beautiful*, Sabin, 1973(5), illus. pl.1.

1795 Painting by Henry Singleton,* *President and Members of the Royal Academy*, see Comparative Groups.

A portrait of Chambers by Singleton exhibited RA 1795(29) was probably connected with this group.

Posthumous

1797 Marble bust by Richard Westmacott. Soane Museum (illus. Harris 1996, p.10; Busco 1994, p.11). Exhibited RA 1797(1129). Commissioned by the Office of Works.

1857 Profile bust by Benjamin Wyon, for a medal minted in 1857 for the Art Union of London (Brown 1987, no.2596). Exhibited RA 1858(1118). Derived from the Westmacott bust; example in the NPG reference collection (D 2911). (Harris 1970, p.173, attributed the medal in error to William Wyon).

1909 Stone bust by Gilbert Bayes. Victoria and Albert Museum, south front.

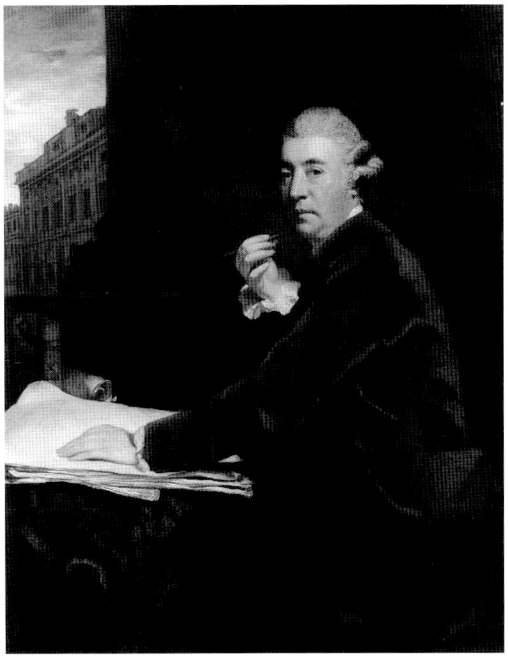

CHAMBERS by Joshua Reynolds 1778-80 (Royal Academy of Arts, London)

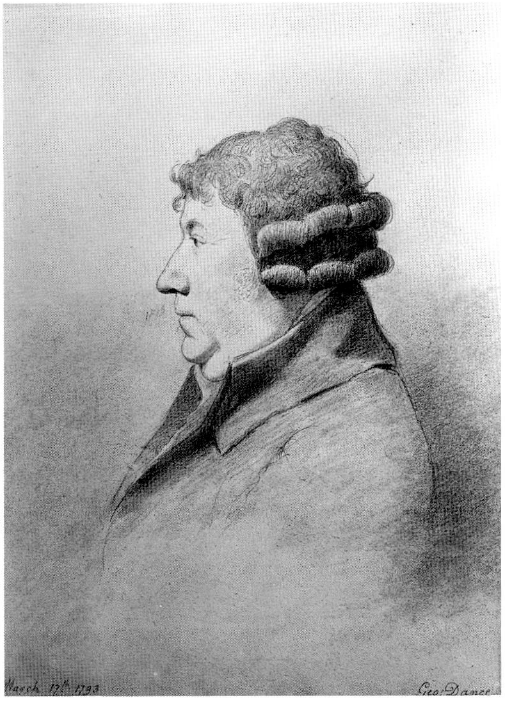

CHAMBERS by George Dance 1793 (Royal Academy of Arts, London)

DOUBTFUL PORTRAIT

Miniature by W.S. Lethbridge (1771-1831), leaning over a table on which are *Mitchells Plans & Views and Chambers Architecture*, exhibited *Miniatures from the Hothfield Heirlooms*, Soho Square, London, 1936(95).

CHARLEMONT, James Caulfeild, 1st Earl of 1728-99

Irish patriot and patron; suc. as 4th Viscount Charlemont [I] 1734; travelled in the near East and Italy 1747-54; FRS 1755; Earl of Charlemont [I] 1763; commanded the Ulster volunteers 1781; KP 1783; first president of the Royal Irish Academy 1786.

'the most public-spirited, and at the same time the best-natured, and the best bred man in Ireland' (Edmund Burke, 1785).

'of the middle size, or rather above it; but he stooped considerably, especially towards the latter part of his life; the effect, I believe, of ill health. When he appeared with his blue ribband, and in full dress at the levee, his air and deportment were exactly those of a Foreign Ambassador of the highest rank. His eyebrows were large and black. His features ... even before he reached middle life ... became expanded, strong, and more expressive than handsome' (Francis Hardy, 1812).

176 JGD after RICHARD LIVESAY [c.1782]

Canvas 68 x 50 (26¾ x 19¾) lined; original canvas indistinctly inscribed verso: *General Earl of Charlemont / Copy from the Original in M Walcots possession, by JGD 1784*. Cleaned and restretched 1999; the surface is abraded, and there are several minor losses.

Blue-grey eyes, grey powdered hair, wearing the light blue ribbon of St Patrick, and the irregular uniform of a volunteer general:[1] red coat with black facings and gold trim, cream waistcoat and breeches, his black hat with a gold trim on the floor beside him with his sword; he sits in a green chair, his right hand resting on papers inscribed *ULSTER VOLUNTEERS* (see note 3 below), lying on a table covered with a green cloth; on the far wall are four medallions lettered *VALOUR*, *HIBERNIA RESURGENS*, *CONCORDE* and *MODERATION* (see note 3 below); in the distance troops are drilling.

Collections: By descent to the 3rd Earl of Charlemont,[2] from whom purchased 1864.

Engraving: J. Dean 1785 (*Painted by R. Livesay ...*).[3]

The original portrait, presumably that now in the National Gallery of Ireland (4051)[4] and evidently painted for 'Mr Walcot', celebrated Charlemont's command of the Ulster Volunteers and his leadership of the national Volunteer movement. The movement initially led to the Irish parliament obtaining greater legislative independence in 1782, but Charlemont's plea for moderation subsequently reduced their role.[5]

NPG 176 is dated 1784, the year before the publication of Dean's mezzotint; it is almost the same size, and it appears possible that 'JGD' was the engraver himself, who is known to have painted occasionally.[6]

1 So described by Maj. N.P. Dawnay (February 1952; NPG archive).
2 Who wrote to Scharf, 28 May 1864 saying that the portrait 'was painted from life by I believe Livesay, but at all events by the artist who painted the portraits of the first Knights of St Patrick at the time of the Institution of the order [i.e. J.K. Sherwin] ... [of several portraits he had of his grandfather] this is the only full length & the only painting which represents him in the Uniform of General in Chief of the Volunteers of 82 & with the star & ribbon of the order of S.P.' (NPG archive).
3 CS 5. The papers on the table inscribed: *To General Earl of Charlemont Dublin; Thanks of Parliament to the Volun*[teers]; the date *11 Feby 1782* follows *Ulster Volunteers*. The plaques on the wall inscribed: *Adsur / toribus / Libertatis / publicae; Hibernia resurgens, Concordia and Moderationi*.
4 From the collection of the 6th Earl of Arran; sold Sotheby's, 23 June 1971, lot 100.
5 See for example, J. Kelley in M. McCarthy ed. *Lord Charlemont and his Circle*, 2001, pp.18-29.
6 Cf. Waterhouse 1981, p.104.

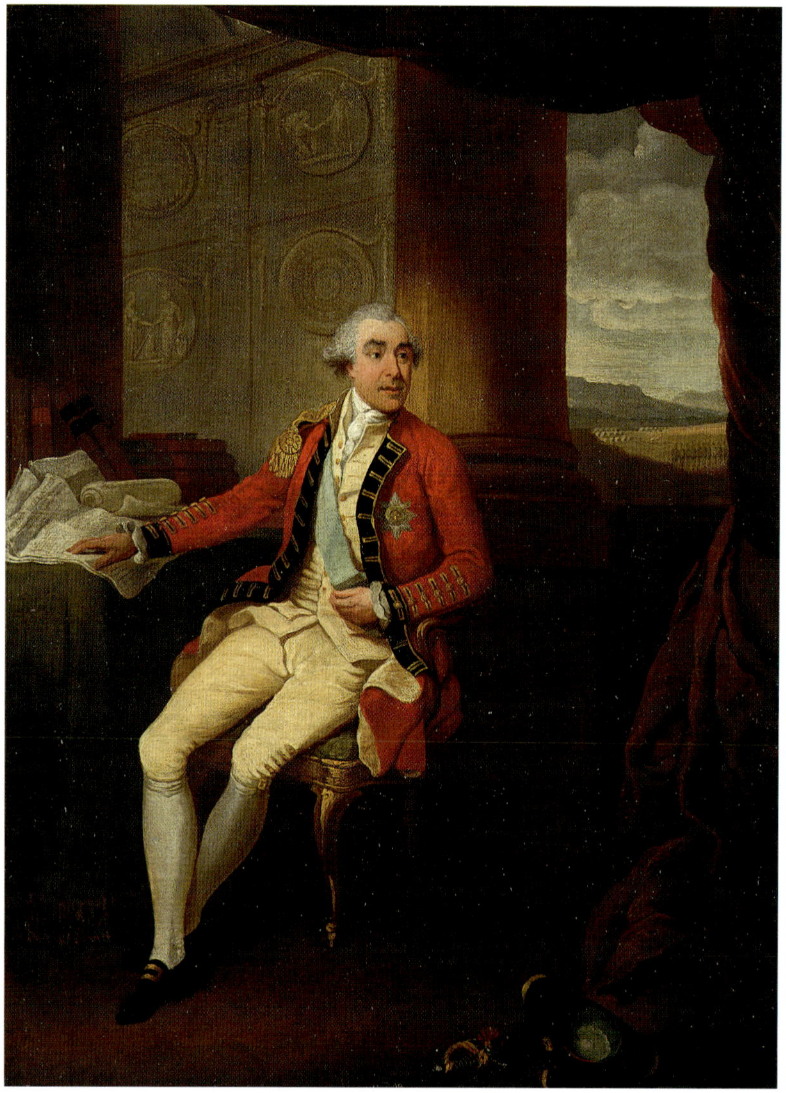

1st Earl of CHARLEMONT
NPG 176

ICONOGRAPHY

In Rome 1750-54

1750-51 Caricature drawing by P.L. Ghezzi,* seated at table with Joseph Leeson jr. Philadelphia Museum of Art (1978.70.290).

Charlemont also appeared in other (rather less informative) caricature groups painted in Rome 1750-51 by Joshua Reynolds:

a) *The Parody of the School of Athens*, playing a flute (NG of Ireland, 734; Mannings 2000, no.1962); engraved J. Scott 1878

b) Group of four figures, in which Charlemont wears the Irish shamrock (NG of Ireland, 737; Mannings 2000, no.1965).

1753-56 Painting by Pompeo Batoni,* three-quarter length standing. Yale Center for British Art (B1974.3.26; Clark 1985, no.190). Painted in Rome. A second (whole-length) portrait by Batoni, painted at the same time, remains untraced.

Ireland and England

1757-62 Payments to Joshua Reynolds by Charlemont suggest two three-quarter length portraits painted between 1757 and 1762 (Mannings 2000, no.326). Identified and illus. by J. Coleman in M. McCarthy ed., *Lord Charlemont and his Circle*, 2001, pp.41-44, as an untraced half length of Charlemont, and a half-length oval of his brother, Francis Caulfeild.

c.1759 Painting by William Hogarth, unfinished half length. Smith College, Northampton, Mass. (illus. R. Paulson, *Hogarth*, 1993, III, f.p.300). Engraved J. Haynes 1782 *from an original Portrait by Hogarth in the Possession of Mr Saml Ireland*; anon. circular plate 1784 (*European Mag.*). A comparable, but weak, small half-length version, was called Hogarth when in the Charlemont collection (photograph, NPG archive, as Sir Herbert Hughes-Stanton collection).

c.1781 Anon. engraving, equestrian whole length, as commander-in-chief of the Ulster Volunteers (NG of Ireland; 11.188).

1784 Painting by Richard Livesay, see NPG 176.

c.1785 Miniature attributed to Richard Cosway. Sotheby's, 30 June 1980, lot 148. Copied in enamel by Henry Bone 1814 for Mrs Caulfield; preparatory drawing in the NPG Bone albums (*Bone* 1999, no.101); exhibited SKM 1865(2610) lent Hon. Mrs Caulfield [*sic*].

1788 Miniature by Horace Hone, bust-length oval in old age, wearing the badge of St Patrick. Sotheby's, 20 July 1981, lot 101, with an enamel replica inscribed verso: *This Enamel copied from a Water Colour Picture the same size which Earl Charlemont sat for and from which picture the medal was made, for the Irish Royal Academy. The Original Picture and this Enamel were both painted by Horace Hone ... The water-colour ... in Dublin in the year 1788 and this Enamel in London in the year 1805*. Replicas by Hone dated 1789 in the Royal Collection (illus. Walker 1992, no.229) and exhibited RA 1807(849). The type was engraved T. Nugent 1790; L. Schiavonetti 1810; B. Smith 1814 and 1822; derivative small plates by K. Mackenzie 1799, S. Freeman, Holl, and J. Heath 1810 (described as from a painting by Hamilton; Strickland 1913, I, p.198, alleged that a drawing from the Hone miniature by John Comerford was made for Heath's engraving).

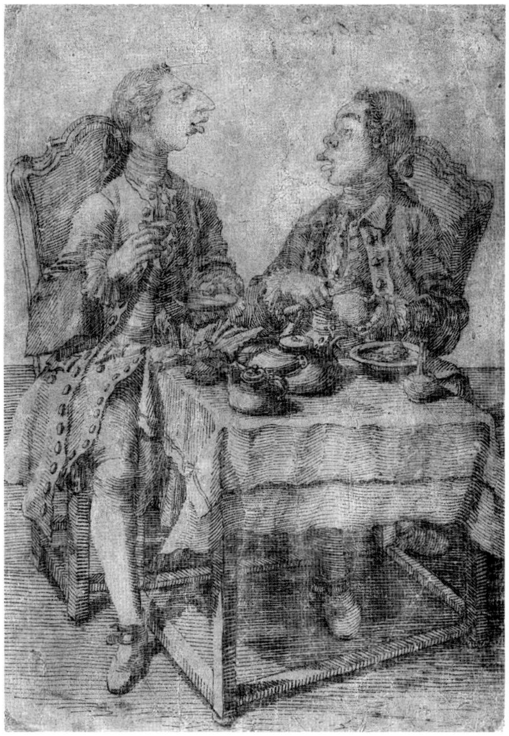

1st Earl of CHARLEMONT (right) with Joseph Leeson by P.L. Ghezzi 1750-51 (Philadelphia Museum of Art)

1790 Bronze medallion by William Mossop (Brown 1980, no.267). The medal made for the Royal Irish Academy of which Charlemont was the first president. Mossop's wax model, made from the Hone miniature of 1788, is in the NG of Ireland (8164).

1790 Painting by Martin Quadal, half-length seated with the ribbon of St Patrick. NG of Ireland (1763).

1795 Drawing by George Dance, profile bust, with badge of St Patrick, dated August 1795. Bayham Abbey (SSB 91/41). Engraved W. Daniell* 1814 (*Dance Portraits*, as *John Earl of Charlemont*).

Posthumous

c.1820 Painting by William Cuming, the head derived from the Hone miniature of 1788, three-quarter length seated, with Nollekens's statue of Minerva beyond. NG of Ireland (187); originally painted for the Dublin Library in D'Olier Street. A version with the Royal Irish Academy, exhibited *Great Irishmen*, Belfast, 1965(39).

1820 Medal by W.S. Mossop (Brown 1980, no.1043). Said to have been taken from the head by William Cuming (see *Irish Portraits*, NPG, 1969, p.98); intended as one of a series of forty Irish celebrities.

Charlemont appears in several narrative scenes, including: *The Irish House of Commons* by Francis Wheatley, 1780 (Leeds CAG; illus. *Wheatley* 1970,

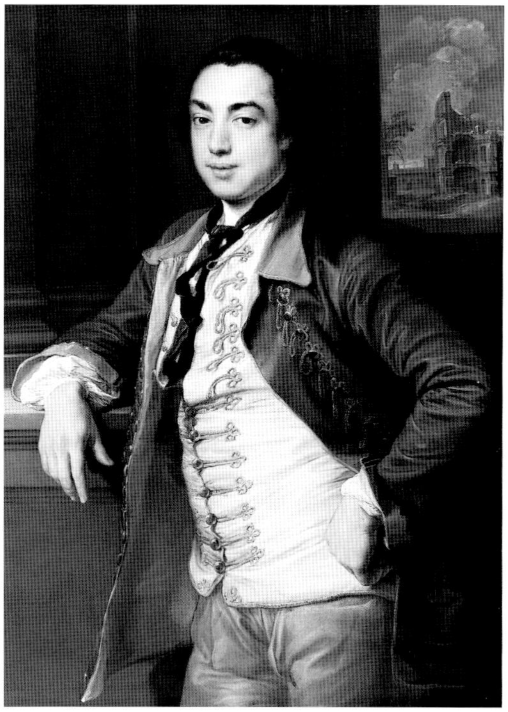

1st Earl of CHARLEMONT by Pompeo Batoni 1753-56 (Yale Center for British Art)

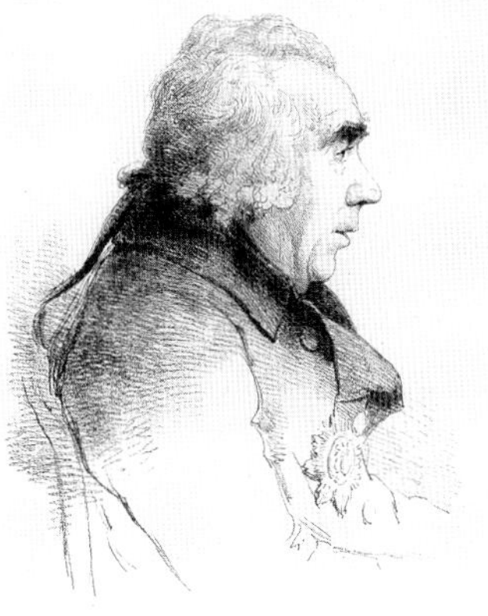

1st Earl of CHARLEMONT W. Daniell after George Dance 1795 (NPG D 12053)

p.36); *Lord Charlemont at the Provincial Reviews in Phoenix Park, Dublin, 3 June 1782*, anon. engraving 1783 (NG of Ireland; 11,870), and the *Installation Banquet of the Knights of St Patrick, Dublin, 1783*, by J.K. Sherwin (NG of Ireland, 396).

DOUBTFUL PORTRAITS

Painting by James Russell, *Group of British Connoisseurs in Rome* (Yale Center for British Art, B1981.25.272; illus. *Grand Tour*, Tate Gallery, 1996, no.43); painting by A.R. Mengs (NG Prague, DO 4561) has been identified as showing Charlemont with a personification of Architecture (see *Mengs*, Kenwood, 1993, no.4); miniature by George Chinnery, engraved for *Walker's Hibernian Mag.*, March 1800, as 'an original likeness'.

CHARLOTTE, Queen 1744-1818

Princess Charlotte Sophia [Sophie Charlotte], 2nd surv. dau. of Duke Charles Lewis of Mecklenburg-Strelitz; m. George III on 8 September 1761; they were crowned jointly on 22 September; between 1762 and 1783 she bore fifteen children, of whom only the last three failed to achieve their majority; d. 17 November 1818.

'of a middling stature, and rather small, but her shape fine, and carriage graceful; her hands and neck exceedingly well turned; her hair auburn; her face round and fair; the eyes of a light blue, and beaming with sweetness; the nose a little flat, and turned up at the point; the mouth rather large, with rosy lips, and very fine teeth' (John Watkins, 1819).

Abbreviation

Levey 1977: M. Levey, *A Royal Subject, Portraits of Queen Charlotte*, National Gallery, 1977

224 studio of ALLAN RAMSAY [1762]

Canvas 148 x 108 (58¼ x 42½) lined; cleaned 1991.

Grey eyes, fair hair, in coronation robes; with a jewelled necklace, pale blue gown trimmed with ermine and silver floral decoration; silver skirt embroidered with gold; pearl bracelets on both wrists; the crown of silver and dark grey velvet; a pale-red table cloth and pink drapery hanging above.

Collections: Purchased from J. McLachlan 1866.

Exhibitions: National Gallery -1920; *Scottish Art*, RA, 1939(61).

Reference: Smart 1999, no.192fg.

A reduced studio version of Ramsay's whole-length coronation portrait painted in 1762, which remains in the Royal Collection[1] and was never engraved. For the distribution and execution of the many copies of Ramsay's portraits of the King and Queen, see George III, NPG 223.

The original in the Royal Collection shows the head turned slightly to the left, tightly-curled powdered hair, a pearl necklace and no bracelets. Subsequent portraits vary in detail. The earliest copies, for example in the Guildhall Art Gallery (39) and at

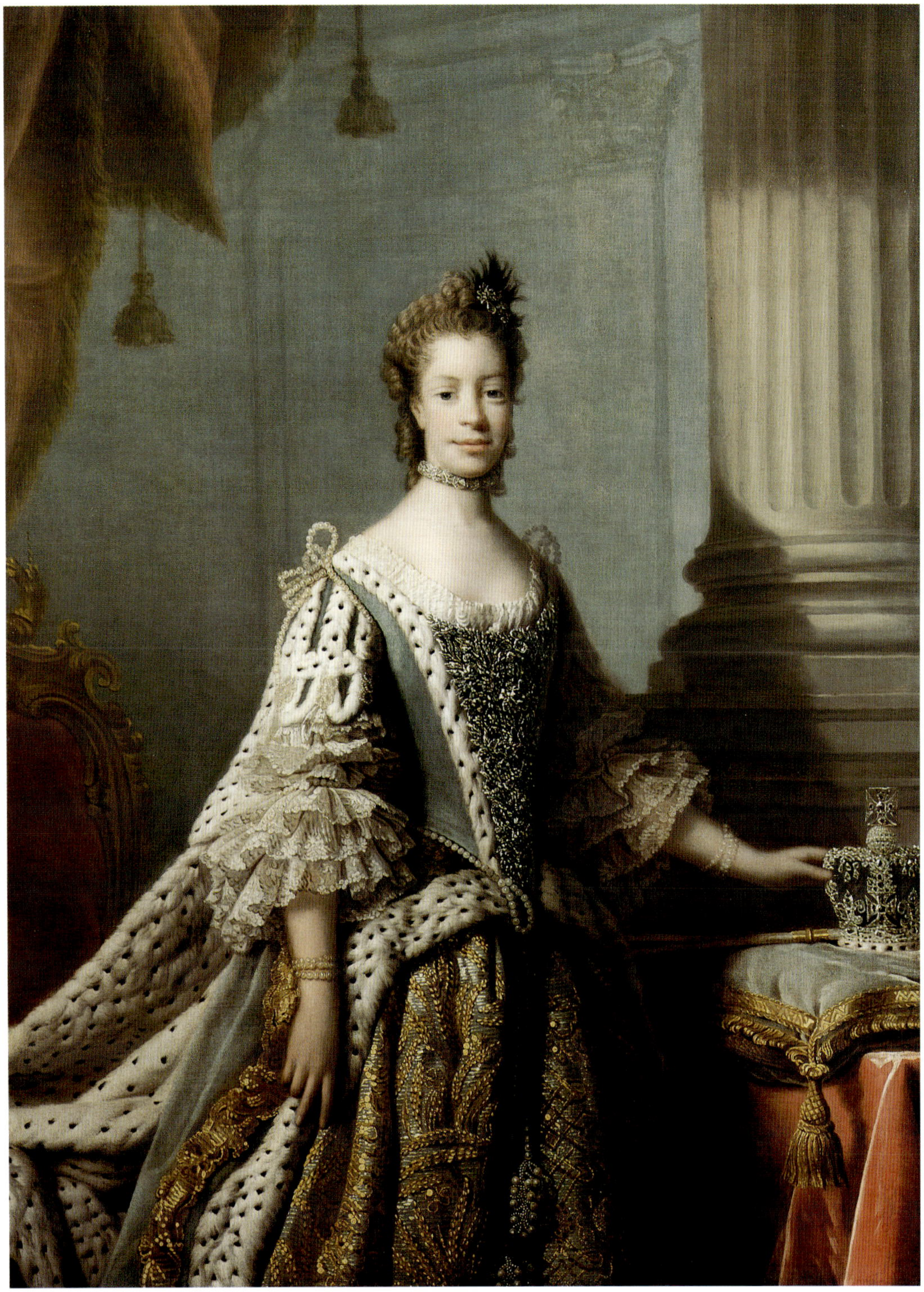

Queen CHARLOTTE *NPG 224*

Ragley, and most subsequent examples, show auburn hair with two rows of curls and the head turned slightly to the right, as in NPG 224. The jewellery varied, generally between a necklace of precious stones and bare wrists or, as in NPG 224, with pearl bracelets. A version at Badminton exceptionally shows her hair much darker and a pendant on her right wrist. A miniature half-length copy by Samuel Finney is in the Victoria and Albert Museum (Evans 114) and another in the Royal Collection.[2]

1 Millar 1969, no.997; Smart 1999, no.85.
2 Walker 1992, no.225.

6290 HENRY BONE after WILLIAM BEECHEY [c.1793]

Enamel on copper 7 x 5.7 (2¾ x 2¼); signed bottom right: *HBone.* and inscribed verso: *Her Most Gracious / Majesty: / Painted Aug. 1801 by / Henry Bone Enamel / painter to H.R.H. the / Prince of Wales.* The back of the casing engraved: *H.M. / Queen Charlotte / wife of George III / 1744-1801* and *by H. Bone.*

Grey eyes, greying hair, clear complexion, wearing a pearl necklace and a white dress.

Collections: Hon Frederic H.A. Wallop (d.1953), by whom lent to the Victoria and Albert Museum 1927-49; his nephew Alan Evans, by whom bequeathed to the National Gallery 1974; lent to the NPG until permanently transferred in 1994.

Exhibition: *Gillray*, Tate, 2001(100b).

Reference: Walker 1998, no.79.

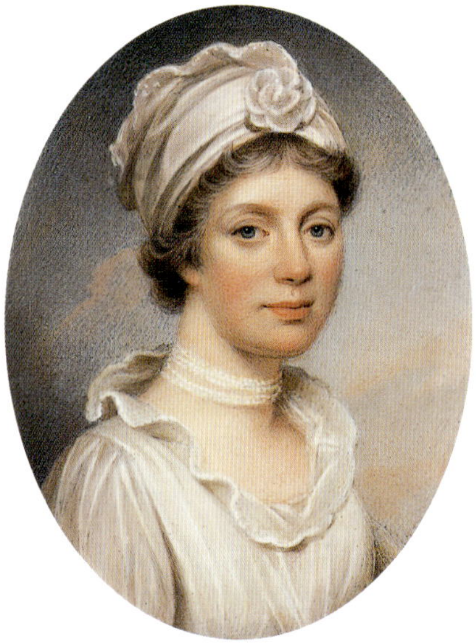

Queen CHARLOTTE *NPG 6290*

An accomplished copy of a miniature now attributed to George Place,[1] which in turn derived from a Beechey sketch engraved by W. Evans in 1809 as *From an Original Picture by* [Beechey] *in his own Possession.*[2] Beechey's portrait very probably dated from soon after his appointment as Portrait Painter to the Queen in 1793 and it anticipated the whole length of 1796 (see below). The Place miniature and NPG 6290 show a simpler dress and a slightly different hair styling.

Two more copies by Bone in the Royal Collection are also dated August 1801,[3] one identified by Walker as that exhibited RA 1802(532); another dated 1801 is in the Victoria and Albert Museum (944.1868).[4] Another miniature version of the Beechey by W. Thomson is in the Royal Collection.[5]

For other enamels of the Queen by Bone see below under 1782 Gainsborough, 1796 Beechey, 1803 Edridge and 1814 Edridge.

1 Formerly at Stanton Harcourt (illus. Walker 1992, fig.27), said to have been given by Queen Charlotte to the 2nd Earl Harcourt.
2 Evans's drawing, dated 1808, sold Sotheby's, 19 July 1979, lot 109. The Beechey sketch was probably that in the Beechey sale, Christie's, 9 June 1836 (see Walker 1992, p.272).
3 Walker 1992, nos.746-47.
4 Walker 1992, p.272, lists further copies, incuding one illus. J. de Bourgoing, *Minaturen*, 1919, pl.18.
5 Walker 1992, no.908.

2788 attributed to ISAAC ROBERT CRUIKSHANK after HENRY MEYER [1818]

Brown and grey wash with traces of pencil on paper 19.7 x 14 (7¾ x 5½).

A plumed lace scarf over her head.

Collections: Presented by Godfrey Brennan 1935.

Exhibitions: *Princes & Palaces*, Orleans House, Twickenham, 1973-74(40); *A Royal Subject*, NG London, 1977(17).

The attribution of this slight drawing to Cruikshank rests solely on the circumstancial evidence of an otherwise inaccurate letter of 1870.[1] Copied from an engraving by Henry Meyer published on 1 December 1818, two weeks after the Queen's death,[2] NPG 2788 omits the background detail. Meyer's engraving, described as 'from an original drawing', shows a head related to that in Beechey's whole length of 1796 (see below), although the eyes are averted and the ruff collar is of a later period; it certainly does not reflect the appearance of the Queen in her seventies.

1 Formerly attached to the frame: *On showing this portrait of Queen Caroline (Wife of George III IV) to George Cruikshank, in London, May 17, 1870, he informed me that he had little doubt that it was the production of his father, Isaac Cruikshank.* [signed] *W Beles.*
2 *European Mag.*, November 1818.

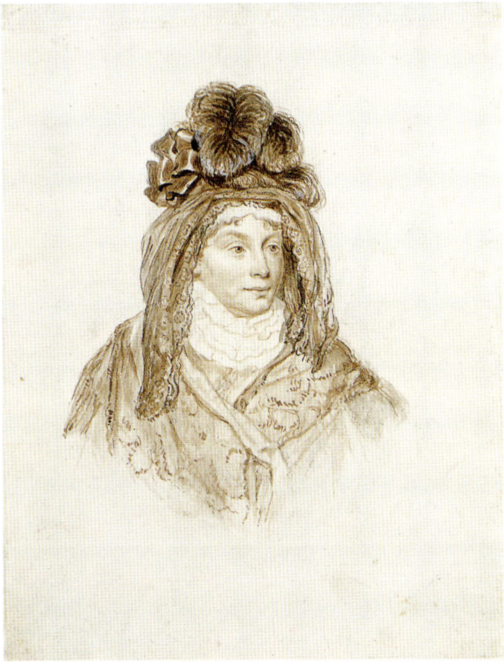

Queen CHARLOTTE *NPG 2788*

ICONOGRAPHY

The principal surveys of Charlotte's iconography are contained in the catalogues of the Royal Collection (Millar 1969 and Walker 1992) and in the National Gallery exhibition catalogue by Michael Levey (Levey 1977).

As Princess Charlotte Sophia

c.1760 Miniature by an unidentified German artist, bust-length oval. Royal Collection (Walker 1992, no.442). Probably sent to the King from Mecklenburg in 1760.

1761 Painting attributed to J.G. Ziesenis, three-quarter length attended by a black servant, gesturing toward the crown of Mecklenburg-Strelitz, a miniature of her father on her right wrist. Formerly in the collection of Queen Mary (illus. H. Clifford Smith, *Buckingham Palace*, 1931, pl.61). A half-length miniature version attributed to Elizabeth Ziesenis in the Royal Collection (Walker 1992, no.426) of which a replica in the Historisches Museum, Hanover, is inscribed *La Reine d'Angleterre peint par Elizabeth Ziesenis 1761*.

As Queen Charlotte

Princess Charlotte was unknown in England before her arrival in September 1761 at the age of sixteen. A spate of ill-informed half-length engravings followed her marriage to the King on 8 September and the coronation on 22 September by, for example, T. Burford, M.P. Hauck, J. Miller (7 November) J.E. Nilson and C. Spooner. Medals celebrating the marriage and coronation were made by John Kirk, Thomas Pingo and J.L. Natter (Brown 1980, nos.10, 30, 66; Eimer 1998, no.19). See also George III.

1761 Mezzotint by J. McArdell after Jeremiah Meyer, half length (illus. Walker 1992, fig.21).

1761 Miniature by J.R., bust length. Royal Collection (Walker 1992, no.296).

c.1761 Painting by Francis Hayman, whole length in coronation robes, painted for the annexe to the Rotunda at Vauxhall Gardens. Listed in the proposed Vauxhall sale, 15-16 June 1840 (Allen 1987, p.171).

c.1761 Unattributed miniature, bust length, wearing a jewelled crucifix (a cross of diamonds was given to the Queen on her arrival in England; Scarisbrick 1994, p.260). Royal Collection (Walker 1992, no.325).

1762 Painting by G.D. Matthieu, three-quarter length seated, the King's miniature on her left wrist. Gripsholm Castle (Katalog, *Porträtt före 1809*, 1951, no.1192).

1762 Painting by Allan Ramsay, see NPG 224.

1762 Miniature by Jeremiah Meyer. Royal Collection (Walker 1992, no.253). Two copies are also in the Royal Collection (Walker 1992, nos.254, 1043).

1762 Mezzotint by Thomas Frye from his own drawing, the likeness taken at a London theatre (CS I, p.516), published 24 May 1762 (after Frye's death). The companion piece of the King engraved by Pether published 1 November 1762. Related but indifferent portraits in oil sold Sotheby's, 14 March 1951, lot 104, and Christie's, 17 June 1966, lot 109. A three-quarter length mezzotint by P. Haid evidently derived from Frye's plate.

1762 Engraving by Richard Cooper, exhibited FS 1762(131).

c.1762[?] Unattributed pastel, resembling the Ramsay pattern of 1762. The Prince of Hanover. With a companion piece of the King.

1762-63 Medals marking the birth of the Prince of Wales, by Thomas Pingo, with facing bust of the King (Eimer 1998, no.26) and J.L. Natter (Brown 1980, nos.25, 76, 77). See also George III.

1762-63 Painting by Allan Ramsay, half length, a fan in her right hand. Private Scottish collection (Smart 1999, no.86). A contemporary version in St John's College, Oxford (Poole, III, p.183).

1763 Model by Lewis Pingo, exhibited FS 1763(162), possibly the wax bust in the British Museum (Eimer 1998, no.144).

1763 Pastel by Katherine Read, exhibited SA 1763(172). Possibly that exhibited *Guelph* 1891, no.75, p.23, lent by the Earl of Chichester.

1763 Miniature by Miss Todderick ('at the Star and Garter Warehouse, Tavistock Street'), exhibited FS 1763(223).

c.1763 Engraving by R. Houston after Robert Pile [presumably Pine] three-quarter length holding the infant Prince of Wales. The head taken from Frye's mezzotint of 1762.

c.1763-65 Unattributed painting, whole length in coronation robes, Queen's College, Oxford (Poole, II, p.134, no.75). The pose resembles the Ramsay pattern of 1762, but is reversed.

c.1764 Painting by Henry Morland, three-quarter length holding an architectural engraving, apparently the ground plan and east and north elevations of Halton's Library in Queen's College (see J.R. Magrath, *The Queen's College*, 1921, II, f.p.68). Queen's College, Oxford (Poole, II, p.133; illus.

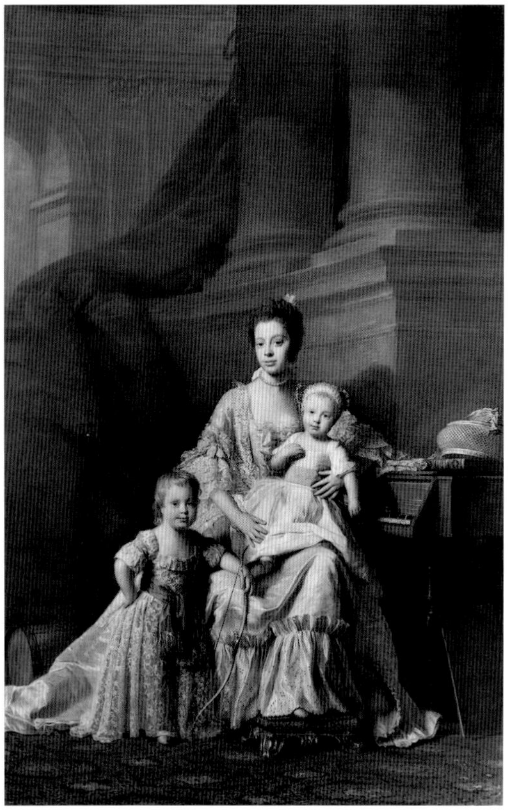

Queen CHARLOTTE by Allan Ramsay 1764-65 (The Royal Collection)

Connoisseur, CXIV, 1944, p.103). Presented in 1765 as by Moreland, somewhat resembling the portrait by Ziesenis of 1761.

A second half-length portrait attributable to Morland, the head comparable with the Oxford portrait, but less conspicuously dressed, was sold Sotheby's, 2 August 1967, lot 292. See also 1767 and 1774 below.

1764-65 Painting by Allan Ramsay,* a domesticated whole length with her two eldest sons. Royal Collection (Millar 1969, no.998; Smart 1999, no.87). Versions are at Badminton, Lancaster House (GAC 2555/2), and in the Museum of Art, Baltimore.

c.1765 Painting by Johann Zoffany, at her dressing table with her two eldest sons - Frederick in oriental dress, George as Telemachus. Royal Collection (Millar 1969, no.1199).

c.1765 Two profile drawings by William Hoare. Sotheby's, 11 November 1993, lot 25. Part of an album of drawings by Hoare compiled 1761-83.

c.1765 Miniature attributed to Richard Collins, profile, set in a tortoiseshell box. Royal Collection (Walker 1992, no.172). The hairstyle recurs in the Henry Morland portrait of c.1764.

c.1765? Wax by Stephana. Royal Collection (illus. Pyke 1973, pl.275).

1766 Miniature by Ozias Humphry half-length, looking curiously unregal. Royal Collection (Walker 1992, no.231). Probably that exhibited SA 1767(747 as Queen Charlotte 'painted from the life'). A miniature version by Edward Shiercliffe sold Christie's, 11 May 1994, lot 29.

c.1766 Painting attributed to Johann Zoffany, three-quarter length seated wearing the King's miniature on her right wrist. Holburne Museum, Bath (*A Gift to the Nation*, Bath, 1991, no.40). The composition compares, in reverse, with the portrait of the Queen seen hanging in the background of Zoffany's *George, Prince of Wales, and Prince Frederick*, in the Royal Collection (Millar 1969, no.1200).

1767 Painting by Francis Cotes, whole length, the sleeping Princess Charlotte in her arms. Royal Collection (Millar 1969, no.718). Engraved W.W. Ryland 1770. A half-length pastel version, signed and dated 1767, probably preceding the whole length, is in the Royal Collection (Millar 1969, no.717), exhibited SA 1767(32), and another at Syon House. A miniature attributed to Samuel Cotes of the Queen's head, derived from the Francis Cotes composition, is in the Royal Collection (Walker 1992, no.207).

1767 Painting by Angelica Kauffmann, three-quarter length, engraved T. Burke 1772, *Raising the Genius of the Fine Arts* (illus. Roworth 1992, p.144; *Kauffmann* 1998, p.159). A version sold New York, 21 February 1916, lot 331, and a half-length pastel of the Queen alone is in a private collection. A miniature copy by J.H. Hurter sold Christie's, 11 July 1985, lot 431.

1767 Painting by Henry Morland exhibited FS 1767(198).

1769 Drawing by H.D. Hamilton, bust length with black lace shawl and lace cap. The Prince of Hanover. A version dated 1771 is in the Royal Collection (Oppé 1950, no.288, pl.6; *Kings and Queens*, Queen's Gallery, 1982-83, no.66) and an unattributed miniature enamel version is in the Gemäldegalerie, Berlin (299).

1769 Painting by Nathaniel Dance,* whole-length standing in robes of state. Uppark. Exhibited RA 1769(31) with a companion piece of the King. Versions belong to the Prince of Hanover, and a three-quarter length version of the Queen alone was on the Munich art market 1931.

1770 Painting by Johann Zoffany, with the King and their children, see George III 1770.

c.1770 Medal by Julien Colibert (Brown 1980, no.27, as 1761, but Colibert came to England in 1769).

c.1770? Etching by J. Spilsbury, half length, *Printed for Thomas Simes – Captain in the Queen's Royal Regiment of Foot.*

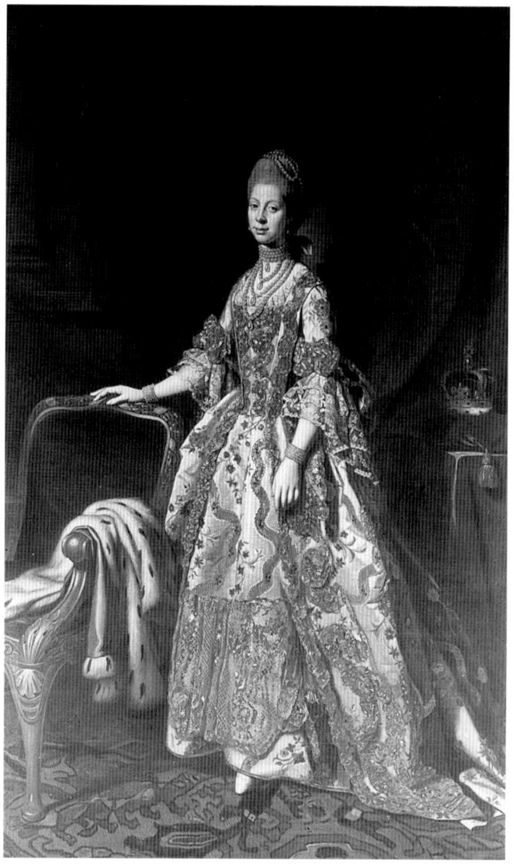

Queen CHARLOTTE by Nathaniel Dance 1769 (Uppark, The National Trust)

1771 Painting by Johann Zoffany,* three-quarter length with a black shawl, a miniature of the King on her right wrist. Royal Collection (Millar 1969, no.1196). Engraved R. Houston 1772. An indifferent half-length adaptation in the Royal Collection (Millar 1969, no.1214) and a miniature copy by L-F. Aubry (Walker 1992, no.941); other copies at Somerset House (GAC 0/325/50) and, of the head, sold Christie's, 24 February 1933, lot 46.

c.1771 Painting attributed to Johann Zoffany, a standing version of the 1771 composition. The Prince of Hanover. With a companion piece of the King, both of high quality.

c.1771 Painting on copper by Johann Zoffany, bust length in robes of state. Royal Collection (Millar 1969, no.1198).

1772 Painting by Johann Zoffany, whole-length seated, with her two brothers and Prince William and Princess Charlotte. Royal Collection (Millar 1969, no.1207). Exhibited RA 1773(320). The figure of the Queen alone recurs in a painting attributed to Zoffany in the Tryon Palace, New Bern, North Carolina.

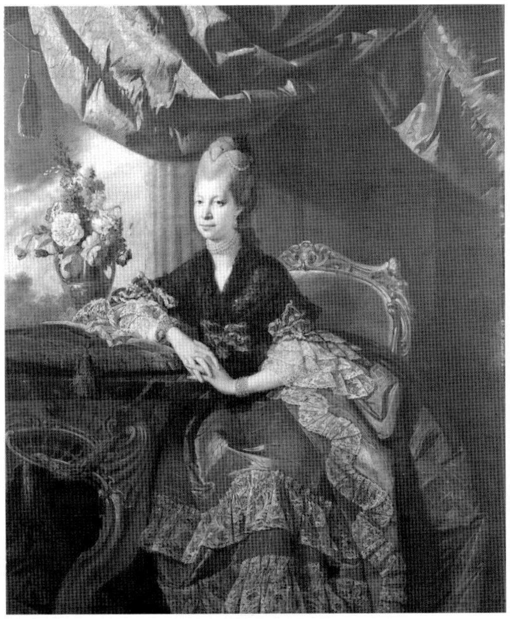

Queen CHARLOTTE by Johan Zoffany 1771 (The Royal Collection)

c.1772 Miniature by Jeremiah Meyer, bust length with white lace cap. Royal Collection (Walker 1999, no.255). Drawing in the Ashmolean Museum, Oxford (1361 Meyer Album; Brown 1982, p.461). A version attributed to Meyer also in the Royal Collection (Walker 1992, no.269), of which a replica was set into a ring in 1827 (illus. Ward 1981, no.261). The cap recurs in Hamilton's drawing of 1769 and the miniature by Hurter of 1780.

A bust-length miniature in the Royal Collection, attributed to Richard Collins (Walker 1992, no.173), resembles the Meyer.

1773 Enamel by W.H. Craft, whole length. British Museum (MLA 1891.2.17.17)

1773–74 Medals by John Kirk (Brown 1980, nos.168, 184).

1774 Painting by Henry Morland, exhibited FS 1774(201).

before 1775 Painting by Mary Benwell, half length, engraved R. Houston.

1775 Unattributed lead statue. Queen's Square, London (illus. J. Blackwood, *London's Immortals*, 1989, p.45). Formerly identified as Queen Anne.

1776 Painting by Benjamin West, three-quarter length with Princess Charlotte. Royal Collection (Millar 1969, no.1142; Erffa & Staley 1986, no.562). Exhibited RA 1777(362). Engraved V. Green 1778. A preparatory drawing by West for the figure of the Queen is in the Royal Collection (Oppé 1950, no.640, pl.3).

c.1776 Painting by Benjamin West, half-length seated. Earl of Elgin (Erffa & Staley 1986, no.553).

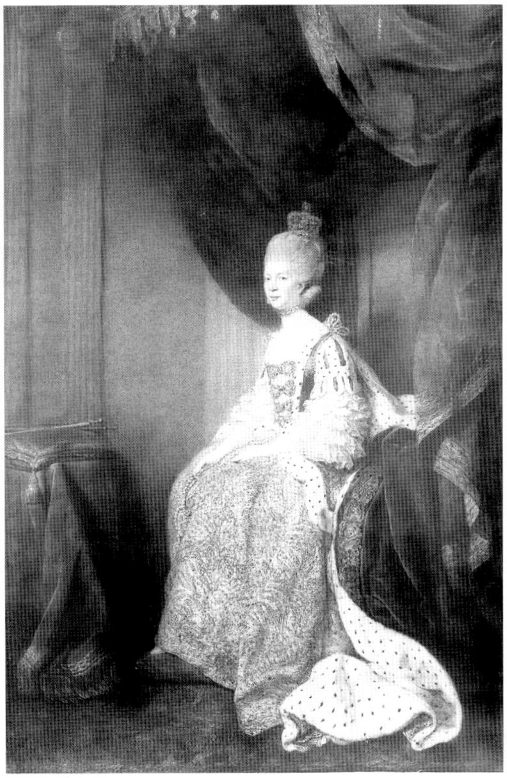

Queen CHARLOTTE by Joshua Reynolds 1779 (Royal Academy of Arts, London)

Engraved V. Green 1790. A replica, dated 1777 in the Yale Center for British Art (B1977.14.155; Erffa & Staley 1986, no.555) and a version, with a work-basket on the table beside her, is in the Berger collection, Denver, Colorado (illus. *Cat.*, 1998, p.141).

c.1776 Painting on copper by Benjamin West, seated with the King. Private collection (Erffa & Staley 1986, no.559).

c.1776 Wedgwood medallion, with the King, attributed to William Hackwood after Isaac Gosset (illus. Reilly 1973, p.168). An undated wax by Isaac Gosset sold Sotheby's, 22 April 1982, lot 109. Variant examples of the Wedgwood medallion are in the British Museum and the Victoria and Albert Museum.

c.1777 Wedgwood medallion, modelled by John Bacon sr. (T. Clifford, *Apollo*, CXXII, 1985, p.294), previously attributed to William Hackwood (Reilly 1973, p.96).

1778 Painting by Nathaniel Dance, whole length in coronation robes with a distant view of Westminster Abbey. Hermitage Museum, St Petersburg (illus. *Hermitage* 1997, p.38 as 1778). The composition relates closely to the Ramsay coronation portrait; the companion piece of the King was copied from the

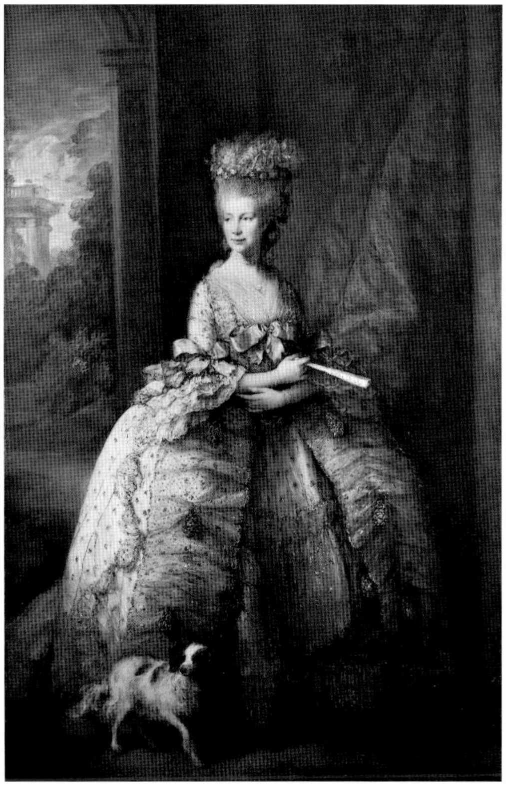

Queen CHARLOTTE by Thomas Gainsborough 1781 (The Royal Collection)

Dance portrait of 1776 (see George III). A half-length version was at Bayham Abbey (SSB 91/11).

1779 Painting by Anna Liszewska, three-quarter length, the head comparing closely with that by Zoffany of 1771. The Prince of Hanover. An autograph version, inscribed as painted at Brunswick in 1779, with differing hair style and background, sold Sotheby's, 13 November 1996, lot 57 with a companion piece of the King.

1779 Painting by Joshua Reynolds,* whole length seated in robes of state. Royal Academy (Mannings 2000, no.718). For the distribution of the many copies, see George III.

1779 Painting by Benjamin West, whole length, her thirteen children behind her. Royal Collection (Millar 1969, no.1139; Erffa & Staley 1986, no.556). Exhibited RA 1780(130). A reduced version with the Historical Society, Pennsylvania (Erffa & Staley 1986, no.557). See also West 1782.

1780 Stone medallion by Joseph Wilton for Somerset House (façade).

1780 Miniature by J.H. Hurter, bust-length. Royal Collection (Walker 1992, no.237).

c.1780? Wax by Thomas Engleheart. Royal Collection (illus. Pyke 1973, pl.89).

1781 Painting by Thomas Gainsborough,* whole length. Royal Collection (Waterhouse 1958, no.130; Millar 1969, no.775). Exhibited RA 1781(168). 'Tis actual motion, and done with such a light, airy, facility' (Northcote); 'the only happy likeness we ever saw portrayed of Her Majesty' (Levey 1977, p.15). Engraved G. Dupont 1790, whose preparatory oil sketch was formerly with the Countess of Athlone. An oval bust-length version by Gainsborough also in the Royal Collection (Millar 1969, no.777).

For the distribution of versions paired with Gainsborough's portrait of the King, see George III. Of the Queen alone there are versions in the Royal Collection by William Hopkins, attributed to Gainsborough Dupont (see also c.1794 below), and two reduced copies (Millar 1969, nos.809-12), together with related miniatures attributed to J.H. Hurter and Richard Collins (Walker 1992, nos.242, 326); a miniature copy by Hurter is in the Gilbert collection (illus. Coffin & Hofstetter 2000, no.30). A half-length copy is at Penshurst, and a derivation at Powis Castle.

1782 Painting by Thomas Gainsborough, bust-length painted oval. Royal Collection (Waterhouse 1958, no.132; Millar 1969, no.779). Replica in the Metropolitan Museum of Art, New York (49.7.55), and a copy in the Victoria and Albert Museum (91.1879). In the Royal Collection an enamel miniature by Henry Bone 1804, and two miniature copies attributed to Richard Collins (Walker 1992, nos.749, 170-71); further miniature copies, by Robert Bowyer, Richard Crosse, William Grimaldi, and Anne Mee, are listed by Walker (1992, p.85).

1782 Painting by Benjamin West, whole length, her fourteen children behind her. Royal Collection (Millar 1969, no.1140; Erffa & Staley 1986, no.558). Composition reversed from West's portrait of 1779, see above.

1782 Engraved silhouette by W. Turner, whole length (McKechnie 1978, no.937; Levey 1977, p.17).

1782 Drawing by John Downman, half-length profile. Formerly in the E.M. Hodgkins collection (illus. Williamson 1907, f.p.viii). Replica dated 1784 sold Sotheby's, 26 November 1998, lot 11; another, undated, sold Sotheby's, 11 July 1985, lot 89.

1783 Anon. wax, exhibited FS 1783(382).

1783 Drawing by John Downman, half length. Formerly in the collection of Lord Ronald Sutherland Gower (illus. R.S. Gower, *Bric à Brac*, 1888, p.84). Inscribed by the artist, verso, *I also drew a whole length of the Queen for the Duchess of Ancaster, and two others* (see 1784 Downman below).

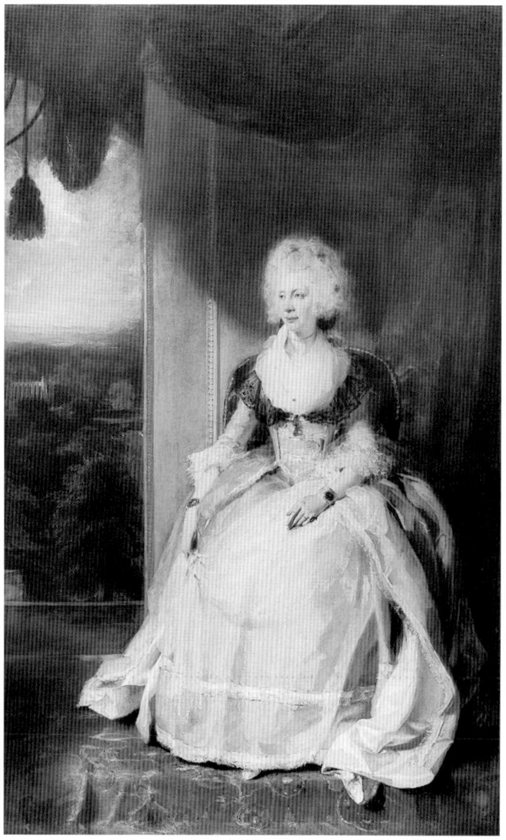

Queen CHARLOTTE by Thomas Lawrence 1789 (National Gallery, London)

A second drawing by Downman dated 1783 is in the Fitzwilliam Museum, Cambridge (PD.24-1971).

1784 Drawing by John Downman, whole-length seated. Christie's, 9 July 1991, lot 55. Apparently derived from the drawing of 1783, see above.

c.1785 Wedgwood medallion by William Hackwood from a model by Isaac Gosset (illus. Reilly 1973, p.96).

c.1785 Drawing by Richard Cosway, seated whole length, the head alone finished. Bonham's, 10 April 2002, lot 370 (illus. G. Barnett, *Richard & Maria Cosway*, 1995, pl.iiic).

1787 Watercolour by John Downman, half-length oval, her crown beside her. Royal Collection (*Gainsborough & Reynolds* 1994, no.40).

1787 Painting by Thomas Stothard, *George III and his Family*, engraved J. Murphy 1794. A similar painting, now attributed to Richard Livesay (and formerly to Stothard) is at Upton House.

c.1787 Marble bust attributed to the studio of John Bacon sr. Southill (illus. *Whitbread* 1984, p.43). Presented to Samuel Whitbread c.1787 with a bust of the King derived from a Bacon type of 1774.

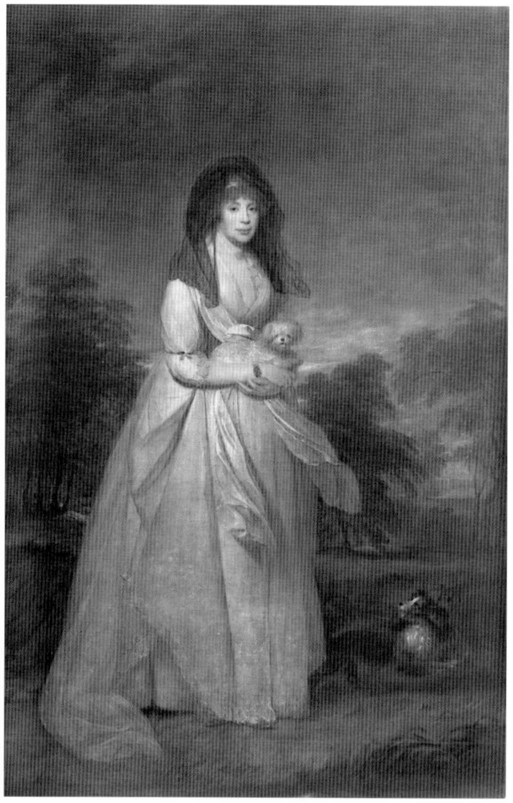

Queen CHARLOTTE by William Beechey 1796 (The Royal Collection)

1788 Medal by Wilmore, Alston & Co (Brown 1980, nos.278-79).

1789 Painting by Thomas Lawrence,* whole length with a distant view of Eton College Chapel. NG London (4257; Egerton 1998, pp.194-99). Exhibited RA 1790(100). A study for the head in the Lawrence sale, Christie's, 18 June 1831, lot 13. Lawrence received a single sitting at Windsor on 28 September 1789.

1789 Painting by Richard Livesay, half-length seated. Sotheby's, 16 May 1984, lot 188. A later inscription supplies the attribution and date.

1789 Painting by Benjamin West, see George III 1789.

1789 Medal by C. James and Thomas Wyon sr. (Brown 1980, no.304).

c.1789 Miniature attributed to Anne Mee, bust length. Royal Collection, with two replicas (Walker 1992, nos.875-77). Miss Foldsone (Mrs Anne Mee) drew the Queen in November 1789 and 'at different times through life she attended the Royal family to take their miniatures' (*Journals of Mrs Papendiek*, 1887, II, pp.143-44).

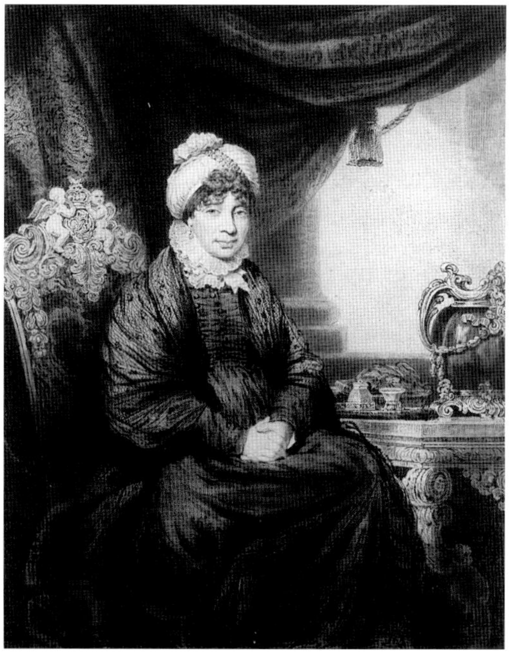

Queen CHARLOTTE S.W. Reynolds after Henry Edridge 1814 (NPG D 9174)

1790 Medals by Thomas Wyon sr. and C.H. Küchler with conjoined busts of the King and Queen (Brown 1980, nos.338-40).

1791 Engraving by J. Collyer from a painting by John Russell, bust length in a striped dress.

c.1791 Painting by Benjamin West, with the Royal family, receiving the Duchess of York. Untraced (Erffa & Staley 1986, no.576). Related to the painting attributed to Richard Livesay at Upton House, see 1787 above.

1792 Silhouette by James Lind, bust length. Royal Collection (illus. McKechnie 1978, no.519).

c.1793 Painting by William Beechey, half length with white dress and cap. Engraved W. Evans 1809. Copied in enamel by Henry Bone, see NPG 6290.

1794 Miniature by Edward Miles, bust length. Royal Collection (Walker 1992, no.270). The Queen sat to Miles on 4 April 1794.

c.1794 An undated MS account of *Portraits Painted for the King by Gainsborough Dupont* (NPG archive, *Autograph letter: D*) lists whole-length portraits of the King and Queen painted for the Duke of York, the Commissioners House at Portsmouth, and Windsor Castle, and half lengths for Windsor Lodge.

1795 Miniature by Richard Cosway, bust length. Royal Collection (Walker 1992, no.174).

1795 Medal by C.H. Küchler (Brown 1980, no.389).

1795 Wax model by Samuel Percy. Royal Collection. Another wax of the Queen on a sofa with a dog, also dated 1795, is in an American private collection. An unspecified wax bust of Charlotte by Percy sold Christie's, 10 June 1993, lot 235 from Stanton Harcourt.

1796 Coade stone medallion by John Bacon sr. Trinity House, London (façade).

1796 Painting by William Beechey,* whole length, holding a Maltese dog. Royal Collection (Millar 1969, no.659). Exhibited RA 1797(92). Engraved for Boydell 1803 and by T. Ryder 1804. Versions in the Courtauld Gallery and at Upton House; a three-quarter length version, formerly in the collection of W.L. Elkins, sold Sotheby's, 10 November 1995, lot 25; a half length dated 1799 painted for Mr Ruyfsen sold Sotheby's, 14 July 1999, lot 97, and another formerly at Burley-on-the-Hill; reduced copy with the Prince of Hanover. Enamel by Henry Bone 1799 in the Royal Collection (Walker 1992, no.748), preparatory drawing in the NPG Bone albums (*Bone* 1999, no.111, fig.116), with two oval half-length miniatures by William Grimaldi (Walker 1992, nos.815-16); another sold Sotheby's, 9 April 1992, lot 208. Head only 'perhaps by Lady Beechey' Royal Collection (Walker 1992, no.328), and another by François Ferrière sold Christie's, 16 February 1965, lot 38; a pastel copy of the head, attributed to John Russell, is in a private collection.

1799 Engraving by F. Bartolozzi after William Beechey, bust length, the King's miniature worn at her breast, as *Patroness of Botany and of the Fine Arts* (Walker 1992, fig.19; Levey 1977, p.6).

c.1801 Wax profile by Catherine Andras. Sotheby's, 22 April 1982, lot 309.

1802 Medal attributed to William Mossop, conjoined busts of the King and Queen (Brown 1980, no.529).

1803 Drawing by Henry Edridge, whole-length seated. Royal Collection, where there is also a duplicate dated 1804 (Oppé 1950, nos.198-99, pl.10). A half-length miniature copy attributed to John Hopkins in the Royal Collection (Walker 1992, no.833); another by Paul Fischer, dated 1823, sold Sotheby's, 10 June 1993, lot 173, from Stanton Harcourt.

1807 Painting by P.E. Stroehling, whole length with a distant view of Windsor. Royal Collection (Millar 1969, no.1094).

1807 Medal by Thomas Wyon sr. and T. Martyn, with conjoined busts of the King and Queen (Brown 1980, no.628).

1809 Life mask by Marie Tussaud (O. Hedley, *Queen Charlotte*, 1975, p.321, fig.25).

1809 Silhouette print by H.W. Holden, conjoined busts of the King and Queen. Royal Collection (McKechnie 1978, no.845, where dated 'before 1810').

1809 Medal attributed to P. Kempson, with conjoined busts of the King and Queen (Brown 1980, nos.643-45).

c.1809 Silhouette by Hinton Gibbs, bust length. Royal Collection (McKechnie 1978, no.1038).

c.1810? Silhouette by William Hamlet sr., bust length. Private collection (McKechnie 1978, no.1059).

1814 Drawing by Henry Edridge, engraved S.W. Reynolds* 1819, three-quarter length seated in dark dress, probably that exhibited RA 1815(435). The face closely resembles that in the Edridge drawing of 1803. A bust-length enamel by Henry Bone was made for Princess Elizabeth in 1815; preparatory drawing in the NPG Bone albums (*Bone* 1999, no.112, fig.114), and another was listed in the Hanover collection in 1914 (Williamson 1914, no.5); a three-quarter length enamel by him is in the Royal Collection, dated March 1821 (Walker 1992, no.750), preparatory drawing in the NPG Bone albums (*Bone* 1999, no.113, fig.117); another dated 1820 was sold Christie's, 28 November 1978, lot 59. An enamel by Henry P. Bone dated 1837 is in the Royal Collection.

1816 Wax profile by Peter Rouw, Christie's, 5 October 1976, lot 35. Other examples sold Sotheby's, 5 July 1990, lot 194; 30 October 1985, lot 206; 8 December 1988, lot 308; Christie's, 16 October 1973, lot 24, and 16 July 1980, lot 8.

1817 Miniature by H.D. Thielcke, bust length, comparable with the Edridge of 1814. The Prince of Hanover (illus. Williamson 1914, no.6). An extended three-quarter length seated version by Thielcke formerly at Frogmore (illus. Williamson 1914, pl.viiia).

1817 Anon. engraving after Lucius Gahagan, bust length (illus. Levey 1977, p.23). Gahagan had seen the Queen at Bath in December 1817.

1817 Medal attributed to P. Kempson celebrating the Queen's visit to Bath (Brown 1980, no.934).

1818 Unattributed drawing, engraved H. Meyer, see NPG 2788.

1818 Marble bust by Peter Turnerelli, head covered, a medallion of the King at her breast. Leeds CAG (T. Friedman, *Leeds Arts Calendar*, 75, 1974, pp.12-17; Levey 1977, p.23). The *Literary Gazette* announced the completion of the bust a week after the Queen's death, stating that sittings had begun in 1809 and that the Queen had 'actually wrought a part of it'.

1818 Medals by Thomas Kettle, T. Wharton, and attributed to P. Kempson, marking the death of the Queen (see Brown 1980, nos.963-66, 1009).

CHEESMAN, Thomas 1760–1835

Engraver and draughtsman, pupil of Bartolozzi; exhibited RA 1802–34.

780 attributed to FRANCESCO BARTOLOZZI c.1777

Canvas 37 x 29 (14½ x 11½) lined, with additional strips of canvas top and bottom making the overall height 40 (15¾); varnish much discoloured; repaired horizontal tears behind shoulder and above right arm, and an old damage in the centre of the jacket.

Grey eyes, grey powdered hair, wearing a green coat with a white neckcloth.

Collections: Mme Vestris (the artist's grand-daughter); Messrs Rawlins; bt. from Mr Rayner 1885 by T. Humphry Ward,[1] and presented by him 1888.

Exhibition: RA 1887(8).

Identity, attribution and date are derived from the label on the verso, but the likeness does not seem to disagree with the drawing by Edridge listed below. The painting is a standard plate size, but no engraving is recorded.

1 Provenance taken from a label verso: *Portrait of Thomas Cheesman, engraver, at 17. By his master, / Francesco Bartolozzi, R.A. / Bought by me in 1885 from Mr Rayner, of Francis A ... / He had it of Messrs Rawlins, who had it (many ... ago) of Madame Vestris, who was Bartolozzi ...*

ICONOGRAPHY

c.1777 Painting by Francesco Bartolozzi, see NPG 780.

c.1795–1800 Drawing by Henry Edridge,* three-quarter length seated, chalk in hand. British Museum (1867.4.13.533).

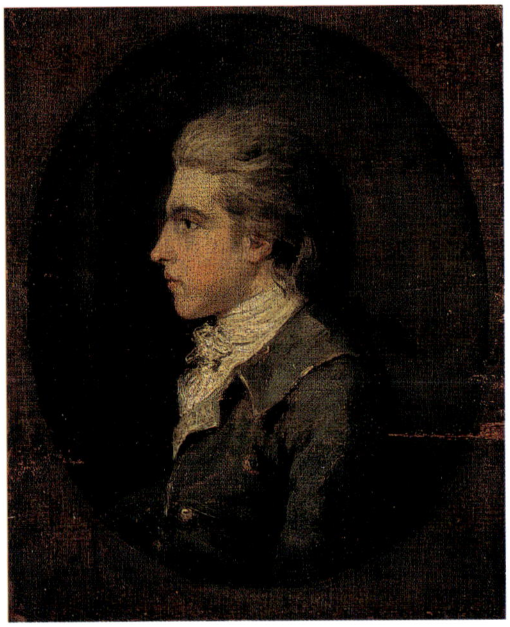

CHEESMAN NPG *780*

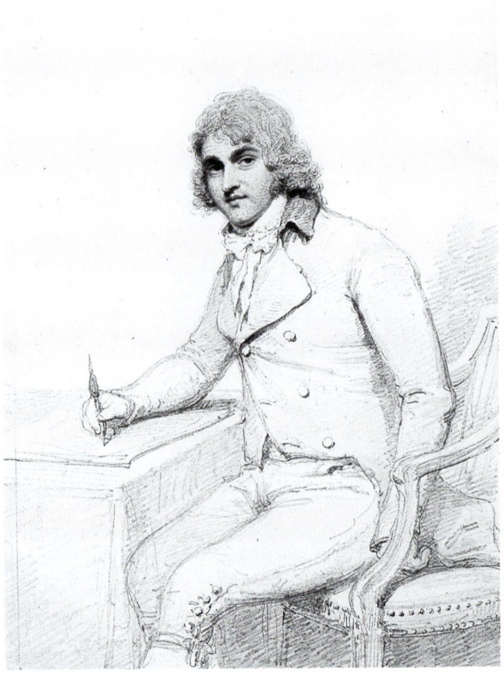

CHEESMAN by Henry Edridge c.1795–1800 (British Museum)

CHILDREN, George 1742–1818

Electrician; a senior partner of the Tunbridge Bank, he retired after 1802 to devote himself to the study of galvanic electricity with his son, John George Children (1777–1852); following the collapse of the bank in 1816 his last years were spent in penury.

5150 ARCHER JAMES OLIVER c.1806

Canvas 75.5 x 62 (29¾ x 24½) lined; cleaned 1974; the surface is rubbed and there is a damage in the lower part of the coat.

Blue-grey eyes, golden-brown hair, wearing dark blue coat with yellow waistcoat and white neckcloth; he sits in a red-upholstered chair.

Collections: By descent to John C. Children, by whom presented, 1977.[1]

Engraving: Lithograph by A. Gauci (as aged 64).

The dating derives from the inscription on Gauci's lithograph.

1 Scharf saw the portrait in Halsted, Kent, on 23 October 1886, giving just a written description 'Mr Children a banker painted by A.J. Oliver' (TSB 33/71).

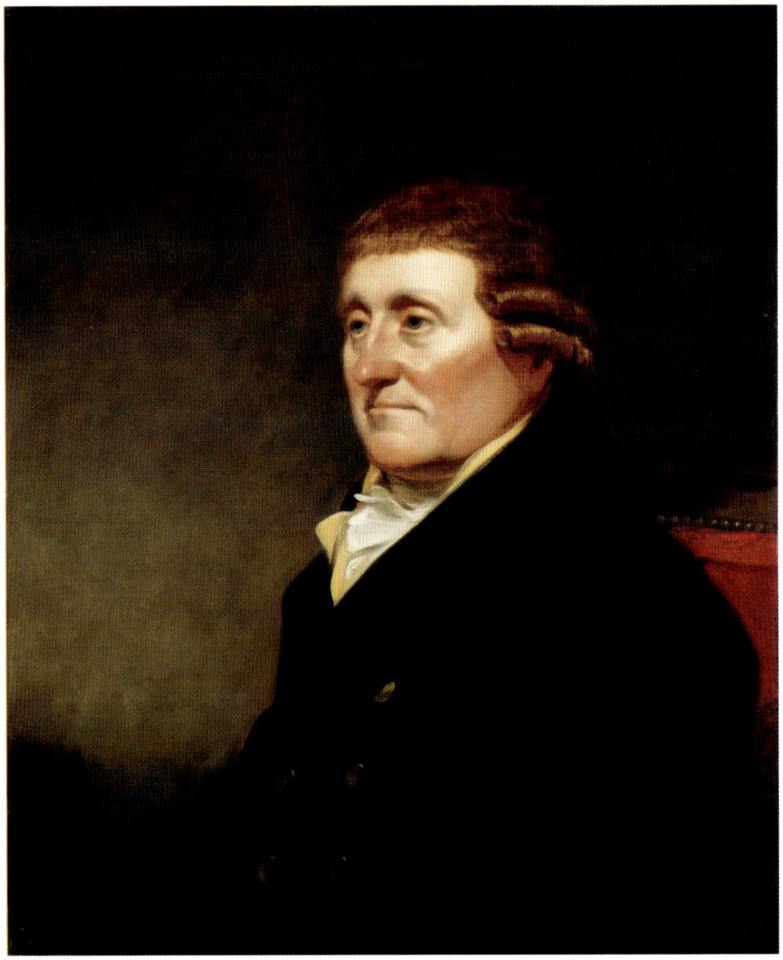

CHILDREN NPG *5150*

CHOLMONDELEY, George James Cholmondeley, 1st Marquess of 1749-1827

Suc. as 4th Earl of Cholmondeley 1770; in Italy 1771-72, 1775, 1781-82 and 1792-93; as great-nephew of the 3rd Earl of Orford, inherited Houghton Hall 1797; cr. 1st Marquess of Cholmondeley 1815; chamberlain to the Prince of Wales 1795-1800 and lord steward of the Household 1812-21; KG 1822; a profligate member of Brooks's, 'extremely fond of luxury and display' (*CP*).

2076 see Groups, *Mr Fox and his Friends* by WILLIAM LANE c.1813

ICONOGRAPHY

1772 Painting by Pompeo Batoni,* half length in scarlet uniform. Private collection (Clark 1985, no.343). A second half length by Batoni was in the Strawberry Hill sale, 22nd day, 19 May 1842, lot 34 (Clark 1985, no.344).

1779-81 Painting by J.S. Copley,* *The Death of Chatham*, see Comparative Groups.

1780 Painting by Joshua Reynolds,* whole length in peer's robes. Private collection (Mannings 2000, no.362). Exhibited RA 1780(32).

c.1813 Drawing by William Lane, *Mr Fox and his Friends*, see Groups NPG 2076.

1820 Painting by T.C. Thompson, exhibited RA 1820(383).

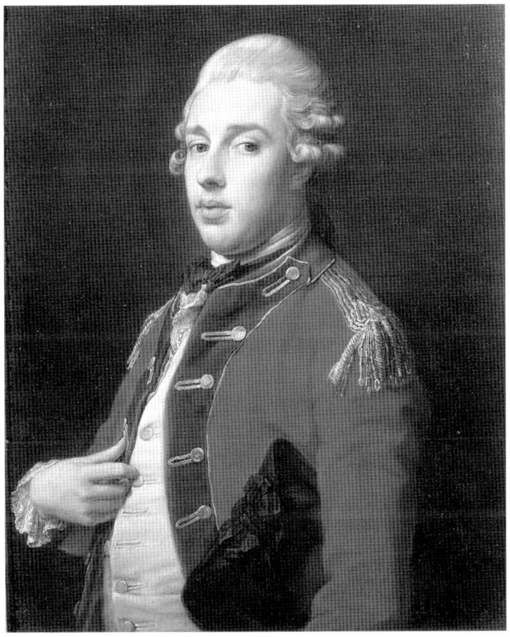

1st Marquess of CHOLMONDELEY by Pompeo Batoni 1772 (Private Collection)

1825 Painting by John Simpson, half length, own white hair, wearing Garter badge, exhibited RA 1825(306). Engraved W. Brett. The head resembles that by William Lane in *Mr Fox and his Friends* of c.1813, see Groups NPG 2076.

Undated Painting by G.H. Harlow, elderly, full-faced bust, engraved J. Posselwhite.

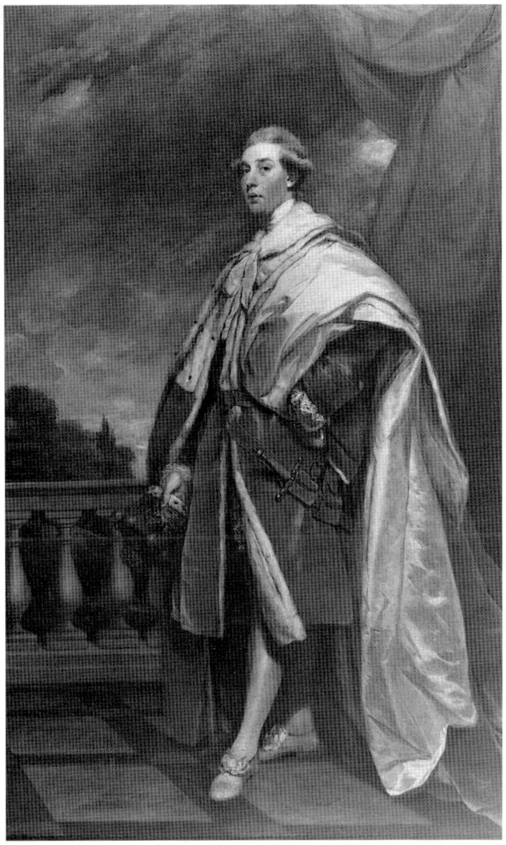

1st Marquess of CHOLMONDELEY by Joshua Reynolds 1780 (Private Collection)

CIPRIANI, Giovanni Battista 1727-85

Painter; b. Florence, he came to London with William Chambers and Joseph Wilton 1756; foundation member of the RA 1768, where he exhibited 1769-79; also exhibited FS 1783; much employed as a decorative painter by Chambers and a close associate of Bartolozzi, who designed his monument (now untraced).

'As a man, he was very elegant in his manners, with most liberal sentiments, ever ready to assist those who solicited his instructions' (Edward Edwards, 1808).

3186 see Groups, *Carlini, Bartolozzi and Cipriani* by JOHN FRANCIS RIGAUD 1777

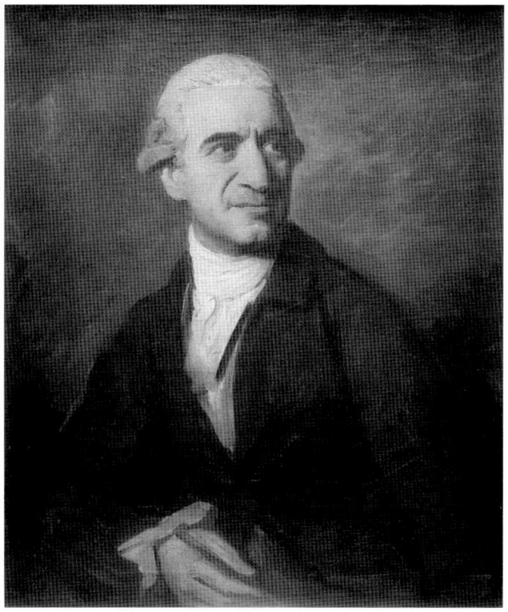

CIPRIANI by Nathaniel Dance c.1775 (Royal Academy of Arts, London)

ICONOGRAPHY

c.1760-65? Unattributed drawing, bust length, inscribed *J.B. Cipriani RA* and with a reinforced inscription: *The Father (a Painter) given me by his son.* Christie's, 18 March 1986, lot 13.

c.1765-70 Painting by J.H. Mortimer,* *Caricature Group*, see Comparative Groups.

c.1770 Drawing by Francesco Bartolozzi, whole-length seated, painting. Royal Collection (Oppé 1950, no.50; illus. *Connoisseur*, XCII, 1933, p.76). On the same sheet as Cipriani's drawing of Bartolozzi asleep (Oppé 1950, no.125).

1772 Painting by Johann Zoffany,* *The Academicians of the Royal Academy*, see Groups NPG 1437.

c.1775 Unfinished painting by Nathaniel Dance,* half length, holding a porte-crayon. Royal Academy. Exhibited NPE 1867(521). Described as 'an admirable likeness' (Farington, 20 November 1816).

1777 Painting by J.F. Rigaud,* with Bartolozzi and Carlini, see Groups NPG 3186. In 1789 Earlom engraved a half-length oval, lettered after Rigaud, the head copied from this group, the rest perhaps invented.

1783 Drawing by Francesco Bartolozzi, bust-length profile, engraved 1788 and 1791 (pub. M. Bovi; illus. *Art Journal*, 1890, p.110).

CLINTON, Henry Fiennes, see NEWCASTLE

COBB, James 1756-1818

Employed in the London office of the East India Company from 1771, he wrote a number of essentially indifferent pieces for the theatre, performed principally at Drury Lane between 1779 and 1809.

3900 GEORGE DANCE c.1800-05

Pencil and wash on paper 24.5 x 18.7 (9⅝ x 7⅜) laid down on paper; faded and a blue stain round an old damage behind the head; a dark wash on the coat, lower right, and round the edges of the lapel evidently added by another hand.

Collections: The artist's grandson, the Rev George Dance; his sale, Christie's, 1 July 1898, lot 36; Walker's Galleries, from whom purchased 1954.

Engraving: W. Daniell (*Dance Plates*).

Exhibition: *New Year's Exhibition*, Walker's Galleries, 1953(29).

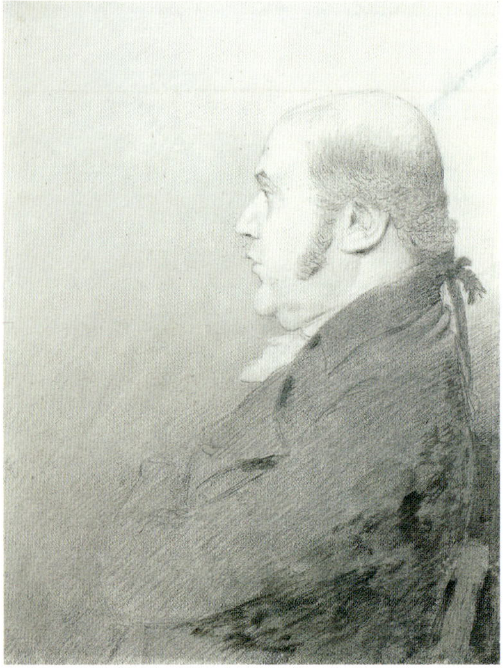

COBB NPG *3900*

NPG 3900 is rather more worked than usual for a Dance drawing. A copy by William Daniell, inscribed *J. Cobb*, sold Sotheby's, 11 July 1991, lot 102.

ICONOGRAPHY

c.1796 Painting by Samuel Drummond, half-length oval, engraved J. Chapman 1796 (*European Mag.*).

c.1800-05 Drawing by George Dance, see NPG 3900.

c.1803 Painting by Edward Burch, half-length oval, engraved W. Ridley★ 1803 (*Monthly Mirror*). The painter's name beneath the engraving is badly scratched; it has also been read, unconvincingly, as Adam Buck (see Strickland 1913, I, p.119).

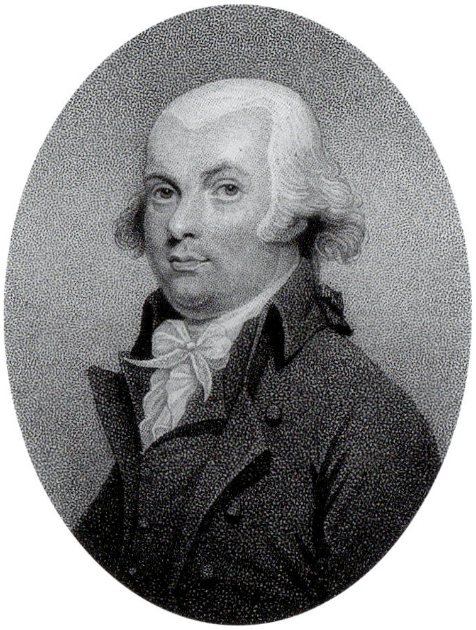

COBB W. Ridley 1803 after Edward Burch (NPG *D 13795*)

1809 Engraving by T. Blood, half length (for Mrs Inchbald, *Collection of Farces*, 1809). The head compares with that drawn by Dance, NPG 3900.

COBHAM, Richard, Lord, see TEMPLE

COKE, Thomas 1747-1814

Nonconformist minister; b. Brecon; DCL Oxford 1775, he had turned to methodism by 1777; in America 1784-91, discharging episcopal functions in methodist societies; d. en route to India.

'like Zaccheus, little of stature, being of about five feet and an inch in height; ... strong, vigorous and handsome ... His face was remarkably pleasing, and continued so, notwithstanding the increase of years' (Jonathan Crowther, 1817)

'He looked a mere boy when he was turned fifty, with such a smooth apple face, and little round mouth' (William Wilberforce, 1808)

1434A HENRY EDRIDGE 1799

Pencil and grey wash on paper 17.7 x 14 (7 x 5½) laid down on paper; signed and dated, bottom left: *E. 99*.

The upright volume behind him lettered *HOLY BIBLE*.

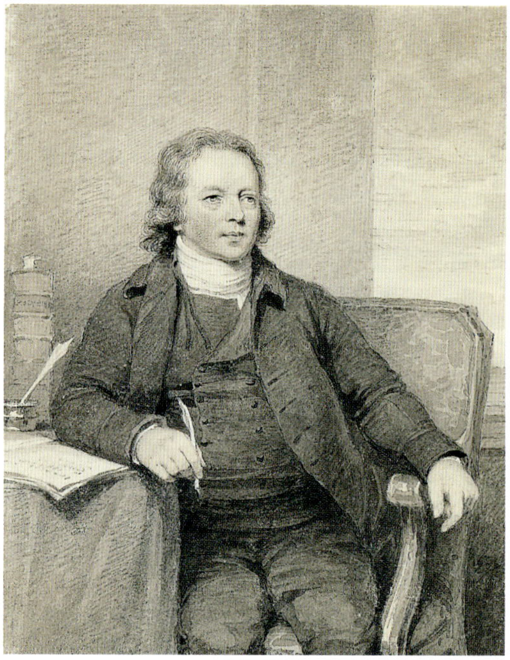

COKE NPG *1434A*

Collections: Christie's, 2 April, 1906, lot 24 (as the Rev George Whitefield),[1] purchased.

Engravings: W. Ridley (*The Revd. Thomas Coke L.L.D.*) 1801;[2] S. Freeman 1815 (with a simplified background, as *Rhodes, Leeds, Pinxt.*).

1 A confusion with the G. Whitefield (whose name was written on the verso of the print sold with NPG 1434A) who published Ridley's engraving in 1790.

2 Illus. front, J. Vickers, *Thomas Coke*, 1969.

ICONOGRAPHY

1779 Engraving, half-length oval 'of an impetuous young man with animated features' (*Arminian Mag.*; see J. Vickers, *Thomas Coke*, 1969, p.41). Probably similar to the anon. plate, half-length oval to right in gown and bands, lettered ... *Aetatis.33*.

1783 Anon. engraving, small bust-length oval, gown and bands, lettered *Aged 36*.

1790 Drawing by Henry Edridge, three-quarter length seated, engraved W. Ridley 1790. A variant half-length also engraved by Ridley (oval).

1799 Drawing by Henry Edridge, see NPG 1434A.

Undated anon. oval engraving, half length seated, looking overweight, in gown and bands, an open book before him (illus. S. Drew, *Thomas Coke*, 1817, front.; J.W. Etheridge, *Thomas Coke*, 1860, front.).

An epitaph carved by J.E. Thomas is in the Dr Coke Memorial Church, Brecon (cf. J.W. Etheridge, *Thomas Coke*, 1860, pp.448-49).

COLE, Thomas c.1730-96

Of Melbourne St Andrews, Dorset; Eton and Queen's College, Oxford; LL.B. 1751; vicar of Dulverton, Somerset, from 1764; d. Westminster.

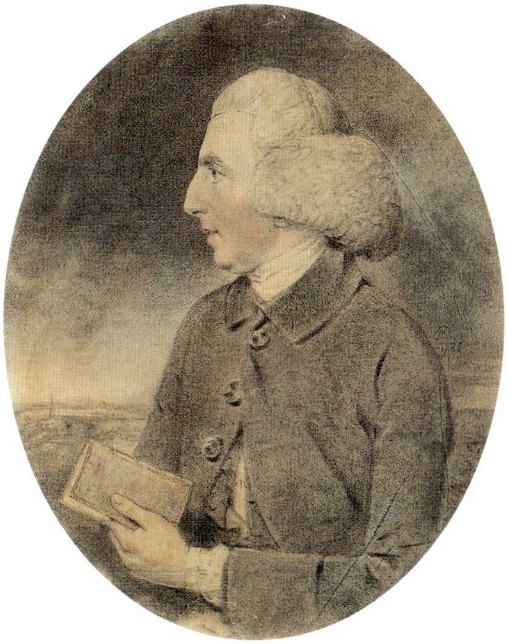

COLE NPG *1719A*

1719A JOHN DOWNMAN 1780

Watercolour and pencil on paper, irregularly-cut oval 21.5 x 17.7 (8½ x 7) laid down on paper; signed and dated *JD/1780* behind the head; much faded and the surface cracked in several places; a distant view of a church spire to the left.

Grey eyes, dark bushy eyebrows, white powdered wig, wearing a grey coat.

Collections: Bequeathed by the sitter's great-grandson, William Comyns Clifton (d.1913) and accepted for the reference collection.

COLMAN, George 1732-94

Playwright; b. Florence, where his fa. was British envoy; manager of the Covent Garden theatre 1767-74 and the Theatre Royal, Haymarket, 1777-86; co-author with Garrick of *The Clandestine Marriage* 1766; insane during his last four years.

'His manner was calm, neat and unforced, not at all loud and decisive; but had the temperance and smoothness and dignified ease of one who remembered that he was a gentleman' (James Boaden, 1825).

'He was extravagant and ostentatious, but preserved during his life the esteem and affection of the best men of his day' (*DNB*).

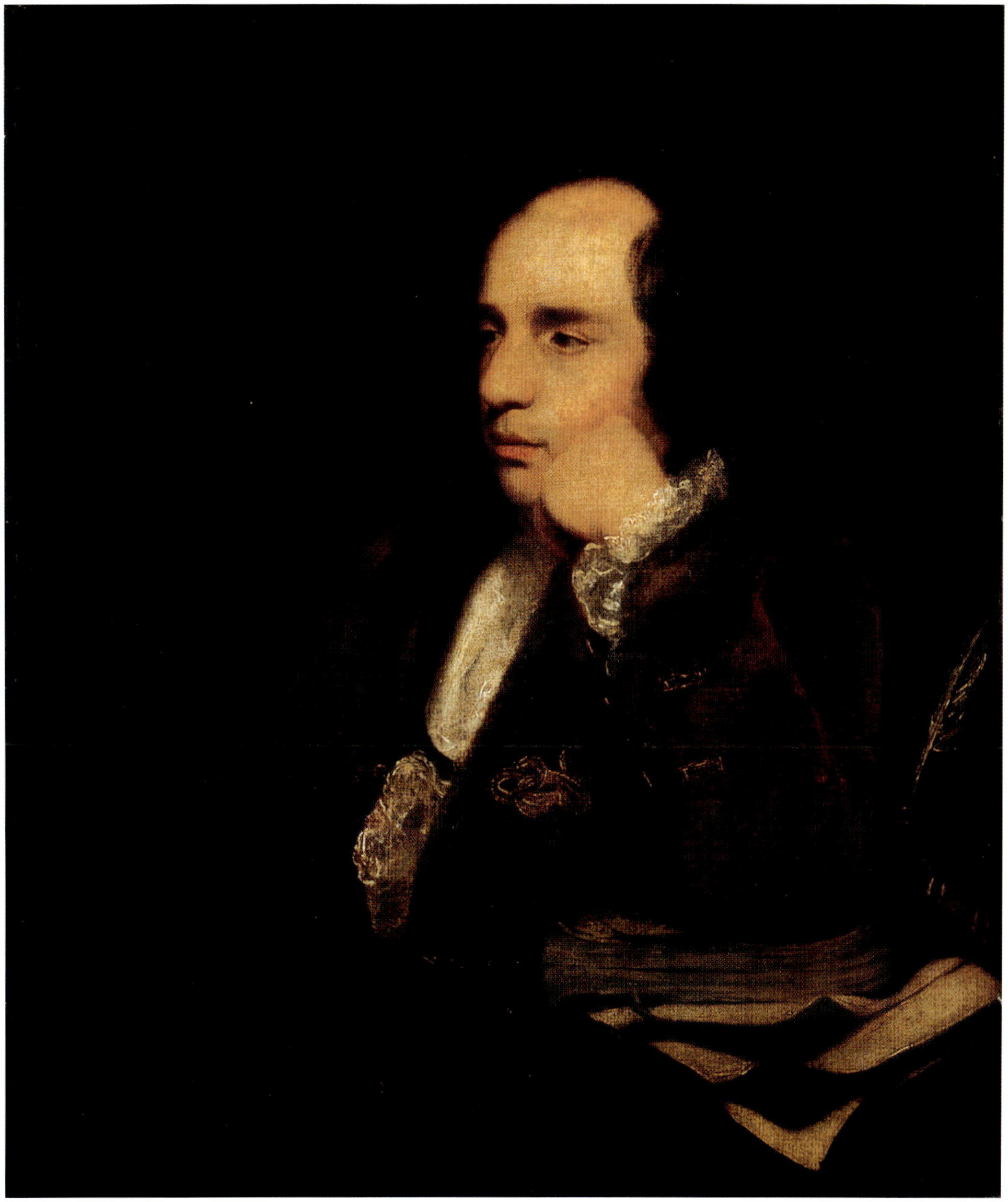

COLMAN NPG *1364*

1364 after JOSHUA REYNOLDS [1768-70]

Canvas 75.5 x 63 (29¾ x 24¾) lined; in poor condition, the surface rubbed and retouched and the varnish discoloured.

Brown eyes, dark hair, deep red coat trimmed with black fur.

Collections: Thomas Turton, Bishop of Ely; his sale, Christie's, 14 April 1864, lot 331 as 'Unknown artist, Oliver Goldsmith, his arm resting on a book'; C.J. Huth sale, Christie's, 19 March 1904, lot 48 as Goldsmith by Dance ('from the collection of the Bishop of Ely'), bt. Leggatt for the NPG.

Reference: Mannings 2000, no.396b.

The original portrait, painted for the 1st Baron Mulgrave,[1] was last sold Sotheby's, 8 April 1998, lot 101, and is in poor condition.[2] When it was exhibited at the RA in 1770, hung with Reynolds's *Goldsmith* and *Johnson*

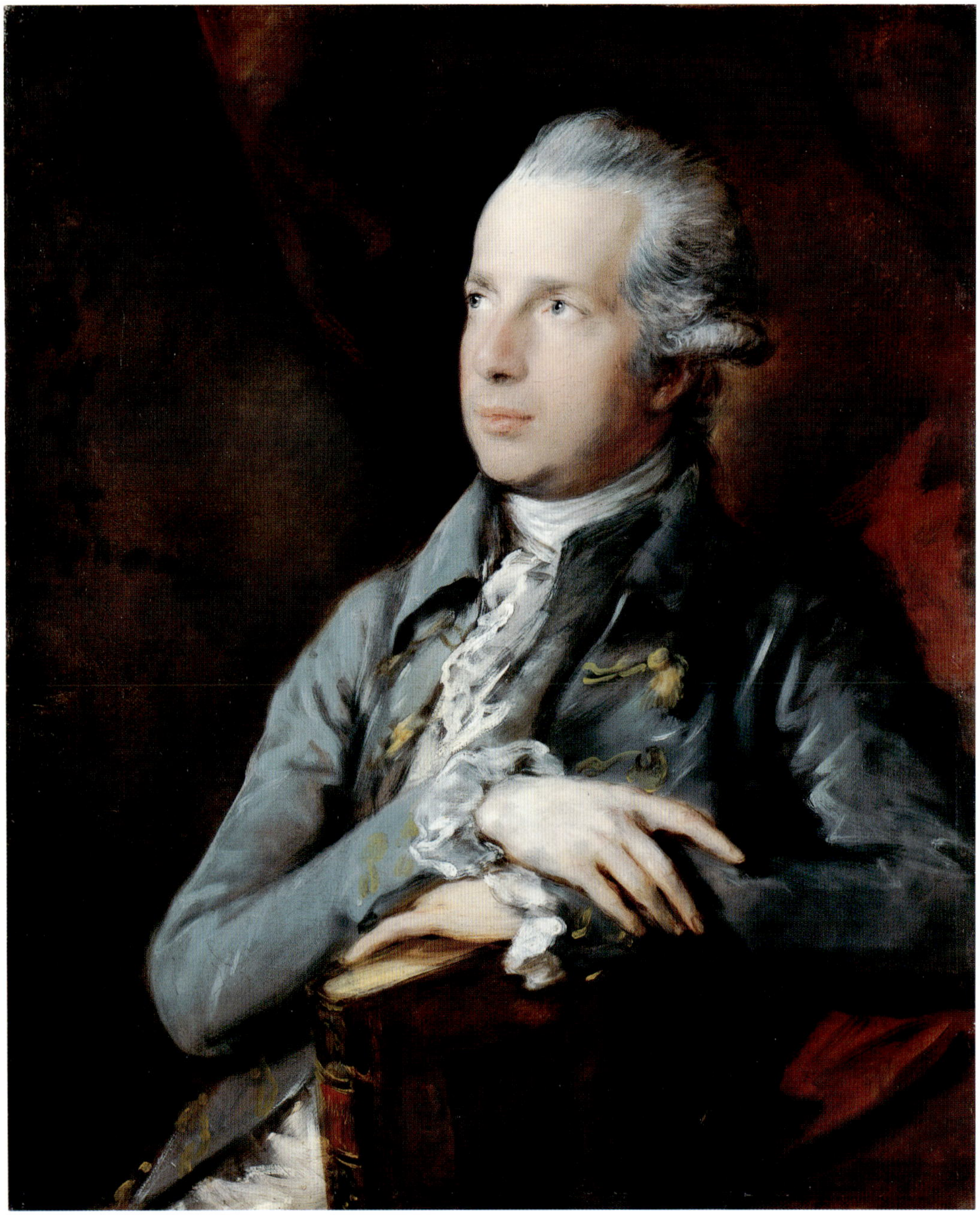

COLMAN *NPG 59*

(both now in a private collection), an anonymous satirist wrote: 'but what the deuce brought Coly there? ... Now may the touch of Reynolds save/The mungrel's likeness from the grave:/Drawn by the hand of such deserving,/ Even frogs and toads are worth preserving'.[3]

Other copies are in the Garrick Club,[4] at Buscot Park and sold Bonham's 7 December 1990, lot 126 (from the Gow collection); Haydon recounted how John Jackson made 'a really wonderful copy' from the Mulgrave portrait.[5]

1 Mannings 2000, no.396; engraved G. Marchi 1773, other plates include those by N. Schiavonetti 1807, E. Scriven 1813 and S. Fisher 1841.
2 Northcote 1819, p.158, described it being force-dried by a fire when it was covered by a fall of soot and dust. Reynolds, observing a picture [the same?] on which soot had fallen, is supposed to have remarked on the 'fine, cool tint' and scumbled the dirt into the flesh (B.R. Haydon, *Autobiography*, 1926 ed., II, p.390).
3 *Wal. Corr.*, XLI, pp.400-01.
4 Ashton 1997, no.125.
5 B.R. Haydon, *Autobiography*, 1926 ed., I, p.23; John Jackson's preparatory drawings for the engraving by E. Scriven are in the British Museum (1861.5.18.210 dated 1802, and 1856.7.12.959 dated 1810).

59 THOMAS GAINSBOROUGH c.1778

Canvas 75.5 x 63 (29¾ x 24¾) lined; cleaned 1975.

Blue eyes, powdered hair, wearing a pale blue coat with gold trim, grey waistcoat, white breeches; a deep red curtain behind him.

Collections: Bought from the sitter's son, George Colman (d.1836), on 30 November 1836 by Charles Webb;[1] John Webb, from whom purchased 1859.

Engravings: J. Scott 1874; as a bust-length oval: anon. 1785 (*from an original Picture by Gainsborough*; *European Mag*.,); J. Hall 1787; A. Smith 1802; T. Cheesman (as after de Loutherbourg) 1807.

Exhibitions: National Gallery -1920; *Georgian Playhouse* 1975(93); *La peinture britannique*, Bordeaux, 1977(15); *Gainsborough*, Paris, 1981(49); *Royal Opera House Retrospective*, RA, 1982(196); *Treasures* 1995-96(15); *Gainsborough*, Ferrara, 1998(18).

Reference: *Gainsborough* 1953, p.23; Waterhouse 1958, no.161.

Probably painted in 1778, when Gainsborough was decorating the King's Theatre, Haymarket (opposite the Theatre Royal, where Colman was manager).[2] Boaden later recalled how on first meeting Colman, in about 1781, he had been 'very much struck with the exact resemblance of his portrait, by Gainsborough, which hung over the fire-place in his sitting room'.[3]

1 As recorded in an old label verso.
2 See *The Georgian Playhouse*, 1975, no.93.
3 At 28 Soho Square; J. Boaden, *Life of Kemble*, I, 1825, p.288.

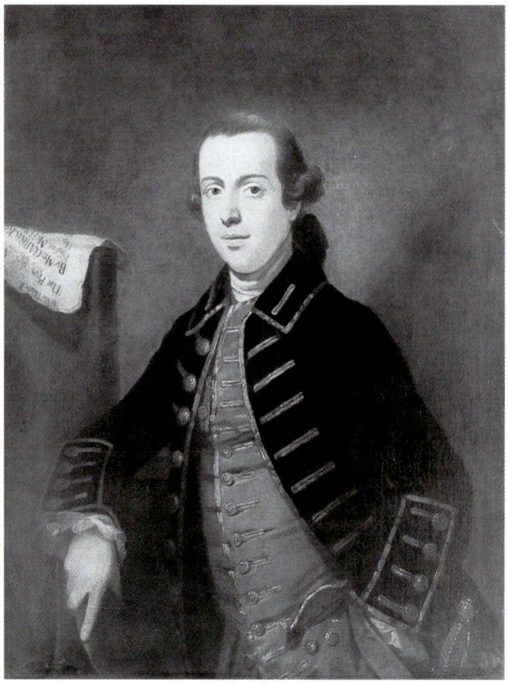

COLMAN after Johann Zoffany c.1764 (Garrick Club)

ICONOGRAPHY
See also the *Harvard Catalogue*, I, pp.271-72, and Highfill, III, p.420.

1761 Miniature by Nathaniel Hone, bust-length oval. Sotheby's, 14 February 1957, lot 22.

c.1764 Painting by Johann Zoffany, half length, with a playbill for *The Provok'd Wife* by him. Pawsey & Payne 1992, from Sotheby's, 10 July 1985, lot 51, and 18 November 1988, lot 59 (illus. Williamson 1920, f.p.224, with wrong identity). Engraved E. Smith 1822 (illus. Highfill, III, p.406). A version is in the Garrick Club* (Ashton 1997, no.126) in which the book on the left is inscribed: *Coke on Literature*.

1768-70 Painting by Joshua Reynolds, see NPG 1364.

c.1778 Painting by Thomas Gainsborough, see NPG 59.

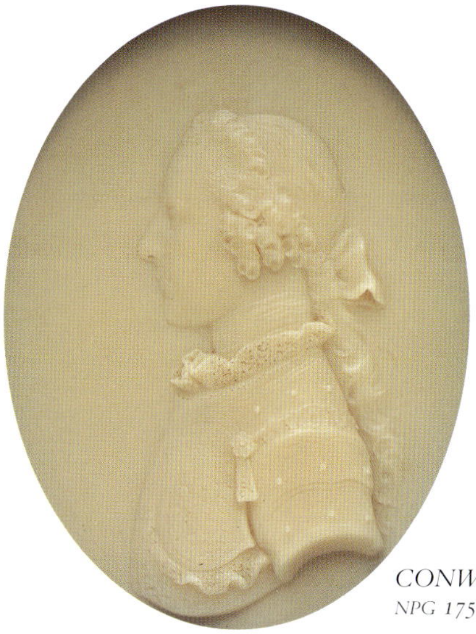

CONWAY
NPG 1757

CONWAY, Hon. Henry Seymour 1719-95

Soldier and statesman, yr. bro. of the 1st Marquess of Hertford and cos. of Horace Walpole; served at Culloden and in the Seven Years War; colonel 1746, major-general 1756, lieutenant-general 1759, general 1772, field-marshal 1793; MP 1741-84, secretary of state 1765-66; governor of Jersey from 1772.

'He had already passed his sixtieth year, yet his figure and deportment were exceedingly distinguished; nor did he want abilities; but his enunciation, embarrassed and often involved, generally did injustice to his conceptions' (Sir Nathaniel Wraxall, 1815).

1757 ISAAC GOSSET 1760

Cream wax 10 x 7.5 (4 x 3) oval; an imperfect take from the mould, with repairs around the drapery and throat when it was finished in Gosset's studio; the impression number *6* painted on the reverse of the cast.[1] The oak backboard is inscribed (probably in a contemporary hand): *Gen. Henry Conway 1760*.

Collections: [by descent from the 1st Viscount Sydney] at Frognal, by descent to Robert Marsham-Townshend (d. 1914), nephew of the last Lady Sydney; Frognal sale, Knight, Frank & Rutley, 10 June 1915, lot 575, bt. Leggatt for the NPG.

A Gosset medallion was listed at Clumber House in 1914,[2] and it is conceivable that the Tassie medallion listed in the early 19th century was another, or an enamel copy.[3]

1 Notes by V.J. Murrell 1968.
2 Clumber cat., 1923, no.386.
3 Gray 1894, no.86 as unseen.

ICONOGRAPHY
c.1742 Painting attributed to J-B. Van Loo,* standing three-quarter length in armour, gesturing towards a distant battle. Ragley Hall (illus. *Guide*, 1982, p.16).

c.1744 Miniature by Christian Zincke, bust-length oval, wearing a blue coat over breastplate. Wallace Collection (M314; illus. *Cat. of Miniatures*, 1980, p.83). Closely related to, and possibly the basis for, the 1746 portrait by Eccardt (who also copied Walpole's portrait from Zincke).

1746 Painting by J.G. Eccardt, half-length oval, wearing breast plate beneath dark coat. Christie's, 10 February 1900, lot 34, from Strawberry Hill. Engraved W. Greatbach 1857 (illus. *Wal. Corr.*, XXXVII, f.p.234).

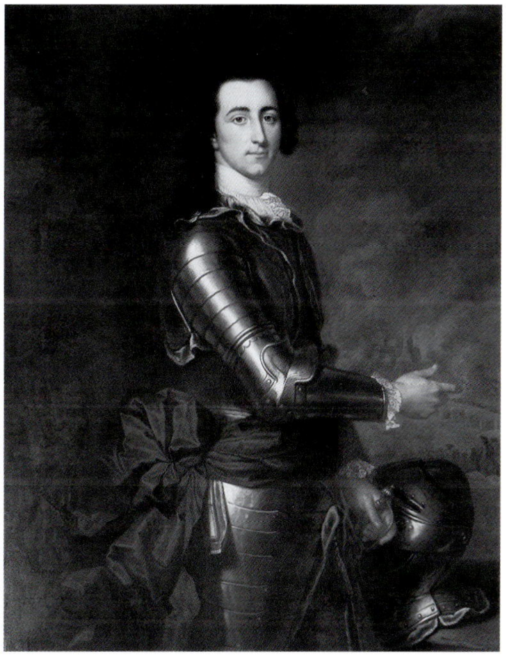

CONWAY attributed to J-B. Van Loo c.1742 (Private Collection)

Apropos this portrait, Conway observed to Horace Walpole that it was 'a pretty indifferent thing to posterity whether my eyebrow is more or less arched or the hollow over my eye more or less conspicuous' (*Wal. Corr.*, XXXVII, p.234).

c.1750 Painting by Bartholomew Dandridge, standing three-quarter length. Houghton Hall (illus. *Wal. Corr.*, XXXVII, f.p.12); listed in Horace Walpole's will (*Wal. Corr.*, XXX, p.371).

c.1754 Painting by J.G. Eccardt, whole length in Van Dyck costume with his wife Lady Ailesbury and daughter Anne (b.1749). Private collection (illus. *Rococo*, Victoria and Albert Museum, 1984, p.257). Hanging in the Blue Bedchamber at Strawberry Hill by May 1754 (*Wal. Corr.*, XXXV, p.174), the composition taken from Watteau's *La Cascade*. See Orford NPG 988.

1760 Wax by Isaac Gosset, see NPG 1757.

1765-67 Unattributed painting, three-quarter length standing, wearing breastplate, his right hand on a copy of the Free Port Bill. Commissioned for the Faneuil Hall, Boston, Mass., in 1765 (with a portrait of Isaac Barré) and delivered in 1767. Engraved C. Heath 1798 (bust-length oval, without painter's name). A copy attributed to G. Berwick (but possibly

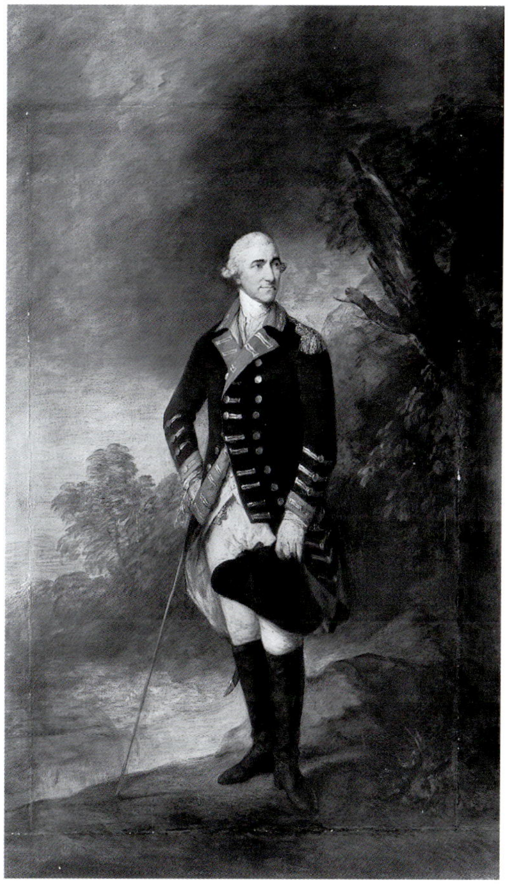

CONWAY by Thomas Gainsborough 1780 (Inverary Castle)

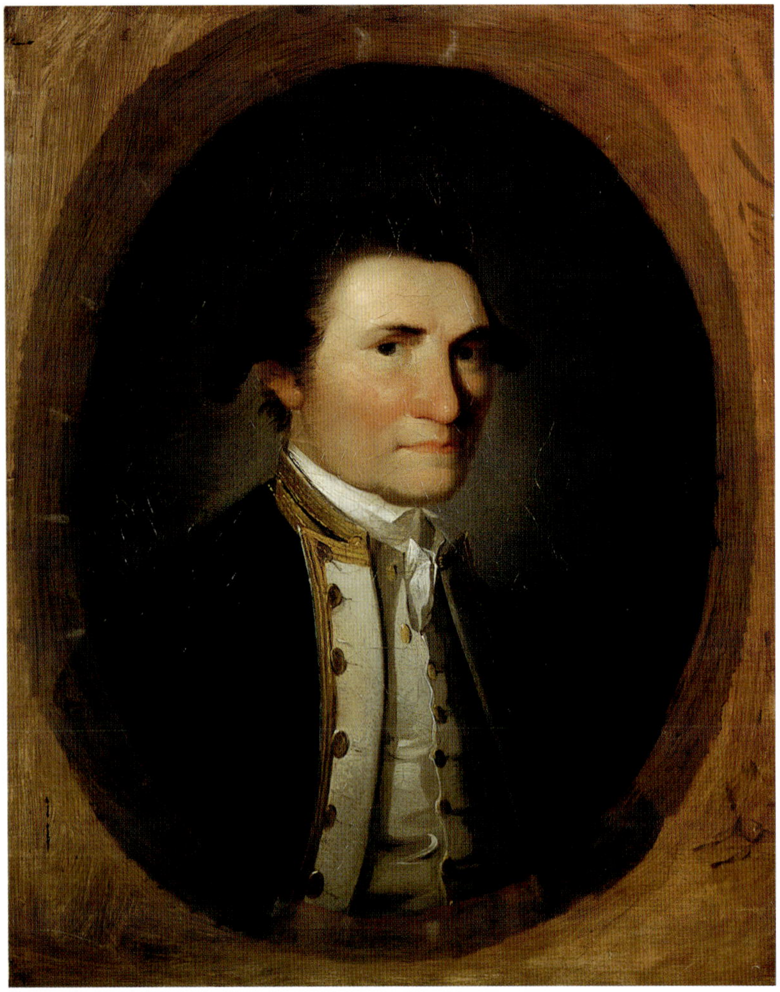

COOK NPG *26*

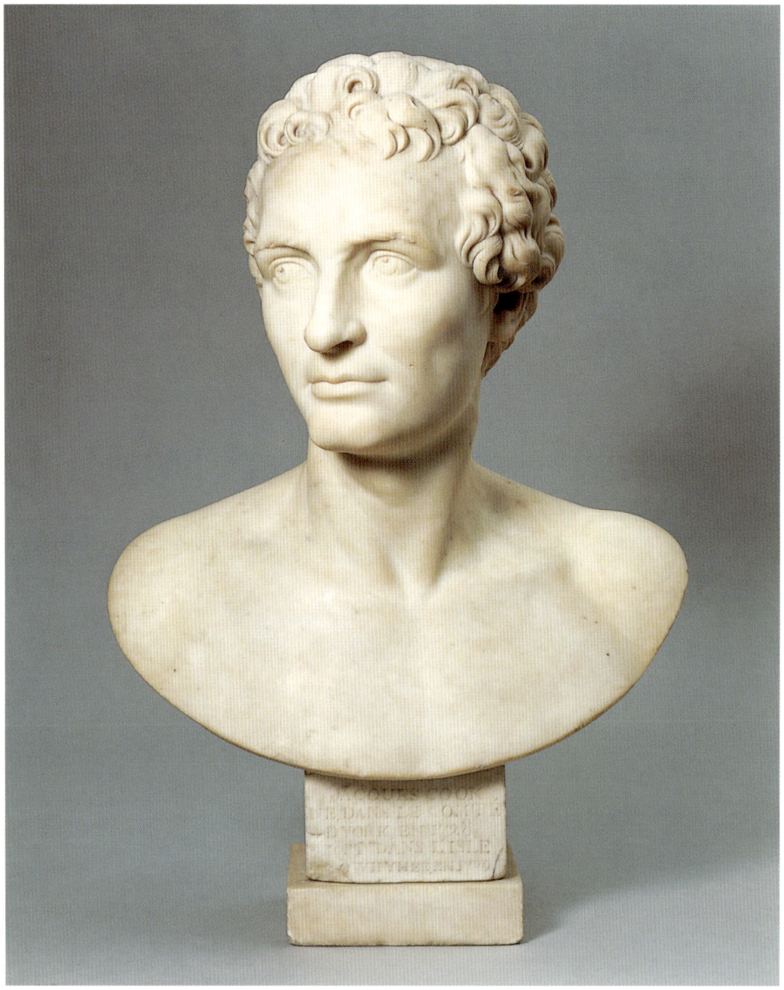

COOK NPG *984*

Ranelagh Barrett?) is in the Lewis Walpole Library, Farmington (W.S. Lewis, *Horace Walpole*, 1960, pp.xvii-xviii, illus. p.33), exhibited *Guelph* 1891, no.335 as a copy by G. Berwick of a portrait by Reynolds painted 'at the request of the citizens of New York'.

1780 Painting by Thomas Gainsborough,* whole length in general's uniform. Inverary Castle. Exhibited RA 1780(14). Engraved G. Dupont 1780; half-length plates by Angus 1782, and anon. 1782 (*London Mag.*). Version, possibly a replica, with Jersey Museums Service; engraved R. Josey 1874 (from *the original Picture belonging to the States of Jersey*).

DOUBTFUL PORTRAITS

Paintings: by Joshua Reynolds c.1762, Ragley Hall (Mannings 2000, no.408; engraved C.A. Tomkins 1768); another sold Anderson, New York, 16 November 1933, lot 5 (Mannings 2000, no.409); attributed to Thomas Gainsborough, exhibited NPE 1867(462) lent by the Duke of Argyll.

Miniature by Richard Cosway (Victoria and Albert Museum; D.99), and a drawing by John Smart, sold Christie's, 15 February 1937, lot 39.

COOK, James 1728–79

Mariner; made voyages to the South Pacific 1768–71 (in the *Endeavour*) and 1772–75 (*Resolution*), and to the North Pacific 1776–79 (*Resolution*), when he was murdered by natives at Hawaii; commander 1771; captain 1775; FRS 1776; '[my] ambition leads me not only farther than any other man has been before me, but as far as I think it possible for man to go' (Cook's *Journals*).

'He was certainly six feet. I should rather guess that he exceeded that height. He was raw boned, with a very small head, and capable of enduring the greatest fatigue' (Molesworth Phillips, 1826).

26 JOHN WEBBER 1776

Canvas 43 x 35 (17 x 13¾), the oval image 37.5 x 29 (14¾ x 11½) lined 1858; cleaned 1984; the bottom of the painted oval frame is laid over the figure; pentimenti to the outlines of the shoulders, and a general fine craquelure in the head.

Blue-grey eyes, dark hair, wearing a captain's full-dress uniform, white neckcloth, dark blue coat with white lapels and waistcoat, gold buttons, white neckcloth.

Collections: Purchased from J.H. Burn 1858.

Engravings: F. Bartolozzi 1784; [J.P.] Haid 1788; J.A. Selb.

Exhibitions: *Captain Cook*, Portland, Ore., 1968(2, as by Lionel Cust after John Webber, *sic*); *Captain Cook*, Birmingham, 1979; *First Impressions*, British Museum, 1988; *John Webber*, Manchester, Bern, 1996(11).

Reference: Joppien & Smith, III, p.646(3-451).

Webber, primarily a view painter, accompanied Cook to the North Pacific in 1776-79. According to the inscription on Bartolozzi's plate, this portrait was *Painted at the Cape of Good Hope, by J. Webber*, indicating a date between mid-October and November 1776.

Lot 88 in the Webber sale, Christie's, 2nd day, 15 June 1793, 'Captain Cook's Portrait and a small ditto', bought by 'Segr.' (probably the dealer William Seguier, d. 1844), probably comprised NPG 26 and Webber's larger portrait of 1782, see below. An early, reduced, version was sold Christie's, 8 April 1998, lot 114, and a copy was made in 1985 for the Cook museum at Whitby.

For other portraits by Webber, see below, 1777 and 1782.

984 LUCIEN LE VIEUX 1790

Marble bust *all'antica* 58.4 (23) high; damage to the nose repaired 1973; incised beneath left shoulder: *Le Vieux ft 1790*. The original socle inscribed: *JACQUES COOK / NÉ DANS LE COMTÉ / D'YORK EN 1728 / MORT DANS L'ISLE / D'OWHYHÉE EN 1779*.

Collections: Phillips and Neale, a house sale, Portland Place, c.1893;[1] F.C. Bentinck, from whom purchased 1895.

Exhibitions: National Maritime Museum, 1971-2000; *Mutiny on the Bounty*, National Maritime Museum, 1989(6).

An idealised classical bust, unlike any authentic image of Cook, apparently derived from that carved by Auguste Pajou for the marquis de Laborde in 1788, see below.

1 Letters from F.C. Bentinck to Lionel Cust, 3 May 1895: 'I saw this bust at a Sale of effects in a house in Portland Place about two years ago', and to Mrs A. Esdaile, 13 September 1928: 'I happened to see this bust at Phillips & Neale's Auction Rooms included in one of their weekly sales of furniture' (copies in NPG archive). It was not the Charles Magniac sale, Phillips & Neale, 8-9 June 1893 (as David Scrase has kindly informed me).

ICONOGRAPHY

There were just three basic portraits of Cook, by Hodges 1775-76, Dance 1776, and Webber 1776, of whom only Dance was a portrait painter. Cook iconography is therefore an austere study - but after his death his image was much in demand and many unreliable portraits were produced, while others acquired his name.

A. Klenman, *The Faces of Captain Cook, a numismatic memoir*, 1983, illustrates medals from 1772-1979. A useful listing of secondary material relating to Cook iconography in Australian Libraries appears in M.K. Beddie, *Bibliography of Captain Cook*, 1970, pp.501-12, 530-617.

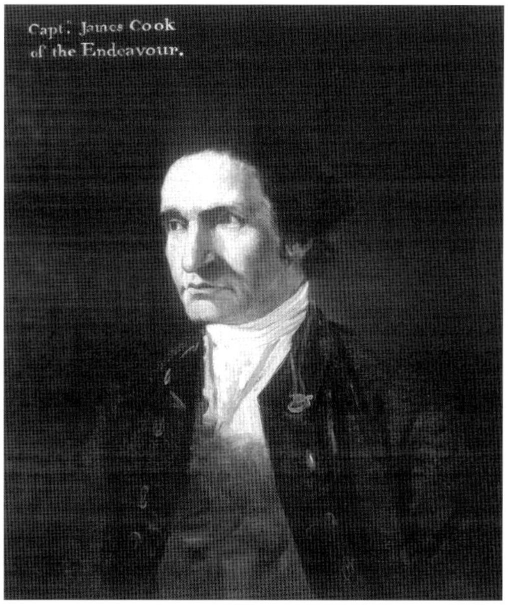

COOK by William Hodges 1775-76 (National Maritime Museum, London)

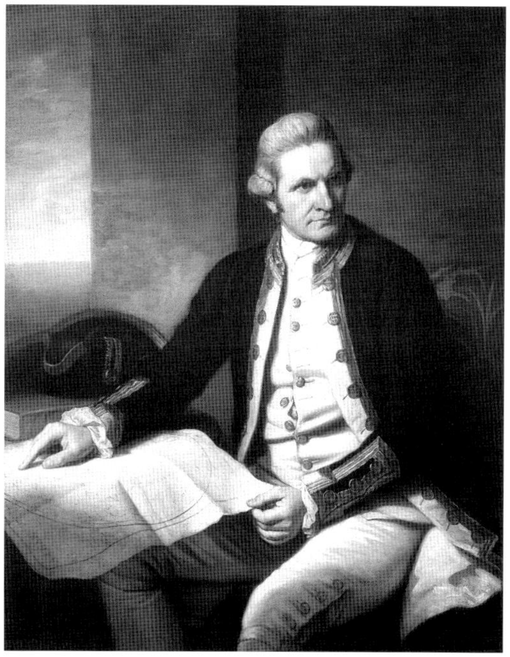

COOK by Nathaniel Dance 1776 (National Maritime Museum, London)

1775-76 Painting by William Hodges,* half length in captain's uniform. National Maritime Museum (BHC 1802). Hodges sailed with Cook on his second voyage 1772-75 and the portrait was probably painted in London between August 1775 and July 1776. Adapted for an engraving by J. Basire 1777 (exhibited FS 1778, no.14), from whose plate derived others by J. Tookey 1784, Thornton 1784 (*from the Original Picture in the Possession of G.W. Anderson*), and Gabriel.

A version was exhibited Manchester 1857(modern masters 110) lent John Garland, and a copy by Michele Cornè 1803 is in the Peabody Museum, Salem, Mass. (illus. *Connoisseur*, CLXXXI, 1972, p.209).

1776 Painting by Nathaniel Dance,* three-quarter length seated in captain's full-dress uniform. National Maritime Museum (BHC 2628). Commissioned by Joseph Banks and presented by his executor, Sir Edward Knatchbull, to the Painted Hall, Greenwich, 1829. Engraved J.K. Sherwin 1778; I.F. Bolt 1788; T. Holloway 1790; P. Roberts, and W. Holl; many reduced plates, including one by J. Collyer 1780 *from a painting by Mr Dance in the Possession of Joseph Banks Esq*. Painted in May 1776, the most competent and reliable image of Cook: 'the plate engraved by Sherwin, after a painting by Dance, is a most excellent likeness of Captain Cook; and more to be valued, as it is the only one I have seen that bears any resemblance to him' (D. Samwell, *Death of Captain James Cook*, 1786, p.23).

Copies include those in the NPG, Canberra; Australia House, London (made in 1928); AG of New South Wales, Sydney; and those sold Christie's, 8 April 1986, lot 68; Christie's, 1 March 1990, lot 152; Christie's, 8 April 1998, lot 108 (bust-length miniature); an extended version was with Colnaghi c.1907.

1776 Painting by John Webber, see NPG 26.

1777 Painting by John Webber. Drawn at Tahiti at the request of King Otoo, and last seen there in 1791 (Joppien & Smith, III, 3-454).

Posthumous

1777-84 Painting by James Barry, *Commerce*, part of the *Progress of Human Culture*, in which 'the late Captain Cook of amiable memory' appears in the centre left foreground. Royal Society of Arts, London (Pressly 1981, no.25). Engraved J. Barry 1791. The head derived from the Dance portrait of 1776.

1778 'Antique marble profile of a man, pressed into service as an ideal likeness of Cook' on the base of the Cook monument at Stowe.

by 1779 Wedgwood medallion, attributed to John Flaxman (see also 1784 below), derived from Basire's engraving after Hodges (illus. Reilly 1973, p.111).

1780 Model for a monument to Captain Cook by Thomas Banks, the corpse stretched over a globe, attended by Britannia. Banks sale, Christie's, 22 May 1805, lot 104. Exhibited RA 1780(474). Never executed, the design was etched, probably by Banks himself (illus. Bell 1938, pl.iv).

1780 Wax portrait by J.F. Vandermeulen, exhibited SA 1780(277).

1780 Cook Memorial medal, the verso inscribed: *Courage and Perseverance*, or: *Kill'd by the Indians* (illus. A. Klenman, *The Faces of Captain Cook*, 1983, K3, K4)

1782 Painting by John Webber, dated three-quarter length, in captain's full-dress uniform, the head copied from NPG 26. NPG Canberra; from Trinity House, Hull, 1844-1983 (Joppien & Smith, III, 3-452). Probably the portrait from the Webber sale, Christie's, 2nd day, 15 June 1793, lot 88 (see NPG 26 above).

An undated, slightly extended and less gainly version, with telescope in left hand and hat in right, is in the Museum of New Zealand, Wellington (Joppien & Smith, III, 3-453); from Cook's widow (d. 1835), by whom given to Greenwich Naval Hospital 1824, but returned to her in 1829 when the Dance portrait of 1776 was presented (letters in NPG archive). Mrs Cook disliked one of Cook's portraits (possibly this one) which she thought made Cook look severe, 'and she was "hurt" by the idea that he was severe' (J. Beaglehole, *Life of Captain Cook*, 1974, p.695). Beaglehole illustrates the Wellington portrait, f.p.696, dating it 1776, which is surely a mistake (cf W. Hauptmann, *John Webber*, Bern, Manchester 1996, p.139).

1784 Wax profile by John Flaxman, half length. Private collection. Closely resembling the Wedgwood medallion modelled by Flaxman the same year (illus. Reilly 1973, p.111).

1784 Memorial medal by Lewis Pingo (Brown 1980, no.258; Eimer 1998, no.64). Produced for the Royal Society, commissioned by Joseph Banks; resembling the Flaxman 1784 profile. Engraved anon. 1785.

1788 Marble bust by Auguste Pajou, *all'antica* undraped, on the pedestal of a monument designed by Hubert Robert. Erected in the parc de Méréville, Etampes, commissioned by Jean-Joseph de la Borde; transferred to the Château de Jeurre 1887; the bust offered for sale 1938-39 (see H. Stein, *Pajou*, 1912, pp.136-38; correspondence and photographs in NPG archive).

1790 Marble bust by Lucien Le Vieux, see NPG 984.

before 1791 Medallion by James Tassie, derived from the Dance portrait of 1776 (Gray 1894, no.87). Plaster replica Scottish NPG (PG 487), cast from a medallion belonging to Jeffery Whitehead in 1894.

The several depictions of the death of Cook include the unfinished painting by Johann Zoffany, c.1795 (National Maritime Museum; BHC 0424).

Later statues and monuments include: 1844 model for a statue of Cook by W.G. Nicholl, exhibited Westminster Hall 1844, 'a tame crabbed looking person' (Gunnis 1968, p.271); 1864-67 unattributed stone medallion, Bradford Wool Exchange; 1867 statue by W.F. Woodington, formerly Liverpool Exchange (illus. Cavanagh 1997, p.302); 1878 bronze statue by Thomas Woolner, Hyde Park, Sydney NSW. (illus. A. Woolner, *Thomas Woolner*, 1917, f.p.280); c.1900 stone statue by L-J. Chavalliaud, formerly Liverpool, Palm House (illus. Cavanagh 1997, p.202); 1912 bronze statue by John Tweed, Whitby, West Cliff (illus. Bennett, *Discovering Statues*, 1968, p.64); bronze replica at St Kilda, Australia; a bronze statuette in the Royal Ontario Museum (951.53); 1914 bronze statue by Thomas Brock, London, The Mall (illus. Byron 1981, p.23); 1994 bronze statue by Anthony Stones, National Maritime Museum.

DOUBTFUL PORTRAITS

See Unidentified Portraits NPG 1414. Lithograph by Albert Hoffay 1827, allegedly after Reynolds, dedicated to the Duke of Clarence.

COOTE, Sir Eyre, KB 1726-83

Army officer; b. Limerick; went to India 1754; defeated the French at Wandewash 1760 and Pondicherry 1761; save for a brief return to Madras 1769-70, he was in England 1762-77; MP 1768-80, KB 1771; returned to India 1777 as lieutenant-general, commander-in-chief at Calcutta, and his successful campaign against Hyder Ali included a victory at Porto Novo 1781; d. Madras.

'A bodily frame of unusual vigour and activity, and mental energy always awake, were restrained from excessive action by a patience and temper which never allowed the spirit of enterprise to outmarch the dictates of prudence. Daring valour and cool reflection strove for the mastery in the composition of this great man' (Mark Wilks, 1810).

124 attributed to HENRY ROBERT MORLAND [c.1763]

Canvas 75.5 x 62 (29¾ x 24½) lined; cleaned 1971.

Grey eyes, grey powdered hair, wearing a gilded silver gorget engraved with the crown and cypher of George III,[1] and the uniform of a colonel of the 84th Foot[2] - red coat with black facings and gold trim, buff waistcoat with gold trim, black hat with gold trim under his arm; pink officer's sash over his coat which bears the star of the Bath (evidently added and conveniently half-hidden by the lappet of the coat collar).

Collections: Purchased from S. Stroud, Bayswater, 1861.

Exhibition: *The Raj*, NPG, 1990-91(108) but not shown.

NPG 124 is one of several versions of the portrait by Henry Morland, showing Coote as colonel of the 84th Foot, a rank he held 1759-63,[3] indicating a date soon after his triumphal return to England late in 1762. The star of the Bath, which he received in 1771, was evidently added.

Morland's authorship is confirmed by Philip Dawe's mezzotint published in July 1782 (*H. Morland pinxit*), which shows a similar but oval image, differing in the omission of the right hand and hat, the replacement of the officer's sash with the Bath ribbon beneath his coat, the suggestion of greyer hair, and an open sky background. The publication of this print coincided with the exhibition of a portrait of *General Sir Eyre Coote* by Morland at the Society of Artists in 1782, no.26. The publication by James Walker in 1783 of a second related (reversed) bust-length engraving, made *From a Painting in the possession of G. Hesse Esqr* (and without the Bath insignia), suggests that Morland's 1782 exhibit was of the 1763 pattern, doubtless brought out (with the Bath insignia added) to mark Coote's military successes against Hyder Ali the previous year.[4]

Other versions are in the National Army Museum (7112-49) and in an Irish private collection.[5] Another, a painted oval, omitting the right hand and without the star of the Bath, was sold Christie's, New York, 8 November 1985, lot 96; this, or another, belonged to family descendants in 1968.[6]

1 See G. Bernard Hughes, *CL*, CXXXVII, 1965, p.1081.
2 As identified by Maj. N.P. Dawnay, note of September 1968 (NPG archive); he emphasised that this uniform of 1759-63 was obsolete before Coote received the Bath in 1771.
3 The regiment was disbanded in October 1763 (H.C. Wylly, *Sir Eyre Coote*, 1922, pp.119-20).
4 Cf. *GM*, LI, 1781, p.592, announcing in December 'our great success in the East Indies' under Sir Eyre Coote, whose further successes were anounced in March 1782 (*GM*, LII, 1782, p.204).
5 Exhibited *Great Irishmen*, Belfast, 1965(48).
6 Examined in the NPG in 1968 (NPG archive).

ICONOGRAPHY

[*Caveat*: Eyre Coote's nephew, General Sir Eyre Coote (1759-1823), who suc. to his estates at Weston Park, Hants., KB 1802, GCB 1815]

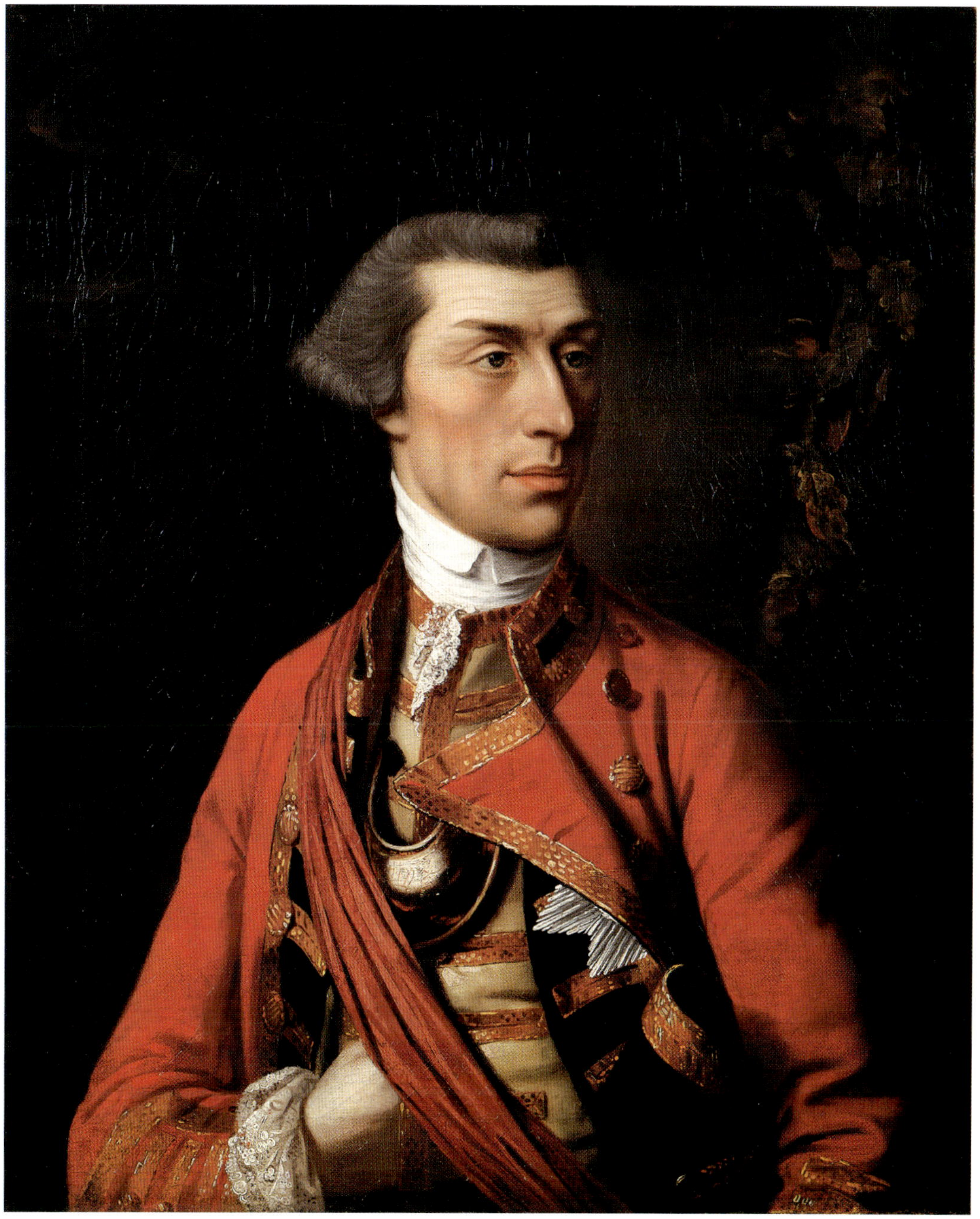

COOTE NPG 124

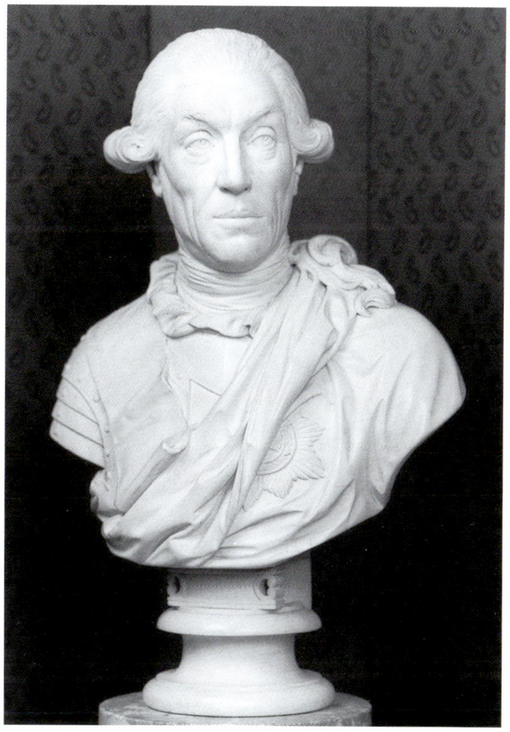

COOTE *by Joseph Nollekens 1779 (National Army Museum, London)*

Many Coote family portraits at Queniborough Old Hall, Leics., were dispersed after 1960.

c.1763 Painting by H.R. Morland, see NPG 124.

c.1763 Unattributed drawing, half-length oval, full face, wearing a gorget and officer's sash. Untraced. Engraved (each plate identified as Col. Coote): A. Benoist (*from an Original Drawing in the Possession of the Publisher of this Magazine*), F-G. Aliamet and A. Walker.

c.1764 Painting by Francis Hayman, *The Surrender of Pondicherry in 1761*, with Coote mounted on the left. Melanesia International Trust; from Queniborough Old Hall (illus. *The Raj*, NPG, 1990-91, p.91; see Allen 1987, no.50). Coote also appeared in Hayman's *Britannia distributing Laurels to the Victorious Generals* of c.1764, painted for Vauxhall Gardens, now untraced (not engraved).

1770 Pastel by H.D. Hamilton, bust-length oval, with the ribbon of the Bath added. Formerly at Queniborough Old Hall (with pendant pastel of his wife).

c.1770-79 Painting by Nathaniel Dance, see 1783 Zoffany below.

1779 Marble bust by Joseph Nollekens, with wig, wearing armour beneath a cloak with the ribbon and star of the Bath. National Army Museum.

c.1780? Unattributed painting, three-quarter length standing, wearing a red coat with two epaulettes and the ribbon and star of the Bath, white waistcoat and breeches. Oriental Club, London (illus. *Historical Portraits*, I, f.p.184). The head closely resembles that by H.R. Morland (see NPG 124) with the hair whitened.

c.1782 Painting by William Lawranson, small bust-length oval, wearing scarlet coat with blue facings and one epaulette, with the ribbon and star of the Bath. Formerly at Queniborough Old Hall. Engraved J. Walker 1782 as Lt.-Gen. Sir Eyre Coote by W. Lawranson *from an original picture in the Possession of John Purling*. The pose resembles that of the Hamilton pastel of 1770.

1783 Painting by J.T. Seton, whole-length standing in his tent, wearing a red coat with blue facings and one epaulette, and the ribbon and star of the Bath. India Office, British Library (illus. Archer 1986, no.57, pl.ix). Painted in Calcutta where engraved by C.J. Garbrand in May 1783 (Archer 1979, p.443n13).

A bust-length miniature based on the Seton portrait was sold Christie's, 26 June 1979, lot 58 (as 'Indian School').

1783 Paintings by Johann Zoffany and Nathaniel Dance:

Two pictures of Coote and Col. Claude Martin (who had deserted from the French to the English side at Pondicherry in 1760) and two pictures of Coote alone, were listed in Martin's collection at his death in Bengal in 1800 (Archer 1979, p.448n60). Since Zoffany arrived in India in 1783 and Coote died in April that year, the artist probably worked from engravings or from a portrait in Martin's collection by Nathaniel Dance, described as 'a remarkable likeness', which Henry Hudson was intending to engrave when he died in 1795 (Archer 1979, p.448n62). Dance could only have painted Coote in England between 1767-69 or 1770-79. In the Warren Hastings sale, Daylesford House, Farebrother, Clark & Lye, 22-27 August 1853, lot 923 was described as 'Zoffany/ A fine whole length portrait of Sir Eyre Coote, with despatches etc.' (conceivably of the Seton pattern, see 1783).

There was evidently a tendency to attribute portraits of Coote to Zoffany; two versions of the Morland pattern were published as Zoffany (Williamson 1920, pp.100, 188), and see Hickey 1822.

Posthumous

1788 Marble statue by Thomas Banks commissioned by the East India Company 1784. India Office, British Library (Archer 1986, no.123, pl.xxx).

1789 Monument by Thomas Banks, incorporating a profile medallion. Westminster Abbey (Bell 1938, pl.ix). Commissioned by the East India Company 1784. Engraved J. Condé 1790.

c.1790 Wedgwood medallion modelled by E.G. Mountstephen 1788 and based on the Nollekens bust of 1779 (illus. Reilly 1973, p.112). Previously misidentified as King Ferdinand of Sicily by Flaxman. A bronze version in the National Museum of Wales.

1795 Painting by Robert Home, commissioned by the citizens of Madras. Painted presumably from engravings and the artist's memories of his uncle (Archer 1979, p.307). According to Wilks writing in 1810, 'no sepoy who had served under him ever entered the room [at Madras] without making his obeisance to *Coote Bahadur*' (Wilks, *Historical Sketches of the South of India*, 1869 ed., I, pp.252). See 1822 below.

1822 Painting by Thomas Hickey, whole length, wearing red coat with blue facings and the ribbon and star of the Bath, with his native orderly and a servant. Formerly in Government House, Madras (illus. H.D. Love, *Descriptive List of Pictures in Government House and the Banqueting Hall*, Madras, 1903, f.p.168). Painted 'with the aid of a dilapidated portrait by Home, the face being taken from a canvas by Zoffany' (*ibid.*, p.168).

COPLEY, John Singleton 1737-1815

Painter, b. Boston, Mass., whence he dispatched works for exhibition in London at the SA 1766-72; in 1774 he came to Europe, spending a year in Italy before settling in London 1775; exhibited RA 1776-1812; ARA 1776 and RA 1779; d. London.

'Very thin, pale, a little pock-marked, prominent eyebrows, small eyes, which, after fatigue, seemed a day's march in his head' (George Carter, 1774).

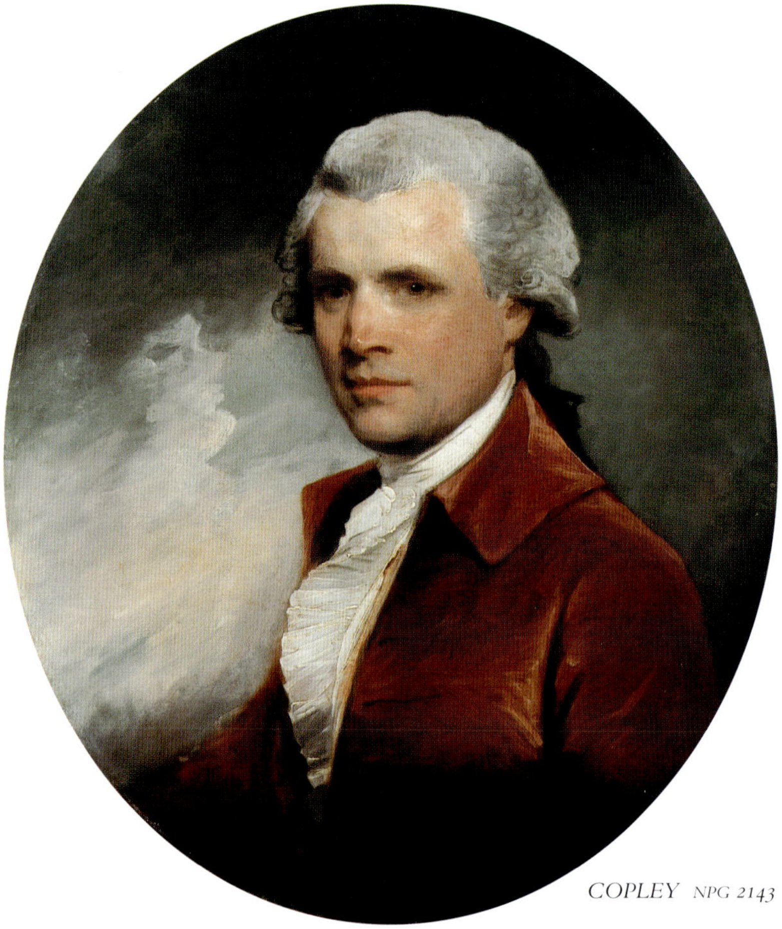

COPLEY NPG 2143

2143 GILBERT STUART 1783-84

Canvas 70 x 59.5 (27½ x 23½) oval, lined; cleaned 1975.

Brown eyes, grey powdered wig, wearing a red coat with white neckcloth.

Collections: Josiah Boydell;[1] J.S. Copley; his son, Lord Lyndhurst (d.1865); Lady Lyndhurst (d.1901), who bequeathed it in trust to her daughter, Georgina, Lady Du Cane (d.1927), and thence to the NPG, where received in 1927.

Engraving: W.C. Edwards 1830 as Gainsborough (*from the original in the possession of Lord Lyndhurst*).

Exhibitions: Boydell Gallery, London, 1784; *British Painting in the Eighteenth Century*, Montreal, Toronto, Toledo, 1957-58(66); *Stuart*, Washington, Rhode Island, 1967(11); *This New Man*, Smithsonian, 1968; *1776*, National Maritime Museum, 1976(353).

Reference: Park 1926, no.190.

Described by Copley's son, Lord Lyndhurst, as the 'best and most agreeable likeness of [my father] ever produced',[2] NPG 2143 was commissioned in 1783 by Josiah Boydell for his new London gallery at 90 Cheapside, one of a series of fifteen portraits of painters and engravers connected with his firm (see

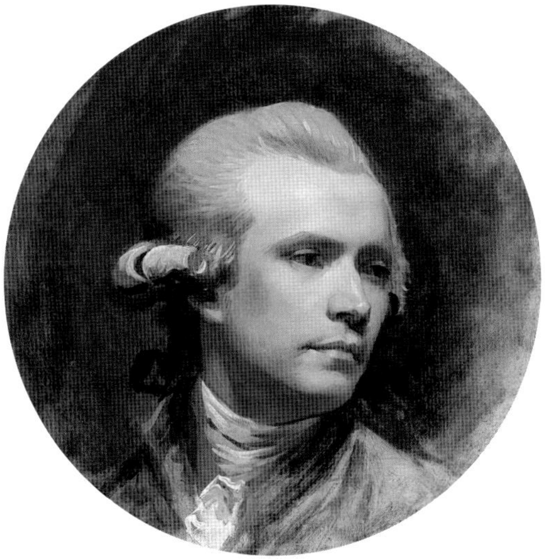

COPLEY Self portrait 1780–84 (National Portrait Gallery, Washington)

also Hall NPG 693). The majority were finished by April 1784. On 6 August the *Morning Herald* announced that Copley's

> celebrated picture of the death of Major Pierson is fixed up in Mr. Boydell's gallery. The frame in which it is placed is a beautiful piece of carved work. Three ovals are placed on top of the frame, in the centre of which is Mr. Copley's portrait, painted by that able artist, Mr. Stuart. The portrait of Mr. Heath, who is to engrave the subject, is on one side of the frame, and that of Mr. Josiah Boydell, who is to make the drawing, on the other.[3]

The Death of Major Pierson (250 x 280) is now in the Tate Gallery; Stuart's circular portraits (each 60 diameter) of James Heath and Josiah Boydell are now identified as those respectively in the Wadsworth Atheneum and the Museum of Art, Rhode Island School of Design.[4] It is not clear when NPG 2143 became detached, but *The Death of Major Pierson* remained with Boydell until his death in 1805; it was acquired after the Boydell sale of 1806 by Copley, probably with NPG 2143. A copy made by Robert S. Chase in 1947 is with the Bostonian Society, Boston, Mass.

1 Not identifiable in the Boydell sale, Christie's, 8 March 1806, lot 98.
2 Whitley 1932, p.48. There was little competition.
3 Quoted by Whitley 1932, *loc. cit.*, and Prown 1966, II, p.307.
4 The three are illus. together, with an Adam sketch for the design of the frame, in *Copley* 1995b, p.68. Robert Adam's designs are discussed in greater detail by E. Harris, *Furniture History*, XXVI, 1990, pp.93–95, figs.1, 2.

ICONOGRAPHY

Self-Portraits

1769 Pastel, half length. Winterthur Museum (illus. *Copley* 1995a, front., p.36). Miniature replica in the Manney collection (illus. *Copley* 1995a, pp.49, 252). A pendant to a pastel in Winterthur of his wife (he m.1769) and probably given to her.

1776–77 Painting, *The Copley Family*, in which the artist appears in the background. NG Washington (1961.7.1; illus. *Copley* 1995b, pp.22, 93). Oil sketches for the composition are in the NG Washington and the Museum of Fine Arts, Boston, Mass.

1780–84 Painting,* bust-length circular. NPG Washington (77.22).

Undated Painting, circular. Lyndhurst sale, Christie's, 5 March 1864, lot 75; with Charles Amory of Boston, Mass., 1872, and probably destroyed by fire that year (Prown 1966, II, p.415).

By other Artists

c.1780–85 Drawing by Paul Sandby, profile head, one of the series of heads drawn at print sales. Royal Collection (Oppé 1947, no.417/4, fig.21). Engraved anon.,* *Sketches taken at Print Sales*, see Comparative Groups.

1783–84 Painting by Gilbert Stuart, see NPG 2143.

1793 Drawing by George Dance,* profile bust to left, dated 30 March 1793. Royal Academy. Engraved W. Daniell (*Dance Plates*).

1795 Painting by Henry Singleton,* *President and Members of the Royal Academy*, see Comparative Groups.

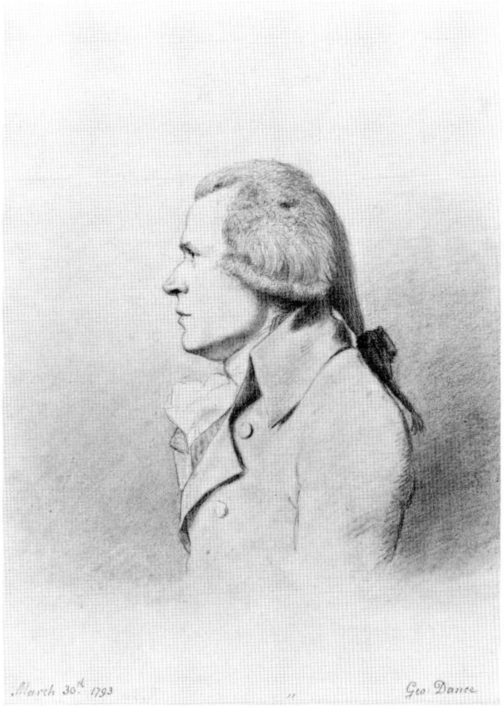

COPLEY by George Dance 1793 (Royal Academy of Arts, London)

CORNEWALL, Folliott Herbert Walker 1754–1831

Prelate; Dean of Canterbury 1793–97; Bishop of Bristol 1797–1803, of Hereford 1803–08 and of Worcester 1808–31.

'He was possessed of fair scholarship, strong good sense, polished manners, and an amiable temper' (*GM*, 1831).

5324 WILLIAM OWEN 1813

> Bevelled oak panel 56 x 45 x 1 (22 x 17¾ x ⅜); slight convex warp; some retouching of craquelure in the darks and background areas.
>
> Blue eyes, grey powdered wig, wearing a Bishop's rochet and chimere; brown background.
>
> *Collections*: Commissioned by the sitter and paid for in 1813 (see below); by descent in the Cornewall family at Delbury Hall[1] to Ada M. South, great-granddaughter of the sitter (d.1958); brought to London 1905;[2] her children, Elsie M.S. South, and Cecil Andrew South, by whom presented 1980.

A receipt from William Owen, dated 23 June 1813 *Receiv'd of Porteus Esq ninety four pounds ten shillings for amount of the Bishop of Worcester* was presented with the portrait.[3] It helps to confirm an attribution for the unique portrait type of Cornewall, but it is difficult to interpret the sum of ninety guineas (which clearly covers more than one painting). NPG 5324, which descended through the Bishop's family, should perhaps be accounted the original, and there were similar panels at Buxted in 1905 from the collection of Lord Liverpool (Charles Jenkinson, 1st Earl, had been a particular friend of the Bishop),[4] and another at Powis Castle in 1957,[5] the home of the Bishop's cousin, the 1st Earl of Powis.

There is a copy at Hartlebury Castle, the Bishop's last official residence, and an indifferently extended half-length version in the Deanery at Canterbury;[6] a pastel copy by Miss Lancaster Lucas was formerly at Kirkham Abbey,[7] and an unidentified version was exhibited by A.C. Hooper in 1882.[8]

1 The panel is inscribed in ink verso: *This Picture belongs to Delbury Hall* and *This picture belongs to Delbury hall / J H Cornewall / 28th April 184*[0]. For the Cornewall descent, see Liverpool & Reade, *House of Cornewall*, 1908, pp.137–41; NPG 5324 illus. p.viii.
2 Hawkesbury 1906, p.51. An author's annotation in Hawkesbury 1904a (NPG copy), under Buxted no.13, refers to the portrait at Delbury [NPG 5324] being 'brought to London to be sold'.
3 From Cornewall's account book, now NPG archive; Porteus was, presumably, the Bishop's agent.
4 Hawkesbury 1905, p.51; previously wrongly identified as Bishop Jenkinson of St David's (author's annotation of Hawkesbury 1904a, under Buxted no.13; NPG); Buxted had by then passed to Lord Portman (and by 1925 some of these portraits were with the

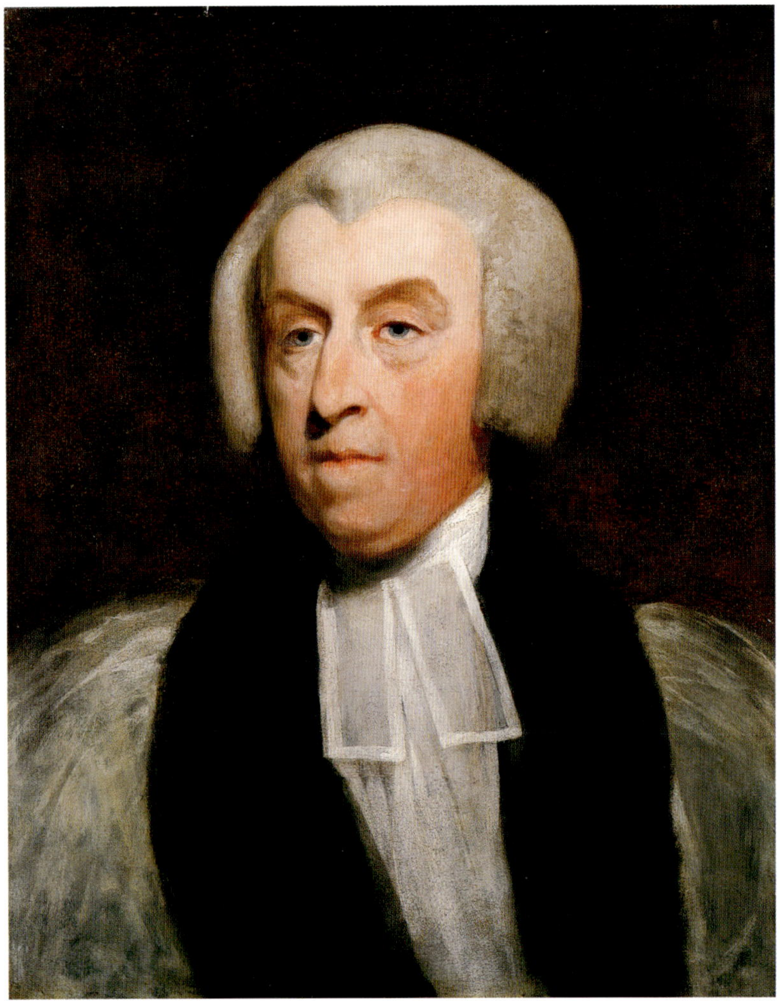

CORNEWALL NPG 5324

4th Viscount Portman in Bournemouth). The 1st Earl of Liverpool of the 2nd creation [Cecil George Savile, i.e. Lord Hawkesbury] was one of the principal buyers at the Delbury Hall sale in 1906 (according to a letter from C.A. South, September 1980; NPG archive).

5 Steegman, I, p.268, no.88.

6 Illus. Ingamells 1981, fig.58. The above account differs from that given in Ingamells 1981 when, alas, a reference was misunderstood and the NPG portrait unknown.

7 In Lord Hawkesbury's/Lord Liverpool's collection (Hawkesbury 1905, p.51).

8 *Worcestershire Exhibition* 1882 (History Section 151, cat., p.29); a written description in the NPG archives clearly indicates a version of NPG 5324.

999 see Groups, *The Trial of Queen Caroline* 1820 by GEORGE HAYTER 1820-23

CORNWALLIS, Charles Cornwallis, 1st Marquess 1738-1805

General and diplomat; sty. Lord Brome until suc. as 2nd Earl Cornwallis 1762; cr. Marquess Cornwallis 1792; KG 1786; major-general 1775, general 1793; surrendered at Yorktown 1781; governor-general of India 1786-93 and 1805, defeating Tipu Sultan at Seringapatam in 1792; lord-lieutenant of Ireland 1798-1800; d. India.

'Manly, affable, and good-natured; of an excellent judgement, and has a degree of application to business beyond what you would suppose' (John, 1st Baron Teignmouth, d.1834).

'You will have heard that soon after I left England I was elected a Knight of the Garter, and very likely laughed at me for wishing to wear a blue riband over my fat belly' (Lord Cornwallis, 1786).

281 THOMAS GAINSBOROUGH 1783

Canvas 75 x 63.5 (29½ x 25) lined; inscribed upper left: *CHARLES EARL CORNWALLIS. 1783*; small loss on chin, the head very thinly painted.

Blue eyes, powdered hair, lieutenant-general's uniform, bright red coat, with blue revers and gold trim, gold buttons and gold epaulette on his right shoulder. Within a painted oval; brown spandrels.

Collections: Francis, Lord Rawdon (later Marquess of Hastings, d.1826); his heirs' sale, Philips, 26 February 1869, lot 215, bt. Graves for the NPG.

Engraving: J. Scott 1884.

Exhibitions: RA 1783(45); *The Past We Share*, Dallas, 1967(17); *1776*, National Maritime Museum, 1976(537); *Battle of Yorktown*, Yorktown, Va., 1981; *The Raj*, NPG, 1990-91(152).

Reference: *Gainsborough* 1953, p.24; Waterhouse 1958, no.168.

Cornwallis had returned from his American campaigns in January 1782. Early in 1783 he and Lord Rawdon, a fellow officer from the American war, were sitting to Gainsborough for their portraits, for presentation to each other. Cornwallis's picture was hung in the Royal Academy exhibition that year and was considered a good likeness.[1] According to the provenance, NPG 281 was this portrait; the version in the Royal Collection, painted for the Prince of Wales, was presumably painted soon after[2] and differs only in the set of the shoulders which are inclined to the right.

1 This account is taken from Whitley 1915, pp.194-95.

2 Waterhouse 1958, no.167; Millar 1969, no.799; *Gainsborough & Reynolds* 1994, no.21.

4316 JOHN SMART 1792

Pencil and grey wash on paper 13.8 x 12.8 (5⅜ x 5) oval; scattered staining in the coat, the lower half of head and top centre; laid down on grey-washed paper 18.5 x 17 (7¼ x 6⅝), stained, and inscribed in a contemporary hand below: *The Right Honorable / Charles Earl Cornwallis Knight of the most Noble/order of the Garter / Governor General and Commander in Chief / in India // John Smart delineavit / Madras 1792.*[1]

Collections: Sir Bruce Ingram (d.1963); Colnaghi, from whom purchased 1963.

Exhibition: *Master Drawings* 1993-95(28).

Reference: Walker 1998, no.69.

The branch of laurel on the painted roundel must refer to Cornwallis's victory over Tipu Sultan in the Third Mysore War which ended in March 1792; Tipu's Palace at Seringapatam appears in the background.[2] Smart was in India from September 1785 to April 1795, living mainly in Madras, and NPG 4316 is one of several por-

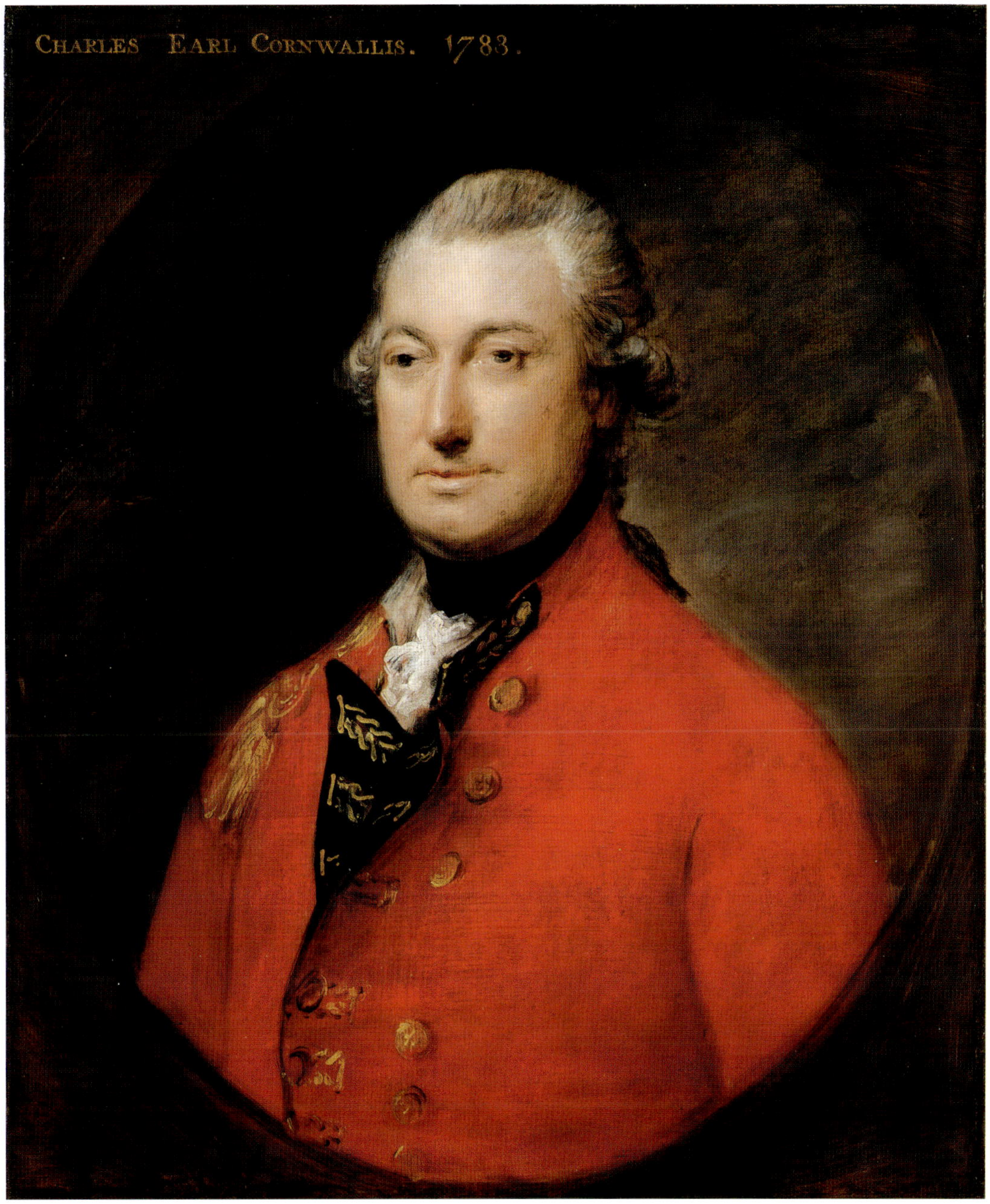

1st Marquess CORNWALLIS NPG *281*

traits he drew of Cornwallis. In order of date these are:

a) 1787 Christie's, 15 May 1903, lot 28 (signed and dated, wearing Garter insignia).

b) 1791 C.H. Moore 1942 (photograph NPG archive).

c) 1792 E.M. Hodgkins 1904 (illus. Williamson 1904, II, pl.lxx, no.9).

d) 1792 Fitzwilliam Museum, Cambridge (3922; illus. Bayne-Powell 1985, p.202, and G. Reynolds, *Cambridge Miniatures*, 1998, p.103.).

e) 1792 location unknown (illus. Archer 1979, p.392).

f) 1792 NPG 4316.

g) 1792 exhibited RA 1879 (case P 23) and *Guelph* 1891(974), on each occasion lent J. Whitehead.

h) 1794 E.B.H. Travers, sold Sotheby's, 27 November 1972, lot 169.

Of these a) and g) are otherwise unknown; the heads of b), d), e), f) and h) appear identical, and c) shows a similar head reversed. Smart sent a miniature of Cornwallis for exhibition at the RA 1793(180), and an undated miniature on a gold locket was sold

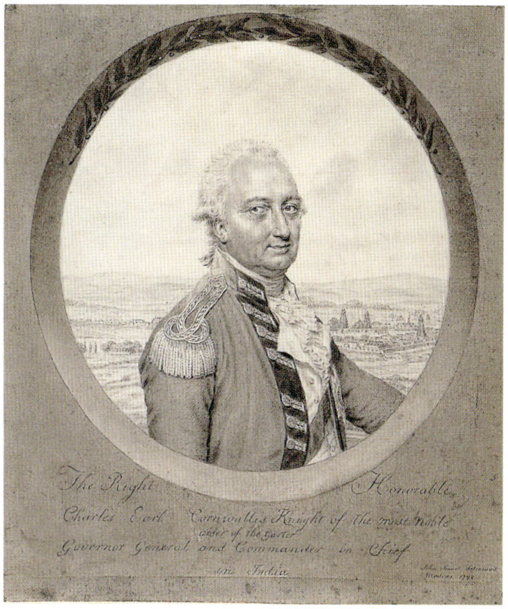

1st Marquess CORNWALLIS NPG *4316*

Christie's, 8 July 1914, lot 120.[3] A miniature copy from Smart by Samuel Andrews, who was in India c.1791-1807 and in 1794 moved into a house in Madras once occupied by Smart,[4] was sold Bonham's, 12 June 1995, lot 170.[5]

1 The spacing is less than perfect; was Smart anticipating Cornwallis's elevation as Marquess which was announced in London on 8 October 1792 (and presumably not known in India before February 1793)?

2 Cf. the contemporary views of Seringapatam illus. *The Tiger and the Thistle*, NG of Scotland, 1999, pp.45, 46, 65.

3 Another, said to have been dated 1793, was exhibited at 158b New Bond Street in 1911 with a pendant of Lady Cornwallis also dated 1793 - but she had died in 1779.

4 See Archer 1979, p.396; her account mentions an unlocated miniature by him of Cornwallis.

5 Another miniature resembling the Smart pattern, inscribed *Found in Charles Thackery's book, May 1794*, sold Bonham's, 24 November 1999, lot 246.

ICONOGRAPHY

1742 Painting by an unknown artist, whole-length seated, as a boy, with his brother Henry (1740-61). Audley End.

1761 Painting by Joshua Reynolds,* three-quarter length seated in uniform, as Lord Brome. Private collection (Mannings 2000, no.422). Engraved C. Knight (half length) 1780.

before 1776 by H.D. Hamilton, half-length oval, assumed by Strickland (*Wal. Soc.*, II, 1913, p.104) to have been a pastel. Engraved F. Bartolozzi 1781 (lettered *Earl Cornwallis, Lieutenant General*); D. Berger 1787 (German title); anon. 1781 as *Admiral Kempenfelt*; A. Rosenthal. The same head was used for a half-length oval plate by W. Grainger 1791, lettered as from a drawing by W.H. Brown (for *The Senator*).

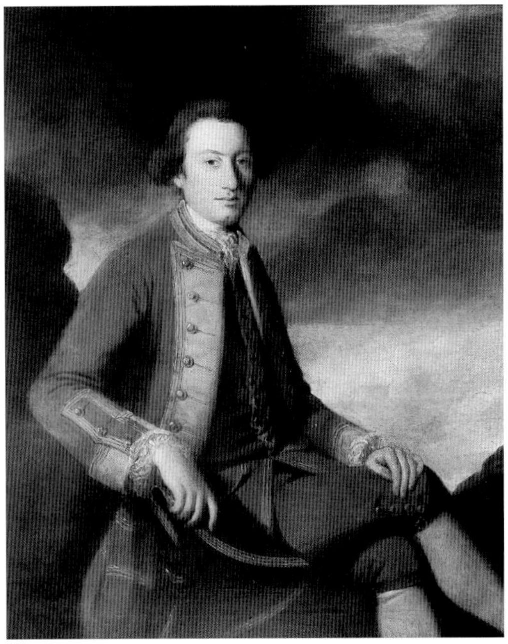

1st Marquess CORNWALLIS by Joshua Reynolds 1761 (Private Collection)

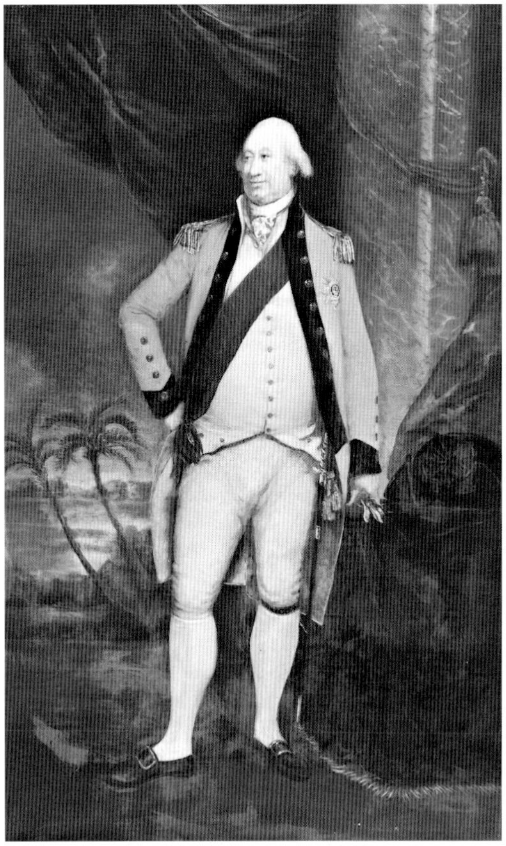

1st Marquess CORNWALLIS by A.W. Devis c.1792-93 (British Library)

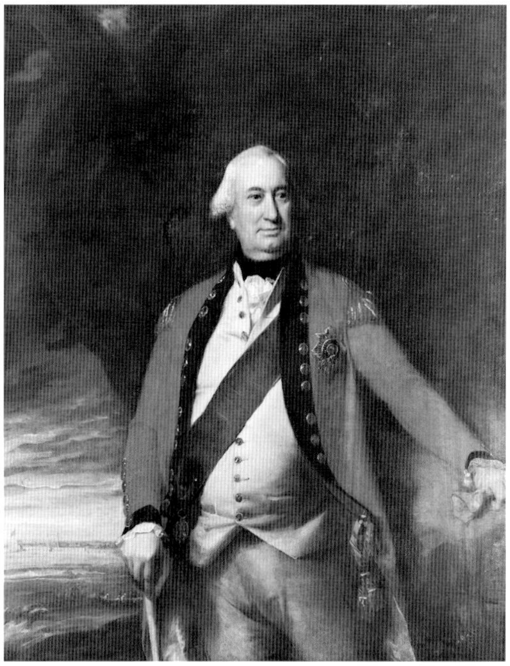

1st Marquess CORNWALLIS by J.S. Copley 1794 (Guildhall Art Gallery, London)

From 1776 to 1781 Cornwallis was in America, save a brief visit to England in 1778-79; he was then in England 1782-86.

1782 Gouache by Daniel Gardner, oval, inscribed and dated, whole-length standing in uniform as lieutenant-general, wearing hat. Christie's, 6 June 2002, lot 14. Engraved J. Jones 1793 (rectangular); F. Haward 1784 (half-length oval, a later state altered to *Gen. Burgoyne* by F. Bartolozzi; see Williamson 1921, pp.20, 61).

c.1782 Gouache by Daniel Gardner, three-quarter length standing in uniform of lieutenant-general with pink sash, right hand on hip, wearing hat. Christie's, 28 November 2000, lot 23, from the Berger collection, Denver (illus. *Berger Collection*, Denver, 1998, p.204). Exhibited *Gardner*, Kendal, 1962(5) as *Maj. Leggatt*, framed as an oval.

c.1782 Gouache by Daniel Gardner, whole-length standing in uniform as lieutenant-general, hat in hand. Giffords Hall, Suffolk, in 1967. Anon. half-length oval engraving.

1783 Painting by Thomas Gainsborough, see NPG 281.

Cornwallis was in India 1786-93.

1787 Miniature by John Smart, see under NPG 4316.

1792 Painting by Robert Home, whole length in uniform with Garter insignia, the treaty with Tipu Sultan of March 1792 lying on the table. Formerly in the Banqueting House, Madras (illus. Archer 1979, p.302), commissioned by the inhabitants of Madras in May 1792.

1792 Medals by C.H. Küchler (Brown 1980, no.363) and W. Mainwaring (Brown 1980, 6no.373; Foskett 1964, fig.72).

1792-94 Miniatures by John Smart, see NPG 4316.

c.1792-93 Paintings by Arthur William Devis, whole lengths, painted following Cornwallis's return to Madras in March 1792 after the Third Mysore War:

a) in military uniform with Garter insignia, right hand on hip, standing in a tent with British and Indian soldiers in the mid-distance. Formerly in Government House, Calcutta, commissioned by the inhabitants of Calcutta, July 1792 (photograph in NPG archive presented by the Secretary of State for India 1887). Engraved H. Hudson, Calcutta, 1794 (illus. Archer 1979, p.259).

b) in military uniform* with Garter insignia, right hand on hip, two palm trees in the left mid-distance. India Office, British Library. Painted for William Larkins, probably the portrait Devis exhibited RA 1796(282).

c) wearing parliamentary robes over a dark grey coat with red cuffs, grey breeches and waistcoat. Spink 1983, descended through the Kennaway family. A half-length version sold Christie's, 5 June 1925, lot 34 as Beechey.

d) a half-length engraving after A.W. Devis by F. Bartolozzi 1799 (dedicated to Lady Louisa Browne, the sitter's daughter-in-law) does not exactly agree with any of the preceding, but closely resembles Heath's engraving after Comerford, see 1809.

Cornwallis was in England 1794-1805, save for his Irish sojourn in 1798-1800. In 1805 he was sent to Calcutta but died that year at Ghazipore.

1793-98 Marble statue by John Bacon sr., completed by his son John Bacon jr., whole length *all'antica*, holding a sword and an olive branch. India Office, British Library (Archer 1986, no.121, pl.xxx), commissioned by the East India Company. Engraved L. Sailliar [Sahler] 1802 from a drawing by Bacon *taken from his original bust* (see 1798).

A larger version of the monument, completed by John Bacon jr. in 1803, is in the Victoria Memorial Hall, Calcutta (illus. *Apollo*, CXX, 1984, p.53; Groseclose 1995, p.106). Engraved G. Dawe 1803.

1794 Painting by J.S. Copley,* three-quarter length, in military uniform with ribbon and badge of the Garter, a distant view of Seringapatam. Guildhall

AG, London (59), presented by John Boydell 1795. Engraved B. Smith 1798; J. Hopwood 1806; W. Holl jr. 1832; S. Freeman 1833. Cornwallis received the Freedom of the City of London on his triumphal return to England in 1794; Boydell paid for this portrait on 5 June 1795, and by 18 June it was hanging in the Corporation's Common Council Chamber. Copies by Samuel Lane in the Oriental Club, by T.W. Jones c.1839 in Dublin Castle, and by Lancelot Speed 1890 at Clare College, Cambridge.

1794 Painting on copper by Henry Walton, half length. Moyse's Hall Museum, Bury St Edmunds (*Walton* 1999, no.32, as 1792; illus. *Walton*, Norwich, 1963, pl.ix). Engraved J. Ogborne, 1 July 1795 (illus. *Connoisseur*, XXV, 1909, p.143). Farington saw the portrait on 9 January 1795; Walton lived close to Brome, the Cornwallis seat in Suffolk.

1795–1800 Monument, 'a mark of gratitude of the East India Company, for the military services of the gallant veteran', by Thomas Banks, whole length in parliamentary robes, left hand on hip; the pedestal includes a bas-relief of Cornwallis receiving the sons of Tipu Sultan. Fort St George Museum, Madras (Bell 1938, pl.xxxiii; Groseclose 1995, pp.64–65). Begun in 1795, busts exhibited RA 1796(872, probably the model) and RA 1800(1096, marble), see Bell 1938, pp.135–36.

A profile medallion bust was engraved F. Eginton 1802 as after Thomas Banks.

1798 Marble bust by John Bacon sr. Squerryes. Exhibited *Treasures from Kent Houses*, Canterbury, 1984(48) when identified as that exhibited RA 1798(966), but this could equally have been the bust at Audley End or that in the Victoria Memorial Hall, Calcutta. Previously described as a replica from the India Office statue (see 1793–98 above) and exhibited Kenwood 1959(7) as by Thomas Banks (see Whinney 1964, p.181).

1799 Painting by William Beechey, whole length in Garter robes. Audley End. Exhibited RA 1799(89). Engraved J. Ward 1799; E.P. Lightfoot.

1801 Painting by T.H. Cutbush, half length, wearing a blue coat. Government Art Collection, presented by the artist 1801 (Walker 1976, p.18).

c.1803 Painting by John Hoppner, half length, own white hair, wearing military coat with Garter badge. Untraced. Engraved H. Meyer 1804 (oval) *from the last painted Portrait of His Lordship*; J. Davis 1812; D. Edwin 1812; W.C. Edwards 1835.

On 1 August 1803 Cornwallis wrote that he had given Hoppner 'a long sitting' when he was last in London 'which has, in my opinion, much improved the picture' (Cornwallis, *Corr.*, 1859, III, p.499). This may refer to a second portrait by Hoppner which uses the same body but shows the head turned more to the front and leaning slightly to the left. Untraced, engraved J. Wright 1820; W. Holl jr. 1858.

This second Hoppner type agrees substantially with a miniature by William Grimaldi in the Royal Collection, dated 1812 (Walker 1992, no.820), which differs only in showing the Garter ribbon over the coat and in slightly extending the figure downwards (without hands); Walker suggests it was a copy of 'the large miniature' by Grimaldi sent to the sitter's son in India in 1810.

The many less important engravings of Cornwallis include a half-length profile with ermine [perhaps after a wax?] published 1781; a half length after T. Prattent 1786 and a profile bust by Simon de Koster engraved J. Stow 1801.

Posthumous

c.1805? Medallion attributed to James Tassie (illus. J.P. Smith, *James Tassie*, 1995, p.65). Another(?) medallion, described as Wedgwood, exhibited *Guelph* 1891(1569) lent J.L. Propert.

c.1805? Wax by Catherine Andras. Christie's, 23 May 1967, lot 5.

1806 Miniature by Richard Bull, exhibited RA 1806(753).

1807–11 Monument by J.C. Rossi, whole-length figure in Garter robes, three Indian figures round the pedestal. St Paul's Cathedral. A finished sketch exhibited RA 1810(872), half-size models of the ancillary figures RA 1811(927), and a model of the statue RA 1814(764), three years after the date inscribed on the statue. Engraved S. Rawle 1819 (*European Mag.*).

1807–13 Monument by John Flaxman, medallion with Britannia and two grieving Indian figures. St John's Church, Penang. Destroyed during Second World War (*Wal. Soc.*, XXVIII, 1940, pl.xviia, p.89; Groseclose 1995, p.63). Commissioned by the citizens of Penang [Prince of Wales Island]; the model was paid for in 1807. Exhibited RA 1812(896). The original plaster is in University College, London.

before 1809 Miniature[?] by John Comerford, bust length; engraved J. Heath 1809 as from *an original painting by Commuford in possession of Sir J[onah] Barington*, see above c.1792–93 A.W. Devis.

1811 A statue by John Bacon jr. (Groseclose 1995, p.133n20). A half-sized model 'of a statue to be erected in Bombay' exhibited RA 1811(924).

1811 Engraved gem by William Brown, exhibited RA 1811(699).

1812–23 Memorial by John Flaxman, a profile head with a Brahmin and a Muslim on each side. Ghazipur, Uttar Pradesh (illus. *Apollo*, CXX, 1984, p.54).

1837 Medal by E.W. Wyon, exhibited RA 1837(1140).

1867 Statue by W.G. Nicholl (listed by Gunnis 1968, p.272 as India Office, but untraced).

Cornwallis was portrayed in many history pictures, principally celebrating his victory over Tipu Sultan in the Third Mysore War (in preference to his defeat at Yorktown). The many interpretations of Cornwallis with the Sons of Tipu Sultan *include (besides untraced pictures by James Northcote and Edward Bird, see Archer 1979, p.421) the following (listed alphabetical by artist):*

Mather Brown 1792 (private collection, India; Evans 1982, no.245); copy in the Bowes Museum, Barnard Castle (illus. *The Tiger and the Thistle*, NG of Scotland, 1999, p.48).

Mather Brown 1793 (Oriental Club; Evans 1982, no.237; Archer 1979, p.422 as c.1793); reduced version in the Victoria Memorial Hall, Calcutta (illus. Archer 1979, p.408), another sold Christie's, 20 June 1969, lot 28.

George Carter 1792 (Victoria Memorial, Calcutta; illus. Archer 1979, p.278).

A.W. Devis 1793–1805 (private collection; illus. Archer 1979, p.263); a larger version in a second private collection (illus. Archer 1979, p.265). One of these exhibited RA 1802(128).

Robert Home c.1793–94 (National Army Museum, 7611.86; illus. Archer 1979, p.309; *The Raj*, NPG, 1990–91, no.157); exhibited RA 1797(244).

Henry Singleton 1793 (Christie's, 13 July 1984, lot 107; illus. Archer 1979, p.422); exhibited RA 1793(93).

Robert Smirke (Yale Center for British Art, B1976.7.70).

COSWAY, Richard 1740-1821

Painter and virtuoso; principal painter to the Prince of Wales from 1785; ARA 1770, RA 1771; exhibited SA 1760 and 1767-69, FS 1761-66, RA 1770-1806; m. 1781 the Italian painter Maria Hadfield (1759-1838) who later founded a girls' college at Lodi.

'The artist cultivated a highly fashionable personal appearance as a macaroni or dandy, which expressed both his highly extrovert personality and also may have been an attempt to conceal his physical shortcomings, both in terms of his lack of height and his pronounced facial features' (Stephen Lloyd, 1995).

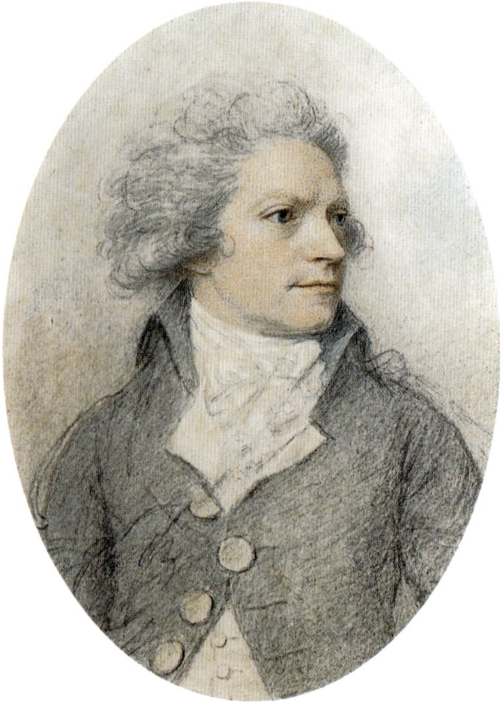

COSWAY NPG *304*

Abbreviation: Gipponi 1998
T. Gipponi ed., *Maria e Ricardo Cosway*, Turin, 1998

304 SELF PORTRAIT c.1790

Pencil and wash on paper 10.5 x 7.9 (4⅛ x 3⅛); the preliminary drawing shows his left arm stretched out, and his right hand raised as if holding a brush.

Collections: Maria Cosway; Mrs Williamson; presented by Mrs Georgiana M. Zornlin[1] 1870.

Exhibition: *Cosway* 1995(112).

Reference: Walker 1998, no.75.

To judge by the alterations, this is the original drawing from which several versions derived. It has been dated c.1790 by Lloyd,[2] and a miniature copy by Henry Stubble in the Huntington Art Collections, San Marino, Calif., is dated 1792.[3] Versions in pencil include those sold Sotheby's, 19 June 1969, lot 117 (from E.M. Hodgkins collection);[4] Christie's, 27-28 April 1983, lot 350, described as a copy of NPG 304 'perhaps by James Heath Millington', and see NPG 1678 below.

1 She wrote to Scharf, 14 May 1870, explaining that the picture 'was given me by a Mrs Williamson who was an intimate friend of Cosway and of his sister Miss Cosway by whom it was bequeathed to my friend Mrs Williamson' (NPG archive).
2 *Cosway* 1995, p.123.
3 No.24.27; illus. *Cat. of Miniatures by Richard Cosway* ... [belonging to] *Edward Joseph*, 1885, no.1.
4 Illus. Foskett 1979, p.360, pl.104d.

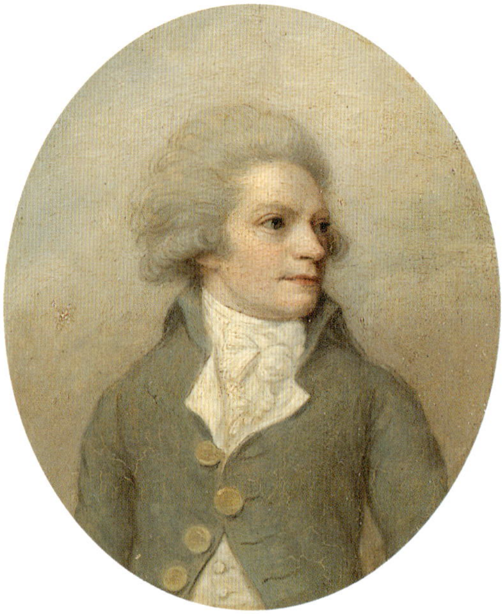

COSWAY NPG *1678*

1678 after RICHARD COSWAY [c.1790]

Mahogany panel 15.5 x 13.5 x 0.8 (6⅛ x 5¼ x ¼), the oval image 10.5 x 9 (4¼ x 3⅝); there are small losses above the shoulder (centre left), and in the coat by his sleeve (below left); there is a general fine craquelure.

Clear brown eyes, grey powdered hair, wearing a grey coat with gold buttons and a white waistcoat; there is a thin yellow line round the image and the surround is painted black.

Collections: Presented by Heber Mardon 1912.

Apparently a contemporary version of NPG 304, but not by Cosway himself; it differs in detail, principally in the hair and the more dramatic lighting of the head.

ICONOGRAPHY

'Dicky Cosway has published a great many likenesses of his own dear self, but whether to commemorate the beauties of his person, or to give posterity the eternal similitude of so amiable a man, it is difficult to say.' (*Morning Post*, 16 June 1788)

Self Portraits

c.1770 Painting, three-quarter length standing, wearing Rubensian dress. Attingham Park (illus. *Face to Face*, Liverpool, 1994, p.73).

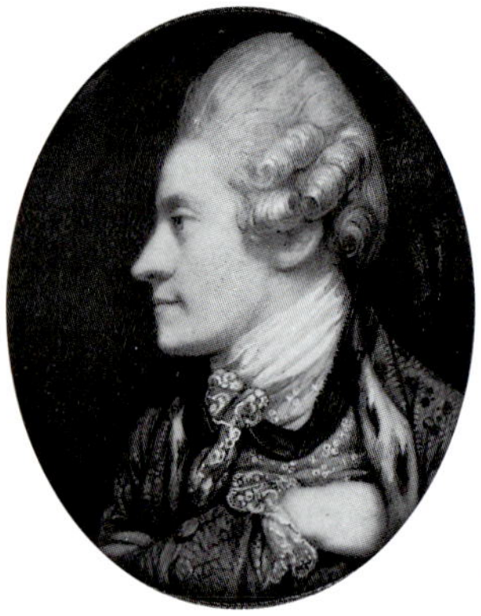

COSWAY Self portrait c.1770 (Metropolitan Museum of Art, New York)

c.1770 Miniature,* bust length in profile, arms folded. Metropolitan Museum of Art, New York (62.49; Reynolds 1996, no.130).

c.1770-75 Painting, half-length oval in Van Dyck dress with a black plumed velvet hat. Private collection (by descent from the artist).

c.1780 Drawing, half length. Fondazione Cosway, Lodi (illus. Gipponi 1998, p.55).

1780-85 Painting, half length. Fondazione Cosway, Lodi (illus. Gipponi 1998, p.95).

1784 Etching, seated in a garden in Rubensian dress, with his wife and a servant (illus. *Cosway* 1995, pl.35; *Face to Face*, Liverpool, 1994, p.74).

c.1785 Drawing, seated in a garden in Rubensian dress, with his wife. Fondazione Cosway, Lodi (illus. *Cosway* 1995, pl.33; Gipponi 1998, f.p.36). Inspired by the Rubens self portrait with his first wife in Munich.

c.1785 Drawing, half length in Rubensian dress with black plumed hat. Fondazione Cosway, Lodi (illus. Gipponi 1998, f.p.36).

c.1785-90 Miniature, bust length in Elizabethan dress. NG of Ireland (3024; illus. *Cosway* 1995 pl.63; Caffrey 2000, p.76).

c.1785-90 Drawing, lying reading beneath a tree, wearing a broad-brimmed hat. Christie's, 17 November 1981, lot 76.

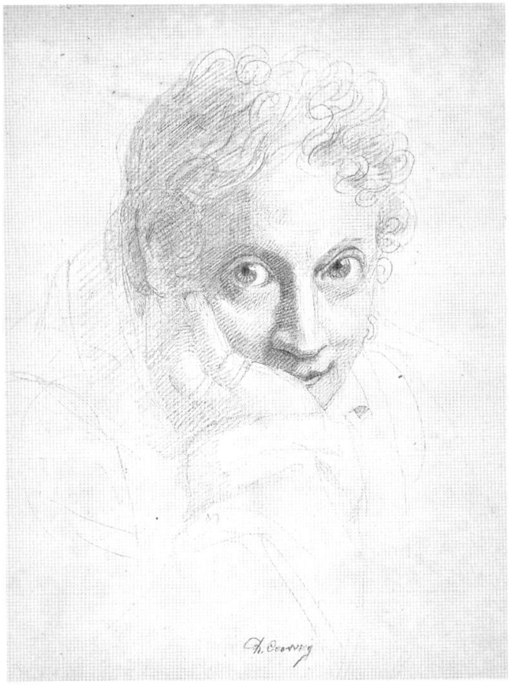

COSWAY *Self portrait c.1790 (Private Collection)*

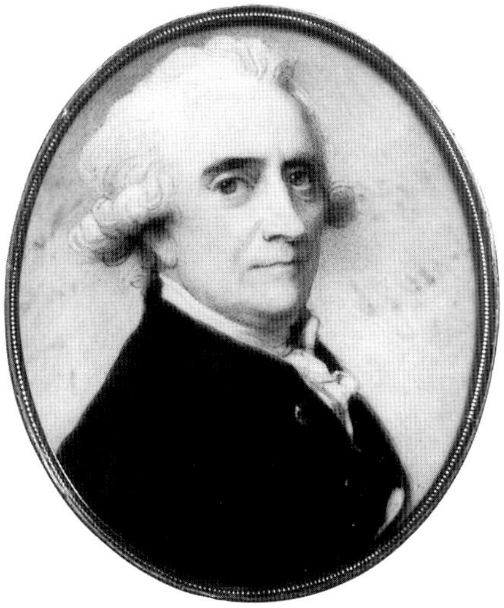

COSWAY *Self portrait c.1805-10 (Fitzwilliam Museum, Cambridge)*

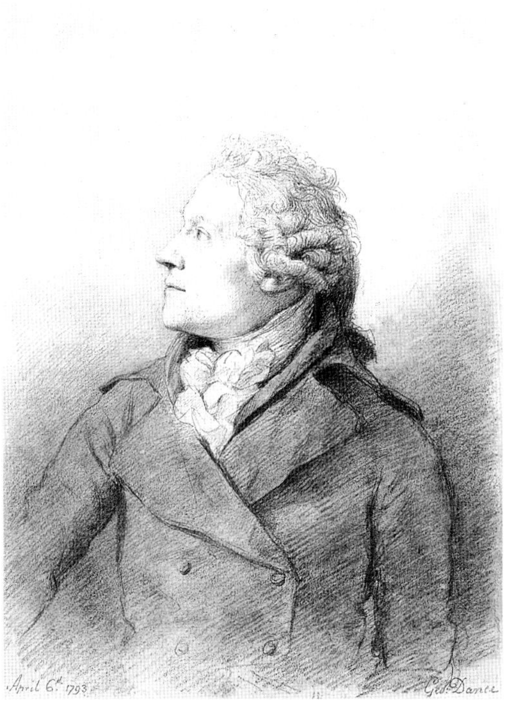

COSWAY *by George Dance 1793 (Royal Academy of Arts, London)*

1786 Drawing, whole-length seated, wrapped in a cloak, wearing a broad-brimmed plumed hat, the *Vita di Rubens* at his side. Engraved M. Bova [Bovi] 1786 and lettered *Rdus Cosway Armiger R.A. Primarius Pictor Serenissimi Walliae Principis* (illus. *Cosway* 1995, pl.39; Gipponi 1998, p.55).

c.1788 Drawing, half length in 'Spanish' seventeenth-century dress. Huntington Art Collections, San Marino, Calif. (27.141; illus. *British Portrait Drawings*, Huntington, 1982, no.15). Engraved J. Clarke 1788; E. Scriven 1832; W.C. Edwards 1833.

1789 Drawing, whole length in Rubensian costume, with his wife. Engraved R. Thew 1789, the first state entitled *Abelard and Eloisa* (illus. Gipponi, front.).

c.1789 Drawing, whole-length standing in Rubensian costume, contemplating busts of Michelangelo and Rubens. Fondazione Cosway, Lodi (illus. *Cosway* 1995, pl.40; Gipponi 1998, f.p.60).

c.1790 Drawing, bust length. Private collection, USA (*Cosway* 1995, pl.73 as c.1800; Gipponi 1998, p.47 as c.1790).

c.1790 Drawing, whole length, in Rubensian dress with a plumed hat, leaning on a pedestal bearing a bust of Rubens. Fondazione Cosway, Lodi (illus. Gipponi 1998, f.p.192).

c.1790 Drawing, see NPG 304 and NPG 1678.

1800 Etching, whole-length seated wearing a plumed hat, with his wife, *Coppia in lettura* (illus. Gipponi 1998, p.183).

1804-05 Miniature, bust length, wearing black seventeenth-century dress. Pierpont Morgan Library, New York, from the Whitehead sale, Christie's, 5 August 1915, lot 650 (Williamson 1906, II, no.269, pl.lxxxvii). Compares quite closely with the c.1805-10 type below.

c.1805 Drawing, at an easel. British Museum (1945.2.8.191/307), from a sketchbook (see *Cosway* 1995, no.188).

c.1805 Drawing, half length between two Masonic columns, pointing to the Star of David. Worcester Art Museum, Mass. (1921.57; illus. Williamson 1905, front.) Lloyd has explained that in 'later life Cosway was a practising magician and faith healer, who claimed to have prophetic powers' (*Cosway* 1995, p.127).

c.1805-10 Miniature,* bust length with a white wig. Fitzwilliam Museum, Cambridge (PD.203.1961). A version sold Phillips, 16 July 1996, lot 178.

1806 Drawing as Esau standing between the columns of the Temple of Jerusalem. Uffizi, Florence (3257), presented by the artist's widow 1824 (illus. *Firenze e l'Inghilterra*, Florence, 1971, no.52).

By other artists

1772 Painting by Johann Zoffany,* *The Academicians of the Royal Academy*, see Groups NPG 1437.

c.1780-85 Drawing by Paul Sandby, profile head almost obscured by a slouch hat, one of the series of heads drawn at print sales. Royal Collection (Oppé 1947, no.417/3). Engraved anon.,* *Sketches taken at Print Sales*, see Comparative Groups.

1781 Anon. etching, *A Smuggling Machine, or, a Convenient Cos/au/way for a Man in Miniature*, showing Cosway's profile emerging from his wife's hoops (George 6102; illus. Smith 1920, II, f.p.329).

c.1790 Unattributed medal (illus. *Cosway* 1995, p.17; Brown 1980, no.341).

c.1790? Drawing by Elias Martin. Nationalmuseum, Stockholm (102/1884). Exhibited *Elias Martin*, London 1963(42). Martin was in London 1768-80 and 1788-91.

1793 Drawing by George Dance,* half length, dated 6 April 1793. Royal Academy. Engraved W. Daniell 1811 (*Dance Portraits*); a Daniell tracing in the Yale Center for British Art (B1977.14.4193).

1795 Painting by Henry Singleton,* *President and Members of the Royal Academy*, see Comparative Groups.

A portrait of Cosway by Singleton, exhibited RA 1797(275), was probably connected with this larger group (cf. Thomas Sandby and Johann Zoffany).

Posthumous

1821 Monument by Richard Westmacott jr. with profile medallion surrounded by the figures of Art, Taste and Genius. St Mary's, Marylebone (illus. Busco 1994, p.155). Engraved C. Picart.

1909 Sculpture by Ernest Gillick, Victoria and Albert Museum (south front).

DOUBTFUL PORTRAITS

Painting by William Beechey, engraved H. Meyer after a drawing by W. Evans; 'self-portraits' in the Yale Center for British Art (B1977.14.4976); sold Christie's, 14 November 1991, lot 90, and a miniature, sold Christie's, 12 July 1988, lot 192 (illus. Williamson 1905, f.p.66).

COWPER, William 1731-1800

Poet, author of *The Task* 1785 and a translation of Homer 1791; following a breakdown in 1763 he lived a withdrawn, evangelical life with the widowed Mary Unwins, mainly in Buckinghamshire.

'To say the truth, when a man has once turned his mind inside out for the inspection of all who chuse to inspect it, to make a secret of his face seems but a little better than a selfcontradiction' (William Cowper, 1793).

'he was of middle stature, rather strong than delicate in the form of his limbs; the colour of his hair was a light brown, that of his eyes a bluish-grey, and his complexion ruddy. In his dress he was neat, but not finical' (William Hayley, 1812).

Abbreviation: Russell 1963

N. Russell, 'Bibliography of William Cowper to 1837', *Oxford Bibliographical Society*, NS XII, 1963

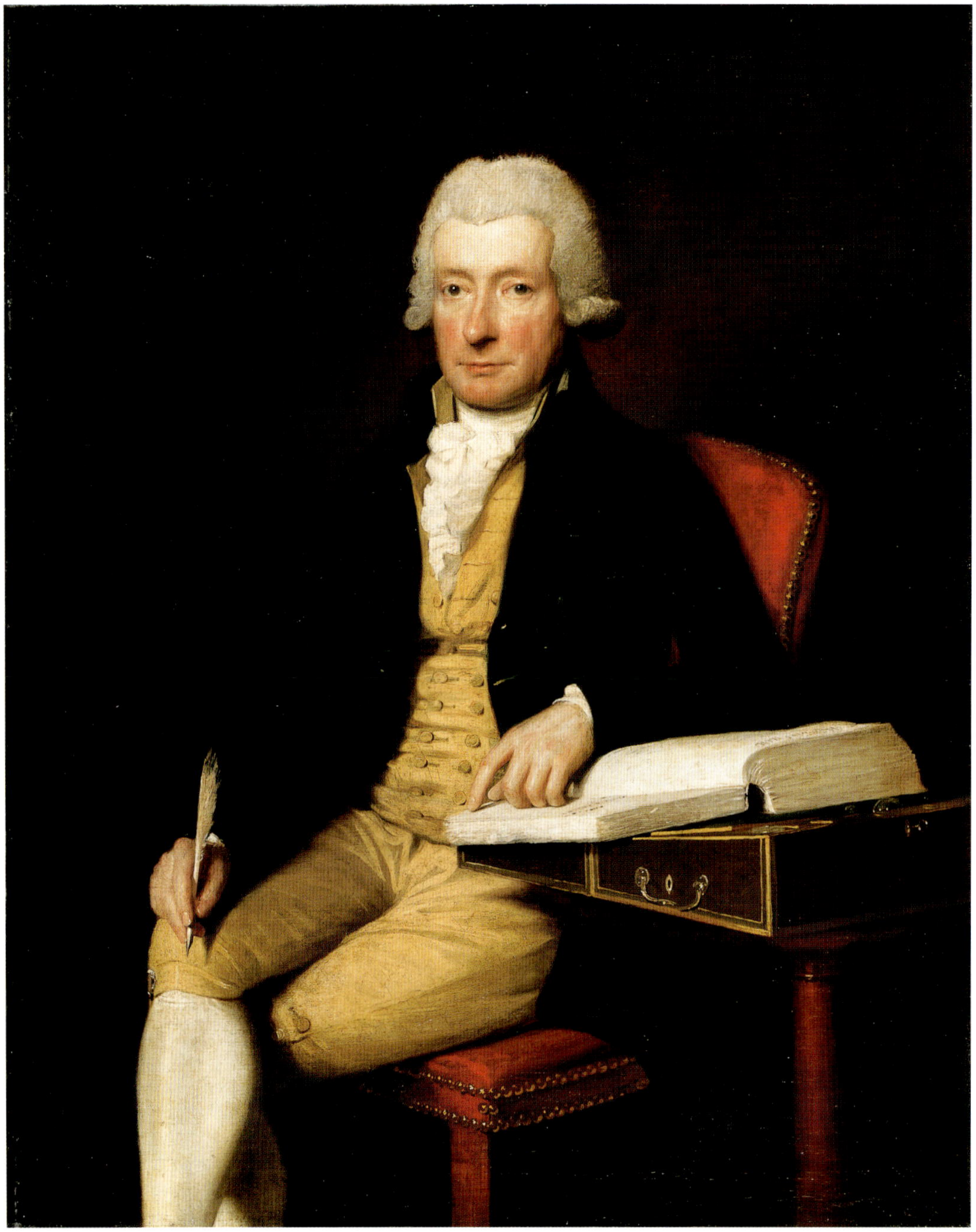

COWPER *NPG 2783*

2783 LEMUEL FRANCIS ABBOTT 1792

Canvas[1] 126 x 100 (49½ x 39½) lined 1976; areas of craquelure above his right thigh and in the shadow on the left side of coat; minor retouchings in the desk. Original canvas inscribed verso: *The / Author of the Task &c./ in the sixty first year of his age/ represented with astonishing like ness by / Lemuel Francis Abbott / who painted this portrait in the month of July / 1792 / at Weston Underwood in Buckinghamshire / according to the engagement of it's highly gratified possessor / John Johnson.*

Grey eyes, white hair, green 'archery' coat, white neckcloth, buff waistcoat and breeches, white stockings, seated in a red chair, beside a polished wood table with lectern on which lies a notebook, the left-hand page headed *HOMERS ILIAD.*

Collections: Commissioned by the Rev John Johnson for his aunt, Mrs Anne Bodham (d.1846);[2] Rev William Cowper Johnson (d.1893); Rev William Cowper Johnson II (d.1916), from whose widow purchased 1935.

Engravings: W.C. Edwards 1823;[3] R. Cooper 1824 (half length).

Exhibition: *Guelph* 1891(353) lent Rev W. Cowper Johnson.

Reference: Russell 1963, pp.287-88.

NPG 2783 was commissioned for the poet's cousin, Mrs Anne Bodham, by her nephew John Johnson, who had apparently first attempted to employ Thomas Lawrence.[4] Abbott, whom Cowper found 'a sober, quiet man',[5] painted him wearing the 'Green and buff ... colours in which I am oftener seen than in any others, and are become almost as natural to me as a parrot, and the dress was chosen indeed principally for that reason';[6] on his desk (given him by his cousin Theadora Cowper),[7] Abbott painted the bound manuscript of Homer's *Iliad* (referring to Cowper's continuing revision of his translation published in 1791).[8]

The progress of the portrait is well documented in Cowper's letters. Abbott came up from London to Weston Underwood, where Cowper was living with the invalid Mrs Unwin, arriving on 12 July 1792.[9] 'You never heard of him, you say. It is very likely, but there is nevertheless such a painter and an excellent one he is'.[10] Three days later Cowper quipped 'Abbot is painting me so true, / That (trust me) you would stare, / And hardly know, at the first view, / If I were here, or there';[11] after six days he was complaining that his 'whole time' was 'engaged to the Painter',[12] then on 21 July he announced that 'Tomorrow will be my last sitting';[13] he had 'been sitting these ten days' and he was 'heartily glad that my sitting time is over'.[14] Abbott was to complete the portrait on 23 July and depart on 25 July.[15]

It was much admired within the poet's circle. For Cowper himself the likeness was 'the closest imaginable' and he thought it would give 'as much pleasure, nay perhaps, even more, than a sight of the Original'.[16] Johnson, who had commissioned it, had already said on 19 July that it was 'a most enchanting likeness', and that friends were 'crazy to have prints of it';[17] the inscription on the verso of NPG 2783 provides further evidence of his pleasure. Finally on 29 July Cowper announced 'To morrow it goes to town, and will hang some months at Abbot's, when it will be sent to its due destination in Norfolk'.[18] It remained in Abbott's London studio in Caroline Street from August 1792 until March 1793, by which time it had 'been a spectacle long enough'.[19] Cowper then became resigned to the fact it was to be shown at the Royal Academy; 'after having been exhibited in [Abbott's] room so long, I care not where I am exhibited next. The Public at large are welcome to a sight of me'.[20] But the application arrived too late, 'only by a day or two'.[21]

For a comparison made in 1838 between the portraits by Abbott and Romney, taken within a month of each other, see NPG 1423 below.

A copy was made for the Johnson family in 1935 and remains in the mid-nineteenth-century frame previously on NPG 2783; 'a big frame which has a valuable old pedigree of Cowper, as big as the Picture, - inside it the picture itself, in a narrow frame, being hinged to open like a door in the big frame'.[22]

1 Canvas stamp, visible before relining: *T Poole / High Holborn / London*; and *856* [143 145].
2 She was also the niece of Cowper's mother; in 1800 John Johnson was presented by Mrs Bodham to the livings of Yaxham and Welborne (Cowper, *Letters*, III, 1982, p.xxvii); the inscription on NPG 2783 suggests it reverted to him before his aunt's death.
3 John Johnson thought it was 'indifferently copied and engraved' and the plate by Cooper was preferred for the early editions of Cowper's *Private Corr.* (see Russell 1963, p.204n2).
4 Cowper, *Letters*, IV, 1984, pp.142n3, 156; 25 July 1792, to William Bull. Mrs Bodham had also sat to Abbott.
5 *Ibid.*, p.148, 15 July 1792, to William Hayley.
6 *Ibid.*, p.186; 29 August 1792, to Samuel Rose.
7 Russell 1963, p.287. In February 1786 Cowper had received 'a most elegant writing desk. It is of Cedar and mounted with silver. Lady Hesketh sent it, but assured me she is not the giver' (Cowper, *Letters*, II, 1981, p.481).
8 On 10 July 1793 he was 'at the end of the 22d book' (Cowper, *Letters*, IV, 1984, p.366); his subsequent illnesses delayed publication until after his death.
9 Cowper, *Letters*, IV, 1984, pp.148n3, 156 (see below).
10 *Ibid.*, p.156; 25 July 1792, to William Bull.
11 *Ibid.*, p.148; 15 July 1792, to William Hayley.
12 *Ibid.*, p.150; 18 July 1792, to Samuel Teedon.
13 *Ibid.*, p.153; 21 July 1792, to Lady Hesketh.
14 *Ibid.*, p.156, 25 July 1792, to William Bull.
15 *Ibid.*, p.153; 22 July 1792, to William Hayley.
16 *Ibid.*, pp.152-53, 21 July 1792, to Lady Hesketh.
17 Russell 1963, p.287; to his sister Catherine, 19 July 1792.
18 Cowper, *Letters*, IV, 1984, p.160; 29 July 1792 - 'Every creature that has seen it has been astonish'd at the strong resemblance.... It is a half-length, as it is technically but absurdly call'd, that is to say it gives all but the foot and ancle'.
19 *Ibid.*, pp.178, 300; to Joseph Johnson, 21 August 1792 and 3 March 1793.
20 *Ibid.*, p.322; 11 April 1793, to Joseph Johnson.
21 *Ibid.*, p.335; 21 May 1793, to Lady Hesketh.
22 W.H. Cowper Johnson, 10 June 1935 (NPG archive). The pedigree is mentioned by Russell 1963, p.287n2.

806 WILLIAM HARVEY after L.F. ABBOTT [1792]

Pencil and watercolour on paper 26.5 x 18 (10½ x 7), a pencilled 'frame' 23.5 x 16.5 (9¼ x 6½); laid down on paper; faded ink inscription along the bottom edge *WILLIAM COWPER ESQ TAKEN FROM LIFE W HARVEY*; a hole by his right shoulder, some staining lower right.

Blue coat, yellow waistcoat and breeches; the head is also tinted, but the hands and desk are left as pencil outlines.

Collections: Presented by the Rev W.J. Loftie 1888.

Harvey drew the vignettes and portraits for Robert Southey's *Life and Works of William Cowper*, published in fifteen volumes 1835-37. NPG 806 is a copy, presumably from the engraving by W.C. Edwards, after the Abbott portrait NPG 2783; the blue tint of the coat disagrees with the green of the original. It was not engraved for the *Life and Works*, Romney's head being preferred, but the faded inscription matches the typeface used for the inscriptions on the portraits in those volumes.[1]

1 Cf. Russell 1963, f.p.245.

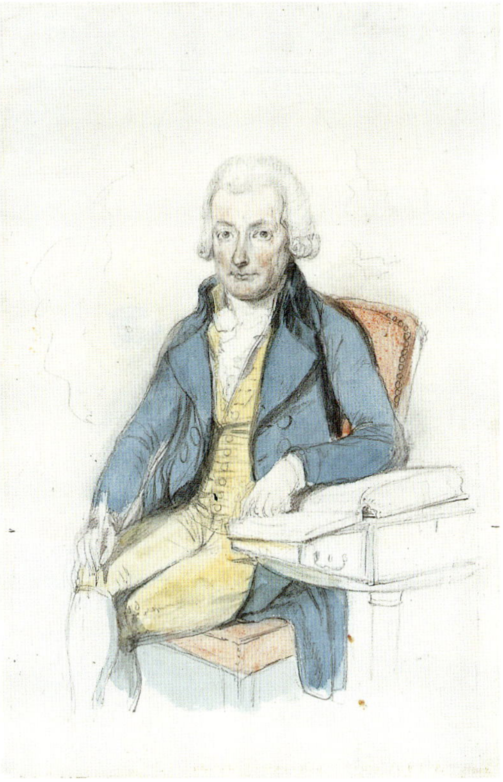

COWPER NPG *806*

1423 GEORGE ROMNEY 1792

Pastel on off-white laid paper 57 x 47 (22½ x 18½); 'repaired' by Nowlam, London, February-April 1905; labels on backing board:[1] *William Cowper The Poet / Drawn from the life / by George Romney / 1792*.

Grey eyes, wearing a white cap, and a grey-green coat; 'the face is a plain, everyday sort of face, with ruddy, weather-beaten cheeks, and a wide, gentle mouth. ... But out of this face glance a pair of eyes which change its whole expression; startled, speaking eyes.'[2]

Collections: William Hayley, by whom bequeathed to the Rev John Johnson (d.1833); his son, H.R. Vaughan Johnson, from whose widow, Hon Cecilia Vaughan Johnson, purchased 1905.

Engravings: W. Blake 1802; C. Watson 1805; Roffe 1814; J. Kennerley 1817; Radclyffe 1817; W. Holl sr. (small oval) 1819; anon. 1823; W. Darton 1823; W. Wise and G.W. Hutin 1825; H. Cook 1833; R. Bell 1834; L. Stocks 1835 from a drawing by William Harvey (elaborated to include his left hand on a closed book and a sofa arm beneath his right arm).

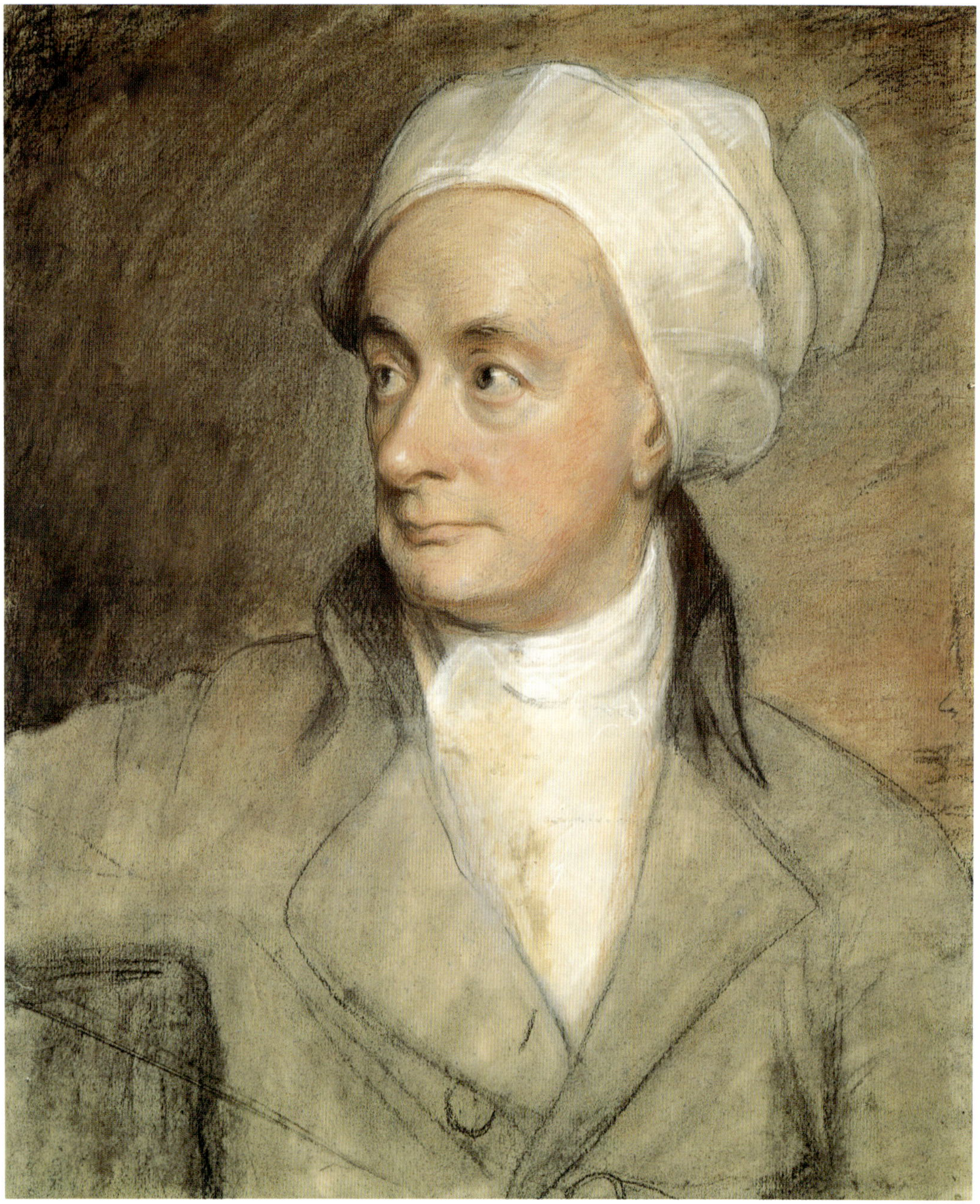

COWPER NPG *1423*

Exhibitions: NPE 1868(777); *British Portraits*, RA, 1956-57(665); *Master Drawings* 1993-95(38); *Romney*, Liverpool, NPG, 2002(137).

Reference: Romney 1830, pp.226-28; Ward & Roberts 1904, II, pp.34-35; Chamberlain 1910, pp.175-82; Russell 1963, pp.288-90.

The circumstances of this remarkable portrait are well documented in Cowper's letters. His portrait by Abbott (NPG 2783) being finished, Cowper and his companion Mary Unwins left Weston Underwood on 1 August 1792 for Eartham,[3] the Sussex home of his friend William Hayley, which they had reached by 5 August.[4] Romney had joined them by 16 August[5] and on 25 August Cowper announced that 'Romney has drawn me in crayons; by the suffrage of all here, extremely like'.[6] According to Hayley, for whom the portrait was made, Romney came to consider it 'as the nearest approach that he had ever made to a perfect representation of life and character'; he had much wanted to 'execute a portrait of a person so memorable, and in drawing it he was peculiarly desirous of making the nearest approach to life, that he possibly could: for this purpose he chose to make use of coloured crayons, a mode of painting in which he had indeed little experience'.[7] Hayley greatly admired the portrait, considering that Romney had produced 'a resemblance so powerful that spectators who contemplated [it] with the original by its side, thought it hardly possible for any similitude to be more striking or more exact'; but Hayley also allowed that for some 'more conversant with the colloquial, than with the poetic countenance of Cowper' the portrait might seem 'to border on extravagance of expression'.[8]

Cowper, who did not otherwise much care for portraiture, addressed a sonnet to Romney:[9]

To George Romney, Esq. on his picture of me in crayons, drawn at Eartham in the sixty-first year of my age, and in the months of August and September, 1792.

Romney! Expert infallibly to trace,
On chart or canvas, not the form alone,
And 'semblance, but, however faintly shown,
The mind's impression too on ev'ry face,
With strokes that time ought never to erase:
Thou hast so pencil'd mine, that though I own
The subject worthless, I have never known
The artist shining with superior grace.
But this I mark, that symptoms none of woe
In thy incomparable work appear:
Well! I am satisfied it should be so,
Since, on maturer thought, the cause is clear;
For in my looks what sorrow could'st thou see
While I was Hayley's guest, and sat to thee?

Both artist and poet had a melancholic cast of mind and Romney, said Hayley, had soon appreciated Cowper's 'genius, benevolence and ... misfortunes'.[10] Forty years later the poet Bernard Barton reflected that 'such a picture will hardly ever be taken again unless a mad painter should again have a mad poet for his sitter'. He had just seen the Abbott and Romney portraits, NPG 1423 and NPG 2783, hanging together in the Johnson's house; while he found the Abbott 'a beautifully executed painting, with a mild pleasing expression of countenance', it was the Romney 'that rivets your attention and engrosses your thought and feeling'.[11]

A copy of NPG 1423 by A.E. Dyer is in the County Hall, Hertford; another was made in 1905 by Frank Nowlan[12] and sold to B. Vaughan Johnson after the sale of NPG 1423; a miserable example belonged to W. Harvey of Peckham in the late nineteenth century. A watercolour copy by Romney's pupil Isaac Pocock, dated 1799,[13] was sold Christie's, 13 April 1878, lot

132, bought by John Murray. William Blake, who engraved NPG 1423 in 1802, also made a small copy of the head dated 1801 (private collection) and three others undated (Library of Congress, Washington; Widener Library, Harvard, and the Ashmolean Museum, Oxford);[14] he used Romney's head again for the tempera head of Cowper in the series of poets which he painted for William Hayley's study at Felpham (now in Manchester City Art Gallery).[15]

1 Stamped: *Hogarth picture frame maker to Her Majesty & HRH the Prince of Wales .. 96 Mount Street, Grosvenor Square London.*
2 D. Cecil, *The Stricken Deer*, 1930, p.15.
3 Cowper, *Letters*, IV, 1984, p.158; 27 July 1792, to Thomas Carwardine.
4 *Ibid.*, p.163; 5 August 1792, to Samuel Teedon. For Hayley, see NPG 662 (Walker *Regency*, I, pp.240-41, II, pls.552-53).
5 *Ibid.*, p.173, 16 August 1792, to John Newton.
6 *Ibid.*, p.182, 26 August 1792, to Lady Hesketh.
7 Hayley 1809, pp.177, 181.
8 *Ibid.*, pp.177-78.
9 Cowper, *Letters*, IV, 1984, p.226, 28 October 1792, to William Hayley (see also pp.192, 217 and 222).
10 Hayley 1809, p.177. On 28 November 1792 Cowper confessed to Romney that he had been 'a poor creature ever since I saw you; dispirited to the greatest degree and incapable of mental exertion' (Cowper, *Letters*, IV, 1984, p.245).
11 Letter to John Linnell, 8 August 1838 (A.T. Story, *John Linnell*, 1892, p.193); I owe this remarkable quotation to Alex Kidson.
12 Nowlan made his copy between May and August 1905; from February he had been conserving NPG 1423 (letters NPG archive). Charles Fairfax Murray had offered to make a copy for Johnson if the portrait was bought by the NPG (B. Vaughan Johnson to L. Cust, 17 August 1905).
13 Copied at Eartham, see SSB 93/2.
14 M. Butlin, *Paintings and Drawings of William Blake*, 1981, nos.351-54; pls.457-60. Russell 1963, pp.301-02.
15 Butlin, *op.cit.*, no.343, pl.452.

ICONOGRAPHY

Cowper was a reluctant sitter. After sitting to Abbott and Romney within a period of eight weeks he wrote (29 Aug. 1792): 'I have now I think been sufficiently a subject of the pencil, and comfort myself frequently with the thought that I have no more pennance to undergo of that kind'; a month later (24 Sept. 1792) he was still more emphatic: 'I have now been sufficiently copied, and hope to have nothing more to do with painters', and five months later (10 Feb. 1793) he was being perfectly realistic: 'The painters having made two good hits, it would be folly to try them again, therefore I purpose never to do it' [Cowper, *Letters*, IV, 1984, pp.186-87, 200, 291].

Cowper's portraiture has been scrupulously surveyed in Russell 1963, pp.285-307.

A portrait of Cowper as a child with a bow and arrow, was mentioned in a letter of 13 October 1801 from John Johnson to William Hayley (Russell 1963, p.303). A miniature of him as a child was known in 1834 and another had belonged to Theadora Cowper (Russell 1963, p.303; W.B. Donne to Scharf, 22 May 1868, NPG archive).

1791 Drawing by John Higgins, profile with a tie wig and cravat, from a shadow picture (illus. *Saturday Review of Literature*, 28 November 1931; see Russell 1963, pp.285-86).

c.1791 Silhouette by James Andrews, bust length. Cowper Museum, Olney (illus. Russell 1963, f.p.286).

1792 Painting by Lemuel Francis Abbott, see NPG 2783 and NPG 806.

1792 Painting by George Romney, see NPG 1423.

*'Yet once more is my patience to be exercised', wrote Cowper (5-6 October 1793), 'and once more I am made to wish that my face had been made moveable, to put on and take off at pleasure, so as to be portable in a band-box and sent to the artist' (*Letters, *IV, 1984, p.411).*

1793 Drawing by Thomas Lawrence, half length with cap (Garlick 1964, p.222; Russell 1963, pp.290-98). Private collection; commissioned by Samuel Rose. Exhibited RA 1795(596). Engraved F. Bartolozzi 1799 (a private plate, published in 1805; illus. Russell 1963, f.p.294); W. Blake 1802; C. Watson 1806 and many times thereafter; plates by W. Ridley 1803 and D. Lundin 1803 assemble the Lawrence head with, apparently, the Abbott wig and coat. Replica in the Cowper Museum, Olney. Pencil copy by John Constable 1804 (Louvre; illus. G. Reynolds, *Early Paintings and Drawings of Constable*, 1996, pl.239); another, anon., NPG reference collection (D159).

A small drawing by Lawrence of a profile head of Cowper, in the Denham Album, Yale University Library, was probably made at the same time.

Posthumous

1801-c.1804 Watercolour and tempera painting by William Blake, see NPG 1423.

c.1813 Painting by John Jackson, half-length seated at table. Christie's, 16 July 1998, lot 44, from Panshanger (Russell 1963, pp.298-301). Curiously described in the Panshanger cat., 1885, p.229, as 'after a chalk drawing from life'; a Cowper descendant alleged that Jackson had been dissatisfied with his copy of the Abbott portrait and had proceeded to draw his own (note of 26 April 1966; NPG archive). Exhibited NPE 1867(807). Engraved J. Bull 1825; W. Raddon 1824 (variant).

A version engraved H. Meyer 1816, 'from an Original Picture by F. Abbot in the Possession of the Revd John Johnson LLD'; also engraved W. Holl 1835; S. Freeman 1834; G. Stodart (head only).

Posthumous tributes also include a model by W.C. Marshall for an unexecuted monument in Poets' Corner, Westminster Abbey, exhibited RA 1849(1232); memorial windows incorporating the figure of Cowper in Westminster Abbey (by Clayton & Bell 1875) and in SS.Peter & Paul, Olney (1973); a medallion by J. Nesfield Forsyth for All Saints, Lower Edmonton, exhibited RA 1889(2079); and a late and sorry-looking Wedgwood bust, illus. *Connoisseur*, XXIII, 1909, p.61.

DOUBTFUL PORTRAIT

Pastel by John Russell, illus. Williamson 1894, f.p.54, as Cowper, but copied from Rosalba Carriera's Philip, Duke of Wharton.

CRAMER, Wilhelm 1746-99

Violinist and composer; b. Mannheim, he came to London in 1772 on the invitation of J.C. Bach and led the Handel Commemoration Concerts in Westminster Abbey in 1784 and 1787.

6198 THOMAS HARDY 1794

Canvas 75.5 x 62 (29¾ x 24½) lined; *pentimenti* above his right shoulder; the background area very thin and retouched.

Brown eyes, powdered hair, a wart on his left cheek; wearing a grey coat; pink drapery across the back of the green-upholstered chair.

Collections: John Bland 1794;[1] Christie's, New York, 21 May 1992, lot 238; Lane Fine Art, from whom purchased 1993.

Engravings: T. Hardy 1794 (as in the collection of J. Bland, the publisher of the engraving); J.F. Schröter.

Exhibition: RA 1794(240).

NPG 6198 was presumably commissioned by John Bland. An old black-painted inscription, *William Cramer / Painted by T Hardy 1794*, on a batten, said to be part of the original stretcher, is attached to the back of the frame.

1 Music publisher, see *Handel*, NPG, 1985, no.245.

ICONOGRAPHY

c.1770? Painting by an unknown artist (probably German), seated three-quarter length, playing the violin. Royal College of Music, London; from Christie's, 19 December 1974, lot 1, and William

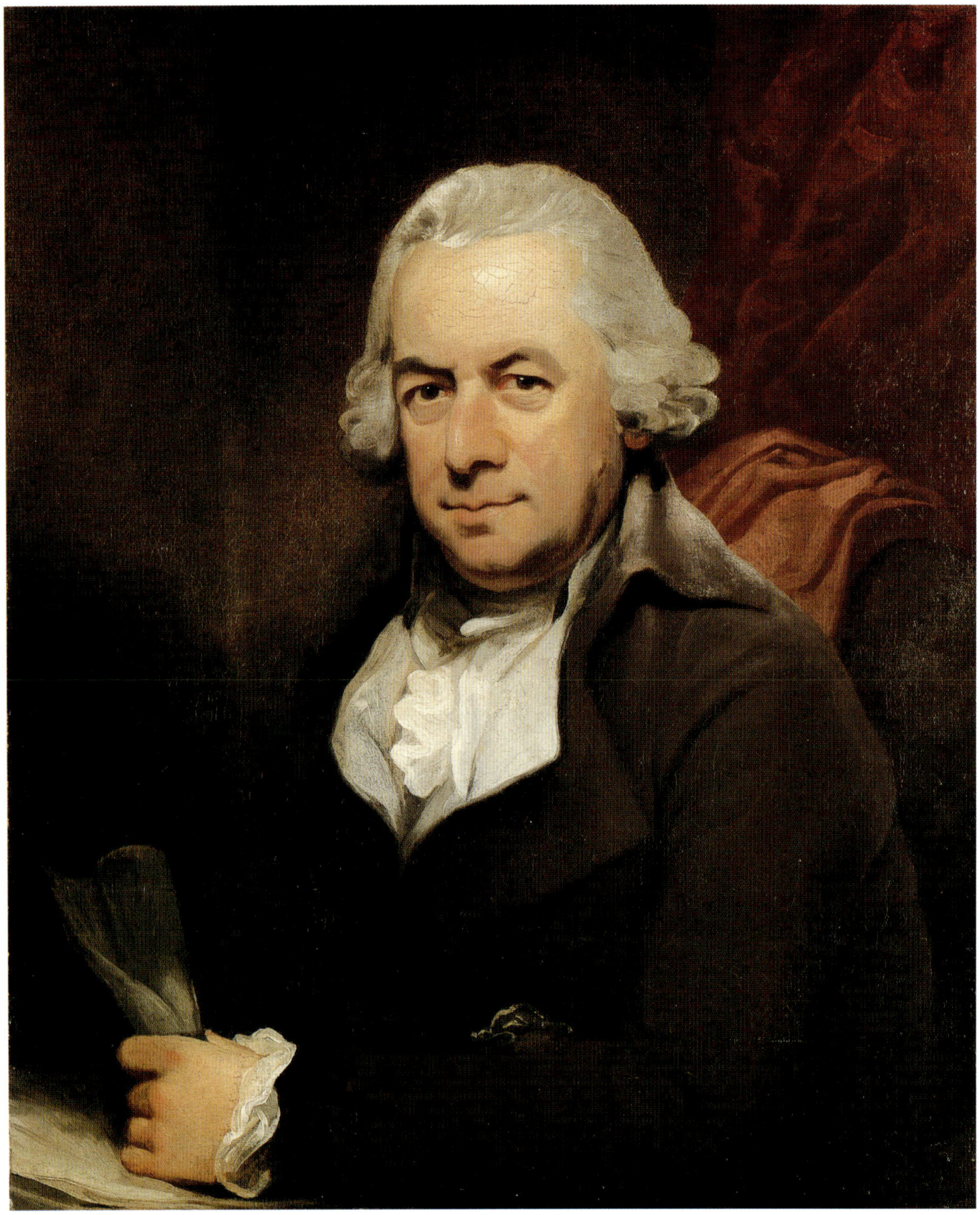

CRAMER NPG 6198

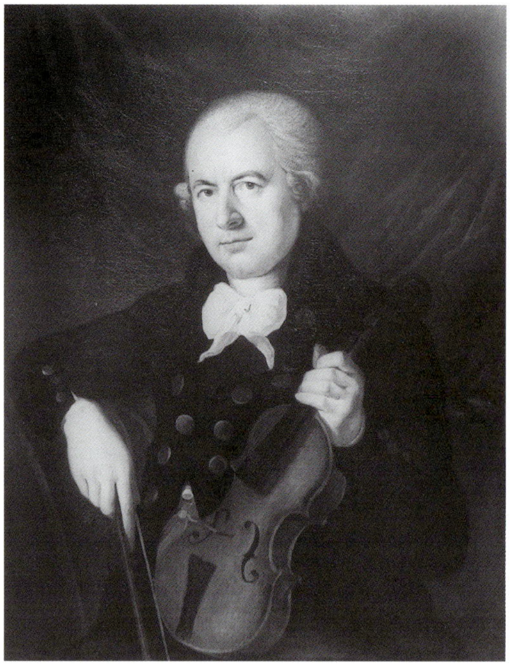

CRAMER unknown artist c.1770? (Royal College of Music, London)

Hill (violin makers) 1917 (when described as 'in the style of Gainsborough'). Presumably also the portrait of Cramer exhibited *Music Loan Exhibition*, London, 1904, lent W.E. Hill & Sons (cat., p.228, unrealistically attributed to William Davison, fl.1813–43).

1778 Drawing by James Roberts, half-length oval in profile. Private collection 1984 (Phillip's, 4 June 1979, lot 84).

1794 Painting by Thomas Hardy, see NPG 6198.

1797 Miniature by George Place, half-length oval, exhibited RA 1797(1025). Engraved T. Bragge 1803.

CRANLEY, George, 1st Baron, see ONSLOW

CREWE, John Crewe, 1st Baron 1742–1829

MP 1765–1802; in Italy 1761–62; Dilettante 1764; founder member of the Whig Club 1784; Baron 1806; the friend and patron of Fox, at whose funeral he was observed to shiver 'from head to foot'.

2076 see Groups, *Mr Fox and his Friends* by WILLIAM LANE c.1813

ICONOGRAPHY

1761 Painting by Joshua Reynolds. Untraced (Mannings 2000, no.447).

1762 Painting by Pompeo Batoni,* three-quarter length standing, a bust of Minerva behind him. Private collection (Clark 1985, no.248). Painted in Rome, where Crewe arrived in December 1761.

1765 Painting by George Stubbs, mounted on a bay hunter. Christie's, New York, 4 June 1982, lot 176; with the Crewe family until 1969.

1777 Two drawings by John Downman, half length. Fitzwilliam Museum, Cambridge (1806, 1807).

1789 Painting by Joshua Reynolds, half length. Private collection (Mannings 2000, no.448).

c.1810 Painting by Thomas Lawrence, half length. Private collection (Garlick 1989, no.221). Engraved W. Say* (the proof in the British Museum, 1852.10.9.1333, identified as *Lord Crewe 1819*).

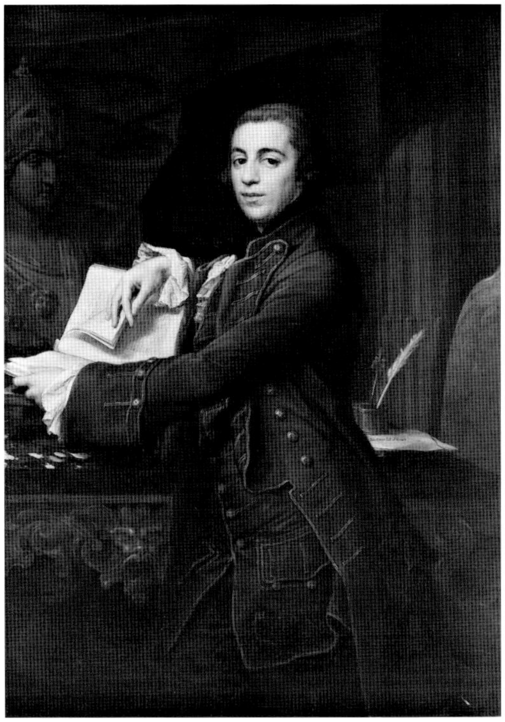

1st Baron CREWE by Pompeo Batoni 1762 (untraced)

1811 Portrait by William Lane, exhibited RA 1811(795, 'Lord Crewe and Dudley North Esq'), presumably the source for the head by Lane in *Mr Fox and his Friends*, see below.

c.1813 Drawing by William Lane, *Mr Fox and his Friends*, see Groups, NPG 2076.

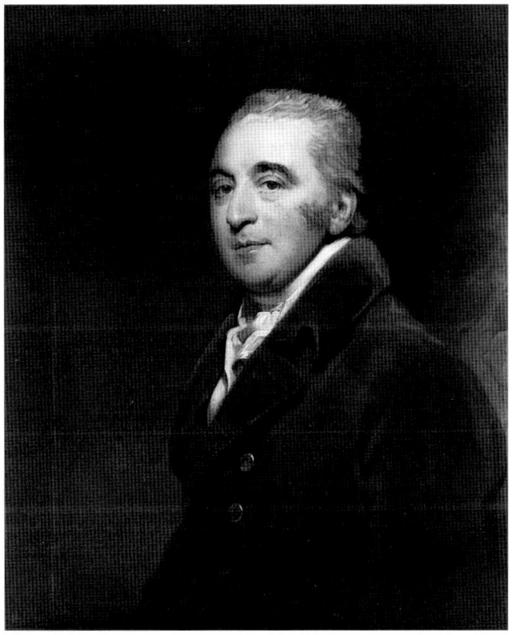

1st Baron CREWE W. Say after Thomas Lawrence c.1810 (NPG D 1535)

Undated A painting by George Romney and a drawing by Henry Edridge formerly belonged to the Crewe family at Madeley - the latter was possibly one of the drawings of the five friends of Fox from the St Anne's Hill House sale, see Lansdowne 1796, Upper Ossory 1798, and Groups NPG 2076.

Undated Etching by J.G. Wood, half-length profile.

CUMBERLAND, Richard 1732-1811

Writer and diplomat; crown agent for Nova Scotia, Ulster secretary in Ireland 1760 and unofficial ambassador to Spain 1780-81; author of *Anecdotes of Eminent Painters in Spain* 1782, some forty plays of uneven merit, including *The West Indian* 1771, and three novels, of which *Henry* appeared in 1795.

'an old gentleman of distinguished appearance, ... [his] grey brows gave a dullish expression to his eyes, the nose prominent and well-shaped, was more than usually distant from the somewhat compressed mouth, which relaxed into a smile of the blandest courtesy as he peered round the room ...' (Horace Smith, 1847).

19 GEORGE ROMNEY c.1771-76

Canvas 126 x 100 (49½ x 39½) lined; cleaned 2001; x-radiography shows his right hand was first painted hanging down limply, and the book painted over a roll of paper.

Grey eyes, grey powdered hair, wearing a crimson coat edged with brown fur and a pale yellow waistcoat with a green and gold trim; his chair is covered with an ochre cloth; on the table, covered by a turkey rug, a light blue book and a bronze group.[1]

Collections: By descent to the sitter's daughter-in-law, Lady Albinia Cumberland (d.1850);[2] her son, Captain Richard Cumberland, from whom purchased 1857.

Exhibitions: *Romney*, Kenwood, 1961(17); *Faces as Art*, NPG, 1976; *Romney*, Liverpool, NPG, 2002(37).

Reference: Ward & Roberts 1904, II, p.37.

Cumberland had initially regarded Romney as 'a second Corregio', believing he would rank 'with the first masters of the highest province and best age of painting'.[3] Romney 'was uniformly kind and affectionate to me', he wrote, 'and certainly I was zealous in my services to him'.[4] Their friendship latterly may have cooled, but Cumberland was to write Romney's obituary for the *European Magazine*. He sat to Romney several times for his portrait (see below), NPG 19 being the most formal, showing the writer in search of inspiration. Cumberland's wife and children also appeared in a series of Romney half-lengths of c.1772 and 1776-81.[5]

The dating of NPG 19 is difficult, as Kidson has demonstrated.[6] There are related compositional studies dateable 1770-71 in three Romney sketchbooks;[7] some years later, after Romney's Italian sojourn of 1773-75, John Romney listed a 'half length' [i.e. 127 x 101] of Cumberland in 1776[8] (though no sittings are recorded that year). In NPG 19 the head and left hand are relatively tightly executed, while the right hand and the upper left area have been vigorously reworked in a broad, loose manner. This disparity suggests the picture evolved over a period of time; it may have been the portrait exhibited in 1771, reworked after the Italian visit.[9]

In 1859, as they considered NPG 19 in the newly opened National Portrait Gallery, Lord Lansdowne told Sir William Stirling Maxwell how Cumberland was known to have clapped and hissed at the same time while watching a new play by a rival; his professional jealousy was well known (as befitted a man who furnished Sheridan with the character of Sir Fretful Plagiary in *The Critic*).[10]

1 Ill-defined, but possibly a casual reference to the Ludovisi Mars. R. Asleson (in A. Kidson ed., *Essays on Romney*, 2002, p.164) believes it to be from 'the central figure in the ... Laocoön'.
2 According to her son (letter of 28 February 1856; NPG archive), she had kept the portrait 'for about sixty years in the apartments in Hampton Court Palace'.
3 Northcote, *Reynolds*, 1813, p.145; Romney 1830, p.313.
4 Cumberland, *Memoirs*, 1807, II, p.214. Odes to Romney by Cumberland of 1776 are printed in part in Romney 1830, pp.313-19, and Ward & Roberts 1904, II, pp.37-38. Romney is said to have given Cumberland portraits and in 1781 was able to lend him money (Chamberlain 1910, pp.52-53).
5 Five listed in Ward & Roberts 1904, II, pp.38-39, of which *Mrs Cumberland and her Son* and *George Cumberland* are now in the Tate Gallery. Another of *The Misses Cumberland* exhibited *Romney* 2002(38).
6 *Romney* 2002, pp.91-93.
7 Two in the Royal Academy, 781a & 781b; NPG archive sketchbook, p.35; see Kidson, *Romney* 2002, pp.92, 93n13.
8 Ward & Roberts 1904, II, p.37.
9 NPG 19 has been variously dated in the past, e.g. Ward & Roberts 1904, II, p.37 as probably 1776; Chamberlain 1910, p.332 as 'shortly after his return from Italy'; *Romney*, Kenwood, 1961(17) as c.1768; Cross 2000, p.39, as c.1772.
10 Note by Stirling Maxwell attached to the back of a portrait, said to be of Cumberland, still at Pollok House (see Doubtful Portrait); the play in question was perhaps *The Will* by Frederick Reynolds (see S.T. Williams, *Richard Cumberland*, 1917, p.258).

ICONOGRAPHY

c.1768-1771 Paintings by George Romney.

a) half length* in blue coat, a quill in his right hand. Huntington Art Collections, San Marino, Calif. (44.103; *Huntington 2001*, no.90). Exhibited NPE 1867(589) lent E. Clough Taylor. Possibly b) below.

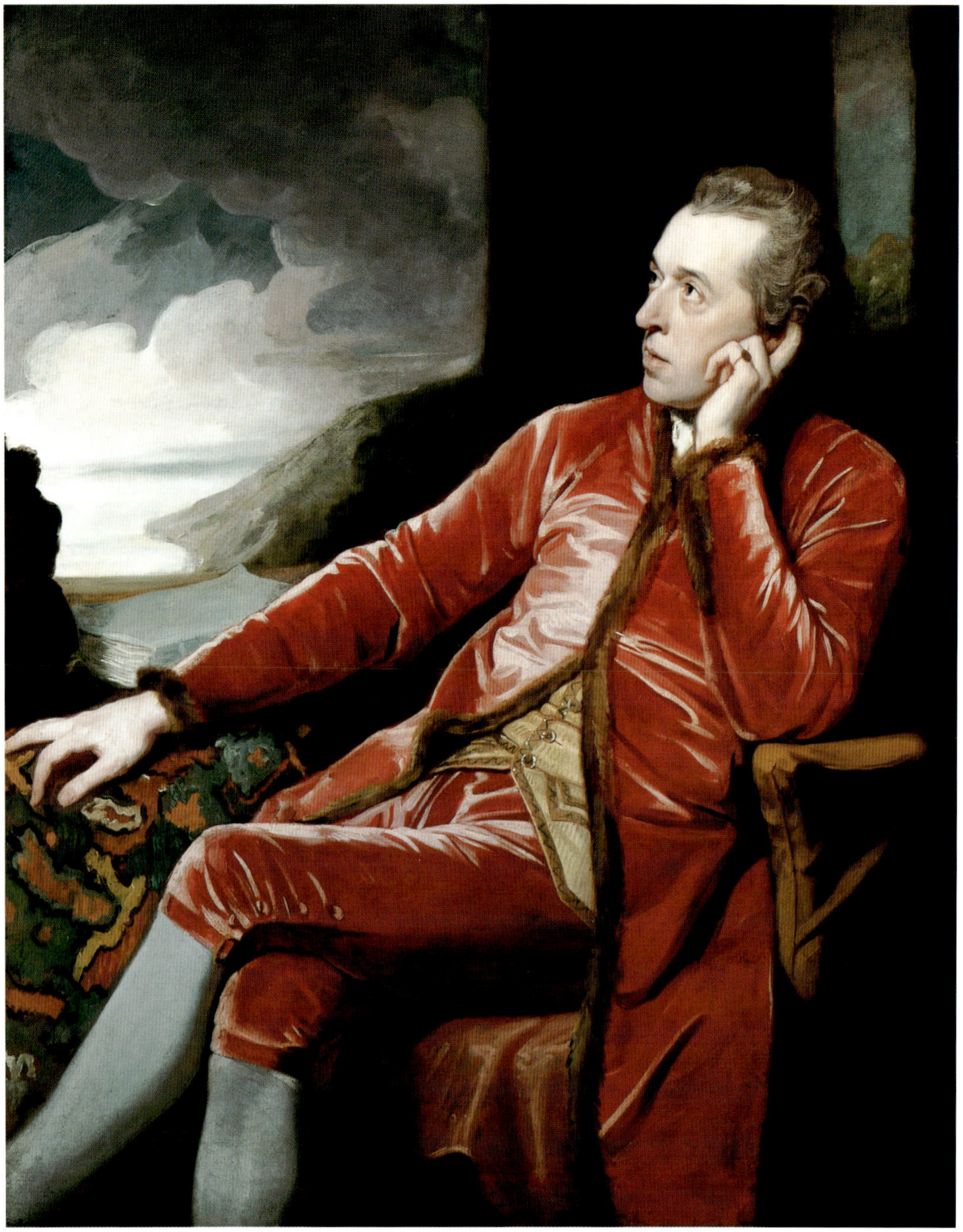

CUMBERLAND NPG 19

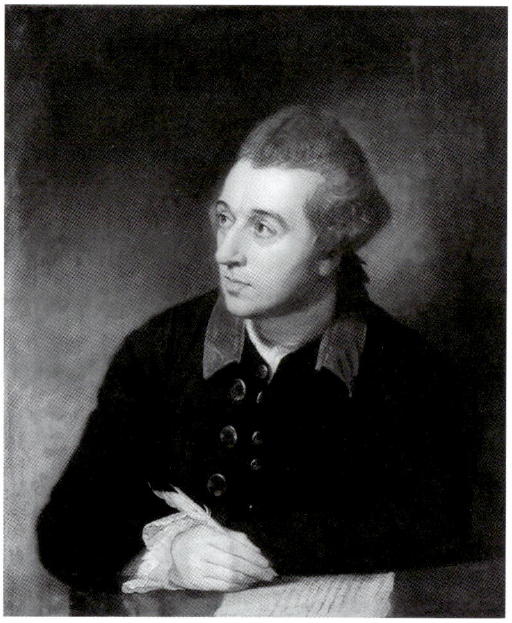

CUMBERLAND by George Romney c.1768-71
(Huntington Art Collections, San Marino, California)

b) wearing a 'blue coat with a red cape'. Seen in Romney's studio (together with *The Leigh Family* of c.1767-68) by Garrick who thought it 'very like', but advised that he must be given 'something to do; put a pen in his hand, a paper on his table, and make him a poet' (Cumberland, *Memoirs*, 1807, II, pp.213-14, where he also records paying Romney ten guineas for a half-length portrait). Garrick had little respect for Cumberland as a dramatist (see Northcote, *Reynolds*, 1813, pp.144-45: 'Damn his dish-clout face!').

c) toga'd half length, showing the left hand. Engraved W. Evans 1805 and J. Hopwood (oval) 1806. Tentatively associated by Ward & Roberts with the portrait Garrick saw (see b above). A version, probably not autograph, is in the Tate Gallery (T63), from the collection of Capt. T.B. Cumberland.

d) toga'd half length, head almost in profile. New York art market 1927 (Ward & Roberts 1904, II, p.37, no.2). Engraved V. Green 1771; W. Ridley (oval) 1797; J. Rogers 1825. See 1771 below.

e) exhibited SA 1771(142 'a gentleman three-quarters' [which would usually imply 76 x 63, but which might, exceptionally, refer to the length of the figure, see Kidson, *Romney* 2002, p.93n14]). Identified as 'Mr Cumberland, author of the West Indian, Comedy' by Walpole, who also commented that 'the nose seems quite to project' (*Wal. Soc.*, XXVII, 1939, p.76). Possibly d) above, or NPG 19.

f) see NPG 19.

1806 Painting by Joseph Clover, half-length seated. Untraced. Engraved E. Scriven 1806 from a picture in the possession of Henry Fry. Probably the portrait exhibited RA 1806(195).

1806-11 Painting by Joseph Clover, half length. Tunbridge Wells Council. Engraved E. Scriven 1814 as in the possession of the sitter's daughter, from a drawing by J. Jackson.

c.1809 Drawing by William Lane, half length, engraved J. Neagle 1802; W. Ridley 1809 (*European Mag.*); R. Cooper; Holl (small oval).

DOUBTFUL PORTRAIT

A small half-length oval, attributed to Romney, at Pollok House, Glasgow (no.56).

DALE, David 1739-1806

Philanthropist and industrialist; pioneer of the Glasgow cotton trade, he built mills at New Lanark, initially in partnership with Richard Arkwright; a benevolent administrator and a preacher in the free church which he founded.

'In person, Mr Dale was short and corpulent ... He was of a cheerful temperament, of easy access, lively and communicative; and, when in company of friends, he freely relaxed all formal restraints' (Andrew Liddell, 1855).

5810 JOHN HENNING 1803

Glass paste 6 (2⅜) high; incised on the truncation: *David Dale Glasgow / John Henning fec*[?] *1803*; an illegible ink inscriptions on the original backing begins: *For Mr Kelly ...* [1]

Collections: [Kelly, see above]; purchased from Daniel Shackleton, Edinburgh, 1985.

Engravings: J. Thomson 1822; Freeman (half length) after 1806.

Dale withdrew from active business in 1800, retiring to Rosebank, near Glasgow; in 1801 Henning came to Glasgow, where he was patronised by both Dale and Scott Moncrieff, then directors of the Royal Bank of Scotland.[2]

1 A later early 19th-century inscription on the paper lining reads: *David Dale Esqre. / Henning Fecit / This beautiful ... was/ engraved by Thomson, and / published by Henry Fisher/ Caxton, London 1822.*
2 *Henning* 1977, n.p..

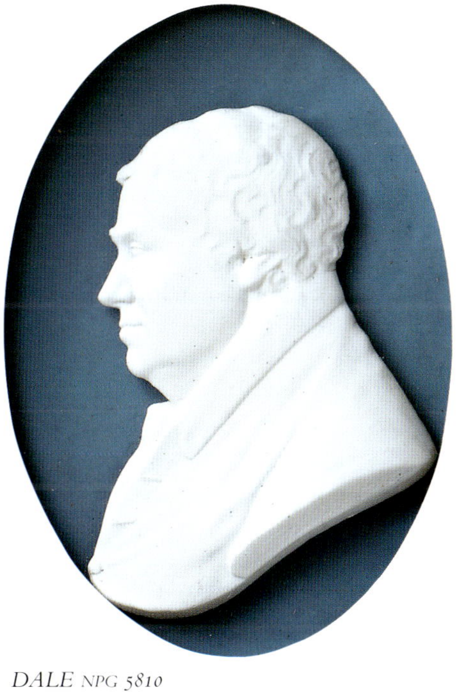

DALE NPG *5810*

ICONOGRAPHY

A small portrait 'of no great artistical merit, was etched, which, however, is said to be a fair likeness. His name was not given, but the portrait was entitled, 'The Benevolent Magistrate'. It was copied into 'Kay's Edinburgh Portraits' [but not in the NPG library copy] and also into 'Stewart's Views of Glasgow in Former Times'.' (*Biographical Dictionary of Eminent Scotsmen*, V, 1855, p.174).

1791 Medallion by James Tassie (Gray 1894, no.103, pl.xii), example in the Scottish NPG (PG 2219). Engraved anon. (half length; the NPG copy bears the pencilled date *1797*).

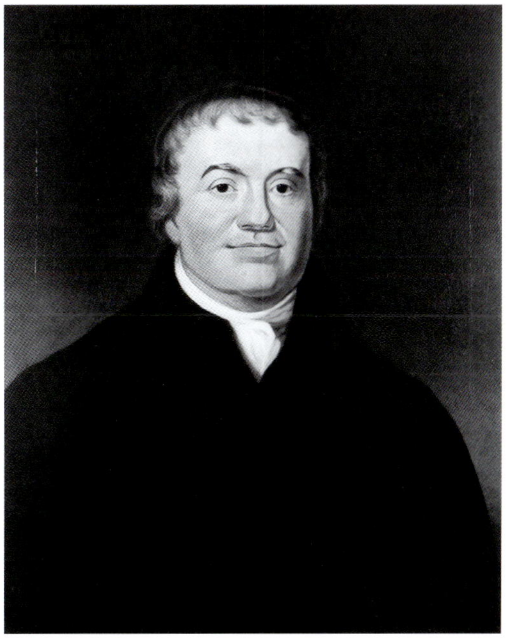

DALE unknown artist c.1800? (Glasgow Art Gallery)

c.1800? Unattributed painting,★ half length. Glasgow AG (333). Previously attributed to Hugh William Williams.

1803 Medallion by John Henning, see NPG 5810.

DANCE, Nathaniel 1735-1811

Painter; s. of the architect George Dance sr. (the architect George Dance jr. was his yr. bro.); in Italy 1755-65; foundation member of the RA 1768, exhibiting 1769-76; retired professionally in 1776, and m. 1783 a wealthy widow, Mrs Dummer (née Bishop, of Parham); resigned from the RA 1790; MP 1790-1811; by royal licence took the name of Holland, 4 July 1800; Bt 27 November 1800.

'reserved in his habits, but very accessible to good humour, and though he could not be unconscious of his superior talents and knowledge, he had none of the silly pride charged upon him' (John Taylor, 1811).

3626 SELF PORTRAIT c.1773

Canvas 75.5 x 63 (29¾ x 24¾) lined and cleaned 1977; there remain slight traces of a previous oval slip frame; the verso of the original canvas bears an early inscription: *Portrait of / Nathl Dance R.A. / afterwards / Sir Nathl. Holland Bart ./ Painted / by himself.*

Brown eyes, grey hair, wearing a white neckcloth, green waistcoat and a deep red coat with brown fur collar.

Collections: By descent to Miss Mary Sibyll Dance (great granddaughter of the sitter's brother, George Dance jr.), by whom bequeathed 1948.

Exhibitions: *Kauffmann* 1968(3626); *George Dance*, Geffrye Museum, 1972(7); *Dance* 1977(35).

NPG 3626 was dated c.1773 by Goodreau on stylistic grounds.[1] Dorothy Stroud had previously associated it with the self portrait requested by the Society of Dilettanti in 1777;[2] Dance had been elected to the Society that year and in May it was agreed that he should be allowed 'to present the Society with his own Picture painted by Himself, Sir J. Reynolds Painter to the Society having waved His right to paint the same', but the portrait had not been delivered when Dance resigned in 1784.[3]

1 *Dance* 1977, no.35.
2 *George Dance*, 1971, p.93, pl.22, and see *George Dance*, Geffrye Museum, 1972, no.7.
3 L. Cust, *History of the Society of Dilettanti*, 1898, p.224.

ICONOGRAPHY

1760 A self portrait for his actor brother, James Love Dance, was proposed while Dance was in Rome (Dance letters, 2 November and 17 December 1760; RIBA).

1764 Drawing by Angelica Kauffmann, half length, porte-crayon in right hand. Victoria and Albert

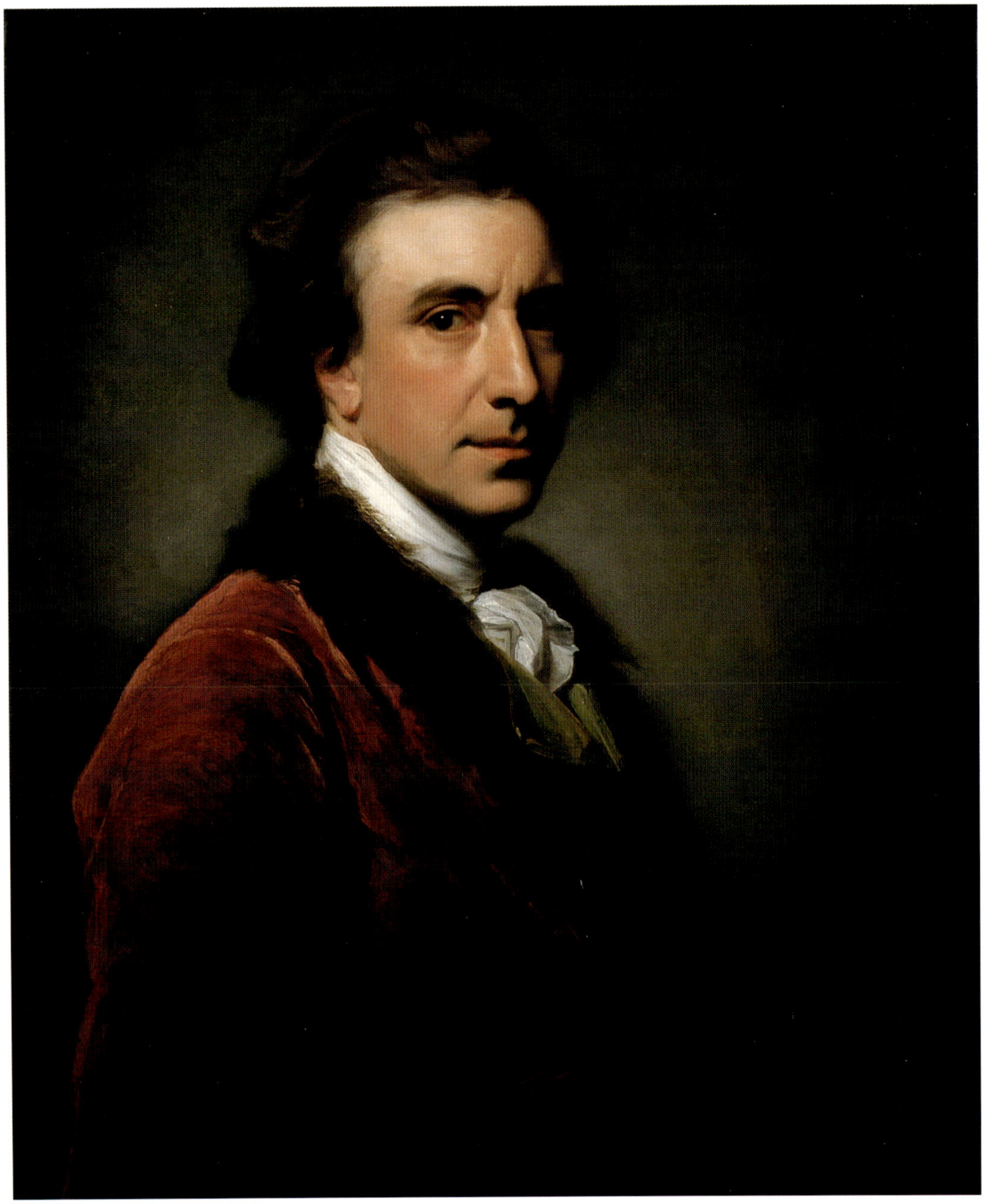

DANCE NPG *3626*

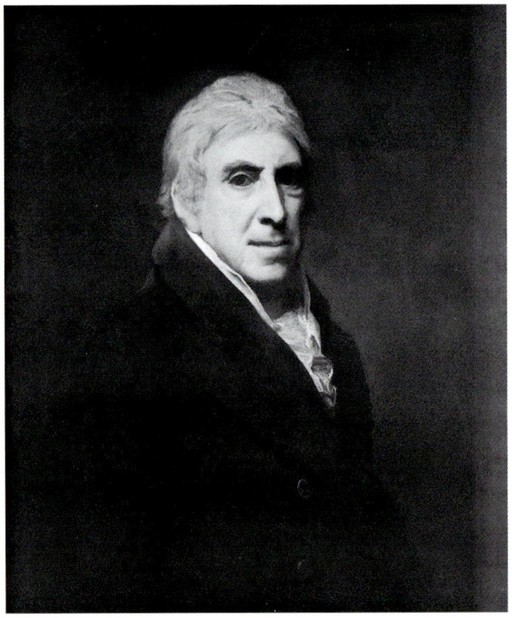

DANCE Self portrait c.1800 (untraced)

Museum (Vallardi sketchbook, E.384.1927, no.40; illus. *Burl. Mag.*, CXIX, 1977, p.109). Dance was a close friend of Kauffmann in Rome, and the identification appears plausible.

c.1773 Painting, self portrait, see NPG 3626.

c.1800 Painting,* self portrait, half length, white hair. Sotheby's 21 March 1945, lot 85, from the collection of Mary Sibyll Dance (see *Connoisseur*, LXV, 1923, p.30; letters in NPG archive). The features may be reconciled with those in NPG 3626 and Dance was still occasionally painting as late as 1807 (Farington, 2 November 1807).

DOUBTFUL PORTRAIT

Bust-length 'self portrait', exhibited NPE 1868(770) lent Lady Abinger.

DANCER, Daniel 1716-94

Miser, of Pinner, who inherited eighty acres in Middlesex; ate one meal a day, bound his feet in straw, while his house stood unrepaired for fifty years; d. attended by Maria, Lady Tempest, who inherited his wealth but died soon after, having caught a chill while nursing him; Mr Boffin (*Our Mutual Friend*) affected much admiration for him.

4369 RICHARD COOPER c.1790?

Pencil on paper 15 x 12.5 (5⅞ x 4⅞), some staining round the edges and a general fading; a horizontal split in the paper runs through his shoulder; inscribed/ signed, in pencil, verso: *Danl Dance the Miser / Rd Cooper delt.*

Collections: Presented by James Byam Shaw 1964.

Engravings (all reversed and all omitting his left hand): J. Chapman (oval) 1801; anon. (oval) published by James Cundee 1806 (an accompanying vignette shows Lady Tempest visiting him); R. Page 1821.

The quality of this mean drawing seems appropriate. The identity may be confirmed by the posthumous engravings, none of which, however, names the artist. The *Rd Cooper* named in the inscription was probably the miniaturist Richard Cooper who exhibited at the RA between 1793 and 1799. An extended engraving by G. Scott, published in 1805, shows Dancer three-quarter length seated in a sparse interior, his left hand covering coins on a table.

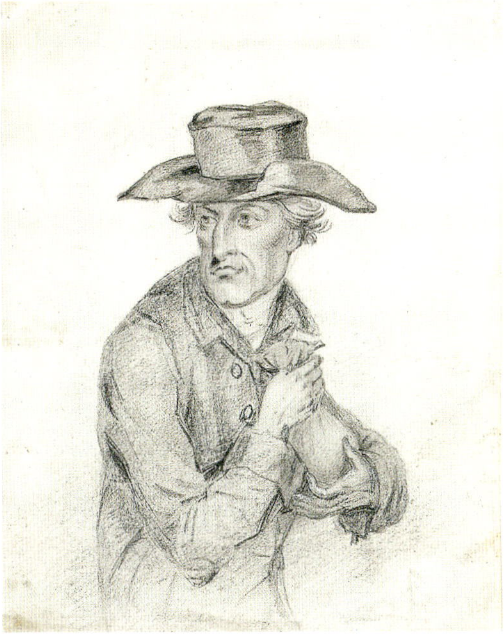

DANCER NPG *4369*

DOUBTFUL PORTRAIT

Unattributed pen and wash drawing, possibly late eighteenth-century (NPG reference collection, D2132), a whole-length scraggy, miserly figure in a run-down interior, inscribed in pencil *Daniel Dancer*.

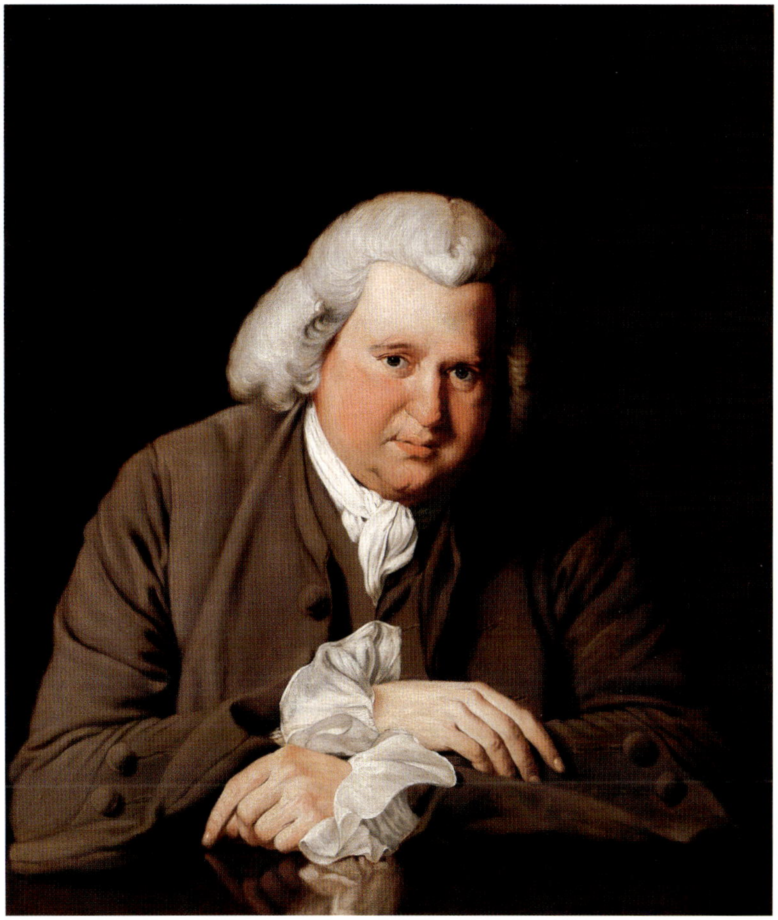

DARWIN NPG *88*

DARWIN, Erasmus 1731-1802

Physician, scientist and poet; practised in Lichfield 1756-81 and in Derby from 1783; FRS 1761; co-founder with Matthew Boulton of the Lunar Society in Birmingham 1766; wrote the didactic poem, *The Botanic Garden* 1789-92; grandfather of Charles Darwin.

'Darwin, never handsome or personally graceful, with extremely impeded utterance; with hard features or a rough surface; older much in appearance than in reality; lame and clumsy!' (Anna Seward, 1781).

'He was somewhat above middle size, his form athletic, and inclined to corpulence; his limbs too heavy for exact proportion. The traces of a severe small pox; features, and countenance, which, when they were animated by social pleasure, were rather saturnine than sprightly; a stoop in the shoulders ... gave, at that early period of life, an appearance of nearly twice the years he bore' (Anna Seward, 1804).

Abbreviation

Keynes 1994: M. Keynes, 'Portraits of Erasmus Darwin, FRS, by Joseph Wright, James Rawlinson and William Coffee', *Notes and Records, Royal Society, London*, 48, 1, 1994, pp.69-84

88 after JOSEPH WRIGHT of Derby [1770]

Canvas 75.5 x 63 (29¾ x 24¾); lined; cleaned 1977.

Grey eyes, white powdered wig, wearing a white neck-scarf and shirt and a dull grey-green coat with matching buttons.

Collections: The sitter's illegitimate daughter, Mary Parker (d.1859);[1] Anna Maria Jerome [née Day], from whom purchased, through her cousin Josephine Vickery, 1859.[2]

Exhibitions: *Regency Portraits*, Kenwood, 1986; *Apples to Atoms* 1986-87; *Darwin und Darwinismus*, Dresden, 1994(2/3); *Romantic Icons*, Grasmere, 1999(8).

Reference: Nicolson 1968, under no.51; Keynes 1994, p.72.

NPG 88 is not of prime quality; in 1860 it was plausibly suggested that it could be by James Rawlinson of Derby who 'was very successful in his copies' of Wright's work.[3] Wright's original portrait, now in Darwin College, Cambridge,[4] was described by Anna Seward as 'a simply contemplative portrait of the most perfect resemblance';[5] since it was not listed in Wright's account book it was conceivably painted for the sitter in payment for medical treatment.[6]

Another contemporary version, descended from the sitter's brother, William Darwin, is in a private collection;[7] a weak version (wearing a grey suit, the arms resting on a closed book) is in the Johnson Birthplace Museum, Lichfield. The Wedgwood medallion and the relief in Lichfield Cathedral, described below, were based on the Wright head.

1 Her mother was Mary Parker (1753-1820), who m. Joseph Day of Birmingham in 1782; see note 2.

2 Scharf sketched the portrait on 10 November 1859 'at Mrs Vickery's' (TSB 3/49). Josephine Vickery wrote to the NPG (12 December 1859): 'it would be difficult for me to give any information or particulars as to relationship - of the late owner - by letter but I should be happy to give you a Viva Voce explication'. A.P. Booth told Scharf that the NPG picture came from 'Mrs A.M. Day probably the wife of a son or a Daughter' of the Mr Day who had married Mary Parker (23 November 1860; NPG archive), see note 1. Elizabeth Greaves confirmed that Mary Parker had had a portrait of Erasmus Darwin by Wright which she gave to a relative and which was sold to the NPG (letter to Charles Darwin, 14 December 1877; Down House MSS).

3 P. Booth to Scharf, 23 February 1860 (NPG archive); the same letter said that Mrs Booth 'remembers her Mother saying that a copy of Wright's own portrait (with a broad hat) by Rawlinson was equal to the original, & she was herself an artist & a woman of superiour taste & talent'.

4 Nicolson 1968, no.50; exhibited *Wright* 1990(144); by descent from the sitter's second illegitimate daughter, Susan Parker (Mrs Hadley, 1772-1856) and Charles Darwin, see Keynes 1994, pp.71-2.

5 A. Seward, *Erasmus Darwin,* 1804, p. 21.

6 Keynes 1994, p.71. The portrait was engraved as an oval by W. Bromley 1795 (another state lettered H. Wheelwright), *from an original drawing*; by J.T. Wedgwood in 1820 *from a Picture by Wright in the possession of Mrs Darwin*; M. Alpin 1825.

7 Nicolson 1968, no.51.

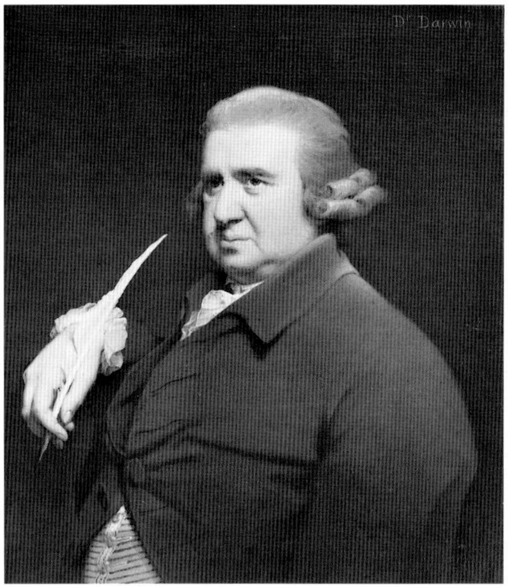

DARWIN by Joseph Wright of Derby 1792 (Private Collection)

ICONOGRAPHY

1770 Painting by Joseph Wright of Derby, see NPG 88.

1780 Wedgwood medallion attributed to William Hackwood, after the Wright portrait of 1770 (illus. Reilly 1973, p.118).

1783 Enamel on Wedgwood earthenware by George Stubbs, half-length oval. Wedgwood Museum, Barlaston. Exhibited *Stubbs and Wedgwood*, Tate Gallery, 1974(12). The circumstancial evidence outweighs the visual in favour of this identification (see B. Tattersall, *Apollo*, CI, 1975, pp.34-35).

c.1785 Silhouette attributed to Francis Torond, playing chess with his son Erasmus. Private collection (illus. *CL*, CLI, 1972, p.360).

1792 Painting by Joseph Wright,* half length, a quill in his raised right hand, 'a straight but severe likeness'. Private collection, commissioned by Sacheverell Pole, the sitter's stepson (Nicolson 1968, no.52; *Wright* 1990, no.145). Engraved J.R. Smith 1797; reduced oval plate by Holl 1800.

Wright painted copies (see Nicolson 1968, I, pp.192-93) for Sir Brooke Boothby (unidentified) and Jedediah Strutt (private collection), the latter showing the right hand turned more toward the spectator, as do all the other known versions; other replicas are at Down House and in Derby MAG, the latter showing the yellow waistcoat unstriped.

A copy attributed to James Rawlinson in Wolverhampton AG (unstriped waistcoat); an early copy at St John's College, Cambridge (Christie's, 18 April 1986, lot 115), omitting the right hand; later copies with the Royal Society of Medicine, London, and the Royal Masonic School for Boys, Bushey.

A miniature formerly at Down House resembles Holl's oval engraving of 1800; Darwin had presented a miniature of himself to the Rev Robert Clive (d.1792), see S. Felton, *Portraits of English Authors on Gardening*, 1830, p.164.

c.1793? Pastel by James Sharples, small half length. Bristol CMAG (*Cat. of the Sharples Coll.*, Bristol, 1910, no.23). A related pastel by Ellen Sharples dated 1816 is on loan to Down House (*English Heritage Review*, 1999, p.37); she had recorded copying her husband's small portrait in June-July 1803 (Knox 1930, p.117).

1800 Silhouette in the manner of Richard Jordan, profile bust. Private collection (illus. *CL*, CLI, 1972, p.359).

c.1800? Painting by James Rawlinson, half length. On loan to Darwin College, Cambridge (illus. Keynes 1994, p.78). Engraved J. Heath 1804; F. Holl 1807 (*from the original in the possession of Dr Thornton*, i.e. Dr R.J. Thornton's *Linneaus Gallery*, see Milne NPG 5180); M. Haughton 1807; R. Cooper 1823. Versions at Down House and sold Sotheby's, 17 April 1957, lot 151.

1801 Painting by S.J. Arnold, seated reading a letter, engraved B. Pym 1801 (illus. A. Desmond & J. Moore, *Darwin*, 1991, f.p.44). An unsatisfactory likeness.

1802 Painting attributed to James Rawlinson, half-length oval, writing at his desk. High View Community School, Breadsall, Derby. Taken from an ink drawing by Rawlinson, signed and dated 1802, sold Sotheby's, 11 December 1992, lot 68.

Posthumous

1804 Coade stone bust by W.J. Coffee, lifesize. Derby MAG (described in the *Monthly Mag.*, 1804, p.557). A bronze cast was engraved H. Meyer 1820 when in the possession of Dr Sacheverell Darwin; another made in 1967 is at Down House (illus. D. King-Hele, *Erasmus Darwin,* 1999, f.p.86, pl.1).

Undated Alabaster bust attributed to George Moneypenny. Darwin College, Cambridge, from the Mechanics Institute, Derby; Christie's, 7 December 1993, lot 92 as attributed to W.J. Coffee (illus. Keynes 1994, p.80). An unprepossessing likeness.

1886 Relief medallion by E. Onslow Ford, derived from the Wright portrait of 1770. Lichfield Cathedral.

DOUBTFUL PORTRAIT

Darwin has been unconvincingly identified in Joseph Wright's *Experiment with the Air Pump* (NG London); see D. King-Hele, *Erasmus Darwin*, 1998, pp.83, 184.

DASHWOOD, Sir Francis, 2nd Bt, see LE DESPENCER

DAY, Thomas 1748-89

A 'splenetic, capricious, yet bountiful philanthropist' of radical persuasions, a disciple of Rousseau; author of the children's tale *Sandford and Merton* 1783-89, an advocacy of radical education.

'Mr Day looked the philosopher. Powder and fine clothes were, at that time, the appendages of gentlemen. Mr Day wore not neither. He was tall and stooped in the shoulders, full made, but not corpulent; ... his features interesting and agreeable amidst the traces of a severe small pox. There was a sort of weight upon the lids of his large hazle eyes . . . beneath the shade of sable hair, which, Adam-like, curled about his brows' (Anna Seward, 1804).

2490 JOSEPH WRIGHT of Derby 1770

Canvas 125 x 101 (49¼ x 39¾) lined; cleaned 1990.

Grey eyes, black hair, wearing a silver Van Dyck suit with slashed sleeves, a white unbuttoned shirt, and a light brown wrap; in his left hand a number of unbound and illegible printed sheets; behind him, a stormy sky broken by a flash of lightning over a mountainous landscape.

Collections: Richard Lovell Edgeworth by 1789 (see below); by descent at Edgeworthstown House, Co. Longford,[1] to Mrs Rose B. Montagu, from whom bt. 24 August 1930 by Harold Hill, Newcastle-upon-Tyne;[2] Sotheby's, 10 December 1930, lot 115 with Edgeworth's 1789 letter (see below) and a copy of the engraving by Meyer;[3] purchased from Hill 1931.

Engraving: H. Meyer 1820 (for R.L. Edgeworth's *Memoirs*).

Exhibitions: *Georgian Essex*, Dagenham, 1958(309); *Lunar Society*, Birmingham, 1966(55); *Johnson and the Midlands*, Lichfield, 1984(26); *Looking into Paintings*, Arts Council, 1987(4); *Wright* 1990(60); *Gainsborough*, Tate Gallery, 2002-3(106).

Reference: Nicolson 1968, no.57.

The circumstances of this portrait were described (poetically) by Anna Seward in 1804:[4]

> In the course of the year 1770, Mr Day stood for a full-length picture to Mr Wright of Derby. A strong likeness and a dignified portrait were the result. Drawn as in the open air, the surrounding sky is tempestuous, lurid, and dark. He stands leaning his left arm against a column inscribed to Hambden. Mr Day looks upward, as enthusiastically meditating on the contents of a book, held in his dropped right hand. The open leaf is the oration of that virtuous patriot of the senate, against the grant of ship-money, demanded by King Charles the first. A flash of lightning plays in Mr Day's hair, and illuminates the contents of the volume.

Seward's description was substantially repeated in 1862 by Day's biographer John Blackman, who further specified that it was painted in Derby in August 1770 and added references to 'the poetry of nature in the background, the surrounding sky tempestuous and dark, to image forth his gloomy view of society, as he saw it revolving around'.[5] Neither version of this picture bears any inscription, and the references to John Hampden appear fanciful[6] (Egerton[7] even suggested 'we can be virtually certain' that the book he holds 'is by Rousseau, and probably a copy of *Emile*'). It is, as Alistair Smith first remarked,[8] the portrait of a visionary stoic, in which Van Dyck is recalled not just by the costume (a totally imaginary Van Dyck undress),[9] but by the composition, with the figure casually reclining against a classical column[10] (such elegance is in complete contrast to Wright's *Erasmus Darwin*, painted in the same year, cf. NPG 88).

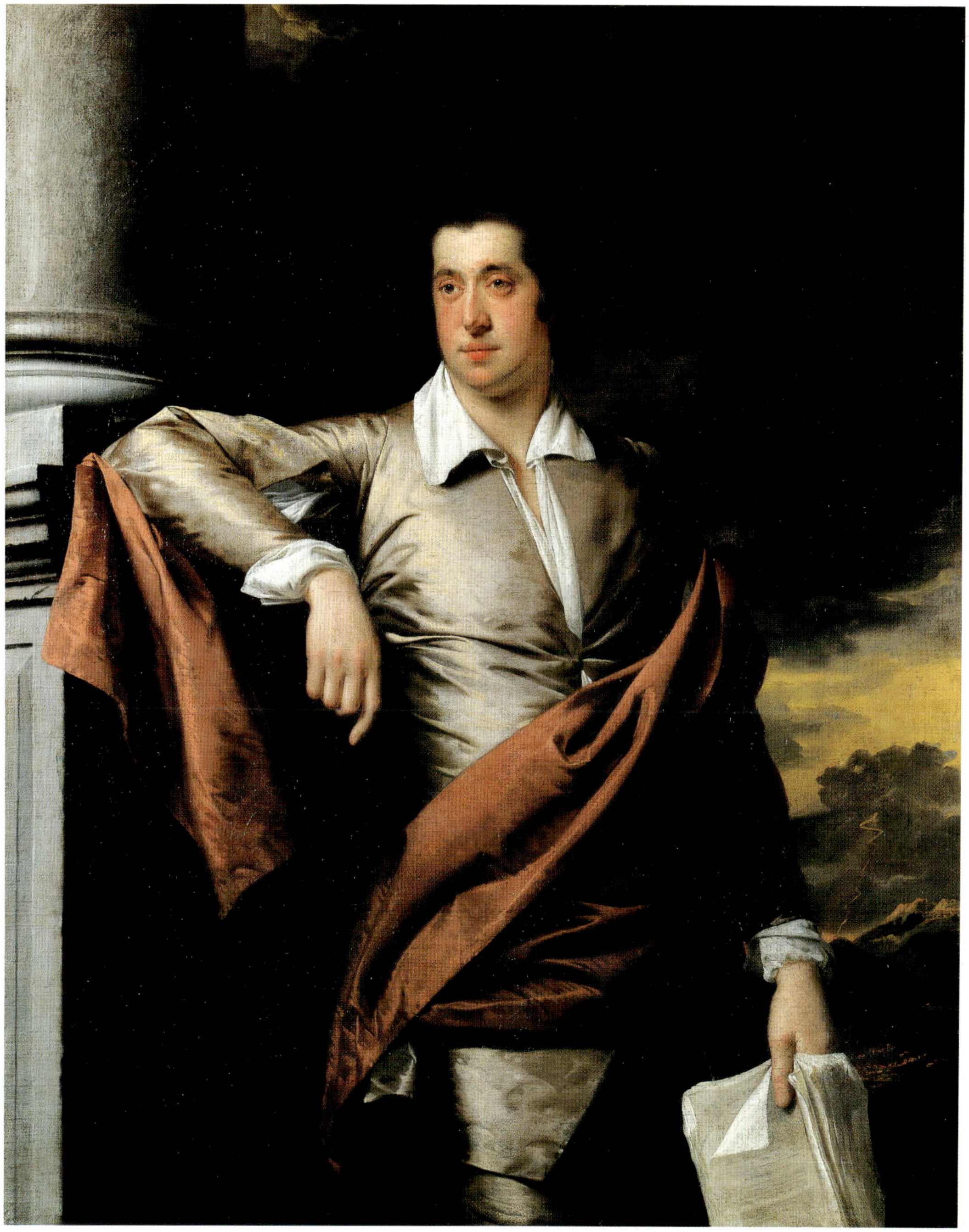

DAY NPG *2490*

Wright's accounts of c.1770 list two half lengths of Mr Day at £42,[11] the second being presumably the replica of NPG 2490 acquired by Manchester City Art Gallery in 1975.[12] NPG 2490 was apparently painted for Richard Lovell Edgeworth, one of Day's closest friends. Three weeks after Day's sudden death (the result of being thrown from a horse which he was resolved to tame through gentleness), Edgeworth wrote to Thomas Lowndes: 'I have an excellent picture of Mr Day by Wright; if Mrs Day should wish for it, it is at her service - She may be sure no other person shall have it but one of my own children'.[13] Mrs Day, it appears, did not take the picture, which remained at Edgeworthstown House until 1930.

1 Where it was recorded by J. Blackman, *Memoir of Thomas Day*, 1862, p.67.
2 The copy of a receipt from Rose B. Montagu, 24 August 1930, for £100 for a 'Picture of Thomas Day by Wright of Derby' is on file.
3 Bought 'Halliwell', 5gns., which might suggest the picture had been withdrawn, but Sotheby's archive does not say so (I am grateful to David Moore-Gwyn for this information).
4 Anna Seward, *Memoirs of the Life of Dr Darwin*, 1804, p.20.
5 J. Blackman, *Memoir of Thomas Day*, 1862, p.66.
6 Despite allegations in the Birmingham Lunar Society 1966 exhibition cat.
7 *Wright* 1990, p.119.
8 *Looking into Paintings*, Arts Council, 1987, p.8.
9 A. Ribeiro, *Dress worn at Masquerades in England 1730-90*, 1984, p.198.
10 Cf. the black-haired Abbé Scaglia, NG London (6575); Titian's *Benedetto Varchi* in Vienna is similarly posed and holds a book by his side. Wright's composition was also compared, by Nicolson, with Reynolds's *Lord Fortescue* of 1756 and, by Egerton, with Kneller's *Anthony Henley*, engraved by John Smith c.1690.
11 Nicolson 1968, I, p.194.
12 Illus. Nicolson 1968, no.58, as in the collection of Lord Belper.
13 21 October 1789, printed in *Memoirs of Richard Lovell Edgeworth*, II, 1821 ed., p.89; the original letter bt. from Hill in 1931 (NPG archive).

DOUBTFUL PORTRAITS

Wright's whole-length *Indian Captain* (Yale Center for British Art, B1981.25.713) was once identified as Thomas Day; a half-length version sold Sotheby's, 18 November 1970, lot 43.

Posthumous conjectural engravings by M. Bovi from a drawing by J.G. Wood 1791, and by J. Condé 1794.

DELANY, Mrs Mary, *née* Granville 1700-88

'A model of female excellence' (Burke); m. 1) 1717 Alexander Pendarves (c.1665-1724), 2) 1743 Patrick Delany (1685-1768), Dean of Down 1744; after his death she spent much time at Bulstrode with Margaret, Duchess of Portland, through whom she became a Royal favourite; on the Duchess's death in 1785 she was given a house near Windsor; made paper mosaic flowers (much of her *hortus siccus* now in the British Museum) and practised as an amateur painter.

'a person finely proportioned, she had a most lovely face of great sweetness, set off with a head of fair hair, shining and naturally curled, with a complexion which nothing could out-do or equal ... Her eyes were bright indeed, I never could tell what colour they were ... [she was] almost the only woman I ever saw whose lips were scarlet, and her bloom [was] beyond expression' (Dean Patrick Delany, 1759).

Abbreviation

Hayden 1980: R. Hayden, *Mrs Delany her life & Flowers*, 1980

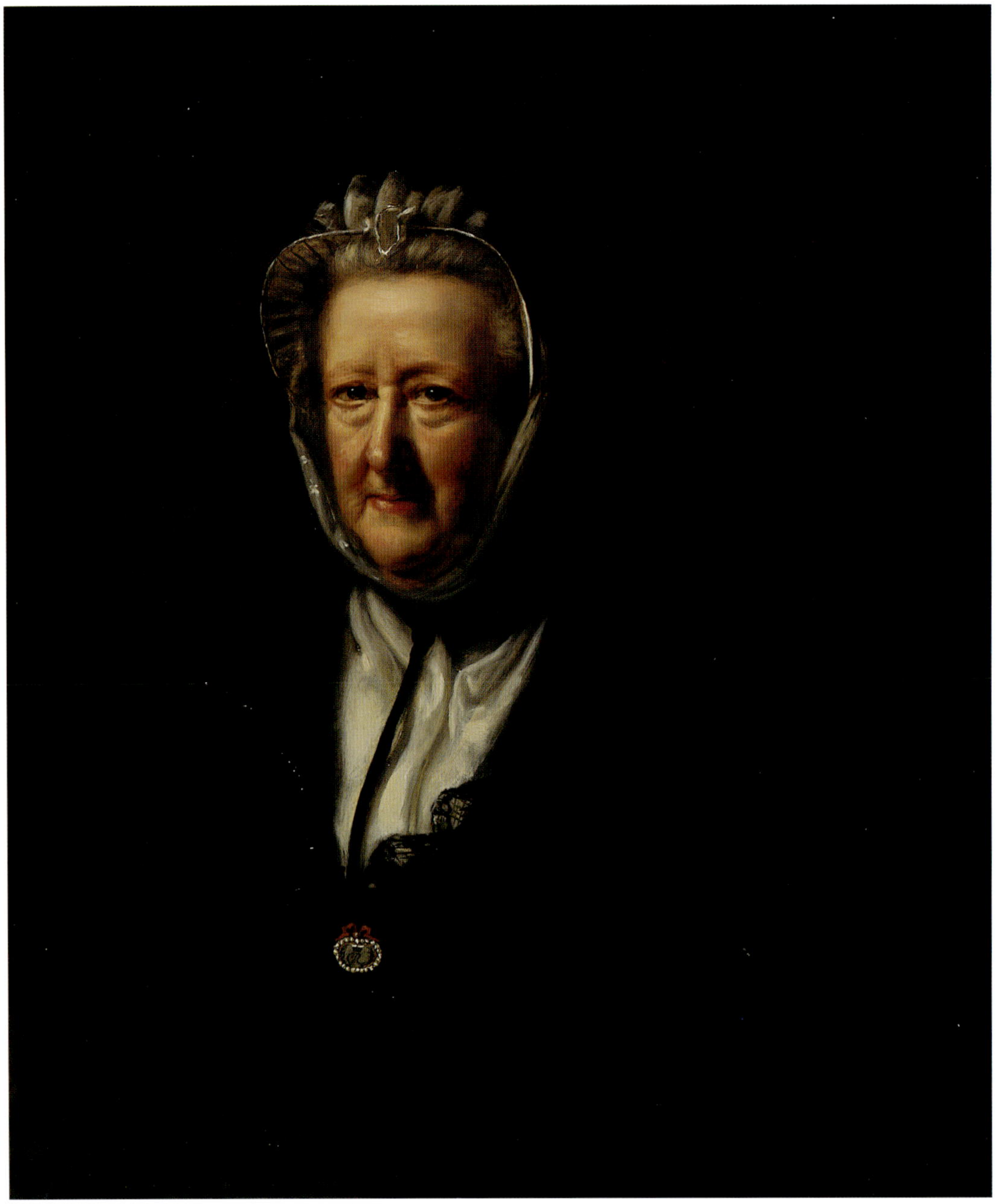

DELANY NPG *1030*

1030 JOHN OPIE 1782

Canvas 75 x 62 (29½ x 24½), lined; fine overall craquelure.

Light brown eyes, white hair, wearing widow's dress of a black lace shawl, white bonnet and a black cloak; from a black ribbon round her neck hangs the heart-shaped locket, inscribed *CR* beneath a crown, surrounded by pearls and containing a hair of Queen Charlotte which had been given her, together with a cameo of the King, by Their Majesties.[1] Within a painted oval.

Collections: Commissioned by Mary, Countess of Bute (d.1794); the Marquess of Bute [presumably the 2nd Marquess] to the sitter's great-niece, Mrs Georgina Mary Ann Waddington;[2] her daughter, Augusta, Lady Llanover, by whom bequeathed 1896.[3]

Engraving: J. Brown 1861 (Delany 1861-62, I, front.).

Exhibitions: *Opie*, Plymouth, 1957(22); *Opie*, Arts Council, 1962-63(22); *Designs for English Picture Frames*, Wiggins, London, 1987(40); *Mrs Delany's Flower Collages*, Bath, 1988; Beningbrough 1979–.

Reference: Rogers 1878, p.89; Earland 1911, pp.36, 273; Millar 1969, under no.975; Simon 1997, pp.113-14, 165.

NPG 1030 is virtually a replica of the portrait in the Royal Collection, for which the eighty-two year old Mrs Delany sat at the command of George III and Queen Charlotte early in 1782.[4] On 14 February Walpole wrote that Opie 'has done a head of Mrs Delany for the King - *oui vraiment,* it is pronounced like Rembrandt, but as I told her, does not look older than she is, but older than she does';[5] it was doubtless the picture 'of an old lady' which Opie mentioned in a letter of 11 March as painted for the King and Queen.[6] Lady Bute then induced Mrs Delany to sit a second time to Opie, for NPG 1030, 'that he might paint a portrait of her from life in exactly the same dress and position'.[7] In the event there are some very slight differences in the folds of the head scarf and cloak.

NPG 1030 remains in the frame which Horace Walpole designed for Lady Bute following the death of Mrs Delany in April 1788.[8] Elaborately carved, the principal ornaments were described by Lady Llanover as emblematic of Mrs Delany's accomplishments; 'at the top are a group of musical instruments, interspersed with sprays of bay and laurel, and at the bottom a palette forms the centre, with a miniature easel, pencils and brushes'; on the palette is written a commemorative text by Walpole (completed on 13 May 1788):

> *Mary Grenville / Niece of Lord Lansdown / Correspondent of Dr Swift, / Widow / of Mr Pendarvis, / and of Dr Delany Dean of Downe. / Her piety and Virtues, her excellent understanding, / and her Talents and Taste in Painting & Music, / were not only the Merits, Ornaments & comforts / of an uniform life, / but the Blessings that crowned & closed / the termination of her existence / at the uncommon age of 88.*

A third version, formerly in the Wellesbourne collection, with further slight differences in the disposition of the cloak and shawl, was sold in 1955;[9] miniature derivations include those formerly in the collection of Sir Arthur Harford and with R.A.E. Herbert in 1984;[10] a pencil copy was sold Sotheby's, 19 November 1992 (within lot 232).

1 Described and illus., *Delany* 1861-62, I, 1861, front., and VI, p.489.
2 This provenance given in *Delany* 1861-62, VI, p.498 ('The picture and the frame were given by the late Marquis of Bute to the Editor's mother').
3 With a portrait by Mrs Delany of her sister Mrs Anne D'Ewes which was declined by the Trustees.
4 Millar 1969, no.975; engraved anon. 1842 *from the original Painting at Hampton Court.*
5 To William Mason; *Wal. Corr.*, XXIX, p.185.
6 Rogers 1878, p.24; Wolcot also mentioned 'the portrait of a lady which [Opie] painted expressly for [the King].' (*ibid.*, p.23).
7 *Delany* 1861-62, VI, p.497.
8 See Simon 1997.
9 Illus. R. Granville, *The Granville Family,* 1895, f.p.452; exhibited *Birmingham Houses,* 1938(115); Sotheby's, 6 July 1955, lot 164 as Opie (see Millar 1969, sub no.975; Earland 1911, p.273).
10 Listed respectively in Steegman, II, p.29, no.25, and p.152, no.28.

ICONOGRAPHY

c.1730 Unattributed painting, half length. Private collection (illus. *Handel*, NPG, 1985, no.156; Hayden 1980, p.37 an oval detail). Version in widow's dress with Lady Llanover in 1878 (SSB 96/65).

1740 Miniature by C.F. Zincke, as Mrs Pendarves, bust-length oval. Christie's, 8 March 1995, lot 21. Exhibited SKM 1865(2525) lent Mrs Greville Howard. Set in the lid of a gold portrait box which has three other miniatures by Zincke of the Duchess of Portland, Mrs Elizabeth Montagu and another. Mrs Delany was sitting to Zincke in April 1740 (E.J. Climenson, *Montagu Corr.*, I, 1906, p.45).

c.1740? Drawing by Lady Catherine Hanmer (d.1741), three-quarter length at her easel. Private collection (illus. Hayden 1980, p.94).

c.1740-45 Painting formerly attributed to Van Aken, small bust-length painted oval. Sotheby's, 13 February 1980, lot 193.

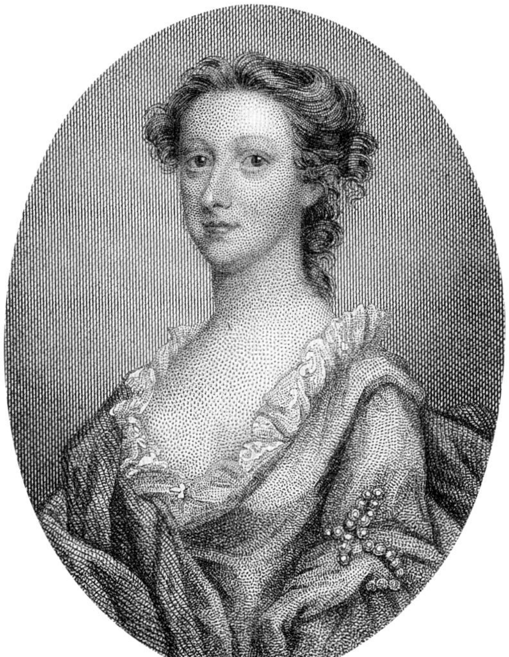

DELANY J. Brown after a miniature attributed to Lucius Barber c.1745-50 (NPG D 13796)

c.1745-50 Miniature enamel attributed to Lucius Barber, bust-length. Formerly in the collection of R.A.E. Herbert (Steegman, II, p.152, no.27). Engraved J. Brown 1861,* *from an enamel picture given to Erskine Sandford to the Baroness de Bunsen* (*Delany* 1861-62, II, front.). A miniature enamel by Rupert Barber listed by Strickland (1913, I, p.22) and another 'possibly by Barber' illus. Hayden 1980, p.77. Mrs Delany patronised and encouraged 'Mr Barber' in Dublin; in March 1746 'Barber' had 'just finished another picture of me in enamel' and he was making copies for her that same year (*Delany* 1861-62, II, pp.429, 421) and in 1755 (*Delany* 1861-62, III, p.385).

1782 Painting by John Opie, see NPG 1030.

c.1785 Drawing attributed to John Hoppner,* half length, with black hat. Victoria and Albert Museum (E.580.1929).

Silhouettes of Mrs Delany in old age illus. *Connoisseur,* XXV, 1909, p.219 (Wellesley collection); *ibid.*, XC, 1932, p.292 (Royal Collection), and Hayden 1980, p.172.

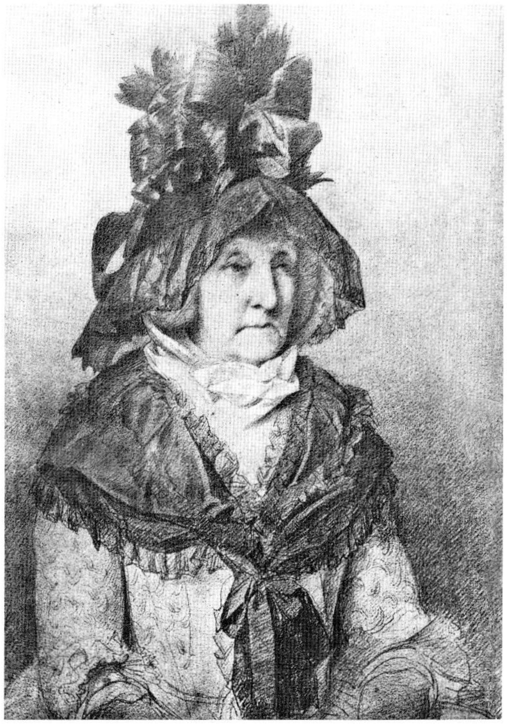

DELANY attributed to John Hoppner c.1785 (Victoria and Albert Museum)

DOUBTFUL PORTRAITS

Scharf recorded a bust-length portrait with Lady Llanover in 1888 (TSB 34/51; he had previously thought it might show Mrs Delany's mother; SSB 96/64v; 1878); he also noted an unattributed half length identified as Mary Granville at Longleat in 1862 (SSB 65/62), not in the 1881 Longleat cat. An unattributed half length of c.1725, wearing a hood, with R.A.E. Herbert, described as Mrs Delany (Steegman, II, p.150, no.11); another in the Royal Collection (illus. *CL*, CXXXIII, 1963, p.1273, as Mrs Delany), but see Millar 1969, no.1231.

DE LOUTHERBOURG, Philippe Jacques 1740-1812

Painter; b. Strasbourg, studied in Paris, where he exhibited 1763-71; *académicien* and *peintre du roi* 1766; came to London 1771; exhibited RA 1772-1812; RA 1781; scene-painter at Drury Lane 1772-81; in 1781 he devised the *Eidophusikon*, a peep-show, imitating 'Natural Phenomena, represented by Moving Pictures'; practised as a faith healer 1789; historical painter to the Duke of Gloucester 1807.

A polygraphic reproduction [mechanical painting] from one of his landscapes, *Summer*, probably produced at Boulton's Soho Manufactory, is in the NPG reference collection (D4446; illus. *Burl. Mag.*, CXII, 1970, p.497, fig.16, and see *Burl. Mag.*, CXIII, 1971, p.158).

'The person and appearance of De Loutherbourg were those of a gentleman of baronial rank and dignity; his manners were conciliating and urbane' (*British Gallery of Contemporary Portraits*, 1822).

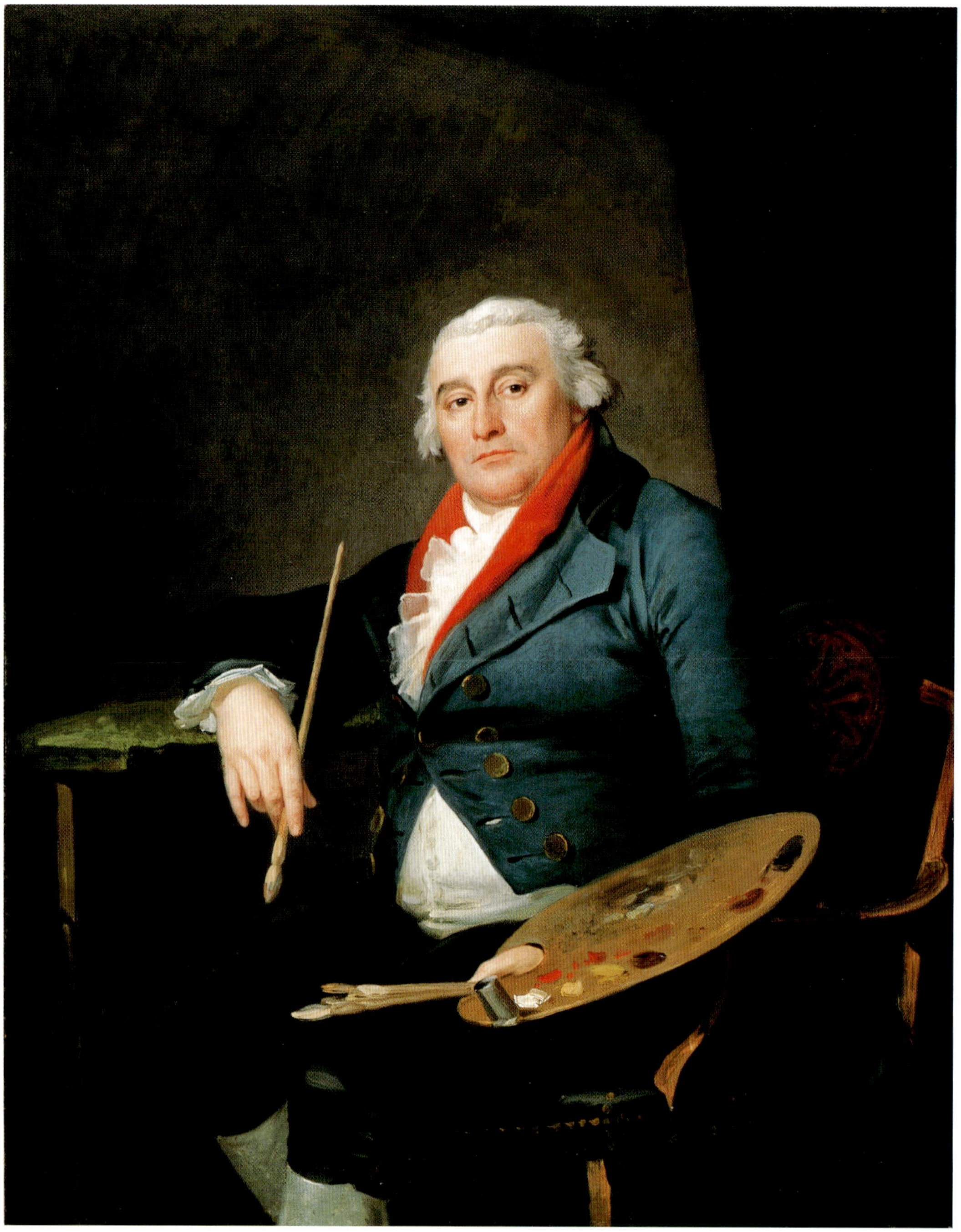

DE LOUTHERBOURG NPG *2493*

2493 SELF PORTRAIT c.1805-10

Canvas 126.5 x 101 (49¾ x 39¾); lined; cleaned 1973 and strip-lined 1997.

Brown eyes, white hair; wearing a red scarf, blue coat, red waistcoat and black breeches; round the edge of his palette (from the left): flake white with vermilion above, yellow ochre, brown ochre, raw umber, burnt umber and ivory black; in the centre a flesh tint.[1]

Collections: Mrs De Loutherbourg (see Engraving below); C.H. Woolford, Edinburgh, 1910;[2] F.B. Daniell, London, from whom purchased 1931.

Engraving: R. Page 1814 (half-length oval) *from the Original Picture in the Possession of Mrs Loutherbourg* (for the *Encyclopaedia Londinensis*).

Exhibitions: *British Self Portraits*, Arts Council, 1962(41); *De Loutherbourg*, Kenwood, 1973(1); *Panoramania*, Barbican, 1988(90); *Sehsucht*, Bonn, 1993(III.i).

NPG 2493 is dated according to the apparent age of the sitter; it is the only known painted self-portrait by De Loutherbourg. Might the distinctive arm-rest have been the 'rising arm rest with stuffed top' in the De Loutherbourg sale (Coxe, 18 June 1812)?

1 See F. Schmid, *Burl. Mag.*, CVIII, 1966, pp.520-21.
2 Inscribed photograph in NPG archive.

ICONOGRAPHY

1778 Painting by Thomas Gainsborough, half length. Dulwich Picture Gallery (Waterhouse 1958, no.456). Exhibited RA 1778(408). De Loutherbourg was a particular friend of Gainsborough (who admired the *Eidophusikon*) and drew his portrait probably at the same time (Yale Center for British Art; B1986.29.61). A pencil copy was on the London art market in 1991.

1795 Painting by Henry Singleton,* *President and Members of the Royal Academy*, see Comparative Groups.

1798 Drawing by Sarah Singleton, half length. Christie's, 12 February 1974, lot 32. Engraved anon. 1798.

c.1800 Miniature by Richard Cosway, bust-length oval. Sotheby's, 7 May 1946, lot 68, from the Ashcroft collection (illus. *Connoisseur*, LXXV, 1926, p.137, and XCIV, 1934, p.224). Copy by John Jackson, *from a miniature picture in the Possession of Mrs de Loutherbourg*, engraved H. Meyer 1813. Cosway shared De Loutherbourg's interest in the supernatural: 'Mr Cosway as well as Mr De Loutherbourg has had a call' (*Gazetteer*, 20 February 1790).

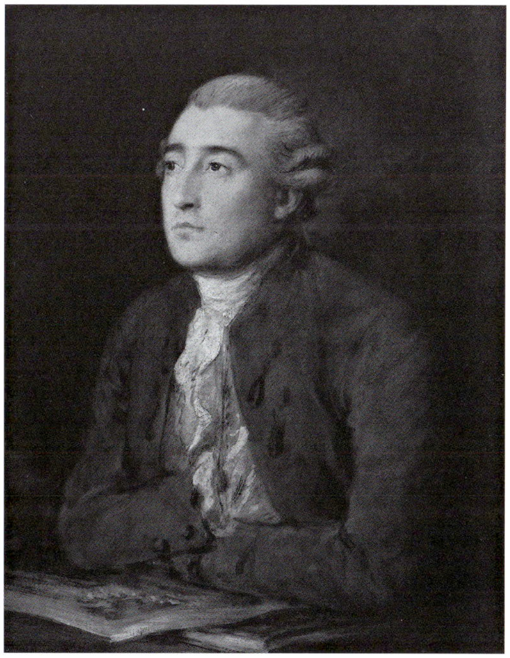

DE LOUTHERBOURG by Thomas Gainsborough 1778 (Dulwich Picture Gallery)

1801 Miniature by W.P.J. Lodder (De Loutherbourg's pupil), exhibited RA 1801(725).

c.1805-10 Painting by De Loutherbourg, see NPG 2493.

De Loutherbourg is said to appear as a tiny skater in his *Winter Morning* 1776 (private collection, Paris, 1973) and in the 'Landscape in which the artist has introduced a portrait of himself with his gun and dog' sold Foster's, 28-29 May 1829 (see *De Loutherbourg*, Kenwood, 1973, under nos.1 and 22).

DOUBTFUL PORTRAITS

Painting attributed to Hoppner, from the Deland Museum of Art, Florida, sold Phillips, 6 July 1999, lot 17, alleged to show De Loutherbourg and his wife; drawing c.1770 formerly identified as a self portrait in the Hessisches Landesmuseum, Darmstadt (cf. *De Loutherbourg*, Kenwood, 1973, under no.1).

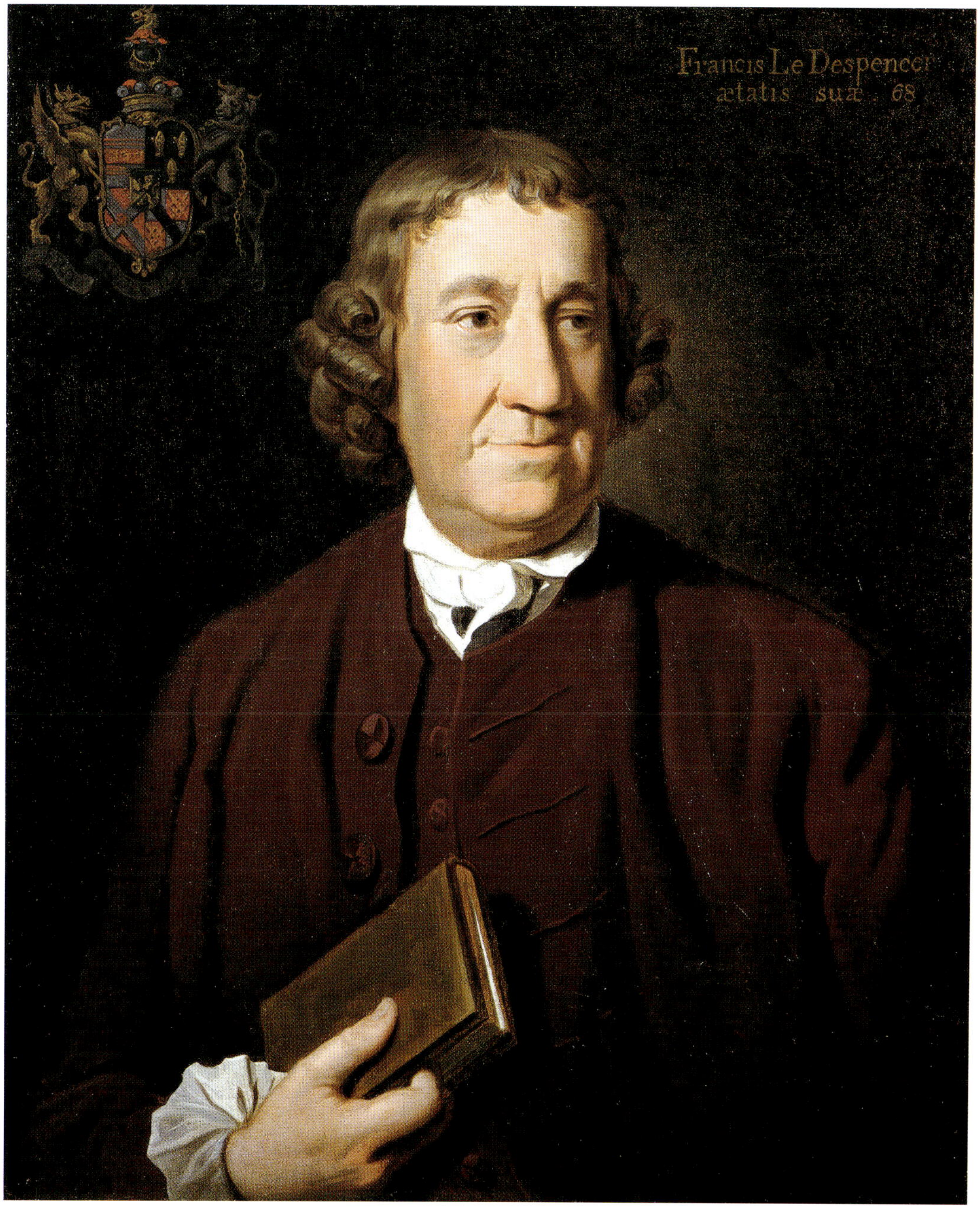

15th Baron Le DESPENCER NPG *1345*

LE DESPENCER, Francis Dashwood, 15th Baron 1708-81

Politician and dilettante, of West Wycombe, Bucks.; suc. as Sir Francis Dashwood 2nd Bt 1724; travelled extensively in Europe and the Middle East in 1726, between 1730 and 1733 and in 1739-41; FRS 1746; MP 1741-63; chancellor of the exchequer 1762-63, postmaster-general 1766-81; suc. as 15th Baron Le Despencer 1763.

'He was a man of sense, without eloquence; and of humour, without good humour; naturally inclined to adventures, and had early in life made a voyage to Russia, dressed like Charles the Twelfth, in hopes of making Czarina Anne fall in love with him' (Horace Walpole, *Memoirs of George II*).

Dashwood 'who loved to know, and who cultivated a roughness of speech, affected to know no more than what he had learnt from unadorned understanding' (*ibid.*).

1345 NATHANIEL DANCE 1776

Canvas 75 x 62 (29½ x 24½) lined; cleaned 2000.

Brown eyes, light hair, wearing a brown suit; inscribed top right: *Francis Le Despencer / aetatis suae.68.* and with the arms of Lord Le Despencer top left (quarterly, Dashwood, Fane, Neville and Spencer, with crest and motto *PRO MAGNA CHARTA*).[1]

Collections: Purchased from Archibald Ramsden 1903.

NPG 1345 appears to be a replica of the portrait by Dance at West Wycombe which is inscribed *NDance pinxt / 1776.*[2] A version from Mereworth Castle (which also belonged to the Dashwood family) was sold Christie's, 2 February 1973, lot 64;[3] this or another was sold from Frankham in Sussex by Christie's, 25 September 1989, lot 312. Each of these portraits bears the arms and inscription seen on NPG 1345.

1 *Quarterly, 1st, ar. on a fess betw. two double cotises gu. three griffins' heads erased or,* for Dashwood; *2nd a az. three dexter hand gauntlets with their backs forward or,* for Fane; *3rd, gu. on a saltire ar. a rose of the field, barbed and seeded ppr.,* for Neville; *4th, quarterly, ar. and gu. in the 2nd and 3rd quarters a fret or, over all a bend sa.,* for Spencer. *Crest – out of a ducal coronet or, a saracen's head affrontee ppr. wreathed about the temples ar. and sa. Supporters – Dexter, a griffin, wings elevated or, collared and line reflexed over the back sa. the collar charged with three escallops ar.; sinister, a bull ar. pied sa. armed, hoofed, collared, and chain reflexed over the back or.*

2 Illus. NT Guide, *West Wycombe*, 2001, p.51. The 8vo. book in his hand was described in the NT Guide, 1984, p.16, as possibly a copy of the abridged Book of Common Prayer which Lord Le Despencer and Benjamin Franklin produced at West Wycombe in 1773 (see *Franklin at West Wycombe*, American Philosophical Society, Pa., 1977, pp.16–20).

3 Exhibited Sabin, *English Portraits*, 1976(17) illus.

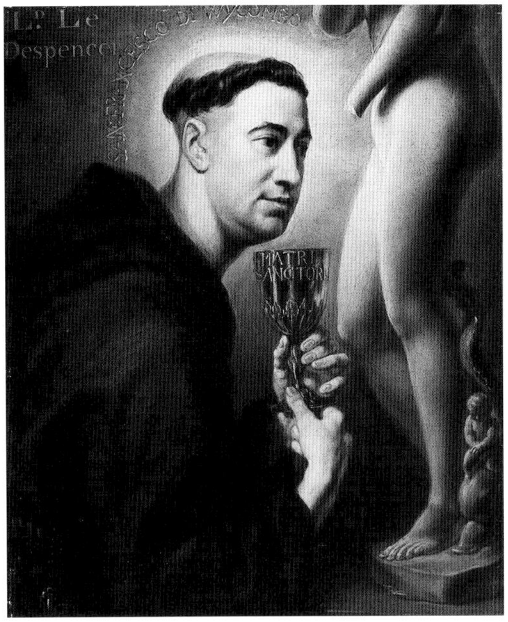

15th Baron Le DESPENCER by George Knapton 1742 (Society of Dilettanti)

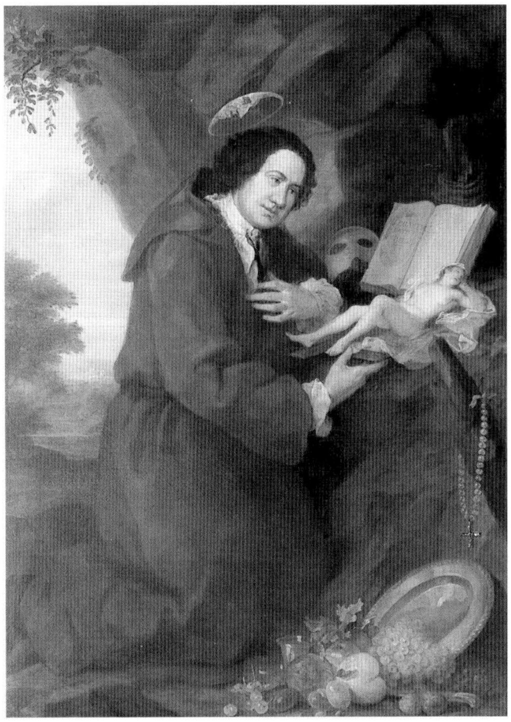
15th Baron Le DESPENCER by William Hogarth c.1745? (Private Collection)

ICONOGRAPHY

Many of the surviving portraits show Sir Francis Dashwood *en travesti*—as a Turkish Pasha, referring to his Divan Club; as Pope, evoking his profane escapades in Rome, or as St Francis, referring to his Franciscan Brotherhood at Medmenham Abbey where he 'officiated as High Priest, habited in the dress of a Franciscan Monk, pouring a libation from a Communion cup to the mysterious object of… homage'.

c.1730–31 Painting by Bartolomeo Nazari, called *Lord Boyne in the Cabin of his Ship*, in which the seated Dashwood points to a map. Versions at West Wycombe (illus. NT Guide, *West Wycombe*, 2001, p.23); National Maritime Museum (BHC 2567; exhibited *Grand Tour*, Tate Gallery, 1996, no.57), and elsewhere. There is some doubt concerning the identities of the figures, but Dashwood appears to be identified from his portrait by Carpentiers of 1739, see below.

1739 Painting by Adriaen Carpentiers, half length. West Wycombe. Engraved J. Faber 1753 (illus. B. Kemp, *Sir Francis Dashwood*, 1967, f.p.70). A version sold Phillips, 16 July 1975, lot 321, had been offered to the NPG in 1952.

1742 Painting by George Knapton,* half length as St Francis, his halo inscribed *San Francesco di Wycombo*, holding a chalice inscribed *Matri Sanctoru …*, closely considering a Medici Venus. Society of Dilettanti, London. In 1736 Dashwood was elected to the Society, 'a club for which the nominal qualification is having been to Italy, and the real one, being drunk: the two chiefs are Lord Middlesex and Sir Francis Dashwood, who were seldom sober the whole time they were in Italy' (*Wal. Corr.*, XVIII, p.211).

c.1742? Painting by Adriaen Carpentiers, half length as a Pope, inscribed *Innocens Pont: opt. Max:.* West Wycombe (illus. NT Guide, *West Wycombe*, 2001, p.50). Following the death of Pope Clement XII in 1740 while Dashwood was in Rome, he instigated a mock conclave.

c.1742? Painting by Adriaen Carpentiers, half length dressed in Divan Club costume with turban and ermine-lined cloak; inscribed verso: *El Faquir Dashwood Pasha.* West Wycombe (illus. NT Guide, *West Wycombe*, 2001, p.249). The Divan club (for those who had visited Turkey) was founded by Dashwood and Lord Sandwich on their return to England in 1741.

c.1742 Unattributed painting, three-quarter length, dressed as St Francis. West Wycombe (illus. F. Dashwood, *The Dashwoods*, 1987, f.p.88). Possibly by George Knapton.

c.1745? Painting by William Hogarth,* whole-length kneeling figure as St Francis, the halo above his head containing the head of Lord Sandwich, worshipping a naked Venus. Private collection. Engraved Platt. Probably painted for Dashwood's close friend Gustavus, Lord Boyne, who d.1746. A copy sold Christie's, SK, 14 December 1983, lot 44.

1761 Painting by Adriaen Carpentiers, half length, grey hair. West Wycombe (illus. F. Dashwood, *The Dashwoods*, 1987, f.p.88 where misdated), from the Ditchley sale, Sotheby's, 24 May 1933, lot 3.

1776 Painting by Nathaniel Dance, see NPG 1345.

1779 Bust by Thomas Scheemakers. Le Despencer employed Scheemakers at both Mereworth and West Wycombe in 1779–80 and the sculptor's bust of his patron is said to have been exhibited in 1779 (presumably FS 1779, no.147, 'a nobleman'; cf. NT Guide, *West Wycombe*, 2001, p.12). A plaster cast or casts of a bust of Le Despencer appeared in the Scheemakers sale, Christie's, 21 May 1805 (Gunnis 1968, p.344).

A plaster bust of the elderly Le Despencer attributed to Scheemakers is at West Wycombe, together with two casts.

1810 Bust of 'the late Lord Le Despencer' by John Bacon jr., exhibited RA 1810(895).

DOUBTFUL PORTRAIT

Gunnis 1968, p.26, listed a bust of c.1780 by John Bacon sr. in the Mausoleum at West Wycombe; this appears to be the marble bust of a virtuoso, since removed to the House, which is neither obviously by Bacon nor of Lord Le Despencer (I am grateful to Alastair Laing for this advice; see also NT Guide *West Wycombe*, 2001, p.45).

DEVIS, Arthur 1712-87

Portrait painter, b. Preston, Lancs.; settled in London by 1742; exhibited FSA 1761-63, 1767-70, 1775 and 1780, and President 1768; retired to Brighton 1783.

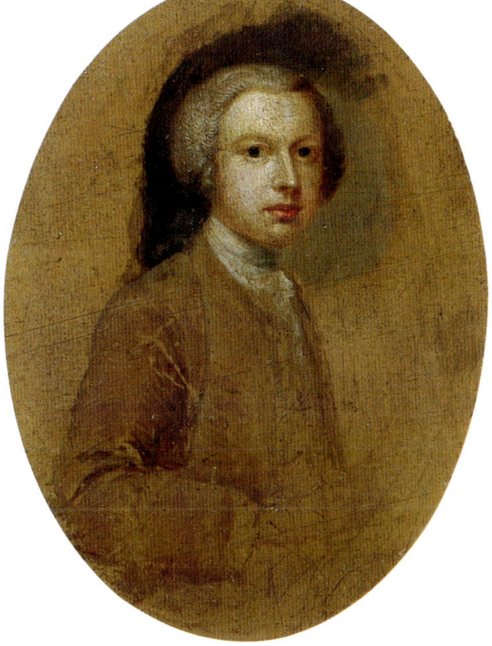

DEVIS NPG *6153*

6153 SELF PORTRAIT c.1742-44

Oak panel 9.3 x 6.8 x 0.7 (3⅝ x 2¾ x ¼) oval, the grain running diagonally; unfinished; some abrasion and slight scratching, with minor losses round the edges.

Brown eyes, powdered hair, wearing a light brown coat; brown background.

Collections: Private collection, Newburyport, Me.; Marvin Sadik Fine Arts, Falmouth, Me., from whom purchased 1991.

Reference: Walker 1998, no.43.

An undocumented and previously unrecognised self portrait, NPG 6153 was identified by Ellen D'Oench who indicated a comparison with Devis's self portrait miniature of c.1742 see below, suggesting it might be a little later.[1]

1 Letter to M. Sadik, 18 April 1991.

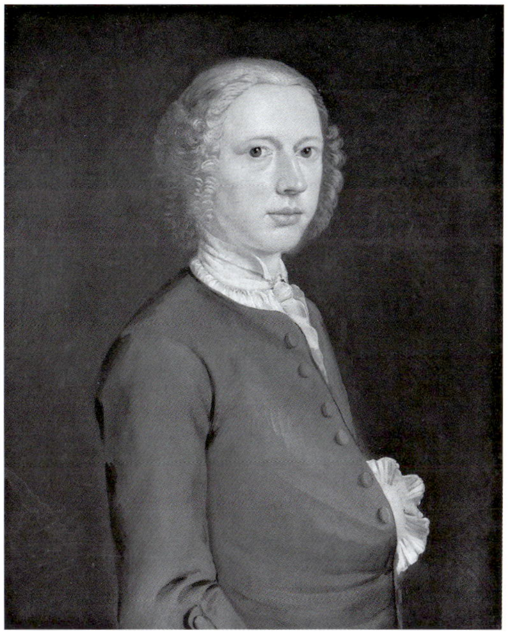

DEVIS Self portrait c.1737-38 (Harris Museum and Art Gallery, Preston)

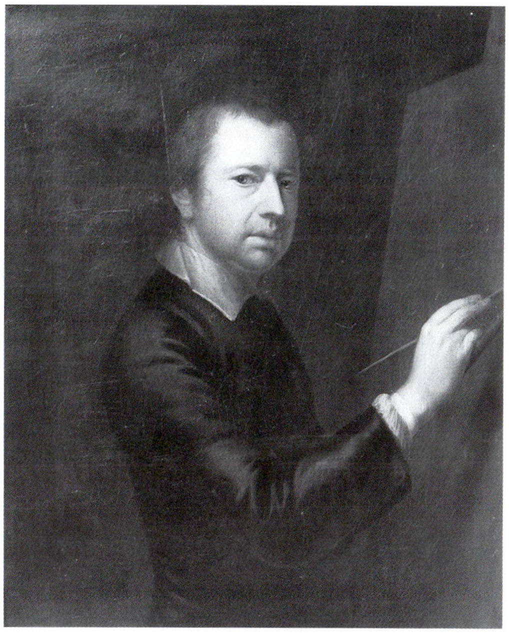

DEVIS Self portrait c.1754-55 (Harris Museum and Art Gallery, Preston)

ICONOGRAPHY

Self Portraits

c.1737-38 Painting,★ half length. Harris MAG, Preston (*Devis* 1980, no.47; *Devis* 1983, no.1).

1742 Painting,★ half length. Harris MAG, Preston, given by the sitter to his father in 1742 (*Devis* 1980, no.49; *Devis* 1983, no.2).

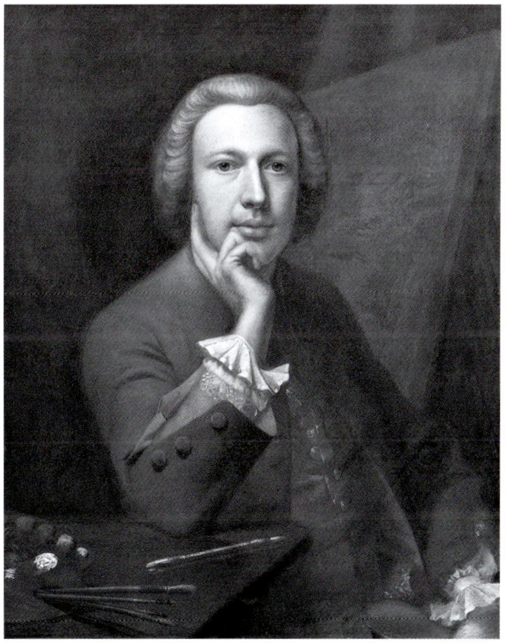

DEVIS Self portrait 1742 (Harris Museum and Art Gallery, Preston)

c.1742 Miniature on copper, bust-length oval. Harris MAG, Preston (*Devis* 1980, no.48; *Devis* 1983, no.58). A pendant to a miniature he drew of his wife (also in the Harris MAG).

c.1742-44 Miniature on panel, see NPG 6153.

c.1754-55 Painting,★ half length, painting at his easel in Van Dyck dress. Harris MAG, Preston (*Devis* 1980, no.50; *Devis* 1983, no.33).

By other Artists

1764 Unattributed miniature, bust-length oval. Harris MAG, Preston (illus. S.H. Pavière, *The Devis Family of Painters*, 1950, pl.7; on p.13 he suggested an attribution to Richard Corbould, see c.1788 below, who in 1764 was thirteen years old).

1787 Drawing by Anthony Devis (the sitter's half brother), profile. Harris MAG, Preston (illus. *Devis* 1983, no.61).

c.1788 Miniature by Richard Corbould, sleeping head lying in death, inscribed: *Behold the virtuous man ...*, set in a model tomb commissioned by his daughter Ellin. Harris MAG, Preston (*Devis* 1983, fig. xi). Corbould was Devis's son-in-law.

DOUBTFUL PORTRAIT

Miniature 'self-portrait' drawing, as a double of the Young Pretender; Harris MAG, Preston (illus. *Devis* 1983, no.66b).

DEVONSHIRE, Georgiana, Duchess of, *née* Spencer 1757-1806

A leader of Whig society; dau. of the 1st Earl Spencer, m. 1774 the 5th Duke of Devonshire who from 1784 shared the favours of Lady Elizabeth Foster, whom he eventually m. 1809 - a *ménage à trois* founded on mutual admiration and a love of high fashion.

'The Duchess of Devonshire effaces all, without being a beauty; but her youth, figure, flowing good nature, sense and lively modesty, and modest familiarity, make her a phenomenon' (Horace Walpole, 1775).

'her beauty ... lay in the amenity and grace of her deportment, in her irresistible manners and the seduction of her society. Her hair was not without a tinge of red, and her face, though pleasing, yet had it not been illuminated by her mind, might have been considered as an ordinary countenance' (Sir Nathaniel Wraxall, 1815).

1041 ascribed to JOSHUA REYNOLDS c.1759-61

Canvas 61 x 48.5 (24 x 19) lined; the darks and her hair upper right much disfigured with shrinkage craquelure; a fine craquelure in the dress; very broadly painted: the right side of the dress and her right arm and hand unresolved.

Light brown eyes (but her left eye a black blob), fair hair, white head dress with a blue stripe, wearing a blue-striped white dress with blue waistband; red background, grey spandrels; perhaps the hint of a chair lower right. Within a painted oval.

Collections: Farrer; John Heugh sale, Christie's, 10 May 1878, lot 234, bt. Wigzell; G.R. Burnett sale, Christie's, 18 March 1882, lot 114, bt. Colnaghi;[1] Lord Ronald Sutherland Gower, the sitter's great-grandson,[2] by whom presented 1896.

Exhibitions: *Fair Children*, Grafton Gallery, 1895(161); Beningbrough 1979-.

Reference: Graves & Cronin, III, p.922; Simon 1997, pp. 64, 161; Mannings 2000, no.1680.

A broadly painted sketch with a much disfigured surface, NPG 1041 is difficult to assess. It relates directly to the Reynolds double portrait of *Lady Spencer and her Daughter*★ (see below 1759-61), and was sold in 1878 as a sketch for it.[3] Mannings, however, who dates NPG 1041 c.1759 (but the sitter is surely older than two?), reserves slight doubts concerning the attribution; Waterhouse considered it an old copy,[4] and Graves & Cronin noted that 'the title rests in the statement of Mr Farrer; but there is no record whatever of the picture'. A version, the same size but without the painted oval, was sold Christie's, 28 November 1969, lot 129.

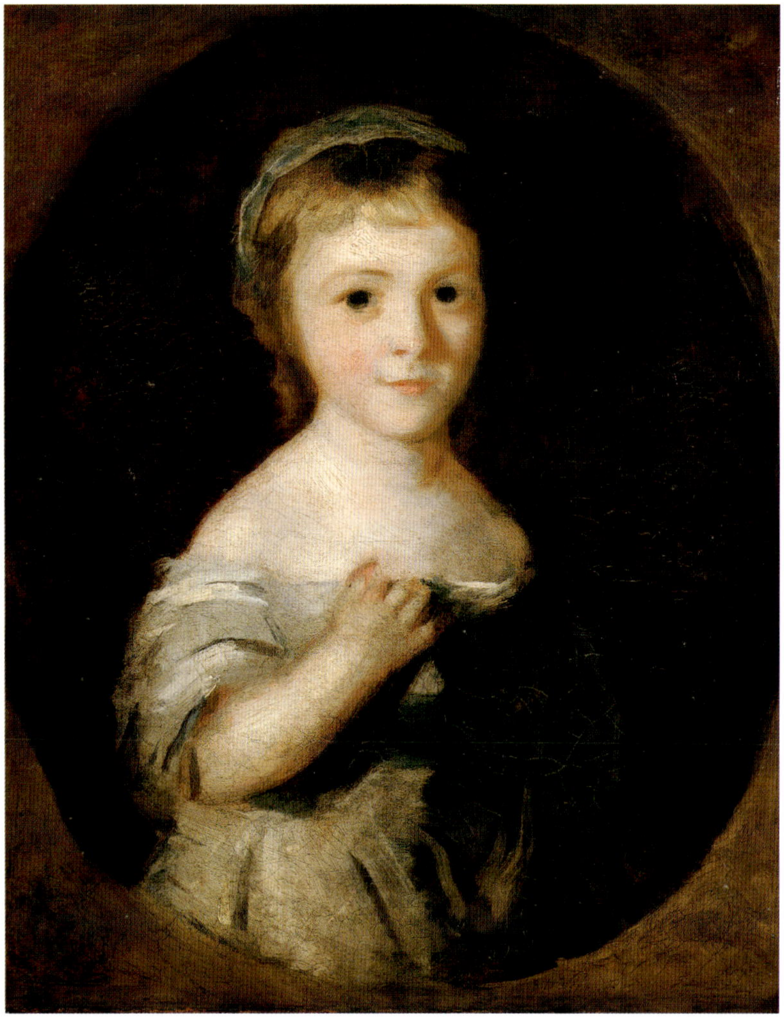

Georgiana, Duchess of DEVONSHIRE NPG *1041*

1 A. Mackay to Lord Ronald Sutherland Gower, 20 March 1882, confirmed the provenance as 'formerly the property of Mr Henry Farrer the previous history is unknown. It was bought at the sale of Mr Fs effects - & sold to Mr John Heugh - then to Mr G R Burnett, the distiller at whose sale the 18th March 1882 it was bought' (NPG archive). But NPG 1041 is not identifiable in the Farrer sales of 1866-68 (L.29211, 29685, 30453); lot 104 in his sale of 15 June 1866 (L.29211) was a portrait of the Duchess by Hoppner 'in a white dress with landscape background'. The account repeated in R.S. Gower, *Bric à Brac*, 1888, p.66.

2 Illus. at Gower Lodge, Windsor, in sitting room no.2, R.S. Gower, *Bric à Brac*, 1888, f.p.6.

3 A view last repeated by J. Steegman, *AQ*, XXI, 1958, p.249.

4 In his annotated copy of Graves & Cronin (Paul Mellon Centre, London). K. Garlick described NPG 1041 as 'a somewhat doubtful sketch' (*Wal. Soc.*, XLV, 1976, p.68).

ICONOGRAPHY

The 'numerous indubitable portraits of her vary so immensely that, but for documentary evidence, it would seem impossible that all represent the same person.' (C.F. Bell; MS note interleaved in his copy of V. Foster, *The Two Duchesses*, 1898, f.p.84; NPG).

In addition portraits of Georgiana have frequently been confused with those of Lady Elizabeth Foster (her successor as Duchess); W. Roberts, *MA*, XXV, 1901, pp.368-73, began their disentanglement. Their respective likenesses are best established by the documented double portraits by Downman of 1785 and 1787 and by Guérin of 1791. Georgiana had golden-red hair, a full face with a firm chin; Elizabeth dark hair, a straight nose, large dark eyes and a slightly receding chin. The principal portraits of the mature Georgiana are those by Angelica Kauffmann (c.1774), Gainsborough (1783), and the three by Reynolds (c.1775-76, 1784 and c.1785-89).

1758 Pastel by Katherine Read, as a baby (inscribed 'one year old') looking at a rose held by her mother. Althorp (*Wal. Soc.*, XLV, 1976, p.66, no.517). Possibly the unattributed miniature, 'as a child', exhibited SKM 1865(923) lent Spencer.

1759-61 Painting by Joshua Reynolds,★ whole-length standing, held by her mother. Althorp (Mannings 2000, no.1677). Engraved J. Watson 1770; R. Purcell; J.S. Paul 1771. Unfinished preparatory sketch

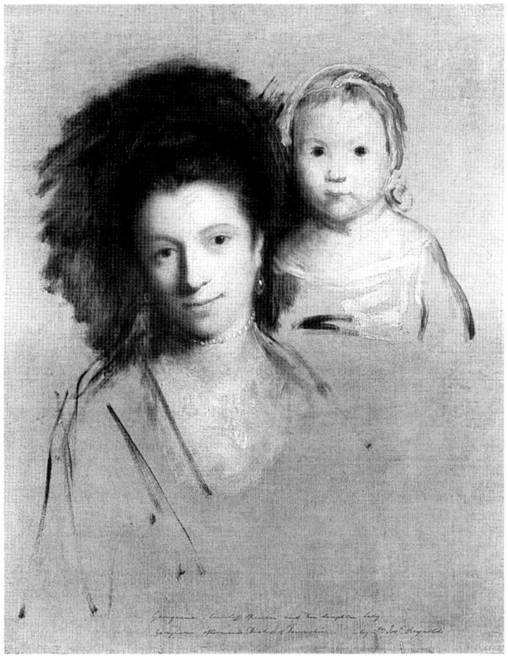

Georgiana, Duchess of DEVONSHIRE by Joshua Reynolds 1759-61 (Chatsworth)

at Chatsworth (Mannings 2000, no.1678); reduced version formerly at Castle Howard (Hawkesbury 1904, no.238). See also NPG 1041.

1763 Painting by Thomas Gainsborough,* three-quarter length standing, in white. Althorp (Waterhouse 1958, no.631, pl.76). Painted in Bath. Engraved R. Josey (oval); V. Lhuillier 1877. Oval version sold Christie's, 29 October 1988, lot 118. Small copy at Castle Howard by G.D. Tomlinson (Hawkesbury 1904, no.21); another sold Lawrence, Crewkerne, 10 November 1983, lot 233.

c.1765 Pastel by Katherine Read, bust length, wearing a bonnet. Althorp (*Wal. Soc.*, XLV, 1976, p.66, no.513, as aged seven or eight).

c.1766 Pastel by Katherine Read, bust length, with her brother George and sisters Henrietta and Charlotte. Althorp (*Wal. Soc.*, XLV, 1976, p.66, no.517).

1771 Pastel by H.D. Hamilton, bust-length oval. Chatsworth.

c.1773 Painting by R.E. Pine, half-length holding a lyre, with flowers in her hair. Althorp (*Wal. Soc.*, XLV, 1976, p.63, no.499, described as aged sixteen).

c.1774 Painting by Angelica Kauffmann, whole-length seated with her brother and sister (George, 2nd Earl Spencer and Henrietta, Countess of Bessborough). Althorp (illus. *Wal. Soc.*, XLV, 1976, pl.19). The ladies alone, against a slightly different background, engraved W. Dickinson (illus. *Connoisseur*, L, 1918, p.203). An oval miniature of the

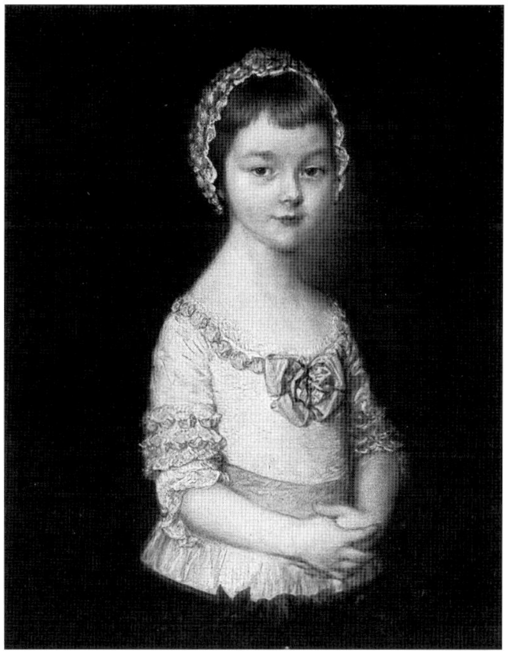

Georgiana, Duchess of DEVONSHIRE by Thomas Gainsborough 1763 (Althorp)

Duchess alone, in a rose-coloured dress, described as after Kauffman, sold Christie's, SK, 14 December 1999, lot 11. See also Hurter 1779 below.

c.1775 Miniature by Jeremiah Meyer, half length, a veil on her head, unfinished. Royal Collection (Walker 1992, no.266). Previously attributed to Richard Cosway (cf. Williamson 1905, f.p.100). A similar bust-length miniature by Meyer, the face alone finished, is also in the Royal Collection (Walker 1992, no.267); version sold Sotheby's, 13 February 1978, lot 80.

c.1775-76 Painting by Joshua Reynolds, whole-length standing in a landscape. Huntington Art Collections, San Marino, Calif. (25.20; Mannings 2000, no.327; *Huntington* 2001, no.73). Engraved V. Green 1780; S. Freeman 1822 (three-quarter length); S.W. Reynolds; W. Read 1836 (three-quarter length); S. Cousins 1878. Reversed copy sold Christie's, SK, 15 September 1994, lot 17.

1776 Anon. engraving, half-length oval, *Court Beauties no.10*, pub. R. Baldwin 1776.

1777-84 Painting by James Barry, *Distribution of Premiums in the Society of Arts*, part of the *Progress of Human Culture*, in which the Duchess appears standing centre right. Royal Society of Arts, London (Pressly 1981, no.26). Engraved J. Barry 1791. A study for the head appeared in the artist's sale, Christie's, 10 April 1807, lot 109.

1778 Drawing by Lady Diana Beauclerk, three-quarter length profile, seated. Mrs D.V. Garstin, America (illus. *Wal. Corr.*, XXVIII, f.p.386). Engraved F. Bartolozzi 1778; R. Laurie 1779; R. Stewart 1779; T. Watson 1782; W. Humphrey; J. Newton; Macklin. 'A Castalian nymph conceived by Sappho and executed by Myron would not have more grace and simplicity' (Walpole, 18 April 1778; *Wal. Corr.*, XXVIII, p.386). Watercolour copy in the Royal Collection (illus. *Connoisseur*, LXIII, 1922, p.1; Oppé 1950, no.60).

1779 Miniature by J.H. Hurter, bust-length oval, closely based on the head by Angelica Kauffmann of 1774, sold Sotheby Parke-Bernet, Monaco, 25-26 June 1976, lot 384. Another dated 1779 is in the Gilbert collection (illus. Coffin & Hofstetter 2000, no.29).

1780 Miniature by J.H. Hurter, bust-length oval, with extravagantly dressed hair. Madresfield. Exhibited *British Portrait Miniatures*, Edinburgh, 1965(396).

1781 Miniature by J.H. Hurter, bust-length oval. Madresfield (illus. Foskett 1979, p.335, pl.94g).

1781 Engraving *from the life* by J.K. Sherwin, oval, half-length seated. A derivative engraving pub. E. Hedges 1783 (illus. *MA*, XXV, 1901, p.369).

1782 Miniature by J.H. Hurter, bust-length oval. Madresfield (SSB 92/13). Hurter also copied the Reynolds portrait of the Duke of the Devonshire in 1782.

1782 Painting by Maria Cosway, whole length as Cynthia from *The Faerie Queen* (iii, 43). Chatsworth (illus. *Cosway* 1995, p.104, see no.229). Exhibited RA 1782(17). Engraved V. Green 1783 (half length).

1782 Miniature by Richard Cosway, bust length in white with a pearl necklace. Royal Collection (Walker 1992, no.192). Versions at Chatsworth and J.P. Morgan sale, 2nd day, 25 June 1935, lot 275 (illus. Williamson, 1906, II, no.268, pl.lxxxv).

A closely related miniature at Althorp, without the necklace and a greater décolleté, engraved G.T. Stubbs 1782 (illus. *MA*, XXV, 1901, p.368). A similar head appears in the Cosway miniature at Chatsworth showing the Duchess(?) as Venus holding a silver bowl, exhibited BFAC 1889(iv 42, pl.xvii), and in a Cosway miniature in the Huntington Art Collections, San Marino, Calif., of the Duchess 'holding her infant son' [but evidently a daughter, either Georgiana b.1782 or Harriet b.1785], exhibited BFAC 1889 (xl 37, pl.xvii).

The Duchess sat to Cosway frequently and a substantial bill for work executed between 1776 and

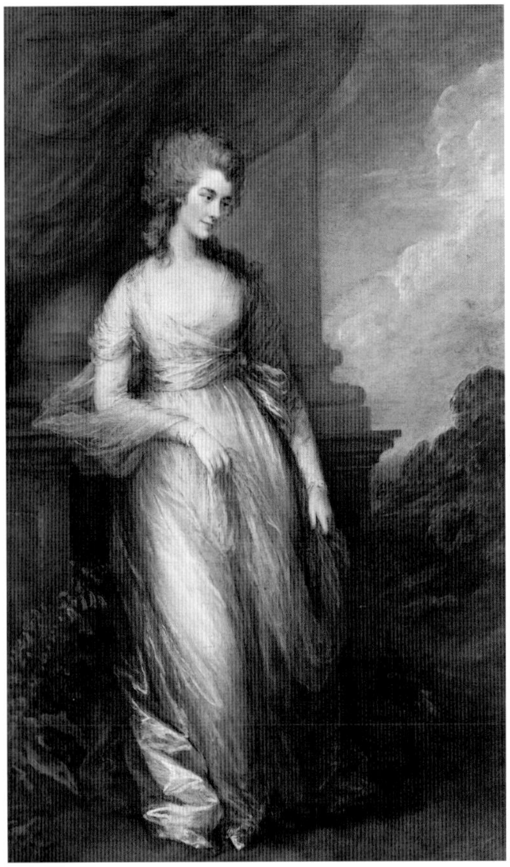

Georgiana, Duchess of DEVONSHIRE by Thomas Gainsborough 1783 (National Gallery of Art, Washington)

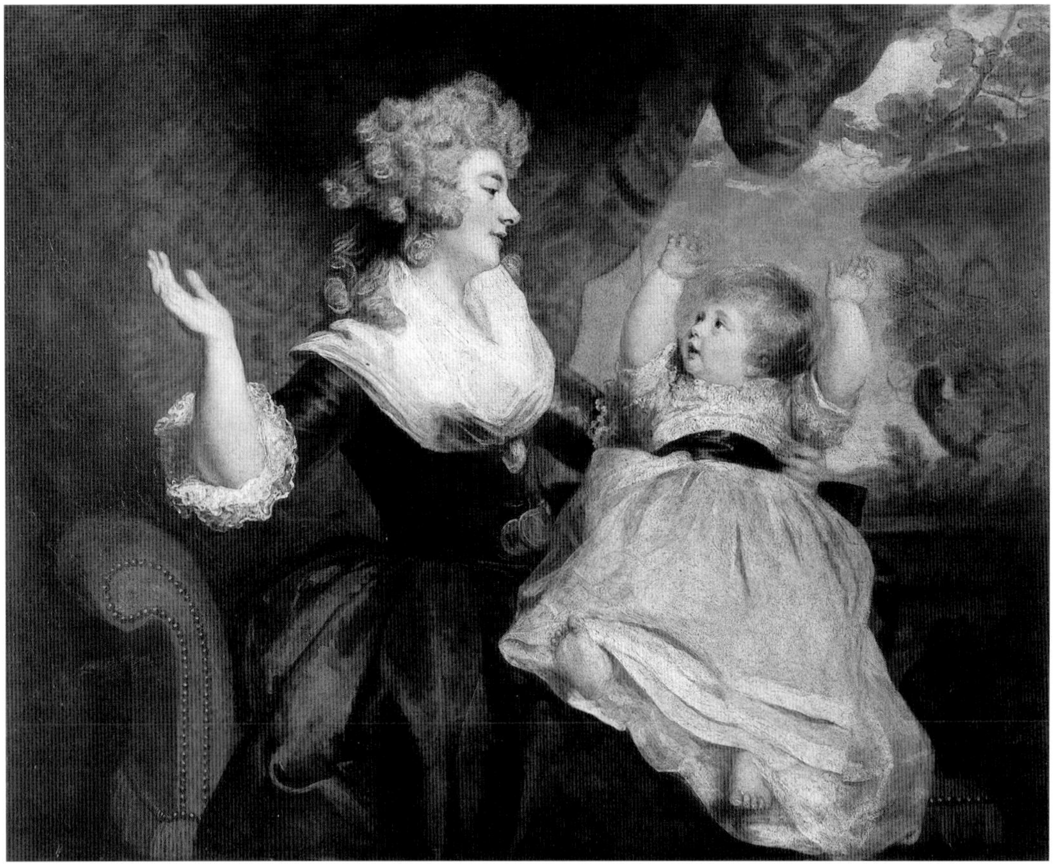

Georgiana, Duchess of DEVONSHIRE by Joshua Reynolds 1784 (Chatsworth)

1789 remained unpaid in 1820 (*Cosway* 1995, p.118 under no.54); see also below, c.1785 and 1786.

1782 Drawing by Thomas Lawrence, bust-length oval. Chatsworth. Drawn at Bath when the artist was thirteen years of age (illus. *Pickpocketing the Rich*, Bath, 2002, no.54).

1782 Wedgwood medallion, the model attributed to John Flaxman (illus. Reilly 1973, p.122).

1783 Medallion by Robert Stewart, exhibited SA 1783(309).

1783 Miniature by James Nixon, half-length with loose hair, engraved F. Bartolozzi 1783 (illus. *MA*, XXV, 1901, p.368) and I.B. Martin.

1783 Painting by Thomas Gainsborough,* whole-length standing. NG Washington (1937.1.93; Waterhouse 1958, no.194) formerly at Althorp. Probably RA 1783(78). Engraved W.W. Barney 1808; H. Meyer from a drawing by J. Jackson 1814; R.B. Parkes. Reduced copy by G.D. Tomlinson 1858 at Castle Howard (Hawkesbury 1904, no.623); a three-quarter length copy by John Rising exhibited *Guelph* 1891(336) lent Lord Hartington.

A closely related half-length drawing attributed to Ozias Humphry dated 1782, sold Christie's, 16 November 1982, lot 78; a half-length oval miniature copy by Henry Spicer at Chatsworth.

1783 Miniature by Ozias Humphry, half-length seated. Althorp. Exhibited SKM 1865(949, 'a profile sketch from nature') and BFAC 1889(xxxii 43).

In 1784 the Duchess's extravagant canvassing on behalf of Fox and the Whigs attracted much attention and she was, for example, frequently caricatured by Thomas Rowlandson (George describes nine within nos.6520-63)

1784 Painting by Joshua Reynolds,* seated three-quarter length with her infant daughter, Lady Georgiana. Chatsworth (Mannings 2000, no.329). RA 1786(166) Engraved G. Keating 1787. Copy by William Etty in the Royal Collection (Millar 1969, no.1041); a miniature copy by Samuel Shelley, J.P. Morgan sale, Christie's, 3rd day, 26 June 1935, lot 440; other unattributed miniature copies exhibited SKM 1865(2726) lent A.G. Ponsonby, and sold Christie's, 12 May 1998, lot 20; an enamel by H.P. Bone exhibited RA 1845(689) and another by William Grimaldi (Grimaldi 1873, p.29, no.246); a pastel copy by William Lane 1809 sold Christie's, 5-7 March 1904, lot 104 from Raynham (Duleep Singh 1928, ii, p.199, no.9).

1784 Drawing by John Downman, oval half length. Fitzwilliam Museum, Cambridge (2314.15). Another dated 1784 in the British Museum (1967.10.14.194; illus. R.S. Gower, *Bric à Brac*, 1888, f.p.82) with an undated half length (1967.10.14.203). Another was listed at Castle Howard (Hawkesbury 1904, no.467).

1785 Drawing by John Downman seated in a garden, Lady Elizabeth Foster standing by her. Ickworth. Engraved E. Tily (illus. Williamson 1907, pl.19).

1785 Curious casts in wax of the Duchess, 'intended as ornaments for mansions, public libraries, etc', were being sold by Austin, Drawing Master, St James's Street, London, in 1785 (*Morning Herald*, 22 April 1785).

c.1785 Painting by George Romney 'a beautiful whole-length of the amiable Duchess of Devonshire' was reported in his studio in 1785 (Whitley 1928, II, p.63). Seven sittings by the Duchess are listed between 1788 and 1794; 'each time he commenced a new picture, but none proceeded beyond the first sitting' (Romney 1830, p.149;

Ward & Roberts 1904, II, p.45).

c.1785 Painting attributed to John Downman, half length, her left hand holding the brim of her hat. Chatsworth. Exhibited BFAC 1932(155 as ascribed to Downman). Scharf had puzzled over the attribution, settling for Downman in 1870 (SSB 85/21), as described by the 6th Duke of Devonshire in his *Handbook to Chatsworth and Hardwick*, 1844, p.209.

c.1785 Miniature by Richard Cosway, bust-length, an unfinished head. Fitzwilliam Museum, Cambridge (PD 961-1963; illus. Bayne-Powell, 1985, p.40); from Lord Wharncliffe.

c.1785-89 Painting by Joshua Reynolds, unfinished half-length profile, wearing a black hat. Chatsworth (Mannings 2000, no.328). A 'finished' version with Scott & Fowles, New York, 1952.

1786 Miniature by Richard Cosway, bust-length, wearing large white bonnet. Chatsworth (illus. *Cosway* 1995, pl.61, no.76).

1786 Three half-length miniatures by Andrew Plimer:

a) seated to right, in white holding a bouquet, sold Christie's, 27 November 1984, lot 149, from J.P. Morgan (illus. Williamson 1903, f.p.89)

b) to left, sold Christie's, 27 November 1979, lot 48, from E.M. Hodgkins (illus. Williamson 1903, f.p.22)

c) to right in white, sold Christie's, SK, 27 October 1998, lot 45.

1787 Watercolour by John Downman, whole-length standing, wearing white. Chatsworth (illus. *Romantic Women Writers*, Grasmere, 1994-95, no.24). Engraved F. Bartolozzi 1788 (as a half-length oval; reissued 1797) as after *an original drawing for the Scenery at Richmond House Theatre* (illus. *Connoisseur*, X, 1904, p.130); J. Collyer (illus. Williamson 1907, p.27). A preliminary drawing, an *Outline, the Duchess of Devonshire, 1787. A whole length for the Duke of Richmond* is in the British Museum (1936.11.16.31/21). A related chalk drawing of the head alone sold Christie's, 17 October 1971, lot 100. A 'Head by Downman' was listed at Hardwick (Hawkesbury 1903, no.245).

1787 Drawn and engraved *from the life* by P. Wray, bust-length oval wearing a large plumed hat (*European Mag.*; illus. *MA*, 1901, XXV, p.368).

1788 *Portraits of Four Ladies of Quality* (Devonshire, Richmond, Duncannon, etc) by John Downman, exhibited RA 1788(451).

1788 A portrait of the Duchess belonging to the Duke of Portland was sent from Mansfield Woodhouse to London on 23 July 1788, since very tentatively identified with a small whole length attributed to Angelica Kauffmann at Welbeck (*Portland Cat.* 1936, no.553).

1790 Drawing by Thomas Rowlandson, with her sister Lady Duncannon, singing accompanied by a lutenist. Yale Center for British Art (B1975.3.141).

c.1790-95 Miniature attributed to Samuel Shelley, half length with turban. Sotheby's, 5 June 2001, lot 5, from the J.P. Morgan collection (Williamson 1906, II, no.349, pl.CVI, as Andrew Plimer).

1791 Miniature by J-U. Guérin, three-quarter length standing with Lady Elizabeth Foster. Wallace Collection (M177, illus. *Cat. of Miniatures*, 1980, p.168). Painted at Passy in November 1791. A copy sold Sotheby's, 20-31 October 1988, lot 244, and a bust-length of the Duchess alone by Horace Hone 1812 in the Gilbert collection (Coffin & Hofstetter 2000, no.25).

1793 Painting by Hugh Robinson, made in Rome (Ingamells 1997, pp.295, 815).

c.1795? Enamel miniature by Thomas Peat, bust-length oval. Louvre (RF30921; illus. *d'Outre Manche*, Paris, 1994, p.213, no.132). Another, bust length, in a landscape, sold Christie's, Geneva, 28 April 1976, lot 151; another, signed and inscribed, at Chatsworth (*Treasures from Chatsworth* 1979, no.24).

In 1796 the Duchess lost the sight of her right eye, which was said to droop thereafter. In 1799 Elizabeth, Lady Holland, rather wickedly described the Duchess: 'Her figure is corpulent, her complexion coarse, one eye gone, and her neck immense. How frail is the tenure of beauty' (Journal, 1908, p.244).

1800 Drawing by [Samuel] Drummond, bust-length oval, two large plumes in her hair; engraved W. Ridley 1800.

c.1800-05 Drawing by Henry Edridge, bust length, her hair dressed in a white turban. Holker Hall. The profile somewhat resembles that drawn by Humphry in 1783.

1805 Anon. engraving *from an original Drawing*, half-length profile, hair dressed with a dark band, pub. R. Philips 1805 (*Public Characters of 1806*; illus. D.M. Stuart, *Dearest Bess*, 1955, f.p.86).

The Duchess appeared in a number of group portraits, including:

The Finding of Moses painted and engraved by J.K. Sherwin 1789 ('The Princess Royal is the Egyptian infanta, accompanied by the Duchesses of Gloucester, Cumberland, Devonshire, Rutland, Lady Duncannon, etc ...', *Wal. Corr.*, XXIX, p.185; illus. V. Foster, *The Two Duchesses*, 1898, f.p.278).

The Three Witches from Macbeth, pastel by Daniel Gardner of c.1790, with Lady Melbourne on the left and Mrs Anne Damer on the right. Christie's, 10 July 1990, lot 85 (illus. Williamson 1921, f.p.44). A second version of the composition (illus. Williamson 1921, p.36) was listed at Panshanger (cat., 1885, p.475, as by Anne Damer).

The Shakespeare Gallery, watercolour by Francis Wheatley 1790 (Victoria and Albert Museum; 1719.1871).

DOUBTFUL PORTRAITS

Paintings: by Gainsborough, Chatsworth House Trust (Waterhouse 1958, no.195; see Whitley 1915, pp.199-200); a copy by Gainsborough Dupont in the NG Washington (1970.17.119; Hayes 1992, pp.66-67 as the Duchess of Devonshire).

attributed to John Hoppner, formerly Hardwick Hall ((Hawkesbury 1903, no.89; SSB 74/52).

Miniatures: attributed to Richard Cosway (illus. Williamson 1897, f.p.46) probably shows Louisa Dorothea Holroyd (Williamson 1897, pp.106, 123, 124, listed Cosway miniatures of Georgiana in the collections of Lord Tweedmouth, F. Woodroffe and Lord de Mauley).

by Andrew Plimer, formerly at Castle Howard (illus. Williamson 1903, f.p.90) copied in enamel by Henry Bone 1795 (see *Bone* 1999, no.159) shows Elizabeth, Duchess of Devonshire.

attributed to Ozias Humphry, sold Bearnes, Torquay, 15 January 1986, lot 13 (somewhat resembling a small bust-length oval painting called Downman at Chatsworth).

by Antonio Fattori, formerly at Castle Howard (illus. I. Leveson Gower, *A Face without a Frown*, 1944, f.p.129).

by Anne Mee, Royal Collection (Walker 1992, no.865; showing some resemblance to the Duchess's daughter Harriet, 1785-1862, who m. Lord Granville 1809); a drawing apparently after Mee by William Lane, dated 1809, sold Phillips, 13 January 1969, lot P9.

Drawings: by William Lane listed at Castle Howard (Hawkesbury 1904, p.76, no.633); a similar miniature formerly at Holland House (cat., 1904, p.193, no.4) was described as based on a picture by Angelica Kauffmann in the collection of Claud Ponsonby, but see Walker 1992, no.865; 'by Lady Elizabeth Foster 1791', in the collection of Lord Dormer (illus. D.M. Stuart, *Dearest Bess*, 1955, f.p.86); a curiosity.

DEVONSHIRE, William Cavendish, 5th Duke of 1748-1811

Suc. as 5th Duke 1764; in Italy 1768-69; KG 1782; the phlegmatic husband successively of Georgiana Spencer and Elizabeth Foster and the patron of Fox, who died in his house at Chiswick; once described as 'a jewel not yet well polished'.

2076 see Groups, *Mr Fox and his Friends* by WILLIAM LANE c.1813

ICONOGRAPHY

1765 Miniature by Nathaniel Hone, half length in a blue coat. Welbeck. Described by the sitter's sister as 'a most shocking thing' (*Welbeck Abbey Miniatures,* 1916, p.156, no.227).

1765 Painting by Arthur Devis, the artist chosen by the sitter's tutor. 'I am much afraid it will be frightful' wrote Lord John Cavendish (*Devis* 1980, pp.31, 81).

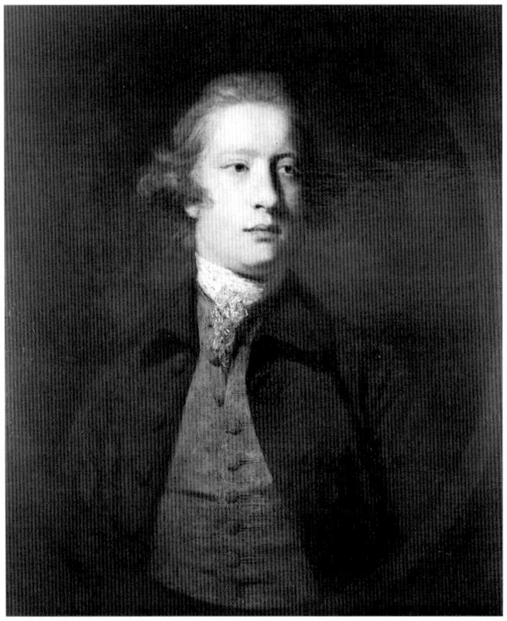

5th Duke of DEVONSHIRE by Joshua Reynolds 1766-67 (Private Collection)

1766-67 Painting by Joshua Reynolds,* half length. Private collection (Mannings 2000, no.336). Exhibited NPE 1867(474) lent Lord Crewe.

1767 Pastel by Francis Cotes, half length. Formerly at Welbeck Abbey (Johnson 1976, no.208).

In Italy (April 1768-May 1769)

1768 Painting by Thomas Patch, *The Music Lesson,* whole-length, morose and seated, with Henry Lyte, William Fitzherbert and an Italian music master. Private collection (illus. *Wal. Soc.*, XXVIII, 1940, f.p.50, pl.x). Painted in Florence.

1768-69 Painting by Anton von Maron, three-quarter-length standing. Chatsworth. Painted in Rome. In 1845 the 6th Duke of Devonshire wrote that the 'face was so very bad that Elizabeth, Duchess of Devonshire, had it altered by (I believe) Mr Rising, the cleaner of pictures – from Sir Joshua' (Ingamells 1997, p.296).

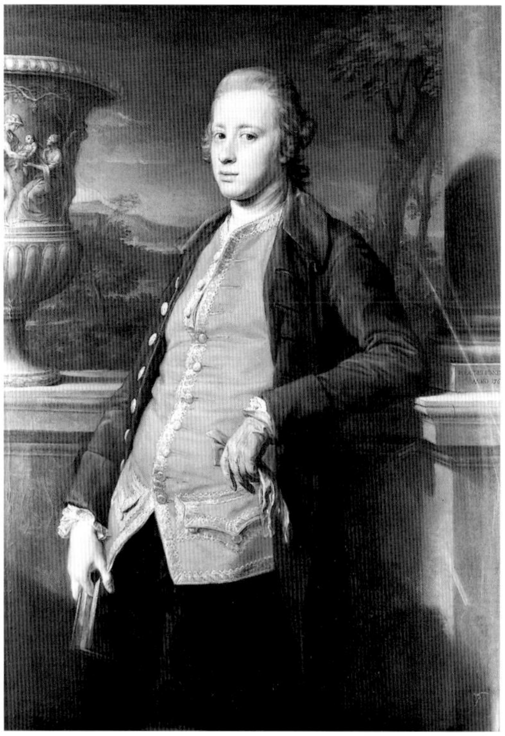

5th Duke of DEVONSHIRE by Pompeo Batoni 1768 (Chatsworth)

1768 Painting by Pompeo Batoni,* three-quarter-length standing. Chatsworth (Clark 1985, no.321). Painted in Rome.

England

1775 Painting by Joshua Reynolds, half length, with a high-collared brown coat. Althorp (Mannings 2000, no.337). Engraved J.R. Smith 1776. A copy, perhaps by Hayter, formerly at Hardwick. Watercolour copy by William Grimaldi (Grimaldi 1873 p.29, no.245) and a pastel by William Lane, the head only finished, private collection (formerly at Raynham Hall; Duleep Singh, II, p.199, no.10), presumably a preparatory study for *Mr Fox and his Friends,* see Groups NPG 2076.

Miniature copies by Henry Bone: exhibited RA 1811, no.321; NG of Ireland, 19.274; Christie's, 20 June 1967, lot 5; Castle Howard sale, Sotheby's, 2nd day, 12 November 1991, lot 546); Bone's preparatory drawing in the NPG Bone albums (*Bone* 1999, no.158); by J.H. Hurter 1782 (Madresfield; Foskett 1979, p.334, pl.94e); by Andrew Plimer 1786 (Sotheby's, Monaco, 23-24 June 1976, lot 13); by Richard Cosway (Buxton Museum), another formerly in the Sutherland collection, and by Ozias Humphry, Chatsworth (Williamson 1917, p.240).

1779-81 Painting by J.S. Copley,* *The Death of Chatham*, see Comparative Groups.

1793 Drawn and engraved by C.T. Warren 1793, bust-length, elderly and overweight.

Posthumous

1812 Draped marble bust by Joseph Nollekens. Examples bearing the date 1812 are in the Royal Collection (illus. *Princes as Patrons*, Cardiff, 1998, p.81), at Chatsworth, Chiswick House and the North Carolina Museum of Art, Raleigh (see *North Carolina Museum of Art Bulletin*, XIV, i, 1977, pp.1-13). A workshop example also dated 1812 sold Sotheby's, 21 April 1988, lot 287.

c.1813 Drawing by William Lane, *Mr Fox and his Friends*, see Groups NPG 2076.

DIBDIN, Charles 1745-1814

Entertainer; b. Southampton; London debut 1760, becoming best known as a writer of sea songs (such as *Tom Bowling*); 'the spirited strains of Dibdin [were] no mean auxiliary to the English government [during the French wars]' (Herman Melville); he wrote *A Complete History of the English Stage* 1800, a *Tour through Scotland and England* 1808, and a rather cantankerous autobiography 1803.

'he sang, and accompanied himself on an instrument, which was a concert in itself; he was, in fact, his own band. A few lines of speaking happily introduced his admirable songs, full of wit and character, and his peculiar mode of singing them surpassed all I ever heard' (John O'Keeffe, 1826).

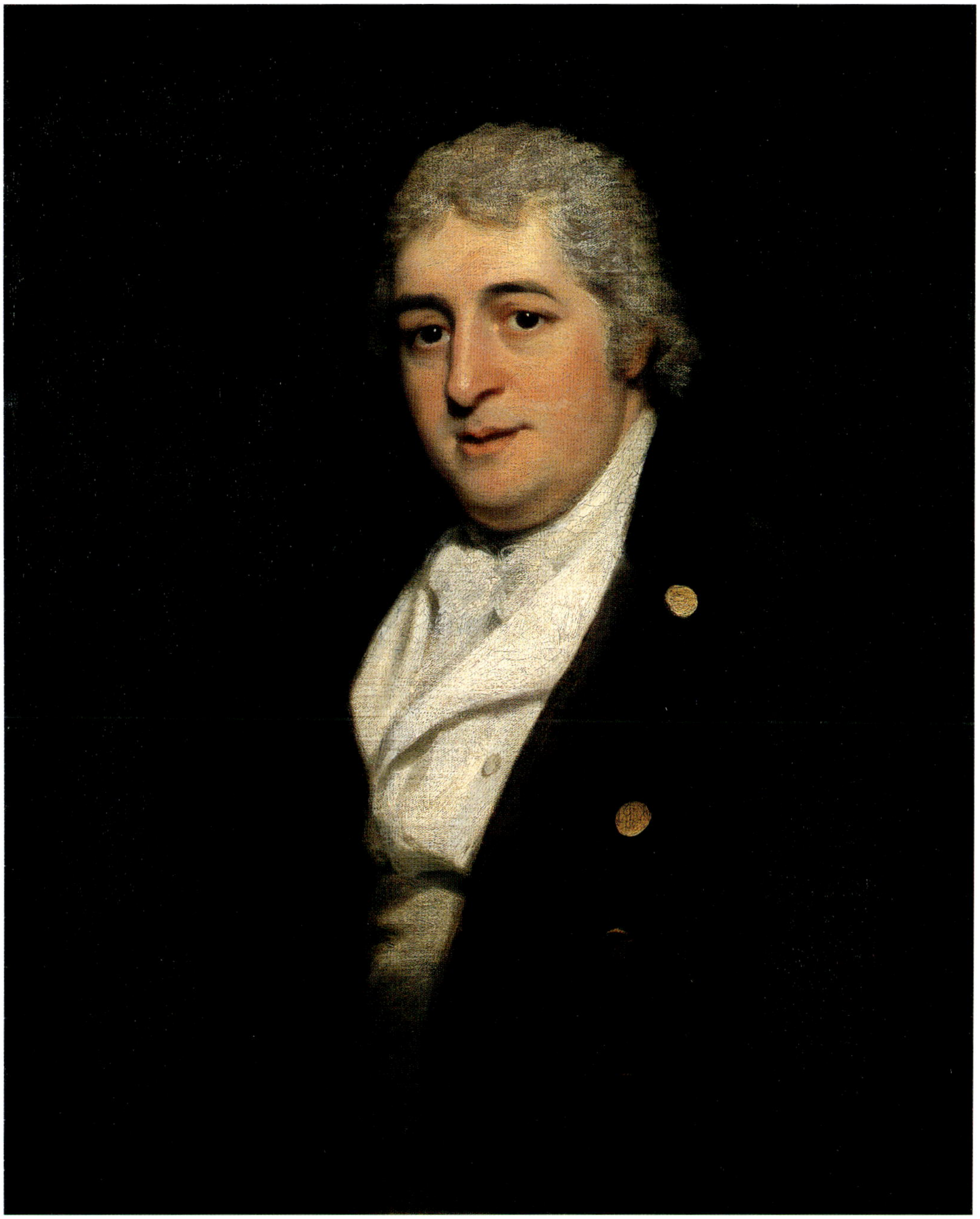

DIBDIN *NPG 103*

103 THOMAS PHILLIPS 1799

Canvas 75.5 x 63 (29¾ x 24¾) lined, the surface a little rubbed,[1] as seen in the hair and neckcloth; signed and dated, lower left: *TP* (monogram)/ *1799*.

Brown eyes, grey powdered hair, wearing a white neckcloth and waistcoat, and a dark brown coat with black collar and brass buttons.

Collections: John Hutchinson;[2] Samuel John Egbert Jones, from whom purchased 1860.

Engravings: J. Young 1799; W. Greatbach 1838; A. Dick 1838 (vignette); G. Stodart.

Exhibitions: NPE 1868(10); *Royal Naval Exhibition*, Chelsea, 1891(497).

Reference: *Phillips Sitter Book*, March 1799, no.92.

A three-quarters of Dibdin is entered in the Phillips sitter book in March 1799; a marginal note indicates that it was exhibited with the five other portraits listed that month, but it seems the Dibdin was never shown in the artist's lifetime.[3]

1 In 1860 it had 'never been cleaned but coming to me in a very filthy state I have washed it with water only and rubbed over it a little megilp attenuated with poppy oil' (E. Niemann to Scharf, 28 May 1860; NPG archive).

2 'It came to me from the late Mr John Hutchinson for many years the friend of the Dibdins. I have no doubt it was either a present to him as a slight compensation for that friendly assistance he was accustomed to yield them up to the termination of their lives, or he had become its purchaser when they wanted money' (S.J.E. Jones to Dr E. Niemann, 7 May 1860; NPG archive).

3 The sitter book is not scrupulous, e.g. the *Miss Sabine* entered for March 1799 had been exhibited RA 1798(290), but four of the portraits listed that month are identifiable at the RA in 1799.

ICONOGRAPHY

See also the *Harvard Catalogue*, I, pp.364-65, and Highfill, IV, pp.375-76 (listing further portrayals of Dibdin in character).

1794 Painting attributed to Samuel De Wilde, half length. Private collection, by descent in the sitter's family. Engraved W. Ridley 1794 (oval; as after C. Wilde); an anon. reversed print puts the Kearsley head of 1795 on the Wilde body.

c.1794 Watercolour by Robert Dighton, bust-length oval, signed and inscribed. Sotheby's, 23 February 1978, lot 78. Engraved anon. 1794. Dighton illustrated some of Dibdin's songs 1790-95.

1795 Painting by Thomas Kearsley, half length. Corporation of Southampton. Exhibited *Guelph* 1891(268) and presumably the portrait exhibited RA 1795(188). Engraved B. Smith 1801 (illus. Highfill, IV, p.361), and see 1794 above.

1799 Painting by Thomas Phillips, see NPG 103.

c.1800 Painting by S.J. Arnold,* half-length seated;

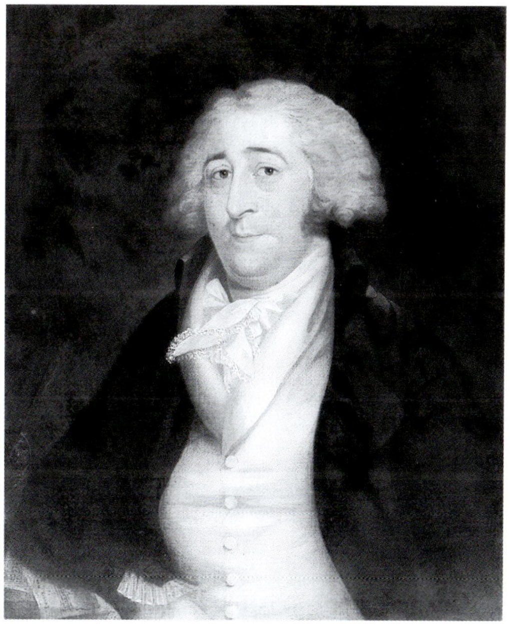

DIBDIN by S.J. Arnold c.1800 (Garrick Club)

Lovely Nan inscribed on paper on table (a song by Dibdin first performed in 1796). Garrick Club (Ashton 1997, no.154).

c.1802 Painting by A.W. Devis, half length; engraved B. Smith 1803 (for the *Professional Life of Mr Dibdin*; illus. *CL*, CLXII, 1977, p.1276); J. Heath 1809; W. Hawkins (reversed); H.B. Hall; C. Phillips (for *Pocket Selection of Dibdin Songs*).

1809 Painting by Samuel Drummond, half length, hair cut short at the sides, engraved W. Ridley 1809 (*European Mag*.).

1829 Marble bust on a monument by Robert Sievier, classically draped, a mourning figure below and an inscription (*author of the national naval ballads*). Royal Naval College, Greenwich. Sievier exhibited the mourning figure alone BI 1827(467).

A miniature said to show Dibdin was lent by Henry Melton to the *Royal Naval Exhibition*, Chelsea, 1891(1897), and an unspecified sculpture was shown by J. Milo Griffiths (2861). An undated and unattributed pastel portrait was in the Dibdin library sale, Worrall & Co., Liverpool, 13-14 May 1987, lot 350.

DOUBTFUL PORTRAITS

Paintings by John Downman, sold Sotheby's, 29 May 1963, lot 97, from the Ionides collection; attributed to J.T. Seton c.1790, called *The Dibdin Family*, sold Sotheby's, 13 July 1988, lot 48 (illus. Williamson 1920, f.p.152 as Zoffany; C. Saumarez Smith, *18th-century Decoration*, 1993, p.341 as c.1790); unattributed, Royal College of Music (illus. P. Scholes, *Oxford Companion to Music*, 1938, pl.53); attributed to William Beechey, formerly with Knoedler, London (illus. privately printed pamphlet, W. Roberts, *Charles Dibdin by Beechey*, 1922); by William Owen, Museum of Fine Arts, Boston, Mass. (97.444).

DODD, William 1729-77

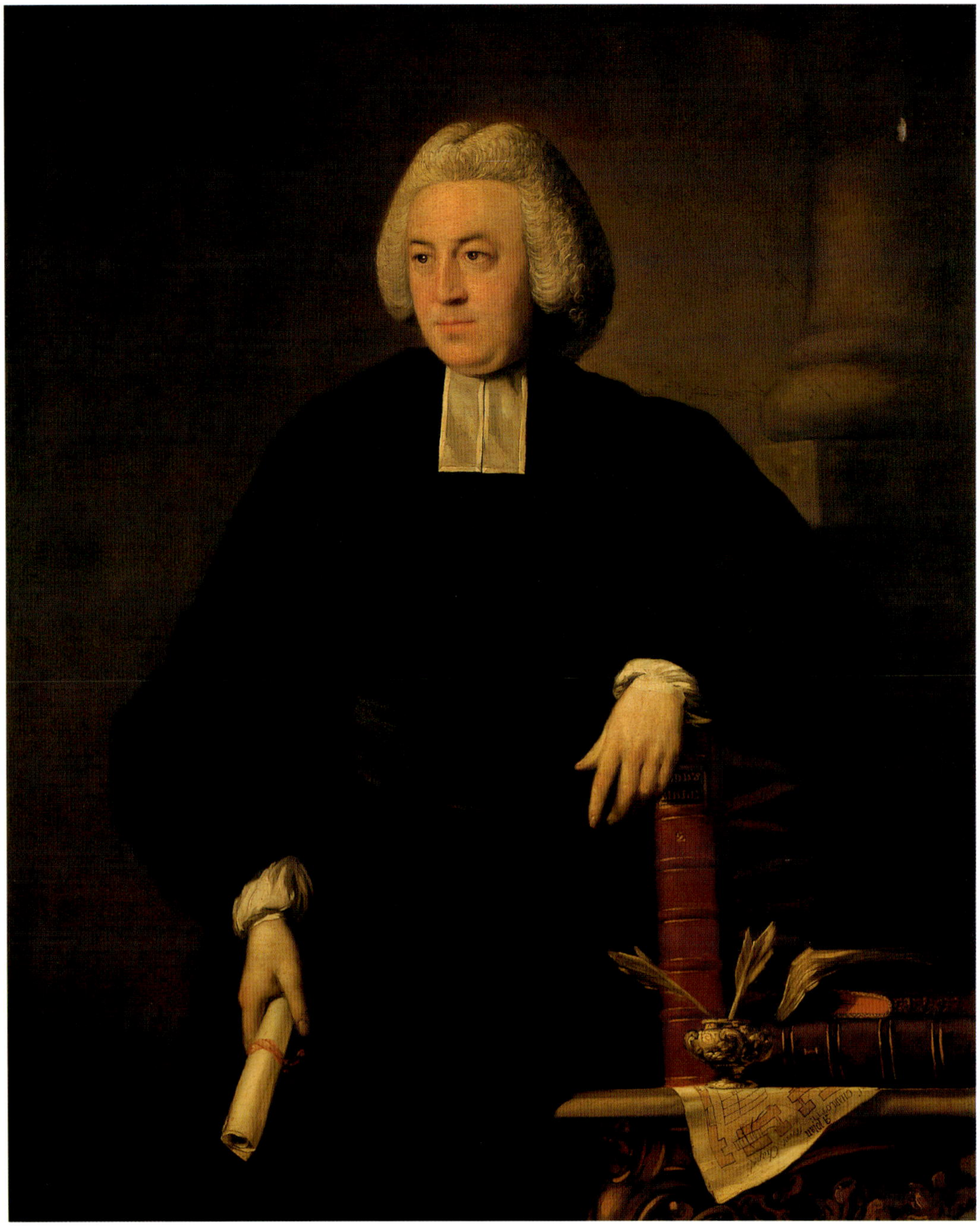

DODD NPG *251*

Extravagant parson and forger; chaplain of the Magdalen Hospital at Streatham ('the mother Penitentiary of the Empire') 1758-77; private tutor to Philip Stanhope (later 5th Lord Chesterfield); built the Charlotte Chapel, Pimlico, 1768; his many publications included *Beauties of Shakespeare* 1752 and a Biblical commentary 1770; in 1777 he forged a bond for £4,200 in Lord Chesterfield's name, for which crime he was hanged, despite pleas for clemency from Dr Johnson.

'with a cambric handkerchief in one hand and a diamond ring on the other ... he waves this way and that way, and he courtsies, and he bows, and he bounces, ... but then his Wig, Madam! I am sure you must admire his dear wig; not with the bushy brown buckles hanging and dropping like a Newfoundland spaniel, but short, rounded off at the ear to show his plump cherry cheeks, white as a curd, feather-topped, and the curls as close as a cauliflower' (Samuel Foote, 1774).

'it is droll that a young comely divine should have fallen into the sin, not of Mary the Penitent, not of her host Simon the Pharisee, but of Simon Magus, the founder of Simony' (Walpole, 29 January 1774; *Wal. Corr.*, XXXII, p.185).

251 JOHN RUSSELL 1769

Canvas 124.5 x 100 (49 x 39½) lined. Signed, bottom left: *JR*[monogram]*ussell Pinxt/ 1769*; inscribed verso: *Revd W. DODD.LL.D./ Preacher at the Magdalen,/ 1774./ From whence this Picture bt. 1867*. There are some discoloured retouchings, a small tear upper right, and the varnish is discoloured.

Brown eyes, powdered wig, wearing black clerical dress; his right hand rests on [*D*]*ODD'S/BIBLE*, two volumes of which are displayed; a silver quill stand on an architectural plan inscribed *A PLAN of Charlotte Street Chapel*.

Collections: Bought from Horace Rodd c.1857 by Mrs A. George,[1] from whom purchased 1867.

Exhibitions: NPE 1867(821 lent Mrs George); *Georgian Essex*, Dagenham, 1958(311).

Reference: Williamson 1894, pp.23, 155.

On 22 July 1768 Russell wrote: 'Set off for Wilton to dine with the famous Dr Dodd, as he is to sit for his picture'; he afterwards stayed with Dodd at Whitton, near Twickenham, and on 16 January 1769 Dodd was sitting for his portrait.[2] Both the books and the plan displayed in NPG 251 were topical: Dodd's Charlotte Chapel had just opened in Pimlico, while *Dodd's Bible* refers to his *Commentary* published in three volumes in 1770, having been issued in numbers from 1765. The 5th Lord Chesterfield, Dodd's eventual victim, also sat to Russell in 1769 (Ranger's House, Blackheath).[3]

1 Who told Scharf (letter 13 December 1867; NPG archive) she had bought the portrait 'of Mr Horace Rodd about ten years since'. NPG 251 was described in the NPE 1867 cat. as having been brought from the Magdalen in 1774; Williamson 1894, p.23, gave the previous provenance as the Magdalen Chapel, the Charlotte Street Chapel in 1774, and the Rev H.S. Cotton, ordinary of Newgate (Scharf remembered having seen the portrait at 1 Newgate Street). H.F.B. Compston, *Magdalen Hospital*, 1917, p.137, stated there was no record of Russell's portrait having been at the Magdalen.

2 Williamson 1894, pp.22-23.

3 *Ibid.* See the 4th Lord Chesterfield's *Letters*, ed. B. Dobrée, VI, 1932, no.2557.

ICONOGRAPHY

1769 Painting by John Russell, see NPG 251.

1772 Painting by Thomas Hickey, presented by the artist to the Magdalen Hospital; it was given to the sitter's widow in 1782 (H.F.B. Compston, *Magdalen Hospital*, 1917, pp.137-38).

1773 Painting by Thomas Gainsborough, half length in gown and bands. Prince of Wales Museum, Mumbai [Bombay] (Waterhouse 1958, no.198; illus. Hayes 2001, p.121). Engraved T.L. Atkinson 1884. 'The ladies say it is very handsome as it is ... Lord, says, one, what a lively eye that gentleman has' (Gainsborough, 24 November 1773, to Mrs Dodd; Hayes 2001, p.121).

The remaining images of Dodd are inconsistent engravings produced in a hurry during his trial and sentence. He was convicted on 22 February 1777 and hanged on 27 June.

The most substantial was an oval half length mezzotint in wig, gown and bands, published by W. Humphrey, 24 May 1777,* on which a number of later prints were based, e.g. those by Freeman (oval) and Graves; a head by T. Trotter *from an Original Portrait painted from the Life* (later impressions dated 1787 and 1788) shows a different wig.

A bust-length oval, engraved by John Goldar from a drawing by [Daniel?] Dodd, also shows a weeping

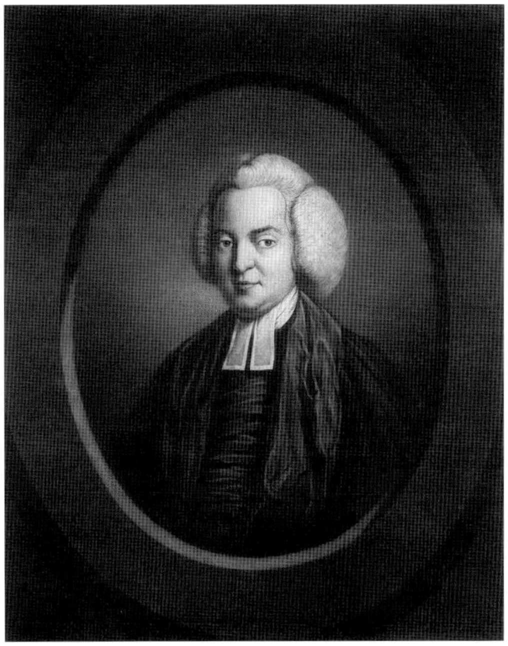

DODD *anon. mezzotint, published by W. Humphrey 1777 (NPG D 13740)*

putto, a view of the Magdalen Hospital and a book lettered *Dodd on Miracles*. A quite different head appears in an anon. engraving, bust-length oval to right with gown and bands lettered *The Unfortunate Clergyman Now under Sentence of Death in Newgate*.

An anon. plate, whole length, his hands raised before him, is lettered *Taken from the Life in Newgate the Morning of his Execution*, and the same head appears in the bust-length plate by Daniel Berger, lettered *an Morgen seiner Hinrichtung nach dem Leeben gezeichnet*. Another anon. plate showed Dodd with his arms bound on the morning of his execution (pub. A. Hamilton).

Posthumous

1777 Death mask. A cast in the Department of Anatomy, University of Edinburgh, from the Edinburgh Phrenological Society (*Death Masks and Life Masks*, Edinburgh University, [1988], p.31).

1798 Engraving by W. Ridley *from an original drawing*, bust-length oval in gown and bands. Several crude reductions were made from this type.

1865 Anon. engraving, whole length standing in a silk robe (P. Fitzgerald, *A Famous Forgery*, 1865, front.).

DOUBTFUL PORTRAITS

Miniature by Samuel Shelley dated 1774, three-quarter length in gown and bands, sold Christie's 10 July 1991, lot 121. An unattributed and untraced miniature, exhibited *Guelph* 1891(1041) and BFAC 1889(XVIII 15), was in the Whitehead sale, Christie's, 2nd day, 5 August 1915, lot 654.

DOLLOND, Peter 1730-1820

Optician, of Huguenot descent; a silk weaver in Spitalfields with his father John Dollond FSA (d.1761), but their interest in the science of optics led them to set up their own successful shop in 1750; although not mathematically gifted, Peter developed his father's achromatic and refracting telescopes (observing from Greenwich the transit of Venus in 1769).

1075 see Groups, *Men of Science living in 1807-08* by JOHN GILBERT, FREDERICK SKILL and WILLIAM & ELIZABETH WALKER 1858-62

ICONOGRAPHY

c.1790 Painting by John Hoppner,* half length, a mounted glass behind him. Yale Center for British Art (B1981.25.367). Engraved J. Thomson 1820 (*European Mag.*). See Groups NPG 1075.

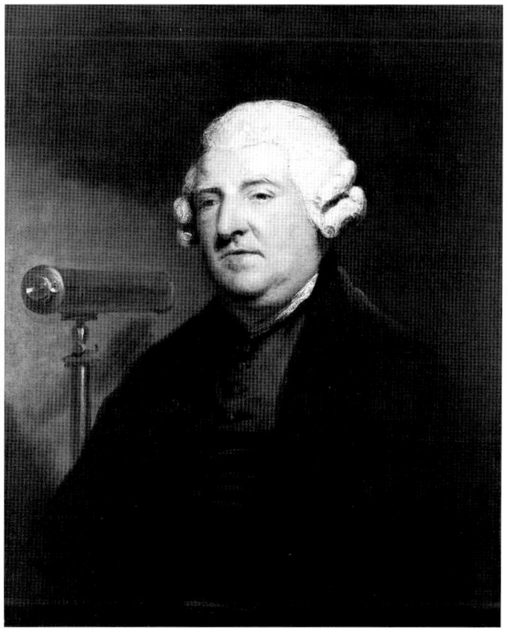

DOLLOND *by John Hoppner c.1790 (Yale Center for British Art)*

DOUBTFUL PORTRAIT

The untraced portrait of 'Mr Dolland, optician to his Majesty' exhibited by Benjamin Wilson SA 1761(134) was probably of John Dollond who d. 1761, within months of his royal appointment.

DOUGHTY, William 1757-80/82

Painter and engraver; b. York, where patronised by Canon William Mason; studied under Reynolds 1775-78; exhibited RA 1776-79; published eight mezzotints (five after Reynolds) 1779-80; worked briefly in York and in Ireland before sailing for India, but d. in Lisbon.

'a very pretty young man, Doughty, [in the summer of 1778] a pupil of Sir Joshua's, he is now brushing away for himself in Little Titchfield Street' (Robert Potter, 1779).

'of a jealous, sulky temper, arising probably from despondency' (James Northcote; *Conversations with James Ward*, 1901).

2513 SELF PORTRAIT c.1776

Canvas 23 x 19 (9 x 7½) lined and cleaned 1973; brown-painted canvas is wrapped round the stretcher, perhaps indicating an original size of 24 x 20 (9½ x 8); the original stretcher was inscribed in a contemporary hand: *Mr Doughty a Pupil of / Sir Joshua Reynolds* and *Mary Brook*.

Grey eyes, powdered hair tied with a black ribbon, wearing a green coat.

Collections: [William Mason (see below)] Mary Brook (see above); E. Gurney of Ashford, from whom purchased 1931.

Exhibition: *Mason* 1973(103).

Reference: J. Ingamells, *Apollo*, LXXX, 1964, pp.33, 35.

NPG 2513 probably dates from 1776. On 28 July that year Doughty told Northcote that William Mason had visited him and seemed 'well pleased with me. My own picture he liked so well that he desired a copy of it. but I offered him the original which he did me the honour to accept'.[1]

1 Whitley 1928, II, pp.303-04.

ICONOGRAPHY

c.1776 Painting attributed to William Doughty, half length, the head alone finished. Sotheby's, New York, 25 January 2001, lot 151 as Reynolds; indistinctly inscribed. The features closely correspond to those in NPG 2513.

c.1776 Painting by William Doughty, see NPG 2513.

1779-80 Mezzotint by William Doughty,* showing the head and pose of NPG 2513, but in Van Dyck costume and with a dramatically lit background (CS 1).

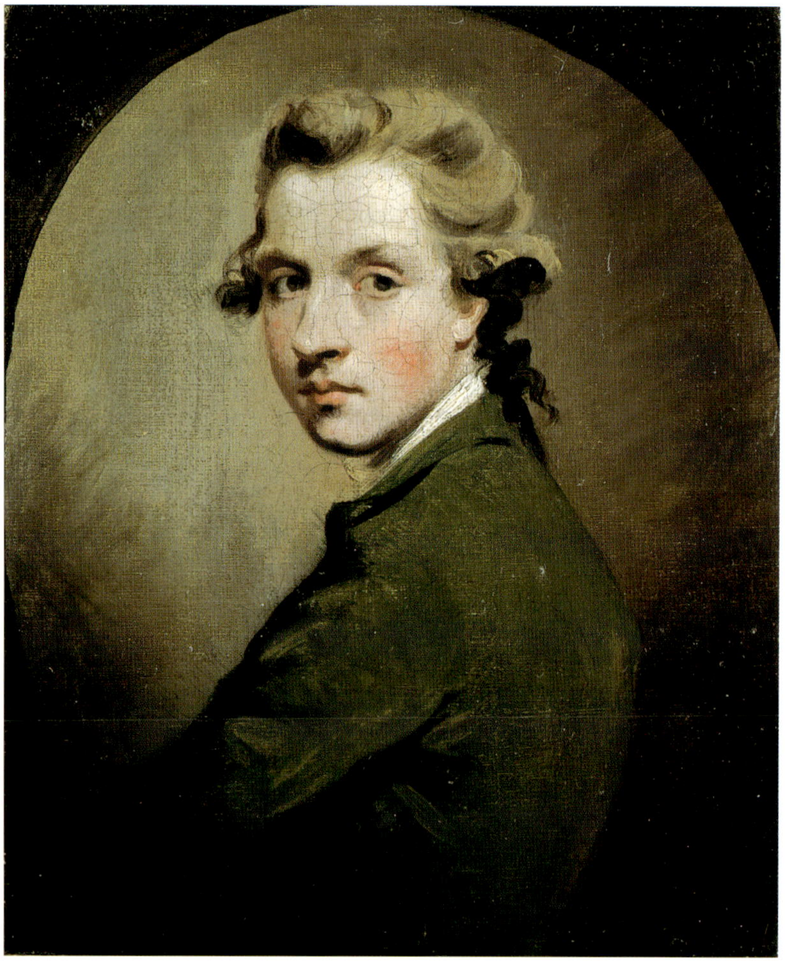

DOUGHTY NPG *2513*

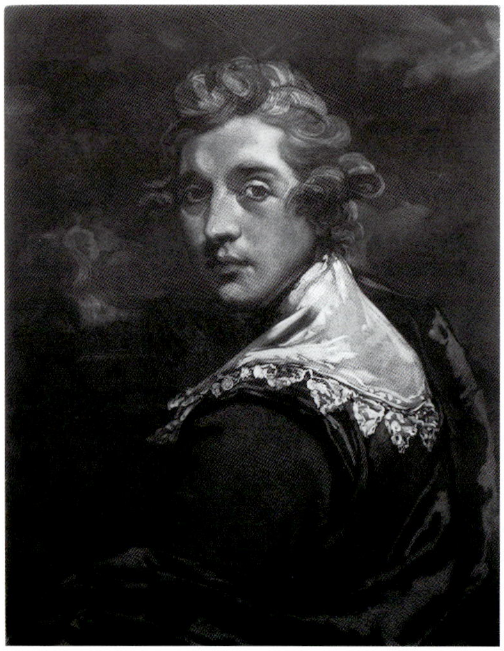

DOUGHTY Self portrait mezzotint 1779-80 (NPG D 13741)

DUNCANNON, Frederick, Viscount, see **BESSBOROUGH**

DUNNING, John, see **ASHBURTON**

EGERTON, Francis, see **BRIDGEWATER**

EDGEWORTH, Richard Lovell 1744-1817

Natural philosopher, author and inventor, of Edgeworthstown House, Co. Longford; FRS 1781; four times married (the third time to the dau. of Daniel Augustus Beaufort), his twenty-two children included the novelist Maria Edgeworth; friend of Erasmus Darwin and Thomas Day.

'a man eccentric, talkative to a tiresome degree; but possessing considerable talent' (F.N.C. Mundy, 1813).

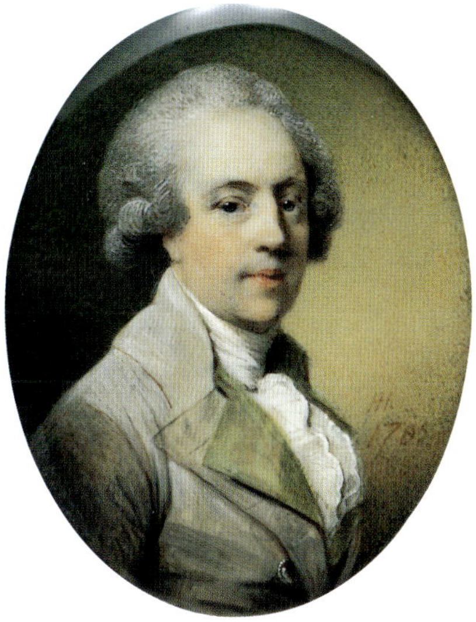

EDGEWORTH NPG 5069

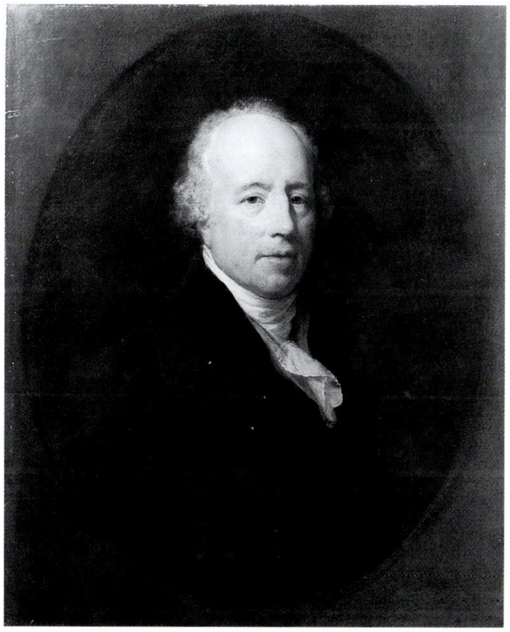

EDGEWORTH by H.D. Hamilton c.1795 (National Gallery of Ireland)

5069 HORACE HONE 1785

Watercolour and bodycolour on ivory 7.7 x 6 (3 x 2⅜); signed and dated lower right: *HH/1785*; cleaned 1935.[1] Label inside frame is inscribed, in brown and black watercolour: *Richard Lovell Edgeworth / Horace Hone / Pinxit 1785*.

Blue-grey eyes, powdered wig, grey coat, green waistcoat.

Collections: By descent from the sitter; in 1870 with his granddaughter, P.E. Gibbons;[2] Helena Gibbons by 1935;[3] Miss Alice Blandford, by descent to her niece, Mrs John Fletcher,[4] by whom sold Christie's, 10 February 1976, lot 34,[5] bt. Leggatt for the NPG.

Exhibition: *Master Drawings* 1993-95(27).

Reference: Walker 1998, no.72.

Probably painted in Dublin where Edgeworth was working from 1782.

1 Label verso: *Mildew removed in Oct 1935 by Mrs Minney-Wynn during my ownership his (Helena Gibbons) Grt Grt grand daughter.* A second inscription, verso, reads: *This miniature of [Edgeworth] was opened & cleaned Oct.r 1935 . . . Helena Gibbons present owner had cleaning done & mildew removed*
2 Label verso: ... *left in Mrs Cornegies / care 1870 belongs to / P E Gibbons/ Grandaughter / of the above / R L Edgeworth*.
3 See note 1.
4 Mrs Fletcher wrote that the miniature was left to her mother (née Beddoes) by an aunt called Miss Alice Blandford (note in NPG archive).
5 Sold with five other Edgeworth family miniatures; see also NPG 5070, *Thomas Beddoes* by S.T. Roche (Walker *Regency*, I, p.31, II, pl.66).

ICONOGRAPHY

1780 Miniature by John Smart (listed by Foskett 1964, p.66); see also doubtful portraits below.

1785 Miniature by Horace Hone, see NPG 5069.

1787 Drawing by Adam Buck, with his third wife, Elizabeth, née Sneyd, and ten children, oval. Christie's, 16 December 1969, lot 170. Anon. lithograph, NG Ireland (11,508). A later oval copy in a private collection 1967.

c.1790 Drawing by John Comerford, whole length, hat in left hand. NG Ireland (7883; illus. *Comerford* 1999, p.13).

c.1795 Painting by H.D. Hamilton,* half length. NG Ireland (1350). Engraved A. Cardon 1812. On 7 January 1811 John Comerford completed a portrait of 'Edgworth' 'after Hamilton' (NPG archive; see *Comerford* 1999, p.68).

1803 Plaster plaque by John Henning. Examples Scottish NPG (PG 2135) and exhibited *Great Irish Women*, Belfast, 1965(62) lent Mrs Colvin.

1811 Portrait by John Comerford, see c.1795 above.

DOUBTFUL PORTRAITS

Unattributed portrait, called *The Edgeworth Family - Richard Lovel and Maria Edgeworth*, exhibited Dublin 1872(NPG section, no.416), lent Edgeworth; miniature by John Smart, dated 1807, sold Bonham's, 22 November 1993, lot 124.

EGMONT, John Perceval, 2nd Earl of 1711-70

Politician; sty. Viscount Perceval 1733-49, suc. as 2nd Earl of Egmont [I] 1749; cr. Baron Lovel and Holland [GB] 1762; MP 1731-62; first lord of the Admiralty 1763-66; FRS 1764; m. 1) 1737 Catherine (1719-52), dau. of the 5th Earl of Salisbury; 2) 1756 Catherine (1731-84), dau. of the 6th Earl of Northampton (cr. Baroness Arden 1770).

'He is very bold and resolved, master of vast knowledge, and speaks at once with fire and method' (Horace Walpole, 1750).

'... when his ambition and lust of parliament were out of the question, he was humane, friendly, and as good-humoured as it was possible for a man to be who was never known to laugh; he was once indeed seen to smile, and that was at chess' (Horace Walpole, *Memoirs of George II*).

2481 THOMAS HUDSON 1759

Canvas 126 x 100 (49½ x 39½) lined; cleaned 1976; pentimenti show the top of the chair was at first higher; inscribed, top left: *IOHN.EARL.OF.EGMONT.BARON. / LOVELL.AND.HOLLAND.&c.1759*.

Pale brown eyes, powdered wig; his Earl's coronet in his right hand; beneath his Peer's coronation robes he wears a blue-grey coat with gold trim and a white satin waistcoat with gold trim; turquoise chair and dark green curtain.

Collections: By descent in the sitter's family; Egmont sale, Christie's, 12 December 1930, lot 88, bt. Leggatt for the NPG.

Engravings: J. McArdell 1764; anon. (bust length; *Universal Mag.*); anon. 1802 (bust length); Freeman 1807 (bust length).

Exhibition: Beningbrough 1979–.

The inscription, apparently written after 1770 (see note 2), gives the date 1759; the companion piece, showing the seated Countess, Egmont's second wife, holding their infant son Charles (b.1756),[1] is inscribed in a similar hand with the date 1st October 1758.[2] Both portraits were engraved by McArdell in 1764-65. A full-size copy was also in the Egmont sale, Christie's, 12 December 1930, lot 89.

1 Egmont sale, Christie's, 24 February 1933, lot 50; with Lane Fine Art, London, 1993.
2 *CATHARINE DR. OF CHARLES COMPTON. & SISTER OF CHARLES COMPTON EARL OF NORTHAMPTON, COUNTESS OF EGMONT. WITH MASTER CHARLES PERCEVAL HER SON 1ST OCTOBER 1758 AET 2. CREATED BARONESS OF ARDEN, IN HER OWN RIGHT & TO HER HEIRS MALE 1770.*

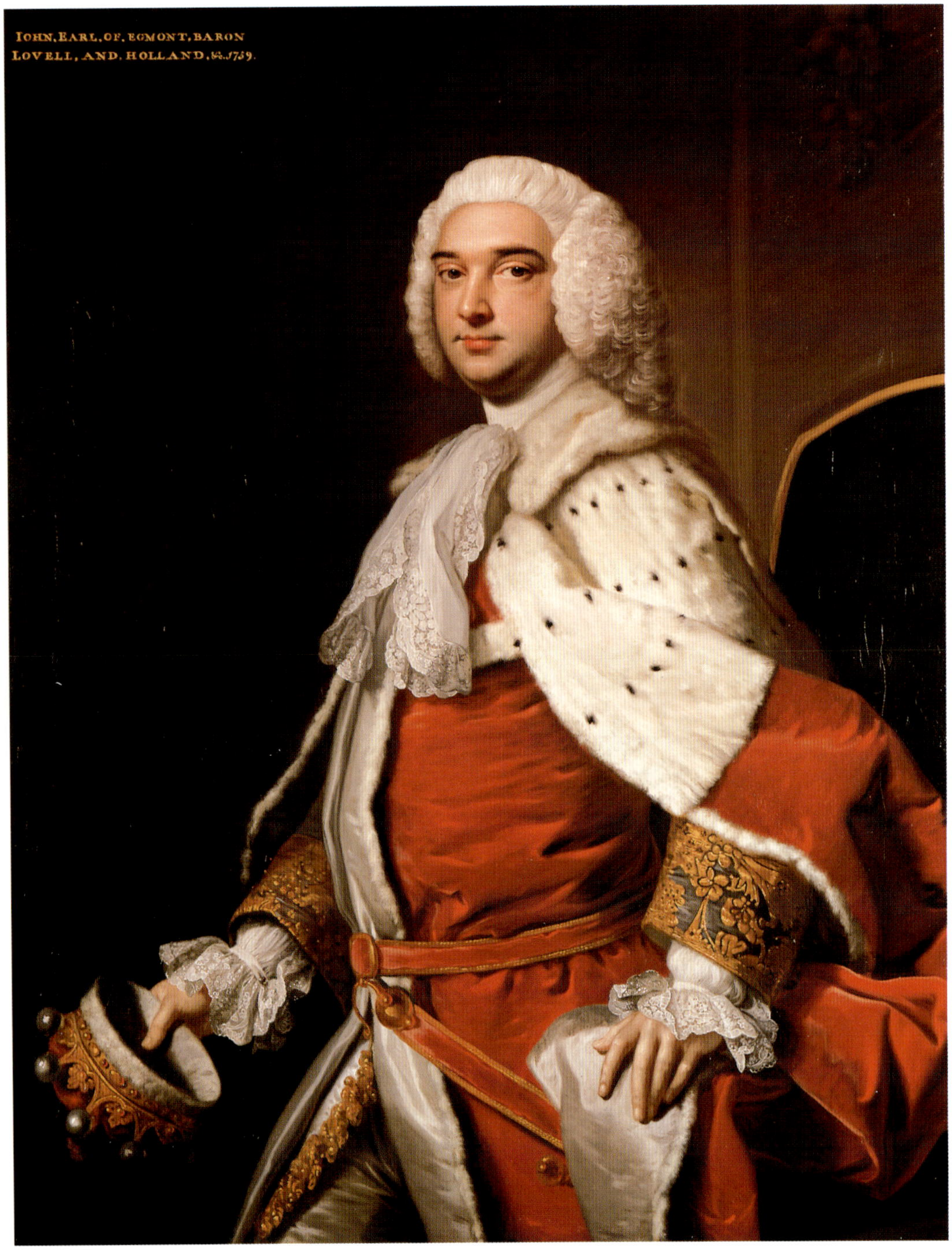

2nd Earl of EGMONT NPG *2481*

ICONOGRAPHY

1742 Painting by C.F. Zincke, bust-length oval, the arms of Yvery with supporters below. Engraved J. Faber 1744 (with a companion plate of the Countess) for *The History of the House of Yvery* 1743, a genealogical volume perceived as a prodigious exercise in vanity (see below).

c.1742 Painting by Francis Hayman, three-quarter length standing, with Kanturk Castle in the background and the Egmont shield of arms (incorporating Perceval, Salisbury and Northampton). NG of Ireland (4489; illus. Allen 1987, no.6, p.33). Engraved J. Faber. The figure was quoted in the satirical plate *Vain Glory,* 1744 (George 2615), showing Egmont by a pile of books and inscribed *Genealogy from Wm ye Conqueror Fifty two Ways* (see above).

1756 Painting by Joshua Reynolds,* three-quarter length standing in the grounds of Enmore Castle, Somerset, with his second wife, Catherine (whom he m. 1756). Cartwright Hall, Bradford (Mannings 2000, no.1430). Engraved R. Josey 1876.

1759 Painting by Thomas Hudson, see NPG 2481.

1770 Painting by Hugh Barron, whole-length standing with his wife and eight children (three boys, one infant, four girls). Egmont sale, Christie's, 12 December 1930, lot 69 (illus. Waterhouse 1981, p.41). Exhibited SA 1770(4).

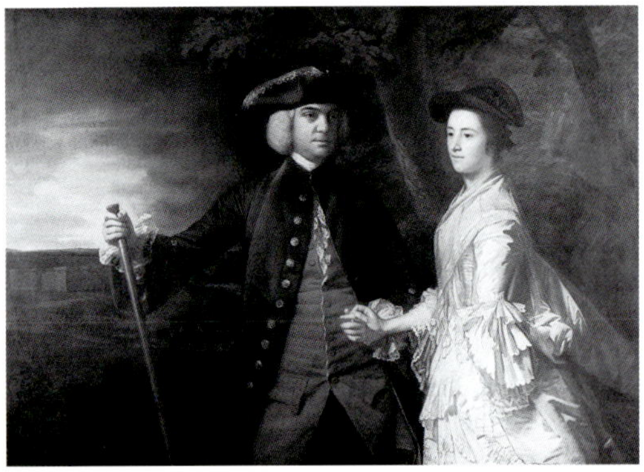

2nd Earl of EGMONT with his second wife, Catherine, by Joshua Reynolds 1756 (Bradford Art Galleries and Museums)

DOUBTFUL PORTRAITS

An unattributed painting of a boy (with the Egmont arms with label for difference for the eldest son), sold Bonham's, 11 October 1973, lot 64, from the Egmont sale Christie's, 24 February 1933, lot 43, probably shows John James Perceval (b.1738), Egmont's eldest son by his first wife. Painting by Thomas Hudson, three-quarter length, c.1745–50, at Cowdray Park.

EGREMONT, Charles Wyndham, 2nd Earl of 1710–63

Politician; suc. his father as 3rd Bt 1740; suc. his uncle, the 7th Duke of Somerset, as 2nd Earl of Egremont 1750; MP 1735–50; secretary of state 1761–63.

Egremont 'died suddenly ... he used no exercise and could not be kept from eating ... a day or two before he died, he said, 'Well, I have but three turtle dinners to come, and if I survive them, I shall be immortal' (Horace Walpole, 1763).

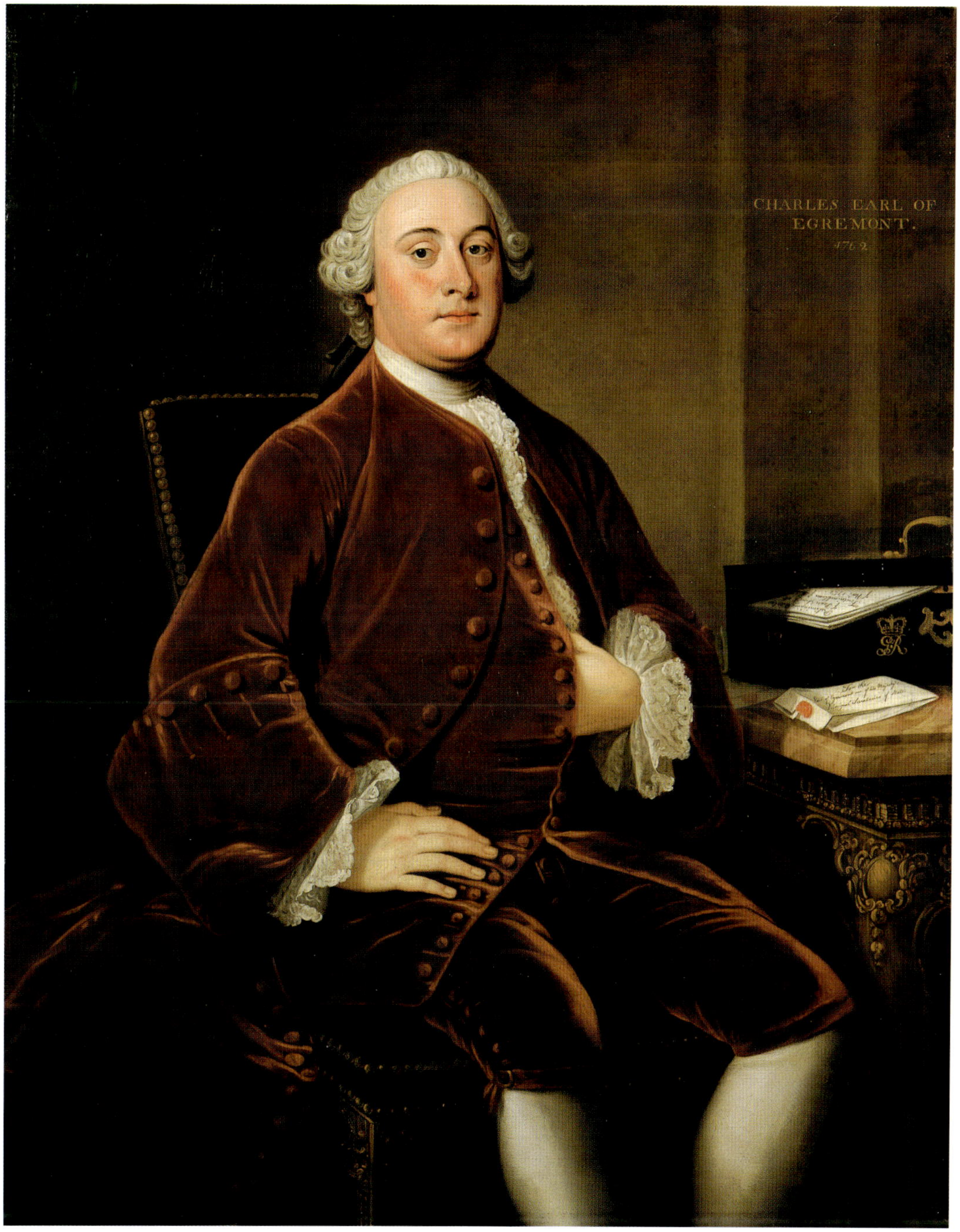

2nd Earl of EGREMONT NPG 4589

4589 WILLIAM HOARE 1762

Canvas 125.5 x 100.5 (49½ x 39½) lined; several small losses and discoloured retouchings; *pentimenti* above despatch box which was originally higher. Inscribed, centre right: *CHARLES EARL OF / EGREMONT / 1762*.

Blue grey eyes, powdered wig and black hair ribbon, wearing a red-brown suit, white stockings; blue-upholstered chair and a green curtain to the left; on the pink-marble-topped table lies a folded paper inscribed: *To the / Earl of Egremont one of his Majesty's / Principal Secretaries of State*; from the blue dispatch box, which bears the Royal crest and the number 12, projects a sheet inscribed: *Preliminary Articles / of Peace Sign'd at / Fontainebleau ye 3rd / of Novr 1762*.

Collections: Anon. sale, Christie's, 20 October 1967, lot 18, bt. Leggatt for the NPG.

NPG 4589 appears to be an autograph version of the Hoare portrait at Petworth,[1] for which there is a finished chalk study in the British Museum (1894.4.17.10); it differs in the substitution of a blue chair for a green sofa, and the inclusion of a table bearing diplomatic papers witnessing Egremont's prominent part in the negotiations of the peace with France after the Seven Years War.

1 Illus. *Apollo*, CV, 1977, p.346; Petworth cat., 1920, p.55, no.538*; engraved E. Harding 1799. Hoare's bill to the 2nd Earl of Egremont (Petworth MSS), listing half lengths of the Earl and his Countess, a full length of their two children, and four fancy pictures, was paid on 27 September 1763 (*Hoare* 1990, no.20a, p.41); the paintings of the Countess and children also remain at Petworth.

ICONOGRAPHY

c.1720? Painting attributed to Charles d'Agar, full length as a boy, a bow in his right hand; inscribed. Petworth (cat., 1920, p.40, no.493 as English School, the present convincing attribution by Alastair Laing).

c.1750? Painting ascribed to William Hoare,* half length. Petworth (cat., 1920, p.55, no.563, where described in error as a copy of the Hoare portrait of 1762). The head closely resembles that in another half-length of Egremont at Petworth, a copy by Thomas Phillips, wearing a brown coat and yellow vest (cat., 1920, p.94, no.265, as from a lost original, evidently based on the earlier 'Hoare' type).

1762 Painting by William Hoare, see NPG 4589.

An unidentified painting of Egremont was in the Stowe sale, 22nd day, 13 September 1848, lot 177, bt. Crole.

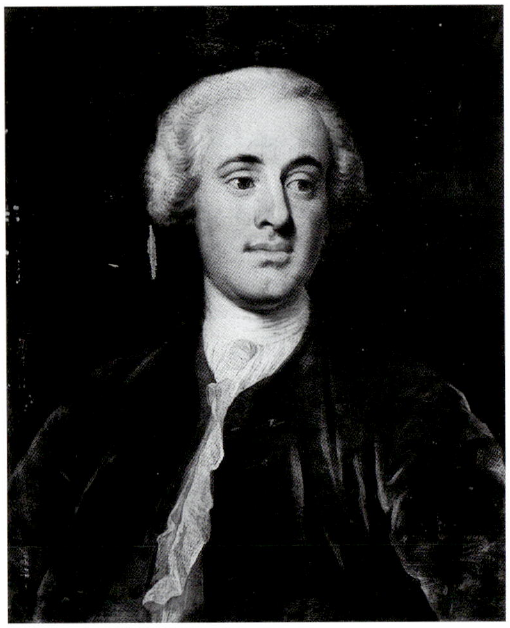

2nd Earl of EGREMONT ascribed to William Hoare c.1750? (Petworth House, The National Trust)

DOUBTFUL PORTRAITS

Painting at Dulwich Picture Gallery (561), now attributed to William Hoare, was formerly identified as Egremont; the portrait of Lord Halifax with his two secretaries, a version of which is NPG 3328, was once thought to include Egremont, but see Kerslake *Early Georgian*, I, pp.116–18.

ELIOTT, George Augustus, see HEATHFIELD

ELLIS, Welbore, see MENDIP

EUSTON, Augustus Henry, Earl of, see GRAFTON

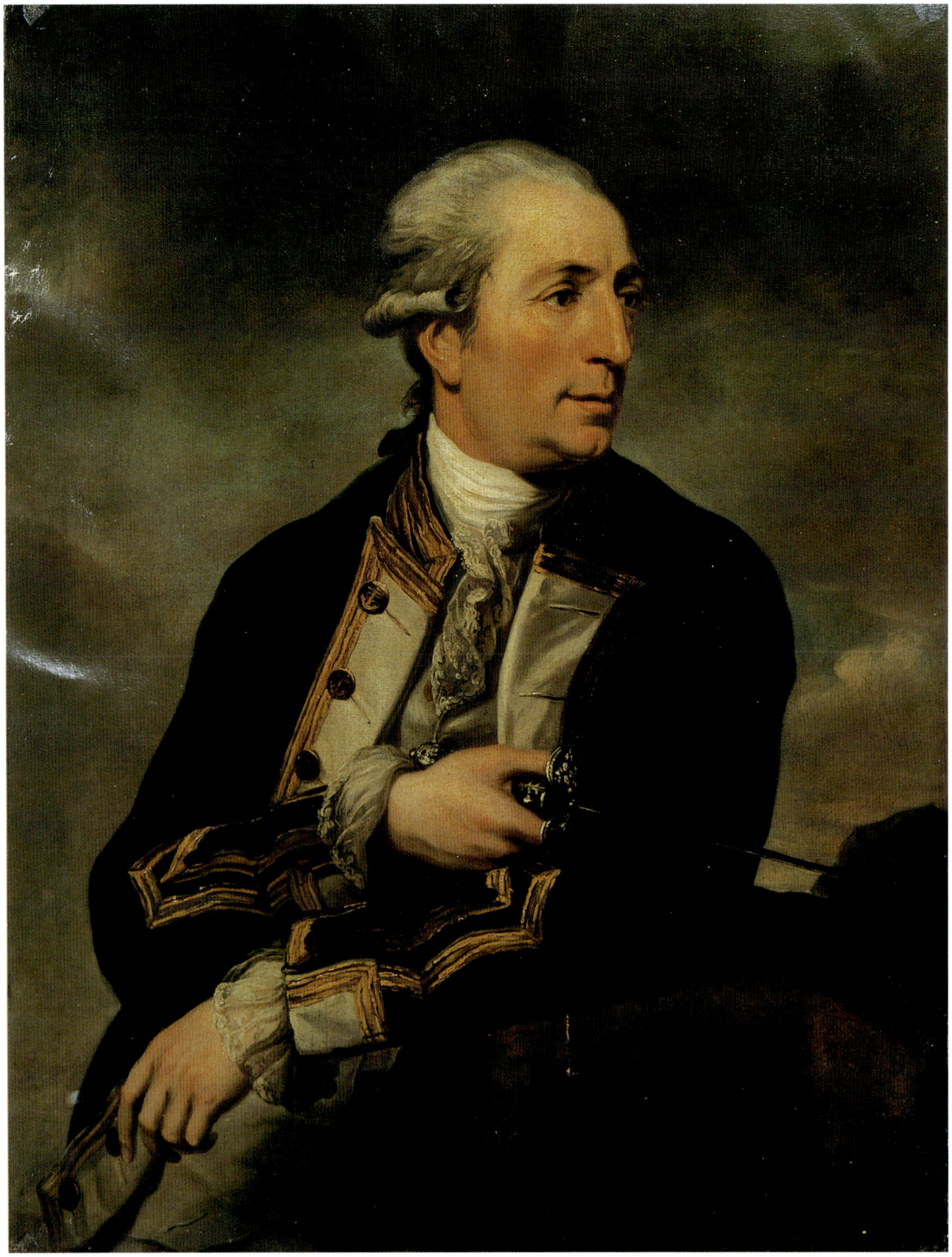

FARMER NPG 2149

FARMER, George 1732–79

Naval officer; captain 1771; killed in an action against the French off Cape Ushant on 6 October 1779, when his frigate, the *Quebec*, was destroyed by the *Surveillante*. 'To excite an emulation in other officers' and to render his fate 'rather to be envied than pitied', the Admiralty made his son a Baronet and gave pensions to his widow and nine children.

2149 CHARLES GRIGNION junior 1778

Canvas 91.5 x 71 (36 x 28); in poor condition, the unlined, sagging, canvas detached from the original stretcher along the top and left-hand edges; much discoloured varnish; a small vertical tear below his left sleeve and paint losses along the lower edge.

Brown eyes, powdered hair, wearing a captain's uniform.

Collections: By descent to the sitter's granddaughter, Miss Sophia Aphra Farmer (d.1875);[1] her executor, George Boydell, from whom bt. 1877 by Henry Taylor; bequeathed by him 1927.[2]

Engraving: J. Murphy 1780 (... *Charles Grignion Jur pinxit 1778* and *in an Action with a French Frigate of Superior Force after having silenced her Fire, Gloriously perished* ...).

Exhibitions: RA 1778(133, 'Portrait of a Naval officer, Kit-cat');[3] Grosvenor Museum, Chester, c.1925;[4] Royal Naval Museum, Portsmouth, 1975-2002.

A finished chalk drawing by Grignion is in the British Museum (1868.8.8.1282), the same size as the mezzotint plate by Murphy. A version of NPG 2149 was sold Christie's, 17 February 1984, lot 94, from the collection of the Rev O.F. Raymond, possibly the replica with W.M. Sabin in 1926.[5] A reduced and pedestrian oval version, probably copied from Murphy's engraving, belonged to Leonard O'Malley in 1912;[6] this or another was in a private collection, Montreal, in 1955;[7] a crude derivative enamel (set in the lid of a patch-box) was sold Sotheby's, Sussex, 10 June 1990, lot 2998.

1 E.B. Barker of Chester, one of her executors, sent Scharf a photograph of NPG 2149 on 6 July 1875.
2 A label written by Taylor, previously on the verso of NPG 2149, reads: *the original picture purchased by me Henry Taylor 13 Jany 1877 from my Partner George Boydell the nephew (by marriage) and Executor of Miss Sophia Aphra Farmer of Newgate House, Chester, the Granddaughter of Capt. Farmer.* See also *NQ*, 7/iv, 1887, pp.473-74.
3 Identified as Farmer by Henry Taylor in his MS notes (NPG archive), but the evidence is not known.
4 A newspaper cutting on file refers.
5 Note by C.K. Adams (NPG archive).
6 Photograph NPG archive.
7 Photograph NPG archive.

DOUBTFUL PORTRAIT

Unattributed portrait sold Bearne's, 25-27 October 1994, lot 642.

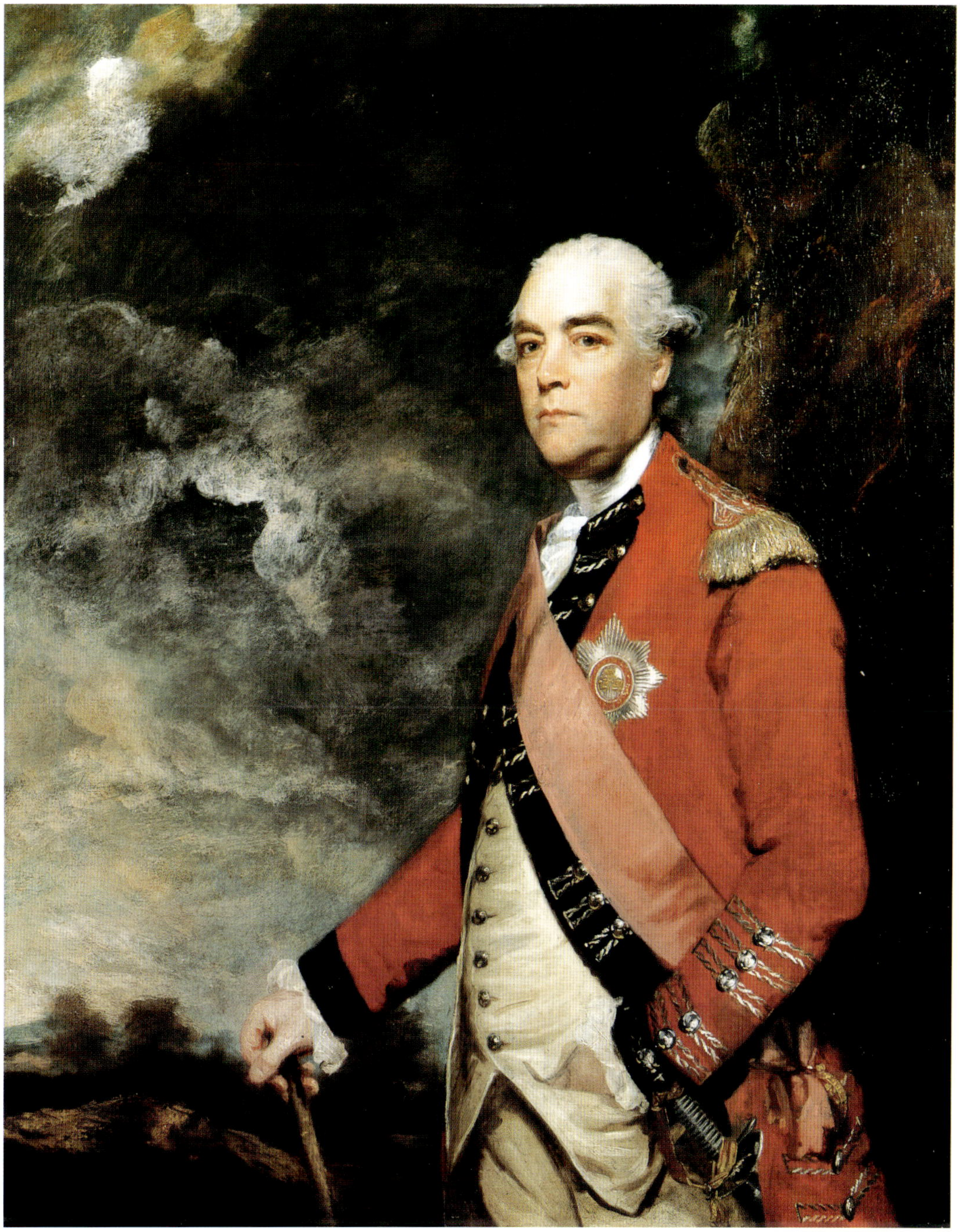

FAWCETT NPG 5515

FAWCETT, Sir William, KB 1728-1804

Army officer; served in Germany during the Seven Years War; studied French and German, translating three of the military texts of Field-Marshal Saxe 1757-59; colonel 1772, major-general 1777, lieutenant-general 1782 and general 1796; KB 1786 and PC 1799. 'His manners were formed with equal strength and softness; and to coolness, intrepidity and extensive military knowledge, he added all the requisite talents of a man of business, and the most persevering assiduity, without the least ostentation' (*GM*, 1804).

5515 JOSHUA REYNOLDS 1784-85

Canvas 127 x 101.5 (50 x 40) relined and partially cleaned 1984; marked craquelure in the upper right area; the ribbon of the Bath is painted over the buttons.

Grey eyes, white hair, wearing the uniform of a lieutenant-general: red frock with dark blue lapels and silver trim; silver epaulettes; white vest and breeches.

Collections: By descent in the sitter's family:[1] W.W. Fawcett by 1884;[2] Knoedler, New York (before 1941); Mrs F.E. Guest sale, New York, 25 September 1968; Parke Bernet, New York, 18 May 1972, lot 158; Sotheby's, New York, 17 June 1982, lot 102, bt. Agnew, from whom purchased.

Engravings: J. Ward 1801; S.W. Reynolds.

Exhibitions: RA 1785(175);[3] *Reynolds*, Grosvenor Gallery, 1883-84(58) lent W.W. Fawcett; RA 1895(9) lent R.A. Fawcett; Metropolitan Museum of Art, New York, 1957-61 lent by Mrs Guest.

Reference: Graves & Cronin, I, p.299; Waterhouse 1941, p.76; Mannings 2000, no.599.

Fawcett's only known appointment with Reynolds was on 8 January 1784, but the pockets books for 1783 and 1785 are missing. 'General Fosset' paid Reynolds 100 gn. in August 1785[4] and the portrait had been shown at the RA in April that year. The ribbon and star of the Bath, awarded Fawcett in 1786, were added to the finished portrait. Copies were sold Christie's, 18 October 1985, lot 195, and Sotheby's, 10 April 1991, lot 121.

1 On 23 November 1801 the sitter described NPG 5515 as having been 'drawn some years since by the late Sir Joshua Reynolds, and in the possession of Mrs Farrer' (letter from A. Chisslett, 1 August 2000; NPG archive).
2 NPG 5515 was sketched by Scharf in the collection of 'Mr Fawcett', Spring Lodge, Sydenham, 12 February 1863 (TSB 7/71).
3 Graves & Cronin quote a contemporary review from the *Morning Herald*: 'No.175. Portrait of an officer, General Fawcett.'
4 Cormack 1970, p.152.

ICONOGRAPHY

c.1770 Painting by J.G. Ziesenis,* bust length in officer's uniform, red coat with dark lapels trimmed with gold. Sotheby's, 19-20 February 1997, lot 216.

1784-85 Painting by Joshua Reynolds, see NPG 5515.

c.1786-90 Miniature attributed to Philip Jean, bust length with the badge of the Bath, wearing scarlet military coat with blue facings and silver epaulettes. Christie's, 19 February 1980, lot 63.

Undated Anon. bust-length silhouette, formerly in the Nevill Jackson collection (illus. *Connoisseur*, XC, 1932, p.363).

As adjutant-general, Fawcett stands in the foreground of William Beechey's *George III at a Review*, see George III 1797-98.

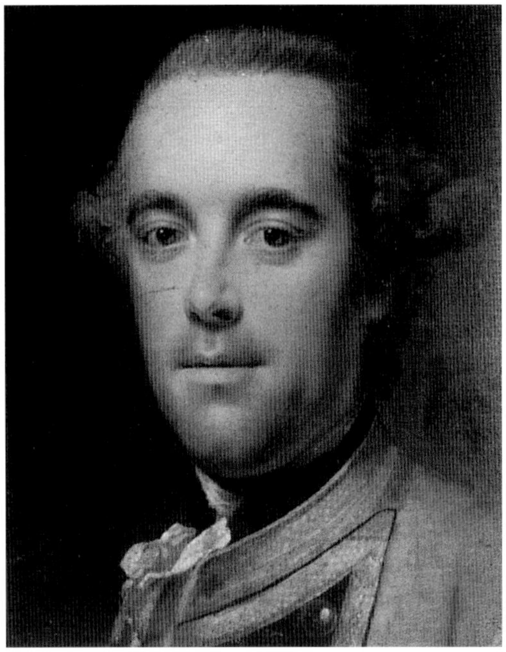

FAWCETT by J.G. Ziesenis c.1770 (Sotheby's)

DOUBTFUL PORTRAIT

Pastel by John Russell, sold Georges Petit, Paris, 10-11 December 1928, lot 50.

FIELDING, Sir John, Kt 1721-80

Magistrate; half-bro. of the novelist Henry Fielding (1707-54), whom he first assisted; went blind in 1741; published pamphlets on aspects of law and social welfare 1755-71; promoted the idea of a police force and a stipendiary magistracy, and a pioneer of child welfare; Kt 1761.

'a venerable Elderly Gentleman with hoary locks and blind (as Justice is represented to be) having a black fillet over his eyes, of a mild deportment, ready apprehension and great penetration, as his queries to the prisoners manifest' (Samuel Curwen, 1775).

'Sir John had a bandage over his eyes, and held a little switch or rod in his hand, waving it before him as he descended from the bench. The sagacity he discovered in the questions he put to the witnesses, and a marked and successful attention as I conceived, not only to the words, but to the accents and tones of the speaker, supplied the advantage which is usually rendered by the eye' (Dr Thomas Somerville, 1779).

3834 NATHANIEL HONE 1762

Canvas 125 x 99.5 (49¼ x 39¼) lined; scattered retouchings; signed, lower left: *N Hone 1762*.

White hair, a dark blue band above his sightless eyes; he wears a white collar and neckcloth, a blue-grey coat with gold trim, a gold-embroidered waistcoat, black breeches and white stockings; he holds a light-blue-covered pamphlet in his left hand and there is a ruby ring on the little finger of his right hand; the chair is green; on the table a black leather-bound book lettered in gold *HOLY BIBLE* and a calf-bound book lettered in gold in a red panel *STATUTES / AT LARGE / VOL.1* / and in a green panel *MAGNA CHARTA HENR*.

Collections: [Female Orphan Asylum, later the Royal Female Orphanage, Lambeth] Royal Female Orphan Asylum, Beddington, by 1866;[1] placed in storage with the Whitgift Foundation, Croydon, 1945-52; purchased from the Royal Female Orphanage by the friends of C.F. Bell and presented 1952.[2]

Engraving: J. McArdell (before 1765).[3]

Exhibitions: Probably SA 1762(39 Sir John Fielding, half length); *Casanova*, Venice, 1998-99(163).

The earlier history of NPG 3834 is not completely established, but it was presumably the portrait exhibited by Hone in 1762. By 1866 it belonged to the Royal Female Orphanage, a charity originally founded in Lambeth (as the Female Orphan Asylum) by Fielding in 1758, when he became a governor of the Magdalen Hospital. The pamphlet in his hand probably refers to his *Account of the Origin and Effects of a Police* ..., published in 1758, which had appended a first plan for the rescue of 'deserted girls'. NPG 3834 also celebrated Fielding's knighthood, an honour he had solicited in 1757, and received from the King on 1 October 1761.[4]

1 Where the portrait was noticed by H.F.B. Compston, *The Magdalen Hospital*, 1917, p.41.
2 On his eightieth birthday, a number of Bell's friends had given him a sum of money to acquire a work of art to be presented to a gallery of his choice. Bell had been a Trustee of the NPG 1910-40.
3 McArdell died in 1765; his print differs only in the placing of the titles on the books, and in the added words *Plan of* to the scroll.
4 See R. Leslie-Melville, *Life and Work of Sir John Fielding*, 1934, pp.112-27, 131-32.

ICONOGRAPHY

1757 Miniature attributed to Nathaniel Hone, half length wearing dark band above his eyes, with his first wife and adopted daughter (illus. R. Leslie-Melville, *Fielding*, 1934, f.p.6).

1762 Painting by Nathaniel Hone, see NPG 3834.

1769 Painting by James Williams, exhibited FS 1769(240, 'A deception'), see *Wal. Soc.*, XXVII, p.82.

1771 Bust by James Paine jr., exhibited SA 1771(224).

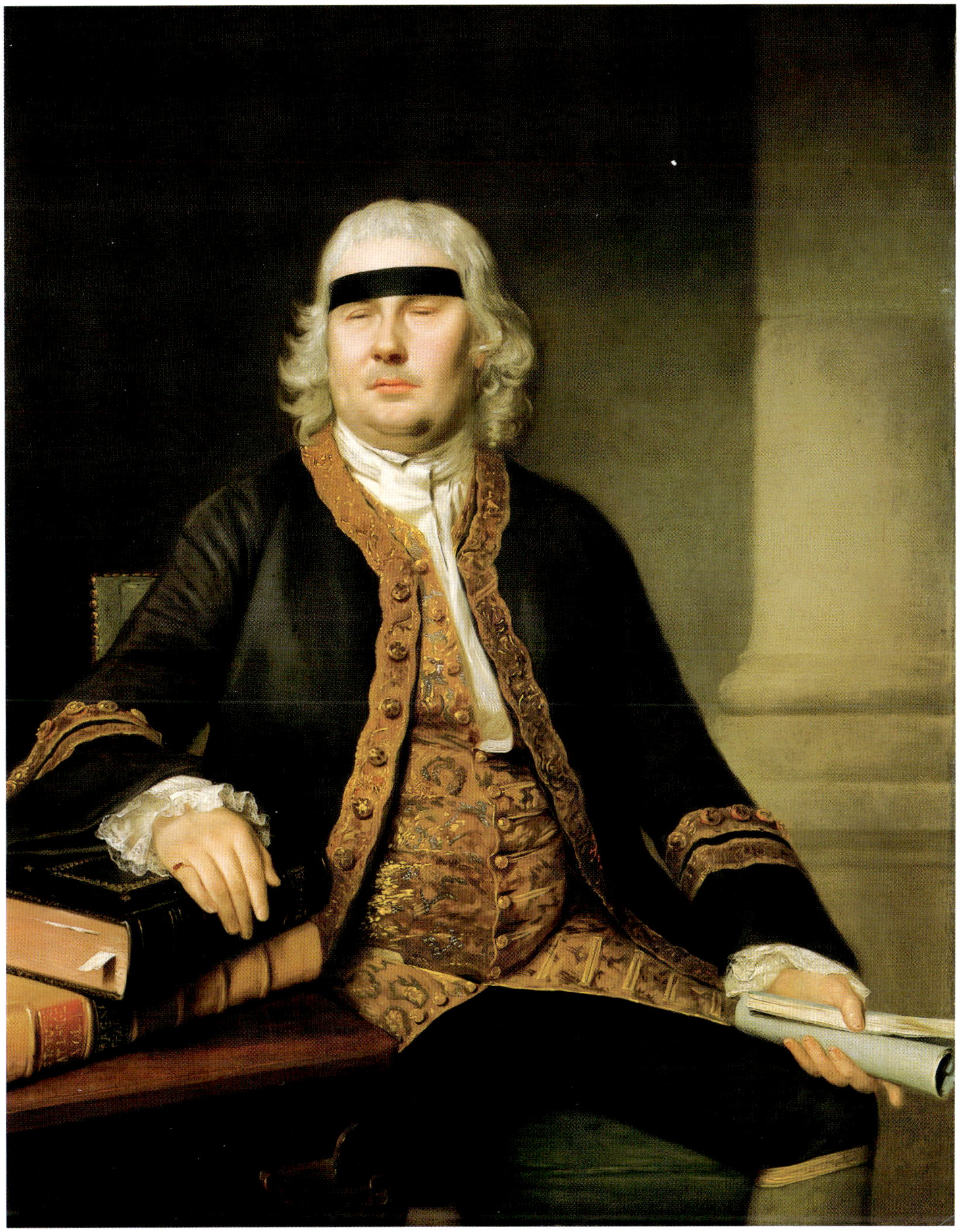

FIELDING NPG 3834

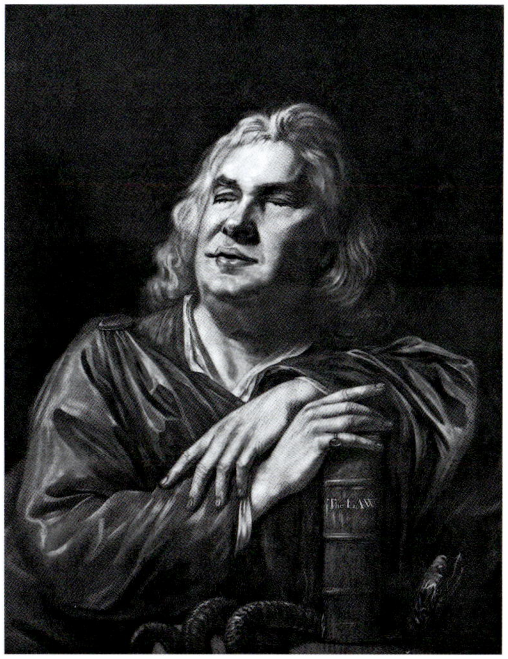

FIELDING J.R. Smith after Nathaniel Hone 1773 (NPG D 18430)

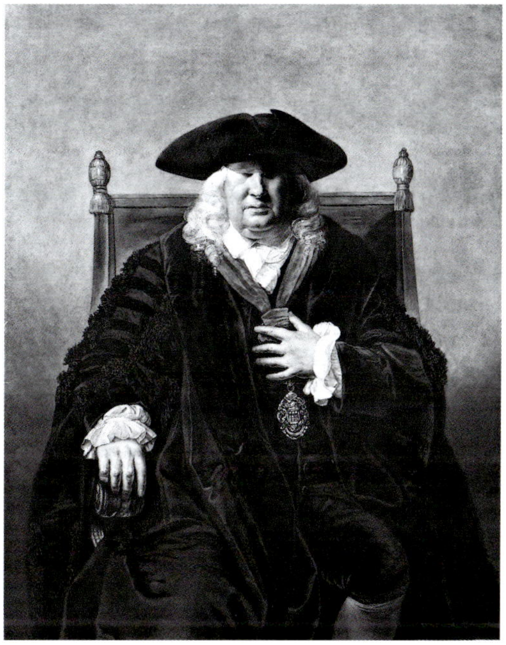

FIELDING W. Dickinson after M.W. Peters 1778 (NPG D 18431)

1773 Painting by Nathaniel Hone, half length, bareheaded, wearing a deep red cloak, his arms resting on a copy of *The Law* which weighs down a serpent. Middlesex Guildhall Collection. Engraved J.R. Smith 1773* (exhibited SA 1774, no.267).

1774 Medal, bust derived from the 1773 Hone portrait; inscribed on the reverse: CAECUS LATENTES SCRVTATVR. SENEX VIOLENTOS COERCET. (Brown 1980, no.187).

1774 Engraved on stone by John Kirk, a head, exhibited SA 1774 (under 129).

c.1774 Anon. engravings: bust-length oval with dark band above his eyes; and, reversed, with a portrait of Lady Fielding (presumably his second wife, whom he m. 1774).

1778 Painting by M.W. Peters, three-quarter length seated, a band above his eyes, as Chairman of the Quarter Sessions for the City of Westminster, exhibited RA 1778(231). Engraved W. Dickinson 1778.. (seen in S. De Wilde's *The Village Lawyer* in the Garrick Club; Ashton 1997, no.40). A half-length miniature version sold Christie's, 20 March 1990, lot 136, and Phillips, 22 April 1991, lot 108.

A busto by Charles Harris, large as life, was advertised in his trade cat. of c.1793 at two guineas.

FINCH, Lady Charlotte, *née* Fermor 1725-1813

Royal governess, 2nd dau. of the 1st Earl of Pomfret; when in Italy with her parents in 1741 Walpole considered her 'the cleverest girl in the world; speaks the purest Tuscan, like any Florentine'; m. 1746, as his second wife, William Finch (1691-1766), 2nd s. of the 7th Earl of Winchilsea; governess to the Royal children 1762-92.

6205 JOHN ROBINSON 1744

Canvas 125.5 x 101 (49½ x 39¾) lined; areas of retouching upper left remain discoloured, and the rock supporting her right elbow is no longer clear (although apparent in Major's engraving).

Grey eyes, dark hair, pearl ear ring; she wears a lilac-coloured dress trimmed with white lace and pearls, and a yellow cloak; gold bracelets on her wrists; an inscription added, lower left: *LADY CHARLOTTE FARMOR DAUR. / OF THOS. EARL OF POMFRET, / & WIFE OF THE RT. HONBLE. / WILLIAM FINCH. 2D. SON OF DANIEL / EARL OF / WINCHILSEA & / NOTTINGHAM.*

Collections: By descent in the Finch family at Burley-on-the-Hill, to Maj. James Hanbury;[1] his sale, Christie's, 20 June 1947, lot 81, bt. Reaney and deposited in the NPG; accessioned 1993.[2]

Engraving: T. Major 1755 (bust-length oval, inscribed in English and German).

Exhibition: *Coronation Exhibition*, Leicester, 1937(9).

Reference: P. Finch, *History of Burley-on-the-Hill*, 1901, II, p.34 as Dahl; A.C. Sewter, typescript catalogue of Burley-on-the-Hill, [1937], NPG archive, p.39, no.2 as Dahl or Robinson, and *Burl. Mag*, LXXVII, 1940, pp.62, 64, as Vanderbank.

The identity of the sitter and the attribution are securely based on the inscribed print by Thomas Major. Although Sewter had correctly attributed NPG 6205 to Robinson at the Leicester exhibition in 1937, he mistakenly published it in 1940 as one of Vanderbank's best portraits. Robinson (d.1745) perhaps derived his composition from a drawing by Alexander Vanhaecken (NG of Scotland, D 2172); it recurs, with minor variations in the left hand, in another of his portraits known only through a (presumably reversed) plate by John Faber.[3]

Lady Pomfret recorded going with her daughter, Charlotte, 'to set for her picture' in April 1744,[4] surely NPG 6205; Robinson also painted three-quarter lengths of Charlotte's sister Lady Sophia (1721-45) and her husband whom she married in 1744, the 2nd Earl Granville.[5]

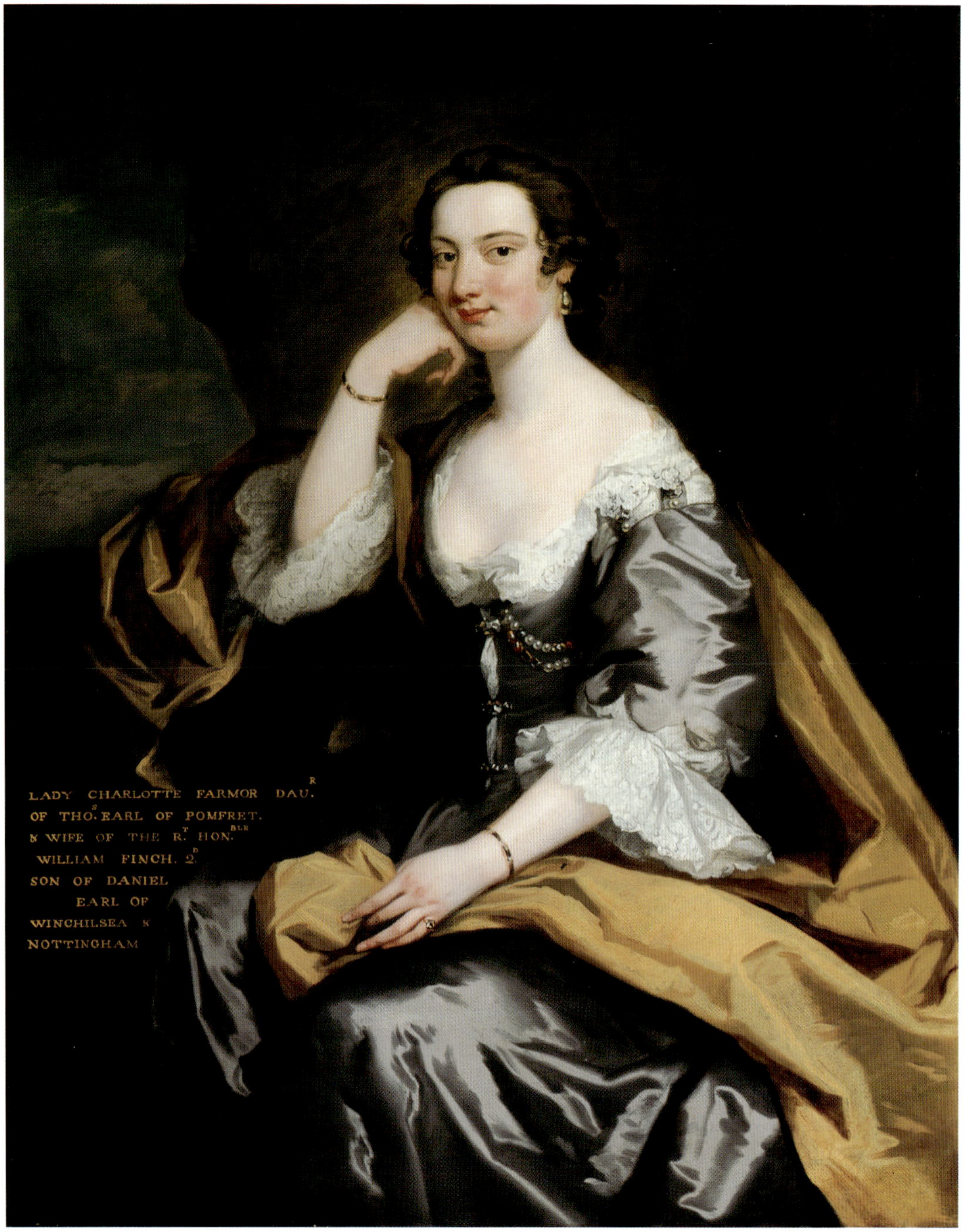

Lady Charlotte FINCH NPG *6205*

1 Whose mother was Gwendolen, dau. of G.H. Finch of Burley-on-the-Hill.
2 The portrait had been deposited in 1947, presumably for the frame.
3 CS 129; reworked with the title *The Amorous Beauty* (illus. B. l'Anson, *The Finch Family*, 1933, f.p.84, as of Lady Charlotte Finch).
4 Lady Pomfret's MS Diary, Leicester RO (information from Jill A. Shefrin).
5 Burley-on-the-Hill sale, Christie's, 20 June 1947, lots 84, 85.

ICONOGRAPHY

c.1735-40 Painting attributed to Thomas Hudson, half length as a girl, a goldfinch in her left hand. 15th Earl of Winchilsea sale, Christie's, 9 May 1947, lot 15 with another 'Hudson' of Lady Mary and Heneage Finch as children.

1744 Painting by John Robinson, see NPG 6205.

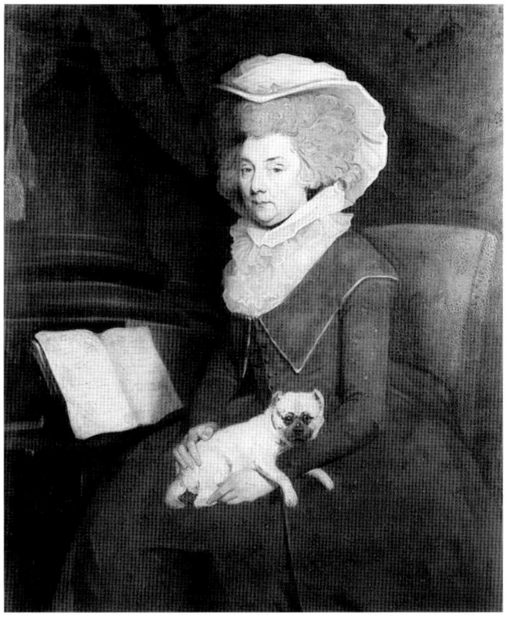

Lady Charlotte FINCH by William Hopkins 1787 (UK Government Art Collection)

c.1770-72 Painting by Johann Zoffany, standing behind Queen Charlotte who is accompanied by her two brothers and three of her children. Royal Collection (Millar 1969, no.1207). Exhibited RA 1773(320). Another Zoffany of c.1765 in the Royal Collection, of the young Princes George and Frederick with Queen Charlotte, probably shows Lady Charlotte reflected in a mirror (Millar 1969, no.1199); the Queen later gave her 'a Picture in small Size done by Zoffani in Oyl, of the P. of Wales & P. Frederick' (O. Hedley, *Queen Charlotte*, 1975, p.93).

c.1774 Wedgwood medallion, modelled by Joachim Smith (illus. Reilly 1973, p.137).

1775 Miniature by William Sherlock, half length, wearing a white cap. Sotheby's, 18 December 1986, lot 45.

1785 Pastel by Thomas Lawrence, bust length, with a large white bonnet. Sotheby's, 20 May 1953, lot 20 (*Lawrence* 1964, p.261). Drawn at Bath. A copy was in the Burley-on-the-Hill sale, Christie's, 20 June 1947, lot 22 (illus. P. Finch, *Burley-on-the-Hill*, 1901, I, f.p.285 as an unattributed watercolour on kid); described by Sewter (typescript cat. of Burley-on-the-Hill, NPG archive, [1937], p.32, no.16) as copied from 'a larger portrait by Mr Mee [*sic*]' (but cf. c.1802 below).

1787 Painting by William Hopkins,* three-quarter length seated, a pug dog in her lap. Government Art Collection (GAC 3810), from the Burley-on-the-Hill sale, Christie's, 20 June 1947, lot 75 as Northcote.

c.1802 Miniature attributed to Henry Edridge, bust-length oval, wearing a blue dress and white cap. Royal Collection (Walker 1992, no.807, who notes a previous attribution to Mrs Mee). Copies recorded by J.[or T.] H. Murton dated 1802 (formerly with G.F. Deane); by Princess Elizabeth (Royal Collection; Walker 1992, no.809) and attributed to her (Bonhams, 13 June 1994, lot 122).

1807 Engraving by K. Mackenzie after W.M. Craig, bust-length oval, wearing white bonnet and a fur-trimmed dark dress (*Lady's Monthly Museum*).

A monument to Lady Charlotte by Francis Chantrey is at Burley-on-the Hill.

FITZMAURICE, William, Viscount, see LANSDOWNE

FITZPATRICK, John, see UPPER OSSORY

FITZPATRICK, Hon. Richard 1747-1813

Army officer; 2nd s. of the 1st Earl of Upper Ossory; MP 1770-1813; a leader of fashion, bro.-in-law of Fox, under whom he served as secretary of war in 1783 and 1806-07; founder member of the Whig Club 1784; served in America 1777-78; general 1803.

745 see Groups, *The House of Commons 1793-94* by KARL ANTON HICKEL 1793-95

2076 see Groups, *Mr Fox and his Friends* by WILLIAM LANE c.1813

ICONOGRAPHY

c.1750 Painting by George Knapton, as a child with his brother and sister. Woburn Abbey (illus. *Manners & Morals*, Tate Gallery, 1987, no.195).

1773 Painting(?) by H.D. Hamilton, exhibited SA 1773(130).

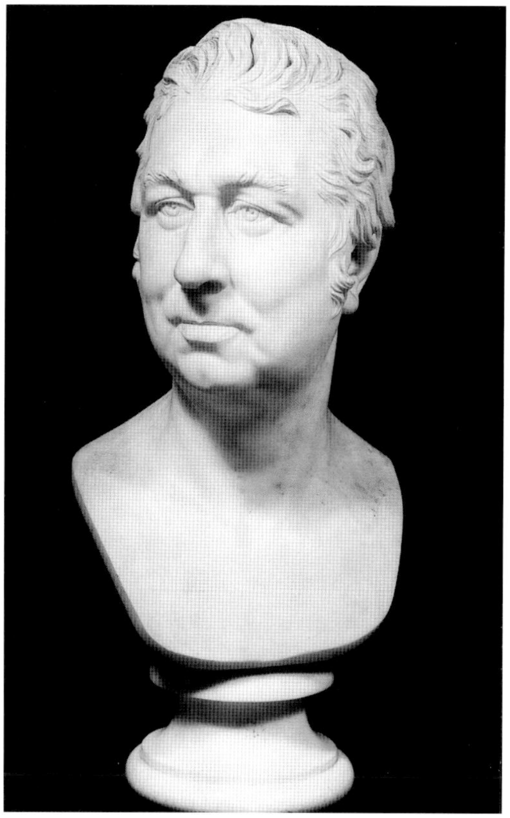

FITZPATRICK by Joseph Nollekens 1803 (formerly Woburn Abbey)

c.1780? Silhouette painted on glass, bust length, wearing military hat (illus. Wellesley, *One Hundred Silhouette Portraits*, 1912, pl.18).

1793-95 Painting by K.A. Hickel, *The House of Commons 1793-94*, see Groups NPG 745.

1803 Bust by Joseph Nollekens.* Formerly in the Temple of Liberty, Woburn Abbey. Exhibited RA 1804(949). A plaster, formerly at Holland House, was sometime lent to Kenwood.

Posthumous

c.1813 Drawing by William Lane, *Mr Fox and his Friends*, see Groups NPG 2076.

1814 Portrait by William Lane exhibited RA 1814(472 'the late General Fitzpatrick') with another of his brother Lord Ossory. Probably connected with the half-length drawing by William Lane, engraved H.R. Cook, the source of the image in Groups NPG 2076, see above.

FITZROY, Augustus Henry, see GRAFTON

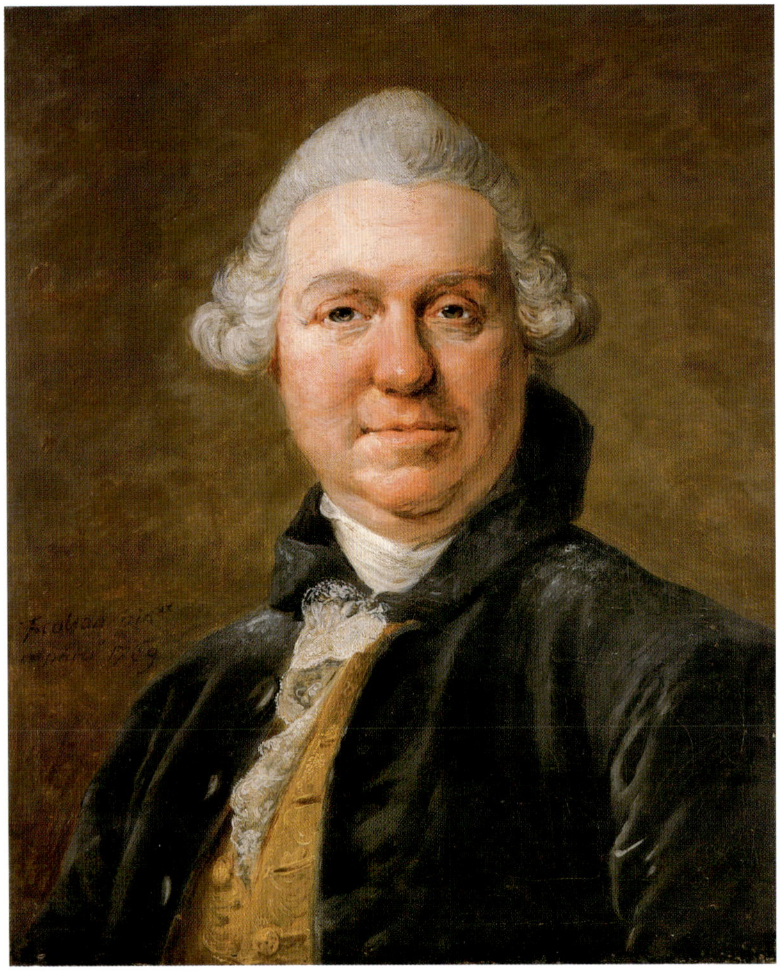

FOOTE NPG 4904

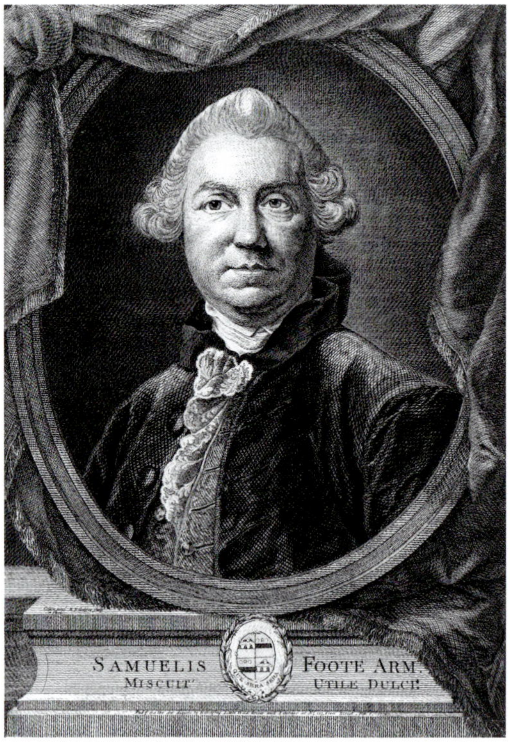

FOOTE R.B. Godfrey after J-F. Colson 1769 (British Museum)

FOOTE, Samuel 1720-77

Actor and playwright; in 1766 a fall from a horse led to the amputation of his (right?) leg; built the new Haymarket theatre 1767 and wrote a number of farces 1770-76 on topical events; famed for his cutting repartee.

'Foote was in his person about the middle size, rather clumsily made; with a broad fleshy face, that would be reckoned both vulgar and unmeaning, but for a certain archness in his eye, which at once overcame all other appearances, and instantly proclaimed him the genuine humourist' (William Cooke, 1805).

4904 JEAN-FRANÇOIS COLSON 1769

Canvas 54 x 45 (21¼ x 17¾) lined; cleaned 1989; repaired tears round head; signed, lower left: *F Colson pinxt / a paris 1769.* [the inscription indistinct]; the original canvas was inscribed verso: *Original Portrait of/ the Celebrated Dramatic Author / Samuel Foote Esq.*[1]

Blue-grey eyes, powdered hair, white neckcloth, blue-grey velvet coat, gold embroidered waistcoat.

Collections: Bonham's, 4 April 1968, lot 30, bt. Christopher Wood; Christie's, 23 June 1972, lot 99, bt. Kenyon for the NPG.

Engravings: R.B. Godfrey 1770 (oval); W. Ridley 1794 (oval); C. Watson 1805 (oval); S. Freeman, 1809 (Inchbald's *Farces*); W. Read; Orme & Butler 1888 (Doran's *Annals of the English Stage*).

Exhibition: *Georgian Playhouse* 1975(91).

This vigorous study was painted early in 1769 in Paris; having spent the winter there, Foote returned to London in February that year.[2] In 1805 his biographer wrote that while there were several prints of Foote in dramatic and private character, none of which were unlike, the most perfect likeness was 'the French print published immediately after one of his trips from Paris, and which is prefixed to these memoirs,'[3] i.e. the print by Godfrey* as copied for the *Memoirs* by Caroline Watson. Godfrey's elaborate print, exhibited in 1770,[4] was surely devised by Foote, whose pretence is apparent both in the title, *SAMUELIS FOOTE ARM. / MISCUIT UTILE DULCI*,[5] and in the elaborate quartered coat of arms with motto, *QUE SERA SERA* - both otherwise unrecorded for the Foote family.[6]

Foote was a frequent visitor to Paris, where in 1775 he remarked that 'the French were quite astonished at his figure and manner, and at his dress, which he obstinately continued exactly as in London'.[7]

1 A modern handwritten label recorded this inscription on the original canvas.
2 Highfill, V, p.344.
3 W. Cooke, *Memoirs of Samuel Foote*, 1805, II, p.i. In mistakenly calling it a French print, Cooke probably confused it with Brookshaw's plate after Cotes which was published in Paris in 1773 and shows a closely comparable head.
4 SA 1770(209).
5 Foote was armigerous, see below; the tag comes from Horace *Ars Poetica*, 343, *omne tulit punctum qui miscuit utile dulci* (he who blends profit with delight wins general approbation).
6 The Foote arms given in *Burke's General Armory* were: *vert a chev betw. three doves ar*, a motto *qui sera sera* is cited for Edgell, Folkes, Bettenson and Wolferstan (by Washbourne 1847 and Elvin 1860); the arms appearing in the print are quarterly, *1 & 4, or., a vair gu., sa. and az.; 2 & 3 or, a fesse sa. with a mullet gu. betw. two guzes.*
7 *Boswell*, II, p.403n.

ICONOGRAPHY

See also the *Harvard Catalogue*, II, pp.47-49, and Highfill, V, pp.357-59 (listing further portrayals of Foote in character).

c.1745-50? Miniature by Thomas Worlidge, half length with long curled wig. Victoria and Albert Museum (P.9.1942; illus. Foskett 1972, II, pl.395, no.956).

1764 Painting by Charles Maucourt, half-length seated. Sotheby's, 13 December 1992, lot 107.

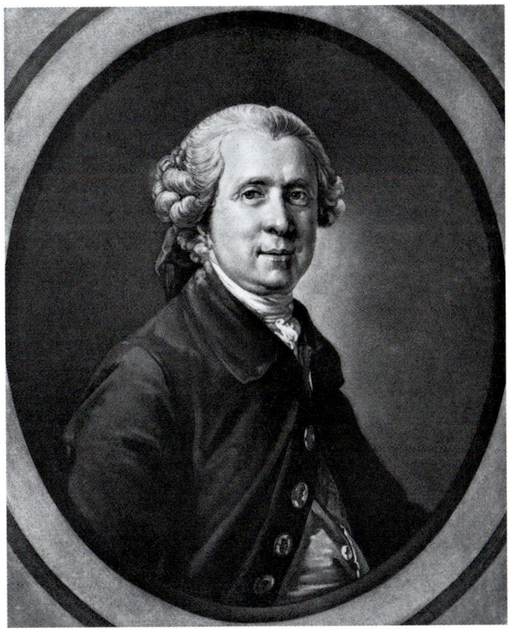

FOOTE R. Brookshaw after Francis Cotes 1765 (NPG D 10598)

1765 Painting by Francis Cotes, half-length oval; engraved R. Brookshaw 1773,* lettered *F. Cotes Pinxt Londini 1765. R. Brookshaw fecit Paris 1773.*

c.1765–70 Painting by J.H. Mortimer, *Caricature Group*, see Comparative Groups.

1767 Painting by Joshua Reynolds, three-quarter length standing. Lincoln sale, Christie's, 31 March 1939, lot 46 (Mannings 2000, no.656). Engraved T. Blackmore 1771; S.W. Reynolds. Versions are in the Garrick Club (Ashton 1997, no.229; engraved W. Greatbach 1857) and two in private collections, one described as a copy by George Romney (Mannings 2000, no.656a).

1769 Painting by J-F. Colson, see NPG 4904.

c.1770 Painting by Thomas Gainsborough, half length. Private collection, Canada (Waterhouse 1958, no.263; illus. *Gainsborough in Canada*, Fredericton, 1991, no.13). From the artist's Bath period, the identity based on a tale that the artist gave a portrait of Foote to Walter Wiltshire, from whom the provenance of this picture may be traced, but the sitter appears suspiciously dapper.

c.1770–75 Drawing, formerly attributed to Francis Cotes, bust-length as Mrs Cole in Foote's *The Minor* (British Museum, 1859.2.12.19; Johnson 1976, no.13).

1778 Bust by John Bacon sr., exhibited RA 1778(5).

Thomas Hudson's sale, 26 February 1785, lot 7 contained portraits of Barry and Foote, presumably

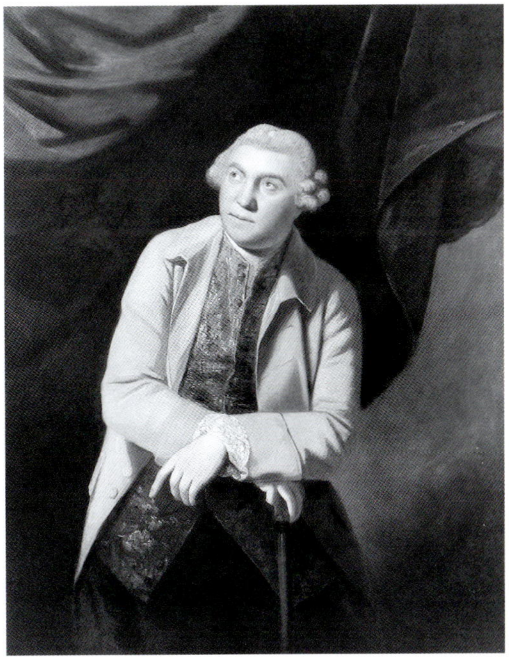

FOOTE after Joshua Reynolds 1767 (Garrick Club)

Spranger Barry and Samuel Foote (Miles 1977, II, pp.31, 83); a portrait called Foote by Hudson was sold Christie's, 22 July 1871, lot 173. A portrait by R.E. Pine was sold Christie's, 19 May 1911, lot 118.

Depictions of Foote in character include two paintings by Johann Zoffany: as Sturgeon in Foote's *The Mayor of Garratt*, 1764 (private collection; engraved J.G. Haid 1765, illus. Highfill, V, p.342); and as Dr Hellebore in Foote's *The Devil upon Two Sticks* (private collection; illus. *Zoffany* 1977, no.50; engraved J. Finlayson 1769, illus. Highfill, V, p.345).

DOUBTFUL PORTRAITS

Painting by Gainsborough (Waterhouse 1958, no.777; illus. *Connoisseur*, CXXVIII, 1951, p.214); miniatures by J.H. Bogle, exhibited SKM 1865(1046) lent Mrs Vivian, and by William Naish, sold Christie's, 3 September 1984, lot 218.

FOURDRINIER, Henry 1730–99

6091 see Groups, *The Fourdrinier Family*, attributed to JOHN DOWNMAN c.1786

FOX, Charles James 1749–1806

Parliamentarian and statesman, 2nd s. of the 1st Baron Holland; MP 1768–1806; foreign secretary 1782; secretary of state 1783 and 1806.

'His features, in themselves, dark, harsh, and saturnine, like Charles II, derived a sort of majesty from the addition of two black and shaggy eyebrows, which sometimes concealed, but more frequently developed, the workings of his mind ... His figure, broad, heavy, and inclined to corpulency, appeared destitute of elegance or grace, except the portion conferred on it by the emanations of intellect' (Sir Nathaniel Wraxall, 1815).

From the time of the American wars Fox assumed a blue coat and yellow waistcoat, imitating the 'buff and blue' colours of Washington's army. These colours became the 'uniform of the Fox club' and the 'the badge of the entire Whig party' (George, 6th Earl of Albemarle, 1852).

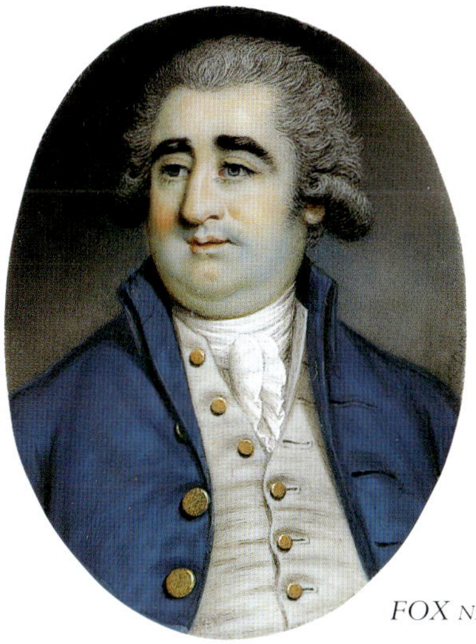

FOX NPG *6292*

6292 THOMAS DAY 1787

Watercolour and bodycolour on ivory 6.7 x 5.1 ($2\frac{5}{8}$ x 2); signed and dated *T.D.1787* in the right-hand margin. The back of the silver-gilt case engraved: *Rt. Hon Charles James Fox / Thomas Day / 1787.*

Grey eyes, powdered hair, blue coat, silver waistcoat, white neckcloth.

Collections: Hon Frederic H.A. Wallop (d.1953), by whom lent to the Victoria and Albert Museum 1927–49; his nephew Alan Evans, by whom bequeathed to the National Gallery 1974; lent to the NPG until permanently transferred in 1994.

Engravings: J. Jones 1787 (with a Greek inscription from Aristophanes, *Acharnians*, 1:531, 'he lightened, he thundered, he set all Greece in turmoil');[1] anon.

Exhibition: *Gillray*, Tate, 2001(100d).

Reference: Walker 1998, no.64.

1 For this identification I am grateful to Prof. Geoffrey Waywell.

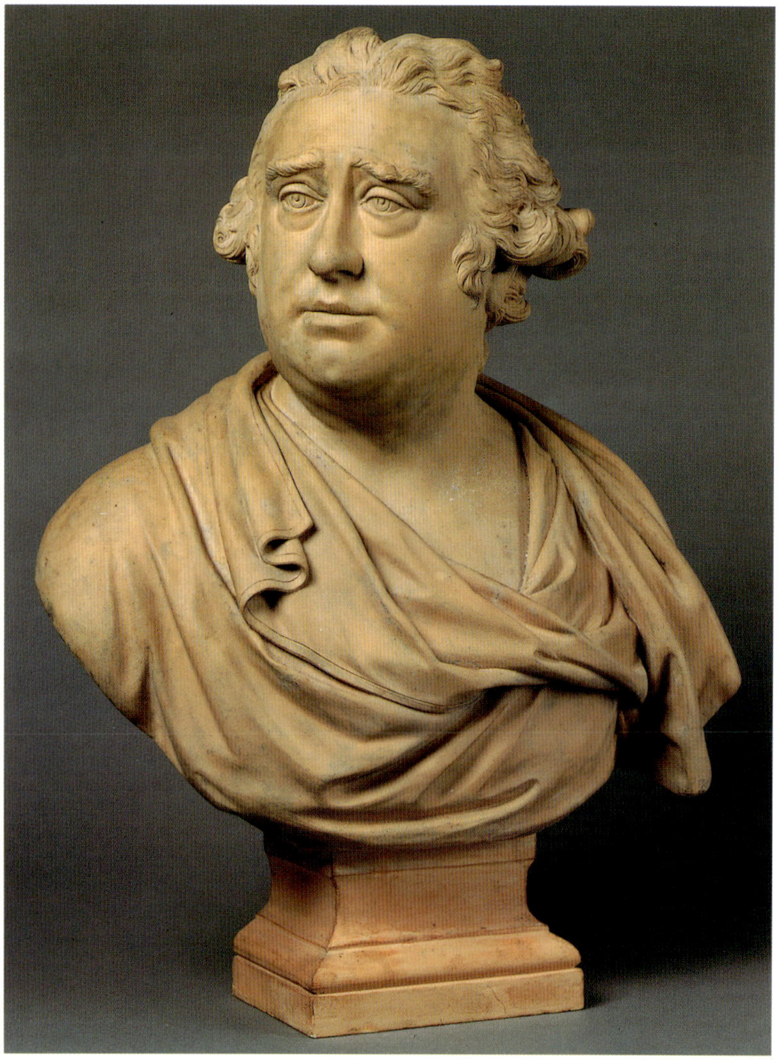

FOX NPG *139*

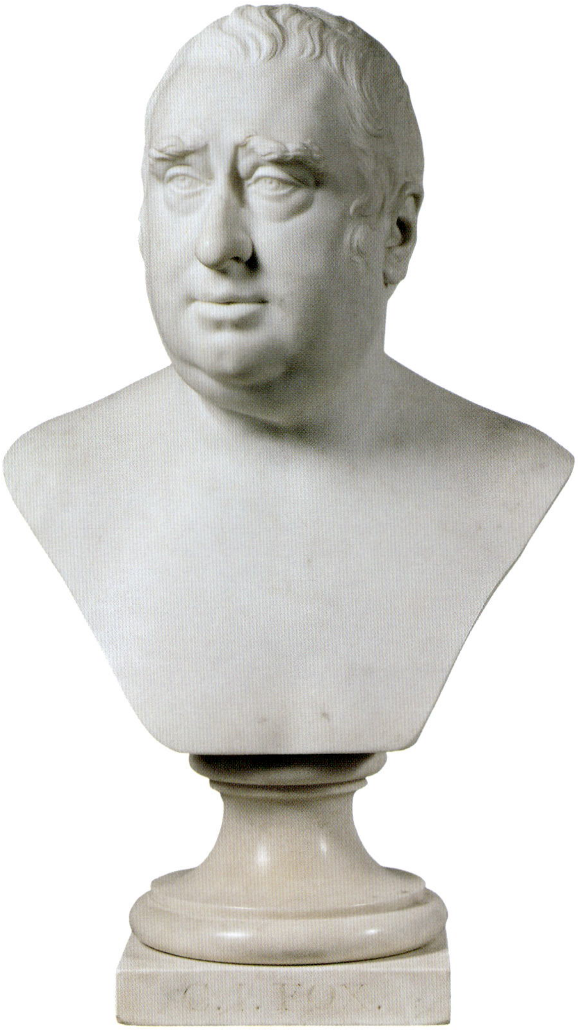

FOX NPG *3887*

139 after JOSEPH NOLLEKENS 1791

Terracotta 65 (25½) high; traces of a black and grey deposit on the surface; probably a cast.[1]

Collections: Purchased from Farrer 1862.

Exhibition: *The Shadow of the Guillotine*, British Museum, 1989 (85).

For a general discussion of the almost innumerable Nollekens busts of Fox, see NPG 3887 below.

NPG 139 is a copy of the first model, the original of which was exhibited RA 1791(632) and sent to St Petersburg in September 1791 at the request of the Empress Catherine who, wishing to acknowledge Fox's friendly diplomacy during the Russo-Turkish war, placed it in the Hermitage Museum (where it remains), while a bronze cast, taken in 1792, was placed between busts of Cicero and Demosthenes in the colonnade gallery at Tsarskoye Selo.[2] An engraving of the bust by William Pether, published on 1 January 1792, was dedicated to the Empress. The bust had originally been modelled for the 4th Earl Fitzwilliam's Mausoleum at Wentworth Woodhouse dedicated to the 2nd Marquess of Rockingham; Fitzwilliam ceded the bust to Catherine and took the second bust, also dated 1791. In 1796 Lord Fitzwilliam gave Mrs Armistead another example of this bust (currently on loan to the NPG).

The many other examples include those at Holkham (made for Thomas Coke, dated 1792),[3] the Yale Center for British Art (B1977.14.16; made for Lord Robert Spencer, 1792), Howick Hall (made for the 2nd Earl Grey, 1792), in a private collection (made for the 3rd Lord Holland, 1793), with the Thirlestane Castle Trust (1793), in the Walters Art Gallery, Baltimore, and in the Philadelphia Museum of Art. Several busts, including that given to Mrs Armistead in 1796, had inscribed on the socle a quatrain by Richard Fitzpatrick, Fox's brother-in-law.

A marble copy by E.H. Baily dated 1832 is in a private collection, and a bronzed plaster is one of several copies in Brooks's, London.

1 Note in NPG archive from Malcolm Baker, June 1988. There are structural holes in the top of the head and behind each shoulder.
2 See *British Art Treasures from Russian Imperial Collections*, 1996, no.54. In 1791 Fox had dissuaded the British government from sending ships to the Baltic. The marble in the Hermitage illus. *British Art Journal*, II, 2000–01, p.125.
3 Illus. Whinney 1964, pl.121.

743 KARL ANTON HICKEL 1794

Canvas 133 x 114 (52½ x 45) lined; many minor retouchings, prominently discoloured in the sky area.

Grey eyes, white hair, wearing a black top hat, dark blue coat and yellow waistcoat, with black breeches and white stockings; he sits on a green garden seat and

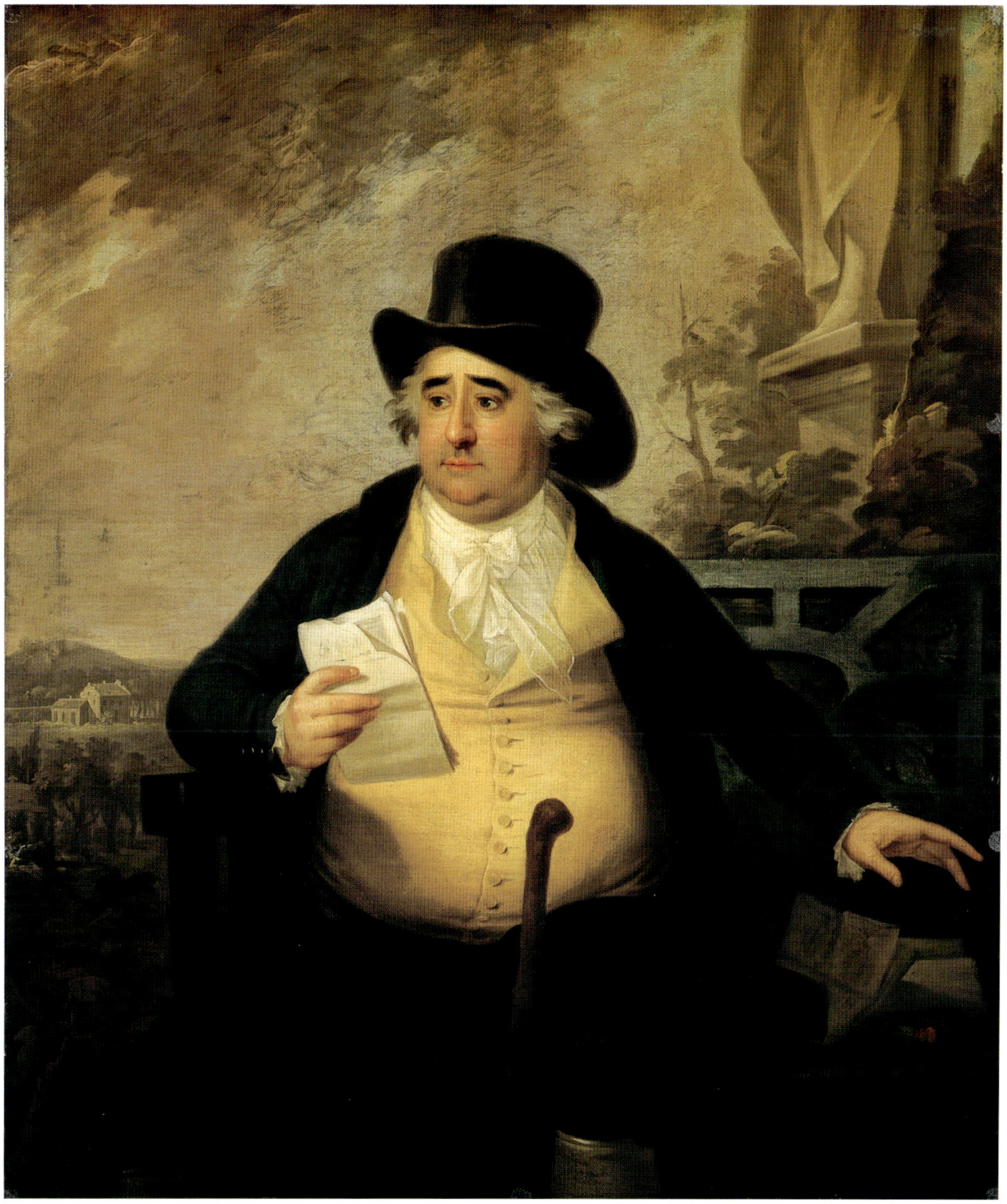

FOX NPG *743*

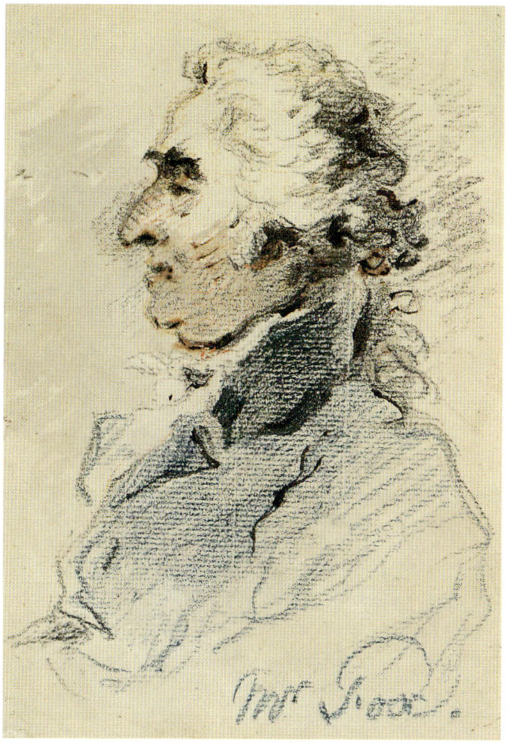

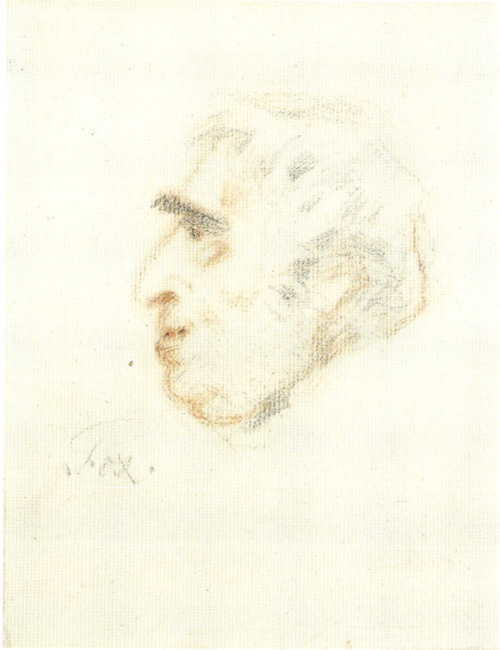

FOX NPG *1310A (above), 1310B (below)*

a female statue stands behind him; for the distant houses, see below.

Collections: Mr Desvignes, of Lewisham;[1] Christie's, 2 April 1885, lot 115; Graves, from whom purchased 1885.

Engraving: J.G. Huck.

Exhibition: *Romantic Icons*, Grasmere, 1999(14).

Lord Canning recorded that Fox had sat to Hickel by May 1794[2] and in July Hickel told Farington he had spent four days with Fox at St Anne's Hill, near Chertsey in Surrey.[3] The house had been acquired c.1778 by Mrs Armistead, subsequently Mrs Fox, and by 1794 Fox, then largely withdrawn from active politics, was enjoying this country retreat, 'the seat of true happiness',[4] where he had access to 'Nightingales, Flowers, Litterature, History etc'.[5] NPG 743 evokes his pleasurable life, although the distant house differs somewhat from early-nineteenth-century depictions and plans of St Anne's Hill House.[6]

Farington added that Hickel was to paint two Parliamentary groups, 'The Majority being conspicuous in one with Pitt speaking. - The Minority in the other with Fox speaking'. In both these compositions of 1793–95 the figure of Fox derived closely from NPG 743; the first is NPG 745, see below, and the second is known only through a sketch in a private collection.[7]

A half length of Fox by Hickel, 'Painter to His Imperial Majesty', was engraved by John Young in 1797, the head closely resembling that in NPG 743.

1 As annotated by Scharf in his sale cat.
2 See Walker *Regency*, I, p.599.
3 Farington, 25 July 1794.
4 6 March 1795; *Memorials and Corr. of Charles James Fox*, III, 1854, p. 100.
5 L.G. Mitchell, *Charles James Fox*, 1992, p.178.
6 Cf. a map of Chertsey of 1814 and a watercolour of the house by John Hassell of 1822 (both in the Chertsey Museum). See E.W. Brayley, *History of Surrey*, 1850, pp.236-8, 242. The house was demolished in 1937.
7 Illus. Walker *Regency*, II, pls.1511-12.

745 see Groups, *The House of Commons 1793-94* by KARL ANTON HICKEL 1793-95

1310 UNKNOWN ARTIST c.1795-1800

A Blue, black and red crayon, with some grey wash 15.8 x 11 (6¼ x 4⅜) inscribed bottom right in blue: *Mr Fox*.

White hair, wearing a blue coat.

B Black and red crayon with some pencil 13.7 x 10.8 (5⅜ x 4¼) inscribed below left in pencil: *Fox*.

Collections: Presented by the Hon Philip Stanhope (later Lord Weardale) 1902.

Exhibition: *Bicentennial Center Opening*, Yorktown, Va., 1976.

These profiles, suggesting a benign and a forceful Fox, are doubtless by the same hand. The inscriptions appear to be written by different hands.

3887 JOSEPH NOLLEKENS [1802]

Marble 70 (27½) high overall, the bust 50 (19¾) high; inscribed on the back: *Nollekens Ft / 1805* and, on the side of the base: *C.I. FOX.* and *Carolus eloquii nostro Demosthenis aevo/Unicus adfertor.*[1]

Collections: Commissioned by William Smith MP (1756-1835); by descent to P. Leigh-Smith, by whom presented 1953.

Exhibition: *Return to Life*, Leeds, Edinburgh, NPG, 2001(5).

Nollekens's busts of Fox 'brought him into more notice than any other of his productions',[2] and when Abbott painted his portrait c.1797 (NPG 30)[3] a bust of Fox (as NPG 139) was prominently displayed. The Empress Catherine of Russia was alleged to have had 'no fewer than twelve busts of Mr Fox in marble, all executed by Mr Nollekens, to give as presents',[4] and others were placed in temples dedicated to the liberty and friendship embodied by Fox.[5] By August 1803 Nollekens had executed fourteen,[6] and in June 1807 he had eight to execute and had already made twenty-one;[7] he charged one hundred guineas for each. By 1817 Lorenzo Bartolini in Florence had imported casts from which he was supplying marble busts at 22 guineas each.[8]

NPG 3887 represents the later model (for the earlier, see NPG 139 above), the short hair agreeing with the 'Crops and Democrats' fashion of the 1790s,[9] and echoing Fox's comparison of himself at that time with Brutus watching the Roman republic give way to the despotism of the Caesars.[10] The first example was carved in 1802 for the 5th Duke of Bedford for his Temple of Liberty at Woburn[11] and was, presumably, that shown at the RA 1802(1073). NPG 3887 was carved for William Smith, to whom Fox wrote on 29 November 1804: 'I will if I can let Nollekens have one sitting, but I own I think the Bust he has done is so good & meets with such universal approbation, that it is a pity to have it altered in the slightest degree'. On 24 June 1811 Nollekens signed a receipt for £73.10 from Smith.[12]

There were two types of this second model, with or without classical drapery. Examples without drapery, as NPG 3887, include those at Wistow (acquired by Sir Henry Halford in 1807) and Dalmeny (1809); examples with drapery include those at Castle Howard (1803), the Victoria and Albert Museum (A.1.1945), the Royal Collection (1808), Brooks's, London (1810), the Walker Art Gallery, Liverpool (4156) and at Chatsworth (1811). This type of bust is shown in William Lane's *Whig Statesmen and their Friends*, see Groups NPG 2076.

Unspecified Nollekens busts were sent to the 8th Lord Kinnaird at Rossie Priory[13] and the 1st Baron Yarborough at Brocklesby Park;[14] another was at Strawberry Hill.[15] An ivory bust by Benjamin Cheverton after Nollekens was exhibited RSBA 1835(794).

1 'Charles, alone in our time revived the oratory of Demosthenes'. J. Kenworthy-Browne informs me that this is copied in a MS list of Nollekens inscriptions in the Beinecke Library, Yale University (Osborn shelves d 174, f.122).
2 Smith 1920, I, p.73.
3 See Walker *Regency*, I, pp.368, II, pl.887.
4 Smith 1920, II, p.12n.
5 N. Penny, 'The Whig Cult of Fox in early nineteenth-century Sculpture' *Past and Present*, 70, February 1976, pp.94-105.
6 Farington, 14 August 1803.
7 *Ibid.*, 6 June 1807. Whinney 1964, p.269n14 said 'at least 50 replicas [of the second type of bust] are known'. Kenworthy-Browne recorded four plaster busts of Fox in the Nollekens sale in 1823 (*CL*, CLVII, 1975, p.1510). Four examples are in the GAC, of which two are in British Embassies in Brasilia and Washington (768 & 4615; see Walker, 1976, p.25).
8 H. Matthews, *Diary of an Invalid*, 1820, p.59.
9 Farington, 16 November 1795.
10 L.G. Mitchell, *Charles James Fox*, 1992, p.155.
11 See J. Kenworthy-Browne, 'The Temple of Liberty at Woburn Abbey', *Apollo*, CXXX, 1989, p.27ff. (the inscribed date of the Woburn Fox is 1802 as Kenworthy-Browne has kindly informed me).
12 Both receipt and letter were also presented by Mr P. Leigh Smith in 1953 and are now in the NPG archive.
13 A.H. Millar, *Historical Castles & Mansions of Scotland*, 1890, pp.21, 38.
14 Waagen, IV, p.71.
15 Sale, 19th day, 16 May 1842, in lot 26.

2076 see Groups, *Mr Fox and his Friends* by WILLIAM LANE c.1813

ICONOGRAPHY

'Mr Fox spoke of the Arts and said Commerce must support them. He entertains the highest opinion of Sir Joshua Reynolds, -- and thinks very favorably of Northcote & Opie. -- Of West he spoke with contempt & thinks slightly of the works of Fuseli' (Farington, 18 September 1794).

1751 Painting by William Hoare as a child 'aged three' with a dog. Private collection (illus. L.G. Mitchell, *Charles James Fox*, 1992, f.p.148), from Lady Dimsdale's sale, Christie's, 1 May 1875, lot 153, as Reynolds.

1762 Painting by Joshua Reynolds, three-quarter length, with his aunt Lady Sarah Bunbury and cousin Lady Susan Fox Strangways, the composition inspired by Latin verses by the eleven-year-old Fox. Private collection (Mannings 2000, no.677). Engraved J. Watson 1762. A reduced version showing Fox whole length and an extended landscape is in the same collection. The figure of Fox alone engraved W. Read 1859 as after Ozias Humphry (conceivably from the unattributed miniature of Fox as a boy of thirteen formerly at Holland House; cat., 1904, p.193, no.2); a miniature attributed to Humphry after Reynolds exhibited *Guelph* 1891(1066) lent J. Whitehead.

1762-63? Painting by Joshua Reynolds, half length. Sotheby's, New York, 11 April 1984, lot 21A (Mannings 2000, no.672). Studio version at Eton College.

c.1775-80 Drawing by H.D. Hamilton, half-length oval. Private collection.

1778 Chalk drawing by John Downman. Fitzwilliam Museum, Cambridge (1949). Said to have been made for 'the beautiful Mrs Crewe' (Williamson 1907, p.liv). A small painting on copper by Downman, dated 1778, sold Christie's, 21 December 1950, lot 70/1, conceivably shows Fox (illus. Waterhouse 1981, p.113).

1782 Painting by Joshua Reynolds,★ three-quarter length. Holkham (Mannings 2000, no.674). Painted for the 1st Lord Crewe who gave it to the Earl of Leicester. Exhibited RA 1784(108). Engraved J. Jones 1784. The most familiar painted image of Fox and the most copied. Fox had insisted that a draft of his India Bill be included on the table, despite that fact that the Fox-North coalition ministry had ended before the picture was completed.

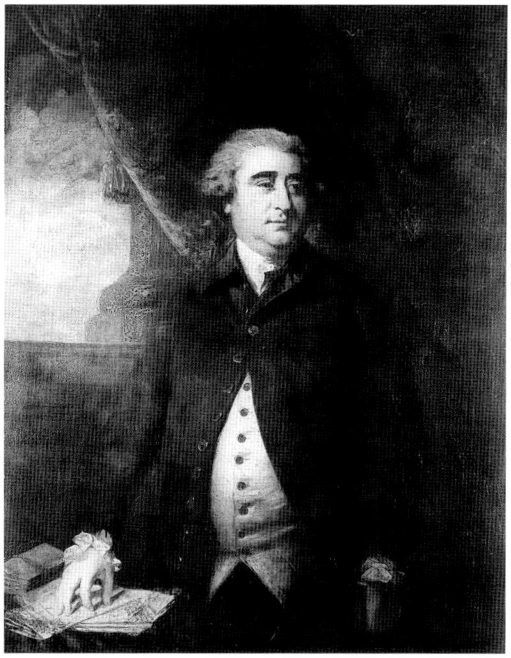

FOX by Joshua Reynolds 1782 (Holkham Hall)

A replica for Mrs Armistead (Mrs Fox) paid for in 1789 is now in a private collection. Versions recorded with the Marquess of Bute in 1861 (SSB 60/115) and at Euston Hall (Farrer 1908, p.108, no.23). Two copies are at Hertford College, Oxford (Poole, III, pp.273-74) and another was sold Christie's, 17 October 1986, lot 113. Of many reduced copies, examples are at Castle Howard, Somerset House (GAC 2177), the Palace of Westminster, and Pembroke College, Oxford (Poole, III, p.247). Others were at Hopetoun House (sold Christie's, 19-20 July 1993, lot 528), in the Keppel collection (Christie's, 19 June 1911, lot 7) and at West Harling Hall. Named copyists include G.P.A. Healy (Versailles); John Jackson (formerly at Panshanger and at Trentham Hall); John Rising (examples at Petworth, Hardwick, and Milton), and Paterson (Christie's, 5 February 1842, lot 96).

Pastel copies were made by Samuel Cotes (Phillips, 17 March 1998, lot 4) and William Lane 1808 (Royal Collection; Millar 1969, no.1042). A drawing by Lane was in the St Anne's Hill House sale, Phillips, 26 November 1924, lot 509. A watercolour copy by Lady Diana Beauclerk was formerly at Holland House (cat., 1904, p.30, no.177a).

Miniature copies include examples by William Bate dated 1831 (Scottish NPG, PGL 834; illus. *Comerford* 1999, p.57); by Henry Bone dated 1792 (Sotheby's, 28 April 1981, lot 229) and 1818 (formerly at Woburn Abbey; SSB 89/17), and by Charles Muss dated 1820 (Louvre; formerly at Holland House, see cat., 1904, no.282, and a third sold Christie's, 27 February 1968, lot 68). An unattributed miniature version sold Sotheby's, 18 December 1995, lot 143 (with another of Edmund Burke after Romney).

1782 Painting by Richard Cosway, bust length, untraced, etched by Cosway (*Cosway pinxt ad vivum et sculpt*, 4 June 1782; illus. T. Gipponi ed., *Maria e Ricardo Cosway*, 1998, p.71). One of only two plates etched by Cosway (*Cosway* 1995, no.80).

1782 Etching by J. Sayers, *Vox Populi*, whole length standing, fists clenched (George 6054).

c.1782? Engraving by J. Strutt after a painting by *Gavinus Hamilton*, half length, pub. 1 July 1794. Possibly H.D. Hamilton was meant; crayon portraits of Fox by H.D. Hamilton (who was in Italy 1782-91) were formerly at Carton and at Castletown in Ireland (*Wal. Soc.*, II, 1913, p.106).

1783 Drawing by Nathaniel Dance, see Guilford 1783.

before 1784 Painting given by Fox to the Corporation of Tain on his election as member for the Northern Burghs in 1784; sent to Edinburgh in November 1856 for conservation (J. Barron, *Northern Highlands in the Nineteenth Century*, III, 1913, p.362; information by courtesy of Helen Smailes).

c.1784 Unattributed painting, half length. Fogg Art Museum, Cambridge, Mass. (1934.65; illus. Fogg Art Museum, *European Paintings*, 1990, p.140). Variously attributed to West or Abbott; conceivably by J.S. Copley. The distant view of St Paul's Covent Garden presumably refers to the Westminster elections of May 1784, when the church portico was the setting for violent political meetings; it was later proposed that Westmacott's monument to Fox should stand there.

c.1784? Miniature by Joseph Daniel. Christie's, 17 March 1987, lot 120 (previously Sotheby's, 18 December 1972, lot 75, as Abraham Daniel).

c.1784? Painting by Thomas Hickey, see Burke c.1784.

c.1785 Wash drawing by Lady Diana Beauclerk, three-quarter length seated. Sotheby's, 4 May 1972, lot 203. Other drawings by her of Fox were formerly at Woolbeding (illus. *CL*, CII, 1947, p.330) and Holland House (cat., 1904, no.195 mistakenly described as after Reynolds).

c.1785 Miniature attributed to Richard Crosse. Christie's, 21 October 1997, lot 79. See c.1791 below.

1787 Miniature by Thomas Day, see NPG 6292.

1789 Medals by W. Lutwyche and Thomas Wyon sr. (Brown 1980, nos.323-25).

c.1790 Wedgwood medallion attributed to John Flaxman (illus. Reilly 1973, p.144). See also medallion by Tassie, before 1791 below.

c.1790-95 Unattributed miniature. Royal Collection (Walker 1992, no.355).

1791 Marble bust by Joseph Nollekens, see NPG 139.

before 1791 Medallion by James Tassie, modelled by W. Whitley (Gray 1894, no.134). Plaster in the Scottish NPG (PG 298). Closely resembling the Wedgwood medallion of c.1790.

A cameo and a cornelian modelled by Barnet are listed by Raspe 1791, nos.14187-88.

c.1791 Miniature by Richard Crosse. Royal Ontario Museum, Toronto (illus. *Portrait Miniatures in the Royal Ontario Museum*, 1981, p.35). Closely resembling the portrait by Reynolds of 1782 but with a double row of buttons on the waistcoat. Crosse received two payments from 'Mr Fox', on 27 February 1783 and 25 February 1791 (*Wal. Soc.*, XVII, 1929, pp. 75, 80).

1793-95 Painting by K.A. Hickel, *The House of Commons 1793-94*, see Groups NPG 745.

1793-95 Painting by K.A. Hickel, *The Opposition 1793-94*, whole length, addressing the House. Private collection (illus. Walker *Regency*, II, pl.1511-12). Sketch for a projected large canvas.

c.1793-96 Intaglio by Nathaniel Marchant (*Marchant* 1987, p.75, no.135). Exhibited RA 1797(1003). Fox 'sat in so restless and unsteady a manner that Marchant could make nothing of [tracing a silhouette] (Farington, 15 December 1798). P. Ettinger, *Burl. Mag.*, XLV, 1924, p.88, described an unsigned intaglio on sardonyx attributed to Karl Leberecht.

1794 Painting by K.A. Hickel, see NPG 743.

1794 Medal by W. Whitley (Brown 1980, no.388).

c.1795-1800 Miniature by Harold Credoe, sold Christie's, 15 May 1979, lot 87 (illus. Foskett 1972, II, pl.66, no.187).

c.1795-1800 Unattributed drawings, see NPG 1310A & B.

1796 Drawing by Henry Edridge, seated. Private collection (illus. L.G. Mitchell, *Charles James Fox*, 1992, f.p.149). Engraved C. Turner 1806 from a drawing belonging to Mrs Fox (presumably that in the St Anne's Hill House sale, Phillips, 3rd day, 26 November 1924, lot 505). A close variant, differing only in background detail, and also dated 1796, in a private Scottish collection.

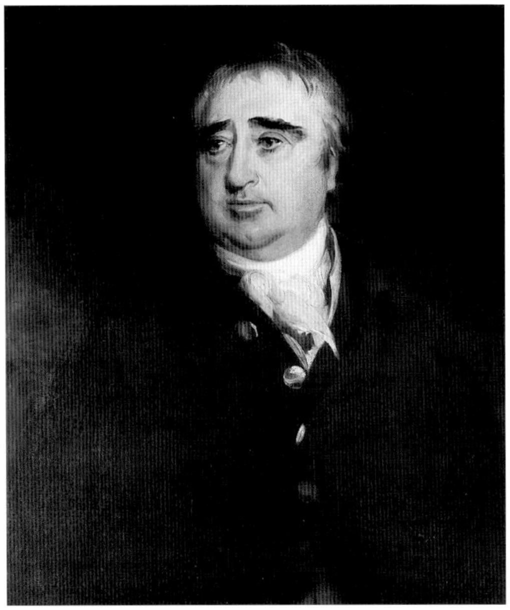

FOX by Thomas Lawrence 1800 (Private Collection)

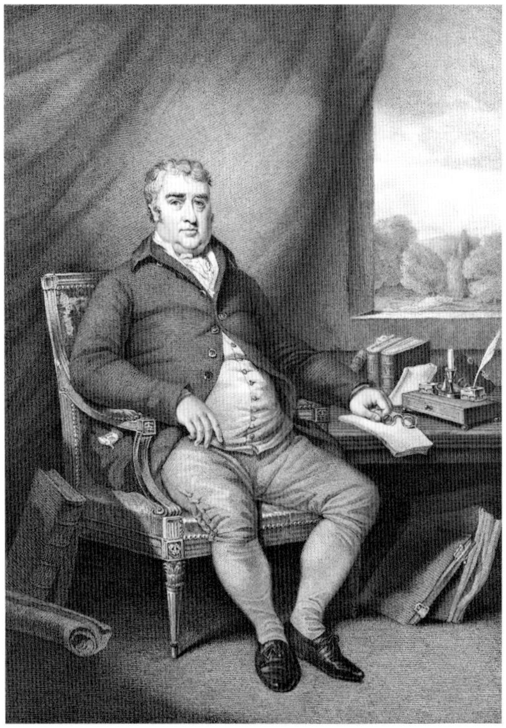

FOX S.W. Reynolds after J.R. Smith 1802 (NPG D 18432)

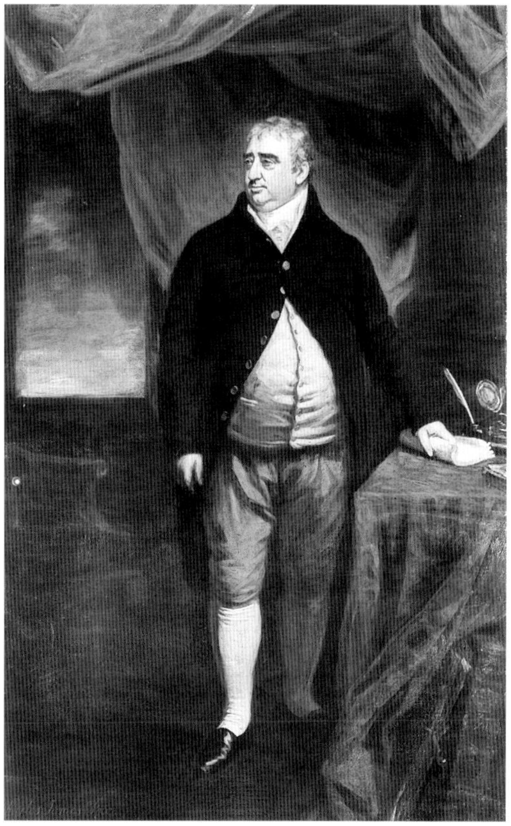

FOX by John Opie 1804 (Holkham Hall)

c.1796 Drawing by Henry Edridge, half-length seated. British Museum (1891.5.11.41). Edridge exhibited drawings of Fox RA 1796(685) and 1798(719).

1797 Wooden bust by George Leader. Sotheby's, 8-9 December 1988, lot 301.

1798 Painted terracotta bust by Lawrence Gahagan. Government Art Collection (0.86). Another, without drapery, dated 1800, in the Athelstan Museum, Malmesbury. A plaster cast, attributed to Garrard after Gahagan, sold Sotheby's, 10 December 1987, lot 210.

1798 Miniature by Henry Bone, three-quarter length seated. Christie's, 14 October 1998, lot 133. The composition repeats Lawrence's *Lord Auckland* (1792; Christ Church, Oxford), substituting Fox's head.

1799 Painting by J.T. Barber, bust length, engraved by A. Mackenzie 1799.

1799-1800 Medals by J.G. Hancock (Brown 1980, nos.467, 488).

1800 Painting by Thomas Lawrence,* half length. Private collection (Garlick 1989, no.307). Lawrence was painting Fox at St Anne's Hill in November 1800 (Farington, 4 November 1800). He supplied a version to Mr Bouverie in 1806 and a copy by John Simpson was in the Lawrence sale, 18 June 1831, under lot 79. Fox's nephew said the portrait 'was the worst ever painted of so eminent a man by so eminent an artist' (G.O. Trevelyan, *Macaulay*, 1961 ed., I, pp.196-97); it was copied by Samuel Lane (Farington, 5, 12 March 1801) and miniatures by Horace Hone were based upon it, examples exhibited RA 1810(631) and 1812(679); others dated 1810 (Christie's, 11 July 1985, lot 390), and 1811 (Brooks's, London); an undated version sold Phillips, 10 November 1998, lot 215.

c.1801 Wash drawing by Robert Dighton, profile. Palace of Westminster (Walker 1988, I, p.129). A bust-length oval by 'Dighton' engraved R. Newton 1801.

1802 Marble bust by Joseph Nollekens, see NPG 3887.

1802 Pastel by J.R. Smith, whole-length seated at table, *Principles of the Wigs* [*sic*] at his side. Exhibited RA 1802(346). Engraved S.W. Reynolds 1802, re-issued 1806* with an open window replacing the books on the table. Probably the 'large crayon' by J.R. Smith of Fox seated in his library, in the St Anne's Hill House sale, Phillips, 3rd day, 26 November 1924, lot 514. Pastel versions sold Christie's, 10 July 1984, lot 153, and 14 July 1999, lot 60; another in Brooks's, London; a three-quarter length in oils, said to be dated 1808, sold Christie's, 27 June 1980, lot 134.

A posthumous portrait by Thomas Phillips (Sotheby's, 16 May 1990, lot 57), dateable 1808 from the *Phillips Sitter Book* (no.266 'composed from various'), was based closely on Smith's picture. A 'small square miserable' copy by William Allan sold Christie's, 18 July 1874, lot 96.

1802 Drawing by E.F. Burney, engraved W. Holl *from a Drawing by Burney in 1802* and H. Meyer, with a different head, *from a drawing by Burney in 1806.*

1802 Marble bust by Anne Seymour Damer. Louvre (illus. Farington, V, f.p.1848). Exhibited RA 1803(1018). Fox, unhappily, seems to resemble Napoleon, Farington remarking it was 'not a very good likeness' (11 September 1802).

1803 Painting by James Lonsdale, exhibited RA 1803(438).

c.1803 Wax medallion by Samuel Percy. Fitzwilliam Museum, Cambridge. Possibly that exhibited RA 1803(1027); waxes by Percy sold Sotheby's, 16 May 1957, lot 96, and Christie's, 10 June 1993, lot 236, from Stanton Harcourt.

1804 Painting by John Opie,* whole length. Holkham. Exhibited RA 1805(82). Opie is said to have used Nollekens's bust to complete his portrait, Fox proving a distracted sitter (Smith 1920, II, p.221). Three-quarter length versions in Brooks's, London; at Temple Newsam, Leeds; North Carolina Museum of Art, Raleigh; University of Western Ontario, and sold Sotheby's, 16 July 1975, lot 64, and 14 July 1999, lot 40. A copy sold Sotheby's, 14 July 1999, lot 39.

Henry Bone copied the composition in 1805 (Royal Collection; Walker 1992, no.779); a preparatory drawing, dated July 1805, in the NPG Bone albums (*Bone* 1999, no.206), and copied the head alone (Berkeley Castle). A Bone enamel of 1818 was set in a snuff box for the Duke of Bedford (preparatory drawing NPG; *Bone* 1999, no.208), and there are other preparatory drawings by him, reduced versions, in the NPG Bone albums (*Bone* 1999, no.205, dated September 1805, and no.207, dated 1818). An enamel copy by William Bone is in the NG of Ireland (5578; illus. Caffrey 2000, p.134) and a miniature copy by William Derby was recorded at Knowsley (SSB 63/1).

1805 Wax bust by Catherine Andras. Victoria and Albert Museum (414.1362.1885; illus. Rackham 1930, pl.75). A model exhibited RA 1805(762). Engraved anon. 1807. Other examples sold Sotheby's, 30 November 1964, lot 80 (dated 1805), and Bonham's, 21 November 1996, lot 3.

c.1805? Painting by Henry Richter, engraved S. Freeman.

1806 Painting by Samuel Drummond, half length, engraved W. Ridley 1806.

1806 Death mask taken by Joseph Nollekens (Farington, 19 September 1806). A cast in the Department of Anatomy, University of Edinburgh, from the Edinburgh Phrenological Society (*Death Masks and Life Masks*, Edinburgh University, [1988], p.5).

c.1806? Miniature enamel attributed to J.L. Richter, in old age. NG of Ireland (3587).

Undated miniature by Nathaniel Plimer sold Christie's, 17 March 1987, lot 70. A miniature by 'A. Plimer' was formerly at Holland House (cat., 1904, p.193, no.3).

Unattributed drawing, half-length seated. Victoria and Albert Museum (E.3276.1948).

Watercolour miniature and a pencil outline by William Grimaldi (Grimaldi 1873, pp.22, 49, nos.134, 160).

Posthumous

1806 Commemorative medals by T. Webb, W. Whitley, Peter Wyon, and anon. (Brown 1980, nos.604-609).

1807 Enamel by Miss Jones, exhibited RA 1807(879).

1807 Bust by George Garrard. Uppark, destroyed by fire 1989 and replaced with a copy. Exhibited RA 1807(1099).

1808 Wax by Peter Rouw. Exhibited RA 1808(790). Examples in the Victoria and Albert Museum (1063.1871), and formerly at Holland House.

1810 Bust by W.J. Coffee (Gunnis 1968, p.109).

1813 Impression from an intaglio by J. Warwick, exhibited RA 1813(551).

c.1813 Drawing by William Lane, *Mr Fox and his Friends*, see Groups NPG 2076.

1815 Monument by Richard Westmacott jr., Fox supported by Liberty, mourned by Peace and thanked by Africa. Westminster Abbey (illus. Whinney 1964, pl.169; Busco 1994, p.70). Alternative designs by Thomas Stothard in Manchester CAG and in the Victoria and Albert Museum (7344; illus. J.Physick, *Designs for British Sculpture* 1969, p.166).

1816 Statue by Richard Westmacott jr., whole-length seated, the Magna Carta in his right hand. Bloomsbury Square, London (illus. Busco 1994, p.73). Engraved S.W. Reynolds and W. Ward 1817. A bronze model formerly at Holland House. The head based on Nollekens's 1801 bust. Separate marble busts by Westmacott sold Christie's, 28 January 1988, lot 189, and formerly at Alscot Park; bronze busts sold Sotheby's, 15 July 1998, lot 38 (as Nollekens), and in Brooks's, London.

c.1820? Marble bust by Federico Nicolini. National Maritime Museum. Formerly at Clandon Park (SSB 111/34a). Similar to the draped 'Roman' Nollekens of 1802.

1831 Marble bust by William Behnes. The Prince of Hanover.

1857 Marble statue by E.H. Baily. Palace of Westminster (illus. Read 1982, p.83). Model exhibited RA 1857(1210).

FRANCIS, Sir Philip, KB 1740-1818

Politician, reputedly the author of *The Letters of Junius* 1767-72; a member of the council of Bengal 1774-81, he became a dedicated opponent of Warren Hastings; MP 1784-1807; KB 1806, GCB 1815.

'Acrimony distinguished and characterised him in everything. Even his person, tall, thin, and scantily covered with flesh; his countenance, the lines of which were acute, intelligent, and full of meaning; the tones of his voice, sharp yet distinct and sonorous; his very gestures, impatient and irregular, eloquently bespoke the formation of his intellect' (Sir Nathaniel Wraxall, 1815).

'His figure was tall, erect, and well proportioned, but with no remarkable muscular development. His whole mien and carriage were calculated to attract notice in any circle and under any circumstances; yet it might be said that both face and figure were but half seen in repose' (J. Parkes & H. Merivale, 1867).

334 JAMES LONSDALE 1806-10

Canvas 76 x 63 (30 x 24¾) lined; cleaned 1990.

Brown eyes, white hair, wearing a white collar and neckcloth, yellow waistcoat, dark grey coat with gold buttons and the ribbon and star of the Bath.

Collections: By descent to the sitter's grandson, J.G. Francis,[1] from whom purchased 1871.

Engraving: Freeman 1810 (*Monthly Mirror*) and 1816.

When he offered NPG 334 in 1871, Francis alleged it was 'much better than the one at Holland House, and very superior to the picture now at Byfleet.'[2] The Holland House portrait was engraved by T. Lupton in 1817 as Lonsdale and, less elaborately, by H. Adlard in 1867 as Hoppner;[3] in 1904 it was catalogued as 'a replica' by Lonsdale of NPG 334.[4] The Byfleet version was that lent by H.R. Francis to the NPE 1867(767) as by Hoppner.[5]

The Holland House portrait was conceivably Lonsdale's original, while the Byfleet picture appears to be a copy; NPG 334 differs slightly from both of them, principally in the disposition of the coat and waistcoat collars.

1 In a letter to Lord Stanhope, 13 October 1871 (NPG archive) he wrote that 'It has been in my possession for more than thirty years. My father deceased in 1837.' He wrote twice more to Stanhope, with increasing urgency, concerning the sale, being evidently strapped at the time.
2 Letter to Lord Stanhope, 13 October 1871 (NPG archive).
3 As front. to H. Merivale, *Memoirs of Philip Francis*, 1867.
4 NPG cat., 1904, no.19.
5 According to the annotated volume of illustrations of the NPE 1867 in the NPG archive; illus. *The Francis Letters*, ed. B. Francis & E. Keary, n.d., I, front.).

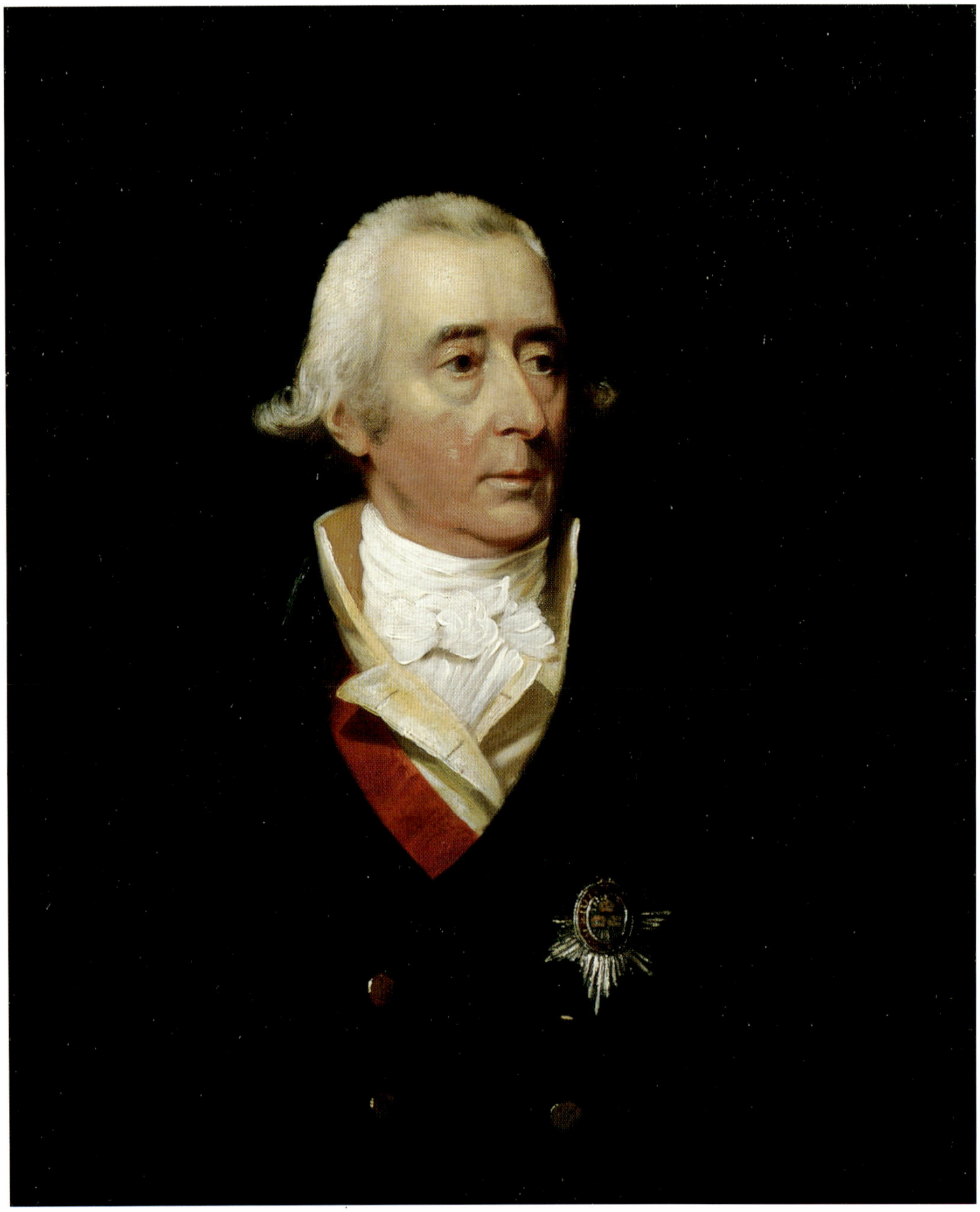

FRANCIS NPG *334*

ICONOGRAPHY

c.1770? Pastel by an unknown artist, half-length profile (illus. *The Francis Letters*, ed. B. Francis & E. Keary, n.d., II, front.).

1788 Caricature etching by J. Sayers, whole-length standing, lettered *I hate Alonzo / Zanga* [from Dr Yonge's *The Revenge*] referring to his contest with Hastings (George 7292; illus. J. Parkes & H. Merivale, *Sir Philip Francis*, 1867, II, front.).

1794 Caricature etching by J. Sayers, bust-length profile as *François Philippeaux / citoyen actif & sans culotte*, referring to his sympathy for the French Revolution (George 8455).

1806–10 Painting by James Lonsdale, see NPG 334.

DOUBTFUL PORTRAITS

Miniatures by John Smart 1781 (Victoria and Albert Museum; 479.1907), and unattributed (Bonham's, 24 November 1999, lot 66).

FRANKLIN, Benjamin 1706-90

Statesman, scientist and printer; b. Boston, Mass.; in England 1724–26 and 1757–62; published *Experiments and Observations on Electricity* 1751; FRS 1756; LL.D St Andrew's 1759, DCL Oxford 1762; ambassador extraordinary for the American colonies in London 1766–75 and in Paris 1776–85; returned to America in 1785; president of the executive of Pennsylvania 1785–88.

'He was fat, square built, and wore his own hair, thin and gray: but he looked healthy and vigorous. His head was remarkably large in proportion to his figure, and his countenance mild, firm, and expressive' (Deborah Logan, 1868).

Abbreviations

Nini 2001: A.C. Baiardi & B. Sibille, eds., *J B Nini*, exh. cat. Urbino, Blois, 2001.

Sellers 1962: C.C. Sellers, *Benjamin Franklin in Portraiture*, 1962.

Storelli 1896: A. Storelli, *Jean Baptiste Nini. Sa Vie Son Oeuvre*, 1896.

722 JEAN-BAPTISTE NINI 1777

Cast terracotta 12.1 (4¾) diameter; incised on the truncation: *NINI F 1777* with an armorial device, a coronet (*'une couronne de fantaisie'*) above a shield displaying a hand holding a rod drawing lightning; lettered: *.B.FRANKLIN. AMERICAIN.* and *1777*; surface rubbed in places revealing black underlay; verso, a small impressed fleur-de-lys.

Collections: Presented by Charles Seidler 1884.

Engravings: J. Hopwood; W. Grainger; J. Heath (from a medallion in the possession of Dr. Lettsom).

Reference: Storelli 1896, no.lxi; Sellers 1962, pp.344–46; *Nini* 2001, no.94.

Showing Franklin soon after his arrival in Paris: 'my thin gray strait hair, peeps out from under my only coiffure, a fine Fur Cap, which comes down to my Forehead ... Think how this must appear among the Powder'd Heads of Paris! I wish every gentleman and Lady in France would only be so obliging as to follow my Fashion'.[1] The fur cap, which Nini had heard of but not seen, was copied from an engraved portrait of Rousseau,[2] the profile from a drawing by the amateur artist Thomas Walpole. On 11 December 1777 Franklin told the artist's father, 'From a sketch ... which was drawn by your ingenious & valuable Son, they have made ... Medallions in *terre cuit*. A Dozen have been presented to me.'[3]

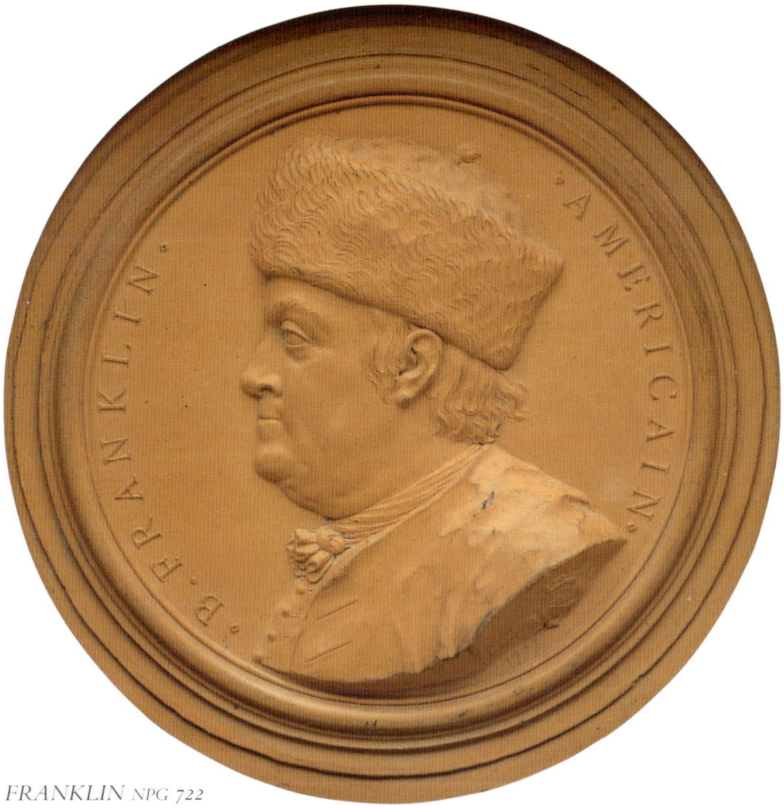

FRANKLIN NPG *722*

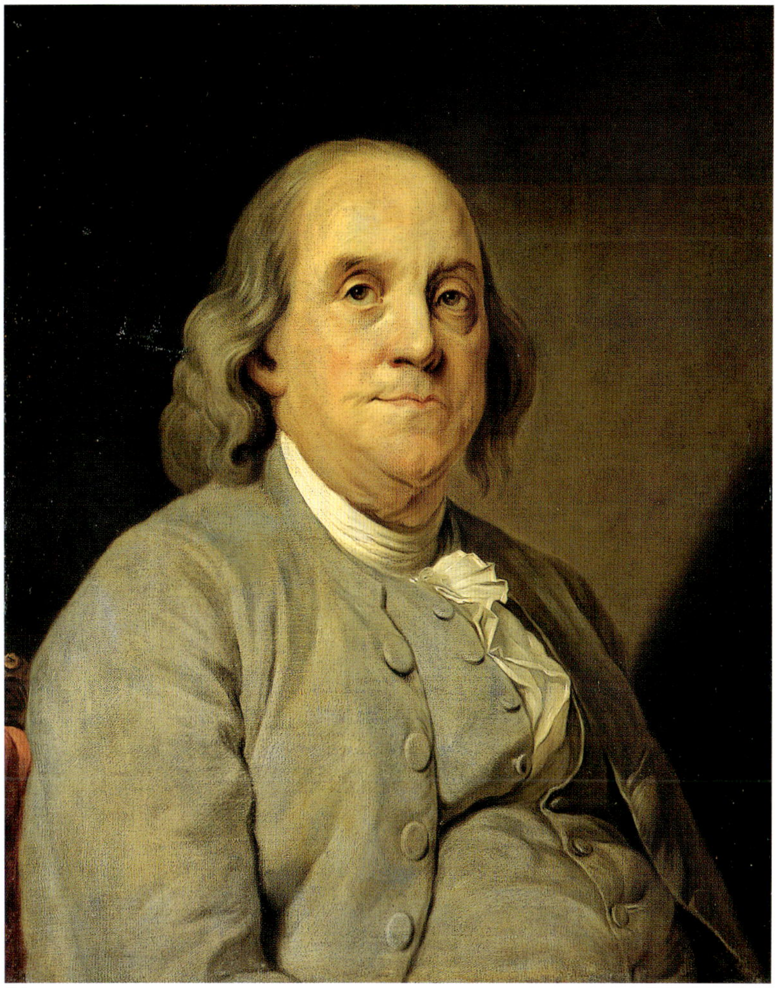

FRANKLIN NPG *327*

The medallion was mass-produced, Storelli describing it as being '*expédié par milliers en Amerique*'; undelivered consignments were discovered in the 19th century at the Château de Chaumont where the Leray factory, of which Nini had been manager, had been located.[4] The medallion was also produced in a smaller size (diameter c.9cm.),[5] and was copied by Wedgwood.[6] A much rarer type by Nini differs only in the addition of Franklin's spectacles,[7] and another of 1777 adds a '*bonnet de liberté*'.[8] In 1778, when Franklin became an accredited foreign representative at the French court, a more orthodox image was deemed desirable, and hat and spectacles disappeared, see below.

1 Franklin to Emma Thompson, 12 January 1777 (Sellers 1962, pp.99-100).
2 By Allan Ramsay (illus. Smart 1999, no.451).
3 Sellers 1962, p.345 (the banker Thomas Walpole).
4 Storelli 1896, p.23.
5 Storelli 1896, no.lxii.
6 Illus. Reilly 1973, p.147.
7 Storelli 1896, no.lxiii; Sellers 1962, p.346; *Nini* 2001, no.93.
8 Storelli 1896, no.lxv; *Nini* 2001, no.91.

327 after JOSEPH-SILFRÈDE DUPLESSIS [1778]

Canvas 72 x 58 (28¼ x 22¾); lined in 1871;[1] the varnish is discoloured; a repaired tear upper left and minor background losses; signed and dated, illegibly, lower right [*G: Menrr. 17, 5*]

Brown eyes, grey hair, light blue-grey suit; glimpse of a red-upholstered chair on the extreme left.

Collections: Henri Stettiner, London, from whom purchased 1871.

Exhibition: *The Past We Share*, Dallas, 1967(14).

Reference: Sellers 1962, p.275, no.9.

One of many derivations from the pastel by Duplessis in the New York Public Library which is generally dated 1778[2] (and which shows no chair back). A version in oils by Duplessis in the National Portrait Gallery, Washington (87.43), which once belonged to Franklin's friend and neighbour in Paris, Mme. Brillon, includes the red chair back – which led Sellers to suggest that NPG 327 may once have been owned by her.[3]

The signature and date on NPG 327 defy interpretation; copyists of this type of Franklin portrait by Duplessis included Jean Valade, Alexandre Roslin, Marie Lavoisier[4] and François Baricolo[5] (to whom NPG 327 was once attributed).[6] Miniature versions include examples attributed to François Dumont[7] and Lorentz Sparrgren (Christie's, 18 December 1990, lot 65). For the version with a red coat painted by Joseph Wright in 1782 and for the more celebrated Duplessis oval portrait of Franklin of 1778, wearing a fur-collared red coat, see below.

1 Original canvas was inscribed: *Benjamin Franklin, <né> a L'amerique Sept.le; Mort au Même pays en 1790.*
2 Illus. Sellers 1962, pl.25.
3 Sellers 1962, pp.272 no.5, 275 no.9.
4 *Ibid.*, pp.253, 258, 273.
5 With the Rev T. Davis Lamb, London, in 1865 (TSB 9/79); dated 1783; see also Sellers 1962, pp.275, 422-23.
6 NPG cats. 1888-1914; it was described as by or after J. Wright in 1925, and thereafter as after Duplessis.
7 Sellers 1962, pp.267-69, pl.25; for an example in the Gilbert collection, see Coffin & Hofstetter 2000, no.83.

ICONOGRAPHY

'Numberless are the prints & medals we have seen of you' (Georgiana Shipley to Franklin, 1 May 1779; Sellers 1962, p.267).

'A variety of [clay medallions] have been made of different sizes; some to be set in the lids of snuffboxes, and some so small as to be worn in rings; and the numbers sold are incredible. These, with the pictures, busts and prints, (of which copies upon copies are spread everywhere) have made your father's face as well known as that of the moon . . .' (Franklin to his daughter, 3 June 1779; Sellers 1962, pp.107-08).

A discriminating survey of Franklin's formidable iconography was made by Sellars in 1962; the ensuing list is generally confined to the more important images.

London 1757-62

1757 Miniature by C. Dixon. Museum of Fine Arts, Boston, Mass. (Sellers 1962, pl.2). Sent by Franklin to his wife in January 1758.

1759 Painting by Benjamin Wilson, half length, with lightning striking a church spire in the left background. White House, Washington (illus. Kloss 1992, p.55; Sellers 1962, pls.2, 3). Wilson painted two replicas, the second c.1765, for Dr Thomas Bond, and a three-quarter length version was with Knoedler, New York, 1962; engraved J. McArdell 1761 (Sellers 1962, pl.2); J. Chapman (oval) 1806; S. Freeman; W. Haines (half length) 1806. Like Franklin, Wilson had experimented with electricity and lightning conductors.

1762 Painting by Mason Chamberlin, three-quarter length seated, lightning to the left. Philadelphia Museum of Art (illus. Sellers 1962, pl.4). Commissioned by Col. Philip Ludwell. Exhibited SA 1763(19). Engraved E. Fisher 1763; F.N. Martinet 1773; J. Lodge (bust length). A replica, since destroyed, painted for Franklin's son 1764. Copy by George D. Leslie (Yale University AG); a 19th-century miniature copy (private collection, Philadelphia, probably from the Wellesley collection; Sellers 1962, pp.226-27); an anon. medal of 1777, bust length wearing a cap (Sellers 1962, pl.5), taken from Lodge's engraving.

c.1762-72 Painting by Matthew Pratt, half length. American Scenic and Historic Preservation Society, Yonkers, NY (Sellers 1962, pl.3). Derived from the Wilson half length of 1759.

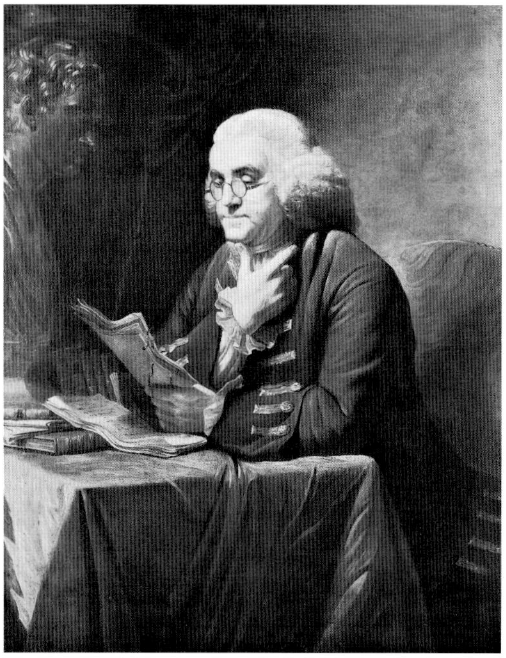

FRANKLIN by David Martin 1766 (Pennsylvania Academy of Fine Arts)

London 1764-75

1766 Wax profile by Isaac Gosset (Sellers 1962, p.294). American Philosophical Society, Philadelphia, and Dr Philip Bate 1962 (Sellers 1962 pl.9). Copied as a Wedgwood medallion and cameo (illus. Reilly 1973, p.146, as c.1775 and after Patience Wright); by James Tassie (Gray 1894, no.135; Sellers 1962, pl.9) and for a medal formerly attributed to William Mossop (Sellers 1962, pl.9).

1766 Painting by David Martin, half-length seated at table, wearing glasses. White House, Washington (Sellers 1962, pl.8; Kloss 1992, p.56). Exhibited SA 1767(99). Replica of 1767 in the Pennsylvania Academy of Fine Arts, Philadelphia,* bequeathed by Franklin; another dated 1772 with Dr A.J. Alexander, Lexington, Ky., in 1962. Copied by C.W. Peale (American Philosophical Society, Philadelphia) and reduced copies at Chevening and Brocklesby Park; a miniature enamel copy by Jeremiah Meyer in the Buccleuch collection (illus. Foskett 1972, II, pl.232, no.582).

1770 Painting by Henry Bembridge, exhibited RA 1770, no.14 (Sellers 1962, pp.190-92).

1772 Wax busts by Patience Wright, life size (Sellers 1962, pp.426-29). In 1781 in Paris Wright also made a wax head of Franklin for Elkanah Watson, now destroyed.

Undated Painting by Caleb Whitefoord, untraced; 'acknowledged to bear a strong and striking likeness' (D. Allen, *Connoisseur*, CXC, 1975, p.197). Whitefoord was Franklin's neighbour in London and he also attended the Paris peace commission in 1782.

Paris 1776-85

From 1776 Franklin continually wore spectacles.

1777 Plaster bust by Claude Dejoux. Musée de la Coopération Franco-Américaine, Château de Blérancourt, Aisne (Sellers 1962, pl.15), probably antedating the Caffiéri bust.

1777 Plaster bust by L-P. Dufourny de Villiers. D.A. Bernstein, Sound Beach, Conn., in 1930 (Sellers 1962, pl.15).

1777 Medallions by J-B. Nini, see NPG 722.

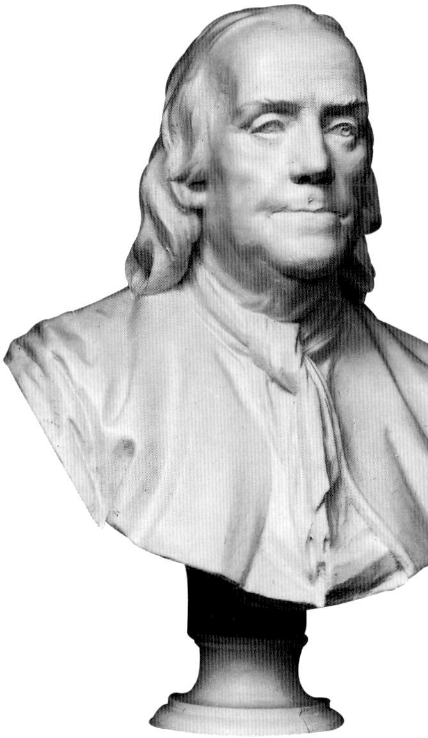

FRANKLIN by J-J. Caffiéri 1777 (Royal Society of Arts, London)

1777 Terracotta bust by J-J. Caffiéri, with long hair and neckcloth. Bibliothèque Mazarine, Paris (Sellers 1962, pl.16). Casts include those with the Institut de France (1785); Royal Society of Arts, London (c.1777-90),* and Bowdoin College, Brunswick, Maine, c.1785; four were bought by Franklin for his family, and others ordered for Sir Edward Newenham, Dublin (1783), William Carmichael (1785), and the Pennsylvania Hospital, Philadelphia.

Marble copies include, in Philadelphia: at the American Philosophical Society, and with the Home [formerly Franklin] Insurance Co.; in Washington: at the NPG (69.61) and the White House (illus. Kloss 1992, p.359); the Public Library, Boston, Mass.; the Detroit Institute of Arts and in the Huntington Art Collections, San Marino, Calif.

A number of derivative Sèvres medallions 1778-79 (Sellers 1962, pls.12-14), frequently engraved; copied by James Tassie as an intaglio seal, and at Wedgwood (illus. Reilly 1973, p.147).

1777 Painting by J-B. Greuze, half length in fur-collared coat. Sotheby's, New York, 30 January 1998, lot 120 (illus. *AQ*, XXVI, 1963, p.2). An oval replica with the American Philosophical Society, Philadelphia, and preliminary pastel study with the Dept. of State, Washington DC (Sellers 1962, pl.22).

Pastel copies by Simon Petit (exhibited Salon de la Correspondence 1781, no.7) and J-S-L. Piot (musée Cantonal, Lausanne); copies in oil by G.P.A. Healy (Versailles) and Joseph Gaye (Sotheby's, 20 March 1978, lot 51); miniature copies by Louis de Broux 1777 (French private collection) and by *D.C. 1785* (Sotheby's, 16 May 1957, lot 37, inscribed *d'apres Duplessis*).

1777 Drawing by C-N. Cochin, half length with fur hat, engraved A. de Saint Aubin (illus. Sellers 1962, pl.10). Copied by John Trumbull (Yale University AG). Enamel copy in the Victoria and Albert Museum (414.1810.1885; Rackham 1924, pl.45) from the engraving by G. Cooke. A medal by J.M. Lageman 1790 derived from the Cochin portrait.

1778 Painting by J-S. Duplessis, oval, similar to NPG 327 but wearing a red coat with brown fur collar. Metropolitan Museum of Art, New York (32.100.132; Sellers 1962, pl.24). Exhibited Salon 1779(128). Engraved J. Chevillet 1778 (Sellers 1962, pl.27); P.A. Tardieu 1795, and J. Thomson 1834. Duplessis exhibited another version Salon 1801(128).

The many copies include those at Boston, Mass., in the Athenaeum (Sellers 1962, pl.26) and Public Library; in Philadelphia, in the Independence Hall (Sellers 1962, pl.26) and Mutual [formerly Franklin] Assurance; at New York, with the Historical Society and in the Metropolitan Museum of Art, New York (95.21); others are in Yale University Library, the Fogg Art Museum (1943.235) and the Huntington Art Collections, San Marino, Calif. (pastel), and in France in the musées at Douai and Brest.

Miniature versions attributed to A.N.B. Graincourt (Philadelphia Museum of Art), and by Francis Lainé (exhibited RA 1786, no.283; see Sellers 1962, pl.24).

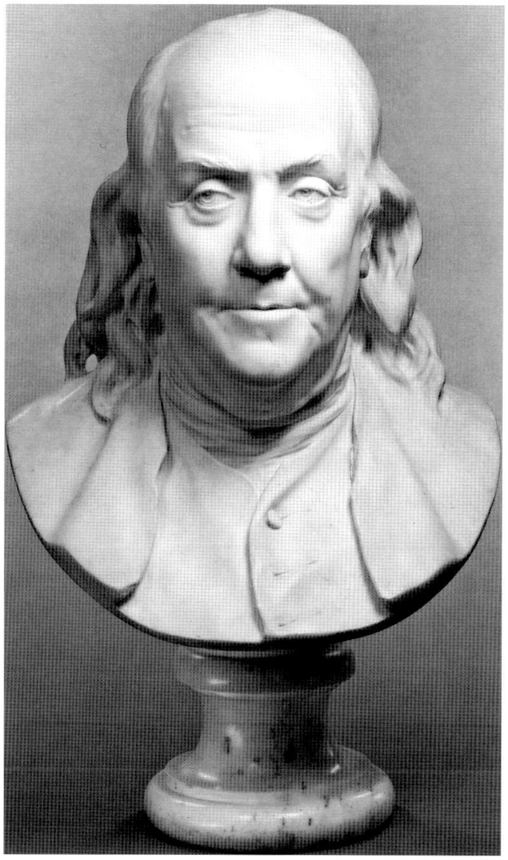

FRANKLIN by J-A. Houdon 1778 (Metropolitan Museum of Art, New York)

1778 Pastel by J-S. Duplessis, see NPG 327.

1778 Terracotta bust by J-A. Houdon, wearing coat and waistcoat showing one button and two empty buttonholes. Louvre (Sellers 1962, pl.18). Exhibited Salon 1779(221). Franklin was given four casts; others include those in the American Academy of Arts and Sciences, Cambridge, Mass.; Schlossmuseum, Gotha; City Art Museum, Saint Louis, and Museum of Art, Toledo, Ohio.

Examples in marble in the Metropolitan Museum of Art, New York, dated 1778(72.6),* the Philadelphia Museum of Art, dated 1779, and sold Sotheby's, 5 December 1996, lot 78, dated 1778. There are bronze versions, for example, in the White House, Washington; the American Embassy, London, and in the Bodleian Library, Oxford (Poole, I, p.109).

A drawing by Houdon of Franklin was sold Sotheby's, 23 March 1978, lot 179. A 'death mask', probably the life mask taken by Houdon in Paris in 1785, was allegedly sold for 10 francs in 1828 (illus. *Harper's Mag.*, XXIV, 1892, p.910; Sellers 1962, pl.44).

The bust was also copied by John Flaxman c.1801, showing four buttons on waistcoat; plaster cast with the American Philosophical Society, Philadelphia (Sellers 1962, pl.21) – apparently the source for the marble busts by Hiram Powers, see 1848-49 below.

1778 Painting by J-F. de L'Hospital, half-length oval. University of Pennsylvania, Philadelphia (Sellers 1962, pl.22). Sellers recorded three copies.

c.1778 Painting attributed to C-P-A. Van Loo, half-length oval with fur-collared coat. American Philosophical Society, Philadelphia (Sellers 1962, pl.23). Variant, without the fur collar, engraved P.M. Alix c.1790 (Sellers 1962, pl.23); pastel copy by L.M.D. Guillaume with the Virginia Historical Society, Richmond.

c.1778 Painting by Anne Rosalie Filleul, half length showing right hand, his glasses on a table. French private collection 1962 (Sellers 1962, pl.23). Engraved L-J. Cathelin, exhibited Salon 1779(263).

1778-79 Wedgwood medallions, modelled by William Hackwood 1778, produced in several sizes (Sellers 1962, pl.11); a variant, with longer hair at the neck, also attributed to Hackwood (illus. Reilly 1973, p.145, as c.1775); another was produced in 1779, with a smaller variant (illus. Reilly 1973, p.148).

1778-79 Terracotta medallions by J-B. Nini from a drawing by Anna Vallayer-Coster, classical profiles to left (Nini 2001, nos.95-98).

a) with longer hair, inscribed: *eripuit coelo fulmen sceptrumque tirannis*

b) with shorter hair, inscribed in French.

1779 Stone bust by P-F. Berruer, life size. Formerly with J. de Saint Pierre (illus. *Gazette des Beaux-Arts*, XVIII, 1928, p.169). Apparently derived from the bust by Dejoux, see 1777.

1779 Drawing by C-J. Notté, exhibited Salon de la Correspondance 1779:'*portrait de M. le docteur Franklin, dessiné au crayon, avec des allégories*'.

1780 Painting by Stephen Elmer, half-length seated at table. Private collection, New York (Sellers 1962, pl.13). Engraved T. Ryder 1782.

c.1780-81 Drawing by L-C. de Carmontelle, whole-length seated. Private collection, New York (Sellers 1962, pl.28). Engraved by F.D. Née 1781. A closely related drawing by Gaspard Duché de Vancy was also engraved by Née.

1782 Pastel by Joseph Ducreux, exhibited Salon 1782(88).

1782 Painting by Joseph Wright adapted from the Duplessis portrait of 1778, the features altered from the life. Yale University AG (Sellers 1962, p.415, no.2; see *Wright* 1985, pp.84-89, nos.9-13). Engraved W. Angus 1783. Replicas in Boston Public Library; Corcoran AG, Washington; Royal Society, London (presented by Caleb Whitefoord 1791); versions in the Pennsylvania Academy of Fine Arts, Philadelphia; from the Northbrook collection, sold Sotheby's, 31 January 1951, lot 98; a miniature copy by J-T. Perrache sold Christie's, 21 April 1998, lot 40 (cf. Foskett 1972, II, pl.268, no.662).

Used by Benjamin West for his unfinished *Signing of the Preliminary Treaty of Peace of 1782* in which Franklin appears with John Jay, John Adams, Henry Laurens and his own grandson William T. Franklin (Winterthur Museum; Erffa & Staley 1986, no.105).

c.1782 Miniature by J-B. Weyler, examples on ivory and in enamel in the Louvre (33126 and 35727; Sellers 1962, pl.34, and front.). Replicas in the Gilbert collection (illus. Coffin & Hofstetter 2000, no.60), Sotheby's, 10 November 1986, lot 197, and Christie's, Geneva, 15 May 1990, lot 251. Related enamels, both signed *D.C. 1785*, formerly with Wildenstein, New York (Sellers 1962, pl.34) and sold Sotheby's, 16 May 1957, lot 37 inscribed *après Mr Weyller.*

1783 Pencil drawing inscribed *M. Perier ce 4 janvier 1783*, profile bust to right, wearing hat. Walters AG, Baltimore (Sellers 1962, pl.13). A pastel copy, with spectacles added, in the Metropolitan Museum of Art, New York.

1783-84 Medals: by J-F. Bernier 1783, commissioned by the Masonic Lodge of the *Neuf Soeurs*, Paris, of which Franklin had been *Venerable* (Sellers 1962, pp.193-94) and by Augustin Dupré 1784 (C. Saunier, *Augustin Dupré*, 1894, p.21, pl.iv).

America 1785-90

1785 Painting by C.W. Peale, bust-length oval, wearing spectacles; unfinished (Sellers 1962, pl.37). Pennsylvania Academy of Fine Arts, Philadelphia. Engraved C.W. Peale 1787 (Sellers 1962, pl.37). Unlocated miniature copies by William Mercer and Rembrandt Peale. Enlarged replica painted in 1789 with an elaborate quotation in view on table ['In every stroke of lightning. I am of opinion that the stream of electric fluid ...']; Historical Society of Pennsylvania, Philadelphia.

1787 Wooden bust by William Rush. Yale University AG (Sellers 1962, pl.38). Rush also carved two ship's figureheads of Franklin, one on the *Franklin* (Sellers 1962, pp.358-59). A derivative bronze in the White House, Washington (illus. Kloss 1992, p.359).

c.1787 Painting by R.E. Pine, bust length, wearing spectacles. Franklin Institute, Philadelphia (Sellers 1962, pl.37; *Pine* 1979, p.57).

c.1787 Miniature by John Ramage. British Society for International Understanding, London (Sellers 1962, pl.37).

c.1789 Silhouettes by Joseph Sansom (Sellers 1962, pl.39) and A-A-C-F. Edouart (illus. E.F. Nevill Jackson, *Silhouette, Notes and Dictionary*, 1938, pl.54).

Posthumous

1790-91 Marble statue by Francesco Lazzarini, the head from the Caffiéri bust of 1777. Library Company, Philadelphia, taken down in 1879 and replaced with a copy by Lewis Iselin jr. 1959 (Sellers 1962, pp.203-04).

1791 Bust by J-A. Houdon, exhibited Salon 1791(484, among '*onze morceaux de Sculpture Bustes tant en marbre qu'en terre cuite, Plâtre & Bronze*'). Provisionally associated with the draped plaster *all'antica* in the Boston Athenaeum (Arnason 1975, fig.119, and see p.54); another in the musée des Beaux-Arts, Angers.

A marble version, bearing a signature and the enigmatic date 1780, is in the Nelson-Atkins Museum of Art, Kansas (Sellers 1962, pl.21); there is a closely resembling marble by Domenico Menconi of c.1862 (American Philosophical Society, Philadelphia; Sellers 1962, pl.21).

1793 Terracotta statuette by F-M. Suzanne, standing by a broken column. Metropolitan Museum of Art, New York (Sellers 1962, pl.29). Exhibited Salon 1793(62). Copied in marble, bronze and other metals.

Nineteenth-century images include the marble bust by Hiram Powers 1848-49 (Yale University AG; illus. Wunder 1991, II, p.151; Sellers 1962, pl.21), of which there are many replicas; the statue by Powers of 1861-62 (US Capitol, Washington DC; illus. Wunder 1991, ii, pp.150-1), and another by John J. Boyle (University of Pennsylvania).

GAGE, Hon. Thomas 1721-87

Army officer; 2nd s. of the 1st Viscount Gage; went to America as lieutenant-colonel in 1754; governor of Montreal 1760-63; major-general 1761; commander-in-chief, North America, 1763-75, but in England 1773-74; lieutenant-general 1770; governor of Massachusetts Bay 1774-75; resigned in 1775, finding himself 'in a position of too great importance for his talents'.

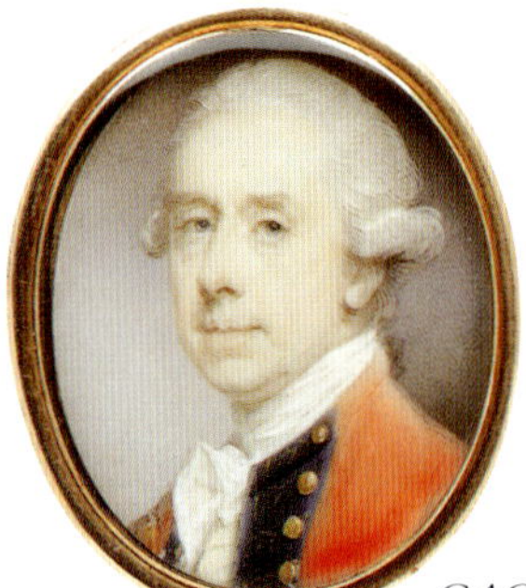

GAGE NPG *4070*

4070 JEREMIAH MEYER c.1775

Watercolour and bodycolour on ivory 4.8 x 3.8 (1⅞ x 1½). The back of the gold case is engraved: *Honble. Lieut. General / Thomas Gage / by / J. Meyer.R.A.*

Clear grey eyes, white powdered hair, wearing a general's uniform, red coat with dark blue facings and gold buttons, a gold epaulette on his right shoulder.

Collections: Sabin, London, c.1935, bt. E. Peter Jones, Chester, by whom presented 1958.

Exhibition: *1776*, National Maritime Museum, 1976(54).

Reference: Walker 1998, no.54.

Probably painted after Gage's return from America late in 1775,[1] but it might also date from his period of leave in England between April 1773 and April 1774.[2] Stylistically NPG 4070 compares closely with the miniature of William Chambers (NPG 4040) and of an unknown man dated 1775.[3]

1 'Will you not smile at Gage being recalled and made Generalissimo?' (Walpole, 27 October 1775; *Wal. Corr.*, XLI, p.313).
2 For these dates see C.E. Carter ed., *Corr. of General Thomas Gage 1763-75*, II, 1933, p.157.
3 Illus. Foskett 1972, II, pl.232, no.583.

ICONOGRAPHY

c.1768-69 Painting by J.S. Copley,* three-quarter length in the uniform of a major-general, pointing to a distant battlefield. Yale Center for British Art (B1977.14.45). Painted in New York. Exhibited *Copley* 1995a, no.66, irregularities in the uniform being noted.

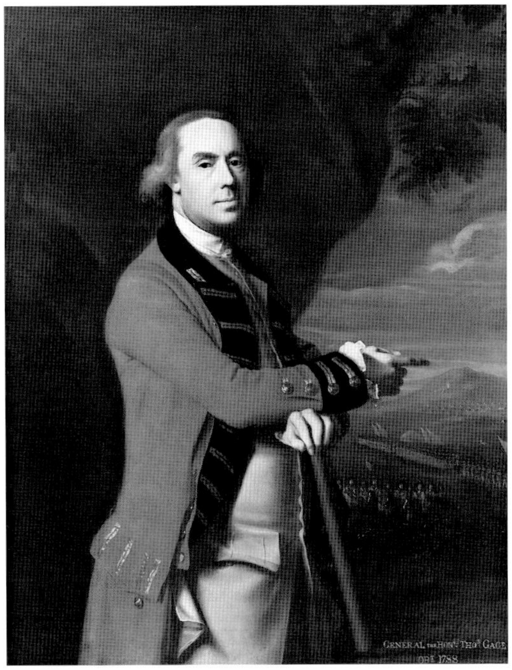

GAGE by J.S. Copley 1768-69 (Yale Center for British Art)

1773 Painting by Hugh Barron, whole-length standing in the uniform of a major-general (the uniform resembles that seen in the Copley portrait of 1768-69, with the addition of piping on the waistcoat and a waistband, but without the trim on the coat pocket). Firle Place. Presumably painted in 1773 when Gage was in England (see NPG 4070 above), and before October, when Barron left to spend six years in Italy.

c.1775 Miniature by Jeremiah Meyer, see NPG 4070.

c.1775 Painting by David Martin,* whole-length standing in uniform of a lieutenant-general, his hat in his right hand. Firle Place. Martin's companion portrait of Mrs Gage (Margaret Kemble of New York, whom Gage m.1758) at Firle Place is dated 1775.

Undated Anon. engraving, bust-length oval, as major-general with epaulette on his left shoulder, lettered *1st Military Governor of Montreal*.

An unattributed miniature exhibited SKM 1865(1090) lent Lord Abingdon.

DOUBTFUL PORTRAIT

A miniature at Firle Place attributed to Meyer has been identified as Gage, but the sitter is described as wearing a blue uniform with cream facings.

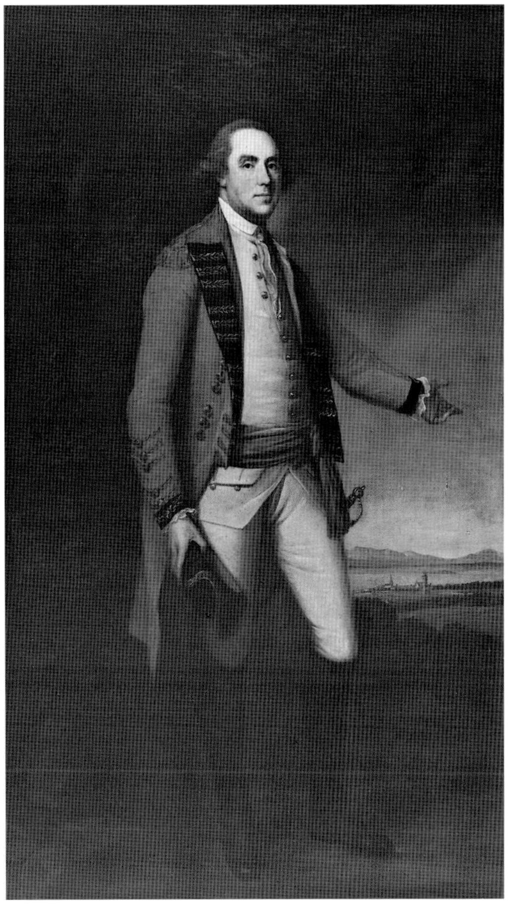

GAGE by David Martin c.1775 (Firle Place)

GAINSBOROUGH, Thomas 1727-88

Painter; worked in London 1746-48, Suffolk 1748-59, Bath 1759-74 and London 1774-88; foundation member of the RA 1768; exhibited SA 1761-68, RA (irregularly) 1769-83, and FS 1774 and 1783; in portraiture, he observed, there must be 'Variety of lively touches and surprising effects to make the Heart dance'.

'His cranium is so crammed with genius of every kind that it is in danger of bursting upon you, like a steam-engine overcharged' (David Garrick; E. Hardcastle, *Wine and Walnuts*, 1824).

'James Christie, the auctioneer, often declared that the presence in the rooms of Gainsborough and Garrick, with their banter and good humour, added fifteen percent to his commission on a sale' (Hayes 2001).

4446 SELF PORTRAIT c.1758-59

Canvas 75 x 62 (29½ x 24½) lined; some abrasion particularly apparent in the background and jacket; some retouching lower left.

Blue-grey eyes, chestnut hair, brown coat with gold buttons, black neckcloth and white shirt. The waistcoat buttons do up the opposite way to the coat, as was usual out of London.[1]

Collections: Mrs Sophia Lane (the artist's niece); her son Richard Lane; his sale, Christie's, 26 February 1831, lot 51, bt. in; bt. from Dunsford by the 2nd Baron Northwick 1832; by descent at Northwick Park to Capt. E.G. Spencer Churchill; purchased from the Spencer Churchill Estate by the Government through the Land Fund and allocated to the NPG 1965.

Exhibitions: *Pictures lent by owners resident in the County*, Gloucester, 1934(21); *Gainsborough*, 45 Park Lane, London, 1936(4); *Gainsborough*, Tate Gallery, 1953(16); *Sudbury's Heritage*, Sudbury, 1975; *Gainsborough's Family*, Sudbury, 1988(12); *The Harvest Waggon*, Birmingham, 1995(4); *Gainsborough*, Ferrara, 1998(7); *Gainsborough*, Tate Gallery, Washington, Boston, Mass., 2002-03(26).

Reference: Northwick Catalogue, 1864, no.126; T. Borenius, *Northwick Catalogue*, 1921, no.284; *Gainsborough* 1953, p.45; Waterhouse 1958, no.291; J. Kerslake, *Connoisseur*, CLXI, 1966, pp.160-61.

Apparently painted in Suffolk, just prior to Gainsborough's move to Bath in 1760. Gainsborough painted a half length of his wife at much the same time (Gemäldegalerie, Berlin; 2200),[2] but they face the same way and do not appear to be pendants.

1 Comment by Aileen Ribeiro on file.
2 Waterhouse 1958, no.297; exhibited *Gainsborough's Family*, Sudbury, 1988, no.14.

1107 FRANCESCO BARTOLOZZI after THOMAS GAINSBOROUGH [1787-88]

Black and red crayon with pencil and grey wash on paper 20 x 17 (7⅞ x 6¾); oval portrait 19 x 16.3 (7½ x 6½); laid down on paper; the original sheet is stained, in part the consequence of an old oval slip frame; small damage in the cheek and some abrasion around it; there is a pencil border 19.5 x 16.5 (7¾ x 6½) within which the image is squared up (twelve horizontal divisions, fifteen vertical), the grid now hardly perceptible.

Collections: Bought from George Crozier of Carnforth, Lancs., 1897.[1]

Reference: Hayes 2001, p.175.

Preparatory drawing for Bartolozzi's stipple engraving after Gainsborough's self-portrait in the Royal Academy, London (see below 1787-88),* published by Boydell on 1 January 1798. The indecision in the oval

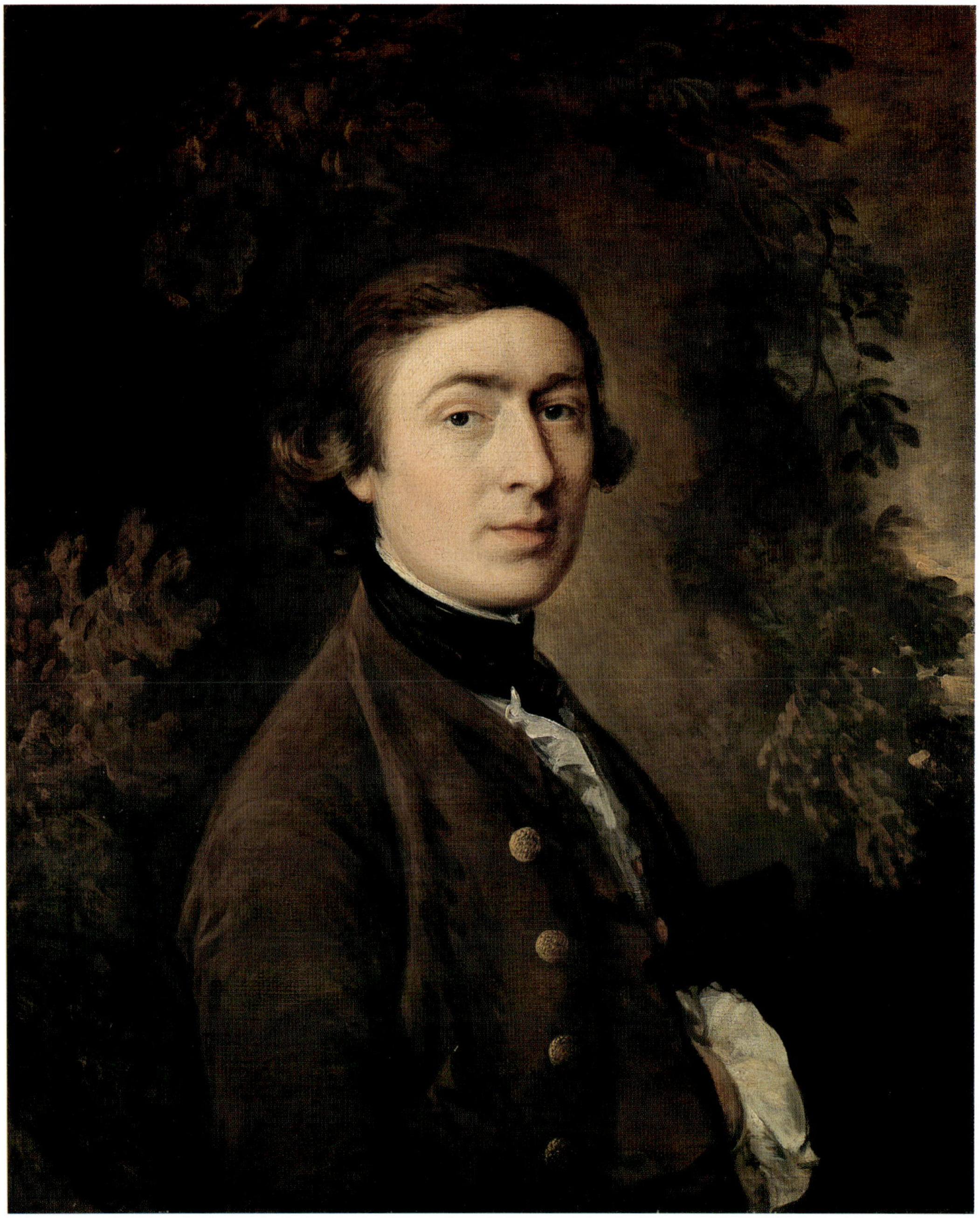

GAINSBOROUGH NPG *4446*

border on the right-hand side is exactly as Gainsborough left it.[2]

It is generally assumed that the Royal Academy self-portrait was that which Gainsborough was painting for his friend Karl Abel, who died in 1787 before it was completed. In 1788 Gainsborough directed that no plaster cast, model, or likeness whatever of himself be taken after his death, but he allowed that 'if Mr Sharp, who engraved Mr Hunter's Print [see NPG 77], should chuse to make a print from the ¾ sketch which I intended for Mr Abel painted by myself, I give free consent'.[3] William Sharp did not engrave the portrait, and Bartolozzi's print may lack the presence Gainsborough anticipated.

1 Crozier offered the drawing for sale in his capacity as an executor; he subsequently mentioned 'the ladies interested in the sale' (letters of 16 and 28 October 1897; NPG archive).

2 Illus. *Gainsborough's Family*, Sudbury, 1988, p.75.

3 Unaddressed letter of 15 June 1788 (Hayes 2001, p.175), and see Farington, 29 January 1799, when Gainsborough's daughter recalled her father forbidding any cast or drawing of his face after his death, and directing that 'no engraving should be made unless by Sharp who engraved the portrait of John Hunter and that He might but only from a picture painted by himself, in the possession of Mr Abel [*sic*], the musician, his particular friend'.

ICONOGRAPHY

A very useful illustrated survey is provided by H. Belsey, *Gainsborough's Family*, Gainsborough's House, Sudbury, 1988.

Self Portraits (paintings)

c.1740 standing three-quarter length, holding palette. Private collection. Exhibited *Gainsborough*, Tate Gallery, Washington, Boston, Mass., 2002-03(1). The identity is probably correct.

c.1748 with his wife and small daughter in a landscape. National Gallery (6547; Waterhouse 1958, no.296; Egerton 1998, pp.64-71). The daughter has been identified as Mary who was buried on 1 March 1747/8.

1754 unfinished, bust length with hat. Houghton Hall (Waterhouse 1958, no.290).

c.1758-59 see NPG 4446.

c.1786 half-length painted oval, in blue coat. Holkham (Waterhouse 1958, no.295). Version sold Christie's, 15 April 1994, lot 23; another Old Hall Gallery, Rye, 1992, probably by Gainsborough Dupont.

1787-88 half-length painted oval,* in green coat. Royal Academy (Waterhouse 1958, no.292), presented by the artist's daughter 1808. Engraved F. Bartolozzi 1798, for whose preparatory drawing, and further discussion, see NPG 1107 above; H. Meyer from a drawing by John Jackson, 1810 (related drawings by Jackson are in the Victoria AG, Bath, and the Fitzwilliam Museum, Cambridge).

A replica, completed by Dupont, in the Courtauld Gallery (Waterhouse 1958, no.293). A reversed bust-length crayon drawing with W.H. Pfungst 1910 (photograph in NPG archive) possibly a fabrication from Gainsborough self portraits.

By other Artists

c.1772 Painting by Johann Zoffany,* unfinished bust-length oval. Tate Gallery (N 1487), lent to the NPG 1934-93. Probably painted as a study for Zoffany's *Academicians* (see Groups NPG 1437), from which however Gainsborough (with George and Nathaniel Dance) chose to be omitted. According to Fulcher 1856, p.205, C.H. Weigall took a medallion from this portrait.

Posthumous

1790 Painting by Gainsborough Dupont, exhibited RA 1790(471).

1858 Medal by E. Ortner (Brown 1980, no.2653). Exhibited RA 1858(1110). Art Union laudatory medal, an example in the NPG reference collection (D 28410).

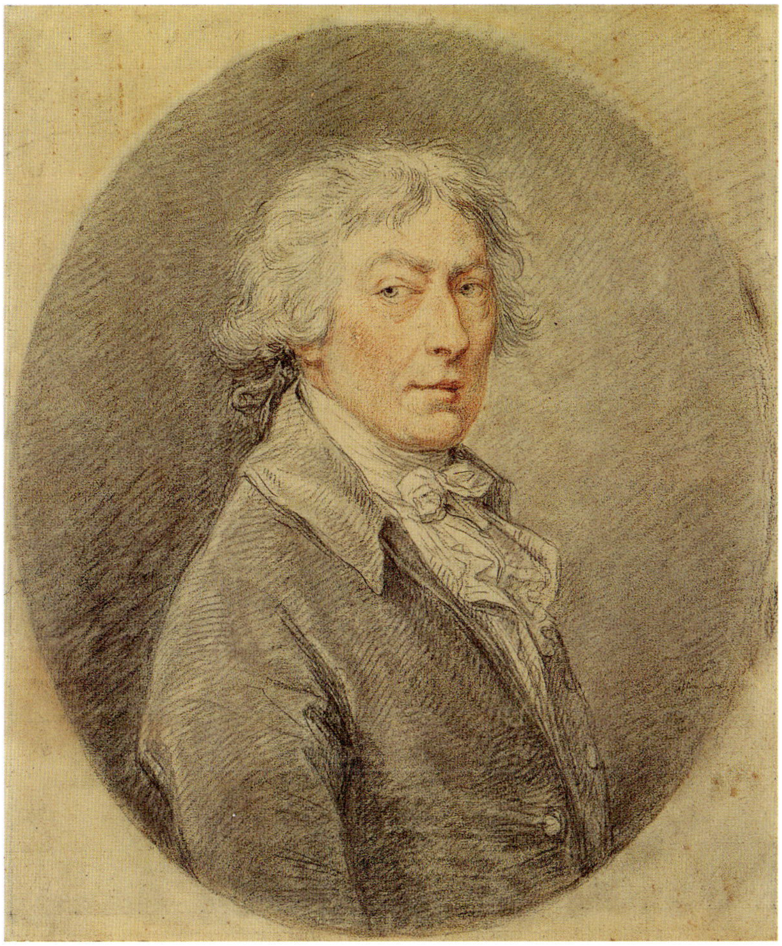

GAINSBOROUGH NPG 1107

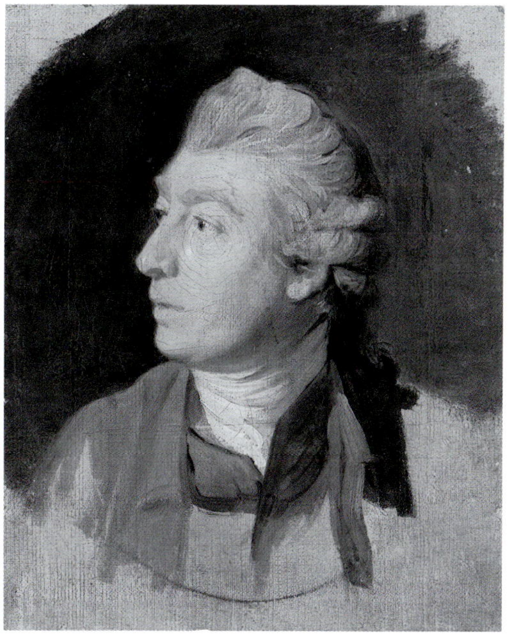

GAINSBOROUGH by Johann Zoffany c.1772 (Tate Gallery)

engraved R. Lane 1825 in reverse), the other ascribed to Fuseli (Victoria and Albert Museum, P.1.1914).

1906 Marble statue by Thomas Brock. Tate Gallery. A life-size plaster exhibited *Franco-British Exhibition*, London, 1908(1308), and a bronze cast in Burlington House.

1909 Sculpture by S.N. Babb. Victoria and Albert Museum, south front.

1913 Bronze statue by Bertram Mackennel. St Peter's church, Sudbury, Suffolk. Mackennel exhibited a bronze statuette of Gainsborough RA 1916(1900).

DOUBTFUL PORTRAITS

Painting by Gainsborough, *Conversation in a Park* c.1746 (Louvre; Waterhouse 1958, no.752, and see Thomas Sandby); painting variously attributed to Zoffany or William Hoare (Museum of Art, Santa Barbara, Calif.; illus. Williamson 1920, f.p.242 as Zoffany; Hayes 1975, fig.3 as attributed to Hoare), possibly shows Daniel Webb (1719?-98).

Two drawings of a left-handed artist sketching in a landscape: one by Gainsborough of c.1750-5 (British Museum, 1988.3.5.59; Egerton 1998, p.66;

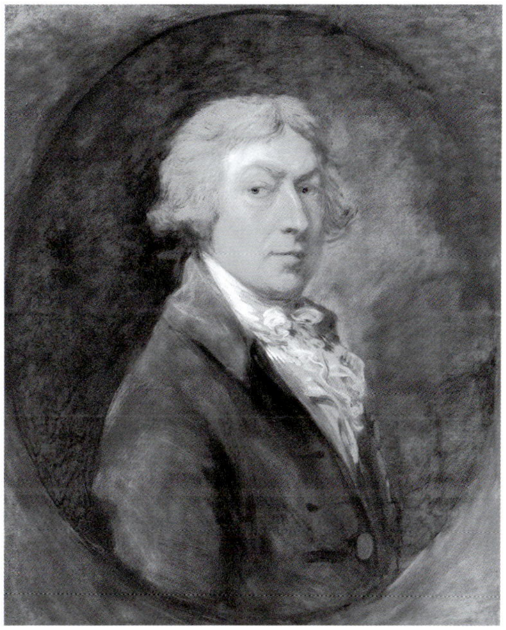

GAINSBOROUGH Self portrait 1787-88 (Royal Academy of Arts, London)

GARDNER, Alan Gardner, 1st Baron 1742-1808

Naval officer; captain 1766; commander-in-chief, Jamaica, 1786-89; a lord of the Admiralty 1790-95; MP 1790-1806; rear-admiral 1793; Bt 1794, following his bravery under Lord Howe in the Caribbean; vice-admiral 1794, admiral 1799; commander-in-chief Ireland 1800-02; cr. Baron [I] 1800 and Baron [GB] 1806.

'[his son] spoke of the late Lord Gardner's extraordinary regularity. . . before He died He was, though only 66 years, eight months, and eight days old, the Oldest looking man He had ever seen. His constitution was quite worn out' (Farington, 1809).

'a zealous and brave man, with the worst nerves possible, and full of doubts as to the precision of other men' (Lord St Vincent, 1801).

745 see Groups, *The House of Commons 1793-94* by KARL ANTON HICKEL 1793-95

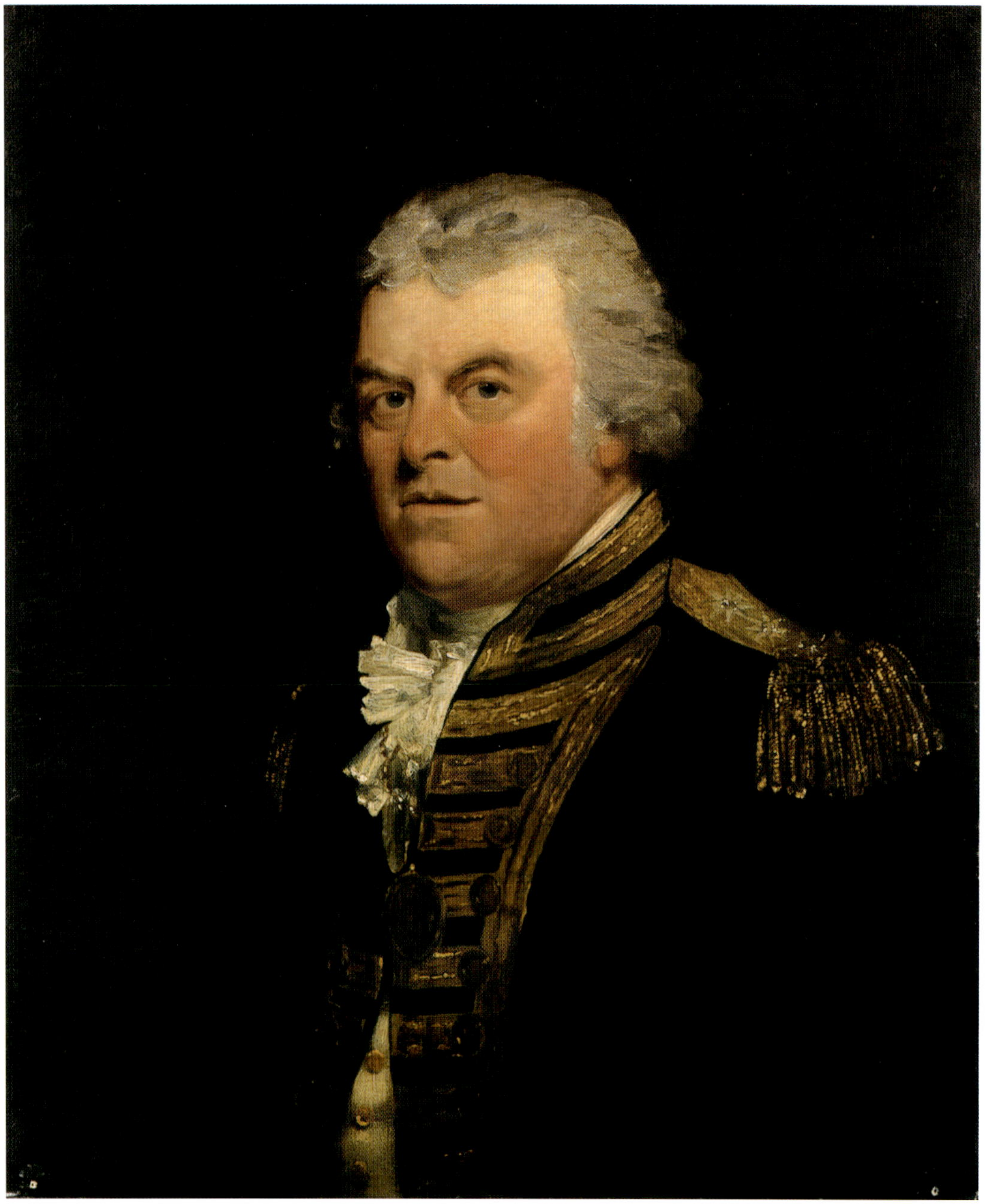

1st Baron GARDNER NPG *2103*

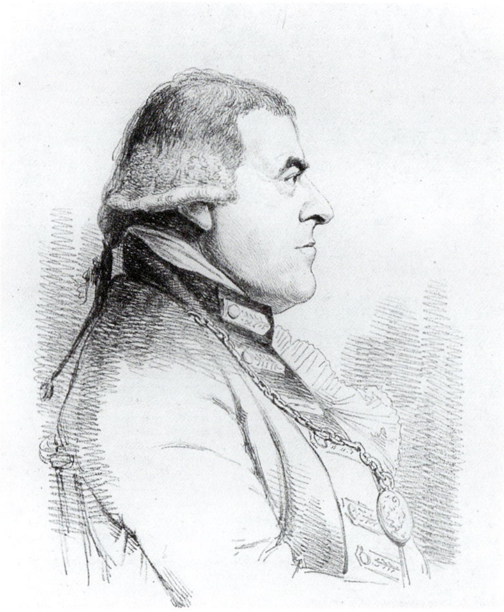

1st Baron GARDNER *W. Daniell after George Dance 1794* (NPG D 12126)

2103 THEOPHILUS CLARKE 1799

Canvas 75 x 63 (29½ x 24¾) lined; the face area is rubbed and there are discoloured retouchings.

Blue-grey eyes, grey hair, in admiral's full-dress uniform, wearing a campaign medal (which is illegible, but is presumably for the action of 1 June 1794[1]).

Collections: Purchased from Leggatt 1925.

Engravings: B. Reading 1799 (as *Sir Alan Gardner Bt, Admiral of the Blue, & M.P. for the City of Westminster.*); anon. (small oval as *Admiral Gardiner*).

Exhibition: RA 1799(276).

1 Commemorated in the great canvas by P.J. De Loutherbourg in the National Maritime Museum (BHC 0470).

ICONOGRAPHY

c.1780? Drawing by Ozias Humphry, bust-length oval in private dress, inscribed with identity. Formerly in the collection of G.C. Williamson (illus. Williamson 1918, p.80).

c.1782 Painting called John Downman, bust-length oval, in captain's uniform. Christie's, 20 May 1977, lot 22. Engraved, the uniform altered to flag officer's undress, W. Ridley 1802 (from an unattributed painting *in the possession of Dobree Esq 1782*; Pierson 1794 (*European Mag.*).

1794 On 17 July 1794 Farington introduced Bowyer to Admiral Gardner 'to compare Stuarts portrait with the Admiral', implying Stuart had painted him. Gilbert Stuart certainly painted the Admiral's brother Henry (Farington, 20 December 1802).

1794 Drawing by George Dance, half-length profile with tie wig, engraved W. Daniell* 1809 (*Dance Portraits*). Presumably the portrait by Dance exhibited RA 1795(582). Gardner first sat to Dance on 18 July 1794 (Farington).

1794 Gardner sat to Robert Bowyer on 21 July 1794 (Farington).

1794 Painting by K.A. Hickel,* half-length painted oval. National Maritime Museum (BHC 2704). Gardner sat to Hickel on 22 July 1794 ('They think the portrait like'; Farington), for inclusion in Hickel's *House of Commons* (NPG 745), see Groups NPG 745

1796 Drawing by G.K. Parker, engraved G. Murray, half-length oval, in admiral's uniform, wearing campaign medal (*Lady's Pocket Mag.*).

1799 Painting by Theophilus Clarke, see NPG 2103.

c.1799? Painting by William Beechey, half length in admiral's full-dress uniform. Engraved Fenner &

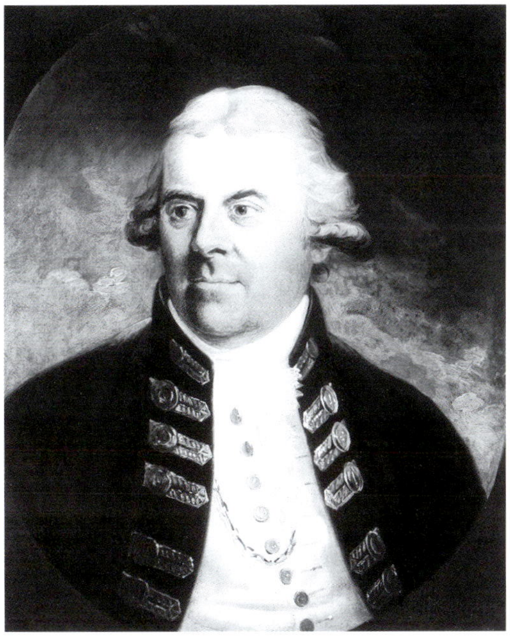

1st Baron GARDNER by K.A. Hickel 1794 (National Maritime Museum, London)

Co 1832. Oval version exhibited NPE 1867(613) lent Lord Gardner; a version with Lt.-Col. Cornwall in 1928. Copy in the National Maritime Museum (BHC 2703), exhibited *Royal Naval Exhibition*, Chelsea, 1891(338) unattributed.

c.1800 Silhouette, painting on glass by Charles Rosenberg, bust length to left. Bonham's, 9 November 1995, lot 87.

Undated miniature by J.H. Hurter, in naval uniform, was exhibited SKM 1865(59) lent Lord Cremorne.

GARRICK, David 1717-79

Actor, playwright, producer; came to fame with his *Richard III* at Goodman's Fields 1741; joint patentee of Drury Lane in 1747; 'celebrated men ... have had their applause at a distance; but Garrick had it dashed in his face, sounded in his ears, and went home every night with the plaudits of a thousand in his *cranium*' (*Boswell*, iii, p.263).

'*Garrick est d'une stature médiocre, plutôt petite que grande. Il a la physionomie agréable et spirituelle, et un jeu prodigieux dans les yeux. Sa vivacité est extrême.*' (Baron Friedrich Melchior von Grimm, 1765).

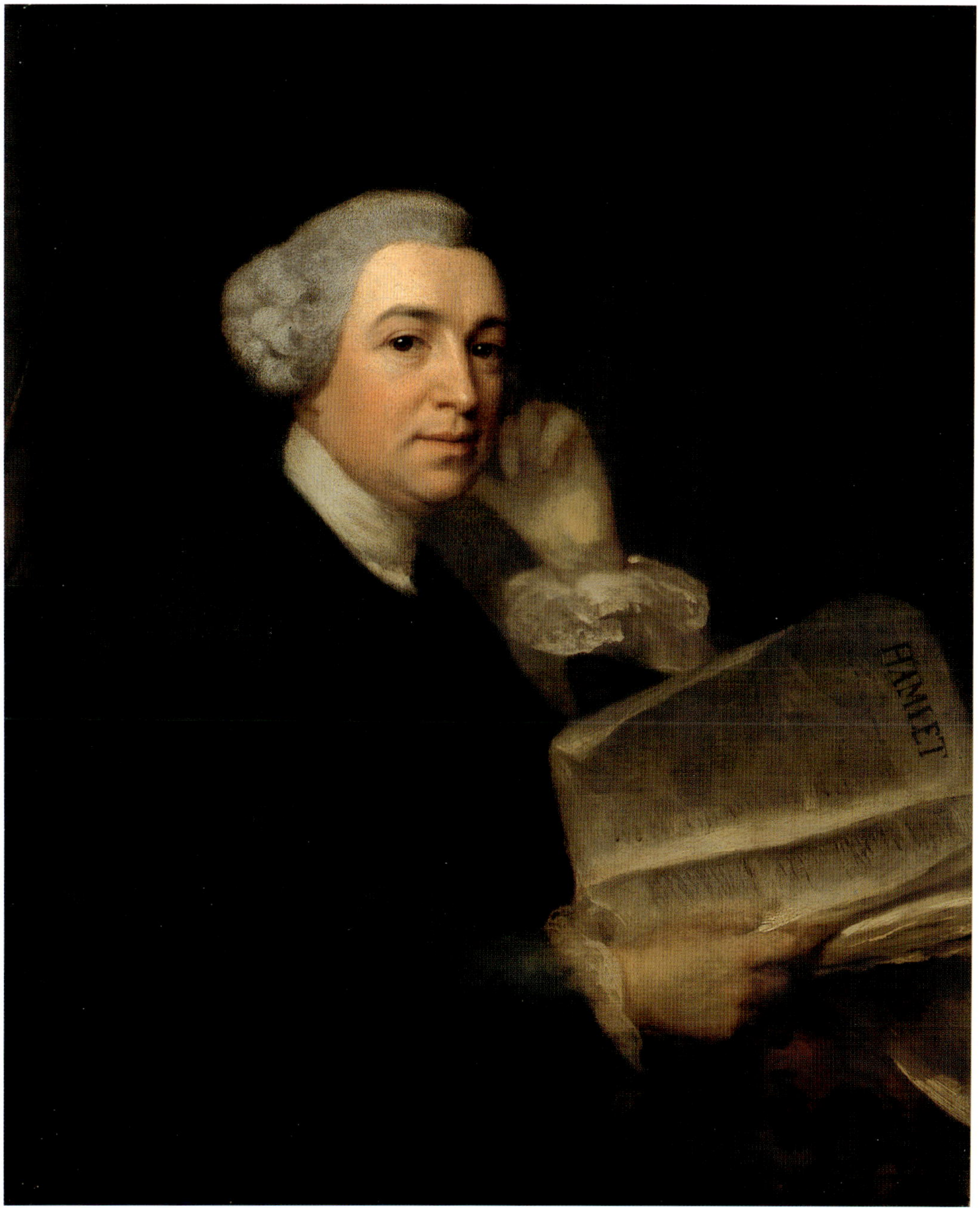

GARRICK NPG *6249*

6249 BENJAMIN WILSON c.1752-55

Canvas 75.5 x 62 (29¾ x 24½) lined; the surface is rubbed, particularly apparent in the hands; a *pentimento* shows his right thumb was lowered.

Brown eyes, grey powdered hair, wearing a blue coat and holding an open folio *HAMLET* above a skull; he sits in a dark blue chair.

Collections: Kenyon family since c.1830;[1] by descent to the 5th Baron Kenyon,[2] by whom bequeathed 1993.

Exhibitions: *Art Treasures*, Wrexham, 1876 (308), as by Richard Wilson; *Richard Wilson*, Tate Gallery, 1925(41) as by Richard Wilson; *Pictures from Welsh Private Collections*, Cardiff, 1951(62); *Works of Art from Private Collections*, Manchester, 1960(130).

The head sufficiently resembles that in the Liotard pastel of 1751 (see below) for the traditional identification to be acceptable. Wilson, a collector of Rembrandt etchings, appears to have based the composition on that of *Lieven van Coppenol*.[3]

Between 1753 and 1761 Wilson painted several theatrical portraits of Garrick (see below) before being

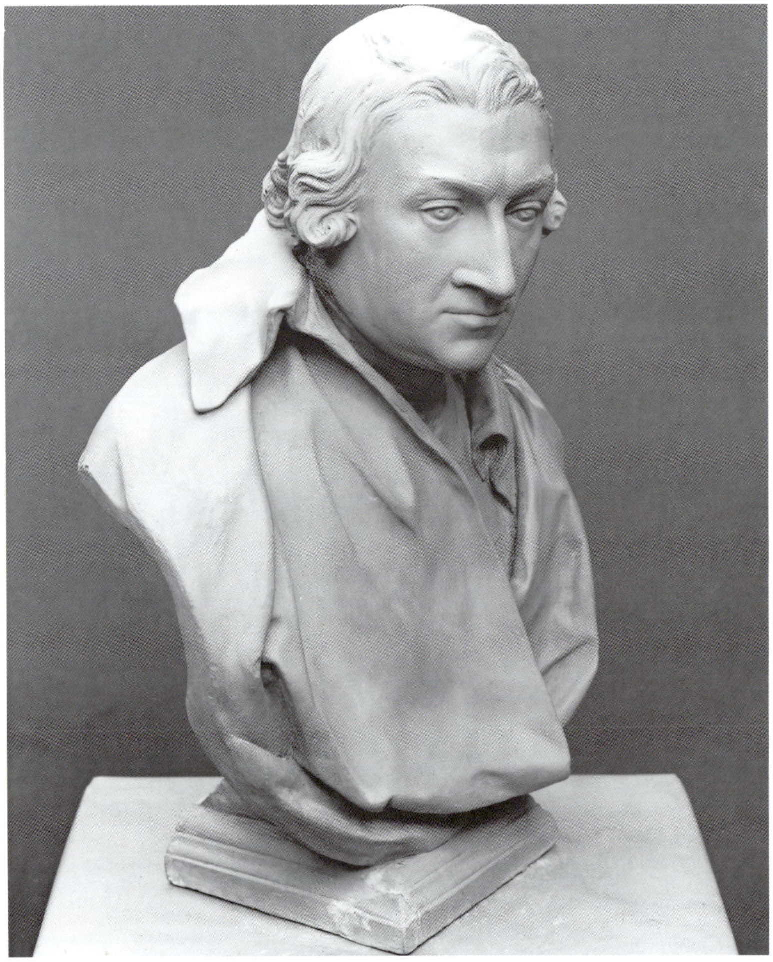

GARRICK NPG 707A

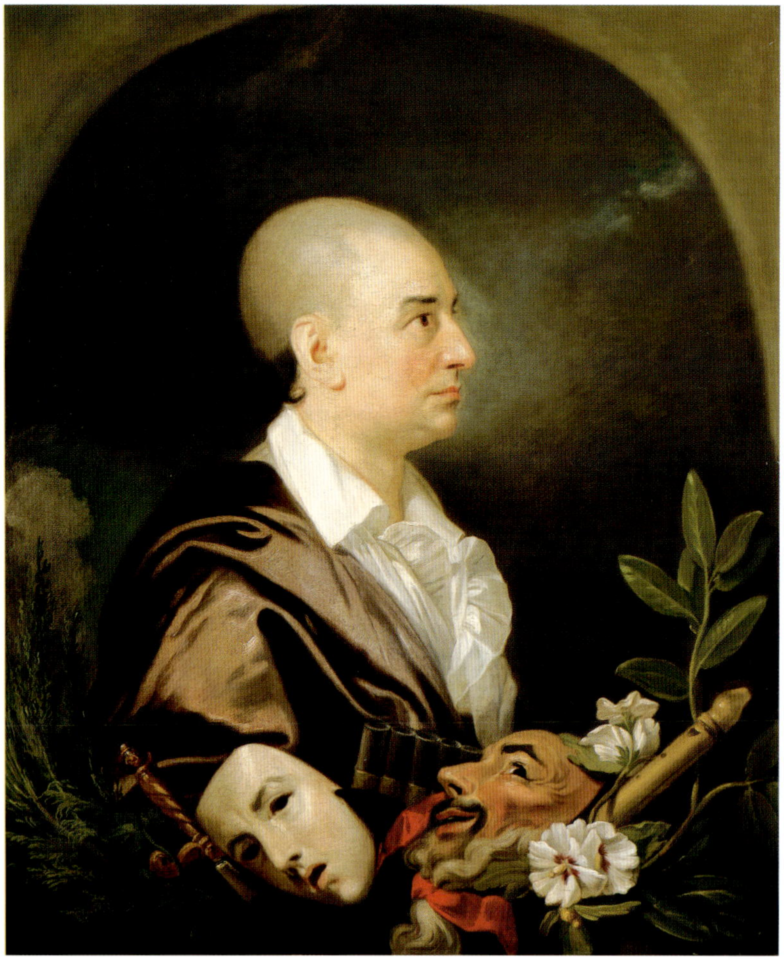

GARRICK NPG 1167

overtaken by his assistant Zoffany. 'We all love Wilson', Garrick later wrote, 'but You will find him with all his knowledge, & Philosophy, as Simple as a Child'.[4] Two half-length portraits called Garrick and attributed to Benjamin Wilson in the Garrick Club are less convincing likenesses.[5]

1 W.G. Constable, *Richard Wilson*, 1953, p.66, no.11.
2 Listed at Gredington by Steegman, I, p.159, no.70.
3 C. White ed., *Rembrandt in England in the 18th century*, 1983, no.58. Rembrandt's plate illus. *All the Etchings of Rembrandt*, 1977, B 283.
4 ?May 1767; *Garrick Letters* 1963, II, p.576, no.463.
5 Ashton 1997, nos.246 and 251.

707A after LOUIS-FRANÇOIS ROUBILIAC c.1758

Plaster painted terracotta 63.5 (25) high; mould lines visible on the face; small losses at the edges of the drapery and some surface marking.

Collections: Presented by Sir Theodore Martin KCB 1883.

Roubiliac is seen finishing a bust of Garrick (presumably in terracotta) in the portrait by Andrea Soldi dated 1757/8 in the Garrick Club.[1] A marble bust was in Mrs Garrick's sale, Christie's, 23 June 1823, lot 72.

Roubiliac made a gilt-bronze plaque of Garrick dated 1758,[2] and four plaster medallions, three wax medallions and two terracotta busts were in Roubiliac's sale, Langford's, 12-15 May 1762. He also made in 1758 the celebrated statue of Shakespeare for Garrick's Temple at Hampton (now in the British Museum).

1 Ashton 1997, no.727.
2 Garrick Club; Ashton 1997, S15.

1167 studio of JOHANN ZOFFANY [1763]

Canvas 75 x 63 (29½ x 24¾) lined 1977; the original canvas inscribed verso: *Mary Bradshaw* eleven times, with the date *December the 31st: 1763*. Heavily ironed, a spill down through shoulder; retouchings in the upper background.

Dark brown eyes, a wisp of black hair below the ear, purple cloak; beneath the portrait, emblems of Garrick's diverse roles: rosemary and laurel, Pan pipes, flute and sword, masks of comedy and tragedy, the latter with a red ribbon.

Collections: Given by the sitter to Mrs Mary Bradshaw 1763;[1] Mrs David Garrick, who bequeathed to her husband's nephew, Nathan Egerton Garrick, 'the Portrait of my late Husband without a wig, by Zoffany, which I bought after his death of Mrs Bradshaw, to whom it had been given as a present';[2] his son, Nathan David Garrick, by whose widow bequeathed to the National Gallery 1885 (no.1197); lent to the NPG 1900; ownership transferred to the Tate Gallery 1954 and to the NPG 1957.

Exhibition: Beningbrough 1979–.

Reference: Davies 1946, p.13, no.1197, as British School; Mander & Mitchenson 1955, pp.65-72, 189.

The profile, inevitably, resembles the head of Garrick painted by Zoffany in 1762 in *Mr and Mrs Garrick taking tea at Hampton*. NPG 1167 is a version of the portrait in the Ashmolean Museum, Oxford (A1219), from the collection of Thomas Harris, manager of the Covent Garden Theatre,[3] at whose sale, Christie's, 12 July 1819, lot 55, it was said to have been painted for George Colman the elder, the circumstances being described as follows:

to avoid the different changes in countenance, with which Garrick used to amuse himself while sitting for this portrait, Zoffany took this likeness concealed in an antechamber, during the times of Garrick's shaving his head, his constant custom in the afternoon.

The portrait was engraved by J.S. Müller [J. Miller] in 1769,[4] and a copy in miniature by Anne Louisa Lane (formerly in the collection of Lord Olivier) was engraved by James Heath in 1819;[5] an anonymous lithograph was published in 1824.[6]

Garrick had departed for the Continent in September 1763 and was abroad when, according to the inscription cited above, NPG 1167 was given to Mrs Bradshaw. It was once attributed to the Irish engraver and miniaturist Luke Sullivan.[7] A version showing a red silk drape round Garrick's shoulders is in an American private collection; another with darkish hair added is in the Maugham collection in the National Theatre,[8] resembling an engraving by Miller of 1790. Another profile of Garrick with his wig by Zoffany was engraved by John Hall,[9] who also exhibited a 'print of Mr Garrick', SA 1763(168).

Garrick became an enthusiastic patron of Zoffany, whom he discovered in 1762 working as an assistant to Benjamin Wilson, see NPG 6249. In August that year Garrick declared he would do Wilson's 'German friend all ye good offices in my Power; he was warmly recommended to me by my Acquaintance, is a Man of merit, & well behaved in my family', and, he added, 'providence has blessed him with Genius.'[10]

1 The date assumed from the inscriptions on the original canvas.
2 As quoted by Mander & Mitchenson 1955, p.65. Zoffany had already painted Mary Bradshaw on stage with Garrick in 1762, see below.
3 Illus. *The Ashmolean*, 37, 1999, p.10; Mander & Mitchenson 1955, p.69 when in the collection of Mrs J.C. Conway.
4 Once erroneously identified as a plate to Smollett's 1757 *History of England* (cf. Davies 1946), but see Mander & Mitchenson 1955, pp.65–66.
5 Both illus. Mander & Mitchenson 1955, pp.70, 72.
6 The 1819 sale description was reprinted below the lithograph; the painting then belonged to George McKenny (Mander & Mitchenson 1955, p.67).
7 Cf. *Connoisseur*, LXXXV, 1930, p.217. Presumably because Sullivan was said to have painted his wife, see Mrs Garrick.
8 Mander & Mitchenson 1980, no.10.
9 Illus. Mander & Mitchenson 1955, pp.70, 71.
10 *Garrick Letters* 1963, I, p.363, no.292.

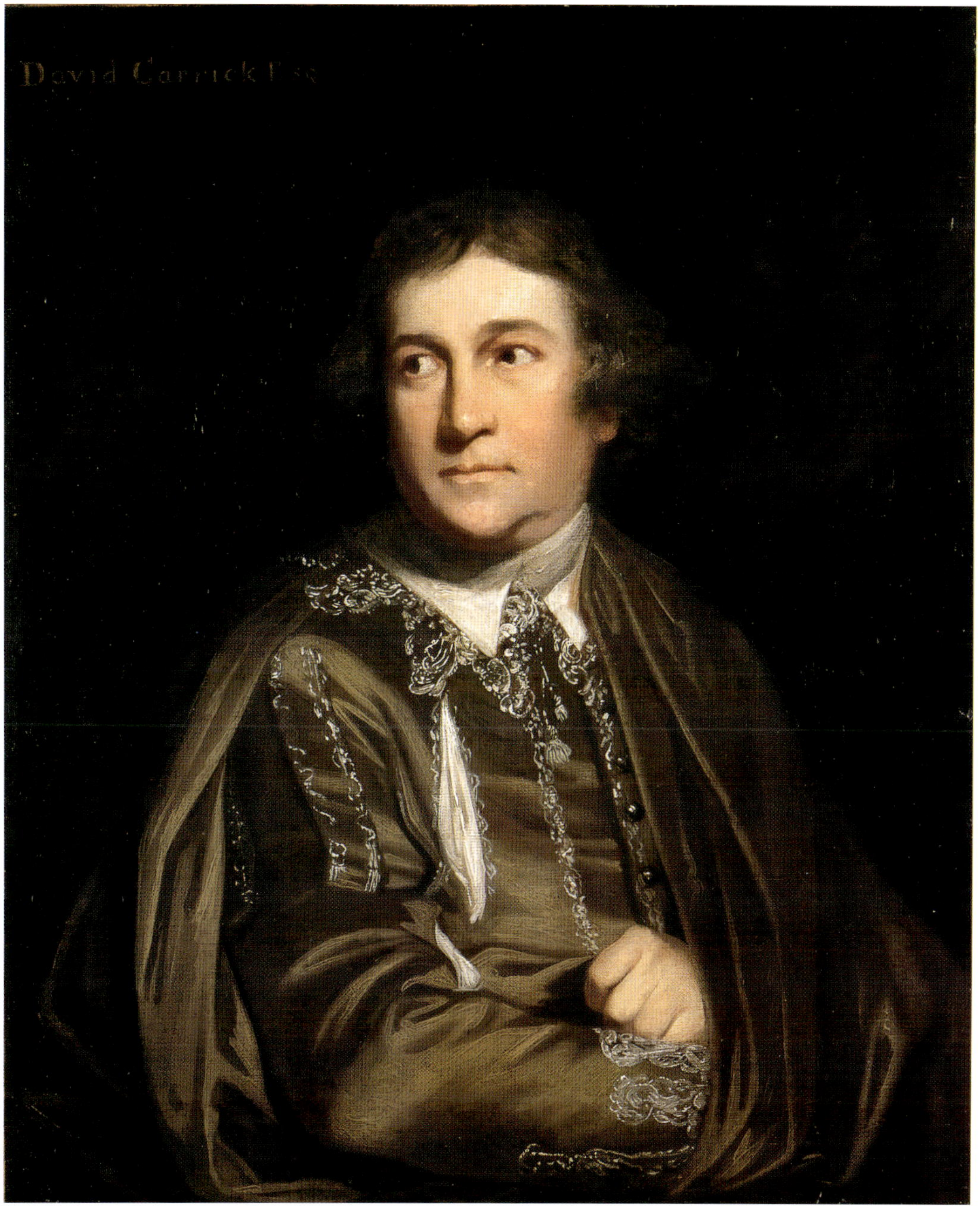

GARRICK NPG *4504*

4504 after JOSHUA REYNOLDS, as *Kitely in Every Man in his Humour* 1768

Canvas 75 x 62 (29½ x 24½) inscribed, upper left: *David Garrick Esq*.; cleaned and lined 1990.

Brown eyes, brown hair, wearing grey-green Van Dyck costume with silver trim.

Collections:[1] Stephen, 2nd Baron Holland; 2nd Earl of Upper Ossory; his nephew, the 3rd Baron Holland (d.1840); his son, Gen. Charles Richard Fox;[2] Christie's, 27 June 1863, lot 62, bt. in; Fox sale, 4 July 1874, lot 21, bt. Graves for Louis Huth; his sale, Christie's, 20 May 1905, lot 123; acquired by Norman Wolfe in the late 1920s; presented by Mrs Jenny Wolfe 1966.

Exhibitions: *Art Treasures*, Manchester 1857(BPG 286); *Reynolds*, Grosvenor Gallery, 1883–84(143); *The Gothick*, Brighton, 1975(D2); *Johnson and the Midlands*, Lichfield, 1984(48); *Casanova*, Venice, 1998(275).

Reference: Graves & Cronin, I, p.350; Mannings 2000, no.704a.

A contemporary copy of some quality after the Reynolds in the Royal Collection dated 1768, which was given by the artist to Edmund Burke and acquired by the Prince Regent in 1812.[3] Garrick had revived Ben Jonson's play in 1751, making some adjustments to the original text; Kitely became one of his best roles (he last performed it in April 1776). Finlayson's engraving of the original picture identified the scene as Act II, scene i, which is set in a hall in Kitely's house and contains four long speeches by Kitely, including the lines 'Yea, every look, or glance, mine eye ejects, Shall check occasion'.

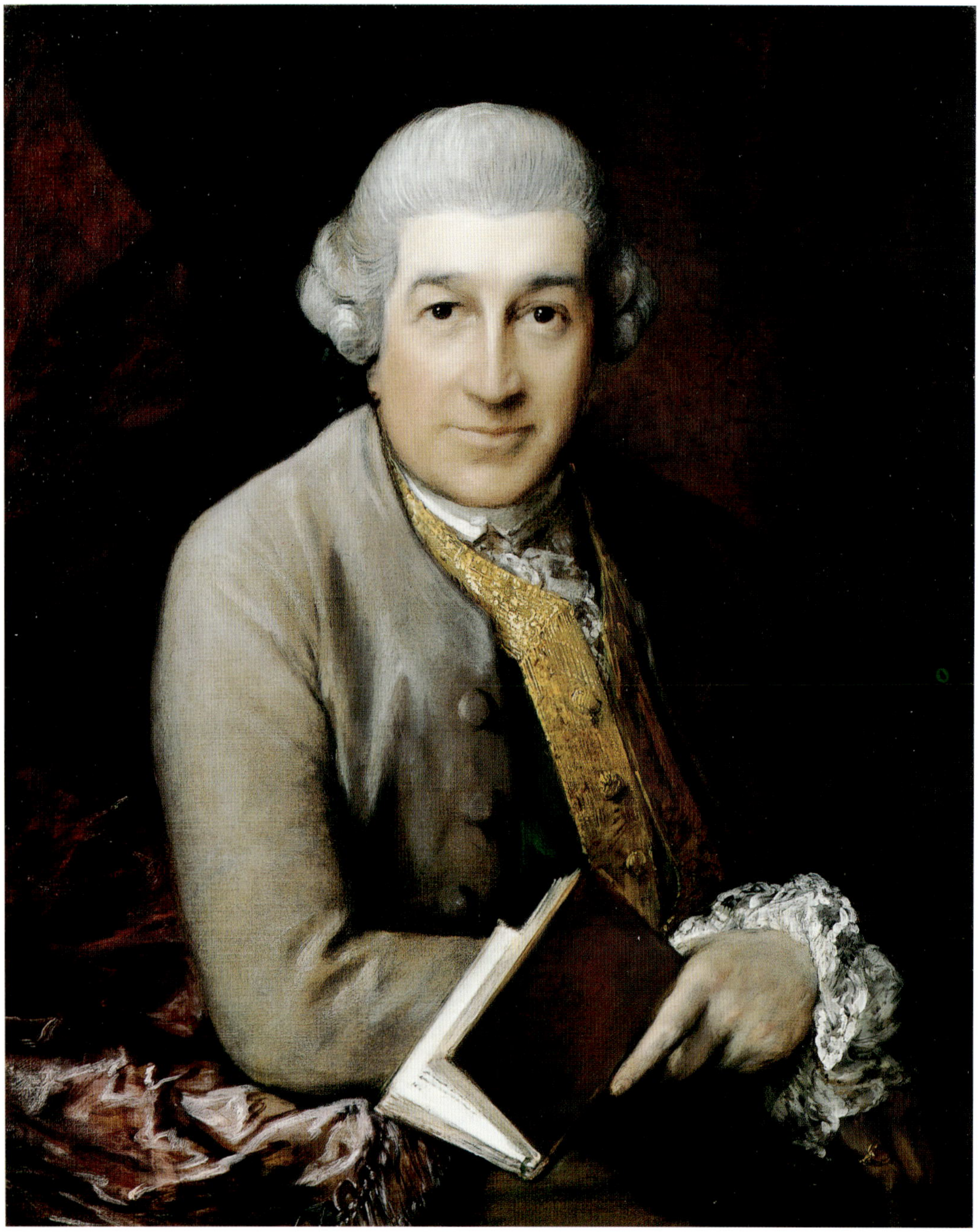

GARRICK NPG *5054*

5054 THOMAS GAINSBOROUGH 1770

Canvas 75 x 62 (29½ x 24½); lined 1975; the paint is very thin in his right sleeve; drying cracks in the right background area have been retouched.

Deep brown eyes, grey powdered wig, wearing a pale grey coat and green waistcoat trimmed with gold; a red-stone ring on his right little finger; a purple drape to the left.

Collections: [Mrs Garrick, see below]; Albany Wallis (1713?-1800, Garrick's executor); bequeathed to Lady Ann Bayly; her son, Gen. Lewis Bayley Wallis (c.1776-1848); through his adopted daughter to her husband, Sir Belford Hinton Wilson KB; by descent to R. Bayly Wallis Wilson; his (anon.) sale Christie's, 16 June 1900, lot 105,[1] bt. Agnew for the 1st Baron Masham, by descent to the 1st Earl of Swinton; purchased from the Trustees of the Swinton Settled Estates 1975.

Engraving: Joseph Collyer 1776, oval.

Exhibitions: RA 1770(86); BI 1814(64) lent Gen. Wallis; *Art Treasures*, Manchester 1857(BPG 284) lent Sir Belford Wilson; *Yorkshire Loan Exhibition*, York, 1934(9); *Masterpieces from Yorkshire and Durham*, Leeds, 1936(25); *Gainsborough*, 45 Park Lane, London, 1936(12); *Garrick*, Buxton, 1981; *Evenings of English Music*, Pushkin State Museum, 1983; *Johnson*, Arts Council, 1984(72); *Gainsborough's Circle at Bath*, Bath, 1988(14).

Reference: *Gainsborough* 1953, p.9; Waterhouse 1958, no.305.

This intimate characterisation within a half-length format may be compared with Gainsborough's contemporary portraits of *J.C. Bach*, NPG 5557, and *John Henderson*, NPG 980. When exhibited at the RA in 1770, Horace Walpole remarked that NPG 5054 was 'Very like',[2] although Gainsborough, like other artists (see below, Portraits in Character, Hogarth, c.1745), did not find Garrick an easy sitter. According to his obituarist in the *Morning Chronicle*,

> when he was sketching the eyebrows and thought he had hit upon the precise situation and then looked a second time at the model he found the eyebrows lifted up to the middle of the forehead; and when he looked a third time they were dropped like a curtain, close over the eye. So flexible and universal was the counenance of this great player that it was as impossible to catch his likeness as it is to catch the form of a passing cloud.[3]

On 22 June 1772 Gainsborough told Garrick his portrait was to go from Bath to London 'on Wednesday next' and asked pardon for having kept the picture so long from Mrs Garrick:

> It has indeed been of great service in keeping me going, but my chief reason for detaining it so long

A studio version was sold Sotheby's, 12 April 1995, lot 63;[4] copies were sold Christie's, 18 December 1925, lot 81, attributed to James Northcote, and Sotheby's, 30 October 1957, lot 70; a miniature copy was exhibited BFAC 1889(xix 3) and *Guelph* 1891(1050), lent J. Whitehead.

1 Old label verso: *This picture belonged to Stephen Lord Holland & then [to the Earl of Up]per Ossory who left it to Hen[ry Lord Holland] in 1818, and was afterwards left [ ] Fox 1840*. Another: *David Garrick by Sir Joshua Reynolds. From the collection of the late General C.R. Fox.*

2 Waagen IV, 233, saw it in the the library of General Fox in Kensington, describing it as 'spirited'.

3 Millar 1969, no.1021; *Gainsborough & Reynolds* 1994, no.5; Mannings 2000, no.703. Engraved J. Finlayson 1769; J. Scott 1864.

4 Mannings 2000, no.704 (said to have been commissioned by Bennet Langton).

was the hopes of getting one copy like, to hang in my own Parlour, not as a show Picture, but for my own enjoyment, to look when I please at a Great Man, who has thought me worthy of some little notice; but not one copy can I make which does not as much resemble Mr Garrick's Brother as Himself - so I have bestow'd a drop of excellent Varnish to keep you out, instead of a falling tear at parting and have only to beg of Dear Mrs Garrick to hang it in the best light she can find out, and to continue puffing for me in the manner Mr Keate informs me She does - That you may long Continue to delight & surprise the World with your Original Face whilst I hobble after with my Copy.[4]

It is assumed that NPG 5054 was the portrait sent to Mrs Garrick.[5] Gainsborough's own copy remains unidentified. A second copy was made for Garrick's business adviser, James Clutterbuck;[6] in a second undated letter Gainsborough told Garrick 'I will never consent that any body makes a present of your Face to Clutterbuck but myself, because I always intended a Copy (by my own hand) for Him', adding 'and for the Original, it was to be my present to Mrs Garrick'.[7]

In 1859 Scharf noted that NPG 5054 was superior to a version in the Schomberg collection (sold by Paul Mellon, Sotheby's, 18 November 1981, lot 184);[8] other versions were formerly at Tockenham Manor;[9] sold Robinson and Fisher, 16 May 1928, lot 162, and on the London art market in 1969.

A miniature copy by William Essex was sold Christie's, 18 December 1973, lot 62, and enamel copies by him were exhibited at the RA 1857(656), SBA 1858(816) and RA 1860(856).[10]

1 For this provenance see also Mannings 2000, no.1816 (Reynolds's portrait of Albany Wallis). The Wilson sale in 1900 also included, lot 106, a *Mrs Garrick* by Gainsborough, see Mrs Garrick under Doubtful Portraits.
2 Graves RA, III, p.191.
3 Whitley 1915, p.45.
4 Hayes 2001, pp.105-06.
5 Mrs Garrick lived twenty-two years longer than Wallis, and why she should give such a portrait away is not at all clear; in her sale, Christie's, 23 June 1823 (L.10483), there was no Gainsborough portrait of her husband, but in an Appendix to the sale an unattributed portrait of him fetched the high price of 45 gns. Wallis, according to his unsympathetic obituary (*GM*, LXX, 1800, ii, pp. 908-9), had 'paid his addresses to [Garrick's] relict' and raised Garrick's monument in Westminster Abbey, see 1797 below.
6 English private collection; Waterhouse 1958, no.306.
7 Hayes 2001, p.85.
8 TSB 2/91A, 92. See Waterhouse 1958, no.307.
9 Duleep Singh, II, p.420, no.46.
10 A letter from Essex to George Scharf, 14 May 1860 (NPG archive), confirmed that the enamel exhibited in 1860 was taken from the portrait belonging to the Wilson family, i.e. NPG 5054.

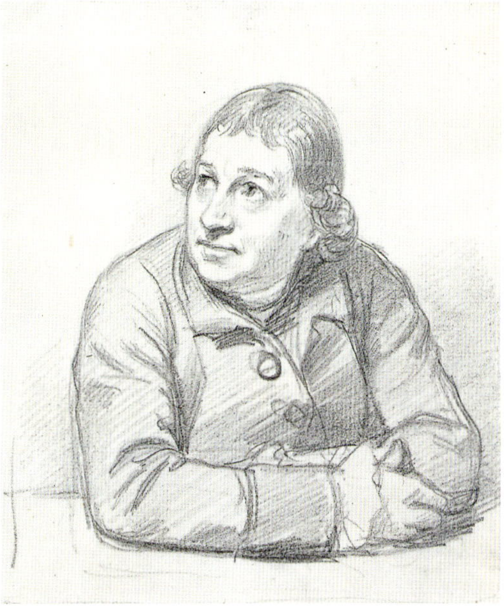

GARRICK *NPG 3639*

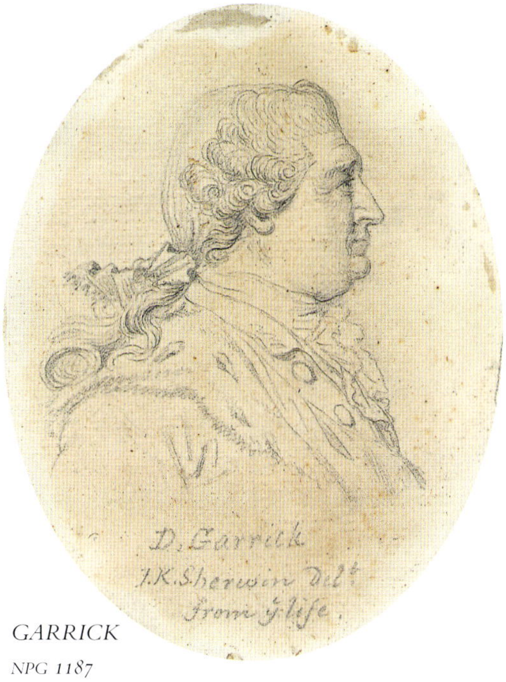

GARRICK
NPG 1187

3639 NATHANIEL DANCE 1771

Pencil on paper laid down on paper 13.6 x 11.4 (5⅜ x 4½) a repaired horizontal tear across his left shoulder.

Collections: Inscribed verso: *drawn by Dance of* [sic] *the breakfast Table // These two pencil drawing by Dance* [see also *Mrs Garrick* NPG 3640]- *hung up in Garrick's study- and at Mrs Garrick's death passed to Mrs J.G. Payne - née Garrick his niece - and at Mrs Paynes death came into the possession of her Godchild Miss Desirée D'Enville - my first wife - Mr Garrick always considered it the best likeness ever made of him. Mrs Garrick, née Violette is in her night Cap. / W.E. Image / Herringswell / House* [Mildenhall, Suffolk]. Presented by Miss Katherine R. Image, granddaughter of William Edmund Image, 1948.

Engraving: Mrs Dorothea Solly by 1829, lithograph (in reverse).

Exhibition: *Dance* 1977(28).

The pendant drawing of Mrs Garrick [see NPG 3640] is inscribed on the backboard verso: *Dance delint. / March 16 / 1771*. On 25 July 1829 J.T. Smith saw in Garrick's Villa 'two drawings of Mr and Mrs Garrick, by Dance', presumably NPG 3639 and 3640, 'of which there are lithographic engravings by Mrs Solly, the daughter of the Rev Mr Racket, with impressions of which that lady honoured me for my wife's illustrated copy of the *Life of Dr Johnson*'.[1] Both drawings have previously been attributed to George Dance,[2] but the similarity of the David Garrick to Nathaniel's half-length portrait of 1773 establishes the latter's authorship. At the time he made these drawings Dance was also painting his full-length of *Garrick as Richard III* (see below). A similar drawing of Garrick in the Folger Shakespeare Library is inscribed *David Garrick from a Sketch in Pencil made by the late George* [sic] *Dance, Esqr - - - - - - by Mrs Saml. Solly Daughter of the Revd Thomas Rackett*.

1 Smith 1905, p.290. The lithograph of Garrick illus. Phillips sale cat., 19 March 1992, p.5.
2 Cf. D. Stroud, *George Dance*, 1971, pls. 55a, 55b.

1187 JOHN KEYSE SHERWIN c.1774

Pencil on paper laid down on paper 8.9 x 7 (3¾ x 2¾) the paper generally discoloured; inscribed below in pencil: *D. Garrick / I.K. Sherwin Delt. / from ye life*. A label on the frame verso: *This is Sherwin's original drawing from / which he engraved* [a] *print*.

Collections: W.McJ. Croy of Reading, by whom sent to Christie's in December 1898; transferred to Foster's for sale;[1] purchased from Graves 1899.

Engraving: J.K. Sherwin c.1774.[2]

Exhibition: *Garrick and his Contemporaries*, Stratford-upon-Avon, 1969(53).

The profile compares with those of 1772 by Lewis Pingo and Benjamin Van der Gucht (see below). Sherwin completed his apprenticeship with Bartolozzi in 1774, and NPG 1167 presumably dates from that time.

1 Identified by an inscription on the frame verso: *789W*; I am grateful to Margie Christian for this information.
2 A second anonymous engraving of this type, within a drawn oval, shows different drapery.

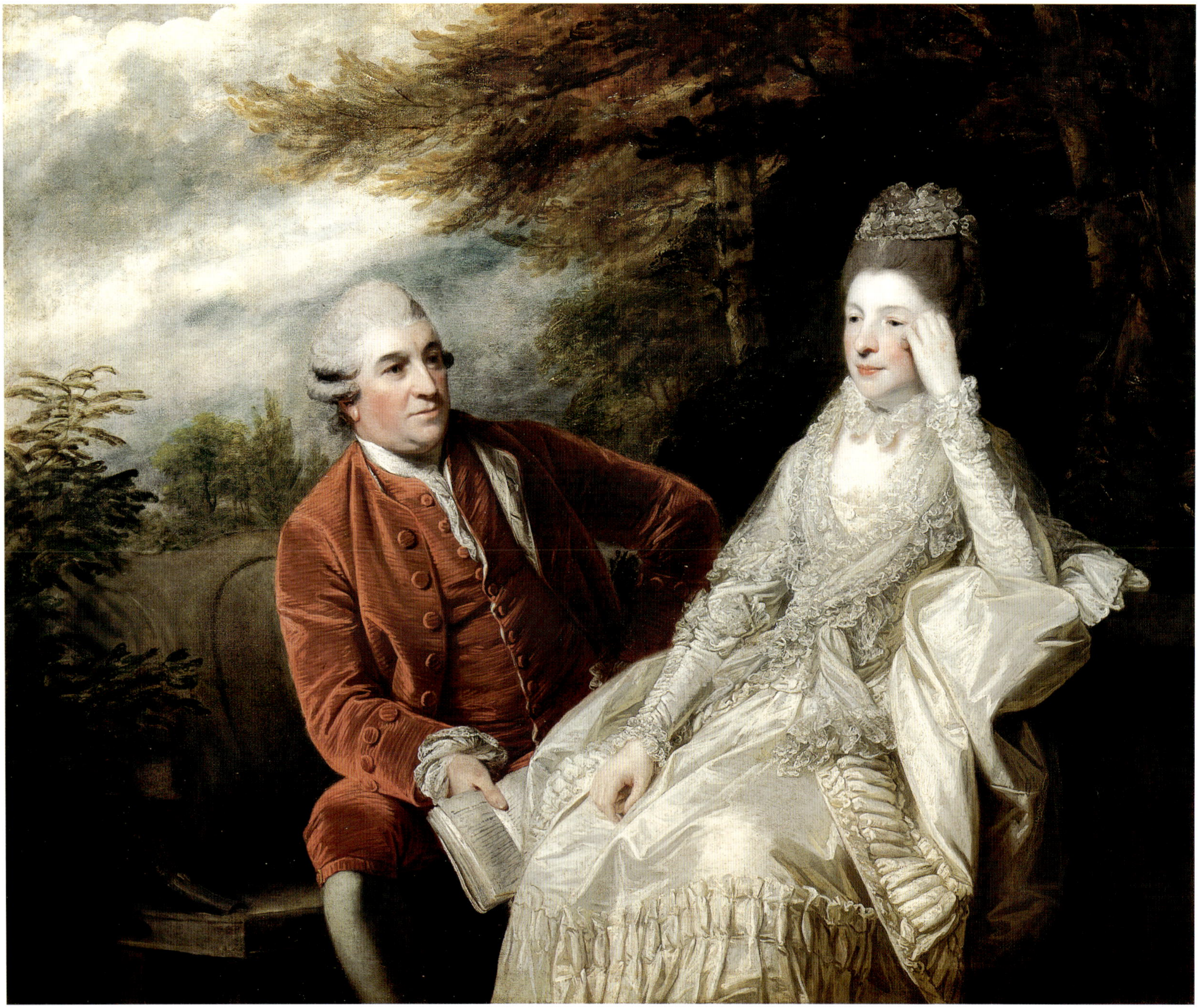

GARRICK with Mrs GARRICK NPG 5375

5375 JOSHUA REYNOLDS, *with Mrs Garrick* 1772–73

Canvas 139.5 x 169 (55 x 66½) lined; cleaned 1981; *pentimenti* show Garrick's arms widened and his right leg lowered; Mrs Garrick's head-dress originally taller and the fourth finger of her right hand longer; the arm of the seat has been lowered.

Garrick has brown eyes, a grey powdered wig, and wears a red corded velvet suit, the coat and waistcoat with a white lining. Mrs Garrick has blue-grey eyes, and is dressed in white satin.

Collections: the Hon Thomas Fitzmaurice paid Reynolds 150 gn. for *Mr and Mrs Garrick* on 17 January 1775;[1] his grandson the 5th Earl of Orkney; his sales Christie's, 11 May 1860, lot 194, bt. in, and Christie's, 15 June 1861, lot 108, bt. W.O. Foster; by descent to the executors of Maj.-Gen. Edward H. Goulburn (d.1978); Christie's, 21 November 1980, lot 111, withdrawn; purchased by private treaty 1980.

Exhibitions: RA 1773(238); BI 1860(151); NPE 1868(837); *Reynolds*, 45 Park Lane, London, 1937(82); *Garrick, Johnson and the Lichfield Circle*, Lichfield, 1953(7); *Johnson and the Lichfield Circle*, Lichfield, 1959(8); *Reynolds*, Birmingham, 1961(55); *Treasures* 1995–96(14).

Reference: Graves & Cronin, I, pp.351–52, & IV, p.1318; Waterhouse 1941, p.63; Simon 1997, pp.95, 163; Mannings 2000, no.707.

Garrick appears to have just finished reading to his wife who reflects upon his words; the setting has been described, inevitably, as the Garricks' villa at Hampton.[2] On 19 November 1772 James Northcote told his brother that Reynolds was 'painting Mr and Mrs Garrick in one picture'.[3] Reynolds's pocket books record appointments for David Garrick in 1772 on 29 October and 3, 5 and 6 November; and for his wife on 16, 20, 27 and 29 October and 4 November. In 1773 Mrs Garrick sat on 17 April. Ribeiro has observed that Garrick's velvet suit was rather old-fashioned by this time; the style (the three garments made of the same fabric) was one favoured in his youth; by contrast Mrs Garrick, who has artificially whitened skin and rouged cheeks, wears the newly fashionable long-sleeved gown.[4]

The figure of Garrick alone was copied on a kit-cat canvas once owned by Sir James Mackintosh,[5] etched by W. Boucher in 1894 as from a painting by Gainsborough [*sic*] belonging to Mrs Kaye. A reduced copy of NPG 5375 was sold Christie's, 30 July 1981, lot 256.

1 Cormack 1970, p.152; listed in his collection by Malone 1797, I, p.xxxvi.
2 Leslie & Taylor 1865, I, p.436.
3 Whitley 1928, II, p.293.
4 Ribeiro 2000, pp.128–29.
5 Graves & Cronin, IV, p.1318.

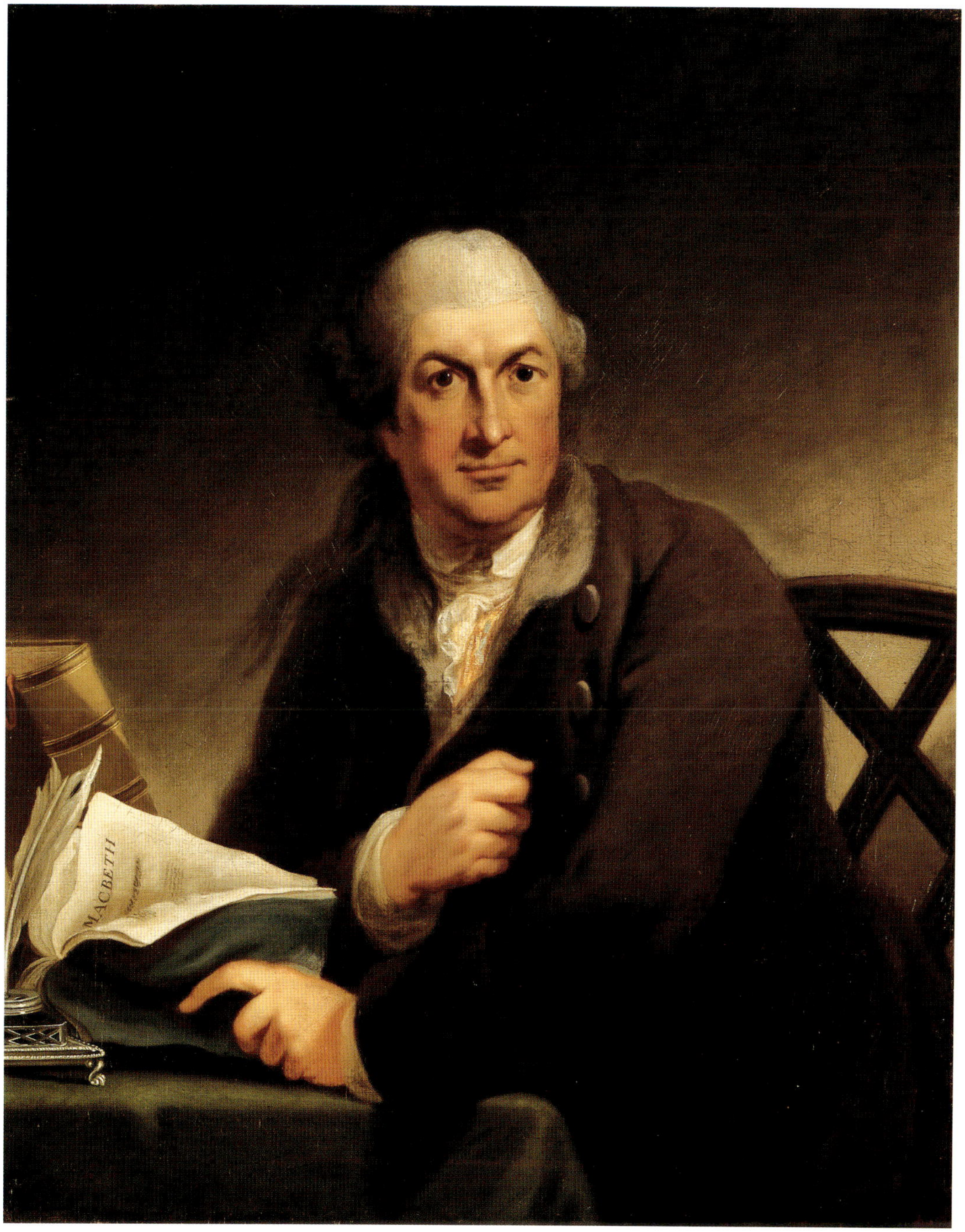

GARRICK *NPG 82*

82 ROBERT EDGE PINE c.1775

Canvas 90 x 72.5 (35½ x 28½); lined; cleaned 1985; *pentimenti* in right thumb and left hand. The title page of the blue-covered book in his left hand inscribed *MACBETH.*

Brown eyes, white hair, wearing a fur-lined purple coat and a gold and light blue waistcoat; a green cloth on the table.

Collections: Sir Richard Sullivan (d.1806), 1st Bt, of Ember Court, Thames Ditton;[1] his son Sir Charles Sullivan, 3rd Bt; sold Christie's, 18 June 1859, lot 26 as Romney, 'Portrait of Garrick, Painted for Sir Richard Sullivan', bt. Farrer for the NPG.

Engravings: W. Dickinson 1778 (a proof bears the scratched date 1 December 1776);[2] R. Cooper 1815. Reduced plates by W. Holl 1819, C.T. Warren 1824 and J. Rogers.

Exhibitions: *Johnson and the Lichfield Circle*, Lichfield, 1959(9); *Samuel Johnson, Londoner*, Royal Exchange, London, 1964; *Pickpocketing the Rich*, Bath (Holburne), 2002 (41).

NPG 82 has some claim to be an original portrait by Pine, although such status should not be overvalued. When sold in 1859 it was said that when Garrick was in Bath

> Sir R Sullivan saw his portrait in the Artist's studio & asked leave to have a copy – Mr Garrick refused, but generously offered to sit specially to oblige Sir Rd Sullivan The faithfulness of this likeness is confirmed by rather a romantic incident Mrs Garrick so deciding declared it to be the best likeness of her husband, that once a year during her widowhood, she obtained permission of Lady Sullivan to closet herself for some hours with this picture as the tenderest & most faithful remembrance of her dcd husband![3]

Pine was living in Bath between 1772 and 1779. A reduced copy in pastel is in the Theatre Museum and an enamel copy by William Essex was exhibited RA 1838(663), possibly that dated 1835 in the Victoria and Albert Museum (938.1868).

The same head recurs in a number of variant portraits of Garrick by Pine, their frequency suggesting 'a fascination that went beyond simple economics'.[4] They were painted, it would appear, between 1775 and 1780; in July 1775 Garrick paid Pine for two oval burnished gold frames[5] and in 1780 Pine exhibited at the RA a *Portrait of Mr Garrick*.[6] Apart from NPG 82 seven types of Pine portrait may be identified.

a) Three-quarter length seated to left, table to right, an open book held up in his right hand, the chair with curved back. Engraved by W. Skelton, published 1 November 1818, *from an undoubted original Picture in the possession of the Widow of the late George Wilson*. Skelton also engraved in 1818 a miniature of Garrick after Pine (with George Daniels in 1865).

b) Half-length oval, in a blue coat, holding in his left hand across his body a well-thumbed paper-bound text; Folger Shakespeare Library.[7]

c) Half length, in a red coat, his left hand stretched out across his breast; versions in the New York Public Library[8] and in the Garrick Club.[9] This type has been associated, too tenuously, with Garrick's farewell performance as Don Felix in *The Wonder*, the gesture recalling his final epilogue.[10] The pose was incorporated in Pine's whole-length canvas of 1782, *Mr Garrick speaking the Ode to Shakespeare* (also known as the *Apotheosis of Garrick*) engraved by C. Watson in 1783.[11]

d) Half-length standing, in a blue coat with a red collar, his right hand held across his body. Garrick Club.[12]

e) Half length, in a blue coat, a copy of *Macbeth* in his right hand. Versions at Christ Church, Oxford,[13] and sold Sotheby's, 14 February 1962, lot 172.

f) Bust-length oval, without hands. Versions in the Yale University Art Gallery, at Newbury House, and with M. Sylvester, Canada, 1961.

g) Face mask alone, without hair, engraved anonymously, published on 4 April 1779, giving the semblance of a death mask.[14] Garrick was buried in Westminster Abbey on 1 February 1779.

1 'painted for my father - original- and said by Mrs Garrick to be the best likeness ever made' (Sir Charles Sullivan to Scharf, 9 June 1858; NPG archive); see also note 3.
2 A *trompe l'oeil* painting by J. Collier incorporating this engraving sold Christie's, 17 June 1983, lot 206.
3 Letter, written in a poor hand, sent at the behest of Sir Charles Sullivan from the Land & Auction Offices, 7 June 1858, to Scharf (NPG archive); most portraits of Garrick were at one time or another declared to be the best likenesses of him. See also note 1.
4 Pressly 1993, p.216.
5 MS sold Phillips, 19 March 1992, lot 15.
6 *A Portrait, in the character of Jaques, Shakespeare's As you Like it*, also shown by Pine at the RA in 1780 is sometimes assumed to have shown Garrick who, however, was not known for that role.
7 Pressly 1993, no.120, as probably the portrait exhibited RA 1780.
8 On loan from the New-York Historical Society; illus. M.W. England, *Garrick and Stratford*, 1962, f.p.56.
9 Ashton 1997, no.239.
10 When he addressed his audience: 'the deepest impression of your kindness will always remain here (Putting his hand on his breast) fixed and unalterable' (cf. *Georgian Playhouse* 1975, no.90).
11 See *Pine* 1979, pp.111, 117; illus. *Georgian Playhouse* 1975, no.62, and *Theatre: The Age of Garrick*, Courtauld Institute, 1994, no.54.
12 Ashton 1997, no.240.
13 Poole, III, p.72.
14 Illus. *Garrick Letters* 1963, III, p.1265.

ICONOGRAPHY

See also the *Harvard Catalogue*, II, pp.84-106, and Highfill, VI, pp.81-103 (listing further portrayals of Garrick in character). For a general survey of Garrick iconography, see E. Wind, 'Portraits of Actors - Garrick', in *Hume and the Heroic Portrait*, 1986, pp.34-42.

When Garrick was in Paris in November 1764 he wrote to his brother in London: 'I am so plagu'd here for my Prints or rather Prints of Me - that I must desire You to send me by ye first opportunity six prints from Reynolds's picture, You may apply to ye Engraver he lives in Leicester fields, & his name is Fisher, he will give you good ones, if he knows they are for Me - You must likewise send me a King Lear by Wilson, Hamlet do Jaffier & Belv[idera] by Zoffani, speak to him for two or 3, & what Else he may have done of Me - There is likewise a print of Me, as I am, from Liotard's picture Scrap'd by MacArdel, send me 2 or 3 of them, speak to MacArdel, & any other prints of Me, if tolerable, that I can't remember' (*Garrick Letters* 1963, I, p.433, no.343).

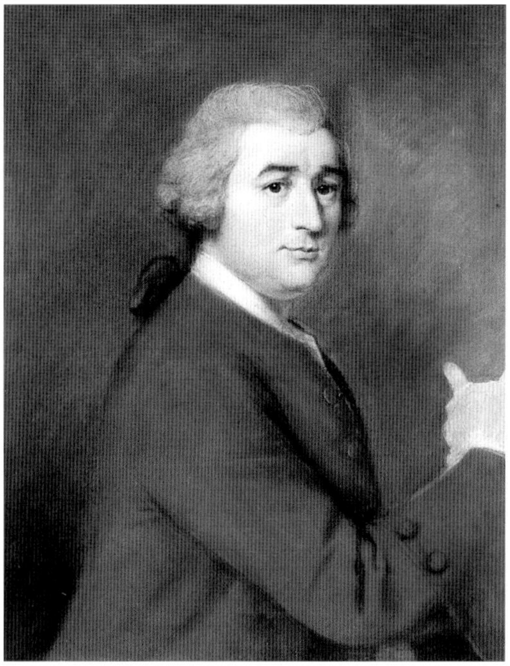

GARRICK by J-E. Liotard 1751 (Chatsworth)

1745 Painting by Arthur Pond, bust length; engraved J. Wood 1745 (illus. Pressly 1993, p.249); N. Parr 1747; J. McArdell.

c.1745 Painting by Francis Hayman, whole-length seated with William Windham of Felbrigg. Private collection (illus. Allen 1987, no.17).

1746 Drawing by William Hogarth, whole-length figure seen in profile and from the back, compared with similar views of the actor James Quin. Royal Collection (Oppé 1950, no.351, pl.61). Engraved T. Cook 1808.

1751 Pastel by J-E. Liotard,* half length. Chatsworth. Engraved J. McArdell as *from an Original Picture Painted at Paris 1751*. Drawn in Paris, with pendant of his wife. Copy in Drury Lane Theatre, London.

c.1751 Drawing doubtfully attributed to Benjamin Wilson, half length. Folger Shakespeare Library. Formerly attributed to Gainsborough. The likeness closely resembles that in the Liotard pastel of 1751. Conceivably the drawing in the Garrick sale, 5 May 1825, lot 133, 'portrait framed and glazed in black lead pencil by Liotard of the late David Garrick'.

c.1752-55 Painting by Benjamin Wilson, see NPG 6249.

1757 Painting by William Hogarth,* three-quarter length seated, his wife behind him, the *Prologue to Taste*, written by Garrick for Samuel Foote's comedy, before him. Royal Collection (Millar 1963, no.560). Garrick did not approve this picture, which was given to his widow by Hogarth's widow.

1758 Gilt-bronze plaque by L-F. Roubiliac. Garrick Club (Ashton 1997, S15), see NPG 707A.

c.1760? Pastel by F-X. Vispré, half length. Garrick Club (Ashton 1997, no.245). A replica in the Bromley-Davenport sale, Sotheby's, 11 June 1947, lot 3 with a pendant of Mrs Garrick.

1761 Painting by Thomas Hudson, half-length seated, engraved J. Dixon (illus. *Thomas Hudson*, Kenwood, 1977, no.64). Exhibited SA 1761(54). Versions sold Christie's, 27 July 1928, lot 143 (illus. A.E. Garnier, *Garniers of Hampshire*, 1900, f.p.22), and 28 July 1967, lot 376 as *Colonel Verelst* by Gainsborough.

1762 Two paintings by Johann Zoffany, with Mrs Garrick in their gardens at Hampton. Lord Lambton (illus. *Zoffany* 1977, nos.11, 12).

1762 Painting by Joshua Reynolds,* whole length between the figures of Comedy and Tragedy. Rothschild Family Trust, Waddesdon (Mannings 2000, no.700). Exhibited SA 1762(88). Engraved E. Fisher 1762.

Reduced copies in the National Theatre (Maugham Collection; Mander & Mitchenson 1980, no.11), the Garrick Club (Ashton 1997, no.242), Lulworth Manor, and the National Museum, Havana. Daniel Dodd exhibited a crayon drawing of *Garrick between Tragedy and Comedy*, FS 1767(94), and F.P. Nodder a version made of hair, SA 1775(185).

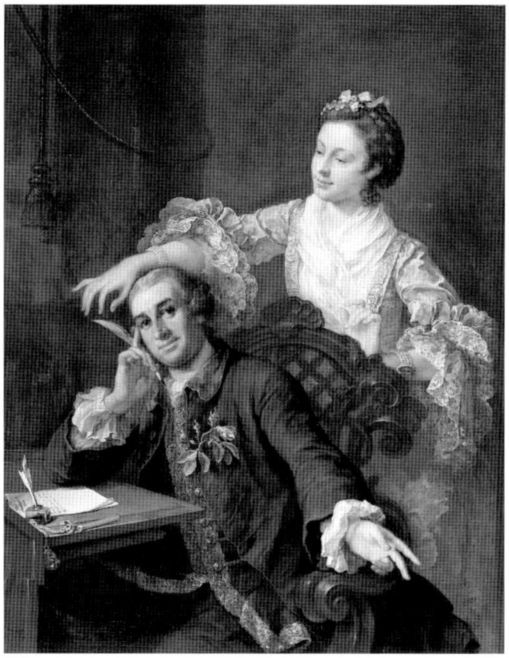

GARRICK with Mrs Garrick by William Hogarth 1757 (The Royal Collection)

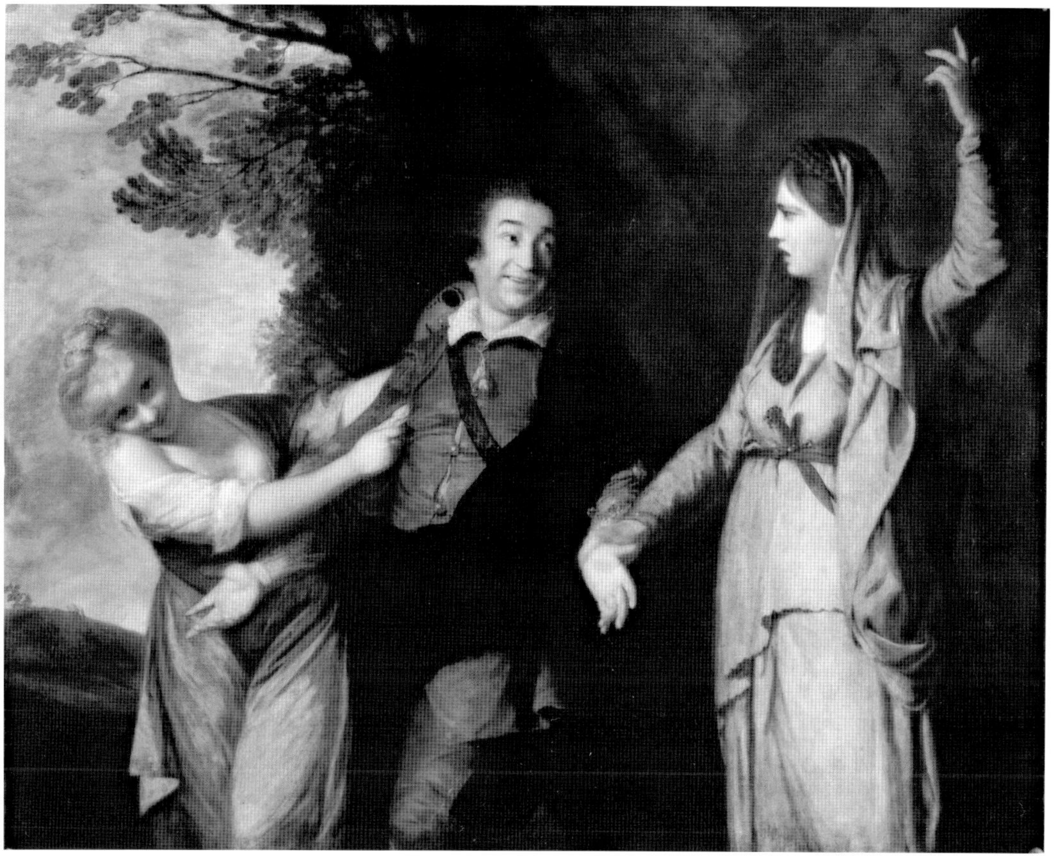

GARRICK between Comedy and Tragedy, by Joshua Reynolds 1762 (Waddesdon Manor, Rothschild Family Trust)

1762 Bust by John Nost jr., exhibited FS 1762(178). Nost is said to have taken a life mask of Garrick, of which the masks in the Garrick Club (Ashton 1997, S13) and the Folger Shakespeare Library are probably examples. From this mask he made the bust, of which a plaster cast has been identified in the Garrick Club (Ashton 1997, S11). Copies of Nost's bust were 'in every Barber's shop window, as a block for wigs' (Smith 1920, II, p.207), and it provided the pattern for the bust supplied by Hoskins & Grant to the Wedgwood factory in 1777 (Reilly 1973, p.159; and see Ashton 1997, S12).

1763 Painting by Johann Zoffany, see NPG 1167.

c.1763 Painting by Johann Zoffany, bust length unfinished. Garrick Club (Ashton 1997, no.249). Previously attributed to Hogarth and Reynolds.

1764 Painting by Pompeo Batoni, half-length holding the Vatican edition of the *Comedies of Terence*. Ashmolean Museum, Oxford (Clark 1985, no.266). Painted in Rome. A reduced copy in the Garrick Club (Ashton 1997, no.234).

1764 Painting by Angelica Kauffmann, half-length seated. Burghley House (176; illus. Roworth 1992, p.101). Exhibited FS 1765(217). Painted in Naples. Reduced version sold Sotheby's, 24 January 1951, lot 87.

1764 Marble bust by Joseph Nollekens. Althorp. Modelled in Rome and, according to Smith (1920, I, p.8), the first bust Nollekens modelled; Garrick paid for it in gold. A plaster was with A. Forbes Sieve-King, London, 1925.

1764 Painting by Nathaniel Dance, done in Rome, as reported in London in April 1764 (Walpole *Anecdotes* V, p.29).

1765 Bust by J-B. Lemoyne, exhibited Paris salon 1765 when described by Diderot: '*c'est Roscius commandant à ses yeux, à son front, à ses joues, à sa bouche à tous les muscles de son visage*' (*Salons*, ed. J. Seznec and J. Adhémar, II, 1960, p.213).

1766 Painting by Thomas Gainsborough, whole length leaning against a plinth bearing the bust of Shakespeare. Destroyed by fire 1946, formerly in the Town Hall, Stratford-upon-Avon (Waterhouse 1958, no.304). Exhibited SA 1766(51), and reworked for the Stratford Corporation on the occasion of the Stratford Shakespeare Jubilee in 1769. Reduced copies include examples in the Folger Shakespeare Library (Pressly 1993, no.109), and at Charlecote; an enamel copy by William Essex 1856 is in the Victoria and Albert Museum (1587.1871).

1768 Painting by Benjamin Van der Gucht, bust length. Sold Sotheby's, 17 June 1981, lot 61 (illus. *Early Journals and Letters of Fanny Burney*, I, 1988, p.149). It bears an uncomfortable resemblance to the head by Batoni, see 1764 above.

1769–73 Intaglio by Nathaniel Marchant, a bust of Shakespeare behind him. A sulphur impression exhibited SA 1773(168). A second intaglio by Marchant reproduced Garrick's bust alone (illus. *Marchant* 1987, figs.139–40).

1770 Painting by Thomas Gainsborough, see NPG 5054.

1771 Drawings by Nathaniel Dance, see NPG 3639.

1772 Painting by Benjamin Van der Gucht, half length looking at the Shakespeare Jubilee Medal. Althorp. Exhibited RA 1776(309). Engraved J. Saunders 1773. Painted to mark Garrick's stewardship of the Shakespeare bicentenary celebrations at Stratford-upon-Avon in 1769. Versions at Parham Park (illus. Highfill, VI, p.45) and in the Johnson Birthplace Museum, Lichfield; a reduced version on copper, from the collection of Lucy Porter, with A.D.H. Pennant 1953; another in the Garrick Club has a paper inscribed *Prologue* replacing the Shakespeare medal (Ashton 1997, no.244). A red wax medallion by Tassie after the Van der Gucht portrait, and a red wax study showing the bust alone, were with J. Whitehead in 1894 (Gray 1894, no.146); plaster replicas of each in the Scottish NPG (PG 474, PG 1903; illus. Highfill, VI, p.46).

1772 Wax medallion by Lewis Pingo. Exhibited FS 1772(152), with another of Mrs Garrick (*Wal. Soc.*, XXVII, 1939, p.75). Engraved by Isaac Taylor as *Mr Pingo's Seal for the Theatrical Fund* (Eimer 1998, nos.136, 136a). Used as pattern for silver and copper medals (Brown 1980, no.160; Eimer 1998, no.48), and for a Wedgwood medallion in 1773 (illus. Reilly 1973, p.159).

1772 Medallion by John Kirk, the 'Tribute Medallion' (Brown 1980, no.161). Exhibited SA 1773(151).

1772 Wax bust by Patience Wright (C.C. Sellers, *Benjamin Franklin in Portraiture*, 1962, p.427).

1772–73 Painting by Joshua Reynolds, with Mrs Garrick, see NPG 5375.

1773 Medallions by John Kirk (Brown 1980, nos. 172, 173) and Wedgwood, see 1772 Lewis Pingo.

1773 Painting by Nathaniel Dance, half-length seated, a copy of *Macbeth* in his hand; engraved J. Hall 1773 when in Lord Mansfield's collection. A studio version, given by Garrick to John Taylor in 1774, in the Folger Shakespeare Library (Pressly 1993, no.106). A crayon drawing in the William Salt Library, Stafford, exactly reproduces this portrait, and see NPG 3639.

c.1774 Drawing by J.K. Sherwin, see NPG 1187.

c.1774 Wax profile by Gardener. Garrick Club (Ashton 1997, S16). Other examples in the Royal Collection and sold Christie's, 11 December 1978, lot 134.

c.1775? Wax medallion by Robert Stewart. Victoria and Albert Museum (A.37.1970; illus. Pyke 1973, pl.276).

1775–80 Portraits by R.E. Pine, see NPG 82.

1776 Medal by John Kirk, commemorating Garrick's farewell to the stage on 10 June 1776 (Brown 1980, no.204). Exhibited SA 1776(221 and 223).

1776 Painting by Joshua Reynolds,* 'The Prologue Portrait', half length seated; a paper inscribed *The Prologue* before him. Private collection (Mannings 2000, no.705). Exhibited RA 1776(241).

Of many versions, one painted for Henry Thrale's library at Streatham House is in the Hyde Collection; another once belonging to Edmund Burke was in the Duke of Bedford's sale, Christie's, 19 January 1951, lot 132; a third painted for Topham Beauclerk is in an English private collection, and a fourth from the Lansdowne collection is in the Folger Shakespeare Library (Pressly 1993, no.121; Mannings 2000, no.706).

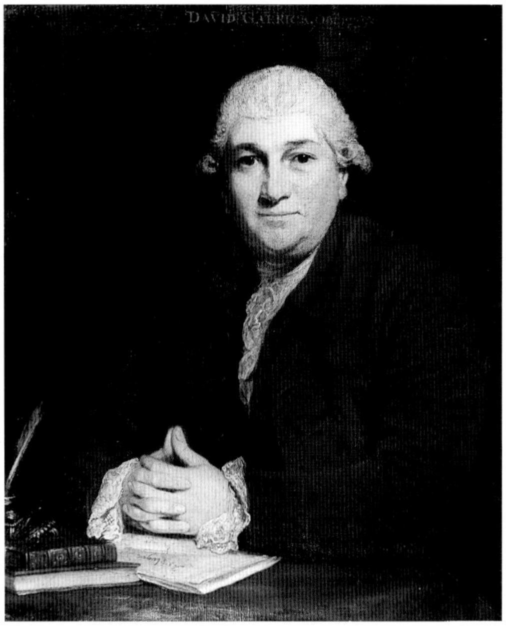

Garrick by Joshua Reynolds, 1776 (Private Collection)

Copies are in the Royal Collection (Millar 1969, no.1043), the Garrick Club (Ashton 1997, no.241), the Folger Shakespeare Library (Pressly 1993, no.122) and the Hereford City Museum. A bust-length miniature copy by Samuel Shelley dated 1777 was in the collection of Lord Churchill in 1883 (SSB 105/50a); another by Anne Lane, incorporating hair, is in the Garrick Club (Ashton 1997, no.235).

1777 Drawing by Edward Edwards, half-length oval, unfinished; signed and dated. Victoria and Albert Museum (F.61).

1777 Wedgwood medallion, see Nost 1762.

c.1777 Unattributed painting, half length, wearing a dark fur-trimmed coat. Huntington Art Collections, San Marino, Calif. (19.4; *Huntington* 2001, no.104).

c.1778 Drawing by E.F. Burney, whole-length seated, the head alone finished. British Museum (Ec 3.71).

1779 Painting by Benjamin Van der Gucht, exhibited RA 1779(334), as 'the last picture he sat for'. This reference has also been associated with a forlorn portrait in the Garrick Club (Ashton 1997, no.243).

1779 Carved gemstone by William Brown, exhibited RA 1779(27).

Undated Miniatures exhibited BFAC 1889(xix 8, attributed to G. Engleheart) lent J. Whitehead; BFAC 1889(xxxvi 73) and *Guelph* 1891(1912) lent J. Lumsden Propert, and *Guelph* 1891(720) lent the Earl of Carlisle.

Terracotta statuette of Garrick as Roscius, attributed to John Nost. Brighton MAG (illus. *CL*, CLV, 1974, p.260). Possibly the cast of *Garrick as Roscius* bought from Nost by Sir Watkin Williams Wynn in February 1778 (see *Georgian Playhouse* 1975, no.63), or the unattributed cast given by Mrs Garrick to George Garrard ARA, seen in Garrick's villa in 1825 (Smith 1905, p.290).

Wax medallion by E.M. Diemar. Private collection (Pyke 1973, p.39). Garrick frequently sat to 'Demar, the wax modeller, who did hundreds of profiles of him' (Smith 1920, II, p.207).

Anon. enamel medallion, Victoria and Albert Museum (414.1417.1885; illus. Rackham 1924, pl.45).

Posthumous

1779 Death mask. Department of Anatomy, Edinburgh University, from the Edinburgh Phrenological Society (*Death Masks and Life Masks*, Edinburgh University, [1988], p.11). Engraved R.E. Pine with the eyes added.

c.1782 Painting by George Carter,* *The Immortality of Garrick*, see Comparative Groups.

1785 Bust by Phillipson. Phillipson sale, Christie's, 12 December 1785.

c.1793 Marble bust by Richard Westmacott sr., Lichfield Cathedral (illus. 1851 ed. of Boswell's *Johnson*, III, p.250), placed near Westmacott's bust of Samuel Johnson which was installed 1793. Another in the Royal Collection (sent from Carlton House to Windsor in 1828, also with a companion bust of Johnson).

c.1793 Medallions at half a guinea and bustos at 7 shillings and 6 pence, by Charles Harris (advertised in his trade cat. of c.1793).

1797 Marble monument by Henry Webber in Westminster Abbey (illus. Whinney 1964, pl.130B).

1825 Portrait by W.S. Lethbridge, exhibited SBA 1825(496).

1826 Intaglio by C.H. Weigall, exhibited RA 1826(933).

1831 Bust by Lucius Gahagan. Garrick Head Hotel, Bath.

Portraits in Character

'The essence of Garrick's method was the direct communication of emotion which should be impressed on the whole body as well as the face. Communication was directed to the heart, and intensity was conveyed through highly expressive physiognomy and body-language, as can be glimpsed from Hogarth's painting of Garrick as Richard III.' (D. Bindman, *Roubiliac and the Eighteenth-century Monument*, 1995, pp.35-36).

1741 Painting by Thomas Bardwell, as Richard III in Shakespeare's *Richard III*. Russell-Cotes AG, Bournemouth (Kirby Talley 1978, no.54). A variant picture, then in the collection of the Earl of Clarendon, engraved J. Ogborne 1810.

c.1741 Pastel by Bartholomew Dandridge, as Richard III in Shakespeare's *Richard III*. Johnson Birthplace Museum, Lichfield.

c.1745 Painting by William Hogarth, as Richard III in Shakespeare's *Richard III*. Walker AG, Liverpool (634; illus. D. Bindman, *Hogarth*, 1981, p.108). Engraved by W. Hogarth and C. Grignion sr. 1746. Hogarth wrote of it: 'Painted from Mr Garrick big as the life, & ... sold for two hundred pounds on account of its likeness, which was the reason it was call'd Mr. Garrick in the Character of Richard the 3d - and not any body else' (Oppé 1950, p.63), but the 'constant and complete mobility' of Garrick's face caused him much difficulty; he attempted it several times, finally sewing in a face painted on a separate canvas (R. Paulson, *Hogarth*, 1992, II, p.250).

c.1747 Painting by Francis Hayman, as Ranger in Hoadly's *The Suspicious Husband*, with Mrs Pritchard as Clarinda. Yale Center for British Art (B1976.7.35; illus. Allen 1987, no.39, pl.viii). Replica in the Museum of London (illus. Highfill, VI, p.23).

1752 Painting by Thomas Worlidge, as Tancred in Thomson's *Tancred and Sigismunda*. Garrick Club (Ashton 1997, no.247). Engraved by Worlidge 1752. A bust-length version in the Theatre Museum (D.14; Ashton 1992, no.7) and a half-length version sold Christie's, New York, 25 March 1983, lot 159. Related drawings are in the Garrick Club (Ashton 1997, nos.238 and 248) and with the Royal Shakespeare Memorial Theatre, Stratford-upon-Avon.

1753 Painting by Benjamin Wilson, as Romeo, with Anne Bellamy as Juliet, in Shakespeare's *Romeo and Juliet*. Yale Center for British Art (B1975.5.29). Versions in the Theatre Museum (S.1452.1986; Ashton 1992, no.8) and at Stourhead. An etching by Wilson shows the half-length figure of Garrick from the larger composition.

1754 Engraving by J. McArdell from a painting by Benjamin Wilson, as Hamlet in Shakespeare's *Hamlet* (illus. Pressly 1993, p.234).

1760 Painting by Francis Hayman, as Richard III in Shakespeare's *Richard III*. National Theatre (Maugham Collection; Mander & Mitchenson 1980, no.2). Exhibited SA 1760(25). Copy by T. [but probably J.] Boultbee 1806, sold Christie's, 26 May 1989, lot 188.

1761 Engraving by J. McArdell from a painting by Benjamin Wilson, as Lear in Shakespeare's *King Lear*, with Havard and Bransby as Edgar and Kent (illus. Mander & Mitchenson 1957, p.44).

1762 Painting by Johann Zoffany, as the Farmer in *The Farmer's Return*, an interlude by Garrick, with Mary Bradshaw. Lord Lambton (illus. *Zoffany* 1977, no.10). Exhibited SA 1762(138). Studio versions in the Yale Center for British Art (B1981.25.731), and sold Christie's, 20 November 1981, lot 123.

1763 Painting by Johann Zoffany, as Jaffier in Otway's *Venice Preserv'd*, with Susanna Cibber as Belvidera. Lord Lambton (illus. *Georgian Playhouse* 1975, no.22). Exhibited SA 1763(137). Versions in the National Theatre (Maugham Collection; Mander & Mitchenson 1980, no.3), in the Garrick Club (Ashton 1997, no.252) and in the Museum of Fine Arts, Budapest.

1763-65 Painting by Johann Zoffany, as Sir John Brute in John Vanbrugh's *The Provok'd Wife*. Wolverhampton AG. Engraved J. Finlayson 1768. Exhibited SA 1765(167). Studio version with Lord Normanby, and a study for the figure of Garrick is in the National Theatre (Maugham Collection; Mander & Mitchenson 1980, no.6).

1764 Drawing by L-C. de Carmontelle as a tragic and comic actor. Musée Condé, Chantilly (illus. E. Wind 1986, *Hume and the Heroic Portrait*, 1986, pl.30).

1766 Painting by Johann Zoffany, as Lord Chalkstone in Garrick's *Lethe*, with Ackman and Bransby. Birmingham MAG (illus. Mander & Mitchenson 1955, p.20). Exhibited SA 1766(198). A version in the National Theatre (Maugham Collection; Mander & Mitchenson 1980, no.7), and there are three versions of the figure of Garrick alone: in the Garrick Club (Ashton 1997, no.250), formerly with W.H. Hearst (illus. Mander & Mitchenson 1955, p.22), and in a private collection.

1768 Painting by Joshua Reynolds, as Kitely, see NPG 4504.

1768 Painting by Johann Zoffany, as Macbeth in Shakespeare's *Macbeth*, with Mrs Pritchard. The Maharajah of Baroda. Version in the Garrick Club (Ashton 1997, no.253).

1769 Engraving by J. McArdell from a painting by Johann Zoffany, as the Auctioneer in Foote's *Taste*.

1770 Painting by Johann Zoffany, as Abel Drugger in Jonson's *The Alchymist*, with Burton and Palmer as Subtle and Face. Sotheby's 29 November 2001, lot 11, from Castle Howard (illus. *Zoffany* 1977, no.59). Exhibited RA 1770(212). Two studies for the figure of Garrick are in the Ashmolean Museum, Oxford; Garrick alone engraved J. Dixon 1791 (illus. Highfill, VI, p.12).

1771 Painting by Nathaniel Dance as Richard III in Shakespeare's *Richard III*. Stratford-upon-Avon Town Council (illus. *Dance* 1977, no.29). Exhibited RA 1771(54). Engraved by J. Dixon 1772, exhibited SA 1772(67), who also exhibited a drawing after Dance's figure SA 1772(66).

Of many copies, there are reduced versions in the Garrick Club (Ashton 1997, no.237, as by Henry Morland), the Folger Shakespeare Library (Pressly 1993, no.107), Northampton MAG, and in the National Theatre (Maugham Collection; Mander & Mitchenson 1980, no.12). A miniature version attributed to Dance, 'sketched from the pit', exhibited SKM 1865(2939) lent William Meyer.

1774 Painting by P-J. De Loutherbourg as Richard III in Shakespeare's *Richard III*, exhibited RA 1774(166). Photograph in the Emery Walker archive (NPG).

1774 Painting by P-J. De Loutherbourg as Don Juan in Beaumont and Fletcher's *The Chances*. Theatre Museum (D.70; Ashton 1992, no.9). Exhibited RA 1774(163). A watercolour dated 1774 in the Victoria and Albert Museum (P.46.1935). One of several reduced versions is in the Garrick Club (Ashton 1997, no.236).

DOUBTFUL PORTRAITS

See NPG 6249 note 5. Paintings by Nathaniel Dance (Christie's, 18 June 1954, lot 154); called Gainsborough (Phillips, 24 November 1998, lot 7); attributed to Nathaniel Hone (Sotheby's, 12 July 1989, lot 52); attributed to P. Longhi, *Garrick in the Green Room* (Lady Lever AG, Port Sunlight, LL 3526); by J.B. Van Loo (National Theatre; Maugham Collection). Silhouette in the Scottish NPG (PG 1449).

With Mrs Garrick: unattributed painting c.1760, (Royal Shakespeare Collection, on loan to the Victoria and Albert Museum, RSC.6.2001); miniature by James Scouler (Victoria and Albert Museum; P.5.1951).

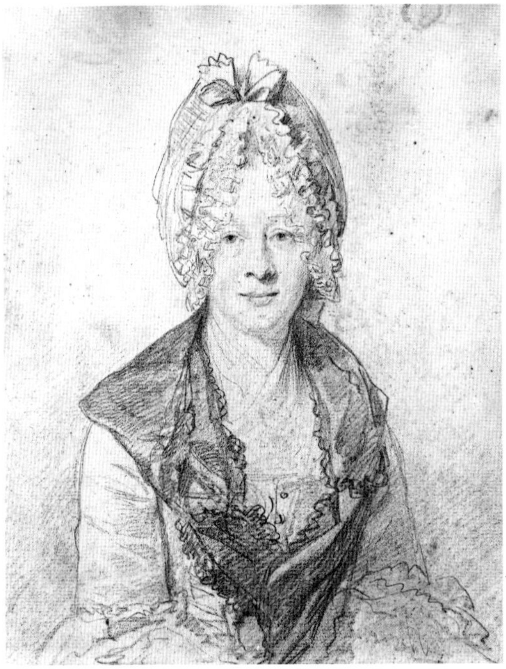

Mrs GARRICK NPG *3640*

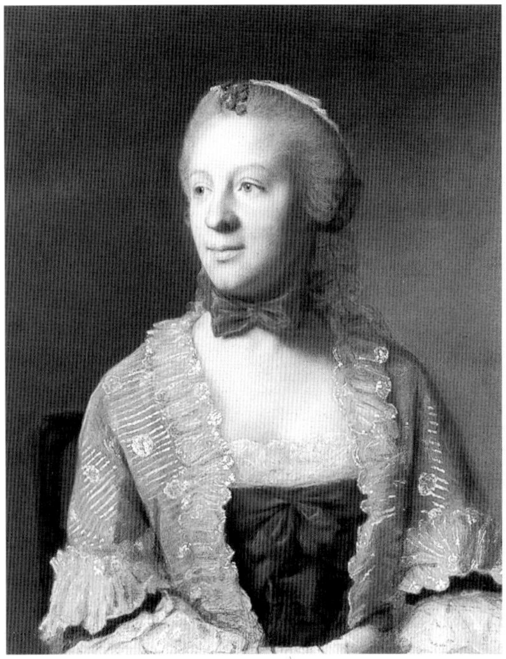

Mrs GARRICK by J-E. Liotard 1751 (Chatsworth)

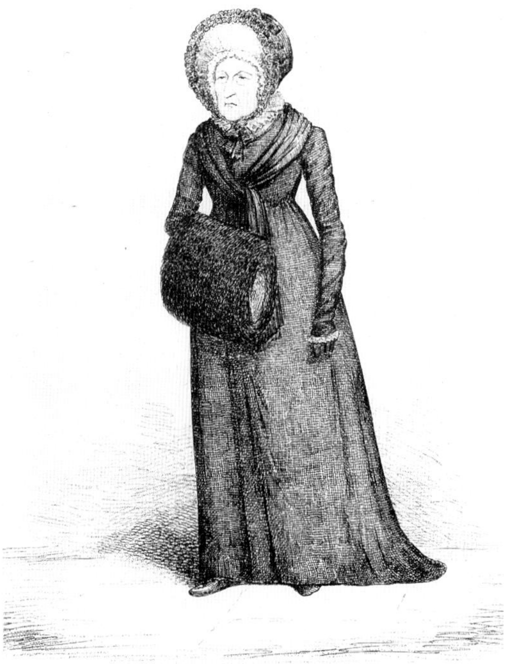

Mrs GARRICK drawn and etched by I.R. Cruikshank 1820 (British Museum)

GARRICK, Mrs Eva Maria, *née* Veigel 1724-1822

Dancer; b. Vienna, came to England 1746 and performed as Madame Violette, patronised by the Earl and Countess Burlington; her professional career ended with her marriage to David Garrick 1749; she retained a Teutonic accent and, according to Mrs Delany, seemed 'never to depart from a perfect propriety of behaviour, accompanied with good sense and gentleness of manners.'

3640 NATHANIEL DANCE 1771

Pencil on paper 13.6 x 11.4 (5⅜ x 4½)

Collections: see NPG 3639 David Garrick; stolen 1968.

Engraving: see NPG 3639 David Garrick.

See NPG 3639, the companion drawing of David Garrick.

5375 JOSHUA REYNOLDS, *with David Garrick* 1772-73, see David Garrick

ICONOGRAPHY

See also the *Harvard Catalogue*, II, p.107, and Highfill, VI, pp.111-12.

pre-1749 Pastel attributed to William Hoare, of which there are two versions: Sotheby's, 14 July 1994, lot 75, descended from Garrick's niece, Arabella Garrick (Mrs Schaw); Chatsworth (where attributed to George Knapton), presumably descended from the Earl and Countess of Burlington.

1749 Anon. engraving, half length as *Mademoiselle Violetti* (*London Mag.*, a pendant to an engraving of the Pond portrait of her husband).

1751 Pastel by J-E. Liotard,* half length. Chatsworth. Drawn in Paris, with pendant of her husband.

1753-55 Pastel by Katherine Read, half length. Victoria and Albert Museum (P.10.1963; illus. Archer 1979, p.119), by descent from Arabella Garrick. Engraved W. Sherlock 1802; a drawing in the Garrick Club (Ashton 1997, no.254) is closer to the engraving than the pastel (illus. Highfill, VI, p.110). A half-length painting derived from the Read pattern was listed at Tockenham Manor as a pendant to Gainsborough's 1770 portrait of David Garrick (Duleep Singh 1928, II, p.420, no.47).

1757 Painting by William Hogarth,* with her husband, see David Garrick.

c.1760 Painting unconvincingly attributed to Johann Zoffany, half length. Robinson & Fisher, 7 May 1914, lot 110, descended from Arabella Garrick (illus. *Garrick Letters* 1963, I, f.p.117), probably correctly identified.

c.1760? Pastel by F-X. Vispré. Bromley-Davenport sale, Sotheby's, 11 June 1947, lot 3 with a pendant of David Garrick.

1762 Paintings by Johann Zoffany, with her husband, see David Garrick.

1771 Drawing by Nathaniel Dance, see NPG 3640.

1772 Wax medallion by Lewis Pingo, exhibited FS 1772(153), see *Wal. Soc.*, XXVII, 1939, p.75.

1772-73 Painting by Joshua Reynolds,* with her husband, see David Garrick NPG 5375.

1795 Miniature by George Engleheart, sold Sotheby's, 28 April 1988, lot 48 (Williamson 1902, pp.30, 98).

1820 Drawing by I.R. Cruikshank, small whole length, dated September 1820; etched by him* on her death in October 1822.

DOUBTFUL PORTRAITS

While apparently sharing the early provenance of Gainsborough's portrait of David Garrick NPG

5054, a portrait called Mrs Garrick by Gainsborough in the Grand Rapids Art Museum, Michigan (exhibited *Art Treasures*, Manchester, 1857, BPG 285; sale Christie's, 16 June 1900, lot 106), appears to be by Nathaniel Hone and not to show Mrs Garrick; a miniature copy by Horace Hone dated 1771 sold Christie's, 28 October 1980, lot 86.

Attributed to Gainsborough (private collection; Waterhouse 1958, no.308). Miniature by Luke Sullivan 1761, sold Bonham's, 20 November 1997, lot 63; unattributed portraits in the Garrick Club (Ashton 1997, nos.255-56), with two unattributed wax busts (Garrick Club; Ashton 1997, S14, S17).

See also Doubtful Portraits under David Garrick.

GEORGE III 1738-1820

King of Great Britain and Ireland; 1st s. of Frederick, Prince of Wales (d.1751); cr. Prince of Wales 20 April 1751; suc. his grandfather as King 25 October 1760; m. 8 September 1761 Princess Charlotte Sophia of Mecklenburg-Strelitz; d. 29 January 1820 (eleven weeks after his Queen).

'a tall, well-built man, in later life inclining to stoutness, with a good leg. ... The most prominent features of his face were a high forehead, protruding eyes, a large nose, thick lips, and a dimpled chin. ... His complexion was ruddy. His face was not handsome but he had a steady and open expression which commanded respect. ... He cared little for clothes or for fashion, and dressed much the same as an old man as he had when young' (John Brooke, 1974).

'in the flower and bloom of youth George had a handsome, open and honest countenance; and with the favour that attends outward accomplishments of his age, he had none of those vices that fall under the censure of those who are past enjoying them themselves.' (Horace Walpole, *Memoirs of George III*).

1165 RICHARD WILSON, *as Prince George, with his brother Prince Edward (1739-67) and tutor Dr Francis Ayscough (1700-63)* c.1749

See Kerslake *Early Georgian*, I, pp.9-11, II, pl.39.

The reduced version listed by Kerslake in the collection of Mrs Thomas Parrington is now in the Yale Center for British Art (B1981.25.689); another is in the Tate Gallery (N 1880). John Faber engraved the figure of Prince George alone in 1751, the year he became Prince of Wales (reversed, and wearing a richly-decorated coat, illus. W.G. Constable, *Richard Wilson*, 1953, pl.7b).

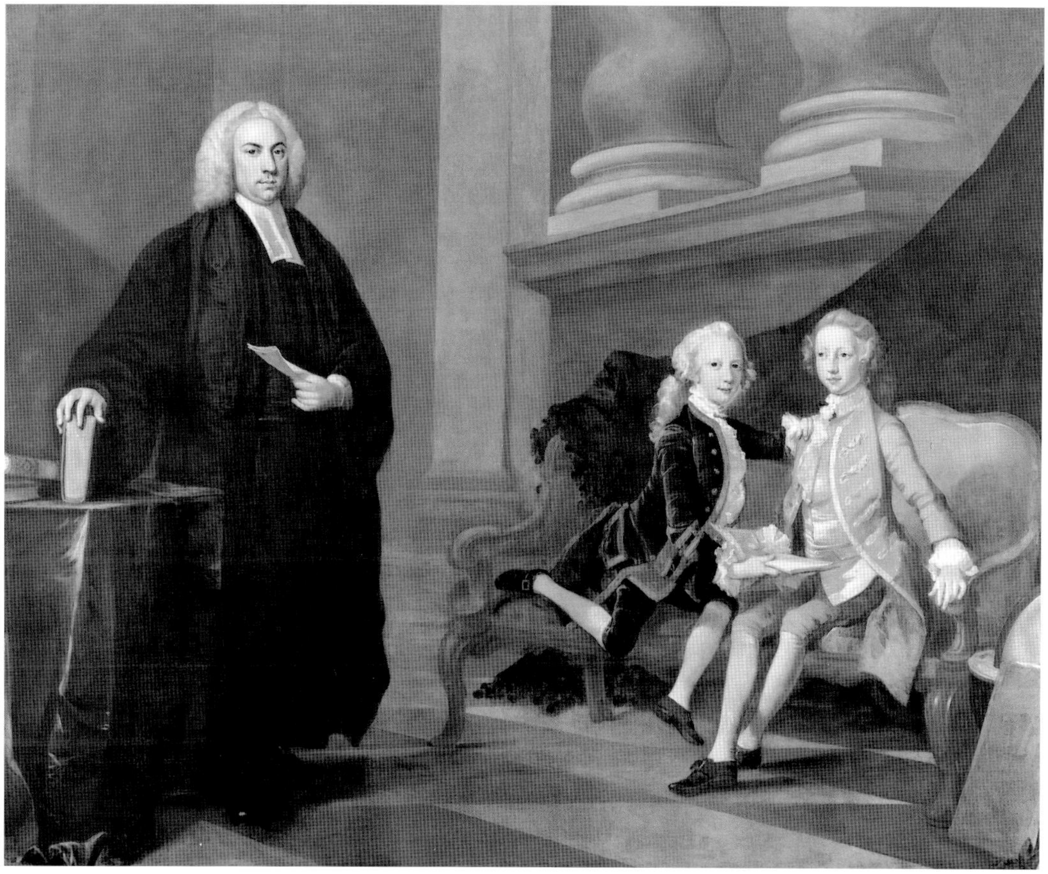

GEORGE III as Prince of Wales (right) with his brother Prince Edward and their tutor Dr Francis Ayscough NPG 1165

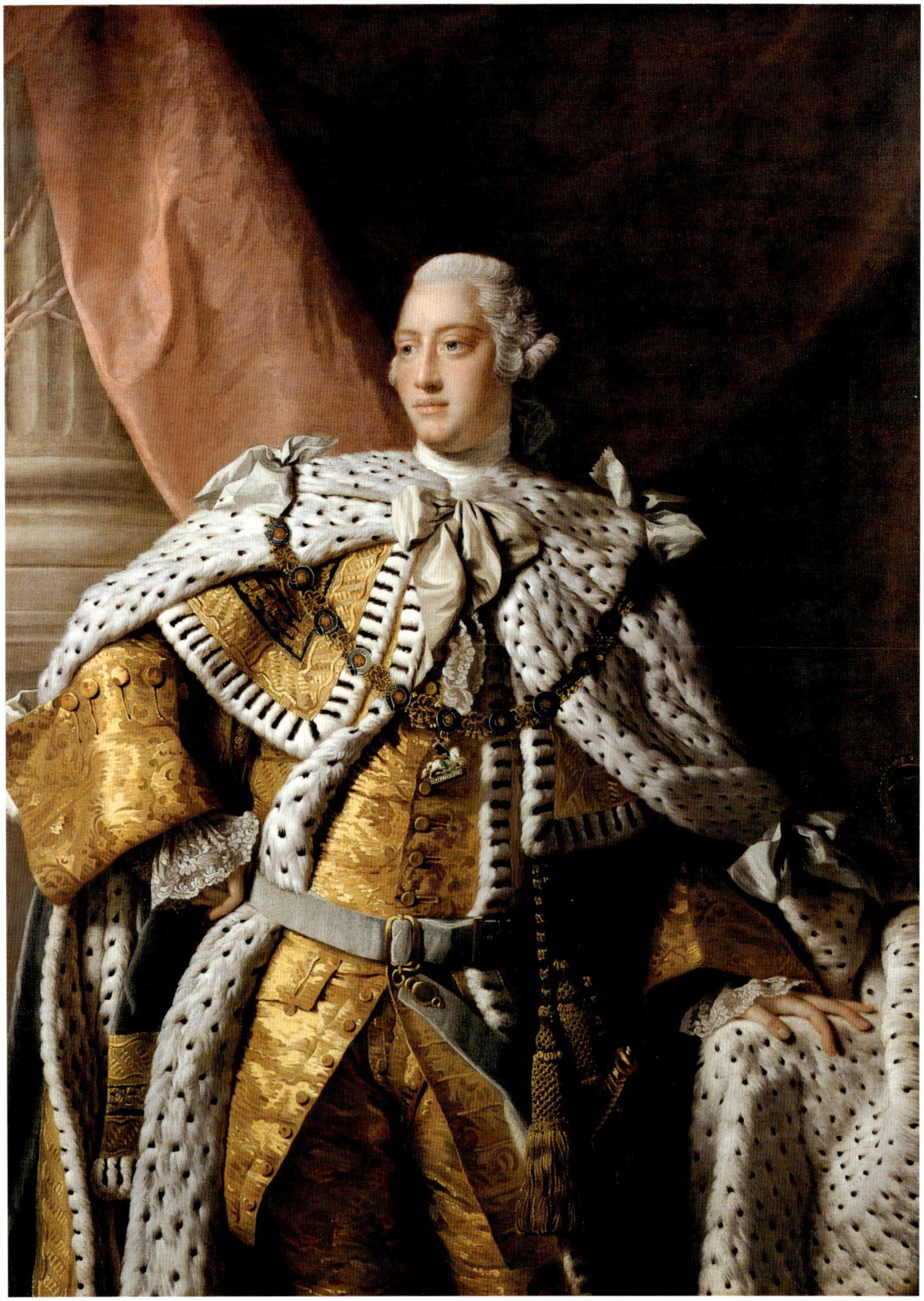

GEORGE III NPG *223*

223 studio of ALLAN RAMSAY [1761–62]

Canvas 146 x 108 (57½ x 42½) lined.

Blue eyes, white powdered hair, in coronation robes over a damask-patterned gold suit with a blue-grey sword belt, wearing the Collar of the Garter; a pink curtain behind him.

Collections: Purchased from J. McLachlan 1866.

Exhibitions: *Scottish Art*, RA, 1939(63); *The Past We Share*, Dallas, 1967(15); *Treasures* 1995–96(13).

Reference: Smart 1999, no.192fg.

A reduced studio version of Ramsay's celebrated whole-length coronation portrait which he was working on in December 1761 and had finished by March 1762, when Walpole commented it had been 'painted exactly from the very robes which the king wore at his coronation. The gold stuff and ermine are highly finished; rather too much for the head does not come out as it ought'.[1] The original portrait remains in the Royal Collection[2] and was engraved by W.W. Ryland in 1767. There are good early whole-length versions, for example, in the Archbishop's Palace at Armagh, Stratfield Saye, and the Guildhall Art Gallery (38).

Ramsay was to be concerned with the replication of his coronation portraits of the King and Queen (see NPG 224) for the rest of his life. Copies were required by the Privy Purse for the Royal residences and by the Lord Chamberlain for 'Nobility Ambassadors and Governors of Provinces', which then included the American colonies. Records survive of one hundred and seventy portraits of the King and one hundred and fifty of the Queen; nearly one hundred of each are known today.[3] Although Ramsay told Lord Bute in 1762 that he intended 'to give the last painting to all of them',[4] his resolution proved impractical; 'portraits of His Majesty in every stage of their operation' came to crowd his studio, eagerly sought by 'distant corporations and transmarine colonies' so that 'with all the assistance he could procure he could by no means satisfy the diurnal demands'.[5] These assistants included David Martin, the young Philip Reinagle, J.G. Eccardt and George Roth, but it is impossible to distinguish their hands; NPG 223 and NPG 224, good early studio versions, were probably finally touched by Ramsay himself.

Ramsay's portraits were distributed until his death in 1784, by which time the King's age had doubled from twenty-three to forty-six, and there are rare examples of a 1771 Zoffany head being grafted on to a Ramsay body.[6] Ramsay also painted two half-length profile portraits of the King wearing Court and informal dress, see below c.1761–62.

1 Walpole *Anecdotes* V, p.56.
2 Millar 1969, no.996; Smart 1999, no.192.
3 Cf. J. Simon, *Burl. Mag.*, CXXXVI, 1994, pp.451–55; Smart 1999, pp.88–90, 111–21.
4 Yale University Library, Tinker cat., no.1707 (quoted Smart 1999, p.112).
5 J. Moser, *European Mag.*, LXIV, 1813, p.516.
6 Smart 1999, no.192fc (Sotheby's, 13 November 1996, lot 44).

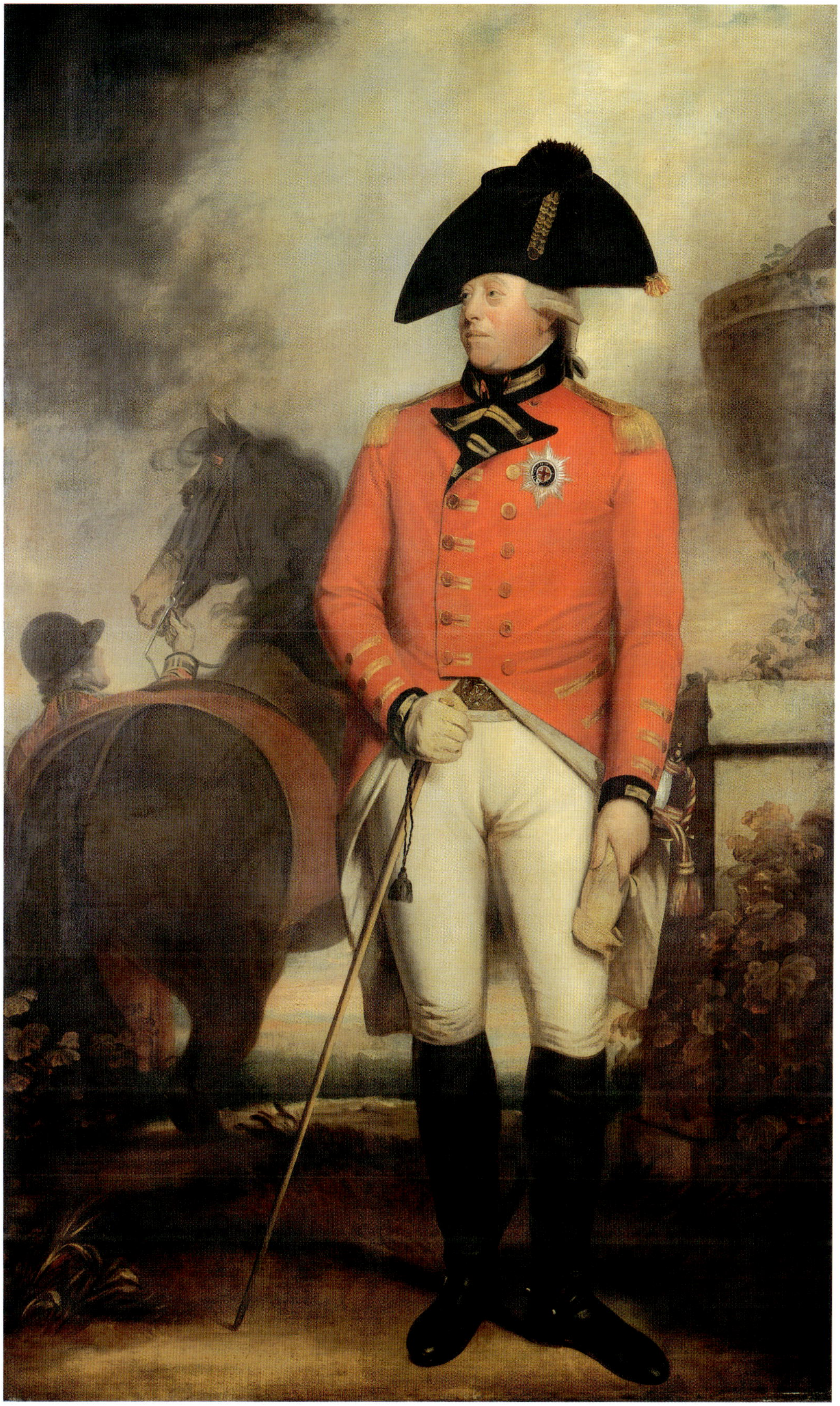

GEORGE III NPG 2502

2502 studio of WILLIAM BEECHEY [1799–1800]

Canvas 237 x 147 (93½ x 58) lined; the surface slightly rubbed and the varnish somewhat discoloured; two repaired damages in the lower left area.

Wearing the red coat with the star of the Garter and white breeches of a General Officer.

Collections: George, Duke of Cambridge; his sale Christie's, 11 June 1904, lot 52 (unattributed); Miss Lillie Belle Randell, by whom bequeathed 1931 in memory of her sister, Mrs Cornelius Garrison (d.1925).[1]

Exhibitions: War Office, 1931–41; *Meet the Family*, Welsh Arts Council, 1972–73(25); *George III*, Yorktown, Va., 1977; Cumberland Lodge, Windsor, 1984–; *Act of Union Bicentenary*, Belfast, 2001.

A thinly painted studio version of Beechey's whole length portrait in the Royal Collection,[2] exhibited RA 1800(69). It omits the soldiers in the mid-distance, but shows the large ornate garden urn in the right foreground, now invisible in the Royal Collection picture, but which appears in the engraving by Benjamin Smith published in 1804.[3] Other whole-length versions show variations in the background: one at Hatfield includes Hatfield House; a distant view of Windsor Castle appears in a three-quarter length version sold American Art Association, 3 February 1938, lot 67,[4] and a different view of the Castle appears in a version sold Christie's, 17 June 1966, lot 102; a reduced whole length, with an equestrian statue in the background, is in the National Maritime Museum (BHC 2711), and a version, formerly with Major E. Christie-Miller, shows the King wearing the blue uniform of Royal Horse Guards.[5]

Half-length versions, besides NPG 6250 (below), include those at the Deakin University Museum of Art, Malvern, New South Wales; the National Library of Australia, Canberra; the Royal College of Physicians, London,[6] and in the Weymouth Museum.

A fine whole-length enamel copy dated 1801 by Henry Bone,[7] together with a bust length of 1801,[8] are in the Royal Collection, with other miniature versions by Richard Collins, Samuel Cotes and William Grimaldi.[9]

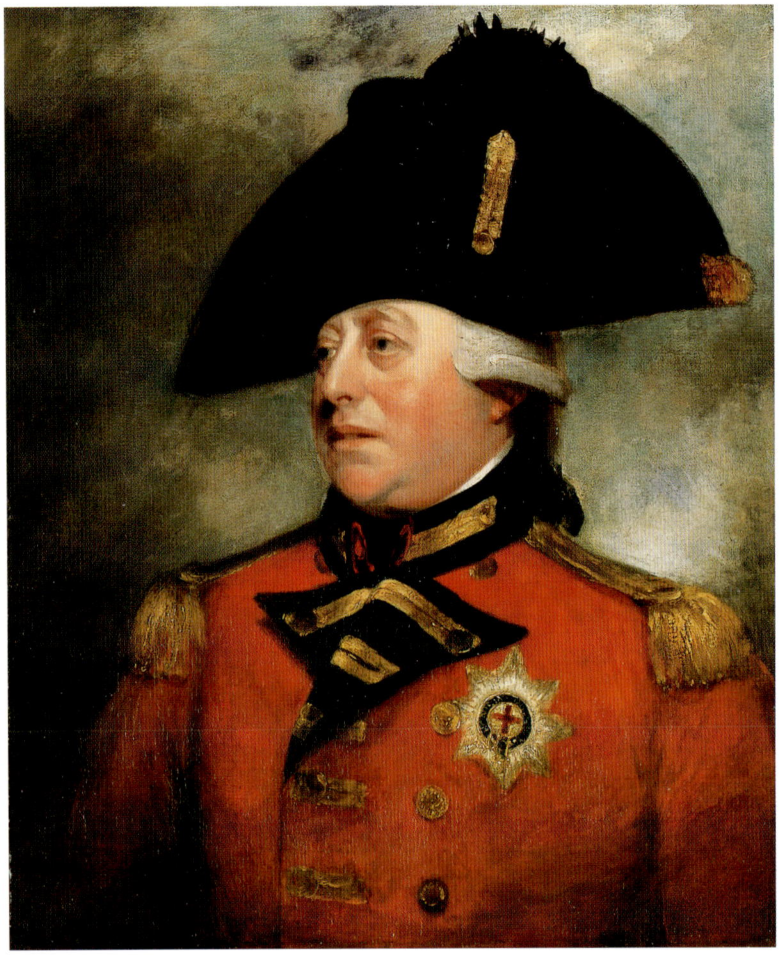

GEORGE III NPG *6250*

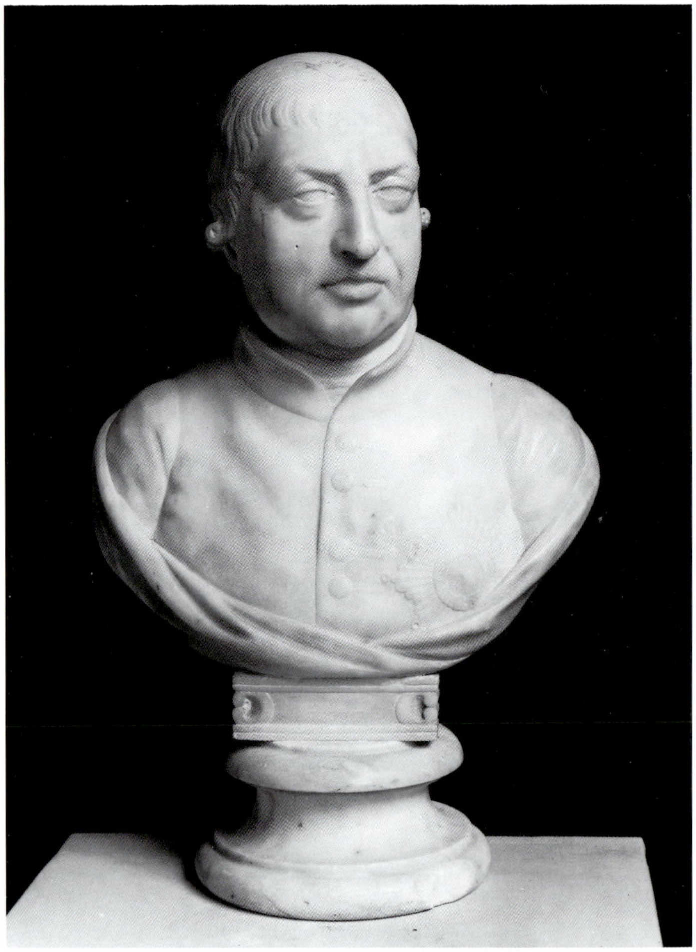

GEORGE III NPG *3903*

1 An ink label verso suggests Mrs Garrison (see Newcastle NPG 2504 note) may have bought the picture after the Cambridge sale: *Mrs L.W. Garrison - W.1 King George 3rd by Sir Wm Beechey from the collection of H.R.H. the Duke of Cambridge 13/8/04 P206.*
2 Millar 1969, no.658.
3 Several half-length plates were engraved between 1804 and 1820; O'Donoghue, II, p.301, lists ten.
4 Illus. Roberts 1907, f.p.106. Another three-quarter length version is at Schloss Greinburg.
5 Another reduced copy belongs to the Prince of Hanover.
6 Illus. *Cat. of Portraits*, 1977, p.119.
7 Preparatory drawing in NPG Bone albums (*Bone* 1999, no.216).
8 Walker 1992, nos.744-45. A half-length enamel by Henry Bone sold Christie's, 6 July 1965, lot 33.
9 Walker 1992, nos.169, 205, 811-12, 323-24. Other miniature versions include half-lengths by Grimaldi (cf. Grimaldi 1873, pp.8, 9, 23, 32) and by S.G. [S. Cotes?], dated 1807 (Bonham's, 12 July 1993, lot 195).

6250 studio of WILLIAM BEECHEY [1799-1800]

Canvas 75.5 x 63.5 (29¾ x 25) lined; surface cleaned 1994.

Grey eyes, white powdered hair, wearing the uniform of a general officer with the bdge of the Garter.

Collections:[1] Presented by the artist to the Royal Female Orphanage, 1809; Shaftesbury Society; Leggatt, 1970; the 5th Baron Kenyon, by whom bequeathed 1993.

A bust-length version of the Beechey whole-length, see NPG 2502 above; a competent head is supported by the most pedestrian body.

1 Label on the back of the frame reads: *Presented by the Artist to the Royal Female Orphanage (of wh. The DK of Wellington was a Patron) 1809. From the Collection of the Shaftesbury Society / Leggatt Bros. 6/1970.*

3903 PETER TURNERELLI 1809

Marble bust 43 (17) high; incised at back of base: *P. Turnerelli / Fecit 1809.*

Collections: Purchased from Herman Hornek, London, 1954.

An example of the Jubilee bust, marking the fiftieth anniversary of the King's accession. Turnerelli, sculptor in ordinary to the Royal Family since 1801, received sittings from the King in 1809 and exhibited the original bust at the RA 1810(883); Benjamin West had recommended contemporary dress 'as it appeared to him an erroneous idea, to dress every bust in the habit of a Roman senator'.[1] According to the *European Magazine* it was 'universally admired' and Turnerelli 'had nearly eighty copies to execute in marble, for the nobility and several of the principal corporate bodies of the empire, seven of which were expressly ordered by the Royal Family'.[2] A small model 'of the National Bust' was shown at the RA 1812(908) and dated examples include those at Lancaster House (1810; GAC 2673), Frogmore and the City Art Centre, Edinburgh (1812), Penicuik (1813), Apsley House (1814), and the Huntington Art Collections, San Marino, Calif. (1815); an undated bust is in the Victoria and Albert Museum (A.62.1965).

1 *European Mag.*, LXXIX, 1821, i, p.393; the article illus. with an engraving after Samuel Drummond of Turnerelli with the Jubilee bust.
2 *Ibid.*, p.389.

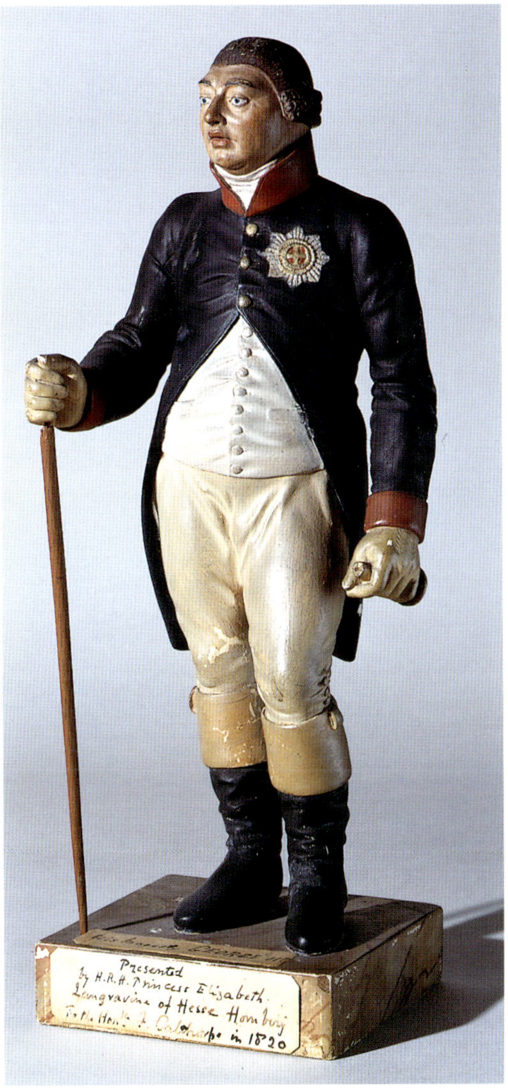

GEORGE III *NPG 4383*

4383 FRANCIS HARDENBERG 1820

Painted plaster statuette 28 (11) high, on a marbled wooden base; the paint is rubbed on the coat and there are small losses on the breeches, gloves and boots; a label on the back of the base reads: *Pubd. May 8th 1820, by / F. Hardenberg, 19 Mount St. / Grosvenor Sqre. London.*

Blue eyes, dark wig, wearing the Windsor uniform of a dark blue coat with red collar and cuffs, white waistcoat and breeches; a glass in his left hand and a (separate) stick in his right.

Collections: *His Majesty GEORGE III Presented / By H.R.H. Princess Elizabeth / Langravina of Hesse Homberg / To the Honble. F. Calthorpe*[1] *in 1820* (label verso); presented by E. Bullivant through the National Art Collections Fund 1964.

Published within three months of the King's death; another example of this statuette is in the Athenaeum. Hardenberg also exhibited a marble bust of the King in 1820, and a closely comparable statuette was made by Lucius Gahagan in 1811, see below.

1 Frederick Calthorpe (1790–1868), later 4th Baron Calthorpe

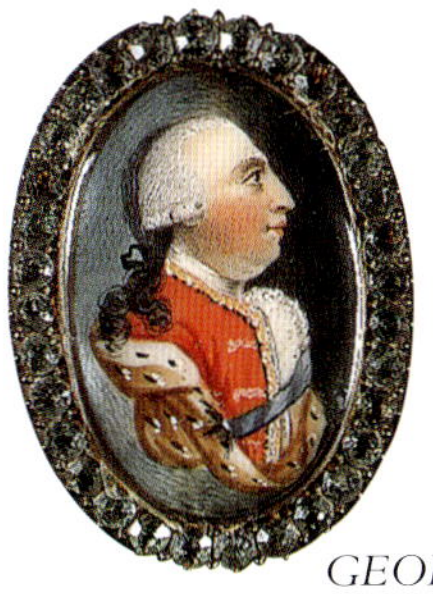

GEORGE III *NPG 6288*

6288 UNKNOWN ARTIST C.1809

Watercolour and bodycolour on ivory 3 x 1.9 (⅞ x ¾); signed [?] below left [*GJ*]?.[1] The locket case engraved verso: *George 3 / was born 4.June 1738. / ascended the British Throne / 25 Octr. 1760. / The / Grand National Jubilee / celebrated 25. Octr. 1809*

Dark eyes, white powdered wig, improbably giving way to a black queue; red cloak trimmed with ermine and gold, with the blue ribbon of the Garter.

Collections: Hon Frederic H.A. Wallop (d.1953), by whom lent to the Victoria and Albert Museum; his nephew Alan Evans, by whom bequeathed to the National Gallery 1974; lent to the NPG until permanently transferred in 1994.

Exhibition: Gillray, Tate, 2001(100c).

The inscribed case may imply NPG 6288 was produced for the 1809 Jubilee, but it has somewhat the air of a caricature and ultimately derives from such accessible sources as the Wedgwood medallion of 1776 or the medal by J.G. Hancock of 1801 (see below). A comparable bust appears in an unattributed miniature in the Draper Gift, Kenwood.[2]

1 This has been associated with James Gillray, which seems unlikely.
2 *Miniatures at Kenwood*, 1997, no.33.

ICONOGRAPHY

The principal surveys of George III's iconography are contained in the catalogues of the Royal Collection (Millar 1963 and 1969 and Walker 1992). The following list includes the more important images of the King as well as those portraits which appeared in contemporary exhibitions, but cannot claim to be comprehensive; history pieces and satires are generally omitted, and the two hundred and fifty contemporary medals are treated with discrimination.

As Prince George 1739–51

1739 Painting by J.B. Van Loo, with his mother Augusta, Princess of Wales. Royal Collection (Millar 1963, no.538, pl.191).

c.1742 Painting attributed to George Knapton, *The Children of Frederick, Prince of Wales*, including Prince George as Cupid. Royal Collection (Millar 1963, no.577).

c.1744 Unattributed drawing, seated on the floor reading. Royal Collection (Oppé 1950, no.713, fig.60).

1746 Painting by Barthélemy du Pan, with his brothers and sisters. Royal Collection (Millar 1963, no.572, pl.213). Engraved J. Faber, T. Ryley.

c.1749 Painting by Richard Wilson, see NPG 1165.

c.1750 Unattributed painting, whole-length standing in rich blue costume with Garter ribbon. Schloss Greinburg.

As Prince of Wales 1751–60

1751 Painting by George Knapton, whole length with his mother, brothers and sisters. Royal Collection (Millar 1963, no.573, pl.212). The figure of the Prince of Wales repeated in a separate painting, presumably by George Knapton, in the Victoria and Albert Museum (W.35.1972).

A drawing by Knapton in the Huntington Art Collections, San Marino, Calif., shows the Prince with his brother Edward, Duke of York, and Simon, 1st Earl Harcourt (their tutor 1751–52).

1752 Wax by Isaac Gosset (Vertue, III, p.160).

1753 Miniature by J-E. Liotard, in red coat with the ribbon and star of the Garter. Christie's, 21 October 1997, lot 14.

1754 Engraving by J. McArdell after David Luders, bust length with the ribbon and star of the Garter.

c.1754 Pastel by J-E. Liotard, half length. Royal Collection (Millar 1963, no.581, pl.215). Miniature versions in the Royal Collection (Walker 1992, no.729), the Dutch Royal Collection dated 1754 (illus. Foskett 1972, II, pl.212, no.533) and with the Prince of Hanover. A copy in enamel by Henry Bone dated 1818 is in the Royal Collection (Walker 1992, no.743) and his preparatory drawing, dated 1811, is in the NPG Bone albums (*Bone* 1999, no.215, fig.130). Related versions include a pastel at Wykeham Abbey, and paintings at Cairnbulg Castle and the Royal Collection (a bust-length oval; Millar 1969, no.1216).

1755 Engravings by B. Baron and G. Bockman after J.A. Adolphe, on horseback with ribbon and star of

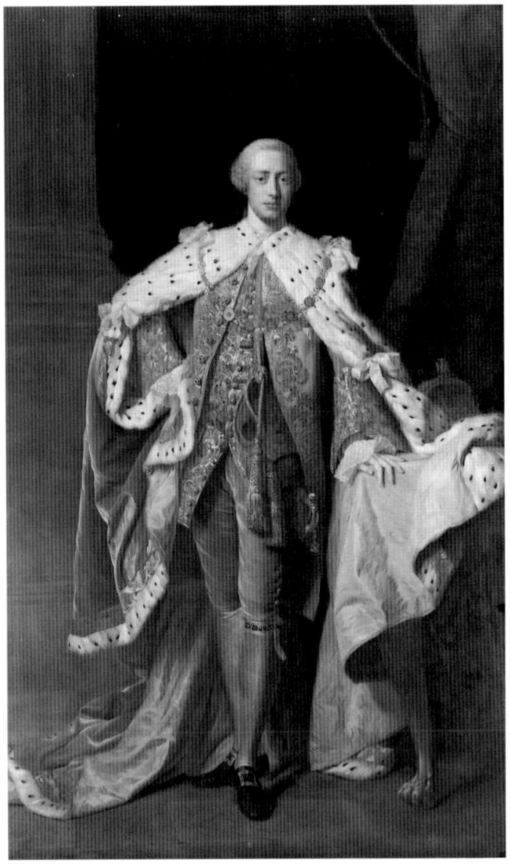

GEORGE III by Allan Ramsay 1757-58 (Private Collection)

the Garter. Drawing by Bernard Baron sold Sotheby's, 16 November 1989, lot 35.

1757-58 Painting by Allan Ramsay,* whole length in robes of state. Private collection, commissioned by the Earl of Bute (Smart 1999, no.191). Engraved W.W. Ryland 1761. Versions at Marlborough House and, reduced, at Ickworth and the Bank of England. Miniature adaptations include one attributed to Jeremiah Meyer in the Royal Collection (Walker 1992, no.249) and another attributed to Gervase Spencer, sold Christie's, 3 July 1996, lot 60, and Sotheby's, 28 April 1999, lot 313. A three-quarter length mezzotint by R. Houston also derives from this type.

1757-60 Engraving by H.J. Tyroff after Richard Wilson, half length, with ribbon and star of the Garter (illus. W.G. Constable, *Richard Wilson*, 1953, pl.7a).

1759 Painting by Joshua Reynolds, three-quarter length with ermine-trimmed cloak and the ribbon of the Garter. Royal Collection (Millar 1969, no.1011; Mannings 2000, no.715). The head appears to be derived from the Liotard of c.1754.

1759 Drawn and engraved by Jonathan Spilsbury, bust length, *from an original painting in the possession of Thos Jefferys*, published June 1759. Reissued, with added ribbon and star of the Garter, as George III.

1759 Medal by Thomas Pingo, celebrating the majority of the Prince of Wales (Eimer 1998, no.13). Exhibited FS 1761(153). Portrait re-used for further medals in 1760-62 (see Brown 1980, nos.1, 3, 30, 71, 82; Eimer 1998, nos.16-19, 27).

c.1760 Painting by Henry Morland, half length with Garter ribbon. Engraved R. Houston as Prince of Wales, a later state as George III (also used for the King's Address, 18 November 1760); a three-quarter length version engraved J.E. Nilson.

As King 1760-1820

George succeeded to the throne on 25 October 1760; he married Princess Charlotte of Mecklenburg-Strelitz [see Charlotte] on 8 September 1761 and they were crowned on 22 September. Over fifty medals were struck celebrating the Royal marriage and the coronation, including those by John Kirk, J. Abraham, J.U. Hans, J.L. Natter, E. Thomason and T. Ward (see Brown 1980, nos.10-19, 21-26, 28, 29, 31-64).

1760 Miniature profile bust by Jeremiah Meyer, believed to have been drawn from memory, set in a pearl bracelet and sent to Princess Charlotte in Strelitz as an engagement present (Walker 1992, fig.20). Queen Charlotte wears this miniature in her portraits by Matthieu 1762, attributed to Zoffany c.1766, Zoffany 1771, West 1776, Lawrence 1789 and Beechey 1796 (see Charlotte). Two other versions by Meyer are in the Royal Collection, one dated 1767 (Walker 1992, nos.250-51) and another, also set in a ring, is in the British Museum (Hull Grundy 1984, no.311). A comparable profile by Meyer, resembling the Pingo medal of 1759, engraved in 1761 by J. McArdell, I. Simson, and as *C. Spooner delint. et fecit.*

Studies by Meyer for a portrait of the King are in the Meyer Album in the Ashmolean Museum, Oxford (1361; Brown 1982, p.461). In 1761 Meyer was awarded a Gold Medal by the Society for the Encouragement of Arts for the best drawing of a profile of the King, for the purpose of having a dye cast from it (E. Edwards, *Anecdotes of Painters*, 1808, p.159; Walker 1992, p.xv).

1760 Medals celebrating the King's accession by John Kirk (Brown 1980, no.4) and see 1759 Thomas Pingo.

c.1760-62 Unattributed pastel, profile bust to right. The Prince of Hanover. A pair of unattributed pastels of the King and Queen, the latter resembling the Ramsay type, is in the same collection.

c.1760-65 Paintings by David Morier, equestrian portraits of the King attending military reviews, of slight iconographic worth.

Morier exhibited SA 1762(71) a portrait of the King on a brown horse attended by the Marquess of Granby and other Officers; four of his portraits are in the Royal Collection (Millar 1969, nos.952-955) and others include those sold Christie's, 12 July 1991, lot 11; Bonham's, Knightsbridge, 6 July 1995, lot 182, and Sotheby's, 25 November 1998, lot 34.

1761 'A profile drawn from Memory' by Henry Morland, exhibited SA 1761(72).

1761 Model in wax by Spang, exhibited SA 1761(161).

1761 Models in wax by Isaac Gosset exhibited SA 1761(147) and FS 1761(100). A Wedgwood medallion after Gosset (illus. Reilly 1973, p.163) was probably taken from one of these. Undated wax by Gosset in the Victoria and Albert Museum (A.57.1970). See also under 1774 and 1776.

1761-62 Painting by Allan Ramsay, whole length in coronation robes, see NPG 223.

c.1761 Painting by Francis Hayman, whole length in coronation robes, painted for the annexe to the Rotunda at Vauxhall Gardens; listed in the proposed Vauxhall sale, 15-16 June 1840 (Allen 1987, p.172).

c.1761 Enamel miniature attributed to Francis Sykes, with ribbon of the Garter. Royal Collection (Walker 1992, no.312). Engraved J. Basire; J. Miller (reversed) 1761. Derived from a mezzotint medallion by J.J. Haid, published shortly after the coronation.

c.1761-62 Painting by Allan Ramsay, half length profile with the star of the Garter. Private collection, commissioned by the Earl of Bute (Smart 1999, no.193).

A similar half-length by Ramsay painted c.1762-63, differing in having a richly-embroidered red coat, is in a private collection (Smart 1999, no.194). Engraved R. Houston, J. Watson and W. Woollett. Versions include examples at St John's College, Oxford (Poole, III, p.184), the Salisbury Guildhall, and a miniature derivation in the Royal Collection (Walker 1992, no.319).

1762 Painting by Andrea Casali, as Augustus, exhibited FS 1762(45).

1762 Engraving by W. Pether after an *ad vivum* drawing by Thomas Frye, see Charlotte (CS 17-18), bust length, with quilted coat and the collar of the Garter. The companion plate of the Queen engraved by Frye himself. Half-length portraits which may be ascribed to Frye, sold Christie's, 19 December 1975, lot 136, and Sotheby's, 8 November 1978, lot 215.

1762 'A head in crayons', by Henry Morland, exhibited SA 1762(72).

1762 Painting by John Miller, 'a head', exhibited SA 1762 (190).

1762 Miniature by Henry Millington, with ribbon and star of the Garter, dated. Royal Collection (Walker 1992, no.284). Presumably that exhibited by Millington FS 1762(114).

1762 Medal by Thomas Pingo, celebrating the birth of the Prince of Wales, with facing bust of the Queen (Brown 1980, no.77; Eimer 1998, no.26).

1763 Model in profile by Lewis Pingo, 'from the life', exhibited FS 1763(161), probably to be associated with the Pingo wax in the British Museum (1993.5.47.1; cf. Eimer 1998, no.144).

c.1763 Painting by John Shackleton, three-quarter length in robes of state. Guildhall, Lincoln. Probably the portrait exhibited FS 1763(200). Shackleton remained the King's Painter until his death in 1767, although Ramsay, whom the King called 'his Painter', effectively filled that office.

1764 Marble bust by John Nost jr. Yale Center for British Art (B1977.14.22).

A bronze statue by Nost, formerly in the City Hall, Dublin, was presented in 1765 (described by Thackeray as 'a pert statue ... in a Roman toga simpering and turning out his toes'; Strickland 1913, II, p.484). Another marble bust by Nost is in the Victoria and Albert Museum (A.3.1957).

1764 Medal by John Nost jr. (Brown 1980, no.89).

1765 Medal by Thomas Pingo, the Royal Military Academy medal (Brown 1980, no.93; Eimer 1998, no.33).

c.1765? Miniature by Charles Dixon, profile with ribbon and star of the Garter. Sotheby's, 28 February 1977, lot 152.

1766 Lead equestrian statue by Beaupré under the direction of Joseph Wilton, 'in the character of Marcus Aurelius'. Formerly Berkeley Square, London. A marble statue in Roman armour by Wilton, formerly at the Royal Exchange, London, was dismantled by 1829 (Whinney 1964, pp.139, 265n27). Another gilded lead equestrian statue by Wilton, over life-size, commissioned by the General Assembly of New York in 1766, erected in 1770 and destroyed in 1776 (the head returned to England). A life-size marble head of George III, once displayed in the public market, Montreal, and now in the McCord Museum, McGill University (E. Miles, *American Colonial Portraits 1700-76*, NPG Washington 1987, pp.301-03), is conceivably also by Wilton.

1766 Wax model of a medallion by George Parbury, exhibited SA 1766(211).

1767 Miniature by Murray, exhibited FS 1767(214).

1767 Miniature by Jeremiah Meyer, half-length. Christie's, 21 November 2000, lot 15. See also 1760.

c.1767-69 Wax by Lewis Pingo. Royal Society of Arts, London (Pyke 1981, pl.219a; Eimer 1998, no.147).

c.1767-70 Painting attributed to Richard Brompton, three-quarter length standing in coronation robes, left hand on orb. Formerly at Langley Park (listed as Ramsay in Duleep Singh 1928, I, p.381, no.40, and Smart 1999, no.192w). The date proposed allows for the return of Brompton, to whom the portrait is tentatively attributed, from Italy in 1767.

c.1767? Painting by Henry Morland, exhibited FS 1767(197). Probably the half length in robes of state, engraved R. Houston and C. Spooner.

1768 Engraving by William Brown, exhibited SA 1768(139).

1768 Medal by John Kirk (Brown 1980, no.112).

1769 Painting by Nathaniel Dance,* whole length standing, with ermine robes, left hand resting on the crown. Uppark. Exhibited RA 1769(30) with a companion piece of the Queen. Versions are in the collection of the Prince of Hanover and a three-quarter length of the King alone was formerly at Thoresby Hall (exhibited Spencer House, London, from 1991). A reversed engraving of the head by W. Daniell for the *Dance Plates*, once thought to be after George Dance.

1769 Drawing by H.D. Hamilton, bust length. Royal Collection (Oppé 1950, no.283, pl.5).

1769 Model of an equestrian statue in Roman costume, by Agostino Carlini. Royal Academy (illus. *Apollo*, LXXXIX, 1969, p.45). Exhibited RA 1769(9). Engraved W. Bromley 1798 from a drawing by E.F. Burney. Reduced models by Carlini listed at the RA, Royal Collection (Windsor) and formerly at Audley End (Gunnis 1968, p.81).

1769 Sculpture by William Brown, exhibited SA 1769(220).

1769 Medallion by John Bacon sr., exhibited RA 1769(1).

1769 Medal by Thomas Pingo, the Royal Academy prize medal (Brown 1980, no.132; Eimer 1998, no.42). A similar medal by Barnett or John Westwood sr. 1772 (Brown 1980, no.165).

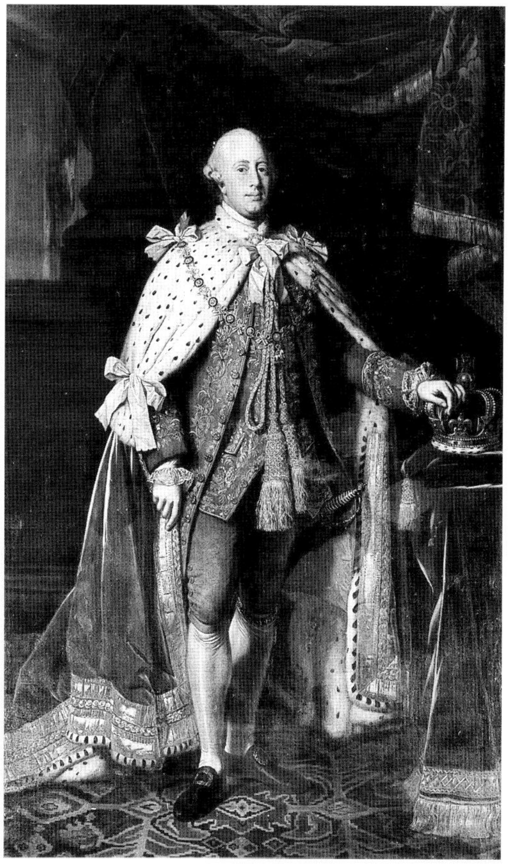

GEORGE III by Nathaniel Dance 1769 (Uppark, The National Trust)

1770 Painting by Johann Zoffany, whole-length standing in Van Dyck costume with the Queen and their six small children. Royal Collection (Millar 1969, no.1201). Exhibited RA 1770(211). Engraved R. Earlom 1770. Zoffany's preliminary sketch also in the Royal Collection (Millar 1969, no.1202) and there is a small copy at Clarence House. Three Derby biscuit porcelain groups modelled by John Bacon sr. in 1772 derived from the Zoffany composition (illus. *Apollo*, CXXII, 1985, p.297).

1770 Painting in imitation of a print by James Williams, exhibited FS 1770(267).

1770 Medal by John Kirk, celebrating the tenth anniversary of the King's reign (Brown 1980, no.137).

1770 Wax by Lewis Pingo, exhibited FS 1770(204).

c.1770 Medal by Julien Colibert (Brown 1980, no.27, as 1761, but Colibert came to England in 1769).

1771 Painting by Johann Zoffany,* three-quarter length seated in a General Officer's coat, the 'Farmer George' portrait. Royal Collection (Millar

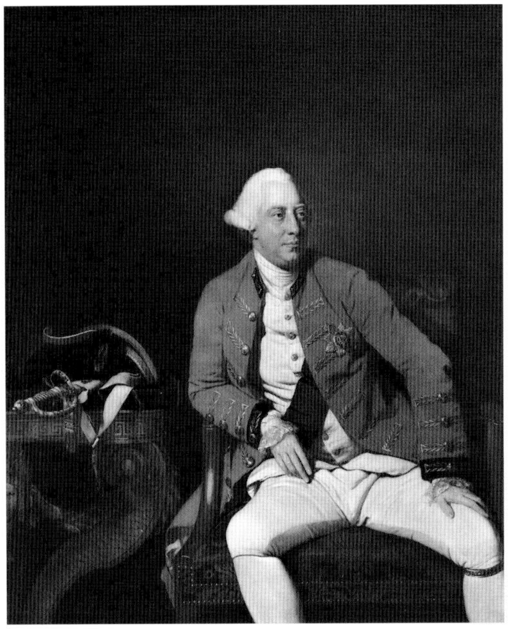

GEORGE III by Johann Zoffany 1771 (The Royal Collection)

1969, no.1195). Engraved R. Houston 1772. Exhibited RA 1771(230). Contemporary copies in the Royal Collection (Millar 1969, no.1213), at Aske, Schloss Celle, and formerly Dalton Hall (by Mason Chamberlin; illus. A.M.W. Stirling, *The Hothams*, 1918, II, f.p.150 as William Chamberlain); a poor copy at Somerset House (GAC 0.643). Daniel Dodd painted a half-length version (illus. NPG, W. Roberts photo archive).

Miniature derivations include a bust length by Princess Amelia and a three-quarter length by L-F. Aubry in the Royal Collection (Walker 1992, nos.143, 940); miniature copies by Henry Edridge sold Phillips, 17 March 1998, lot 163a, and by Thomas Cheesman, Christie's, 29 November 1989, lot 175.

Zoffany re-used the head for a half-length portrait, painted on copper, in robes of state (Royal Collection; Millar 1969, no.1197, illus. *Zoffany* 1977, no.68), first exhibited at Cox's Museum, London, in 1772. See also Liszewska 1779 and Chalmers c.1780.

c.1771 Painting attributed to Johann Zoffany, a standing version of the 1771 composition. The Prince of Hanover. With a companion piece of the Queen.

1771 William and Mary College medal by Thomas Pingo (Brown 1980, no.154; Eimer 1998, no.47).

1772 Enamel by Pasquier, 'from memory', exhibited RA 1772(184)

1772 Painting by M.F. Quadal, 'His Majesty reviewing the artillery, on horseback', exhibited RA 1773 (224). Probably Quadal's *George III at a Review* dated 1772 in the Royal Collection (Millar 1969, no.995).

1772 Painting by William Shuter, head with festoons, exhibited SA 1772(285).

1772 Proof medal by John Kirk, exhibited SA 1772(150, 156). Further medals by Kirk were exhibited SA 1773(150), 1775(127) and 1777(222).

1772 Impression from a wax seal by John Pingo, exhibited FS 1772(149), see Eimer 1998, no.132.

1772 Medallion by J.F. Moore, exhibited FS 1772(262).

1773 Marble bust by Agostino Carlini. Royal Academy (illus. Gunnis 1968, f.p.1123; *Apollo*, LXXXIX, 1969, p.45). Exhibited RA 1773(376).

1773 Marble bust by Joseph Nollekens. Royal Society, London (illus. Gunnis 1968, f.p.273; Whinney 1964, pl.128A). Exhibited RA 1774(190).

1773 Bust in composition by Thomas Pether, exhibited FS 1773(144).

1773 Marble medallion by John Moore jr., exhibited FS 1773(126).

1773 Enamel by W.H. Craft, whole length. British Museum (MLA 1891.2.17.16)

1774 Portrait by Henry Morland, exhibited FS 1774(200).

1774 Marble bust by John Bacon sr.* Christ Church, Oxford (Poole, III, p.85). Exhibited RA 1774(3). Versions include those at Windsor, dated 1775 (illus. Gunnis 1968, f.p.16); Göttingen University, and Society of Antiquaries, dated 1780. Copies by Francis Chantrey dated 1837 in the Royal Collection (made for the Pantheon at Kew; *Chantrey* 1994, no.276a), and by W.F. Woodington dated 1846 at Eton College. A version with differing drapery, attributed to Bacon's studio, was presented to Samuel Whitbread c.1787 with a bust of the Queen (illus. *Whitbread* 1984, p.43).

1774 Miniature by Henry Millington, exhibited FS 1774(116).

1774 Wax by Isaac Gosset, exhibited SA 1774(93). This was presumably the Gosset wax used at Wedgwood for medallions modelled by William Hackwood c.1775 and 1776 (Reilly 1973, pp.163-64, 168). See also 1776.

1774 Medals by G.M. Moser and Thomas Kirk (Brown 1980, nos.183, 197).

1775 Medal by Lewis Pingo, exhibited FS 1775, no.213 (Brown 1980, no.265; Eimer 1998, no.54).

c.1775 Miniature by Jeremiah Meyer, bust length. Royal Collection (Walker 1992, no.252).

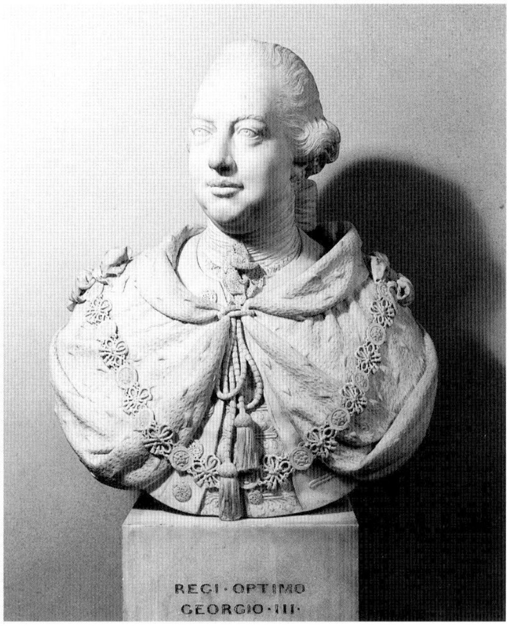

GEORGE III by John Bacon senior 1774 (Christ Church, Oxford)

1776 Painting by Nathaniel Dance, whole length in coronation robes, the crown on a table to the left. Drapers' Company, London (who commissioned the portrait). Versions in the Hermitage Museum, St Petersburg (illus. *Hermitage* 1997, p.38 as 1778) with a companion piece of the Queen, and at Gripsholm Castle; a half length was at Bayham Abbey (SSB 91/11). An unattributed miniature in the Royal Collection uses the same head (Walker 1992, no.320).

c.1776 Wedgwood medallion, with the Queen, the model attributed to William Hackwood after Isaac Gosset (illus. Reilly 1973, p.168).

c.1776 Painting on copper by Benjamin West, seated with the Queen. Private collection (Erffa & Staley 1986, no.559). The head of the King resembles that in the single portrait by West of c.1776, see below.

c.1776 Painting by Benjamin West, half-length seated. Earl of Elgin and Kincardine (Erffa & Staley 1986, no.547). Engraved E. Fisher 1778. A reduced version on copper sold Sotheby's, 2 March 1983, lot 44 (Erffa & Staley 1986, no.548). A preparatory drawing by West is in the Royal Collection (Oppé 1950, no.639, pl.2).

c.1776-78 Miniature by George Engleheart, with ribbon and star of the Garter. Royal Collection (Walker 1992, no.217). An enamel replica also in the Royal Collection (Walker 1992, no.219). Engleheart is believed to have painted at least twenty-five portraits of George III, both from sittings and after Gainsborough; his Fee Book lists portraits in 1776, 1778, and each year from 1783 to 1788 (Williamson 1902, p.43).

1777 Painting by J.B. Gianelli, whole length on horseback, exhibited SA 1777(202).

1777 Medallion portrait by Julien Colibert, exhibited RA 1777(59), see Brown 1980, no.2.

c.1777 Wedgwood medallion, modelled by John Bacon sr. (T. Clifford, *Apollo*, CXXII, 1985, p.294), previously attributed to William Hackwood (Reilly 1973, p.167).

1779 Painting by Anna Liszewska, three-quarter length in red suit, the head comparing closely with that by Zoffany of 1771. The Prince of Hanover. An autograph version, inscribed as painted at Brunswick in 1779, with slight variation in the background, sold Sotheby's, 13 November 1996, lot 57 with a companion piece of the Queen.

1779 Painting by Joshua Reynolds,* whole-length seated in robes of state. Royal Academy (Mannings 2000, no.717). Engraved W. Dickinson and T. Watson 1781. Reynolds was to succeed Ramsay as the King's Painter in 1784 and his portraits were duplicated in some quantity (see Mannings 2000 under no.718). Pairs of the King and Queen are in the Royal Collection (Millar 1969, nos.1035-38) and, for example, at Attingham, Bath (Guildhall), Belton House, Devizes (Assembly Rooms), Lancaster House (GAC 2554/1, 2555/2), Hatfield House, Holyrood, Sudbury Hall and the Los Angeles Museum of Art. Versions of the King alone in the Royal Collection (Millar 1969, no.1039), the National Maritime Museum (BHC 2712), and in the Guildhall, Worcester.

When Thomas Lawrence succeeded Reynolds as King's Painter in 1792 he made further copies (Cormack 1970, pp.167-68; Garlick 1989, p.193), of which a pair is in the British Embassy, Rome (GAC 9412/1 &2); in 1804 Samuel Woodforde made a copy of the King for the town of Doncaster (Farington, 30 June 1804).

1779 Painting by Benjamin West, whole-length standing in military coat holding a scroll recording troop dispositions. Royal Collection (Millar 1969, no.1138; Erffa & Staley 1986, no.549). RA 1780(116). A small version, in which the King wears a hat, belongs to the Historical Society of Pennsylvania (Erffa & Staley 1986, no.550).

A three-quarter length portrait in armour, derived from the 1779 portrait, is in the Cleveland Museum of Art (Erffa & Staley 1986, no.551), possibly that exhibited RA 1783(73).

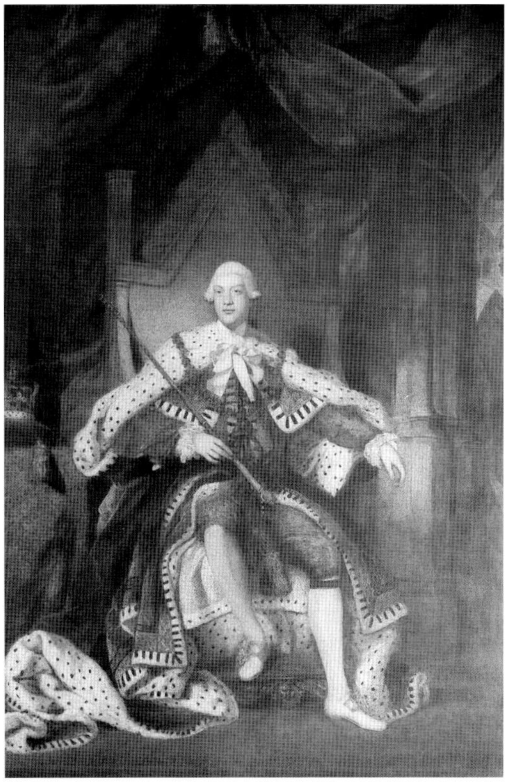

GEORGE III by Joshua Reynolds 1779 (Royal Academy of Arts, London)

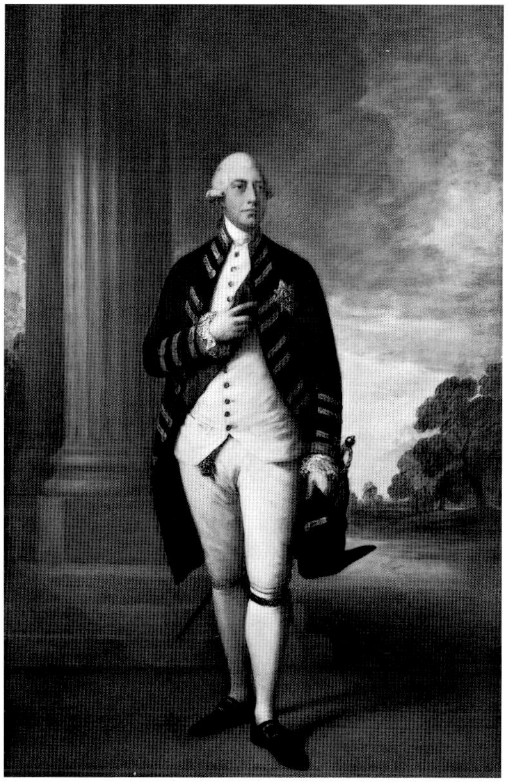

GEORGE III by Thomas Gainsborough 1781 (The Royal Collection)

1779 Marble bust by 'Adam Nost' [identified by Gunnis 1968, p.282, as John Nost jr.], exhibited RA 1779(220).

1779 Enamel by John Ford, exhibited RA 1779(92).

1780 Stone medallion by Joseph Wilton for Somerset House (façade).

c.1780? Wax by Thomas Engleheart. Royal Collection (illus. Pyke 1973, pl.89).

c.1780 Painting by George Chalmers, whole length in coronation robes (as in the Ramsay of 1761-62, see NPG 223), left hand on hip. Trinity House, Hull. The head closely resembles that in the Zoffany portrait of 1771. Chalmers was working in Hull 1778-81.

1781 Painting by Thomas Gainsborough,* whole length in Windsor uniform. Royal Collection (Waterhouse 1958, no.309; Millar 1969, no.774). Exhibited RA 1781(146). Engraved G. Dupont 1790.

Gainsborough's portraits of the King and Queen, which effectively replaced those of Allan Ramsay (despite the presence of Reynolds as the King's Painter), were much copied. Pairs include those at Hatfield House, Abingdon Town Hall (dated 1794), Horse Guards (GAC 12374 & 12375), two with the Prince of Hanover (one by Dupont); others sold Christie's, 11 June 1948, lot 109, and 2 May 1986, lot 148. Copies by C.W. Hanneman at Audley End (1786), Hartlebury Castle(1790), and Worcester Guildhall (1789), and by G.P.A. Healy at Versailles; reduced copies in pastel by R. de la Houlière 1791 sold Christie's, 31 March 1950, lot 25 (the King alone, Sotheby's, 16 November 1989, lot 36) and in pencil by E.F. Burney in the Huntington Art Collections , San Marino, Calif..

Of the King alone, three-quarter length copies at Eton and sold Christie's 21 May 1984, lot 66; a reduced half length in the Royal Collection (Millar 1969, no.776), and a bust length sold Christie's, 24 July 1987, lot 204.

Miniature bust-length copies in the Royal Collection by J.H. Hurter 1781; Richard Collins 1790, 1792; William Grimaldi and other unidentified hands (Walker 1992, nos.236, 165-68, 813, 321); Walker also lists further miniature copies by Collins dated 1788, 1812 and 1816, Richard Crosse, Robert Bowyer, Richard Livesay and J. Simpson (Walker 1992, pp.83-84). One by Crosse 1792 is in the Gilbert collection (illus. Coffin & Hofstetter

2000, no.82); half-length miniatures by Collins and Crosse sold Sotheby's, 31 July 1961, lots 45 and 70, and by Hurter dated 1782, Bonham's, 25 March 1997, lot 22. Derivative head drawn and engraved by P.W. Tomkins 1801, and a closely-related drawing by William Berczy engraved by G.S. and J.G. Facius 1791.

1782 Painting by Thomas Gainsborough, half length in Windsor uniform. Royal Collection (Millar 1969, no.778). Exhibited RA 1783 (134). A copy given by the King to Sir Herbert Taylor, and others have been recorded at Wistow and Arolsen; further examples sold Christie's, 11 June 1904, lot 88, and Christie's, 15 December 1993, lot 25.

1782 Portrait by Henry Morland, exhibited FS 1782(1).

1782 Wax portrait by Sylvester, exhibited FS 1782(225).

1783 Unattributed wax, exhibited FS 1783(382).

c.1783-88 Miniature by George Engleheart, bust length as general, with ribbon and star of the Garter. Royal Collection (Walker 1992, no.218).

1785 Painting by Thomas Gainsborough, three-quarter length in Windsor uniform. Museum Naradowe, Warsaw (illus. Millar 1969, fig.9). Painted for the King of Poland; the composition resembles that of the Dupont whole lengths, see 1794 below.

c.1785 Two Wegwood medallions (illus. Reilly 1973, pp.166-67), from models by Edward Burch. Closely related medals by Burch appeared in 1785 and 1788 (Brown 1980, nos.266, 291) and an undated wax relief by him sold Sotheby's, 10 June 1993(255).

1786 Model in wax by R. Santler, exhibited RA 1786(301).

1787 Painting by Thomas Stothard, *George III and his Family*, engraved J. Murphy 1794. A similar painting, now attributed to Richard Livesay (and formerly to Stothard), is at Upton House. See also under c.1791 below.

1787 Watercolour by John Downman, half-length oval, derived from the Gainsborough whole length of 1781. Royal Collection (*Gainsborough & Reynolds* 1994, no.39).

1788 Bronze statue by John Bacon sr., *King George III and the River Thames*. Somerset House, London (illus. J. Newman, *Somerset House*, 1990, p.29).

1788 Medals by R.W., C. James and J. Davies, marking the King's visits to Cheltenham and Worcester in July and August (Brown 1980, nos.271-77); another by C. James, marking the centenary of the 1688 revolution (Brown 1980, no.286).

Between November 1788 and February 1789 the King suffered the first attack of a genetic disorder, now recognised as porphyria; his recovery was publicly celebrated on 10 March. Twenty medals were then struck, including those by C. James, J. Milton, J. Davies and Lewis Pingo (Brown 1980, nos.294-313).

1789 Painting by Benjamin West, with the Queen, bust-length profiles. Royal Collection (Millar 1969, no.1141; Erffa & Staley 1986, no.560), originally intended for the canopy above the throne in the Audience Chamber at Windsor Castle. Reduced version in a private collection (Erffa & Staley 1986, no.559).

1789 Painting by Solomon Williams (Strickland 1913, ii, p.538).

1789 [Wax?] portrait by Charles Peart, exhibited RA 1789(592).

1789 Medals by J. Davies, W. Cragg and C. James marking the King's tour in July and August through Lyndhurst, Southampton, Weymouth, Plymouth and Bath (see Brown 1980, nos.314-20).

c.1789 Silhouettes by William Locker (illus. *CL*, CXXXI, 1962, p.182) and William Wellings (illus. P. Hickman, *Two Centuries of Silhouettes*, 1971, p.33).

c.1789 Painting attributed to Gainsborough Dupont, whole length, derived from the Gainsborough 1781 pattern. Royal Collection (Millar 1969, no.808).

c.1789-90 Wedgwood medallion (illus. Reilly 1973, p.166) from a wax by Henry Burch jr., possibly that exhibited SA 1790(44); a wax model by him was given by the King to Elizabeth, Countess of Pembroke, in 1789 (illus. Pyke 1973, pl.41).

1790 Painting by Mather Brown, whole length in Windsor uniform. Sotheby's, 19 November 1986, lot 60 (Evans 1982, no.67). Sir Richard Arkwright bought a whole length of George III by Brown in 1790 (R.S. Fitton, *The Arkwrights*, 1989, p.201).

1790 Medals by Thomas Wyon sr. and C.H. Küchler, with conjoined busts of the King and Queen (Brown 1980, nos.338-40).

1790 Cameo portrait by W. Whitley, exhibited RA 1790(676).

c.1790 Engraving by C. Tomkins, on horseback, with the Duke of York and the Prince of Wales.

c.1790? Medallions by James Tassie. Three patterns are recorded (Gray 1894, no.150): a laureate bust with toga; a laureate head without drapery, and wearing a tye-wig and ribbon of the Garter, probably c.1790 (see Scottish NPG, PG 400, PG 485, PG 1371 and PG 1904).

c.1790? Wedgwood medallions from unknown models (illus. Reilly 1973, p.165).

1791 Proof from a gem portrait by Edward Burch, exhibited RA 1791(279).

c.1791 Painting by Benjamin West, with the Royal family, receiving the Duchess of York. Sold Robins, 20-22 June 1829, lot 102. Related to the painting by Richard Livesay at Upton House (Erffa & Staley 1986, no.576), see 1787 above.

1792 Painting attributed to John Hoppner, whole length in Garter robes. Municipal Hall, Taunton (Taunton Deane Borough Council), presented by Sir Benjamin Hammett 1792. A version belongs to Fife Council, and a 'copy of Hoppner' is in the British Embassy at Athens (GAC 0.6).

1792 Painting by Thomas Lawrence,* whole length in Garter robes with a distant view of Windsor. Herbert AG, Coventry (CH 23; Garlick 1989, no.324). Exhibited RA 1792(65). Engraved W. Holl 1829. Replicas are in the Royal Collection (Millar 1969, no.871); St George's Hall, Liverpool, and formerly Patshull House. A half-length version sold Sotheby's, 23 March 1966, lot 81. Samuel Lane made a copy in 1809 (Farington, 6 March 1810).

Following the death of Lawrence in 1830, a number of claims were made on his estate for undelivered portraits of the King (*Lawrence* 1964, pp.272-73).

1792 Silhouette by J. Lind, bust length. Royal Collection (McKechnie 1978, no.518).

1793 Medal by C. Twigg (Brown 1980, no.370).

1794 Painting by Gainsborough Dupont, whole length in robes of state. Royal Collection (Millar 1969, no.766). Derived from the Gainsborough whole length of 1781 and probably the portrait exhibited RA 1794(85). A version at Trinity House, London, painted in 1795; another in the Royal Collection (Millar 1969, no.767), given by the King to the Prince of Wales in 1795, was modified by John Simpson to show the robes of the Garter. A whole-length variant is at Powis Castle and a bust-length copy at Belton House.

An undated MS account of 'Portraits Painted for the King by Gainsborough Dupont' (NPG archive, *Autograph letter: D*) lists, besides the whole length for the Prince of Wales (see above), whole-length portraits of the King and Queen painted for the Duke of York, the Commissioners House at Portsmouth and Windsor Castle, and half lengths for Windsor Lodge.

c.1794 Painting attributed to Gainsborough Dupont, whole length in robes of state. Walker AG, Liverpool (2998). Another in the Guildhall, Worcester. Closely related to the 1794 Dupont portrait but showing the ermine worn over a suit (instead of the

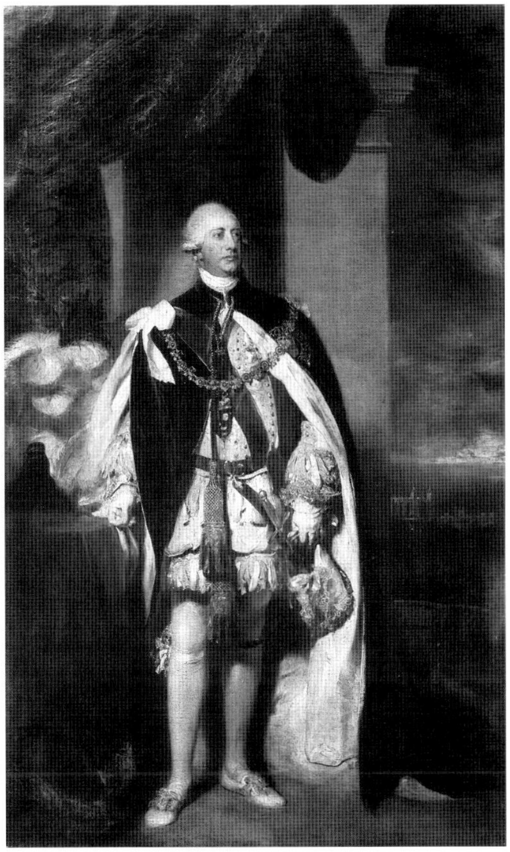

GEORGE III by Thomas Lawrence 1792 (Herbert Art Gallery and Museum, Coventry)

Windsor uniform), the left hand on hip and the right holding the sceptre.

1795 Wax portrait by Samuel Percy. Royal Collection. Other waxes by Percy at Brighton MAG, and sold Sotheby's, 30 November 1964, lot 69, and 15 December 1980, lot 7, and see 1804 below.

1795 Statue by Anne Seymour Damer. Registrar's Office, Edinburgh.

c.1795 Unattributed bronze bust. Ashmolean Museum, Oxford (Penny 1992, III, no.615).

c.1795 Engraving by H. Meyer 1823, bust length in Garter robes, 'from a likeness taken in his 57th year'. Resembling the Lawrence head of 1792.

1796 Painting by Philip Jean, whole length in robes of state. Exhibited RA 1796(723), RA 1797(896). Farington thought 'very indifferent' (2 April 1796); intended 'for some public office in Jersey ..., principally made up from Sir Joshua Reynolds's picture in the Council Room of the Royal Academy' (E. Edwards, *Anecdotes of Painters*, 1808, p.275). Possibly the unattributed whole-length seated portrait of the King in the Bishop's Palace at Fulham.

1796 Coade stone medallion by John Bacon sr. Trinity House, London (façade).

1797 Painting by Thomas Stewart, exhibited RA 1797(812). Farington considered it 'to be a copy from Gainsborough', and Stothard 'not only not original, but very bad' (Farington, 9, 12 April 1797).

1797 Painting by James Northcote, whole-length equestrian. Crown Court, Lancaster (*Northcote* 1996, no.562). Exhibited RA 1807(154 'painted for the Palatine of Lancaster and presented by Jas. Ackers Esq. The high sheriff Ann Dom 1800'). Lawrence had previously failed to supply the portrait (Farington, 17 July 1800, 8 September 1806). A later version completed in 1812 in the Royal Marines Museum, Portsmouth. Reduced versions in an American private collection, and sold Sotheby's, 2 August 1972, lot 85.

1797 Miniature by Robert Bowyer, bust length. Engraved by J. Fittler 1797 (illus. Walker 1992, fig.23; see Oppé 1950, p.108).

1797–98 Painting by William Beechey, on horseback wearing General's uniform, reviewing the 3rd Dragoon Guards and the 10th Light Dragoons, his party including the Prince of Wales. Destroyed by fire 1992, formerly Royal Collection (Millar 1969, no.660). Exhibited RA 1798(178). The King alone engraved W. Ward 1799. Replaced at Windsor in 1995 with a copy sent by the Government of Canada; other copies at Plas Newydd, the National Army Museum and in the Louvre. Of several reduced copies, one is in the collection of Count Kielmansegg, another in the Sterling and Francine Clark Art Institute, Williamstown, and a third in the Government Art Collection (2670). A watercolour by Beechey is in the Victoria and Albert Museum (134.1890; illus. Millar 1969, fig.1).

Reduced version of the King alone in the Royal Collection (Millar 1969, nos.675–76) and copies include those at Rockingham Castle, Althorp, and the Weymouth Museum; others sold Mallans, 25 April 1995, lot 54; Christie's, SK, 27 November 1997, lot 275, and Sotheby's, 18 September 1997, lot 65 as James Ward.

A full-size version in a private collection, the horse painted by James Ward, the figure copied from Beechey by William Hopkins, engraved J. Ward (C.R. Grundy, *James Ward*, 1909, pp.63–64; *CL*, CXV, 1954, p.1229); an enamel version by Henry Bone sold Sotheby's, 11 July 1991, lot 284; preparatory drawing, dated 1819, in the NPG Bone albums (*Bone* 1999, no.217).

1798 Medal celebrating the naval victories of 1798 (the Battle of the Nile) by C.H. Küchler (Brown 1980, no.458).

1799 Medal by J-P. Droz (Brown 1980, no.465).

1799–1800 Painting by William Beechey, see NPG 2502 and NPG 6250.

1800 Medals by C.H. Küchler and P. Kempson, celebrating the King's survival of an assassination attempt on 15 May; another by G.V. Bauert (Brown 1980, nos.482–86, 495). Medal by John Milton exhibited RA 1800(893), cf. Brown 1980, no.461.

c.1800 Painting by R.B. Davis, on horseback as a Horse Guards[?] officer with distant view of Windsor. Christie's, 12 February 1954, lot 99. In 1806 C. Turner engraved Davis's *George III in his Travelling Chariot*.

The King suffered a recurrence of his illness for four weeks in February-March 1801. His recovery was marked by a medal by J.G. Hancock (Brown 1980, no.503).

1801 Wax relief by Catherine Andras. Hatfield House. Another dated 1820 in the British Museum and other examples in the National Maritime Museum (MNTO 167) and the Metropolitan Museum of Art, New York.

1801 Medal by C.H. Küchler, marking the Union with Ireland, and medals by P. Kempson & S. Kindon, Henry Kettle, and C.H. Küchler, marking the Preliminaries of the Peace of Amiens (Brown 1980, nos.513–15, 523–25, 527).

1802 Medal attributed to William Mossop, with conjoined busts of the King and Queen (Brown 1980, no.529). See also 1810 below. Medal by C.H. Küchler marking the Peace of Amiens (Brown 1980, nos.534–35).

c.1802 Silhouette by Charles Rosenberg, bust length with spectacles. Royal Collection (illus. McKechnie 1978, no.1159).

1803 Drawing by Henry Edridge, whole length. Royal Collection (Oppé 1950, no.197, pl.11). Engraved A. Cardon 1812 and, the head alone, W. Sharp 1822. A copy of the head in miniature by Edridge is also in the Royal Collection (Walker 1992, no.805).

1803 Engraving by C.T. Warren from a drawing by Richard Corbould, profile in Windsor uniform; also engraved by R. Page 1820.

c.1803 Miniature attributed to George Place, bust length in Windsor uniform. Royal Collection (Walker 1992, no.288).

c.1803 Miniature by George Place, as general of the Blues with the ribbon and star of the Garter. Royal Collection (Walker 1992, no.286). Resembling the

Beechey (see NPG 2502). Two copies are in the Royal Collection (Walker 1992, nos.289-90); others attributed to Richard Collins sold Sotheby's, 6 October 1980, lot 147, and 12 March 1984, lot 91, and a variant, very doubtfully attributed to Richard Cosway, is at Schloss Altshausen (Walker 1992, p.144).

1804 Coade stone statue, whole length in Roman armour at Taplow Court, 'very poor' (Farington, 2 January and 21 September 1804).

1804 [Wax?] by Samuel Percy, exhibited RA 1804(957).

1805 Medals by Thomas Webb and John Westwood jr. (Brown 1980, nos.601, 599).

c.1805-10 Drawing by Richard Cosway, profile. Private collection (*Cosway* 1995, p.127, no.157).

By October 1805 the King was virtually blind

1806 Painting by James Northcote, whole-length seated in Garter robes. Commissioned by John Fisher, Bishop of Salisbury (*Northcote* 1996, no.542). Engraved by W. Say. A copy by James Holmes at Temple Newsam, Leeds.

1806 Medal by G.F. Pidgeon (Brown 1980, no.620).

c.1806-07 Silhouette by William Hamlet sr., bust length in Windsor uniform. Private collection (illus. McKechnie 1978, no.1060).

1807 Painting on copper by P.E. Stroehling, whole-length standing in Windsor uniform, dated 18 November 1807. Royal Collection (Millar 1969, no.1093).

1807 Engraving by E. Scriven from a drawing by Thomas Uwins, bust length in robes of state.

1807 Medal by Thomas Wyon sr. and T. Martyn, conjoined busts of the King and Queen; another of the King by P. Kempson & S. Kindon (Brown 1980, nos.628-31).

c.1807-08 Silhouette by William Hamlet jr., whole length in Windsor uniform, with spectacles. Private collection (illus. McKechnie 1978, no.823).

1808 Medal by J. Phillip (Brown 1980, no.632).

The fiftieth year of the King's reign, 1809, was marked by some thirty medals, including those by J. Barber, Peter Wyon, Thomas Wyon sr., Thomas Halliday, and P. Kempson (see Brown 1980, nos.641-47, 649, 651-56). Turnerelli produced a Jubilee bust and statues appeared in Weymouth and Southampton.

1809 Marble bust by Peter Turnerelli, see NPG 3903.

1809 Plaster bust by Lucius Gahagan. Christie's, 26 June 1980, lot 4.

1809 Statue in artificial stone in state robes, designed by James Hamilton. The Esplanade, Weymouth. Engraved E. Scriven 1811 (described as Coade & Sealey's monument to the King erected at Weymouth & Melcombe Regis); the statue was painted in 1949. A second unattributed statue, in Roman armour, installed at Bargate, Southampton.

1809 Life mask taken by Marie Tussaud (A. Leslie & P. Chapman, *Madame Tussaud*, 1978, p.140).

1809 Drawing by Charles Rosenberg, whole length in Windsor uniform, engraved by J.C. Stadler 1810.

1809 Silhouette by H.W. Holden, conjoined busts of the King and Queen. Royal Collection (McKechnie 1978, no.845, where dated 'before 1810').

c.1809 Painting by Thomas Lawrence, three-quarter length in robes of state. Royal Collection (Millar 1969, no.872). The head resembles that in Lawrence's earlier portrait of 1792.

c.1809 Marble bust by Edward Smyth. NG of Ireland (8038; illus. *Apollo*, LXXXIV, 1966, p.309).

c.1809 Miniature by an unidentified artist, half length in robes of state. Royal Collection (Walker 1992, no.910). Possibly derived from a drawing by M.C. Wyatt which was engraved J. Heath 1809 (illus. Walker, *loc. cit.*); for Wyatt's bust, see 1810 below.

c.1809 Unattributed miniature, three-quarter length, in robes of state. Packington Hall. The head reminiscent of Turnerelli's bust of 1809, see NPG 3903.

c.1809 Silhouette by John Miers (illus. *CL*, CXXXI, 1962, p.182).

c.1809 Unattributed miniature, see NPG 6288.

The Golden Jubilee of 1810 was commemorated with medals by Thomas Halliday, N. Hyde, C.H. Küchler, W.S. Mossop and Thomas Wyon sr. (Brown 1980, nos.680-87, 700). The fiftieth anniversary was publicly celebrated on 25 October 1810, but the same day marked a recurrence of the King's illness.

1810 Bronze bust by M.C. Wyatt. British Embassy, Lisbon (GAC 156). Exhibited RA 1811(943).

1810 Coade stone crowned bust. Lincoln Castle (illus. *Burl. Mag.*, CXXXVIII, 1996, p.17); the remains of the statue by Joseph Panzetta made for the Coade factory, originally placed on the Dunston Pillar, Lincs. See also 1811 below.

1810 Miniature by Robert Bowyer, bust length with star of the Garter. Engraved J. Godby 12 May 1820 as *taken from the life in the Year 1810* (illus. Walker 1992, fig.29). See Oppé 1950, p.108.

1810 Impression from a medal by Thomas Wyon sr., exhibited RA 1810(644).

1810 Wax medallion by William Mossop, dated 1810, inscribed *wax design for medal of George III on his 50th year of reign, W. Mossop Senior* [d.1803]. Sotheby's, 10 June 1993, lot 222, from Stanton Harcourt.

1810-14 Marble bust by Francis Chantrey AG of South Australia, Adelaide (*Chantrey* 1994, no.19). Chantrey had received two sittings in 1810. Versions of 1814 with the Royal College of Surgeons, London (engraved M. Gauci 1820, exhibited RA 1814, no.794; illus. LeFanu 1960, pl.16) and in the Goldsmiths' Hall, London.

On 6 February 1811 the Regency Bill was passed and from 1812 the King, ill and virtually blind, led a solitary existence. From this time his portraits must have been derivative.

1811 Painting by Thomas Stewardson, half length, engraved G. Clint.

1811 Statue by Peter Turnerelli, exhibited RA 1811(944). Presumably related to the half-life-size standing figure in robes, sceptre in right hand, dated 1813, in King's College, London; a bust-length derivation, dated 1818, at the National University of Ireland, Maynooth.

1811 Bronze statuette by Lucius Gahagan. Phillips, 20 June 1989, lot 136. Other examples sold Christie's, 22 October 1974, lot 95; Sotheby's, 21 October 1988, lot 199. A painted plaster version dated 1818 sold Christie's, 21 July 1988, lot 23. (illus. *Connoisseur*, CLXXX, 1972, p.233). For a related statuette by Francis Hardenberg, see NPG 4383.

1811 Study by George Garrard for an equestrian statue to commemorate the Jubilee, exhibited RA 1811(922) with a model (942).

1811 Coade stone statue. Portland Square, Bristol (destroyed 1817). See also 1810.

1811 Miniature by A.E. Chalon, half length in Windsor uniform. Engraved A. Cardon 1811, from the collection of the Duke of Sussex.

1811-15 Colossal statue by Francis Chantrey, standing in robes of state. Guildhall London, destroyed 1940; commissioned by the City of London (*Chantrey* 1994, no.15, fig.11). Plaster head in the Ashmolean Museum, Oxford (Penny 1992, III, no.638).

c.1811 Engraving by G. Testolini after Thomas Stothard, whole length in robes of state.

c.1811? Painting by Edward Bird, whole length in robes of state. Bristol Corporation. Exhibited Bristol Institution 1826 ('a poor thing by Bird'; S. Richardson, *Edward Bird*, Wolverhampton 1982, no.75). The composition appears to derive from the Testolini engraving after Stothard, see above.

1812 Drawing attributed to Robert Bowyer, whole-length standing on a dais. Royal Collection (Oppé 1950, no.716).

1812 Small statue 'to be executed in bronze' by W. 'Tallemach' [i.e. Tollemache], exhibited RA 1812(906).

1812 Bust by Peter Turnerelli, life-size laureate, with Roman drapery bearing the badge of the Garter; examples in the Bank of England and the British Library are dated 1812; Newark Town Hall; Victoria and Albert Museum (A.11.1937); Trinity College, Dublin, and formerly at Trinity House, London (dated 1813; destroyed 1941).

1812 Wax portrait by W. Cramphorn, exhibited RA 1812(912).

1812 Wax by Peter Rouw. Stanton Harcourt (Pyke 1973, p.123). Other wax laureate profiles by Rouw sold Christie's, 16 October 1973, lot 24, and 16 July 1980, lot 8, dated 1817 (cf. illus. *CL*, CXXXI, 1962, p.658). Rouw also exhibited a portrait medallion RA 1820(951) following the death of the King.

1812 Painted silhouette by John Field. Sotheby's, 22 February 1985, lot 184.

c.1812 Silhouette by William Hamlet sr., whole length in Windsor uniform. Private collection (illus. McKechnie 1978, no.1067).

1813 Painting by Benjamin West, three-quarter length seated in robes of state. Bishopthorpe Palace, York, commissioned by the Archbishop of York (Erffa & Staley 1986, no.552). Derived from West's portrait of 1776.

1813 Whole-length statue by John Bacon jr., designed by Thomas Kirk, in robes of state. Royal Bank of Dublin. Anon. engraving 1821 (*European Mag.*).

1813 Plaster by Peter Turnerelli, model for an equestrian statue. Soane Museum, London (illus. *Irish Georgian Society Bulletin*, x, 1967, p.4).

1813 Marble statue by Peter Turnerelli, half-life-size. King's College, London, see 1811.

1814 Medals by John Westwood jr. and Thomas Wyon jr. (Brown 1980, nos.828, 844).

1815 Colossal marble bust by J.C. Rossi. County Hall, Carlisle. Exhibited RA 1815(868).

1815 Impression from a medal die by Thomas Wyon sr., exhibited RA 1815(830).

1816 Painting by Edmund Bristow, on horseback in Windsor Park. Christie's, 16 March 1984, lot 83. Derived from Beechey's figure of 1797–98, see above.

1816 Onyx cameo by Benedetto Pistrucci. British Museum (Hull Grundy 1984, no.897). A jasper cameo head of the King by Pistrucci was commissioned in 1816 by Sir Josph Banks who presented it to the Queen (see H.B. Carter, *Sir Joseph Banks*, 1988, p.516). Waxes by Pistrucci dated 1817, 1818 and 1820, used for the coinage, are in the Museo Numismatico della Zecca, Rome.

1817 Marble busts of the King were being replicated by Lorenzo Bartolini in Florence at £22 each (H. Matthews, *Diary of an Invalid*, 1820, p.59).

1817 Portrait (medallion?), by Smith, exhibited RA 1817(972).

1817 Engraving by H. Meyer, bearded *in his 80th year … from an original drawing taken from the life in 1817*. Another, reversed, engraved W. Lowry, 6 November 1817, *drawn by M. Wyatt*.

1817 Medals celebrating the anniversary of the King's accession, by William Wyon and Thomas Wyon sr. and Alexis Depaulis (Brown 1980, nos.932–33).

c.1817 Miniature attributed to H.D. Thielcke, in Windsor uniform. Royal Collection (Walker 1992, no.907). Engraved H.D. Thielcke 1819.

1818 Impression from a die by Thomas Wyon sr., exhibited RA 1818(1009).

1819 Engraving by R. Cooper after J.M. Wright, half length in general's uniform with the star of the Garter.

Posthumous: the King died on 29 January 1820.

1820 Engraving by T. Illman after William Derby, half length in Windsor uniform, published 14 February 1820.

1820 Anon. engraving published 1 March 1820, three-quarter length seated, wearing a cap, with short white beard, *From an Original Drawing taken at the Age of 82 in the 60th year of his Reign.*

1820 Miniature by Charles Muss, three-quarter length seated with long white beard. Royal Collection (Walker 1992, no.893). Inscribed as being after John Jackson. Engraved S.W. Reynolds, published 24 February 1820. An enamel version by Joseph Lee is in the Royal Collection and a painting by him dated 1821 was sold Sotheby's, 29 March 1976, lot 9, as after John Jackson (see Walker 1992, p.385).

Comparable mezzotint by C. Turner, three-quarter length seated, with white beard, both hands on chair arms.

1820 Bust by J.E. Carew, exhibited RA 1820(1034).

1820 Statuette by Francis Hardenberg, see NPG 4383.

1820 Marble bust by Francis Hardenberg, with classical toga (illus. *CL*, CXCIII, 3 June 1999, p.145) and another by William Spence and Samuel Franceys (both in private collections).

1820 Sixteen medals marking the death of the King, including those by J. Marrian, Thomas Kettle and Thomas Wyon sr. (see Brown 1980, nos. 458, 991–1005, 1009). A medallion portrait by Peter Rouw was exhibited RA 1820, no.951, with another, from a dye by William Wyon, no.950.

1821 Model by Richard Freebairn, exhibited RA 1821(1165), showing the King 'under his afflicting malady' (*Literary Gazette*, 1822, p.346).

1821 Bronze equestrian statue by Robert Henderson, exhibited RA 1821(1140). Possibly the bronze statuette dated 1821 in the Victoria and Albert Museum (A.4.1937).

1822 Equestrian statue by Richard Westmacott, in Roman dress. London Road, Liverpool, commissioned by the City in 1809, executed 1818–22 (illus. Busco 1994, pp.66–67).

1831 Bronze equestrian statue by Richard Westmacott, in Roman dress, the granite pedestal by Jeffry Wyattville. Windsor Great Park (illus. Busco 1994, p.69). Executed 1824–31. An undated marble bust with Roman drapery and the star of the Garter, at Belton House, signed Westmacott RA, appears to relate to this monument.

1836 Bronze equestrian statue by M.C. Wyatt. Cockspur Street, London (illus. J.M. Robinson, *The Wyatts*, 1979, p.183). Commissioned in 1822, unveiled 1836.

Undated Unattributed lead laureate bust. Royal Collection. Exhibited *Kings and Queens*, RA 1953(243). Probably after 1800.

Unattributed bronze bust. Victoria and Albert Museum (A.51.1932)

Wax by Guion. Stanton Harcourt (Pyke 1973, p.60).

GIBBON, Edward 1737-94

Historian; lived in Lausanne 1753-58 and 1783-93; wrote the *History of the Decline and Fall of the Roman Empire*, 1776-88: 'the scope of information is vast, and the Style generally possesses the property that is styled Magic, when applied to painting' (Rennell); FRS 1788.

'His face is one of the most singular spectacles in physiognomy on account of the irregular proportions of the individual parts of the whole. The eyes are so small that they afford the strongest contrast with the high and splendidly arched brow; the rather snub nose almost disappears between the extremely prominent cheeks, and the large double chin hanging far down makes the already elongated oval of the face still more striking' (Friedrich Matthisson, 1802).

'I heard [Soames Jenyns] very innocently remark, when Gibbon published his history, that he wondered any body so ugly could write a book' (Richard Cumberland, 1807).

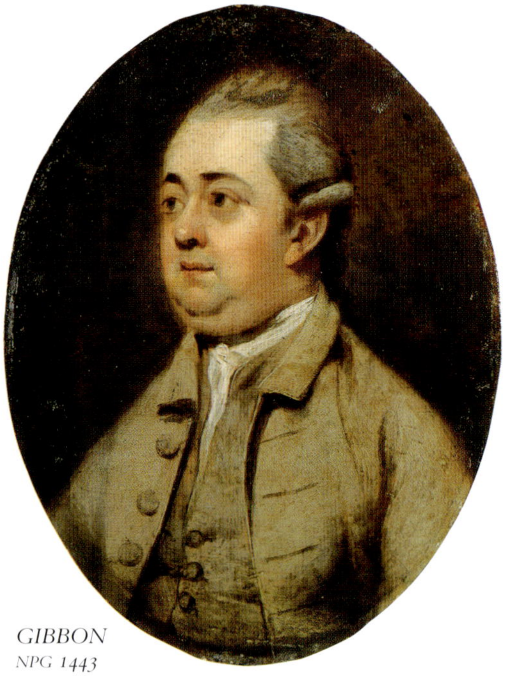

GIBBON
NPG 1443

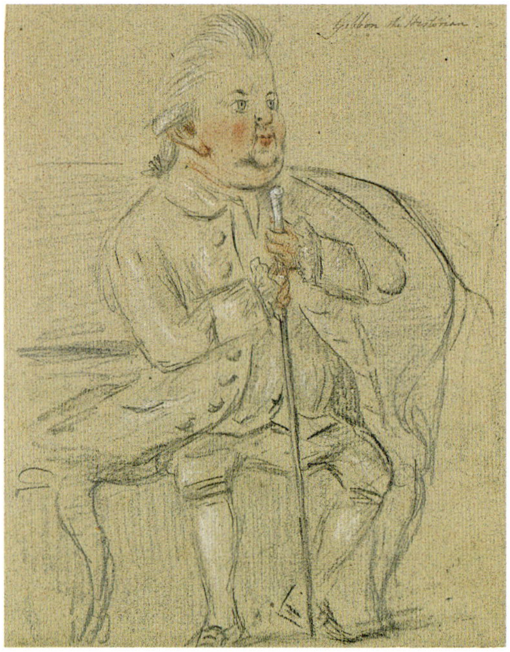

GIBBON NPG 4854

1443 HENRY WALTON 1773

Mahogany panel 23.5 x 18.5 (9¼ x 7¼) the thickness of the panel varies from 1 at the bottom to 0.4 at the top; some retouching evident in the jacket and background areas; the whole thinly painted and the surface slightly rubbed.

Blue eyes, grey powdered hair, grey coat, waistcoat and buttons, white shirt; grey-green background.

Collections: [see below] given by the sitter to his step-mother, Mrs Dorothea Gibbon, 1773,[1] by whom bequeathed to the 1st Baron Sheffield 1796,[2] thence by descent to the 3rd Baron Sheffield, by whom sold Christie's, 30 June 1906, lot 149, bt. by the NPG.

Engravings: See below.

Exhibitions: *Gibbon Commemorative Exhibition*, London, 1894; OP 1906(129) lent by Lord Sheffield; *Walton*, Norwich, 1963(2).

Reference: *Walton* 1999, nos.61, 66.

Sold by the 3rd Baron Sheffield in 1906, NPG 1443 was almost certainly the portrait Gibbon had sent his step-mother at Bath in July 1773 and which she in turn bequeathed to Lord Sheffield in 1796.[3] On 13 July Gibbon told Mrs Gibbon she would be receiving 'by the Bath Coach a representation, which is said to be very like a person, whom I believe is not indifferent to you'. Henry Walton was then being patronised by a number of Gibbon's circle: J.B. Holroyd (later Lord Sheffield) and his wife, John Thomas Batt, Sir John Russell, George Wilbraham, Booth Grey and Godfrey Bagnall Clarke.[4]

Four other oval versions are known, of which the picture at Magdalen College, Oxford,[5] and another in a private collection painted for George Wilbraham,[6] show the grey suit seen in NPG 1443. The others show Gibbon wearing an embroidered silk waistcoat and a green coat, either partly open, as in the portrait with the Government Art Collection (GAC 16642),[7] or wide open as in the example in a Swiss private collection.[8] An unspecified version, 'after Walton', was sold Christie's, 11 September 1997, lot 36.

An engraving by James Fittler published in 1815 and lettered *from the original Portrait* [with] *Lord Sheffield, Painted by Mr Warton* [*sic*] *in the year 1774*, shows the head of NPG 1443 (but with a different wig tie), on the body of the Reynolds portrait of 1779 (then at Sheffield Place).[9]

1 See Gibbon, *Letters*, 1956, I, p.370. This provenance was first proposed by C.F. Bell in a letter to the *TLS*, 20 June 1929.
2 See J.H. Adeane, *The Girlhood of Maria Josepha Holroyd [Lady Stanley of Alderley]*, 1896, p.369.
3 At Sheffield Place c.1804 Harding listed four portraits of Gibbon, one by Walton which he inaccurately called 'the last likeness taken of him' (Harding, I, f.13). It is curious that Sheffield did not himself have already a copy of the Walton portrait, although he owned the Reynolds portrait of 1779, see below.
4 Gibbon, *Letters*, 1956, I, pp.370, 379, 382; D.M. Low, *Gibbon*, 1937, p.111. Harding listed Walton's copies of his portraits of Batt and Sir John Russell at Sheffield Place c.1804 (Harding, I, ff.9, 11, 13).
5 Given in 1937, see *Walton* 1999, no.63; from the Porten family, through the Rev Thomas Burningham and his daughter Mrs Onslow; illus. G. de Beer, *Gibbon*, 1967, p.73. According to C.F. Bell 'totally ruined by violent scrubbing' (NPG archive). The portrait was stolen in June 1991 and subsequently recovered.
6 *Walton* 1999, no.62; exhibited NPE 1867(664) lent G.F. Wilbraham, the cat. describing the coat as 'grey' and saying the portrait was one of a set of four by Walton, the others being of Grey, Clark and Wilbraham himself. The photograph from the 1867 exhibition suggests a crude picture.
7 *Walton* 1999, no.64; ex Sotheby's, 15 July 1964, lot 133 as Downman, and 13 July 1988, lot 52.
8 *Walton* 1999, no.65; painted for Georges Deyverdun; illus. Gibbon, *Letters*, 1956, II, front.
9 *Walton* 1999, p.59. Other engravings listed by O'Donoghue as after Walton (by B. Reading 1788, W. Ridley 1794 and G. Murray 1796) relate to the Reynolds portrait of 1779, see below.

4854 UNKNOWN ARTIST c.1785-90

Black chalk with white heightening, the hands and ears in sanguine, with pink crayon on the cheeks, on laid grey paper 19 x 15 (7½ x 5⅞); verso, a chalk sketch of blossom and the inscription: *The Decline & Fall of the Roman Emp*

Both hands holding a silver-topped cane before him; inscribed top right: *Gibbon the Historian*.

Collections: Mrs D.F. Walpole of Oaklands, Sheringham, who gave it in 1965 to R.W. Ketton Cremer, by whom bequeathed 1971.

This amateur drawing, showing Gibbon towards the end of his life, seated in characteristic pose, his legs wide apart due to his gout,[1] was found loose in an album of drawings (some bearing dates from 1793) by a member of the Walpole of Wolterton family, although it seems to be by a different hand.[2] It bears some resemblance to a drawing by Lavinia, Countess Spencer, in the British Museum (1890.5.12.10), see below.

1 As seen, for example, in the drawing by M.V. Brandoin of 1785-90, engraved by C. Constans, and cf. G. de Beer, *Gibbon*, 1967, pp.93, 141.
2 The album contains drawings of Bavarian peasants as mentioned by R.W. Ketton Cremer, in his letter of 12 October 1965 (NPG archive); he added 'I think the insertion of the drawing in this volume may have been accidental'.

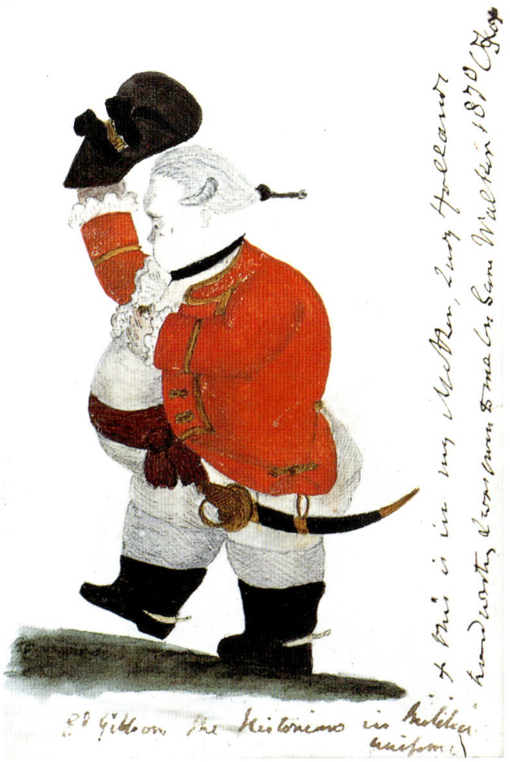

GIBBON *NPG 3317*

3317 UNKNOWN ARTIST c.1825

Watercolour on thin card 15.5 x 10.5 (6⅛ x 4⅛); painted on the verso of an official invitation to Lord Holland from the Prince Leopold to a reception at Marlborough House on Friday 13 May;[1] inscribed below: *Ed Gibbon the Historian in Militia uniform* and up the right-hand margin: *this is in my Mother, Lady Hollands*[2] */ handwriting & was given to me by Sam Walker 1870 CFox*.

Black hat in his hand, black collar, gold-laced red coat, purple sash, black boots, a scimitar at his waist.

Collections: 3rd Baron Holland (d.1840); Sam Walker; Gen. Charles Richard Fox (d.1873) 1870; Bernard Halliday, bookseller, Leicester in 1935,[3] when offered to the NPG; it was declined, but subsequently [1946?] acquired.[4]

Exhibition: *Garrick and his Contemporaries*, Stratford-upon-Avon, 1969(54).

A whimsical, posthumous caricature. Gibbon served as a captain with the South Hampshire militia 1759-62 (and attended annual training camps between 1766 and 1770, when he resigned), the 'habits of a sedentary life' being 'usefully broken by the duties of an active profession'. But he was apparently not then the corpulent figure of later life, being described in 1757 as 'a thin little figure, with a large head'.[5]

1 Prince Leopold (1790-1865) of Saxe-Coburg. Annotated by Charles Richard Fox (1796-1873, Lord Holland's illegitimate son by Lady Holland): 'This must be in some year between 1817 & 1830'; 1825 was the only year within that period in which 13 May was a Friday.

2 Elizabeth, *née* Vassall (1771-1840), who m. 2) 1797 Henry Holland, 3rd Baron Holland.

3 Item 426 in Halliday's cat.196, 1935.

4 Offered with fourteen miscellaneous drawings (which are in the NPG reference collection); on 20 December 1935 C.K. Adams told Halliday that the drawings 'will not be required for this Gallery, but I think it is possible that one of the Trustees might be interested in them' (NPG archive). It is assumed that an unidentified Trustee acquired them and subsequently presented them, according to the accession number, in 1946.

5 See Gibbon, *Autobiography*, Everyman ed., n.d., pp.65, 102-04; *Letters*, I, p.200n.

ICONOGRAPHY

c.1759? Miniature by Penelope Carwardine. Private collection (illus. Gibbon, *Letters*, 1956, I, f.p.112). Probably the miniature set in a gold box which Gibbon gave Daniel Pavillard before 1763 (Gibbon, *Letters*, 1956, I, p.151n4) and the portrait of Gibbon 'aged 21' listed at Sheffield Place c.1804 (Harding, I, f.9).

1773 Painting by Henry Walton, see NPG 1443.

1779 Painting by Joshua Reynolds,* half length with fur-trimmed coat and waistcoat. Dalmeny (Mannings 2000, no.725), at Sheffield Place until 1896. Exhibited RA 1780(18). Engraved J. Hall 1780 and frequently thereafter; an enamel version, painted over the print by Hall is in the Victoria and Albert Museum (414.1409.1885).

A version attributed to James Northcote was with C.W. Traylen, Guildford, 1981, formerly with Lord St Germans. Copy sold Sotheby's, 22 February 1928, lot 22 as Walton from the Sheffield collection; other copies in pastel by J-S-L. Piot in the musée de Lausanne (illus. M. Bishop, *Blake's Hayley*, 1951, f.p.160) and sold Christie's, 19 March 1975, lot 124; miniature copies by Edward Miles (Sotheby's, 15 March 1982, lot 145); J. Watts (seen by Scharf in 1882 when with William Baker; TSB 30/23), and attributed to Henry Bone (with Hallam Murray 1896). A drawing after Reynolds by Henry Edridge c.1795 was engraved W. Ridley 1799.

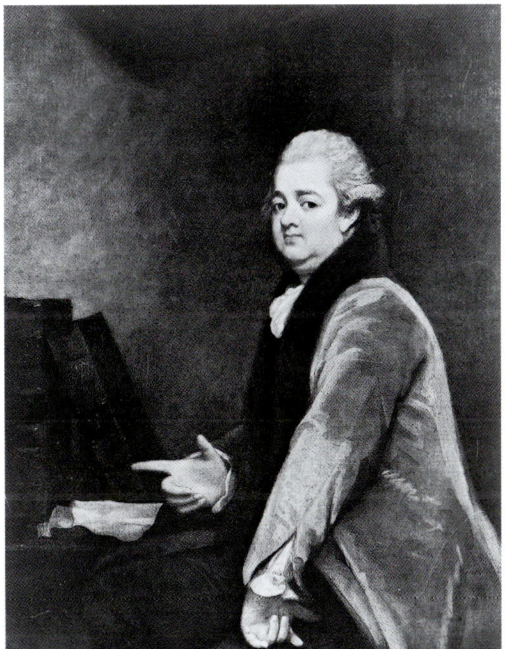

GIBBON NPG *by Joshua Reynolds 1779 (The Earl of Rosebery)*

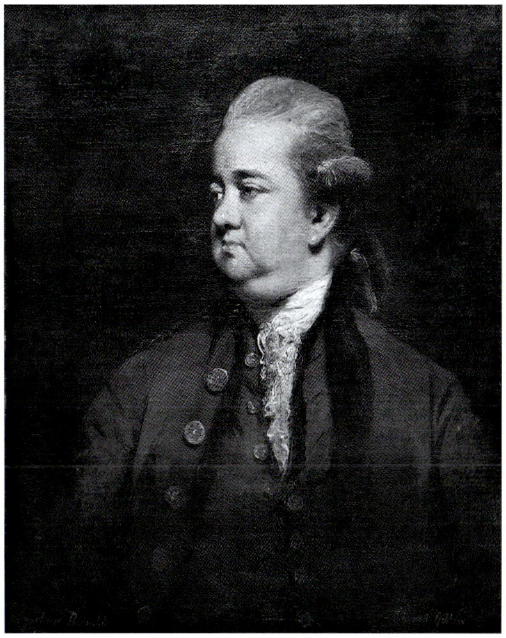

GIBBON *by George Romney 1783 (Private Collection)*

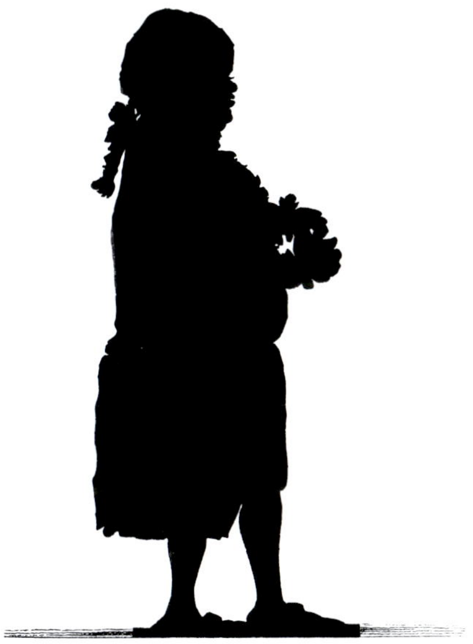

GIBBON *anon. silhouette 1791 (NPG archive)*

1783 Painting by George Romney,* three-quarter length seated, pointing to books on a table. Private collection. Painted for Hayley 'the countenance exquisitely painted ... but the subordinate parts ... very far from being entitled to praise' (Hayley 1809, pp.90-91). Small watercolour copy by Isaac Pocock sold Christie's, 3 April 1878, lot 131 (SSB 93/2).

c.1783? Wedgwood medallion (illus. Reilly 1973, p.173). Resembling a (reversed) engraving by B. Reading published in 1788 (*European Mag.*).

c.1790? Drawing attributed to Thomas Lawrence, bust-length profile. Private collection (illus. *Boswell*, NPG, 1967, no.101 as James Boswell).

1791 Silhouette, whole-length standing, with Lord Sheffield. Private collection (illus. G. de Beer, *Gibbon*, 1967, p.101). Others show Gibbon whole-length seated or standing taking snuff* (see D.M. Low, *Gibbon*, 1937, f.p.172).

1793 On 15 July 1793 Joseph Banks and Samuel Lysons were going to persuade Gibbon to sit to George Dance (Farington).

A portrait of Gibbon by the 1st Earl Lucan was at Sheffield Place c.1804 (Harding, I, f.9).

Undated Engraving by Torchiana, *Odoardo Gibbon*, whole-length seated on a rock, from a drawing by Bosio (presumably J.B.F. Bosio).

Amateur drawings, by Lady Diana Beauclerk c.1780? and Lavinia, Countess Spencer, c.1785, are in thre British Museum (illus. *A Noble Art*, British Museum, 2000, nos.181-82); another called Gibbon by George Townshend c.1775 (*ibid.*, no.180) may show Lord North, see Guilford; a drawing by 'the Hon. William Wallace' shows Gibbon at table with Mme. De Silva at Geneva in 1791 (Holland House Cat., 1904, no.225; illus. G. de Beer, *Gibbon*, 1967, p.108); a caricature by the Rev. James Douglas, *The Luminous Historian* 1788 (illus. G. de Beer, *Gibbon*, 1967, p.106) 'gave great offence to Mr Gibbon, whose outer man Nature has not bestowed so much care upon, as that nobler counterpart, the mind' (Angelo 1904, I, p.332). See also NPG 3317.

DOUBTFUL PORTRAIT

Drawing by Thomas Patch, whole length, part of a sketchbook; Yale Center for British Art (B1977.14.309P).

GILBERT, Thomas c.1719-98

Politician, of Cotton, Staffs.; MP 1763-95; his many pamphlets principally addressed the subject of poor relief - his name should be 'written in letters of gold, for the uncommon pains he had taken to assist the poor'; he also campaigned for improved road and canal transport.

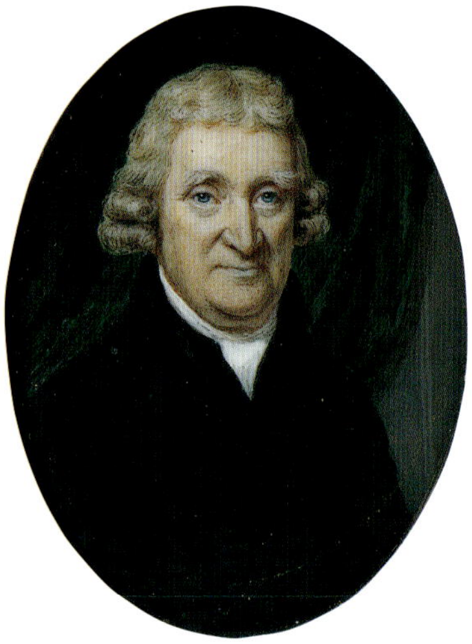

GILBERT NPG *6070*

6070 UNKNOWN ARTIST c.1790

Watercolour and bodycolour on ivory 7.2 x 5.5 (2⅞ x 2⅛)

Blue eyes, grey powdered hair, wearing a black coat; a green curtain in the background.

Collections: By descent to the sitter's great-grandson, F.H. Gilbert in 1932,[1] thence to S.F. Anderton, The Hague, from whom purchased 1988.

The only known portrait of Gilbert; the identification is based on family tradition.

1 When it was considered doubtful whether Gilbert was 'of sufficient fame for this Gallery' (H.M. Hake, 18 February 1932).

GILPIN, Sawrey 1733-1807

Animal painter, yr. bro. of William Gilpin; studied under Samuel Scott 1749-56 and later patronised by the Duke of Cumberland; exhibited SA 1762-83, RA 1786-1807; ARA 1795, RA 1797.

'[a] cripple below - [he] wheels about very easy & cheerful, social & likes to tell stories and tells them well ... always wakes abt 3 in morning & eats apple, piece of bread &c. which removed irritation' (Joseph Farington, 1799).

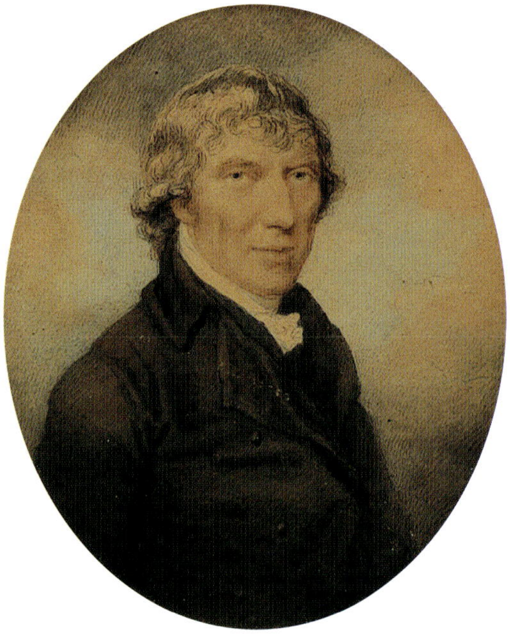

Sawrey GILPIN NPG *4328*

4328 WILLIAM SHERLOCK c.1785

Watercolour 14.2 x 12.1 (5⅝ x 4¾) considerably faded; a *pentimento* shows changes to the outline of his left arm; a scratch runs across his right shoulder; inscribed verso, possibly added by the artist:[1] *Mr S. Gilpin, R A / Painted by / W Sherlock.*

The fading of the colours complicates description: probably grey eyes and light hair, wearing a grey coat.

Collections: Presented by A.A. Appleby 1963.

Sherlock copied Walton's portrait of Sawrey's brother, William Gilpin, in 1783 or 1785 (see NPG 4418) which conceivably indicates the date of NPG 4328.

1 That is, NPG 4328 appears to date from before 1797 when Gilpin was elected RA.

ICONOGRAPHY

c.1785 Watercolour by William Sherlock, see NPG 4328.

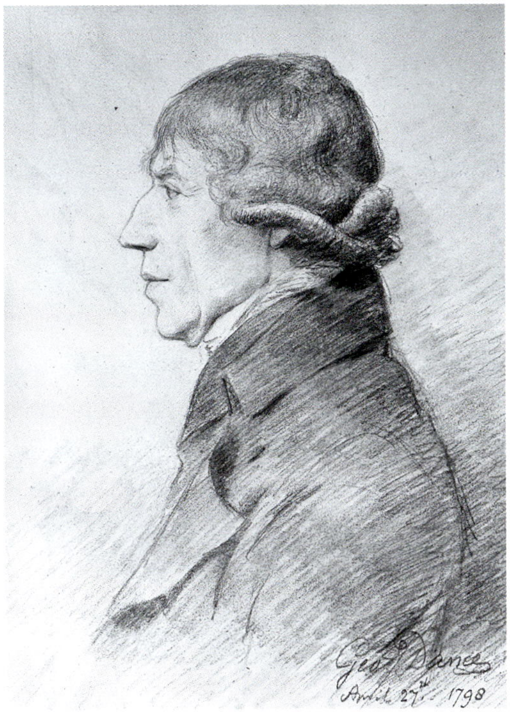

Sawrey GILPIN by George Dance 1798 (Royal Academy of Arts, London)

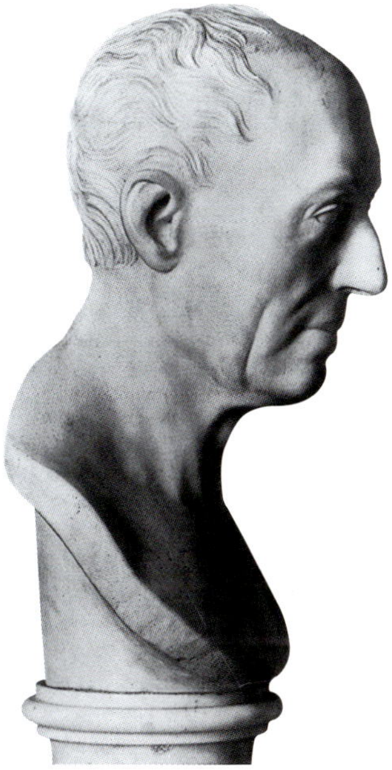

Sawrey GILPIN by George Garrard 1808 (Southill Chattels Trust)

c.1785-90 Painting attributed to Sawrey Gilpin, half length, with fair hair. Private collection, USA (not in the Gilpin sale, Foster's, 20 April 1915).

1798 Drawing by George Dance,* profile bust, dated 27 April 1798. Royal Academy. Engraved W. Daniell 1810 (*Dance Portraits*); tracing by Daniell in the Yale Center for British Art (B1977.14.4183). A second undated profile by Dance is in the British Museum (1859.5.28.69).

1803 Plaster bust by George Garrard, undraped *all'antica*. Burghley House. Presumably the bust by Garrard exhibited RA 1806(815).

Posthumous

1808 Marble bust by George Garrard, undraped, *all'antica*, with receding hair. Southill. Inscribed *carved by order of Sl Whitbread ...* .

DOUBTFUL PORTRAIT

In 1808 there was a portrait of 'Gilpin' in the library at Muncaster Castle, Cumberland (Farington, 14 October 1808).

GILPIN, William 1724-1804

Writer and philanthropist, bro. of Sawrey Gilpin; by 1752 a schoolmaster at Cheam, Surrey; published *Essay on Prints* 1768; vicar of Boldre, Hants., 1777; between 1769 and 1782 made numerous sketching tours, whose subsequent publication made him the unwitting champion of the picturesque.

'His figure is apostolical, his head bald - a short man' (Samuel Rogers, 1792).

'His face, somewhat fat, with a roundish bald head, chiefly expresses a grave and cheerful benevolence, spiced with some hint of mental alacrity' (P. Walker, 1873).

4418 HENRY WALTON 1781

Mahogany panel 25.5 x 20.5 x 0.7 (10 x 8 x ⅜), horizontal grain; slight horizontal craquelure, more prominent in the left background; cleaned 1982; verso, a vertical strip of canvas 11 (4¼)wide, the whole covered with black paint and varnish; signed and dated, bottom left: *H. Walton / 1781*.

Blue eyes, fair hair, wearing a white collar, dark grey coat and black vest, his right hand on a stick. Within a painted oval.

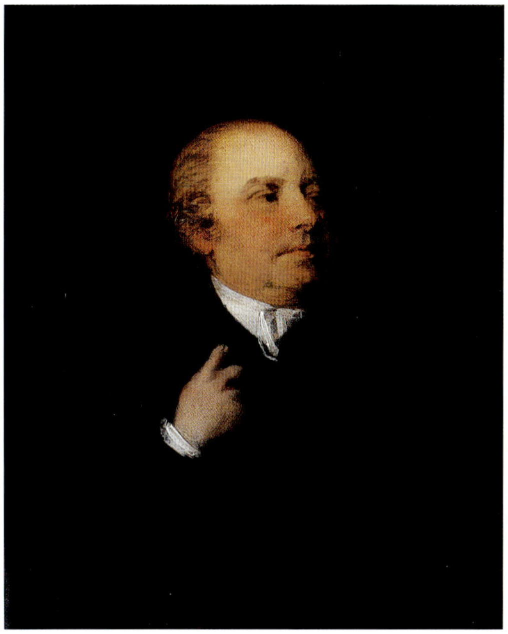

William GILPIN NPG *4418*

Collections: [passed from the sitter's second son, the Rev W. Gilpin (d.1848); to his eldest son C.B. Gilpin (d.1891), to his niece Elizabeth Mary Gilpin, to her son E.B. Benson (d.1940) and to his nephew F.A.G. Benson (b.1883), from whom stolen c.1945]; E.J. Duckett, Sevenoaks, c.1945; J. Maas, London, from whom purchased 1964.

Engravings: G. Clint 1805 (as *Painted by H. Walton Esqr ... Engraved by G. Clint / From a Picture, the only one Painted in the Year 1781 - & in the possession of Mrs Gilpin*); G. Measom 1851.

Exhibitions: Maas Gallery, Nov.-Dec. 1964(120); *The Arrogant Connoisseur*, Manchester, 1984(198).

Reference: *Walton 1999*, no.68.

When Clint's mezzotint was published in 1805, the *Monthly Magazine* declared that it gave 'a very strong resemblance to the original, as the countenance is animated, and the general effect interesting; considered as a whole, it is a very well engraved mezzotinto'.[1] A miniature copy by William Sherlock, dated 1783 or 1785,[2] remains with the sitter's descendants, and several miniature copies were made for the family by Mrs R.G. Benson (20th century);[3] a full-size copy is in Tullie House, Carlisle.[4]

Evelyn Bell[5] suggested that NPG 4418 is a smaller version of a 'larger portrait' engraved by Clint,[6] now lost, but sharing the same provenance up to E.F. Benson (see above); but Clint's figure appears identical with that in NPG 4418.

1 *Monthly Mag.*, XX, 1805, p.361.
2 Sherlock also painted William's brother, Sawrey Gilpin, c.1785, see NPG 4328.
3 See C.P. Barbier, *Gilpin*, 1963, p.87.

4 Illus. *Cumberland Artists*, 1971, p.6; C.P. Barbier, *Samuel Rogers and William Gilpin*, 1959, front.
5 *Walton* 1999, no.69.
6 The engraving illus. W.D. Templeman, *William Gilpin*, 1939, front. C.P. Barbier, *Gilpin*, 1963, p.87n, refers to the 'good engraving after the original portrait'.

ICONOGRAPHY

1781 Painting by Henry Walton, see NPG 4418.

1805 Bust by George Garrard, exhibited RA 1805(780).

A pastel portrait was recorded in Walhampton Park, 'a house which [Gilpin] often visited' (P. Walker, *Rambles*, 1873, p.34).

DOUBTFUL PORTRAIT

Miniature by William Sherlock 1806 in a private collection (illus. Caffrey 2000, p.57, no.105) may show one of Gilpin's nephews.

GLYNN, John 1722-79

Politician and lawyer; serjeant-at-law 1763; defended Wilkes against charges of sedition in 1763, 1764 and 1768; MP for Middlesex 1768-79 and a leading member of the Society for the Bill of Rights; recorder of London 1772.

1944 see Groups, *John Glynn, John Wilkes and John Horne Tooke*, after RICHARD HOUSTON [1769]

ICONOGRAPHY

1769 Engraving by R. Houston, with Wilkes and Horne Tooke, see Groups NPG 1944.

c.1769 Anon. engraving, whole length in bands, holding a paper lettered: *Wilkes Esqr / The King Res* (for the *Political Register*). Three anon. engravings, bust-length ovals, in gown and bands (one for the *Universal Mag.*).

c.1770 Painting formerly attributed to Johann Zoffany, standing behind Wilkes, see Wilkes c.1770.

An unspecified portrait exhibited Exeter 1873(103) lent Mrs Glynn.

GOLDSMITH, Oliver 1728-74

Novelist and playwright; b. Pallas, Co. Longford, came to London 1756; published *The Vicar of Wakefield* 1766, *The Deserted Village* 1770 and *She Stoops to Conquer* 1773.

'something under middle size; his limbs on which he prided himself, sturdy and well shaped; his habits active. ... His complexion was pale, his forehead and upper lip rather projecting, his face round, pitted with the small pox, and marked with strong lines of thinking. ... His eyes were of grey or hazel colour and possessed considerable expression; and he always ... wore a wig. ... Although not prepossessing on first appearance, the moment he became at ease the native good humour and benevolence of his disposition broke forth' (Sir James Prior, 1837).

130 studio of JOSHUA REYNOLDS [1769-70]

Canvas 75.5 x 63.5 (29¾ x 25) lined; cleaned 1968.

Brown eyes, mousy hair, deep purple fur-collared cape, black jacket.

Collections: By descent from the sitter to his brother-in-law, Daniel Hodson of Lishoy; his daughter, Mrs Neligan; her son, Dr William Hodson Neligan (d.1859) of Athlone,[1] by whose three executors offered for sale, Dublin, 1861; purchased through Robert H. Boyce 1861.[2]

Exhibitions: NG of Ireland 1897-1916; *Georgian Playhouse* 1975(92).

Reference: Graves & Cronin, I, p.369; Mannings 2000, no.737b.

A contemporary studio copy of the Reynolds portrait in a private collection which was exhibited at the RA in 1770 and first engraved by Giuseppe Marchi in 1770.[3] A replica by Reynolds, dated 1772, formerly at Woburn Abbey (and from the Piozzi sale 1816), is now in the National Gallery of Ireland (4600).[4] Reynolds 'was intimately acquainted with Dr Goldsmith. They unbosomed their minds freely to each other, not only in regard to the characters of their friends, but what contributed to make men's company desired or avoided'.[5] When Goldsmith died it was 'the severest blow Sir Joshua ever received - he did not paint all that day',[6] and it was Reynolds who 'fixed upon the place where Goldsmith's monument now stands, over a door in the Poets' Corner'[7] in Westminster Abbey. Goldsmith, in turn, had dedicated to Reynolds his celebrated poem *The Deserted Village* in 1770.

Despite Goldsmith's 'dish-clout' face,[8] his portrait was much admired. 'I have seen nothing on canvas more touching', wrote Leslie, for whom it recalled 'all that is known of the sufferings of the tenderest and warmest of hearts';[9] Frances Reynolds considered it 'a very great likeness ... the most flattered picture she ever knew her brother to have painted';[10] Catherine Horneck thought it conveyed 'a good idea of his face; it was painted as a fine poetical head for the admiration of posterity, but as it is divested of his wig and with the shirt collar open, it was not the man as seen in daily life'.[11] But when at home Goldsmith 'usually wore his shirt collar open' and he is shown as a writer; Hilles stressed how Reynolds painted Goldsmith as 'essentially a simple person, unpretentious and unaffected'.[12]

NPG 130 was described by Prior in 1837 as a 'copy', 'very indifferently executed', but in 1861 he told Scharf 'it was then, as it appears now, impaired by time and neglect and shewed disadvantageously';[13] the folds of the cloak appear more strongly lit than in the original or the replica in Dublin. Other copies include those with Trinity College, Dublin;[14] the Royal College of Physicians of Ireland, Dublin; Sir Torquil Munro sale, Christie's, 25 September 1942, lot 65; Stirling of Keir sale, Christie's, 22-24 May 1995, lot 480 (head only, inscribed *Northcote*), and see NPG 828 below. In 1837 Prior listed additionally versions in a private collection in Salisbury (from the collection of Archdeacon Coxe) and with a Mr Bacon of the Middle Temple, London.[15] Northcote repeated the composition in his portrait of Joshua Hunt of 1776.[16]

1 In whose collection mentioned by Prior in 1837 (*Life of Goldsmith*, II, p.536) and Maria Edgeworth in 1842 (letter of 18 June 1842 to W.H. Neligan; copy NPG archive).
2 Provenance as given by Robert H. Boyce in letters (addressed from Pembroke Dock) to Scharf (NPG archive): he brought the sale to Scharf's attention 'having become possessed by marriage of a share in [the picture] and [as] requested by the other claimants' (26 January 1861); 'I have only a third share in the picture. My wife's father died intestate & his widow (a second wife) admitted all the property has been sold except the above portrait, it was placed for auction lately in Dublin but withdrawn on the representation of my brother in law' (1 March 1861). The executors had asked £1,000 before finally accepting £150.
3 Mannings 2000, no.736.
4 *Ibid.*, no.737.
5 Hilles 1952, p.26.
6 *Conversations of Northcote*, ed. W. Hazlitt, 1949, p.112.
7 Northcote 1819, I, p.326.
8 So described by Garrick (Northcote 1819, I, p.234)
9 Leslie & Taylor 1865, I, p.360.
10 Quoted *Reynolds* 1986, p.247.
11 J. Prior, *Goldsmith*, 1837, II, p.380. He later told Scharf these comments came from 'a long conversation of 1833 or 1834' (letter of 3 May 1861; NPG archive).
12 Hilles 1952, p.26. *Reynolds* 1986, p.248.
13 Letter of 3 May 1861 (NPG archive).
14 Illus. Crookshank & Webb 1990, p.154.
15 J. Prior, *Life of Goldsmith*, 1837, II, p.536.
16 Illus. *Burl. Mag.*, CXXXVI, 1994, p.235.

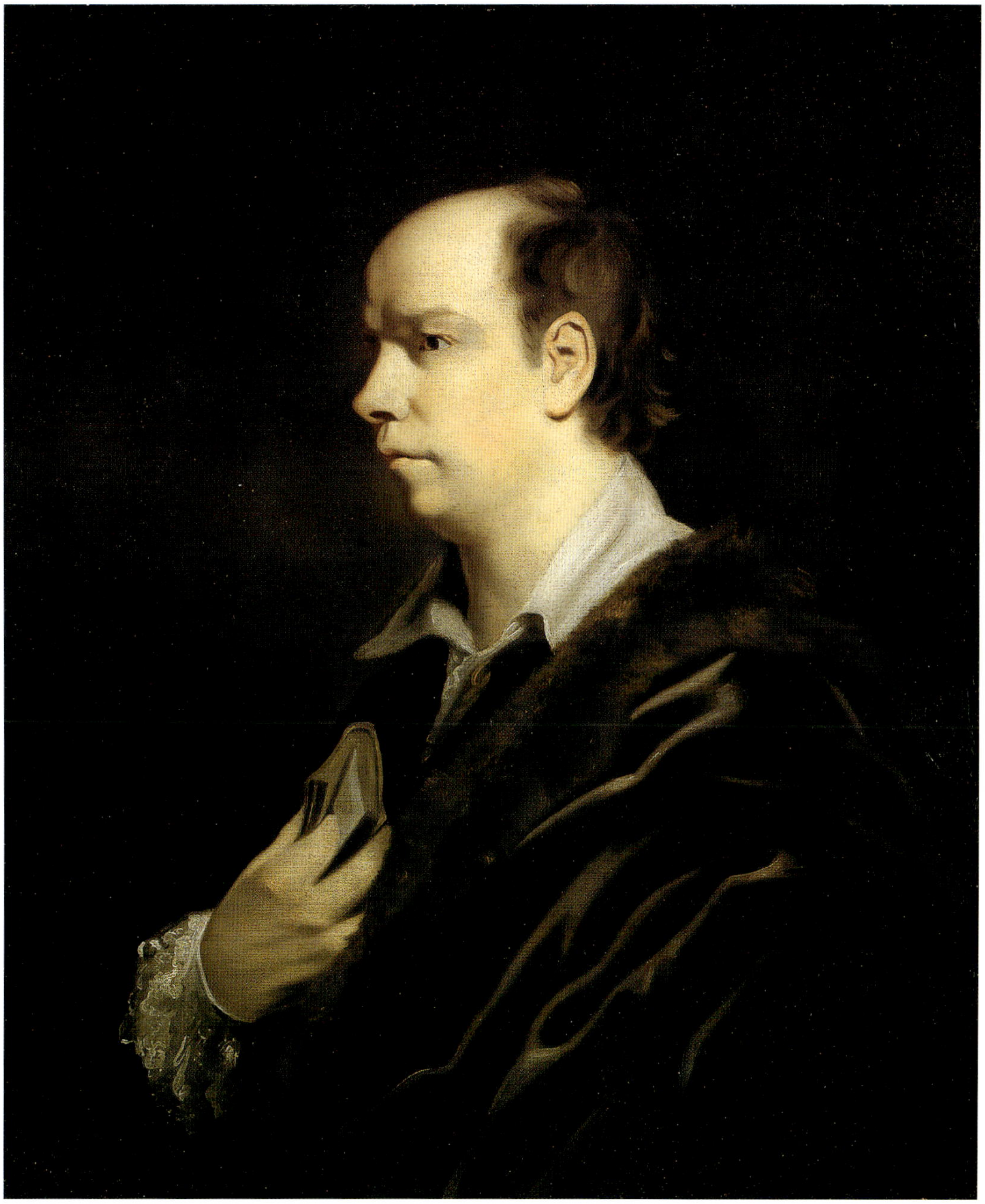

GOLDSMITH NPG 130

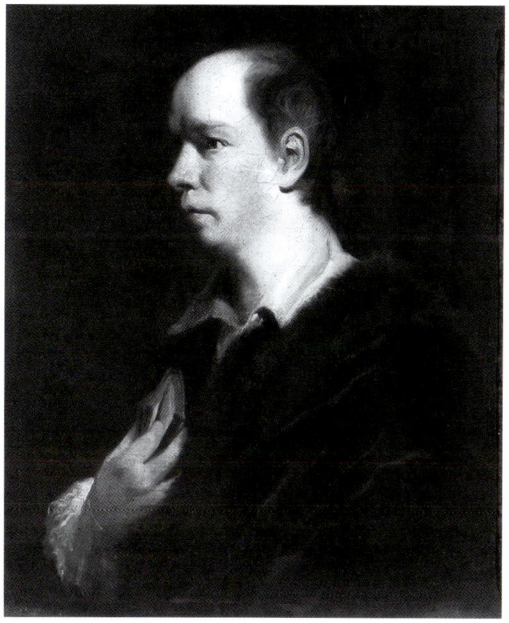

GOLDSMITH NPG 828

676 UNKNOWN ARTIST c.1770?

Watercolour and chinese white on laid paper 12 x 9.8 (4¾ x 3⅞), the image 7.5 x 4.5 (3 x 1¾); the outline modified with white overlay; inscribed verso in pencil: *Original drawing / by O. Humphrey.*[1]

Collection: Sir Theodore Martin KCB, by whom presented 1883.

Exhibition: *Samuel Johnson, Londoner*, Royal Exchange, London, 1964.

Reference: Williamson 1918, p.243, ascribed to Humphry.

Acquired as a silhouette by Ozias Humphry, but it is hardly good enough to be by him; the identification of Goldsmith may be correct.

1 The original backboard had a label: *Portrait of Oliver Goldsmith / From the life / By / Ozias Humphrey his / friend*

828 after JOSHUA REYNOLDS [1769-70]

Canvas 74 x 62 (29¼ x 24½) lined; varnish much discoloured and a marked overall craquelure.

See NPG 130 above; the cloak a deep red.

Collections:[1] Bought in Tewkesbury[2] by Dr Leifchild, 'a well-known Congregational Minister', and bequeathed by him 1890.

Exhibition: NG of Ireland 1916-82.

Reference: Graves & Cronin, I, p.369; Mannings 2000, no.737c.

An indifferent copy of the Reynolds portrait, for which see NPG 130.

1 Graves & Cronin associated NPG 828 with the half length in the Caleb Whitefoord sale, Christie's, 4 May 1810, lot 91, and with the portrait bt. in by Kelsall, Christie's, 22 May 1813, lot 112.
2 When 'rolled up' (L.G. Holland, Sketchbook no.3, f.75; NPG archive).

ICONOGRAPHY

A brief survey of Goldsmith's iconography appeared in A. Dobson, *The Poetical Works of Goldsmith*, 1927, Appendix A, pp.259-61.

1769-70 Painting by Joshua Reynolds, see NPG 130 and NPG 828.

1770 in January 1770 Goldsmith sent his cousin Jenny a miniature of himself: 'the face you well know is ugly enough, but it is finely painted'. This has been associated with the drawing engraved Cook 1780 (K. Balderston ed., *Goldsmith, Collected Letters*,

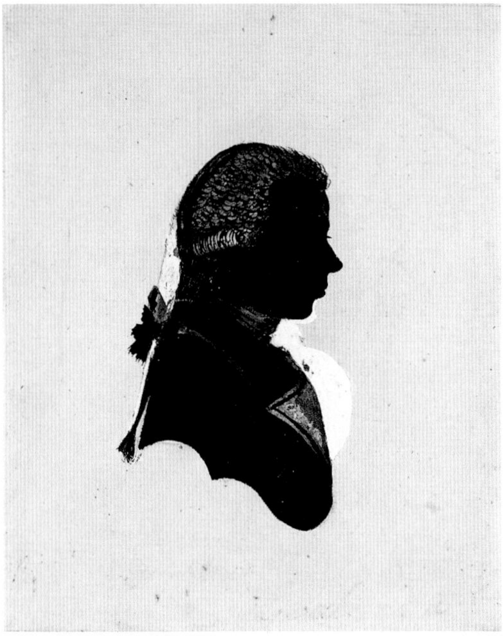

GOLDSMITH NPG *676*

1928, p.85); anon. (*Universal Mag.*), and P. Audinet 1795 (*Biographical Mag.*).

Caleb Whitefoord had an 'admirable miniature' of Goldsmith 'by Reynolds' which belonged to his descendants in 1898 (*Whitefoord Papers*, 1898, p.xxvii).

c.1770 Watercolour by an unknown artist, see NPG 676.

c.1772 Drawing by Henry Bunbury whole-length walking, his hat in his right hand, etched J. Bretherton 1772 as *The Full Blown Macaroni* (Stephen 4714).

c.1772 Etching by Henry Bunbury, half length, inscribed by Horace Walpole. Lewis Walpole Library, Farmington (illus. *Eighteenth-century Studies*, IX, i, 1975, f.p.42, fig.2).

c.1772? Drawing by Henry Bunbury, half-length oval, etched J. Bretherton 1776 (illus. A. Dobson, *Poetical Works of Goldsmith*, 1927, f.p.259). The artist's sister-in-law thought 'nothing can exceed its truth', and Prior described it as 'an excellent though not flattering likeness, yet presenting great benevolence of expression, and conveying the best idea of his countenance' (J. Prior, *Life of Goldsmith*, 1837, II, pp.380, 536).

A second bust-length profile (without hands), by Bunbury was also etched by Bretherton.*

1774 Miniature by Joseph Saunders, exhibited SA 1774(247).

1774 Painting, probably a miniature, by John Ford, exhibited FSA 1774(387).

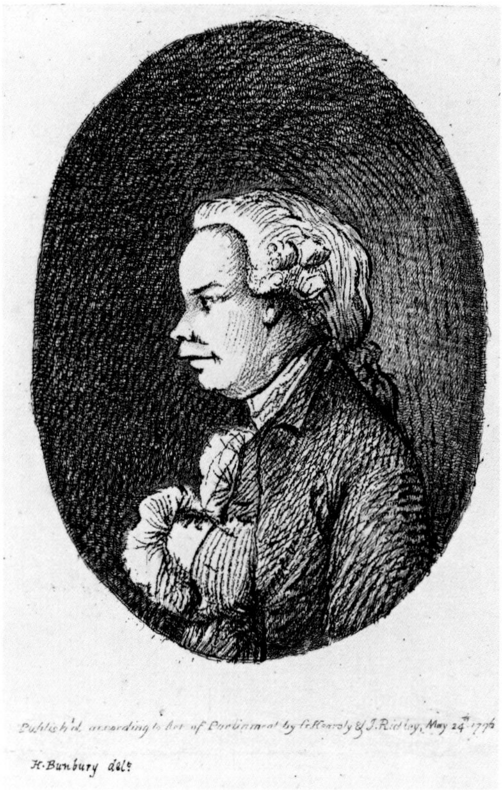

GOLDSMITH J. Bretherton after Henry Bunbury c.1772 (NPG D 17847)

Posthumous

1774–76 Monument by Joseph Nollekens, incorporating a medallion portrait derived from the head by Reynolds. Westminster Abbey. Johnson was composing the epitaph in June 1776. Engraved E. Finden 1836 and J. Cochran *from the original drawing by J. Nollekens*.

1777–84 Painting by James Barry, *Elysium*, part of the *Progress of Human Culture*, in which Goldsmith appears behind Samuel Richardson. Royal Society of Arts, London (Pressly 1981, no.27). Engraved J. Barry 1791. The head apparently based on the Reynolds portrait of 1769–70.

c.1800 Medal by John Woodhouse (Brown 1980, no.187a).

1827 Marble bust by William Behnes.* Trinity College, Dublin. Plaster in the Irish Museum of Modern Art, Dublin; another was exhibited Crystal Palace (Phillips 1854, no.410).

1861–65 Monument by J.H. Foley, whole-length standing. Trinity College, Dublin (illus. Read 1982, pp.36, 166; Crookshank & Webb 1990, p.60). Engraved G. Stodart 1865. Statuette sold Sotheby's, 15 July 1998, lot 79. A version in the Royal Collection. Modello exhibited RHA 1861(599) and RA 1861(981).

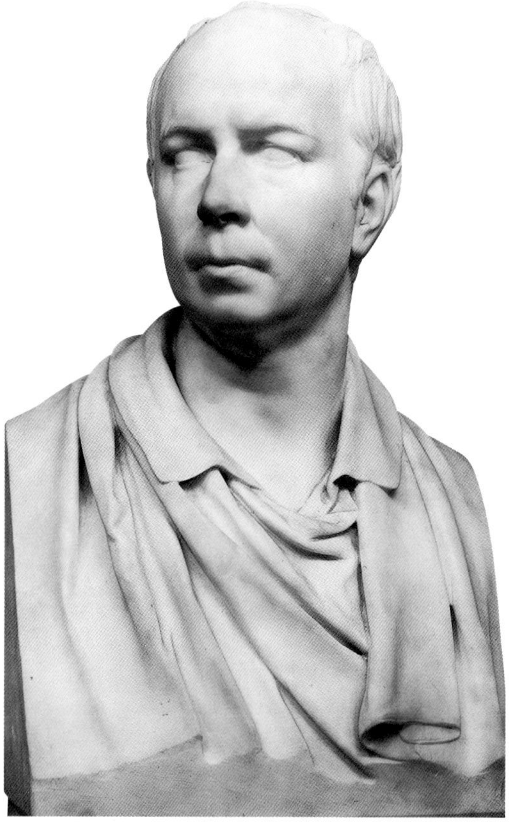

GOLDSMITH by William Behnes 1827 (Trinity College, Dublin)

DOUBTFUL PORTRAITS

Painting in the possession of the Rev Mr Williams, engraved Wainwright; W. Ridley 1799; J.C. Bock 1800, and F. Fleischmann.

For the portrait sold Christie's, March 1904, lot 48 as Goldsmith by Dance, see Colman, NPG 1364.

GORDON, Lord George 1751–93

Maverick 3rd s. of the 3rd Duke of Gordon; MP 1774–80; president of the Protestant Association 1779, whose petition he presented to Parliament on 2 June 1780, occasioning the anti-catholic Gordon Riots; acquitted of treason 1781; sentenced to five years imprisonment for libel 1788, by which time he was converted to Judaism; d. in Newgate jail.

'In his person he was thin, his features regular, and his complexion pale. His manners were gentle, his conversation agreeable, and he had the appearance as well as the deportment of a man of quality. There was, however, something in his cast of countenance and mode of expression that indicated cunning, or a perverted understanding, or both' (Sir Nathaniel Wraxall, 1815).

Abbreviations

Rubens 1935: A. Rubens, *Anglo-Jewish Portraits*, 1935

Rubens 1954: A. Rubens, *A Jewish Iconography*, 1954

4603 JAMES TASSIE 1781

Amethyst glass intaglio 7.6 (3½) high, stamped, in reverse: *LORD GEORGE GORDON / Tassie F. 1781.*

Collections: K.E. Houston sale, Sotheby's, 15 January 1968, lot 90, bt. Nora Breen, from whom purchased 1968.

Reference: Gray 1894, no.159.

The image was presumably based upon the contemporary engravings by Trotter and Lodge, see below; it was engraved by C. Knight 1783 and copied by Wedgwood, perhaps after 1787.[1]

1 Reilly 1973, pp.175–76, where described as based on the painting by de Fleur, engraved by Trotter, see below.

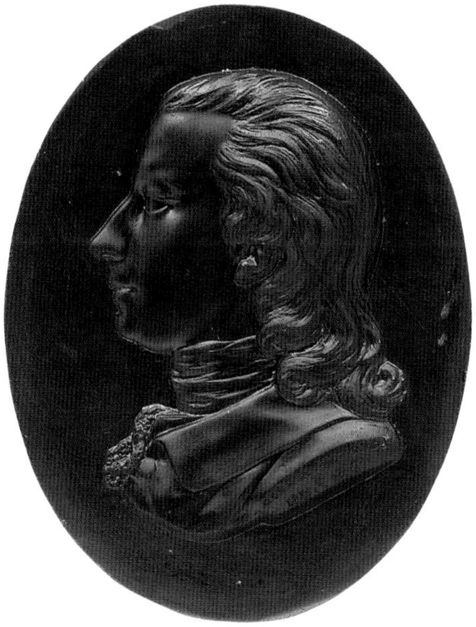

Lord George GORDON NPG *4603*

ICONOGRAPHY

Further engravings and caricatures of Gordon are catalogued in Rubens 1935, nos.125–41, and Rubens 1954, nos.124a–141a.

1780 Medal by T. Spence (Brown 1980, no.227).

1780 Drawn and engraved by R. Bran* (*drawn from the life*), whole-length standing, pointing to *The Protestant Petition* (George 5694; Rubens 1935, no.125.

1780 Anon. engraving, oval profile with vignette of the Tower below (*Westminster Mag.*).

c.1780 Gouache attributed to Daniel Gardner, small three-quarter length seated, a dog in his lap. Arbury (illus. *Palace of History*, Glasgow, 1911, I, f.p.60 as by Alexander Skirving). Exhibited Birmingham 1934(192) as by Gardner.

c.1780 Painting by I. de Fleur, half-length profile, engraved T. Trotter (Rubens 1935, no.131). A comparable profile was published by R.S. Kirby in 1805.

1781 Anon. medal, bust length, *The Trial of Lord George Gordon* (Brown 1980, no.240, illus.). An engraved bust of 1781 (*Universal Mag.*; Rubens 1935, no.126) shows a similar head, which is only tenuously related to the Tassie/Gardner likenesses.

1781 Drawn and engraved by C. Hall, bust-length oval, celebrating Gordon's acquittal (Rubens 1935, no.127).

1781 Engraving by J. Lodge, half-length oval (Rubens 1954, no.131a).

1781 Medallion by James Tassie, see NPG 4603.

1785 Anon. caricature etching, *Lord George Riot made a Jew*, showing Gordon circumcised (George 8249; Rubens 1954, no.133a).

1787–88 Anon. mezzotint, halflength as a Jew, with beard and hat (illus. Rubens 1935, no.139, illus. f.p.48).

A number of anon. caricatures showing him as a Jew were published at this time, e.g. *Birmingham Moses*, *Wandering Jew* and *Dining in Newgate* (Rubens 1935, nos.134, 136–37; George 7209, 7423–24).

1787 Anon. etching, whole length with beard and long coat, pub. I. Wallis (Rubens 1935, no.135).

c.1787 Miniature by Solomon Polack, engraved G. Wilson,* half-length oval with beard and hat. A ms note by the engraver on the verso of the BM copy (li 3–93, portrait series Cl.ii, P4) has: *The Painting from which this is done was executed in Water colours of the same size by Mr Polack, from Lord George Gordon*

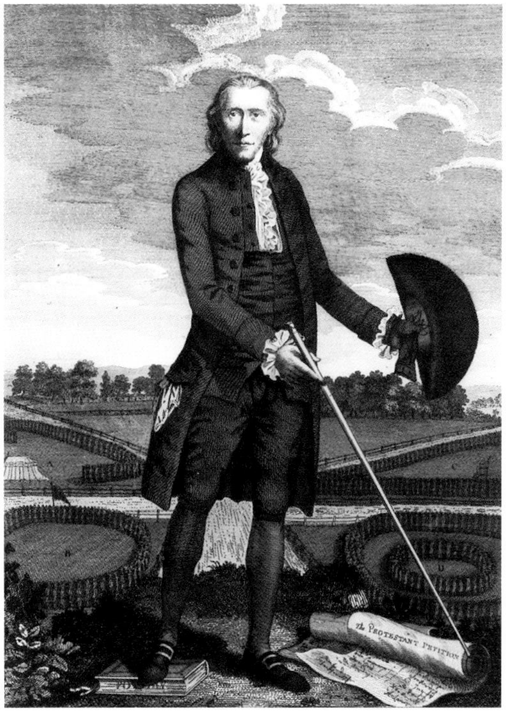

Lord George GORDON drawn and engraved by R. Bran 1780 (NPG *D 2793*)

while in Newgate: & is allowed to be the best likeness of him extant (Rubens 1935, no.138).

after 1787 Wedgwood medallion, see NPG 4603.

1793 Etching by Richard Newton, *Promenade in the State Side of Newgate*, including Gordon with beard and hat (illus. D. Alexander, *Richard Newton* 1997, p.37).

DOUBTFUL PORTRAIT

Drawing, signed and dated T. Heseltine 1759, as a child (untraced; Rubens 1955, p.123, no.141a).

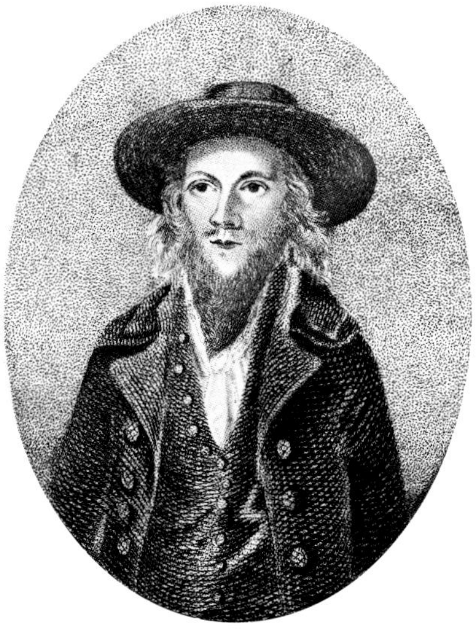

Lord George GORDON G. Wilson after Solomon Polak c.1787 (British Museum)

GRAFTON, Augustus Henry Fitzroy, 3rd Duke of 1735-1811

Statesman; sty. Earl of Euston 1747; suc. his grandfather 1757 as 3rd Duke of Grafton; MP 1756-57; prime minister 1768-70; KG 1769; lord privy seal 1771-75 and 1782-83; Newmarket, the hunt and his mistress Nancy Parsons easily distracted him from his statesman's role.

'Of a reserved nature and an imperious disposition, vacillating and inconsistent in devising measures, ... [preferring] indolence to exertion' (J.H. Jesse, 1867).

4899 POMPEO BATONI 1762

Canvas 75 x 61.5 (29½ x 24¼) lined; painted on a red ground.

Blue eyes, dark hair, wearing the red coat with silver trim of the western batallion of the Suffolk Militia and holding a spontoon over his right shoulder; within a painted oval.

Collections: Commander Henry Forrester; his sale, Christie's, 1 June 1934, lot 65, bt. Walton; Christie's, 15 June 1951, lot 126, bt. in; Christie's, 19 October 1951, lot 120, bt. in; Bearnes & Waycotts, Torquay, 25 July 1972, lot 438, bt. Leggatt for the NPG.

Engravings: Anon. 1805; J. Watson 1806; J. Cook 1845 (variant, without the spontoon, his right hand in his vest).

Exhibition: *Faces as Art*, NPG, 1976; Beningbrough 1979-.

Reference: Clark 1985, no.255.

Grafton was in Italy for a second time in 1761-62 accompanied by his Duchess; they travelled allegedly for the sake of her health, but the motif was more probably an attempt to retrieve a floundering marriage. They were in Rome from 1 February to 11 April 1762 when NPG 4899 was painted. In Turin the Duke had been privileged to wear the royal hunting uniform; here he wears that of the Suffolk militia.[1]

A version at Euston Hall, using the same face mask and scarf, attributed by Clark to the 'Maron hand', shows Grafton holding a halberd, his left hand on his right wrist.[2]

1 For his tour of Italy see Ingamells 1997, pp.415-16.
2 See Clark 1985, p.288.

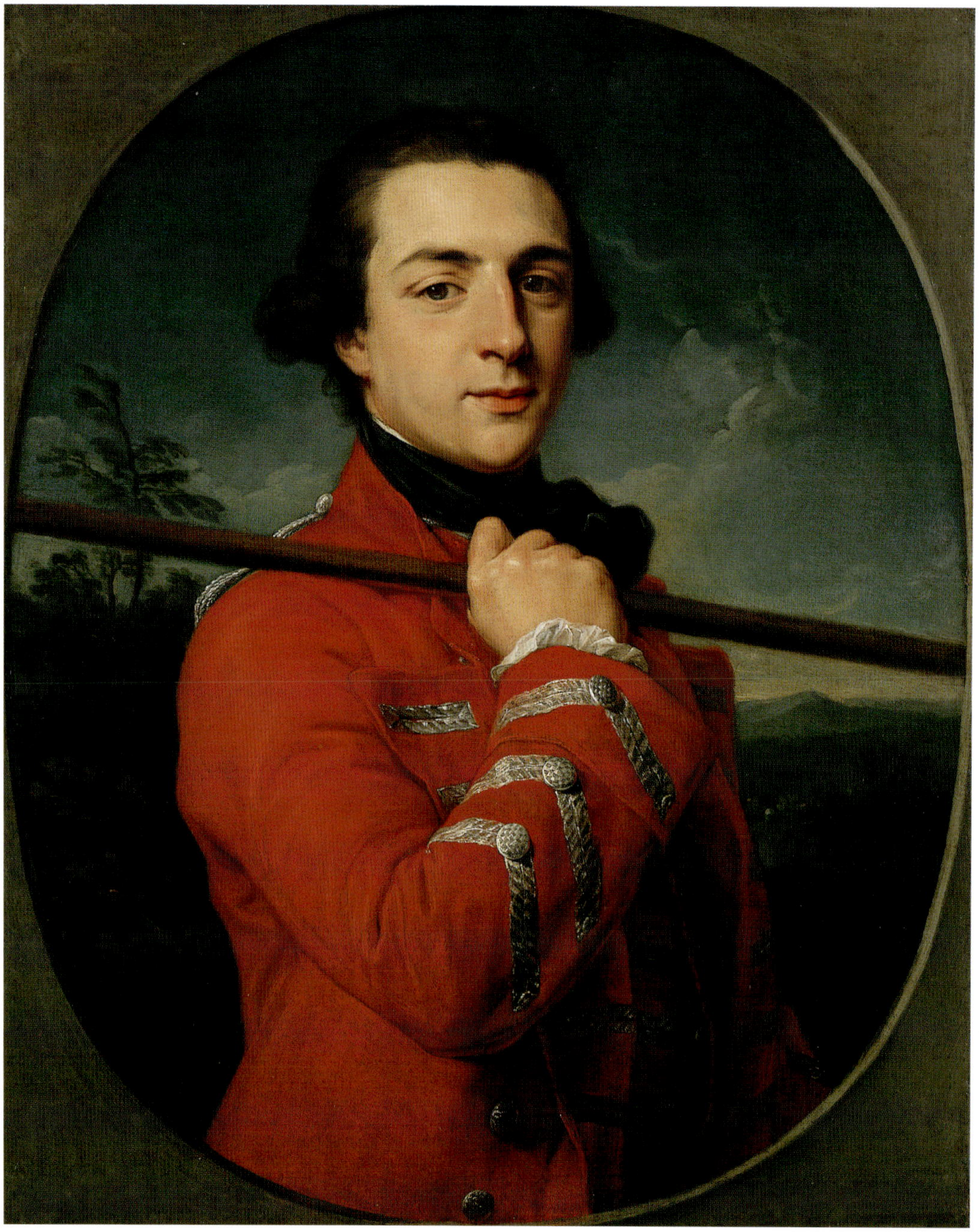

3rd Duke of GRAFTON NPG *4899*

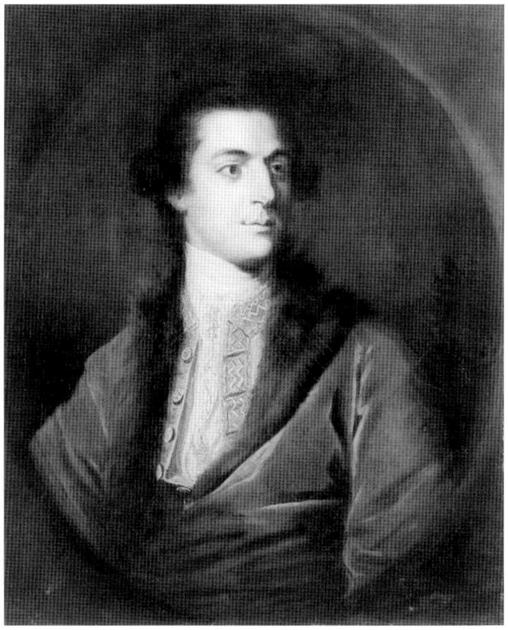

3rd Duke of GRAFTON by Joshua Reynolds 1759 (Sotheby's)

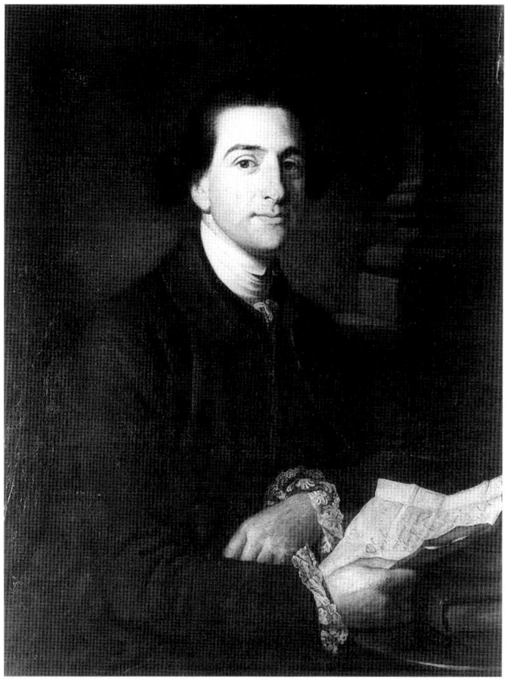

3rd Duke of GRAFTON by Nathaniel Dance c.1766 (Euston Hall)

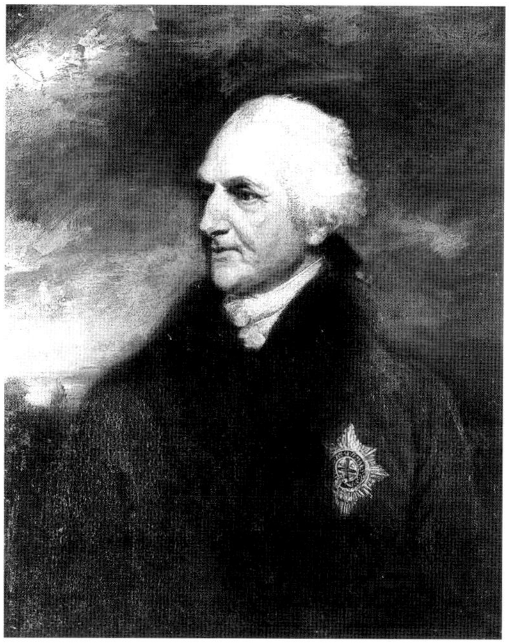

3rd Duke of GRAFTON by John Hoppner 1805 (Euston Hall)

ICONOGRAPHY

c.1753–54 Unattributed painting, whole-length standing. Euston. Probably painted during Grafton's first tour in Italy in 1753–54; formerly attributed to Hudson.

1755–58 Painting by Joshua Reynolds; sittings took place in February and March 1755 and January 1758 (Mannings 2000, no.636).

1759 Painting by Joshua Reynolds,* half-length painted oval, wearing a fur-collared red coat. Private collection (Mannings 2000, no.637).

1762 Painting by Pompeo Batoni, see NPG 4899.

c.1766 Painting by Nathaniel Dance,* half length, holding a letter signed *ND*. Euston. Dance, who probably met Grafton in Rome in 1762, had returned to England by June 1766.

1776 Painting by R.E. Pine, three-quarter length, wearing Garter robes, holding *Motion for Address for 1776*. Euston (drawn by Scharf 1881; SSB 102/70). The *Motion* proposed that diplomacy might prevent war with the American colonies.

c.1780 Miniature attributed to Jeremiah Meyer, bust-length oval wearing Garter star. Euston.

c.1780–85 Wax relief by Isaac Gosset, medallion profile. Walters AG, Baltimore (75.23). The identification is plausible but undocumented.

1782 Two etchings by J. Sayers, each whole length:

a) with hat and stick, the Garter star on his coat;

b) with folded arms (George 6060; illus. A.S. Turberville, *English Social History*, 1929, p.261). A drawing for or from the latter sold Sotheby's, 8 June 1978, lot 108.

1793 Engraving by C.T. Warren, bust-length (for *The Senator*).

1794 Etching by J. Sayers, profile bust titled *Egalité* (George 8457).

1798 Engraving by W. Ridley, bust-length profile. There is a similar undated engraving by H. Richter.

1801 Etching by Robert Dighton, *A Noble Duke, taken on the Steyne at Brighton*, whole length (George 9742).

1805 Painting by John Hoppner,* half length with Garter star. Euston. Exhibited RA 1805(122). Engraved C. Turner 1805; H.R. Cook 1807; T. Wright 1820; E. Bocquet. Version formerly at Bayham Abbey (illus. *Connoisseur*, XXI, 1908, p.76) and copies listed with the Duke of Grafton in 1931 and with Mrs Hore-Ruthven in 1962 (Steegman, II, p.11, no.31).

1805 Engraving by Kennerley, bust length with Garter star.

c.1805 Silhouette on glass by Charles Rosenberg, bust length. Christie's, 11 October 1977, lot 21 (*100 Silhouette Portraits from the Wellesley Coll.*, 1912, pl.xv). Another, reversed, showing Garter star, sold Christie's, 27 November 1984, lot 17 (as the 4th Duke).

An unspecified portrait listed at Ragley in 1797 (Musgrave MSS 6391, f.217).

Grafton appears as an incidental figure in a painting of c.1780 attributed to a follower of Hugh Barron, *A Hunt Breakfast*, sold Christie's, 11 November 1999, lot 52 (illus. Williamson 1920, f.p.156, as Zoffany), and his head appears in the stained-glass windows by M.E. Ainmiller 1855–58 in Peterhouse chapel, Cambridge.

DOUBTFUL PORTRAITS

A half-length pastel of c.1755 in a Scottish private collection and an unattributed miniature at Woburn Abbey (SSB 110/22, 29).

GRAHAM, Mrs Catharine Macaulay, see MACAULAY

GRANGER, James 1723-76

Biographer, iconomaniac; vicar of Shiplake, Oxford, 1746-76; compiled the *Biographical History of England* 1769 and ultimately, according to Walpole, drowned 'his taste for portraits in the ocean of biography'.

'He was a perfectly well bred worthy man, possess'd of great talents and a clear understanding, which never failed to enliven those who were in company with him' (Dr Philip Hayes, post 1776).

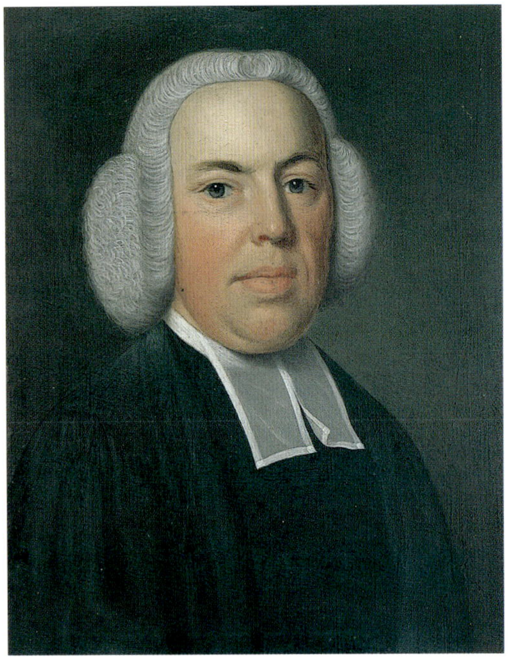

GRANGER NPG 2961

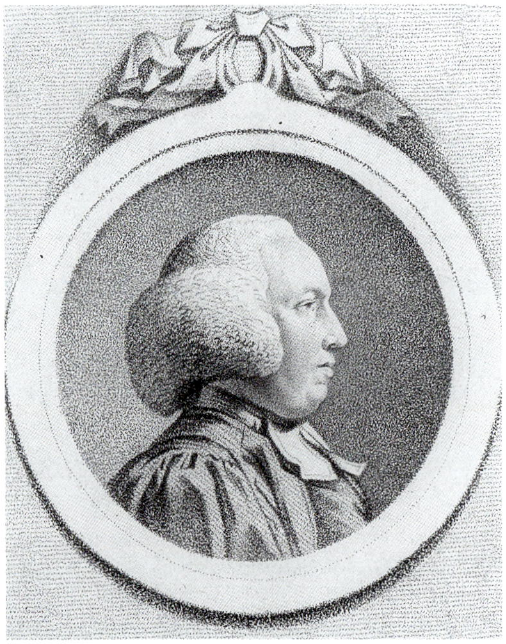

GRANGER D.P. Pariset after P-E. Falconet 1768 (NPG D 13798)

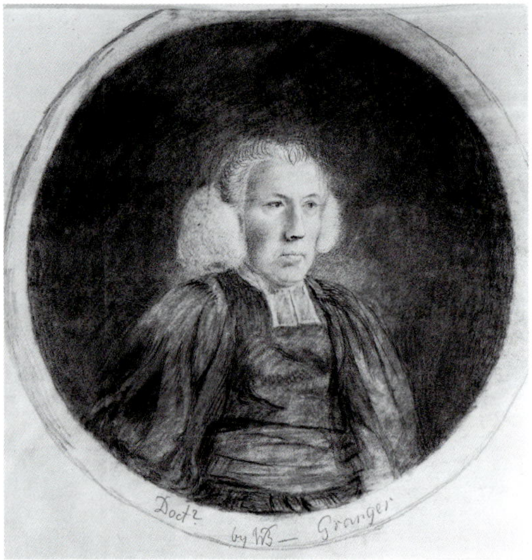

GRANGER by William Baillie before 1776 (Huntington Art Collections, San Marino, California)

2961 JOHN CORNISH 1765

Copper 18.9 x 15 (7½ x 6); minor flaking by chin lower left and on vertical edges; a contemporary inscription on the old backboard read: *Joan:s Cornish Pinxt Oxon:/ 1765* and *Revd Mr Granger/ Shiplake.*[1]

Blue-grey eyes, powdered wig, wearing a black gown and bands.

Collections: By descent from the sitter's brother John (who m. Mary Lunn), to Mrs Dorothy Lunn in 1932 and Henry T. Lunn, by whom presented 1938.

The identification and attribution of NPG 2961 derive from the contemporary inscription quoted above. The extreme modesty of Granger's portraiture is perhaps explained by his statement that 'My name and person are known to few, as I had the good fortune to retire early to independence, obscurity, and content'.[2]

1 As copied by C.K. Adams 1932; the backboard was apparently not with the picture when it was presented in 1938.
2 Granger, *Biographical History*, preface, 1769.

ICONOGRAPHY

1765 Painting by John Cornish, see NPG 2961.

1768 Drawing by P-E. Falconet, medallion, engraved D.P. Pariset 1768* (front. for the first edition of the *Biographical History* 1769); this print is seen in the 1782 portrait by L.F. Abbott of Sir William Musgrave (British Library), who had commissioned the Falconet drawing.

1775 Drawing by W.W. Ryland, medallion profile, resembling the Falconet head of 1768, engraved C. Bretherton for the 1775 edition of Granger's *Biographical History*. Copied by S. Freeman 1803 for the 1804 edition and anon. (and badly) for the 1811 edition.

before 1776 Drawing by William Baillie,* half-length oval in gown and bands, looking older than in the Falconet head of 1768. Huntington Art Collections, San Marino, Calif. (extra-illustrated Bull Granger, xxxiv, f.1r).

A 'very good' portrait, given him by the sitter's widow, belonged to the sitter's brother, John Granger of Basingstoke, in 1803 (*GM*, LXXIII, 1803, ii, p.895).

Posthumous

1895 Stone bust by F.C. Thomas, in gown and bands. National Portrait Gallery, north front.

GRANVILLE, Mary, see DELANY

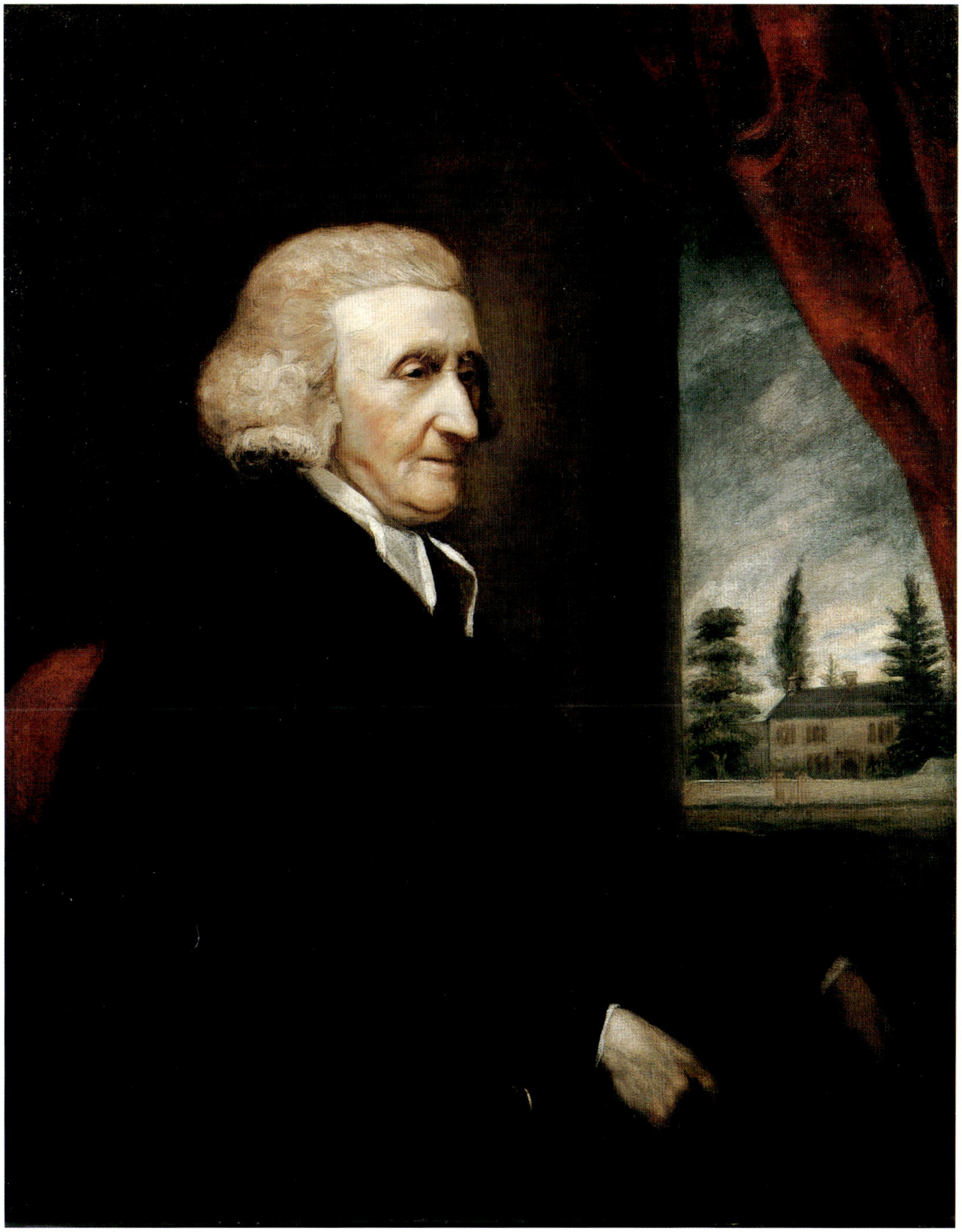

GRAVES NPG 5281

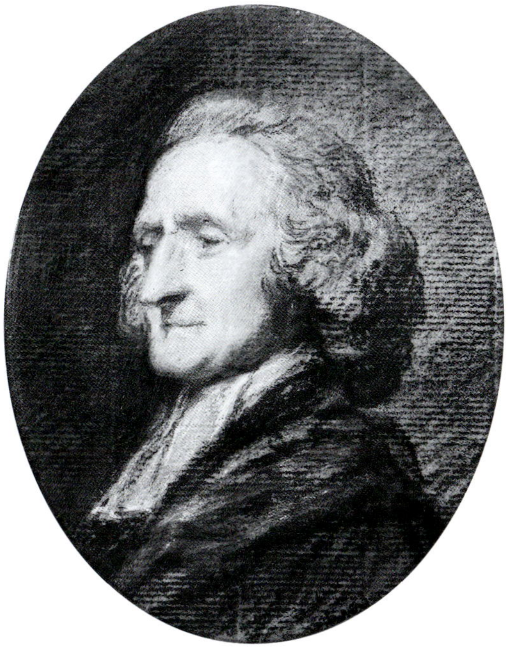

GRAVES by Thomas Gainsborough c.1786 (Pierpont Morgan Library, New York)

GRAVES, Richard 1715-1804

Poet, classicist and novelist, author of the humorous and anti-methodist *Spiritual Quixote* 1772; rector of Claverton, Somerset, from 1750.

'in frame he was short and slender, and he was eccentric in both dress and gait, but his features were expressive and his conversation was marked by a sportive gaiety' (*DNB*).

5281 JAMES NORTHCOTE 1799

Canvas 90 x 72.5 (35½ x 28½) lined; cleaned 1980; the surface is worn (e.g. his left hand) and bituminous in the lower area; there are *pentimenti* round the head which was at one time cut out [an area 46 x 36 (18 x 14)]; indistinctly signed and dated above his left hand: *J. Northcote / pinxt / 1799.*[1]

Dark brown eyes, powdered wig, wearing clerical gown and bands, seated in a red-upholstered chair; a deep red curtain to the right.

Collections: Prince Hoare[2] in 1800; Charles Roberson by 1868; Graves 1872;[3] Graves family at Bradenham Manor, Bucks., until c.1948 when inherited by Richard Goddard-Wilson (d.1979);[4] Phillips, 26 November 1979, lot 85, bt. Leggatt for the NPG.

Engravings: S.W. Reynolds 1800;[5] W. Ridley 1800; Ridley & Holl 1806 (half-length oval); anon. (octagonal).

Exhibitions: RA 1800(116); NPE 1868(884) lent Charles Roberson.

Graves, shown in his eighty-fourth year, had remained an 'amiable, well-read, and lively old man', retaining 'the easy air, light step, and brisk movement, of a stripling'.[6] The house in the background was presumably the Claverton parsonage described by Nichols as a 'very good substantial building, much enlarged and improved by Mr Graves. The garden, though not large, is a pretty rural spot, strongly marked by that classic elegance of taste which distinguished the late proprietor as an author.'[7]

1 As recorded in the Reynolds engraving of 1800 and by Scharf in 1872 (TSB 18/36).
2 A pupil of Richard Graves and a close friend of Northcote.
3 Henry Graves offered it for sale to the NPG that year (when sketched by Scharf; TSB 18/36).
4 This later provenance given in a letter from Mrs Goddard-Wilson, 11 June 1980 (NPG archive).
5 As in the possession of Prince Hoare.
6 *Public Characters of 1799-1800*, p.391.
7 Nichols *Anecdotes*, III, p.135.

ICONOGRAPHY

c.1786 Chalk drawing by Thomas Gainsborough,* bust-length oval wearing bands. Pierpont Morgan Library, New York (1957.12; Hayes 1970, no.55). Engraved G. Dupont 1790; Hibbart, n.d.; J. Basire, from a drawing by D. Parker, 1812 (Nichols *Anecdotes*, III); J. Scott 1884.

c.1795? Pastel by James Sharples, profile bust. Bristol CMAG (*Cat. of the Sharples Coll.*, Bristol, 1910, no.41; illus. Knox 1930, f.p.111). The original probably dates from before 1796 when Sharples first went to America, but he was again in England 1802-09.

1799 Painting by James Northcote, see NPG 5281.

c.1800 Anon. caricature, whole length, with hat and stick (*Public Characters of 1799-1800*; 'his personal figure is very happily caught by the annexed etching', but the print is omitted from the NPG copy).

GREEN, Valentine 1739-1813

Engraver and antiquarian; exhibited SA 1766-72 and RA 1774-1806; mezzotint engraver to the King 1773; ARA 1774; FSA 1775; engraved pictures from the Düsseldorf Gallery 1789-95, an enterprise abruptly ended by war which ultimately caused him considerable hardship; Keeper of the BI 1805; published a history of Worcestershire 1796.

1260 LEMUEL FRANCIS ABBOTT 1788

Canvas 76 x 63 (30 x 24¾) lined, the surface heavily ironed; retouching in the head.

Grey eyes, white hair, wearing a red waistcoat with gold trim and a dark grey coat.

Collections: Purchased from Colnaghi 1900.

Engravings: V. Green 1788;[1] J. Fittler (circular) 1795;[2] Freeman (oval) 1809.

Exhibitions: RA 1788(431); *Seeing is Deceiving*, Manchester, 1984.

When he engraved NPG 1260 in 1788 Green was at the height of his powers; he had begun the twelve plates illustrating events in the history of the Queens of England (*Acta Historica Reginarum Angliae* 1786-92) and the following year he began the Düsseldorf pictures, a privilege accorded by the Duke of Bavaria.[3]

1 Illus. A. Whitman, *Valentine Green*, 1902, front.
2 Front. for Green's *History & Antiquities of Worcester*, 1796.
3 See A. Whitman, *Valentine Green*, 1902, pp.16-17, 160-73.

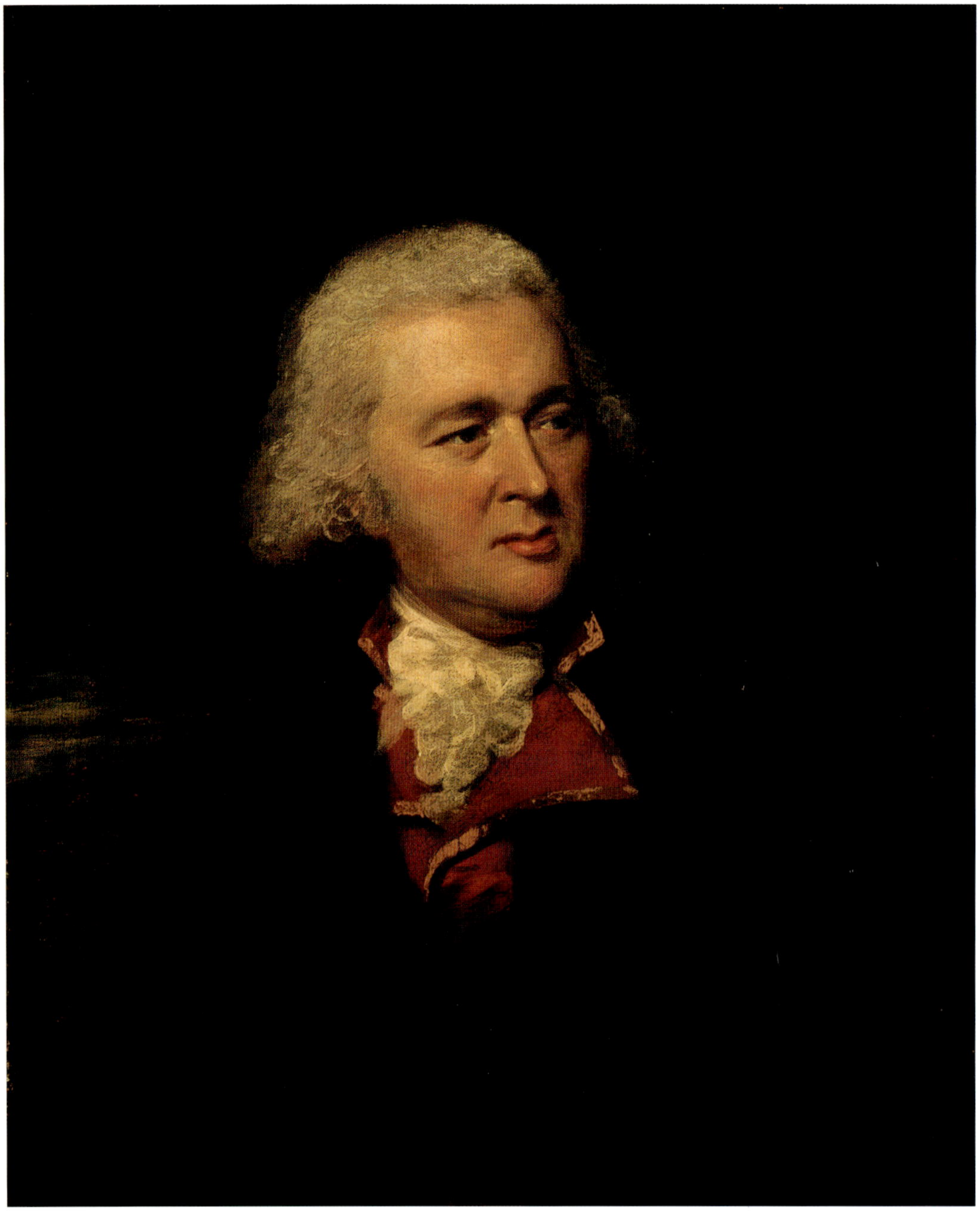

GREEN NPG 1260

ICONOGRAPHY

c.1780-85 Drawing by Paul Sandby, profile head, one of the series of heads drawn at print sales. Royal Collection (Oppé 1947, no.417/6). Engraved anon.,* *Sketches taken at Print Sales*, see Comparative Groups.

1788 Painting by L.F. Abbott, see NPG 1260.

c.1800-5 Drawing by Thomas Phillips, half-length seated, his left hand in his lap, inscribed with identity. Private collection (in a sketchbook).

1806 Drawing by A.E. Chalon, *Students at the British Institution 1806*, with Green, as Keeper, in the foreground (one of sixteen figures). British Museum (1879.6.14.757).

1808 Model for a bust by George Garrard, exhibited RA 1808(884).

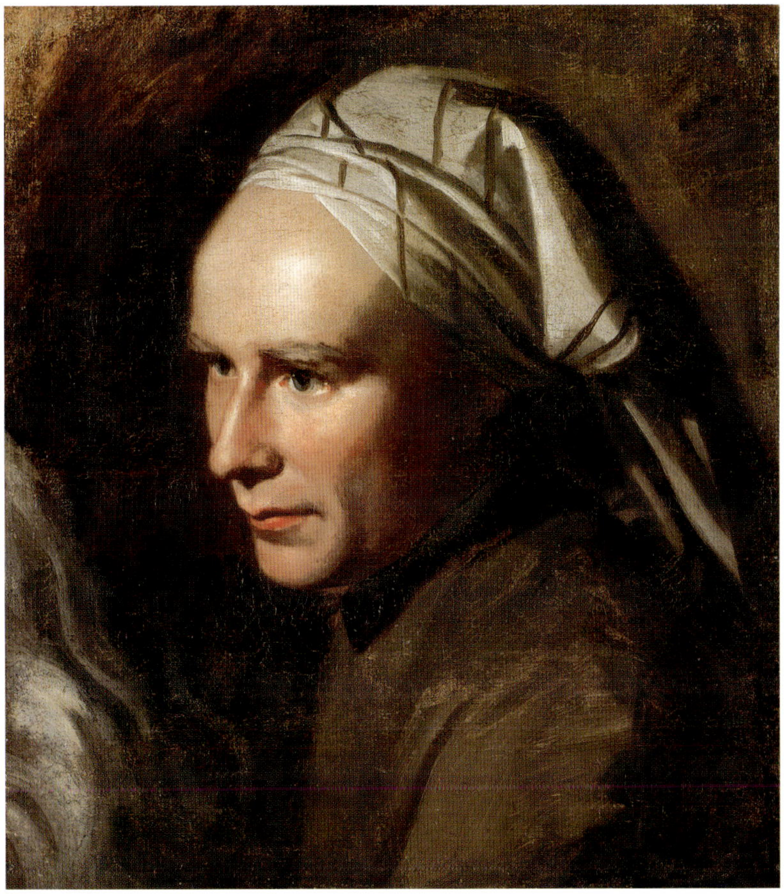

GREENE *NPG 972*

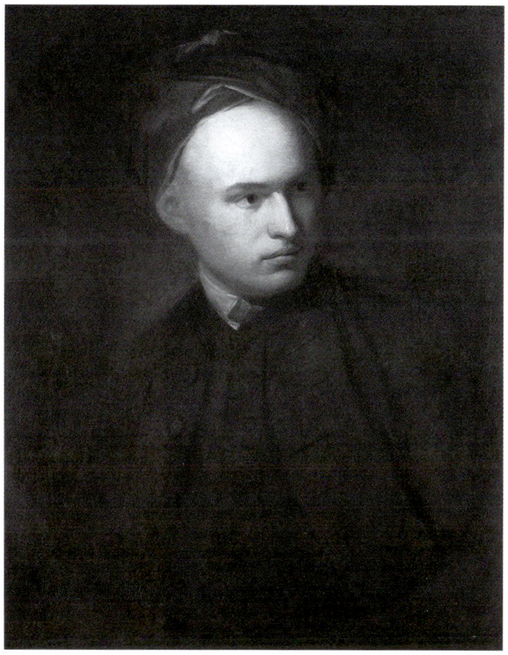

GREENE by George Romney c.1763 (Abbot Hall Art Gallery, Kendal)

GREENE, Thomas 1737-1810

Attorney; b. Slyne, Lancs., attending the same school as George Romney at Dendron; in practice in London by 1762; travelled in France in 1764 with Romney and remained the artist's patron and tolerant financial adviser; FSA and FRS 1798; his travel diary of 1764 and MS life of Romney are in the Preston CRO.

972 GEORGE ROMNEY c.1762-63

Canvas 43 x 38.5 (17 x 15¼) lined and cleaned 1996; there are a number of losses, principally in the neck-cloth, across the chest and round the edges.

Blue eyed, pink complexion, head dress is white with green and brown stripes; wearing a grey-green coat; in the area lower left perhaps white hair, or flax.

Collections: Miss Elizabeth Romney;[1] Romney sale, Christie's, 24 May 1894, lot 174 'Romney, A Head, possibly Cowper',[2] bt. Agnew; presented by Sir George Scharf, 1894,[3] as of William Cowper.

Reference: Ward & Roberts 1904, II, p.35; N. Russell, 'Bibliography of William Cowper to 1837', *Oxford Bibliographical Society*, NS XII, 1963, p.304; A. Kidson, *Romney* 2002, p.15.

NPG 972 was accepted in 1894 as a portrait of William Cowper, an identity first rejected by Roberts in 1900.[4] It is a fragment from a larger painting,[5] costume and composition suggesting an historical subject. Dated 1762-63 by Kidson, who also first suggested that the model could be Thomas Greene, on comparison with his portrait by Romney in the Abbot Hall Art Gallery, Kendal (see below);[6] there is a pronounced similarity in the clean-cut features.

1 See Romney, NPG 959, Collections, note 1.
2 Scharf annotated his sale cat. (NPG archive): 'tattered, no frame'. Lawrence Romney recalled that the picture 'had been for years on one of the attics at Whitestock Hall, and was covered with house dirt, and part of the paint had peeled off. When looking over the sketches and other pictures in preparation for the 1894 sale, I thought it might well be meant for a portrait of Cowper, but as I was not certain, I had it catalogued merely as 'A Head (possibly Cowper)'; see Chamberlain, 1910, p.177.
3 'Scharf tried to persuade his Trustees to buy it, but they would not, and so he purchased it himself ... had it done up, and presented it' (Chamberlain 1910, p.177).
4 W. Roberts, *Athenaeum*, 17 February 1900, pp.215-16. NPG 972 was nonetheless illus. as Cowper in, for example, *Leisure Hour*, April 1900, p.482, and Milford's first edition of Cowper's *Poems*, 1907.
5 Conservator's report by Anne Broomfield, October 1996; NPG archive.
6 Letter of 7 June 2000; NPG archive.

ICONOGRAPHY

c.1762-63 Painting by George Romney, see NPG 972.

c.1763 Painting by George Romney,* half length. Abbot Hall AG, Kendal, on permanent loan from the Provincial Insurance plc; from Whittington Hall (Ward & Roberts 1904, II, p.64, no.1).

c.1773 Miniature by Ozias Humphry, bust-length oval. Private collection (illus. *Greene* 1986, no.9). Humphry was in Italy with Romney 1773-77.

1794-95 Painting by George Romney, half length, painted as a gift for the sitter. Formerly Whittington Hall (Ward & Roberts 1904, II, p.64, no.2; illus. *Greene* 1986, no.7).

A portrait by George Dance is listed in *Greene* 1986 (n.p.).

DOUBTFUL PORTRAIT

'A portrait of Mr Green' by Romney, belonging to 'a Lady of Title', was sold Robinson & Fisher, 1 March 1900, lot 52, bt. Leggatt.

GRENVILLE, Richard, see TEMPLE

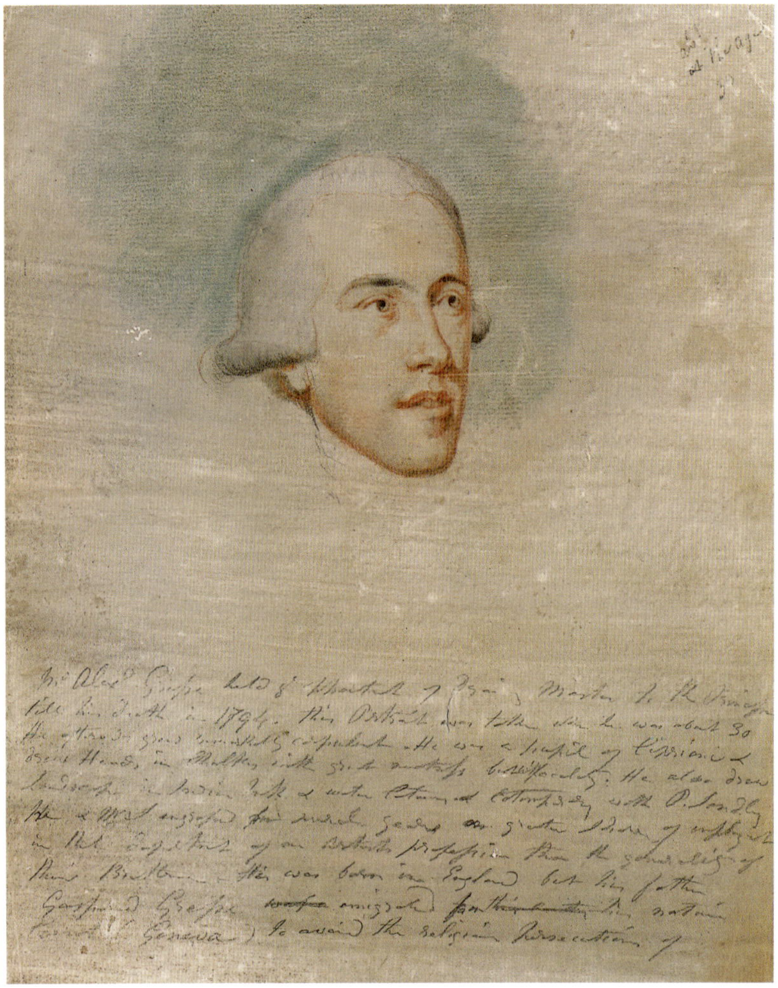

GRESSE NPG 4196

GRESSE, John Alexander 1741-94

Drawing master, b. London of a Swiss father; studied under Scotin, Major, Cipriani and Zuccarelli, before becoming drawing master to the Queen and Princesses by 1777; studio sale Christie's, 10 April 1794.

'though a good-natured and friendly-hearted man, Gresse was very irritable, and could not patiently endure the least observations upon the stupendosity of his figure' (Henry Angelo, 1828).

4196 UNKNOWN ARTIST c.1770

Black and sepia crayon with coloured washes, on paper 28.5 x 22 (11⅛ x 8¾), the head 9 (3½) high; the sheet, bearing the watermark IVILLEDARY,[1] is stained and rubbed, with a small hole centre right; there is an illegible (modern) pencil inscription top right [. . . /30], and a contemporary pencil inscription below: *Mr Alexr Grasse held ye appointment of Drawing Master to the Princesses till his Death in 1794. this Portrait was taken when he was about 30. He afterwards grew remarkably corpulent. He was a pupil of Cipriani & drew in Heads in Chalks with great neatness but with facility. He also drew Landscape in Indian Ink & water Colour cotemporary with P. Sandby. He & Mr S engrossed for several years greater share of imployment in that department of an Artists profession than the generality of their Brethren. He was born in England but his father Gaspard Grasse emigrated from his native Country (Geneva) to avoid the religious persecution of* [sic].

Collections: Presented by E. Daly Lewis 1947.

Dated according to the evidence of the inscription. The donor plausibly suggested NPG 4196 may have been a self-portrait,[2] although the inscription does not encourage the idea.

1 Probably indicating a date of 1758-60, cf. Churchill, nos.407, 409, 411.

2 Letter of 3 July 1947 (NPG archive). The Gresse sale, Christies, 7-12 April 1794, included some heads by Gresse: 'A head in black and red chalk' and '4 heads' (day 3, lots 51, 73), and 'A head in crayons' (day 4, lot 46).

GRIFFITH, Mrs Elizabeth, *née* Griffith 1727-93

Actress, playwright and novelist; stage début Dublin 1749-51 as Miss Kennedy; m. 1751 Richard Griffith (1716-88), her *Letters between Henry and Frances* 1757 publishing their courtship correspondence; played at Covent Garden 1753-54 and settled in London c.1756; subsequently wrote dramatic poems and plays, several translated from the French.

4905 see Groups, *Portraits in the characters of the Muses* by RICHARD SAMUEL 1778

ICONOGRAPHY

See also J.M.S. Tompkins, *The Polite Marriage*, 1938, p.195.

1778 Painting by Richard Samuel, *Portraits in the characters of the Muses*, see Groups NPG 4905.

1775-80 Drawing by the Rev J. Thomas, engraved MacKenzie 1801,* bust-length oval with a head scarf (*Lady's Monthly Mag.*). She appears a little younger than in the anon. engraving of 1780.

1780 Anon. engraving, pub. Fielding & Walker 1780, bust-length oval within an elaborate surround (masks, a lute, and books titled *Letters of Henry and Frances* [1757] / *Del*[*icate*] *Distress* [1769-70] / *Lady Barton* [1771] / *Morality and Shakespeares Drama* [1775]).

Tompkins also mentions now untraced portraits of her by 'Pyne' [presumably R.E. Pine] at Hendersyde Hall (light-brown hair and a long nose) and a youthful pencil drawing by Giles Hussey made in Ireland.

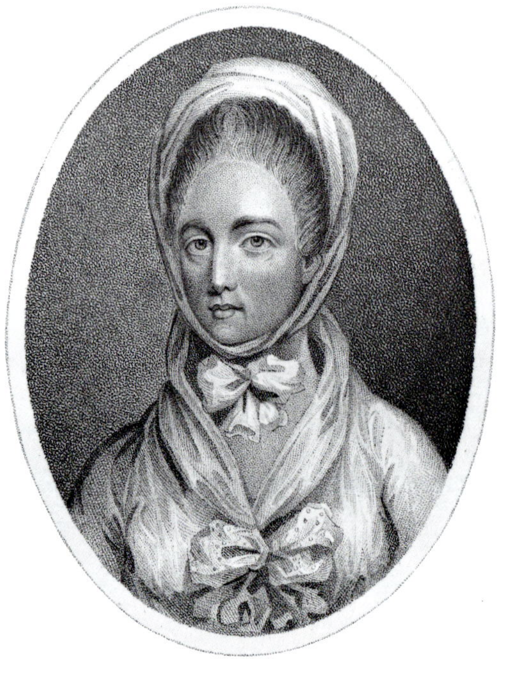

GRIFFITH *Mackenzie after the Rev. J. Thomas 1775-80* (NPG D 8995)

GUILFORD, Frederick North, 2nd Earl of 1732-92

Statesman; 1st s. of the 1st Earl of Guilford and half bro. of Brownlow North; sty. Lord North 1752, suc. as 2nd Earl of Guilford 1790; MP 1754-90; chancellor of the exchequer and leader of the House 1767-82, prime minister 1770-82; KG 1772; chancellor of Oxford University 1773; FSA 1776; by 1787 he was almost blind but, said Walpole, he retained 'his spirits, good humour, wit, sense and drollery.'

'Nothing could be more coarse or clumsy or ungracious than his outside. Two large prominent eyes that rolled about to no purpose (for he was utterly short-sighted), a wide mouth, thick lips, and inflated visage, gave him the air of a blind trumpeter. A deep untuneable voice, which, instead of modulating, he enforced with unnecessary pomp, a total neglect of his person, and ignorance of every civil attention, disgusted all who judge by appearance' (Horace Walpole, *Memoirs of George II*).

6180 POMPEO BATONI 1753-56

Canvas 92.5 x 73 (36¼ x 29¾) lined; cleaned 1992; minor retouchings round head and in his left hand; the canvas may have been slightly reduced in height,[1] but the ink well on the left was originally cut through (confirmed by the selvage of the original canvas).

Blue-grey eyes, his own fair hair tied with a long black ribbon, wearing a sage-green frock coat with coral-coloured collar and cuffs, buff silk waistcoat and brown knee breeches and grey stockings; he sits in a purple chair.[2]

Collections: By family descent at Guilford House, London, and Waldershare Park to the 9th Earl of Guilford; purchased from the Countess of Guilford by private treaty sale with the aid of the National Art Collections Fund 1992.

Exhibition: *Batoni*, Kenwood, 1982(8).

Reference: Clark 1985, no.192; *NACF Review 1992*, p.40.

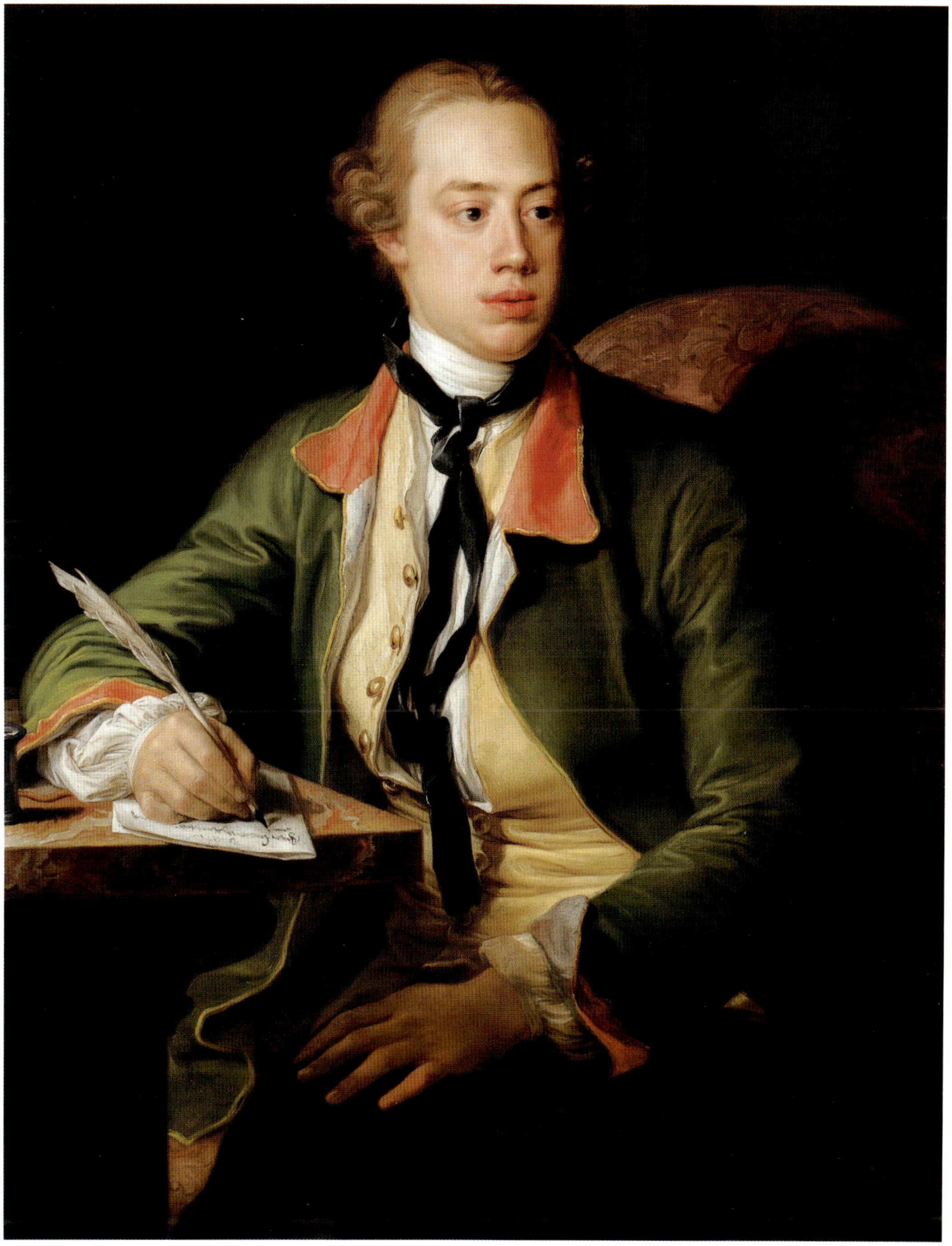

2nd Earl of GUILFORD NPG *6180*

In 1752-53 Lord North travelled in Italy with his step-brother William, 2nd Earl of Dartmouth.[3] By January 1753 they were in Rome, where both sat to Batoni for three-quarter length portraits, Dartmouth's an orthodox standing pose[4] and NPG 6180 one of Batoni's first seated three-quarter compositions. The portraits took some time to complete, and it was not until 1 May 1756 that Thomas Jenkins was able to write from Rome to Lord Dartmouth that he had 'at last received from Signor Pompeo Lord North's portrait with your Lordship's and it shall be sent away at the first opportunity'.[5] Walpole later saw both portraits in the Countess of Guilford's house in Grosvenor Square, with other Batoni three-quarter lengths of Sir Edward Dering and Lord Bolingbroke.[6]

Batoni also made half-length miniature versions in watercolour of each portrait which were dispatched from Rome late in 1754;[7] Walpole later recorded that 'Mr George Montagu [c.1713-80] has two heads in water-colours, painted by Pompeio at the same time, of lord Dartmouth and lord North.'[8] North's miniature was sold from Wroxton Abbey, Sotheby's, 27 July 1923, lot 139.[9]

1 The average size of Batoni's three-quarter length portraits at this time was 98 x 73 (cf. Clark 1985, nos.154-61, 163, 175, 179-81, 187, 190-91, 195-96).
2 See Ribeiro 2000, pp.122-23.
3 Dartmouth's widowed mother m. North's widowed father; Brownlow North was their son; see Ingamells 1997, p.277.
4 Private collection; Clark 1985, no.195.
5 *HMC 15th Report*, app. i, 1896, p.171.
6 Walpole *Anecdotes* V, 1937, pp.18-19. All four sitters were bound, as Francis Russell has expressed it, by 'close if complicated family ties' (*CL*, CLIII, 1973, p.1610). See also Clark 1985, nos.192, 195, 217 and pp.46, 369.

7 Jenkins, Rome, 30 March 1755, acknowledging a letter from Lord Dartmouth of 27 December 1754: 'The case addressed to the Hon. Miss Legge, was that which contained the music, your Lordship's and Lord North's miniatures and some other articles' (*HMC 15th Report*, app. i, 1896, p.169). The Dartmouth miniature is in a private collection in Rome (Clark 1985, no.194).
8 Walpole *Anecdotes* V, 1937, p.19.
9 Clark 1985, no.193.

3627 NATHANIEL DANCE 1773-74

Canvas 125.5 x 100 (49½ x 39½) lined;[1] cleaned 1970; minor retouchings in the head.

Blue eyes, white powdered hair with a black ribbon; wearing a chancellor's black gown with gold facings[2] and the ribbon of the Garter over a light brown suit; white stockings.

Collections: By family descent at Wroxton Abbey; the Trustees of the North Settled Estates sale, Christie's, 19 March 1948, lot 1, bt. Leggatt for the NPG.

Engravings: T. Burke 1775, reissued 1785; E. Bocquet (half length); W.H. Mote 1833 (after a drawing by William Derby, from the original belonging to Hon Georgiana North); Holl (bust-length oval).

Exhibitions: BI 1820(51) lent by the Earl of Guilford;[3] NPE 1867(641) lent Col. North; *Dance* 1977(36).

The standard portrait of Lord North, skillfully accommodating his physical clumsiness and the dignity of his office as chancellor of the University of Oxford. He had been installed in July 1773[4] (having received the Garter the previous year), and the first of many engravings of the portrait was published on 23 May 1775. A medal by John Kirk after Isaac Gosset was also struck in 1775 to mark the election of the new chancellor, see iconography.

NPG 3627 appears to be wholly by Dance, but may be a replica of the portrait at Waldershare Park.[5] Many copies are recorded, including those at the Bodleian Library, Oxford (given in 1805);[6] Trinity College, Oxford (bought in 1817);[7] the Carlton Club; Dalmeny (Rosebery sale, Christie's, 5 May 1939, lot 36), and another was offered by Graves to the NPG in 1891.[8] A half-length version was engraved by R.H. Cromek in 1802 from a picture belonging to Sir Grey Cooper (d.1801).[9]

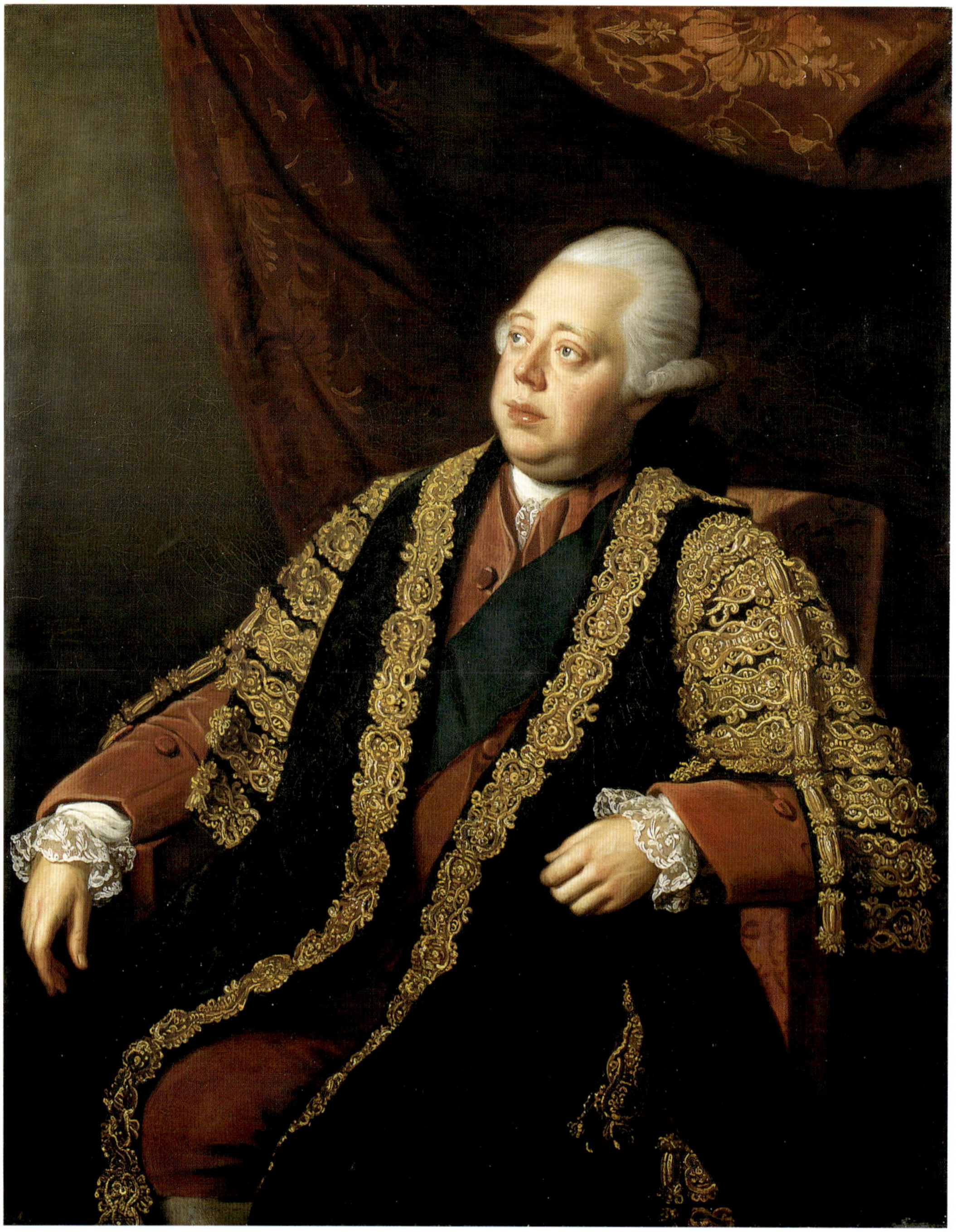

2nd Earl of GUILFORD NPG *3627*

1 The lining canvas inscribed in a 19th-century hand: *Fredk. / 2nd Earl of Guildford*.
2 The gown might equally apply to the chancellor of the University of Oxford or to the chancellor of the exchequer; Huddesford's whole-length portrait of North's predecessor at Oxford, Lord Lichfield (illus. OP 1906, f.p.69) shows a rust-coloured suit beneath the chancellor's gown.
3 It is possible that this was the portrait now at Waldershare Park.
4 Cf. *Wal. Corr.*, XXXII, p.137n10.
5 Exhibited *The Dye is now Cast*, NPG Washington, 1975 (138), illus. fig.97. Listed in 1866 as a 'replica of one at Wroxton Abbey [i.e. NPG 3627]' (Scharf transcript of 1866 Waldershare cat., no.90).
6 Poole, I, p.110.
7 Poole, III, p.135.
8 TSB 36/49; after it was declined Graves had it collected from the NPG, Scharf noting that 'it was put openly on the top of a cab and the driver went in the direction of Victoria Street & not to Pall Mall'. Another version was sold Sotheby's, 18 December 1974, lot 121 (withdrawn).
9 Other reduced versions were sold Phillips, 30 January 1990, lot 33; Sotheby's, 11 July 1984, lot 207, and Bonham's, 25 October 1990, lot 93; see also NPG 276 below.

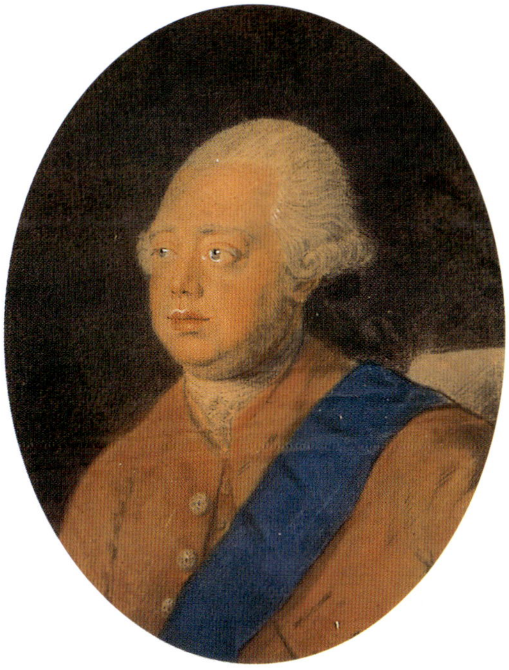

2nd Earl of GUILFORD NPG *276*

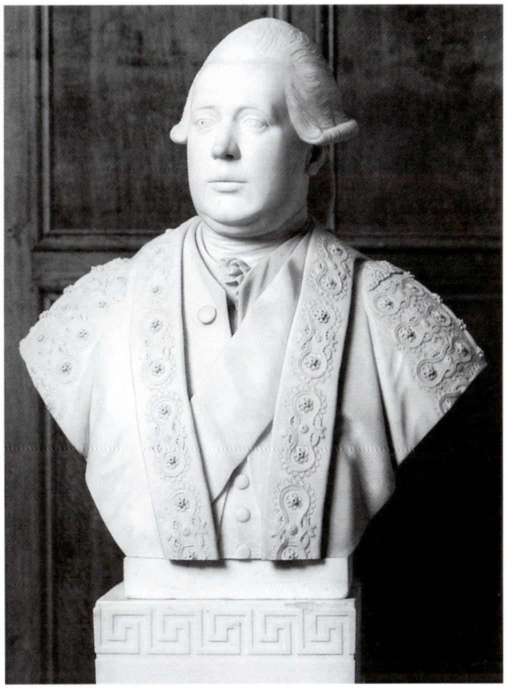

2nd Earl of GUILFORD by John Bacon senior c.1775? (Examination Schools, Oxford)

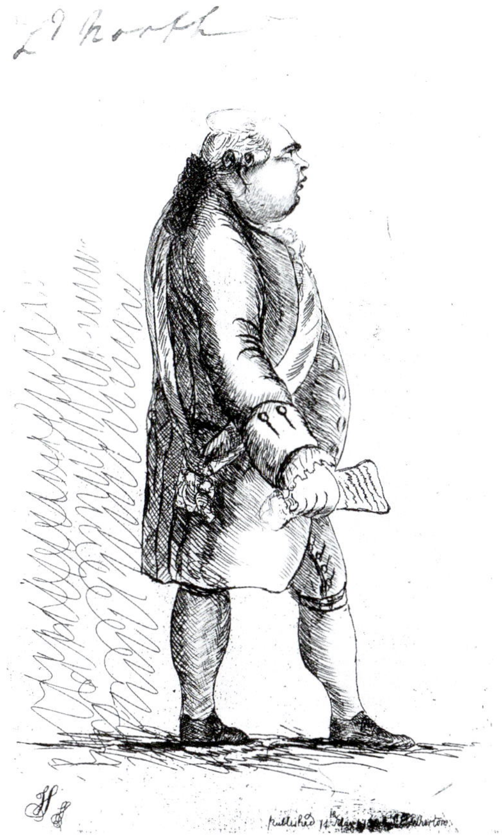

*2nd Earl of GUILFORD etched by J. Sayers 1782 (*NPG *D 2827)*

276 after NATHANIEL DANCE [1773–74]

Pastel on paper 24 x 19 (9½ x 7½) oval; horizontal creases run across the shoulders.

Light brown eyes, powdered hair, brown suit with brass buttons and the blue ribbon of the Garter; black background.

Collections: Purchased from T.H. Parker 1869.

See NPG 3627, of which this is a rather wretched derivation. It was apparently taken from Burke's second engraving, published on 20 September 1775, showing the same head, but with a plain coat wearing the ribbon and badge (here omitted) of the Garter.[1] A better miniature version, sold from Wroxton Abbey, Sotheby's, 27–28 July 1922, lot 138, is in the British Museum (Hull Grundy 1984, no.495).[2]

1 Cf. CS 7. There was also a reduced (inferior) oval plate by R. Pollard – possibly related to the unattributed half-length 'sketch' of North, wearing a red coat, in the Sheffield Park sale, Christie's, 11 December 1909, lot 70.

2 A similar miniature, with the Garter ribbon but without the badge, was sketched by Scharf at Wroxton Abbey in 1866 (SSB 59/165).

ICONOGRAPHY

1743 Painting by Enoch Seeman, one of three young boys, with his step bro., William, Viscount Lewisham (b.1731, later Earl of Dartmouth) and half-bro., Augustus Francis North. Private collection, from the Wroxton Abbey sale, Christie's, 11 July 1930, lot 75.

1753 Painting by Thomas Jenkins, three-quarter length. '… before sending away the portraits he had drawn of lord Dartmouth and Lord North, he [Jenkins] found many defects, which it was too late to remedy' (Jenkins to Dartmouth, Rome, 1 June 1754); on 30 March 1755 he wrote that drawings by 'Pompeo, Wilson, and myself were sent by the French courier' (*HMC 15th Report*, app. i, 1896, pp.168–69). Dartmouth's portrait, now untraced, illus. *Apollo*, XCIX, 1974, p.420.

1753–56 Painting by Pompeo Batoni, see NPG 6180.

1757 Painting by Joshua Reynolds, half length. Private collection (Mannings 2000, no.1344). Copy sold Sotheby's, 9 February 1955, lot 124.

1761 Painting by Allan Ramsay, half length, wearing a red suit with (clearly added) the ribbon and badge of the Garter (received in 1773). Parke-Bernet, Los Angeles, 9 March 1977, lot 827 (illus. Smart 1999, no.407), from the Sheffield Park sale, Christie's, 11 December 1909, lot 116 as Reynolds. Engraved J. Jones 1787 (as *A Ramsay fecit 1761…*).

c.1763 Painting by Joshua Reynolds, half-length painted oval. Petworth (Mannings 2000, no.1345).

1772 Caricature, *Boreas*, three-quarter length standing (George 4969).

1773–74 Painting by Nathaniel Dance, see NPG 3627 and NPG 276.

1775 Medal by John Kirk after Gosset (see below), exhibited SA 1775 (127) as chancellor of Oxford University (Brown 1980, no.200). Another, or the same, exhibited SA 1777(222). A Wedgwood medallion of c.1782 was based on the 1775 medal (illus. Reilly 1973, p.179).

c.1775 Wax by Isaac Gosset. Sotheby's 2 June 1975, lot 132.

c.1775? Marble bust by John Bacon sr.,★ wearing the chancellor's robe and Garter ribbon. Examination Schools, formerly Bodleian Library, Oxford, bequeathed by G.J. Williams 1806 (Poole, I, p.110). Probably related to the plaster bust with Garter ribbon in the Sheffield Park sale, Christie's, 11 December 1909, lot 126.

1777 Wax by Robert Stewart, exhibited SA 1777(299).

1779–81 Painting by J.S. Copley,★ *The Death of Chatham*, see Comparative Groups. A drawing from the head of North attributed to Bartolozzi is in the Metropolitan Museum of Art, New York (55.106.8; illus. *Metropolitan Museum of Art Bulletin*, XIV, 1956, p.126).

c.1780 Medallion by James Tassie, as chancellor of Oxford University (Gray 1894, no.287). Cast in the Scottish NPG (PG 506).

1782 Etching by J. Sayers,* whole length (George 6063).

*Lord North's long reign as prime minister ended in March 1782; short-lived governments of Rockingham (March to July 1782) and Shelburne (July 1782 to April 1783) were succeeded, for eight months before the advent of Pitt the younger, by the coalition government of North and Fox, an unlikely partnership which gave rise to a host of political satires – including the etchings by J. Sayers: A Coalition Medal (George 6183) and a whole length of North with Fox (*Fred O'Daub fecit; *George 6192), and a drawing by Nathaniel Dance,* Immortales et sempiterne amicitiae, *the prancing figures of Fox and Burke, sold Phillips, 4 November 1985, lot 25 (see also under Edward Gibbon 'Amateur Drawings').*

1798 Engraving by W. Ridley 1798 half length. Plate reissued as by Hopwood 1805, and two reduced anon. plates derived from it. Very near the Sayers etching of 1782.

Pencil drawing by William Grimaldi (Grimaldi 1873, p.49, no.151).

DOUBTFUL PORTRAITS

Painting, three-quarter length, offered to NPG 1882 by C.H. Waters (TSB 4/66), later cut down to an irregular half length, and last sold Sotheby's, New York, 17 July 1997, lot 128.

Miniature attributed to E. Vaughan, 16 November 1976, lot 5 as 'Thomas, 2nd Earl of Guildford'.

Drawings by J.S. Copley in the Boston Athenaeum (illus. *Apollo*, CII, 1975, p.469, as Lord North, and Prown 1966, II, p.439, and fig.405 as Ralph Brocklesby; by C. Corbould, engraved C.T. Warren 1791, bust-length oval to left (*The Senator*); by John Downman in the Victoria and Albert Museum (P.4.1923; probably of his son).

Wax attributed to Samuel Percy, sold Christie's, 11 December 1978, lot 135, appears too thin to be North and probably shows Frederick, 5th Earl of Guilford.

Engraving after O. Neale, bust length, somewhat resembling the head of North in the satire, *The Colossus of the North*, 1774 (George 5242).

GUNNING, Elizabeth, see ARGYLL

GWYN, Mrs Mary, *née* Horneck c.1752-1840

With her sister Catherine, well-known in the circle of Oliver Goldsmith (who called her 'Jessamy Bride' and her sister 'Little Comedy'); m. 1779 General Francis Gwyn (d. 1821), equerry to George III, and made a lady of the bedchamber to Queen Charlotte; her reminiscences provided much of Goldsmith's first biography (by Prior 1837).

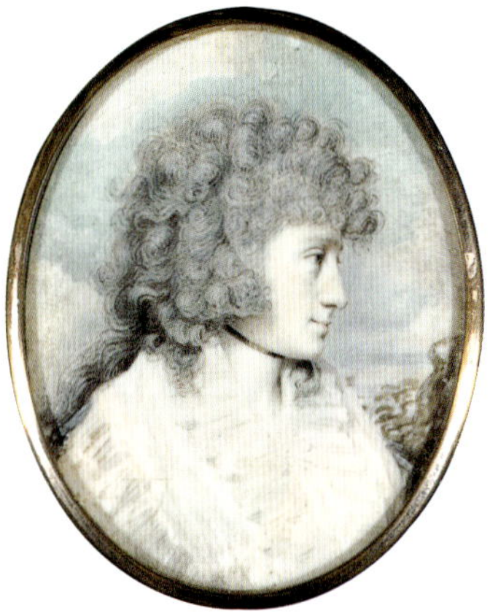

GWYN NPG *3152*

3152 attributed to HENRY EDRIDGE c.1795

Watercolour and bodycolour on ivory 6.2 x 4.9 (2½ x 2); framed as a double-sided locket with verso a memorial urn made of pearl, wire, seed pearls and blue Bristol beads, with a tree made of fair hair.

Dark eyes, grey powdered hair, wearing a thin black neckband and a white dress.

Collections: [Possibly the unattributed miniature in a blue enamel locket, set with diamonds, in the Miss Gwyn sale, Christie's, 29 June 1889, lot 19]; anon. sale, Sotheby's, 6 May 1943, lot 104, bt. H.J. Parker, from whom purchased 1943.

An accomplished but unsigned portrait, sold as Edridge in 1943, when the attribution was accepted by Carl Winter.[1] The head compares closely with the portrait of Mrs Gwyn by Hoppner engraved in 1791 (see below), though apparently rather older.

1 Letter of 21 July 1943 (NPG archive). V.J. Murrell later tentatively suggested Downman.

ICONOGRAPHY

1765-67 Painting by Joshua Reynolds, half-length profile, with her sister Catherine. Two versions:

a) unfinished, showing Catherine full face. Private collection (Mannings 2000, no.937).

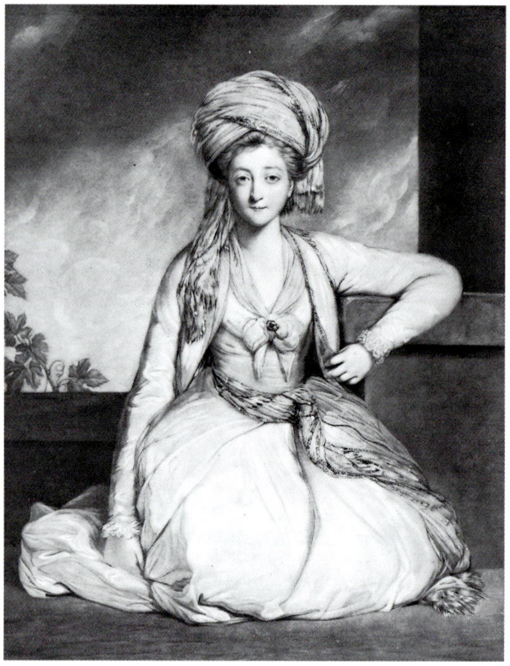

GWYN R. Dunkarton after Joshua Reynolds c.1775 (NPG D 18006)

b) showing Catherine looking down (Mannings 2000, no.938). Engraved S.W. Reynolds. Versions are in private collections and at Somerley; a copy by Robinson Elliott is in the Laing AG, Newcastle-upon-Tyne.

c.1775 Painting by Joshua Reynolds, 'sitting as if in a Turkish mosque'. Cliveden (Mannings 2000, no.936). Exhibited RA 1775(230). Engraved R. Dunkarton 1778.* A reduced copy by E.F. Burney sold Sotheby's, 9 July 1980, lot 114 (presumably the unattributed miniature after Reynolds from the Miss Gwyn sale, Christie's, 29 June 1889, lot 20), and Mannings lists others at Somerley, the Philbrook Museum of Art (Tulsa), and formerly at Farnley Hall.

c.1775 Etching by Henry Bunbury, the Misses Horneck seated playing chess, watched by their brother, Mary wearing the 'Turkish' headdress seen in the Reynolds portrait of c.1775. The artist was Mary's brother-in-law.

c.1780 Pastel and gouache by Daniel Gardner (unfinished), with her sister Catherine. Leicester MAG (illus. Gardner 1972, no.60), from the Miss Gwyn sale, Christie's, 29 June 1889, lot 27.

c.1780 Painting by Daniel Gardner, half length, with her sister Catherine as *The Merry Wives of Windsor*. Castle Museum, Nottingham (1904.32), from the Miss Gwyn sale, Christie's, 29 June 1889, lot 28. Engraved W. Dickinson 1780 (illus. *Connoisseur*, XXVIII, 1910, p.8).

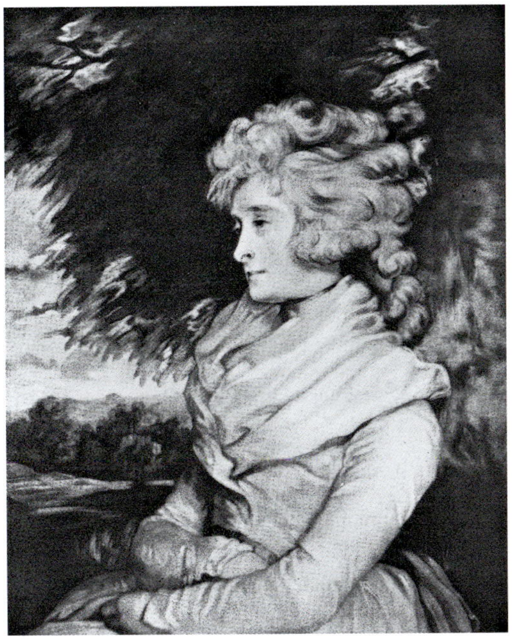

GWYN J. Young 1791 after John Hoppner (NPG Archive)

c.1790 Painting by John Hoppner, half-length seated in a landscape. Florence Gould sale, Sotheby's, New York, 25 April 1985, lot 81 (illus. *Connoisseur*, XXVIII, 1910, p.9, and XLVII, 1917, p.2), from the Miss Gwyn sale, Christie's, 29 June 1889, lot 29. Exhibited NPE 1867(569) lent Robert Gwyn. Engraved J. Young 1791.*

c.1795 Miniature attributed to Henry Edridge, see NPG 3152.

c.1805 Drawing by John Hoppner, three-quarter length seated with a dog in her lap (Courtauld Gallery, Witt coll. 2318).

1818 Painting by J.P. Davis, exhibited RA 1818(423, 'Mrs Gwynn').

Undated Drawing by John Downman, oval profile. Miss Gwyn sale, Christie's, 29 June 1889, lot 18, and presumably the drawing of 'Mrs Gwyn' listed by Williamson 1907, p.lxi, as from a dismembered sketchbook.

DOUBTFUL PORTRAITS

A half-length by Hoppner in the Taft Museum of Art, Cincinnati (1931.403), from the Miss Gwyn sale Christie's, 29 June 1889, lot 30, now identified as Catherine Horneck.

In 1791 George Engleheart listed a 'Miss Horneck' and a 'Miss E. Horneck' among his sitters, but it is hardly likely that Mrs Gwyn would then be so described (Williamson 1902, pp.28, 100); miniatures by him alleged to show Mrs Gwyn were exhibited BFAC 1889 (xvii 23 & 25, lent J. Whitehead, no.23 illus. pl.xx), and were tentatively identified in the Engleheart collection by Williamson (1902, illus. f.p.34 and p.35).

Miniatures attributed to Daniel Gardner (illus. Williamson 1921, f.p.56) and lent by Frederic Wallop to the Wembley Palace of Art 1924(V.99), and by Maria Cosway, sold Christie's, 15 October 1963, lot 84.

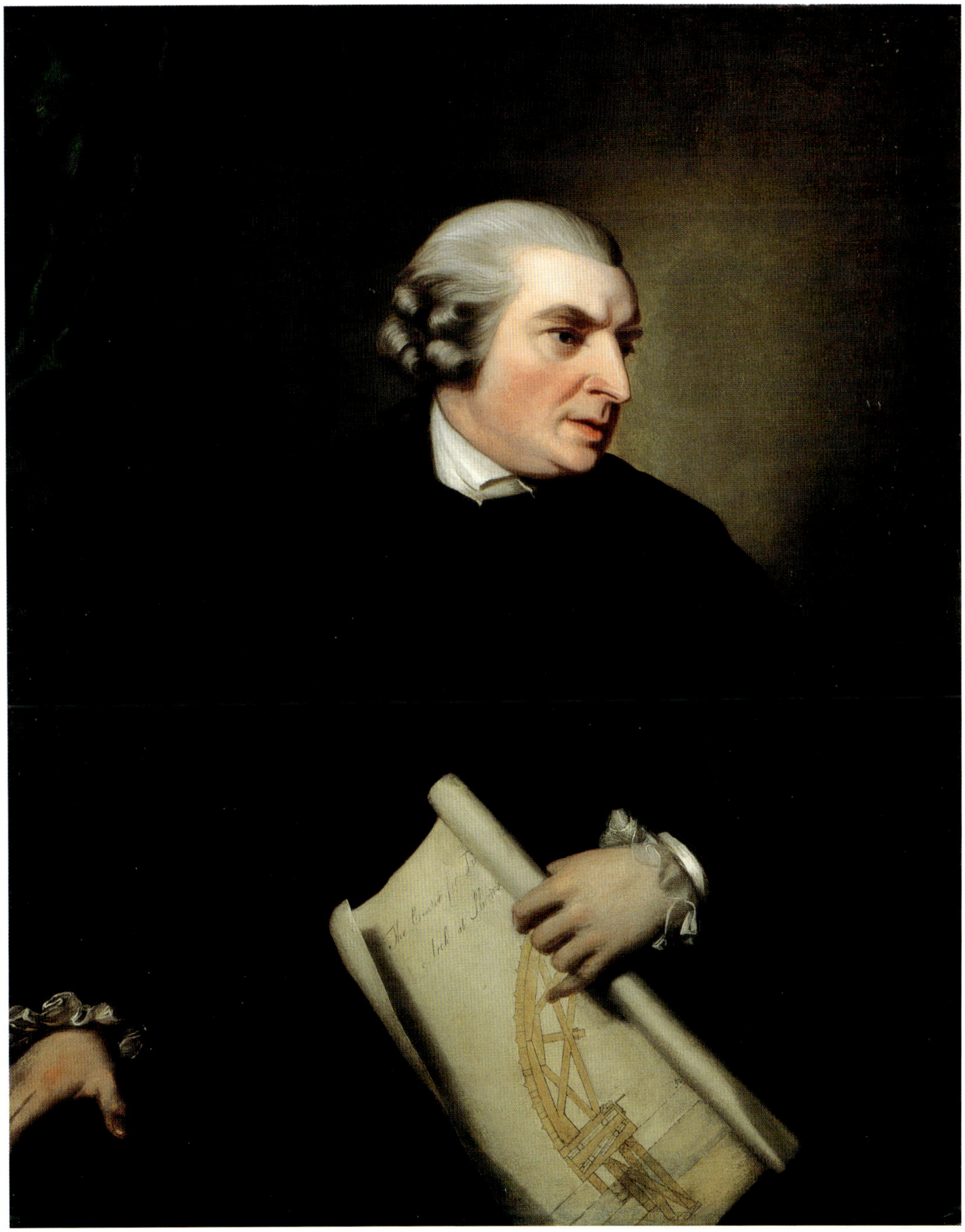

GWYNN NPG 4680

GWYNN, John 1713-86

Architect; one of the three founder architects of the RA 1768; author of *Essay on Design* 1749 and *London and Westminster Improved* 1766.

'lively, quick and sarcastic, of quaint appearance and odd manners' (Hugh Owen, c.1825).

4680 UNKNOWN ARTIST c.1770

Canvas 90 x 73 (35½ x 28¾) lined; repaired tears across the head below the eyes and down the right background area.

Grey eyes, powdered hair, wearing a white collar, dark purple suit and white collar; holding a drawing inscribed: *The Center for ... / Arch at Shrews ...* (see below); a green curtain upper left.

Collections: Purchased from Bernard Weinreb 1969.

Engraving: Anon. etching (bust length, with illegible letters faintly scratched letters below).[1]

The drawing refers to Gwynn's English Bridge at Shrewsbury, built 1769-74. An unfinished version of this portrait, once attributed to Zoffany, is in the Museum at Shrewsbury (0.159);[2] the anonymous etching, cited above, is crude.

1 Illus. *Boswell's Johnson*, ed. R. Ingpen, 1907, I, p.217.
2 Listed Williamson 1920, p.233; the attribution doubtless derived from Gwynn's presence in Zoffany's *Academicians*, see below.

ICONOGRAPHY

c.1770 Unattributed painting, see NPG 4680.

1772 Painting by Johann Zoffany,* *The Academicians of the Royal Academy*, see Groups NPG 1437.

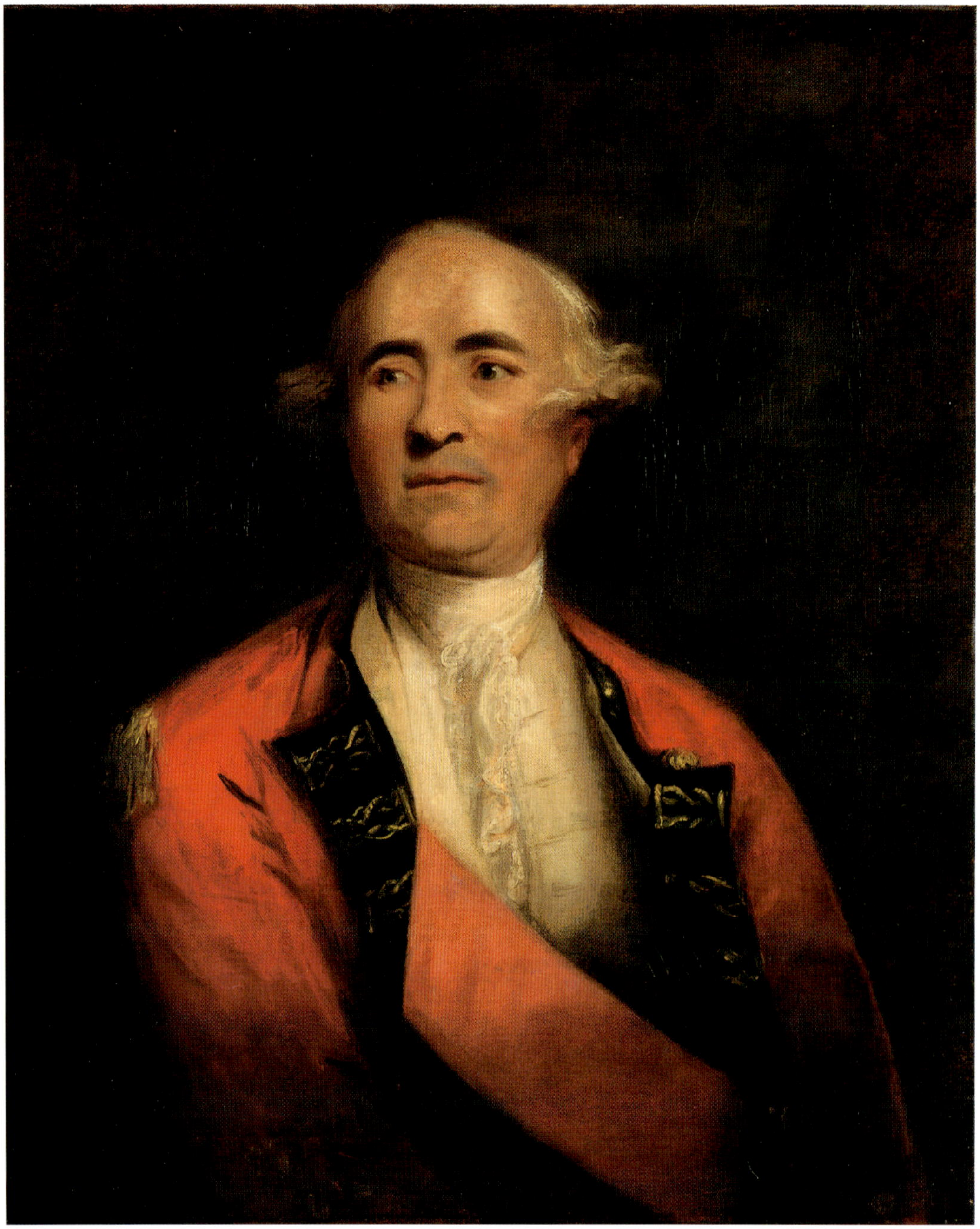

HALDIMAND NPG *4874*

HALDIMAND, Sir Frederick, KB 1718-91

Governor of Canada; b. and d. in Switzerland; after serving with the Dutch, he joined the British army; in 1758 he went to America, where promoted major-general 1772 and lieutenant-general 1777; governor of Canada 1778-84 (his appointment as governor of Gibraltar erroneously announced in 1787); KB 1785.

4874 studio of JOSHUA REYNOLDS [c.1778]

Canvas 75.5 x 63 (29¾ x 24¾) including additional strips on each vertical side (6 and 8 wide, 2⅜ and 3⅛, left and right); lined; cleaned 1974; considerably retouched.

Grey eyes, white hair, wearing a white collar and neckcloth, and a lieutenant general's bright red coat with dark blue lapels and gold trim, and the ribbon and star of the Bath; only the gold tassel of his epaulette is visible.

Collections: Western family, Felix Hall;[1] Lever Gallery, London, 1939; N.C.E. Ashton 1954 (when first offered to the NPG); B.E. Wheeler 1965; W.A. Fields, London, from whom purchased 1972.

Exhibition: *Georgian Canada*, Toronto, 1984(129).

Reference: Mannings 2000, no.799a.

In June 1778 Reynolds was paid 35 gn. for a portrait of 'General Haldeman' and 25 gn. for a copy; in December 1779 he received a further 25 gn. for 'General Haldeman, a copy'.[2] There is no Reynolds pocket book for 1778 and no sittings by Haldimand are recorded. It is not known who made the payments to Reynolds, but Haldimand was appointed governor in Canada in June 1778, and did not return to England until November 1784. The original portrait, now untraced, showing Haldimand without the Bath insignia, descended through Samuel Holland to C.D. Cahoon, Massachusetts, in 1913.[3]

It seems unlikely that NPG 4874 is one of the two replicas, although the condition makes it difficult to judge. Like all known versions it shows Haldimand wearing the Bath insignia to which he became entitled in September 1785; they were, therefore, either additions or indications of a version painted after 1785. Other versions are:

a) with the Haldimand family in Montreal since at least 1889.[4]

b) In 1968 in a private collection, descended from J.A. Haldimand through Henry Pasteur.

c) In 1872 with Mrs Sophia Romilly (1809-77), the sitter's great niece; she then claimed to have the original portrait and said that the two replicas painted by Reynolds then belonged to her brother Mr Marcet in Geneva and his son Dr Marcet in London.[5]

d) Sold New York, 21 April 1971, lot 168;[6] formerly with E.C. Hogan 1872;[7] bt. T.B. Walker 1905 for the Walker Art Center, Minneapolis; exhibited *Pageant of Canada*, Ottawa, 1967(126).

e) In 1963 in a private collection, Norway; apparently a copy.

1 Provenance as given by Mr Lever of the Lever Gallery (note of 20 December 1938; NPG archive). The mother of the 1st and only Baron Western (1767-1844) was dau. of William Bollen, Agent for Massachusetts; the last Western Bt. d.1917; Felix Hall was damaged by fire in 1930.

2 Cormack 1970, p.155.

3 Cf. Mannings 2000, no.799.

4 Illus. J. Winsor, *History of America*, VIII, 1889, p.136, and recorded in the family's collection in 1978 (NPG archive).

5 Letter to Scharf, January 1872 (NPG archive). Scharf's sketch of the Romilly portrait (TSB 23/44) suggests it was that later on the London art market as *Charles Townshend* (photograph NPG archive, showing the same two buttons on the sleeve).

6 Mannings 2000, no.799b.

7 According to later annotations made in Scharf's sketchbook (TSB 23/44) this was also the Romilly portrait, but the details do not agree.

HALL, John 1740-97

Engraver; pupil of Simon Ravenet; historical engraver to George III 1785.

'By possessing a superior mind, and always associating with persons of worth and high literary talents, and being a man of the strictest integrity, Mr Hall was highly respected through life by everyone who know him' (J.T. Smith, 1828).

3992 attributed to WILLIAM LAWRANSON c.1775-80

Pastel on grey Ingres-type paper 59 x 46.5 (23¼ x 18⅜) laid down on linen; faded, with some abrasion by the head, upper right, and across the torso.

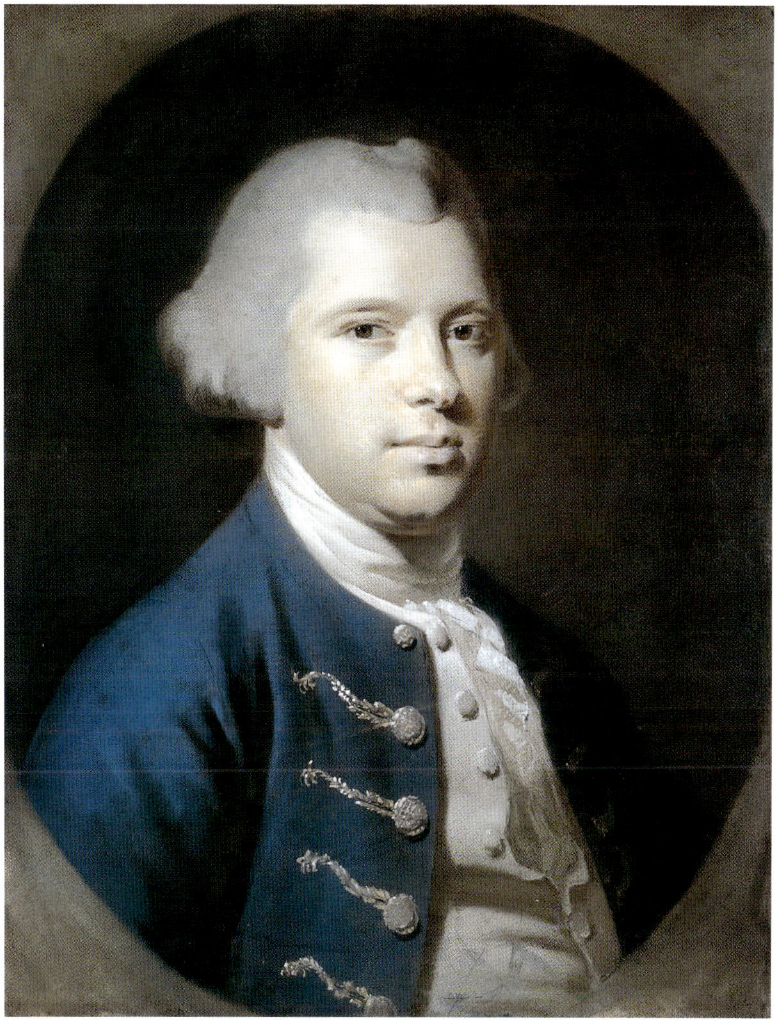

HALL NPG *3992*

Brown eyes, grey powdered hair, wearing a lace neckcloth, a blue coat with silver trim and a silver waistcoat; within a drawn oval.

Collections: By descent through the sitter's son, Dr G.W. Hall, Master of Pembroke College, Oxford, to the sitter's great-great-granddaughter, Miss J.M. Grubbe of Blythburgh [later Mrs Hubbard], by whom presented 1956.[1]

A note in a MS history of the Hall family compiled in 1900 recounts:

> This crayon drawing ... was the work, according to tradition, of William Laurenson, a personal friend of Hall, and was executed between the years 1770 and 1780 when the subject was about 38 years old.[2]

It goes on to point out that Lawranson drew crayon portraits of Sarah Gilles (Hall's sister-in-law), besides Benjamin West and Woollett (see NPG 693 below) '& other celebrities in the world of Art'.

1 The provenance is additionally borne out by the early 19th century label formerly on the verso: *John Hall, Engraver born Decr 21 / 1740 died April 7 - 1797. / There is a portrait of him painted / by Stuart, in the Boydell / Gallery*, and by the account in the family history, see below.

2 The volume, compiled by W.J. Grubbe in 1900, remains in a private collection; a subsequent, but less convincing, note suggests that the portrait may have been by Richard [*sic*] Cotes RA, Laurenson's master [*sic*].

693 GILBERT STUART 1785

Canvas 90 x 70 (35½ x 27½) lined in 1893; cleaned 1977.

Brown eyes, grey powdered hair, wearing a white shirt and a light brown coat with brass buttons; in his right hand he holds up a proof of his engraving of Benjamin West's *Penn's Treaty with the Indians*; he sits in a red chair and on the table before him covered by a purple cloth, lie a porte-crayon, a chisel case and stone.

Collections: Commissioned by John Boydell; Henry Graves (who succeeded to Boydell's business), by whom presented to the National Gallery 1850 (NG 220); lent to the NPG 1883; ownership transferred to the Tate Gallery 1954 and to the NPG 1957.

Exhibitions: Boydell Gallery, London, 1786; NPE 1867(537); *Georgian Essex*, Dagenham, 1958(317);

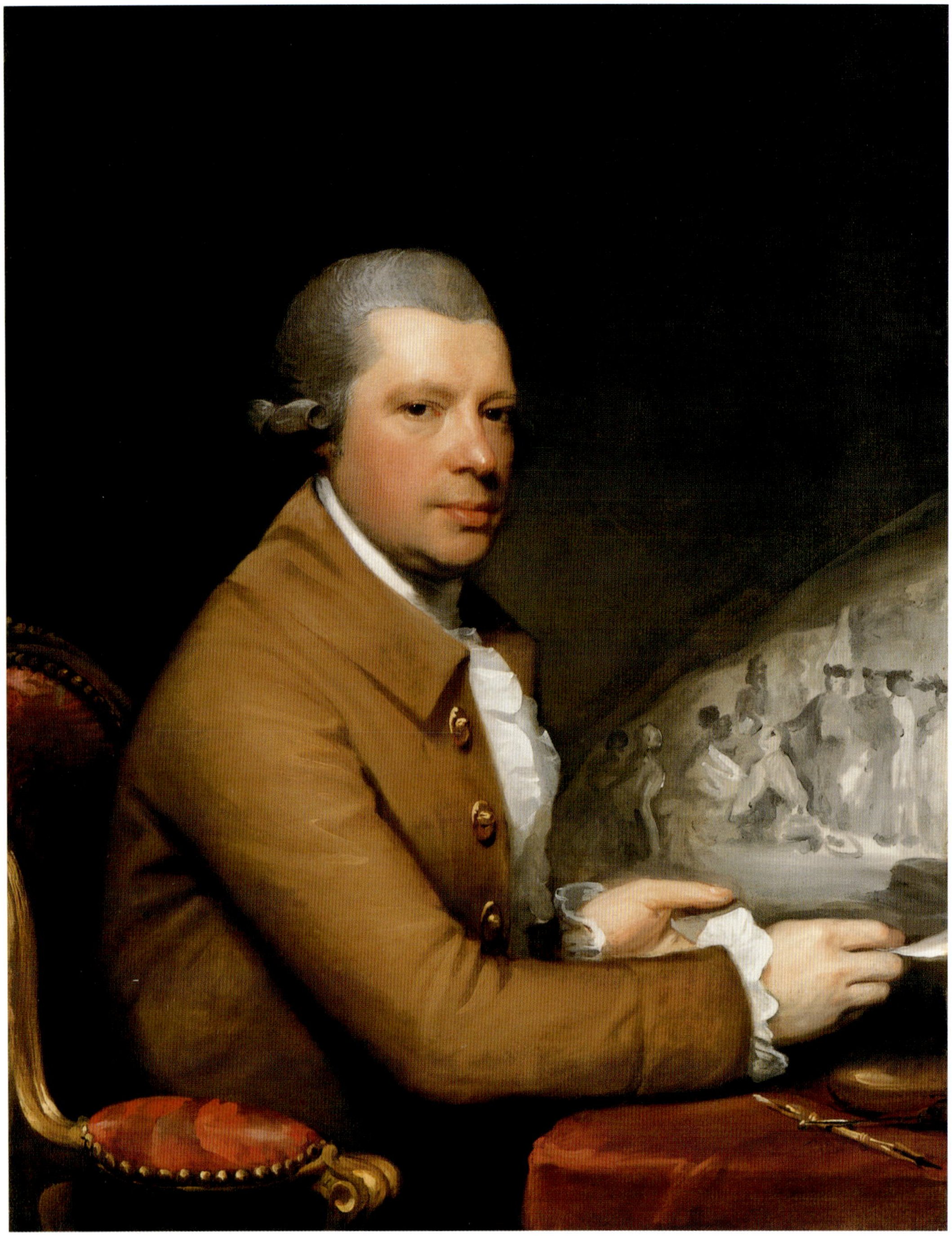

HALL NPG 693

Return to Albion, Washington, 1979; *Artists at Work* 1981-82(7).

Reference: Park 1926, no.367; Whitley 1932, pp.55, 62; Davies 1946, p.145; Erffa & Staley 1986, pp.207-08.

One of the series of portraits of painters and engravers Stuart painted for Boydell, their patron, all of which were exhibited in Boydell's rooms in Cheapside in 1786 (cf. Copley, NPG 2143).[1] Park stated that NPG 693 was painted in 1785, which seems very likely; this was also the year of Hall's appointment as historical engraver to the King on the death of Woollett. He is shown holding a proof of his print of West's *Penn's Treaty with the Indians*,[2] which was published in 1775, and the portrait complements Stuart's *William Woollett* (exhibited 1783; Tate Gallery), who is shown in front of West's *Death of Wolfe*, which he had engraved in 1776. These two engravings after West by Hall and Woollett were hugely successful and launched Boydell on his career of patronage; 'no Engravers could possibly be more cheerfully attentive to the remarks of the painter whose works they were copying, than Woollett and Hall were to those of Mr West' wrote J.T. Smith in 1828, and 'no prints from the works of one master surpass, or even equal, those by [these] two Historical-Engravers'.[3]

1 Whitley 1932, p.55.
2 Park, Whitley and Erffa & Staley agree that Hall is holding an impression of his plate. A squared-up drawing by Hall, the same size as his plate, is with the Historical Society of Pennsylvania, and a reduced version of the painting, by West himself, the same size as Hall's plate, belongs to the Chicago Historical Society.
3 Smith 1920, II, p.307.

ICONOGRAPHY

c.1775-80 Pastel attributed to William Lawranson, see NPG 3992.

c.1780-85 Two drawings by Paul Sandby, profile heads, each inscribed *Hall Engraver*, among the series of heads drawn at print sales. Royal Collection (Oppé 1947, no.417/8 & 9). One of the heads appears in the anon. engraving,★ *Sketches taken at Print Sales*, see Comparative Groups.

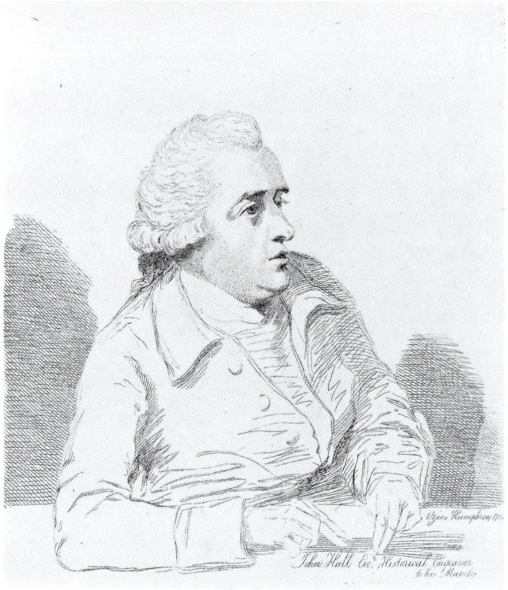

HALL Mrs D. Turner after Ozias Humphry 1784 (NPG D 18002)

1784 Drawing by Ozias Humphry, half length, resting his arms on a table with a rolled paper in his hands. Royal Academy (illus. Williamson 1918, f.p.2). Etched by Mrs Dawson Turner.★

1785 Painting by Gilbert Stuart, see NPG 693.

c.1797 Anon. engraving, oval, published posthumously.

Undated miniatures by Richard Cosway, described as early and signed, and another unattributed were with the sitter's descendants in 1900 (H.W. Lewer, *Essex Review*, XXIII, 1914, p.100).

HAMILTON, Elizabeth, Duchess of, see ARGYLL

HAMILTON, Elizabeth, Baroness, see ARGYLL

HAMILTON, Emma, Lady, *née* Amy Lyon 1765-1815

Courtesan; as Emily Hart, the mistress of Sir Harry Featherstonhaugh 1781; as Emma Hart, mistress of Charles Greville 1782-85; in 1786 went to Naples to join Sir William Hamilton, Greville's uncle, whom she m. in London 1791; from 1798 mistress of Horatio (Lord) Nelson, by whom she bore a daughter, Horatia, in 1801; d. Calais, deeply in debt.

'I find her not so beautiful as I expected, but certainly extremely handsome and her figure uncommonly fine. She was well dressed and there is something in her manner very good humoured and a great desire of pleasing' (Lady Palmerston, 1793).

'Her face is beautiful; she is all Nature and yet all Art; that is to say her manners are perfectly unpolished, of course very easy, though not with the ease of good breeding, but of a barmaid' (Sir Gilbert Elliot, 1796).

Abbreviation

WR: 'Portraits of Emma Hart, Lady Hamilton', H. Ward & W. Roberts, *Romney, A Biographical and Critical Essay with a Catalogue Raisonné of his Works*, 1904, II, pp. 179-88 (a numbered list)

4448 GEORGE ROMNEY c.1785

Canvas 61 x 51 (24 x 20) lined; cleaned 1987; craquelure most apparent within the impasted whites of the forehead and scarf.

Grey eyes, reddish-brown hair, vermilion lips, wearing a white scarf and dress which are rapidly brushed in.

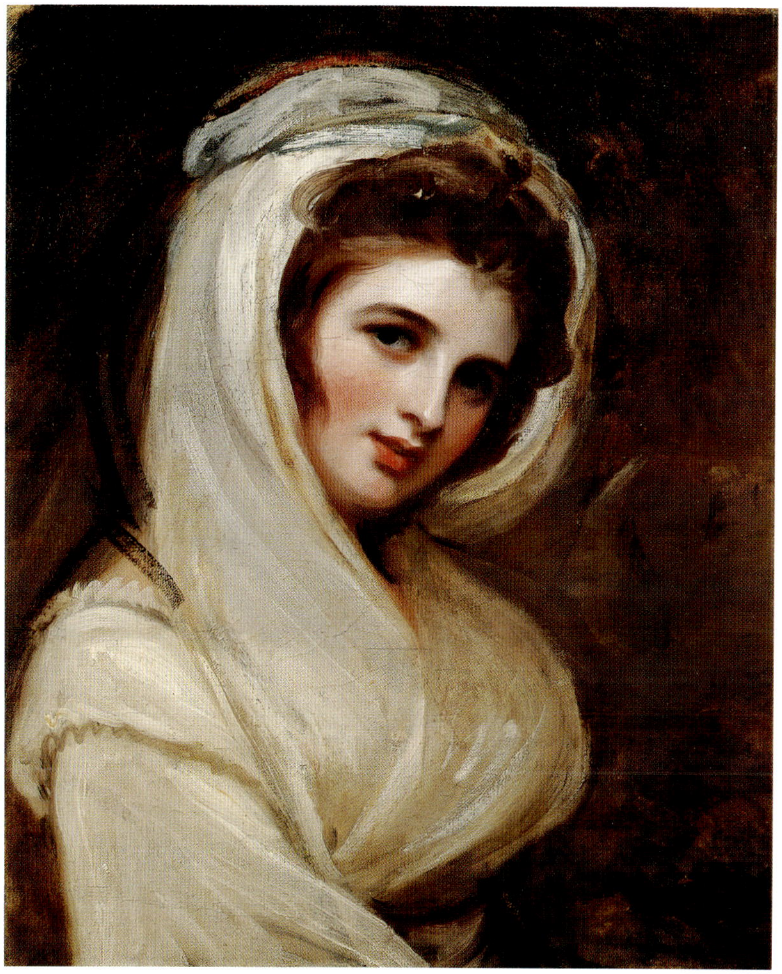

Emma, Lady HAMILTON
NPG 4448

Collections: Rev John Romney sale, Christie's, 10 May 1834, lot 93, bt. Norton for the 2nd Baron Northwick; by descent at Northwick Park to Capt. E.G. Spencer Churchill; purchased from the Spencer Churchill Estate in a private treaty sale with the aid of the National Art Collections Fund 1965.

Exhibitions: BI 1854(143); *Hamilton* 1972(16); *Regency Portraits*, Kenwood, 1986; *Romantic Icons*, Grasmere, 1999(26).

Engraving: J. Skelton 1849 (the costume more finished).

Reference: Northwick Catalogue, 1864, no.141; WR 39a; T. Borenius, *Northwick Catalogue*, 1921, no.366.

For Romney, Emma Hamilton was 'the divine lady. I cannot give her any other epithet, for I think her superior to all womankind'.[1] She first sat to him as Mrs Hart in April 1782, probably for the picture engraved in 1784 as *Nature*, now in the Frick Collection, New York; by March 1786 over one hundred sittings are listed, even though Romney's diary for 1785 is missing.[2] In March 1786 she left London for Naples, but when she briefly returned with Sir William Hamilton in 1791 she sat to Romney a further thirty-four times between 2 June and 6 September, the day of her marriage (when Romney's diary records two appointments: 'Mrs Hart 9' - 'Lady Hamilton 11'). There were no further sittings, and on 20 December 1791 Emma wrote to Romney from Naples: 'You was the first dear friend I open'd my heart to, you ought to know me, for you have seen and discoursed with me in my poorer days, you have known me in my poverty and prosperity'.[3]

Romney's pictures of Emma almost invariably show her playing parts or modelling *têtes d'expression*. 'Her features', Hayley once observed, 'like the language of Shakespeare, could exhibit all the feelings of nature, and all the gradations of every passion, with a most fascinating truth, and felicity of expression'.[4] Reynolds, Lawrence, Gavin Hamilton, Angelica Kauffmann and Vigée Le Brun, for example, each painted her as Muse or Bacchante and Emma's private appearance remains an enigma;[5] only the modest pastel by Johann Schmidt of 1800 seems to convey a still likeness.

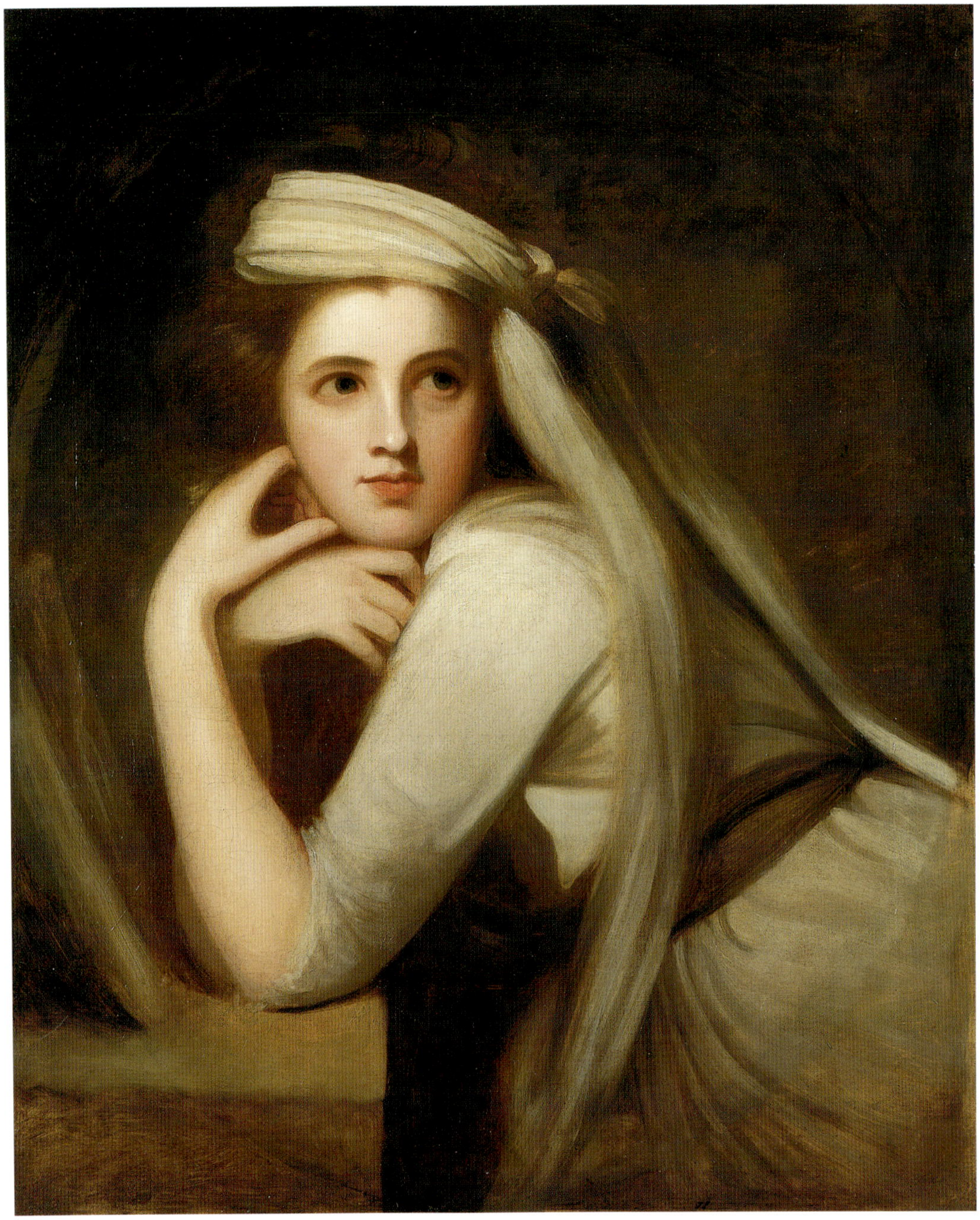

Emma, Lady HAMILTON NPG *294*

NPG 4448, a spirited sketch, probably dates from 1785; the cast of the head recurs, for example, reversed in Romney's celebrated *Emma in a Straw Hat* of c.1785 in the Huntington Art Collections, San Marino, Calif., and a similar head-scarf in *The Spinstress* of c.1784–85 at Kenwood (see below). A bust-length oval version of NPG 4448 called *Daphne* was formerly in the Tennant collection (WR 39b), and a three-quarter length studio elaboration was sold Sotheby's, 10 November 1993, lot 50 (WR 39d). A double portrait, in which the head from NPG 4448 appears on the left and that of Emma as a Nun (WR 21) on the right, was sold Christie's, 3 July 1964, lot 88. There are derivative oval engravings of 1803 by J. Condé (the head wreathed in vine leaves) and James Hopwood.

1 Letter of 19 June 1791, quoted in Hayley 1809, p.158.
2 Cross 2000, p.228n151, quoting Watson 1974 (see below); cf. Ward & Roberts 1904, II, p.179.
3 Quoted by P. Jaffé, *Hamilton* 1972, p.10.
4 Hayley 1809, p.119.
5 Cf Sterne's *Sentimental Journey* (the remise door): 'thou cheatest us seven times a day with thy pictures and images, yet with so many charms dost thou do it, and thou deckest out thy pictures in the shapes of so many angels of light,'tis a shame to break with thee'.

294 GEORGE ROMNEY c.1785

Canvas 75 x 62 (29½ x 24½) lined; cleaned 1976; a painted oval border, upper left, and the other spandrels thinly painted; previously framed as an oval.

Dark brown eyes, rich auburn hair, dressed in white with a darker sash at her waist; on the ledge to the left a book (or mirror, see below) is suggested.

Collections: James Green (1771–1834); his son, Benjamin Richard Green (1806–76), from whom purchased 1870.[1]

Exhibitions: *Kauffmann* 1968(407); *Faces as Art*, NPG, 1976; *Joseph Haydn*, Eisenstadt, 1982(781); *Treasures* 1995–96(17); *Muses, Madonnas and Maidens*, Tokyo, 2001(B22).

Reference: WR3g (*Lady Hamilton as a Bacchante*).

See NPG 4448. A kit-cat version, sold Sotheby's, 15 July 1998, lot 50, as *Lady Hamilton as a Bacchante*, shows a mirror on the table to the left. Other closely related compositions include the *Medea* in the Norton Simon Foundation, Los Angeles,[2] *The Comic Muse* with Leggatt in 1948 (WR 8b), and the *Bacchantes* with the University of Missouri (79.103), and with Sir Philip Antrobus in 1989.[3]

1 Benjamin Green then wrote that NPG 294 had been acquired by his family 'about half a century ago having been purchased by my father at a sale as a portrait of Lady Hamilton by Romney' (NPG archive). His father was a portrait painter.
2 *Hamilton* 1972, no.17 illus.; a version sold Sotheby's, 27 June 1973, lot 13.
3 WR 38; illus. *Connoisseur*, XII, 1905, p.264.

2941 RICHARD COSWAY c.1801

Pencil and watercolour on paper 23.2 x 14.1 (9⅛ x 5½), a small tear in the upper left corner; laid down on paper; the face mask alone is coloured; minor repairs top right and at her waist to the right.

The eyes are grey; there is the suggestion of a classical pillar to the left.

Collections: Bequeathed by H.W. Murray 1938.

Exhibitions: *Kauffmann*, 1968(181); *Hamilton* 1972(92); *Van Dyck in Check Trousers*, Edinburgh, 1978(48); *The Artist's Model*, Nottingham, Kenwood, 1991(35); *Cosway* 1995(102).

Probably drawn following Emma's final return from Naples in November 1800, NPG 2941 shows her in an attitude derived from classical sculpture (see Appendix below). Other miniatures of Emma attributed to Cosway and listed by Williamson,[1] are not convincingly identified.

1 Williamson 1905, pp.111, 122 and f.p.108.

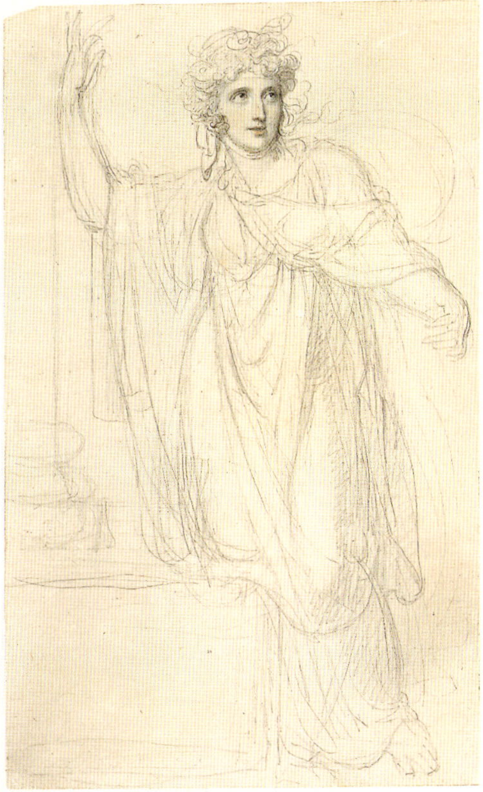

Emma, Lady HAMILTON NPG 2941

ICONOGRAPHY

See NPG 4448. Aspects of Emma's iconography have been surveyed by P. Jaffé (*Hamilton* 1972); I. Jenkins and K. Sloan (*Vases & Volcanoes* 1996); J.C. Watson, 'The Paintings of Emma Hart by George Romney: a study of their significance in relation to his historical works', MA thesis, Oberlin, 1974, and see Appendix below.

Paintings by George Romney (see under NPG 4448) include the following of some iconographical interest:

1782 Half length as *Nature*, a spaniel in her arms. Frick Collection, New York (04.1.103; WR 20; see *Romney* 2002, no.168), commissioned by Charles Greville. Engraved J.R. Smith 1784. Enamel copy by J. Lee exhibited RA 1825(439).

c.1782 Whole length as *Circe*, her wand in her right hand, her left arm raised. Private collection (WR 6; illus. *Connoisseur*, XII, 1905, p.249; see *Romney* 2002, pp.167-68). Bust-length version in the Tate Gallery (N 5591; *Romney* 2002, no.98).

1783 Three-quarter length with a dog, as a *Bacchante*. Private collection, commissioned by Sir William Hamilton (WR 3a; illus. *Vases & Volcanoes* 1996, p.267). Engraved C. Knight 1797.

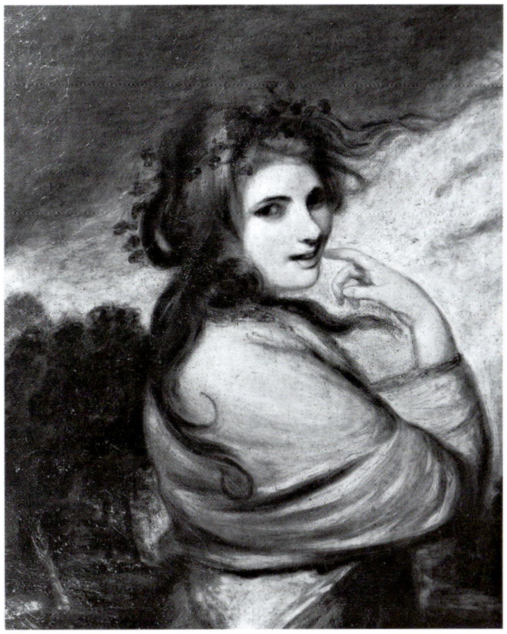

Emma, Lady HAMILTON after Joshua Reynolds 1784 (Waddesdon Manor, The National Trust)

c.1784 Whole-length seated as *The Spinstress*. Kenwood (WR 29; *Romney* 2002, no.108). Commissioned by Charles Greville.

c.1785 Three-quarter length seated, wearing a straw hat ornamented with a large black ribbon and tied round with a white scarf. Huntington Art Collections, San Marino, Calif. (24.5; WR 10; *Huntington* 2001, no.92; Romney 2002, no.109). Commissioned by Charles Greville. Engraved J. Jones 1785. A variant, without the hat but with the head scarf, engraved W. Read 1815.

c.1785 See NPG 4448 and NPG 294 above.

c.1786 Three-quarter length seated, looking upwards, with large black hat and falling white ruffled collar. Private collection (WR 19; *Romney* 2002, no.110). A half-length variant, with plumes in her hat, in a private collection (WR 45 and WR 4, illus. f.p.184).

before 1786 Whole-length seated as *St Cecilia*, wearing white, her hands joined in prayer. Christie's, 21 November 1975, lot 68 (WR 24a; illus. F. Fraser, *Emma, Lady Hamilton*, 1986, f.p.118). Engraved G. Keating 1789. A related half-length composition at Kenwood.

1784 Painting by Joshua Reynolds, half length as a *Bacchante*. Private collection (Mannings 2000, no.815), commissioned by Sir William Hamilton. Engraved J.R. Smith 1784. Exhibited RA 1784(342 with wrong title, 'Boy Reading'). Copies include those by John Rising* (Waddesdon Manor), Thomas Sully 1837 (Philadelphia Museum of Art), and anon. (formerly in a Canadian private collection, destroyed by fire; illus. J. Watson, *Reynolds in Canada*, 1988, p.79). Enamel copy by Henry Bone, Sotheby's, 11 November 1993, lot 41, exhibited RA 1803(634).

In March 1786 Emma left London for Naples where she arrived on 26 April and took up residence with Sir William Hamilton in the Palazzo Sessa.

1786 Painting by Gavin Hamilton, three-quarter length as a *Sybil*. Private collection (illus. *Hamilton* 1972, pl.ii). Gavin Hamilton escorted Emma on her journey to Naples.

1786 Painting by Gavin Hamilton, three-quarter length as *Hebe*. London art market 1972 (illus. *Hamilton* 1972, pl.iii). Version at Burghley House (no.366), engraved D. Cunego, exhibited *Kauffmann* 1968(274) as possibly a copy by Hamilton after Kauffmann.

In 1787 Emma described the Palazzo Sessa as being 'full of painters painting me. [Sir William] as now got nine pictures of me, and 2 a painting. Marchant is cutting my head in stone ... There is another man modeling me in wax, and another in clay. All the artists is come from Rome' (Ingamells 1997, p.456).

1787 Sardonyx by Nathaniel Marchant (illus. Marchant 1987, no.138, fig.141). Probably exhibited RA 1789(344). A chalcedony profile by Marchant, set in a gold ring, in the Metropolitan Museum of Art, New York, illus. *Vases & Volcanoes* 1996, p.209. Emma's seal (illus. H. Gamlin, *Nelson's Friendships*, 1899, II, p.178) apparently derived from Marchant's gem.

c.1788 Painting by Wilhelm Tischbein, half-length profile as a *Sybil*. Stiftung Weimarer Klassik, Weimar (illus. *Vases & Volcanoes* 1996, p.88).

1788 Painting by Wilhelm Tischbein, as *Iphigenia*, with Orestes. Private collection (illus. *Connoisseur*, CXCI, 1976, p.120).

c.1789-90 Painting by H.D. Hamilton, as *Three Muses*, half-length figures. Lennoxlove (illus. *Vases & Volcanoes* 1996, p.263). Exhibited *Kauffmann*, 1968(281 as by Gavin Hamilton). A miniature, attributed to Samuel Shelley, derived from the right-hand head, sold Christie's, 23 May 1989, lot 159.

1790 Painting by Elisabeth Vigée Le Brun, as *Ariadne*, whole-length recumbent on a sea shore. Private collection (illus. *Vigée Le Brun*, Fort Worth, 1982, p.88). Miniature versions by Henry Bone in the Wallace Collection (M21, illus. *Cat. of Miniatures*, 1980, p.312; exhibited RA 1803, no.634), and in the Victory Museum, Portsmouth; preparatory drawing dated 1803 in the NPG Bone albums (*Bone* 1999, no.246).

A copy by T. Fall is in the National Maritime Museum, with another set in a lacquer box.

1790 Charcoal sketch on panel by Elisabeth Vigée Le Brun, bust length. Syon House sale, Sotheby's, 14 May 1997, lot 226 (illus. *Vases & Volcanoes* 1996, p.270; *Vigée Le Brun*, Fort Worth, 1982, p.100), from the Earl of Warwick's collection.

In May 1791 Emma returned from Naples to London, with Sir William Hamilton.

1791 Paintings by George Romney (see under NPG 4448):

Three-quarter length seated, wearing a plumed hat, *The Ambassadress*. Jack S. Blanton Museum of Art, Austin, Tex. (WR 30; Romney 2002, p.201). Engraved T.G. Appleton.

Half length with white turban over her distinctive auburn hair, her left hand at her waist. Huntington Art Collections, San Marino, Calif. (26.109; illus. Huntington 2001, no.93 as c.1791).

On 7 July 1791 Romney wrote of other pictures he was to do of Emma: 'I have begun, the Joan of Arc, a Magdalen, and a Bacchante, for the Prince of Wales; and another I am to begin as a companion to the Bacchante'. The Joan of Arc was never finished (Hayley 1809, pp.159, 172) and Romney's surviving pictures from their last meeting, showing Emma as Calypso, Cassandra, Comedy and The Magdalen, are fancies rather than portraits.

1791 Painting by Thomas Lawrence,* whole length as *La Penserosa*. Duke of Abercorn (Garlick 1989, no.370a). Exhibited RA 1792(1). A related drawing, bust length to left wearing a turban (British Museum, 00.5.22; illus. *Vases & Volcanoes* 1996, p.19) was engraved C. Knight 1792. A second drawing by Lawrence, showing her with a turban, her right hand raised to her shoulder, was engraved, and has also been called Lady Charlotte Bury (Sotheby's, 11 April 1991, lot 31).

Other drawings by Lawrence which appear to show Emma include *Painting* (a brush in her right hand, her hair dressed with flowers), sold Christie's, 15 June 1971, lot 52, and the *Portrait of a Lady*, sold Sotheby's, 15 June 2000, lot 6.

c.1791 Painting by Thomas Lawrence, half-length oval as a *Bacchante*. Formerly Broadlands Collection (Garlick 1989, no.370b). Painted over a design by Reynolds within a border of flowers by J.B. Monnoyer.

c.1791 Marble bust by Joseph Nollekens, as *Niobe*. Ashmolean Museum, Oxford (*Visitors Report* 1965, pp.56–57, illus. f.p.50). The identification is plausible, but undocumented.

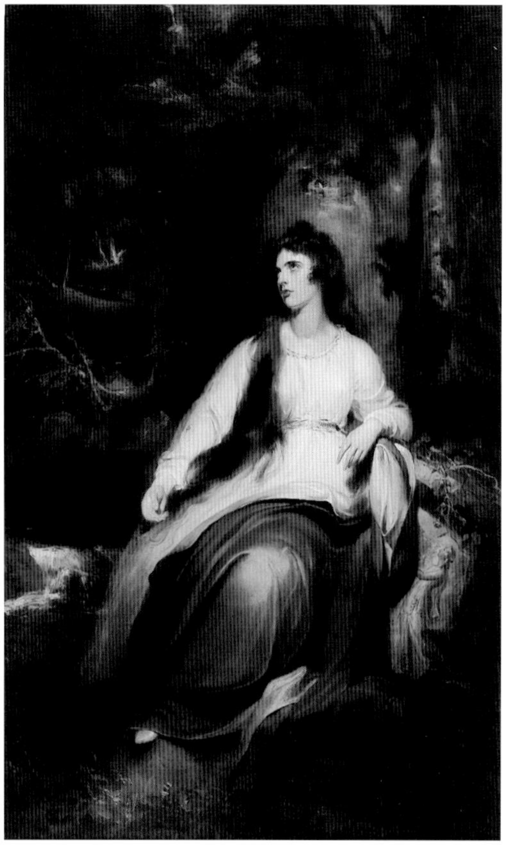

Emma, Lady HAMILTON by Thomas Lawrence 1791 (The Duke of Abercorn)

c.1791 Miniature by Samuel Shelley, bust-length oval. Sabin 1905 (*Burl. Mag.*, VIII, 1906, p.130, illus. f.p.135). Perhaps correctly identified.

c.1791 Miniature by Mrs Anne Mee. Huntington Art Collections, San Marino, Calif.

In September 1791 Emma, now Lady Hamilton, returned with Sir William Hamilton to Naples, where they arrived in December.

1791 Etching by D. Vivant-Denon, half-length profile. British Museum (1989.11.4.430; illus. *Vases & Volcanoes* 1996, p.258). Made in Venice. Etched J. Suntach as *Madame Hart*. Anon. miniature copy in the Holburne Museum, Bath (illus. Bayne-Powell 1995, p.84).

1791 Painting by Domenico Pellegrini, half length, a dog in her lap. Sotheby's, 13 November 1996, lot 62 (illus. Waterhouse 1981, p.272).

1791 Painting by Angelica Kauffmann, three-quarter length as the *Comic Muse*. Private collection (illus. *Kauffmann* 1998, p.263). Engraved R. Morghen 1797 (illus. *Vases & Volcanoes* 1996, p.273) and H. Meyer 1815 (half length).

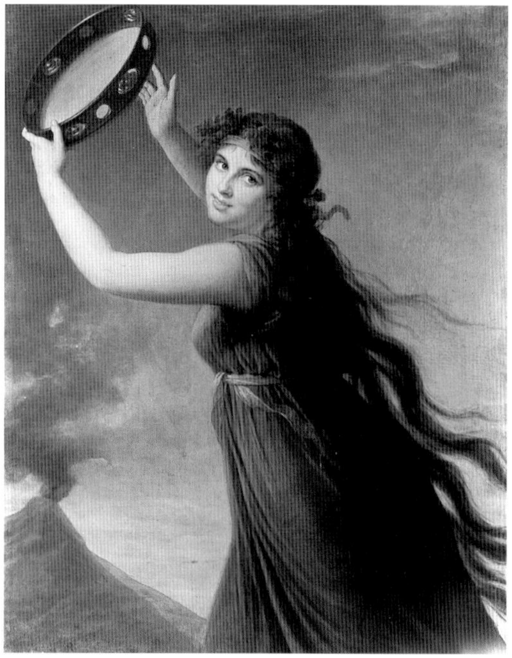

Emma, Lady HAMILTON by Elisabeth Vigée Le Brun c.1791 (Lady Lever Art Gallery, Port Sunlight)

c.1791 Painting by Elisabeth Vigée Le Brun,* three-quarter length as a *Bacchante*.Lady Lever AG, Port Sunlight (LL 3527).

c.1791 Painting by Elisabeth Vigée Le Brun, three-quarter length as a *Sybil*. Sotheby's, New York, 11 January 1996, lot 154. A version dated 1792 is in a British private collection (illus. *Vigée Le Brun*, Fort Worth, 1982, p.101). Engraved Grevedon. A half-length version was given by the artist to Sir William Hamilton (see *Vases & Volcanoes* 1996, p.271).

1792 Paintings by Alexander Day, copies in oil and miniature from a portrait of Lady Hamilton, as described by the artist in a letter to Sir William Hamilton, 13 January 1792 (Ingamells 1997, p.286).

1792 Miniature drawing by Harriet Carr, half-length oval. Francis Wellesley sale, Sotheby's, 2nd day, 29 June 1920, lot 214.

c.1795? Engraved gem by Filippo Rega. A cast glass intaglio version by James Tassie is in the British Museum (MLA 1867.7.8.1; illus. *Vases & Volcanoes* 1996, p.304).

1796 Painting by Angelica Kauffmann, small whole-length seated. Victoria and Albert Museum (579.1875; illus. *Kauffmann* 1968, pl.53). Painted in Naples.

1797 Marble bust by Christopher Hewetson. On 10 June 1797 Robert Fagan wrote that 'Hewetson is at Naples doing Sir William and Lady's busts' (*Hewetson* 1958, p.53).

1798 Painting by Guy Head. Emma threw a palette at the artist as he tried to explain with his stammer that her foot was too large for a sandal and he was therefore giving it a slipper (Pryse Lockhart Gordon, *Personal Memoirs*, 1830, II, p.384). A heavy-featured bust-length profile by Head, then with E.J. Mallough, was engraved B. Reading 1817, displaying the arms of Hamilton in the title and of Nelson within the image. A closely related profile engraving, published G. Andrews 1804.

A similar profile, flowers in her hair which hangs loose over her shoulder, lettered: *Grignon deli: Vinc: Aloja Sculp:* titled *hamilton*. Charles Grignion was in Italy 1784-1802.

In 1798 Sir William Hamilton listed fourteen portraits of Emma in the Palazzo Sessa, three each by Tischbein and Romney, two each by Vigée Le Brun and Gavin Hamilton, and others by Reynolds, Kauffmann and Head (Ingamells 1997, p.458).

On 10 June 1800 Emma, with Sir William Hamilton and Lord Nelson, left Naples and, travelling through Germany, reached London on 9 November.

1800 Pastel by Johann Schmidt,* half length in white, wearing the order of the Knights of Malta (given her by the Czar of Russia at Nelson's request in 1799). National Maritime Museum (PR 63/75). Painted at Dresden and inscribed verso by Emma: Nelson 'thought he could not be victorious if he did not see it in the midst of Battle'. The companion piece of Nelson is also in the National Maritime Museum.

c.1801 Drawing by Richard Cosway, see NPG 2941.

c.1802 Enamel miniature attributed to W.H. Craft, bust length. Christie's, 7 June 1966, lot 16.

1803 Portrait by Henry Edridge, exhibited RA 1803(346).

1803 Drawing by W.M. Bennet, half-length oval, wearing hat with a feather, engraved K. Mackenzie.

1803 Miniature by Harriet Beckford, half-length roundel, her head covered. Ernest Salaman 1930 (illus. *Connoisseur*, LXXXVI, 1930, p.178).

1803-05 Drawings by Thomas Baxter. Merton sketchbook, National Maritime Museum. Baxter visited Nelson's home at Merton making several informal studies of Emma, some dated 1803 (a half-length seated with Charlotte Nelson illus. F. Fraser, *Emma, Lady Hamilton*, 1986, f.p.246). A miniature by Baxter set in a snuff box is also in the National Maritime Museum.

c.1803? Miniature by John Dunn, half-length oval, with vine leaves in her hair. Christie's, bt. in before 1964. Showing Emma much overweight, as in the Guy Head profile of 1798.

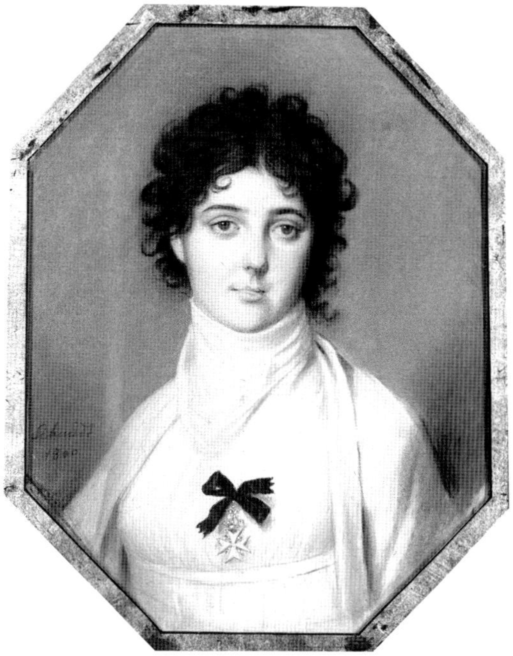

Emma, Lady HAMILTON by Johann Schmidt 1800 (National Maritime Museum, London)

1804 Painting by J.J. Masquerier, seated by a window at night with a view of Mount Vesuvius, exhibited RA 1804(67). Engraved W. Say 1806 (illus. *Connoisseur*, LX, 1921, p.221).

APPENDIX

Although they cannot count as portraiture Emma's 'Attitudes' performed in Naples largely determined how she was perceived. 'With the assistance of one or two Etruscan vases and an urn, [she] became a Sybil, then a Fury, a Niobe, a Sophonisba drinking poison, a Bacchante drinking wine, dancing and playing the tambourine, an Agrippina at the tomb of Germanicus, and every attitude of almost every different passion ... a painter had cried with pleasure the whole time' (J.B.S. Morritt 1796; Ingamells, 1997, p.458). The 'Attitudes' were frequently drawn, e.g. by Pietro Antonio Novelli 1791; Friedrich Rehberg 1794 (engraved by Tommaso Piroli); William Artaud, and Wilhelm Tischbein (see *Vases & Volcanoes* 1996, pp.88, 92n79).

For further discussion of the 'Attitudes', see *Vases & Volcanoes* 1996, pp.256, 259-61; U. van de Sandt, 'Le attitudini di Lady Hamilton Emma Hart a Venezia nel 1791', *Saggi e Memorie dell'Arte*, XXII, 1998, pp.301-16, and U. Ittershagen, *Lady Hamiltons Attitüden*, Mainz, 1999.

HAMILTON, Sir William, KB 1730-1803

Diplomat, vulcanologist and antiquary; at Naples as British envoy extraordinary 1764-67 and minister plenipotentiary 1767-1800; FRS 1766; KB 1772; visited London in 1772, 1776-77, 1783-84, 1791, finally returning in 1800; m. 1) 1758 Catherine Barlow (d.1782), 2) 1791 Emma Hart.

'tall and meagre, with a dark complexion, a very aquiline nose, ... [and] such an air of intelligence, blended with distinction, in his countenance, as powerfully attracted and conciliated all who approached him' (Sir Nathaniel Wraxall, 1815).

'With the courage of the elder Pliny, but with better fortune, he has explored the terrific scenes of devastation which Aetna and Vesuvius have of late years presented; scenes which appal the brave to view, and which the timorous shudder even to contemplate' (*European Mag.*, 1784).

589 DAVID ALLAN 1775

Canvas 228 x 181 (89¾ x 71¼); lined; cleaned 1980 and areas of local flaking treated 1996; inscribed on the paper lying on the floor, bottom left: *Painted by D. Allan / & by him humbly presented / to the British Museum. / Anno.Dom..1775.-*

Blue-grey eyes, grey powdered hair, wearing the ceremonial dress of a Knight of the Bath: gold collar and badge, pink cape over a silk white suit, the ostrich-plumed hat on a chair at his side. He holds diplomatic papers resting against a table with carved lion-headed supports of a Pompeian type and bearing on a side panel the crest of the Dukes of Hamilton (to whom Hamilton was related)[1] displayed as a badge. To the right a glass fronted cabinet in the form of a Roman *lararium* (such as had been found at Pompeii), crowned with an acroterial statue of Jupiter and bearing a head of Medusa in relief on the pediment; it contains items from the Hamilton Collection, including an ornate Apulian vase,[2] a bronze statuette of Athena Promachos, and a bronze tripod and bowl. Through the window a view of the smouldering Vesuvius.

Collections: Presented by the artist to the British Museum 1775, where received on 1 March 1776; transferred to the NPG 1879; on loan to the British Museum from 1982.

Exhibitions: *Kauffmann* 1968(106); *Hamilton* 1972(28); *The indefatigable Mr Allan*, Edinburgh, Glasgow, Dundee, Alloa, 1973(41); *The Order of the Bath*, Tower of London, 1981; *The Arrogant Connoisseur*, Manchester, 1982(172); *Vases & Volcanoes* 1996(1).

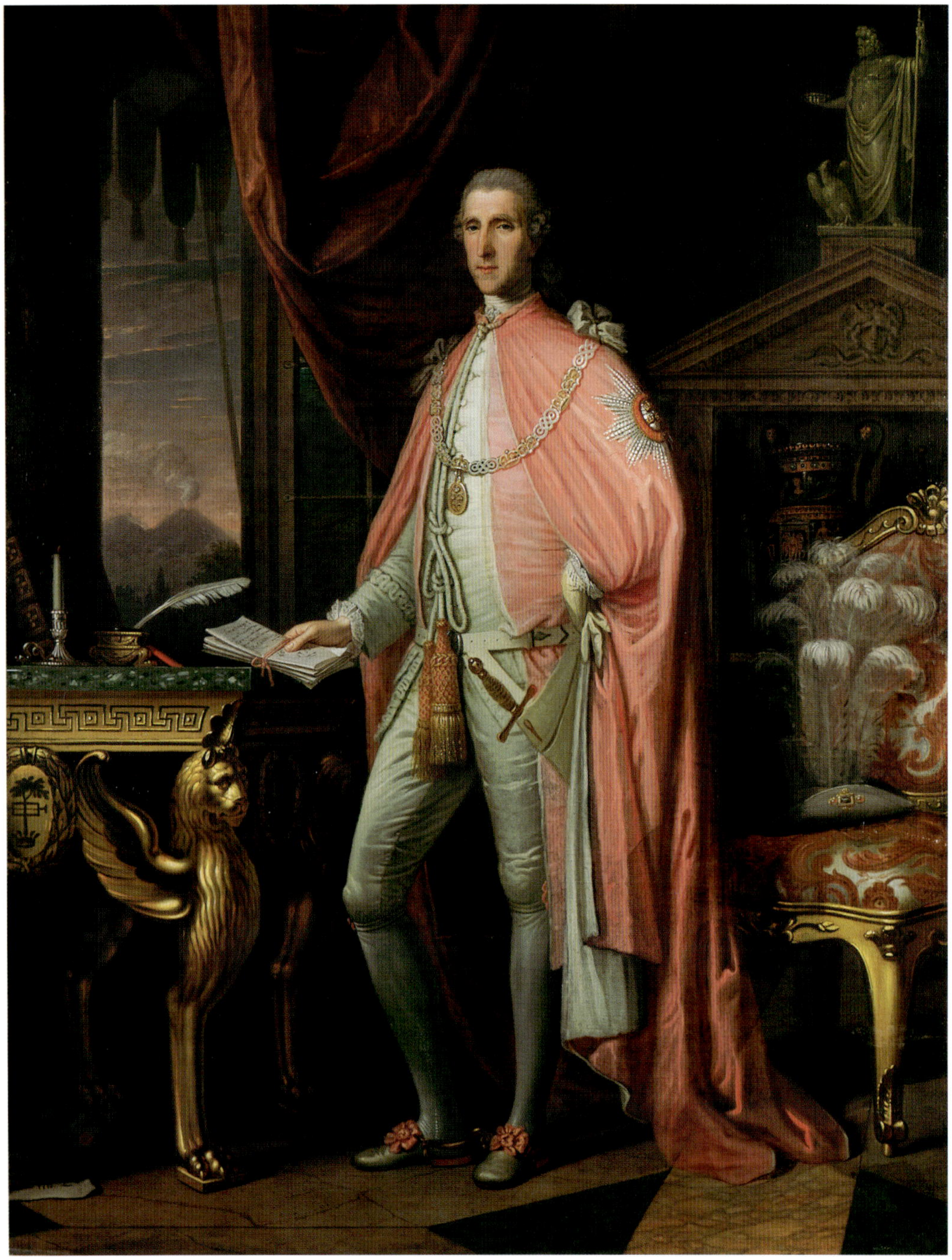

Sir William HAMILTON NPG *589*

Reference: T.C. Gordon, *David Allan*, 1951, p.22; J.R. Fawcett Thompson, *Connoisseur*, CLXXIII, 1970, pp.250–53.

Set, presumably, in the Palazzo Sessa, Hamilton's official residence at Naples, this formal portrait of a distinguished diplomat makes careful reference to ancestry, rank, honours, taste and generosity. It is in marked contrast to the informal portrait of the Hamiltons which Allan had previously painted at Posilippo (see below), and with the later full length by Reynolds (NPG 680).

The circumstances of the portrait are well documented. In 1772 the British Museum had purchased the Hamilton Collection of antiquities, gathered in Naples since 1764, for £8,400. On 6 October 1775 the young Scottish artist David Allan, then on his second visit to Naples during a Grand Tour which had started in 1767, wrote to Dr Maty, Secretary of the Museum, offering the portrait which he had painted out of 'Gratitude and Regard' for Hamilton, 'a true lover and Promoter of the fine Arts and protector of Artists, of which I have had the honor of a very particular share':

> I have indeavoured to do his portraite as well as I can; And considering his great ingenuity and merit in making such a Noble Collection of interesting and beautiful monuments of Antiquity which are at present rightly placed in the B. Museum has induced me to think a portrait of the worthy collector might very properly find a place in that collection, on this consideration I have ventured to offer the picture to the Directors, which if they thought the weak performance worthy of being put up with this collection, woud do me an honnor and be of service to me as the work woud be seen, and I should be very happy if the picture should not be thought unworthy of their acceptance.[3]

The portrait was accepted and on 1 March 1776 the Museum's General Committee were told it was in London.[4] But the artist's hopes of his work being seen were soon to be disappointed. In February 1782 Hamilton presented to the British Museum his portrait by Reynolds (NPG 680) and Allan's portrait was consigned to storage, which it only left upon being transferred to the NPG in 1879.

1 *Out of a ducal coronet, an oak fructed and penetrated transversely in the main stem by a frame-saw.* Hamilton was the 4th son of Lord Archibald Hamilton, who was 7th son of the 3rd Duke of Hamilton. His mother was a daughter of the 6th Earl of Abercorn.

2 The decoration is shown in reverse; Allan evidently copied the reversed engraving from d'Hancarville's *Antiquités Etrusques, Grecques et Romaines*, I, 1766, pl.54 (as first indicated by J.R. Fawcett Thompson, *Connoisseur*, CLXXIII, 1970, p.252); see *Vases & Volcanoes* 1996 (2).

3 BM archive, OL & P, I, f.293 (as quoted in *Vases & Volcanoes* 1996, p.106).

4 BM archive, CM, p.150.

680 JOSHUA REYNOLDS 1776–77

Canvas 255 x 175 (100 x 71) lined; the surface is somewhat rubbed and there is a drying craquelure in darker areas; pentimenti show that the tree, top left, originally spread further to the left.

Blue-grey eyes, powdered hair, wearing a deep maroon jacket with the star of the Bath and holding open on his lap the first volume of d'Hancarville's *Antiquités* (open at pl.71 which bears a Greek dedication to Hamilton);[1] it is presumably the second volume which lies open on the floor; on the right Greek antiquities from the Hamilton collection in the British Museum: a red-figured hydria, a wine jug, two drinking horns and a bronze sword;[2] beside him on the floor stand folio volumes inscribed *VLCAN/ /DIICARA* and *PRINTS / PASTE*.[3]

Collections: Commissioned by the sitter and presented to the British Museum 1782; transferred to the National Gallery 1843 (NG 185); ownership transferred to the Tate Gallery 1954 and to the NPG 1957.

Engravings: H. Hudson 1782 (dedicated to the Trustees of the British Museum), later states 1787, 1788; S.W. Reynolds.

Exhibitions: BI 1831(114); *English Taste in the 18th century*, RA, 1955(403); *Hamilton Collection*, British Museum, 1972(49); *Civiltà del 700 a Napoli 1734-99*, Naples, 1979(180); *Vases & Volcanoes* 1996(51); *Viaggio in Italia*, Genoa, 2001(vii.36).

Reference: Graves & Cronin, II, pp.423–24, IV, pp.1329–31; Waterhouse 1941, p.68; Davies 1946, p.116; *Vases & Volcanoes* 1996, pp.176–81; Mannings 2000, no.823.

Commissioned by Hamilton with the intention that it should accompany his collection of antiquities in the British Museum, rather than the Allan portrait (NPG 589). Sittings took place during his residence in England from summer 1776 to autumn 1777; there is no sitter book for 1776 but there are eight appointments in June 1777, some of which may have been for the Dilettanti group portrait (for which Reynolds used the same head, see below 1777). In February 1782 NPG 680 was hanging in the British Museum,[4] although Reynolds did not receive his 100 guineas for 'Sir William Hamilton, Museum Picture', until September 1784.[5]

Since 1775, when Allan had painted his formal portrait (NPG 589), Hamilton's achievements as a collector and scientist had been lavishly published, in the first two volumes of d'Hancarville's *Antiquités Etrusques, Grecques et Romaines*, and the first two volumes of Hamilton's vulcanological studies, the *Campi Phlegraei*. Reynolds refers to these publications in presenting the elegant connoisseur, an altogether appropriate image for the British Museum.

Although catalogued by Davies in 1946 as Reynolds, NPG 680 was subsequently listed in the concise NPG catalogues of 1949, 1970 and 1981 as a studio copy[6] (the size and intricacy of the composition inevitably led to some studio collaboration).

Two related oil sketches, possibly contemporary copies, are recorded in private collections; one the same size as the Hudson engraving, the other exhibited *Lady Hamilton* 1972, no.29.[7]

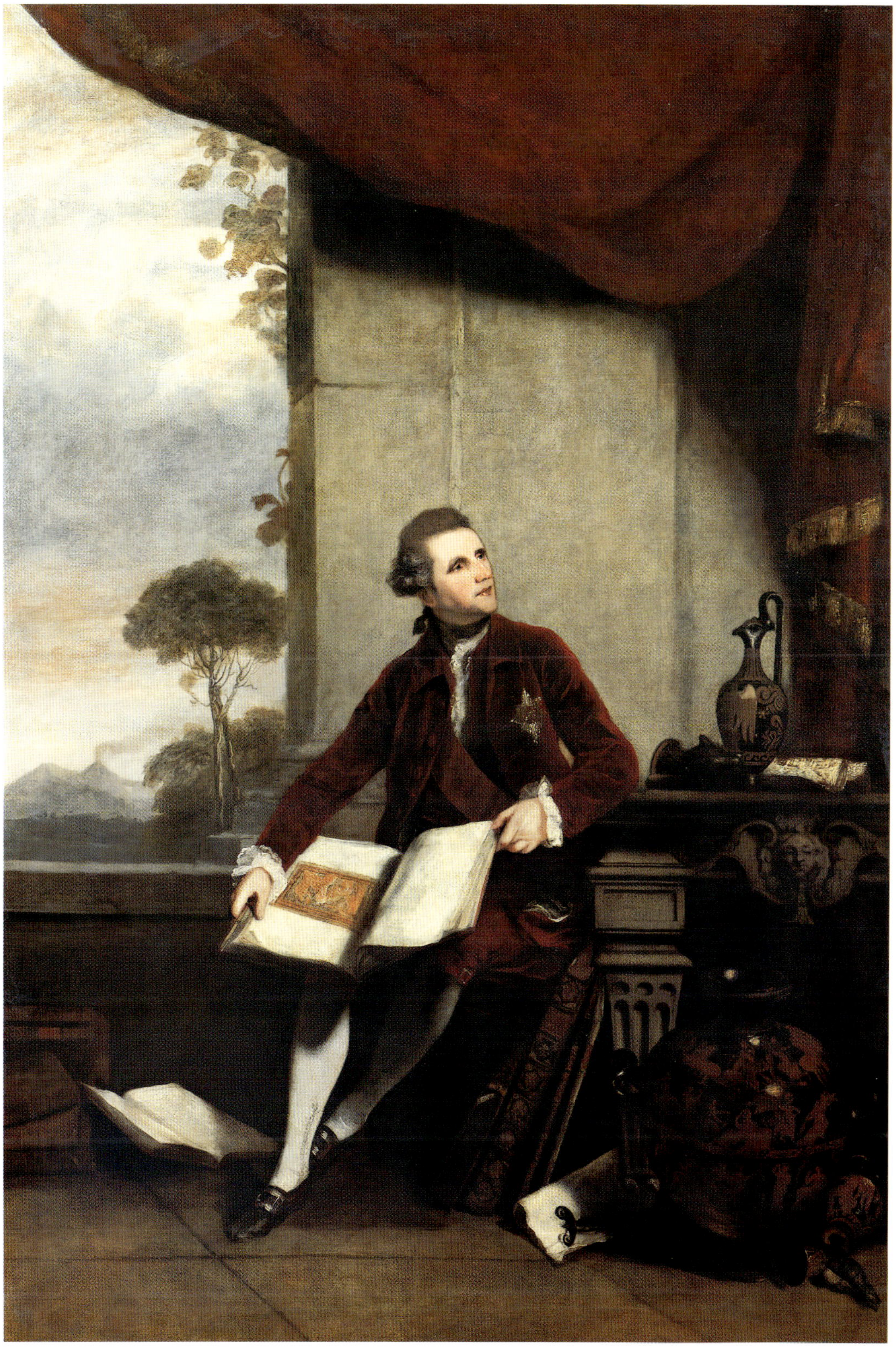

Sir William HAMILTON NPG *680*

1 *Vases & Volcanoes* 1996, p.179.
2 *Ibid.*, nos.55–57.
3 Possibly referring to Hamilton's *Campi Phlegraei* (vols. I & II published in 1776) with their illustrations by Pietro Fabris (cf. *Vases & Volcanoes* 1996, p.165).
4 Where it was varnished, with the agreement of Reynolds and Hamilton, on 2 July 1782 (*Vases & Volcanoes* 1996, p.176).
5 Cormack 1970, pp.154–55. Apparently a special price; at the same time Hamilton paid his contribution to the Dilettanti group portrait (35 gn.).
6 The result of a review of all the Reynolds portraits in the NPG undertaken by C.K. Adams, J. Steegman and H.M. Hake in 1937. NPG 680 was illustrated as a studio work, for example, *Connoisseur*, CLXXIII, 1970, p.253; *CL*, CXXXIV, 1963, p.1338, and J.R. Fawcett Thompson, *Connoisseur*, CLXXIII, 1970, p.253. It reverted to Reynolds in *Vases & Volcanoes* 1996(51) and Mannings 2000, no.823.
7 Respectively Mannings 2000, nos.823a and 823b.

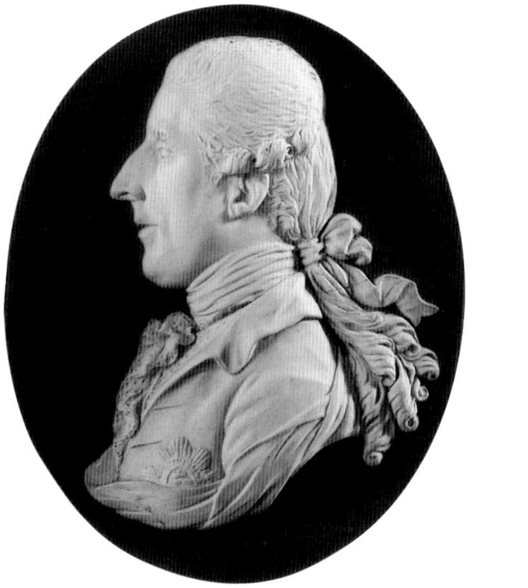

Sir William HAMILTON Wedgwood 1772 (Wedgwood Museum, Barlaston)

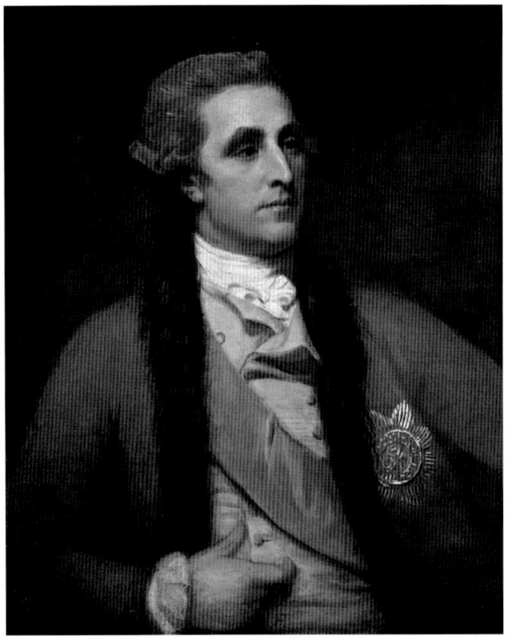

Sir William HAMILTON by George Romney 1783 (National Gallery of Art, Washington)

ICONOGRAPHY

1757-58 Painting by Joshua Reynolds, half-length seated. Toledo Museum of Art (Mannings 2000, no.822). 'Painted by Sr Joshua Reynolds when he married', i.e. 1758, and given by the sitter to his niece, Mrs Mary Dickenson, in 1785 (E. & F. Anson, *Mary Hamilton*, 1925, pp.253-54); it may have been reworked by Reynolds, and is dated 1757-72? by Mannings.

1768 Painting by Anton von Maron, 'Maronne, Portrait in full length of Sir William and the late Lady Hamilton [243 x 183]'. Untraced, commissioned by Hamilton. Dispatched from the Palazzo Sessa in 1798 (B. Fothergill, *Sir William Hamilton*, 1969, p.441; *Vases & Volcanoes* 1996, pp.88, 92n75).

1770 Painting by David Allan, interior at Posilippo with Hamilton whole-length seated in a green coat (to which the star and ribbon of the Bath have been added), his (first) wife playing the harpsichord. Blair Castle (illus. *Vases & Volcanoes* 1996, p.14). A replica, also dated 1770, is in a Scottish private collection, and a version was sold Christie's, 26 June 1925, lot 1.

1771 Painting by Pietro Fabris, a musical concert at Lord Fortrose's house in Naples: Hamilton playing the violin with the young Mozart and his father behind him. Scottish NPG (PG 2611; illus. *Vases & Volcanoes* 1996, p.128). Fabris, the protégé of Hamilton, for whom he illustrated the *Campi Phlegraei*.

1772 Wedgwood medallion modelled by Joachim Smith,* with the star of the Bath (Reilly 1973, p.182); another version from the same model, the drapery reduced along the bottom edge, engraved anon. 1784 (*European Mag.*), and see 1779 below.

1775 Painting by David Allan, see NPG 589.

1776 Marble bust by Michael Foy, with the star of the Bath. Basil Deighton in 1924 (illus. *Burl.Mag.*, XLV, 1924, p.87).

1776-77 Painting by Joshua Reynolds, see NPG 680.

1777-78 Painting by Joshua Reynolds,* *The Society of Dilettanti*, see Comparative Groups.

1779 Wedgwood medallion, remodelled on a larger scale from the Smith medallion of 1772 (illus. Reilly 1973, p.183 and p.256, pl.ix; *Vases & Volcanoes* 1996, p.160). The medallion was issued paired with that of the French antiquary and collector, the comte de Caylus.

1783 Painting by George Romney,* half length with the star and ribbon of the Bath. NG Washington (1970.17.133). Painted in London in November-December 1783. Engraved W. Sharp 1794.

1784 Medallion by James Tassie. Scottish NPG (PG 133; Gray 1894, no.177).

c.1784 Drawing by Dominique Vivant-Denon, bust length. Private collection (illus. *Vases & Volcanoes* 1996, p.127). Hamilton also appeared in an etching by Vivant-Denon, *Le corps diplomatique à Naples*, 1784 (illus. *Vases & Volcanoes* 1996, p.126).

c.1789-90 Painting by H.D. Hamilton, bust length. Lennoxlove (illus. *Vases & Volcanoes* 1996, p.264). Engraved W.T. Fry *from an original Drawing made at Naples, by C. Grignon* (illus. *ibid.*, p.296). A finished chalk study (illus. *ibid.*, p.262), probably connected with the engraving by G. Morghen c.1790 (illus. *ibid.*, p.296), sold Sotheby's, Castle Howard, 2nd day, 12 November 1991, lot 531 as H.D. Hamilton. Miniature copies at Lennoxlove and the Victory Museum, Portsmouth; enamels by W.H. Craft, in the British Museum (1890.8.10.21; dated 1802), the Ashmolean Museum, Oxford (illus. Walker 1997, p.65), and sold Sotheby's, 1 March 1965, lot 35 (dated 1802).

c.1795? Chalcedony intaglio by Filippo Rega. National Maritime Museum (illus. *Vases & Volcanoes* 1996, p.104).

1797 Marble bust by Christopher Hewetson, perhaps unfinished. On 10 June 1797 Robert Fagan wrote that 'Hewetson is at Naples doing Sir William and Lady's busts' (*Hewetson* 1958, p.53).

1802 Painting by William Beechey, exhibited RA 1802(170), a half length commissioned by Lord Nelson, who wrote to Beechey on 28 December 1801 (letter sold Sotheby's, 5 June 1944, lot 202).

1805 Enamel on china by Thomas Baxter, exhibited RA 1805(520).

DOUBTFUL PORTRAITS

Paintings ascribed to Ozias Humphry, sold Sotheby's New York, 17 July 1998, lot 42; attributed to H.D. Hamilton, sold Sotheby's, 4 July 2001, lot 46.

HAMILTON, William 1751-1801

Decorative, history and portrait painter; in Italy 1767; ARA 1784, RA 1789.

3089(7) WILLIAM DANIELL after GEORGE DANCE [1793]

Pencil with the outlines drawn over in red crayon, on paper 25.5 x 20 (10 x 7⅞) laid down on paper, on card; irregular perforations round the edges, slight staining; inscribed below in pencil: *Gavin Hamilton / Artist* ('Gavin' in a different hand); NPG stamp lower left.

Engraving: W. Daniell (*Dance Plates*) see Appendix II.

Collections, Reference: see Appendix II.

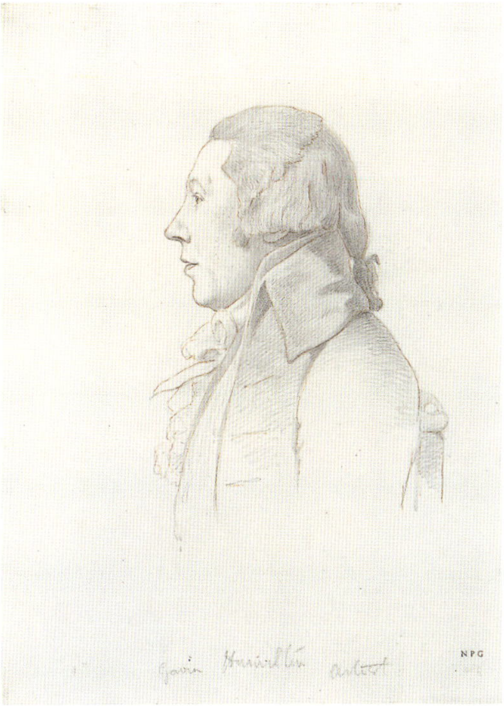

William HAMILTON NPG *3089(7)*

Dance's original drawing in the Royal Academy is dated 31 March 1793. Daniell's engraving was published as Gavin Hamilton, but this identity is impossible on grounds of age and the sitter is securely identified as William Hamilton.[1]

1 Cf. *Treasures of the Royal Academy*, RA 1963(93), and Farington, 11 January 1799.

ICONOGRAPHY

c.1785 Drawing, 'circular portrait sketch', by Thomas Lawrence. Untraced. Exhibited SKM 1865(2956), lent Mrs Denham, as 'about 1785'.

1793 Drawing by George Dance, see NPG 3089(7).

1795 Painting by Henry Singleton,* *President and Members of the Royal Academy,* see Comparative Groups.

DOUBTFUL PORTRAITS

A half-length portrait signed *W.H. 1787*, sold Christie's, 17 February 1939, lot 73. The drawing by John Comerford, sold Christie's, 3 April 1962, lot 101, as William Hamilton, shows H.D. Hamilton.

HARCOURT, William Harcourt, 3rd Earl 1743-1830

Army officer and courtier; 2nd s. of the 1st Earl Harcourt; MP 1768-74; colonel 16th Light Dragoons ('Harcourt's Black Horse') 1779, major-general 1782, lieutenant-general 1793 and general 1798; served in Havana 1762, America 1776-77 and Flanders 1793-95; first governor of the Royal Military College at Sandhurst 1801-11; suc. bro. as 3rd Earl 1809; groom of the bedchamber 1766-1808; GCB and field-marshal 1821.

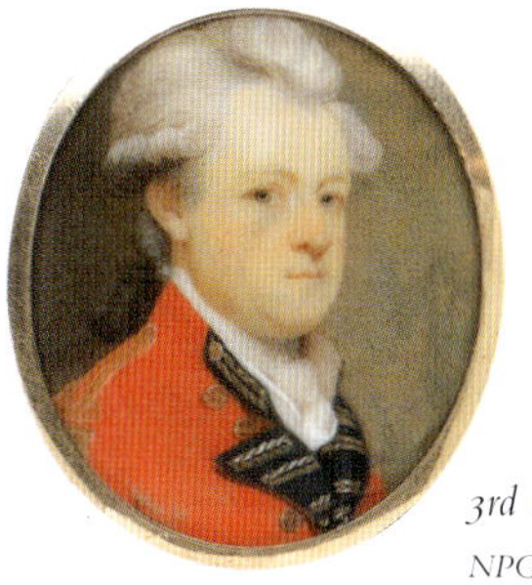

3rd Earl HARCOURT
NPG *5561*

5561 attributed to RICHARD COLLINS c.1780

Watercolour and bodycolour on ivory 4.5 x 3.7 (1¾ x 1½)

Blue eyes, white powdered hair with a black ribbon, as colonel of the 16th Light Dragoons,[1] wearing the red coat with blue facings and silver and gold trim, with brass buttons and gold epaulette.

Collections: Anon. sale, Christie's, 8 December 1982, lot 239, bt. in, and 28 February 1983, lot 195, bt. Leggatt for the NPG.

The back of the frame is incised *WILLIAM 3RD EARL HARCOURT B.1743.D.1830.*, and the likeness has been copied from the Reynolds group portrait of 1780, see below. NPG 5561 was sold in 1982-83 as by Richard Collins, an attribution which is stylistically possible but unproved.

1 With the distinctive split fringe to the epaulette, cf. *JAHR*, XXXVI, 1958, p.33.

999 see Groups, *The Trial of Queen Caroline 1820* by GEORGE HAYTER 1820-23

ICONOGRAPHY

c.1758 Drawing by Paul Sandby, whole-length as a Hussar with shako. Private collection. Of little value as a portrait.

1780 Painting by Joshua Reynolds, three-quarter length in the uniform of an aide-de-camp to the King, with his older brother George, the 2nd Earl, and his Countess. Private collection (Mannings 2000, no.833). Engraved C. Tomkins.

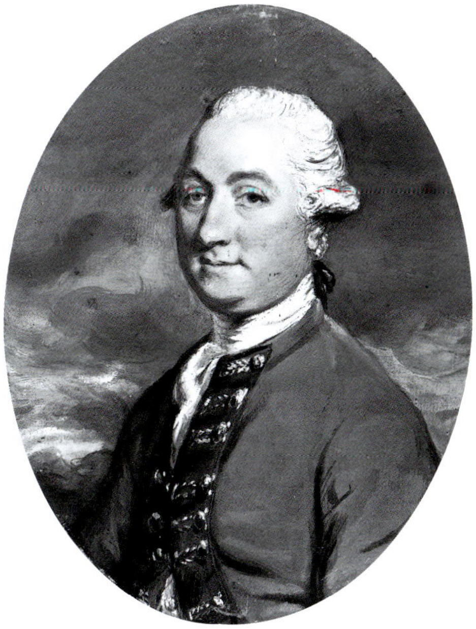

3rd Earl HARCOURT by Daniel Gardner c.1795 (Private Collection)

c.1780 Miniature attributed to Richard Collins, see NPG 5561.

c.1795 Drawing (gouache and pencil) by Daniel Gardner,* half length oval as field officer. Private collection. Another at Hartwell House in 1921.

1818 Painting by Henry Edridge, three-quarter length seated in Peer's robes, engraved S.W. Reynolds.*

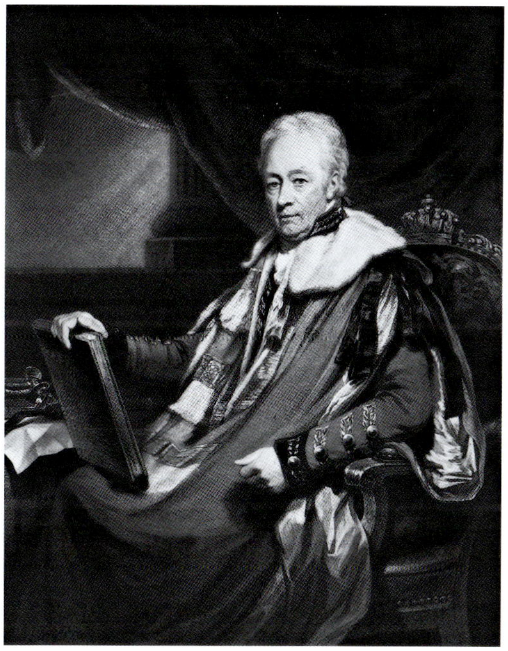

3rd Earl HARCOURT S.W. Reynolds after Henry Edridge 1818 (NPG D 2568)

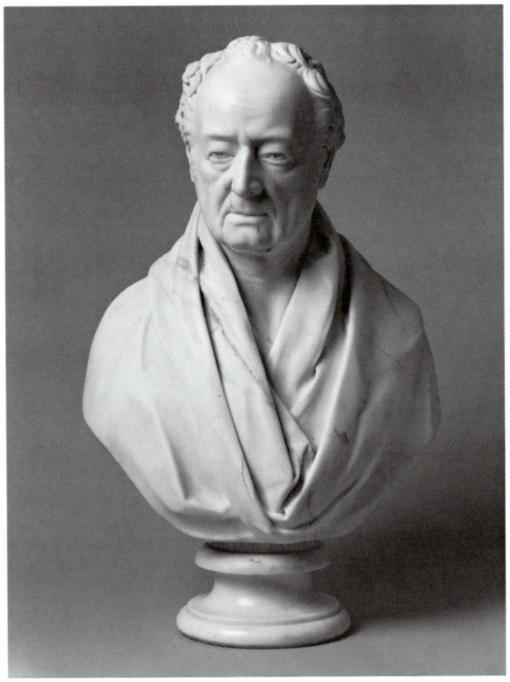

3rd Earl HARCOURT by R.W. Sievier 1828 (The Royal Collection)

1820-23 Painting by George Hayter, *The Trial of Queen Caroline*, see Groups NPG 999.

1822 Marble bust by R.W. Sievier, with toga and star of the Bath. Sotheby's, 10 June 1993, lot 704 (illus.), from Stanton Harcourt. Presumably the bust exhibited RA 1822(1036).

1824 Plaster bust by R.W. Sievier, wearing court dress with Bath collar and star. Private collection.

1828 Marble bust by R.W. Sievier,* draped with a gown. Royal Collection. A plaster copy from Stanton Harcourt dated 1829 sold Sotheby's, 10 June 1993, lot 709.

1832 Monument by R.W. Sievier, whole length in Peer's robes. St George's Chapel, Windsor. Exhibited RA 1832(1177). The plaster model is in St Michael's church, Stanton Harcourt (illus. *CL*, XC, 1941, p.631; Gunnis 1968, f.p.353).

DOUBTFUL PORTRAIT

Painting attributed to Robert Hunter, c.1765, three-quarter length in military uniform, private collection.

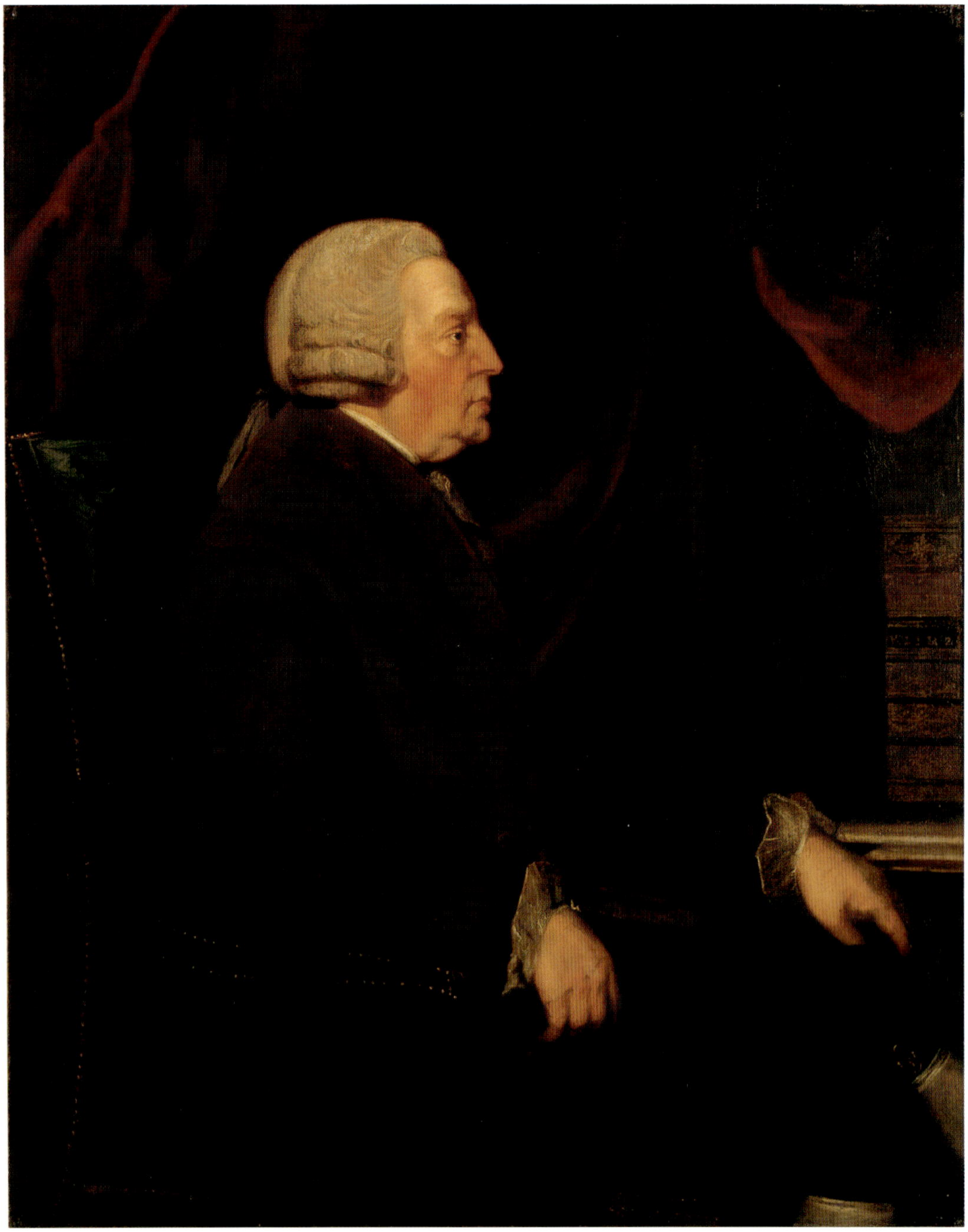

HARRIS NPG 186

HARRIS, James 1709-80

Classical scholar, whose works included *Hermes, or A Philosophical Enquiry concerning Universal Grammar*, 1751; FRS 1763; MP 1761-80, lord of the Admiralty 1763, lord of the Treasury 1763; secretary and comptroller to the Queen 1774-80; his s. cr. Baron Malmesbury 1788 and Earl of Malmesbury 1800.

'There always appeared to me something of affectation in [his] manner of writing ... but all his writings are imbued with learning; and all breathe that philanthropy and amiable disposition, which distinguished him as a man' (James Boswell, 1785).

attributed to FRANCES REYNOLDS c.1777

Canvas 126.5 x 101 (49¾ x 39¾) lined; pentimenti in his right hand (which was slightly higher) and at the back of his head (an unresolved area).

Blue-grey eyes, white powdered wig, wearing a brown coat, green breeches and white stockings; he sits in a green chair, a deep red curtain behind him; on the table stands a book lettered: *ARISTOTEUS/LOGIC ET ETHIC/ VOL 1 & 2.*

Collections: By descent in the sitter's family to the 3rd Earl of Malmesbury, by whom presented 1865.

Reference: Graves & Cronin, IV, p.1335 as Reynolds; Ward & Roberts 1904, II, p.71, as Romney.

NPG 186 may be associated with an entry in the sitter's diary, 24 February 1777, in which he recorded sitting to Mrs Reynolds.[1] It is a poor picture, hesitantly executed,[2] the head apparently derived from a now untraced wax medallion by Gosset (see below). In the later nineteenth century the attribution wavered unrealistically between Reynolds[3] and Romney.[4] There is an exact copy at Wadham College, Oxford,[5] and a small watercolour copy remains with the sitter's descendants.

1 D. Burrows, letter of 15 February 1999 (NPG archive); R. Wendorf, *Reynolds*, 1996, p.78, lists Harris among Frances Reynolds's sitters.
2 C.F. Bell first suggested it had been 'cobbled together' from different sources (undated letter; NPG archive).
3 Graves & Cronin, II, p.440, and see note 5 below.
4 See Ward & Roberts 1904, II, p.71; Poole, III, p.226, no.54.
5 Poole, III, p.226, inscribed verso: *James Harris Esq, Author of Hermes 1780. Painted by Sir Joshua Reynolds*; it was however engraved as by Romney (G.H. Every 1866).

ICONOGRAPHY

c.1745 Painting by Joseph Highmore, three-quarter length standing by a table. Private collection. Engraved C. Bestland 1801* (see A.S. Lewis, 'Joseph Highmore', D.Phil. thesis Harvard, UMI, 1979, II, no.79).

c.1750? Painting by F.M. Newton, half length. Offered to the NPG in 1857 from an unrecorded source (TSB 1/25).

c.1776 Wax medallion head by Isaac Gosset. An engraving by C. Bestland 1801 *from a model by Gosset*, describing the sitter as aged 67 [i.e. 1776], incorporates background detail comparable with NPG 186 (front. *The Works of James Harris*, I, 1801; illus. *Connoisseur*, XCIII, 1934, p.296); a comparable profile engraved by W. Evans 1803 (*Drawn & Engraved by Wm Evans*) giving the sitter's age as 60, shows a different tie to the hair and a more flamboyant neckcloth.

The Gosset wax may also have furnished the pattern for the following profiles of Harris (none of which, however, acknowledged such a source): drawing attributed to Joseph Highmore (Tate Gallery, T 4223; illus. *Tate Gallery Acquisitions 1986-88*, pp.32-33); engravings by F. Bartolozzi 1776 (*F. Bartolozzi del. et sculp.*) and W. Ridley 1802, giving the sitter's age as 67 (*European Mag.*).

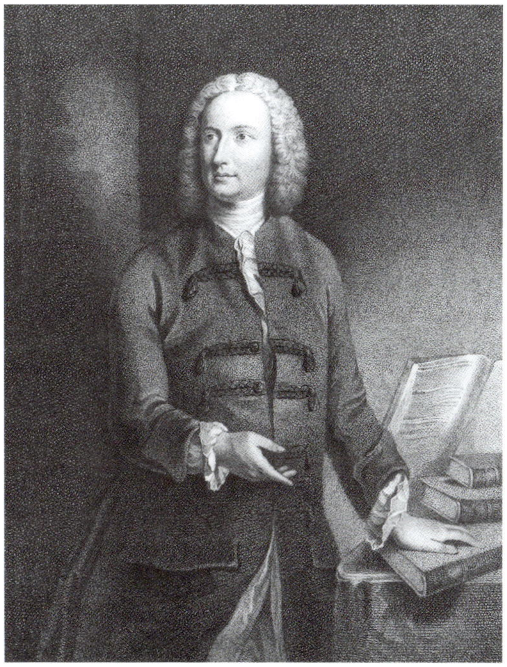

HARRIS C. Bestland after Joseph Highmore c.1745 (NPG D 3231)

c.1777 Painting attributed to Frances Reynolds, see NPG 186.

1777-84 Painting by James Barry, *Distribution of Premiums in the Society of Arts*, part of the *Progress of Human Culture*, in which Harris appears as a profile head centre right. Royal Society of Arts, London (Pressly 1981, no.26). Engraved J. Barry 1791.

c.1780 Medallion portrait (held by a mourning woman) by John Bacon sr. on the Harris monument in Salisbury Cathedral.

DOUBTFUL PORTRAIT

A small half-length painting attributed to Joshua Reynolds and described as having been painted in 1775, sold Greenwood's, 14 April 1796, lot 66, was listed in the collection of Lord Malmesbury in 1899 (Graves & Cronin, II, p.440).

HARRISON, John 1693-1776

Horologist; in 1735 received a Parliamentary award for a timepiece to ascertain longitude at sea and in 1749 the Copley Gold Medal from the Royal Society; sailed to the West Indies 1761-62 and 1764 demonstrating the efficacy of his chronometer, for which he received £10,000 from the Government in 1765 and a further £8,750 in 1773.

'he seems to have lacked the ability to win the sympathy of others, or to exercise sufficient patience and amiability to make his own foibles and deficiencies in temperament acceptable' (Humphrey Quill, 1966).

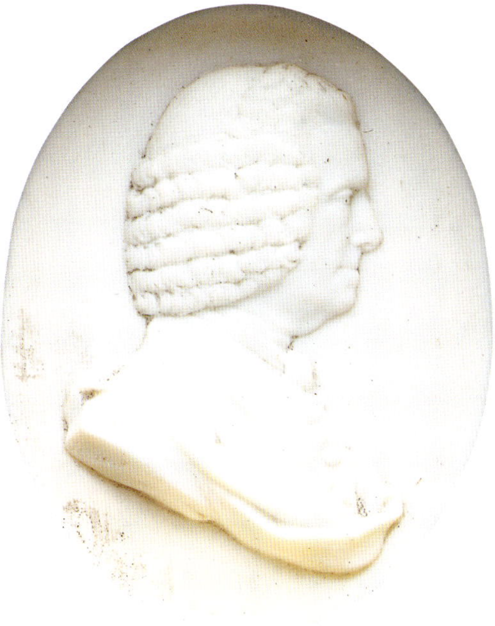

John HARRISON
NPG 4599

4599 JAMES TASSIE 1775

Glass paste 7.5 (3) high, incised on the truncation: *Tassie. F.*; there is some surface discolouration. A label (apparently early 19th-century) attached to the back of the glass paste reads: *John Harrison / 1775 / Inventor of the Chronometer*, with later annotations: *182* and *£7.10*.

Collections: K.E. Houston sale, Sotheby's, 15 January 1968, lot 97, bt. Michael Denton, from whom purchased 1968.

Engraving: B. Reading 1788 (*European Mag.* 1789).

Exhibition: *John Harrison*, Lincoln, Wakefield, 1993(62).

Reference: Gray 1894, no.182.

Another example of this medallion from the Tassie family collection, now with the Clockmakers' Company, London, was dated 1775 in the Tassie sale in 1882.[1] The date 1775, as also given in the label on the back of NPG 4599, fits well with Harrison's biography:

in 1773 Parliament had finally acknowledged his achievement and in 1775 he published his *Description concerning such Mechanism as will afford a ... Mensuration of Time ...*; James Cook returned that year from his second Pacific voyage, enthusing over the chronometer.

An enamel copy was incorporated in a late eighteenth-century watch made by Harrison's grandson, John Barton.[2]

1 *Corporation of London, Cat. and Supp.*, 1910, no.911.
2 Private collection; illus. H. Quill, *John Harrison*, 1966, f.p.231.

ICONOGRAPHY

1765-66 Painting by Thomas King,* three-quarter length seated, a watch in his right hand. Science Museum, London (500), from the sitter's direct descendants. Engraved P.J. Tassaert 1768 (with minor alterations, to show Harrison's chronometer, known as the H4, on the table; illus. L. Jordanova, *Defining Features*, NPG, 2000, p.60); W. Holl (half length, after Tassaert) 1835.

1775 Medallion by James Tassie, see NPG 4599.

DOUBTFUL PORTRAITS

Medals by John Kirk of 1761, 1771 and 1773 (Brown 1980, nos.67, 156, 205), with a draped bust inscribed *IOANNES HARRISON*. which bears no resemblance to Harrison.

A painting by Joseph Wright of Derby of Dr John Harrison, engraved J.R. Smith, has sometimes been mistaken for the horologist (see Nicolson 1968, no.74).

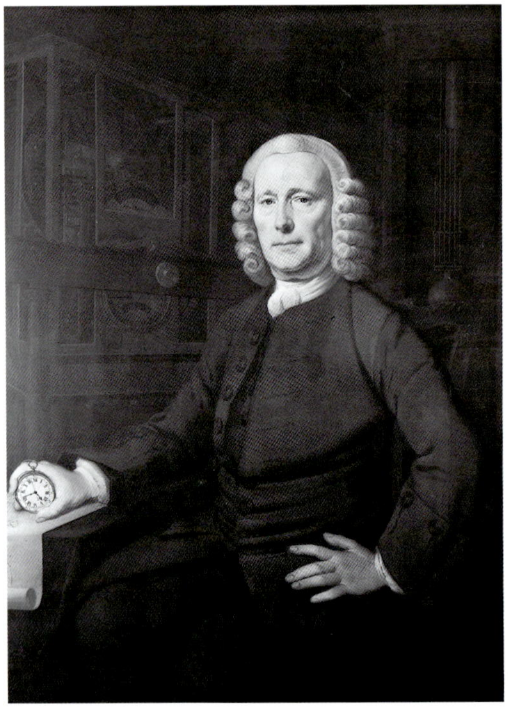

John HARRISON by Thomas King 1765-66 (Science Museum, London)

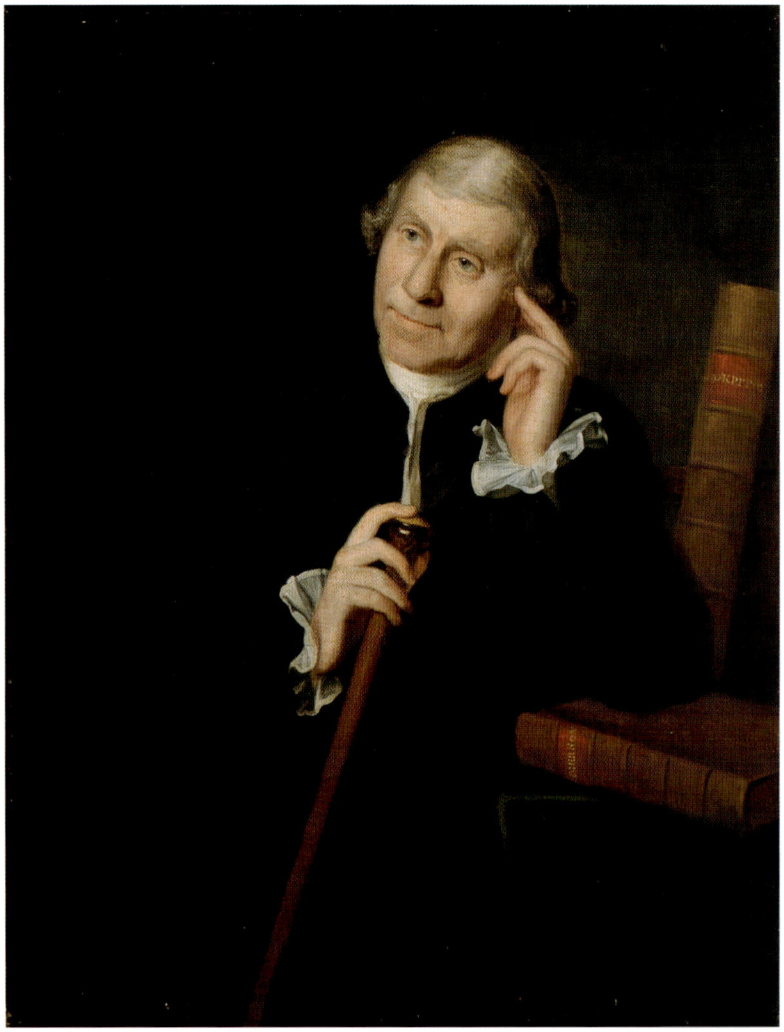

Robert HARRISON NPG *4898*

HARRISON, Robert 1715-1802

'Philosopher Harrison', mathematician and linguist; master of Trinity House school, Newcastle, from 1757, when he published, with Isaac Thomson, a *Short Account of a Course of Natural and Experimental Philosophy...*; his later years were spent in retirement at Durham.

4898 WILLIAM BELL 1791

Canvas 90 x 70.5 (35½ x 27¾); lined; cleaned 1972; there are worn areas in and around the head.

Blue-grey eyes, grey hair, wearing a blue coat, black satin waistcoat and black breeches; on the green-covered table two leather-bound books lettered *EMERSON* and *THEOCRITUS* (the latter in Greek).

Collections: Debenham Coe, London, 9 August 1972, lot 48, bt. Leggatt for the NPG.

The unique portrait of Robert Harrison, who is sufficiently identified by an old faded and label on the stretcher: ... *Harrison / nat 13th May 1715 ... Oct 1802 / Wm Bell Newcastle 1791*, as well as by the combination of books displayed: Emerson (the mathematician William Emerson, 1701-82), and Theocritus, referring to his mathematical and linguistic abilities.

HASTINGS, Warren 1732-1818

Governor-general of Bengal 1774-84; served with the East India Company 1750-65 and 1769-84, rising from clerk at Madras to governor of Bengal, an office he performed without undue regard for colonial justice; impeached and tried at Westminster 1787-95 on charges of corruption, but acquitted; FRS 1801.

'In his person he was thin but not tall, of a spare habit, very bald, with a countenance placid and thoughtful, but when animated full of intelligence' (Sir Nathaniel Wraxall, 1815).

In 1788 'he stood five foot six, but weighed only eight stone ten' (Keith Feiling, 1954).

Abbreviations

Grier 1905: S.C. Grier, *Letters of Warren Hastings to his Wife*, 1905

Knapp 1951: Sir Arthur Knapp, *A Catalogue of the known Portraits of Warren Hastings,* [1951], typescript NPG [a revision of his catalogue in A. M. Davies, *Warren Hastings*, 1935, pp.566-70]

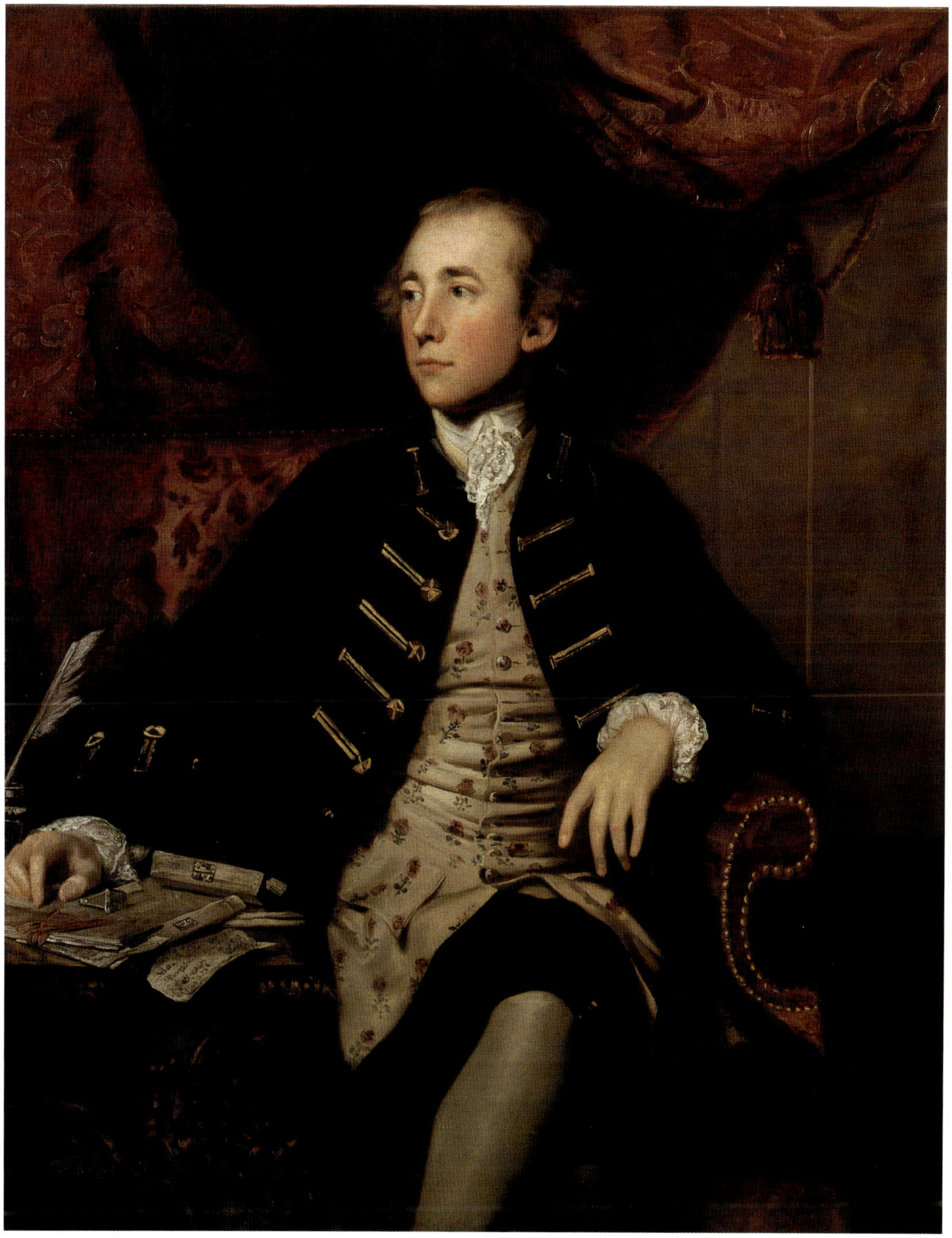

HASTINGS NPG *4445*

4445 JOSHUA REYNOLDS 1766-67

Canvas 126 x 101 (49½ x 39¾) lined.

Grey eyes, light brown hair; wearing a dark-blue coat with gold trim, a pale cream sprigged waistcoat (probably of Indian origin), black velvet breeches and white stockings; on the table papers (illegibly inscribed), a silver seal and (apparently Persian) documents.[1]

Collections: [presumably the portrait of Hastings by Reynolds 'sold under an extent from the Crown', Squibb's, 21 June 1817, lot 111] G. Watson Taylor by 1823; his sale, Robins, 15th day, 25 July 1832, lot 148, bt. Newton, who sold it to the 2nd Baron Northwick; by descent at Northwick Park to Capt. E.G. Spencer Churchill; accepted by the Government in lieu of tax from the Spencer Churchill Estate and allocated to the NPG 1965.

Engravings: J. Watson 1777; J.M. Zell 1786; J.C. Edwards 1834; T.W. Knight c.1834; H. Davis.

Exhibitions: BI 1823(36) lent G.W. Taylor; BI 1854(149) lent Northwick; *Worcestershire exhibition*, Worcester, 1882 (Fine Art Section 70); *Reynolds*, Grosvenor Gallery, 1883-84(102); *Hastings Bicentenary*, British Museum, 1932-33; *Reynolds*, 45 Park Lane, London, 1937(57); *Bicentenary Exhibition*, RA, 1968-69(129); *Anniversary Exhibition*, Nationalgalerie, Berlin, 1980; *Reynolds*, RA, 1986(66); *The Raj*, NPG, 1990-91(132).

Reference: Northwick Catalogue, 1864, no.211; Graves & Cronin, II, pp.449-51; T. Borenius, *Northwick Catalogue*, 1921, no.358; Waterhouse 1941, p.58; Knapp 1951, p.1, no.1; J. Kerslake, *Connoisseur*, CLXI, 1966, pp.160-61; Mannings 2000, no.861.

Painted during Hastings's stay in England between June 1765 and March 1769. He had come back from his first period in India a widower and in poor health, to find his young son had died in England; when he returned to India in 1769 his London clothes were too small.[2] In 1766 Reynolds's pocket books list appointments for Hastings on 3, 7, 12 and 18 March, 14 and 28 April, 5 May and 19 June; a further appointment occurred on 9 February 1767. The portrait was paid for on 9 October 1766 and cost seventy guineas.[3] Ribeiro has commented on Hastings' semi-formal attire, his clothes of different colours and fabrics: the blue silk and woollen coat with a velvet collar, the black velvet breeches, and the printed cotton (probably Indian) waistcoat.[4]

It is not clear who first owned NPG 4445. It appears that Hastings did not take it back to India,[5] since Watson's mezzotint, inscribed *Warren Hastings Esqr, Governor General of Bengal, &c & &c*, was not published until 20 March 1777, after Hastings's activities in Bengal had excited public interest.

A portrait described as Hastings by Reynolds, now untraced, was bought in 1868 by Graves from 'Holmes of Birmingham' and sold to Edward Akroyd.[6]

1 Joan Lancaster of the India Office (letter of 16 March 1966 in NPG archive) wrote 'I am told that the documents and the seal (very stylised) appear to be Persian'. Christopher Gandy (note of 21 April 1986 in NPG archive) commented that in India at this time such seals were 'usually inscribed in Persian letters including the owner's English name'.
2 K. Feiling, *Warren Hastings*, 1954, pp.55-56. Hastings m. 1756 Mrs Mary Buchanan (d.1759) in India; their two children were Elizabeth (d.1758) and George (d.1764).
3 Cormack 1970, p.123.
4 A. Ribeiro & V. Cumming, *History of Costume*, 1989, p.151, and Ribeiro 2000, pp.124-25.
5 See *Reynolds* 1986, no.67.
6 Graves & Cronin, II, p.450.

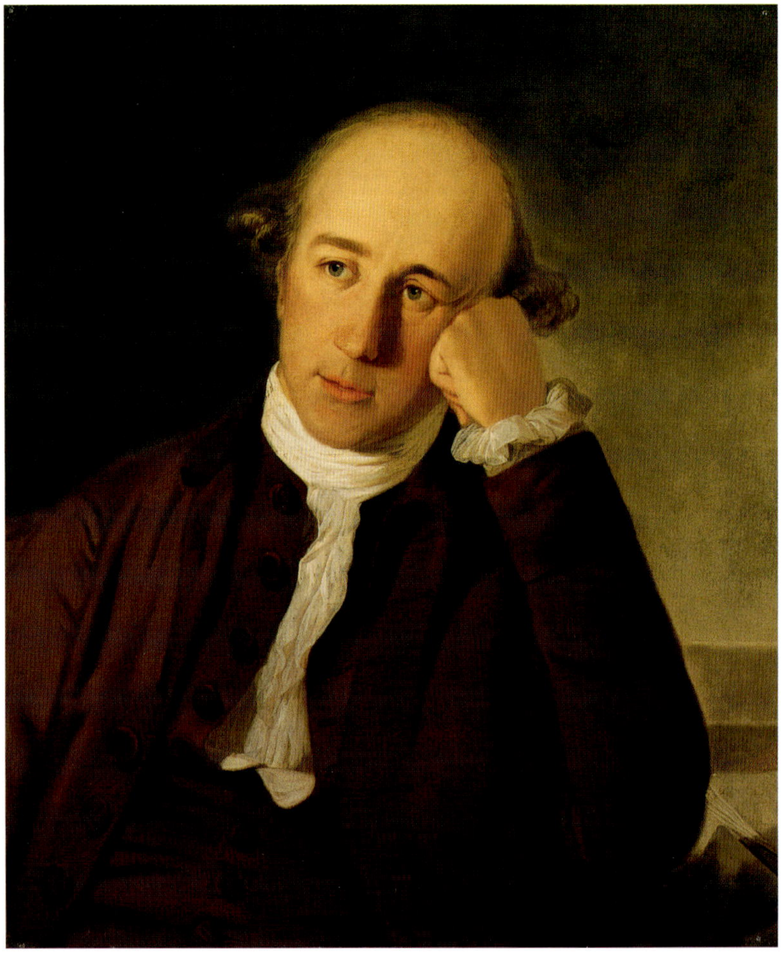

HASTINGS NPG *81*

81 TILLY KETTLE c.1772

Canvas 69 x 61 (27¼ x 24) lined.

Grey eyes, fair hair, wearing a reddish-brown suit.

Collections: Given by the sitter to Sir Richard Sullivan (d.1806), 1st Bt, of Ember Court, Thames Ditton;[1] his son Sir Charles Sullivan, 3rd Bt; sold Christie's, 18 June 1859, lot 29 as Romney, purchased.

Engraving: W. Angus 1782 (from a painting belonging to Mrs Maitland; *European Mag.*).

Exhibitions: Royal Dublin Society, Dublin, 1861 (Ancient Masters 490); NPE 1867(688); *Hastings*, Westminster School, 1932(4); *British in India*, Brighton, 1973(B20).

Reference: *Kettle* 1927, pp.71-72, 92-93; Knapp 1951, p.2, no.2.

Kettle painted Hastings twice in Calcutta. The more substantial portrait, a seated whole length dated 1769-72 by Milner, belongs to the Asiatic Society Museum, Calcutta;[2] a near-contemporary half-length copy by Thomas Palmer is in the East India Club, London.[3] NPG 81 uses a closely comparable head and, although dated 1772-76 by Milner, could be contemporary with the whole length; a three-quarter length version descended from John Stewart, Judge Advocate of Bengal 1773-76, also belongs to the East India Club.[4]

1 '... given to my father by Warren Hastings himself' (Sir Charles Sullivan to Scharf, 9 June 1858; NPG archive); his father was in India with Hastings from 1768 to c.1782.
2 Illus. Archer 1979, p.90.
3 Knapp 1951, p.2, no.4.
4 *Ibid.*, p.2, no.3.

3823 THOMAS LAWRENCE 1786

Pastel on vellum 31.8 x 26.7 (12½ x 10½) oval; in poor condition, having previously been affected by mould and severely rubbed in the background area. Originally inscribed verso in the artist's hand: *Be pleas'd to keep / this from the damp & from / the Sun TLawrence Pinxt / 1786* (this sheet is now separately preserved).

White powdered hair, white cravat and waistcoat, reddish-brown coat.

Collections: Descended from the sitter; Daylesford House sale, Farebrother, Clark & Lye, 22-27 August 1853, lot 820, bt. Sir Thomas Phillips;[1] by descent to his grandson T.F. Fenwick (d.1938);[2] bt. in Cheltenham 1952 by Mrs F. Dodgson Wilkinson, from whom purchased 1952.

Exhibition: 'Earls Court 1895, lent by an art dealer'.[3]

Reference: Knapp 1951, pp.16-17, no.10; Lawrence 1964, p.262.

Drawn at Bath, where the young Lawrence was living 1780-87, and sold in 1853 as a companion piece to Lawrence's portrait of Sir Elijah Impey, NPG 821.

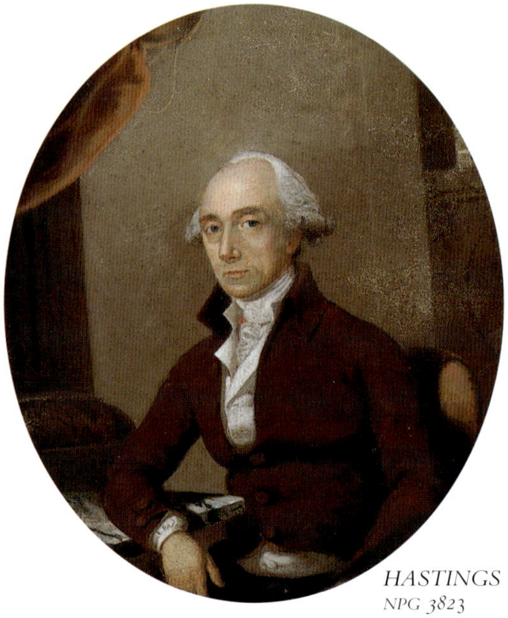

HASTINGS
NPG *3823*

1 A printed label and an ink inscription verso identify this purchase.
2 A MS label verso reads: *On no account is the paper on the back of this picture to be removed / T.F. Fenwick.*
3 Knapp 1951, p.17.

6286 RICHARD COSWAY 1787

Watercolour and bodycolour on ivory 5.5 x 4.7 (2¼ x 1⅞); signed and inscribed verso: *Rdus Cosway / R:A. / Primarius Pictor / Serenissimi Wallia / Principis / Pinxit / 1787*, with lockets of fair hair in the back of the case. 'Originally set in diamonds but these were removed by Mr Woodman-Hastings and paste substituted'.[1]

Blue eyes, white hair, wearing a blue coat with brass buttons, cream waistcoat and white stock.

Collections: Mrs Warren Hastings; W.H. Woodman

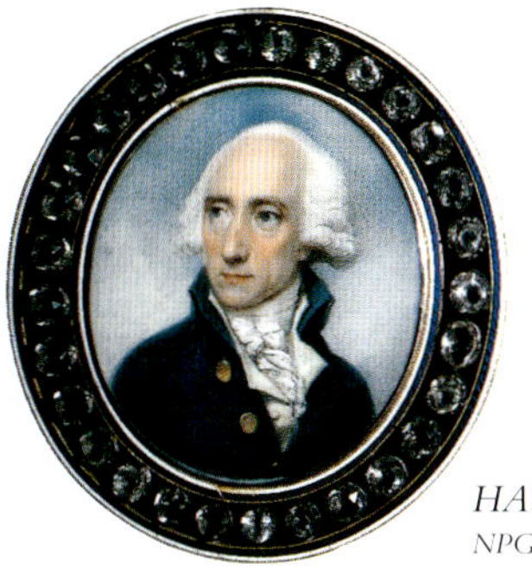

HASTINGS
NPG 6286

Hastings, who sold it; bt. on the London art market in 1926 by the Hon Frederic H.A. Wallop (d.1953), by whom lent to the Victoria and Albert Museum 1927-49; his nephew Alan Evans, by whom bequeathed to the National Gallery 1974; lent to the NPG until permanently transferred in 1994.

Exhibition: *Cosway* 1995(65).

Reference: Knapp 1951, p.14, no.1; Walker 1998, no.67.

Hastings was impeached in May 1787, the year NPG 6286 was drawn, and his trial was to begin in February 1788. Maria Cosway then told Thomas Jefferson that 'Mr H [Hastings] was with Mr Cosway at the very moment the trial was going on'.[2]

A version in a plain oval frame, 'given by the sitter to William Byam Martin, Commissioner at Calcutta, in the 1780s',[3] was with Miss H.D. Layton, Oxford, in 1954.

1 Knapp 1951, p.14.
2 Quoted by G. Barnett, *Richard and Maria Cosway*, 1995, p.102.
3 Note in NPG archive.

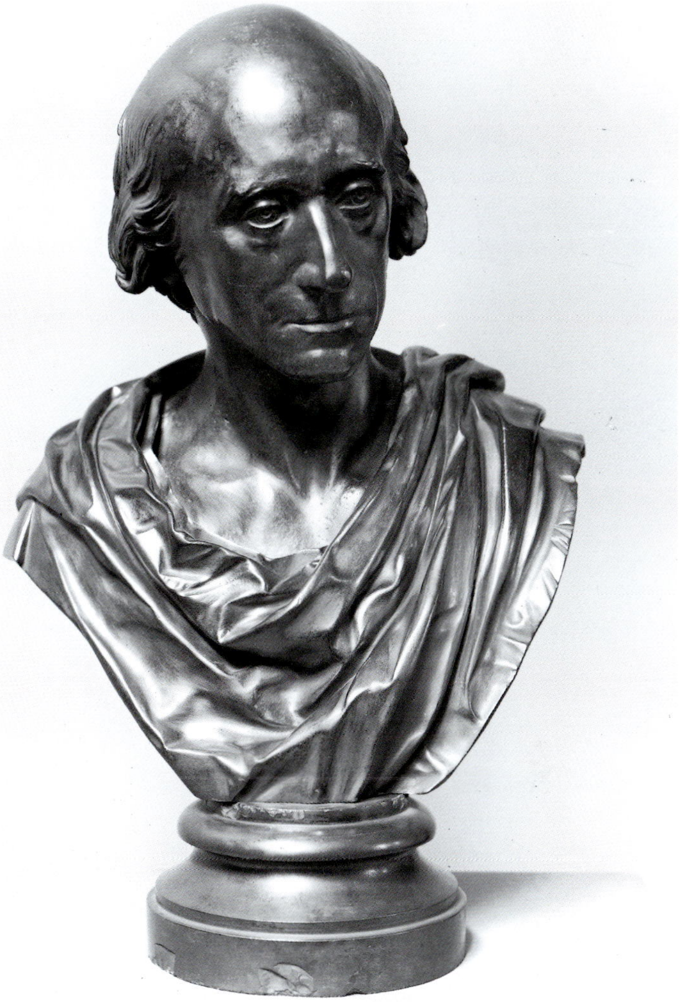

HASTINGS NPG *209*

209 THOMAS BANKS 1794 [1790]

Bronze bust 49.5 (19½) high; incised verso: *Warren Hastings Esqre 1794*; some small losses in the lacquer; standing on a separate stone base 10 (4) high.

Collections: [Warren Hastings; his godson Warren Hastings Frith of Lesley, Hants.];[1] John Marshall of Southampton, who had purchased it 'a few years ago from a family related to [Hastings]',[2] from whom purchased 1866.

Reference: Bell 1938, pp.79-81, 102-03; Knapp 1951, p.20, no.2.

Banks 'entertained the highest veneration' for Hastings, frequently expressing his admiration 'of the fine expression of his features, and more particularly of the uncommonly grand form of his forehead, which, with that of Horne Tooke, he considered the finest he had seen in modern heads'.[3] Hastings had promised to sit to Banks in December 1789, and sittings are listed in his Diary between 1 and 5 February 1790, the 5th being 'the last day', when the model was presumably completed. Hastings paid Banks 'for the bust & 5 casts £73.10.0' on 14 April 1791.[4]

This first bust by Banks was produced in two forms, the marble with the shoulders complete, and the bronze with the shoulders cut, as NPG 209. The marble, dated 1790, belongs to the India Office (British Library);[5] a terracotta is in the Victoria Memorial Hall, Calcutta, and another was with Mrs Shortt in 1938; a bronze cast (bearing the inscribed date 1790, but see below), was sold Christie's, New York, 16 April 1994, lot 1, and a plaster also belongs to the India Office (British Library).[6]

NPG 209, differing from the preceding with its cut shoulders, is dated 1794 and appears to have been the subject of two letters from Banks to Hastings. On 27 December 1794 he wrote: 'I have at last succeeded in Obtaining a Cast of yr Bust in bronze, tho not altogether to my mind I beleive it is as good as can be got done at any London foundry - the expences attending the making three or four Moulds & the casting & repairing together, make it necessary for me to charge you thirty five pounds...'. On 9 January 1795 he wrote again saying he had begun the bronze 'by advice of Mr Cockerell who thought I might get something by sending some to India & I imagin'd it might be your wish to have one also & therefore made trial but finding the doing them attended with a good deal of trouble & expence I have giv'n up the idea of sending any to India & if I have been under a Mistake with respect to that which I sent to yr house I am willing to withdraw it'.[7] A plaster cast was presented to Westminster School by a descendant of Cockerell.[8]

Banks produced a second marble bust for Lord Lansdowne in 1796, the right shoulder bare, the socle inscribed *INGRATIA PATRIA* (Foreign Office; GAC 2680/1).[9] Sittings were given in October and December 1796; a profile engraving by T. Gaugain (from a drawing by Simon de Koster) was published 10 October 1797 and another by the same artists showing a full-face view was published in 1798.[10] The 'Bust of Mr Hastings' exhibited at the RA in 1799(1081) was presumably this second type. On 12 January 1798 Banks told Hastings he had 'but one cast from the last Bust I made of you' and a new mould costing five guineas was required.

An 'original' terracotta of one of Banks's busts was in William Tassie's sale, Christie's, 12 July 1805, lot 207. A plaster cast from an unspecified model by Banks belonged to Captain D.M. Anderson in 1935. In Banks's sale, 22 May 1805, lot 5 was a 'Mask of Mr Hastings'; lots 53 and 54 were busts of Hastings in terracotta; lot 55 another with 'the Mould of Ditto', and lot 56 'Ditto in different Drapery, and Mould of Ditto'.

In 1792 Banks had also modelled two chimney-pieces for Daylesford, incorporating Persian and Indian motifs.[11]

1 See Bell 1938, pp.80, 103. An undated note in Scharf's hand in the NPG archive records the death of Warren Hastings Frith, son of Col. Frith, at Lesley, Hants, 'about 6 years ago'.
2 Letters from Marshall of 1, 8 November 1865, 6 March 1866 (NPG archive); the bust was acquired with 'a granite polished column'.
3 Bell 1938, pp.80-81 (quoting Mrs Forster to Allan Cunningham, 1 March 1830, from *The Builder*, XXI, 3 January 1863, p.5).
4 *Ibid.*, p.79.
5 *Ibid.*, pl.xxxi; dated 1790, illus. Whinney 1964, pl.139A as 1799; Archer 1986, no.124; engraved J. Condé 1792.
6 Archer 1986, no.125.
7 Bell 1938, pp.102-03 (quoting BL, Add. MS. 9173, ff.292, 306). The architect Samuel Pepys Cockerell had designed Daylesford for Hastings.
8 Bell 1938, p.80; Knapp 1951, p.20, no.4.
9 Bell 1938, pp.110-11, 115-16.
10 *Ibid.*, pl.xxxi.
11 *Ibid.*, pp.88-89, pls.xxii, xxiii.

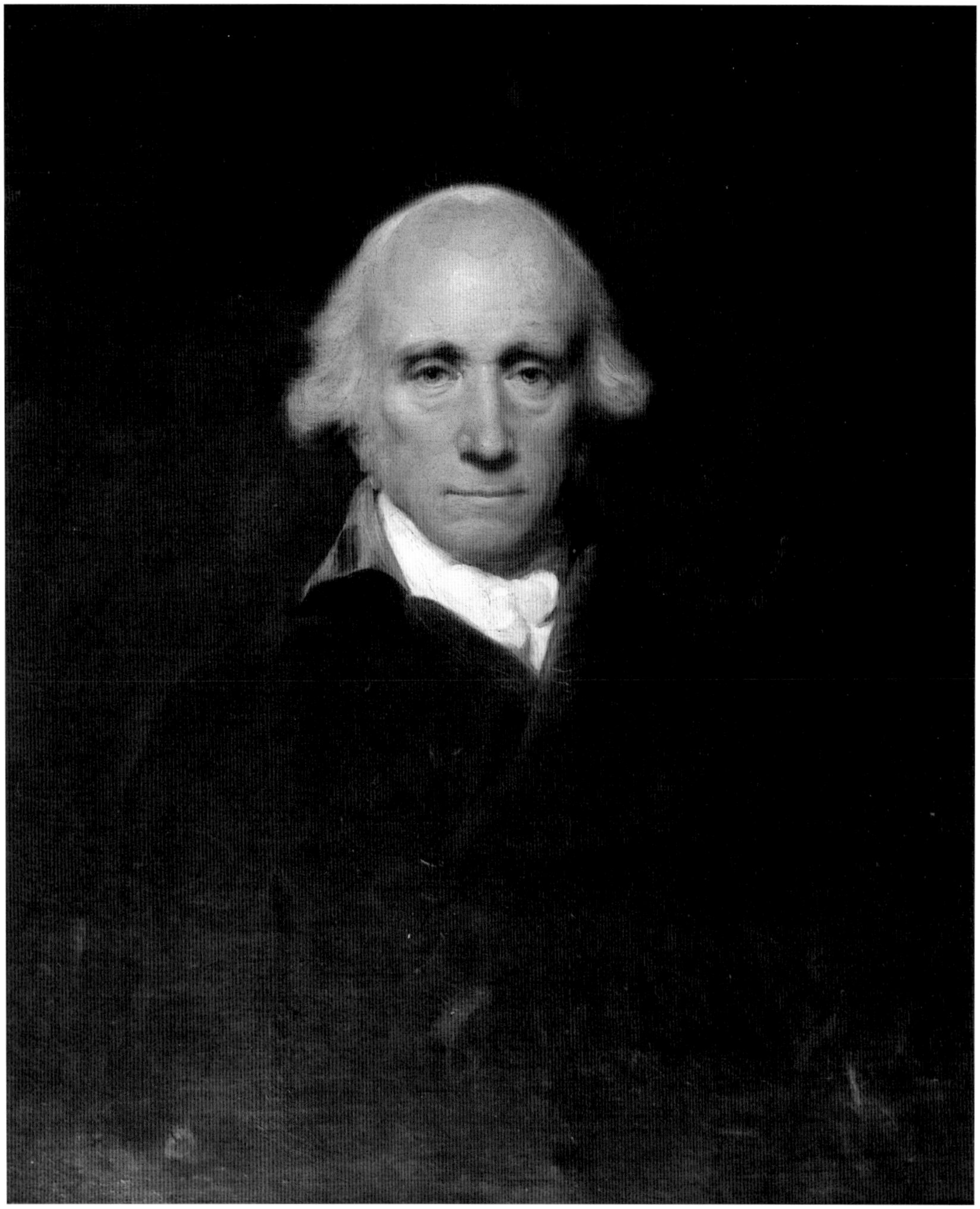

HASTINGS NPG 1845

1845 LEMUEL FRANCIS ABBOTT 1796

Canvas 74 x 62 (29 x 24½)

[not available for examination]

White hair, grey-blue eyes, dark-blue coat.

Collections: Mrs Warren Hastings; by descent to her great-niece, Miss Marian Winter, by whom bequeathed 1919.

Engraving: H. Robinson 1832 (as Reynolds).

Exhibitions: Victoria Memorial Hall, Calcutta, 1919-87; British High Commission, New Delhi, 1987-.

Reference: Knapp 1951, p.7, no.19.

Sittings to Abbott are recorded in Hastings's Diary on 10 August, 7 October and 15 December 1796 (the last two coinciding with sittings to Thomas Banks) and 'it is clear that upon several occasions the painter was at work on his picture at the same time as the sculptor on his bust'.[1] The original portrait, for which Hastings paid 15 guineas,[2] was given to David Anderson[3] and remains with his descendants, together with a letter from Hastings to Anderson of 13 January 1797:

> To Sr Joshua Reynolds I more than once mentioned my desire of sitting to him at a very early period. What prevented it then, I do not recollect, but well remember the subsequent causes; his long illness, loss of sight & death. After that event I could meet with no artist with whose skill I was satisfied, till accident brought me acquainted with Mr Abbot, and after many patient sittings in the course of two years, if not more, & much change in the original similitude, I at length obtained from him one more which, whether well executed or not, has appeared to me to bear a stronger resemblance of me than any that I have yet seen ... It was sent off last friday (the 6th, I believe) by the Edinburgh waggon.

Anderson told Hastings on 3 February: 'I am delighted with it beyond expression ... it is the strongest resemblance I ever saw'. Hastings gave further sittings to Abbott for a portrait for his wife, identified as NPG 1845.[4] Following all the vituperation of his public trial which had ended in 1795, Abbott's benign portrait prompted Hastings to compose some ironic verse, including the lines

> And such in all his attributes array'd
> Behold him here on Abbot's canvas spread!
> 'Tis true, to vulgar sense they lie conceal'd,
> To Burke, and men like Burke, alone reveal'd.[5]

Hastings distributed several copies of the portrait. In 1928 one originally given to his step-son, Sir Charles Imhoff, was with Mrs E.F.A. Wansborough (*née* Woodman-Hastings); others then belonged to the descendants of Sir Elijah Impey (see below), Nathaniel Halhed, and of Hastings's ward, Sir John D'Oyly.[6] Copies were also painted for a William Cowper (by 1797) and Edward Baber, Bengal colleagues.[7] Another in the Victoria Memorial Hall, Calcutta, apparently descended from Sir Thomas Plumer, one of the counsel for Hastings's defence at his impeachment.[8]

A fine version, possibly that descended from Elijah Impey, was sold Christie's, 15 April 1994, lot 24, and another on 20 December 1957, lot 58 as Lawrence. Reduced versions were with Ulric Blyth in 1932 as Raeburn[9] and sold Christie's New York, 16 April 1994, lot 2.[10] Two miniature copies were made by Henry Bone: one for 'Mr Minhoff' (presumably Sir Charles Imhoff),[11] the other dated 1800;[12] one of these was presumably the Warren Hastings miniature exhibited by 'H. Berne', RA 1800(896). A miniature version in the Victoria and Albert Museum (P.7.1915), showing a glimpse of a chair at the extreme left, is attributed to Ozias Humphry.

For other portraits of Hastings attributed to Abbott, see below c.1796-97 and 1797.

1 Bell 1938, p.110 (citing the Hastings Diaries, BL, Add. MS 39883).
2 Knapp 1951, p.7, no.18.
3 Illus. A.M. Davies, *Warren Hastings*, 1935, front. See Evan Cotton, *Bengal Past & Present*, XLIV, ii, 1932-33, pp.113-19.
4 Knapp 1951, p.7, nos.18, 19, quoting the Hastings Diary, 'after the portrait for Anderson was finished he gave further sittings for a portrait intended for Mrs Hastings'.
5 Quoted *in extenso* in A.M. Davies, *Warren Hastings*, 1935, pp.565-66.
6 Knapp 1951, pp.8-10, respectively nos.21, 20, 22 and 28. The D'Oyly portrait sold Christie's, 28 June 1929, lot 48, as Beechey, and Sotheby's, 18 December 1946, lot 29 as H.J. Simpson after Beechey.
7 See principally Evan Cotton (at note 3); Knapp 1951, p.22, no.1.
8 Knapp 1951, p.8, no.23. Christie's, 11 July 1885, lot 71, as Lawrence, and called Hoppner in 1909.
9 Illus. *CL*, LXXII, 1932, p.661; Knapp 1951, p.11, no.32.
10 Probably the 'small head' attributed to John Simpson listed by Knapp 1951, p.10, no.29, as in the possession of Edward Impey. Knapp listed another version of the Abbott type (p.10, no.27) belonging to Sir George Sutherland.
11 Presumably Knapp 1951, p.15, no.5, as Henry Bone 1799 in the collection of Miss A.M. Woodman-Hastings; the preparatory drawing in the NPG Bone albums (*Bone* 1999, no.248).
12 Preparatory drawing dated 1800 in the NPG Bone albums (*Bone* 1999, no.247).

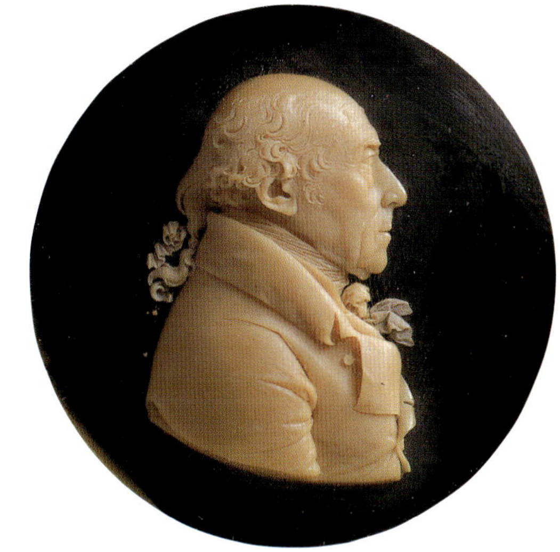

HASTINGS NPG 5065

5065 PETER ROUW 1806

Pink wax profile portrait 6.5 (2½) high, set on a black-painted glass 11 (4⅜) diameter; incised on the truncation: *Pr Rouw / Sculpr London 1806*. Inscribed in ink on the backing paper: *Portrait of the / Right Honble Warren Hastings / Peter Rouw / Sculptor-Modeller of Gems / & Cameos, to his R.H: The / Prince Regent / 22 Carmarthen Street / Fitzroy Square.*[1]

Collections: [2nd Viscount Halifax (1839-1934)]; bt. 'at a sale of Lord Halifax's effects' by J.R.G. Marchetti; his cousin, J.D.H. Woodfield of Halifax, c.1945;[2] Sotheby's, 15 December 1975,[3] lot 2, bt. Cyril Humphris for John Harris, from whom purchased 1976.

Exhibition: RA 1806(627).

Another wax medallion by Rouw, dated 1805, is in the Victoria Memorial Hall, Calcutta, and a version was sold Phillips, 17 July 1985, lot 244 as after Peter Rouw.

1 Copied (in the early 19th century?) from the original backing of which only a torn fragment remains, but sufficient to show it was in the same hand as the inscription on the backing of Rouw's Duke of Bridgewater, NPG 4276 - presumably the hand of Rouw (who officially received his Royal appointment in 1807).
2 Provenance as given verbally by Mr Woodfield in November 1980: at the time of the sale the wax had been in his possession 'for over 30 years'; he inherited it from his cousin, who had 'acquired it from a sale of Lord Halifax's effects'.
3 The wax by Thomas Poole of Robert Hall (NPG 5066) came from the same sale (see Walker *Regency*, I, p.232).

390 THOMAS LAWRENCE 1811

Canvas 91 x 71 (35¾ x 28) lined; inscribed on the left chair arm: *Warren Hastings / Aged 79*. Pentimenti visible on his right hand and shoulder.

Blue eyes, white hair, wearing a black suit; a red drape behind him.

Collections: Painted for the sitter's step-daughter, Mrs Marian Barton;[1] by descent to J.P. Fearon (d.1873); Francis Fearon, from whom purchased 1874.

Engraving: W. Say 1813.

Exhibitions: RA 1811(194); *Art Treasures*, Manchester, 1857 (BPG 291, as Reynolds); NPE 1867(850) lent J.P.Fearon;[2] *British Paintings*, Roumania and Hungary, 1972-73; *Indian Summer*, Cheltenham, 1985; *Pickpocketing the Rich*, Bath (Holburne), 2002(55).

Reference: Knapp 1951, p.13, no.36; K. Garlick, *Lawrence*, 1954, p.42; *Lawrence* 1964, p.104; Garlick 1989, no.397.

Although Hastings was rather small and at the time of this portrait 'his life was in the sere,' Lawrence 'often spoke in admiration of the severity of dignity and grandeur in his appearance'; his expression used to be, 'What a fine lion-like repose there is about him!'[3] A modern copy by W.B. Morris is in the Oriental Club, London.

1 *Née* Brisco; previously mistakenly described as the wife of Hastings's aide-de-camp (Grier 1905, p.403n2).
2 Labels for both the 1857 and 1867 exhibitions remain on the stretcher.
3 D. Williams, *Life and Corr. of Thomas Lawrence*, 1831, I, p.311n.

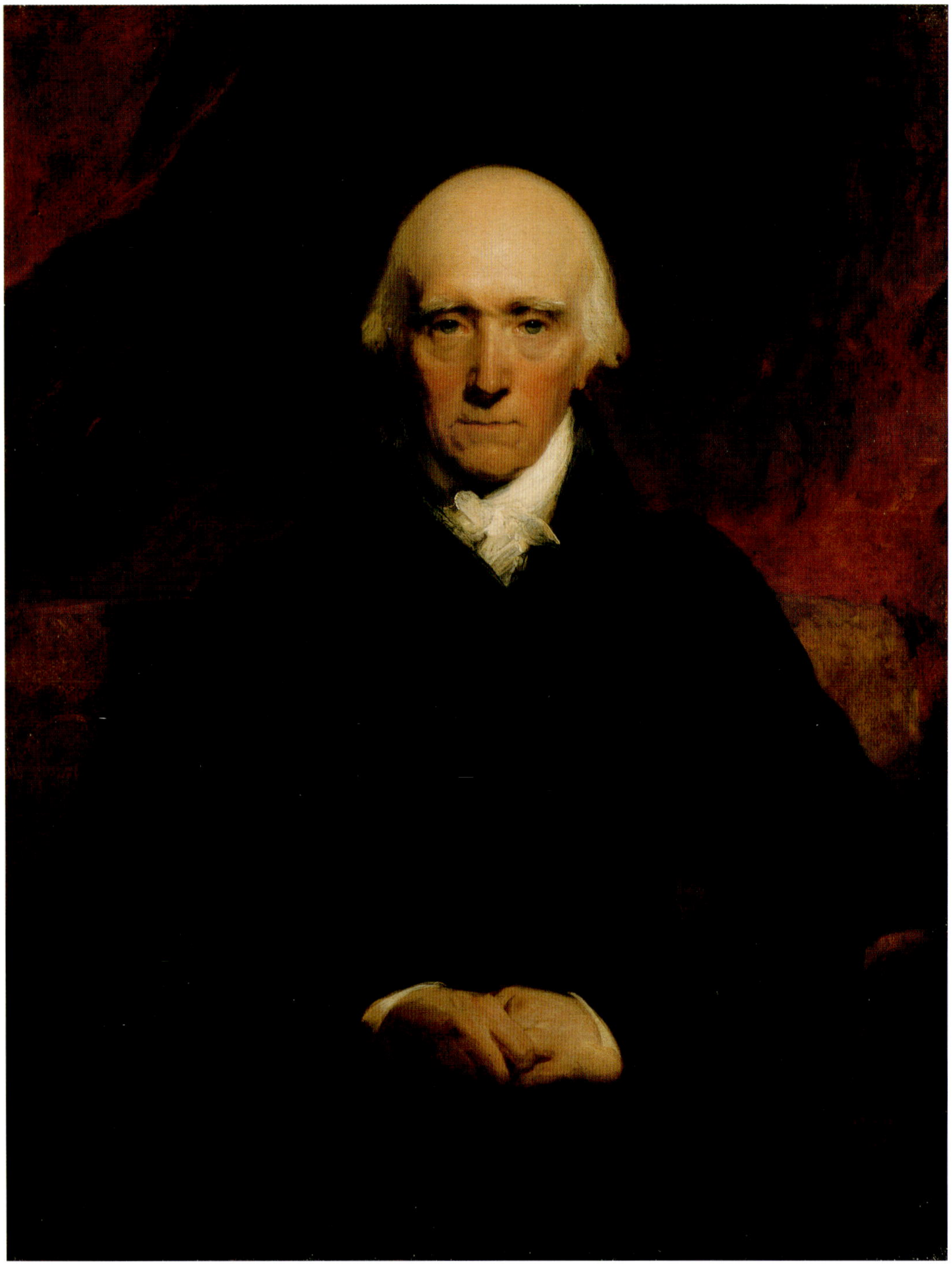

HASTINGS NPG *390*

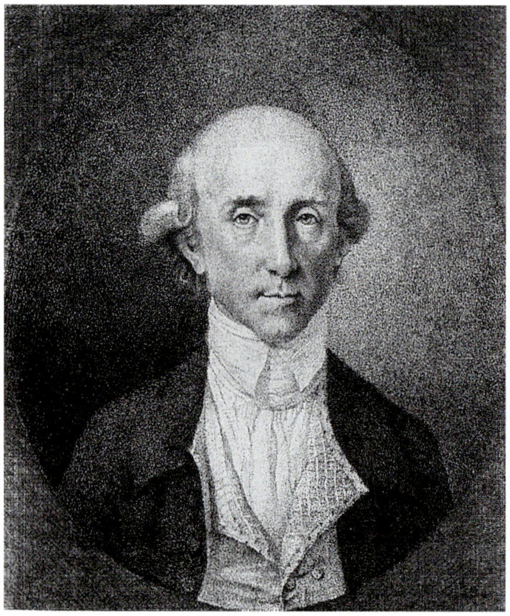

HASTINGS R. Brittridge after Johann Zoffany 1784 (Christie's)

ICONOGRAPHY

Shortly after Hastings had returned home in 1784, George Thompson, his secretary in Calcutta, wrote to him 'both you and Mrs Hastings should set to Gainsborough. For God's sake do so, and if the Picture is a good one have some Mezzotinto's scraped from it. They will be 1000 times more valuable to your Friends, and creditable to you than the many bad Pictures which are now extant of you' (Grier 1905, pp.247-48).

1766-67 Painting by Joshua Reynolds, see NPG 4445.

In India

c.1769-72 Paintings by Tilly Kettle, see NPG 81.

1780-81 A profile bust-length portrait of Hastings appears in Reynolds's *Richard Barwell and his Son*, formerly at Daylesford (Mannings 2000, no.129).

c.1782 Gouache by an unknown Mughal artist, whole length with an Indian attendant. India Office (British Library; illus. *The Raj*, NPG, 1990-91, no.134).

1783-87 Painting by Johann Zoffany, whole length with his second wife and her *ayah* with a distant view of Alipore, their country residence near Calcutta. Victoria Memorial Hall, Calcutta (illus. *Zoffany* 1997, no.99; Archer 1979, p.140 and pl.iv). Hastings m. 1777 Marian Chapuset, Baroness Imhoff (1747-1837), as his second wife (there were no children); she left India in January 1784, but the picture was still awaited in 1787. A version belonged to C.P. Hastings in 1935 (Knapp 1951, p.3, no.9).

1784 Painting by Johann Zoffany, half length. Leger in 1995, descended from Sir Elijah Impey. Exhibited *British Paintings Watercolours & Drawings*, Leger, 1995 (cat. p.68). Engraved R. Brittridge,* Calcutta, August 1784. Copies in the East India Club, London, and, in gouache, by a painter of the 'Company School' in the Victoria Memorial Hall, Calcutta (illus. P. Vaughan ed., *The Victoria Memorial Hall, Calcutta*, 1997, p.108). Hastings was said to have given many sittings to Zoffany in January 1784 (K. Feiling, *Warren Hastings*, 1954, p.310) and Zoffany's account to Hastings of 1785 included a 'Three Qr Portrait of Mr Hastings' and two copies, one already sent to Benares (Archer 1979, p.152). A preparatory chalk drawing is in a private collection (exhibited *Hidden Treasures*, Ashmolean Museum, Oxford, 1993, no.27 as by Humphry). A related anon. engraving after Zoffany, the body turned slightly to the right, is dated 1786 (Knapp 1951, p.18, no.5).

The Flaxman medallion made for Wedgwood derived from this portrait, see c.1785-90 below.

1784 Painting by J.T. Seton, three-quarter length seated. Untraced. Engraved J. Jones 1785 (illus. Archer 1979, p.115), R. Dalton 1797. A whole-length version, including a globe behind the sitter, painted in Calcutta for Sir Thomas Metcalfe, was acquired by the Victoria Memorial Hall, Calcutta, 1934. Another, painted in Bengal for Sir John D'Oyly, reduced to a three-quarter length in 1934 when on the London art market, presumably that sold Sotheby's, 12 June 2003, lot 13. A miniature copy of the head attributed to John Smart (illus. *Apollo*, XI, 1930, p.403), and attributed to Diana Hill by Knapp 1951, p.15, no.6 (where said to have been sold Sotheby's, 1 May 1930).

1784-85 Painting by A.W. Devis, whole length, a bust of Clive behind him. Rashtrapati Bhavan, New Delhi (illus. Archer 1979, p.242). Commissioned for William Larkins, accountant-general in Bengal 1777-93, who thought 'every other part but the face is a mere daub' (Grier 1905, p.421); presented to the NPG by the Secretary of State for India, 1885, but returned to the India Office 1902. Engraved H. Hudson, Calcutta, 1794. A copy by Miss Hawkins 1885 is in Government House, Calcutta, and another by Sephton was in the Town Hall, Calcutta.

A similar but smaller portrait, a scroll on the table inscribed *In memory and great friendship Mr Hastings has presented this painting to Beniram Pandit and Bissumber Pandit, 1st February 1785* (Hastings left for England on 7 February) is in a private collection, Benares (Knapp 1951, p.5, no.12). Devis's account for his two whole-length portraits is printed in Archer 1979, p.242.

A reduced copy commissioned by Lord Dalhousie c.1856 was sold from Colstoun, Sotheby's, 22 May 1990, lot 253; a three-quarter length version from Harewood was sold Christie's, 29 June 1951, lot 60 as Hudson, and a half length, originally belonging to Thomas Davies, Hastings's secretary in Bengal, and exhibited in 1878, 1879 and 1882 as Zoffany, sold Sotheby's, 15 July 1987, lot 70 (Knapp 1951, p.3, no.10).

Hastings returned to England in 1784 and in 1788 his trial began in London, the prosecution led by Edmund Burke.

c.1785-90 Wedgwood medallion, modelled by John Flaxman evidently from the Zoffany half length; previously attributed to Charles Peart (illus. Reilly 1973, p.186; Reilly 1994, p.339).

1786 Pastel by Thomas Lawrence, see NPG 3823.

1787 Miniature by Richard Cosway, see NPG 6286.

1789 Miniature on ivory by Ozias Humphry, three-quarter length seated, unfinished. Victoria and Albert Museum (996.1897; illus. Archer 1979, p.202). Engraved (as a finished picture) E. Finden 1836. Described in 1981 in error as after John Hoppner (due, presumably, to the similarity with the portrait now attributed to Abbott and formerly to Hoppner, see c.1796-97 below). Hastings was sitting to Humphry on 4 and 5 July 1789 (Archer 1979, p.203).

c.1789 Miniature on ivory by Ozias Humphry, half length. F.H. Turner 1950 (illus. Williamson 1918, f.p.118). Engraved W. Greatbach 1841. The head closely resembles that of the 1789 miniature; a similar miniature (once attributed to Grimaldi) said to have been given by Hastings to Anna Maria Scott on her marriage to John Reade in 1796, belonged to E.B. Reade in 1950 (Knapp 1951, p.14, nos.2 and 3).

1790 Bust by Thomas Banks, see NPG 209.

1790 Miniature attributed to Robert Bowyer. The Duke of Buccleuch. Hastings gave several sittings to Bowyer in 1790 (Knapp 1951, p.16, no.7; H.A. Kennedy, *Early English Portrait Miniatures in the Collection of the Duke of Buccleuch*, 1917, pl.lxiv as unknown).

1791 Enamel on Wedgwood biscuit earthenware by George Stubbs, whole length on his Arabian mare. Private collection (illus. *Stubbs*, Tate Gallery, 1984, no.130). Painted for Hastings's secretary at Calcutta, George Nesbitt Thompson, who described it as a poor likeness (Grier 1905, p.438n1). A similar, slightly smaller, enamel is in the Victoria Memorial Hall, Calcutta (Knapp 1951, p.6, no.15) and a replica, oil on panel, is at Dalmeny (illus. *Apollo*, CXIX, 1984, p.417). A watercolour of the head alone, attributed to Stubbs, illus. *Stubbs*, Hall & Knight, New York, 2000, p.61; engraved G.T. Stubbs 1795.★ An inscribed watercolour copy by G.T. Stubbs dated 1796, sold Robinson & Fisher, 21 February 1935, lot 74 as *A Huntsman*.

In 1787 Stubbs had been painting the Arab horse (K. Feiling, *Warren Hastings*, 1954, p.348), presumably *Hastings' Arabian Horse* engraved by G.T. Stubbs in 1798 (exhibited *Hastings*, Westminster School, 1932, no.42).

1793 Drawing by Richard Corbould, engraved B. Crosby 1793; B. Granger 1796.

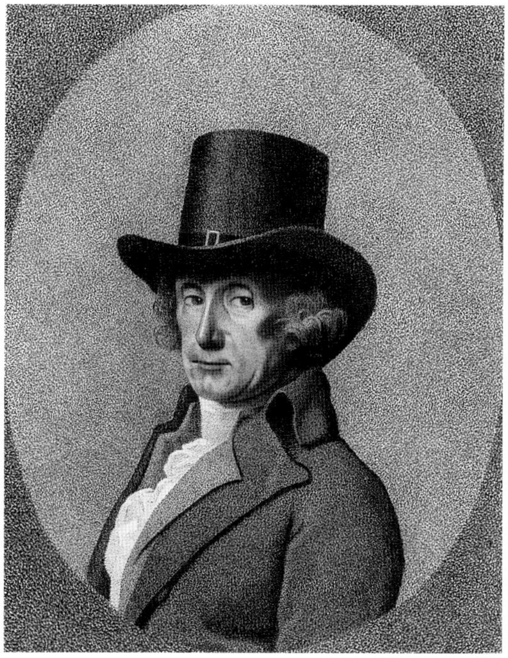

HASTINGS G.T. Stubbs after George Stubbs 1791 (NPG D 13799)

1795 Painting by George Romney, whole length. India Office, British Library (Walker 1976, p.32; Archer 1986, no.56, pl.ix). Painted for William Larkins, see 1784-85 above.

1796 Painting by L.F. Abbott, see NPG 1845.

1796 Bust by Thomas Banks, see under NPG 209.

c.1796-97 Painting attributed to L.F. Abbott, three-quarter length seated. AG of New South Wales, Sydney (illus. *Cat. of British Paintings*, [1987], p.126, as Masquerier), from the collection of Warren Hastings Anderson, the sitter's godson. Previously attributed to Masquerier and Hoppner (*Burl. Mag.*, III, 1903, f.p.129), but the head very closely resembles the 1795 Abbott pattern.

1797 Painting attributed to L.F. Abbott, half length. Engraved by W. Bromley 1797 (with two supporting Indian figures drawn by Thomas Stothard). Knapp 1951, pp.8-9, nos. 24, 25, recorded two versions of the original painting, variously attributed to Devis, Hoppner, Stuart and Abbott; one is now in the Palace of Westminster (from the collection of Lord Teignmouth), the other, from Stratton Park (Lord Northbrook), appears to have been the portrait with blue coat and red waistcoat with the Vose Galleries, Boston, Mass., in 1977. A third version, wearing a brown coat and looking to the left, with a glimpse of a red chair to the right, with Sotheby's in 1993, descended from James Peter Auriol (Knapp 1951, p.9, no.26, as c.1796; illus. A. M. Davies, *Warren Hastings*, 1935, f.p.418).

Miniatures by W.H. Craft (Sotheby's, 28 February 1972, lot 85) and William Bone (Sotheby's, 25 November 1974, lot 13) closely resemble the engraved portrait.

1800 Bust by J.C. Rossi, 'rising out of the sacred Flower of the Lotus' in artificial stone on a pedestal dedicated 'to the genii of India ... particularly the Immortal Hastings' set in an imitation Hindu temple designed by Thomas Daniell at Melchet Park, near Romsey, Hampshire, for John Osborne. Destroyed c.1850. Engraved J. Sewell 1803 (*European Mag.*, XLII, 1802, ii, pp.448–49; C. Lawson, *Private Life of Warren Hastings*, 1896, pp.248–49). A pencil drawing by William Daniell relates to this bust (P. Rohatgi, *Portraits in the India Office Library*, 1983, p.98).

1801 Painting by Robert Fulton, half length, engraved W. Nutter (Knapp 1951, p.18, no.4).

1804 Painting by W.M. Craig, half length. Christie's, 26 June 1925, lot 5, from the collections of the Earl of Morton and Lord Churston. Exhibited RA 1804(614). Hastings recorded seven sittings to Craig in 1804 (Knapp 1951, p.22, no.3).

1805–06 Waxes by Peter Rouw, see NPG 5065.

1806 Painting by William Beechey, half-length seated, a quill in his right hand. Phillips, 3 June 1997, lot 50, from the collection of the Duke of Gloucester. Hastings sat to Beechey in April 1806 'for a portrait he was giving to the Duke of Gloucester' (K. Feiling, *Warren Hastings*, 1954, p.387); the Duke acknowledged 'a remarkably fine painting as well as extremely like' (Knapp 1951, p.12, no.34).

1806 Painting by J.J. Masquerier, whole-length seated. Oriental Club, London, presented by Sir Charles Forbes 1829. Exhibited RA 1809(231). Engraved S. Freeman 1815 and Holl (illus. A.F. Baillie, *The Oriental Club & Hanover Square*, 1901, p.232). A sketch was in the Masquerier sale, Christie's, 19 January 1877, lot 27.

1811 Painting by Thomas Lawrence, see NPG 390.

1813–14 Painting by William Beechey, half length, holding an envelope addressed to Daylesford. Phillips, 19 May 1981, lot 40. Engraved W. Skelton 1817 from the original in the collection of William Leake. According to Knapp 1951, p.13, no.37, the portrait was finished at Daylesford on 10 June 1814. A variant, without papers on the desk or in his hand, inscribed verso *painted for Sir Henry Halford Bart. 1813/by Sr Wm Beechey RA*, sold Sotheby's, 12 March 1969, lot 59a.

1815 Portrait by W.M. Bennett, exhibited RA 1815(127).

Posthumous

1821 Marble bust by Samuel Manning. Westminster Abbey. Exhibited RA 1821(1106, 'Bust, in marble, of the late Right Hon. Warren Hastings; part of a monument to be erected in Westminster Abbey'). Miss M. Hastings Rainford, a direct descendant, had a 'black' bust believed to be a model for this monument (Knapp 1951, p.21, no.9). The monument incorporating Manning's bust was designed by John Bacon jr. (dated 1818 by Gunnis 1968, p.31). A similar bust with different drapery, his right shoulder bare, sold Christie's, 15 December 1982, lot 334 (unattributed and unidentified). It was presumably a cast of Manning's bust which was exhibited Crystal Palace (Phillips 1854, no.451 as by Bacon).

1823 Marble statue by John Flaxman. India Office, British Library (Walker 1976, p.32; illus. Archer 1986, no.133).

1830 Marble statue by Richard Westmacott jr. Victoria Memorial Hall, Calcutta (illus. *Apollo*, CXX, 1984, p.53); the head exhibited RA 1828(1213).

1867 Statue by Theodore Phyffers. India Office, London (Knapp 1951, p.21, no.13).

Undated Unattributed drawing, half-length seated, sold Christie's, 1 March 1989, lot 18.

Silhouette by John Field, sold Sotheby's, 24 October 1977, lot 42.

Paste medallion attributed to James Tassie with Spink in 1986. A paste cameo by William Tassie belonged to Capt. D.M. Anderson in 1935 (Knapp 1951, p.21, no.10).

HAWARD, Francis 1759–97

Engraver; studied at the RA 1776 and elected Associate Engraver 1783, at which time he changed his manner from mezzotint to stipple.

1233 OZIAS HUMPHRY 1794

Pastel on heavyweight laid paper 58.5 x 45.5 (23 x 18) laid down on linen; some abrasion in the lower areas; the execution is vigorous with bold hatching in the hair and face.

Blue eyes, white powdered hair, wearing a dark brown coat, white neckcloth and a buff waistcoat; a green curtain on the left.

Collections: Bequeathed by Charles Drury Edward Fortnum 1899.[1]

Reference: Williamson 1918, pp.243–44.

The only surviving portrait of Haward, identified by an early 19th-century label on the stretcher: *This / Portrait of Francis Haward. A.R.A. / 1794. Engraver to H.R.H. the Prince of / Wales etc. Painted by / Ozias Humphry Esq R.A.* It is assumed that 1794 refers to the date of the pastel (Humphry's activity as a pastellist was confined to the years 1791–97).

1 Fortnum (1820–99), collector, Trustee of the British Museum and benefactor of the Ashmolean. The (original) frame bears verso neatly painted in red the letters *P.S.EF.* which remain unexplained.

HAWKESBURY, Charles, Baron, see LIVERPOOL

HAWKINS, Sir John, Kt 1719–89

Writer and magistrate; Kt 1772 as 'the best magistrate in the kingdom'; compiled a *General History of Music* 1776, and wrote the first life of Dr Johnson, incorporated in Johnson's *Works* 1787–89, of which he was an editor.

5020 UNKNOWN ARTIST c.1781

Ink on paper 15.5 x 9.5 (6 x 3¾) the silhouette 7 (2¾) high; inscribed in ink verso: *Sir John Hawkins Knt. Aetat Suae* LXII.; laid down on card; the paper is stained and there are retouchings within the silhouette and in the surround.

Collections: Bought in 1969 by Mrs Edna Gray, by whom presented 1975.

Engraving: Lambert 1822 (reversed) as *Aetat Suae* LXII

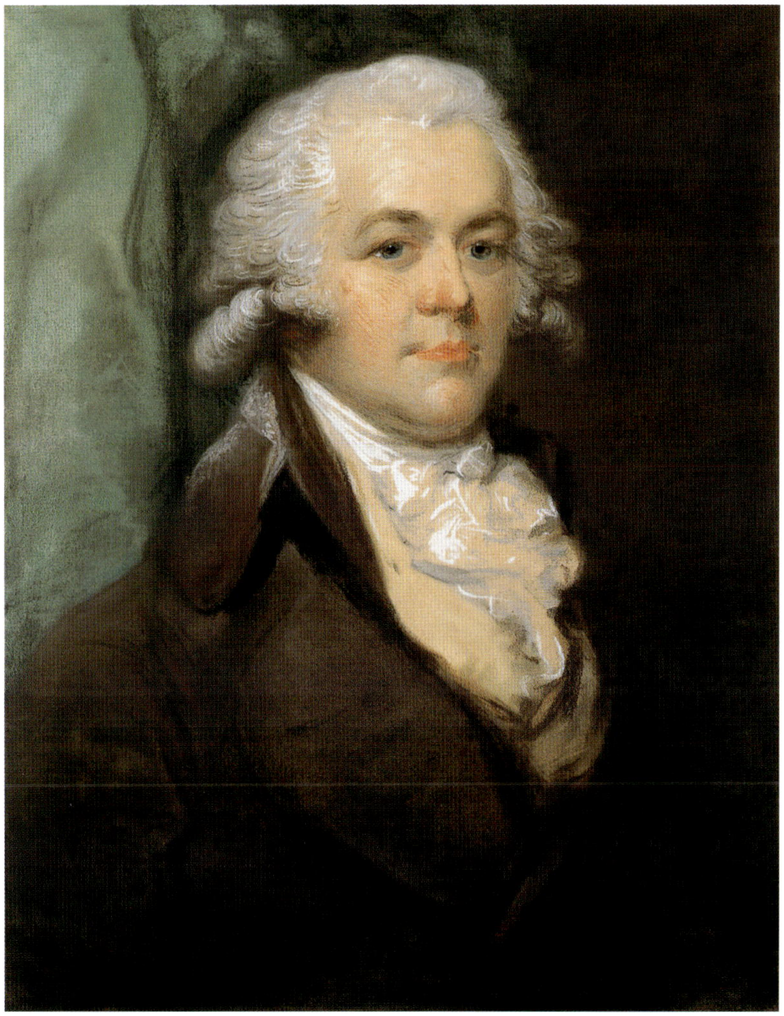

HAWARD NPG 1233

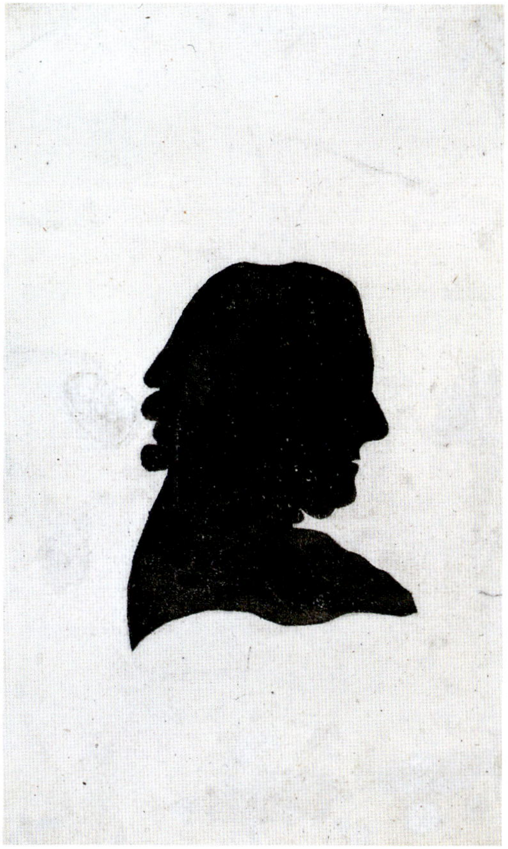

HAWKINS NPG 5020

(front. for L.M. Hawkins, *Anecdotes, Biographical Sketches and Memoirs*, 1822).

The origin of NPG 5020 was explained by the sitter's daughter; 'my father had always refused, even to my mother's request, to sit for his picture. He treated such a solicitude for being remembered, as foppery, for which he entertained the most unqualified contempt. We had therefore nothing approaching nearer to a portrait, than an outline taken by a friend by candlelight'.[1] An identical silhouette was with Limner Antiques, London, in 1985.

1 M.L. Hawkins, *Anecdotes*, 1822, p.137.

ICONOGRAPHY

c.1781 Unattributed drawing, see NPG 5020.

1786 Painting by James Roberts,* half length holding a book, his *History of Music* on the shelves behind him. Faculty of Music, Oxford (Poole, I, pp.162–63, illus., as dated 1786). Engraved R. Clamp 1794, from a drawing by S. Harding (*Biographical Mirrour*). Exhibited NPE 1867(571, as dated 1785); *Johnson*, Arts Council, 1984, no.16; and see *Handel*, NPG, 1985(215).

Commissioned for the Music School by Dr Philip Hayes, a patron of the young James Roberts, but according to the sitter's daughter, Hawkins was painted 'as he never looked, dressed as he never dressed, and employed as he never was employed; for he is represented smirking in a velvet coat, with a volume in his hand which ... must be one of the last new novels then printed. The artist vowed it was 'a capital likeness'...' (M.L. Hawkins, *Anecdotes*, 1822, pp.137–38).

DOUBTFUL PORTRAIT

A grey-wash drawing by G.P. Harding, sold Sotheby's, 28 July 1980, lot 308.

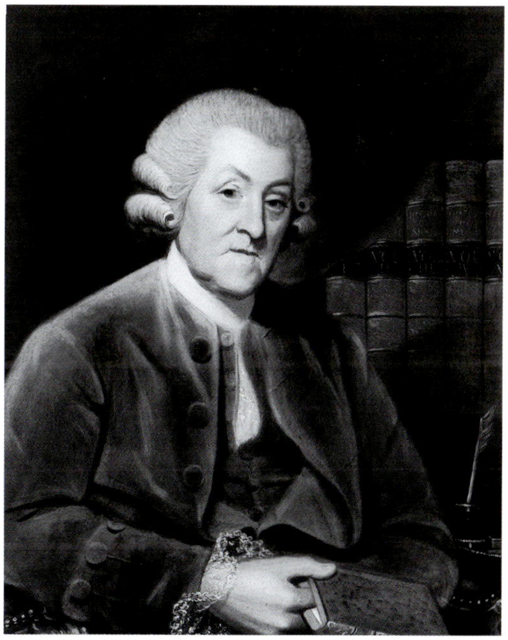

HAWKINS by James Roberts 1786 (Faculty of Music, Oxford)

HEARNE, Thomas 1744-1817

Watercolourist; exhibited FS and SA 1763-83 and RA 1781-93 and 1806; visited the West Indies 1771-75, and subsequently made many tours in Great Britain; his patrons included Sir George Beaumont, Richard Payne Knight and Thomas Monro who considered him 'superior to everybody in drawing'.

'a man of purer dignity does not exist' (Sir George Beaumont, 1816).

1653 HENRY MONRO 1812

Pastel on grey Ingres-type paper 71 x 57 (28 x 22½) drummed to an oak panel; the vertical edges deckled, the top and bottom edges turned round the panel; the surface is cockled and generally rubbed; the most prominent abrasion runs down across the cheek through the coat lapels.

Pale blue eyes, white hair, wearing a dark grey coat, a small green paint jar in his left hand.

Collections: F.T. Monro (d.1912); W.E. Monro,[1] from whom purchased 1912.

Exhibition: RA 1812(766), see below.

NPG 1653 may reasonably be identified as the drawing of Hearne exhibited by Monro at the RA in 1812. Hearne was a close friend of Thomas Monro, the artist's father,[2] and the portrait descended through the Monro family. In 1912 W.E. Monro wrote that there was 'some doubt as to whether it was drawn by my great grandfather [i.e. Thomas Monro - the writer seems to have been unaware of Henry Monro] about the year 1800 or by Hearne himself',[3] but Hearne is not known for pastel portraits, while in his very short career Henry Monro exhibited two at the RA in 1808 and 1811.

By 1812 Hearne was not in good spirits. Farington, who regularly reported on his welfare, had noted in 1806 that he appeared 'undressed and squalid, which in one advancing in years should not be', and by 1811 he had a 'general disinclination to exertion. He said that which He best liked to do was to remain at home & finish up His old drawings'.[4] Perhaps that is what Monro shows him doing, as he holds a paint jar in his hand.

1 Who wrote that the portrait had been 'in my family for a number of years' (W.E. Monro, 5 April 1912; NPG archive).
2 They were buried side by side at Bushey.
3 Letter of 15 April 1912 (NPG archive).
4 Farington, 7 November 1806 and 1 July 1811.

ICONOGRAPHY

1783 Miniature by John Smart. Possibly the 'self portrait' formerly in the Wicander collection (cat., 1920, no.302, pl.116), identified by A. Jaffé, *AQ*,

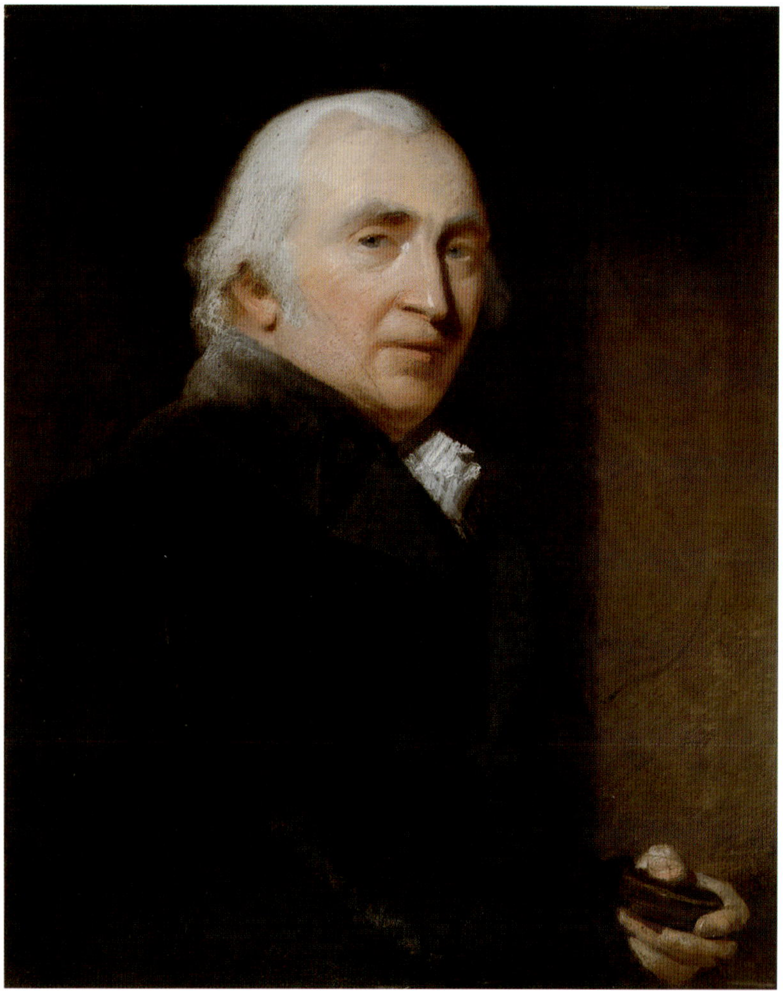

HEARNE NPG *1653*

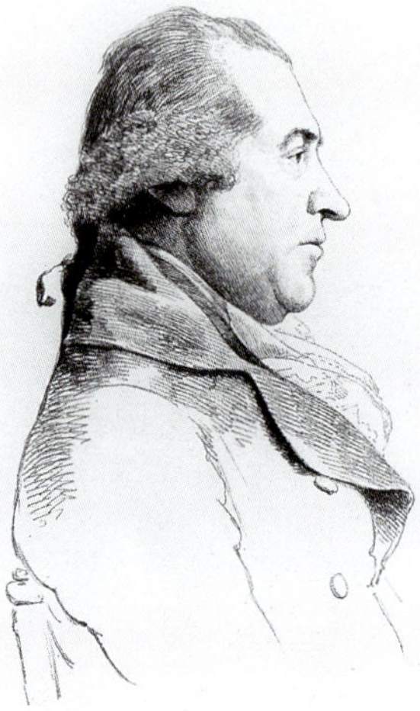

HEARNE W. Daniell after George Dance 1795 (NPG D 12145)

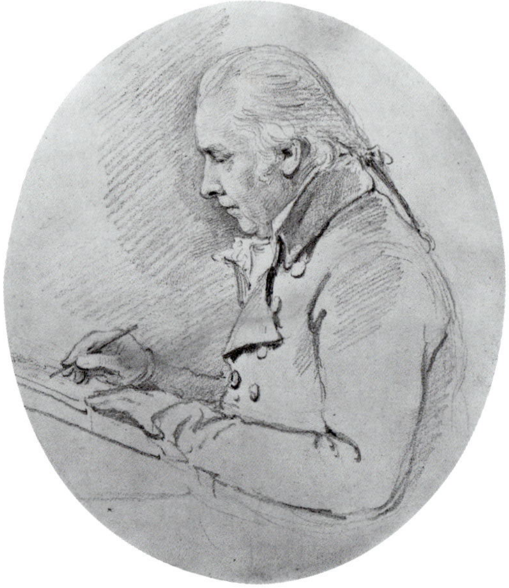

HEARNE by Henry Edridge 1800-01 (Private Collection)

XVII, 1954, pp.254–55, as Hearne from the Dance drawing, see 1795 below.

1795 Pencil drawing by George Dance, profile bust, dated 11 January 1795 (recorded by Farington). Presumably the drawing of 1795 in the Dance sale, Christie's, 1 July 1898, lot 65 ('Hearne – doctor'). Engraved W. Daniell* 1809 (*Dance Portraits*).

Versions attributed to Dance sold Christie's, 12 November 1968, lot 38, and (reversed) in a private collection (illus. *Hearne*, Bolton, 1985, p.2); two copies by W. Daniell are in the Yale Center for British Art (B1975.4.1120 & 1127).

1800–01 Four drawings by Henry Edridge:
a) whole-length seated, sketching in Ashtead Churchyard, Surrey, dated 1800. Victoria and Albert Museum (D.542.1906; illus. *Hearne*, Bolton, 1985, p.94).
b) half-length seated sketching, circular.* Private collection. Exhibited *Monro and the Monro Academy*, Victoria and Albert Museum, 1976(81).
c) seated sketching in a field, indistinctly dated 1801. British Museum (1845.8.18.1.2).
d) seated looking up from a book of landscape views. British Museum (1867.4.13.525).

c.1800 Drawing attributed to Thomas Monro, sketching at table. Yale Center for British Art (B1975.4.852).

1812 Pastel by Henry Monro, see NPG 1653.

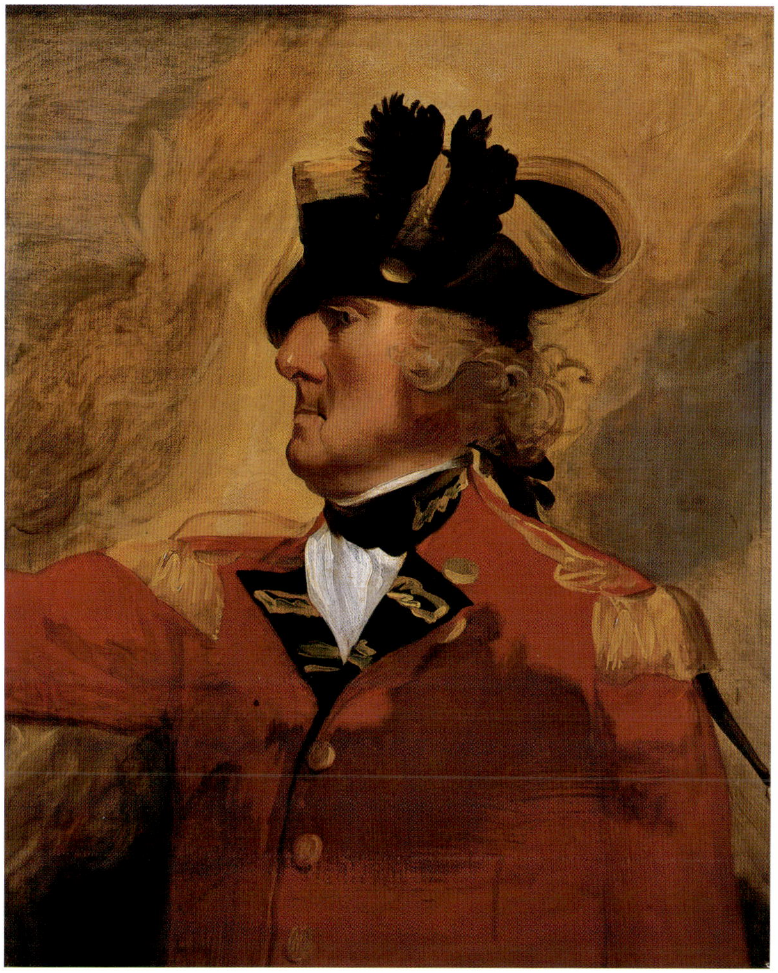

1st Baron HEATHFIELD
NPG 170

HEATHFIELD, George Augustus Eliott, 1st Baron 1717–90

Army officer; 7th s. of Sir Gilbert Eliott of Roxburgh; served in the War of the Austrian Succession and the Seven Years War (in Europe and Havana); lieutenant-general 1763; commander-in-chief Ireland 1774–75 and governor of Gibraltar 1775–87; for his defence of Gibraltar 1779–83 he was made KB 1783; cr. Baron Heathfield 1787.

'General Eliott was remarkable for an abstemious mode of living, seldom tasting anything but vegetables, simple puddings, and water; and yet was very hale, and used constant exercise' (John Drinkwater, 1786).

1752 see Groups, *The Siege of Gibraltar 1782* by GEORGE CARTER 1784

170 JOHN SINGLETON COPLEY 1787

Canvas 70 x 59 (27½ x 23¼) lined 1880; unfinished sketch; surface imprint from a previous framing at 65 x 56 (25½ x 22).

Clear grey eyes, grey hair with a black ribbon, in the uniform of an officer of the 15th Light Dragoons; black cockade and hat with gold trim, red coat with black collar, dark blue lapels.

Collections: The artist's son, Lord Lyndhurst; his sale, Christie's, 5 March 1864, lot 57, purchased.

Exhibitions: NPE 1867(486); *Romantic Art in Britain*, Detroit, Philadelphia, 1968(45).

Reference: Prown 1966, II, pp.327, 402, 419; *Copley* 1995b, pp.40–42.

Described by Prown as a 'vigorous and virile oil sketch', NPG 170 is a portrait study for Copley's *Defeat of the Floating Batteries* (see below 1791),* commissioned by the Corporation of London in 1783 and completed in 1791. For an account of the action, see Groups 1752. The final composition was determined early in 1787, when Copley was asked 'to wait on the illustrious characters whose portraits he wishes to have'.[1] In the finished picture Eliott appears mounted on a grey, marshalling the British troops, his right arm outstretched. A second sketch, showing the complete mounted figure, was sold Christie's, 15 November 1996, lot 26.

1 Prown 1966, II, p.326. In August 1787 Copley was still seeking portraits of de la Motte, Dachenhausen, Hugo and Schleppegrell (*ibid.*, p.327).

6079 JEAN-PIERRE DROZ [1787]

Bronze medal 6 (2⅜) diameter.

Obverse: profile bust to left in uniform with badge of the Bath (the motto clearly legible), inscribed: *GEORGE AUGUSTUS ELIOTT GOVERNOR OF GIBRALTAR*. and *J.P. DROZ F.*

Reverse: Hercules standing between two pillars, the left on the coast of Africa, the right by the rock of Gibraltar, inscribed: *FORTITER ET RECTE* and in the exergue: *XIII SEPT / MDCCLXXXII. / DROZ F.*

Collections: Glendining's, 22 November 1989, lot 163, bt. Baldwin for the NPG.

Reference: Brown 1980, no.247 (as 1782).

Eliott had returned to England from Gibraltar in June 1787[1] and Droz arrived in London in September to stay until 6 October.[2] By 3 October Lord Heathfield (as he had become) had sat four times to Droz who had made 'a sketch' and on 22 October Droz wrote from Paris that the portrait was finished, meaning

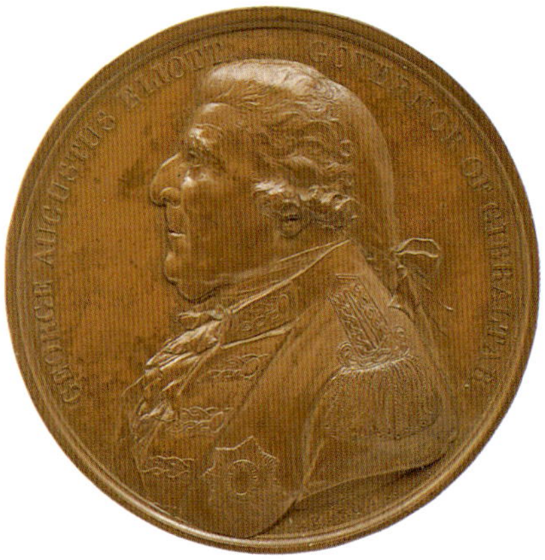

1st Baron HEATHFIELD NPG 6079

probably that he had made a satisfactory wax model. A year later, in October 1788, Droz called on Lord Heathfield in London and found his portrait a close resemblance. Droz's wax model of the head belonged to Matthew Boulton in 1790 and it appears that the medal may not have been cast until 1816-20.

1 His last letter from Gibraltar was dated 21 May 1787 and on 6 July he was created Baron Heathfield.

2 The following account is entirely taken from J.G. Pollard, *Numismatic Chronicle*, 7th ser., VIII, 1968, pp.263-64 (largely based on corr. between Droz and Matthew Boulton).

ICONOGRAPHY

Apart from two early portraits, Heathfield's portraiture was the consequence of his gallant defence of Gibraltar. His appearance in several of the historical scenes is specific enough to be included here.

c.1745-50? Unattributed miniature, bust-length oval (illus. *Connoisseur*, LXXXI, 1928, p.168).

c.1765? Painting by Nathaniel Hone, half length, engraved R. Pollard 1782 *from the Original Picture in the Possession of Willm Fuller* (the sitter's daughter Anne m. John Fuller in 1777); W. Angus (as after [W.?] Miller) 1782 (*European Mag.*); J.E. Mansfeld (Vienna).

1782 Drawing by G.F. Koehler, *General Eliott and his aide-de-camp, Lieutenant G.F. Koehler, in the King's Bastion during the action at Gibraltar*, whole-length figure, in uniform, pointing with his right hand, engraved T. Malton 1785? (illus. Prown 1966, II, fig.494). The figure of Eliott was separately engraved by F. Gregori, with minor alterations (his right hand tucked into his coat, standing before a sheer rock face) and several engravings were based on the head alone: by W. Angus 1785 (circular); J. Beugo 1794; J. Chapman 1796 (to right); R. Scott (to right and showing the star of the Bath on the wrong side), and an anon. print, *Cock of the Rock*, the hat badge made to resemble a cock's comb.

A Wedgwood medallion of c.1786 (illus. Reilly 1973, p.189) also derived from the Koehler head.

1784 Painting by George Carter, *The Siege of Gibraltar*, see Groups NPG 1752.

1787 Painting by Joshua Reynolds,* three-quarter length standing, in the uniform of the 15th Light Dragoons with the star of the Bath and the key of Gibraltar in his hands. National Gallery (111; Mannings 2000, no.578; Egerton 1998, pp.228-33). Exhibited RA 1788(115). Engraved R. Earlom 1788 and several times in the 19th century. Copies include those at the Guildhall AG, London (63); at Bodorgan, Anglesey, and a miniature by H. Bone which belonged to J.T. Smith in 1828 (see Mannings 2000, nos.578a-d).

From Reynolds's portrait Samuel Percy modelled a wax bust (examples sold Sotheby's, 10 June 1993, lot 212 from Stanton Harcourt; Sotheby's, 12 December 1996, lot 205, and Christie's, 2-3 July 1996, lot 161) and Peter Turnerelli a plaster bust, commissioned by the sitter's son (exhibited Colnaghi, *English Ancestors*, 1983, no.64).

1787 Painting by J.S. Copley, see NPG 170.

1787 Medal by J-P. Droz, see NPG 6079.

c.1787 Painting by Antonio Poggi, three-quarter length standing in uniform with hat and star of the Bath. Sotheby's, 21 April 1983, lot 76. Engraved F. Bartolozzi 1788, J. Chapman (bust length). A smaller version in the National Army Museum (7681), the same size as the Bartolozzi plate. A drawing by Poggi, head only with hat, in the Scottish NPG (PG 2048; exhibited *British Portraits*, RA, 1956-57, no.654 as Copley) was possibly made in 1783 when Poggi visited Gibraltar, although the attitude much resembles the Reynolds portrait of 1787. A closely comparable bust-length miniature by W. Thick was sold Christie's, 8 December 1982, lot 240.

1788 Painting by Mather Brown,* half length looking half right in uniform with the star of the Bath. Detroit Institute of Arts (70.953; Evans 1982, no.84). Exhibited RA 1791(241).

1788 Painting by Mather Brown, whole length in uniform with the star of the Bath, left arm extended. Pelham House, Lewes, East Sussex County Council (Evans 1982, no.85). Exhibited RA 1792(138).

c.1788 Drawing attributed to Johann Zoffany, half-length oval, resting a short sword across his left arm. Governor's Residence, Gibraltar (GAC 16246; illus. Williamson 1920, f.p.134).

1789 Painting by John Trumbull, *The Sortie made by the Garrison of Gibraltar, 26 November 1781*, shows Eliott standing in profile, right arm extended. Metropolitan Museum of Art, New York (1976.332; illus. Trumbull 1982, p.57). Engraved W. Sharp 1799. A version is in the Cincinnati Art Museum.

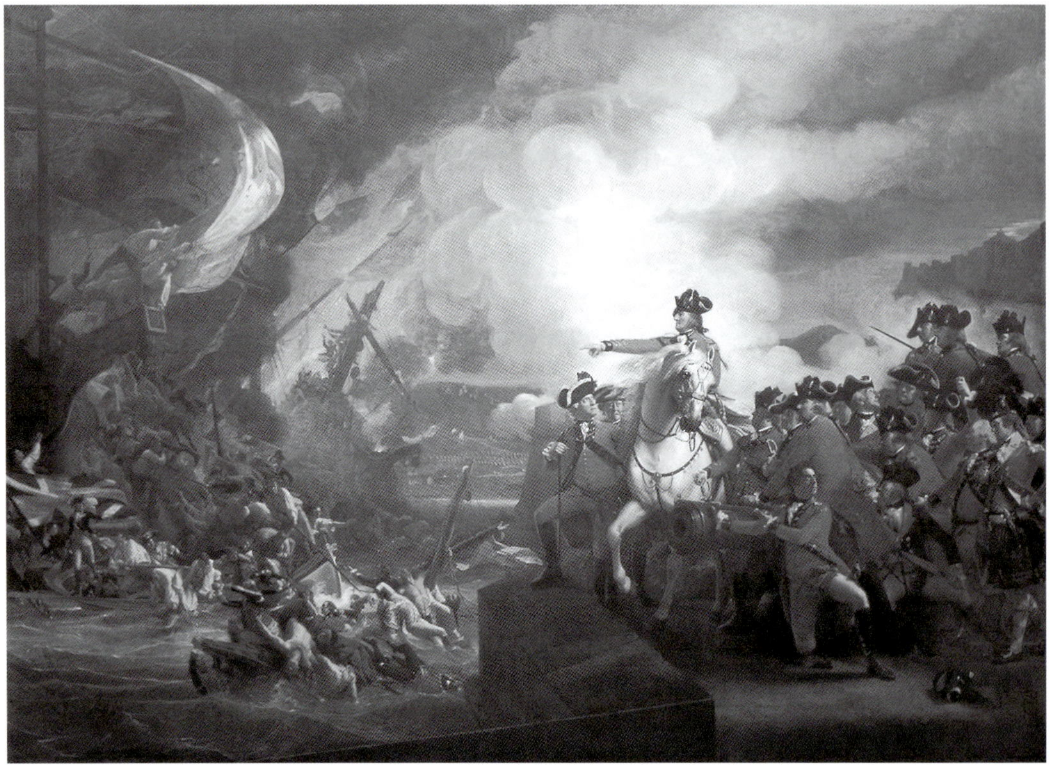

The Defeat of the Floating Batteries by J.S. Copley 1791 (Guildhall Art Gallery, London)

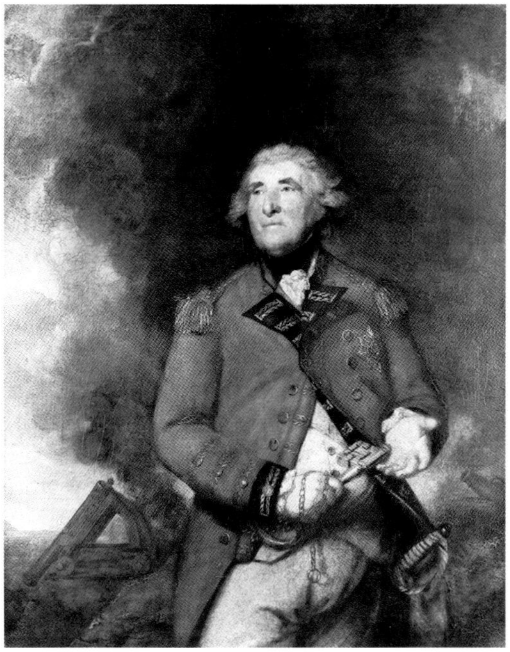

1st Baron HEATHFIELD by Joshua Reynolds 1787 (National Gallery, London)

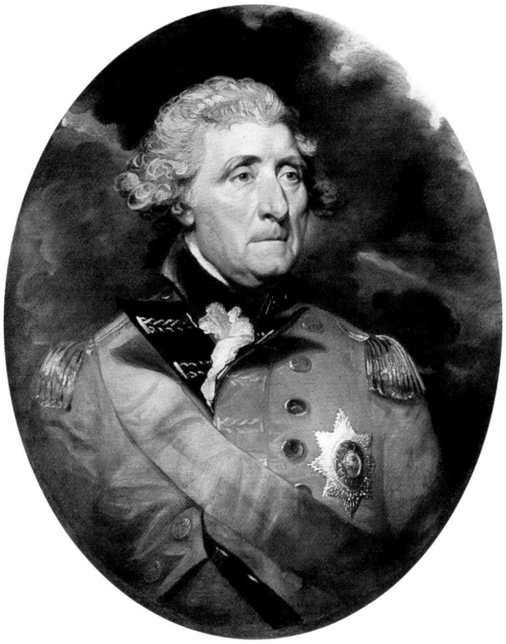

1st Baron HEATHFIELD by Mather Brown 1788 (Detroit Institute of Arts)

1790 Engraved caricature by I. Cruikshank 1790, showing Heathfield seated with gouty feet in uniform, his hat pulled well down, training cats (of which he was inordinately fond) to drill (George 7651; illus. J. Russell, *Gibraltar Besieged*, 1965, f.p.180).

1791 Painting by J.S. Copley, *The Defeat of the Floating Batteries on 13 September 1782*,* with Eliott mounted as the central figure. Guildhall AG, London (43), commissioned by the Corporation of the City of London 1783 (Prown 1966, II, pp.447-57, with numerous preliminary sketches). Engraved W. Sharp 1810. Oil sketch in the Foundling Hospital; copies of 1810 in the Tate Gallery (N 787) and of 1906 by G.V. Shepton in the Bomann Museum, Celle.

Undated A pastel by H.D. Hamilton, 'half length wearing uniform', was sold Sotheby's, 4 July 2001, lot 155.

Posthumous

1795 Heathfield monument by John Bacon sr., with a medallion portrait. Church of St Andrew, Buckland Monochorum, Devon.

1823-26 Statue by J.C. Rossi. St Paul's Cathedral (illus. Gunnis 1968, f.p.289). Rossi's 'Monument to be erected in St Paul's' exhibited RA 1824(991) and his 'Model of the statue in St Paul's' exhibited RA 1826(1018).

DOUBTFUL PORTRAITS

Several portraits, rushed out in 1782-83, bear no relation to the authentic images of Reynolds, Poggi and Koehler; they include engraved heads by Js.H (1782) and anon. (with pronounced beak nose, 1783); whole-length engravings pub. R. Sayer, *The victorious Governor of Gibraltar* (illus. McGuffie, 1965, f.p.173) and by Martin after P. De Glim (1783); medallions by J. Weber, in armour (Brown 1980, no.249), and Terry (Brown 1980, no.246), and a Wedgwood medallion (illus. Reilly 1973, p.188), said to derive 'from a medal'.

HENDERSON, John 1747-85

Actor; won a drawing prize at the Society of Arts 1761; first played at Bath 1772-77; played at Drury Lane 1777-78 and at Covent Garden from 1779; also performed at Dublin 1778 and 1779, Liverpool 1782 and 1783 and Edinburgh 1784; buried in Westminster Abbey.

'As an actor he had many disadvantages to cope with. His height was below the common standard. He had an uncompacted frame. His limbs were ill proportioned; they were too short; he had not much of that flexibility of countenance which anticipates the tongue ... His temper was placid, and under very uncommon government' (John Ireland, 1786).

'his person was without either dignity or grace, and his eye, though well placed for expression, wanted colour, as his face, though rather handsome, was too fleshy to shew all the muscular action, in which expression resides' (James Boaden, 1825).

980 THOMAS GAINSBOROUGH c.1773-75

Canvas 75.5 x 63 (29¾ x 24¾) lined; cleaned and relined 1986; the flesh areas are rubbed and *pentimenti* show alterations to the left hand, book and collar; background has been reworked to the left of the head.

Clear grey eyes, grey powdered hair, wearing a blue coat with a red collar, white neckcloth and cuffs.

Collections: By descent to the sitter's granddaughter, Miss Julia Carrick Moore, by whom presented 1895.

Engravings: J. Jones 1783; R. Josey 1875.[1]

Exhibitions: BI 1817(64) as Reynolds, lent Mrs Henderson;[2] *Genial Company*, Nottingham, Edinburgh, 1987(29); *Gainsborough's Circle at Bath*, 1988, Bath, 1988(15); Gainsborough's House, Sudbury, 1962-.

Reference: *Gainsborough* 1953, p.56; Waterhouse 1958, no.360, on both occasions as datable 1777 and exhibited RA 1780(194).

Gainsborough and Henderson met at Bath, where Henderson made his stage debut in October 1772. Gainsborough came to admire his ability and, from the 'sincere desire I have of seeing you a great and happy man', urged him to study Garrick as much as he could and not to 'eat so devilishly'.[3] Three letters from Henderson mention portraits by Gainsborough. On 3 August 1773 he told John Palmer, the manager of the Bath Theatre, that Gainsborough was 'a varlet, he promised me a miniature from the picture of mine, but wits and genius, if they get nothing else from the court, learn their d—d tricks of promising and forgetting';[4] on 24 February 1775 he asked Mrs John Ireland if she had yet seen his picture at Gainsborough's: 'I intend it for my dearest Jack [John Ireland],[5] because I think it very like . . .'[6], and on 12 February 1777 he wrote from Bath to John Ireland: 'I hope too, that Gainsborough will let you have my head — don't you think it's a very fine likeness.'[7] The first letter confirms a portrait of 1773 (though strictly speaking not necessarily by Gainsborough); the others confirm a portrait or portraits by Gainsborough in 1774-75 and 1776-77. These letters have hitherto been taken to imply two portraits, one of 1773, the other of c.1777,[8] but there is much confusion.

Two may be identified today: NPG 980 and one known only through a half-length oval engraving by John Jones published on Henderson's death in 1786 (which appears to show an older head). As described below, an untraced portrait by Gainsborough of Henderson 'studying' was exhibited at the RA in 1780, and two further portraits, somewhat resembling this 1786 engraving, have been attributed to Gainsborough.[9]

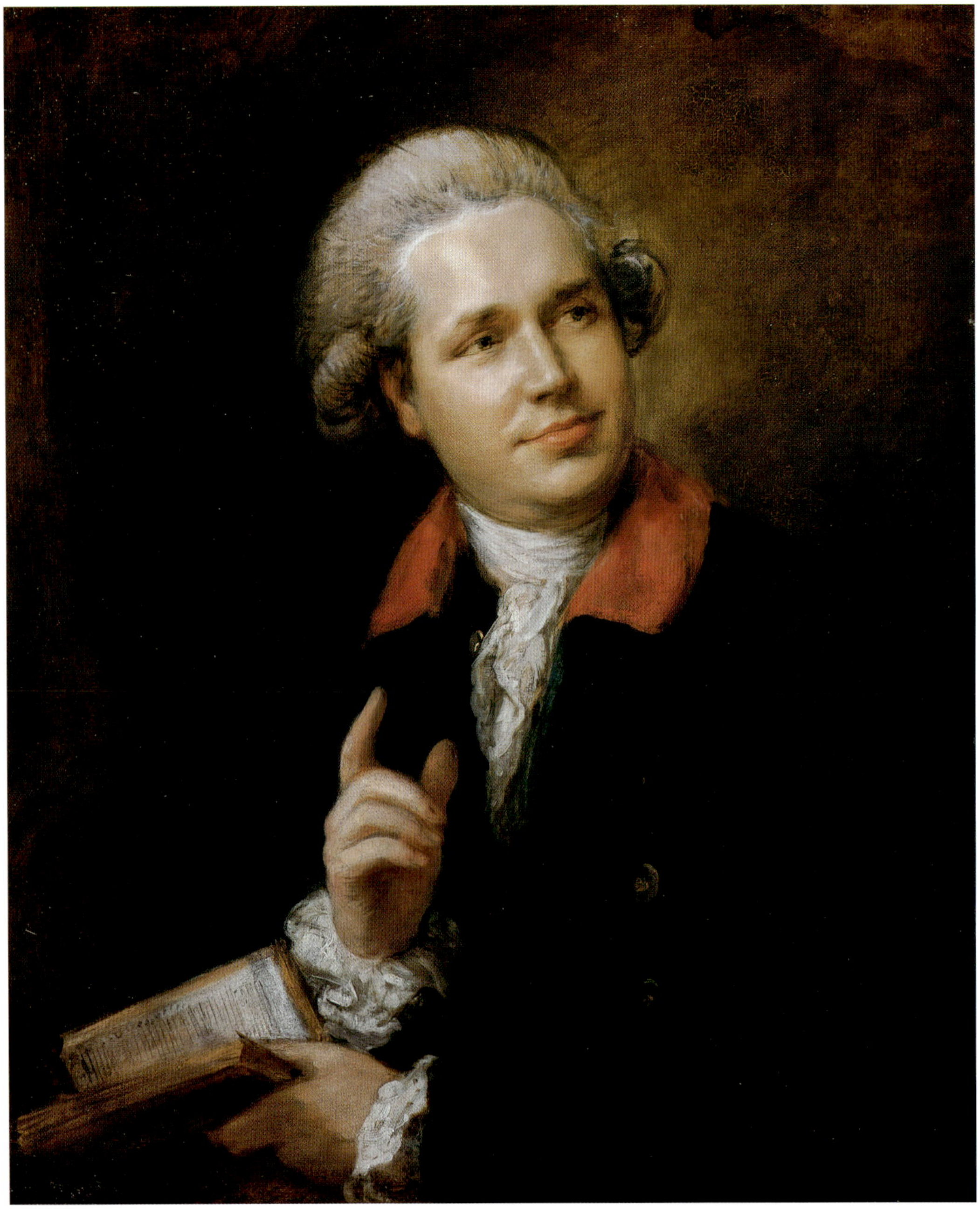

HENDERSON NPG *980*

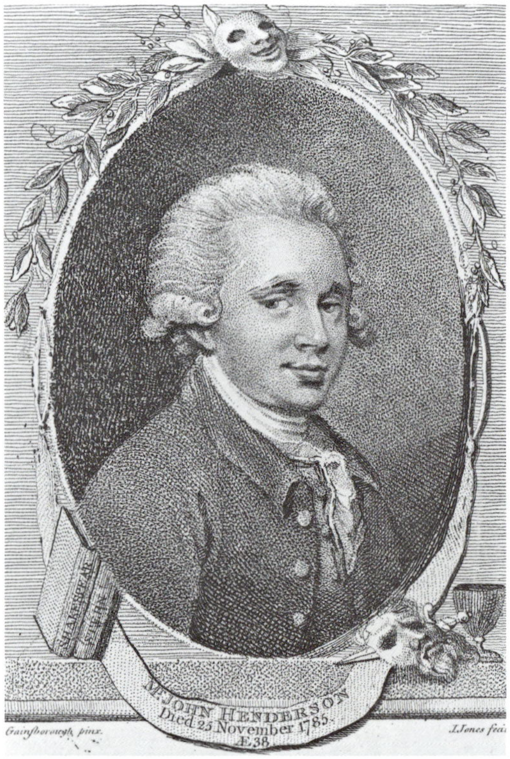

HENDERSON J. Jones 1786 after Thomas Gainsborough (NPG D *18096*)

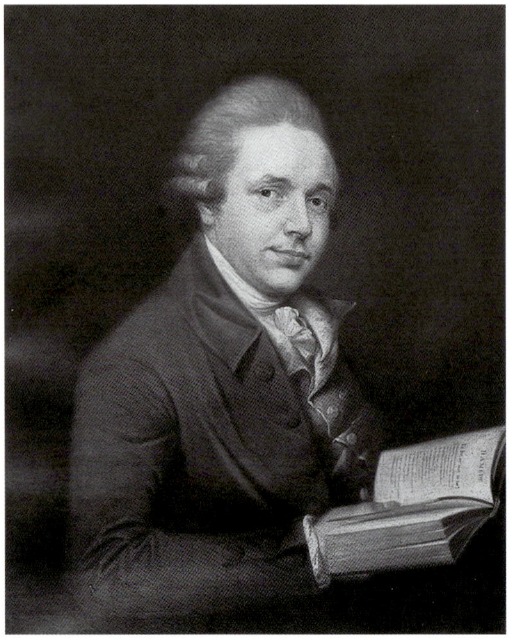

HENDERSON after Thomas Gainsborough c.1777? (Garrick Club)

Although no longer in prime condition, it is clear that NPG 980 was a freely handled, informal portrait (the book has no legible text), and probably that mentioned by Henderson in 1773 and 1775; stylistically it could easily belong to Gainsborough's late Bath period.[10] Waterhouse however believed it might be a portrait painted in 1777 and shown at the RA in 1780.[11] It remains unexplained why it was not engraved until 1783 (for what is easily the most impressive print of Henderson). Two versions are recorded: one in the Treat Gallery, Bates College, Lewiston, Maine, the other, called Gainsborough Dupont, was with Ehrich, New York, in 1933.

1 Described as *In the collection of the Henderson family*.
2 There is no portrait of Henderson by Reynolds; Fulcher 1856, p.218, listed the BI portrait as Gainsborough, and the provenance of NPG 980 implies that it was the portrait in question.
3 Hayes 2001, pp.117 (Bath, 27 June 1773); a second letter to Henderson is dated 18 July 1773 (*ibid.*, pp.117–18).
4 J. Ireland, *Letters and Poems by the late Mr. John Henderson with Anecdotes of his Life*, 1786, p.125.
5 John Ireland (d.1808), later the biographer of Henderson and Hogarth, who had probably introduced Henderson to Gainsborough (see Whitley 1915, p.86).
6 Ireland, *op. cit.*, p.177.
7 *Ibid.*, p.194.
8 Cf. *Gainsborough* 1953, p.56 and Waterhouse 1958, nos.360–61.
9 An otherwise unidentified 'Gainsborough' portrait of Henderson, 61 x 56 cm., was exhibited at the Grosvenor Gallery, 1885(142) lent Andrew Mackay.
10 Hugh Belsey also prefers a date in the early 1770s (letter of 1 October 2001; NPG archive).
11 Waterhouse 1958, no.360; followed, for example, by Highfill, VII, p.261, no.4; Hayes 2001, p.204.

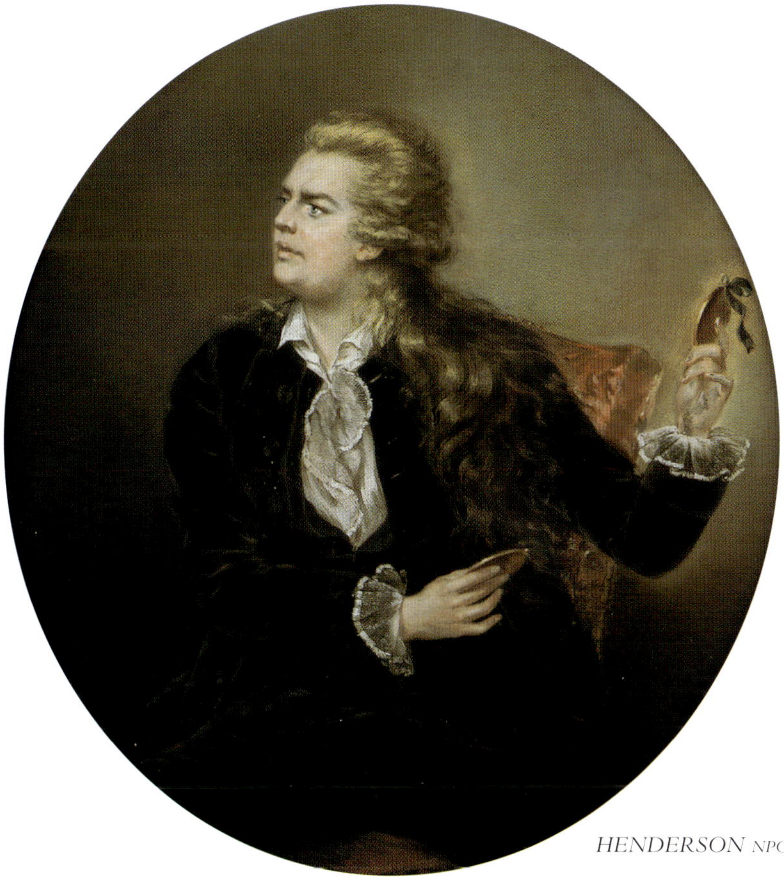

HENDERSON NPG 1919

1919 ROBERT DUNKARTON, *as Hamlet* 1776

Pastel 45 x 41 (17½ x 16¼) sight, oval; the left hand is rubbed; signed lower left: *R Dunkarton / pinxt 1776*.

Blue-grey eyes, fair flowing wig, wearing a black velvet suit with a white shirt; seated in a pink damask chair, holding oval miniatures in each hand (only the backs are shown).

Collections: Glyn family (of Gaunt House, Dorset), sale Christie's 17 March 1877, lot 4;[1] John Heugh sale, Christie's, 10 May 1878, lot 72, bt. 9½ gn.;[2] with Edmund Robert Wodehouse (d.1914) in 1893;[3] Ernest E. Leggatt, by whom presented 1919.

Exhibitions: RA 1776(91); *Georgian Playhouse* 1975(38).

Henderson is portrayed as Hamlet: 'Look here, upon this picture, and on this, -- / The counterfeit presentment of two brothers' (*Hamlet*, III, iv). Henderson had played Hamlet in Bath since 1772 and Garrick saw him in the part there in April 1775, meanly describing his performance as 'a mixture of Tragedy Comedy pastoral farce & nonsense'.[4] The drawing of his left arm is not above criticism.

1 Sketched by Scharf in his copy of the sale cat.
2 TSB 38/7-8; an old label verso also identifies this sale and records the price fetched of 9½ gn.
3 *Ibid*.
4 *Garrick Letters* 1963, III, p.1001, no.903.

ICONOGRAPHY

See also the *Harvard Catalogue*, II, pp.217-19, and Highfill, VII, pp.261-63 (listing further portrayals of Henderson in character).

1773 Painting by Thomas Beach,* half length. Garrick Club (Ashton 1997, no.292). The likeness agrees with the engraved Gainsborough portrait of 1777-80 and Beach also painted Henderson and Jackson in *Richard III*, exhibited, SA 1774(18).

c.1773-75 Painting by Thomas Gainsborough, see NPG 980.

1776 Pastel by Robert Dunkarton, see NPG 1919.

c.1777? Painting attributed to Thomas Gainsborough,* half-length seated at table, an open book in his hand inscribed *HAMLET / To be or not to be*. Untraced. A copy in the Garrick Club (Ashton 1997, no.293) In 1953 Waterhouse believed the head engraved by Jones in 1786 (see below, c.1780) derived from this pattern (but the relationship is not exact) and he considered the Garrick Club picture to be after a lost Gainsborough original (Gainsborough 1953, p.56). W. Armstrong, *Gainsborough* 1898, p.110, considered this portrait to show Henderson 'some years older' than NPG 980, but Waterhouse thought it looked younger. See below, 1780 Gainsborough.

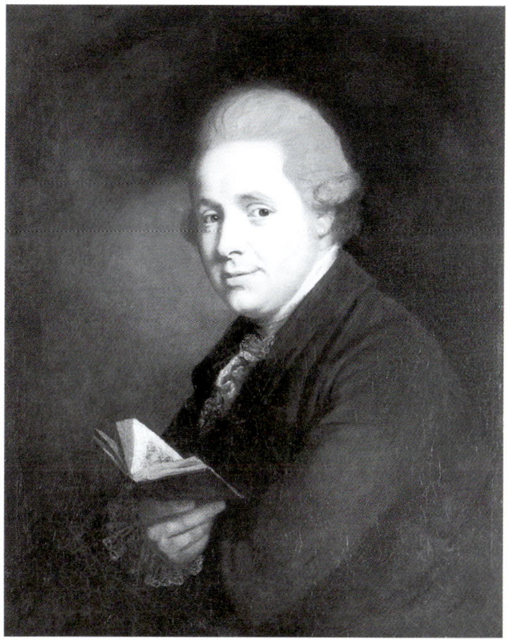

HENDERSON *by Thomas Beach 1773 (Garrick Club)*

Reduced oval half-length versions on panel in the Garrick Club (Ashton 1997, no.294 as after Gainsborough), and sold Robinson & Fisher, 16 May 1928, lot 163.

c.1779 Painting ascribed to Benjamin Wilson (but not by him), three-quarter length in black as Hamlet with Richard Wilson as Polonius. Garrick Club (Ashton 1997, no.296). The two actors played together in *Hamlet* in April 1779. A version of this 'somewhat

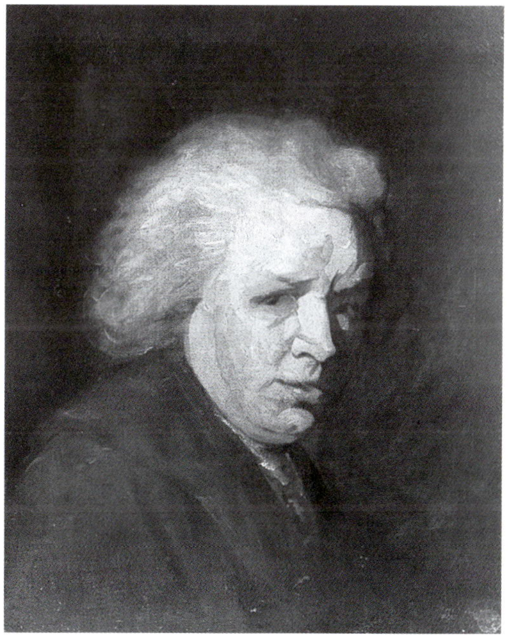

HENDERSON *by Gilbert Stuart 1785 (Victoria and Albert Museum)*

unsatisfactory picture' with whole-length figures is in the National Theatre (Maugham Collection; Mander & Mitchenson 1980, no.16).

1780 Painting by Thomas Gainsborough, studying. Untraced. Exhibited RA 1780 (291, see Graves RA, III, p.192; Whitley 1915, p.167). The Garrick Club portrait of c.1777, see above, would fit this brief description; T. Mulvany ed., *Life of James Gandon*, 1846, p.201, mentioned Henderson's portrait by Gainsborough showing him 'in the act of studying of passage, in which he appears deeply interested'.

1780 Painting by George Romney, as Macbeth, half length in armour with a red mantle, with Banquo and the three Witches. Christie's, 28 June 1890, lot 116 (Ward & Roberts 1904, II, p.76). Engraved J. Jones 1787 (illus. Pressly 1993, p.227; Cross 2000, p.128). For Romney and Henderson, see *Romney* 2002, pp.216-17.

Reduced versions in the Garrick Club (Ashton 1997, no.297), the Folger Shakespeare Library (illus. Pressly 1993, p.225), and sold Sotheby's, 26 January 1996, lot 76. Versions showing the figure of Macbeth alone sold Anderson, New York, 18 May 1933, lot 29 (three-quarter length); Sotheby's, 14 July 1976, lot 112 (half length), and Windsor AG, Ontario (half length; illus. *Romney in Canada*, 1985, p.62).

1780 Miniature by John Smart, bust-length oval, wearing a brown coat. Madresfield Court (illus. Williamson 1904, ii, pl.lxxii; *The Art of the Country House*, Tate Gallery, 1998, no.25).

c.1780 Unattributed painting, half length. Untraced. Engraved anon. 1786 (CS, IV, p.1732, no.82 with the comment 'this picture has been stated to be by Gainsborough'). The head at a comparable angle to the c.1777 Gainsborough listed above, with the body turned more to the right.

Two closely related paintings (or possibly one), showing his left hand resting on an upright folio on a table sold Christie's, 8 July 1938, lot 119 as Gainsborough and Christie's, New York, 7 December 1977, lot 55 as attributed to Gainsborough.

c.1780 Painting by Thomas Gainsborough, engraved J. Jones 1786* (bust-length oval; *European Mag.*, December 1785). Waterhouse 1958, no.361, as a lost original of 1772-73, but Henderson appears decidedly older than in NPG 980.

c.1781? Wax portrait by E.G. Mountstephen. Victoria and Albert Museum (414.1368.1885; illus. Rackham 1924, pl.79).

1785 Painting by Gilbert Stuart,* sketch of the head, as Iago. Theatre Museum (D.26; Ashton 1992, no.12). Engraved F. Bartolozzi 1786 (oval; illus. Highfill, VII, p.255); W. Read. The head was used by Ramberg in his whole length drawing of Henderson as Iago, engraved J. Thornthwaite 1785 (illus. Burnim 1998, p.55).

c.1785 Miniature by Gilbert Stuart, bust-length oval. Francis Wellesley sale, Sotheby's, 5th day, 2 July 1920, lot 765 (Park 1926, no.394, illus. III, p.239; *Connoisseur*, LI, 1918, p.69). Engraved J. Coyte 1787 as Mr Henderson *from an original painting*.

Undated Wax by Samuel Percy in his sale Christie's, 31 January 1800 (Gunnis 1968, p.300; Pyke 1973, p.104).

DOUBTFUL PORTRAITS

Painting attributed to Zoffany, Christie's, 27 July 1895, lot 31 (sketch in NPG archive); miniature by Daniel Gardner (Williamson 1921, p.129, as Wellesley collection); drawing by Romney, Francis Wellesley sale, Sotheby's, 4th day, 1 July 1920, lot 676.

A painting attributed to William Hamilton in the Garrick Club (Ashton 1997, no.295) shows Samuel Ireland (cf. O'Donoghue, II, p.604).

HENLEY, Robert Henley, 1st Baron, see NORTHINGTON

HERBERT, John 1723-99

Factor with the East India Company at Sumatra in 1755; in 1773 he arrived as chief of a new settlement at Balambangan (a small island near Borneo); dismissed on suspicion of fraud in 1775, when the island had been recaptured by the Sultan of Sulu (who had first granted it to England in 1763); Herbert escaped to Madras and reached London in 1778; he returned to India in 1781 and d. at Dacca.

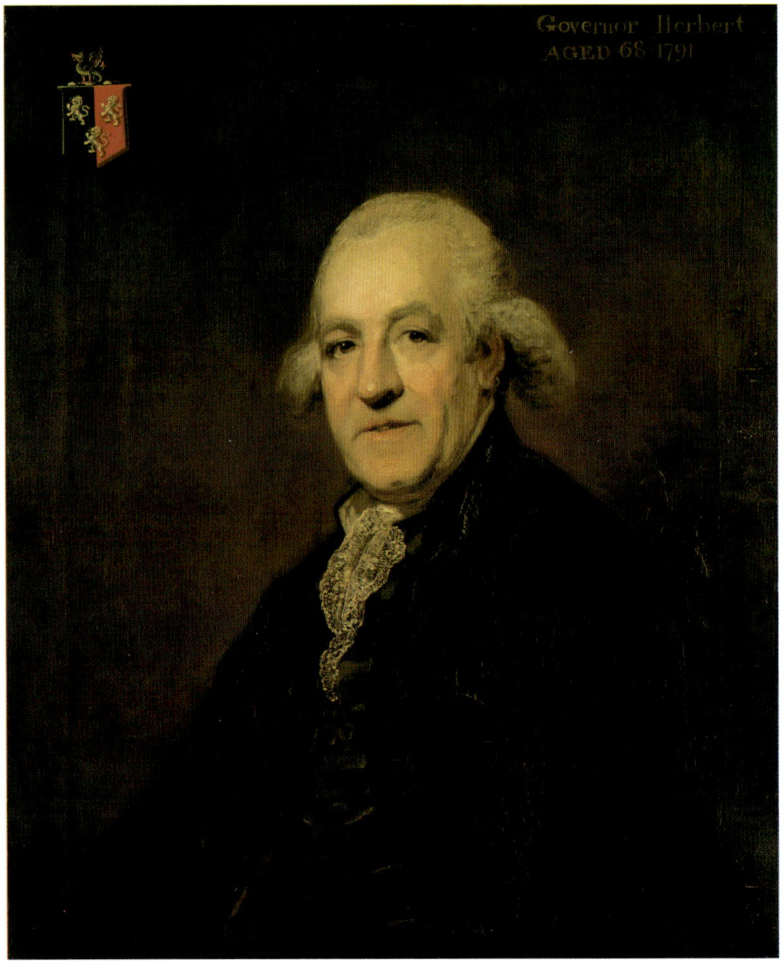

HERBERT NPG 547

547 ARTHUR WILLIAM DEVIS 1791

Canvas 76 x 63.5 (30 x 25); pronounced drying craquelure and the varnish is discoloured; inscribed, upper right: *Governor Herbert / AGED 68 / 1791*; inscribed verso: *John Herbert Esq.re Father of Mrs. B.W. Page /*[1] *painted by Davis at Calcutta.*

Brown eyes and white hair, wearing a black suit and waistcoat with a white lace neckcloth; arms of Herbert of Pembroke and Montgomery upper left.[2]

Collections: Presented by the sitter's son-in-law, Admiral B.W. Page (d.1845), to the British Museum, whence transferred to the NPG 1879.

Exhibitions: National Gallery, 1899; India Office, 1927-45.[3]

Reference: W. Foster, *Wal. Soc.*, XIX, 1931, p.26.

The inscriptions on the portrait (incorporating the title of 'Governor' and the display of the Pembroke arms) suggest both Herbert's pretence and the fraudulence which led to his dismissal at Balambangan.

1 Eliza Herbert (d. 1834) m. 1) Philip Manington (Superintendent of Penang 1794-96), 2) 1796 Adm.B.W. Page (c.1765-1845) whose portrait by Robert Hannah belongs to the Ipswich Corporation.
2 *Per pale, az. and gu. three lions ramp. ar. crest wyvern vert holding a sinister hand couped at wrist gu.*
3 NPG 547 appeared in the NPG cats. of 1898 and 1946, but not in the intervening editions 1900-1932.

HERVEY, Augustus, see BRISTOL, 3rd Earl of

HERVEY, Frederick, see BRISTOL, 4th Earl of

HEWITT, James, see LIFFORD

HIGHAM, Charles, Lord, see ROCKINGHAM

HILL, Sir Richard, 2nd Bt 1732-1808

Polemicist, writer of religious pamphlets; 1st s. of Sir Rowland Hill of Hawkstone Park, Salop., whom he suc. as 2nd Bt 1783; he was twice in Italy 1756-57 and 1791; MP 1780-1806, 'one of the most upright, disinterested and honest men who ever sat in Parliament'.

'his manners were quaint and puritanical, his address shy and embarrassed. He possessed, however, a most benevolent disposition' (Sir Nathaniel Wraxall, 1815).

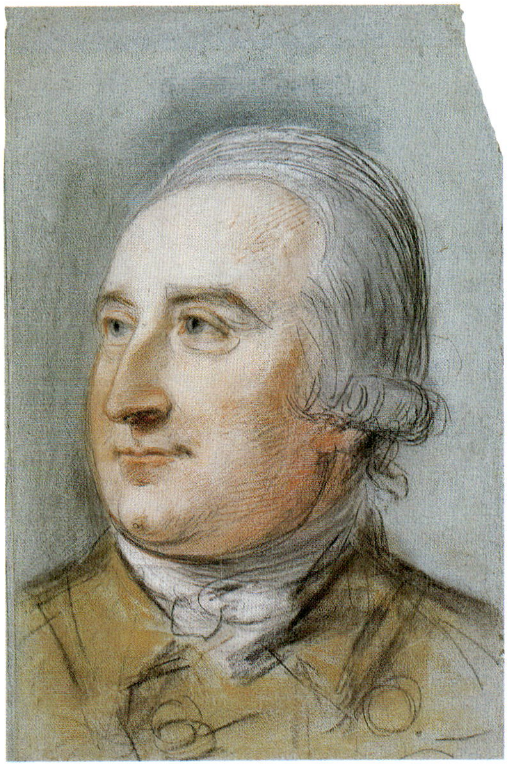

Sir Richard HILL NPG *1465*

1465 JOHN RUSSELL c.1780-83

Pastel on blue laid paper (with watermark Churchill, no.406) 38.5 x 27 (15¼ x 10⅝) uneven; remounted 1998; inscribed verso: *Sir R Hill* (pencil) and: *Sir Richard Hill. Bart. M.P ./ of Hawkstone Park. Shropshire* (ink).

Pale blue eyes, grey powdered hair, lime-green jacket.

Collections: Sir Edward Durning-Lawrence,[1] by whom presented 1907.

Exhibition: *Russell*, Imperial Institute, South Kensington, 1894(46) lent Lawrence.

Reference: Williamson 1894, pp.52, 151.

Russell, a Methodist convert, stayed with the Hills at Hawkstone in 1780; see Rowland Hill below.

1 In 1894 Williamson, *loc. cit.*, recounted that Edward Lawrence (cr. Bt. 1898, when he assumed the additional name of Durning) had bought a large portfolio of original Russell sketches at a sale 'some time since'.

745 see Groups, *The House of Commons 1793-94* by KARL ANTON HICKEL 1793-95

HILL, Rowland 1744-1833

Evangelist, 6th s. of Sir Rowland Hill, 1st Bt, of Hawkstone Park, Salop.; an unorthodox preacher, ordained 1773, but never attained Anglican priesthood; a chapel was built for him at Wotton, Glos., and another in 1783 in London, the Surrey Chapel, where he was buried; founded the London Missionary Society 1799.

'He was rather above the middle height in stature, and when young was remarkably thin, though wonderfully strong and active. His countenance was expressive of the complexion of his mind, and the play upon his lips and piercing look of his small grey eyes, denoted both intelligence and humour. When between fifty and sixty years of age his fine upright figure, combined with a high-bred, gentleman-like deportment, caused him to be the subject of general admiration' (Edwin Sidney, 1834).

Abbreviation

Sidney 1834: E. Sidney, *Life of Rev Rowland Hill*, 1834

1464 JOHN RUSSELL c.1780-83

Pastel on blue laid paper 31.5 x 26.5 (12⅜ x 10⅜) maximum, unevenly cut edges; laid down on board 1998; inscribed, upper left: *Revd R Hill.*

Blue eyes, grey hair, white neckcloth and black coat.

Collections: Sir Edward Durning-Lawrence,[1] by whom presented 1907.

Exhibition: *Russell*, Imperial Institute, South Kensington, 1894(47) lent Lawrence.

Reference: Williams 1894, pp.52, 151.

Russell, a Methodist convert, first heard Rowland Hill preach in 1772, and his diary records visiting Mr (later Sir) Richard Hill at Hawkstone in August 1780.[2]

NPG 1464 would appear to be a preparatory study for the standing three-quarter length pastel of Hill, his right hand pointing at an open Bible, engraved by J. Collyer* in 1783.[3] Derivative bust-length ovals were also engraved by I. Lovelace 1790 and I. Farn 1796.

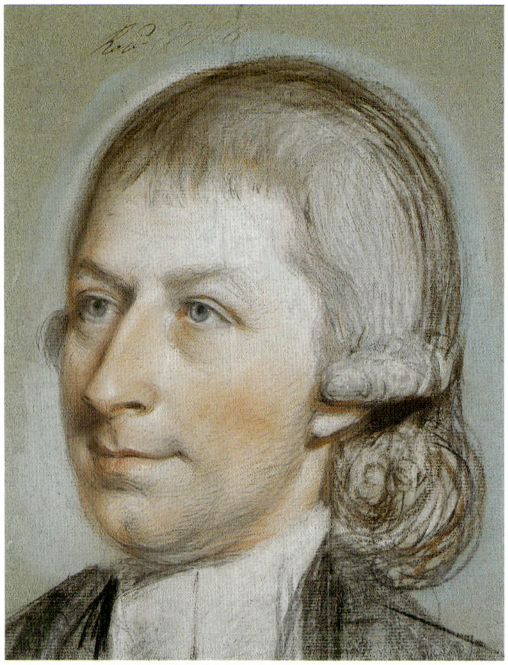

Rowland HILL NPG *1464*

1 In 1894 Williamson, *loc. cit.*, recounted that Edward Lawrence (cr. Bt. 1898, when he assumed the additional name of Durning) had bought a large portfolio of original Russell sketches at a sale 'some time since'.
2 When he found the discussion of Wesley a little too much (Williamson 1894, pp.46, 51).
3 Russell's 'portrait of a clergyman' exhibited RA 1782(370) drew the contemporary comment: 'Sure this should be the resemblance of good Sir Rowland Hill?' (Whitley 1928, II, p.394). Sir Rowland Hill, 1st Bt, who d. August 1783, was not a clergyman and spent his later ears trying to moderate his sons' enthusiasm.

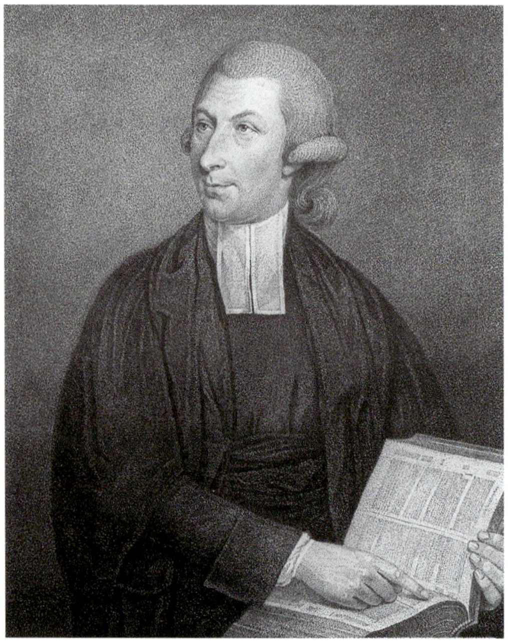

Rowland HILL *J. Collyer 1783 after John Russell* (NPG D *13800*)

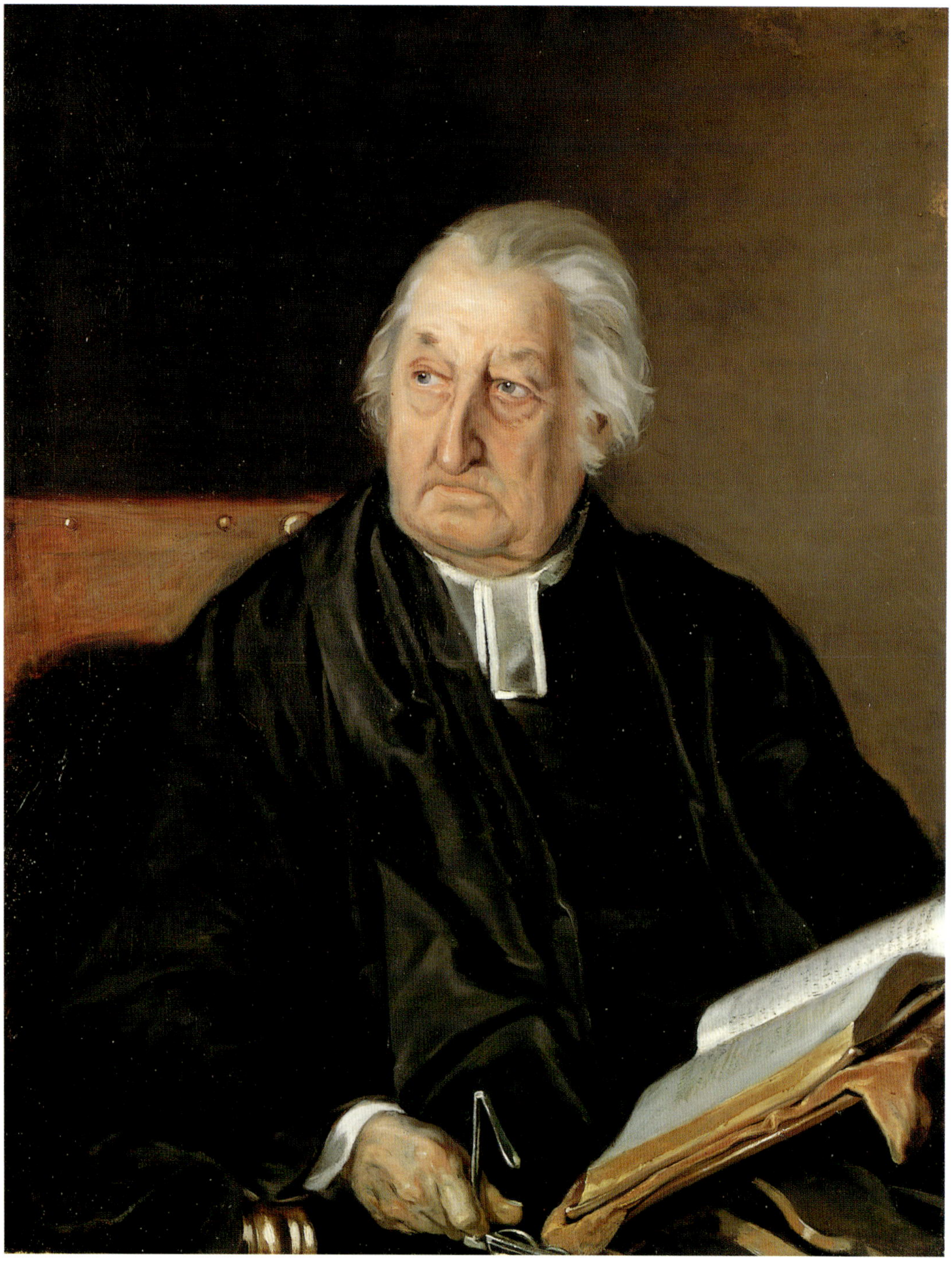

Rowland HILL NPG *5397*

5397 SAMUEL MOUNTJOY SMITH 1828

Canvas 91.5 x 71 (36 x 28); signed and dated, lower right: *S.M. Smith / 1828.*

Blue eyes, own white hair, seated in a pink backed chair, wearing black gown and bands, his spectacles in his right hand and an open book with a gilt fore-edge resting on a lectern covered with a pink cloth.

Collections: Presented by the Rev J.C. Hill, Newport, 1981.

Engravings: T. Lupton 1828; H. Robinson 1834 (*from a portrait in the possession of General the Lord Hill*).

This may be a copy of the 1828 portrait copying the signature as well; it is very breezily painted. A version is in New College, London, and another anonymous engraving uses the same head in a half-length wearing a black 'biretta'.

1401 UNKNOWN ARTIST c.1850?

Painted plaster 38.5 (15⅛) high, including socle 8 (3⅛) high; the surface is chipped on the right at the bottom of the gown and is generally grimy.

Collections: George Pool;[1] bt. Draper; his son, Francis Draper, by whom presented 1905.[2]

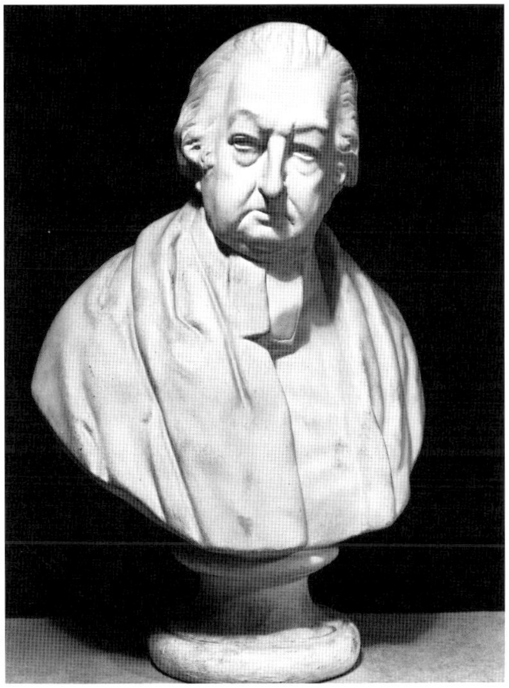

Rowland HILL NPG *1401*

A slight, posthumous image, probably modelled from the engraving by H. Robinson after S.M. Smith (see NPG 5397). 'Vigo of High Holborn' [A.L. Vago?], or the antiquary John Smith have previously been suggested as the modeller.[3]

1 Of 77b Great Queen St., London.
2 Francis Draper was the framemaker for the NPG; the provenance as given by him in a letter of 13 June 1905 (NPG archive).
3 Anon. [probably c.1910] note, and conversation of John Smith's grandson with C.K. Adams, 6 December 1940; both NPG archive.

ICONOGRAPHY

c.1765-70 Anon. engraving, half-length oval standing preaching his arms raised, lettered *Rowland Hill M.A. of the University of Cambridge*.

c.1770-75 Anon. engraving, pub. Carrington Bowles, three-quarter length standing preaching in open fields.

1773 Anon. engraving, bust-length profile, pub. Carington Bowles 1773 (CS, IV, p.1732, no.83). Deriving from this head, a reduced anon. plate for the *Gospel Mag.* 1774, and the *New Spiritual Mag.* 1784.

1774 Drawn (*from the life*) and engraved by J. Wilson, half-length standing.

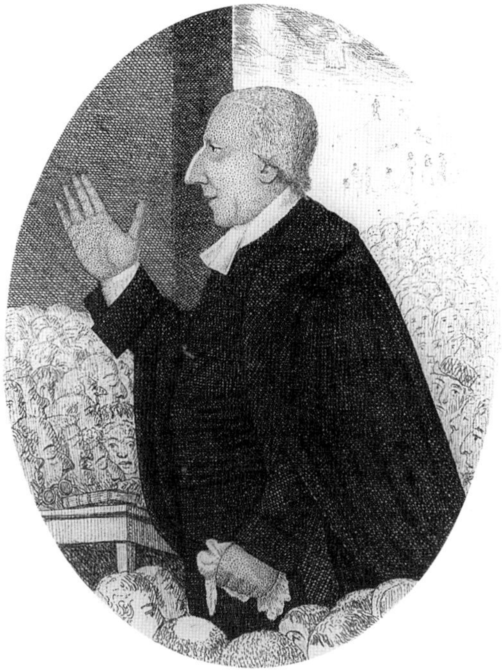

Rowland HILL etching by J. Kaye 1798 (NPG D 13801)

c.1780-83 Pastels by John Russell, see NPG 1464.

before 1791 Unattributed miniature, bust-length oval. Royal Collection (Walker 1992, no.257). Engraved anon. 1791, lettered *Minister of the Gospel Surry Chapel* (*Christian Mag.*). Closely related to the head by Russell NPG 1464.

1792 Drawing by I. Lovelace, three-quarter length seated, a paper in his left hand, engraved Springsguth 1792. The head related to a bust-length oval *I. Lovelace del. et sculpt. 1790*.

1798 Etching by J. Kay,* half-length oval, preaching (*Kay's Portraits* 1842, I, p.333). Looking older than his years; taken on the occasion of Hill's first visit to Scotland (he returned in 1799 and 1824).

1799 Painting by Theophilus Clarke, half length in gown and bands, engraved W. Bond 1799 (illus. Smith 1905, f.p.161).

1802 Painting by Joseph Robinson, half length in civilian dress, exhibited RA 1802(803). Engraved R.M. Meadows 1803, the book inscribed *Village Dialogues* [published 1801]. A similar head with longer hair, wearing gown and bands, engraved S. Freeman 1815.

c.1807 Pastel by James Sharples, profile head. Bristol CMAG (*Cat. of the Sharples Coll.*, Bristol, 1910, no.40). Ellen Sharples recorded in January 1808 copying her husband's portrait of Hill 'lately executed'; there had been 'many copies previosuly done of him' (Knox 1930, p.119).

1808 Bust-length oval profile, within a view of the Wotton Chapel drawn by J. Ker; engraved J. Barlow 1808; J. Chapman.

1811 Wax by T.R. Poole. Sotheby's, 10 June 1993, lot 229. See also 1820 below.

1814 Painting by Michael Keeling, half length in gown and bands. Exhibited NPE 1867(57) lent by the 2nd Viscount Hill. A related reversed engraving by T. Blood 1813.

1814 Painting by Samuel Drummond, exhibited RA 1815(289). Engraved T. Blood 1814; J. Jenkins, half length in gown and bands.

1817 Drawing by John Linnell, half-length seated, engraved S. Freeman 1817. Linnell's diary records this drawing and a duplicate in 1817 (see D. Linnell, *The Life of John Linnell*, 1994, p.386).

1820 Wax by T.R. Poole. Sotheby's, 21 October 1968, lot 99. See also 1811 above.

1822 Painting by William Derby, half-length seated in gown and bands, exhibited RA 1822(548). Engraved S. Freeman 1825 and 1831, the earlier probably the print in circulation during the winter of 1826-27 which 'met with so large a share of the public approbation that I fear the print recently published by you will meet with a dull sale, at least in this metropolis' (see Sidney 1834, p.330).

1827 Drawing by M. Rebecca Sheppard [M.R.S], three-quarter length seated, engraved J. Linnell. Hill told Miss Sheppard 'you have hit me off very correctly' (see Sidney 1834, pp.326-30).

1828 Painting by S.M. Smith, see NPG 5397.

1829 Bust by N. Palmer, exhibited RA 1829(1169).

Posthumous

1833 Bust by R. Harper, exhibited SBA 1833 (838).

1833 Anon. medal, draped bust (Brown 1980, no.1650).

1833 Death mask by J.S. Deville. 'One of the most beautiful casts I ever saw was taken of [Hill] after his decease, by the well-known phrenologist Deville, ... this beautiful bust, in possession of the celebrated phrenologist ... made an indelible impression on my memory' (Sidney 1834, pp.404-05).

c.1833 'Drawn from Life & on stone by G.M.Z.', medallion head to left in gown and bands, inscribed: ... *Obiit 11th April 1833 aetat 89 years*.

c.1850? Unattributed bust, see NPG 1401.

Undated Portrait bust from the Coade manufactory (Gunnis 1968, p.106).

Painting attributed to Opie, small seated half length, with long white hair, Sotheby's, 9 May 1951, lot 60 (cf. Rogers 1878, p.109); pastel, Sotheby's, Summers Place, 10 February 1998, lot 1175; painting by John Downman, exhibited RA 1804(448), described as *Rev Mr Hill aet 94 1803* (Williamson 1904, p.lx); half-length figure by Charles Harris, see *Statues of Charles Harris* 1985 (photocopy in NAL); engraving by H. Brocas (1762-1837), listed by Strickland 1913, I, p.90.

HILL-TREVOR, Anne, see MORNINGTON

HINCHLIFFE, John 1731-94

Prelate; in Italy 1761-62; DD 1764 Trinity College, Cambridge; headmaster of Westminster School 1764, resigning after three months through ill-health; tutor to the 5th Duke of Devonshire 1764-66; Master of Trinity College, Cambridge 1768-88; Bishop of Peterborough 1769-94; Dean of Durham 1788-94; known for the pronunciation of his consonants.

5563 NATHANIEL HONE 1757

Canvas 74.5 x 61.5 (29¼ x 24¼) lined; cleaned 1983; a general craquelure particularly evident in the darker areas; signed, lower left: *NH / 1757*. Inscribed verso: *John Hinchliffe / afterwards Bp. Of Peterboro' / By Hone / H.J.H. 20th June 1839*.[1]

Brown eyes, grey powdered hair, in black academic dress worn over a deep-blue suit; a red-fore-edged book in his left hand (which is unfinished).

Collections: [H.J. Hinchliffe] Sotheby's, 2 March 1983, lot 45, bt. Leggatt for the NPG.

Reference: A. Le Harivel, *Nathaniel Hone*, 1992, pp.11, 13.

Painted in the year Hinchliffe received his MA from Cambridge.

1 H.J.H. was presumably Henry John Hinchliffe (1768-1848), the sitter's son.

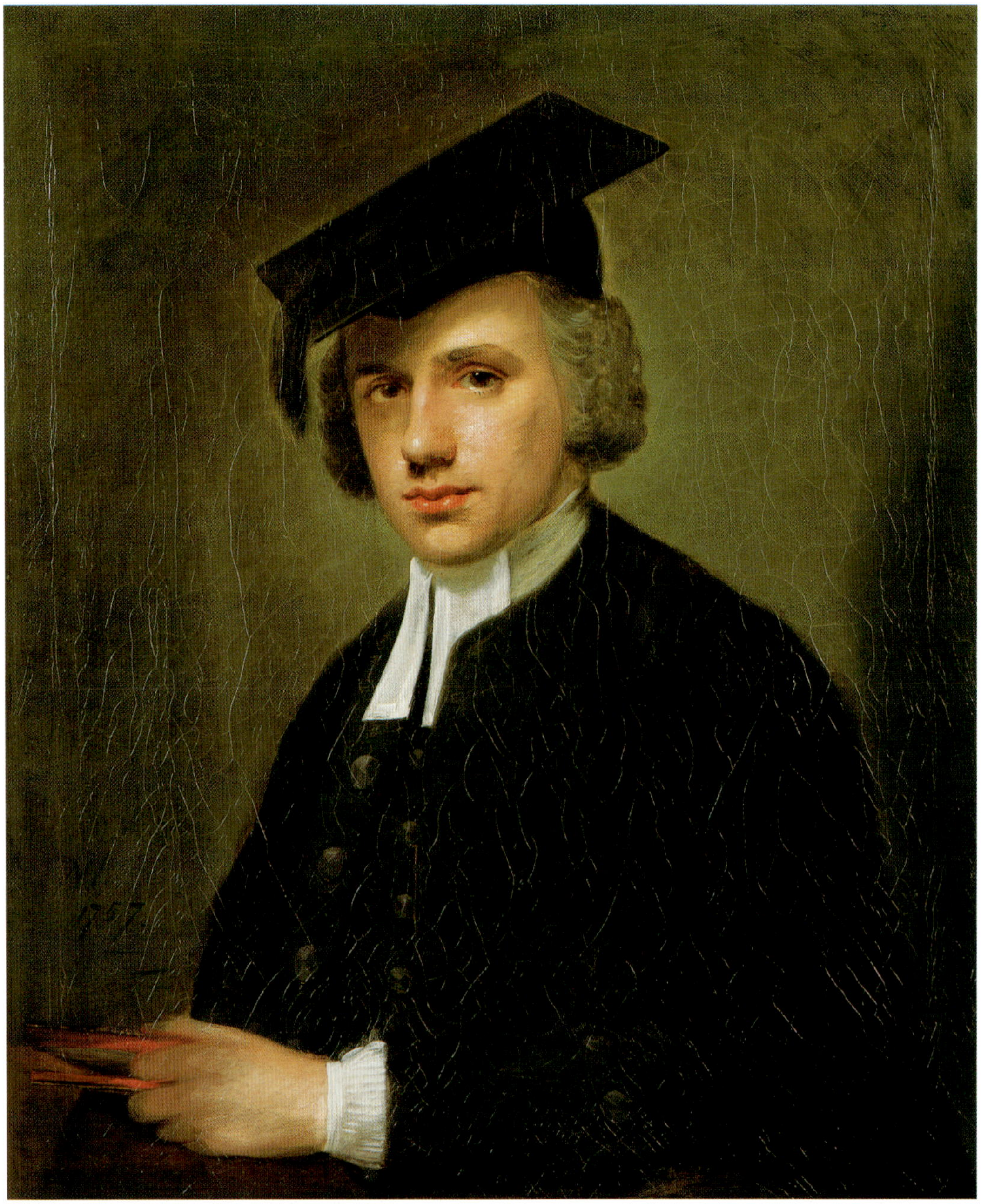

HINCHCLIFFE NPG 5563

ICONOGRAPHY

1757 Painting by Nathaniel Hone, see NPG 5563.

1758 Miniature enamel by Nathaniel Hone, exhibited SKM 1865(2971) lent Emilius Clayton.

1764 Painting by Nathaniel Hone, half length in gown and bands. Private collection. Exhibited SA 1765(52). A replica in the Bishop's Palace, Peterborough (inscribed with his arms as Bishop: for Hinchliffe, *a wyvern betw. three fleur-de-lys)*.

1777 Drawing by John Downman, half length, wearing a Bishop's rochet and chimere. Fitzwilliam Museum, Cambridge (1802). Three drawings by Downman of Mrs Hinchliffe, also dated 1777, are in the same collection (1803-1805).

1779-81 Painting by J.S. Copley,* *The Death of Chatham*, see Comparative Groups. A preliminary drawing of Hinchliffe's head,* inscribed: *To the corner of the eye 5 feet 2½ inches.* Wadsworth

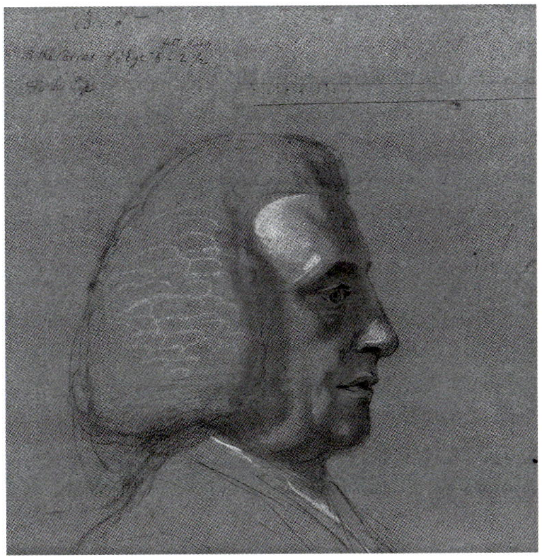

HINCHLIFFE by J.S. Copley 1779-81 (Wadsworth Atheneum, Hartford)

Athenaeum, Hartford, Conn. (1947.365); a copy of the head attributed to Bartolozzi is in the Metropolitan Museum of Art, New York (55.106.3; illus. *Metropolitan Museum of Art Bulletin*, XIV, 1956, p.122).

1781 Painting by Benjamin Van der Gucht, half length in rochet and chimere. Bishop's Palace, Peterborough (illus. Ingamells 1981, fig.128). Exhibited RA 1781(165). Engraved anon. 1781 pub. I. Walker, and anon. 1781 (reversed bust-length oval).

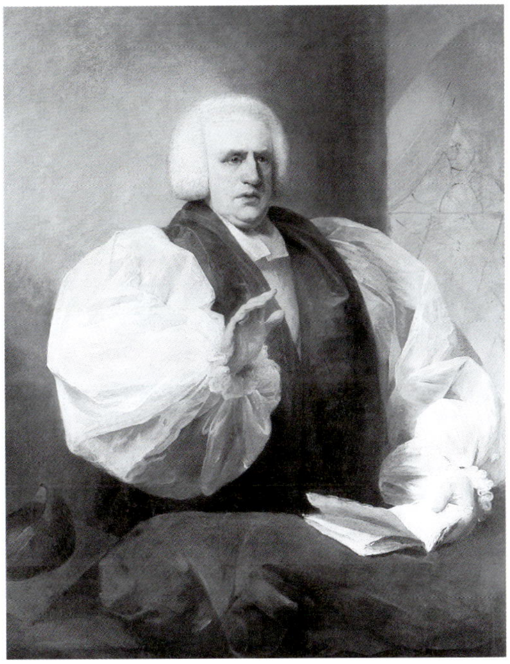

HINCHLIFFE by M.W. Peters 1787-88 (Trinity College, Cambridge)

1787-88 Painting by M.W. Peters,* wearing rochet and chimere, preaching from a raised pulpit. Trinity College, Cambridge. Exhibited NPE 1867(671). Engraved J. Young 1788.

1793 Engraving by W.H. Brown, *drawn from the life*, bust-length oval (*The Senator*).

Undated two drawings by John Greenwood, profile heads. British Museum (1866.7.14.22 & 23).

DOUBTFUL PORTRAIT

Anon. engraving of c.1781, bust-length roundel *accurately engraved from an Original Picture taken from the Life*.

HOLLAND, Charles 1733-69

Actor; played at Drury Lane from 1755 and at Bristol, with William Powell, 1767-69; d. in London of smallpox, George Garrick, David's brother, being one of his executors; he had a certain reputation for gallantry.

'his figure is agreeable; his features well-proportioned, and pleasingly disposed. Some tones of his voice, which is not strong, remind us of that of Mr Garrick, which it resembles' (anon. critic, c.1758-60).

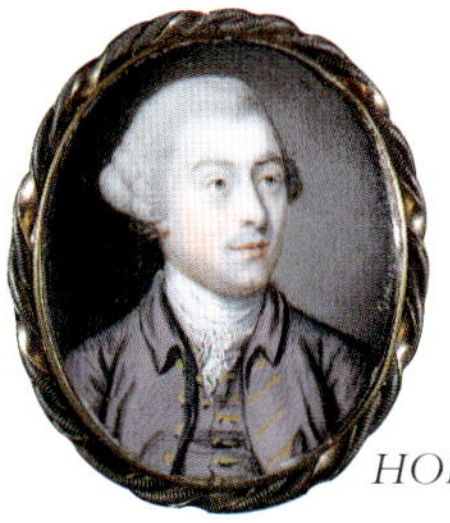

HOLLAND NPG 6287

6287 J.H. 1760

Watercolour and bodycolour on ivory 4 x 3.2 (1½ x 1¼); signed *J.H. 1760* lower right. The unusual frame is of a gilt twisted ribbon and silver rope pattern.

Brown eyes, light powdered hair, wearing a pale purple suit.

Collections: Alan Evans, bequeathed to the National Gallery; lent to the NPG 1974 until permanently transferred 1994.

Reference: Walker 1998, no.47.

The signature has hitherto been interpreted as that of Joseph Hutchinson who was aged thirteen in 1760. A similar head appears in the painting by H.B., c.1765-70, in the Garrick Club, see below.

ICONOGRAPHY

1760 Miniature by J. H., see NPG 6287.

1760 Miniature by Charles Handyside, 'Mr Holland in the character of Tancred' [in *Cymbeline*], exhibited SA 1760(24).

c.1760 Engraving by J.S. Müller [J. Miller], bust-length oval (illus. Highfill, VII, p.367).

1762 Painting by P.E. Hauck, 'Mr Holland in the character of Jachimo in Cymbeline', exhibited SA 1762(37).

c.1765-70 Painting by H. B.,* half-length painted oval, engraved J.R. Smith 1771 as *H B pinxt*. Copy in the Garrick Club (Ashton 1997, no.301) attributed to Hugh Barron.

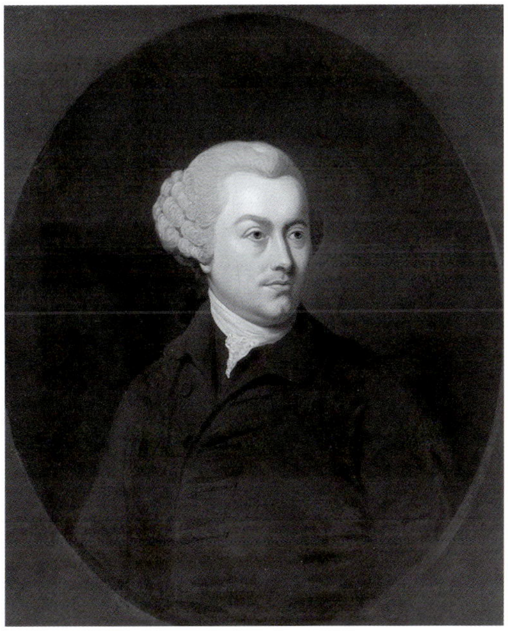

HOLLAND by H.B. c.1765-70 (Garrick Club)

A similar head appears in another engraving by J.R. Smith, three-quarter length, right hand in his waistcoat, left in his pocket (illus. Highfill, VII, p.369).

1769-70 Bust by William Tyler on Holland's monument. St Nicholas, Chiswick. The monument engraved anon. c.1770 (with a blank panel left for an epitaph by Garrick).

DOUBTFUL PORTRAIT

Pastel by P.M. Barrat, dated 1772, Christie's, 12 February 1954, lot 57.

HOLLAND, Sir Nathaniel, 1st Bt, see DANCE

HOLROYD, John, see SHEFFIELD

HOME, John 1722-1808

Dramatic poet, of Leith, Edinburgh, a kinsman of David Hume; fought against the Jacobites 1745; minister of Athelstaneford, East Lothian, 1746, but he offended the Scottish kirk as a dramatist and resigned 1756; the success of his tragedy *Douglas* 1756 eventually led to patronage from the King and Lord Bute; his last work, *History of the Rebellion of 1745*, appeared in 1802.

'John Home was an admirable companion ... he was very handsome and had a fine person, about 5 feet 10½ inches, and an agreeable catching address; he had not much wit, and still less humour, but he had so much sprightliness and vivacity ... that he was truly irresistible and his entry to a company was like opening a window and letting the sun into a dark room' (Alexander Carlyle, 1860).

320 HENRY RAEBURN c.1795-1800

Twill canvas 75 x 62 (29½ x 24½) lined 1871; discoloured varnish; a repaired tear by his left arm; the original canvas was painted on the verso.[1]

Grey eyes, white hair; wearing a brown suit with brown buttons.

Collections: by descent to George Home and his nephew Charles Home, from whom purchased 1871.

Engraving: J.G. Mitchell, after 1822 (*from an original picture ... in the possession of Geo. Home ...*).

Home here appears slightly older than in the more ambitious kit-cat portrait by Raeburn (see below). The latter is generally identified as that exhibited at the RA in 1792 and is the better-known through engravings. A copy of NPG 320 is in the Scottish NPG (PG 1378).

1 'the back of the picture having been painted over, probably with the notion that such treatment would preserve the picture from damp' (J.L. Rutley, 3 March 1871; NPG archive).

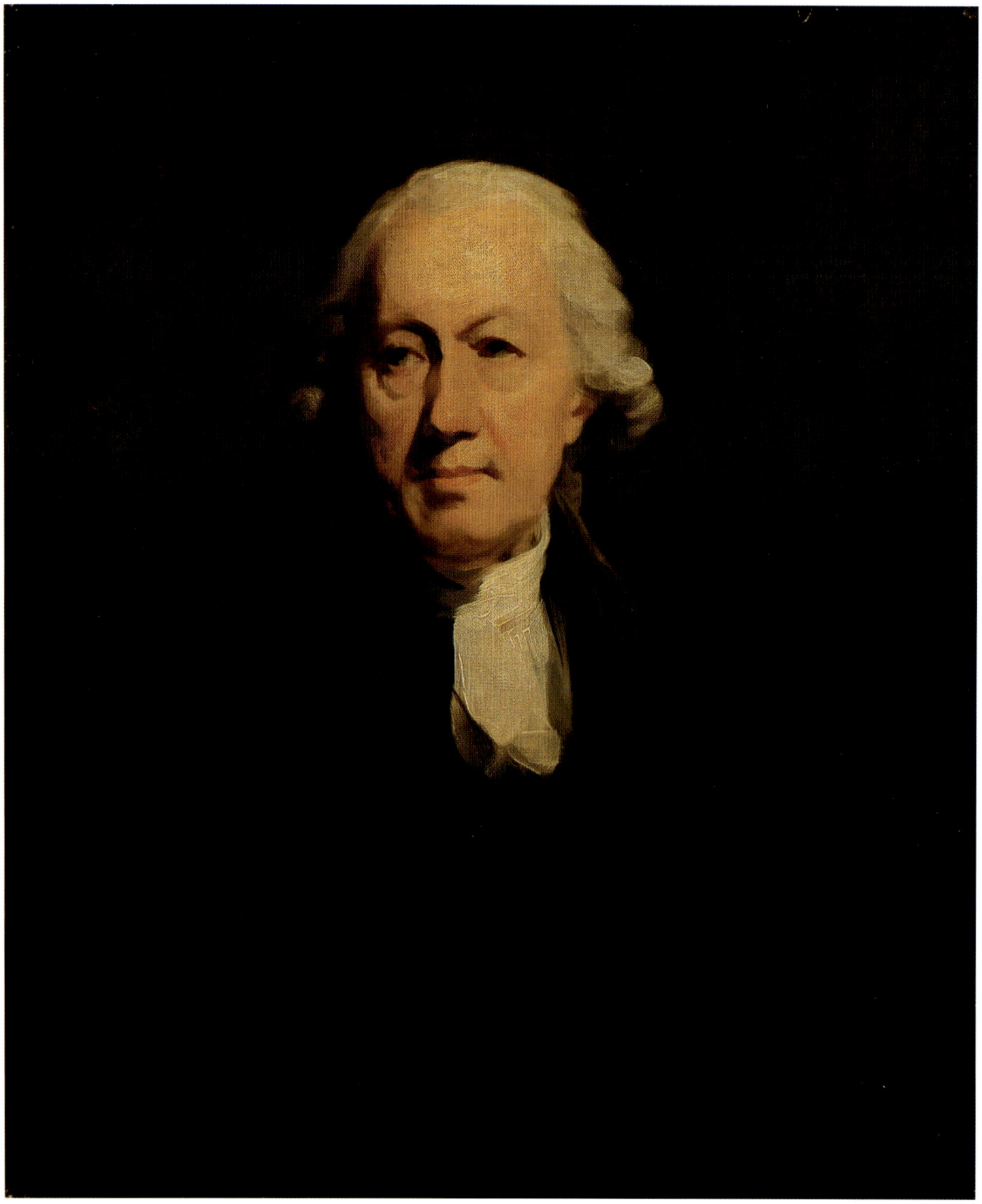

HOME NPG *320*

ICONOGRAPHY

1762 Painting by William Millar, half length. Scottish NPG (PG 1564).

1791 Medallion by James Tassie* (Gray 1894, no.192). Example Scottish NPG (PG 1253). Engraved W. Ridley 1804 (*European Mag.*).

1792 Painting by Henry Raeburn, kit-cat, seated. Christie's, Monaco, 15 June 1990, lot 34. Almost certainly the portrait exhibited RA 1792(395), see NPG 320 above; engraved A. Birrell 1799; C. Watson 1816 (from a drawing by W. Evans, from an original in the possession of Sir John Macpherson); Haig; J. Rogers 1855.

Another version by Raeburn sold Phillips, 15 December 1987, lot 48; a crude-looking version, exhibited NPE 1868(823) lent Lord Binning, sold Christie's, 18 March 1921, lot 51, and a weak bust-length sold Sotheby's, 12 November 1958, lot 191. A version showing an ink well on a table to the left, engraved J. Stewart 1822 (as then belonging to Sir G. Warrender).

c.1795-1800 Painting by Henry Raeburn, see NPG 320.

1797 Painting by Anthony Stewart, half-length oval, his own short hair; engraved E. Mitchell 1797.

1799 Painting by Samuel Drummond, half-length oval; engraved W. Ridley 1799.

Undated Unattributed miniature. Scottish NPG (PG 1209).

DOUBTFUL PORTRAITS

Painting by John Hoppner, called John Home of Wedderburn, half length, formerly with Knoedler, London (Witt photo). Anon. oval half-length engraving in gown and bands, c.1750.

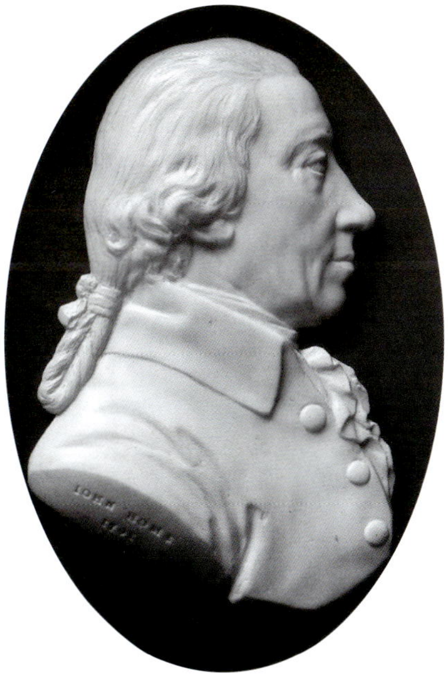

HOME by James Tassie 1791 (Scottish National Portrait Gallery)

HONE, Nathaniel 1718-84

Painter and miniaturist; b. Dublin; m. 1742 in York Mary Earle, an heiress; settled in London by 1748; ceased miniature painting in the 1760s, turning to life-size oils; a director of the SA 1766, where he exhibited 1760-68; foundation member of the RA 1768; in 1775 he exhibited his 'Pictorial Conjurer, Displaying the Whole Art of Optical Deception' (National Gallery of Ireland), a thinly-veiled criticism of Reynolds's plagiarisms.

'[a] tall, upright, large man, with a broad-rimmed hat and a lapelled coat buttoned up to his stock, with measured and stately steps' (J.T. Smith, 1828).

1878 SELF PORTRAIT c.1755

Enamel on copper 3.2 x 2.8 (1½ x 1⅛) oval; signed verso: *Nat Hone / Pictor / NH Pinx*.

Blue eyes, white powdered air, wearing a golden yellow coat and waistcoat.

Collections: bequeathed by H.V. Metcalfe[1] 1920.

Exhibition: *Kauffmann* 1968(286).

Reference: A. Le Harivel, *Nathaniel Hone*, 1992, p.27 as c.1750.

A date of c.1755 is suggested on comparison with the dated miniature of 1749, see below, which appears to show a younger man.

1 Possibly a descendant; Hone's niece Mary married a Dr Metcalfe.

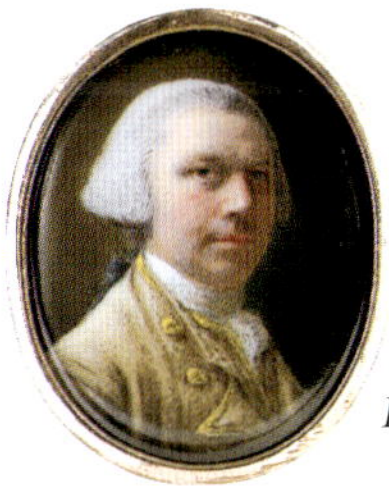

HONE NPG 1878

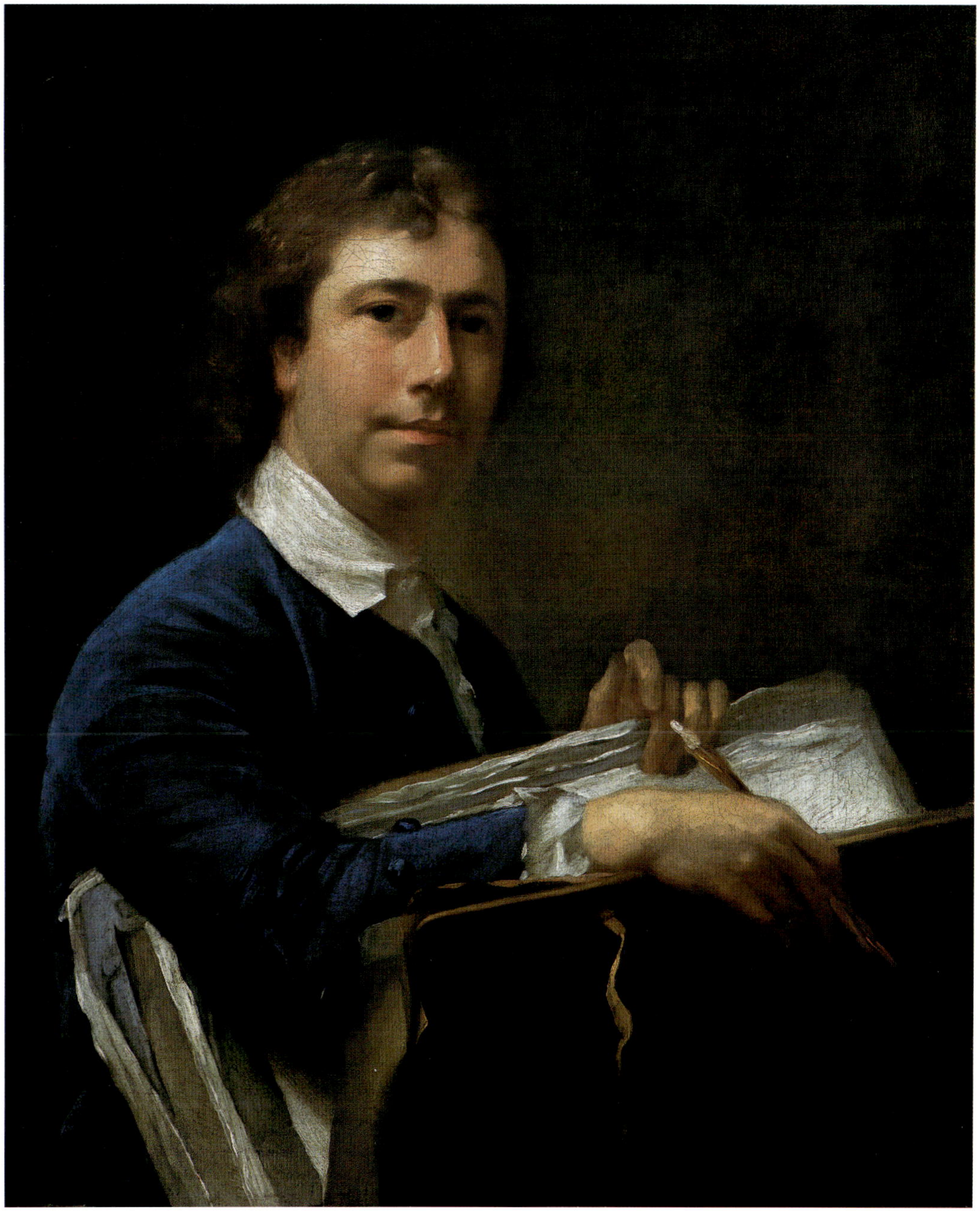

HONE NPG 177

177 SELF PORTRAIT c.1760

Canvas 75 x 61.5 (29½ x 24¼); lined; cleaned 1989; the surface is worn and there is an old damage behind the left hand.

Grey eyes, brown hair; wearing a dark blue coat; the folder contains blue and white sheets.

Collections: Purchased from J.H. Chance (framemaker) 1864.

Reference: A. Le Harivel, *Nathaniel Hone*, 1992, p.22.

Acquired in 1864 as probably a portrait of the painter Richard Wilson,[1] but by 1879 it was described as Nathaniel Hone,[2] an identification which is above suspicion. NPG 177 appears contemporary with the self portrait in the National Gallery of Ireland (1003), see below.

1 Letters from J.H. Chance, 23 March 1864 and his agent H. Merritt, 24 March 1864; NPG archive.
2 NPG cats. 1866 as Wilson, and 1879 as Hone.

ICONOGRAPHY

Self Portraits

'Hone was a vain man and his numerous Self Portraits show his limited range at its fullest' (E.K. Waterhouse, *Painting in Britain 1530-1790*, 1953, p.183).

1747 Painting, half length wearing a fur cap with a chain over his left shoulder; engraved by Hone, lettered *ipse pinxit 1747* ... (illus. *Rembrandt in 18th century England*, New Haven, 1983, pl.12, and see p.29).

1749 Miniature, half-length oval in Van Dyck dress, fingering a miniature at his breast. Christie's, 26 June 1980, lot 90. Exhibited SKM 1865(245) lent G.A. Larby.

Another enamel miniature, said to be signed and dated 1749, exhibited SKM 1865(1940) lent J.H. Anderdon.

1749 Miniature, bust-length wearing a beaver hat, a gold chain over his right shoulder. Clarke collection (illus. *Clarke Collection Miniatures*, Scottish NPG, 2001, no.33). The features do not readily agree with those seen in other self-portrait miniatures of 1747 and 1749.

c.1750-60 Chalk drawing, half-length oval, at his drawing board. British Museum (1890.10.3.16). A similarly posed painting, not apparently by Hone, sold Christie's New York, 15 January 1986, lot 74.

c.1755 Miniature, see NPG 1878.

c.1760 Painting, see NPG 177.

c.1760 Painting,* standing half length before an easel, supporting a folio with his left hand. NG of Ireland (1003). Engraved E. Fisher. A replica exhibited *British Self Portraits*, Arts Council, 1962(25) lent Mrs Arnold Willis.

c.1760-65 Painting, half-length pointing to his first wife's portrait behind him. NG of Ireland (196). A comparable portrait of his first wife dated 1760, sold Christie's, 27 March 1981, lot 142.

1760-69 Miniature, half length, wearing a scarlet coat with gold lace. Christie's, 11 December 1957, lot 48 as dated *176* .

c.1765 Painting,* half-length painted oval, wearing a broad-brimmed hat, in Van Dyck dress. Royal Academy. Exhibited NPE 1867(524); *British Self Portraits*, Arts Council, 1962(26); *Genial Company*, Nottingham/Scottish NPG, 1987(43).

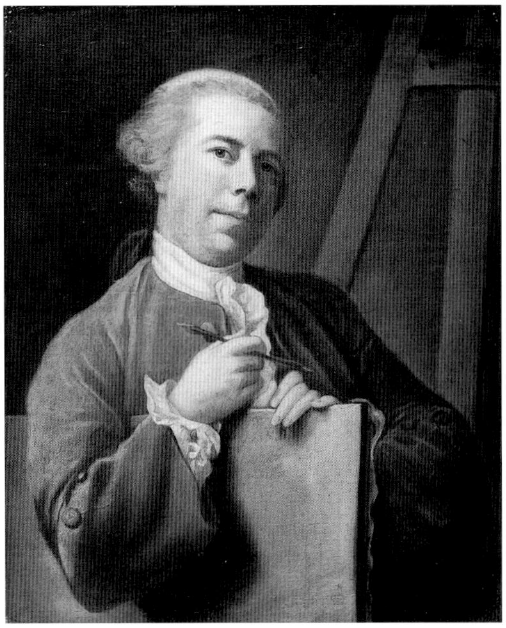

HONE *Self portrait c.1760 (National Gallery, of Ireland)*

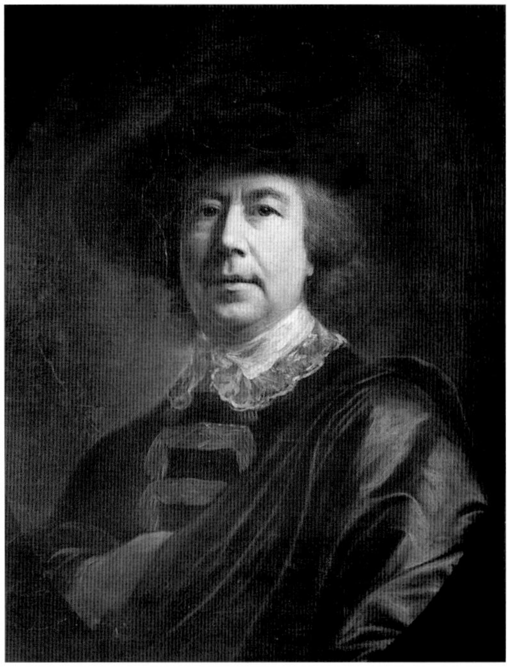

HONE *Self portrait c.1765 (Royal Academy of Arts, London)*

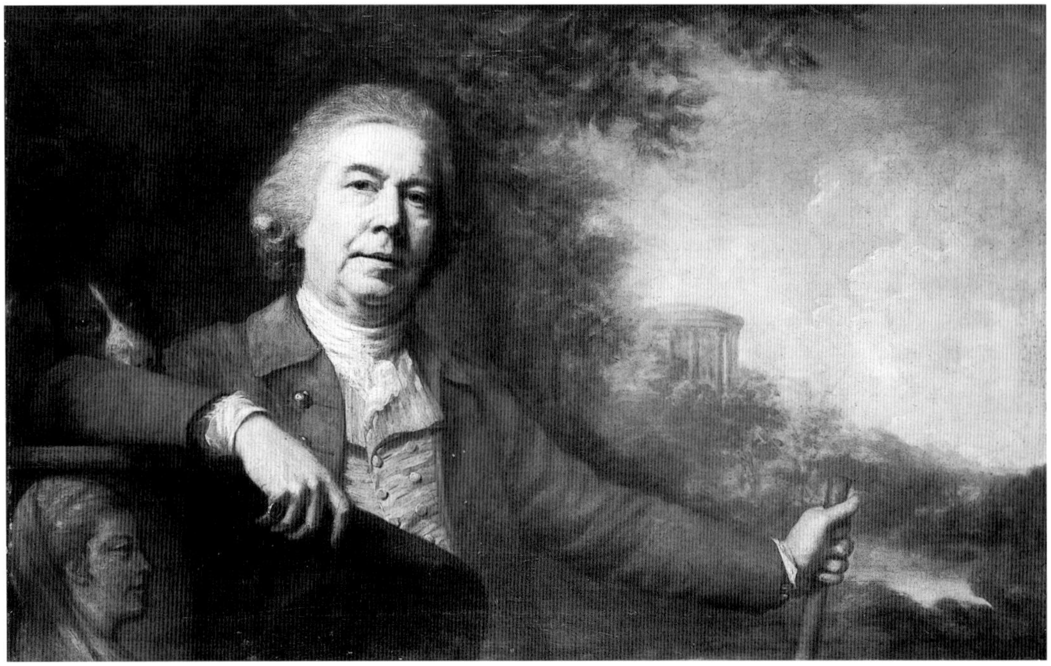

HONE *Self portrait c.1775 (National Gallery of Ireland)*

c.1775 Painting,* half-length seated in a landscape, his right arm resting on a bas-relief of his [first] wife; a distant view inspired by the temple of Tivoli. NG of Ireland (886). Exhibited *British Self Portraits*, Arts Council, 1962(27). It is probable that the bas-relief indicates the death of Hone's first wife, see 1778 below.

1778 Painting, half length wearing a broad-brimmed hat. Manchester CAG (1928.75). Probably the self portrait exhibited RA 1779(144). In 1777 Hone remarried a Mrs Tinswood of Petworth (d.1791).

Undated Mezzotint, half length wearing a turban, laughing and pointing (CS 4). Possibly late 1740s.

Portraits by other artists

1772 Painting by Johann Zoffany,* *The Academicians of the Royal Academy*, see Groups NPG 1437.

c.1780-84 Drawing by Paul Sandby, profile head, one of the series of heads drawn at print sales. Royal Collection (Oppé 1947, no.417/10, fig.24). Engraved anon.,* *Sketches taken at Print Sales*, see Comparative Groups.

DOUBTFUL PORTRAITS

Two miniatures of c.1750, bust-length ovals in Van Dyck costumes (Rosenbach Foundation, Philadelphia); miniature of an elderly man (Walters sale, Parke-Bernet, New York, 30 November-4 December 1943, lot 787); drawing, signed *NH 1764*, a young man drawing (British Museum, 1890.10.13.17), probably shows one of the artist's sons.

HOOLE, John 1727-1803

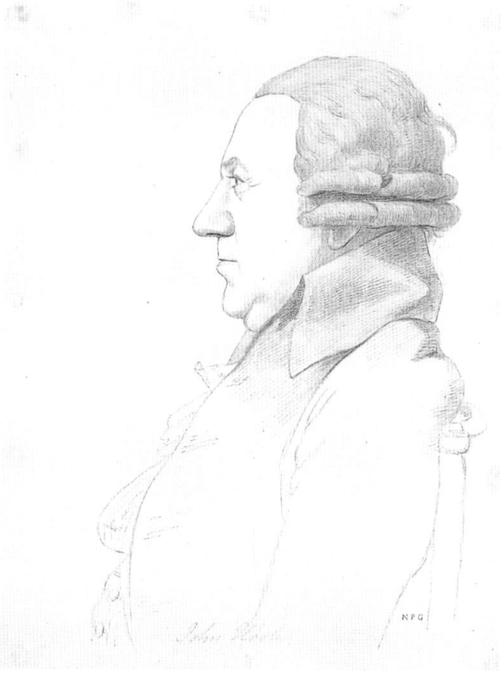

HOOLE NPG *3089(9)*

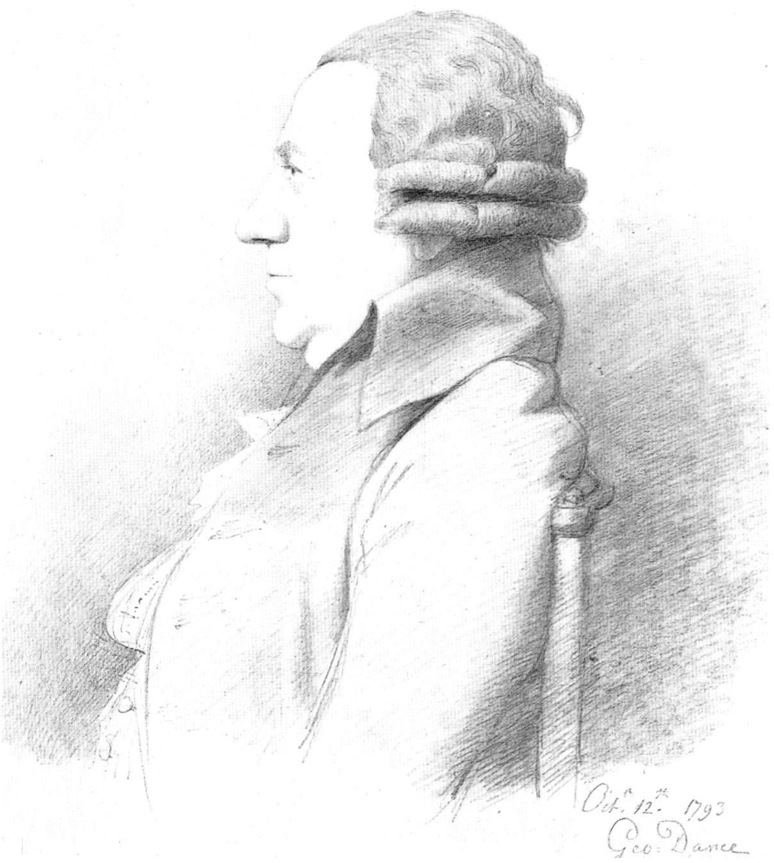

HOOLE NPG *1143*

Translator of Tasso's *Gerusalemme liberata* 1763 and Ariosto's *Orlando Furioso* 1773, 1785; until 1785 an accountant in the East India House, of which he was once termed 'the great boast and ornament'.

'His character may be comprised in a few words: gentle, unassuming, and affectionate' (William Daniell, 1814).

1143 GEORGE DANCE 1793

Pencil with traces of pink on the cheeks and lips, on paper 31 x 23 (12¼ x 9⅛) faded and stained; signed and dated in pencil lower right: *Octr.12th.1793 / Geo: Dance*; laid down on a contemporary washed mount lettered: *JOHN HOOLE*.

Collections: The artist's grandson, the Rev George Dance; his sale Christie's, 1 July 1898, lot 71, bt. Colnaghi for the NPG.

Engraving: W. Daniell 1810 (*Dance Portraits*).

3089(9) WILLIAM DANIELL after GEORGE DANCE [1793]

Pencil with the outlines drawn over in red crayon, on paper 25.5 x 19.5 (10 x 7¾) laid down on paper, on card; irregular perforations round the edges, slight staining; inscribed below in pencil: *John Hoole*; NPG stamp lower left.

Engraving: See NPG 1143 above.

Collections, Reference: see Appendix II.

For Dance's original drawing, see NPG 1143.

ICONOGRAPHY

1768 Painting by Frances Reynolds (Leslie & Taylor 1865, I, p.92). A painting called Hoole, school of Reynolds, standing three-quarter length by a bust, sold Sotheby Parke Bernet, New York, 6 December 1980, lot 55, remains unverified.

1784 Drawing by Ozias Humphry, half-length seated

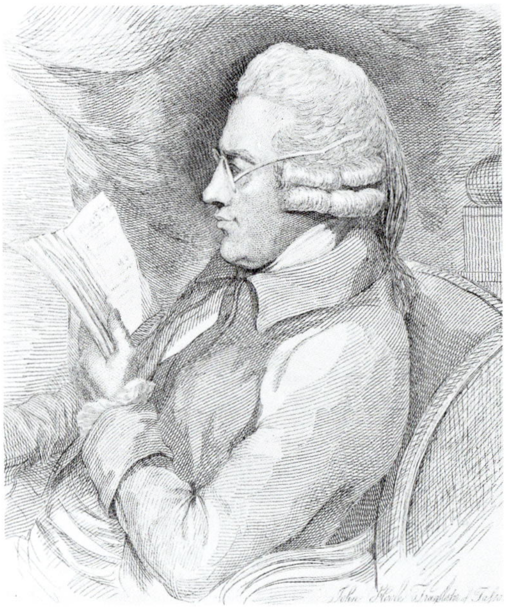

HOOLE *Mrs D. Turner after Ozias Humphry 1784 (NPG D 18001)*

reading. Francis Wellesley sale, Sotheby's, 30 June 1920, lot 462. Pencil copy in the Victoria and Albert Museum (E.1112.1927), etched by Mrs Dawson Turner.*

1792 Engraving by A. Smith, half-length oval, with wig and spectacles (*European Mag.*).

1793 Drawing by George Dance, see NPG 1143.

HORNE, John, see TOOKE

HORSLEY, Samuel 1733-1806

Prelate; Bishop of St David's 1788-93, Rochester 1793-1802 and St Asaph 1802-06; Dean of Westminster and Dean of the Order of the Bath 1793-1802; FRS 1767 and secretary 1773-76; apart from theological tracts, published the works of Isaac Newton 1785 and papers on astronomy and Euclid; member of Dr Johnson's Club 1783.

[at the age of seventeen] 'his eyes and his complexion dark as a raven, his nose even set, his brows begin to shew that they are somewhat capable of assuming his father's frown' (William Cleghorn, 1750).

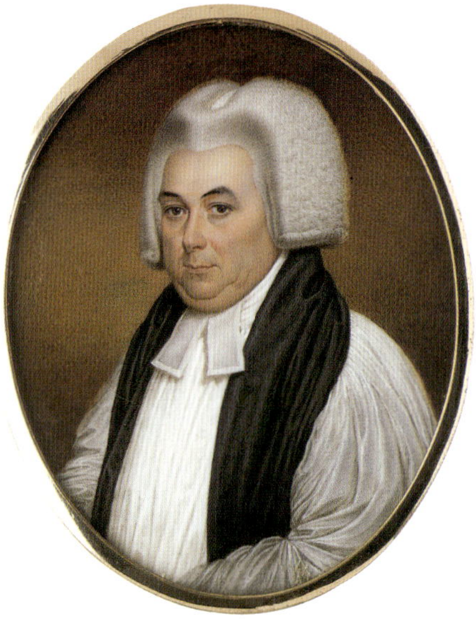

HORSLEY NPG 155

155 WALTER STEPHENS LETHBRIDGE c.1803

Watercolour and bodycolour on ivory 8.5 x 6.8 (3⅜ x 2⅝). The original backing paper had affixed the trade label of *W.S. Lethbridge / Artist / 30 / Southampton Street / Strand.*

Brown eyes, white powdered wig, wearing a Bishop's rochet and chimere.

Collections: Purchased from William Mannin[1] 1863.

Exhibition: RA 1803(870).

NPG 155 was presumably the miniature Lethbridge exhibited at the RA in 1803. In 1863 Mannin said it was painted 'not long before the Bishop's death, and was ... exhibited at the Royal Academy'; he also said that Lethbridge had offered it for sale to the Bishop's family without success (they 'having several other portraits of the Bishop in their possession').[2]

A half-length canvas copy is in the Westminster Deanery.[3]

1 Who was 'intimately acquainted' with Lethbridge; 'shortly after' the latter's death NPG 155 (with NPG 156, see John Wolcot) 'came into my possession, in which they have remained ever since' (Mannin to Scharf, 26 January 1863; NPG archive).
2 W. Mannin to Scharf, 26 January 1863; NPG archive.
3 Exhibited NPE 1867(625); accurately listed as 'bad' by Harding, II, p.131.

ICONOGRAPHY

1788-93 Miniature by S.T. Roche, half length in rochet and chimere (without the badge of the Bath, i.e. before 1793). Mrs Morris in 1822. Engraved J. Stow 1822 from a drawing by G.P. Harding (*Deans of Westminster*).

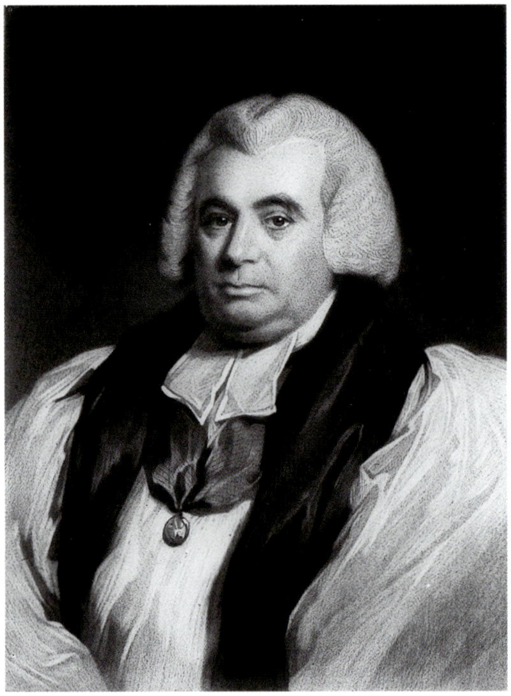

HORSLEY S.W. Reynolds after Mrs Barou 1799 (NPG D 3100)

1799 Miniature by Mrs Barou, bust length in rochet and chimere, with the badge of the Bath. Bayne-Powell sale, Sotheby's, 11 October 1994, lot 123 (illus. Foskett 1979, p.188, pl.43d). Exhibited RA 1799(719). Engraved S.W. Reynolds,* without artist's name.

c.1799 Drawing by Robert Dighton, half-length oval in rochet and chimere with the badge of the Bath,

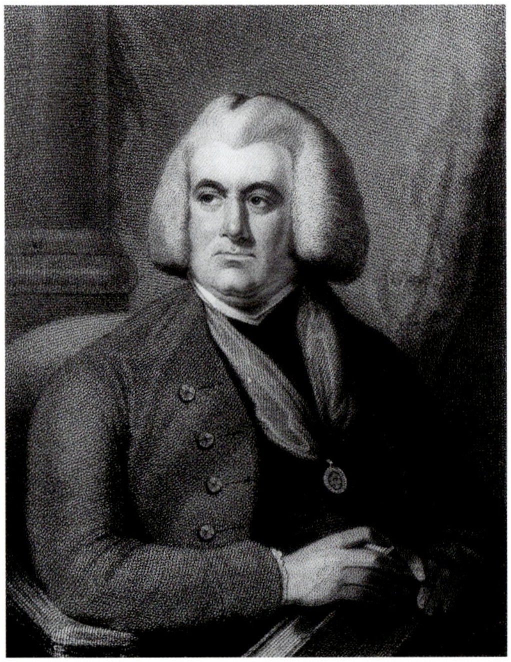

HORSLEY J. Godby after Ozias Humphry before 1802 (NPG D 13742)

engraved W.S. Leney 1799. A bust-length engraving by J. Owen 1799 (*Public Characters 1798-99*) evidently derived from Leney's print.

before 1802 Painting by James Green, half-length seated in rochet and chimere, wearing the badge of the Bath. Engraved H. Meyer 1813; T.A. Dean; H. Meyer (reduced).

before 1802 Painting by Ozias Humphry, half-length seated, a book in his hands, in private dress, wearing the ribbon and badge of the Bath. Engraved J. Godby;* T. Blood 1813 (*European Mag.*).

1802 Drawn and etched by Robert Dighton, whole length, in private dress; re-issued 1809.

c.1803 Miniature by W.S. Lethbridge, see NPG 155.

An unattributed miniature exhibited BFAC 1889(xxxviii 1) lent Miss Horsley Whiteman.

Horsley appears in a caricature drawing of 1795 by G.M. Woodward (d.1809) in the Royal Collection (Oppé 1950, no.682), *A Friendly discussion of Politics or Miracles of Human Wisdom and Understanding.*

HOWARD, Charles, see NORFOLK

HOWARD, John 1726?-90

Philanthropist, prison reformer and traveller; FRS 1756; high sheriff of Bedfordshire 1773, when he began his humanitarian enquiry into the condition of prisons at home and abroad; published *State of Prisons in England and Wales* 1777; d. in southern Russia where he was visiting military hospitals.

'the first thing that struck an observer ... was a stamp of extraordinary vigour and energy on all his movements and expressions. An eye lively and penetrating, strong and prominent features, quick gait, and animated gestures, gave promise of ardour in forming, and vivacity in executing his designs' (John Aikin, 1792).

'Howard's personal appearance was by no means prepossessing, but rather the contrary. In his smile, however, there was an indescribable sweetness and benevolence. ... He was below the middle stature, very thin, with a pale, and somewhat sallow complexion. His features were large, his eye keen and penetrating, and his whole countenance such as indicated much intelligence, energy, and decision. ... His dress was stiff and singular, giving him the appearance of a foreign, rather than an English gentleman. His whole deportment showed that what he undertook he executed with promptness and dispatch' (Thomas Taylor, 1836).

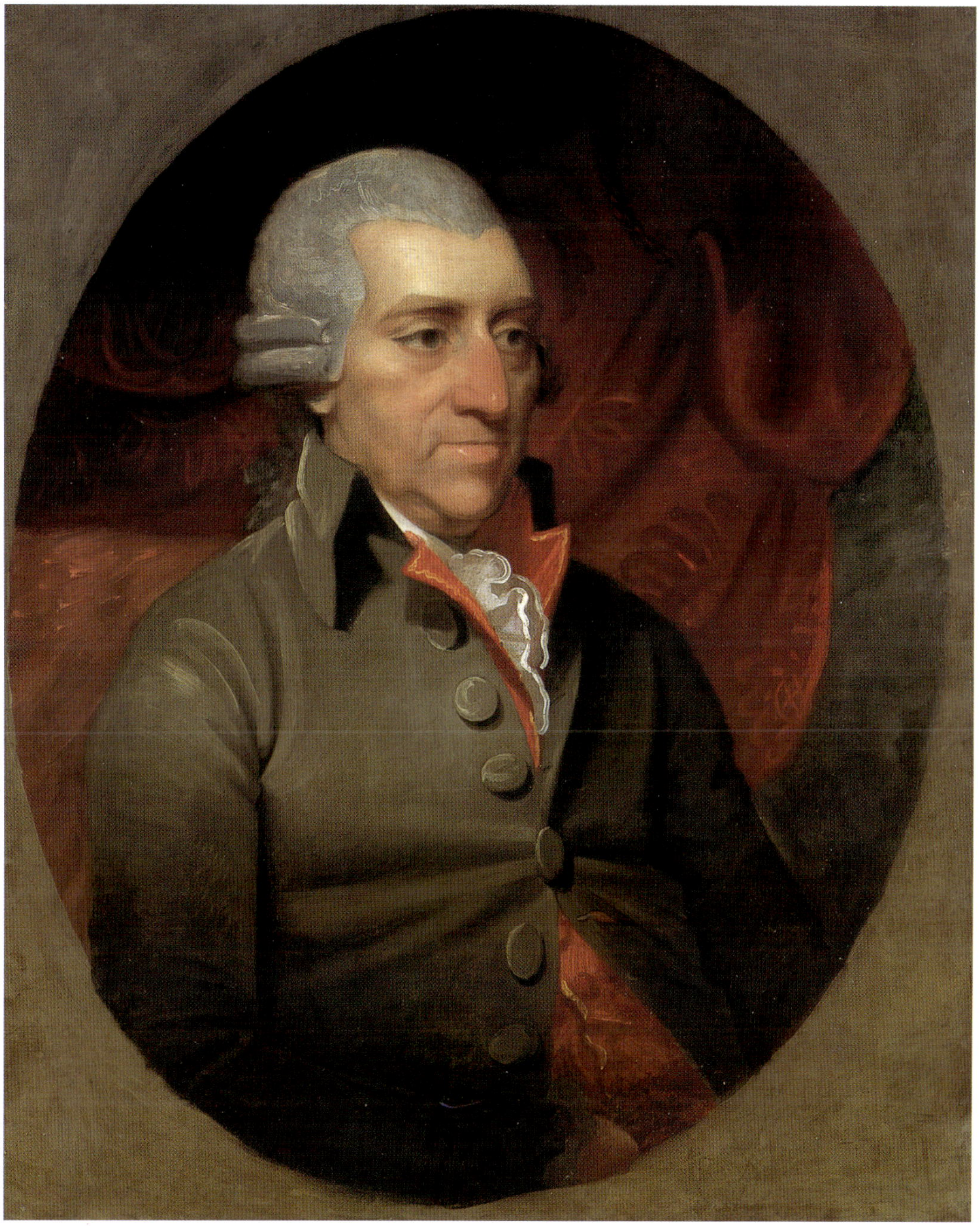

HOWARD NPG *97*

Abbreviations

Aikin 1792: Dr J. Aikin, *A View of the Character and Public Services of the late John Howard*, 1792

Brown 1823: J.B. Brown, *Memoirs of the Public and Private Life of John Howard*, 2nd ed., 1823

Field 1850: J. Field, *Life of John Howard*, 1850

97 MATHER BROWN [1789]

Canvas 74.5 x 61.5 (29¼ x 24¼) lined; cleaned 1984; a re-worked area, lower right, is not elucidated by x-radiography.

Grey eyes, powdered hair, wearing a green coat, red waistcoat with gold trim, and a white cravat; a red curtain behind; the spandrels are grey.

Collections: Purchased from the Rev Robert Ainslie 1860.

Engravings: see below.

Exhibitions: NPE 1867(815); *La scienza e la colpa*, Turin, 1985.

Reference: Evans 1982, no.96.

There is no satisfactory portrait of Howard. The casts taken of his face at his death are untraced and there was otherwise 'no portrait of him extant but what was taken by stealth'.[1] A dissenter, he held strong views about portraiture; he had found in his travels in Italy many monuments 'to humble the pride of Man and shew how Luxury and Wickedness will sink a Nation'[2] and when in 1787 friends had raised a subscription for his statue[3] he reacted strongly. 'I cannot', he wrote, 'without violating all my feelings, consent to the execution of your design. It would be to me a cruel punishment ... I must always view with pain and abhorrence every attempt of my friends to bring me forward to public view and public approbation'.[4] In 1792 his friend and biographer John Aikin wrote that all portraits published in other books were totally unlike and the frontispiece to his own biography (by Holloway, see below) although something of a caricature, did show exactly Howard's expression when in a serious, attentive mood.[5]

NPG 97 is a reduced version of a three-quarter length by Mather Brown, now untraced,[6] which was engraved by E. Scott, the print published on 14 September 1789, two months after Howard had set out on his last, fateful voyage. The print shows Howard seated by a fluted column, holding in his right hand a half-rolled plan lettered *Plan of a Lazaretto* (he had been visiting the Italian fever hospitals in 1786). Evans has plausibly suggested[7] that Brown's portrait was prompted as a commercial venture instigated by the engraver, and the cruder derivative plates of 1790 suggest the viability of such a scheme.[8] These engravings, however, fall among those portraits dismissed by Aikin as 'totally unlike'.

A crude version at Southill, which evidently belonged to Howard's close friend Samuel Whitbread, is inscribed: *Can we forget the generous MAN / Who touch'd with human woe redressive sought / Into the horrors of the gloomy jail.*

1 Brown 1823, p.533.
2 See Ingamells 1997, p.528.
3 See *GM*, LVI, 1786, i, p.360, ii, 627-32; proposed by 'Anglus' who urged that 'no time is to be lost; for, if it be not executed before his return, Mr Howard's humble sense of his own merits would most certainly prevent it'; the subscription was raised through the printer Nichols; Flaxman, Hickey and Sanders sought 'instructions of any of Howard's friends, intimately acquainted with his features'.
4 T. Taylor, *Memoirs of John Howard*, 1836, pp.301, 303.
5 Quoted in Whitley 1928, II, p.360. What was George Crabbe remembering when he said his father's 'highly marked countenance' was not unlike that of Howard (*Life of Crabbe, by his son*, 1947 ed., p.7)?
6 Evans 1982, no.95.
7 Evans 1982, p.89.
8 For example, the two by T. Cook and J. Wooding, both pub. April 1790 (i.e. on the news of Howard's death). There is also a later French lithograph by de Villain from a drawing by A. Maurin.

ICONOGRAPHY

For general comments on Howard's iconography, see above, and Whitley 1928, II, pp.359-60.

Contemporary Inventions

1786 Medallion head, engraved T. Prattent. 'No picture of Mr Howard having ever been painted, a gentleman has undertaken to draw one from memory' (*European Mag.*, X, 1786, p.317). A crude anon. engraving derived from this plate.

1788 Anon. engraving, bust length, wearing a hat, *Taken from Nature, March 1788* from a drawing sent from Dublin - 'a pencilled likeness ... drawn from the life (unknown to Mr Howard) while at my house, by a young and ingenious artist' (*GM*, LX, 1790, ii, p.685).

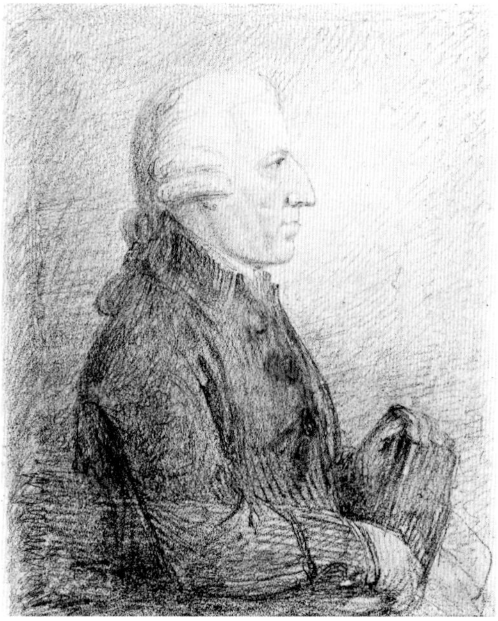

HOWARD by Thomas Holloway c.1788 (British Museum)

c.1788 Drawing by Thomas Holloway,* half-length profile, an upright book in his lap. British Museum (1939.3.3.5). A drawing copied by stealth 'by an artist of some eminence in his day ... considered by his surviving friends and domestics to be a very striking resemblance' (Brown 1823, p.533; and see NPG 97). Engraved reversed 1791 (showing button holes, not buttons) for Aikin 1792, see below; T. Holloway 1791 (T. Holloway *ad vivum delin. et sculp.*); the following not reversed and showing buttons: H. Adlard 1822; S. Freeman 1823; Fry 1836 (re-issued 1850); anon. 1855; Blanchard (reversed); R. Starling jr. (including a chair back); G. Scharf (lithograph).

Aikin 1792, p.209, described the drawing as sketched originally in London, engraved in Dublin, and copied for his book: 'it is somewhat of a caricature, but has very exactly the expression of his countenance when in a very serious attentive mood'. Sir Richard Phillips in the *Monthly Mag.* said the portrait of Howard prefixed to Aikin's Biography 'was engraved by Manning (a young artist of great promise who died soon after) from a sketch made by himself in St Mary's Church, Dublin' (Whitley 1928, II, p.360). Howard had been in Ireland several times between 1775 and 1788.

1789 Painting by Mather Brown, see NPG 97.

1790 According to Aikin 1792, p.210, before Howard's interment in Russia, two plaster casts were taken of his face, by direction of Prince Potemkin, the one for himself, and the other for Mr Howard's servant; the latter later purchased by 'the elder Mr Whitbread' (Brown 1823, p.592).

after 1790 Monument in Kherson, Russia (where Howard died), an obelisk bearing a medallion bust (illus. *ILN*, LXX, 1877, p.292). An undated Russian medal (reproduction in NPG archive) appears to relate to this medallion portrait.

Posthumous Inventions

1795 Monument by John Bacon sr.,* whole length *all'antica*, holding a scroll lettered *Plans for the Improvement of Prisons*. St Paul's Cathedral. Engraved J. Basire 1796 (*GM*); H. Adlard 1833; anon. 1828 and 1849. A bust by Bacon is above the entrance to Shrewsbury Prison.

Howard had told his son that should he die abroad 'let there be only a plain strip of marble placed under that of my wife Henrietta's, with this inscription - John Howard, died - aged -: My hope is in Christ' (Field 1850, p.380).

1873 Medal by A.B. Wyon, marking the centenary of Howard's election as Sheriff of Bedfordshire, exhibited RA 1875(1285) for the Statistical Society (Brown 1987, no.2970).

before 1882 Plaster medallion by T. Butler. Royal College of Physicians, London (illus. *Cat. of Portraits*, 1964, p.227).

1890 Statue by A. Gilbert, Bedford, Market Hill (M.H. Spielmann, *British Sculpture Today*, 1901, p.80). A bronze model is in the Tate Gallery (N 5885).

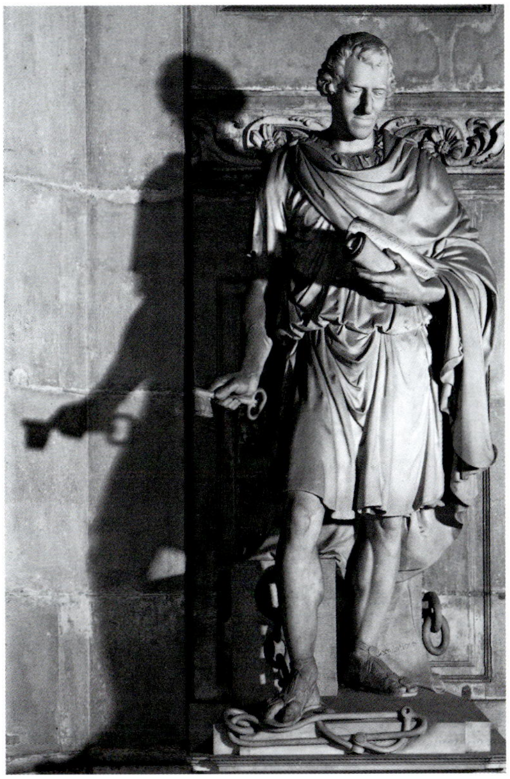

HOWARD by John Bacon senior 1795 (St Paul's Cathedral, London)

c.1900 Wedgwood medallion (illus. Reilly 1973, p.195).

Several history pieces celebrated Howard, principally Francis Wheatley's *Howard visiting and relieving the miseries of a Prison*, 1787 (private collection), engraved J. Hogg 1790, exhibited *Treasure Houses*, Washington, 1985(484); and Thomas Marshall's *Howard visiting prisons in Italy in 1786*, 1859 (Walker AG, Liverpool, 2979).

Many compositional drawings were made by George Romney for a painting, *Human Misery*, suggesting the figure of Howard visiting prisons abroad; see *Romney* 2002, nos.130-31.

A drawing by John Flaxman for a proposed Howard monument is in the Kunsthalle, Hamburg (illus. D. Bindman, *Flaxman*, 1979 p.117 no.135).

DOUBTFUL PORTRAITS

Paintings by David Martin in the Dean Orphanage Edinburgh 1972; by H. Burch, exhibited *Guelph* 1891(327) lent John Harley; miniature of c.1765 in the Royal Collection (Walker 1992, no.358). An engraving by W. Hincks 1783 after T. Collopy, lettered *John Howard Esqr.*, shows Bishop Hussey (cf. Strickland 1913, I, p.192).

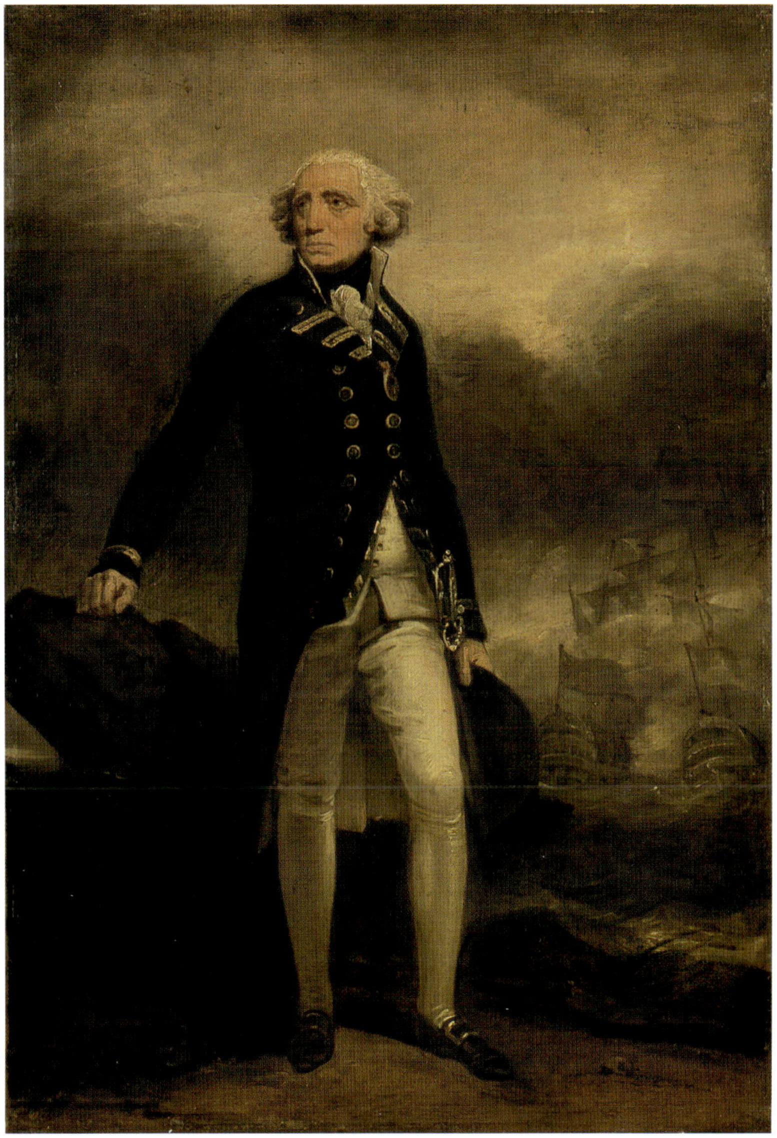

1st Earl HOWE NPG 75

HOWE, Richard Howe, 1st Earl 1726-99

Naval officer; MP 1757-82; suc. as 4th Viscount Howe 1758; served in the Seven Years War; rear-admiral 1770, vice-admiral 1775; commanded naval forces in the American war 1776-78; admiral of the blue and cr. Earl Howe 1782; relieved Gibraltar 1782; first lord of the Admiralty 1783-88; vice-admiral of England 1792-96; defeated a French fleet off Ushant, 'The Glorious 1st of June', 1794; KG 1797.

'his countenance was of a serious cast, strongly marked and dark; at the same time there was a shyness and awkwardness in his manner, ... [but] the expression of his features [soon] assumed a very different and an animated character, assuming that benign aspect which corresponded with his disposition' (Sir John Barrow, 1803).

'his profile bore, indeed, a very strong resemblance to George I, from whom, by his mother, he descended' (Sir Nathaniel Wraxall, 1815).

Abbreviation

Howe 1988: A. French, ed., *The Earl and Countess Howe by Gainsborough*, exh. cat., Kenwood, 1988

75 HENRY SINGLETON c.1795

Canvas 58 x 40.5 (22¾ x 16) lined; retouched in the background area and in the hair; *pentimenti* and a surface dent round and across the shoulders.

Blue eyes, his own white hair, wearing the uniform of an admiral, his hat in his left hand, the King's 1794 medal on a pink ribbon at his breast;[1] behind him a French and British ship in combat.

Collections: Bought 'from an artist many Years ago' by (William) Frederick Harrison,[2] from whom purchased 1859.

Engraving: S.W. Reynolds 1799.[3]

Exhibitions: *Regency Portraits*, Kenwood, 1986; *Howe* 1988(A32).

NPG 75 shows the elderly hero standing against a background of stormy skies and naval engagements (there is more than a touch of Lear on the heath about his staring eyes).[4] Possibly a reduced version of a lost painting, NPG 75 may have been painted expressly for engraving, being the same size as the plate by S.W. Reynolds published in 1799 (ten weeks after Howe's death), but the absence of Garter insignia presumably indicates that it was painted before 1797.

1 His actual medal illus. *Howe* 1988, p.90; it was presented to him on 26 June 1794.
2 Letter of April 1859; NPG archive. Frederick's brother Robert Harrison was the London Library Librarian 1857-93.
3 Published 1 November 1799 (Howe had died on 5 August); see A. Whitman, *S.W. Reynolds*, 1903, pp.54-55, no.155.
4 Compare Singleton's *Sir Edward Vernon* (National Maritime Museum, BHC 3070), another small whole-length, engraved in 1791.

3313 after JOHN DE VAERE [1798]

Coloured wax relief 5.7 x 3.8 (2¼ x 1½); incised (rather crudely) beneath the right arm: *J.FLAXMAN.* and painted in yellow on the glass beneath: *HOWE*; the colours much deteriorated.

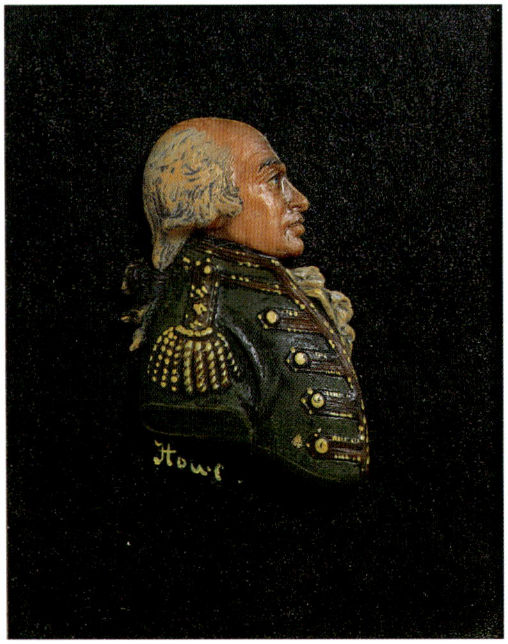

1st Earl HOWE NPG *3313*

Blue eyes, white hair, the coat now green and the trim a tarnished brown.

Collections: Purchased from E. Linton Coombe 1946.

Exhibition: *Bicentennial Center Opening*, Yorktown, Va., 1976.

A crude, reduced copy of the wax medallion made by John de Vaere for the Wedgwood factory in 1798 and produced as a plaque c.1800.[1]

1 Illus. Reilly 1973, p.195, and see Reilly 1994, pp.242, 397n101, where dated c.1800-10; probably produced 1800 following Howe's death in August 1799.

ICONOGRAPHY

'A mezzotinto portrait of him was taken by a foreign artist, without his knowledge, he was amazed when it was presented to him, but hung it up in his cabin, and for a long time this caused him to be known as "Black Dick"' (CS, I, p.135).

In 1796 George Dance wished to take a profile drawing of him, but 'Lord Howe felt modest about sitting' (Farington, 7 May 1796).

1758 or later, Painting by Arthur Devis, of Howe and his wife. Devis sale, 11 June 1822, lot 89 (*Devis* 1980, p.84, no.86).

1763-64 Painting by Thomas Gainsborough,* whole length in the undress uniform of a commodore. Private collection (Waterhouse 1958, no.386). Exhibited *Art Treasures*, Manchester 1857 (BPG 299). Companion to the whole length of his wife at Kenwood.

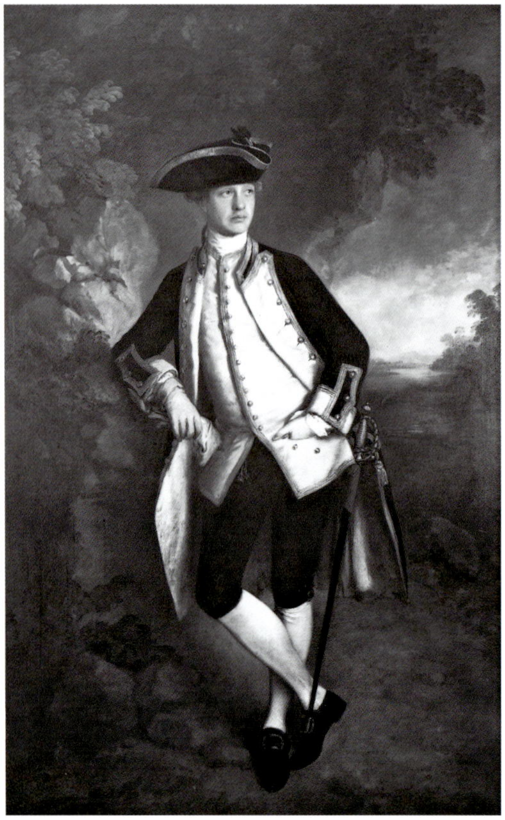

1st Earl HOWE by Thomas Gainsborough 1763-64 (Private Collection)

1777 Engraving by 'Corbutt' [C. Purcell], standing three-quarter length in naval uniform, pub. J. Morris (illus. *Howe* 1988, p.82). Re-issued 1794.

1778 Engraving by J. Watson, half-length oval in uniform, showing Howe apparently c.1765 (illus. *Howe* 1988, p.66) A painted copy is at Penn House.

1780 Miniature by John Smart (listed by Foskett 1964, p.68).

1782 Drawn and engraved by Benjamin Killingbeck, whole-length standing on the shore in admiral's uniform. Re-issued in 1794. The head somewhat resembles that in Watson's engraving of 1778.

c.1790 Painting by J.S. Copley,* bust-length in admiral's undress uniform. National Maritime Museum (BHC 2790). Exhibited NPE 1867(730) lent Earl Howe. Engraved R. Dunkarton 1794; F. Bartolozzi 1802 (within a larger plate, *Commemoration of the Victory of June 1st 1794*; illus. *Howe* 1988, p.89); W. Sharp 1810; J.T. Wedgwood; E. Finden 1837 (half length). Directly related to the portrait exhibited in 1791, and see Barrington, NPG 5519. Versions with the Howe family, Lord Sligo, and the Empire Trust Co., New York, in 1966. Copies by Peter Mequignon (engraved R. Cooper; R. Laurie 1794); J. Harrison 1850 (United Services Club, London) and G.F. Clarke c.1880 (Admiralty House, Portsmouth); a miniature copy by Edward Miles is in the Royal Collection (Walker 1992,

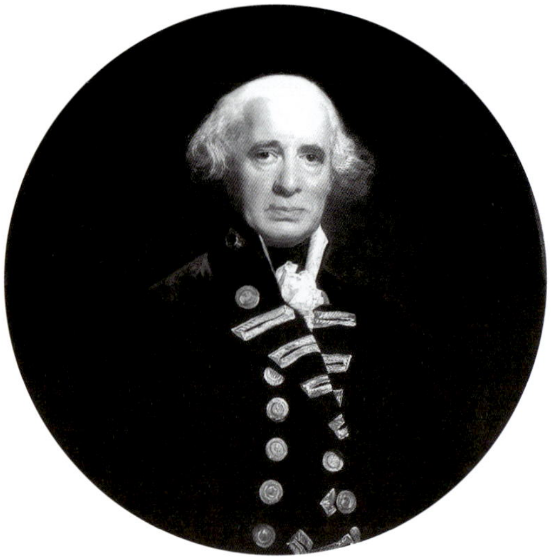

1st Earl HOWE by J.S. Copley c.1790 (National Maritime Museum, London)

no.279), and another was sold Christie's, 23 October 1989, lot 93.

An engraving by W. Ridley 1794, uses the Copley head, but the body is turned to the left and the left arm extended.

Copley was also said to have painted Howe in full-dress uniform with epaulettes, the ribbon of the Garter, and the King's gold medal and chain; versions with Lord Sligo and at Penn House in 1922 (*Connoisseur*, LXIV, 1922, p.245); not listed in Prown 1966, but possibly referring to a portrait by Mather Brown, see 1794 below.

1791 Drawing by Godefroy, bust-length oval, engraved J. Pass.

1794 Painting by Mather Brown, *Lord Howe on the deck of the Queen Charlotte*, at the death of Captain Neville. National Maritime Museum (BHC 2740). Engraved D. Orme 1795. Howe's head separately engraved D. Orme 1795 (*European Mag.*) and 1798; G. Murray 1794 (badly for the *Pocket Mag.*); G. Gabrielli 1875 (*Eton Portraits*).

The 1798 Orme engraving was apparently the basis for the unattributed portrait in the National Maritime Museum (BHC 2789) which Evans 1982, p.247, suggests may be by Orme, who also copied Brown's picture, see *Rule Britannia*, Sotheby's, 1986(91).

c.1791-94 A half-length portrait by Mather Brown, described as similar to that by Copley, remains at Penn House (*Howe* 1988, p.70), and see under Copley above.

1794 Medals by William Barnett, exhibited RA 1795(535), and C.H. Küchler, celebrating Howe's victory of 1 June 1794 (Brown 1980, nos.382-83; both illus. *Howe* 1988, p.91).

1794 Painting by Gainsborough Dupont, whole-length standing. Trinity House, London. Exhibited NPE 1868(877). Engraved V. Green 1799 in *British Naval Victors* (half length with added Garter ribbon and badge; illus. *Howe* 1988, p.89); W.T. Fry 1831 & 1837, W. Greatbach 1878 (half length); H. Robinson 1832 (three-quarter length); a three-quarter length copy by George Kirtland c.1800, Guildhall AG, London (62).

1794 'Painted in Crayons' by Simon de Koster, half length, map and sword before him, engraved T. Burke from the original then with Sir Charles Saxton.

c.1795 Painting by Henry Singleton, see NPG 75.

c.1795 Miniature by François Ferrière, bust length as Admiral. Christie's, 24 November 1964, lot 104. Exhibited *British Portrait Miniatures*, Edinburgh, 1965(278) lent R. Graham.

1798 Wax medallion by James De Vaere, see NPG 3313.

1798-99 Paste medallion by James Tassie (Gray 1894, nos.196-97; illus. *Howe* 1988, p.71) comparable with the medal by Barnett of 1794. Examples dated 1798 and 1799, Scottish NPG (PG 476, 477).

1799 Medal by Thomas Wyon sr. (Brown 1980, no.468). An impression from a medal die by W. Wyon, one of 'Mr Mudie's series of National Medals', exhibited RA 1819(1111).

Undated Pastel by H.D. Hamilton; with Capt. Conolly, Castletown, in 1913 (*Wal. Soc.*, II, 1913, p.107).

Miniature by Thomas Hazelhurst, 'in blue coat and white cravat', exhibited *Hothfield Heirlooms*, London 1936(20) lent Lord Hothfield.

Unattributed wax profile, sold Christie's, 27 September 1989, lot 64.

Posthumous

c.1800 Wedgwood medallion (illus. Reilly 1973, p.195), see also NPG 3313.

c.1800 Wax bust by Thomas Wyon sr., in admiral's uniform. Formerly E.J. Pyke collection (illus. *CL*, CXXXI, 1962, p.658).

1802 Modello by Thomas Banks, standing figure in Roman dress attended by two allegorical figures, for an unexecuted monument. Soane Museum (illus. Bell 1938, pl.xxxviii).

c.1802 Painting on copper by Edward Bird, oval study for a memorial to Lord Howe, Wolverhampton AG (505).

1803-11 Monument by John Flaxman.* St Paul's Cathedral. Engraved J. Hall 1812; S. Rawle after E.F. Burney 1818. J.C.F. Rossi had also made a model for Howe's St Paul's monument (Farington, 27 April 1802).

1809 Colossal plaster bust by Francis Chantrey. National Maritime Museum (*Chantrey* 1994, no.1). Exhibited RA 1809(789). Ordered by the architect David Alexander, with similar busts of Duncan, St Vincent and Nelson, to be placed outside the Royal Naval Hospital, Greenwich; replaced c.1870 by a stone imitation.

Life-size version, ordered in 1810 for Trinity House, London, probably destroyed during the Second World War.

History pictures incorporating Lord Howe include: *The Triumph of Britannia*, by Francis Hayman 1762, containing a medallion portrait of Howe obscured by a triton, painted for Vauxhall Gardens and since destroyed, engraved S. Ravenet 1765 (illus. Allen 1987, p.65); *Howe being presented with Sword of State by George III*, watercolour by Isaac Cruikshank c.1794, Guildhall AG, London (243); *Lord Howe on the Queen Charlotte, 1 June 1794*, by John Frost 1795, Sotheby's, 12 March 1969, lot 82; *Lord Howe accepting the French surrender, 1 June 1794*, by Samuel Drummond c.1795, Christie's, 13 March 1970, lot 162; *George III presenting a sword to Earl Howe on board the Queen Charlotte* by H.P. Briggs 1828 (National Maritime Museum, BHC 0476; illus. *Howe* 1988, p.10).

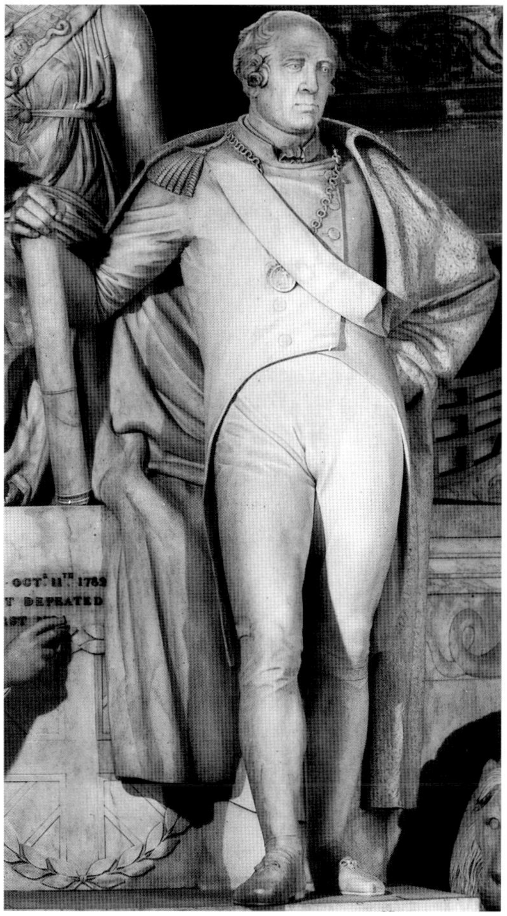

1st Earl HOWE by John Flaxman 1803-11 (St Paul's Cathedral, London)

DOUBTFUL PORTRAITS

Unreliable engraved portraits include: W. Angus 1782, *Lord Viscount Howe* (*European Mag.*); J.Brown 1815 after W.M. Craig, bust-length medallion; E. Smith (for McGregor's *History of the French Revolution*).

HULL, Thomas 1728-1808

Actor and playwright; played in Dublin and Bath before appearing in 1759 at Covent Garden, where he stayed; founded the Covent Garden Theatrical Fund 1765; an intimate friend of William Shenstone, whose select letters he edited in 1778.

4625 UNKNOWN ARTIST c.1765

Canvas 76 x 63.5 (30 x 25) lined; cleaned 1979.

Blue eyes, powdered toupée wig, wearing deep red coat with dark fur trim, a bright red waistcoat with gold trim, a quill in his right hand, his left holding a sprig of laurel above a bust of William Shenstone which stands before a green curtain; on the paper the heading *Elegy*.

Collections: Guy Bolton (b.1884); Christie's, 8 June 1951, lot 53 (as by Zoffany and with a bust of Garrick); Capt. L.F. Plugge, London, from whom stolen; Phillips, 30 September 1968, lot 97 (as by J. Wright), bt. Leggatt for the NPG; returned in November 1968 to Capt. Plugge; sold Sotheby's, 20 April 1977, lot 277 (as by Barry), bt. Leggatt for the NPG.

The laurel held above Shenstone's bust[1] and Hull's evident intention to compose an Elegy, suggests that NPG 4625 was painted soon after the poet's death in 1763.[2] The wig and coat with deep close cuffs also suggest a date within the 1760s. NPG 4625, an unsophisticated portrait with an oversized head, defies attribution;[3] it may be compared with a portrait of Thomas Worlidge (d.1766), sold Christie's, 11 May 1951, lot 126,[4] and the little-known Daniel Bond (1725-1803), a painter within the Shenstone circle,[5] should not be discounted.

1 It may be compared with the engraved front. to Shenstone's *Works*, I, 1764; see Kerslake *Early Georgian*, II, pl.726. Shenstone had been considering a bust of himself in 1754 when he encountered a sculptor from Stratford making busts at 2 gn. each (M. Williams ed., *Letters of William Shenstone*, 1939, pp.409-10).

2 Walker 1992, under no.359, suggested a date of c.1765.

3 Having previously been sold, with some optimism, as Barry, Zoffany and Wright, see Collections above.

4 Attributed, unconvincingly, to Tilly Kettle; it is more like Edward Penny (as Malcolm Rogers observed), without meriting such an attribution.

5 Who painted an untraced portrait of Shenstone which belonged to Hull (M. Williams ed., *Letters of William Shenstone*, 1939, p.379n2), presumably the portrait in Hull's possession which was engraved anon. and published by Bagster in 1777. A portrait of Juliana Ludford by Bond was sold Christie's, 1 December 2000, lot 29, but he is otherwise known as a painter of classicising landscapes.

3899 GEORGE DANCE 1799

Pencil with traces of pink in the flesh areas, on paper 25.3 x 19 (10 x 7½) laid down on paper; faded; signed and dated bottom right: *Geo.Dance / March 16t.1799*.

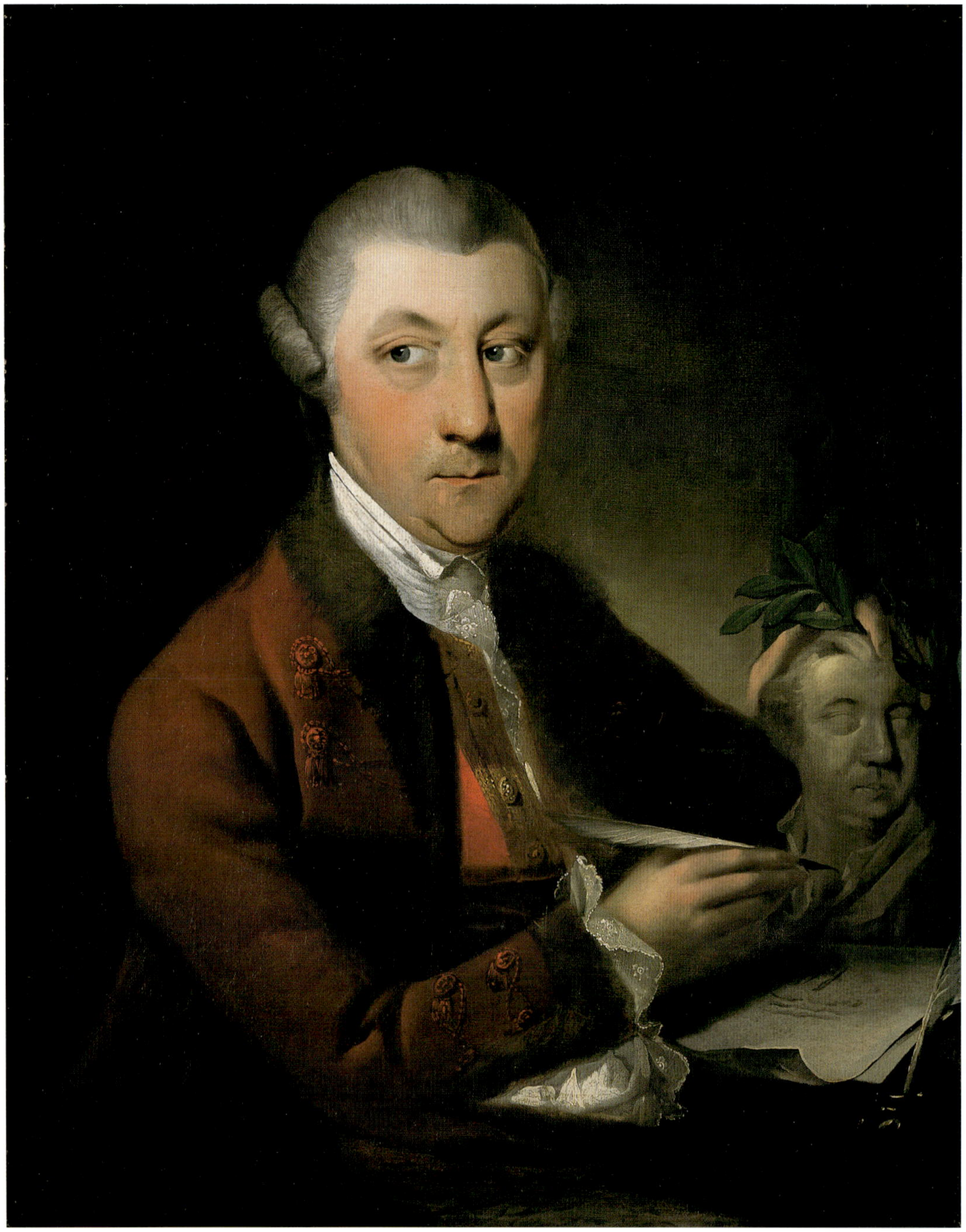

HULL NPG *4625*

Collections: The artist's grandson, the Rev George Dance; his sale, Christie's, 1 July 1898, lot 74; Walker's Galleries, from whom purchased 1954.

Engraving: W. Daniell (*Dance Plates*).

Exhibition: *Early English Water-Colours*, Walker's Galleries, 1954(30).

ICONOGRAPHY

See also the *Harvard Catalogue*, II, pp.265-66, and Highfill, VIII, p.40 (listing further portrayals of Hull in character).

c.1765 Unattributed miniature, bust-length oval. Royal Collection (Walker 1992, no.359 as c.1765).

c.1765 Unattributed painting, see NPG 4625.

1777 Drawing by John Downman,* half length. British Museum (1967.10.14.181/167), labelled *Mr Hill* [sic] *the Actor 1777*. One of six drawings Downman made for *my design from Mason's Play of Caractacus* [in which Hull played the part of Mador], *but which I had not time to make a picture of as I intended* (inscription beneath the last drawing in the same sketchbook).

c.1782 Painting by George Carter, *The Immortality of Garrick*, see Comparative Groups.*

c.1795 Painting by John Graham,* three-quarter length seated, with an outsized head. Garrick Club (Ashton 1997, no.311). Engraved W.S. Leney 1797 (illus. Highfill, VIII, p.38; Burnim 1998, p.162).

1799 Drawing by George Dance, see NPG 3899.

Paintings of Hull in character include: scenes from Moore's *Gamester* by De Wilde and Mather Brown 1782 (Garrick Club; Ashton 1997, nos.310, 682), and Zoffany's *Provok'd Wife* (see Garrick 1763-65).

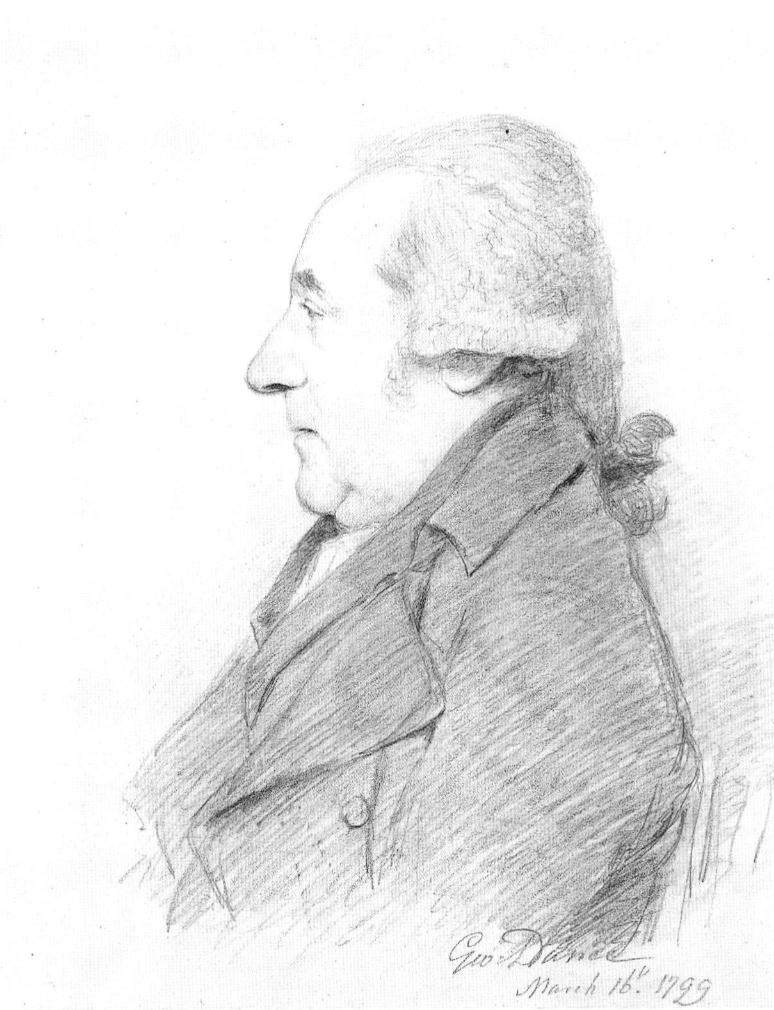

HULL NPG *3899*

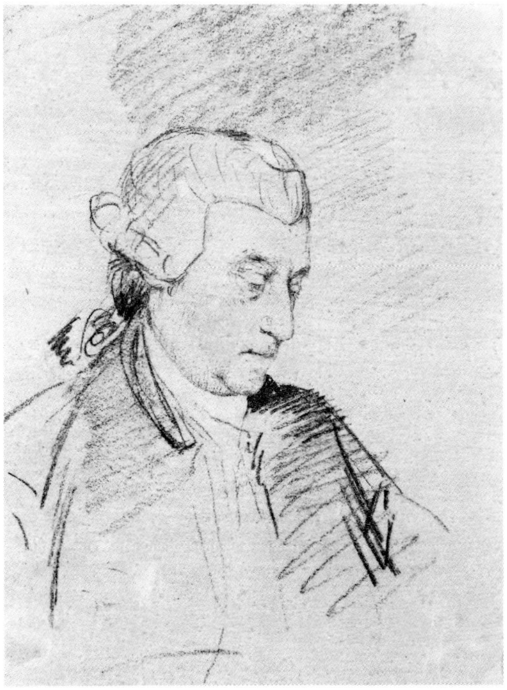

HULL by John Downman 1777 (British Museum)

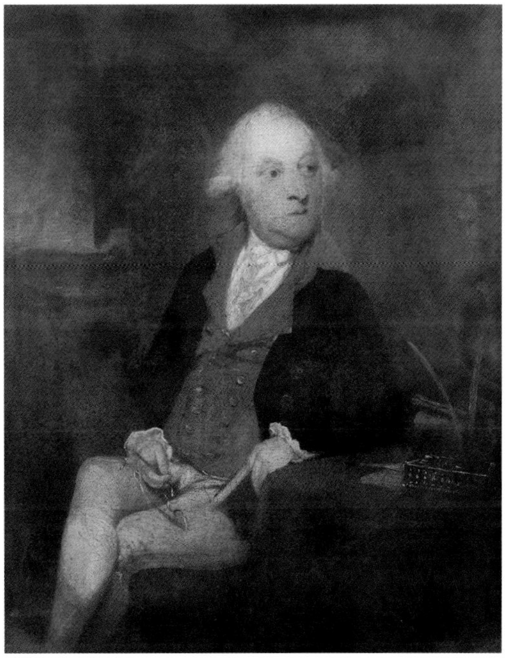

HULL by John Graham c.1795 (Garrick Club)

HUME, David 1711-76

Philosopher; secretary to the British embassies in Vienna and Turin 1748 and Paris 1763-66; his works include the *Treatise of Human Nature* 1739-40, the *Essays Moral and Political* 1741-42, and the *History of England* 1754-62; 'to reduce life to exact rule and method is commonly a painful, oft a fruitless occupation', he wrote, but it was 'one of the most amusing in which life could possibly be employed'.

'Nature, I believe, never yet formed any Man more unlike his real Character than David Hume. ... His face was broad and fat, his Mouth wide, and without any other Expression than that of Imbecility. His eyes vacant and spiritless, and the Corpulence of his whole Person was far better fitted to communicate the Idea of a Turtle-eating Alderman than of a refined Philosopher' (James, 1st Earl of Charlemont).

'All the pretty women had a great run on him, and ... the fat Scottish philosopher was pleased with their society. This David Hume is an excellent man; he is naturally placid; he listens attentively, he sometimes speaks with wit, although he speaks little; but he is clumsy, he has neither warmth, nor grace, nor charm of humour, nor anything that properly appertains to the chirping of those charming little mechanisms known as pretty women' (Baron Friedrich Melchior von Grimm, 1766).

Abbreviation

Mossner 1954: E.C. Mossner, *Life of Hume* 1954

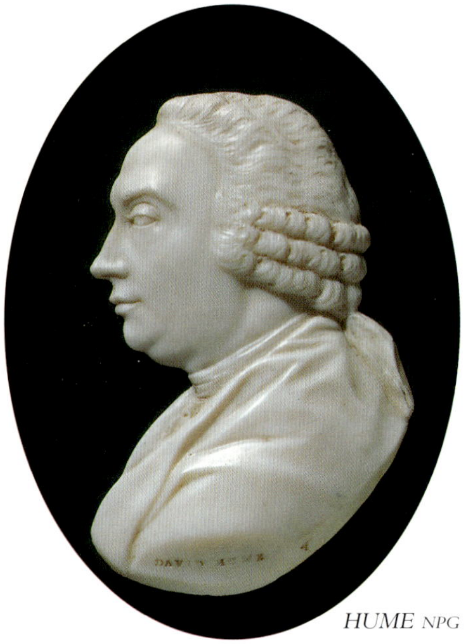
HUME NPG 4897

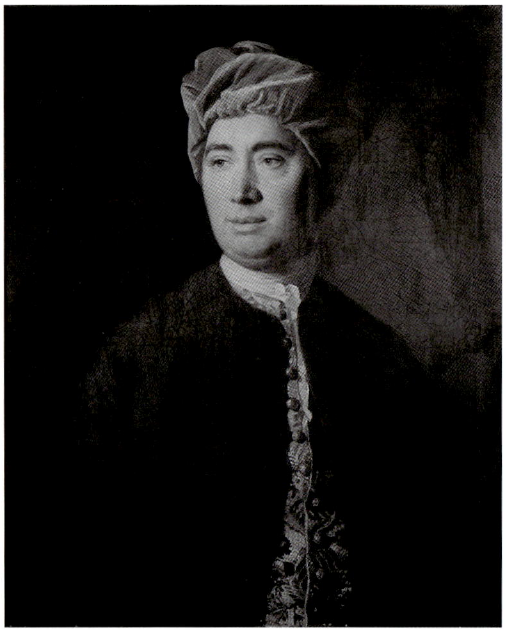
HUME by Allan Ramsay 1754 (Private Scottish Collection)

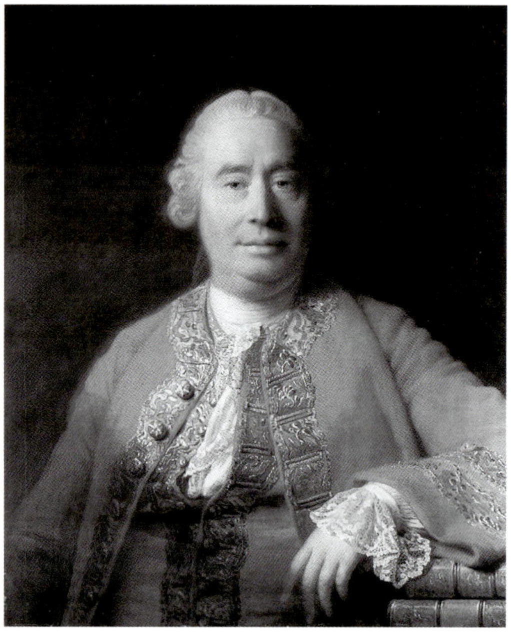
HUME by Allan Ramsay 1766 (Scottish National Portrait Gallery)

4897 JAMES TASSIE c.1791

Glass paste 7.6 (3) high, incised on truncation: *DAVID HUME* and *T.*; set on glass.

Collections: Sotheby's, Gleneagles, 24 August 1972, lot 108, bt. Leggatt for the NPG.

Reference: Gray 1894, no.198.

This posthumous image apparently derives from the engraved profile by Cochin of 1764 (see below). Tassie had produced a medallion of Hume's kinsman, the dramatist John Home, in 1791. A second type by Tassie, showing Hume *all'antica* with short hair and a drape over his bare shoulder, is represented in the Scottish NPG (PG 1196).[1]

1 Gray 1894, no.199.

ICONOGRAPHY

1754 Painting by Allan Ramsay,* half length. Private collection (Smart 1999, no.278). In 1754 Ramsay, Hume and Adam Smith founded the Edinburgh Select Society. Copy by William Millar of 1758 in the University of Edinburgh, previously exhibited in the Phillimore Ives Memorial Gallery, Stellenbosch, 1951.

Paris October 1763- February 1766

1764 Drawing by C-N. Cochin, profile head. Fogg Art Museum, Cambridge, Mass. (illus. *AQ*, XXV, 1962, p.403). Engraved S.C. Miger 1764 (illus. *Apollo*, XCVII, 1973, p.5); J. Basire 1765 (without wig and wearing a beret); A.B. Duhamel; anon. c.1800 (extended to half length).

1764-65 Drawing by L-C. de Carmontelle, whole-length seated, the head seen in profile, reading. Scottish NPG (PG 2238; illus. *CL*, CLVII, 1975, p.823).

London 1766-68 and Edinburgh 1769-76

1766 Painting by Allan Ramsay,* half length, richly dressed in a scarlet coat. Scottish NPG (PG 1057 (Smart 1999, no.279). Engraved D. Martin 1767; other dated plates include those by A. Smith 1806, W. Finden 1822 and T. Woolnoth 1825. George III considered the portrait 'very like', but 'the dress rather too fine'; Charlemont commented that Hume looked 'like a Grocer of the Trained Bands ... disguised in Scarlet, while his broad face was rendered still broader by a smart Wig a la militaire'. A version formerly at Oxenfoord Castle (cat., 1911, no.99), and a miniature copy sold Christie's, 23 October 1989, lot 21.

1766-69 Painting attributed to David Martin, half length. Christie's, New York, 11 January 1989, lot 28.

c.1770 Miniature by John Donaldson, bust-length oval, engraved S. Ravenet (within a stone frame, an open book below; later impression reversed without book); W. Walker c.1780; other dated plates include: P. Audinet (copied by J. Collyer 1788); A. Smith 1794 (*From an original drawing*; *Biographical Mag.*); W. Ridley 1794 (from a drawing by R. Richards); W. Holl 1819.

Later derivative plates by H.R. Cook 1823, R. Page 1825 and W.H. Worthington alleged an original by Joshua Reynolds.

Posthumous

1776 Anon. medal (Brown 1980, no.206).

c.1791 Medallion by James Tassie, see NPG 4897.

1792 Anon. silhouette profile, dated January 1792. British Museum (1980.U.895).

1866-70 Statue by Matthew Noble. Burlington House, London (rear facade).

1901 Statue by J.P. Macgillivray. Scottish NPG (north-west tower). A bronze modello belongs to the Royal Society, Edinburgh (see C. Waterston, *Portrait Prowl*, Royal Soc., Edinburgh, 1997, p.12).

1997 Bronze statue by Alexander Stoddart, the head ultimately derived from the Cochin profile. Royal Mile, Edinburgh.

DOUBTFUL PORTRAITS

Paintings: from the 'circle of Ramsay', Christie's, Keir Mains, 22-24 May 1995, lot 466 (exhibited *Art Treasures*, Manchester, 1857, BPG 313); unattributed, Scottish NPG (PG 578); so-called Reynolds, Christie's, 19 March 1859, lot 103 (Scharf sketch in sale cat.; illus. *Connoisseur*, LIX, 1921, p.227); signed and dated *EE* (monogram) *1774*, with Farrer, May-June 1862, and offered to the NPG (TSB 7/22; and SSB 62/99).

Watercolour by Lady Abercromby, Edinburgh University (head only illus. *Cullen and the 18th century Medical World*, 1993, p.14; cf. D. Talbot Rice & P. McIntyre, *Edinburgh University Portraits*, 1957, no.70).

HUNTER, John 1728-93

Surgeon, bro. of William Hunter; came to London from Lanark in 1748, studying with and assisting his brother; sailed to Belleisle 1761 and Portugal 1762, before practising in London from 1763; FRS 1767; surgeon at St George's Hospital 1767; surgeon extraordinary to the King 1776 and deputy surgeon general to the army 1786; he assembled a museum to illustrate life in its entirety, subsequently acquired by the Royal College of Surgeons, London.

'in person [he] was of middle height, vigorous, and robust, with high shoulders and rather short neck. His features were strongly marked, with prominent eyebrows, pyramidal forehead, and eyes of light blue or grey. His hair in youth was a reddish yellow ... impatient, blunt and unceremonious ... but candid and unreserved to a fault' (*DNB*).

Abbreviation

Taylor 1993: S. Taylor, *John Hunter and his Painters*, Royal College of Surgeons of England, 1993

1712 LIFE MASK [c.1785]

Plaster 20.5 (8) high

Collections: Presented by Messrs D. Brucciani & Co. 1913.

See NPG 4288 below.

4288 LIFE MASK [c.1785]

Bronze cast of the life mask 20.5 (8) high.

Collections: Presented by the Royal College of Surgeons, London, 1962.

NPG 1712 and NPG 4288 are taken from the life mask belonging to the Royal College of Surgeons, London.[1] NPG 4288, which is less subtle than the plaster NPG 1712, is one of three bronze casts made by the firm of Morris Singer in 1962; another was presented to the Hunterian Museum in Glasgow, and the third retained by the College.

Hunter described having such a mask taken: 'when I had plaster of Paris applied to my face to make a mould, in the taking it off, it produced a kind of suction on the fore part of the nose'.[2] It is not clear exactly when this mask was taken; William Norris, in his Hunterian Lecture in 1825, alleged that it was Reynolds who had asked Hunter 'to let a caste be taken from his face', a story elaborated by Keith in 1919.[3]

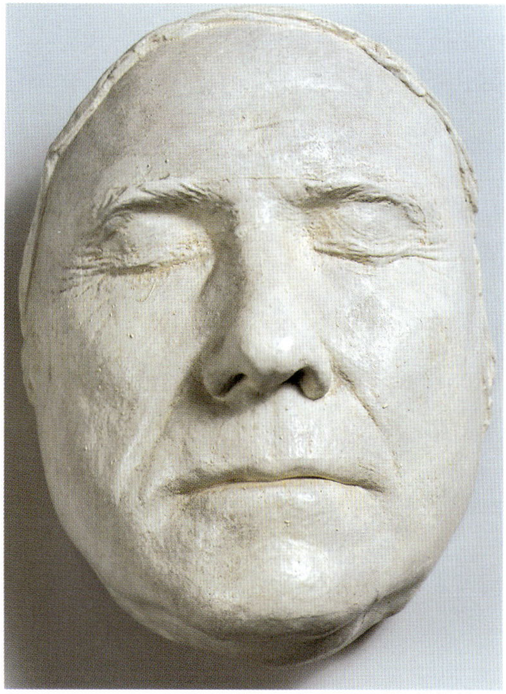

John HUNTER NPG *1712*

1 LeFanu 1960, p.42(127); illus. Taylor 1993, fig.3.
2 J. Hunter, *A Treatise on the Blood* ..., 1794, p.65; the *Treatise* was 'first arranged' in 1762 but continually revised; the date of 1781 is mentioned in the final text.
3 W. Norris, *Hunterian Oration*, 1825, p.35; Sir A. Keith fancifully suggested (*Lancet*, 18 October 1919, p.710) that Reynolds's request was made in order to get rid of the straggly beard seen in one version of the 1786 portrait (see NPG 77, n19).

77 JOHN JACKSON 1813 after JOSHUA REYNOLDS [1786]

Canvas 142 x 110.5 (56 x 43½) made up of four components: a vertical strip, 39.5 (15½) wide added on the right; the left section of three pieces, the top 26.5 (10½), centre 97 (38), and bottom 18.5 (7½) deep;[1] lined; the canvas joins are retouched and there is shrinkage craquelure in the thicker reds; a repaired damage above the head to the left.

Grey eyes, white hair, wearing a red velvet suit with a white lining, and white stockings; he sits in a green chair; a preparation of the lungs under a bell glass; the open book shows on the left-hand page a series of forelimbs, from the simplest foot to the human hand, and on the right a series of skulls from the human to the least developed; the paper beneath his elbow shows radiating lines; the two closed books are not titled [but in the original portrait they are *Natural History of Fossils* and *Natural History of Vegetables*[2]]; on a ledge beneath the jar an example of a spliced spine by an ossified prop; on the wall the feet of the skeleton of the Irish giant Charles Byrne.[3]

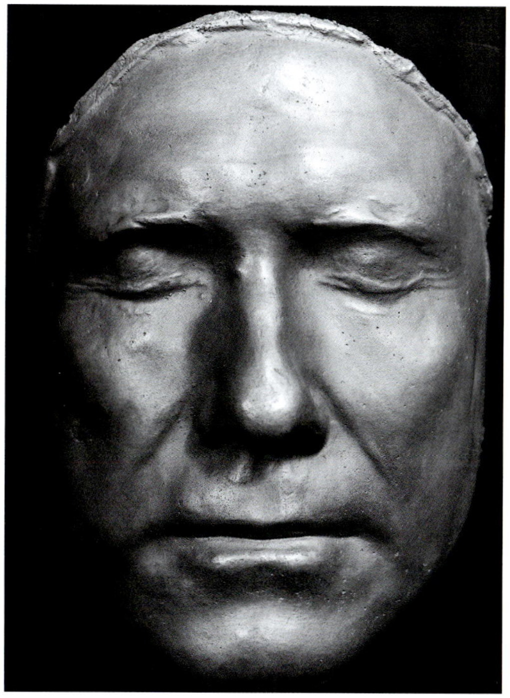

John HUNTER NPG *4288*

Collections: Sir Charles Bell, professor of surgery at the University of Edinburgh;[4] his widow, Marian, Lady Bell, from whom purchased 1859.

Exhibitions: *Apples to Atoms* 1986-87; *The Room in View*, NPG, 1996-98.

Reference: Graves & Cronin, II, pp.495-96; Mannings 2000, no.973c.

Copied from the portrait by Reynolds belonging to the Royal College of Surgeons, London,[5] which was exhibited RA 1786(223) and engraved by William Sharp in 1788;[6] in 1865 Taylor observed that it was then 'so irretrievably ruined by darkening and cracking, that the knowledge of what it had been seemed likely to be preserved to us by [NPG 77]'.[7] According to Hunter's early biographer Everard Home,[8] friends had long wished to have an engraving of him, but he was reluctant to pay for a portrait; it was only to oblige his (and his wife's) friend the engraver William Sharp, that sittings took place[9] in 1786; it was said that after some difficulty with the pose, Hunter 'fatigued, fell into a train of thought ... absorbed in his own reflections', which Reynolds promptly seized.[10] He sat again to Reynolds in 1789, when the head was slightly modified,[11] as is demonstrated by close comparison of the portrait with the Sharp engraving of 1788 - a curious episode; few would agree to have their portraits altered to reflect the effects of illness.[12] Sharp's print was particularly admired; J.T. Smith said he had 'immortalised himself' by it, and Hunter took fifty copies.[13]

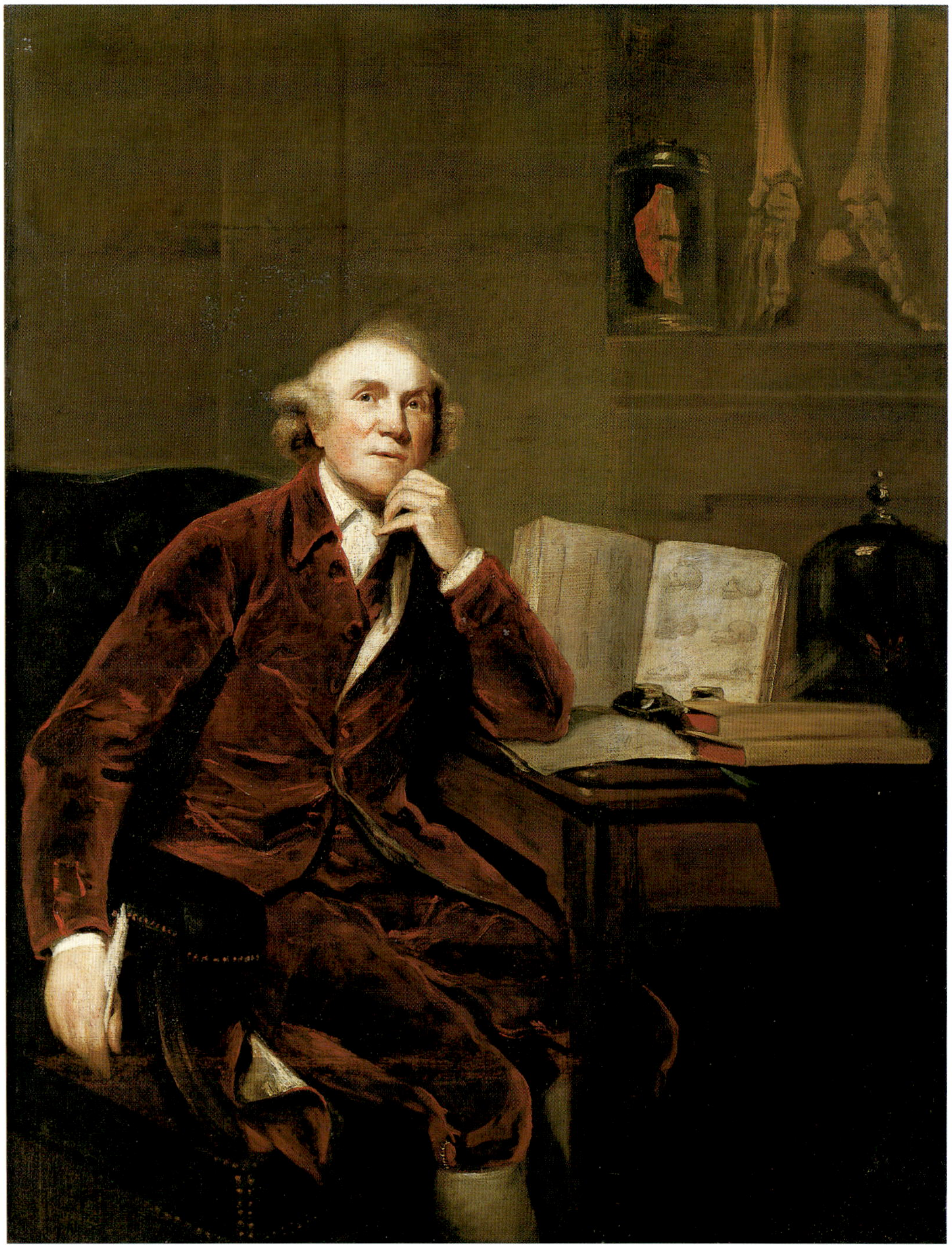

John HUNTER NPG *77*

John Jackson was well-regarded as a copyist. Charles Bell, for whom NPG 77 was made, wrote to his brother on 6 October 1813:[14]

> I have got a beautiful copy of Sir Joshua Reynolds' finest portrait – John Hunter, namely. It is admitted to be nearly as fine as the admired original. There is a man, Jackson, who has a wonderful talent for copying Old Masters. He charges more for a copy than Raeburn does for painting a portrait.

C.R. Leslie recalled that in the autumn of 1813 he and Jackson were both engaged in copying Reynolds's portrait of John Hunter, then on public exhibition at the British Institution, and later, when he saw Jackson's copy in Sir Charles Bell's house, 'had I not been told what it was, I might have mistaken it for the original'.[15] Jackson also made a half-length drawing from the Reynolds portrait which was engraved by R. Cooper in 1814.[16]

Other copies of the Reynolds portrait are: at Oriel College, Oxford;[17] by H.W. Pickersgill c.1850 (three-quarters) in St Bartholomew's Hospital, London (with an anonymous kit-cat copy); St George's Hospital, Tooting; a bust-length enamel miniature by Henry Bone 1798,[18] a variant by H.M. Allen (half length with a wispy beard),[19] and a (damaged and reduced) copy by Muller 1854, are with the Royal College of Surgeons, London; a version without the open book, and the 'prime' version of the bearded half length, are in the Apothecaries' Hall, London, and two nineteenth-century copies (one by Stewart Watson) belong to the Royal College of Surgeons, Edinburgh.[20]

1 That is, an extended kit-cat canvas.
2 These appear indicative rather than specific titles.
3 He was drawn by Thomas Rowlandson (Royal Society of Surgeons, London; illus. LeFanu 1960, pl.52), the drawing engraved (George 6856).
4 A label formerly verso reads: *This Portrait of John Hunter was copied by John Jackson R.A. from the original by Sir Joshua Reynolds in the possession of the Royal College of Surgeons, London, in the year 1816* [but see below], *for Sir Charles Bell: and it was in his possession till his death April 29th 1842.*
5 Mannings 2000, no.973 [NPE 1867(832)].
6 Also engraved as a half length by W. Sharp 1788; later prints include those by R. Cooper 1814, J. Kennerly 1823, S.W. Reynolds 1833 and W.O. Geller 1836.
7 Leslie & Taylor 1865, II, p.475. In 1809 Farington had described the original as 'utterly gone by cracking &c' (10 June).
8 Sir Everard Home (1756–1832), Hunter's brother-in-law and executor.
9 J. Hunter, *A Treatise on the Blood ...*, 1794, pp.xxxiv–xxxv. In 1785 Hunter had moved to Leicester Square becoming a near-neighbour of Reynolds.
10 Leslie & Taylor 1865, II, p.475.
11 X-radiographs taken by the NPG in 1959.
12 Hunter's health had not been good; he suffered increasingly from angina and gout; in May 1788 he had had 'a very severe indisposition for three weeks' (S. Paget, *John Hunter*, 1897, pp.168, 181).
13 *Ibid.*, p.180 (where Hunter is also described as 'a great admirer' of Sharp's work; Smith 1920, I, p.267. Sharp's print was also, apparently, admired by Gainsborough, see Gainsborough NPG 1107.
14 *Sir Charles Bell's Letters*, 1870, p.208. On 12 August he had singled out the Hunter portrait within the Reynolds exhibition at the British Institution as being 'admirable' (*ibid.*, p.207).
15 C.R. Leslie, *Autobiographical Recollections*, 1860, I, pp.77–78.
16 *British Gallery of Contemporary Portraits*, 1822, I, p.70.
17 Poole, II, pp.89–90.
18 Exhibited RA 1798(797); his preparatory drawing in the NPG Bone albums (*Bone* 1999, no.294).
19 Illus. Taylor 1993, fig.2; the beard grown during an outbreak of a rash (J. Kobler, *The Reluctant Surgeon*, 1960, p.265). The portrait has been whimsically described as the first by Reynolds, who then devised the idea of taking a face mask so that Hunter would have to shave (see NPG 4288n3); it passed from Hunter's widow to James Weatherall; thence to his nephew Thomas Knight, by whom presented to the Apothecaries, 1857 (see Taylor 1993, p.1).
20 Reduced copies include one with Spink in 1976, and those sold Christie's, 12 April 1995, lot 485, and another 11 March 1999, lot 33.

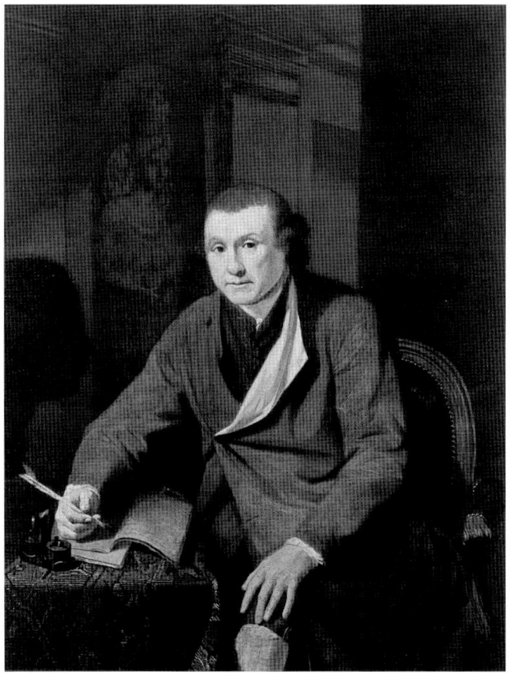

John HUNTER by Robert Home c.1775-79 (Royal College of Surgeons of England)

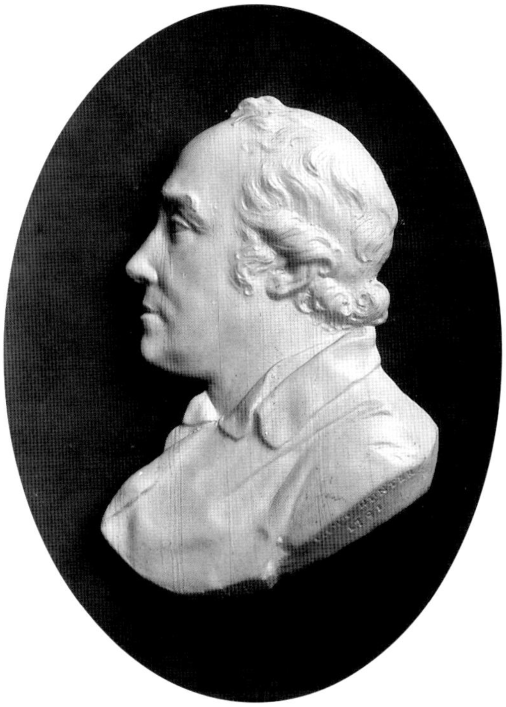

John HUNTER by James Tassie 1791 (Scottish National Portrait Gallery)

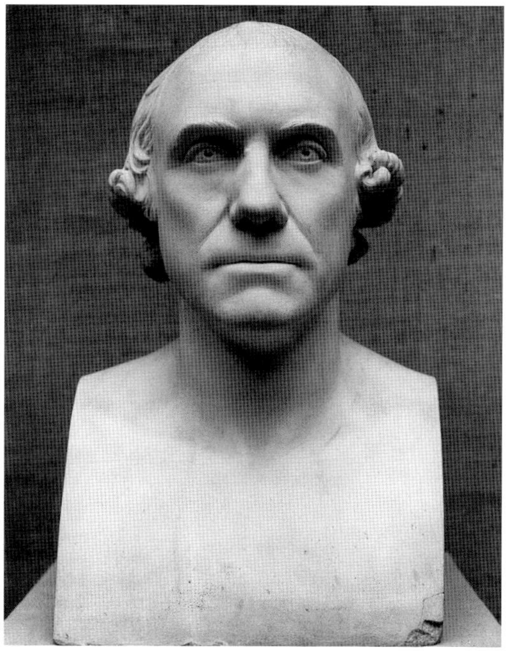

John HUNTER by John Flaxman c.1800-05 (Royal College of Surgeons of England)

ICONOGRAPHY

c.1770 Painting by Robert Home [the sitter's brother-in-law], three-quarter length seated in a landscape. Royal Society, London (illus. *Royal Society* 1980, p.183; Taylor 1993, fig.5). Engraved H. Cook c.1838. A copy by Dorofield Hardy with the Royal College of Surgeons, London.

c.1775-79 Painting by Robert Home,* three-quarter length seated. Royal College of Surgeons, London. Engraved H. Cook 1838.

1785 Prize medal of the Lyceum Medicum by L. Milton, designed by John Flaxman (illus. Bindman 1979, nos.168, 175; Brown 1980, no.262).

c.1785 Plaster life mask. Royal College of Surgeons, London, see NPG 1712 and NPG 4288.

1786 Painting by Joshua Reynolds, see NPG 77.

1786 Engraving by R. Stewart, half length.

1791 Medallion by James Tassie (Gray 1894, no.202). Examples in wax and porcelain in the Royal College of Surgeons, London, and Scottish NPG* (PG 263); listed in copper and bronze by Brown 1980, no.354. Engraved J. Caldwall and, far less capably, by J. Corner 1793 (*European Mag.*); H. Adlard 1861.

1793 Drawing by Nathaniel Dance, half-length seated, much resembling the Tassie medallion. Royal College of Surgeons, London (illus. *AJ*, 1890, p.51; Taylor 1993, fig.7). Inscribed verso: *Drawn by Sir Nathaniel Holland 1793 -- late Dance.* Lithograph (*from a pencil drawing by Sir Nathaniel Holland*) pub. M. & N. Hanhart from a drawing dated 1849 by T.H. Maguire. A related painting was with Sotheby's, March 1996 (bust-length to left, thin white hair, purple coat).

1793 Bust-length oval head, engraved C. Josi. Published 1 December 1793 and inscribed *European Magazine* -- where it was not used, a poor plate by J. Corner (see Tassie 1791) appearing instead.

Posthumous

c.1800-05 Marble bust by John Flaxman,* undraped, based on the life mask. Royal College of Surgeons, London. A silhouette engraving by G. Maile 1818 was taken from the Flaxman bust (see LeFanu 1960, p.42).

1820 Marble bust by Francis Chantrey, draped. Royal College of Surgeons, London (illus. LeFanu 1960, pl.23; *Chantrey* 1994, nos.19b, 108b). Two plaster casts also belong to the College; another in the Ashmolean Museum, Oxford (Penny 1992, III, no.723). Derived in part from the life mask, see NPG 1712 and NPG 4288.

1828 Painting by J. Wilson from a posthumous bust by Chantrey, exhibited RA 1828(1090).

1850 Medal by L.C. Wyon, bust taken from the Reynolds portrait (Brown 1987, no.2395).

Later sculptures include statues by Henry Weekes 1864 (Royal College of Surgeons, London; illus. LeFanu 1960, pl.22); Matthew Noble 1872-74 (Burlington House, London, rear facade); Henry Pinker 1886 (Museum of the History of Science, Oxford), and J.P. Macgillivray 1906 (Scottish NPG, north-east tower).

Half-length bronze by Alfred Gilbert 1893 (St George's Hospital, Tooting; illus. *Gilbert*, RA, 1986, no.82). Busts by Thomas Woolner 1874 (Leicester Square, London); Alfred Drury c.1880 (St George's Hospital, Hyde Park Gate, London); A.L. Vago c.1883 (Royal College of Surgeons, London); Ismond Rosen 1944 (Royal Society of Medicine; illus. Cat., 1988, p.67) and Nigel Boonham 1979 (Lincoln's Inn Fields, London; illus. Byron 1981, p.145).

Plaster bas-relief by John Tweed c.1895 (Royal College of Surgeons, London; illus. LeFanu 1960, pl.23)

DOUBTFUL PORTRAITS

Unattributed painting, half-length holding a skull, Royal College of Surgeons, London (illus. Taylor 1993, fig.9); painted over an 18th-century portrait; the head somewhat resembles Zoffany.

Medal by E.W. Wyon, 'the late John Hunter', exhibited RBA 1835(785) probably showed another sitter of the same name.

HUNTER, William 1718-83

Anatomist, bro. of John Hunter; came to London from Lanark in 1741; physician to the Queen 1764 and professor of Anatomy at the Royal Academy 1768; FRS 1767; formed a considerable collection of natural history, antiquities, books and pictures, bequeathed to Glasgow University, now the Hunterian Museum.

'the polite scholar, accomplished gentleman, the complete anatomist and probably the most perfect demonstrator as well as lecturer the world has ever seen' (Joseph Adams, 1817).

Abbreviation

Kemp 1975: M. Kemp ed., *Dr William Hunter at the Royal Academy of Arts*, 1975

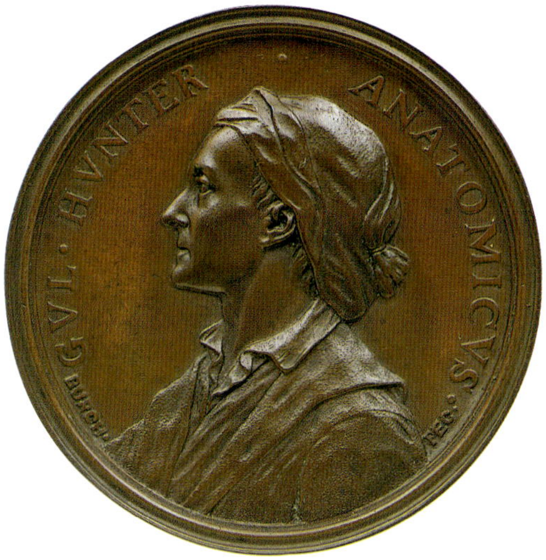

William HUNTER NPG *6012*

6012 EDWARD BURCH 1774

Bronze medal 8 ($3\frac{1}{8}$) diameter with the original fitted case

Obverse: draped bust to left wearing cap, inscribed: *GVL.HVNTER . ANATOMICVS*. and below: *BURCH.FEC.*

Reverse: a classical vase bearing a scene of a surgical operation,[1] inscribed: *OLIM. / MEMINISSE. / IVVABIT.* [Virgil, *Aen.*, i, 203] and date *1774*.

Collections: Purchased from Mrs Neddy Allen 1988.

Reference: Brown 1980, no.188.

The size and style recall earlier Florentine medallists such as Soldani and Selvi, examples of whose work were bought by Hunter and remain in the Hunterian Museum.[2] Burch also made wax écorchés for Hunter.[3]

1 The original in silver, based on a design by William Kent, is in the Hunterian Museum.
2 Compare Spink, *Important Collection of Renaissance and Baroque Medals and Plaquettes*, 1996, no.515.
3 See Kemp 1975, pls.8, 9, pp.16-17.

ICONOGRAPHY

In 1768 Hunter wrote that he was 'pretty much acquainted with most of our best artists and live in friendship with them'.

c.1764 Painting by Allan Ramsay,* three-quarter length seated. Hunterian AG, Glasgow (Smart 1999, no.283). A copy and a bust-length oval miniature version (possibly by Nathaniel Hone, see below) are with the Royal College of Physicians, London (illus. *Cat. of Portraits*, 1977, p.135). Ramsay's preparatory drawing is in the NG of Scotland (D 2017; Smart 1999, fig.728).

1765 Miniature by Nathaniel Hone, bust-length oval. Christie's, 23 June 1958, lot 70. Resembles the Ramsay portrait of c.1764. Presumably the miniature exhibited SA 1765(55).

1769 Painting by Mason Chamberlin,* half-length. Royal Academy, London, presented by the artist (illus. Kemp 1975, pl.7). Engraved as half length J. Collyer 1783; B. Smith from a drawing by M. Haughton, 1817. Exhibited NPE 1867(829). The head closely resembles that by Zoffany in *Hunter lecturing at the Royal Academy*. Half-length oval miniature copy, ascribed to G.M. Moser, Hunterian AG, Glasgow.

c.1770 Painting by R.E. Pine, seated at table. Royal College of Surgeons, London (illus. LeFanu 1960, pl.18). Engraved J. Thomson 1838.

c.1771 Drawing attributed to Charles Grignion jr.,* bust-length profile, wearing spectacles. Hunterian AG, Glasgow (illus. Kemp 1975, pl.5). Probably drawn as Zoffany was making sketches for his *Academicians* of 1772 (see also Wilton NPG 4314).

1772 Painting by Johann Zoffany,* *The Academicians of the Royal Academy*, see Groups NPG 1437.

c.1772 Painting by Johann Zoffany, *Dr William Hunter lecturing at the Royal Academy*. Royal College of Physicians, London (illus. *Cat. of Portraits*, 1964, p.233).

1774 Medal by Edward Burch, see NPG 6012.

1777-84 Painting by James Barry, *Distribution of Premiums in the Society of Arts*, part of the *Progress of Human Culture*, in which Hunter appears lower right. Royal Society of Arts, London (Pressly 1981, no.26). Engraved J. Barry 1791.

1780 Drawn and engraved by J. Thornthwaite, oval half-length seated. Re-issued 1812.

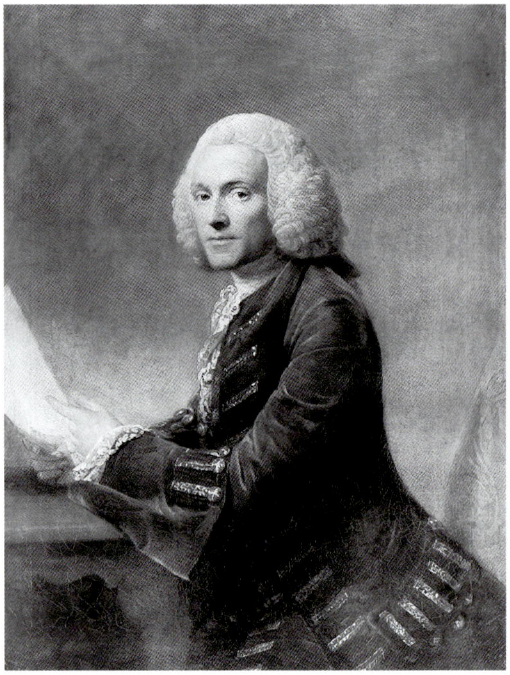

William HUNTER by Allan Ramsay c.1764 (Hunterian Art Gallery, Glasgow)

c.1780 Miniature attributed to Richard Crosse, half-length oval. Royal College of Physicians, London (illus. *Cat. of Portraits*, 1964, p.235).

c.1780 Painting attributed to James Barry, half length. Royal College of Physicians, London (illus. *Cat. of Portraits*, 1977, p.137; Pressly 1981, no.51). The body is evidently by an inferior hand, but the head relates directly to that of Hunter in the *Distribution of Premiums* (see 1777-84).

1783 Medal by Thomas Pingo (Brown 1980, no.224; illus. Eimer 1998, no.63). Engraved W. Read; W. Angus from a drawing by Millar, inscribed 'from a model in the possession of Mr Pingo of the Tower' (*European Mag*.; illus. L. Jordanova, *Defining Features*, NPG, 2000, p.24).

Posthumous

1783 Death Mask. Hunterian Museum, Glasgow (illus. *British Medical Journal*, CCIXC, 1985, p.1787).

1785 Gemstone[?] by William Brown, exhibited RA 1785(362).

1785 Miniature by John Bogle, exhibited RA 1785(281).

1787 Painting by Joshua Reynolds standing three-quarter length to left. Hunterian AG, Glasgow (Mannings 2000, no.976). Engraved S. Freeman 1855; J. Smith. A posthumous portrait largely derived, according to contemporary description, from the portraits by Zoffany and Mason Chamberlin and from Hunter's death mask (Whitley 1928, II, p.83). Two copies belong to the

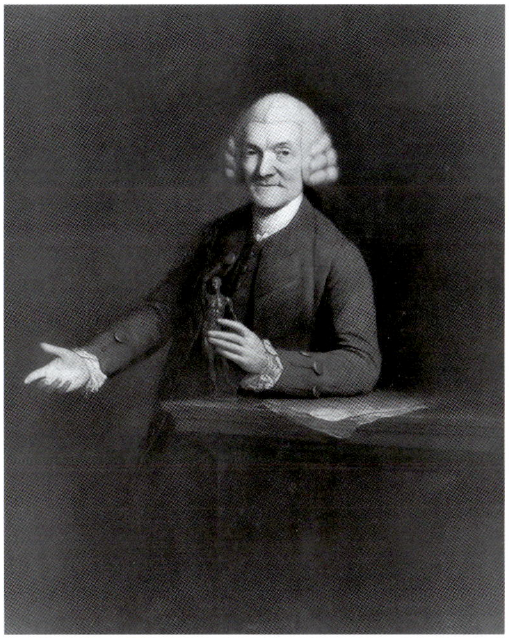

William HUNTER by Mason Chamberlin 1769 (Royal Academy of Arts, London)

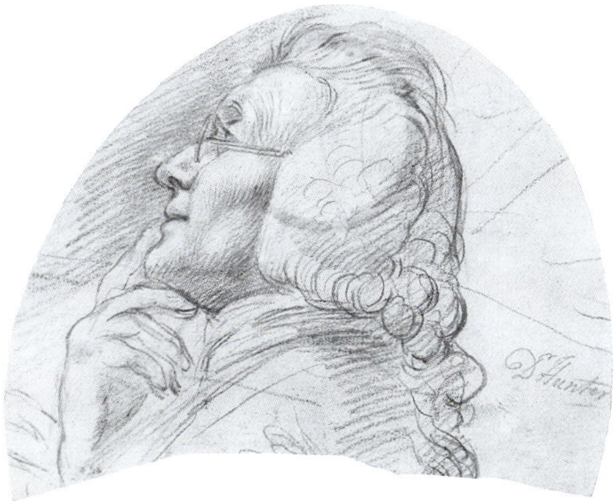

William HUNTER by Charles Grignon junior c.1771 (Hunterian Art Gallery, Glasgow)

Royal College of Surgeons, London, and another to the Royal Faculty of Physicians and Surgeons, Glasgow (formerly attributed to Pine); a small copy by J.G. Gilbert is in Glasgow AG (553).

DOUBTFUL PORTRAITS

Silhouette, seated writing (Royal College of Surgeons, London) engraved c.1834; drawing by Elias Martin, *A Lecture on Anatomy* (Nationalmuseum, Stockholm, 61/1909);

A painting by Cosmo Alexander (Newport Historical Society, RI; illus. *AQ*, XXVI, 1963, p.321) shows another William Hunter.

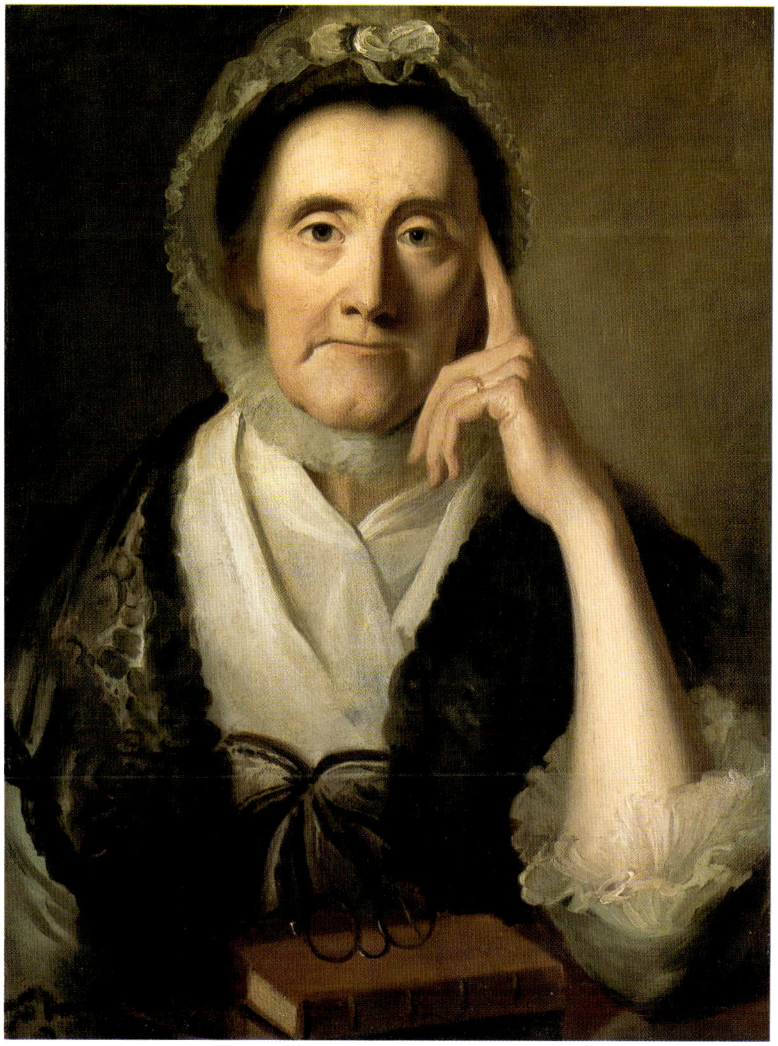

Selina, Countess of HUNTINGDON NPG 4224

HUNTINGDON, Selina, Countess of, *née* Shirley 1707-91

'Patriarchess of the Methodists'; dau. of the 2nd Earl Ferrers, m. 1728 Theophilus Hastings, 9th Earl of Huntingdon (d.1746); of her seven children, five had died by 1763; converted to Methodism by 1739 and through her peeress's privilege established 'Lady Huntingdon's Connexion', appointing her own nonconformist chaplains and building her own chapels; her crusade against worldliness often considered to be 'much at variance with high rank and good breeding'.

Abbreviation

Schlenther 1997: B.S. Schlenther, *Queen of the Methodists*, 1997

4224 UNKNOWN ARTIST c.1780

Oil on card on panel 56 x 42.5 (22 x 16¾); the card is wrapped round the panel and the painting was evidently larger originally; an old horizontal tear runs from the chin to the left edge; a pentimento on her left forearm.

Grey eyes, black hair with a white bonnet, wearing a grey dress white fichu and a black lace shawl.

Collections: Given or bequeathed to John Elkington;[1] by descent to his great-grandson, John St C. Elkington, by whom presented 1961.

A slightly reduced version of a half-length painted oval in a private collection, which has been tentatively attributed to James Millar of Birmingham.[2] The sitter appears slightly older than in the engraved Russell half length of 1776 (see below); in both portraits her head leans on her left hand, the pose recurring in the portrait by Bowyer engraved in 1790.

1 According to J. St C. Elkington (letter of 28 June 1961; NPG archive), together with a Chippendale chair and a trowel, both allegedly used by Lady Huntingdon in Birmingham. Notes of a conversation between C.K. Adams and Elkington in March 1950 record that Lady Huntingdon herself made the gift or bequest: the Elkingtons, electro-plating manufacturers, were an Unitarian family of Birmingham; but all her possessions were left to four self-perpetuating Trustees, Lady Anne Erskine, Thomas and Janetta Haweis and John Lloyd (Schlenther 1997, p.183).

2 An attribution favourably discussed in correspondence between John Kerslake and Sir Gyles Isham in 1968; NPG archive.

ICONOGRAPHY

c.1738 Painting by Andrea Soldi,* seated three-quarter length, with two children identified by an inscription as Fernando (b.1732) and Elizabeth (b.1731). Sir Rupert Bromley. Dated by the apparent ages of the named children.

1745 Painting by Andrea Soldi, three-quarter length seated, with her husband and two of their children, Selina (b.1737) and Henry (b.1739). Cheshunt Foundation, Westminster College, Cambridge (illus. *Brycheiniog*, XV, 1971, f.p.94, pl.1C, reversed; Schlenther 1997, f.p.82, pl.1, reduced). Said to have been dated 1745 which agrees with the apparent ages of the named children. An undated letter to Lady Huntingdon from her daughter Elizabeth mentions going 'to Soldie to see my Dear Papa's and your picture ... I never saw anything more like than Br Henry and Sister Selina and papa but as for you Mama he has made you a sad figure and he has tied a purple Hankerchief round about the Neck of your black Velvet gown' (Huntington Library, San Marino, Calif.; HA 1040B).

after 1746 High-relief medallion portrait by J.M. Rysbrack, set on her husband's monument (he d. 1746). Hastings Chapel, St Helen's Church, Ashby-de-la-Zouch (illus. *Architectural History*, XXIX, 1986, p.160; Schlenther 1997, f.p.82, pl.2).

1773 Painting by John Russell, whole-length standing, a white veil on her head, a crown of thorns in her right hand, her foot on her coronet. Engraved anon. 1773,* the print described by Walpole as showing 'much pompous humility' with the Countess resembling 'an old basket-woman' (*Wal. Corr.*, XXXV, p.346). The original painting appears to have been dispatched to Lady Huntingdon's colony in Georgia, America, and mercifully lost *en route*, see c.1776 below.

c.1776 Painting by John Russell, half-length painted oval. Cheshunt Foundation, Westminster College, Cambridge. Engraved anon. 1776 (*Gospel Mag.*), and 1784 (*Spiritual Mag.*). Williamson 1894, p.139, described this as a second portrait by Russell, the first having been lost on its way to America (see 1773 above).

c.1780 Unattributed painting, see NPG 4224.

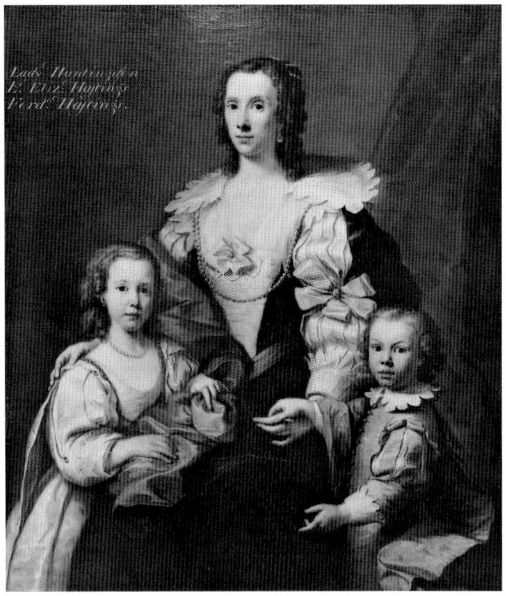

Selina, Countess of HUNTINGDON by Andrea Soldi c.1738 (Sir Rupert Bromley)

c.1785 Pastel by Samuel Cotes, half-length oval. NG of Ireland (3020).

c.1785–90 Unattributed painting, half length, drawing a curtain with her left hand (the head appears to resemble that by Bowyer of 1790). Woburn Abbey in 1884 (SSB 110/18), but not in the Woburn *Biographical Cat.*, 1892.

1790 Painting by Robert Bowyer, half-length seated, her left elbow resting on *Galatians vi*. Engraved J. Fittler 1790; J. Cross 1824 from a drawing by F. Hurlstone (showing two closed books on the table and a half-open book in her right hand); R. Page 1819 (half length, her elbow resting on closed books). Reduced bust-length oval version engraved Malpas 1798 (cover of *A Collection of Hymns*). A variant half-length oval, holding a sheet of paper in her right hand, engraved D. Lundin 1804.

1790 Drawn and engraved by C. Blackberd, half-length oval, *Aged 83*.

1790 Etching by J. Kay, half-length oval (*Kay's Portraits* 1842, II, f.p.16).

c.1790? Silhouette by Hinton Gibbs. Bonham's, 8 November 1993, lot 5.

Undated Ink drawing by Benjamin West,* *Countes of Huntingdon*. NG Washington (B-30, 828).

Posthumous

1791 Medal by W. Mainwaring (Brown 1980, no.351).

1791 Caricature, *The Tears of Methodism* (George 7962; illus. Schlenther 1997, pl.5), published to mourn the death of a 'well-meaning misguided countess'.

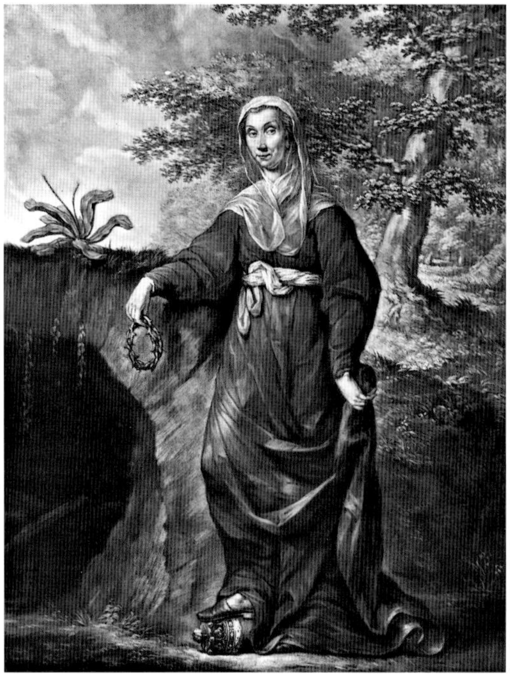

Selina, Countess of HUNTINGDON, anon. after John Russell 1773 (NPG D 3128)

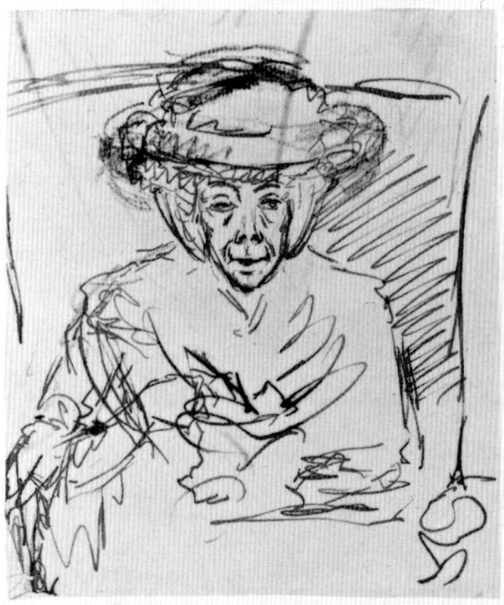

Selina, Countess of HUNTINGDON by Benjamin West (National Gallery of Art, Washington)

DOUBTFUL PORTRAITS

Paintings formerly attributed to Henry Morland (Holborn Hall, Gray's Inn Road, London, in 1924), and formerly attributed to William Hogarth (Walters AG, Baltimore).

HUTTON, Charles 1737-1823

Mathematician; b. Newcastle, he opened a mathematical school at Jesmond 1760; wrote *The Schoolmaster's Guide* 1764 and many essays, primarily in the field of applied mathematics; professor of mathematics at the Royal Academy, Woolwich 1773-1807; FRS 1774; LL.D. Edinburgh 1779.

'He is remarkable for his unassuming deportment, for the simplicity of his habits, the mildness and equability of his temper, and the permanency and warmth of his personal attachments' (*GM*, 1823).

5783 BENJAMIN WYON 1823

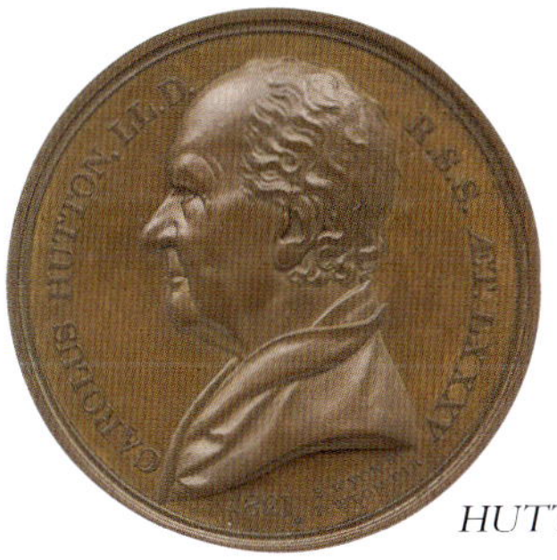

HUTTON NPG *5783*

Bronze medal 4.4 (1¾) diameter

Obverse: profile bust to left, inscribed: *1821 CAROLUS HUTTON, LL.D. R.S.S.*[1] *AET.LXXXV* and below: *B.WYON SC./T.WYON DIR*

Reverse: a globe suspended from a weighing bar and a quadrant with a cannon (see below), inscribed: *FULMINA BELLI/ PONDUSQ.TERRAE/ AESTIMATA*

Collection: Mrs Neddy Allen, from whom purchased 1985.

Engraving: J. Thomson; H. Fisher 1823.[2]

Reference: Brown 1980, no.1158.

The inscribed date, 1821, derives from Gahagan's bust (see below), on which the likeness is evidently based,[3] but Wyon's medal was only finished in time to be distributed at Hutton's funeral in January 1823,[4] and an impression was exhibited at the RA that year (no.1007). Benjamin Wyon, the modeller, was then in his twenty-first year. The medal had been commissioned from money left over from the subscription for the bust,[5] the Committee agreeing in 1822 that the balance should be used

> to engrave a Die, for striking off Medals, (one of which to be given in a Case to each Subscriber,) to contain, on the *Obverse*, the Head of Dr. Hutton, in profile, with an appropriate Legend of Name, Age, & c. -- *On the Reverse*, Emblems of two Philosophical Discoveries by Dr. Hutton; the one on the Density or Weight of the Earth, and the other on the Exact Force or Strength of Gunpowder; with an appropriate Motto, &c.[6]

The reverse celebrates Hutton's *Force of fired gunpowder, and the initial Velocities of Cannon balls* 1776-78, and his *Mean Density of the Earth* 1778 (revised 1821).

1 That is, FRS (regalis societatis socius).
2 See R. Burgess, *Portraits of Doctors & Scientists in the Wellcome Institute of the History of Medicine*, 1973, p.182.
3 The socle of the Gahagan bust is inscribed: *HUTTON, LL.B.R.S.S./ OB. 1821, AET.85*, the '*OB.*' an unfortunate error.
4 *GM*, XCIII, 1823, i, p.232; *European Mag.*, LXXXIII, 1823, i, p.486.
5 The subscription raised over £168 (£115 from individuals at £1 each and 51 gn. from five public bodies): lists printed in the *Tribute of Respect to Charles Hutton ... by the Presentation of his Bust in Marble*, [1822], pamphlet 8pp. (copy in NPG archive).
6 As quoted in the *Tribute*, see note 5.

ICONOGRAPHY

1804 Painting by Henry Ashby, exhibited RA 1804(34).

1804 Miniature by Miss M. Byrne, exhibited RA 1804(754). Engraved C. Knight, and a version engraved W. Read.

1812 Painting by Henry Ashby, three-quarter length; engraved C. Turner 1812 as *Aetat 75, 1812* (half length); anon. 1824.

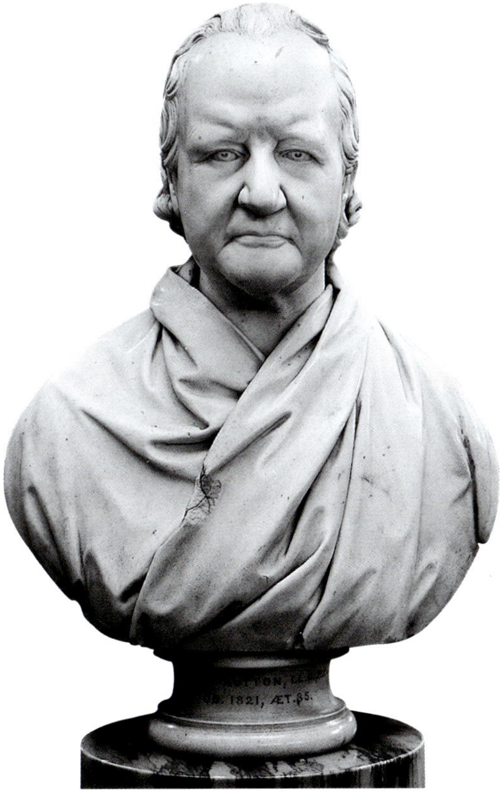

HUTTON by Sebastian Gahagan 1822 (Literary and Philosophical Society of Newcastle upon Tyne)

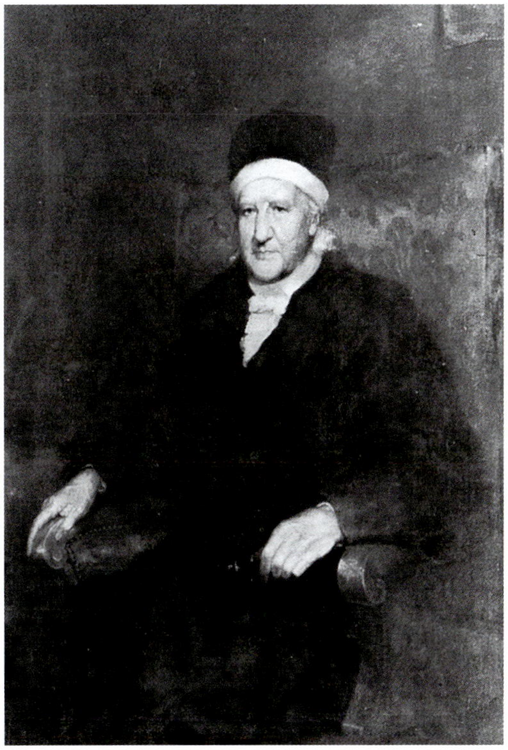

HUTTON by Andrew Morton 1823 (Literary and Philosophical Society of Newcastle upon Tyne)

1821 Painting by Henry Ashby, exhibited RA 1821(408).

1822 Marble bust by Sebastian Gahagan,* with loose drapery (see NPG 5783). Newcastle Literary & Philosophical Society. Commissioned by subscription for the sitter who bequeathed it to the Society. Exhibited RA 1822(1034). Engraved J. Thomson 1823 from a drawing by W. Derby (*European Mag.*). The plaster model was completed in 1821 and the marble bust presented to the sitter on 21 September 1822. Casts were obtained by 'many of Dr. Hutton's friends, and still continue to be supplied by the sculptor' (*GM*, XCIII, 1823, i, p.232).

1823 Painting by Andrew Morton,* three-quarter length seated. Newcastle Literary & Philosophical Society (illus. *Art for Newcastle*, 1984, p.94). Exhibited RA 1823(236).

1823 Medal by Benjamin Wyon, see NPG 5783.

1824 Anon. engraving, half length, writing at table; the head apparently derived from the 1812 Ashby portrait.

DOUBTFUL PORTRAITS

Gunnis 1968, p.95, listed a bust of Hutton by Francis Chantrey belonging to the Newcastle Literary Society, but it does not appear in the Chantrey Ledgers and was apparently a confusion with the bust by Gahagan described above.

IMPEY, Sir Elijah, Kt 1732-1809

Judge; recorder of Basingstoke 1766-73; Kt 1774 on his appointment as the first chief justice of the supreme court of Bengal, where he joined his old acquaintance Warren Hastings; recalled in 1783 for investigation, but escaped impeachment, finally resigning in 1787; MP 1790-96; a scholar, accomplished in Latin, French, Persian and Hindustani.

335 JOHANN ZOFFANY c.1771-72

Canvas 124.5 x 99 (49 x 39) lined; the face is rubbed and there is extensive crazing within the discoloured varnish.

Blue-grey eyes, grey hair, wearing a light-brown gown with dark-brown fur trim over a grey waistcoat; a deep-red curtain to the left.

Collections: Bequeathed by the sitter's godson, Sir Roderick Impey Murchison 1872.[1]

Exhibition: National Gallery -1920.

Reference: Williamson 1920, p.221.

Impey here appears appreciably younger than in Zoffany's Indian portraits of 1783-84 (see below), indicating a date prior to his departure for Bengal in 1774 and prior to Zoffany's departure for Italy in June 1772. Such contact may explain how, on his arrival in India in 1783, Zoffany immediately received further sittings.

1 Bequeathed with portraits of Lady Impey by Zoffany and a Raeburn of his Father, both of which were rejected.

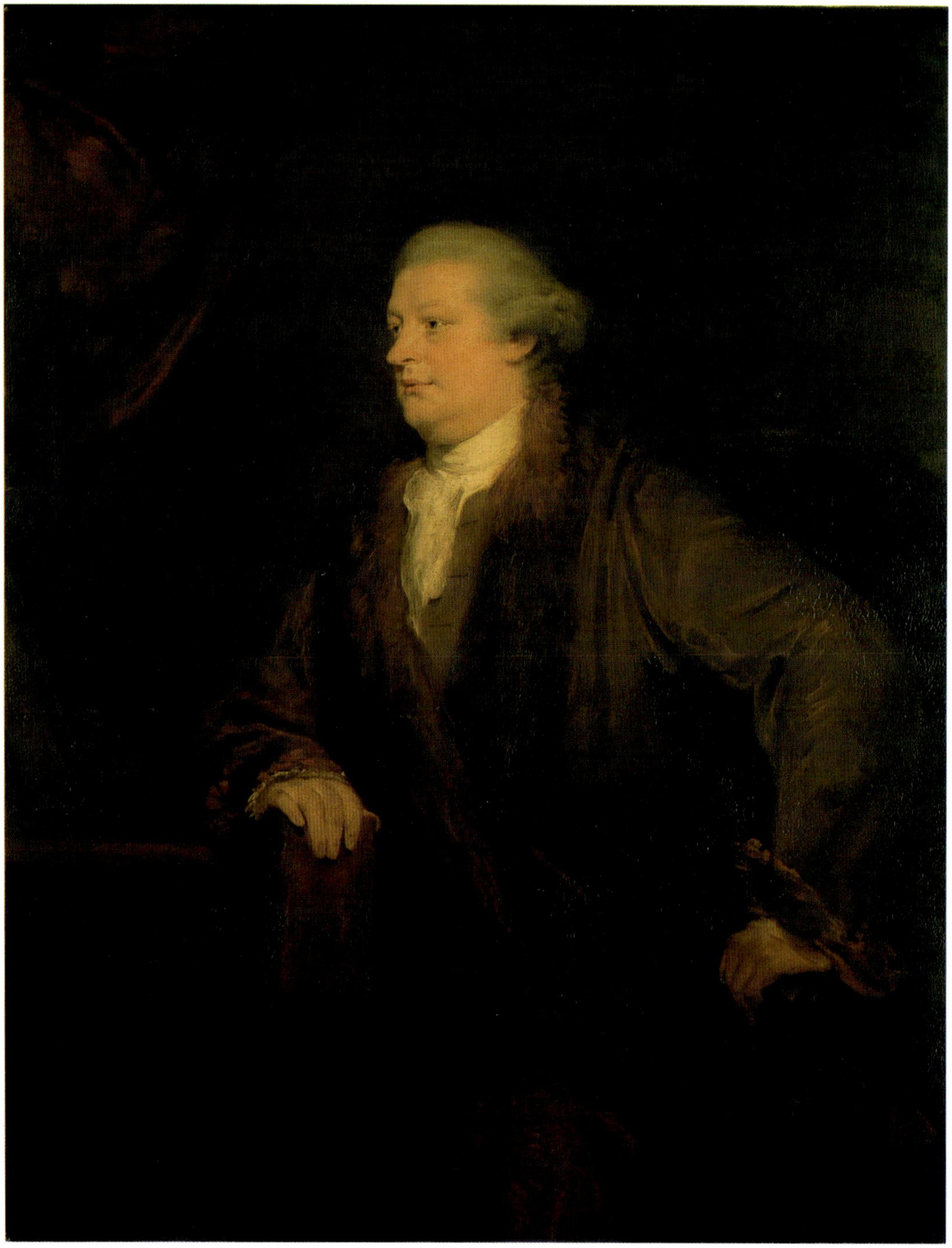

IMPEY NPG *335*

821 THOMAS LAWRENCE 1786

Pastel 32.5 x 27.5 (12¾ x 10¾) oval; the lower edges are scuffed from a previous mount; some spotting. A label, formerly on the back of the frame (now separately conserved), in the artist's hand: *Be pleas'd to keep / this from the Sun & Damp - / TLawrence Pinxt./Aet 16.1786.*

Blue eyes, white powdered wig; wearing a royal blue coat with metal buttons, a beige waistcoat and white neckcloth; he sits on a red chair; behind him a brown curtain above the window.

Collections: Warren Hastings; Daylesford House sale, Farebrother, Clark & Lye, 22-27 August 1853, lot 821;[1] Mrs Charlotte Hartree; her children, William, Charles & John Hartree and Mrs Isabella Rayner, by whom presented 1889.

Exhibition: *Pickpocketing the Rich*, Bath (Holburne), 2002 (56).

Reference: *Lawrence* 1964, p.262.

Sold from the Hastings collection in 1853 as the companion piece to Lawrence's pastel of Warren Hastings, see NPG 3823. A signed and inscribed duplicate, sold Christie's, 17 February 1956, lot 2, is now in a private collection.

1 Old label, formerly verso, *Bought at the sale of Warren Hastings Effects at Daylesford - August/53*, and surely lot 821 (*companion* [to lot 820, see Hastings NPG 3823] *portrait of a Gentleman in a blue dress*).

ICONOGRAPHY

c.1770 Miniature by Ozias Humphry, bust-length oval. Christie's, 10 November 1993, lot 50. Impey's name appears in Humphry's fee book in 1768 and 1770; he later encouraged the artist to make his Indian visit in 1785-87.

c.1771-72 Painting by Johann Zoffany, see NPG 335.

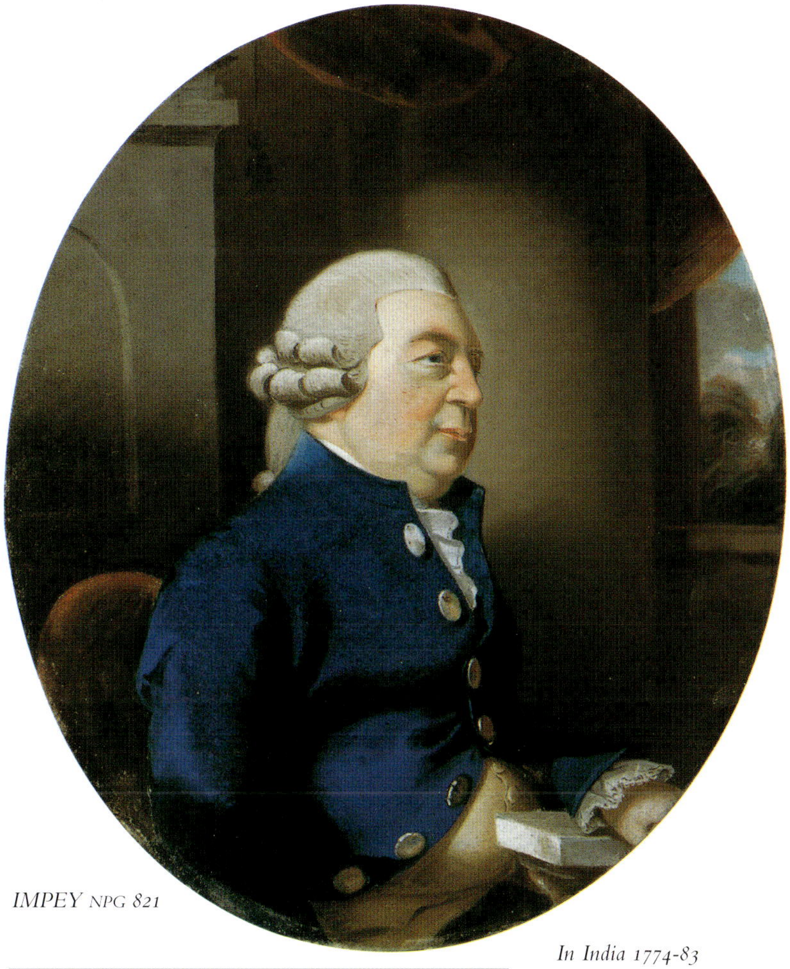

IMPEY NPG 821

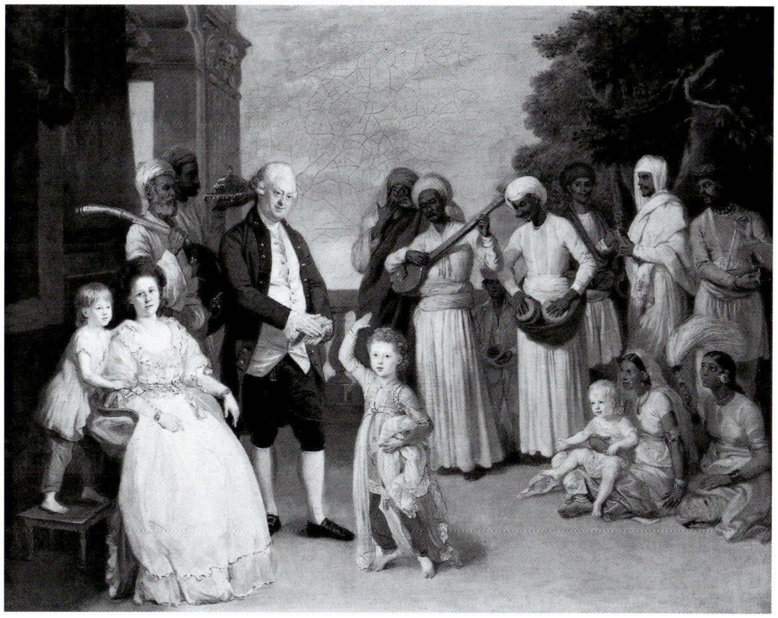

IMPEY with his Family, by Johann Zoffany 1783-84 (Museo Thyssen-Bornemisza, Madrid)

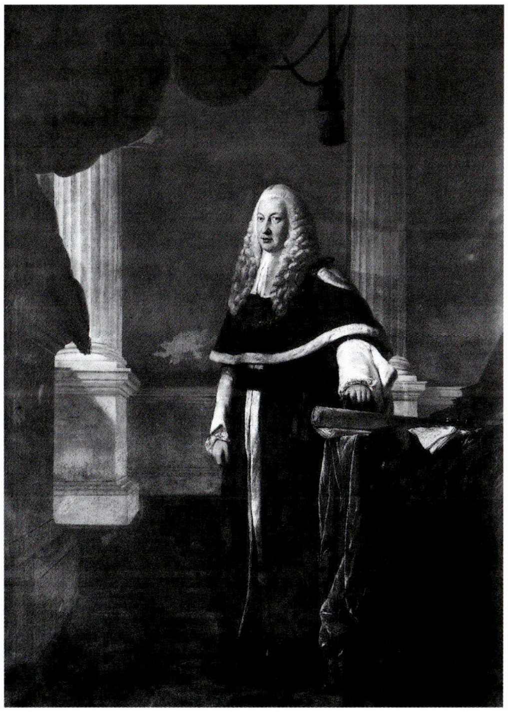

IMPEY by Tilly Kettle 1775 (NPG archive)

In India 1774-83

1775 Painting by Tilly Kettle,* whole-length standing in Judge's robes. Destroyed, formerly High Court Dacca, Bangladesh. Kettle served on the jury for the Nand Kumar trial in 1775, one of Impey's first and most complex cases.

c.1775 Painting by Tilly Kettle, three-quarter length seated in judge's robes. Victoria Memorial Hall, Calcutta, since 1928 (illus. Archer 1979, p.89). Engraved Carlos 1846 (half length).

1783 Painting by Johann Zoffany, whole-length standing in judge's robes. High Court, Calcutta (illus. Archer 1979, p.138). Zoffany arrived in Calcutta on 15 September 1783 and Impey left for England that December. A platinotype is in the India Office (illus. *The Raj*, NPG, 1990-91, no.128).

1783 Painting by Johann Zoffany,* half-length painted oval in private dress. Private collection (illus. Archer 1979, p.135).

1783-84 Painting by Johann Zoffany,* *The Impey Family listening to strolling musicians*, in which Impey stands whole length in private dress with his wife and three children. Thyssen-Bornemisza Museum (445). The picture must have been completed after the Impeys left India (see under 1783 above).

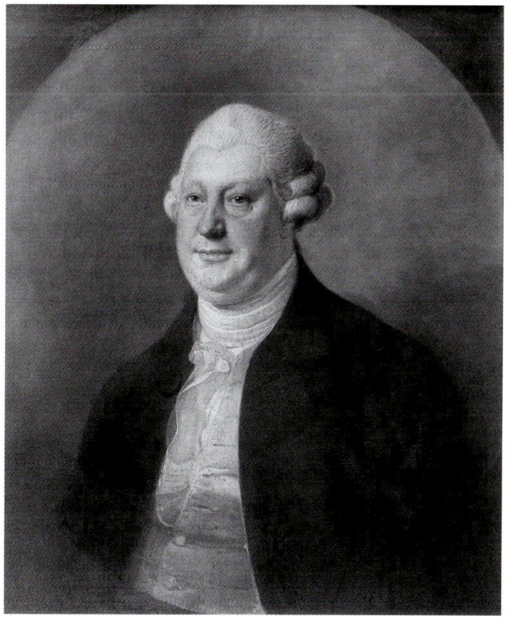

IMPEY by Johann Zoffany 1783 (Sotheby's)

In England 1784–

1786 Drawing by Thomas Lawrence, see NPG 821.

1798 Silhouette by Tiberius Cavallo, with his family (eleven figures and a dog; see McKechnie 1978, p.382). Probably that sold Sotheby's 12-21 October 1987, lot 2409.

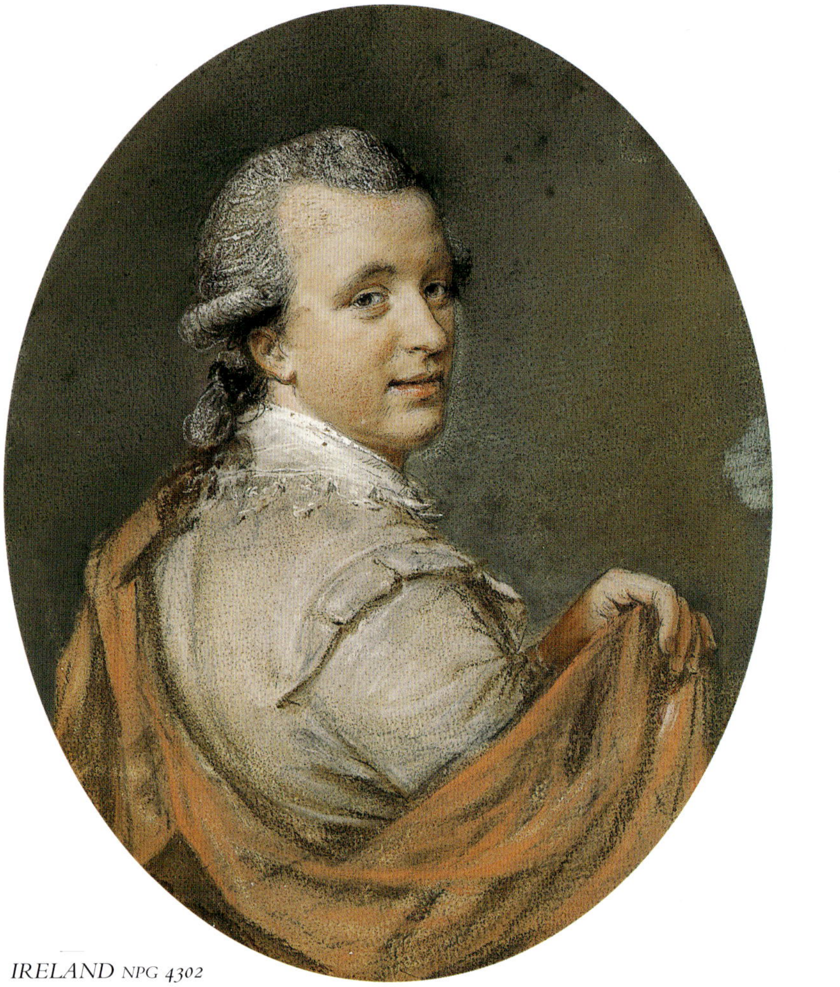

IRELAND NPG *4302*

1799 Miniature by John Smart (listed by Foskett 1964, p.69). Smart had been in India 1785–95.

1802 A bust by J.C.F. Rossi, exhibited RA 1802(1075).

DOUBTFUL PORTRAITS

Paintings attributed to Gilbert Stuart (illus. *Connoisseur*, XLVIII, 1917, p.37), and by Philip Simpson, sold Christie's, Glasgow, 23/29/30 November 1995, lot 834.

IRELAND, Samuel 1744[1]–1800

Engraver; weaver in Spitalfields who turned to dealing in prints and drawings while practising as a self-taught artist and engraver; exhibited RA 1784 and contributed to the *Graphic Illustrations of Hogarth* 1794; his later career centred on the defence of his (putative) son W.H. Ireland (1777–1835) against charges of forgery (as the 'Shakespeare' play *Vortigern* of 1796).

1 The evidence for this date is the inscription on the verso of NPG 4302, see below.

4302 HUGH DOUGLAS HAMILTON 1776

Pastel on grey paper 26.5 x 21 (10½ x 8¼) oval; retouching in the wig, forehead and the left side of the head, and some grey spot staining in background area; further damp staining below left and an abrasion centre right edge; a label formerly on frame verso inscribed: *Samuel Ireland / Born 1744 / and in another hand: Sl.Ireland. / Drawn by / Hamilton. / 1776.*; the original wooden backboard inscribed in a contemporary hand: *Hamilton 1776.*

Grey eyes, grey powdered hair, wearing a light grey Van Dyck costume with an orange drape.

Collections: [by descent from the sitter to][1] Mrs Gwendoline May Butt; her sale, P.H. Inman, Hove, 6–7 September 1960, lot 167; Sotheby's, 20 February 1963, lot 43 (as by William Hamilton), bt. Leggatt for the NPG.

Engraving: S. Ireland.

Exhibition: *Master Drawings* 1993–95(31).

Ireland's undated etching from this portrait (in the same sense and inscribed *Hamilton pinxt. S. Ireland fect.*) shows minor differences in the collar, ear and hair.

1 Mrs Butt was said to be Ireland's great-granddaughter (MS note on her sale cat., NPG).

ICONOGRAPHY

1760 Unattributed miniature, bust length. Butt sale, P.H. Inman, Hove, 6–7 September 1960, lot 172.

c.1770 Painting on copper, attributed to John Downman, half-length oval in Van Dyck dress. Christie's 2 June 1961, lot 32 (previously Butt sale, P.H. Inman, Hove, 6–7 September 1960, lot 143; a companion piece, the same lot, sold as John Ireland). A weaker variant was in a private collection in 1987.

1776 Pastel by H.D. Hamilton, see NPG 4302.

DOUBTFUL PORTRAIT

Painting attributed to William Beechey, half length holding a folio volume lettered *HOGARTH*, Ehrich Galleries, New York, 1920 (not listed in Roberts 1907).

IRWIN, Sir John, KB 1722–88

Army officer; b. Dublin; colonel 1761; MP 1762–83; governor of Gibraltar 1766–68; lieutenant-general 1772; KB 1779; commander-in-chief Ireland 1775–82; general 1782; his last years were spent abroad in some financial difficulty; d. in Parma.

'His person, manners and conversation were all made for the drawing-room, ... his figure, tall, graceful, and dignified, set off by all the ornaments of dress, accompanied by a ribband and star, rendered him conspicuous in every company ... no man better knew the value of external figure aided by manner' (Sir Nathaniel Wraxall, 1815).

682 FRANCIS WHEATLEY, *reviewing Troops in Dublin* 1781

Canvas 242 x 182 (95¼ x 71½) lined; a horizontal seam 63 (24¾) from the top; there are minor losses in the central horse's neck and in the trees above; signed and dated, bottom centre left: *F. Wheatley px / 1781.*

On the left General Irwin's horse attended by his (presumably liveried) servant wearing a black hat, green coat with silver-trim and brown boots, holding a saddle cloth bearing the motto and crest of the Bath. The foreground staff officers (who remain unidentified) have black hats, red coats with epaulettes and blue facings, white gloves, white breeches and black boots. The standing officer with the stick in his right hand wears a purple sash, as does the mounted officer behind him. On the right, Irwin stands against another's horse (which bears a gold saddle cloth), receiving a dispatch; he wears the ribbon and badge of the Bath and the two embroideries round the cuff indicate his rank of lieutenant general.[1]

Collections: W.H. Hughes, Balham; Christie's, 22 December 1877, lot 105; Graves, from whom purchased 1882.

Exhibitions: NG of Ireland, 1897–1934; *Wheatley*, Aldeburgh, Leeds, 1965(7); *Bicentenary Exhibition*, RA, 1968–69(*hors catalogue*).

Reference: Webster 1970, no.36.

NPG 682 was painted in Dublin, where Wheatley resided in 1781 when Irwin was commander-in-chief. No other portrait of Irwin is now known; he was made colonel of the 3rd regiment of horse in Ireland in 1780 (and, according to Wraxall, was given the sixth Dragoon Guards by the King). As commander in Ireland Irwin enjoyed 'very ample appointments and advantages'; in 1781 he gave a banquet in Dublin for the Lord Lieutenant, Lord Carlisle, at which 'he displayed on the table, as the principal piece in the dessert, a representation of the fortress of Gibraltar, invested by the Spanish forces, executed in confectionery ... together with the works, batteries, and artillery of the besiegers, which threw sugar plumbs against the walls'.[2]

NPG 682 had previously been variously identified. It was sold in 1877 as *George III and staff at a Review*; in 1882 it was offered to the NPG as *The Encampment in Hyde Park during the Gordon Riots with portraits of Lord Amherst, Genl Conway, Alderman Turner, &c.*,[3] and in 1888 it was catalogued as a *Military Group of Officers, believed to include Lord Amherst and Field Marshal Conway*. In 1896 it was identified as a *Review of Troops in the Phoenix Park, Dublin, by General Sir John Irwin, KB*,[4] a title which now appears correct, although the identification of Phoenix Park is probable rather than topographical. More recently NPG 682 was very tentatively, but it seems mistakenly, associated with a painting exhibited by Wheatley at the Society of Artists in 1783(320), the *Review of the Irish Volunteers in the Phoenix Park, Dublin*.[5]

1 Cf. Maj. N.P. Dawnay, *JSAHR*, XXXI, 1953, p.71.
2 Wraxall, III, pp.91–92. Irwin had himself been governor of Gibraltar 1766–68. See also Groups NPG 1752.
3 As described by Henry Graves, letter to Scharf, 19 March 1883; NPG archive.
4 F.R. Falhirer, letter of 28 June 1896 (NPG archive), first suggested the subject was a review by General Sir John Irwin in Phoenix Park, Dublin; he emphasised that it had nothing to do with the Irish Volunteers who were disbanded in 1781 and not reviewed that year; Lord Carlisle, the lord-lieutenant, was not KB.
5 As recounted in Webster 1970, p.129. Wheatley's *Irish Volunteers at College Green* 1779 (NG of Ireland), illus. Webster 1970, fig.35, shows different uniforms, and see note 4.

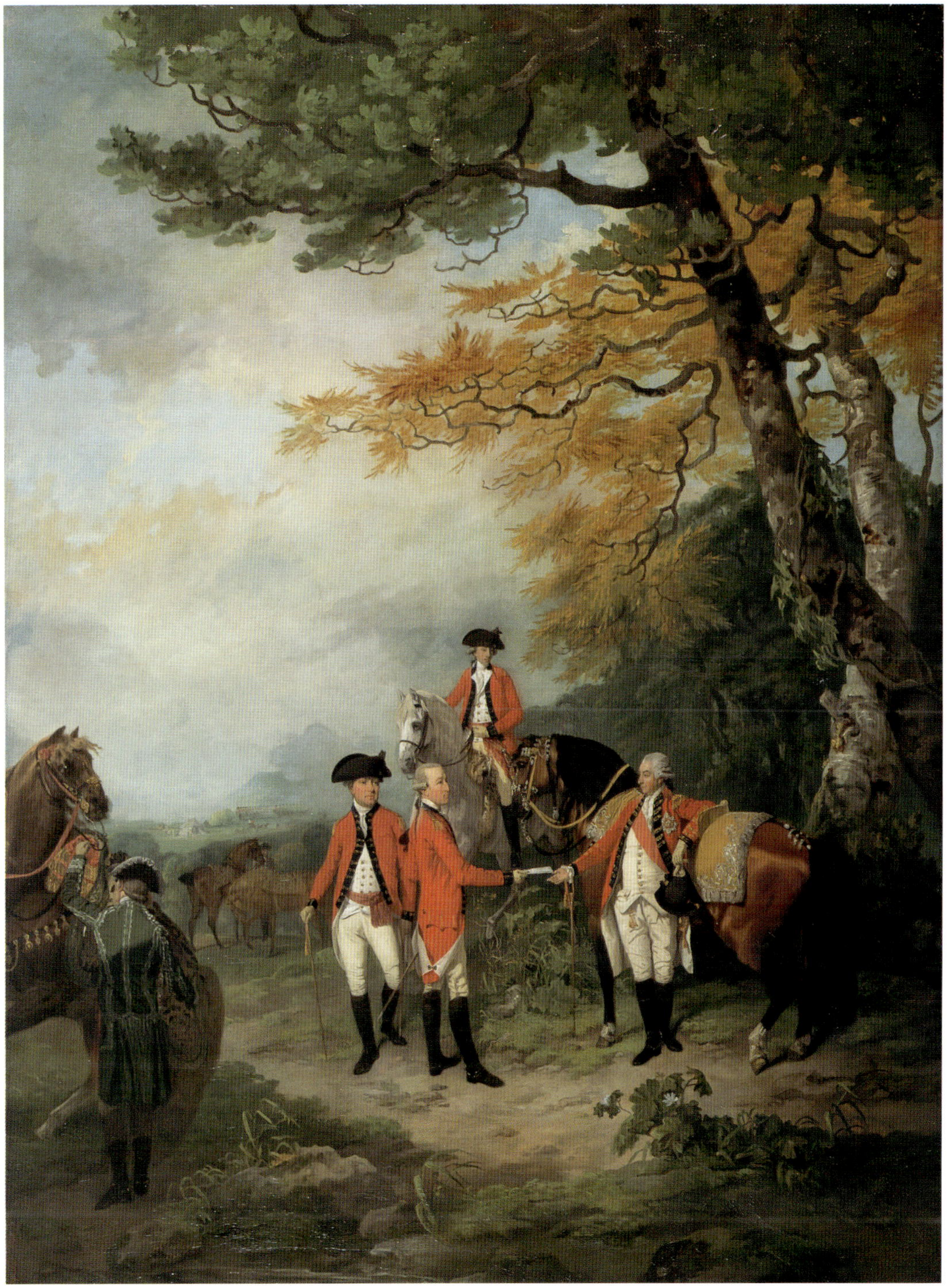

IRWIN NPG *682*

ICONOGRAPHY

1761 Painting by Joshua Reynolds. A.I. Dasent in 1896 (Mannings 2000, no.993). In a letter of 1 July 1896 to Lionel Cust (NPG archive) Arthur I. Dasent (author of the Irwin entry in *DNB*) said this portrait probably showed Alexander Irwin, but Reynolds's sitter books have 'Coll. Erwin', indicating John Irwin.

1781 Painting by Francis Wheatley, see NPG 682.

JEFFERYS, James 1751-84

Historical painter, s. of the painter William Jefferys of Maidstone; apprenticed to the engraver William Woollett; RA schools 1772; exhibited SA between 1771 and 1774 and RA 1774-75 and 1783; in Italy 1775-78 on a three-year travelling scholarship from the Society of Dilettanti and may have stayed until 1781, when he is next recorded in England.

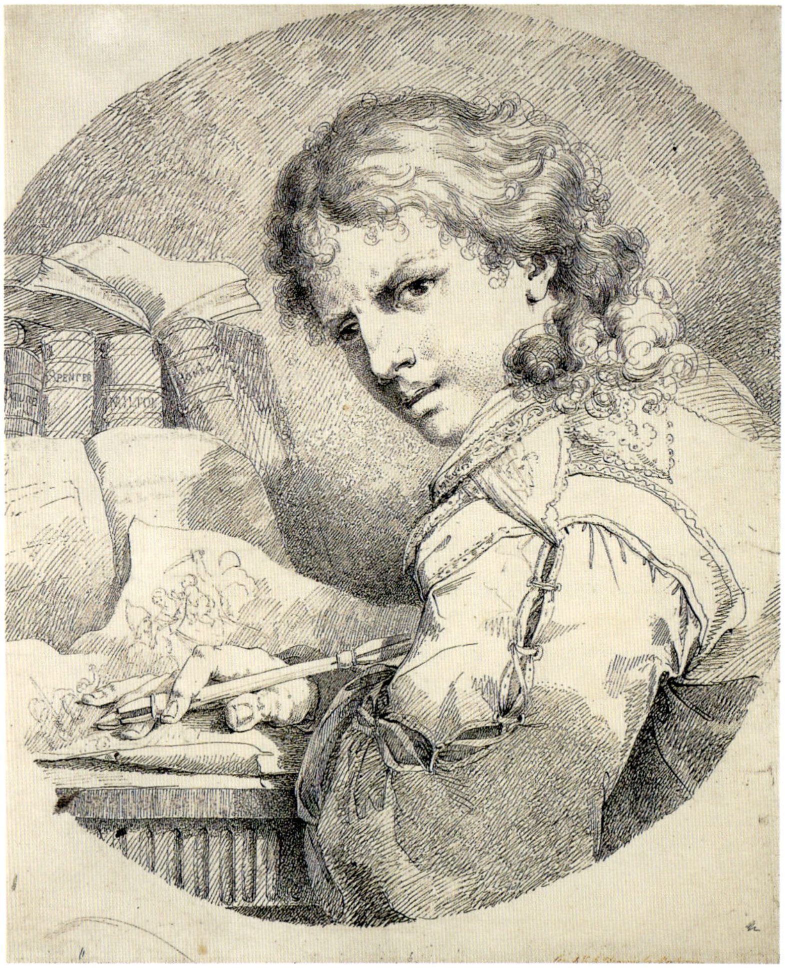

JEFFERYS NPG *4669*

4669 SELF PORTRAIT c.1774-75

Ink and pencil 47.5 x 41 (18½ x 16¼); some slight staining; indistinct watermark (somewhat resembling Churchill, no.515).

Wearing a fanciful seventeenth-century costume and drawing a Biblical subject, the *Massacre of the Innocents*; the standing books are titled (from the left): *NATURE SPENCER* [*sic*] *MILTON HOMER*; above them an open book inscribed on the fore-edge: *ADDISON on the Pleasures of the Imagination*, and on a leaf: *Paper iv & v / on Greatness*; leaning against these volumes another inscribed [*SHA*]*KESPEARE Midsummer Night's Dream* and, below, *And as the Youthful Imagination bodies/forth the forms of things* [*unknown*];[1] a separate, later, inscription, in the bottom right margin: *Pen & Ink drawing by Mortimer.*

Collections: [probably John Newington Hughes sale, Sotheby's, 18 February 1848, either lot 53 'Masterly Pen Sketches, Anatomical Studies, by Mortimer 33', or lot 57 'Pen and other Sketches, by Mortimer, and others 13'];[2] George Hilder Libbis; Miss Nell Hilder Libbis; Sotheby's, 13 March 1969, lot 67, bt. Colnaghi, from whom purchased with the aid of the National Art Collections Fund 1969.

Exhibitions: *British Romantic Painting*, Paris, 1972(195 as Mortimer); *British Portraits*, Tokyo, 1975; *Fuseli Circle in Rome*, New Haven, 1979(82 as Jefferys); *Artists at Work* 1981-82(28); *Master Drawings* 1993-95(29); *Face to Face*, Liverpool, 1994(24).

Reference: J. Sunderland, *Burl. Mag.*, CXI, 1969, p.518 (as Mortimer); J. Sunderland, *Burl. Mag.*, CXII, 1970, pp.526, 528, 531 (as Mortimer); J. Sunderland, *Burl. Mag.*, CXIX, 1977, pp.279-81 (as of Jefferys and probably by him); *Mortimer* 1986, p.221(R15, as not by Mortimer).

NPG 4669 was sold in 1969 with a companion drawing (now in the Yale Center for British Art; B1977.14.6227),[3] showing the artist from behind in the act of writing a letter, a youthful credo:

> Hon^d Sir - July 26 - I flatter myself I have abilities for the Art of Painting wch I hope will appear by the Drawing I send you, but indeed there are so many young Persons pursuing the same Art, that I think it will be a prudent Step to drop it intirely, & get into any kind of Business you shall think, proper, I make no doubt but you will comply with my desire more especially when you inform yourself how much the Proffession is disgrac'd by the Folly and Vice of many of the Proffessors.

This letter, addressed to Brenchley, the artist's patron in Maidstone,[4] together with the books carefully displayed in NPG 4669, defines a proud, young history painter, who could add the word 'Youthful' to a Shakespearean quotation to increase its pertinence. In each portrait the artist is shown with a historical drawing (*The Massacre of the Innocents* and *Pride led by the Passions*, from Spenser's *Faery Queen*). Such evidence implies that both portraits date from the ambitious, earlier part of Jefferys' short career, just prior to his departure for Italy in July 1775.

Both portrait drawings had been sold in 1969 as by J.H. Mortimer, whose manner they closely imitate. Even the Shakespearean quotation had been (accurately) used by Mortimer beneath his etching, *Poet*, published in May 1775 (an image comparable with NPG 4669),[5] and the possible derivation of NPG 4669 from a self-portrait by Salvator Rosa is wholly within the Mortimer tradition.[6] But the discovery of the work of James Jefferys in 1976[7] led to a convincing reattribution, as was carefully described by John Sunderland in 1977 and Nancy Pressly in 1979.[8]

1 *Midsummer Night's Dream*, V, I, 14-15; 'Youthful' is the artist's addition.
2 John Newington Hughes (1776-1847), a Kentish antiquary and twice mayor of Maidstone, was said to own drawings Jefferys made at Rome 'and other pen drawings' (see T. Clifford & S. Legouix, *Burl. Mag.*, CXVIII, 1976, p.153); none appeared in his sale, but, for example, NPG 4669 is inscribed *Mortimer*.
3 See P.J. Noon, *English Drawings & Miniatures*, New Haven, 1979, no.71.
4 The name written on the drawing in front of the artist; John Brenchley (1725-91) a Maidstone brewer.
5 The original, reversed, drawing (Huntington Art Collections, San Marino, Calif.) illus. *Mortimer* 1986, fig.160.
6 Sunderland (*Burl. Mag.*, 1970, *loc. cit.*), cites as a possible source a portrait by Salvator now in the Ringling Museum of Art, Sarasota, FL (as *A Poet*).
7 T. Clifford & S. Legouix, *Burl. Mag.*, CXVIII, 1976, pp.148-57.
8 Sunderland, *Burl. Mag.*, 1977, *loc. cit.*; Pressly, in the *Fuseli Circle in Rome*, New Haven, 1979(82).

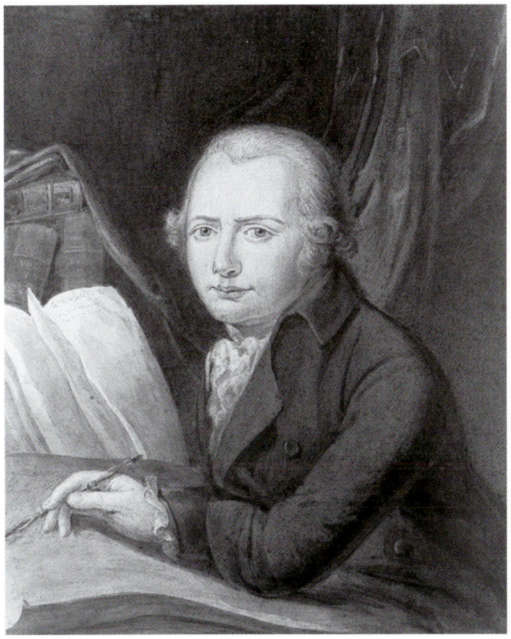

JEFFERYS after W. Jefferys c.1774 (Maidstone Museum and Bentlif Art Gallery)

ICONOGRAPHY

c.1774 Painting by William Jefferys, the sitter's father, half-length seated, an open book inscribed *Spencer* [*sic*] propped up before him with other volumes; in poor condition. Book Trust, London, on loan to the Maidstone MAG (a reduced watercolour copy* is in the same collection).

c.1774–75 Self-portrait drawings, see under NPG 4669.

JENKINS, Thomas 1722–98

Art-dealer and banker; b. Rome, studied painting in London, returning to Rome 1751; practised briefly as a painter before turning to an increasingly profitable and slightly unscrupulous trade in art and antiquities; FSA 1757; a favourite with Clement XIV (Pope 1769–74), he set up as a banker in 1776; by 1780 English travellers regarded him as an unofficial ambassador; returned to England 1798 but d. the same year.

'by purchasing and selling, at his Own Prices, Old Pictures, Antique Gems & Statues with the Profits of a lucrative banking house – he was enabled to vie with the Roman Nobility in Splendor & magnificence –' (Thomas Jones, 1780).

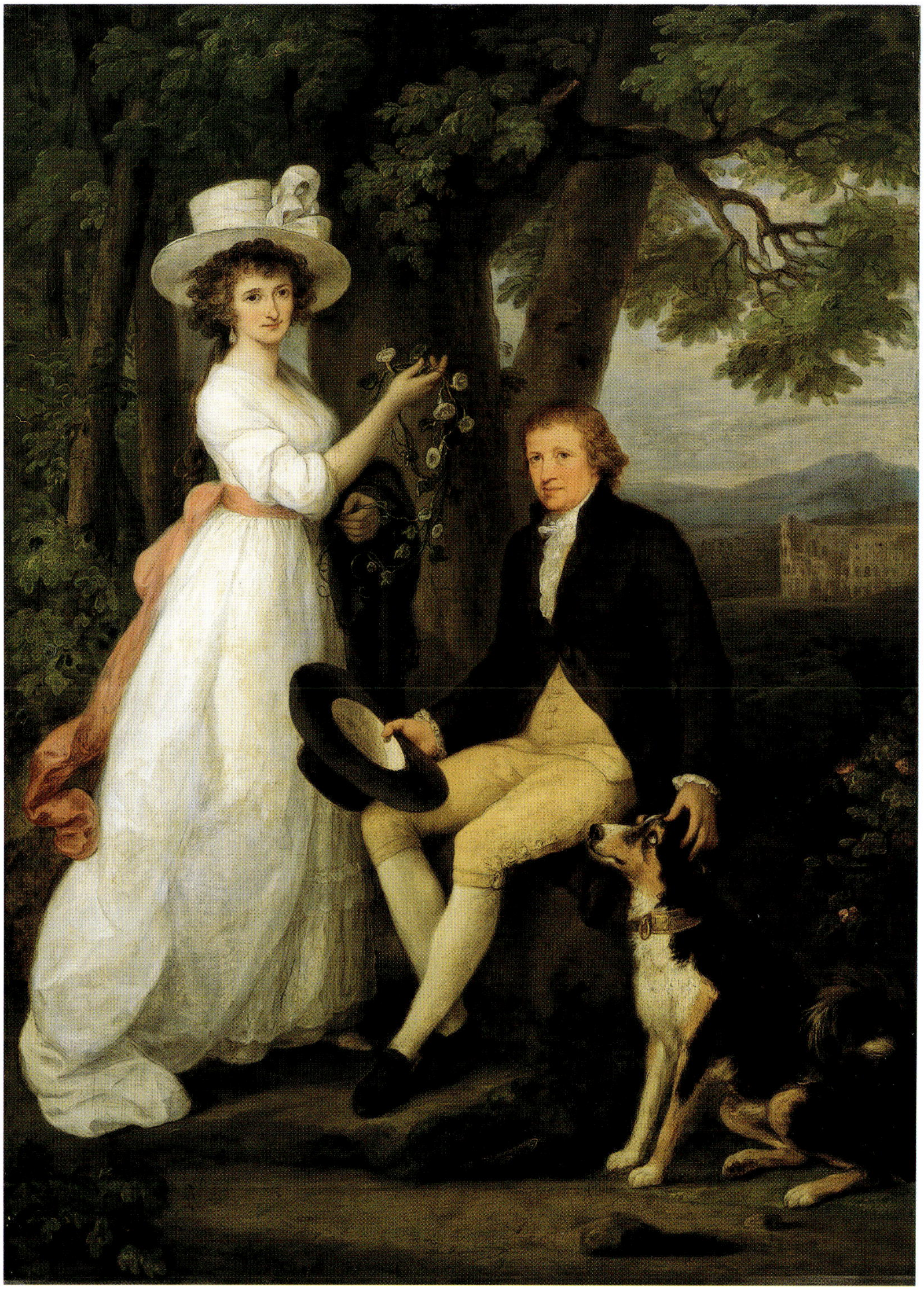

JENKINS with his Niece NPG 5044

5044 ANGELICA KAUFFMANN, *with his Niece Anna Maria Jenkins* 1790

Canvas 128 x 94 (50½ x 37); lined, and strip-lined 1998; old retouchings in the background area and some discolouration in the varnish; signed, bottom centre, in black: *Angelica Kauffman. / Pinx: Roma, / 1790.*

Seated in a landscape outside Rome with a distant view of the Colosseum, Jenkins has blue-grey eyes, fair reddish hair; he wears a black coat and hat, a yellow waistcoat and breeches, with white stockings and black shoes. His niece, Anna Maria, stands by him; she has brown eyes, brown hair, and wears a white hat, a white dress with a pink waist band and white slippers; she holds a bunch of white convolvulus.

Collections: R.W.M. Walker; Christie's, 20 July 1945, lot 92 (as 'Mr and Mrs Jenkins'); Frost & Reed; Phillips, 10 July 1972, lot 44; J.A. Lewin; Christie's, 20 June 1975, lot 113, bt. Leggatt for the NPG.

Exhibitions: *British Artists in Rome*, Kenwood, 1974(11) lent J.A. Lewin; *The Arrogant Connoisseur*, Manchester, 1982(180); *Travels in Italy*, Manchester, 1988(14); *Kauffman*, Brighton, York, 1993(15); *Kauffmann* 1998(167).

Reference: Williamson 1924, pp.85, 158.

Noted by the artist in her memorandum of paintings[1] as:

Roma 1790. Per il Sigr. Tomaso Jenkins Inglese Un quadro alto palmi 6 - largo palmi 4.6. - Il Ritratto del sudetto e quello della sua nipote Anna Maria con il ritratto pure d'un grosso cane favorito - La figura intiera di circa 3. palmi e mezzo - in sito campestre con vedutta in lontano del Colosseo - il detto quadro fu dipinto per amicizia e fù regalatta la pitricce d'una bellma. testa antica di marmo all naturalle, in Bassorilievo su fondo oscuro, in guisa di cameo - rapresenta uno de nipoti d'Augusto, ma di eccellente maestro e perfetate. conservatta - e di più due belle gemme cioé un cameo antico ed un'ametista con bellmo. intaglio dell b. Vergine Maria, gema ovalle di onzie due legata in oro d'apendersi in guisa di gioielo al seno.

In 1782 Kauffmann had bought a carriage from Jenkins, who was acting as her banker at least from 1785 to 1795.[2]

Anna Maria Jenkins lived with her uncle in Rome 1788-94, until her marriage to Giovanni Martinez, Jenkins's neighbour; she was described at the time as 'a tall slender damsel out of powder & tho' very English not the style of the fashionable World in England'.[3]

1 RA Library, London. Published by C. Knight, *La 'Memoria delle piture' di Angelica Kauffman*, Lucca, 1998, pp.52-53 ['Rome 1790. For Mr Thomas Jenkins, Englishman. A picture 6 palmi high and 4.6 palmi wide, a portrait of the above and of his niece Anna Maria, with a large pet dog. Full length figures about 3½ palmi in a landscape setting with a distant view of the Colosseum. This picture painted out of friendship, the artist being given a beautiful ancient life size marble head, a bas relief set on a dark background like a cameo, of one of the nephews of Augustus, by an excellent artist and wonderfully preserved, and two lovely jewels, an antique cameo and an amethyst on which is engraved the image of the Blessed Virgin, an oval of 2 onzie set in gold, to be worn as a pendant round the neck'].
2 Ingamells 1997, p.555.
3 Elizabeth Gibbes MS journal, Rome, 1789-90; see Ingamells 1997, p.553.

ICONOGRAPHY

c.1752-53 Drawing by Richard Wilson, three-quarter length seated. Pierpont Morgan Library, New York (illus. *Apollo*, XCIX, 1974, p.419; *Wilson*, Tate Gallery, 1982, no.24). Wilson and Jenkins had arrived together in Rome late in 1751 and shared lodgings on the Piazza di Spagna 1752-53.

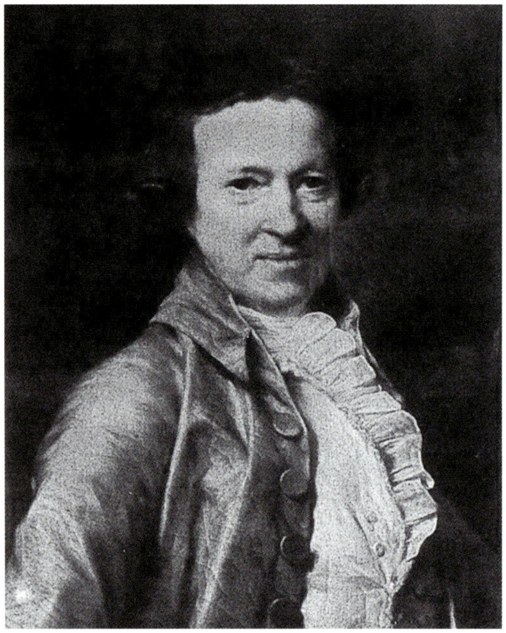

JENKINS by Anton von Maron 1791 (Accademia di San Luca, Rome)

1790 Painting by Angelica Kauffmann, see NPG 5044.

1791 Painting by Anton von Maron,* half length. Accademia di S. Luca, Rome. Jenkins had been elected to the Accademia (as a painter) in 1761.

JENKINSON, Charles, see LIVERPOOL

JENNINGS, Henry Constantine 1731-1819

Virtuoso and eccentric, of Shiplake, Oxon.; in Italy c.1753-61, when he purchased the celebrated marble 'dog of Alcibiades' (British Museum) which he sold in 1778, due to debts accrued principally through horse racing; collected portraits, prints, shells and stuffed birds, and published a number of essays, including *A Free Enquiry into the Enormous Increase of Attornies* 1785 and *Thoughts on the Rise and Decline of the Fine Arts* 1798.

'[his] figure was short, thin, and much bent by age; and he was very singular in his dress. The crown of his hat fitted his head as close as a *pitch-plaster*, his coat was short, of common cloth, and ... regularly buttoned up from his waist to his chin. ... He stepped astride in consequence of the bowness of his legs, and generally attracted notice by striking his walking stick hard on the stones with his right arm fully extended, while his left swung low before him' (J.T. Smith, 1845).

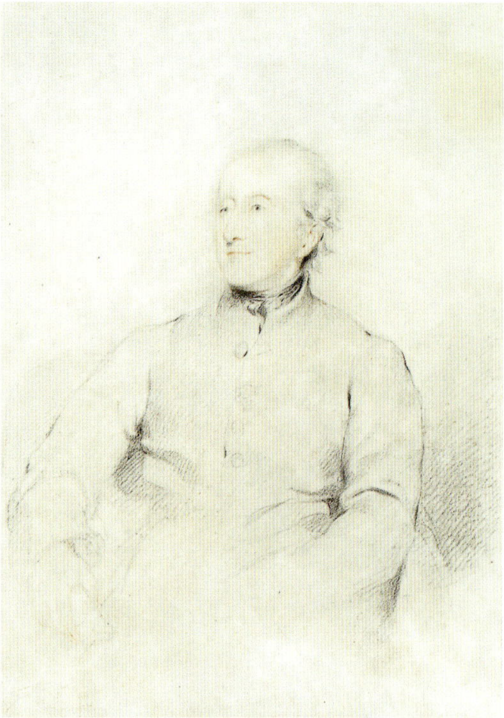

JENNINGS NPG 5711

5711 THOMAS LAWRENCE c.1799

Black and red chalk 32 x 23 (12½ x 9), the red confined to the flesh areas; the sheet bears the watermark *E & P*;[1] it is lightly stained after over-cleaning,[2] and the drawing has been rubbed; the original mount, removed during subsequent conservation, is inscribed: *Sir Thomas Lawrence fecit*[3] *Henry Constantine Jennings Esqr.*

Collections:[4] By descent from the sitter's daughter Elizabeth, who m. 1805 William Locke II of Norbury Park; their daughter, who m. the 3rd Baron Wallscourt, thence to the 5th Baron (d.1920); his daughter, Mrs Leycester Storr, Cowes, IOW; Sotheby's, 7 July 1983, lot 85; Clarendon Gallery, London, from whom purchased 1984.

Probably drawn in 1799 when Lawrence painted the sitter's daughter;[5] the engraved portrait of 1815 appears to show an older figure.

1 Similar to that of Edmunds & Pine (Churchill, p.52).
2 As was acknowledged at the time of purchase in 1984.
3 Lawrence was knighted in 1815, which implies this inscription is not contemporary.
4 The earlier part of this provenance is deduced from the fact that NPG 5711 belonged to Lord Wallscourt before 1920 (photograph in NPG archive; *D'Arblay*, V, iv, p.466).
5 Garlick 1989, no.440; private collection.

ICONOGRAPHY

c.1799 Drawing by Thomas Lawrence, see NPG 5711.

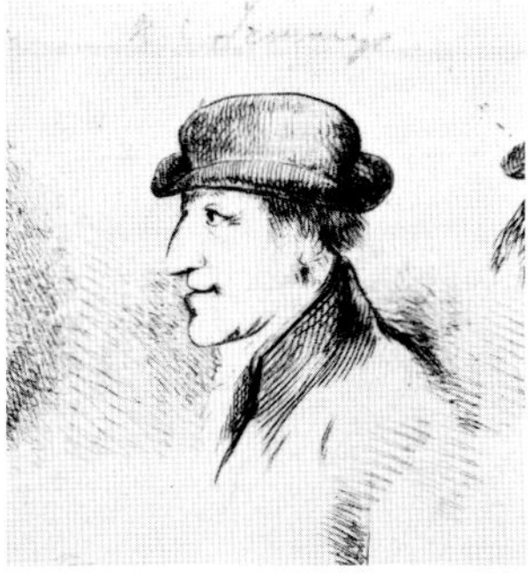

JENNINGS Portraits from Sketches made at Rare Print Sales anon. engraving 1814 after Beugo (detail; British Museum)

1814 Engraving after [John?] Beugo,* *Portraits from Sketches made at Rare Print Sales*, including Jennings.

1815 Engraving by E. Dorrell, half length, looking at a pastoral print on a table (illus. *Jnl. of the History of Collections*, 14, no.2, 2002, p.215), reissued 1829 (Faulkner's *Chelsea*). A version, showing the stick under his right arm and the print in his hands, engraved R. Cooper 1820 as *The Remarkable Virtuoso*.

DOUBTFUL PORTRAIT

'Master H.C. Jennings' painted by P. Condé, exhibited RA 1806(763).

JOHNSON, Samuel 1709-84

Critic, essayist, novelist, poet; b. Lichfield; LLD Dublin 1769, DCL Oxford 1775; author of *Dictionary of the English Language* 1755 and *The Lives of the Poets* 1776-79.

'... the oddest and most peculiar fellow I ever saw. He is six feet high, has a violent convulsion in his head, and his eyes are distorted. He speaks roughly and loud, listens to no man's opinions, thoroughly pertinacious of his own. Good sense flows from him in all he utters, and he seems possessed of a prodigious fund of knowledge, which he is not at all reserved in communicating; but in a manner so obstinate, ungenteel, and boorish, as renders it disagreeable and unsatisfactory' (Rev William Dodd, 1750).

'his Heighth was five Foot eleven without Shoes, his Neck short, his Bones large & His Shoulders broad ... his Sight was near, and otherwise imperfect ... his eyes of a light blue colour' (Mrs Hester Thrale, later Mrs Piozzi, 1777).

'the scrophula, or king's evil ... disfigured a countenance naturally well formed, and hurt his visual nerves so much that he did not see at all with one of his eyes' (James Boswell, 1791).

1597 JOSHUA REYNOLDS 1756-57

Canvas 127.5 x 101.5 (50¼ x 40); lined and cleaned 1976, when a complex series of additions was confirmed, see below.

Blue-grey eyes, powdered wig, wearing a brown coat and waistcoat with dark-grey breeches; the chair covered with green and white check, the table with a green cloth. Johnson habitually wore 'clothes of the darkest and dirtiest colours, and, in all weathers, black stockings'.[1]

Collections: Given by Reynolds to Boswell, probably in 1789 (see below); the *Public Advertiser*, 18 June 1791, announced that 'Sir Joshua Reynolds, with a munificence truly princely, has ... presented Mr. Boswell with the large portrait of Dr Johnson'; Boswell sale, Sotheby's, 3 June 1825, lot 3293 as 'painted for the late James Boswell of Auchinleck', bt. John Graves of Southwark and sold by him to James M. Morrison;[2] thence by descent to Charles Morrison (d.1909); presented anonymously 1911.

Engravings:[3] J. Heath 1791, lettered ... *From the original Picture in the Possession of James Boswell ... Publish'd 10 April 1791* (fourth state); J. Baker 1793 (showing one book only); E. Mitchell 1817 (ditto); H. Meyer 1818; R. Graves c.1820 (reduced); R. Josey 1880.

Exhibitions: NPE 1867(557) lent Charles Morrison; *Reynolds*, Grosvenor Gallery, 1883-84(97); *Boswell*, NPG, 1967(12); *Johnson*, Arts Council, 1984 (39); *Romantic Icons*, Grasmere, 1999(4).

Reference: Graves & Cronin, II, pp.518-19; Boswell, IV, pp.448, 463; Waterhouse 1941, p.41; K.K. Yung in *Johnson*, Arts Council, 1984, pp.78-83; I.S. Lustig in *The Age of Johnson*, 1987, pp.161-80; Mannings 2000, no.1011.

Painted in 1756-57 and later modified, as discussed below. Johnson had published his *Dictionary of the English Language* in 1755 and he met Reynolds soon after;[4] the ensuing friendship was of great significance for them both. The date of 1756 given on James Heath's engraving of NPG 1597 may indicate when the picture was begun; there is no Reynolds sitter book for 1756, but appointments in 1757 for 'Mr Johnson' on 25 January, 1, 3 and 10 February, and 30 April are associated by Mannings with the portrait. In 1789 Reynolds gave it to Boswell who wished to have it engraved for his *Life of Johnson* (published on 16 May 1791). Boswell was less concerned with the quality of the portrait than with its novelty, believing that a portrait of Johnson by Reynolds 'from which no engraving has yet been taken' would lend his biography distinction.[5] He originally described it as 'unfinished, though I cannot help thinking it a striking likeness'.[6] In the published text of the *Life of Johnson*, Boswell mischievously modified this account to read:

> [on first meeting Johnson in 1763] I found that I had a very perfect idea of Johnson's figure, from the portrait of him painted by Sir Joshua Reynolds soon after he had published his Dictionary, in the attitude of sitting in his easy chair in deep meditation, which was the first picture his friend did for him, which Sir Joshua very kindly presented to me, and from which an engraving has been made for this work.[7]

But Boswell first met Reynolds in 1769[8] and it is most unlikely that he knew the portrait in 1763.

Soon after March 1789 NPG 1597 was sent to the engraver James Heath whose plate evolved through four states, differing in detail from NPG 1597 as it is now seen.[9]

*a) a 'finished' portrait with a bushier wig, buttons added to the waistcoat, and the left lapel of the coat turned back; a plain wooden table replaces that covered with a green cloth; on it an inkwell with a second quill and three books, one lettered on the spine *Johnson's English Dictionary A-K*.

*b) heavier eyebrows, the chair now also visible behind Johnson's left shoulder and a door knob behind his left arm. An annotation by Boswell on an example of the second state (which he thought the first) in the Hyde Collection indicates that

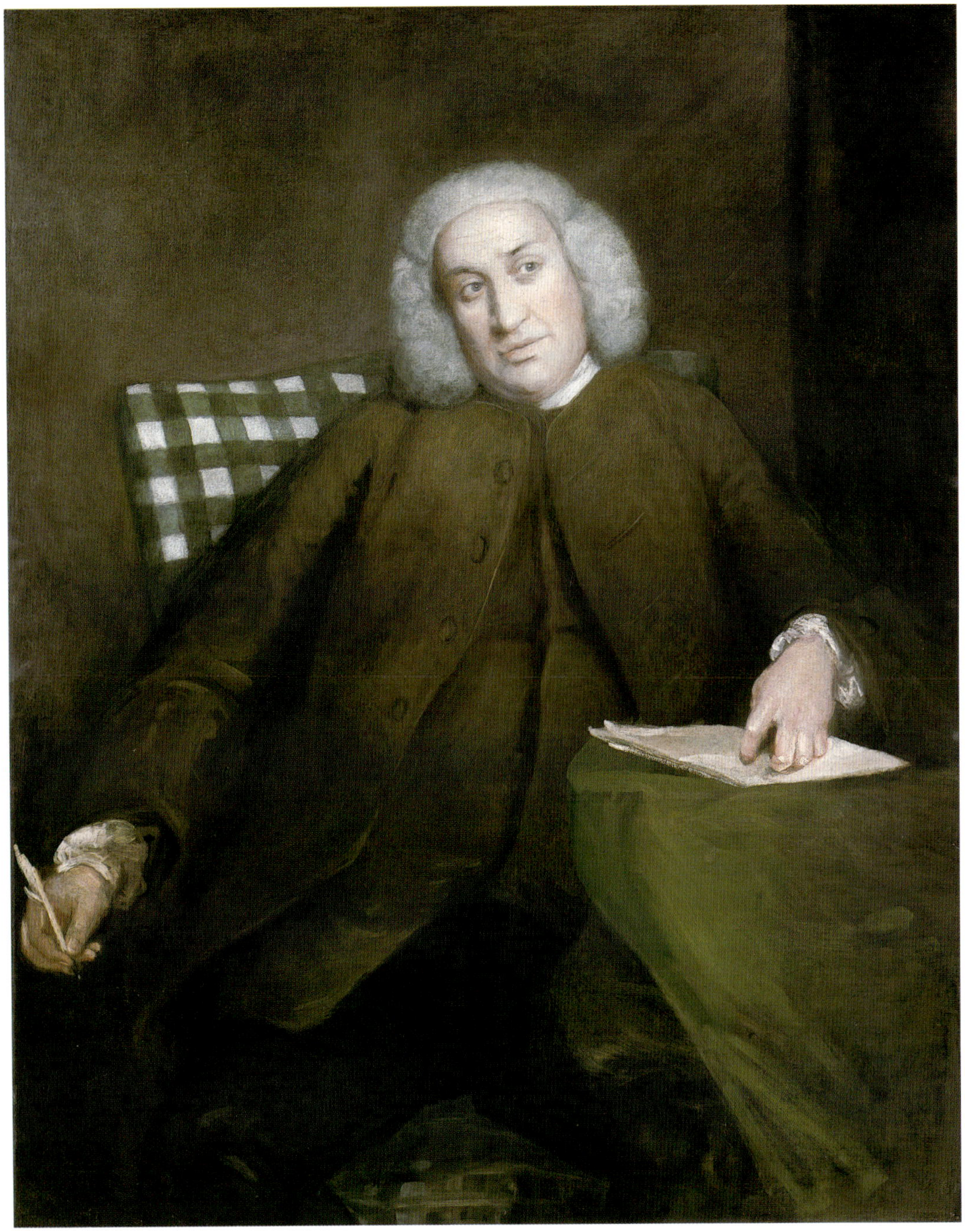

JOHNSON NPG *1597*

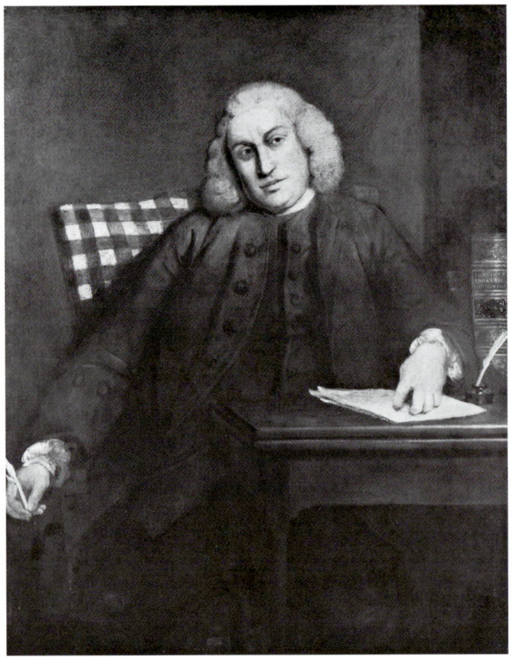

JOHNSON NPG *1597 before cleaning*

further, more subtle alterations were then made: *Mr Heath the Engraver thought it was finished. He went with me to Sir Joshua Reynolds's who suggested that the countenance was too young and not thoughtful enough. Mr Heath therefore altered it so much to its advantage that Sir Joshua was quite satisfied …*[10]

*c) incorporating Reynolds's suggestions, the abstracted gaze marginally shifted towards the spectator, shadows round the eyes and a frown on the forehead; a chair arm below the right wrist.

Reynolds understood that the meditative Johnson of 1756 did not compare with the burly pedagogue[11] suggested, for example, by the many copies and engravings of the Reynolds portrait of 1772. An example of this third state (Hyde Collection) was annotated by Boswell: *Second* [sic] *Impression of Dr Johnson's Portrait after the Plate had been improved by Sir Joshua Reynolds's suggestions. Mr Heath afterwards gave it a few additional touches*[12]

*d) as finally published in 1791, virtually the same as c), with slight additional touches on the coat and breeches.

The evolution of Heath's engraving is thus well documented, but not that of NPG 1597. Recent technical analysis has confirmed that changes were made so that the 'unfinished' painted portrait agreed with Heath's final engraving, but how many of these changes were made for the engraving, or how many from it, and which, if any, had been made sometime before, is no longer clear. Those changes described above in Heath's first proof must have been made to the painting by 1789, presumably by, or under the supervision of, Reynolds (whose eyesight began to suffer in 1789) -but whether all were done at that time, or whether some had been done long before (as the table, inkwell and books – the stock accessories of a literary portrait, cf. Orford NPG 6520), is not clear. The changes described in the second and third proofs of Heath's plate must have been transferred to the painting in or after 1791. It was not then a particularly pretty sight.

Adverse comment mainly concerned the condition. In 1825 it was 'completely faded';[13] in 1854 Waagen, exceptionally, found the execution 'broad and masterly', but described Johnson as being 'at an advanced period of life and evidently suffering from illness';[14] in 1867 the complexion was 'quite pale' and the whole was 'not worthy of Reynolds',[15] and in 1884 the portrait was described as having been 'painted on'.[16] When the picture was cleaned in 1976 the

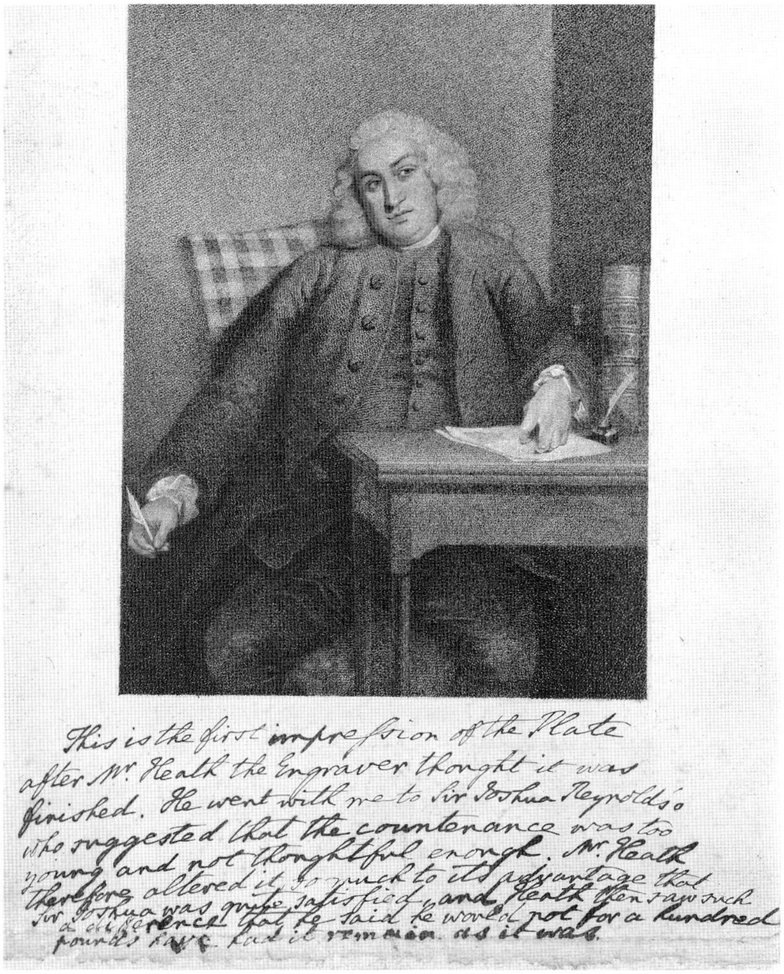

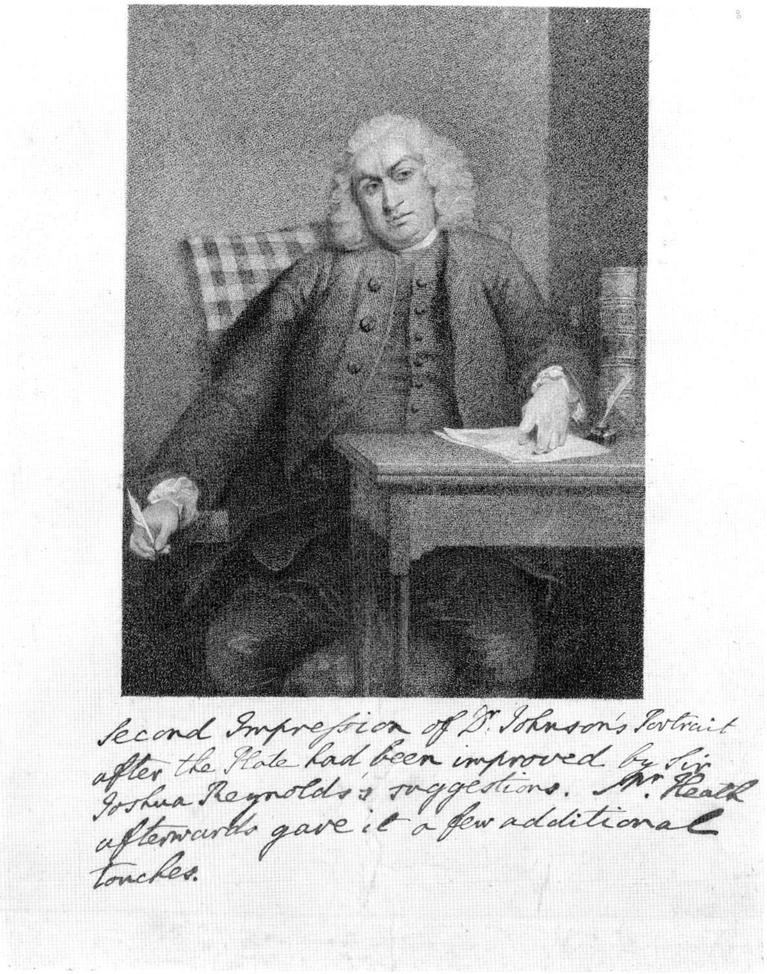

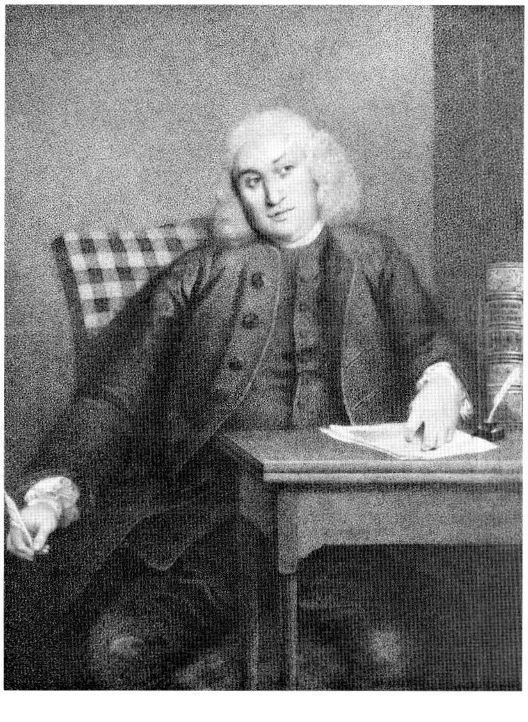

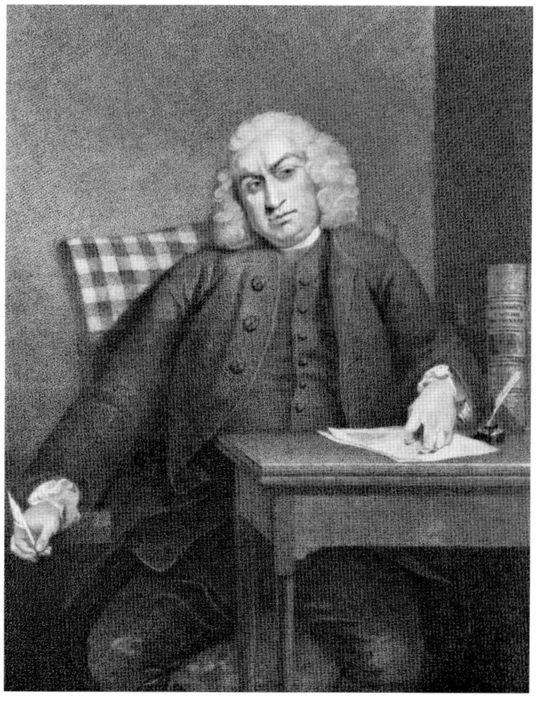

JOHNSON J. Heath 1791 after NPG *1597;*

1st state (below left, formerly Herman Liebert collection)
2nd state (upper left, Hyde Collection)
3rd state (upper right, Hyde Collection)
4th state (lower right, NPG archive)

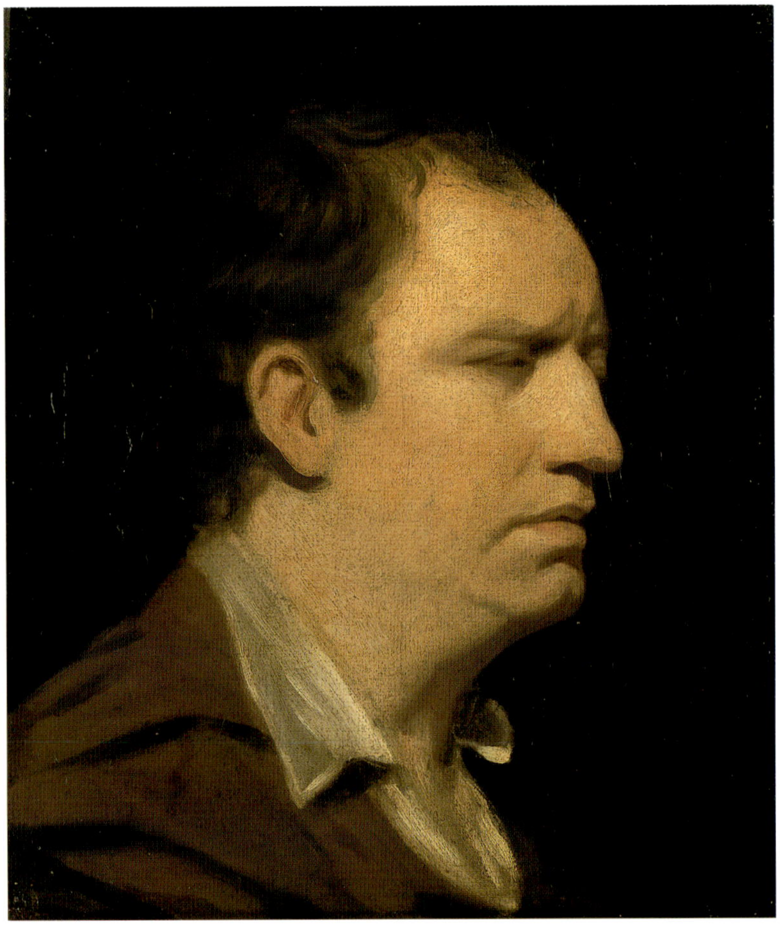

JOHNSON NPG 1445

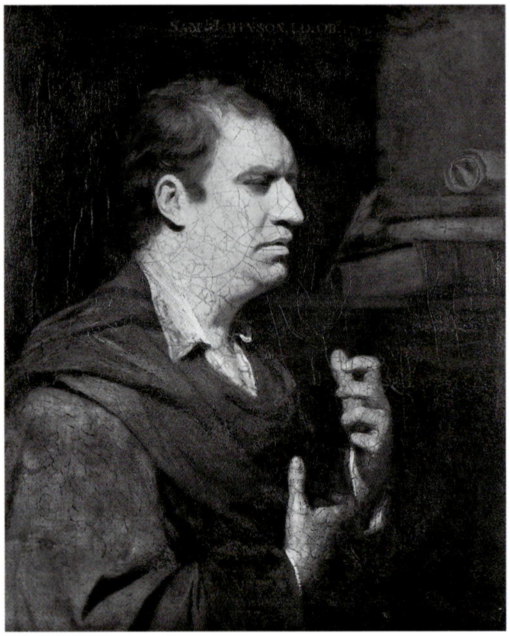

JOHNSON by Joshua Reynolds 1769 (Private Collection)

post-1757 alterations were removed, but the books and the ink-well were painted over with a water-based pigment.[17]

A half-length, apparently nineteenth-century, pastel copy is in the Johnson Birthplace Museum, Lichfield. A related half-length miniature in the Hyde Collection, showing Johnson in a mauve suit, was engraved by E. Finden in 1830 as 'from a miniature worn as a bracelet by Mrs Johnson' - who, however, died in 1752.[18]

1 Sir John Hawkins, *Life of Samuel Johnson*, 1787, p.327n.
2 Listed in 'Mr Morrison's gallery, at Basildon' by Leslie & Taylor 1865, i, p.147n.
3 See Boswell, IV, p.463.
4 Writing in 1786-87 Reynolds recalled 'thirty years intimacy' with Johnson; see Hilles 1952, p.66.
5 Announcement in the *Public Advertiser*, 24 March 1789, quoted by Lustig (*loc. cit.*, pp.171-72), who suggested it was probably devised by Boswell himself; it described how the portrait had been due to be delivered to James Heath 'last week' but 'most happily was delayed', thus avoiding a fire on the engraver's premises on 20 March.
6 In the first draft of his *Life of Johnson* (MS Yale M144, ff.207-08), quoted in *Johnson*, Arts Council, 1984, p.80.
7 Boswell, I, p.392.
8 See F. Brady, James Boswell, *The Later Years 1769-1795*, 1984, p.36; *Johnson*, Arts Council, 1984, p.80.
9 See note 5. These engravings were carefully discussed by K.K. Yung in *Johnson*, Arts Council, 1984, nos.40-43.
10 See *Johnson*, Arts Council, 1984, no. 41.
11 As discussed by R. Wendorf, *The Elements of Life*, 1990, pp.256-58.
12 See *Johnson*, Arts Council, 1984, no.42.
13 Lady Boswell to William Murray, 8 July 1825 (MS Yale, Talbot inv., no.4, f.11), quoted by Lustig, *loc. cit.*, p.176.
14 Waagen, IV, p.106.
15 Report made by the NPG at the 1867 National Portraits Exhibition (NPG archive).
16 Grosvenor Gallery exhibition cat.
17 Cleaning was described by the restorer, Bettina Jessell, in *The Conservator*, 5, 1981, pp.36-40. Lustig (*loc. cit.*, p.177) was not alone in urging the NPG 'to uncover the books and inkpot with quill and give us again 'Dictionary' Johnson'.
18 Cheney sale, 29 April 1885, lot 301; Dr Harwood of Lichfield; Lord Rosebery. Puffed in *GM*, LXXXVIII, 1818, i, p.194, but see Boswell, IV, p.458

1445 after JOSHUA REYNOLDS [1769]

Canvas[1] 45 x 38 (17¾ x 15); discoloured varnish and retouchings.

Brown hair, wearing a light brown coat.

Collections: Sir Henry Ellis (d.1869); presented, as a study for the original picture, by T. Humphry Ward[2] 1906.

Exhibitions: *Samuel Johnson, Londoner*, Royal Exchange, London, 1964; *Johnson and The Thrales*, Bowood, 1984 (1).

Reference: Mannings 2000, no.1013b.

A reduced and indifferent mid-19th-century copy from the Reynolds in a private collection★ completed in 1769 and known as the 'Johnson Arguing' portrait.[3] It illustrates Johnson's mental concentration; Reynolds himself wrote how, when Johnson was excluded from conversation, 'he remained but a few moments without speaking or listening. His mind appeared to be preying on itself; he fell into a reverie accompanied with strange antic gesticulations'.[4]

A studio version, painted before 1771 for Lucy Porter, Johnson's step-daughter, is in the Houghton Library, Harvard, and a copy in the Tate Gallery (N 4506).[5] A copy in crayon by Ozias Humphry was etched by Mrs Dawson Turner c.1825,[6] and Boswell listed 'a beautiful miniature in enamel' by Humphry from the original portrait.[7] An unattributed miniature copy is in the collection of the Duke of Buccleuch.[8]

1 Mannings notes that it is a machine-woven mid-19th century canvas.
2 Who wrote, 5 July 1906: 'I have it from the collection of the late Sir Henry Ellis, [chief librarian] of the British Museum' (NPG archive).
3 Mannings 2000, no.1012. Exhibited RA 1770(150); first engraved J. Watson 1770.
4 Hilles 1952, p.70.
5 Respectively Mannings 2000, nos.1013 and 1013a (and for the latter see also Davies 1946, pp.128-29, no.4506).
6 Illus. Williamson 1918, f.p.88.
7 *Boswell*, IV, p.421n.
8 Illus. C. Holme & H.A. Kennedy, *Portrait Miniatures in the collection of the Duke of Buccleuch*, 1917, pl.lxvii.

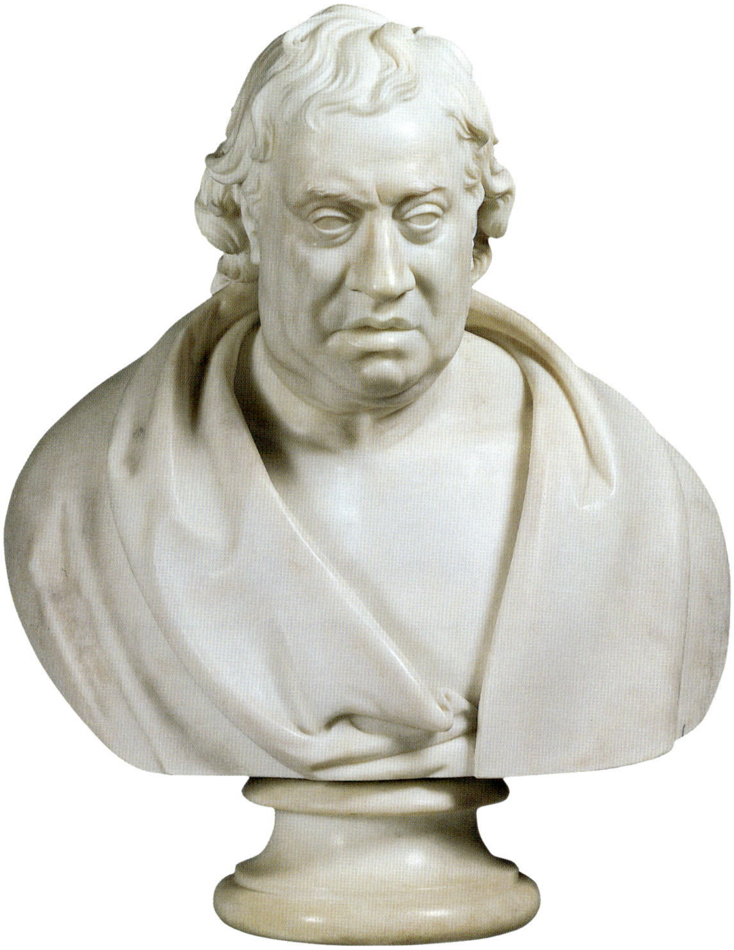

JOHNSON NPG *996*

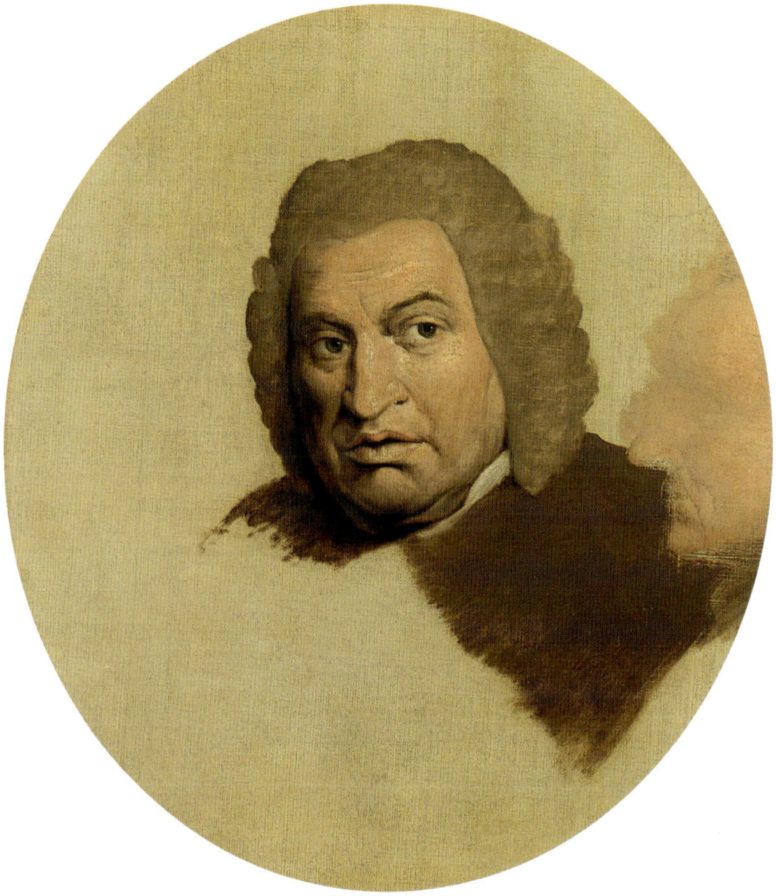

JOHNSON NPG *1185*

996 EDWARD HODGES BAILY 1828, after JOSEPH NOLLEKENS 1777

Marble bust 68.6 (27) high; inscribed: *E.H. BAILY, R.A./ AFTER NOLLEKENS,/ 1828.* Cleaned 1993.

Collections: Commissioned (with busts of George Canning, Isaac Newton and the Duke of Wellington) by Robert Vernon, by whom presented to the National Gallery 1847; lent to the NPG 1895; ownership transferred to the Tate Gallery 1954 and to the NPG 1957.

Exhibitions: *Boswell*, NPG, 1967(87); *Robert Vernon's Gift*, Tate Gallery, 1993(3); Beningbrough 1979- .

Reference: H.W. Liebert, *Johnson's Head: the story of the Bust of Dr Samuel Johnson ...*, Grolier Club, [1960], n.p.; K.K. Yung, *Johnson*, Arts Council, 1984, p.125.

Baily's bust derives directly from that by Joseph Nollekens, exhibited RA 1777, of which he owned a cast.[1] The head has lost much of the subtlety of Nollekens's carving, the drapery has been greatly simpified and the shoulders widened.

No marble original of the Nollekens is known. Johnson sent a cast to his step daughter Lucy Porter in 1777-78 and writing to her on 27 February 1778 said that 'My bust was made for the exhibition, and shown for the honour of the artist'.[2] The likeness was not approved by Mrs Thrale, Frances Reynolds or Mrs Garrick, and Johnson himself was displeased by the hair which Nollekens had insisted upon to make him resemble 'an ancient poet'.[3] The mould was acquired by James Deville from the Nollekens sale, Christie's, 3 July 1823, and the first cast was bought by Francis Chantrey, who considered it 'by far, the finest head' ever made by Nollekens.[4] A marble copy by John Bacon sr. was bequeathed to Pembroke College, Oxford, by Samuel Whitbread in 1796. A lead cast is in the Victoria and Albert Museum (A.63.1926);[5] a nineteenth-century marble copy is at Willey Park and an indifferent version is in Westminster Abbey;[6] a terracotta by A.L. Vago is in the Athenaeum, London, and plaster casts are, for example, at the Yale Center for British Art (B1990.17) and Johnson's Birthplace Museum, Lichfield (two, one bronzed).

An anonymous, provincial painting, possibly late-eighteenth century, in the Johnson Birthplace Museum, Lichfield, shows Bennet Langton contemplating Nollekens's bust.[7]

1 See *Robert Vernon's Gift*, Tate Gallery, 1993, no.3.
2 Redford, III, pp.54, 108-09.
3 'Modelled from the flowing locks of a sturdy Irish beggar'; Smith 1920, I, p.49; II, p.51.
4 Smith 1920, II, p.69.
5 Illus. *Johnson*, Arts Council, 1984, no.91; *Boswell*, IV, f.p.555.
6 Presented by G.F. Tite 1938; acquired from the Peel Heirlooms sale, Robinson & Fisher, 10 May 1900, lot 150, unattributed.
7 Illus. *Johnson*, Arts Council, 1984, no.59.

1185 JAMES BARRY 1778-80

Canvas, oval 59.5 x 52 (23½ x 20½), lined.

Blue-grey eyes, grey wig, dark brown coat; to the right a profile head has been overpainted.

Collections: Barry's sale, Christie's, 10-11 April 1807, lot 102 'A Portrait (the Head only) of Samuel Johnson, A striking likeness', bt. Manson;[1] bt. in 1842 by George Tomlinson (d.1863), Bishop of Gibraltar;[2] his daughter, Miss May Tomlinson, from whom purchased 1899.

Engraving: A. Smith (pub. J. Manson, 1 March 1808, and exhibited RA 1808, no.568, as *fac-simile of a study, now in the possession of Mr. Manson, by the late J. Barry Esq* ...).

Exhibitions: Garrick, *Johnson and the Lichfield Circle*, Lichfield, 1953(1); *Johnson*, Birmingham, 1959(181); Dr Johnson's House, London, 1973-75 and 1976-83; *Georgian Playhouse* 1975, no. 94; *Barry*, Tate Gallery, 1983 (44); *Johnson*, Arts Council, 1984(92).

Reference: Pressly, 1981, no.50 (as 1778-80).

Barry, who admired Johnson's 'consistent, manly, and well spent life'[3] painted this vivid study for 'The Distribution of Premiums in the Society of Arts', one of the six vast murals which make up *The Progress of Human Culture*, painted for the Society in the Adelphi between 1777 and 1784.[4] In the finished mural Johnson appears between the Duchesses of Rutland and Devonshire; the present study appears to show on the right (for all its masculinity) the erased profile of Mrs Elizabeth Montagu to whom, in the finished canvas, Johnson points (as she presents a young girl displaying her handiwork to the Duchess of Northumberland). When Smith's engraving was published in 1808 it was puffed as being 'a speaking likeness, and by much the best portrait of Dr Johnson which has yet been set before the public: it makes all others, notwithstanding that those after Reynolds and Opie are among their number, look sottish, blinking, or imbecile'.[5]

1 The NPG copy of that sale cat. bound in with Barry's *Works* is annotated *since engraved*. That the buyer was Manson seems apparent from the engraving, as described above.
2 An obscured label on the stretcher reads: *Johnson/ by Barry now in/ the possession of the/ Bishop of Gibraltar Decr 1842*. Tomlinson had been made Bishop in August that year.
3 J. Barry, *Works*, 1809, II, p.339.
4 Pressly 1981, no.26; engraved J. Barry 1791.
5 *The Review of Publications of Art*, 1808, I, pp.221-22 (quoted in *Barry* 1983, p.98).

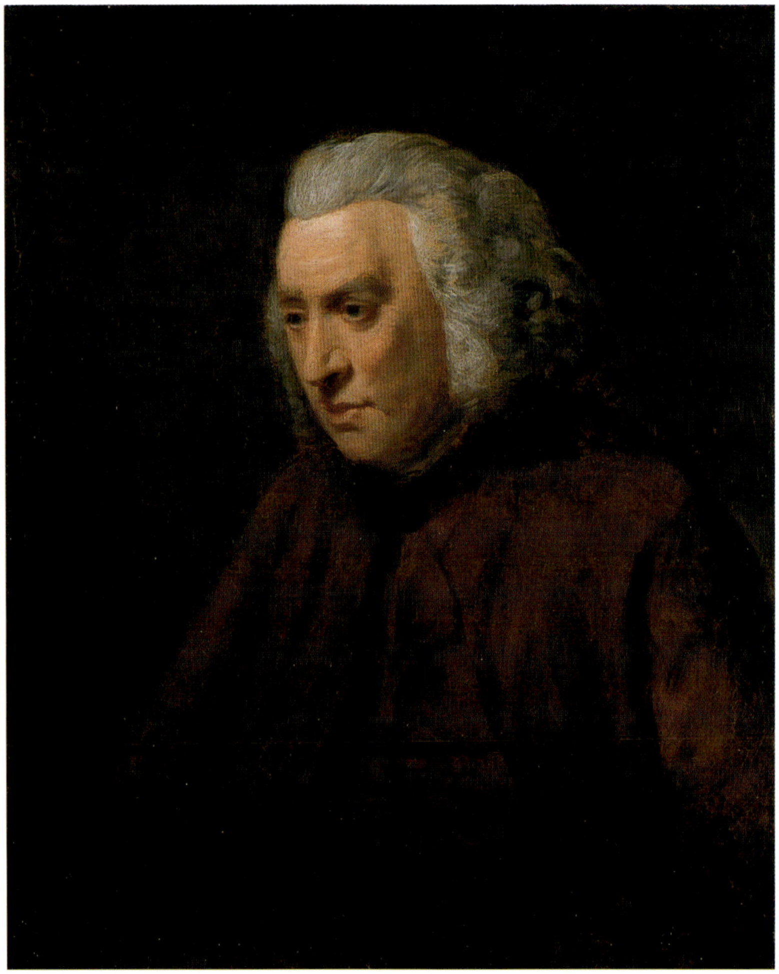

JOHNSON NPG *1302*

1302 after JOHN OPIE [1783-84]

Canvas 49.5 x 40.5 (19½ x 16) lined.

Blue eyes, grey wig, wearing a brown coat and waistcoat.

Collections: Bt. in Tunbridge Wells by Lord Ronald Sutherland Gower 1901, and presented by him that year.[1]

Exhibitions: *Johnson and the Lichfield Circle*, Lichfield, 1959(58); *Johnson and the Midlands*, Lichfield, 1984 (58).

NPG 1302 is a thinly-painted version, possibly contemporary, of the Opie portrait of 1783-84 in the Houghton Library, Harvard;[2] it differs only in showing the eyes less hooded.

Johnson told Mrs Thrale he had sat for his picture on 16 June 1783, and that evening had suffered a stroke. [3] On 7 August Michael Lort wrote that Johnson was recovered, 'and gone to Mr Langton's at Rochester. Before he went he sat to Opie, the famous self-taught Cornish painter, for his picture, and who I am told has given a just but not flattering likeness'.[4] On 3 September 1783 Johnson wrote he had sat to Opie 'as long as he desired, and I think the head is finished, but it [is] not much admired. The rest he is to add when he comes again to town.'[5] According to Sir John Hawkins, in 1784 Johnson 'resumed sitting to Opie for his picture, which had been begun the year before, but, I believe, was never finished'.[6]

A replica is in an English private collection.[7] Copies in London include those in the Athenaeum and at Dr Johnson's House (an oval).[8] A miniature copy by William Patten was sold Christie's, 15 October 1996, lot 153; a weak half-length portrait, derived from the Opie type, is in Trinity College, Oxford,[9] and a pencil head by Cosway was said to derive from the Opie.[10]

1 Illegible Christie's stencils remain on the stretcher, and the frame bore the inscription *by Gainsborough* in 1901.
2 Illus. Redford, III, front.; engraved C. Townley 1786.
3 Redford, IV, p.151
4 *Johnson*, Arts Council, 1984, p.132 (from Nichols *Illustrations*, VII, p.459).
5 Redford, IV, p.193.
6 Sir John Hawkins, *The Life of Samuel Johnson*, 1787, p.569.
7 Exhibited *Johnson*, Arts Council, 1984, no.99; engraved J. Heath 1786 (*from an Original Painting by Opie in the Possession of Mr Harrison*).
8 Others include two in private English collections, and one sold Christie's, 5 June 1888, lot 83, said to have come from the King's Head Collection at Lancaster, where it was mentioned by Dickens in *The Uncommercial Traveller*.
9 Poole, III, p.134, attributed to Frances Reynolds, illus. OP 1906, f.p.72; see also 1783 below.
10 Rogers 1878, p.117.

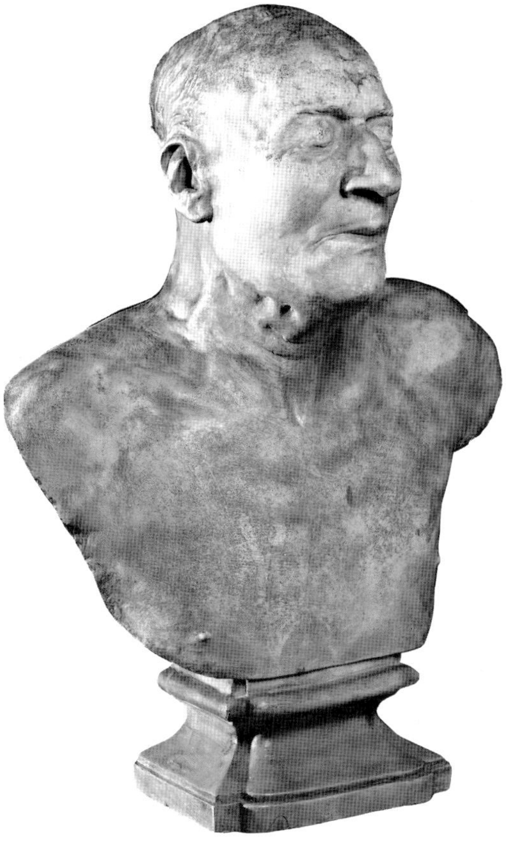

JOHNSON NPG *4685*

4685 CAST INCORPORATING DEATH MASK 1784

Painted plaster 51 (20) high, on a plaster socle 11 (4¼) high.

Collections:[1] William Cruikshank (Johnson's physician); his daughter Mrs A. Thomas; given in 1844 to her son-in-law, William Hutchins; given in 1864 to the Royal Literary Fund, by whom presented 1969.

Exhibition: Johnson, Arts Council, 1984(105).

William Cruikshank, who had attended Johnson at his death, told his daughter that NPG 4685 was 'from a cast after [Johnson's] death' and that 'all Dr Johnson's friends had one of them'.[2] Immediately after Johnson's death, Joshua Reynolds had 'ordered Mr [James] Hoskins, in St Martin's Lane, caster of figures to the Royal Academy, to make a plaster of Paris cast from his face',[3] and a 'plaister bust of Dr Johnson moulded after his death' was in the Thomond sale, 26 May 1821, lot 48. A cast of the death mask is preserved in the Department of Anatomy, University of Edinburgh,[4] and two plaster casts from NPG 4685** were taken by Brucciani for the NPG in 1878.[5]

In 1796 a correspondent of the *Gentleman's Magazine* recorded seeing a death mask of Johnson 'some time since' at 'Mr Coade's, the artificial stone maker, near Westminster Bridge'.[6]

1 Taken from corr. copied from The Royal Literary Fund (including letters from Mrs A. Thomas to W. Hutchins, n.d., and from Mrs Isabella Hutchins to Scharf 28 November [1877?]).
2 Letter from his daughter Mrs A. Thomas, [n.d., probably 1844], to her son-in-law, William Hutchins, see note 1 above.
3 *The Beauties of Johnson*, 1797 ed., p.xcix. See also Thomas Tyers, *Biography of Dr Samuel Johnson*, 1785 ed., p.22: Johnson's 'face and shoulders were moulded and taken off since his death ... by Hoskins of St Martin's-lane, from which a bust is made' (quoted *Johnson*, Arts Council, 1984, p.137).
4 *Death Masks and Life Masks*, Edinburgh University, [1988], p.17.
5 NPG 498A and 498B, the latter exhibited *Samuel Johnson, Londoner*, Royal Exchange, London, 1964.
6 *GM*, LXVI, 1796, i, p.298.

621 JOSEPH EDGAR BOEHM 1881

Painted plaster 44.5 (17½) high, incised on the base *Dr. Samuel Johnson* and signed *J.E.B.*

Collections: Presented by the artist 1881.

A small-scale half-length modello, derived from the portrait by Reynolds (see NPG 1445 above). In a letter to George Scharf of 8 March 1881 Boehm wrote that 'if the proposal of the sketch of Dr Johnson should take some day the form of a lifesize half figure I would do it in consideration for the Gallery [if?] it is to find it's place, for Two hundred Guineas. It is quite half a statue! you know'(NPG archive).

621A JOSEPH EDGAR BOEHM 1881

Clay bust 28.6 (11¼) high

With head-dress, wearing an open coat.

Collections: Presented by the artist, 1881.

See NPG 621 above.

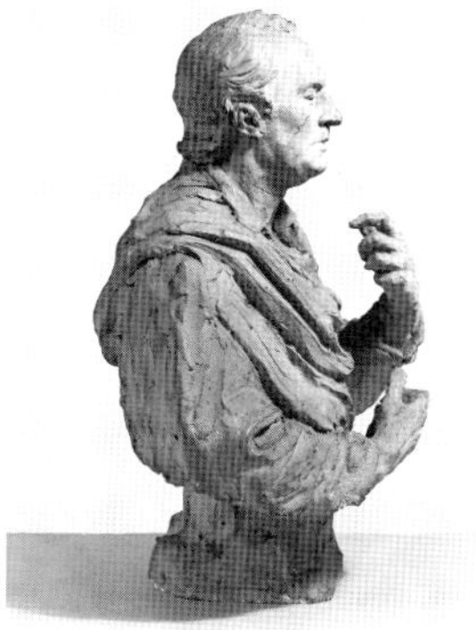

JOHNSON NPG *621*

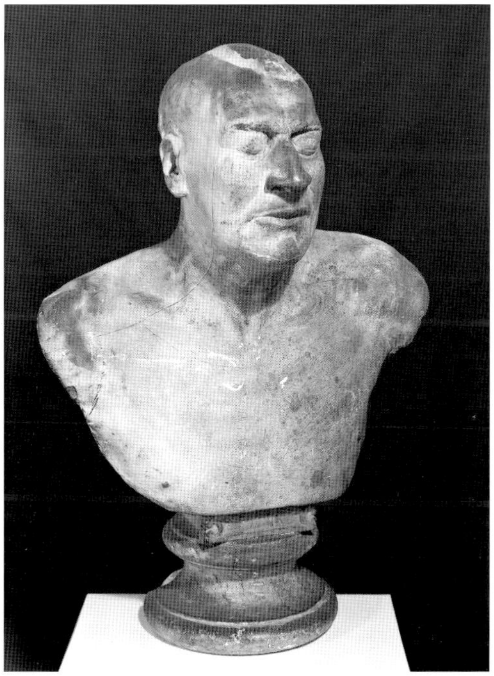

JOHNSON NPG *498A*

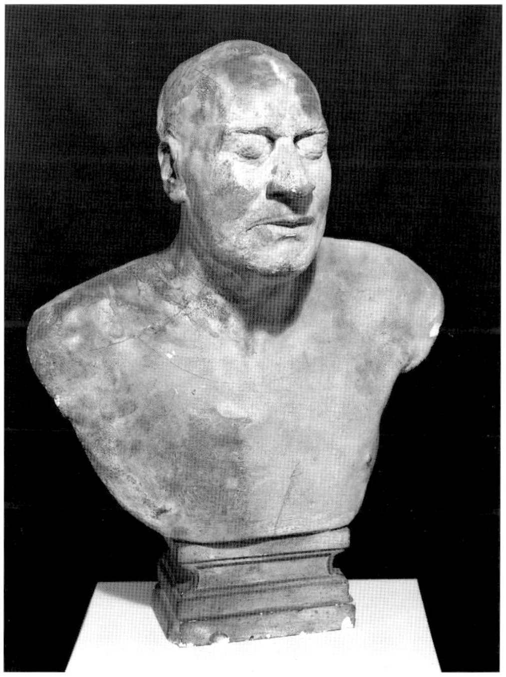

JOHNSON NPG *498B*

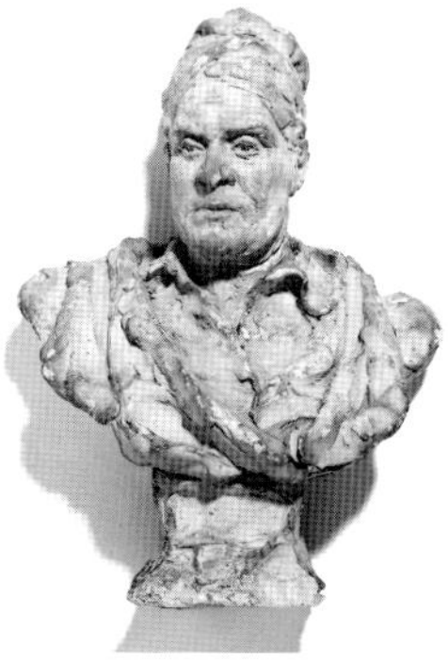

JOHNSON NPG *621A*

ICONOGRAPHY

Johnson's portraiture has been surveyed by L.F. Powell, 'The Portraits of Johnson' in *Boswell*, IV, pp.447–64; by David Piper, 'The Development of the British Literary Portrait up to Samuel Johnson', *Proc. of the British Academy*, 1968, pp.71–72; H.W. Liebert, 'Portraits of the Author: Lifetime Likenesses of Samuel Johnson', *English Portraits of the Seventeenth and Eighteenth Centuries*, William Andrews Clark Memorial Library, University of California, 1974, pp.47–70, and by K.K. Yung in *Johnson*, Arts Council, 1984.

1756–57 Painting by Joshua Reynolds, see NPG 1597.

1769 Painting by Joshua Reynolds, see NPG 1445.

1769 Drawing, probably by John Taylor, profile. Pembroke College, Oxford. Inscribed: *Done by permission of Dr Sam Johnson himself for the Revd H. Bright 1769* and *The head of Dr Johnson from a seal of the Revd G. Strahan.* Apparently *the original drawing* engraved by P. Lamborn in May 1772 (illus. *Cambridge Bibliographical Soc.*, III, 1962, p.311) and by I. Taylor. Taylor made two drawings of Johnson at Oxford, one of which was for Sir Robert Chambers who went to India in 1773 (Smith 1905, pp.318–19).

1775? Painting by Joshua Reynolds, half length, holding a book close to his eyes. Loren R. Rothschild, California (Mannings 2000, no.1016). Engraved J. Hall 1787. The least satisfactory of Reynolds's portraits of Johnson. The dating is uncertain; Northcote 1819, II, pp.3–4, gave 1775, but a copy of Hall's engraving in the British Museum (1838.7.14.29) is inscribed 'the head was painted by Sir Joshua from memory after the death of the Doctor'.

An unfinished version is in the Hyde Collection, inscribed as made by Gilbert Stuart for Johnson's friend William Bowles (illus. G. Austin ed., *Four Oaks Library*, 1967, f.p.51). Miniature copies by William Essex exhibited RA 1846(738) and RA 1860(858), the latter presumably that dated 1859 (illus. *Connoisseur*, CCII, 1979, p.140).

1777 Bust by Joseph Nollekens, see NPG 996.

1778 Painting by Joshua Reynolds, half length. Tate Gallery (N 887; Mannings 2000, no.1014). Painted for Henry Thrale's library at Streatham. Engraved W. Doughty 1779.

Several versions are recorded; one from the collection of Topham Beauclerk is in a private English collection (Mannings 2000, no.1015); three are at Pembroke College, Oxford (Poole, III, pp.243–44), others at Gunby Hall, and in the Hyde Collection. Reduced versions include examples at Dunvegan Castle and formerly with Sir Russell Brain.

A copy by E.F. Burney sold Sotheby's, 6 March 1940, lot 22 (see Burney 1991, I, pp.290–91n17). A miniature copy by W. Hatfield in the Ashmolean Museum, Oxford (dated 1780) and another, unattributed, sold Christie's, 27 March 1985, lot 312.

A version, showing a stick in the left hand, with Courage Ltd, has been unnecessarily attributed to Opie. A 'Sketch in chalks from the life, by Frye', sold Christie's, 5 June 1888, lot 82, derived from this type (Scharf sketch, NPG archive).

1777–84 Painting by James Barry, *Distribution of Premiums in the Society of Arts*, part of the *Progress of Human Culture*. Royal Society of Arts, London. See NPG 1185.

1778–80 Painting by James Barry, see NPG 1185.

1782 Drawn and etched by Thomas Trotter,* profile head, *from the Life*. Fanny Burney thought the print 'as like him as it can look' (*New Light on Dr Johnson*, ed. F.W. Hilles, 1959, p.330). Originally intended as the frontispiece for Kearsley's *Beauties of Samuel Johnson*, 1782, but rejected by George Steevens as 'a very ugly head' (Smith 1920, I, p.127). Subsequently used by Flaxman in 1784, see below.

A drawing, probably after Trotter's etching, with Canon Henry Blagden, Oxford, in 1909 (illus. A.M. Broadley, *Johnson and Mrs Thrale*, 1910, f.p.14), apparently that sold Bonham's, 28 November 1990, lot 13, as by Blaydon.

1782 Drawing by Thomas Trotter, half-length seated. Hyde Collection (illus. Redford, IV, front.) Etched by Trotter 1786, *from the original Drawing in the possession of Mr John Simco, taken from the life, a Short time before his decease, and Etched by T. Trotter* (2nd ed. of Kearsley's *Beauties of Samuel Johnson*). Trotter engraved a slightly larger plate from what appears to be the same drawing in 1792, *From an original drawing by T. Trotter, in the Possession of the Revd Dr Farmer.*

This or another drawing 'from the life' exhibited by Trotter RA 1785(565). Trotter's 1786 engraving of Dr Johnson in his travelling dress appears to derive from it, see below.

Johnson sat twice to Trotter 'at Mr Kearsley's request' (*Beauties*, 1797 ed., pp.xciii, xcix).

1782 Drawing by J. Harding, half length, etched by Trotter 1782 (as *Drawn from the Life by J. Harding*). Closely resembling the Trotter drawing of 1782.

1782 Painting by Johann Zoffany, perhaps unfinished. The *Morning Herald*, 6 January 1783, announced Johnson had sat twice to him; Johnson recorded an appointment with 'Zaftanie' on 31 December 1782

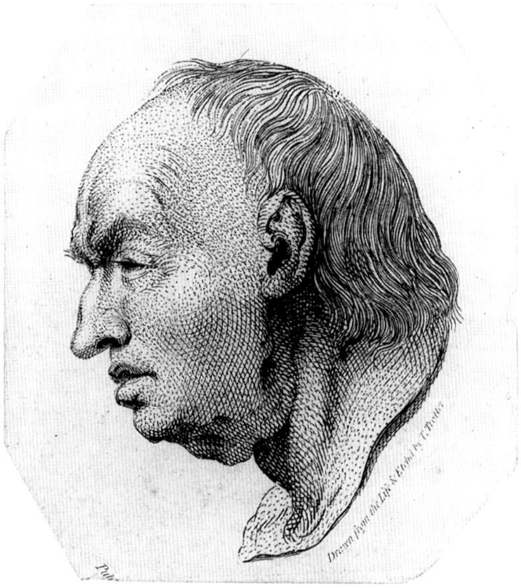

JOHNSON etching by T. Trotter 1782 (NPG D 13814)

(*Boswell*, IV, p.454) but Zoffany set out for India on 17 January 1783 (see Whitley 1928, II, pp.17–18).

(A so-called Zoffany allegedly of Johnson, half-length, leaning on his left hand, an open book before him, sold Christie's, 26 February 1868, lot 115).

1783 Painting by Frances Reynolds. On 20 August 1783 Johnson said the portrait was finished and was to be engraved (Redford, III, p.278n1; IV, pp.186–88). It was not well received; in 1819 it was in the collection of John Hatsell in London (Northcote 1819, II, p.159).

Generally identified, but without proof, as the portrait in the Albright-Knox AG, Buffalo, N.Y., which is comparable with the disputed Reynolds 1775 pattern, but shows Johnson holding a leather-bound book. A similar portrait, with Courage Ltd, may be by Theophila Palmer (Mrs Gwatkin) since it bears a label: *by the niece of Sir Josh. Reynolds* [*18*]*62 T.W. Guillod.* Frances Reynolds's portrait has also been associated with a version of the 1783–84 Opie, see NPG 1302 (and note 9) and Boswell, IV, p.456.

There is a crude engraving by I.I. de Claussen 1813 of a related portrait (*I Northcote R.A. Pinxt*).

1783–84 Painting by John Opie, see NPG 1302.

1784 Drawing by James Roberts, three-quarter length seated. On loan to Pembroke College, Oxford (illus. *Burl. Mag.*, LI, 1927, pp.266–67). A carbon copy also in Pembroke College (Poole, III, pp.244–45). Said to have been taken by Roberts for Miss Adams, daughter of Dr William Adams whom Johnson visited in 1784.

1784 Wedgwood medallion by John Flaxman, evidently based on Trotter's etching of 1782 (illus. Reilly 1973, p.199). Flaxman's invoice to Wedgwood dated 3 February 1784 (Reilly 1994, p.340). A wax model illus. D.R. Reilly, *Portrait Waxes*, 1953, fig.40. A comparable but later wax medallion by William Wyon, sold Sotheby's, Sussex, 19-27 July 1988, lot 1901.

A second Wedgwood medallion portrait of Johnson, the likeness not striking, listed in 1788 (illus. Reilly 1973, p.199). Gunnis 1968, p.211, said that James Hoskins had supplied Wedgwood with a bust of Johnson in 1775.

c.1784 Unattributed painting, half length. James P. Magill Library, Haverford College, Haverford, Penn. (illus. *Johnson*, Arts Council, 1984, no.103; see Mannings 2000, after no.1016). The likeness is unmistakable and closely resembles the death mask. An attribution to Opie cannot be dismissed, although Boswell listed only one portrait of Johnson by him (*Boswell*, IV, 421n2). Versions sold Christie's, 14 April 1864 (343, unattributed and described as 'copied from the portrait in the Painted Hall at Greenwich'[presumably a mistaken reference to Barry's painting in the Society of Arts, see NPG 1185]); and in private collections in Detroit 1969 (illus. *Connoisseur*, CIII, 1939, p.203), and London 1953. A reduced copy on copper in the Johnson's Birthplace Museum, Lichfield.

Posthumous

1784 Death mask, see NPG 4685.

1785 Drawn and engraved by Francesco Bartolozzi, profile. A similar engraving *from an original drawing* published 15 November 1786 by W. N. Gardiner, and a third by Freeman was published 1813 from an *original drawing by Bartolozzi*. A portrait at the Johnson Birthplace Museum, Lichfield, apparently copied from the Bartolozzi, has needlessly been attributed to William Hoare. A red wax impression from an intaglio (NPG reference collection, D7040) appears to derive from the Bartolozzi design.

1786 Engraving by T. Trotter, whole length walking, *Dr Johnson in his Travelling Dress as described in Boswells Tour, Drawn from the Life and Engrav'd by T. Trotter* (illus. *Johnson*, Arts Council, 1984, no.76). A later derivative plate by E. Finden 1835, whole length, left hand raised, *From an Original Painting in the possession of Mr Archdeacon Cambridge*.

1790 'Proof from gem' by Edward Burch, exhibited RA 1790(297).

1793 Marble bust by Richard Westmacott sr. Lichfield Cathedral, placed near Westmacott's bust of David Garrick. The likeness is not convincing, but the intended identity is beyond dispute. Another is in the Royal Collection (with a companion bust of Garrick).

1796 Marble statue by John Bacon sr.* St Paul's Cathedral. A plaster cast was exhibited Crystal Palace (Phillips 1854, no. 425a). A chalk study for the pose, attributed to Bacon, sold Sotheby's, 13 November 1997, lot 14.

1812-26 Engraved gem by James Wicksteed, exhibited RA 1812(644), and intaglios by James Wicksteed, exhibited RA 1822(954), and by C.H. Weigall, exhibited RA 1826(933).

Later busts include those by John Woodley 1842 (marble, sold Sotheby's, 2 July 1971, lot 82, the head close to the Nollekens type); by Augustus Saint-Gaudens 1874 (marble in the R.W. Norton Gallery, Shreveport, La.; plaster in the Berger collection, Denver, Colorado); by J.E. Boehm 1881, see NPG 621 and 621a above, and an undated marble, with tightly curled wig and buttoned coat (Sotheby's, 31 October 1985, lot 289; a related small bronze sold Sotheby's, 19 November 1996, lot 270).

Later statues include those by R.C. Lucas 1838 (Lichfield market place) and by Percy Fitzgerald 1910 (St Clement Danes, London), 'it should be removed' (Boswell, IV, p.472); a modello in the Hyde Collection).

DOUBTFUL PORTRAITS

Alleged miniatures by Samuel Shelley, exhibited *Guelph*, 1891 (733) lent J.L.G. Mowatt, and by John Smart jr. (Williamson, 1904, II, p.4). A portrait attributed to Reynolds in the Johnson Birthplace Museum, Lichfield (engraved G. Zobel).

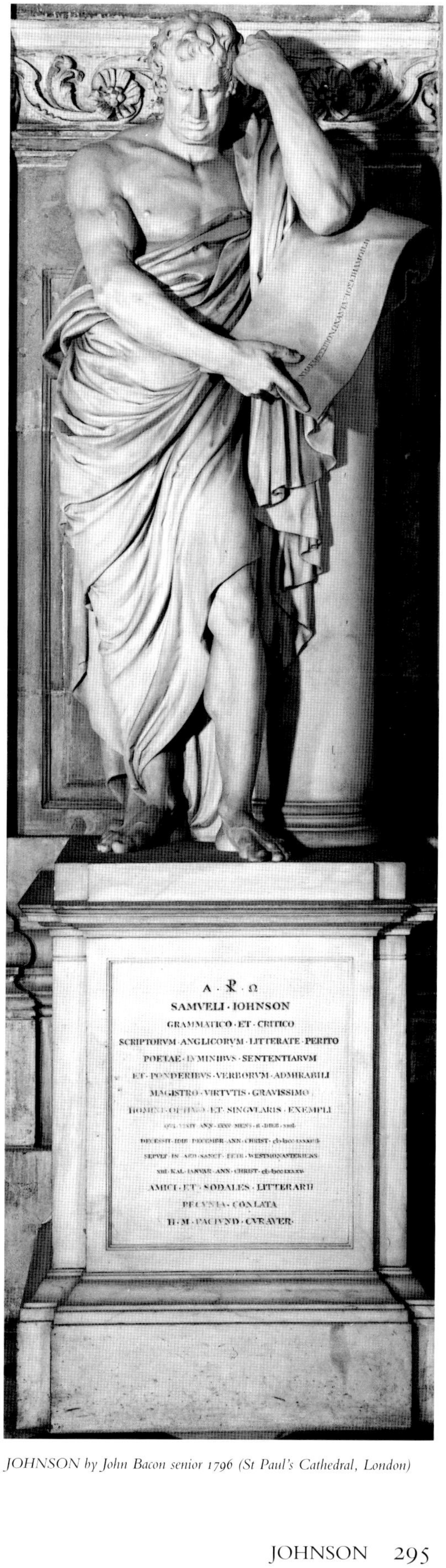

JOHNSON by John Bacon senior 1796 (St Paul's Cathedral, London)

JONES, John Paul 1747-92

Naval adventurer; b. John Paul in Kirkbean, Dumfries; assumed the name of Jones 1775 and joined the American navy, for whom he terrorized British coastal waters; made *chevalier du mérite militaire* in Paris 1780; returned to America 1781; served briefly in Russia 1788 under Potemkin, returning in 1790 to Paris, where he was buried. In 1913, by order of the American President, he was reburied in a marble sarcophagus in the US Naval Academy at Annapolis, Md.

'Eccentricities and Irregularities are to be expected from him – they are in his Character, they are visible in his Eyes. His voice is soft and still and small, his eye has keeness and Wildness and softness in it' (John Adams, 1779).

'he is small of stature, well proportioned, soft in his speech, easy in his address, polite in his manners, vastly civil, understands all the etiquette of a lady's toilette as perfectly as he does the mast, sails and rigging of his ship. Under all this appearance of softness he is bold, enterprising, ambitious and active' (Mrs John Adams c.1785).

Abbreviations

Morison 1960: S.E. Morison, *John Paul Jones*, 1960

TJP: *The Papers of Thomas Jefferson*, Princeton (reference is made to vols. XIII, 1956; XIV, 1958; XV, 1958, and XVI, 1961)

4022 AUGUSTIN DUPRÉ 1789

Bronze medal 5.6 (2¼) diameter.

Obverse: profile bust bareheaded in uniform, inscribed: *JOANNI PAVLO JONES CLASSIS PRAEFECTO. COMITIA AMERICANA.*

Reverse: the engagement between the *Bonhomme Richard* and the *Serapis*, inscribed: *HOSTIVM NAVIBVS CAPTIS AVT FVGATIS* and in the exergue: *AD ORAM SCOTIAE XXIII SEPT. / MDCCLXXVIIII*

Collections: Presented by Cyril Hughes Hartmann 1957.[1]

Engravings: J. Jacquemart 1878 (obverse and reverse).

Exhibition: *Bicentennial Center Opening*, Yorktown, Va., 1976.

Reference: C. Saunier, *Augustin Dupré*, 1894, pp.25-26, 114; *TJP*, XVI, 1961, pp.71, 76nn15-17; Brown 1980, no.222.

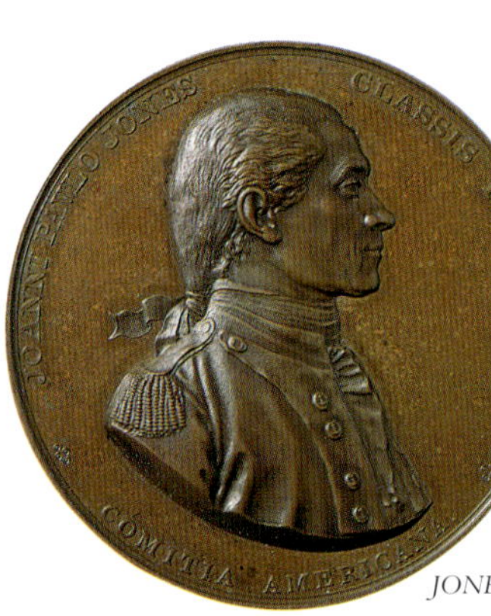

JONES NPG 4022

In July 1787 the American Congress voted that a medal in gold be struck and presented to the Chevalier John Paul Jones 'in commemoration of the valour and brilliant services of that Officer'. Jefferson in Paris was directed to commission it,[2] but it was not until 13 February 1789 that he ordered from Dupré 350 examples '*en or, argent ou bronze*' to be ready by 15 April 1789.[3] On 23 March he told Jones his medal would be done during the summer and the distribution would be: 'one of gold or silver (as the case may be) to the person who is the subject ... one of silver to every sovereign and one of copper to every university of Europe (Gr. Britain excepted) 200 copies to Congress and one apeice to La Fayette, Rochambeau, Destaing, and Degrasse'.[4] Jones had previously written to Jefferson from Russia on 29 August/9 September 1788 saying, with customary bravado, that he would want 'four Gold Medals as soon as the Dies are finished. I must present one to the United-States, another to the King of France, and I cannot do less than offer one to the Empress [Catherine of Russia]. As you will keep the Dies for me, it is my intention to have some more Gold Medals struck; therefore I beg you, in the mean time not to permit the striking of a single Silver or Copper Medal'.[5]

Dupré took Jones's likeness from Houdon's bust and his preparatory drawing is at Blérancourt.[6] For the reverse, he was sent an engraving of the celebrated action of September 1779 when Jones in the *Bonhomme Richard* successfully engaged the British man o'war *Serapis* off Flamborough Head; the engraving was apparently made from a wax by Reynaud,[7] though it also much resembles the print of the battle by Lerpinière and Fittler after Richard Paton.[8] For the inscription Jefferson had consulted the Académie Royale[9] who allowed one error, Flamborough Head not being off the coast of Scotland. The dies remain in the hôtel de la Monnaie and were used to make a fresh strike in gold for the chapel crypt in Annapolis MD, near Jones's body.[10]

A Wedgwood medallion was cast from the obverse in 1906;[11] a very similar wax profile attributed to the otherwise unrecorded 'Capri', was sold Bonham's, 14 June 2000, lot 136, and a variant in the Boston Public Library has been described as a study for the medal by Dupré.[12]

1 When accepted by the Trustees for the reference collection.
2 *TJP*, XVI, 1961, pp.63, 77, and XII, 1955, p.266.
3 *TJP*, XIV, 1958, pp.545-55. An example had been 'lately received' in Paris on 15 December (*TJP*, XVI, p.34).
4 *TJP*, XIV, 1958, p.687.
5 *TJP*, XIII, p.585.
6 Musée national de la coopération Franco-Américaine; illus. *TJP*, XVI, 1961, pl.XX (f.p.52).
7 There are some errors of detail (see Morison 1960, pp.238, 353; *TJP*, XIII, p.586). Jones had certainly employed the French medallist Reynaud (Morison 1960, p.352); he mentioned a French medallist, without naming him, who had 'executed three Medals for me in Wax', one of the battle between the *Bonhomme Richard* and the *Serapis*, which he thought might help with the new medal, though it was 'by no means to be Copyed' (*TJP*, XIII, p.586; an engraving illus. *TJP*, XVI, pl.XXI, f.p.52); Jefferson sent it to Dupré who, he said, would 'avail himself of so much of the design as is good' (*TJP*, XIV, 1958, p.687).
8 Illus. Morison 1960, f.p.232.
9 *TJP*, XVI, p.65.
10 Morison 1960, p.354.
11 Illus. Reilly 1973, p.201, and see Reilly 1994, p.275.
12 Illus. Morison 1960, f.p.153.

ICONOGRAPHY

1776 Silhouette by Jean Millette, half length. Franklin D. Roosevelt Library, New York (illus. Morison 1960, f.p.9).

1779 Engraving by J.E. Haid, three-quarter length standing in uniform with tricorne hat, a telescope in his right hand, inscribed ... *Commander of a Squadron in the Service of the Thirteen United States of North America 1779*. The example in the NPG Washington (67.54) listed as by Haid; similar plates are given to R. Brookshaw (see below), or unattributed (CS, IV, p.1735, no.97). A close version by Joh. Lorenz Rugendas and a reduced version, head only, engraved C. Bogerts from a drawing by J. Buys. A copy in oil (30 x 25 cm.), inscribed *John Paul Jones 1779*, was sold Sotheby's, 4th day, 21 June 1928, lot 861, bt. Maggs, as the original of the mezzotint by R. Brookshaw, and a related enamel was last sold Christie's, 25 July 1977, lot 22.

1780 Bust by J-A. Houdon, bare-headed, in uniform wearing the croix du mérite militaire. Plaster dated 1780 commissioned by the Masonic Loge des Neuf Soeurs, Paris, exhibited Salon 1781(261). Two terracottas were in the Houdon sales of 1795 and 1828. A marble dated 1781 is in the US Naval Academy Museum, Annapolis, Md. (formerly in the collection of the duc de Nemours; illus. Arnason 1975, fig.126).

Bronze casts include those in the NPG Washington (71.8), the Corcoran AG, Washington, and the

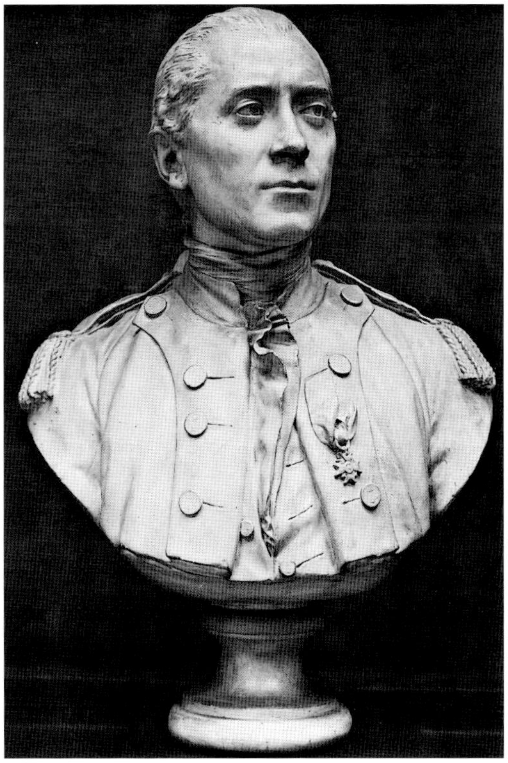

JONES by J-A. Houdon 1780 (musée national du château de Versailles)

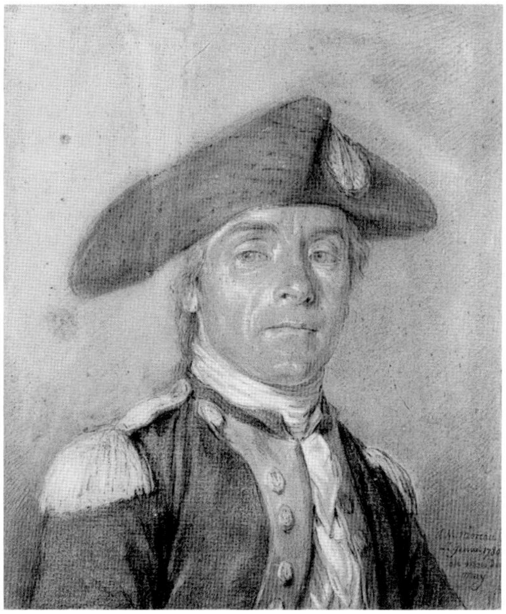

JONES by J-B. Moreau 1780 (Louisiana State Museum) detail

Addison Gallery of American Art, Andover, Mass.

Jones sent plasters to Washington, Franklin, Lafayette, d'Estaing, Baron Grimm, Roger Morris and Jefferson (this last received by February 1786; now Museum of Fine Arts, Boston, Mass.; illus. Arnason 1975, pl.63); he sent eight more to America in 1789 and another was commissioned by the State of North Carolina in March 1791 (see *TJP*, XV, 1958, pp.xxxvii-xxxviii, 122, 376, 437-38, 551, 591). Today plasters include those in the Pennsylvania Academy of Fine Arts, Philadelphia; the National Academy of Design, New York; the Metropolitan Museum of Art, New York; Versailles;* the musée de Blérancourt, and the Scottish NPG (PG 669).

1780 Drawing by J-M. Moreau le jeune,* half length in naval uniform with hat, with an inscription below ... *dessiné d'apres nature au mois de may, 1780, à Paris* ... Louisiana State Museum, Patterson, La. Engraved J-B. Fosseyeux 1781.

1780 Unattributed painting, bust-length, in uniform without medals; a copy by G.P.A. Healy, commissioned in 1846, is at Versailles (illus. *Peintures*, 1995, I, p.454).

1780 Miniature, bust length, in blue coat with yellow facings, wearing the *croix du mérite militaire*. NPG Washington (73.10). Versions are in the US Naval Academy Museum, Annapolis, Md., and in the Hermitage Museum (illus. A.C. Buell, *Paul Jones*, 1900, I, front.). Engraved anon. (illus. Morison 1960, f.p.280).

Said to have been painted in Paris by the 'Countess Lavendal' [Constance de Lowendal, comtesse de Turpin de Cerissé, or Charlotte-Marguerite de Bourbon, comtesse de Lowendahl], who drew 'his picture (a striking likeness) ... and presented it to him', making him 'like a second Narcissus, in love with his own resemblances' (*Memoirs of Rear-Admiral Paul Jones*, 1830, II, p.254; Morison 1960, p.279).

A second, less reliable, account described a miniature 'painted on ivory by a Dutch artist named Van der Huydt, to whom Jones gave sittings in 1780, and was presented by him to the duc de Chartres; two or three replicas were made by Van der Huydt, one given to the comtesse de la Vendahl' (A.C. Buell, *Paul Jones*, 1900, II, p.337).

c.1780 Wax medallion attributed to J-M. Renaud, bust length in uniform with the *croix du mérite militaire*. Scottish NPG (PGL 104; illus. *Proc. of the Soc. of Antiquaries of Scotland*, XL, 1906, p.79). Sent by Jones from Paris to a Mrs Belches in Scotland, with a covering letter of 29 August 1786 (*ibid.*, pp.77-78) and possibly one of the three wax medals Jones mentioned in 1789, see NPG 4022, note 7. The head resembles that in the 1780 miniature listed above.

1781 Painting by C.W. Peale, bust-length oval, in blue coat with red facings, wearing the *croix du mérite militaire*. Independence National Historical Park, Philadelphia (illus. Morison 1960, f.p.280; see *Selected Papers of C.W. Peale*, I, 1983, p.441n6). Engraved J.B. Longacre 1852. Jefferson thought it a very bad likeness (Morison 1960, p.311). A miniature copy was made by either James or Anna Peale.

c.1781 Painting by C-J. Notte, half length, standing on deck in uniform during the engagement between the *Bonhomme Richard* and the *Serapis*. Engraved C. Guttenberg (NPG Washington, 79.201). A related painting in a private collection in 1949 (photograph NPG archive). The head was evidently the ultimate source for the oval half length engraved J. Chapman 1796, without hat, pistols in his belt.

Morison (1960, p.8n) recorded a wax portrait with light brown hair in the US Naval Academy Museum, Annapolis, Md., and another miniature in the Masonic Library, Boston, Mass. A.C. Buell, *Paul Jones*, 1900, II, p.338, described a full-length portrait by 'Chapelle', standing on his quarter deck in full uniform, a glass in left hand, the head taken from the Houdon bust.

1789 Medal by Augustin Dupré, see NPG 4022.

DOUBTFUL PORTRAITS

There were many propagandist images of Jones, whose appearance prior to 1780 remained generally unknown. A medallion engraving (illus. Morison 1960, f.p.72) was said to be from a sketch taken by Simon Fokke in Amsterdam in October 1779. The American journal, *The King*, 8 July 1905, pp.471, 473 (NPG archive), illustrated four engravings of Jones, bearing no relationship to his appearance as documented by Houdon: a profile head inscribed: *Ce marin Anglois Eut merité d'être François*; two whole-length oval prints, as Commodore and Captain in the American navy, possibly of Dutch origin, and a whole length, sabre in hand, published in London in 1780.

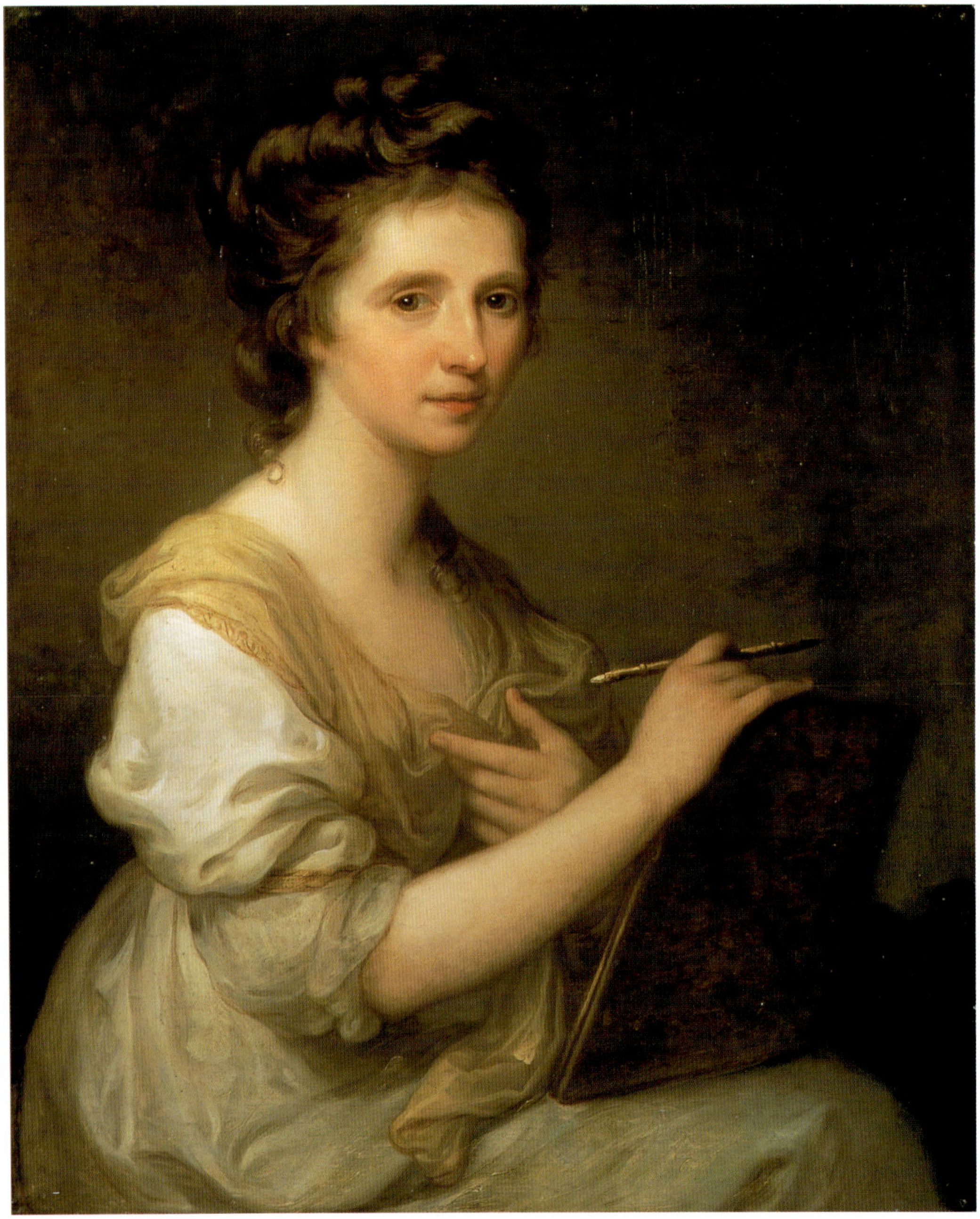

KAUFFMANN NPG *430*

KAUFFMANN, Angelica 1741-1807

Painter; b. Chur (Coire), Switzerland; studied in Italy before leaving Venice for England 1766, where Reynolds and Dance were sometime enamoured of her; foundation member of the RA 1768; m. 1781 Antonio Zucchi (d. 1795), the Italian decorative painter, and moved to Rome; Goethe and Herder were among her friends; Canova directed her funeral in Rome.

'At the age of ten she spoke English and French as familiarly as if they were her native language [and] could read Spanish with equal ease ... she was quite mistress of the Italian, and of German which was her native tongue. She has an agreeable person, a sweet and open countenance, of a very modest, engaging deportment, and was no small proficient in music' (Dr John Morgan, 1774).

Abbreviations

Hommage an Kauffmann 1992: O. Sandner, *Hommage an Angelika Kauffmann*, exh. cat., Liechtenstein, Milan, 1992

Rosenthal 1996: A. Rosenthal, *Angelika Kauffmann, Bildnismalerei im 18. Jahrhundert*, 1996

430 SELF PORTRAIT c.1770-75

Canvas 76 x 63.5 (30 x 25) lined; scattered retouchings; a small loss below centre.

Brown eyes, brown hair, wearing a white dress with a yellow shawl, a porte-crayon in her right hand which rests on an upright leather-bound folder.

Collections: [By descent to Johann Kauffmann; Georg Kauffmann 1859];[1] 3rd Earl of Morley; his sale Christie's, 3 June 1876,[2] lot 34, purchased.

Exhibitions: *Kauffmann*, Kenwood, 1955(20); *Kauffmann* 1968(4); *Women Artists 1550-1950*, Los Angeles, 1977(49); *Eva und die Zukunst*, Hamburg, 1986(224); *Travels in Italy*, Manchester, 1988(92); *Hommage an Kauffmann* 1992(4); *Mirror, Mirror*, NPG 2001 (n.n.); Beningbrough 1979–

Reference: Williamson 1924, p.197.

Ribeiro has pointed out how the fanciful, part classical 'renaissance', costume emphasises Kauffmann's status as an artist and, perhaps, her disdain for the intricacies of high fashion.[3] NPG 430 has been dated between 1770 and 1775;[4] the elegant pose, not unrelated to the Reynolds portrait of c.1777, was subsequently developed in the self portraits sold Sotheby's, 14 June 2001, lot 2, of 1775-80, at Chur of c.1780, and in Munich of 1784 (see below).

1 NPG 430 was sold in 1876 with a certificate in German signed by Georg Kauffmann, Dornbirn, 3 August 1859 [trans.]: 'I the undersigned hereby declare that according to documents in our family the portrait of Angelica Kauffmann was painted by Sir Joshua Reynolds the English painter and given by him to Angelica. At her death it came by Will to my late Uncle Johann Kauffmann who left it by Will to me. I declare this to be the truth'. But see the Reynolds portrait of c.1777-78 below. There was a second portrait of Kauffmann at Saltram, see self portraits c.1765-70 below.

2 For this sale of part of the Saltram collection, see NT, *Saltram Guide*, 1988, p.63.

3 Ribeiro 2000, p.16.

4 Rosenthal 1996, p.324, as 1770-75; Kauffmann 1998, pp.224, 231, as 1770.

4905 see Groups, *Portraits in the characters of the Muses* by RICHARD SAMUEL 1778

ICONOGRAPHY

Self Portraits

c.1753 Painting, aged thirteen, half length as a singer. Tiroler Landesmuseum, Innsbruck (illus. *Kauffmann* 1998, p.226).

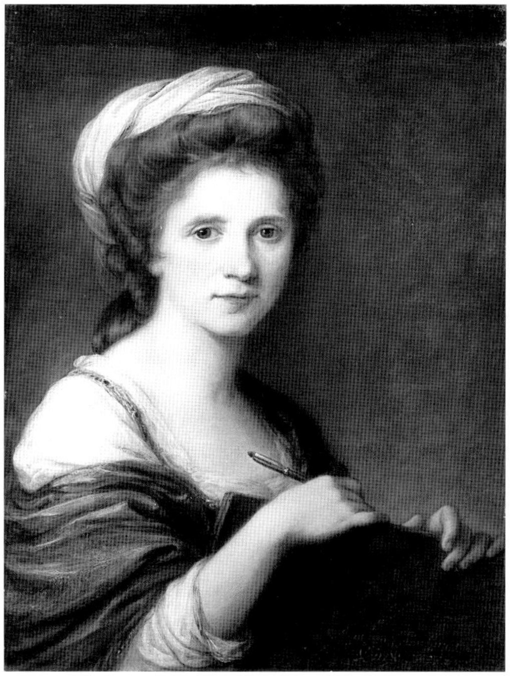

KAUFFMANN *Self portrait c.1780 (Bündner Kunstmuseum, Chur)*

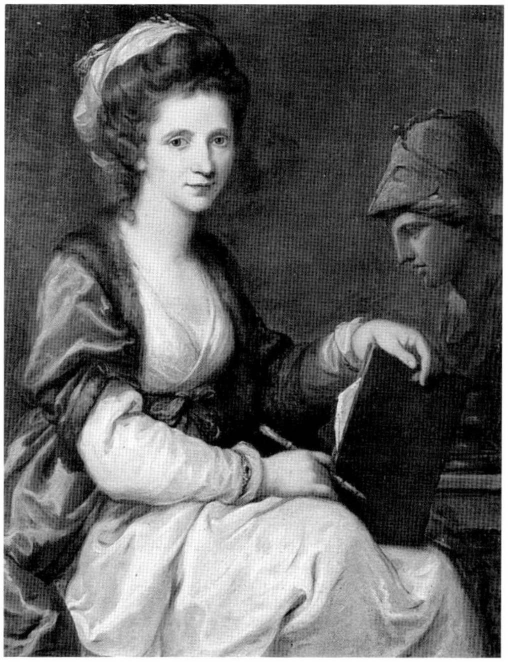

KAUFFMANN *Self portrait 1784 (Neue Pinakothek, Munich)*

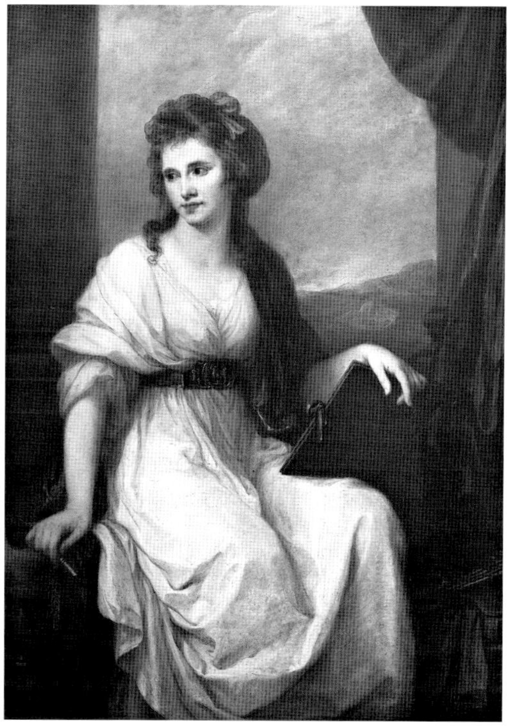

KAUFFMANN *Self portrait 1787 (Galleria degli Uffizi, Florence)*

c.1757-59 Painting, three-quarter length seated in Bregenz peasant costume. Uffizi Gallery, Florence (4444; illus. *Kauffmann* 1998, p.227). Copy in Vorarlberger Landesmuseum, Bregenz (illus. Rosenthal 1996, p.328, fig.125).

1762-66 Drawing, half-length oval, wearing a lace cap. Victoria and Albert Museum (Vallardi sketchbook, E.398.1927; illus. *Kauffmann* 1998, p.197).

c.1763-64 Painting, half-length oval. Pennsylvania Academy of Arts, Philadelphia (illus. *Kauffmann* 1998, p.22; Rosenthal 1996, p.103, fig.18). There was also an etched self portrait of 1764 (listed *Kauffmann* 1998, p.436).

c.1765-70 Painting, three-quarter length seated, wearing a turban, playing a viol. Saltram. In poor condition, but the eighteenth-century inscription of sitter and artist provides serious evidence.

c.1770-75 Painting, see NPG 430.

1771 Drawing, half length, porte-crayon in her left hand (a mirror image). Yale Center for British Art (B1977.14.5552; illus. *Kauffmann* 1998, p.239; Rosenthal 1996, p.315, fig.116).

1773 Painting, half length, wearing a red Grison costume, brushes and palette in her left hand. Private collection (illus. *Kauffmann* 1998, p.229). Copy sold Christie's, 25 March 1966, lot 25.

1775-80 Painting, half-length painted oval, wearing a turban, a porte-crayon and case in her right hand. Sotheby's, 14 June 2001, lot 2 (illus. Rosenthal 1996, p.325, fig.122). The pose closely resembles NPG 430. A copy is in the Museum of Fine Arts, Montreal (140.1996; illus. *Collage*, Montreal, Spring 1998, p.13).

c.1780 Painting,* three-quarter length seated, wearing a fur-trimmed red cloak, a portfolio in her left hand, porte-crayon in her right, a bust of Minerva at her side. Bündner Kunstmuseum, Chur.

c.1780 Painting, half length, porte-crayon in right hand, wearing a rose-coloured dress, with white front trimmed with gold. Formerly Holland House (cat., 1904, no.116). Exhibited, *British Self Portraits*, Arts Council, 1962(48). Miniature copy in the Bowes Museum, Barnard Castle.

1781 Painting, bust-length in Bregenz peasant costume, black hat and a black fur-trimmed cape. Tiroler Landesmuseum, Innsbruck (illus. *Kauffmann* 1998, p.232; Rosenthal 1996, p.326, fig.123). Engraved A. Testa.

1782 Painting, oval, whole-length seated, as Design, listening to the inspiration of Poetry. Kenwood (illus. *Kauffmann* 1998, p.242; Rosenthal 1996, p.331, fig.128). Engraved T. Burke 1787.

1783 Miniature, three-quarter length seated holding a drawing, inscribed *Kaufman Angelica à son amie Adelina Rosalba. For ever, Bologne. 1783*. Exhibited BFAC 1889(x 29, pl. xxiv) lent J. Whitehead.

1784 Painting,* half length, wearing a white turban, her right hand holding a porte-crayon. Neue Pinakothek, Munich (1056); painted for Count Firmian. Copies include a drawing by Hermann Römer, Sotheby's, Munich, 18 May 1988, lot 3, and a poor miniature by Joseph Pastorini (illus. Williamson 1924, f.p.2).

1787 Painting,* three-quarter length, a portfolio in her left hand and porte-crayon in her right, the belt of her white dress bearing two cameo plaques of Minerva. Uffizi Gallery, Florence (1928). Engraved P. Audouin. Miniature copy by Leopoldi Galli (half-length oval), sold Christie's, 25 September 1997, lot 130. Versions with Leger 1929; in the Globe Theatre, London; Hatchlands (Cobbe Collection), and Christie's, 26 April 1985, lot 98.

1792 Painting, standing three-quarter length, hesitating between female figures emblematic of Music and Painting. Pushkin Museum, Moscow (illus. *Kauffmann* 1998, p.234), painted for Princess Holstein-Beck of Russia. Replica at Nostell Priory dated 1794 (illus. Rosenthal 1996, p.340, fig.136).

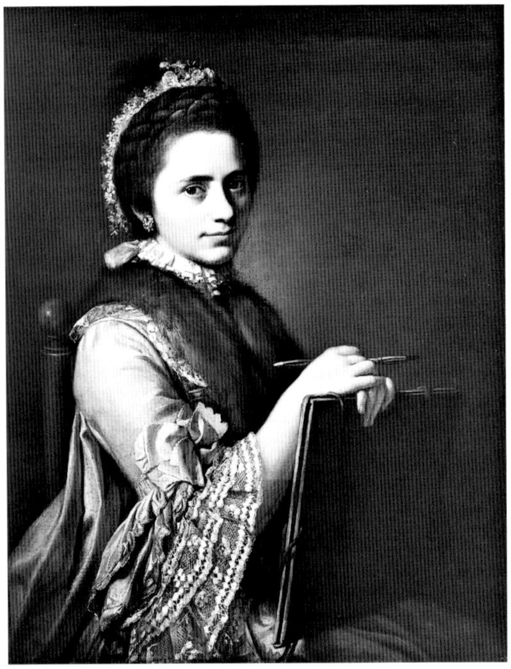

KAUFFMANN by Nathaniel Dance c.1764 (Burghley House Collection)

1802 Drawing, bust length with a white turban. Private collection (illus. *Kauffmann* 1998, p.225).

By other Artists

c.1764 Painting by Nathaniel Dance,* half length, wearing a bonnet and holding an upright portfolio. Burghley House.

c.1766-67 Drawing by Nathaniel Dance, whole-length seated, with her brushes, mahlstick and palette in her left hand, her right on her heart, turning to Joshua Reynolds who sits at her side. Harewood (illus. *Reynolds*, RA, 1986, no.170; Rosenthal 1996, p.193, fig.49). A separate drawing of Kauffmann alone is in the British Museum (1898.7.12.72; illus. *Dance* 1977, no.14d).

c.1766-67 Drawing attributed to Nathaniel Dance, seated wearing a bonnet, a small Belvedere torso on the table before her. NG of Scotland (illus. *Kauffmann* 1998, p.18). Mischievously parodied by Robert Dighton 1772 as *The Paintress* (illus. *Kauffmann* 1998, p.19; Rosenthal 1996, p.210, fig.52).

1772 Painting by Johann Zoffany,* *The Academicians of the Royal Academy*, see Groups NPG 1437.

c.1777-78 Painting by Joshua Reynolds,* half length, a lock of hair over her right shoulder. Private collection, formerly at Althorp (Mannings 2000, no.1026). Left by Kauffmann in her will to her cousin Johann Kauffmann, a bequest apparently confused with the earlier history of NPG 430, see above. Engraved (as an oval) F. Bartolozzi 1780; E. Morace. A copy by Kauffmann 1794 is in an Austrian private collection (illus. *Kauffmann* 1998, p.190). Versions include those at the Lady Lever AG, Port Sunlight; in the Accademia di S. Luca, Rome, and in a private collection (illus. Rosenthal 1996, p.185, fig.44).

1778 Painting by Richard Samuel, *Portraits in the characters of the Muses*, see Groups NPG 4905.

1789 Watercolour by J.G. Schütz, Kauffmann in the gardens of the Villa d'Este in a group which includes Goethe, Herder, and the Duchess Anna Amalia of Saxe-Weimar. Goethe-Nationalmuseum, Weimar. Copy in Goethe Museum, Düsseldorf (illus. *Kauffmann* 1998, p.342).

1794 Wax medallion by F. Möglich, engraved J.F. Bause 1794, and Rauch.

1795 Painting by Henry Singleton,* *President and Members of the Royal Academy*, see Comparative Groups.

1796 Silhouette by C.H. Tatham, profile bust. Sotheby's, Monaco, 5 December 1992, lot 203. Another, differing principally in the hair ribbon, private collection, Rome (illus. Williamson 1924, f.p.183, and Riccio 2000, p.45 mistakenly attributed to Joseph Bonomi).

1796 Marble bust by Christopher Hewetson. Parish church of Schwarzenberg (illus. *Hommage an Kauffmann* 1992, pp.107, 257; and see *Kauffmann* 1998, p.106).

c.1804 Silhouette by C.L. Duttenhofer, whole-length seated at her easel with a bust of Minerva. Schiller Museum, Marbach (illus. *Kauffmann* 1998, p.343).

1809 Bust by (her cousin) J.P. Kauffmann. Protomoteca Capitolina, Rome (illus. D.M. Mayer, *Kauffmann*, 1972, no.4).

DOUBTFUL PORTRAITS

Self portraits provisionally identified by Rosenthal 1996, figs.17 (miniature), 61, 119, 120, 130, and pl.7 (cf. *Kauffmann* 1998, p.224n3); a slight so-called self-portrait drawing exhibited *English Drawings*, Colnaghi 1964(24).

Painting by Daniel Gardner, Government Art Collection (Sotheby's, 24 November 1999, lot 51), engraved R. Josey c.1870 (illus. *Connoisseur*, CXVIII, 1946, p.24), a version at Southside House, Wimbledon.

Miniature by John Smart, signed and dated 1764, listed in Foskett 1964, p.69 as called Kauffman, but the date is impossible.

Drawings by Richard Cosway (Cosway Foundation, Lodi; illus. Gipponi, *Cosway*, 1998, p.13) and

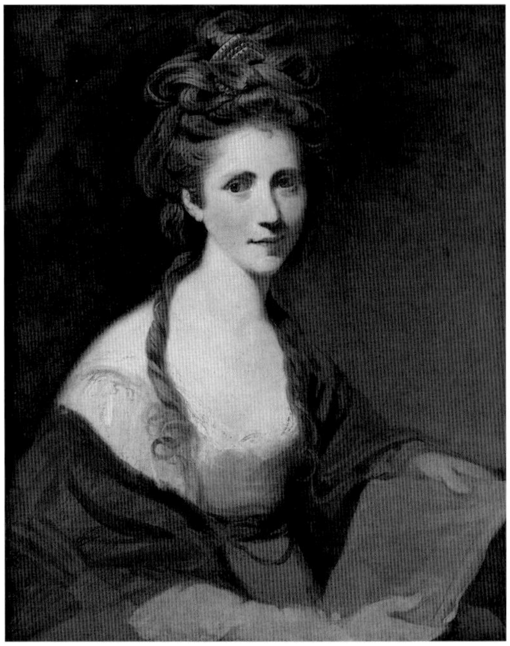

KAUFFMANN by Joshua Reynolds c.1777-78 (Christie's)

Francesco Bartolozzi (Lempertz, Cologne, 15 May 1999, lot 1243); attributed to John Hoppner (with Zeitlin & Ver Brugge, Los Angeles, 1977), and by Benjamin West c.1763 (Friends Historical Library of Swarthmore College, Swarthmore, Pa.; illus. *American Art Jnl.*, XII, 2, 1980, p.9).

Engravings by W. Ridley 1809 (*European Mag.*) and, reversed, by T. Woolnoth 1821; by T. Burke (illus. *Connoisseur*, LX, 1921, p.206).

The identity is founded on the provenance. Although Russell's signature appears genuine and a date has been read, NPG 4213 evidently derives from the earlier three-quarter length portrait by Andrea Soldi, see below.

1 This provenance was given by Mary Simms in letters of 19 January and 6 February 1961.

ICONOGRAPHY

c.1760 Painting by Andrea Soldi,* three-quarter length seated by his harpsichord. Christie's, 13 July 1984, lot 112 (as 'a Musician'); formerly with Miss Musgrave, London, in 1915. The approximate date of the portrait is based on comparison with Soldi's few dated works of this period. In his Will Kelway left his own portrait to his 'faithfull friend' Ann Phillips (*DNB*).

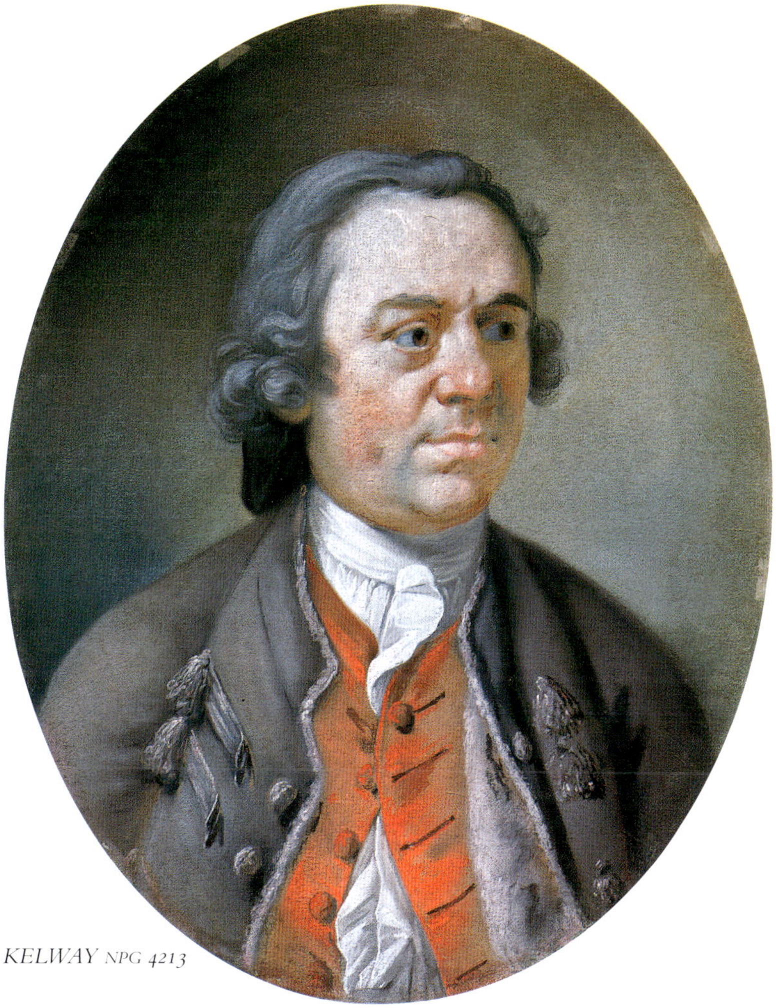

KELWAY NPG *4213*

KELWAY, Joseph c.1702-1782

Musician; organist of St Michael, Cornhill, 1730, and of St Martin-in-the-Fields 1736; harpsichord master to Queen Charlotte 1761; published *Six Sonatas for the Harpsichord* c.1764.

4213 JOHN RUSSELL 1776 after ANDREA SOLDI [c.1760]

Pastel on paper 61 x 48 (24 x 19) oval, laid on canvas; signed *I. Russell* in light green above shoulder, with the date *1776* faintly visible in black below; discordant touches of brown and blue on the face.

Brown eyes, grey powdered hair with black ribbon, wearing a grey coat, pink waistcoat and white shirt.

Collections: [Commissioned by George III for Samuel Wesley, his Court Musician, together with pastels of Handel, Corelli and see Boyce NPG 4212; thence to the Simms family 'in payment of a debt'[1]] Miss Leat, Yelverton, 1915; Mrs Mary Simms, Yelverton, from whom purchased 1961.

Exhibition: Beningbrough 1979-.

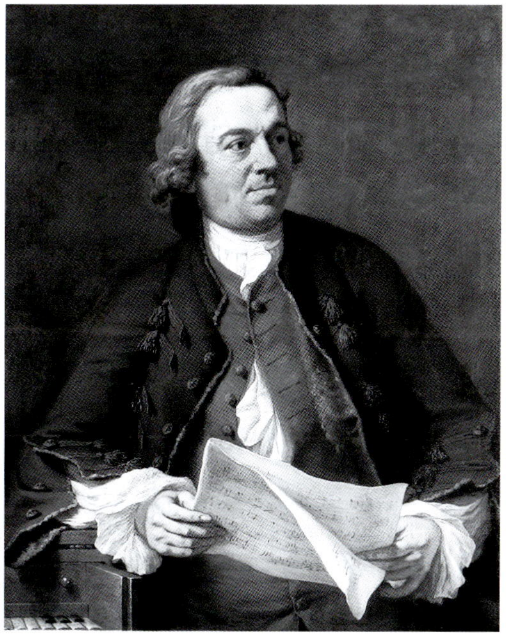

KELWAY by Andrea Soldi c.1760 (Christie's)

KEMBLE, Sarah, see SIDDONS

KEMPENFELT, Richard 1718-82

Naval officer; b. London of a Swedish father; served in the West Indies 1741-46 and East Indies 1757-64; travelled in Europe in the later 1760s; as Philotheorus, published hymns and poems 1777; rear-admiral 1780; captured twenty French vessels off Ushant 1781; his tragic death by drowning at Spithead on 29 August 1782, while his ship was being refitted, was commemorated by William Cowper in the *Loss of the Royal George* ('Toll for the brave').

'a man of great stature, spare and upright, and of a swarthy complexion. He wore a stiff queue of enormous length, and his whole attire was so plain that he was once mistaken for the clerk of his own flag ship' (E.H. Locker, 1831).

1641 RALPH EARL 1783

Canvas 127 x 101 (50 x 39¾) strip-lined; cleaned 1991; minor retouchings in the sky and in his left elbow; signed lower left, on the anchor: *R. Earl Pinxt 1783.*

Grey eyes, grey powdered buckle-wig, wearing the full-dress uniform of a flag officer: dark-blue coat with gold facings, white waistcoat with gold trim and white breeches; holding a wooden telescope in his right

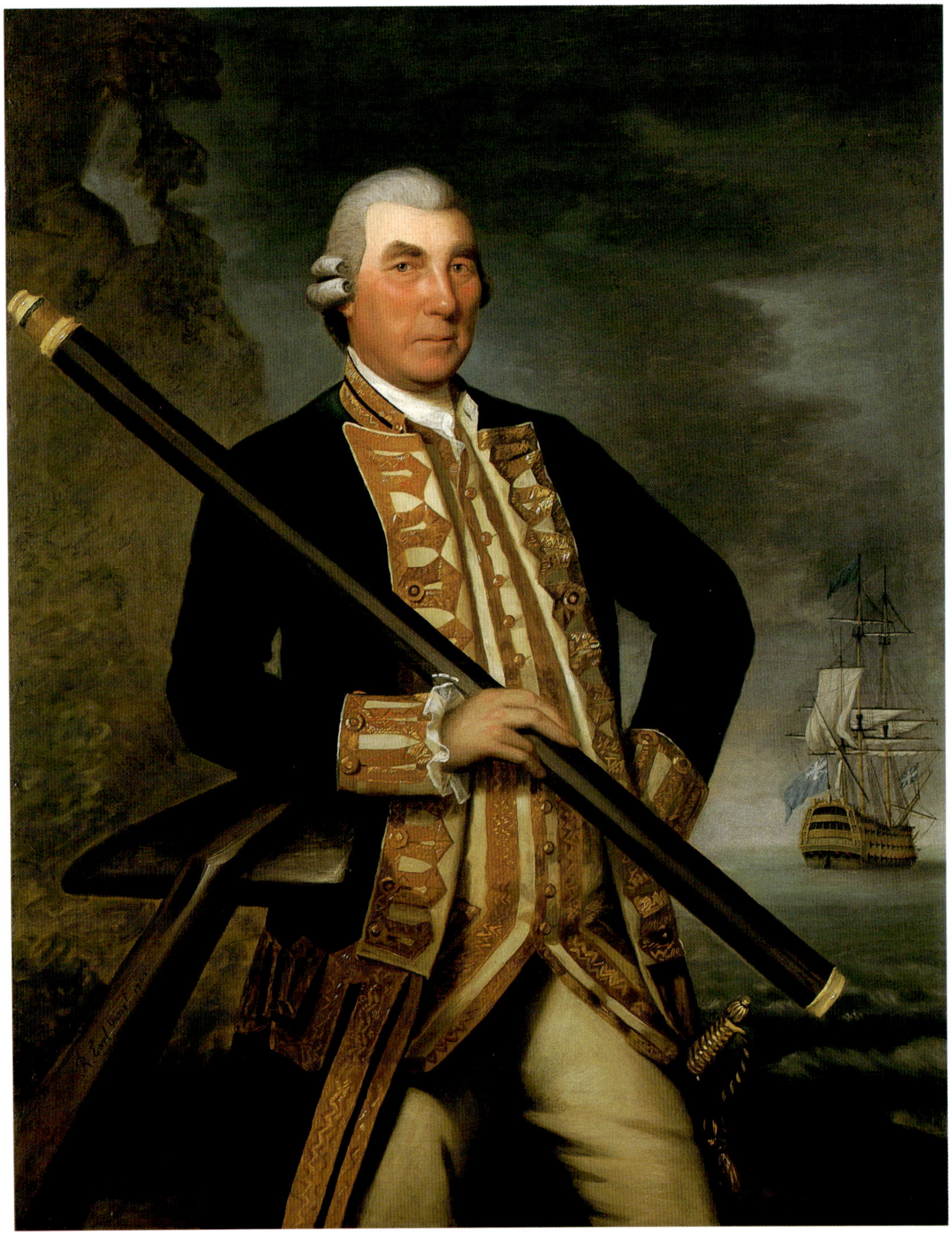

KEMPENFELT NPG *1641*

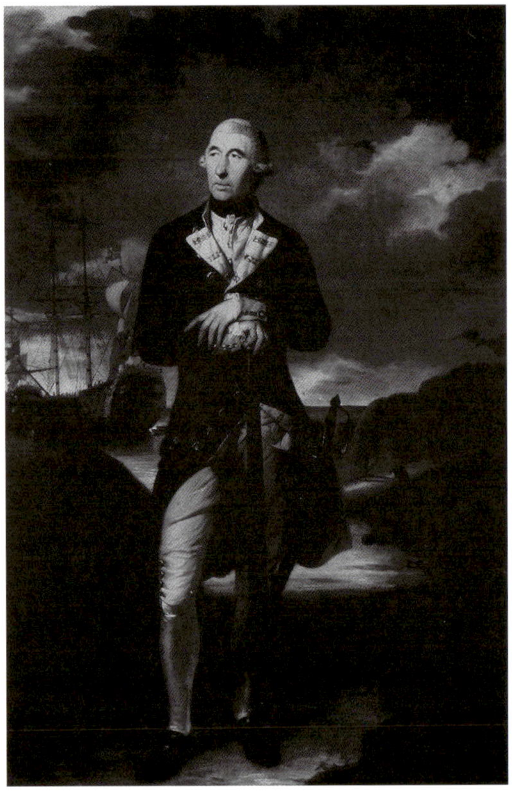

KEMPENFELT by Tilly Kettle 1781–82 (National Maritime Museum, London)

hand, resting his elbow on an anchor; the distant three-decker, resembling the *Royal George* (see below), flies a plain blue flag on the main mast[1] and blue flags quartered with a white cross fore and aft.

Collections: Graves 1889;[2] John Glen, London, 1911; Leggatt, from whom purchased 1912.

Exhibition: *Ralph Earl*, Washington, Hartford, Fort Worth, 1992(12).

Although dated 1783, after Kempenfelt's death, the head is vigorously painted, suggesting it was painted from the life, i.e. before April 1782 when Kempenfelt departed for Spithead on his last voyage. It has been observed that the likelihood of an American artist being commissioned to paint a portrait of a deceased English hero is remote, but if he had already painted the head he would undoubtedly have received commissions.[3] The rest of the composition, imitating Gainsborough's portrait of the 3rd Earl of Bristol and displaying a carefully-described uniform, is more pedestrian. The distant three-decker appears to derive from the mezzotint by Richard Earlom (published on 22 October 1782 after Kettle's whole-length portrait), identified as the *Royal George* (see below).

1 Normally indicating an admiral of the blue; the flag of a rear-admiral of the blue would fly from the mizzen (third) mast, as in the Kettle portrait (M.S. Robinson, letter of 24 January 1947 on file). Kempenfelt hoisted his flag as rear-admiral of the blue on 7 April 1782 on the *Royal George* at Spithead.
2 Where sketched by Scharf in 1889 (TSB 35/37).
3 As first proposed by W & S. Sawitzky, *Worcester Art Museum Annual*, VII, 1960, p.24.

ICONOGRAPHY

1768 Painting by Tilly Kettle, Admiral Samuel Cornish in his cabin with his secretary Thomas Parry, issuing orders to Kempenfelt, who stands on the left in captain' uniform. Private collection, commissioned by Thomas Parry, formerly at Highnam Court (illus. Kettle 1927, pl.xxi; Williamson 1920, f.p.40 as Zoffany). Exhibited SA special exhibition 1768(58) and 1769(75). Kempenfelt served as flag-captain under Cornish at the reduction of Manila in 1762.

1781-82 Painting by Tilly Kettle,★ whole length wearing an undress flag officer's uniform. National Maritime Museum (BHC 2828), bequeathed by the sitter's brother. Exhibited RA 1782(5); NPE 1867(735). Engraved as a three-quarter length with a different background by R. Earlom 1782, showing the blue flag on the mizzen (third) mast (as befitted a rear-admiral of the blue) and the boat called *Royal George*, though this lettering is half erased. A copy of Earlom's print painted by H. Paterson 1841 is in Admiralty House, Portsmouth. The figure alone was engraved as a half length by W. Ridley 1802, H. Robinson 1837, and served as the basis for several anon. and second-rate prints published following Kempenfelt's death.

1782 Anon. engraving, *From an original Painting*, crude bust-length oval in flag-officer's coat (*London Mag.*).

1783 Painting by Ralph Earle, see NPG 1641.

A monument by John Bacon jr. 1808, incorporating Kempenfelt's soul bound for heaven, is in Westminster Abbey.

DOUBTFUL PORTRAITS

Unattributed half-length in captain's uniform, with Woodward of Cheltenham in 1891 (TSB 36/19) and with Drummond, London, 1991; by 'Van der Gucht', bust-length in civilian dress, sold Christie's, 3 March 1967, lot 141.

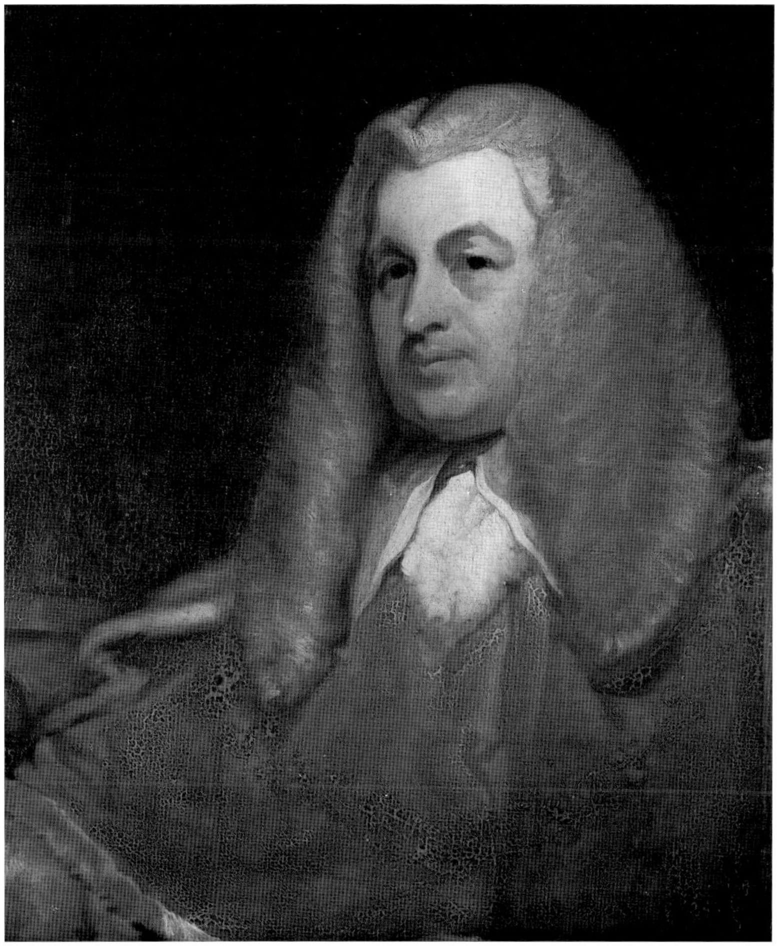

1st Baron KENYON NPG *469*

KENYON, Lloyd Kenyon, 1st Baron 1732-1802

Lord chief justice; b. Gredington, Flints.; came to London 1750; called to the Bar 1756, working for Dunnington and Thurlow; chief justice of Chester 1780; KC 1780; MP 1780-88 and briefly attorney-general 1782-83 and 1783-84; master of the rolls 1784-88 and chief justice of the King's Bench 1788-1802; Bt 1784 and Baron 1788.

'In person he was about five feet ten inches in height, spare of figure, stern in countenance, chary of speech' (*DNB*)

'Little conversant with the manners of polite life, Kenyon retained ... all the original coarse homeliness of his early habits. Irascible in his temper ... destitute of all refinements in dress or external deportment, parsimonious even in a degree approaching to avarice, he nevertheless more than balanced these defects ... by strict morality, probity, and integrity' (Sir Nathaniel Wraxall, 1815).

469 WILLIAM DAVISON 1839-40 after G. ROMNEY and M.A. SHEE [1792]

Canvas 75 x 63 (29⅝ x 25) lined 1919; a strip 2 (¾) wide appears to have been added to the right-hand edge; the robe, collar, darker shadows and lower parts of the black background are badly disfigured by a wide shrinkage craquelure. The original canvas inscribed verso: *W.DAVISON/61 L[E]ICESTER/ SQU[A]R/ Kenyon.*[1]

Brown eyes, wearing the full white wig of the chief justice of the King's Bench, with the white fur hood, white-fur-trimmed red gown and gold SS collar.

Collections: Painted for the Serjeant's Inn, Society of Judges & Serjeants-at-Law, by whom presented 1877.

Exhibition: Law Courts, London, 1966-.

Reference: Ward & Roberts 1904, II, p.88.

A copy painted in 1839-40 from a half-length presented in 1821 by the sitter's son to the Middle Temple,[2] where it was described in 1834 as by Romney.[3] The Minutes of the Middle Temple Society, 8 November 1839, record that Lord [the 2nd Baron] Kenyon had requested the loan of this portrait 'for the purpose of

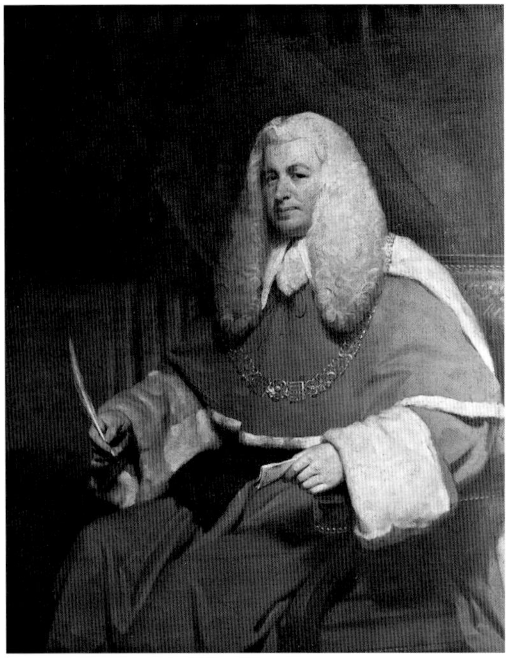

1st Baron KENYON by George Romney 1777-78 (Lord Kenyon)

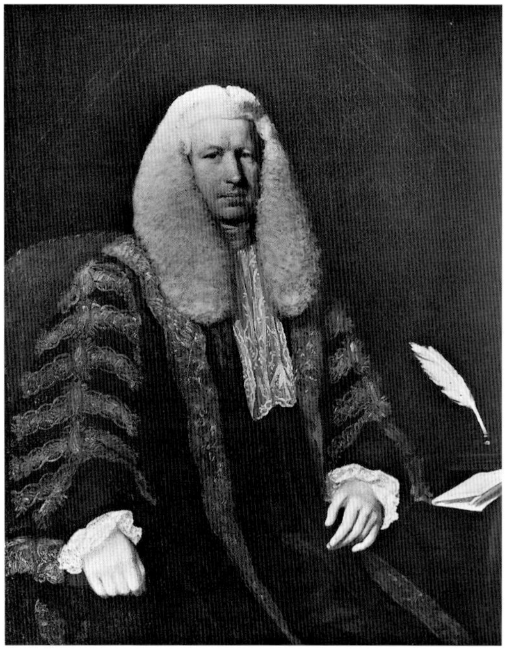

1st Baron KENYON by John Opie 1788 (Lord Kenyon)

taking a copy thereof to be placed in Serjeant's Inn Hall; It is ordered that the portrait be lent to Mr Davison & that he be allowed to take it home for the purpose of copying it'.[4] On April 1840 the Serjeant's Inn acknowledged the receipt of the portrait.[5]

The Middle Temple half length had itself been copied from the three-quarter length portrait formerly at Gredington (of which a version was sold Sotheby's, 25 November 1998, lot 45).[6] It was engraved by Holl in 1804 as by Romney,[7] but a reduced version of Holl's plate published in 1833 and 1847 was lettered as after Shee. This inconsistency is explained by the fact that Kenyon sat just once, on 21 March 1792, to Romney, who received 60 gn. for the portrait (confirming a three-quarter length), but of this sum 35gn. went to Shee for finishing the painting.[8]

1 Recorded by C.K. Adams in 1919.
2 See B. Williamson, *Cat. of Paintings and Engravings in the possession of the Hon Society of the Middle Temple*, 1931, p.19.
3 On the occasion of it being cleaned (letter from B. Williamson, 14 June 1926; NPG archive).
4 Minute Book O, p.624, 8 November 1839, transcript in NPG archive.
5 *Cat. of the Portraits in Serjeant's Inn*, 1868, p.4, no.16.
6 Described as given by the sitter in 1791 to his niece, later Mrs H.G. Boutes.
7 And, for example, listed as Romney by Steegman, I, p.154, no.20.
8 Ward & Roberts 1904, I, p.125, II, p.88. Shee was to acquire Romney's studio in Cavendish Square in 1798.

ICONOGRAPHY

1777-78 Painting by George Romney,* half length, wearing the black gown and bands of the King's counsel. Gredington (Steegman, I, p.153, no.18). Engraved R. Stewart 1781 as *Lloyd Kenyon Esqr Chief Justice of Chester*. The angle of the head is identical to that in the later Romney/Shee portrait.

1779 Drawing by the ten-year-old Thomas Lawrence, bust length profile. Gredington (illus. *Burl. Mag.*, XCIII, 1951, pp.252-53).

1788 Painting by John Opie,* three-quarter length seated as master of the rolls. Gredington (Steegman, I, p.154, no.19, pl.26). Exhibited RA 1789(187); NPE 1867(837). Engraved J. Fittler 1789 (with Kenyon's new appointment as chief justice added and the arms of Lord Kenyon combined with those of his wife, Kenyon of Peel Hall).

c.1788 Engraving by D. Orme, bust-length oval as master of the rolls.

after 1788 Engraving by T. Cook, bust-length oval, as lord chief justice, with elaborate surround.

after 1788? Wax portrait of 'Lord Kenyon' by Samuel Percy. Percy sale, Christie's, 31 January 1800 (Pyke 1973, p.104).

1792 Painting by George Romney, completed by M.A. Shee, see NPG 469.

1795 Anon. engraving, very poor, bust-length oval, lettered *Chief Justice of the Court of the Kings Bench*.

1798 Engraving by J. Chapman, bust-length oval in judge's robes, derived from the Romney/Shee pattern.

KEPPEL, Augustus Keppel, Viscount 1725-86

Naval officer; 2nd s. of the 2nd Earl of Albemarle; sailed round the world with Anson 1740 and undertook a diplomatic mission to Tunis 1749; served in America 1754-55 and West Indies 1761-64; captain 1744, rear-admiral 1762, vice-admiral 1770 and admiral 1778; MP 1755-82; lord of the Admiralty 1765-66; commander in the Channel 1778-79 when the French fleet escaped off Ushant, for which he was court martialled; his acquittal led to widespread rejoicing; first lord of the Admiralty 1782-83; cr. Viscount 1782.

'[he had] neither dignity in his person nor intelligence in his countenance, the features of which were of the most ordinary cast; and his nose, which, in consequence of an accident that befell him in the course of his professional life, had been almost laid flat, gave him an equally vulgar and unpleasant air' (Sir Nathaniel Wraxall, 1815).

Low of stature [with a] fractured bridge to his nose [by which] his face was seriously and permanently disfigured; yet the fascination of his smile, and the lively and benevolent expression of his eyes, redeemed the countenance from extreme plainness' (Thomas Keppel, 1842).

Abbreviation

Keppel 1842: T. Keppel, *The Life of Augustus Viscount Keppel*, 2 vols., 1842

5572 JOSHUA REYNOLDS c.1765

Canvas 75.5 x 62 (29¾ x 24½) lined; cleaned 1984.

Brown eyes, grey hair, wearing a flag officer's undress uniform of a dark blue coat with gold facings and white vest with gold facings.

Collections: Edward Wright, Newark, in 1835;[1] 1st Baron Burton (1837-1909); by descent to the Trustees of Lord Burton's 1983 Grandchildren's Settlement; Michael Tollemache, from whom purchased 1983.

Engravings: W. Doughty 1779; S.W. Reynolds; J. Chapman 1800 (oval).

Exhibitions: *British Art*, Grosvenor Gallery, 1889(40) lent Lord Burton; *Two Centuries of British Painting*, Vienna, Prague, Bratislava, 1969.

Reference: Graves & Cronin, II, pp.540-44; Waterhouse 1941, p.52; Mannings 2000, no.1041.

Reynolds painted seven portraits of Keppel between 1749 and 1785, but their relationship was based on friendship rather than patronage. They were of an age (Reynolds just two years older) and initially shared the interest of Lord Mount Edgcumbe, on whose suggestion Captain Keppel took Reynolds with him to the Mediterranean in 1749 as a guest on his ship the *Centurion*; 'I had the use of his cabin', wrote Reynolds, 'and his study of books, as if they had been my own, and when he went ashore he generally took me with him ... as if I had travelled as his equal'.[2] Reynolds's Italian studies, followed by his dramatic whole-length portrait of Keppel (see below), launched his distinguished career.

NPG 5572 is a replica of the portrait now in the National Maritime Museum[3] which was probably painted for Lord Rockingham. It appears likely that NPG 5572 was still in Reynolds's studio in 1779 when it was engraved by William Doughty (see NPG 179). A miniature copy of the head, attributed to James Smith, is in the Royal Collection,[4] and another, signed *A.R.*, was sold Christie's, 21 November 2000, lot 24.

1 A pencil annotation of 1835, apparently by William Cotton III, in a set of Hodgson & Graves *Engravings from the Works of Sir Joshua Reynolds* (I, p.80), Cottonian Collection, Plymouth (noted by Mannings 2000, no.1041).
2 To Lord Mount Edgcumbe, after May 1750 (Ingamells 2000, p.9).
3 BHC 2820; Mannings 2000, no.1040.
4 Walker 1992, no.311.

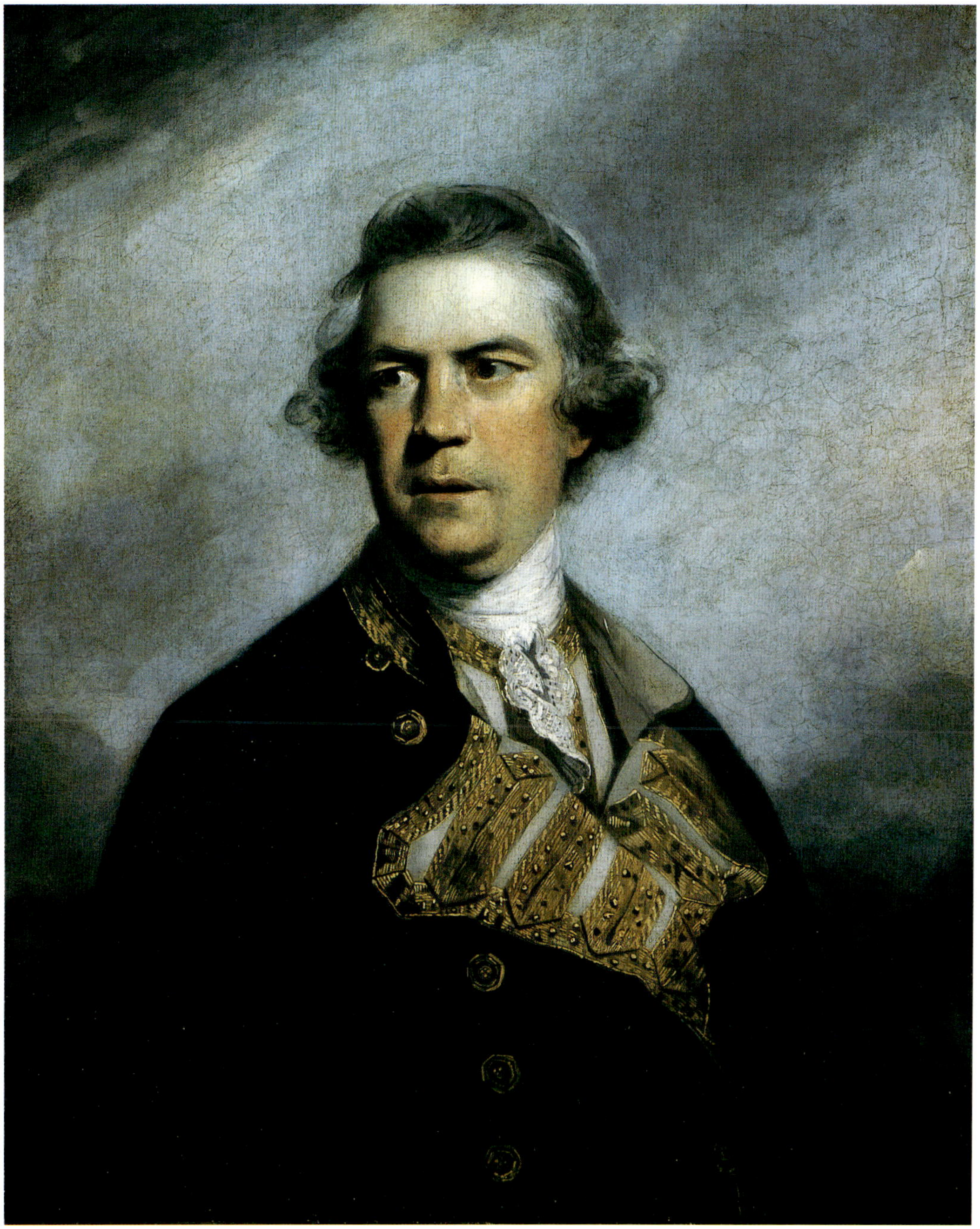

1st Viscount KEPPEL NPG 5572

179 JOSHUA REYNOLDS 1779

Canvas 125.5 x 100 (49½ x 39½) lined.

Clear blue eyes, powdered wig, wearing a flag officer's undress uniform of dark blue coat with gold facings and white vest with gold facings.

Collections: John Dunning, 1st Baron Ashburton; his son, whose widow (d.1835) bequeathed her husband's estates to her maternal cousin, the 10th Baron Cranstoun; purchased from Lord Cranstoun 1864.

Exhibitions: BI 1833(23); NPE 1868(843); *Royal Naval Exhibition*, Chelsea, 1891(342); *War at Sea*, Yorktown, Va., 1978.

Reference: Graves & Cronin, II, p.542; Waterhouse 1941, p.71; Mannings 2000, no.1044 (and see no.1042).

Upon Keppel's honourable acquittal from his court-martial on 11 February 1779, Reynolds immediately had his pupil William Doughty make a mezzotint from the last portrait he had painted of his friend, see NPG 5572. 'I have taken the liberty', he told Keppel, 'without waiting for leave, to lend your picture to an engraver, to make a large print from it'.[1] Keppel's successful defence lawyer, John Lee, then asked for his portrait (rather than accepting his proffered gift of £1000), suggesting that Nathaniel Dance 'takes excellent likenesses'.[2] Keppel, predictably, preferred to sit to Reynolds who then created this defiant image, set against a threatening sky, the right hand firmly holding the sword which had been restored to him.

NPG 179 is one of four replicas which Keppel gave to those who had supported him during his ordeal. He was sitting spasmodically to Reynolds between 27 May 1779 and July 1780, and in September 1779 Reynolds had entered in his Ledger: 'Admiral Keppell, for four half lengths £400',[3] the price indicating that he regarded each as an autograph work (despite some studio intervention). The four replicas are:

a) the portrait received by John Lee, together with a miniature (see below), on 18 November 1779; he considered it beautifully painted, and 'a very exact likeness'; now in the National Maritime Museum, and considered to be the original portrait.[4]

b) NPG 179, given to John Dunning (Lord Ashburton).

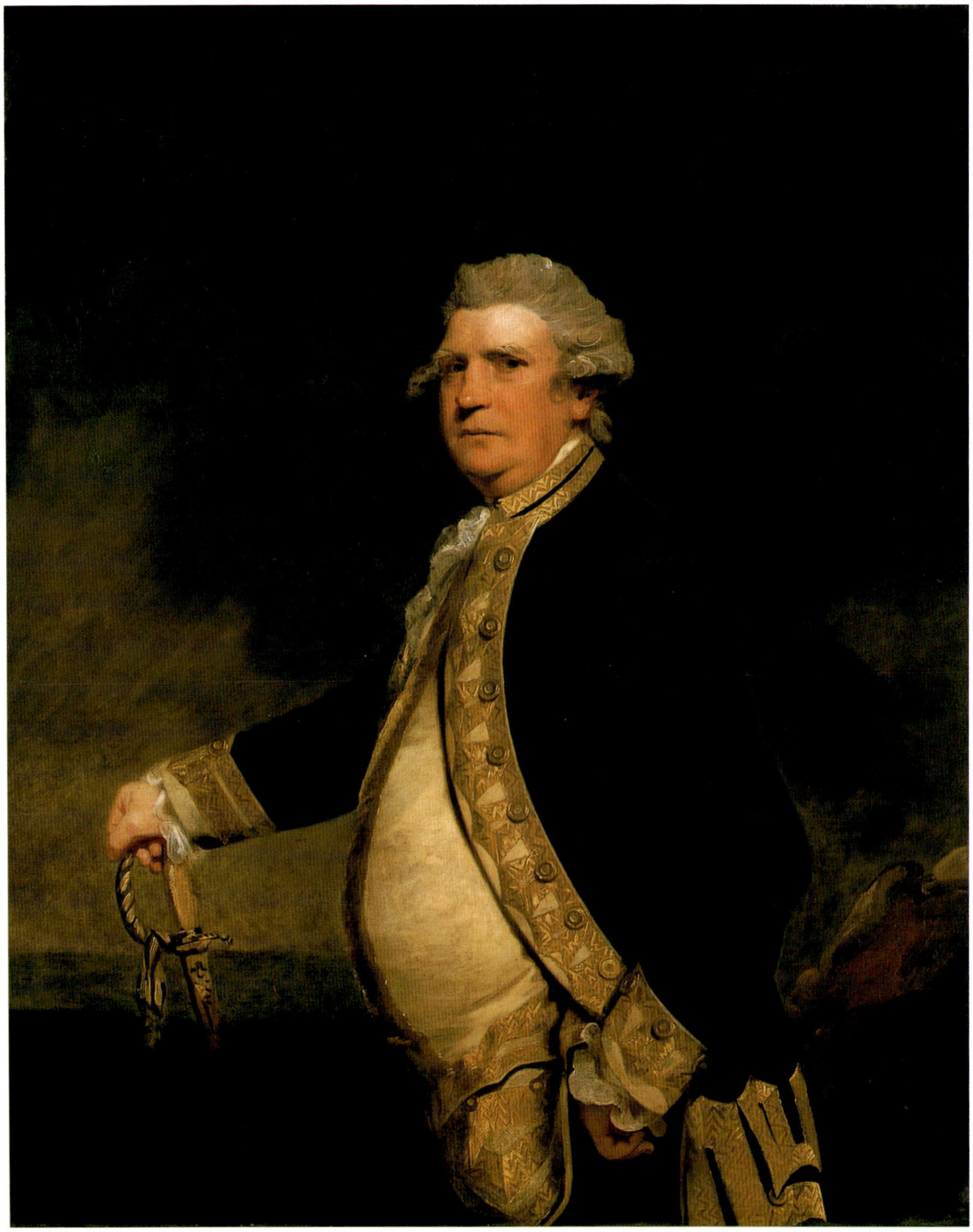

1st Viscount KEPPEL NPG *179*

On 23 February 1779 Keppel told Dunning that his acquittal was 'in a great measure [due] to your good counsel and assistance, together with that of Mr Lee and Mr Erskine'.[5]

c) The portrait given to Edmund Burke some time before 6 November 1779 when Burke told Keppel that 'whenever [my son] sees that picture, he will remember what Englishmen, and what English seamen were'; now in a private collection.[6]

d) The portrait that belonged to the 6th Earl of Albemarle by 1883, now in a private collection.[7]

Another version, probably somewhat later in date, is at Berkeley Castle.[8] Half-length versions include those in the Hessische Hausstiftung at Friedrichschof;[9] sold Parke-Bernet, New York, 4-5 December 1941, lot 86, as Copley, and with Knoedler, New York, in 1975.[10] A pastel version with Derek Hand in 1968. Miniature versions include one by Samuel Shelley 1779 with Mrs George Keppel in 1949, and those sold Christie's, 15 July 1949, lot 112; 19 June 1973, lot 45 (withdrawn), and 13 December 1983, lot 63. A miniature copy had been sent to John Lee in November 1779 (see above) and an entry in the Reynolds Ledger on the same page as Keppel's account for the four half-lengths, reads: '20 Guineas for four miniatures paid'[11] which may, or may not, refer to such copies.

1 12 Feb.1779, the day after Keppel's acquittal (Ingamells 2000, p.81).
2 Keppel 1842, II, p.217.
3 Cormack 1970, p.157 ('half length' meaning our three-quarter length).
4 BHC 2822 (Mannings 2000, no.1042). *Keppel* 1842, II, p.262.
5 *Keppel* 1842, II, p.213; the letter enclosed a gratuity of £1000 (such as he also sent to Lee, see above, and Erskine, who accepted it) which Dunning declined: 'no pecuniary consideration can add to the respect and esteem with which I have the honour to subscribe myself, Your faithful and obedient servant' (1 Mar.1779; *Keppel* 1842, II, pp.213-15).
6 *Burke Corr.*, IV, p.169 (Burke to Keppel, 6 Nov.1779); Mannings 2000, no.1043.
7 Mannings 2000, no.1045.
8 *Ibid.*, no.1046.
9 *Ibid.*, no.1047.
10 *Ibid.*, nos.1046a & b.
11 Cormack, p.157.

ICONOGRAPHY

c.1745 Unattributed miniature, bust-length oval in captain's uniform. Bathurst Collection 1920 (illus. *Bathurst Miniatures*, n.d., no.13; NPG archive).

1749 Painting by Joshua Reynolds, three-quarter length standing in Captain's undress uniform. National Maritime Museum (BHC 2821; Mannings 2000, no.1036).

1752-53 Painting by Joshua Reynolds,* whole length in Captain's undress uniform (but with grey facings). National Maritime Museum (BHC 2823; Mannings 2000, no.1037). First engraved by E. Fisher 1759 and J. Collyer 1786. According to Northcote the setting referred to the wreck of Keppel's ship, the *Maidstone*, off the Britanny coast in 1747 (see Mannings, *loc. cit.*, and *Keppel* 1842, I, pp.95-96, 146-47).

1759 Painting by Joshua Reynolds, three-quarter length standing, wearing a flag officer's undress uniform. Woburn Abbey (Mannings 2000, no.1038). The Duke of Bedford was Keppel's brother-in-law. An autograph version, showing a captain's uniform, is in a private collection (Mannings 2000, no.1039); engraved E. Fisher 1760; E. Harding (half length) 1802; H.T. Ryall 1833.

1762 Painting by Francis Hayman, *The Triumph of Britannia*, with a medallion portrait of Keppel. Destroyed (Allen 1987, nos.79, 98), painted for Vauxhall Gardens. Engraved S. Ravenet 1765.

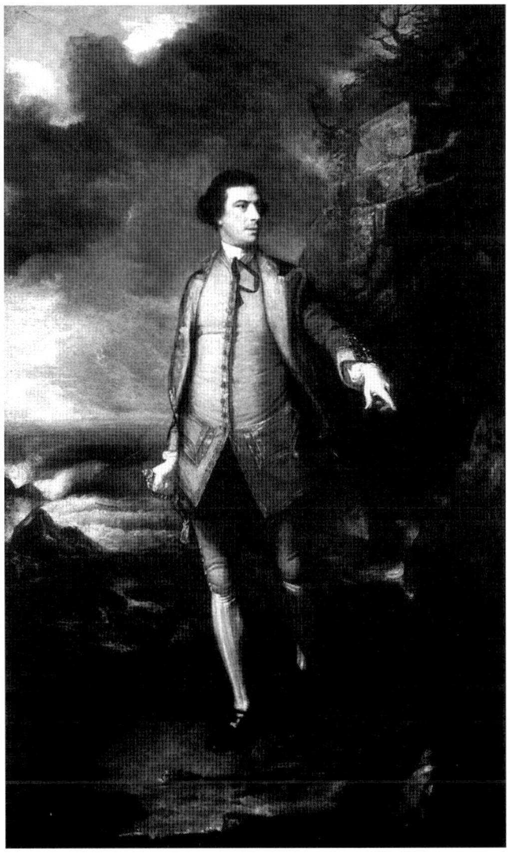

1st Viscount KEPPEL by Joshua Reynolds 1752-53 (National Maritime Museum, London)

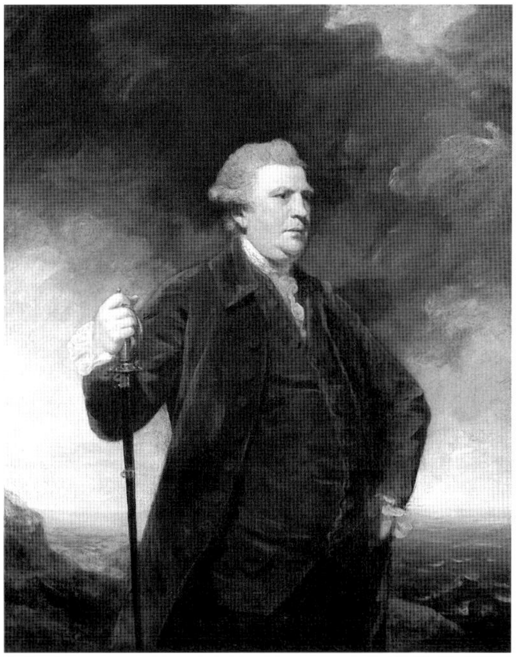

1st Viscount KEPPEL by Joshua Reynolds 1781-83 (Tate Gallery)

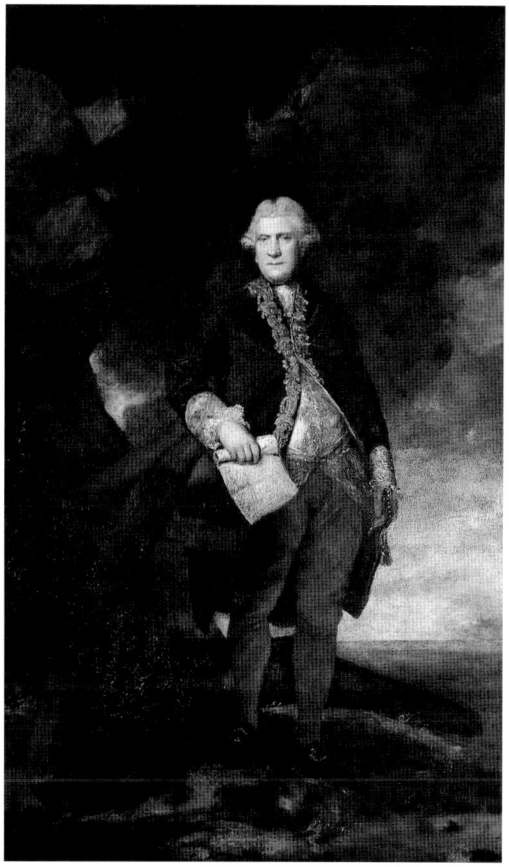

1st Viscount KEPPEL by Joshua Reynolds 1785 (The Royal Collection)

c.1765 Painting by Joshua Reynolds, see NPG 5572.

1765 Pastel by Francis Cotes, bust-length oval in flag officer's undress uniform. Private collection (Johnson 1976, fig.57). Exhibited SA 1765(21).

1776 Painting by George Romney, half length in dark blue coat with gold piping. Goodwood. Engraved W. Dickinson 1779 (*from the original in the possession of the Duke of Richmond*); W. Ridley 1802 (oval). A copy exhibited NPE 1868(846) lent by the Rev W.A.W. Keppel, sold Sotheby's, 24 June 1931, lot 89. A version showing a flag officer's undress uniform sold Parke-Bernet, 24 March 1938, lot 52.

1777 Marble bust by Giuseppe Ceracchi, draped, *all'antica*. Belvoir Castle. Exhibited RA 1777(51) and considered 'extremely like' by Walpole. Engraved R.S. Marcuard 1782. Another dated 1779 was at Wentworth Woodhouse.

Following Keppel's acquittal on 11 February 1779 the portrait of this popular naval hero was in great demand.

1779 Painting by Joshua Reynolds, see NPG 179.

1779 Painting by Robert Stewart, bust-length profile, engraved R. Stewart.

1779 Wax portrait by Lewis Pingo, exhibited FS 1779(201).

1779 Bust from the life by Thomas Scheemakers, exhibited FS 1779(148). A cast of a bust of Keppel was in his sale, 21 October 1805.

1779 Three medallions by James Tassie (Gray 1894, nos.210-12):

a) with uniform coat and drape below. Cast in the Scottish NPG (PG 414). Engraved J. Caldwall 1779, exhibited FS 1779(34); re-issued 1782. A variant, with the truncation just below the neck, based on a gem engraved by Brown after the Tassie medallion (Gray 1894, no.213), was presumably similar to the sulphur impression by William Brown, exhibited RA 1780(238).

b) classical profile head to right, dated 1779 (cast in the Scottish NPG, PG 505).

c) classical profile head to left, the head looking older than in b) above (cast in the Scottish NPG, PG 519).

1779 Wedgwood medallion, probably modelled by William Hackwood (illus. Reilly 1973, p.205, and see Reilly 1994, p.341). Engraved anon. (*Murray's History of the American War*).

1779 Four medals (Brown 1980, nos. 214-16, 221), evidently celebrating the acquittal of 11 February 1779, each bearing a bust-length portrait resembling heads of Keppel engraved by Cook 1779 from a drawing by Daniel Dodd; by I.H., and anon. plates of 1778.

1779 Medal by Truels Lyng (Brown 1980, no.220), apparently derived from the Wedgwood or Tassie pattern.

c.1780 Unattributed pastel, bust-length oval in flag officer's undress uniform, sketched by Scharf in 1877 (NPG reference collection), when it belonged to a Mr Parker. Williamson 1894, p.148, listed an otherwise unknown (larger) pastel by John Russell, belonging to the Rev J.C. Jackson.

c.1780 Pastel by H.D. Hamilton, bust-length oval. Private collection.

c.1780 Marble bust, in flag officer's undress uniform. Private collection. Exhibited *Rule Britannia*, Sotheby's, January 1986(136, attributed to Agostino Carlini).

1781-83 Painting by Joshua Reynolds,★ three-quarter length standing, in a red suit. Tate Gallery (N 886; Mannings 2000, no.1048).

1782 Wax portrait by Lewis Pingo, exhibited FS 1782(167).

1782 Miniature by James Smith, exhibited RA 1782(254).

1782 'a model of Lord Keppel' by Thomas Scheemakers, exhibited FS 1782(239).

c.1782 Wedgwood medallion, the face much fuller and the eyes smaller than the 1779 medallion (illus. Reilly 1972, p.206; see Reilly 1994, p.341).

1783 Painting by Benjamin Killingbeck, exhibited SA 1783(145).

1783 Wax model by an unnamed artist, exhibited FS 1783(387).

1784 Etching by J. Sayers, whole-length standing (George 6638).

1785 Painting by Joshua Reynolds,* whole-length standing, in admiral's full-dress uniform. Royal Collection (Millar 1969, no.1024; Mannings 2000, no.1049). Engraved E. Scriven 1814 (head only). Half-length versions at Chequers, and sold Christie's, 23-24 February 1989, lot 132.

Undated Miniatures: bust-length oval, heavy features (Woburn Abbey; SSB 110/22, 26); another exhibited SKM 1865(1105) lent by the Rev W.A.W. Keppel.

DOUBTFUL PORTRAITS

Paintings: bust length, 'aged 25 c.1770', given by the Duke of Bedford to T.K. Keppel, was listed in The Grange, Old Buckenham, by Duleep Singh (I, p.50); another attributed to George Knapton, three-quarter length standing in captain's uniform, at Tapley Park, Devon, in 1931.

KER, John, see ROXBURGHE

KERRICH, Thomas 1748-1828

Antiquary, s. of Dr Samuel Kerrich, vicar of Dersingham, Norfolk; upon graduating at Magdalene College, Cambridge, 1771, he travelled abroad on a scholarship, spending four years in Rome;[1] vicar of Dersingham 1784 and Hemisby 1786; University Librarian 1797 and FSA 1805; prebend of Lincoln 1798 and of Wells 1812; a residuary legatee of the sculptor Joseph Nollekens 1823; he bequeathed historical portraits to the Society of Antiquaries; paintings, books and prints to the Fitzwilliam Museum, Cambridge, and manuscripts to the British Museum.

1 William Cole, 23 May 1778 (*Wal.Corr.*, II, pp.83); Nichols 1831, p.811, said he spent six months in Paris and two years in Rome.

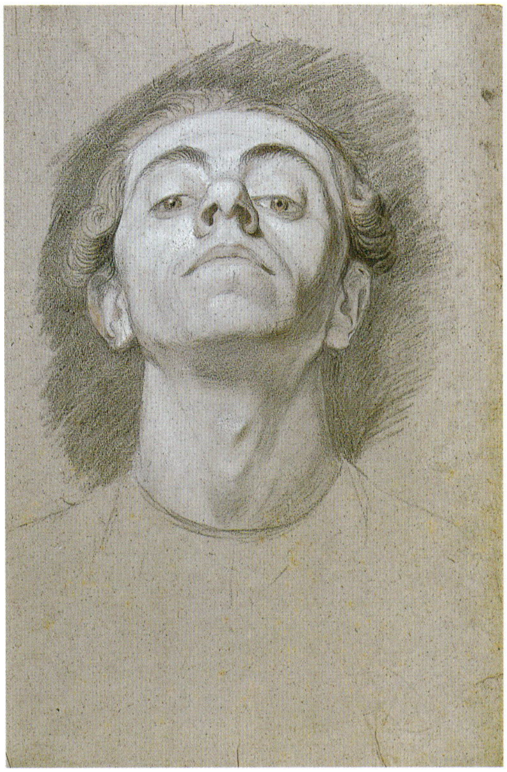

KERRICH NPG *6531*

Abbreviation

Nichols 1831: 'Rev Thomas Kerrich, F.S.A.', in Nichols *Illustrations*, VI, 1831, pp.807-29

6531 SELF PORTRAIT 1774

Black chalk with white and red heightening on grey paper[1] 43.5 x 29.5 (17 x 11½) irregular; some slight staining and the outer areas are wrinkled; signed in ink verso: *T. Kerrich/ ipse fecit/ L'Arricia 1774.*

Collections: Hugh Wyatt, a descendant of one of the artist's daughters;[2] Sotheby's, 22 March 2000, lot 128, 'Property of a Descendant of the Artist', bt. Hazlitt, Gooden & Fox, from whom purchased with the aid of the National Art Collections Fund 2000.

The least orthodox of a number of accomplished self-portrait drawings which Kerrich made in Italy.[3] When he went abroad in 1771 his mentor William Cole described him as 'an ingenious young man, a brother antiquary, and a most excellent draftsman',[4] and in the course of his travels one of his drawings obtained a silver medal from the Academy of Painting at Antwerp.[5] After his return to Cambridge Kerrich continued to draw both antiquarian subjects and portraits,[6] Cole even suggesting that

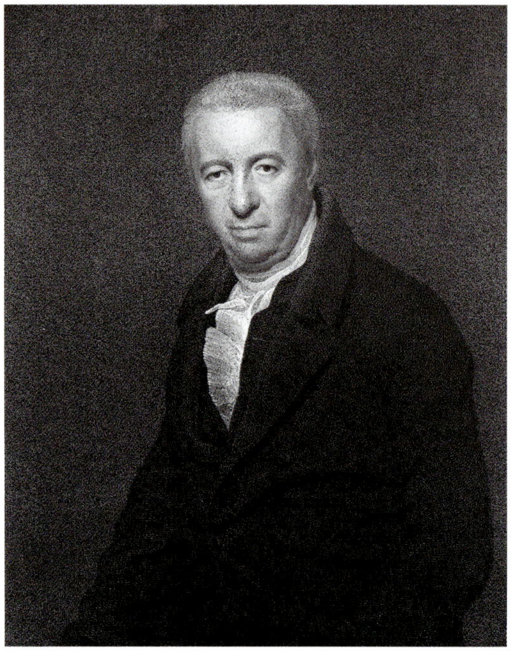

KERRICH G.S. Facius after H.P. Briggs 1815 (NPG D 8389)

as his fortunes are very small and his genius very great, I took the liberty, when I sat to him for my picture at his room in college last autumn, to tell him that I thought he had better give up his design of going into orders . . . and take up with the better profession of a face painter, for which he seems admirably calculated.[7]

In the event, bolstered by several benefices, Kerrich pursued a productive antiquarian career.

1 Watermark similar to Churchill, nos.368 and 373.
2 I am grateful to Sir John Guinness for this identification (letter 10 Jan. 2001, NPG archive).
3 One dated 1775, sold Sotheby's 22 March 2000, lot 137 (and at least two more were in that sale - lots 129, 135-37 and 142 each comprising a folio/album of Kerrich drawings); others include those sold Christie's, 11 February 1987, lot 125; and 21 March 1989, lot 87, dated 1774.
4 The Rev Wm. Cole, 17 Nov. 1771 (Nichols 1831, p.811n).
5 Nichols 1831, p.812.
6 See Nichols 1831, p.814 (list of etchings by Kerrich c.1782-85); p.816 (list a portrait drawings engraved by G.S. Facius).
7 Not dated (*Wal. Corr.*, II, p.83n8), but probably 1780 since Kerrich drew a portrait of Cole in 1779 (*ibid.*, p.182n16) cf. the drawing in the British Museum (1972-U-536), illus. *A Noble Art*, British Museum, 2000, no.156.

ICONOGRAPHY

1769 Drawing, self portrait, bust length. Sotheby's, 8 April 1998, lot 15.

1774-75 Drawings, self portraits, see NPG 6531.

1815 Painting by H.P. Briggs. Formerly with Mrs F.M. Hartshorne. Engraved G.S. Facius 1815,* P. Audinet 1831 (Nichols *Illustrations*, VI, f.p.552). A replica is in Magdalene College, Cambridge (T.D.

Atkinson, *Cambridge Described & Illustrated*, 1897, p.433, as 1795).

c.1820? Etching by Mrs Dawson Turner, 'somewhat older' than in the Briggs portrait (Nichols 1831, p.817).

DOUBTFUL PORTRAIT

A painting by Pompeo Batoni of c.1773-74 in a private collection, South Africa (illus. Duleep Singh, I, f.p.168), which includes a letter inscribed *A Monsieur T. Kerrich, Gentilhomme Anglais à Rome*, must show Thomas Kerrich (d.1809) of Geldeston Hall, Norfolk, although it has been identified as the antiquarian (cf. Clark 1985, no.379; Ingamells 1997, p.574). It is implausible that a travelling academic, subsequently described as being of 'small fortune', should have been able to sit to Batoni in Rome, and it was presumably Kerrich of Geldeston who met Lord Coke in Turin in 1772 (see *Coke of Norfolk and his Friends*, 1908, I, pp.104, 110-14). I am grateful to Lady Wedgwood who first raised this important question of identity.

LANSDOWNE, William Petty, 1st Marquess of 1737-1805

Statesman; 2nd s. of the 1st Earl of Shelburne; suc. as 2nd Earl 1761; cr. Marquess of Lansdowne 1784; served in the Seven Years War; colonel 1760 and general 1783; MP 1760-61; KG 1782; first lord of trade 1763; secretary of state 1768 and 1782; prime minister 1782-83; his independent, liberal ideas made him politically unpopular; a considerable patron of the arts, he gathered an outstanding collection of books, manuscripts and antiquities.

'a man of coarse manners, but a man of abilities and information. I don't say he is a man I would set at the head of a nation, though perhaps he may be as good as the next Prime Minister that comes' (Samuel Johnson, 1783).

'Affable, polite, communicative, and courting popularity, ... [his] personal courage was indisputable. Splendid and hospitable at his table, he equally delighted his guests by the charms of his conversation and society. ... But the confidence which his moral character inspired did not equal the reputation of his abilities. His adversaries ... asserted that unless all the rules of physiognomy were set at defiance, his very countenance and features eloquently indicated falsehood' (Sir Nathaniel Wraxall, 1815).

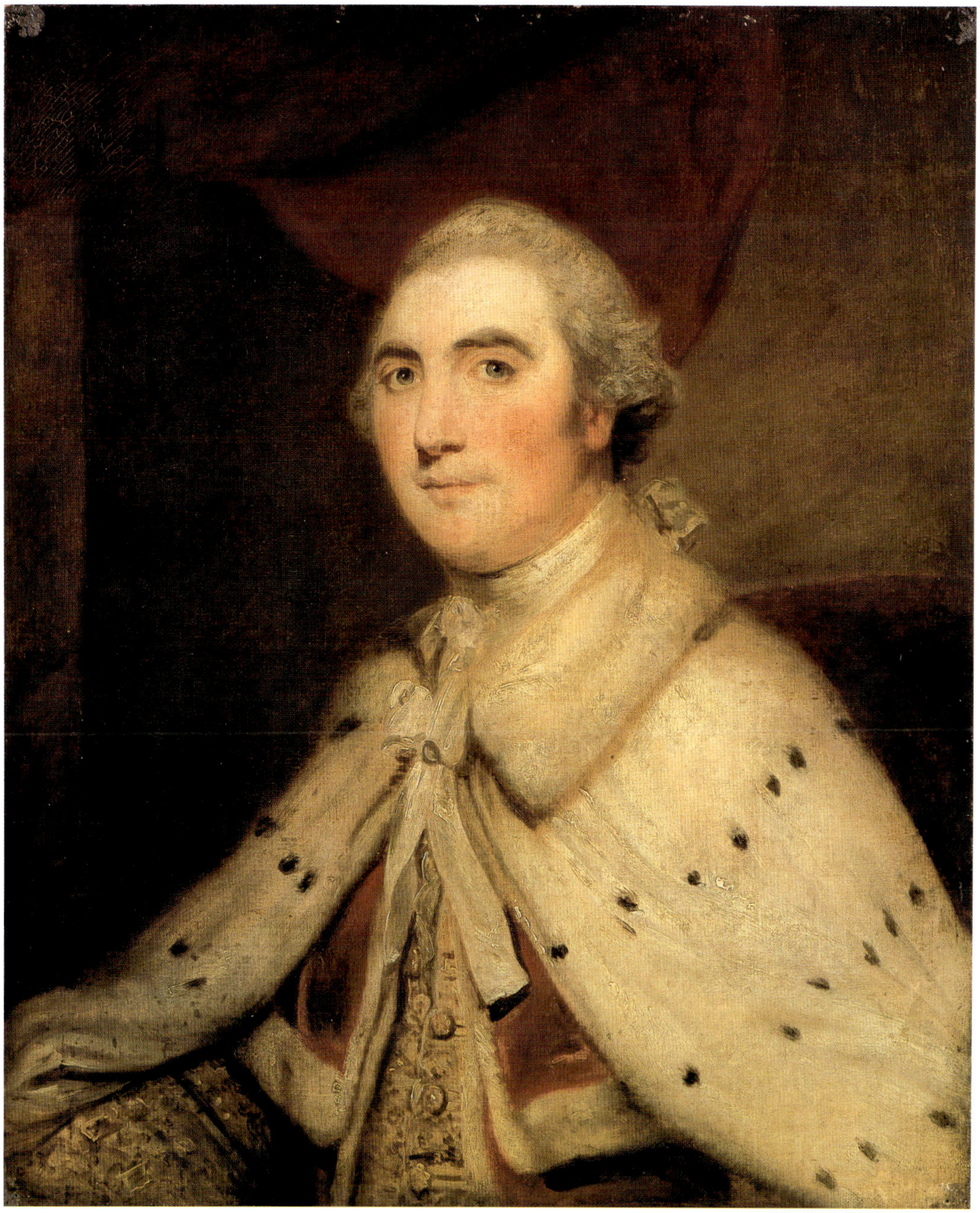

1st Marquess of LANSDOWNE NPG *43*

43 after JOSHUA REYNOLDS [1766]

Canvas 75.5 x 63 (29¾ x 24¾) lined 1858; discoloured varnish and retouchings in head, cape and upper left area; pentimento above his left arm.

Grey eyes, powdered hair with a white ribbon, wearing a white neckcloth and bands, and ermine robes over a red suit trimmed with ermine; gold waistcoat; deep red velvet chair.

Collections: Presented by the sitter's son, the 3rd Marquess of Lansdowne, 1858.

Reference: Mannings 2000, no.1442b.

Before presenting NPG 43, Lord Lansdowne sent this portrait of his father to be lined, maintaining, that 'it was the first ever painted of him'.[1] But NPG 43 is a reduced copy from the Reynolds three-quarter length, of which there are several versions, showing Shelburne (as he then was) seated at table in his peer's robes, his right hand resting on a paper. The earliest, dateable 1766, at Dalmeny, was originally given to Colonel Barré,[2] and there are replicas at Bowood, probably painted in 1767,[3] and Saltram, dateable 1767–70.[4]

1 Undated letter to Scharf c.10 June 1858 (NPG archive).
2 Mannings 2000, no.1440 (engraved S.W. Reynolds 1824).
3 *Ibid.*, no.1442.
4 *Ibid.*, no.1441.

ICONOGRAPHY

1764 Painting by Joshua Reynolds, three-quarter length seated at table. National Museum, Havana (Mannings 2000, no.1439).

1766 Painting by Joshua Reynolds, see NPG 43.

1778 Silhouette sent by Shelburne to the Abbé Morellet, with others of Dunning (Lord Ashburton), Col. Barré and Townsend (*Lettres de Morellet*, ed. D. Medlin & J-C. David, I, 1992, pp.387, 425).

1779–81 Painting by J.S. Copley,* *The Death of Chatham*, see Comparative Groups.

1780 Anon. engraving, bust-length oval profile, as *Lord Shelburne* within an elaborate surround; a similar, but reversed, print published 1780.

c.1780? Anon. engraving, bust-length oval profile, with pig tail, without Garter insignia, as *Earl of Shelburne*.

1782 Etching by J. Sayers, whole-length standing with ribbon of the Garter (George 6062).

c.1784 Painting by Gilbert Stuart, being sought by J.M. Gérard de Rayneval late in 1784 (*Lettres de Morellet*, ed. D. Medlin & J-C. David, I, 1992, pp.549, 552) and listed among Stuart's portraits in *The World*, 18 April 1787 (Whitley 1932, p.60). A half-length oval, wearing a red/brown coat with powdered hair was sold from Burley-on-the-Hill, Christie's, 20 June 1947, lot 90, as Lansdowne by Stuart. On his first visit to Stuart's studio the painter concluded 'from his shabby black dress and respectful politeness' that Lansdowne was 'some poet or author from Grubb Street' (R. McLanathan, *Gilbert Stuart*, 1986, p.55). In 1796 Lansdowne received the celebrated whole-length portrait of Washington by Stuart, known as the Lansdowne portrait, see Washington.

c.1787 Painting by Thomas Gainsborough, half-length oval with ribbon and badge of the Garter. Probably sent to France in 1787 (Waterhouse 1958, no.428). Engraved F. Bartolozzi, Gainsborough considering the plate did not show Lansdowne's 'cheerful Countenance', making it 'long instead of

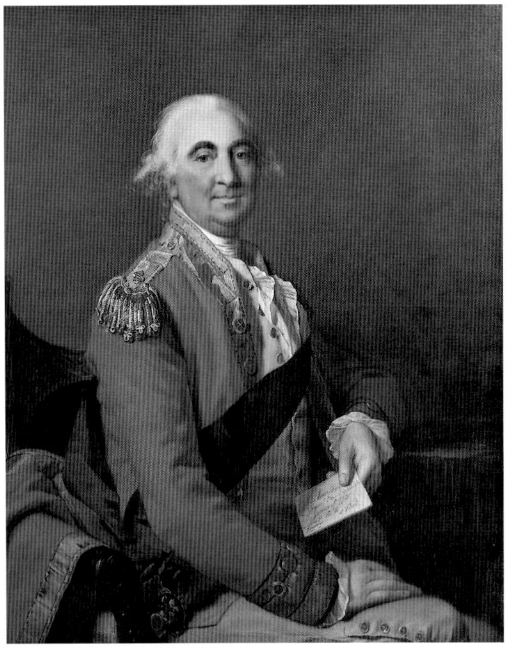

1st Marquess of LANSDOWNE by J.L. Mosnier 1791 (Bowood House)

round' (Hayes 2001, pp.167–68, illus.); Kennerley 1805. Copy at Hughenden Manor (Disraeli had regarded Lansdowne as a 'most accomplished statesman'); another sold Sotheby's, 23 November 1973, lot 38.

1787–88 Painting by Joshua Reynolds,* three-quarter length seated in peer's robes, with Col. Barré (centre) and Lord Ashburton (left), see Ashburton. Enamel copy of the figure of Lansdowne by Henry Bone exhibited RA 1807(739), examples in Royal Collection (Walker 1992, no.780), and at Meickleour House (preparatory drawings in the NPG Bone albums; *Bone* 1999, nos.307–08). A copy of the figure of Lansdowne alone was formerly at Holland House (cat., 1904, no.142).

1791 Painting by J.L. Mosnier,* three-quarter length seated in a general's uniform with Garter ribbon, the lesser George tied to his sash; a letter in his left hand addressed to *His Excellency Lt General Baron de Schlaffen Governor of Wesel … Lansdowne*. Bowood, ex Meikleour House. Lansdowne corresponded with Baron von Schlieffen (1732–1825), an ambassador in London in 1789, from 1760.

1791 Drawing by W.H. Brown, bust-length oval with Garter badge; engraved C.T. Warren (*The Senator*).

1794 Etching by J. Sayers, caricature bust, inscribed: *Chauvelin* (George 8456), a comparison with the Jacobin *ci-devant* marquis de Chauvelin.

1796 Drawing by Henry Edridge, three-quarter length seated at table. Formerly at Holland House; one of the five friends of Fox by Edridge from the St Anne's Hill House sale, Phillips, 3rd day, 26 November 1924, lots 505–507. Presumably the portrait by Edridge exhibited RA 1797(521).

1798 Engraving by W. Ridley, half-length oval with Garter ribbon and star.

c.1800 Unattributed painting, three-quarter length seated in a library with Garter ribbon and star. William L. Clements Library, University of Michigan, Ann Arbor MI, presented by the 6th Marquess of Lansdowne.

LAUDERDALE, James Maitland, 8th Earl of 1759–1839

Statesman; sty. Viscount Maitland until suc. as 8th Earl of Lauderdale (S) 1789; MP 1780–89, a supporter of Fox; cr. Baron Lauderdale (GB) 1806; KT 1821.

'a violent tempered, shrewd, eccentric man, with a fluent tongue, a broad Scottish accent, and a taste for political economy' (*DNB*).

928 after THOMAS GAINSBOROUGH [c.1785]

Mahogany panel 14.6 x 11 x 0.4 (5¾ x 4⅜ x ⅛) prominent horizontal craquelure and discoloured varnish; light brown painted spandrels.

Blue eyes, powdered wig, white neckcloth, yellow waistcoat, blue coat.

Collections: Miss Clark;[1] bt. in Bath by Mackay; bt. from Colnaghi by Lord Ronald Sutherland Gower 1879 and presented by him 1892.[2]

Exhibitions: *Gainsborough*, Grosvenor Gallery, 1885(4 as a self portrait); *Loan Exhibition*, Ipswich 1887(888 as a self portrait).

Received in 1892 as a self portrait by Gainsborough, and previously identified as Pitt by Reynolds or Sir J. Bassett by Gainsborough,[3] NPG 928 is a copy of the Gainsborough half length of Lauderdale, now in Stanford University.[4] A small oval version, attributable to Gainsborough Dupont,[5] the same size as NPG 928, belonged to Lady Hillingdon in 1936[6] and there is a copy at Thirlestane.

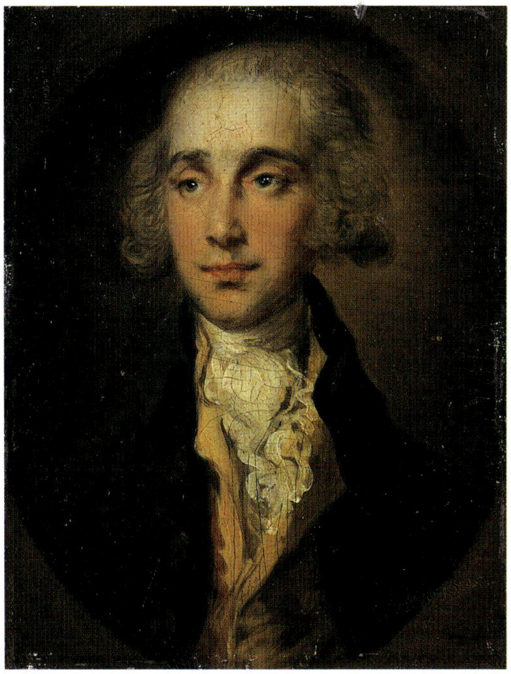

8th Earl of LAUDERDALE NPG *928*

1 Fulcher 1856, p.205: 'His own portrait' belonging to Miss Clark 'The size of a large miniature'; she appears to have owned several paintings by Gainsborough in the 1850s and 1860s, see Davies 1946, p.183.
2 Provenance from an old label verso: *Portrait of T Gainsborough by himself mentioned in Fulcher's Life of the artist as size of a large miniature belonging to Miss Clarke Bought by me at Colnaghi's May 1879 from Mr McKay who had purchased it at Bath/ Ronald Gower*. See R.S. Gower, *Bric à Brac*, 1888, p.70.
3 The panel retains early nineteenth-century labels verso: *Pitt/by Sir Jha Reynolds* and *Sir J Bassett* (and see note 6 below).
4 Waterhouse 1958, no.431; illus. *Gazette des Beaux Arts*, CXI, 1978, March *supp.*, p.49, no.218.
5 A typescript by Waterhouse (NPG archive), based on the 1936 Gainsborough exhibition, identified this picture as having belonged to Richard Dupont; sold Wheeler & Westoby, Sudbury, 29 May 1874, lot 142, and Christie's, 14 June 1875, lot 77 as from the collection of Gainsborough Dupont.
6 Exhibited as 'Sir J. Bassett' *Conversation Pieces*, 25 Park Lane, 1930(118), and *Gainsborough*, 45 Park Lane, 1936(85).

999 see Groups, *The Trial of Queen Caroline 1820* by GEORGE HAYTER 1820-23

ICONOGRAPHY

c.1785 Painting by Thomas Gainsborough, see under NPG 928.

before 1795 Painting by Thomas Lawrence, untraced (K. Garlick, *Sir Thomas Lawrence*, 1954, pp.45, 67 no.41).

1803 Marble bust by Joseph Nollekens. Scottish NPG (PG 1364) with a plaster (PG 348). The original bust was made for the Temple of Liberty at Woburn Abbey (see *Apollo*, CXXX, 1989, pp.27-32).

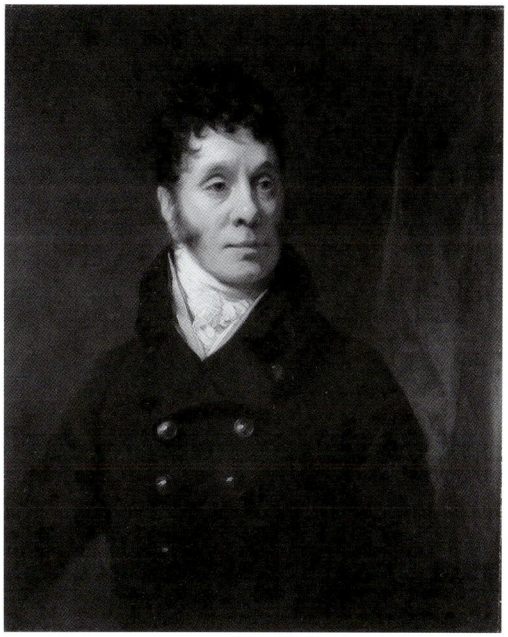

8th Earl of LAUDERDALE by Thomas Phillips 1806 (Scottish National Portrait Gallery)

1806 Medallion by John Henning. Scottish NPG (PG 212 paste, and (PG 1538 porcelain), with two related drawings (PG 119, 397).

1806 Painting by Thomas Phillips,* half length. Scottish NPG (PG 756).

1820-23 Painting by George Hayter, *The Trial of Queen Caroline*, see Groups NPG 999.

1826 Marble bust by Thomas Campbell. Thirlestane.

1829 Painting by Colvin Smith, whole length in Thistle robes. Thirlestane.

1834 Plaster statuette, seated in Thistle robes. Thirlestane.

LE DESPENCER, see DESPENCER

LEEDS, Francis Osborne, 5th Duke of 1751-99

Statesman; 3rd s. of the 4th Duke of Leeds and Lady Mary Godolphin; sty. Marquess of Carmarthen 1761; Dilettante 1774; MP 1774-75; to House of Lords as Lord Osborne (his father's barony) 1776; FSA 1776; ambassador to Paris 1783; foreign secretary 1783-91; suc. as 5th Duke 1789; KG 1790 but never installed; pall-bearer at Reynolds's funeral.

'the prettiest man in his person, the most polite and pleasing in his manners' (Mrs Elizabeth Montagu, 1777).

'highly accomplished, of the most pleasing manners, of very elegant deportment, of a lofty mind, and of considerable talents ... endowed with a very independent mind' (Sir Nathaniel Wraxall, 1815).

801 attributed to BENJAMIN WEST c.1769

Canvas 70.5 x 91 (27¾ x 35¾) lined 1895.

Blue-grey eyes, fair hair with black silk ribbon, dressed for a masked ball, holding his mask by a silk frill in his right hand; wearing a white silk domino over a red silk suit, both trimmed with gold lace; his black hat decorated with gold braid and white ostrich feathers is on the table beside him; a green figured damask curtain in the background.[1]

Collections: By descent to the 3rd Earl of Chichester,[2] by whom presented 1888.

Exhibition: *Masquerade*, Museum of London, 1983.

Reference: Graves & Cronin, I, pp.151-52 (as Reynolds), and IV, p.1277 (as Knapton); Erffa & Staley 1986, p.496n2.

An elaboration of West's half-length graduation portrait of Lord Carmarthen (as he then was) painted in 1769 (see below). It was accepted in 1888 as by George Knapton, the attribution to West being proposed in 1970.[3] Although Erffa & Staley in 1986 thought it 'probably not by West', the head is taken directly from the 1769 half length by West formerly at Stanmer Park (see below), while the consistently competent execution and impeccable provenance suggest it probably is by him.

1 Described in Ribeiro 2000, pp.126-27.
2 The sitter's daughter, Frances, m. Thomas Pelham, 2nd Earl of Chichester. Scharf sketched NPG 801 at Stanmer Park in 1886 (TSB 33/51).
3 Note by John Kerslake on file.

ICONOGRAPHY

Attributions for the 5th Duke's portraits have wavered considerably: the NPG West was called Reynolds and

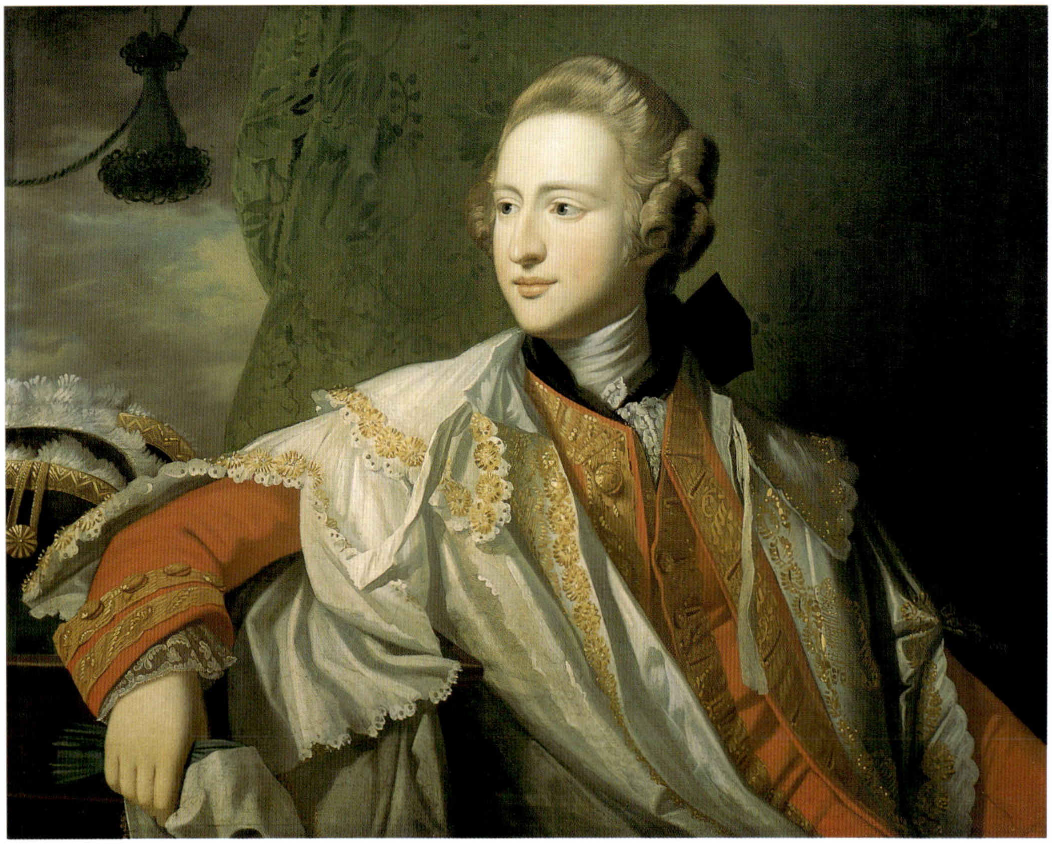

5th Duke of LEEDS NPG *801*

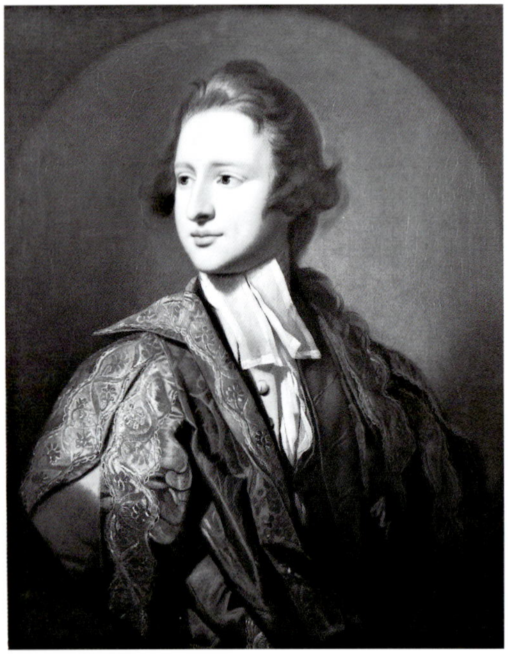

5th Duke of LEEDS by Benjamin West 1769 (Sotheby's)

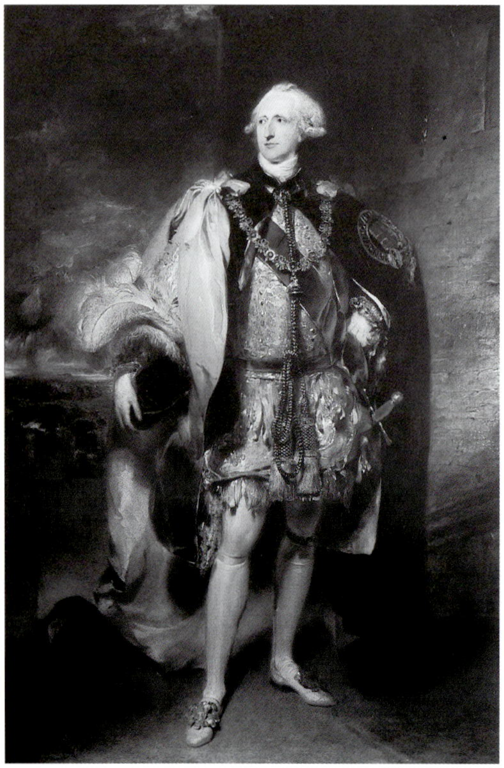

5th Duke of LEEDS by Thomas Lawrence 1796 (Private Collection)

Knapton, and versions of the youthful Reynolds were given to Allan Ramsay and Nathaniel Hone.

1764 Painting by Joshua Reynolds, half-length painted oval. Private collection (Mannings 2000, no.1367; Christie's, 22 April 1983, lot 89). A version (once called Ramsay) from Stanmer Park, sold Christie's, 17 March 1967, lot 83; another, with a red coat, sold American Art Association, 14 January 1938, lot 51, as Nathaniel Hone.

1769 Painting by Benjamin West,* half-length painted oval, wearing bands and a nobleman's blue academic gown with gold facings. Sotheby's, 17 June 1970, lot 47, and 17 November 1971, lot 77 (Erffa & Staley 1986, no.600). Carmarthen, as he then was, graduated MA at Christ Church, Oxford, on 30 March 1769. A version, apparently autograph, the hair as in NPG 801, sold Sotheby's, 18 November 1992, lot 45, from Lord Chichester's collection (sketched by Scharf at Stanmer Park in 1888; SSB 117/26). See also NPG 801.

1777-78 Painting by Joshua Reynolds,* *The Society of Dilettanti*, see Comparative Groups.

1796 Painting by Thomas Lawrence,* whole-length standing in Garter robes. Formerly at Brocklesby Park, commissioned by the Foreign Office on the resignation of Leeds in 1791 (Garlick 1989, no.475). Exhibited RA 1796(103). Engraved R.M. Meadows 179[7?] (illus. A. Bolton, *John Soane*, 1927, f.p.90); anon. half length.

Undated Wax profile by Samuel Percy, in his sale, Christie's, 31 January 1800 (Pyke 1973, p.104).

DOUBTFUL PORTRAITS

Miniature by Richard Cosway, and a half-length painting attributed to L.F. Abbott, both in a private collection (formerly E.W. Balfour Melville) and both showing a dark 'military' coat with gold-trimmed button holes.

Three watercolour miniatures by William Grimaldi 1789 of *Francis Godolphin V Duke of Leeds* after Reynolds, half-length oval to right, in a scarlet velvet coat with Garter ribbon (Grimaldi 1873, pp.15, 45) were probably of the 4th Duke who d.1789 (cf. Mannings 2000, no.1370).

LENNOX, see RICHMOND and LENNOX

LENNOX, Mrs Charlotte, *née* Ramsay 1720-1804

Writer: b. New York, where her father was governor; sent to England 1735; m. c.1747 Alexander Lennox; in 1748 described by Walpole as 'a poetess, and deplorable actress'; her first novel *Harriot Stuart* 1750 earned Johnson's praise; later works included a successful novel *The Female Quixote* 1752, an unsuccessful play *The Sister* 1769, and some ill-chosen literary criticism; d. in straitened circumstances.

4905 see Groups, *Portraits in the characters of the Muses* by RICHARD SAMUEL 1778

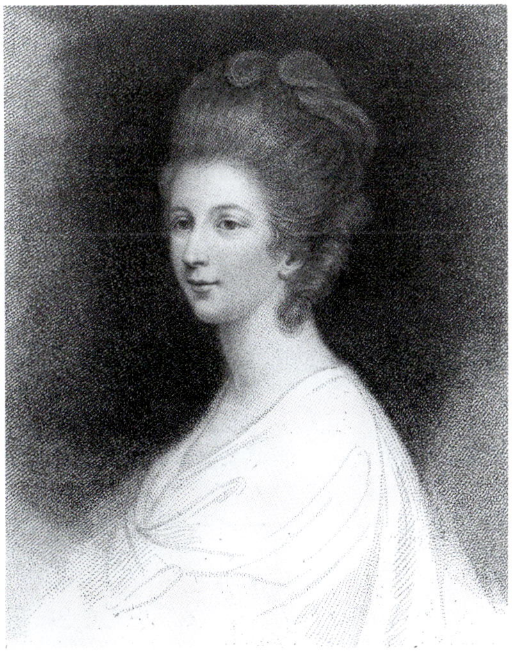

LENNOX F. Bartolozzi after 'Joshua Reynolds' (NPG D 13802)

ICONOGRAPHY

1770s Painting called Joshua Reynolds, half length, engraved F. Bartolozzi 1792; H.R. Cook 1813.

DOUBTFUL PORTRAIT

Painting by William Beechey, sold Christie's, 18 November 1960, lot 63.

LEWES, Sir Watkin, Kt 1740?-1821

MP 1781-96; alderman 1772, sheriff 1772-73 and lord mayor 1780-81 of the City of London; Kt 1773; his career facilitated by his marriage to Rebecca Popkin, a Welsh heiress.

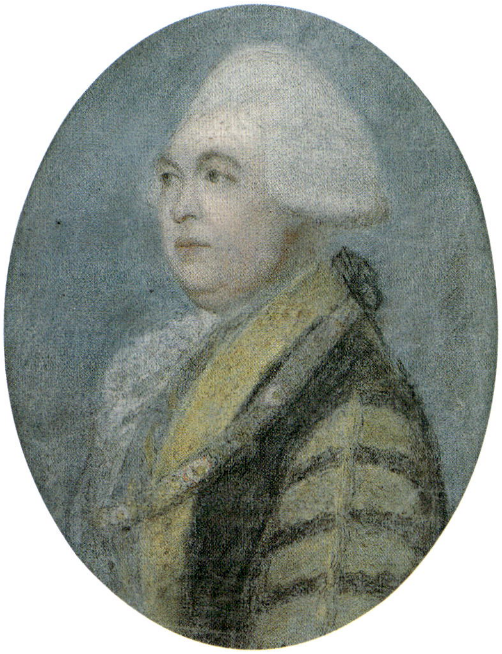

LEWES NPG *2439*

2439 after DANIEL DODD c.1780

Pastel on blue paper, irregular oval 31.5 x 25.5 (12½ x 10), the image 27 x 21.5 (10½ x 8½); laid down on paper 1984; rubbed and faded; a repaired tear centre-left edge, and a horizontal fold cuts across the base of the figure; inscribed in margin below in ink (perhaps a late 18th- or early 19th-century hand): *Sir Watkin Lewes*.

Brown eyes, white powdered wig, wearing the black and gold mayoral state robe with the SS collar.

Collections: Discovered by G. Scharf 'in one of the drawers of the table desk when I took office' at the NPG in Great George Street 1863; registered in 1929.

A sorry object, NPG 2439 relates directly to the drawing by Daniel Dodd engraved by C.T. Warren (in reverse) for *The Senator* in 1791 as *Sir Watkin Lewes, member for the City of London* - although he is shown in the mayoral robes which he wore only in 1780-81.

ICONOGRAPHY

1773 Painted and engraved by William Dickinson,* three-quarter length oval as sheriff of London

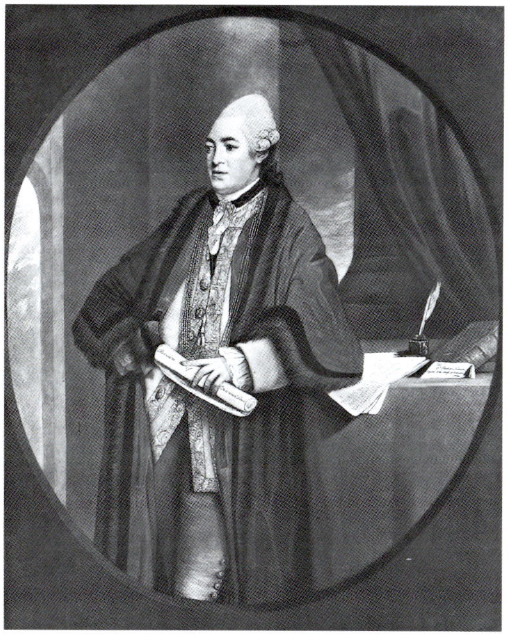

LEWES painted and engraved by William Dickinson 1773 (NPG archive)

wearing his robes, holding papers inscribed *Revision of Criminal Law*.

c.1780 Drawing by Daniel Dodd, see NPG 2439.

c.1781 Painting by T. Hill, engraved W. Skelton, profile bust to left, as lord mayor (Lambert's *London*, 1806, p.638).

1793 Miniature by F. Allison, exhibited RA 1793(373).

LEWIS, William Thomas c.1746-1811

Actor-manager; played in Ireland before coming in 1773 to Covent Garden where he played thirty-five consecutive seasons, specialising in fashionable and flippant characters; deputy manager 1782-1803; in 1803, in partnership with Thomas Knight, he reopened the theatre at Liverpool.

'Mr Lewis is an excellent stage figure, not tall, but neat and well proportioned. He has a pair of lively eyes, and a very pleasing countenance' (*Covent Garden Mag.*, 1773).

'... gay, fluttering, hare-brained Lewis, the greatest comic mannerist perhaps that ever lived' (William Hazlitt).

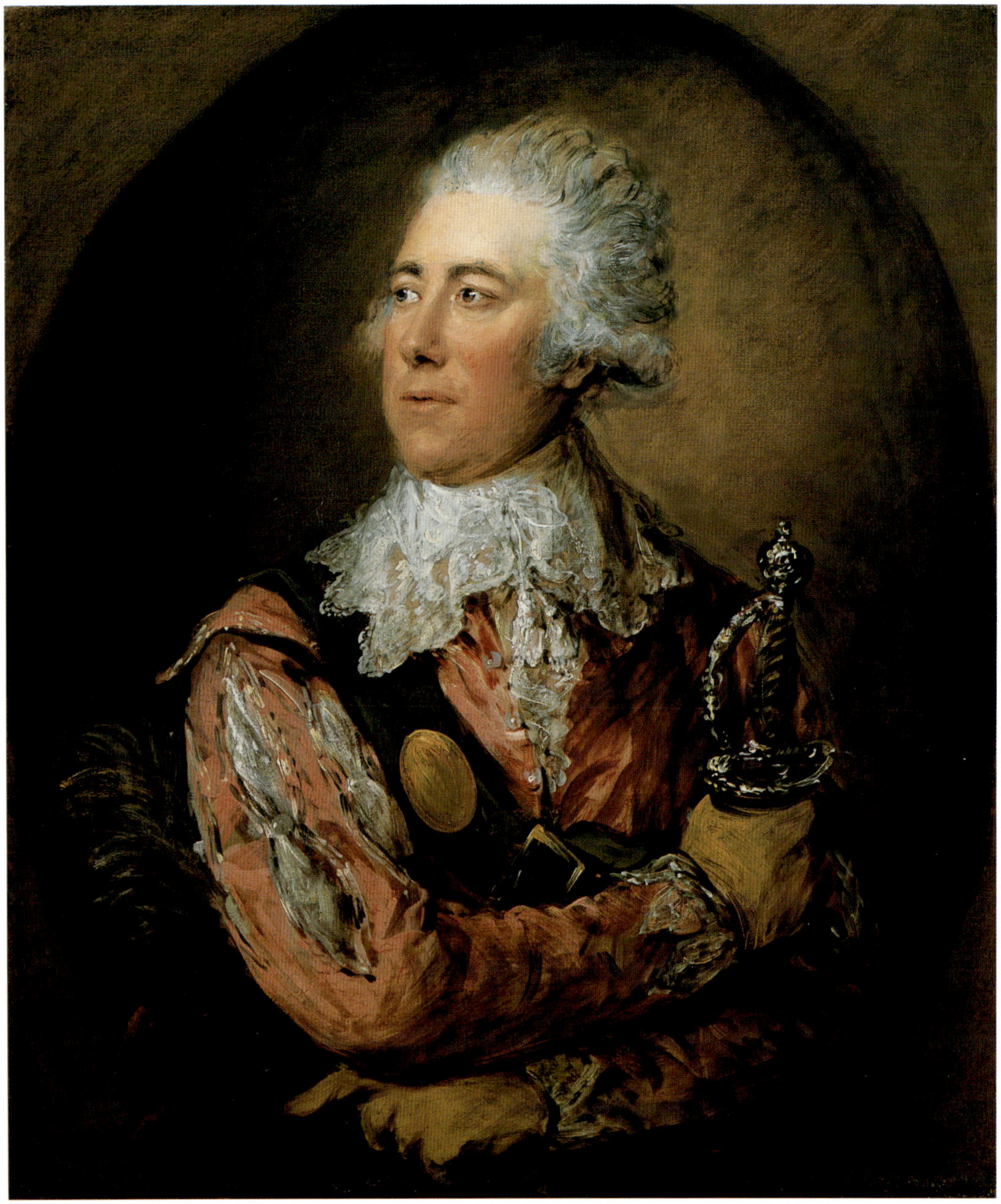

LEWIS NPG *5148*

5148 GAINSBOROUGH DUPONT, *as Mercutio in Romeo and Juliet* 1794

Canvas 72.5 x 63 (28½ x 24¾) lined; cleaned 1978, some glazes had been previously damaged; a pentimento round his left shoulder; a horizontal strip 2.5 (1) wide along the bottom edge was originally a tacking margin before lining.[1]

Brown eyes, white powdered hair, wearing pink Van Dyck costume with yellow gloves, a black sword-belt bearing a pearl button; a black-plumed hat with a thin red ribbon in his left hand; within a painted oval.

Collections: Thomas Harris (see below); his sale, Robins, 12 July 1819, lot 18 ('Dupont, Lewis as Mercutio'); anon. sale, Christie's, 25 July 1891, lot 100 ('Gainsborough, William Thomas Lewis, the Actor'), bt. Nathan, presumably for Sir Charles Tennant (1823-1906) who lent it for exhibition that year; by descent through the Barons Glenconner to the Hon Colin Tennant; sold by the Trustees of his Children, Sotheby's, 6 July 1977, lot 22, bt. Leggatt for the NPG.

Exhibitions: RA 1795(273, 'Dupont, Portrait of Mr Lewis'); RA 1891(46 as Gainsborough); *Loan Collection*, Glasgow, 1902(114 as Gainsborough); *Les Arts du Théâtre de Watteau à Fragonard*, Bordeaux, 1980(18); *Royal Opera House Retrospective*, RA, 1982(124).

Reference: Tennant Catalogue, 1896, n.p. (as Gainsborough, Lewis as the Marquis in *The Midnight Hour*); *Gainsborough* 1953, p.68 (as late Gainsborough or Dupont); Waterhouse 1958, p.42 (as Dupont).

NPG 5148, a loose and vigorous portrait, was one of a series commissioned from Gainsborough Dupont in 1793-94 by Thomas Harris, manager of the Covent Garden Theatre from 1774.[2] Harris, 'considering Dupont as wanting employ commissioned him to paint portraits of the Actors of that Theatre and only to proceed with the commission when he had no others',[3] the actor John O'Keeffe adding that the subjects were to be 'the principal performers of Covent Garden theatre, in their most distinguished characters'.[4] Twenty-three or twenty-four portraits are recorded; besides NPG 5148, twelve are now in the Garrick Club[5] and one in the Norton Gallery, West Palm Beach.[6]

On 22 March 1794 the *Morning Herald* announced that Dupont had completed twelve portraits, including Lewis as Mercutio in *Romeo and Juliet*, a role he had played on three occasions in the 1793-94 season.[7] Both the attribution and the identity as Mercutio were subsequently lost (see Collections and Exhibitions above). In 1896 the Tennant catalogue stated it showed Lewis as the Marquis in Mrs Inchbald's *The Midnight Hour*, probably because the then well-known whole length by Shee in the National Gallery showed him in that role (see below). Lewis was again shown as Mercutio by Samuel De Wilde in 1809 (see below), on this occasion wearing a silver costume with a blue cloak, a falling lace collar and a sword belt.

1 Clearly shown in the illus. in the Tennant cat., 1896, n.p.
2 This account is based on J. Hayes, *Connoisseur*, CLXIX, 1968, pp.221-27. See also G. Ashton, *Royal Opera House Retrospective*, 1982, pp.69-79.
3 Farington, 21 April 1795.
4 John O'Keeffe c.1793 in his *Recollections*, 1826, quoted by Ashton 1982, p.70.
5 See Ashton 1997, nos.87, 120, 210, 306, 603, 460, 597, 633, 677, 683, 701, 796. Another by Singleton, no.333, was presumably added to the set after Dupont's death.
6 Illus. *Connoisseur*, CLXIX, 1968, p.227. Another matching half length by Dupont in the Royal Collection of Mme Bacelli, who played at the King's Theatre (Millar 1969, no.769), was not apparently painted for Harris, since it belonged to George IV in 1816.
7 Quoted by J. Hayes, *Connoisseur*, CLXIX, 1968, p.223, and see Ashton 1982, p.71, no.124.

ICONOGRAPHY

See also the *Harvard Catalogue*, III, pp.52-55, and Highfill, IX, pp.290-92 (listing further portrayals of Lewis in character).

1783 Coloured wax by Calvert, exhibited SA 1783(53).

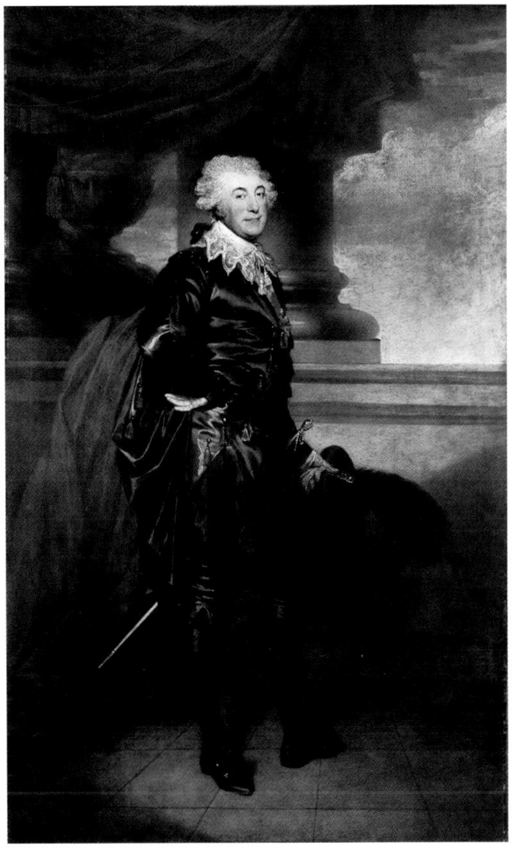

LEWIS by M.A. Shee 1792 (National Gallery, London)

1787 Painting by Mather Brown, bust-length oval, holding a tragic mask, exhibited RA 1787(66); visible in J.H. Ramberg's engraving of that exhibition. Engraved J. Corner 1788 (*European Mag.*; illus. Egerton 1998, p.412).

1792 Painting by M.A. Shee,* whole length as the Marquis in Mrs Inchbald's *The Midnight Hour.* National Gallery, London (677). Exhibited RA 1792(205); NPE 1868(109). Engraved J. Jones 1792; H.R. Cook 1812.

1793 Miniature by William Naish, half length; exhibited RA 1793(430). Engraved W. Hinton; C. Townley. An unfinished half-length painting in the Garrick Club, a monocle in his left hand, shows a comparable head; it has been associated with Naish, and very tentatively with Gilbert Stuart (Ashton 1997, no.427). A cruder, unattributed half length, with shorter white hair, belonged to J. Drakeford Lewis in 1935.

1794 Painting by Gainsborough Dupont, see NPG 5148.

c.1795 Anon. engraving, half-length oval, the head resembling Shee's 1792 portrait.

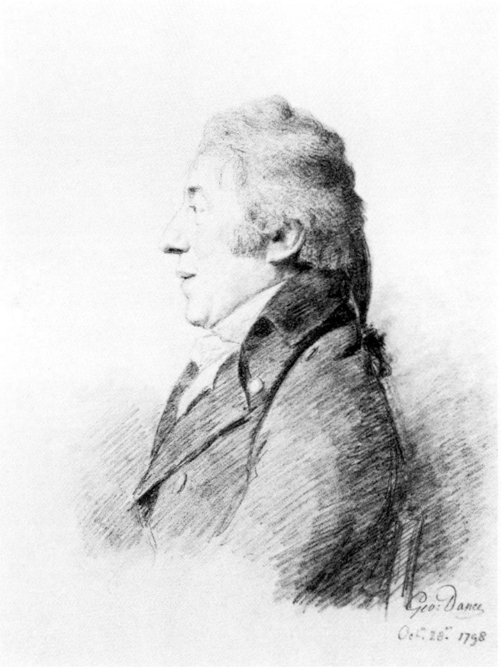

LEWIS by George Dance 1798 (British Museum)

1798 Drawing by George Dance,* profile to right, dated 28 October 1798. British Museum (1898.7.12.25). Exhibited RA 1799(456). Engraved W. Daniell 1810 (*Dance Portraits*).

1798 Miniature by George Chinnery, bust-length oval, engraved W. Ridley 1798 (also published the same year as by A. Pope).

c.1800 Painting by M.A. Shee, half length. Garrick Club (Ashton 1997, no.428). From the Thomas Harris sale (lot 40), for which see NPG 5148.

Other depictions of Lewis in character include: painting by Zoffany, as Tanjore in Reynolds's *Speculation* 1795-96 (Garrick Club; Ashton 1997, no.429); two paintings by De Wilde, as Copper Captain in Beaumont and Fletcher's *Rule a Wife and have a Wife* (engraved J. Thornthwaite 1791, illus. Burnim 1998, p.182) and as Pharnaces in Hoole's *Cleonice* (Garrick Club; Ashton 1997, no.426; engraved P. Audinet 1795, illus. Burnim 1998, p.183); two drawings by De Wilde in the Garrick Club (Ashton 1997, nos.424-25) show him as Diddler in Kenney's *Raising the Wind* and as Mercutio in *Romeo and Juliet* (engraved J. Condé 1791; said to have been the last portrait taken of Lewis).

DOUBTFUL PORTRAIT

Thomas Lawrence exhibited a painting of Mr Lewis, RA 1789(536), which may, or may not, have been the actor (Garlick 1989, no.491).

LIFFORD, James Hewitt, 1st Viscount 1712-89

Lord chancellor of Ireland; b. Coventry, called to the Middle Temple 1742; serjeant-at-law 1754; King's serjeant 1759; MP 1761-66, a supporter of Chatham; justice of the King's bench 1766; lord chancellor of Ireland from 1767, an appointment derided by Lord Mansfield, but which he filled effectively, being regarded in Dublin as 'a most worthy, honest and amiable man'; Baron Lifford [I] 1768 and Viscount Lifford [I] 1781.

4249 UNKNOWN ARTIST [c.1775]

Black and white chalk on grey paper, irregular oval 14 x 10.5 (5½ x 4) maximum; inscribed in pencil verso: *113/262/ Lord Lifford/ Lord Chancellor/ of Ireland/ by Samuel Lover/ IHRA/ the artist & poet/ Fosters Sale/ 1881.*

Wearing the long wig of a lord chancellor.

Collections: Samuel Lover; his sale, Foster's, 23 March 1881, lot 113 ('a portfolio of 262 pencil sketches and drawings by Mr. Lover'); anon. sale, Knight, Frank & Rutley, 30 August 1961, lot 41, bt. Leggatt for the NPG.

The legal wig identifies a chancellor and the oval shape of the head agrees with Madden's portrait of Lifford as engraved in 1775. Previously (according to the evidence of the provenance) accepted as a copy by

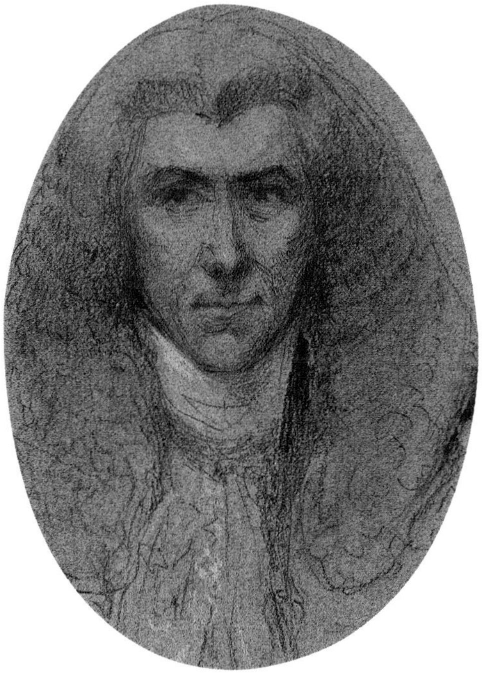

1st Viscount LIFFORD NPG 4249

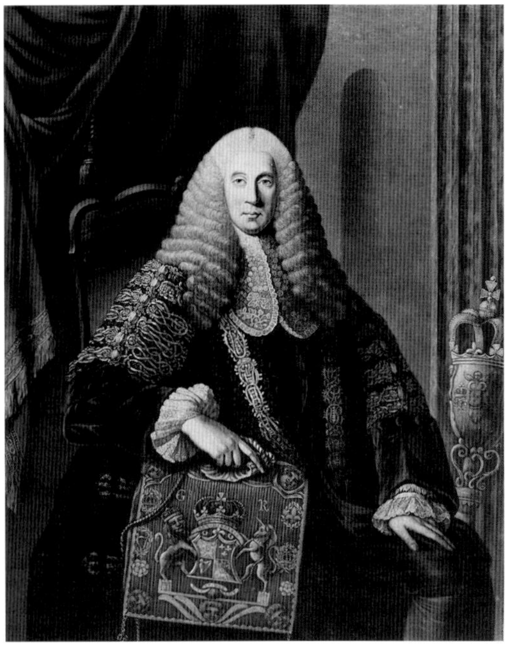

1st Viscount LIFFORD W. Dickinson 1775 after Wyndham Madden (National Gallery of Ireland)

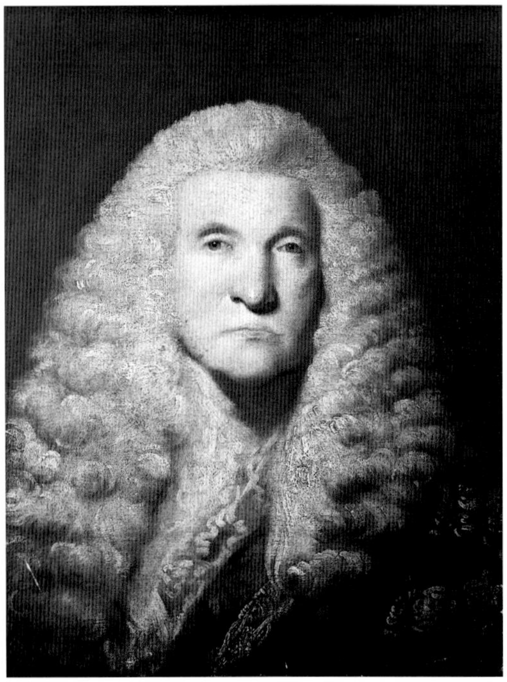

1st Viscount LIFFORD by Joshua Reynolds 1788 (Smithsonian American Art Museum, Washington)

the nineteenth-century Irish artist Samuel Lover from an unknown portrait of Lifford, but NPG 4249 appears to be a freshly-observed drawing, with the eyes askance, owned rather than executed by Lover.

ICONOGRAPHY

Undated Painting by George Romney, three-quarter length seated in chancellor's robes. Formerly with Lord Lifford (Ward & Roberts 1904, II, p.94).

c.1775 Unattributed drawing, see NPG 4249.

c.1775 Painting by Wyndham Madden, three-quarter length seated in chancellor's robes. Engraved W. Dickinson 1775.*

1788 Painting by Joshua Reynolds, whole-length seated in chancellor's robes. Private collection (Mannings 2000, no.898). Engraved R. Dunkarton 1790 (Mannings 2000, fig.1541). Exhibited RA 1789(225); NPE 1867(849) lent Viscount Lifford. Half-length copies in the National Collection of Fine Arts, Washington (1956.11.46);* by R.L. West in the NG of Ireland (54); sold Sotheby's, 6 April 1993, lot 116, and with Mrs George P. Miller in 1955.

LINCOLN, Henry, 9th Earl of, see NEWCASTLE

LINLEY, Elizabeth, see SHERIDAN

LIVERPOOL, Charles Jenkinson, 1st Earl of 1727-1808

Statesman; private secretary to Lord Bute 1761-63; lord of the Treasury 1767-73, president of the board of trade 1786-1804; FRS 1794; cr. Baron Hawkesbury 1780 and Earl of Liverpool 1796.

'He was above the common height, but his lank limbs and figure were destitute of elegance or of grace. The expression of his countenance was not destitute of deep intelligence. Reflection and caution seemed to be stamped on every feature, while his eyes were usually, even in conversation, directed towards the earth' (Sir Nathaniel Wraxall, 1815).

'pleasant in his voice and manner, though eminently ugly, long, and lean, with strange sort of eyes, oddly thrown up or cast down, but never looking like the eyes of any other man' (Mrs Hester Piozzi).

5206 GEORGE ROMNEY 1786-88

Canvas 150 x 113 (59 x 44½) lined; when exhibited in 1867 the picture was said to be 'much repaired and repainted'; cleaned by Lewis & Simmons 1925 and at the NPG in 1979;[1] the dark areas, below right, show a wide craquelure. X-radiography indicates a reworking of the area behind and above the chair.

Brown eyes, powdered wig, wearing a purple velvet coat with a black collar and gold buttons, a white waistcoat with gold trim and buttons, and white stockings; he sits in a red-upholstered chair, holding a snuff box in his left hand. The table is covered with a Turkish rug; the paper beneath his hand inscribed: *A/ Bill/ for/ The [fur]ther [Increase and]/ Encouragement of Ship/ and Navigation/ 26 Geo.III/ 17[8]6*; the three upright papers: *[Green]land [Whale] Fish[ery] 1786; Southern Whale Fishery 1786*, and *New Foundland Fishery 1786*.[2] The standing leather volume has a red title panel, illegibly inscribed, with a green band below.

Collections: By descent to Lady Louisa Cotes (dau. of the 3rd Earl of Liverpool); John Cotes by 1867; C.C. Cotes by 1905; Col. C.J.C. Grant of Pitchford Hall, by whom sold Christie's, 11 May 1923, lot 110, bt. G.P. Bennett; Lewis & Simmons, London, 15 December 1925, bt. Comm. L.D. Beaumont, Paris; his widow, Mrs H. Beaumont, Monte Carlo; Sotheby's, 19 July 1978, lot 31, bt. Leggatt for the NPG.

Engraving: J. Murphy 1788.

Exhibition: NPE 1867(785) lent John Cotes.

Reference: Ward & Roberts 1904, II, pp.73-4.

Lord Hawkesbury sat to Romney on 9, 11 and 19 August 1786 and 31 March, 5 April and 18 July 1787; his portrait was 'sent home' on 9 May 1788 and he paid fifty guineas for it on 10 May.[3] The papers on the table refer to four acts of 1786 concerning overseas trade, see note 2 below, but in the engraving by Murphy they are differently described.[4] Other painted versions of the portrait follow NPG 5206: a copy at University College, Oxford (where Jenkinson proceeded MA in 1752),[5] and two late nineteenth-century copies which belonged to the family in 1905, one by May Lancaster Lucas,[6] probably identifiable with a copy now in another private collection,[7] the other a half-length by Constance Pitcairn, now untraced.[8]

1 When the broad craquelure in the lower dark areas was very pronounced and much overpainting was removed.
2 These papers refer to four Acts, largely devised by Jenkinson as president of the Board of Trade, which received the Royal assent, respectively, on 27, 13 and 16 June, and 22 May, 1786 (*Journals of the House of Commons*, 41, 1803, pp.562, 939, 459-60, 833, 598, 899, 765, 907).
3 Ward & Roberts 1904, II, p.74.
4 The leaning book bears a title panel: *Report on Commercial Intercourse with America* (apparently a general reference to the following acts); the three papers beneath his right hand are lettered: *Newfoundland Fishery 1786, Greenland and Southern Whale Fishery*, and *Act for P... the further Increase & Encouragement of Shipping & Navigation*.

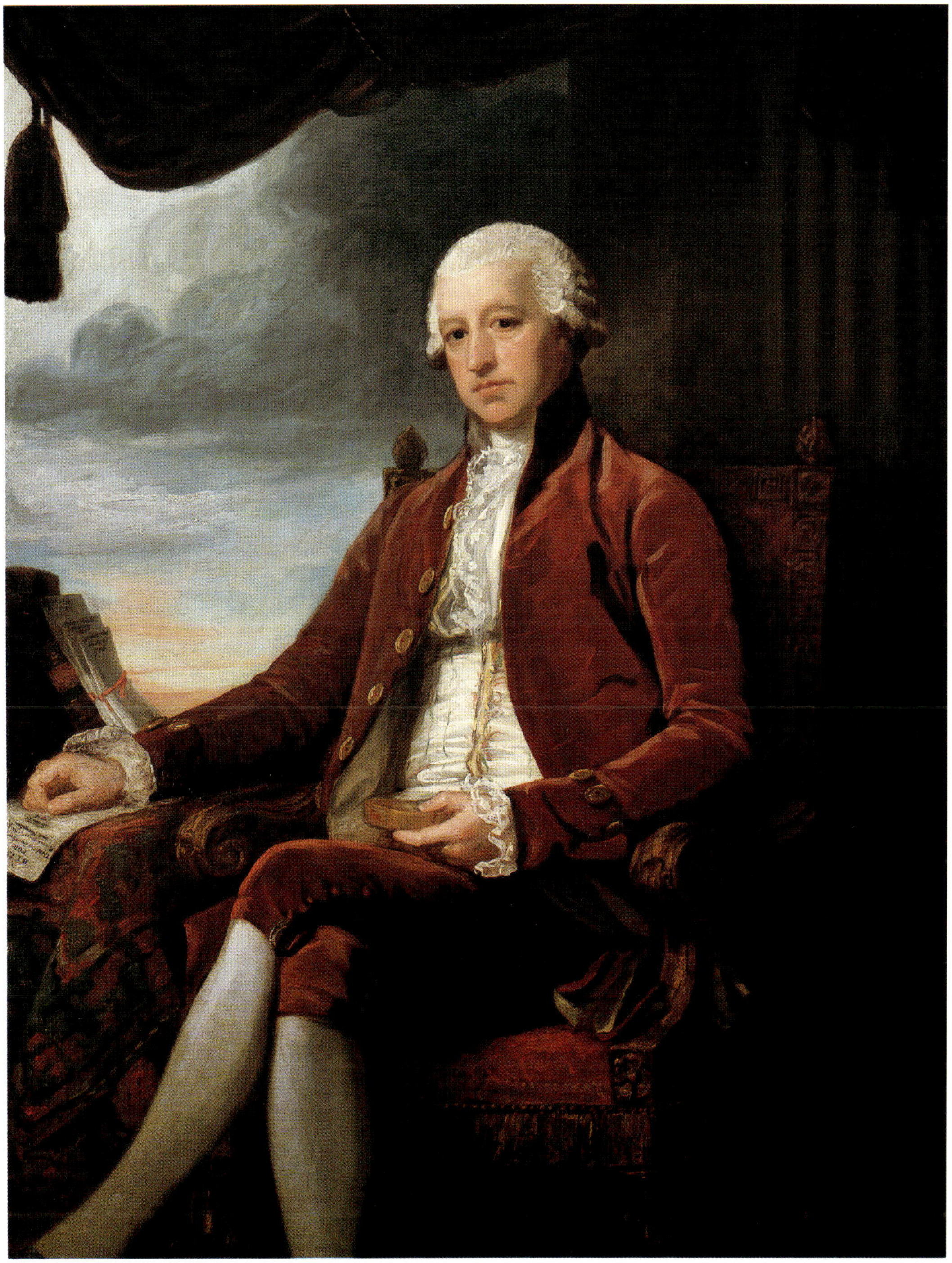

1st Earl of LIVERPOOL NPG 5206

5 Poole, II, p.10 (the 'original slightly larger now with C.C. Cotes').
6 Hawkesbury 1906, p.5, no.17.
7 Inscribed verso: *please return to Lady Louisa Coates*; sold by Lord Caledon from Tyttenhanger c.1966. The 1st Earl of Liverpool's daughter was the mother-in-law of the 3rd Earl of Caledon.
8 Hawkesbury 1906, no.116, pl.xxviii.

ICONOGRAPHY

1763 Painting by Joshua Reynolds,* whole length, attending the 3rd Earl of Bute, see Bute.

1784 Wedgwood medallion modelled by John Flaxman (illus. Reilly 1973, p.217). Engraved anon. 1785 (*European Mag.*).

1786-88 Painting by George Romney, see NPG 5206.

1791 Engraving by C.T. Warren from a drawing by Charles Benazech, half-length oval (*The Senator*).

1802 Drawing by Henry Edridge. Lord Liverpool, London, in 1905 (Hawkesbury 1906, p.120, no.504), presumably the half length with dark coat, high-buttoned waistcoat and white neckcloth, engraved by W. Evans 1808 (described as from an original drawing belonging to the Earl of Liverpool), and by Ridley & Blood 1809. A painting by Edridge, wearing black with a white neckcloth, was in the same collection (Hawkesbury 1906, p.50, no.72).

An unattributed pencil head, a 'head in oval', and an unattributed bust, listed in Lord Liverpool's collection in 1905 (respectively Hawkesbury 1906, pp.80, no.187; 88, no.202; 69, no.154/1).

LONG NORTH, Dudley, see NORTH, Dudley

LOUTHERBOURG, see DE LOUTHERBOURG

LOVEL and HOLLAND, Lord, see EGMONT

LYNCH, Sir William, KB c.1730-85

Eldest s. of John Lynch, Dean of Canterbury; MP 1762-80; envoy to Sardinia at Turin 1769-79, but he was in England 1772-74 and from 1776; KB 1771.

3090(9) UNKNOWN ARTIST [c.1774]

Pencil and brown wash on paper (watermarked *J Whatman 1844*) 38.5 x 28 (15 x 11), the figure 15 x 15 (6 x 6); inscribed below in pencil: *Sir Wm. Lynch K.B.*

Wearing the badge of the Bath.

Collections: Purchased from Appleby 1940.

A mid-19th century copy from an unattributed portrait showing Lynch as envoy to Sardinia. A version from the F. D. Brockman collection was sold

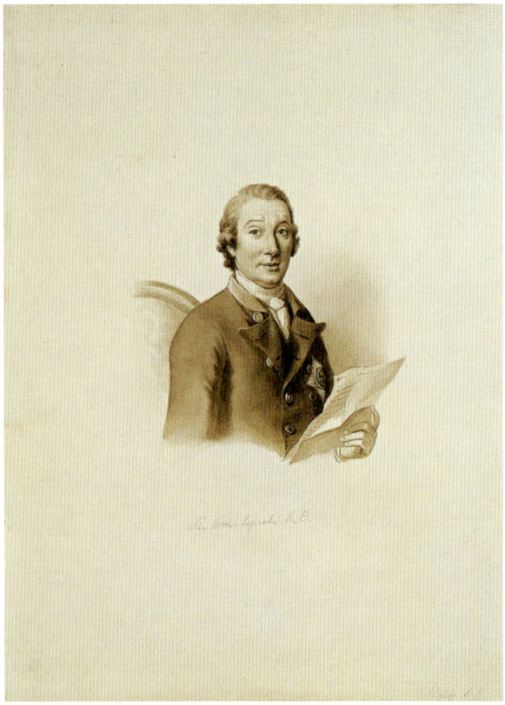

LYNCH NPG *3090(9)*

Christie's, 31 July 1931, lot 14 (attributed to Tilly Kettle; wearing a green coat with a red collar); a pastel version (unattributed; wearing a blue coat with red collar and cuffs) is at Longleat[1] (Lynch had been patronised by Lord Weymouth), and a third version was in an English private collection 1991.[2] An unspecified portrait was with Lord Carteret at Haynes House, Bedford, in 1797.[3]

1 Cat., 1881, no.116.
2 Note in the NPG archive.
3 Musgrave MSS 6391, f.2v.

LYTTELTON, Thomas Lyttelton, 2nd Baron 1744-79

Profligate of contradictory temper; in Italy 1763-65 and 1769-71; MP 1768-69; suc. as 2nd Baron Lyttelton 1773; it was alleged that a dream warned him three days in advance of his sudden, early death - 'it is the ghost story, after all, which makes his lineaments worth preserving in the National Portrait Gallery' (*Westminster Gaz.*, 1900).

1446 attributed to RICHARD BROMPTON c.1775

Canvas 72.5 x 61.5 (28½ x 24¼) lined; a repaired damage above the head and small losses around the mouth; pentimenti over his right arm (not elucidated by x-radiography) suggesting the arm may have first been by his side and that the vent of his robe may have reached his shoulder; his left shoulder has also been modified.

Brown eyes, grey powdered hair, wearing red, ermine-lined Baron's robes, the ermine guard trimmed with gold lace; the paper in his right hand has no legible inscription.

Collections: By descent to the 8th Viscount Cobham, by whom presented 1906.

Exhibition: *Guelph* 1891(158 as After Gainsborough) lent Lord Cobham.

Reference: Hagley Hall Catalogue, 1900, no.121, as Gainsborough.

Accepted in 1906 as an 'old copy after Gainsborough',[1] NPG 1446 is a weak portrait, a slightly skewed head sitting uneasily on an altered body. Lyttelton had previously been represented in the collection by a similar-sounding half length ('in red velvet with powdered hair') attributed to Richard Brompton[2] - who painted the head of the whole length of Lyttelton formerly at Hagley Hall (and who exhibited a half length 'Nobleman in the robes of the house of lords' at the SA 1773, no.44). It is probable that Brompton at least began NPG 1446.

1 An old MS label formerly on the stretcher had *Rt. Hon. Thos, Lord Lyttelton/Painted by Thomas Gainsborough* and a note in the NPG archive recorded that the original canvas had, verso: *Thos Gainsborough*.
2 NPG 1166, from the (illegal) bequest of Sir John James Hamilton, 2nd Bt, 1892 (who m. Marianna Augusta Cockburn); returned by the NPG in 1900 and sold by the Beneficiaries of Sir James Cockburn, 10th Bt (1867-1947), Christie's, 25 June 1900, lot 10 as by R. Brompton; now untraced.

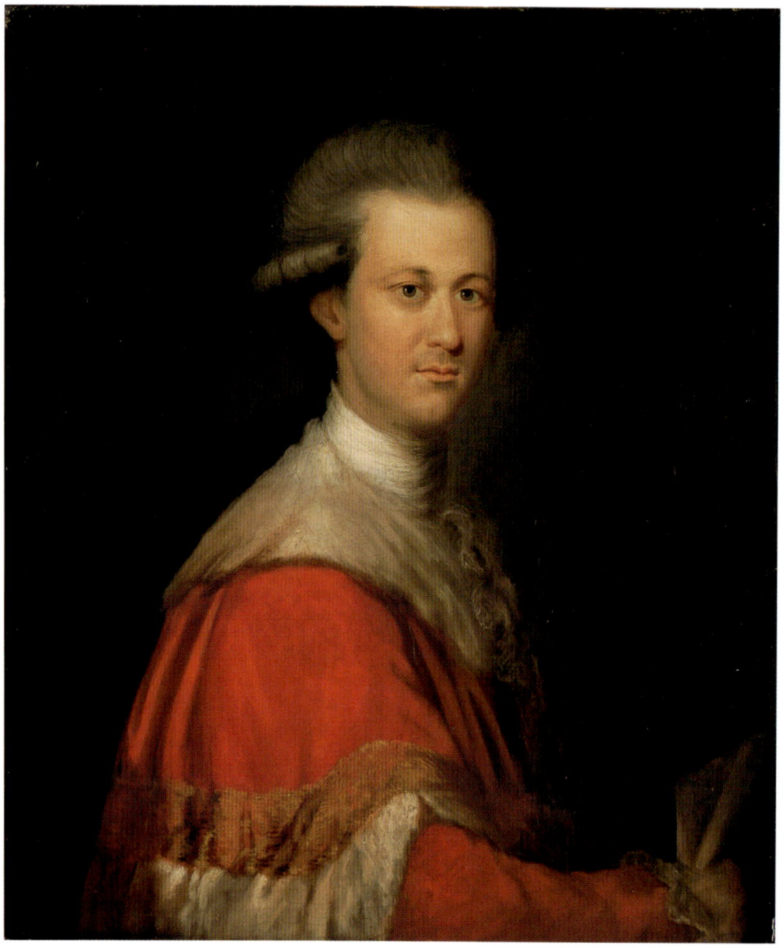

2nd Baron LYTTELTON
NPG *1446*

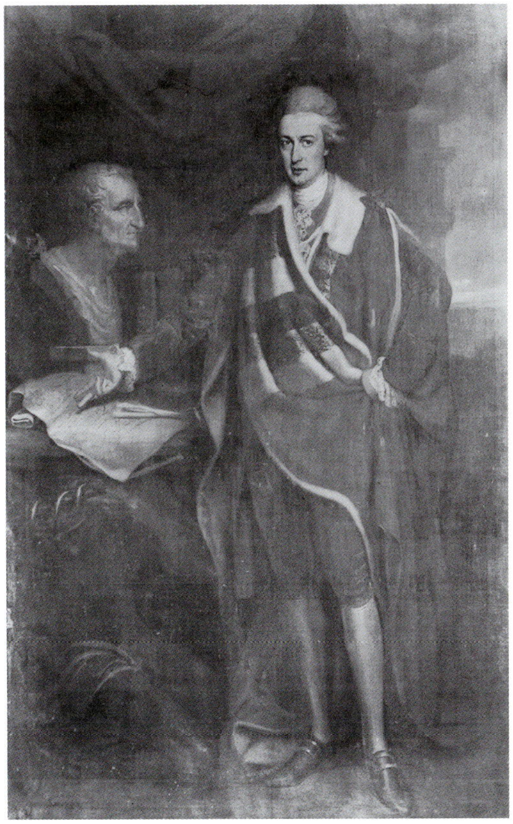

2nd Baron LYTTELTON by Richard Brompton and Richard Cosway c.1775 (formerly Hagley Hall)

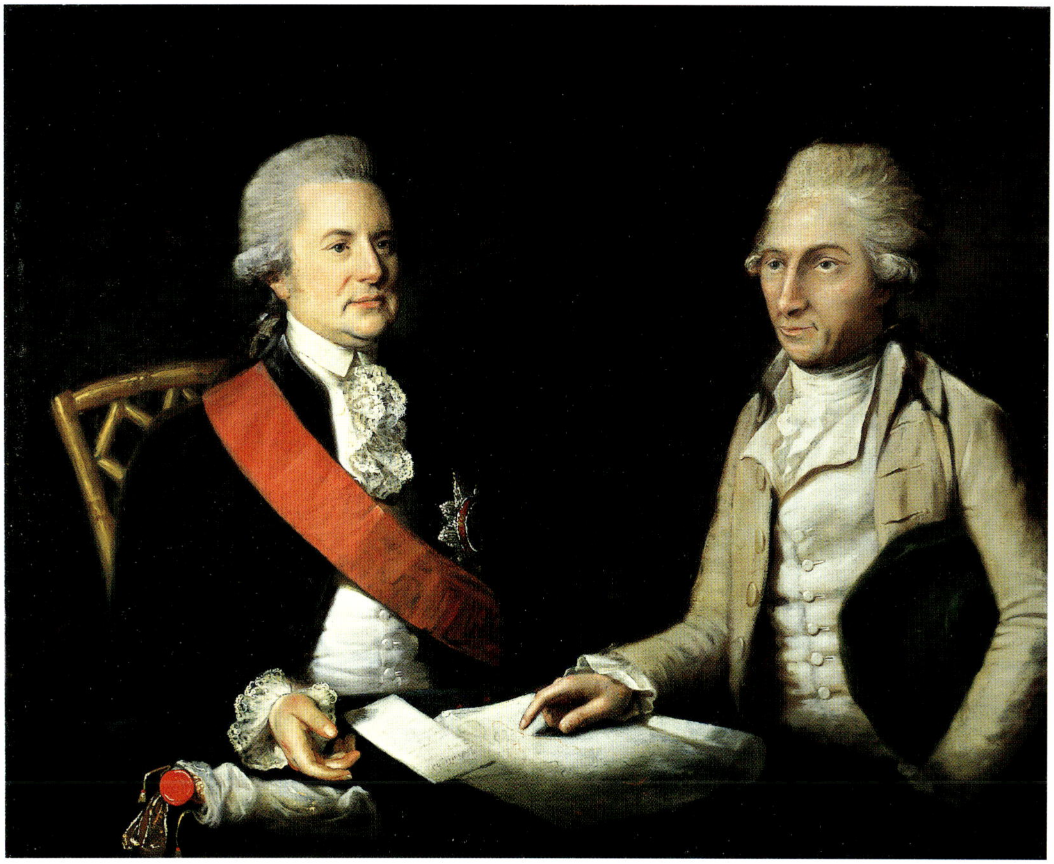

Earl MACARTNEY (left) and STAUNTON NPG *329*

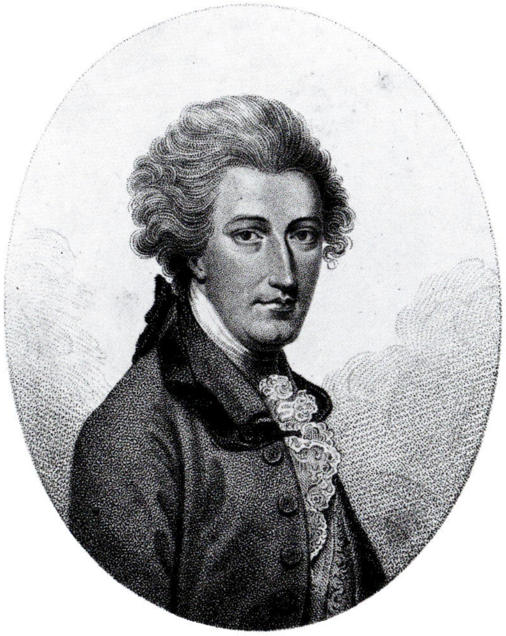

2nd Baron LYTTELTON C. Townley after Richard Cosway 1780 (British Museum)

ICONOGRAPHY

c.1771 'Drawn at Rome after the manner of the Old Roman coins & Medals by Pompeo Battoni'. Formerly at Hagley Hall (MS list by R. Colt Hoare, n.d. [after 1787], no.47).

c.1775 Painting by Richard Brompton and Richard Cosway,* whole-length standing, in Baron's robes, a bust of Demosthenes beside him. Formerly at Hagley Hall (MS list by R. Colt Hoare, n.d. [after 1787], no.8: 'Thomas Lord Lyttelton - a whole length - head by Brompton finish'd by Cosway'). Exhibited NPE 1867(795) lent Lord Lyttelton.

c.1775 Painting attributed to Richard Brompton, see NPG 1446.

c.1775-79 Miniature by Richard Cosway, bust-length oval. Hagley Hall (illus. *Cosway* 1995, no.20, pl.15). Engraved anon. 1806.

1780 Painting by Richard Cosway, half length in Peer's robes, his right hand raised in horror at the portent of death. Engraved C. Townley 1781.*

MACARTNEY, George Macartney, Earl 1737-1806

Diplomat; travelled in Europe 1761-64; Kt 1764; envoy extraordinary to St Petersburg 1764-67; Kt of the White Eagle of Poland 1766; MP 1768-69, 1774-76, 1780-81; MP[I] 1768-76 and chief secretary in Ireland 1769-72; KB 1772; governor of Grenada 1775-79 and Madras 1781-85; FRS 1792; plenipotentiary Peking 1792-94; visited the exiled French King in Verona 1795-96; governor of the Cape of Good Hope 1796-98; cr. Baron 1776 [I], Viscount 1792 [I], Earl [I] 1794, and Baron [GB] 1796, his titles becoming extinct on his death.

'[in 1766 he was] considered among the handsomest and most accomplished young men of his day. His features were regular and well proportioned, his complexion wore the glow of health, and his countenance was open, placid, and agreeable ... [in his maturity] his person was somewhat above the middle size and rather corpulent ... his manners were engaging, and his carriage easy and dignified' (Sir John Barrow, 1807).

Abbreviations

Barrow 1807: J. Barrow, *Public Life ... of the Earl of Macartney*, 2 vols., 1807

Robbins 1908: H.H. Robbins, *Our First Ambassador to China, an Account of the Life of George, Earl of Macartney*, 1908

Roebuck 1983: P. Roebuck ed., *Macartney of Lisanoure*, 1983

329 LEMUEL FRANCIS ABBOTT, *with George Staunton* c.1785

Canvas 101 x 127 (39¾ x 50) lined;[1] cleaned and restored 1985; there are considerable losses: within a square area between the two figures affecting Macartney's left shoulder and Staunton's right, and the head of Staunton on the right is entirely repainted; there are pentimenti around his collar; in Macartney's figure there are pentimenti around his left shoulder and hair ribbon; above Staunton an inscription *Sir George Staunton/ Baronet/ 1783* had been overpainted.

Macartney on the left with his secretary, George Staunton, on the right; on the table a red-wax sealed silk bag, a letter headed *Instructions* and an illegible map to which Staunton points.

Macartney: blue eyes, grey powdered hair, wearing a blue coat with the ribbon and badge of the Bath; sitting in a bamboo chair.

Staunton: grey eyes, white hair, wearing a cream jacket and white vest, a green hat under his arm.

Collections: Macartney's widow, Jane (d.1828), by descent at Lissanoure Castle to his great nephew, George Macartney Hume (d.1869);[2] Lissanoure Castle sale, 12 May 1850, bt. S. Macartney Caldwell;[3] Sir Maziere Brady (d.1871), sold Dublin 1871;[4] C.H. Waters,[5] from whom purchased November 1871.

Exhibitions: *Irish Industrial Exhibition*, Dublin 1853(324 as Reynolds) lent S.M. Caldwell; *China und Europe*, Berlin, 1985(14/2); *Britain's First View of China*, British Museum, 1992.

NPG 329 shows Lord Macartney as governor of Madras with his private secretary George Staunton, whom he had first met in Grenada in 1775. It is a much-damaged version of the double portrait formerly belonging to the Staunton family and now in an American private collection,[6] in which the map is inscribed *Mangalore* and the folded document *Instructions/ for/ making Peace/ with Tippoo Sultan*. In September 1783 Macartney sent Staunton with two other envoys (Sadleir and Huddleston) to Seringatapam to negotiate a settlement in Mysore, where Tipu Sultan with his father, Hyder Ali (d.1782), had harassed the British. Staunton succeeded in this mission at the cost of ceding the port of Mangalore, where the treaty was signed on 11 March 1784. Macartney was much impressed with Staunton's diplomatic skill, telling Fox that he was a man 'most capable of rendering essential service to the State of India'.[7] Staunton's treaty was subsequently modified by Warren Hastings.

NPG 329 had been called Reynolds in 1850 and it was offered in 1871 as Gainsborough,[8] but Scharf convincingly attributed it to Abbott, remembering that the Staunton version had previously been offered in 1860 as Abbott.[9] NPG 329 particularly commemorates Staunton's success, combining Macartney's instructions of September 1783 with a reference to Mangalore. The Staunton version also suggests that Staunton's head was painted with rather more interest than Macartney's; the heads relate uncomfortably and neither looks at the other. Abbott, who was never in India, had arrived in London in 1784 and first exhibited at the RA in 1788; Staunton returned from India in 1784 and Macartney in 1785, and their double portrait as Indian officials must date soon after. Apart from the regrettable differences in condition, there are minor variations between the two versions: NPG 329 shows the folded document lying on the table instead of in Macartney's right hand; Macartney's waistcoat buttons are more visible, and the back of his bamboo chair is of a different pattern.

Abbott also painted a separate (related) half length of Macartney, see below.

1 A label formerly on the verso reads: *Received Augt 29 1850 from S.M. Caldwell Esqre the sum of Sixteen Pounds for cleaning and restoration a Picture by Sir Joshua Reynolds - J. Caldwell.*
2 See Robbins 1908, p.456; Roebuck 1983, p.306.
3 A label formerly on the verso reads: *This Picture by Sir Joshua Reynolds was Purchased by me at Lissanoure Castle Co Antrim Ireland May 12 1850 when a Sheriffs sale took place at the suit of A Clarke against George Macartney Esqr/ S Macartney Caldwell.*
4 This ownership is implied by Scharf; among his papers relating to NPG 329 is a note that the Brady sale, Christie's, 1 July 1871, did not include 'the Macartney one. That was sold afterwards at Dublin'.
5 The London dealer (cf. Walker *Regency*, I, pp.98, 201).
6 Descended through the Staunton family; with Sir George Staunton in 1850, when he told Macartney he had a duplicate of their picture (letter from Sir George Staunton to S. Macartney Caldwell dated May 27 1850 copied on a label formerly on the back of NPG 329); offered to the NPG in 1860, see note 3, as Abbott; Capt. G.S. Lynch-Staunton sale, Christie's, 8 July 1927, lot 70, as Abbott; Dr D.B. Bache, USA (d.1994); London art market.
7 Quoted in Robbins 1908, p.145.
8 NPG *Offers 1865-71*, 23 November 1871.
9 NPG *Offers 1857-64*, 11 January 1860, from C.M. Lynch, 'Painted by Abbott'.

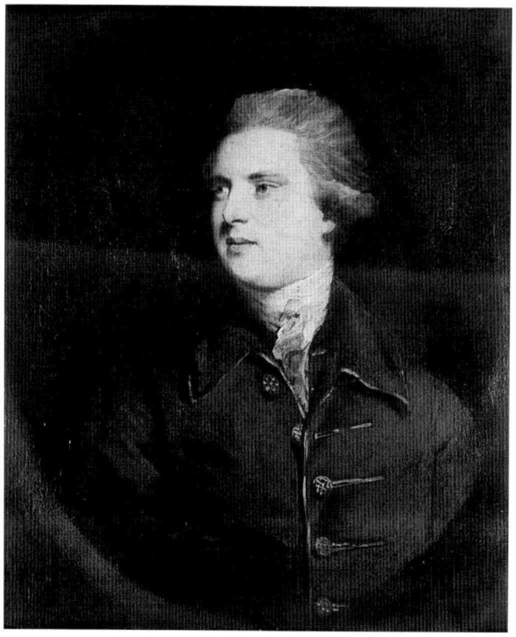

Earl MACARTNEY by Joshua Reynolds 1764 (Petworth House, The National Trust)

ICONOGRAPHY

c.1758 Painting by Robert Hunter, half length in a fur-trimmed cloak, 'aged 21'. with C.G. Macartney 1908 (illus. Robbins 1908, f.p. 12; Roebuck 1983, p.13). Offered to the NPG by the sitter's grand nephew in 1867.

1761 Drawing by Thomas Patch, whole-length seated. Private collection (illus. *Apollo*, LXXXV, 1967, p.353). A later inscription identifies *Lord Macartney*.

1764 Painting by Joshua Reynolds,* half-length painted oval. Petworth (Mannings 2000, no.1164). Engraved S.W. Reynolds 1820. A copy in Philadelphia Museum of Art (828).

Copy by Thomas Phillips at Petworth (Petworth cat., 1920, p.95, no.282, as painted in 1799 after the Reynolds portrait of 1764), exhibited RA 1800(322); another copy dated 1800 formerly at Holland House (cat., 1904, no.31). *Phillips Sitter Book* also records a portrait of Macartney painted for the Earl of Upper Ossory in 1800.

Copy by Malcolm Stewart 1905 in Government House, Cape Town.

c.1770 Pastel by Gustav Lundberg, half length, wearing the Polish Order of the White Eagle. Ulster Museum, Belfast (89; illus. Robbins 1908, front.).

c.1775 Unattributed miniature, bust-length oval, an illegible badge at his breast. with C.G. Macartney 1908 (illus. Robbins 1908, f.p.52, with a miniature

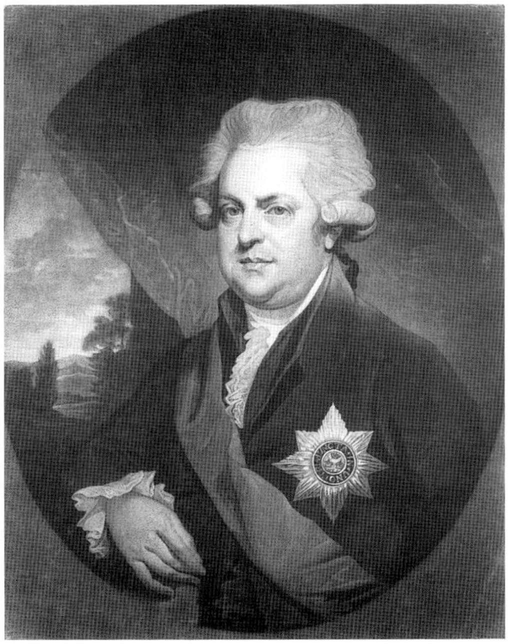

Earl MACARTNEY H. Hudson after Mather Brown 1789 (NPG D 13744)

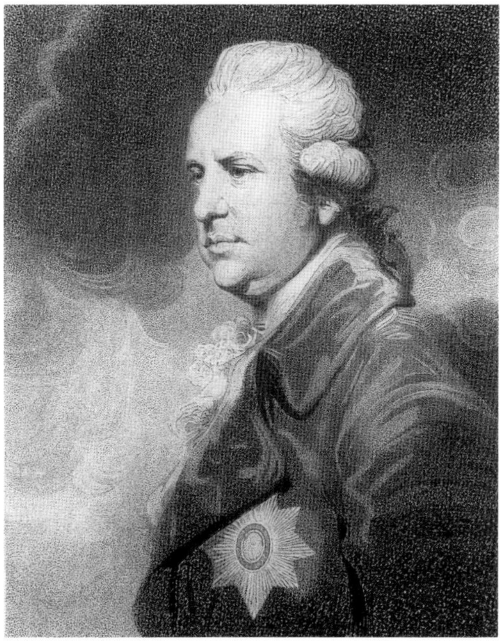

Earl MACARTNEY J. Singleton after Ozias Humphry c.1796 (NPG D 13803)

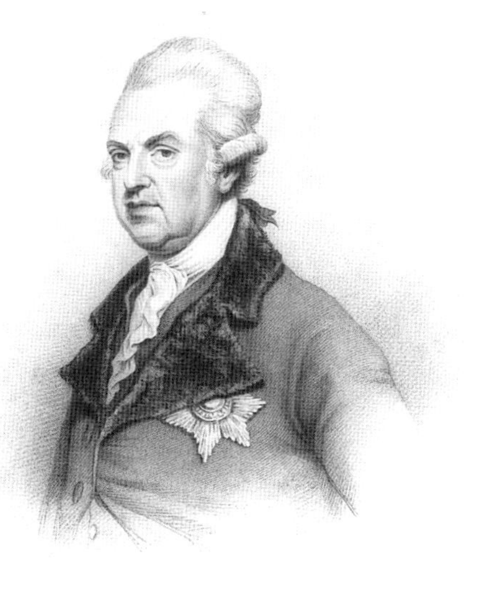

Earl MACARTNEY G.S. Bartolozzi after Henry Edridge c.1802 (NPG D 13743)

of his wife, an enamel version of which, signed and dated *I. Tayler...1786*, was sold Sotheby's, 7 November 1986, lot 235). An anon. half-length engraving 1781 (*London Mag.*) appears to derive from this miniature (although his badge is wrongly shown as that of the Garter).

1783 Painting by Johann Zoffany. Painted in Madras and mentioned by Macartney in a letter of introduction he wrote for Zoffany, who spent six weeks at Madras in July/August 1783 (Archer 1979, p.133).

c.1785 Painting by L.F. Abbott, *Lord Macartney and George Staunton*, see NPG 329.

c.1785 Painting by L.F. Abbott, half length, wearing the ribbon and badge of the Bath. Parke-Bernet, New York, 21 February 1945, lot 76, from Lord Portarlington's collection. The head somewhat resembles that seen in NPG 329.

1789 Painting by Joshua Reynolds. Untraced. Five sittings listed in 1789 with a payment of 50gns in July (Mannings 2000, no.1165).

1789 Painting by Mather Brown, half-length oval, with ribbon and badge of the Bath. Untraced. Engraved H. Hudson 1790* (Evans 1982, no.117). A pair of small half lengths by Brown of Macartney and his wife were listed in the Bute collection at Mount Stuart in 1931.

c.1789 Painting by Mather Brown, whole-length sketch standing in Peer's robes with badge of the Bath. Scone Palace (Evans 1982, no.118).

c.1789? Painting attributed to Mather Brown, half length, in the robes of the Bath. Col. H.T.W. Clements in 1969 (illus. Roebuck 1983, p.209); probably also the portrait in the Braemer sale, Paris, 3-5 June 1913, lot 88 as Hoppner.

1790 Painting by William Beechey, exhibited RA 1790(87). A half length by Beechey belonged to Col. H.P. Close, London.

1792 Pencil drawing attributed to William Alexander, bust-length profile, a badge on his right side, on board the *Lion* during his Chinese embassy. British Library (illus. Roebuck 1983, p.223). Alexander was the official draughtsman to the Chinese embassy 1792-94, and Thomas Hickey (see below) the painter (Archer 1979, p.218).

1792 Painting by Thomas Hickey, three-quarter length seated, with the ribbon and badge of the Bath. Probably RA 1792(391). Engraved J. Hall 1796 (illus. Roebuck 1983, p.223); R. de Launay (bust length). A half-length version sold Christie's, 15 June 1866, lot 26 signed and dated 1792 (TSB 3/8; also tracing by Scharf of 1859); another sold Sotheby's, 12 July 1989, lot 176 (as attributed to L. Abbott) and a third in the Brooks Museum of Art, Memphis (illus. *Sixty Paintings*, Memphis, 1966, no.22 as Copley).

1792 Painting by Simon de Koster, whole-length standing, in the robes of the Bath, his plumed hat at his side, pointing to China on a map. Bennett's, Dublin, 15 March 1898, lot 195, and probably Christie's, 7 May 1898, lot 86, as dated 1792 (listed by McKay & Roberts 1909, p.159 as Hoppner). Engraved C. Townley 1793 (illus. Robbins 1908, f.p.196).

1792-94 Etching by James Gillray, *Reception of the Diplomatique and his Suite at the Court of Pekin* 1792 (George 8121). Two drawings by William Alexander in the British Library, made during Macartney's Chinese mission in 1792-94, show Macartney in audience with the Emperor of China (illus. *Europa und die Kaiser von China*, Berlin, 1985, p.176) and a whole-length Macartney wearing the robes of the Bath which he wore for this audience (illus. *Connoisseur*, CC, 1976, p.125).

1795-97 Painting by an unidentified Italian artist, three-quarter length standing, with the ribbon and badge of the Bath, a letter on a table by him inscribed *Verona*. Sotheby's, 8 January 1964, lot 206.

c.1796 Pastel by Ozias Humphry, half length, with badge of the Bath. Private collection, USA, 1967 (illus. H.S. Berry-Hill, *Chinnery & China Coast Paintings* 1970, front.). Engraved J. Singleton 1796* (*European Mag.*); anon. (bust length) 1802 (*Public Characters 1802-03*). Previously attributed to John Russell (cf. Williamson 1894, p.161, and

Williamson 1917, p.246). An oval miniature version sold Sotheby's, 28 April 1988, lot 77, with the badge of the Garter.

1801 Portrait by Henry Edridge, exhibited RA 1801(379).

c.1802 Drawing by Henry Edridge, engraved L. Schiavonetti, as half-length oval with badge of the Bath, described as from a full-length drawing by Edridge *in his 65th year ... perhaps as a strong a character as the pencil is capable of producing* (Barrow 1807, I, p.370). Half-length chalk copy by G.S. Bartolozzi (British Museum, 1876.7.8.2365), engraved by him 1817.* A drawing by Edridge exhibited *Arts, Industries & Manufactures*, Dublin 1872(National Portrait Gallery 332) lent Lord Spencer (Althorp cat., 1851, no.500).

Unidentified portraits include those lent by Arthur Hume to the Dublin Exhibition of *Arts, Industries & Manufactures*, 1872 (National Portrait Gallery 183), and listed at Somerley attributed to Gilbert Stuart.

DOUBTFUL PORTRAITS

Paintings: attributed to John Hoppner, half length, versions in the Burdett-Coutts sale, Christie's, 4 May 1922, lot 35, and Lee sale, Knight, Frank & Rutley, 9 April 1930, lot 235; anon., oval profile head, exhibited NPE 1867(566) lent Lord Houghton; attributed to Francis Cotes, half length, sold Puttick & Simpson, 25 May 1930, lot 133; anon., half length in red coat with the badge of the Thistle, Sotheby's, New York, 22 May 1997, lot 165 attributed to Zoffany, and Sotheby's, New York, 8 January 1998, lot 110.

MACAULAY, Mrs Catharine,[1] *née* Sawbridge 1731-91

Radical historian; m. 1) 1760 George Macaulay, a Scottish physician (d.1766), 2) 1778 William Graham, a quack Bath doctor, some twenty-six years her junior; her *History of England from the accession of James I*, 1763-83, attracted much attention and was translated into French 1791-92; acclaimed in Paris 1777 and America 1784-85, but at home she became an isolated figure.

1 *Catherine Macaulay* is the name printed on the title page of vol. I of her *History.*, but *Catharine* is printed on the title page of vols. iii and v. She was called Catharine on the engraved portraits by Spelsbury and Williams; her current biographer Bridget Hill calls her Catharine Macaulay.

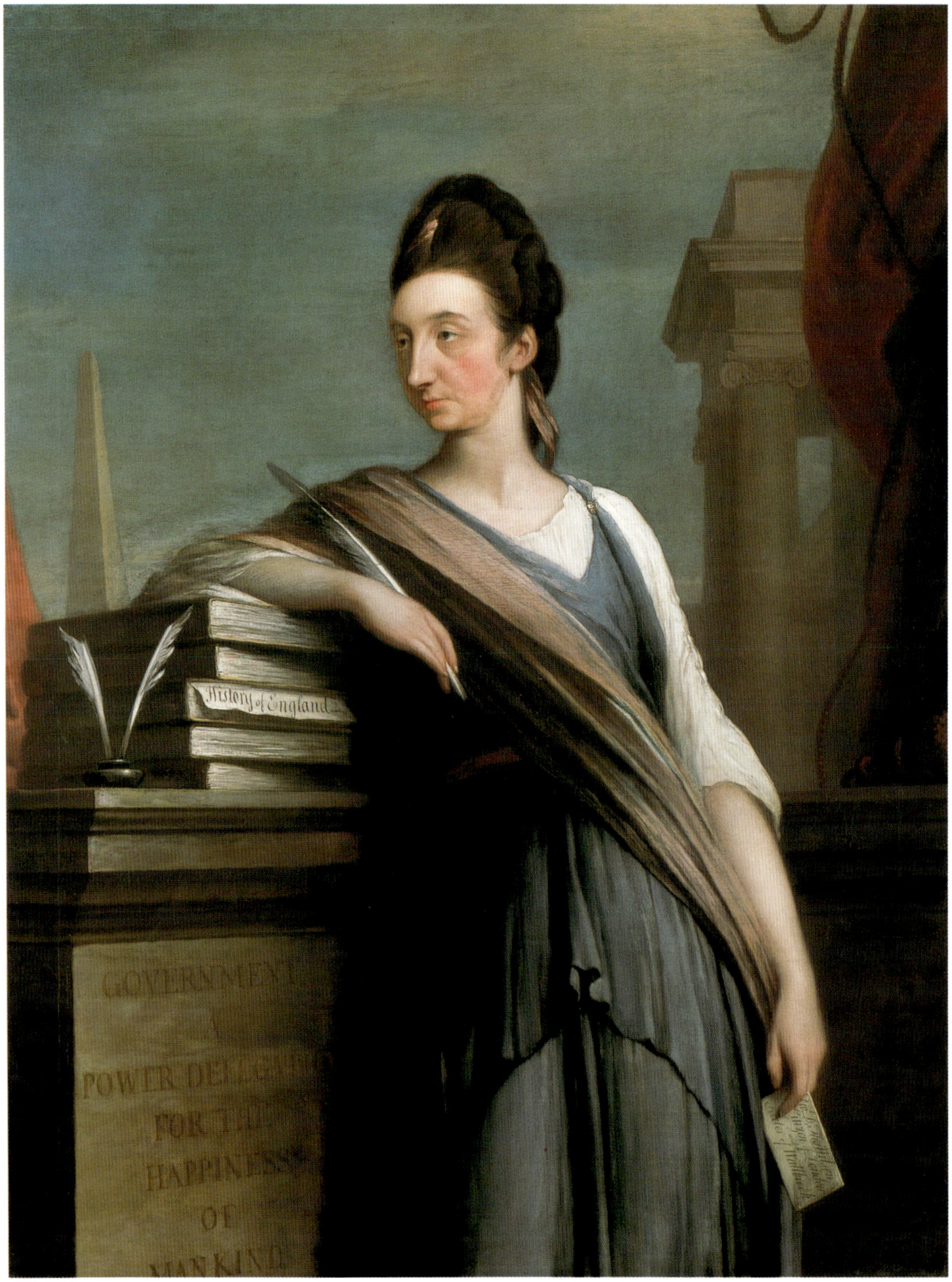

MACAULAY NPG 5856

'above the middling size, inclining to tall; her shape slender and elegant; the contour of her face, neck, and shoulders, graceful. The form of her face was oval, her complexion delicate, and her skin fine; her hair of a mild brown, long and profuse; her nose between the Roman and the Grecian; her mouth small, her chin round ... her eyes beautiful as imagination can conceive, full of penetration and fire, but their fire softened by the mildest beams of benevolence; their colour was a fine dark hazel, and their expression the indication of a superior soul' (Mrs Elizabeth Arnold, 1769).

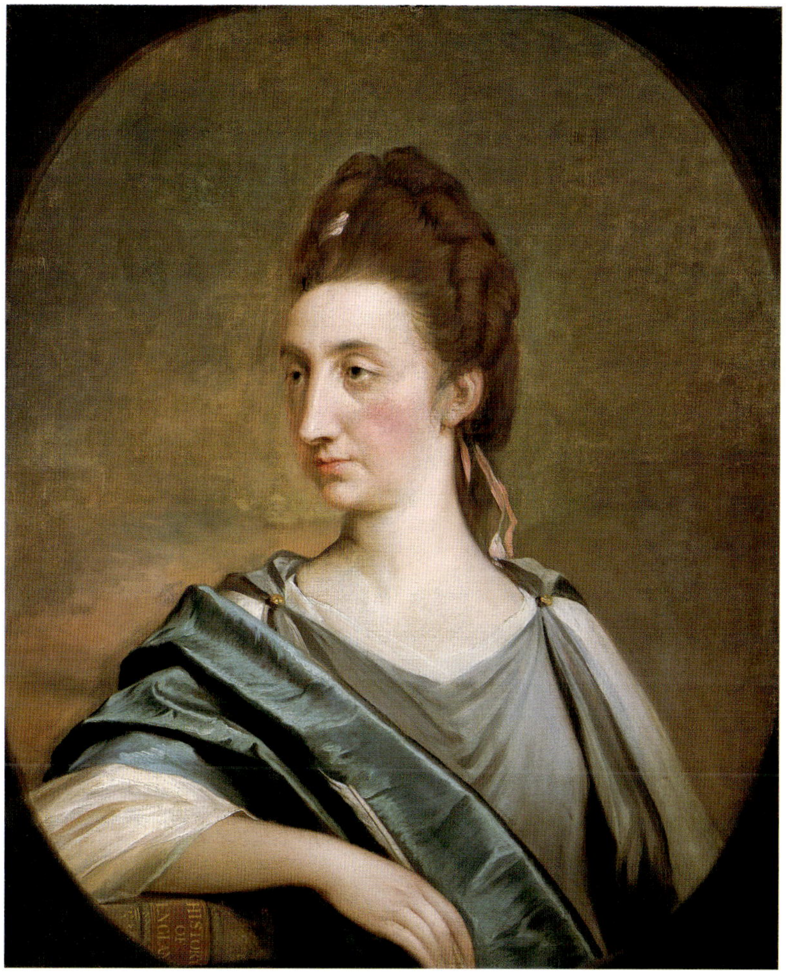

MACAULAY NPG 1357

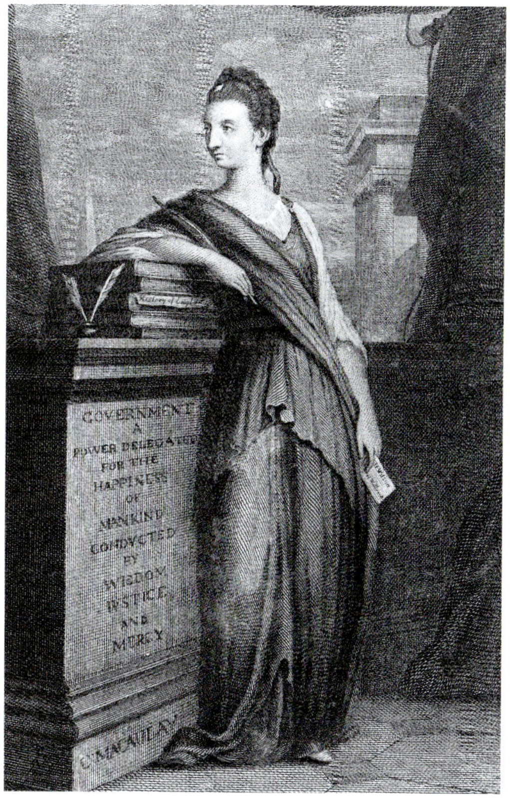

MACAULAY *J. Caldwall after R.E. Pine c.1775* (NPG D 18086)

Abbreviation

Hill 1992: Bridget Hill, *The Republican Virago, The Life and Times of Catharine Macaulay, Historian*, 1992

5856 ROBERT EDGE PINE c.1775

Canvas 136 x 104 (53½ x 41) lined; painted canvas is wrapped round the stretcher, the original canvas being some 123 cm wide, showing the far edge of the pedestal (see below); pentimenti indicate her right shoulder was lowered and there was a domed building beyond the portico on the right.

Brown eyes, brown hair with a purple ribbon, wearing a white tunic, a blue-grey dress and the purple scarf of a Roman senator; the paper in her left hand is inscribed: *Revd. Dr: Thos Wilson/ Citizen of London/ and/ Rector of Wallbrook.*; a quill in her right hand; five uniform volumes lie on the plinth, the middle with a slip inscribed: *History of England*; the plinth is inscribed: *GOVERNMENT/ A/ POWER DELEGATED/ FOR THE/ HAPPINESS/ OF/ MANKIND*; bright red curtain to the left and a dark red curtain on the right.

Collections: [Probably commissioned by the Rev Thomas Wilson, see below]; by descent within the sitter's family to Matthew Fortescue-Brickdale; sold Christie's, 22 November 1985,[1] lot 121, bt. in; purchased from Christie's, 1985.

Engravings: J. Caldwall (without artist's name) as whole length with, added to the inscription on the pedestal: */CONDUCTED/ BY/ WISDOM/ JUSTICE/ AND/ MERCY/ C MACAULAY.* – presumably the engraving of *Mrs Macauly* Caldwall exhibited FSA 1778(30); anon. reversed (whole length) with, below, the approximate arms of Sawbridge of Olantigh.[2]

Exhibition: *Pickpocketing the Rich*, Bath (Holburne), 2002(40).

Reference: B. Allen in *British Portraiture 1660-1960*, 1991, pp.200-01.

Cut down from the whole-length composition seen in Caldwall's engraving of 1778,* NPG 5856 now presents a mildly eccentric composition, with the head uncomfortably high within the canvas. It remains nonetheless of interest as a doctrinaire portrait of a remarkable woman.

It was painted in Bath, where Mrs Macaulay, then a relatively wealthy widow, had moved for her health in 1774. She had published the first five volumes of her *History of England* between 1763 and 1771 (as seen in NPG 5856; the sixth and seventh appeared in 1778 and 1783) and was already a celebrated figure. In Bath she met the widowed Thomas Wilson, absentee rector of St Stephen's Walbrook and nearly thirty years her senior, who quickly became her champion, giving her commodious lodgings at Alfred House, adopting her daughter in April 1775, pledging an inheritance,[3] and rendering himself 'truly ridiculous by the unaccountable frolicks of his attachment'.[4] The relationship ended with Mrs Macaulay's second marriage in November 1778.

Both Macaulay and Wilson were 'zealous for liberty' and friends of Wilkes, and so was the artist Pine, who was living in Bath 1772-79.[5] A Spartan picture, NPG 5856 shows Mrs Macaulay in a Roman setting, dressed as a Roman matron but wearing a senator's purple scarf, attributes synonymous with republican sympathies.[6] In 1772 her younger brother, the radical politician John Sawbridge, had been painted by Benjamin West as a Roman tribune.[7] In NPG 5856 prominent reference is made to her *History of England*, to Thomas Wilson and to a concept of democracy, through the inscription on the pedestal. The same (unidentified)[8] inscription appears on the scroll in the monument to Mrs Macaulay which Wilson commissioned from J.F. Moore[9] (see below). All of which suggests that NPG 5856, which descended through the sitter's family, may have been commissioned by Wilson, though that is unproven. Mrs Macaulay's continued interest in Pine is indicated by a letter from George Washington, telling her of the artist's activities in Philadelphia in 1787.[10]

Although sold in 1985 as by Pine, NPG 5856 was subsequently attributed to Chamberlin,[11] before reverting to Pine in 1990.[12] The execution seems entirely characteristic of Pine. It remains curious, however, that the untraced whole-length portrait of Macaulay by Chamberlin exhibited at the RA in 1774 was then described as

> bold, animated, and a good likeness of the original, but the under parts of the drapery are not cast full enough to give the whole sufficient ease; the general disposition of the picture, however, is very characteristic, she is drawn leaning on a term, supporting the volume of the history of England, on which is the following inscription: GOVERNMENT/ A power, delegated for the happiness of mankind,/ conducted by/ Wisdom, Justice and/ Mercy.[13]

An early 19th-century label on the verso of NPG 5856 states it was painted by Chamberlin.[14]

1 With two other Sawbridge family portraits - of Stephen Beckingham, Mrs Macaulay's brother-in-law, and Dorothy Sawbridge Beckingham, her niece.
2 *Or, two bars az. each charged with a barrulet dancettée ar.*, crest a head, bearded and hatted, and motto *WISDOM AND FORTIT*[*UDE*]); neither crest nor motto recorded in Burke's *General Armory*.
3 As recounted by Hume, 13 May 1776 (*Letters*, II, 1932, p. 321). Wright of Derby painted a double portrait of Wilson and Catherine Sophie Macaulay in 1776 (illus. *Bath History*, VI, 1996, p.138), see also Hill 1992, p.83 and f.p.114, pl.10.
4 *European Mag.*, IV, 1782, p.332.
5 For Pine's residence in Bath, see S.L. Sloman, *Bath History*, VI, 1996, p.139; for his radicalism, see J. Sunderland, *Burl.Mag.*, CXVI, 1974, pp.322-26; by 1772 he had painted portraits of Wilkes and the radical MP Richard Oliver.
6 See the engraved portraits of Mrs Macaulay of 1765 and 1770 described below.
7 Destroyed (but engraved), see Erffa & Staley 1986, no.694.
8 E.g. Hill 1992, p.100, quoted without attribution; it is given to Macaulay in the contemporary engraving by Caldwall (see above).
9 He had previously made monuments for the radical William Beckford sr.
10 16 November 1787 (*NQ*, 5/ix, 1878, p.421).
11 See NPG, *Complete Illus. Cat.*, 1981, p.371.
12 B. Allen and D. Solkin, for example, urged the Pine reattribution (letter of 23 July 1990; NPG archive).
13 Quoted by Susan Sloman, *Pickpocketing the Rich*, Bath (Holburne), 2002, p.21.
14 *Catherine Wife of George/Macaulay M.D. & daughter of /John Sawbridge Esqr of Olantigh/Kent. Sister to Mrs Beckingham/ Author of The History of England/ & other works -/Painted by Mason Chamberlayne.* Susan Sloman has speculated on whether Chamberlin was unable to produce replicas of his 1774 picture and Pine produced a similar portrait instead (*Pickpocketing the Rich*, p.21).

1357 ROBERT EDGE PINE c.1775

Canvas 75.5 x 63 (29¾ x 24¾) lined; retouching in the background, a pentimento on the right sleeve.

Grey-brown eyes, light brown hair with pink ribbon, wearing a white tunic, a pale blue-grey dress and blue silk scarf; a quill in her right hand, her right arms resting on a volume titled *HISTORY OF ENGLAND*.

Collections: Purchased from C.W. Radeke 1904.[1]

Exhibition: Beningbrough 1979–

NPG 1357 appears an autograph work by Pine, and derives closely from NPG 5856.

1 Radeke wrote: 'I own amongst a number of old family portraits which have been handed down in my family for generations, also one which is not of the family but represents the Historian Mrs Markham ... by Angelica Kaufmann.' (6 January 1904; NPG archive). It was immediately identified by Lionel Cust as Mrs Macaulay.

4905 see Groups, *Portraits in the characters of the Muses* by RICHARD SAMUEL 1778

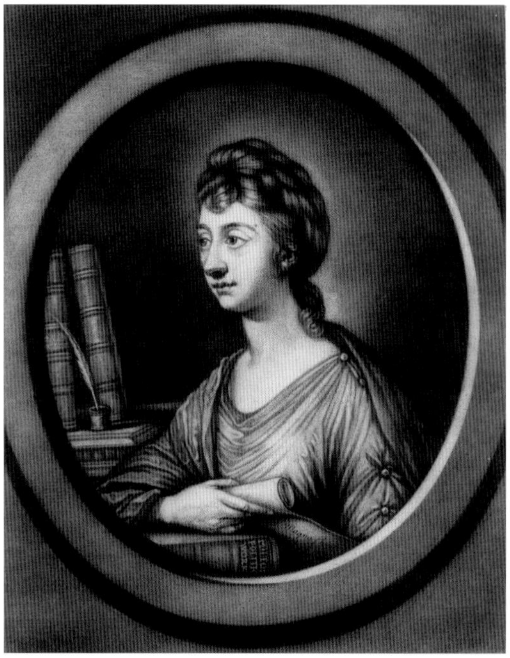

MACAULAY J. Spelsbury after Katherine Read 1764 (NPG D 13745)

ICONOGRAPHY

1764 Pastel? by Katherine Read, half-length seated, a scroll inscribed *Magna Charta* in her right hand which rests on a volume titled *MILTON/POLITIC/ WORKS*; engraved J. Spelsbury [Spilsbury],* a later reversed engraving 1812 pub. Vernon Hood & Sharpe. See also 1770 below.

1765 Drawing by G.B. Cipriani, engraved J. Basire, profile medallion bust lettered *CATHARINA MACAULAY*, with a small roundel below of four Romans with axe and fasces, inscribed *BRUTUS* (illus. Hill 1992, f.p.114, pl.1). Frontispiece for the third volume of Mrs Macaulay's *History*, published in 1767, in imitation of a Roman coin in honour of the republican Brutus, showing the head of Liberty; the small roundel represents the reverse of this coin, showing Brutus's four sons led to execution for having conspired with the deposed King Tarquin.

1770 Engraving by J.M. Williams, half-length oval, *In the Character of a Roman Matron lamenting the lost Liberties of Rome, from an original painting by Miss Read.* Williams exhibited an engraving of 'Mrs Macauley, in the character of a Roman Matron', SA 1773(360).

1772 Wax bust by Patience Wright; '[Mrs Macaulay] may live by the fingers of Mrs Wright as long as in her republican history, wherein she has given us a picture of her mind; but Mrs Wright has preserved to us the person of this celebrated and patriot female' (*London Mag.*, XLIV, 1775, pp.53, 556; *Wal. Corr.*, XXXII, p.98 and n24). Wright had come from America, see also Garrick and Wilkes.

1772 Painting by P-E. Falconet, small whole length, exhibited SA 1772(99).

1773 Painting by Richard Atkinson, exhibited SA 1773(1), 'indifferent & little like' (*Wal. Soc.*, XXVII, 1939, p.60).

1774 Painting by Mason Chamberlin, whole length, exhibited RA 1774(34), see NPG 5856.

c.1775 Painting by R.E. Pine, see NPG 5856 and NPG 1357.

1777 Statue by J.F. Moore,* Roman classical figure, quill in right hand, a scroll in her left, the base inscribed *HISTORY*. Warrington Reference Library; formerly in St Stephen, Walbrook, commissioned by Thomas Wilson, rector, unveiled in September 1777 (*GM*, XLVII, 1777, p.458) but removed soon after (Mrs Macaulay not being a parishioner). Engraved anon., the scroll inscribed: *GOVERNMENT IS A POWER DELEGATED FOR THE HAPPINESS OF MANKIND* and a long inscription on the base (see Hill 1992, p.100-01).

c.1777 [Painting?] by Bonnieu, engraved [J.J.?] Hubert, half-length oval within an elaborate frame; presumably published during or soon after her visit to Paris in 1777. A more modest version engraved Marais *le jeune* c.1792 [*Mme. Macaulay/ Histoire*

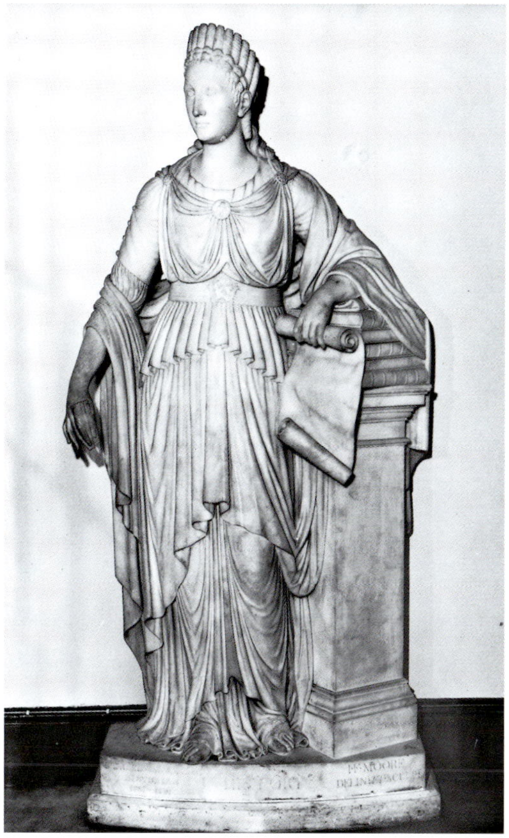

MACAULAY by J.F. Moore 1777 (Warrington Library, Cheshire)

d'Angleterre] presumably for the French translation of her *History* (illus. Hill 1992, f.p.114, pl.6).

1778 Painting by Richard Samuel, *Portraits in the characters of the Muses*, in which Macaulay is alleged to appear; see Groups NPG 4905.

1778 Engraving by J. Caldwall, exhibited FS 1778(30), see NPG 5856.

1791 Medallion portrait on her monument in All Saints church, Binfield, Berks.

DOUBTFUL PORTRAITS

A half-length portrait attributed to Gainsborough, exhibited *Gainsborough*, Grosvenor Gallery, 1885(206) lent E.P. Roberts, from the collection of Mrs D. Arnold, Macaulay's sister-in-law; listed in W. Armstrong, *Gainsborough*, 1898, p.199. In 1899 J.J.G. Graham, a great nephew of Mrs Macaulay, wrote that he knew of only two portraits of her; 'one I possess, either a Romney or a Gainsborough; the other was bought at a sale of Mrs Dr Arnold's effects (the said Dr Arnold was a nephew of Mrs Macaulay's second husband), and is now in the possession of Mr E.P. Roberts.' (*NQ*, 9/iv, 1899, p.238).

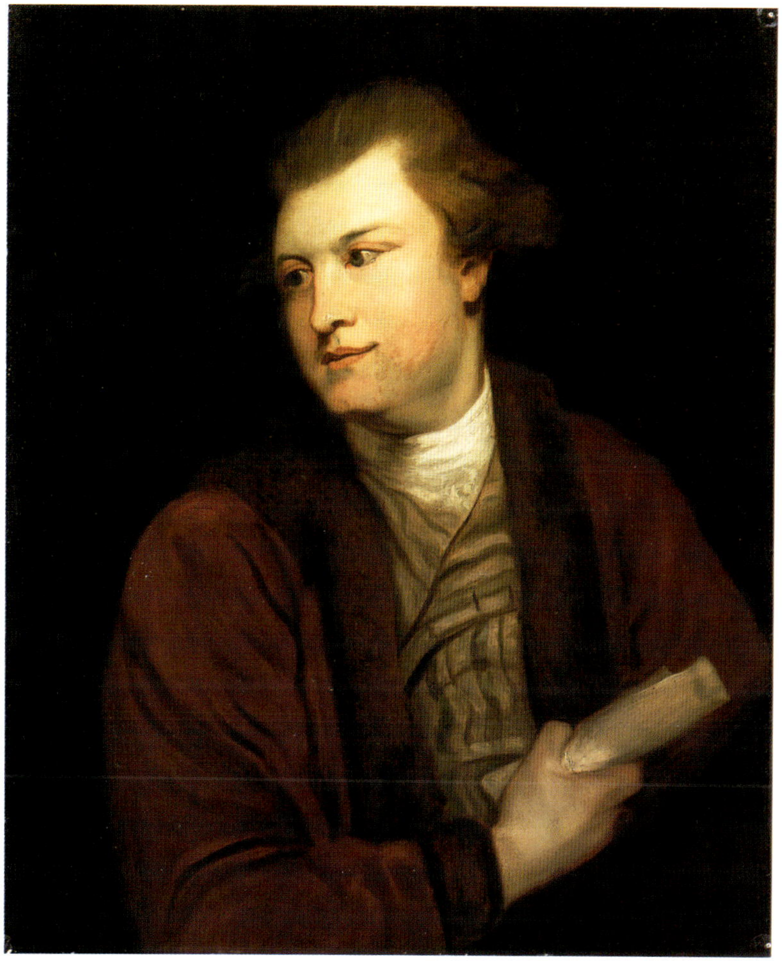

MACPHERSON
NPG *983*

MACPHERSON, James 1736-96

Miscellaneous writer; b. Ruthven, Inverness; published *Fragments of Ancient Poetry collected in the Highlands* 1760, Ossian's *Fingal* 1762 and *Temora* 1763; through Lord Bute, his literary sponsor, made secretary of West Florida 1764-66; published *A History of Great Britain* 1775; as London agent for the Nawab of Arcot from 1778, wrote a history of the East India Company 1779; MP 1780-96; buried, on his own direction, in Westminster Abbey.

'He was good-looking, of a large size, with very thick legs, to hide which he generally wore boots, though then not in fashion. He appeared to me proud and reserved ...' (Alexander Carlyle, recalling 1759).

'[He] was a handsome man, - six foot three inches in height, of a fair and florid complexion, the countenance full, and somewhat inclining to the voluptuous in expression, but marked by sensibility and acuteness' (Robert Carruthers, 1843).

983 after JOSHUA REYNOLDS [1772]

Canvas[1] 76 x 63 (30 x 24¾) lined 1895; abrasion below the chin, prominent retouchings in the face, and a damaged area upper left; discoloured varnish.

Blue eyes, brownish hair, wearing a red coat with a dark fur collar over a silver waistcoat striped with green.

Collections: Presented by Henry Willett 1895.

Reference: Mannings 2000, no.1168a.

A weak copy of the Reynolds portrait at Petworth painted in 1772.[2] Other copies sold Sotheby's, 14 May 1986, lot 189, and in the Scottish National Portrait Gallery (PG 1439). An oval miniature copy attributed to Ozias Humphry was sold Christie's, 18 December 1979, lot 59,[3] presumably related to the 'small enamel portrait of Macpherson, the duplicate of one painted for the Nabob of Arcot, also by Sir Joshua' seen in the Macpherson home, Balavil House [Belleville], c.1840.[4]

1 The linen stamp copied on the lining canvas: *D 30 17 70* [?].
2 Mannings 2000, no.1168; engraved J.K. Sherwin 1775; C. Knight 1805; J. Fittler 1805, and W. Bond 1806 and 1813.
3 Probably that exhibited SKM 1865(1252), lent Lea.
4 R. Carruthers, *The Highland Notebook*, 1843, p.307.

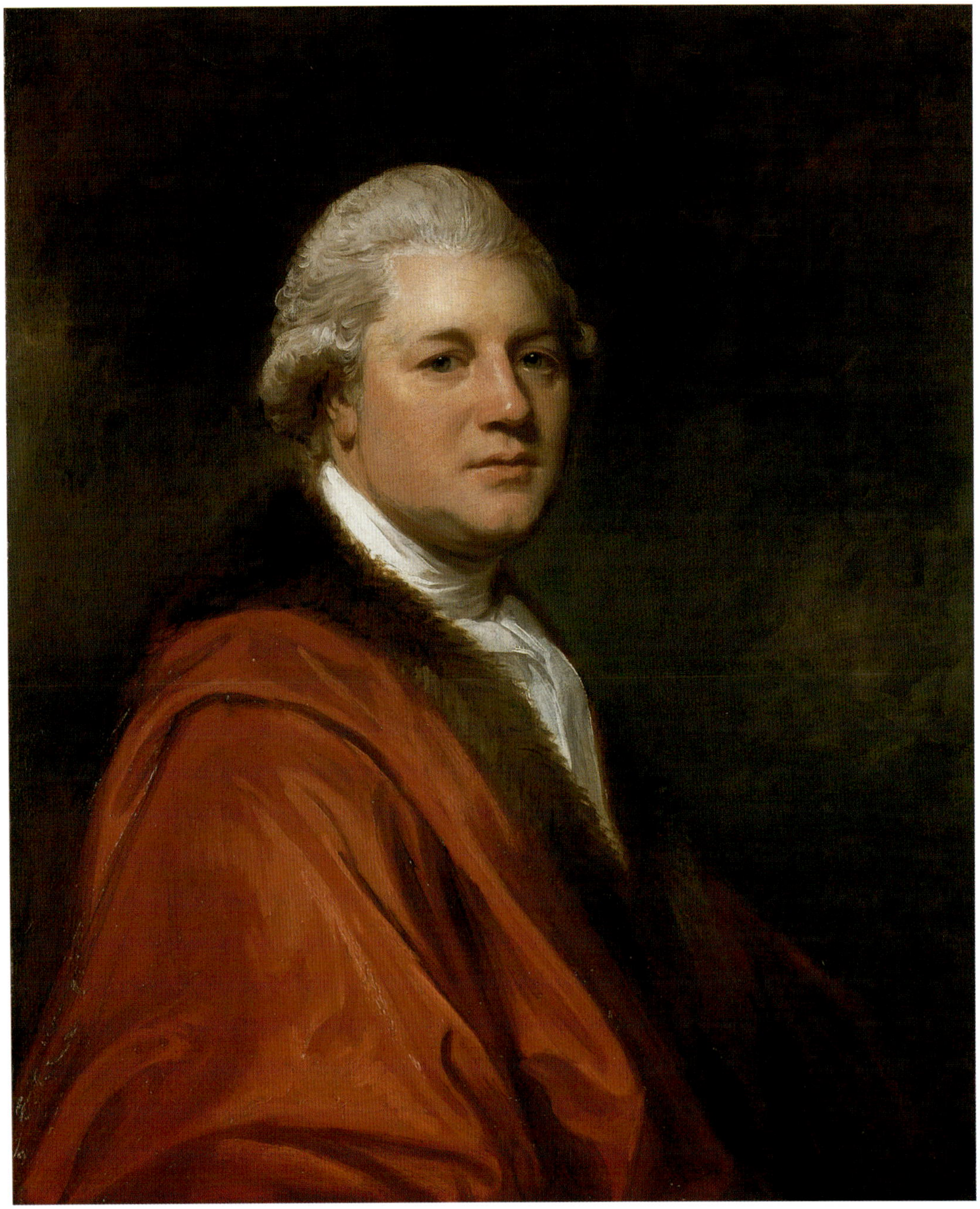

MACPHERSON NPG 5804

5804 GEORGE ROMNEY 1779–80

Canvas 76 x 63.5 (30 x 25) lined; original canvas inscribed verso: *J Maxton Graham Cultoquhey Portrait of James McPherson Esq Romney.*

Blue-grey eyes, white powdered hair, wearing a red silk gown with black fur trim.

Collections: Painted for Sir Richard Sullivan (d.1806), 1st Bt of Ember Court, Thames Ditton; his son Sir Charles Sullivan, 3rd Bt; sold Christie's, 15 June 1859, lot 28,[1] bt. Graves for James Maxton Graham;[2] by descent to R. Maxton Graham; sold Sotheby's, 21 March 1979, lot 93, bt. Agnew, from whom purchased 1985.

Exhibitions: NPE 1867(775); *Scottish Portrait*, Edinburgh, 1884(320); *The Portrait Surveyed*, Agnew, 1980(33); *Romantic Icons*, Grasmere 1999(10).

Reference: Ward & Roberts 1904, II, p.99.

Richard Sullivan, who paid Romney 18gn. for NPG 5804 in 1784, had published *An Analysis of the Political History of India* in 1779, the year Macpherson published his *History of the East India Company*. Macpherson's sittings to Romney in August 1779 and January and February 1780 possibly included a second portrait, see below.

1 Label formerly on the stretcher: *James Macpherson Esq/The Translator of Ossian/ Painted by Romney/ This Picture was painted/ for Sir Richard Sullivan Bart./ and sold with his Collection/ of Pictures by his son/ Sir Ch Sullivan Bt/ by Christie & Manson in/ 1859*. It was sketched by Scharf at Ember Court, 28 May 1858 (SSB 51/49a).

2 Whose name is inscribed on the verso of the original canvas (see above); Graham acquired the portrait since his relative, Lord Lynedoch had been the pupil of Macpherson (Ward & Roberts 1904, II, p.99).

ICONOGRAPHY

1772 Painting by Joshua Reynolds, see NPG 983.

1772 Painting by David Martin, kitcat, exhibited SA 1772(201).

1779–80 Painting by George Romney, see NPG 5804.

c.1779–80? Painting by George Romney, half-length seated. By descent to C. Brewster Macpherson in 1904 (illus. B. Saunders, *James Macpherson*, 1895, front.).

c.1800 Marble memorial pillar with a medallion portrait of Macpherson. Kingussie (Highlands and Islands).

MAITLAND, James Maitland, Viscount, see LAUDERDALE

MALONE, Edmond 1741–1812

Literary critic and editor; b. Dublin (yr. bro. of Richard, cr. Lord Sunderlin 1785); after practising at the Irish bar settled in London 1777; elected to Johnson's Club 1782; assisted Boswell in editing the life of Johnson; DCL Oxford 1793; edited the works of Goldsmith 1780, Shakespeare 1790, and Dryden 1800.

'I weighed at ... Oct. 4th, 1791, eleven stones two pounds. Height five feet six inches and a half' (Edmond Malone, 1791)

'His countenance had most pleasing expression of sensibility and curiosity. When I saw him, his dress was unlike that of most other gentlemen of the time. He wore a light blue coat, white silk stockings, and I think buckles in his shoes. His hair was white and tied behind.' (a lady, quoted by Prior 1860).

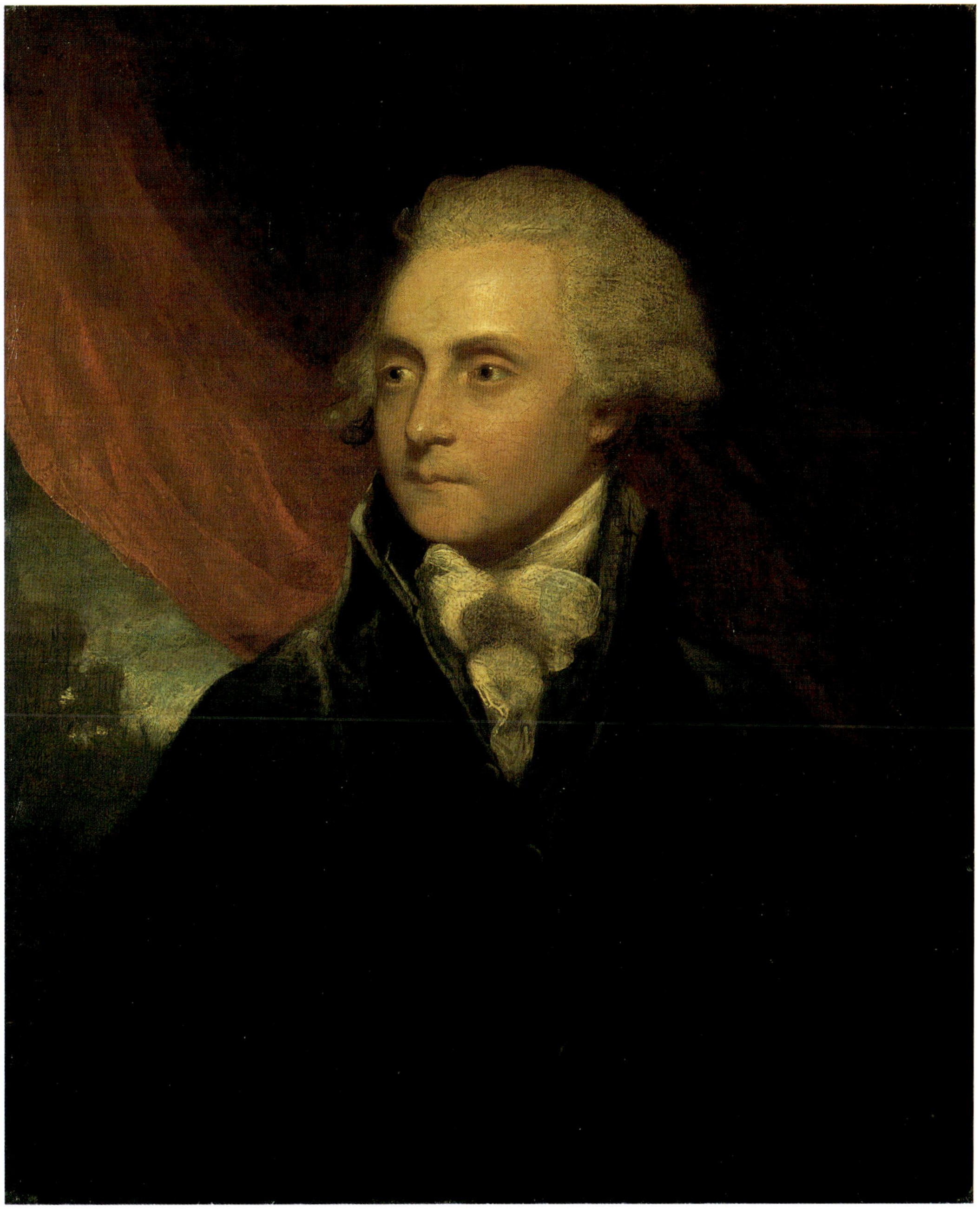

MALONE NPG *709*

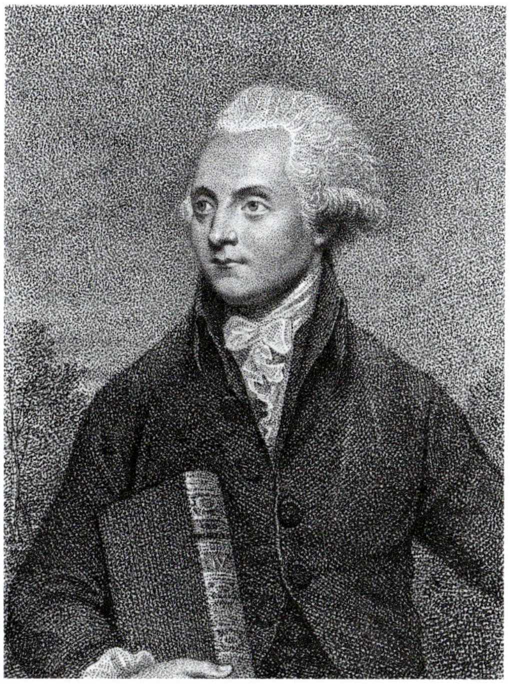

MALONE F. Bartolozzi 1787 after Joshua Reynolds (NPG D 5194)

Abbreviation

Prior 1860: J. Prior, *Life of Edmond Malone*, 1860

709 JOSHUA REYNOLDS 1778 and c.1786

Canvas 75 x 62 (29½ x 24½) lined; heavily restored; discoloured retouchings in the numerous wide drying cracks and further repaired losses in the coat and curtain; the varnish is discoloured. X-radiography shows alterations in the background, head, shoulders and in the lower left area (see below). An old inscription on wood is attached to the stretcher: *Edmond Malone Painted by Sir Joshua Reynolds in 1778- Retouched in 178*[9?].

Grey eyes, grey powdered wig; wearing a blue-grey coat and white neckcloth; a red curtain behind him.

Collections: By descent from the sitter's elder brother, Richard, Lord Sunderlin, who m. Dorothea Rooper, to the Rev W.H. Rooper (c.1808–95), from whom bt., 19 April 1883,[1] by Sir William Agnew,[2] and presented by him 1883.

Engravings: F. Bartolozzi, 3rd state dated 1787 (book in his right hand, sky behind him, see below); C. Knight 1791 (as NPG 709, see below); R. Page 1813 (half-length oval with plain background); S.W. Reynolds (as the Bartolozzi); J.C. Armytage 1860 (as the Bartolozzi); J. Scott 1865 (as NPG 709).

Exhibitions: Probably RA 1779(225, 'a gentleman'); NPE 1867(565) lent Rooper; *Reynolds*, Grosvenor Gallery, 1883–84(148) lent Agnew; *Boswell*, NPG, 1967(96); *Reynolds*, Plymouth, 1973(48); *Johnson*, Arts Council, 1984(70).

Reference: Graves & Cronin, II, pp.609–10; Waterhouse 1941, p.70; Mannings 2000, no.1180.

According to the painter's sister Frances, Malone was 'the greatest friend and admirer of Sir Joshua that he ever had perhaps',[3] while for Malone 'from the time of our first being acquainted, [Reynolds] always showed me great kindness and partiality'.[4] Prior recalled that the two men were 'of similar stature and weight, and although of considerable difference in age, each fond of testing his physical vigour as a pedestrian'.[5] Malone was one of Reynolds's three executors[6] and the first editor of his literary works (1797).

Malone recalled[7] Reynolds taking 'very particular pains in drawing my picture. I think I did not in the whole sit for it less than twelve or fourteen times. He painted first in the year 1778, when I sat seven or eight times.[8] Again, about ten years afterwards, he repainted it, making several alterations in the hair, drapery, &c'.[9] The original appearance of NPG 709, prior to the repainting, is preserved in the engraving by Bartolozzi (the third state published in 1787)* and remains legible by x-radiography; the hair was fuller on the top of the head, the shoulders and collar were were lower, the background was open sky and in his crooked right arm he carried a quarto volume (which Bartolozzi lettered *Old Worthies/IV* - illegible on the x-radiograph). It was also in 1786 that Reynolds was asking Malone to 'run your eye over my Discourse ... in regard to grammatical correctness, the propriety of expression, and the truth of the observations'.[10]

The differing engravings of the portrait (as listed above) led some earlier writers to suppose two distinct portraits.[11] A copy of NPG 709 was in a private collection in New York in 1990, and another was formerly with A.S. Drey, Munich.[12]

1 Date taken from Mannings 2000, no.1180.
2 A note of 4 July 1883 in the NPG archive reads: 'On the steamboat returning from the Tower of London [June 1883] Mr Agnew made an off-hand offer of the portrait'; William Agnew had told Scharf that it was 'purchased by my firm from Malone's descendant . . . the Rev W.H. Rooper'.
3 To Elizabeth Reynolds, 1 December 1796 (Yale Center for British Art, MS Reynolds 57).
4 Prior 1860, p.433.
5 *Ibid.*, p.65.
6 Each of whom was left £200 'to be laid out, if they should think proper, in the purchase of some picture at the sale of [Reynolds] collection, to be kept for his sake' ([Malone], *Testimonies to the genius and Memory of Sir Joshua Reynolds*, 1792, pp.112-13).
7 Prior 1860, p.434.
8 Malone paid Reynolds 35 gn. for his portrait in July 1778 (Cormack 1970, p.159); there is no sitter book for that year, but ten appointments with Malone between February and July 1779 may have been sittings (as opposed to social engagements).
9 In August-September 1786 Reynolds pocket book shows five appointments for Malone which may have been sittings.
10 Letter of 15 December 1786; Ingamells 2000, p.177.
11 For example, Graves & Cronin, II, pp.609-10.
12 Mannings 2000, nos.1180a & b.E. Hamilton, *Engraved Works of Sir Joshua Reynolds*, 1884, p.179, listed a second portrait then belonging to Col. Anthony Malone.

ICONOGRAPHY

1778 and c.1786 Painting by Joshua Reynolds, see NPG 709.

1797 Ozias Humphry. Untraced. On 9 October 1797 Lord Charlemont wrote from Dublin to Malone saying he had received as a gift from the artist 'a portrait of you by Humphry, as like as possible, and as well painted as I would wish him to paint ... It is the exact resemblance of an absent friend' (*Charlemont Papers*, HMC, II, 1894, p.309).

1811 Miniature by G. Chase, exhibited RA 1811(711).

MALTON, Charles, Earl of, see ROCKINGHAM

MANSFIELD, William Murray, 1st Earl of 1705-93

Judge; KC and solicitor general 1742; attorney-general 1754 and lord chief justice 1756-88; an outstanding advocate who defined much of English commercial law; cr. Baron Mansfield 1756, Earl of Mansfield 1776; d. at Kenwood, which he had bought in 1754.

[in 1777] 'the roses and lilies had not yet forsook his cheeks; and the lustre of his complexion was augmented by means of eyes that seemed to sparkle with genius. His person, if somewhat below the exact standard of beauty, was yet exquisitely formed; his motions were graceful; his dress neat, becoming, and appropriate' (Alexander Stephens, 1813).

Abbreviations

Holliday 1797: J. Holliday, *Life of William late Earl of Mansfield*, 1797

Lord Mansfield 1971: J. Jacob, *The true resemblance of Lord Mansfield*, Kenwood, 1971

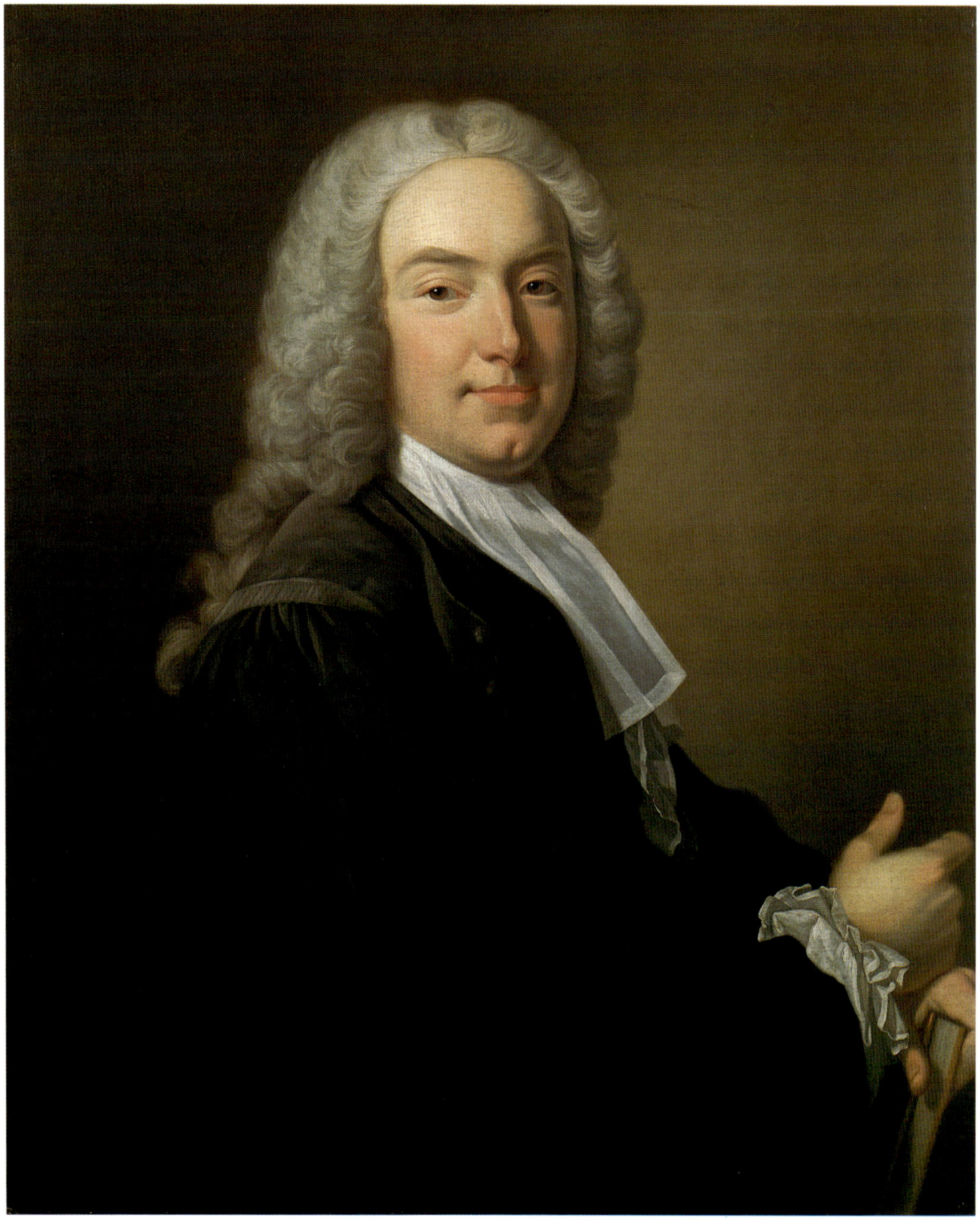

1st Earl of MANSFIELD NPG *474*

474 JEAN-BAPTISTE VAN LOO 1737–38

Canvas 75.5 x 63 (29¾ x 24¾) lined; pentimenti on the white bands.

Brown eyes, powdered wig, wearing white bands and a black 'bar' gown over a black coat.

Collections: John Holliday (c.1730–1801), Lincoln's Inn; Sir William Horne Kt (d.1860), Lincoln's Inn, by whom presented 1839 to the Hon Society of Judges and Serjeants-at-Law; presented by the Society 1877.

Engraving: J. Basire 1797 (for Holliday's *Life* see below).

Exhibition: *Lord Mansfield* 1971(12).

Reference: Holliday 1797, p.281.

Van Loo's portrait was described in 1797 by its first known owner, the barrister John Holliday, as being 'in high preservation in the chambers of the Author ... in Lincoln's Inn;' full of 'vivacity and spirit', it showed 'Mr Murray, when a young barrister, in his maiden bar gown, about the year 1734'. The engraving of 1797, listed above, is lettered: *J. Bapt. Vanloo Pinxt.1732/ The Honourable William Murray/ Aetat 28.* But since Van Loo only arrived in London in December 1737 (and left in October 1742), a date of 1737–38 seems more likely. NPG 474 was attributed to Ramsay when first acquired.[1]

Versions are at Kenwood[2] and Scone Palace, the latter differing in detail, with his right index finger pointing and the left shoulder just visible. A portrait of Lord Mansfield 'when a very young man beginning to study the Law ... without date or name', conceivably of this pattern, was at Witley in 1796.[3]

Van Loo used the face mask for three other portraits of Murray, see below.

1 NPG cats.; first given to Van Loo in the 15th edition 1920.
2 Illus. *English Heritage, Collections Review*, III, 2001, p.47.
3 Musgrave MSS 6391, f.239v.

172 JOHN SINGLETON COPLEY 1782–83

Canvas 225 x 147 (88½ x 58) lined; repaired tear in the paper lying on the table and minor losses in his right knee and in the top left background; slight pentimenti on his right shoulder and in the chair legs; signed bottom right: *J.S. Copley. pinx.*

Grey eyes, grey full-bottomed legal wig, wearing a black suit and an Earl's parliamentary robes; the manuscripts on the table are deliberately illegible; above the door, behind him, is a bust, probably of Pope (see below).

Collections: Sir Francis Buller, 1st Bt (d.1800); the artist's son, Lord Lyndhurst; his sale, Christie's, 5 March 1864, lot 81, purchased.

Exhibitions: RA 1783(5); *Copley*, Metropolitan Museum of Art, New York, 1936–37(39); Royal Courts of Justice, London, 1958–85; *Copley*, Washington, New York, Boston, 1965–66(76); *Lord Mansfield*, Kenwood, 1971(53).

Reference: Prown 1966, II, pp.426–27; *Copley* 1995b, pp.50–52.

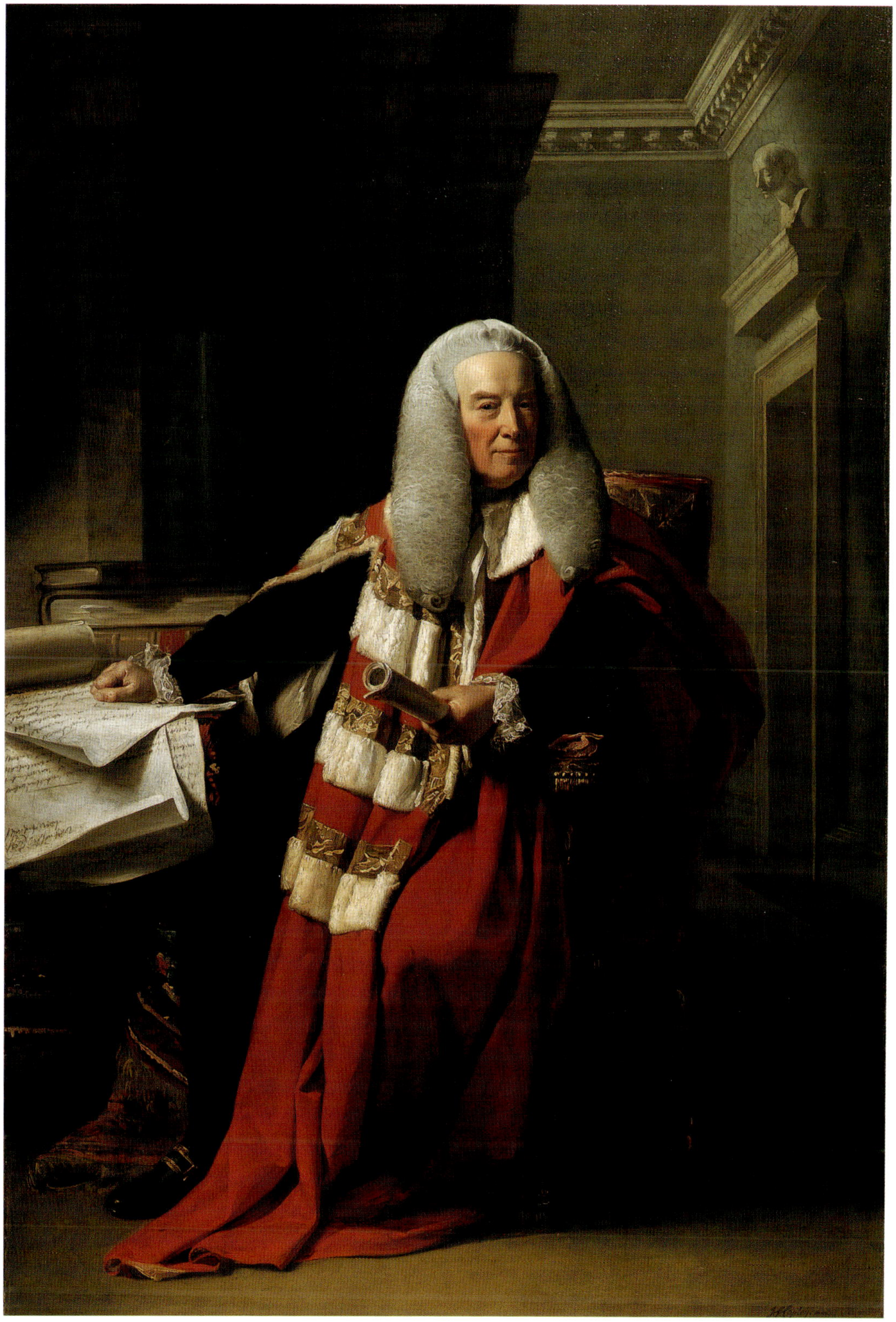

1st Earl of MANSFIELD NPG *172*

Although NPG 172 passed to Lord Lyndhurst, the artist's son, the *Morning Chronicle*, 30 April 1783, asserted that it had been commissioned by Mr Justice Buller, who had greatly benefited from Mansfield's patronage;[1] Holliday alleged that Mansfield sat 'no less than four times to Copley, out of respect to Mr Justice Buller'.[2]

Ultimately derived from the impassive figure of Mansfield in Copley's *Death of Chatham* (see p.533), NPG 172 is an animated and powerful portrait. A number of compositional drawings reveal Copley's initial uncertainty; while the figure was always whole length, looking right, robed and seated, the body and arms were variously disposed.[3] The bust perched oddly above the door behind him is presumably intended for Pope, his 'friend and favourite',[4] of whom Mansfield had an unidentified bust at Kenwood.[5] When the portrait was shown at the RA in 1783, the *Public Advertiser* congratulated Lord Mansfield on the 'apparent amelioration of his taste. As long as we can remember he has been in the worst hands, Ramsay, Martin and so on ... we do not despair of soon seeing him the Patron of Painters worth patronizing, Romney, Gainsborough and Reynolds'.[6]

A three-quarter length version from Inworth Hall was sold Phillips, 19-20 September 1951, lot 26; a miniature copy by William Birch dated 1785 is in the Harvard Law School and another, the date illegible, was sold Christie's, Geneva, 28 April 1976, lot 156.

1 Sir Francis Buller, see NPG 458. Mansfield eased his legal promotion and was to leave him £2,000. See W.L. Pressly in *Copley* 1995b, p.52, and *Lord Mansfield* 1971, no.26.

2 As John Jacob commented (*Lord Mansfield* 1971, introduction, n.p.), this may have been confusing Mansfield with Camden, who sat four times to Dance.

3 Illus. Prown 1966, II: Yale University AG (fig.430); Museum of Fine Arts, Houston (fig.431); Mead Art Museum, Amherst, Mass. (fig.432); Cleveland Museum of Art (fig.434); British Museum, 1913.5.28.20 (fig.435), and unlocated (fig.433).

4 Holliday 1797, p.284. Pope addressed Mansfield in his Imitation of *Horace's Epistle I*, vi: 'Grac'd, as thou art, with all the power of words,/So known, so honour'd, at the House of Lords' (48-49).

5 D. Lysons, *Middlesex*, III, 1795, p.349 ('in the breakfast parlour is a bust of Pope'); W.K. Wimsatt, *The Portraits of Pope*, 1965, p.235. The bust formerly at Kenwood is now identified as that by Roubiliac in Leeds CAG, see *Lord Mansfield* 1971, no.3, and M. Baker in *Return to Life*, exhibition cat., NPG etc., 2000, p.29; the socle does not agree with that shown in NPG 172, but it is unnecessary to seek such a detail in what was evidently intended by Copley to be a generalised reference.

6 Whitley 1928, I, p.362. A portrait by Ramsay, Martin's teacher, remains untraced, but see NPG 474, which was once attributed to him.

ICONOGRAPHY

There have been two surveys of Mansfield's portraiture: J. Holliday, *Life of William late Earl of Mansfield*, 1797, pp.281-84 and J. Jacob, *The true resemblance of Lord Mansfield*, exhibition catalogue, Kenwood, 1971. The first is eccentric and at times demonstrably at fault, the second exemplary.

c.1737-38 Painting by J-B. Van Loo, see NPG 474.

c.1737-38 Painting by J-B. Van Loo, seated three-quarter length, the head agreeing with NPG 474. Kenwood (1296), ex Christie's, 12 April 1991, lot 10. Engraved A. Baillie. Other versions at Scone Palace (illus. *Lord Mansfield* 1971, n.p.), Glynde Place, Raby Castle and Crarae.

A 'full-length' portrait by Van Loo, which by 1797 had passed from James Booth (Mansfield's Catholic conveyancer) to the Duke of Norfolk (Holliday 1797, p.282), may have been of this type, together with the three-quarter length copy by Ranelagh Barrett 'after Venloe' at Dupplin Castle in 1799 (Musgrave MSS 6392, f.55), and the portrait Holliday described as by Hudson ('animated likeness' and 'inimitable drapery') painted for Hoskins of Lincoln's Inn and belonging to Smith 'an eminent solicitor in Chancery'.

A curious variant at Gosford House shows the same composition but with a profile head which closely resembles that drawn by Falconet in 1768; exhibited *Lord Mansfield* 1971, no.42 as Martin; formerly at Christ Church, Oxford, where dated 1757 (when Martin was twenty) and disposed of in 1770 (Poole, III, pp.73-74), when replaced by the Martin whole length, see below.

c.1737-38 Painting by J.B. Van Loo, half-length, his left hand in his waistcoat, his hat under his arm. Versions at Crarae, Welbeck (*Portland Cat.* 1936, no.478; exhibited *Art in Nottinghamshire*, Nottingham, 1937, no.481 as by William Hoare), and Kenwood (attributed to J.G. Eccardt after Van Loo; *English Heritage Collections Review*, III, 2001, p.39), the versions showing different wigs. The figure is closely adapted from Van Loo's seated three-quarter length.

c.1737-38 Painting by J-B. Van Loo, three-quarter length seated, in undress with velvet turban. Royal College of Physicians, London (illus. *Cat. of Portraits*, 1964, p.29, and 1977, p.151). In 1964 identified as John Arbuthnot and attributed to Jervas. Version in the Clarendon collection (Gibson 1977, no.97), and a weak half-length, the book lettered *Cicero*, sold Christie's, 25 May 1984, lot 106.

1743 Marble bust by J.M. Rysbrack. Scone Palace (illus. *Lord Mansfield* 1971, no.36; *Sculpture and Scotland 1540-1990*, 1991, p.141). Presumably the 'bust of his Lordship, when young, in the hall' at Kenwood in 1795 (D. Lysons, *Middlesex*, III, 1795, p.349).

1757 Unattributed painting, dated 1757, listed at Christ Church, Oxford (Poole, III, p.74), see under Van Loo c.1737-38.

1768 Drawing by P-E. Falconet, engraved anon. (*GM*).

1770 Painting by David Martin,★ half-life size whole length, seated, wearing a Baron's coronation robes, his right hand on an open *Cicero*, a bust of Homer behind him. Scone Palace. A replica, showing slight variations in the hands, is at Kenwood (exhibited *Lord Mansfield* 1971, no.67). The type engraved D. Martin 1775 (as painted in 1770), the plate not agreeing in every detail with these versions. The bust of Homer had been presented him by Pope; it recurs in the Jervas portrait of Pope (NPG 112) and is now in Scone Palace (exhibited *Lord Mansfield* 1971, no.5). Holliday 1797, p.281, described a full length by Martin in coronation robes, inscribed with a six-lined latin motto, belonging to Mansfield's physician, Dr Turton, at his house in the Adelphi; a portrait by Martin of 1770 listed at Dupplin Castle in 1799 (Musgrave MSS 6391, f.49).

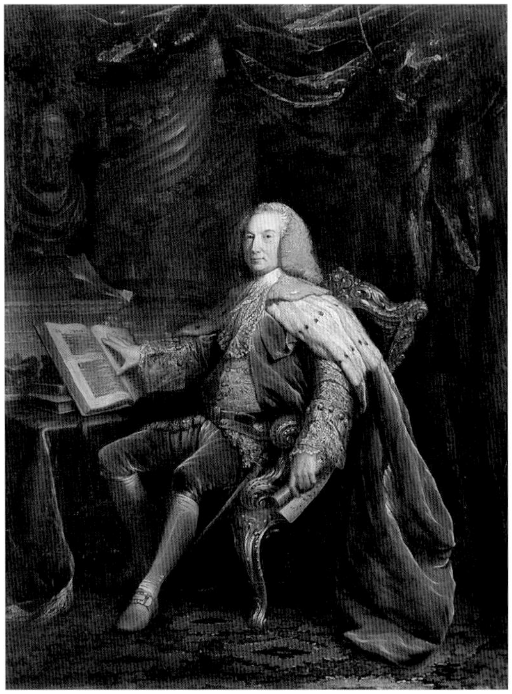

1st Earl of MANSFIELD by David Martin 1770 (The Earl of Mansfield)

A three-quarter length version (110 x 136, as if cut from a life-size whole length), sold Sotheby's, 11 July 1984, lot 39. Another, with plain columns and the book lying on the table, belongs to the Faculty of Advocates, Edinburgh (illus. J.L. Caw, *Scottish Portraits*, II, pl.lxxvi; exhibited *Lord Mansfield* 1971, no.17). A half-length version sold Christie's, 23 March 1979, lot 116. A three-quarter length watercolour copy was listed at Clumber House (cat., 1923, no.445). An oval chalk drawing for the head is in the Scottish NPG (PG 1445).★

c.1775 Painting by Johann Zoffany, *Merchant of Venice with Macklin as Shylock* (Tate Gallery) portrays Mansfield as one of the Venetian magnificos on the extreme left (see C. Hughes, *Burl. Mag.*, CXXIII, 1981, pp.290-95).

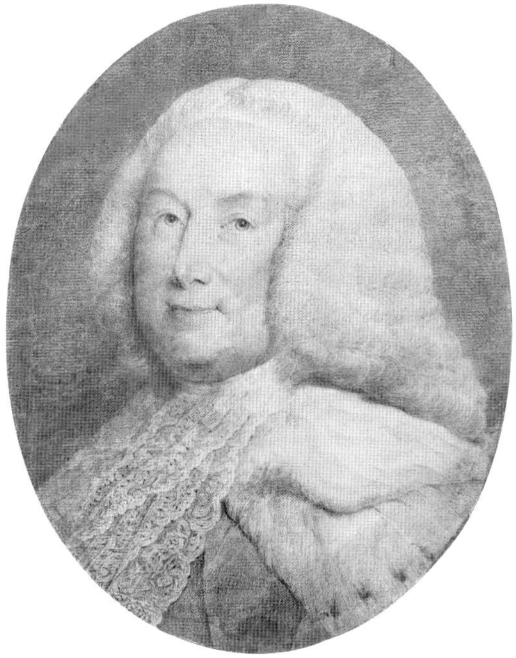

1st Earl of MANSFIELD by David Martin 1770 (Scottish National Portrait Gallery)

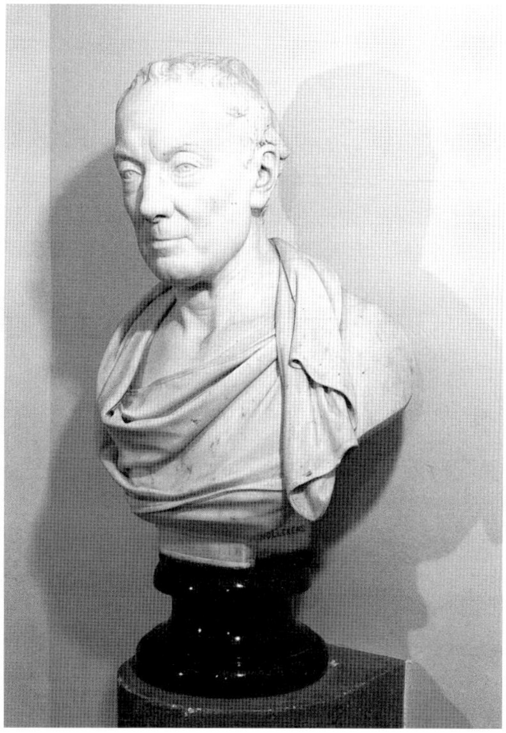

1st Earl of MANSFIELD by Joseph Nollekens 1779 (Trinity Hall, Cambridge)

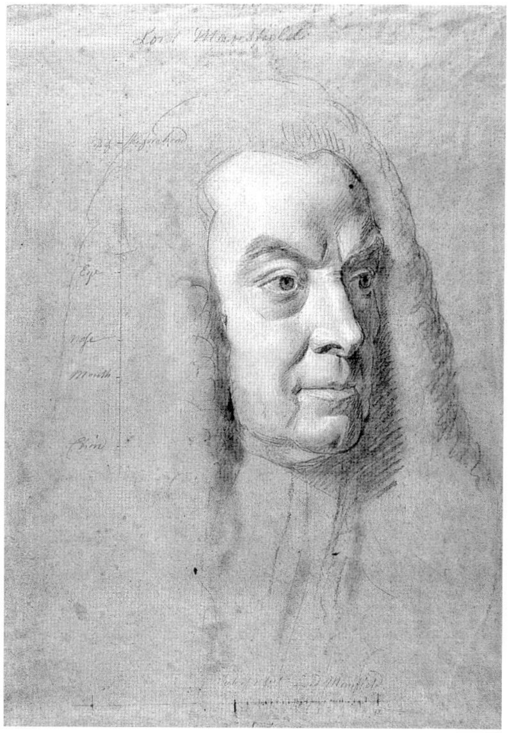

1st Earl of MANSFIELD by J.S. Copley 1779-81 (Boston Athenaeum)

1776 Painting by David Martin, essentially repeating the 1770 design, but life size and with the coronation robe of an Earl (Mansfield received his Earldom in 1776). Scone Palace; originally in the library at Kenwood and the the most imposing of Martin's many Mansfield portraits. Exhibited *Lord Mansfield* 1971, no.92. Replica at Christ Church, Oxford; a half life-sized version dated 1777 is in the Scottish NPG (PG 598). A copy by Wendy Norris 1992 is now in the library at Kenwood.

c.1776 Painting by David Martin, standing three-quarter length in a library (with busts of Socrates and Homer above the shelves). W.M. Sabin 1934 (illus. *CL*, CXLIX, 1971, p.1166). Probably the portrait described by Holliday 1797, p.283, as belonging to John Way of Acton, 'in the grave yet elegant dress in which his Lordship was presented to the late most unfortunate French king and queen at Versailles in 1774, viz in a well-dressed tie-wig, a black velvet coat, and a handsome white embroidered waistcoat'.

1776-77 Medals by John Kirk, exhibited SA 1776(220) and 1777(222).

1779 Marble bust by Joseph Nollekens. Kenwood. Exhibited RA 1779(217); *Lord Mansfield* 1971(48). Close variants at Trinity Hall, Cambridge,* 'a very strong, expressive, and animated likeness' (Holliday 1797, p.284) and Belvoir Castle (dated 1790). A plaster at Hartlebury Castle (J. Nankivell, *The Collection of Portraits at Hartelbury Castle*, 1953, p.22, unattributed).

1779 Medallion by James Tassie, as chief justice, inscribed on truncation *uni aequus virtuti* (Gray 1894, no.251). Examples Kenwood and Scottish NPG (PG 2589; illus. *Sculpture and Scotland 1540-1990*, 1991, p.148). Engraved anon. (pub. in Perth) 1788; T. Holloway 1793; W. Ridley 1798 (for *Junius* 1799 ed.); J. Hopwood 1805. Copied by Wedgwood (Reilly 1973, p.227).

A second classical medallion by Tassie exists in three variants, differing slightly in size, one without drapery (Gray 1894, nos.252-54).

1779-81 Painting by J.S. Copley,* *The Death of Chatham*, see Comparative Groups. Of Mansfield's portrait it was said: 'perhaps one of the finest portraits on the scale in which he is drawn in the known world' (*Gazetteer*, 7 May 1781). 'Almost as much unmoved as the senseless body itself', Mansfield was criticised for his coolness towards Chatham which 'the Painter has very properly expressed ... by fixing him in his Chair, while the whole House is on Tip-Toe' (*St James's Chronicle*, 9-12 June 1781). A drawing for Mansfield's head is in the Boston Athenaeum;* another, apparently made after the head and attributed to Bartolozzi, is in the Metropolitan Museum of Art (illus. *Metropolitan Museum of Art Bulletin*, XIV, 1956, p.124).

1781 Wax medallion by Isaac Gosset, wearing parliamentary robes. Hartlebury Castle (J. Nankivell, *The Collection of Portraits at Hartelbury Castle*, 1953, p.22).

1782-83 Painting by J.S. Copley, see NPG 172.

1785 Painting by Joshua Reynolds,* seated three-quarter length, in the robes and full-bottomed wig of the lord chief justice - 'his countenance much changed since he lost his teeth'. Scone Palace (Mannings 2000, no.1318). Engraved F. Bartolozzi 1786; H. Meyer 1812 from a drawing by John Jackson, and many times thereafter. A replica destroyed by fire at Belvoir Castle 1816. A copy attributed to John Jackson c.1812 at Kenwood; other copies Georgetown University Law Center, Washington DC; Sotheby's, 16 May 1990, lot 45, and on loan to the Law Courts (GAC 0.131). Reduced bust-length copies in Harvard Law School and the Scottish NPG (PG 312, by Mason 1866). Enamel copies by William Birch, dated 1788 and 1793, at Kenwood (Draper collection), and dated 1793 in the Ashmolean Museum, Oxford; at Crarae; sold Christie's, 2 May 1961, lot 77, and 10 November 1993, lot 25, and Bonham's, 25 November 1998, lot 107. Enamel by Henry Bone, exhibited RA 1803(634); example at Kenwood (Draper collection); preparatory drawing, dated 1803, in the NPG Bone albums (*Bone* 1999, no.339).

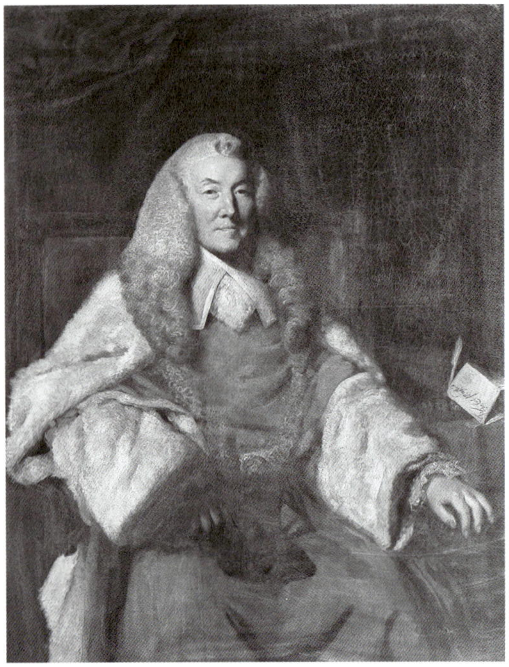

1st Earl of MANSFIELD by Joshua Reynolds 1785 (The Earl of Mansfield)

before 1793 Painting by William Grimaldi, three-quarter length seated in private dress, engraved J. Jones 1797 (for Holliday's *Life*), the original then belonging to a Dr Combe (see *Lord Mansfield* 1971, no.81).

1793 Miniature by J. Hutchison [Hutchinson], exhibited RA 1793(362).

Undated Wax by Samuel Percy. Brighton MAG. Others sold Christie's, 31 January 1800 and 18 July 1857 (Pyke 1973, pp.104-05).

Posthumous

1801 Monument by John Flaxman, Westminster Abbey (illus. Whinney 1964, pl.146). Engraved J. Godby 1812. The figure based on the Reynolds portrait of 1786. Painted by J.P. Neale, exhibited RA 1817(997). A cast exhibited Crystal Palace (Phillips 1854, no.448).

1855 Marble statue by E.H. Baily. Palace of Westminster.

Mansfield appears as a tiny gesturing figure in Wootton's *View from Caen Wood House over London* 1755 (private collection; exhibited *Wootton*, Kenwood, 1984, no.32). An unattributed painting of Mansfield as attorney-general, Strawberry Hill sale, 18th day, 14 May 1842, lot 105, may have related to the Wootton composition.

Holliday also listed an unspecified portrait belonging to Andrew Moffat and formerly with Caleb Whiteford (p.283), and a miniature belonging to George Brooks of Grosvenor Square (p.284).

MARKHAM, William 1719-1807

Prelate; headmaster of Westminster school 1753-65; royal chaplain 1756; Dean of Rochester 1765-67; Dean of Christ Church 1767-77; Bishop of Chester 1771-77, preceptor to the Prince of Wales 1771-76, and Archbishop of York 1777-1807; a 'warlike metropolitan archbishop' (Walpole).

'a tall portly man and 'high he held his head' ... His business was rather in courting the great than in attending to the school ... He had a great deal of pomp, especially when he lifted his hand, waved it, and repeated Latin verses' (Jeremy Bentham).

'in his person [he] is tall and graceful, and in his manners and address extremely dignified. He is supposed to have always rather too much indulged a constitutional indolence, and to this is owing that so little has been contributed to the instruction of the public by a man of such superior abilities and attainments' (*Public Characters of 1805*).

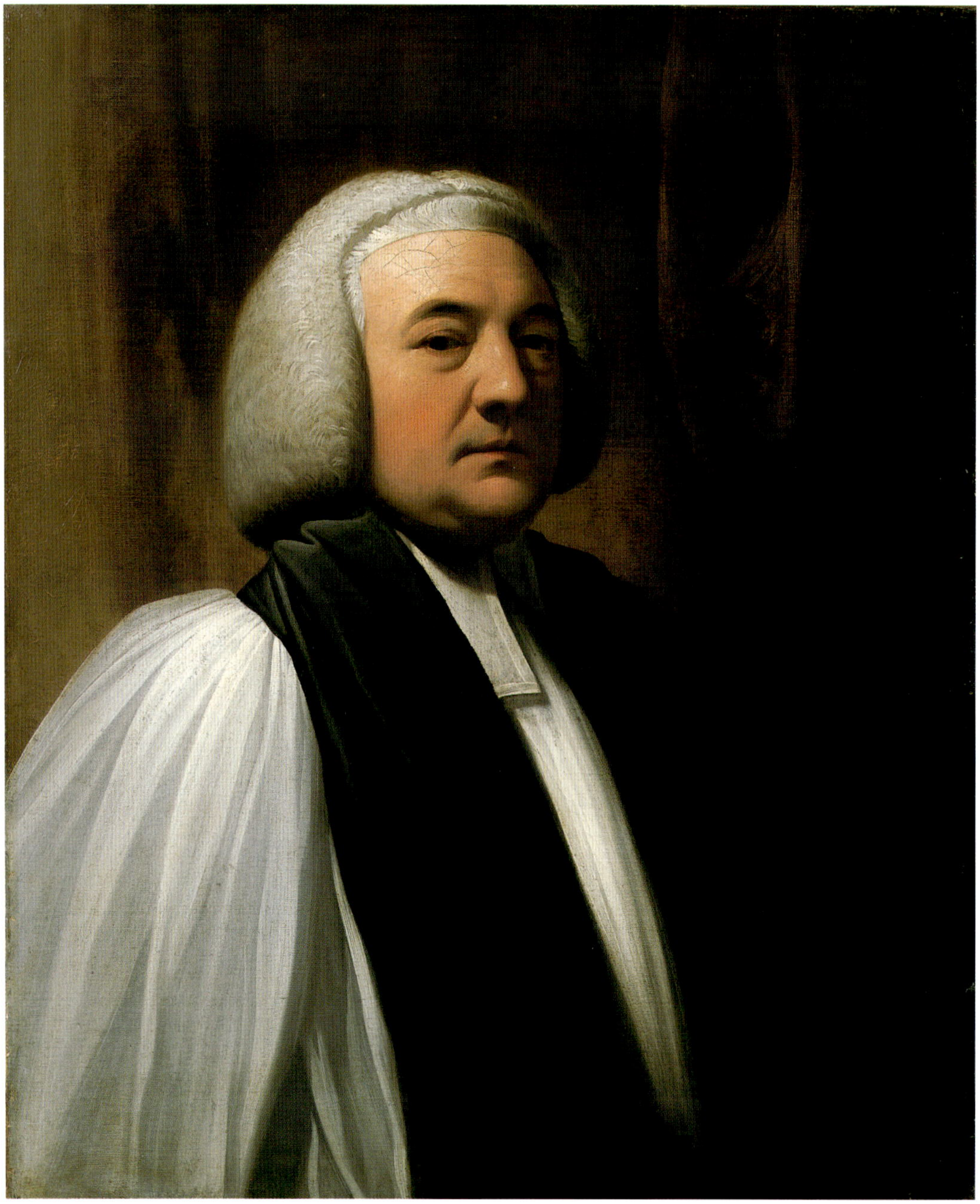

MARKHAM NPG 4495

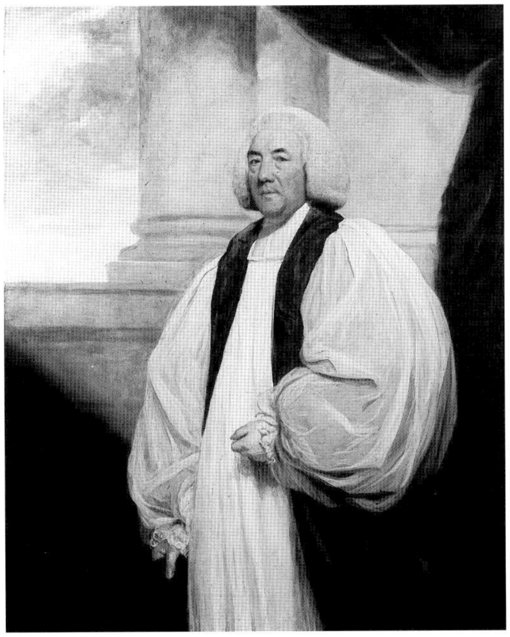

MARKHAM by Joshua Reynolds 1777 (Christ Church, Oxford)

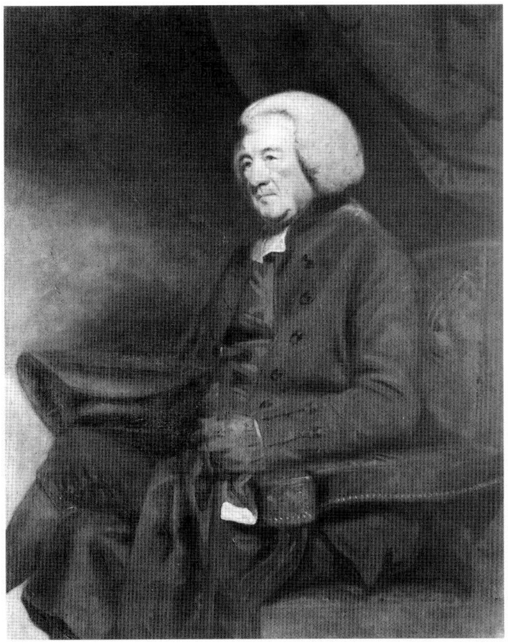

MARKHAM by John Hoppner 1799 (The Royal Collection)

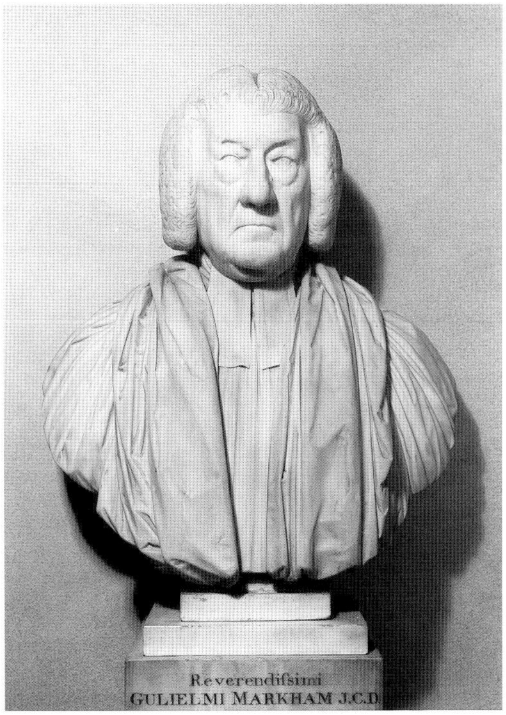

MARKHAM by John Bacon junior 1804 (Christ Church, Oxford)

4495 BENJAMIN WEST c.1775

Canvas 76 x 63.5 (30 x 25);[1] unlined; marked craquelure in the face; an old ink label on the stretcher: *Wm. Markham/ Archbishop of York/ when Bishop of Chester/ by Sir Benn West.*

Grey eyes, white wig, wearing Bishop's rochet and chimere; a brown curtain on the right.

Collections: By descent in the sitter's family to P.G. Markham,[2] from whom purchased, though Colnaghi, 1966.

Exhibitions: Leeds 1868(3241) lent Col. W.T. Markham; Art Gallery, Christchurch, New Zealand, 1965, lent P.G. Markham.[3]

Reference: Ingamells 1981, p.287; Erffa & Staley 1986, no.655.

When headmaster of Westminster, Markham was among the first to welcome Benjamin West in England, introducing him to Burke and Johnson in 1763, and to a number of distinguished Bishops in 1765 (Newton of Bristol, Johnson of Worcester and Drummond of York).[4] Markham is not known to have acquired works from West, other than NPG 4495 which, according to the label cited above, was painted between 1771 and 1777 while he was Bishop of Chester; it evidently precedes the Reynolds of 1777 (see below).

1 The adjustable stretcher, without a cross bar, is original, see Rica Jones, *The Conservator,* XV, 1991, p.14.
2 C. Markham, *Markham Memorials*, 1913, II, p.49; letter from P.G. Markham, Waikato, New Zealand, 25 September 1966 (NPG archive).
3 The picture was taken to New Zealand in 1938, see note 2.
4 J. Galt, *Life and Works of Benjamin West*, 1820, II, pp.6–7, 9.

ICONOGRAPHY

1759 Painting by Joshua Reynolds, half length in gown and bands. Christ Church, Oxford (Mannings 2000, no.1220). Engraved E. Fisher.

c.1775 Painting by Benjamin West, see NPG 4495.

1777 Painting by Joshua Reynolds,* three-quarter length in rochet and chimere. Christ Church, Oxford (Mannings 2000, no.1221). Exhibited RA 1778(247); NPE 1867(717). Engraved J.R. Smith 1778; S.W. Reynolds (and in reduced form by C.T. Warren 1792, J. Hopwood 1807). A studio version at Bishopthorpe Palace and copies at Powderham Castle and Christ Church, Oxford.

1779–81 Painting by J.S. Copley,* *The Death of Chatham*, see Comparative Groups.

1790–94 Painting by George Romney, three-quarter length in private dress. Christie's, 16 July 1982, lot 63. Sittings took place between May 1790 and April 1794 (Ward & Roberts 1904, II, p.100). Engraved J. Ward 1800. A replica was in Romney's sale, 27 April 1807, lot 31.

1795 Ozias Humphry, exhibited RA 1795(422) and 'much approved' (Farington, 18 April 1795).

1799 Painting by John Hoppner,* three-quarter length seated in private dress. Royal Collection (Millar 1969, no.847). Exhibited RA 1799(84). Engraved J. Heath 1807–10 (he exhibited a plate after Hoppner RA 1830, no.983, and see C. Baker, *British Art Jnl.*, II, 2001, pp.36–38). Copies at Westminster School, Bishop's House at Chester, and Scone Palace. Miniature by William Grimaldi with the Markham family in 1913 (Grimaldi 1873, nos.326–28); two enamel copies by Henry Bone, one exhibited RA 1800(896), another in the Royal Collection (Walker 1992, no.781); preparatory drawings in the NPG Bone albums (*Bone* 1999, nos.341–42, figs. 137, 140).

1804 Bust by John Bacon jr.,* with wig and bands. Christ Church, Oxford (Poole, III, p.79). Exhibited RA 1804(939). Another dated 1813 at Windsor Castle (illus. *Connoisseur*, CXXXII, 1953, p.118; Gunnis 1968, f.p.16). Examples were with the Markham descendants and at Kenwood in 1913; a plaster is in York Minster Library.

1805 Drawing by Henry Edridge, exhibited RA 1805(637).

Minor images include: a crude anon. bust-length circular engraving 1783 (*accurately drawn from an original picture*; *New Christian Mag.*); and two caricatures, by Burnet 1782 *A Bp Laud charging his Clergy* (head taken from the later Reynolds; George 5958), and anon., *An Arch Prelate in Boots or The Church Militant* 1778, whole length with shield and sword marked *Yorks Sermons*.

MASKELYNE, Nevil 1732-1811

Astronomer and priest; ordained 1755; FRS 1758; observed the transit of Venus from St Helena 1761; tested Harrison's chronometer in 1763 as chaplain on the *Louisiana*; astronomer royal 1765; DD 1777 and associate member of the French Académie 1802; his publications included the *British Mariner's Guide* 1763 and *Observations made on the mountain Schehallien* 1775 (concerning the density of the earth); his sister m. Robert Clive of India.

'in character [he] was modest and somewhat timid in receiving visits of strangers, but his ordinary conversation was cheerful and often playful' (William Walker, 1862).

1075 see Groups, *Men of Science living in 1807-08* by JOHN GILBERT, FREDERICK SKILL and WILLIAM & ELIZABETH WALKER 1858-62

ICONOGRAPHY

c.1775 Drawing attributed to John Russell, bust length with wig. Private collection. See Groups NPG 1075.

1785 Painting by L.F. van der Puyl, three-quarter length seated in clerical gown, holding a diagram lettered *PRISMATIC MICRO*[*SCOPE*], above a book lettered: [*MASK*]*ELINE'S*/ *OBSERVATIONS*/ *GREENWICH*; a distant view of the Greenwich Observatory. Royal Society (illus. *Royal Society* 1980, p.214). Exhibited NPE 1867(817). Engraved E. Scriven (bust length).

1801 Miniatures by William Theed and Mary Byrne, bust-length ovals in gown and bands. Private collection.

1804 Pastel by John Russell, half-length oval, with a distant view of the Greenwich Observatory. Private collection (illus. M. Arnold Forster, *Basset Down*, 1950, p.39). Engraved anon. 1804 (*European Mag.* 1805); R. Page 1815.

DOUBTFUL PORTRAIT

Painting by John Downman 1779, half length, National Maritime Museum (BHC 2854), but Howse subsequently doubted the identity (letter, 19 April 1997; NPG archive).

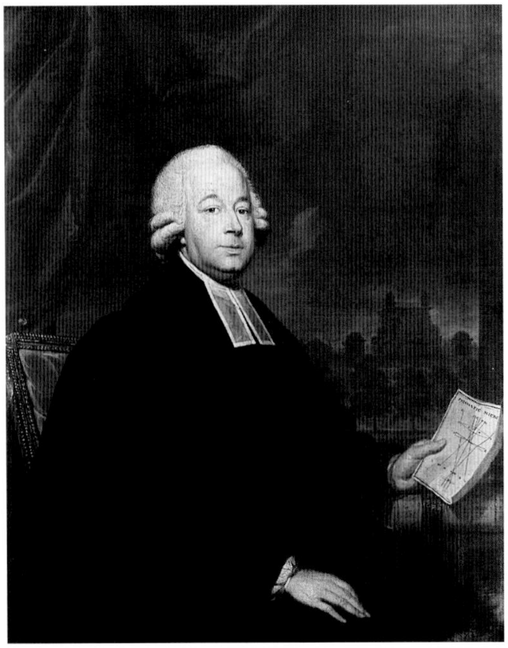

MASKELYNE by L.F. van der Puyl 1785 (The Royal Society)

MASON, William 1725-97

Virtuoso; rector of Aston, Yorks., 1754-97 and precentor of York 1762-97; friend of Joshua Reynolds who annotated his translation of Du Fresnoy's *Art of Painting* 1783; wrote dramatic poems *Elfrida* 1772 and *Caractacus* 1776, and *The English Garden* 1772-81; biographer of Thomas Gray and William Whitehead; an altarpiece painted by him, *The Good Samaritan*, remains at Nuneham.

'a little, fat old man of hard-featured countenance' (Mrs Anne Fletcher, c.1788).

4806 WILLIAM DOUGHTY 1778

Canvas 76 x 62 (30 x 25); relined 1993.

Blue eyes, powdered grey hair, wearing a grey coat; a reddish-brown curtain behind; within a painted oval, black spandrels.

Collections: Lord Campden;[1] Phillips, 13 April 1970, lot 156, bt. Leggatt for the NPG.

A replica of the oval painting in York City Art Gallery (510), exhibited RA 1778(87), and given by Mason to the 2nd Earl Harcourt.[2] Mason seems not to have liked it: 'It makes me look like Le Beck's head in the Strand. All my relations who saw it ... cry shame on it', Mason wrote;[3] but he was soon reminded by the poet William Whitehead that he was 'grown grey-haired & intolerably fat'.[4] The following year Doughty made his fine mezzotint from the Reynolds portrait of 1774, see below.

1 As indicated by an ink label on the stretcher: *Wm Mason/ Reynolds/ Coll. of Lord Campden*, presumably a Viscount Campden who succeeded as Earl of Gainsborough.
2 Illus. York CAG, *Cat. of Paintings*, II, 1963, pl.29; engraved A. Warren 1820 from a drawing by J. Thurston.
3 To Lord Harcourt, 20 June 1778 (*Harcourt Papers*, VII, p.590); Le Beck painted by Kneller and engraved A. Miller 1739, looking decidedly overweight.
4 As Mason told Lord Harcourt in an undated letter of 1779 (*Harcourt Papers*, VII, p.60).

2690 JOHN BACON senior c.1797

Pen and pencil on paper 30 x 18 (11¾ x 7); signed below in ink: *John Bacon R.A.* and inscribed up the right-hand side in ink: *about 8 ft high and 4ft 6 wide*.

Design for Mason's monument in Westminster Abbey incorporating a medallion head of Mason.

Collections: Acquired 1934.

Exhibition: *Mason* 1973(117).

The medallion was copied for the monument to Mason in All Saints, Aston (Yorks.). Another drawing for the monument by Bacon is in the Victoria and Albert Museum (E.1529.1931).[1] Bacon died in August 1799 and the monument in Westminster Abbey, installed in 1800, was completed by his son, John Bacon junior.[2]

1 Illus. J. Physick, *Designs for English Sculpture 1680-1860*, 1969, p.162.
2 Illus. *ibid.*, p.163.

ICONOGRAPHY

A general, partially illustrated, iconography appears in *Mason* 1973, pp.21-23.

Thomas Gray in a letter of April 1760 wrote that Mason was 'sitting (as usual) for his picture' (*Corr. of Thomas Gray*, 1935, II, p.664), but no certain portrait of him before 1765 survives.

1759 Painting by Benjamin Wilson, showing 'what a pretty sort of fellow I was ... *my hair tyed up ... a poet about town*' (Mason 1759; *Mason* 1973, p.21).

c.1765 Two silhouettes by Francis Mapletoft: seated at his easel, and a bust. Pembroke College, Cambridge (illus. *Mason* 1973, p.20; *Cambridge Portraits*, Fitzwilliam Museum, 1978, no.41).

1767 Painting by P-E. Falconet,* half-length oval. Sotheby's, 10 June 1993, lot 867, from Stanton Harcourt. Mason holds the epitaph he wrote on the death of his wife in March 1767.

c.1770 Unattributed miniature, bust-length oval; exhibited SKM 1865(552) lent T.S.B. Eastwood (sketched by Scharf in NPG copy of the cat.).

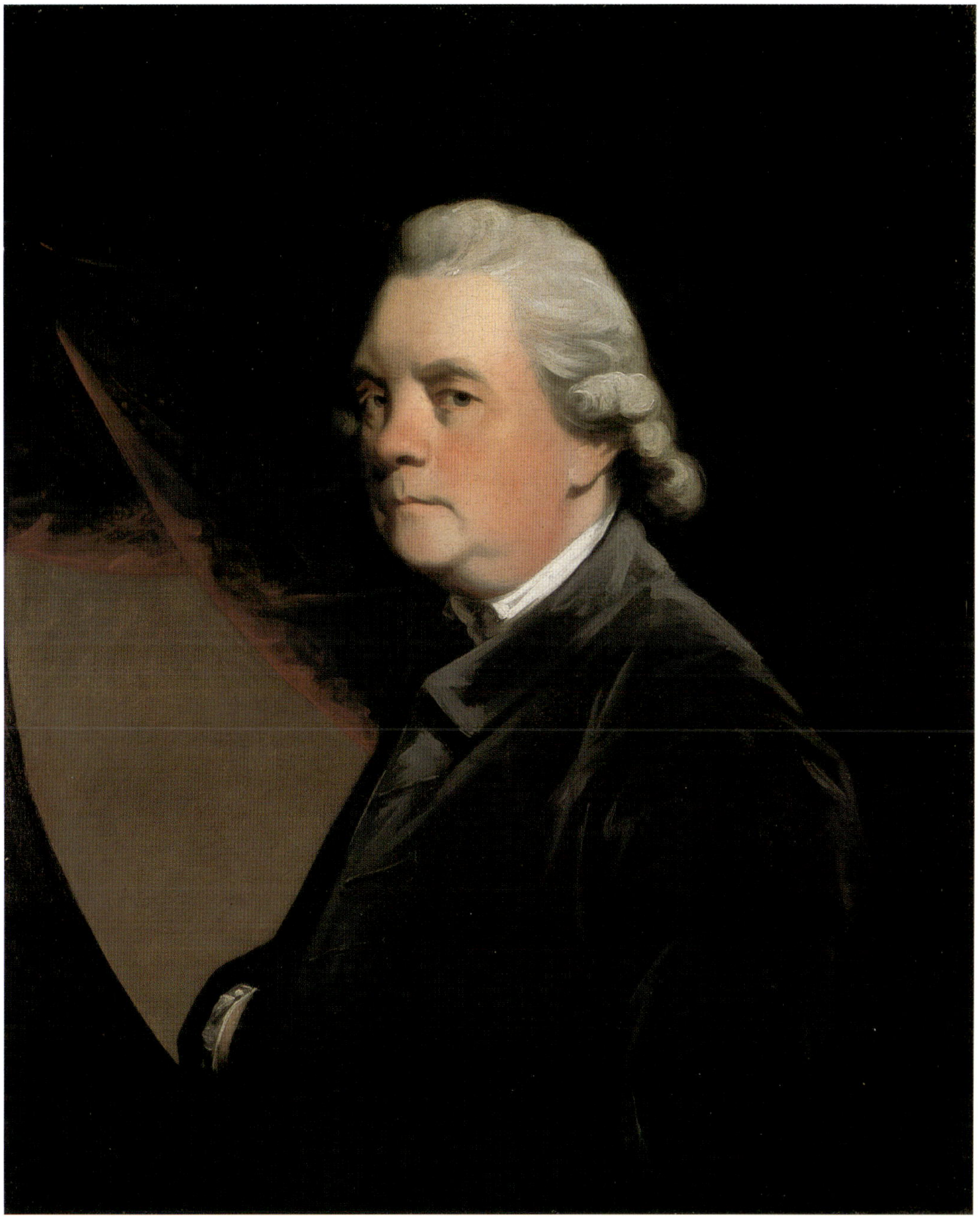

MASON NPG *4806*

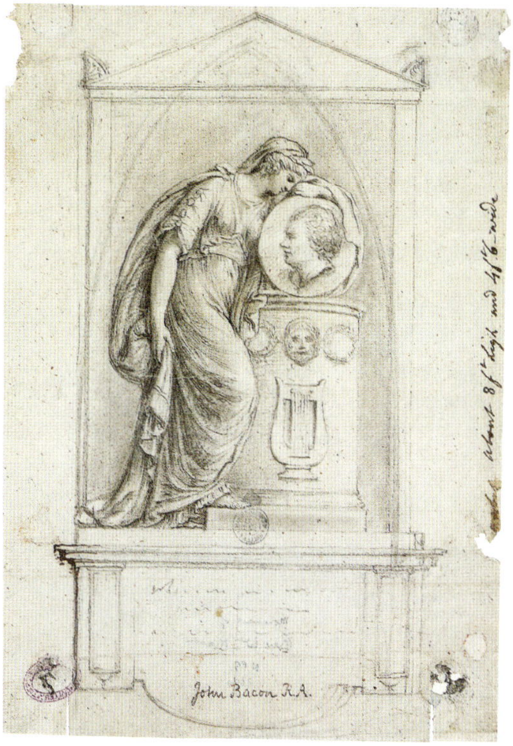

MASON NPG *2690*

1771 Drawing by Lewis Vaslet, halflength, etched by C. Carter 1771.* Gilpin considered it a 'strong likeness, but not a pleasing one' (1781; *Mason* 1973, p.22). Copied by Edward Burch as a Tassie medallion (Raspe 1791, no.14285, as after Verelst) and the source of several engravings: a half-length oval *from an original painting* by W. Ridley 1799; others, reversed, by R. Page and Holl; a pencil copy on silk, incorporating Mason's own hair, in the Victoria AG, Bath.

1774 Painting by Joshua Reynolds,* half length. Pembroke College, Cambridge (Mannings 2000, no.1227). Engraved W. Doughty 1779; J. Watson; S.W. Reynolds; E. Scriven 1813. Reynolds, wrote Mason, 'has taken a great deal of pains with it & says it is the best head he ever painted' (*Mason* 1973, p.22). Among many copies are those at the Lewis Walpole Library, Farmington; York Minster Library (by William Staveley); Wilberforce House and the Ferens AG, Hull, and in an English private collection; others sold Christie's, 20 November 1970, lot 180; 18 May 1990, lot 233, and Sotheby's, 5 September 1989, lot 349, and 9ff. July 1990, lot 1921.

1777–84 Painting by James Barry, *Elysium*, part of the *Progress of Human Culture*, in which Mason appears alongside the poet Gray. Royal Society of Arts, London (Pressly 1981, no.27). Engraved J. Barry 1791.

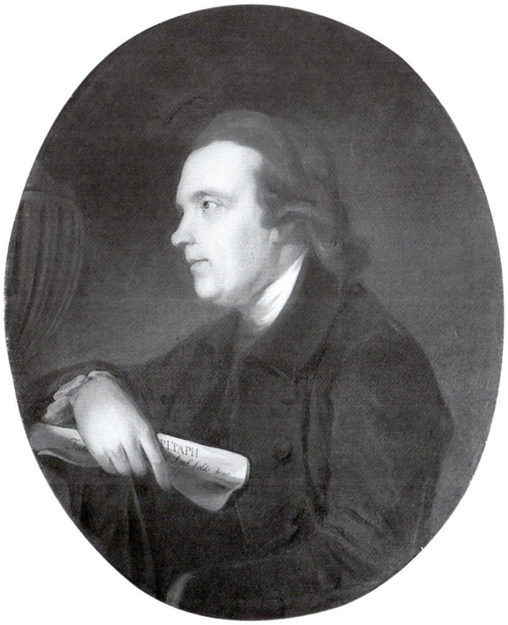

MASON by P-E. Falconet 1767 (Sotheby's)

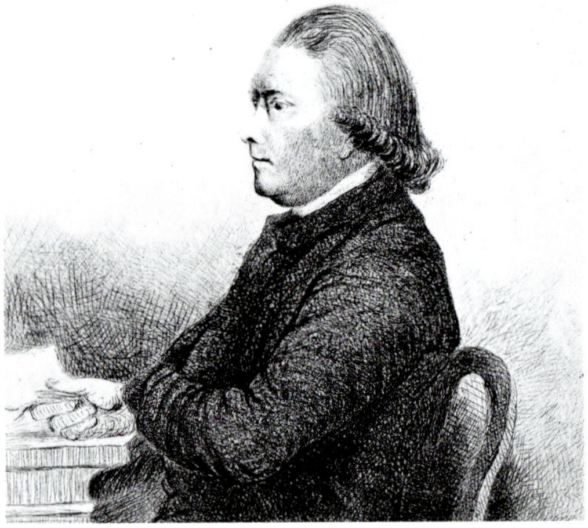

MASON C. Carter after Lewis Vaslet 1771 (NPG D 18115)

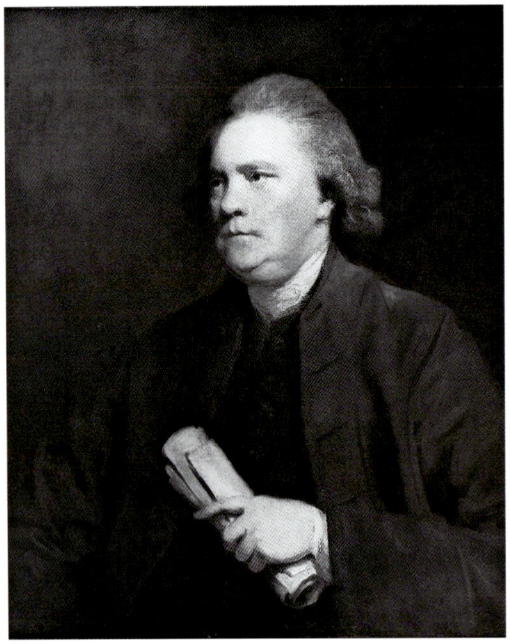

MASON by Joshua Reynolds 1774 (Pembroke College, Cambridge)

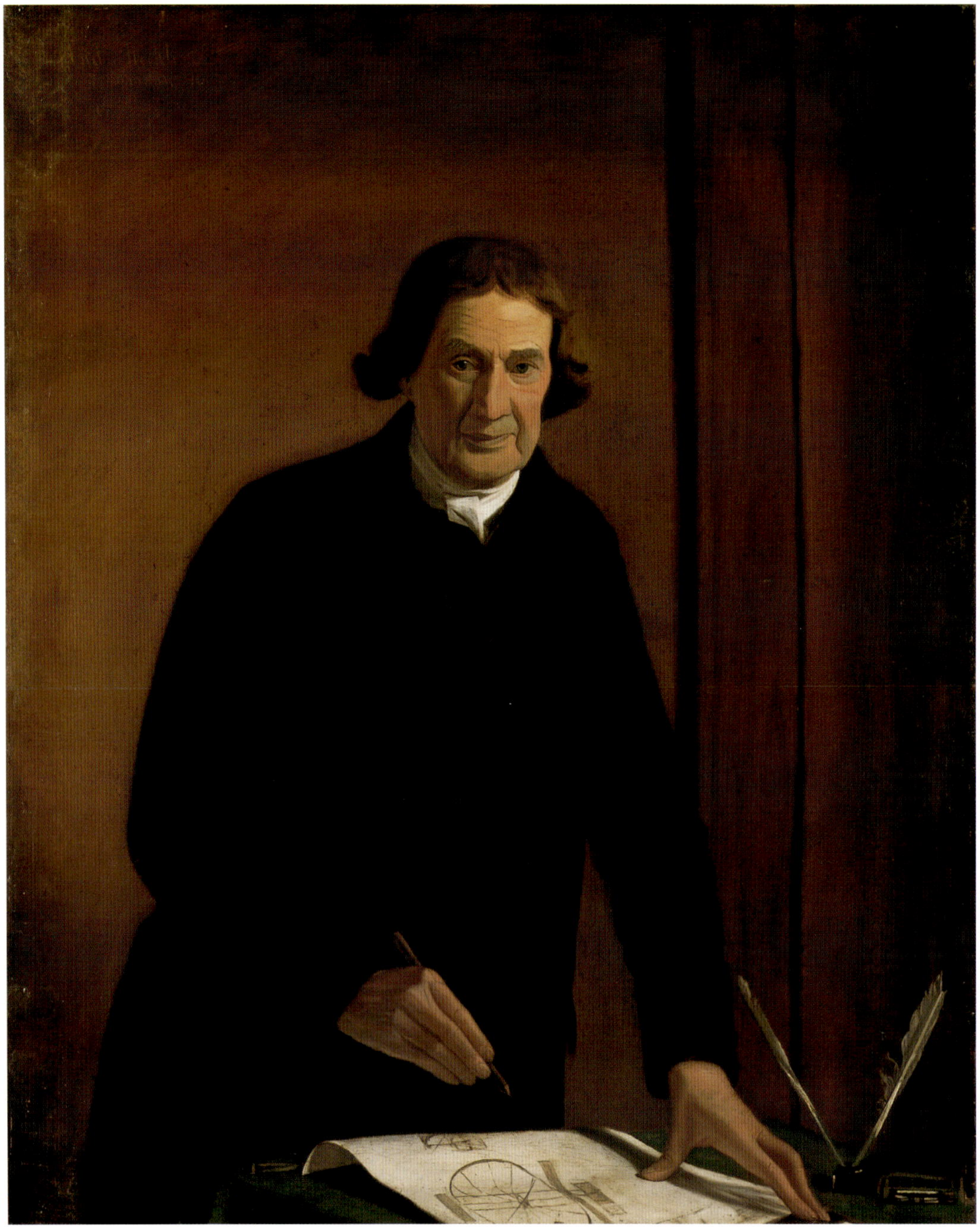

MEIKLE NPG *5001*

The head apparently based on Falconet's portrait of 1767.

1778 Painting by William Doughty, see NPG 4806.

1783 Unattributed bust-length profile, engraved W. Angus 1783 (*European Mag.*).

c.1790 Medallion by James Tassie, half-length seated profile (Raspe 1791, no.14285). An example with Roy Davids in 1999 also inscribed Edward Burch.

Undated A 'coloured drawing' of Mason was in the Strawberry Hill sale, 11th day, 6 May 1842, lot 109.

In 1778 an anon. caricature, *Abelard and Eloisa*, showed Mason simpering before Mrs Elizabeth Montagu (Stephens 4557 as c.1770; detail illus. *Mason* 1973 cover).

Posthumous

1800 Monument by John Bacon sr.& jr. Westminster Abbey, see NPG 2690.

1803 Wax by Catherine Andras, exhibited RA 1803(823).

DOUBTFUL PORTRAIT

See Unidentified Portraits NPG 1393.

MEIKLE, Andrew 1719–1811

Inventor of the threshing machine; farmer and miller at Houston Mill, near Dunbar, in 1768 he obtained a patent for a machine for dressing grain; at the second attempt he invented a 'drum thrashing-machine' (separating corn from straw) patented in England 1788 and produced in some quantity from 1789, though at little personal profit; invented a means for rapidly furling windmill sails; 'a capital player on the Northumbrian bagpipes'.

5001 A. REDDOCK c.1790-1800

Canvas 124.5 x 100.5 (49 x 39½) lined; some losses down the left-hand edge and considerable retouching throughout; inscribed top left: *Andw. Meikle/ of the Thrashing Machine/ 93 years/ 1811*.

Blue-green eyes, dark brown hair; wearing a black coat and waistcoat, holding a sharpened pencil in his right hand; a green cloth covers the table on which stand an ink well with two quills, a diagram of a threshing machine and a separate paper lettered: *PLA.. / THRASH..*

Collections: Anon. sale,[1] Bonham's, 15 August 1974, lot 8, bt. Brian Sewell, from whom purchased 1974.

Engraving: T.D. Scott (half-length oval), 1862 (for Smiles *Lives of the Engineers*, II).

The unique and unsophisticated portrait of Meikle, identified by the inscription (the date of which is presumably commemorative rather than actual) and the working drawings on the table before him. The painter, identified through the 1862 engraving (lettered *Ruddock*), is otherwise known for two Scottish portraits.[2]

1 Printed label on stretcher has: *Lunn's Stores/ Edinburgh No.5*. The label of Doig, Wilson & Wheatley on the frame.
2 Letter from Robin Hutchison, 19 March 1976; he suggested that Reddock [or Reddoch] looked toward Raeburn and mentioned a portrait of James Dalyell, 5th Bt of the Binns, inscribed *A. Reddock/ Falkirk*.

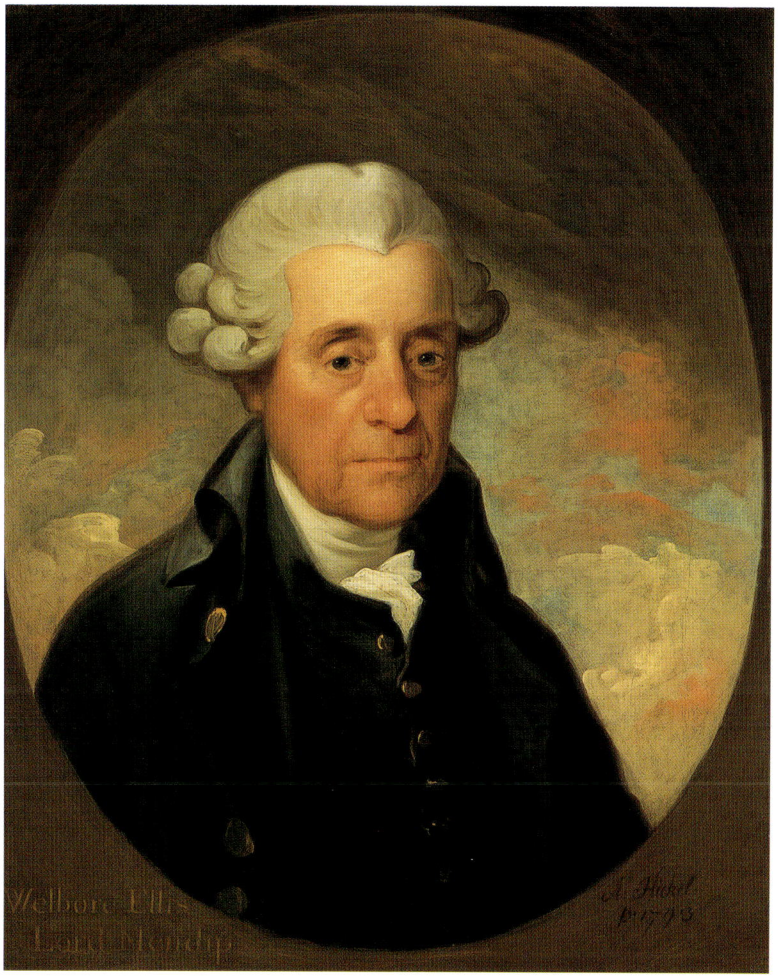

1st Baron MENDIP NPG *3993*

MENDIP, Welbore Ellis, 1st Baron 1713-1802

Statesman; s. of Welbore Ellis, Bishop of Meath; travelled in Italy 1739-40; FRS 1745; MP 1741-94, acquiring the reputation of a placeman; lord of the Admiralty 1747-55, vice-treasurer of Ireland 1755-62 and 1770-77, secretary of war 1762-65, treasurer of the navy 1777-1782 and secretary of state for America 1782; cr. Baron Mendip 1794.

'in his figure, manner, and deportment the very essence of form, he regularly took his place on the Treasury bench dressed in all points as if he had been going to the drawing-room at St James's' (Sir Nathaniel Wraxall, 1815).

'ridiculed for his diminutive stature, not redeemed by any loftiness of mind' (Philip, 5th Earl of Stanhope, 1854).

3993 KARL ANTON HICKEL 1793

Canvas 60.5 x 50 (23¾ x 19¾) lined;[1] cleaned 1956; some discoloured retouchings in head and coat; signed, bottom right: *A: Hickel./ p.: 1793*, and inscribed bottom left: *Welbore Ellis/ Lord Mendip*.

Blue-grey eyes, white powdered wig, wearing a blue coat and waistcoat with brass buttons; within a painted oval.

Collections: By descent from the sitter: his heir the 2nd Viscount Clifden of Gowran,[2] to Anne, daughter of the 3rd Viscount (who m. the 3rd Baron Annaly); her sale, Christie's, 4 May 1945, lot 141;[3] Christie's, 23 July 1954, lot 146; Christie's, 1 June 1956, lot 102, bt. Leggatt for the NPG.

Preparatory for Hickel's *House of Commons*, see Groups NPG 745; the sitter moved to the House of Lords in 1794.

1 Stamped verso: *W. Morrill/ Liner*.
2 Presumably the portrait of Lord Mendip listed at Gowran Castle, Kilkenny, in 1826 by J.P. Neale (*Seats*, 2nd series, vol. III).
3 As identified by E.K. Waterhouse (letter of 8 December 1956; NPG archive).

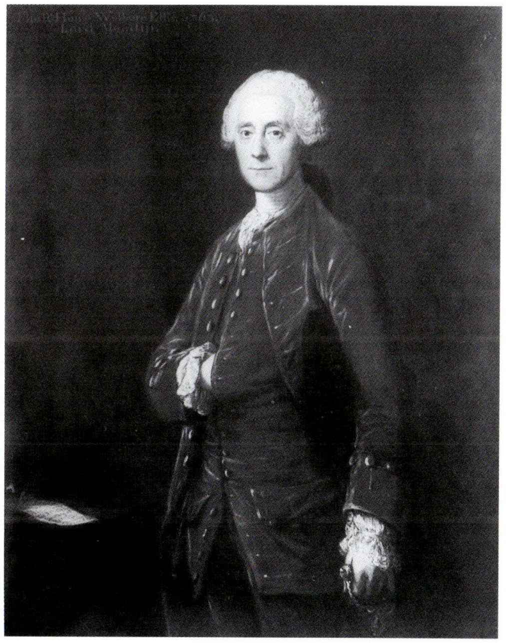

1st Baron MENDIP by Thomas Gainsborough 1763 (Christ Church, Oxford)

745 see Groups, *The House of Commons 1793-94* by KARL ANTON HICKEL 1793-95

ICONOGRAPHY

1763 Painting by Thomas Gainsborough,* three-quarter length standing. Christ Church, Oxford (Poole, III, p.76; Waterhouse 1958, no.478). Exhibited NPE 1867(489). Engraved J. Whessell; C. Tomkins 1868.

1780 Medallion by James Tassie. A cast in the Scottish NPG (PG 479; Gray 1894, no.265).

c.1791 Miniature by Jeremiah Meyer, bust length. Somerley (where seen by Scharf in 1883; SSB 105/41). Engraved C. Watson 1791.

1793 Painting by K.A. Hickel, see NPG 3993.

1793-95 Painting by K.A. Hickel, *The House of Commons 1793-94*, see Groups NPG 745.

METCALFE, Philip 1733-1818

Distiller and philanthropist; MP 1784-1806; FRS 1790; treasurer (1794-1808) and secretary (1797-1808) of the Society of Dilettanti; Dr Johnson enjoyed Metcalfe's 'excellent table and animated conversation', and Metcalfe acted as treasurer to the committee responsible for Johnson's monument in St Paul's; an executor of Joshua Reynolds, with whom he had travelled in Flanders and Holland in 1781.

'A shrewd, sensible, keen and very clever man' (Fanny Burney, 1782).

2001 POMPEO BATONI c.1766-67

Canvas 73 x 61 (28¾ x 24) lined (c.1850?);[1] cleaned 1982.

Blue-grey eyes, a black hair-ribbon; wearing a bright red coat with gold facings and a red waistcoat, his black hat in his hand; a view of the Colosseum in the background.

Collections: Henry Metcalfe, sold Christie's, 15 June 1850, lot 46 (as Reynolds), bt. Metcalfe; by descent within the Metcalfe family at Hawstead House,[2] to Col. T.G. Booth; his widow Mrs Frances Booth (*née* Metcalfe), by whom presented 1923.

Exhibition: Beningbrough 1982–.

Reference: Clark 1985, no.306.

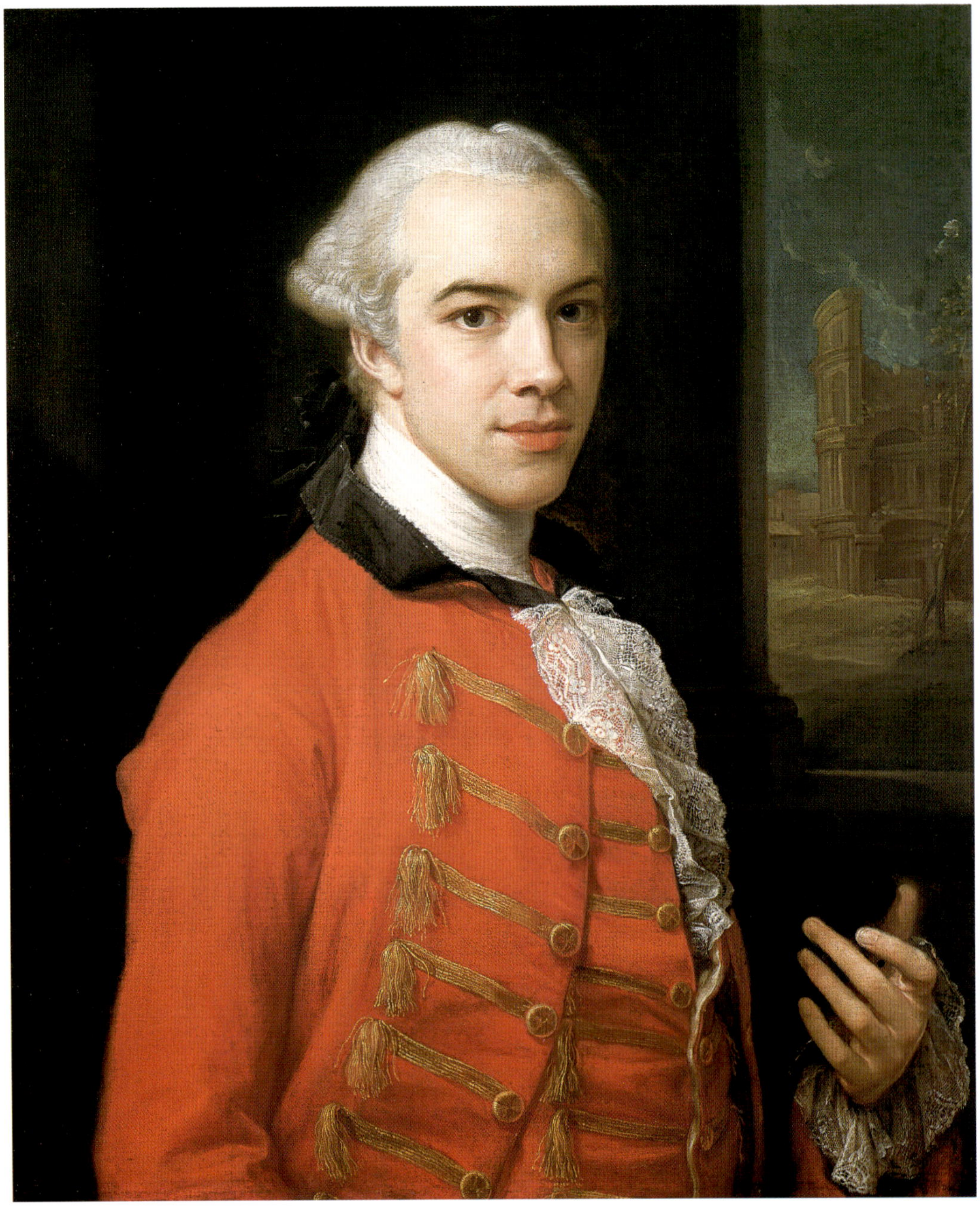

METCALFE NPG 2001

NPG 2001 is the only evidence for Metcalfe's visit to Rome, but the identity, based upon the provenance and inscription appears secure. The proposed date is that given on stylistic grounds by Clark in 1985.

1 The ink inscription on the verso of the lining canvas (and presumably copied from the original canvas): *Philip Metcalf. FRS - FSA - MP./by ~~J. Reynolds~~: P. Battoni-Battoni*, must have been altered in, or soon after, 1850, the attribution being amended from Reynolds to Batoni at the Christie's sale that year (Graves & Cronin, II, p.639).

2 Farrer 1908, p.169, no.24.

ICONOGRAPHY

c.1766-67 Painting by Pompeo Batoni, see NPG 2001.

1801 Drawing by Edmund Scott, bust-length oval. Engraved W. Evans 1801 as *Aetat.68* (with Metcalfe arms: *ar. three cows pass. sable with crest a hound sejant ppr. posing the forefoot on an escutcheon or*).

MILLER, Patrick 1731-1815

Pioneer of steam navigation; b. Glasgow; director 1767 and deputy governor 1790 of the Bank of Scotland; bought an estate at Dalswinton, Dumfries, 1785 and spent much of his later life experimenting in agriculture, ordnance, and ship design; he devised multiple and flat-bottomed hulls, propulsion by paddle-wheels and the Symington steam engine.

2009 attributed to GEORGE CHALMERS c.1770

Canvas 75.5 x 63 (29¾ x 24¾) lined and cleaned 1924; the flesh areas are rubbed and there is much retouching, with losses in his right sleeve and above and to the left of the head; varnish discoloured.

Grey eyes, powdered white hair, wearing a brown coat with gold trim (oak leaves and berries motif), white lace cuffs and neckcloth; brown background.

Collections: [sale of the Dalswinton estate c.1821;[1] Miss Gregan by 1859, see below] Miss Murphie, Cresswell House, Dumfries, by 1896; her niece, Mary G. Livingstone, from whom purchased 1923.

Exhibition: *Burns*, Glasgow, 1896(117) lent Miss Murphie.

The identity rests on the alleged provenance; Miller is shown as banker rather than inventor, considerably younger than in his other surviving portraits. The attribution to Chalmers (who was active in Edinburgh between 1760 and 1776) seems first to have been made in 1923, when the portrait came to the NPG, it having previously been called Nasmyth.[2]

NPG 2009 was possibly the portrait used as a source for the mid-19th century group portrait of *Men of Science living in 1807-08* (see Groups NPG 1075), in which case it was, c.1860, 'in the Portrait Gallery of the South Kensington Museum' - and doubtless the portrait which, according to *DNB*, had been lent by a Miss Gregan of Dumfries to the Patent Office in 1859-60; see also Iconography c.1790 below.

1 According to the letters from Mary Livingstone of 15 October and 5 December 1923 (NPG archive).
2 *Ibid.*

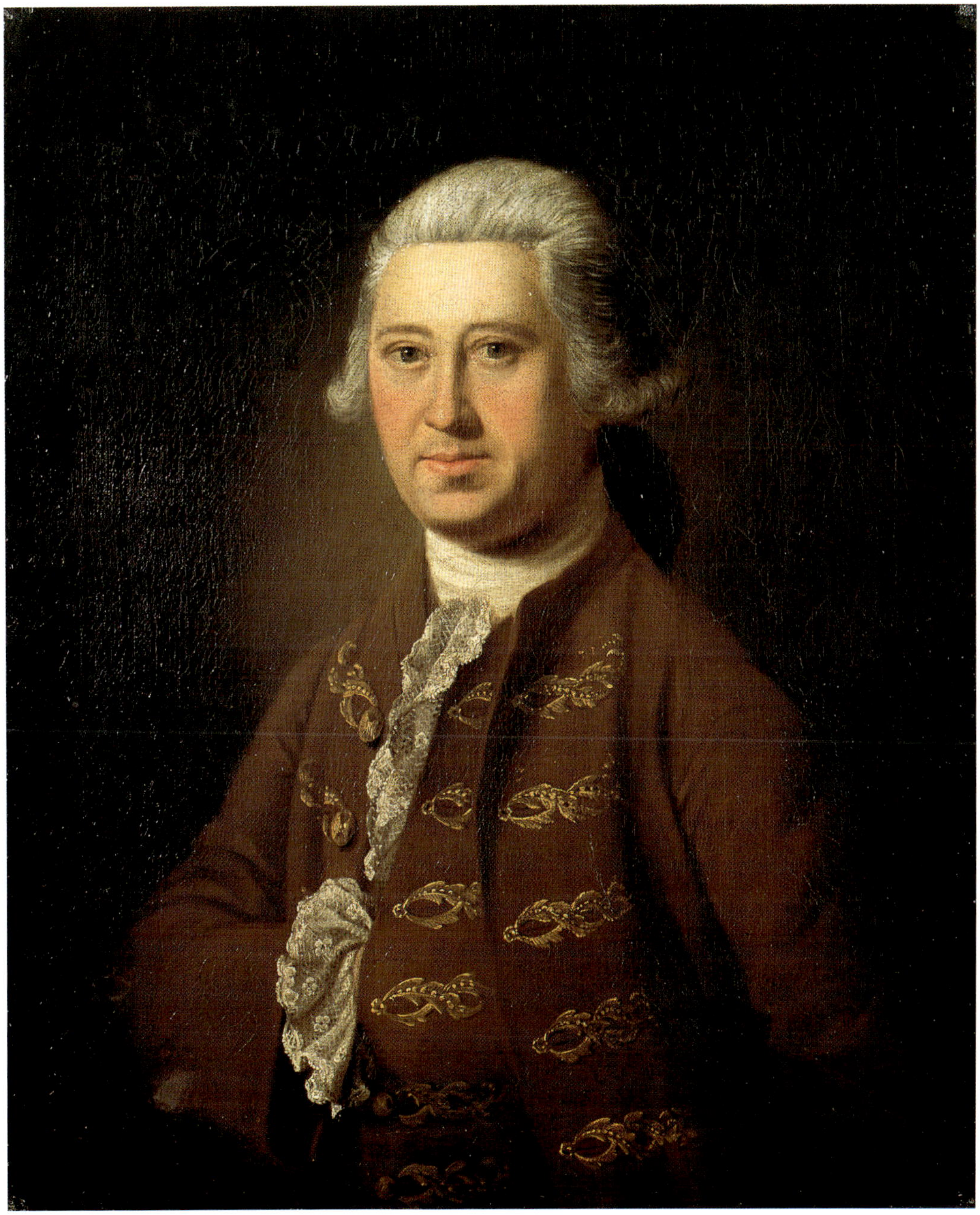

MILLER NPG *2009*

1075 see Groups, *Men of Science living in 1807-08* by JOHN GILBERT, FREDERICK SKILL and WILLIAM & ELIZABETH WALKER 1858-62

ICONOGRAPHY

c.1770 Painting attributed to George Chalmers, see NPG 2009.

1789 Medallion by James Tassie.* Plaster replica in the Scottish NPG (PG 385; Gray 1894, no.270). Perhaps the medallion presented by the Misses Nasmyth to the Patent Office (Cat. 1858, no.54) was by Tassie, but see Henning 1809 below.

c.1790 Painting attributed to Alexander Nasmyth, profile, half-length seated. Maj. G.G. Macfarlane in 1930 (illus. C. Carswell, *Burns*, 1930, f.p.342), possibly that listed in Cooksey 1991, p.66, N25. A copy presented to Bennet Woodcroft in 1861 by Mrs Beatrice Bairnsfather, the sitter's great-granddaughter, formed part of his gallery of inventors' portraits at the Patent Office which was transferred to the Science Museum in 1883;* see Groups NPG 1075.

Alexander Nasmyth was Miller's intimate friend; he made the plates for Miller's 1787 pamphlet concerning the Triple Vessel driven by a waterwheel and his son, James Nasmyth, remembered that 'my father painted Mr Miller's portrait as well as those of several members of his family' (*Autobiography*, 1883, p.27).

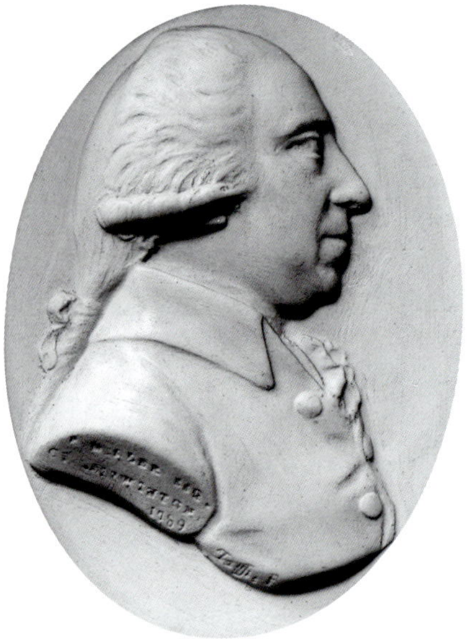

MILLER by James Tassie 1789 (Scottish National Portrait Gallery)

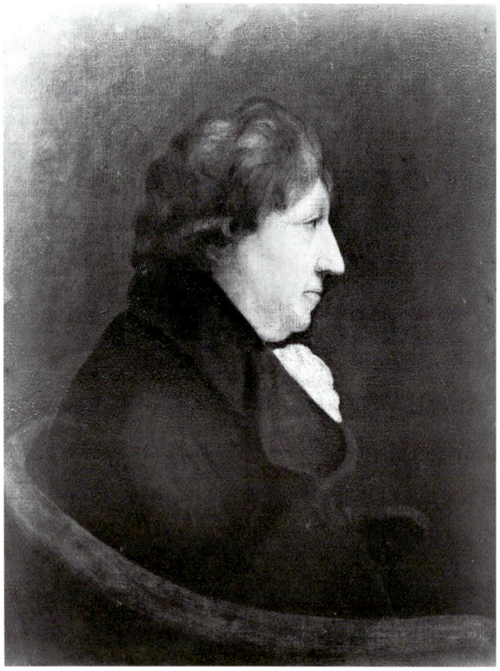

MILLER after Alexander Nasmyth c.1790 (Science Museum, London)

1809 Medallion by John Henning. Paisley MAG (illus. *Henning* 1977, n.p.).

DOUBTFUL PORTRAIT

Painting by Alexander Nasmyth of 1782, said to show Patrick Miller with his family in a park, apparently shows Miller's children (Sotheby's, 20 March 1963, lot 95; illus. Cooksey 1991, p.59, N7).

MILNE, Colin 1743-1815

Botanist and priest; b. Aberdeen; LLD Edinburgh; by 1773 he was living in Deptford, where he was lecturer to the Old and New Church and founded in 1783 the Royal Kent Dispensary (later the Miller Hospital, Greenwich); prominent member of the Royal Humane Society; rector of North Chapel, Sussex; published a *Botanical Dictionary* 1770 and *Institutes of Botany* 1771-72, parts of an incomplete translation of Linnaeus.

5180 JOHN RUSSELL 1803

Pastel on paper 60 x 44.5 (23½ x 17½) laid down on board; signed in pencil, top left: *J. Russell R.A. pinxit./ 1803* -; slight spotting in the hair and there is some rubbing along the right-hand and bottom edges.

Blue eyes, white hair, wearing gown and bands, holding with his right hand a leather-bound LINNAEI/ GENERA/ PLANTARM.

Collections: Dr Robert John Thornton (c.1768-1837); offered in Thornton's Royal Botanical Lottery 1811;[1] Thornton's sale Christie's, 2 July 1813, lot 23, bt. Swift; for sale in the European Museum, London 1814 (cats. of April 1814, lot 497, and 29 August 1814, lot 497);[2] Miss M.J.C. Gray; Christie's, 22 November 1977, lot 101, withdrawn; purchased from Miss Gray 1977.

Engraving: Holl 1804 (oval, lettered . . . *AUTHOR OF THE BOTANICAL DICTIONARY;* the book titled *BOTANICAE/DICTIONAR*).

Exhibition: *Dr Thornton's Exhibition*, Bond Street, London, 1804(48).

NPG 5180 was one of six pastel portraits by Russell commissioned by Dr Thornton for his extravagant *New Illustration of the Sexual System of Linnaeus*, pub-

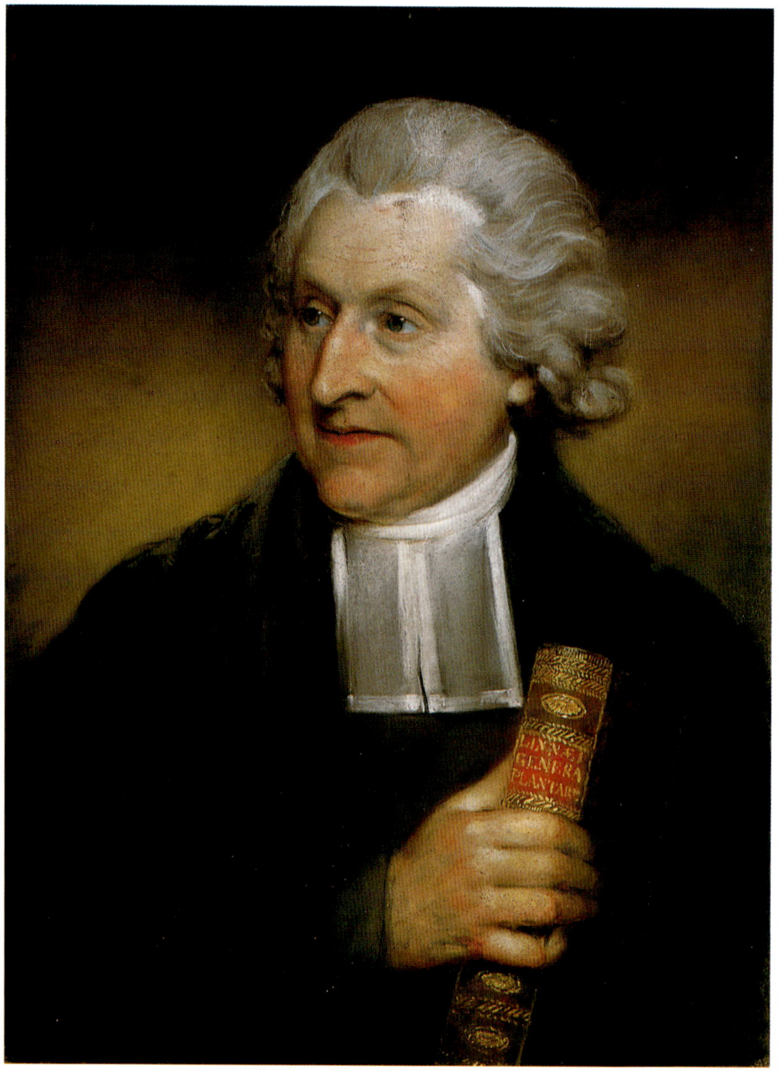

MILNE NPG 5180

lished in parts between 1799 and 1807. The dispersal of the many pictures he commissioned was both protracted and unremunerative.

1 An early-19th century ink label, formerly verso, reads: *John Russell.R.A./ Portrait of Rev Dr. Colin Mylne. F.R.S./ B.1743. d.1815./ This is one of the Pictures in the Linnaeus Gallery/ & was disposed of with others in the Great Lottery by Dr. Thornton in 1811.*

2 There is then a long gap in the provenance; listed as 'missing' by Williamson 1894, p.130.

MOLINI, Pietro 1729/30-1806

Editor; b. Tuscany; served in the British navy as a naturalised Englishman, and later travelled in Italy with the Duke of Gloucester; editor of the Baskerville edition of Ariosto; his family maintained the firm of Molini, Polidori & Molini, booksellers in Haymarket; buried in St Pancras catholic burial ground.

3089(12) WILLIAM DANIELL after GEORGE DANCE [1795]

Pencil with the outlines drawn over in red crayon, on paper 25.5 x 20 (10 x 7⅞) laid down on paper, on card; vertical score marks run up through the shoulder behind the head; irregular perforations round the edges, slight staining; inscribed below in pencil: *Molini*; NPG stamp in reverse, lower left (showing through from the verso).

Engraving: W. Daniell (*Dance Plates*).

Collections, Reference: see Appendix II.

Dance's original drawing of *Signor Molini* in the Royal Academy is dated 25 January 1795.

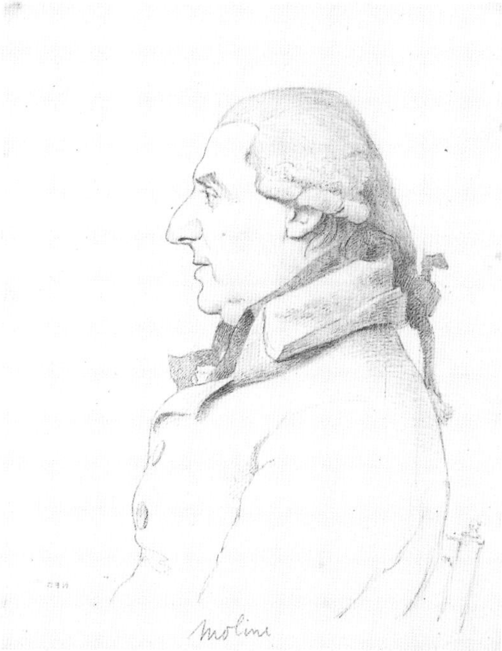

MOLINI NPG *3089(12)*

MONTAGU, Edward Wortley 1713-76

Eccentric traveller, 1st s. of Edward and Lady Mary Wortley Montagu, bro. of Mary, Countess of Bute; with his parents in Constantinople 1716-18; after running away to sea, he was commissioned in the army 1743-48; in London in 1750 Walpole observed that 'his parts are not proportionate, but his expense is incredible'; FRS 1750; MP 1747-68, without ever speaking, his seat used as security against creditors; left England 1762, travelling in the Middle East 1763-65 and 1768-73 as an enthusiastic archaeologist, and spending much time in Venice; d. Padua.

'His mother ... describes him as an excellent linguist, a thorough liar, and so weak-minded as to be capable of turning 'monk one day, and a Turk three days after'' (*DNB*).

3924 attributed to JEAN BAPTISTE VANMOUR, *as a little boy with his Mother and her retinue at Constantinople* c.1717.

See Kerslake *Early Georgian*, I, pp.188-89; II, pl.549.

4573 MATTHEW WILLIAM PETERS 1775

Canvas 115.5 x 85 (45½ x 33½) lined; pentimenti above his right elbow and left shoulder; scattered retouchings in the face and a marked drying craquelure in the more impasted passages of the costume; signed, centre right: *Peters. Px.*

Blue eyes, thin grey beard, wearing a turban with red, dark green and gold decoration, a black gown and a richly figured gold scarf; a gold-handled dagger hangs from his red belt by a gold cord; a Turkey rug over the table to the left.

Collections: William, 2nd Viscount Courtenay 1776 (see engravings); 3rd Viscount Courtenay sale, Christie's, 27 April 1816, lot 78 ('Peters, Portrait of Wortley Montagu, In his Asiatick Dress, painted with the rich and golden effect of Rembrandt's colouring; a very surprising effect of this painter'), bt. by the 2nd Marquess of Stafford (Duke of Sutherland 1803);[1] by descent to Elizabeth, Countess of Sutherland (niece of the 5th Duke of Sutherland), and sold Christie's, 7 July 1967, lot 91 (as 'The Turk'),[2] bt. Leggatt for the NPG.

Engravings: J.R. Smith 1776 (the second state lettered: ... *From the original Painting, In the collection of the Right Honourable Lord Viscount Courtenay. Published Augt. 15th, 1776* ...);[3] G. Murray 1820.

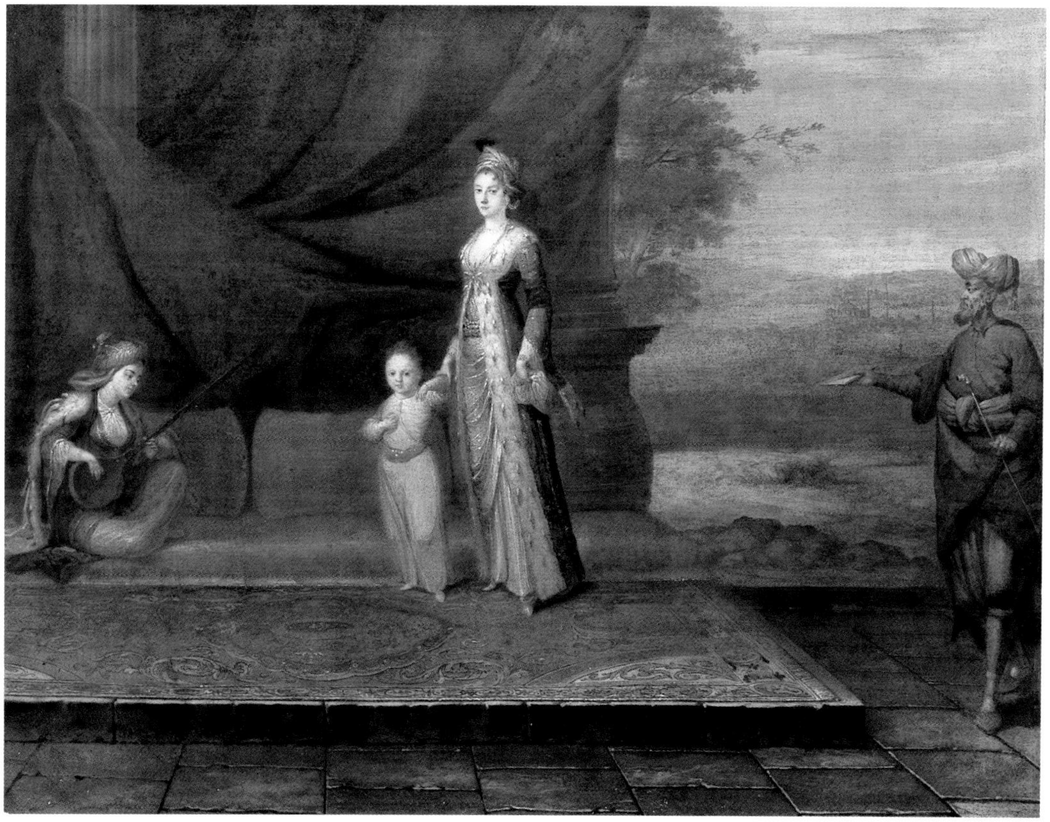

Edward MONTAGU with his Mother NPG *3924*

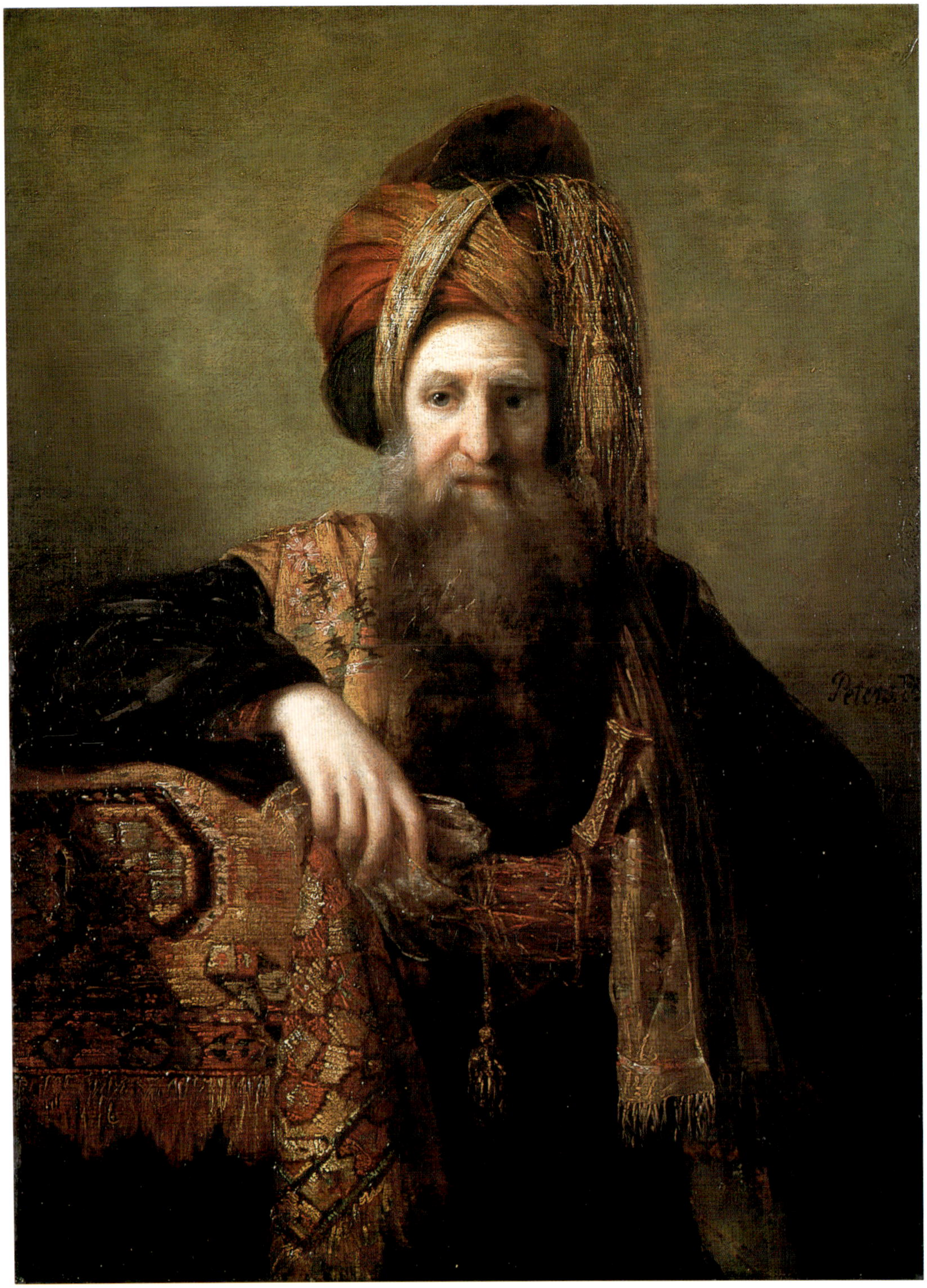

Edward MONTAGU NPG 4573

Exhibitions: RA 1776(222, 'in his dress as an Arabian Prince'); BI 1817(90) lent by the Marquis of Stafford; *Van Dyck in Check Trousers*, Edinburgh, 1978(10); *Visions of the Ottoman Empire*, Edinburgh, 1994.

Reference: C. White, *Rembrandt in England in the 18th Century*, 1983, no.28.

Wortley Montagu lived in Venice from July 1773 until his death in April 1776. When the Duke of Hamilton visited him there he found him 'wonderfully prejudiced in favour of the Turkish character and manners, which he thinks infinitely preferable to the European, or those of any other nation'; Nichols described him 'living in Venice with the manners, the habit, and the magnificence of a Turk'.[4] Peters had been in Venice for a year from March 1772 and intended to leave Rome for Parma in April 1775; NPG 4573 suggests he may have returned to Venice before returning to England in 1776. Romney, who was in Venice in March-April 1775, also painted Montagu there, see below.

A small sketch resembling NPG 4573 was with the Marquess of Bute in 1913.[5]

1 Listed in the drawing room of Trentham Hall in 1820 (J.P. Neale, *Seats*, III, 1820, n.p.).
2 When said to have come from the collection of Mrs W. Carpenter - which Christie's can no longer explain; it evidently didn't.
3 This inscription implies that Courtenay bt. the painting at the RA exhibition in 1776. Smith's mezzotint was exhibited SA 1777(287); illus. Lady Victoria Manners, *Peters*, 1913, pl.viii.
4 Nichols *Anecdotes*, iv, pp.650, 652.
5 Lady Victoria Manners, *Peters*, 1913, pp.9, 55 (differing 'in some respects' from Smith's mezzotint); exhibited Graves' Galleries, London, 1910(15).

ICONOGRAPHY

c.1717 Painting attributed to J-B. Vanmour, see NPG 3924.

1764 'By a Gentleman, Portrait of Edward Wortley Montagu, Esq., with a view of part of the written Mountains in Arabia', exhibited SA 1769(365, *hors catalogue*). William Watson wrote to Montagu on 25 September 1775 saying he would be 'very glad to see your portrait. I have more than once visited that representing you near the Written Mountains', i.e. in the Sinai Peninsula which Montagu had visited in 1764 (Nichols *Anecdotes*, IV, pp.646-47).

c.1775 Painting by Pietro Longhi, seated in Turkish dress attended by a black servant. Private collection, Venice (illus. T. Pignatti, *Longhi, L'opera completa*, 1974, no.207).

1775 Painting by George Romney,* three-quarter length standing in oriental dress with dark beard. Private collection. Painted in Venice. Engraved G. Fiesinger 1793; J. Condé 1793 (both bust length). Romney painted a replica (with Lord Wharncliffe in 1961; engraved W. Greatbach 1837) and a version was at Highcliffe Castle in 1949. Romney also drew a 'head in crayons' based on the three-quarter length (*Romney* 1830, p.123). A half-length copy sold Sotheby's, New York, 8 July 1999, lot 55.

1775 Painting by M.W. Peters, see NPG 4573.

Undated Anon. miniature, exhibited *Guelph* 1891(749) lent Lord Wharncliffe.

DOUBTFUL PORTRAITS

The marble bust by Peter Scheemakers, 1766, in the Wren Library at Trinity College, Cambridge

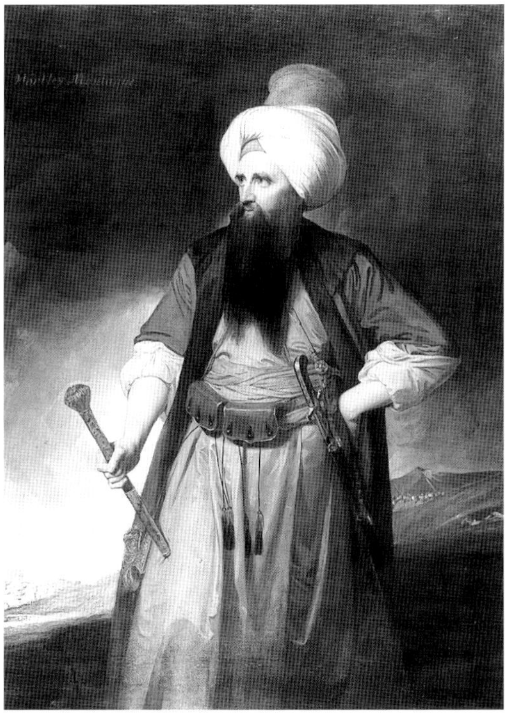

Edward MONTAGU by George Romney 1775 (formerly owned by the Earl of Warwick)

(illus. D. McKitterick, *Wren Library*, 1995, pl.78, p.135) is of Edward Wortley Montagu (1678-1761) *père*. An anon. three-quarter length in oriental costume, with Berry Hill Galleries, New York, in 1957, exhibited NPE 1867(406) lent F. Vernon Wentworth.

MONTAGU, Mrs Elizabeth, *née* Robinson 1720-1800

Literary hostess, regarded by Johnson as 'Queen of the Blues'; m. 1742 Edward Montagu (d.1775), g.s. of the 1st Earl Sandwich; wrote *Essay on the Writings and Genius of Shakespeare* 1769, which established her literary reputation; built Sandleford 1781 and Montagu House 1782 (22 Portman Square).

'in her youth her beauty was most admired, in the peculiar animation and expression of her blue eyes, with high-arched dark eye-brows, and in the contrast of her brilliant complexion with her dark brown hair. She was of the middle stature, and stooped a little, which gave an air of modesty to her countenance, in which the features were otherwise so strongly marked, as to express an elevation of sentiment befitting the most exalted condition. As she advanced in age her appearance was distinguished by [a] superiority of demeanour.' (Matthew Montagu, 1809).

Abbreviations

Blunt 1923: R. Blunt ed., *Mrs Montagu, her letters and friendships 1762-76*, 1923

Climenson 1906: E.J. Climenson ed., *Elizabeth Montagu; her correspondence 1720-1761*, 2 vols., 1906

4905 see Groups, *Portraits in the characters of the Muses* by RICHARD SAMUEL 1778

ICONOGRAPHY

1740 Miniature by Christian Zincke, bust-length oval, as Anne Boleyn, set in a box (see Mrs Delany). Christie's, 8 March 1995, lot 21. SKM 1865(2526) lent Mrs Greville Howard (illus. Climenson 1906, I, front.). Engraved R. Cooper 1809.

1744 Painting by Edward Haytley, with her husband in the grounds of Sandleford Priory. Leger 1978.

1749 Painting by William Hoare, half-length painted oval, wearing a purple and white dress with lace collar and veil. Christie's, 30 June 1888, lot 39 as 'Mrs Montague' (sketch by Scharf in sale catalogue). On 8 May 1749 Mrs Montagu wrote that her husband had made her put a masquerade dress on one side 'to be painted in when I see Mr Hoare again. His picture is thought like but the face too thin for my full jaws', and in 1750 she wrote that if Hoare pleased 'to send my face to Hill Street, it will meet with a kind reception; it is a young face to be sure, but the retrospect to 18 is so pleasant I shall find no fault with it' (Climenson, I, pp.265, 272). The portrait appears to have been commissioned by Lord Hardwicke and to have been at Wimpole; it was 'improved' by Hoare in 1784 (Blunt 1923, II, pp.168-69).

c.1750 Painting by Edward Haytley, whole length standing in a park. Private collection.

1762 Painting by Allan Ramsay, three-quarter length seated, her elbow resting on the third volume of Hume's *History*. Private collection (Smart 1999, no.371).

1775 Painting by Joshua Reynolds, seated three-quarter length. Untraced (Mannings 2000, no.1270). Mrs Montagu thought there was 'a good deal of flattery in the likeness' (Blunt 1923, II, p.293).

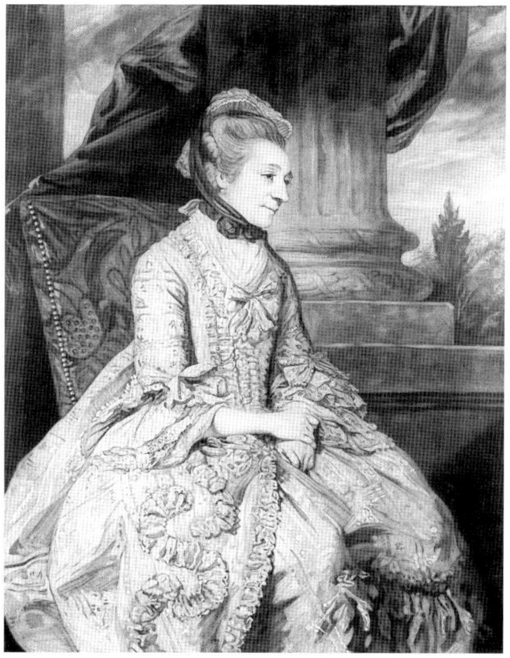

Elizabeth MONTAGU J.R. Smith after Joshua Reynolds 1775 (NPG archive)

Engraved J.R. Smith 1776;* F. Bartolozzi 1792 (bust length) and many other small derivative plates. Miniature copy by H. Edridge exhibited SKM 1865(214) lent C.B. Carruthers. A derivative bust length with a fur collar, drawn by Rivers engraved W. Ridley 1800.

1775 Wedgwood medallion (illus. Reilly 1973, p.246). Engraved T. Holloway 1776 (facing a bust of Mrs Barbauld, with an elaborate surround) and 1785; W. Ridley 1800 (*European Mag.*). A 'cameo', presumably the Wedgwood medallion, was being distributed in 1776; the original model was possibly by Joachim Smith (cf. Blunt 1923, I, pp.308-09); on 3 July 1775 Wedgwood wrote that the medallions of Mrs Montagu and Mrs Barbauld were not modelled as a pair 'neither in size nor character' (see Barbauld).

c.1775-80 Painting by Frances Reynolds, half length much resembling the portrait by Joshua Reynolds, engraved C. Townley (illus. Climenson 1906, II, front.).

1777-84 Painting by James Barry, *Distribution of Premiums in the Society of Arts*, part of the *Progress of Human Culture*, in which Mrs Montagu appears as a profile head in the centre. Royal Society of Arts, London (Pressly 1981, no.26). Engraved J. Barry 1791.

1778 Painting by Richard Samuel, *Portraits in the characters of the Muses*, see Groups NPG 4905.

1787 Engraving by R. Lowry, bust-length oval wearing a bonnet with broad ribbon.

DOUBTFUL PORTRAITS

Nasty octagonal engraved half length, head in stern profile, *Mrs Montague*, pub. I.W.H. Pyne 1815.

Painting by Nathaniel Hone, half length, formerly at Brent Eleigh Hall, Suffolk, 1908 (Farrer 1908, p.47, no.15).

MONTAGU, John, see SANDWICH

MOORE, John 1729-1802

Physician and writer; b. Stirling; studied in Glasgow and served as a military surgeon during the War of the Austrian Succession; later studied in Paris; MD Glasgow 1770; travelled in Europe 1772-78 with the 8th Duke of Hamilton and his own son John (later the hero of Corunna); settled in London 1778; his books included *View of Society and Manners in Italy* 1781, *Medical Sketches* 1786, the novel *Zeluco* 1786, and a *History of the French Revolution* 1795.

1148 GEORGE DANCE 1794

Pencil with touches of red on the lips and cheek, on paper 25.4 x 18.9 (10 x 7½) laid down; faded with repaired damages across the neckcloth and lapel; signed and dated in ink, bottom left: *July 10th. 1794/ Geo: Dance*; contemporary washed mount lettered: *MOORE*.

Collections: The artist's grandson, the Rev George Dance; his sale, Christie's, 1 July 1898, lot 95, bt. Colnaghi for the NPG.

Engraving: W. Daniell 1808 (*Dance Portraits*).

A copy with the Royal College of Physicians, London,[1] exactly agrees with the engraving by Daniell and was probably made by him.

1 Illus. *Cat. of Portraits*, 1964, p.311; unsigned; inscribed *Dr Moore*, bottom centre.

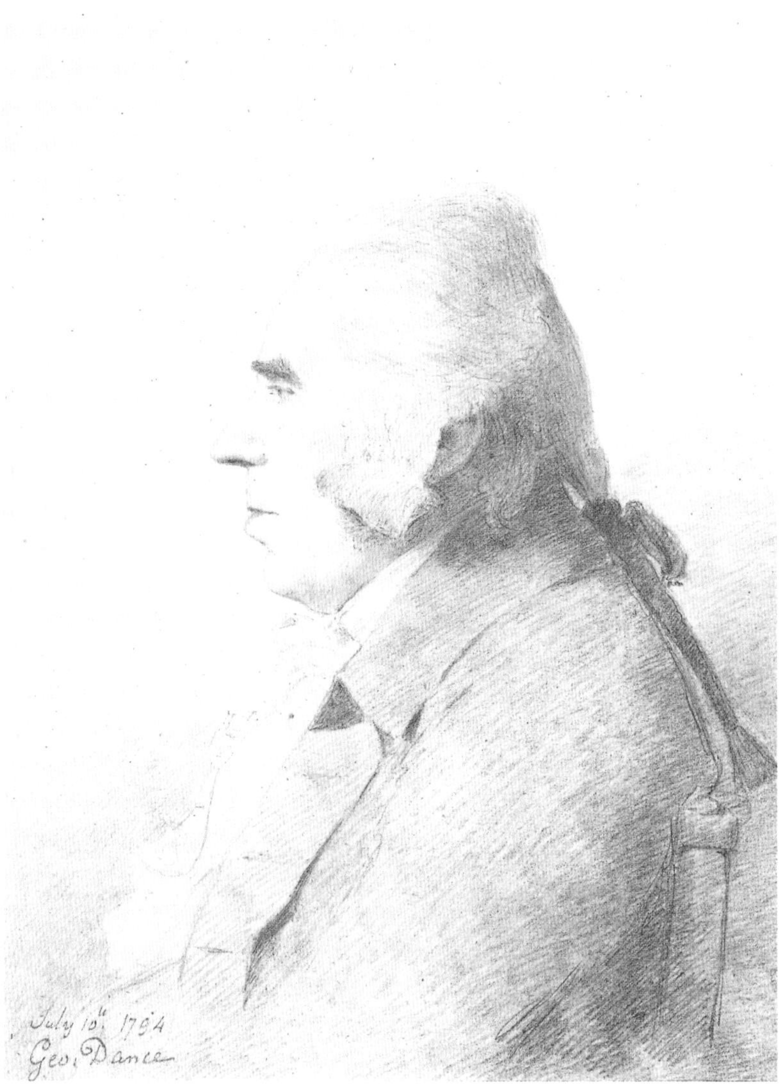

Dr John MOORE
NPG 1148

ICONOGRAPHY

1774 Painting by Jean Preud'homme, standing leaning against a chair, with his son and the 8th Duke of Hamilton. Royal Museum of Scotland (illus. *Burl. Mag.*, CXXXIV, 1992, p.563; *NACF Review 1992*, pp.148-49). Painted in Geneva.

1775-77 Painting by Gavin Hamilton, seated, bareheaded gesturing towards the Duke of Hamilton, centre, and his son, right. Scottish NPG (PG 3265; illus. *Grand Tour*, Tate Gallery, 1996, no.15). Painted in Rome. The figure of Dr Moore was separately engraved W.H. Lizars 1820.

c.1780 Anon. engraving from a drawing, half length, pub. 24 Nov. 1804, titled *John Moore M.D.* (illus. *British Medical Jnl.*, 21 Sept. 1929, where described as from a plate 'dug up', cleaned and pulled by W.M. Harris of Kendal).

1790 Painting by Samuel Drummond, bust-length oval, engraved W. Bromley (*European Mag.*).

c.1790? Wedgwood medallion (illus. Reilly 1973 p.250). Probably a private commission (cf. Reilly 1994, p.362).

1790-91 Painting by Thomas Lawrence,* half length. Scottish NPG (PG 571; Garlick 1989, no.571). Engraved G. Keating 1794. Exhibited RA 1791(375).

1794 Drawing by George Dance, see NPG 1148.

c.1795? Drawing by William Lock, half length, with long white hair, engraved J. Hopwood (for *Mooriana*, 1803, where described as 'a masterly drawing of the Doctor, sketched at a time posterior to his picture by Lawrence, by the bold and faithful pencil of W. Locke, jun....').

1798 Etching by E.P., profile half length, verging on caricature.

DOUBTFUL PORTRAITS

Painting by Antoine Vestier, 1794-95, half length, musée Carnavalet, Paris (illus. *Apollo*, CVI, 1977, p. 445); painting by Cochrane of Rome, half length in a dark suit looking left, engraved J. Cochran 1855 *from an original in the possession of Charles Macintosh...*, evidently of Dr Moore's son, despite the inscription.

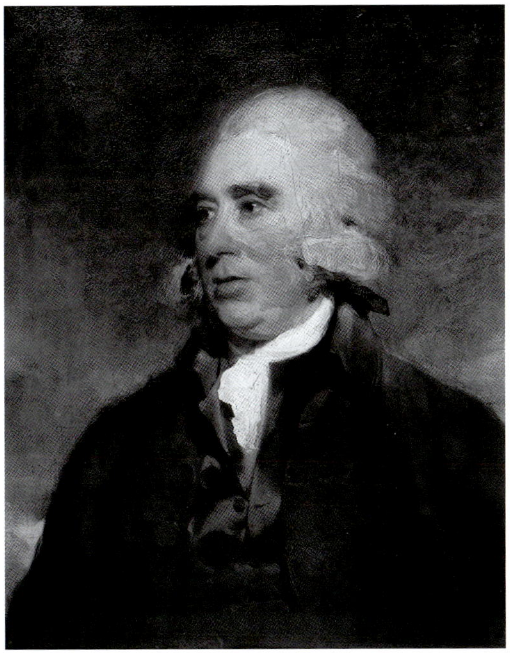

Dr John MOORE by Thomas Lawrence 1790-91 (Scottish National Portrait Gallery)

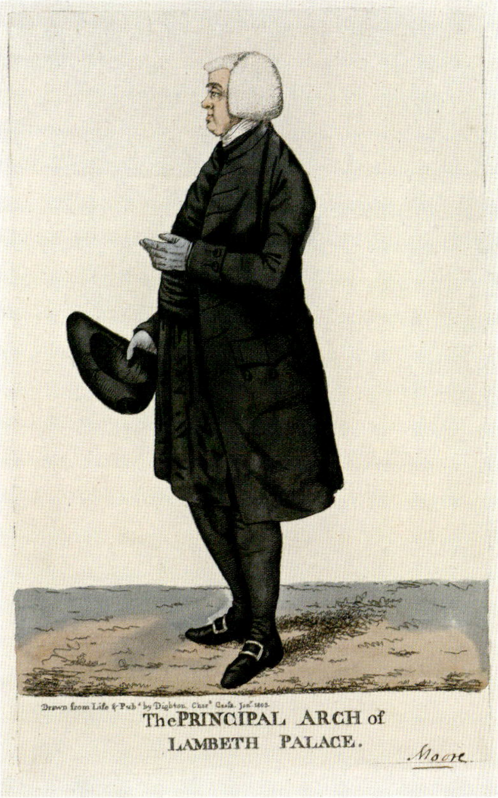

Archbishop John MOORE NPG *982E*

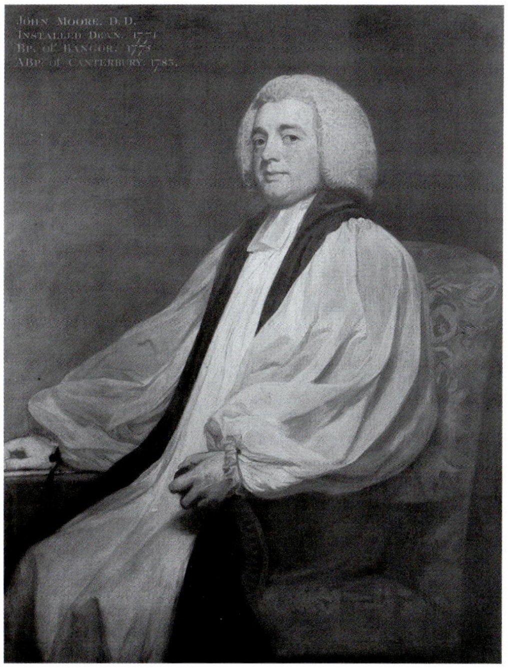

Archbishop John MOORE by George Romney 1776-83 (The Deanery, Canterbury)

MOORE, John 1730-1805

Prelate; patronised by the Duke of Marlborough, canon of Christ Church 1763, Dean of Canterbury 1771-75, Bishop of Bangor 1775-83, and Archbishop of Canterbury 1783; a promoter of the Sunday school movement and of missionary enterprise; his patronage was particularly directed towards his own family.

982E ROBERT DIGHTON 1803

Hand-coloured etching, plate 27.5 x 17.7 (10¾ x 7); lettered: *Drawn from Life & Pub by Dighton, Charg Cross. Janr. 1803.* THE PRINCIPAL ARCH OF LAMBETH PALACE. inscribed in ink, bottom right: Moore over faint traces of a scratched *Mo...*

Whole length standing to left in civilian dress, his tricorne hat in his right hand.

Collections: 'Taken from NPG portfolios' (first catalogued 1909).

ICONOGRAPHY

1776-83 Painting by George Romney,* three-quarter length seated in rochet and chimere. Deanery, Canterbury. Exhibited NPE 1867(792). After a single sitting in 1776, '*ABC*' received ten in 1780 and one each in 1781-83; payment was made to Romney in 1783.

1788-90 Painting by George Romney,* three-quarter length seated in rochet and chimere. Lambeth Palace. There were five sittings in 1788 and one in 1790; payment was made to Romney in 1792. Engraved J. Jones 1792; J. Owen 1798 (bust; *Public Characters 1798-99*); C. Bestland 1803 (half length); Holl 1800 (bust-length oval). Copies by Thomas Heaphy in the Old Vicarage, Bangor; by Thomas Stewart at Christ Church, Oxford (Poole, III, p.77), and by S.P. Hall 1913 at Pembroke College, Oxford (Poole, III, p.247).

1794 Painting by Thomas Lawrence,* three-quarter length standing in rochet and chimere. Southampton CAG (Garlick 1989, no.570). Exhibited RA 1794(115).

1796 Painting by William Hamilton, whole-length standing in rochet and chimere. Lambeth Palace. Exhibited RA 1796(13).

1801 Engraving, *Dighton del. Pye fct.*, half length in rochet and chimere (*Orthodox Churchman's Mag.*, 1801).

1803 Drawing and etching by Robert Dighton, see NPG 982e.

1804 Painting by Henry Ashby, exhibited RA 1804(486).

1804 Drawing by Henry Edridge, bust length in rochet and chimere, exhibited RA 1804(559). Enamel copy by Henry Bone dated 1805, in the NG of Ireland (3619); his preparatory drawing in the NPG Bone albums (*Bone* 1999, no.362, fig.143).

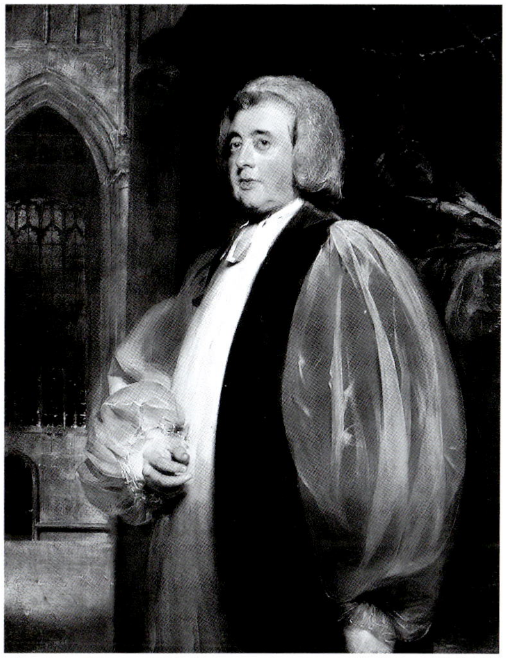

Archbishop MOORE by Thomas Lawrence 1794 (Southampton City Art Gallery)

MORE, Hannah 1745-1833

Philanthropist, author; b. Stapleton, Bristol, the youngest of five sisters; published five plays, including *Percy*, and poetry 1773-79, frequenting London literary society; until 1789 a schoolteacher in Bristol with her sisters; thereafter she founded Sunday schools in Somerset and wrote on religious, moral and educational subjects.

Abbreviations

Hopkins 1947: M.A. Hopkins, *Hannah More and her Circle*, 1947

Roberts 1835: W. Roberts ed., *Memoirs of the Life and Correspondence of Mrs Hannah More*, 3rd ed., 4 vols., 1835

4905 see Groups, *Portraits in the characters of the Muses* by RICHARD SAMUEL 1778

6533 UNKNOWN ARTIST 1805

Pencil on paper 9 x 6.6 (3½ x 2⅝) irregular, laid down on paper, the support bearing a contemporary ink inscription: *Miss Hannah Moore/1805*.

Collections: B. Issler, Cheltenham, c.1976; John Somers, from whom purchased 2000.

An amateur sketch from a notebook whose contents otherwise included views in Ireland and a drawing of Maria Edgeworth (NPG 6534) inscribed *C.H. fecit*.

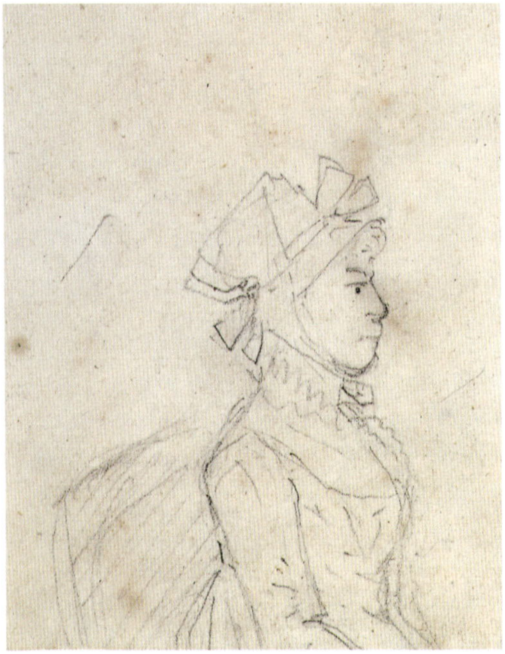

MORE NPG *6533*

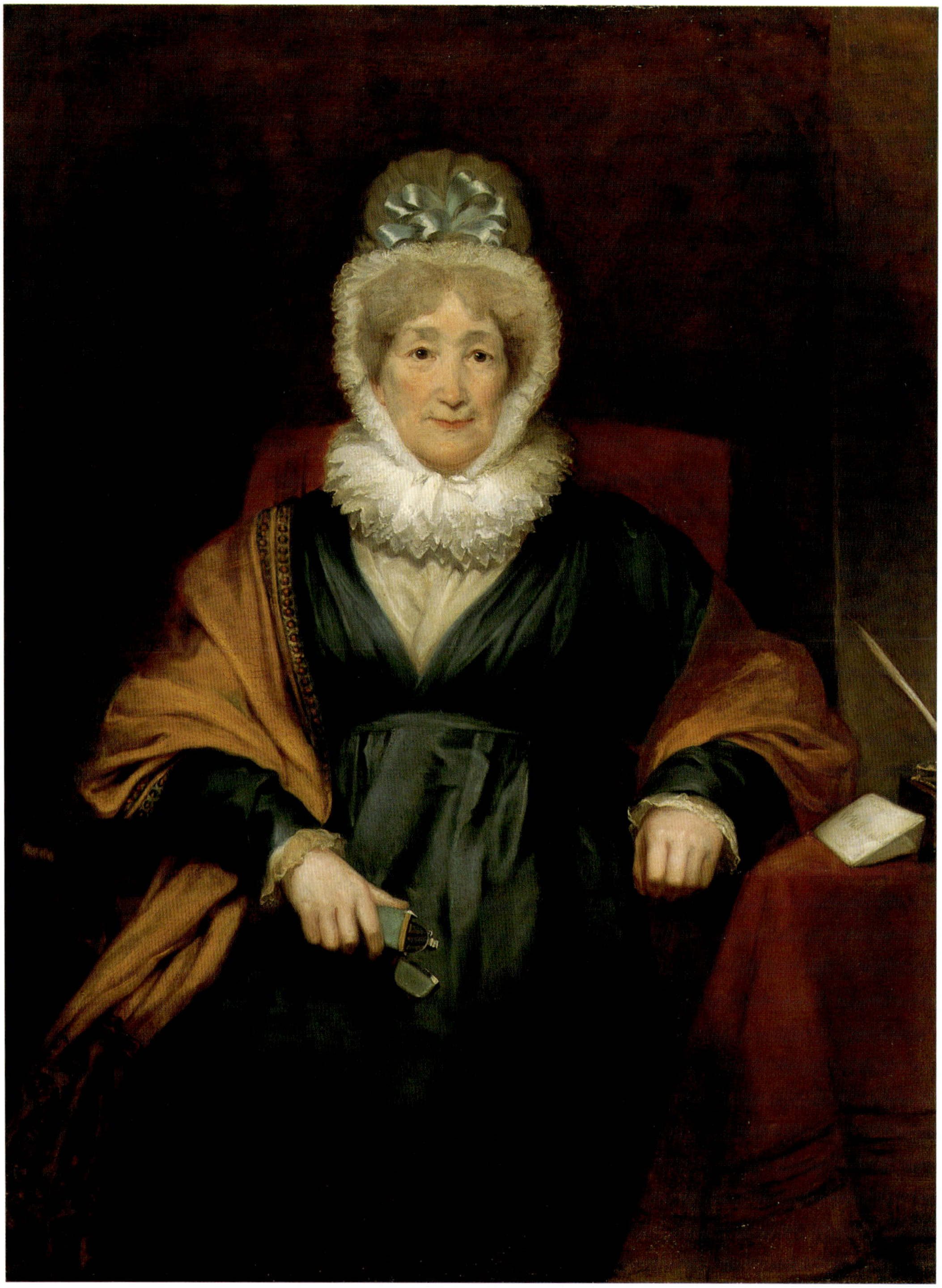

MORE NPG *412*

412 HENRY WILLIAM PICKERSGILL 1821

Canvas 127 x 94.5 (50 x 37¼) harshly lined 1875; cleaned 1986; the surface is generally worn, particularly in the lower area; there are pentimenti in the chair back and above the chair arm on the left; on the right a vertical grey strip is difficult to construe; the imprint of the previous arch-topped slip frame remains visible.

Brown eyes, grey hair, wearing a white bonnet with blue silk ribbon, a blue dress over a white blouse, a gold wrap round her shoulders with a green, red and white border; a light blue spectacle-case in her right hand; she sits in a dull-red upholstered chair (a vertical stripe appears on the left); to the right a table, with a red cloth, ink, quill, and a folded paper inscribed *W. Wilberforce*.[1]

Collections: Purchased from the artist's sale, Christie's, 17 July 1875, lot 342.

Engravings: (all from the Acland original, see below) W.H. Worthington 1824; W. Finden 1831; J. Jenkins 1846; anon. (bust-length oval).

Exhibitions: *Romantic Women Writers*, Grasmere, 1994-95(11); *Art on the Line*, Courtauld Gallery, 2001(282).

The genesis and the anguish of Pickersgill's portrait were several times described in Hannah More's letters. She didn't want to sit: 'I have opposed it with all my might. Morally and physically it is grievous to me', she complained,[2] but in October 1821 she had to explain that

> An ardent friend, Sir Thomas Acland, who by the most affectionate tyranny, is sure to carry every thing his own way, has actually, against my vehemently-repeated refusal, sent down Mr Pickersgill from London, and your poor old friend is condemned, sorely against her will, and on the verge of eternity, to see 'the lack-lustre eye', and corrugated visage, snatched a little while from oblivion. The picture is for Sir Thomas, and at his expense. Besides the fatigue of sitting four hours a-day to a painter, I object, in a moral point of view, that so much time out of my little fragment of life should be so spent.[3]

Pickersgill stayed in her house, Barley Wood in Wrington, Devon,[4] and in the event painted two portraits, the second for Lovell Gwatkin, as she wrote on 16 October 1821:

> You know it was my hard fate to sit for two portraits, lest the one friend should think his a copy of the other. It happens that each proprietor likes his own best. I believe the painter has made the best of my withered visage. You are aware with what extreme reluctance I submitted to the operation.[5]

As it now appears, NPG 412 differs from the original Acland portrait at Killerton,[6] as engraved by Worthington, as follows:

a) the striped material on the chair back is just visible on the left but not on the right, where the size of the chair back has been much reduced.

b) There is no candle holder on the table.

c) The richly patterned tablecloth is much plainer.

d) The grey strip on the right of NPG 412 does not appear in the original, which shows a large dark drape sweeping across the whole background, with a glimpse of sky on the extreme left above the chair arm.

While a-c may conceivably be explained by the indifferent condition, d cannot, indicating that NPG 412 is a slightly simplified version. What happened to Lovell Gwatkin's portrait is unclear, but NPG 412, evidently a third version, was retained by Pickersgill and appeared in his studio sale in 1875. A modest half-length version in poor condition was owned by Mrs O.G.A. Phillips in 1953; an enamel after Pickersgill by Thomas Roth was exhibited RA 1824(619); an unattributed miniature is in the Bristol Art Gallery, and another by Mrs Purcell was sold Sotheby's, 29 April 1968, lot 476.[7] Examples of a biscuit statuette based on the Pickersgill portrait are in Brighton Art Gallery[8] and at Killerton.

1 With whom she had been well acquainted since 1786; he was an inspiration to her; see, for example, Hopkins 1947, pp.158-59.
2 To the Misses Roberts, October 1821; Roberts 1835, IV, p.169.
3 To Sir William Pepys; Roberts 1835, IV, p.177.
4 To Hart Davis, 16 October 1821; Roberts 1835, IV. pp.167-68.
5 To the Misses Roberts; Roberts 1835, IV, p.168. Roberts identifies the two portraits as being for Acland and Lovell Gwatkin, p.168n.
6 Exhibited RA 1822(159); NPE 1868(146) lent Sir T. Dyke Acland.
7 Presumably this was the miniature, described as a duplicate of the Bristol one, listed Hopkins 1947, p.266, as belonging to C.B. Pigot, illus. f.p.19.
8 As recorded by Scharf in 1884 (SSB 92b/23 & 39).

4501 AUGUSTIN EDOUART 1827

Cut black paper silhouette, maximum size 18.5 x 24.4 (7¼ x 9½) laid down on white paper 22 x 27 (8¾ x 10½) which has a grey wash below and is signed in brown ink below left: *Augt Edouart fecit 1827* and inscribed above in pencil: *Correct likeness of the celebrated Mrs Hanna More taken from nature in her Study at Barley wood the 12th June 1827 - by A. Edouart.*[1]

Collections: Sotheby's, 25 July 1966, lot 15, bt. Woollett for the NPG.

Exhibition: *Cardinal Newman*, NPG, 1990(27).

1 Edouart's trade label formerly on the verso, as illus. McKechnie 1978, p.306, fig.397.

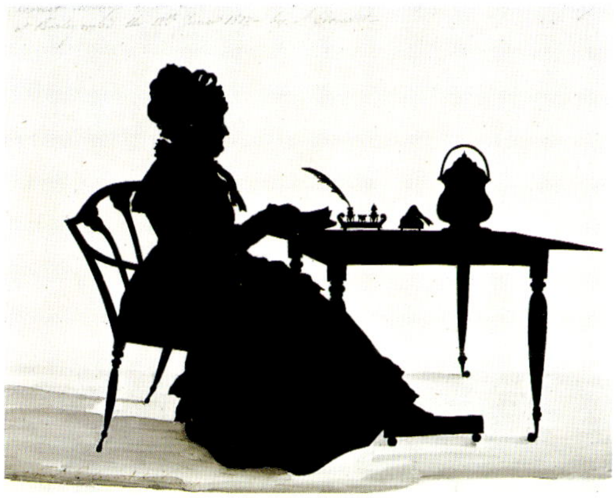

MORE NPG 4501

ICONOGRAPHY

1778 Painting by Richard Samuel, *Portraits in the characters of the Muses*, see Groups NPG 4905.

1778 On 5 March 1778 Hannah More told Mrs Gwatkin: 'nothing but your great partiality for me could make you think it worth having. Be that as it will, I shall most readily obey you by sitting to [Daniel] Gardiner before I leave town' (Roberts 1835, I, p.139).

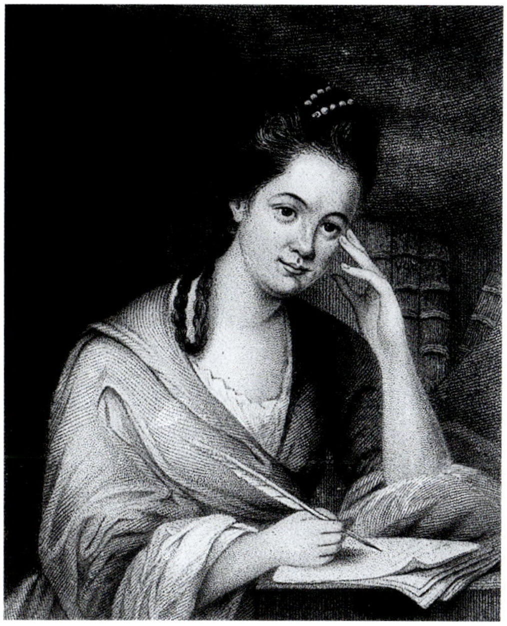

MORE E. *Scriven after Frances Reynolds 1780* (NPG D 13788)

1780 Painting by Frances Reynolds, half-length seated writing. Bristol CMAG (K313; illus. I. McIntyre, *Garrick*, 1999, f.p.466). Exhibited NPE 1868(158) lent Rev T.F. Simmons. Engraved E. Scriven 1838* (*from a drawing by Miss Simmons after a Picture presented to her by Mrs More/ Painted by Miss Reynolds Sister of the late President of the Royal Academy*). Dr Johnson interrupted one of Hannah More's sittings to Mrs Reynolds in 1780 (Roberts 1835, I, p.175).

1786 Painting by John Opie,* half length with grey powdered hair. Girton College, Cambridge; from the Kimbolton sale, 18 July 1949, lot 90. Exhibited NPE 1868(150) lent by the Duke of Manchester. Engraved J. Chapman, W. Finden 1834 (*from the Picture painted by Opie in 1786 now in the Possession of Lady Olivia B. Sparrow*), R. Woodman 1838, anon. (reversed), A. Halbert 1845. Miniature copy by [John] Roberts, engraved C. Heath 1798 (reversed; illus. Hopkins 1947, front.), in the Strawberry Hill sale, 11th day, 6 May 1842, lot 51 (*Strawberry Hill,*

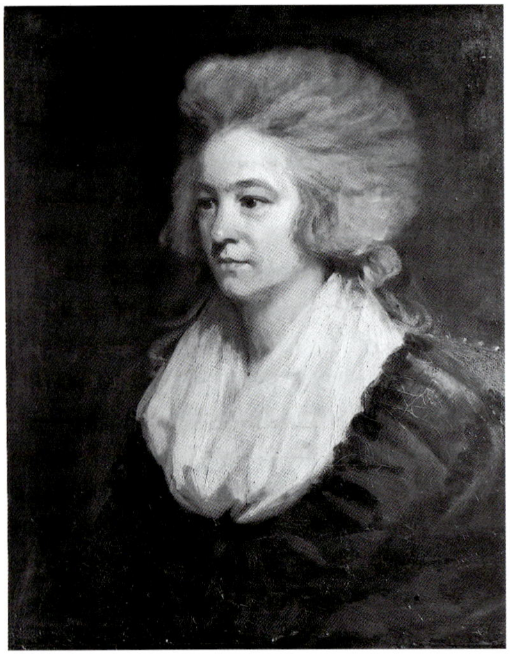

MORE by John Opie 1786 (Girton College, Cambridge)

1784, p.93). A matching drawing is in the Toronto Reference Library. More told Mrs Edward Boscawen, who commissioned the portrait, that she had 'such a repugnance to having my picture taken, that I do not know any motive on earth which could induce me to it but your wishes' (Roberts 1835, II, p.37).

1798 Anon. bust-length oval. Engraved W. Ridley 1798, 1799; Maguire (pub. P. Wogan and W. Porter).

1805 Unattributed drawing, see NPG 6533.

1809 Painting by Edward Bird, a small half-length panel. Untraced, with H.L. Nightingale 1863 (TSB 8/1a, 2). Engraved J. Godby 1809;* W.T. Fry 1819; W. Read (version); G. Parker 1826. Hannah More did not apparently care for this portrait; in 1819, on the publication of her *Works* by Cadell & Davies with the Fry engraving as the frontispiece, she advised Miss Roberts: 'you will not, I think, when you see Cadell, express to him your admiration of my sweet portrait, but rather inquire if no steps can be taken for its abolition' (Roberts 1835, IV, p.34).

1813 Drawing by J. Slater, half-length seated, engraved E. Scriven (*from a drawing by Mr Slater taken at Barley Wood in November 1813*; illus. Hopkins 1947, f.p.18). On 27 December 1813 Hannah More wrote: 'Good old Mr Bean asked me to sit to his son-in-law Mr Slater, of Newman Street, who was then in Clifton. I opposed it with all my might, but in vain. I sat at last to him; but as one sits down to a tooth-drawer. It is small, but they say extremely like . . . But the worst part is to come, I was forced to consent to its being engraved, without which it could not have been profitable to the painter. It is such a folly! At my age too. It has quite mortified me' (Roberts 1835, III, p.419).

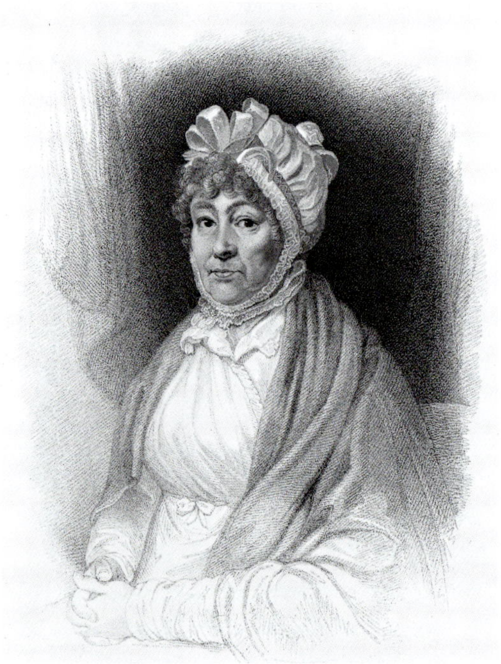

MORE J. Godby after Edward Bird 1809 (NPG D 5299)

1815 Anon. engraving (pub. John Bell) of a related portrait, half length with bonnet.

1821 Painting by H.W. Pickersgill, see NPG 412.

c.1825 Unfinished drawing by John Jackson, bust length. British Museum (1856.7.12.957). Jackson had made drawings for the engraving of Bird's portrait, see 1809 (cf. TSB 8/1b, 2).

c.1825 Plaster statuette by Lawrence Gahagan, seated, teaching a young girl at her side. Private collection.

1827 Silhouette by Augustin Edouart, see NPG 4501.

Mrs Hannah More and her favourite Squirrel, 'the old lady at a Chippendale table, the squirrel upon it', an unattributed picture described by E.M. Forster (*Abinger Harvest*, 1940 ed., p.234).

Stone bust wearing bonnet and full collar in the church porch Wrington, Avon (illus. *CL*, XCI, 1942, p.459), facing a similarly crude bust of John Locke (who was born there).

A 'Scottish School' miniature, bust-length profile to right with lace cap, sold Christie's, 19 September 1983, lot 232.

MORNINGTON, Anne, Countess of, *née* Hill 1742-1831

Mother of the Duke of Wellington, dau. of the 1st Viscount Dungannon; m. 1759 the 2nd Baron Mornington (Earl of Mornington 1760; 1735-81); Mrs Delany thought 'her education not finished enough for her to make any considerable figure' but, despite her husband's extravagance, her five sons each achieved distinction; a severe figure in later life, it was said that her letters to her sons could have been read aloud at Charing Cross.

[at the age of sixteen] 'a fine young woman altogether; rather a little clumsy, but fine complexion, teeth, and nails, with a good deal of modesty and good-humour' (Mrs Delany, 1758).

2665 THOMAS LAWRENCE c.1820

Pencil and red crayon on paper 22 x 17.5 (8¾ x 6⅞), the head 5 (2) high.; an illegible and truncated pencil annotation bottom right [perhaps *J.E.*?].

Collections: [Probably Matthew Hutchinson's sale, Christie's, 22 February 1861,[1] lot 84 'Lawrence, Head of the Countess of Mornington'];[2] Henry Farrer, by whom presented 1861.[3]

Exhibition: *Lawrence*, New Haven, Fort Worth, Richmond, 1993(57).

Anne, Countess of MORNINGTON NPG 2665

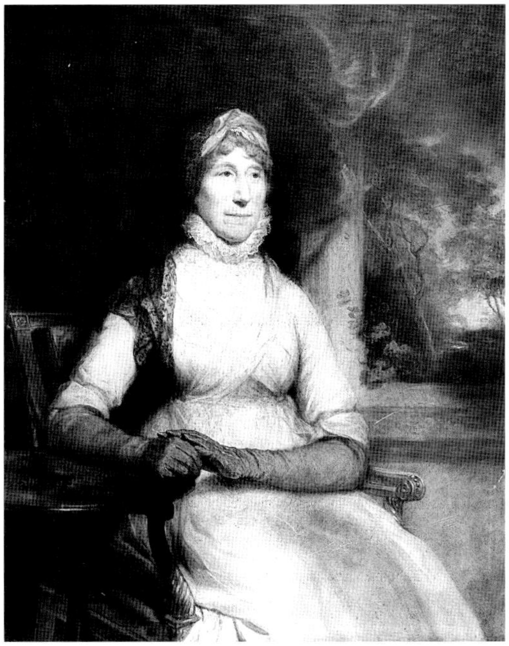

Anne, Countess of MORNINGTON by William Owen 1813 (untraced)

The likeness agrees satisfactorily with that in the Rochard watercolour of c.1820, see below. Another watercolour of Wellington's mother in a private collection bears a false Lawrence signature.[4]

1 Hutchinson, from Blackheath, was selling more than 50 drawings by Lawrence, together with 7 paintings by him bought at the Lawrence sale; two of his own copies after Lawrence were also in this sale.
2 Garlick had previously supposed this might be of Catherine (d. 1825) who m. 1812 the 4th Earl of Mornington (*Lawrence* 1964, p.238).
3 But not accessioned until 1934.
4 See W. Armstrong, *Lawrence*, 1913, p.186; *Lawrence* 1964, p.238.

ICONOGRAPHY

1760 Pastel by Robert Healy, oval whole length, feeding peacocks. Stratfield Saye. Exhibited *Irish Portraits*, NPG, 1969(73).

c.1760 Pastel by Robert Healy, half length. Stratfield Saye.

c.1781 Pastel by John Russell, half length, wearing white 16th-century 'deuil blanc'. Badminton. Probably correctly identified.

1813 Painting by William Owen, three-quarter length seated. Stratfield Saye (illus. *Apollo*, CII, 1975, p.24). Version formerly at Chequers.*

c.1820 Miniature by George Chinnery, half length. NG of Ireland (2685).

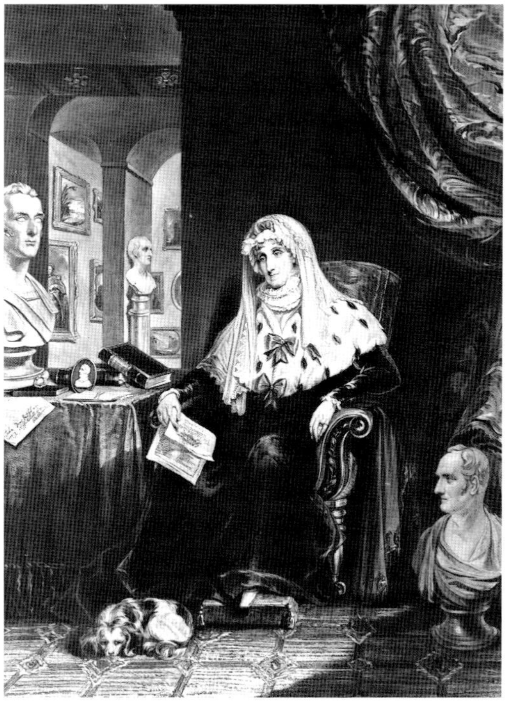

Anne, Countess of MORNINGTON T. Hodgetts after Lady Burghersh 1838 (NPG archive)

c.1820 Watercolour attributed to S.J. Rochard, seated at table. Stratfield Saye (illus. C. Hibbert, *Wellington*, 1997, f.p.112).

c.1820 Drawing by Thomas Lawrence, see NPG 2665.

1838 Painting by Priscilla, Lady Burghersh [daughter of the 3rd Earl Mornington], whole-length seated, holding the *London Gazette* with the news of Waterloo. Apsley House. Exhibited NPE 1867(823) lent by the Countess Dowager of Westmorland. Engraved T. Hodgetts 1839.*

An undated miniature by Henry Edridge, exhibited RA 1879(6p), BFAC 1889(xvii 1), *Guelph* 1891(1026), lent J. Whitehead. An unidentified portrait exhibited *Arts, Industries & Manufactures*, Dublin 1872(National Portrait Gallery 343) lent Rev G.H. Reade.

DOUBTFUL PORTRAITS

Miniature by Andrew Plimer (illus. *Connoisseur*, LI, 1918, p.68), half length wearing white, exhibited NPE 1867(435) lent by the Duke of Wellington; wash drawing, half length, a winged putto at her side (Stratfield Saye).

MORRIS, Charles 1745-1838

Song-writer; served in America before joining the 2nd Life Guards in London, where in 1785 he became 'punch-maker and bard' of the Sublime Society of Beef Steaks; he received an annuity from the Prince of Wales; *A Collection of Songs by the inimitable Captain Morris* appeared in 1786 and his *Lyra Urbanica* posthumously in 1840; 'many of his convivial songs will live, and much that he ought not to have written is already forgotten' (*GM*, 1838).

739 JAMES LONSDALE c.1814

Canvas 75.5 x 62 (29¾ x 24½) lined; retouchings in the coat and head, with some blistering in the lower area; an old damage in the upper left area; discoloured varnish.

Brown eyes, short white hair, wearing a white collar and cravat, dark blue coat with brass buttons (the uniform of the Society of Beef Steaks);[1] in his right hand a paper inscribed *A Bit of a Thing*; a rust-coloured drape above and to the right.

Collections: Painted for Henry Frederick Stephenson MP (1790-1858); his son, Sir Augustus Keppel Stephenson QC,[2] by whom presented 1885.

The interest of this portrait is confined to the history of the Sublime Society of Beef Steaks, which flourished from 1735 to 1867.[3] Lonsdale (elected 1819) was painter to the Society and Morris (elected 1785, retired 1831) the Bard, 'the life and soul of the Society'. The donor's father (elected 1813) was treasurer and secretary until his death in 1858 (and his son had been elected in 1849). Lonsdale painted seven portraits of members for the Society, all dispersed in 1869. NPG 739 was painted expressly for the secretary, probably at the same time as the three-quarter length given to the Society (see below 1814), to judge by the apparent age. In 1884 the donor admitted that NPG 739 was 'a bad [painting]'[4] and it was first rejected by the Trustees but, 'further particulars of [Morris's] life & of his political influence having been obtained', it was accepted.[5]

1 'The blue coat with brass buttons, the buff waistcoat, the tights and hessians', as described by W. Arnold, *The Life and Death of the Sublime Society of Beef Steaks*, 1871, p.31.
2 Letter to Scharf, 4 November 1884: 'painted by Lonsdale for my father & ... now come into my possession on the recent death of my mother' (NPG archive).
3 See W. Arnold, *op. cit.*, 1871, see note 1, from which this account has been taken.
4 Letter to Scharf, 27 November 1884 (NPG archive). Stephenson presented at the same time Lonsdale's portrait of Sir William Bolland (another member of the Beef Steaks and shown in the Society's uniform), NPG 730, see Walker *Regency*, I, p.55, II, pl.119.
5 Meetings of 19 November 1884 and 2 May 1885; the reasons for their change of mind may seem tenuous.

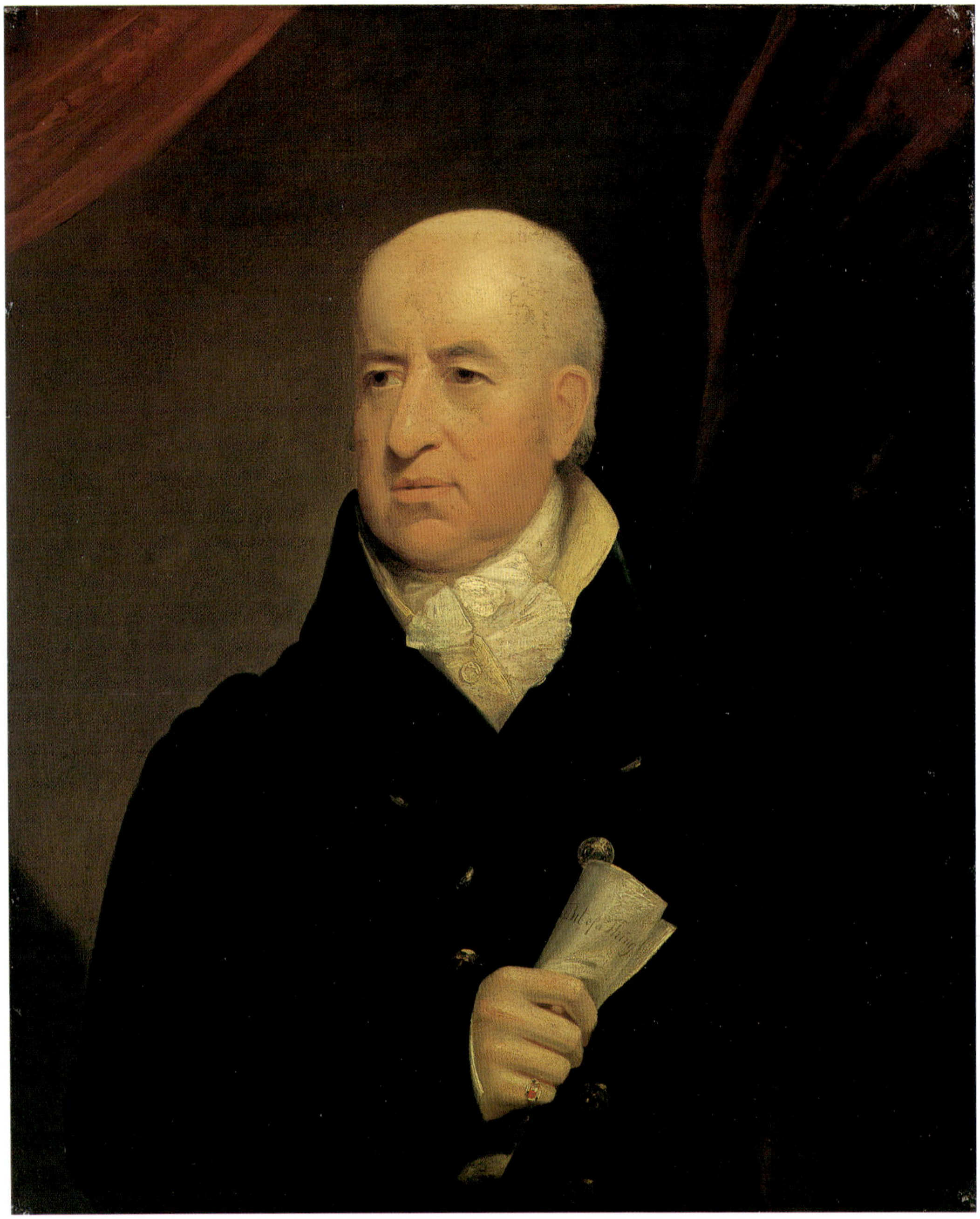

MORRIS NPG 739

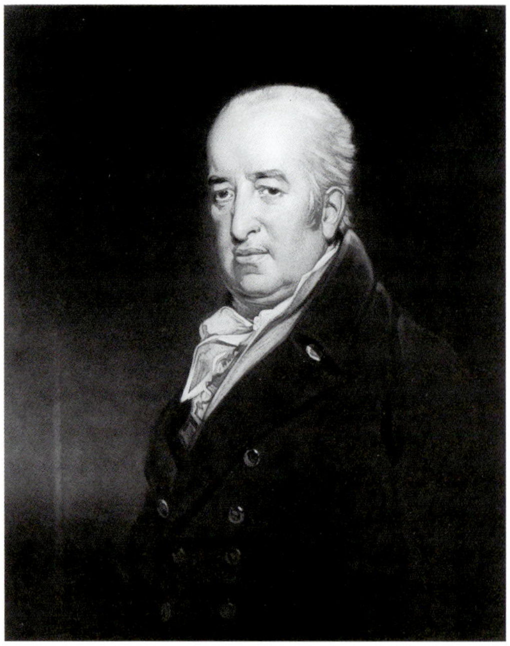

MORRIS T. Hodgetts after A.J. Oliver 1807 (NPG D 13747)

DOUBTFUL PORTRAIT

Unattributed portrait, half-length young man holding a large sheet, with F. Simpson, Brighton, 1916 (photograph NPG archive).

ICONOGRAPHY

1807 Painting by A.J. Oliver, half length. Exhibited RA 1807(91). Engraved T. Hodgetts 1808;* W. Greatbach 1840 (from a picture *in the possession of the family*).

1814 Painting by James Lonsdale, three-quarter length in the same Society uniform as NPG 739, a paper in his left hand inscribed *The Holy Alliance*. Christie's, 13 March 1997(36), from the Beef Steak sale, Christie's, 7 April 1869, lot 60, bt. Lord Dalhousie (a member), thence by descent at Hopetoun. Presumably the picture Lonsdale exhibited RA 1814(572) as Capt Morris. In 1997 the frame retained the Society's cypher of Beef and Liberty.

c.1814 Painting by James Lonsdale, see NPG 739.

Morris's sympathies with the Prince of Wales led to his appearance in several satires; he was portrayed by James Gillray in 1790 and 1797 (George 7710 and 9023).

MORTIMER, John Hamilton 1740-79

Painter; b. Eastbourne; exhibited SA 1762-77, FS 1763-64 and RA 1778-79; President SA 1774-76; the last decade of his short life was somewhat intemperate and increasingly given to the production of banditti scenes in the manner of Salvator Rosa.

'a man of fine personal appearance, of great gaiety of manners, and a most delightful companion. He had moreover, an excellent heart ... a tall, elegantly formed man' (Henry Angelo, 1828).

234 after JOHN HAMILTON MORTIMER [c.1765]

Canvas 75 x 63 (29½ x 24¾) lined; the surface is rubbed; numerous retouchings particularly on the right and in the foreground areas.

The seated Mortimer has brown eyes, dark hair, wearing a light grey coat, brown breeches and grey stockings; the boy has brown eyes, dark hair and wears a red waistcoat and grey coat; a green folder stands by the chair.

Collections: R. Twining 1857; Miss Elizabeth Twining, by whom presented 1867.

Exhibitions: *Art Treasures*, Manchester, 1857 (modern masters 88) lent R. Twining; *Artists at Work* 1981–82(6).

Reference: *Mortimer* 1986, no.32a.

A pedantic copy of Mortimer's somewhat incomplete *Self portrait with Joseph Wilton and a Student* of c.1765 (Royal Academy),[1] with the figure of Wilton omitted. The setting possibly evokes the sculpture gallery of the Duke of Richmond in Whitehall which Wilton had directed until 1761; Mortimer copied there from 1758 until c.1762 and the classical bust carried by the boy resembles the Chrysippos type.[2]

A copy of NPG 234, previously recorded, is now untraced.[3]

1 *Mortimer* 1986, no.32, fig.49. Mortimer's head alone engraved A. Van Assen 1810.
2 Cf. G.A. Richter, *The Portraits of the Greeks*, 1984 ed., pp.101–08.
3 *Mortimer* 1986, p.132, under no.32.

ICONOGRAPHY

Self Portraits

c.1762 Painting, half length. Untraced, formerly with descendants of the artist (illus. *Mortimer* 1986, no.7, fig.22). Mortimer exhibited a self portrait SA 1762(74).

c.1765 Painting,* whole-length seated holding a gun, with his father (Thomas 1697–1774) and brother (Charles 1734–1803). Yale Center for British Art (B1981.25.466; illus. *Mortimer* 1986, no.29). A version exhibited *First Hundred Years*, RA, 1951–52(45), sold Bonham's, 13 December 1984, lot 207.

c.1765 Painting[?], engraved V. Green 1779, half length holding a palette (*Mortimer* 1986, no.30).

c.1765 Painting, see NPG 234.

c.1765–70 Painting,* *Caricature Group*, see Comparative Groups.

c.1775–78 Painting,* bust length, in character with turban. Towner AG, Eastbourne (*Mortimer* 1986, no.107). Copy in the Tate Gallery (T1041); another sold Christie's, New York, 25 November 1998, lot 46. A related pen drawing in the Victoria and Albert Museum (E.328.1961) probably connected with the etching by R. Blyth 1782 (illus. *Mortimer* 1986, fig.1); also engraved W. Watt 1833.

DOUBTFUL PORTRAITS

A portrait of an elegantly dressed young artist sketching by a tomb (Royal Academy), long attributed to Richard Wilson and called a portrait of Mortimer, is now considered to be an unknown artist painted by Mortimer, and a drawing in the British Museum (1859.7.9.70), exhibited as a self-portrait in 1974, probably shows James Paine (*Mortimer* 1986, nos.44, 168).

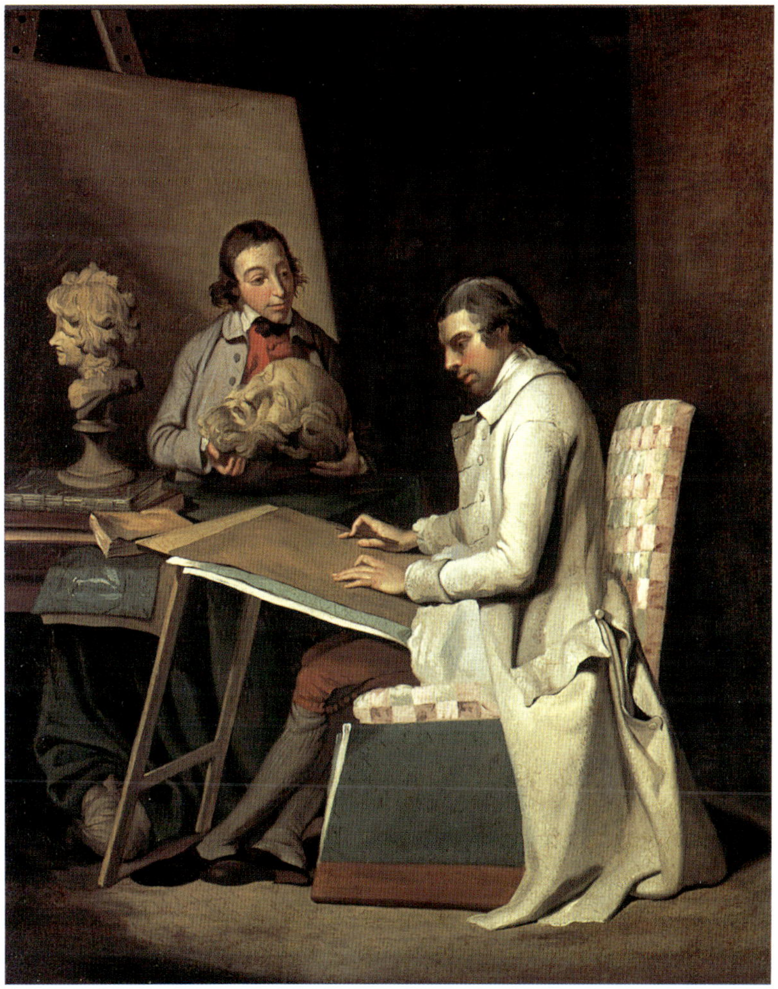

MORTIMER NPG *234*

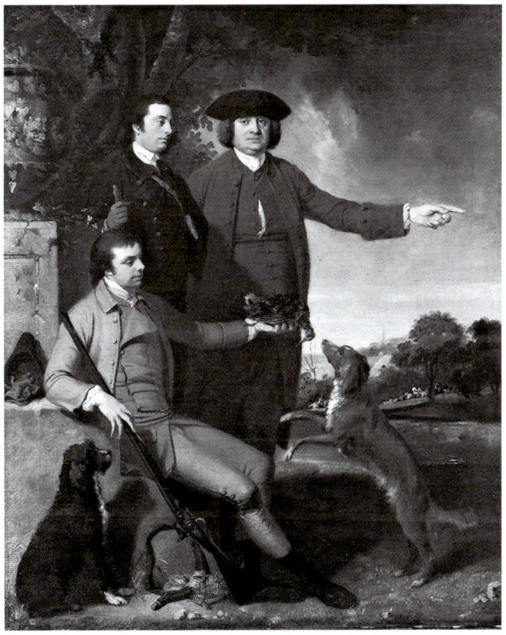

MORTIMER Self portrait with his father and brother c.1765 (Yale Center for British Art, Paul Mellon Collection)

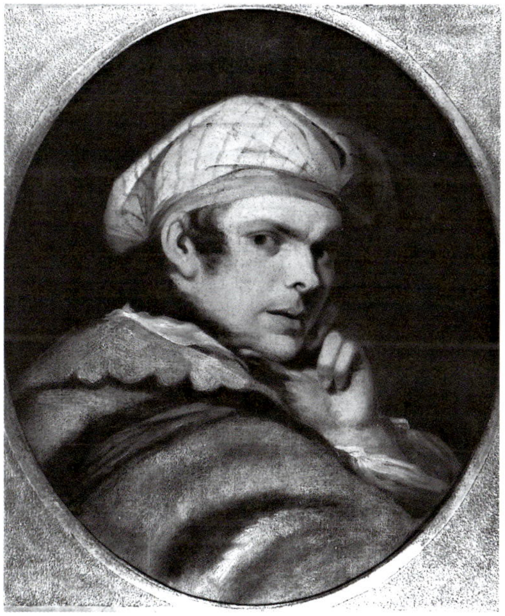

MORTIMER Self portrait c.1775–78 (Towner Art Gallery, Eastbourne)

MULGRAVE, Constantine John Phipps, 2nd Baron 1744-92

Naval officer; lieutenant 1762 and captain 1765; MP 1768-74, 1776-90; FRS 1771; led an expedition to the Arctic 1773; suc. as 2nd Baron Mulgrave [I] 1775; lord of the Admiralty 1777-82; served in the Channel during the American war; joint paymaster-general of the forces 1784-90; cr. Baron Mulgrave [GB] 1790.

'as he was formed on rather a heavy colossal scale, the Opposition, to distinguish him from his [brother Charles, also an MP] denominated him 'Ursa Major'' (Sir Nathaniel Wraxall, 1815).

1094 UNKNOWN ARTIST c.1775

Canvas 122 x 100 (48 x 39½) cleaned and lined 1973; the surface is abraded, the red ground showing through in the background areas.

Grey eyes, brownish hair, wearing a captain's uniform, blue coat with white revers, gold trim and brass buttons, white waistcoat with gold trim, white breeches and stockings; holding an ice-spear with wooden and metal points.

Collections: By descent from the sitter at Mulgrave Castle through his cousin, the 1st Viscount Normanby (d.1831), to the 3rd Marquess of Normanby; his sale, Christie's, 8 May 1897, lot 103, bt. Colnaghi, from whom purchased 1897.

In 1773, by Royal command, a voyage was made 'to see how far navigation was practicable towards the North Pole'.[1] Captain Phipps in the *Racehorse* was given command, accompanied by Captain Lutwidge in the *Carcass*, and he was additionally charged with making 'such observations of every kind as might be useful to navigation, or tend to the promotion of natural knowledge'.[2] Between 3 July and 22 August he explored the ice-bound coasts around Spitsbergen, within 10 degrees of the North Pole, returning to England in September. The following year he published a detailed, illustrated account,[3] evidently consulted by the painter of NPG 1094 - John Cleveley's plate of the *Racehorse and Carcass on 7 August 1773* showing a similar team of men hauling a boat across the ice. Phipps's head may be based on an original study, unlike his stance[4] and the menacing sky.[5]

A replica, with minor variations in the background, remains with family descendants. Haydon recounted seeing this, or NPG 1094, in Lord Mulgrave's collection in 1808:

> We were loitering about the picture of Lord Mulgrave's brother blocked up in the ice, in the Arctic expedition in which Nelson sailed as a middy. Lord Mulgrave, holding the lamp, said: 'What is that my brother has got hold of? Is it a boat hook?' 'No. My Lord!' said [George] Colman [the younger], in his half-throttled, witty voice; 'it is the North Pole!'[6]

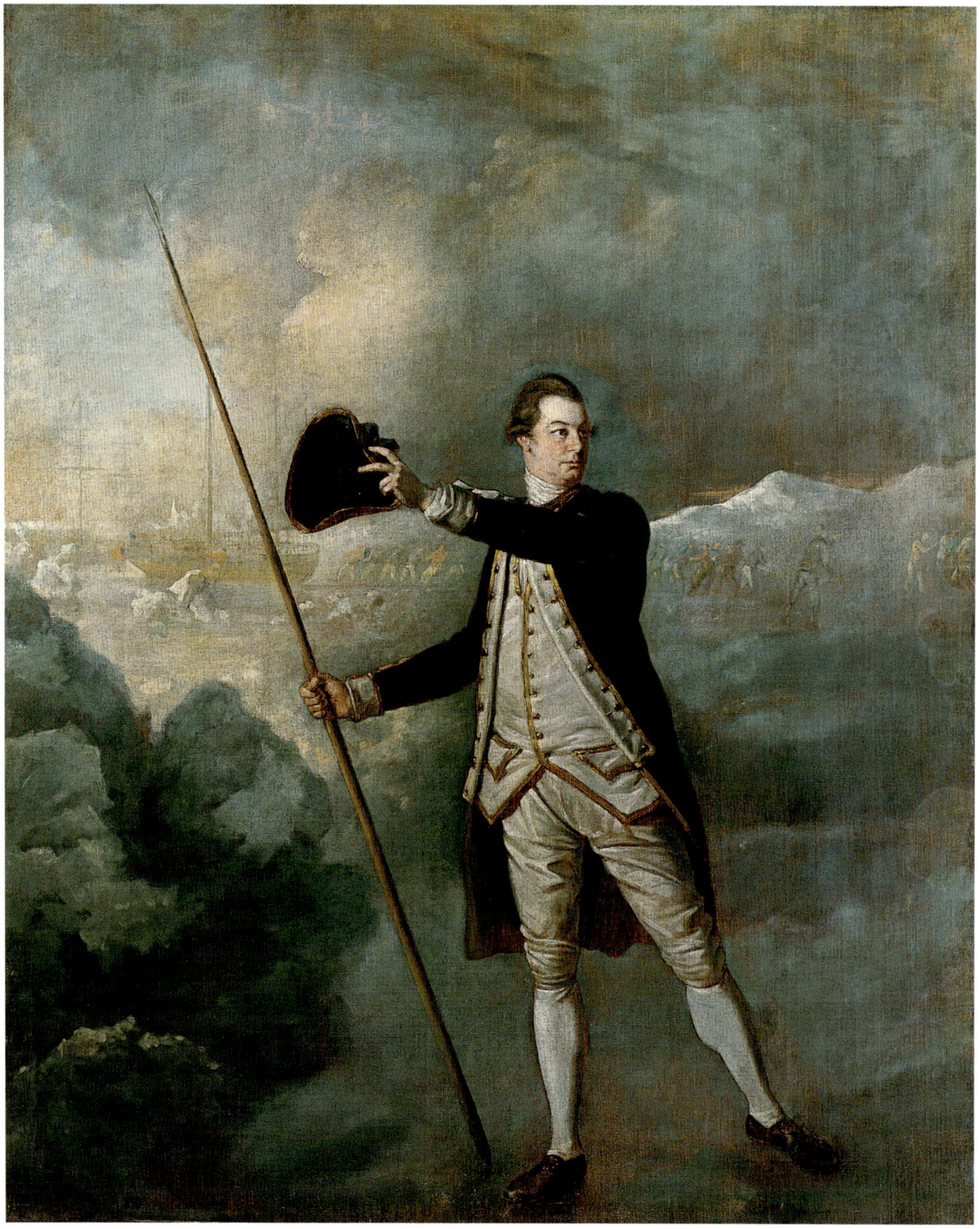

2nd Baron MULGRAVE NPG *1094*

1 Phipps 1774 (at note 3), p.10.
2 *Ibid.*, p.20.
3 C.J. Phipps, *A Voyage towards the North Pole*, 1774, of which pp.1-76 contain Phipps's journal and pp.77-253 detailed appendices ('an account of all the experiments and observations'); reprinted in J. Pinkerton, *Voyages and Travels*, I, 1808, pp.538-94, and partly in *GM*, XLIV, 1774, pp.420-24.
4 Perhaps ultimately inspired by the Prima Porta *Augustus* in the Vatican Gallery.
5 Phipps 1774 (at note 3), p.71, recorded that the arctic sky 'was in general loaded with hard white clouds'; there was just one day of foul weather.
6 B.R. Haydon, *Autobiography*, 1926 ed., i, p.79.

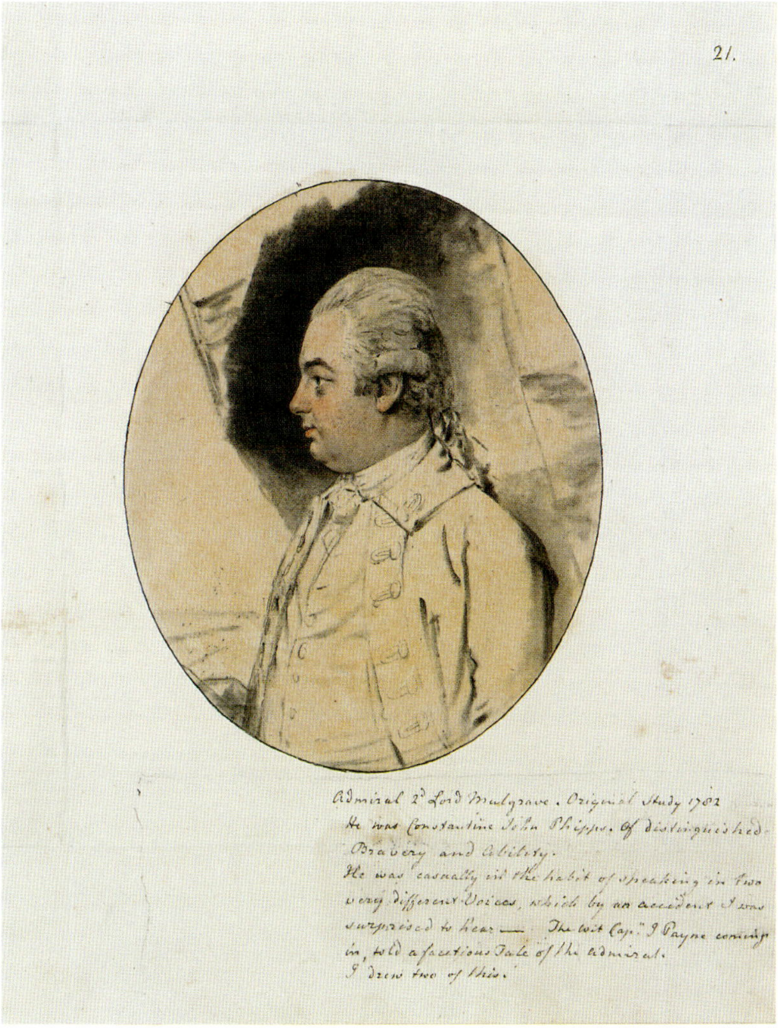

2nd Baron MULGRAVE
NPG *966*

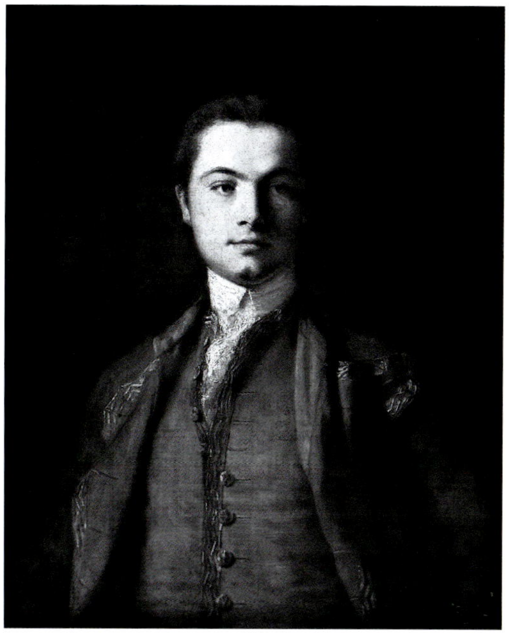

2nd Baron MULGRAVE by Joshua Reynolds 1764 (Montreal Museum of Fine Arts)

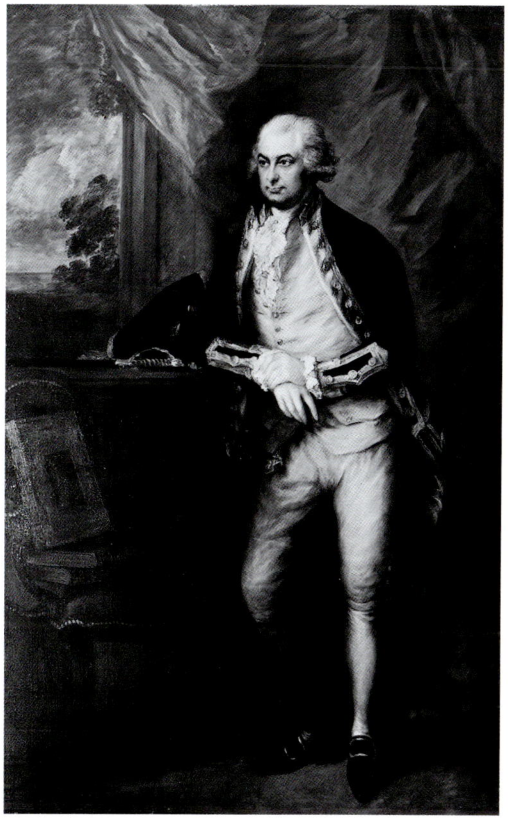

2nd Baron MULGRAVE by Thomas Gainsborough 1785-86 (Mulgrave Castle)

966 JOHN DOWNMAN 1782

Watercolour and pencil on paper, the oval image 20.7 x 17 (8¼ x 6¾); yellow staining within the image apparently from an old adhesive; the whole sheet 36 x 28 (14¼ x 11) was previously folded over to 25.5 x 21.5 (10 x 8½); inscribed by the artist in ink lower right, written over an erased pencil inscription: *Admiral 2d Lord Mulgrave. Original study 1782/ He was Constantine John Phipps. Of distinguished/ Bravery and Ability./ He was casually in the habit of speaking in two/ very different Voices, which by an accident I was surprised to hear - The wit Capn.Payne coming in, told a facetious tale of the Admiral.*[1] */ I drew two of this.* Numbered *21* top right.

Brown eyes, grey powdered hair with a queue.

Collections: Purchased from Colnaghi 1894.

Part of Downman's inscription is borne out by Wraxall, who remarked upon Mulgrave's 'singularity of physical conformation, possessing two distinct voices, the one strong and hoarse, the other shrill and querulous'.[2]

1 Mulgrave was not an admiral, but a lord of the Admiralty (1777-1782).
2 Wraxall, II, p.173.

ICONOGRAPHY

1764 Painting by Joshua Reynolds,★ half length. Montreal Museum of Fine Arts (1963.1399; Mannings 2000, no.1446).

1772 Painting by Thomas Gainsborough, half-length oval. Mulgrave Castle (Waterhouse 1958, no.508). Exhibited RA 1772(97). Engraved anon. 1774.

c.1775 Painting by an unknown artist, see NPG 1094.

1777-78 Painting by Joshua Reynolds,★ *The Society of Dilettanti*, see Comparative Groups.

c.1779 Painting by Ozias Humphry, half length. National Maritime Museum (GH 27). Exhibited NPE 1867(745). Engraved anon. 1782 with elaborate surround including upright book lettered *Philoso/Trans/ Vol./I* and an unrolled paper lettered: *Journal of a Voyage to the North Pole* (another state has: *Memoirs of the Royal Society*). Replica sold

Sotheby's, 9 July 1947, lot 96, and a bust-length miniature copy sold Christie's, 13 February 1962, lot 8.

1782 Drawing by John Downman, see NPG 966.

1785-86 Painting by Thomas Gainsborough,* whole-length standing, in Captain's uniform. Mulgrave Castle (Waterhouse 1958, no.509). Engraved W. Ridley 1802 and anon. 1802 (both bust-length ovals). A replica, cut down to half length, sold Sotheby's, 14 November 1990, lot 142 (Waterhouse 1958, no.510). Half-length versions were with Knoedler 1922 (oval) and Baroness Burton; a three-quarter length version sold Christie's, 11 April 1980, lot 146.

DOUBTFUL PORTRAITS

Painting by Edward Alcock, sold Phillips 24 January 1995, lot 24; painting by N. Hone, sold Christie's, 29 September 1977, lot 267.

MUNRO, Sir Hector, KB 1726-1805

Army officer, s. of Hugh Monro of Novar; served in India 1760-65, hailed as the liberator of Bengal after his victory at Buxar 1764; MP 1768-1802; major-general 1777 (East India Company); returned to India 1778 as commander at Madras, capturing Pondicherry, but during the campaign against Hyder Ali he was replaced by Eyre Coote 1780 and returned home 1783; KB 1779; major-general 1782 (British army), colonel of the Black Watch 1787, lieutenant-general 1791 and general 1792.

1433 attributed to DAVID MARTIN 1785

Canvas 122 x 95 (48 x 37½) lined; the surface is abraded and there are scattered retouchings; repaired tears to left of head and in the canon; pentimenti round his head and outstretched left hand; signed and dated on the canon: [*D.* or *C.*] *W.P.* [?]/ *pnxt 1785*, and inscribed *G.R.III.*/[*B*]*UXAR.*/ *PONTDECHEREY.*[1]

Brown eyes, white hair tied with a black ribbon, wearing a major-general's uniform[2] of a red coat with gold trim, blue-tabbed collar and epaulette, a white waistcoat and breeches with black boots; in addition he wears a steel gorget, a purple sash and the ribbon of the Bath. The attendant horseman wears a black hat, a light-grey coat with yellow collar and a yellow waistcoat. In the distance the nearer troops wear blue coats and black hats, the further red coats and black hats.

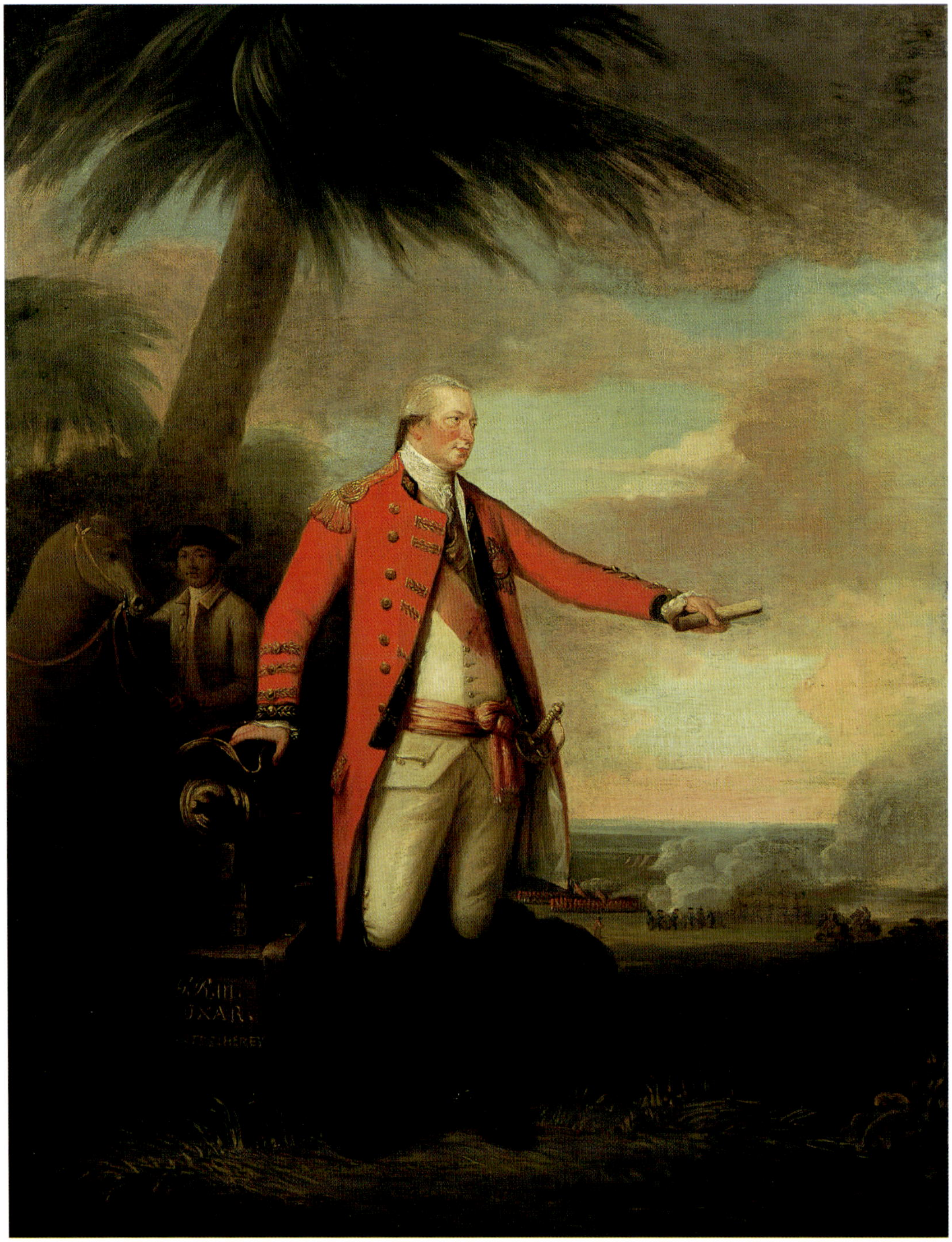

MUNRO NPG *1433*

Collections: Purchased from the Brook Street Gallery 1906.

Exhibition: *Cornchest for Scotland*, Edinburgh, 1986 (n.n.).

The indistinct signature, as Jacob Simon recently indicated, recalls that of David Martin who, after he had been made the Prince of Wales's Limner in Scotland in 1785, used the suffix *P.P.W* after his name,[3] and an attribution to Martin is not impossible.

1 The normal contemporary English spelling was Pondicherry (cf. *GM*, XLIX, 1779, p.153).
2 See Maj. N.P. Dawnay, *JSAHR*, XXXI, 1953, pp.70, 72.
3 See *David Martin Bicentenary Exhibition*, St Andrews, 1997, nos.18-23, 25-27.

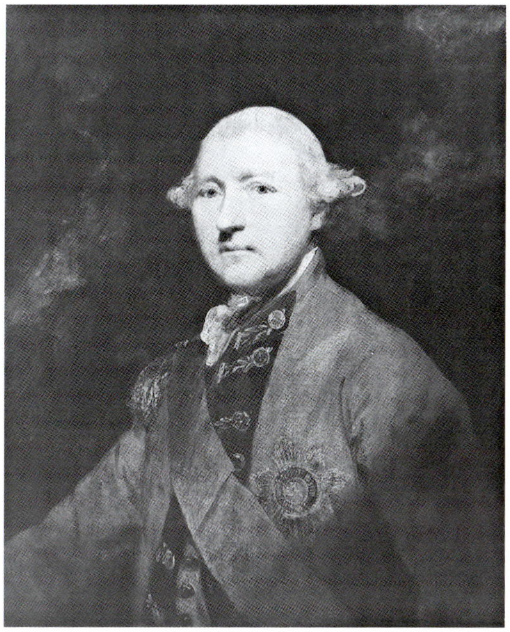

MUNRO by Joshua Reynolds 1785 (untraced)

ICONOGRAPHY

c.1778-80 Painting by George Willison, whole length. Private collection (Archer 1979, p.442n19). Willison was in India 1774-80.

1785 Painting by Joshua Reynolds,* half length, with ribbon and badge of the Bath. Untraced (Mannings 2000, no.1311). Exhibited RA 1785(89).

1785 Unattributed painting, see NPG 1433.

1796 Medallion by James Tassie (Gray 1894, no.278). Plaster in the Scottish NPG (PG 468).

DOUBTFUL PORTRAIT

Painting by Francis Cotes dated 1763, when Munro was in India (Johnson 1976, no.125).

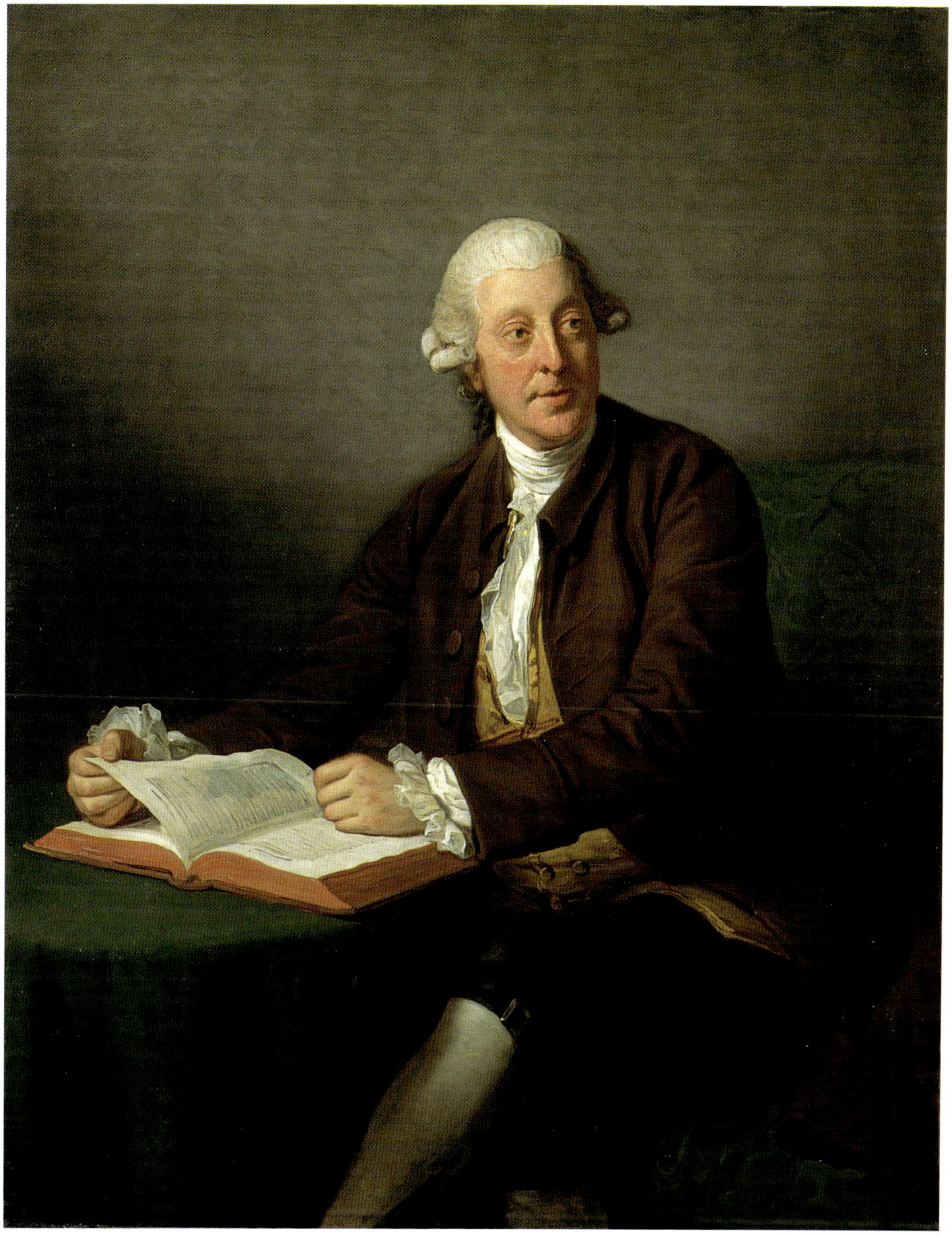

MURPHY NPG 10

MURPHY, Arthur 1727-1805

Writer, actor and barrister; pupil of Foote, he retired from the stage after two years in 1756, when his first play, *The Apprentice,* was staged; his last, *The Rival Sisters*, appeared in 1793; called to the Bar in 1762, he retired from practice in 1788; published translations of Horace and Tacitus and wrote a biography of Garrick 1801.

'Before his sickness about ... 1792, he was of a fine form, neither corpulent nor thin. He was tall and graceful, and his limbs were proportionately adjusted: his bones small; his hands and fingers delicate, and his shoulders rather narrow: the contour of his face was oval, and marked a little with small pox; his nose was acquiline: his eyes light and full: his complexion fair' (Jesse Foot, 1811).

10 NATHANIEL DANCE 1777

Canvas 129.5 x 103 (51 x 40½) lined; cleaned 1977.

Brown eyes, white powdered wig with a black tie, wearing a brown coat, yellow waistcoat with gold trim, black breeches and white stockings; the table cloth and chair upholstery are green.

Collections: 'Miss Thrales' by 1805 (see Engravings), probably Hester Thrale (1764-1857), later Viscountess

Keith;[1] Colnaghi 1857, from whom purchased 1857.

Engravings: T. Cook 1786 (for Murphy's *Works*); W. Ridley 1805 *from an Original Picture by Nathl Dance Painted in the Year 1786* (*European Mag.*); W. Ward 1805 (*from an Original Picture in the Possession of Miss Thrales*); P. Condé 1811 as *Aetatis 50*; Hall (*Biographical Mag.*); E. Scriven 1815; J. Romney 1817.

Exhibitions: NPE 1867(843); *Arts, Industries & Manufactures*, Dublin, 1872(National Portrait Gallery 141a); *Dance* 1977(42); *Johnson*, Arts Council, 1984(82).

Despite the engraver Ridley's assertion that NPG 10 was painted in 1786 (four years after Dance had retired from professional practice), it is generally dated 1777, as stated by Condé (see above). William Ward's mezzotint of 1805 agrees exactly with NPG 10 and gives the owner as 'Miss Thrales', but it is unlikely that it was originally painted for one of the Thrale daughters (the eldest of whom was thirteen in 1777). If NPG 10 was painted for Mrs Piozzi (for whom Murphy was 'a mighty pleasing Man'), it may have reached Streatham before the Reynolds portrait (see below). For a related oil sketch attributed to Dance, see below c.1777.

A copy is in the Yale University Art Gallery (1930.108). A version, differing only in showing an oval buckle on the breeches,[2] was with Peter V. Crooks (Washington DC) in 1973; another was with S.R. Christie-Miller in 1913,[3] possibly the portrait with W.M. Withers in 1911.[4]

1 The oldest of the Thrale daughters, who m. Viscount Keith as his second wife in 1808. In 1805 two other daughters remained unmarried: Sophia (1771–1824), who m. Henry Hoare in 1807, and Susanna 1770–1858, who did not marry, and to whom Murphy had dedicated a translation from Vanière (*The Bee*, 20 March 1799). In 1816 Mrs Piozzi wrote that her daughters 'have a very fine Portrait of Mr Murphy full Length painted by Dance' (30 May 1816, to Sir James Fellowes; *Piozzi Letters*, V, 1999, p.493).

2 Engraved J. Neagle 1811 (pub. J. Stockdale).

3 He then believed it showed Boswell (NPG archive).

4 He alleged it was signed and dated 1791 and came from the collections of Braine [?] & St Helens [Lord St Helens, Alleyne Fitzherbert, 1753–1839] (NPG archive). One of these two versions was presumably the Murphy by Dance sold Christie's, 13 November 1830, lot 43, bought Stockdale.

ICONOGRAPHY

See also the *Harvard Catalogue*, III, pp.245–46, and Highfill, X, p.399.

1773–79 Painting by Joshua Reynolds, half length. Christie's, 14 December 1917, lot 72; from the Thrale and Peel collections (Mannings 2000, no.1312).

1777 Painting by Nathaniel Dance, see NPG 10.

c.1777 Painting called Nathaniel Dance, half length, a quill in his right hand. NG of Ireland (959; illus.

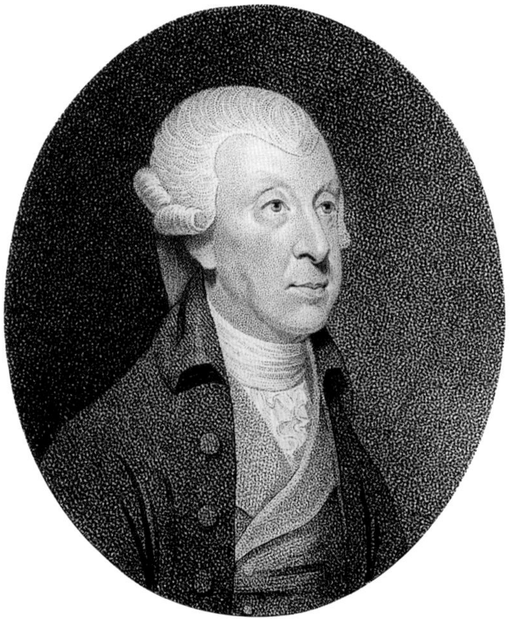

MURPHY W. Ridley after Samuel Drummond 1798 (NPG D 13805)

Highfill, X, p.392). Engraved E. Scriven 1815, from a drawing by John Jackson after *the original by Dance in the collection of Mr Davies* (possibly of Cadell & Davies who published the print in the *British Gallery*, 1822); the Jackson drawing is now NG of Ireland (2169). The fundamental pose resembles that of NPG 10 and it is conceivably a preliminary oil sketch.

c.1790? Pastel by Ozias Humphry, half length. American Art Association, New York, 25 October 1934, lot 35, and previously Christie's, 8 June 1928, lot 15; said to have descended from the artist (cf. Williamson 1918, p.220).

1798 Painting by Samuel Drummond, bust-length oval, engraved W. Ridley;* Evans.

1799 Medallion by T.R. Poole, engraved by P. Condé as *Aetatis 72*, i.e. 1799 (illus. Highfill, X, p.393).

Posthumous

1806 Bust by Peter Turnerelli, *all'antica*, but showing warts on his right cheek and below lower lip, exhibited RA 1806(852). Engraved E. Scriven 1807.

MURRAY, Hon. James 1719–94

Army officer and colonial governor, 5th s. of the 4th Baron Elibank [S]; lieutenant-colonel 1751, major-general 1762, lieutenant-general 1772, general 1783; fought in the Seven Years War under Prince Ferdinand and under Wolfe at Quebec; first governor of Canada 1760–66; governor of Minorca 1774–82, until surrendering to the French; both his governorships ended with official enquiries, followed by honourable acquittals.

3122 UNKNOWN ARTIST c.1767

Canvas 127 x 101.5 (50 x 40) lined c.1890;[1] somewhat rubbed; pentimenti on his right sleeve, left cheek and lower part of the coat; small tear bottom right.

Grey eyes, white powdered wig with a black ribbon, wearing the uniform coat of a major-general,[2] bright red coat with gold trim and blue cuffs, and buff/silver waistcoat with gold trim; Abraham Heights, Quebec, seen in the distance.

Collections: By descent to the sitter's great-great grandson, Gen. E.R.B. Murray, by whom bequeathed 1942.

Exhibitions: *Pageant of Canada*, Ottawa, 1967(103); *Georgian Canada*, Toronto, 1984 (77); *Eighteenth-century Montreal*, Montreal, 1993.

A slightly reduced derivative version, showing sky and a rampart wall in the left background, belongs to the Canadian High Commission in London. Two later copies are recorded: one made c.1910 for the National Archives of Canada, Ottawa,[3] another in the Sigmund Samuel collection, Toronto, by 1952 (slightly reduced all round).

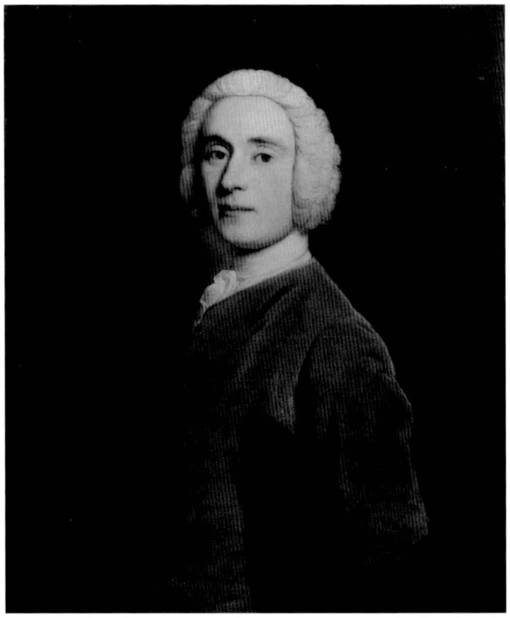

MURRAY by Allan Ramsay 1742 (Scottish National Portrait Gallery)

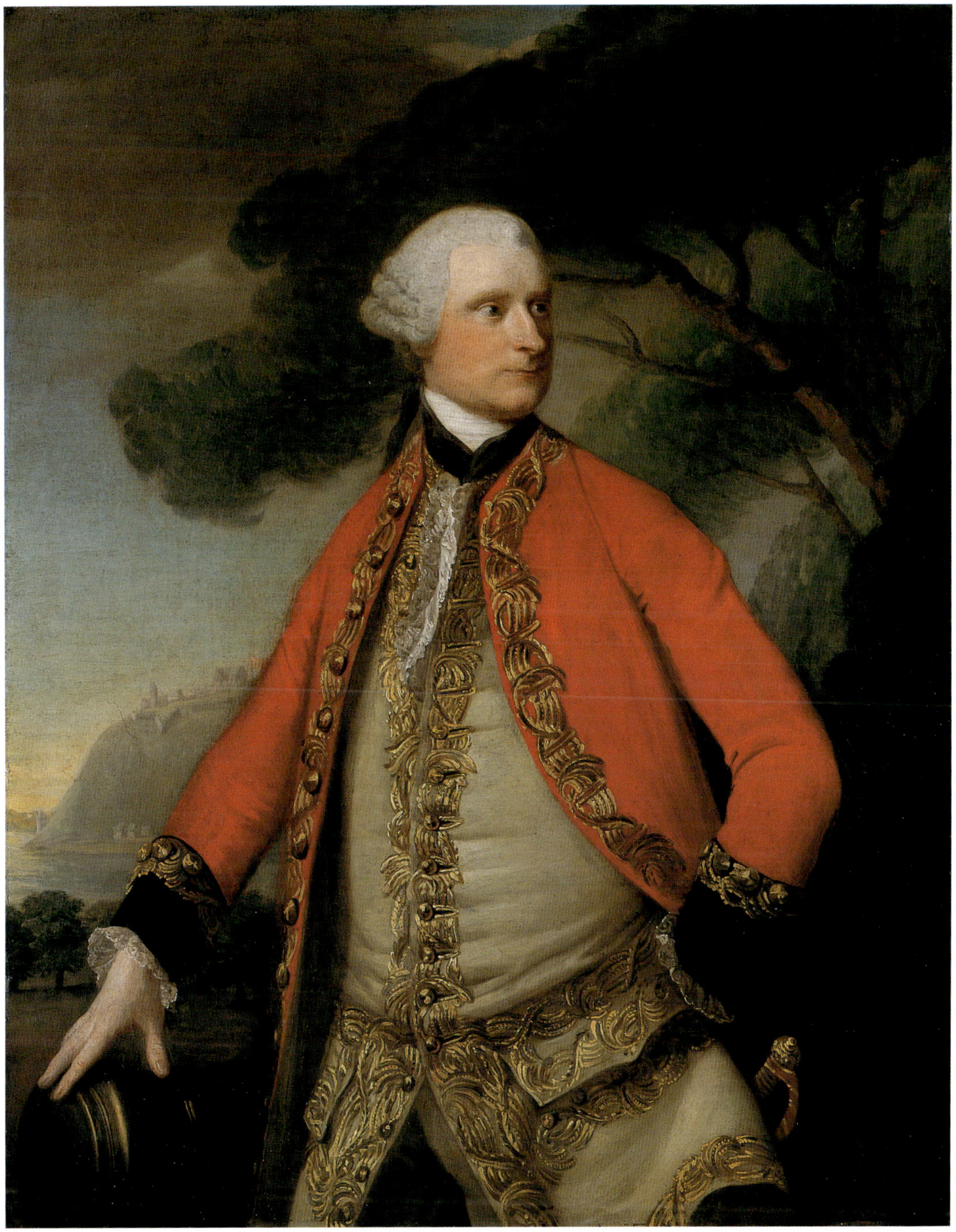

MURRAY NPG *3122*

1 Letter from Enid Vaughan of February 1940 'the canvas was stretched in Ireland some fifty years ago'.
2 The uniform coat was introduced in 1767; the waistcoat should be buff - the white pattern was only introduced in 1772, the month Murray was promoted to lieutenant-general (note by Maj. N.P. Dawnay, 1951, on file).
3 According to a letter of February 1940 from Enid Vaughan (NPG archive; she was secretary to the testator's brother).

ICONOGRAPHY

1742 Painting by Allan Ramsay,* half length. Scottish NPG (PG 2215; Smart 1999, no.388).

c.1767 Painting by an unknown artist, see NPG 3122.

1783 Anon. engraving, half length profile, pub. S.A. Cumberlege (*Universal Mag.*).

Murray's court-martial in 1782 for alleged misconduct during the siege of Minorca aroused popular interest and prints then published included one by James Gillray (George 6041; illus. *Gillray*, Tate, 2001, nos.7a, 7b).

MURRAY, William, see MANSFIELD

MYLNE, Robert 1733-1811

Architect and civil engineer, b. Edinburgh; travelled in France and Italy 1754-59; designed the bridge at Blackfriars (opened 1769; demolished 1868); FRS 1767; surveyor of the cathedrals at St Paul's and Canterbury 1766-67; his peculiarities 'were chiefly connected with a high independence of spirit, and an inflexible sense of duty and justice' (Nichols *Anecdotes*, IX, p.233).

'a man of austere manners ... [and] violent temper, [who] appeared to have a contempt of every art but his own, and for every person but himself' (James Elmes, 1847).

'a rare jintleman, but as hot as pepper and as proud as Lucifer' (anon., one of Mylne's workmen).

1150 GEORGE DANCE 1795

Pencil on paper 25.8 x 19.2 (10⅛ x 7½) faded, with slight damages above the head; signed and dated in pencil, bottom right: *Geo Dance/ 1795*, the date reinforced; laid down on a contemporary washed mount lettered: *ROBERT MYLNE*.

Collections: The artist's grandson, the Rev George Dance; his sale, Christie's, 1 July 1898, lot 97, bt. Colnaghi for the NPG.

Engraving: W. Daniell 1810 (*Dance Portraits*).

1075 see Groups, *Men of Science living in 1807-08* by JOHN GILBERT, FREDERICK SKILL and WILLIAM & ELIZABETH WALKER 1858-62

ICONOGRAPHY

1757 'Whilst [Mylne] was at Rome in 1757, a good portrait of him was painted by [Richard] Brompton, which was engraved at Paris by V. Vangeliste 1783, inscribed "Robert Mylne, Architect, Engineer, Surveyor, aetat. xxiv. F.R.S.;" [illus. R. Mylne, *Scottish Masons*, 1897, f.p.281] and a copy of it is here attached' (Nichols *Anecdotes*, IX, 1815, p.233). Profile bust to right with banded hair. Brompton is not otherwise recorded in Rome until 1758.

c.1760? Pastel as a young man. Miss J.M.H. Mylne, Ware, in 1966.

1795 Drawing by George Dance, see NPG 1150.

1796 Miniature by his daughter, bust profile. Miss J.M.H. Mylne, Ware, in 1966. Engraved H. Adlard

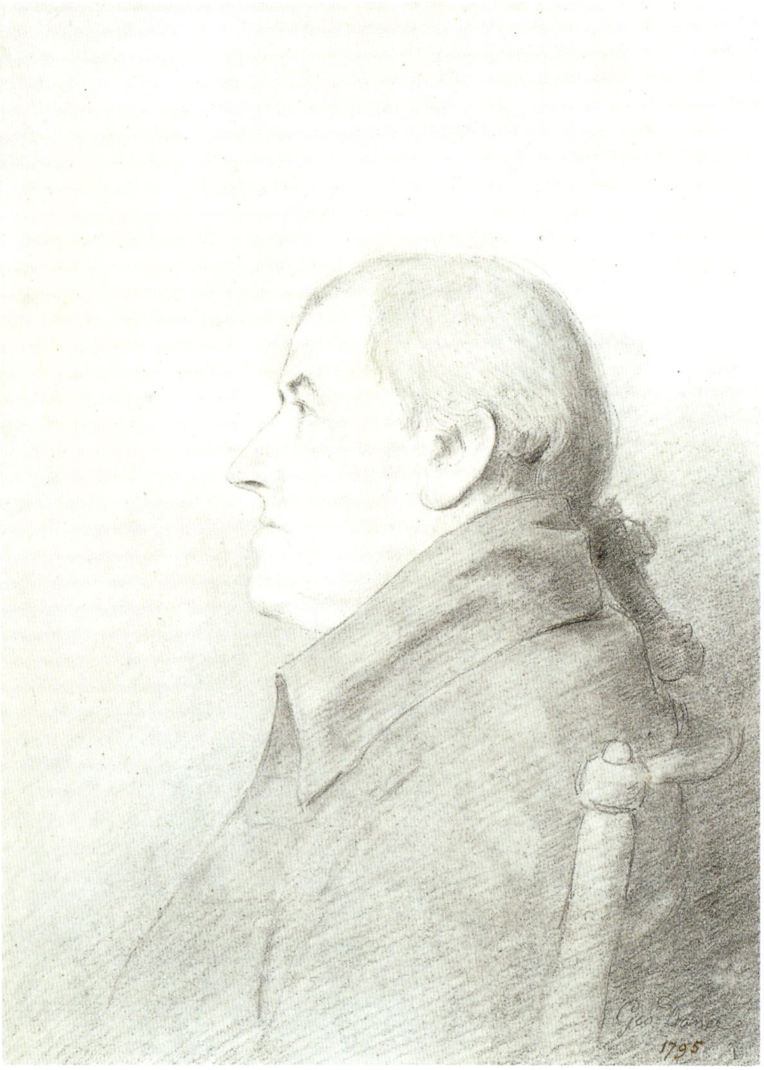

MYLNE NPG *1150*

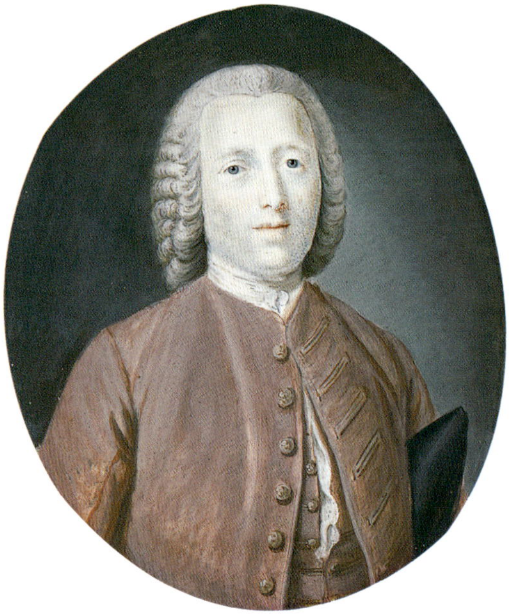

NEEDHAM NPG *4889*

1860 (with arms: *or, a cross moline az. square pierced of the field betw. three mullets of the second,* motto: *tam arte quam marte*; illus. *CL*, CXLIV, 1968, p.402). See Groups NPG 1075.

Anon. engraved satire 1760, *Just Arriv'd from Italy The Puffing Phoenomenon* [i.e. Mylne] *with his Fiery Tail turn'd Bridge builder* ... (concerning the building of Blackfriars Bridge and the alleged support of Mylne by Lord Bute); a reversed version *Arriv'd from Italy* 1760 (Stephens 3733-34).

NASSAU de ZUYLESTEIN, William Henry, see ROCHFORD

NEEDHAM, John Turberville 1713-81

Catholic priest and scientist, b. London; studied at Douai and ordained at Cambrai 1738; FRS 1746; FSA 1761; tutor to British travellers in France and Italy 1751-67; elected to the *académie des sciences* in Paris 1768; director of the literary society, later the Imperial Academy, Brussels, from 1769; his publications treated hieroglyphics, honey-bees and electricity; Boswell found him 'a learned, accurate, easy man'.

4889 JEAN-BAPTISTE GARAND 1755

Water- and body-colour on paper 13 x 11.5 (5⅛ x 4½) oval; the flesh area faded, the blue stippled shadows very apparent; inscribed verso, in the hand of Charles Townley: ... *Turberville Needham/ [fe]llow of the Royal and Antiquarian Societies in London. Correspondent/ of the Academy of Sciences in Paris/ President of the Royal Academy at Bruxelles,/ and author of various Philosophical, moral/ and Physical essays.// Painted by Monsieur Garand, when Mr Needham/ was Governor at Paris 1755.*

Blue eyes, white powdered wig, wearing a purple suit, his black hat under his left arm.

Collections: Charles Townley (1737-1805), by descent to the 3rd Lord O'Hagan; his sale, Christie's, 19 May 1939, lot 4, bt. Labey for Francis R.D. Needham;[1] sale after his death, bt. Paul Rich, Farnham Common, from whom purchased 1972.

Exhibition: *Richard Challoner*, Westminster Cathedral, 1981(168).

Townley, whose remarkable collection of classical sculpture is preserved in the British Museum, was educated at Douai (like his fellow-catholic Needham), and introduced to Parisian society before he returned to England c.1758. The inscription on NPG 4889, which must have been written after 1769 (when Needham became director of the Brussels academy), may imply that Needham was his tutor in Paris in 1755 (when Townley was eighteen-years old).

1 Ink inscription on the frame verso: *From the pictures of the 3rd Lord O'Hagan, sold at Christie's May 19 1939 and bought by Francis R.D. Needham of Welbeck Abbey.*

DOUBTFUL PORTRAIT

The miniature by Henry Edridge in the Holburne Museum, Bath, exhibited SKM 1865(753) lent Sir T.W. Holburne, described as 'after Reynolds', cannot show the same Needham.

NEWCASTLE, Henry Clinton, 2nd Duke of 1720-94

Courtier, 2nd s. of the 7th Earl of Lincoln; suc. as 9th Earl 1730; travelled in Italy 1739-41; a succession of Court appointments accrued from his uncles, Henry Pelham, whose daughter he married, and Thomas Pelham, Duke of Newcastle-under-Lyme, whom he suc. by special patent as 2nd Duke 1768, taking the additional name of Pelham; FRS 1747, KG 1751.

2504 studio of WILLIAM HOARE c.1752

Canvas 237 x 146 (93¼ x 57½) lined; cleaned 1982; *pentimenti* round the column, upper right, suggest there was once a drape around it.

Blue eyes, white powdered wig, in ceremonial Garter robes, his plumed hat on the green tablecloth by his side.

Collections: Lord Edward William Pelham-Clinton (d.1907);[1] Miss Lillie Belle Randell,[2] by whom bequeathed in memory of her sister, Mrs Cornelius Garrison (d.1925), 1931.

Exhibition: Foreign Office 1932-82.

NPG 2504 was given as a portrait of the 1st Duke of Newcastle (see note 1), the correct identification first appearing in the NPG Summary catalogue of 1970.

It is a studio version of the portrait belonging to the University of Nottingham, formerly at Clumber House,[3] which shows an arched window on the left, as does Hoare's elaborate chalk drawing of the finished painting in the British Museum (1894.4.17.4).[4] Hoare painted several portraits for the Pelham family,[5] and it was reported in March 1752 that he had been 'sent for ... to draw Mr. Pelham's whole family, they preferring him to any Painter in London.[6]

A half-length version was sold Christie's, SK, 8 June 2000, lot 42 (as a 'Gentleman by a Follower of Hudson').

1 As stated in a note from G.B. Croft Lyons, a friend of Miss Randell, to Milner, c.June 1925 (NPG archive): 'Thomas Holles Pelham Duke of Newcastle 1693-1768 in Peers-robes formerly the property of General Pelham Clinton'; and see *NPG 75th Annual Report*, 1932, p.3.

2 Daughter of a Missouri landowner who had lived with her sister Mrs Cornelius Garrison (d. 1925) in Grosvenor Square.

3 Clumber House cat., 1923, no.76; illus. *The Newcastles of Clumber*, University of Nottingham, 1992, front.

4 Described by Binyon, II, p.314, no.14, as Frederick, Prince of Wales.

5 See Kerslake *Early Georgian*, I, pp.193-94(NPG 757), 208-09(NPG 221); see also *Hoare* 1990, no.14a.

6 Letter from John Brown, 7 March 1752, to Humphrey Senhouse; E. Hughes, *North Country Life*, II, 1965, p.93; and cf. Vertue, III, p.161.

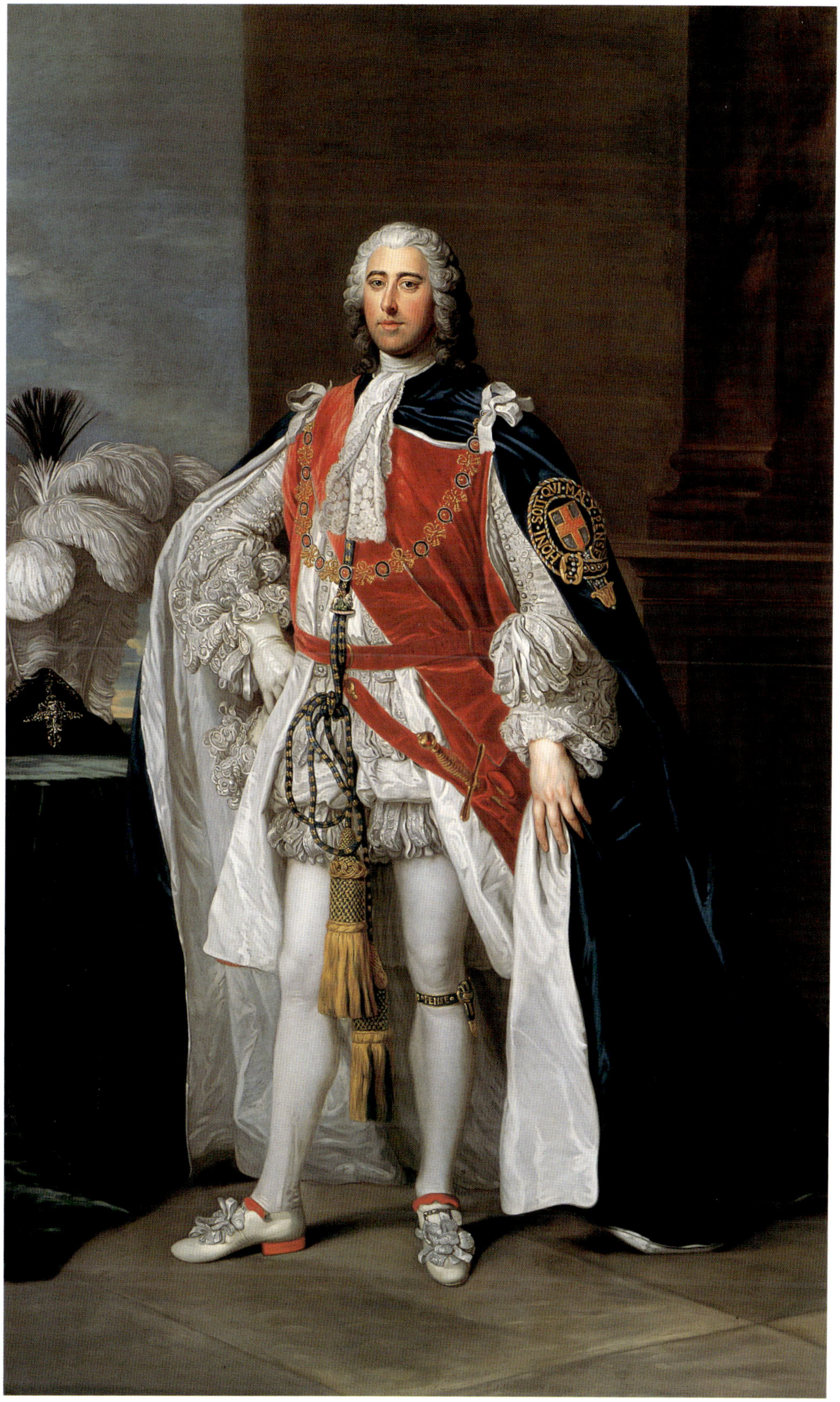

2nd Duke of NEWCASTLE NPG *2504*

ICONOGRAPHY

1741 Pastel by Rosalba Carriera,* bust length. University of Nottingham, formerly at Clumber House (cat., 1923, no.335). Drawn in Venice, pendant to a pastel of Horace Walpole (who wears an identical coat; see Orford), with whom Lincoln spent much time in northern Italy.

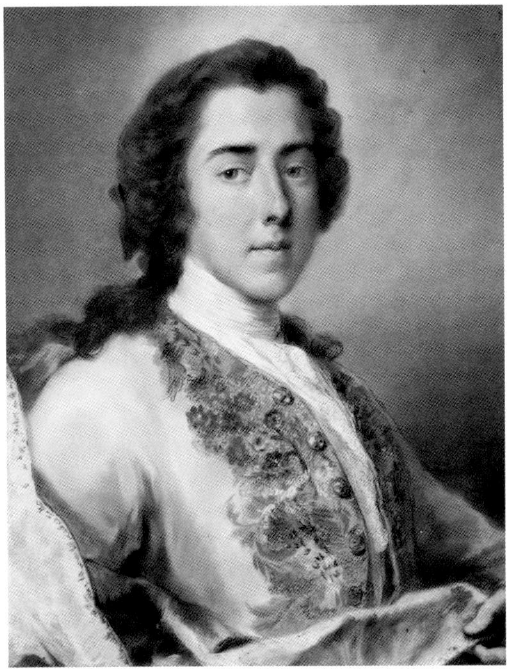

2nd Duke of NEWCASTLE by Rosalba Carriera 1741 (University of Nottingham)

c.1750 Painting by Arthur Devis, the 9th Earl of Lincoln with his wife and son Lord George Clinton (1745–52). Sotheby's, 29 May 1963, lot 94 (*Devis* 1983, no.40). A pastel by Hoare exactly repeated the Devis figure of the Countess as a half length.

c.1752 Painting by William Hoare, see NPG 2504.

c.1760 Pastel, probably after William Hoare, half length with the Garter ribbon over his left shoulder. Sotheby's, 19 February 1964, lot 35 (as George III by John Russell), from Lord Harrington's collection. Perhaps a version of the half-length pastel by William Hoare, wearing an orange velvet coat with embroidered front and the ribbon and star of the Garter, formerly at Clumber House (cat., 1923, no.304).

1770 Drawing by P-J. Lion, bust-length circular. Private collection. formerly at Clumber House (cat., 1923, no.356, with a pendant drawing of his second wife). Lent to Birmingham MAG 1958.

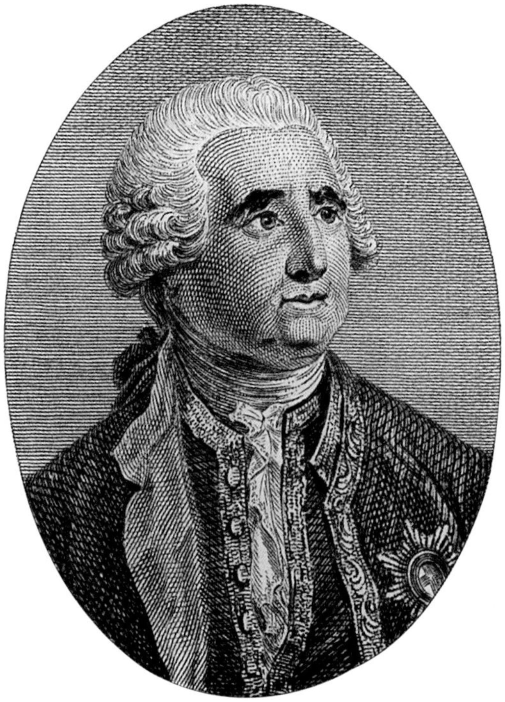

2nd Duke of NEWCASTLE C.T. Warren 1792 after W.H. Brown (NPG D 13806)

1788 Painting by Francis Wheatley, *The Return from Shooting*, showing the 2nd Duke on horseback with Clumber House in the distance. Graves AG, Sheffield (illus. Webster 1970, p.99) from Clumber House (cat., 1923, no.134). Exhibited RA 1789(17); NPE 1867(649) lent by the Duke of Newcastle. Engraved F. Bartolozzi 1792.

1792 Drawing by W.H. Brown, bust-length oval, engraved C.T. Warren 1792* (*The Senator*).

Other portraits, now untraced, were listed in the Clumber House cat., 1923: painting attributed to Charles Jervas of the three children of the 7th Earl of Lincoln (no.77); painting attributed to Enoch Seeman, whole length as a youth, (no.275); unattributed pencil and coloured drawing of five heads in profile of the 9th Earl, his Countess and their three sons (no.450).

DOUBTFUL PORTRAIT

Miniature by André Rouquet, bust-length oval without Garter, sold Sotheby's, 20 July 1981, lot 97 (Foskett 1979, p.171, pl.39g).

NICHOLSON, Ann, see ALLAN

NORFOLK, Charles Howard, 11th Duke of 1746-1815

Whig politician and voluptuary; FRS 1767; sty. Earl of Surrey 1777; suc. as 11th Duke and Earl Marshal 1786; FSA 1779 and president 1793; renounced catholicism to become MP 1780-86; lord of the Treasury 1783; a friend of Fox and the Prince of Wales; from 1789 he restored Arundel Castle, acting largely as his own (Gothick) architect.

'His person large, muscular, and clumsy, was destitute of grace or dignity, though he possessed much activity. He might indeed have been mistaken for a grazier or butcher by his dress and appearance; but intelligence was marked in his features, which were likewise expressive of frankness and sincerity' (Sir Nathaniel Wraxall, 1815).

'As he advanced in age he increased in bulk; [in 1814] such was his size and breadth, that he seemed incapable of passing through a door of ordinary dimensions. Yet he had neither lost the activity of his mind nor that of his body' (*ibid.*).

5294 THOMAS GAINSBOROUGH 1784-86

Canvas 230 x 151 (90½ x 59½) lined; the coronet, robes, arms and baton were added to the original composition (see below); discoloured varnish with a marked shrinkage craquelure, particularly in the blacks and in the gold drapery to the right, with numerous discoloured retouchings; a repaired damage by his left foot; pentimenti suggest changes in the bottom-left area and in his right hand and baton.

Blue eyes, short dark hair, wearing dark purple Van Dyck dress with black breeches, gold garters and gold buckles on his shoes; he holds the Earl Marshal's gold baton in his right hand; grey, gold-fringed gloves on and in his left hand; his Peer's robes to the left and, to the right, a ducal coronet and the Norfolk arms[1] displayed on a stone pediment.

Collections: By descent at Arundel Castle; accepted by H.M. Treasury in lieu of capital transfer tax and allocated to the NPG 1980.

Engraving: J.K. Sherwin 1790.

Exhibition: Arundel Castle 1980-.

Reference: Gainsborough 1953, p.80; Waterhouse 1958, no.517.

The complex paint structure of NPG 5294 would confirm that it is the portrait Gainsborough was working on between 1784 and 1786. He exhibited an incomplete portrait of Lord Surrey in Schomberg House in July 1784; 'the head only is finished. His Lordship is to be painted in a dress of the last century'.[2] The portrait

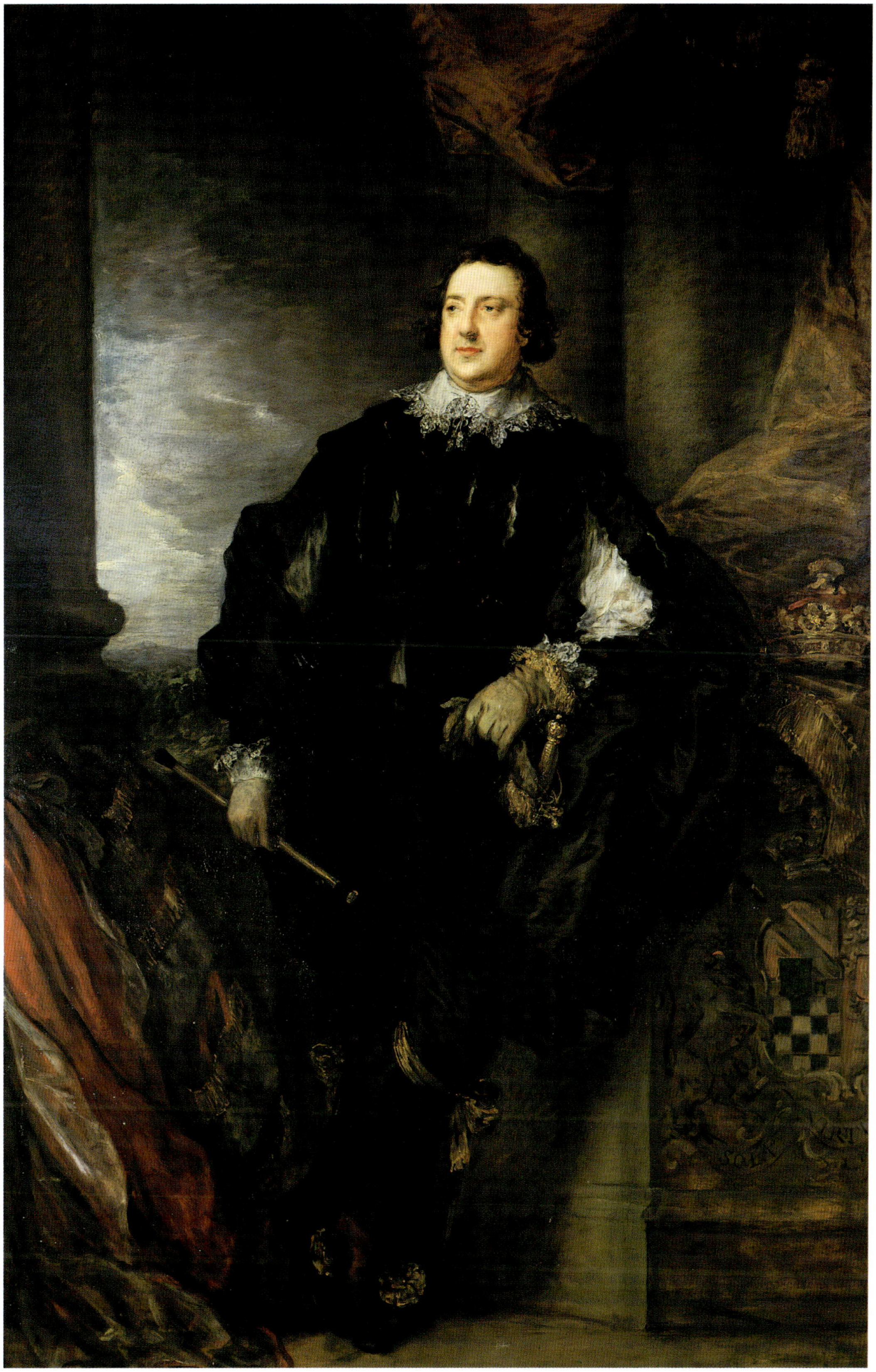

11th Duke of NORFOLK NPG 5294

was still in hand in April 1786; Gainsborough exhibited it in the autumn of that year, when it was considered a fine portrait, though the costume was twice criticised: once for not being crimson, and once for detracting from the likeness.[3] Lord Surrey had been nominated in 1782 deputy Earl Marshal to his father, whom he succeed as 11th Duke on 31 August 1786. NPG 5294 shows him as a Duke and Earl Marshal, with his coronet, robes, arms and baton, all of which must have been added to the original composition.

1 Perfunctorily painted to show: quarterly, 1st, HOWARD; and 3rd, WARREN, but the 2nd and 4th quarterings for BROTHERTON and FITZALAN, are scarcely legible; below, the motto: SOLA VIRTU[S INVICTA]; there is also a dark illegible escutcheon of pretence, presumably intended for SCUDAMORE of Holm Lacy, of which the Duke's second wife, Frances, was heiress [*de facto: quarterly, 1 & 4 gu., three stirrups leathered and buckled or; 2 & 3 or, a cross pattée fitchée gu.*].

2 Whitley 1915, p.227.

3 *Ibid.*, pp.259, 265.

ICONOGRAPHY

'At a time when men of every description wore hair powder and a queue, [Norfolk] had the courage to cut his hair short and to renounce powder, which he never used except when going to court', and his dress was 'most singular, and always the same, except when he went to St James's, namely, a plain blue coat of a peculiar dye approaching to purple' (Wraxall, III, pp.361, 364).

1767 Miniature by Nathaniel Hone, 'in the dress of the 16th-century', exhibited SKM 1865(1399) lent Philip Henry Howard. Probably the miniature with T.E. Spence in 1960.

c.1767 Unattributed portrait with his first wife (Mariana Coppinger, m. 1767, d.1768) listed at Greystoke Castle c.1820 (Harding, III, p.75).

c.1775 Painting attributed to Nathaniel Dance, half length in Van Dyck dress. Bonham's, 29 October 1987, lot 72.

c.1775 Painting by Henry Walton, bust-length oval. Private collection (*Walton* 1999, no.100).

1782 Etching by J. Sayers, whole length (George 6058).

1783 Anon. engraving, bust-length oval, his own short dark hair (as *Earl of Surry* [sic]).

1784-86 Painting by Thomas Gainsborough, see NPG 5294.

1792 Painting by Arthur Morris, exhibited RA 1792(179).

c.1795 Pastel by Daniel Gardner, unfinished half-length oval. British Museum (1914.4.6.8; illus. *Portrait Drawings*, British Museum, 1974, p.85).

1799 Painting by Thomas Lawrence,* three-quarter length standing. Arundel Castle (Garlick 1989, no.605). Exhibited RA 1799(76).

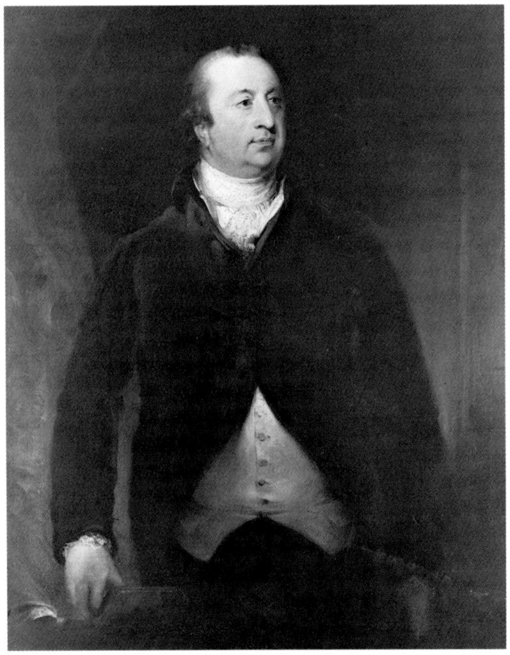

11th Duke of NORFOLK by Thomas Lawrence 1799 (Arundel Castle)

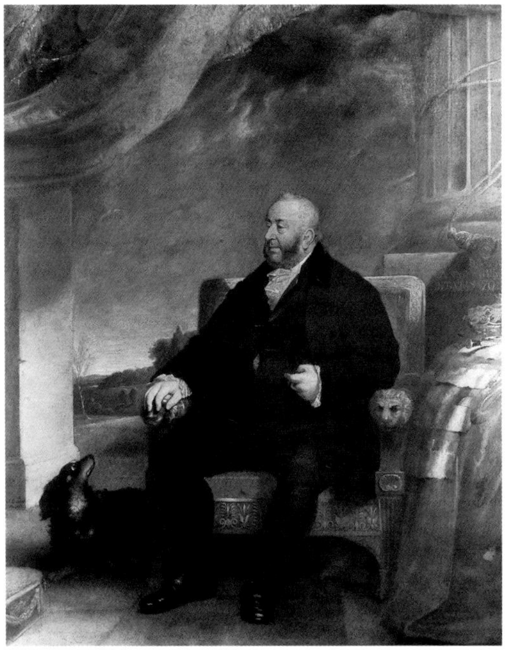

11th Duke of NORFOLK by James Lonsdale 1815 (Arundel Castle)

1800 Painting by John Hoppner, three-quarter length seated in Ducal robes, with the Earl Marshal's baton. Phillips, Scotland, 18 May 1994, lot 230 (previously Christie's, 30 June 1906, lot 137). Engraved anon., from the portrait then belonging to Henry Howard of Corby Castle, the Duke's executor (see McKay & Roberts 1909, p.184).

1811 Miniature by W.C. Ross, half-length seated, a miniature in his hand; engraved T. Williamson 1813 as President of the Soc. of Antiquaries, from the picture belonging to Dr Taylor. Presumably the miniature exhibited RA 1811(401).

1815 Painting by James Lonsdale,* whole-length seated in private dress. Arundel Castle. Exhibited RA 1815(318). Engraved C.T. Warren 1817 (bust-length). A version in Ducal robes sold Sotheby's, 4 June 1980, lot 324, included a crowned bust on a pedestal.

Posthumous

1816 Painting by A.J. Oliver, exhibited RA 1816(84).

1817 Bust by L.A. Goblet, exhibited RA 1817(1039).

Some of the stained-glass windows installed by the Duke in the course of his restoration of Arundel (removed by the late nineteenth century), showed him playing historical roles: as *Baron Robert Fitzwalter* (design by A.J. Oliver exhibited RA 1803, no.251), as *Solomon* entertaining the Queen of Sheba (design by William Hamilton exhibited RA 1790, no.176) and as a *Duke of Norfolk* witnessing the signing of the Magna Carta (designed by James Lonsdale).

The many caricatures of the Duke included etchings by Robert Dighton, *A View of Norfolk* 1796 (George 8866; illus. *Connoisseur*, XIV, 1906, p.232) and *Members of the Whig Club* 1798 (George 9216); by James Sayers, *The Comet* 1789 (George 7508) and *Worshipping the Sun* 1804 (George 10258), and by James Gillray, *Dissolution of Partnership* 1809 (George 11214).

NORTH, Anne, see SHEFFIELD

NORTH, Hon. Brownlow 1741-1820

Prelate; 2nd s. of the 1st Earl of Guilford, half bro. of the prime minister Lord North (2nd Earl of Guilford), by whom he was much favoured; fellow of All Souls 1763; canon of Christ Church 1770; Dean of Canterbury 1770-71; Bishop of Coventry and Lichfield 1771, Worcester 1774, and Winchester 1781 (and Prelate of the Garter); restored Farnham Castle; 'possessed of much higher abilities than has generally been supposed; which might, perhaps, be owing to his deafness' (*GM*, 1820).

5709 WILLIAM MINEARD BENNETT 1813

Pencil on paper 26 x 22 (10¼ x 8¾) laid down on paper, marked fading within an area 21.5 x 18 (8½ x 7) exposed by a previous mount; some staining round the edges; signed and dated, centre right: *W.M. Bennett/Delt 1813*. Conserved 1984 when backing paper with the watermark *J Whatman 1810* was removed.

Wearing private dress with the badge of the Prelate of the Garter.

Collections: Purchased from A.J. Stirling 1983.

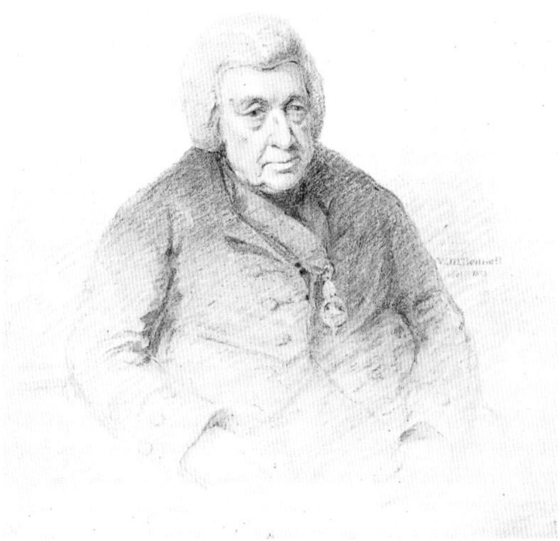

Brownlow NORTH NPG *5709*

ICONOGRAPHY

c.1763 Painting by Tilly Kettle, half length wearing academic gown and bands. Museum of Art, Baltimore (illus. *Connoisseur*, CXVI, 1945, p.111), from Merton Hall.

1776 Painting by George Romney,* three-quarter length, in rochet and chimere. The Deanery, Canterbury.

c.1785-90 Painting formerly ascribed to Henry Howard, half-length seated, in private dress wearing the badge of the Prelate of the Garter. Wolvesey, Winchester.

1793 Painting by Hugh Robinson, painted in Rome (Ingamells 1997, p.712).

c.1796 Silhouette on glass by Charles Rosenberg, *Church King & Constitution*, whole-length standing in private dress, with George III and Lord Loughborough. Private collection (illus. *Silhouettes*, NPG, 1972, no.39).

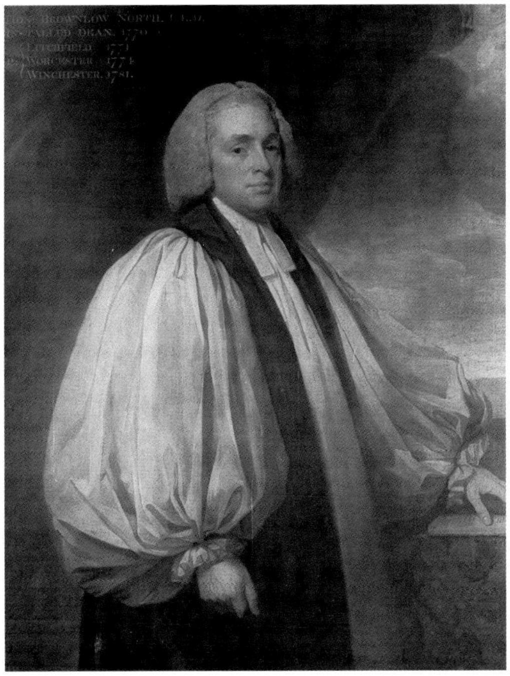

Brownlow NORTH by George Romney 1776 (The Deanery, Canterbury)

1798 Painting by Henry Howard, three-quarter length standing as Prelate of the Garter. Wolvesey, Winchester (illus. Ingamells 1981, fig.210). Exhibited RA 1798(69). Engraved W. Bond and anon. 1815. Version from the Guilford collection sold Christie's, 24 November 1972, lot 57; another sold Christie's, 27 July 1928, lot 142; a third illus. *CL*, CXLVI, 1969, p.1091. A half-length version was at Waldershare Park in 1956. Half-length portraits by Howard at Highclere Castle 1878 (Ingamells 1981, p.314) and in the Wroxton Abbey sale, Tipping's, 3rd day, 24 May 1933, lot 715, may have been of this type, but see also 1818.

c.1810? Silhouette by John Field. Sotheby's, 16 October 1978, lot 115.

1813 Drawing by W.M. Bennett, see NPG 5709.

1815 Bust by Peter Turnerelli, exhibited RA 1815(881).

1818 Painting by Henry Howard,* three-quarter length seated as Prelate of the Garter. All Souls, Oxford. Exhibited RA 1818(92). Engraved S.W. Reynolds 1819. Copy by William Dixon 1864 in Trinity College, Oxford; a half-length copy at Hartlebury Castle.

Posthumous

1822-25 Marble by Francis Chantrey, kneeling figure in high relief, part of North's monument in Winchester Cathedral (*Chantrey* 1994, no.146b).

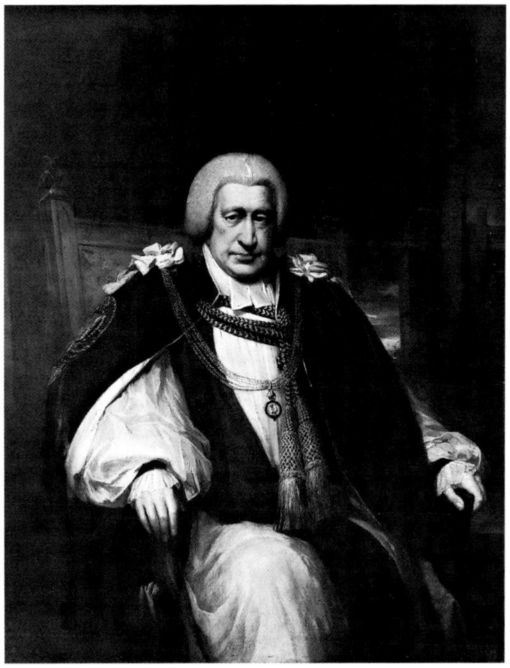

Brownlow NORTH by Henry Howard 1818 (All Souls College, Oxford)

DOUBTFUL PORTRAITS

Painting by Enoch Seeman 1743 of three young boys, once thought to include Brownlow North, but see 2nd Earl of Guilford, under 1743. An unspecified portrait listed at Sheffield Place in 1804 (Harding, I, p.13).

NORTH, Dudley Long 1748-1829

MP 1780-1821; s. of Charles Long of Hurts Hall, Suffolk; in 1789 he took the name of North on inheriting the estates of North of Little Glemham, but in 1812 he resumed the name of Long in addition to North; a zealous adherent of Fox, he was described by Samuel Johnson as 'a man of genteel appearance and that is all'.

2076 see Groups, *Mr Fox and his Friends* by WILLIAM LANE c.1813

ICONOGRAPHY

1803 Portrait by William Lane, exhibited RA 1803(581, 'Mr & Mrs D. North').

1811 Portrait by William Lane, exhibited RA 1811(795, 'Lord Crewe and Dudley North Esq'). Presumably the source for the head in *Mr Fox and his Friends*, see below.

c.1813 Drawing by William Lane, *Mr Fox and his Friends*, see Groups, NPG 2076.

Undated Bust by Joseph Nollekens, see 1833 below.

Miniature by Richard Cosway, formerly with W.C. Elwes (Williamson 1897, p.108).

Posthumous

1833 Statue by John Gibson, whole-length seated on a Grecian chair. Little Glemham church, Suffolk. Carved in Rome the head from 'a cast of the likeness modelled by Nollekens'; the original was lost at sea, but was insured and Gibson carved another (T. Matthews, *Gibson*, 1911, pp.74-75). Engraved O.U.

NORTH, Frederick, Lord, see GUILFORD

NORTHINGTON, Robert Henley, 1st Earl of c.1708-1772

Statesman; solicitor-general 1751-54 and attorney-general 1754-56 to the Prince of Wales (later George III); MP 1747-57; lord keeper of the Great Seal 1757-61 (the last person to hold this title) and lord chancellor 1761-66; lord president of the council 1766-67; Kt 1756, cr. Baron Henley 1760 and Earl of Northington 1764; renowned for his temper and intemperance, he was valued by George III as a lawyer of firm judgment.

2166 studio of THOMAS HUDSON [1760-61]

Canvas 126 x 100.5 (49½ x 39½) lined; the varnish is discoloured and there are scattered retouchings.

Grey eyes, white powdered wig; holding the great seal, wearing the lord chancellor's black gown with gold trim; red-velvet chair with the carved coronet of an Earl.

Collections: By descent to the 6th Baron Henley, by whom presented 1927.[1]

Exhibitions: NPE 1867(446) lent by the 3rd Baron Henley.[2] Royal Courts of Justice 1966-.

Reference: Miles 1977, no.141.

NPG 2166 is a studio version of the portrait by Hudson exhibited at the SA in May 1761(51, 'the present

Lord Chancellor') and engraved (undated) by James McArdell.[3] This was either the portrait now at All Souls, Oxford,[4] or that belonging to the sitter's descendants in 1972. NPG 2166 which, according to the provenance, was painted for the sitter's family, differs from both these portraits in displaying on the back of the chair an Earl's coronet, to which Henley became entitled in 1764. Another version, similar to NPG 2166, was with Leger in 1970, and a half length also remained with the sitter's descendants in 1972.

The only known portrait of Northington, the image was engraved as a half length by James Miller c.1760 (as *Lord Henley, Keeper of the Great Seal*; the plate intended for Smollett's *History of England*, II, 1760); anon. before 1764 (as *Lord Henley, Lord Chancellor*); anon. 1764-66 for the *General Mag.* (as *Lord Northington, Lord Chancellor*), and by W.C. Edwards 1831.

1 The sitter's dau. m. 1783 the 1st Baron Henley; the Northington title became extinct in 1786. In a letter of 26 May 1927 (NPG archive), Lord Henley described NPG 2166 as 'a replica, which I found under an old staircase here [at Watford Court]'.
2 The Arundel Society photograph of the portrait in that exhibition (NPG archive) just reveals the Earl's coronet on the back of the chair which, together with the fall of the lace cuff, distinguishes NPG 2166 from other versions.
3 Miles 1977, II, p.153, suggested it was painted between January and May 1761, following Henley's appointment as lord chancellor in January, but he had been entitled to bear the Great Seal from 1757 and Miller's crude engraving, based on the Hudson portrait, was to have been published in 1760 (see above).
4 Bearing the inscribed date 1761; Poole, II, p.193, no.46; exhibited Kenwood 1979(63), illus.

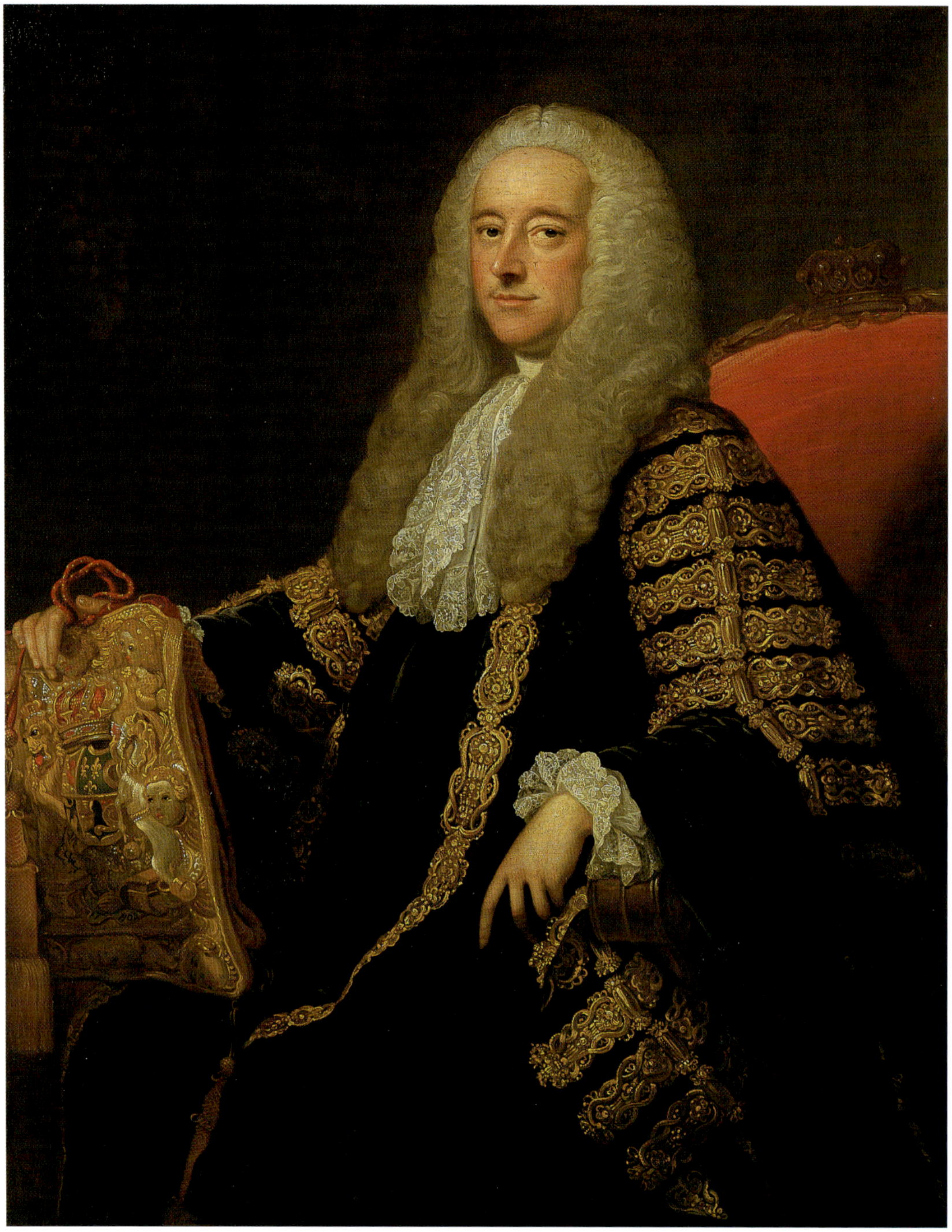

1st Earl of NORTHINGTON NPG *2166*

NORTHUMBERLAND, Hugh (Smithson) Percy, 1st Duke of 1715-86

Courtier and philanthropist; suc. his gd. fa. as 4th Bt Smithson 1733; FSA and FRS 1736; MP 1740-50; as s.-in-law of the 17th Earl, he suc. as 18th Earl of Northumberland 1750 and took the name of Percy in lieu of Smithson; his wife Elizabeth Seymour suc. as Baroness Percy 1750; Trustee of the British Museum 1753; KG 1757; lord-lieutenant of Middlesex 1762; viceroy of Ireland 1763-65; cr. Duke of Northumberland 1766; his properties included Alnwick Castle, Albury Park, Northumberland House and Syon House.

'with a princely fortune, he sustained his exalted rank through life with the greatest dignity, generosity and splendour' (*GM*, 1786).

4954 JAMES TASSIE 1780

Glass paste profile 8.2 (3¼) high, incised on truncation: *HU. DUKE OF/ NORTHUMBERLAND 1780 T*; set on dark glass.

Collections: K.E. Houston sale, Sotheby's, 15 January 1968, lot 117, bt. Sanders of Oxford; Christie's, 22 May 1973, lot 5, bt. Leggatt for the NPG.

Reference: Gray 1894, no.292.

Tassie's portrait is taken from a medal by John Kirk, exhibited in 1772 (see below) with minor variations (e.g. in the hair ribbon); Tassie's head in turn provided the pattern for the Wedgwood medallion, first advertised in 1787.[1] A plaster is in the Scottish National Portrait Gallery (PG 441).

1 Reilly 1973, p.260; Reilly dates the medal 1766, but see below under 1772.

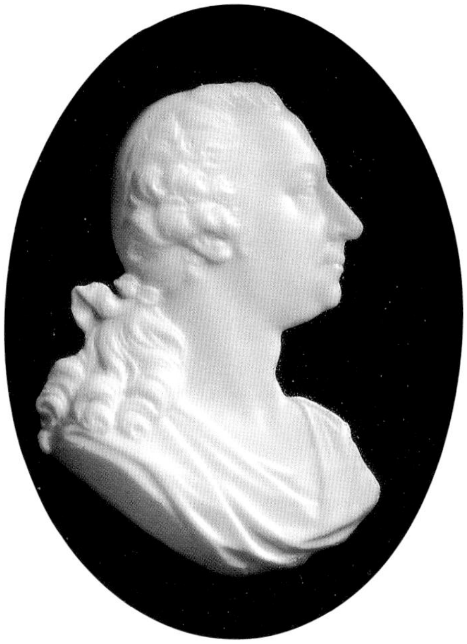

1st Duke of NORTHUMBERLAND NPG 4954

ICONOGRAPHY

c.1730–35 Painting attributed to Charles Phillips, *The Henry V Club* or *The Gang*, in which Sir Hugh Smithson sits on the left, with Frederick, Prince of Wales, William O'Brien and four others. Royal Collection (Millar 1963, no.535).

1756 Painting by Joshua Reynolds, half length, in Peer's robes with Garter collar. Alnwick Castle (Mannings 2000, no.1433). The Earl of Northumberland was nominated KG in November 1756 and invested in March 1757.

1761 Painting by R.E. Pine,★ whole length standing, laying the foundation stone of the Middlesex Hospital. Middlesex Hospital, London. Exhibited FS 1761(78).

1762 Painting by Joshua Reynolds, whole length wearing peer's robes with Garter collar, as founder of the first Westminster Guildhall. Middlesex Guildhall Collection (Mannings 2000, no.1434).

c.1763 Painting by Allan Ramsay, half length, with the ribbon and star of the Garter. Albury Park (Smart 1999, no.411). Engraved W.H. (sometimes assumed to be William Hoare) 1764 (the head reversed); Aliamet, and anon.

1764 Medal, see 1772 below.

1765–66 Painting by Joshua Reynolds, whole length, using the 1762 head and much of that pose, but differing in showing Garter rather than Peer's robes. Dublin Mansion House (illus. *Irish Arts Review*, XV, 1999, pp.154–56). Northumberland agreed the Dublin commission in August 1765 and paid for the picture in May 1766. Engraved E. Fisher (bust length); G.H. Every (illus. G. Brenan, *House of Percy*, 1902, II, f.p.428). A copy is at Alnwick Castle, framed with the pendant portrait of the Duchess.

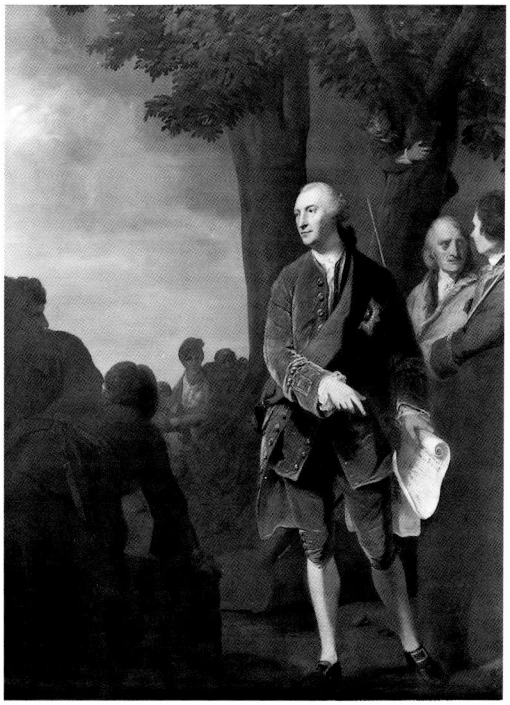

1st Duke of NORTHUMBERLAND by R.E. Pine 1761 (Middlesex Hospital)

In November 1763 Walpole had referred to the Northumberlands in Dublin as 'their Vice-Majesties of Ireland' scattering 'pearls and diamonds about the streets' (Corr., XXXVIII, p.235).

before 1766 Marble bust by Joseph Wilton, with open-collared shirt. Syon House (illus. *Treasure Houses*, Washington, 1985, p.16).

1766 Medal, see 1772 below.

after 1766 Pastel by Daniel Gardner, small whole length in Garter robes. Private collection. The composition ultimately derived from the Reynolds whole length of Lord Rockingham at St Osyth's Priory (Mannings 2000, no.1858).

1768 Drawing by P-E. Falconet, bust-length oval, engraved D.P. Pariset.

1768 Coade stone, oval medallion. Britwell House sale, Sotheby's, 20 March 1979, lot 144.

1771 Pastel by H.D. Hamilton, half length. Alnwick Castle. Engraved J. Finlayson 1771 (feigned oval).

1772 Medal by John Kirk, exhibited SA 1772(157). Brown 1980, nos.106–07, lists similar medals dated 1764 and 1766 (and see NPG 4954).

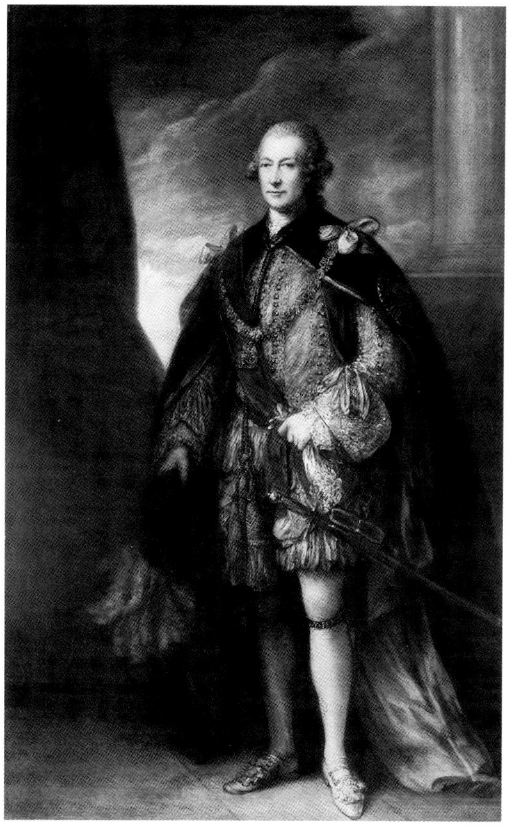

1st Duke of NORTHUMBERLAND by Thomas Gainsborough 1783 (Middlesex Guildhall)

1779 Pastel by James Sharples, oval half-length profile. Christie's, 9 April 1991, lot 48. Engraved C.H. Hodges 1784. Presumably the pastel of Northumberland exhibited by James Sharples, RA 1779(168), see Knox 1930, pp.111–12.

1780 Profile by James Tassie, see NPG 4954.

c.1780 Drawing by Pierre Violet, medallion, engraved I.J. Van den Berghe.

1783 Painting by Thomas Gainsborough,★ whole length in Garter robes. Middlesex Guildhall Collection (Waterhouse 1958, no.519). Exhibited RA 1783(153). Engraved G. Dupont.

There are three closely related half-length painted-oval portraits by Gainsborough, with the Garter ribbon and star, probably based on separate sittings; the best appears to be that at Albury Park (Waterhouse 1958, no.520; illus. *Gainsborough*, Tate Gallery, 2002, no.168); others are in the NG of Ireland (129; Waterhouse 1958, nos.521; illus. *Apollo*, XCIX, 1974, p.137) and in the Northumberland collection at Prince's Gate.

c.1784–86 Painting by James Barry,★ whole length, in Garter robes, as Master of the Horse. Syon House (Pressly 1981, no.64). Northumberland's appoint-

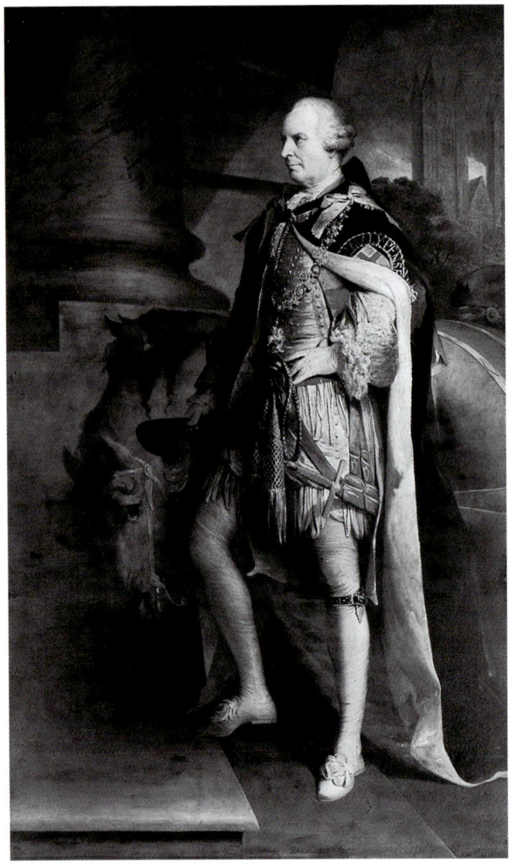

1st Duke of NORTHUMBERLAND by James Barry 1784-86 (Syon Park)

ment as Master of the Horse, at a time when he had both gout and the stone, had particularly amused Walpole (*Corr.*, XXXIV, p.210); the distant prospect of Westminster Abbey may allude to Northumberland's burial there, indicating a posthumous completion.

1787 Wedgwood medallion (illus. Reilly 1973, p.260), see NPG 4954.

1787 Painting by G. van der Puyl, whole-length seated receiving the standing Henry Selby. Albury Park (illus. *Albury Park*, 1951, p.21 as Zoffany). Exhibited RA 1787(74).

Undated Three miniatures identified as the 1st Duke of Northumberland are listed by J.J. Foster, *Cat. of Miniatures belonging to the Duke of Northumberland*, 1921, nos.50, 54 and 121, each apparently c.1770, the first two attributed to Peter Lens (nos.54 and 121 illus. pl.xii); according to Foskett 1972, I, p.380, one of these may be by Jeremiah Meyer.

A drawing by Thomas Bewick in the British Museum appears to have been copied from a miniature (1882.3.11.1423).

ONSLOW, George Onslow, 1st Earl of 1731-1814

Courtier; s. of Arthur 'Speaker' Onslow (see Kerslake, *Early Georgian*), and nephew by marriage of the 1st Duke of Newcastle; MP 1754-74, first a champion of Wilkes and latterly a loyal courtier; lord of the Treasury 1765-77; cr. Baron Cranley in May 1776 and suc. his cos. as 4th Baron Onslow in October 1776, after which he briefly but extravagantly made improvements at Clandon; comptroller 1777-79 and treasurer of the Household 1779-80, and lord of the bedchamber from 1780, while maintaining the friendship of the Prince of Wales; cr. Earl of Onslow 1801.

5212 JOHN FIELD c.1800-10

Silhouette on paper, the figure 6 x 4 (2¼ x 1½) maximum; inscribed verso: *Lord Onslow.*

Collections: Eric Quayle; Sotheby's, 16 October 1978, lot 120, bt. Leggatt for the NPG.

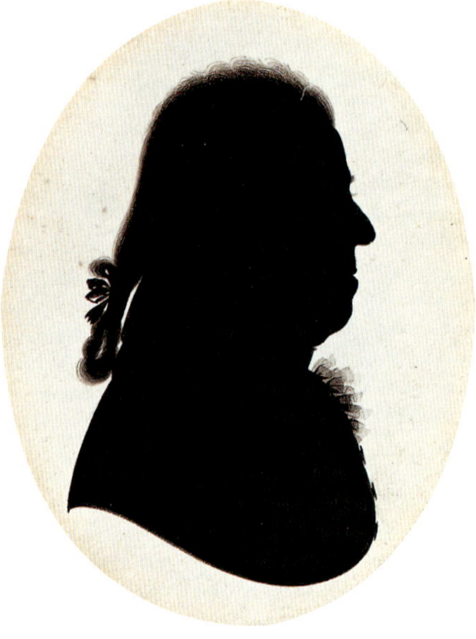

1st Earl of ONSLOW NPG 5212

ICONOGRAPHY

[*Caveat*: his cousin, George Onslow (1731-92), MP 1760-84, the subject of several satires, as *Little cocking George*, (George 4855, and cf. George 6065)]

c.1750 Pastel formerly attributed to John Russell, half length wearing mortar board and gown. Lord Onslow. Version in oil sold Christie's, 23 April 1954, lot 87 as Reynolds. A traditional identification.

1779-81 Painting by J.S. Copley,* *The Death of Chatham*, see Comparative Groups.

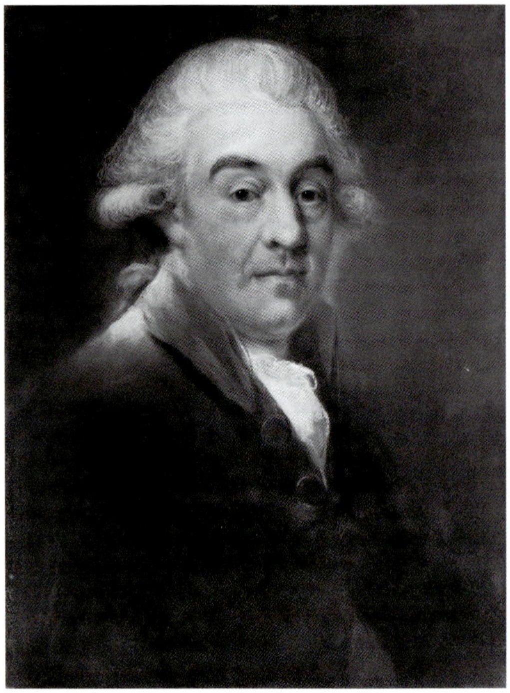

1st Earl of ONSLOW by John Russell c.1790 (Sotheby's)

c.1780 Unattributed painting, half length, wearing peer's robes. Clandon Park.

c.1790 Pastel by John Russell,* half length, wearing Windsor uniform. Sotheby's, 22 March 2000, lot 87.

1792 Drawn and engraved by C.T. Warren, *George, Lord Onslow*, bust-length (*The Senator*).

1798 Silhouette by Charles Rosenberg , whole length with cocked hat and sword. Bonham's, 24 November 1999, lot 313.

c.1800-10 Silhouette by John Field, see NPG 5212.

1813 Painting by Thomas Stewardson, whole-length seated in Windsor uniform. Clandon (indistinctly illus. *CL*, LXII, 1927, p.401). Exhibited RA 1813(160, 'painted for the Magistrates of the county of Surrey'). Engraved W. Ward. A half-length kit-cat version also at Clandon, lent by Lord Onslow (illus. C.E. Vulliamy, *The Onslow Family*, 1953, p.176).

ORAM, Edward fl.1766-99

Landscape painter, s. of the painter William Oram (1704-77); exhibited landscapes at the SA 1766 and RA 1775-90 and 1798-99; sometime the assistant of De Loutherbourg, he painted scenery for the Royalty Theatre which flourished in 1788-89 (see John Palmer).

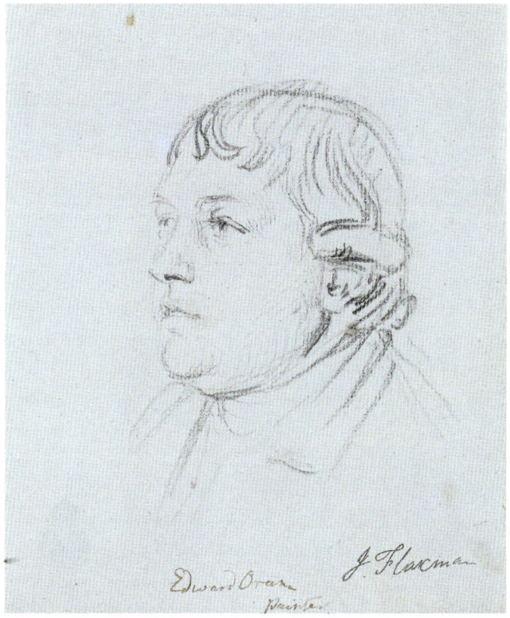

ORAM NPG *3112*

3112 JOHN FLAXMAN c.1780

Black crayon on paper 17.5 x 14.5 (6⅞ x 5¾); some staining; inscribed bottom right: *J. Flaxman* and below, centre: *Edward Oram/painter.*

Collections: Purchased from Appleby 1941.[1]

Exhibition: *Kauffmann* 1968 (*hors catalogue*).

No other portrait of Oram is known and the identification is based on the contemporary inscription. It was presumably drawn at the time when both Flaxman and Oram were being patronised by the Rev Anthony Stephen Mathew (1733-1824) and his bluestocking wife, an episode described by J.T. Smith and Gilchrist with 'infuriating vagueness'.[2] For their house at 27 Rathbone Place 'Loutherbourg's assistant, *young* Oram' painted a window 'in imitation of stained glass' and Flaxman furnished 'models in putty and sand, of figures in niches in the Gothic manner'.[3] NPG 3112 may be compared with Flaxman's drawings of Mathew and his daughter Harriet,[4] which have been dated c.1780, the former bearing an identical 'signature' to NPG 3112.[5]

1 Unnamed among 'a miscellaneous lot of portrait drawings' (*Trustees Minutes*, 6 February 1941, and *Statement of Expenditure*, 3 April 1941 (NPG archive).
2 Iolo A. Williams, *Burl. Mag.*, CII, 1960, p.246.
3 J.T. Smith, *Book for a Rainy Day*, 1845, p.83; A. Gilchrist, *Life of William Blake*, 1863, I, pp.44-45; *NQ*, CXCVI, 1951, pp.162-63. Oram's last recorded address, in 1799, was 5 Gresse Street, Rathbone Place.
4 In 1960 these drawings were, respectively, in the collections of Iolo A. Williams and E. Croft Murray; illus. *Burl. Mag.*, CII, 1960, p.251.
5 Williams, *loc. cit.*, pp.246, 249; it is possible that these 'signatures' may have been added by Flaxman's adopted daughter, Maria Denman. A drawing of Mathew's son, Henry William Mathew, also dateable c.1780, belonged to Iolo Williams in 1960.

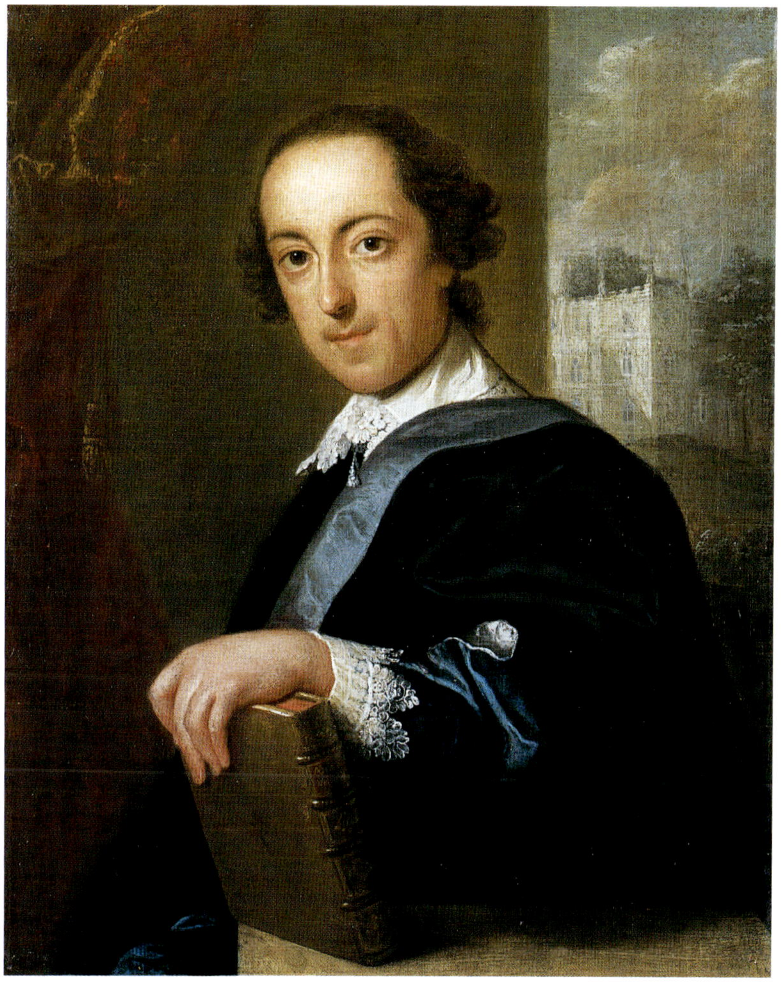

4th Earl of ORFORD
NPG *988*

ORFORD, Horace Walpole, 4th Earl of 1717-97

Virtuoso, 4th s. of the prime minister Sir Robert Walpole, 1st Earl of Orford; published *Anecdotes of Painting in England* 1762-71; suc. his nephew as 4th Earl 1791.

'His figure was ... not merely tall, but more properly *long* and slender to excess; his complexion and particularly his hands, of a most unhealthy paleness. I speak of him before the year 1772. His eyes were remarkably bright and penetrating, very dark and lively: - his voice was not strong, but his tones extremely pleasant' (Laetitia-Matilda Hawkins, 1822).

Abbreviation

Walpole 1970: C.K. Adams & W.S. Lewis, 'The Portraits of Horace Walpole', *Wal.Soc.*, XLII, 1970, pp.1-34

988 JOHN GILES ECCARDT 1754

Canvas 40.5 x 33 (16 x 13) the paint surface is rather rubbed, particularly evident in the background areas; a paper on the stretcher inscribed by the sitter:[1] *Horace Walpole/ youngest Son of Sr R. Walpole/ by Eckardt/ 1754.*

Brown eyes, dark brown hair, wearing Van Dyck costume, a black cloak lined with silver blue silk over blue breeches and tunic with white bobbin lace collar and cuffs;[2] his left hand holds a copy of the *Aedes Walpol*[*ianae*]; a red curtain to the left, a distant view of Strawberry Hill to the right.

Collections: By descent from the sitter; Strawberry Hill sale, 22nd day, 19 May 1842, lot 28 ('... an exceedingly clever original picture; it has been highly esteemed from its likeness to Horace Walpole, and from it the Portrait in the Catalogue has been taken'), bought by the Rev Horace George Cholmondeley (d.1851); his son-in-law, Canon Francis Vansittart Thornton (d.1895); purchased through Colnaghi 1895.

Engravings: Anon. 1798 (head only finished) and 1807; L. Du Pont 1809-10 (on a silver button);[3] W. Greatbach 1840; G.H. Madeley 1842, 'from a Painting at Strawberry Hill, by Eckhardt, in 1754'.

Exhibitions: NPE 1867(377) lent Rev F.V. Thornton; *English Taste in the 18th century*, RA, 1955-56(313); *Walpole and Strawberry Hill*, Orleans House, Twickenham, 1980(10).

Reference: *Walpole* 1970, A10.

One of six portraits commissioned by Walpole from Eccardt between 1746 and 1754 which hung together in his blue bed-chamber at Strawberry Hill. Their compositions derived from Watteau, Rubens and Van Dyck, and they were shown in black and gold frames, 'carved after those to Lombard's prints from Vandyck, but with emblems peculiar to each person'.[4] The other portraits were of Richard Bentley (NPG 5885) and Thomas Gray (NPG 989), both after Van Dyck; Sir Charles Hanbury Williams (untraced); General Henry Seymour Conway and his Wife, in the manner of Watteau (private collection), and Charles Churchill and his Wife, in the manner of Rubens (Lewis Walpole Library, Farmington). On 18 May 1754 Walpole told Bentley that all the portraits were installed, one in each wall panel; 'mine', he added, 'is to match yours [i.e. NPG 5885]'.[5] NPG 988 had evidently not then been started, but it was completed by the end of the year (according to Walpole's label quoted above).

The pose of NPG 988 is taken from Van Dyck's portrait of Simon Vouet as engraved by Robert van Voerst;[6] Walpole described NPG 988 as 'from Vandyke, leaning on the *Aedes Walpolianae*: behind him a view of Strawberry Hill'.[7] The House is seen from the east, showing two new rooms, the great parlour and the refectory with, above it, the library, which were completed in 1754. The *Aedes*, Walpole's catalogue of his father's pictures at Houghton, was his first book, published in 1747.

A version showing Strawberry Hill with the east battlement surmounted with a cross (added between 1754 and 1764) is in an English private collection; in 1762 Mrs Mary Shepherd bequeathed 'The picture of Horace Walpole' to a direct ancestor of the present owner.[8] A copy in another English private collection is possibly by Thomas Stewart ('a portrait of Lord Orford, copied from Echard by Stuart, in 1787' was in Strawberry Hill in 1807);[9] another is at Marble Hill.[10] A miniature copy in watercolour by G.P. Harding was sold Sotheby's, 16 December 1974, lot 61.

1 The hand identified by W.S. Lewis, see *Walpole* 1970, p.12; a label in the same hand was on the verso of NPG 989, Thomas Gray (see Kerslake *Early Georgian*, I, p.106).
2 A. Ribeiro, *The Art of Dress*, 1995, p.184.
3 Illus. L.S. Albert & K. Kent, *The Complete Button Book*, 1949, f.p.398.
4 These frames remained with the portraits in 1842, but by 1867 NPG 988 and NPG 989 had been reframed. The Conway portrait alone retains its original frame.

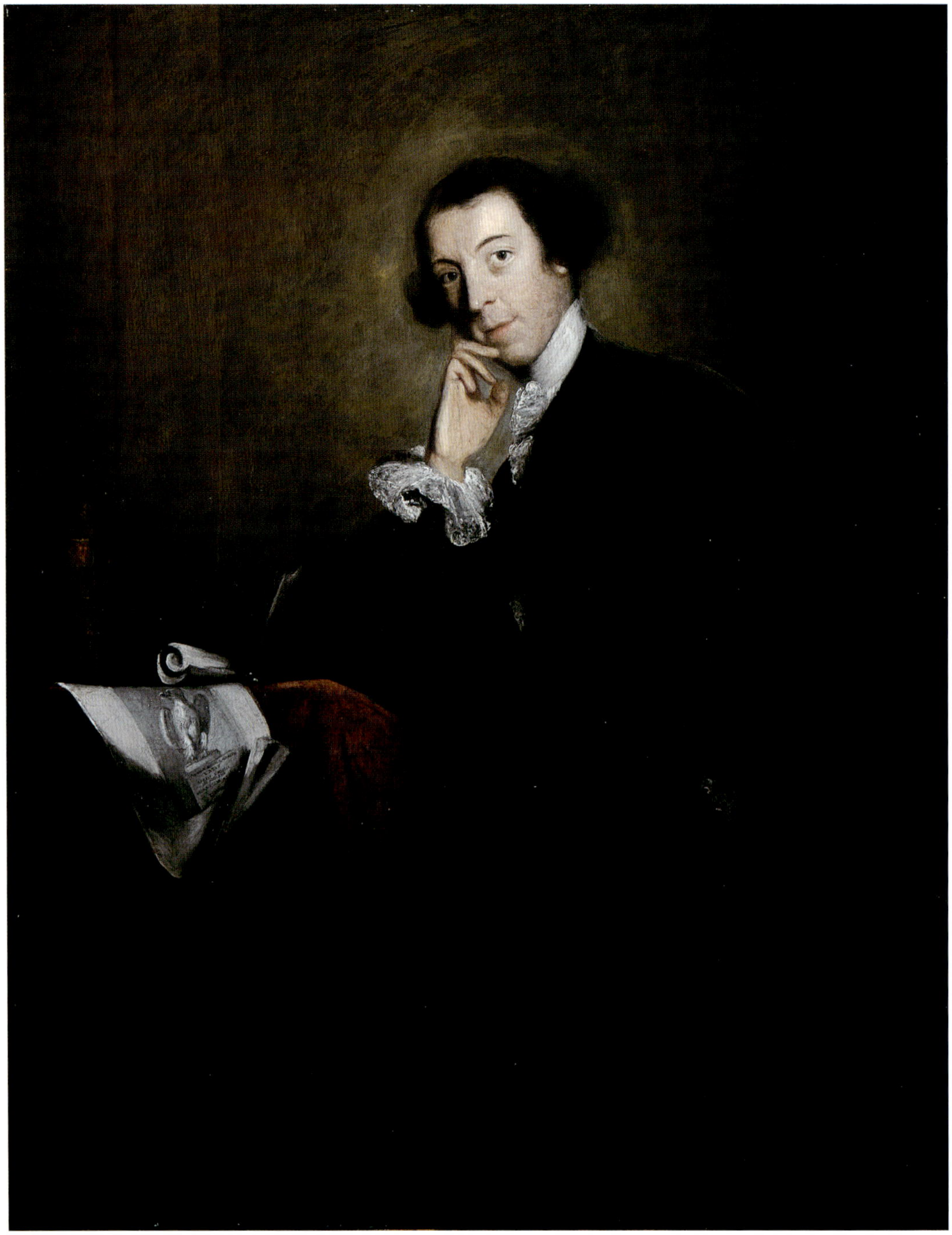

4th Earl of ORFORD NPG *6250*

5 *Wal. Corr.*, XXXV, p.174.
6 New Hollstein, *Van Dyck*, II, 2002, no.100; Vouet leans on a copy of the *Trattato della Nobilita dell'Pittura*.
7 *Description of Strawberry Hill*, 1784, p.29.
8 See *Walpole* 1970, A10.1, pl.9; exhibited *Mason* 1973(14).
9 *Walpole* 1970, A10.2; probably the portrait sold Sotheby's, 15 March 1978, lot 21.
10 *Walpole* 1970, A10.3; illus. *NACF 2000 Review*, p.97 (Sotheby's, 30 November 2000, lot 105); *English Heritage, Collections Review*, III, 2001, p.38.

6520 JOSHUA REYNOLDS 1756-57

Canvas 127 x 100.5 (50 x 39½) lined; cleaned 1998; minor pentimenti round the hand and head, and the engraving is painted over the red table cloth; varying craquelure in the head, table cloth and in the right background; some retouching in the head, hand and cloth, and a repaired tear upper right; the lower areas are now darkened and the books and quill much rubbed.

Dark brown eyes, dark brown hair, a dark blueish-grey velvet coat with a plum-coloured waistcoat; a crimson tablecloth on which lies an engraving of Walpole's Roman eagle, the inscription cursorily copied: *AQUILAE SIGNUM ..ARMOR..V../ VETVS/ OPERIS EXIMII/ IN A..E..DIB..S/ HORATII WALPOLE/ LONDINI* (see below).

Collections: Painted for Grosvenor Bedford (1708–71)[1] and sold by his descendants after 1847 (when the picture was declined by Robert Peel)[2] and before 1857 to the 3rd Marquess of Lansdowne (d.1863);[3] by descent to the 8th Marquess who gave it to his son, the Earl of Shelburne; sold by the Trustees of the Bowood Settlement and bought with the aid of the Heritage Lottery Fund, the National Art Collections Fund and the Dame Helen Gardner Bequest, 2000.

Engravings: J. McArdell 1757 (? see below); W. Bromley 1826 (as in the possession of G.C. Bedford).

Exhibitions: *Reynolds*, 45 Park Lane, London, 1937(80); *Le Livre anglais*, Bibliothèque nationale, Paris, 1951(499); *Lansdowne Collection*, Agnew, 1954(41); *Age of Rococo*, Munich, 1958(167); *Ramsay, his Masters and Rivals*, Edinburgh, 1963(83); *Lady Suffolk and her Friends*, Marble Hill, 1966(15); *Mason* 1973(42); *Pittura Inglese 1660–1840*, Milan, 1975(107); *Walpole and Strawberry Hill*, Orleans House, Twickenham, 1980(9).

Reference: *Catalogue of the Lansdowne Collection*, 1897, p.86, no.40; Graves & Cronin, III, pp.1024–25 (with incorrect provenance); Waterhouse 1941, p.41; *Walpole* 1970, A13.2; J. Miller, *Catalogue of Paintings at Bowood*, 1982, p.15; Mannings 2000, no.1819.

'Mr Walpole's picture ... from which there is a mezzotinto print in 1757, by MacArdal, standing in a pensive posture by a table, on which is his fine antique eagle in a print, is very like him', commented the Rev William Cole in 1765, 'except that it is a little too plump for him'.[4] He is portrayed as a writer with his quill (he was already known as a copious correspondent) and as a collector with one of the engravings by Charles Grignion senior[5] of the antique marble eagle from the Boccapaduli Palace which he had acquired from Rome in 1745.[6]

NPG 6520 is one of three autograph versions, each painted, apparently, in 1756–57; there is no sitter-book for 1756, and in 1757 a single appointment for Walpole on 30 August need not imply a sitting. The other versions are in the Art Gallery of Ontario, Toronto,[7] descended from Charles Churchill, the sitter's brother-in-law, and at Ragley,[8] probably descended from Francis Seymour Conway, later 1st Marquess of Hertford, Walpole's first cousin. The Toronto portrait was delivered to Churchill in January 1757[9] and differs from the other two in that the print of the eagle is seen upside down (i.e. so that Walpole could appreciate it, but not the spectator) and without an inscription. The Ragley version is signed *J. Reynolds pinxit 1757*. On 9 November 1757 Walpole asked Grosvenor Bedford, his recently appointed deputy at the Exchequer and the first owner of NPG 6520, to retrieve 'my picture' from the engraver McArdell (who had been publicising what had been commissioned by Walpole as a private plate);[10] McArdell's plate is dated 1757 and, since it shows the eagle right way up, was taken from either NPG 6520 or the Ragley version. Late in January 1758 Reynolds noted in his pocket book *Send home Mr Walpole* and again on 1 February *Send* [bill?] *to Mr Walpole*, the latter doubtless referring to the signed receipt, dated 1 February 1758, now preserved in the Lewis Walpole Library, Farmington: *Received of the Honble Horatio Walpole Esq. the sum of forty-eight guineas for two half-length portraits of himself being in full of demands by me.*

There has been much discussion as to which of the three is the prime version. In 1857 Cotton listed NPG 6520; in 1865 Leslie & Taylor, unaware of the Toronto version, stated that 'Lord Hertford had the original, and the Marquess of Lansdowne the duplicate [NPG 6520]';[11] in 1941 Waterhouse allowed 'there is much confusion over the Walpole portraits', and chose to list NPG 6520; in 1973 he illustrated the Ragley version;[12] in 1970 Lewis and Adams considered the Toronto version as 'doubtless' the first; in 1986 Penny considered the Toronto version the first, Ragley the second, and NPG 6520 an early copy, probably by Reynolds.[13] The condition of the three portraits has always complicated their assessment (the Toronto picture appears to have suffered from overcleaning), but the cleaning of NPG 6520 in 1998, when the finely painted head and minor pentimenti were revealed, led Penny[14] to accept it as autograph, while Mannings, who had never doubted its quality, considered it 'probably the first version of the design ... repeated in the Toronto and Ragley versions'.

A copy of NPG 6520 by C.M. Newton was given in 1888 to King's College, Cambridge.[15]

1 See Cotton 1857; Lansdowne cat., 1897. For the Grosvenor Bedford family, see *Wal.Corr.*, XLII, pp.491–92. Walpole has been tentatively identified in a Hayman portrait of Grosvenor Bedford and his family of c.1741 (*Hayman* 1987, pp.5, 86–7, pl. I), lot 28 in the Grosvenor Bedford sale, see note 3.

2 Peel wrote to the dealer John Smith on 24 December 1847 declining the offer (*Walpole* 1970, p.17).

3 Cotton 1857, p.77 'lately purchased from the [Bedford] family by Lord Lansdowne'. The F. Grosvenor Bedford sale, Christie's, 1 March 1861, contained 'A highly interesting Collection of Walpoleana, the property of the late Grosvenor Bedford, Esq. of the Exchequer, Whose Family had been connected with that of Sir Robert Walpole, by early private friendship, and subsequently Official Employment, from 1700 to 1797'; Walpole portraits from this sale are listed in the Iconography below.

4 W. Cole [1765], *Journal of My Journey to Paris*, 1931, p.55.

5 Grignion made two plates of the eagle from drawings by Samuel Wale, both, apparently, published in 1755; one showing the bird on the elaborate classical pedestal it retains to this day (illus. *Wal. Corr.*, XIX, f.p.66), the other as shown in NPG 6520 (illus. *Vases and Volcanoes*, no.136). The full inscription on the latter reads: *VETVS AQVILAE SIGNVM MARMOREVM/ OPERIS EXIMII/ ANNO MDCCXXXXII/ IDIBVS OCTOBRIS/ ROMAE PROPE THERMAS ANTONINIANAS/ IN HORTI BVCCAPADVLIIS/ AD RADICES AVENTINI EFFOSVM:/ NVNC IN AEDIBVS/ HORATII WALPOLE/ LONDINI*. See *Wal. Corr.*, XX, p.485, & XXXV, p.252.

6 Now at Gosford; see *Treasure Houses*, Washington, 1985(244).

7 *Walpole* 1970, A13; Mannings 2000, no.1820.

8 *Walpole* 1970, A13.1; Mannings 2000, no.1821; engraved: J. Barlow 1796, Le Coeur 1798 (bust length), G. Scharf 1825 and S.W. Reynolds; exhibited: *Reynolds*, Birmingham, 1961(22); *Reynolds* 1986(28); *Family & Friends*, Norwich, 1992(58).

9 *Send home Mr Walpole to Mr Churchill* written in Reynolds's pocket book at the beginning of January.

10 *Wal. Corr.*, XL, p.117.

11 Leslie & Taylor 1865, i, p.169.

12 E.K. Waterhouse, *Reynolds* 1973, pl.16.

13 *Reynolds* 1986, under no.28.

14 Letter of 15 November 1998 (NPG archive). See also J. Simon, *NACF 1999 Review*, p.106.

15 T.D. Atkinson, *Cambridge Described & Illustrated*, 1897, p.372.

1161 GEORGE DANCE 1793

Pencil on paper 25 x 19 (9⅞ x 7½) faded and with a small loss in the coat collar; signed and dated in pencil: *July 13th. 1793*, bottom left, and *Geo. Dance*, bottom right; laid down on a contemporary washed mount lettered: *EARL OF ORFORD*.

Collections: The artist's grandson, the Rev George Dance; his sale, Christie's, 1 July 1898, lot 139, bt. Colnaghi for the NPG.

Engraving: W. Daniell 1808 (*Dance Portraits*).

Exhibitions: *Garrick and his Contemporaries*, Stratford-upon-Avon, 1969(56); *George Dance*, Geffrye Museum, 1972(97); *Walpole and Strawberry Hill*, Orleans House, Twickenham, 1980(230); *La revolution française et l'Europe*, Paris, 1989(232); *John Joseph Merlin*, Kenwood, 1985(A12).

Reference: *Walpole* 1970, A17.

Farington and Dance visited Strawberry Hill on 13 July 1793, when Farington recorded that 'in the forenoon Mr Dance made a drawing of [Walpole's] profile an excellent resemblance. – Lord Orford is now in his 76th year, infirm in his body, but lively & attentive in mind'. On 29 April 1794 Farington wrote that Walpole was 'much mortified' to learn that Dance's drawing was on public exhibition, 'thinking it wd. appear at his time of life an instance of vanity', but the report was false.

A version of NPG 1161, inscribed *This is by George Dance from the collection of Miss M. Dance the great granddaughter*,[1] is in the Lewis Walpole Library, Farmington. A copy of Daniell's engraving by J.T. Smith was sold Sotheby's, 11 February 1971, lot 197.

1 Mary Sibyll Dance (d.1948), see Dance, NPG 3626.

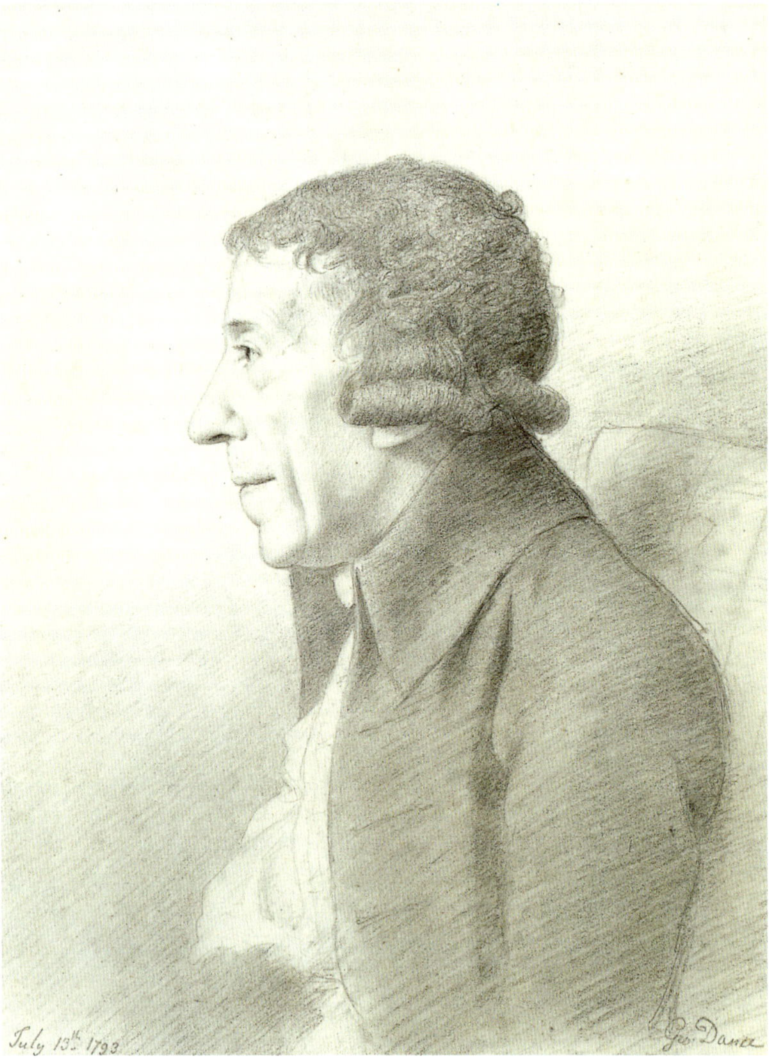

4th Earl of ORFORD NPG *1161*

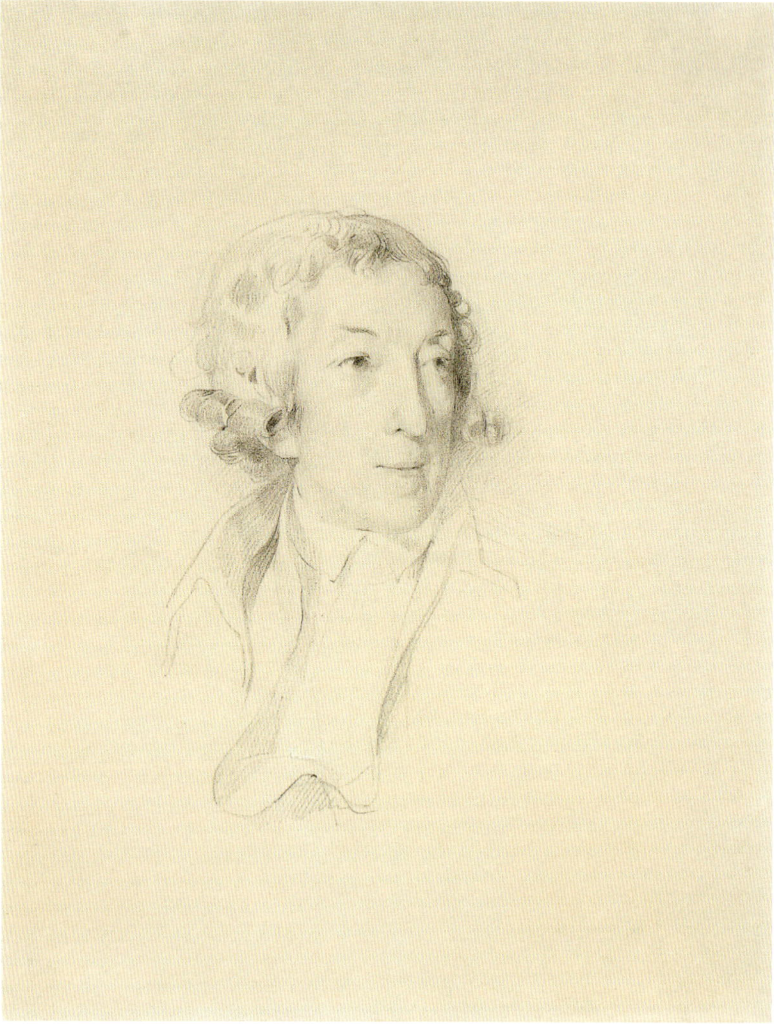

4th Earl of ORFORD NPG *3631*

3631 THOMAS LAWRENCE 1795

Pencil on paper 25.5 x 19.5 (10 x 7¾) laid down on paper; repaired tear bottom centre; the previous mount was inscribed in an early 19th-century hand: *Horace Walpole Earl of Orford/ by Sir Thos Lawrence.*

Collections: Samuel Lysons (1763-1819); Lysons sale, Knowles, Gloucester, 21 April 1887, lot 317, bt. Sir Spencer Walpole (d.1907); presented by his daughter Mrs Maud C. Holland 1948.

Engravings: T. Evans 1798, inscribed *T. Lawrence R.A. ad vivum del. 1796* (for Walpole's *Works*); H. Meyer from a drawing by W. Evans 1811; J. Thomson 1822.

Exhibitions: *Mason* 1973(43); *British Portraits*, Tokyo, 1975-76; *Hyenas in Petticoats*, Grasmere, 1997(17).

Reference: *Lawrence* 1964, p.239; *Walpole* 1970, A18.

Lysons considered it 'a most characteristic and excellent likeness',[1] and Lord Glenbervie wrote of Evans's engraving that 'It is a head, a mere outline, but the most striking likeness I ever saw, for the features and expression'.[2] A copy by Harriet Elizabeth Onslow 1797 is in the Huntington Art Collections, San Marino, Calif.

Farington recorded (18 August 1795) that at this time Lawrence intended 'to draw & form a collection' of distinguished persons and that 'Lord Orford is the first He has made, with this view'.

1 D. Lysons, *Environs of London*, II, 1810ed., p.783n61.
2 Lord Glenbervie, *Diaries*, 1928, I, p.140.

ICONOGRAPHY

Walpole's portraiture was surveyed by C.K. Adams and W.S. Lewis in 1970 (*Walpole* 1970). Portraits whose identity Adams and Lewis rejected, or considered doubtful, are here generally omitted, together with some pictures in which Walpole's likeness is incidental.

c.1720 Crayon drawing 'when a child, in a white frock, drawn about the year 1720'. Strawberry Hill sale, day 22, 19 May 1842, lot 10 (*Walpole* 1970, A1).

c.1725-26 Wash drawing by Bernard Lens, whole-length seated at a desk, inscribed by the sitter: *Drawn from the life by Lens,/ who was Master Horace Walpole's/ drawing master.* Lord Waldegrave (*Walpole* 1970, A2, pl.1).

1729 Painting by William Hogarth, whole length by a sundial. Lord Lonsdale (illus. *Walpole* 1970, B3). From the Grosvenor Bedford sale, Christie's, 1 March 1861, lot 33 as 'Horace Walpole by Le Mercier'. Presumably the portrait referred to in the Houghton MSS *pay'd Mr Howgarth for Mester Haurris*

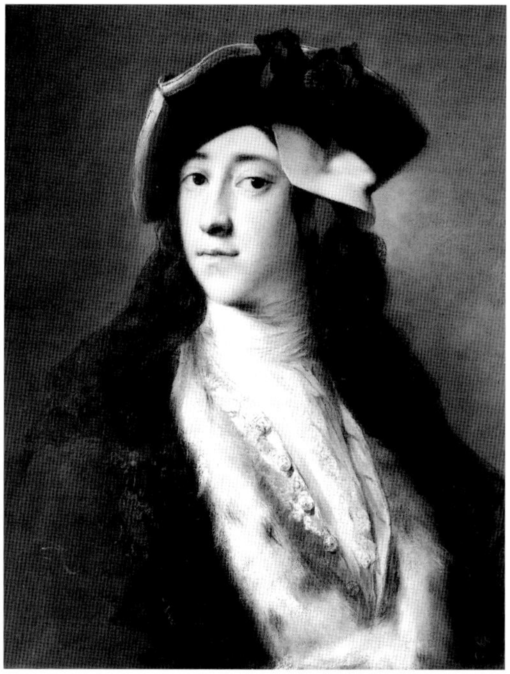

4th Earl of ORFORD by Rosalba Carriera 1741 (Private Collection)

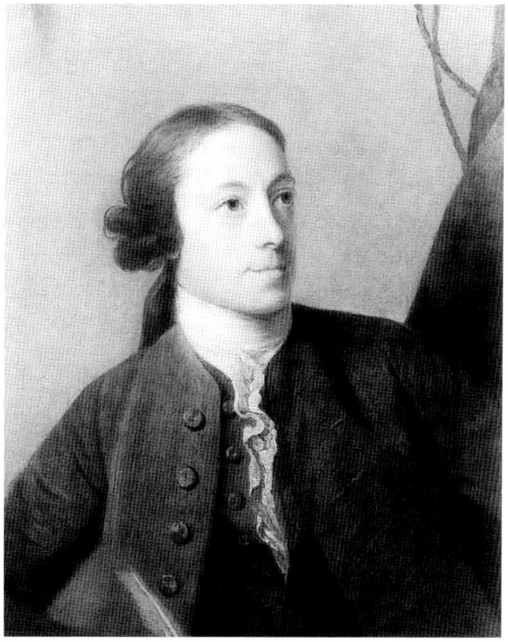

4th Earl of ORFORD by Allan Ramsay c.1759 (Lewis Walpole Library, Yale University)

[i.e. Horry's] *picture 05-05-00, 10 October 1729* (as kindly communicated by John Cornforth).

c.1729 The miniature of Walpole set in a ring, listed in the will of Mrs Mary Shepherd (d.1762), is possibly that in the Buccleuch collection, engraved J. Stephenson 1861 as by Zincke (*Walpole* 1970, B4, pl.24b, as by Zincke or Lens) and copied by G.P. Harding 1801 (Lord Waldegrave) as of Walpole. Two miniatures by Zincke of Walpole, 'in early childhood' and 'when a child' were lots 34 and 36 in the Grosvenor Bedford sale, Christie's, 1 March 1861.

1734–35 Painting by Jonathan Richardson, three-quarter length. Lord Waldegrave (*Walpole* 1970, A4, pls.2,3). Copies in a private collection and formerly at Eton; a miniature copy by William Prewett 1735 in the Buccleuch collection (*Walpole* 1970, pl.4a).

c.1736 Pastel by George Knapton, bust length. Houghton in 1736 (*Walpole* 1970, A5). An unattributed pastel portrait of Walpole was in the Grosvenor Bedford sale, Christie's, 1 March 1861, lot 27.

1741 Pastel by Rosalba Carriera,* bust length. Houghton Hall (*Walpole* 1970, A6; A. Moore ed., *Houghton Hall*, 1996, p.109). Drawn in Venice, where Madame Suares exclaimed that never in her life had she seen 'a portrait of such perfection and verisimilitude'. Pendant to a portrait of the 9th Earl of Lincoln (who wears an identical coat; see Newcastle). A sketch by Rosalba was in the Strawberry Hill sale, day 21, 18 May 1842, lot 1.

1745 Miniature by C.F. Zincke, bust length. Lord Waldegrave (*Walpole* 1970, A7, pl.4b), from the Strawberry Hill sale, day 14, 10 May 1842, lot 36. Engraved T.A. Dean 1861. A version sold Christie's, 27 June 1978, lot 34.

1745 Painting by John Robinson which Walpole thought 'very ill painted' (to Hanbury Williams, 6 August 1745). Possibly the half length in King's College, Cambridge (*Walpole* 1970, B6, pl.26a) and the portrait once belonging to Charles Bedford, copied by G.P. Harding 1801 (Lord Waldegrave) and attributed to Worlidge, presumably lot 32 in the Grosvenor Bedford sale, Christie's, 1 March 1861, as Richardson.

1750 Miniature by Nathaniel Hone. Whitehead sale, 2nd day, Christie's, 5 August 1915, lot 321.

c.1750 Painting by J.G. Eccardt, half length. Private collection (*Walpole* 1970, A9, pl.7). A version, possibly a copy by Edward Edwards, with Lord Mersey in 1937. Watercolour copy by G.P. Harding 1801 in the Grosvenor Bedford sale, Christie's, 1 March 1861, lot 21, probably that now in the Lewis Walpole Library, Farmington. A related copy by John Carter 'From an unfinished Painting', presumably by Eccardt, is in the Huntington Art Collections, San Marino, Calif. (*Walpole* 1970, A9.1, pl.6).

1754 Painting by J.G. Eccardt, see NPG 988.

1755–59 Pen and wash drawing by J.H. Muntz, whole length seated in his library at Strawberry Hill. Private collection (*Walpole* 1970, A11, pl.11). The figure alone engraved W. Greatbach 1842 *from a drawing by Muntz in the possession of Sir Alexander Johnston*.

1756–57 Painting by Joshua Reynolds, see NPG 6520.

c.1759 Painting by Allan Ramsay,* half length. Lewis Walpole Library, Farmington (*Walpole* 1970, A14; Smart 1999, no.529). A three-quarter length preparatory drawing is in the NG of Scotland (D 240; *Walpole* 1970, pl.18; Smart 1999, fig.689). A copy by Thomas Gogain from Stanton Harcourt sold Sotheby's, 10 June 1993, lot 870, and a copy of the Gogain was in an English private collection in 1970.

1768 Drawing by P-E. Falconet, profile bust, engraved by D.P. Pariset 1768 (*Walpole* 1970, A15, pl.20).

c.1770? Three caricatures of Walpole, drawn by John Carter, 'after breakfast', 'before dinner' and 'after dinner'. Huntington Art Collections, San Marino, Calif. (illus. Riccio 2000, p.11).

1793 Drawing by George Dance, see NPG 1161.

1795 Drawing by Thomas Lawrence, see NPG 3631.

A stone bust by Frederick Thomas 1895 is on the east front of the National Portrait Gallery.

DOUBTFUL PORTRAITS

See Unidentified Portraits NPG 116. A Rosalba pastel in the Lady Lever AG, Port Sunlight (illus. *Women's Works*, Liverpool, 1988, p.73), bears some resemblance and came from Wolterton (as Sir John Guinness has kindly informed me), but is probably not of Walpole; another, engraved J. Cochran 1835 as Walpole, and existing in several versions, shows Gustavus, 2nd Viscount Boyne (see *Walpole* 1970, pp.27–29, C5, C9).

OSBORNE, Francis Godolphin Osborne, Lord, see LEEDS

OSSORY, John, 1st Baron, see UPPER OSSORY

PAINE, Thomas 1737-1809

Democrat, author of *Common Sense* 1776 and *The Rights of Man* 1791; lived in America 1774-87; France 1787; England 1787-92 with visits to Paris in 1790 and 1791; Paris 1792-1802, and America 1802-09; d. New York.

'Tall and slim about five feet eight inches' (William Carver, c.1757).

'He is better in print than in the flesh; he has all the wit and egoism of the model Englishman. His blazing-red face dotted with purple blotches make him ugly, although he appears inspired and his eyes are full of fire' (George Forster, 1793).

'He has a red and rugged face, which looks as if it had been much hackneyed in the service of the world. His eyes are black and lively, his nose somewhat aquiline and pointing downward. It corresponds in colour with the fiery appearance of his cheeks' ('Dr Mitchill', c.1803).

Abbreviations

Conway 1892: M.D. Conway, *Thomas Paine*, 1892

Conway 1897: M.D. Conway, in *The Athenaeum*, 26 June 1897

Conway 1898: M.D. Conway in *The Truth Seeker*, 29 January 1898

897 AUGUSTE MILLIÈRE c.1876 after GEORGE ROMNEY [1792]

Canvas 43 x 33 (17 x 13); discoloured varnish and overall craquelure, an uneven surface due to there being the portrait of a lady underneath; inscribed verso: *No 1/ Portt of/ Thomas Paine// Aug. Milliere/ 72 Prince of Wales Road/ Kentish Town*

Brown eyes, brown, greying hair, brown coat; the papers on the left read: *Rigts/ of/ Man* and *Common/ Sense*.

Collections: [Nathan; Holyoake][1] bt. in 1891 by Henry Willett[2] by whom presented 1892.

Exhibition: Thetford, Guild Hall, 1951.

Millière wrote in 1896 that he had painted NPG 897 'nearly twenty years ago ... from an old engraving of the Original Portrait painted by Romney,'[3] presumably the plate by William Sharp published in 1793.[4] The original Romney portrait remains untraced;[5] according to Conway, it was painted for Dr Thomas Cooper (1759-1840) a Manchester radical, who emigrated to America.[6] It was painted in June and July 1792, when Paine was awaiting trial in London following the publication of *The Rights of Man* and effigies of him were being burned throughout the country. Paine simply

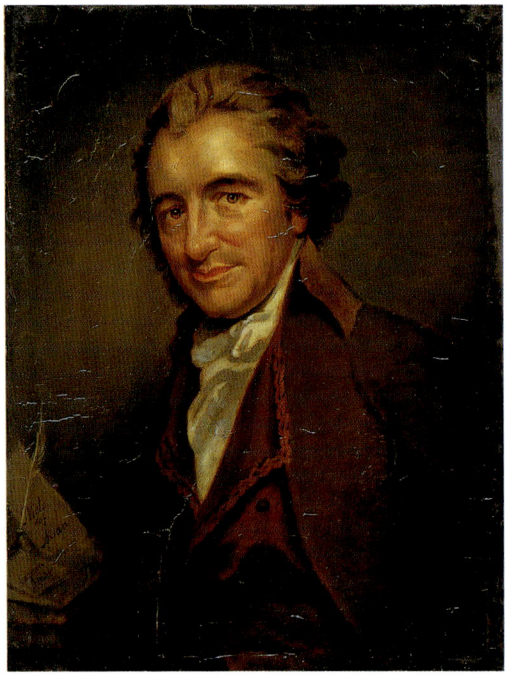

PAINE NPG *897*

announced that he was 'very quietly sitting to Mr Romney, the painter'.[7] The sittings had been arranged by his friend (and biographer) Clio Rickman, who considered the portrait 'perhaps the greatest likeness ever taken by any painter'.[8] Later John Romney declared it 'one of the finest heads ever produced by pencil', adding that 'if Paine had not been notorious by his mischievous writings, this portrait alone would have rescued his name from oblivion'.[9]

Romney's portrait was also engraved by C.T. Warren 1791, F. Bonneville 1796, A. Easto (head only), T.A. Dean 1830, and A. Krause; a crude bust-length version, reversed, etched by John Kay c.1794, was described as *taken from a miniature painted in America, and sent home to the artist by a friend*.[10] Copies were painted in America by J.W. Jarvis in 1803 and C.W. Jarvis in 1857;[11] by Clark Mills (NG Washington) and Bass Otis in 1859 (Independence National Historical Park, Pa.).[12] A dependant miniature 'by Romney', without the hands and with a fur-collared coat, allegedly painted for Outram Henfrey, was offered to the NPG in 1865 and 1894.[13] Two small copies, with an added right hand supporting a book, are recorded in private collections,[14] and a small whole-length extrapolation was with W.W. Bartlett, Brighton, in 1904.

1 Millière wrote that his picture was sold 'along with other rubbish in a lot, by auction, and bought by a Mr Nathan for a triffle [sic]' (letter of 26 October 1896; NPG archive).
2 Who said (letter of 20 April 1892; NPG archive) he had bought it 'last year'; he had been told it came 'from one of the Holyoakes who died & treasured it greatly' (letter of 24 April 1892; NPG archive) - the radical author George Jacob Holyoake (1817-1906, who was twice married) may have been related.
3 Letter of 26 October 1896; NPG archive.
4 Illus. Cross 2000, p.171; NPG 897 differs only in the height of the sheet inscribed, by Millière, *Rigts* [sic] *of Man*.
5 Ward & Roberts 1904, II, p.115.
6 He emigrated 'about a hundred years ago' [i.e. 1797] and became president of South Carolina College; Conway 1897, p.848 (he went on to associate it with an indifferent copy after Romney).
7 Quoted by J. Keane, *Tom Paine*, 1996, p.341.
8 T.C. Rickman, *Life of Thomas Paine*, 1819, p.14.
9 Romney 1830, pp.223-24.
10 *Kay's Portraits* 1842, II, f.p.184.
11 Both listed by Conway 1892, p.481, in American private collections.
12 Conway 1898, p.71.
13 By members of the Henfrey family; illus. TSB 9/38 (23 March 1865). In 1865 a Trustee had objected to the acquisition as long as he himself remained on the Council.
14 One in a painted oval with *The Rights of Man* (Dublin collection 1938), the other with *Sense*, illus. and exhibited *Up in Arms*, Belfast 1998(56).

ICONOGRAPHY

Paine's biographer, Moncure D. Conway, became much involved with his iconography, although he did not see his way too clearly; his accounts were published in his *Thomas Paine*, 1892, II, pp.473-81; *The Athenaeum*, 26 June 1897, *The Freethinker*, 3 October 1897, and *The Truth Seeker*, 29 January 1898 (all in NPG archive).

In America

1779-80 Painting by C.W. Peale, three-quarter length seated at table, holding sheet inscribed *To the Cause of Liberty and my Country*. Commissioned by Henry Laurens 1779 and taken in August 1780 to London, where engraved J. Watson 1783* and W. Angus

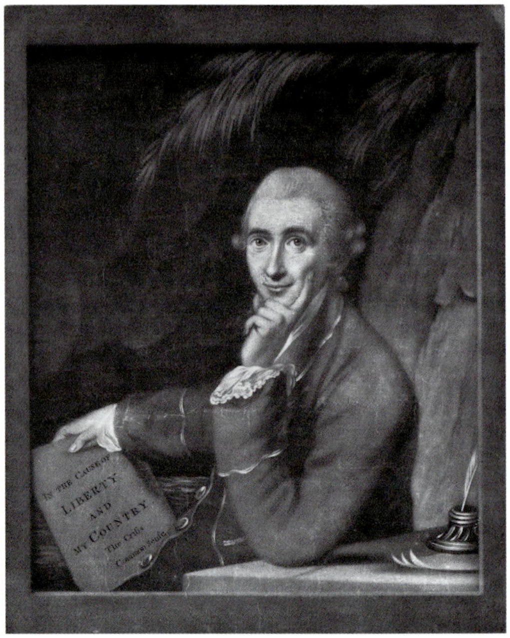

PAINE by J. Watson after C.W. Peale 1779-80 (National Portrait Gallery, Washington)

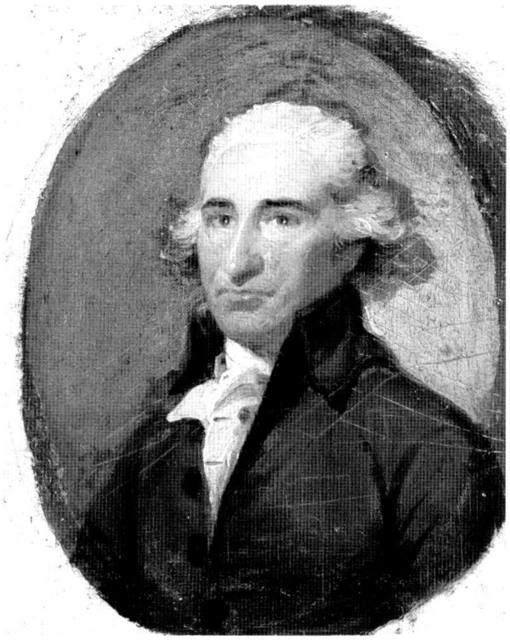

PAINE by John Trumbull 1788 (Monticello, Thomas Jefferson Foundation)

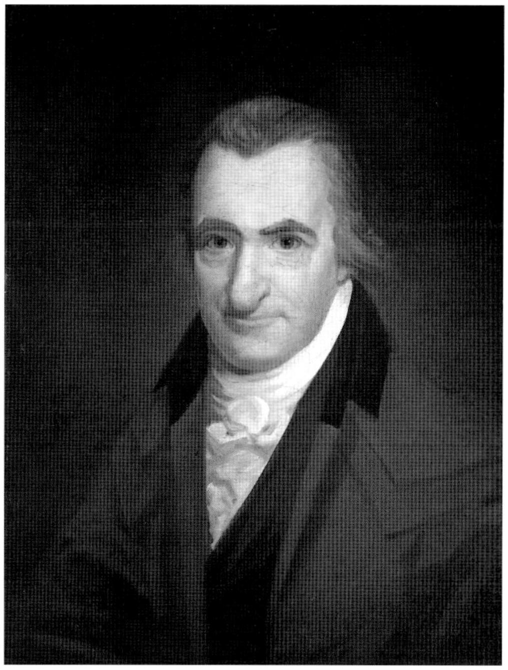

PAINE by J.W. Jarvis c.1806-07 (National Gallery of Art, Washington)

1791. A replica in the Peale Museum 1784, remains untraced (*Peale Papers*, I, 1983, pp.468n2, 635n). There were apparently at least two other versions: one engraved 1791 (published J. Ridgway, London) as *The Picture by Peel of Philadelphia in the Possession of T.B. Hollis Esqr.*, and Conway 1897, p.848, stated that another belonging to Joseph Jefferson had been destroyed by fire.

A related drawing inscribed *A Drawing from which Mr Bassett engraved his plate. I knew Thomas Paine, and positively declare this to be a great likeness Geo B Ba.. rell, Thetford*, is in the Norfolk County Library.

In England

Mather Brown was commissioned by Thomas Jefferson in 1787 to paint Paine, but apparently didn't (Evans 1982, no.137).

1788 Miniature by John Trumbull,* bust length. Thomas Jefferson Foundation, Monticello, Charlottesville. Painted for Thomas Jefferson.

1792 Painting by George Romney, see under NPG 897.

1792 Ink and wash drawing by Samuel Collings, three-quarter length seated with an open copy of the *Rights of M.* NPG Washington (9043). Engraved J. Barlow 1792 as *Collings ad vivum delt.*

In Paris

1792 Engraving by 'Pelegrini' [?D. Pellegrini], *Louis XVI's address to the Bar 26 December 1792*, in which Paine appears in the crowded Convention wearing a top hat (illus. J. Keane, *Tom Paine*, 1996, f.p.410).

1793 Medal (illus. Brown 1980, no.365). Possibly modelled by Samuel Percy in whose sale, Christie's, 31 January 1800, there was a wax portrait of Paine (Gunnis 1968, p.300).

c.1793 Drawing by C. Schule, half length; engraved A. Schule (illus. J. Keane, *Tom Paine*, 1996, f.p.410).

1796 Anon. engraving, standing pointing to a scroll lettered *The Rights of Man* (for Baxter's *History of England*).

1800 Miniature by H. Richards, rather stout, broad-faced, engraved K. Mackenzie (Conway 1892, II, p.478).

In America

1803 Drawing 'done from the Life in America 1803', profile bust caricature, engraved J. Godby 1805 (illus. J. Keane, *Tom Paine*, 1996, f.p.410, as from a drawing by Edward Stacey).

c.1806-07 Painting by J.W. Jarvis,* half length. NG Washington (1950.15.1). Engraved J.R. Ames. Version sold Christie's, 8 January 1894, lot 86.

1806-07 Drawing by William Constable showing 'the ravages of age'. Dr C.J. Grece, Redhill, in 1892 (Conway 1892, II, p.479).

Posthumous

1809 Death mask taken by J.W. Jarvis, the nose somewhat distorted. New York Historical Society, a cast with the Norfolk Museums Service (illus. *Harper's Mag.*, XXIV, 1892, p.912; *Family and Friends*, Norwich, 1992, p.140).

1809 Plaster bust by J.W. Jarvis, derived from his painting, the death mask, and memory. New York Historical Society (illus. *Cat. of American Portraits*, 1974, II, p.596).

1964 Bronze statue by Charles Wheeler. Thetford (illus. *CL*, CXXXV, 1964, p.1422).

1997 Bronze figure by Lawrence Holofcener. Sotheby's, 14 July 1999, lot 65.

DOUBTFUL PORTRAITS

Painting, formerly attributed to William Owen, inscribed *Thomas Paine London 1790*, sold Sotheby's, 8 May 1951, lot 354; another attributed to Owen, sold Sotheby's, 25 September 1974, lot 114; drawing attributed to A. de Saint-Aubin in the Fitzwilliam Museum, Cambridge (PD.101-1961); watercolour, inscribed *Thomas Paine A Drawing from the life/ taken at New York Octr 1783*, with B.F. Stevens & Brown in 1942. A wax seal, profile head to right, purporting to show Paine c.1772 remains a curiosity (illus. Conway 1892, II, front., and see I, p.33).

PALEY, William 1743-1805

Priest and philosopher, of Christ's College, Cambridge; Archdeacon of Carlisle 1782; author of *The Principles of Moral and Political Philosophy* 1785 and *Evidences of Christianity* 1794.

'a thick, short, square-built man, with a face which, though animated and cheerful, could not but, at first sight, appear ugly; with bushy brows, snub nose and projecting teeth; with an awkward gait and movement of the arms; a decent and dignified but by no means excessive protuberance of the belly .. he spoke with a very broad northern dialect' (H.D. Best, 1829).

3659 GEORGE ROMNEY 1789-91

Canvas 152 x 122 (60 x 48) unlined (with illegible canvas stamp); the canvas is slack, with a prominent shrinkage craquelure in the darks (the bottom of his coat, his hat and the topmost areas); a repaired tear lower centre; there has been some reworking of the background, so that, for example, the fishing lines, seen in Jones's engraving and described in the NPE 1868 catalogue, are no longer visible.

Brown eyes, white powdered wig, wearing black clerical dress; to the left a brown background, with open sky to the right.

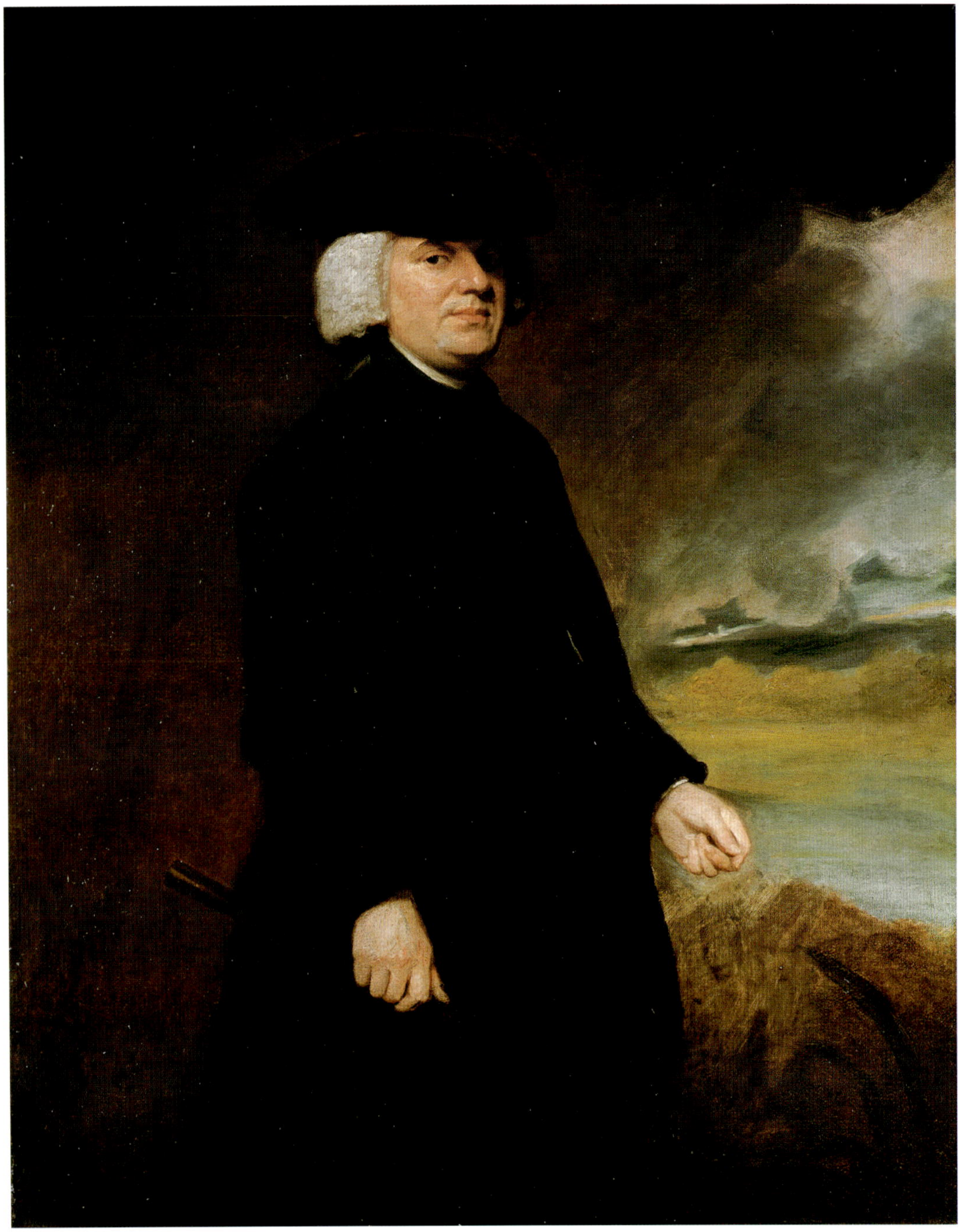

PALEY NPG *3659*

Collections: Edward Law, 1st Baron Ellenborough (d.1818); by descent to the 8th Baron Ellenborough; Sotheby's, 11 June 1947, lot 98; F.B. Daniell, London, from whom purchased 1949.

Engravings: J. Jones 1792;* R. Graves (bust length); G.B. Shaw (and see NPG 145 note 2).

Exhibition: NPE 1868(833) lent by the Earl of Ellenborough.[1]

Reference: Ward & Roberts 1904, II, p.116.

According to Paley's son, NPG 3659 was commissioned by John Law, Bishop of Clonfert,[2] whom Paley had succeeded as Archdeacon of Carlisle in 1782. Sittings are recorded in July and August 1789, but Romney's diaries show that the portrait was delivered to 'Mr Law' in Bloomsbury Square on 24 January 1791 and paid for on 6 April by 'Ed. Law', i.e. John's brother Edward, later 1st Baron Ellenborough.[3]

The slightly incongruous image of a formally-dressed archdeacon fishing was variously explained. Romney's son said that when Paley first went to sit, accompanied by John Law, then Bishop of Clonfert, his dress being considered unsuitable 'he was prevailed with to put on the Bishop's hat, and, I believe, his coat also'; he was then shown with his fishing rod in his hand to indicate 'his attachment to a contemplative amusement, not inconsistent with the sacred functions of his profession'.[4] Paley's son explained that his father enjoyed fishing 'to his heart's content' at Appleby, Cumbria, where he lived after 1782, and

> it might be probably from his eagerness for this amusement .. that Mr Law struck out his intention of having his picture taken in his fishing trim; but it was not carried into execution till some time after, when Dr Law was advanced to an Irish bishopric. To say nothing of the preposterous figure of a fisherman in a buzz wig and an archdeacon's hat, which was scarcely worn on state occasions, it is probable that neither Romney, who painted it, nor Dr Law who insisted on having it painted in that guise, knew much of fishing, or recollected how little that very peculiar kind of pike fishing would be recognised on canvas even by fishermen.[5]

According to the provenance NPG 3659 is Romney's original portrait, but there are two other three-quarter length versions. One was exhibited by the Rev Robert Vanbrugh Law in 1868,[6] and the other, listed by Maxwell and Gower as the original portrait,[7] descended in the Paley family who still owned it in 1924;[8] it was presumably one of these two which was sold at Bonham's, 24 February 1977, lot 17.

For half-length versions, see under NPG 145 below.

1 Who suc. as 2nd Baron Ellenborough in 1818; cr. Earl of Ellenborough 1844; d.s.p. 1871, the Earldom becoming extinct.
2 E. Paley, *William Paley*, 1825, p.93.
3 Ward & Roberts 1904, II, p.116 (sittings on 10, 14, 16, 18, 20, 27 July and 3, 6 August).
4 Romney 1830, p.212.
5 E. Paley, *William Paley*, 1825, p.93. Paley's anecdote of Romney then begrudging the Bishop of Clonfert his purchase was strongly denied by John Romney (Romney 1830, pp.212-13n).
6 Exhibited Leeds 1868(3183) illus. Hailstone 1869, II, no.168; this exhibition coincided with the NPE 1868 exhibition, to which NPG 3659 was already lent. R.V. Law (1799-1884) was the 1st Lord Ellenborough's nephew.
7 H. Maxwell, *Romney*, 1902, p.186(295); R.S. Gower, *Romney*, 1904, p.123 (295).
8 Exhibited RA 1889(135) lent John Paley; with G.A. Paley (d.1941), Ampton Hall, 1905 (Farrer 1908, p.4, no.14, illus. f.p.4); in 1924 J. Sweetland, *née* Paley, wrote that 'the original was still in our family' (letter of 7 August; NPG archive).

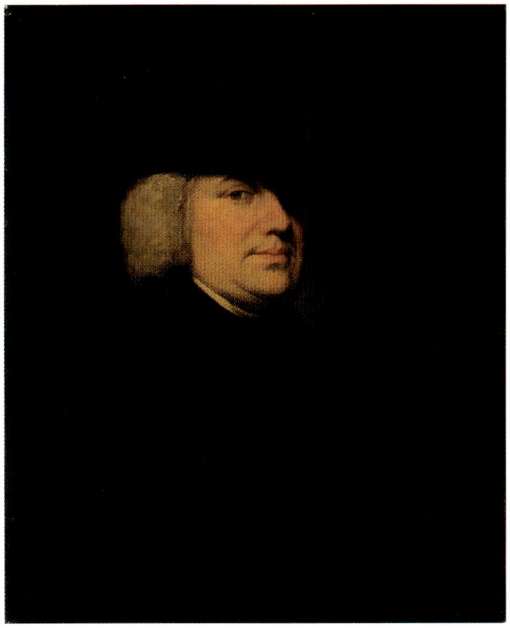

PALEY NPG *145*

145 after ROMNEY [1789–91]

Canvas 75 x 61.5 (29½ x 24¼) lined; varnish much discoloured.

Grey eyes, powdered wig, black hat with a red ribbon, dark blue coat.

Collections: Bt. in Bristol by Christopher Knight Watson,[1] from whom purchased 1862.

A pedestrian copy from NPG 3659. A previous attribution to Beechey, made by Scharf in 1862, was doubtless based on several half-length engravings from the Romney portrait being described as after 'Beechy',[2] but the attribution was immediately questioned.[3] In 1985 Goodison showed that the half-length version in Christ's College, Cambridge, was a documented copy from Lord Ellenborough's Romney made by Beechey in 1809.[4] Another weak half-length version was in a private collection in 1960.

1 1844–1901, secretary of the Society of Antiquaries 1860–82; he told Scharf (letter of 8 April 1862; NPG archive) that he had bought the portrait 'somewhat rashly, on the representation of a friend who wrote to tell me that a 'portrait of my Grandfather Bishop Watson [Richard Watson, 1737–1816] was on sale at Bristol'.

2 By F. Engleheart 1810, T. Ranson 1819 and 1822, and J. Gellatly; a second state of Engleheart's plate altered Beechey's name to Romney. Other half-length plates by J. Hopwood 1805 and S. Freeman gave no painter's name.

3 Letters from John Burton and Lord Ellenborough, *NQ*, 3/ii, 1862, pp.388, 416.

4 J.W. Goodison, *Cat. of the Portraits in Christ's, Clare and Sidney Sussex Colleges*, Cambridge, 1985, p.31(64), and see Roberts 1907, p.229.

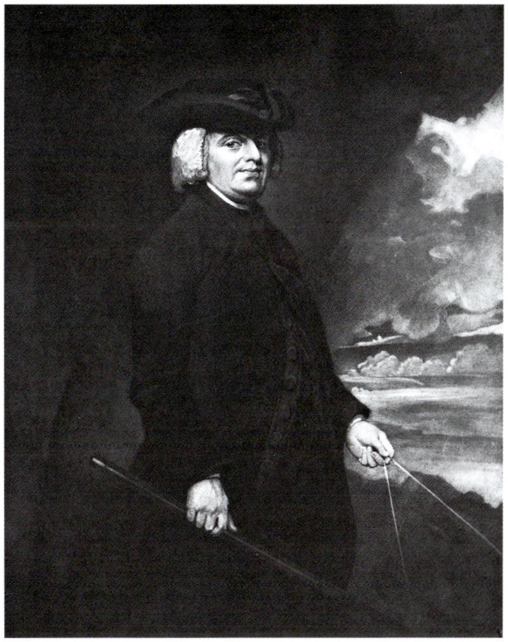

PALEY J. Jones after George Romney 1789–91 (NPG D *9534*)

ICONOGRAPHY

1769 Painting by 'Vandermyn' (presumably Frans Van der Mijn), signed and dated 1769, half length in gown and bands. Fornham House in 1908 (Farrer 1908, p.120, no.19). Presumably the portrait recorded by G.M. Meadley (*Memoirs of William Paley*, 1810, p.88) with John Law, painted about 1769 by 'Vandermyn, a Cambridge artist' and then belonging to Dr John Ord (of Fornham House).

1789–91 Painting by George Romney, see NPG 3659 and NPG 145.

c.1790–1800 Painting by Samuel Drummond, bust-length oval, engraved by W. Ridley 1805 (*European Mag.*).

A caricature by Henry Bunbury of Paley with Richard Watson, designed 'to excite the risible faculties of the residents of the university', listed in the *Universal Mag.*, III, 1805, p.289.

Stained-glass portraits of Paley are at Christ's College, Cambridge, at Giggleswick school, Yorkshire, and in the vestry of St Alfege's church, Greenwich (as listed by M.L. Clarke, *Paley*, 1974, p.135).

PALMER, John 1742–98

Actor-manager, 'plausible' John Palmer (from Wycherley's *Plain Dealer*); played at the Haymarket 1762 and later that year at Drury Lane, where he was to perform regularly, initially under Garrick; built the Royalty Theatre in Wellclose Square, London, which ran from 1787–98, but left him greatly in debt; d. on stage at Liverpool; a popular, versatile actor, and an improvident man.

'the figure of John Palmer rose nearly to the height of six feet, and was finely adjusted between spareness and corpulency; his shoulders and chest were broad; his legs were in some measure what they called bowed ...; his countenance was fair and open, ... his eye was blue, his nose aquiline; his forehead high; his hair light; his voice firm and powerful' (*Monthly Mirror*, 1798).

2086 HENRY WALTON, *as Count Almaviva in The Spanish Barber* 1779

Canvas 75 x 50 (29½ x 19¾) lined; discoloured varnish, with retouched craquelure in the cloak, vest and background area immediately round the figure.

Light brown hair, wearing a red cloak over a green and pink striped suit, with white stockings with brown shoes and a white-plumed grey hat.

Collections: John Palmer; C. Wylie; sold Christie's, 7 February 1910, lot 71, bt. Pollard; John Lane,[1] by whom bequeathed 1925.

Engraving: Anon. 1788 (*Count Almaviva. Spanish Barber, half length oval, from an original painting by Walton in the Possession of Mr Jno. Palmer Esqr*).[2]

Exhibitions: RA 1779(338 'a scene in the Spanish Barber, Act 1, Scene 1'); *Walton*, Norwich, 1963(13).

Reference: C.H. Collins Baker, *Connoisseur*, XLVIII, 1917, p.136; *Walton* 1999, no.122.

George Colman's *The Spanish Barber, or the Fruitless Precaution*, a three-act comic opera adapted from *Le Barbier de Seville* by Beaumarchais, was first performed at the Haymarket in August 1777 with Palmer in the leading role as Count Almaviva; in act 1, scene i, Almaviva duly appears on his own, as specified in the RA catalogue of 1779 (see above).

1 For whose collection of British portraits, see C.H. Collins Baker, *Connoisseur*, XLVIII, 1917, p.127.

2 The plate made for the *General Mag. & Impartial Review* was published in April 1788 was evidently a puff for Palmer's Royalty Theatre.

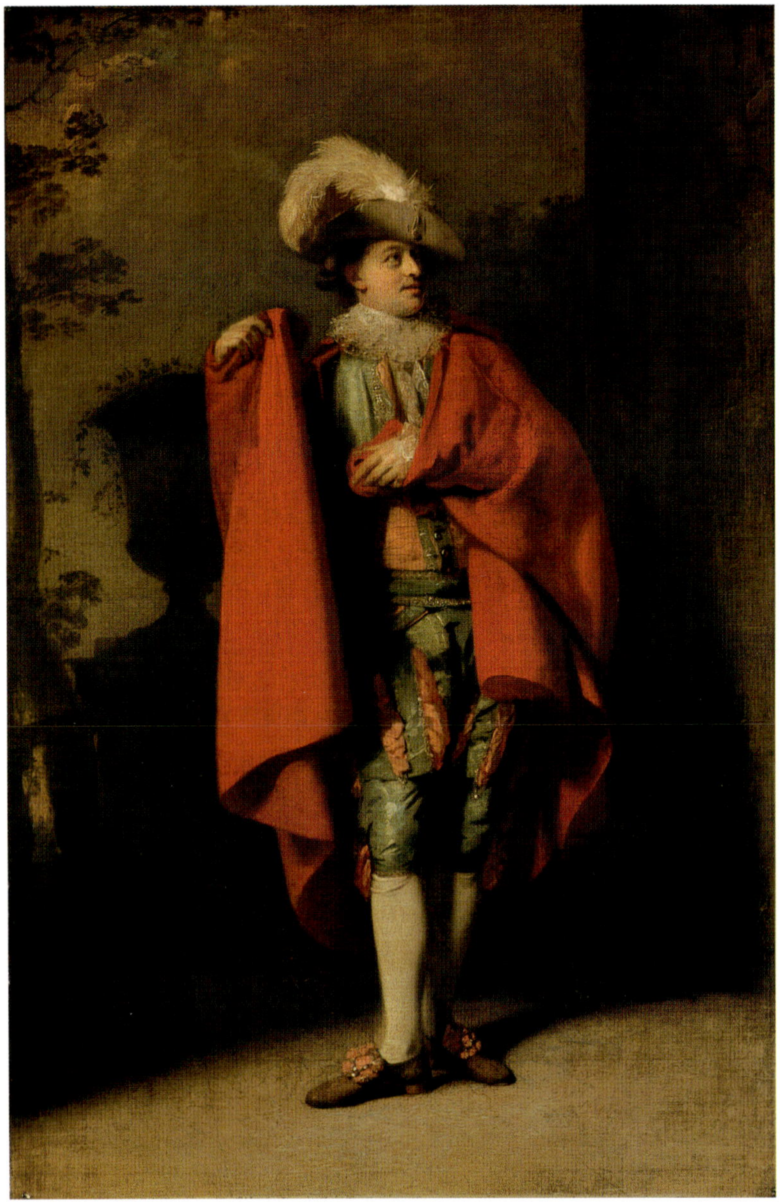

PALMER NPG *2086*

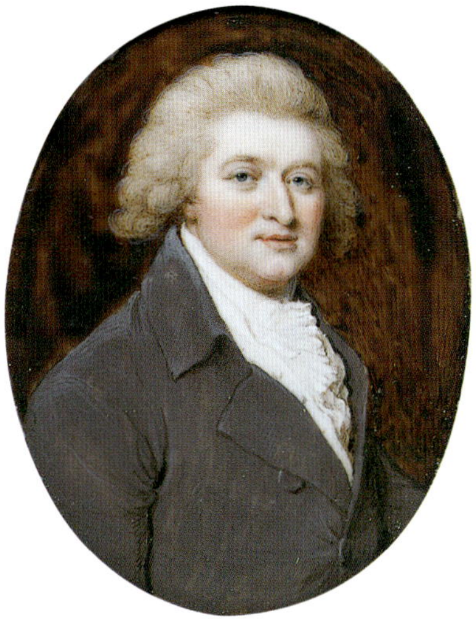

PALMER NPG *6167*

6167 UNKNOWN ARTIST c.1785-90

Watercolour and bodycolour on ivory 7.5 x 5.8 (2⅞ x 2¼); wooden backing inscribed in ink: *portrait of* [*the/ late*] *Jo Palmer /never exhibited*.

Blue eyes, powdered hair, wearing a grey coat and white neckcloth.

Collections: Moses Lazarus; given by the Misses Sarah and Josephine Lazarus to the Metropolitan Museum of Art, New York, 1888; de-accessioned 1990; Christie's, 4 March 1992, lot 78 attributed to Thomas Hull, bt. Leggatt for the NPG.

The identity is corroborated by the engraved oval pastel of 1786 by John Russell in the Garrick Club (see below). Unattributed while at the Metropolitan Museum of Art, NPG 6167 was sold in 1992 as by Thomas Hull, apparently as the result of a confused association with Hull's miniature of another John Palmer (1742-1818) exhibited in 1827;[1] a miniature of 'John Palmer' by Hull c.1795 was sold Sotheby's, Chester, 17-19 November 1987, lot 4035.[2]

1 See NPG 4929 (Walker Regency, I, p.382, II, pl.919).
2 Not seen by the compiler.

ICONOGRAPHY

[*Caveat*: the actor John 'Gentleman' Palmer (1728-68), and John Palmer (1742-1818), inventor of mail coaches]

See also the *Harvard Catalogue*, III, pp.290-92, and Highfill, XI, pp.175-77 (listing further depictions of Palmer in character).

1779 Painting by Henry Walton, see NPG 2086.

1779 Drawing by Robert Dighton, bust-length oval, engraved R. Laurie (illus. Highfill, XI, p.162).

c.1782 Painting by George Carter,* *The Immortality of Garrick*, see Comparative Groups.

c.1785-90 Unattributed miniature, see NPG 6167.

1786 Pastel by John Russell,* half length. Garrick Club (Ashton 1997, no.649). Exhibited RA 1786(152). Engraved J. Collyer 1787.

c.1790 Unattributed drawing, half length, wearing a Shakespeare favour. Garrick Club (Ashton 1997, no.650).

1792 Drawn and engraved by John Condé (*Thespian Dictionary* 1793).

1798 Painting by L.A. Arlaud, half-length oval, engraved W. Byrne (with the announcement of Palmer's death on 2 August 1798).

1798 Engraving by W. Ridley from a drawing 'taken in the Liverpool theatre', half-length oval in the title role of *The Stranger*, which Palmer was playing at his death (illus. Highfill, XI, p.167).

1799 Engraving by J. Chapman, bust-length oval.

Undated Pastel by John Russell, in the title role of *Comus* (Williamson 1894, p.156, when with Mrs Gough Nicholls).

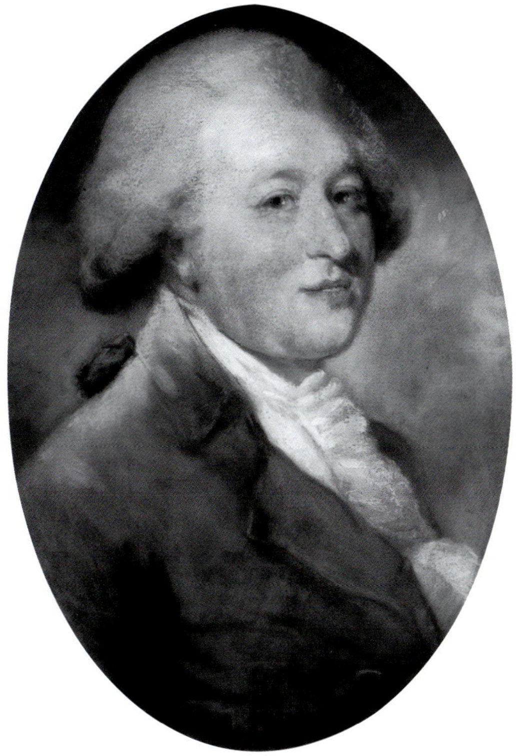

PALMER by John Russell 1786 (Garrick Club)

Undated Painting by Mary Benwell, half-length, engraved J. Corner (oval).

Paintings of Palmer in character include: Zoffany, as Face in Jonson's *The Alchymist*, see Garrick; Zoffany also drew a single figure of Palmer in *The Alchymist*, engraved 1771 (illus. *Georgian Playhouse* 1975, no.42); Thomas Parkinson, as Iachimo in *Cymbeline* 1778 (Garrick Club; Ashton 1997, no.651); James Roberts, as Surface in *School for Scandal* 1779 (Garrick Club; Ashton 1997, no.3); by De Wilde, as Don John in Beaumont and Fletcher's *The Chances* (National Theatre, Maugham Collection; Mander & Mitchenson 1980, no.23; engraved J. Thornthwaite 1791; illus. Burnim 1998, p.201), and as Don Carlos in Cibber's *Ximena* (engraved J. Thornthwaite 1792; illus. Burnim 1998, p.200); by James Saxon, as Col. Cohenberg in Cobb's *Siege of Belgrade*, 1796 (presumably the painting in the Garrick Club; Ashton 1997, no.648).

DOUBTFUL PORTRAITS

See Simpson, NPG 1485. Painting by Johann Zoffany, once called *John Palmer and his Family*, Tate Gallery, shows Mr & Mrs Richard Dalton (cf. *Zoffany* 1977, no.32).

PATCH, Thomas 1725-82

Painter and etcher, b. Exeter; he went to Italy in 1747 and studied under Joseph Vernet in Rome; in 1755 he was banished because, thought Lord Charlemont, of his 'oddities and loose way of talking in all companies'; he moved to Florence, where he became the close friend of the British resident Sir Horace Mann, who thought him 'really a genius'.

4081 attributed to THOMAS PATCH c.1745

Watercolour and bodycolour on card 9.7 x 7.5 (3¾ x 3); apart from the figure itself and an adjoining area to the right, the surface is thinly varnished. The original backing vellum inscribed in ink in an early nineteenth-century hand: *Thomas Patch/Painter & Engraver/ third son of/John Patch Senr-/Surgeon at Exeter/ died unmarried/ in Italy* and: *John Patch's senr Surgeon/ Portrait is in y Hospital/*[*Exeter*]; on the back of the vellum a pencil drawing apparently of a half-length figure with long hair seen from behind.

Blue eyes, powdered hair, wearing a red coat with a black collar.

Collections: By family descent to Blanche Patch;[1] H. O'Nians, from whom purchased 1958.

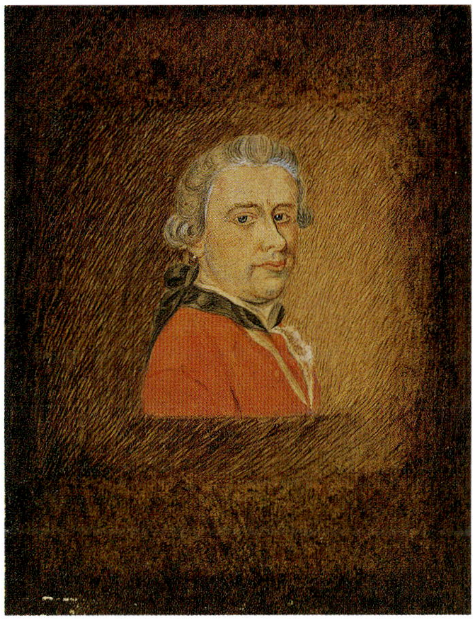

PATCH NPG 4081

The identification was accepted by Watson.[2] Although previously listed as by an unknown artist, the pose suggests a self portrait (and the dense background cross-hatching recurs in other drawings by Patch),[3] while the sitter's apparent age and the family provenance further suggest NPG 4081 was made in Exeter before Patch's departure for Italy in 1747.

1 Information from Francis Watson, November 1958 (NPG archive); Blanche Patch (c.1880-1966) was for nearly forty years George Bernard Shaw's secretary.
2 Note by C.K. Adams, November 1958 (NPG archive).
3 Cf. the profile of a lady in the British Museum (1874.7.11.179), illus. *Apollo*, XXVI, 1937, p.218.

ICONOGRAPHY

c.1745 Drawing attributed to Thomas Patch, see NPG 4081.

1751 Painting by Joshua Reynolds, *Parody of the School of Athens*, caricature group in which Patch may appear on the extreme right. NG of Ireland (734; Mannings 2000, no.1962). Patch was listed by Reynolds amongst his subjects for this group, but this figure has also been recognised as Reynolds himself. Painted in Rome.

1768 Engraving by Thomas Patch,* whole-length seated, measuring a mask on a table (*Twenty-five Caricatures* 1771).

1772-77 Painting by Johann Zoffany,* *The Tribuna, Florence* (see Introduction) with Patch in the right foreground holding Titian's *Venus of Urbino*. Royal Collection (Millar 1969, no.1211). George III took exception to the inclusion of Horace Mann and Patch 'who were considered as men addicted to improper practises' (Farington, 15 December 1804).

The iconography of Patch is otherwise confined to self portraits lurking within the caricature groups he painted in Florence, including the following:

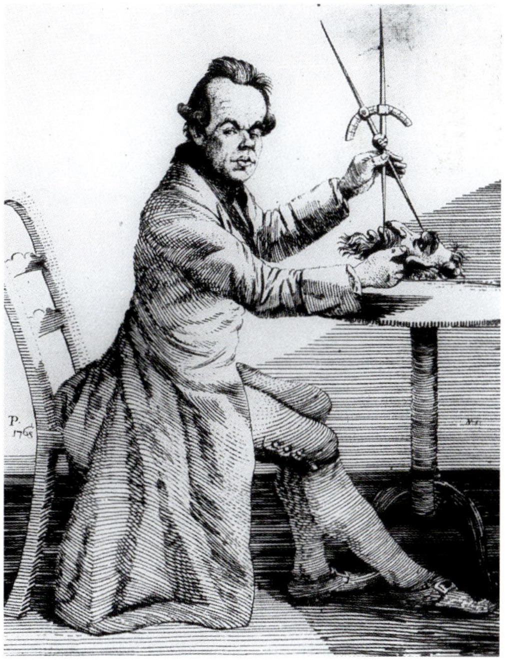

PATCH engraved self portrait 1768 (NPG archive)

before 1760 *The Cognoscenti*, with a half-length picture of Patch dressed as a cavalier in Spanish costume. Petworth.

1760 *The Punch Party*, with a bust of Patch mounted on the wall. Dunham Massey (illus. *Patch* 1940, no.1, pl.ixb).

1760 *The Punch Party*, with a bust of Patch above the mantelpiece. Yale Center for British Art (B1976.7.187; illus. Waterhouse 1981, p.269).

1760 *Antiquaries at Pola*, in which a fragmentary marble head lying on the ground caricatures the artist. Dunham Massey (illus. *Patch* 1940, no.2, pl.ixa).

after 1760 *A Gathering at Horace Mann's, Florence*, with a whole-length self portrait at his easel painting a satyr. Lewis Walpole Library, Farmington (illus. *Patch* 1940, no.6, pl.xa; *Wal. Corr.*, XXI, f.p.543).

c.1760-61 *A Gathering of Dilettanti in a Sculpture Hall*, with Patch mounted on steps measuring the *Medici Venus*. Brinsley Ford collection (*Wal. Soc.*, LX, i, 1998, pl.85).

1761 *The Punch Party or The Golden Asses*, with Patch extreme right on a statue of a donkey, the plinth inscribed from Macchiavelli ... *questo Asin ci cappi E sentirassi come il mondo e guasto....* Chatsworth. A version in the Lewis Walpole Library, Farmington (illus. *Grand Tour*, Tate Gallery, 1996, no.41).

c.1761 *A Caricature Group*, with two painted caricatures of the artist, one with a lion's body in a cage, the other with a bull's body in a landscape; the bust on a wall bracket might also represent him. Royal Albert Memorial Museum, Exeter (illus. *Apollo*, XXVI, 1937, p.221). Patch engraved the 'bull' self portrait separately (*Twenty-five Caricatures* 1771).

c.1768 *The Music Lesson*, with a half-length self portrait at his easel. Tissington (*Patch* 1940, no.9, pl.xb; *CL*, CLX, 1976, p.287).

1770 *Group in the Artist's studio in Florence*, with a self portrait at his easel painting commedia dell'arte figures. Lewis Walpole Library, Farmington (illus. *Apollo*, LXXXV, 1967, p.349; *Grand Tour*, Tate Gallery, 1996, no.42).

1774 *A Musical Party*, with Patch standing on the extreme right holding a folio volume inscribed *Le Regole del FISONOMIZARE FIRENZE 1774*. Floors Castle. In the *Regole* Patch expounded the possibility of drawing a head without seeing the subject, from a knowledge of a person's nationality, character and beliefs.

DOUBTFUL PORTRAITS

Drawing by Thomas Patch, Royal Albert Memorial Museum, Exeter (5.1943).

PENDARVES, Mrs Mary, see DELANY

PERCEVAL, Viscount, see EGMONT

PERCY, Hugh, see NORTHUMBERLAND

PETTY, William, see LANSDOWNE

PHELPS, Richard c.1718-85

Painter, from Porlock, Somerset; collaborated with the amateur artist C.W. Bampfylde (see below) and exhibited SA 1764; an album of his portrait drawings is in the British Museum and three portraits (dating from before 1766) are at Dunster Castle; d. Porlock, 12 July 1785 aged 67.

1797A RICHARD PHELPS 1771

Charcoal on grey Whatman paper 32 x 27 (12½ x 10¾) faded, with some spotting and yellow staining; creases in the collar and in the lower right corner; inscribed verso: *Richd. Phelps/ Drawn by himself in 1771 Aged 52 years.*

Collections: Presented by Francis Wellesley 1917.

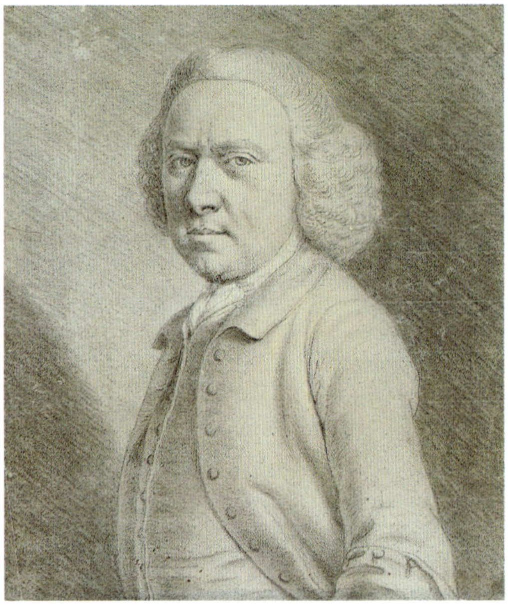

PHELPS NPG *1979A*

ICONOGRAPHY

[*Caveat*: Richard Phelps (c.1720-71) diplomat and traveller]

1746? Painting by Richard Phelps and C.W. Bampfylde (1720-91),* signed by both artists, the latter on a grey hunter, the former as a groom with a bay hunter, at Hestercombe, Somerset, which Bampfylde inherited in 1750. Guy Morrison, London. The date was read as 1746, which seems too early; Bampfylde exhibited at the SA and RA between 1763 and 1783.

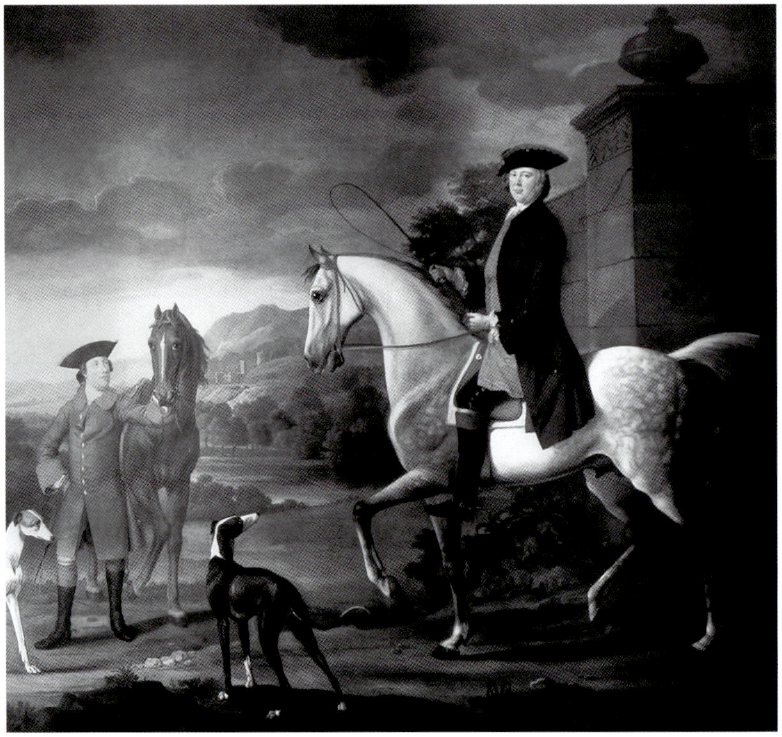

PHELPS standing with C.W. Bampfylde by Richard Phelps and C.W. Bampfylde 1746? (Guy Morrison, London)

1771 Drawing by Richard Phelps, see NPG 1797A.

1779 Drawing by Richard Phelps, half-length oval. Ashmolean Museum, Oxford (1472; Brown 1982, p.494). Looking slightly fuller in the face and less forbidding than in NPG 1797A.

PHILLIP, Arthur 1738-1814

Naval officer and colonial governor; b. London, s. of a language teacher from Frankfurt; served in the Mediterranean 1756 and at Havannah 1762, retiring from the navy in 1763; served with the Portuguese navy 1774-78, rejoining the British fleet in 1778; governor of New South Wales 1786-93, where he founded a convict settlement; an 'intelligent, active and persevering' governor, he returned to England in poor health; rear-admiral 1801 and vice-admiral 1810; d. Bath.

'Well I remember his little figure, ... his face shrivelled, and thin aquiline nose, under a large cocked hat, gathered up in a heap, his chin between his knees, sitting under the mainmast ... ' (Captain Landman, 1796).

1462 FRANCIS WHEATLEY 1786

Canvas 91 x 70 (35¾ x 27½) lined; pentimenti lower left-hand edge of coat and down his right leg; signed and dated on the rocks, lower left: *FW:/1786*.

Brown eyes, wearing a captain's undress uniform, black hat, blue coat with brass buttons, white breeches.

Collections: Miss Harriet Lane; Mrs Elizabeth Gayton, by whom bequeathed 1907.[1]

Engraving: H. Macbeth-Raeburn c.1900.[2]

Exhibitions: *Wheatley*, Aldeburgh, Leeds 1965(11); *First Impressions*, British Museum, 1988; *Coming of Strangers*, Sydney, 1988.

Reference: Webster 1970, no.49.

NPG 1462 was presumably painted following Phillip's appointment in August 1786 as governor of New South Wales and before he sailed for Botany Bay on 13 May 1787. The setting is non-descript (the boat cannot be identified), but Phillip's stepping ashore is wholly appropriate. A second portrait of Phillip by Wheatley, a well-characterised head, is also dated 1786 (see below).

1 Of Queens Road, Peckham; the picture had been in her house since 1860 when Harriet Lane died there 'and is believed to have been in her [Lane's] possession many years' (letter from Messrs Freshfields, Mrs Gayton's solicitors, 18 May 1907; NPG archive). Colin Dean (letter of 16 October 1989; NPG archive) said 'there appears to have been' an Ellen Gay[i]ton, a contemporary, who was related to Phillip.

2 Example sold Christie's, SK, 10 November 1988, lot 151.

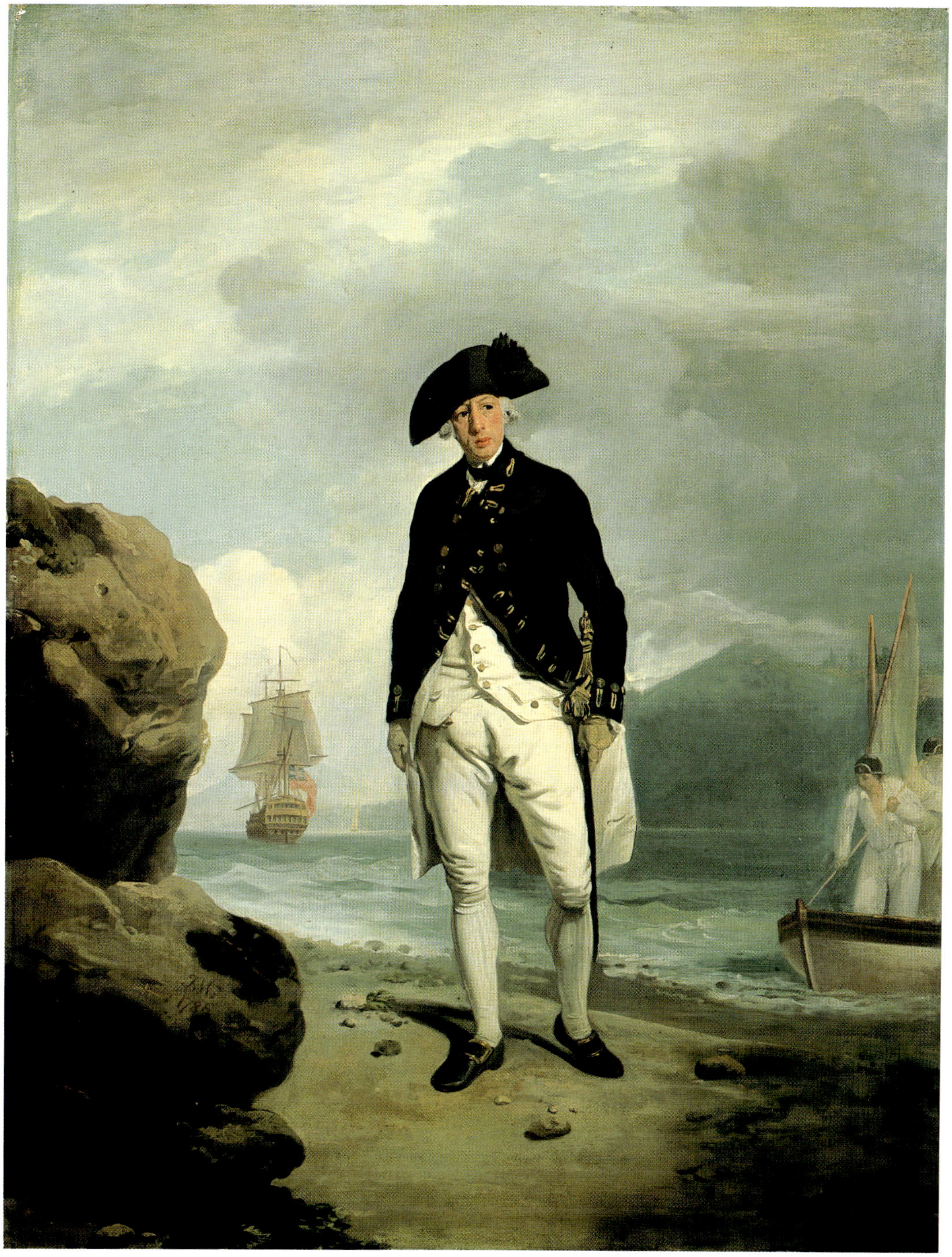

PHILLIP NPG *1462*

ICONOGRAPHY

1786 Painting by Francis Wheatley, see NPG 1462.

1786 Painting by Francis Wheatley, small half-length oval, dated 1786, holding a plan marked *New South Wales 1787*. State Library, Sydney, New South Wales (illus. Webster 1970, no.50, p.97). Engraved W. Sherwin 1789, with the plan dated *1788*; R. Page 1812; Ermer.

Posthumous

1932 Bronze bust by Charles Hartwell, in naval uniform. Cannon Street, London. Originally part of the Phillip memorial in the church of St Mildred, Bread Street, London, unveiled in 1932 and destroyed during the war. Hartwell exhibited a second bronze bust of Phillip, RA 1933(1684).

PHIPPS, Constantine John, see MULGRAVE

PIGOT, George Pigot, 1st Baron 1719–77

Governor of Madras; joined the East India Company in Madras 1737, becoming governor 1755–63; the fortune he acquired included the celebrated Pigot diamond (sold in 1802 for 9,500 gn.); MP 1765–77; Bt 1764, cr. Baron Pigot of Patshull [I] 1768; his wealth exhausted, he returned to Madras as governor 1775–76, but was deposed by his Council and d. in confinement; his persecutors were to be heavily fined; a man of 'shallow abilities, of great spirit ... excessive vanity and overbearing despotism'.

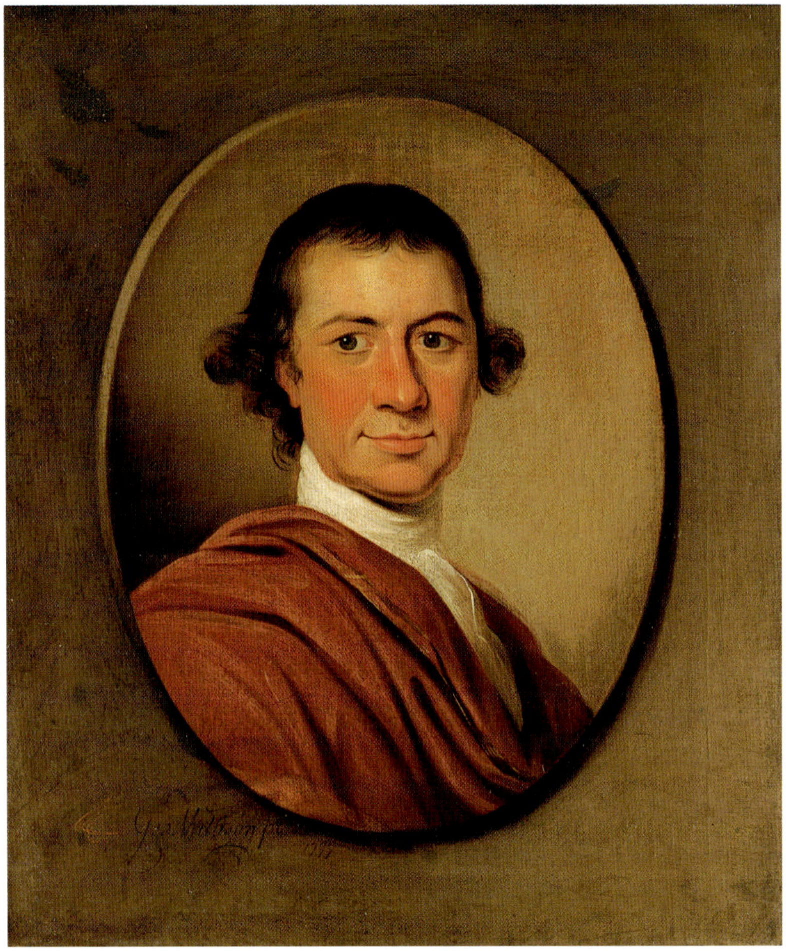

Baron PIGOT NPG *3837*

3837 GEORGE WILLISON 1777

> Canvas 68.5 x 58.5 (27 x 23) lined; signed, lower left in spandrel: *Geo. Willison pinx/ 1777*; pentimenti show an alteration to his left shoulder, and show the painted oval to have been an addition: his right arm originally across the foreground area, his right shoulder at the left edge, a drapery hanging top left and his left arm bottom right.
>
> Blue eyes, dark hair, wearing a red cloak.
>
> *Collections*: Purchased from Mrs Cavil Elborne, Peterborough, 1952.
>
> *Exhibition*: *The Raj*, NPG, 1990–91(141).[1]

Willison was based in Madras in 1777 when he painted NPG 3837. Pigot died there on 11 May, in confinement in the Garden House, near Fort St George (where he had been moved the month before, having previously been detained at St Thomas's Mount, some nine miles from Madras). The alterations to NPG 3837 (the painted oval surround appears to be laid over an orthodox rectangular composition) might suggest it was unfinished at Pigot's death, but the head certainly suggests a live sitting.[2]

Willison also painted in 1777 a three-quarter length canvas incorporating a similar portrait of Pigot on a pedestal supported by the figure of Fame and mourned by a weeping female, with a view of Madras in the distance;[3] it remained in Madras until 1973, and Archer has proposed that it was commissioned by the Raja Tulsaji of Tanjor, whom Pigot had restored to his throne.[4]

1 The cat. entry, however, begins to describe the portrait by Tilly Kettle, see below.
2 Cf. Archer 1979, pp. 104–05.
3 He had previously used this device in an emblematic portrait of the Duke of Queensberry, engraved in 1770.
4 See Archer 1979, p.106; in 1985 with the Malcolm Innes Gallery, London. Mrs Elborne, the former owner of NPG 3837, also owned a 'memorial portrait' of Pigot in 1952 (letter of 31 August 1952; NPG archive).

ICONOGRAPHY

1769 Painting by George Stubbs, whole-length on horseback. Private collection (illus. *Stubbs*, Tate, 1984, no.106). Engraved B. Green 1769.

1769 Painting by Tilly Kettle,* three-quarter length seated at table. Hartnoll & Eyre, London, 1975. Pigot was in England in 1769, and Kettle completed the portrait in Madras where he arrived in June (*ibid.*, pp.67, 104).

1777 Paintings by George Willison, see NPG 3837.

c.1777? Painting by John Powell, engraved Scawen as a half-length oval. A poor likeness, probably posthumous.

DOUBTFUL PORTRAIT

Unattributed painting, whole length, with Lane Fine Art in 1994 (from a direct descendant of the sitter).

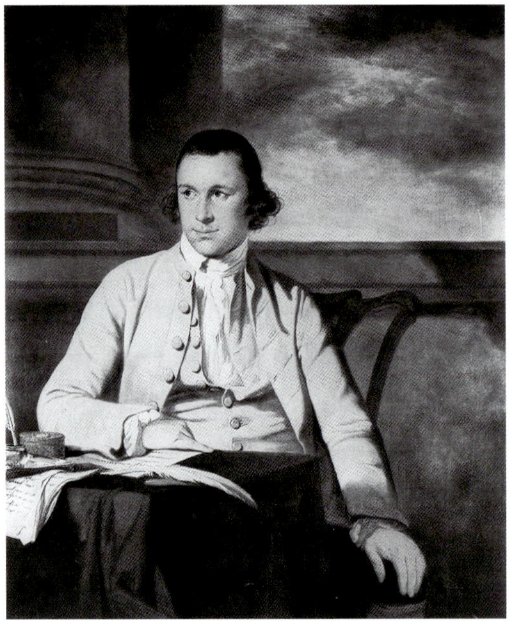

Baron PIGOT by Tilly Kettle 1769 (untraced)

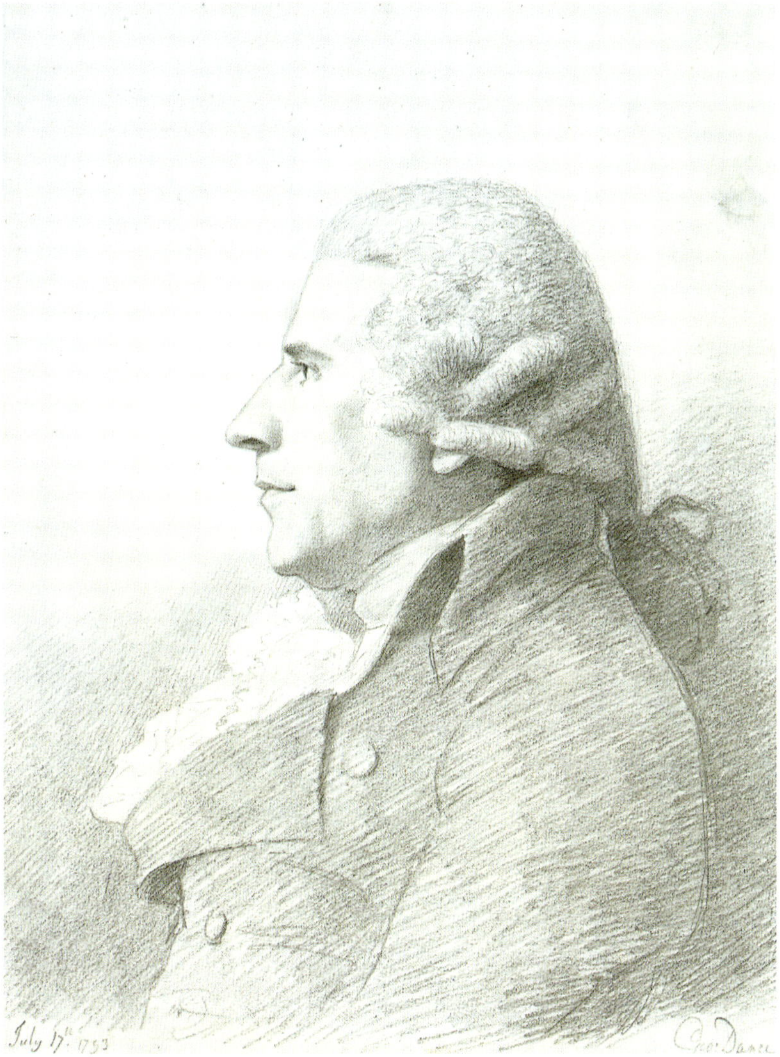

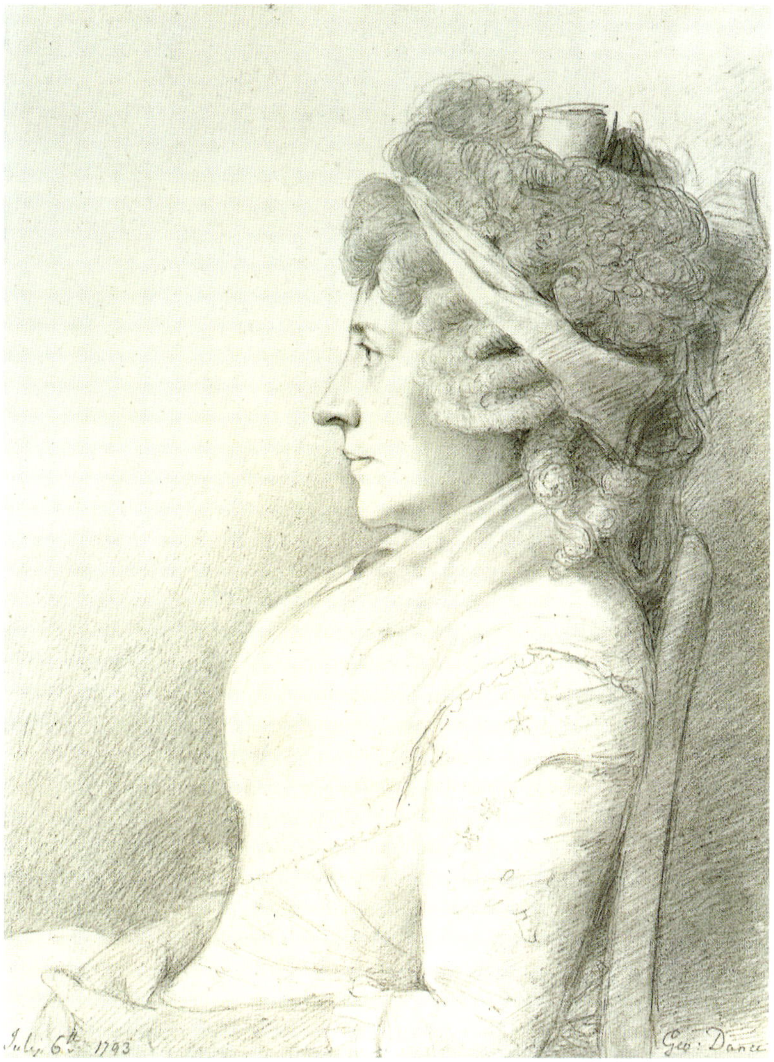

Gabriel PIOZZI NPG 1152 *Mrs PIOZZI* NPG 1151

PIOZZI, Gabriel 1740-1809

Musician; b. Qinzano near Venice; came to London c.1776; m. 1784 the widowed Mrs Thrale, see Mrs Piozzi; naturalised 1793.

'He is a very obliging unaffected man, and as much English as a foreigner can be in manner and way of thinking' (Joseph Farington, 1793).

1152 GEORGE DANCE 1793

Pencil with traces of pink on the cheek and lips, on paper 25.3 x 18.8 (10 x 7⅜) some staining and a small damage upper right; signed and dated in pencil: *July 17th. 1793* bottom left, and *Geo: Dance.* bottom right; laid down on a contemporary washed mount lettered in pencil: *PIOZZI*.

Collections: The artist's grandson, the Rev George Dance; his sale, Christie's, 1 July 1898, lot 106 bt. Colnaghi for the NPG.

No engraving appears to have been published. See the pendant drawing of Mrs Piozzi, NPG 1151.

ICONOGRAPHY

1785-86 Gabriel Piozzi's portrait was twice painted in Italy; one was last recorded with Enrico Piozzi in Brescia in 1892, the other is now in the Hyde Collection,* see Mrs Piozzi, NPG 4942.

DOUBTFUL PORTRAIT

See Unidentified Portraits NPG 761a.

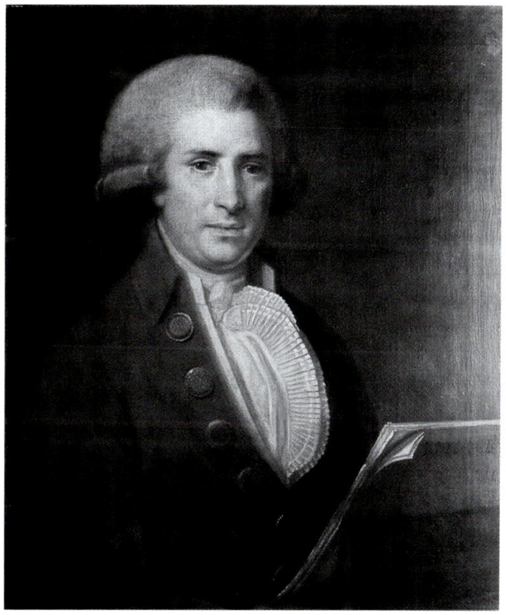

Gabriel PIOZZI unknown artist 1785-86 (Hyde Collection)

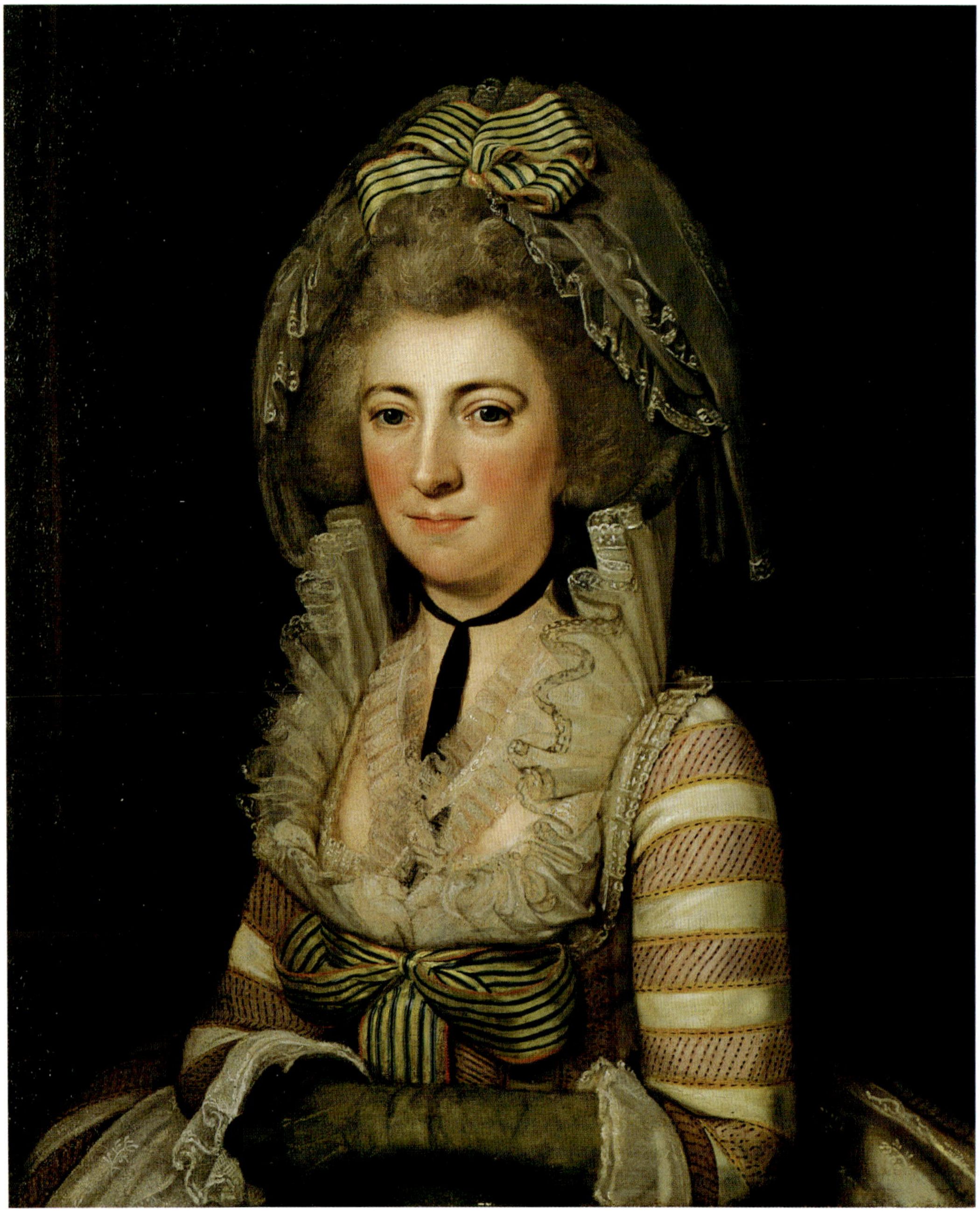

Mrs PIOZZI NPG *4942*

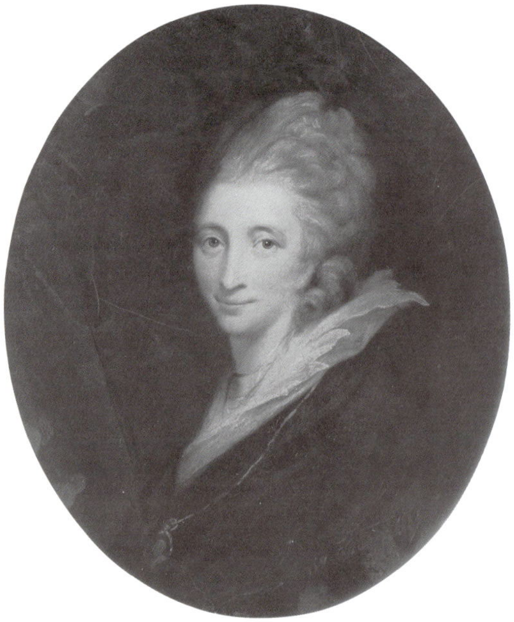

Mrs PIOZZI by R.E. Pine 1781 (Scottish Courage Ltd)

PIOZZI, Mrs Hester, *née* Salusbury 1741-1821

Miscellaneous writer and close friend of Dr Johnson; b. Bachycraig, Flintshire, m. 1) 1763 the brewer Henry Thrale (d.1781), 2) 1784 Gabriel Piozzi (see NPG 1152).

'less than five feet in height, plump and deep-chested, with large muscular hands ... her eyes were fine and expressive, light grey in colour; her hair was chestnut brown' (J. L. Clifford, 1952).

'Short, plump and brisk' (James Boswell, 1791).

Abbreviation

Queeney Letters: Marquess of Lansdowne ed., *The Queeney Letters, being letters addressed to Hester Maria Thrale by Doctor Johnson, Fanny Burney and Mrs Thrale-Piozzi*, 1934

4942 UNKNOWN ITALIAN ARTIST 1785-86

Canvas 76 x 63.5 (29¼ x 24½) considerable losses in the background areas and the lower left corner; restored and relined 1976.

Grey hair, grey-blue eyes, fresh complexion; she wears a *dormeuse* cap, a ribbon in her hair and at her waist with blue and black stripes and red edges; a standing collar of silk gauze *à la Médici*, with a black silk ribbon at her neck; her silk dress is striped with pink-banded yellow-edged panels and she has black net gloves.[1]

Collections: Mrs Beryl Salusbury Whitaker, a family descendant;[2] Lawrence, Crewkerne, 22 March 1973, lot 351, bt. Leggatt for the NPG.

Exhibition: *Ivory, Feathers and Lace*, Museum of London, 1986.

Mrs Piozzi and her husband were in Italy from October 1784 to September 1786; from 24 October to November 1785 and 27 February to 19 April 1786 they were at Rome, where they sat for their portraits.[3] NPG 4942, a pedestrian work, was apparently one of these, and the pendant portrait of Gabriel Piozzi may be identified with that now in the Hyde Collection.[4]* While these portraits descended through the Salusbury-Piozzi family in England, another pair were left behind in Italy, and were last recorded in the collection of Enrico Piozzi at Brescia in 1892.[5] Mrs Piozzi's description of her Roman portrait seems more appropriate for the latter; she told her daughter: 'We sate for our Pictures in Rome as I said I would - but such *Objects*! mine particularly, that

I have done nothing but beg they might be burned ever since; as a Red-haired old Hag in a white Bed-gown, is neither 'Ornamento' of *one* Country, nor 'Grazia' of *another*'.[6]

1 Her costume is decribed in Ribeiro 2000, pp.143-44.
2 Who also sold in 1973 portraits of Sir John Salusbury Piozzi, the Piozzi's adopted son, and of his wife (lot 352).
3 Cf. Ingamells 1997, pp.770-71.
4 Illus. Clifford 1952, f.p.308; *Piozzi Letters*, I, p.213; from the collection of George Augustus Salusbury (1822-93), great nephew of Gabriel Piozzi.
5 Illus. Piozzi, *Glimpses of Italian Society*, 1892, f.p.4, and Clifford 1952, p.285.
6 Verona, 27 September 1786 (*Piozzi Letters*, I, p.215 and see p.216n14).

1151 GEORGE DANCE 1793

Pencil with traces of pink on the lips and cheek, on paper 25.4 x 19 (10 x 7½) faded; signed and dated in pencil: *July 6th 1793* bottom left, and *Geo: Dance*. bottom right; laid down on a contemporary washed mount lettered: *HESTHER LYNCH PIOZZI.*

Collections: The artist's grandson, the Rev George Dance; his sale, Christie's, 1 July 1898, lot 105, bt. Colnaghi for the NPG.

Engraving: W. Daniell (*Dance Plates*).

Exhibitions: *Johnson*, Birmingham, 1959(184); *George Dance*, Geffrye Museum, 1972(89); *George Dance*, Bath, 1982; *Johnson and the Midlands*, Lichfield, 1984(44); *Master Drawings* 1993-95(39), withdrawn for *Romantic Women Writers*, Grasmere, 1994-95(*hors catalogue*).

On 19 July 1793 Mrs Piozzi wrote that 'Mr Dance the Profilist is making a Collection of celebrated Heads; I have sate, but nobody knows me they say, so I am to sit again'.[1] She was presumably referring to NPG 1151, which is dated 6 July, but she did not mention the pendant drawing of Gabriel Piozzi, NPG 1152, which is dated 17 July. On 20 July Joseph Farington, accompanied by Samuel Lysons and George Dance, breakfasted with Mr Piozzi at Streatham, and 'Mr Dance made drawings of Mr & Mrs Piozzi', presumably a second, untraced, pair. Copies of the NPG drawings (repeating the inscribed dates) were sold Sotheby's, 21 November 1978, lots 270-71.

Ribeiro has contrasted Mrs Piozzi's appearance in NPG 1151 with that in the earlier portrait, NPG 4942: the wide frizzed coiffure is retained but the dress is much simpler, a *robe à l'anglaise*.[2]

1 *Piozzi Letters*, II, p.128.
2 Ribeiro 2000, p.144.

ICONOGRAPHY

MS notes by C.F. Bell are inserted in his copy of *Hester Lynch Piozzi* by James L. Clifford, 1941, which he bequeathed to the NPG.

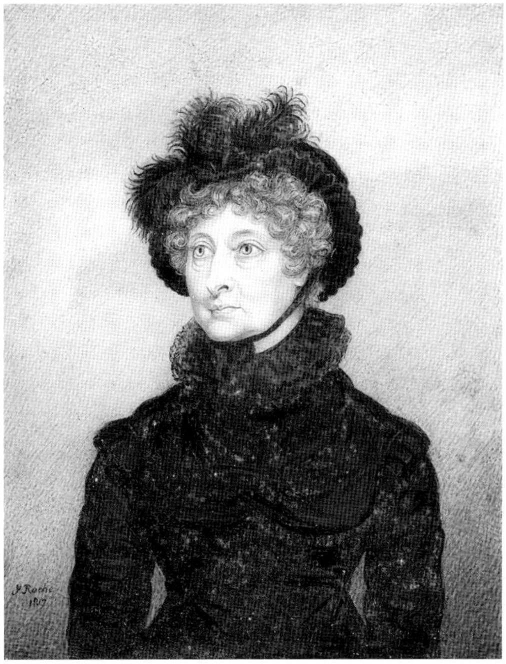

Mrs PIOZZI by S.T. Roche 1817 (National Museums & Galleries of Wales)

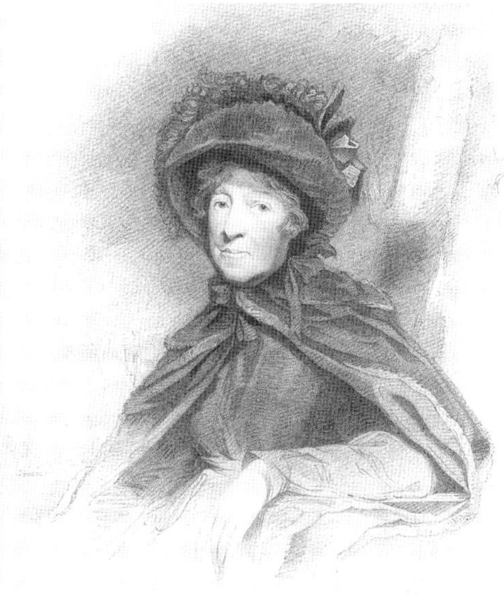

Mrs PIOZZI H. Meyer after John Jackson 1810 (NPG D 13807)

1766-73 Portrait by P-E. Falconet, wearing a black jacket with 'such a Noble Negligence' (*Queeney Letters*, p.208).

c.1777 Painting by Joshua Reynolds, seated with her eldest daughter Hester (b. 1764). Beaverbrook AG, Fredericton (illus. *Johnson*, Arts Council, 1984, p.115; Mannings 2000, no.1750). Mrs Thrale's head engraved E. Finden 1835. At the same time Reynolds painted Henry Thrale (Hyde Collection), both portraits to hang in the library at Streatham.

1778-84 'My Portrait by some of the Burneys', presumably E.F. Burney, had belonged to Dr Johnson, who left it to Francis Barber (*Thraliana* 1942, II, p.690n3; *Piozzi Letters*, V, pp.197, 199n7).

c.1780? Anon. silhouette (illus. *NPG Burney Diaries*, II, ii, p.285).

c.1780 Miniature by Richard Cosway. University of Texas at Austin (Harry Ransom Humanities Research Center, Carlton Lake Art Collection, 70.33; illus. Hyde 1977, p.15). On 7 July 1784 Mrs Piozzi mentioned that Dr Dobson 'wanted to borrow my Miniature painted by Cosway' (*Queeney Letters*, p.157).

1781 Painting by R.E. Pine,* half-length oval, in widowhood wearing a miniature, presumably of her late husband (Henry Thrale d. 4 April 1781). Courage Ltd. Engraved T. Holloway 1786, without painter's name (*European Mag.*, accompanying extracts from the *Florence Miscellany*); H.R. Cook 1813 as Reynolds (illus. *Piozzi Letters*, II, front.).

On 25 August 1781 Mrs Thrale and Fanny Burney visited Pine and saw a picture 'of Mrs Thrale. ... not like, I think, but a mighty elegant portrait' (*Burney Diary*, 1904, II, p.33).

1782 Miniature by S.T. Roche, bust length. Francis Wellesley sale, Sotheby's, 4th day, 1 July 1920, lot 673 (illus. *Connoisseur*, xlix, 1917, p.43).

1785-86 Two paintings by unknown Italian artists, see NPG 4942.

by 1788 Painting by George James, 'in a green hat'. Untraced. On 18 July 1788 Mrs Piozzi wrote that 'Mr James has made a very fine Portrait indeed of Your faithful Friend' (*Piozzi Letters*, I, pp.268, 269n6 and see p.251n3; *Thraliana* 1942, I, p.584n3).

1793 Drawings by George Dance, see NPG 1151.

1798-99 Miniature by J.T. Barber, bust-length oval. Sold Lawrence, Crewkerne, 13 September 1973, lot 384 (illus. *Dr Johnson and the Fair Sex*, 1895, p.67). Exhibited RA 1799(690). Engraved W. Ridley 1798 (*Monthly Mirror*).

1800 Painting by Pierre Violet, wearing a fur boa, engraved M. Bovi 1800. The engraving, which was compared to the 'Witch of Endor', used as the title page for Mrs Piozzi's *Retrospection*, 1801 (Clifford 1952, p.401; *Piozzi Letters*, III, pp.245, 246n5).

1810 In a letter of 19 February 1810 Mrs Piozzi referred to 'an admirable Miniature of my *Black Bonnet*' (*Piozzi Letters*, IV, pp.268, 270n1, where identified as the drawing by Jackson, see below; but see 1811).

1810 Drawing by John Jackson, half length, in mourning. Dr Johnson's House, London (illus. Clifford 1952, f.p.406). Engraved H. Meyer 1811.* 'Jackson painted her picture in May' 1810 (Clifford 1952, p.430n3). A small version in oil, plausibly attributed to Jackson, showing a paper in the left hand, is in the Hyde Collection (illus. *Piozzi Letters*, IV, front.).

*All subsequent portraits show Mrs Piozzi in black, a dress she forsook only for her eightieth birthday fête, when she wore white (Hyde 1977, p.310). According to M.E. Lucy (*Charlecote and the Lucys*, 1958, p.258), while she lived at Brynbella in Denbighshire [from 1794], Mrs Piozzi wore black satin with a turned-up hat of the same, a wig of brown curls and rouge - at that time completely abandoned for general use.*

1811 Unattributed miniature, bust-length profile wearing a black bonnet. Johnson Birthplace Museum, Lichfield (from Lawrence, Crewkerne, 13 September 1973, lot 382).

c.1815-20 Miniature by W.M. Bennett, with a white cap. A.D.H. Pennant, Nantlys, in 1957 (illus. Hyde 1977, p.317). A miniature copy by Sophia Merrik Hoare 1822.

c.1815-20? Miniature by Charles Jagger painted for William Augustus Conway (Hyde 1977, p.310).

1817 Miniature by S.T. Roche,* half length with black bonnet. National Museum and Gallery, Cardiff, from Lawrence, Crewkerne, 13 September 1973, lot 381. Mrs Piozzi enjoined Roche 'to introduce a trivial deformity of the lower jaw on the left side, where ... she had been severely hurt by her horse treading on her', and the picture was considered 'the essential of resemblance, perfect' (E. Mangin, *Piozziana*, 1833, pp.9-10). She had commissioned Roche to paint her portrait for Sir James Fellowes; in 1817 a copy of it was given to the Rev Edward Mangin, and a second copy was given to Lady Salusbury in December that year (Hyde 1977, pp.297, 302, 307); it was presumably one of these which was sold Sotheby's, 26 June 1978, lot 233.

1820 Painting by James Hopwood, half length, engraved J. Thomson 1820 (illus. Hyde 1977, p.311 described as Mrs Piozzi at her eightieth-birthday fête).

DOUBTFUL PORTRAITS

The portrait illustrated in Clifford 1952, front., as Hester Thrale is of an unidentified American lady by J.S. Copley (Los Angeles Museum). The anecdote that, as a child, Hester Salusbury posed for Hogarth's *Lady's Last Stake* remains unsubstantiated (*Piozzi Letters*, IV, pp.282, 285n12).

PONSONBY, Frederick, see BESSBOROUGH

PRATT, Charles, see CAMDEN

PRESCOTT, Robert 1725-1816

Army officer and colonial governor; served in Canada under Wolfe and in Martinique under Monckton 1761; served in America 1775-77 and in the West Indies from 1778 as lieutenant-colonel; governor of Martinique 1794, as lieutenant-general; governor of Canada and Nova Scotia 1796-1807; general 1798; came home in 1799 in poor health, spending his last years at Battle in Sussex.

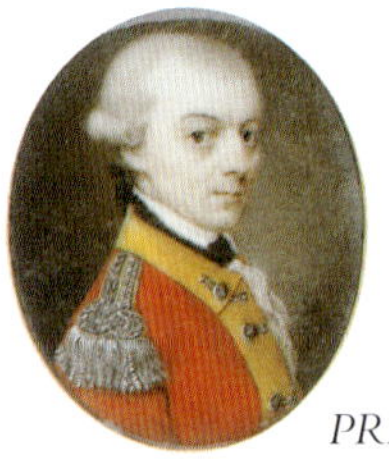

PRESCOTT NPG *3963*

3963 JOHN BOGLE 1776

Watercolour and bodycolour on ivory 3.5 x 3 ($1\frac{3}{8}$ x $1\frac{1}{8}$); signed bottom right: *J B/1776*. The back of the gold case is engraved: *General Robert Prescott./ Governor of Canada,/ returned to England 1799./ Died Dec.21.1815.*

Brown eyes, white powdered hair with a black ribbon, wearing a red coat with yellow facings and a silver epaulette, as lieutenant-colonel of the 28th Foot.[1]

Collections: Mrs Fuller-Maitland, Turriff; How of Edinburgh, from whom purchased 1955.

Exhibitions: *Pageant of Canada*, Ottawa, 1967(128); *1776*, National Maritime Museum, 1976(570); *Georgian Canada*, Toronto, 1984(240).

In 1776 Bogle was exhibiting at the RA from a London address and he is not known to have visited America. Prescott must have returned to England that year, after the battle of Fort Washington and before the expedition to Philadelphia in 1777. Bogle subsequently produced at least two replicas, in which the uniform is altered to that of a general officer: one dated 1780 sold Sotheby's, Geneva, 9 November 1959, lot 73, the other dated 1789 sold Christie's, 30 April 1996, lot 105.[2]

1 I am most grateful to Andrew Cormack for help in identifying this uniform; cf. *Georgian Canada* exhibition cat., Toronto, 1984.
2 Illus. *Secret Passion to Noble Fashion*, Bath (Holburne), 1999(56).

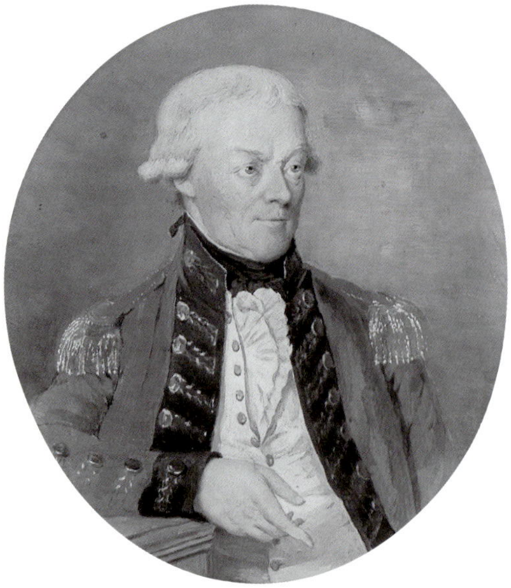

PRESCOTT by William Berczy c.1800 (Sotheby's)

ICONOGRAPHY

1776 Miniature by John Bogle, see NPG 3963.

c.1800 Miniature by William Berczy,* half-length oval wearing general's uniform (cf. *JSAHR*, XXXI, 1953, p.75). Sotheby's, 23 November 1966, lot 24 (illus. Waterhouse 1981, p.50). Engraved J. Young.

PRICE, James 1752-83

'Alchemist'; b. James Higginbottom, changing his name to Price in 1781 in accordance with the will of a relative who left him a fortune; FRS 1781; MD 1782; in May 1782, at Stoke, near Guildford, he converted mercury into silver and gold (proved genuine on assay); published *An Account* in 1782; under pressure from the Royal Society, he was to repeat his experiments in 1783, but took his own life that August.

1942 JOHN RUSSELL c.1782

Pastel on paper 60 x 45 ($23\frac{1}{4}$ x $17\frac{1}{2}$) laid down on paper; the surface is slightly rubbed; conserved c.1900[1] and 1936.

Brown eyes, powdered hair with a black ribbon, wearing a light brown coat.

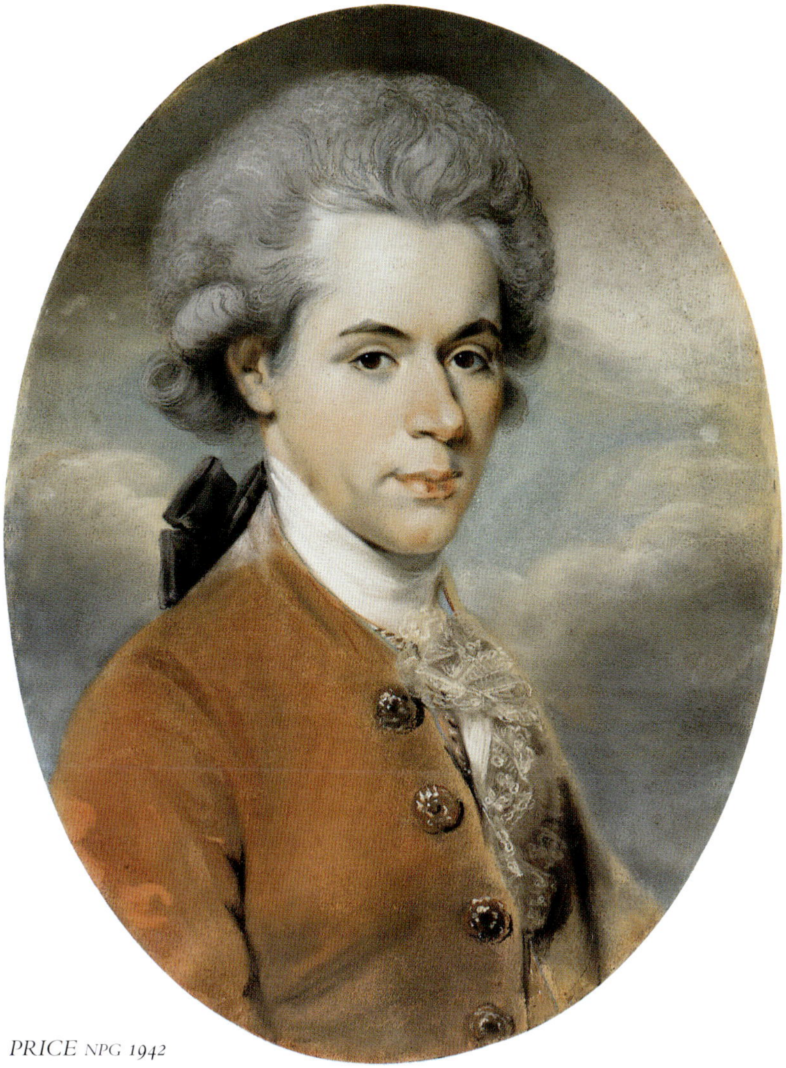

PRICE NPG *1942*

Collections: Rev J. Penfold of Croydon,[2] by whom presented to the Guildford Institute, Borough Hall, Guildford, 1850;[3] purchased from the Guildford Institute 1922.

Exhibitions: *Surrey Art Loan Exhibition*, Guildford, 1884;[4] *Russell*, Imperial Institute, South Kensington, 1894(35).

Reference: Williamson 1894, p.148.

The only known portrait of Price, whose identity rests on the testimony of previous owners; Russell was born in Guildford, where Price conducted his first experiments.

1 T. Whitburn, letter in the *Surrey Times*, 2 February 1902.
2 Russell painted a pastel of a Mrs Penfold, c.1780 (Williamson 1894, p.158) who may, or may not, have been related.
3 T. Whitburn, *List of Pictures belonging to Guildford*, 1888, p.44.
4 As recorded by Whitburn, see note 1.

PRIESTLEY, Joseph 1733-1804

Scientist and dissenting minister; LL.D Edinburgh 1764; FRS 1766; friend and correspondent of Franklin, published a *History of Electricity* 1767; by 1774 he had defined oxygen; librarian to Lord Lansdowne 1772-80; his radical sympathies led to the destruction of his home during the Birmingham Riots of 1791; emigrated to America 1794 and d. in Northumberland, Pa.; 'if we choose one man as a type of the intellectual energy of the eighteenth century we could hardly find a better than Joseph Priestley' (F. Harrison).

'Dr Priestley was about the middle stature, or five feet eight inches high. He was slender, and well proportioned; his complexion was fair, his eyes grey and sparking with intelligence, and his whole countenance was expressive of the benignity of his heart. He often smiled but seldom laughed' (J. Corry, 1804).

Abbreviations

Bolton 1892: H. C. Bolton, 'The Likenesses of Priestley in oil, ink, marble, and metal', in *Scientific Correspondence of Joseph Priestley*, 1892, pp.173-94

Priestley 1983: J. McLachlan, *Joseph Priestley: iconography of a great Yorkshireman*, 1983

Priestley 1994: V.A. Livingston, 'Joseph Priestley in the Public Eye: Reconstructing the Man through Portraits and Caricatures', *Joseph Priestley in America 1794-1804*, exh. cat., Susquehanna and Carlisle, Pa., 1994, pp.30-35

Yates 1860: J Yates, *Memorials of Dr Priestley from the Christian Reformer*, 1860, with numerous corrections and additions ['a descriptive catalogue of portraits and relics of Priestley, exhibited that year at Dr Williams's Library'; *DNB*]

175 ELLEN SHARPLES [c.1797]

Pastel on buff-coloured laid paper 24 x 18.7 (9½ x 7⅜) maximum, the edges cut unevenly, laid down on card; the window of the mount 21.5 x 16.5 (8½ x 6½) has abraded the margins.

Blue eyes, greying hair, black suit, white collar and neckcloth; blue background with the hint of a curtain.

Collections: William Taylor; his step-daughters, the Misses Eaton, of Liverpool and Leamington, by whom given to the sitter's grand-daughter, Miss Catharine I. Finch of Birmingham, who gave it to James Yates (1789-1871)[1] 1860; presented by him, with a portrait of George Washington [NPG 174], 1864.

Exhibitions: *Priestley*, Dr Williams's Library 1860(17); *Apples to Atoms* 1986-87.

Reference: Yates 1860, no.17 (as by Mrs Sharples); Bolton 1892, p.182 (as by Mrs Sharples); Knox 1930, p.101 (as by Mrs Sharples).

After reaching America in 1794 Priestley settled in Northumberland, Pa.; the Sharples portraits show him a lonely man, soon after losing his wife (1796) and youngest son (1795).

For the complexities of the Sharples practice, see Washington NPG 174. Taylor's step-daughters (see Provenance) were 'not sure whether his pastels of Priestley and Washington were the work of Mr or Mrs Sharples, but as her name is on the back there seems no doubt they are hers';[2] Yates described NPG 175 (rather too confidently?) as 'drawn at Philadelphia by Mrs Sharples soon after Dr Priestley's arrival there'.

The original portrait was drawn in America, where the Sharples arrived in 1796, two years after Priestley. Copies include those in the NPG Washington

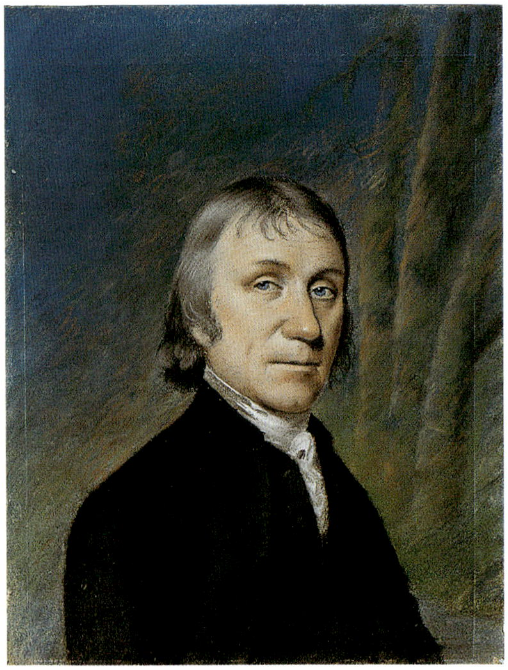

PRIESTLEY NPG *175*

(NPG.77.160),[3] two in the Sharples collection in Bristol Art Gallery[4] and NPG 2904, see below. An indifferent copy in oils belonging to James Walton was exhibited in America in 1886-87.[5] Ellen Sharples recorded copying her husband's portrait of Priestley in December 1804;[6] she exhibited two miniatures of him RA 1807(851 and 920), probably copies of this same pattern, although there was also a Sharples profile (see below c.1797).

1 The distinguished unitarian and antiquary, treasurer of the appeal for the Stephens statue of Priestley at Oxford in 1860 and a collector of Priestley MSS, which he bequeathed to the Royal Society (see Bolton 1892, p.192). The provenance is given in a letter to Yates from Catharine Finch, 11 December 1860 (NPG archive).
2 Letter from Catharine Finch to J. Yates, 11 December 1860 (NPG archive); but Mrs Sharples's name is no longer visible on the back of either the Priestley or the Washington (NPG 174).
3 Attributed to James Sharples.
4 Knox 1930, pp.99, 100 (one by Ellen Sharples, the other by either James or Ellen or both); *Cat. of the Sharples Coll.*, Bristol, 1910, nos.22, 66 (one by James Sharples, the other by Ellen).
5 Bolton 1892, p.182; Knox 1930, p.64; photograph in the NPG archive.
6 Knox 1930, p.118.

2904 ELLEN SHARPLES [c.1797]

Pastel on buff-coloured laid paper 23.7 x 18.8 (9⅜ x 7⅜) irregular oval; some staining in the lower areas and spotting in the face; a small damage repaired centre right; on the verso, the black chalk outline of a half-length male figure.

Blue eyes, own grey hair, wearing a black suit with white collar and neckcloth.

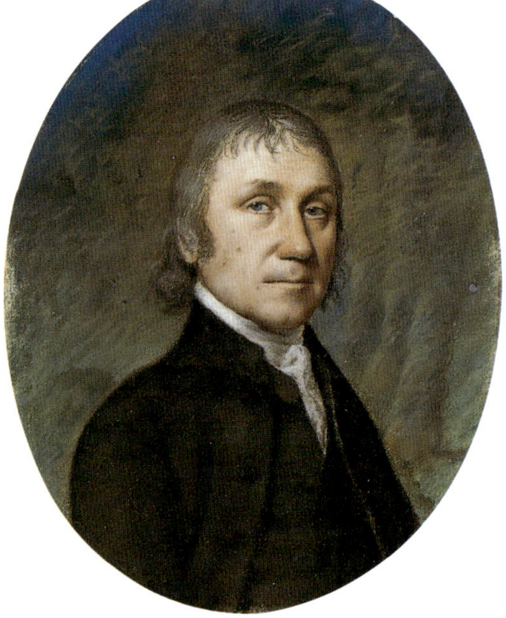

PRIESTLEY NPG *2904*

Collections: Given by the artist to William Russell (1740-1818) of Birmingham; by descent to T.H. Russell by whom, with his sister Mrs Alexander Scott, presented, together with a portrait of George Washington [NPG 2903], 1936.[1]

Reference: Bolton 1892, p.182 (as by Mrs Sharples, belonging to Dr W.J. Russell, London).

See NPG 175. A nineteenth-century label, formerly on the verso, described NPG 2904 as by Mrs Sharples.

1 Provenance as given to Hake by T.H. Russell in November 1936. William Russell was the friend of Priestley in Birmingham and in America, and of the Sharples (with whom in 1794 he had been captured at sea by the French as they sailed to America, where they later met again); see S.H. Jeyes, *The Russells of Birmingham in the French Revolution and in America 1791-1814*, 1911, pp.2, 8-13, 44-49, 86, 89, 92, 169, 203.

175A PHIPSON 1804

White metal medallion 5.1 (2) diameter

Obverse: profile bust to right, wearing a drape over his coat, inscribed: *JOSEPHUS PRIESTLEY.* and below: *PHIPSON FECIT*

Reverse: inscribed: *MAGNUS CHRISTIANUS PHILOSOPHUS* and: *APR: VIII/ BRITANNIAE/ LITORA LINQUENS/ COLUMBIAM ADVENIT/ JUNII IV/ MDCCXCIV.* with added inscription below: *NATUS 13 MART 1733, MORT. 6 FEB. 1804.*

Collections: Presented by James Yates (see NPG 175) 1864.

Reference: Yates 1860, no.42; Bolton 1892, p.190; Brown 1980, no.565.

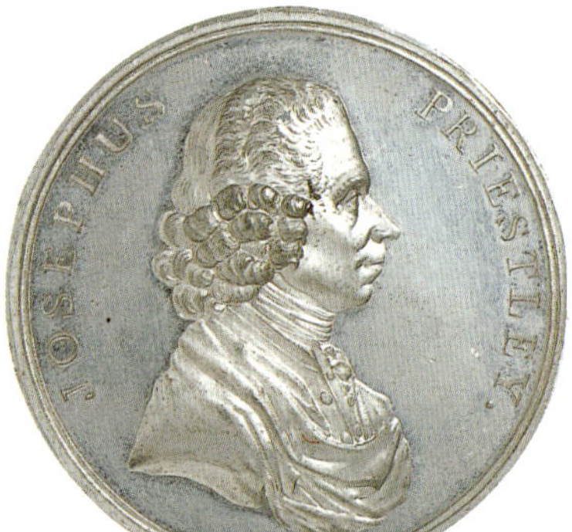

PRIESTLEY NPG *175A*

Phipson worked in Birmingham and doubtless knew Priestley. This medal was first struck to commemorate Priestley's arrival in America in 1794,[1] the inscription being expanded on his death in 1804. A variant inscription (*i decus, i, nostrum mel[l]ioribus utere fatis*; *Aeneid*, VI, 546) is also recorded.[2] An indifferent engraving by J. Hopwood 1804 appears to derive from Phipson's medal.[3]

1 Brown 1980, no.381.
2 *Priestley* 1983, p.53
3 Illus. *Priestley* 1983, p.42.

175B THOMAS HALLIDAY 1804

Bronze medallion 5.1 (2) diameter

Obverse: profile bust to left wearing academic gown, inscribed: *JOSEPH PRIESTLEY LLD.F.R.S.: AC. IMP. PETROP. R. PARIS. HOLM. TAURIN. ITAL. HARLEM. AUREL. MID. PARIS. CANTAB. AMERIC. ET PHILAD. SOCIUS.*[1] and on the truncation: *HALLIDAY F.*

Reverse: inscribed with the text of a tablet composed by Dr Samuel Parr for the New Meeting House at Birmingham: *THIS TABLET IS CONSECRATED TO THE MEMORY OF THE REV. JOSEPH PRIESTLEY ... UNITARIAN CHAPEL/ BIRMINGHAM.*[2]

Collections: Presented by James Yates (see NPG 175) 1864.

Reference: Yates 1860, no.46; Bolton 1892, p.191; Brown 1980, no.563.

Another bronze example is in the NPG reference collection (D7056). The medal was restruck in 1904 to mark the centenary of Priestley's death. Halliday, a Birmingham resident and a friend of Priestley, also made a small bust (copy in Dr Williams's Library) of which several plaster copies were made,[3] and see below c.1780-91.

1 Elliptically referring to his membership of the Academies in St Petersburg, Paris, Stockholm, Turin, Haarlem, Orleans, Cambridge and Philadelphia.
2 Quoted in full by Bolton 1892, p.189.
3 Bolton 1892, p.188.

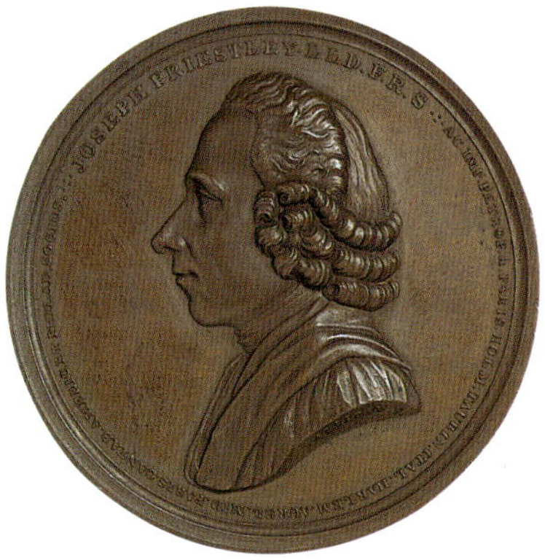

PRIESTLEY NPG *175B*

ICONOGRAPHY

'Priestley's likeness was being incessantly reproduced. In the houses of Dissenters it was a conspicuous ornament, and after he had given to the world his discovery of oxygen the resemblance of this great man, either as a full-size medallion, or as a bust, was largely bought by continental savants' (E. Meteyard, *Wedgwood*, 1865, II, p.451).

1762 Silhouette, bust (Yates 1860, front., no.6 as 1762; illus. *Proc. of the Leeds Philosophical Soc.*, II, xii, 1934, f.p.555).

c.1763-65 Unattributed painting, half length ('The Leeds Portrait'). Royal Society (Yates 1860, no.4; illus. *Royal Society* 1980, p.244; *Priestley* 1983, p.16). Probably showing Priestley as tutor at the Warrington Academy. A version belongs to the Municipal Library, Warrington (illus. A.R. Orange, *Priestley*, 1976, p.11).

c.1779 Medallion by Giuseppe Ceracchi, with neckcloth, produced for the Wedgwood factory. Example Dickinson College, Carlisle, Pa. (illus. *Priestley* 1983, p.47; *Priestley* 1994, p.34). Manufactured in two sizes (cf. illus. Reilly 1973, p.283; Hermitage, *English Art*, 1979, no.246; *Priestley* 1994, p.35). A pink plaster medallion by Bemi in Birmingham MAG relates closely.

The Wedgwood bust was the ultimate source of several essentially indifferent engravings, including those in the *Westminster Mag.* 1782, by W. Angus in the *Literary Mag.* 1792, G. Murray 1794, P.A. Tardieu (after 1804) and E. Mackenzie 1805.

c.1779 Wedgwood medallion, remodelled from Ceracchi's bust, probably by William Hackwood, showing an unbuttoned shirt collar. Used for larger medallions, as in the Brooklyn Museum of Art (illus. Reilly 1973, p.284; Reilly 1989, p.123) and the source of an engraving by W. Bromley 1791 (illus. *Priestley* 1983, p.39).

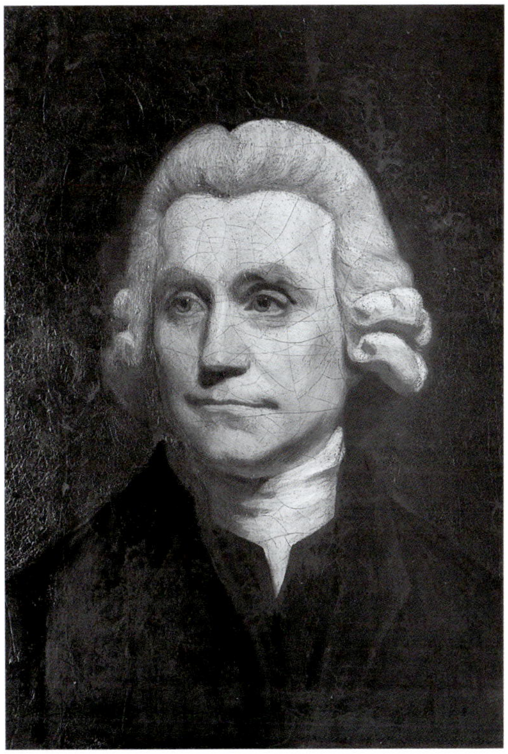

PRIESTLEY by John Opie c.1783 (Royal Brompton Hospital)

c.1780-91 Plaster bust by P. Bemi. Dickinson College, Carlisle, Pa. (illus. *Priestley* 1994, p.34). Bemi at one time was Thomas Halliday's assistant, and has been credited with the design of Halliday's bust of Priestley, see NPG 175B.

1783 Painting by J.H. Fuseli, three-quarter length seated. Dr Williams's Library, London (Schiff 1973, no.761; illus. *Priestley* 1983, p.20). Engraved C. Turner 1836. A half-length pencil copy by Moses Haughton in the British Museum (1888.12.11.5).

1783 Medal by J.G. Hancock, bewigged bust with unbuttoned shirt collar (Brown 1980, no.251). A white metal example is in the NPG reference collection (D7057). A comparable bust recurs on a medal inscribed *PRIESTLEY CITIZEN OF THE WORLD* with on the reverse emblems of liberty (illus. *Priestley* 1994, p.42).

c.1783 Painting by John Opie, half length. Manchester College, Oxford. Engraved J. Caldwall 1801. Said to have been painted in the house of the publisher Joseph Johnson (Yates 1860, no.12; Bolton 1892, p.174). A bust-length version in the Royal Brompton Hospital, London.*

1789 Miniature by John Hazlitt, engraved W. Nutter 1789 (Yates 1860, no.14; illus. *Priestley* 1983, p.45).

1789 Painting by James Millar, half length. Royal Society (illus. *Royal Society* 1980, p.247; *Priestley* 1983, p.25). Exhibited RA 1790(172). Version by Millar, with his right hand tucked into his waistcoat, Manchester College, Oxford (illus. OP 1906, f.p.74).

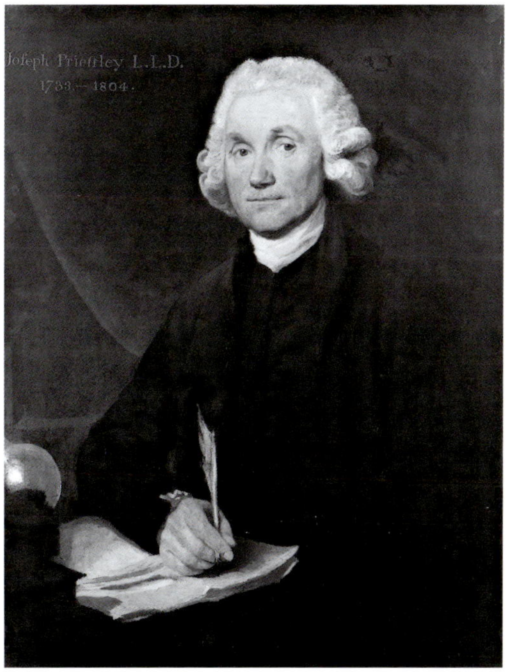

PRIESTLEY by William Artaud 1794 (Dr Williams's Library, London)

1794 Medal by William Phipson, see NPG 175A.

1794 Painting by William Artaud,* half-length seated. Dr Williams's Library, London (Yates 1860, no.15; illus. *Priestley* 1983, p.27). Presumably the portrait exhibited RA 1794(315). Engraved T. Holloway 1795. A small copy with the Royal Society (illus. *Royal Society* 1980, p.247). A drawing by Peter Holland, similar but inferior to the Artaud portrait, was with Thomas Thornely, Liverpool, in 1860 (Yates 1860, no.8; Bolton 1892, p.177).

In America

c.1797 Pastel by James Sharples, oval half-length profile. Sotheby's, 22 April 1982, lot 97. Engraved anon. 1804 (for Priestley's *Notes on Scripture*), anon. 1805 (oval). Yates 1860, no.18, described a profile of Priestley in crayons belonging to his sister, and in a letter to Miss Eaton (James Taylor's step-sister, 13 December 1860; NPG archive) said it had belonged to his father and was probably bought by James Taylor.

c.1797 Pastels by James and Ellen Sharples, see NPG 175 and NPG 2904.

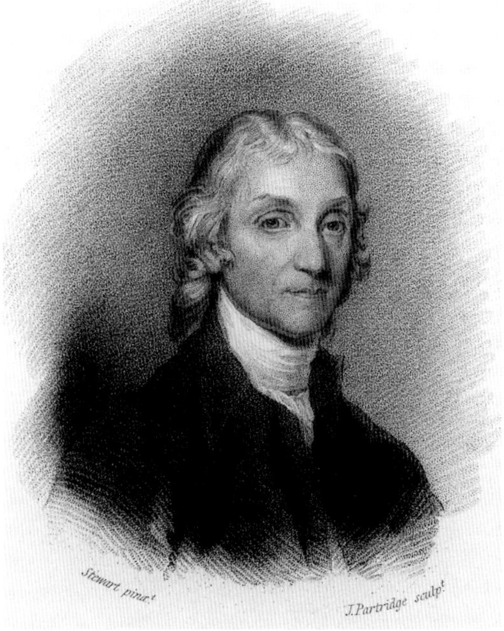

PRIESTLEY J. Partridge after Gilbert Stuart c.1800 (NPG D 13808)

c.1800 Painting by Gilbert Stuart, half length. Private collection; illus. *Retratos ingleses em Portugal,* II, Lisbon, 1969, no.22; *Priestley* 1983, p.32). Commissioned by the American Philosophical Society, Pa., but sold by the artist to T.B. Barclay, a Liverpool merchant, and said to have been completed in England by William Artaud (Yates 1860, no.20; Bolton 1892, pp.177-80; Park 1926, II, no.680), who made several copies. Engraved J. Partridge 1806* and 1815, W. Holl 1835 (when in Barclay's collection), C. Cook 1859, A. Rosenthal 1921 (illus. *Priestley* 1994, p.33). Reduced copies include those in Birmingham MAG (732'40), Warrington MAG, and Yale University AG. A miniature, evidently based on the Stuart portrait, belongs to the Pennsylvania Historical and Museums Commissions (illus. *Priestley* 1994, p.32). Yates 1860 lists two copies by Artaud and two other 'small copies' (nos.21-24).

c.1801 Painting by Rembrandt Peale, half-length painted oval. New York Historical Society (illus. *Peale* 1992, p.49). Replicas with American Philosophical Society, Pa., and Dickinson College, Carlisle, Pa. (illus. *Priestley* 1994, p.32). Engraved J. Reich before 1892. In 1804 C.W. Peale's Philadelphia Museum contained a portrait of Priestley among the 'two rows of Portraits of distinguished Personages, painted from the life, by C.W. Peale and his Son Rembrandt' (*Charles Willson Peale, Selected papers*, II, 2, 1988, p.763).

Posthumous

1804 Memorial medals by William Phipson and Thomas Halliday, see under NPG 175A & 175B.

1804 Medallion by Peter Rouw for the Priestley memorial tablet. Five Ways, Edgbaston, Birmingham (Yates 1860, no.49; illus. *Priestley* 1983, p.50). Based on Ceracchi's Wedgwood medallion of c.1779. Plaster versions in Birmingham MAG and Dr Williams's Library, London.

1807 Miniature by Ellen Sharples, exhibited RA 1807(920), see NPG 175.

1849 Imitation cameo by Mary Anne Nichols, exhibited RSBA 1849(553).

1867 Medallion by William Waite, exhibited Birmingham Midland Institute, April 1867 (Bolton 1892, p.192).

1888 Medal, centenary of the church of the Messiah Sunday schools, with draped busts of Priestley (based on Hancock's medal of 1783) and Dr Henry Crosskey (Brown 1987, no.3362).

Later statues include those by E.B. Stephens 1860 (Oxford Museum History of Science); F.J. Williamson 1874 (Chamberlain Square, Birmingham, illus. Priestley 1983, p.57; a small plaster replica with the Institute of Chemistry, London, and a plaster modello in Birmingham MAG); by Alfred Drury 1899 (City Square, Leeds, illus. Priestley 1983, p.59; a reduced bronze version in the Ashmolean Museum, Oxford); by Frances Darlington 1912 (Market Place, Birstall, Yorkshire; a model in Huddersfield AG and a plaster belongs to Warrington MAG); by Gilbert Bayes 1915 (Institute of Chemistry, London). A stone head by W.B. Fagan 1928 is on the ICI Building, Millbank, London.

Priestley also appears in the Warrington stained glass window of 1896 at Manchester College, Oxford.

DOUBTFUL PORTRAITS

A silhouette called the Priestley Family, sold Phillips, 18 April 1978, lot 55. Drawing by H.D. Hamilton, half-length oval wearing a bonnet, Huntington Art Collections, San Marino, Calif. (63.52.94).

QUICK, John 1748-1831

Actor; London debut at the Haymarket theatre 1766 and played regularly at Covent Garden 1767-98, specialising in low comedy; the original Tony Lumpkin in *She Stoops to Conquer* 1773, the role which made his reputation; a particular favourite with George III.

1355 THOMAS LAWRANSON 1789

Canvas 75 x 63 (29½ x 24¾) lined; the surface is rubbed; many retouchings, and repaired tears across and above the hat and in the chest; discoloured varnish.

Brown eyes, grey hair, wearing a grey hat, green coat and white waistcoat with gold trim.

Collections: Coley in 1861;[1] Hughes & Tillmann, London, from whom purchased 1904.

Engraving: anon. 1789 (oval, *from an original painting by Lawrenson*).

1 Sketched by Scharf 'at Mr Coley's', 2 February 1861 (TSB 5/33), when for sale at 30 gn.

ICONOGRAPHY

See also the *Harvard Catalogue*, III, pp.370-72, and Highfill, XII, pp.223-25 (listing further portrayals of Quick in character).

1780 'Mr Quick' sat to the miniaturist Richard Crosse on 25 November 1780 (Highfill, XII, p.223).

1789 Drawing by Thomas Lawranson, see NPG 1355.

1791 Painting by William Score, half length, presumably the portrait exhibited RA 1792(73). Engraved W. Score 1791; W. Ridley 1793, T. Cheesman 1807 (without hands).

1793 Drawn and engraved by John Condé, bust length (*Thespian Mag.*).

Highfield lists drawings by Sylvester Harding in the Widener Library, Harvard (engraved W.N. Gardiner 1789), and by Samuel De Wilde c.1804 at Holkham Hall.

Depictions of Quick in character include two paintings by Zoffany in the Garrick Club: as Mendoza in Sheridan's *Duenna*, and as Arable in Reynolds's *Speculation* (Ashton 1997, nos.703 and 429); paintings by De Wilde: as Tony Lumpkin in Goldsmith's *She Stoops to Conquer* (engraved P. Audinet 1791, illus. Burnim 1998, p.219); as Don Lewis in Cibber's *Love makes a Man* (engraved P. Audinet 1791; illus. Burnim 1998, p.218); as Vellum in Addison's *The Drummer* (engraved J. Thornthwaite 1792; illus. Burnim 1998, p.220); as Tony Allspice in Morton's *The Way to get Married* c.1796 (Yale Center for British

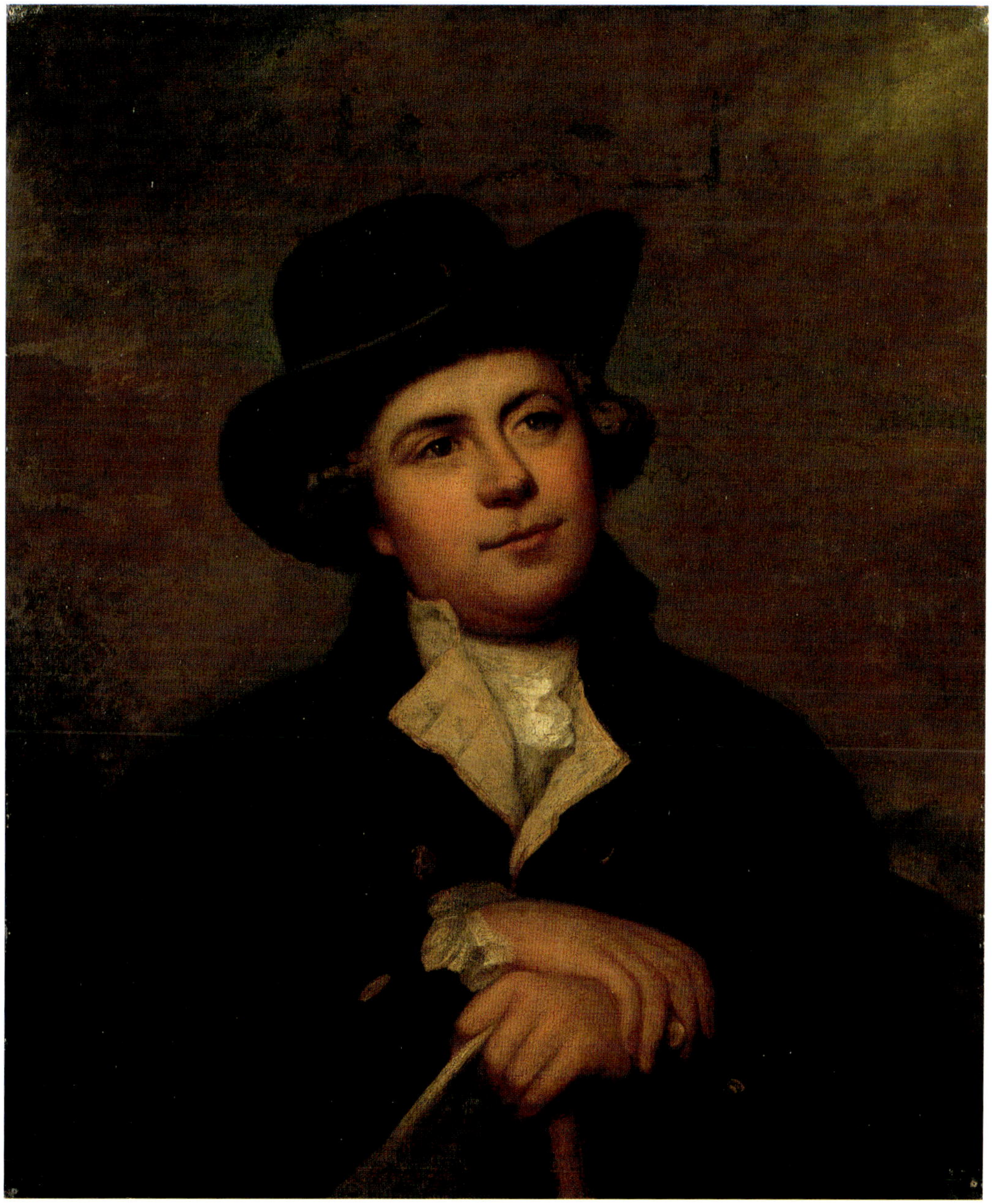

QUICK NPG 1355

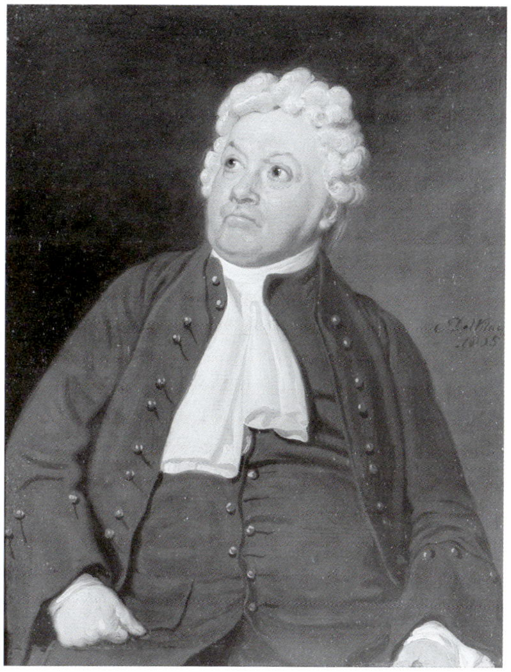

QUICK as Old Doiley by Samuel de Wilde 1788 (Garrick Club)

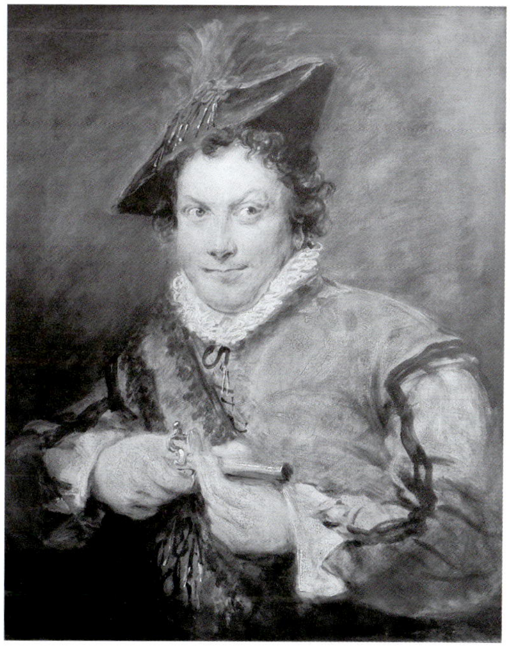

QUICK as Spado by Gainsborough Dupont 1794 (Garrick Club)

Art, B1981.25.237; illus. Mander & Mitchenson 1957, no.172), and as Old Doiley in Cowley's *Who's the Dupe*★ 1805 (Garrick Club; Ashton 1997, no.699); by Gainsborough Dupont, as Spado in O'Keeffe's *Castle of Andalusia*★ 1794 (Garrick Club; Ashton 1997, no.701); by Thomas Parkinson, as Lumpkin in *She Stoops to Conquer* (private collection; exhibited RA 1774, no.356; illus. *Royal Opera House Retrospective*, 1982–83, p.132).

Drawings by John Downman, as Woodcock in Bickerstaffe's *Love in a Village* 1787 (Fitzwilliam Museum, Cambridge; made 'for a group with Mrs Wells as Madge'), and by De Wilde as an unidentified character (Harvard Theatre Collection; illus. Highfill, XII, p.218).

RAIKES, Robert 1735-1811

Philanthropist; suc. his father as editor of the *Gloucester Journal* 1757-1802; campaigned for improvements in prisons and promoted Sunday Schools; his first Sunday school opened in Gloucester 1780, admittance depending only on 'clean hands, clean faces, and the hair combed'; Fanny Burney (in 1788) found him worthy and good-hearted, but 'somewhat too flourishing, somewhat too forward, somewhat too voluble'.

1551 GEORGE ROMNEY 1785-88

Canvas 124.5 x 99 (49 x 39) lined; conserved 1979, but in poor condition; the surface is much rubbed, there is extensive retouching throughout and a marked shrinkage craquelure in the darker areas.

Blue eyes, white hair, wearing a dark blue coat, yellow waistcoat, grey breeches and white stockings; he sits in a red chair, in his right hand a paper inscribed *Sunday Schools*; a red curtain above him and on the table, covered by a green cloth, are books, an inkstand, papers and a silver stamp.

Collections. By descent to Gen. Robert Napier Raikes (d.1909); purchased from his heirs 1909 (as by Beechey).

Engraving: W. Woolnoth 1821, 1828, 1830, etc. (half length); anon. (life-size half-length lithograph).

Reference: Ward & Roberts 1904, II, p.128.

Presumably the 'half-length' portrait of 'Mr Raikes' for which Thomas Raikes paid Romney 50 gn. - £20 in March 1785, the balance in January 1788. The portrait was sent to him in London in April 1788, returned to Romney in March 1794, and then sent to Gloucester.[1] Thomas Raikes (d.1813), a director of the Bank of England, was the sitter's brother, Gloucester the sitter's home.

A half-length version was made for the Dean of Lincoln, Dr Kaye,[2] and another belonged to the sitter's granddaughter, Lady Thompson, in 1910.[3] A whole-length version, incorporating a King Charles spaniel, belonged to Mrs Holloway at Stroud in 1900.[4]

1 Ward & Roberts 1904, II, p.128. Sittings to Romney are impossible to determine: there is no sitter book for 1785, and there were three Raikes sitting to Romney 1785-92 (cf. Ward & Roberts 1904, II, p.129).
2 Ward & Roberts 1904, II, p.128; presumably sent before 1789 when Dr Kaye became Sir Richard Kaye.
3 Raikes's eldest daughter, Ann, m. 1799 Sir Thomas Boulden Thompson, 1st Bt; the owner was presumably Gertrude, Lady Thompson (d.1921), wife of the 2nd Bt. The portrait was seen, but not sold, at Christie's, 8 July 1910 (note in NPG archive).
4 Ward & Roberts 1904, II, p.128; illus. J.H. Harris, *Robert Raikes*, 1899, front.

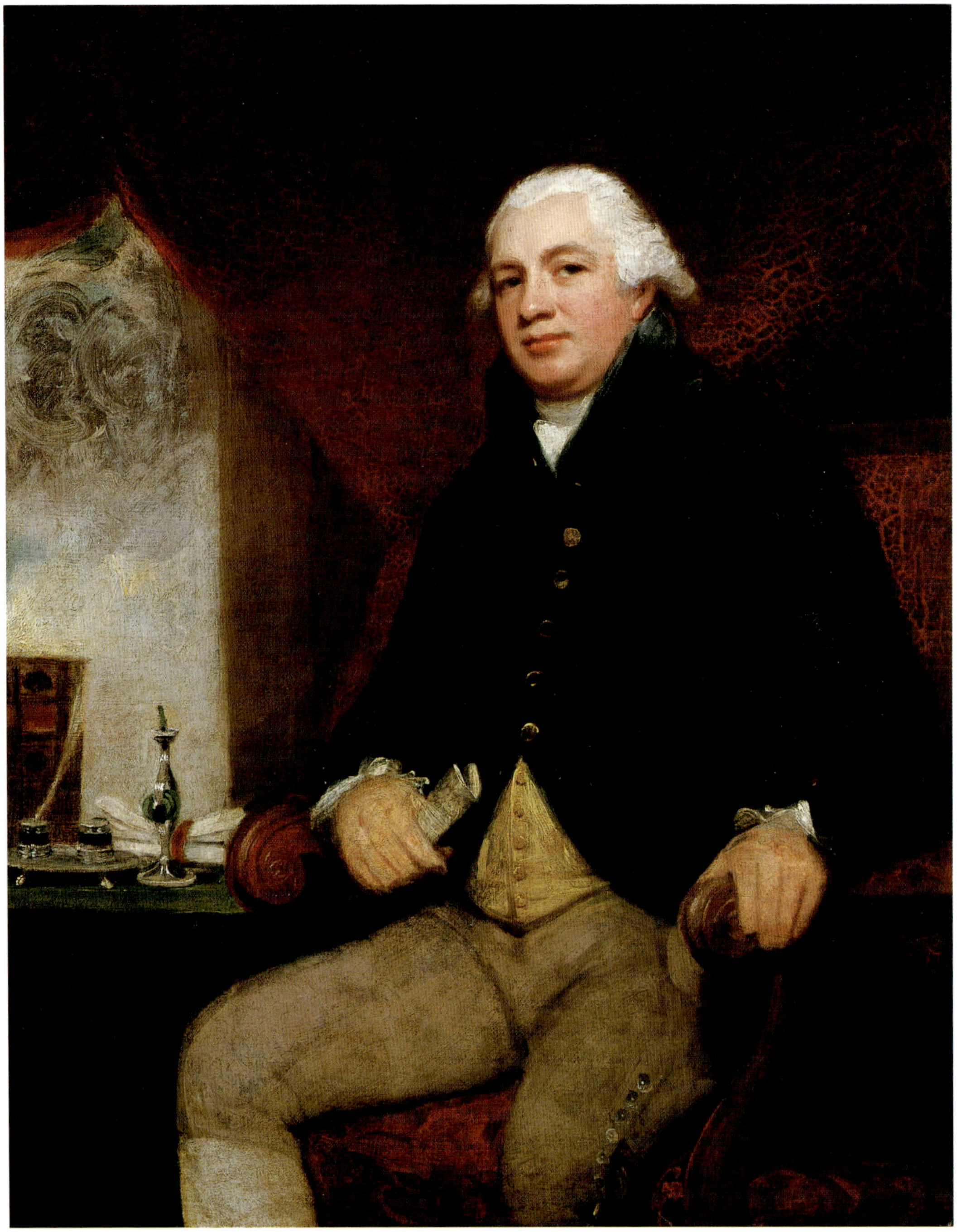

RAIKES NPG *1551*

ICONOGRAPHY

c.1740 Anon. engraving, three-quarter length standing, with his parents, brother and sister.

1785-88 Painting by George Romney, see NPG 1551.

1788 Drawing by Samuel Drummond, bust length, engraved W. Bromley 1788* (*European Mag.*).

c.1795 Engraved silhouette, bust length.

Posthumous

1831 Seven medals, including one by Thomas Halliday and another by T.W. Ingram, each bearing a draped medallion bust of Raikes, marking the Raikes Sunday School Jubilee (Brown 1980, nos.1551, 1553-58). The source of the medallion is unknown; the late 19th century profile engraving by A.W. Strutt presumably derived from it.

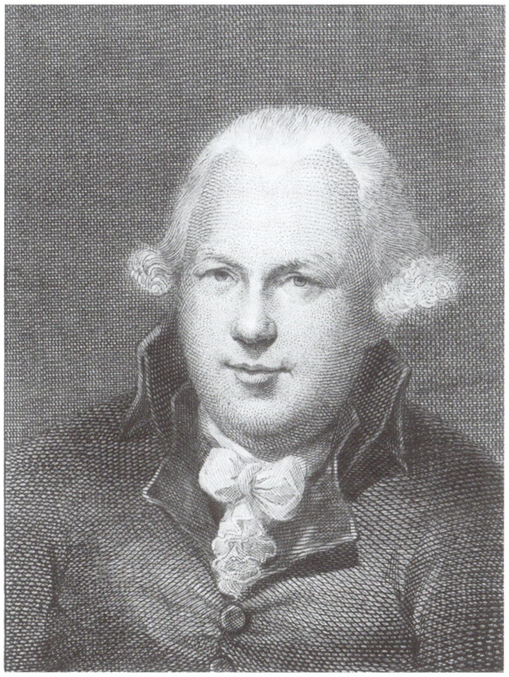

RAIKES W. Bromley after Samuel Drummond 1788 (NPG D 5575)

1880 Bronze statue by Thomas Brock. Embankment Gardens, London. A model exhibited RA 1880(1547). Replicas, cast in 1929, are in Gloucester Park, Gloucester, and at Queen's Park, Toronto.

APPENDIX

Medallion by William Tassie, NPG 2548, purchased in 1932 as of Robert Raikes, shows William Herschel, for whom see Walker *Regency*, I, pp.247-49.

RAMSAY, Charlotte, see LENNOX

RAMSAY, James 1733-89

Abolitionist; b. Fraserburgh, Aberdeen; a ship's surgeon who, after breaking his thigh bone at sea, entered the church, officiating for nineteen years in the West Indies, where he grew concerned over slavery; returned briefly to England 1777, before taking naval chaplaincies 1778-80; settled in Teston, Kent, 1781, writing anti-slavery tracts which effectively began the abolitionist movement; his African servant was buried at Teston in 1787.

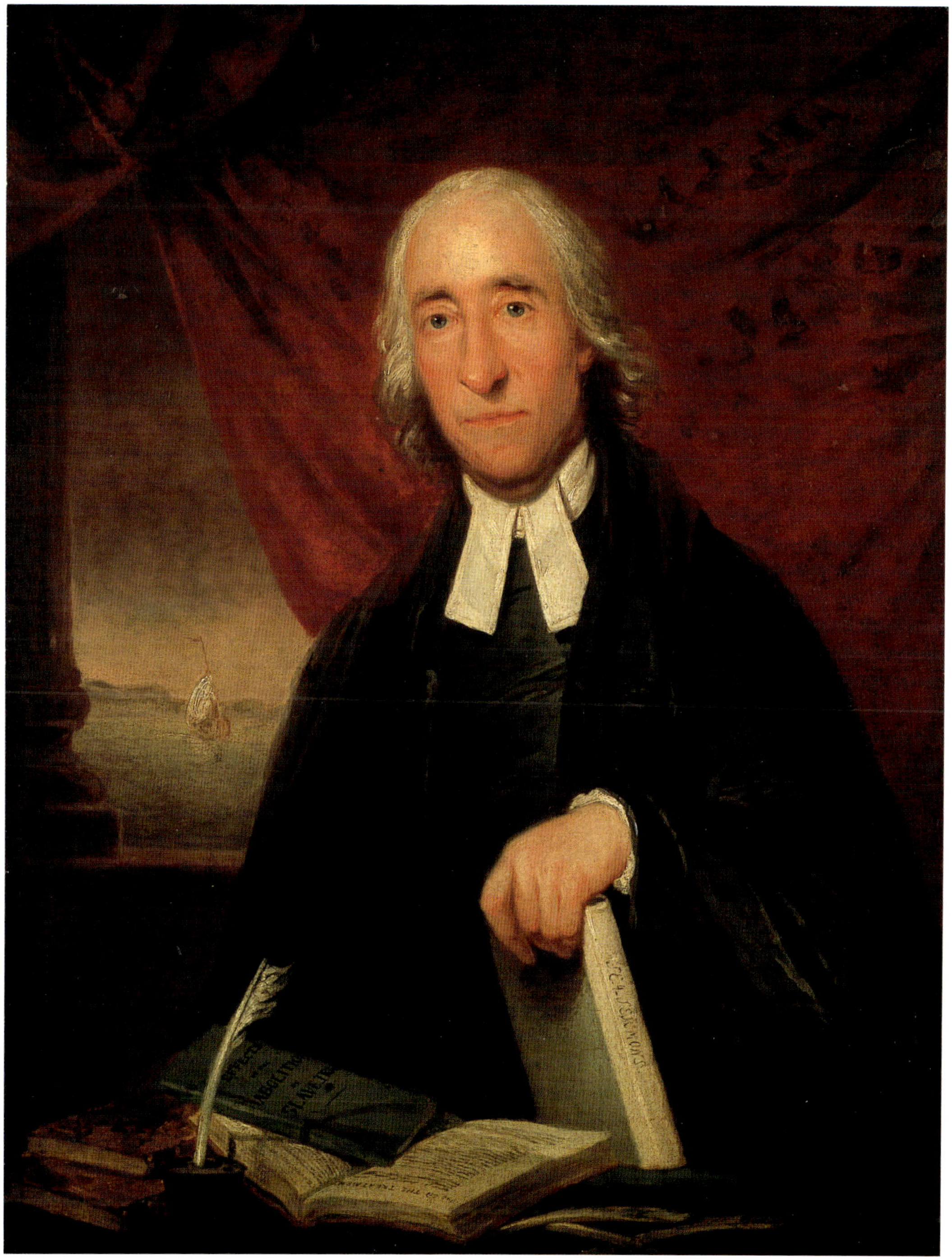

RAMSAY NPG *2559*

2559 CARL FREDRIK VON BREDA 1789

Canvas 89.5 x 69 (35¼ x 27¼) lined; discoloured varnish, scattered retouchings and a pronounced drying craquelure in the darker areas; signed below left: *Breda/ 1789*.

Blue eyes, white hair, wearing gown and bands; a red drape behind him; his left hand rests on *Sea Sermons* [1781] and on the table lies open *On the Treatment Conversion of* [*African Slaves in the British Sugar Colonies* 1784] and a pamphlet *Effects of the Abolition of Slave Trade* [*Enquiry into the Effects of putting a stop to the Slave Trade* 1784].

Collections: The sitter's great-great grandson, Lt.-Col. P.R. Phipps (d.1932);[1] his cousin and executor, Sir Edmund Phipps Kt, by whom presented 1933.

Ramsay died on 20 July 1789 but NPG 2559, dated that year, appears to have been painted from the life.

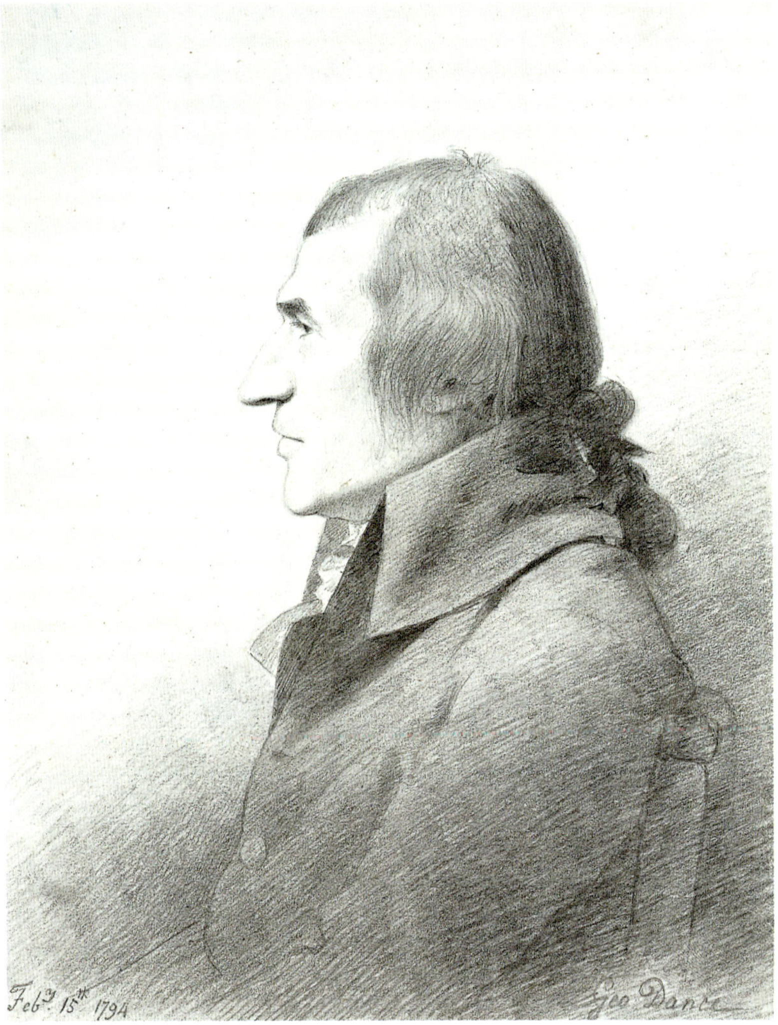

RENNELL NPG *1153*

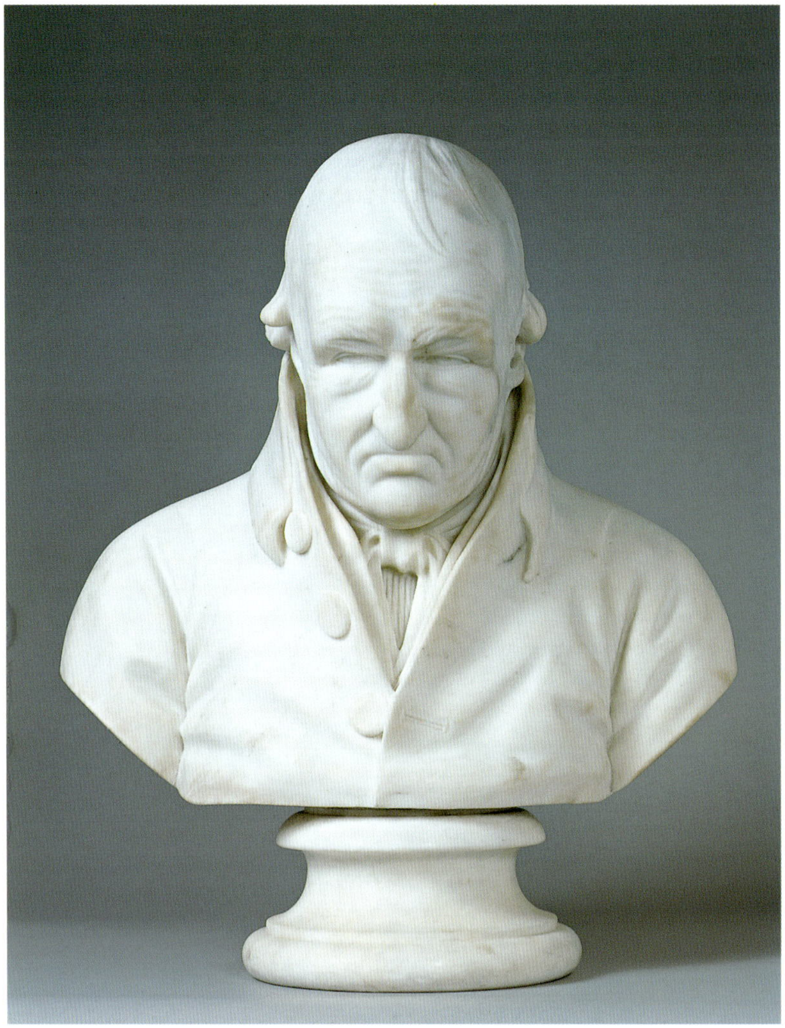

RENNELL NPG *896*

Three other versions have descended through the family: one with Phylis Green in 1957;[2] another, signed, and with an enclosed architectural background, at Chilston Park,[3] and a less finished version, also with an enclosed background, belonged to the Duke of St Albans at Newtown Anner, Clonmel, in 1957.[4] This last was presumably the portrait said to have been painted by Mrs Bouverie, a neighbour of Ramsay at Teston,[5] which in 1894 was said to belong to the Duke of St Albans.[6] A miniature copy was with Sir Edmund Phipps in 1933.[7] There is also an unlettered, bust-length engraving of Ramsay, wearing bands, the head not unrelated to NPG 2559 (conceivably based on a drawing by von Breda).[8]

1 Possibly the portrait of Ramsay sold in Oxford Street as John Wesley, bt. by a Mrs Dickinson and bequeathed to Pownoll W. Phipps's mother (P.W. Phipps, *Life of Col. Pownoll Phipps*, 1894, pp.122-23).

2 Given to her father by Mary Warde, a direct descendant.

3 Illus. *CL*, CXII, 1952, p.2099 (and see pp.2096-99 for the descent).

4 As described by Lady Beatrix Beauclerk (letter of 31 March 1933; NPG archive): 'There is very little difference between [this and NPG 2559], but I should say that [NPG 2559] is the better one, & certainly shows more detail. In ours, the books are barely indicated ... and the background shows no distant view'. Sir Edmund Phipps had first described NPG 2559 as a copy of Lady Beauclerk's (letter of 4 October 1932; NPG archive).

5 Mrs Elizabeth Bouverie (c.1726-98) of Teston, cos. of the 5th Earl of Radnor, friend of Hannah More, unm. (*Wal. Corr.*, XXXI, p.294n3).

6 See *DNB*, *ad vocem*, and P.W. Phipps, *Life of Col. Pownoll Phipps*, 1894, pp.122-23. The gift of the portrait recorded in the diary of Lady Osborne (d.1856), the Duchess of St Albans's great-grandmother (letter from the 12th Duke of St Albans, 12 July 1957; NPG archive).

7 Seen by J. Steegman in St James's Court, 7 October 1932 (note on file).

8 Photograph of 1967 in NPG archive from the print in the Vicarage at Yalding, where Ramsay's son-in-law was rector for over forty years.

RENNELL, James 1742-1830

Geographer; joined the East India Company 1763; surveyor-general in Bengal 1764-77; major in the Bengal engineers 1776; published in London the *Bengal Atlas* 1779 and a *Map of India* 1783; FRS 1781; his later works related to the geography of Africa, the Middle East and the Atlantic, and included an edition of the geographical system of Herodotus (1800).

'Major Rennell was of middle height, well proportioned, with a grave, yet sweet, expression on his countenance, which is said to have conciliated the regard of all he spoke with' (Mrs Bayne; C. Markham, *Rennell*, 1895).

1153 GEORGE DANCE 1794

Pencil with trace of pink on the lips, on paper 25 x 19.4 (9⅞ x 7⅝) laid down on paper; signed and dated in pencil (reinforced): *Feby. 15th 1794*, bottom left, and *Geo Dance.*, bottom right.

Collections: The artist's grandson, the Rev George Dance; his sale, Christie's, 1 July 1898, lot 111, bt. Colnaghi for the NPG.

Engraving: W. Daniell 1808.

On 16 December 1794 Farington noted that 'Major Reynell [sic] has expressed great pleasure on his profile [by Dance] being to be engraved. He has given Dance a set of his works'.

*896 UNKNOWN ARTIST c.1820-30

Marble bust 54.5 (21½) high (including socle).

Collections: By descent to the sitter's grandson, James Rennell Rodd (1858-1941),[1] by whom presented 1892.

When presenting this bust James Rodd wrote, disarmingly, that he did not think it was 'of great merit', but it was interesting 'as a good likeness of a remarkable man'; he had been unable to trace the authorship.[2]

1 KCMG 1899, cr. Baron Rennell 1933; for his other Rennell portraits, see below.
2 Letter of 26 April 1892; NPG archive.

ICONOGRAPHY

c.1776 Painting attributed to J.T. Seton, small half-length oval, wearing uniform. James Rodd in 1904 (illus. A. Gaussen, *Later Pepys*, 1904, II, f.p.76).

1794 Drawing by George Dance, see NPG 1153.

1799 Miniature by Edmund Scott, half-length profile, seated, painted for the 2nd Earl Spencer. Engraved A. Cardon 1799; W. Ridley 1802 (*European Mag.*); anon. 1804. A version in oil was with the Lever Gallery, London, in 1938.

c.1820 Wax medallion by Peter Rouw, in old age. Victoria and Albert Museum (A.86.1965).

c.1820-30 Unattributed marble bust, see NPG 896.

1831 Draped marble bust by Jacob Hagbolt, with the down-turned mouth of NPG 896. Westminster Abbey. Exhibited RA 1831(1169). A bronze copy by Hamo Thornycroft in the Victoria Memorial Hall, Calcutta, presented by James Rodd 1903.

1831 Medallion by Jacob Hagbolt, exhibited RA 1831 (1043). Probably the 'beautiful wax model by Hogbolt' presented to the Royal Society by Sir Joseph Hooker.

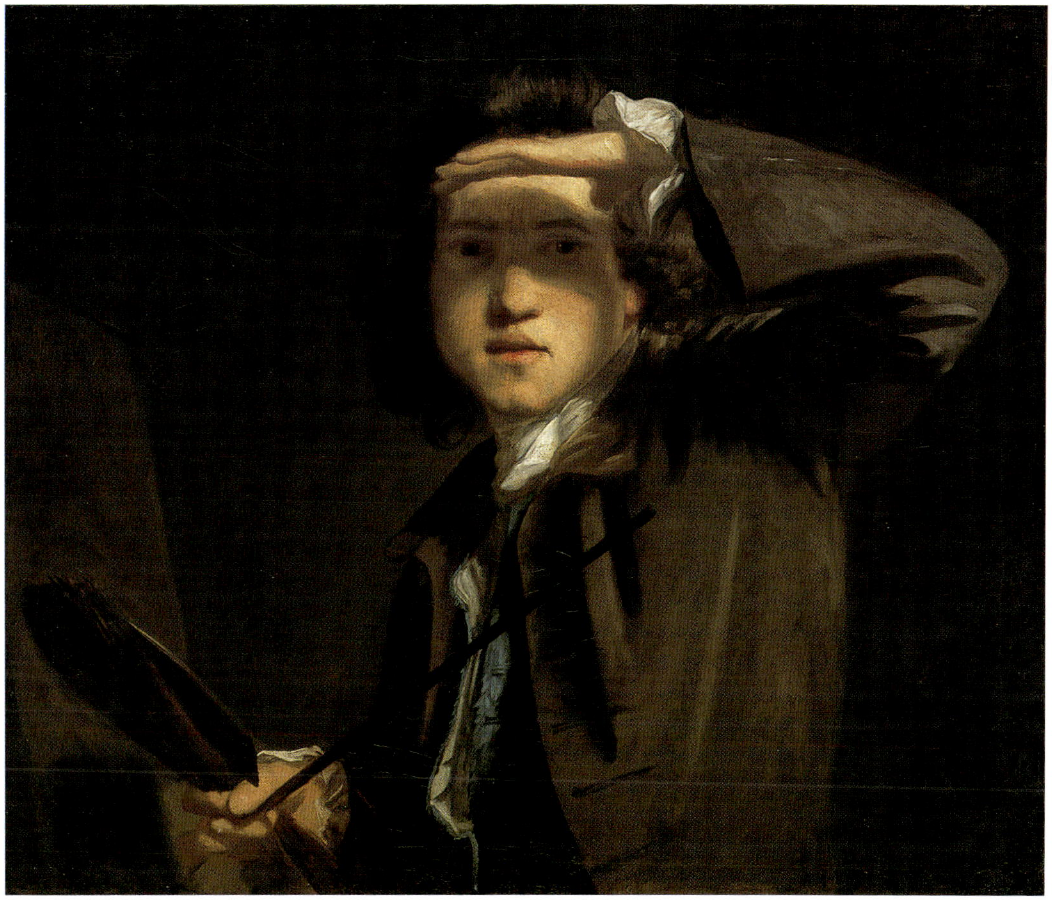

Joshua REYNOLDS NPG 41

REYNOLDS, Sir Joshua, Kt 1723-92

Painter, first President of the Royal Academy 1768; FRS 1761; Kt 1769; DCL Oxford 1773; 'so easy, so uniformly cheerful, so willing to please and be pleased, so fond of the company of literary men, so well read in mankind, so curious an observer of character' (Edmond Malone).

'[I have had] an odd accident ... a fall from a horse down a precipice, which cut my face ... my lips are now spoiled for kissing for my upper lip is so bruised that a great part was cut off' (Joshua Reynolds, 1749).

'His appearance at first sight impressed the spectator with the idea of a well-born and well-bred English gentleman' (Edmond Malone, 1797).

'In his stature, Sir Joshua was rather under the middle size. He was in height nearly five feet six inches, of a florid complexion, roundish blunt features, and a lively pleasing aspect; not corpulent, though somewhat inclined to it, but extremely active' (Joseph Farington, 1819).

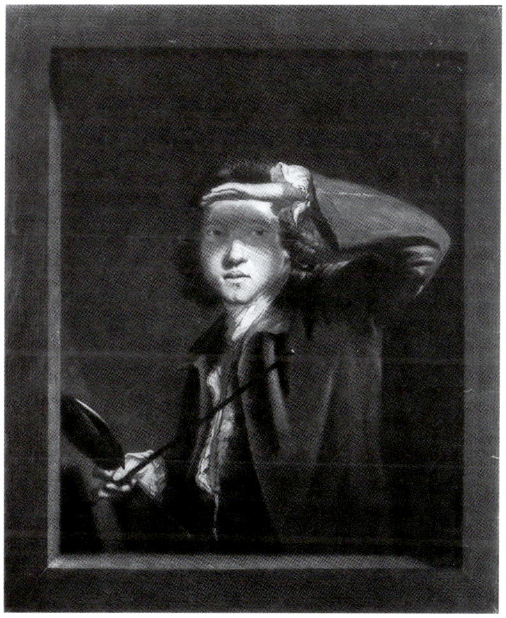

Joshua REYNOLDS self portrait c.1747-49 engraved by S.W. Reynolds 1795 (NPG D 4022)

41 SELF PORTRAIT c.1747-49

Canvas 63 x 75 (24¾ x 29½) cut down from 91 x 75 (36 x 29½) in the early 19th century (see below); lined 1973, cleaned 1982.

Brown eyes, dark hair, wearing a grey frock coat with a velvet collar, and a blue silk waistcoat;[1] an area at the extreme bottom left, with the easel and the artist's right hand, is left unfinished.

Collections: Thomas Lane (c.1742-1817) of Coffleet, Devon, by 1795 (see engravings); Lane sale, Christie's, 24 May 1845, lot 62, bt. B.S. Smith; Joseph Sandars (d. 1857) of Taplow House, Berks;[2] his sale Christie's, 15 May 1858, lot 40, purchased.

Engravings: S.W. Reynolds 1 February 1795 (*From an Original Picture in the possession of Thos Lane Esqr of Coffleet*);* R. Cooper, from a drawing by J. Jackson, 24 June 1813 (reversed, for Northcote's *Memoir of Reynolds*);[3] S.W. Reynolds c.1823 (showing the portrait reduced to its present proportions).

Exhibitions: NPE 1867(517); *Reynolds*, Grosvenor Gallery, 1883-84(148); *British Painting*, Moscow, Leningrad, 1960(17); *La Pittura Inglese*, Rome, 1966(21); *Reynolds*, Plymouth, 1973(27); *La peinture dans la peinture*, Dijon, 1983; *Reynolds*, RA, 1986(13); *Reynolds* 1992(3); *L'âme au corps: arts et sciences*, Paris, 1993-94; *Face to Face*, Liverpool, 1994(29); *Treasures* 1995-96(10); *Mirror Image*, NG, 1998.

Reference: Graves & Cronin, II, pp.790-91; Waterhouse 1941, p.39, as 1753-4; D. Mannings, *Burl. Mag.*, CXVII, 1975, p.219; Mannings 2000, no.2.

The only (undisputed) one of Reynolds's many self-portraits to show him engaged in his trade.[4] The engravings show that between 1808 and c.1823 NPG 41 was reduced along the top and bottom edges to its present shape. The proportions of the 1795 mezzotint suggest the original size was 91 x 75 and that 20 cms. were removed from the top edge and 8 cms from the bottom.[5]

NPG 41 may be dated after Reynolds had left Hudson in London and before his departure for Italy in May 1749, as Malone first suggested[6] and Mannings has argued; the brown and blue of his frock coat and silk waistcoat are indicative of the 1740s.[7] The originality of the composition and the technical assurance had previously suggested a later dating; Leslie and Taylor had hinted that the mouth showed signs of the accident Reynolds sustained in 1749.[8]

A nineteenth-century copy of NPG 41 in its present format is at Stourhead.

1 The palette in his right hand resembles one in the Cottonian Collection, Plymouth CMAG.

2 Corn merchant of Liverpool, s. of Joseph Sandars (1752-1842) of Derby; described as of Johnston House (W. Cotton, *Sir Joshua Reynolds and his Works*, 1856, p.272) and of Taplow House, Berks (Waagen, IV, p.292; perhaps acquired following the death of the 2nd Marquess of Thomond at Taplow in 1846); instrumental in the building of the Liverpool–Manchester railway.

3 Illus. A. Whitman, *S.W. Reynolds*, 1903, f.p.6 (and see no.247); Jackson gave his drawing to David Wilkie on 6 August 1808 (A. Cunningham, *David Wilkie*, 1843, I, p.186). See also *Rembrandt in England in the 18th century*, New Haven, 1983, no.33.

4 See below, self portraits c.1765-70.

5 NPG 41 appears in a reduced oval form in the background of Northcote's *Worthies of England* dated 1828 (Coram Foundation), but this format may have been invented to conform with the other half-length portraits shown in his composition.

6 Malone 1797, I, p.xlvi.

7 See *Reynolds* 1986, p.175.

8 Leslie & Taylor 1865, I, p.34.

987 see Groups, *Chambers, Wilton and Reynolds* by JOHN FRANCIS RIGAUD 1782

ICONOGRAPHY

Self Portraits

Before the comprehensive listing by David Mannings (Mannings 2000), the self portraits had been generally surveyed in Malone 1797, I, pp.xlv-xlvii., by J. Steegman, *Burl. Mag.*, LXXX, 1942, pp.31-34, and by David Mannings in his exhibition catalogue *Reynolds: The Self Portraits*, Plymouth, 1992.

c.1740 Drawing, bust length. Sotheby's, 6 June 2003, lot 1 (illus. *Reynolds* 1992, no.1).

c.1746 Painting, bust length. Private collection (Mannings 2000, no.1). Given by the artist to his niece, Mary Palmer, later Marchioness of Thomond.

c.1747-49 Painting, see NPG 41.

1750 Drawing, bust length. British Museum (1897.6.15.1; illus. *Reynolds* 1992, no.5).

c.1750 Painting, half length. Yale Center for British Art, ex Christie's, 12 June 2002, lot 31, from the Strutt collection.

1751 Painting, *Parody of the School of Athens*, caricature group in which the artist is believed to appear on the extreme right (but this figure has also been recognized as Thomas Patch). NG of Ireland (734; Mannings 2000, no.1962). Painted in Rome.

c.1751-52 Painting,* half length, with broad-brimmed hat. Private collection (Mannings 2000, no.3). Probably painted in Rome.

c.1753-55 Painting,* half length. Tate Gallery (N 889; Mannings 2000, no.4). Northcote thought this the most like of all the self portraits (Davies 1946, p.122).

c.1756 Painting, half length, in red robe with black fur collar. Sold Christie's 24 November 1998, lot 40, from Panshanger (Mannings 2000, no.5). A version in a private collection was given by the Marchioness of Thomond to Sir George Baker (Mannings 2000, no.6).

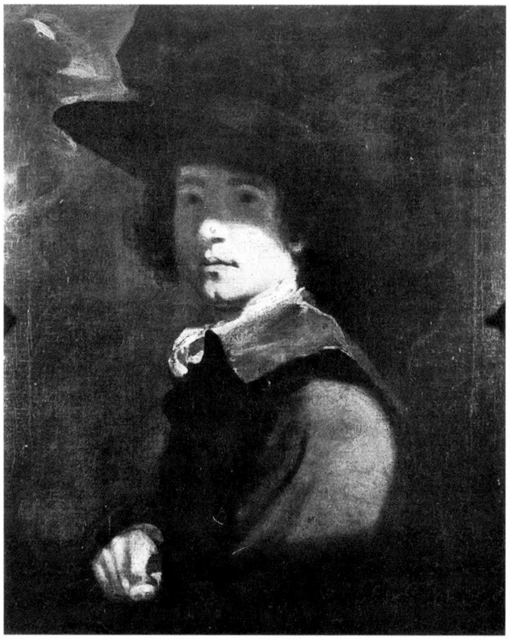

Joshua REYNOLDS Self portrait 1751-52 (Private Collection)

c.1764-67 Painting, half length in dull yellow cape. Plymouth CMAG, Cottonian Collection (Mannings 2000, no.7). Painted for the artist's nephew, Dean Joseph Palmer.

c.1765-70 Painting, seated at his easel. Sold Phillips, 10 July 1990, lot 49 (illus. C. White ed., *Rembrandt in England in the 18th century*, 1983, pl.30). The head possibly by Reynolds. Farington owned a Reynolds self portrait 'as a painter, with a canvass, easel &c before him' (Malone 1797, I, p.xlv), and on 25 March 1801 his 'portrait of Sir Joshua' was to be cleaned and relined by Marchi (Farington).

c.1766 Painting, half length. Society of Dilettanti, London (Mannings 2000, no.8). Reynolds was elected to the Society in 1766. Copies in Auckland AG attributed to James Northcote, and sold Phillips, 3 May 1988, lot 46.

Two other self-portraits in private collections closely resemble this pattern; one bought by Lord Normanton at the Thomond sale, Christie's, 18 May 1821, lot 23, engraved by J. Watson 1770 (Mannings 2000, no.9), the other, a reduced version without the book, at Woburn Abbey (Mannings 2000, no.10).

1773 Painting, half length to left in DCL robes. Private collection (Mannings 2000, no.11). Painted as a gift to the Corporation of Plympton on the artist's election as mayor of Plympton, allegedly 'begun & finish'd in the same day'. Version sold Sotheby's, 27 June 1973, lot 77.

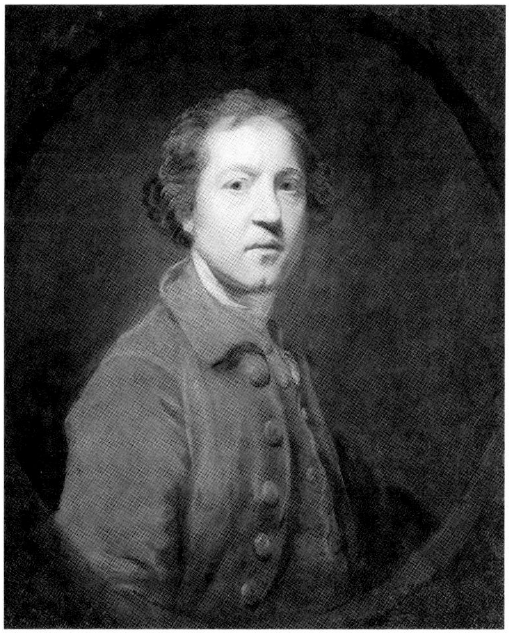

Joshua REYNOLDS Self portrait 1753-55 (Tate Gallery)

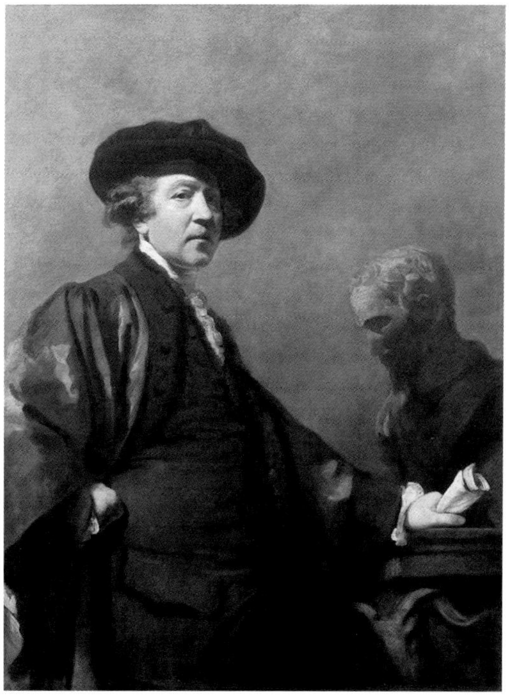

Joshua REYNOLDS Self portrait c.1780 (Royal Academy of Arts, London)

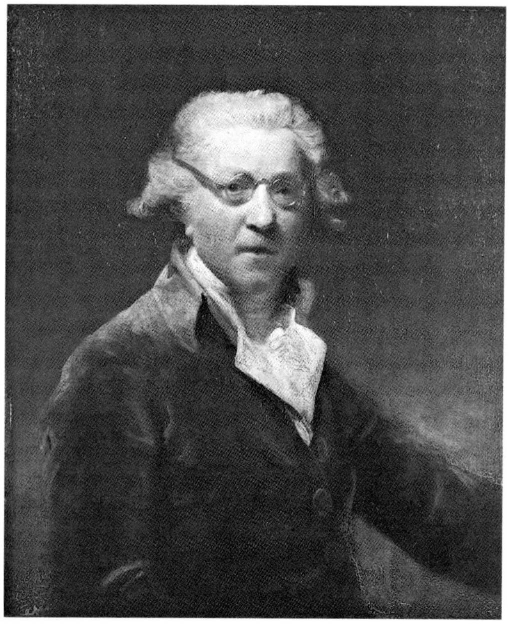

Joshua REYNOLDS Self portrait c.1788 (The Royal Collection)

A reduced version sold Christie's 21 November 1986, lot 100, and of several copies, two attributed to Northcote, one listed at Chesterfield House in 1893 (NPG archive), the other sold Sotheby's, 10 April 1991, lot 137.

c.1773-74 Painting, half length to right in DCL robes. Althorp (Mannings 2000, no.12). Versions include those sold Christie's, 15 April 1994, lot 16a; Christie's, 18 July 1924, lot 127 (from Lord Leverhulme's collection); Christie's, 17 April 1964, lot 131, and another is at Newnham House (see Mannings 2000, no.13a-c).

Miniature copies by Andrew Robertson in the Metropolitan Museum of Art, New York (illus. Reynolds 1996, no.163), by James Nixon in the Fitzwilliam Museum, Cambridge (illus. Bayne-Powell 1985, p.160), and by George Engleheart (illus. Williamson 1902, f.p.52). The image was also adapted by Reynolds for the self portrait as a shepherd in the Adoration scene in the window he designed for New College, Oxford.

1775 Painting, half length to right in DCL robes and cap, a scroll in his right hand. Uffizi Gallery, Florence (1932; Mannings 2000, no.16). Commissioned by the Grand Duke of Tuscany. Replica in a private collection (Mannings 2000, no.17). Versions with the University of Rochester Memorial AG, N.Y.; formerly at Wynnstay, and sold Sotheby's, 17 May 1989, lot 229 (Mannings 2000, nos.16a-c). A copy by James Northcote is in the Government Art Collection (GAC 1973) and a chalk copy was made by him in Florence (illus. Gwynn 1898, f.p.210); a reduced copy by John Powell sold Christie's, 10 April 1992, lot 104, and a miniature copy by Giuseppe Macpherson is in the Royal Collection (Walker 1992, no.661).

There appear to be two preliminary versions of this composition; formerly at Apethorpe (Mannings 2000, no.14), including an open paper in his right hand, engraved by J.K. Sherwin 1784; and in the Tate Gallery (N 306; Mannings 2000, no.15), his left hand at his breast.

c.1775 Painting, half length, his left hand at his ear. Tate Gallery (N 4505; Mannings 2000, no.18). Painted for Henry Thrale's library at Streatham Park. A copy in the Albright-Knox AG, Buffalo N.Y., and another by the artist's niece, Mary Palmer (later Marchioness of Thomond), sold Sotheby's, 8 February 1956, lot 116.

c.1775-80 Painting, three-quarter length seated in DCL robes, holding a paper addressed to the President and Council of the Royal Academy; a bust of Michelangelo behind him. Destroyed by fire 1898 (Mannings 2000, no.19). From the Thomond sale, 19 May 1821, lot 44. Engraved G.H. Every 1866.

c.1780 Painting,* three-quarter length in DCL robes and cap, with a bust of Michelangelo. Royal Academy, London (Mannings 2000, no.21). Engraved V. Green 1780. A replica at Belvoir Castle destroyed by fire 1816. Half-length versions sold Phillips, 6 June 1989, lot 35 (Mannings 2000, no.20), and in a private collection. Of numerous copies, one is in the National Museum, Havana, another (half-length) by R.A. Clack in the Royal Albert Memorial Museum, Exeter, and a pencil copy of the head by B.R. Haydon was sold Sotheby's, 3 October 1968, lot 192. A miniature copy by W.H. Craft is in the Ashmolean Museum, Oxford (illus. Walker 1997, no.87); an enamel copy by Henry Bone in the Royal Collection (dated 1804; Walker 1992, no.783) was copied by Sarah Barett Malden (Louvre).

c.1783 Drawing bust length, expressive of terror. Tate Gallery (N 1834; illus. *Reynolds* 1992, no.21). A study for a background figure in *Mrs Siddons as the Tragic Muse* (Huntington Art Collections, San Marino, Calif.).

c.1785? Painting, half length. Marshall collection sale, Bonham's, 28 March 1974, lot 110. Exhibited: RA 1906(86, as a self portrait). The head appears to have been a self portrait, but the picture is now in poor condition and an attribution difficult.

c.1788 Painting,* half length, wearing spectacles. Royal Collection (Millar 1969, no.1008; *Gainsborough & Reynolds* 1994, no.66; Mannings 2000, no.22). Engraved C. Watson 1789.

Copies of this portrait abound. Good contemporary versions include two in private collections, one sent by Reynolds to the Duke of Leeds in 1790

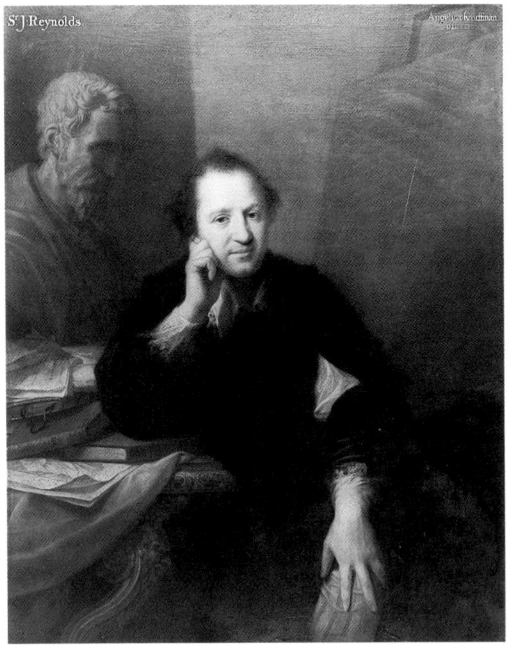

Joshua REYNOLDS by Angelica Kauffmann 1766 (Saltram, The National Trust)

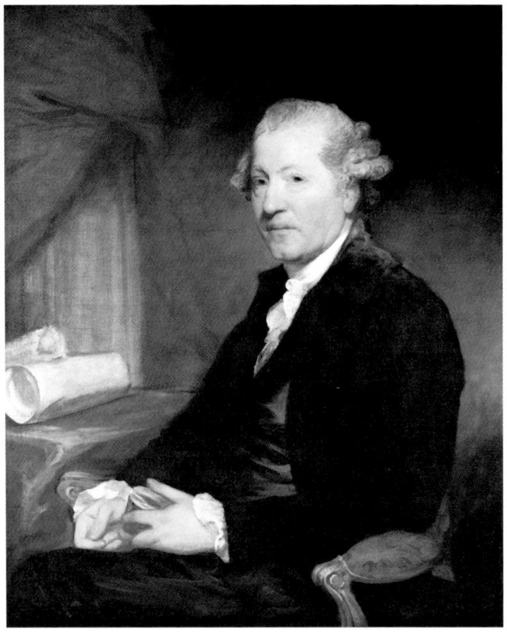

Joshua REYNOLDS by Gilbert Stuart 1784 (National Gallery of Art, Washington)

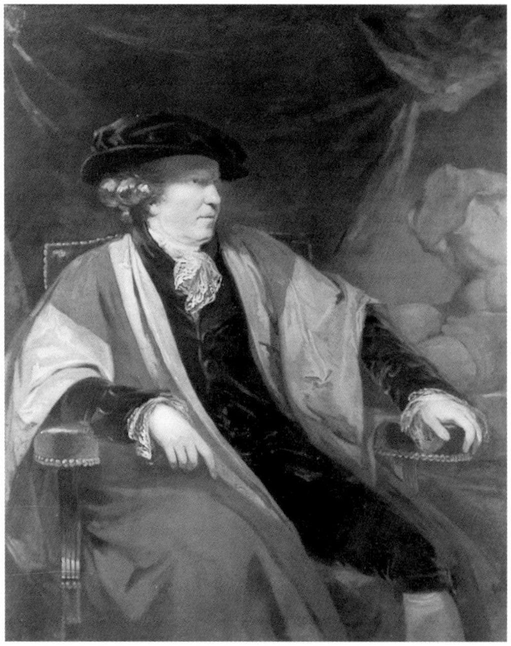

Joshua REYNOLDS by C.F. von Breda 1791 (Royal Academy of Fine Arts, Stockholm)

(Mannings 2000, no.23), the other made for William Mason; a copy made for Edmund Burke is in the Royal Collection (Millar 1969, no.1032) and another for Edmond Malone at Kenwood (Mannings 2000, nos.25, 24). Versions are in the Dulwich Picture Gallery (Mannings 2000, no.26), Apsley House and Petworth (cat. 1920, p.108, no.308).

Copies include examples in the Thyssen-Bornemisza Museum (333), the Toledo Museum of Art, and at Chequers. Named copyists include John Jackson (Holburne Museum, Bath), John Rising (Lord Brownlow's collection), G.P.A. Healy 1845 (Versailles), Rev George Huddesford (illus. *CL*, CIV, 1948, p.1270), and Lady Anne Fitzpatrick (pastel formerly at Holland House; cat., 1904, no.180).

Miniature copies by Henry Bone are in the Royal Albert Memorial Museum, Exeter, the Royal Collection (dated 1809; Walker 1992, no.784); preparatory drawings dated 1804 in the NPG Bone albums (*Bone* 1999, nos.427-28), and sold Sotheby's, 4 July 1989, lot 346 (dated 1792). Another by H.P. Bone dated 1851 is in the Lady Lever AG, Port Sunlight (a duplicate in the Leverhulme sale, Anderson Galleries, New York, 2-4 March 1926, lot 17). Miniature copies by William Grimaldi include: Sotheby's, 26 March 1979, lot 69 (dated 1791); the Royal Collection (dated 1792; Walker 1992, no.822); Christie's, 9 November 1994, lot 28 (dated 1809), and Christie's, 23 May 1989, lot 121 (dated 1811). An unattributed miniature copy is in the Scottish NPG (PG 2323).

c.1788 Painting, half length. Private collection (Mannings 2000, no.27). Given to the artist's niece, Theophila Palmer. Exhibited RA 1790(35). Copies include one in Dr Johnson's House, London.

Portraits by other Artists

These are also summarised in Mannings 2000, pp.591-92.

1766 Painting by Angelica Kauffmann,* three-quarter-length seated, a bust of Michelangelo behind him. Saltram.

c.1767 Drawing by Nathaniel Dance, whole-length seated, with Angelica Kauffmann. Harewood (illus. *Reynolds* 1992, no.27).

1768 Drawing by P-E. Falconet, bust length, engraved by D.P. Pariset (see *Reynolds* 1992, no.28).

1772 Painting by Johann Zoffany,* *The Academicians of the Royal Academy*, see Groups NPG 1437.

1773 Medal by John Kirk (Brown 1980, no.177).

c.1773 Miniature by Ozias Humphry, half length, wearing a brown coat, the frame inscribed 'Painted from Life by his Friend Humphry'. Corsham Court (illus. *Reynolds* 1992, no.29; *The Art of the Country House*, Tate Gallery, 1998, no.22).

1778 Marble bust by Giuseppe Ceracchi, inscribed, probably later, ... *Cirachi sculpsit Roma*. Royal Academy (illus. *Reynolds* 1986, no.172). A terracotta model was formerly also at the RA and a copy is in the Athenaeum, London. J.T. Smith recalled that Ceracchi's bust was 'sold by the figure-casters' (Smith 1920, II, pp.119-21). It has been supposed that the marble may have been acquired by Watson Taylor in 1821 (cf. *Reynolds* 1986, no.172), but see 1785 below.

1782 Painting by J.F. Rigaud, with Joseph Wilton and Sir William Chambers, see Groups NPG 987.

1782 Painting, unfinished, by Thomas Gainsborough. Reynolds sat to Gainsborough in November 1782 but further sittings were prevented by Reynolds's health; he left for Bath and the portrait was not resumed on his return (Malone 1797, I, p.xlvi).

1784 Painting by Gilbert Stuart,* three-quarter length seated. NG Washington (1942.8.21; Miles 1995, pp.172-77). A miniature copy by Charles Bestland in the Ashmolean Museum, Oxford (Walker 1997, no.89).

1785 Marble bust by Thomas Banks. Watson Taylor sale, Robins, 15th day, 25 July 1832, lot 162 ('A bust in statuary marble of Sir Joshua Reynolds, modelled from the life, in 1785, and sculptured by J. Bankes, A.R.' 'A fine original statuary bust' of Reynolds, presumably the same piece, had been bought for G. Watson Taylor at the Thomond sale, 19 May 1821, lot 76, but see also 1778 above.

before 1788 Wedgwood medallion, attributed to John Flaxman; listed in the 1788 Wedgwood cat. (illus. Reilly 1973, p.290).

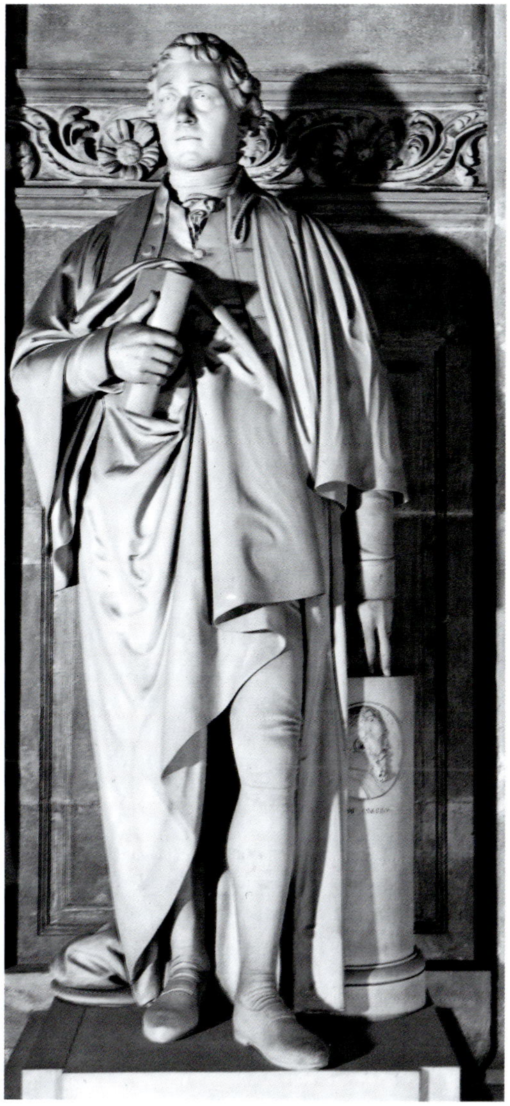

Joshua REYNOLDS by John Flaxman 1813 (St Paul's Cathedral, London)

1791 Wax profile by E.G. Mountstephen. Royal Academy (illus. Pyke 1973, fig.200). Exhibited RA 1791(643).

1791 Painting by C.F. von Breda,* three-quarter length seated in DCL robes. Royal Academy of Fine Arts, Stockholm, by whom commissioned. Exhibited RA 1792(390). Engraved S.W. Reynolds 1796.

1792 Enamel by William Birch, exhibited RA 1792(275).

Undated Medallion by T.R. Poole. Sotheby's, 24 July 1978, lot 57.

J.T. Smith described in Nollekens's house a miniature of Reynolds, 'by Edridge, taken from a picture in the club-room in the Thatched-house Tavern, St James's-street', i.e. the Club which Reynolds and Johnson had founded in 1764 (Smith 1920, I, p.297).

Posthumous

1798 Painting by James Barry, *Elysium*, of 1777-84, part of the *Progress of Human Culture*, in which Reynolds appears below Rubens, pointing to Michelangelo; his head was added in 1798 (i.e. after Barry had engraved his composition in 1791). Royal Society of Arts, London (Pressly 1981, no.27). The head derived from the Reynolds self portraits of the 1770s.

1813 Marble statue by John Flaxman.* St Paul's Cathedral, unveiled in 1813. Flaxman began work in 1805 (Farington, 21 January 1805) and exhibited a model RA 1807(1092). Nollekens had been asked by Lady Thomond to execute a monument to Reynolds but he declined (Farington, 9 March 1803).

1817 Bust by John Bacon jr. Formerly British Institution. Exhibited RA 1817 (1045).

1827 Enamel after a self-portrait by Reynolds by J.W. Higham, exhibited RA 1827(779).

Later statues include those by H.H. Armstead 1860, in the frieze of the Albert Memorial; by E.B. Stephens 1873, Burlington House, façade; by J.B. Philip c.1875, Town Hall, Chelsea, destroyed 1940; two sketch models by Hamo Thornycroft in the Reading MAG; by Reuben Sheppard 1909, Victoria and Albert Museum, south front; eight bronze studies for a statue by F.D. Wood 1916 in the Tate Gallery, and a bronze statue by Alfred Drury 1931 at Burlington House.

Busts include those by William Behnes 1860, Plymouth CMAG (Cottonian Collection; executed from Ceracchi's model; illus. *Reynolds* 1992, no.31a); by Henry Weekes 1874, Leicester Square, London, and by Frederick Thomas 1895, National Portrait Gallery, north front.

A painting by H.W. Phillips 1869 is in the Lecture Theatre of the Victoria and Albert Museum.

DOUBTFUL PORTRAITS

See Unidentified Portraits NPG 927 and NPG 1761B.

REYNOLDS, Richard 1735-1816

Ironmaster and philanthropist; b. Bristol; from 1756 a partner in the Coalbrookdale iron-works of Abraham Darby, whom he succeeded in 1763; he cast cylinders and made the first rotative engine for Boulton & Watt; retired 1789, devoting his life to philanthropy; on his death a Reynolds Society was founded to commemorate the considerable benefits he had discreetly conferred, primarily in Bristol.

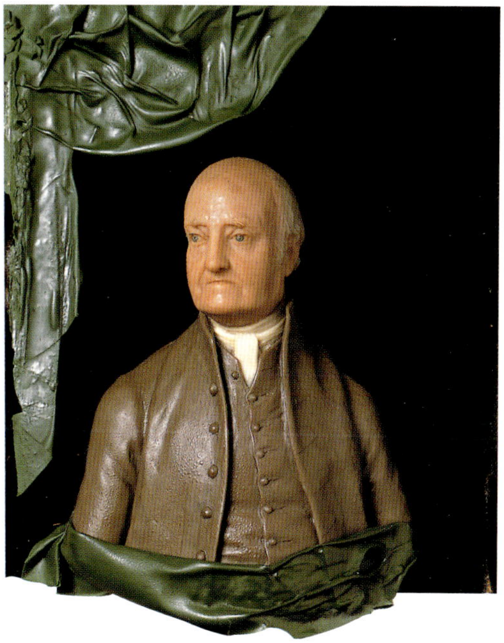

Richard REYNOLDS NPG *4674*

4674 SAMUEL PERCY c.1810

Polychrome wax bust 18 x 14 x 4 (7 x 5½ x 1½), fixed to a brown velvet covered wooden board; repaired and restored 1997; the frame bears a contemporary label inscribed: *Richd. Reynolds.*

Blue eyes, white hair, wearing a white neckcloth and a light brown suit; green drapes above and below.

Collections: Peter Charlesworth, from whom purchased 1969.

Engravings: H. Meyer 1817 (*European Mag.*) *from an original Bust by S. Percy in the possession of George Dillwyn Esqre.*; Freeman.

The apparent age of the sitter and his dress indicate an early 19th-century date, and another example of the wax, in the Leeds City Art Gallery (18/81), has been dated 1810.[1] An unattributed wax portrait of Reynolds was in the Hatfield House, Chilham, sale, 3 December 1964, lot 175.

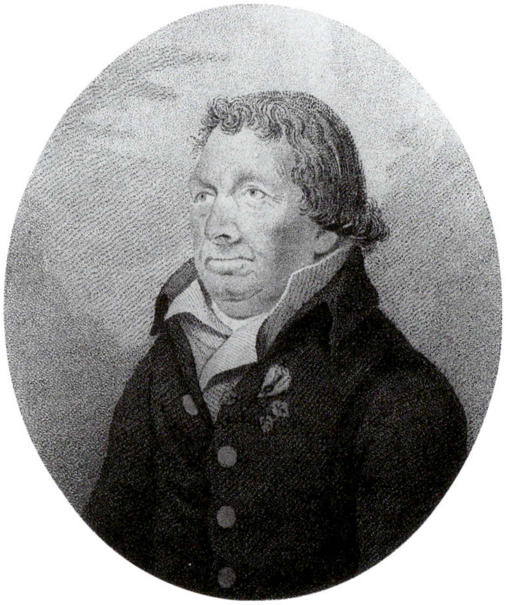

Richard REYNOLDS drawn and engraved by J. Baldrey 1799 (NPG D 13809)

1 Illus. *Leeds' Sculpture Collections, concise cat.*, 1996, p.5. Other examples of the wax were sold Sotheby's, 22 April 1982, lot 312; with D. Mathias in 1973 (Pyke 1973, p.104) and erroneously stated to be in the National Maritime Museum (Pyke 1981, p.32).

ICONOGRAPHY

1798 Miniature by Samuel Shelley, exhibited RA 1798(860).

1799 Painted and engraved by John Baldrey,* half-length oval.

c.1810 Wax by Samuel Percy, see NPG 4674.

c.1815 Engraving by Bottomley, profile, aged 80.

1816? Portrait by William Hobday, three-quarter length seated. with J.B. Braithwaite 1900. Seen by Scharf 1866 'at Mr Webbs, Cooper's Row' and considered 'very poorly painted' (TSB 11/16). Exhibited RA 1817(558); NPE 1867(176) lent S. Gurney. Engraved W. Sharp 1817, anon. 1823. Much resembling the Percy wax, see NPG 4674.

c.1816 Anon. engraving, half length, bald with white hair, wearing a dark suit [the engraving in the NPG has *Bronwhite* written on the verso and *Meyer*].

c.1816 Profile, bust length, engraved J.L. Frost, Bristol.

Posthumous

1852 Engraving by S. Bellin (H.M. Rathbone, *Letters of Richard Reynolds with a Memoir*, 1852).

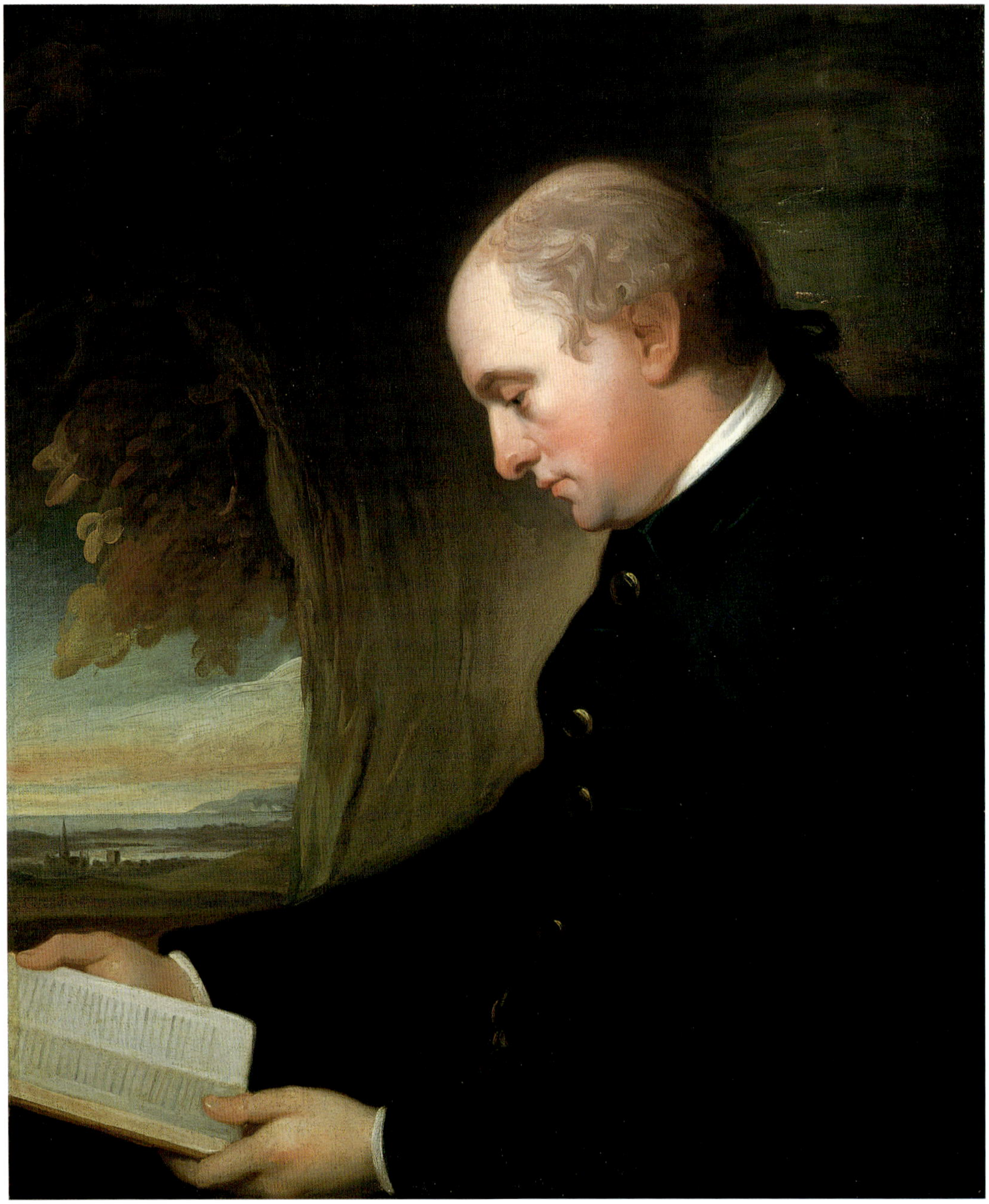

3rd Duke of RICHMOND and LENNOX NPG *4877*

RICHMOND and LENNOX, Charles Lennox, 3rd Duke of 1735–1806

Statesman; suc. as 3rd Duke 1750; FRS 1755; opened an artists' academy in Richmond House, Whitehall 1758 (under the direction of Cipriani and Wilton); served in Germany during the Seven Years War; general 1782, field-marshal 1792; ambassador in Paris 1765; KG 1782; master-general of the Ordnance 1782–95; member of Pitt's cabinet 1784; Wraxall commended his application which compensated for a limited range of ideas.

4877 GEORGE ROMNEY 1775–77

Canvas 80 x 67.5 (31½ x 26½) lined; cleaned 1994.

Dark eyes, grey powdered hair with black ribbon, wearing a blue coat; a distant view of Chichester cathedral from the north east (as seen from Goodwood, but not to be taken too seriously).

Collections:[1] Maj.Gen. Randal Rumley (b.1804); his bro.-in-law, the 7th Earl of Berkeley,[2] his sale 'Phillips, February 1885 [in which there were two portraits – the Duke of Richmond and the Duke of Richmond reading]';[3] Baroness Burdett-Coutts (d.1906); William Burdett-Coutts (d.1921); his sale, Christie's, 4 May 1922, lot 74, bt. Lindsay Fleming; his son John Fleming, by whom sold Sotheby's, 22 March 1972, lot 97, bt. Leggatt for the NPG.

Engravings: See below.

Exhibitions: *Guelph* 1891(70) lent Baroness Burdett-Coutts; *The Dye is now Cast*, NPG Washington, 1975(156); *Bicentennial Center Opening*, Yorktown, Va., 1976.

Reference: Ward & Roberts 1904, II, p.131, no.1; Romney 2002, p.28.

The Duke of Richmond had 'a great regard' for Romney. He had first noticed him studying in the sculpture gallery at Richmond House and had subsequently encouraged him to study in Italy. When Romney returned to London in July 1775 he had some difficulty in re-establishing himself:

> ruin was already beginning to stare him in the face, when, at length, the Duke of Richmond, not forgetful of the encouragement he had formerly given him, came to sit for his portrait. The picture was a three-quarters, and represented his Grace *en profile*, reading. It was universally admired, and he was in consequence commissioned to paint several copies for the Duke's particular friends.[4]

On 25 November 1775 the Duke described his portrait, while urging his friend Edmund Burke to sit to Romney:

> in the midst of Business a little Relaxation is of use, but I have thought of a method even to reconcile Your Business with this sitting, which is by having Mr Romney take Your Portrait while You are writing or Reading whichever you like best. I know the Painters have a nonsensical Jargon that such attitudes throw a Shadow on the face, lose a Part of it, and particularly the eyes which are so necessary to the Countenance. But in truth all this is not founded, and is meant more to flatter the sitter than for any real purpose. Romney has half finished one for me which for my own Conveniency I chose to have reading, and altho' the Brilliancy of my Eyes are lost, I believe you will think it a good and a like Portrait when you see it.[5]

Hayley described the portrait as 'a happy specimen of the improving artist';[6] it is a remarkable, contemplative image of a sitter noted for his vehemence. Romney was to use the same half-length reading profile for his portrait of Samuel Whitbread in 1781-83 (Eton College).

Romney's sitter and account books show that sittings took place on 24 April and 6, 9 November 1776, and 24, 28 January 1777.[7] The original portrait, for which he received 15 gn. on 21 March 1777, was sent to Lady Louisa Lennox (the Duke's third sister, who m. Thomas Conolly) and four copies at 10gn. each were sent to Lady Susan [Sarah] Lennox (the sitter's youngest sister, who m. 1) Sir Thomas Bunbury and 2) George Napier); Mr Adair, Serjeant;[8] Mr Adair, St James's Street, and Mr Peckham; a fifth was apparently sent to William Ogilvie (who m. Emily, the Duke's second sister) on 9 April 1788. NPG 4877 is evidently one of the replicas, and is distinguished by the inclusion of a distant view of Chichester Cathedral. It is no longer clear which is the prime version; versions are at Goodwood[9] and Cirencester,[10] and there are two in American collections, one dated 1778,[11] the other apparently of prime quality.[12] Further, unverified, versions are recorded.[13] None of these versions exactly agrees with the mezzotint by James Watson published on 21 December 1778, which shows lace cuffs; a second state, published on 21 December 1782, shows the Garter star (awarded in April 1782).[14]

Reduced copies include a miniature by Henry Bone, formerly at Holland House;[15] an enamel at Cirencester;[16] a painting by John Milbourn (private collection, from the Strawberry Hill sale, 17th day, 13 May 1842, lot 37); another with H.H. Heldring, The Hague, in 1962, and a third in the Castle Howard sale, Sotheby's, 11-13 November 1991, lot 557.

1 This provenance is based on that given in the Burdett-Coutts sale cat.
2 He m. Caroline, dau. of Admiral Sir George Berkeley (1753-1818) and Emily Lennox (d.1832), 2nd dau. of the 2nd Duke of Richmond (the sitter's father).
3 According to Ward & Roberts 1904, II, p.131; such a sale is not listed by Lugt (it was not Puttick, 19 February 1885).
4 Romney 1830, p.135; see also pp.72-73.
5 *Burke Corr.*, III, p.238.
6 Hayley 1809, p.63.
7 This account taken from Ward & Roberts 1904, II, pp.131-32.
8 Probably James Adair, serjeant at law (d.1798), MP 1780-98.
9 Illus. *Chefs d'oeuvre de Goodwood*, Fondation Mona Bismarck 1992, no.32; engraved W. Evans c.1800.
10 Illus. Bathhurst cat., 1908, p.138,
11 From the Gordon Castle sale 1938; exhibited *Romney*, Kenwood, 1961(24); sold Christie's, 7 July 1967, lot 12.
12 Hon Mrs Cecil Brassey sale, Christie's, 24 March 1950, lot 12, and Sotheby's, 15 March 1978, lot 16.
13 For example, in the Norton AG, West Palm Beach, Fla. (66 x 61 cm.); sold Christie's, 12 December 1903, lot 111, bt. Fairfax Murray; and formerly with Sir Henry Bunbury at Barton Hall, Suffolk.
14 CS 124 also describes the second state as showing more ornate lace ruffles (an overpainted version is at Goodwood). A similar but smaller print by H.R. Cook published in 1807.
15 Cat., 1904, no.435.
16 *Bathhurst Miniatures* (NPG archive), no.31.

ICONOGRAPHY

c.1740 Painting ascribed to Thomas Hudson, half-length oval as a child. Goodwood.

1755 Painting by Pompeo Batoni,★ three-quarter length standing. Private collection (Clark 1985, no.188). Autograph replica at Goodwood. Painted in Rome, where Richmond and his brother Lord George Lennox had arrived by 26 March 1755.

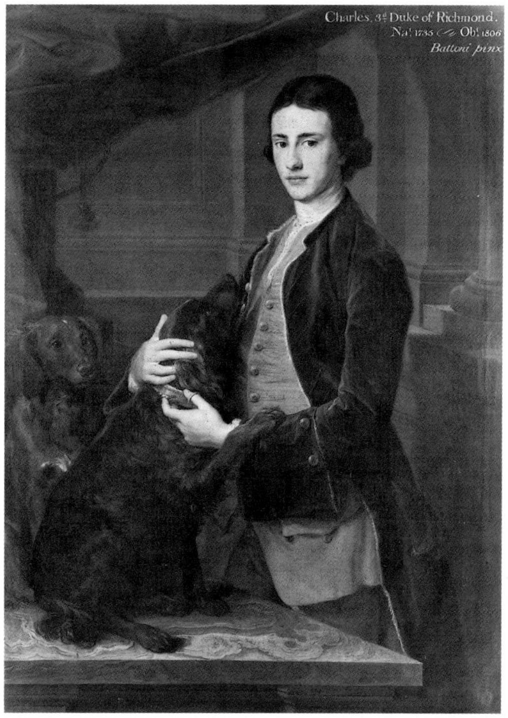

3rd Duke of RICHMOND and LENNOX by Pompeo Batoni 1755 (Private Collection)

1755 Painting by Anton Mengs, three-quarter length standing in Van Dyck costume. Goodwood (S. Roettgen, *Mengs*, 1999, no.218). Painted in Rome, see under 1755 above. Another (described as painted at Rome in 1750) was at Appuldurcombe Park in 1797 (Musgrave MSS 6391, f.83).

1758 Painting by Joshua Reynolds,★ three-quarter length standing. Goodwood (Mannings 2000, no.1113). Reynolds made a copy for General Henry Conway (at whose house Richmond was married in 1757) and supplied a miniature copy, both untraced.

c.1759 Painting by George Stubbs, *The Duke of Richmond with the Charlton Hunt*. Goodwood (illus. *Stubbs*, Tate, 1984, no.28). According to Ozias Humphry this commission from the Duke (for three hunting scenes) was the first 'of considerable importance' that Stubbs received following his arrival in London in 1758.

c.1770 Miniature by Ozias Humphry, bust-length oval. Sotheby's, 9 March 1964, lot 26.

1775-77 Painting by George Romney, see NPG 4877.

1777-84 Painting by James Barry, *Distribution of Premiums in the Society of Arts*, part of the *Progress of Human Culture*, in which Richmond stands in profile on the right. Royal Society of Arts, London

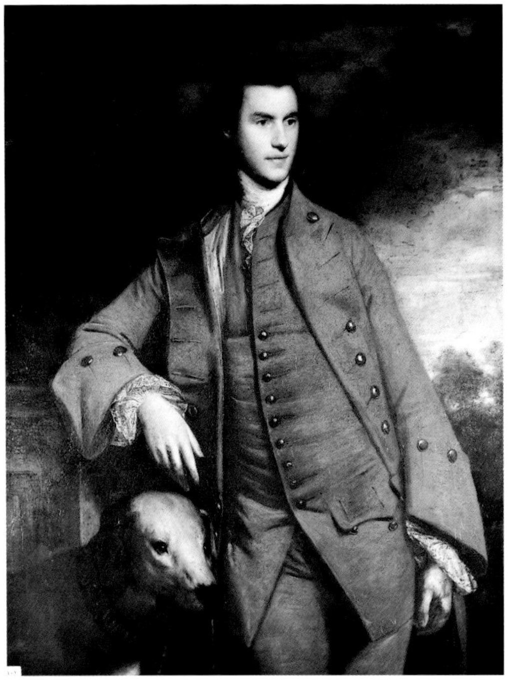

3rd Duke of RICHMOND and LENNOX by Joshua Reynolds 1758 (Trustees of the Goodwood Collection)

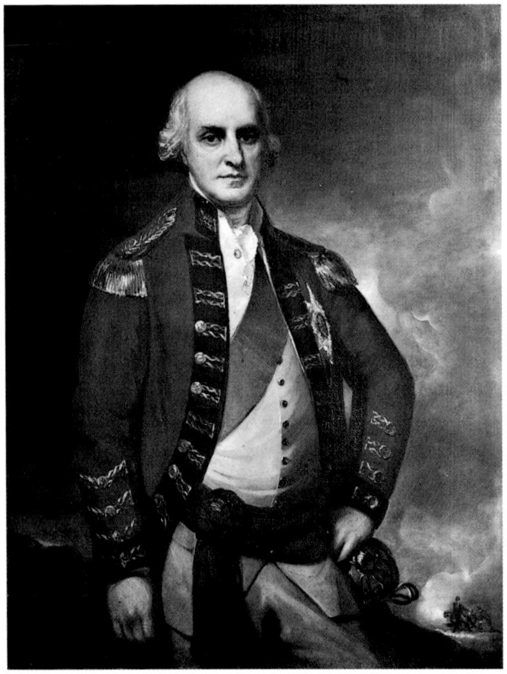

3rd Duke of RICHMOND and LENNOX by George Romney 1795 (Trustees of the Goodwood Collection)

(Pressly 1981, no.26). Engraved J. Barry 1791.

1779-81 Painting by J.S. Copley,* *The Death of Chatham*, see Comparative Groups.

1783 Enamel by Henry Spicer, exhibited SA 1783(255).

1789 Engraving by J. Sayers, whole-length walking.

1795 Painting by George Romney,* three-quarter length standing, in military uniform (presumably that of a field marshal) with Garter ribbon and star. Goodwood (Ward & Roberts 1904, II, p.131, no.3). Sittings took place in January and April-June 1795. Exhibited as Gainsborough, *Guelph* 1891(339). A copy is also at Goodwood.

Undated Wax profiles by Isaac Gosset (Clumber House cat., 1923, no.375) and Samuel Percy (his sale, Christie's, 31 January 1800; Pyke 1973, p.104), and a jasper medallion, bust-length to right (illus. *Franklin and his Circle*, New York, 1936, p.95).

An unattributed marble bust listed at Goodwood in 1839 (W.H. Mason, *Goodwood*, 1839, p.38); a plaster bust by Anne Damer listed at Goodwood as 'Duke of Richmond' (Gunnis 1968, p.120).

DOUBTFUL PORTRAIT

Painting by Johann Zoffany c.1765, with Leggatt 1963 (illus. *Connoisseur*, CLIV, 1963, p.109).

ROBERTSON, William 1721-93

Historian, b. Borthwick, Midlothian; principal of Edinburgh University 1762-92; Royal chaplain in Scotland 1762; historiographer of Scotland 1763; his works included a *History of Scotland* 1759, the *History of Charles V* 1769 and the *History of America* 1777.

'His manner was not graceful in little matters, though his demeanour was dignified on the whole... He was in person above the middle size - his features were strongly marked - his forehead was high and open - the expression of his mouth was that of repose, of meditation, and of sweetness at the same time' (Henry, Lord Brougham, 1846).

'In point of stature Dr Robertson was rather above the middle size; and his form, though it did not convey the idea of much activity, announced vigour of body and a healthful constitution. His features were regular and manly; and his eye spoke at once good sense and good humour. He appeared to greatest advantage in his complete clerical dress; and was more remarkable for gravity and dignity in discharging the functions of his public stations, than for ease or grace in private society' (Dugald Stewart, 1811).

5800 JAMES TASSIE 1791

Glass paste 7 (2¾) high, incised on the truncation: *WILL.ROBERTSON D.D./ 1791/ Tassie F*; set on glass backed in dark blue.

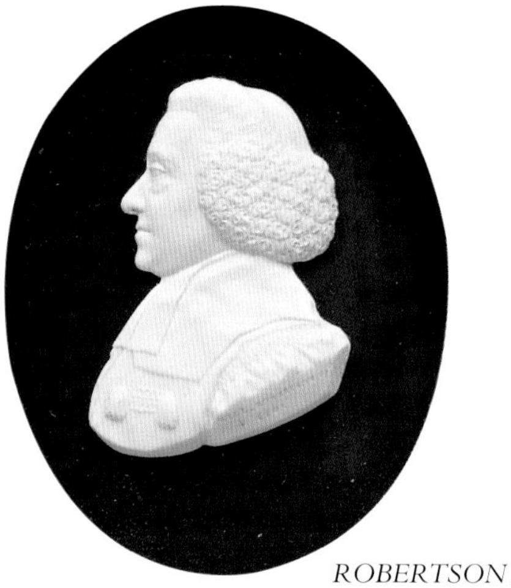

ROBERTSON NPG *5800*

Collections: Christie's, 27 February 1985, lot 30, bt. Leggatt for the NPG.

Engravings: by W. Ridley 1802 (*European Mag.*); C. Picart, from a drawing by John Jackson, 1811 (D. Stewart, *Biographical Memoirs*).

Reference: Gray 1894, no.329.

ICONOGRAPHY

c.1765? Painting attributed to William Millar, half length, in gown and bands. Oxenfoord Castle (cat., 1911, no.98).

c.1772 Painting by Joshua Reynolds,* three-quarter length seated. Scottish NPG (PG 1393; Mannings 2000, no.1528). Exhibited RA 1772(207). Engraved J. Hall, exhibited SA 1772(128); J. Dixon 1772, exhibited SA 1773(97); C. Heath, and many later plates. Copy by H.J. Lintott 1957 with the Gallery of Historians of the Pan American Institute, Mexico City. An 'admirable likeness' according to Stewart, who also remarked in 1796 that it was 'already much faded' (*Biographical Memoirs*, 1811, p.308).

1785 Etching by J. Sayers[?], whole length walking.

1790 Etching by J. Kay, whole-length wearing academic gown and bands (*Kay Portraits* 1842, I, no.xlii).

c.1790 Drawing by Archibald Skirving, bust-length profile, as if copied from a relief medallion. Exhibited *Scottish Portrait Drawings*, Scottish NPG, 1955(171) lent Ian Murray Thomson.

1791 Medallion by James Tassie, see NPG 5800.

1792 Painting by Henry Raeburn,* three-quarter length seated in gown and bands. Edinburgh University, commissioned by the college of Edinburgh. Exhibited NPE 1868(888); *Raeburn*, Edinburgh, London, 1997 (22).

Undated Anon. etching, half-length oval in gown and bands.

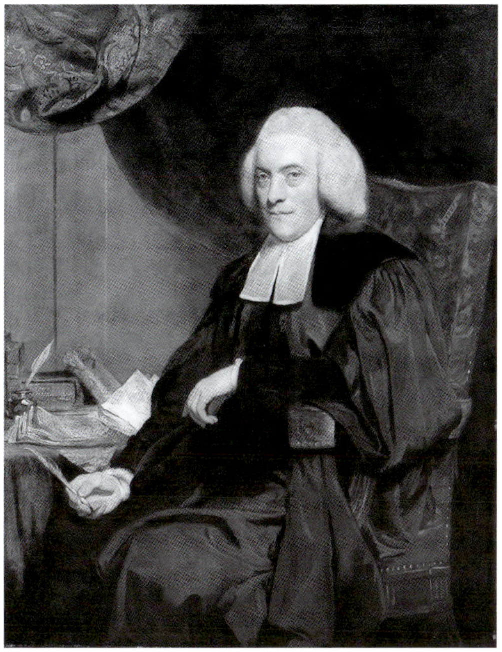

ROBERTSON by Henry Raeburn 1792 (Edinburgh University)

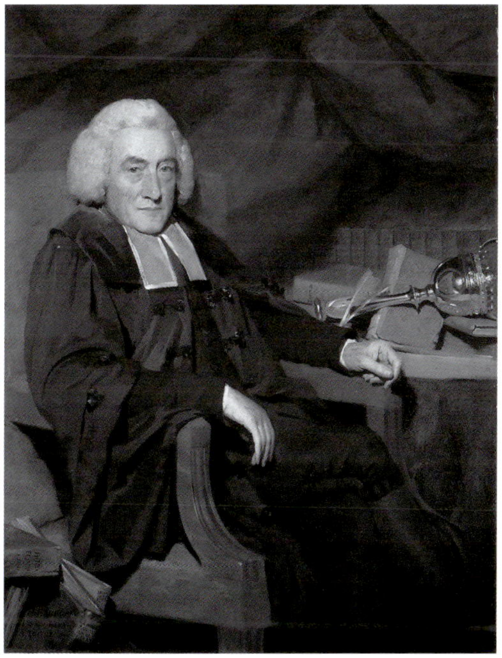

ROBERTSON by Joshua Reynolds c.1772 (Scottish National Portrait Gallery)

DOUBTFUL PORTRAIT

Unattributed ivory exhibited SKM 1865(1441) lent Mrs Littledale (conceivably a Tassie medallion?).

ROBINSON, Elizabeth, see **Montagu**

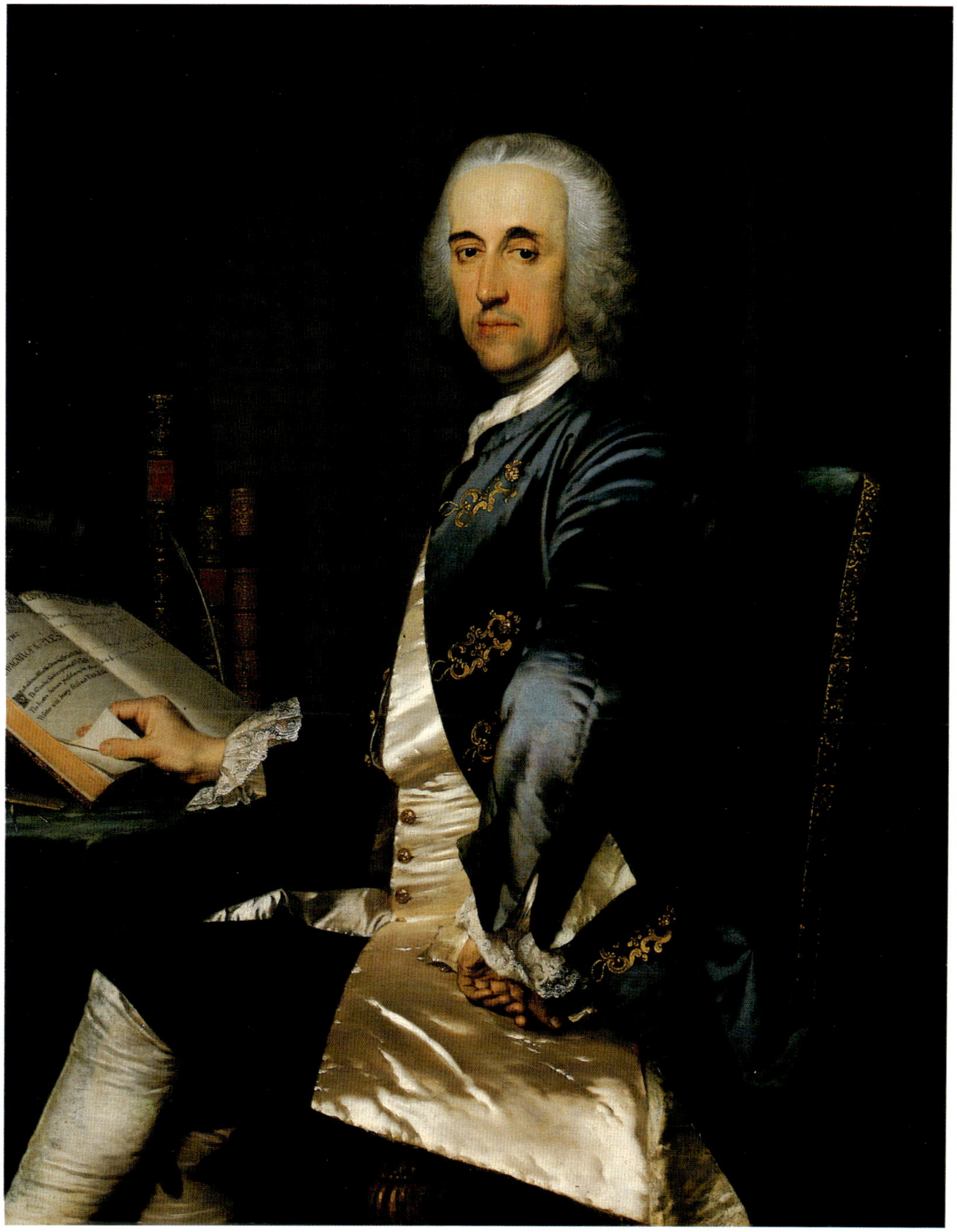

ROBINSON NPG 5275

ROBINSON, Sir Thomas, 1st Bt 1702?-77

'Long Sir Thomas', diplomat and virtuoso, of Rokeby, Yorks.; FRS 1726; MP 1727-34; m. 1728 Elizabeth (d. 1739), dau. of the 3rd Earl of Carlisle and widow of Nicholas, Lord Lechmere; in Italy 1729-30; Bt 1731; an amateur architect, designed the west wing of Castle Howard and rebuilt Rokeby 1725-30; commissioner of excise 1735-42; governor of Barbados 1742-47; master of ceremonies at Ranelagh Gardens; the 'inimitable' cousin of Elizabeth Montagu, accounted 'a man of the town, and a great pest to persons of high rank or in office'.

5275 FRANS VAN DER MIJN 1750

Canvas 125.5 x 100.5 (49½ x 39½) lined; signed lower right: *F. Vander Mijn/ 1750.*; prominent retouchings in the sleeve and forehead; pentimento in his right leg.

Blue eyes, grey powdered wig, wearing a blue satin coat lined with white, white satin waistcoat with gold buttons, black velvet breeches and white silk stockings;[1] on the table, which is covered by a green cloth, are dividers and books entitled *PALLAD/ ARCHI/ VOL/ I* and *SHAKES/ PEAR* and *LADY LECHMERES/ WORKS/ VOL I*; he turns the pages of a manuscript in which may be read *ON THE/COMPAGNIA OF NAPLES/ No boisterous Wind the Growing Spring to blast/ The Glowing Sumer rip'ning all for taste/ The loaden Autumn yielding up her Store/ Winter with hoary frost not Whitn'd Oer*[2]

Collections: Lady Rosamond Cary (d.1985);[3] Leggatt, from whom purchased 1979.

Exhibitions: *English Taste in the 18th century*, RA 1955-56(85) lent Lady Cary; Beningbrough 1981-.

Reference: A. Staring, *Nederlands Kunsthistorisch Jaarboek*, XIX, 1968, p.200(18).

In 1750 Robinson was awarded an annual government pension of £500. NPG 5275 may express his satisfaction, as well as his pretence and learning; richly dressed and elegantly posed, he reads his dead wife's verses,[4] while advertising his appreciation of Palladio and Shakespeare.

1 See Ribeiro 2000, pp.118-19.
2 Lines presumably written by his dead wife, see below.
3 Wife of Sir Robert Cary, Bt (d.1979); her mother was the dau. of the 4th s. of the 4th Baron Rokeby; the 1st Baron Rokeby, cr. 1777, was Bishop Richard Robinson (c.1708-94), the sitter's brother.
4 Vol.I of her works (which appear not to have been printed) stands on the table; he presumably reads from vol.II.

ICONOGRAPHY

[*Caveat*: Sir Thomas ('Short Sir Thomas') Robinson (1695-1770), KB, Baron Grantham 1761; see Kerslake *Early Georgian*, I, pp.103-4]

1729 Painting by William Hogarth, *The Beggars Opera*, Yale Center for British Art (B1981.25.349; illus. *Age of Hogarth*, Tate, 1988, p.80); in which Walpole identified Robinson as the tall man standing on the left wearing a blue coat with gold trimming (Paulson, *Hogarth*, 1971, i, pp.184, 527n23).

1730 Anon. Italian ivory relief, draped bust *all'antica*. Ashmolean Museum, Oxford (WA 1996.384; illus. *Annual Report 1995-96*, pl.vi).

1730 Marble bust by Filippo della Valle,* draped *all'antica*. Westminster Abbey. Possibly carved from a model by Edme Bouchardon; it stands on his monument alongside a bust of his wife, Lady Lechmere, made by Bouchardon in Rome. His Will had stipulated that 'the fine busts made by Bouchardon

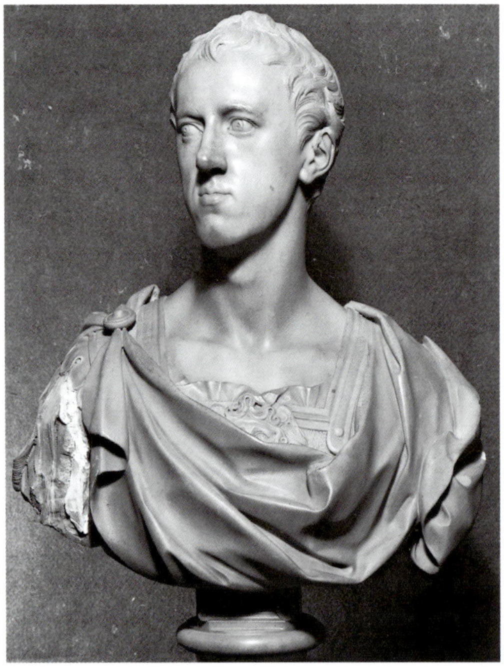

ROBINSON by Filippo della Valle 1730 (Westminster Abbey)

and Philippo della Valle at Rome in [1730] of Lady Lechmere and myself should be placed on his monument (see A. Laing, *Burl. Mag.*, CXLII, 2000, p.755).

1750 Painting by Frans van der Mijn, see NPG 5275.

c.1761 Drawing by Paul Sandby, caricature, whole length with Lord Melcombe. Yale Center for British Art (B1975.4.1385; illus. *Sandby*, New Haven, 1985, p.45).

c.1775 Anon. caricature etching, three-quarter length standing.

DOUBTFUL PORTRAIT

Miniature, manner of Bernard Lens, Christie's, SK, 1 October 1988, lot 58.

ROCHFORD, William Henry Nassau de Zuylestein, 4th Earl of 1717-81

Diplomat; b. St. Osyth Priory, Essex, g.s. of the 1st Earl of Rochford, who had accompanied William III to England; suc. as 4th Earl 1738; envoy to the King of Sardinia, Turin 1749-55; ambassador in Madrid 1763-66 and Paris 1766-68; secretary of state 1768-75; KG 1778 (but not installed); well-intentioned, but untalented.

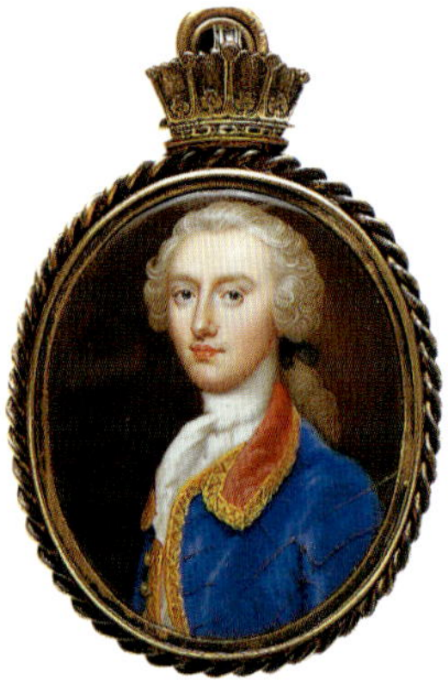

4th Earl of ROCHFORD NPG *5796*

5796 CHRISTIAN FRIEDRICH ZINCKE c.1745-49

Enamel on copper 4.5 x 3.5 (1¾ x 1⅜); the lower right area is cracked and chipped. The gold frame, which bears an Earl's coronet, is engraved verso with the arms of Nassau impaling Younge.[1]

Brown eyes, grey powdered hair, wearing a bright blue coat with a maroon velvet collar and gold braid oak leaves (emblems of the Hanoverian victory at Dettingen in 1743).

Collections: Jeffery Whitehead; his sale, Christie's, 2nd day, 5 August 1915, lot 313; Christie's, 27 March 1985, lot 362, bt. Leggatt for the NPG.

Reference: Walker 1998, no.45.

NPG 5796, painted after the battle of Dettingen in 1743 (see above), seems to show Lord Rochford a little younger than in the portrait engraved after Duprá (see below) of c.1750-55, and was presumably painted in London before his departure for Turin in September 1749.

1 *Sinister; quarterly, 1st az. billettée or, a lion ramp. of the second, for Nassau; 2nd, or, a lion ramp. gu. ducally crowned az., for Dietz; 3rd, gu. a fess ar., for Vianden; 4th gu. two lions pass. guard. in pale or, for Catzenellogen; overall on an escutcheon gu. three zules ar. in chief a label of three points of the last, for Zuyleston. Dexter; vair on a chief gu. three lions ramp. or. for Younge. Supporters - two lions erminois, each ducally crowned az. Motto - spes durat avorum.*

ICONOGRAPHY

Given Lord Rochford's reputation for extravagance (*DNB*), his portraiture is remarkably mean. The portraits now at Brodick Castle, formerly a Hamilton house, were removed from Easton Park in 1919, having descended through Lord Rochford's brother, who m. 1751 the widow of the 5th Duke of Hamilton.

1739 Painting attributed to Thomas Bardwell,* three-quarter length standing in peer's robes. Brodick Castle (E. Miles, *Wal. Soc.*, LIII, 1987, pp.183, 186n13, fig.191y). Previously attributed to Charles Jervas.

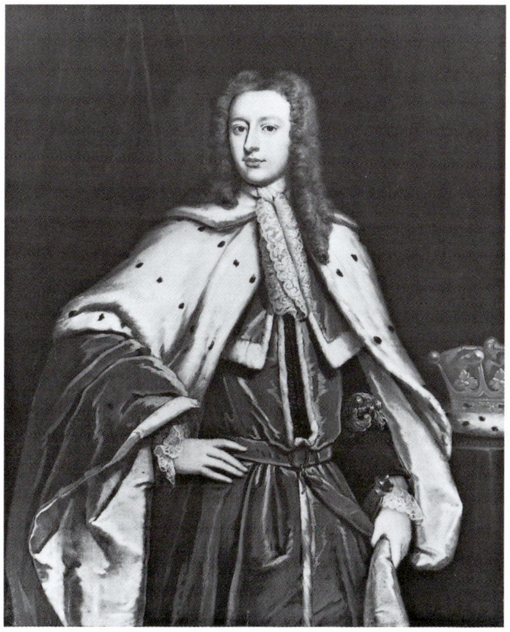

4th Earl of ROCHFORD attributed to Thomas Bardwell 1739 (Brodick Castle, The National Trust for Scotland)

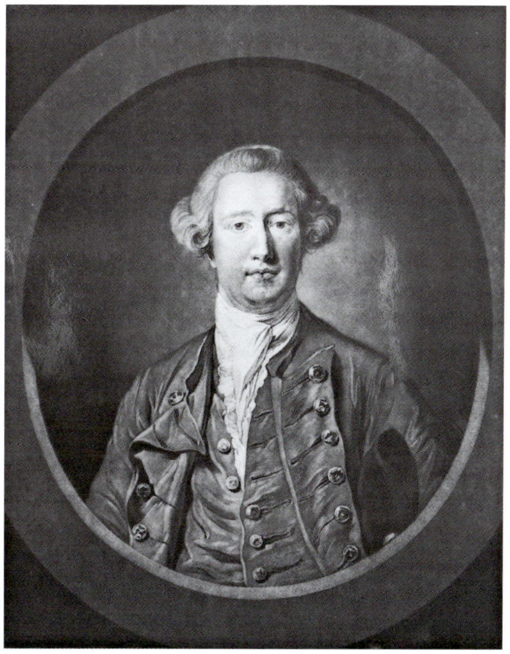

4th Earl of ROCHFORD V. Green 1770 after J-B. Perroneau (NPG D 5829)

1741 Painting by Thomas Bardwell, standing by a dappled horse in the grounds of Easton Park, Suffolk. Brodick Castle (Kirby Talley 1978, no.89). For Easton Park, inherited by Rochford from an uncle in 1741, see J. Harris, *The Artist and the Country House*, 1979, p.319. Bardwell was particularly favoured by Lord Rochford, to whom he dedicated his *Treatise on Painting* 1756.

c.1743 Painting attributed to Thomas Bardwell, half length. Heeze Castle, North Brabant, Netherlands, descended through the Nassau van Zuylesteyn family (Kirby Talley 1978, no.90). The features compare closely with those in the Bardwell portrait of 1741.

c.1745-49 Miniature by C.F. Zincke, see NPG 5796.

c.1750-55 Painting by Domenico Duprá, half length. Engraved R. Houston (illus. *Connoisseur Year Book*, 1958, p.85). Presumably painted in Turin where Duprá was Court Painter and Rochford the British envoy 1749-55.

c.1768 Pastel by J-B. Perronneau, half-length oval, wearing blue suit. Sotheby's, 11 July 2001, lot 210. Engraved V. Green 1770;* a crude derivative plate by J. Lodge 1771 (*London Museum*). Presumably drawn while Lord Rochford was in Paris 1766-68; the composition compares closely with Perronneau's pastel of Abraham van Robais dated 1769 (Louvre).

1770 Painting by P-E. Falconet, exhibited SA 1770(45).

c.1778 Unattributed watercolour, oval half-length profile, in the uniform of Colonel of the West Essex regiment with Garter sash. Private collection, by family descent.

ROCKINGHAM, Charles Watson-Wentworth, 2nd Marquess of 1730-82

Statesman; sty. Lord Higham 1739, Earl of Malton 1746; suc. as 2nd Marquess 1750; FRS 1751; KG 1760; twice briefly prime minister, July 1765 to July 1766 and March 1782 to his death on 1 July 1782; 'having been only known to that public by his passion for horse-races', Walpole commented, 'men could not be cured of their surprise at seeing him First Minister'.

'An amiable and a respectable individual rather than a superior man, nature had not designed him to be the First Minister of a great country' (Sir Nathaniel Wraxall, 1815).

406 after JOSHUA REYNOLDS [1766-68]

Canvas 76 x 62.5 (29¾ x 24½) lined; some small losses (in his left temple, behind his neck and centre left) and the background area is rubbed.

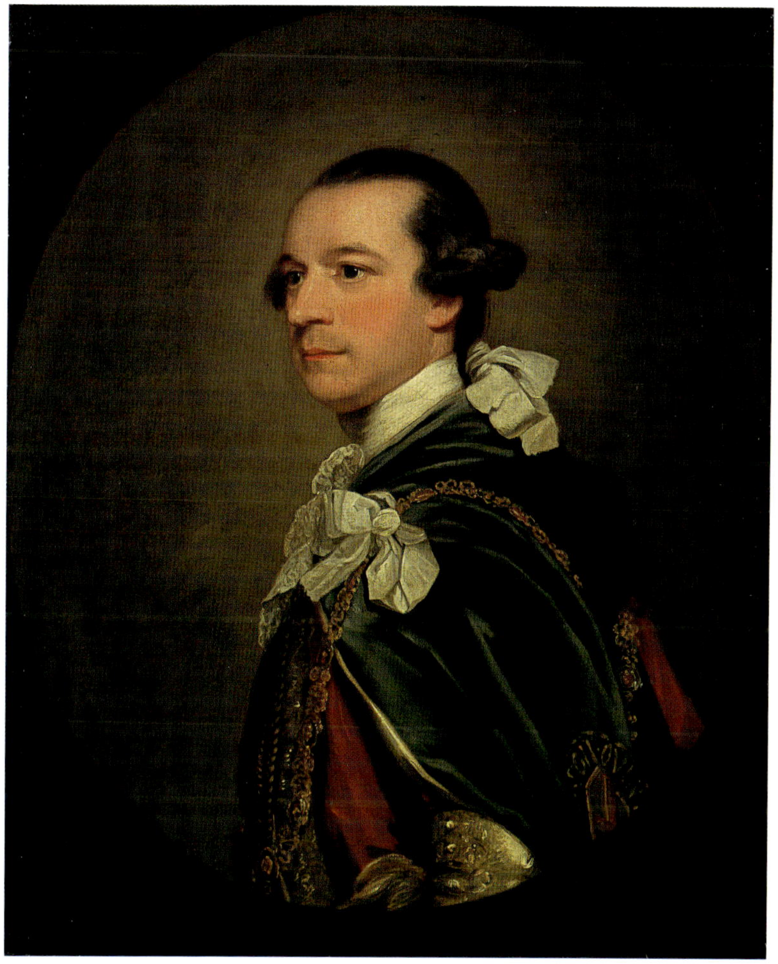

2nd Marquess of ROCKINGHAM NPG 406

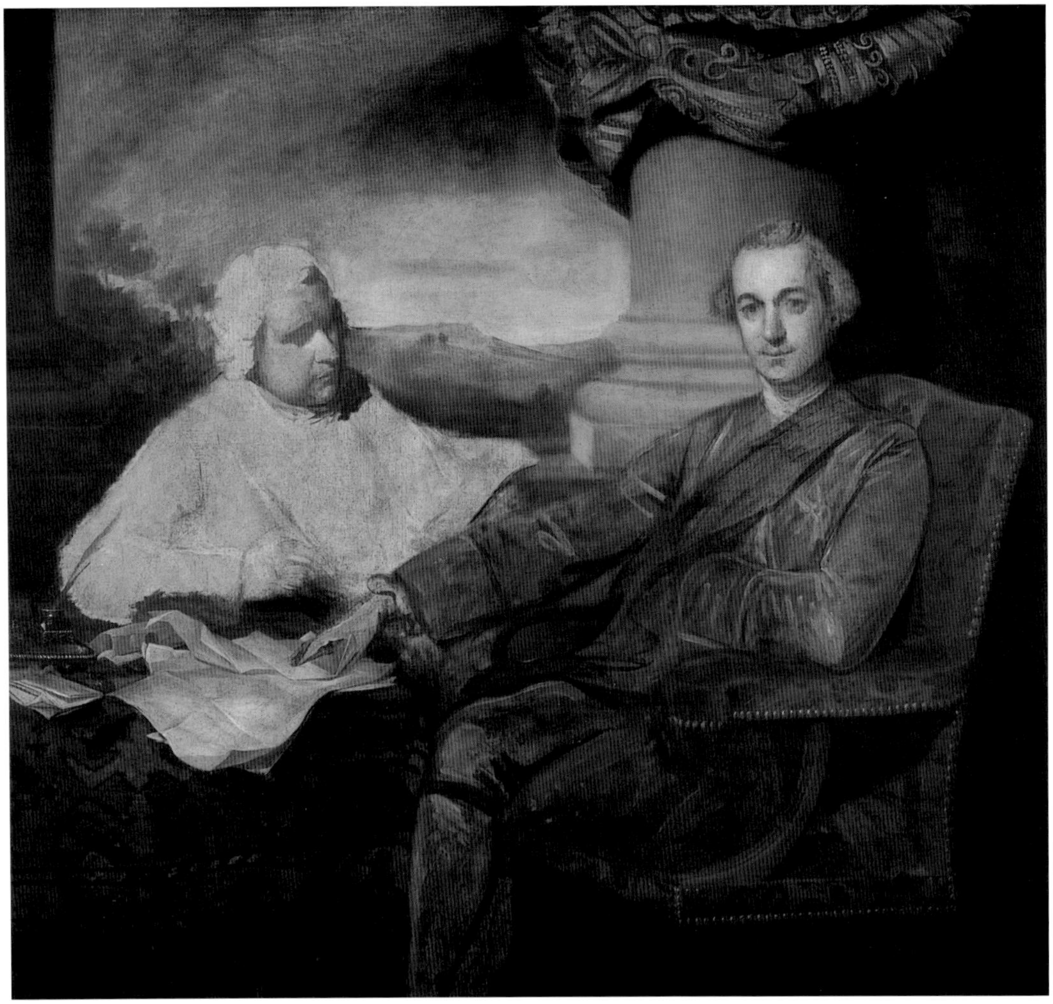

2nd Marquess of ROCKINGHAM (right) with BURKE by Joshua Reynolds 1766-67 (Fitzwilliam Museum, Cambridge)

Blue-grey eyes, lightly-powdered toupée wig, his own dark brown hair hanging behind; wearing the Garter robe; within a painted oval and sometime framed as an oval.

Collections: 'Direct from the studio of Sir Joshua Reynolds to the late Peregrine Wentworth, for whom it was painted; bequeathed to Francis Maude [c.1768-1842] of Hatfield Hall, near Wakefield';[1] his [invalid] son, the Rev Ralph Maude, by whom presented 1875.

Exhibitions: House of Lords 1972-75; *The Dye is now Cast*, NPG Washington, 1975(155); *Bicentennial Center Opening*, Yorktown, Va., 1976.

Reference: Mannings 2000, no.1860a.

A copy from the whole-length portrait by Reynolds now at St Osyth's Priory, painted in 1766-68 and first engraved by Edward Fisher in 1774.[2] Full-length replicas are in the Royal Collection painted in 1781-82,[3] and the York Mansion House painted in 1781-83;[4] a three-quarter length studio version, dating from 1781-83, is at Dalmeny.[5]

Many copies are recorded; whole lengths by Katherine Read 1786 (Jockey Club, Newmarket) and Thomas Phillips 1805 (Doncaster Corporation);[6] half lengths include a pastel attributed to Francis Cotes at Rockingham Castle;[7] in miniature by William Birch in the Gilbert collection dated 1786,[8] and attributed to Samuel Shelley, sold Phillips, 6 July 1987, lot 172. See also Northumberland, Iconography.

1 Letter from Ferguson Branson (acting for the Rev Ralph Maude), 19 March 1875 (NPG archive).
2 Mannings 2000, no.1858.
3 Millar 1969, no.1045; Mannings 2000, no.1859.
4 Mannings 2000, no.1860.
5 *Ibid.*, no.1861.
6 Exhibited Leeds 1868(3170); illus. Hailstone 1869, II, no.151.
7 Others include those at Alnwick and sold Sotheby's, 9 June 1971, lot 159, and 11 June 1996, lot 450; Phillips, 20 November 1990, lot 148, and Christie's, 7 April 1993, lot 105.
8 Illus. Coffin & Hofstetter 2000, no.2; others sold Sotheby's, 1 December 1980, lot 53 dated 1785, and Sotheby's, 22 September 1992, lot 562.

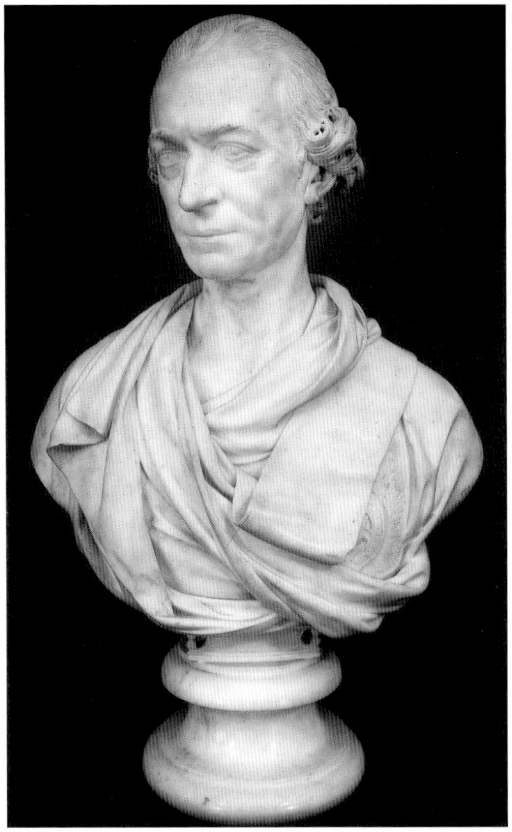

2nd Marquess of ROCKINGHAM by Joseph Nollekens c.1788 (Birmingham Museums and Art Gallery)

ICONOGRAPHY

1738 Painting by Enoch Seeman, half-length painted oval, as Lord Higham. Private collection, by family descent. Possibly the portrait exhibited Leeds 1868(3196) as after Hoppner 'at the age of 16', lent by the Ladies Wentworth Fitzwilliam.

1738 Painting by Charles Phillips, three-quarter length standing holding a shepherd's crook, with his sister Lady Anne Wentworth. Private collection, by family descent.

1752-56 Onyx cameo by Lorenz Natter (illus. *Apollo*, CXX, 1984, p.115, without location).

c.1755 Painting by Benjamin Wilson, three-quarter length standing. Christie's, 11 June 1948, lot 68 (when in poor condition). Painted prior to his investiture as KG in 1760. Engraved R. Houston, and anon. 1782 (half-length oval, with the Garter ribbon and star added; *Universal Mag.*).

1766-67 Unfinished painting by Joshua Reynolds,* three-quarter length seated, with his secretary Edmund Burke. Fitzwilliam Museum, Cambridge (653; Mannings 2000, no.1863). Commemorating Rockingham's short-lived administration of 1765-

66; the composition derived from Van Dyck's group of the *Earl of Strafford and his Secretary* which Rockingham then owned.

1766–68 Painting by Joshua Reynolds, see NPG 406.

1766–68 Painting by Joshua Reynolds, half-length, similar to NPG 406 but showing the Garter collar and star more prominently. Private collection (Mannings 2000, no.1862). Engraved J.K. Sherwin 1797, E. Bocquet 1811.

1776 Painting by Benjamin Killingbeck, a perfunctory whole-length, with his jockey in front of Wentworth Woodhouse. Sotheby's, 6 July 1983, lot 323.

c.1776 Painting by George Romney, commissioned by the Duke of Richmond. Untraced (Romney 1830, pp.135–36)

1779–81 Painting by J.S. Copley,* *The Death of Chatham*, see Comparative Groups.

1782 Etching by J. Sayers, whole length (George 6069).

Posthumous

before 1787 Medallions by James Tassie. Tassie produced three closely-related medallions of Rockingham (Gray 1894, nos.337–39), one wearing a coat with the Garter star and ribbon (examples Victoria and Albert Museum, 414.1318.1885; Scottish NPG, PG 301), another with a cloak, and a third, reduced in size, a simple bust showing only the coat collar (illus. Gray 1894, pl.iii). A Wedgwood medallion of c.1787 (illus. Reilly 1973, p.291) was taken from the first pattern.

Burke thought Tassie 'in his Glass' had made 'the best likeness, I mean the best uncoloured likeness which exists [of Rockingham]' (*Burke Corr.*, V, p.343; 10 July 1787).

Unattributed medallions were with the Earl of Chichester c.1910, and at Sir William Turner's Hospital, Kirkleatham, before 1970 (NPG archive).

1787 Cameo by Edward Burch, exhibited RA 1787(263).

1788 Marble statue by Joseph Nollekens, in peer's robes with Garter collar. Wentworth Woodhouse mausoleum (see *Burke Corr.*, V, p.343). Erected by Lord Fitzwilliam, Rockingham's nephew and heir. Burke recorded that no bust was made of Lord Rockingham during his lifetime, Nollekens's head being 'made from a masque taken from his face after his Death'.

Nollekens produced two patterns of bust using the head from the Wentworth Woodhouse statue and presumably predating it. The more common, with loose classical drapery showing the ribbon and star of the Garter, is represented at Althorp, Dalmeny, Muncaster Castle and Birmingham MAG* (illus. Whinney 1964, pl.123 as c.1784). Another, given to Lord Charlemont in 1788 for his Rockingham Library at Charlemont House, Dublin, belonged to his descendants in London in 1873 (SSB 87/63) and letters from Lady Rockingham to Lord Charlemont described the production of this bust under Lady Rockingham's direction (F. Hardy, *Memoirs of Lord Charlemont*, 1812, II, pp.227–31).

The second type of Nollekens bust, showing different curls on the wig and peer's robes over a Garter ribbon, is represented in the Palace of Westminster (from Wentworth Woodhouse; illus. M. Bond, *Works of Art in the House of Lords*, 1980, p.104) and at Goodwood.

1798 Engraving by W. Ridley, an unsatisfactory bust-length oval, reissued 1805.

Undated Wax bust by Samuel Percy, probably posthumous (illus. *Connoisseur*, XCIV, 1934, p.105).

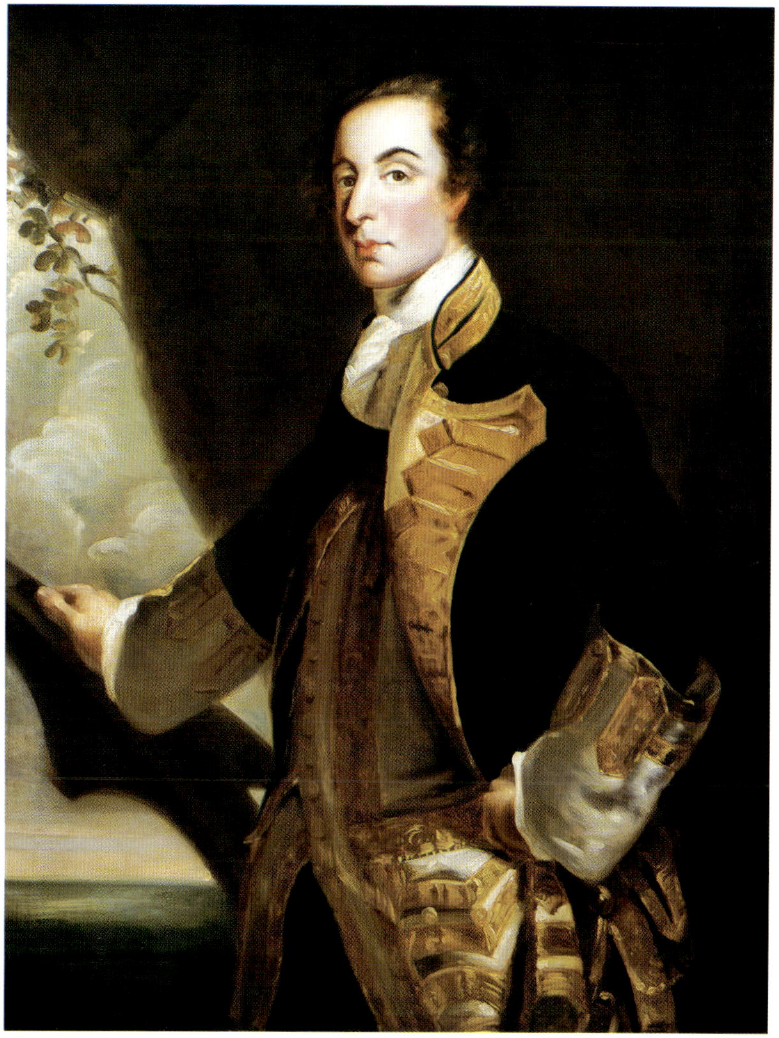

1st Baron RODNEY NPG 1398

RODNEY, George Brydges, 1st Baron 1719–92

Naval officer; governor of Newfoundland 1749–50; MP 1751–54, 1759–74, 1780–82; rear-admiral 1759; commander Leeward Islands 1761–63; Bt 1764; governor Greenwich Hospital 1765–70; commander Jamaica 1771–74; lived in Paris 1775–78 to avoid creditors; admiral 1778; commander Leeward Islands and Barbados 1779, defeating the Spanish at Cape St Vincent 1780, for which he was made KB; captured the island of St Eustatius and defeated the French at Domenica (the Battle of the Saints) 1782; cr. Baron 1782.

'His person was more elegant than seemed to become his rough profession. There was even something that approached to delicacy and effeminacy in his figure; but no man manifested a more temperate and steady courage in action' (Sir Nathaniel Wraxall, 1815).

'in person, Lord Rodney was rather above the ordinary standard. His features were comely and full of expression, his figure elegant and well formed' (G.B. Mundy, 1830).

1398 after JOSHUA REYNOLDS [1756–59]

Canvas 104 x 84 (41 x 33); lined 1976; scattered retouchings.

Brown eyes, dark hair, wearing the uniform of a rear-admiral.

Collections: Purchased from Leggatt 1905.

Exhibitions: *Bicentennial Center Opening*, Yorktown, Va., 1976; *War at Sea*, Yorktown, Va., 1978.

Reference: Mannings 2000, no.1544c.

A crude copy of the original Reynolds at Petworth;[1] the uniform is skimped and the features misleadingly and incompetently softened. The Petworth portrait, first engraved by James Watson in 1762,[2] was possibly begun in 1756 (there is no Reynolds sitter book for that year) and modified in 1759 following his promotion to rear-admiral; he was at sea from August 1759 to February 1761, when he paid Reynolds 10 gn. Another copy was with the Buchholz Gallery, Philadelphia, in 1963.

1 See Mannings 2000, no.1544.
2 Plate reissued with short cuffs 1778, similar to an engraving by W. Dickinson 1780, although each was based upon a different version of the painting, see CS, iv, p.1535.

ICONOGRAPHY

1756–59 Painting by Joshua Reynolds, see NPG 1398.

c.1760 Unattributed painting, half length, dark hair, wearing the uniform of a rear-admiral. National Maritime Museum (BHC2969).

1768 Painting by Hugh Barron, 'A gentleman's family in conversation', exhibited SA 1768(8), see *Wal. Soc.*, XXVII, 1939, p.61.

1780 Painting by Hugh Barron, three-quarter length, in admiral's uniform. Engraved V. Green 1780; reduced versions anon. 1785, J. Chapman 1796, and [R.]Page 1811. Reduced copy sold Christie's, 22 July 1988, lot 217.

c.1780 Drawing by Hugh Barron, bust-length oval, bareheaded in admiral's uniform. Christie's, 12 November 1968, lot 10. Engraved C. Knight 1781; anon. 1815. The head relates closely, in reverse, to that in Barron's three-quarter length portrait, see above.

c.1780 Anon. engraving, bust-length oval, bare-headed, in admiral's uniform; published Fielding & Walker, 1 April 1780; later versions engraved [E.] Harding 1800, and Kirkwood.

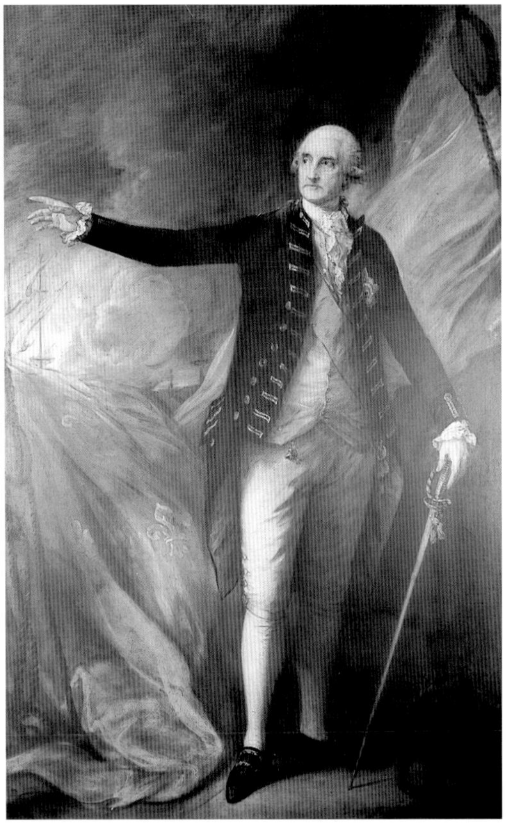

1st Baron RODNEY by Thomas Gainsborough 1783-86 (The Earl of Rosebery)

1780–82 A series of anon. and unsophisticated portraits, in uniform with cocked hat, appeared on medals struck to mark the victories of Cape St Vincent 1780, St Eustatius 1780, and the Battle of the Saints 1782 (Brown 1980, nos.225-26, 229-38, 243-45).

1783–86 Painting by Thomas Gainsborough,* whole length, with the ribbon of the Bath, as the victor in the Battle of the Saints. Dalmeny (Waterhouse 1958, no.583). Engraved G. Dupont 1788. A version attributed to Dupont was in the Groult collection, Bordeaux; a chalk copy in the National Maritime Museum (illus. *Mariner's Mirror*, XXVIII, 1942, f.p.177).

1784 Painting by R.E. Pine, whole-length standing 'in action aboard the *Formidable*, attended by his principal officers [Cranstoun, Dashwood and Douglas]'. Historical Institute, Kingston, Jamaica (illus. Pine 1979, p.18). Exhibited RA 1784(378).

1786 Painting by Gilbert Stuart for Sir John Taylor, Lysson Hall, Jamaica (Whitley 1932, p.59).

1786 Monument by John Bacon sr., whole-length *all'antica*, right arm extended. Spanish Town, Jamaica (illus. *Connoisseur*, LXXVI, 1926, p.37; *Sculpture Journal*, II, 1998, p.48). Commissioned by the Jamaica House of Assembly, Rodney's victory in the Battle of the Saints having saved the island from the French. Whinney (1964, p.168) described it as 'a foolish production in classical dress.'

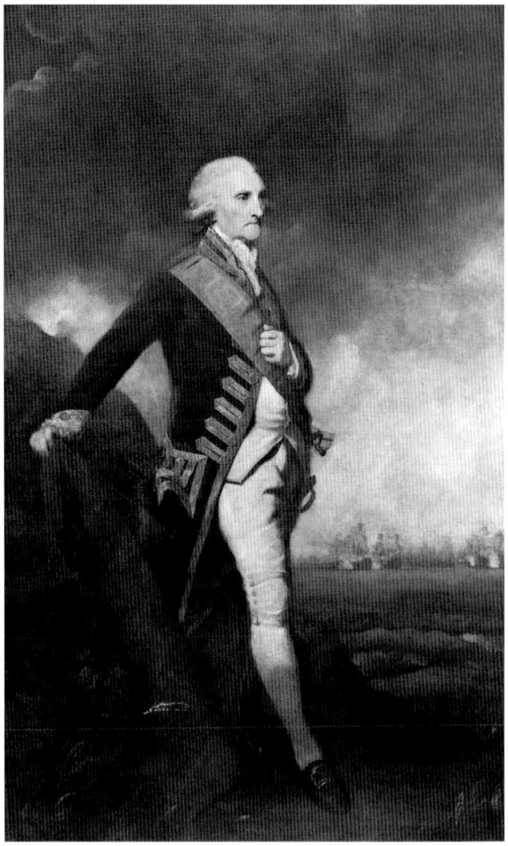

1st Baron RODNEY by Joshua Reynolds 1788 (The Royal Collection)

c.1786? Unattributed bust *all'antica*. Formerly Royal United Services Club, London. The angle of the head similar to the Bacon monument; see also Silvester below.

1788 Bust by Silvester, exhibited RA 1788(656).

1788 Painting by Joshua Reynolds,* whole-length striding, in admiral's full-dress uniform with the ribbon of the Bath. Royal Collection, commissioned by the Prince of Wales (Millar 1969, no.1026; Mannings 2000, no.1545). Exhibited RA 1789(225). Engraved E. Scriven. 'The light falls on each accident of the face, on the sunken eye, the craggy nose, the shrunk grim mouth that disdains false teeth' (D. Piper, *The English Face*, 1957, p.201). Copies by Shepperson 1824 (National Maritime Museum; BHC 2971); G.F. Clarke (formerly with the Admiralty) and Bullock pre-1840 (formerly Royal United Services Club, London); a miniature copy by William Grimaldi in the Royal Collection (Walker 1992, no.823) and a watercolour copy by him is listed (*Grimaldi* 1873, p.49).

1791 Painting by J-L. Mosnier, three-quarter length seated in admiral's full-dress uniform with the ribbon of the Bath. National Maritime Museum (BHC 2970). Exhibited RA 1793(99). Engraved J. Cochran 1833. Copy in the Guildhall AG, London (64; presented c.1793), and a miniature copy by MB 1824 sold Christie's, SK, 24 May 1994, lot 22.

c.1810 A *modello* by John Bacon jr., whole length in contemporary dress. Victoria and Albert Museum (A.20.1931; illus. *Sculpture Journal*, II, 1998, p.54). Convincingly identified by Joan Coutu (*loc. cit.*) as a submission for the St Paul's monument, a commission given to Rossi, see below. A sketch by John Flaxman for a Rodney monument was sold Sotheby's, 26 March 1975, lot 142, perhaps relating to the same commission.

1811 Monument by J.C.F. Rossi, whole-length figure in naval uniform standing between the figures of Fame and History. St Paul's Cathedral (illus. Whinney 1964, pl.161b as 1810-15).

DOUBTFUL PORTRAITS

Paintings by George Beare 1744 (Sotheby's, New York, 14 October 1998, lot 127; previously Christie's, 10 June 1912, lot 96); by Allan Ramsay (Smart 1999, no.447); unattributed (Holburne Museum, Bath; illus. J.D. Spinney, *Rodney*, 1969, f.p.128); unattributed, with William Green, Liverpool, in 1862 (TSB 7/28).

Miniatures sold Christie's, SK, 1 December 1988, lot 42; formerly attributed to Engleheart, Clarke Collection (illus. Williamson 1902, p.26b; *Portrait Miniatures from the Clarke Collection*, Scottish NPG 2001, no.34, as by Abraham Daniel); by Zincke exhibited *Guelph* 1891(1022) lent J. Whitehead.

ROMAINE, William 1714-95

Evangelist, of Huguenot descent; b. Hartlepool; lecturer at St Dunstan's in the West 1749-95; preacher at St George's, Hanover Square, 1750-c.1755 and chaplain to Lady Huntingdon; rector of St Anne's, Blackfriars, 1766-95; a prolific author, his works culminating in *The Life of Faith* 1795; officiated at the marriage of the artist John Russell in 1770.

'his stature was of the middling size, his visage thin and marked ... his eye was quick and keen, yet his aspect benign, and frequently smiling ... he wore a suit of blue cloth always, a grey wig without powder, and generally but a poor one ... his stockings were coarse and blue, as his cloaths' (Thomas Haweis, 1797).

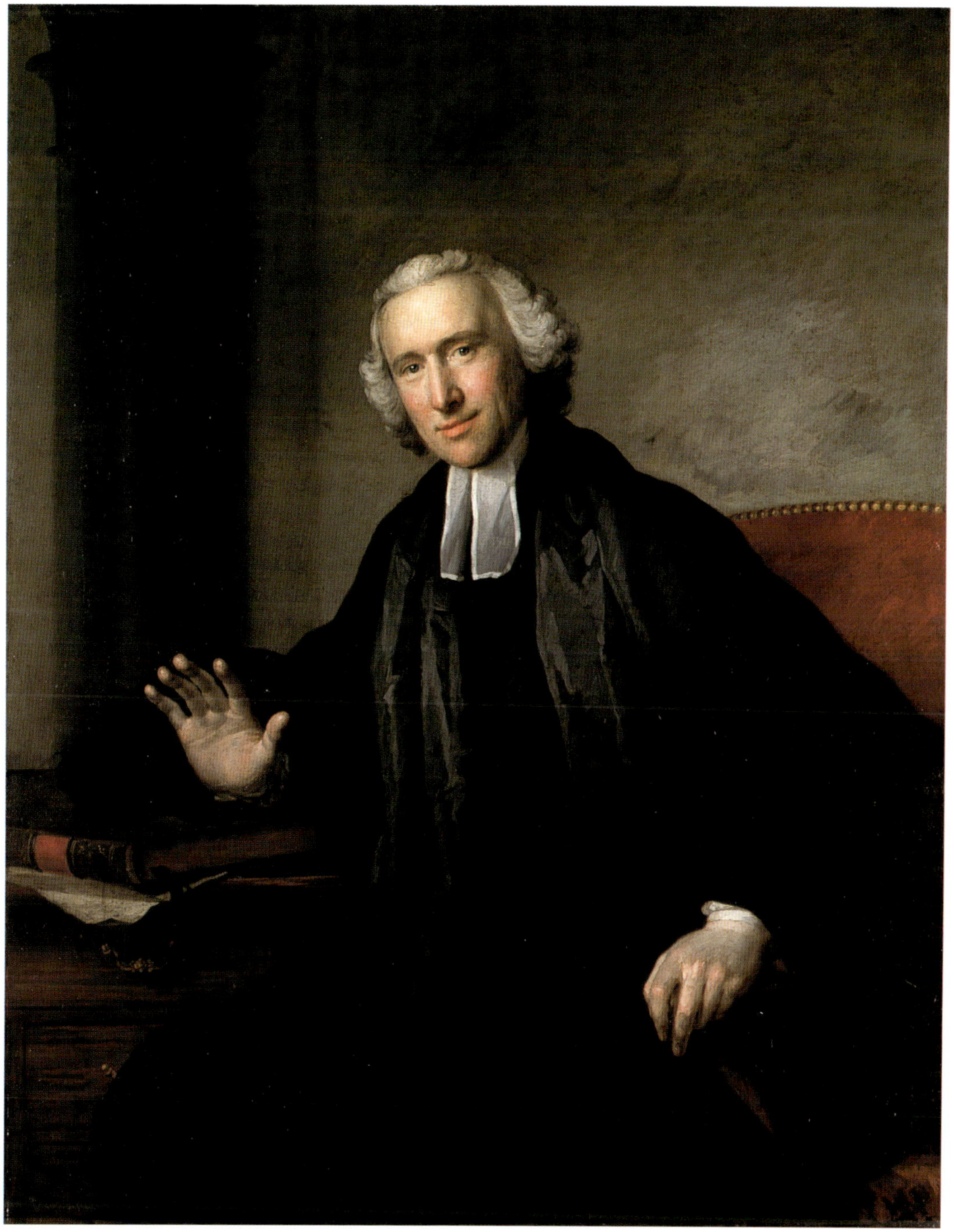

ROMAINE NPG 2036

2036 FRANCIS COTES 1758

Canvas 126.5 x 100.5 (49¾ x 39½) lined; cleaned 1996; pentimento on his right sleeve; signed and dated, bottom left; *FCotes pxt /1758*.

Grey eyes, white powdered wig, wearing black gown and bands, seated in a red chair.

Collections: By descent in the Romaine family to William Colin Romaine, Windsor (d.1924); his sister Gabrielle Enthoven, from whom purchased 1924.

Engravings: R. Houston; C. Corbutt (with added curtain upper right, damasked chair back and IHS on the spine of the book); reduced plate by Corbutt and another of the head alone, pub. John Bowles; anon. (crude half length) 1774.

Exhibitions: NPE 1868(889) lent W.R. Romaine; *Cotes*, Nottingham, 1971(12).

Reference: Johnson 1976, no.87.

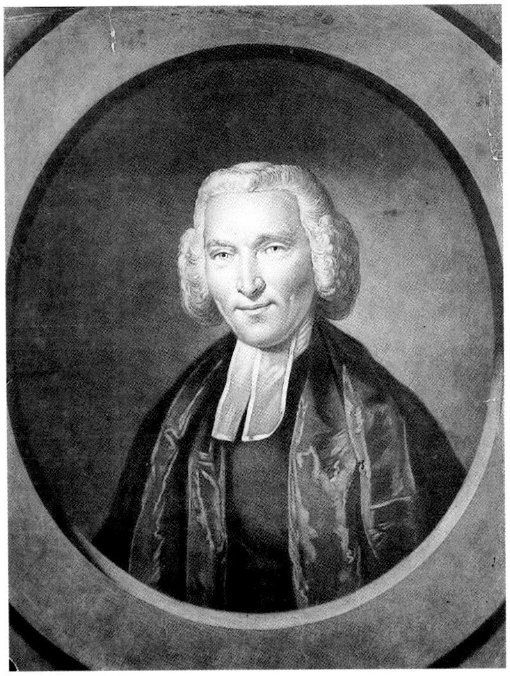

ROMAINE R. Houston after John Russell 1775 (NPG D 13748)

Painted shortly after Romaine had resigned as preacher at St George's Hanover Square, where society had effectively objected to the influx of poorer people anxious to hear his enthusiastic sermons.

ICONOGRAPHY

Apart from the portraits by Cotes and Russell and the bust by John Bacon senior, Romaine's iconography is confined to indifferent engravings, principally for evangelical publications.

1758 Painting by Francis Cotes, see NPG 2036.

c.1760? Anon. engraving, three-quarter length preaching (from Acts XI), lettered ... *Prepare to meet thy God, Amos IV, 12,* pub. R. Sayer, derived from a smaller print of the Rev Thomas Jones (same head and view through window) which appeared as one of four portraits on one plate (of which Romaine after Cotes was another).

1774 Anon. engraving, profile (*Gospel Mag.*).

1775 Painting by John Russell, half-length oval in gown and bands, engraved R. Houston 1775.*

1782 Anon. medal (Brown 1980, no.241).

1784 Anon. engraving, profile (*New Spiritual Mag.*).

c.1785 Miniature attributed to Mrs Avarne, bust-length. Sotheby's, 16 June 1982, lot 215 (one of 13 nonconformist divines). Several bust-length engravings relate to this type: T. Trotter 1786; anon. 1790 (*Christian's Mag.*), 1795 (*Evangelical Mag.*) & 1796; Mackenzie 1807; T. Crabb (19th century).

c.1790 Anon. engraving, half-length preaching.

1795 Two crude engravings pub. G. Thompson, three-quarter length, preaching from Ephesians II, with Romaine arms [*ar. on a fesse sa. three crosses flowered or*] and motto [*I live by the Faith of the Son of God*]: *Drawn from life & Engrav'd B. Reading*, pub. 6 June 1795; *West/ Smith dt.*, with date of death, 26 July 1795, pub. 10 August 1795. Both heads relate to the c.1785 pattern described above.

1795 Engraving by J.W., small profile bust.

Posthumous

1796 Miniature by J. Watts, exhibited RA 1796(594).

1797 Marble bust by John Bacon sr., on monument in St Anne's church, Blackfriars (destroyed 1940). Engraved Rivers 1797, W. Skelton 1797.

1831 Engraving by G.H. Adcock, half length, ultimately derived from the Cotes portrait.

ROMNEY, George 1734-1807

Painter; b. Beckside, Cumbria; exhibited FS 1763-69 and SA 1770-72; travelled in France 1764 with Thomas Greene and in Italy 1773-75; retired to Kendal in 1799, when mentally unstable.

'shy, private, studious and contemplative; conscious of all the disadvantages of a very stinted education; of a habit naturally hypochondriac. With aspen nerves, that every breath could ruffle' (Richard Cumberland, 1807).

'The person of Romney was rather tall, his features were broad and strong, his hair was dark, his eyes indicated much vigour, and still more acuteness of mind. ... His feelings were perilously acute. They made him a man of many frailties, but the primary characteristic of his nature was that true christian charity, which more than compensates for manifold imperfections' (William Hayley, 1809).

2814 SELF PORTRAIT c.1765

Pencil 14.5 x 10.2 (5¾ x 4); cursory figure sketches verso, including a standing woman with child.

Collections: By descent to Miss Elizabeth Romney; her sale, Christie's, 24 May 1894,[1] within lots 135-137 [which comprised drawings and sketches 'Studies for Portraits']; 'acquired from the Great Grand-daughter [*de facto* grand-daughter] of Romney' and sold Sotheby's, 17 January 1898, lot 177, bt. William Ward; M.H. Spielmann by 1904, from whom purchased 1936.

Exhibitions: *Genial Company*, Nottingham, Edinburgh 1987(65); *Romney*, Liverpool, NPG, 2002(9).

Reference: Ward & Roberts 1904, II, p.134 (after no.8).

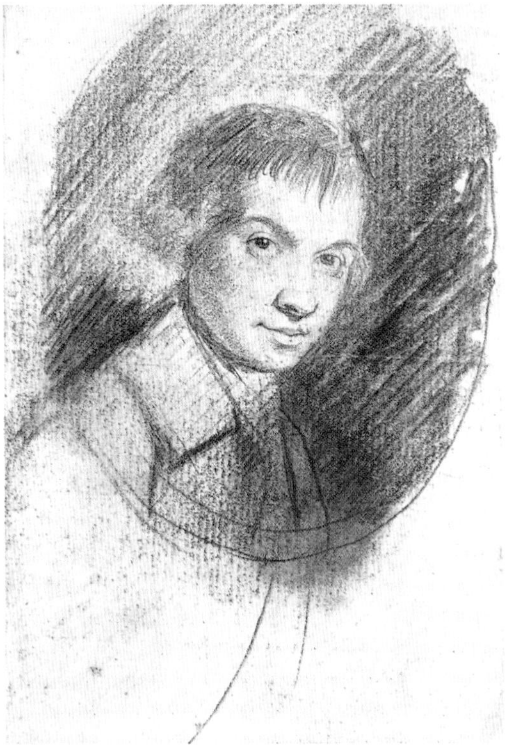

ROMNEY NPG *2814*

Attribution and date are founded on style and provenance, and the identity seems proved both by the likeness and the self-portrait pose. Kidson has associated the figure sketches on the verso with Romney's work c.1764-65.[2]

1 See below, NPG 959, note 1.
2 *Romney* 2002, no.9.

959 SELF PORTRAIT c.1784

Canvas 127 x 101.5 (50 x 40); strip lined 1975.

Brown eyes, greying hair, reddish-brown coat; there are the faintest parallel lines running across the canvas just above elbow level and the incomplete background may hint at a brooding sky.

Collections: Given by the artist to William Hayley, by whom given c.1820 to the Rev John Romney; by descent to Miss Elizabeth Romney;[1] Romney sale Christie's, 24 May 1894, lot 186, bt. Agnew for the NPG.

Engravings: W. Ridley 1803 (small bust-length oval, the drapery finished); C. Watson 1809 (head only); W.T. Fry 1817; T. Wright 1830.

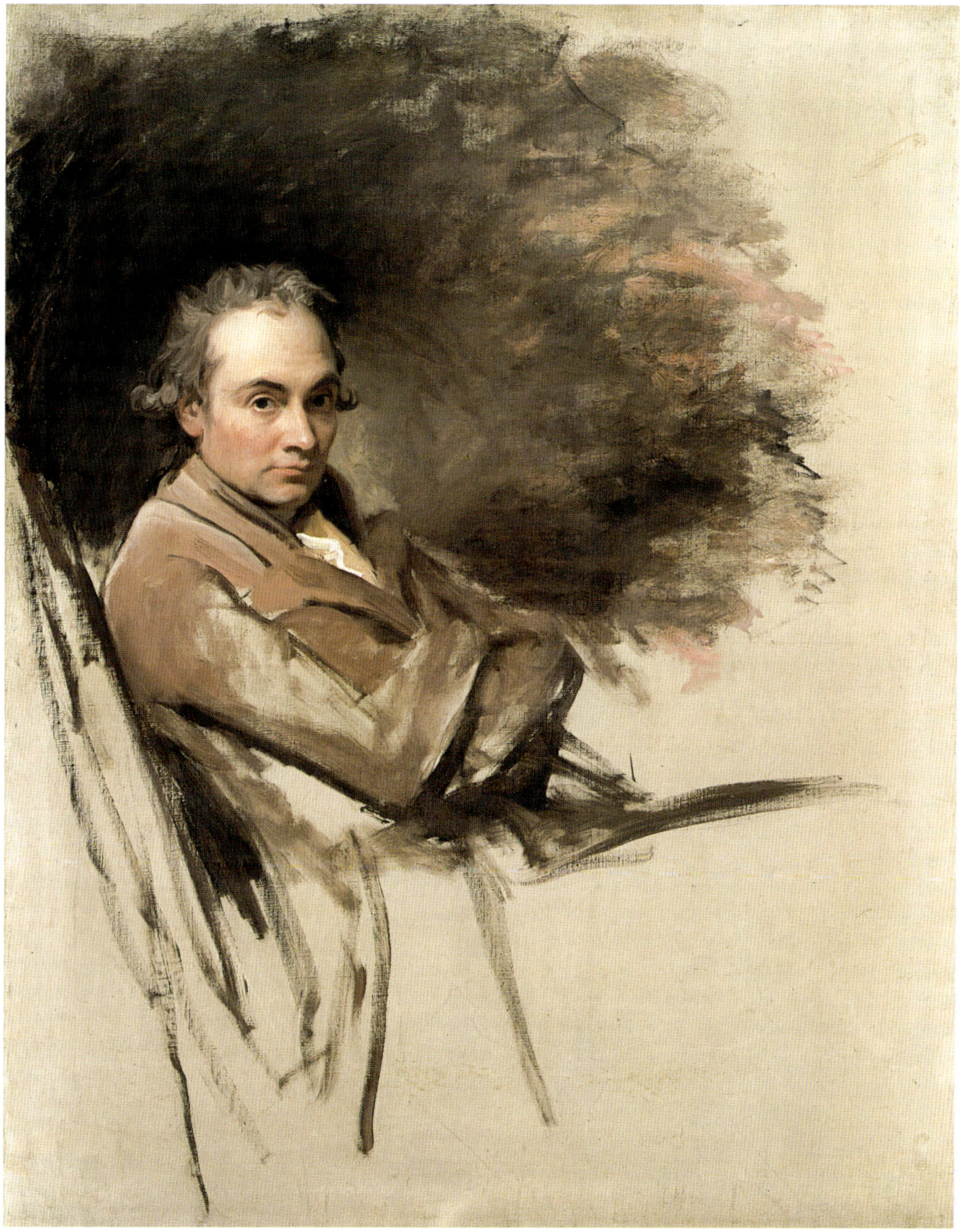

ROMNEY NPG *959*

Exhibitions: BI 1862(193) lent Rev John Romney; NPE 1867(528) lent Rev John Romney; *Romney*, Kenwood, 1961(32); *Hamilton* 1972(3); *Romney*, Leger, 1984(1); *Regency Portraits*, Kenwood, 1986; *Treasures* 1995-96(16); *Romney*, Liverpool, NPG, San Marino, Calif. 2002(106).

Reference: Ward & Roberts 1904, II, p.134, no.1; Chamberlain 1910, pp.121-23, 229, 244, 264, 331.

This remarkable portrait was painted for the artist's friend and subsequent biographer William Hayley. Hayley recalled that it was at his Sussex home, Eartham, in the autumn of 1784 that Romney 'began at my request the striking resemblance of himself in oil, which may be regarded as the best of his portraits ... the frontispiece to this volume [the engraving by Caroline Watson 1809] with the year of his age, forty-nine [i.e. between December 1783 and November 1784]. It well expresses that pensive vivacity, and profusion of ideas, which a spectator might discover in his countenance, whenever he sat absorbed in studious meditation'.[2] Elsewhere he wrote that it showed Romney 'as he appeared in the most active season of his existence'.[3] Twenty years later the artist's son, John Romney, wrote that the portrait was begun in the autumn of 1782 and afterwards given to Hayley 'who did not allow him to finish it, but hurried it off to Eartham without delay'; the portrait was 'extremely like, and full of character' and showed his father at the age of forty eight [i.e. between December 1782 and November 1783].[4] John Romney's account was repeated by Chamberlain in 1910,[5] but neither Hayley nor John Romney was infallible.[6]

Kidson has suggested that, having been started at Eartham and very probably in the autumn of 1784, the portrait was taken back to London where Romney eventually brushed in the torso to satisfy an impatient Hayley;[7] it was not until 11 August 1787 that 'The Picture of Mr Romney was sent to Willm Hayley Esq from the Whit[e] Heart Burrow'.[8]

1 Elizabeth Romney, the last Romney occupant of Whitestock Hall, Ulverton; the house was completed in 1806 by John Romney (1758-1832), the painter's only son, and descended through his son John (1817-75) and grandsons John (b.1851) and Lawrence (b.1857); after monetary difficulties, Whitestock then passed to the grandson's two aunts, Mrs Brooks (d.1889) and Miss Elizabeth Romney (d.1893) who moved from Coniston, the latter bringing with her 'a few good Romney pictures which she had bought from time to time'; the house was finally sold in 1901 (Chamberlain 1910, pp.223, 227-28).

2 Hayley 1809, p.96.

3 *Ibid.*, p.254.

4 Romney 1830, pp.192-93; he also addressed a lamentable sonnet 'To my Father's portrait, painted by himself'.

5 Chamberlain 1910, p.123; he considered John Romney usually more accurate than Hayley.

6 Or generous, e.g. 'Mr Hayley's friendship [with Romney] was grounded on selfishness, and the means, by which he maintained it was flattery ... whatever errors [the artist] may have committed, they were mainly owing to the counsel, or instigation of Mr Hayley' (Romney 1830, p.139).

7 A. Kidson in *Romney* 2002, no.106.

8 The Romney ledger (NPG). On 29 August 1787 *The World* alleged that Romney was with Mr Hayley at Eartham, where 'he is painting, what for some time and place will be the more value, a head of himself' – perhaps a garbled reference to the delivery of NPG 959.

1881 MARY BARRET 1798

Watercolour on ivory 7.2 x 5.8 (2⅞ x 2¼)[1]

Brown eyes, white hair, dark grey coat with white neckcloth.

Collections: Miss Elizabeth Romney;[2] Romney sale Christie's, 24 May 1894, lot 140 ('Portrait of G. Romney, in 1798, by M. Barrett'); Ernest E. Leggatt, by whom presented 1920.

Exhibition: *Cumbrian Characters*, Kendal, 1968(30).

Reference: Walker 1998, no.59.

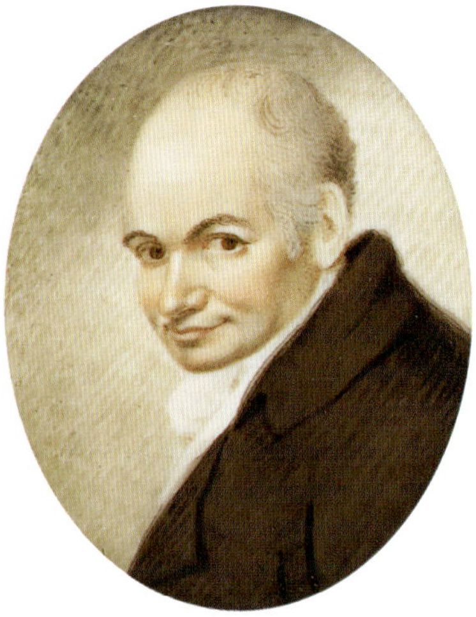

ROMNEY NPG *1881*

The artist was studying under Romney in 1797,[3] and the date of 1798 assigned to NPG 1881 at the Romney sale is entirely appropriate. In 1798 Romney was suffering from 'lassitude of body, and restlessness of mind,' but in May he was 'very chearfully amused by sitting to a lady of the house [of the late Jeremiah Meyer], for his portrait; it was an ex tempore production; a rapid sketch; but a very striking resemblance'.[4] This may refer to NPG 1881, or to another Barret portrait.

1 Old backing inscribed in Ernest Leggatt's hand: *George Romney in 1798 Painted by Miss M Barrett a pupil of Romneys Purchased May 24 1894 at the sale of the late Miss Romney of Whitestock Hall Ulverstone.*
2 See NPG 959, note 1.
3 She was listed 'At Mr Romney's', RA cat., 1797.
4 Hayley 1809, p.281.

ICONOGRAPHY

Self Portraits

1756–57 Painting, sent to his wife from York. 'It was hard and laboured, and had all the appearance of a first essay' (Romney 1830, p.17).

c.1758 Painting, *A Boating Party on Lake Windermere*, Timothy Clode Collection (illus. *Romney* 2002, no.1) including the painter second from the left, whole length wearing a blue suit.

c.1765 Drawing see NPG 2814.

c.1770–75? Painting, half-length with wig and cloak. Romney sale, 24 May 1894, lot 183, as aged 'about 35', but probably older (Ward & Roberts 1904, II, p.134, no.4). Engraved W.T. Fry 1822 after a drawing made by John Jackson in 1817 'from an original Picture by himself in the Possession of his Son, the Revd John Romney'.

c.1778 Watercolour, bust length with hat. Drawn at Eartham (Ward & Roberts 1904, II, p.134, no.3). Engraved C. Watson 1809 (Hayley 1809, pp.86, f.p.332).

c.1778 Painting, half length, head on right hand. Private collection (illus. *Greene* 1986, cover). Unfinished; the head by Romney, the remainder by Michael Keeling.

c.1784 Painting, see NPG 959.

c.1785? Painting, vigorous bust-length sketch. Christie's, 8 June 1995, lot 28. Inscribed verso: *Given to his pupil James Rawlinson.*

1795? Painting,* half length, with his own thin white hair. Metropolitan Museum of Art, New York (15.30.37; Ward & Roberts 1904, II, p.134, no.2). Probably the 'head of himself ... not entirely finished, without spectacles, though he had been in the habit of using glasses for many years' painted in 1795 (Romney 1830, p.239). A version, in which he looks much younger, with Spink 1921.

1796 Two paintings, *Flaxman modelling the bust of Hayley* (Yale Center for British Art; B1981.25.538) and *The Four Friends* (Abbot Hall AG, Kendal), each contain an insignificant head of the artist: 'from an excess of modesty, or from capricious indolence, [Romney] has so slighted each portrait of himself, in the two pictures ... that both may be considered rather as caricatures, than fair likenesses of the painter' (Hayley 1809, p.254). A version of the first, but without Romney's head, is NPG 101 (see Walker *Regency*, I, pp.186–87, II, pl.435).

c.1796 Drawing, bust-length (from a sketchbook in the Huntington Art Collections, San Marino, Calif.; illus *Romney* 2002, no.146). Alex Kidson has plausibly suggested that this 'head of an elderly man with pinched cheeks and staring eyes' may be a self-portrait.

1799 Crayons, wearing spectacles, completed on 6 March. Formerly William Hayley (Hayley 1809, pp.293–94, f.p.332; Ward & Roberts 1904, II, p.134, under no.3). Engraved C. Watson 1809. Painted at Eartham. Copied by Thomas Hayley, 'with such variations, as added to the force of the resemblance; for Romney, by representing himself in a very placid humour, had injured the intelligent animation of his own features' (W. Hayley, *Memoirs*, 1823, II, pp.451–52).

Portraits by other Artists

c.1790? Silhouette by Daniel Walker, profile, markedly receding hair with pig-tail. Miss Walker, Tooting, 1864 (tracing by Scharf in NPG copy of Hayley 1809).

c.1795–97 Plaster medallion by Thomas Hayley, 'in the decline of life'. Chichester RO (illus. Cross 2000, p.184; see Hayley 1809, pp.255, 269 and *Memoirs*, 1823, II, p.357). Engraved C. Watson 1809 from a drawing by Maria Denman (for Hayley 1809).

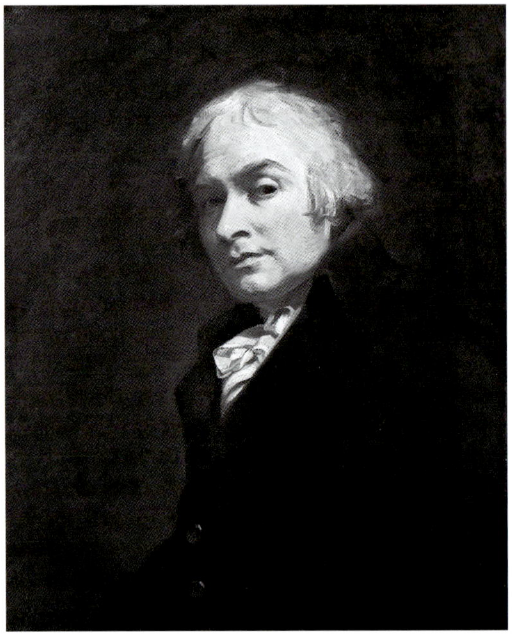

ROMNEY Self portrait 1795? (Metropolitan Museum of Art, New York)

1798 Miniature by Mary Barret, see NPG 1881.

1799 Painting by M.A. Shee, three-quarter length standing, exhibited RA 1799(271). Engraved W. Bond 1810; W.C. Edwards (head only). In 1798 Romney had sold to Shee the lease of his house in Cavendish Square (where he had succeeded Francis Cotes; Hayley 1809, p.290); see also Groups NPG 1106.

A bust of Romney by S.N. Babb 1909 is on the south front Victoria and Albert Museum.

DOUBTFUL PORTRAITS

Doubtful self portraits include those in the Uffizi (774A) and the Louvre (RF1095); the former remains unattributed, the latter is perhaps by George Willison.

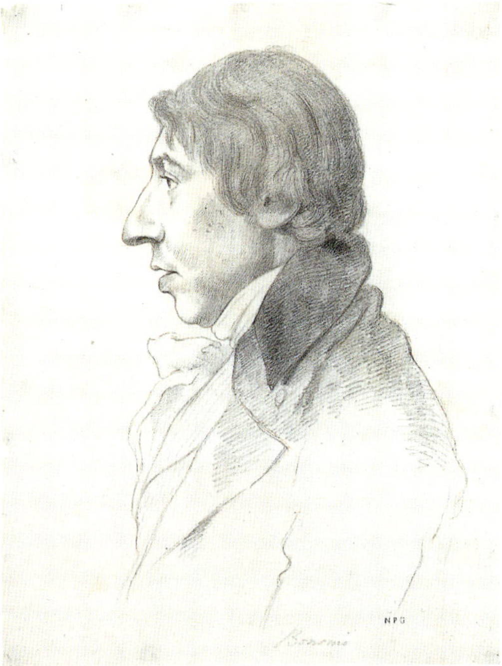

ROSSI NPG *3089(2)*

ROSSI, John Charles Felix 1762–1839

Sculptor; b. Nottingham where his Sienese father practised as a doctor; RA schools 1781; in Rome 1785–88; ARA 1798, RA 1802; exhibited RA 1782–1834; sculptor to the Prince of Wales 1797 and sculptor in ordinary to William IV 1830.

3089(2) WILLIAM DANIELL after GEORGE DANCE [1798]

Pencil with the outlines drawn over in red crayon, on paper 25.5 x 20 (10 x 7⅞) laid down on paper; small damage in the cheek, irregular perforations round the edges and slight staining; inscribed in pencil bottom centre: Bonomi, with the NPG stamp lower right.

Engraving: W. Daniell (*Dance Plates*).

Collections, Reference: see Appendix II.

Dance's original drawing, dated 3 September 1798, is in the Royal Academy. NPG 3089(2) has previously been listed as 'Bonomi',[1] according to the pencil inscription.[2]

1 For example, NPG, *Complete Illus. Cat.*, 1981, p.685.
2 The correct identification made by Kate Jaram in 2002.

ICONOGRAPHY

1798 Drawing by George Dance, see NPG 3089(2)
1824 Painting by W.B. Brown, exhibited RA 1824(271).
1824 Bust by Richard Williams, exhibited RA 1824(1022).
1830 Bust by F.O. Rossi, exhibited RA 1830(1269).
1838 Bust by F.O. Rossi, exhibited RA 1838(1321).

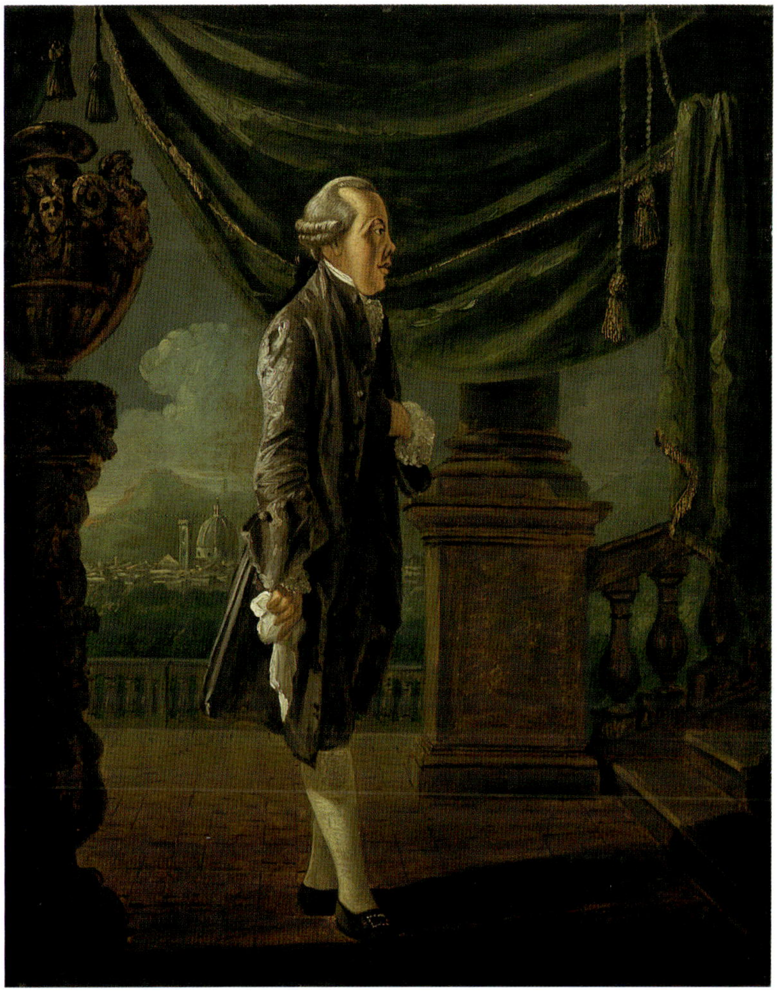

3rd Duke of ROXBURGHE NPG *724*

ROXBURGHE, John Ker, 3rd Duke of 1740–1804

Bibliophile; sty. Marquess of Bowmont before he suc. as 3rd Duke 1755; travelled in Europe 1760–62, when his courtship of Christiana, dau. of the Duke of Mecklenburg-Strelitz, ended as her sister Charlotte became Queen of England; with his 'lofty presence and felicitous address' he remained a friend of the King, being made KT 1768, groom of the bedchamber 1767 and KG 1801, but he preferred retirement, being an 'unwearied reader of romance'; FSA 1797; the sale of his celebrated library lasted forty-five days (18 May–8 July 1812), during which The Roxburghe Club, devoted to 'the common love of rare and curious volumes', was founded.

724 THOMAS PATCH 1761

Canvas 65 x 52 (25½ x 20½) lined and heavily ironed; patches of discoloured varnish, particularly behind his back.

Dark eyes, powdered wig, wearing a grey suit, white silk stockings and black shoes with diamond buckles; a green curtain above him; on the left an exotic column with masks and sphinx, the urn above with a goat's head; distant view of Florence with the Duomo and Campanile.

Collections: Presented by Sir Richard Wallace 1884.

Exhibition: *Italy and the Grand Tour*, Norwich, 1958(94).

Reference: *Patch* 1940, no.12.

In the course of his European travels Roxburghe spent at least four months, from August to November 1761, in Florence where he was well received by Horace Mann and painted three times by Mann's protégé, Thomas Patch. NPG 724 is a loosely brushed caricature, in which, as Ribeiro has observed, Roxburghe stands fashionably posed, showing off a well-turned leg and a fine lace ruffle[1] – but the setting is perfunctory (and the urn not centred on the pedestal). Roxburghe's remarkably retroussé nose, as drawn at least three times by Patch, became quite Roman in later portraits.

1 Ribeiro 2000, p.122.

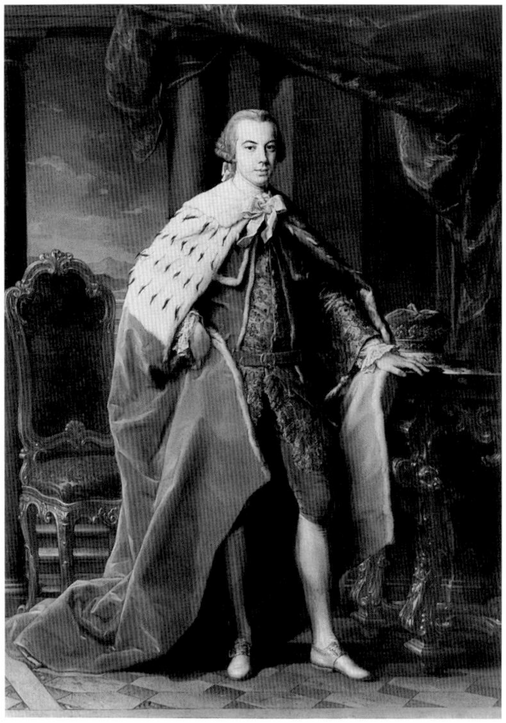

3rd Duke of ROXBURGHE by Pompeo Batoni 1761-62 (Private Scottish Collection)

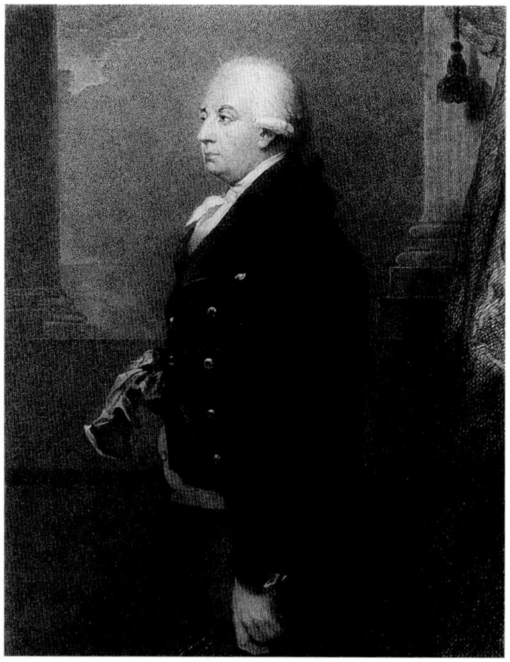

3rd Duke of ROXBURGHE E.C. Wagstaff after William Hamilton c.1800? (NPG D 13810)

ICONOGRAPHY

c.1745 Painting by 'Metyard', half-length painted oval as a child. Floors Castle.

1747 Painting by Thomas Hudson as a boy, whole length, a gun over his shoulder. Lord Mostyn (illus. *Burl. Mag.*, XC, 1948, p.206; Steegman, I, p.194, no.45, pl.35d).

1752 Painting by Thomas Hudson, whole-length seated in a park, with his brother, the Hon Robert Ker. Sotheby's, New York, 28 October 1988, lot 10 (*Hudson*, Kenwood, 1977 fig.3).

In Italy 1760-62

1761 Painting by Thomas Patch, whole-length standing, in Patch's studio with Tabitha Mendes behind him. Formerly at Holland House (*Patch* 1940, no.4; S. Sitwell, *Conversation Pieces*, 1936, pl.89). Miss Mendes, according to Nathaniel Dance, was 'a young Lady of about 4 feet & a half high, and in every respect, with regards to person, one of the ugliest figures I ever saw', but it was alleged in Florence that Roxburghe was to propose to her (Ingamells 1997, p.654), after his disappointing romance in Hanover (see biography above).

1761 Painting by Thomas Patch, *The Punch Party,* or *The Golden Asses*, includes Roxburghe standing centre left, receiving a letter from Sir Horace Mann; on the back wall, in the centre, hangs a picture of Roxburghe (as a monkey?) proposing to Tabitha Mendes (see above). Chatsworth (*Patch* 1940, no.5). A version in the Lewis Walpole Library, Farmington (illus. *Grand Tour*, Tate Gallery, 1996, no.41; see Patch).

Roxburghe has also been identified as the elegant whole-length seated figure with a riding crop in Patch's *Musical Party* of 1774 at Floors Castle (see Patch).

1761 Painting by Thomas Patch, see NPG 724.

1761-62 Painting by Pompeo Batoni,* whole-length standing in peer's robes. Scottish NPG at Floors Castle (Clark 1985, no.239).

Later Years

1788 Painting by John Hoppner, exhibited RA 1788(236). A standing three-quarter-length, in dark blue coat and buff trousers, without insignia, at Floors Castle, has been identified as the 3rd Duke of Roxburghe by Hoppner, but may show the 4th Duke.

1789 Painting by William Beechey, half length, the star of the Thistle just visible under his lapel. Engraved anon. 1816 (Clarke, *Repertorium Bibliographicum*, without names of engraver or artist); W. Say 1819 (Ames, *Typographical Antiquities*, front.). Roxburghe paid Beechey 10 gn. in 1789 (Chamberlain 1910, p.222). A comparable half length, wearing a brown coat with a red collar and the star of the Thistle, offered to the NPG by G.H. Parker in 1868 as Roxburghe by Beechey (TSB 13/66).

1790-95 Painting attributed to William Beechey, half length, white haired wearing a dark blue coat with gold trim and red collar, with the ribbon and star of the Thistle. Floors Castle.

c.1800? Painting by William Hamilton, three-quarter length standing, without insignia, engraved as Roxburghe by E.C. Wagstaff 1832.*

DOUBTFUL PORTRAIT

Unattributed painting, Scottish NPG (PG 288).

RUSSELL, Lord John, see **BEDFORD**

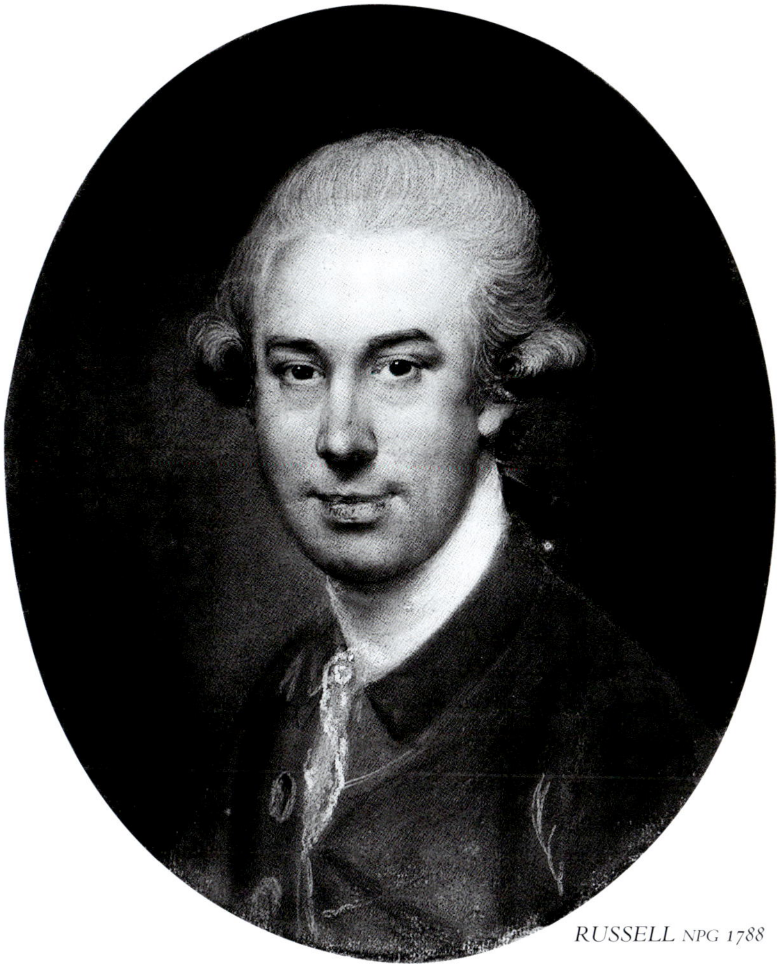

RUSSELL NPG 1788

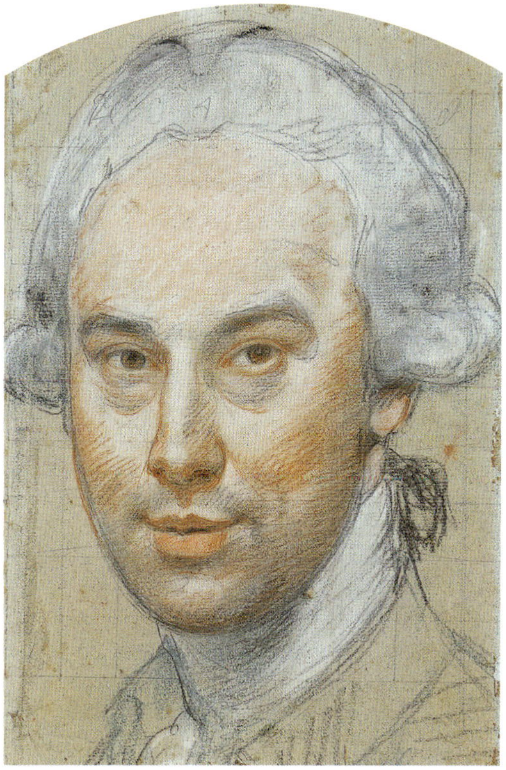

RUSSELL NPG 3907

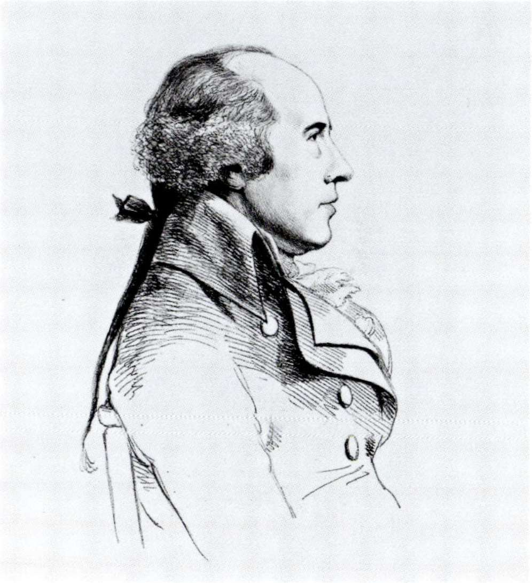

RUSSELL W. Daniell after George Dance 1793 (NPG D 12098)

RUSSELL, John 1745-1806

Pastellist, b. Guildford; dramatically converted to Methodism 1764; studied under Francis Cotes c.1765-67 and at the RA schools 1770; exhibited SA 1768 and RA 1769-1806; published *Elements of Painting in Crayons* 1772 (revised 1777); ARA 1772, RA 1788; Crayon Painter to the King 1790; he made a study of the surface of the moon, completing a lunar relief map in 1795 (Museum of the History of Science, Oxford).

1788 SELF PORTRAIT c.1780

Pastel 30.5 x 25.5 (12 x 10); the surface rubbed.

Collections: By descent to the Misses E.A. & B.M. Russell, Guildford,[1] from whom purchased 1917; stolen in 1960.

Exhibition: *Russell*, Imperial Institute, South Kensington, 1894(79).

Although NPG 1788 was described by the vendors as being in 'absolutely perfect condition', Milner found it 'not nearly so fine as I had imagined'.[2] Dated according to the sitter's apparent age; he appears appreciably younger than in the self portrait of 1794 (see below). Previously and wrongly associated with a so-called miniature of Russell traditionally attributed to Francis Cotes,[3] NPG 1788 relates directly to the elaborate study NPG 3907, see below.

1 Born, respectively, in 1842 and 1844, they were described in 1894 as 'the only surviving children of Samuel, seventh child of William Russell, youngest brother of the artist' (Williamson 1894, p.23 and f.p.172). NPG 1788 had on backboard: *Portrait of John Russell R.A./ by Himself// E.A. & B.M. Russell/ Aldersey Place/ Guildford.*

2 J.D. Milner, letters of 26 March and 12 June 1917 (NPG archive). NPG 1788 was illus. *MA*, XV, 1892, p.75, and Williamson 1894, p.18.

3 Illus. as such Williamson 1894, p.8 (then belonging to the Misses E.A. & B.M. Russell); an old photograph of NPG 3907 in the *Russell Album* is captioned 'after the miniature by Coates'; perhaps Samuel Cotes was intended.

3907 SELF PORTRAIT c.1780

Black, white and red chalk, with some pencil, on grey paper 33.5 x 22.5 (13¼ x 8¾); an area 25.5 x 20.5 (10 x 8) squared up in pencil in 1 in. squares, numbered across the top and down the left-hand side; some fading, staining and spotting.

Brown eyes.

Collections: By descent to Miss E.M.F. Wood,[1] by whom bequeathed 1954.

Exhibition: *British Self Portraits*, Arts Council, 1962(52).

A squared-up study, relating directly to the oval pastel self portrait NPG 1788, although slightly larger.

1 Sister-in-law of Herbert Russell, the artist's great-grandson.

ICONOGRAPHY

c.1760 Drawings by the youthful John Russell, a half-length profile and a crude half length dated 1760. Sotheby's, 16 July 1992, lot 25.

c.1780 See NPG 1788 and NPG 3907.

1793 Drawing by George Dance, profile bust, dated 13 April 1793. Royal Academy. Engraved W. Daniell* (*Dance Plates*); a tracing by Daniell in the Yale Center for British Art (B1975.4.1132).

1794 Pastel by John Russell, half length, a porte-crayon in his hand. Private collection (illus. Williamson 1894, f.p.62; I.C. Rhodes, *John Russell*, 1986, cover).

1795 Painting by Henry Singleton,* *President and Members of the Royal Academy*, see Comparative Groups.

DOUBTFUL PORTRAITS

See Unidentified Portraits NPG 3160. Pastels unconvincingly identified as self portraits include: sold Foster's, 22 May 1912, lot 102 dated 1774 (illus. *Connoisseur*, LXV, 1923, p.113); sold Christie's, 21 July 1939, lot 5; exhibited *Many Faces*, Spink, 1997(8), and dated 1791 (illus. Williamson 1894, pp.78, 168).

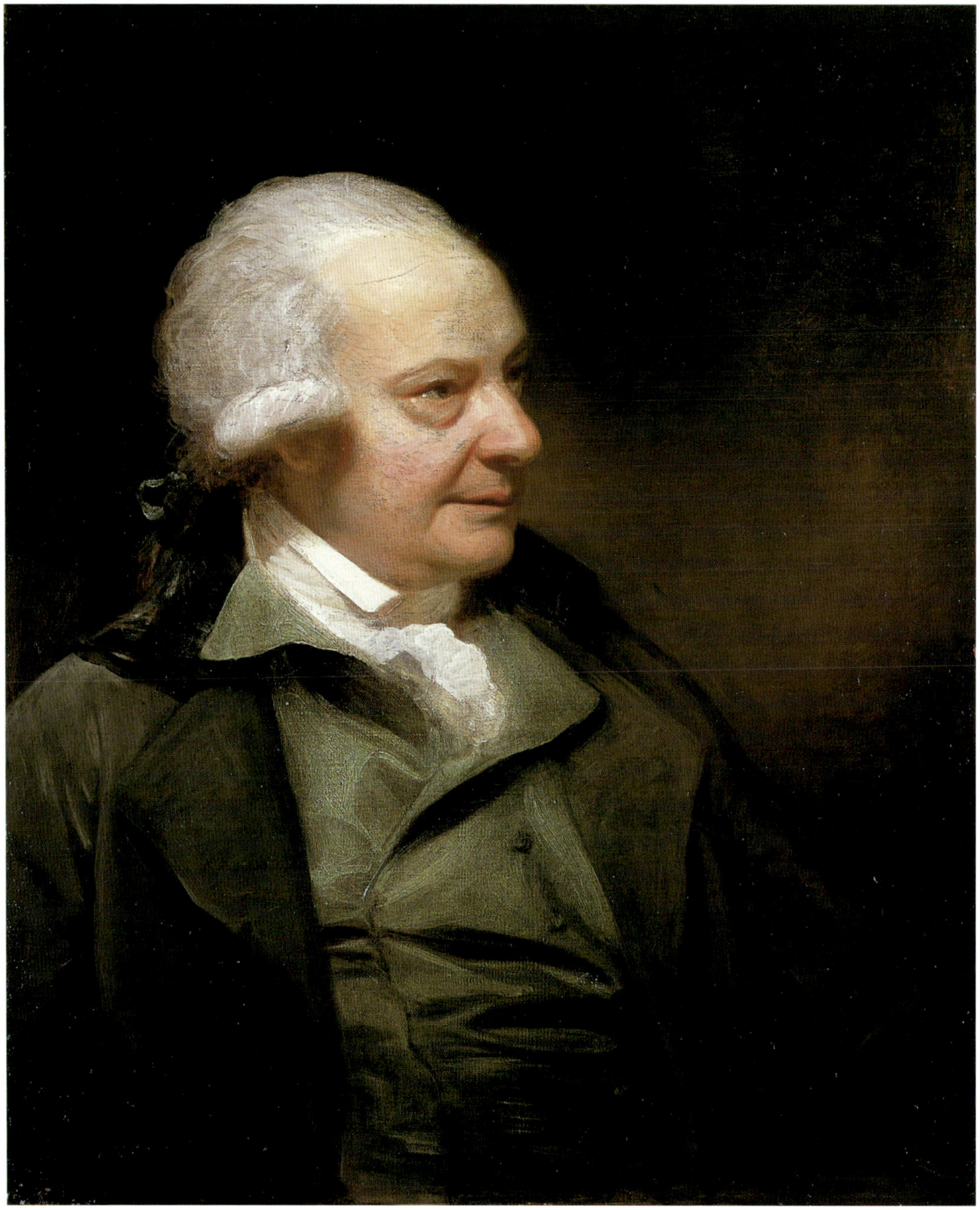

Paul SANDBY NPG *1379*

ST JOHN, St Andrew St John, 14th Baron 1759-1817

Whig politician, of Melchbourne Park, Beds., MP 1780-1805 when he suc. his bro. as 14th Baron; FRS and FSA 1808.

2076 see Groups, *Mr Fox and his Friends* by WILLIAM LANE c.1813

ICONOGRAPHY

c.1813 Drawing by William Lane, *Mr Fox and his Friends*, see Groups NPG 2076.

Unattributed miniature of 'St. Andrew Thirteenth Baron St. John, born 1759, died 1817' exhibited SKM 1865(2540) lent by the Hon Mrs MacLeod of MacLeod.

SALUSBURY, Hester, see PIOZZI

SANDBY, Paul 1731-1809

Landscape painter and printmaker, b. Nottingham, ygr. bro. of Thomas Sandby; came to London c.1746; as a draughtsman to the Board of Ordnance worked on the survey of Scotland 1747-52; exhibited SA 1760-68; foundation member of the RA 1768, where he exhibited 1769-1809; chief drawing master at the Royal Military College, Woolwich, 1768-97; toured Wales 1770, 1771 and 1773, an album of Welsh views 1775 being his first aquatints; less fashionable in his later years, he asked the RA for financial aid in 1799.

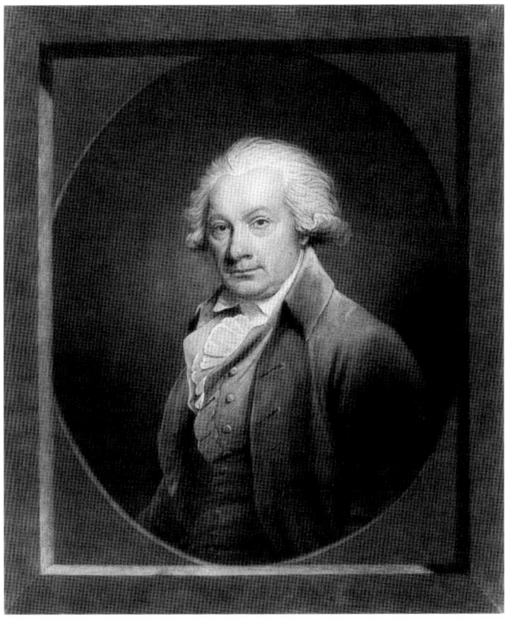

Paul SANDBY S.W. Reynolds 1794 after William Beechey (NPG D 13816)

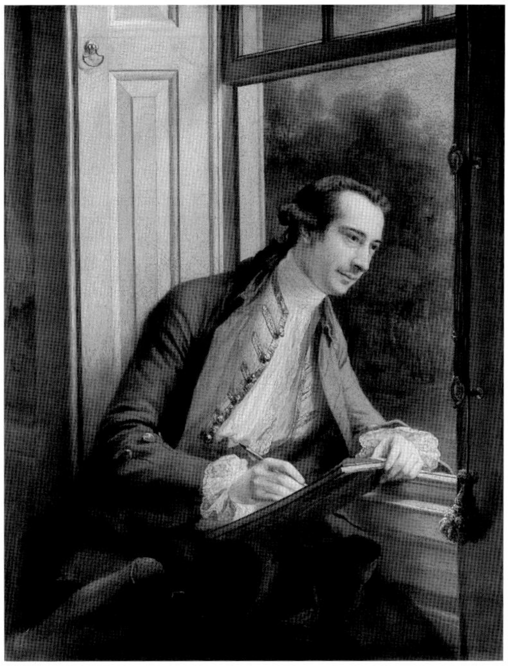

Paul SANDBY by Francis Cotes 1761 (Tate Gallery)

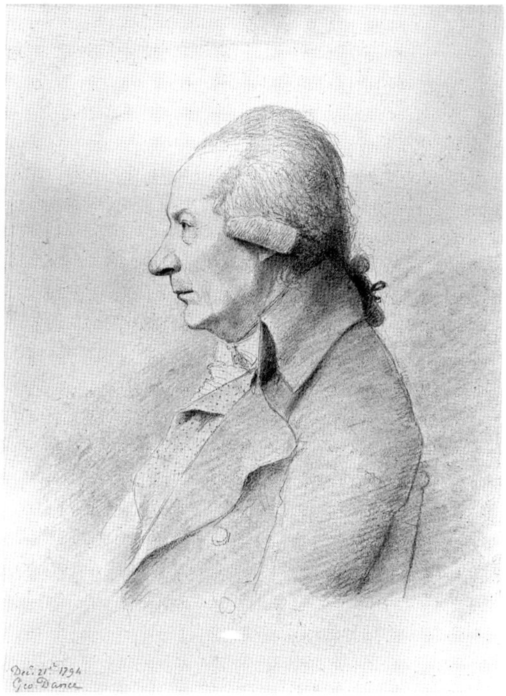

Paul SANDBY by George Dance 1794 (Royal Academy of Arts, London)

Abbreviation

Sandby 1892: W. Sandby, *Thomas and Paul Sandby*, 1892

1379 WILLIAM BEECHEY c.1789

Canvas 75.5 x 62.5 (29¾ x 24½); the head and neck-cloth abraded.

Blue eyes, white powdered wig, wearing a dark green coat with a velvet collar, bright green waistcoat.

Collections: By descent to William Arnold Sandby,[1] by whom bequeathed 1904.

Engraving: H. Landseer 1809 from a drawing by W. Evans.[2]

Exhibitions:[3] [RA 1789(241), see below]; RA 1888(22) lent W. Sandby [28 Westbourne Park West];[4] *Thomas and Paul Sandby*, Reading, Bolton, 1972(2); *Mason* 1973(72).

Beechey was a close friend of 'father Sandby' who advised him 'on all matters relative to his profession ... encouraged and protected him in and out of the Academy', and witnessed his marriage in February 1793.[5] A second half-length portrait by Beechey was engraved by S.W. Reynolds in 1794,★ facing left with head turned to front, wearing a crimson coat and white waistcoat; it was lent by William Sandby to the NPE 1867(509), when it was clearly in a very poor state.[6] William Sandby recorded that one of these 'two very admirable portraits, [painted] later in life (when he was seventy-two)' was presented to Sandby and the other was kept by Beechey 'until his death, when it came into the [Sandby] family'.[7] It is not clear which was exhibited by Beechey at the RA in 1789.

1 Author of the Sandby monograph 1892; probably a grandson of Thos. Sandby's dau. Harriot (1763–1832), who m. her cousin, Paul Sandby's son Thomas William (d.1832); his obituary in *The Times*, 1 June 1904, referred to 'his kinsmen', Thomas and Paul Sandby.
2 The drawing now in Nottingham Castle MAG (04-479).
3 An unexplained label on the verso of NPG 1379 reads: *1886/ March 24th /No.4// William Sandby Esqre/ ? portrait of Paul Sandby, R.A., at 72./By Sir William Beechey, R.A.*
4 The label remains verso.
5 Chamberlain 1907, pp.29, 184.
6 Photograph NPG archive, showing severe shrinkage craquelure throughout the head.
7 *Sandby* 1892, p.193.

ICONOGRAPHY

1761 Painting by Francis Cotes,★ three-quarter length drawing by an open window; dated. Tate Gallery (N 1943; Johnson 1976, no.95), transferred from NPG 1919. Exhibited SA 1761(21). Engraved E. Fisher 1763. A weak wash drawing copy dated 1804 in the NPG reference collection (D 18). Cotes exhibited a pendant of Sandby's wife, Anne, SA 1760(13), sold Sotheby's, 9 April 1997, lot 33.

1767 Drawing by R. Pollard, half-length profile wearing cocked hat; engraved 1780 (*Sandby* 1892, p.193).

1767 Drawing by P-E. Falconet, bust-length tondo. Ashmolean Museum, Oxford (553; Brown 1982, p.273, pl.xxiii). A similar drawing by Falconet, dated 1768, in the British Museum (1868.8.8.1967), appears to be that engraved D.P. Pariset 1769.

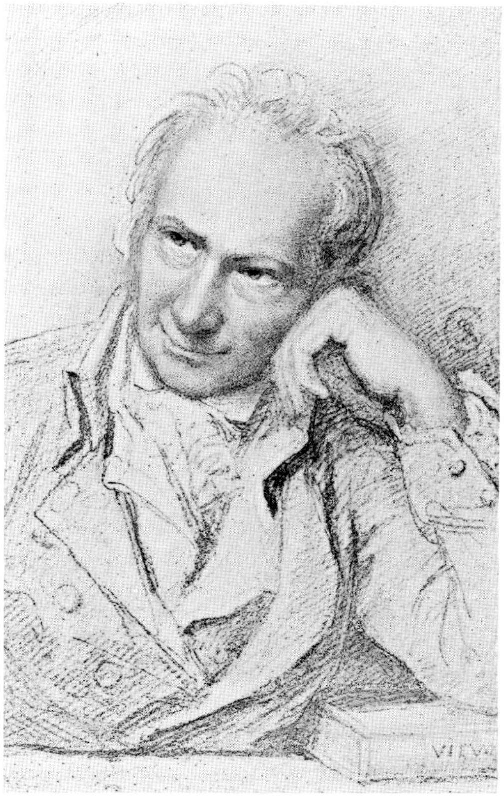

Paul SANDBY photogravure after Richard Cosway 1804 (NPG archive)

c.1770? Drawing by William Parry, whole-length seated sketching beneath a parasol. Royal Collection (Oppé 1950, no.473; H.B. Carter, *Sir Joseph Banks*, 1988, p.122).

1772 Painting by Johann Zoffany,* *The Academicians of the Royal Academy*, see Groups NPG 1437.

1787 Miniature by Philip Jean, half-length oval. Private collection (illus. *Burl. Mag.*, CVII, 1965, p.538). Engraved J. Thomson 1796 (*European Mag.*). Presumably the miniature of 'Mr Sandby' exhibited RA 1788(315). See Serres NPG 1909.

c.1789 Two paintings by William Beechey, see NPG 1379.

c.1790 Wash drawing by Paul Sandby, bust length. Christie's, 24 March 1959, lot 128 (illus. *CL*, CXXV, 1959, p.822; *Connoisseur*, CXLIII, 1959, p.265).

1792 Wax by G. Leader, exhibited RA 1792(779).

1794 Drawing by George Dance,* profile bust, dated 21 December 1794. Royal Academy. Engraved W. Daniell 1809.

1795 Painting by Henry Singleton,* *President and Members of the Royal Academy*, see Comparative Groups.

1800 Engraving by J. Owen, outline profile head (*Public Characters of 1800-01*).

1804 Drawing by Richard Cosway, half length, head on left hand. Nottingham Castle MAG (1945-175).* Presented by Cosway to Sandby's son in the hope he would find it a 'tolerable resemblance of that good man and accomplished artist' (*Sandby* 1892, p.194). Version by Mrs Barber sold Sotheby's, 26 March 1979, lot 103.

Posthumous

1882 Bust by Onslow Ford, derived from NPG 1379. Royal Institute of Painters in Water-Colours, Piccadilly (façade).

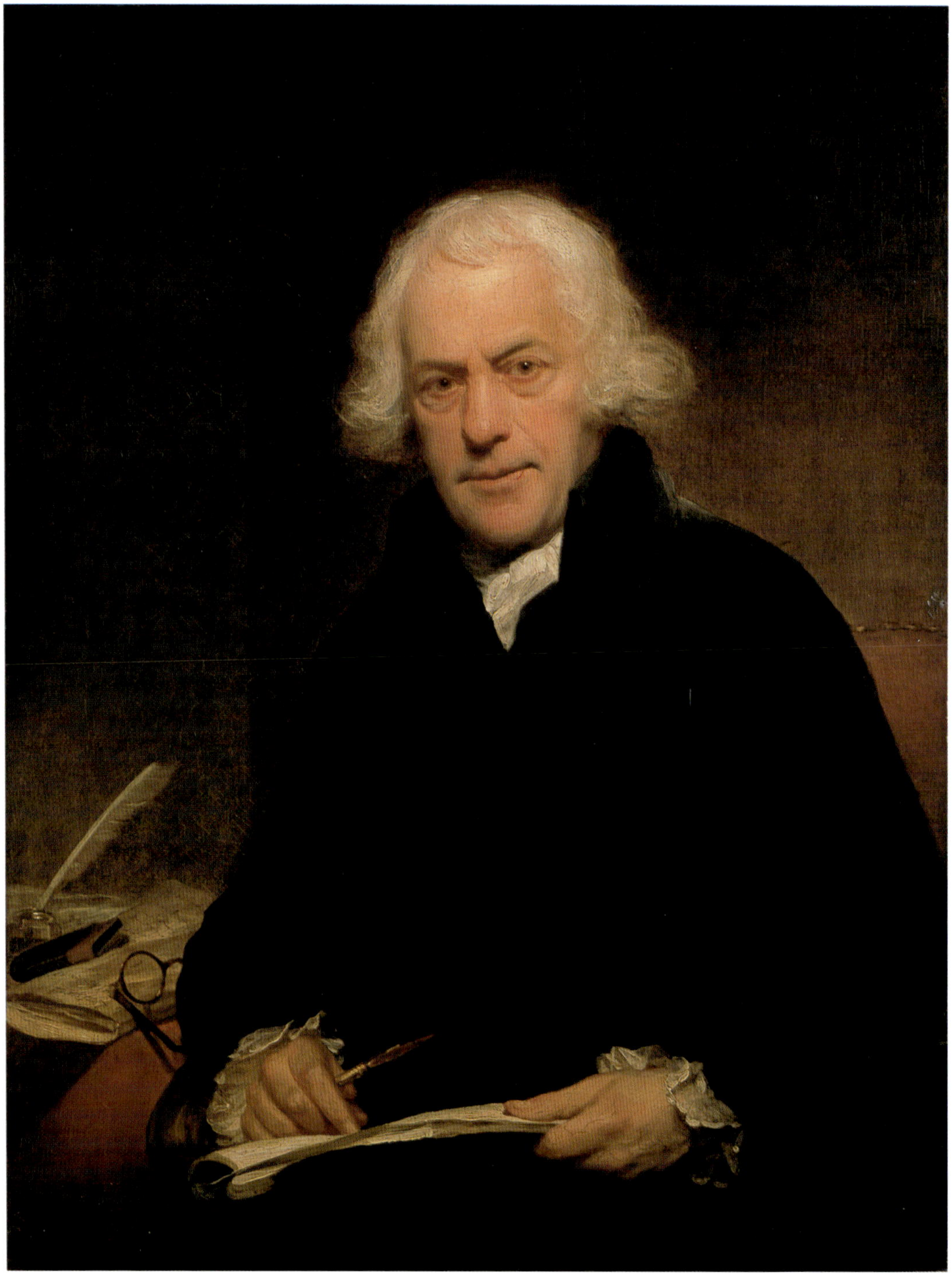

Thomas SANDBY NPG *1380*

SANDBY, Thomas 1721-98

Architect, b. Nottingham, older bro. of Paul Sandby; left Nottingham for London 1742, joining the Board of Ordnance, for whom he worked in Scotland 1745 attracting the patronage of the Duke of Cumberland; appointed deputy Ranger, Windsor Great Park 1746; architect of the King's Works 1777; foundation member of the RA 1768 and first Professor of Architecture; 'universally esteemed [and]... one of the gentlest and best of human beings' (*GM*, 1798).

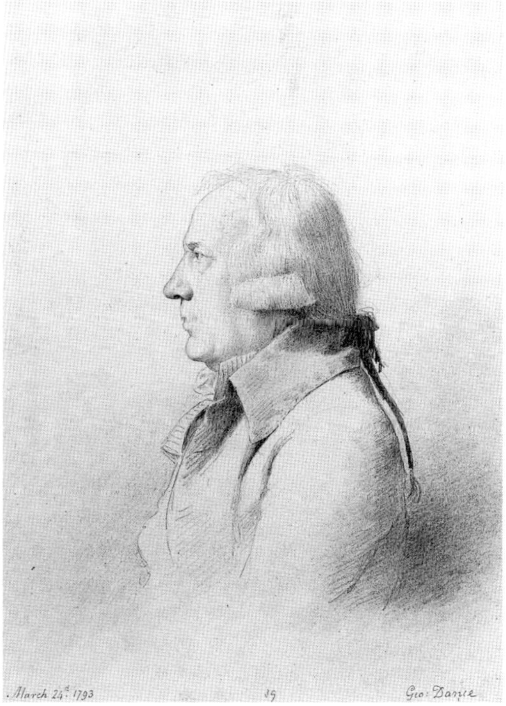

Thomas SANDBY by George Dance 1793 (Royal Academy of Arts, London)

1380 WILLIAM BEECHEY 1792

Canvas 89.5 x 69 (35¼ x 27¼) lined; prominent craquelure in the head and numerous retouchings; signed bottom left: *WB.1792*.

Brown eyes, white hair, wearing a dark coat and waistcoat, seated in a red chair, in his right hand a porte-crayon with red chalk; to the left on a table, his quill, spectacle case and spectacles.

Collections: By descent to William Arnold Sandby (see NPG 1379), by whom bequeathed 1904.

Exhibitions: RA 1792(111); *Thomas and Paul Sandby*, Reading, Bolton, 1972(1).

For Beechey's close friendship with Paul Sandby, see NPG 1379. When exhibited at the RA in 1792 NPG 1380 was described as 'the best in the room, in our minds, for the true simplicity of the art, the sober and unaffected style which attracts and satisfies more than the tinselled glittering of the French School'.[1] A version without the spectacles, inscribed *Dr Hawkesworth* [probably for John Hawkesworth, 1715-73, the friend of Samuel Johnson], belonged to T.L. Metters in 1964. NPG 1380 was copied by W. Evans,[2] preparatory for an engraving for Cadell's contemporary portraits, but a print was never published.[3]

1 Chamberlain 1907, p.40 (quoting Humphry Ward's press cuttings).
2 Drawing in Nottingham Castle MAG (04-478); cf. NPG 1379.
3 Sandby 1892, p.195.

ICONOGRAPHY

1762 Painting by F. Van der Mijn, 'Mr Sandby', exhibited FS 1762(55).

1772 Painting by Johann Zoffany,★ *The Academicians of the Royal Academy*, see Groups NPG 1437.

c.1780 Watercolour by William Hamilton, half length at table in a green coat. Christie's, 24 March 1959, lot 2.

c.1790 Silhouette by James Lind, bust length (illus. Oppé 1947, tailpiece). Lind, physician to the Royal Household, was a neighbour in Windsor from the late 1770s. Another silhouette by him of Sandby was sold Christie's, 24 March 1959, lot 3.

1792 Painting by William Beechey, see NPG 1380.

1793 Drawing by George Dance,★ profile bust, dated 24 March 1793. Royal Academy. Engraved W. Daniell (*Dance Plates*); tracing by Daniell in the Yale Center for British Art (B1977.14.4187).

1795 Miniature by François Ferrière, 'Mr Sandby', exhibited RA 1795(524). Possibly that sold Sotheby's, 26 March 1979, lot 104.

1795 Painting by Henry Singleton,★ *President and Members of the Royal Academy*, see Comparative Groups. The figure of Thomas Sandby alone engraved anon. A portrait by Singleton, bust-length profile, was exhibited by William Sandby NPE 1867(516) when described as painted in 1793 and a study for Singleton's 1795 group; presumably also the portrait exhibited RA 1797(222), cf. Richard Cosway and Johann Zoffany.

Several drawings by Paul Sandby have been said to include his brother Thomas, but they hardly signify as portraits (e.g. Oppé 1947, nos.102, 253, 385; Christie's, 26 May 1959, lot 113, of which a copy is in the Albertina, Vienna, and Sotheby's, 1 April 1976, lot 175).

DOUBTFUL PORTRAIT

Painting by Gainsborough c.1746 in the Louvre (Waterhouse 1958, no.752), which has been doubtfully called a self portrait, was engraved G. Sanders 1878 as *Mr & Mrs Sandby*, and exhibited as such RA 1877(69) and *Gainsborough*, Grosvenor Gallery, 1885(9).

SANDWICH, John Montagu, 4th Earl of 1718-92

Statesman; suc. his grandfather as 4th Earl 1729; travelled in Europe and the Middle East 1737-39; FRS 1740; FSA 1746; served with the army in Holland; colonel 1745; lord of the Admiralty 1744-46 and first lord 1749-51, 1763 and 1771-82; minister plenipotentiary at the treaty of Aix-la-Chapelle 1748; secretary of state 1763-65 and 1770-71.

'he was tall, of a vigorous frame, apparently designed for longevity, and his physiognomy full of expression; but conviviality rather than forethought or profound reflection characterised his features. A distinguished votary of wit, conviviality, and pleasure ...' (Sir Nathaniel Wraxall, 1815).

Abbreviation

Voyage 1799: *A Voyage performed by the late Earl of Sandwich round the Mediterranean in the years 1738 and 1739, written by himself*, 1799

1977 JOSEPH HIGHMORE 1740

Canvas 119.5 x 93.5 (47 x 36¾) lined; scattered darkened retouchings, craquelure marked in the flesh areas; discoloured varnish; signed below left: *Jos Highmore pinx:/1740*.

Dark grey eyes, wearing a blue cap below his turban, a red kaftan beneath a blue coat trimmed with rat-tailed ermine; in his deep-blue belt with red and gold decoration, a gold-handled dagger; on the table covered with a Turkey rug, a paper with drawings of pyramids; on the right a distant view of the minarets and dome of the Hagia Sophia.

Collections: 'A Lady of Rank', sold Christie's, 11 June 1870, lot 145 (as Lady Mary Wortley Montagu);[1] presented anonymously 1923.

Exhibitions: *Highmore*, Kenwood, 1963(12); *The Dye is now Cast*, NPG Washington, 1975(159); *Bicentennial Center Opening*, Yorktown, Va., 1976; Beningbrough 1979-.

Reference: A.S. Lewis, 'Joseph Highmore', D.Phil. thesis Harvard, UMI, 1979, II, no.151.

NPG 1977 celebrates Lord Sandwich's voyage to the Middle East in 1738-39. In July 1738 he had left Leghorn with William Ponsonby (later 2nd Earl of Bessborough) and the French artist Liotard (see below) to visit Athens, Constantinople, Cyprus and Egypt. In his account of the voyage, published posthumously in 1799 and dedicated to the King as 'an early performance of a long-tried and faithful Servant', he described how, besides copying inscriptions

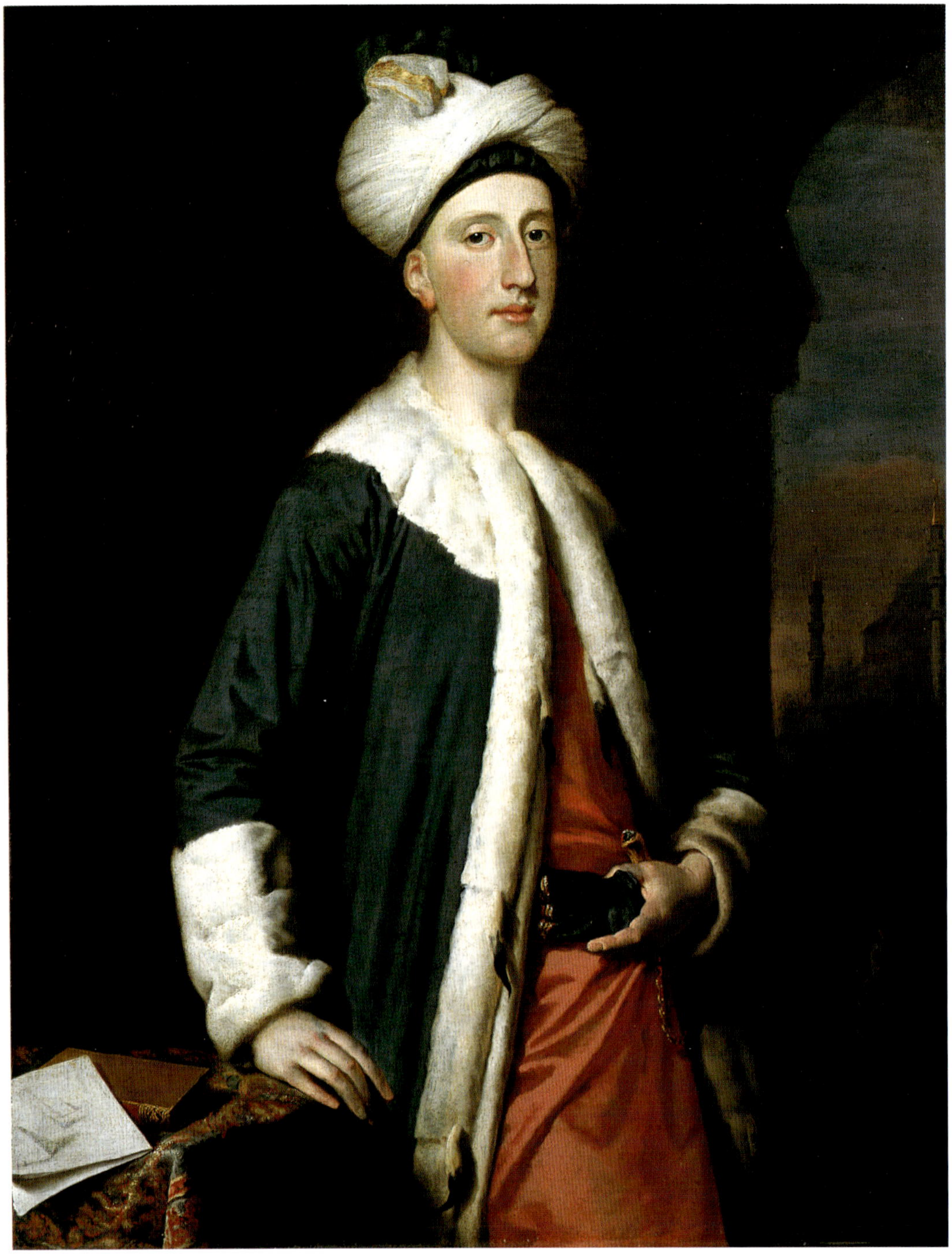

4th Earl of SANDWICH NPG *1977*

and taking 'plans and drafts of the pyramids, and all ancient buildings', he had returned with

> two mummies and eight embalmed ibis's from the catacombs of Memphis; a large quantity of the famous Egyptian papyrus; 50 intaglios; 500 medals ... marble vase from Athens ... and a very long inscription ... on both sides of a piece of marble of about two feet in height.[2]

On his return Sandwich was elected FRS; he became the first President of the Egyptian Society in 1742 and founded, as 'Vizir', the Divan Club for Turkish travellers in 1744.[3]

Both Sandwich and Ponsonby were painted whole length in Turkish costume by Liotard (see below). NPG 1977 shows a blue cloak,[4] where Liotard showed green; in the background are the dome and minarets of Hagia Sophia,[5] and drawings of the pyramids, as described in the *Voyage*, lie on the table.[6] An earlier depiction of an English adaptation of Turkish dress is seen in the portrait by J.B. Vanmour of Lady Mary Wortley Montagu in Constantinople c.1717 (NPG 3924).[7]

1 The anonymous donor still believed in 1923 that it showed Lady Mary (letters in NPG archive).
2 *Voyage* 1799, p.iii; the marble inscription he gave to Trinity College, Cambridge.
3 N.A.M. Rodger, *The Insatiable Earl*, 1993, p.7; see J. Sweetman, *The Oriental Obsession*, 1988, pp.63-64.
4 A similar cloak is worn by Ponsonby in his portrait by Liotard (Stansted; illus. *Liotard, opera completa*, 1978, no.48, tav.vii).
5 The minarets agree with the engraving by John Cooke in the *Voyage* 1799, f.p.131, presumably copied from drawings made during the voyage.
6 Cf. the [six] engravings of the pyramids in the *Voyage* 1799, f.p.456-61.
7 See Kerslake *Early Georgian*, I, p.188-89, II, pl.549.

182 after JOHANN ZOFFANY [c.1764]

Canvas 75 x 62.5 (29½ x 24½) lined and heavily ironed; flaking and some losses, lower right; two repaired tears upper right background; discoloured varnish.

Blue eyes, white powdered wig with a black ribbon, wearing a deep red coat with a black collar and gold trim; within a painted oval.

Collections: Christie's, 9 July 1864, lot 111, purchased.

Exhibition: *Wilkes*, British Museum, 1969.

NPG 182 is adopted from Zoffany's three-quarter length portrait of Lord Sandwich painted for Trinity House, London, on, or soon after, his appointment as first lord of the Admiralty in 1763. NPG 182 uses the same head, but the perfunctory body and costume are different.

The Trinity House portrait showed him holding a letter conspicuously addressed to himself in his new position at the Admiralty;[1] a version in which the letter is addressed to *His Majestie's Principal Secretary of State*, remains with the sitter's descendants,[2] together with a whole-length adaptation, seated on a terrace, his right hand on his hip, a book in his left.[3] A bust-length version is in a private collection.

1 Destroyed 1939-45; illus. Williamson 1920, f.p.38; engraved V. Green 1774 (illus. *Zoffany* 1977, no.17).
2 Illus. *Sandwich Papers*, IV, 1939, front.; lent to the Foreign Office 1958 by Lord Hinchingbrooke; apparently the picture seen at Knowsley in 1866 by Scharf (SSB 77/79).
3 Inscribed with the date 1764; illus. *Sandwich Papers*, I, 1932 front.

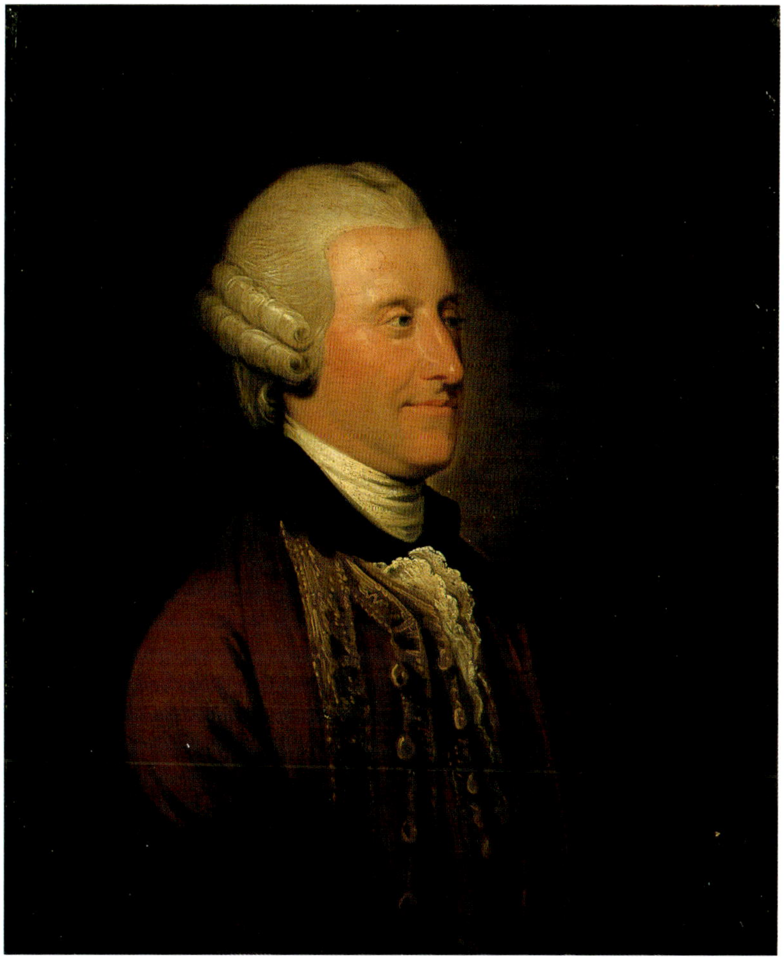

4th Earl of SANDWICH
NPG 182

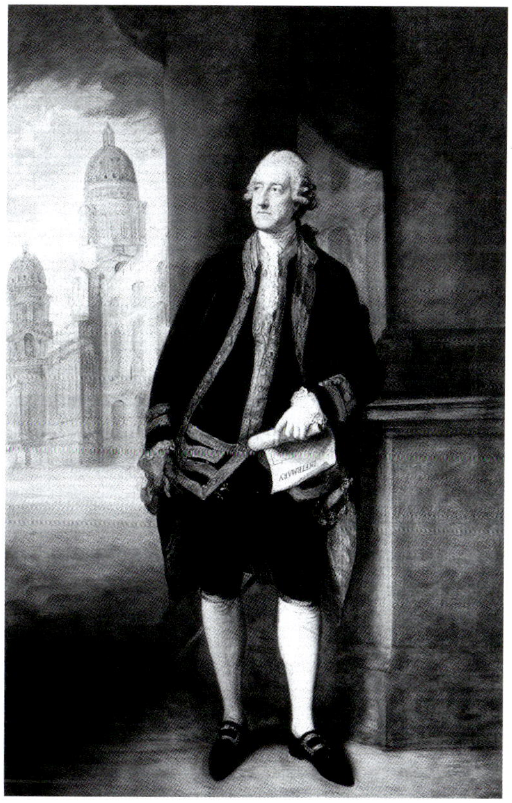

4th Earl of SANDWICH by Thomas Gainsborough 1782 (National Maritime Museum, London)

ICONOGRAPHY

c.1725 Painting attributed to Isaac Whood, as a child in skirts with a bow. Formerly Hinchingbrooke, destroyed by fire 1997.

c.1739 Painting by J-E. Liotard, whole length in Turkish dress. Formerly Hinchingbrooke, destroyed by fire 1997 (illus. *Liotard, opera completa*, 1978, no.45, tav.iv). In 1763 Walpole wrote that it was 'done at Constantinople by Liotard' (*Wal.Soc.*, XVI, 1928, p.49). A miniature copy by Henry Bone was exhibited Wembley, 1924(V.195), lent Lord Sandwich.

1740 Painting by Joseph Highmore, see NPG 1977.

1745 Painting by George Knapton, half length in Turkish dress, a glass in his left hand. Society of Dilettanti (illus. Cust & Colvin, *Dilettanti*, 1898, f.p.110, p.219). Exhibited NPE 1868(930).

The head recurs in a three-quarter length version, wearing a slightly different Turkish costume, at Dunrobin Castle (formerly at Trentham Hall; Harding, II, p.113).

1758 Painting by Joshua Reynolds,* three-quarter length in Peer's robes. Private collection (Mannings 2000, no.1273).

1761 Medal by Thomas Pingo. National Maritime Museum. A trial strike of a medal not issued (Brown 1980, no.9).

c.1764 Painting by Johann Zoffany, see under NPG 182.

1779 Drawn and engraved by Robert Stewart, bust-length oval.

An inferior engraving by O'Neale 1779, bust-length oval (*London Mag.*), a later imprint reversed.

1779–81 Painting by J.S. Copley,* *The Death of Chatham*, see Comparative Groups.

by 1781 Wedgwood medallion (illus. Reilly 1973, p.298), resembling an engraving by J. Corner 1787 (*European Mag.*), of which a cruder version had been engraved anon. 1782.

1782 Painting by Thomas Gainsborough,* whole length. National Maritime Museum (BHC 3009; Waterhouse 1958, no.599). Exhibited RA 1783(190); NPE 1867(719). Engraved J.K. Sherwin; J. Scott; J. Collyer 1799 (oval). Copy by

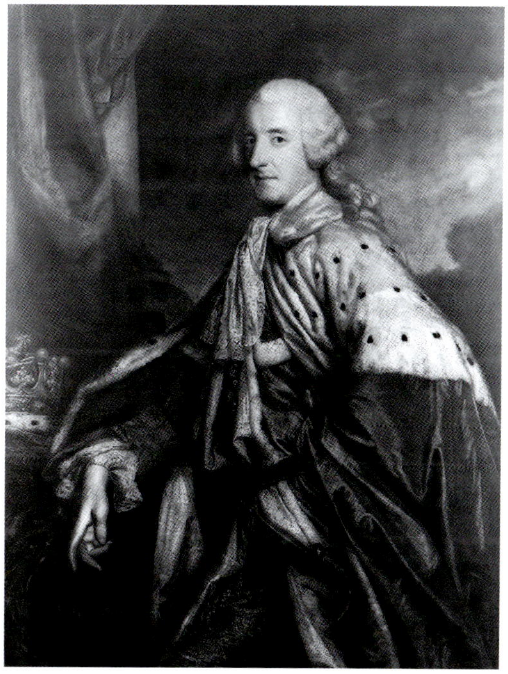

4th Earl of SANDWICH by Joshua Reynolds 1758 (Private Collection)

Thomas Beach [1793] at Huntingdon Town Hall, with long inscription, lower right (illus. *Connoisseur*, CXXXV, 1955, p.241).

1782 Engraving by J. Sayers, whole length (George 6076).

1782 Wax by Lewis Pingo, exhibited FS 1782(159).

c.1782-85 Painting by Thomas Gainsborough, half length. Marquise de Ganay sale, Paris, 8-10 May 1922, lot 47 (Waterhouse 1958, no.600).

1787 Painting by John Opie, whole length in peer's robes. Formerly Royal Naval Barracks, Stonehouse (illus. *Sandwich Papers*, IV, 1938, p.272; Rogers 1878, p.155). Exhibited RA 1787(218). Copy by F. Lane in a private collection. A half-length derivation, in private dress, in the same private collection, and another was with Lord Wharncliffe in 1954.

1790 Drawing by John Nixon, showing Sandwich as one of the five directors at the 1790 Handel Commemoration. Private collection (illus. *Handel*, NPG, 1985, no.244).

c.1791 Painting by Thomas Beach, whole length, wearing peer's parliamentary robes. Private collection.

The many caricatures of Sandwich include the *Holy Order of St Almac* 1773 (George 4642), *A Sandwich* 1788 (George 7421) and a drawing in the Townshend Album (NPG 4855, no.23), see Appendix III.

SAWBRIDGE, Catharine, see **MACAULAY**

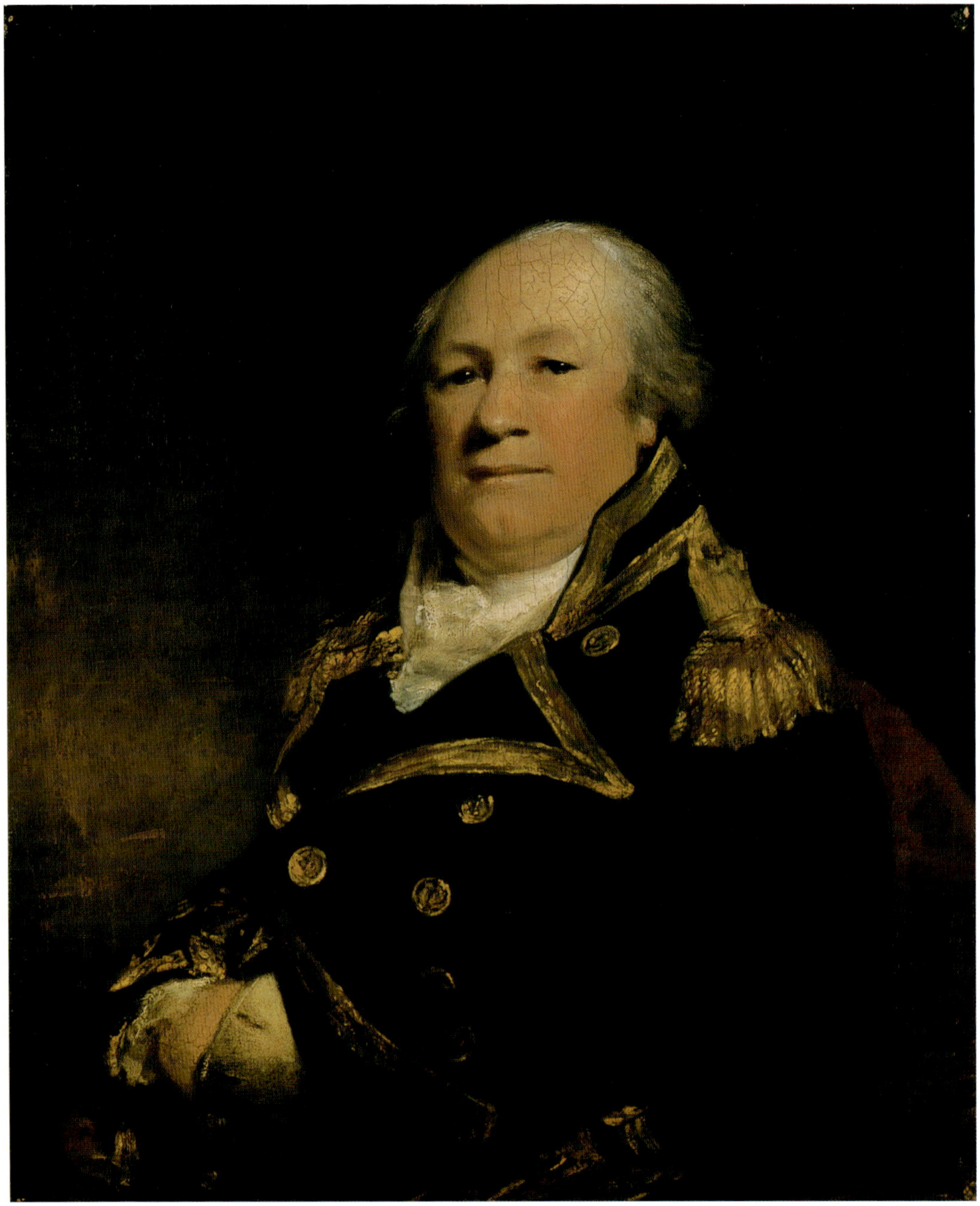

SCHANCK NPG 1923

SCHANK, John 1740-1823

Naval engineer; b. Fifeshire, entered the navy 1758, serving in the West Indies and America, fitting out a flotilla for the Canadian Lakes; captain 1783; agent general West Indies 1794, superintendant of naval transport for the Duke of York's Dutch expediton of 1799, and in charge of the coastal defences of Britain 1799; inventor of the sliding keel and the floating bridge; retired in 1802 with failing eyesight; promoted rear-admiral 1805, vice-admiral 1810 and admiral 1821.

1923 JOHN JAMES MASQUERIER 1799

Canvas 76 x 63.5 (30 x 25) lined; a marked wide craquelure in the darks and retouchings in the jacket and background areas; pentimenti behind the head and collar and along his right sleeve.

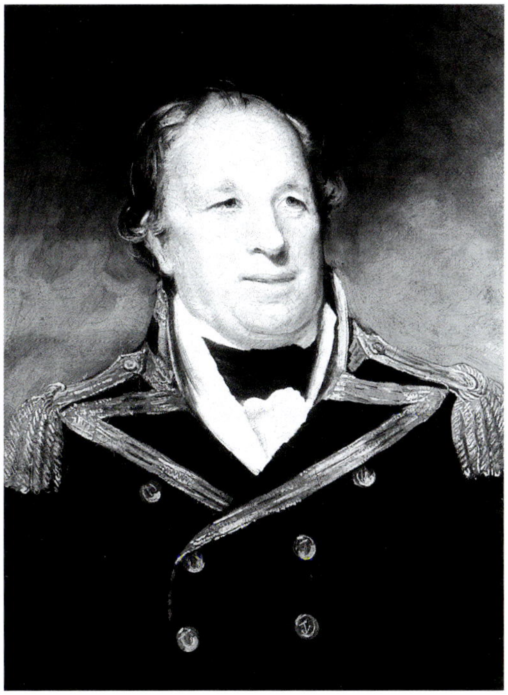

SCHANCK unknown artist c.1795-1800 (National Maritime Museum, London)

Grey eyes, white hair, wearing captain's uniform, dark-blue coat with gold trim.

Collections: By descent from the sitter to Lt. Col. H.A. Schank, by whose wish presented 1921.[1]

Engraving: C. Turner 1799.[2] .

An identical portrait by Masquerier was in the Burdett-Coutts collection in 1917.[3]

1 The presentation made through his widow Mrs M.M. Schank, who described him as 'the last of his race' (letter of 25 October 1921; NPG archive).
2 A. Whitman, *Turner*, 1907, no.512, quotes Turner's diary, 14 September 1799: 'Began to scrape Capt Schank'
3 Illus. *Connoisseur*, LII, 1918, p.10; not in the Burdett-Coutts sale, Christie's, 4 May 1922.

ICONOGRAPHY

c.1795-1800 Painting by an unidentified artist,* half length in captain's uniform, with slightly more hair than in NPG 1923. National Maritime Museum (BHC 3014). Engraved anon. 1805 (*European Mag.*).

1799 Painting by J.J. Masquerier, see NPG 1923.

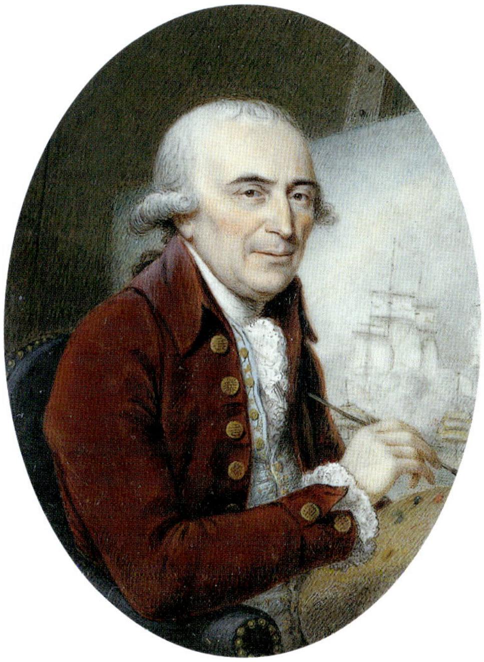

SERRES NPG 1909

SERRES, Dominic 1719-93

Painter; b. in Gascony; captured on a Spanish ship, he was brought to England; m. 1749 in London; exhibited FS 1761-64, SA 1765-68; foundation member of the RA 1768, where he exhibited 1769-93; appointed Marine Painter to the King 1780 and RA Librarian 1792.

Abbreviation

Russett 2001: A. Russett, *Dominic Serres*, 2001

1909 PHILIP JEAN 1788

Watercolour and bodycolour on ivory 10.6 x 8.2 ($4\frac{1}{8}$ x $3\frac{1}{4}$); some retouching in the sleeve and by the lower right edge, where a signature, *P . .* may be discerned. Inscribed in ink on paper lining verso: *Portrait of Dominick/ Serres RA by P. Jean* and *P Jean pinxt/1788*.

Brown eyes, grey powdered hair, wearing a deep red coat and light blue waistcoat, brush in right hand, palette in left; seated in a blue chair at his easel.

Collections: R. Cole, 1865; Miss Serres Brock, from whom purchased 1921.

Exhibitions: RA 1788(315); SKM 1865(2869) lent R. Cole; *First Hundred Years*, RA, 1951-52(596).

Reference: Walker 1998, no.52; Russett 2001, p.189.

In 1787 Jean had painted a closely comparable miniature, the same size, of Serres' neighbour Paul Sandby, and see below.

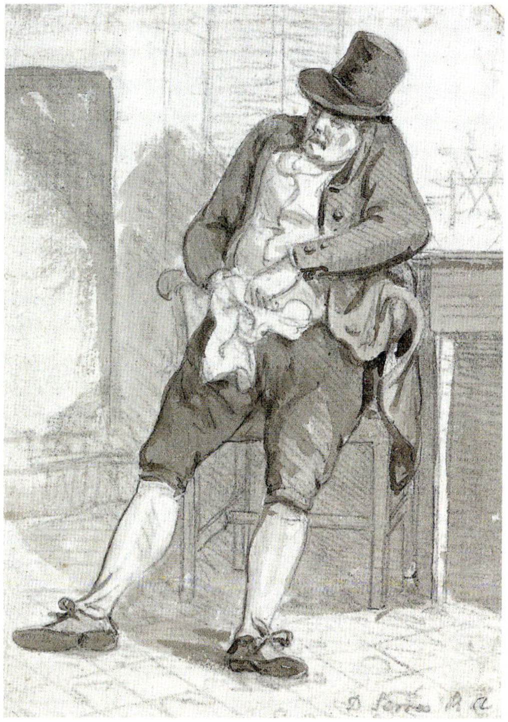

SERRES NPG 650A

650A PAUL SANDBY 1792

Pencil and wash on paper 16.8 x 12 ($6\frac{5}{8}$ x $4\frac{3}{4}$) laid down on paper; some staining; inscribed in pencil, bottom right: *D Serres R A*; the old mounting board was inscribed: *Portrait of Dominic Serres R.A./ a year before his death./ ob. 1793*.

Collections: Presented by William Hudson 1881.

Described by the donor as 'amusing rather than interesting',[1] this appears to be one of the drawings made by Serres' friend and neighbour (from 1780) in St George's Row, Paul Sandby. Another more finished drawing, showing Serres asleep in a chair, was last sold Sotheby's, 10 July 1997, lot 17,[2] and a reversed and cruder copy was sold Christie's, 26 May 1959, lot 96.

1 Letter of 3 October 1884; NPG archive.
2 Illus. Russett 2001, p.183, and see p.189.

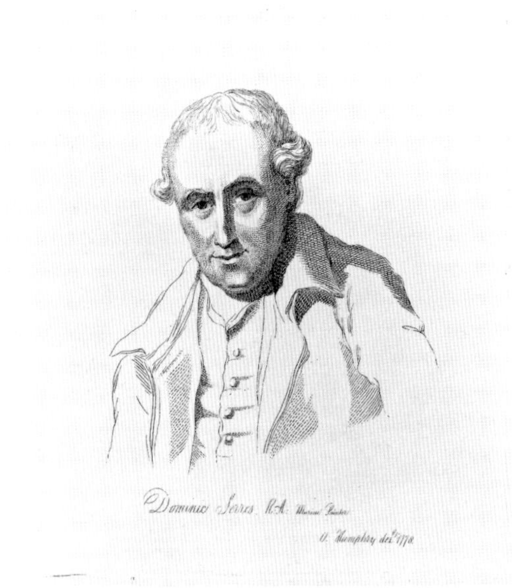

SERRES *Mrs D. Turner after Ozias Humphry 1778* (NPG D 9494)**

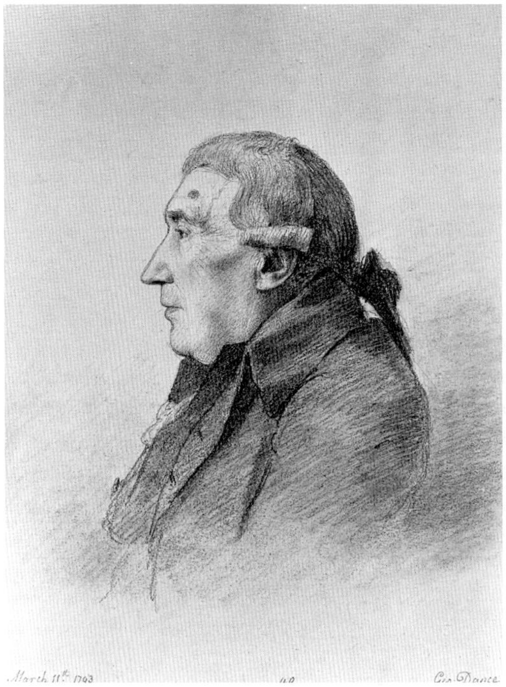

SERRES *by George Dance 1793 (Royal Academy of Arts, London)*

ICONOGRAPHY

1772 Painting by Johann Zoffany,* *The Academicians of the Royal Academy*, see Groups NPG 1437.

1778 Drawing by Ozias Humphry, half length. Puttick & Simpson 25 May 1917, lot 150. Engraved by Mrs Dawson Turner.*

1782 Painting by Gilbert Stuart, 'in the act of fresh pointing his pencil', exhibited RA 1782(164); see Russett 2001, p.146.

1788 Miniature by Philip Jean, see NPG 1909.

1788 Painting by William Beechey, exhibited RA 1788(429).

c.1790 Painting called 'circle of Thomas Hickey', small whole-length seated by a rocky coast. Sotheby's, 31 October 1990, lot 280, and Sotheby's, Sussex, 20 May 1991, lot 264 (illus. Russett 2001, p.147).

1792 Drawings by Paul Sandby, see under NPG 650A (and Doubtful Portraits below).

1793 Drawing by George Dance,* profile bust, dated 11 March 1793. Royal Academy. Engraved W. Daniell (*Dance Plates*); a tracing by Daniell in the Yale Center for British Art (B1977.14.4190).

A drawing for a projected monument to Serres, including a small oval bust-length portrait 1794 (*Town and Country Mag.*; illus. Russett 2001, p.219).

DOUBTFUL PORTRAITS

The wash drawing by Paul Sandby dated 1792, with a cartouche by Dominic's daughter, Joanna Serres, sold Sotheby's, 4 July 2001, lot 173, as Serres, must show his son Dominic (fl.1778–1804).

A painting said to be of Serres belonged to Col. M.H. Grant in 1948.

SEWARD, Anna 1742–1809

Writer, the 'Swan of Lichfield', dau. of Thomas Seward, prebendary of Lichfield; copious poetess and correspondent, the friend of Erasmus Darwin and Walter Scott (who was to edit her verse, while confiding that most of it was 'absolutely execrable'); six volumes of selected letters 'that, after I had written them, appeared to me be worth the attention of the public', were published on her instruction in 1811.

'a handsome likeness of those full-length pictures of Queen Elizabeth, where the painters gave her majesty all the beauty they could, consistent with the character of her face. The Muse laughs at herself as fat and lame; yet the connoisseurs in woman would still pronounce her handsome' (William Hayley, 1781).

'Her eyes were auburn, of the precise shade and hue of her hair, and possessed of great expression' (Walter Scott, 1810).

Abbreviation
Letters 1811: *Letters of Anne Seward written between the years 1784 and 1807*, 6 vols., 1811

2017 TILLY KETTLE 1762

Canvas 75.5 x 62 (29¼ x 24½) lined; cleaned 1977, the background areas and the right side of her hair very worn; signed bottom right: *T. Kettle/ Pinx. 1762.*

Brown eyes, dark brown hair, wearing a pearl necklet above a black velvet collar, and a white dress with a purple gown with dark fur edging; each page of her open book is headed *MILTON* and two of the pages are numbered *112* and *114*; green tablecloth.

Collections: Passed to the sitter's nephew, Thomas White of Lichfield, thence by descent to his grandson Leonard Jauncey White-Thomson, Bishop of Ely (d.1933), of Broomford Manor, Exmouth;[1] Christie's, 1 February 1924, lot 148, bt. Leggatt for the NPG.

Engraving: A. Cardon 1811 (*from the original picture painted in 1762 by Kettle in the possession of Thomas White Esqr. Lichfield*).

Exhibitions: *Garrick, Johnson and the Lichfield Circle*, Lichfield, 1953(15); *Johnson and the Lichfield Circle*, Lichfield, 1959(15); *Johnson*, Royal Exchange, London, 1964; Beningbrough 1979–94; *Johnson and the Midlands*, Lichfield, 1984(31); *Romantic Women Writers*, Grasmere, 1994–95(8).

Reference: *Kettle* 1927, p.81.

The earliest dated painting by Kettle; the pose appears indebted to the Reynolds portrait of Kitty Fisher painted in 1759.[2] It was presumably coincidental that in

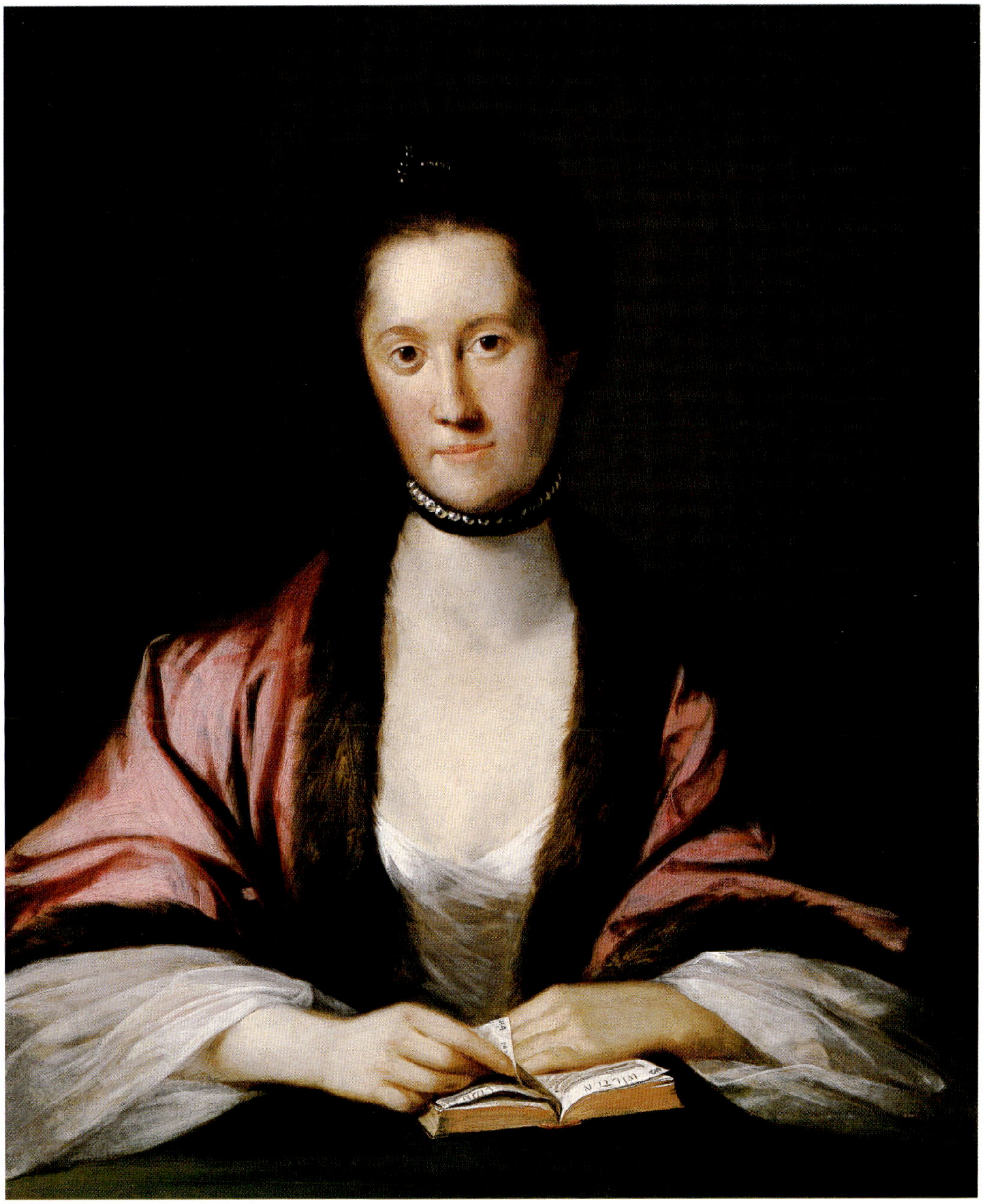

Anna SEWARD NPG *2017*

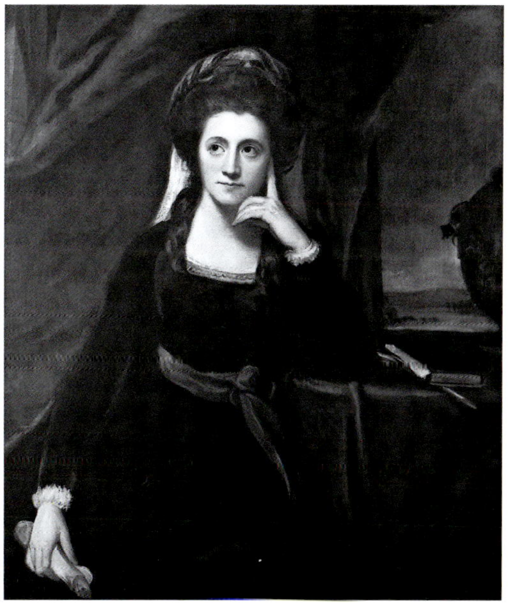

Anna SEWARD by George Romney 1782-86 (Robert Hull Fleming Museum, University of Vermont)

1762, the year it was painted, Anna Seward had met an officer called Taylor, whose departure from Lichfield the same year she regarded 'with tender, but not visibly impassioned regret'.[3] Kettle also painted a matching halflength of her younger sister, Sarah (d.1764).[4] When Romney's three-quarter length arrived in Lichfield (see below), Anna Seward wrote: 'I keep [the portrait] by poor Kettle, for which you know I sat at Nineteen, as a foil to Titiano's [Romney's], and am diverted with people taking it for my mother's picture, after they have looked at Romney's'.[5]

1 He also once owned the miniature by Meyer, see below.
2 At Petworth; it had been engraved in 1759 (Mannings 2000, no.611).
3 In 1764, after they had met again in London, an engagement was quashed by Anna's father, on the basis of Taylor's inadequate income.
4 *Kettle* 1927, pl.xivb; wearing a white dress with a blue cloak, scated writing; lot 149 in the White-Thomson sale cited above.
5 *Letters* 1811, II, p.194 (to William Hayley, 9 November 1788); her allusion to 'poor Kettle' refers to his death in 1786, in relative poverty *en route* to India.

ICONOGRAPHY

Anna Seward described her attitude to portraiture in a letter of 2 March 1796, addressed to Mrs T. (*Letters* 1811, IV, p.174):

> As to an actual picture, ... it was always my resolve never to sit for one between the periods of forty and sixty ... A portrait, where any portion of youthful appearance can be preserved, may be pleasing, and it may be interesting in the mellow tints of venerable age; but the hardness of middle life is detestable on canvas, or ivory.
>
> I sat for a miniature to Smart, twenty-five years ago. He was esteemed eminent, and I sat to Miers six years after ... [he] took immense pains with my picture; he made it a very fine one, but he did not make it like; and Smart's had still less resemblance. Both of them were long since given away. Ten years ago Romney painted me nearly at full length. It is a graceful, expressive portrait, and some people think it like, others deny the resemblance.

1762 Painting by Tilly Kettle, see NPG 2017.

c.1771 Miniature by John Smart, see above.

c.1777 Miniature by Jeremiah Meyer bust-length oval. Private collection. See above.

1782-86 Painting by George Romney,* seated three-quarter length; on the table a book inscribed AMERICA (possibly an oblique reference to her *Monody on the death of Major André in America*, published in

1781). Robert Hull Fleming Museum, Burlington, Vt. (1953.9; Ward & Roberts 1904, II, p.141). See above. Presumably the portrait painted for William Hayley who, by 1785, had placed it between busts of Pope and Prior at Eartham (*Letters*, 1811, I, p.23); in Hayley's sale, Christie's, 15 February 1821, lot 133, was 'Sketch of a portrait of Miss Seward' (originally printed as 'Mrs Siddons', but altered in the Christie's copy of the cat.). Seward met Romney at Eartham in 1782, when he began her portrait and she marked the occasion with dated verses (Hayley 1809, p.90; Romney 1830, pp.187-91); her name appeared in Romney's ledgers on 11 June 1786, and Romney's rough list that year noted a half length [127 x 101] and a copy for Hayley.

A version completed for Seward's father in 1788, with a plainer background and a paper on the table, is now in the Forsyth County Public Library, Winston Salem, N.C. (illus. Chamberlain 1910, p.45; Boswell, *Applause of the Jury*, 1981, f.p.228). Seward wrote that this second portrait was generally considered 'still more pleasing than the first, and the more like me for having that smile ... also from the hair being more gracefully disposed ...' (31 May 1788; Romney 1830, p.202; see also *Letters* 1811, II, pp.117, 126).

The type was engraved J. Chapman 1823 (a pedestal replacing the table on the right) and there are bust-length engravings by W. Ridley 1797, W. Woolnoth 1821, and anon.

1799 Engraving by J. Chapman, half-length oval with head-dress. Anon. version 1804.

DOUBTFUL PORTRAITS

'Miss Seward £15.15' was listed, and struck through, in Wright of Derby's sitter book (Nicolson 1968, I, p.218). Wright's portrait of her father is at Down House.

Painting attributed to John Hoppner, half length wearing an open white dress. Metropolitan Museum of Art, New York (06.1242), exhibited NPE 1868(140 as Anna Seward by Opie) lent W. Percival Boxall.

Drawing by John Downman, half length, engraved H. Landseer, lettered *Here only weak Against the charms of Beauty's powerful glance.*

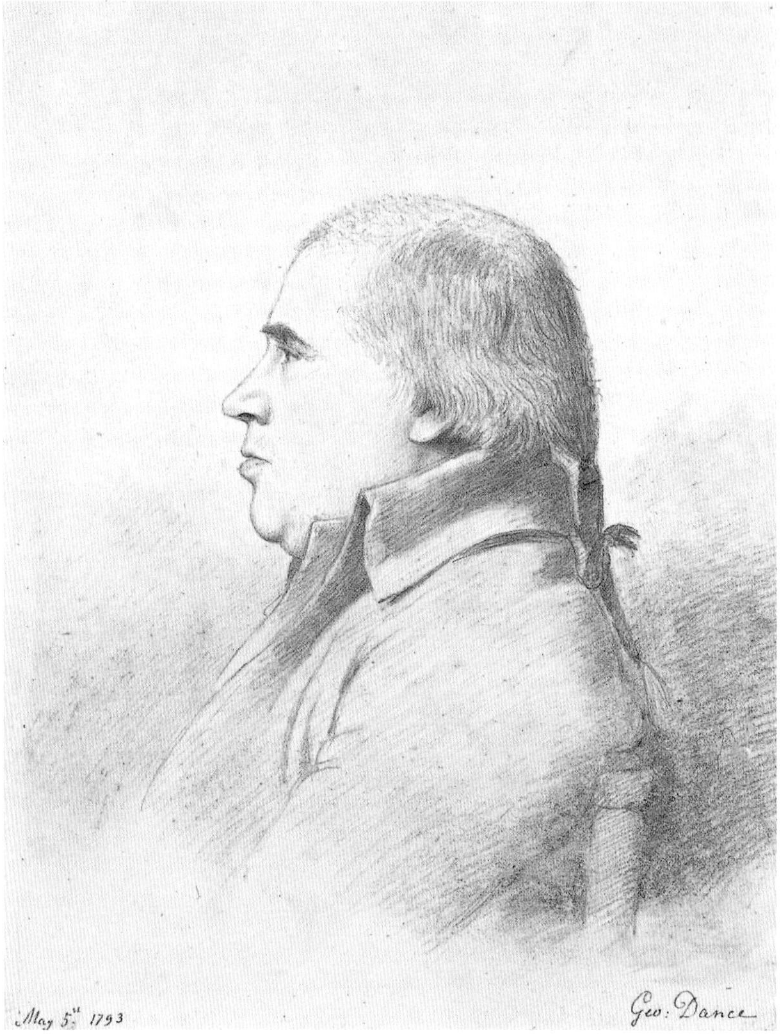

William SEWARD
NPG 1157

SEWARD, William 1747-99

Writer and hypochondriac, of independent means; said to have travelled in Italy; the friend of Samuel Johnson who thought him abrupt, but with an excellent understanding; 'he dwelt much in locomotion, and often passed from place to place in search of happiness' (*GM*, LXIX, 1799, i, p.439); FRS 1779, FSA 1779; his *Anecdotes of Some Distinguished Persons* 1795-97 and *Biographiana* 1799 were much admired.

1157 GEORGE DANCE 1793

Pencil with traces of pink on the lips and cheek and some grey wash in the background, on Whatman paper 25.4 x 19.1 (10 x 7½) some staining and a repair lower right; a vertical pencil rule runs up the left-hand edge; signed and dated in pencil: *May 5th.1793*, bottom left, and *Geo: Dance*, bottom right; laid down on a contemporary washed mount lettered: SEWARD.

Collections: The artist's grandson, the Rev George Dance; his sale, Christie's, 1 July 1898, lot 123, bt. Colnaghi for the NPG.

Engraving: W. Daniell 1809 (*Dance Portraits*).

ICONOGRAPHY

1793 Drawing by George Dance, see NPG 1157.

1799 Painting by J.G. Wood, half length and stout. Engraved W. Holl 1799; W. Ridley 1799 (*European Mag.*).

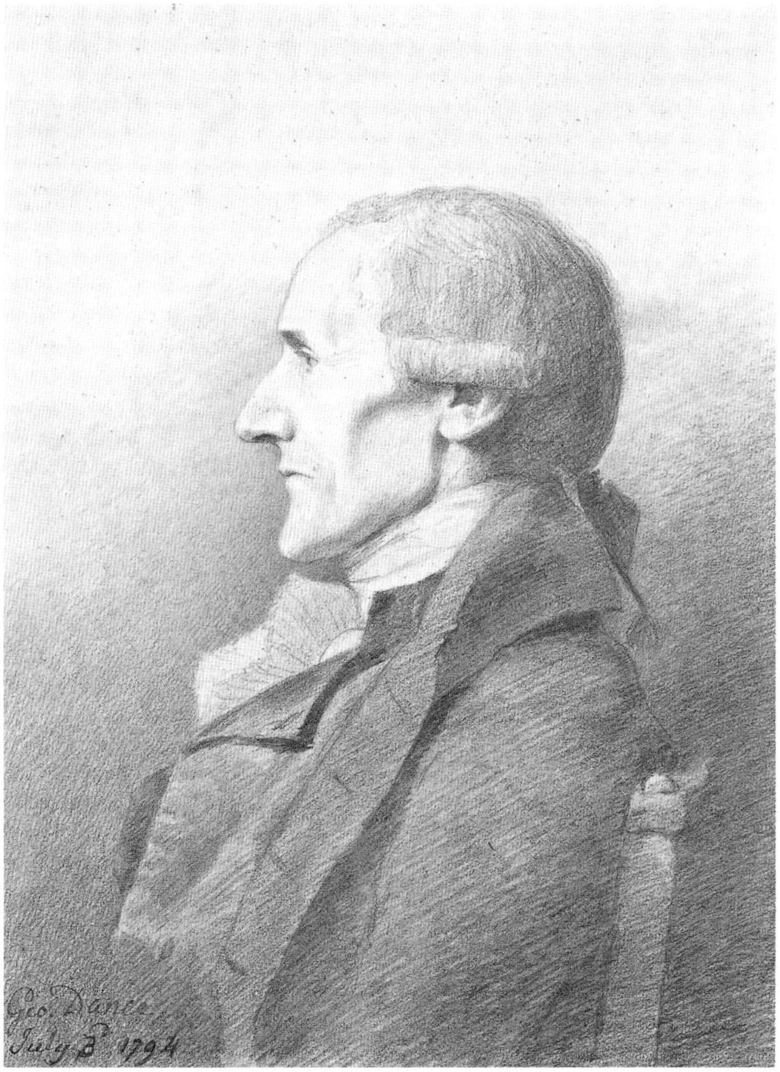

SHARP NPG 1158

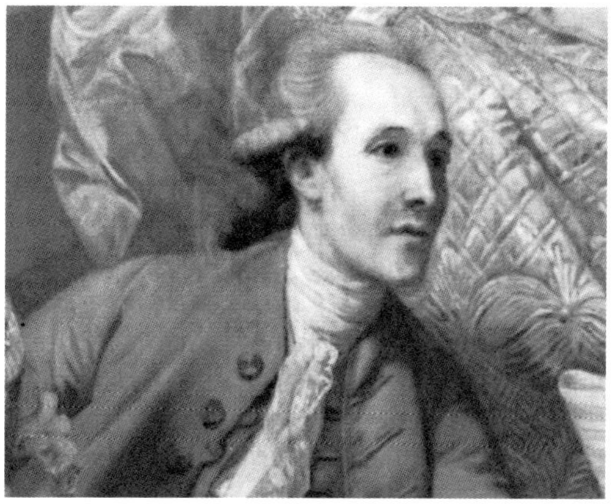

SHARP detail from The Sharp Family by Johann Zoffany 1779-81 (Private Collection)

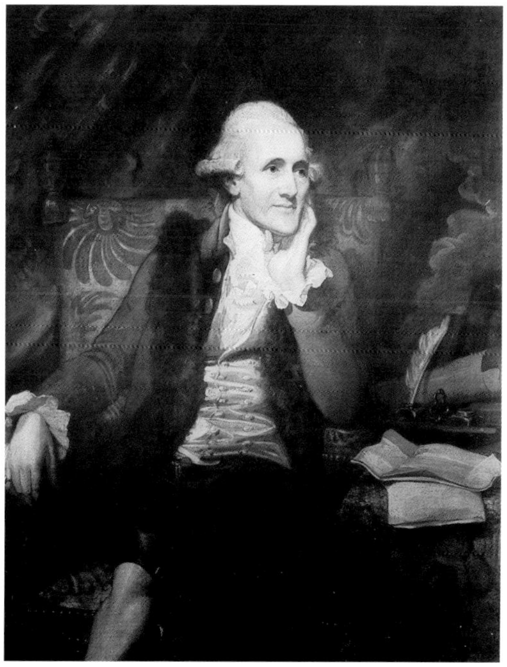

SHARP by Mather Brown 1790 (Private Collection)

SHARP, Granville 1735-1813

Philanthropist, 9th s. of Thomas Sharp, Archdeacon of Northumberland; served in the ordnance department 1758-76; a campaigner for civil rights, chairman of the society for the abolition of slavery 1787; wrote *Remarks on the Uses of the Definitive Article in the Greek Text of the New Testament* 1798, founded the British and Foreign Bible Society in 1804 and latterly believed Napoleon to be the 'Little Horn' mentioned in the Book of Daniel.

1158 GEORGE DANCE 1794

Pencil on paper 25 x 18.6 (9⅞ x 7⅜) faded; signed and dated in pencil, bottom left: *Geo: Dance/ July 3d 1794*, the date reinforced in ink; laid down on a contemporary washed mount lettered: *GRANVILLE SHARP*.

Collections: The artist's grandson, the Rev George Dance; his sale, Christie's, 1 July 1898, lot 124, bt. Colnaghi for the NPG.

Engravings: W. Daniell 1809 (*Dance Portraits*); T. Blood 1817; JS [James Sayers?] 1820; J. Pass 1827; G. Adcock 1833.

Exhibition: RA 1795(612).

ICONOGRAPHY

1779-81 Painting by Johann Zoffany,* *The Sharp Family on the Thames at Fulham*, with Granville Sharp, seated centre left, holding two flageolets. Private collection on loan to the NPG (L 169; illus. *Zoffany* 1977, no.87). Exhibited RA 1781(85). From the 1750s Sharp's musical brothers and sisters performed fortnightly as an orchestra, their water concerts on the Thames becoming celebrated.

1790 Painting by Mather Brown,* three-quarter length seated, wearing a fur-trimmed coat. Private collection (Evans 1982, no.165). Exhibited RA 1790(201); NPE 1867(798) lent T.B.L. Baker. A second portrait, described as Sharp by Brown, a half-length figure in the uniform of the Putney Volunteers, sold Christie's, 8 May 1931, lot 135.

1794 Drawing by George Dance, see NPG 1158.

1805 Painting by L.F. Abbott, half length, his left arm resting on four books, a paper in his left hand, engraved C. Turner 1805.

1808 Wax profile by Catherine Andras. Sotheby's, 30 November 1964, lot 81. Exhibited RA 1809(667). Engraved W. Worthington 1810. Plaster in the Scottish NPG (PG 455).

1816 Monument by Francis Chantrey, incorporating a profile head. Westminster Abbey, commissioned by the African Institution, which Sharp had helped to found in 1807 (*Chantrey* 1994, no.39a). A related bust-length silhouette pub. T. Stackhouse.

1818 Silhouette by Longmate, bust length, engraved 1818 (*GM*; illus. *Connoisseur*, LXXVII, 1927, p.10).

1826 Marble bust by Francis Chantrey. Destroyed 1940, formerly Guildhall, London; commissioned by the City of London (*Chantrey* 1994, no.183a). Engraved S. Cousins 1827. Plaster in the Ashmolean Museum, Oxford (Penny 1992, III, no.757).

DOUBTFUL PORTRAIT

Painting by an unidentified artist, half length to right with his own dark hair, bearing the date 1816, offered to the NPG in 1937 as Granville Sharp.

SHEFFIELD, Anne, Countess of, *née* North 1764-1832

Dau. of the prime minister, Frederick, 2nd Earl of Guilford, she m. 1798, as his third wife, John, 1st Baron Sheffield (see NPG 2185).

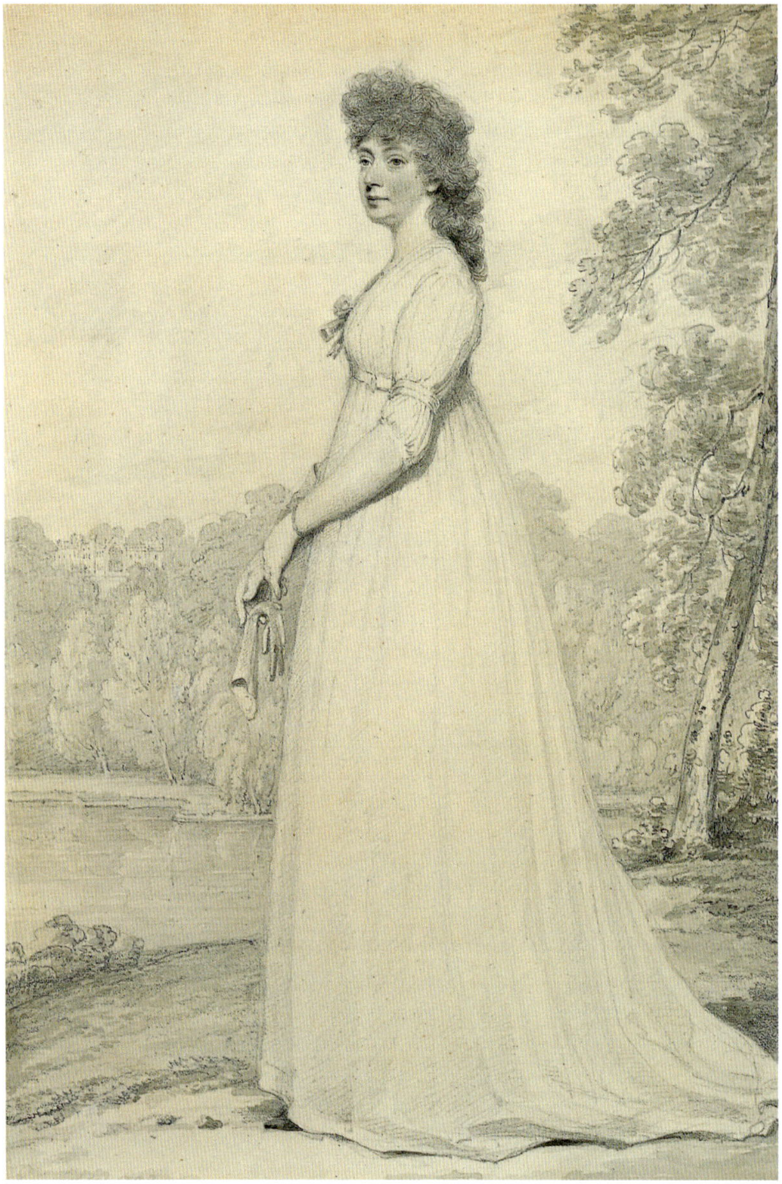

Anne, Countess of SHEFFIELD NPG *2185A*

2185A HENRY EDRIDGE 1798

Pencil and wash 27 x 18 (10½ x 7⅛) signed, bottom left: *Edridge 1798*; there is general fading; laid in a plain white window mount.

In the left distance a view of Sheffield Park from the south east.

Collections: See NPG 2185.

The view of Sheffield Place recurs in the earlier drawing by Edridge of 1795 of Maria Josepha, Sheffield's eldest daughter (illus. J.H. Adeane, *Girlhood of Maria Josepha Holroyd*, 1896, f.p.234).

ICONOGRAPHY

1779 Painting by Catherine, Lady Glenbervie, whole length. Sheffield sale, sold Christie's, December 1909, lot 111. Lady Glenbervie was the sitter's sister.

1798 Drawing by Henry Edridge, see NPG 2185A.

c.1798 Miniature attributed to Henry Edridge, half length. Sotheby's, 18 July 1988, lot 72.

after 1798 Painting by John Hoppner, three-quarter length. Sheffield sale, Christie's, 11 December 1909. A 'sketch' sold Sotheby's, 22 February 1928, lot 21.

DOUBTFUL PORTRAITS

A half length attributed to Hoppner, sold Knight, Frank & Rutley, 15 February 1929, lot 42 as Anne, Countess of Sheffield, shows Sheffield's second wife, Lucy (1763-97), dau. of the 1st Earl of Chichester. Other versions of this portrait sold Christie's, 11 December 1909, lot 74 as Beechey; Sotheby's, 17 January 1996, lot 197 as M.A. Shee; a half length sold Christie's, 17 November 1967, lot 48 as Hoppner.

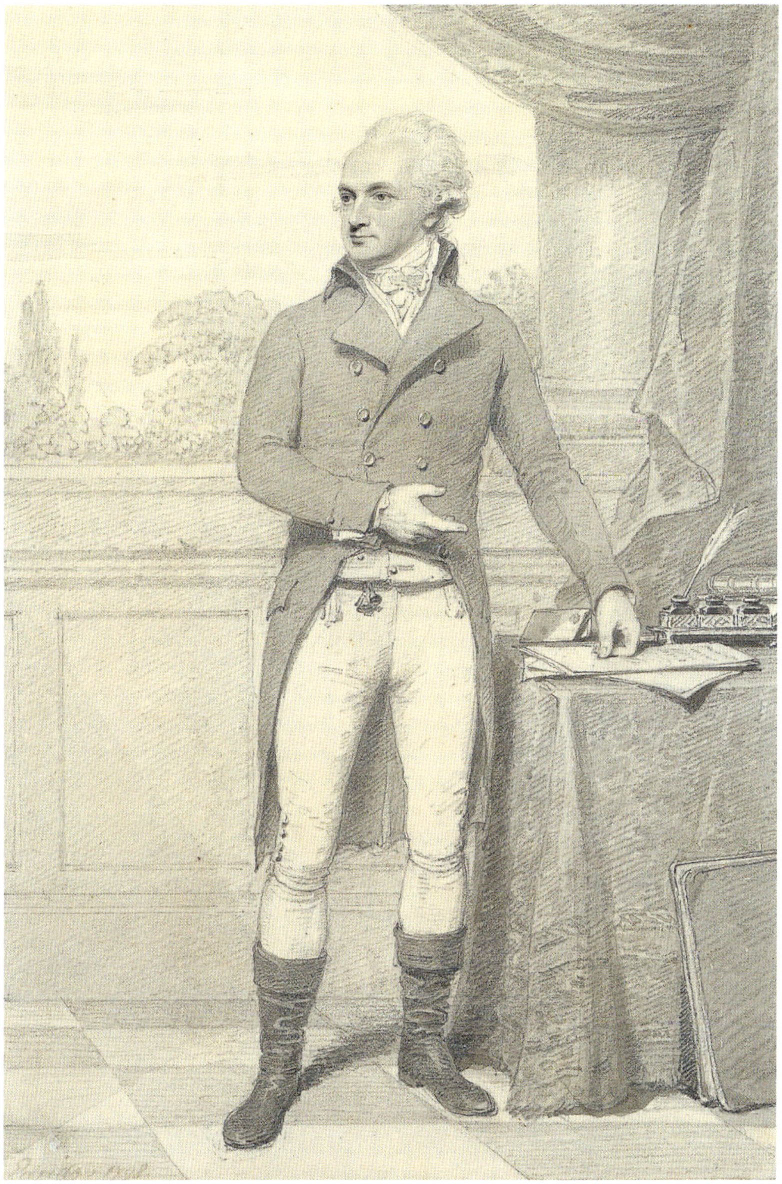

1st Earl of SHEFFIELD NPG *2185*

SHEFFIELD, John Baker Holroyd, 1st Earl of 1735-1821

Statesman; served with 21st Dragoons 1760-63; travelled in Europe 1763-66; MP 1781-84, 1790-1802, an accomplished spokesman on commerce and agriculture; cr. Baron Sheffield of Dunamore [I] 1781, Baron Sheffield of Roscommon [I] 1783, Baron Sheffield [GB] 1802, and Earl of Sheffield [I] 1816; FRS 1783; friend and editor of Edward Gibbon, whom he first met at Lausanne in 1764.

'friendly, honourable, well informed, and sedulous' (William, 1st Baron Auckland, 1806).

'always employed for himself, his friends, and the public, and always persuading himself that he wishes for leisure and repose' (Edward Gibbon, 1792).

745 see Groups, *The House of Commons 1793-94* by KARL ANTON HICKEL 1793-95

2185 HENRY EDRIDGE 1798

Pencil and wash on paper watermarked *1794* 26.5 x 18 (10½ x 7⅛) laid in a grey-washed paper mount; signed, bottom left: *Edridge 1798*; there is general fading and a repaired tear bottom left; his right foot was redrawn.[1]

Collections: By descent at Sheffield Place[2] to the 3rd Earl of Sheffield (d.1909); sold by a legatee, Sotheby's, 22 February 1928, lot 8, bt. Meatyard for the NPG.

Exhibition: RA 1799(629).

A small oval portrait in oils of Lord Sheffield by Edridge was sold Sotheby's, 22 February 1928, lot 33 (together with portraits of his two daughters Louisa and Maria).

1 Label formerly verso of Henry Brookes, 28 Coventry Street, supplier of drawing paper, picture and glass frames etc.
2 Where listed c.1804 (Harding, I, p.10).

ICONOGRAPHY

1764-65 Pastel by Thomas Hickey, whole-length standing before Roman ruins. Sheffield sale, Christie's, 11 December 1909, lot 3, unattributed (but cf. Harding, I, p.9, as 'Lord Sheffield in the uniform of the Royal Forresters Hickey'). If painted in Italy, as the Roman ruins might suggest, the portrait must be dated 1764-65 when Holroyd, Ridley (see below) and Hickey were together in Rome. Holroyd was a Cornet in the 21st Dragoons (Royal Forresters) from April 1760, and Captain from December 1761.

1764-65 Painting by Thomas Hickey, whole length, with Col. Richard Ridley. Sheffield sale, Christie's, 11 December 1909, lot 84 as Hickey 1766 (Harding, I, p.15, as 'Lord Sheffield & Col. Ridley reading. painted at Rome Hickey', indicating a date of 1764-65, see above).

1769 Portrait by John Smart. Sheffield Place c.1804 (Harding, I, p.9) with a companion piece of his first wife Abigail, the latter presumably the miniature dated 1769, sold Sotheby's, 11 November 1993, lot 12.

c.1775 Painting by George Romney, half length. Liechtenstein collection, Vienna (from the Sheffield sale, Christie's, 11 December 1909, lot 117).

1777 Painting by Angelica Kauffmann, whole length in Van Dyck dress with a plumed hat. Private collection; Sheffield sale, Christie's, 11 December 1909, lot 94. Engraved J.R. Smith 1777.

1780 Pastel by John Downman, half-length oval. Sheffield sale, Christie's, 11 December 1909, lot 6 sitter unidentified (illus. J.H. Adeane, *Girlhood of Maria Josepha Holroyd*, 1896, f.p.112).

1788 Painting by Joshua Reynolds, half length in Peer's robes. London art market (Mannings 2000, no.918). Painted for Edward Gibbon; Sheffield sale, Christie's, 11 December 1909, lot 114. Exhibited RA 1788(23). Engraved J. Jones 1789.* Version with Earl of Chichester at Stanmer in 1886 (TSB 33/63); copy by Henry Edridge 1795 (J.H. Adeane, *Girlhood of*

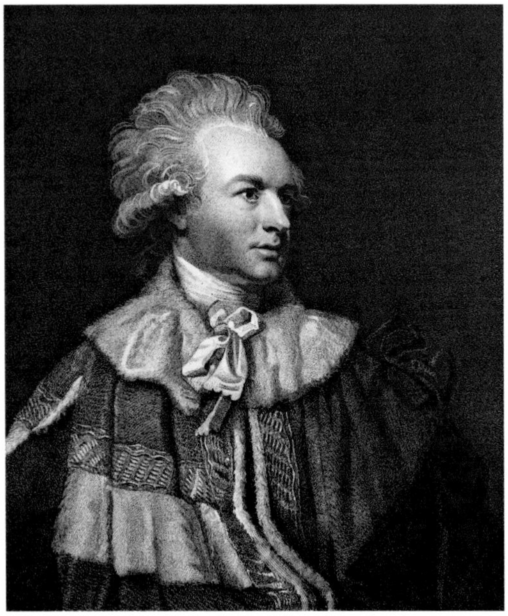

1st Earl of SHEFFIELD J. Jones after Joshua Reynolds 1788 (NPG D 6894)

Maria Josepha Holroyd, 1896, p.334); miniature copy by William Grimaldi 1788, New Orleans Museum of Art (illus. P.P. Bardo, *English and Continental Portrait Painting*, 1978, p.67, no.61; Grimaldi 1873, p.37, no.402, with a pencil drawing, p.47, no.97).

1791 Silhouette, whole-length standing, with Edward Gibbon. Private collection (illus. G. de Beer, *Gibbon*, 1967, p.101).

1793-95 Painting by K.A. Hickel, *The House of Commons 1793-94*, see Groups NPG 745.

1798 Drawing by Henry Edridge, see NPG 2185.

1806 Painting by M.A. Shee,* whole length. Parliament Building (assembly hall), Fredericton, New Brunswick. Commissioned by the House of Assembly, New Brunswick, for Province Hall. Exhibited RA 1806(29), Farington commenting (10 April 1806) 'very indifferent'.

c.1815-20 Miniature by C. Borckhardt,* white hair, white neckcloth, black coat. Victoria and Albert Museum (Evans 71).

1820 Painting by George Beechey, half length. Sotheby's, 22 February 1928, lot 20 as Sir W. Beechey. Exhibited RA 1821(434).

DOUBTFUL PORTRAITS

Two weak anon. bust-length oval engravings of 1783 (paired with a 'Miss Charlotte F - r') and 1784 (*European Mag.*).

A pastel attributed to H.D. Hamilton, Myers Galleries, exhibited *Italy & the Grand Tour*, Grosvenor House Fair, n.d., no.9. Painting attributed to M.W. Peters, half length in Van Dyck dress, sold Christie's, 10 November 1961, lot 125 (bearing the Sheffield arms).

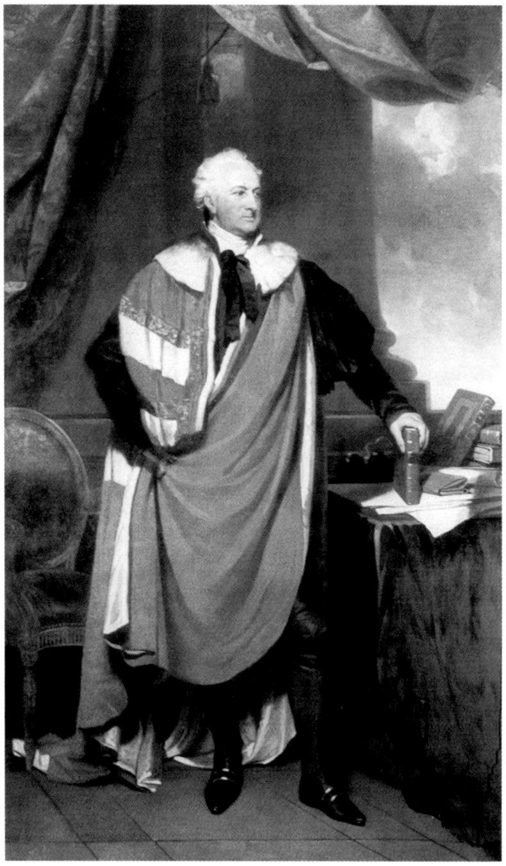

1st Earl of SHEFFIELD by M.A. Shee 1806 (Legislative Assembly of New Brunswick, Fredericton)

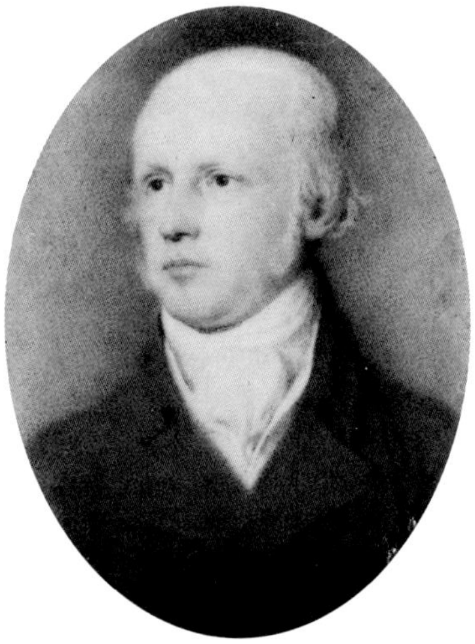

1st Earl of SHEFFIELD by C. Borckhardt c.1815-20 (Victoria and Albert Museum)

SHELBURNE, William, 2nd Earl of, see LANSDOWNE

SHERIDAN, Mrs Elizabeth, *née* Linley 1754-92

Singer, famed for her voice and her beauty; eldest dau. of Thomas Linley, musician of Bath; first performed at the age of twelve; in 1772 she sang before the King; m. 1773 R.B. Sheridan, after which she stopped singing in public; she assisted Sheridan at the Drury Lane Theatre and publicly supported Fox; d. of consumption in Bath.

'a late Bishop used to say that "she seemed to him the connecting link between woman and angel"' (Thomas Moore, 1825).

'She is really beautiful; her Complection, a clear, lovely, Animated Brown, with a blooming colour on her Cheeks; her Nose, that most elegant of shapes, Grecian; fine, luxurious, easy setting Hair, a charming Forehead, pretty mouth, & most bewitching Eyes. With all this, her Carriage is modest & unassuming, & her Countenance indicates diffidence, & a strong desire of pleasing; a desire in which she can never be disappointed' (Fanny Burney, 1773).

Abbreviation

Dulwich 1988: G. Waterfield ed., *A Nest of Nightingales; Thomas Gainsborough, The Linley Sisters*, Dulwich, 1988

4905 see Groups, *Portraits in the characters of the Muses* by RICHARD SAMUEL 1778

ICONOGRAPHY

1768 Painting by Thomas Gainsborough, 'a large Picture of Tommy Lindley & his Sister' (Hayes 2001, p.51). Generally equated with the *Beggar Boy and Girl* which Gainsborough sold to the Duke of Dorset in 1784, now Sterling & Francine Clark Institute, Williamstown, Mass. (Waterhouse 1958, no.801; Dulwich 1988, pp.8, 62).

1772 Painting by Thomas Gainsborough,* whole length standing in a landscape with her sister Mary (Mrs Tickell). Dulwich Picture Gallery (Waterhouse 1958, no.450; Dulwich 1988, pp.45, 64). Exhibited RA 1772(95); 'I was just finishing her picture for the Exhibition' wrote Gainsborough (31 March 1772), when she married Sheridan. A bust-length oval ver-

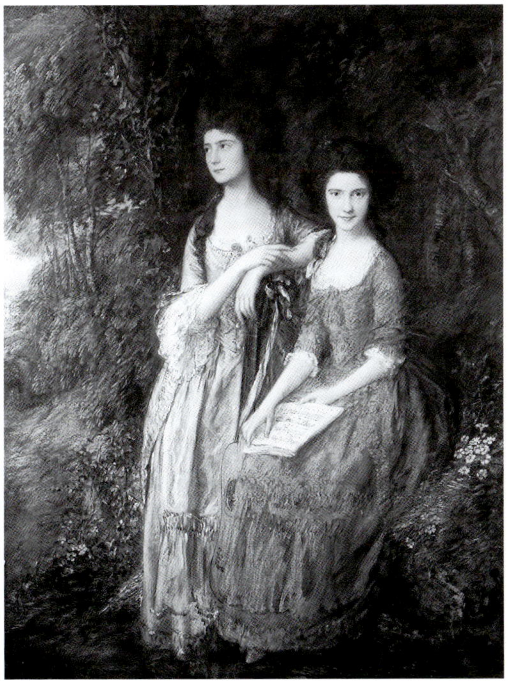

SHERIDAN (left) with her sister by Thomas Gainsborough 1772 (Dulwich Picture Gallery)

sion of Elizabeth's head, attributed to Gainsborough Dupont, in the White House, Washington DC; a copy called Ozias Humphry sold Bonham's, 20 November 1997, lot 65a.

The half-length oval by Gainsborough c.1775 in the Philadelphia Museum of Art (E24-4-13; Waterhouse 1958, no.449; Dulwich 1988, p.58) closely imitates the Dulwich head.

1775 Painting by Joshua Reynolds, whole length as St Cecilia seated playing an organ. Waddesdon Manor (Mannings 2000, no.1614). Engraved W. Dickinson 1776; T. Watson 1779; S.W. Reynolds. Exhibited NPE 1867(665) lent Lord Lansdowne. Copied by Beechey and a half-length pastel version by Ozias Humphry is in the Victoria AG, Bath (Dulwich 1988, p.75).

1778 Painting by Richard Samuel, *Portraits in the characters of the Muses*, see Groups NPG 4905.

1779 Drawing by Ozias Humphry, profile bust to left, looking down. Victoria AG, Bath (Dulwich 1988, p.74). This head recurs in the engraving by J. Ogborne 1779 (as Attention) and in the untraced pastel by Humphry exhibited RA 1796(490), known through the engraving by H. Meyer 1816 (Dulwich 1988, p.75).

1783 Painting by Thomas Gainsborough, whole length, exhibited RA 1783(140), possibly the Washington portrait below.

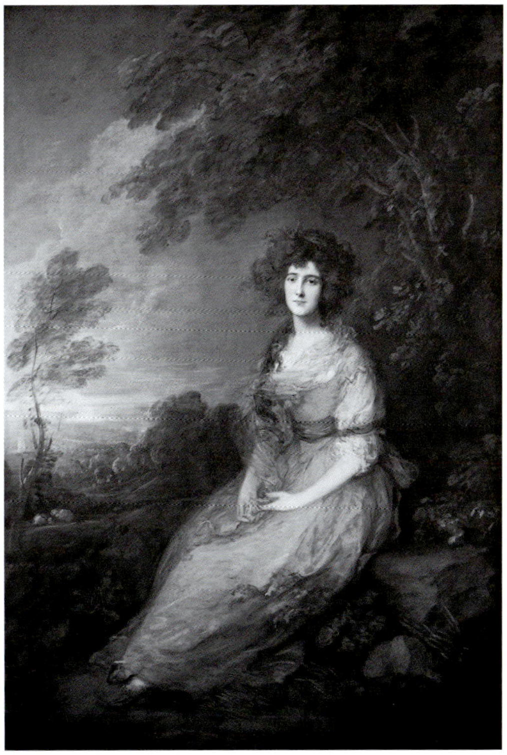

SHERIDAN by Thomas Gainsborough 1785-87 (National Gallery of Art, Washington)

1785-87 Painting by Thomas Gainsborough,* whole-length seated to left in a landscape. NG Washington (1937.1.92; Waterhouse 1958, no.613; Dulwich 1988, pp.44,77; Hayes 1992, pp.103-06). Engraved R. Lane 1825; an unpublished plate by G. Dupont.

DOUBTFUL PORTRAITS

Miniature by Richard Cosway of c.1780 in the Holburne Museum, Bath (Bayne-Powell 1995, no.69); versions illus. J.L. Propert, *History of Miniature Art*, 1887, f.p.114; W. Sichel, *Sheridan*, 1909, I, f.p.320, and Williamson 1905, f.p.52 (reversed). Mrs Sheridan did not apparently like Cosway; in her informal will, as quoted by Sichel, II, pp.222-23, she left to her friend Mrs Canning a portrait of herself 'to be painted by anyone but Cosway'.

Her identity as the model for *Charity*, one of the three theological virtues in the windows of New College, Oxford, designed by Reynolds, is academic (Mannings 2000, no.2116). She has also been recognised in paintings by Benjamin West (Erffa & Staley 1986, no.697), a miniature formerly at Hardwicke House, Hawstead (Farrer 1908, p.161, no.109) and in an engraving after Mrs Crewe, *Maternal Instruction* (illus. W. Sichel, *Sheridan*, 1909, II, p.220).

SHIRLEY, Lady Selina, see HUNTINGDON

SIBTHORP, Humphry 1713-97

Botanist, of Canwick Hall, Lincs.; as Sherardian Professor of Botany at Oxford from 1747 he delivered one indifferent public lecture; a correspondent of Linnaeus who dedicated to him the genus *Sibthorpia*; FRS 1788; his son John (see Walker *Regency*) was a more eminent botanist.

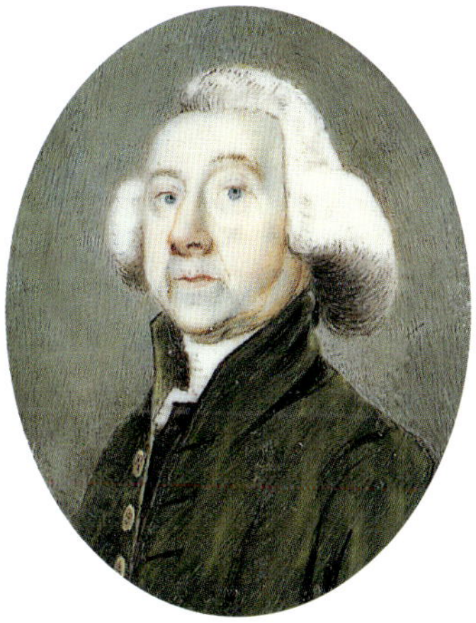

SIBTHORP NPG 4408

4408 UNKNOWN ARTIST c.1780

Watercolour and bodycolour on ivory 7.1 x 5.4 (2¾ x 2⅛); the whites in the hair and neckcloth have flaked away and the face and coat have been retouched; pentimento above his left shoulder.[1]

Blue eyes, white powdered 'physical' wig, wearing a green coat, his black waistcoat just visible.

Collections: By descent to Hon Mrs Dudley Pelham, Canwick Hall, Lincs., by whom presented 1964, together with a miniature of his son John Sibthorp (NPG 4409).

Reference: Walker 1998, no.61 (as c.1794).

Dated by the dress and apparent age of the sitter, NPG 4408 appears not to be by the same hand as the miniature of his son, NPG 4409 (see Walker *Regency*, I, pp.453-54, II, pl.1093.).

1 The previous backing paper (NPG archive), cut from an envelope franked 1859 and addressed to *Mrs Hill/5 Cumberland Place/New Road*, bears an ink inscription: *Doctor Humphrey Sibthorp/Professor of Botany/at Oxford/ died at Instow/ North Devon/ 1797*.

SIDDONS, Mrs Sarah, *née* Kemble 1755-1831

Tragedienne; dau. of a theatrical manager Roger Kemble, sister of the actor John Philip Kemble; m. 1773 William Siddons.

'Her height was above the middle size, but not at all inclined to the *embonpoint*. Her face is peculiarly happy, the features being finely formed, though strong ... Her eye is brilliant and varying like the diamond ...' (James Boaden, 1827).

'Damn the nose, there's no end to it!' (Thomas Gainsborough).

Abbreviation

Asleson 1999: R. Asleson ed., *A Passion for Performance, Sarah Siddons and her Portraitists*, exh. cat., Getty Museum, 1999

50 GILBERT STUART 1787

Canvas 76 x 63.5 (30 x 25) lined, cleaned 1975; craquelure apparent in the lower sleeve, minor losses in the hair and some rubbing in the dress and turban.

Dark blue eyes, powdered hair, large white turban with a white rosette, wearing a pale grey-blue dress with a white fichu and sash, holding a book.

Collections: [the father of Horace Twiss, her nephew, commissioned a portrait from Stuart];[1] family possession[2] descending to John Thadeus Delane,[3] by whom presented 1858.

Exhibitions: *The Gothick*, Brighton, 1975(D16); *Treasures* 1995-96(18); 10 Downing Street, 1996-98; *Muses, Madonnas and Maidens*, Tokyo, 2001(B23).

Reference: Roberts 1907, p.46, f.p.230 as Beechey; Park 1926, no.765 as c.1785; Asleson 1999, pp.48-49; Evans 1999, pp.39-40.

NPG 50 may be compared with the 1782 portrait by Thomas Beach in the demonstration of modest sensibility (and see also Beechey, NPG 5159 below). Accepted for the collection with an attribution to Beechey, but an attribution to Stuart, first proposed in 1914 by C.H. Hart,[4] has since found acceptance. In 1932 Whitley plausibly associated NPG 50 with the announcement in the *World*, 18 April 1787, that Stuart's portrait of Mrs Siddons was

> not yet finished, but if finished with as much spirit and delicacy as it exhibits while this account is writing of it, there will be no inferiority even to the *first* head of Kemble[5] ... [Stuart] dives deep into mind, and brings up with him a conspicuous draught of character and characteristic thought - all as sensible to feeling and to sight as the most palpable projections in any feature of a face.[6]

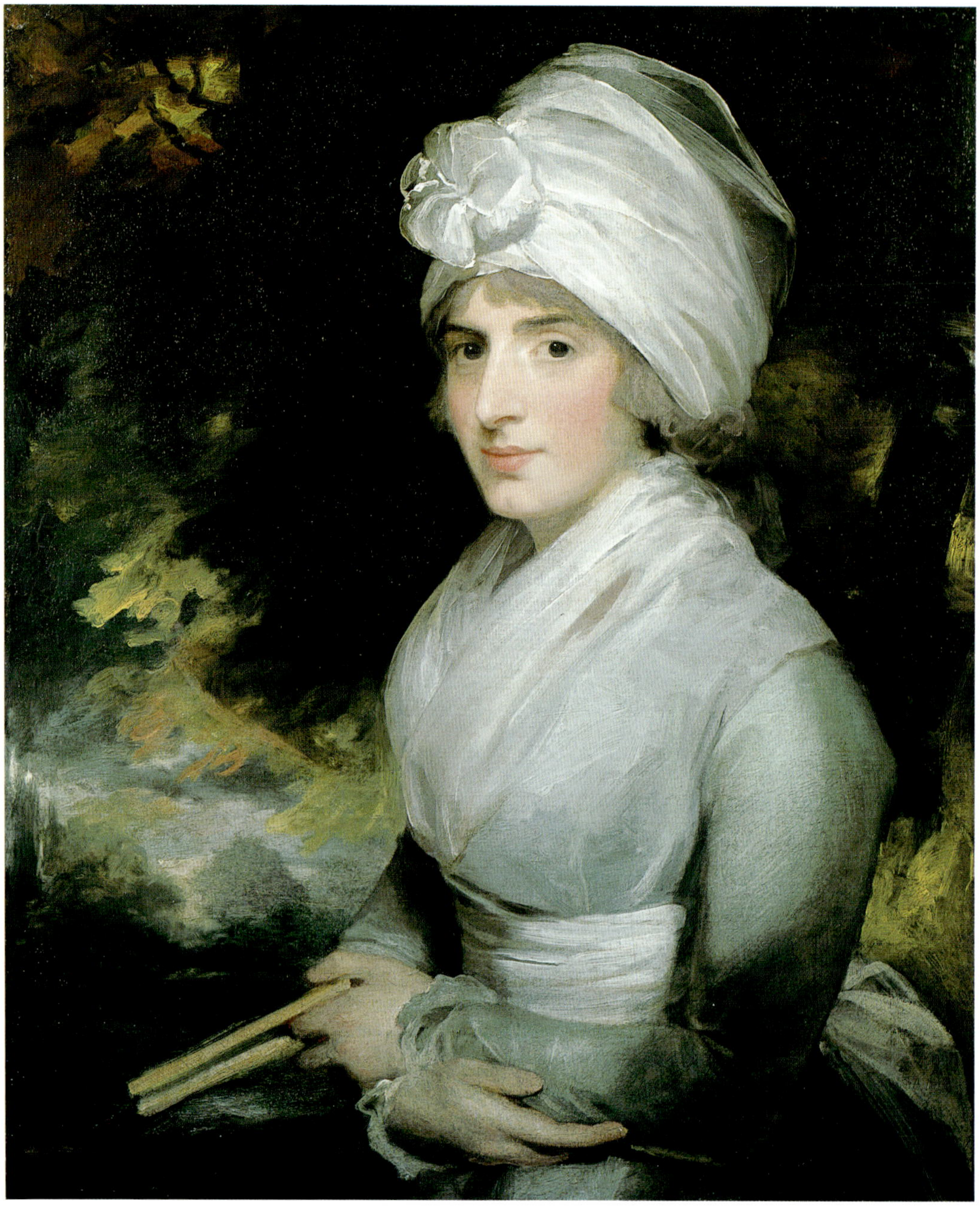

SIDDONS NPG *50*

A copy by W. Horn Rosenberg was sold Christie's, 14 December 1905, part lot 187 as after Beechey, and a version is in an American private collection.[7]

1 Whitley 1932, p.60.
2 Park 1926, no.765, suggested that NPG 50 'was probably the picture sold in London in 1829 for two guineas as by Stuart and of Mrs Kemble'; but Mrs Siddons was then still alive and NPG 50 appears to have remained with her direct descendants; a portrait of Mrs Siddons now identified as Romney, see 1783 below, was sold in 1829 as by 'Stewart' (see J. Watson, *Apollo*, CXXXVI, 1992, pp.149, 151).
3 1817-79, editor of *The Times*, he married a daughter of Horace Twiss, nephew of J.P. Kemble. He wrote to Scharf, 21 July 1859, saying that NPG 50 had been in the Kemble family since it was painted 'and came into my hands through the late Mr Horace Twiss whose mother was a Kemble' (NPG archive).
4 As described by Park 1926, no.765.
5 An untraced head, as Macbeth, see Whitley 1932, p.53.
6 Quoted in Whitley 1932, pp.59-60.
7 A portrait once called Mrs Siddons and formerly attributed to Stuart, but probably by Hoppner, was sold Christie's, 16 July 1909, lot 136 (illus. *The Masterpieces of Hoppner*, 1926, p.57, and see McKay & Roberts, *Supplement*, 1914, p.47 (NPG annotations).

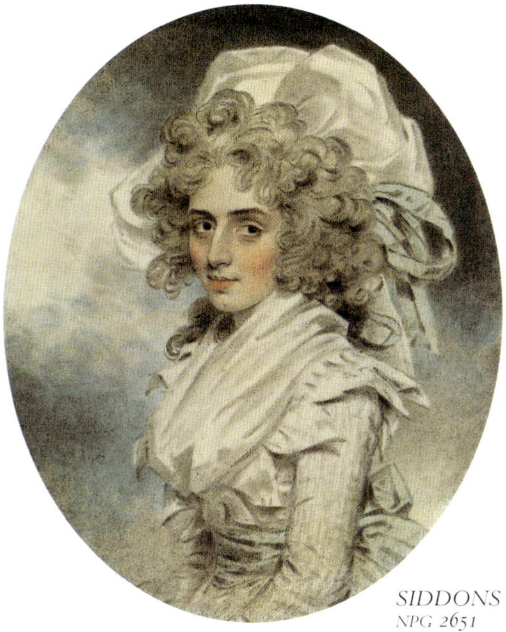

SIDDONS
NPG 2651

2651 JOHN DOWNMAN 1787

Coloured chalk on paper 21.3 x 17.8 (8⅜ x 7) laid down on paper; signed and dated lower left: *J Downman/ del/ 1787.*

Dark eyes, grey powdered hair, rouged complexion; wearing a white hat, a white dress with grey stripes, a white frilly fichu and a hair-ribbon and waistband of silver-blue.

Collections: Henrietta, Lady Brooke (d.1911), by descent to Mrs D.E. Knollys, by whom presented 1934.

Engravings: see below.

Exhibitions: RA 1788(463, 'Portraits of two celebrated Actresses' [Sarah Siddons and Elizabeth Farren, see NPG 2652]); *Downman*, 18 Carlton House Terrace, 1893(68) lent Henrietta, Lady Brooke; *Bicentenary Exhibition*, RA, 1968–69(527); *Georgian Playhouse* 1975(107); *Master Drawings* 1993–95(35).

Reference: Asleson 1999, pp.79–80.

Inscribed by the artist, on a separate paper now mounted with the drawing: *Mrs Siddons 1787. Original/ The great Tragic Actress/I drew this for the Duke of Richmond, but/he preferred the Duplicate./Off the Stage I thought her face more/inclined to the Comic.* In 1787 Downman had collaborated with Mrs Siddons in private theatricals organised by the 3rd Duke of Richmond, providing portraits of contemporary beauties as stage scenery.[1] Downman's discovery of 'the comic' in Mrs Siddons features led to NPG 2651 being criticised when shown at the RA, as being a portrait of 'a pastoral coquette'.[2]

The second version, mentioned by Downman, also signed and dated 1787, was last sold Christie's, 10 July

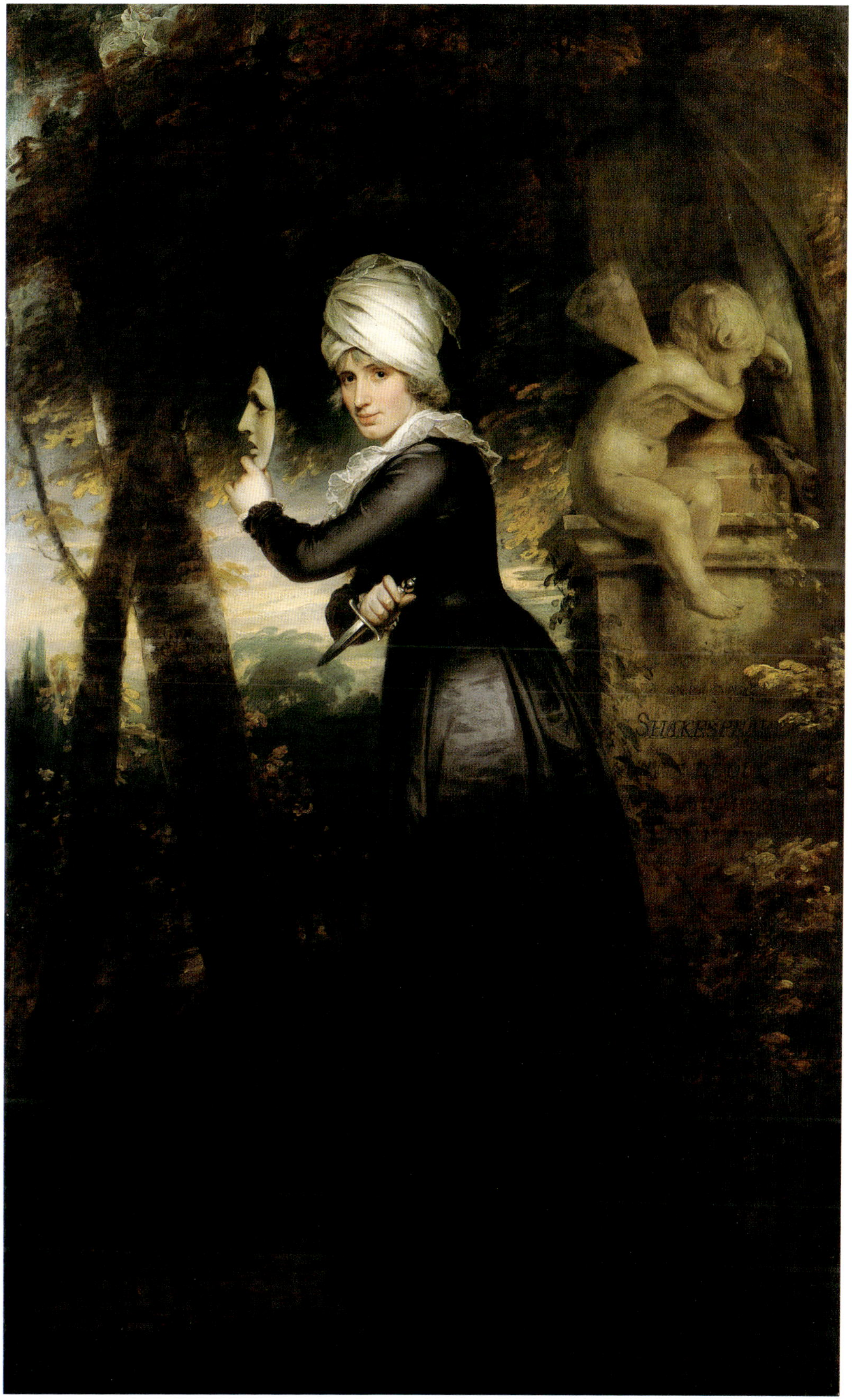

SIDDONS NPG 5159

1990, lot 84. Slight variations (in, for example, the top of her hat and the fold of her waistband) indicate it was this second version which was engraved by P.W. Tomkins in 1797.[3]

An enamel copy by Henry Bone was in an English private collection in 1970 (yellow dress, purple ribbon in hair). A miniature copy was last sold Phillips, 11 November 1991, lot 7a.

1 Asleson 1999, p.79; see S. Rosenfeld, *Temples of Thespis*, 1978, p.36.
2 *St James's Chronicle*, 24 May 1788.
3 Illus. Williamson 1907, pp.12, 37.

5159 WILLIAM BEECHEY, *with the Emblems of Tragedy* 1793

Canvas 246 x 152 (96 x 59½) lined[1] and strip lined 2001; cleaned 1997; a repaired tear upper right above the putto's head; signed and dated *WB p./ 1793* on the tree trunk.

Dark brown eyes, grey powdered hair, highly coloured complexion; a dagger in her right hand, a tragic mask in her right; wearing a black dress, a white turban topped with lace, white frilled muslin collar; a grieving putto sits on the pedestal inscribed: *Shakespeare/ Dedit/ Loqui*.

Collections: Artist's sale, Christie's, 11 June 1836, lot 67, bt. in; studio sale, Rainy's, 19 July 1839, unsold; the 4th Earl Brooke (1818–93) by 1860; Trustees of Lord Brooke's Settlement sale, Christie's, 22 March 1968, lot 75; Dr D.M. MacDonald, by whom presented 1977.

Exhibitions: RA 1794(127, 'Mrs Siddons with the Emblems of Tragedy'); BI 1860(121) and BI 1867(139), lent by the Earl of Warwick; RA 1878(229, as Reynolds); *Guelph* 1891(354, as Reynolds); *Fair Women*, Grafton Gallery, 1894(79, as Reynolds?); *The Collection of Dr D.M. Macdonald*, Leggatt, 1970(1); *Regency Portraits*, Kenwood, 1986; *Art on the Line*, Courtauld Gallery, 2001(64).

Reference: Graves & Cronin, III, p.900; Roberts 1907, pp.45–46, 266; Asleson 1999, pp.75–76.

Beechey's portrait conveys Mrs Siddon's eminence as a Shakespearean tragedienne through emblem rather than attitude or performance, thus contrasting with the great Reynolds whole length of 1784. It was criticised at the RA in 1794 by Pasquin: 'the attitutude is affectedly disgusting. It conveys the semblance of a gipsy in sattin, disporting at a masquerade, rather than the murder-loving Melpomene. As a portrait the figure is too thin for the original'.[2] Ironically NPG 5159 came to bear an attribution to Reynolds between 1878 and 1894 (see above) which was dismissed by Graves & Cronin in 1900.

The head closely resembles that painted by Gilbert Stuart in 1787, see NPG 50 above. A reduced version, probably a preliminary sketch, the pedestal prominently inscribed *Sacred/ to/ the Memory/ of/ Will:/ Shakespere* was in the collection of Mrs Arthur Bull at Brynderwen, Usk, in 1962.[3]

1 Stretcher stamped *F. Leedham Liner*, indicating a date c.1880.
2 Quoted by Roberts 1907, pp.45–46.
3 Steegman, II, p.125, no.5. Possibly the small copy of *Mrs Siddons as the Tragic Muse* sold Christie's, 26 May 1821, lot 17.

5460 JOHN HENNING 1807

Enamel 5.8 (2¼) maximum diameter, the figure 4 x 3.5 (1½ x 1⅜); incised on shoulder: *1807/* HENNING/F

Collections: Purchased from Agnew 1981.

Exhibition: *Sculpture and Works of Art*, Agnew, 1981(10).

Henning exhibited a medallion of Mrs Siddons at the Association of Scottish Artists, Edinburgh, in 1808. A copper mould and a plaster cast are in the Paisley Art Gallery and another cast is in the Scottish National Portrait Gallery (PG 537). A related drawing by him was sold Sotheby's, 15 March 1984, lot 25.[1] In 1810 Henning exhibited a bust of Mrs Siddons in Edinburgh. These were apparently the items he again exhibited at the RSBA in 1824: no.343 a 'Bust of Mrs Siddons' and no.515 a 'Portrait of Mrs Siddons fifteen Years ago; A Study for a Medallion (drawing)'.

Benjamin West, in speaking 'very favourably' of Henning's work, singled out his 'life size [drawing] of Mrs Siddons and her small Medallion'.[2]

1 Illus. *Henning* 1977, n.p.
2 Henning to William Mure, 9 January 1844; quoted in *Henning* 1977, n.p.

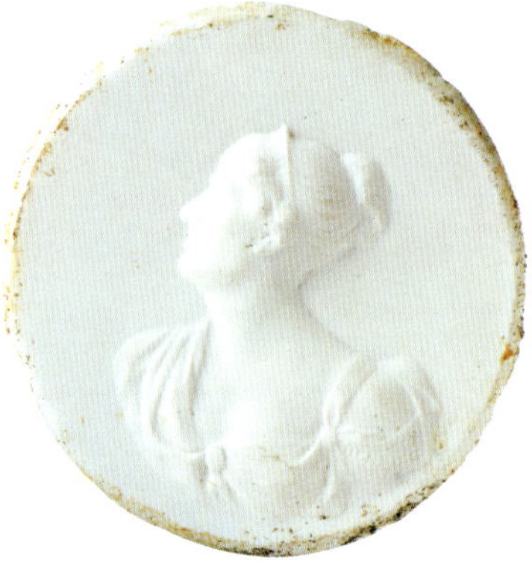

SIDDONS NPG 5460

642 THOMAS CAMPBELL 1843

Marble high relief 116 x 95 (45¾ x 37½), the figure 82 (32¼) high; some staining and minor abrasion; small chip in plinth and the outside edges of the surround.

Holding a scroll in her left hand, and wearing a coronet.

Collections: Bought from the studio sale of Thomas Campbell (d.1858) by James Thomson Gibson-Craig, by whom presented 1881.

Exhibition: RA 1856(1295, 'Mrs Siddons; alto relievo in marble').

Campbell's first proposal for the monument to Mrs Siddons in Westminster Abbey, for which the actor William Macready had long campaigned.[1] This first design of a 'half length figure. In alto-relievo, in a niche' was ready in 1843, and in 1844 it was confirmed that it would be placed in Westminster Abbey, although it could not be 'considered as sufficiently important; but the sum subscribed was singularly small'.[2] But on 28 June 1845 Campbell promised to send Macready a drawing of a grander design, evidently the full-length version of NPG 642. On 27 February 1846 Macready advised Campbell of 'a defect in the proportion; he admitted it, and promised to add length to the form below the bust'. By December 1846 Campbell had completed the model, 'seven feet in height, ideally draped, and holding in the hand a scroll', and the statue was installed in the Abbey in October 1849.[3]

On 9 April 1881 Gibson-Craig, the former owner of NPG 642, wrote that 'All who have seen the statue & what I now offer, much prefer the alto relievo':

> When I used to pass through London, I generally called at Campbell's Studio & I several times tried to purchase the Alto relievo, but he never would part with it. After his decease, there was a sale of his works,[4] when I sent an order, and secured it.[5]

1 See *The Diaries of William Charles Macready 1833–51*, 1912, II, pp.95, 117, 123, 217, 298, 325.
2 *Art Union*, 1843, p.247, and 1844, p.8.
3 *Athenaeum*, 1846, p.1273; *ILN*, 6 October 1849, p.229.
4 Not listed in Lugt.
5 Letter to Scharf (NPG archive).

ICONOGRAPHY

See also the *Harvard Catalogue*, IV, pp.56–67, and Highfill, XIV, pp.37–67 (listing further portrayals of Siddons in character). For an overall view, see Asleson 1999, to which the following account is deeply indebted.

Mrs Siddons remained unmistakeable in her tragic roles, and many portraits and depictions of her in character are included below.

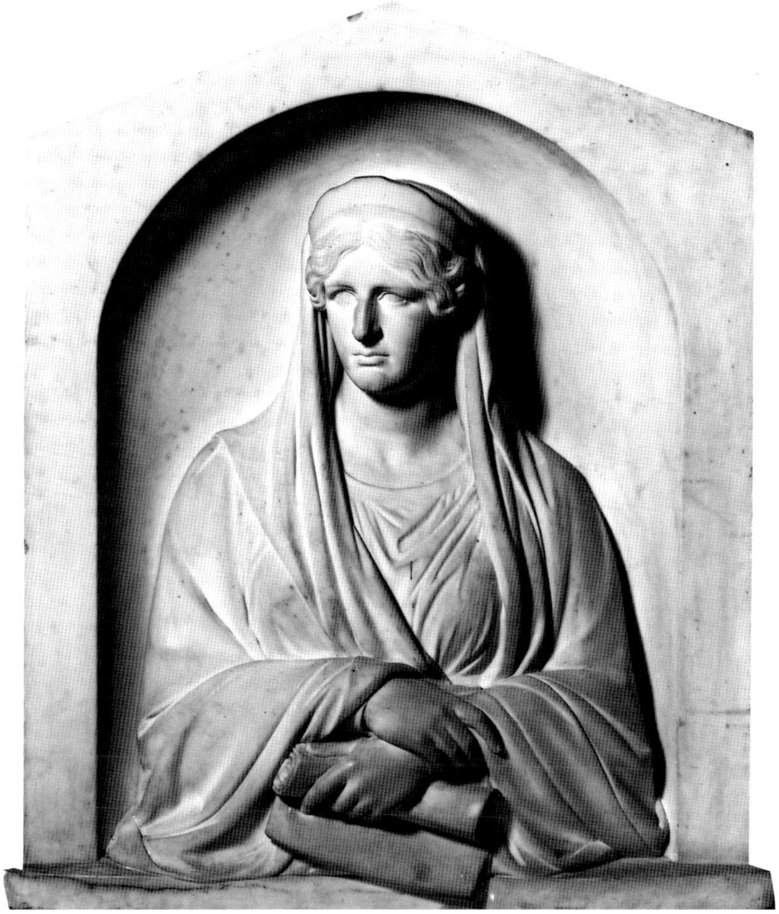

SIDDONS NPG *642*

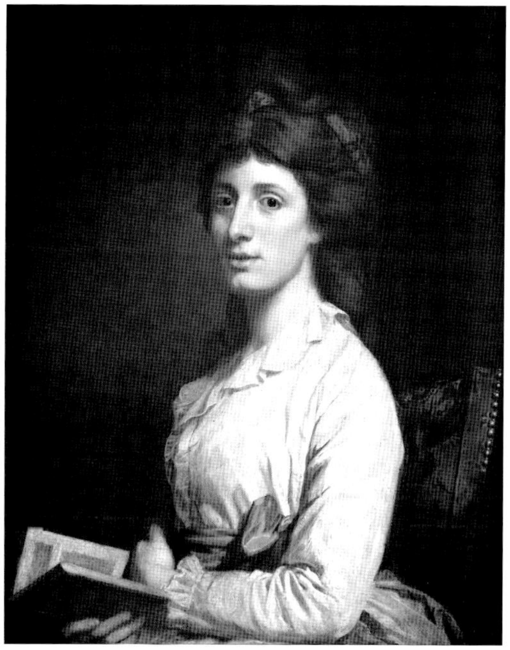

SIDDONS by Thomas Beach 1782 (Auckland Art Gallery, Toi o Tamaki)

1780 Painting by William Hamilton, whole length as Euphrasia in Murphy's *The Grecian Daughter*. Stratford Town Hall (illus. Asleson 1999, p.57). Exhibited RA 1780(339). Engraved J. Caldwall 1788 and 1789. Reduced versions sold Sotheby's, 16 February 1966, lot 127; Christie's, 13 April 1927, lot 107, and in a private collection.

An unfinished head attributed to William Hamilton (Theatre Museum, D.76; Ashton 1992, no.11) may have been a preliminary study, the head at the same angle as in the Reynolds of 1784.

1782 Drawings made at Bath by the thirteen-year-old Thomas Lawrence: half-length pastel as Zara in Congreve's *Mourning Bride*, private collection 1964, engraved J.R. Smith 1783 (illus. Asleson 1999, p.44); a profile drawing, Beinecke Library, Yale University, probably the basis for the engraving by T. Trotter 1783 of Euphrasia in Murphy's *Grecian Daughter* after Lawrence (illus. Asleson 1999, pp.60-1); bust-length oval in riding habit, engraved F. Jukes 1783 *from a crayon painting*; watercolour copy, inscribed *By Horace Hone ARA from a Painting by Lawrence of Bath 1782*, in the Garrick Club (Ashton 1997, no.745).

1782 Painting by William Hamilton, whole length with her eight-year-old son Henry, as Isabella in Garrick's *Isabella*. Exhibited RA 1785(98). Engraved J. Caldwall 1785 (illus. Asleson 1999, p.54). Versions formerly with Sir William Fitzherbert (exhibited *Midland Houses*, Birmingham, 1938, no.133); with Mrs R. Butler 1975, and Garrick Club dated 1784 (Ashton 1997, no.749, from the Nettlefold collection). A bust-length version dated 1783, from Stanton Harcourt, is in a private collection (Asleson 1999, p.8; see G. Ashton, *Apollo*, CXIV, 1981, pp.88, 92n3).

In the general enthusiasm to see this picture before it was finished 'carriages thronged to the artist's door; and, if every fine lady who stept out of them did not actually weep before the painting, they had all of them, at least, their white handkerchiefs ready' (T. Campbell, *Life of Mrs Siddons*, 1834, I, p.191; Asleson 1999, p.28).

The same subject by Thomas Stothard engraved by W. Sharp 1783, echoes Hamilton's composition (illus. Asleson 1999, p.54).

1782 Painting by Thomas Beach, whole length as Melancholy from Milton's *Penseroso*. Sotheby's, 10 November 1993, lot 61 (illus. Asleson 1999, p.50). Exhibited SA 1783(24). Engraved W. Dickinson 1782.

1782 Painting by Thomas Beach,* half length holding a book. Auckland AG. Exhibited SA 1783(28). Engraved W. Ridley 1791.

1782 Painting by J.K. Sherwin, half length as Euphrasia in Murphy's *Grecian Daughter*. Theatre Museum (D.77; Ashton 1992, no.10). Engraved J.K. Sherwin 1782 (illus. Asleson 1999, p.60) and W. Holl 1800. Another version in a Scottish private collection.

1783 Paintings by George Romney. Mrs Siddons sat to Romney between February and May 1783 (Ward & Roberts 1904, II, pp.142-43). A whole length, bought from the artist in 1785, was subsequently cut down (see Asleson 1999, pp.66-69, 93-94n73). Two half-length versions, leaning on her right hand, are in private collections, one showing ivy leaves in her hair (illus. Highfill, XIV, p.6; *Romney* 2002, no.104), the other a turban (Sotheby's, 16 November 1983, lot 50) (both illus. J. Watson, *Apollo*, CXXXVI, 1992, pp.147, 149); a miniature copy of the latter belonged to Mme Belloc in 1893 (SSB 127/67).

Another canvas by Romney, *Sidonian Recollections*, c.1785-90, shows three wildly tragic heads, Princeton University Art Museum (illus. Asleson 1999, p.45).

1783 Painting by R.E. Pine, whole length as Euphrasia in Murphy's *Grecian Daughter*, engraved C. Watson 1784 (illus. Asleson 1999, p.62).

1783 Miniature by Richard Crosse, three-quarter length, hands clasped. Victoria and Albert Museum (P.146.1929; illus. *Portrait Miniature in England*, 1998, p.94, pl.63). Exhibited RA 1783(334).

1783 Enamel by William Birch, bust-length oval, as Isabella in Garrick's *Isabella*. Christie's, 3 December 1963, lot 146. Exhibited RA 1783(325). Copy sold Phillips, 1 October 1986, lot 268.

1783 Portrait by James Turner, exhibited SA 1783(297).

1783 Painting by John Bateman, half-length oval profile. Engraved T. Burke 1783. Resembling Hone's 1784 miniature.

1783 Painting by Thomas Beach, whole length as Calista in Rowe's *Fair Penitent*, exhibited SA 1783(25).

On 11 February 1784 Mrs Siddons told Lord Hardwicke that she was 'much honoured by [his] wishing a resemblance of her, and will as soon as possible sit to Mr Collins [Richard Collins?], *but at present she is under the hands of three painters which with her other avocations fully employs her' (Whitley 1928, p.35).*

1784 Painting by Joshua Reynolds,* whole length as *The Tragic Muse*. Huntington Art Collections, San Marino, Calif. (21.2; Mannings 2000, no.1619; Asleson 1999, pp.97-140; H. McPherson, *Eighteenth-Century Studies*, XXXIII, 2000, pp.401-30; *Huntington* 2001, no.79). Exhibited RA 1784(190). First engraved F. Haward 1787 (exhibited RA 1787, no.512). The pose derived from Michelangelo's *Isaiah* or Domenichino's *St John the Evangelist* (Glyndebourne), despite a wealth of Siddons anecdote; it was later used by De Wilde in his painting of her as Medea. A studio version dated 1789, painted for Noel Desenfans, is in Dulwich Picture Gallery (Mannings 2000, no.1620; Asleson 1999, pp.128-36); a bust-length version was sold Sotheby's, 22 April 1964, lot 31.

The numerous copies include those sold Christie's, 12 July 1990, lot 82, from Langley Park; by Charles McLagan (Herbert AG, Coventry), by Mary, Lady Buckingham (private collection), and, reduced, by Moses Haughton 1799 (exhibited *Mrs Jordan*, Kenwood, 1995, no.39), and William Harness (Christie's, 4 May 1922, lot 71); a three-quarter length copy belongs to the Royal Academy of Dramatic Art, London; copies in miniature include those by Henry Collen (Christie's, 27 November 1985, lot 162) and an enamel by J. Haslem (RA 1838, no.660); a small watercolour copy by Julia Knight 1837 sold Sotheby's 24 September 1997, lot 379.

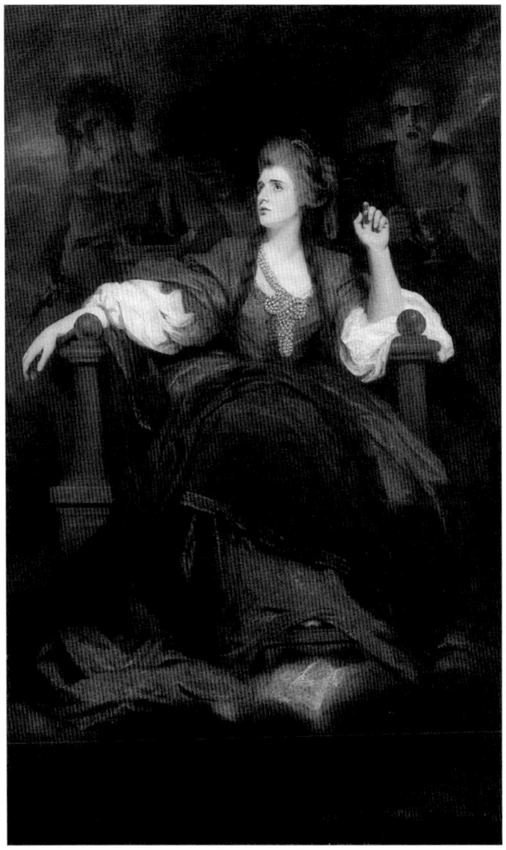

SIDDONS by Joshua Reynolds 1784 (Huntington Art Collections, San Marino, California)

1784 Silhouette by John Miers (illus. J. Woodiwiss, *British Silhouettes*, 1961, p.21). There were at least two other silhouettes by Miers, examples sold Bonham's, 21 February 1996, lot 86, and illus. *CL*, XCVII, 1945, p.726.

1784 Wedgwood plaque modelled by John Flaxman (Reilly 1973, p.306; Reilly 1994, p.351). The model of the Queen in the Wedgwood chess set of 1783-85 was also said to derive from Mrs Siddons (Reilly 1994, p.188).

1784 Enamel miniature by Horace Hone, half length. NG of Ireland (7318; illus. Asleson 1999, p.20; Caffrey 2000, pp.95-97). Engraved F. Bartolozzi 1785; G.H. Phillips 1825. A pastel copy by Thomas Lawrence, dated 1786 in the Tate Gallery (N 2222; illus. *Pickpocketing the Rich*, Bath, 2002, no.58) and a copy in enamel exhibited RA 1822(554).

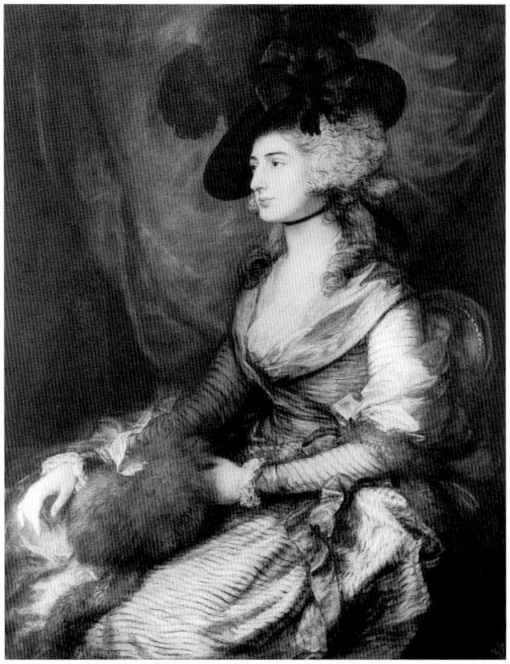

SIDDONS by Thomas Gainsborough 1785 (National Gallery, London)

Closely related miniatures by Hone sold Sotheby's, 4 December 1985, lot 201, dated 1785; and dated 1786, with oriental head dress and fur tippet, sold Sotheby's, Geneva, 25/27 May 1993, lot 9 (illus. Asleson 1999, p.20).

Another half-length type, dated 1784, with the Royal Shakespeare Memorial Theatre, Stratford-upon-Avon (illus. *RS Theatre Gallery* [1981], p.24).

Hone exhibited further miniatures of Mrs Siddons, RA 1795(387) and RA 1804(487 as 'Mrs Siddons in the year 1785').

c.1784 Miniature by Jeremiah Meyer. Sotheby's, 11 July 1991, lot 277 (a silhouette by Miers on the verso).

c.1784 Painting by William Hamilton, three-quarter length with a plumed hat as Zara from Congreve's *Mourning Bride*. Sotheby's, 5 February 1947(78). A half-length version sold Christie's, 21 November 1975, lot 51.

'Perhaps Mrs Siddons has given greater exertions to the pencils of artists than any lady in the dramatic world' (Morning Herald, *12 March 1785)*

1785 Painting by Thomas Gainsborough,* three-quarter length seated with large black hat. NG London (683; Waterhouse 1958, no.617; Egerton 1998, pp.114-19). Drawing Cleveland Museum of Art (Hayes 1970, no.64; illus. Egerton 1998, p.116). After being acquired by the National Gallery in

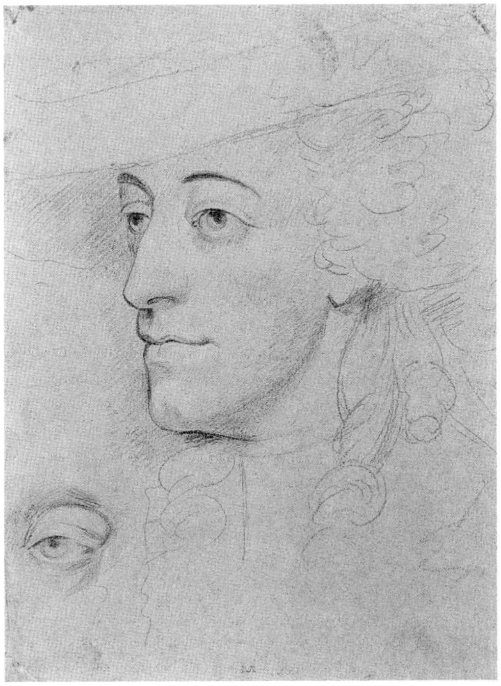

SIDDONS by David Martin c.1785 (National Gallery of Scotland)

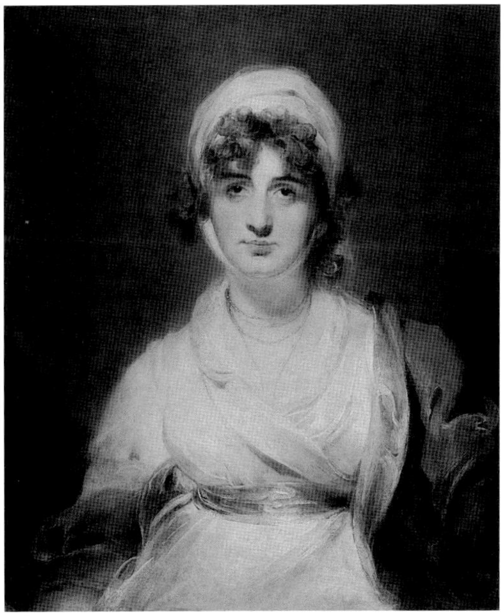

SIDDONS by Thomas Lawrence 1803-04 (Tate Gallery, London)

1862 the portrait was much copied. First engraved R. Graves 1869. Copies include examples in the Theatre Royal, Bristol, and in the Folger Shakespeare Library (Pressly 1993, p.197); an enamel by W.B. Ford was exhibited RA 1863(879).

1785 Model in enamel for a gem by William Lane, exhibited RA 1785(266).

1785 'Model in small for a statue executing in marble, with a likeness of Mrs Siddons', by John Hickey, exhibited RA 1785(637). See also 1786.

1785 Portrait by Alexander Pope, exhibited RA 1785(112).

c.1785 Painting attributed to Daniel Gardner, whole length in character with another actress. Mrs Hart sale, Christie's, 28 November 1927, lot 85. An undated entry in a Gardner sketchbook listed a *Mrs Siddons 3' 9 x 2' 11*. A crayon portrait of *Mrs Siddons as the Tragic Muse* belonged to G.H. Gardner in 1856 (Williamson 1921, pp.48, 151-2).

c.1785 Miniature by Richard Cosway, bust-length oval. Private collection (illus. *ILN*, 7 June 1890). In 1785 'Cosway's delicate small whole length' was nearing completion, probably the drawing of *Mrs Siddons as Tragedy* now in a private collection (Highfill, VI, p.23; Egerton 1998, p.117).

c.1785 Chalk drawing by David Martin,* half length wearing broad-brimmed hat. NG of Scotland (Egerton 1998, p.118).

1786 Painting by Thomas Beach, as Lady Macbeth three-quarter length, with J.P. Kemble. Garrick Club (Ashton 1997, no.390). Exhibited RA 1786(199); Beach exhibited a second portrait of Mrs Siddons alone in the same exhibition, no.381.

1786 Statuette by John Hickey, as Cassandra, whole-length standing. Sotheby's, New York, 11 January 1995, lot 163. Exhibited RA 1786(616). Copy sold Christie's, 15 March 1798, lot 44 'after the original by Mr Hickey in the collection of Earl Fitzwilliam'.

1786 Watercolour by William Hamilton, whole length, a book in her right hand. Victoria and Albert Museum (D.24).

1787 Paintings by Gilbert Stuart and John Downman, see NPG 50 and NPG 2651.

1787 Pastel by John Russell, half-length seated in white with silver-blue ribbons. Private collection (illus. *Connoisseur*, XV, 1906, f.p.145). Exhibited RA 1787(156).

c.1787 Pastel by J.J. Masquerier, bust-length oval. Christie's, 14 June 1977, lot 216.

1790 Portrait by J. Loggan, exhibited RA 1790(685).

1790 Pencil drawing by Thomas Lawrence, half length, left hand on chair back (illus. Asleson 1999, p.82). Etched by the artist, 'an experiment which failed' (*Lawrence* 1964, p.243). Fine Arts Museums of San Francisco.

1790s Drawing by Thomas Lawrence, profile, wearing a high-crowned hat. Garrick Club (Ashton 1997, no.744). Engraved W. Nicholls 1810.

c.1790 Painting by John Opie, bust length. Private collection (illus. Highfill, XIV, p.30; Asleson 1999, p.42).

1791 Watercolour by William Hamilton, whole length as Jane Shore. Victoria and Albert Museum (D.25).

c.1791 Painting by Samuel De Wilde, whole length as Isabella in Garrick's *Isabella*. Phillips, 21 June 1994, lot 37 (illus. Asleson 1999, p.17). Engraved W. Leney 1792 (illus. Burnim 1998, p.228).

1792 Bust by J.C. Rossi, exhibited RA 1792(744).

1793 Painting by William Beechey, see NPG 5159.

1793 Drawing by William Hamilton, whole length, wearing a cap. Christie's, 14 December 1971, lot 54.

1794 A cast of a bust by Anne Seymour Damer, as Melpomene, with vine leaves in her hair, exhibited RA 1795(733). Terracotta version, dated 1794, private collection (illus. *Hidden Treasures*, Oxford, 1993, p.47).

1795 See under 1784 Hone.

1796 Painting by Thomas Lawrence, half length in white. Private collection (Garlick 1989, no.715b). Exhibited RA 1797(166). Engraved C. Turner 1826. Described by a contemporary as 'unquestionably the most exact in point of similitude that has ever appeared of that admirable actress' (Whitley 1928, II, p.214).

A second similar half length in a private collection (Garlick 1989, no.715d), possibly the 'Lawrence's ¾ head of Mrs Siddons' which Farington noted (17 May 1796) had pleased the Kemble family.

A third similar half length is in the Tate Gallery* (N 785; Garlick 1989, no.715c; Asleson 1999, p.7). Engraved J. Heath 1799. Enamel copy by Henry Bone 1798 (Royal Collection, Walker 1992, no.786; preparatory drawings, dated 1798, in the NPG Bone albums (*Bone* 1999, nos.472-73, fig.151). Copies include those in the Museum of London and the Fogg Art Museum (1977.190). So-called Lawrence sketches sold Sotheby's, 18 November 1981, lot 187; Christie's, 29 January 1982, lot 88, and Sotheby's, Bridge House, 14-15 July 1982, lot 36.

1796 Bust by Thomas Banks, exhibited RA 1796 (873 'Bust of Melpomene') identified in the *True Briton*, 26 April 1796 (Highfill, XIV, p.66, no.362).

1797 Painting by G.F. Joseph, as *The Tragic Muse*, exhibited RA 1797(203).

1797 Drawing by Thomas Lawrence, bust-length profile. Private collection. Exhibited *Lawrence*, New Haven, Fort Worth, Richmond, 1993(59). A replica in the Pierpont Morgan Library dated 1798.

1800 Bust by George Bullock, exhibited in the artist's Birmingham studio 1800, possibly a wax (C. Wainwright, *George Bullock*, 1988, pp.145-46, no.73).

c.1800? Chalk drawing attributed to Thomas Lawrence, half length. Private collection. A copy by Prince Hoare sold Sotheby's, 1 August 1974, lot 247.

1802 Drawing by Samuel De Wilde, profile head dated 1 April 1802, on a sheet with other heads. Yale Center for British Art (B1975.4.1640). An undated chalk drawing by De Wilde, half length in profile with a lyre, exhibited *De Wilde*, Northampton, 1971(57) from a private collection.

1802 Bust by Benjamin Papera supplied to Wedgwood (Reilly 1989, II, p.457).

1803-04 Painting by Thomas Lawrence,* whole length. Tate Gallery (N 188; Garlick 1989, no.715e). Exhibited RA 1804(193). Engraved W. Say 1820. Fanny Kemble thought the portrait 'like a handsome cow in a coral necklace', but Mrs Siddons considered it 'more like me than anything that has been done' (Whitley 1930, p.218). A half length pastel copy in the Garrick Club (Ashton 1997, no.747).

c.1804 Drawing by Thomas Lawrence, head, as *The Tragic Muse*. Private collection (illus. Asleson 1999, p.86).

1806 Miniature by Elizabeth Paye, exhibited RA 1806(636).

1807 Drawing and medallion by John Henning, see NPG 5460.

1808 Colossal bust by George Bullock, exhibited RA 1808, no.916 (C. Wainwright, *George Bullock*, 1988, p.146, no.75).

c.1810 Plaster bust by Mrs Siddons herself. Victoria and Albert Museum (D.3329; illus. Asleson 1999, p.67 as c.1790; see also D. Bilbey with M. Trusted, *British Sculpture 1470-2000*, Victoria & Albert Museum, 2002, pp.358-59, where dated '1820s?'). A plaster with slight differences is in the Theatre Museum (S.86.1978).

Mrs Siddons began modelling in clay in 1789, assisted by her friend Anne Seymour Damer (T. Campbell, *Life of Mrs Siddons*, 1834, II, pp.166-67; Asleson 1999, p.28). A medallion portrait was engraved W. Ridley 1796 as *after a Medallion modelled by Mrs Siddons*.

1812 Miniature by P. Henderson, exhibited RA 1812(634).

1812 Plaster by Joachim Smith. Drury Lane Theatre (illus. Highfill, XIV, p.48; Asleson 1999, p.27). Exhibited RA 1813 (916). Replica at Guy's Cliff (Gunnis 1968, p.357) and a cast in the Royal Shakespeare Memorial Theatre, Stratford-on-Avon.

c.1812 Life mask. Soane Museum (illus. L. Hutton, *Portraits in Plaster*, 1894, p.47; Highfill, XIV, p.54, as 'believed to have been taken about the time of her retirement', i.e. 1812).

1813 Painting by G.H. Harlow, small whole length as Lady Macbeth. Garrick Club (Ashton 1997, no.743; Asleson 1999, p.11). Engraved R.J. Lane 1813. A preparatory drawing in a private collection is dated 1813; other drawings are in the Huntington Art Collections, San Marino, Calif. (illus. Asleson 1999, p.88) and in a second private collection.

c.1814 Painting by G.H. Harlow, whole length as Lady Macbeth. Bob Jones University, Greenville (illus. Highfill, XIV, p.27; Asleson 1999, p.87). Exhibited BI 1814(93). Engraved C. Rolls. R. Cooper 1822. A reduced version in the Garrick Club (Ashton 1997, no.742).

c.1814 Pencil drawing by G.H. Harlow, half length, a book in her right hand. Private collection.

1819 Drawing by Peter Contencin, bust length in Murphy's *Grecian Daughter*. Christie's, 31 July 1979, lot 55. Two drawings attributed to Cotencin, heads in profile, are in a private collection.

1819 Painting by Thomas Barber, exhibited RA 1819(465).

1826 Chalk drawing by John Hayter, profile head. British Museum (1913.5.8.9).

1830 Painting by H.P. Briggs,* three-quarter length seated, with Fanny Kemble. Boston Athenaeum. Exhibited RA 1832(343). An oil study for the head of Mrs Siddons was with G.H. Willett, London, in 1920.

Undated Watercolour by W.J. Newton, three-quarter length with her brothers Charles and J.P. Kemble. Sotheby's, 17 January 1996, lot 216.

Posthumous

1843 Marble relief by Thomas Campell, see NPG 642.

1849 Marble statue by Thomas Campbell, Westminster Abbey, see NPG 642.

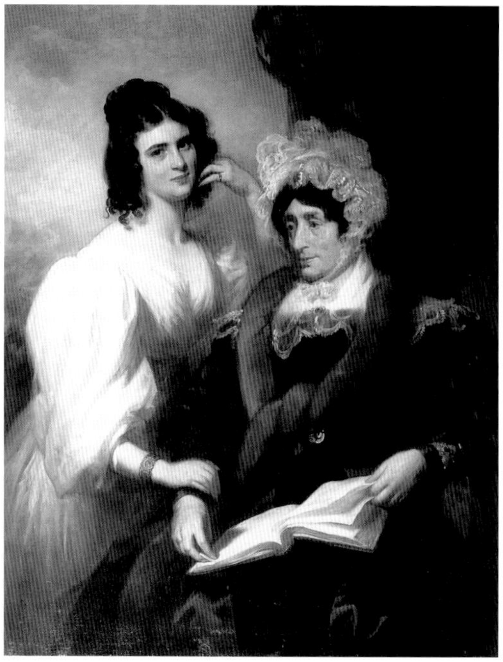

SIDDONS with her niece by H.P. Briggs 1830 (Boston Athenaeum)

1897 Statue in white marble by L-J. Chavalliaud, whole-length seated, as *The Tragic Muse*. St Mary's churchyard, Paddington Green, London (illus. Byron 1981, p.196).

DOUBTFUL PORTRAITS

Painting by Romney (Ashmolean Museum, Oxford; see Romney 2002, no.105). Miniatures by Cosway including one engraved J. Brown 1862 as Mrs Siddons 'aged 27' (T.S. Whalley, *Journals & Corr.*, I, 1852, f.p.361) and another in the Huntington Art Collections, San Marino, Calif. (from the E.M. Hodgkins collection).

Although Mrs Siddons was said to have been one of Hoppner's first sitters (W. Sandby, *History of the Royal Academy*, 1862, I, p.308) such a portrait remains untraced.

A Wedgwood medallion (illus. Reilly 1973, p.306).

SIMPSON, John c.1738-before 1789

Of Bradley Hall, Durham, the son of John Simpson (1710-86), alderman of Newcastle, and Anne, *née* Clutterbuck; matriculated at Christ Church, Oxford, aged 18 in 1756; m. 1768 Lady Anne Lyon, 2nd dau. of the

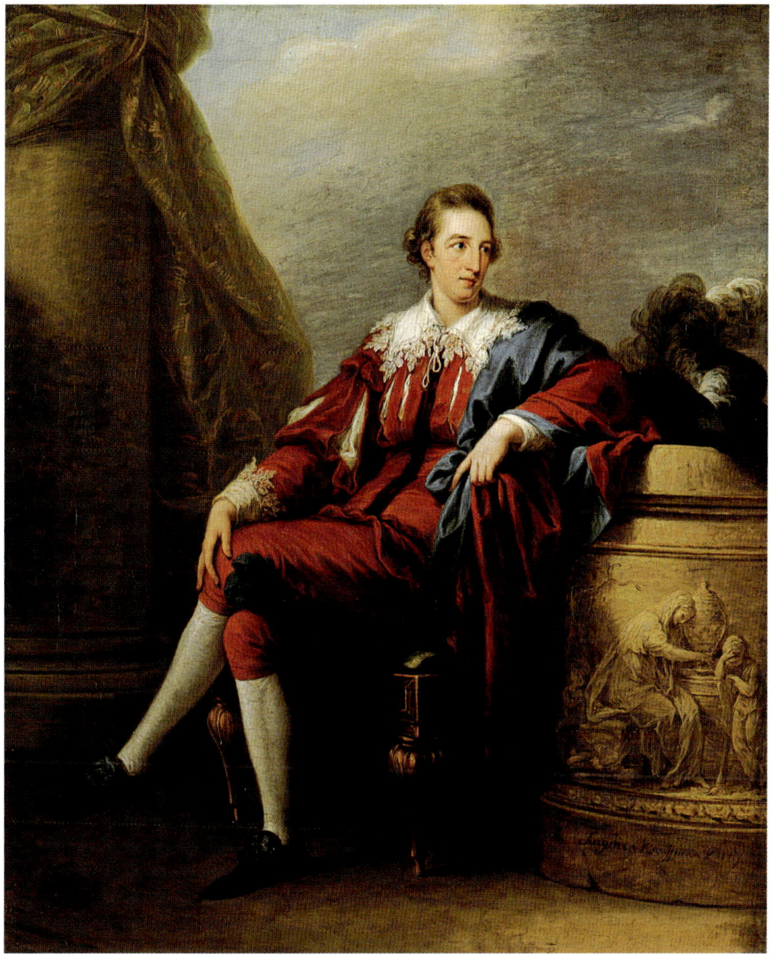

SIMPSON NPG *1485*

8th Earl of Strathmore; their only son John (c.1772-96) matriculated at Trinity College, Oxford, in 1789 as the son of John Simpson deceased; of their three daughters, Maria m. 1796 the 1st Baron Ravensworth (their 6th dau. m. 1833 the 4th Earl of Hardwicke) and Frances m. 1799 Sir John Paul, 1st Bt.

1485 ANGELICA KAUFFMANN c.1777

Canvas 75 x 62 (29½ x 24½) lined; *pentimenti* round both the legs and between chair and plinth;[1] inscribed (or possibly a reinforced signature), bottom right: *Angelica Kauffman pinx*.

Blue eyes, brown hair, wearing a blue drape over a red Van Dyck costume, white stockings with blue rosettes at the knee and on the brown shoes; green chair and a green drape above; his black, plumed hat rests on a the pedestal bearing a classical relief of a grieving woman.

Collections: By descent from Sir John Paul, 1st Bt., the sitter's son-in-law, to Aubrey John Dean Paul (1827-90; suc. as 3rd Bt. 1868); his sale Christie's, 5 July 1855, lot 4[2] (as John Simpson by Kauffmann), bt. Watson; Charles Davis, by whom presented 1908 (as John Palmer).

Exhibitions: Laing Art Gallery, Newcastle, 1925-94.

Reference: Williamson 1924, p.197.

Simpson is an intruder within the National collection, NPG 1485 having been accepted in 1908 as a portrait of the actor John Palmer (*q.v.*), although it had previously been sold as a portrait of Simpson. The correct identity had been established by 1924[3] and in 1925 the portrait was lent to Newcastle (see above).

A replica is in a private collection in Sussex.[4] Both derive from the signed three-quarter length by Kauffmann dated 1777, formerly with the sitter's descendants, which otherwise differs principally in showing a large urn to the right instead of the hat, and no slashes in the costume.[5] A miniature by John Smart, sold Christie's, 14 October 1998, lot 160, apparently derived from Kauffmann's composition. Kauffmann also painted three-quarter length portraits of his mother, dated 1767 (the year her husband sat to Reynolds), and of his wife.[6]

A silhouette inscribed John Simpson was sold Bonham's, 2 February 2000, lot 4.

1 No alteration in the composition can be read by X-radiography.
2 The Christie's day book says the pictures came 'from Mr Gambart'; I am grateful to Margie Christian for this information.
3 Following Milner's visit to Eslington in 1922, see note 6.
4 Earl of Hardwicke sale, Christie's, 27 June 1924, lot 140; exhibited *Sussex and the Grand Tour*, 1986(27).
5 Illus. A. Ribeiro, *The Art of Dress*, 1995, p.209, as with the Trafalgar Galleries; Williamson 1924, p.203; Eslington Park sale, Anderson & Garland, 2nd day, 6 November 1951, lot 490; Christie's, 28 January 1983, lot 41.
6 Both were sketched at Eslington Park by J.D. Milner in 1922 (TSB 43/n.p.); Eslington Park sale, Anderson & Garland, 2nd day, 6 November 1951, lots 491, 489; Williamson 1924, p.203.

SMART, John 1742/3-1811

Miniaturist; studied at Shipley's Academy in St Martin's Lane; exhibited SA 1762-83 and RA 1797-1811; vice-president 1777 and president of the Incorporated Society of Artists 1778; worked in India 1785-95, principally in Madras.

Abbreviation

Jaffé 1954: A. Jaffé, 'John Smart, Miniature Painter: his life and iconography', *AQ*, XVII, 1954, pp.242-54

3817 UNKNOWN ARTIST c.1795-1800

Canvas 91 x 70.5 (35¾ x 27¾) lined; a horizontal mark suggests it was once folded just above the head; small damage bottom edge centre and scattered retouchings.

Blue eyes, white hair, wearing a dark green coat and yellow waistcoat, a porte-crayon in his right hand; a miniature of a lady appears in front of the portfolio, bottom left.

Collections: By descent from the artist to his great-granddaughter, Mrs Lilian M. Dyer, Bexhill,[1] from whom purchased 1952.

Smart's numerous self-portraits confirm the identity and indicate the date, but the attribution remains uncertain. Smart's descendants believed NPG 3817 to be by Smart himself[2] and it was acquired by the NPG as a self portrait; the drawing of the hand, together with the composition of the lower half of the picture - 'in neither of which Smart excelled' - suggested to Jaffé in 1954 'a unique attempt by Smart at a self portrait in oil'.[3] An attribution to L.F. Abbott, first proposed in 1953,[4] is perhaps easier to accept, but remains conjectural.

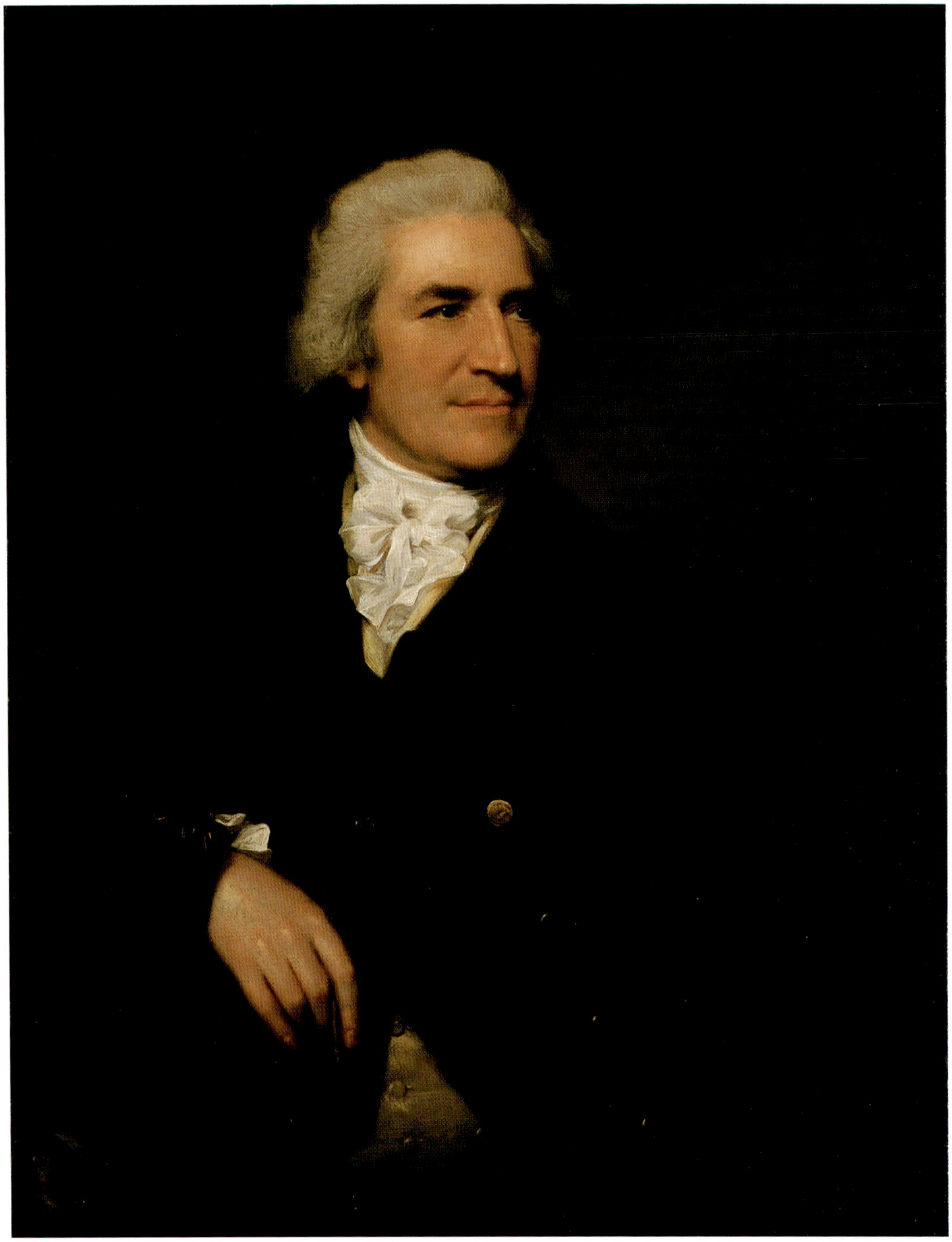

SMART NPG *3817*

1 The descent is illustrated in the Smart family tree printed in Foskett 1964, f.p.90, and see p.53.
2 Mrs L. Dyer wrote that her mother 'always told me it was a portrait of himself, painted by himself' (letter of 23 November 1951; NPG archive).
3 Jaffé 1954, p.254. Foskett 1964, pl.3, also believed it to be a self portrait.
4 Within the NPG, on comparison with other Abbott portraits in the Collection.

ICONOGRAPHY

[*Caveat*: John Smart (1756–c.1813) painter, exhibited RA 1786–1813 from an Ipswich address]

Self-portrait miniatures

1762 Crayons, exhibited SA 1762(103).

c.1783 Drawing, bust-length profile. Michael Jaffé in 1964 (Foskett 1964, fig.5).

1783 Half-length oval. Mrs H. Kahn in 1964 (Foskett 1964, fig.4). Replica with the Rev Howard A.L. Grindon, Cleveland, 1954.

1786 Half-length oval.* Museum of Fine Arts, Boston, Mass. (54.935). Painted in India.

1793 Drawing, half-length profile. H.A. Machen in 1954 (Jaffé 1954, pp.245 fig.3, 252). A similar, but oval, drawing sold Sotheby's, 19 October 1981, lot 184.

1797 Half length* wearing a green coat. Victoria and Albert Museum (P.11.1940; K. Coombs, *Portrait Miniature in England*, 1998, p.93).

1802 Half-length oval. Cleveland Museum of Art (52.95; Foskett 1964, fig.6). A slightly smaller replica dated 1803 was with A. Jaffé in 1954 (Jaffé 1954, p.254).

1810 A self portrait dated 1810 listed by Foskett 1964, p.73.

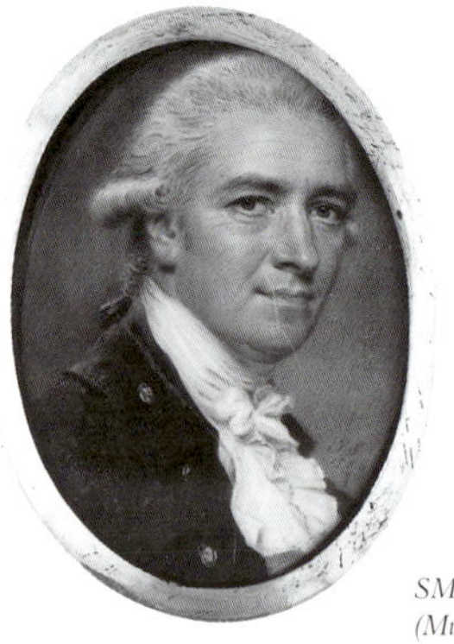

SMART Self portrait 1786 (Museum of Fine Arts, Boston)

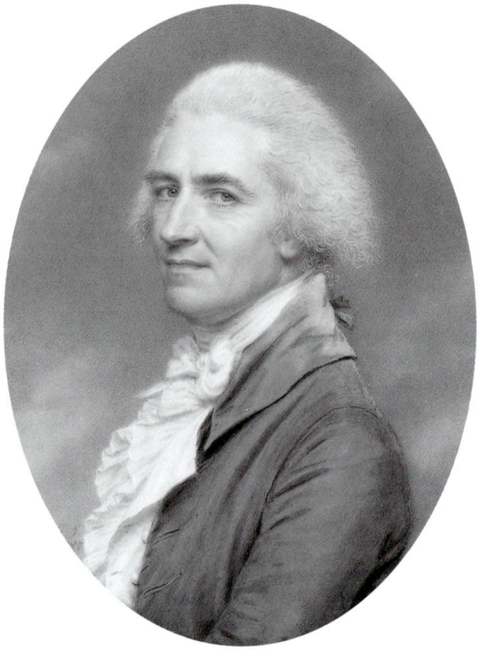

SMART Self portrait 1797 (Victoria and Albert Museum)

Portraits by other artists

1777 Medal by John Kirk from a model by Joachim Smith, inscribed: *JOH: SMART. PICT: EFFIG: MINUT:* (Jaffé 1954, pp.243, 245 fig.1, 252; Brown 1980, no.153, as uncertain date; M.H. Grant, *British Medals since 1760*, 1938, p.7 as 1777). Probably struck to celebrate the year Smart was elected Vice-President of the Incorporated Society of Artists (cf. Foskett 1964, p.8).

1780 Painting by Richard Brompton, half length, sketching. Starr Foundation, Kansas (Jaffé 1954, pp.246 fig.5, 253; Foskett 1964, pl.1), by descent within the artist's family, sold Christie's, 17 December 1936, lot 47. Exhibited SA 1780(7), identified by Whitley 1928, II, p.368. Brompton (d.1782) succeeded Smart as President of the Incorporated Society of Artists in 1780.

c.1784-85 Painting by Mather Brown, half length. Joslyn Art Museum, Omaha (Evans 1982, no.169; Jaffé 1954, pp.246 fig.6, 253 as Gilbert Stuart and as singularly failing 'to convey the keen and vigorous man Smart was'; Foskett 1964, pl.2 as Stuart), by descent within the artist's family, sold Christie's, 25 July 1934, lot 204 as Reynolds. Preliminary drawing* in the Scottish NPG (PG 2254; Evans 1982, no.368).

c.1795-1800 Painting by an unknown artist, see NPG 3817.

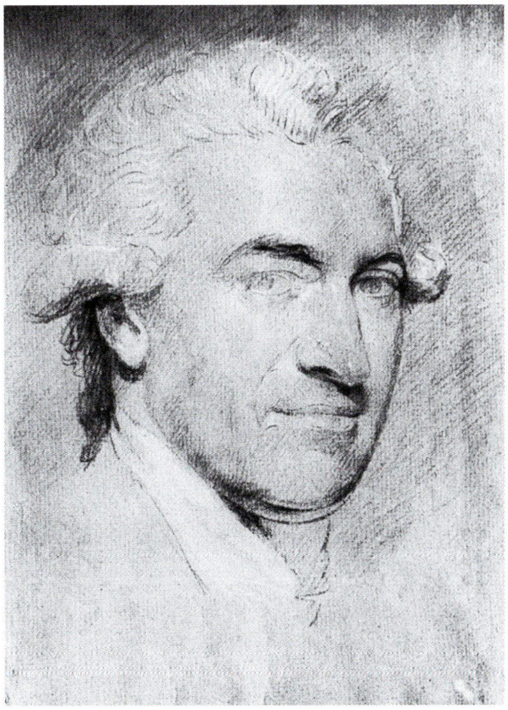

SMART by Mather Brown c.1784-85 (Scottish National Portrait Gallery)

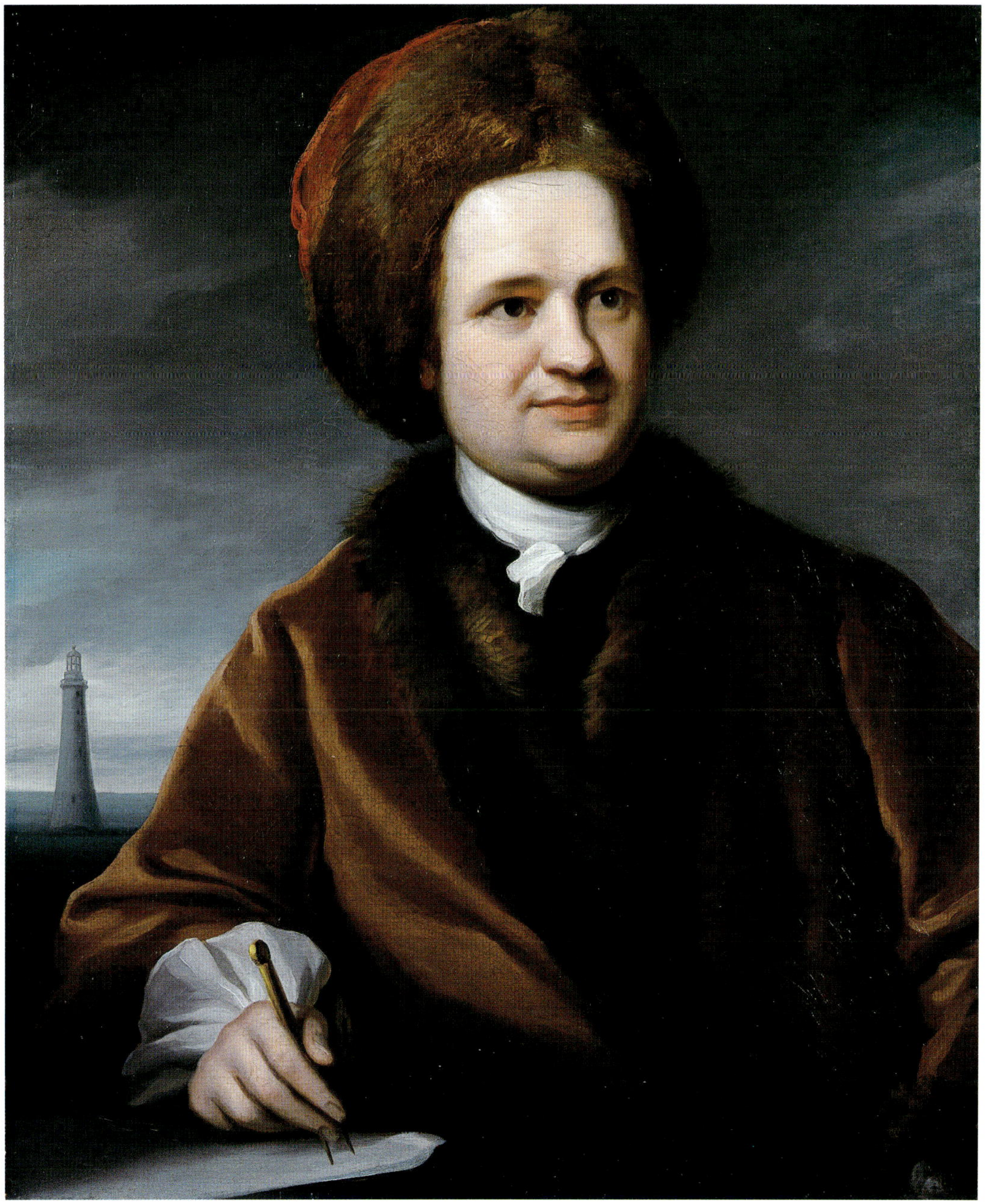

SMEATON NPG *80*

DOUBTFUL PORTRAITS

Profile silhouette on ivory (Jaffé 1954, pp.245 fig.4, 253, as 'so unlike Smart's [profile] that it must, I think, represent a relation ...'; illus. *Connoisseur*, LXXIV, 1926, p.196); painting called a self portrait, Dulwich Picture Gallery, no.639. Smart has also been identified as the model for the figure of Carmine in Robert Smirke's painting from *The Conquest*, exhibited RA 1796(94), see Jaffé 1954, pp.250 figs.11 & 12, 254. Unattributed drawing c.1810-20 of two heads (Yale Center for British Art; B1977.14.5999).

SMEATON, John 1724-92

Civil engineer of Austhorpe, Leeds; FRS 1753, contributing various papers on marine navigation, air pumps and the steam engine; his masterpiece was the third Eddystone lighthouse, completed in 1759 (replaced in 1882); designed bridges, advised on drainage schemes, and planned the Forth and Clyde canal, completed in 1790; James Watt declared that Smeaton's 'example and precepts have made us all engineers'.

'he had a warmth of expression, that might appear to those who did not know him well, to border on harshness ... he would sometimes break out hastily ...' (John Holmes, 1793).

'In person he was of middle stature, broad and strong made, and possessed originally of a vigorous constitution. In his manners he was simple, plain, and unassuming ... He spoke in the dialect of his native county, and was not ashamed to admit it' (Samuel Smiles, 1862).

80 GEORGE ROMNEY after RHODES [c.1779]

Canvas 75.5 x 63.5 (29¾ x 25) cleaned and lined 1977; wide craquelure in face and collar.

Brown eyes, wearing a red fur-trimmed hat, a brown fur-trimmed gown over a black waistcoat; dividers in his right hand and a view of the Eddystone lighthouse in the distance.

Collections: See below: either the sitter's daughter, Mrs Jeremiah Dixon, gave it to Mary Sullivan, or it was painted for her husband, Sir Richard Sullivan (d.1806), 1st Bt.; Sir Charles Sullivan, 3rd Bt,[1] of Ember Court, Thames Ditton;[2] sold Christie's, 18 June 1859, lot 27, purchased.

Reference: Ward & Roberts 1904, II, p.144.

A version of the three-quarter length portrait, belonging to the Royal Society, London (see below). Pose, face, collar and right hand are identical, but the working dress is changed to an elegant informal attire and the distant Eddystone lighthouse is better placed in the distance. NPG 80 was acquired as by an unknown artist, but from 1862 was catalogued as 'probably by Rhodes', on the basis of a comment made by a Mr Longbottom in the NPG visitors' book on 21 November 1860:

> Smeaton's portrait is either painted by Rhodes of Halton near Leeds one mile from Smeaton's birth place or is it a copy of Rhodes' likeness painted if I remember aright between 1774 and 1784. Some years ago about 1836 I saw the original by Rhodes in the possession of Mr Bywater then steward of Temple Newsam now the seat of Meynell Ingram Esq. Rhodes was a schoolfellow of Smeaton's & died & was buried in Leeds in 1790, I believe his son is still living & has some celebrity as a local artist.[3]

In 1904 Ward & Roberts showed that in 1779 Romney had made a copy of Mr Smeaton for Mr Sullivan;[4] Romney's account with Sullivan shows on 26 June 1784 that 18 gn. was owing for 'a copy of Mr Smeaton'.[5]

From this curious and sometimes conflicting evidence, it appears most likely that NPG 80 is the copy made by Romney for Richard Sullivan (for whom he also painted in 1779 the portrait of Macpherson, NPG 5804, who also wears a fur-trimmed gown). His son Sir Charles Sullivan was demonstrably mistaken in parts of his descriptions of the portraits sold in 1859 (see Garrick NPG 82 and Hastings NPG 81), and perhaps the alleged provenance of NPG 80 (see above) was also mistaken (or even confused with that of the Royal Society portrait?).

NPG 80 has been distinguished by being copied as a shop sign (as the *Smeaton Stores* in Rye, Sussex).

1 Who told Scharf (letter of 9 June 1858) that the Smeaton portrait, 'considered an admirable likeness, was given to my Mother [née Mary Lodge, of Leeds] by her friend - Mrs Dixon - Smeaton's Daughter'. For Mrs Dixon see S. Smiles, *Lives of the Engineers*, 1862, II, p.86n1.
2 Where NPG 80 was seen and sketched by Scharf, 28 May 1858 (SSB 51/48a).
3 Possibly related to the Leeds artist Joseph Rhodes 1782-1854 (for whom, see Thomas Coke, NPG 1434A), whose only son John N. Rhodes (1809-42) was also a painter.
4 Ward & Roberts 1904, II, p.144; they were also dismissive (without reasons) of the Rhodes attribution for NPG 80 and of the alleged provenance from Mrs Dixon. Sullivan may still have been in India in 1779 (cf. *Commons 1754-1790*, III, p.511, and *Commons 1790-1820*, V, p.321).
5 MSS, Huntington Library, San Marino, Calif.

ICONOGRAPHY

c.1775-80 Painting by an unknown artist,* possibly Rhodes (see above), three-quarter length seated, left hand in breeches pocket, the Eddystone lighthouse behind him. Royal Society, London. Formerly attributed to J. Richardson (Royal Society cats. of 1860, p.60, and 1912, p.13). Reduced version sold Bonham's, 7 December 1990, lot 130; a copy by Louisa Wren sold Sotheby's, 27 April 1983, lot 31.

There has been some confusion as to how the Royal Society acquired their two portraits of Smeaton, this by Rhodes and the other by Brown (see 1783 below). The Society's cats. of 1860 and 1912 said both were given by Smeaton's friend Alexander Aubert FRS, who indeed presented the Brown in 1799 (as contemporary engravings confirm); the 1980 Catalogue said that the Brown was bequeathed by the sitter's daughter, Mrs Dixon, which is certainly wrong; perhaps this was the provenance of the 'Rhodes' portrait.

c.1779 Painting by George Romney after Rhodes, see NPG 80.

1783 Painting by Mather Brown,* half length with a watermill wheel behind him. Commissioned by one of Smeaton's clients, Mr Hilbert (Evans 1982, pp.93-94; no.170). A weak version was with M. Cusack in 1930.

A copy, in which the Eddystone lighthouse replaced the waterwheel, was commissioned by Smeaton's friend Alexander Aubert FRS c.1788 and presented to the Royal Society 1799 (Evans 1982, p.94; no.171).* Exhibited *Art Treasures*, Manchester, 1857(BPG 257); NPE 1867(678). The many engravings include those by W. Bromley 1790, 1792, 1798, and R. Woodman (*from an original picture ascribed to Mortimer in the possession of the Royal*

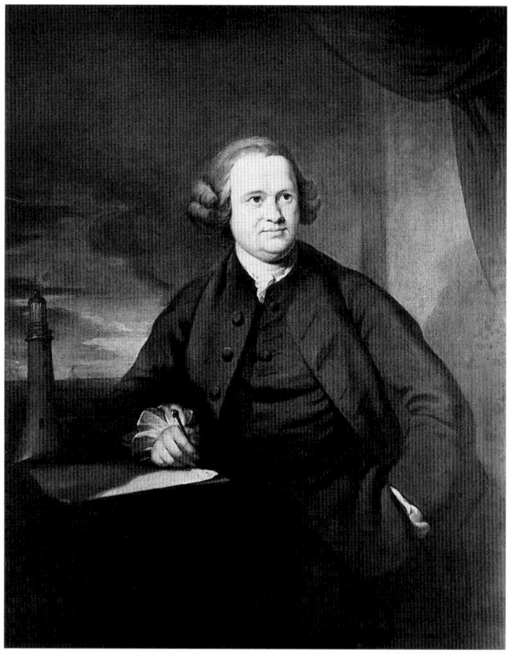

SMEATON by 'Rhodes' c.1775-80 (The Royal Society)

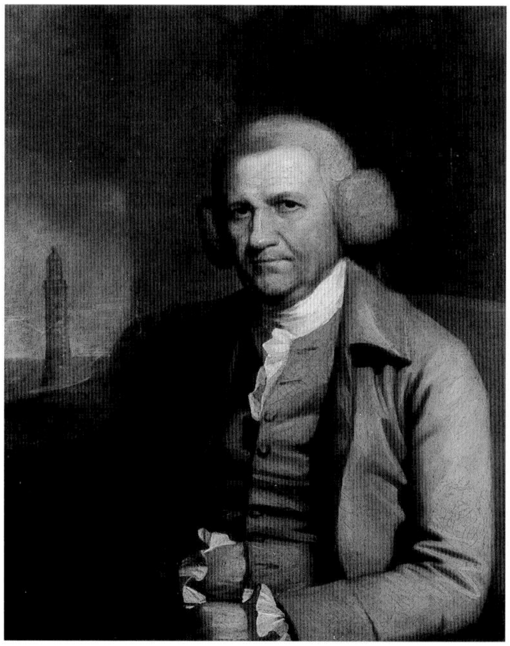

SMEATON after Mather Brown 1783 (The Royal Society)

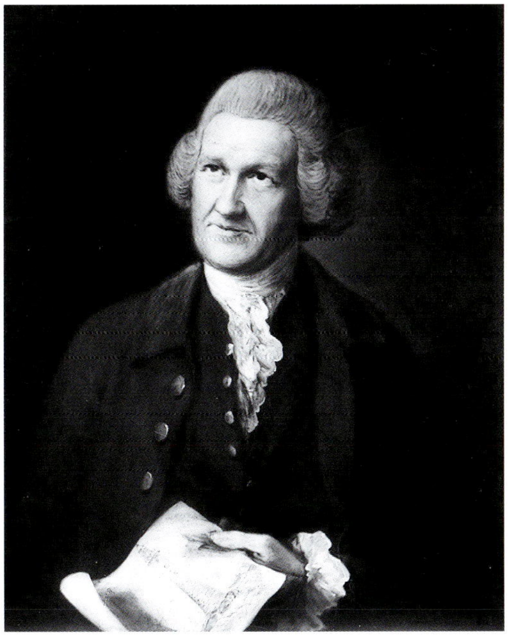

SMEATON by Thomas Gainsborough c.1786-88 (Southill Chattels Trust)

Society). Copies sold Sotheby's, 1 November 1991, lot 434 (reduced); 18 September 1997, lot 73, and 12 February 1998, lot 211.

A version of either the Brown or the 'Rhodes' type, with 'the Eddystone Lighthouse seen in the background', was formerly with Robert Napier, West Shandon, Glasgow (cat., 1865, p.59, no.559].

c.1786-88 Painting by Thomas Gainsborough,* half-length, holding a drawing of the Eddystone lighthouse. Southill (Waterhouse 1958, no.623). Smeaton had designed a bridge and constructed underground cisterns for the brewer Samuel Whitbread, with whose descendants the portrait remains. Engraved mid-19th century from a drawing by Margaret Tekusch *from a picture in the possession of the Institution of Civil Engineers/ The Original by Gainsborough belonging to William Whitbread*. A version, the paper bearing a plan of Ramsgate Harbour (Aubert, see under Mather Brown 1783 above, was Chairman of Ramsgate Harbour development), was in the McCormack sale, American Art Assoc., New York, 3 December 1936, lot 70.

Posthumous

1897-1902 Bust by Henry Fehr. Institution of Civil Engineers, London.

The tablet to Smeaton at Whitkirk, Leeds, by Robert Cooke 1792 displays a model of the Eddystone lighthouse (illus. S. Smiles, *Lives of the Engineers*, 1862, II, pp.89-90).

SMITH, Adam 1723-90

Political economist; b. Kirkcaldy; taught logic and moral philosophy at Glasgow 1751-63, publishing the *Theory of Moral Sentiments* 1759; travelled in France and Switzerland 1764-66 with the 3rd Duke of Buccleuch; FRS 1767; withdrew to Kirkcaldy 1767-73 where he wrote *The Wealth of Nations* 1776; commissioner of customs for Scotland in Edinburgh 1778-90.

'in stature he somewhat exceeded the ordinary size, and his countenance was manly and agreeable' (William Smellie, 1800).

'I am a beau in nothing but my books' (Adam Smith).

Abbreviations

Ross 1995: I.S. Ross, *The Life of Adam Smith*, 1995

Smith 1894: J.M. Gray 'The Portraits of Adam Smith', in J. Bonar, *Catalogue of the Library of Adam Smith*, 1894; reference is here made to the 2nd ed. of 1932, pp.xx-xxviii

3237 JAMES TASSIE 1787

Glass paste 7 (2¾) high, incised on the truncation: *ADAM SMITH/IN HIS 64TH YEAR/1787* and *Tassie F.*; set on a dark glass.

Collections: Sotheby's, 18 April 1945, lot 110, bt. Leggatt for the NPG.

Engravings: B.L. Prevost 1796; anon. 1796 (*Scots Mag.*); J. Beugo 1801; W. Ridley 1802 (*European Mag.*); J. Horsburgh 1828; R.C. Bell 1872; J. Brown; W. Holl. Engravings by Mackenzie 1809 and by C. Picart from a drawing by John Jackson 1811 show the coat elaborated (D. Stewart, *Biographical Memoirs*, 1811).

Reference: *Smith* 1894, pp.xxi-xxiii; Gray 1894, no.356.

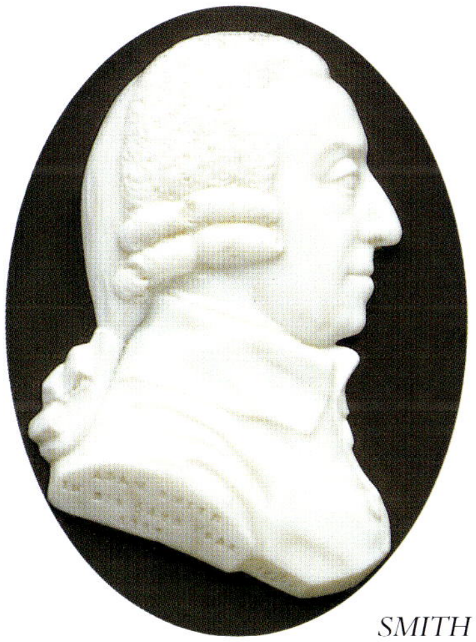

SMITH NPG 3237

In 1793 Dugald Stewart, who had known Smith, stated that 'the medallion of Tassie conveys an exact idea of his profile, and of the general expression of his countenance'; it is the only satisfactory likeness of Smith and was conceivably modelled from the life.[1]

It was copied in Wedgwood paste,[2] and a reduced version in enamel was described by Gray as taken from a gem engraved by Thomas Warner after Tassie;[3] a derivative bust by Boog appeared on a Scottish penny token of 1797.[4]

1 D. Stewart, *Biographical Memoirs*, 1811, p.117; Ross 1995, p.410.
2 Illus. Reilly 1973, p.309.
3 Smith 1894, p.xxiii; Gray 1894, no.358.
4 Illus. Forrer, I, 1904, p.215.

1242 after JAMES TASSIE [1787]

Plaster cast 7 (2¾) high, incised on the truncation: *ADAM SMITH/IN HIS 64TH YEAR/1787* and *Tassie F.*

Collections: Presented by James L. Caw 1899.

See NPG 3237.

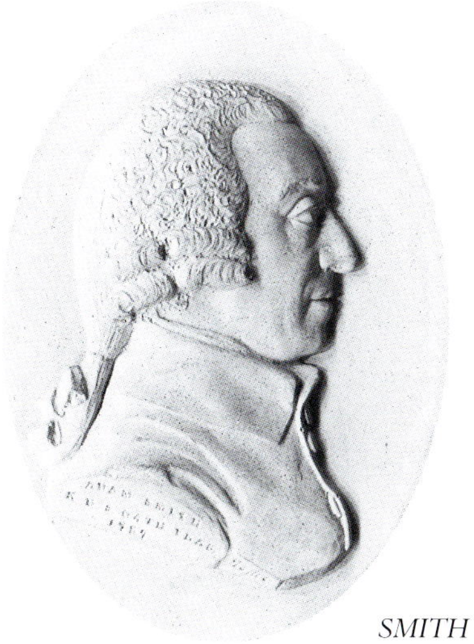

SMITH NPG 1242

ICONOGRAPHY

Dugald Stewart stated that Smith 'never sat for his picture' (*Biographical Memoirs*, 1811, p.117) and, the Tassie medallion apart, his iconography is very meagre.

1787 Medallion by James Tassie, see NPG 3237 and NPG 1242.

1787 Medallion by James Tassie, undraped profile *all'antico* (Gray 1894, no.357; illus. Ross 1995, front.). Example Scottish NPG (PG 157). A similar bust used in a medal of 1787 attributed to John Milton (Brown 1980, no.268).

1787 Etching by J. Kay, whole-length profile, his stick over his shoulder, 'as a soldier carries his musket', standing between Lord Rockville and Commissioner Brown (*Kay Portraits* 1842, I, no.xxxiii).

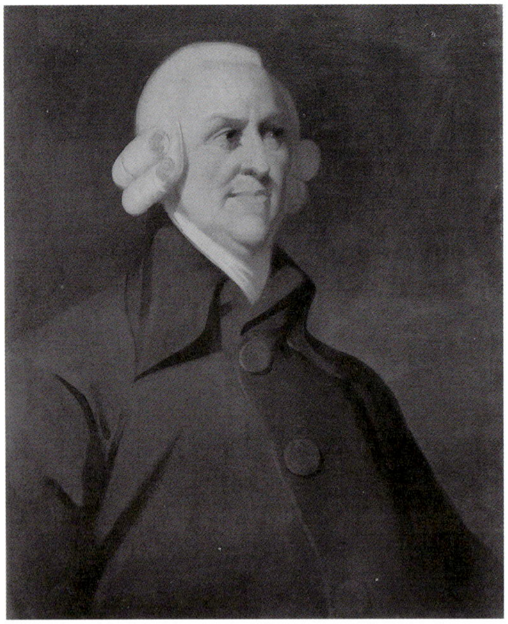

SMITH unknown artist c.1790? (Scottish National Portrait Gallery)

1790 Etching by J. Kay, whole-length profile, standing by a table, 'The Author of the Wealth of Nations' (*Kay Portraits* 1842, I, no.xxxiv).

c.1790? Painting by an unknown artist,* half length, with wig and dark-blue coat. Scottish NPG (PG 1472). Approximately the same age as in the Tassie profile and probably a posthumous derivation from it (cf. *Smith* 1894, p.xxv-vi).

Posthumous

The many busts and statues include:

1845 Marble bust by Patric Park (Glasgow AG). 1851 Marble bust, by Carlo Marochetti (Town Hall, Kirkcaldy); reduced bronze version in Balliol College, Oxford (illus. *Portraits of Balliol College*, 1990, p.26). c.1867 Marble statue by Johann Gasser (Hunterian Museum, Glasgow), and a number of reduced plaster versions. 1869 Statue by William Theed (rear façade of Burlington House, London). 1879 Statuette by Joseph Durham as a young man, seated meditating (*Smith* 1894, p.xxviii). 1887 Statuette by Charles Macbride 1887, used by H.S. Gamley 1904 for the figure of Smith on the north-west tower of the Scottish NPG. 1888 Marble bust by D.W. Stevenson (Wallace Monument, Stirling).

An unspecified plaster cast, 'formerly in the collection of Sir Thomas Lawrence', exhibited Crystal Palace (Phillips 1854, no.426).

DOUBTFUL PORTRAIT

Painting by Tyron Collopy, three-quarter length seated to right, his left hand raised, a copy of *The Wealth of Nations* on the table. Royal Museum of Scotland (see *Smith* 1894, pp.xxvi-vii).

SMITH STANLEY, James, see STRANGE

SMITHSON, Hugh, see NORTHUMBERLAND

SNELLING, Thomas 1712-73

Numismatist; a prominent dealer in Fleet Street, his numerous papers included *A View of the Silver Coin of England* 1762 and *Thirty-three Plates of English Medals* 1776 (published by his son, Thomas Snelling, who continued his business); a sale of his stock was held at Langford's, 31 January-3 February 1774.

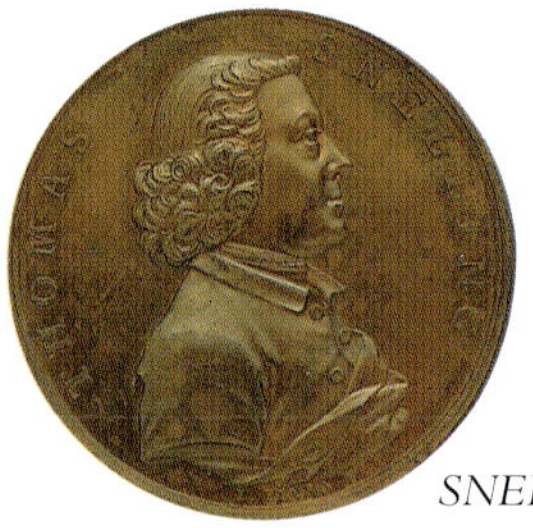

SNELLING NPG 6078

6078 LEWIS PINGO 1773

Bronze medal 3.9 (1½) diameter

Obverse: profile bust to right, inscribed: *THOMAS SNELLING* and *L.PINGO F.*

Reverse: inscribed: *MERVISTI* with added engraved inscription: *THE GREAT MEDALLIST OF HIS TIME* and (within a wreath) *OBIIT/ DIE II MAII/ MDCCLXXIII/ AETAT/ LXI*

Collections: Glendining's, 22 November 1989, lot 144, bt. Baldwin for the NPG.

Engravings: C. Hall 1776.

Reference: Brown 1980, no.180 (without engraved inscription); Eimer 1998, no.49.

A commemorative medal, probably commissioned by Snelling's son, Thomas Snelling, NPG 6078 is the only recorded example with the inscription *the great medallist of his time*. An etching by John Thane appears a crude derivation of Pingo's medal, but it is dated 1770 and suggests, therefore, a common (undiscovered) source.

ICONOGRAPHY

1770 Engraving by J. Thane, see NPG 6078.

1773 Medal by Lewis Pingo, see NPG 6078.

1773 Medal by William Rawle, bust *all'antico*, with inscription on reverse ... *numismatum explorator* ... (Brown 1980, no.178, illus.; H. Blackmore, *Apollo*, CXXVII, 1988, pp.97, 99).

1773 Medal by John Kirk, with inscription on reverse: *Let the art he loved and understood preserve his memory* (Brown 1980, no.179; illus. C. Eimer, *Introduction to Commemorative Medals*, 1989, no.68).

DOUBTFUL PORTRAITS

A medallion by James Tassie listed by Gray (1894, no.363, as not seen); another was of Snelling's daughter (Gray 1894, no.364).

SPENCER, Lady Georgiana, see DEVONSHIRE, Duchess of

SPENCER, Lord Robert 1747-1831

Whig parliamentarian; 3rd s. of the 3rd Duke of Marlborough; MP 1768-99, 1802-07 and 1817-20; a member of Brooks's and a serious gambler, his 'political conduct was governed entirely by his close personal friendship with Fox' (*Commons 1754-90*).

2076 see Groups, *Mr Fox and his Friends* by WILLIAM LANE c.1813

ICONOGRAPHY

c.1754 Painting by Thomas Hudson, *The Family of the 3rd Duke of Marlborough*, in which Lord Robert appears as a small child on the right. Blenheim (illus. *Apollo*, XCV, 1972, p.48).

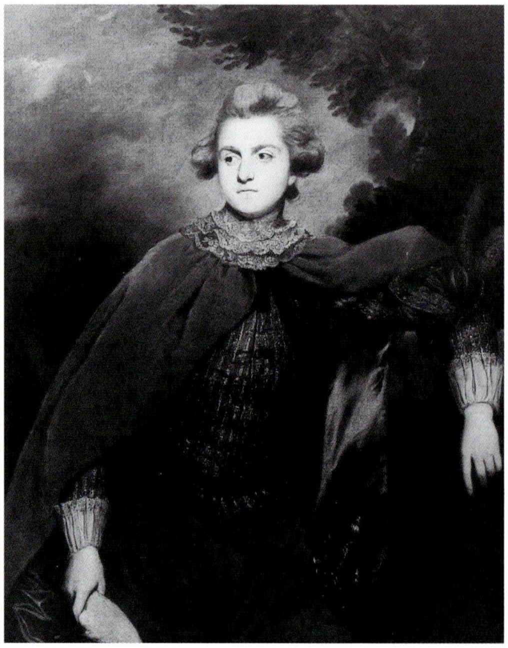

Lord Robert SPENCER by Joshua Reynolds 1769 (Sotheby's)

1758 Painting by Joshua Reynolds, as a boy, half length, in van Dyck dress. Blenheim (Mannings 2000, no.1671).

*1769 Painting by Joshua Reynolds, three-quarter length standing in masquerade costume. Private Collection, from Woolbeding (Mannings 2000, no.1672).

1791 Drawing by W.H. Brown bust-length oval, engraved W. Grainger 1791 (*The Senator*).

1803 Bust by Joseph Nollekens. Formerly in the Temple of Liberty, Woburn Abbey (illus. *Apollo*, CXXX, 1989, p.31). Exhibited RA 1804(951).

c.1813 Drawing by William Lane, *Mr Fox and his Friends*, see Groups NPG 2076.

DOUBTFUL PORTRAIT

A drawing of 1796 by Henry Edridge, formerly at Holland House, provisionally identified as Spencer; one of the five friends of Fox from the St Anne's Hill House sale, Phillips, 3rd day, 26 November 1924, lots 505-507 (cf. Lansdowne 1796 and Upper Ossory 1798).

SPODE, Josiah I 1733-97

Potter; worked with Thomas Whieldon 1749-54 before setting up independently at Stoke; creator of bone china and underglaze blue printing; described as 'mild, modest and unobtrusive'; his business was much enlarged by his son.

4586 UNKNOWN ARTIST c.1790-95

Watercolour and bodycolour on ivory 7.6 x 6 (3 x 2⅜)

Grey eyes, grey hair, wearing a yellow waistcoat and dark grey coat.

Collections: By descent to Josiah Spode IV (d.1893) of Hawkesyard House,[1] who bequeathed his estate to the Dominican Order; transferred to Woodchester Priory, whence acquired by B. Weinreb, from whom purchased 1967.[2]

Apparently the unique image of Spode I. The identity is based on the provenance, and the apparent age of the sitter in relation to the apparent date of the miniature; the existence of two versions, differing only in detail, in the Spode Museum, Stoke-on-Trent,[3] is also reassuring.

1 Cf. A. Hayden, *Spode and his Successors*, 1925, p.19.
2 Provenance from a note supplied by Weinreb in 1967.
3 Letter from L.R. Whiter, Spode Museum, 28 September 1967 (NPG archive); one illus. A. Hayden, *Spode and his Successors*, 1925, f.p.16, and in the Museum guide, *Tradition-Spode-Copeland*, 1960, pl.7.

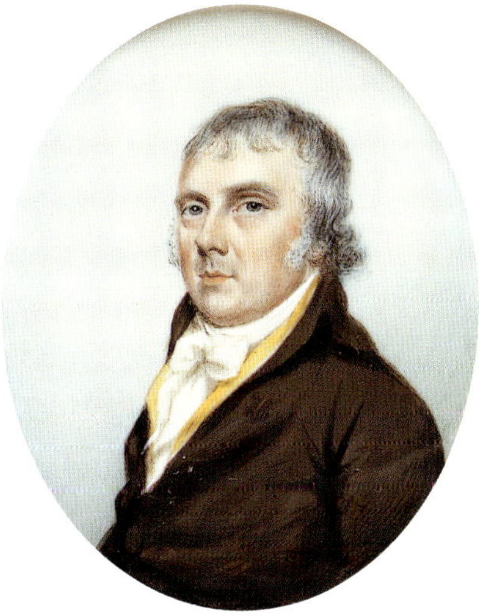

SPODE I NPG 4586

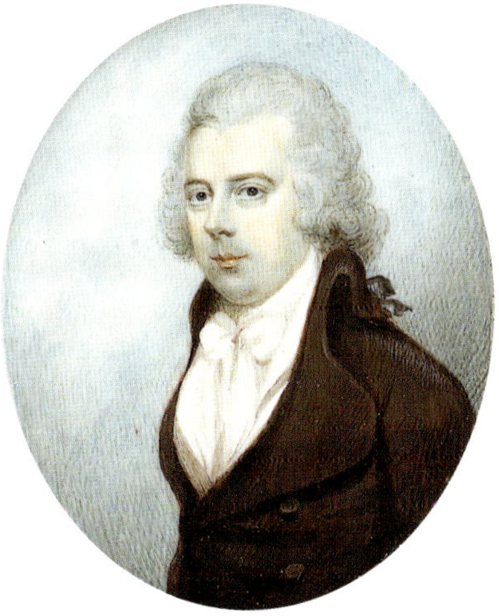

SPODE II NPG 4587

SPODE, Josiah II 1754-1827

Potter, the most successful china manufacturer of his time; worked with his father, Josiah I, and expanded the factory, setting up London showrooms, assisted by William Copeland, and introducing stone china and felspar porcelain; on his father's death, he returned to Stoke, leaving Copeland with the London business; appointed potter to the King 1806; d. at his mansion at Penkhull, Staffs.

4587 UNKNOWN ARTIST c.1785-90

Watercolour and bodycolour on ivory 7.6 x 6.3 (3 x 2⅜)

Blue-grey eyes, light powdered hair, wearing a dark brown coat; light blue background.

Collections: By descent to Josiah Spode IV (d. 1893) of Hawkesyard House, who bequeathed his estate to the Dominican Order; transferred to Woodchester Priory, whence acquired by B. Weinreb, from whom purchased 1967.[1]

The identification is traditional, although not readily reconcilable with those portraits cited in the Iconography below. NPG 4587 is probably not by the same hand as NPG 4586.

1 Provenance from a note supplied by Weinreb in 1967.

ICONOGRAPHY

c.1800 Unattributed painting, whole-length standing in riding habit. Potteries MAG, Stoke-on-Trent.

1806 Painting by Michael Keeling, half-length standing by a pillar, engraved W. Greatbach (illus. A. Hayden, *Spode and his Successors*, 1925, f.p.112.

1821 Painting by William McCall, half length, a paper in his left hand. Potteries MAG, Stoke-on-Trent (illus. Spode Museum guide, *Tradition-Spode-Copeland*, 1960, pl.10). Said to have been presented by the sitter to his daughter Mary on the occasion of her marriage in 1821.

An earthenware bust, perhaps of c.1800, is in the Potteries MAG, Stoke-on-Trent (illus. A. Hayden, *Spode and his Successors*, 1925, f.p.108).

STANLEY, James, see STRANGE

STAUNTON, Sir George Leonard, 1st Bt 1737-1801

Diplomat; MD Montpellier 1758; practised in the West Indies 1762-70 and 1772-79, where he met George Macartney, becoming his aide-de-camp 1779; secretary to Macartney at Madras 1782-84, successfully negotiating with the French and Tipu Sultan in Mysore; Bt [I] 1785; FRS 1787 and honorary DCL Oxford 1790; minister plenipotentiary with Macartney in China 1792-96, accompanied by his son (Sir George Thomas Staunton, 1781-1859); published an account of the mission in 1797.

329 LEMUEL FRANCIS ABBOTT, *with Lord Macartney* c.1785, see Lord Macartney

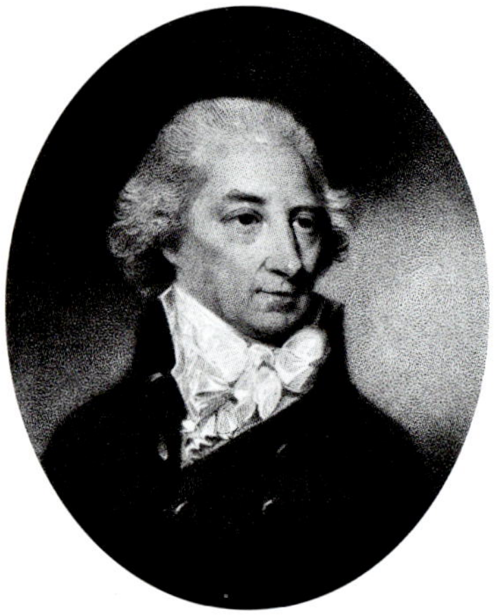

STAUNTON C. Picart after George Engleheart c.1792 (British Museum)

ICONOGRAPHY

c.1780 Unattributed miniature, half-length oval in green coat. Sotheby's, 27 November 1972, lot 37. The head appears to agree with that shown in Abbott's double portrait with Macartney (see Macartney NPG 329).

c.1785 Painting by L.F. Abbott, *Lord Macartney and George Staunton*, see Macartney NPG 329.

c.1792 Miniature by George Engleheart, bust-length; engraved C. Picart* 1823 as aged 55 (private plate for *Memoir of the Life and Family of the late Sir George Leonard Staunton*, 1823).

1792-94 Drawings by William Alexander, made during Macartney's Chinese mission in 1792-94. British Library. Staunton and his son with Macartney in audience with the Emperor of China. (illus. *Europa und die Kaiser von China*, Berlin, 1985, p.176), and a whole-length Staunton wearing the robes of a Doctor of Laws of Oxford University which he wore for this audience (illus. *V & A Album 4*, 1985, p.302).

Posthumous

1824 Monument by Francis Chantrey, with bas-relief showing Staunton whole-length seated, addressing an Indian. Westminster Abbey (*Chantrey* 1994, no.84a).

STEEVENS, George 1736-1800

Literary critic, miscellaneous writer and bibliophile; FRS and FSA 1767; edited the works of Shakespeare 1773 (4th edition 1793); collected Hogarth prints, collaborating with Nichols in *Biographical Anecdotes of Mr Hogarth* 1781; capricious and mischievous, in 1789 he faked a monument to the anglo-saxon King 'Hardyknute' which was duly engraved; he was, said Dr Parr, 'one of the wisest, most learned, but most spiteful of men'.

STEEVENS NPG 1160

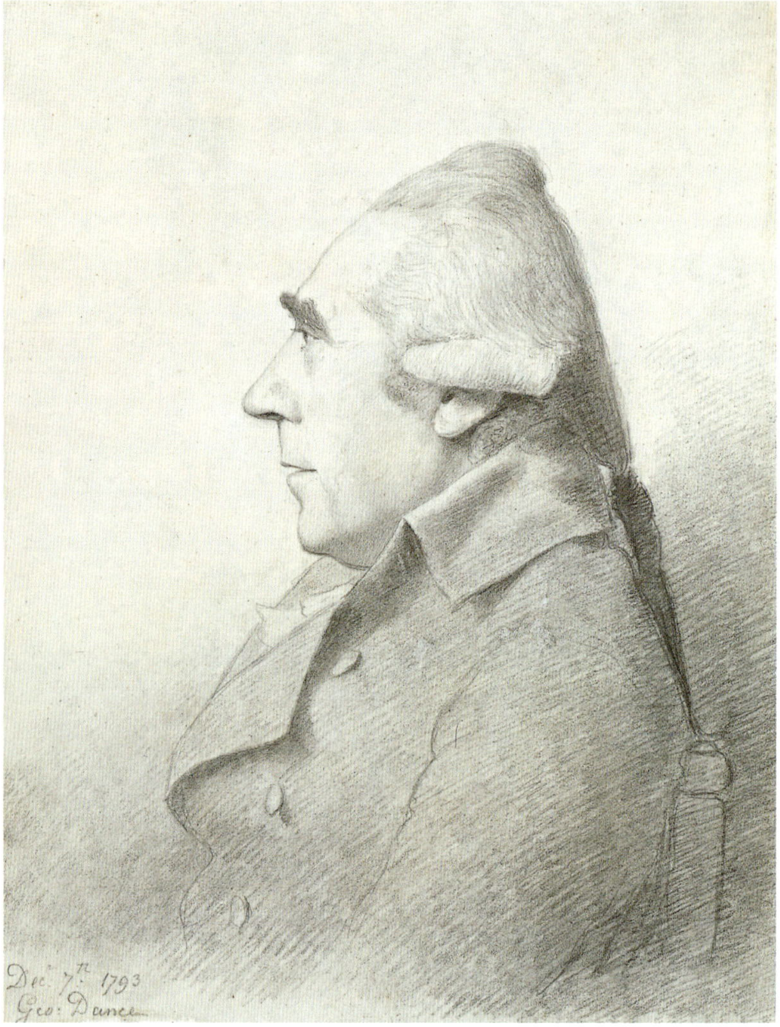

1160 GEORGE DANCE 1793

Pencil on paper 30 x 23.3 (11¾ x 9¼) faded with some staining; a repaired vertical tear across the coat collar and old damages on the shoulder and down the right-hand edge; signed and dated in pencil bottom left: *Decr. 7th. 1793/ Geo: Dance*; laid down on a contemporary washed mount lettered: GEORGE STEEVENS.

Collections: The artist's grandson, the Rev George Dance; his sale, Christie's, 1 July 1898, lot 134, bt. Colnaghi for NPG.

Engravings: W. Daniell 1802, 1808 (*Dance Portraits*); W. Hawksworth 1848.

Another slightly smaller but almost identical drawing by Dance was with Sabin in 1973.[1]

1 Exhibited, *Sublime and the Beautiful*, Sabin, 1973(25), illus. pl.2.

ICONOGRAPHY

According to one obituary Steevens 'never would sit for his picture' (*GM*, LXX, 1800, i, p.178), but in 1812 John Nichols (*Anecdotes*, II, p.658) wrote that

A capital portrait of Mr Steevens was accidentally discovered, a few years since, which he had looked all London through to find, but to no purpose. It was the intention of the Original to serve this inimitable likeness as he had before done a miniature of himself by Myres, and a whole-length, in the character of Barbarossa, which Mr Steevens played in a private theatre with great eclat. Fortunately the third and last picture of this extraordinary man escaped the ravage of the self-destroyer. It was painted by Zoffanii before he went to India, and sold, with many others, to a Mr Clark, in Princes-street, having been left in the Painter's hands, who got rid of all his portraits when he set out to his Eastern expedition [*such a sale is not recorded by Lugt; a half-length portrait by Zoffany was in Richard Clark's sale (L.7634), Christie's, 15 September 1809, lot 17a*]. From this picture an excellent print was engraved for sale, at the expence of Sylvester Harding, in whose family the plate now remains.

1774 Painting by Johann Zoffany, kit-cat seated with

two dogs. Christie's, 20 April 1990, lot 31. Inscribed (after 1800) as painted in 1774. Engraved W. Evans 1800;★ T. Hodgetts 1816 (half-length oval). A crude drawing of the head, probably connected with one of the engravings, is in the Garrick Club (Ashton 1997, no.772). The identification of this portrait was entirely due to Nichols (see above); presumably he was right.

c.1775-80 Miniature attributed to Jeremiah Meyer, bust-length oval. Philippa Steevens, Philadelphia, in 1960, a collateral descendant. Presumably the miniature listed in *DNB* as with Mrs Inglis of Cheltenham, a great-granddaughter of Mrs Collinson, Steevens's cousin and housekeeper (and see Nichols above).

Engravings by J. Sayers, bust 'from memory' and half-length oval. Steevens was so exasperated at receiving an etching of his face ('though not a very good likeness'), taken by stealth by Sayers that 'he threatened to cane the fellow' (Smith 1920, I, pp.64-65).

1793 Drawing by George Dance, see NPG 1160.

1800 Monument by John Flaxman whole-length bas relief, seated, contemplating the bust of Shakespeare. Formerly St Matthias, Poplar, London (illus. *Flaxman*, RA, 1979, no.117). Engraved H. Moses 1811; G. Cooke 1812 (reissued 1828). Steevens's father had been a governor of the East India Company, for whom the church of St Matthias was built.

DOUBTFUL PORTRAIT

Painting by E. Haytley, small whole length, Sotheby's, 30 April 1980, lot 360.

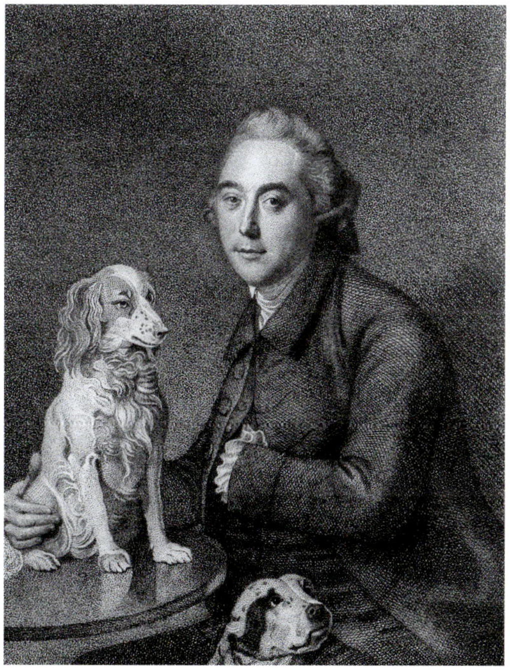

STEEVENS W. Evans after Johann Zoffany 1774 (NPG D 13811)

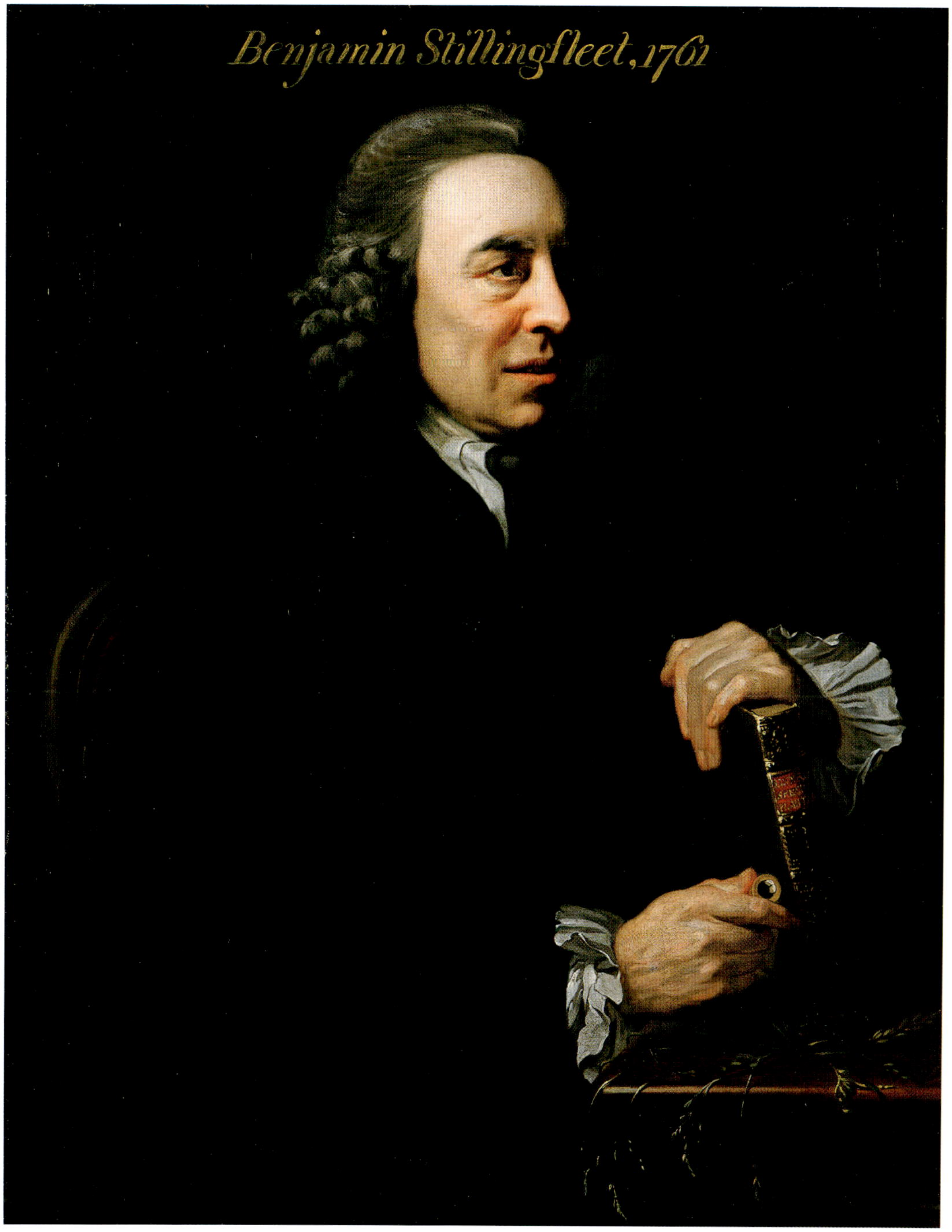

STILLINGFLEET NPG *6477*

STILLINGFLEET, Benjamin 1702-71

Virtuoso and botanist; from 1724 tutor to his 2nd cos., William Windham of Felbrigg, with whom he travelled in Europe 1738-40; moved to Robert Price's estate at Foxley 1746, and turned to the study of botany; one of the first English advocates of the Linnaean system, he published *Observations on Grasses* appended to his *Miscellaneous Tracts* (translations from Linnaeus) 1759; a 2nd ed. 1762 included illustrations by Price; he also aspired as a writer and musician; the blue worsted stockings he wore at the salons of learned ladies first evoked the term 'bluestocking'.

6477 JOHANN ZOFFANY c.1761

Canvas 90.5 x 70.5 (35½ x 27¾) lined; repaired tears in his right hand and in the background; inscribed above *Benjamin Stillingfleet, 1761*.

Brown eyes, grey powdered hair, wearing a dark blue coat with blue buttons; seated in a red chair; the leather-bound book is titled: *LINNAEI/ SPECIES/ PLANTAR*[*UM*]*// TOM/ I*; he holds a magnifying glass and specimens of grasses lie on the table.

Collections: Probably painted for Robert Marsham; Marsham family, Rippon Hall, Heveningham, Norfolk, by 1910;[1] 2nd Viscount Camrose by 1955; his executors sale, Christie's, 11 June 1999, lot 47, withdrawn; private treaty purchase 1999.

Exhibition: *Norfolk and the Grand Tour*, Norwich, 1985(70) as after Zoffany.

Stillingfleet at sixty appears as an engaging, open-mouthed botanist. As well as his magnifying glass, he holds a volume of Linnaeus's *Species Plantarum* (1753), in which the Linnaean system of classification,[2] which he championed, was first defined, and the grasses on the table define his particular study – besides Zoffany's delight in botanical illustration.[3]

NPG 6477 is one of the earliest of Zoffany's English portraits. He had arrived in 1760, and his first sitters included a number of friends who had first met on the Continent in 1738-41: Stillingfleet (then with his charge William Windham, who d.1761), Richard (Aldworth) Neville and Robert Price (d.1761) of Foxley (who had all belonged to 'The Common Room', a lively group in Geneva 1740-41), and Robert Marsham (who had met Windham and Stillingfleet in Lyons in 1738).[4] Zoffany painted Neville[5] and Price[6] in 1761, and his portraits of Marsham (also a botanist)[7] and Stillingfleet are presumed to date from the same period.

A contemporary version, apparently a replica, in the Berger Collection, Denver,[8] in which the grasses are disposed differently on the table, descended through the sitter's nephew, William Locker, and was three times engraved.[9] NPG 6477, previously considered a version of the Berger portrait,[10] was very probably commissioned by Robert Marsham (see above); their portraits by Zoffany were together at Rippon Hall until at least 1910.[11]

1 Duleep Singh 1927, II, p.248, no.40.
2 Viz. of identifying a plant by using a second or trivial name in addition to the generic name.
3 Cf. *Zoffany* 1977(no.9), and, for example, the plants in his portrait of Garrick, NPG 1167.
4 See A.W. Moore in *Norfolk and the Grand Tour*, 1985, pp.41-47.
5 Private collection; exhibited *Zoffany* 1977(no.7).
6 Untraced; engraved J. Basire 1810.
7 Private collection; engraved E. Edwards (illus. *Norfolk and the Grand Tour*, Norwich, 1985, p.42).
8 Illus. *Berger Collection*, Denver, Colo., 1998, p.129; from the Locker Lampson sale, Christie's, 14 December 1928, lot 88; Robinson & Fisher, 26 March 1936, lot 103; Christie's, 27 January 1950, lot 163; Sotheby's, 9 April 1997, lot 34.
9 By V. Green 1782 (half-length roundel; illus. *CL*, CLXIII, 1978, p.832; Nichols *Anecdotes*, II, p.338, said that 'the original plate [by Green] having been purposely destroyed, the impressions from it are very rare'); Robert Shipster c.1772 (half length; from the picture with William Locker; illus. *Norfolk and the Grand Tour*, Norwich, 1985, p.42), and J. Basire 1810 (Nichols *Anecdotes*, II; oval, from the picture with E.H. Locker).
10 When the portraits were placed side by side in 1986 and examined by John Hayes and Mary Webster it was apparent that NPG 6477 was the original.
11 The Marsham portraits listed in Duleep Singh 1927, II, pp.245-46, nos.24-29.

DOUBTFUL PORTRAIT

A whole length at Felbrigg, previously described as Stillingfleet and attributed to Frans van der Mijn, is now believed to show James Dagnia (c.1709-55) by John Shackleton (I am most grateful to Alastair Laing for this information).

STRAHAN, William 1715-85

Printer and publisher; b. Edinburgh, came to London 1738, working first with the printer Andrew Millar and later in partnership with Thomas Cadell; printed the *Monthly Review* from 1749 and Johnson's *Dictionary* 1755; much respected by his authors (who also included Gibbon, Hume, Macpherson, Robertson and Adam Smith); MP 1774-84 and master of the Stationers' Company from 1774.

'Living in times not the purest in English annals, he escaped unsullied through the artifices of trade and the corruption of politics. In him a strong and natural sagacity, improved by extensive knowledge of the world, served only to render respectable his unaffected simplicity of manners (Nichols *Anecdotes*).

4202 JOSHUA REYNOLDS 1780

Canvas 90 x 70 (35½ x 27½) lined; partially restored 1984; a wide shrinkage craquelure in the darker areas, less marked in the face;[1] pentimenti round the chair back and the hands and cuffs.

Blue eyes, white powdered wig, wearing a dull red suit and silver waistcoat.

Collections: By descent to Mrs Arthur Lemon (*née* Strahan), 1897; Mrs W. Strahan, from whom purchased 1961.

Engravings: J. Jones 1792; C.A. Tomkins 1866.

Exhibitions: RA 1783(230); BI 1833(33) lent E. Snow Strahan; *Guelph* 1891(195) lent Mrs A. Lemon; *Johnson*, Arts Council, 1984(38).

Reference: Graves & Cronin, III, pp.940-41; Waterhouse 1941, p.74; Mannings 2000, no.1717.

Strahan sat to Reynolds on seven occasions in May and June 1780, and NPG 4202 was paid for on 30 May 1780 (£40) and June 1783 (£38.19).[2] Reynolds had originally intended to exhibit it in 1781, but did not do so until 1783, when it was described as 'well executed but much too flattering'.[3]

A copy by William Beechey was given to the Stationers' Company by Andrew Strahan in 1815;[4] another is in a private collection.

1 Cleaning before 1914 was arranged by 'the artist Ouless'; the portrait was exposed to fire in 1940 (letters from Mrs W. Strahan, December 1960-April 1961; NPG archive).
2 Cormack 1970, pp.163, 164.
3 *Morning Post*, 1783, as quoted by Mannings, *loc. cit.*
4 Mannings 2000, nos.1717a.

ICONOGRAPHY

1764 Miniature by Luke Sullivan, bust-length oval. Private collection, by descent from the sitter.

c.1775 Painting by Mason Chamberlin,* three-quarter length seated, a paper in his right hand. Yale Center for British Art (B1981.25.269). Engraved after 1785 as *the late Mr Strahan, Chamberlayne pinxt/ Leney sculpt* (oval).

1780 Painting by Joshua Reynolds, see NPG 4202.

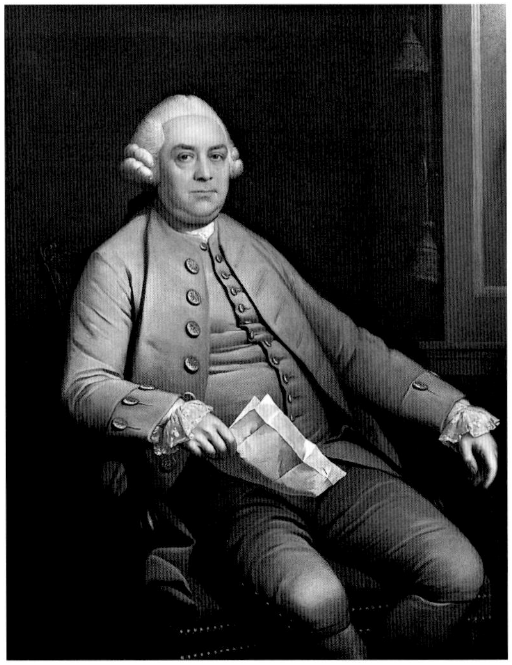

STRAHAN by Mason Chamberlin c.1775 (Yale Center for British Art)

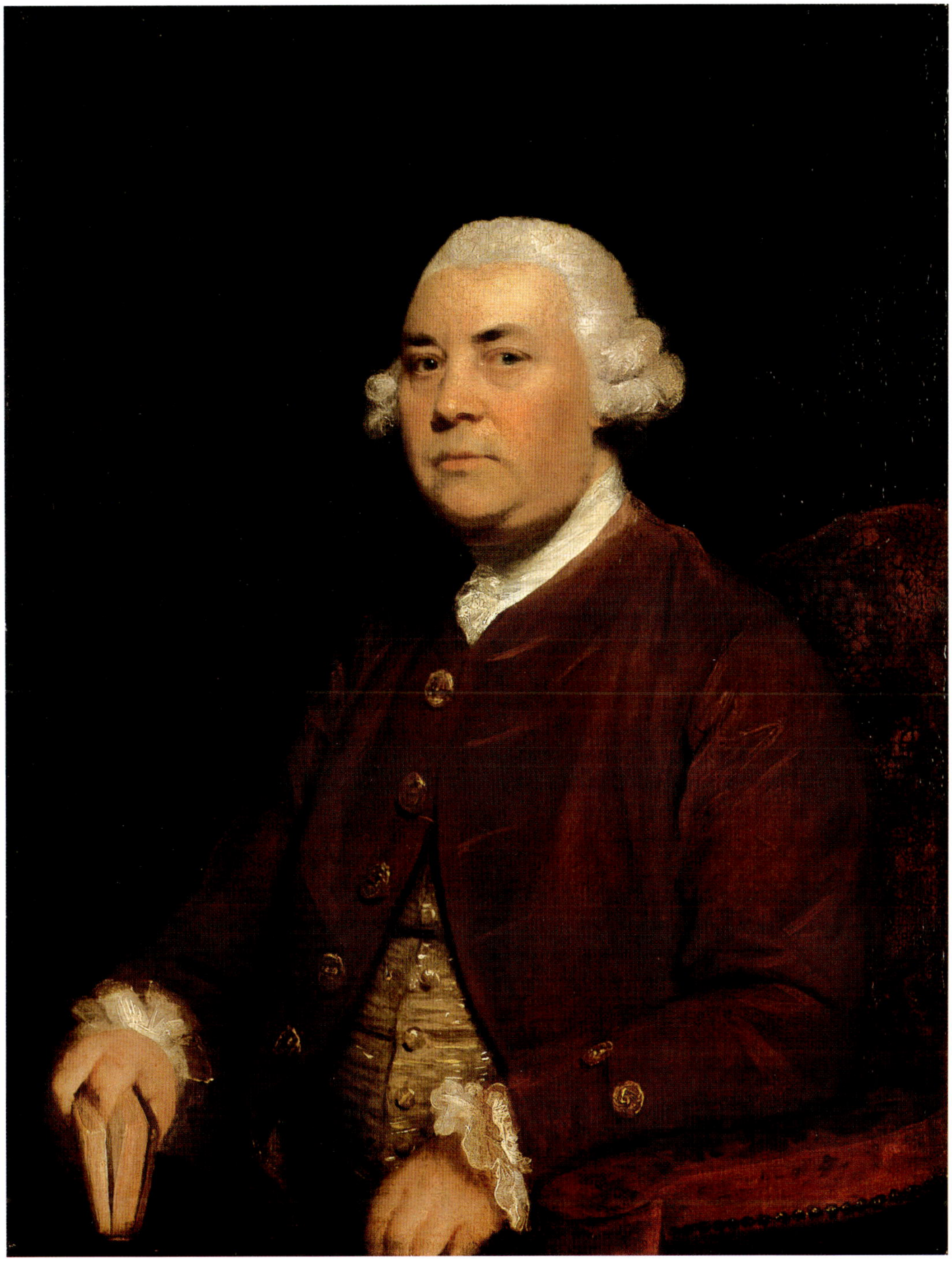

STRAHAN NPG *4202*

STRANGE, James Smith Stanley, Lord 1717-71

Parliamentarian, 1st s. of the 11th Earl of Derby; m. 1747 an heiress, Lucy Smith of Weald Hall, Essex, assuming the additional name of Smith; MP 1741-71, generally acting independently; chancellor of the Duchy of Lancaster 1762-71; Walpole described him as 'a busy young Lord, very disinterested, often quick, as often injudicious, and not the less troublesome for either'.

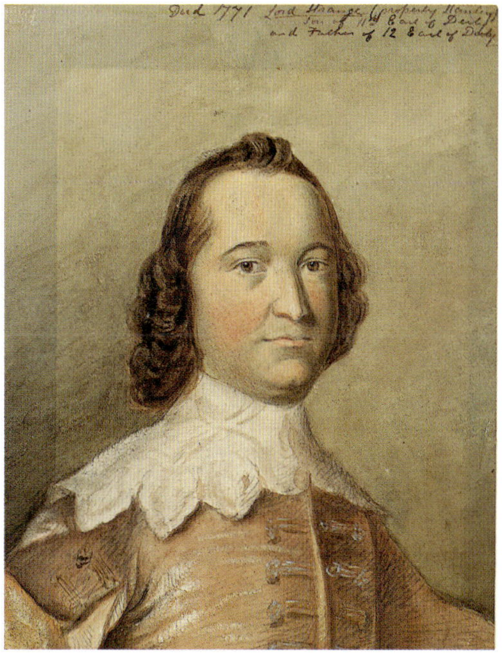

Lord James STRANGE NPG *2424*

2424 WILLIAM DERBY after THOMAS HUDSON [c.1749]

Watercolour and pencil on paper 20.3 x 16 (8 x 6¼) laid down on paper; an area 18 x 13 (7¼ x 5¼) is faded through exposure; inscribed in ink, top right: *Died 1771 Lord Strange (properly Stanley)/ son of 11th Earl of Derby/ and Father of 12 Earl of Derby*; and verso (now concealed), above: *The Right Honble Lord Strange/ Died 1771/ Original at Knowsley* and below: *W. Derby del.*

Brown eyes, dark hair, wearing pink Van Dyck masquerade costume.

Collections: Unknown, accessioned 1929.

Derby made small watercolour copies for the 13th Earl of Derby of all the known portraits of the Stanley family.[1] NPG 2424 is copied from Hudson's three-quarter length portrait at Knowsley[2] showing Lord

Strange in masquerade dress, holding a mask in his left hand; Derby also drew a squared-up outline of the whole portrait (NPG archive).[3]

The composition compares closely with Hudson's William Bouverie, Earl of Radnor, which is dated 1749.[4] There appear to be three contemporary versions: one on the London Art market in 1986,[5] another from Sizergh Castle sold at Christie's, 4 May 1951, lot 26,[6] and a third sold Christie's, 20 November 1987, lot 87. A copy by James Cranke was sold Sotheby's, 29 July 1964, lot 303, and a half-length copy was in a private collection in 1992.

1 'Exquisitely bound in many volumes' (*AJ*, IX, 1847, p.88). Twelve small water-colour copies by Derby are listed in the 1876 Knowsley cat., identified as studies for Lodge's *Portraits of Illustrious Personages of Great Britain* (1835 ed.).
2 Exhibited NPE 1867(317); *Painting & Sculpture in England 1700-1750*, Liverpool, 1958(23).
3 *Drawings by William Derby*, p.33; an album purchased from Charles Derby, the artist's son, 1893, containing many squared-up drawings of Stanley portraits.
4 Illus. *Hudson*, Kenwood, 1977, no.43.
5 Exhibited *The British Face*, Colnaghi, 1986(20).
6 This appears to be the version subsequently sold Bonham's, 4 July 1968; Christie's 2 August 1973, lot 118, and 29 September 1977, lot 126.

ICONOGRAPHY

1721 or 1729? Painting by Hamlet Winstanley, as a boy, whole length in a landscape holding a lance. Knowsley (cat., 1875, no.179, reproducing the signature and date which might be read as 1729).

1746 Painting by Edward Haytley, small whole length in costume. Private collection (illus. *Haytley*, Leger, 1978, fig.1).

c.1749 Painting by Thomas Hudson, see under NPG 2424.

1773 Painting by Edward Penny, 'full length' inscribed. formerly in the Assembly Rooms, Manchester (J. Britton, *Beauties of England and Wales*, IX, 1807, p.269).

STUART, Mrs Elizabeth, *née* Blackstone 1762-99

Second wife of James Stuart whom she m. 1779 (she was then seventeen and he sixty-six); after his death in 1788 she saw to the publication of the second volume of the *Antiquities of Athens*, assisted by William Newton.

55B UNKNOWN ARTIST c.1790

Watercolour and bodycolour on ivory 5.7 x 4.8 (2¼ x 1⅞)

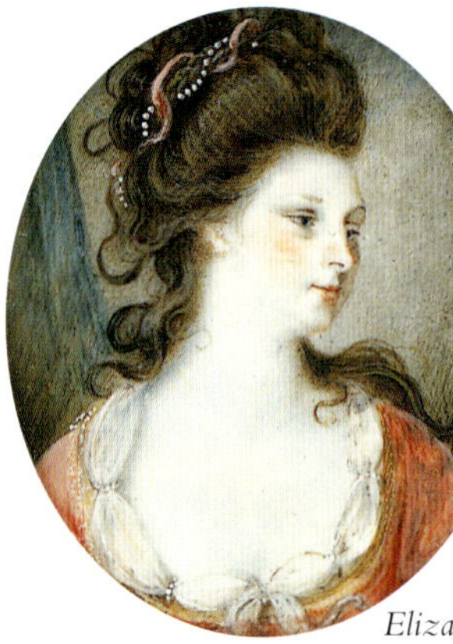

Elizabeth STUART
NPG 55B

Blue eyes, dark hair dressed with pearls and a pink ribbon, wearing a plum-coloured dress.

Collections: Presented by the sitter's son, Lt. James Stuart RN, 1858.

The original backing is inscribed: *Mrs Elizabeth Stuart/ the Wife of/ James Stuart Esq/ surnamed/ Athenian/ Born: 12 August 1762/ Maried* [sic] *at the Age 17/ Died 30 Novemr 1799*.

Dated by the sitter's dress and apparent age. Presented by her son, with the miniature of her husband (NPG 55A), as 'painted at the same time by the same artist',[1] but NPG 55B is of lower quality and appears to have been painted later as a pendant (there is a comparably discreet architectural setting).

1 Letter to Scharf, 29 November 1858 (NPG archive).

STUART, James 1713-88

'Athenian Stuart', painter and architect; studied in Italy 1742-51; with Nicholas Revett, travelled in Greece and Turkey 1751-54; they published the *Antiquities of Athens* 1762 (vol. 2 1789); Dilettanti 1751 and (nominally) Painter to that Society 1763-68; FRS 1758; exhibited FSA 1765-83, mostly architectural views; an arbiter of Grecian taste, but his architectural practice was slight; somewhat intemperate in his later years (according to Mrs Montagu).

'his stature was of the middle size, but athletic; of robust constitution, and a natural courage invincible by terror; and a bold perseverance, unshaken by the most poignant difficulties' (Nichols *Anecdotes*).

'Mr Stuart, though short, was not a fat, but rather a heavy-looking man, and his face declared him to be fond of what is called friendly society' (J.T. Smith, 1828).

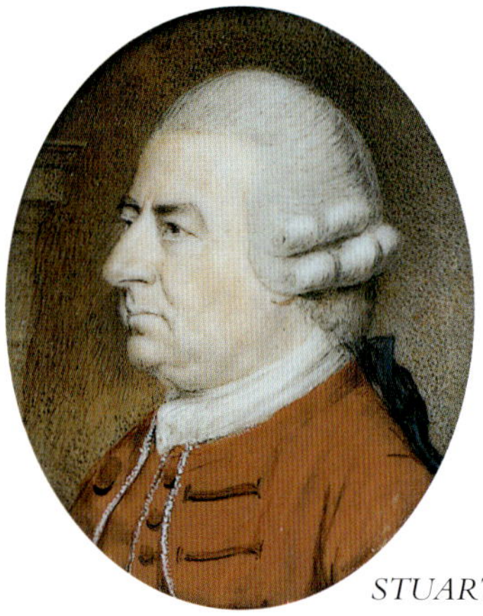

STUART *NPG 55A*

55A attributed to PHILIP JEAN c.1780

Watercolour and bodycolour on ivory 5.4 x 4.4 (2⅛ x 1¾)

Clear grey eyes, white powdered wig, wearing a brown suit with silver piping.

Collections: Presented by the sitter's son, Lt. James Stuart RN, 1858.[1]

Dated by the sitter's dress and apparent age. The attribution to Jean was first proposed by Basil Long in 1928.[2]

1 He had written to Scharf, 11 August 1858, saying that 'It may add to the interest thereof that it should be presented in the year 1858 by a man whose father was born in the reign of Queen Anne' (NPG archive).
2 Letter to Hake, 15 March 1928 (NPG archive). The donor had touchingly believed it to be by Reynolds: 'my Father being eminent in Art & Science would doubtless have employed the first rate Artist' (letter to Scharf, 29 November 1858; NPG archive).

ICONOGRAPHY

c.1730 Drawing, self portrait, porte-crayon in his hand. Royal Institute of British Architects, London (illus. D. Watkin, *Athenian Stuart*, 1982, pl.1). Possibly the crayon portrait of himself 'at the age of thirteen or fourteen' mentioned in *DNB* (where also said to have won an award from the Society of Arts, founded in 1754 when Stuart was passed forty).

c.1748 Painting by Samuel Provan, half length, engraved W.C. Edwards* (*Proben pinxt Roma ... From a picture in the possession of Richard Brettingham ...*). A later state of 1827 prints the artist's name as Proven. Provan is recorded in Rome in 1748 (Ingamells 1997, p.789).

c.1770 Painting formerly attributed to Joshua Reynolds (Graves & Cronin, III, 1899, p.943), half length, with turban and large loose cloak, engraved S.W. Reynolds 1795.

by 1773 Wedgwood medallions, one draped, the other with coat* (Reilly 1973, p.315).

c.1780 Drawing called George Dance, half-length profile, head and dress resembling NPG 55A. Copied

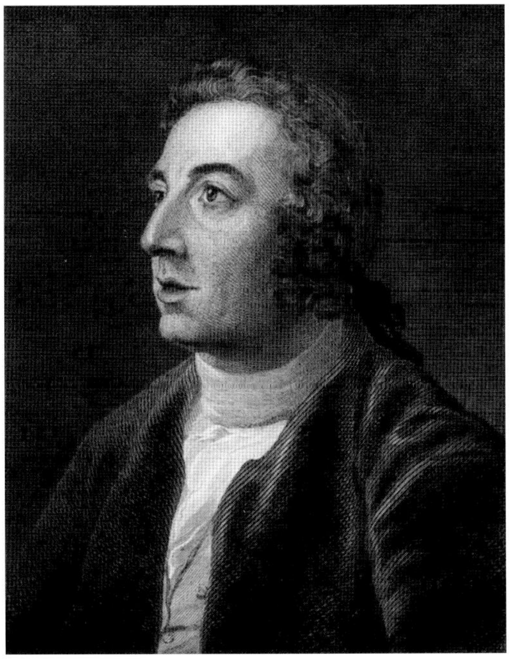

STUART W.C. Edwards after Samuel Provan c.1748 (NPG D 13811)

by John Henning (Victoria and Albert Museum, E.581.1929; illus. *Henning* 1977, n.p.).

c.1780 Miniature attributed to Philip Jean, see NPG 55A.

Posthumous

1789 Drawn and engraved Charles Knight, bust length *all'antico*, pub. by his widow (Nichols *Anecdotes*, IX, p.147n).

1789 Engraving by J. Basire, three-quarter length seated drawing, wearing a fur hat; reissued 1794 for the anon. *Rudiments of Ancient Architecture*, 2nd ed.

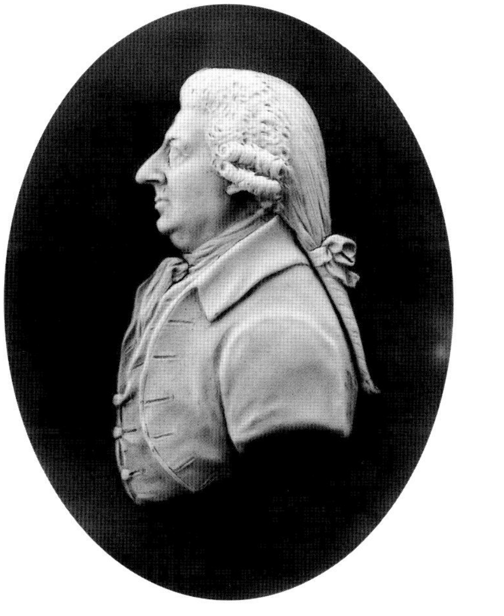

STUART Wedgwood pre-1773 (Wedgwood Museum, Barlaston)

STUART, John, see BUTE

STUBBS, George 1724–1806

Painter and engraver; b. Liverpool, where he studied under Hamlet Winstanley; portrait painter in Yorkshire 1745-53; in Italy 1754; worked at Horkstow, Lincs., 1756-58, preparing *The Anatomy of the Horse* (engravings published 1766); settled in London c.1760; exhibited SA 1762-74, RA 1775-1803; President SA 1772; ARA 1780, but his election as RA in 1781 was never ratified since he failed to deposit a diploma picture.

'Mr Stubbs's habits of life were almost as extraordinary as his intellectual attainments. ... He was always a very early riser; and his constitution continued robust to the last ... [he] was remarkably abstemious; eating little food, and drinking only water, for the last 40 years (*GM*, 1806).

He weighed 13 stone 12 lbs on 22 December 1782, according to Joseph Banks's scales (J. Egerton, *Stubbs, anatomist and painter*, 1976).

Abbreviations

Stubbs 1984: J. Egerton, *Stubbs*, exh. cat., Tate Gallery, 1984

Stubbs 2000: *Fearful Symmetry, George Stubbs, painter of the English Enlightenment*, exh. cat., Hall & Knight Ltd, New York, 2000

1399 after OZIAS HUMPHRY [1777-79]

Watercolour and pencil with some gum arabic on thin card 51 x 40.5 (20 x 16);[1] a small loss bottom centre right; some spotting and minor areas of abrasion.

Collections: Stubbs's son, George Townly Stubbs (d.1815), to the Stamfords;[2] A. Stamford, London; his widow, Mrs A. Stamford, from whom purchased 1905.

Engraving: W. Nicholls 1809 (*Sporting Mag.*).

Exhibitions: *Stubbs & Wedgwood*, Tate 1974(5); *Stubbs* 1984(2); *Stubbs* 2000(30, facsimile).

Reference: B. Taylor, *Apollo*, LXXXI, May 1965, supp. pp.3-4.

The head derives from a chalk study by Humphry dated 1777.[3] The composition was indifferently engraved (slightly reduced) by William Nicholls in 1809[4] as *Humphry pinx.*,'from a picture in the possession of Mrs Spencer'- doubtless the 'Three Quarter Length Oil Picture, being a Portrait of the late Mr George Stubbs, senior, painted by Humphry', bequeathed by Stubbs's companion Mary Spencer to a Mrs Mary Dean.[5] NPG 1399, hitherto attributed to Humphry,[6] would appear to be a copy of this lost portrait; the execution is pedantic (and the card support suggests a working drawing).[7] A small oval half-length version by W.H. Craft, dated 1779 (see below), shows an almost identical head and may also derive from the lost Humphry portrait.

Stubbs is shown holding his *Phaeton and the Chariot of the Sun*, of which he kept an enamel painting on copper dated 1775 in his studio until his death[8] – although the *Phaeton* shown in NPG 1399 is clearly larger.[9] Stubbs evidently prized this subject which, although considered an 'un-natural fiction' by Wedgwood, was also produced as a Wedgwood plaque in 1783.[10]

1 An old ink inscription verso: *21 x 1* [5?] *5/8*.
2 '[It] came direct from Townley [*sic*] Stubbs to the Stamfords. They have also two very large enamels by Stubbs of a lion & Tiger fighting & A Horse & Lion fighting size about 24" by 18" oval (letter from [T?] Winter of Reigate, acting for Mrs Stamford, 28 February 1905; NPG archive); the Stamfords had 'always believed it to be by Stubbs himself' (*idem.*, 3 April 1905).
3 Private collection (illus. *Stubbs* 1984, no.1); Humphry had only returned to London from Italy in October 1777. Giovanni Fontana carved a bas-relief from this drawing for Joseph Mayer, the biographer of Stubbs.
4 Illus. Lennox-Boyd 1989, p.4.
5 Her Will quoted in *Stubbs* 1984, p.26; Mary Spencer died in 1817.
6 Williamson 1917, p.244, even suggesting that it was the drawing exhibited by Humphry RA 1794(374), see Iconography 1794.
7 Jacob Simon points out that the good neo-classical frame could imply a late eighteenth-century date for NPG 1399.
8 Private collection, 37.5 x 46; illus. *Stubbs* 2000, no.27; for Stubbs's concern with the subject, see nos.25-29.
9 Lennox-Boyd 1989, p.379, supposed that a later and larger ceramic version may be depicted.
10 Wedgwood comment from B. Taylor, *Wedgwood Soc.*, IV, 1961, p.220; for the plaques, see further F. Milner, *Stubbs* [in] *Merseyside Collections*, 1987, p.19, and *Stubbs* 2000, no.29.

4575 SELF PORTRAIT 1781

Enamel on Wedgwood biscuit earthenware[1] 69 x 52.5 x 1.5 (27¼ x 21 x ⅝) some specks and flaws in the enamel caused by firing; signed, lower right: *Geo Stubbs/ pinxit 1781* and inscribed verso (the inscription also fired): *Geo. Stubbs painted by himself for his friend Richard Thorold/ of the Inner Temple London.1781*.

Grey eyes, grey powdered hair tied with a black ribbon, wearing a brown smock, his brush in his right hand.

Collections: Painted for Richard Thorold, FRS (d.1792);[2] Sir John Astley, 3rd Bt (d.1894), Elsham Hall, Lincs.,[3] sale c.1893, bt. by a Mr Heely;[4] by descent to Mrs Muriel Heely of Alford, Lincs.; Christie's, 12 July 1967, lot 81, bt. Leggatt, from

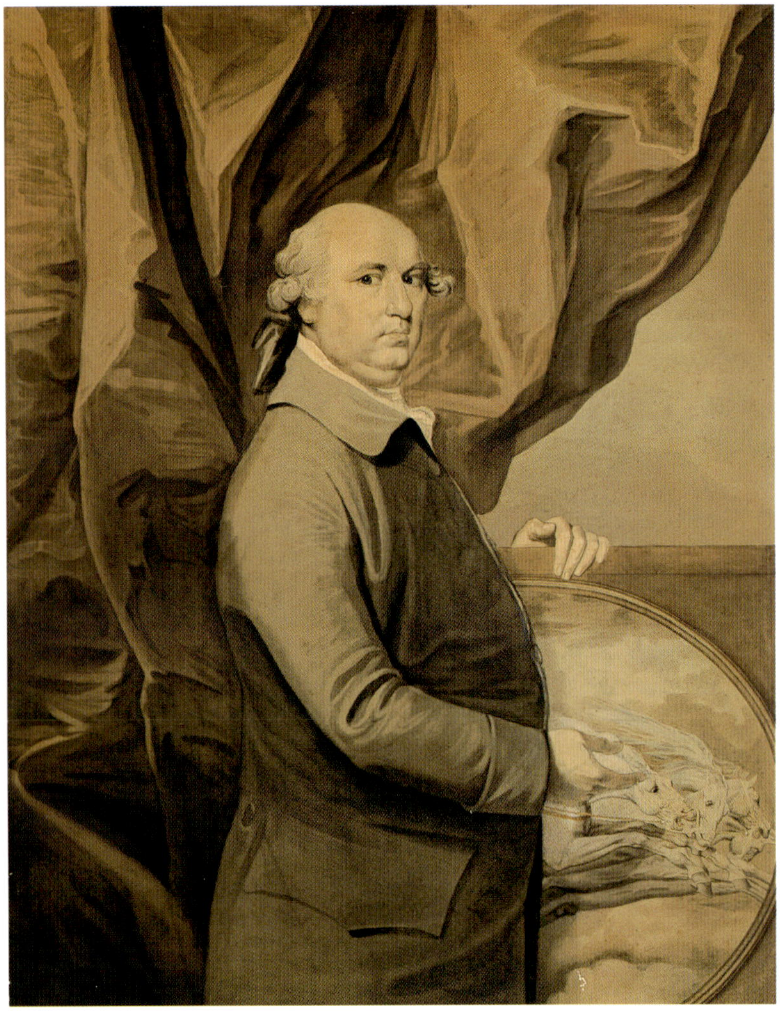

STUBBS NPG *1399*

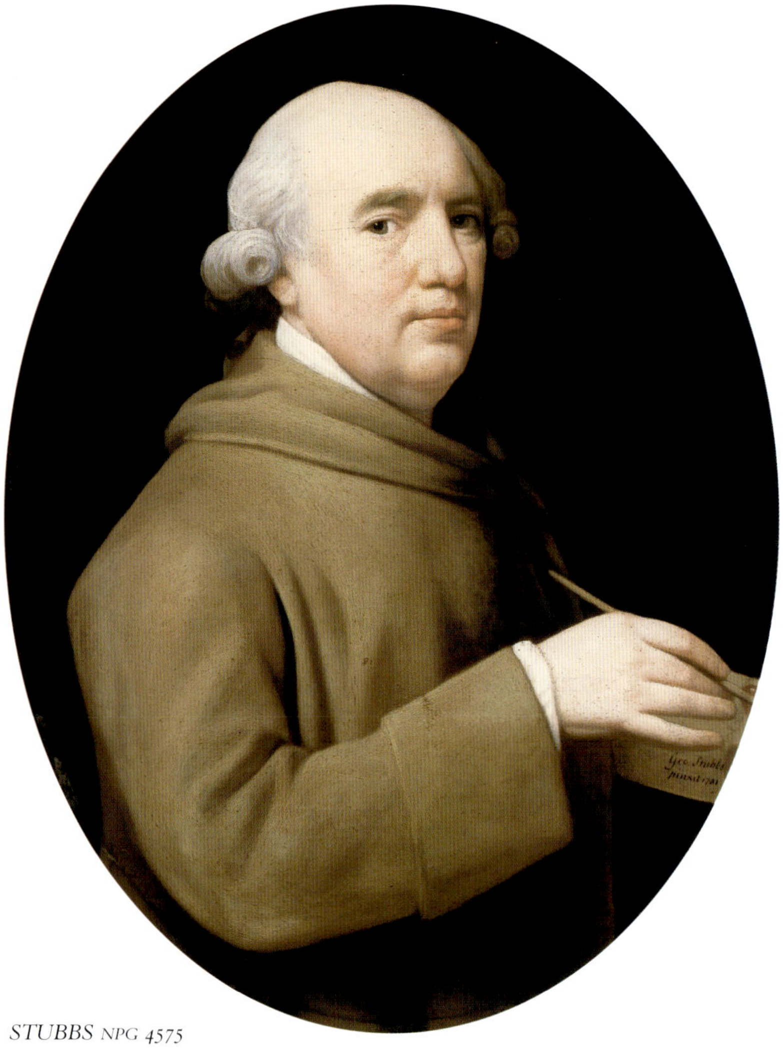

STUBBS NPG *4575*

whom purchased with the aid of an anonymous donor and the National Art Collections Fund 1967.

Exhibitions: RA 1782(173); *Stubbs*, Liverpool, 1951(27 as Josiah Wedgwood) lent Mrs Muriel Heely; *Stubbs*, Whitechapel, 1957(12) lent Mrs Muriel Heely; *Stubbs & Wedgwood*, Tate, 1974(B in the catalogue, but not lent); *Stubbs* 1984(4).

Reference: B. Taylor, *Wedgwood Soc.*, IV, 1961, p.209; B. Taylor, *Apollo*, LXXXI, May 1965, supp., pp.3-4; Simon 1997, pp.96, 163.

When exhibited at the RA in 1782 the *Public Examiner* (1 May 1782) commented that 'The Portrait, as large as life, on this Enamel of Stubbs, is the Effigies of himself, and if the white had not been so cadaverous, it would have been a vera effigies'.[5] When the portrait re-emerged in 1951 it was thought to show Josiah Wedgwood (see Exhibitions above), but it was correctly identified by Taylor in 1957.[6] A finished preparatory pencil drawing, just under half size and squared-up for enlargement, is in the Yale Center for British Art (B2001.2.1262).[7]

ICONOGRAPHY

A survey of the engraved portraits of Stubbs is given in Lennox-Boyd 1989, p.379; a preliminary Stubbs iconography was published by B. Taylor, *Apollo*, LXXXI, May 1965, supp., pp.3-4.

c.1755 Painting, identified as a self portrait, miniature half-length oval, dark hair, wearing a light green coat. Christie's, 26 March 1976, lot 82; lent to the Fitzwilliam Museum, Cambridge, 1984 (see *Burl.Mag.*, CXXVII, 1985, pp.67, 85, illus., as a self portrait). Undocumented and perhaps to be regarded with slight reservation; the black hair is unexpected, but the likeness seems unmistakeable and the pose is evidently that of a self portrait.

1769 Drawing by P-E. Falconet, medallion profile. Engraved D.P. Pariset 1769 (illus. Lennox-Boyd 1989, f.p.1); B. Reading 1792. A related wash drawing attributed to Falconet was sold Christie's, 12 November 1968, lot 51.

1 R. Emmerson, *Apollo*, CL, August 1999, p.51, has shown that the Wedgwood clay tablets made for Stubbs received a light glaze to provide a smooth surface for painting.

2 Of Barnetby-le-Wold, Lincs., described as 'of considerable knowledge in antiquity, and a very ingenious mechanic' (*GM*, LXII, 1792, i, p.387); see also J. Egerton, *Stubbs, anatomist and animal painter*, Tate, 1976, p.29, and note 3 below. Ozias Humphry, c.1797, recorded Stubbs's 'portrait of himself in Enamel (painting) by a commission from Mr Thorold ... half the Size of Life' (*Stubbs* 2000, p.205); mistakenly printed in J. Mayer, *Early Exhibitions of Art in Liverpool*, 1876, p.125, as 'painted for Mrs Therold'.

3 Sir John Astley m. 1858 Eleanor Corbett (d.1897), an only child, of Elsham Hall, where they lived from 1859; Astley's financial instability is demonstrated throughout his biography, *Fifty years of my Life*, 1894, edited by his 'close friend' Richard Thorold, presumably a descendant of the Richard Thorold for whom NPG 4575 was painted.

4 Mrs Heely said the picture was bought by either her husband's grand or great-grand father in 'about 1893 or 1894' at the Elsham Hall sale (note of a conversation with David Piper, 11 April 1967; NPG archive); the sale was presumably on the death of the intemperate Sir John Astley in 1894. There was apparently a second Elsham Hall sale c.1928: Miss C. Soames, an Astley descendant, wrote in 1968: 'My uncle some 40 odd years ago decided to sell the contents of Elsham Hall ... [but] I do not remember the Stubbs portrait' (5 January 1968; NPG archive).

5 Quoted by Kidson 1999, p.159n9; Kidson very tentatively supposed the exhibited portrait may have been the equestrian self portrait of 1782 in the Lady Lever AG, Port Sunlights, but the contemporary description would seem to deny this.

6 *Stubbs*, Whitechapel 1957(12).

7 Illus. *Stubbs* 1984, no.3.

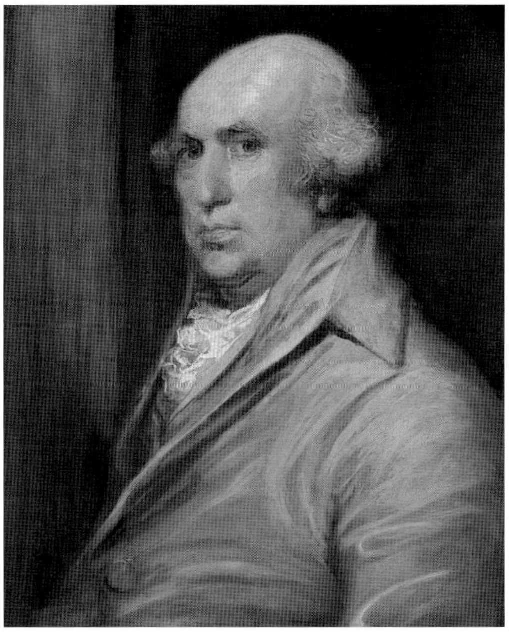

STUBBS by Ozias Humphry 1794 (Walker Art Gallery, Liverpool)

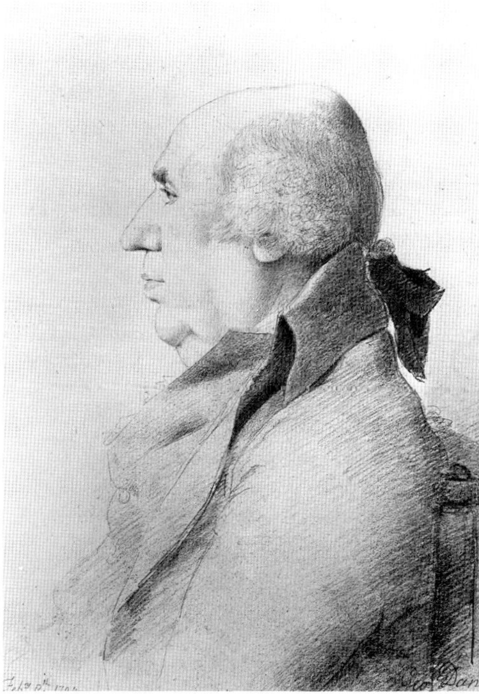

STUBBS by George Dance 1794 (Royal Academy of Arts, London)

c.1770? Drawing, in the manner of George Dance, half-length seated at table etching. Royal Collection (illus. Oppé 1950, p.39, no.169; *Stubbs* 2000, p.54). A drawing from the Oppé collection of a comparable head, now in the Tate Gallery (T 0857) attributed to Nathaniel Dance, appears not to show Stubbs (cf. Oppé, *loc. cit.*).

A comparable, larger, drawing was formerly in the Oppé collection (exhibited *Oppé Collection*, Bath, 1958, no.131).

c.1773-75 Drawing by Thomas Orde, engraved in reverse by J. Bretherton, profile head, rather unhappily stuck on a three-quarter length seated figure painting with the left hand (illus. Lennox-Boyd 1989, p.3).

1777 Drawing by Ozias Humphry, bust length, see NPG 1399.

1777-79 Portrait by Ozias Humphry, three-quarter length standing, see NPG 1399.

1779 Enamel by W.H. Craft, half-length oval, his left hand resting on a portfolio, the pose identical to that in NPG 1399. Yale Center for British Art (B2001.2.72; illus. *Stubbs* 2000, p.186). The date of 1779 recorded in NPG archive from Appleby, 1953. See NPG 1399.

1781 Painting, enamel on Wedgwood biscuit earthenware, self portrait, see NPG 4575.

1782 Painting, enamel on Wedgwood biscuit earthenware, self portrait, mounted on a white hunter. Lady Lever AG, Port Sunlight (illus. Kidson 1999, pl.vi). Formerly called Josiah Wedgwood (cf. NPG 4575).

1794 Pastel by Ozias Humphry,* half length. Walker AG, Liverpool (2442). Exhibited RA 1794(374). Farington recorded Stubbs sitting to Humphry on 3 February 1794. Copied by H. Bone: preparatory drawing dated 1810 in the NPG Bone albums (*Bone* 1999, no.499, fig.154) and enamel, exhibited RA 1811(321), Burdett-Coutts sale, Christie's, 3rd day, 11 May 1922, lot 422.

1794 Drawing by George Dance,* profile bust, dated 8 February 1794. Royal Academy. Engraved W. Daniell 1802 (*Dance Plates*); tracing by Daniell in the Yale Center for British Art (B1977.14.6145).

1801 Painting by Thomas Stewart, exhibited RA 1801(98 'Mr Stubbs'), presumably George Stubbs.

SUCKLING, Maurice 1725-78

Naval officer, of Woodton, Norfolk; lieutenant 1745 and captain 1755, fighting with distinction in the West Indies 1757; comptroller of the navy 1775-78 and MP 1776-78; uncle of Lord Nelson.

2010 THOMAS BARDWELL 1764

Canvas 126.5 x 101 (49¾ x 39¾) lined; X-radiography shows an area round his (rather fudged) left hand was reworked; overall craquelure and discoloured retouchings in the face and cravat;[1] signed bottom left: *TBardwell.f.1764*; inscribed, bottom right: *MAURICE SUCKLING/by Bardwell/1764*.

Brown eyes, white powdered wig, wearing captain's uniform; on the table ink well, quill, wax and illegibly inscribed papers.

Collections:[2] Given by the sitter to his nephew, Horatio Nelson; his daughter Lady Charlotte (who m. 1810 the 2nd Bn. Bridport); their son, 1st Viscount Bridport, Cricket St Chard, from whom bt. in June 1896 by Capt. T. Suckling RN (d.1922), Barsham, Norfolk,[3] and Highwood, Hants., bequeathed by him, subject to the life interest of his wife, and received 1924.

Reference: Kirby Talley 1978, no.102.

Bardwell painted several members of the Suckling family.[4] NPG 2010 was described in 1905 as showing Captain Suckling 'seated in front of the portrait (also by Bardwell) of his cousin, young Robert Suckling, of Woodton, and ... probably executed at Woodton-hall a few months before that officer's marriage with his cousin, the Hon. Mary Walpole'[5] - which took place on 20 June 1764. Farrer in 1905 made no mention of Robert Suckling's portrait being visible.[6] Was it identified just by the frame in the left background? NPG 2010 has been relined and no evidence survives of the canvas having been reduced; the position of Bardwell's signature, bottom left, seems against it, and the figure of Suckling is far too small to fit a whole-length composition.[7] The other Suckling portraits by Bardwell were three-quarter lengths.

A modern half-length copy was acquired by the National Maritime Museum in 1948 (BHC 3045)[8] with unattributed portraits of Suckling's parents.

1 A technical analysis of the painting was published in 1975: M. Kirby Talley & K. Groen, 'Thomas Bardwell and his Practice of Painting', *Studies in Conservation*, XX, 1975, pp.44-108; NPG 2010 is specifically mentioned on pp.52-53, 57-58, 71-72, 76-77, 84-90; illus.: detail of signature p.52, and X-ray photographs of the cuffs and head pp.85, 100. See also F. Schmid, *Technical Studies in the Field of the Fine Arts*, ix, 1941, 3 p.156.
2 This provenance recorded in a label formerly attached to the frame of NPG 2010.
3 Where listed in 1905 (Farrer 1921, I, p.62, no.14).
4 See Kirby Talley 1978, p.94, and nos.100-103, 140, 147.
5 'F.S.' in *Norfolk and Norwich Notes and Queries*, 3rd ser., Jan. 1905,

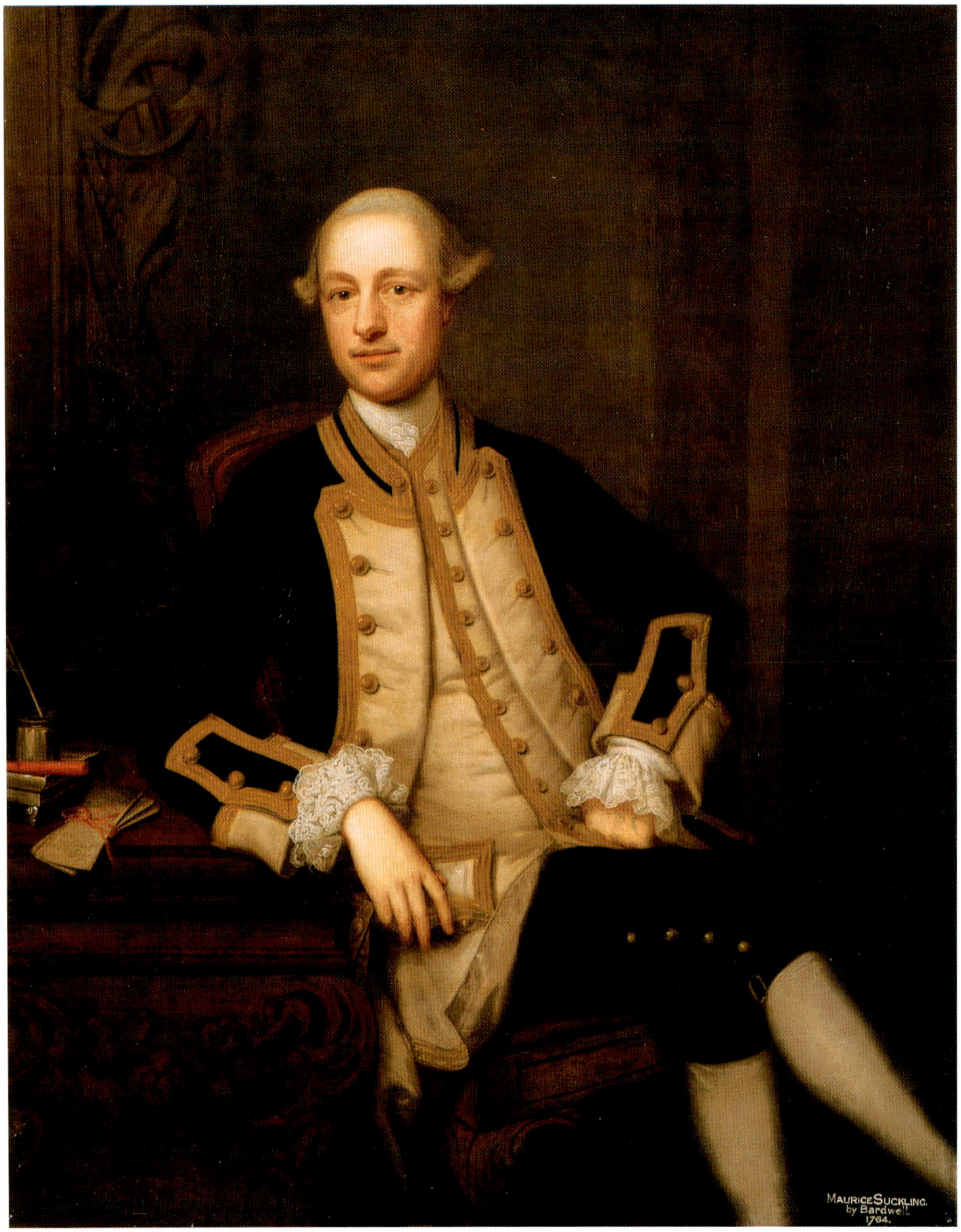

SUCKLING NPG *2010*

pp.111-12, and repeated by E. Mann, *Old Bungay*, 1934, pp.213-14; as quoted by Kirby Talley 1978, no.102.

6 Farrer 1921, I, p.63, no.19; Kirby Talley 1978, no.103; painted in 1756 and last recorded with the Suckling family in 1930.

7 Bardwell sometimes used a 140 x 119 (55 x 47) canvas (e.g. Kirby Talley 1978, nos.5,6 & 73), but this still would not allow a recognisable portrait to appear in the frame shown in NPG 2010.

8 H. Nelson-Ward, a cousin of Thomas Suckling, commissioned a copy of NPG 2010 in 1924 (letters of 11 & 16 April 1924; NPG archive).

ICONOGRAPHY

c.1760? Painting by an unidentified artist, half-length, his own thin hair, wearing captain's undress uniform. Thomas Suckling, Barsham Hall, 1905 (listed by Farrer 1928, I, p.62, no.13). Engraved W. Ridley 1805 (*Naval Chron.*) with Suckling arms (*per pale gu. and az. a three bucks trippant or; crest a roebuck courant az.*).

1764 Painting by Thomas Bardwell, see NPG 2010.

SURREY, Charles, Earl of, see NORFOLK

TAYLOR, Sir Robert, Kt 1714-88

Architect; apprenticed to the sculptor Henry Cheere before going to Rome c.1742; turned to architecture c.1750 and built up a profitable practice; surveyor to the Bank of England by 1764; governor of Greenwich Hospital; Sheriff of London 1782-83; Kt 1782; he left a considerable fortune for the foundation of an institution at Oxford for the study of modern European languages (the Taylorian).

1323 UNKNOWN ARTIST [c.1782]

Watercolour on paper 23 x 18.5 (9 x 7¼); two small surface damages upper right; faint ruled pencil lines define an area 21 x 17.7 (8¼ x 7), presumably for framing; inscribed in ink, verso: *Sir Robert Taylor Architect Founder of the Taylor Institution/ Died in 1788.*

White powdered wig, wearing the robes of the sheriff of London, a red gown trimmed with sable with the gold chain of office, over a brown jacket; the curious quatrefoil in the right background may refer to the arms of Richard I (three lions *passant guardant*) set in the west window in the London Guildhall (destroyed in 1940).[1]

Collections: Purchased from John Glen 1902.

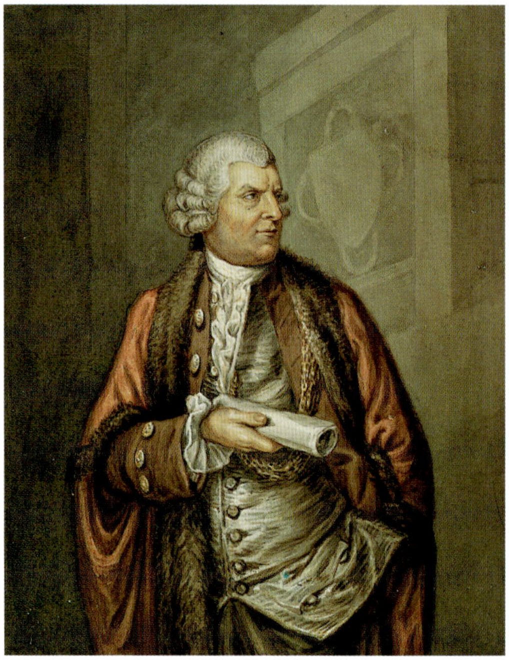

TAYLOR NPG *1323*

Purchased as by Ozias Humphry,[2] but NPG 1323 is a weak, anonymous copy of the three-quarter length portrait in the Taylorian, Oxford, presented by the sitter's son in 1835, the only known type of portrait of Taylor.[3] A version, in which he wears civilian dress, belongs to the Royal Institute of British Architects.[4] The head recurs (back row, right foreground) in a painting by William Miller, *The Swearing in of Nathaniel Newman as Lord Mayor of London 1782* (Guildhall Art Gallery, 55), engraved B. Smith. On the basis of the Guildhall picture, the Oxford portrait has been attributed to William Miller, an unproven but likely hypothesis.[5] A half-length oval engraving of the Oxford portrait was made as a private plate by Edmund Scott in 1789.[6]

1 Slightly more visible in the Taylorian portrait.
2 Listed in Williamson 1918, p.245, as attributed to Humphry.
3 Poole, I, 1912, p.220, illus. pl.xxxiii, f.p.220.
4 Exhibited NPE 1868(886).
5 Cf. M. Binney, *Sir Robert Taylor*, 1984, pl.1 (NPG 1323, but described as belonging to the RIBA).
6 Listed by O'Donoghue as after (W. Miller), without explicit evidence.

TEMPLE, Ann, Countess, *née* Chambers 1709-77

Poetess; dau. and coheir of Thomas Chambers of Hanworth; m. 1737 Richard, 2nd Earl Temple, bringing him a great fortune; she was forty 'before she discovered in herself a turn for genteel versification' and her *Select Poems* were printed at Strawberry Hill in 1764; according to Lord Shelburne, her husband 'did not seem to find the least resource in her conversation, but was inconsolable at her death'.

246 HUGH DOUGLAS HAMILTON 1770

Pastel on paper 24.5 x 19.5 (9¾ x 7¾);[1] general rubbing and a conspicuous repaired damage lower left; signed, lower right: *H.D. Hamilton fect 1770*.

Brown eyes, wearing a white lace cap with a black lace head scarf, blue dress with white lace.

Collections: Horace Walpole (4th Earl of Orford); Strawberry Hill sale, 18th day, 14 May 1842, lot 89, bt. Forster; T. Parker, from whom purchased 1867.

Engravings (all of rectangular format): W. Birrell 1798 *from a Portrait by Hamilton in the Collection at Strawberry Hill*; reduced version anon. 1801; W. Greatbach 1857 from a drawing by G.P. Harding[2] (another state has Hamilton's name instead of Harding's).

A replica, signed and dated 1771, showing the front of the dress slightly more finished, is in a private collection.

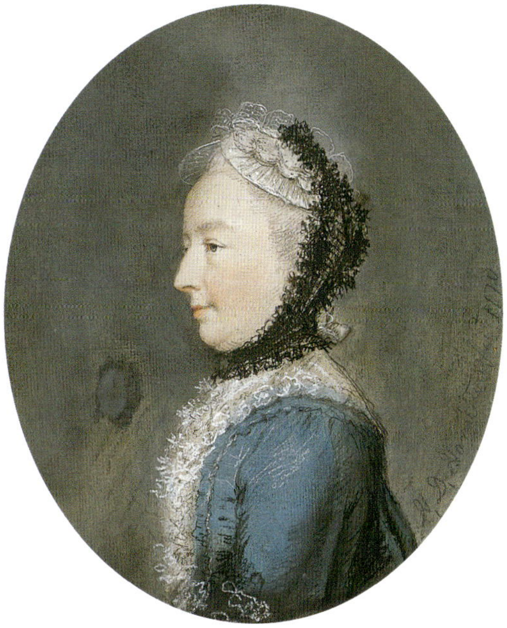

Ann, Countess TEMPLE NPG 246

1 The oval drawn area does not reach the bottom of the sheet. A traced template of 1867 (preserved in the archive) shows a larger oval 27.5 x 22 (10¾ x 8¾) marked 'original size of drawing'; the margin between it and the present size (which occurs round the left and upper edges) is marked 'The drawing was reduced to this extent'.
2 Probably the drawing by G.P. Harding sold Bonham's, 25 November 1998, lot 47.

ICONOGRAPHY

1760 Painting by Allan Ramsay,* three-quarter length seated profile, holding a shuttle and knotting bag. Trustees of the Chevening Estate (Smart 1999, no.508).

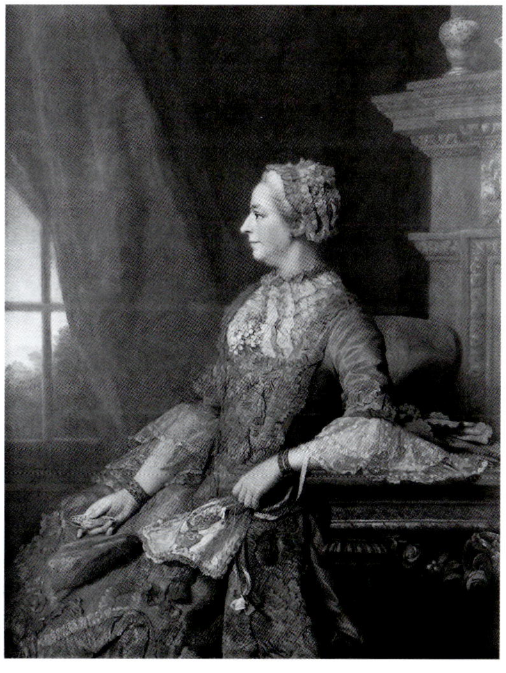

Ann, Countess TEMPLE by Allan Ramsay 1760 (Private Collection)

1770 Pastel by H.D. Hamilton, see NPG 246.

A portrait of 'Ann Countess Temple (Hudson)' was in the Stowe sale, 22nd day, 13 September 1848, lot 207, bt. Gore Langton.

TEMPLE, Richard Grenville-Temple, 2nd Earl 1711-79

Statesman, travelled in Europe 1729-33; MP 1741-52; sty. Lord Cobham 1749 (his mother had inherited Lord Cobham's estate); suc. as 2nd Earl 1752, when he assumed the added name of Temple and inherited the estates of Wotton and Stowe; devoted to his brother-in-law, William Pitt, he was lord privy seal 1757-61 and twice declined the position of prime minister in 1765; KG 1760; much of his later life was spent embellishing Stowe.

'In his person he was tall and large, though not inclined to corpulency. A disorder, the seat of which lay in his ribs, bending him almost double, compelled him in walking to use a sort of crutch; but his mind seemed exempt from decay. His conversation was animated, brilliant, and full of entertainment' (Sir Nathaniel Wraxall, 1815).

258 WILLIAM HOARE c.1757-60

Canvas 125.5 x 100.5 (49½ x 39½) lined; discoloured varnish; isolated areas of craquelure, most prominent around his right eye; the Garter sash is clearly an addition.

Blue eyes, white powdered wig, his hair tied with a blue ribbon, wearing a dove-grey velvet suit, with the blue ribbon of the Garter; seated on a red chair; with his left hand he points to an architectural plan[1] on a table, with behind it, the purse of the lord privy seal; inscribed upper left: *RICHARD EARL/ TEMPLE./ 1760*; a purple curtain to the right.

Collections: By descent to the sitter's great-grand-nephew, the 3rd Marquess of Buckingham; Stowe sale, Christie's, 21st day, 12 September 1848, lot 84, bt. S.M. Peto; E.L. Betts, Preston Hall, Kent; Christie's, 30 May 1868, lot 20 ('from Stowe'), purchased.

Engravings: J. Watson (see below); R. Houston (see below) and a second reduced plate; reduced ovals by C. Townley 1757; C. Watson 1806; A. Walker; anon. (*Universal Mag.*).

Exhibition: Crown Estates Office 1986-.

An unsophisticated portrait, in which the hands and purse are particularly slipshod. The inscribed date of 1760 is slightly misleading. The first state of Houston's undated engraving omitted the Garter regalia and the purse (thereby revealing more of the architectural

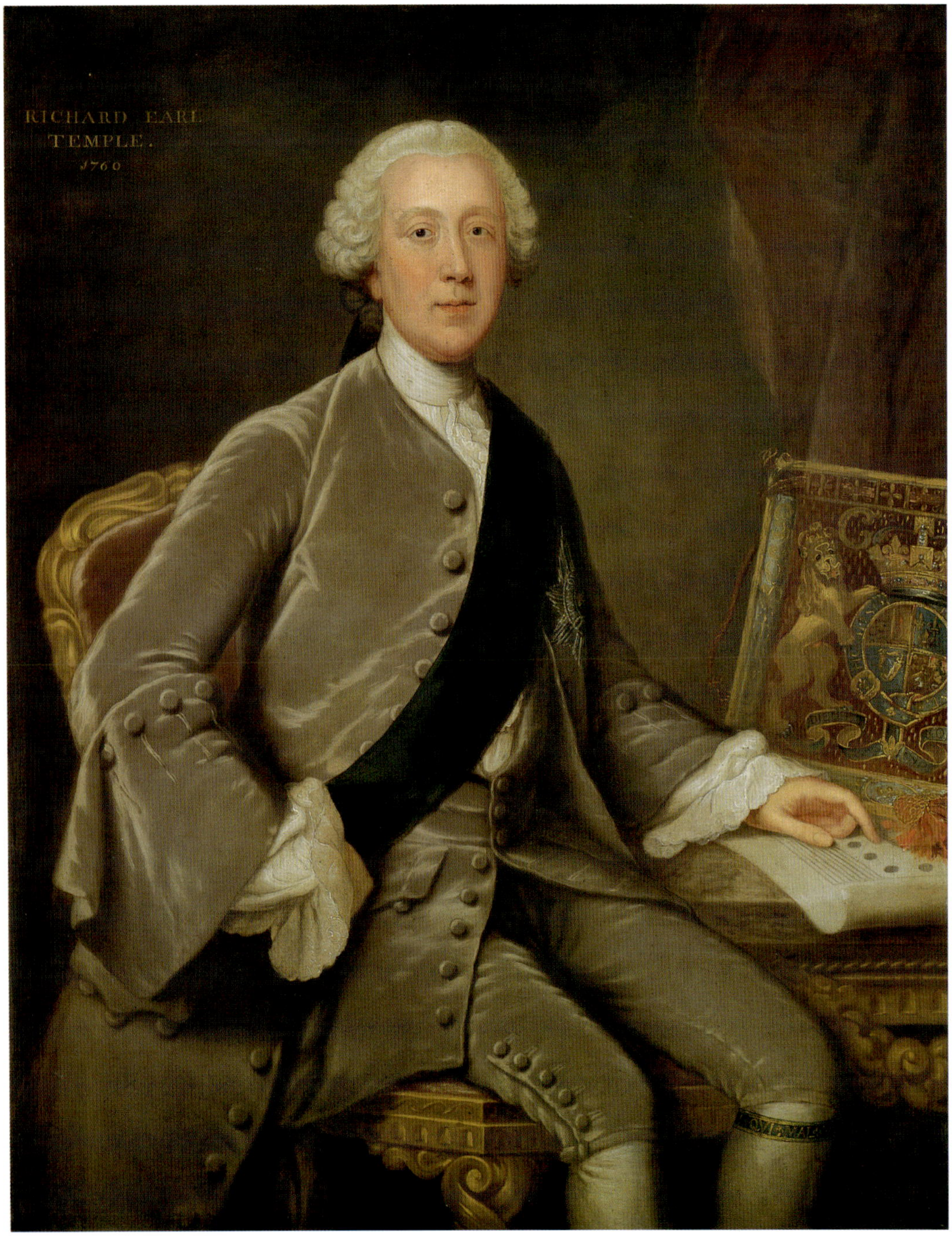

2nd Earl TEMPLE NPG 258

plan), the letterpress describing Temple as lord privy seal; the second state introduced the Garter regalia, while still omitting the purse; the title omitted lord privy seal (an office he resigned in 1761), substituting the lord lieutenancy of Buckingham, an office he held 1758-63. Watson's undated print copied this second state, but omitted the Garter round the knee, the letterpress describing Temple as lord privy seal. These variations indicate Hoare's original portrait was completed after June 1757 when Temple became privy seal and before February 1760 when he became a Knight of the Garter; the Garter regalia was then added. The Garter ribbon seen in NPG 258 hangs differently from that seen in the Houston and Watson prints. An identical version belonging to the Trustees of the Chevening Estate[2] clearly shows the Garter ribbon painted over the coat and may therefore be the original, in which case NPG 258 is a replica, presumably of 1760, as inscribed.

1 Possibly the Grecian Temple at Stowe (begun c.1748 and probably designed by Richard Grenville himself; completed by G.B. Borra in 1762), see *Apollo*, XCVII, 1973, p.571. Watson's print shows more of the plan than NPG 258.

2 Having descended by the marriage of the sitter's niece to the 3rd Earl Stanhope. Seen by Scharf at Chevening in 1862 (SSB 65/112 -blue-grey eyes); illus. *Apollo*, XCVII, 1973, p.588; exhibited *Manners and Morals*, Tate, 1987(219).

ICONOGRAPHY

1731-32 Pastel by Rosalba Carriera half length. Private collection. Inscribed as painted in Venice when the sitter was 19 years old. (B. Sani, *Carriera*, 1989 no.184, fig.160, and see F. Russell, *Burl. Mag.*, CXXXI, 1989, p.857).

c.1740 Bust by Peter Scheemakers, from the Temple of Friendship at Stowe. Stowe sale, Christie's, 6th day, 21 August 1848, lot 766 (unattributed), bt. Sir Alexander Grant.

c.1757-60 Painting by William Hoare, see NPG 258.

1762 Painting by Allan Ramsay,* whole-length standing in Garter robes. NG Melbourne (Smart 1999, no.509). The noble pose belies Temple's physical awkwardness.

c.1775-76 Painting by Joshua Reynolds, three-quarter length standing in Garter robes. Private collection (Mannings 2000, no.765). Exhibited RA 1776(237). Engraved W. Dickinson 1778; S.W. Reynolds.*

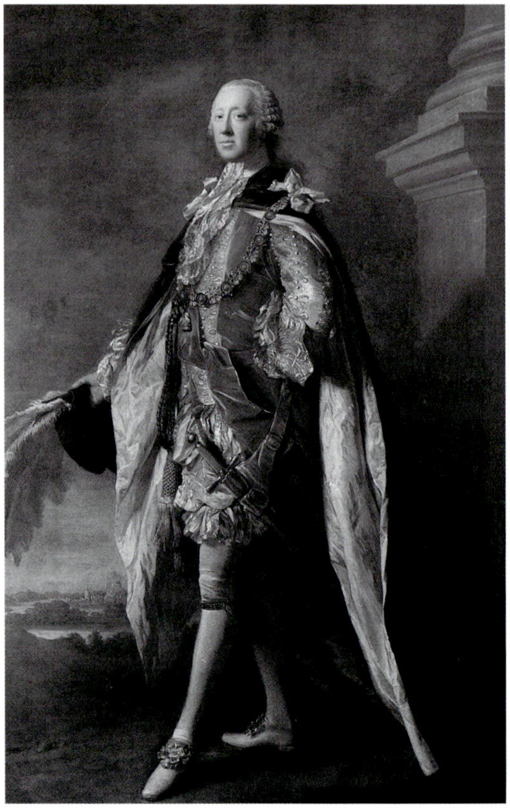

2nd Earl TEMPLE by Allan Ramsay 1762 (National Gallery of Victoria, Melbourne)

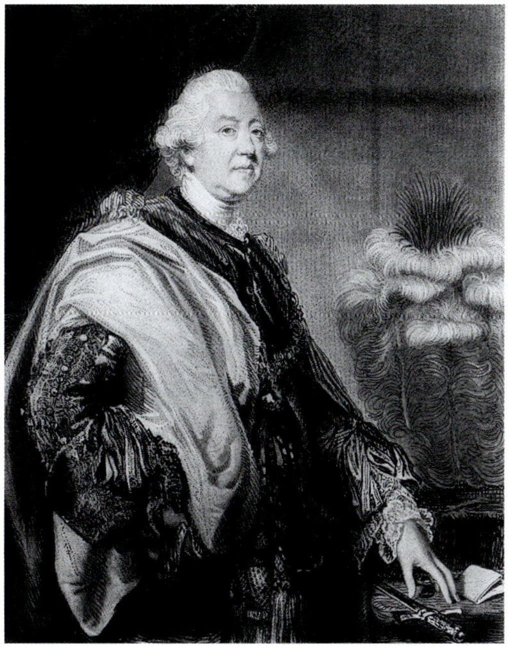

2nd Earl TEMPLE S.W. Reynolds after Joshua Reynolds c.1775-76 (NPG D 13812)

1779-81 Painting by J.S. Copley,* *The Death of Chatham*, see Comparative Groups.

Miniature by C.F. Zincke exhibited *Guelph* 1891(1013) lent J. Whitehead.

DOUBTFUL PORTRAITS

Unlettered oval engraving (*London Mag.* 1782; bust-length oval engraved Ridley & Holl, *Earl Temple*, 1797 (for a 1798 edition of Junius).

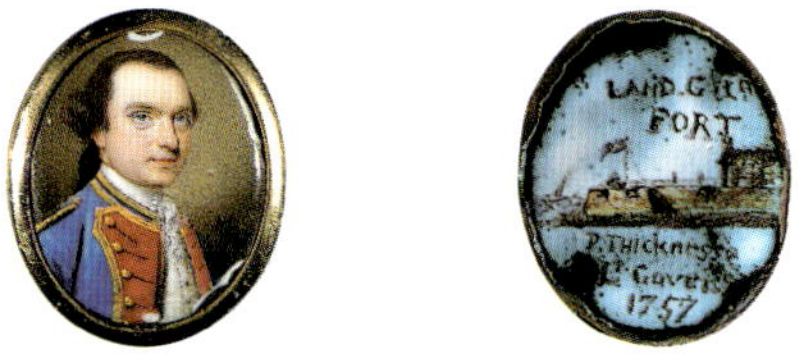

THICKNESSE NPG *4192 and verso*

THICKNESSE, Philip 1719-92

Querulous soldier and dilettante; served in Georgia and Jamaica 1735-40; commissioned in a regiment of marines 1741, serving in the Mediterranean 1744-45; lieutenant-governor of Landguard Fort, Suffolk, 1753-66, where he patronised the young Gainsborough; thereafter lived principally in Bath; published *Journey through France and part of Spain* 1777 and the *Sketch of the Life and Paintings of Thomas Gainsborough* 1788.

'he was extremely handsome; his conversation was entertaining; his talents undisputed ... [with] a high and delicate sense of honour ... susceptible in the extreme of everything that bordered on insult and rudeness' (*GM*, 1809).

4192 NATHANIEL HONE 1757

Enamel on copper 3 x 2.5 (1⅛ x 1); signed lower right *NH/1757*; the edges of the enamel are chipped (upper left, top centre and upper and lower right). Verso a crudely enamelled view of Landguard Fort* lettered: *LAND.GU^{A}/FORT* (above) and *THIcknesse/ L^{T}. GOVER^{O}./ 1757* (below).

Blue eyes, dark brown hair with a black ribbon, wearing a uniform (presumably that of the lieutenant-governor of Landguard Fort)[1] of a rich blue coat with maroon facings and gold piping, with a thin gold epaulette.

Collections: Mrs D. Asher; Sotheby's, 19 December 1960, lot 72, bt. Leggatt for the NPG.

1 Thicknesse married in 1763 wearing 'the private uniform' of Col Sir Armine Wodehouse's Batallion of Militia, in which he was a volunteer (Nichols *Anecdotes*, IX, p.260n).

ICONOGRAPHY

1757 Miniature by Nathaniel Hone, see NPG 4192.

c.1763 Drawing by William Hoare,* three-quarter length standing. British Museum (1894.4.17.9). A record by Hoare of his now untraced painting; there is a similar drawing by him of his painting of the third Mrs Thicknesse (Ann Ford, also painted by Gainsborough).

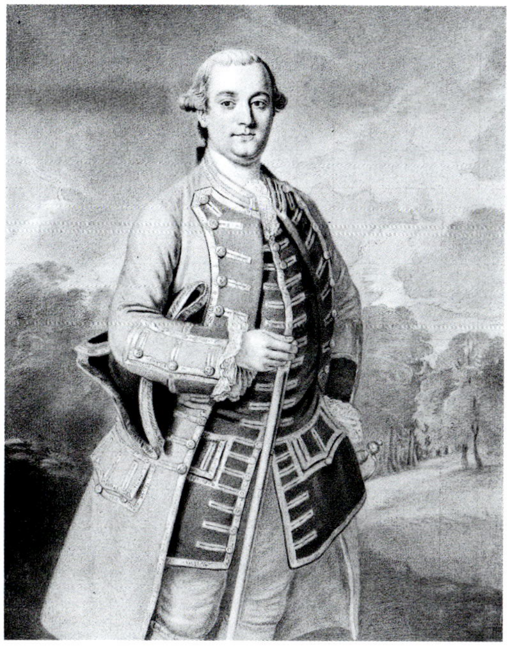

THICKNESSE *by William Hoare c.1763 (British Museum)*

1790 Engraving by James Gillray, bust-length oval, looking sour (illus. Gainsborough 2000, p.119; front. to Adair's *Curious Facts not contained in the Memoirs of Philip Thicknesse*; George 7722). A similar head appears in Gillray's satire of Thicknesse, *Birth of Minerva* 1790 (George 7721).

1790 Silhouette by S.W. Fores, bust length (front. to Thicknesse *Memoirs*, iii, 1791).

Thicknesse also alleged that in 1774 Gainsborough began a whole-length portrait of him with a Newfoundland dog at his feet, in exchange for the gift of Mrs Thicknesse's viola da gamba; it was never finished and Gainsborough returned the viola da gamba (Fulcher 1856, pp.91-97; P. Gosse, *Dr Viper*, 1951, pp.251-56). Whitley 1915, pp.99-101, and most subsequent writers have treated the episode as imaginary.

DOUBTFUL PORTRAIT

Painting by Francis Hayman, whole-length reclining in a landscape, Art Museum, St Louis, Mo. (Waterhouse 1958, no.659, as Gainsborough; illus. Hayman 1987, pp.41, 174, no.53).

THRALE, Mrs Hester, see PIOZZI

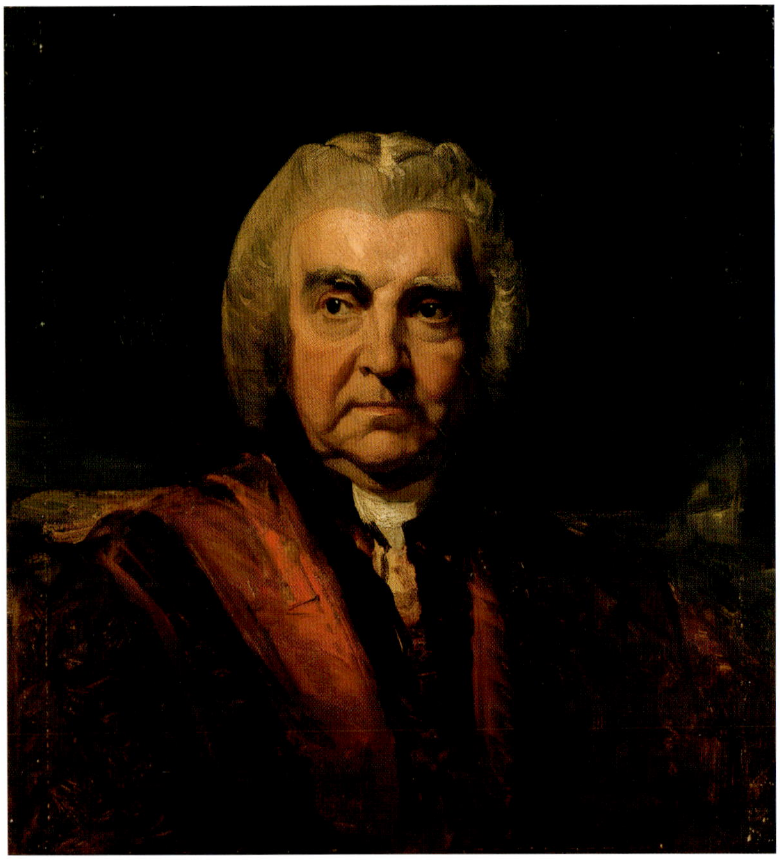

1st Baron THURLOW NPG 395

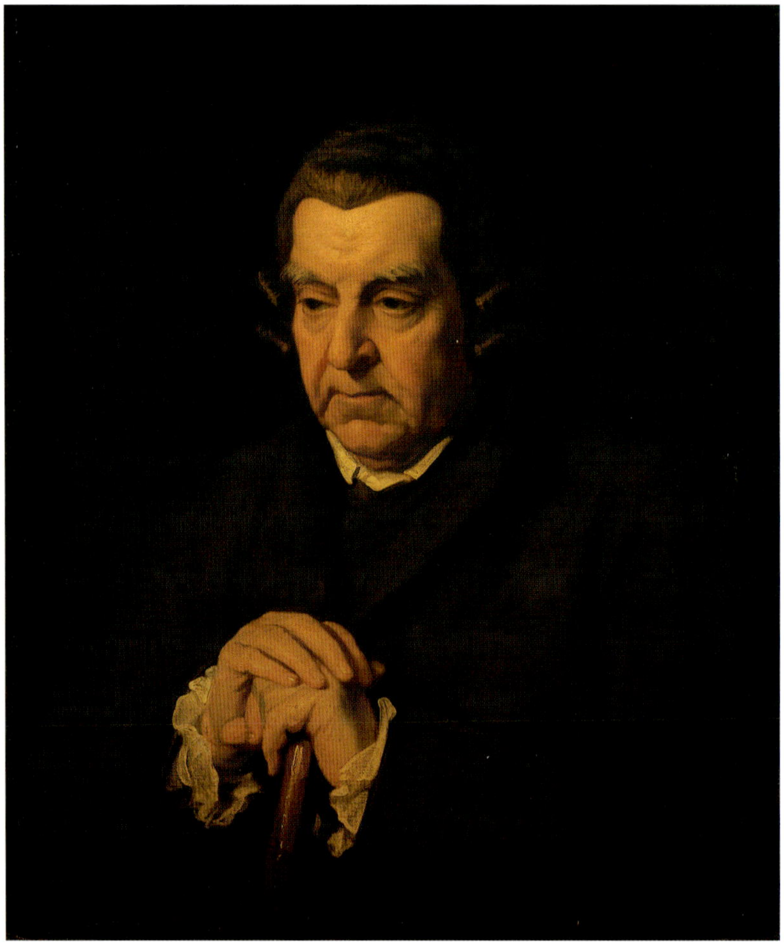

1st Baron THURLOW NPG 249

THURLOW, Edward Thurlow, 1st Baron 1731–1806

Lord chancellor; MP 1765–78; KC 1762; solicitor-general 1770–71; attorney-general 1771–78; cr. Baron Thurlow 1778; lord chancellor 1778–82; a powerful personality, according to Walpole coarse in his manners and indelicate in his pleasures.

'Bold, stern, inflexible, his sombre countenance was generally clothed in terrors. His look was calculated to appal the guilty, while, from his bushy eyebrows, he seemed to scowl dismay even on innocence' (Alexander Stephens, 1813).

'No man could be so wise as Thurlow looked' (C.J. Fox).

395 studio of THOMAS LAWRENCE [1803]

Canvas 66.5 x 62 (26¼ x 24½) lined; the marks of an earlier, smaller slip-frame, 55 (21¾) wide, on the surface.

Brown eyes, powdered grey wig, wearing a black coat beneath a red gown; the lower area is unresolved.

Collections: [possibly the unfinished portrait of Thurlow in the Lawrence sale, Christie's, 18 June 1831, lot 59, bt. Eckford (d.1840)]; J. Gibbons, sale 5 June 1850, lot 29, bt. Woodgate; Christie's, 19 January 1856, lot 110, bt. Waters; 'a gentleman from Blackheath' [William Angerstein], sale Christie's, 20 June 1874, lot 48,[1] bt. Colnaghi, from whom purchased 1874.

Exhibition: Office of Works (Foreign Office; House of Lords) 1900–41.

The vigorously sketched head relates directly to the portrait by Lawrence now in the Royal Collection which was exhibited at the RA 1803(21), see below, but the surround is less accomplished, and the red legal gown worn over the dark coat is peculiar to NPG 395. In 1881 it was described as 'probably by Richard Evans',[2] Lawrence's pupil, but this cannot be proved.

1 This provenance was established by Scharf from chalk inscriptions on an 'old twilled canvas on back'; his sketch of the verso made on 27 June 1874 (SSB 19/82) also indicates a length of 'prepared canvas uncoloured' wrapped round the lower stretcher bar.

2 By Scharf in the NPG cat. of 1881.

1264 THOMAS PHILLIPS 1806

Canvas 126 x 101 (49½ x 39¾) lined, the surface flattened, varnish discoloured; signed, lower right: *TP*[monogram] *1806*.

Brown eyes, powdered wig, wearing a brown suit, the coat lined with grey and with brass buttons, white stockings; sitting in a red-damask covered chair.

Collections: Anon. sale, Christie's, 1 June 1900, lot 113; presented by Lawrence J. Baker 1900.

Exhibition: Royal Courts of Justice 1966–.

A slightly simplified version of NPG 1264 was engraved by Charles Turner in 1808. The plate is inscribed, within the image, bottom right: *aet:74:1806* and differs in showing an arched window on the right and a soft hat and two upright leather-bound books on the table covered with a Turkey rug (see c and d below). Phillips painted several further versions: one signed and dated 1807, in the Palace of Westminster, shows a top hat on the the table with the two upright books behind it and a large fluted column on the right; it was probably the portrait exhibited at the RA 1806, no.103 (see e and f below); two further versions are signed and dated 1808 (see h and i below), one in the Inner Temple, showing a single book lying on the table (as in NPG 1264),[1] the other, virtually identical, sold Christie's, 22 November 1968, lot 179.

The portraits of 1806-08 appear to use the same face mask which, in 1823,[2] was compared with that of an earlier portrait by Phillips (presumably that of 1802, see a below; now untraced); the heads had been painted 'at the distance of three or four years; the first at [Phillips's] house in George Street, Hanover Square, the last at his Lordship's who was then aged, petulant, and infirm - it was but a few months before his death. They were esteemed admirable likenesses'; Thurlow had compared the last with his reflection in a mirror and remarked that 'you have been very faithful, and I have a still higher opinion of your art'.

The *Phillips Sitter Book*, which is not a scrupulous document, listed nine portraits of Thurlow, including five copies (note: ¾ = 76 x 63; *h.l.* = 127 x 101; *l.h.l.* = 140 x 112):

a) March 1802 '*h.l.*' (no.153) '*for exhibition*' (i.e. RA 1802, no.350)

b) April 1806 '*¾*' (no.224) '*2nd time*' '*for exhibition*' (i.e. RA 1806, no.18)

c) August 1806 '*h.l.*' (no.232) '*3rd time*'[3]

d) November 1806 '*h.l.*' (no.238) '*Copy for Ld Erskine*'[4]

e) April 1807 '*h.l.*' (no.243) '*3rd time*'

f) July 1807 '*l.h.l.*' (no.253) '*copy for Mr Thurlow*'

g) August 1807 '*h.l.*'(no.254) '*copy for Mr Ray*'[5]

h-i) 1808 two '*l.h.l.*' (after no.268) two copies for the '*present Ld*[6] *and for Mrs Browne his daughter*'.

1 Sketched by Scharf, SSB 80/22, 33.
2 *Somerset House Gazette*, 13 December 1823, p.149.
3 It would appear that NPG 1264 was either c) or d), the other being the three-quarter length portrait exhibited *Art Treasures*, Manchester, 1857 (BPG 306) and NPE 1867(784) when described as dated 1806 - on each occasion lent by Chancellor Thurlow (the Rev Charles A. Thurlow, 1803-73, chancellor of the diocese of Chester, s. of Edward S. Thurlow).
4 Thomas, Lord Erskine (1750-1823), Lord Chancellor 1806-07 ('Baron Ego of Eye').
5 Engraved as a half length by J. Godby 1809 from a drawing by W. Evans. Farington mentioned Evans's drawing (4 August 1808). Similar half-length engravings, i.e. not associable with a particular Phillips pattern, by Holl (small oval) and anon. 1822.
6 Edward, 2nd Baron Thurlow (1781-1829).

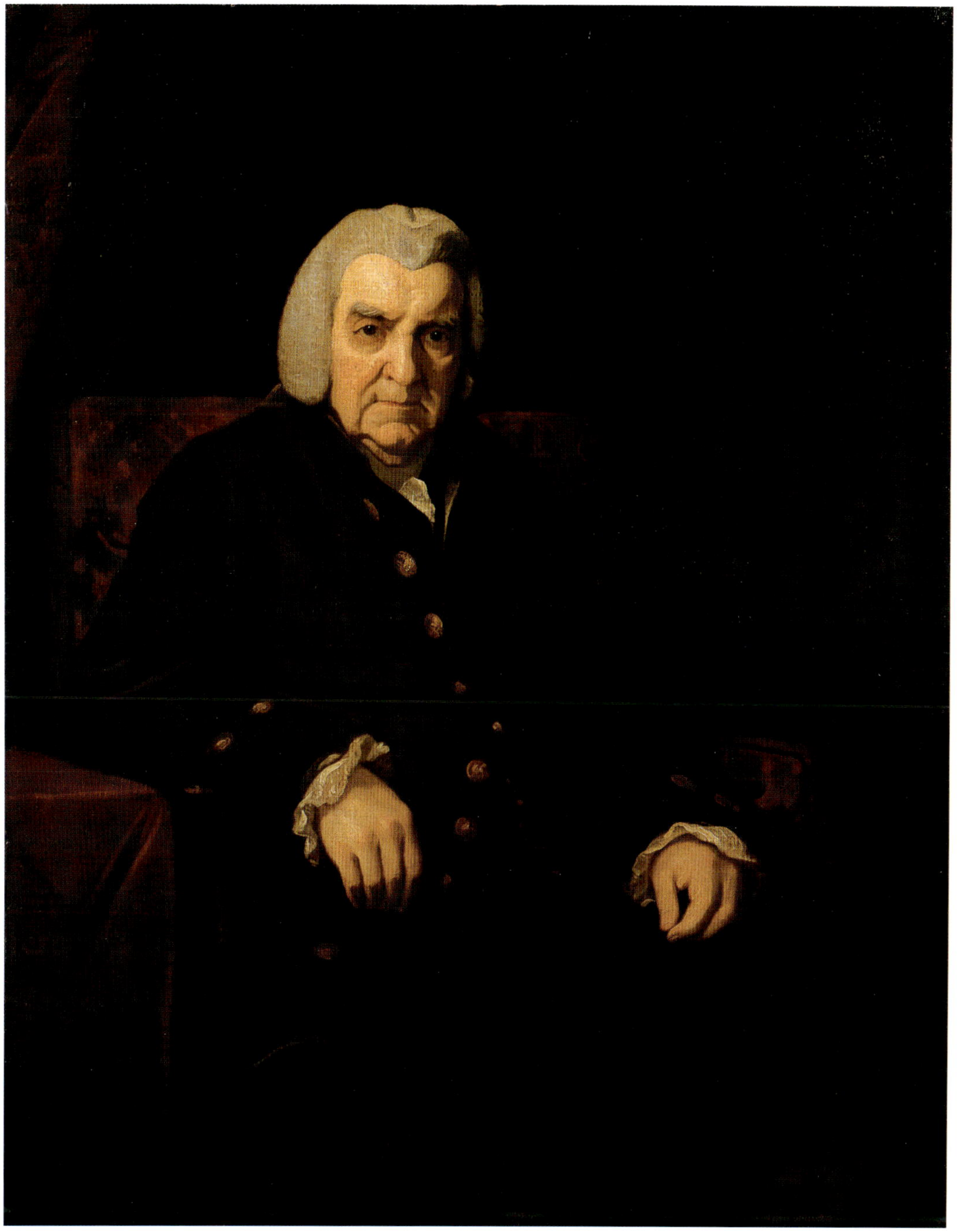

1st Baron THURLOW NPG 1264

249 THOMAS PHILLIPS c.1807

Canvas 75.5 x 63 (29¾ x 24¾) lined; thick discoloured varnish makes the condition difficult to assess; the top and sides show a darker surrounding strip, presumably indicating a smaller slip-frame.

Brown eyes, brown wig, wearing a green suit, his hands resting on the top of his stick.

Collections: Painted for the sitter's daughter, Maria (d.1816) who m. Sir David Cunynghame, 5th Bt;[1] Sir David Cunynghame, 6th Bt, from whom purchased 1867.

Exhibition: Office of Works (Houses of Parliament; House of Lords) 1911-41.

See NPG 1264 above.

1 Cunynghame wrote, 13 September 1867, that the portrait was 'painted by J. Phillips father 1805. It has never been out of the family. It was painted by [Thurlow's] desire for his daughter' (NPG archive).

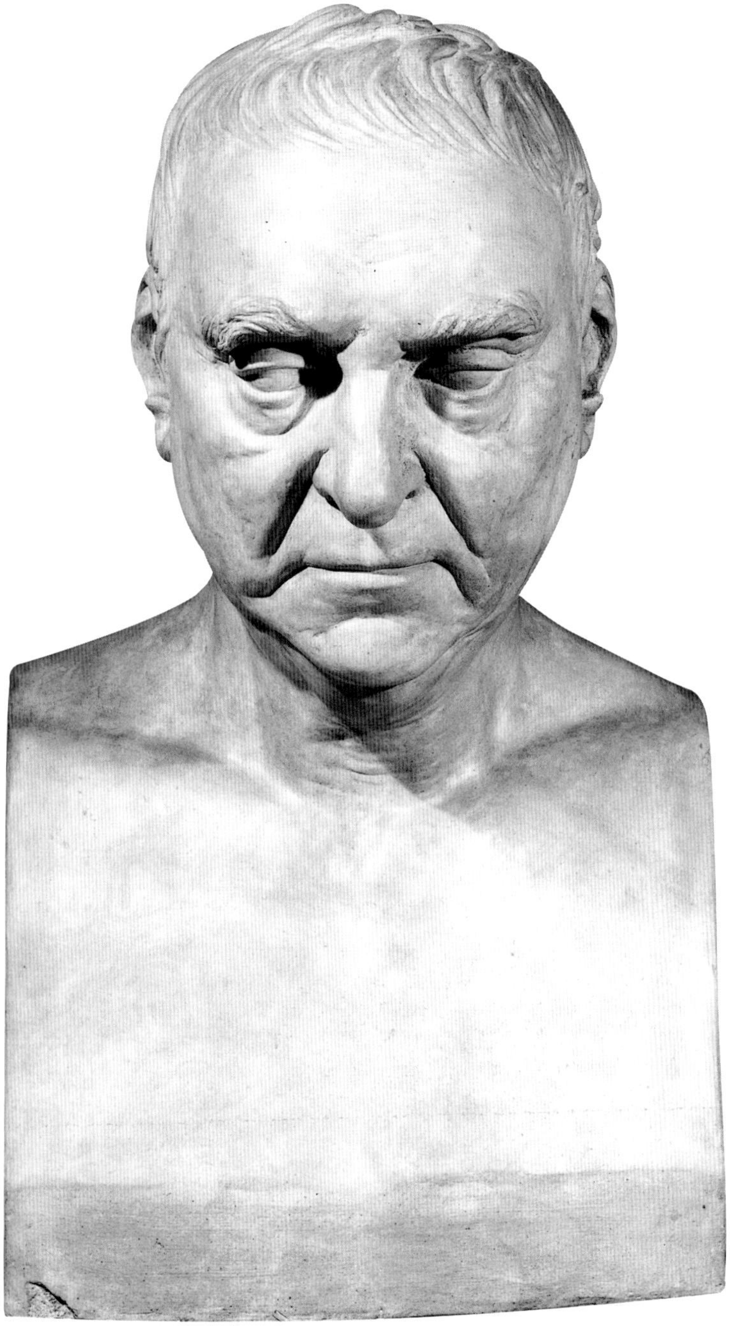

1st Baron THURLOW NPG *5238*

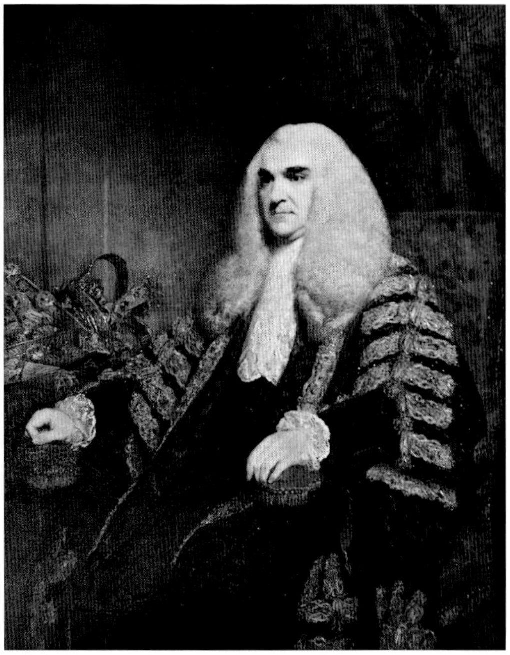

1st Baron THURLOW *by Joshua Reynolds 1781 (Longleat)*

5238 JOHN CHARLES ROSSI 1809

Artificial stone 51 (20) high; painted cream; inscribed *ROSSI* on left side of the base; the paint surface is uneven and there is a chip below left front; incised on side of truncation: *ROSSI*.

Collections: Phillips, 22 January 1979, lot 294, as unknown man, bt. Rogers, from whom purchased 1979.

Rossi exhibited busts of Thurlow at the RA in 1801(1000) and 1809(875). Both were probably taken from the same model, although the latter shows the head slightly more tilted. Two marbles, each with the incised date 1801, are in the Royal Collection.[1] Rossi's 1809 exhibit was described as a bust of Thurlow 'in marble intended for his monument in the Temple church', but only a plaster, identical with NPG 5238, remains in the Inner Temple.[2]

1 In 1969 one was at Windsor, the other at Buckingham Palace (Courtauld Institute photographic survey, B69/488 & 409).

2 By the end of the nineteenth century it had been moved out of the church and stood 'neglected in the vestry', bearing a latin inscription composed by Dr Routh (*DNB*).

ICONOGRAPHY

1773 Miniature by John Smart (Foskett 1964, p.74). An unattributed ivory miniature of Thurlow was exhibited SKM 1865(372) lent by the Rev Edward Thurlow.

1779 Engraving by R. Stewart, bust-length oval profile, in judicial wig.

1779–81 Painting by J.S. Copley,* *The Death of Chatham*, see Comparative Groups.

1781 Painting by Joshua Reynolds,* three-quarter length seated as lord chancellor. Longleat (Mannings 2000, no.1751). Exhibited RA 1782(158), NPE 1867(637). Engraved F. Bartolozzi 1782, L. Schiavonetti 1796, S.W. Reynolds, and many small derivations. A miniature bust-length version in a private collection and weak versions sold Christie's New York, 22 March 1978, lot 79, and Sotheby's, New York, 15 October 1987, lot 72; a copy by Dorofield Hardy c.1911 in the Carlton Club.

1781 Anon. engraving, bust length in dark legal dress with bands and wide cap, pub. E. Hedges.

c.1781 Painting by George Romney, whole-length standing in chancellor's robes. Christie's, 27 October 1961, lot 52, from Dunrobin Castle. Engraved W. Dickinson 1800. A reduced version, formerly

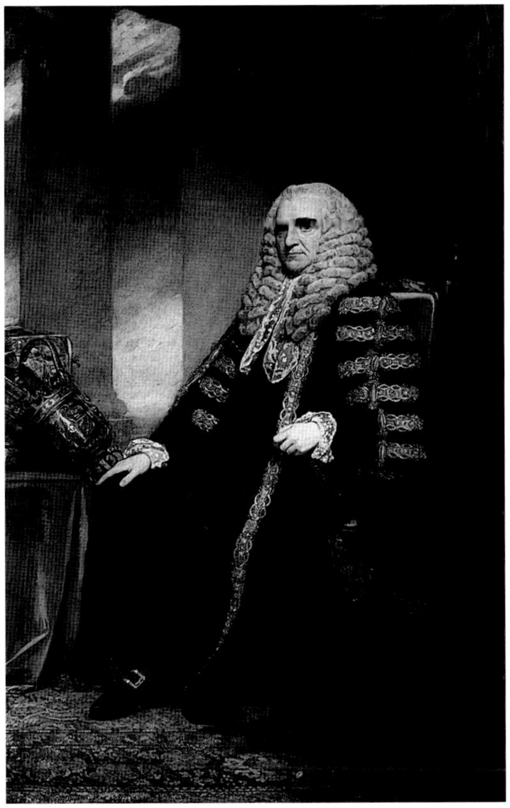

1st Baron THURLOW by George Romney c.1784 (Palace of Westminster)

with Thomas Johnes at Hafod, is presumed to have been destroyed in the fire of 1807; a small tinted drawing by Romney of the head, copied from the Dunrobin picture, was given to Sir Richard Jebb.

Another Romney type, tentatively identified as Thurlow, half length, wearing a short white wig, sold Christie's, 31 January 1975, lot 214.

Thurlow sat 24 times to Romney between November 1780 and January 1784 (Ward & Roberts 1904, II, p.157) and towards the end of his life he recalled that 'at one time there were two factions contending for superiority; the Reynolds faction, and the Romney faction: I was of the Romney faction' (Farington, Reynolds, *1819, pp.90-91).*

1783 Wax medallion by Robert Stewart, exhibited SA 1783(308).

c.1784 Painting by George Romney,* whole-length seated in chancellor's robes. Palace of Westminster, from Lord Kenyon.

1789 Medal by Thomas Wyon sr. (Brown 1980, no.331).

1789-91 Caricatures: by J. Sayers dating mostly from 1789. The most celebrated caricature to include Thurlow was probably James Gillray's *Weird Sisters* of 1791 (George 7937).

c.1791? Drawing by W.H. Brown (fl.1790-91), half length in civilian dress, engraved J. Hopwood.

1792 Painting by Samuel Collings, half length, wearing dark legal dress with wide hat, engraved J. Condé 1792 with arms and motto (*ar., on a chev. betw. two chevronels sa. three portcullises with chains and rings of the field: JUSTITIAE SOROR FIDES*)

c.1792 Anon. etching, bust length in legal dress with wide hat.

1795 Anon. half-length oval engraving, civilian dress, short wig, with arms and motto (see 1792 above).

1797 Bust by Thomas Hayley (Hayley 1809, p.269).

before 1800 Wax by Samuel Percy. Brighton MAG (C.288 frame 2). An example in the Percy sale, Christie's, 31 January 1800.

c.1800 Painting by John Hoppner, 'at an advanced age' (Farington, *Reynolds*, 1819, p.90), Hoppner sale, Christie's, 31 May 1823, lot 29 (with four other portraits).

1801 Bust by J.C. Rossi, see NPG 5238.

1802 Painting by Thomas Phillips, exhibited RA 1802(350), see NPG 1264.

1803 Painting by Thomas Lawrence, three-quarter length seated. Royal Collection (Millar 1969, no.914; Garlick 1989, no.766). Exhibited RA 1803(21). See NPG 395.

1805 Wax medallion by Catherine Andras, exhibited RA 1805(762). Examples in the Fitzwilliam Museum, Cambridge (Pyke Bequest 1997) and the Victoria and Albert Museum (A.119.1965; A.136.1965).

1806-08 Paintings by Thomas Phillips, see NPG 249 and NPG 1264.

Posthumous

1809 Bust by J.C. Rossi, see NPG 5238.

1830 Bust by J.E. Carew, mentioned in the case the sculptor brought against the executors of the 3rd Earl of Egremont (Gunnis 1968, p.80).

DOUBTFUL PORTRAITS

A marble bas-relief, half length as Lord Chancellor, in the collection of Lady Rockley 1937, probably shows Lord Camden.

TOOKE, John Horne 1736-1812

Radical; b. John Horne; vicar of New Brentford, Essex, 1760-73; abroad in 1763 and 1765, when he met Wilkes; founded a separate Constitutional Society 1771; took up philology 1773, publishing *Diversions of Purley* 1786 and 1805; in 1777 and 1794 he was arrested for statements concerning the revolutions in America and France, being acquitted on the second occasion; assumed the added surname of Tooke (an admirer) 1782; MP 1801-02 (although in orders).

'he lost the sight of his right eye [c.1746], a defect, which although visible for some years after, yet became wholly imperceptible' (Alexander Stephens, 1813).

'he was five feet eight inches and a half high. His face was short and rather oval ... Nature had formed him strong and athletic ... his hair, towards the end of his life, was generally combed loosely over the temples, and cut close behind. His eye was eminently expressive; it had something particularly keen, as well as arch in it; [he was] lively and full of pleasantry in general conversation; on politics alone, he was bitter, vituperative, and inflexible' (*Ibid.*).

Abbreviation

Stephens 1813: A. Stephens, *Memoirs of John Horne Tooke*, 2 vols., 1813

1944 see Groups, *John Glynn, John Wilkes and John Horne Tooke*, after RICHARD HOUSTON [1769]

13 THOMAS HARDY 1791

Canvas 76 x 63 (30 x 24¾) lined; cleaned 1981; the surface is flattened and the paint thin, particularly in the flesh areas.

Grey eyes, white powdered hair with a black ribbon, wearing a brown coat with brass buttons, a gold and orange vest, white lace ruffles and cuffs.

Collections: Mr Tyson,[1] at whose death bt. by the antiquarian John Britton (1771-1857), as by Gainsborough; purchased from his widow, Mrs Ellen Britton, 1857.

Engraving: Anker Smith 1791.

Exhibitions: NPE 1867(647); *Chantrey*, NPG, Sheffield, 1981.

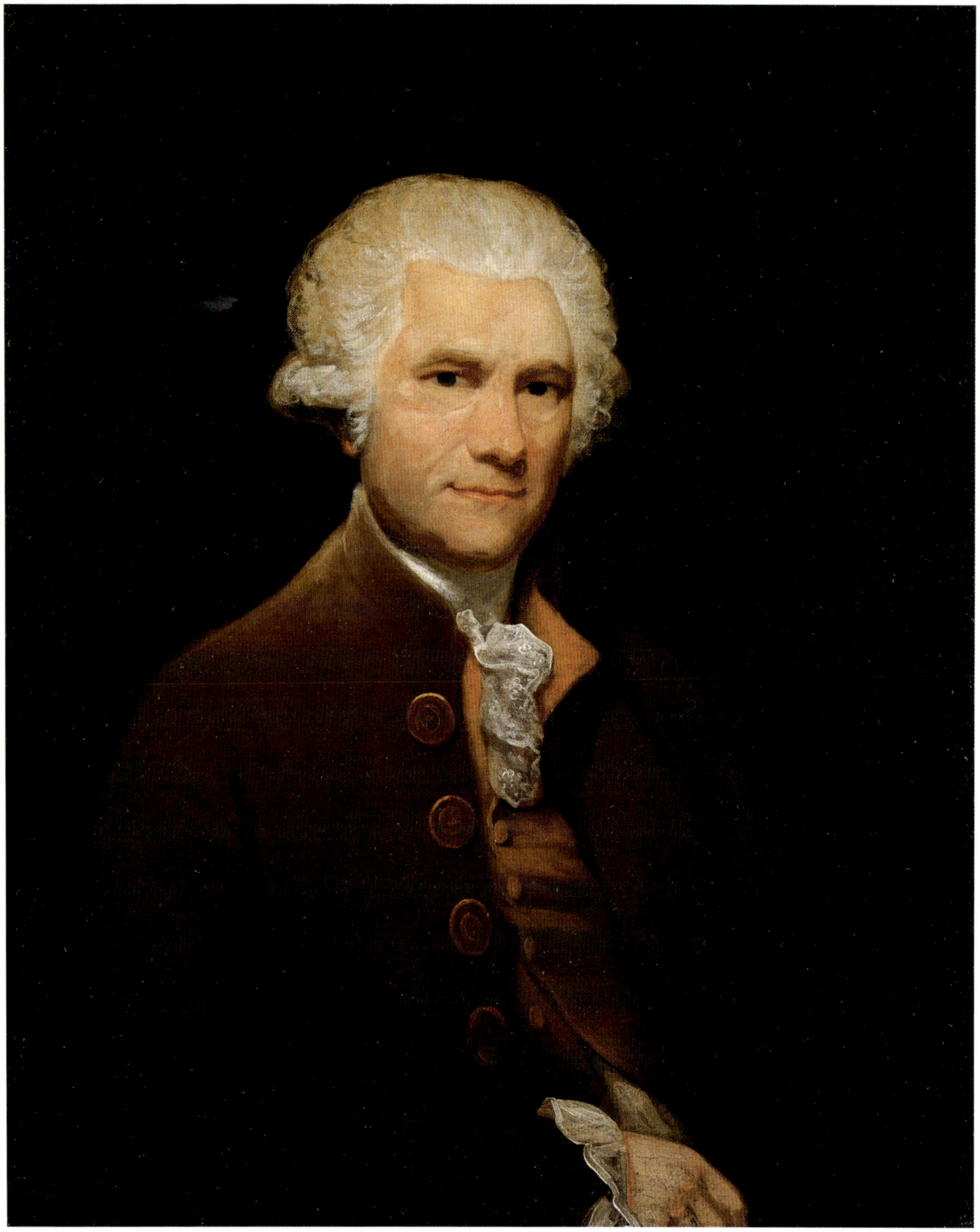

TOOKE *NPG 13*

A reduced copy, signed and dated *Simon Raven 1795*, was in the collection of Bernard Tate in 1963.

1 'a literary gentleman, residing in the neighbourhood of Bristol many years' (Mrs E. Britton to Sotheby, 17 May 1857; NPG archive).

316A(122) FRANCIS CHANTREY c.1810

Ink and pencil on paper 37 x 28 (14½ x 11) inscribed in pencil, bottom left: *John Horne Took* and in ink verso: *Measured Drawing of John Horne To...*; the widest part of the head measured as *8¾*.[1]

Collections: Chantrey's executor George Jones RA, by whose widow presented in 1871.[2]

Reference: Walker *Regency*, I, pp.624, 629.

Walker commented that this drawing appears to be *ad vivum* and not drawn with the *camera lucida*.

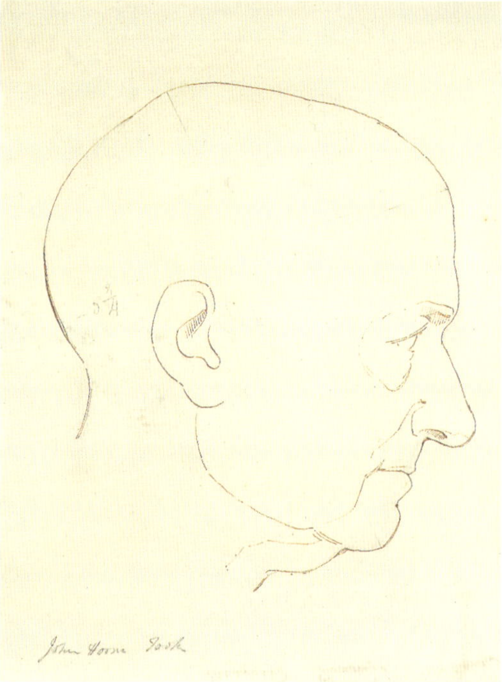

TOOKE *NPG 316A(122)*

Chantrey was pleased to comment that Tooke's head 'possessed a complete resemblance to the bronze of Voltaire', remarking that 'all the parts were well defined and highly finished, so as to exhibit a flowing curvilinear surface, combined with a marked character'.[3] The plaster bust (see below), exhibited at the RA in 1811, first established Chantrey's reputation as a portrait sculptor. Tooke had been his mentor in his early days in London and Chantrey always spoke of him 'as one of the wisest and most judicious friends he ever encountered',[4] who had warned him to avoid 'even the appearance of leaning towards any party in politics'.

1 Chantrey told Stephens 1813, II, p.447, that 'the width of the os occipitis, was exactly six inches and three quarters; the os frontis five inches and a quarter; the greatest width between the extremities of both, eight inches and three quarters'.
2 See Walker *Regency*, I, pp.624-25.
3 Stephens 1813, II, p.447; see also note 1.
4 *Fraser's Mag.*, XLI, 1850, p.456.

ICONOGRAPHY

'... when a young man, he was accustomed to dress genteelly; and as he possessed a good person and agreeable manners, displayed much of the look and mien of a person of fashion. ... Of late years he has left off powder, and this circumstance adds not a little to the appearance of age ... he is still remarkably clean and neat in everything respecting his person' (*Public Characters of 1801-02*, pp.115-16).

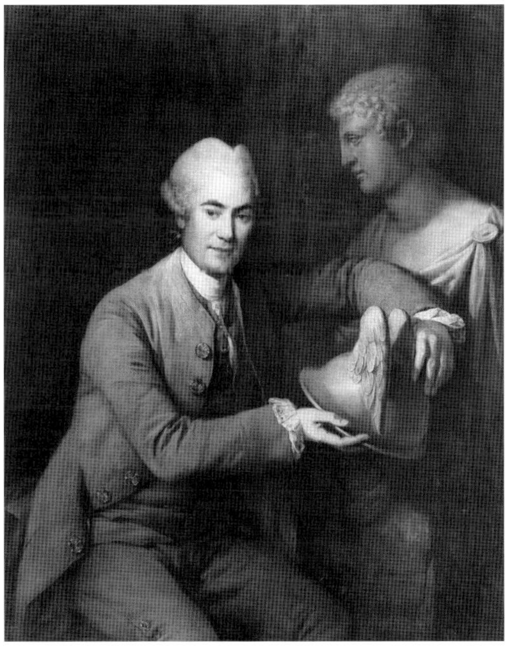

TOOKE by Richard Brompton 1777 (Manchester Art Gallery)

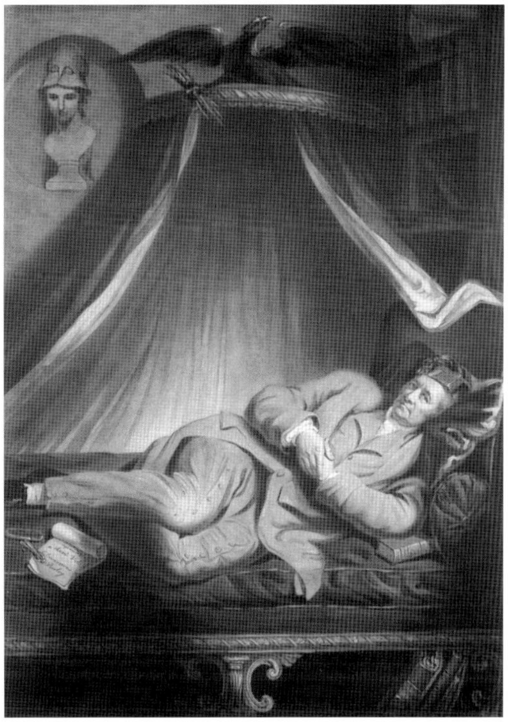

TOOKE W. Ward after J.R. Smith 1811 (NPG D 13749)

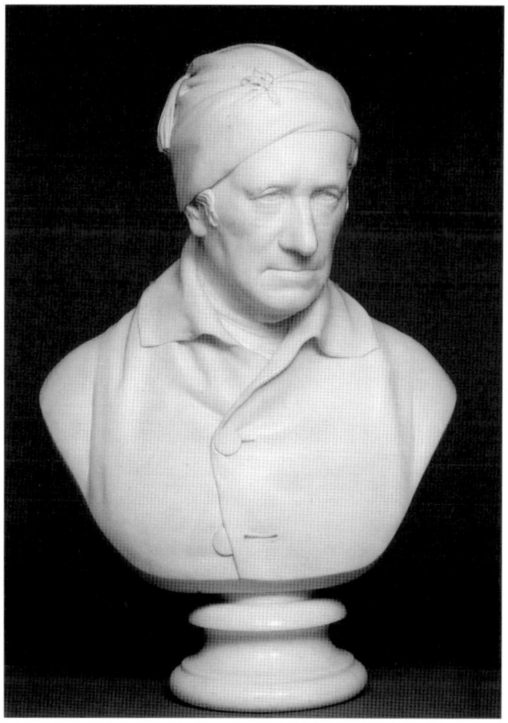

TOOKE by Francis Chantrey 1820 (Fitzwilliam Museum, Cambridge)

1769 Engraving by Richard Houston, seated at table with John Wilkes and John Glynn, see Groups NPG 1944.

c.1769 Anon. mezzotint, half-length oval, with wig, gown and bands (CS, IV, p.1733, no.87). Similar to the profile seen in Groups NPG 1944.

1777 Painting by Richard Brompton,* three-quarter length, seated holding Mercury's winged helmet. Manchester CAG (1913.16). Stephens (1813, II, pp.502-03) described it as a full length painted while he was a prisoner in the King's Bench; Tooke had had the frame regilded a few months before his death. Engraved J. Corner 1791 (half length, without wig; *European Mag.*).

1791 Painting by Thomas Hardy, see NPG 13.

1792 Anon. engraving, bust length, with curled wig, *from an original painting* (*Literary Mag.*); copy in stipple 1828 (*Encyclopaedia Londinensis*).

1793 Medallion by James Tassie (Gray 1894, no.388; Scottish NPG, PG 586).

1794 Drawing by Cruikshanks [Isaac Cruikshank?], engraved G. Murray, half-length oval, with wig.

1794 A number of medals were produced marking the acquittal in November of Tooke, Hardy and Thelwall from charges of sedition (cf. Brown 1980, nos.377, 380); two unattributed bronze medals, one showing Tooke bust-length to left with the inscription *BRITISH JUSTICE DISPLAYED* ... , the other with a profile bust to right and the inscription *TRIED FOR HIGH TREASON* ..., are in the NPG reference collection (D7051 & D7052).

1795 Anon. mezzotint, half-length oval, lettered *John Horn Tooke Esqr*, pub. 12 September 1795 (CS, IV, p.1746, no.145a). An anon. engraving, half-length seated, with wig, appears to date from the same time.

c.1795-1800 Silhouette by John Field, bust. Sotheby's, 16 October 1978, lot 117.

1797 Engraving by W. Ridley, bust-length oval, with wig (*Junius*, 1797ed., II, f.p.128). Copied by Hopwood 1805.

1798 Drawing by I. White, bust length, his own dark hair, engraved M. Tomkins.

1800 Bust by Thomas Banks, draped, with his own hair. From the Burdett-Coutts collection (see Bell 1938, pp.137-38). Engraved E. Bocquet (three quarters); anon. (profile) for *Public Characters of 1801-02*). The bust is seen in the background of *Sir Francis Burdett, 5th Bt*, by William Ross (NPG 2056; see Walker *Regency*, II, pl.164). Stephens 1813, II, p.503, said that the Burdett bust was 'intended as a present to St John's College, Cambridge', but he attributed it to Bacon sr.

c.1800 Stipple engraving by H. Richter, bust length, his own white hair.

1803 A frame with five portraits including Tooke, by Samuel Percy, exhibited RA 1803(1027).

1810 Plaster bust by Francis Chantrey (*Chantrey* 1994, no.81b), exhibited RA 1811(945); 'an old man, wasted by sickness, with a night cap on his head, totally unlike his former self - but *fearfully* like him at the present moment' (Stephens 1813, II, p.411). Chantrey sent J.R. Smith a plaster in 1810 (a bust appears in a pastel by Smith of Tooke's illegitimate daughters, Mrs Mary Harte and Miss Charlotte Tooke, sold Sotheby's, 16 November 1989, lot 43). Casts dated 1810 are in the Ashmolean Museum, Oxford (Penny 1992, III, no.773) and the Yale Center for British Art (B1977.14.2). A cast from an intaglio by R. Clint from Chantrey's bust, exhibited RA 1827(989).

A marble bust, commissioned by Watson Taylor in 1818 and completed in 1820, is in the Fitzwilliam Museum, Cambridge* (*Chantrey* 1994, no.81b). In 1810 Tooke commissioned his own tombstone (Ealing churchyard) from Chantrey and wrote his own epitaph (*Chantrey* 1994, no.24b). For a drawing by Chantrey c.1810, see NPG 316A/122.

1811 Pastel by J.R. Smith, whole-length recumbent on a sofa wearing a night cap, beneath a tent-like canopy surmounted by the eagle of Zeus, a bust of Athene on the wall beyond; at his feet a manuscript inscribed *The third vol. Diversions of Purley* (never published);

other books are lettered *Manu/scripts* and *Sanctius*. Formerly with Walter Bromley-Davenport. Exhibited RA 1811(333). Engraved W. Ward 1811.*

Tooke was frequently portrayed in caricature, of which the following provide stimulating likenesses: *The Parson of Brentford* 1769 (George 4225) and *The Macaroni Parson* 1769 (George 4827); *Guy Faux setting Fire to the Pillars of the London Tavern* 1773 (George 5104); *Protheus on Privileges* 1791 (George 7825; illus. E S Turner, *Unholy Pursuits*, 1998 p.193); *The devil hauling Tooke, Hardy and Thelwall into Hell* by H. Wigstead (d.1793), seen by Farington on 8 June 1796; *Two Pairs of Portraits* 1798 by James Gillray (George 9270).

DOUBTFUL PORTRAITS

Unverified portraits of Tooke include a painting by John Opie listed by Earland 1911, p.319, as 'about July 1803' and painted for Lt.-Col. Harwood, and a miniature by Samuel Collins, exhibited BFAC 1889 (xvii 40) and *Guelph* 1891(1037) lent J. Whitehead.

TOPLADY, Augustus Montague 1740-78

Hymnologist and calvinist who long maintained a bad-tempered public controversy with John Wesley; ordained 1762, vicar of Broad Hembury, Devon, from 1768; his books included *Poems on Sacred Subjects* 1759 and he is perhaps still remembered for the hymn *Rock of Ages*, composed in 1775; editor of the *Gospel Magazine* 1775-76.

3138 after J.R. SMITH 1777

Black, white and sepia crayon with grey wash 32 x 25 (12½ x 9¾) laid down on thin card; in poor condition, scattered tiny holes and a general splashing with a dark [water?] colour; inscribed, lower left, in ink: *355*; verso, in ink: *Rev Augustus Montague Toplady, A.B.*, and, in pencil: *by J R Smith*.

Collections: Purchased from Appleby 1943.

Apparently a contemporary copy from the portrait drawn and engraved by J.R. Smith published in 1777,[1] in which the book on the table is lettered *Holy Bible*.

1 CS 164; J. Frankau, *John Raphael Smith*, 1902, no.351.

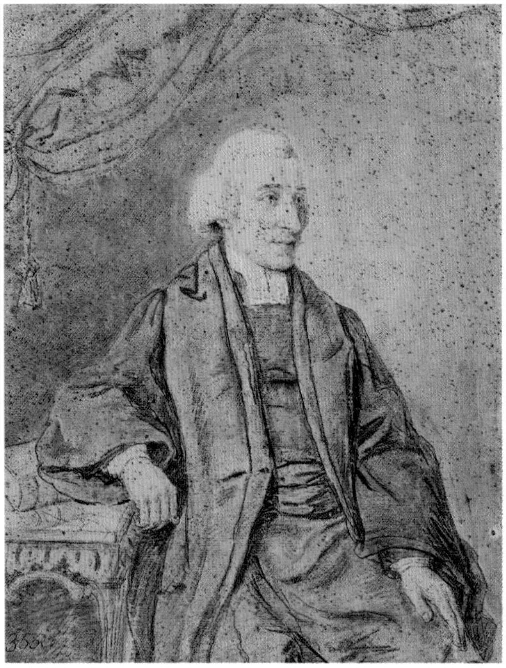

TOPLADY NPG *3138*

ICONOGRAPHY

1777 Drawing by J.R. Smith, see NPG 3138.

The following are all weak posthumous engravings showing Toplady in gown and bands.

1783 Painting by J.C. Garbrand, bust-length oval, engraved T. Trotter 1783, from an original picture in the possession of William Hussey of Kensington (another impression for the *Christian Mag.* 1791).

1784 Anon. engraving, pub. A. Hogg, bust-length oval (*New Spiritual Mag.*).

1794 Painting by C.R. Ryley, standing three-quarter length, a book in his right hand, engraved C. Blackberd; a half-length version engraved E. Scriven 1840.

1801 Engraving by Mackenzie, half-length oval (*Gospel Mag.* 1801).

TOWNSHEND, Lord John 1757-1833

Whig politician, of Balls Park, Herts., 2nd s. of the 1st Marquess Townshend; MP 1780-84, 1788-90, 1793-1818; a follower of Fox, under whom he served as a lord of the Admiralty in 1782 and 1783 and joint paymaster general 1806-07; both his brothers were deranged and he was himself described as mad, though never enough to be confined.

2076 see Groups, *Mr Fox and his Friends* by WILLIAM LANE c.1813

ICONOGRAPHY

c.1764 Pastel attributed to Francis Cotes, with his older brother George, as boys. Formerly at Raynham Hall (Duleep Singh, II, p.238, no.18).

1771-72 Painting by Angelica Kauffmann, *The 1st Marquess Townshend with his Family*, John seated with one of his sisters in his lap. Private collection (illus. *Kauffmann* 1998, p.213).

1788 Painting by Joshua Reynolds,* half length. Sotheby's, 28 November 2002, lot 173, from Raynham Hall (Mannings 2000, no.1767). Engraved J. Jones 1789. Exhibited NPE 1867(646) lent by the Marquess Townshend.

c.1790 Painting ascribed to Thomas Lawrence, half length. Christie's, 24 July 1969, lot 73.

c.1813 Drawing by William Lane, *Mr Fox and his Friends*, see Groups NPG 2076.

1821 Miniature by Elizabeth Reynolds, exhibited RA 1821(733).

1832 Bust by J.E. Carew, exhibited RA 1832(1153).

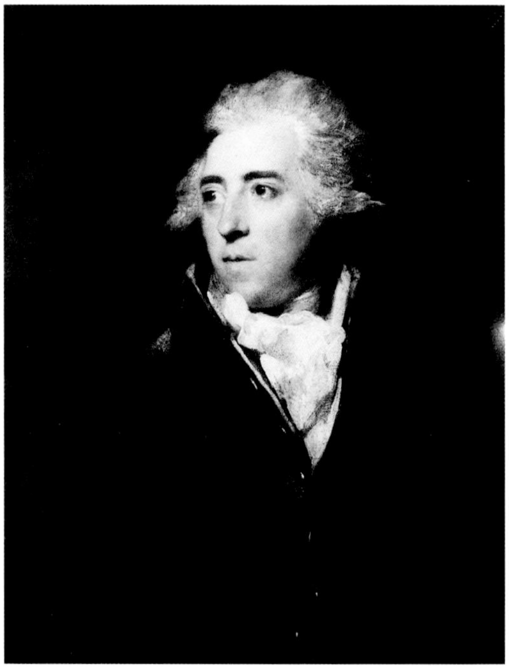

Lord John TOWNSHEND by Joshua Reynolds 1788 (Sotheby's)

UPPER OSSORY, John Fitzpatrick, 2nd Earl of 1745-1818

Whig politician; suc. as 2nd Earl of Upper Ossory [I] 1758; MP 1767-94; FRS 1780, FSA 1793; cr. Baron Upper Ossory [GB] 1794; though he loved gaming and Newmarket, he 'had good sense without vanity, and good nature without weakness' (*CP*); one of the pall-bearers at Joshua Reynolds's funeral; older bro. of Richard Fitzpatrick.

2076 see Groups, *Mr Fox and his Friends* by WILLIAM LANE c.1813

ICONOGRAPHY

c.1750 Painting by George Knapton, as a child with his brother and sister. Woburn Abbey (illus. cat., II, 1892, pt. I, f.p.I).

1763 Painting by Richard Brompton, *Edward Duke of York with his Friends in Venice*, includes Lord Ossory in the centre of a group of three on the right. Royal Collection (Millar 1969, no.689). A repetition, formerly at Ampthill, was painted for Lord Ossory, exhibited SA 1767(14).

1767 Painting by Joshua Reynolds, three-quarter length seated. Lord Castletown in 1899 (Mannings 2000, no.633). Engraved S.W. Reynolds 1820. Version sold Christie's, 4 November 1949, lot 95. A watercolour copy by William Skelton* formerly at Holland House (cat., 1904, no.474).

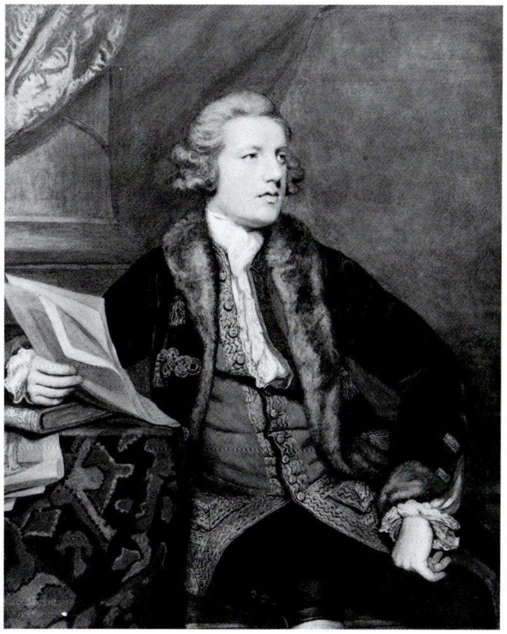

2nd Earl of UPPER OSSORY W. Skelton after Joshua Reynolds 1767 (Private Collection)

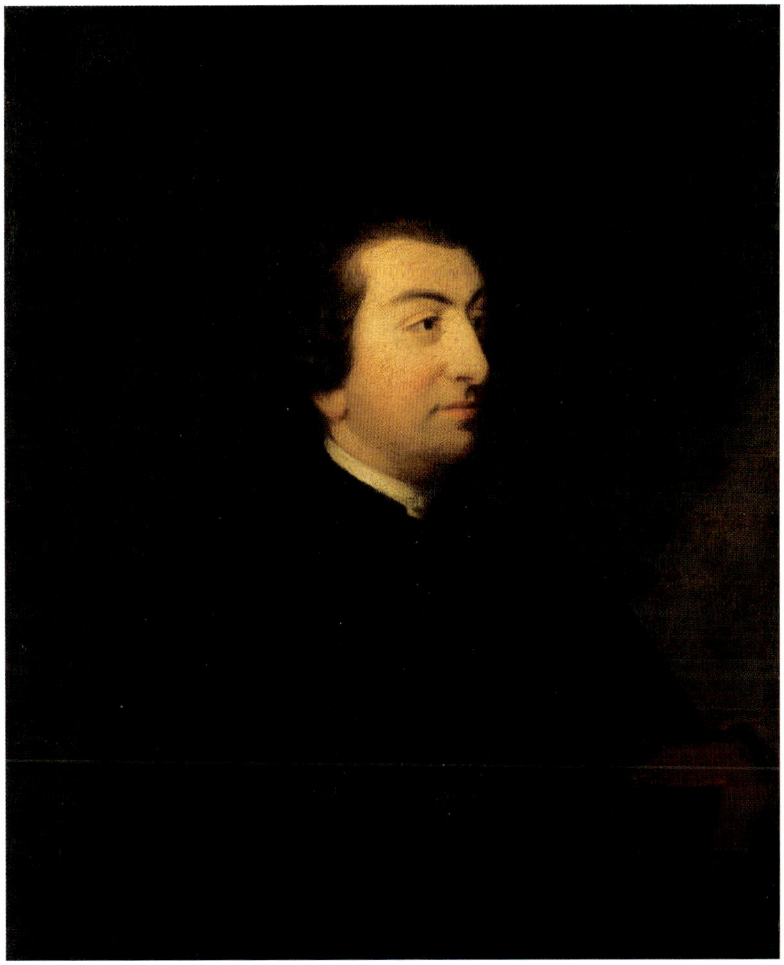

TYRWHITT NPG *2942*

TYRWHITT, Thomas 1730-86

Classicist and literary critic; deputy secretary at war 1756-62 and clerk of the House of Commons 1762-68; his comments on Shakespeare were used by Steevens; published an edition of Chaucer's *Canterbury Tales* 1775-78; exposed the Chatterton forgeries 1777; FRS 1771; his classical criticism included books on Aesop, Strabo and Aristotle.

2942 after BENJAMIN WILSON [1788]

Canvas 75 x 62 (29½ x 24½) lined; discoloured varnish and extensively retouched.

Brown eyes, brown hair, wearing a green coat.

Collections: Presented by the wish of the Rev H.M. Tyrwhitt (d.1937), through his son T. Tyrwhitt, 1938.

NPG 2942 is a simplified copy of the untraced portrait by Benjamin Wilson, engraved by John Jones in 1788, showing a curtain in the left background and a bookcase on the right. It was also engraved on a smaller scale by James Heath (with a plain background; *from the picture in the possession of the Shute Barrington, Bishop of Durham*) and again by John Jones 1792 (without the bookcase, for *Shakespeare Illustrated* 1793).

ICONOGRAPHY

1788 Painting by Benjamin Wilson, see NPG 2942.

1790 Engraving by T. Holloway, *Shakespearean Critics*, in which Tyrwhitt appears with Johnson, Richard Farmer and Thomas Edwards (for Malone's *Shakespeare*).

An unattributed miniature of Tyrwhitt was lent by Jeffery Whitehead to the BFAC 1889(xviii 13).

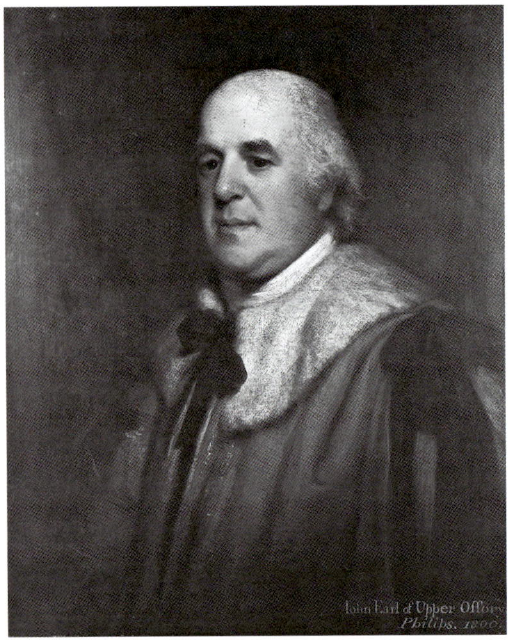

2nd Earl of UPPER OSSORY by Thomas Phillips c.1800 (Christie's)

A drawing, formerly at Holland House (cat., 1904, no.278), was inscribed verso: *an original sketch of Ld Ossory, done by Sir Joshua Reynolds at Ampthill, Given to me* [Lord Holland] *by Lord Ossory.*

1798 Drawing by Henry Edridge, three-quarter length seated. Formerly at Holland House, from the St Anne's Hill House sale, Phillips, 3rd day, 26 November 1924, lot 506 (one of the five friends of Fox by Edridge, lots 505-507). A copy in the Lewis Walpole Library, Farmington.

1800 Painting by Thomas Phillips, half length in peer's robes. Formerly at Ampthill. A reduced version in a private collection (from Christie's, 30 May 1974, lot 293).*

1806 Drawing by William Lane, half-length seated. Formerly at Holland House (cat., 1904, no.87). Engraved W. Skelton. The source for NPG 2076.

c.1813 Drawing by William Lane, *Mr Fox and his Friends*, see Groups NPG 2076.

1814 Portrait by William Lane, exhibited RA 1814(472) with another of his brother General Robert Fitzpatrick; see Groups NPG 2076.

1818 Medallion incorporated in his monument by Richard Westmacott jr. in St James's, Grafton Underwood, Northants. (illus. Busco 1994, p.136).

Undated Silhouette by Charles Rosenberg, sold Christie's, 12 May 1993, lot 56.

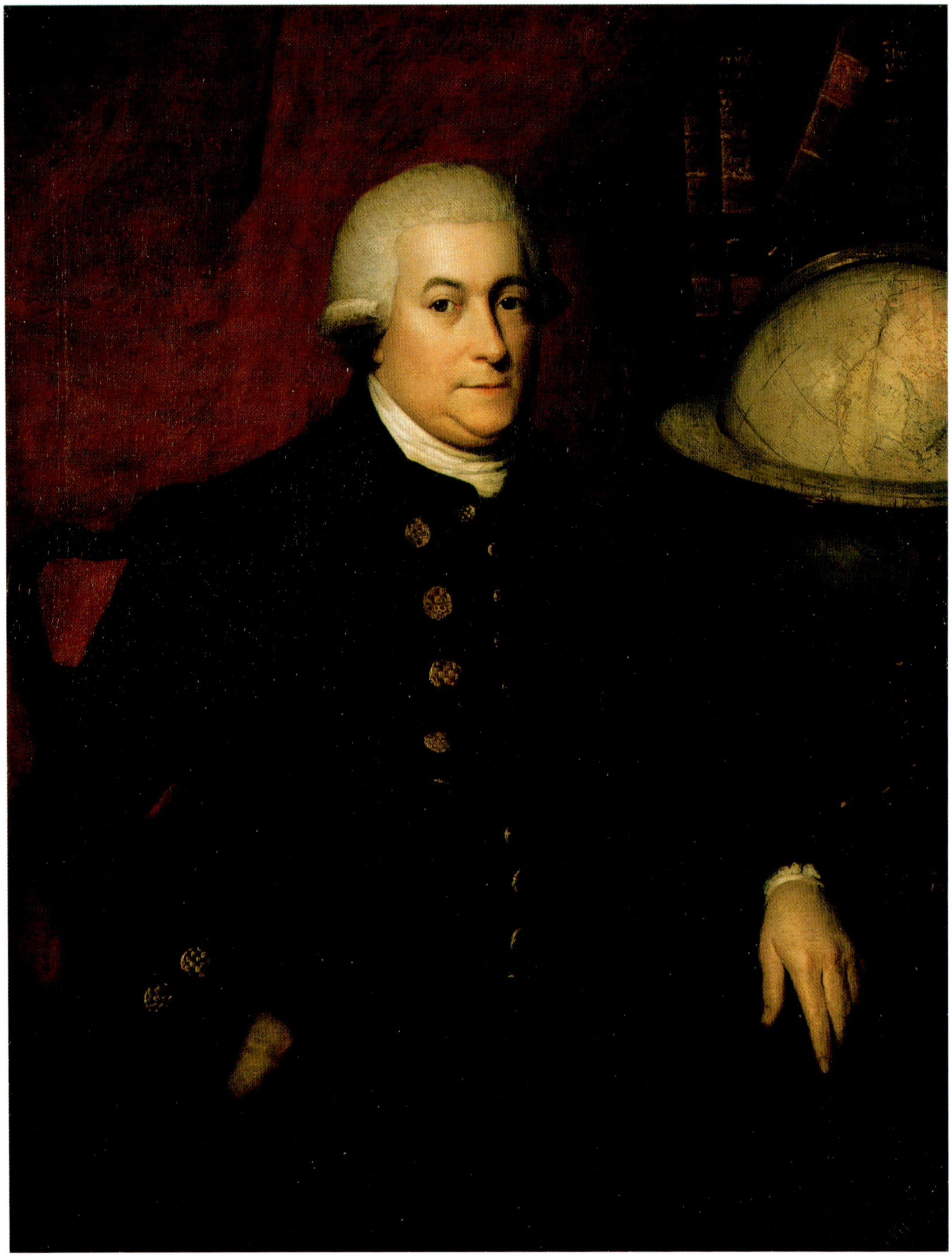

VANCOUVER NPG *503*

VANCOUVER, George 1757-98

Naval officer; b. King's Lynn, Norfolk; accompanied Cook on his second and third Pacific voyages 1772-75 and 1776-79; lieutenant 1780, serving in the Channel and the West Indies; commander 1790; surveyed the north-west coast of America 1791-95, his achievement overshadowed by the outbreak of the French wars and by criticism of his high-minded sense of discipline; in poor health, he retired to Petersham; his travel diary, *A Voyage of Discovery to the North Pacific Ocean*, appeared posthumously in 1798.

503 UNKNOWN ARTIST c.1796–98?

Canvas 111 x 87 (43¾ x 34¼) lined 1895; the surface is worn.

Grey eyes, white powdered wig, wearing a green coat and waistcoat with brass buttons, seated on a green-upholstered wooden chair; a red curtain to the left; the books on the right are, on the top shelf: *COOK'S VOYAGE, Anson's/ Voyage, Magellan/ Voyage, Ba/nk/Voy* ...; second shelf: *Com/ Voyage, Drake/ Voy*...; *HOLY BIBLE* by his left wrist, on the globe *Vancouver* (in pink lettering) was prominent but has been almost erased; otherwise lettered *NORTH AMERICA* *Cook Track/ Gulf/ Car*....

Collections: Thomas Ford, Islington;[1] Christie's, 29 June 1878, lot 77, purchased.

Exhibitions: *Pageant of Canada*, Ottawa, 1967(131); *Capt. George Vancouver*, Vancouver BC, 1987.

Acquired as an unattributed portrait, NPG 503 was tentatively attributed to L.F. Abbott in 1881; listed as by an unknown painter in 1920, but reattributed to Abbott 1932–81; in 1981 it reverted to anonymity and the sitter's identity was also doubted.[2] An attribution to Abbott is untenable, but the identity of Vancouver is possibly correct.

There is no authenticated portrait of Vancouver, only a caricature by James Gillray, showing the back view of an overweight figure.[3] NPG 503 shows a heavy man, evidently a Pacific explorer: the book-titles recall the great explorers (they are not real titles and the cryptic reference to Banks, see above, might even reflect that strained relationship[4]) and the globe shows Vancouver's route and has Vancouver marked. The prominent Bible is appropriate for Vancouver's high-mindedness. The likelihood is that this is a portrait of Vancouver painted between 1796 and 1798 (as both Watt and Kaye Lamb have argued),[5] although it seems strange that no engraving was made of it for his *Voyage of Discovery* published in 1798.

Later copies of NPG 503 as Vancouver, include those by R.L. Allridge (1890, Vancouver Museum); by W. Bright Morris (1914, Town Hall, King's Lynn); R. Swan (Maritime Museum of British Colombia), and anonymous (Bishop Museum, Honolulu, inscribed *English Navigator and a true friend of the Hawiians*).

Imaginative statues of Vancouver are in front of the City Hall, Vancouver, by Charles Marega 1936; on the Parliament Building, Victoria BC, and a bronze by Vernon March 1911 was sold Christie's, 11 December 1979, lot 260.

1 In a letter to Christie's, 20 March 1878, Ford said the portrait had belonged 'many years since' to a West Indian planter called Brooke, and was supposed to be by Gainsborough (NPG archive). Is it worth supposing that the alleged previous owner of NPG 503 might conceivably have been related to the Robert Brooke (fl. 1764–d.1802), governor of St Helena, who had advised Vancouver on his return journey?

2 In successive editions of the NPG cats.

3 Illustrating the episode in Conduit Street, when Lord Camelford, who had been severely disciplined by Vancouver during the American voyage, attacked him (George 8823).

4 Banks once said of Vancouver that 'his manner towards me was not such as I am used to receive from persons in his situation' (J. Gascoigne, *Banks and the English Enlightenment*, 1994, p.38); on the Pacific voyage Vancouver eventually placed Archibald Menzies, the botanist sponsored by Banks, under open arrest.

5 G. Vancouver, *A Voyage of Discovery* ..., IV, ed. W. Kaye Lamb [*Hakluyt Soc.*] 1984, pp.1612–13; J. Watt, *Canadian Bulletin of Medical History*, IV, 1987, pp.45–48.

VEIGEL, Eva, see Mrs GARRICK

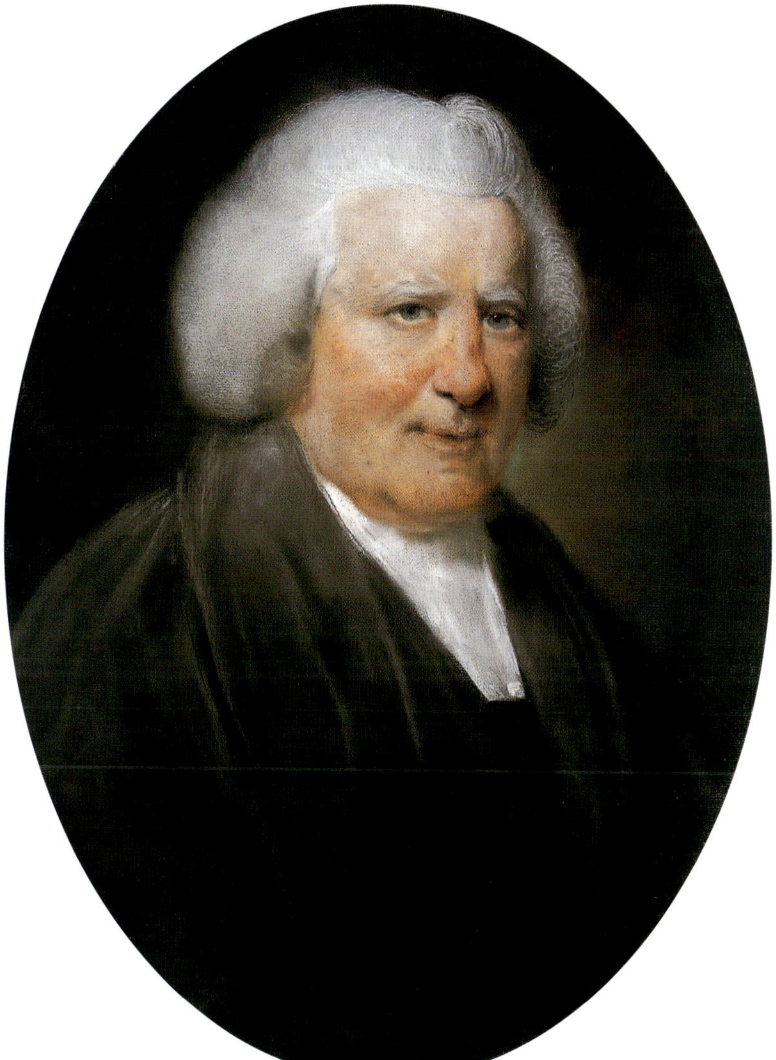

VENN NPG *3161*

VENN, Henry 1725–97

Evangelist; Jesus College, Cambridge, MA 1749; ordained 1749; curate at Clapham 1754–59, vicar of Huddersfield 1759–71 and Yelling, Hunts., 1771–97; one of the leaders of the evangelical revival, author of the *Compleat Duty of Man* 1763.

3161 JOHN RUSSELL 1787

Pastel on paper 62 x 47 (24½ x 18½) oval, the edges uneven; rubbed, lending the face a blotchy complexion, signed in pencil, lower right: *J Russell pt /1787*.

Collections: By descent to the sitter's great-great-nephew, the Rev E.J. Elliott, rector of Broadwater, Worthing; his widow, Mrs E.H. Elliott, by whom bequeathed 1943.

Engraving: anon. (rectangular)

Russell was a particular friend of both the Elliotts of Clapham and the Venns, evangelist families related by marriage (see Williamson 1894, pp.44-45).

ICONOGRAPHY

1770 Painting by Mason Chamberlin,* half length in gown and bands. Formerly with the Rev J.H. Venn, Queens' College, Cambridge. Engraved G. Adcock 1834 (from a picture in the possession of E.B. Venn), another state lettered *Revd John Venn* (his son, 1759-1813, a leader of the Clapham sect).

1787 Pastel by John Russell, see NPG 3161.

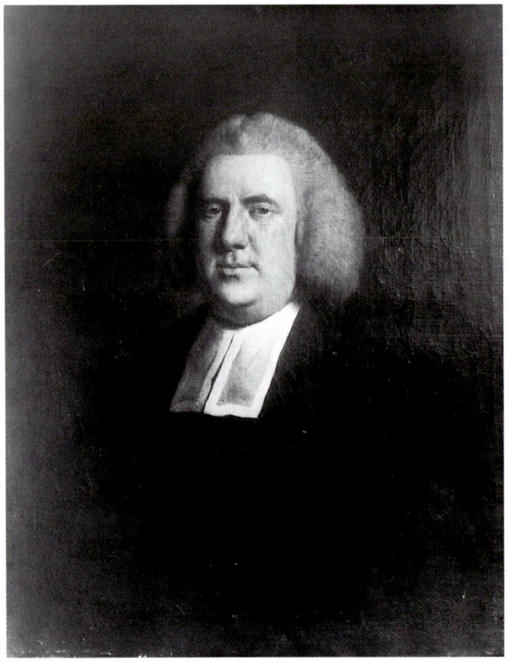

VENN by Mason Chamberlin 1770 (Queens' College, Cambridge)

VESEY, Mrs Elizabeth, *née* Vesey 1715?-91

Bluestocking, dau. of Thomas Vesey, Bishop of Ossory; m. 1) William Handcock MP [I], 2) before 1746 Agmondesham Vesey (d.1785) MP [I], a member of Johnson's Club; Mrs Vesey's 'select and delicate' literary parties were of some repute in the period 1770-84; she became deaf and short-sighted and her last years were impaired by loss of memory.

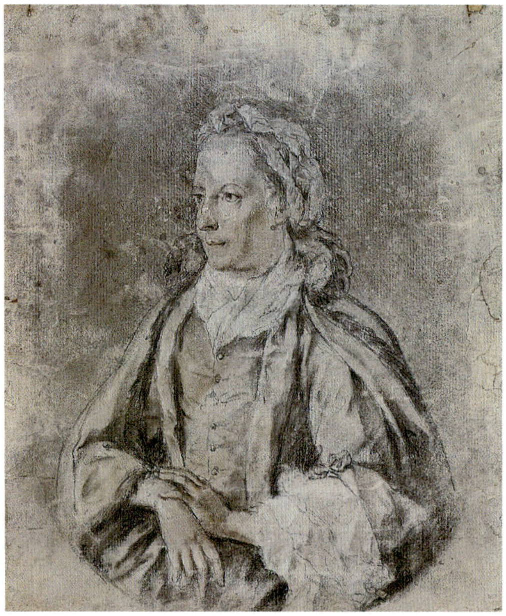

VESEY NPG 3131

'[she had] no personal advantages of manner, and studied no ornament of dress. Simplicity, accompanied by a sort of oblivious inattention to things passing under her very sight, characterised her ... [her] forgetfulness extended to such a point that she sometimes hardly remembered her own name' (Sir Nathaniel Wraxall, 1815).

3131 UNKNOWN ARTIST c.1770?

Black crayon with touches of sepia and grey wash on paper 25.5 x 21.5 (10 x 8½), mounted as an oval 22.5 x 18.8 (8⅞ x 7⅜); badly stained, rubbed and spotted; the original wooden backboard (now separately preserved) inscribed: *Mrs Vesey/ Mrs Shilleto*

Wearing a bonnet, a cape with a fur collar and a buttoned bodice.

Collections: St Clement Danes, London;[1] [the Rev Pennington-Bickford (1874-1941), vicar of St Clement Danes[2]] bt. from a barrow in Lambeth by G.F. Gilmour, by whom presented 1943.

The identity rests on the inscription and the existence of a second very similar but reduced drawing identified as Mrs Vesey;[3] the provenance of NPG 3131 is also supportive. The eccentric costume makes dating hazardous, and the suggested date is based on her possible age.

1 Gilmour described NPG 3131 as bought 'with a lot of odds and ends from St Clement Danes' (letter of 10 February 1943; NPG archive).
2 The indirect descendant of the Rev Montagu Pennington (1762-1849) who, according to *DNB*, owned a crayon portrait of Mrs Vesey; he was the nephew and executor of Elizabeth Carter, whose correspondence he published in 1809, including her extensive letters to Mrs Vesey.
3 Oval half length formerly in the collection of Lord Treowen (1851-1933); illus. *NPG Burney Diaries*, I, i, f.p.153.

DOUBTFUL PORTRAIT

Painting attributed to Henry Morland, half length of a nun, wearing a black head scarf, reading a book, inscribed verso in an early 19th-century hand with identity; Sotheby's, 18 December 1968, lot 276.

VINCENT, William 1739-1815

Headmaster of Westminster school 1788-1802; Vincent Square, which he preserved as a playground for the school, was named after him; Dean of Westminster (and Dean of the Bath) 1802-15, directing restoration work in the Henry VII chapel from 1807; a respected classical scholar, specialising in ancient geography.

1434 HENRY EDRIDGE 1809

Pencil and watercolour 27.8 x 23.5 (11 x 9¼), an area 22.5 x 17.5 (8¾ x 6¾) faded through exposure; a small hole below left; signed (very faintly) bottom left: *H E June 1809*; contemporary ink inscription verso: *Dr Vincent, Dean of Westminster/ by. H. Edridge. June 1809.*[1]

As Dean of Westminster, in civilian dress, wearing a black coat.

Collections: Christie's, 2 April 1906, lot 22, purchased.

Engraving: C. Picart 1810; Holl (bust-length oval).

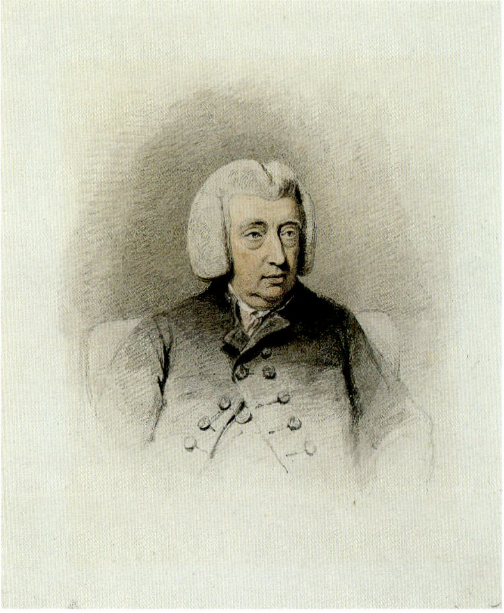

VINCENT NPG 1434

1 With a much later biographical note in pencil: *Dr. Vincent. Eminent geographer. born - Lime-Street Ward 1739;/ educated Westminster and Trinity Coll. Cambridge; Vicar Longdon, Worcester; rector Allhallows, Johns Westminster and Islip Oxford; dean of Westminster, and head master of the school. Died 1815 - buried Westminster Abbey./ Engraved C. Picart.*

2418 G.P. HARDING after WILLIAM OWEN [1811]

Watercolour and bodycolour on paper 15.2 x 11.5 (6 x 4½) the image 12.3 x 10.7 (4⅞ x 4¼); signed bottom right: *G P Harding.fecit*; the margin below inscribed: *William Vincent D.D./ Dean of Westminster.1802./ From the original Picture by Wm. Owen Esqr. R.A. in the possession of G.G. Vincent.*

As Dean of Westminster and Dean of the Bath; blue eyes, wearing the collar of the Bath (with the motto of the badge in mirror writing), a blue cassock and black coat; seated in a red chair.

Collections: J.B. Nicholls; Sotheby's, 22 October 1929, lot 128 (part); bt. H. Breun for the NPG.

Engraving: J. Stow 1822 (for the *Deans of Westminster*).

NPG 2418 was made expressly for the engraving by J. Stow published on 31 December 1822, see below.

ICONOGRAPHY

1801 Painting by Samuel Drummond, half-length oval, with hat, as headmaster of Westminster. Exhibited RA 1801(682). Engraved W. Ridley 1801 as *Dr Vincent* (*European Mag.*).

1806 Painting by Henry Howard, bust-length oval, as Dean of Westminster. Exhibited RA 1806(11). Engraved C. Turner 1806.*

1809 Drawing by Henry Edridge, see NPG 1434.

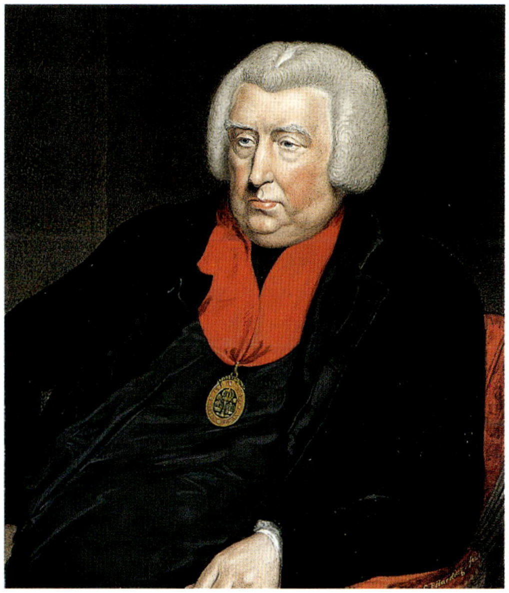

VINCENT NPG *2418*

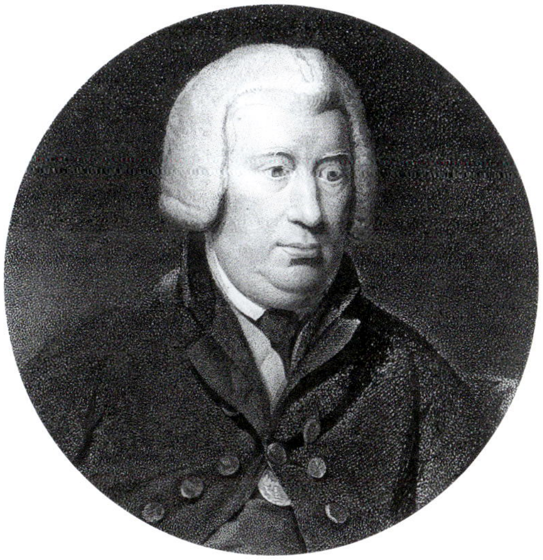

VINCENT C. Turner after Henry Howard 1806 (NPG D *13813*)

1811 Painting by William Owen, seated three-quarter length as Dean of Westminster, a globe by his chair. Exhibited RA 1811(44). Engraved C. Turner 1811, H. Meyer 1812, J. Stow 1822. A reduced version exhibited NPE 1868(186) lent W. Vincent, presumably the picture copied by Harding, see NPG 2418. A half-length version is in the Headmaster's House, Westminster School.

WALKER, Adam 1731-1821

Self-taught inventor and celebrated lecturer; b. Patterdale, Westmorland; from the age of fifteen he taught in Ledsham, Yorks., Macclesfield and Manchester, before setting up as an itinerant lecturer in natural philosophy; settled in London 1778; his inventions included rotatory lights for the Scilly Isles (erected 1790) and his writings the *Cure of Unwholesome Air in large Cities* 1777, and *An Epitome of Astronomy* (26th edition 1817).

'I much admired his mild and gentle, benevolent manners; it seems as if all Romney's intimate friends were truly amiable and feeling like himself' (William Blake, 1804).

'perhaps, there is not any character in the metropolis better known for information, philanthropy, liberality of sentiment and conduct; for ease of address, good nature, good spirits, persevering exertion, and all the more solid qualities, that give value to the character of the philosopher and the man' (*Monthly Mirror*, Highfill, XV).

1106 see Groups, *Adam Walker with his Family* by GEORGE ROMNEY 1796-1801

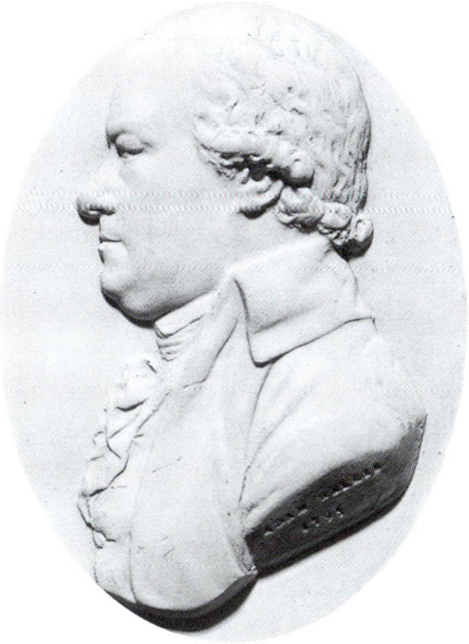

Adam WALKER by James Tassie 1795 (Scottish National Portrait Gallery)

ICONOGRAPHY

c.1758 Painting by George Romney, *Boating Party on Lake Windermere*, in which Walker stands in the boat. Timothy Clode Collection (*Romney* 2002, no.1; Romney 1830, pp.27-28).

c.1760 Painting by George Romney, described by William Blake as 'a whole length canvas about two feet by one and a half; it is the first Romney ever painted' (24 October 1818; A. Gilchrist, *Blake*, 1945 ed., p.184). See also under Groups NPG 1106.

1762 Painting by Christopher Steele, unfinished. Walker's letter to Romney, 12 December 1762 (*Connoisseur*, LIV, 1919, p.93), recalled the chaos left by the precipitate departure of Steele, Romney's former teacher, from Manchester: 'my picture is in the same state you saw it - I do not think the wretch has done a week's work this 6 months'.

c.1790 Painting by George Romney, bust length (see under Groups NPG 1106). Probably that later in the collection of Lord Wavertree (d.1933, indirect descendant).

1792 Painting by Samuel Drummond, half-length oval, engraved anon. 1792 (*European Mag.*).

1795 Medallion by James Tassie (Gray 1894, no.394). Plaster in the Scottish NPG (PG 392).*

1796 Anon. caricature, *A Philosopher* (George 8887), showing Walker as a chemist at his bench with a portrait of Joseph Priestley hanging on the wall.

1796-1801 Painting by George Romney, see Groups NPG 1106.

c.1800 Painting by Henry Howard, three-quarter length standing, his hand on a globe. Offered to the NPG by Miss E.E. Gibson in 1897.

Undated miniature by Mary Barrett, exhibited SKM 1865 (2813) lent W. Sidney Gibson.

WALKER, John 1732-1807

Actor and lexicographer; played in Bristol from 1754 and occasionally at Drury Lane; set up the Crow Street Theatre in Dublin 1758 and appeared at Covent Garden from 1762; from 1768 he turned to the study of elocution and language; his numerous publications included the *Critical Pronouncing Dictionary and Exposition of the English Language* 1791, which had reached a 28th edition by 1826.

5493 HENRY ASHBY 1802

Canvas 129 x 99 (49½ x 39) lined and restored 1983; the surface is worn and there are small tears upper right and left; an area on the extreme left, above the quill, appears to have been reworked.[1]

Blue eyes, white hair, wearing a black suit, an open book in his hand (illegibly inscribed), seated in a red chair; on the green tablecloth to the left, an inkwell and three books: *WALKER'S/ PRONOUNCING/ DICTIONARY* stands on *ELEMENTS/ OF ELOCUTION* which lies on top of *RE.../ GRAMMAR* (see below).

Collections: Dr Thomas Buzzard (d.1919), by descent; Phillips, 26 April 1982, lot 104, bt. Leggatt for the NPG.

Exhibition: RA 1802(149, 'Mr Walker, Professor of Elocution'), see below.

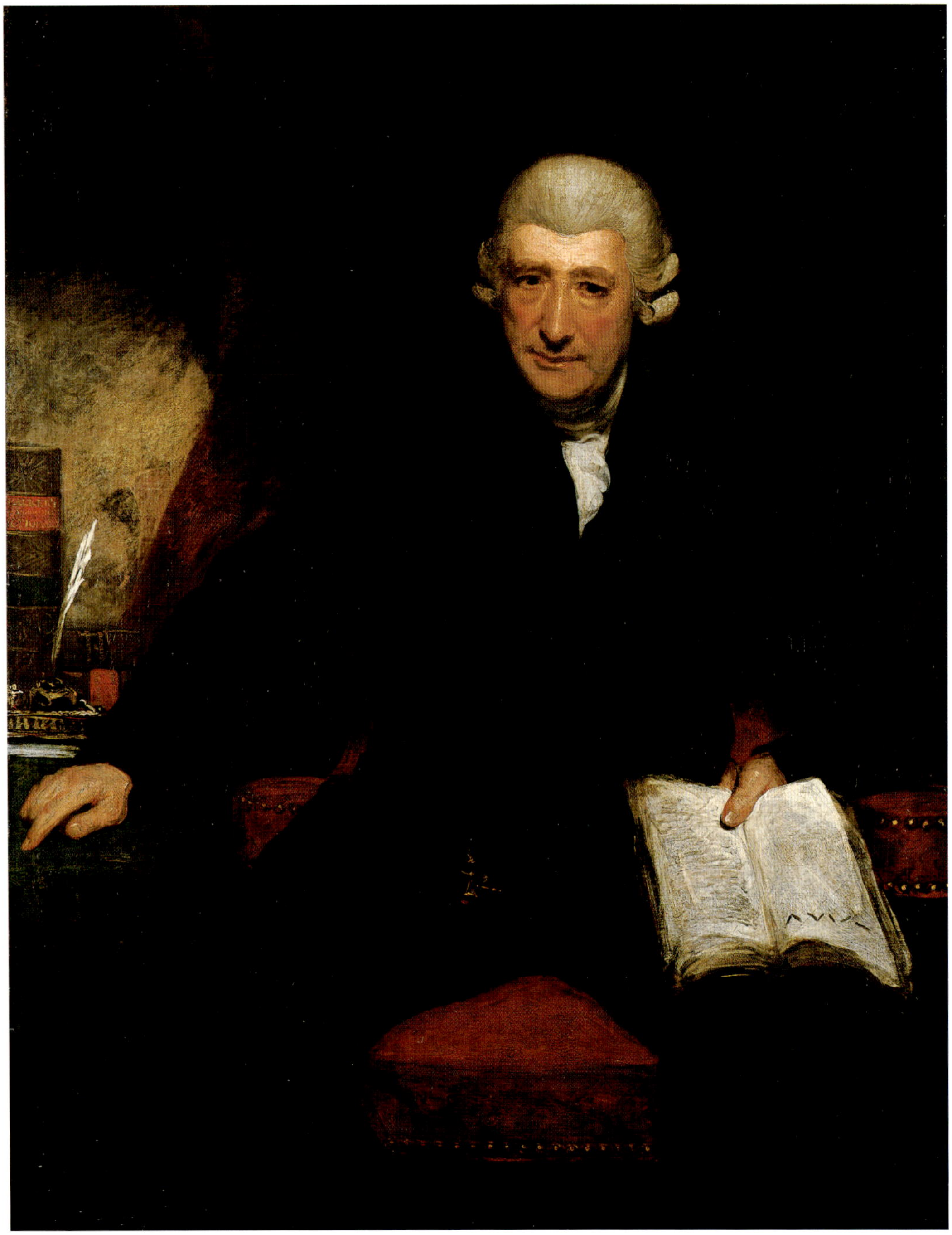

John WALKER NPG 5493

The sitter bears a general resemblance to the earlier engraved miniature by Barry (see below) and is identified by the books on the table, Walker's *Critical Pronouncing Dictionary* of 1791, *Elements of Elocution* of 1781 and the *Rhetorical Grammar* of 1785. The attribution to Ashby is based on comparison with his few known works and it is assumed that NPG 5493 was the portrait of Walker he exhibited in 1802.[2]

1 Not elucidated by X-radiography.
2 Apparent from a note made by Thomas Buzzard on discovering Ashby's portrait listed by Graves in 1905 (copy in NPG archive).

ICONOGRAPHY

c.1785? Miniature by John Barry,* bust-length oval. Victoria & Albert Museum (P69-1931). Engraved (the artist usually described as Jas. Barry) J. Heath; J. Moffat; T. Clerk; J. Sharp (in reverse). An extended version, showing Walker seated, engraved R. Hicks 1825 (illus. Smith 1920, II, f.p.220; Highfill, XV, p.214) and anon.

1802 Painting by Henry Ashby, see NPG 5493.

DOUBTFUL PORTRAIT

Wash drawing, half length, inscribed *Mr Walker vulgo Walker* (NPG reference collection D 6669).

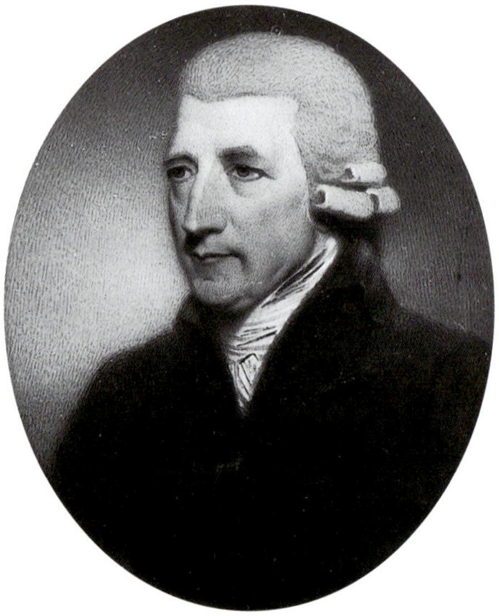

John WALKER by James Barry c.1785? (Victoria and Albert Museum)

WALPOLE, Horace, see ORFORD

WASHINGTON, George 1732–99

Commander-in-chief of United States army 1775–83; first President of the United States 1789–97; commander-in-chief of the United States armies 1798.

'imposing in size, noble and well proportioned, a countenance open, calm and sedate, but without any striking feature, and when you depart from him, the remembrance only of a fine man will remain' (Joseph Mandrillon, 1784).

'The height of his person is about five feet eleven; his chest is full; and his limbs, though rather slender, well shaped and muscular. His head is small . . . His eyes are of a light grey colour; and in proportion to the length of his face, his nose is long' (Isaac Weld, 1796).

Abbreviations

Hart 1904: C.H. Hart, *Catalogue of the Engraved Portraits of Washington*, 1904

Miles 1999: E. Miles, *George and Martha Washington, Portraits from the Presidential Years*, NPG Washington, 1999

Washington 1931: J.H. Morgan & M. Fielding, *The Life Portraits of Washington*, 1931

Wick 1982: W.C. Wick, *George Washington An American Icon*, Smithsonian Institution, 1982

2041 GILBERT STUART [1796]

Canvas 73 x 60.5 (28¾ x 23¾) lined; conserved 1997; retouchings in the face and background areas.

Blue eyes, powdered hair tied with a black ribbon, black coat, white neckcloth.

Collections: Gen. Charles Cotesworth Pinckney (d.1825) of Philadelphia; bequeathed by his daughter, Harriott Pinckney (d.1866), to his nephew, Rev C.C. Pinckney (d.1898); bt. by Justice Horace Gray, Boston, Mass., 1869;[1] sold by his widow 1924 through Knoedler, New York, to Edward S. Harkness, New York, by whom presented 1924.[2]

Reference: M. Fielding, *Gilbert Stuart's Portraits of George Washington*, 1923, p.191, no.70; Park 1926, no.70 (as c.1797); *Washington* 1931, p.294, no.70.

Stuart returned to America from London in 1793, resolved to make a fortune through 'a plurality of portraits' of Washington. Private inadequacies prevented him making a fortune, but his portraits of the President were acclaimed. 'Mr Stewart is justly celebrated as the greatest painter of the age', enthused the New York *Time Piece*, 5 February 1798, 'and Washington is his hobby-horse'; twenty-five years later it was being said that 'the only idea we now have of George Washington, is associated with Stuart's Washington'.[3] It appears that he only received two sets of sittings in 1795 and 1796, but from these four patterns of Washington portrait derived:

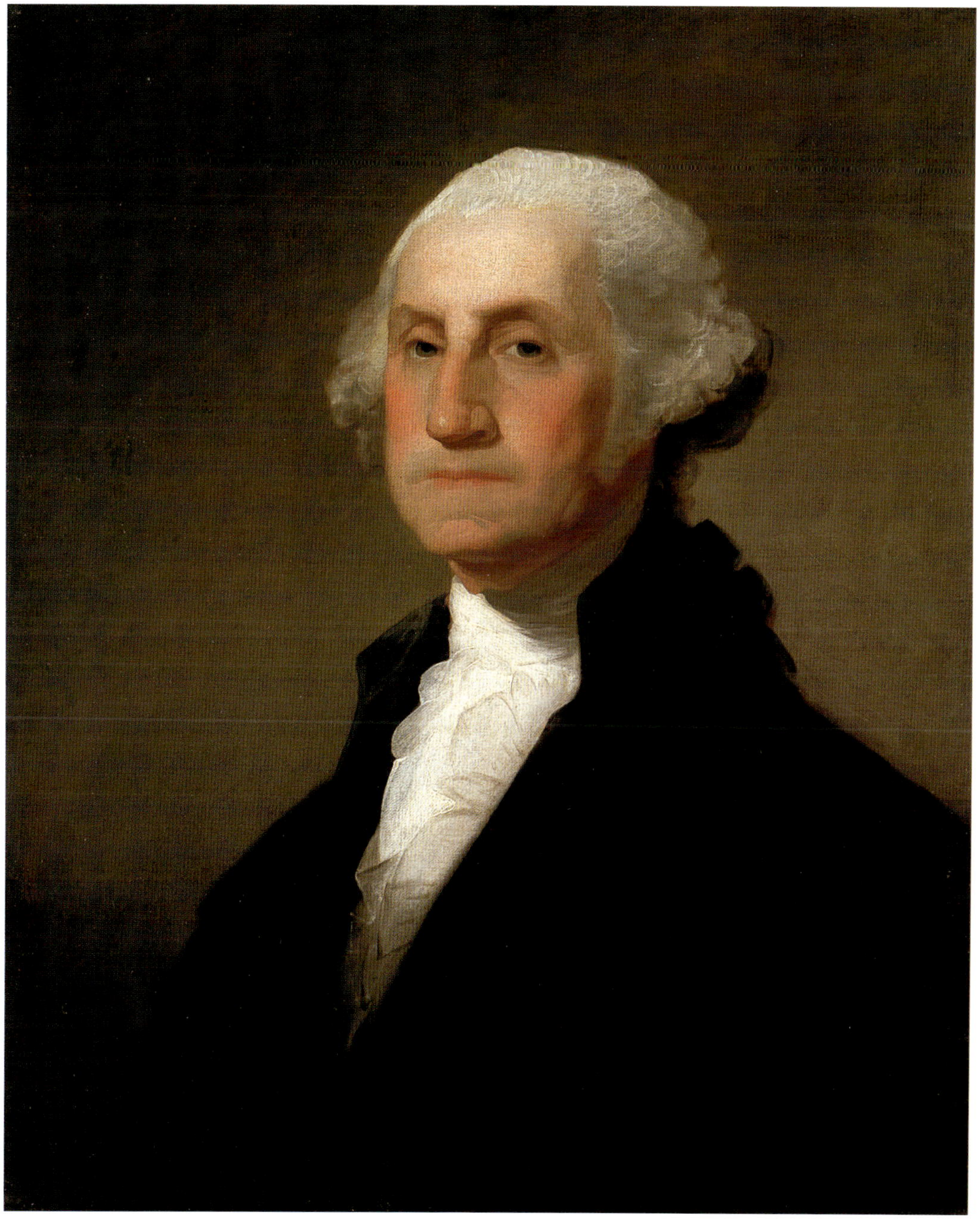

WASHINGTON NPG *2041*

the 'Vaughan' half-length portrait of 1795 (NG Washington)

the 'Athenaeum' portrait of 1796, a fine head on an unfinished three-quarter length canvas (jointly owned by the Museum of Fine Arts, Boston, Mass., and the NPG Washington) – the ultimate portrait of Washington (canonised on postage stamps and dollar bills and which, for different reasons, Stuart termed his hundred-dollar bill) the 'Lansdowne' or 'Tea Pot' portrait of 1796,★ the Athenaeum head on a whole-length standing figure, feet apart and right hand extended (NPG Washington), painted at the behest of Mrs William Bingham for the Marquess of Lansdowne

the 'Munro-Lenox' portrait of 1800, the Athenaeum head on a whole-length standing figure, heels together and his right hand resting on a table (New York Public Library)

the 'Washington at Dorchester heights' of 1806,★ the Athenaeum head on a whole-length standing figure, standing by a white horse (Museum of Fine Arts, Boston, Mass.).

NPG 2041 is an example of the Athenaeum pattern, of which some seventy half-length replicas have been recorded.[4] Three types have been distinguished within this pattern: type A with a short head; type B with smaller eyes and longer lips, and type C with a more pointed chin and darker eyes[5] -- of which NPG 2041 is an example. The provenance suggests an early 19th century date. General Pinckney, the first owner of NPG 2041, had previously commissioned a whole-length portrait of Washington for presentation to the French Directory on his appointment as American minister in Paris in 1796; he never received it and it is now in the White House.[6]

1 This provenance is given in letters from C.C. Pinckney of 2 September 1868 and 25 May 1869 (NPG archive). E. Bryant Johnston, *Original Portraits of Washington*, 1882, p.100, noted the claim that NPG 2041 had been presented by Washington to General Pinckney.
2 Harkness wrote from New York on 2 July 1924 saying that having seen a portrait of Washington in the NPG 'attributed to Gilbert Stuart' [NPG 774], he felt that the Gallery would prefer to have a portrait by Stuart himself (NPG archive).
3 See Evans 1999, pp.60-73.
4 See *Washington* 1931, pp.273-311, 324-46. Hart 1904, nos.345-700, lists 355 engravings of the Athenaeum type. Stuart once said apropos of Washington copies that if 'the General had sat for all these portraits he could have done nothing else; our Independence would have been a secondary matter' (Evans 1999, pp.86, 88).
5 *Washington* 1931, pp.240-47.
6 An irregular saga, for which see, for example, C.M. Mount, *Gilbert Stuart*, 1964, pp.216, 263, 353.

174 ELLEN SHARPLES [1796-97]

Pastel on buff-coloured laid paper 24 x 18.5 (9⅜ x 7¼) laid down on card.

Powdered hair, black coat, white neckcloth; deep blue hatching in the upper left background area.

Collections: William Taylor; his step-daughters, the Misses Eaton, of Liverpool and Leamington, by whom given to the sitter's grand-daughter, Miss Catharine I. Finch of Birmingham, who gave it to James Yates[1] 1860; presented by him, together with a portrait of Joseph Priestley [NPG 175], 1864.

Reference: Knox 1930, no.35 (as by Mrs Sharples).

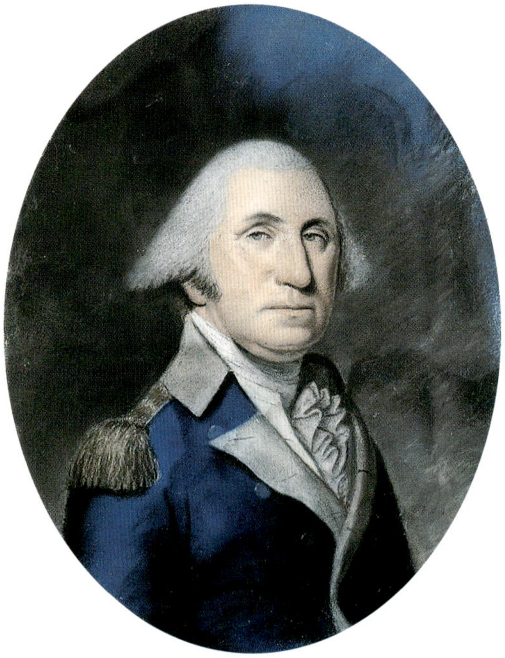

WASHINGTON NPG *2903*

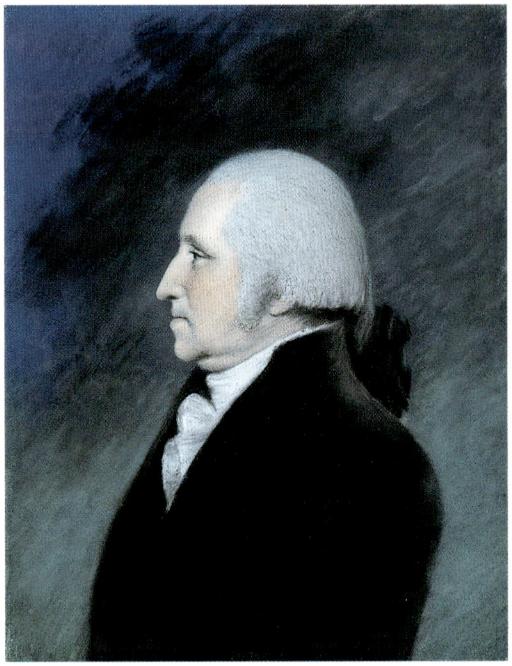

WASHINGTON NPG *174*

James Sharples arrived in New York in 1796 with his third wife Ellen, an amateur artist who became increasingly professional, and they stayed in America until 1801.[2] His pastels, drawn with the aid of a pantograph in finely ground crayon applied with a camel's hair brush on thick grey paper,[3] could be completed within two hours.[4] Charges were $20 for a full face and $15 for a profile.[5] It now seems impossible to distinguish between the hands of husband and wife; it was evidently James who first drew the portraits, but the four in the NPG seem more likely to be copies by Ellen (see Priestley NPG 175 and NPG 2904 and NPG 2903 below).

Washington's sittings, among the last he gave, are undocumented,[6] but Eliza Custis, Washington's granddaughter, considered the Sharples profile 'an admirable likeness, the profile taken by an instrument, and critically exact' and the example in the NPG Washington (76.17) bears a label written by her giving the date as 1797.[7] Copies by Ellen Sharples came to be highly regarded. In December 1804 she wrote that her copies of Washington and Priestley were then 'executed in a very superior style',[8] and she exhibited portraits of Washington and Priestley together at the RA 1807(851); back in New York in 1809 she again described copying the Washington portrait 'drawn by Mr S on our first visit to America'.[9]

Twenty-six copies are illustrated by Knox;[10] examples are in the Wadsworth Athenaeum, the Metropolitan Museum of Art, New York, and in the Sharples collection in Bristol Art Gallery;[11] a single example showing the profile reversed (Knox no.27), belonging to Mrs DeButts in 1931, was then (perhaps questionably) considered the likely original. The type was engraved on five occasions in the late nineteenth century; the plate by H.B. Hall described as *after the portrait painted from the life by Sharpless in 1796*, that by P. Hall as *from the Original portrait in the possession of the Evans family. Painted by Mrs E. Sharpless.*[12]

1 As by Ellen Sharples, see Priestley NPG 175 note 1. This provenance is given in letters to Yates from Catharine Finch of 11 December 1860 and from Miss G. Eaton of 26 December 1860 (NPG archive).
2 They returned in 1809 and James died in New York in 1811. In due course their sons, Felix (c.1786-c.1814) and James jr. (1789-1839), joined the family portrait business (Knox 1930, p.18).
3 Knox 1930, p.12.
4 *Washington* 1931, p.395.
5 Knox 1930, p.9, citing W. Dunlap, *History of the Rise and Progress of Arts of Design in the United States*, 1834, ii, pp.70-71.
6 Miles 1999, p.47. Catharine Finch told James Yates (letter of 11 December 1860; NPG archive) that William Taylor (see provenance), was one of several Birmingham Unitarians who persuaded Priestley and Washington to sit to Sharples, 'each [of the Unitarians] ordering one or more copies'.
7 Miles 1999, pp.47, 49.
8 Knox 1930, pp.13, 118.
9 Knox 1930, p.120.
10 *Ibid.*, nos.15-29, 31-37, 39-41, 43, 45-47; see also *Washington* 1931, pp.398-409.
11 *Cat. of the Sharples Coll.*, Bristol, 1910, no.3.
12 Hart 1904, nos.703-07.

2903 ELLEN SHARPLES [1796-97]

Pastel on buff-coloured laid paper 24 x 19 (9½ x 7½) oval; the surface is abraded and there are stained areas lower right and upper left.

Clear grey eyes, powdered hair, wearing the Continental uniform of blue coat with buff lapels and gold epaulettes and buff waistcoat; dark grey background with deep blue shading upper right.

Collections: Given by the artist to William Russell (1740-1818) of Birmingham;[1] by descent to T.H Russell by whom, with his sister Mrs Alexander Scott, presented, together with a portrait of Joseph Priestley [NPG 2904], 1936.

For the Sharples practice, see NPG 174 above.

The composition approaches that of a miniature of Washington by Walter Robertson, see Iconography 1794, but the cut of the collar (besides the Sharples's movements) confirms a slightly later date. Knox illustrates five copies,[2] of which two are in the Sharples collection in Bristol Art Gallery;[3] another was sold Christie's, 22 May 1973, lot 84. A pencil copy of the head alone by Ellen Sharples is in a folio of her drawings at Bristol.[4] A half-length version in oils belonged to the Hanover Trust Bank, London, in 1968.[5] The type was engraved by Albert Rosenthal in 1900 *from a Sharpless' pastel Owned in Philadelphia*.[6]

1 Provenance as given to Hake by T.H. Russell in November 1936. Russell knew Washington in America, meeting him at Mount Vernon in 1797, see S.H. Jeyes, *The Russells of Birmingham in the French Revolution and in America 1791-1814*, 1911, pp.262, 265; and Priestley NPG 2904 note 1.
2 Knox 1930, nos.49, 51-54. See also *Washington* 1931, pp.409-10.
3 Knox, nos.49, 51; *Cat. of the Sharples Coll.*, Bristol, 1910, nos.1, 72 (both listings agreeing that one was attributable to James Sharples, and the other on ivory was by Ellen Sharples).
4 Knox 1930, no.94 (Sharples collection).
5 Illus. *Connoisseur*, CLXIX, 1968, p.73; cf. Knox 1930, no.48.
6 Hart 1904, no.708.

774 after GILBERT STUART [1800]

Canvas 71 x 49.5 (28½ x 20) lined 1887; cleaned 1971.

Blue eyes, powdered hair, wearing a black suit with black buttons, his black hat on the red-covered table cloth; red upholstered chair, purple drapery in the centre; the books and papers are not lettered.[1]

Collections: William Scholefield (1809-67), Birmingham, who acquired the portrait through his American wife, *née* Miller; his son-in-law, George F. Meredith, 1877,[2] from whom purchased 1887.

Exhibitions:[3] *The Past We Share*, Dallas, 1967(20); *Up in Arms*, Belfast, 1998.

Reference: M. Fielding, *Gilbert Stuart's Portraits of George Washington*, 1923, pp.143-44, no.26; *Washington* 1931, p.321(xviii).

See NPG 2041.

A reduced, uninspired copy of the 'Munro-Lenox' portrait, NPG 774 was once attributed (without real evidence) to the copyist William Winstanley,[4] a British painter settled in New York who probably worked with Stuart in 1796-97 and who forged replicas of his portraits.[5]

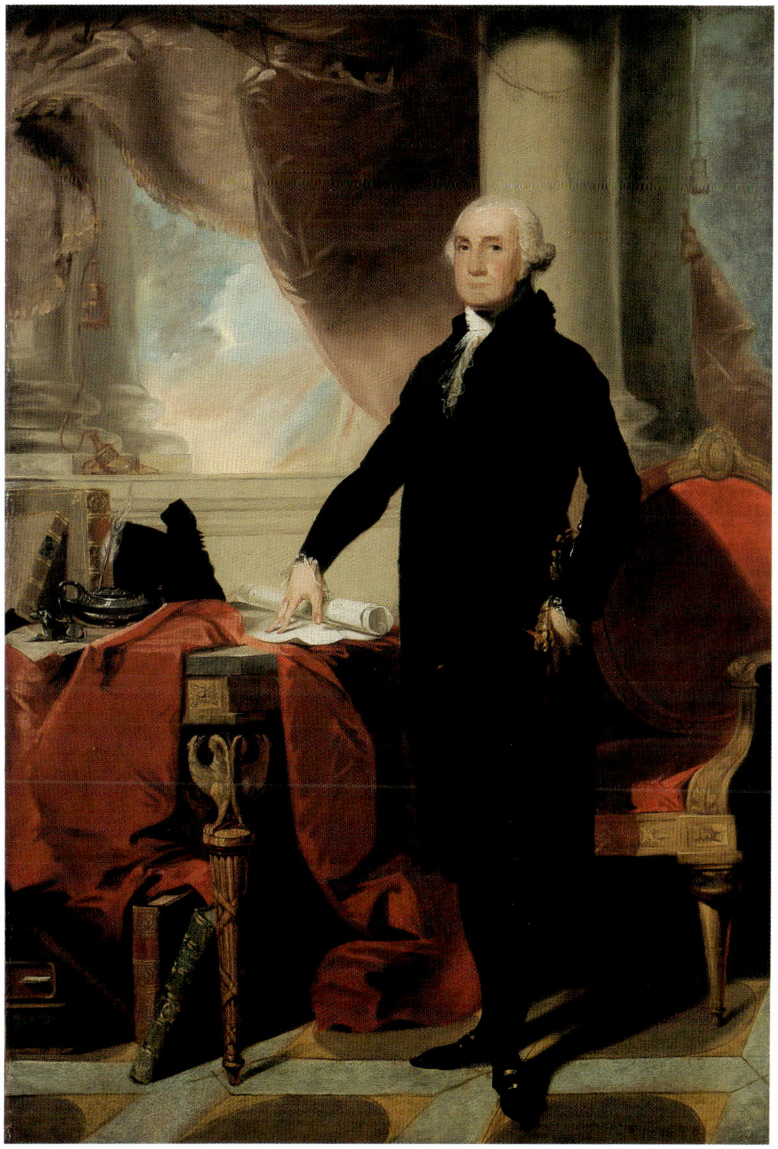

WASHINGTON NPG *774*

1 In Stuart's Lansdowne portrait the three books below the table are inscribed: *GENERAL ORDERS, AMERICAN REVOLUTION* and *CONSTITUTION AND LAWS OF THE UNITED STATES*; the two on the table: *THE FEDERALIST* and *THE JOURNAL OF CONGRESS*; see Kloss 1992, p.66.
2 When Meredith first offered the picture to the NPG, providing the provenance here cited: Scholefield m. in New York in 1828; it was alleged his wife's forebear had served on Washington's staff and had been given the portrait by Washington himself.
3 Meredith also claimed NPG 774 was shown at the Centennial Exhibition in 1876 [the Philadelphia International Exhibition], but that cat. lists, p.210, no.170, only the 'Lansdowne' whole-length Washington lent by J. Delaware Lewis.
4 By C.H. Hart in the Philadelphia *Evening Telegraph*, 3 March 1892, reprinted in *The Collector*, 15 December 1895, p.51 (on file NPG).
5 See Evans 1999, pp.85-86.

ICONOGRAPHY

By 1785 Washington declared that 'I am so hackneyed to the touches of the Painter's pencil, that I am now altogether at their beck, and sit like Patience on a monument, whilst they are delineating the lines of my face'. It was only to get worse for him.

The outstanding likenesses of Washington are those by Houdon of 1785 and Stuart of 1796, but the complete iconography of Washington is a formidable study. In 1904 Hart (Hart 1904) recorded over 700 engraved portraits and in 1931 Morgan & Fielding (*Washington* 1931) listed more than 500 painted portraits of varying distinction. The following list is confined to prime versions.

1772 Painting by C.W. Peale, standing three-quarter length in the Virginia militia uniform (blue coat with scarlet facings). Washington and Lee University, Lexington, Va. (illus. *Washington* 1931, f.p.24). Engraved R. Scot c.1780. C.W. Peale is said to have made 'more than fifty' portraits of Washington in the 1770s and 1780s (Miles 1999, p.39).

In 1775 Washington was made 'General and Commander in chief of the army of the United Colonies'; the War of Independence lasted until 1783. He was now portrayed in the 'Continental' uniform, dark blue coat with buff facings and gold epaulettes, buff waistcoat, blue sash and white knee breeches.

1776 Painting by C.W. Peale, three-quarter length standing in uniform (illus. *Washington* 1931, f.p.26). Brooklyn Museum of Art.

1777 Miniature by C.W. Peale, in uniform. Metropolitan Museum of Art, New York (illus. *Washington* 1931, f.p.46). Another belongs to the Mount Vernon Ladies' Association.

1779 Painting by C.W. Peale,* the 'Continental type', whole-length standing in uniform, his left hand on a cannon, after the Battle of Princeton. Pennsylvania Academy of Fine Arts, Philadelphia (1943.16.2). The first monumental image of Washington; twenty-three versions listed in *Washington* 1931, pp.27-34.

1779 Profile drawing by P-E. du Simitière (c.1736-84) engraved B-L. Prévost (illus. Wick 1982, p.25).

In 1780 Washington ordered that the sash be eliminated from the military uniform and three stars were substituted for rosettes on the epaulettes.

1780 Painting by John Trumbull, small whole-length standing in uniform, hat in left hand. Metropolitan Museum of Art, New York (24.109.88), Painted from memory in London where engraved V. Green 1781. The first authoritative portrait of Washington to be seen in Europe, it was soon copied throughout the Continent.

After his final victory in the War of Independence in 1783, Washington retired to Mount Vernon.

1783 Pastel by William Dunlap, half length in uniform. Capitol, Washington DC (illus. *Washington* 1931, f.p.66).

1783 Painting by Joseph Wright, half length in uniform. Historical Society of Pennsylvania (illus. *Washington* 1931, f.p.70). In 1783 Wright also took a plaster mould or life mask and made a (now untraced) clay bust (*Wright* 1985, pp.93-99).

1784 Painting by Joseph Wright, three-quarter length, in uniform. Massachusetts Historical Society (illus. *Wright* 1985, p.103). Painted for Thomas Jefferson.

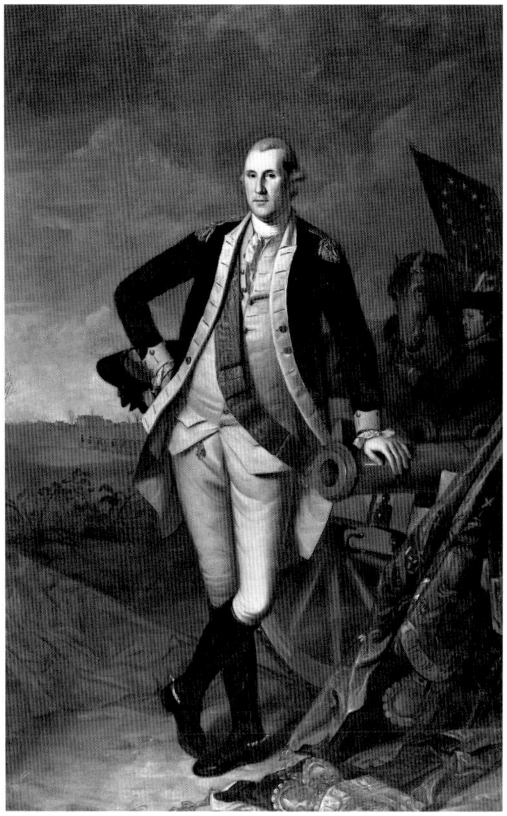

WASHINGTON by C.W. Peale 1779 (Pennsylvania Academy of Fine Arts, Philadelphia)

1784 Painting by C.W. Peale, whole-length standing in uniform, a sword in his right hand. Princeton University (illus. *Washington* 1931, f.p.34).

1784 Painting by C.W. Peale, whole-length standing in uniform, with Lafayette and Col. Tilghman at Yorktown. State House, Annapolis, Md. (illus. *Washington* 1931, f.p.36).

c.1784 Wax medallions by Joseph Wright, laureate bust to right, reduced from the plaster relief of 1783 with the Mount Vernon Ladies' Association (illus. Wright 1985, p.109, and see pp.111, 113). The medallion apparently provided the basis for Wright's profile etching of 1790 (illus. *Wright* 1985, p.127) which was widely copied in prints, medallions and medals (including one of the four Wedgwood medallions, illus. Reilly 1973, p.332; see Wick 1982, p.102).

1785-86 Painting by R.E. Pine, half length, in uniform. Mrs Rolla D. Campbell jr in 1979 (illus. Pine 1979, p.95). Stewart describes two replicas and a pastel copy by the painter's daughter Jane (Pine 1979, pp.92-97).

1785-92 Marble statue by J-A. Houdon, standing in uniform, with fasces and ploughshare. Richmond, Va., Capitol (illus. *Washington* 1931, f.p.110; Arnason 1975, pls.98-101). Commissioned by the State of Virginia, completed in 1792 and erected in 1796. Later bronze casts are at Versailles and in front of the National Gallery, London.

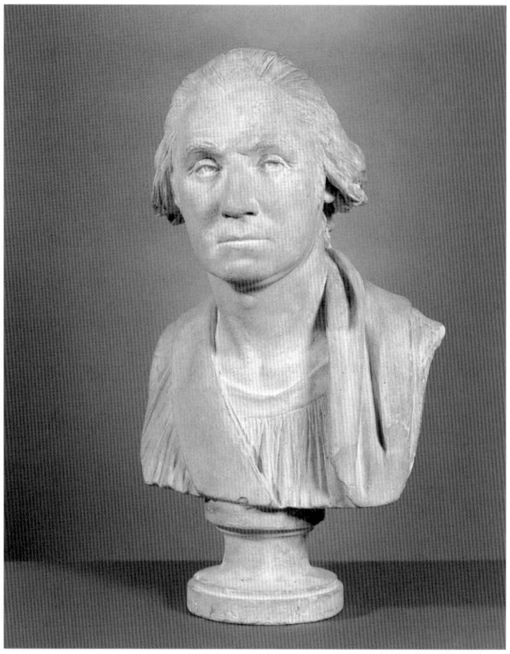

WASHINGTON by J-A. Houdon [c.1785-92] (National Portrait Gallery, Washington)

Houdon took a life mask and modelled a bust at Mount Vernon in October 1785; terracotta busts of 1785 with the Mount Vernon Ladies' Association and of 1786 in the Louvre (Arnason 1975, pls.97a, 97b); a plaster, given by Houdon to Thomas Jefferson, is in the Boston Athenaeum (Arnason 1975, fig.154).

The many busts of this pattern (in terracotta, plaster,* marble, and probably bronze) differ in detail in their Roman costume or the hair (see Arnason 1975, pp.72-77, figs.154-57; *Washington* 1931, pp.96-111).

1787 Painting by C.W. Peale, bust length, in uniform. Pennsylvania Academy of Fine Arts, Philadelphia (illus. *Washington* 1931, f.p.38). Copied by James Peale on a larger canvas with additional figures (Independence Hall, Philadelphia; illus. *Washington* 1931, f.p.126, and New York Public Library) and this, in turn, was adapted many times by his nephew, C.P. Polk who, though he received no sittings, had composed fifty portraits of Washington by 1790 (see Miles 1995, pp.135-37; *Washington* 1931, pp.118-21), including the 'Princeton' portrait, three-quarter length in uniform with a view

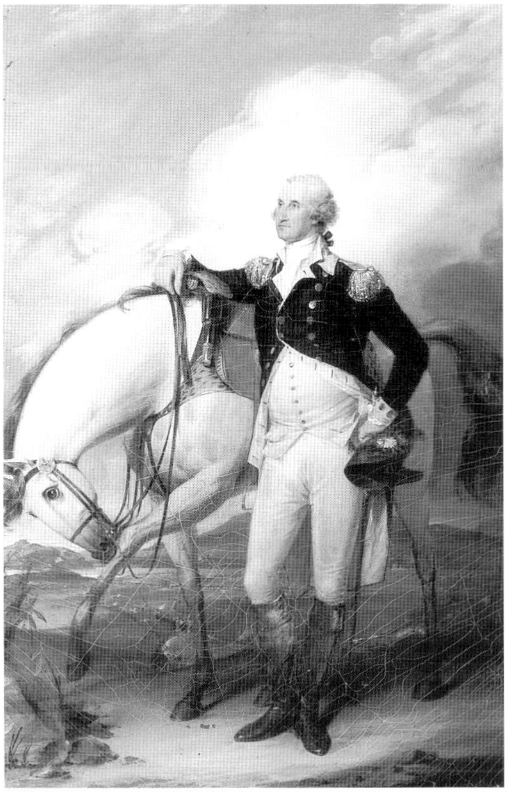

WASHINGTON by John Trumbull c.1790 (Winterthur Museum)

of Nassau Hall (now Princeton College) in the background (NG Washington (1947.13.1).

In 1789 Washington was elected first President of the United States. It was also in this year that he lost his teeth and the artificial ones he was given answered 'very imperfectly the purpose for which they were intended; a marked change occurred in the appearance of his face, more especially in the projection of the under lip' (G.W. Parke Curtis; *Washington* 1931, p.xx).

1789 Painting by Christian Güllager, bust-length painted oval. Massachusetts Historical Society, Boston, Mass. (illus. Miles 1999, p.22).

1789 Miniature by John Ramage, in uniform. Mr & Mrs E.G. Nicholson in 1999. Drawn for Mrs Washington in October 1789 (illus. Miles 1999, p.18).

1790 Painting by Edward Savage, half-length painted oval in uniform. Harvard University, who commissioned the portrait in 1789 (illus. Miles 1995, p.148; Miles 1999, p.22). For Josiah Quincy this was 'the best likeness he had ever seen of Washington, though its merits as a work of art are but small' (Miles 1999, p.50).

1790 Painting by John Trumbull, whole length in uniform standing by his horse. City Hall, New York (illus. *Washington* 1931, f.p.166). A smaller, earlier version is in the Winterthur Museum.* Washington sat to Trumbull between February and July 1790 'for my Picture in his Historical pieces', viz. *The Capture of the Hessians at Trenton, The Battle of Princeton* and the *Surrender of Lord Cornwallis* (all Yale University AG).

c.1790 Miniature signed *WP*, in uniform. Buccleuch Collection (illus. Foskett 1972, II, pl.261, no.642).

1791-95 Bust by Giuseppe Ceracchi (see U. Desportes, *AQ*, XXVI, 1963, pp.141-77). He received a sitting from Washington in 1791 and produced a number of busts *all'antica*, differing in detail, some on a colossal scale, as the terracotta in the musée de Nantes (illus. Evans 1999, p.65). A life-size marble bust dated 1795, declined by Washington, is in the Metropolitan Museum of Art, New York (illus. Miles 1999, p.14).

1791 Miniature by Archibald Robertson, wearing light-brown coat. New York Historical Society (1929.35; illus. Miles 1999, p.27).

1792 Painting by John Trumbull, whole length in uniform standing by his horse at Trenton. Yale University AG (illus. *Washington* 1931, f.p.168; Trumbull 1982, p.121). A similar figure, but with a different background, was painted by Trumbull the same year for the Council Chamber, Charleston City Hall (illus. *Washington* 1931, f.p.170).

by 1793 Painting by Edward Savage, three-quarter length seated. Art Institute of Chicago (illus. Miles 1995, p.151; *Washington* 1931, f.p.176). Engraved E. Savage 1793. Savage used the same head in his *Washington Family* of 1789-96 (NG Washington, 1940.1.2; engraved E. Savage 1798; illus. Miles 1999, p.48).

1793 Miniature by John Ramage, in uniform. Metropolitan Museum of Art, New York (illus. *Washington* 1931, f.p.140). Engraved H.H. Houston c.1796.

1793 Painting by John Trumbull, half length. Yale University AG (illus. *Washington* 1931, f.p.172).

1794 Painting by William Williams, half length with the regalia and jewels of a Master Mason. Alexandria-Washington Lodge, Alexandria, Va. (illus. Miles 1999, p.31). In 1793 Washington's Lodge commissioned Williams to 'Paint him as he is'; the portrait shows a scar on the left cheek, a black mole under the right ear and small-pox scars on his nose and cheeks.

1794 Miniature by Walter Robertson, in uniform. Cincinnati Art Museum (illus. Miles 1999, p.35). Another in the R.W. Norton AG, Shreveport, La. Engraved R. Field 1795 (illus. Wick 1982, p.110).

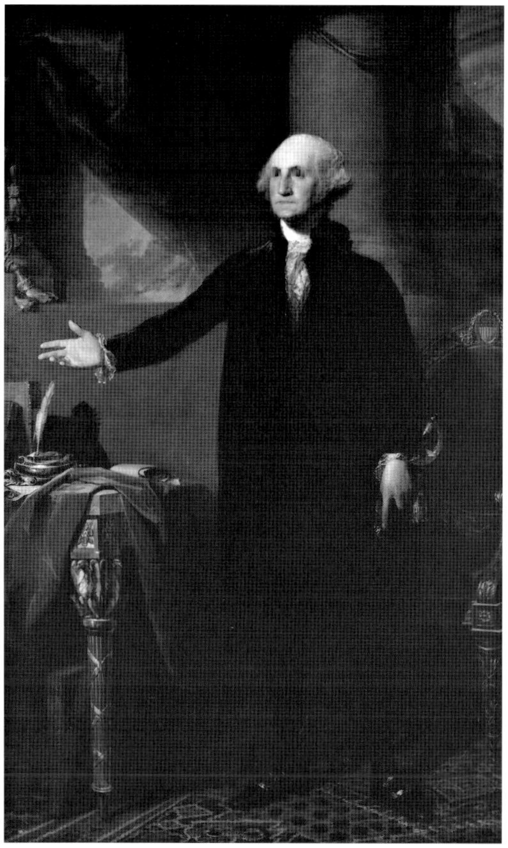

WASHINGTON by Gilbert Stuart 1796 (National Portrait Gallery, Washington)

A miniature version by Robert Field sold Christie's, 20 February 1973, lot 80.

1794 Painting by A.U. Wertmüller, half length. Philadelphia Museum of Art (illus. Miles 1999, p.33).

1795 Painting by Rembrandt Peale, bust length. Historical Society of Pennsylvania, Philadelphia (illus. Peale 1992, p.33; Miles 1999, p.11). Engraved D. Edwin 1800. Peale painted ten copies, the last in 1859 (*Washington* 1931, p.374).

1795 Painting by C.W. Peale, half length. New-York Historical Society (1867.299; illus. Peale 1992, p.33; Miles 1999, p.37).

1795 Painting by Gilbert Stuart, the Vaughan portrait, see under NPG 2041. Two early replicas in the NG Washington (1942.8.27; Miles 1995, pp.201-08) another in the the Frick Collection (18.1.112); first engraved T. Holloway 1798 (Wick 1982, p.59). On 20 April 1795 Stuart listed orders he had received for thirty-nine copies (see *Washington* 1931, pp.227, 250-59).

1796 Painting by Gilbert Stuart, the Athenaeum portrait, see NPG 2041.

1796 Painting by Gilbert Stuart,* the Lansdowne or

'Teapot' portrait, whole-length standing, see under NPG 2041. NPG Washington (2001.13). Autograph replicas in the Pennsylvania Academy of Fine Arts, Philadelphia, and the Brooklyn Museum of Art. First engraved by J. Heath (in London) 1800 (illus. Wick 1982, p.61). The many copies include one in the Lady Lever AG, Port Sunlight, and miniatures by Henry Bone in the Gilbert collection (illus. Coffin & Hofstetter 2000, no.14) and the Holburne Museum, Bath; Bone's preparatory drawings, two dated 1800 and one 1825, in the NPG Bone albums (*Bone* 1999, nos.535-37, fig.160).

c.1796 Painting by Edward Savage, half length in black coat. NG Washington (1960.3.1; illus. Miles 1995, p.159).

1796-97 Pastel by James Sharples, see NPG 174 and NPG 2903.

1798 Crayon drawing by C-B-J-F. de Saint-Mémin, bust length in military coat. J. Carsen Brevoort, Brooklyn, before 1931 (illus. *Washington* 1931, f.p.418). Said to be the last portrait taken from the life.

Posthumous (pre-1845)

'Charles Sumner once remarked that to produce a faithful likeness of George Washington was the noblest project an American sculptor could undertake' (J.S. Ramirez, *American Figurative Sculpture in the Museum of Fine Arts*, Boston, 1986, pp.9-10).

1800 Painting by Gilbert Stuart, the 'Munro-Lenox' portrait, whole length standing, see NPG 2041 and NPG 774. New York Public Library. Replicas were dispatched to the State Houses at Hartford, Conn., and Providence and Newport, R.I. in 1801 (*Washington* 1931, pp.265-69, nos.24-27).

c.1800-10 Marble bust by an unidentified artist. NPG Washington (75.20).

1804 Miniature by R.W. Satchwell, exhibited RA 1804(801).

1806 Painting Gilbert Stuart,* whole length in uniform, standing by white horse, at Dorchester Heights, see under NPG 2041. Museum of Fine Arts, Boston, Mass.

1807 Miniature by Ellen Sharples, exhibited RA 1807(851).

1812 Model of an equestrian statue by John Eckstein, exhibited Philadelphia 1812 (Gunnis 1968, p.139).

1814 Painted wooden statue by William Rush, in civilian dress. Philadelphia Museum of Art, on loan from Independence Hall, Philadelphia (illus., E B Johnston, *Original Portraits of Washington*, 1882, pl.xxviii, f.p.180.

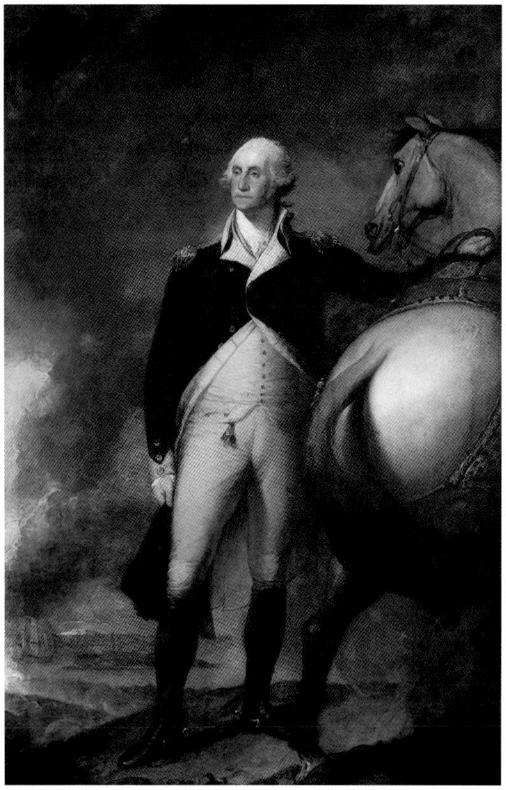

WASHINGTON by Gilbert Stuart 1806 (Museum of Fine Arts, Boston)

1817 Terracotta bust by William Rush, in civilian dress. Valley Forge Museum, Pa. (illus. *William Rush*, Philadelphia, 1937, no.38). Plaster with the New-York Historical Society; a marble copy by J.A. Beck 1856 with the Historical Society of Pennsylvania and a plaster from Beck's marble with the Museum of the Masonic Temple, Philadelphia.

1817-21 Marble statue by Antonio Canova, seated, as a Roman senator. Commissioned by the State of North Carolina for Raleigh. Delivered 1821 and destroyed by fire 1831. The head derived from the bust by Ceracchi (see 1791-95). Six plaster studies remain in the Gipsoteca Canoviana, Possagno (illus. *Canova, opera completa*, 1976, nos.301-06).

1819 Bust by J.B.A. Binon, based on Stuart's portraits (Whitley 1932, pp.162-63).

1820 Sketch for a National Monument by J.C. Rossi, exhibited RA 1820(1024).

1823 Painting by Rembrandt Peale, the 'Pater Patriae' or 'Porthole' portrait, half length to left. Capitol, Washington DC (illus. *Peale* 1992, pl.18), purchased in 1832 on the centenary of Washington's birth. Peale made 'at least seventy-nine copies of this type of head with considerable variation in the accessories' (*Washington* 1931, pp.375-81).

1823 Marble bust by J.C. Herrmann. Dresden, Staatliche Kunstsammlungen (illus. *The Splendor of Dresden*, NG Washington, 1979, p.241). Derived from the head by Canova.

c.1825? Bust by D.A. Olivieri (Gunnis 1968, p.283, citing the Thomas Robson sale of 1835, presumably the Thomas Robinson sale, Southgate, 8-9 October 1835).

1826 Marble monument by Francis Chantrey, standing, a scroll in his right hand. State House, Boston, Mass. (*Chantrey* 1994, no.102a). Exhibited RA 1826(1071). Commissioned by the Washington Monument Association 1819, and intended to furnish a 'a simple manly dignified statue' in contrast to Canova's 'Roman' monument. A plaster model in the Ashmolean Museum, Oxford (Penny 1992, III, no.662; *Chantrey* 1847, no.11).

1832-40 Marble statue by Horatio Greenough, whole-length seated, as Zeus Olympus. NPG Washington (W. Craven, *AQ*, XXVI, 1963, pp.429-38). Originally placed in the Capitol in 1840, placed outside the Capitol 1843 and transferred to the Smithsonian 1908. A marble bust of in the Museum of Fine Arts, Boston, Mass. (95.1385).

1834 Sketch for a statue by J.C. Rossi, exhibited RA 1834(1047).

1838-44 Marble bust by Hiram Powers, derived from the bust by Houdon. Mount Vernon Ladies' Association. Thirty-six commissions for replicas have been listed (Wunder 1991, II, pp. 207-12, 234).

WATSON, Richard 1737-1816

Prelate and scientist; Fellow of Trinity College, Cambridge, 1760; professor of chemistry at Cambridge 1764-71; FRS 1769; his papers were collected as *Chemical Essays* 1781-86; regius professor of divinity at Cambridge; 1771-87; Bishop of Llandaff 1782, a diocese he visited triennially; 'his versatility and power of application were remarkable; what he did he did well up to a certain point, then turned to something else' (*DNB*).

1075 see Groups, *Men of Science living in 1807-08* by JOHN GILBERT, FREDERICK SKILL and WILLIAM & ELIZABETH WALKER 1858-62

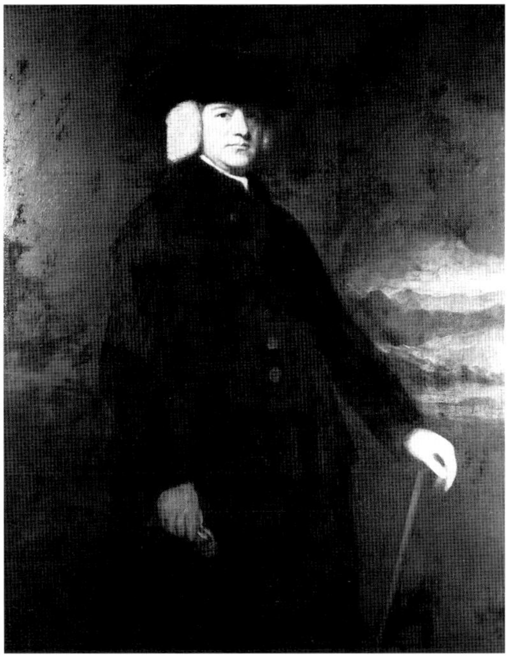

WATSON by George Romney 1787-88 (Trinity College, Cambridge)

ICONOGRAPHY

1769 Painting by Joshua Reynolds, three-quarter length standing in black gown, in his laboratory. National Museum, Havana (Mannings 2000, no.1844). Exhibited NPE 1867(836) lent C. Knight Watson. Offered to the NPG in 1930.

1787-88 Painting by George Romney,*three-quarter length standing as Bishop in civilian dress with hat. Trinity College, Cambridge (Ward & Roberts 1904, II, pp.167-68). 'The delightful conversational talents of this learned divine must have given ... an impulse to the genius of the painter; for certainly a finer portrait was never painted' (Romney 1830, p.199). See Groups NPG 1075. Engraved J. Jones 1793 and 1794, J. Hopwood 1804, H. Meyer 1809, H.R. Cook 1810, W. Holl 1816, W.T. Fry 1817 and F. Engleheart 1823. Version sold Sotheby's, 25 February 1970, lot 110.

1787 Caricature etching by J. Sayers, *Eloquence founded on chemical principles*, whole length in rochet and chimere (George 7147).

1798 Engraving by J. Chapman, bust-length oval in rochet and chimere.

Undated Pastel by James Sharples, bust length. Bristol CMAG (*Cat. of the Sharples Coll.*, Bristol, 1910, no.42).

DOUBTFUL PORTRAIT

Painting attributed to L.F. Abbott, sold Christie's, 20 November 1936, lot 116.

WATSON-WENTWORTH, Charles, see ROCKINGHAM

WATT, James 1736-1819

Engineer, b. Greenock; instrument maker and land surveyor based in Glasgow, increasingly devoted to the improvement of the steam engine; patented the separate condenser 1769; entered into partnership with Matthew Boulton at the Soho Manufactory in Birmingham 1774, where improved steam engines were produced from 1775, and constantly developed; a prominent member of the Birmingham Lunar Society; FRS 1785; Hon LL.D Glasgow 1806.

'I want learning from you of various kinds, and would give you in exchange chearfulness, which by some parts of your letter, you seem to want' (Erasmus Darwin, 1790).

'one of the most complete specimens of the melancholic temperament. His head was generally bent forward or leaning on his hand in meditation, his shoulders stooping and his chest falling in; his limbs lank and unmuscular, and his complexion sallow. ... [His eye and countenance] were calm, as if patiently investigating, or quietly contemplating his object. His utterance was slow and unimpassioned, deep and low in tone, with a broad Scottish accent; his manners gentle, modest and unassuming' (Mary Schimmelpenninck, 1858).

Abbreviations

Muirhead 1858: J.P. Muirhead, *The Life of James Watt*, 1858

Watt 1927: H.W. Dickinson & R. Jenkins, *James Watt and the Steam Engine*, 1927, pp.81-89

186A CARL FREDRIK VON BREDA 1792

Canvas 127 x 102 (50 x 40) lined; signed above table: *Breda p./1792.*; retouchings in the upper right area and in the coat around the waist where there is also some abrasion.

Blue-grey eyes, greying hair, wearing a black coat and seated in a red chair; on the table lies a drawing of a double-acting rotative steam engine, resembling the Watt patent specification of 1769.

Collections: Matthew Piers Watt Boulton of Soho, Birmingham (grandson of Watt's business partner, Matthew Boulton), from whom stolen by his subagent Edward Price; purchased by the NPG from Thomas Scott in 1859 (as NPG 87); when the deception was discovered the portrait was presented to the Gallery by the proper owner, Matthew Piers Watt Boulton, 1865.

Engravings: S.W. Reynolds 1796; anon. (pub. Hodgson, London); E. Mackenzie 1806 (half length).

Exhibitions: *Watt Centenary*, Science Museum, 1919-20; *Regency Portraits*, Kenwood, 1986; *Apples to Atoms* 1986-87; *Treasures* 1995-96(19).

Reference: *Watt* 1927, pp.81-82.

NPG 186A is an autograph replica of the earliest known portrait of Watt. On 7 June 1792 the engineer John Rennie had asked Matthew Boulton and his partner James Watt to sit for their portraits to Mr [Mather] Brown of Cavendish Square in London; Watt replied from Birmingham (9 June) 'I wish you to come this way ... and we can talk about the portrait to which I am rather averse as I think it an honour I do not merit and that my countenance cannot be worth procuring'.[1] In the event Breda painted them both that year in Birmingham (where he also painted William Withering), and mezzotints of his two portraits by S.W. Reynolds were published in December 1796. Mrs Schimmelpenninck recorded that Watt had instructed 'a celebrated Swedish artist', presumably Breda, that rat's whiskers made 'the most pliant and elastic painting-brush'.[2] The portrait of Watt is not without fault, the sitter's raised right arm being unfortunate.

The portrait commissioned by Rennie is now in the Institution of Mechanical Engineers, London,[3] and another signed and dated version is in the Science Museum, London.[4] Later copies were made by a Miss Binnie (Institution of Civil Engineers, London) and by W. Bright Morris 1905, formerly in Andrew Carnegie's collection, and now belonging to the Heriot-Watt University, Edinburgh.

1 Letters cited in *Watt* 1927, p.81.
2 Schimmelpenninck 1858, I, p.41.
3 Sold by Rennie's descendants Christie's 27 March 1936, lot 84; it had previously been offered for sale in 1881 by Mrs M.A. Rennie (Goldsmith, 25-26 October 1881, lot 163, when bought by Theodore Martin, for whom see NPG 663 below) but it had returned to George Banks Rennie in 1907.
4 Sold Bukowski's, Stockholm, 7 April 1987, lot 14, with a pendant portrait of Boulton (now Birmingham MAG).

663 HENRY HOWARD c.1797

Bevelled mahogany panel 19 x 15 x 0.5 (7½ x 6 x ⅛) some scratches across his left shoulder, the edges chipped and abraded.

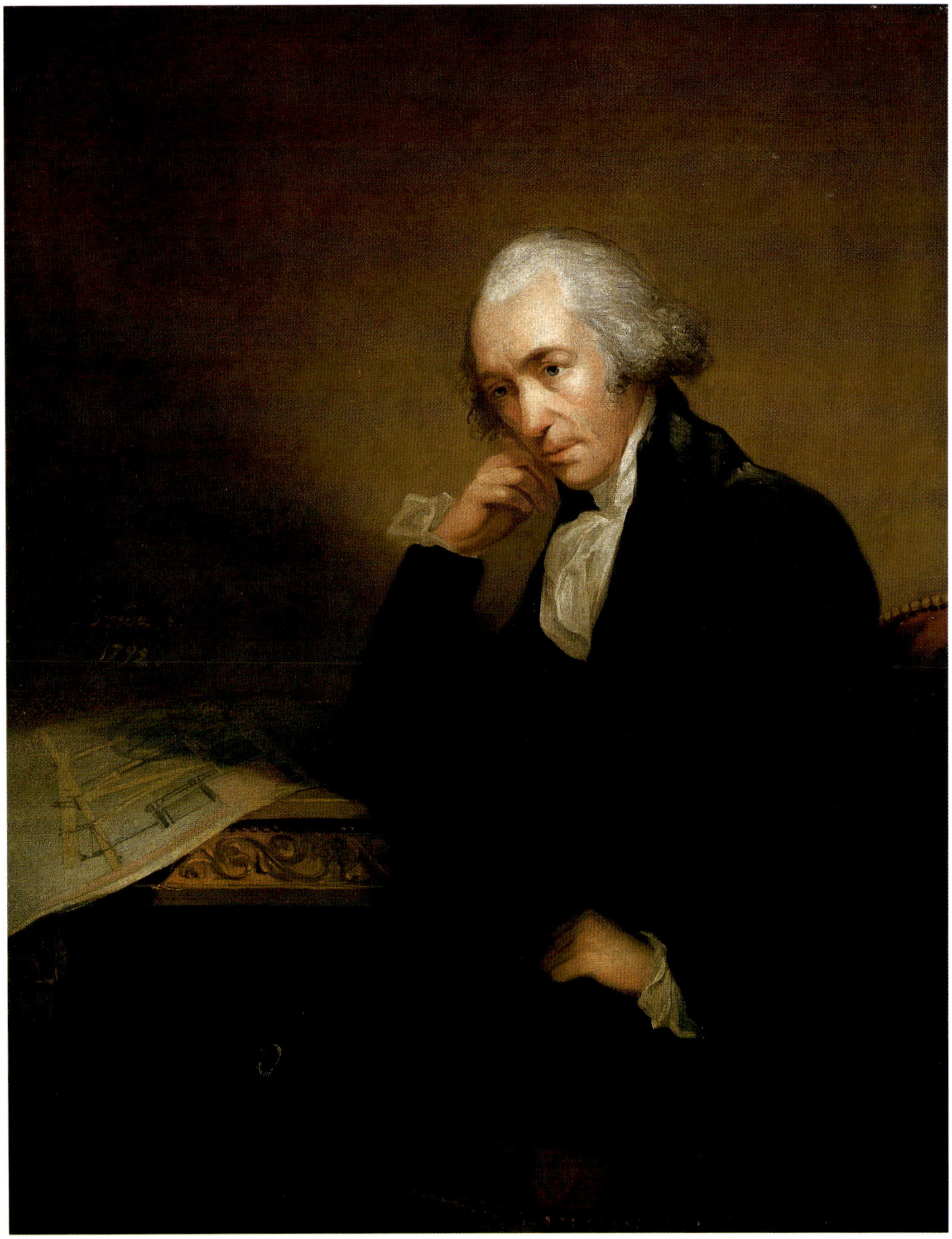

WATT NPG *186A*

Grey eyes, grey wig, plain brown coat, black waist-coat; grey-green background.

Collections: Said to have belonged to John Flaxman (see below);[1] bt. by Sir Theodore Martin at an unidentified Christie's sale through Richard Lane (a mixed lot, 'five heads various'),[2] and presented by him 1882.

Exhibitions: *Watt Centenary*, Science Museum, 1919-20; *Watt Bicentenary*, Science Museum, London, 1936(3); *Chantrey*, NPG, Sheffield, 1981.

Reference: *Watt* 1927, pp.85, 88.[3]

NPG 663 is one of four small bust-length portraits on panel by Howard given to the NPG by Martin in 1882-83, the others being of William Hayley (NPG 662), John Flaxman (NPG 674) and Mrs Anne Flaxman (NPG 675).[4] All, it appears, belonged to John Flaxman,

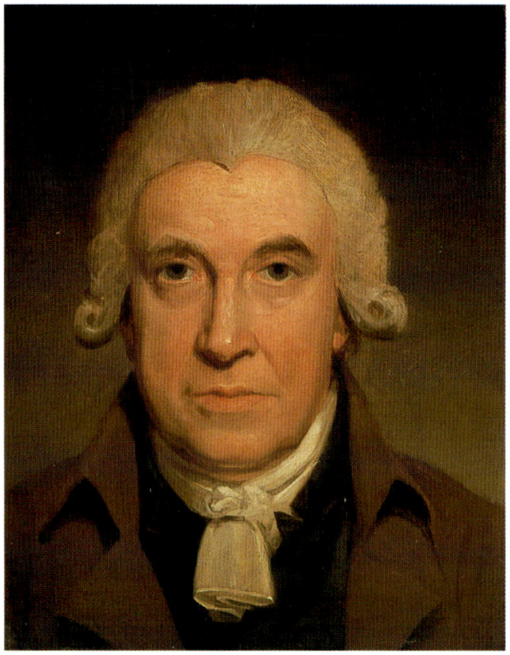

WATT NPG *663*

who had first met the painter in Rome in 1792-94. Martin told Scharf that NPG 662 and NPG 663 had 'belonged to Flaxman & hung on his walls till his death, along with the fine portraits of himself [NPG 674] by Howard, which you have seen in my house'.[5]

All four portraits may be dated c.1797. Howard exhibited a portrait of Flaxman at the RA that year and his comparable bust-length panel of John Constable is dated 1797;[6] in 1882 Scharf described NPG 663 as painted before the artist's election as RA in 1808.[7]

1 Not identifiable in the sales of Flaxman's adopted daughter, Maria Denman, in 1862 and 1876.
2 Letter from Martin to Scharf, 19 August 1882 (NPG archive).
3 Erroneously described as dateable c.1860 (thirteen years after Howard's death), and as based on the Nicholson etching of 1819.
4 See Walker, *Regency*, I, pp.187, 189, 241, II, pls.432, 440, 553.
5 Letter of 19 August 1882 (NPG archive).
6 Exhibited *Constable*, Tate Gallery, 1976(1).
7 NPG *25th Annual Report 1882*, pp.4-5.

183 PETER ROUW 1802

Wax profile portrait 7 (2¾) high, set on a dark glass ground 9.5 (3¾) diameter; the cravat and the queue restored 1902; cleaned 1981; incised on the truncation *P. Rouw/Lo.. 1802*; labels formerly verso: *A Portrait of/ James Watt Eq../ Soho/ Peter Rouw/ Sculptor/ Portland R../ London* and: *A Portrait of/ J. Watt Esqr/ by Peter Rouw/ Sculptor/ Portland Road/ London/ 1802*.

Collections: Purchased from Samuel Pope 1864.

Exhibition: *Regency Portraits*, Kenwood, 1986.

Similar medallions dated 1803 are in the Victoria and Albert Museum (A.27.1941), the Fitzwilliam Muse-

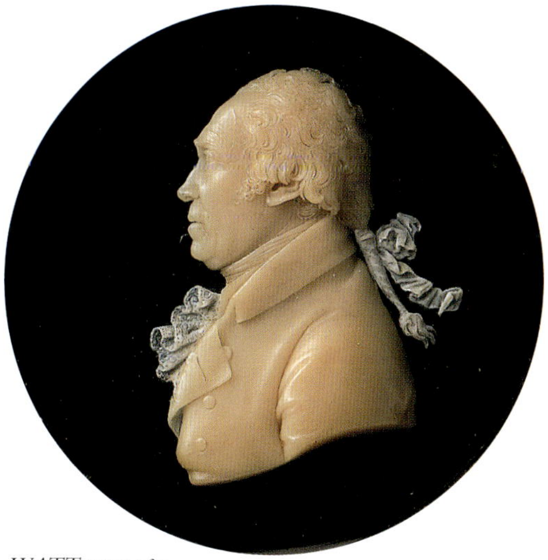

WATT NPG *183*

um, Cambridge (CM.147.1985) and the Birmingham Museum and Art Gallery.[1]

1 See *Watt* 1927, p.83. Another dated 1804 was lent by Mrs Bate to the *Watt Bicentenary*, Science Museum, London, 1936(14).

1075 see Groups, *Men of Science living in 1807-08* by JOHN GILBERT, FREDERICK SKILL and WILLIAM & ELIZABETH WALKER 1858-62

316A(191) FRANCIS CHANTREY c.1814

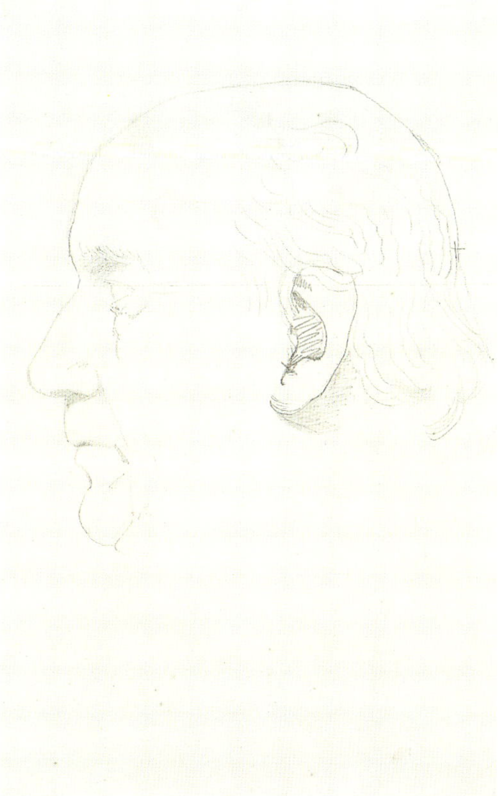

WATT NPG *316A(191)*

Pencil on paper 42 x 27.5 (16½ x 10¾)

Collections: Chantrey's executor George Jones RA, by whose widow presented 1871.

Reference: Walker *Regency*, I, pp.624-25, 629-30.

For Chantrey's busts and monument, see below, 1814-43 and 1824-38. Another drawing of Watt by Chantrey from Doldowlod[1] was sold Sotheby's, 20 March 2003, lot 64.

1 Steegman, II, p.210, no.18.

ICONOGRAPHY

The five statues of Watt by Chantrey, erected by 1838, 'excited the disapprobation of some narrow-minded beings ... [for whom] warriors, and magistrates, and statesmen ... have alone a right to statues' (D.F.J. Arago, *Life of Watt*, 1839, p.90). Less than thirty years later, above the entrance to the Royal Museum of Scotland, the bust of Watt appeared alongside those of Queen Victoria, Prince Albert, Charles Darwin, Isaac Newton and Michelangelo.

A brief survey of Watt's iconography appeared in J.L. Caw, *Scottish Portraits*, 1903, II, pp.75-76.

1792 Painting by C.F. von Breda, see NPG 186A.

c.1797 Painting by Henry Howard, see NPG 663.

1801 Painting by William Beechey,* half-length seated. Sotheby's, 20 March 2003, lot 43 from Doldowlod (Steegman, II, p.209, no.6). Exhibited RA 1802(101). See Groups NPG 1075. Engraved C. Picart 1809;* J. Thomson 1820; T. Wright 1830; C.E. Wagstaff 1833.

In 1809 Watt wrote that 'There is no good portrait of me except that painted by Sir William Beechey, still in his possession, and a copy of it by himself in Mr Tuffen's collection which is more like than the original I having sate again for it' (Muirhead 1858, p.531); Tuffen's replica was sold to Blairman in 1928 by Turner of Godstone, Surrey. A copy by John Partridge is in the Scottish NPG (PG 2612; Muirhead 1858, p.532), lithographed by Schenck & McFarlane 1856 when in the collection of Robert Napier, Glasgow; a copy by A. Wivell 1856 is in the Science Museum.

Copies of varying quality are in the Royal Society, Edinburgh (presented by Watt's son in 1828); the National Maritime Museum (BHC 3084, attributed to Beechey), the Scottish NPG (PG 636) and Birmingham MAG (6'10). See also the enamel version by Henry Bone 1804 below.

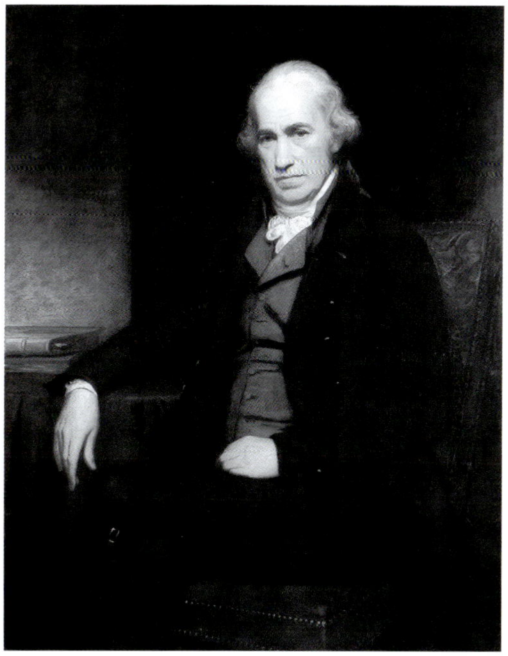

WATT by William Beechey 1801 (Sotheby's)

1802 Medallion by Peter Rouw, see NPG 183.

1804 Enamel by Henry Bone, the Beechey composition extended to three-quarter length. Sotheby's, 20 March 2003, lot 134 from Doldowlod (Steegman, II, p.210, no.19). Exhibited RA 1804(358). Preparatory drawing, inscribed *Mr Watt for Mrs Watt* and dated *8 May 1803*, in the NPG Bone albums (*Bone* 1999, no.538).

c.1805 Pastel by L. de Longastre, half length. By descent from Watt's cousin Robert Muirhead to B.C.L. Whitehead in 1904 (illus. Caw 1903, II, pl.xc). Another was given to Matthew Boulton (Muirhead 1858, pp.531-32).

A pastel by Longastre dated 1805 of Watt's son, James Watt (1769-1848), was at Doldowlod (Steegman, II, p.210, no.17). Bust length pastel portraits of Watt and his wife by 'L. de Large' were sold Bonham's, 16 February 1977, lot 206 (not seen).

1807 Bust by Peter Turnerelli, exhibited RA 1808(865). Commissioned by the sitter; two plasters, one dated 1807, are in the Watt Workshop in the Science Museum, London (*Chantrey* 1994, p.54).

1809 Black chalk drawing by John Henning, profile bust. Scottish NPG (PG 294; illus. *Henning* 1977, n.p.). Made for Lord Jeffrey, exhibited ASA Edinburgh 1810. A small replica formerly in the Watt Memorial Library, Greenock, engraved R. Bell 1856 (G. Williamson, *Memorials of James Watt*,

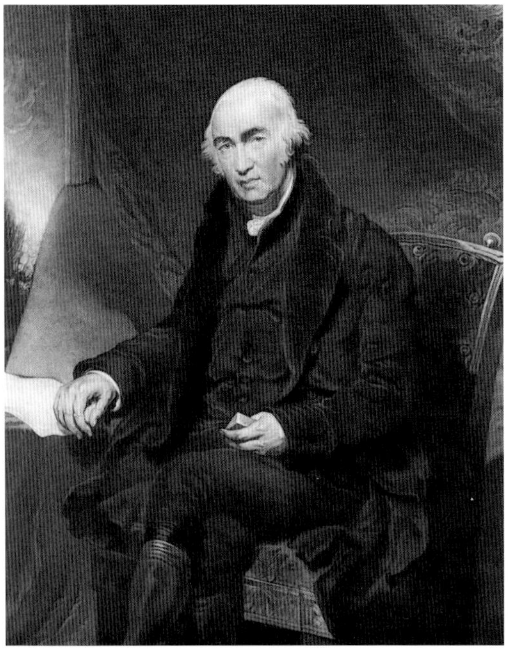

WATT C. Turner after Thomas Lawrence c.1812 (NPG D 18005)

1856). A related porcelain medallion by Henning in the Scottish NPG (PG 419; illus. *Henning* 1977, n.p.), a glass paste profile dated 1809 in the Victoria and Albert Museum (414.1351.1885; illus. Rackham 1930, pl.71).

c.1812 Painting by Thomas Lawrence, three-quarter length seated. Private collection (Garlick 1989, no.797). Exhibited RA 1813(222); Liverpool 1813(31). Engraved C. Turner 1815;* J. Thomson 1815; Blanchard c.1840. A contemporary copy was lent by H.W. Dickinson to the *Watt Bicentenary*, Science Museum, 1936(4), and a small copy by W. Tilbury dated 1828 was sold Sotheby's, 20 December 1961, lot 123; see also 1817–19 J.G. Gilbert below.

1814–43 Marble busts by Francis Chantrey (see *Chantrey* 1994, pp.52–54). The original, probably that exhibited RA 1815(816), remains untraced; a second version, from Doldowlod, dated 1816, is currently on loan to the NPG, ex Sotheby's, 20 March 2003, lot 57 (*Chantrey* 1994, no.36). Engraved S.W. Reynolds 1825, W.C. Edwards, and E. Finden 1839, the latter 'of all the engravings of my father, that by which [he] wished his image should be conveyed to posterity' (Muirhead 1858, p.534). Watt and Chantrey shared an interest in the technology of mechanical carving aids; Watt's 'carving machine' for the production of reduced replicas is preserved in the Science Museum, London.

Replicas include: Glasgow AG 1816; Greenock, Watt College, 1822 (*Chantrey* 1994, no.136b); Birmingham MAG (P80'83) dated 1841 (*Chantrey* 1994, no.301b, as probably commissioned for Lord Brougham in 1839). A cast iron version dated 1818 was formerly in the Darby Engine House, Ebbw Vale, Gwent.

Versions of the bust with cut away shoulders are in the Graves AG, Sheffield (marble), the Scottish NPG (PG 1186) and with Julius S. Held (bronze).

Chantrey's ledgers record payment in January 1821 for 44 casts; examples are in Westminster Abbey (presented by the Institution of Mechanical Engineers 1960); the Science Museum; the Scottish NPG (PG 347), the Ashmolean Museum (Penny 1992, III, no.776) and Birmingham MAG (P2626'85 and P2628'85); one was sent in 1820 to Walter Scott at Abbotsford.

By 1838 Chantrey was complaining that the bust 'was pirated by Italians; and England and Scotland, and even the Colonies, were supplied with unpermitted and bad casts, to the extent of thousands' (Muirhead 1858, p.535).

Of three replicas made by Chantrey's assistant James Heffernan, one is with the Royal Society, London (presented in 1843), and another in the Institut de France, Paris. In 1835 Chantrey had been commissioned to supply a bust to the Institut de France, but it was sold to Campbell in 1840 (*Chantrey* 1994, no.270b). H.C. Fehr made a copy of the bust for the Institution of Civil Engineers in 1896.

Reduced copies in ivory were made by Benjamin Cheverton, using a device similar to Watt's 'carving machine'. A sepia drawing by George Dawe after Chantrey's bust is in the Scottish NPG (PG 126) with another unattributed drawing (PG 1763).

The bust also served for Chantrey's Watt monument, see 1824–38 below, and see NPG 316A(191).

1815 Painting by Henry Raeburn,* bust length. Huntington Art Collections, San Marino, Calif. (63.38; *Huntington* 2001, no.69). Watt sat to Raeburn in Edinburgh in November 1815 and wrote that 'Raeburn has painted a head of me which, though it has not come up to my ideas of my own face, is more comformable to them than any of the others', and he wrote later that it 'is thought like, only it frowns too much'. A copy was made for John Rennie (Muirhead 1858, p.533).

1816 On 31 July 1816 Watt agreed, at John Rennie's instigation, to sit to Archibald Skirving for a pastel portrait (J.P. Muirhead, *Mechanical Inventions of James Watt*, 1854, II, pp.366–7).

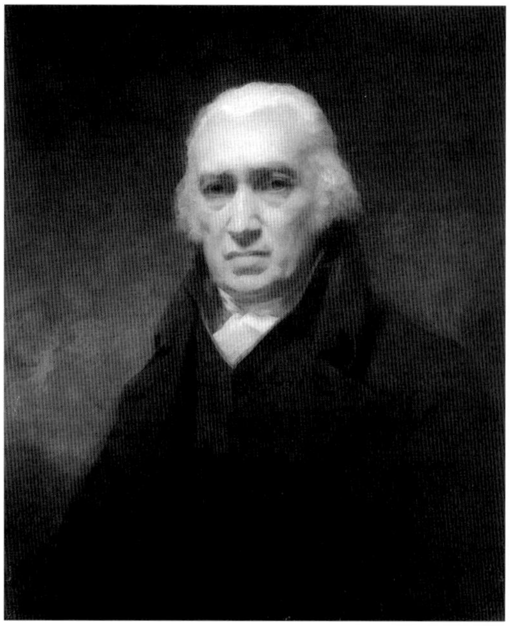

WATT by Henry Raeburn 1815 (Huntington Art Collections, San Marino, California)

1817–19 Painting by J.G. Gilbert, bust length. Hunterian Museum, Glasgow (Muirhead 1858, p.533; Watt 1927, p.85, as c.1818; exhibited *Glasgow Historical Portraits*, 1956, no.12, as 1819). Based, according to the artist, on Chantrey's bust and Lawrence's portrait. A copy commissioned by the sitter's wife was at Doldowlod (Steegman, II, p.209, no.7 as c.1817) and another attributed to Gilbert was sold American Art Association, New York, 8 April 1916.

1818 Drawing by John Jackson, bust length. exhibited RA 1819(529); Watt thought it looked 'peevish' (Muirhead 1858, p.534). Jackson also sketched Chantrey's bust (*Watt* 1927, p.85).

Posthumous

1819 Etching by W. Nicholson, half-length seated, a drawing of a steam engine behind him. An unconvincing likeness (*Watt* 1927, p.85).

1819 Medals struck on the death of Watt by H. Kirkwood for the Watt Club, Greenock; attributed to J. Marrian, and by George Mills, exhibited RA 1821, no.1052 (Brown 1980, nos.981–83).

1824 Monument by Francis Chantrey, whole-length seated holding plan across his knees, 'meditating on the extraordinary power which man wields so easily and profitably'; standing on a base bearing Watt's crest (granted to Watt's son in 1826), a club of Hercules crossed with the caduceus of Mercury (power and ingenuity). St Mary's Church, Handsworth,

Birmingham; commissioned by the sitter's son (*Chantrey* 1994, no.124a; Whinney 1964, pls.182-83; L. Jordanova, *Defining Features*, NPG, 2000, p.65). See Groups NPG 1075. Exhibited RA 1824(1010). Of the plaster model given to Oxford in 1844 only the head and shoulders survive (Ashmolean Museum, Oxford; Penny 1992, III, no.663). The monument was also reproduced on the Chantrey medal by William Wyon of 1846 (Brown 1987, no.2227) and engraved H. Adlard and H. Moses.

There were four later monuments, showing detailed differences; they are more heavily draped; the Westminster and Glasgow (George Square) monuments are over life size, the others on the scale of life:

1830 Glasgow, Hunterian Museum, commissioned by the sitter's son (Chantrey 1994, no.192a). Close variant of the Handsworth monument. The statue is shown in the painting by William Stewart, *Interior of the first Hunterian Museum* (Hunterian AG, Glasgow).

1830 Glasgow, George Square, bronze (*Chantrey* 1994, no.194a). Version of the Westminster statue.

1832 The Westminster Abbey monument,* with drapery covering shoulders and legs. Removed from the Abbey to St Paul's, 1960, and currently Scottish NPG (PGL 370), before going to the Heriot-Watt University, Edinburgh (*Chantrey* 1994, no.193a). Lord Brougham, who composed the original inscription ('... *increased the power of man / and rose to an eminent place* ...'), considered it admirably presented Watt's features 'at once deeply meditative and calmly placid, but betokening power rather than delicacy and refinement' (Caw 1903, II, p.76).

1838 Greenock, Watt Memorial Library (*Chantrey* 1994, no.195a). Commissioned by the citizens of Greenock. Lithographed A. Haenisch and McFarlane. A variant of the Westminster statue, the right leg visible below the knee.

The Chantrey head and monument became a standard source for subsequent images of Watt: marble statuette by William Scoular 1839 (Glasgow AG; S.149), exhibited RA 1840(1169); bronze statue by Peter Slater 1852-54 in Chambers Street, Edinburgh; bronze statue by William Theed 1857 in Piccadilly, Manchester; anon. medal, with motto *ingenio et labore* and crest (Brown 1980, no.984).

1825-84 Watt medals include those by W. Bain, exhibited RA 1825(959), 1828(1098) and 1846(1360); A.J. Stothard, exhibited RA 1826(980); W. Hollins, exhibited Birmingham SA 1827(88); William Wyon, exhibited RA 1836(1041); André Gallé 1839; P-J. David d'Angers 1845; J.S. Wyon,

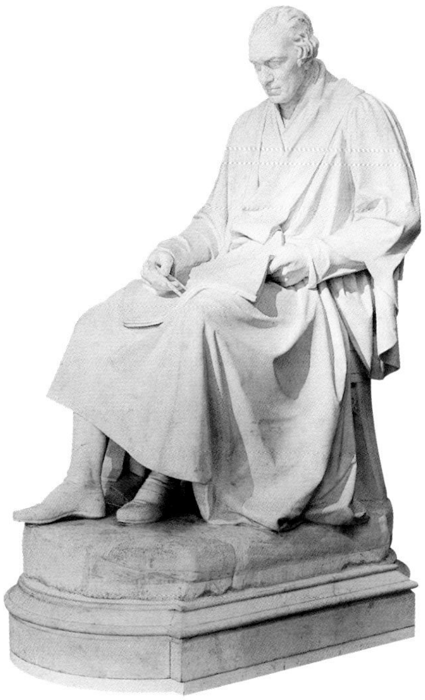

WATT by Francis Chantrey 1832 (Heriot-Watt University, Edinburgh)

exhibited RA 1855(696) and 1858, no.1112 (adapted by the Institution of Civil Engineers for the Watt medal); Joseph Moore 1871 (with Matthew Boulton); Neil Macphail 1871 (for the Scottish Institution of Engineers and Shipbuilders); Allan Wyon 1884 for McGill University, Montreal (see Eidlitz 1928, nos.20, 22, 23, 27, 25, 30, 34, 37; Brown 1987, nos.1261, 985, 1329, 2922, 2923).

Later statues of Watt include those by Alexander Munro 1860 (Oxford Museum of the History of Science; illus. Read 1982, fig.302) and 1868 (Chamberlain Square, Birmingham; a derivative bust in Birmingham MAG (P2631'85); H.C. Fehr 1898 (Watt Memorial School, Greenock; exhibited RA 1899, no.1882; a duplicate in the City Square, Leeds); by William Bloye 1956, with Boulton and Murdoch (Birmingham, Broad Street; illus. J. Bennett, *Discovering Statues, Central and Northern England*, 1968, p.29).

A bust by J.S. Rhind 1859 is on the facade of the Royal Museum of Scotland, Edinburgh, and a marble bust by D.W. Stevenson 1888 on the Wallace Monument, Stirling.

DOUBTFUL PORTRAITS

Paintings attributed to Raeburn, half-length oval of an old man (with William Paterson 1943), and a three-quarter length seated with a model of a steam engine (with Mrs Fredericke 1941).

WEDGWOOD, Josiah 1730-95

Potter and industrialist; founded the Etruria works at Burslem, Staffs., in 1769, taking Thomas Bentley as his business partner; the Wedgwood vases of 1768 were followed by the Frog service for Catherine II of Russia 1773-74 and jasperware 1775; an active promoter of inland waterways and a member of the Lunar Society; FRS 1783; as a consequence of smallpox, his right leg was amputated in 1769.

Abbreviation

Meteyard 1865: E. Meteyard, *The Life and Works of Wedgwood*, 2 vols., 1865

1948 after WILLIAM HACKWOOD [1782]

Cast from original Wedgwood mould, white jasper on black dip 13.3 x 10.4 (5¼ x 4⅛), the figure 8 (3⅛) high; stamped verso: *WEDGWOOD WEDGWOOD* and *BB599*.

Collections: Presented by Josiah Wedgwood & Sons 1922.

Exhibition: *Regency Portraits*, Kenwood, 1986.

A cast made in 1922. Original examples are in the Wedgwood Museum, Barlaston, and the Stoke-on-Trent Museum (Reilly 1973, pp.333-34).

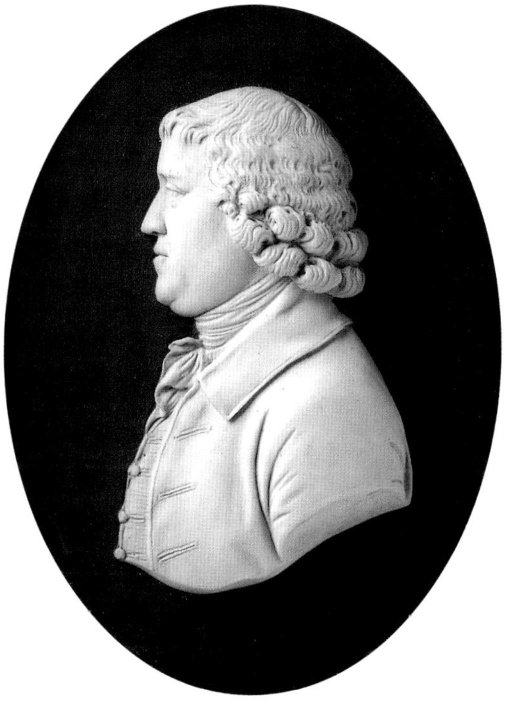

WEDGWOOD NPG *1948*

ICONOGRAPHY

1773-74 Wedgwood medallion modelled by Joachim Smith (illus. Reilly 1973, p.333).

c.1778 Wedgwood medallion attributed to William Hackwood, *all'antica* (illus. Reilly 1973, p.333).

1780 Painting in enamel on earthenware by George Stubbs,* half-length oval, head turned to front, light brown jacket. Wedgwood Museum, Barlaston. Engraved G.T. Stubbs 1795; W. Holl as a rectangle with a pot on a table to the left. Companion piece of Mrs Sarah Wedgwood.

1780 Painting by George Stubbs, seated, wearing a lilac suit and black hat, with his wife and seven children. Wedgwood Museum, Barlaston (illus. A. Burton, *Josiah Wedgwood*, 1976, f.p.137).

1782 Wedgwood medallion modelled by William Hackwood, see NPG 1948.

1782 Painting by Joshua Reynolds,* half length. Wedgwood Museum, Barlaston (Mannings 2000, no.1850). Engraved W. Flaxman 1783; P. Condé 1796 (*copied by Humphreys from a Picture painted by Sir Joshua Reynolds in the possession of Mr Byerley*); later plates include those by S.W. Reynolds and J.T. Wedgwood 1841. The head resembles that painted by Stubbs in 1780. A copy by John Rising sold Christie's, 2 May 1818, lot 86; a bust-length copy at Down House lent by the Darwin Heirlooms Trust (illus. *English Heritage, Collections Review*, II, 1999, p.36).

Posthumous

1803 Marble bust by John Flaxman. St Peter ad Vincula, Stoke-on-Trent (illus. Meteyard 1865, II, p.611). Derivations include a marble roundel and a bust by Arnold Austin c.1940 (Wedgwood Museum, Barlaston; illus. R. Reilly, *Wedgwood* 1989, II, pp.13, 465).

1860 Bronze statue by Edward Davis. Wedgwood Museum, Barlaston.

1864 Marble bust by G.G. Fontana, with cloak. Walker AG, Liverpool (7611). Exhibited RA 1862(1045). After the bust by Flaxman and made for Joseph Mayer (Stubbs's biographer).

1909 Bust by Albert Hodge. Victoria and Albert Museum, London, west façade.

DOUBTFUL PORTRAIT

Miniature, signed by Henry Spicer, sold Christie's, 31 March 1981, lot 70 (from the collection of Robert Bayne-Powell).

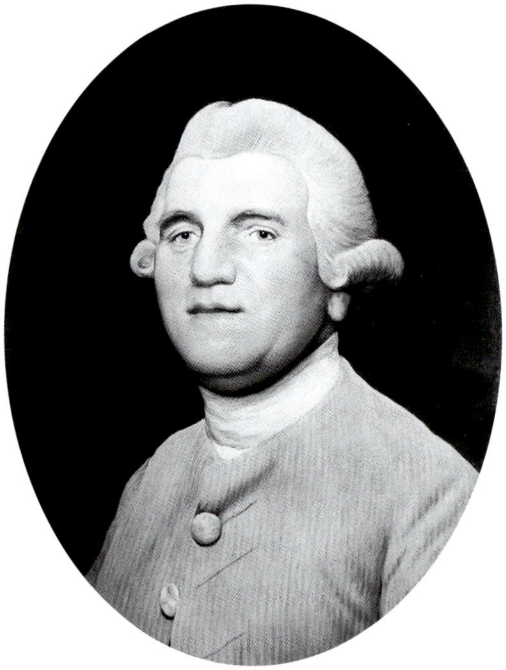

WEDGWOOD by George Stubbs 1780 (Wedgwood Museum, Barlaston)

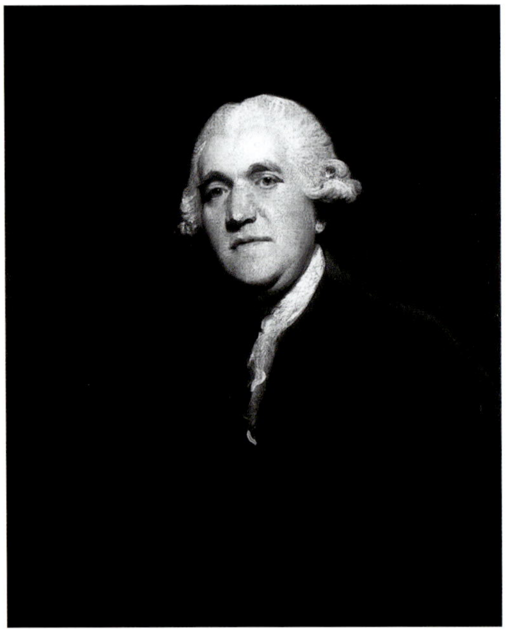

WEDGWOOD by Joshua Reynolds 1782 (Wedgwood Museum, Barlaston)

WHEATLEY, Francis 1747-1801

Painter; trained at Shipley's Academy and RA schools; exhibited SA 1765-77, 1783 and a director in 1774; exhibited RA 1778-1801; ARA 1790, RA 1791; in Dublin, to escape creditors 1779-83; his *Cries of London* 1793-95 achieved considerable popularity through engraving.

'a very personable man, fond of dress, and polite in his manners, which makes him a great favourite with the ladies' (*GM*, 1801).

5037 WILLIAM HAMILTON c.1785

Pencil and watercolour on paper 20.3 x 17.5 (8 x 6⅞) oval; rather faded, with some rubbing round the mouth and eyebrows; signed and inscribed verso: *Portrait of/ Francis Wheatley Esq/ Drawn by/ WHamilton Esqr RA*

Powdered hair, wearing a light blue coat.

Collections: Christie's, 4 March 1975, lot 42, bt. Baskett & Day, from whom purchased 1975.

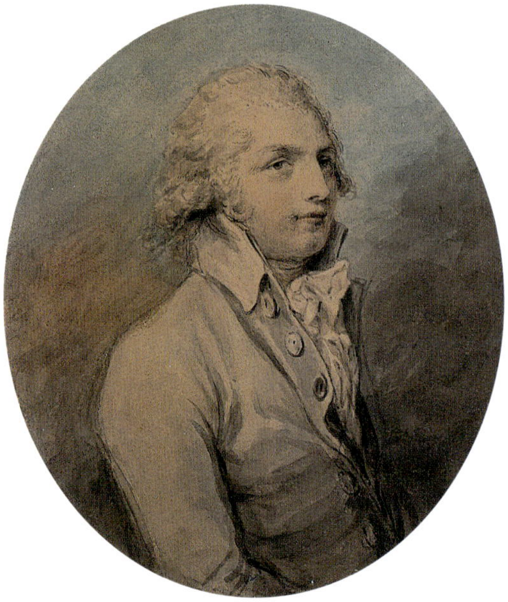

WHEATLEY NPG *5037*

Hamilton and Wheatley were almost exact contemporaries and their work developed along similar lines.

ICONOGRAPHY

c.1785 Drawing by William Hamilton, see NPG 5037.

1793 Drawing by George Dance,* profile bust, dated 17 February 1793. Royal Academy. Engraved W. Daniell 1809 (*Dance Plates*); tracing by Daniell in the Yale Center for British Art (B1975.4.1128).

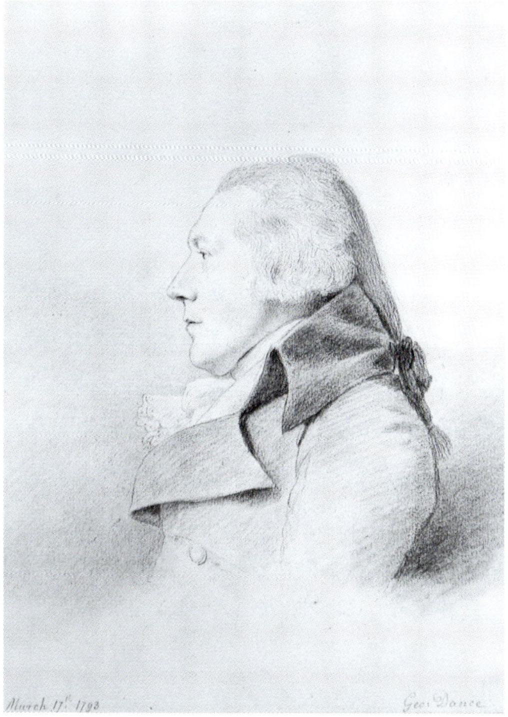

WHEATLEY by George Dance 1793 (Royal Academy of Arts, London)

1795 Painting by Henry Singleton,* *President and Members of the Royal Academy*, see Comparative Groups.

1802 Portrait by Mrs Francis Wheatley, exhibited RA 1802(740) 'Portrait from memory, the late F. Wheatley, Esq. R.A.'

DOUBTFUL PORTRAIT

See Unidentified Portraits NPG 1278.

WHITEFOORD, Caleb 1734-1810

Diplomat and connoisseur; a wine-merchant in London, where he was a neighbour of Benjamin Franklin; secretary at the Paris peace commission 1782; FRS 1784; a founder of the British Institution and a vice-president of the Society of Arts, art critic for the *Public Advertiser* from 1786, but his reputation was principally made by his 'political squibs'; his collection of old master paintings was sold Christie's, 4-5 May 1810.

'what is usually called a slight built man and much addicted when in conversation to shrug up his shoulders. He had a thin face, with little eyes; his deportment was gentlemanly' (J.T. Smith, 1845).

WHITEFOORD NPG 1400

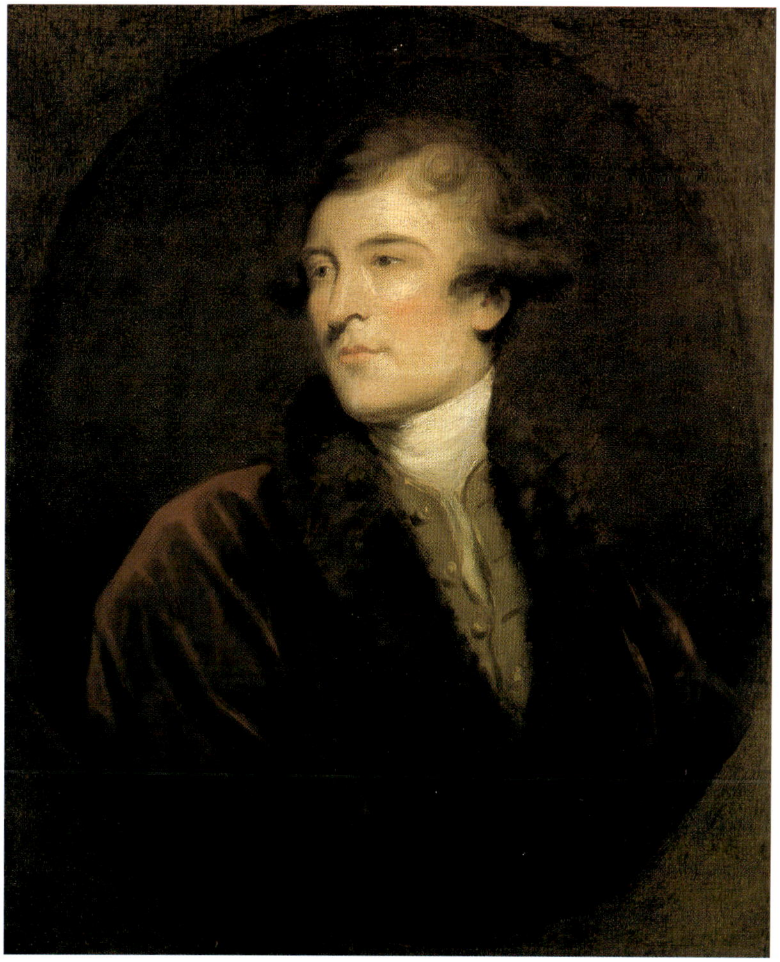

Abbreviation

Allan 1975: D.G.C. Allan, 'Caleb Whitefoord', *Connoisseur*, CXC, 1975, pp.194-99

1400 after JOSHUA REYNOLDS [1773]

Canvas 75 x 62 (29½ x 24½) lined; cleaned 1978; a repaired tear across the chin.

Brown eyes, light brown hair, wearing white neckcloth, deep red-brown coat with sable collar over a beige waistcoat.

Collections: Purchased from W. Holliday 1905.

Reference: Mannings 2000, no.1876b.

NPG 1400 is a copy, probably from the early 19th century, of the portrait by Reynolds painted in 1773, exhibited RA 1775(236), and now in a private collection.[1] The numerous copies include one from the Antrobus collection[2] and a reduced version in the Victoria and Albert Museum (D.68).[3]

1 Mannings 2000, no.1876; engraved J. Jones 1793; S.W. Reynolds (bust length) 1795.
2 Mannings 2000, no.1876a.
3 Further versions sold Christie's, 22 February 1957, lot 134, and Christie's, SK, 7 February 1991, lot 174.

ICONOGRAPHY

1773 Painting by Joshua Reynolds, see NPG 1400.

c.1780-85 Drawing by Paul Sandby, one of the series of heads drawn at print sales. Royal Collection (Oppé 1947, no.417/45). Engraved anon., **Sketches taken at Print Sales*, see Comparative Groups.

1782 Painting by Gilbert Stuart,* half length. Montclair Art Museum, N.J. Exhibited RA 1782(146). Engraved W. Holl 1810, *from the original in the Possession of Mrs Whitefoord*.

1787 Miniature by C. Shirreff, exhibited RA 1787(290).

1795 Drawing by George Dance, profile bust, dated 6 July 1795. Dance sale, Christie's, 1 July 1898, lot 142. Engraved W. Daniell 1809 (*Dance Portraits*(.* A second drawing exhibited *Sublime and Beautiful*, Sabin, 1973(31), illus. pl.2.

c.1798 Drawing by Richard Cosway, half-length oval, engraved P. Condé 1810 (*European Mag.*; illus. Smith 1920, I, f.p.272). On 5 May 1798 James Scott told Whitefoord that Sir Richard Johnstone 'intends to ask Mr Cosway to meet you' (H.A.S. Hewins ed., *The Whitefoord Papers*, 1898, p.246),

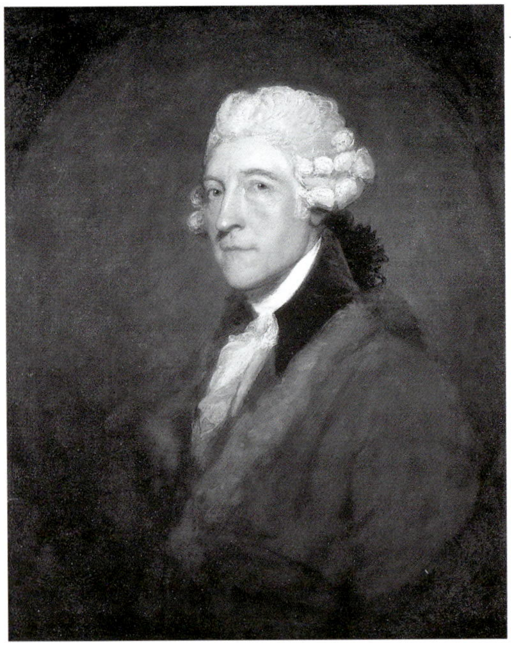

WHITEFOORD by Gilbert Stuart 1782 (Montclair Art Museum, New Jersey)

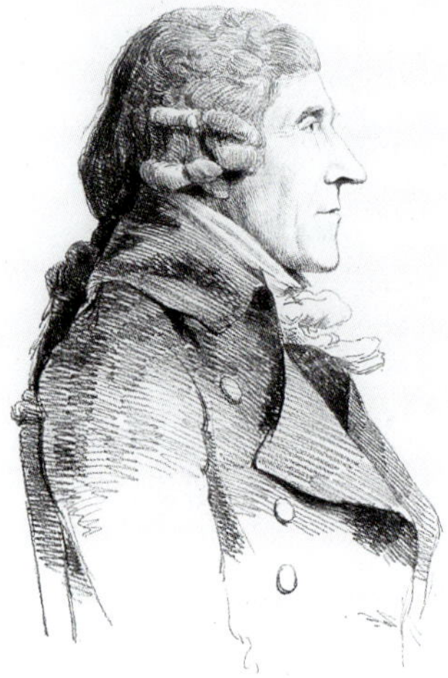

WHITEFOORD by W. Daniell after George Dance 1795 (NPG D 12147)

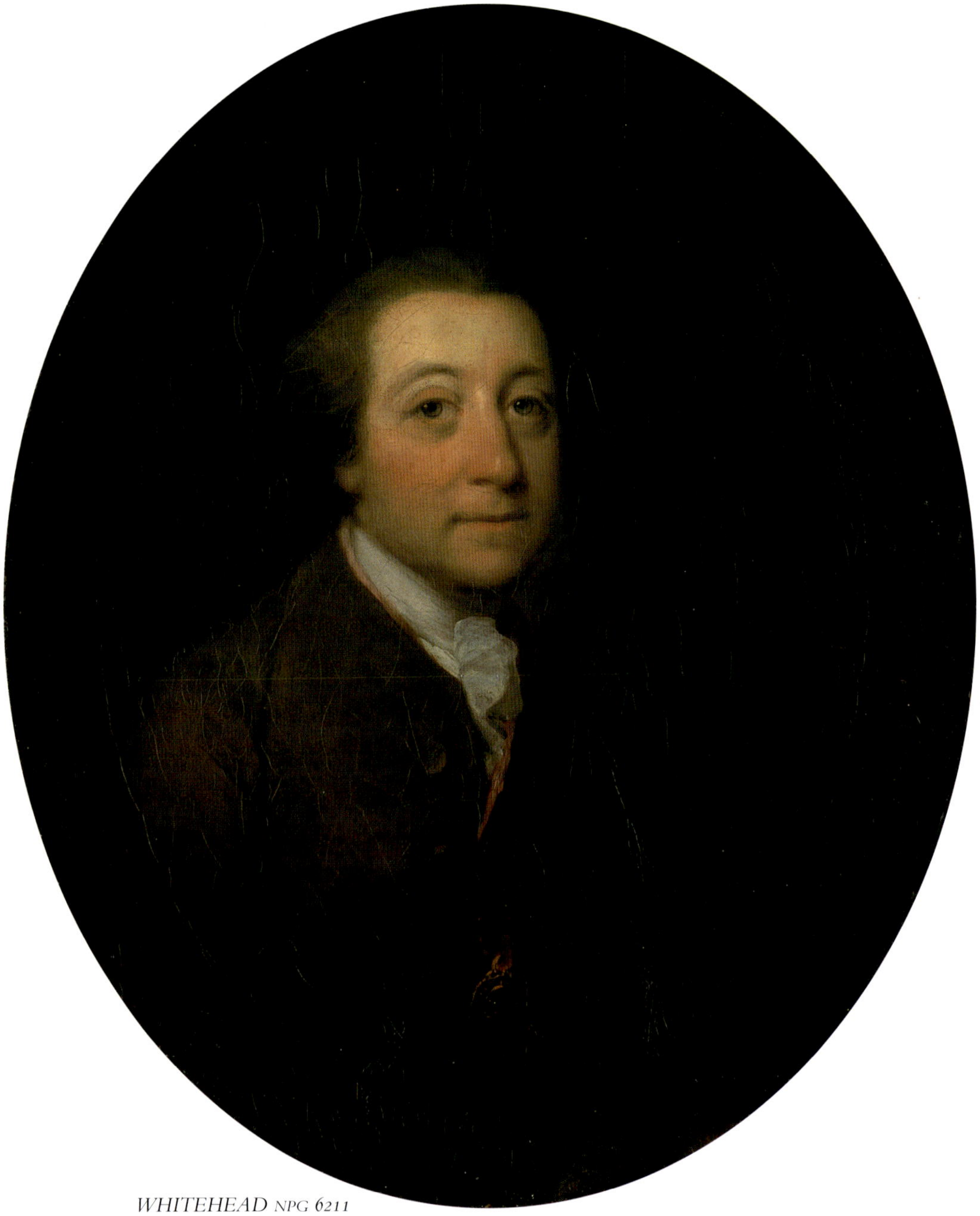

WHITEHEAD NPG *6211*

which may indicate the date of this drawing.

c.1800? Unattributed painting, half-length painted oval. Royal Society of Arts, London (illus. Allan 1975, p.195, as c.1800, but possibly earlier).

Caricatures of Whitefoord as a connoisseur include: *Caleb Curious* 1792 by I. Cruikshank (George 8169); *Connoisseurs examining the collection of George Morland* 1807 (George 10791; illus. Allan 1975, p.196) and *Maecenas in pursuit of the Five Arts* 1808 (George 11076; illus. *Apollo*, CXIX, 1984 p.366), both by Gillray. George also lists (8725) a half-length etching by Dighton.

David Wilkie's *Letter of Introduction* 1813 (NG of Scotland) illustrated an episode in Wilkie's youth when, with a letter of introduction from Sir George Sandilands, he called on Whitefoord in London, only to be snubbed. Wilkie's picture, painted eight years after the event, has some claim to show Whitefoord's elegant study in Argyll Street (Allan 1975, p.198).

WHITEHEAD, William 1715-85

Poet and dramatist; from 1745 tutor to Viscount Villiers (later 4th Earl of Jersey), whom he accompanied on a Grand Tour 1755-56 with Lord Nuneham (later 2nd Earl Harcourt); secretary and registrar of the Order of the Bath 1756 and poet laureate 1757-85; a reader of plays for Garrick; William Mason wrote his brief biography, Boswell observing that 'from a man so still and tame ... conversation worth recording could no more be expected, than from a Chinese mandarin on a chimney-piece'.

6211 BENJAMIN WILSON 1758-59

Canvas 74 x 61 (29¼ x 24¼) oval, lined; cleaned and relined 1994; the head particularly worn; inscribed on the old lining canvas verso: *W. Whitehead Poet Laureate/ by B. Wilson. 1758.*

Grey eyes, brown hair, wearing a brown suit and the ribbon and badge of the Bath; seated in a red chair; four books, one lettered: *Wm. Whitehead Esq./ Poet Laureat./ Register &/ Secretary of ye./ Order of ye./ Bath.*

Collections: Commissioned by the 2nd Earl Harcourt, thence by descent; Harcourt sale, Sotheby's, 10 June 1993, lot 869, bt. Hazlitt, Gooden & Fox for the NPG, and purchased through the Dame Helen Gardner Fund.

Engraving: W. Ensom 1821, from a drawing by J. Thurston (*Effigies Poeticae* 1824).

Exhibitions: NPE 1867(801, as by Richard Wilson) lent Rev W.V. Harcourt; *Guelph* 1891(238, as by Richard Wilson) lent E.W. Harcourt; *Mason* 1973(12).

Reference: W.G. Constable, *Richard Wilson*, 1953, no.135b.

The execution proved a little difficult. On 20 June 1758 Whitehead told his patron Lord Harcourt, who had commissioned the portrait: 'I finished sitting at Wilson's before I came out of town, & the picture seems to me very easy, & amazingly like. He is pleased with it himself, & intends to take great pains in the colouring, &c. He is quite confident that you will like it'.[1] Back in London on 4 November Whitehead wrote again to say that he had called on Wilson: 'what he has done to the picture I cannot tell, but the likeness is considerably lessened. If I have time I am to give him a sitting before your Lordship comes to town'.[2] A week later Mason was writing to Harcourt: 'I saw Whitehead's picture when I was in Town, but it must not go out of Wilson's hands till I see it again, I want several touches about the mouth, &c., & the whole is a tame likeness at present'.[3] Seven months later Whitehead told Harcourt that 'Wilson has made some alterations in my picture, which Mason said were much for the better'.[4] Eventually Harcourt, at least, appears to have been satisfied with the portrait, for on 16 September 1760 Whitehead wrote to him: 'I am glad to find travelling agrees with my picture, I always thought the features like, but the result of the whole not so, perhaps the light you have placed it in is advantageous to it'.[5]

Previously mistakenly attributed to Richard Wilson.[6]

1 E.W. Harcourt ed., *Harcourt Papers*, VII, n.d., pp.215-16.
2 *Ibid.*, p.220.
3 *Ibid.*, p.10 (10 November 1758).
4 *Ibid.*, p.222 (23 June 1759).
5 *Ibid.*, p.227.
6 Exhibited as such in 1867 and 1891, the attribution suspected by W.G. Constable, *loc. cit.*

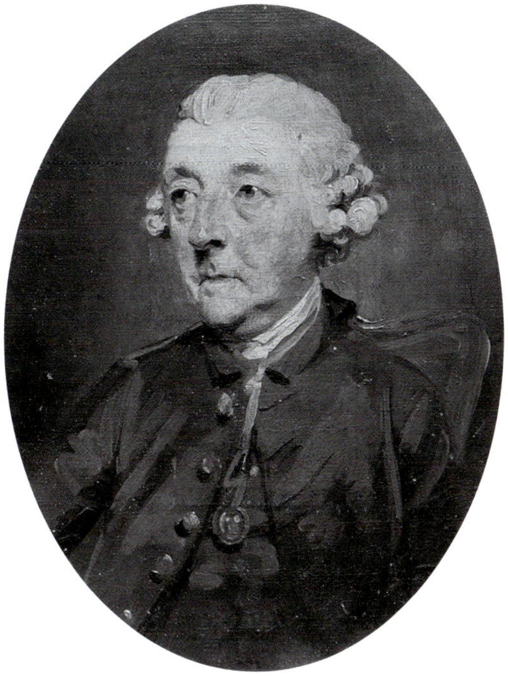

WHITEHEAD by William Doughty 1776 (Victoria and Albert Museum)

ICONOGRAPHY

1754 Painting by Benjamin Wilson, mentioned in a letter from William Mason to Wilson, 22 April 1754 (BM, Add.MS 30,094).

1758-59 Painting by Benjamin Wilson, see NPG 6211.

1776 Painting by William Doughty,* small half-length oval. Victoria and Albert Museum (D.67; illus. *Apollo*, LXXX, 1964, p.34). Engraved J. Collyer 1787 (for Whitehead's *Works*). A copy in a private collection in 1955.

Painting by William Mason, once in his parsonage at Aston, given to the Rev John Mitford in 1853 (*GM*, ns XXXIX, 1853, i, p.338).

WILKES, John 1725-97

Demagogue; MP 1757-64, 1768-69 and 1774-90; arrested in 1763 under a general warrant for a seditious article in the *North Briton, no.45*, but discharged through parliamentary privilege; his continuing provocation (including a pornographic *Essay on Woman*) led to outlawry in 1764; until 1768 he lived abroad; re-elected to Parliament on his return and duly imprisoned 1768-70, in which time he was three times elected MP; finally received back in Parliament 1774; alderman 1769, lord mayor 1774-75 and chamberlain 1779 of the City of London.

'a charming, wicked, honest, jolly, candid sort of fellow' (John Holroyd, 1765).

'in his person he was a little above the middle size: his complexion was somewhat sallow; and before he died he appeared to be affected by a marasmus. His eyes always possessed an unfortunate cast, which exposed him to the impertinence of rude observers and malignant artists' (John Almon, 1805).

'if any man ever was pleasing who squinted, who had lost his teeth, and lisped, Wilkes might be so esteemed' (Sir Nathaniel Wraxall, 1815).

Abbreviation
Almon 1805 J. Almon, *Correspondence of John Wilkes*, 5 vols., 1805

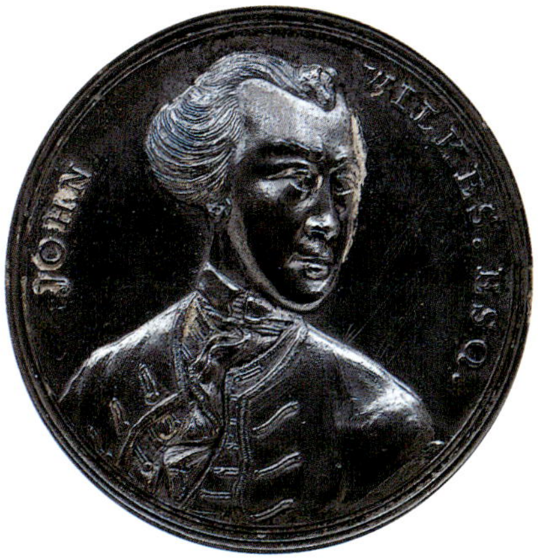

WILKES NPG *1702*

1702 UNKNOWN ARTIST 1768

Silver medal 5.7 (2¼) diameter

Obverse: half-length portrait of Wilkes to right, inscribed: *JOHN WILKES.ESQ.*

Reverse: the figure of Time inscribing a pyramid inscribed: *45/NORTH/BRITON/ MAGNA/CHARTA* and in the exergue: *IN MEMORY OF THE YEAR/ MDCCLXVIII.*

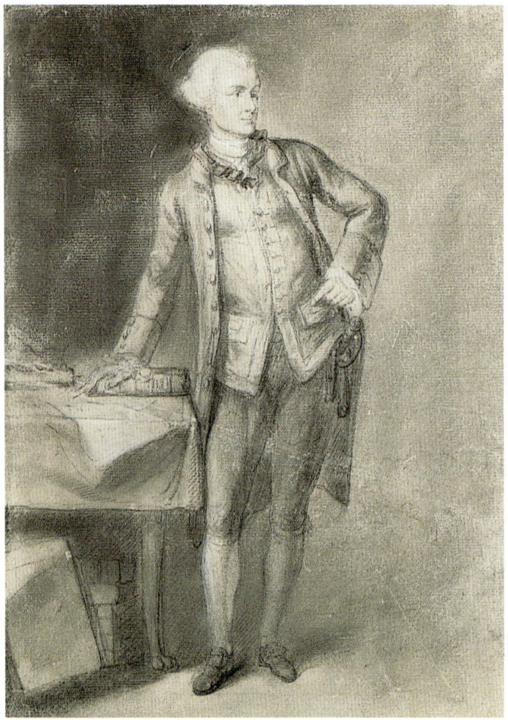

WILKES NPG *284*

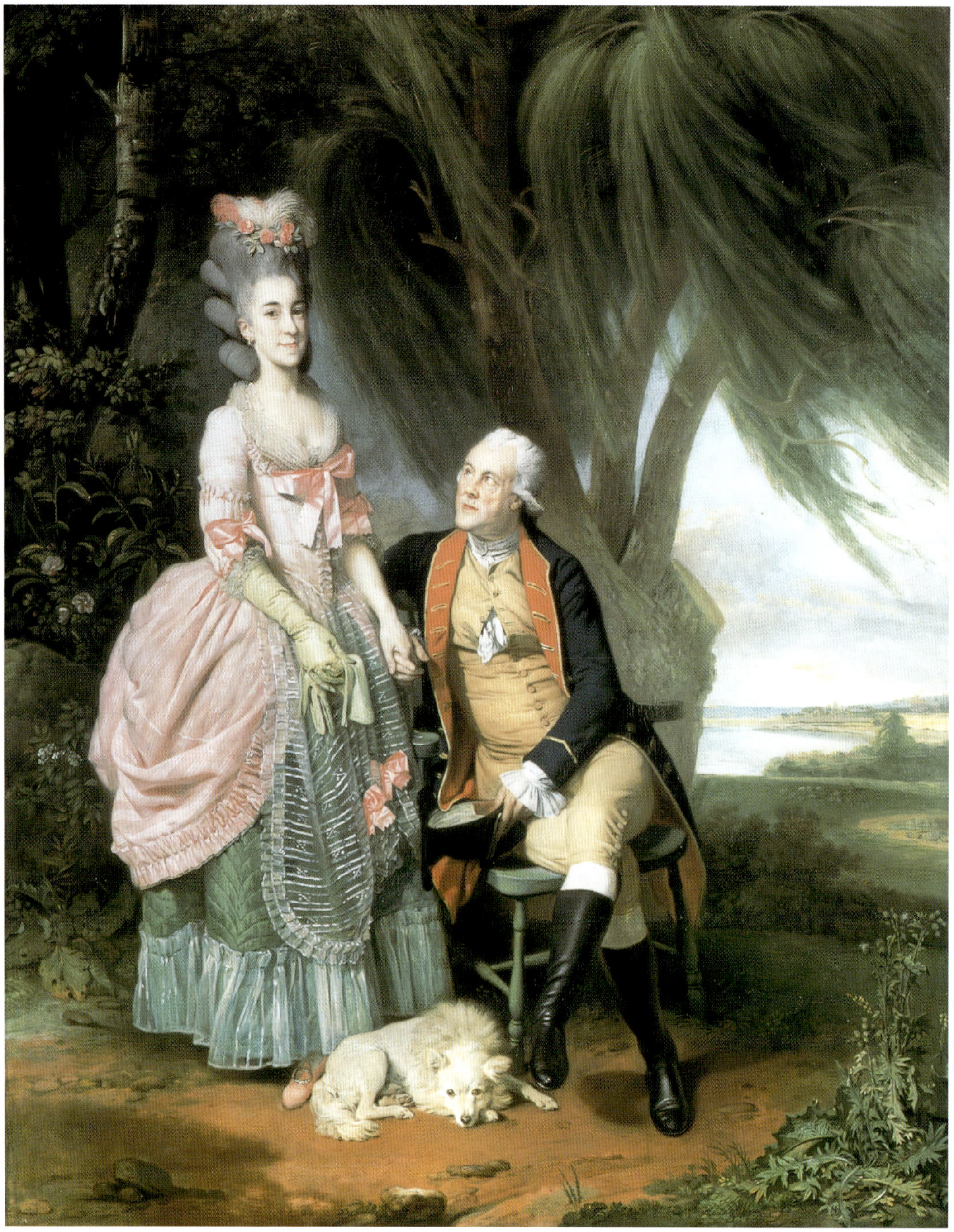

WILKES with his Daughter NPG *6133*

Collections: Purchased from Spink 1913.

Reference: Brown 1980, no.117.

A crude likeness, presumably derived from an engraving after R.E. Pine, see below. One of thirteen medals marking Wilkes's triumphal election for the County of Middlesex in April 1768 (see Brown 1980, nos.113-25).

1944 see Groups, *John Glynn, John Wilkes and John Horne Tooke*, after RICHARD HOUSTON [1769]

284 UNKNOWN ARTIST [1769]

Black and white chalk with grey wash on paper 35.5 x 25.5 (14 x 10) laid down on paper; in poor condition, the surface rubbed, scratched and water-stained; repaired tear above the head.

Holding a quill in his right hand and wearing an ill-defined dark collar (as if for an Order).

Collections: Presented by William Smith 1869.

Exhibitions: *In the Minds and Hearts of the People*, NPG Washington, 1974; *Bicentennial Center Opening*, Yorktown, Va., 1976; *Royal Westminster*, Royal Institution of Chartered Surveyors, London 1981(200).

A competent but damaged drawing, NPG 284 provides one of the kindest heads of Wilkes to survive. It relates directly to a cruder, anonymous mezzotint,[1] dateable 1769, published by R. Sayer, titled . . . *Four times elected Member of Parliament for the County of Middlesex,*[2] *Alderman of the Ward of Farringdon Without…*, but differs principally in omitting the alderman's robe and chair.[3]

NPG 284 has previously always been attributed to Richard Earlom, but it is not at all clear why.

1 The NPG example has 'J. Dixon' written on the back.

2 That is, after 14 April 1769, when Wilkes's fourth election was declared void by the House.

3 The print (CS, IV, p.1749, no.160) also shows the paper on the table lettered: *The Liberty of all Peers & Gentlemen & what touches me more sensibly of all …* [Wilkes's defence plea, 1763; Almon 1805, I, p.117]; another inscribed: *To George Bellas Esqr.* (the Portsmouth lawyer, founder member of the Bill of Rights Society, who chaired the Middlesex election meeting on 14 February 1769).

6133 JOHANN ZOFFANY, *with his daughter* 1779-82

Canvas 126 x 100 (49½ x 39¼) lined; cleaned 1991.

Wilkes has brown squinting eyes, white hair, and wears a dark blue coat with red facings and gold trim (possibly a uniform coat),[1] buff vest, nankeen breeches and black top-boots; he sits in a green chair, holding his black hat in his left hand.

His daughter has brown eyes, her grey hair dressed with red roses and ostrich feathers, pink silk roses and foliage; she wears a green quilted underskirt with a lace apron and a pink and white panelled dress with silver decoration and pink bows on the sleeves; her gloves are pale green and her pink shoes have silver buckles.

Collections: By descent from the sitter to his niece, Dinah Hayley, who m. Sir Robert Baker, 1st Bt;[2] by descent to Sir Robert Sherston-Baker, 7th Bt; Sotheby's, 14 November 1990, lot 47, bt. in; purchased by private treaty sale with the aid of the National Heritage Memorial Fund and the National Art Collections Fund 1991.

Engravings: S. Freeman 1804 (detail bust of Wilkes); S. Freeman 1805 (detail, bust of Mary Wilkes).

Exhibitions: RA 1782(53); NPE 1867(654) lent Sir Henry Baker; *Into View*, Sudbury, 1986(17) lent anon.; *Treasures for Everyone*, NACF exhibition, Christie's, 1997.

Reference: Williamson 1920, pp.73-74, 176-77.

Wilkes's lasting devotion to his daughter Mary (Polly, 1750-1802), his only legitimate child, was one of the less complicated aspects of his character. The fact that Mary seems 'fussily overdressed and lacking in any innate sense of style'[3] may be a reflection of her father's indulgence. Walpole saw NPG 6133 in Zoffany's studio in November 1779: 'A delightful piece of Wilkes looking - no, squinting tenderly at his daughter - it is a caricature of the Devil acknowledging Miss Sin in Milton. I do not know why, but they are under a palm tree, which has not grown in a free country for some centuries'.[4] When it was shown at the RA three years later Walpole found it 'horridly like'.[5] The sleeping pomeranian dog was Zoffany's, and recurs in Zoffany's *Sharp Family* of 1779-81 (on loan to the National Portrait Gallery since 1978; L169).

Mary Wilkes studied in Paris 1763-64 and stayed there again in 1770; well-educated, but evidently plain, she was unmarried; she appeared in an anonymous caricature group, *A Sunday Concert* 1782, smiling at Dr Burney[6] and she also bequeathed her portrait 'done in crayons by Hoare' to Lady Baker;[7] see also Icongraphy below 1763-64.

1 M. Webster suggested it may be the coat of a Chamberlain of the City of London, an office to which Wilkes was elected in 1779 (*Sotheby's Preview*, October 1990, p.19); Ribeiro (2000, p.134) describes it as 'a quasi-military riding coat'.

2 Mary, Wilkes's daughter, directed in her Will: 'I give to my aforesaid cousin, lady Baker, the picture, by Zoffany, of my dear father and myself' (Almon 1805, V, p.114).

3 Ribeiro 2000, p.135.

4 *Wal. Corr.*, XXXIII, pp.137-38; 14 November 1779, to the Countess of Upper Ossory; the tree is palpably not a palm - Williamson (1920, p.74) even suggested the setting 'so far as is known', was Wilkes's country residence, Balcony House, Elysium Row, Fulham.

5 Graves RA.

6 George 6125 (illus. Burney's *History of Music*, ed. F. Mercer, 1934).

7 Almon 1805, V, p.114. There is also a somewhat dubious miniature of her by Ozias Humphry c.1770, in the NG of Victoria, Melbourne (illus. Williamson, 1906, II, no.226, pl.lxxiii; *Connoisseur*, XLVIII, 1917, p.55).

ICONOGRAPHY

Wilkes avoided sitting to Maria Cosway 'by referring her to Buffon's *Histoire Naturelle*, where there was a great likeness of me among the Sapajous and the Sagouins' (Whitley 1928, II, p.117).

He figured prominently in satires and caricatures in 1763-64 and 1768-79, and George lists a further 69 published between 1770 and 1782. From 1763-64 his image was spread in a variety of forms (porcelain, teapots, punchbowls and pub signs). 'Who knows', said Wilkes, 'but a time may come when some future *Horace Walpole* ... may prove that the numerous squinting portraits on tobacco papers, and half penny ballads, inscribed with the name of John Wilkes are a 'weak invention of the enemy', for that I was not only unlike them, but, if any inference can be drawn from the general partiality of the fair sex, the handsomest man of the age I lived in' (J. Ireland, *Hogarth Illustrated*, 1806, II, p.243n).

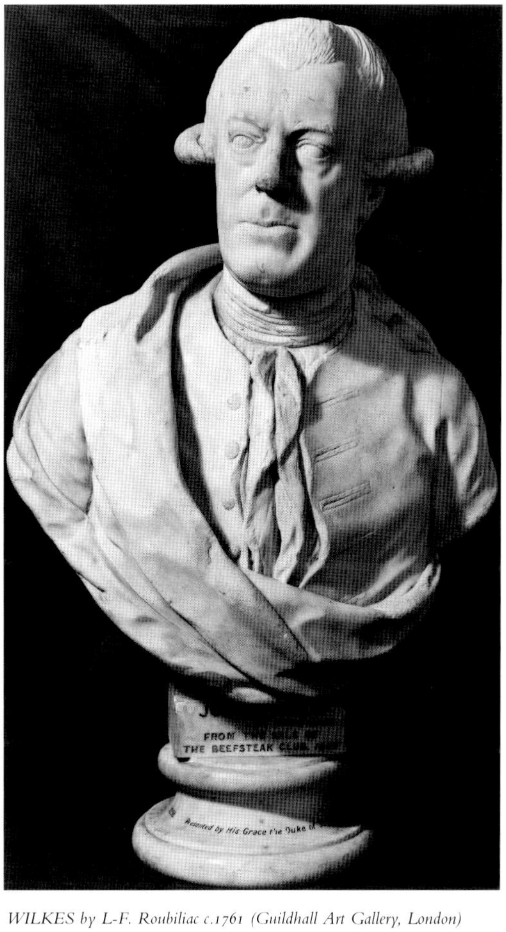

WILKES by L-F. Roubiliac c.1761 (Guildhall Art Gallery, London)

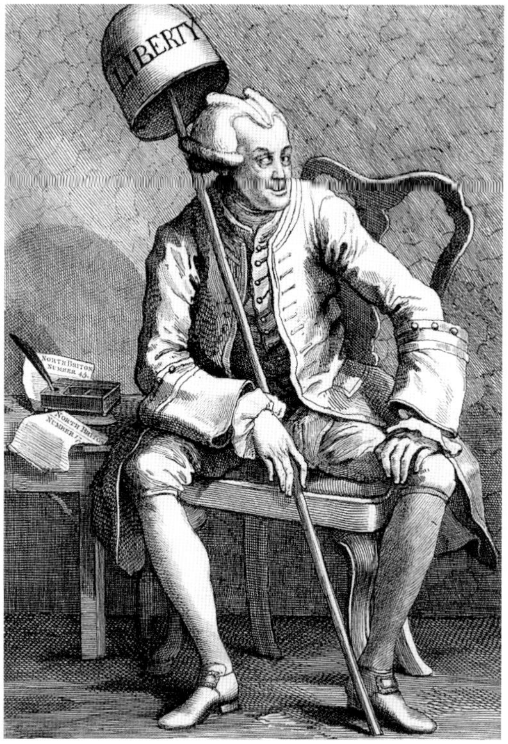

WILKES drawn and etched by William Hogarth 1763 (D 1362)

c.1761 Marble bust by L-F. Roubiliac,* with wig, neckcloth, shirt and drape. Guildhall AG, London (1098), from the Sublime Society of Beef Steaks, sold Christie's, 7 April 1869, lot 92.

1763 Drawing by William Hogarth, whole-length seated, holding the cap of Liberty (much resembling a chamber pot) on a pole over his head, with two numbers of the *North Briton*, 17 and 45, on the table at his side. British Museum (1936.10.15.1; illus. A.P. Oppé, *Drawings of Hogarth*, 1948, pl.89). Etched by Hogarth,* published 16 May 1763 (illus. Paulson 1965, pl.237). Hogarth drew Wilkes in the Court of Common Pleas on 6 May 1763. Wilkes thought Hogarth's portrait 'must be allowed to be an excellent compound caricatura, or caricatura of what nature had already caricatured' (*English Liberty*, pp.367-68), but it

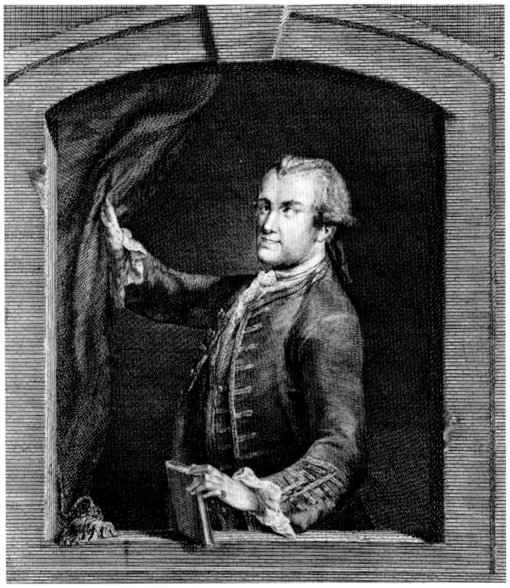

WILKES engraved J.S. Müller 1763 (NPG D 14332)

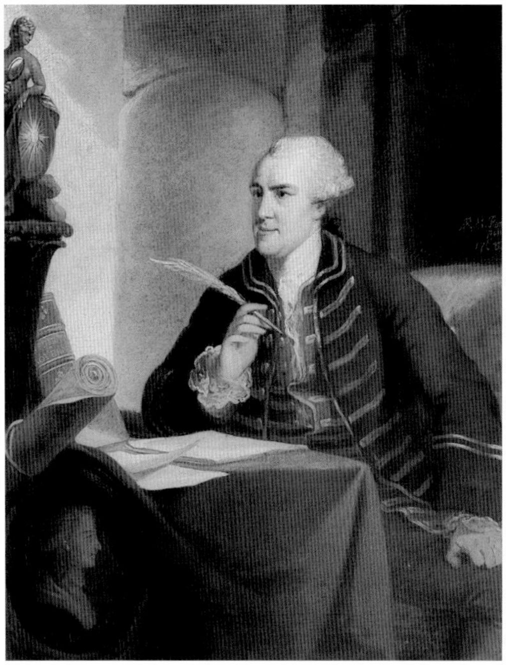

WILKES by R.E. Pine 1768 (Palace of Westminster)

was drawn in a spirit of retribution; Hogarth had criticised Wilkes in his print of *The Times* (Paulson 1965, pls.233-34) and Wilkes had criticised Hogarth in the *North Briton, no.17* (see Paulson 1965, pp.256-57).

1763 Drawn and engraved by J.S. Müller [J. Miller],* half length, at a window drawing back a curtain. Inscribed with lines from Pope: '*Great without title, beyond Fortune bless'd, . . .*' , with the Wilkes arms [*ar., a chev. sa. betw. three eagle's heads erased at the neck ppr.*] and motto (*arcui meo non confido*). Another oval head by Müller was engraved by G. Byrne, and a third inscribed *J. Miller at* [sic] *viv: fect.*

1763-64 Watercolour by L-C. de Carmontelle, whole length with his seated daughter (formerly identified as his mistress, Mme de Corradini). Christie's, 4 July 1995, lot 135. Wilkes was with his daughter in Paris in 1763-64.

1764 Painting by R.E. Pine, three-quarter length seated at table, a quill in his right hand, a medallion of John Hampden in the foreground. Version in the Palace of Westminster* dated 1768 (Walker 1988, I, p.362; illus. Pine 1979, p.16). Engraved J. Watson 1764 (illus. *Connoisseur*, XIV, 1906, p.187); R. Purcell 1764 (inscribed: *patricius pine humanarum Figurarum pictor Pinxit. Purcell nec non fecit*; illus. *Connoisseur*, XIV, 1906, p.187); J. Wilson 1764; Kitchener 1768; W. Dickinson 1768 and 1774 (bust length, costume altered to that of lord mayor); C. Watson 1805 (bust length, for Almon 1805, I, front., inscribed *after a Picture by Pine painted about the Year 1763*); and see Groups NPG 1944. Copy sold Christie's, 13 December 1957, lot 95. For Pine and Wilkes, see J. Sunderland, *Burl. Mag.*, CXVI, 1974, p.322.

1768 Anon. engravings: bust-length oval, supported by the figures of Britannia[?] and Hercules; a three-quarter length standing to right holding Bill of Rights, on an electoral broadsheet; bust-length oval to left (*Universal Mag.*, XLII, f.p.316).

1768 'A fine picture of John Wilkes' exhibited at the Polite Artists of Great Britain, London (Whitley 1928, I, p.193).

1768 Thirteen medals were produced, marking Wilkes's electoral victory (see above NPG 1702), including two by John Kirk and two attributed to John Westwood sr. (Brown 1980, nos.113-25).

1769 Engraving by G. Bockman, half-length oval in fur-lined aldermanic gown (illus. L. Colley, *Britons*, 1994, p.109).

1769 Anon. engraving, see NPG 284.

1769 Engraving by R. Houston, see Groups NPG 1944.

1770 Engraving by J. Dixon, whole-length seated, holding the Magna Charta in his left hand, a picture of *Hercules slaying the Hydra* on the wall behind; on the table beside him papers inscribed *Bill of Rights, To the Gentlemen Clergy & Freeholders of Middlesex* and *The Liberty of all Peers* (see above NPG 284, n3). A later impression published by Carrington Bowles 1775, showing Wilkes as lord mayor, omitting the engraver's name (both states illus. *A Face for Any Occasion*, Scottish NPG, 1976, p.14).

c.1770 Painting formerly attributed to Johann Zoffany, based on the painting by Pine, Wilkes seated, holding a paper referring to his conflict with the secretary of state, Lord Halifax, in 1763, with John Glynn standing beyond him. Formerly with Col. Prideaux-Brune (illus. Williamson 1920, f.p.74).

1771 Painting by R.E. Pine, exhibited SA 1771(125).

1772 Wax bust by Patience Wright (C.C. Sellers, *Benjamin Franklin in Portraiture*, 1962, p.427).

1773 Medal by John Kirk (Brown 1980, no.182).

1774 Anon. medal, as lord mayor (Brown 1980, no.195).

c.1775 Anon. engraving, whole length as lord mayor, pointing with his right hand (*Lady's Mag.*). Another state lettered *Elected Alderman Jan.2 1769* retains the mayoral collar.

1779-82 Painting by Johann Zoffany, see NPG 6133.

1782 Engraving by J. Sayers, whole length, wearing tricorne hat (George 6067).

1796 Engraving by H. Richter, bust length, with some teeth missing, based on the head by Hogarth of 1763 (*Junius*, 1797 ed., II).

A statue by James Butler, unveiled in 1988, stands at the corner of Fetter Lane.

DOUBTFUL PORTRAITS

A medallion by David d'Angers in the musée des Beaux-Arts, Angers, of a John Wilks (cf. J.G. Reuinis, *Medallions of David d'Angers*, 1998, pp.488-89); miniature of a 'Mr Wilks' exhibited by Miss M. Byrne RA 1804(734).

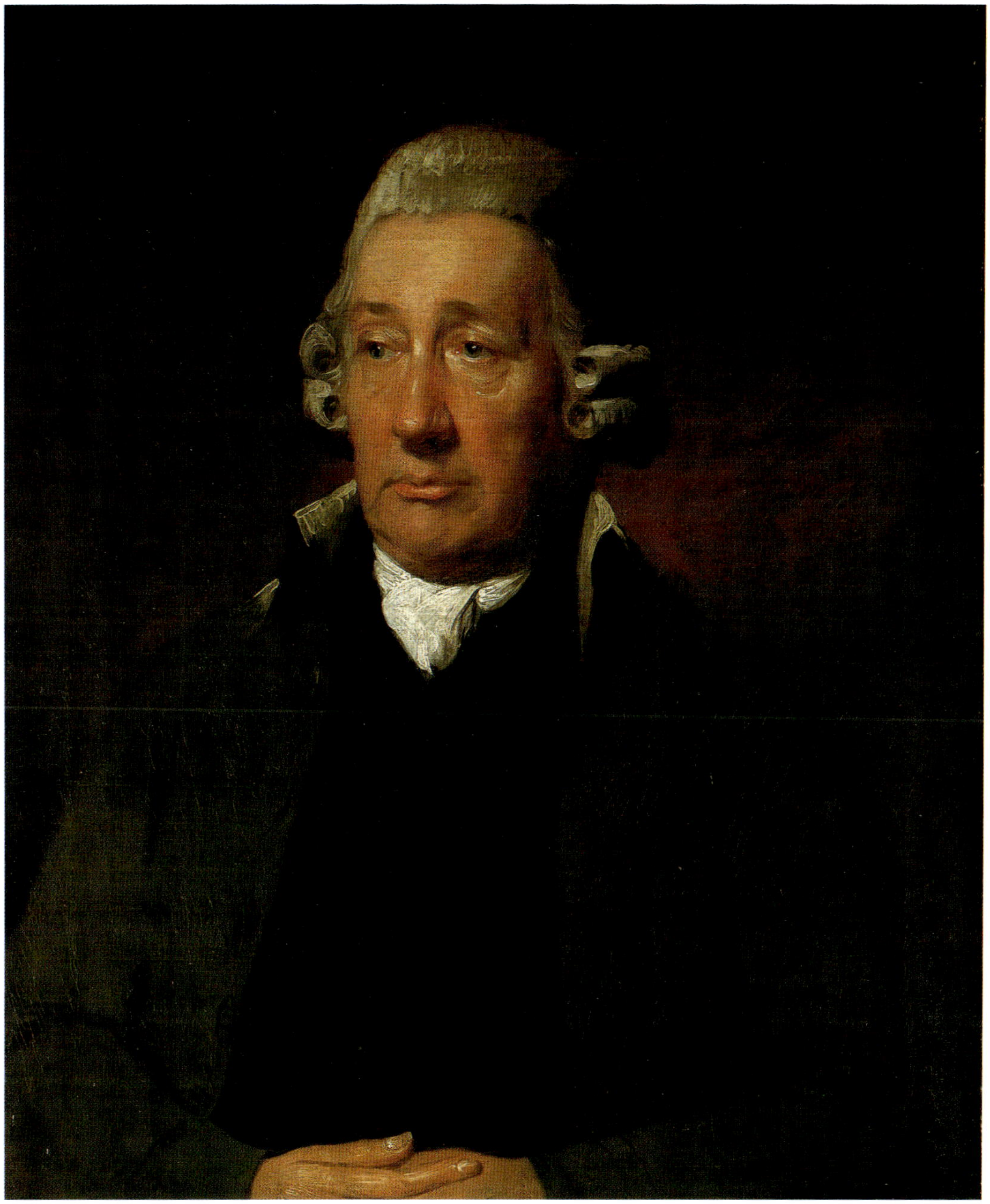

WILKINSON NPG 3785

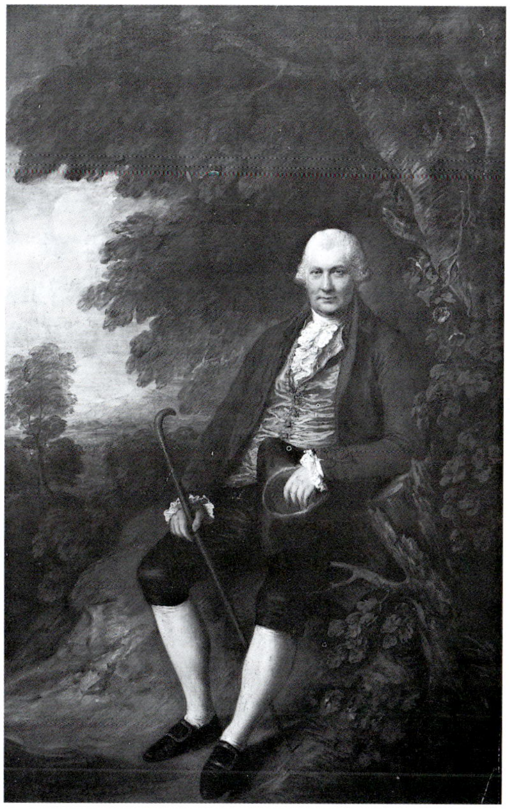

WILKINSON by Thomas Gainsborough c.1776 (Staatliche Museen, Berlin)

WILKINSON, John 1728-1808

Iron master, the 'father of the south Staffordshire iron trade'; ran factories in Lancashire and north Wales, where he was high sheriff for Denbighshire 1799; patented a boring machine for drilling solid iron 1774, essential for the manufacture of cannon and the cylinders of Watt's steam engines; bro.-in-law of Joseph Priestley.

'In person he was strongly built and his voice, even in old age, was deep and sonorous. He was greatly marked by smallpox. A great blot on his character is that his domestic life was ill-regulated' (H.W. Dickinson, 1914).

Abbreviation

Dickinson 1914: H.W. Dickinson, *John Wilkinson*, 1914

3785 after LEMUEL FRANCIS ABBOTT [c.1795?]

Canvas 76 x 64 (30 x 25) lined; old repairs in the upper background area, to the left of the head, and in the waistcoat.

Blue eyes, ruddy complexion, wearing a powdered wig, a dull-green coat and black waistcoat.

Collections: E.H.H. Shorting of Broseley, Salop; C. Marshall Spink 1940; H.W. Dickinson, from whom purchased 1951.

Abbott's original portrait, which remains unidentified, was engraved in 1799.[1] NPG 3785 is not of prime quality; the hands are crudely drawn, the waistcoat skimped and the highlights perhaps too emphatic. Other versions are with the Ironbridge Gorge Museum Trust, Telford (ex Sotheby's, 26 July 1978, lot 149), and the Maelor Museum Service, Wrexham (ex Sotheby's 14 July 1993, lot 70); a third was sold Sotheby's, 4 July 2002, lot 96a. A provincial derivation, the right hand tucked into the waistcoat, is in the Wolverhampton Art Gallery.[2]

1 G. Atkinson 1799 (*from an original Picture by Mr Abbot*; without hands), for the *Agricultural Mag.*, November 1799 (unrecorded by O'Donoghue; a photograph was brought to the NPG by H.W. Dickinson in 1951).

2 Cat., 1974, p.65; illus. Dickinson 1914, front. (detail), and J. Randall, *The Wilkinsons*, 1917, front.

ICONOGRAPHY

c.1776 Painting by Thomas Gainsborough,* whole length, wearing a bright green silk waistcoat, seated in a landscape. Gemäldegalerie, Berlin (1638; Waterhouse 1958, no.722). Although called 'Squire Wilkinson' in 1914, the features are a little difficult to reconcile with Abbott's later portrait; Dickinson (1914, p.55) commented that it was 'too idealized' and failed to convey Wilkinson's forceful character. Copy by Miss Brackenbury 1903 sold Christie's, 20 June 1996, lot 51.

1785 Miniature by John Smart (listed by Foskett 1964, p.76).

1787-93 Copper tokens bearing a medallion portrait, dated between 1787 and 1793 (Dickinson 1914, pp.29-30; *CL*, CX, 1951, p.1371); an example in the NPG reference collection D7054 dated 1793; Wilkinson issued tokens in both silver and copper 'which had a wide currency in Staffordshire and Shropshire' (*DNB*).

c.1795? Painting by L.F. Abbott, see NPG 3785.

after 1808 Monument, a cast-iron obelisk bearing a bust-length medallion portrait. Lindale churchyard, Lancashire, transferred from Castlehead (illus. N. Penny, *English Church Monuments*, 1977, p.170). Wilkinson had stipulated he should be buried in a cast-iron coffin beneath an iron monument of twenty tons weight.

Undated Two untraced portraits listed by Dickinson 1914, p.55: a half length by 'Harper', engraved 'Rejlander' 1849 when in the collection of William Baldwin of Bilston (probably the portrait later belonging to Edward Jones of Wellington and formerly of Brymbo); a painting at Pennybridge Hall of John and Isaac Wilkinson in their foundry at Backbarrow.

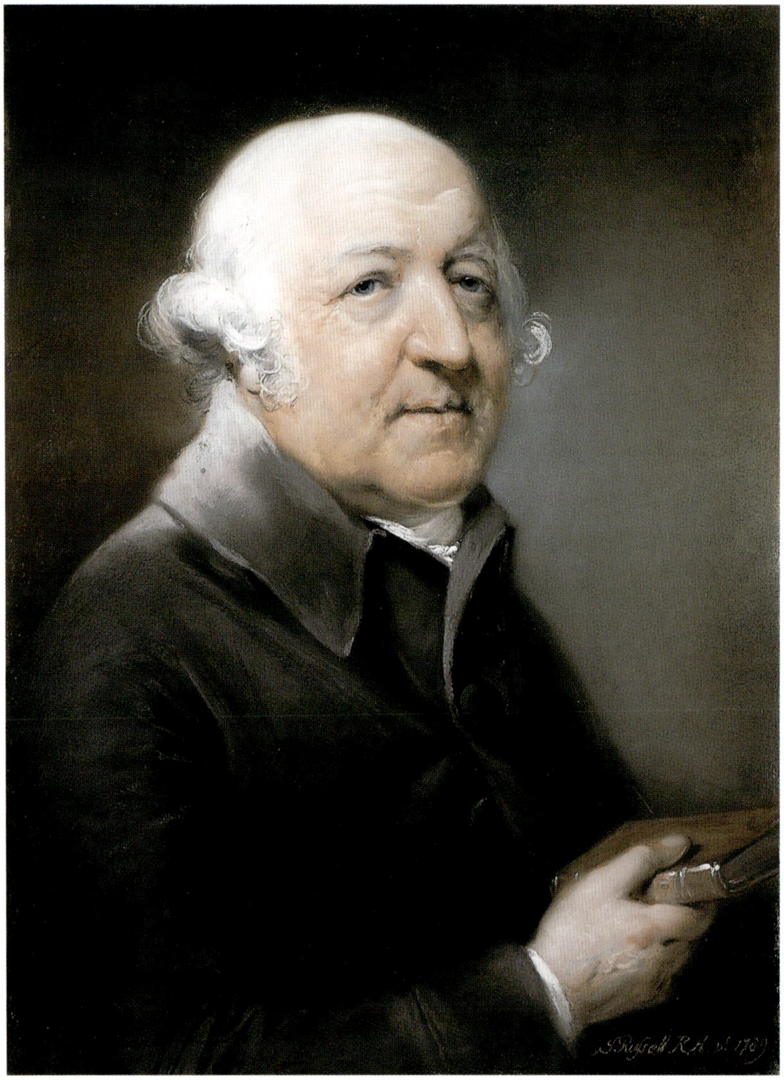

WILLIS NPG *2186*

WILLIS, Francis 1718-1807

Physician; MB and MD Oxford 1759; from 1769 physician in Lincoln, where he treated mental illness; in December 1788 he was summoned to treat George III and on the King's recovery his reputation soared; he built a second house at Shillingthorpe, Lincs., to accommodate his patients; for a few months in 1792 he unsuccessfully treated Maria I, Queen of Portugal, in Lisbon, but he was richly paid.

'Dr Willis is a man of ten thousand; open, honest, dauntless, light-hearted, innocent, and high-minded: I see him impressed with the most animated reverence and affection for [the King]; but it is wholly for his character, - not a whit for his rank' (Fanny Burney, 1789).

'"he had an eye like Mars, to threaten or command" ... his numerous patients, stood as much in awe of this formidable weapon, as of bars, chains, or straight waistcoats' (Frederick Reynolds, 1826).

2186 JOHN RUSSELL 1789

Pastel on paper 61 x 45.5 (24 x 18) signed, bottom right: *J Russell R.A. pt. 1789.*[1]

Blue-grey eyes, white hair, wearing a grey coat, a leather-bound book in his right hand.

Collections: By descent from the sitter to Dr Francis Willis (d.1906) of Braceborough, Lincs.;[2] the Trustees of his Will, from whom purchased 1928.

Engraving: J. Collyer (oval).

Exhibition: RA 1789(156).

A vigorous pastel of Willis in his hour of triumph. On 26 February 1789 the doctors' report from Kew described 'an entire cessation of his Majesty's illness' and on 10 March Parliament sent an address of congratulation to the King on his recovery. The RA exhibition, which opened on 27 April, included three por-

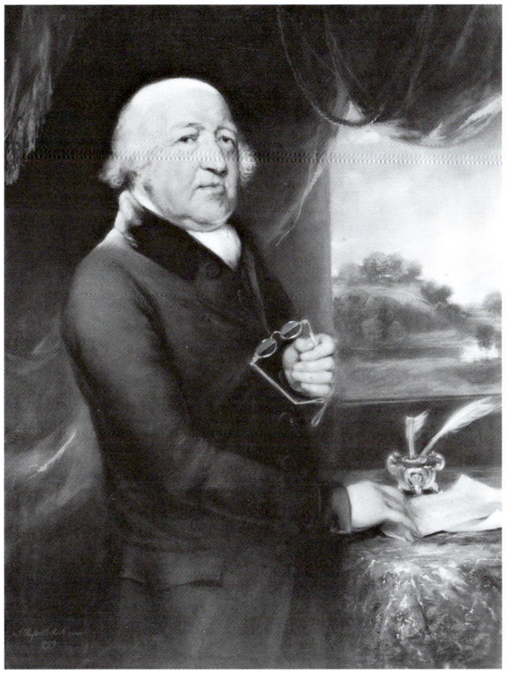

WILLIS by John Russell 1799 (Burghley House Collection)

traits of Willis (NPG 2186, and miniatures by Nixon and Bowyer) and Willis meanwhile had commissioned a medal to celebrate his achievement (see below).

A less lively version was sold Sotheby's, 21 March 2002, lot 102 (possibly the copy or replica of NPG 2186 reported in a Canadian private collection in 1939). A half-length squared-up pencil copy by Henry Bone 1807, presumably preparatory for an untraced enamel, is in the NPG Bone albums.[3]

Willis owned Russell pastels of his wife and four sons all dated 1789,[4] and see below.

1 The original backing had a contemporary ink inscription: *Revd Francis Willis M.D.* (now separately preserved).
2 Listed in his collection by Williamson 1894, p.171.
3 *Bone* 1999, no.552, fig.159.
4 Williamson 1894, p.172; portraits of two of the sons, John and Robert, exhibited RA 1790.

ICONOGRAPHY

1789 Miniature by R. Bowyer, half-length oval, exhibited RA 1789(330); engraved J. Fittler 1789.

1789 Medal by C. James & Thomas Wyon sen., with on the reverse: *BRITONS REJOICE YOUR KINGS RESTORED 1789* (Brown 1980, no.333). Struck at Willis's expense (see 'Porphyria, a Royal Malady', *British Medical Jnl.*, 1968, p.4).

1789 Miniature by James Nixon, half-length oval, exhibited RA 1789(307), engraved F. Bartolozzi.

1789 Pastel by John Russell, see NPG 2186.

1792 Engraving by J. May, bust-length oval. W. Armstrong, *Lawrence*, 1913, p.171, alleged the original was an early work by Thomas Lawrence, an attribution not since repeated.

c.1792 Painting by Richard Livesay, half length, engraved J. Murphy, lettered: *Gravado de Hum Painel pintado por R. Livesay pr a sua Majestade a Rainha de Inglaterra.*

1799 Pastel by John Russell,* three-quarter length standing by a window, glasses in his left hand. Burghley House. Exhibited RA 1800(148). The head almost identical to that in NPG 2186.

c.1800 Unattributed painting, half length, spectacles in his right hand. Mrs C. Nation in 1975.

1803 Plaster bust by George Garrard, undraped, inscribed *Sept. 1803*. Burghley House. Probably the bust exhibited RA 1804(839).

1807 Marble bust by Joseph Nollekens, draped, with books behind him. St Thomas a Becket church, Greatford, Lincs. (illus. *CL*, CXLVI, 1969, p.30). Nollekens also executed the bust of Willis's wife (d.1797) in the same church.

DOUBTFUL PORTRAIT

Samuel Woodforde exhibited a portrait of a Dr Willis, RA 1805(248).

WILSON, Richard 1714-82

Landscape painter; b. Penegoes, Wales; portrait painter in London before going to Italy 1750-57 and turning to landscape; foundation member of both the SA 1760 and RA 1768; exhibited SA 1760-68, RA 1769-80; librarian RA 1776; forthright and intelligent, his lack of 'suavity of manners' contributed to the 'comfortless infirmity' of his last years (Edwards).

'during the latter years of his life, his face became red, and was covered with blotches; he had a remarkable large nose [which] perhaps, may be attributed, in a certain degree to his fondness for a pot of porter, ... he wore a wig tied or plaited behind into a knocker or club, and a triangular cocked hat, according to the costume of the time' (Thomas Hastings, 1824).

Abbreviations

Constable 1953: W.G. Constable, *Richard Wilson*, 1953, pp.67-69 ('Portraits and Self-portraits of Wilson')

Cooper 1948: D. Cooper, 'The Iconography of Richard Wilson', *Burl. Mag.*, XC, 1948, pp.109-16

1305 after A.R. MENGS [1752]

Canvas 59.5 x 50 (23½ x 19¾) lined 1902; repaired tear upper right, discoloured varnish and scattered retouchings; inscribed verso: *A Correct Likeness/ of Richd. Wilson/ af* [sic] *Mengs of Rome/ 1756.*

WILSON NPG *1305*

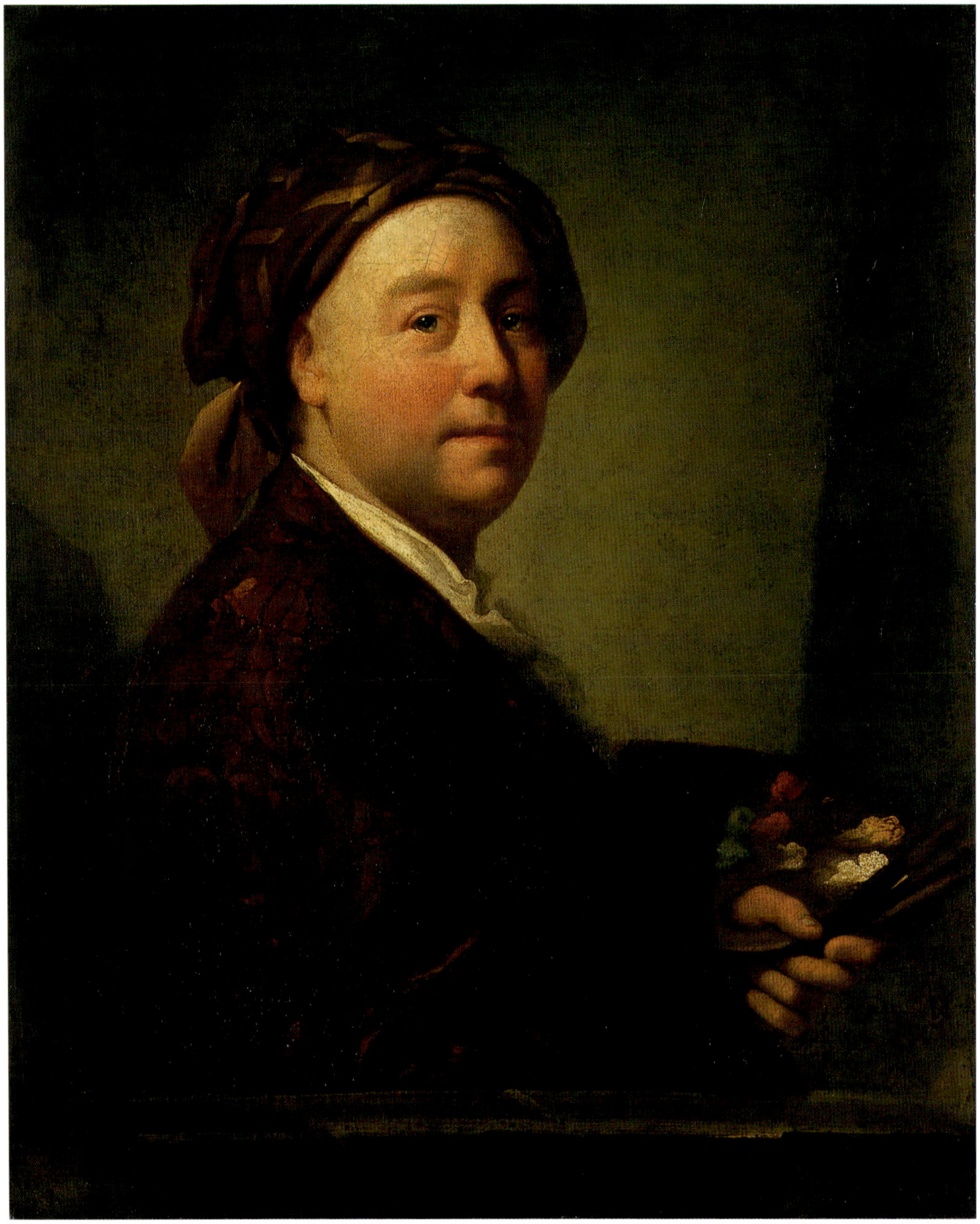

WILSON NPG *1803*

Clear grey eyes; red and green head scarf, wearing a deep brown coat.

Collections: Purchased from Mrs Hughes[1] 1901.

Reference: Constable 1953, p.68; S. Roettgen, *Mengs*, 1999, no.236(WK3, WK5).[2]

A weak half length taken from the Mengs portrait of 1752, see NPG 1803 below; the inscription (copied onto the lining canvas) is probably an inaccurate indication of the source, rather than the date of the copy (although Constable assumed otherwise).

1 A farmer's wife from near Caerwys, Clwyd; her father bt. the picture in Clwyd 'many years ago at a sale' (P.B. Davies-Corke to Cust, 14 August 1901; NPG archive).
2 A slightly confused account, giving two entries for NPG 1305 and one for the Mengs portrait of Charles Hanbury Williams, NPG 383.

1803 EDWARD PENNY after A.R. MENGS [1752]

Canvas 75.5 x 62 (29¾ x 24½) lined;[1] scattered retouchings, a damage below his left ear, and prominent craquelure in the impasted flesh areas on the forehead and nose.

Clear blue-grey eyes, wearing a dark brown turban with yellow strapping, a flowered silk deep red coat; his palette displays turquoise, reds, yellow, white and deep green; a landscape painting on his easel and a stone ledge across the foreground.

Collections: Given by the sitter to Benjamin Booth;[2] his daughter Elizabeth Mary Booth; her sister Marianne, who m. Sir Richard Ford (d.1821), thence by descent to his great-grandson John Ford, by whom bequeathed 1917.[3]

Exhibitions: BI 1814(141) lent Miss Booth; NPE 1868(834) lent F. Clare Ford; *British Art*, Grosvenor Gallery, 1888(128) lent Sir F. Clare Ford.

Reference: Waagen, II, p.226 (as a Wilson self portrait); D. Cooper, *Burl. Mag.*, XC, 1948, pp.109, 111, 113-14 (as Penny); Constable 1953, p.68; *Mengs*, Kenwood, 1993, under no.18; B. Ford, *Wal. Soc.*, LX, i, 1998, p.50; S. Roettgen, *Mengs*, 1999, no.236(WK2).

A close version of the portrait painted in Rome in 1752 by Mengs,* see below, with a number of minor differences: easel, canvas, alcove and chairback are obscured, his right arm and hand are hidden behind a balustrade, the colours on the palette are differently arranged, the lozenge-shaped pattern on the turban is more pronounced and the lighting on the face and background wall is more intense. The attribution of NPG 1803 varied between Wilson and Mengs (cf. note 2) until 1948, when Cooper convincingly equated it with an entry in Benjamin Booth's MSS as 'a [portrait] Of Wilson by his old Friend Penny'.[4]

Perhaps NPG 1803 was made when Wilson sold the original Mengs to Sir Watkin Williams-Wynn (from whose direct descendants it was acquired by Cardiff in 1947); Penny also painted Booth's daughter-in-law, Jane Salwey, Mrs Booth, in 1774.[5] A bust-length drawing in the British Museum (1881.6.11.201), almost a replica of NPG 1803 and on the same scale, once thought to be by Mengs, is now attributed to Penny as a preparatory study for NPG 1803.[6]

1 Stamp verso of F. Leedham Liner.
2 An ink label, formerly verso, in the hand of Sir Richard Ford: *Portrait of Richard Wilson R.A. attributed by tradition in my family to himself: it was given by the artist to my grandfather Benjamin Booth who was his early patron: it [was always considered] to be more likely to [be by Mengs] Richd. Ford.*
3 Presented by Richard Ford as executor for his brother, John, a Trustee of the NPG 1915-17. For John Ford, see *Wal. Soc.*, LX, i, 1998, pp.48-50.
4 Ford MS c.1790-1800 (private collection), quoted by Cooper 1948, p.109.
5 *Wal. Soc.*, LX, ii, 1998, p.379 and fig.206.
6 *Mengs*, Kenwood, 1993, under no.18; S. Roettgen, *Mengs*, 1999, no.236(WK1); illus. Cooper 1948, p.111 as by Mengs.

ICONOGRAPHY

1752 Painting by A.R. Mengs,* half length, painting at his easel, see NPG 1803. National Museum and Gallery, Cardiff (illus. *Mengs*, Kenwood, 1993,

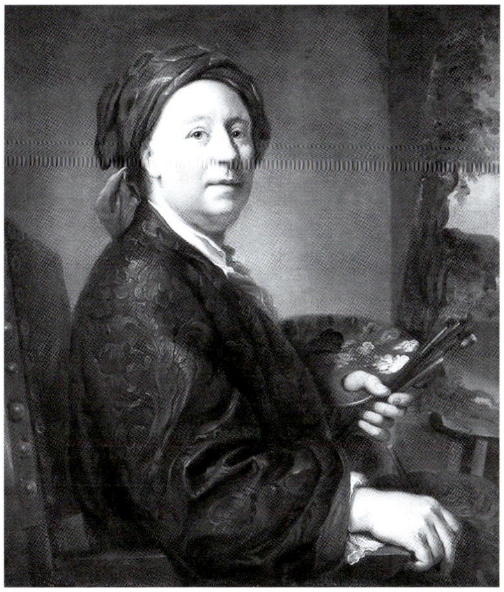

WILSON by A.R. Mengs 1752 (National Museums & Galleries of Wales)

no.18; Roettgen 1999, no.236). Painted in Rome in exchange for a landscape by Wilson. Engraved W. Bromley 1789, 1790; W. Bond 1812 (*From a Portrait copied by John Taylor under the inspection of Wilson, after an original Picture by Raphael Mengs, in the possession of Sir W.W. Wynne*; see Farington, 21 June 1813) and 1824; C. Pye 1822. A copy by William Roos 1846 was offered to the NPG 1871 (TSB 17/79); see also NPG 1305 and NPG 1803 above.

c.1765–70 Painting by J.H. Mortimer,* *Caricature Group*, see Comparative Groups.

1772 Painting by Johann Zoffany,* *The Academicians of the Royal Academy*, see Groups NPG 1437. A pot of porter by his side was painted out after Wilson threatened Zoffany with a thrashing (Constable 1953, p.57).

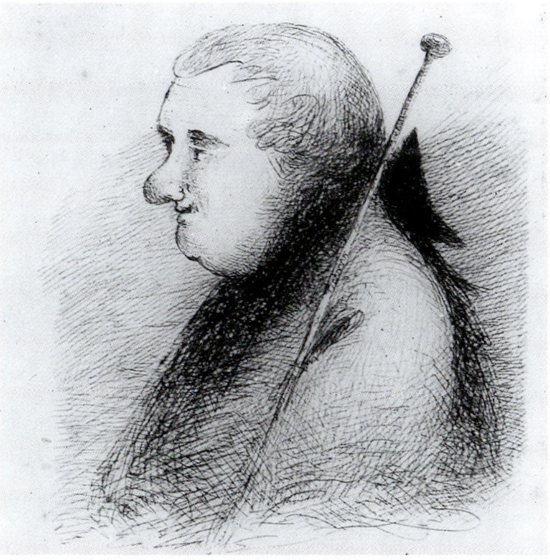

WILSON T. Hastings after George Beaumont c.1775 (British Museum)

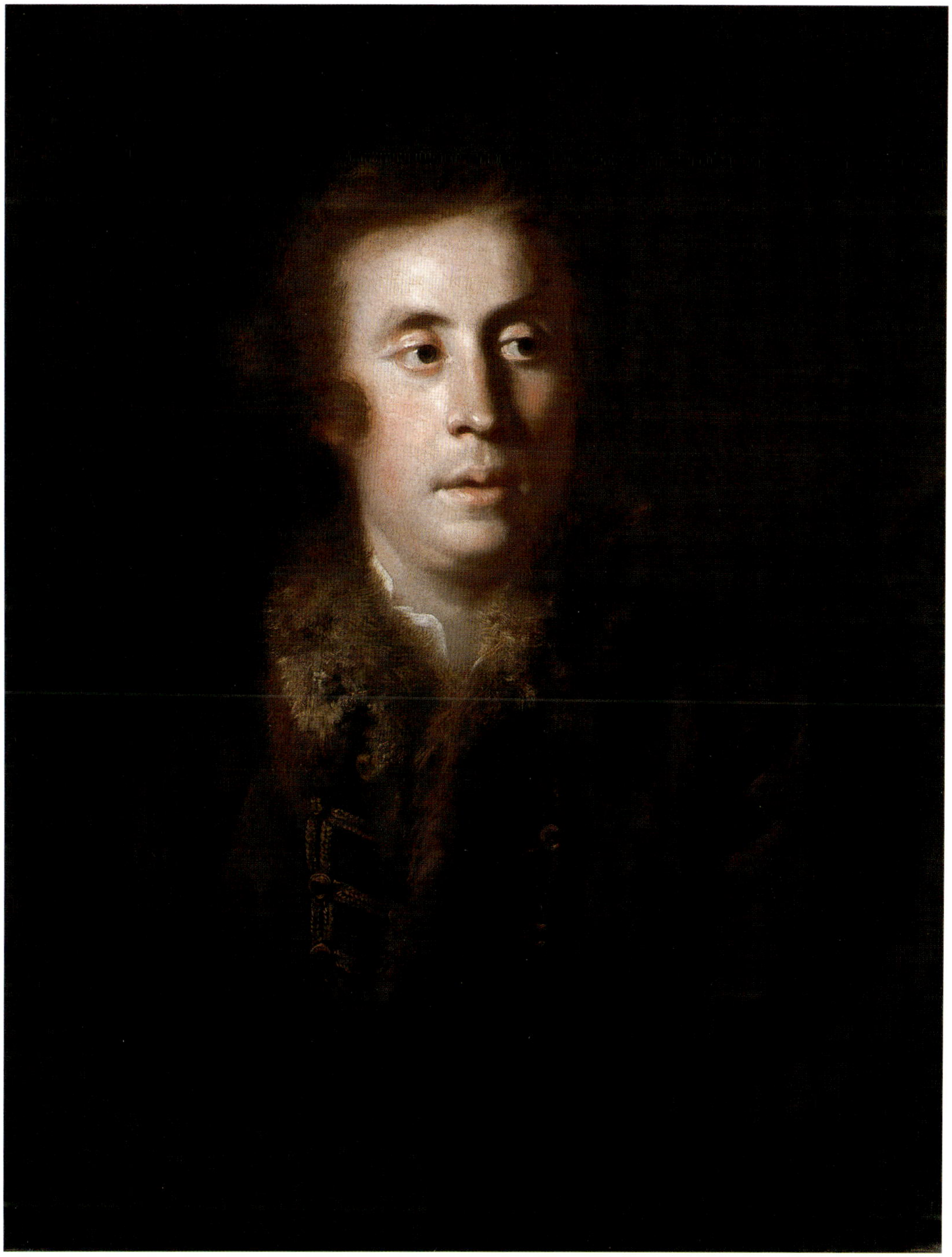

WILTON NPG 4810

c.1775 Drawing by George Beaumont, half length with a mahlstick, etched by T. Hastings 1824.*

DOUBTFUL PORTRAITS

See Unidentified Portraits NPG 1327. A 'self portrait' exhibited Sabin, *English Portrait*, 1976, no.7; painting by an unknown artist, Royal Academy, exhibited NPE 1867, no.523 (illus. Cooper 1948, fig.28; Constable 1953, pl.135c).

WILTON, Joseph 1722–1803

Sculptor; studied in Paris from 1744 and in Italy 1747–55; Sculptor to the King 1761; executed the General Wolfe monument in Westminster Abbey 1773; foundation member of the RA 1768, librarian 1786 and keeper 1790.

'Mr Wilton was in height about five feet ten inches, portly and well-looking: he always dressed in the

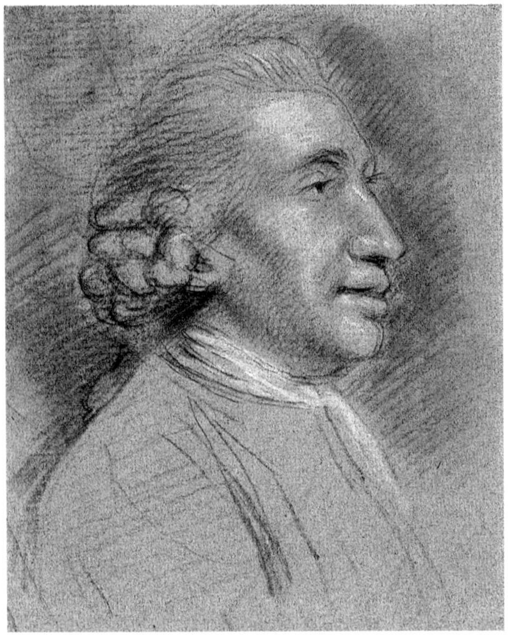

WILTON NPG *4314*

height of fashion, and for many years wore a bag-wig, which, in his latter days, he changed for one with a long tail, and walked, as Gay might have said, with dignity and a gold-headed cane. As to his manners, they were perfectly gentlemanlike, which rendered him an agreeable companion' (J.T. Smith, 1828).

4810 JOSHUA REYNOLDS 1752

Canvas 72.5 x 57 (28½ x 22½) lined; the flesh tones are faded.

Within a scrolled cartouche; blue-grey eyes,[1] reddish hair, wearing a fur-collared brown coat with a gold trim.

Collections: The sitter's daughter, Frances, who m. Sir Robert Chambers, Kt. (1737-1803); by descent to Mrs D. Boyle, from whom purchased 1970.

Engraving: F. Bromley 1862.

Exhibitions: NPE 1867(522) lent G. Wilton Chambers; RA 1884(51) lent G.W. Chambers; *Reynolds*, Birmingham, 1961(9) lent Mrs D. Boyle.

Reference: Graves & Cronin, III, pp.1059-60; Waterhouse 1941, p.38; Mannings 2000, no.1915.

Painted in 1752 in Florence, where Wilton was residing in the course of his Italian sojourn. He had been elected to the Florentine Accademia del Disegno on 9 January and was noticed by the British representative, Horace Mann, as an 'ingenious modest sculptor' whose work was attracting attention amongst 'all the professors as well as connoisseurs here'. Reynolds was in Florence between 10 May and 4 July and was himself elected to the Accademia on 3 September (after his departure).[2]

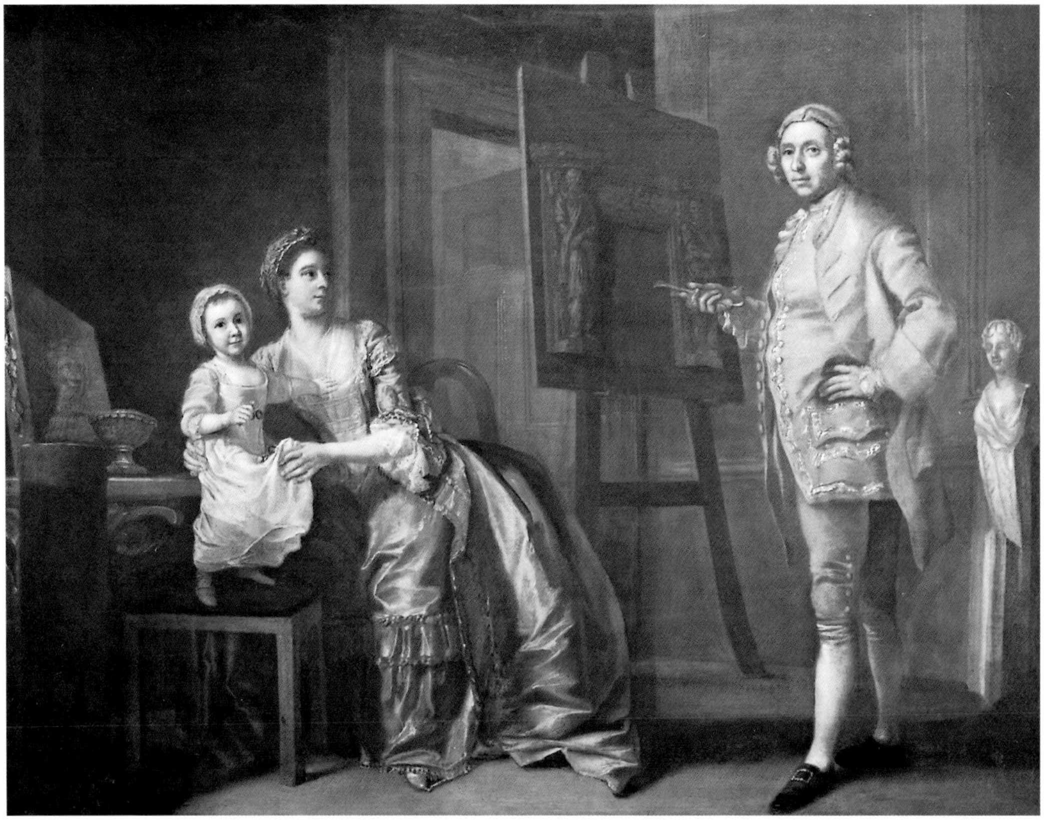

WILTON by Francis Hayman 1760 (Victoria and Albert Museum)

The curiously un-Italian character of the portrait was noticed by Farington:

> While Reynolds remained at Florence, in 1752, he painted a portrait of [Wilton] which was much admired as it was a brilliant display of those qualities in which he so eminently excelled; but of the peculiar merits of the picture, he did not then appear to be sufficiently sensible. 'After studying the finest works of the great masters', he says, 'a new taste and new perceptions began to dawn upon me, but the notions I had of painting when I left England were not eradicated'. No, nor was it necessary they should be so; his mind had become more enlarged it is true, but the bias of his taste was settled, and the portrait of Mr Wilton bore much more affinity to his early productions than to anything he had seen in the Vatican.[3]

1 At the NPE 1867 exhibition the sitter was described as having 'dark sepia' eyeballs and dark silky sepia hair' (NPG archive); perhaps it needed cleaning.

2 For all these comments, see Ingamells 1997, pp.809, 1009.

3 J. Farington, *Memoirs of the Life of Sir Joshua Reynolds*, 1819, pp.35-37.

4314 attributed to CHARLES GRIGNION junior c.1771

Black and white chalk on grey laid paper 13.7 x 11.5 (5⅜ x 4½); verso: an inscription in a contemporary hand *Joseph Wilton/ RA*; the fragment of a chalk drawing of the shoulders of a dark-haired nude figure with the inscription *Julia*, and the Ingram collector's marque above a small *A*.

Collections: Hon Mrs Fitzroy Newdegate, Arbury; Christie's, 14 March 1952, lot 230 (with seven other portrait drawings by Grignion), bt. Colnaghi; Sir Bruce Ingram, from whose executors purchased 1963.

Sold in 1952 with pencil heads of other Academicians - Charles Catton, Tan che-qua (a visiting Chinese painter), Dr William Hunter (see p.277), Joseph Nollekens, John Richards, Benjamin West and Richard Yeo - of which those of Hunter and Catton carried a slightly later inscription saying they had been drawn while they were standing to Zoffany[1] for his *Royal Academicians*★ completed in 1772 (see p.508). All were then said to be by Grignion (aged twenty in 1772), a feasible but unproven attribution.

1 As recorded by Millar 1969, no.1210. A note from the old mount of NPG 4314, presumably by Bruce Ingram, repeats this statement, adding that other drawings 'from this series are in the possession of the Ashmolean Museum, Gilbert Davis Esq, Iolo Williams Esq, and the Hunterian Society Glasgow'.

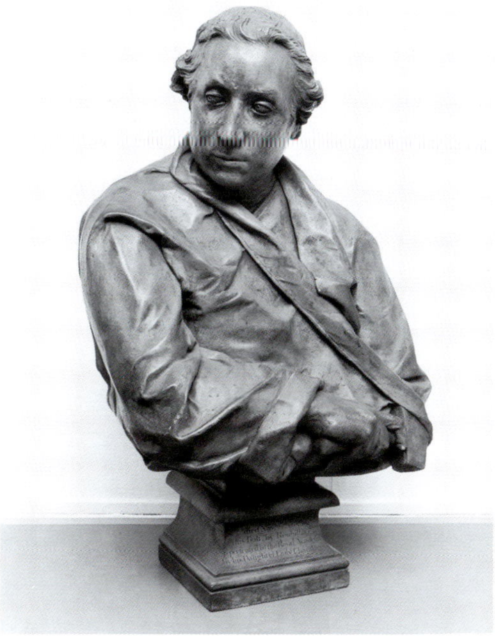

WILTON by L-F. Roubiliac 1761 (Royal Academy of Arts, London)

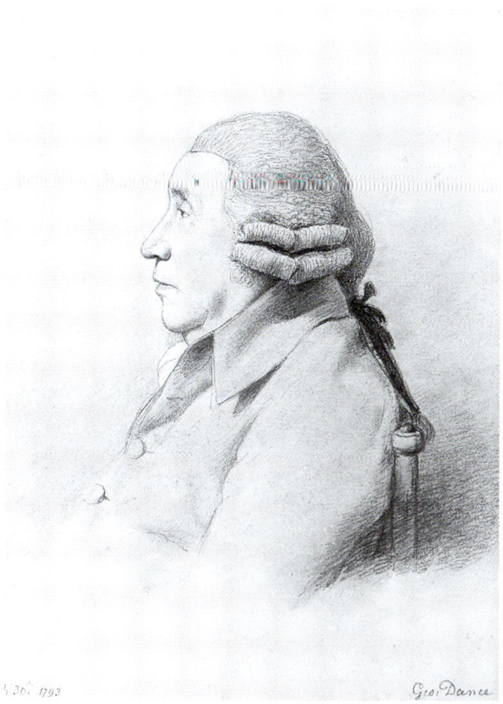

WILTON by George Dance 1793 (Royal Academy of Arts, London)

987 see Groups, *Chambers, Wilton and Reynolds* by JOHN FRANCIS RIGAUD 1782

ICONOGRAPHY

1752 Painting by Joshua Reynolds, see NPG 4810.

1760 Painting by Francis Hayman,* a whole-length sculptor, standing by an easel, with his wife and small daughter. Victoria and Albert Museum (P.7.1985; see B. Allen, *Burl. Mag.*, CXXV, 1983, pp.195-200). The alternative identification of the sculptor Benjamin Carter is less persuasive (J. Wood, *Zeitschrift für Kunstgeschichte*, 62, 1999, pp.404-06).

1761 Bust by L-F. Roubiliac, mallet in right hand. Exhibited SA 1761(154). Cast in the Royal Academy,* exhibited *Rococo*, Victoria and Albert Museum, 1984 (S36.).

In *A Call to Connoisseurs*, 1761, Roubiliac and Wilton were hailed as the 'great and glorious' British sculptors of the age (see M. Baker & D. Bindman, *Roubiliac and the 18th century Monument*, 1995, p.76).

c.1765 Painting by J.H. Mortimer, standing behind the seated Mortimer who is drawing, as a boy brings him a classical bust. Royal Academy (*Mortimer* 1986, no.32, fig.49). See Mortimer NPG 234.

c.1765-70 Painting by J.H. Mortimer,* *Caricature Group*, see Comparative Groups.

c.1771 Painting attributed to Charles Grignion jr., see NPG 4314.

1772 Painting by Johann Zoffany,* *The Academicians of the Royal Academy*, see Groups NPG 1437.

1782 Painting by J.F. Rigaud, with Sir William Chambers and Sir Joshua Reynolds, see Groups NPG 987.

1793 Drawing by George Dance,* half-length profile, dated 30 March 1793. Royal Academy. Engraved W. Daniell 1810 (*Dance Portraits*). Fuseli commented on this drawing: 'How simple are the thinking parts of this man's head, and how sumptuous the manducatory' (Smith 1905, p.204). A less finished version drawing exhibited *Sublime and Beautiful*, Sabin, 1973(32), illus. pl.2.

1793 Pen drawing by John Cawse, heavy whole-length figure, with wig, a stick in his left hand. British Museum (1883.5.12.158).

1795 Painting by Henry Singleton,* *President and Members of the Royal Academy*, see Comparative Groups.

1803 Portrait by T.D. Guest, exhibited RA 1803(711).

WOLCOT, John 1738-1819

'Peter Pindar', satirist, physician and amateur artist; b. Kingsbridge, Devon; physician in Jamaica 1767-72 and ordained 1769; leaving the Church, he practised in the west country 1773-80; as satirist in London, he published *Odes to the Royal Academicians* 1782-85 and the *Lousiad* 1785; *Six Picturesque Views*, aquatints by Alken after Pindar, were published in 1797.

'a thick squat man with a large dark and flat face, and no speculation in his eye' (*DNB*).

830 JOHN OPIE c.1780

Canvas 52 x 42 (20½ x 16½) lined; original size probably 47 x 42, the top edge being unwrapped during lining; in poor condition: overall shrinkage craquelure heavily retouched and discoloured varnish.

Green eyes, dark brown hair wearing a black coat.

Collections: [Mrs Mary Lambe, Bath];[1] Agnew, from whom purchased 1890.

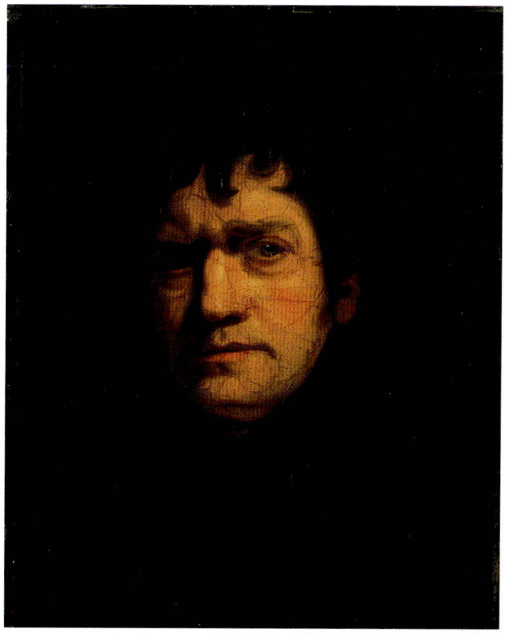

WOLCOT NPG *830*

Although undocumented and in poor condition, this bold sketch appears to show the middle-aged Wolcot; other Opie portraits showed him with a wig, disguising his dark hair. A version in better condition was with Colonel Cree in 1968.[2]

1 Earland, *loc. cit.*, suggested this provenance but Rogers 1878, p.180, described the Lambe portrait as a 'well preserved' bust length 'in a fur cap, sunburnt and swarthy complexion, in black coat, showing very little white cravat', mentioning another version with F. Ouvry.

2 Possibly the version listed by Rogers 1878, p.180, and Earland 1911, p.324, previously with Frederick Ouvry and F.E. Street.

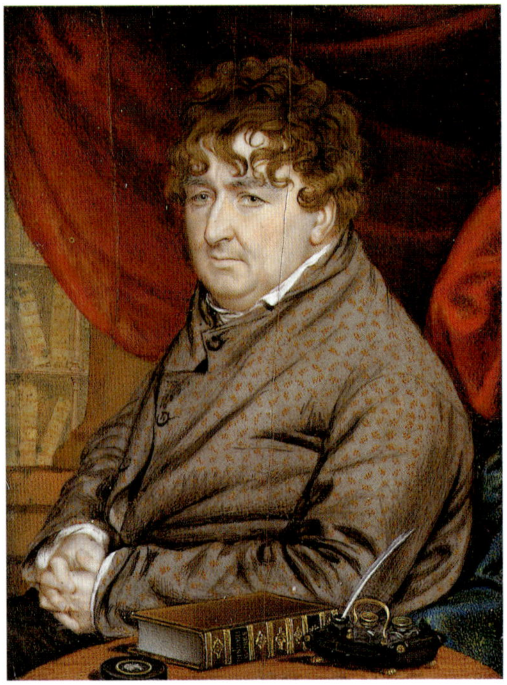

WOLCOT NPG *156*

156 WALTER STEPHENS LETHBRIDGE 1817

Watercolour and bodycolour on ivory 11.3 x 8.5 (4½ x 3⅜) laid down on card; three vertical cracks run from the top edge, two through the head and one through the red curtain to the left; scattered retouchings. The original backing inscribed in ink, in a contemporary hand: *Dr John Wolcot -/son of Alexander & Mary -/ Born May 9 1738 Died* and, below: *WS Lethbridge Pinxit ad vivum /no 391 Strand London / Exhibited in the Royal Academy.1817.*[1]

Grey eyes, fairish wig, wearing a grey suit with a yellow floral pattern, sitting in a blue chair; on the table in front of him a volume titled *PINDAR'S WORKS .OL/V* and a cameo head; a deep red curtain behind him.

Collections: Purchased from William Mannin[2] 1863.

Exhibition: RA 1817(646, with two others).

A version with the Royal College of Physicians, London,[3] signed and dated *Pinxit ad vivum 1817*, shows the standing books arranged slightly differently.

1 Preserved in the NPG archive, with a contemporary MS, also originally behind the miniature: *Written under a Miniature Portrait of John Wolcot M.D. (olim Peter Pindar, Esqr.) taken by that able artist Lethbridge his countryman when the Bard was in his 80th year ... Devonia greets her sons of skill, Who thus their parts so ably fill ....*

2 For whom, see Horsley NPG 155.

3 Illus. *Cat. of Portraits*, 1964, p.447.

ICONOGRAPHY

Portraits by Opie

At the age of fifteen Opie was adopted by Wolcot, who brought him to London in 1781 and carefully promoted his career; 'Wolcot is always with him and is as conceited, vulgar and jawing as ever' Northcote wryly observed in 1782; their business partnership was dissolved in 1783, but they remained friends until 1798 when Opie's second wife, the writer Amelia Alderson, forbade him their house.

c.1780 Drawing, bust length, with wig. Formerly the Rev J.H. de Courcelles (illus. Earland 1911, f.p.10).

c.1780 Painting by John Opie, see NPG 830.

1784 Painting, bust length. Exhibited *Opie*, Arts Council, 1962(26) lent Sir John Seale (cf. Rogers 1878, p.181).

c.1786 Painting, half length with wig. Royal Institute of Cornwall, Truro. Engraved anon. 1794; J. Chapman 1797 (oval, for Pindar's *Works*).

c.1786 Painting, bust-length profile with wig. Exhibited *Opie*, Arts Council, 1963(40) lent Humphrey Woollcombe. Version sold Sotheby's, 4 July 2001, lot 45, from Lord De Dunstanville's collection (Earland 1911, p.324); a similar portrait listed with F.W. Bond in 1878 (Rogers 1878, p.181; Earland 1911, p.324).

1787 Painting, half length with wig. Auckland AG (illus. Auckland *Quarterly*, spring 1956, p.5). Engraved J. Corner 1787 (*European Mag.*). Enamel copy 1801 by P.J. Bone, NG of Ireland (3580).

1787 Painting, half-length seated with wig, right hand on chin. Exhibited NPE 1867(809) lent J. Stirling Taylor. Engraved C.H. Hodges 1787.*

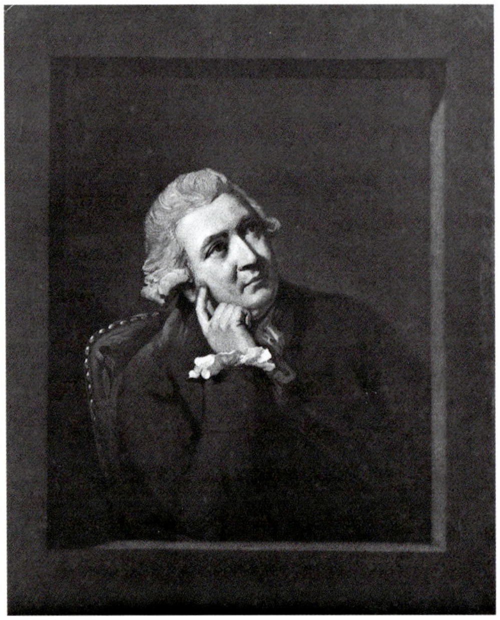

WOLCOT C.H. Hodges after John Opie 1787 (NPG D 4859)

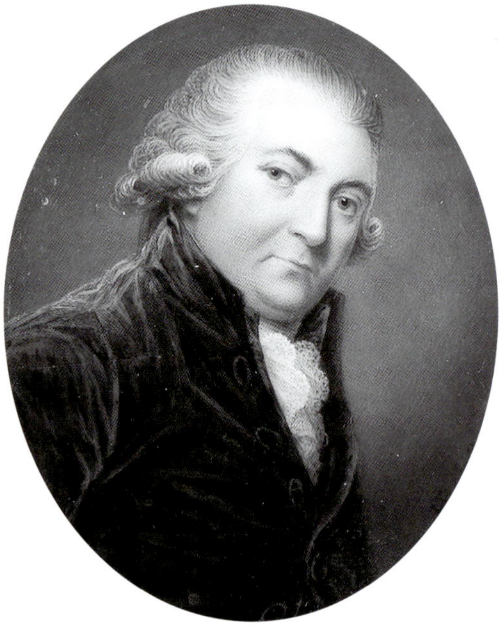

WOLCOT by Henry Bone 1793 (Christie's)

c.1787 Painting, half length with wig, left hand on chin. Christie's, 2 May 1975, lot 164.

1792 Painting, half-length oval, engraved W. Ridley 1792 (*General Mag. & Impartial Rev.*).

1798 Painting, half length, dark hair, engraved K. Mackenzie 1798 & 1802.

after 1800 Painting, bust-length profile, balding. C.J. Sawyer in 1937 (from the Heugh collection, sold Christie's, 13 December 1935, lot 139).

after 1800 Painting, half length, white balding hair. Sotheby's, 28 November 1968, lot 165. Probably correctly identified.

Untraced portraits by Opie with Sir Stafford Northcote (Rogers 1878, p.237).

Portraits by other Artists

1783 Crayon miniature by Ozias Humphry, exhibited SKM 1865(1557) lent J.H. Anderdon.

1789 Drawing by Samuel Collings, bust-length oval with wig, etched by J. Barlow 1789.

1793 Enamel by Henry Bone,* bust-length oval, with wig. Sotheby's, 2 June 1992, lot 686. Presumably the miniature exhibited RA 1794(472), for which a preliminary drawing dated 1793 is in the NPG Bone albums (*Bone* 1999, no.558); a second dated enamel in the Victoria and Albert Museum (706.1904).

1793 Drawing by George Dance,* profile bust, dated 7 July 1793. British Museum (1898.7.12.35). Engraved W. Daniell (*Dance Plates*). A second drawing exhibited *Sublime and Beautiful*, Sabin, 1973(33), illus. pl.2.

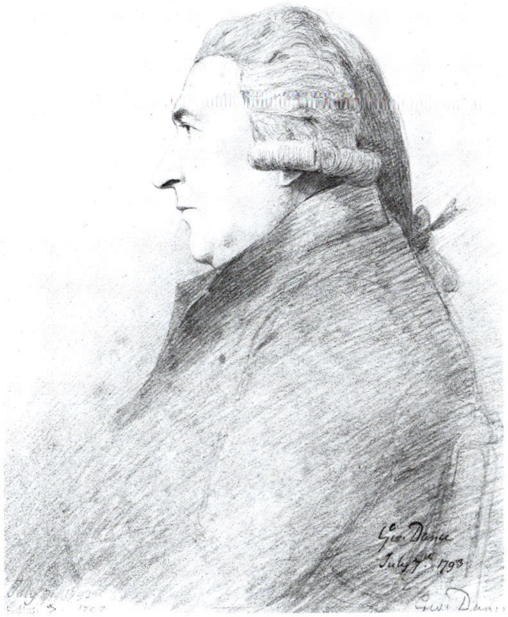

WOLCOT by George Dance 1793 (British Museum)

1795 Painting by J. Barry, half-length oval, engraved P. Roberts 1795.

1800 Painting by Henry Ashby, exhibited RA 1800(107).

1812 Painting by J.R. Smith, half length, dark hair, engraved C. Heath 1812, Carver 1820, W. Holl 1820, C.T. Warren, H.R. Cook (as *T. Uwins del.*) and Halpen.

1817 Miniature by W.S. Lethbridge, see NPG 156.

1819 Drawing by John Taylor, half-length profile with a turban, engraved anon. *a short time previous to his decease* (*Lady's Mag.*).

DOUBTFUL PORTRAITS

Miniature by William Birch, sold Christie's, 20 February 1979, lot 49; the portrait of 'Mr Wolcot' by George Romney, 1779-81 (Ward & Roberts 1904, II, p.174) is unlikely to be Pindar at that time.

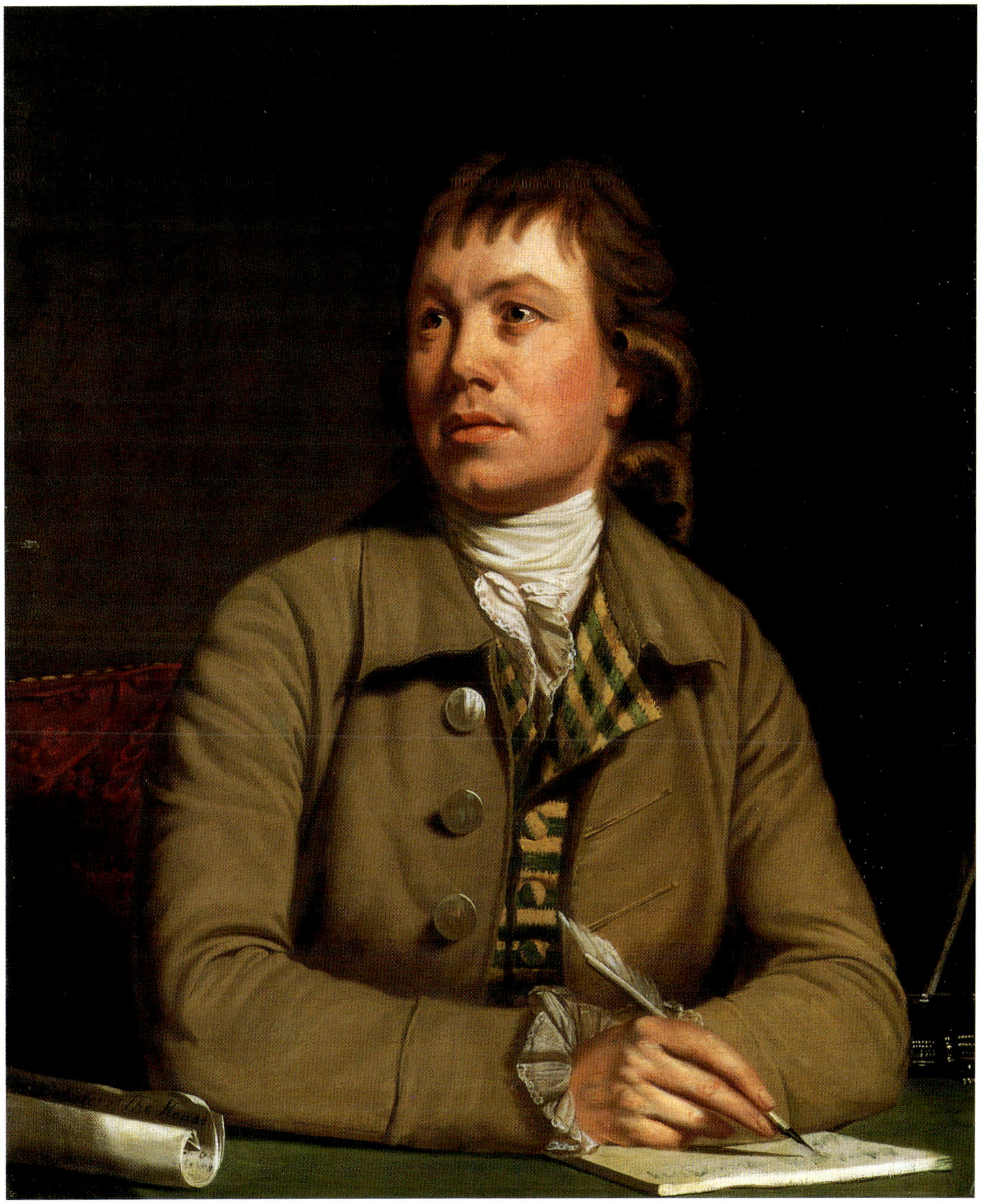

WOODFALL NPG 169

WOODFALL, William 1746-1803

Journalist, celebrated for his parliamentary reporting; edited the *London Packet* 1772-74 and the *Morning Chronicle* 1774-89; founded and edited the *Diary* 1789-93, which first published reports of parliamentary debates the following day.

169 THOMAS BEACH 1782

Canvas 76 x 63.5 (30 x 25) lined 1865; cleaned 1976; signed, lower right above the quill: *T. Beach pinxt./ 1782.*

Brown eyes, light brown hair, light grey coat over a striped green and yellow waistcoat; on the green tablecloth lies a roll of paper headed: *the Debates of the House*.

Collections: By descent to the sitter's great-nephew, H.D. Woodfall, by whom presented 1864.[1]

Engravings: Anon. woodcuts: *ILN*, LXII, 1873, p.353; *London Society*, September 1863.

Exhibitions: [SA 1783 see below]; NPE 1867(687); *Faces as Art*, NPG, 1976.

Reference: H.F. Finberg, *Connoisseur*, LI, 1918, p.141; Beach 1934, p.75.

Beach was working in Bath in 1782 and NPG 169 was probably one of the seven portraits of gentlemen he sent to London for exhibition at the SA the following year.[2] Woodfall's paper, the *Morning Chronicle*, then printed a flattering notice of Beach, describing him as 'illustrious and eminent' among the young artists at Bath, with a 'rich ... natural genius'.[3]

A replica is in the Palace of Westminster.[4]

1 The Trustees hesitated to accept Woodfall; they had declined a portrait of 'Woodfall the Printer of Junius' (i.e. H.S. Woodfall, William's older brother) in 1860; Scharf then told the potential donor of NPG 169 that 'Mr Woodfall did not come within the limits the Trustees have adopted' (2 December 1863; NPG archive); the donor pointed out the previous portrait had been of H.S. not W. Woodfall and, the Board having deferred a decision once, they 'finally' accepted the gift of NPG 169 on 29 February 1864.

2 Whitley 1928, I, p.394; II, p.368, states that one of these was of Woodfall and 'probably [NPG 169]'. Beach 1934, p.75, stated that NPG 169 was the exhibited portrait.

3 Whitley 1928, II, pp.367-68 (also quoted by H.F. Finberg, *Connoisseur*, LI, 1918, pp.139, 141; Beach 1934, pp.16-17).

4 Illus. M. Hay & J. Riding, *Art in Parliament*, 1996, p.48 (from Sotheby's, 18 February 1987, lot 243).

ICONOGRAPHY

1782 Painting by Thomas Beach, see NPG 169.

1792 Miniature by Alexander Pope, exhibited RA 1792(170).

1795 Drawn and etched by Robert Dighton, three-quarter length seated, quill in hand. A variant composition, engraved anon.

1797 Anon. engraving, half-length oval (front. *An Impartial Report of the Debates ...*).

Undated Painting, small whole-length standing, resting his right elbow on a table; exhibited *Caxton*, South Kensington, 1877(3155) lent W. Blades (when seen by Scharf: TSB 23/42).

WRIGHT NPG *4090*

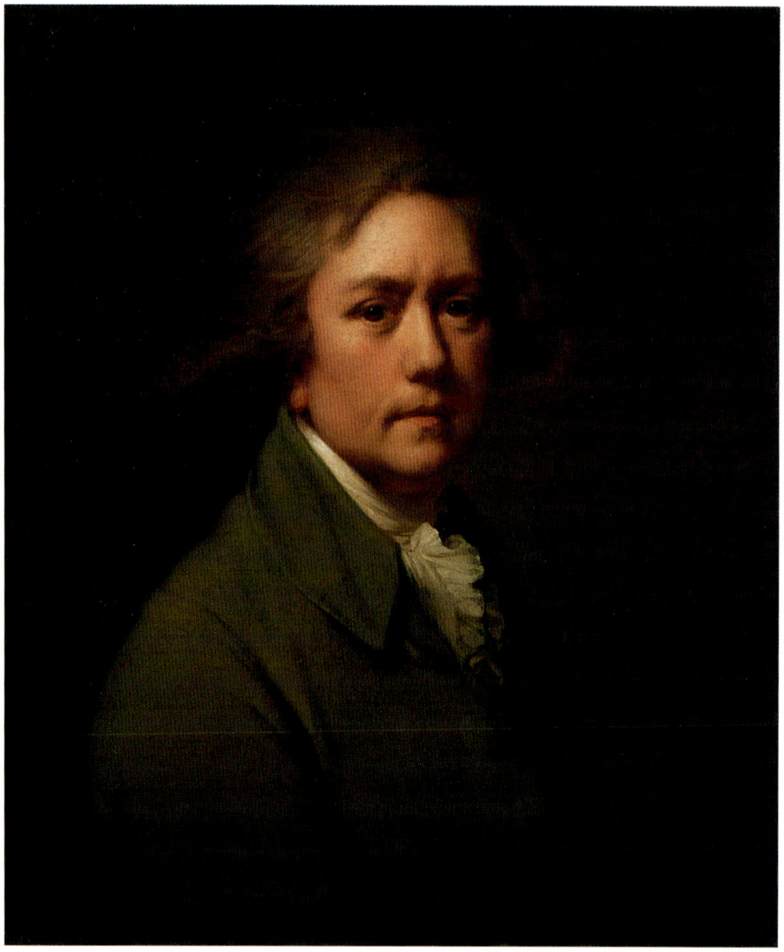

WRIGHT, Joseph, of Derby 1734-97

Painter; studied under Hudson 1751-53 and 1756-57; in Italy 1773-75; exhibited SA 1765-76 and 1791, FS 1778 and 1783, RA 1778-94; elected ARA 1781, but did not accept his RA election in 1784; 'a very respectable character, rather inclined to melancholy, a perfect valetudinarian, who never long enjoyed a firm state of health' (Edwards).

'In his person he was rather above the middle size, and, when young, was esteemed a very handsome man; his eyes were prominent and very expressive' (J. Leigh Philips, 1797).

4090 SELF PORTRAIT c.1785

Canvas 64 x 53.5 (25¼ x 21¼); lined; cleaned 1959; retouchings in the head and coat.

Brown eyes, greying hair, wearing a green coat with a white neckcloth.

Collections: [Probably the artist's daughter Romana, who m. James Cade]; bt. from the Cade family by W. Wright Bemrose c.1900;[1] his son, W.A. Bemrose, from whom purchased 1959.

Exhibitions: *Midland Counties Exhibition*, Derby, 1870(798)[2] lent Miss S.L. Cade; *Joseph Wright*, Derby, 1883(44) lent Miss Cade; Graves' Galleries, London, 1910(32) lent W. Wright Bemrose; Derby, *Wright Bicentenary*, 1934(77) lent W. Wright Bemrose; *Wright* 1990(149).

Although bland in execution and lacking a high degree of finish, NPG 4090 is evidently by Wright (the omission from Nicolson's 1968 catalogue apparently an oversight). Dated c.1782-85 by Egerton, according to the apparent age of the sitter, although it might be later, according to the cut of the coat and the shirt frills,[3] and the pose relates exactly to the 'Yoxall' self portrait painted for Wright's friend Thomas Gisborne in 1793. The essential modesty of the portrait perhaps renders it unlikely that it was the 'Portrait of an Artist' exhibited by Wright in 1785 in Robins's Rooms.[4]

A copy of one of these types was lent H. Fitzherbert Wright to the Wright exhibition at Derby 1934(80).

1 Illus. from his collection, *Connoisseur*, LXXXVI, 1930, p.349.

2 Identified in TSB 17/56.

3 Cf. Wright's *John Holland* dated 1787 (Nicolson 1968, no.85).

4 Cf. Egerton, *Wright* 1990, p.228.

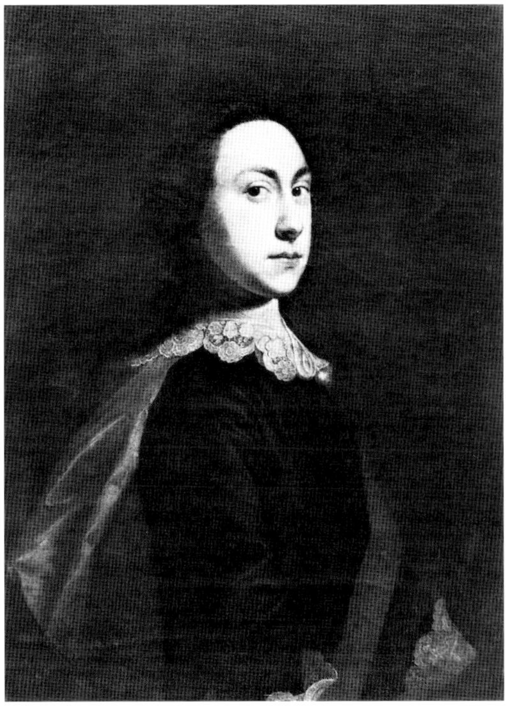

WRIGHT Self portrait c.1753-54 (Derby Museums and Art Gallery)

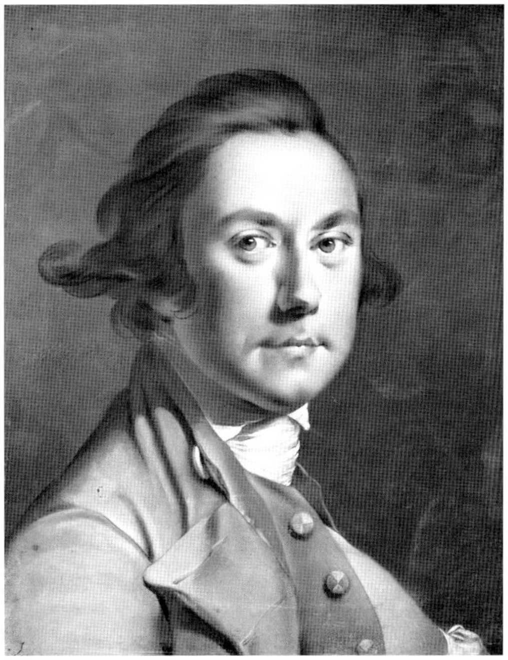

WRIGHT Self portrait c.1765-70 (Derby Museums and Art Gallery)

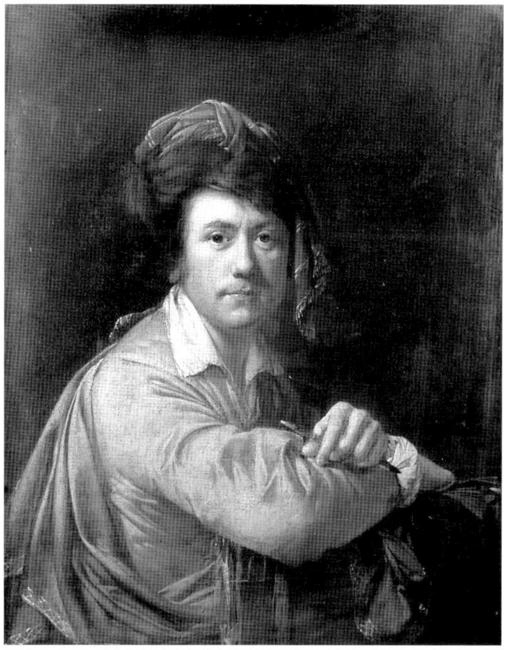

WRIGHT Self portrait c.1772-73 (Private Collection)

ICONOGRAPHY

Self portraits

c.1753-54 Painting,★ half length in Van Dyck costume. Derby MAG (*Wright* 1990, no.1). A related pencil drawing of the head is in the Fitzwilliam Museum, Cambridge (Nicolson 1968, II, pl.7).

c.1760-63? Painting, half length in red Van Dyck costume, a black plumed hat under his right arm. Sotheby's, 16 November 1983, lot 45 (from the collection of Maud, Countess Wharncliffe).

c.1765-70 Charcoal drawing,★ bust length. Derby MAG (DBYMU 1954-219/15; *Wright* 1990, no.43). Inscribed, verso: *Joseph Wright of Derby/ Copied by Wm Pether*. No copy by Pether is known.

c.1767-70 Charcoal drawing of c.1767-70, bust length with fur collar. Derby MAG (DBYMU 1953-186; *Wright* 1990, no.54).

c.1772-73 Painting,★ half length, wearing fur cap, a porte-crayon in his left hand. Private collection (*Wright* 1990, no.94). See also the portrait of c.1776 attributed to Hurlston.

c.1773 Painting, half length, with a striped silk turban, right hand on chin. Private collection (Nicolson 1968, no.169). A copy by John Holland 1800 in a private collection. Copies in the NG Canada (6508), and sold Bonham's, 17 April 1958, lot 104, and 2 October 1958, lot 89.

c.1779-82 Painting half length with a broad-brimmed hat. Formerly Cade collection (Nicolson 1968, no.170). Engraved J. Ward 1807 (illus. *Wright* 1990, P43). Copy by John Holland (private collection; illus. Nicolson 1968, I, fig.8); another copy in Derby MAG. Other versions include those sold American Art Association, 10 January 1929, lot 21 (as Reynolds by Dance); Sotheby's, 10 November 1993, lot 56; Bonham's, 19 March 1997, lot 537; Christie's, 11 April 1997, lot 65 (by the artist's granddaughter, Anna Maria Simpson).

before 1784 Painting with Josiah Wedgwood in 1785 (Nicolson 1968, no.171). Apparently the portrait exhibited as 'Portrait of an Artist', Robins's Rooms 1785(20).

c.1785 Painting, see NPG 4090.

1793 Painting, half length, grey hair and grey coat. Untraced, painted for Thomas Gisborne of Yoxall (Nicolson 1968, no.172); pose and head similar to NPG 4090, but the figure aged by the thinning grey hair. A copy (Nicolson 1968, I, fig.9) in a private collection, differing in not showing shirt frills, bears an inscription verso doubtless copied from the original: *Iosephus Wright,/ Anno Dom: 1793;/ Aetat:59:/ Manu propriâ./ Tabulam hanc/ Amico suo T. G*[*isborne* added]*/ Dono dedit/ Pictor.*

By other Artists

c.1772 Miniature attributed to Samuel Cotes. Private collection.

c.1776? Painting attributed to Richard Hurlston, half length with turban, closely resembling the self portrait of c.1772-73, with a night view of an erupting Vesuvi us. Yale Center for British Art (B1981.25.369). A larger version, from the Arkwright collection, sold Sotheby's, 10 November 1993, lot 54, on loan in Derby MAG in 1994.

1782 Painting by William Tate, half length, a roll of papers in his right hand. Kedleston (illus. Nicolson 1968, I, fig.134).

DOUBTFUL PORTRAITS

See Unidentified Portraits NPG 29. Painting, half length, holding a large drawing of Wright's *Edwin* [of 1777-78] (Royal College of Surgeons, London; on loan to Marble Hill, 2001). Drawings in the Yale Center for British Art (B1977.14.6320; illus. Nicolson 1968, I, p.46; see P.J. Noon, *English Portrait Drawings & Miniatures*, New Haven, 1979, no.72), Derby MAG (Nicolson 1968, no.165), and 'in the possession of John Britton', engraved Graf & Soret as Wright of Derby. Etching, inscribed 'Wright of Derby; etched by himself' (illus. *Wright* 1990, P38; engraved Blake for the *Monthly Mag.*, Sept.1797); a related half-length painting was with J.M. Eardley Simpson in 1958.

WYNDHAM, Charles, see EGREMONT

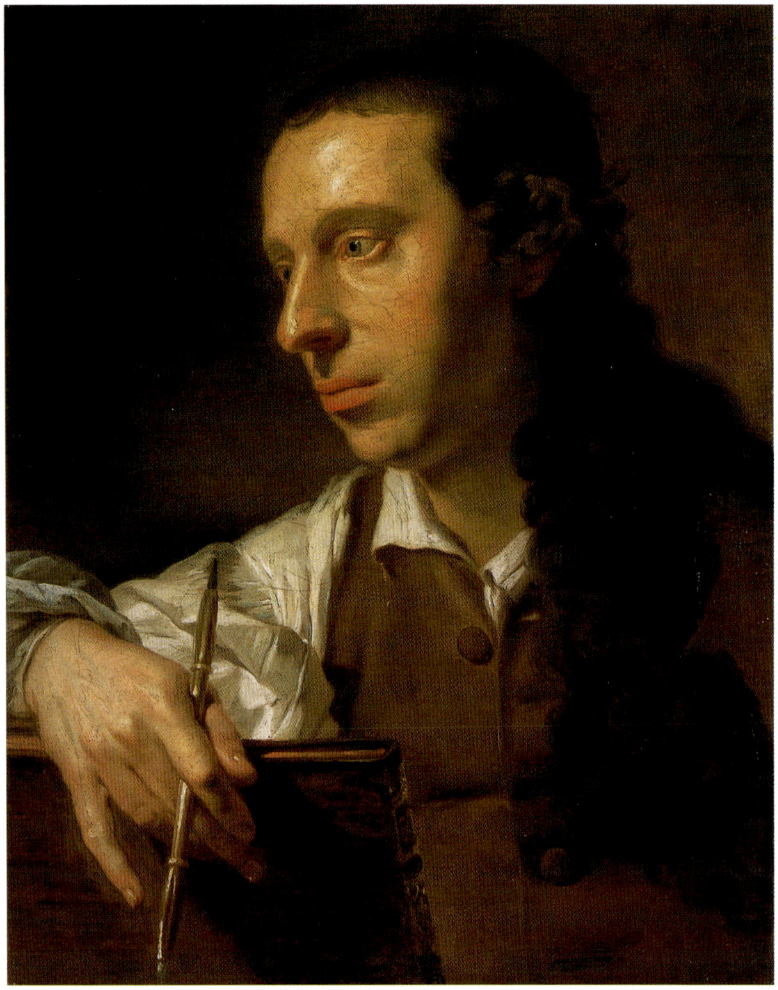

ZOFFANY NPG *399*

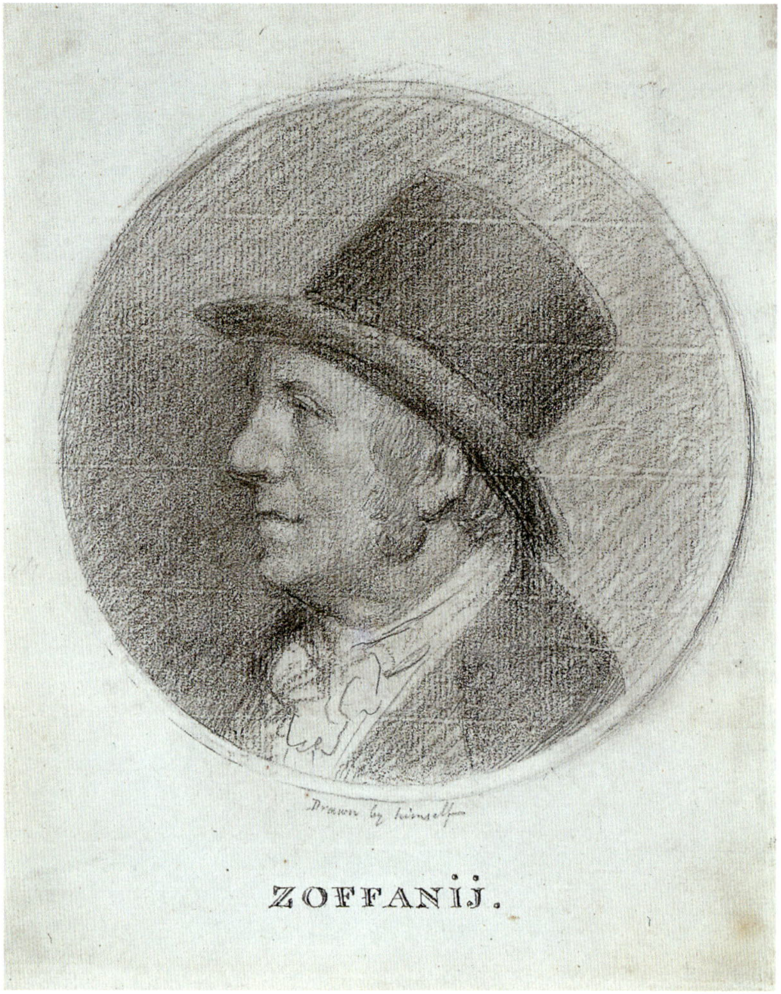

ZOFFANY NPG *2536*

ZOFFANY, Johann 1733-1810

Painter; b. near Frankfurt and trained in Regensburg; Rome 1750-57; came in 1760 to London, where patronised by David Garrick and introduced to the Royal family; exhibited RA 1770-1800; in 1772 Queen Charlotte commissioned him to paint the *Tribuna* in Florence (where Horace Mann called him 'the one-eyed German'); in 1776 in Vienna he was made a Baron of the Holy Roman Empire (he was occasionally called 'Sir' in England thereafter); returned to England 1778; in India 1783-89 making his fortune; returning to London, he gave up painting in 1800.

Abbreviations

Pressly 1987: W. Pressly, 'Genius Unveiled: The Self-Portraits of Johan Zoffany', *Art Bulletin*, LXIX, March 1987, pp.86-101

Pressly 1995: W. Pressly, 'Johan Zoffany as David the Anointed One', *Apollo*, CXLI, March 1995, pp.49-55

399 SELF PORTRAIT 1761

Canvas 54 x 44.5 (21¼ x 17½) lined; the surface is much rubbed; cleaned 1970; signed bottom left: *Zoffany.pinx./ 1761.*[1]

Collections: J. Scotcher (a broker), Ealing, 1873, bt. William Bean, from whom purchased 1875.

Exhibitions: *Zoffany*, Arts Council, 1961(6); *British Self-Portraits*, Arts Council, 1962(34); *Romantic Art in Britain*, Detroit, Philadelphia, 1968(37).

Reference: Williamson 1920, p.221; Pressly 1987, p.97.

The identification of both artist and subject has been doubted,[2] and an element of uncertainty remains. The signature, however, appears original and the features sufficiently resemble those of the self portrait now recognised in Zoffany's *David* of 1756 (see below). Pressly has cautiously observed that 'the attitude of pensive introspection fits with the artist's later self-projections'. A drawing, inscribed *ipse pinxit 1761*, apparently a copy from NPG 399, was in the collection of John Lane in 1924.[3]

1 Under a binocular microscope this signature appeared within the original paint layer although it has been reinforced in places (note in the NPG archive 1985).

2 For example, emphatically by Mary Webster in 1976 (note in NPG archive) and see NPG, *Complete Illus. Cat.*, 1981, p.707 where described as *called* Zoffany by an unknown artist. NPG 399 had previously been accepted as a self portrait by Millar (*Zoffany and his Tribuna*, 1966, p.2).

3 Illus. Williamson 1920, f.p.4; with carefully inscribed title ZOFFANY, as if preparatory for an engraving.

2536 SELF PORTRAIT c.1795

Pencil and black crayon on paper[1] 22 x 17.5 (8⅝ x 6⅞) image 15 (5⅞) diameter; inscribed below: ZOFFANIJ. and in a later hand: *Drawn by himself*

Collections: Presented by Iolo A. Williams 1932.

Exhibitions: *Zoffany* 1977(134); *Genial Company*, Nottingham, Edinburgh, 1987(51).

The date suggested by Webster on comparison with Zoffany's head in Singleton's *Royal Academicians*, see below; Shawe-Taylor suggested Zoffany may have intended a deliberate conceit by showing contemporary dress in a medallion portrait.[2]

1 Watermark comparable to Churchill, no.431 (Strasburg bend and lily) with added scroll below as in Churchill, no.415 (Whatman).
2 *Genial Company*, Nottingham, 1987(51).

ICONOGRAPHY

Self Portraits

1756 Painting,★ as *David with the head of Goliath*, half length, right hand on chin. NG Melbourne (Pressly 1995, p.51).

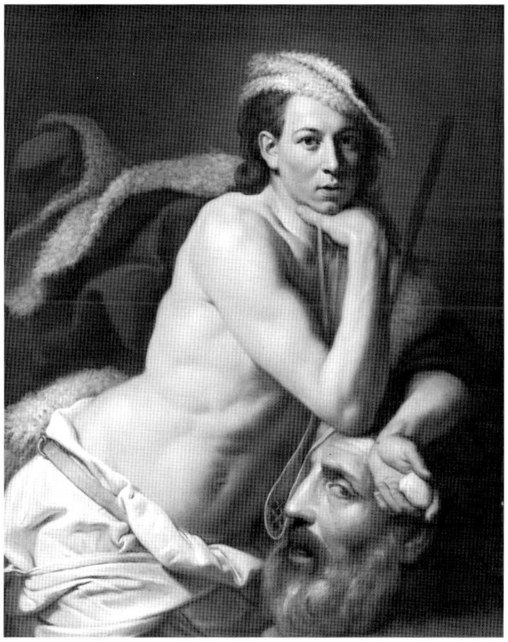

ZOFFANY *Self portrait as David 1756 (National Gallery of Victoria, Melbourne, Australia)*

1757 Painting, *Adoration of the Shepherds*, with Zoffany on the extreme right, hand on heart. Mainfränkisches Museum, Würzburg (Pressly 1995, p.52).

1761 Painting, see NPG 399.

1769 Painting, *William Ferguson as heir to Raith*, with Zoffany seated holding a letter, on the extreme right. Private collection (illus. Zoffany 1977, no.52).

1772 Painting,★ *The Academicians of the Royal Academy*, see Groups NPG 1437.

1772-77 Painting, *The Tribuna, Florence*★ (see Introduction) with Zoffany in the left background holding up Raphael's 'Niccolini-Cowper' *Madonna*. Royal Collection (Millar 1969, no.1211).

1775 Painting,★ half length, right hand on chin. Florence, Uffizi (3293). Zoffany had been elected to the Accademia in Florence in 1773.

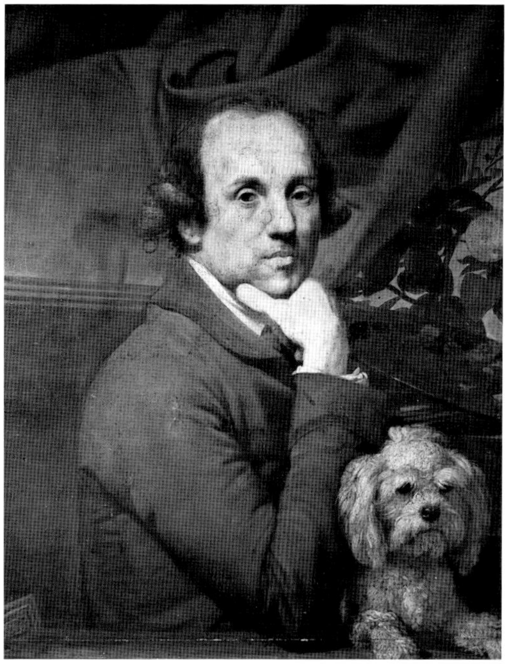

ZOFFANY *Self portrait 1775 (Galleria degli Uffizi, Florence)*

c.1775 Drawing,★ half length, a porte-crayon in his right hand which rests on his chin. British Museum (1927.4.19.1). Version exhibited *English Drawings*, Hazlitt Gooden & Fox, 1990(30).

1776 Painting, half length, wearing a plumed hat, a palette in his left hand. Accademia Etrusca, Cortona (illus. Pressly 1987, p.99). Zoffany was elected to the Accademia in 1777-78. Version sold Sotheby's, 16 May 1990, lot 38.

1776 Painting, half length, an hourglass in his left hand, a skull in his right. Florence, Uffizi (1879; Pressly 1987, p.89). Engraved C. Lasinio; G. Vascellini (from a drawing by Bozzolini). Miniature copy on the German art market 1993.

1779 Painting, half length, his hands inside a Franciscan cowl, as if hesitating to pull it over his head. Galleria Nazionale, Parma. (illus. Pressly 1987, p.93). Painted in Parma, where Zoffany was elected to the Accademia in 1778.

c.1780 Painting, with his daughter[?] and two musicians, his head in the background. Yale Center for British Art (B1977.14.88; illus. Pressly 1987, p.99). For the musicians, see Groups NPG 5179.

1782 Drawing,★ half-length oval to front, a porte-crayon in his right hand held over his drawing board. Ashmolean Museum, Oxford (1919).

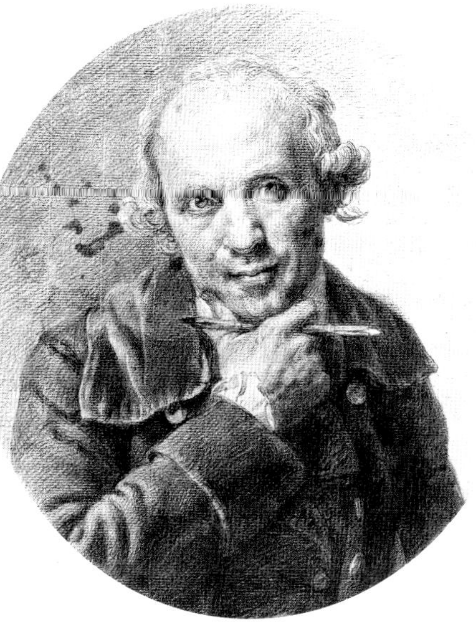

ZOFFANY *Self portrait c.1775 (British Museum)*

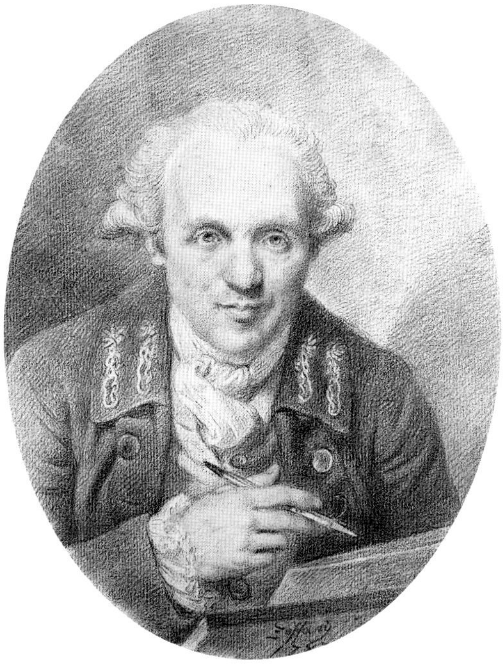

ZOFFANY *Self portrait 1782 (Ashmolean Museum, Oxford)*

1784-86 Painting, *Colonel Mordaunt's Cock Match*, with Zoffany seated in the right background, porte-crayon in hand. Tate Gallery (T 6856; illus. Archer 1979, p.150). Engraved 1792.

1786 Painting, *Colonel Polier with his Friends*, with Zoffany seated centre right, painting a group of Hindus. Victoria Memorial Hall, Calcutta (illus. Pressly 1987, p.100). Painted in Lucknow.

c.1795 Drawing, see NPG 2536.

c.1795-1800 Painting, half-length seated to right wearing spectacles, a palette in his left hand, a hookah in his left. Private collection; Sotheby's, 13 July 1988, lot 189 withdrawn. Previously offered to the NPG in 1868 (TSB 13/57).

c.1795-1800 Painting, seated, with four children, his wife and a nurse (illus. Williamson 1920, f.p.132); sold in two pieces, Christie's, 22 March 1974, lot 52.

Zoffany also showed himself playing very minor roles in two Indian history pictures: the *Embassy of Hyderbeck to Calcutta*, 1796 (engraved R. Earlom 1800; Archer 1979, pp.174-75), and *Death of the Royal Tyger*, c.1785 (engraved R. Earlom 1802; Archer 1979, p.169).

Portraits by other Artists

c.1759 Unattributed painting, standing three-quarter length, with palette and brushes. Mainfränkisches Museum, Würzburg (illus. *Zoffany* 1977, no.5 as by Zoffany; Pressly 1995, p.52 as artist unknown). Inscribed in a later hand: *Joseph Zofanÿ ... London se ipse pinx*.

c.1765 Unattributed miniature, bust-length oval, wearing van Dyck costume. Private collection (illus. Williamson 1920, f.p.128). Exhibited *Zoffany* 1977(136) lent Dr E. Forbes Roberts.

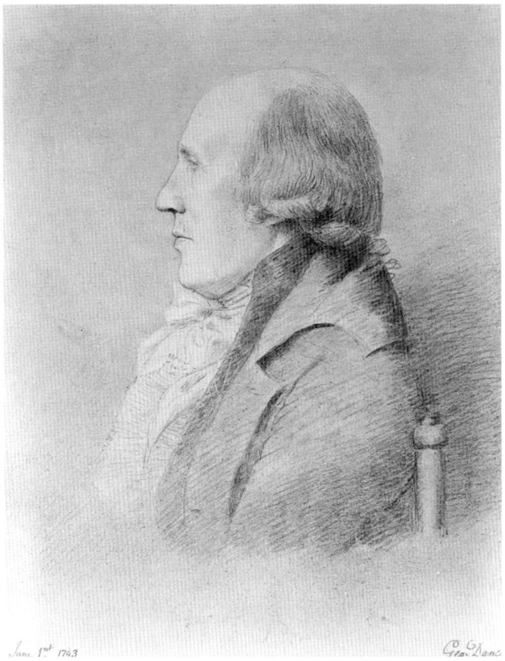

ZOFFANY *by George Dance 1793 (Royal Academy of Arts, London)*

c.1780 Unattributed miniature, bust-length oval. Victoria and Albert Museum (P.2.1954). Exhibited *Zoffany* 1977(137).

c.1790 Unattributed miniature, right hand on chin. Private collection (illus. Williamson 1920, f.p.116). Exhibited *Zoffany* 1977(138) lent Dr E. Forbes Roberts.

1793 Drawing by George Dance,* profile bust to left, dated 1 June 1793. Royal Academy. Engraved W. Daniell 1814 (*Dance Portraits*). A second drawing exhibited *Sublime and the Beautiful*, Sabin, 1973(35).

1795 Painting by Henry Singleton,* *President and Members of the Royal Academy*, see Comparative Groups. A portrait of Zoffany by Singleton exhibited RA 1798(276) was probably connected with this group (cf. Richard Cosway and Thomas Sandby).

DOUBTFUL PORTRAIT

Painting attributed to Zoffany, *An Artist's Studio*, Uffizi, Florence (*Firenze e l'Inghilterra*, Florence, 1971, no.105).

ZUYLESTEIN, William Henry, see **ROCHFORD**

GROUP PORTRAITS

IN ORDER OF ACCESSION NUMBER

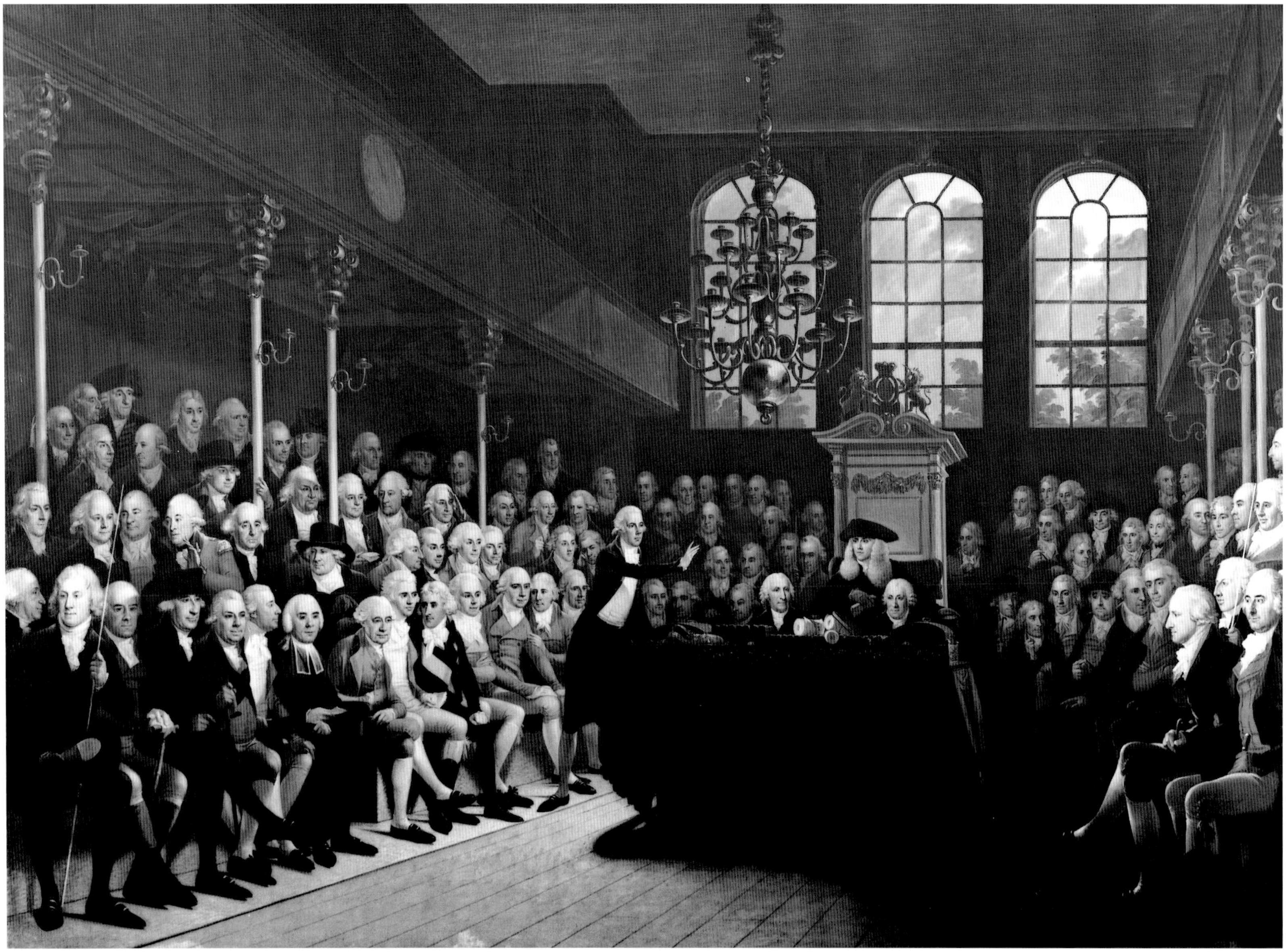

The House of Commons 1793-94 NPG *745*

The House of Commons 1793-94

745 KARL ANTON HICKEL 1793-95

See Walker *Regency*, I, pp.598-604; II, pls.1501-12.

A general view of the House of Commons 1793-94, showing nearly one hundred members, of whom seven feature in this catalogue (references to key and pl. refer to Walker's *Regency* catalogue):

Edmund Burke (1729-97), key 95, pl.1508; his head is seen on the extreme right in the third row, an original, benign and weak likeness. According to Farington (25 July 1794) Burke had insisted on being placed on the opposition side [i.e. with Fox], despite his subsequent change of political opinion induced by the French Revolution.

Hon Richard Fitzpatrick (1747-1813), key ?85, pl.1508, provisionally identified on the right, on the opposition benches behind Fox.

Charles James Fox (1749-1806), key 80, pl.1508, seated on the front bench on the right, the likeness agreeing closely with NPG 743.

Alan Gardner (1742-1808), later 1st Baron Gardner, key no. 21 (although equated by Walker with no. 18), pl.1502.

Sir Richard Hill, 2nd Bt (1732-1808), key 23, pl.1502, appears seated in a broad-brimmed black hat, second row, centre left.

Welbore Ellis, 1st Baron Mendip (1713-1802), key 26, pl.1502, seated on the government front bench, his legs crossed, his right hand in his waistcoat, his suit of a lighter colour than in NPG 3993.

John Baker Holroyd, 1st Earl of Sheffield (1735-1821), key ?37, pl.1502, provisionally identified sitting immediately behind Pitt; the head seems weak and bland.

Sir William Chambers, Joseph Wilton and Sir Joshua Reynolds

987 JOHN FRANCIS RIGAUD 1782

Canvas 120.5 x 146 (47½ x 57½) lined; cleaned 1982; pentiment round Reynolds's left hand. Signed and dated bottom left: *J.F Rigaud/ 1782*.

Collections: Rigaud sale, Peter Coxe, 2nd day, 4 April 1811, lot 81; Montagu Chambers QC (grandson of Sir William); his sale, Christie's, 9 July 1886, lot 109, bt. Wertheimer; James Price sale, Christie's, 15 June 1895, lot 60 (as Reynolds, J. Bacon and Sir W. Chambers), purchased.

Exhibitions: RA 1782(111); RA 1879(172 as Zoffany) lent Montagu Chambers; *Bicentenary Exhibition*, RA, 1968-69(34); *Reynolds* 1992(32); *Chambers*, London, Stockholm, 1996-97; *Art on the Line*, Courtauld Gallery, 2001(9).

Reference: J. Coutu in J. Harris & M. Snodin eds., *Sir William Chambers*, 1996, p.183.

NPG 987 shows, from the left

Sir William Chambers (1723-96): grey eyes, grey powdered wig, wearing the Polar Star on his green coat with silver buttons bearing a gold device; gold brocade waistcoat and grey-green breeches; his right elbow rests on a capital and in his right hand a T-square; he points with his left hand to a plan[1] on which lie dividers.

Joseph Wilton (1722-1803): his dark eyes apparently focused on Chambers's badge of the Polar Star; grey powdered wig, wearing a sandy-brown coat with matching buttons and a yellow green-striped waistcoat; in his right hand a mallet, his left stretched out towards the distant figure of the Apollo Belvedere.[2]

Sir Joshua Reynolds (1723-92): blue eyes, grey powdered wig, wearing a matching coat and waistcoat of red with gold buttons, trimmed with dark fur; he leans on a folio of drawings and sits in a blue-upholstered chair.

Compared with Rigaud's earlier group portrait of the three Italian Academicians (see Groups NPG 3186), the canvas is slightly larger and the composition more successful. The artist's son explained that NPG 987 was 'intended as a companion' and was

> a very interesting group of Sir Joshua Reynolds, the first and distinguished President of the Royal Academy; J. Wilton R.A. Sculptor (afterwards Keeper of the Royal Academy;) and Sir William Chambers R.A. Architect, and Surveyor of the Board of Works: They are represented as in conversation, Sir Joshua in the act of addressing his brother artists, with all the gentleness and suavity for which he was so remarkable, thus giving a perfect idea of his countenance, his expression and character.[3]

He even preferred his father's portrait of Reynolds to

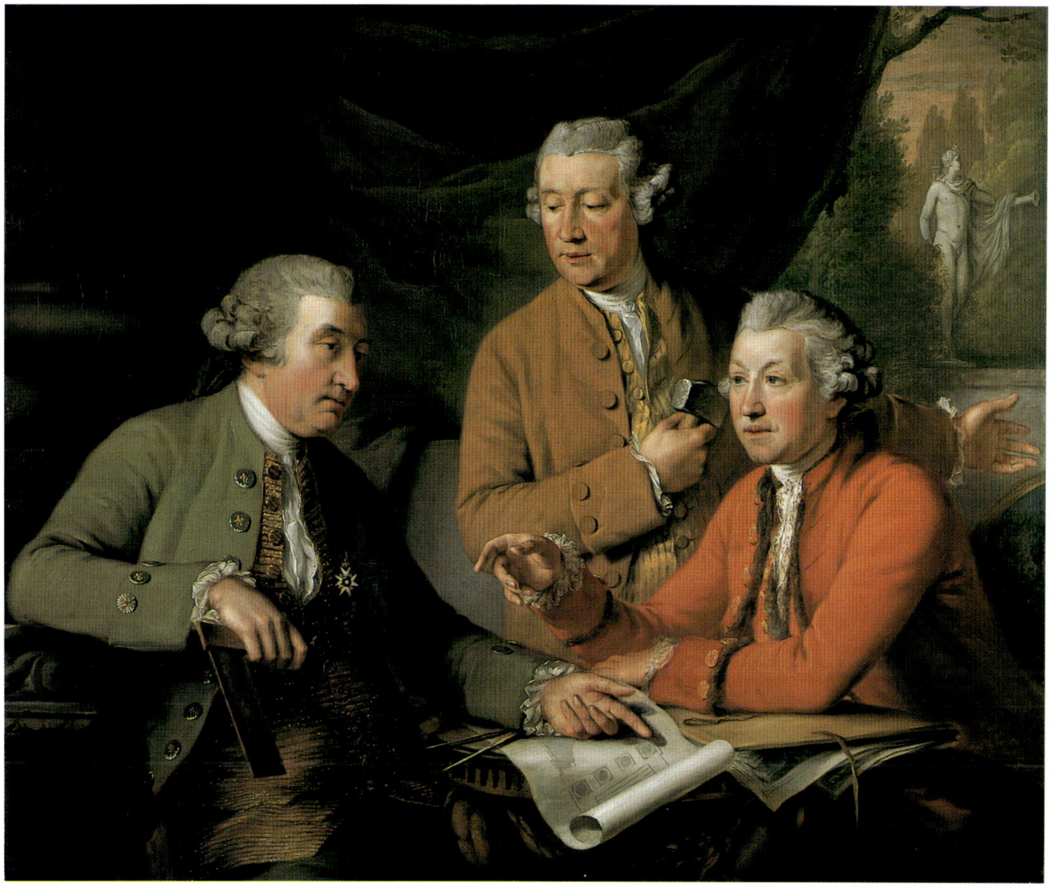

CHAMBERS (left), WILTON and REYNOLDS (right) NPG 987

the self portrait Reynolds presented to the RA (as a Doctor of civil law 1780), as 'a more true representation of his personal appearance, and his peculiar expression' (the Rigaud head somewhat resembles the Reynolds self portrait of 1773, of which, however, there was no early engraving). Of contemporary reviews the *St James's Chronicle*, 2-4 May 1782, agreed that 'They are strong and expressive Resemblances; but the Integrity which led the Artist to copy so exactly the Vulgarity of the President's Countenance will not recommend him to his Favour; and he will probably remain some Time longer among the Associates'. But Rigaud was elected RA in 1784.

This uncommissioned picture portraying three senior Royal Academicians (of similar ages), eminent representatives of the arts of sculpture, architecture and painting, was evidently an exercise in self-advertisement. It may also celebrate the move of the Royal Academy in 1780 to rooms in Somerset House, the masterpiece of Chambers, in which Wilton undertook much decorative carving.[4] Both architect and sculptor had long been distinguished by Royal patronage. The elegant Wilton, to be elected Librarian and Keeper of the Royal Academy in 1786 and 1790 respectively, had been appointed sculptor in ordinary to the King in 1761. Chambers, Knight of the Polar Star, had come to dominate the Office of Works since his initial appointment in 1761; in 1768 he had been the only named appointment (as Treasurer) in the Instrument of Foundation of the Royal Academy. In 1782 he was appointed first surveyor-general and comptroller of the Office of Works. Reynolds, elected first President of the Academy and knighted in 1769, would not be further distinguished by the King until 1784 when he succeeded Ramsay as Principal Painter. He had previously painted the young Wilton in Florence in 1752 (NPG 4810) and had painted Chambers in 1756 (NPG 27) and 1777-80 (a portrait commissioned by the Royal Academy). In 1771 Chambers had designed for him Wick House at Richmond. But the President remained a little in awe of his well-established Treasurer and Wendorf has observed that Rigaud's group hints at uneasiness, the central cluster of gesturing hands suggesting the two are essentially at cross purposes, 'engaged in an administrative stand off'.[5]

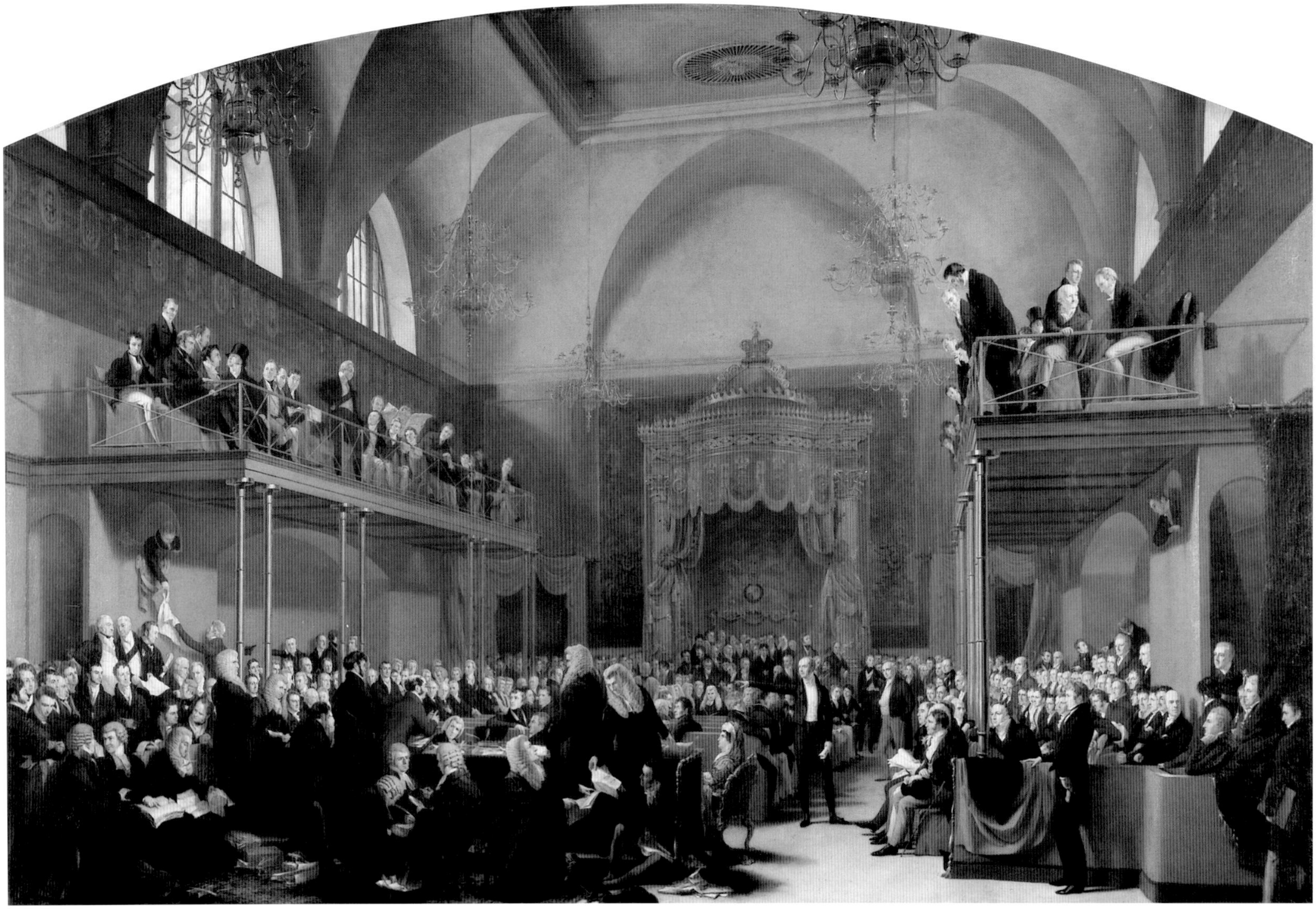

The Trial of Queen Caroline 1820 NPG 999

Each sitter is featured separately in this catalogue.

1 'A plan for a small structure approached by flight of stairs and entered through a lie of four closely packed columns. A casino? A temple? A belvedere to house the Belvedere? The original drawing does not seem to have survived' (N. Bingham, *CL*, CLXXXV, 1991, p.54).
2 Of which he acquired a cast in 1754 and copied for the Duke of Richmond c.1760.
3 Rigaud *Memoir*, p.68.
4 For their collaboration see J. Coutu in J. Harris & M. Snodin eds., *Sir William Chambers*, 1996, pp.175-85.
5 R. Wendorf, *Reynolds*, 1996, p.185.

The Trial of Queen Caroline 1820

999 GEORGE HAYTER 1820-23

See Walker *Regency*, I, pp.608-15; II, pls.1525-32.

The discussion in the House of Lords on a Bill of Pains and Penalties inquiring into the Queen's conduct during her wanderings abroad as Princess of Wales. Hayter's painting contains 186 figures, of whom four feature in this catalogue (references to key and pl. refer to Walker's *Regency* catalogue):

Frederick Ponsonby, 3rd Earl of Bessborough (1738-1844), key 152, pl.1530; his tiny elderly head appears on the right in the second row.

Folliott Herbert Walker Cornewall (1754-1831), key 66, pl.1528; his head appears centre left in the back row. Cornewall also appears in one of Hayter's sketches for the Trial, NPG 1695N (Walker *Regency*, I, p.621; II, pl.1546).

William Harcourt, 3rd Earl of Harcourt (1743-1830), key 46, pl.1528; his head appears on the left, in the second row.

James Maitland, 8th Earl of Lauderdale (1759-1839), key 102, pl.1529; his head appears above and to the left of Queen Caroline.

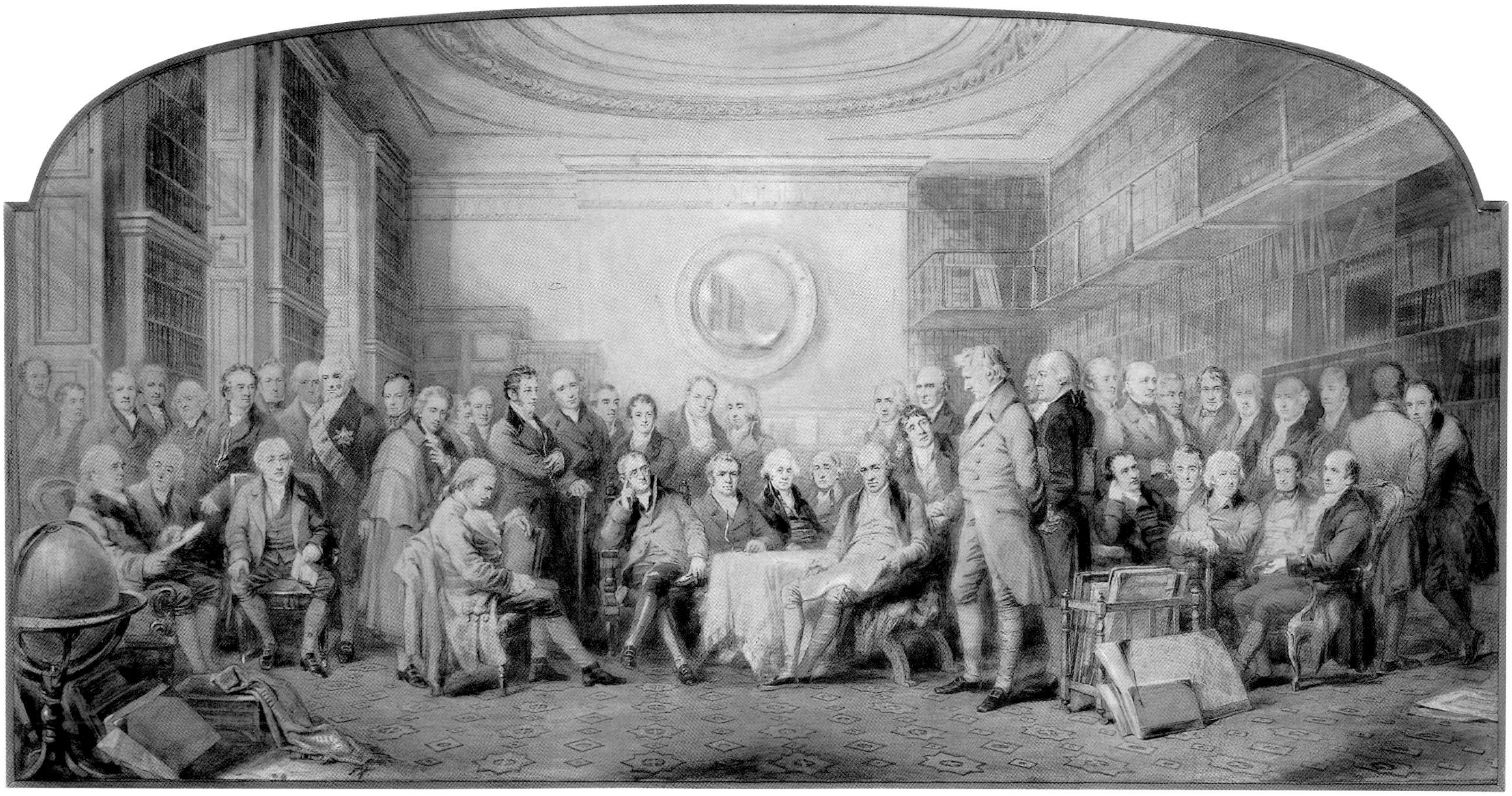

Men of Science living in 1807-08 NPG 1075

Men of Science living in 1807-08

1075 JOHN GILBERT, FREDERICK SKILL and WILLIAM & ELIZABETH WALKER 1858-62

See Walker *Regency*, I, pp.605-08; II, pls.1517-24.

Abbreviation

Walker 1862: W. Walker *Memoirs of the Distinguished Men of Science of Great Britain living in the years 1807-8*, 1862

An imaginary mid-19th century composition showing the scientists assembled in the library of the Royal Institution. Ten of the fifty-four sitters feature in this catalogue (references to key and pl. refer to Walker's *Regency* catalogue):

Sir Joseph Banks (1743-1820), key 13, pl.1519, stands on the left, wearing the ribbon and star of the Bath, the portrait 'taken from the Picture by T. Phillips, R.A., in the possession of the Royal Society' (Walker 1862, p.6).

Sir Samuel Bentham (1757-1831), key 27, pl.1520, stands behind the central table to the left, his likeness 'taken from the Miniature by Murphy, in the Portrait Gallery of the South Kensington Museum' (Walker 1862, p.10).

Matthew Boulton (1728-1809), key 25, pl.1520, is seated in the centre, his likeness taken from 'the Picture by Sir William Beechey, R.A., in the possession of J.W. Gibson Watt, Esq.' (Walker 1862, p.19).

Henry Cavendish (1731-1810), key 18, pl.1519, is seated in the foreground centre left, looking down at the floor, the likeness taken from 'the Drawing by Tomlinson, in the Print Room of the British Museum' (Walker 1862, p.38), now attributed to W. Alexander.

Peter Dollond (1730-1820), key 6, pl.1518, stands in the back row, fifth from the left, the likeness taken from 'the picture by J. Hoppner, R.A.' (Walker 1862, p.72).

Nevil Maskelyne (1732-1811), key 8, pl.1518, is seated in the front row, second from the left, talking to Herschel, his likeness taken from 'the Picture by Russell' (Walker 1862, p.125).

Patrick Miller (1731-1815), key 47, pl.1522, stands in the back row four from the extreme right-hand edge, his likeness taken from the 'Picture by Alexander Nasmyth, in the Portrait Gallery of the South Kensington Museum' (Walker 1862, p.132).

Robert Mylne (1733-1811), key 37, pl.1521, stands centre right in a black coat, his head seen in profile, the likeness taken from 'an original Miniature, lent by R.W. Mylne, Esq., F.R.S' (Walker 1862, p.138).

Richard Watson (1737-1816), does not appear in NPG 1075, but in the engraving by Walker & Zobel he stands in his shovel hat in the centre background beneath the mirror, the likeness taken from 'the Picture by G. Romney, R.A.'(Walker 1862, p.205).

James Watt (1736-1819), key 30, pl.1520, is prominently placed seated just right of centre, the likeness taken from 'the Picture by Sir William Beechey, R.A., in the possession of J.W. Gibson Watt at Doldowlod, and from the Statue by Sir Francis Chantrey, R.A., at Handsworth Church [Birmingham]' (Walker 1862, p.210).

Adam Walker with his Family

1106 GEORGE ROMNEY 1796–1801

Canvas 140 x 170 (55 x 67) lined 1898; restored 1978.

Collections: By descent[1] to the sitter's granddaughter, Miss Ellen Elizabeth Gibson, Durham, by whom bequeathed 1897.

Exhibitions: *Romney*, Kenwood, 1961(41); *Regency Portraits*, Kenwood, 1986.

Reference: Ward & Roberts 1904, II, p.163; Chamberlain 1910, pp.218, 238–39.

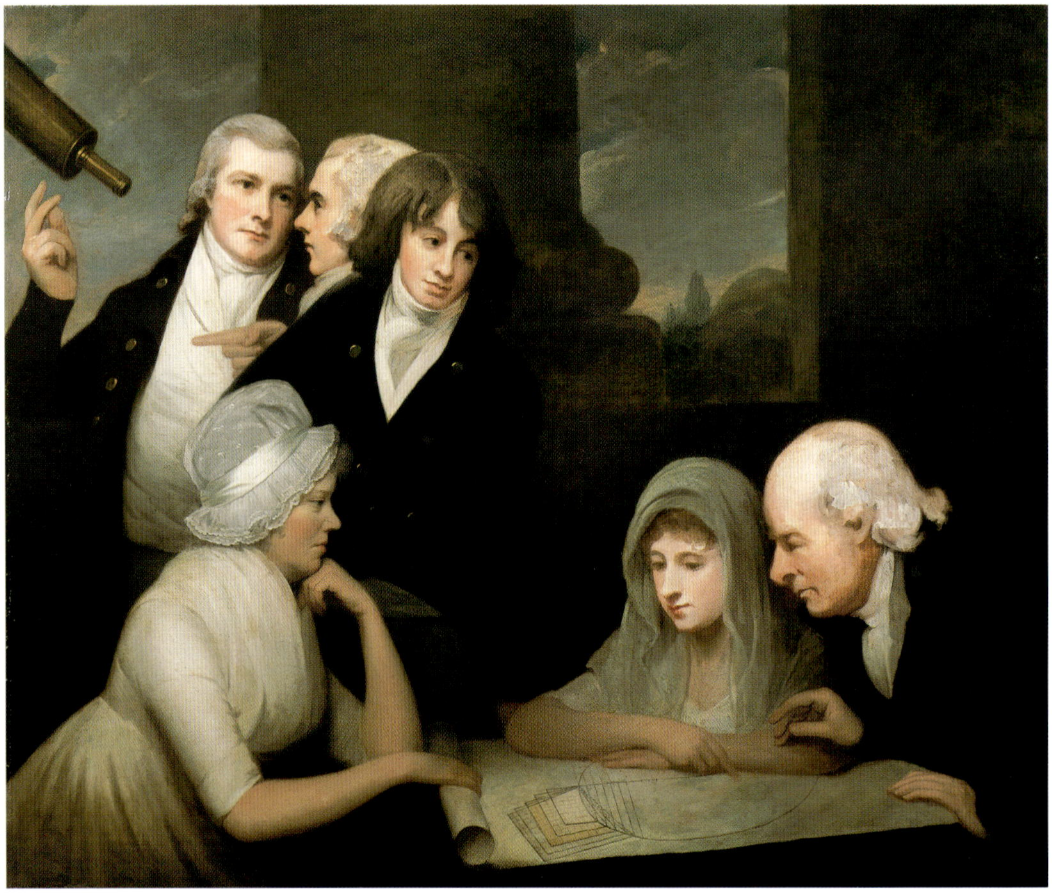

Adam WALKER with his Family NPG 1106

The figures were identified by the donor,[2] as follows:

Adam Walker is seated in the foreground, extreme right: an elderly bald man wearing a blue-grey coat, poring over a diagram.[3]

In the background from the left, his three sons:

William Walker (1766?–1816) who continued his father's lectures; dark brown eyes, grey powdered wig, deep brown coat, pointing to the end of a telescope.

Adam John Walker (1769/70–1839), rector of Bedston, Salop.; with white powdered hair.

Deane Franklin Walker (1778–1865) who suc. his brother William as a lecturer; brown eyes, dark hair, deep blue coat, grey breeches.

In the foreground from the left, his wife and daughter:

Mrs Eleanor Walker (m. c.1764, d. c.1801); blue eyes, grey haired, wearing white.

Eliza Walker (d. 1856) m. Benjamin Gibson of Gosport; brown hair, wearing white.

The uneven execution and the curiously ill-balanced composition of NPG 1106 are explained by its early history. Romney was already beginning to suffer from that 'lassitude of body, and restlessness of mind' which clouded his last years when he began the picture. Hayley recounted how 'Towards the end of 1796, though still dejected, he began a picture of the respectable lecturer in philosophy, Mr Walker and his family, a gentleman endeared to the painter by an intimacy of many years'; on 25 December 1796 Hayley's son told him that 'Romney was preparing to finish the group in what he called his favorite picture of friendship'.[4] On 30 December Farington noted in his diary that Romney had told Sawrey Gilpin 'He will paint no more portraits, the last he has begun, - portraits of Walker the Experimental Philosopher & some of His family'. Apparently he never completed it, for on 27 January 1802 Walker wrote to thank him for his 'last most agreeable present, my family picture. I have got the draperies painted, and a handsome frame, so it is the great lion of my parlour'.[5] On 4 May 1804 William Blake told Hayley he had seen 'the last performance of Romney. It is of Mr Walker and family, the draperies put in by somebody else. It is a very excellent picture, but unfinished. The figures as large as life, half length, Mr. W., three sons, and I believe two daughters, with maps, instruments, &c'.[6] Walker was a lifelong friend of Romney;[7] with his wife he had appeared in one of Romney's earliest paintings, the *Boating Party on Lake Windermere* of c.1758, and he modelled drapery for Romney's *King Lear in the Tempest* c.1761.[8] After Romney's death he told Hayley of their long association, affectionately recalling the painter's pride and impatience, and listing, among the Romney paintings he owned 'my own portrait at full length ... My own head taken fifteen years ago; and my whole family in one piece, one of his last performances. These I hold invaluable'.[9]

For Adam Walker, see also p.467.

1 The Romney Ledger has an entry under no.81: 'Mr Walker, George Street, Hanover Square, half-whole-length; gift, unfinished' (Ward & Roberts 1904, II, p.163).
2 As transcribed by her solicitor, J.G. Wilson, Durham, 13 October 1897; NPG archive.
3 *Athenaeum*, 18 September 1897, p.394, as 'exhibiting an orrery'.
4 Hayley 1809, p.252.
5 Chamberlain 1910, p.218.
6 A. Gilchrist, *Blake*, 1945 ed., p.183.
7 For Walker's friendship with Romney see also Romney 1830, pp.29,30,41–44, and *Connoisseur*, LIV, 1919, p.90.
8 See *Romney* 2002, no.7.
9 Letter of 3 June 1804 from Walker to Hayley; partly transcribed from the MS owned by Mrs Gibson, the donor of NPG 1106, in 1897 (NPG archive). Walker otherwise had by Romney a *Lear and Cordelia*, a copy of a print by Steinkirk ('the first picture he ever attempted'), two landscapes 'of his early production', a marauding piece, *The Vicar of Kendal*, and *A Bacchanalian*.

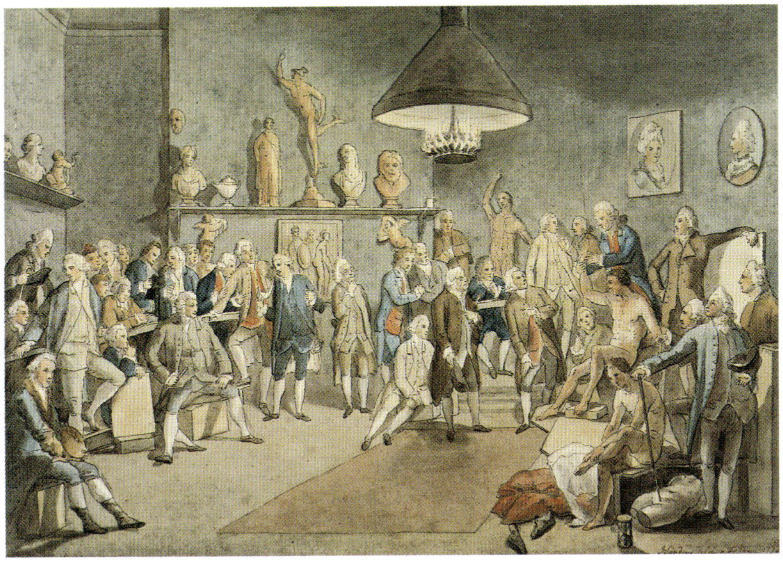

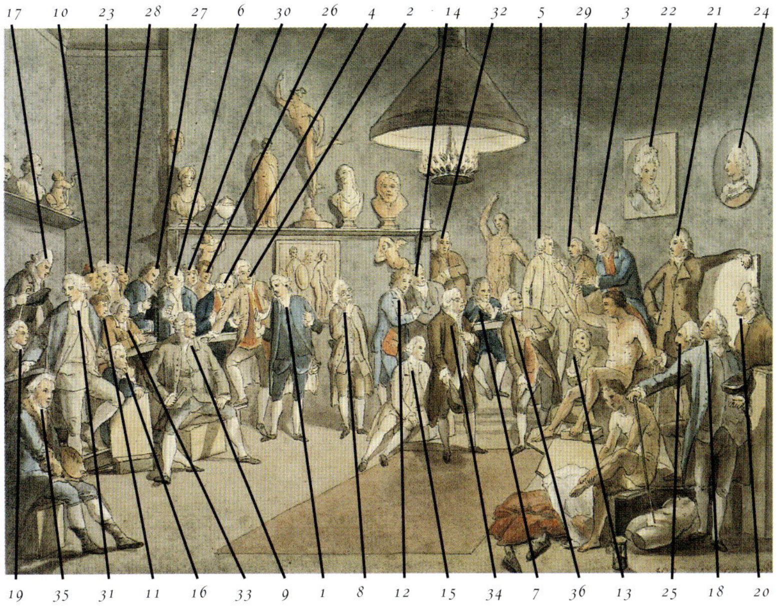

The Academicians of the Royal Academy NPG 1437

The Academicians of the Royal Academy 1772

1437 JOHN SANDERS after JOHANN ZOFFANY [1772]

Watercolour and ink on paper 18.7 x 27.3 (7⅜ x 10¾); laid down; signed bottom right: *J Sanders delin: a Zoffanii 1773* [deletion], with *(97)* above the date; inscribed verso, apparently in the artist's hand: *This Picture was painted by John Zoffany in the year 1770 The names of the artists are on the back of this drawing The Room was that of the R.A. in Pall Mall/ I was admitted a student of this Society Augt 1769 and in the year 1770 gained the Silver Medal for the full Academy figure. J. Sanders.*[1]

Collections: Presented by Alfred Jones of Bath 1906.

Exhibitions: *Kauffmann* 1968(415); *Artists at Work* 1981–82(27a); *Hommage an Angelika Kauffmann*, Liechtenstein, 1992 (*hors catalogue*).

A crude copy of Zoffany's *Academicians of the Royal Academy*★ in the Royal Collection, see p.508, NPG 1437 is of some interest through the inscription stating that the setting was the RA rooms in Pall Mall. In January 1771 the Academy had moved its teaching facilities to Old Somerset House, where it has been assumed Zoffany's painting was set; but the setting has such little character that it is of no real consequence. As a student at the RA Sanders would doubtless have been aware of Zoffany painting the individual portraits probably as early as 1770, and he would certainly have seen the finished painting at the RA in 1772; he would subsequently know the mezzotint by Richard Earlom published on 2 August 1773. NPG 1437 shows differences, for example, in the colours worn by Reynolds, Zuccarelli and William Hunter. A pencil tracing (NPG 1437A) has each figure numbered in red ink and a crude, later ink copy (also NPG 1437A) shows the figures alone with a written key.

The drawing is too slight for the individual figures to be regarded as portraits, but the sitters (and their RA appointments) are listed below in alphabetical order, followed by their numbers in the key.

‡ denotes a sitter separately featured in this catalogue:

George Barret (1732–84), key 11; painter; RA 1768

Francesco Bartolozzi (1727–1815),‡ key 12; engraver; RA 1768

Edward Burch (1730–1814), key 13; medallist; RA 1771; Librarian 1794

Agostino Carlini (c.1718–90),‡ key 14; sculptor; RA 1768; Keeper 1783

Charles Catton (1728–98), key 15; painter; RA 1768

Mason Chamberlin (1722–87),‡ key 16; painter; RA 1768

Sir William Chambers (1726–96),‡ key 2; architect; RA 1768; Treasurer 1768

G.B. Cipriani (1727–85),‡ key17; painter; RA 1768

Richard Cosway (1742–1821),‡ key 18; painter; RA 1771

John Gwynn (1713–1786),‡ key 19; architect; RA 1768

Francis Hayman (1708–76), key 9; painter; RA 1768; Librarian 1770 (see Kerslake *Early Georgian*, I, pp.136–38, II, pls.367–72)

William Hoare (1707–92), key 20; painter; RA 1768

Nathaniel Hone (1718–84),‡ key 21; painter; RA 1768

Dr William Hunter (1718–83),‡ key 8; RA 1768; Professor of Anatomy 1768

Angelica Kauffmann (1741–1807),‡ key 22 painter; RA 1768

Jeremiah Meyer (1735–89), key 23; miniaturist; RA 1768

George Michael Moser (1704–83), key 3; enamellist; RA 1768; Keeper 1768

Mrs Mary Moser (1744–1819), key 24; painter; RA 1768 (daughter of G.M. Moser)

Francis Milner Newton (1720–94), key 4; painter; RA 1768; Secretary 1768

Joseph Nollekens (1737–1823), key 25; sculptor; RA 1772 (see Walker *Regency*, I, pp.368–70, II, pls.887–90)

Edward Penny (1714–91), key 15; painter; RA 1768; Professor of Painting 1768

Sir Joshua Reynolds (1723–92),‡ key 1; painter; RA 1768; President 1768

John Inigo Richards (1731–1810), key 26; painter; RA 1768; Secretary 1788

Paul Sandby (1725–1809),‡ key 27; painter; RA 1768

Thomas Sandby (1721–98),‡ key 6; painter; RA 1768; Professor of Architecture 1768

Dominic Serres (1722–93),‡ key 28; painter; RA 1768; Librarian 1792

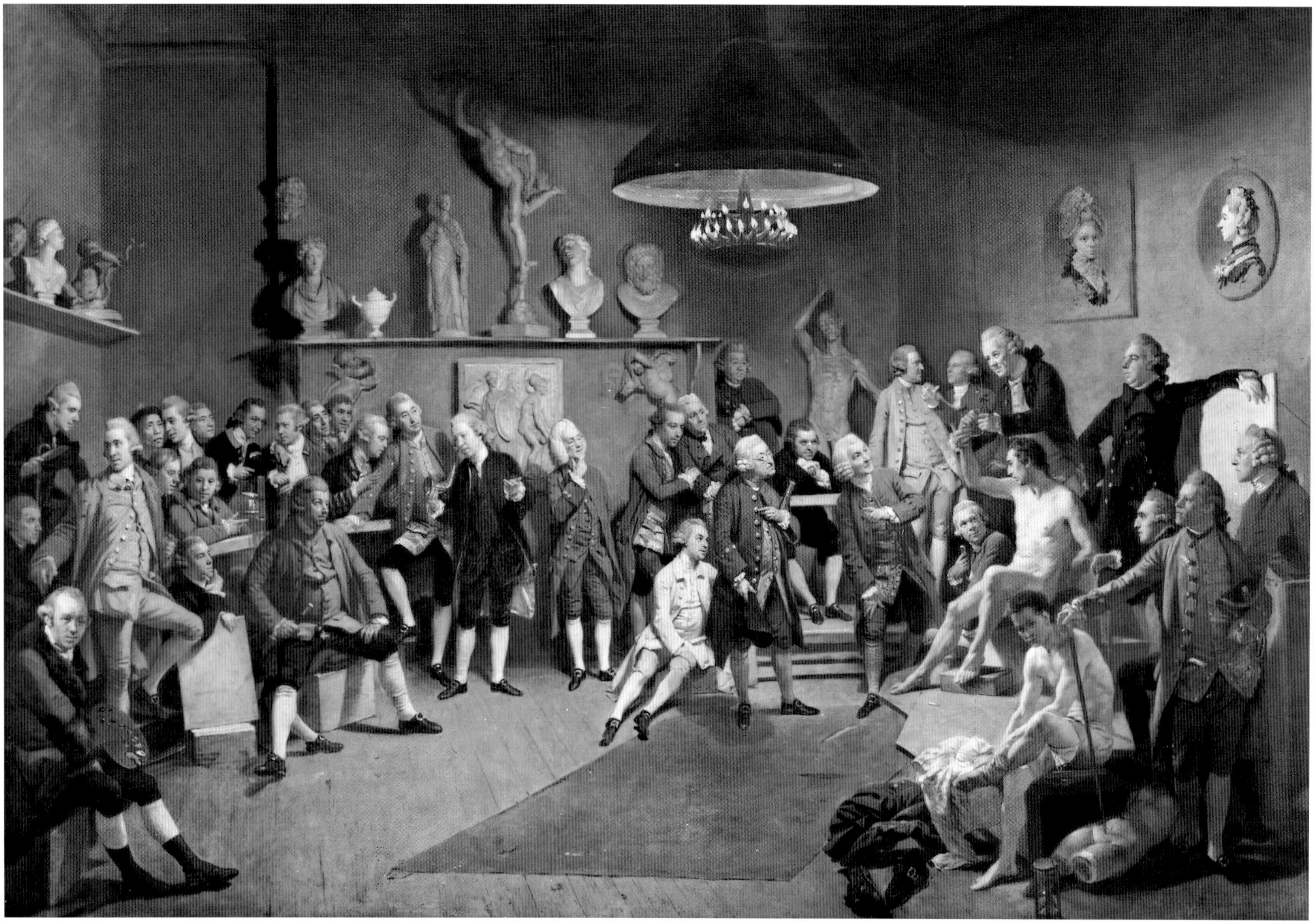

The Academicians of the Royal Academy by Johann Zoffany 1772 (The Royal Collection)

Tan Chet Qua, a Chinese artist who came to England in 1769, key 10

Peter Toms (fl. c.1748-d.1777), key 29; painter; RA 1768

William Tyler (fl. c.1760-d.1801), key 30; sculptor; RA 1768

Samuel Wale (1721-86), key 7; painter; RA 1768; Professor of Perspective 1768 and Librarian 1782

Sir Benjamin West (1738-1820), key 31; painter; President 1792; RA 1768 (see Walker *Regency*, I, pp.543-47, II, pls.1349-59)

Richard Wilson (1714-82),‡ key 32; painter; Librarian 1776; RA 1768

Joseph Wilton (1722-1803),‡ key 33; sculptor; RA 1768; Librarian 1786 and Keeper 1790

Richard Yeo (c.1720-79), key 34; medallist; RA 1768

Johann Zoffany (1733-1810),‡ key 35; painter; RA 1769

Francesco Zuccarelli (1702-88), key 36; painter; RA 1768

There were three absentees: Thomas Gainsborough, and Nathaniel and George Dance.

1 This biographical account is confirmed by the RA Schools register (*Wal. Soc.*, XXXVIII, 1962, no.47); the date of 1770 for the Zoffany painting presumably refers to the time he began to gather individual portraits for the 1772 composition (I am most grateful to Nicholas Savage for his help on this point).

The Siege of Gibraltar 1782

1752 GEORGE CARTER 1784

Gouache on millboard 42 x 56 (16½ x 22); the surface is somewhat spotted.

Collections: O.H. Nicolls in 1906; Alfred Jones of Bath, by whom presented 1915.

Exhibitions: *Military Exhibition*, London, 1901(6) lent Maj.-Gen. O.H. Nicolls of Bognor Regis;[1] *1776*, National Maritime Museum, 1976(560).

Reference: Prown 1966, II, pp.312n, 325, 328-29.

NPG 1752 is a sketch for the large painting in the National Army Museum (1996-07-107)★,[2] which is signed and inscribed: *Gibraltar/ Blockaded June 21.1779/ Firing Began Apl 12.1781/ Floating Batteries Sepr 13.82/ This scene Sepr 14 at Sunrise/ G. Carter pinx. 1784*. Gibraltar had been besieged by the French and Spanish since 1779. In 1782 ten Spanish 'floating batteries' were sent to bombard the island's defences from close range; they began firing on 13 September, but through the following night were all destroyed by General Eliott's shore-based guns.[3] The siege was not finally lifted until February 1783, but the action of 13-14 September 1782 had ensured ultimate British success. After the recent defeat of British troops in America, Eliott's firm resolve caught the public imagination and the destruction of the Spanish batteries was depicted by many artists, from Lt. G.F. Koehler of the Royal Engineers, whose drawing of *Gen. Eliott directing fire on the Spanish Batteries* was soon engraved,[4] to Copley, whose splendid canvas, completed in 1791 (see p.250), was commissioned by the City of London and now hangs in the Guildhall Art Gallery (43).

Copley had accepted the commission on 18 March 1783 (see Heathfield NPG 170),[5] but on 19 March 1783 Carter innocently offered his own candidacy to the Corporation. He claimed to have been working on the subject since the event, to have finished it a month before, and to have engaged to have it engraved; he added that he had consulted state papers and that Sir Roger Curtis, whose portrait was included (but does not appear in Carter's final picture), had superintended the composition. Despite such claims, Carter was still working on his picture in 1784; on 16 August General Eliott in Gibraltar told his London agent Stephen Fuller that 'Mr Carter is here, has taken the Hanoverian chiefs. I sat today, he is very quick, and succeeds in the likenesses I have seen'; and on 9 October he wrote that 'Mr Carter the artist returns by the same ship. He has been very diligent and taken many good likenesses, and several agreeable views of the town and its environs which I heartily wish may reward him for his labours'.[6]

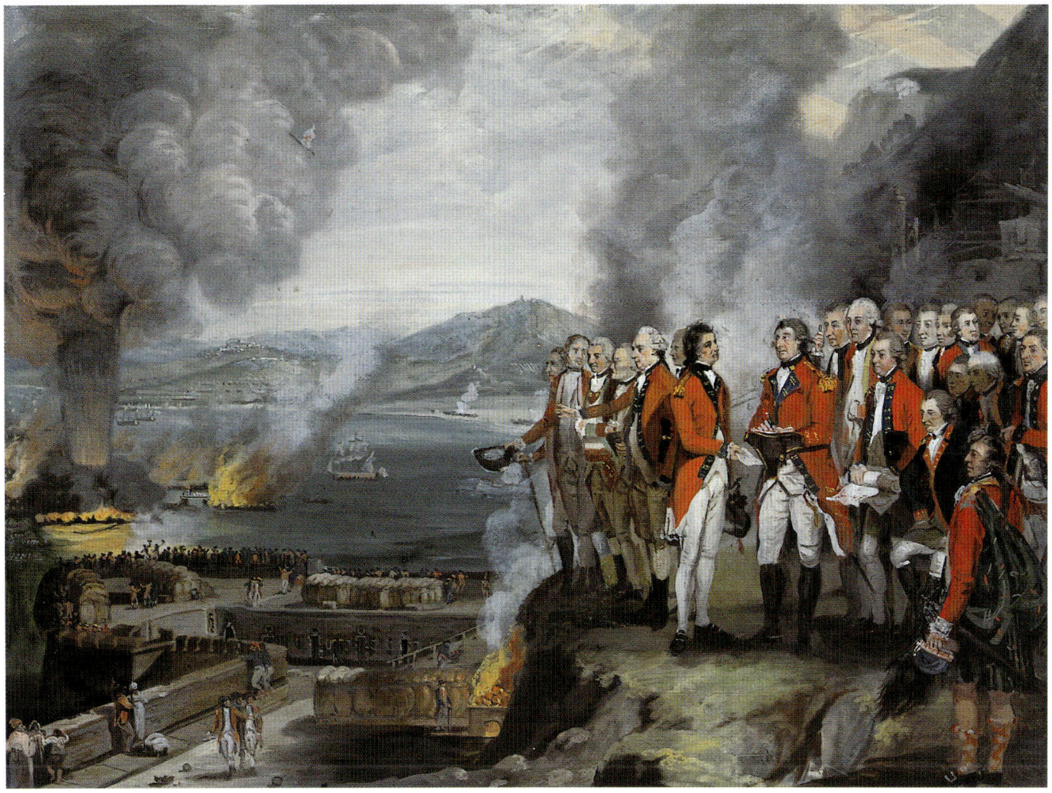

The Siege of Gibraltar NPG 1752

None of the figures in NPG 1752 is clear enough to count as a portrait, although each is named in a numbered key★ painted in grisaille, presumably by Carter, now in the National Army Museum. They are listed below in alphabetical order with their numbers in the key:[7]

Lt.-Gen. Robert Boyd (1710-94), key 5, Lt. Governor and Col. 39th Ft.; KB 1785

Col. Gavin Cochrane, key 9, 58th Ft.

Col. Peter Craig, key 15, 56th Ft.

Lt.-Col. Gustav Friedrich von Dachenhausen, key 20, Reden's Hanoverian Regt.

Maj.-Gen. August de la Motte, key 4, officer commanding the Hanoverian Regts.

Gen. George Augustus Eliott (1717-90), key 8, Governor of Gibraltar; see Heathfield NPG 170 & 6079

Maj. Joseph Eyre, RA, key 22

Col. George Gledstone [*Gledstanes*], key 18, 72nd Ft.

Maj.-Gen. William Green (1725-1811), key 11, Chief Engineer

Maj. George Grove [*Groves*], key 17, RA (wounded on the night of 13 September)

Col. William Hellett [*Kellett*], key 3, 39th Ft.

Lt. Charles (later Gen. Sir Charles) Holloway (1749-1827), key 12, then Lt. ADC to Maj.Green

Col. Ernst August von Hugo (d.1794), key 2, Hardenberg's Hanoverian Regt.

Maj.-Gen. George Lewis (fl.1776-1813), key 23, then Lt.Col. RA

Gen. Vaughan Lloyd (1736-1817), key 16, then Maj. RA

Col. George Mackenzie, key 24, 73rd (Highland) Ft.

Lt.-Col. William Mackintosh, key 19, 97th Ft.

Maj. Philip Martin, RA, key 21

Lt.-Col. John Phipps, RE, key 14 [?Maj.-Gen. Edmund Phipps, 1760-1837, ADC to the Governor of Gibraltar 1782]

Maj.-Gen. William Picton, key 10, 12th Ft. [?Maj.-Gen. John Picton, d. c.1813]

Lt.-Col. von Schreppergill [*Schlippegill, Schlepergrell*], key 1, De La Motte's Hanoverian Regt.

Col. Thomas Trigge, key 13, 12th Ft.

Maj. Charles Valloton [Vallotton], key 7, ADC to the Governor, 56th Ft.

Capt. William Wilson, key 6, ADC to Lt.-Gen. Boyd, 39th Ft.

Carter's composition is largely arranged by rank, the lesser officers to the right and staff officers attended by their ADCs nearer the front (Copley subsequently retained the foreground Scot and the seated Major

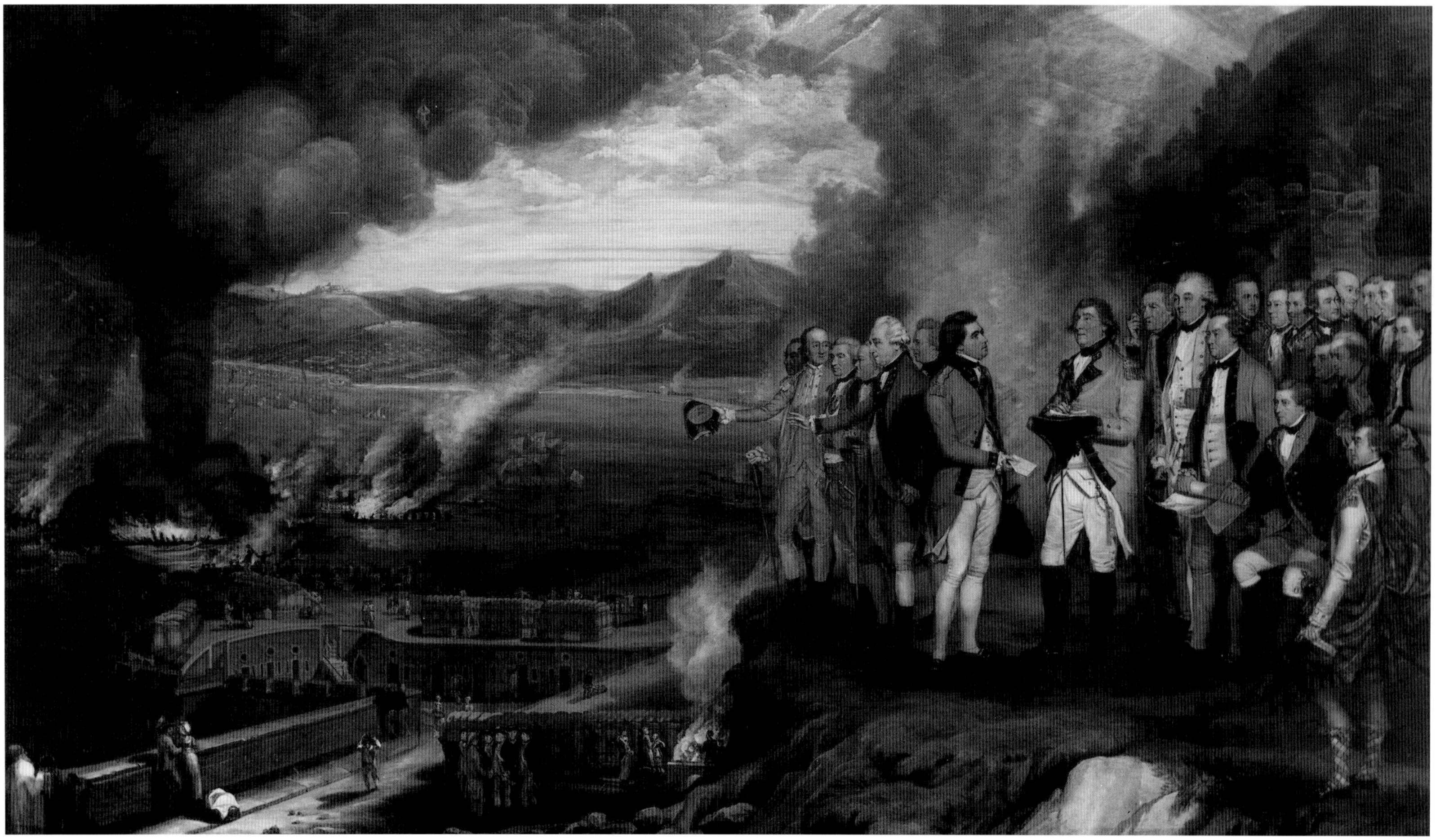

The Siege of Gibraltar, 1784, by George Carter with separate key (National Army Museum, London)

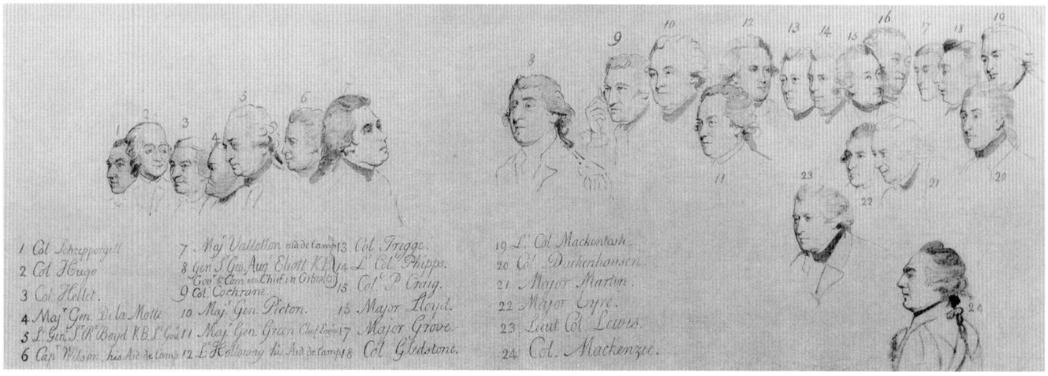

Lewis).[8] Twelve of Carter's officers appear in the Copley composition and five in John Trumbull's *The Sortie made by the Garrison of Gibraltar, 26 November 1781* (Metropolitan Museum of Art, New York).[9]

1 The exhibition label remains on the stretcher.
2 Illus. Prown 1966, II, pl.491 (but described as NPG 1752); *NACF Review 1996*, p.120. See Egerton 1998, pp.230, 233n16; exhibited by Carter in Pall Mall, London, 1785; bt. between 1785 and 1795 by the 6th Lord Balcarres, whose younger brother, Maj. Colin Lindsay of the 73rd Highlanders, was present at the siege (and appeared in Copley's painting); Crawford sale, Christie's, 11 October 1946, lot 43, bt. Barnard, by whom offered to the NPG in 1957.
3 As described, for example, by J. Drinkwater, *History of the Siege of Gibraltar 1779–83*, 1846 ed., pp.134–40.
4 Illus. Prown 1966, II, pl.494; Egerton 1998, p.230. NPG 1752 was previously attributed to G.F. Koehler.
5 Prown 1966, II, pp.311–12.
6 National Maritime Museum, Heathfield MSS 9217, ff.28, 30 (quoted by Prown 1966, II, p.312n1).
7 Variant spellings from J. Spilsbury, *Journal of the Siege of Gibraltar*, 1908 (pub. by the Gibraltar Garrison Library), pp.125–38, Doubtful Portraits II, 'Approximate List of Officers serving at Gibraltar during the Siege'.
8 Prown 1966, II, p.328.
9 Nos.1, 2, 3, 7, 8, 10, 11, 12, 13, 15, 20, 23 and 24 in the Copley, and nos.7, 8, 12, 13 and 24 in the Trumbull.

John Glynn, John Wilkes and John Horne Tooke

1944 after RICHARD HOUSTON [1769]

Canvas 54 x 78 (21¼ x 30¾) lined; old tears in the table cloth top right and across Horne's shoulders, and holes in the painting hanging on the background wall; cleaned 1989.

Collections: Garratt, a picture dealer in the Strand, from whom bt. Evans; his son, G. Evans, in 1862, when offered to the NPG;[1] before 1868 bt. from him by Angela Burdett-Coutts,[2] later Baroness Burdett-Coutts (d.1906); William Burdett-Coutts (d.1921), his sale, Christie's, 4 May 1922, lot 38, bt. Leggatt; presented by the National Art Collections Fund 1922.

Engraving: R. Houston 1769, see below.

Exhibition: *Guelph* 1891(321), lent Baroness Burdett-Coutts; *NACF Exhibition*, Victoria and Albert Museum, 1928.

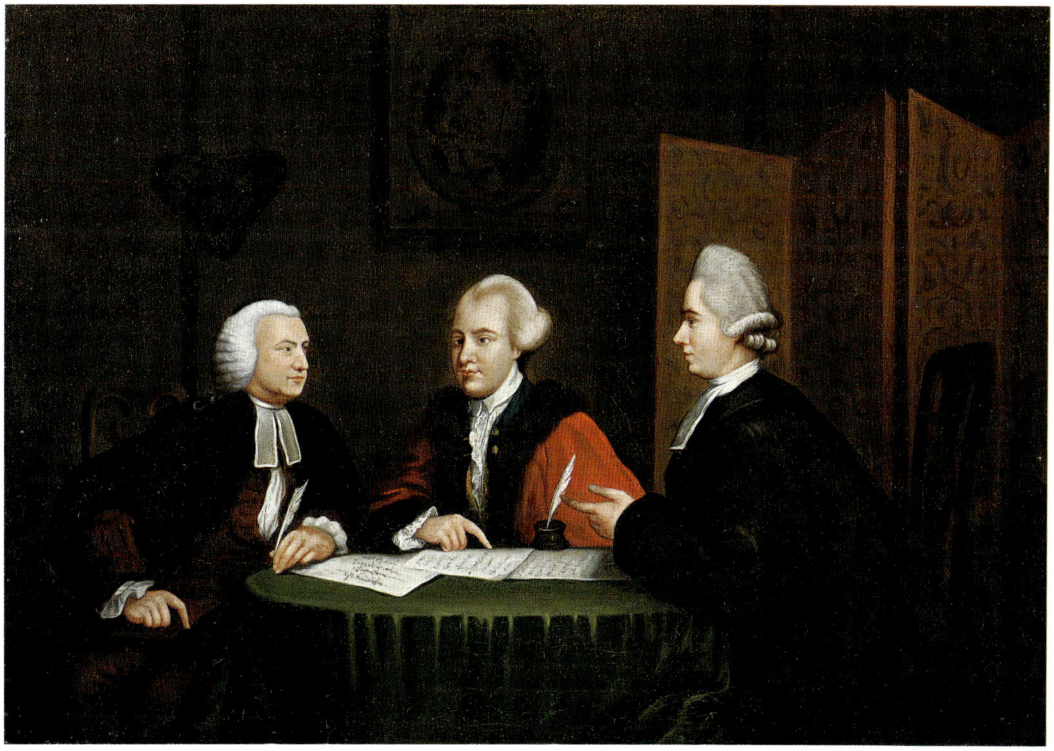

GLYNN (left), WILKES and TOOKE (right) NPG *1944*

NPG 1944 shows from the left:

John Glynn (1722-79), sergeant at law, brown eyes, white powdered wig, with little black top-knot, wearing a black gown over a brown suit, a quill in his left hand; his tricorne hat hangs on the wall behind him.

John Wilkes (1725-97), brown eyes with a pronounced squint, white powdered hair, wearing an alderman's red gown trimmed with black fur over a blue coat with gold buttons and a gold vest; on the wall behind him hangs a painting of the figure of Liberty, holding the cap of liberty on a pole in her left hand.

The Rev John Horne Tooke (1736-1812), brown eyes, white powdered wig, wearing a clergyman's black gown and bands.

NPG 1944 is copied from the Houston print of the three radicals, an imaginary composition published on 6 February 1769.[3] Horne (who in 1782 became Horne Tooke) and Glynn were then Wilkes's most influential supporters (though neither, ultimately, was a friend); the former led the Society of the Supporters of the Bill of Rights which first met in February 1769, resolved to restore Wilkes's solvency and liberty.

When the print was published Wilkes, elected MP for Middlesex in April 1768 and an alderman of the City of London on 2 January 1769, was in the King's Bench prison, charged with sedition and obscenity. Glynn, as a 'Wilkes and liberty' candidate, had just defeated Sir William Beauchamp Proctor in another Middlesex election in December 1768 (necessitated by the death of Wilkes's fellow MP, George Cooke), and Horne had raised his election expenses. The engraving identifies the papers on the table (illegible in NPG 1944): Glynn rests his hand on *Addresses to/ County of Middlesex/ Constitutional Law/ Legal Liberty; Wilkes points to General/ Warrants/ Seizure of/ Papers/ Habeas/ Corpus/ Alteration/ of Records/ Informations/ ex Officio/ Close/ Imprison/ment*, and Horne has before him *Treatise on/ Inclosing/ Commons/ Freedom of/ Elections/ Trial by Jury/ Letters to Sr. J. Gibbons/ and Sir/ W.B. Proctor*;[4] the figure of Liberty in the picture on the wall sits by an unfurled *Magna/ Charta*. They collectively refer to Wilkes's struggle with the law and his arrests in 1763 and 1768, Horne's legal acumen, and Glynn's electoral triumph.

Two of the heads derive from contemporary engravings: Wilkes from one of the many after R.E. Pine which first appeared in 1764 (see p.486), and Glynn from an anonymous bust-length oval published in Smollett's *History of England*, 1763-65. Horne's profile head recurs in an anonymous half-length mezzotint of c.1769 and in two caricatures, *The Macaroni Parson* of c.1769 and *Guy Faux setting fire to the Pillars of the London Tavern* of 1773 (see p.462).

NPG 1944 wholly depends on the mezzotint (it is exactly twice the size), and differs only in pedantic detail, e.g of drapery folds and the patterning of the folding screen. Houston's engraving is inscribed *Richard Houston invt delin et fecit*,[5] but although NPG 1944 has hitherto been attributed to him, it is most unlikely that Houston, otherwise unrecorded as a painter, should either have made such an elaborate preparatory design for a topical derivative plate, or subsequently copied it in oil. On the other hand there must have been a strong market among radicals for copies painted from the print; early in the 19th century the image was being used as a pub sign (*The Three Johns* near Queen's Square, Westminster).[6]

Each sitter is separately featured in this catalogue.

1 Letters from G. Evans, 3 Raymond Buildings, Gray's Inn, to Scharf, dated October 2, 28: 'it was purchased some time back, [by] my late father of Mr Garratt, a picture dealer in the Strand'.
2 As described in a label, signed E.W. Radclyffe, 16 January 1868, formerly attached to the verso of NPG 1944: 'for many years in the possession of Mr Evans's family, of three Staples Inn, Holborn-bars, London, and was bought from that gentleman for Miss Burdett-Coutts'.
3 CS 48; illus. W.P. Treloar, *Wilkes and the City*, 1917, f.p.93.
4 It was rumoured that Gibbons, a ministerial supporter, would oppose Wilkes in the February 1769 Middlesex election; Proctor had been defeated by Wilkes and Glynn in successive Middlesex elections.
5 Misquoted as 'R. Houston pinxit et fecit', *Connoisseur*, XLIX, 1917, p.57.
6 As described in the *Somerset House Gazette*, 1824, II, p.296; perhaps in Bennet Street.

Mr Fox and his Friends

2076 WILLIAM LANE c.1813

Black crayon with red and white heightening on tinted paper 55 x 73 (21¾ x 28¼) maximum (uneven edges), previously folded over a stretcher to give a sight size of 54 x 67.5 (21¼ x 26½); laid down on card; some spotting and a small vertical tear below centre left; the old backboard inscribed [signed?] *W Lane delt/ from Life*.

Collections: By descent at St Anne's Hill House, Chertsey,[1] to the 4th Lord Holland (d.1859); his widow, who devised property to the Hon L.W.H. [Fox] Powys, thence to his nephew, the Hon Stephen Powys; St Anne's Hill House sale, Phillips, 3rd day, 26 November 1924, lot 502 ('Court Scene, by William Lane, the bust of C.J. Fox, and 12 notables'), bt. Leggatt for the NPG.

The title is that given by the first owner, Lord Holland, and the subject is fanciful. It may be regarded as a remote echo of the Temple of Liberty created by the Dukes of Bedford at Woburn Abbey (completed by 1804, in Fox's lifetime) in which the bust of Fox was surrounded by the busts of six of his friends (Lord Robert Spencer, General Robert Fitzpatrick, Lord Holland, James Hare, Charles Grey and Lord Lauderdale).[2] Fox's extraordinary talent for friendship, and the dominance of the Tory party after his death in 1806, made his surviving friends particularly anxious to preserve his memory and broadcast his ideals.[3]

NPG 2076 shows twelve of his disciples,[4] as listed below.

‡ Denotes a sitter separately featured in this catalogue:

Back row from the left:

William Cavendish, 5th Duke of Devonshire (1748–1811);‡ the likeness copied from the portrait by Reynolds of 1776.

William Wentworth Fitzwilliam, 2nd Earl Fitzwilliam (1748–1833); the half-erased head relates to his portrait of 1817 by William Owen (NPG 4979) see Walker *Regency*, I, pp.184–85.

(Bust of Fox‡ copied from the 1802 bust by Nollekens)

John Crewe, 1st Baron Crewe (1742–1829);‡ Lane exhibited his portrait RA 1811(795).

Frederick Ponsonby, 3rd Earl of Bessborough (1758–1844);‡ Lane exhibited his portrait RA 1811(360).

Dudley Long North (1748–1829);‡ Lane exhibited his portrait RA 1811(795).

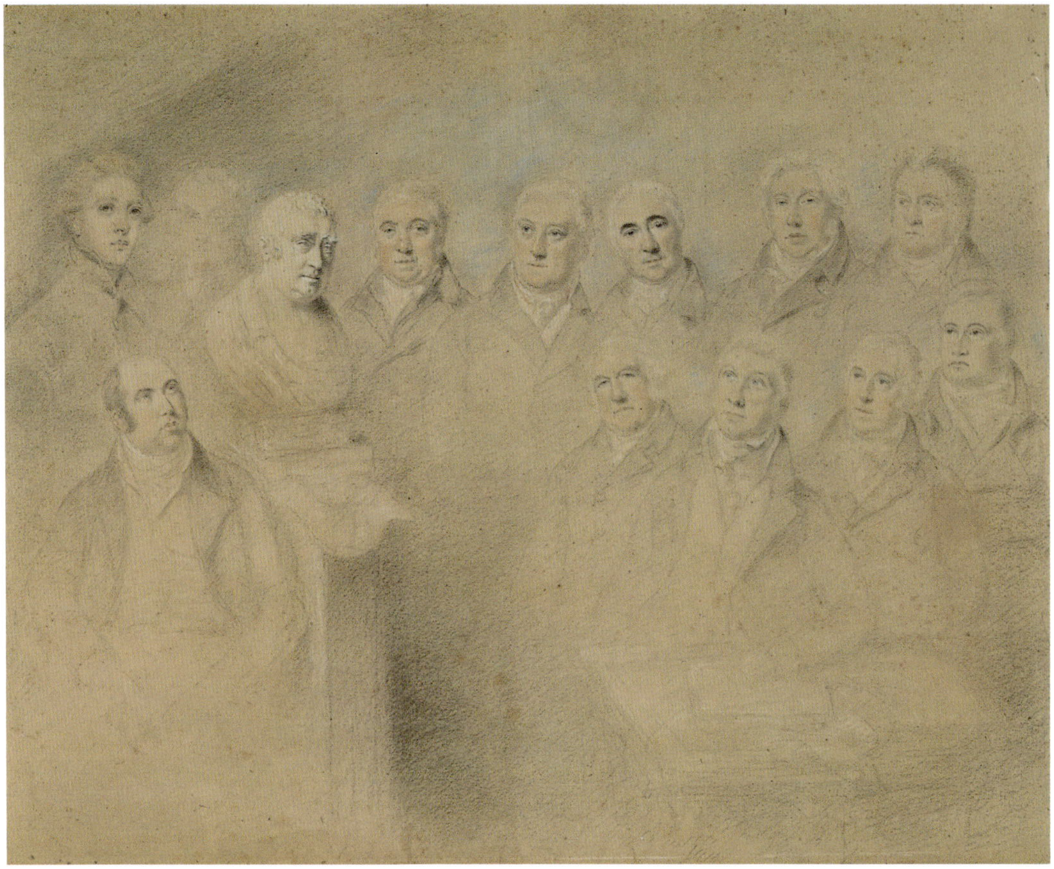

Mr FOX and his Friends NPG 2076

George James, 1st Marquess of Cholmondeley (1749–1827);‡ the likeness corresponds with the portrait by John Simpson exhibited in 1825, six years after Lane's death.

Lord Robert Spencer (1747–1831);‡ the source of this image is untraced.

Front row from the left:

Henry Richard Vassall-Fox, 3rd Baron Holland (1773–1840); the source of this image is untraced (cf. Walker *Regency*, I, pp.256–58).

John Fitzpatrick, 2nd Earl of Upper Ossory (1745–1818);‡ from the drawing by Lane of 1806, formerly at Holland House.

Hon Richard Fitzpatrick (1747–1813);‡ from the drawing by Lane engraved H.R. Cook, probably that exhibited RA 1814(472 'the late General Fitzpatrick').

Lord John Townshend (1757–1833);[5]‡ the source of this image is untraced.

St Andrew St John, 14th Baron St John (1759–1817);‡ the source of this image is untraced.

Fox had died in the Duke of Devonshire's house at Chiswick and the attendants at his death bed included Lord Holland (his nephew), General Fitzprick, Lord Robert Spencer and Lord John Townshend (who had christened his son Charles Fox Townshend). The inscription/signature on the old backboard, *W. Lane delt from Life* must be qualified. Fox is taken from the Nollekens bust of 1802 and the Duke of Devonshire (d. 1811) from the Reynolds portrait of 1776, but the other figures might all derive from original studies by Lane. The death of Fitzpatrick in 1813 may provide a *postquam non*.

A comparable group by Lane showing a group of musicians around a bust of Handel is in the Royal Collection.[6]

1 A label in a late-19th-hand, formerly on the verso, read: *Mr Fox and his friends in chalk by Wm. Lane/ won in a raffle by Lord Holland*, presumably the 3rd Lord Holland.

2 All by Nollekens, see J. Kenworthy Browne, *Apollo*, CXXX, 1989, pp.27–32. Also in the St Anne's Hill House sale were a set of drawings by Henry Edridge, 'Fox and five friends' (lots 505–507).

3 See for example, N. Penny, 'The Whig Cult of Fox in early nineteenth-century Sculpture', *Past and Present*, LXX, 1976, pp.94–106.

4 The identities written in an annotated copy of the St Anne's Hill House sale cat. (NPG archive) and otherwise verifiable.

5 Previously identified as George, 2nd Marquess Townshend (e.g. NPG, *Complete Illus. Cat.*, 1981, p.657).

6 Exhibited RA 1810(544); Oppé 1950, no.408, fig.67.

Agostino Carlini, Francesco Bartolozzi and Giovanni Battista Cipriani

3186 JOHN FRANCIS RIGAUD 1777

Canvas 100.5 x 125.5 (39½ x 49½) lined, cleaned 1981; signed on one of the engravings held by Bartolozzi: *J.F. Rigaud Pinxit 1777*.

Collections: Rigaud sale, Peter Coxe, 2nd day, 4 April 1811, lot 82; probably J.M.W. Turner;[1] by descent to W.C. Turner, his daughter, Mrs M.H. Turner, Hastings, by whom presented 1944.

Engraving: J.R. Smith 1778.

Exhibition: RA 1777(228).

NPG 3186 shows from the left:

Agostino Carlini (c.1718–90): brown eyes, powdered wig, deep red coat and breeches, green gold-trimmed waistcoat, white shirt, a hammer in his right hand which rests on a stone figure (of a River God?).

Francesco Bartolozzi (1727–1815): brown eyes, powdered grey hair, pale green coat, green waistcoat and breeches, a burin in his right hand holding up a portfolio of engravings with his right

Giovanni Battista Cipriani (1727–85): brown eyes, white powdered hair, grey suit with gold buttons, sitting in a red-upholstered chair, painting the wreathed figure of Fame with a trumpet and book on the canvas before him.

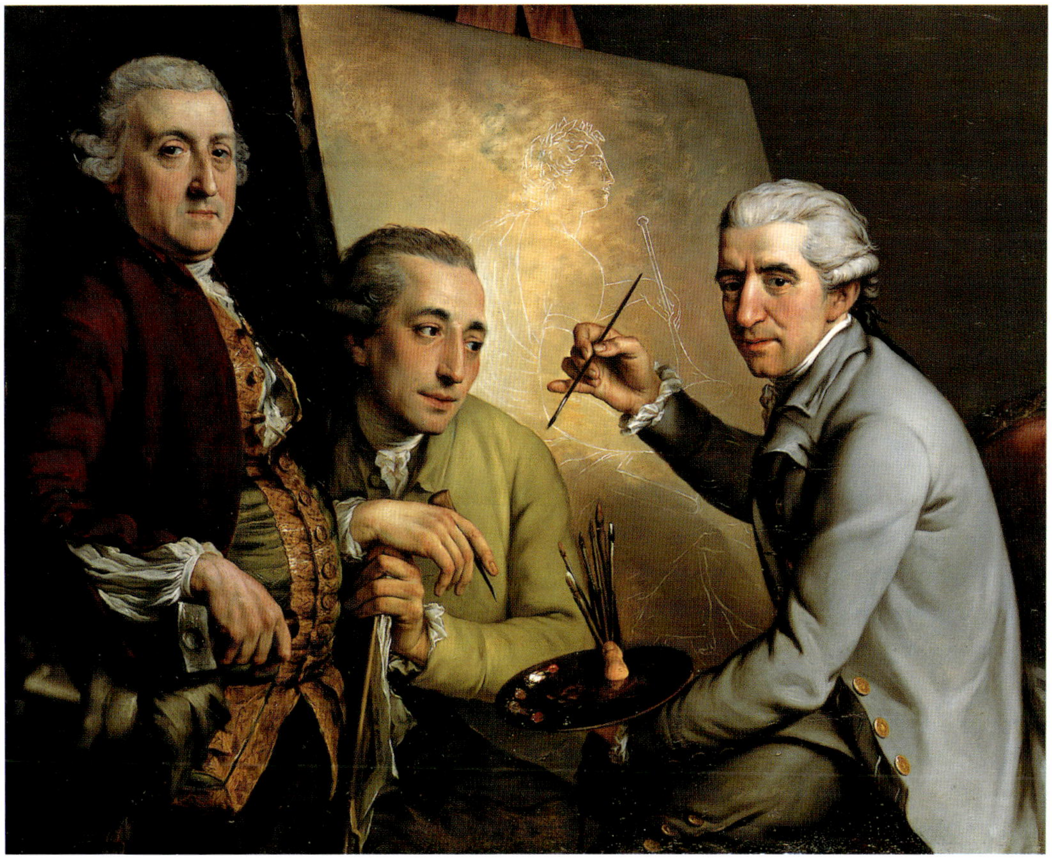

CARLINI (left), BARTOLOZZI and CIPRIANI (right)
NPG 3186

Rigaud, from Turin, had arrived in London in 1771. NPG 3186 shows an Italian sculptor, engraver and painter, each of whom had been a foundation member of the Royal Academy in London in 1768. Spatially the composition is a little awkward, with Bartolozzi perched uncomfortably between his companions, but nonetheless the artist's son considered it

> an interesting group of three Italian Artists Royal Academicians, – Cipriani the painter, Carlini the Sculptor, who held the Office of Keeper of the Royal Academy, and Bartolozzi the engraver; – all extremely like; The two last I well remember, and they were strikingly so. ... The Portrait of Cipriani is, I believe, the only one that was ever taken of that celebrated Artist.[2]

The Florentines Bartolozzi and Cipriani, exact contemporaries, had first met in Hugford's studio in Florence; they then separated, Bartolozzi to Venice to study under Wagner, and Cipriani to Rome where he met Chambers and Wilton, who were jointly responsible for bringing him to London in 1756. When Bartolozzi came to London in 1764 he shared lodgings with Cipriani in Golden Square. Cipriani worked in collaboration with both Chambers and Wilton and his reputation as a decorative artist was greatly facilitated by Bartolozzi's engravings. Carlini, from Genoa, had settled in England by 1760; he also worked for Chambers at Somerset House.

Each sitter is featured separately in this catalogue.

1 In 1837 Turner gave the RA a portrait group by Rigaud of three earlier academicians to be hung in the Council Room, no longer in the RA's collection (Whitley 1930, p.325, quoting RA Council minutes). In a letter of 20 December 1964 C.W.M. Turner of Hampstead, nephew of Mrs M.H. Turner, the donatrix, wrote that her father was a cousin of the artist, 'I think a second or third cousin'.

2 *Rigaud Memoir*, p.61. For further portraits of Cipriani, see p.109.

An Audience with a Sultan

3797 UNKNOWN ARTIST c.1755–65

Watercolour and body colour within ruled border, on paper 51 x 74.5 (20 x 29⅜) laid down on paper; general fading, with scattered losses and slight spotting.

In the throne room of a Palace, a Sultan on his throne wearing a blue-silk robe trimmed with sable; his turban has a red top and bears a black plume (two more ornate turbans stand in a niche in the back wall); he is attended on the left by the Grand Vizier wearing a white kaftan trimmed with sable, his ceremonial hat bearing a gold stripe; on the right stands a beardless man in a rose-coloured kaftan edged with sable.

The Sultan listens to the bowing Dragoman (translator) who wears a round fur hat and light blue tunic beneath his white kaftan.

From the right three Europeans are escorted in for presentation, each wearing a kaftan of honour (which would have been presented by the Master of Ceremonies in the name of the Sultan); the first has silver piping on his black tricorne hat and wears a yellow kaftan trimmed with sable, denoting an ambassador; the second wears a cream kaftan with ermine (considered inferior to sable) and carries before him a red and gold book (the ambassador's credentials); the third wears an orange kaftan with gold trim; each is held by his left arm by an Ottoman court usher wearing silver and gold kaftans with ceremonial headwear.

Beyond them can be seen the backs of four more Europeans.

Collections: Bequeathed by Col. William Agnew Moore 1950 (as *The First British Mission to Persia headed by Sir John Malcolm [at] Teheran in 1807*).

NPG 3797 is a rather crudely painted description of a European Ambassador's reception by the Turkish Sultan in Constantinople.[1] It is one of a number of similar illustrations, and most closely resembles a painting attributed to Antoine de Favray, said to show *The Sultan Osman III receiving the Count de Vergennes, the French Ambassador, on 3 June 1755*,[2] and a watercolour, *The Audience of the Grand Signior* by Francis Smith, in the Royal Collection,[3] engraved by Robert Pranker* in 1769.[4] NPG 3797 evidently dates from the same period. It is not clear what nationality the Europeans are, each being submerged within his kaftan of honour. The British Ambassadors to Turkey within this period were Henry Grenville (1761), Robert Colebrooke (1765) and John Murray (1766).

1 The ritual is described and illus. by M. Beale, *Apollo*, CXXVII, 1988, pp.174–79; the description of NPG 3797 above derives from her account and from the legend of Pranker's 1769 engraving after Francis Smith.
2 Sold Sotheby's, 11 October 1996, lot 232; Favray was in Constantinople 1762–71.
3 Oppé 1950, no.592, pl.70.

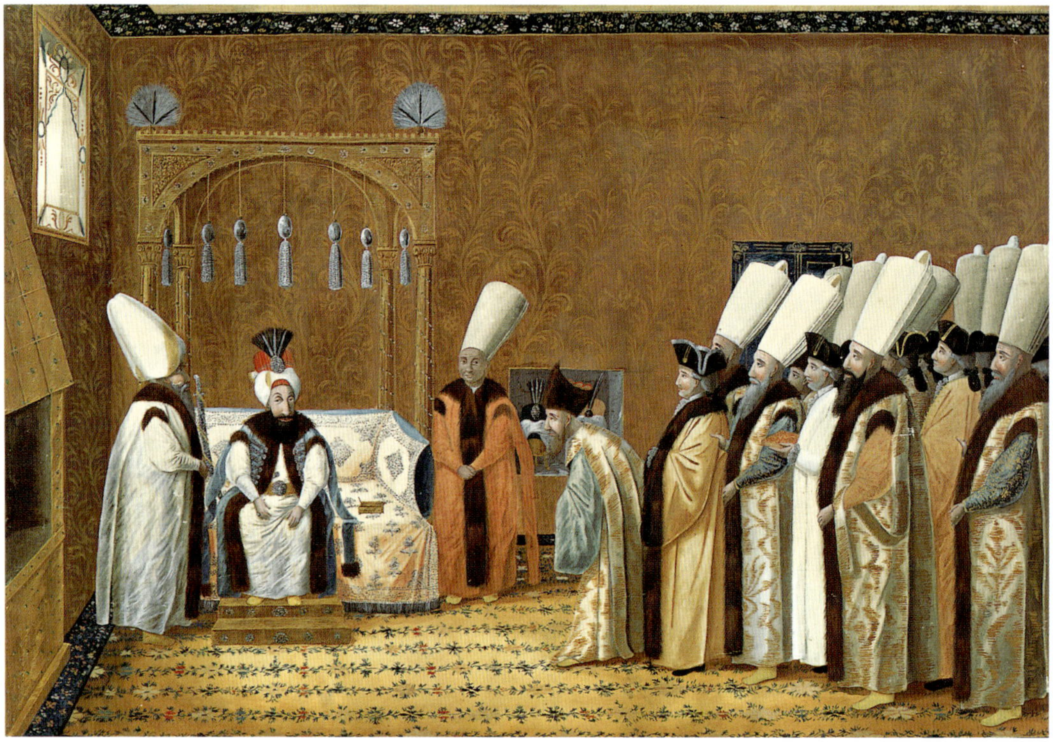

An Audience with a Sultan NPG 3797

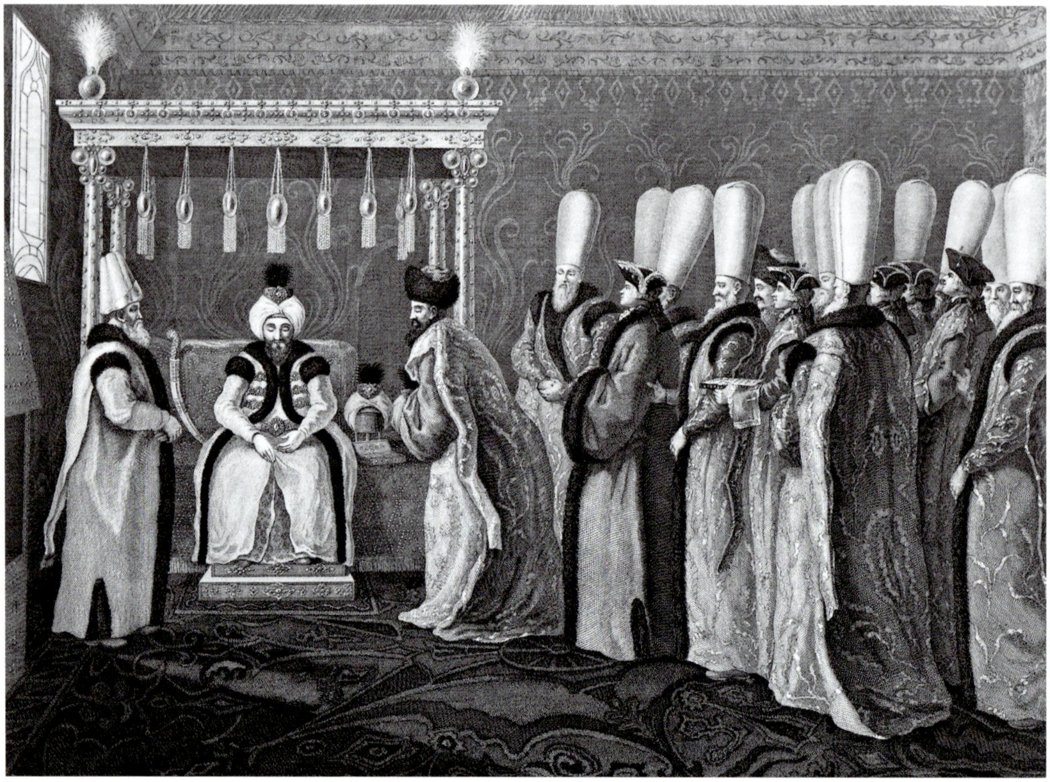

The Grand Vizier giving an Audience to the English Ambassador, R. Pranker 1769 after Francis Smith (NPG D 18007)

4 'from the Collection of Lord Baltimore'; a version is said to have been engraved by J. Fougeron for Lord Baltimore's *Tour to the East in the Years 1763 and 1764*.

Portraits in the Characters of the Muses in the Temple of Apollo

4905 RICHARD SAMUEL 1778

Canvas 130 x 154 (51 x 60½) lined; there is a repaired damage across Apollo's right shoulder and chest, and the surface is generally rubbed with scattered retouchings throughout; signed in monogram lower right: *RS/ 1[77]8*, and lower right on the stone step: *R Samuel/ Pinxit*.

Collections: Purchased from Agnew 1972.

Exhibitions: RA 1779(282 *Portraits in the characters of the Muses in the Temple of Apollo*); Agnew, *Neo-classical Paintings*, 1972(6); *Nest of Nightingales*, Dulwich, 1988(3.9).

Reference: Rosenthal 1996, pp.233–34, fig.67; *Kauffmann* 1998, pp.240–41, fig.126.

On the left: standing fair-haired figure in a brown-red dress and green shawl; a fair-haired figure in a light red dress gesturing towards Apollo; a seated figure at an easel, her hair elaborately dressed, wearing a golden dress with a blue cloak.

In the centre: a standing figure with dark wreathed hair, wearing a pale pink dress with a white drape and blue sash.

On the right: a standing figure with loose brown hair, wearing a light brown drape over a white dress, holding up a bowl in her right hand; next to her a standing figure playing a lute, wearing a dull yellow dress and veil with a blue drape; in front a seated figure holding a scroll, her dark hair dressed with a blue silk turban, wearing a white dress with a golden belt with a cameo clasp; a seated figure with brown hair dressed with a golden brooch and a blue silk veil, wearing a white dress with a green and gold trim; a fair-haired seated figure wearing a white dress with a pink drape looking down at a tablet (illegibly inscribed).

In the centre a statue of Apollo holding a lyre with a small bursting sun in his right hand, a sacrificial stand before him.

The concept of this picture is rather more interesting than its substance. It celebrates the achievements of contemporary women artists and writers, marking the passing of that 'aversion which used to prevail against female claims to literary reputation',[1] and it was presumably the painting exhibited by Samuel at the RA in 1779 (see above). The portraits were not named, but the intended identities may be deduced from a related but crude engraving by Page, *The Nine living Muses of Great Britain*,* made from an earlier drawing by Samuel (it is lettered *Samuel delin. Page Sculp.*), published in November 1777 and printed in *The Lady's Magazine* in 1778.[2]

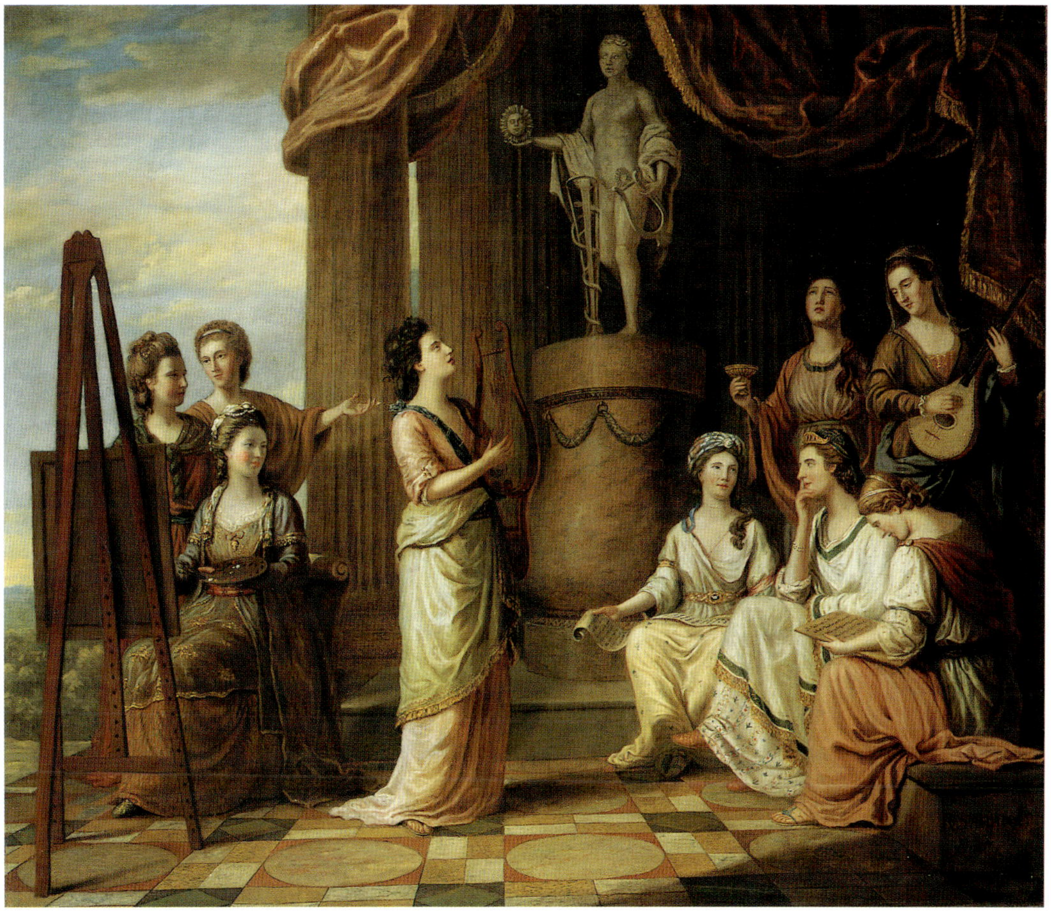

Portraits in the Characters of the Muses NPG 4905

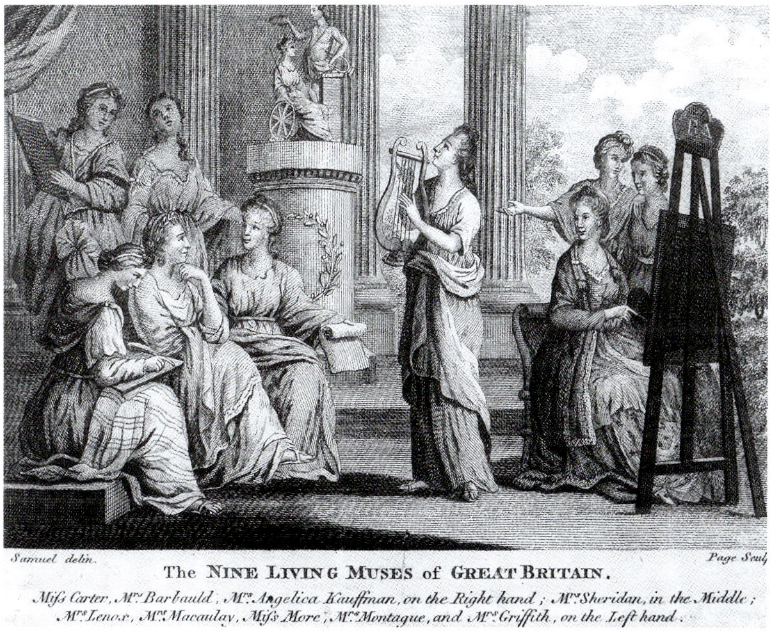

The Nine Living Muses, Page 1777 after Richard Samuel (British Museum)

Apart from a simplified setting, the print shows the same disposition of the nine figures (in reverse), although the faces differ, the attributes of the two standing Muses on the right in the painting have been modified (the cup is omitted and the guitar replaced by a book), and Apollo (who seems to totter on one leg in the painting) crowns the seated figure of Britannia. A key below the print identifies the Muses as: *Miss Carter, Mrs Barbauld, Mrs Angelica Kauffman, on the Right hand; Mrs Sheridan, in the Middle; Mrs Lenox, Mrs Macaulay, Miss More, Mrs Montague, and Mrs Griffith, on the Left hand*. They are listed below in alphabetical order:

Mrs Anna Letitia Barbauld, née *Aikin* (1743–1825), poet and writer

Elizabeth Carter (1717–1806), writer and translator

Mrs Elizabeth Griffith, née *Griffith* (1720?–93), novelist and playwright

Angelica Kauffmann (1741–1807), painter

Mrs Charlotte Lennox, née *Ramsay* (1720–1804), novelist and poet

Mrs Catharine Macaulay, née *Sawbridge* (1731–91), historian

Mrs Elizabeth Montagu, née *Robinson* (1720–1800), literary critic and patron

Hannah More (1745–1833), playwright and poet

Mrs Elizabeth Sheridan, née *Linley* (1754–92), singer

Despite this key, one of the Muses, Mrs Carter, confided to another, Mrs Montagu, that 'by the mere testimony of my own eyes, I cannot very exactly tell which is you, and which is I, and which is any body else'.[3] If Mrs Carter couldn't recognize anyone, neither can we, and the print remains a liability in terms of portraiture. It nevertheless attracted considerable notice[4] and it would appear that NPG 4905 was a necessary (and commercial) attempt to improve upon it.

It is evident that Samuel had not received sittings from his Muses who, in 1777, were aged between 23 and 60. Even though the heads in NPG 4905 are far more personable than those in the engraving, only three plausible likenesses may be suggested:[5] Mrs Sheridan as the central figure with a lyre (she resembles her portrait by Reynolds of 1776 and she is unambigouously identified in the print caption); Angelica Kauffmann at the easel (identified by her profession as much as her likeness), and Elizabeth Montagu as perhaps the central seated figure on the right, her hand on her chin (not dissimilar to her portrait by Reynolds of 1775, engraved in 1776, or the Wedgwood medallion of 1775, while the elegance of the dress would be appropriate). Samuel apparently did not consult contemporary likenesses of Anna Barbauld, Elizabeth Carter or Catharine Macaulay, and he would in any case have had to invent the likenesses of Elizabeth Griffith, Charlotte Lennox and Hannah More, there being no recorded portraits of them by 1777.[6] The Muses are invoked for their number, sex and pedigree rather than their attributes, though Mrs Sheridan with her lyre might be equated with Erato (lyric poetry); Hannah More, whose tragedy *Percy* had been performed in 1774, could have been Melpomene (traditionally shown with dagger and sceptre), and the historian Mrs Macaulay, Clio (traditionally shown with quill and lute, or trumpet and book).[7]

Each of the named sitters is separately featured in this catalogue.

1 *European Mag.*, IX, [March] 1786, p.139.
2 Illus. Dulwich 1988, p.73; S.H. Myers, *The Bluestocking Circle*, 1990, p.277; E. Eger, *Women, Writing and the Public Sphere 1700–1830*, 2001, p.112.
3 Carter, *Letters*, 1817, III, pp.47–48. She was replying to a letter from Mrs Montagu of 24 November 1777, quoted by Eger, pp.122–23, 131n66.
4 For example, Smith 1905, p.79: 1778 'for the honour of female genius, be it here recorded, that, in the Ladies' Pocket Book, published this year, an engraved group of nine whole-length female figures ...'. By 1863 the moment had passed; 'Good Heavens! what a frowsy, drowsy 'party in a parlour', now 'all silent and all damned', wrote Gilchrist (*Life of Blake*, I, pp.45–46), describing the print as 'a flattering apotheosis of nine contemporary female wits', including the 'pious, busy, Hannah More', the 'sprightly fashionable Mrs Montagu', the 'sensible Barbauld' and the 'learned and awful Mrs Carter'.
5 *Romantic Women Writers*, Grasmere, 1994, p.25, and J. Uglow, *Dr Johnson, His Club, and other Friends*, NPG, 1998, pp.9, 30, accepted identifications for all nine muses.
6 See the separate individual entries for these sitters.
7 There were no obvious candidates for the remaining Muses: epic poetry (Calliope), flute-playing (Euterpe), dance (Terpsichore), sacred song (Polyhymnia), astronomy (Urania) and comedy (Thalia).

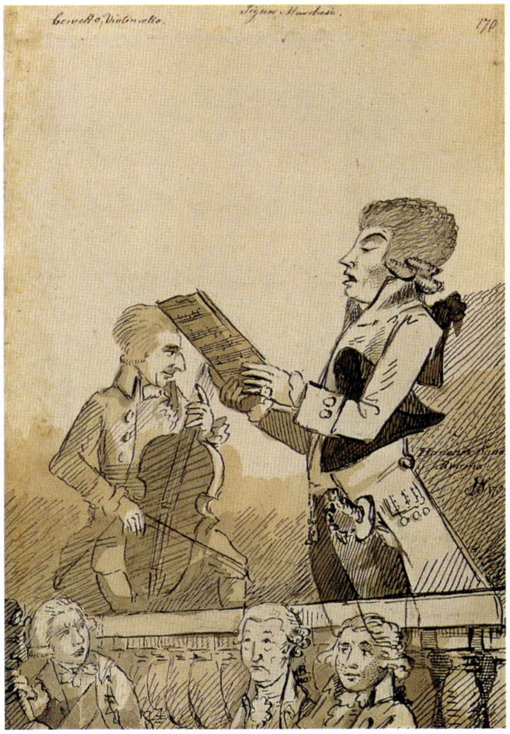

A Bravura at the Hanover Square Concert NPG 5179

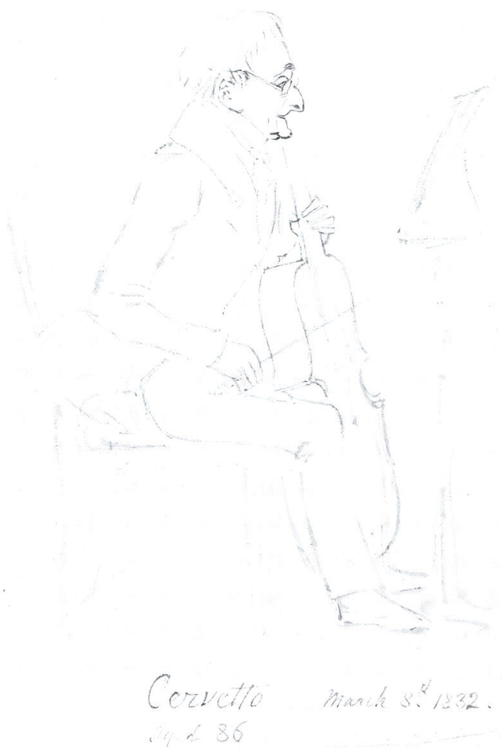

Giacomo Cervetto II by A.E. Chalon 1832 (British Museum)

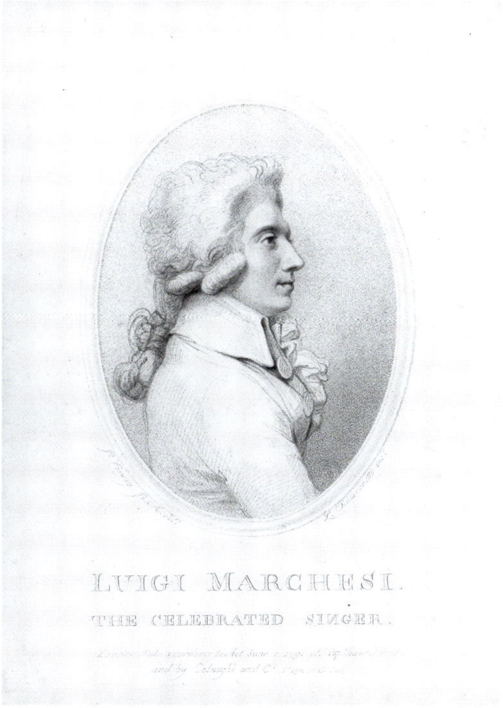

Luigi Marchesi, L. Schiavonetti 1790 after Richard Cosway (NPG D 13804)

A Bravura at the Hanover Square Concert

5179 JOHN NIXON 1789

Pen and wash 23.5 x 17 (9¼ x 6¾) laid down on paper mount, signed in monogram and dated lower right: *JN:1789*, and inscribed immediately above: *Hanover Square/Rooms*; along the top edge, inscribed in a different hand: *Cervetto, Violincello* and *Signor Marchesi* and numbered *170*.

Cervetto on the left playing the 'cello, Marchesi on the right, his hat under his arm, foppishly dressed, with a large ring on his left little finger and a sword; in the foreground a 'cellist with his spectacles on his forehead, and four members of the audience, three looking bored (one wears the ribbon and star of the Garter), and one content.

Collections: The French Hospital of La Providence, Rochester; Christie's, 22 November 1977, lot 49, bt. John Baskett, from whom purchased 1978.

Engraving: Anon. aquatint, pub. William Holland, 27 May 1789, *A Bravura at the Hanover Square Concert* (George 8268).

Exhibition: *Master Drawings* 1993-95(37).

The inscriptions identify:

Luigi Marchesi (1755-1829), a celebrated Italian male soprano who performed throughout Europe and was in London 1788-90. Nixon's caricature fully exploits Marchesi's vanity and affectation, but the likeness may be reconciled with the portrait by Richard Cosway engraved by Luigi Schiavonetti* in 1790.

Giacomo [James] Cervetto II (1749-1837), an Italian 'cellist, was a pupil of Abel in London in 1760, and from 1780 played at the professional concerts at the Hanover Square Rooms. His identity seems confirmed by a second Nixon caricature of 1784[1] and by a drawing of him in old age by A.E. Chalon,* dated 1832 (British Museum; 1922.10.17.5); he has also been identified in a Zoffany group.[2]

The old mount is inscribed below in a near-contemporary hand *Duke of Cumberland 1791*, apparently identifying the left-hand foreground seated figure wearing a (vestigial) Garter ribbon and star as Henry, Duke of Cumberland (1745-90; KG 1767), the rather foolish brother of George III, who was nevertheless musical and owned a collection of musical instruments;[3] the likeness is, however, perfunctory. It has also been suggested that the shadowy profile in the bottom left corner of the drawing evoked Giacobbe Cervetto (1680/81-1783), the 'cellist's deceased father.[4]

The Hanover Square concert rooms in London, a joint venture by J.C. Bach and C.F. Abel (who are separately featured in this catalogue) with the Italian dancer and dancing master G.A. [Sir John] Gallini (1728-1805), had opened in 1775; 'Professional Concerts', run by Professors of Music, were held between 1783 and 1793.

1 Illus. *Master Drawings* 1993-95, no.37; Christie's, 22 November 1977, lot 45 (the same sale as NPG 5179).
2 *Self-portrait with his Daughter*[?] *and two Musicians*, Yale Center for British Art (B1977.14.88), see Zoffany c.1780. A whole-length portrait called Cervetto by Zoffany, sold Christie's, 19 December 1974, lot 9, may also show the younger Cervetto.
3 The title fell into abeyance from 1790 to 1799 when George III's fifth son Ernest (1771-1851) succeeded.
4 See M. Rogers in *Master Drawings* 1993-95, no.37, a full and lively account of Nixon's caricature. Giacobbe has also been identified in the Zoffany group, see note 2 above; his three-quarter length seated portrait by Zoffany sold Sotheby's, 12 June 2003, lot 16.

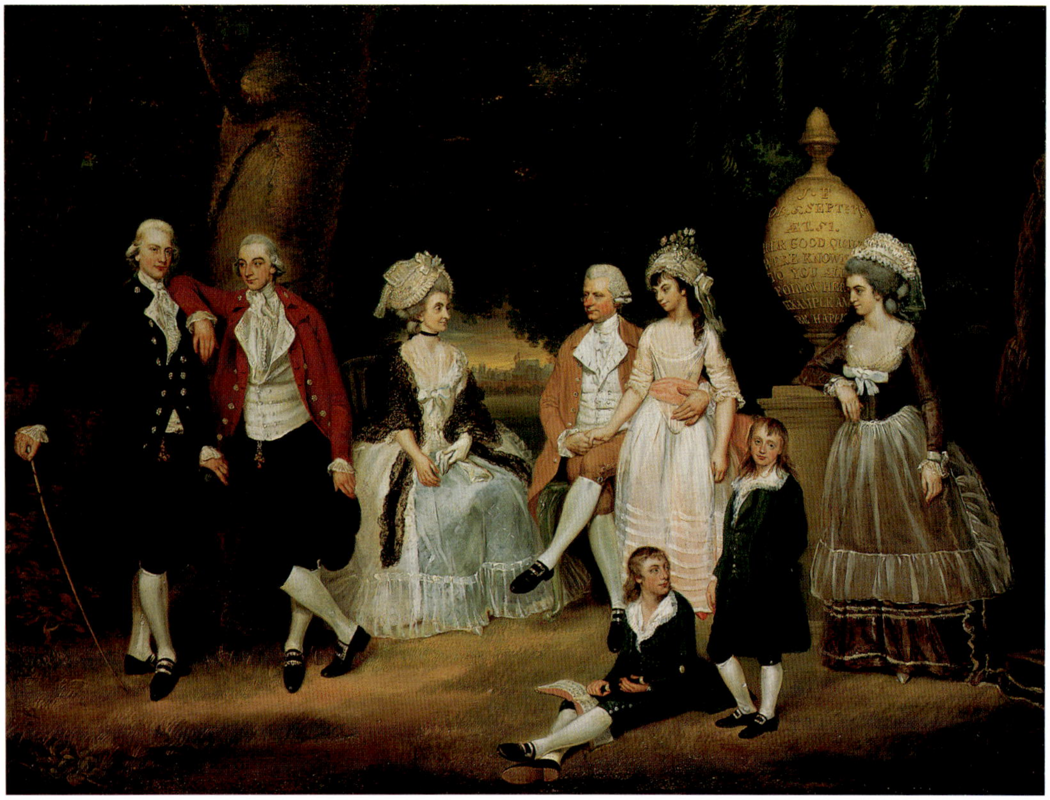

The FOURDRINIER Family NPG *6091*

The Fourdrinier Family

6091 attributed to JOHN DOWNMAN c.1786

Copper[1] 46 x 61.5 (18 x 24¼); cleaned 1990; there is a fine overall craquelure.

The distant central prospect appears to show the Curfew Tower, St George's Chapel and the Round Tower at Windsor.

Collections: By family descent to A. Fourdrinier Fenn 1924; P.A. Fourdrinier Fenn, from whom purchased 1990.

Exhibitions: *The Quiet Conquest*, Museum of London, 1985(259); *Cardinal Newman*, NPG 1990(1).

Henry Fourdrinier (1730-99) sits in a green chair fourth from the left in the back row, with a powdered wig, pale brown suit, white striped waistcoat, white stockings and black shoes.

From the left in the back row:[2]

his son *Charles* (1767-1841)[3] blue eyes, powdered hair, wearing a blue coat with silver buttons, black breeches, his feet elegantly spread; a locket of gold, red and silver hangs at his waist.

His son *Henry* (1766-1854)[4] blue eyes, powdered hair, wearing a red-brown coat with silver buttons, white vest, black breeches, his dark grey hat in his left hand; a locket of gold, red and silver hangs at his waist.

His sister *Mary* (b.1728, d. unm.) in a green wooden chair, grey hair, wearing a white bonnet and black shawl, pale blue underskirt with white panelled dress and white gloves.

An urn commemorates his deceased wife *Jemima*, *née* White (1730-81 who m. 1st William Manning) inscribed: *J.F ./ OB.5 SEPTR.1781 / AET.51. / HER GOOD QUALI*[ties] */ WERE KNOWN / TO YOU ALL/ FOLLOW HER / EXAMPLE AN*[d] */ BE HAPP*[y].

On one side his daughter *Jemima* (1772-1836, m.1799 John Newman, Cardinal Newman was their son) dark brown hair, wearing a white cap, pink underskirt, white dress and pink sash and red shoes.

On the other side his step-daughter *Minerva Manning* (b.1763) grey powdered hair, wearing a white bonnet, purple dress trimmed with silver, a white gauze apron and silver shoes.

In the foreground his fair-haired younger sons, *John Rawson* (b.1770-c.1836) on the left and *Sealy* (1774-1847) on the right, identically dressed in green suits with white stockings and black shoes; John holds a sheet of music and a flute.

Henry Fourdrinier was a paper-maker and stationer in Lombard Street, London, son of the engraver Paul Fourdrinier (d.1758) who came to London from Caen in 1720; his sons Henry and Sealy succeeded to his business, and in 1807 perfected a machine for the manufacture of continuous paper; the considerable costs of their experiments were only partially recovered in 1840, when Parliament made them an award, later supplemented by a subscription raised by the paper trade.

The setting is probably intended to convey the gardens of the Fourdrinier house in Stratford Grove, Putney,[5] although that hardly justifies a distant view of Windsor (if such it is). Miniatures of Henry Fourdrinier and of his sister Mary remained in the family's possession in 1937.[6]

1 Stamped verso: BENJN. ... STOW.

2 These identities are taken from a collotype key furnished by P.A. Fourdrinier Fenn entitled *The Fourdrinier Family Picture [The Original (on Copper - Artist's name not known) was probably painted in, or about, the year 1786*].

3 A miniature of him by James Ross was in a private collection in 1985.

4 For other portraits of him, see Walker *Regency*, I, pp.191, 607; II, pls.1517-24; a miniature of him 'aged about 14 with powdered hair', belonged to the family in 1937 (letter from N.D. Fourdrinier, 24 November 1937; NPG archive).

5 On the death of Henry sr. in 1799, the house was described as having a library, a well-equipped cellar and much household silver and glass, and with a staff including eleven servants, a coachman and gardener (see R. Edwards, 'The Rise and Fall of the Fourdriniers', *The Paper Maker*, October 1968, p.59). See T. Murdoch, *The Quiet Company*, 1985, pp.164, 178, 180. For Henry Fourdrinier see also R.H. Clapperton, *The Paper-making Machine*, 1967.

6 Letter from N.D. Fourdrinier, 24 November 1937 (NPG archive).

UNIDENTIFIED PORTRAITS

IN ORDER OF ACCESSION NUMBER

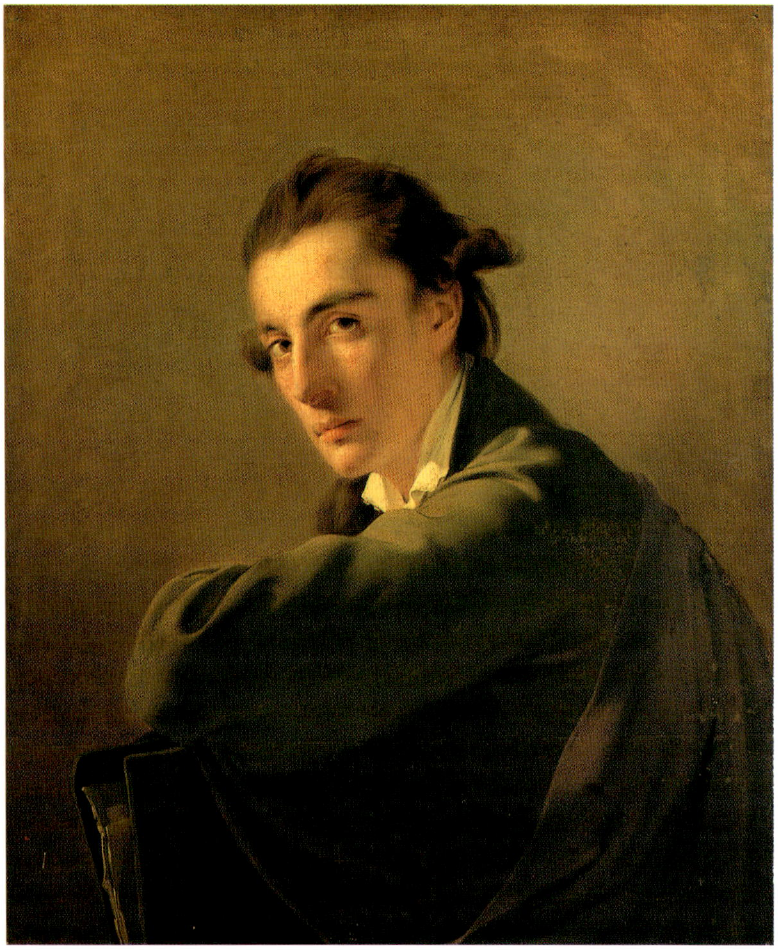

NPG 29

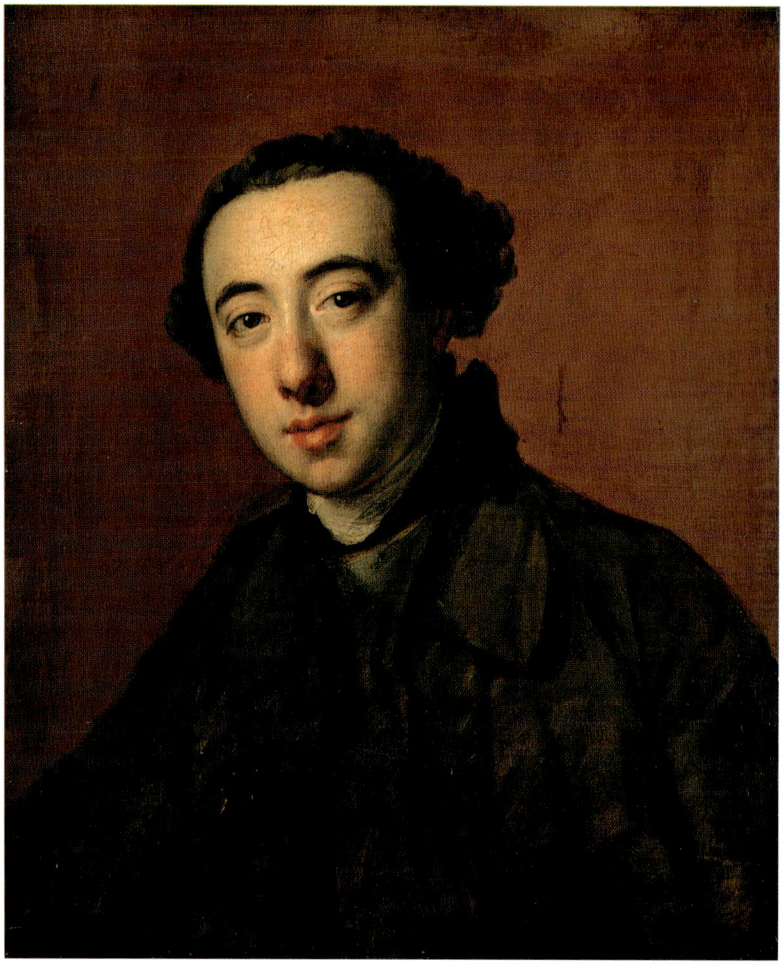

NPG 116

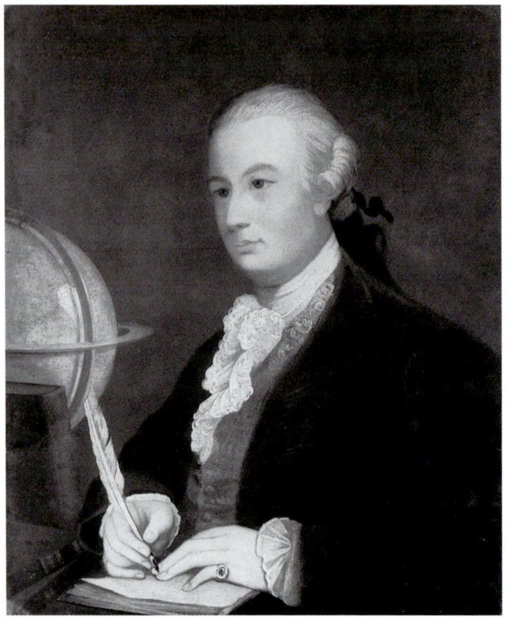

NPG 100

29 UNKNOWN ARTIST c.1765–70

Canvas 75.5 x 64 (29¾ x 25¼); lined; pentimento by his forehead; repaired damage above ear; the surface is rubbed and there are many retouchings. Label verso: *Joseph Wright/ 1775/ painted by himself at Rome/ where he died.*[1]

Brown eyes, brown hair, green coat, brown drape, green folder.

Collections: Deville; Deagostine;[2] Gaetano Polidori; his son-in-law, William Michael Rossetti, by whom presented 1858 (as a portrait of Joseph Wright of Derby).

Exhibition: Derby 1883(50).

Evidently a self portrait of 1765–70, previously identified as Wright of Derby (who is separately featured in this catalogue).[3] A copy was given to Derby Museum and Art Gallery by W. Wright Bemrose, a direct descendant of Wright of Derby.[4] If the sitter was an artist closely connected with Wright c.1765–70, likely candidates would be Richard Hurlston or William Tate, whose features, let alone their work, remain obscure.[5]

1 Recorded by Scharf in 1862.
2 Names given by W.M. Rossetti in a letter to Scharf, 19 February 1858 (NPG archive): he wrote that the picture had descended from his father-in-law, Polidori, who had received it from a Signor Deagostini, who had it from a M. Deville 'who is believed to have been a Hungarian'.
3 Illus. as such by W. Bemrose, *Wright of Derby*, 1885, front.; a collotype (?) published by Bemrose & Co., c.1883 (NPG archive).
4 Exhibited *Wright of Derby*, Derby, 1934 (75).
5 See Nicolson 1968, I, pp.6, 138–40.

100 UNKNOWN ARTIST late 18th century

Canvas 74.5 x 62 (29¼ x 24½) lined; heavily restored.

Brown eyes, white powdered hair with a black ribbon, gold embroidered waistcoat, maroon coat, finger ring on left hand (a blue and pink stone surrounded by brilliants); the books and globe are not inscribed.

Collections: 'From a portion of the family of Bruce' to a Mr Miller, Edinburgh;[1] his sale, Nisbett, Edinburgh, February 1860, bt. Brown & Macindos of Glasgow; E.W. Radclyffe, from whom purchased 1860.

Exhibition: NPE 1867(802).

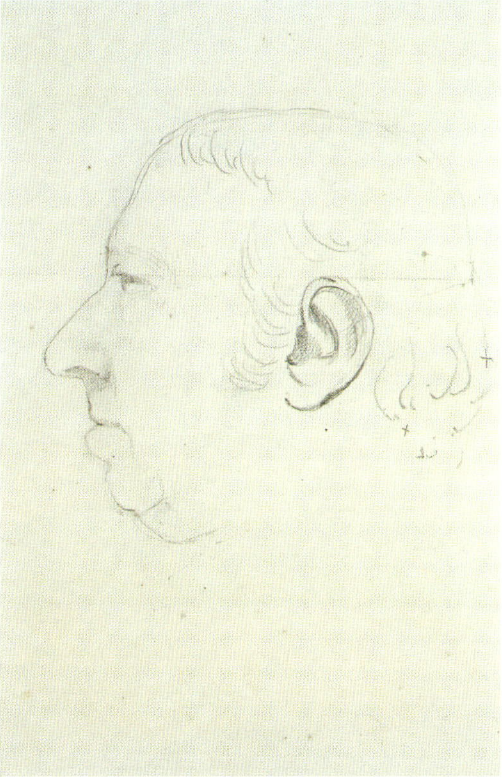

NPG 316A(172)

A very weak picture, acquired as a portrait of the explorer James Bruce (who is separately featured in this catalogue). The head bears a remote resemblance to that of Bruce engraved in 1830 by W.C. Edwards after David Martin, see p.75.

1 The provenance cited was given to Scharf by Radclyffe in his letter of 23 April 1860, in which he also stated the portrait was by [David] Martin (NPG archive).

116 attributed to NATHANIEL HONE c.1765

Canvas 60 x 50 (23⅝ x 19¾) lined 1878; discoloured varnish and retouchings, a drip of paint above his left shoulder.

Grey eyes, very dark hair; wearing a grey-green coat and light green waistcoat which are sketched in.

Collections: Lord Patrick James Herbert Crichton-Stuart (1794–1859); his son Lt.-Col. James Frederick D.C. Stuart, from whom purchased, through T.R. Rutley, 1861.[1]

Reference: C.K. Adams & W.S. Lewis, *Walpole Soc.*, xlii, 1970, p.30, C.10 (as not of Horace Walpole).

Acquired as a portrait of Horace Walpole, 4th Earl of Orford (who is separately featured in this catalogue), but the identification is untenable. W.S. Lewis suggested it might show Horatio Walpole (1723–1809) of Wolterton, later 1st Earl of Orford of the second creation, but comparison with two securely identified portraits by Henry Walton[2] is not conclusive.

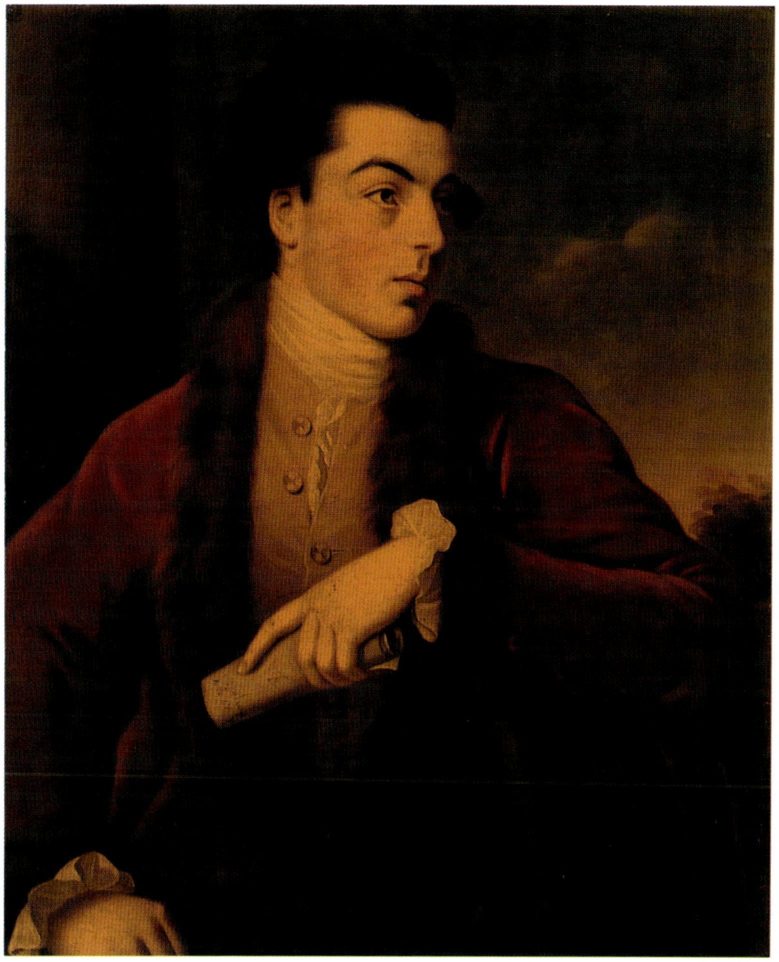

NPG 761A

NPG 116 appears to date from the later 1760s and the traditional attribution to Nathaniel Hone is probably correct; he had painted Lord Mountstuart, father of the first recorded owner. He has also been credited with a miniature once identified as the young Horace Walpole.[3]

1 In a letter of 24 November 1860 (NPG archive), Rutley described the portrait as 'the property of Colonel Stuart. The Picture is from the collection of the late Lord James Stuart of Whitehall Place, in whose family it has been for many years'. Col. Stuart was living at 6 Whitehall Place in 1860.
2 *Walpole Soc.*, XLII, 1970, p.30. *Walton* 1999, nos.144–45, fig.14.
3 Private collection; see *Walpole Soc.*, XLII, 1970, p.32, C.16, as not of Horace Walpole.

316A(172) FRANCIS CHANTREY c.1816–18

Pencil on paper 43.5 x 28.5 (17¼ x 11¼)

Collections: Chantrey's executor George Jones RA, by whose widow presented in 1871.

Reference: Walker *Regency*, I, pp.624–25; *Chantrey* 1994, p.165.

Tentatively identified by Walker as a study for Chantrey's head of Joseph Banks, but the resemblance is not totally convincing.

761A UNKNOWN ARTIST [c.1770]

Canvas 76 x 63.5 (30 x 25) lined 1887; numerous retouchings, the varnish much discoloured.

Brown eyes, black hair, wearing a red coat with fur collar; the inscription on the paper in his hand illegible.

Collections: Perks; Dr Whyatt, by whom presented 1887.[1]

Possibly cut down. Offered as a portrait by Joshua Reynolds of Gabriel Piozzi (who is separately featured in this catalogue), to whom it bears no resemblance, NPG 761A was attributed to Nathaniel Dance by Scharf.[2] First catalogued in 1981.

1 Offered through Shepherd Bros. of London, when Dr Whyatt, 'for many years a physician at Naples' was going abroad; the picture, 'from the collection of Mr Perks' had then been in his family 'for many years' (letters from Shepherds, 30 July, 12 August 1886; NPG archive).
2 *NPG Annual Report* 1887.

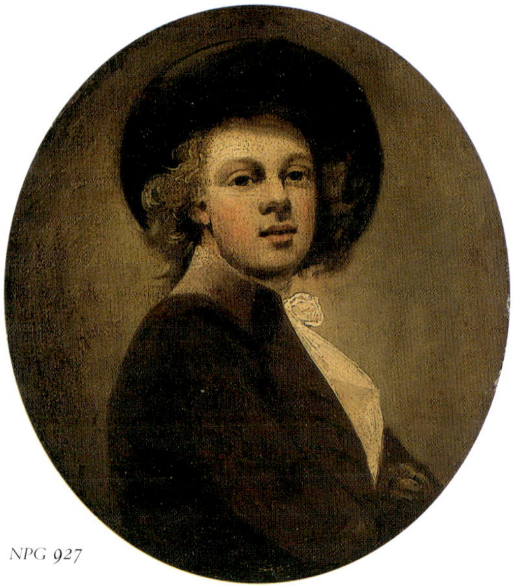

NPG 927

927 UNKNOWN ARTIST [c.1775]

Canvas 20.5 x 18 (8 x 7⅛) oval, lined; discoloured varnish and an old loss upper left.

Blue-grey eyes, fair hair, wearing a black hat and brown coat.

Collections: Mr Johnson, Chichester; his sale, Christie's, 16 ff. November 1874 (787 as a Reynolds self portrait) bought by Lord Ronald Sutherland Gower,[1] by whom presented 1892.

Reference: Graves & Cronin, II, p.794.

Received as a self portrait by Joshua Reynolds (who is separately featured in this catalogue), to whom it bears no resemblance; NPG 927 appears to be a copy from an unidentified self portrait.

1 For this provenance, see R.S. Gower, *Bric à Brac*, 1888, p.68. A label on the stretcher, written by Gower, reads: *Sir Joshua Reynolds/by himself.*

1278 UNKNOWN ARTIST c.1765-70?

Canvas 37.5 x 31 (14¾ x 12¼) lined c.1890; discoloured varnish.

Brown eyes, brown hair, wearing a black hat with silver trim, a brown coat with a pink collar, and light green waistcoat and breeches.

Collections: William Burrough Hill, auctioneer, Southampton,[1] from whom purchased 1900.

NPG 1278 is evidently a self portrait, but a somewhat laboured one, probably the work of an amateur. It was acquired as a portrait of Francis Wheatley[2] (who is separately featured in this catalogue) and was listed as such until 1981.

1 Hill alleged (letter of 21 August 1900; NPG archive) that he had bt. NPG 1278 'about ten years ago' from an artist who had had it 'backlined' and in the course of this operation an inscription was found on the old stretcher 'Portrait of Wheatley by himself', but the stretcher was destroyed.

2 Illus. as such *MA*, XXV, 1901, p.416; W. Roberts, *Wheatley*, 1910, front.

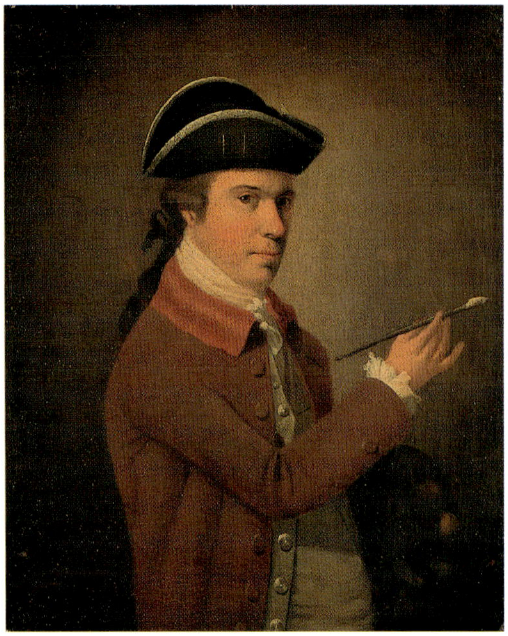

NPG 1278

1327 UNKNOWN ARTIST c.1735

Canvas 75.5 x 62 (29¾ x 24½) lined; much restored, discoloured varnish.

Blue eyes, purple beret, wearing a blue coat; his palette displaying, left to right: blue, green, two umbers, red and yellow; a blank canvas on the easel and a green drape to the left.

Collections: Presented by Sir Hugh Percy Lane 1902.

Reference: D. Cooper, *Burl. Mag.*, XC, 1948, p.115.

NPG 1327 appears in this catalogue because it was once supposed to be a self portrait of Richard Wilson[1] (who is separately featured in this catalogue). But it is an unsophisticated self portrait apparently of c.1735 (Cooper compared the sitter with 'some inmate of Newgate prison'). A similar portrait appears in the background of a portrait of Lancelot Tolson Tilly of c.1735, sold Sotheby's, 7 April 1965, lot 181.

1 Illus. as such A. Bury, *Richard Wilson*, 1947, pl.1.

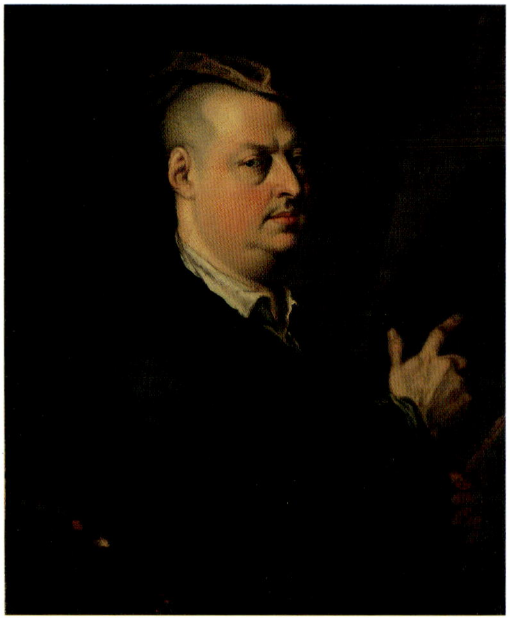

NPG 1327

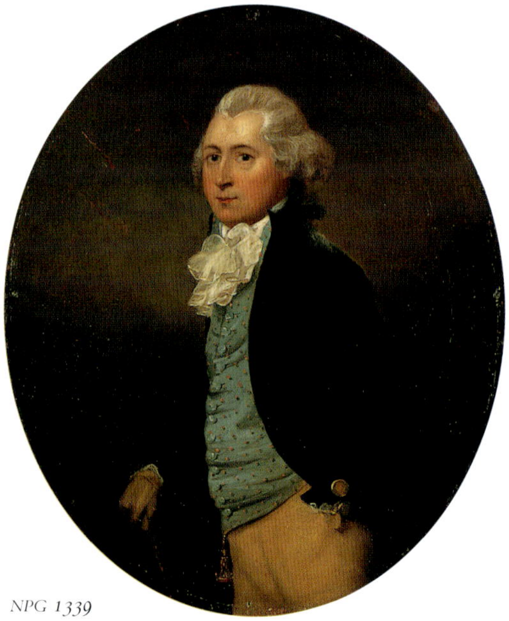

NPG 1339

1339 UNKNOWN ARTIST c.1790

Canvas 45.5 x 38 (18 x 15) lined; discoloured varnish, slight damages upper left in coat and at waist.

Blue-grey eyes, white powdered hair, wearing a blue coat, light green waistcoat with orange dots, yellow breeches, beige gloves, a fob ribbon at his waist.

Collections: Purchased from Leggatt 1903.

A weak portrait, bought as a portrait by J.R. Smith of Christopher Anstey (who is separately featured in this catalogue), but it shows little resemblance to authentic heads of Anstey by Hoare. Another small oval portrait, descended within the Anstey family, showing a head comparable with NPG 1339, but with glasses and without the dandified elegance, described as Christopher Anstey by J.R. Smith, was sold Sotheby's, 12 February 1998, lot 222. NPG 1339 may possibly show one of Christopher Anstey's sons (the Rev Christopher 1755-1827, John 1757-1819, Robert 1760-1818, or Thomas ?1770-1843).

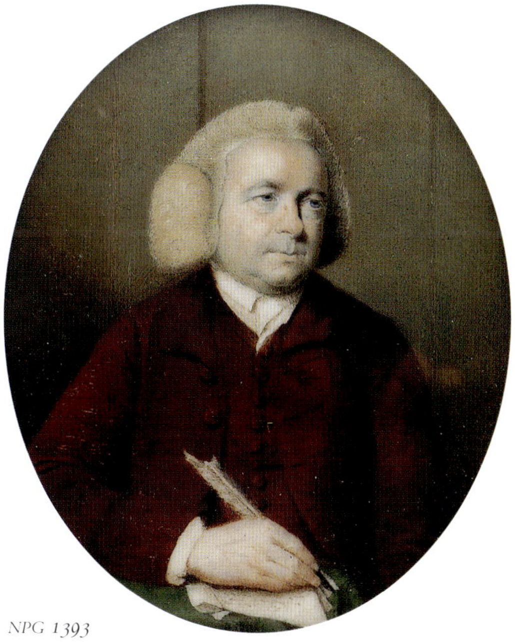

NPG 1393

1393 ascribed to JOHN PLOTT c.1760

Watercolour and bodycolour on ivory 10.6 x 8.7 (4¼ x 3½); some retouchings in the coat and background.

Pale blue eyes, white powdered 'physical' wig, wearing a red-brown suit; there is no legible writing on the paper before him.

Collections: Presented by the 1st Baron Weardale, 1905.

Reference: *Apollo*, XCVIII, 1973, p.372, as Mason; Walker 1998, no.49 (as Mason c.1760).

The identification of the sitter as William Mason (who is separately featured in this catalogue), first suggested by J.D. Milner in 1904,[1] is undocumented and not wholly convincing. That there are missing portraits of Mason from at least 1760 is indicated by a letter from Thomas Gray (see Mason), but no portrait of him before 1765 survives. An attribution to Plott was suggested by Basil Long in 1928.[2]

1 Note on file, 1 December 1904.
2 'The .. Mason reminded me of a miniature by Plott which we have here' (letter of 15 March 1928 in NPG archives); he could only have been referring to Plott's *Mrs Lydia Butt* of 1776.

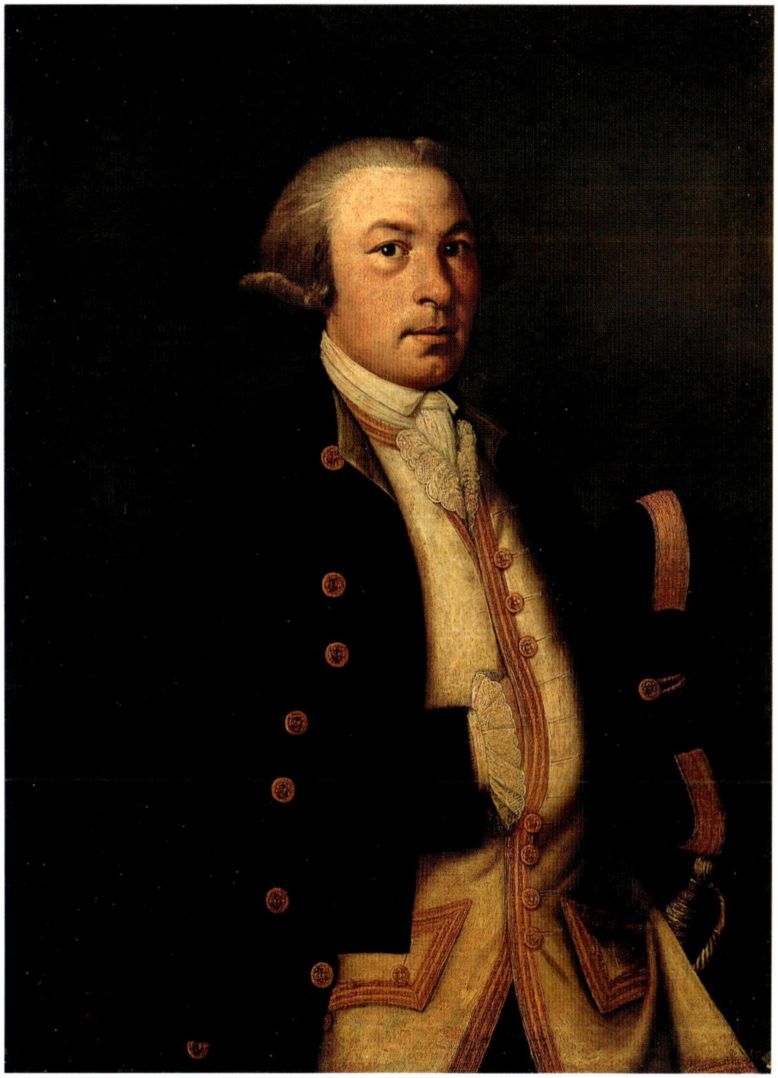

NPG 1414

1414 UNKNOWN ARTIST c.1765

Canvas 92 x 68.5 (36¼ x 27) lined; discoloured varnish; inscribed, bottom left: *James Cook.RN/ Anno 1766/ Atatis 38*; left hand overpainted; verso of original canvas inscribed: *This Portrait of/Jas Cook Marine-/Surveyor/was painted at Newfondland/for Captn Graves the Governor/in the year 1766*.

Brown eyes, powdered hair; the uniform somewhat resembles that of a naval lieutenant:[1] dark blue coat with blue lapels and a white lining, and gold buttons bearing a four-petal rose with an anchor painted over; white neckcloth and waistcoat, the buttons similar to those on the coat.

Collections: [Palisser and Cook-Hervey];[2] John A. East,[3] London, from whom purchased 1905.

Acquired as a portrait of Captain Cook (who is separately featured in this catalogue), but there is no resemblance between NPG 1414 and his three authentic portraits. The 'Captain Graves' of the inscription was governor of Newfoundland 1762–64; Cook made annual surveys of the Newfoundland coast in 1763, 1764, 1765 and 1766. There is a slight resemblance to Captain John Gore (c.1730–90), according to the portrait by John Webber (Nan Kivell collection; Canberra);[4] Gore served as third lieutenant under Cook in 1767–71 and first lieutenant in 1776–9. In 1916 Collins Baker suggested an attribution to Bickeray,[5] an artist otherwise unknown.

1 Comd. May of the National Maritime Museum tentatively suggested, mainly from the cut and length of the waistcoat, that it might show an early lieutenant's uniform (note of 3 November 1953; NPG archive). Cook was promoted lieutenant in May 1768.
2 'The portrait was acquired by purchase & from what I have heard I believe was formerly in the possession of the Palissers & Cook-Herveys who I think were related' (J.A. East, 9 August 1905; NPG archive). Palisser doubtless implied Admiral Sir Hugh Palliser, governor of Newfoundland 1764–69 and an admirer of Cook. Attached to the back of the picture were a facsimile of Cook's *Observations* and a pretentious 19th-century note on Cook's appearance (NPG archive).
3 East had previously offered another portrait of Cook to the NPG in 1902, 'with his hand on a globe and ascribed to Zoffany' (letter from East, 5 February 1902; NPG archive).
4 Exhibited *Captain Cook*, Portland, Ore., 1974(129).
5 *Burl. Mag.*, XXIX, 1916, p.100.

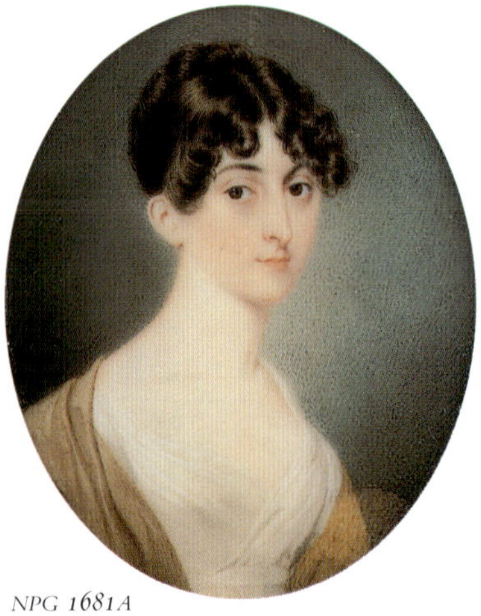

NPG 1681A

1681A JAMES COX DILLMAN ENGLEHEART 1814

Watercolour and bodycolour on ivory 7.9 x 6.4 (3⅛ x 2½); a vertical crack to the left of the head; signed on the original backing paper: *JCD Engleheart/fecit 1814//88 Newman/ Street/ London.*

Brown eyes, dark hair, wearing a dull yellow dress.

Collections: See below; bequeathed by Ellen Mabel Dawson 1912.

NPG 1681A is of interest as a signed and dated miniature by J.C.D. Engleheart, but the identity of the sitter is uncertain. A separate MS note (probably from the mid-19th century), bequeathed with NPG 1681A, reads:

'Bridgeman'.Dau: of James Willyams Esqre: of Carmanton Cornwall who married Lord James O.Brien R.N. Afterwards Marquis of Thomond & died early of decline, & without children -

This Picture by 'Engleheart' of 'Newman St' London, was painted in 1814 - & sent to my Mother Sarah Grylls on Lord Thomonds 2nd marriage. /E. Dawson

This identifies Eliza Bridgeman Willyams (d.1802) who m. 1800, as his first wife, James O'Brien (c.1768-1855), styled Lord James O'Brien from 1809 to 1846, when he suc. as 3rd Marquess of Thomond. But she died twelve years before NPG 1681A was painted, and 'Lord Thomond's' second marriage took place eight years before, in Antigua in 1806. According to the donor's sister 'the Marchioness of Thomonde [presumably meaning Eliza Willyams] was our great-Aunt'.[1]

1 E. Maud Dawson, letter of 7 Aug. 1912 (NPG archive); she also said the miniature had been 'in the family since 1814, the date it was painted' and had always been considered to be by George Engleheart, although she had come to realise it was by his nephew.

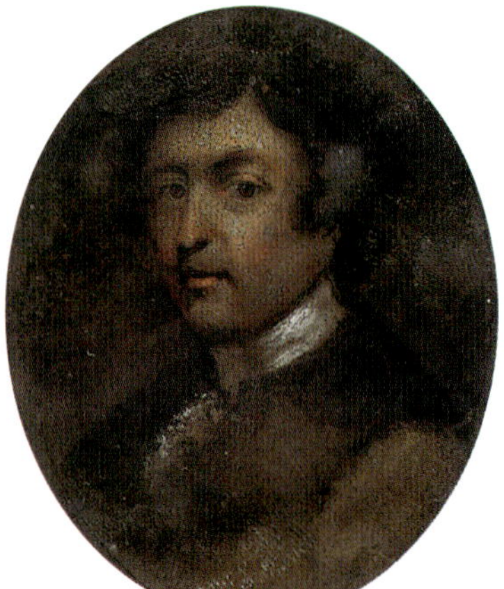

NPG 1761B

1761B UNKNOWN ARTIST [c.1775?]

Oil on copper 6.9 x 5.7 (2¾ x 2¼) much restored.

Black hair, brown eyes, green coat with dark fur collar.

Collections: Presented by the 1st Baron Weardale 1915.

Offered as a portrait of Edmund Burke (who is separately featured in this catalogue), NPG 1761B was accepted as a copy of a self portrait by Reynolds, which it evidently isn't.

1882 GEORGE ROMNEY c.1765?

Canvas laid down on panel 12.2 x 10 (4½ x 4); overall craquelure with some retouching in the hair and coat.

Dark blue eyes, light brown hair, blue coat.

Collections: Miss Elizabeth Romney;[1] Romney sale Christie's, 24 May 1894 [?lot 205, 'unfinished study - Head of one of Romney's Brothers']; Ernest E. Leggatt, by whom presented 1920.

Previously called Peter Romney (1743-77), the younger brother of the painter George Romney, with whom he studied before practising on his own mainly in the north of England.[2] George Romney's double portrait of his brothers (Yale Center for British Art, B1981.25.537)[3] shows Peter with much darker hair, and the identity of NPG 1882 is not secure; a drawing by George Romney, called 'Peter Romney', was sold Christie's, 12 July 1937, lot 6.

1 See Romney NPG 959 note 1.
2 See Romney 1830, pp.271-311.
3 Exhibited FSA 1766(144); illus. RA 1963(254).

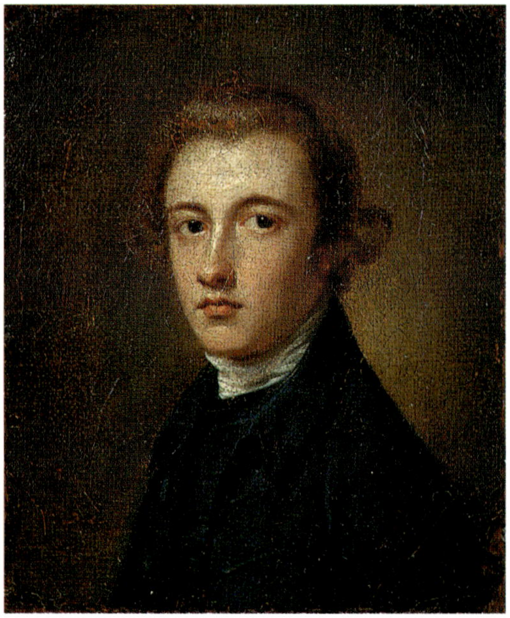

NPG 1882

2355 JOHN WESTBROOK CHANDLER c.1785

Canvas 126 x 96 (49½ x 37¾) lined; the surface is abraded, principally in the lower areas and upper right; signed below centre right: *J W C.*

Blue-grey eyes, grey powdered hair, wearing a bottle-green dress with white scarf and cuffs, a red curtain draped behind her.

Collections: Bequeathed by the 2nd Baron Revelstoke 1929.

Exhibition: Bath Preservation Trust 1976-.

NPG 2355 was bequeathed as the 'Portrait of a Lady said to be Lady Betty Foster [later Duchess of Devonshire] by Chandler'. It is certainly by Chandler, whose signature was subsequently discovered, but doubts concerning the sitter's identity have remained. The features do not readily agree with the Duchess's portraits by Reynolds, Kauffmann and Lawrence, and the identity seems first to have been doubted by C.F. Bell - though he allowed that 'the differences are not perhaps so great as between the different portraits of her predecessor Georgiana.'[1]

The principal interest of NPG 2355 lies in the artist, the natural son of Lord Warwick, he became unstable and died under restraint in 1807.

1 Letter from C.F. Bell, 16 December 1929; NPG archive.

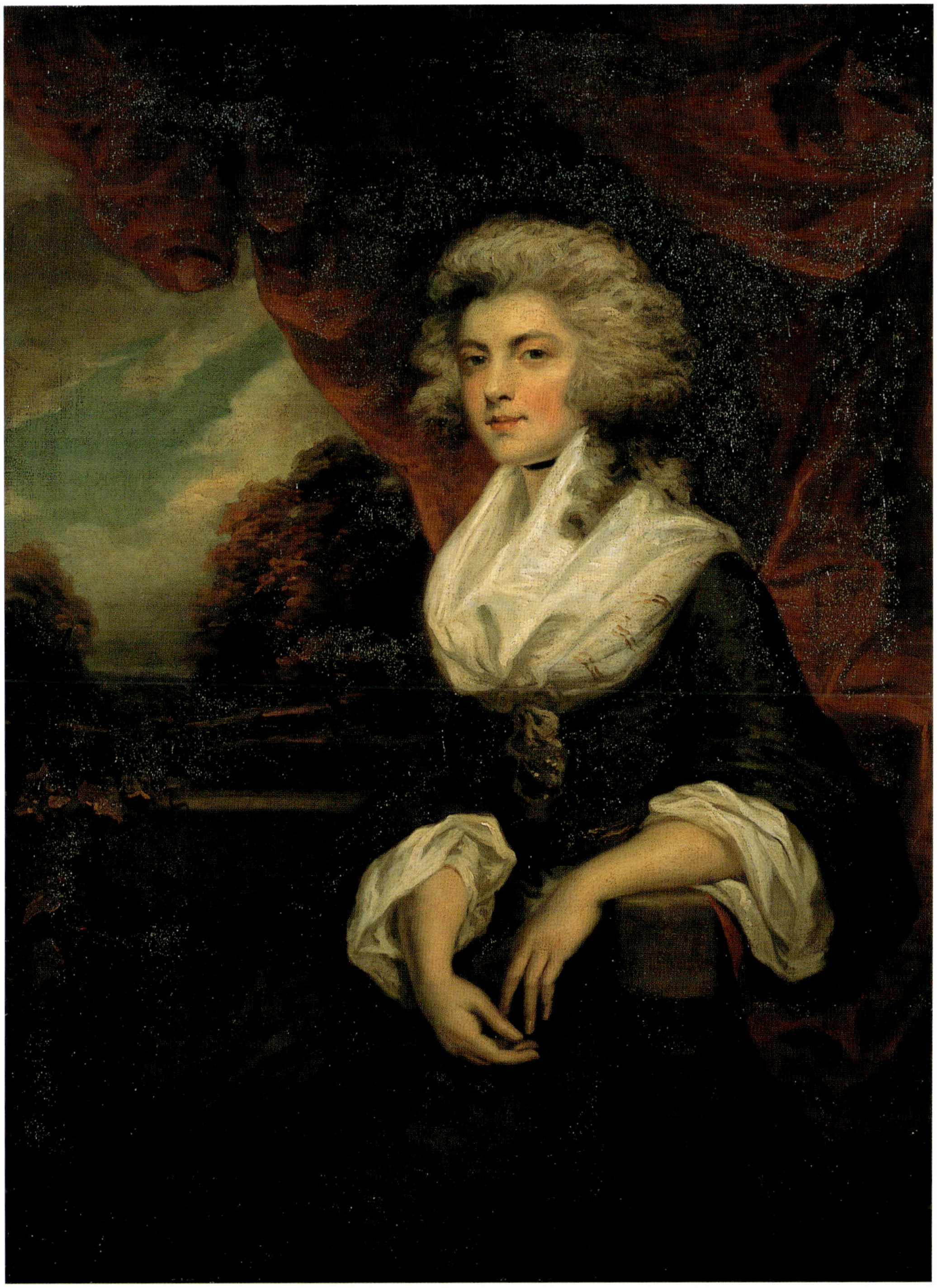

NPG 2355

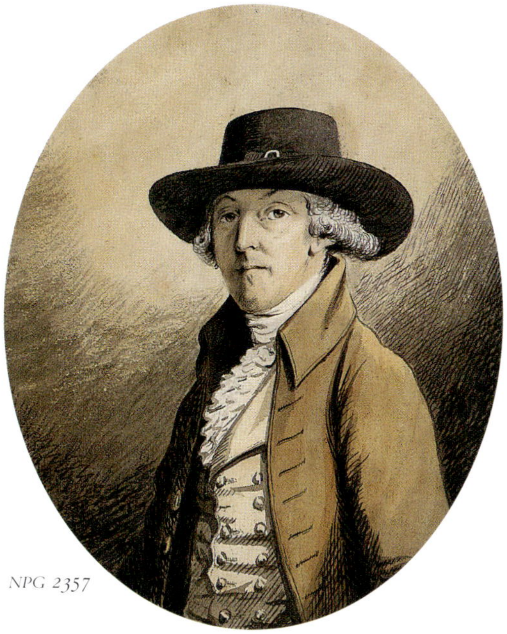

NPG 2357

2357 JCB 1788

Ink and watercolour on paper 15.5 x 12.5 (6 x 5) irregularly cut oval; some fading and staining.

Wearing a black hat with a buckled band and a light-coloured coat.

Collections: Sotheby's, 27 July 1888, lot 62 ('Mr Tattersall', anon.); Sidney Phipson; Sotheby's, 12 June 1929, lot 107 ('Mr Tattersall', signed JCB and with the date 1788), bt. Meatyard for the NPG.

Hitherto called Richard Tattersall (1724-95, the founder of Tattersall's), but NPG 2357 shows a much younger man.[1] It might show his son Edmund (1758-1810), according to the traditional title of 'Mr Tattersall', but the only other image known of him, a caricature by Dighton of 1802,[2] seems to show swarthier features, even allowing for the difference of age. NPG 2357 was sold in 1929 as signed and dated JCB 1788,[3] but no trace of this remains visible; the monogram remains unidentified,[4] while the date seems entirely appropriate.

1 Compare with the portrait of Richard Tattersall by Thomas Beach 1787, engraved J. Jones 1787 (illus. *Pickpocketing the Rich*, Bath, 2002, p.67); the hat he wears identical to that in NPG 2357.
2 *A View in Hyde Park Corner* (George 9901).
3 The framer's label formerly verso inscribed in ink: *Signed JCB 1788*.
4 I.A. Williams very tentatively suggested in 1957 (verbally) I. C. Barrow, one of whose watercolour landscapes is dated 1788.

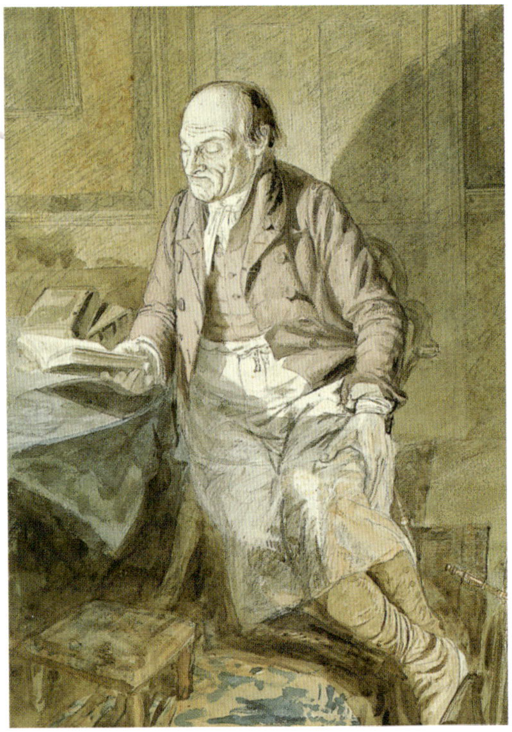

NPG 2430

2430 UNKNOWN ARTIST 19th century

Pencil and watercolour on paper 32.5 x 23.5 (12¾ x 9¼) laid down on paper.

Wearing a pale lilac jacket and white apron.

Collections: Presented by Percy Fitzgerald[1] before 1925.

NPG 2430, which appears to be a late-19th century drawing, was not catalogued until 1981. Called Roger Payne (1739-97), the bookbinder, of whom there is a single contemporary portrait bearing no resemblance to NPG 2430, an etching by Sylvester Harding, published in 1800 and copied by W. Angus 1817 (for T.F. Dibdin, *Bibliographical Decameron*, 1817, II, p.510).

1 A faded inscription on the old backboard reads: *This I believe to be a portrait of Roger Payne [by Rowlandson] I have seen an engraving of it - at least so I think/ Percy Fitzgerald Dec. 1914.*

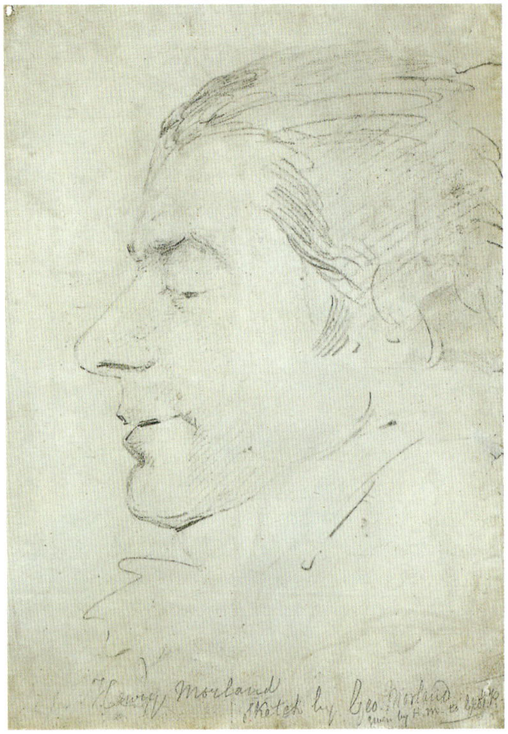

NPG 2905

2905 attributed to GEORGE MORLAND c.1795?

Pencil on paper 27.5 x 19.3 (10¾ x 7⅝) laid down on paper; worn and stained, with repaired tears across the right-hand edge and holes top left and bottom right; inscribed below in pencil in three different hands: early 19th-century: *Henry Morland/ sketch by Geo.*; late 18th century: *Morland*; later 19th century hand: */given by H.M. to Gro...o*

Collections: Purchased from Colnaghi[1] 1936.

The attribution of NPG 2905, a slight sketch of a man of indeterminate age looking rather slyly over his shoulder, and the identity of the sitter depend entirely on the compounded inscription. On comparison with other George Morland drawings, the *Morland* inscription is probably not a signature. NPG 2905 was acquired as a portrait of the artist's father, Henry Morland (c.1719-97), of whom there are no documented portraits,[2] but the inscription could equally refer to the sailor/dealer Henry Morland (c.1760-after 1804), the artist's older brother (and latterly keeper).

1 'from a scrap book' they had bought (note by H.M. Hake, 19 November 1936; NPG archive).

2 Two so-called portraits were: a weak half length of an artist, sold Robinson & Fisher, 6 December 1934, lot 176; and a half-length panel bearing a label *Henry Robert Morland*, signed/inscribed *G. Morland Pinxt 1779*, offered to the NPG in 1934.

3024 UNKNOWN ARTIST c.1775

Black chalk and sanguine on paper 26.5 x 36 (10½ x 14⅛); old fox mark centre left; pencil inscription verso, probably 18th century: *Portrait of Baretti by Sir Joshua Reynolds.*

Collections: William Beckford;[1] Sir William Richard Drake, sale Christie's, 2nd day, 25 May 1892, lot 265 (as by Reynolds of Baretti); M.H. Spielmann, by whom presented 1939.

Acquired as a portrait of Baretti (who is separately featured in this catalogue), but it is doubtful whether

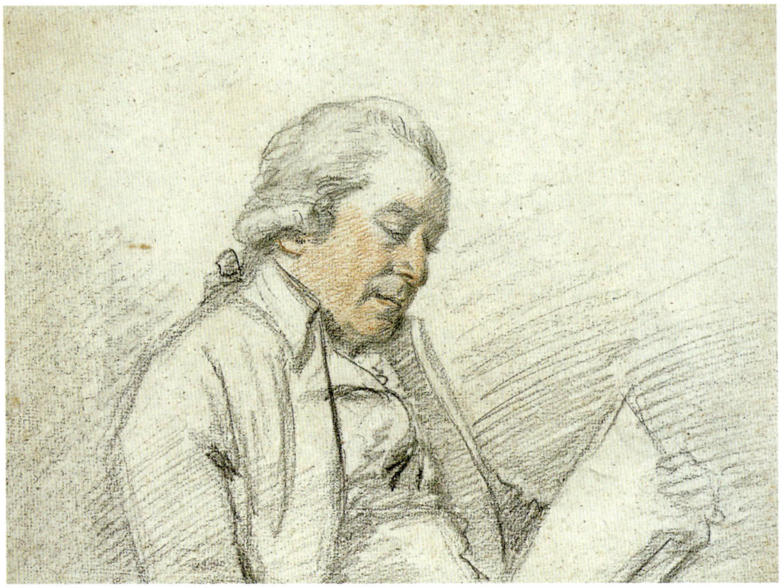

NPG 3024

he could have read a book held at this distance, and the likeness does not compare convincingly with his other portraits. The attribution of this competent drawing to Reynolds cannot be completely dismissed.

1 Provenance apparently endorsed by pencil inscriptions, verso: *599/ Sir Joshua Reynolds/ Portrait of Barretti/ from the sale of Wm. Beckford/ late of Lansdown Crescent Bath* and *J. Barretti/ First Foreign Secretary of R.A./ By Sir Joshua Reynolds. P.R.A./ W. Beckford Colln/ Drake Colln.* The numbers 10 and 24 also appear in pencil. Not identifiable in Beckford sales [e.g. Bath, 24 July-2 August 1848, lot 599].

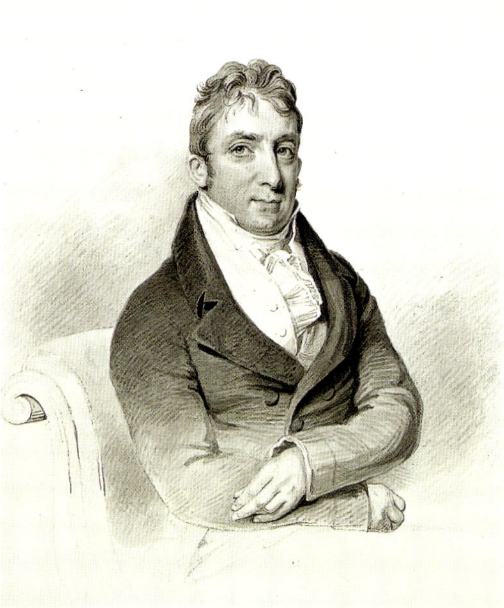

NPG 3160

3160 UNKNOWN ARTIST c.1810-20

Grey wash drawing on white paper 24.5 x 21 (9¾ x 8¼) laid down on paper; an area 22 x 18.5 (8¾ x 7¼) faded through exposure; the original sheet inscribed verso in pencil: [*Romfret*?] *RA/ Wilkins.*

Collections: Mrs M.F. Warner; her sale Sotheby's, 2 June 1943, lot 11 (part lot), bt. Arthur Spencer (of the Siddons Gallery, London), from whom purchased 1943.[1]

Previously called John Russell, the pastellist (who is separately featured in this catalogue), through a misreading of the inscription (the old backing board bore a modern pencil inscription: *Russell R A/ Wilkins*). Probably a preparatory study for an engraving.

1 One of eight drawings, see Chambers NPG 3159.

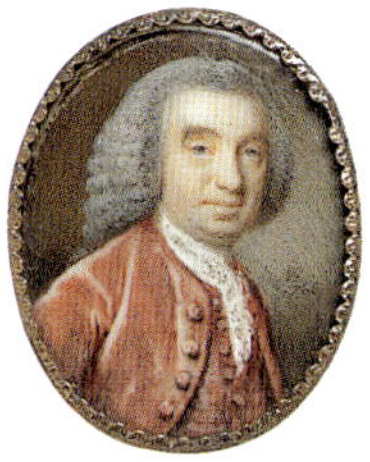

NPG 6283

6283 NATHANIEL HONE 1765

Watercolour and bodycolour on ivory 3.5 x 2.7 (1¼ x 1) oval; signed and dated, lower right: *NH/1765*.

Clear blue eyes, grey powdered wig, wearing a white lace neckcloth and a pale red velvet coat.

Collections: Hon Frederic H.A. Wallop (d.1953), by whom lent to the Victoria and Albert Museum 1927-49; his nephew Alan Evans, by whom bequeathed to the National Gallery 1974; lent to the NPG until permanently transferred in 1994.

Reference: *Smithsonian*, October 1971, p.125 (as Gainsborough); Walker 1998, no.48.

Since at least 1927 identified as the naturalist Peter Collinson (1694-1768),[1] but comparison with his portrait attributed to Benjamin Wilson[2] and the somewhat crabby engravings derived from it, is not conclusive. Nor is the red velvet suit entirely consonant with that distinctive 'simplicity of character' which Collinson is said to have acquired from his Quaker parents (*DNB*); he was otherwise described as 'rather short than tall [with] ... a pleasing and social aspect [and] a temper open and communicative'.[3]

1 Who continued his Quaker father's textile business with America; a friend of Benjamin Franklin; FRS 1728; FSA 1737; he introduced many exotic plant species from America.

2 Holding a paper dated 1767; Mill Hill School, previously sold Christie's, 16 June 1939, lot 13, as Gainsborough. According to Collinson's son Michael (1728-95), his father sat in Bath to Gainsborough in 1767 (N. Brett-James, *Life of Peter Collinson*, 1925, p.284). Offered to the NPG in May 1907 by Hughes & Tillman, together with a half-length version or copy. Four bust-length oval engravings derived from this type: by Trotter 1770, J. Miller 1770, Page, and anon. (*London Mag.*). A half-length painting, inscribed *Peter Collinson Aeta 65 1759 FRS SAS Acad Reg Berol Et suec Soc*, was with Col. H.L. Aylmer, a direct descendant, of Risby Manor, Bury St Edmunds, in 1936.

3 Nichols *Anecdotes*, V, p.312.

COMPARATIVE GROUPS

IN ORDER OF DATE

J.H. MORTIMER, *Caricature Group* c.1765-70 (Yale Center for British Art; B1981.25,467; *Mortimer* 1986, no.34).

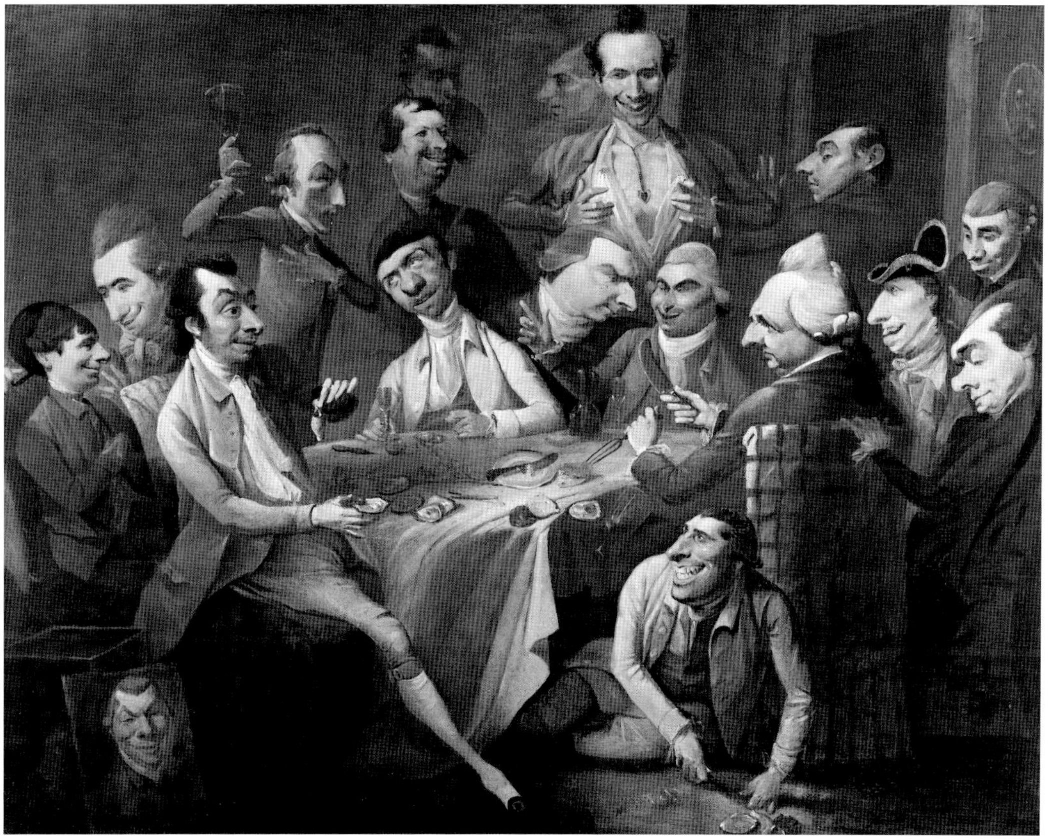

The following, here identified with varying degees of hesitation, appear in this catalogue:

Thomas Arne, standing on the left with raised glass.

Francesco Bartolozzi, behind table, centre, bending over to right.

G.B. Cipriani, second from the left, looking down and left.

Samuel Foote, kneeling on the floor.

J.H. Mortimer, seated extreme left.

Richard Wilson, seated behind table looking up and left (but Wilson more resembles the head immediately above, previously identified as Captain Grose).

Joseph Wilton, seated in gingham-covered chair, right, fork in hand.

JOSHUA REYNOLDS, *The Society of Dilettanti* 1777–78 (Society of Dilettanti; Mannings 2000, no.510). Engraved W. Say 1812.

Sir William Hamilton is seated immediately behind the Greek vase; on the table d'Hancarville's *Antiquités* open at vol. 1, pl.60; Hamilton was elected to the Society in February 1777.

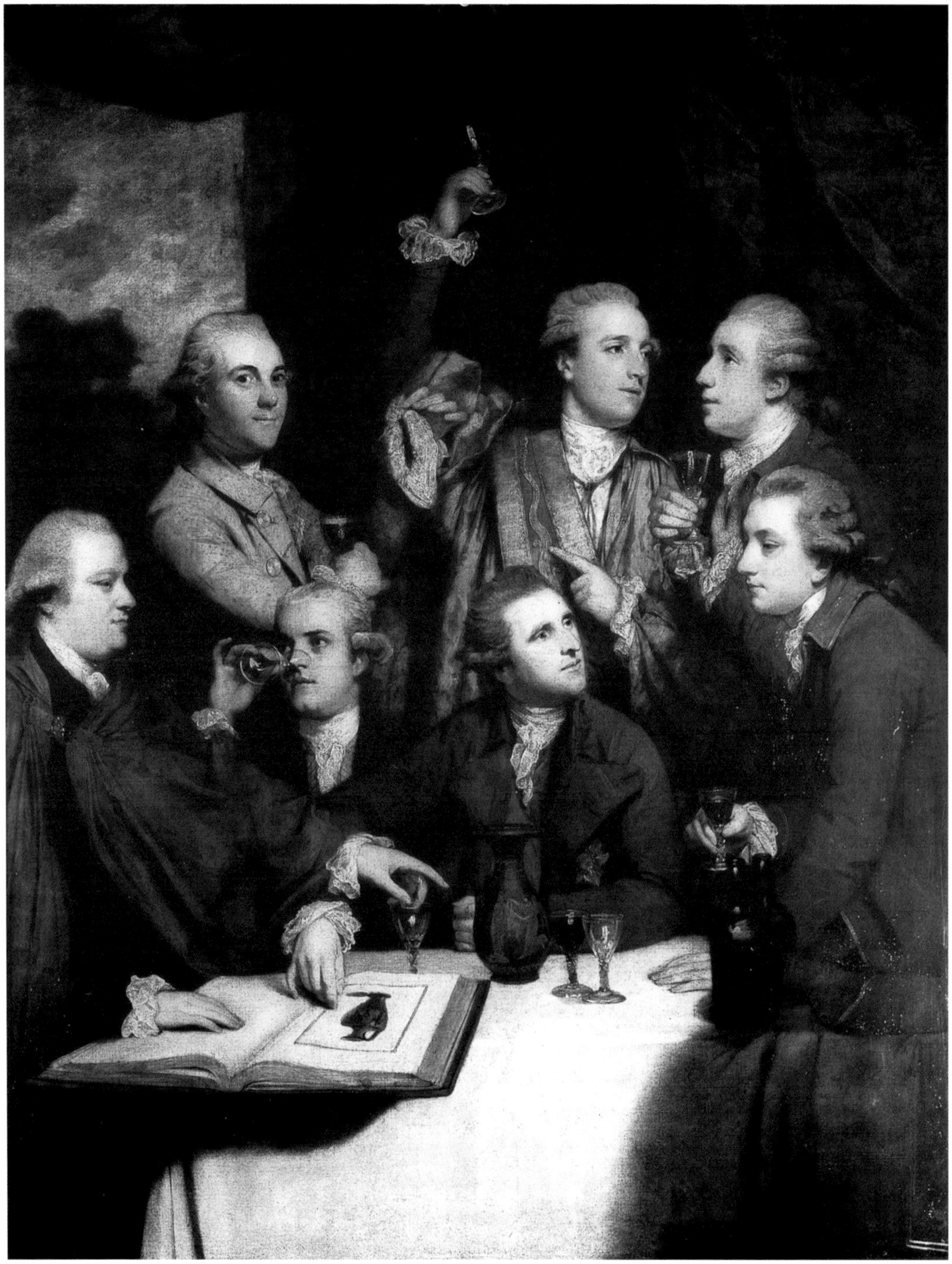

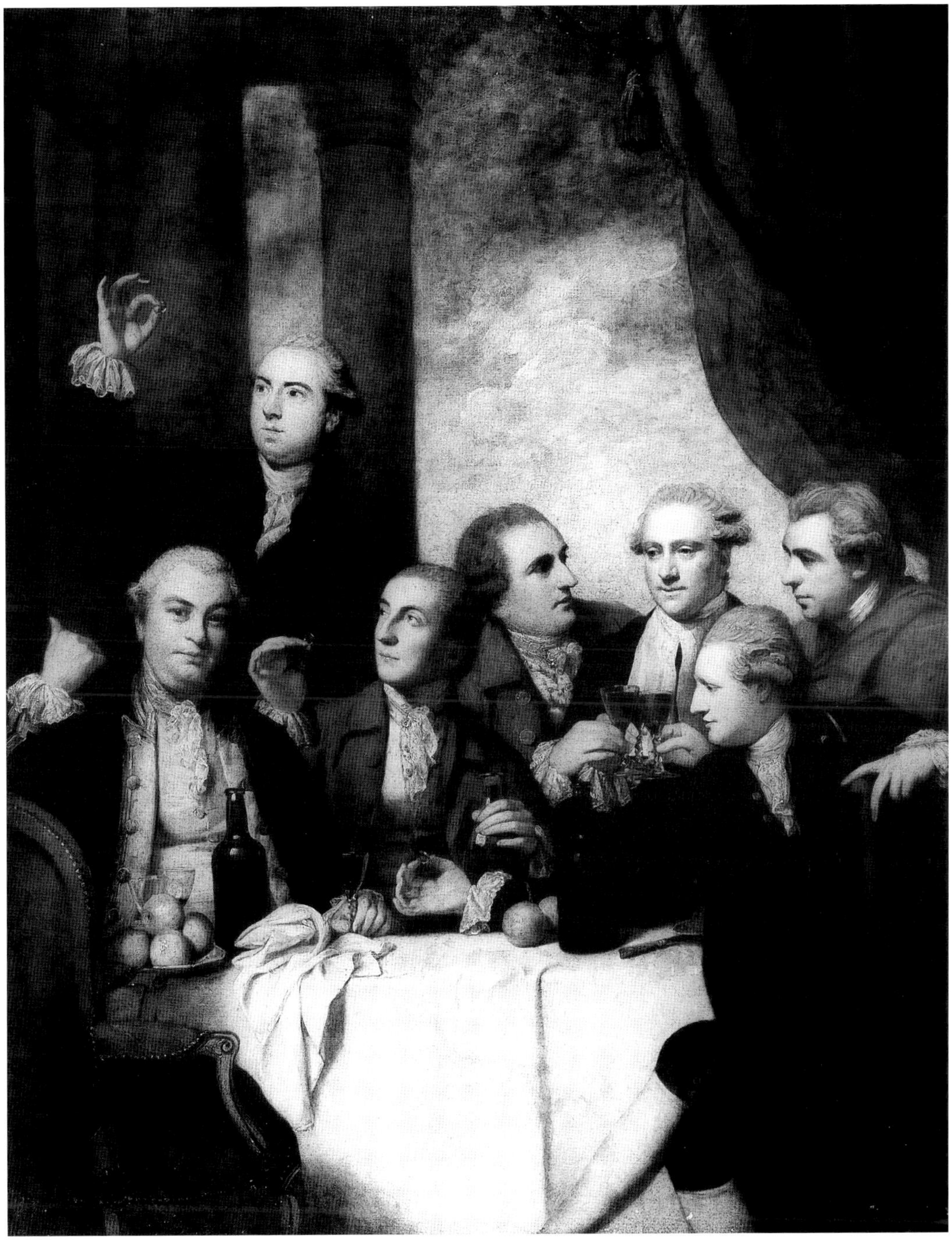

JOSHUA REYNOLDS, *The Society of Dilettanti* 1777–78 (Society of Dilettanti; Mannings 2000, no.511). Engraved C. Turner.

The following appear in this catalogue:

Sir Joseph Banks on the extreme right seen in profile; elected to the Society in 1774, Secretary 1778–97; he sat for this head in 1777.

The 5th Duke of Leeds, as Lord Carmarthen, seated at the front, his right hand across the table holding a gem; elected to the Society in 1774.

The 2nd Baron Mulgrave seated, looking directly to front; elected to the Society in 1775

The following, arranged alphabetically, appear in this catalogue, the numbers taken from the key below:

25 *The 1st Baron Amherst*

32 *The 1st Earl Camden*

31 *The 1st Marquess of Cholmondeley*

43 *The 5th Duke of Devonshire*

12 *The 2nd Earl of Guilford*

17 *Bishop John Hinchliffe*

47 *The 1st Marquess of Lansdowne*

21 *The 1st Earl of Mansfield*

19 *Bishop William Markham*

14 *The 1st Earl of Onslow*

51 *The 3rd Duke of Richmond and Lennox*

52 *The 2nd Marquess of Rockingham*

24 *The 4th Earl of Sandwich*

48 *The 2nd Earl Temple*

10 *The 1st Baron Thurlow*

Key to The Death of Chatham. Anon. 1794 (NPG archive)

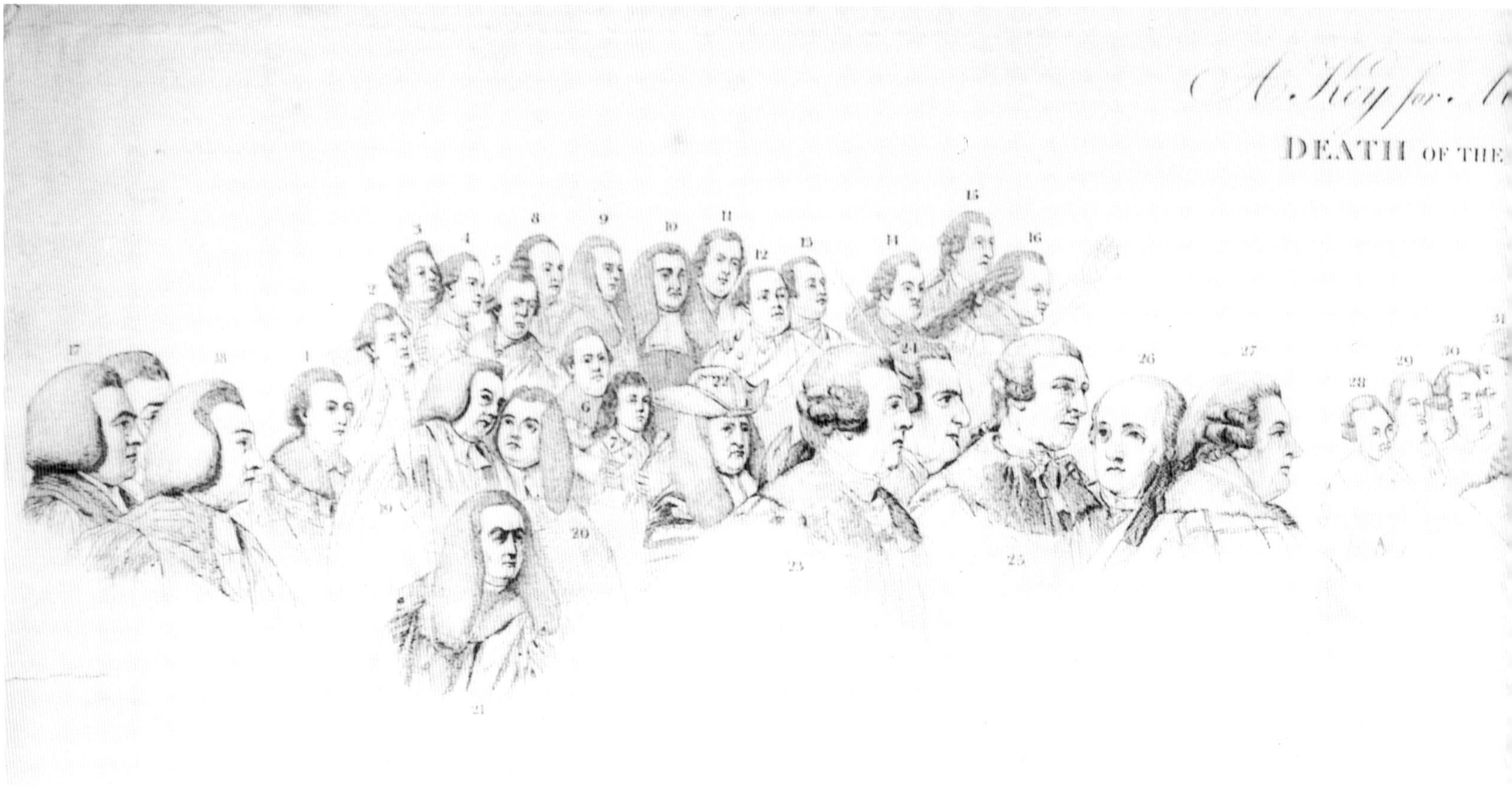

J.S. COPLEY, *The Death of Chatham* 1779–81 (on loan to the NPG from the Tate Gallery, N 100; Prown 1965, II, pp.275–91, 437–40). Engraved F. Bartolozzi 1792.

See Introduction.

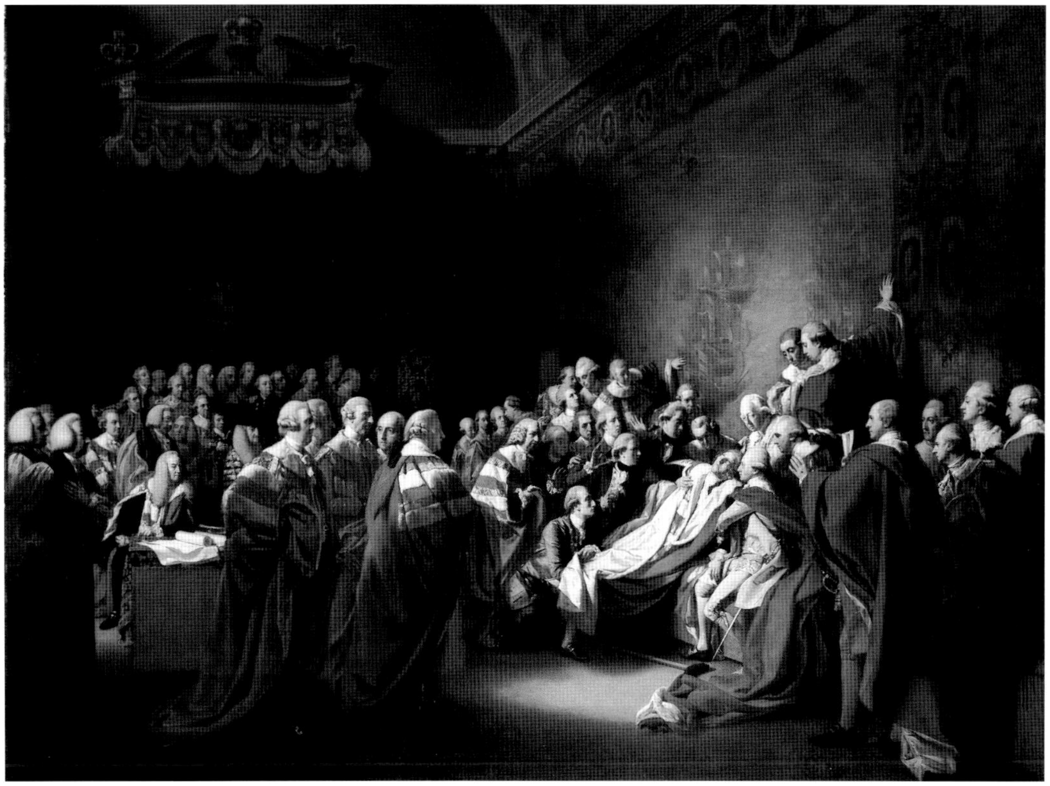

During a discussion in the House of Lords in April 1778 on the State of the Nation, the Duke of Richmond suggested that all British troops should be withdrawn from the America colonies; Chatham opposed this idea but collapsed as he rose to speak a second time.

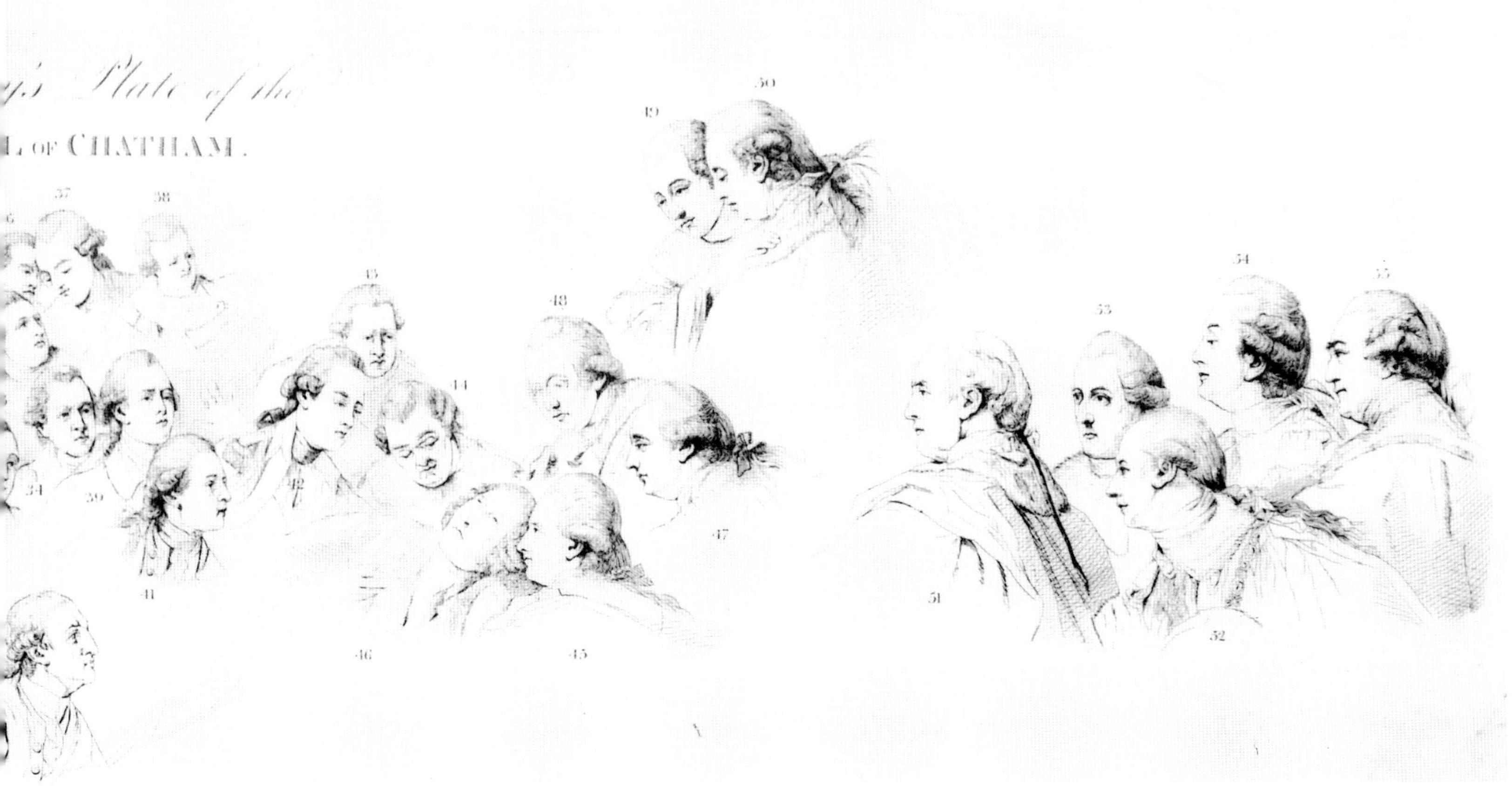

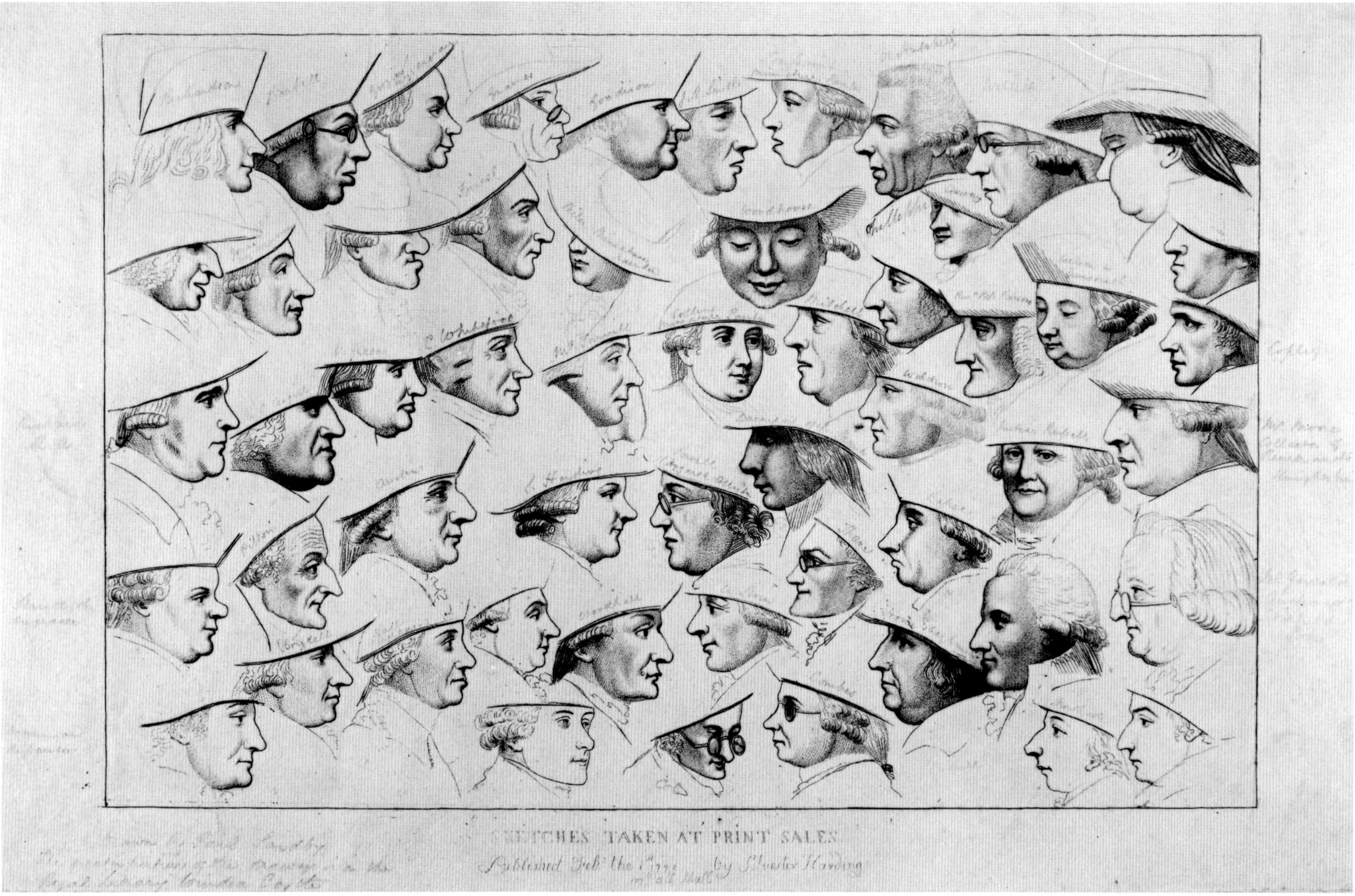

Sketches taken at Print Sales c.1780-86, anon. engraving published by S. Harding 1798, after Paul Sandby (British Museum).

The following appear in this catalogue:

1 *Sir Joseph Banks*
2 *John Boydell*
3 *J.S. Copley*
4 *Richard Cosway*
5 *Valentine Green*
6 *John Hall*
7 *Nathaniel Hone*
8 *Caleb Whitefoord*

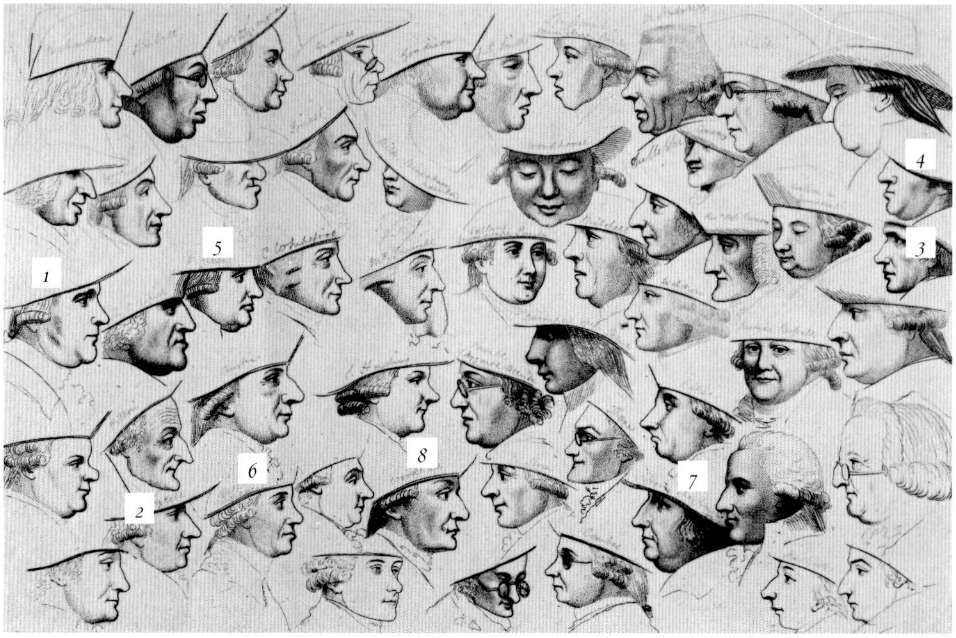

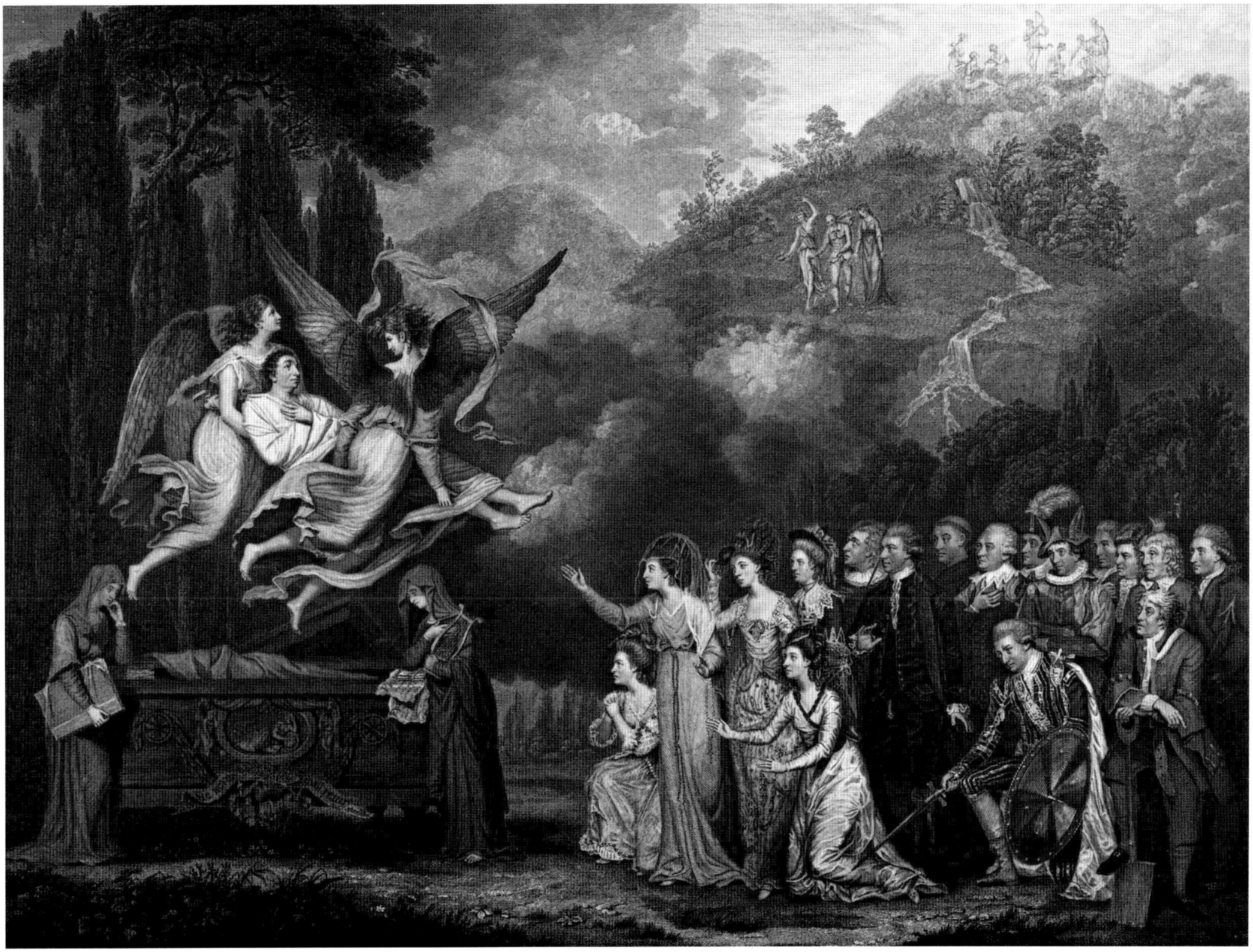

The Immortality of Garrick J. Caldwall and S. Smith 1783 (NPG D 18114) after George Carter. The original painting, exhibited RA 1784(336), belongs to the Royal Shakespeare Memorial Theatre, Stratford-upon-Avon.

A troupe of the leading actors of the day, each shown in a characteristic stage role, mourning the passing of David Garrick. The following appear in this catalogue:

David Garrick is borne aloft on the left

Robert Baddeley standing four from the right, as Dr Caius from *The Merry Wives of Windsor*

Thomas Hull standing six from the right, with plumed hat, as Pisanio in *Cymbeline*

John Palmer kneeling in the right foreground, as Jachimo in *Cymbeline*

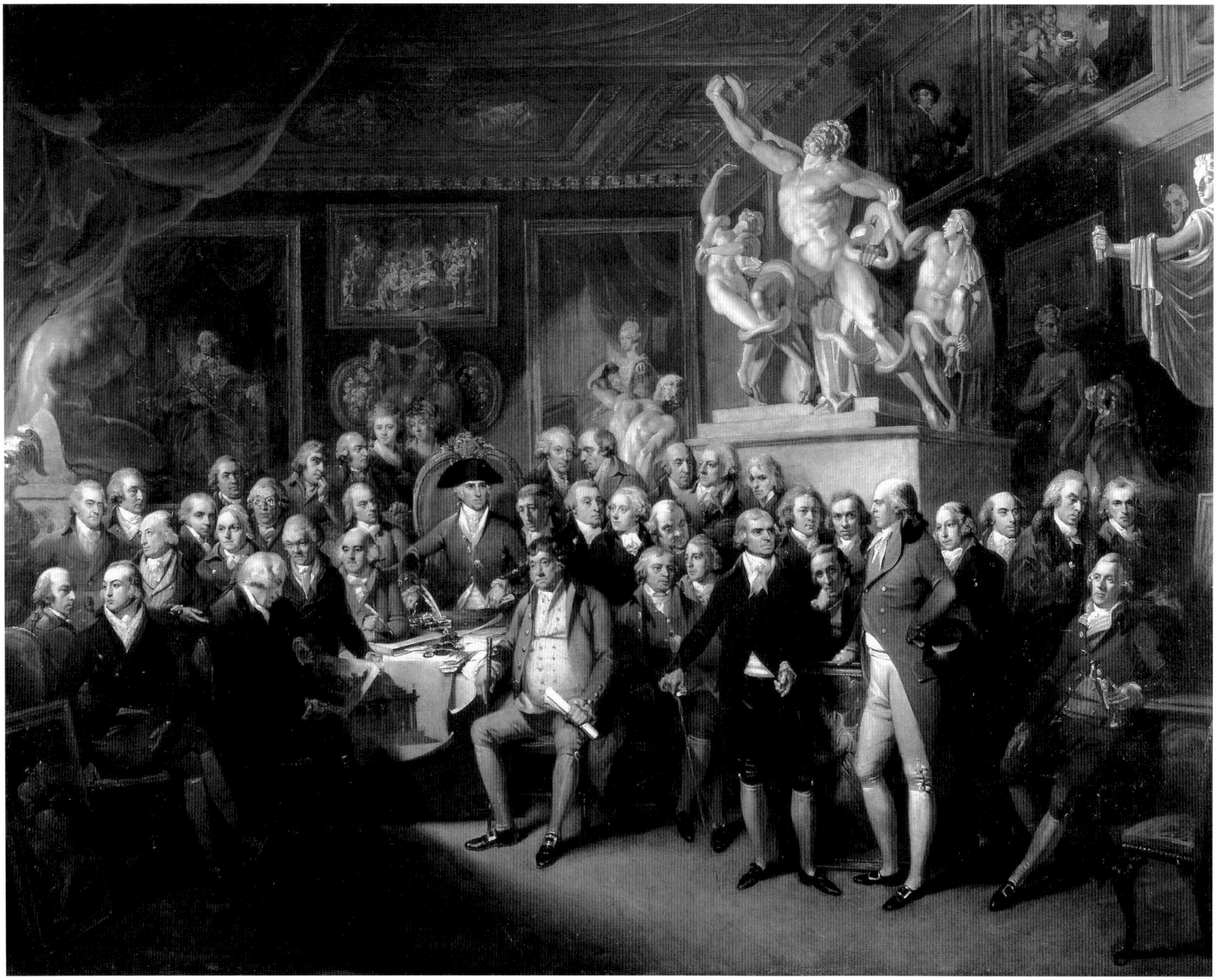

HENRY SINGLETON, *President and Members of the Royal Academy 1795* (Royal Academy of Arts, London). Engraved C. Bestland 1802.

The following appear in this catalogue:

1 *John Bacon*
2 *James Barry*
3 *Francesco Bartolozzi*
4 *Sir William Chambers*
5 *J.S. Copley*
6 *Richard Cosway*
7 *P.J. De Loutherbourg*
8 *William Hamilton*
9 *Angelica Kauffmann*
10 *John Russell*
11 *Paul Sandby*
12 *Thomas Sandby*
13 *Francis Wheatley*
14 *Joseph Wilton*
15 *Johann Zoffany*

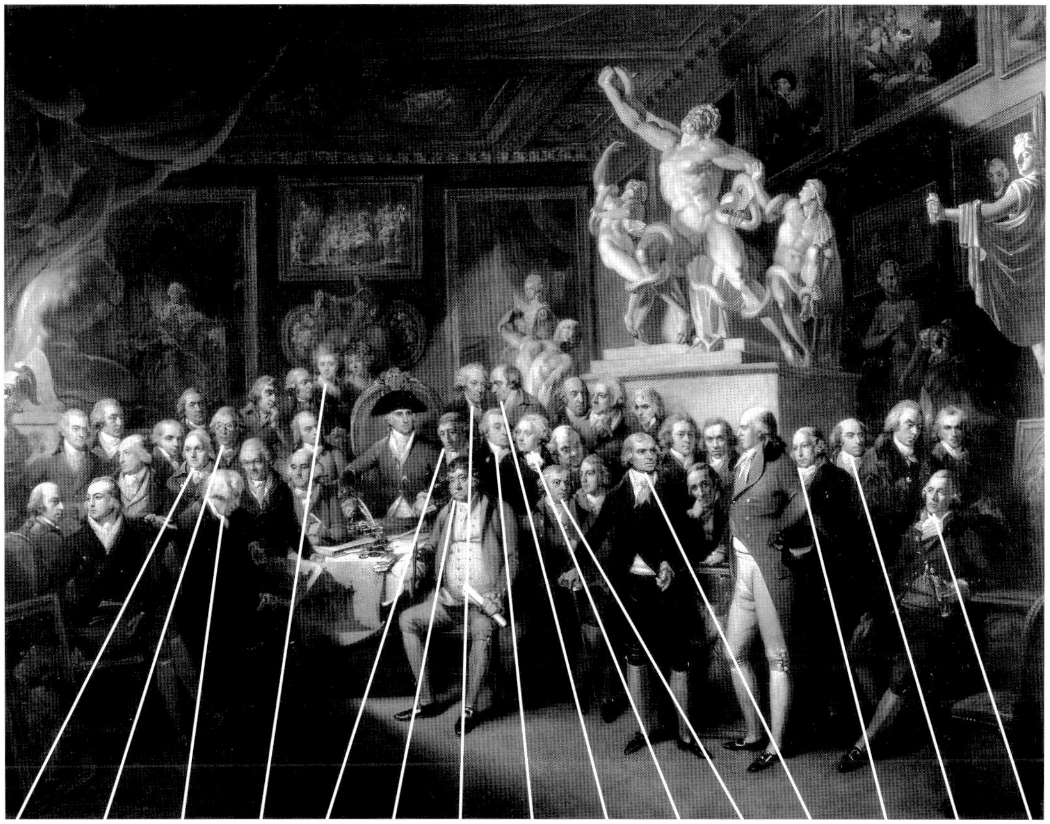

13 14 12 9 3 4 11 7 15 6 2 5 8 10 1

APPENDIX I

PORTRAITS IN THE COLLECTION EXHIBITED AT THE SOCIETY OF ARTISTS AND THE ROYAL ACADEMY

Fifty of the NPG portraits in the preceding catalogue were first seen at the annual exhibitions of the Society of Artists and the Royal Academy, as follows.

Year	no.	Artist, Sitter	(NPG)	medium
Society of Artists				
1762	39	Nathaniel Hone, *Sir John Fielding*	(3834)	oil
1771	128	Francis Parsons, *James Brindley*	(6170)	oil
1783	–	Thomas Beach, *William Woodfall*	(169)	oil
Royal Academy				
1770	86	Thomas Gainsborough, *David Garrick*	(5054)	oil
1773	328	Joshua Reynolds, *David Garrick*	(5375)	oil
1773	239	Joshua Reynolds, *Joseph Banks*	(5868)	oil
1776	91	Robert Dunkarton, *John Henderson*	(1919)	pastel
1776	222	M.W. Peters, *Edward Wortley Montagu*	(4573)	oil
1777	310	John Russell, *William Boyce*	(4212)	pastel
1777	228	J.F. Rigaud, *Bartolozzi, Cipriani, Carlini*	(3186)	oil
1778	133	Charles Grignion jr., *George Farmer*	(2149)	oil
1779	130	William Hoare, *Christopher Anstey*	(3084)	oil
1779	225	Joshua Reynolds, *Edmund Burke*	(709)	oil
1779	338	Henry Walton, *John Palmer*	(2086)	oil
1779	282	Richard Samuel, *Portraits in the Characters of the Muses in the Temple of Apollo*	(4905)	oil
1781	16	Joshua Reynolds, *Charles Burney*	(3884)	oil
1782	10	Joshua Reynolds, *William Beckford*	(5340)	oil
1782	173	George Stubbs, *Self Portrait*	(4575)	oil
1782	53	Johann Zoffany, *John Wilkes*	(6133)	oil
1782	111	Rigaud, *Chambers, Wilton, Reynolds*	(987)	oil
1783	45	Thomas Gainsborough, *Lord Cornwallis*	(281)	oil
1783	5	J.S. Copley, *Lord Mansfield*	(172)	oil
1783	230	Joshua Reynolds, *William Strahan*	(4202)	oil
1785	175	Joshua Reynolds, *Sir William Fawcett*	(5515)	oil
1787	113	Joshua Reynolds, *James Boswell*	(4452)	oil
1788	431	L.F. Abbott, *Valentine Green*	(1260)	oil
1788	315	Philip Jean, *Dominic Serres*	(1909)	miniature
1788	463	John Downman, *Sarah Siddons*	(2651)	drawing
1789	241	William Beechey, *Paul Sandby*	(1379)	oil
1789	156	John Russell, *Francis Willis*	(2186)	pastel
1790	145	Thomas Lawrence, *Mrs Elizabeth Carter*	(28)	drawing
1792	391	Mather Brown, *Sir Francis Buller*	(458)	oil
1792	111	William Beechey, *Thomas Sandby*	(1380)	oil
1794	240	Thomas Hardy, *Wilhelm Cramer*	(6198)	oil
1794	127	William Beechey, *Sarah Siddons*	(5159)	oil
1795	586	George Dance, *James Boswell*	(1139)	drawing
1795	618	George Dance, *Charles Burney*	(1140)	drawing
1795	273	Gainsborough Dupont, *William Lewis*	(5148)	oil
1795	612	George Dance, *Granville Sharp*	(1158)	drawing
1799	629	Henry Edridge, *Lord Sheffield*	(2185)	drawing
1799	276	Theophilus Clarke, *Lord Gardner*	(2103)	oil
1800	116	James Northcote, *Richard Graves*	(5281)	oil
1802	149	Henry Ashby, *John Walker*	(5493)	oil
1803	870	W.S. Lethbridge, *Bishop Horsley*	(155)	miniature
1804	941	Peter Rouw, *Duke of Bridgewater*	(4276)	wax
1806	627	Peter Rouw, *Warren Hastings*	(5065)	wax
1811	194	Thomas Lawrence, *Warren Hastings*	(390)	drawing
1812	766	Henry Monro, *Thomas Hearne*	(1653)	pastel
1817	646	W.S. Lethbridge, *John Wolcot*	(156)	miniature
1829	127	H.W. Pickersgill, *Jeremy Bentham*	(413)	oil

APPENDIX II

3089 (1–12) DANIELL TRACINGS AFTER GEORGE DANCE

Collections: Purchased from Appleby 1940.

Reference: W. Roberts, *MA*, XXII, 1898, pp.656–58; T. Sutton, *Daniells: Artists and Travellers*, 1954, pp.175–79; D. Stroud, *George Dance*, 1971, pp.170–72; Walker *Regency*, I, pp.632–33.

The twelve Daniell tracings in the NPG were part of a collection of more than 150 acquired by Appleby and offered for sale in 1940 (25 are now in the British Museum and 23 in the Yale Center for British Art). In the list below those marked ‡ appear in the main catalogue; the remainder are discussed in Walker *Regency*.

1 ‡Bonomi, Joseph (1739–1808)
2 ‡Carleton, Hugh Carleton, Viscount (1739–1826)
3 Crosdill, John (1751–1825)
4 Earle, Sir James (1755–1817)
5 Fisher, John (1748–1825)
6 ‡Hamilton, William (1751–1801)
7 Hardinge, Sir Richard (1756–1826)
8 ‡Hoole, John (1727–1803)
9 Knyvett, William (1779–1856)
10 Lysons, Samuel (1763–1819)
11 ‡Molini, Peter (1730–1806)
12 ‡Rossi, John Charles Felix (1762–1839)

These tracings were made by the engraver William Daniell preparatory for *A Collection of Portraits sketched from the Life since the Year 1793 by* GEORGE DANCE, *Esq.* R.A. *and engraved in imitation of the Original Drawings by* WILLIAM DANIELL, A.R.A.(*Dance Portraits*). Daniell's engravings (reversed from Dance's drawings) bear dates between April 1802 and April 1814. Seventy-two were bound into two folio volumes published in 1814 (the NPG volumes were bound together, although they retain the two title pages each dated 1814), but they had previously been published in sections. For example, Dance's dedication to Sir George Beaumont (which appeared in volume 1), is dated 1 November 1808; Farington recorded on 15 June 1811 that 'William Daniell called with Dance's 9th No. of Heads', and on 20 April 1814 he noted that the publishers Cadell & Davies 'proposed to publish [Smirke's] Portrait in their next Number of Heads'.

Another bound issue, limited to fifty copies and with additional portraits, was published in 1854 (*Dance Plates*), and a further eighty-four prints are in the British Museum.

APPENDIX III

4855 THE TOWNSHEND ALBUM 1751–58

The Townshend Album contains a collection of seventy-three caricature drawings by George Townshend, 4th Viscount and 1st Marquess Townshend (1724–1807). It was bequeathed to the NPG in 1971 by R.W. Ketton Cremer and was published and fully illustrated by Eileen Harris (*The Townshend Album*, 1974). None of the drawings counts as portraiture in any useful sense, but it would be high-handed not to mention this eccentric and amusing collection. Apart from sitters already treated by Kerslake in his *Early Georgian* catalogue (where the Album was not used), there are twenty-five named sitters who were in their maturity after 1760. They are listed alphabetically below (the bracketed number referring to the page within the Album).

BADEN, August George, Margrave of (1706–71); whole length to left holding stick (36).

BRISTOL, George William Hervey, 2nd Earl of (1721–75), politician; whole length to left walking hat in right hand (7).

BROUGHTON, Jack (1705?–89), boxer; whole length standing to left as a pugilist (29).

BROWN, Riches Repps (d. 1767); corpulent half length figure seated to left (54).

BURLTON, Philip (d. 1790), army surgeon and patron of the turf; on horseback (41).

EVANS, Capt. Thomas (d. 1767) [?], soldier; half length to left (13).

FORTESCUE, Matthew, 2nd Baron (1719–85), politician; half length to left, hat under his left arm (4).

HALLY, Michel Descazeaux du (1710–75), adventurer; whole length to left wearing wide hat (9).

JOHNSTON, Col. James (1721–97), general; head, profile to left (6).

JONES, John ['Jemmy'] (1705–69); on horseback (43).

KNYPHAUSEN, Dodo Heinrich, Freiherr von (1729–89); whole-length walking to left (57), and whole length standing to left (59).

LASCELLES, Mrs; three-quarter length seated, an elderly, skinny lady (14).

MARTINELLI, Vincenzo (1702–85), writer and adventurer; half length to left, bare-headed and hunch-backed (50), bust profile to left (52), and seated smoking a hookah (53).

MELCOMBE, George Bubb Doddington, Baron (1691–1762), politician and literary patron; whole-length corpulent figure to left (21) and a similar drawing (22).

MICHELL, John (1710–66) politician; half length to front (17).

ORFORD, George, 3rd Earl of (1730–91), eccentric; whole length kneeling at prayer (66).

PRESTON, Isaac (1711–68), barrister; as a bear with his own head (56).

PRIME, Sir Samuel (1701–77), lawyer; half length seated at table (45).

PROBYN, John Hopkins (1703–73), lawyer and politician; three-quarter length standing to left (18).

SANDWICH, John Montagu, 4th Earl of (1718–92), first lord of the Admiralty; whole length dressed in motley (23).

SHELLEY, Sir John, 4th Bt (1692–1771), politician; on horseback (44).

SLACK, Jack (d.1778), pugilist; whole length (30).

SMALLWOOD, Thomas?, pugilist; whole length, hat in right hand (34); another drawing, whole length, arms folded (31), is provisionally identified as Smallwood.

TANNER, Rev. Thomas (1718–86), churchman; profile head to left (12).

WINCHILSEA, Daniel Finch, 8th Earl of (1689–1769), politician; whole length back view (24).

INDICES

of names, not including doubtful portraits

1 PAINTERS (including draughtsmen, enamellists and silhouettists)

2 SCULPTORS (including modellers and medallists)

3 ENGRAVERS (including etchers and lithographers)

4 OWNERS and COLLECTIONS

Notes: entries indicate (quantity), NPG number (where relevant) and page
Titles are given in minimal format, sufficient simply to identify the sitter within this catalogue.

1 INDEX OF PAINTERS

2 INDEX OF SCULPTORS

4 INDEX OF OWNERS

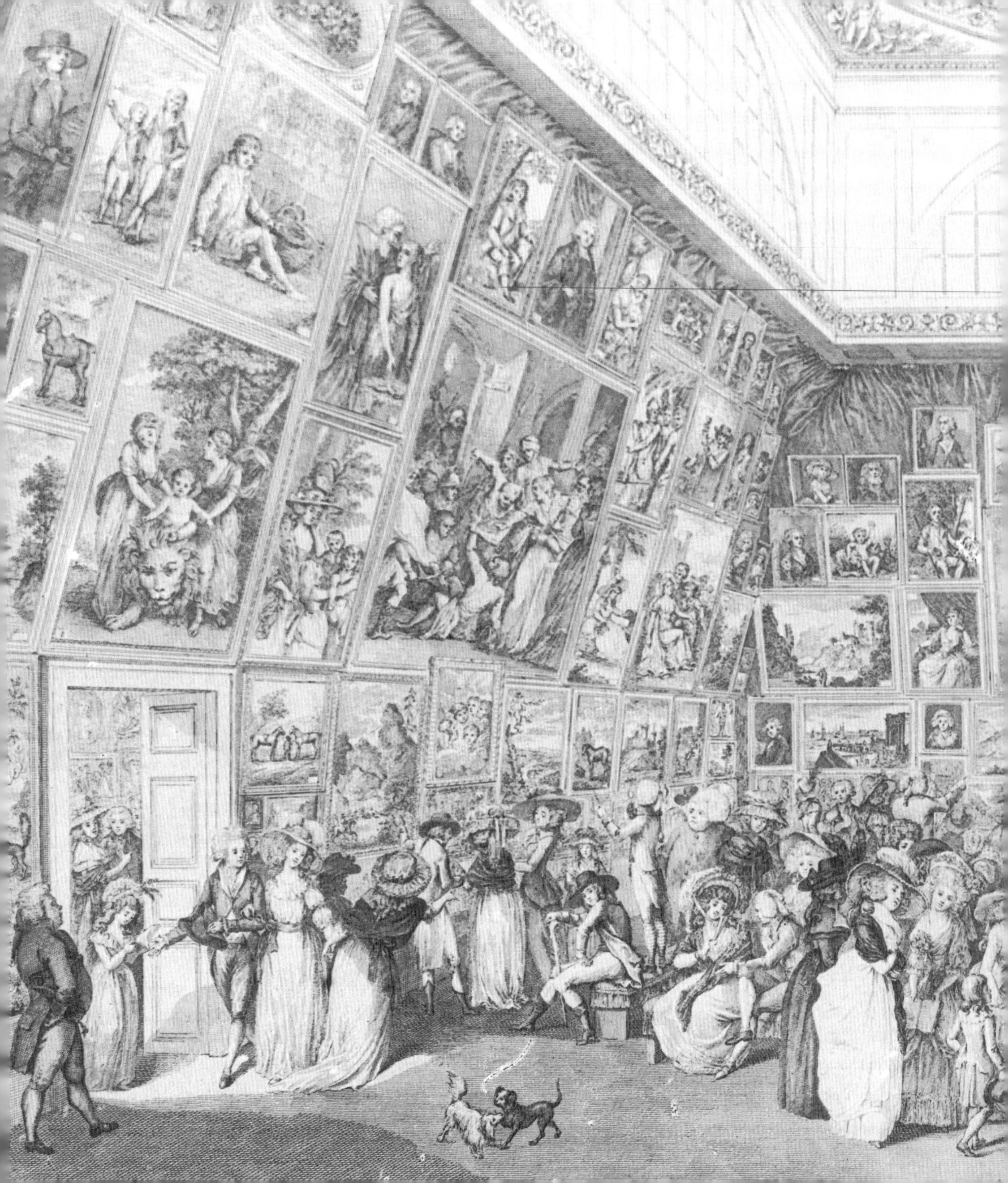